CASES AND MATERIALS

SECURITIES REGULATION

NINTH EDITION

by

JOHN C. COFFEE, JR.
Adolf A. Berle Professor of Law
Columbia University School of Law

JOEL SELIGMAN
Dean and Ethan A. H. Shepley University Professor
Washington University School of Law

Successor
to
Securities Regulation by Jennings, Marsh,
Coffee and Seligman

FOUNDATION PRESS

NEW YORK, NEW YORK

2003

THOMSON
™
WEST

Foundation Press, a division of West Group, has created this publication to provide you with accurate and authoritative information concerning the subject matter covered. However, this publication was not necessarily prepared by persons licensed to practice law in a particular jurisdiction. Foundation Press is not engaged in rendering legal or other professional advice, and this publication is not a substitute for the advice of an attorney. If you require legal or other expert advice, you should seek the services of a competent attorney or other professional.

 TEXT IS PRINTED ON 10% POST CONSUMER RECYCLED PAPER

PREFACE TO NINTH EDITION

With this edition, the names "Jennings" and "Marsh" pass from the title page of this casebook. Their names may be gone in the technical sense, but they are not forgotten. The remaining authors recognize the magnitude of their achievement. Professors Richard Jennings and Harold Marsh defined the architecture of securities regulation as a law school course.

Over the course of eight editions, the Jennings and Marsh team crafted a much respected casebook, which introduced most of the current generation of academics and practitioners to the world of securities regulation, defining its categories and clarifying its fundamental concepts. The original edition of Jennings and Marsh in 1963 was the first casebook on securities regulation, and its publication reflected the emergence of a new course. Those in their position who write the first casebook in a field necessarily shape and define the contents of the standard course. Today, while there are other casebooks in securities regulation, most still follow the structure and organization first laid out by Jennings and Marsh in 1963.

In that light, the current authors have sought to maintain the continuity of the book and avoid disruptive organizational changes. Still, major developments have transpired in securities regulation since the Eighth Edition in 1998. Where once the supremacy of U.S. accounting and disclosure standards was widely acknowledged, that supremacy has now fallen into question. The succession of accounting irregularity and disclosure scandals, beginning with Enron in 2001 and continuing through Tyco, Adelphia, WorldCom and others in 2002, have forced a fundamental re-examination of U.S. securities regulation. Correspondingly, not just auditors, but other gatekeepers, including securities analysts, attorneys, investment bankers, and debt rating agencies, have seen their performance also called into question. The SEC and other regulators (most notably, the new Public Company Accounting Oversight Board (the "Board")) have similarly become the subject of closer scrutiny and harsher criticism than in the past, which criticism culminated in the resignations of SEC Chairman Harvey Pitt and Board Chairman William Webster in 2002. Far more than in the recent past, a sense of crisis overhangs the field today.

These developments have also produced major new legislation: the Sarbanes-Oxley Act of 2002. Written in understandable haste, the Act has given rise to a host of ambiguities and still unresolved issues. Written on the literal edge of these developments, this casebook seeks to interpret and respond to this new legislation in a variety of ways:

First, throughout this edition, a major effort has been made to note and analyze the legislative changes wrought by Sarbanes-Oxley. Necessarily, this effort is incomplete because SEC rules and interpretations remain to be adopted (but they will be noted in subsequent supplements and in special statutory supplement on the Sarbanes-Oxley Act, which is being distributed to all users of this casebook).

Second, increased attention is given to those reforms than the SEC and other regulatory seem to be pursuing: expanded use of the Management Discussion and Analysis of Financial Condition and Results of Operations (the "MD&A"), "real time" disclosure, and new enforcement policies and weapons, including greater use of the criminal sanction.

Third, greater attention is also given to the role of securities analysts and attorneys, as independent investigations involving the allocation of stock in initial public offerings and the integrity of securities research have recently shaken the fields of investment banking and research and may also yet produce significant structural reorganization within the integrated investment banking firm.

Finally, this edition contain new chapters addressing state law and the Investment Company Act. Also, increased attention has been given to the evolution of markets, and in particular technological developments at both the New York Stock Exchange and Nasdaq.. To be sure, these are not new issues, but they have acquired new significance and topicality in recent months.

Professor Coffee wishes to acknowledge the assistance of Brian Jacobs and Benjamin Naftalis of the Columbia Law Class of 2004 in helping to research, edit, cite-check and proofread this edition, and of Ms. Mirna Fermin for diligent secretarial services.

Dean Seligman wishes to express his appreciation to Jerome Duggan, Class of 2002, Mahesh Joshi, Class of 2003, and Stephen Tountas, Class of 2003, and Joanne Margherita for her cheerful and effective reading and secretarial services.

JOHN C. COFFEE, JR.
New York, New York

JOEL SELIGMAN
Saint Louis, Missouri

SUMMARY OF CONTENTS

TABLE OF CONTENTS

SUBDIVISION C.   TRANSACTION EXEMPTIONS AVAILABLE TO
ISSUERS OF SECURITIES

PART IV. CIVIL LIABILITIES UNDER THE FEDERAL SECURITIES LAWS

*

TABLE OF CASES

Principal cases are in bold type. Non-principal cases are in roman type. References are to Pages.

CASES AND MATERIALS

SECURITIES REGULATION

*

PART I

THE CAPITAL MARKETS: AN OVERVIEW

CHAPTER 1

THE INSTITUTIONAL AND REGULATORY FRAMEWORK

SECTION 1. THE GOALS OF SECURITIES REGULATION

The federal securities laws regulate some, but not all, of the financial markets. Chiefly, they focus on those markets that allocate capital, moving it from savers to those who have productive uses for capital and are willing to pay a competitive return. While this capital raising function will be this book's primary focus, financial markets have other functions as well. For example, the derivative markets permit their users to hedge risks (for example, the risks of interest rate or currency fluctuations). Highly diverse in structure and operation, financial markets link very different suppliers of capital with principally corporate borrowers: in some markets, retail investors predominate, while in others they are largely excluded in favor of sophisticated institutional investors. Given these differences, it does not follow that all markets should be regulated equally intensively. In some, private ordering may be feasible, and the need for governmental oversight may seem minimal. Although no simple generalization can explain the historical contingencies that have caused the federal securities laws to apply only to certain markets, American securities regulation clearly varies the intensity of its regulatory supervision depending on the typical investor's need for protection. This Chapter seeks to provide an abbreviated roadmap, first, of the principal financial markets to which the federal securities laws apply; second, of how these markets typically work; and, third, of the interwoven web of regulatory institutions—federal, state, and "self regulatory"—that collectively regulate these markets, usually in cooperation, but sometimes in conflict.

Initially, however, there is an antecedent question: why regulate? The fact that a market is very large does not imply that a federal administrative agency should be created to oversee it. Many markets are adequately controlled simply by the common law of fraud, and, even among financial markets, there are some enormous markets that exist with very little governmental regulation (for example, the currency market or the market for government securities). A distinctive feature of American securities regulation is that it goes beyond simply proscribing fraud and establishes a detailed and mandatory system of affirmative disclosure that, subject to some important exemptions, instructs the issuer what it must disclose and when. Why should securities markets be regulated in this pervasive fashion? This is a topic of some controversy among academics (because some believe the current level of regulation is excessive), but the justifications for such a mandatory disclosure system generally rely on some combination of the following factors:

1. *Consumer Protection.* Historically, the securities markets have long been thought to be affected with a special public interest. The first federal securities laws were passed during the early years of the Great Depression, following the stock market collapse in October 1929. Congress believed not only that investors had been systematically overreached and cheated during the go-go decade of the 1920's,[1] but also that the 1929 stock market collapse had been a principal cause of the Depression and that the Depression had been prolonged by the lack of confidence in the market on the part of investors (with the result that solvent corporations with good prospects could not raise capital).[2] These twin concerns—that investors were vulnerable in a manipulated marketplace *and* that others suffered when investors disinvested in the market—explain why Congress declared in Section 2 of the Securities Exchange Act of 1934 that "transactions in securities as commonly conducted upon securities exchanges and over-the-counter markets are affected with a national public interest which makes it necessary to provide for regulation and control of such transactions."[3]

---

1. The House Report accompanying the Securities Act of 1933 examined the decade after World War I and concluded:

> "Fully half or $25,000,000 worth of securities floated during this period have been proved to be worthless. These cold figures spell tragedy in the lives of thousands of individuals who invested their life savings, accumulated after years of effort, in these worthless securities."

H.R.Rep. No. 85, 73d Cong., 1st Sess. 2 (1933).

2. In recent years, historians have tended to assign greater causal weight to other events, such as the Hawley–Smoot Tariff Act of 1930, in the causation of the De-pression. See John H. Jackson, The World Trading System: Law and Policy of International Relations (1992) at 31. Under this view, the 1929 stock market crash may have precipitated an economic decline, but other developments exacerbated and extended it.

3. Spelling out this critique in more detail on the face of the Securities Exchange Act of 1934, Section 2(3) states:

> "Frequently the prices of securities on such exchanges and markets are susceptible to manipulation and control, ..."

Section 2(4) then adds:

> "National emergencies, which produce widespread unemployment and the dislo-

The political judgment seemed at the time obvious: When Wall Street sneezed (as it did massively in October, 1929), the rest of America could become seriously ill.

Since 1929, there have, however, been other sudden stock market declines (most notably the market collapse in October, 1987, which involved a greater dollar loss but a slightly smaller percentage decline, and the Nasdaq "high tech" bubble, which seemingly burst in 2000). These other crashes have neither lasted as long nor were followed by a general economic decline. Thus, the relationship between stock market volatility and national economic health appears more complex today than it did in the early 1930s.

Yet, the case for paternalism is in some respects today stronger than in 1929. Before the passage of the federal securities laws, only a relatively small percentage of the American public invested in securities (and even less in equity securities). Today, some 84 million Americans (or 43.6% of the adult population) are direct or indirect shareholders,[4] and the percentage of American households that have direct or indirect stock holdings is even higher: 48.8%.[5] Given this heavy investment in equity securities, most recent commentators agree that a stock market crash would have severe consequences for the real economy.[6] The following chart shows that the percentage of U.S. families that own stocks increased by more than thirty percent from 1989 to 1995. Interestingly, the rate of increase is highest at the lower end of the economic scale:[7]

cation of trade, transportation and industry and which burden interstate commerce and adversely affect the general welfare, are precipitated, intensified and prolonged by manipulation and sudden and unreasonable fluctuations of securities prices on such exchanges and markets . . .''.

4. New York Stock Exchange Fact Book (2000) at 55 (citing Federal Reserve Board's 1998 Survey of Consumer Finance). More specifically, some 34 million individuals directly owned shares in publicly traded companies; another 27 million owned shares in equity mutual funds; another 34 million owned shares through self-directed retirement plans; finally, 48 million owned shares through defined contribution pension funds. After adjusting for the overlap in these four categories, the NYSE estimated that 84 million individuals held shares through at least one of these means. See NYSE, SHAREOWN-ERSHIP 2000 at 10 (2000). In contrast, the number of shareholders in Germany in 2000 was estimated at 6.2 million, up from 3.9 million in 1997, but still way below the U.S. on a percentage basis. See Norman Poser,

The Stock Exchanges of the United States and Europe: Automation, Globalization, And Consolidation, 22 U. Pa. J. of Int'l Econ. L. 497 n.3 (2002).

5. Henry T.C. Hu, Investor Beliefs and Government Neutrality, 78 Tex. L. Rev. 777, 805–06 (2000). For detailed data on the growth in stock ownership, see Arthur Kennickell et al., Recent Changes in U.S. Family Finances: Results from the 1998 Survey of Consumer Finances, 86 Fed. Reserve Bull. 1, 15 (table 6) (2000) (showing growth in stock ownership by households); Joseph Tracy et al., Are Stocks Overtaking Real Estate in Household Portfolios? Fed. Reserve Bank N.Y., Current Issues Econ. & Fin., April 1999 at 1–2 (table 1) (showing assets of U.S. households).

6. See Hu, supra note 5, at 794; John Coates IV, The Privatization of the Securities Laws: Private vs Political Choice of Securities Regulation, 41 Va. J. Int'l L. 531, 571 (2001).

7. This chart is extracted from the Federal Reserve Bulletin, January 1997. See also ''The Stock Market,'' 7 The CQ Researcher, May 2, 1997, 385, 392.

All families Income (1995 dollars)	Families with Stock holdings		Share of family's financial assets in stocks	
	1989	1995	1989	1995
	31.7%	41.1%	26.3%	40.4%
Less than $10,000	2.3%	6.0%	10.0%	21.1%
$10,000–$24,999	13.1%	25.3%	10.0%	21.6%
$25,000–$49,999	33.1%	47.7%	20.3%	33.0%
$50,000–$99,999	54.0%	66.7%	25.6%	39.9%
$100,000 and more	79.7%	83.9%	31.4%	47.6%

As this chart shows, a substantial and growing percentage of the American middle class has invested its retirement savings in the stock market and is thus more exposed than in 1929 to the possibility of a severe stock market decline. Particularly after the Enron and Arthur Andersen scandals of 2001–2002, the original Congressional goals of "ensuring honest markets" and "protecting investor confidence" may have more continuing relevance than seemed likely even a few years ago.

2. *The Informational Needs of Investors.* Many markets sell essentially fungible products (wheat, oil, diamonds, etc.) whose grade and characteristics can be specified without great difficulty. Also, most transactions in these markets occur between professionals who expect to do business with each other again and hence value their commercial reputation for honesty and fair dealing. Even in other markets where transactions are not as easily standardized, self-help remedies, including personal inspection, are often available (e.g., one can kick the tires at an automobile showroom or squeeze the tomatoes in the supermarket). Such self-help is less feasible, however, in the case of equity securities. Not only is it impossible for the typical buyer to examine the company, but the value of the security depends heavily on the likely future earnings of the issuing corporation (or other entity). Thus, the investor wants reliable information about the issuer's financial condition, its likely future earnings, its competitive position, the status of its products in their own marketplaces, its prospective contingent liabilities, the background and competence of its management—and a host of other matters. And the investor needs this information to be presented in a relatively standardized and uniform fashion to facilitate comparisons among securities. Absent such disclosures, it is questionable whether most investors would be willing to invest funds in risky enterprises, and it is certain that they would reduce the price that they are willing to pay in direct proportion to their level of uncertainty about the firm's value. Possibly for this reason, the level of disclosure required in securities markets has historically exceeded the level of disclosure generally required by the law of contract or fraud.[8] In short, for the securities market to function efficiently, much more disclosure is required than in most other markets.

3. *Inadequate Incentives to Disclose.* Conceivably, individual securities markets could solve the informational needs of investors without direct governmental intervention, by adopting minimum listing standards for securities traded on them. In fact, the New York Stock Exchange imposed such requirements on its listed companies for several decades prior to the passage of the federal securities laws (although there is some debate as to whether they enforced their own requirements consistently before they became subject to SEC oversight in the 1930s). Still, managers may resist disclosure of adverse information about their firm for any of a variety of self-interested reasons (even

8. See Anthony Kronman, Mistake Disclosure, Information, and the Law of Contracts, 7 J. Legal Stud. 1 (1978) (noting absence of broad disclosure rules under the general law of contracts).

if it were in the long-term interest of the firm to maintain its credibility by disclosing such information). Not only do managers fear that the revelation of adverse information could lead to their ouster (or, at least, to reduced compensation), but they may also fear that disclosure of some forms of information will cause proprietary injury to their firm by alerting competitors, as well as investors, to important developments. Hence, one important rationale for a mandatory disclosure system is that the private costs of disclosure can exceed its social costs, thus leading to lesser disclosure under a private ordering system in which each firm chose its own level of disclosure than under a mandatory system. In short, a socially optimal level of disclosure may only be achievable through mandatory law.[9]

In addition, in a world characterized by competing securities markets, achieving consensus on the format of, and minimum standards for, disclosure has proven difficult—much more so today than in the days when the NYSE had an effective monopoly over trading in companies listed with it. Governmental coordination may be the simplest way to specify a mutually desired common standard.

4. *Allocative Efficiency.* Another important function of the federal securities laws is to ensure the accuracy of securities prices. By "accuracy", economists mean stock prices that conform to the fundamental value of the companies traded.[10] This goal is considered important, even apart from the goal of investor protection, because the capital markets allocate a scarce resource (capital) among competing users. By determining the cost of capital for corporate issuers, the securities markets serve in theory as the nerve center for a capitalist economy, encouraging the flow of capital to firms with superior prospects and penalizing less efficient firms by requiring them to pay more for capital. In this view, the capital markets, and in particular the stock market, promote efficiency and economic growth and thereby benefit all citizens, not simply investors. The more that one takes this view, the more that one can justify a disclosure system having higher costs than rational issuers themselves would voluntarily incur in order to satisfy investors because, from this perspective, there is a public or social benefit that exceeds the private benefits of disclosure.

In recent years, this view has been hotly debated. Some argue that securities markets are characterized by excessive speculative trading, which does not benefit society or improve efficiency but does result in the deadweight loss of high transaction costs (which are estimated to cost investors over $100 billion each year).[11] Others believe that while the goal of "accuracy enhancement" is valid, it must be balanced against the corporate issuer's own interests in confidentiality.[12] Their primary fear is that excessively high disclosure

---

9. For this argument, see Merritt B. Fox, Retaining Mandatory Securities Disclosure: Why Issuer Choice is Not Investor Empowerment, 85 Va. L. Rev. 1335 (1999).

10. See Marcel Kahan, Securities Law and the Social Costs of "Inaccurate" Stock Prices, 41 Duke L.J. 977 (1994); see also Merritt B. Fox, supra note 9; Jeffrey Gordon & Lewis Kornhauser, Efficient Markets, Costly Information, and Securities Research, 60 N.Y.U.L.Rev. 761 (1985); Ronald Gilson &

Reinier Kraakman, The Mechanisms of Market Efficiency, 70 Va.L.Rev. 549 (1984).

11. See Lynn Stout, The Unimportance of Being Efficient: An Economic Analysis of Stock Market Pricing and Securities Regulation, 87 Mich.L.Rev. 613 (1988) (doubting that stock market prices express fundamental values); Stout, Are Stock Markets Costly Casinos? Disagreement, Market Failure and Securities Regulation, 81 Va.L.Rev. 611 (1995).

12. See Edmund Kitch, The Theory and Practice of Securities Disclosure, 61 Brooklyn

standards will result in disclosures that the firm's competitors can exploit. For example, while disclosure of future business plans or new products should enhance the accuracy of securities prices, it may also allow competitors to mimic those plans; over time, this could reduce the incentive to invest in research and development. From this perspective, "accuracy enhancement is only one of a number of conflicting objectives which must be considered . . ."[13]

Controversy also exists over whether the federal securities laws have enhanced market efficiency. Some argue that by arming investors with private causes of action for fraud that give rise to the prospect of significant liability, the federal securities laws "reduce the amount of information that is provided by issuers."[14] This view rests on the premise that market forces alone would elicit a near optimal level of disclosure. This claim overlaps with a lengthy debate about whether, historically, the introduction of the federal securities laws actually increased the amount of disclosure made available to investors.[15] Proponents of mandatory disclosure respond that the most recent empirical evidence shows that mandatory disclosure has improved market efficiency.[16]

5. *Corporate Governance and "Agency Costs."* Disclosure not only informs securities prices, it permits shareholders to gain greater control over their corporate managers. This is an alternative efficiency justification for the mandatory disclosure system established by the federal securities laws, and some commentators see it as the more persuasive justification.[17] Under this interpretation, the principal purpose of mandatory disclosure is to address "agency cost" problems that arise between stock promoters and investors, and between corporate managers and shareholders, by reducing the shareholders' cost of monitoring these agents (in particular, by mandating disclosure of the self-interested use of corporate assets by managers and promoters).[18]

L.Rev. 763 (1995). In essence, this argument is the other side of the coin to Professor Fox's argument that the private costs of disclosure exceed its social costs. See, Fox, supra note 7.

13.   Kitch, supra note 12, at 773.

14.   *Id.* at 770.

15.   Compare George Benston, Required Disclosure and the Stock Market: An Evaluation of the Securities Exchange Act of 1934, 63 Am.Econ.Rev. 132 (Pt. 1) (1973) (concluding that mandatory disclosure system did not produce observable benefits to investors) with Irwin Friend and Randolph Westerfield, Required Disclosure and the Stock Market: Comment, 65 Am.Econ.Rev. 467 (1973) (disagreeing). For an historical assessment of disclosure before and after the passage of the federal securities laws, see Joel Seligman, The Historical Need for a Mandatory Corporate Disclosure System, 9 J.Corp.L. 1 (1983) (collecting evidence of disclosure failures prior to enactment of federal securities laws); see also Joel Seligman, The Transformation of Wall Street: A History of the Securities

and Exchange Commission and Modern Corporate Finance, at 564–65 (1982).

16.   One important recent study has found that the SEC's introduction in the early 1980's of its required "Management Discussion and Analysis of Financial Condition and Results of Operations," which mandated the disclosure of certain forward-looking information, improved the accuracy of share pricing in the U.S. equity markets. See Artyom Durnev et. al., Law, Share Price Accuracy and Economic Performance: The New Evidence (Working Paper 2001).

17.   See Paul Mahoney, Mandatory Disclosure as a Solution to Agency Problems, 62 U.Chi.L.Rev. 1047 (1995).

18.   Agency costs are those costs incurred to control inappropriate behavior in a principal-agent relationship, plus the residual cost of agent opportunism that it is not cost effective to deter or prevent. See Michael Jensen & William Mecking, Theory of the Firm: Managerial Behavior, Agency Costs and Ownership Structure, 3.J.Fin.Econ. 305 (1976).

Proponents of this "agency cost" model argue, however, that it justifies a considerably different disclosure system than that which an "allocative efficiency" model would justify, and they criticize the present-day Securities and Exchange Commission ("SEC") for deviating from the model that they believe makes greater sense.[19]

6. *Economic Growth, Innovation, and Access to Capital.* Not all industrial societies organize their economies around stock markets; indeed, active securities markets may be more the exception than the rule. Germany and Japan represent industrial systems that appear to be more bank-centered than securities market-centered (although each has an active stock market). Yet, there is some evidence that countries with an active stock market experience more rapid economic growth.[20] Even apart from the issue of relative growth rates, a significant qualitative difference is evident in the structure and performance of bank-centered versus market-centered economies: bank-centered systems tend to produce a more centralized system, with greater industrial consolidation and fewer new entrants. In contrast, economies that are organized around securities markets tend to favor new entrants, in particular start-up and venture capital companies that convince the market that a new technological innovation developed by them merits equity capital. Thus, it may not be coincidental that Silicon Valley developed in the United States, not in Germany or Japan. In contrast, in bank-centered systems, there may be pressure for an entrepreneur with a new innovation to merge, or otherwise become affiliated with a larger corporate group as a precondition to bank finance. From this perspective, it is at least a plausible hypothesis that a legal system that facilitates and encourages an active equity securities market may also promote a more decentralized economy and a more rapid pace of technological innovation.

Neither this Chapter nor this Casebook can resolve the foregoing issues, but they are raised here to suggest at the outset the sizable social stakes involved in the design of a securities disclosure system.

SECTION 2.   AN OVERVIEW OF THE FINANCIAL MARKETS

The securities markets are a subset of the broader financial markets that operate both within the United States and internationally. The federal securities laws apply unevenly to these financial markets, sometimes requiring the issuer of the security to enter their mandatory disclosure system, sometimes only prohibiting fraud, and sometimes not applying at all. This contrast is emphasized at the outset for several different reasons:

First, these different markets are increasingly in direct competition; issuers can seek capital in non-securities markets (for example, from commercial banks in direct loans), or they can issue bonds or notes in the U.S. securities

19. See Mahoney, supra note 17, at 1048.

20. For the argument that economies organized around a securities-based capital market are more able to channel capital to emerging firms and to spur economic growth in transitional countries, see Brown, Of Brokers, Banks and the Case for Regulatory Intervention in Russian Securities Markets, 32 Stan. J.Int'l L.Rev. 185 (1996). The recent experience of several Asian countries (most notably Korea, Taiwan, and Singapore) is often cited to support this generalization. Correspondingly, those countries (including some in Eastern Europe) that have experienced difficulties in the transition to capitalism have often had extremely underregulated securities markets, which in some cases have virtually collapsed because of fraud and investor distrust.

markets, or they can seek financing in foreign capital markets. Which markets they choose to enter at any given time will depend on a variety of factors, including (1) the relative cost of capital in the different markets, (2) the time necessary to effect a transaction in a particular market, and (3) the degree of regulatory supervision and legal liability to which issuers subject themselves by entering a particular market.

Second, the line between the securities markets and the other capital markets sometimes becomes uncertain and clearly has shifted over recent years. To some extent, this is the inevitable result of inter-market competition, as each market adapts to competitive pressure by adopting techniques that have proven efficient in other markets.[1] In particular, regulatory conflict has arisen over the status of a host of new financial products known as "derivative instruments"—"swaps," options on other financial instruments, and futures (including particularly futures based on stock market indices). These instruments, which are essentially "side bets," not involving any corporate issuer, are discussed in more detail later in this Chapter, but the relevant point here is that the line between the securities markets and the other financial markets can and has moved.

But why is this line important? Once a financial product is deemed to be a security, three separate and independent legal conclusions typically follow: (1) a mandatory disclosure system becomes applicable to the sale and trading of the instrument (unless the security falls within one of several specified exemptions in the federal securities laws); (2) stiff federal anti-fraud rules apply that are considerably more favorable to the plaintiff than the common law's rules on fraud; and (3) the financial intermediaries who handle transactions in the market for the financial product become subject to close, substantive regulation by the Securities and Exchange Commission ("SEC"). Several chapters will be needed to explain the significance of each of these consequences.

This opening section will attempt to provide an overview that places the securities markets in context by (A) providing a thumbnail sketch of the principal other capital markets; (B) profiling the economic actors—increasingly, institutional investors—who dominate trading in the capital markets; (C) examining the mechanics by which organized trading occurs in these various markets, and (D) surveying the new products now sold in these markets and the process of innovation by which a proliferation of new financial instruments—some securities, some not—have recently entered these markets. The student should understand that this section does not attempt to explain the law of securities regulation (that will come later), but rather focuses on the role of, and relationships among, markets.

A. THE STRUCTURE OF THE FINANCIAL MARKETS: AN OVERVIEW OF THE NON-EQUITY MARKETS

Financial markets perform at least three basic functions: (1) they match lenders and other investors with businesses seeking financing, enabling those

---

1. For example, when a commercial bank today makes a large loan to a corporate borrower, it often turns around and resells participations in all, or virtually all, the loan to other financial institutions (mutual funds, small regional banks and pension funds). As will be seen, this process of distribution by the bank selling the loan participations has elements in common with the traditional underwriting syndication by which underwriters buy and resell debt securities. Although cases have generally held loan participations not to be securities (see infra at pp. 382–384), the line between the loan participation market and the bond market at some point begins to blur.

with surplus funds to earn a favorable return while permitting those unable to finance their operations with internally generated funds to obtain capital; (2) they permit investors to reduce their exposure to risk through various strategies, such as portfolio diversification and hedging (indeed, some markets in what are known as "derivative securities" exist solely to permit investors to minimize specific risks, such as their exposure to interest rate or currency fluctuations); and (3) they provide "liquidity"—an important characteristic that means essentially that investors can anticipate that their decision to trade will not materially change the market price. The term "capital market" is generally used to refer to those markets that deal in longer-term financial instruments (e.g., common and preferred stock, bonds, mortgages, etc.), while the term "money market" describes those markets in which shorter-term debt instruments (typically, having a maturity under one year) are issued and traded.

At the outset of the casebook, it is important to gain some understanding of the diversity of capital markets that now operate in the United States and the differing institutional structure and legal status of each. The remainder of this section will provide a brief overview of the principal financial markets, other than the equity market, that are regulated (at least partially) by the federal securities laws.

1. *The Money Market*. The money market consists of a group of short-term credit market instruments, including negotiable certificates of deposit (CDs), bankers' acceptances, treasury bills, and commercial paper. This market exists because the receipts of businesses, governments and other economic units seldom coincide with their expenditures. Businesses that have short-term surpluses typically hold them in interest-bearing money market instruments, which have low risk. Conversely, businesses that have seasonal cash shortages or that need to finance accounts receivable also typically turn to the money market for short-term credit.[2] The instruments traded in this market usually have a maturity of from one day to one year, are characterized by a high degree of safety, and are commonly issued in units of $1 million or more. Some of the instruments traded in this market are considered securities for purposes of the federal securities laws, but others are not.[3] Corporations typically raise funds in the money market by issuing short-term unsecured promissory notes, called commercial paper. Although commercial paper is normally deemed a security for purposes of the federal securities laws,[4] it is exempt from the "registration requirements" of those laws (meaning that no disclosure document need be filed with the SEC) so long as the maturity of the commercial paper is not greater than 270 days and the proceeds are used for a "current transaction."[5] In recent years, commercial paper has become an increasingly attractive source of financing for corporate borrowers, because typically a creditworthy corporate

---

2. For the standard reference source on the money market, see M. Stigum, The Money Market (3rd ed. 1990); see also T. Cook & T. Rowe, Instruments of the Money Market (6th ed. 1986).

3. See, e.g., Mishkin v. Peat, Marwick, Mitchell & Co., 744 F.Supp. 531 (S.D.N.Y. 1990) (bankers' acceptances and participations therein held not securities); Banco Espanol de Credito v. Security Pacific National Bank, 763 F.Supp. 36 (S.D.N.Y.1991)

(very short-term loan notes held not to be securities).

4. See University Hill Foundation v. Goldman, Sachs & Co., 422 F.Supp. 879 (S.D.N.Y.1976) (describing legal status and marketing procedures in commercial paper market).

5. See § 3(a)(3) of the Securities Act of 1933 (the "1933 Act").

borrower will pay a lower interest rate on commercial paper than commercial banks will charge it on bank loans. The rate on commercial paper is usually a few basis points over the rate on CDs.[6] As a result, the market for commercial paper has doubled over a five year period to almost $400 billion by the end of the 1980s.[7]

Typically, corporate borrowers sell commercial paper through a dealer (Goldman, Sachs and Salomon Brothers, Inc. are the largest of these dealers). For "placing" (or selling a client's commercial paper), a dealer typically charges a commission of between one-tenth to one-eighth of a percentage point at an annual rate; this amounts to around $2.75 to $3.50 per million per day. The process of selling commercial paper is remarkably quick. A seasoned corporate borrower can usually call a dealer in the morning, indicate the amounts and maturities it wishes to sell, and expect the dealer to line up customers and close the transaction that same day. The dealer itself will purchase the paper from the issuer, but then resell quickly to its customers, typically retaining no more than five to ten percent in its inventory. To economize even further on transaction costs, some very substantial users (commercial banks and finance companies) do not use dealers, but directly place their own commercial paper by employing their own sales force.

Because the issuance process is so quick, lenders do not have an opportunity to study financial statements about an issuer; instead, they rely on ratings issued by independent ratings services. These companies (Moody's Investors Services, Inc. and Standard & Poor's Corporation are the best known) charge the issuer for rating its creditworthiness in terms of an established letter grade rating system (Moody's will, for example, rate commercial paper as Prime–1 (P–1), Prime–2 (P–2) or Prime–3 (P–3), or it will deny any rating). These ratings will effectively determine the interest rate on the commercial paper (or deny access to the market if no rating can be earned by the borrower).

Only recently has a secondary market begun to develop for commercial paper. Although an investor who holds commercial paper could usually sell it back to the dealer who placed it with the investor, an inter-dealer trading market has appeared in the last several years, with publicly quoted prices in some cases. Also, in recent years a European counterpart to the commercial paper market has begun to develop (known as the "Euro-paper market").

One other development in the commercial paper market has generalized significance: as banks found that they could not compete with commercial paper in terms of the interest rate charged, they became interested in selling commercial paper for their corporate clients. Although once restricted by federal law from underwriting or dealing in commercial paper, banks won approval from the Federal Reserve Board in the late 1980s to serve as placing agents for their customers.[8] Effectively, this approval meant that they could compete directly with securities dealers in this market.

6. A basis point is one hundredth of one percent. Debt securities tend to be quoted in terms of the number of basis points by which they differ from some agreed upon benchmark (such as the "federal funds" rate on U.S. Treasury securities).

7. See T. Frankel, Securitization: Structured Financing, Financial Asset Pools, and Asset–Backed Securities (1991), at 7.

8. See Securities Industry Ass'n v. Board of Governors of Federal Reserve System, 807 F.2d 1052 (D.C.Cir.1986); see infra at pp. 60 to 66.

2. *The Government Securities Market.* Throughout the world, most national treasuries conduct public auctions at which they sell their notes and bonds. The market in U.S. "government securities" (which includes both securities issued by the U.S. Treasury to finance the national debt and all securities issued by government-sponsored enterprises, such as the Federal National Mortgage Association[9]) represents the world's largest securities market. This market is very different from other major securities markets. First, it is a market for professionals, with relatively little public participation in trading. Treasury securities are sold by the Federal Reserve Bank of New York at regularly scheduled auctions. Generally, anyone can bid at these auctions, and bidders submit offers stating the yield at which they want to purchase securities. The bids are then ranked from the lowest yield to the highest yield required to sell the amount offered at the auction. Those bidders whose bids are accepted pay the price equivalent to the yield they bid.

Secondary trading of treasury securities occurs over-the-counter in investment and commercial banks. Specialized brokers have organized a market in which government bond dealers and some large "buy side" traders trade with each other. These "interdealer brokers" permit their clients to trade on an anonymous basis, which is important in this concentrated a market because dealers do not wish to disclose their trades and trading strategies to their rivals.

Because the government securities market is an extremely concentrated market in which dealers take very large positions, it is potentially more subject to "corners" or "squeezes," which rarely happen in the equity securities market. To "corner" a market means to purchase more than the available supply with the purpose of forcing short sellers (i.e. persons who have sold securities that they do not yet own) to settle with the party who has "cornered" the market on the latter's predictably punitive terms. In 1991, Salomon Brothers Inc. was alleged to have attempted to corner the market in one U.S. Treasury securities auction. Although it escaped criminal prosecution, largely because of its cooperation with the government's investigation, Salomon's chief executive officer resigned and was barred from any further management position in the industry.[10]

As such an episode illustrates, significant contrasts exist between conditions in the government securities market and those in the major stock markets: First, the government securities market has only a limited number of significant actors (although there were some 39 primary dealers in 1991, ten accounted for nearly 90% of all trading). Second, transactions in it can occur at different prices at the same time, because there is no centralized mechanism (such as a stock exchange floor or a computer network linking all traders) through which all buyers and sellers can meet and exchange bids and offers. Third, the principal market makers—the primary dealers—often possess valuable, non-public information about supply and demand imbalances. For example, if a primary dealer knows that its customers intend to buy 80% of the securities being offered in the auction, then it also knows by definition that if it

9. The term "government securities" is defined in Section 3(a)(42) of the Securities Exchange Act of 1934 (the "1934 Act"). "Government securities" are exempt from most provisions of the federal securities laws, other than some anti-fraud rules.

10. See In the Matter of John H. Gutfreund, Securities Exchange Act Rel. No. 34–31554, 1992 SEC LEXIS 2939, 1992 WL 362753 (December 3, 1992).

buys more than 20% for its own account, some of the "shorts" are likely to be "squeezed."

Finally, the government securities market lacks what market experts call "transparency"—namely broad access to real-time pricing information and information about the size of holdings. If, for example, all transactions were visible to all on a single computer screen, it would be far less likely that the market could be manipulated by an intentional "short squeeze." As will be seen shortly, the relative transparency of different capital markets varies considerably, and in the principal stock market, the participant whose role parallels that of the primary dealer—the stock exchange specialist—is not permitted to trade freely for its own account precisely because of the informational advantage it possesses. Proposals for reform of the government securities market have focused on the development of electronic trading and reporting systems that duplicate those now in operation in the equity markets, which will be discussed shortly. In response to the Salomon scandal, the Federal Reserve also announced that it would allow securities dealers who are not primary dealers to submit bids for their clients—a move clearly intended to introduce greater competition into this market.

One last point about the government securities market deserves special emphasis: it is largely beyond the jurisdiction of the Securities and Exchange Commission. Although the Commission has anti-fraud jurisdiction over any sale of government securities, its usual ability to regulate the practices of dealers is expressly limited by statute for this market.[11] Instead, the Government Securities Act of 1986, which established for the first time a regulatory framework for this market, entrusted all rulemaking authority to the Secretary of the Treasury, with the SEC and banking regulators being responsible only for enforcement.[12]

3. *The Municipal Securities Market.* For many years, conditions in the municipal securities market roughly paralleled those in the government securities market—with one important difference: the creditworthiness of local governmental units was often doubtful. Although some SEC anti-fraud rules apply to municipal securities,[13] the Commission lacked authority to require mandatory disclosure with respect to municipal securities or to regulate the conduct of market participants. As a result, while municipal issuers typically prepared an "Official Statement" containing some financial information about themselves, the contents of these documents were unstandardized and uneven. Observers reported that the quality of disclosure in this market and the reliability of the financial information provided about municipal issuers was highly suspect.[14] Investors relied instead on bond ratings supplied by credit

---

11. See Section 15A(f) of the 1934 Act (providing that the National Association of Securities Dealers (or NASD), the principal self-regulatory organization for securities brokers and dealers, lacks jurisdiction with respect to transactions in government securities).

12. The Government Securities Act of 1986 added Section 15C to the 1934 Act, which gave the Treasury Department jurisdiction over such matters as the financial responsibility, record keeping, custody and use of customers' securities by government

securities dealers. See 6 L. Loss and J. Seligman, Securities Regulation (3d ed. 1990) at 3097–3101.

13. Basically, Rule 10b–5 applies to all securities, including municipal securities. See In re Washington Public Power Supply System Securities Litigation, 623 F.Supp. 1466 (W.D.Wash.1985), aff'd, 823 F.2d 1349 (9th Cir.1987).

14. See "Survey Finds Flaws in Financial Data of Cities, Counties," Wall St. J., Oct. 6, 1983 at 38.

rating agencies, whose performance was also subject to much criticism.[15]

In response, Congress in 1975 passed a series of amendments to the Securities Exchange Act of 1934 that established the Municipal Securities Rulemaking Board ("MSRB"). The MSRB is authorized to adopt rules applying to dealers and brokers in municipal securities, but not to regulate the disclosure of municipal issuers, themselves.[16]

This indirect form of regulation allowed Congress to sidestep the politically sensitive issues inherent in potentially curtailing the access of financially strained municipalities to the capital markets. However, the near default of New York City on its bonds in 1974–75 and the later default by the Washington Public Power Supply System revived the debate and refocused concern on the character of the disclosure in this market.[17] On the political level, the problem is that the typical issuer of municipal securities is often quite small (indeed, a decade ago, it was estimated that there were then over 52,000 separate political entities in the United States that had issued municipal securities[18]), and the costs of mandatory disclosure to these diverse issuers might sometimes be high. Equally important, the overall default rate on municipal securities has been well below that on corporate debt.[19]

The debate over the costs and benefits of a mandatory disclosure system in this context seems likely to continue, but intermediate reforms have been adopted. In 1984, the Government Accounting Standards Board ("GASB") was established to promulgate generally accepted accounting principles for municipal issuers.[20] In order to improve disclosure with respect to municipal securities, but constrained in its ability to regulate political entities, the SEC has increasingly focused on underwriters and those who market municipal securities. Initially, pursuant to its authority over brokers and dealers, it adopted Rule 15c2–12 in 1989, which requires underwriters participating in municipal offerings of over $10 million to obtain and review the issuer's disclosure documents and distribute them to investors.[21] Although this obligation was imposed on underwriters, not issuers, it indirectly requires issuers to prepare a mandatory disclosure document. The Commission has also emphasized that underwriters must have a reasonable basis to believe key representations made by the issuers concerning the securities being underwritten.[22] These develop-

---

15. See J. Petersen, The Rating Game: Report of Twentieth Century Task Force on Municipal Bond Ratings (1974).

16. See Section 15B of the 1934 Act; see also Dikeman, Municipal Securities Rulemaking Board: A New Concept of Self–Regulation, 29 Vand.L.Rev. 903 (1976).

17. For recent discussions, see Gellis, Mandatory Disclosure for Municipal Securities: A Reevaluation, 36 Buffalo L.Rev. 15 (1987); Seligman, The Municipal Securities Disclosure Debate, 9 Del.J.Corp.L. 647 (1984).

18. See GAO, Trends and Changes in the Municipal Bond Market as They Relate to Financing State and Local Public Infrastructure (1983) at 2–3.

19. See 3 L. Loss and J. Seligman, Securities Regulation (3rd ed. 1990), at 1163 n. 59.

20. Unlike its counterpart for private issuers, the Financial Accounting Standards Board, the rules, standards and pronouncements of the GASB need only be followed on a voluntary basis. See 3 L. Loss and J. Seligman, supra note 19, at 1171.

21. See Securities Exchange Act Rel. No. 26100 (September 22, 1988) (proposal of rule); Securities Exch. Act Rel. No. 34–26985 (July 10, 1989) (adoption of rule).

22. Securities and Exchange Commission, Staff Report on the Investigation in the Matter of Transactions in Washington Power Supply System Securities (September 22, 1988). For an overview, see Gardner and Doty, The Revolution in Municipal Securities

ments illustrate a familiar pattern in securities regulation: through its enforcement and anti-fraud powers, the SEC can accomplish by the back door what it cannot achieve by the front door—namely, the gradual institutionalization of a mandatory disclosure system within a particular market.

The unresolved issue surrounding the performance of underwriters in municipal securities offerings concerned the standard of care that underwriters had to employ in preparing an offering circular or other disclosure document. This issue came to a head following the bankruptcy of Orange County in California in 1994. Underwriters contended that, although they had an obligation to investigate the securities that they offered, they were immune from suit so long as they complied with the relevant standards followed in their industry. In Securities and Exchange Commission v. Dain Rauscher,[23] however, the Ninth Circuit agreed with the SEC and reversed summary judgment granted for the defendant on this basis, finding that "the standard of care for an underwriter of municipal offerings is one of reasonable prudence, for which the industry standard is one factor to be considered, but is not the determinative factor. . . . "

After an offering is completed, a continuing problem with the municipal securities market is that its issuers are not subject to the same periodic disclosure obligations that public corporations are. Thus, after the issuance of municipal bonds, little continuing information may reach the secondary trading market. To address this problem, the SEC in 1994 adopted rule amendments which prohibit brokers and dealers from (i) purchasing or selling a municipal security unless the issuer agrees to provide certain annual financial information and "event notices" to information repositories, and (ii) recommending the purchase or sale of a municipal security unless they have procedures in place to provide reasonable assurance that they will receive any "event notices" with respect to that security.[24] Again, the same strategy is evident here: placing a regulatory burden on the broker or dealer (who is subject to SEC regulation) to compel a change in behavior by the municipality (who is largely not). In consequence, here as elsewhere, the SEC can accomplish by the back door what it cannot achieve by the front door—namely the gradual adoption of a continuous mandatory disclosure system by municipal issuers.

Probably the most controversial recent SEC action in this field has been the Commission's attempt to restrict practices (known as "pay to play") by which municipal securities underwriters and dealers make political contributions to elected officials and candidates in order to obtain future underwriting business. Such practices obviously invite corruption. In 1994, the Commission approved a rule promulgated by the Municipal Securities Rulemaking Board which restricts political contributions by municipal securities dealers (MSRB Rule G–37). With certain exceptions, MSRB Rule G–37 prohibits dealers from transacting municipal securities business with an issuer within two years after any political contribution to an official of such issuer has been made by the dealer, a professional at the firm, or a dealer-controlled political action committee. A constitutional challenge to the rule was brought by broker-dealer plaintiffs, who asserted that it infringed their First Amendment rights to make

Disclosure Practice, 2 Insights 3 (November 1988).

23.   254 F.3d 852 (9th Cir.2001).

24.   See Securities Exchange Act Rel. No. 34961 (Nov. 17, 1994) (adopting Rule 15c–12). The term "event notice" was broadly used to mean any notice of material events provided by the municipal issuer.

political contributions, but the D.C. Circuit upheld Rule G–37 on the grounds that it was narrowly tailored to advance a compelling governmental interest.[25]

4. *The Corporate Debt Market.* Although seldom the subject of the same publicity or controversy that attends the equity market, the corporate debt market dwarfs the equity market in size. During the 1980s, U.S. business corporations raised $411 billion in the equity markets, but over four times as much ($1.7 trillion) in the bond markets.[26] In 1995, Federal Reserve Board data shows that U.S. corporations issued over $573 billion in bonds, as opposed to only about $100 billion in equity securities.[27] Not only is this a more than a 5 to 1 ratio, but the amount of debt securities thus issued in this one year exceeded the total of all equity securities listed by U.S. corporations during the 1980s. The bond markets thus represent a greater source of capital for corporations than the equity markets. Although basically the same SEC rules and disclosure obligations apply to a corporation publicly issuing debt securities as to one publicly issuing equity securities, nearly half of all debt securities are issued in "private placement" transactions to institutional investors. These transactions are exempt from the SEC's registration requirements (whereas a much smaller percentage of equity issuance by dollar amount occur in private placement or otherwise exempt transactions). The secondary markets for bonds are also quite different from those for equity securities. Although the daily trading volume of bonds is more than double that of common stock, the principal stock exchanges list and trade only a trivial portion of these bonds.[28] Instead, bonds are primarily screen traded in a private and largely unregulated market among dealers.[29] Dealers are linked through computer screen and telephone networks. Although such a market can be very competitive, it again tends to lack relative transparency. The individual customer at most will be aware of the "bid and asked" prices quoted by dealers, but will lack knowledge of recent actual trading transactions. In contrast, the stock market has traditionally reported the actual trading transactions on its tape. In "thin" markets, such as that for high yield (or "junk") bonds, it is not unusual for the same bonds to trade at very different prices with different dealers at the same time.

5. *Derivative Product Markets.* "Derivatives" are contractual instruments that derive their value from the values of underlying instruments or commodities upon which they are based. Derivative contracts include forward contracts, futures, options, and swaps, but only futures and options trade on organized exchanges, and only options normally constitute securities. Historically, the

25. See Blount v. SEC, 61 F.3d 938 (D.C.Cir.1995).

26. See Kamen, Corporate Responsibilities to Bondholders in Institutional Investing: The Challenges and Responsibilities of the 21st Century, (A. Sametz ed. 1991) at 451. This disparity is even greater once one learns that U.S. corporations bought back more of their own stocks during the 1980s than they sold, resulting in a net equity drain of $449 billion for the decade. Id. at 452.

27. See Federal Reserve Bulletin, Vol. 83, No. 6 at Table 1, 46, p. A31 (June 1997).

28. In 1990, the New York Stock Exchange's bond trading amounted to only 0.2% of all bond trading. See Colloton, Bondholder

Communications—The Missing Link in High Yield Debt (1990) at 18. Little increase has occurred since then. The NYSE Fact Book for 2000 indicates that NYSE bond volume in 1999 was only $3.22 billion. Id. at 83.

29. Although the actual market is informal and unregulated in its structure, the brokers who participate in this market are subject to regulation by the National Association of Securities Dealers ("NASD"), which for example regulates the size of commissions. In general, however, there is far less transparency in the reporting of prices and commissions in this market than in the equity market.

exchanges or boards of trade that trade derivative products originated as market centers in which agricultural commodities were traded for future delivery. For example, a buyer might agree to pay a fixed price for a specified quantity of wheat that the seller would deliver in the future. This allowed the seller (typically, a farmer) to lock in a favorable price in advance and also permitted the buyer (perhaps, a cereal manufacturer) to similarly protect its cost of supply from often volatile market changes.

In contrast to the debt or equity markets, the market for "derivative instruments" does not provide capital for issuers; indeed, futures contracts and options contracts do not represent corporate ownership claims and do not necessarily involve the corporation as a contracting or issuing party. Rather, derivative instruments involve side bets on interest rates, currency rates, stock index levels, commodities prices, or similar market prices. When corporations engage in such side bets, they do so not to raise money, but to protect themselves against the risks of adverse changes in these interest rates, currency values, or price levels. Inherently, the transactions in this market are always zero sum; that is, one side's gains equal the other side's losses.

Although the derivative markets began and still trade future contracts on agricultural commodities, this is now a subsidiary activity, because the need to hedge other risks, have created much larger markets. Use of the following types of derivative instruments grew almost exponentially over the last twenty years:

Traded Options. An option gives the buyer the right (but not the obligation) to buy or sell shares of stock (or other financial assets) in the future at a fixed price (known as the "strike price") that is agreed upon today. Although corporations can issue options on their securities, the options traded on the specialized options exchanges are not issued by the corporations that have issued the underlying securities to which the options relate. Therefore, in order to facilitate secondary trading in options, the terms of traded options needed to be standardized.

To achieve standardization, the securities options exchanges created the Options Clearing Corporation ("OCC"), which is jointly owned by them. The OCC is the issuer of all options, and thus it is interposed between buyers and sellers so that there is no contractual relationship between them. This eliminates any risk to the individual buyer or seller that its counter-party might default. An OCC call option conveys the right to buy, and a put option conveys the right to sell, a specified quantity of the underlying security within a fixed period at a specified price. It should be understood that a call option can be bought or sold without any person writing an offsetting put option. Instead, the OCC is the buyer to every seller and the seller to every buyer of traded options. To close out a position, the buyer of an option simply makes an offsetting sale of an identical option, and the seller (or "writer" in the parlance) simply makes an offsetting purchase of an identical option.

An organized secondary market in options was inaugurated by the Chicago Board Options Exchange (CBOE) in 1973. Currently, the CBOE and the American Stock Exchange dominate trading in stock options. Although the SEC acted in 1989 to encourage multiple trading and competition among exchanges in options,[30] exchanges that originate an option contract have tended to

---

30. In May, 1989, the SEC adopted Rule 19c–5 under the 1934 Act, which precludes any exchange from adopting a rule or practice forbidding the multiple listing of stock options. See Securities Exch. Act Rel. No. 34–26870. Options are traded on five

dominate the trading in that option. Only recently has competition among exchanges in the same option contract become more common.

Besides trading options in a particular stock, investors can also acquire an option on a stock index. Such an option may be either on a broad-based index that is a proxy for the market as a whole or on a narrower industry index. The best known and most heavily traded stock index option has been the option on the Standard & Poor's (S&P) 100, which is based on the value of the one hundred stocks in that index and trades on the CBOE.

Futures. A futures contract is simply a contract to buy or sell a financial asset or commodity at a fixed price on a future date. Although futures markets have existed for well over a century to trade agricultural products and other commodities, they expanded their scope in the 1970s to trade contracts on financial assets (such as currencies or bonds). Then, in the 1980s, they began to trade futures on stock market indices (which are simply standardized stock market portfolios). The most popular stock index future is the Standard & Poor's 500 index, which is a contract to buy or sell the value of the S&P 500 index multiplied times $500;[31] this contract trades on the Chicago Mercantile Exchange (CME) and alone accounts for over three-quarters of all trading in stock index futures.[32]

Unlike stock index options, stock index futures create an obligation (not a mere option) to deliver or receive the cash equivalent to a portfolio of stock. Although stock index options expose holders only to the possible loss of the premium they paid for their call or put options, stock index futures involve unlimited risk. Thus, individual investors tend to trade in options (where the risk and return are less), while institutional investors tend to trade futures contracts.[33] Unlike other commodities futures, stock index futures are not settled by physical delivery, but by cash settlement. Thus, the parties quite simply are making a cash bet on the future value of the index on the expiration date.

The rise of stock index trading—both futures and options—is largely explained by its lower transaction costs; it is estimated that index trading transaction costs are only between 5 and 10 percent of the costs of trading in securities.[34] Put simply, one can place a single bet on an index with a dealer in either the futures or options market much more easily than one can assemble a

option exchanges; the American Stock Exchange, the Pacific Stock Exchange, the Philadelphia Stock Exchange, the Chicago Board Options Exchange (CBOE), and the New York Stock Exchange. For an overview, see Seligman, The Structure of the Options Markets, 10 J.Corp.L. 141 (1984); T. Russo, Regulation of the Commodities Future and Options Market (1986 ed.).

31. For example, if the S&P 500's value was 250, the contract would be worth $125,000 (250 × $500). If on the expiration date of the contract the S&P 500 index was 252, the buyer would receive $1,000 (2 points times $500) while if the value fell to 248, the seller would receive $1,000.

32. See 5 L. Loss & J. Seligman, supra note 19, at 2636.

33. This tendency is encouraged by the options market using an index based on 100 stocks, rather than 500. As a result, a stock index option usually costs one fifth of a futures contract. For institutions, the larger size of the contract is desirable because it reduces the number of trades necessary to acquire or liquidate a desired position. Also, there is believed to be greater liquidity in the futures market and thus large trades by an institution will have less of a price impact. See 5 L. Loss & J. Seligman, supra note 19, at 2638–39.

34. See N. Katzenbach, An Overview of Program Trading and Its Impact on Current Market Practices, 8 (NYSE Report 1987).

500–stock portfolio on the New York Stock Exchange. Traders on the futures exchange are also able to receive more credit (or "margin") to finance their transactions than can investors on stock exchanges.[35]

The institutional structure of stock index trading is different from that of securities trading in the stock markets in a variety of respects. All trading on futures exchanges is by an "open outcry" system, as opposed to the auction procedure on a stock exchange. That is, several hundred dealers make and accept offers with each other, without funneling these offers through any central trading post. In contrast, on a stock exchange, the specialist for a particular security serves as, in effect, an auctioneer who must expose each buy or sell offer to the market. Writing in the wake of the 1987 stock market "break," the Presidential Task Force on Market Mechanisms (the "Brady Commission") suggested that the "open outcry system may have the ironic effect of not necessarily exposing a customer bid to all because of the constant tumult and noise in the trading pit."[36] Defenders of the futures exchanges argue in reply that the large number of floor traders in their market gives it greater liquidity than is possessed by either the unitary specialist system of a stock exchange or the multiple dealers in the over-the-counter stock market.

One structural difference between the futures and stock exchanges has particular implications for their relative volatility. On stock exchanges, the specialist is under a legal obligation to maintain a "fair and orderly market" by buying or selling against the direction of the market when there is an order imbalance.[37] No similar person or obligation to engage in stabilizing transactions exists on the futures exchanges. Also, short selling (i.e., the sale of borrowed stock) is restricted on stock exchanges when it would continue a downward price movement,[38] but no corresponding restriction exists on the futures exchanges. Hence, not only are futures exchanges apt to exhibit greater volatility, but the trading of stock indices on futures exchanges may contribute to increased volatility on the stock exchanges as well, because arbitrageurs will logically seek to exploit any difference between the index price on the futures exchange and the individual prices of the component stocks in the index of the New York Stock Exchange.[39] Interestingly, changes in stock index futures

---

35. The "margin rules" are administered by the Federal Reserve under § 7 of the 1934 Act, and restrict borrowing to finance the purchase of securities (but they do not apply to futures). At present, an investor can purchase a futures contract on 25% downpayment (11% if the investor is considered a "speculator" rather than a hedger), but to purchase securities most investors are legally required to make a 50% downpayment (or post similar collateral). See Salwen and McMurray, Futures Shock: Tight Rein if SEC Reigns, Wall St. J., May 17, 1990 at C1; see also, 5 L. Loss & J. Seligman, supra note 19, at 2639.

36. See Report of the Presidential Task Force on Market Mechanisms, VI–20 (1988).

37. Rule 11b–1 under the 1934 Act requires a specialist to "engage in a course of dealings for his own account to assist in the maintenance, so far as practicable, of a fair

and orderly market." Failure to do so can result in the loss of the position as specialist for that security.

38. See Rule 10a–1 ("Short Sales") under the 1934 Act.

39. Index arbitrage is explained later in this Chapter at pp. 54 to 58. Former SEC Chairman David Ruder suggested in Congressional testimony that "the existence of the futures markets, with their relatively low transaction costs and margin requirements, may encourage additional trading in the equity market, with a resultant increase in intraday volatility." See "Black Monday," The Stock Market Crash of October 19, 1987, Hearings Before Senate Comm. on Banking, Hous., & Urban Affairs, 100th Cong., 2d Sess. 515, 516 (1988).

prices have generally preceded corresponding changes on the New York Stock Exchange, suggesting that the stock index markets have become the principal market for "price discovery"—that is, the market in which investor opinions about at least the general state of the economy and the appropriate level of share prices are first registered.[40]

One last difference between stocks and futures involves their regulation: equity securities (including options) are regulated by the Securities and Exchange Commission, while futures (including futures on stock indices) are regulated by the Commodity Futures Trading Commission ("CFTC").[41] As investment banking firms have developed new "hybrid" instruments that defy easy categorization as either futures contracts or equity securities, a regulatory conflict has developed, which will be examined later in this Chapter.

Swaps. This newest and fastest growing instrument requires a transactional explanation. Suppose that you are a U.S. corporation that has borrowed $100,000,000 under a ten year loan at a floating interest rate. Alternatively, suppose the loan must be repaid at maturity in a foreign currency. In either case, you are exposed to a significant risk (if interest rates rise or the value of the dollar falls). You can, however, fix your total liability by agreeing to a "swap" transaction with a large financial institution (typically, a commercial bank). You would agree to pay interest at a fixed rate (say, a small fraction above the current floating rate) to the bank, and it would agree to pay you interest at the floating rate (whatever it was from time to time). Thus, if interest rates rise, you "win"; if they fall, the bank wins. But basically, you pass the risk of rate fluctuations onto a better risk-bearer for a fee.[42] A "currency swap" is similar: you agree to pay the risk-bearing party in dollars and it agrees to pay you the principal and interest on the loan in the foreign currency. Of course, you could also protect your position by buying options on interest rates or foreign currency; but the transaction costs of buying a succession of short-term options for the life of the loan will be higher.

The "swaps market" thus stands as a leading example of a wholly new type of financial contracting that has developed within the two decades. The rate of innovation in the design of new derivative products seems to be increasing. The new products of the 80s were basically financial futures: stock indexes, currency hedging devices, etc. In the 90s, a new stage in the evolution of derivative instruments appears to be dawning as the futures exchanges in particular began to experiment with trading property rights (including possibly environmental allowances to emit sulfur dioxide, insurance futures to allow corporations to hedge health care costs, and energy and electricity contracts). Many of

---

40. See Stoll & Whaley, Stock Index Futures and Options: Economic Impact and Policy Issues (Jan. 1988) at 21.

41. The Commodities Exchange Act (7 U.S.C. § 1–26 (1988)) gives the CFTC exclusive jurisdiction over commodity futures contracts. See generally, P. Johnson & T. Hazen, Commodities Regulation (2d ed. 1989); J. Markham, The History of Commodities Futures Trading and its Regulation (1987); GAO, Securities and Futures: How the Markets Developed and How They Are Regulated (1986). For the most recent and detailed comparison of the differing rules of the SEC and

CFTC, see Appendix SEC–CFTC Comparison in Symposium—New Financial Products, The Modern Process of Financial Innovation, and The Law, 69 Tex.L.Rev. 1273, 1501–1538 (1991).

42. For an excellent overview of "swaps" and their economic and regulatory context, see Hu, Swaps, The Modern Process of Financial Innovation and the Vulnerability of a Regulatory Paradigm, 138 U.Pa.L.Rev. 333 (1989). Although new, the size of the swaps market dwarfs many other financial markets.

these products will and do fall, but each year some innovations survive and become established. Recent legislation now makes possible the trading of futures on a single stock. Thus, investors will soon be able to choose between buying an option on shares of IBM or a futures contract on a similar number of shares.[43]

The appearance of swaps, single stock futures, and other hybrid instruments aggravated the definitional issue of where the line falls between securities and commodities. In the early 1980's, the two then Chairman of the SEC and the CFTC negotiated a compromise (known as the Shad–Johnson Accord) which defined their respective jurisdictions (and prohibited futures on individual securities and narrow indexes). Although Congress adopted their compromise, ambiguous hybrid instruments continue to be developed by a creative industry. The SEC and the CFTC recurrently sparred over these definitional issues, with the SEC arguing that ambiguous instruments were securities and the CFTC claiming that they were instead within its jurisdiction. Still another possibility was that ambiguous instruments were subject to neither agency's jurisdiction. Indeed, in one important 1996 case, a swap transaction between Bankers Trust and The Proctor & Gamble Company was found to fall outside the coverage of both federal and state securities laws and to be exempt by rule from the Commodity Exchange Act.[44] Still, uncertainty remained, because both the SEC and CFTC believed their statutes at least sometimes applied to swaps. To give greater legal uncertainty to transactions that totalled well over several trillion dollars (in notional amounts) and that might have been invalid if swaps were deemed to constitute either securities or futures, the President's Working Group (a consortium of all federal agencies concerned with financial markets) recommended in 1999 that over-the-counter "financial" swaps should be statutorily removed from the jurisdiction of both the SEC ad the CFTC. Its rationale was that financial derivatives are not subject to manipulation in the same way as are derivatives relating to physical commodities, because only the latter are in finite supply and thus only they can be "cornered" or "squeezed." In other words, one can corner either the spot market or the derivatives market for wheat or silver, but not the market for interest rate swaps. Congress obliged by passing the Commodities Futures Modernization Act of 2000 ("CFMA"), but it went further than the President's Working Group had requested by also largely exempting swap contracts on energy and metals. This broad exemption produced feverish trading in these markets in 2000 and 2001, led by EnronOnline, the derivatives trading affiliate of Enron. Currently, investigations are underway into whether the energy market was manipulated during this period, and

---

43. The Commodities Futures Modernization Act of 2000 ("CFMA") eliminated the former prohibition against futures on individual stocks and narrow indexes. This prohibition was based on the premise that insider trading and market manipulation would be easier to effect on the futures exchanges than on the securities exchanges, in part because of the lesser capacity of the CFTC to enforce the prohibition against insider trading. The CFMA requires the SEC and the CFTC to jointly cooperate to enforce the insider trading laws against both securities, options, and futures on securities.

44. See The Procter & Gamble Company v. Bankers Trust Company, 925 F.Supp. 1270 (S.D.Ohio 1996). For a provocative overview of the issues in swaps, (and a critique of the *Procter & Gamble* decision), see Harris, The CFTC and Derivative Products: Purposeful Ambiguity and Jurisdictional Reach, 71 Chicago–Kent Law Review 1117 (1996); Olander & Spell, Interest Rate Swaps: Status Under Federal Tax and Securities Laws, 45 Md. L.Rev. 21 (1986).

Congress is considering whether to cut back on its near complete deregulation of the over-the-counter swaps market.

Still, it is today clear (and unlikely to change) that swaps are not to be considered securities or futures.[45] Non-financial swaps may, however, be again subjected to the antifraud authority of the CFTC.

One other important change was made by the CFMA. It authorizes trading on the futures exchanges in futures on individual securities (for example, a future on General Motor's shares). In part, this authority was a response to competitive developments at foreign exchanges that had begun to trade single-stock futures. The futures industry both feared losing volume to foreign exchanges and resented legislative limitations on its ability to compete with securities products. The SEC had resisted the trading of single stock futures, or futures on narrow stock indexes, fearing the possibility of insider trading abuses. The CFMA responded by giving the SEC concurrent authority to enforce its insider trading laws in such cases.

SECTION 3.   THE EQUITY MARKETS

It is conventional to distinguish the primary market (i.e., issuer transactions in which shares are sold to investors) from the secondary market (trading transactions between investors). The latter secondary market dwarfs the primary market. For example, during 1995, the value of equities traded in public secondary markets came to $5.5 trillion, while the value of the common stock sold in issuer transactions during the same year was $155 billion—a more than thirty to one ratio.[1]

Of course, there must first be issuances in the primary market before a secondary market can arise. Interestingly, the reverse is also generally true: the promise of a secondary market is needed to facilitate primary issuances. As a practical matter, before an issuer can sell its shares to a broad spectrum of the public, it will usually need to be able to assure its prospective investors that some secondary market will provide them with liquidity. When no such secondary market exists (such as in the case of a small start-up company or a family firm), the corporate issuer will usually find it easier to make instead a "private placement" of its securities to a small, select group of sophisticated investors (which group will largely consist of institutional investors). Several exemptions in the Securities Act of 1933 (the "1933 Act") permit such sales to be made without the same disclosure obligations attaching as apply to a "public offering", but generally they also require that the shares so sold be issued only to sophisticated investors and not resold for a defined period to public investors.[2]

A.   THE VENTURE CAPITAL MARKET

As a generalization, start-up companies that have not yet successfully marketed a product or earned significant revenues rarely attempt to enter the

45. Section 2A of the Securities Act of 1933 and Section 3A of the Securities Exchange Act of 1934 both now exempt swaps from the definition of "security."

1. See Report of the Advisory Committee on the Capital Formation and Regulatory Processes. Appendix A at 45–46 (SEC 1996).

2. The principal exemption is Section 4(2) of the 1933 Act. Another motivation for use of this exemption is to avoid the cost, delay and additional legal liability attendant to public offerings under the 1933 Act. The topic of "private placements" is covered in Chapters 5 and 6.

public equity market with an initial public offering ("IPO"). This is less because of legal restrictions, than because of the difficulties in valuing such an infant company that is still at the "concept" stage. At this stage, its product line will have uncertain value, and its management is untested. Instead, such companies in the United States typically receive their start-up capital from venture capital firms in private placements. These firms both have great sophistication in particular high-tech industries and partners who can accept high risk. Also, unlike the more passive investors in public offerings, venture capitalists buy large blocks of stock and negotiate for certain control rights (such as representation on the board of directors and the right to veto certain transactions—for example, they often seek to restrict high executive compensation at this early stage). But such investors are unlikely to acquire absolute majority control, and they tend to invest in the company directly, rather than buying the shares of the actual founders. Their goal is to profit alongside the entrepreneurs in an initial public offering, not to acquire the firm at this unproven stage from the founders.

Typically, venture capitalists buy convertible preferred stock in the early stage company. Later, if the company succeeds, they can convert this senior security into common stock, but if the firm fails or barely becomes profitable, they will receive a priority over the firm's founders for the limited proceeds available for distribution. To a degree, this "two way" play inherent in convertible securities reduces the severity of the valuation problem in start-up companies.[3]

The American venture capital industry originated after World War II and was initially led by firms organized by the Rockefeller and Whitney families. Typically, securities were marketed to wealthy individuals (known popularly as "angel investors"). Over time, large corporations (such as Intel) have come to make substantial, but non-controlling, investments in start-up firms, and these "strategic investors" are a second major source of venture capital. During the 1990's, however, the dynamic growth in this field was largely fueled by the appearance of funds—both mutual funds and unregulated partnerships known as "hedge funds"—that invested on a portfolio basis. That is, a venture capital firm might raise $100 to $200 million by selling partnership interests in a specific partnership (say, "Venture Investments I") that would seek to invest these funds in projects that the general partners would thereafter find. Investors were thus buying into a to-be-determined portfolio, not specific companies. By one estimate, the equity capital in such funds grew from $5 billion in 1990 to over $60 billion in 1999, and the number of such firms grew over the same period from 100 to over 500.[4]

These partnerships are typically formed for a limited period, with the limited partners having the right to withdraw their capital at the end of this period. Hence, these firms both want their investments to proceed quickly to the initial public offering (or "IPO" stage), and they do not typically hold their investments long after the IPO. Instead, venture capital money tends to be recycled into new venture capital investments (except that the less successful venture capital firms fold, as the limited partners decide to reinvest with a

---

3. There are also tax advantages that lead venture capitalists to prefer acquiring convertible preferred instead of common stock at this stage.

4. See John McIlwraith, The Outlook for the Private Equity Market, 51 Case Western Res. L. Rev. 423, 426 (2001); Travis Bradford and Roy Smith, Private Equity Sources and Uses, 10 J. Applied Corp. Fin. 89 (1997).

more successful firm).[5] While these investors invest on a portfolio basis (and may be satisfied if only a minority of their investments make it to the IPO stage), their expectation is that their investments will typically succeed or fail within a relatively brief two to five year period between the date of their investment and the hoped-for IPO. Ultimately, the attractiveness of such investments depends heavily on the strength of the often volatile IPO market. Entry into the public markets is sought for a variety of reasons, including that it will (1) give the issuer greater access to equity capital (and thereby reduce its dependence on debt financing); (2) permit its own founders diversify their investments; (3) enable the venture capital funds to demonstrate their success and then recycle their funds into the next generation of investments; and (4) place a market value on the firm (thus enabling it to use its own shares as a currency for acquisitions).

Firms at the venture capital stage almost invariably share one common characteristic: venture capitalists make their investments in them through convertible preferred stock.[6] Why? Multiple explanations exist: some stress that convertible securities allocate control depending on the portfolio company's success;[7] others see such securities as well suited to align the incentives of entrepreneurs and venture capital investors;[8] and still others stress practical tax advantages.[9] Once the company is ready to enter the public markets via an initial public offering, however, the preferred stock will be converted, and the capital structure of the firm will change dramatically.

B. THE PUBLIC EQUITY MARKETS: AUCTION MARKETS VERSUS DEALER MARKETS

There are two basic kinds of secondary markets for equity securities: (1) the exchange markets; and (2) the dealer markets. The first are "auction" markets in which a "specialist" matches incoming buy and sell orders and intervenes itself only as a buyer or seller of last resort; in contrast, in dealer markets, dealers compete for customers' buy and sell orders and, until recently, every transaction was between a public customer and a dealer (without public buy orders crossing with public sell orders, as they do in auction markets). Yet, while these two different systems operate in very different ways, they are increasingly engaged in head-to-head competition for listings.

As of 1900, there were over one hundred stock exchanges operating in the United States. As information technology improved in the late 19th Century (the most notable innovations being the stock ticker and the telephone), this number began to decline, as markets began to consolidate or close, because high cost informational barriers no longer sheltered them from competition. Today, there are only two major market centers in the United States (the New York Stock Exchange and Nasdaq) plus a handful of smaller exchanges that

5. See Ronald Gilson and Bernard Black, Does Venture Capital Require an Active Stock Market?, 12 J. Applied Corp. Fin. 35 (1999).

6. See George Triantis, Financial Contract Design in the World of Venture Capital, 68 U. Chi. L. Rev. 305 (2001).

7. Erik Berglof, A Control Theory of Venture Capital Finance, 10 J. L. Econ. & Org. 247 (1994).

8. Richard Green, Investment Incentives, Debt, and Warrants, 13 J. Fin. Econ. 115 (1984); William Sahlman, The Structure and Governance of Venture–Capital Organizations, 27 J. Fin. Econ. 473 (1990).

9. Ronald Gilson and David Schizer, Understanding Venture Capital Structure: A Tax Explanation for Preferred Stock (forthcoming in Harvard Law Review 2002).

occupy specialized niches. From a regulatory point of view, the consolidation of exchanges raises an obvious problem: if there is only one dominant exchange for a particular security, monopolistic pricing or other undesirable consequences may result because of the lack of competition. On the other hand, when there are multiple markets trading the same security, there is a danger of market fragmentation. That is, the same stock might trade at different prices in different markets at the same time, because of supply and demand imbalances in each market.

In 1975, in an attempt to achieve both price competition and an integrated market, Congress enacted the 1975 Securities Acts Amendments "to facilitate the establishment of a national market system of securities."[10] A debate has persisted for some time over whether the SEC has been successful in implementing the Congressional vision of a "national market system." Some have applauded its efforts;[11] others criticized it for being too timid,[12] and still others have argued that the fundamental idea of a national market system was flawed and unrealistic.[13] Meanwhile, the technological landscape has changed dramatically with the appearance of new financial institutions, known as Alternative Trading Systems ("ATSs"), which constitute at least partial substitutes for exchanges. This Chapter principally will seek to explain the different institutional mechanisms that are now in active competition.

The following chart provides a useful snapshot of the U.S. equity markets:[14]

U.S. Equity Markets Share and Dollar Volumes
(Based on 1998 data)

	Share Volume	Dollar Volume
Nasdaq	50.3%	39.7%
New York Stock Exchange ("NYSE")	40.9%	51.1%
Third Market (Nasdaq Market–Makers Trading in Exchange–Listed Securities)	4.1%	4.9%
American Stock Exchange	1.9%	1.2%
Regional Stock Exchanges: Boston, Chicago, Cincinnati, Philadelphia and Archipelago (formerly, the Pacific Coast)	2.8%	3.1%
	100%	100%

As of December 31, 2000, Nasdaq listed 4721 issues with a market value of $3.6 trillion, and the NYSE listed 2,862 issues with a market value of $12.3

---

10. See Securities Exch. Act § 11A(a)(2).

11. See Seligman, The Future of the National Market System, 10 J.Corp.L. 79 (1984).

12. See Macey & Haddock, Shirking at the SEC: The Failure of the National Market System, 1985 U.Ill.L.Rev. 315.

13. Poser, Restructuring the Stock Markets: A Critical Look at the SEC's National Market System, 56 N.Y.U.L.Rev. 883 (1981).

14. This table is derived from data set forth in The 1998 Nasdaq Stock Market Fact Book & Company Directory.

trillion.[15] Thus, while Nasdaq has nearly twice the number of stocks listed, the NYSE remains the preferred venue of most major U.S. corporations (and is increasingly becoming an attractive market for foreign corporations as well, as foreign listings now account for 15% of the NYSE's total listed issuers).

Nonetheless, Nasdaq, which was only founded in 1971, has made significant competitive strides towards catching up with the NYSE, as the next table indicates:

Yearly Share Volume (in billions)

Year	Nasdaq	NYSE	Amex
1991	41	45	3
1992	48	51	4
1993	67	67	5
1994	74	73	5
1995	101	87	5
1996	138	105	6
1997	164	133	6
1998	202	170	7
1999	273	204	8
2000	443	262	13

The foregoing chart's focus on trading volume is misleading in one respect, because the NYSE and Nasdaq operate based on very different trading systems, which count transactions differently.[16] Nasdaq is not a physical market in the sense of having an actual location where traders meet. Rather, it is an electronic system for screen trading of securities by telephone and computer, which the National Association of Securities Dealers (NASD) inaugurated in 1971. Today, Nasdaq lists many more companies than the NYSE, although the typical company listed on Nasdaq has a much smaller capitalization and is usually a younger company as well. Thus, the NYSE has a larger dollar volume of trading and remains the market of price discovery for the largest and most important U.S. corporations. No other U.S. competitor has been able to attract significant trading volume in shares of companies listed on the NYSE away from the NYSE.[17] However, as later discussed, a new form of competitor, known as the electronic communications network (or "ECN"), has begun to account for a substantial share of the trading in Nasdaq stocks and may come to do the same in NYSE-listed stocks.

Although the NYSE and Nasdaq are clearly in active competition today, it is not the type of competition that Congress envisioned in 1975 when it passed comprehensive legislation to implement a National Market System. Congress

15. See Marshall E. Blume, The Structure of U.S. Equity Markets (Wharton Working Paper, January 2002).

16. On Nasdaq, most transfers of shares of stock from seller to buyer will consist of two transactions: (1) a sale by the seller to a Nasdaq dealer, and (2) a sale by the Nasdaq dealer to the ultimate buyer. (In contrast, on the NYSE, the typical transactions will be between public to trade at the price). Hence, Nasdaq's system of execution tends to count one transaction as two, and thus the comparison between the Nasdaq's

and the NYSE's share volume can overstate Nasdaq's relative size. The NYSE also has a considerably larger dollar volume because of the typically higher share price of shares listed on it.

17. In 2000, the NYSE captured 82.88% of the consolidated tape volume of NYSE-listed stocks, with the five regional exchanges capturing 8.82% and Third Market traders on Nasdaq gaining 8.30%. See Blume, supra note 15.

anticipated that rival markets would compete to offer superior price quotations in the same stocks to investors, but this has happened to only a very limited degree. Although some Nasdaq dealers do quote prices on NYSE-listed stocks (and they are known as the "Third Market"), as do the Regional Exchanges, they account for only a modest proportion of trading in NYSE-listed securities (roughly 17%).[18] Instead, the NYSE and Nasdaq compete for listings. Companies list on either Nasdaq or the NYSE, but not both (similarly, no companies are listed on both the American Stock Exchange (Amex) and the NYSE). This competition is primarily at the margin between companies with large and small capitalizations. That is, although some very large companies remain listed on Nasdaq (e.g., Microsoft, Intel and Apple Computer), they are primarily computer or high technology stocks that have an affinity with Nasdaq's highly computerized operations. In the past, as a company grew larger, it would usually move its listing from Nasdaq to the NYSE, once it satisfied the higher eligibility standards of the latter. For example, in 1996, some 655 companies made initial public offerings on Nasdaq,[19] and 87% of all newly public companies listed on Nasdaq.[20] Nasdaq is thus the nursery of public corporations (as the Amex once was to a lesser degree). Also, in 1996, however, 96 Nasdaq companies (a record number) defected to the NYSE (as did 22 companies listed on the AMEX.)[21] Historically, this competition for listings worked in one direction only, with Nasdaq and AMEX firms moving up to the NYSE, but none moving in the opposite direction. One reason for this pattern was a former NYSE rule (Rule 500) that required a high supermajority vote of shareholders before a firm could delist from the NYSE. After much criticism of this rule (and some resistance on the part of high tech firms to listing on the NYSE if they could not later reverse this decision), the NYSE announced in 1997 that it would abandon the supermajority vote requirement. In the future, companies may begin to move in both directions.

The competition between Nasdaq and the NYSE is also a contest between different types of markets. The NYSE, as with the other exchanges, is an auction market, while Nasdaq is a dealer market. In an auction market, customers' buy and sell orders can (and often do) cross with each other, with the specialist participating only as a buyer or seller of last resort. When multiple buyers or multiple sellers seek to trade with a "market" order (i.e., an order to buy or sell at the prevailing market price), the specialist will conduct an auction and award the transaction to the highest buyer or the lowest seller (as the case may be). In a dealer market, the investor instead normally buys or sells in a transaction with a dealer, who quotes a "bid/asked" spread (for example, a "bid" or buy price of $9.90 at which it will buy shares up to a specified volume, and an "asked" price of $10 at which it will sell—thus making for a 10¢ spread, which spread is actually unrealistically large today). Different dealers quote different spreads, and the Nasdaq computer will display all these quotations. The highest buy price and the lowest sale price constitute the "national best bid or offer" (or "NBBO"). When a brokerage firm receives an order from a customer to buy (or sell) a Nasdaq security, it is under a legal

18. See supra note 17 for the breakdown.

19. 1998 Nasdaq Stock Market Fact Book & Company Directory at 5.

20. Id. at 1. Some 117 initial public offerings in 1996, were large enough that they listed directly on the NYSE. See Suzanne Wooley, The Booming Big Board, Business Week, August 4, 1997, at 58.

21. See Wooley, supra note 20.

obligation as the customer's agent to make a reasonable effort to find the best available price in the market.[22] To satisfy this duty, the broker checks its Nasdaq computer terminal to determine the best offer (or bid) price and then calls that market maker on the telephone to execute the transaction. Usually different dealers quote the "inside" bid price from those that quote the "inside" asked prices (because one dealer may have a greater interest in buying and the other in selling).

The competition between the NYSE and Nasdaq has generated a long-standing argument about which market system works better for customers. Proponents of dealer markets argue that competition between many dealers making a market in the same stock will produce narrower spreads between the bid and asked quotations and hence superior prices. Proponents of auction markets argue that when customer orders meet customer orders, the public customer benefits because the customer's order can be executed inside the bid/asked spread. That is, the specialist must by law stand aside and allow the public orders to cross, except when there is no other counterparty. In effect, the specialist performs a public utility-like role, providing liquidity when others are unwilling to buy or sell, but otherwise not trading and instead serving as an auctioneer seeking to establish the price at which supply and demand equilibrate. An important difference between stock exchanges and over-the-counter dealer markets is that exchanges provide a centralized forum for trading where all customers' buy and sell orders meet and the highest public buy order is matched against the lowest public sell order.[23]

Whatever the theoretical merits of this debate over auction versus dealer markets, it has recently been it was overshadowed by a major development. First, a scandal that broke in 1994 when evidence surfaced that Nasdaq dealers were collusively maintaining artificially wide bid/asked spreads on Nasdaq stocks. Specifically, two finance professors published an academic study that concluded that Nasdaq market-makers were purposefully avoiding odd-eighth quotes (that is, they would only quote prices in quarter point intervals) in order to widen the spread.[24] Tape recordings subpoenaed by the SEC and the Department of Justice suggested that such a pricing convention had developed and that broker dealers who violated it were subject to threats and intimidation. In 1996, the SEC censured the NASD[25] and forced a formal reorganization under which the latter's regulatory functions were placed in a separate subsidiary, NASD Regulation, Inc., in order to maintain their independence.

This episode led the SEC to try to develop a new source of competition to narrow the bid/asked spread. Recognizing that institutional and public custom-

---

22. This is known as the "duty of best execution." It is discussed later in Chapter 11 and in Securities Exch. Act Rel. Nos. 37619A (September 6, 1996) and 38246 (February 5, 1997).

23. See Norman S. Poser, Restructuring the Stock Markets: A Critical Look at the SEC's National Market System, 56 N.Y.U.L.Rev. 883, 895 (1991).

24. See Paul Christie & William Schultz, Why Do Nasdaq Market Makers Avoid Odd–Eighth Quotes, 49 J.Fin. 1813 (1994) A voluminous literature followed pro-

viding alternative interpretations and theories.

25. See Report Pursuant to Section 21(a) of the Securities Exchange Act of 1934 Regarding the NASD and the Nasdaq Market, 1996 SEC LEXIS 2123 (August 8, 1996). Section 21(a) authorizes the Commission to publish reports of its investigations. This report found that the NASD had failed adequately "to comply with certain NASD rules and, without reasonable justification, to enforce compliance with the Exchange Act and the rules and regulations thereunder." Id. at *1 to *2.

ers could to a degree compete with dealers, and thereby narrow spreads, the SEC developed an ingenious order handling procedure for introducing greater competition into the Nasdaq market. Under its Order Handling Rules, customers can now place a "limit order" to buy or sell a stock at a price between the bid/asked spread.[26] Incoming orders on the other side would then trade with this order as the inside best bid or asked price. For example, if the spread were a very wide $9.80 bid and $10.00 asked, a customer could place a buy limit order at $9.90 and the next incoming sell order would cross with that $9.90 bid price (rather than the lower dealers' best bid of $9.80). In essence, this procedure uses customers to supplement the seemingly limited competition among dealers. Early experience seems to show that these new rules have narrowed the bid/asked spread substantially by introducing a new source of competition (i.e. customers willing to enter limit orders).

A second major development occurred in 1998 when Congress mandated that securities prices be quoted in decimals, not the traditional eights of a point in which securities prices had been quoted for centuries. As securities came to be traded in pennies, the average spread on Nasdaq fell to just over 3¢ in early 2001, thereby reducing the real costs of trading for the retail investor.

C. The New Techonology: Electronic Communications Networks ("ECNs")

The most dynamic and destabilizing recent development in the secondary markets for equity securities has been the explosive growth of electronic communications networks (or "ECNs"). ECNs permit institutional investors and retail customers to trade directly with each other without the intervention of a dealer; thus customers can buy or sell securities at prices between the dealers market's bid/asked spread. ECNs operate simply as order-matching mechanisms and do not maintain their inventory of stocks to satisfy customer demand. Hence, they cannot usually accommodate a buyer or seller who wants to acquire or dispose of a substantial block; nor can they provide much liquidity in time of market stress. Customers typically place limit orders on ECNs, often at a price that is superior to the best price available in the dealer market (i.e., the inside spread price). For example, suppose a customer who wants to buy a stock sees that the lowest "asked" price quoted by a dealer seeking to sell that stock is $10.00 and that the lowest "bid" price is $9.90. By posting a limit order to buy at $9.95, the customer hopes to attract a seller, who would rather sell to it at $9.95 than to a dealer at $9.90. The downside is, however, that no counterparty may be forthcoming, and the market may move adversely to our customer in the meantime (i.e., it may rise to $10.20, meaning that our customer has now lost the opportunity to buy from a dealer at $10.00). Customers may also post limit orders at prices outside the inside bid/asked spread, hoping that some buyers who are seeking to buy or sell a large quantity (often on an anonymous basis) will deal with them in order to avoid moving the price up or down in the dealer market. In all these cases, the parties whose

26. A "limit order" is an order to buy or sell a stock at a specific price. Most customer orders are instead "market orders:" namely, orders to buy or sell at the best available price in the market. Adopted in 1996, Rule 11Ac1–4 ("Limit Order Display Rule") now requires market makers on Nasdaq, and exchange specialists, as well, to display certain customer limit orders (but it does not require a market maker to accept a limit order).

orders cross on an ECN are seeking to eliminate the middleman (i.e., the securities dealer) by trading directly with each other.

Alternative trading systems can take a variety of forms. Some are bulletin board systems at which institutions indicate (often anonymously) a desire to trade a stock at a specific price. Another institution can contact the first (by telephone or computer) and negotiate a price for a transaction between them. Other systems are crossing systems which execute at the midpoint of the bid/asked spread on another exchange. Others use proprietary algorithms to match buy and sell orders, or they run daily auctions, matching buyers and sellers willing to trade at prices that overlap. A important distinction exists between passive systems that execute at the midpoint of another exchange's prices and those (such as the largest alternative trading system, Instinet) on which actual price discovery occurs.

The growth of alternative trading systems has been dramatic over the 1990s, and was largely fueled by the SEC's Order Handling Rules, that were introduced in 1996. By 1997, the SEC estimated that some twenty alternative trading systems accounted for 20 percent of the orders in over-the-counter traded securities and 4 percent in NYSE-listed stocks.[27] More recently, Nasdaq estimates that ECNs now handle as much 30% of the trading on Nasdaq during 2000 and 2001. The growth of ECNs has, of course, taken business away from dealers. In addition, with this growth have come new problems and some basic policy issues. First among these is the issue of transparency. Although brokers-dealers are required to publicly report the price and volumes at which they trade securities within not more than ninety seconds after a transaction is effected in order to inform the market, no similar obligation applies to institutional investors, who can trade between themselves essentially in the dark. An attraction of some alternative trading systems (most notably, Instinet) was that it permitted anonymous trading, in which either the transaction's terms or the institution's identity could be hidden from the market. This may deny other participants in the market knowledge about the most recent transactions, and it can also invite manipulation, if, for example, a market participant buys at ascending prices in one market, but quietly sells at lower prices in another non-transparent market. As a partial solution, the SEC's Order Handling Rules now require an ECN to post its interior bid/asked spread on Nasdaq in order to assure that superior prices on an ECN influence the market as a whole.

More generally, the SEC is concerned that alternative trading systems are not fully integrated into the national market system. Public investors are not permitted to trade in many such systems (in part because of the counter-party risk if there were a customer default). Thus prices may be quoted in this market that are not available to all investors. Finally, there is a regulatory problem: alternative trading systems such as Instinet are competitive rivals to Nasdaq, but are subject to the regulatory supervision of the NASD. The SEC has expressed reservations about letting a competitor have regulatory authority over its rivals. This problem seems to be in the process of correcting itself, however, as the NASD is in the process of turning Nasdaq into a privately-owned free-standing entity that the NASD will neither own nor control.

At present, the sponsors of alternative trading systems are regulated as broker-dealers. However, in 1997, in a Concept Release, the SEC has raised the possibility that such systems (or at least those with high volume) should be

---

27. See Sec.Exch.Act Rel. No. 34–38672 (June 4, 1997).

regulated as securities exchanges under § 6 of the Securities Exchange Act of 1934.[28] Already, some ECNs have applied to become formal exchanges, and in late 2001, the SEC approved the application of Archipelago to convert from an ECN into an electronic exchange.[29]

D. THE NATIONAL MARKET SYSTEM

Although the character of the equity securities market in the United States has rapidly evolved over the last decade, many of the basic features that distinguish it from other capital markets in the U.S. and other equity markets around the world were established roughly a quarter century ago. In 1975, Congress directed the SEC to facilitate the establishment of a "national market system" in conformity with certain enumerated statutory objectives.[30] The structure of the system was not specifically defined in the Act, and no blueprint was drawn up in advance for its implementation. Nonetheless, the SEC envisaged the term "national market system" "as a comprehensive reference to those regulatory and technological steps which the Commission and the securities industry must take in order to integrate the mechanisms for trading qualified securities and the trading behavior of investors and securities professionals in order to achieve a nationwide interactive market system."[31] In other words, rather than having a single central trading floor such as the New York Stock Exchange where all bids and offers for securities would be brought, the goal of this legislation was to achieve efficient linkages between the various exchange trading floors and the dealer markets conducted over-the-counter. The SEC pursued this goal throughout the 1970's and achieved the following milestones.

The Consolidated Tape. The SEC's initial efforts to foster a national market system were directed toward the implementation of a system wide communication system. Previously, trading in NYSE-listed securities on other exchanges or in the over-the-counter market was not reported on the NYSE tape. Thus, the SEC focused first on creating a consolidated transaction tape as a means of increasing the visibility of the regional exchanges and market makers in the over-the-counter market. In 1976, a consolidated system for AMEX listed stocks was installed.[32] As a result, there is today a "moving ticker" which consolidates volume and price information on all sales of NYSE-listed securities and another tape covering AMEX securities. These computerized electronic reporting systems consolidate all transactions in NYSE or AMEX equity shares from all national securities exchanges, Nasdaq (where an increasing number of NYSE securities are traded), Instinet (the leading fourth market broker-dealer), and the third market.

Consolidated Quotation System. The next and more ambitious step by the SEC to foster competition was the consolidated quotation system. By consolidating the bid and asked quotations of different exchanges and market makers

---

28. Id.

29. See Securities Exchange Act Release No. 44983 (November 1, 2001). Archipelago had earlier entered into a joint venture agreement with the former Pacific Coast Exchange, pursuant to which Archipelago would manage the latter. Thereafter, the Pacific Coast Exchange changed its name to the Archipelago Exchange.

30. See Section 11A(a)(2) of the Securities Exchange Act of 1934.

31. Securities Exchange Act Release No. 13662 (June 23, 1977), 12 SEC Dock. 947, at 952.

32. Securities Exchange Act Release No. 34–15671 (Mar. 22, 1979), [1979 Transfer Binder] (CCH) Fed.Sec.L.Rep. ¶ 82,016, at 81,563.

onto a single reporting system, the SEC hoped to foster price competition in the form of tighter bid and asked spreads. In 1978, the SEC adopted Rule 11Ac1–1, which initially required all exchanges and market makers to publish "firm" bid and offer quotes and to indicate the size of the order (i.e., 100, 200 or 500 shares) that they were willing to buy or sell at that price. A "firm" quotation is simply one that the market maker is obligated to observe (that is, buy or sell at its indicated quotation) up to its indicated size limitation. Securities information vendors would then make this information available to both market professionals and public users.

However, the adoption of this mandatory "Quote Rule" failed to achieve its intended objective of creating a mechanism for linking market centers so that orders could be automatically routed to and executed in the market center with the best price. Under the rule, each market center was required to establish mechanisms for collecting from exchange specialists and third market makers bids, offers and quotation sizes with respect to any reported security and to make these available to quotation vendors for dissemination in other market centers. Subject to certain exceptions, the specialist or third market maker furnishing a quotation was obligated to execute any round lot order presented to it at a price at least as favorable as the bid or offer in any amount up to its published quotation size. Nonetheless, the system failed to realize its objective because most regional exchange specialists and third market makers were unable to provide firm quotes in all securities that they traded. Regional exchange specialists typically make a market in a number of stocks, but receive only a small order flow in stocks listed on a primary market (i.e., the NYSE or Amex). Thus, they frequently engage in a policy of "derivative pricing," duplicating the price quotations of the primary market specialist and attempting to compete by charging lower execution or clearance fees. Sometimes, they employ "autoquote" computer devices that simply adjust their quotations to the primary market's quotation, but as a result they could not supply "firm" continuous two-sided quotations throughout the trading day. In 1982, the SEC recognized that regional exchanges could not afford to supply firm quotations and relaxed the firm quotation rule, so that generally only the specialist in the primary market is required to disseminate firm quotations.

A significant number of stocks listed on the NYSE and AMEX may be traded off these exchanges by exchange members who act as market makers in such transactions. This permission was granted by Exchange Act Rule 19c–3 which freed brokers and dealers who were exchange members from all stock exchange off-board trading restrictions with regard to securities which were listed on an exchange after April 26, 1979, the date when Rule 19c–3 was originally announced. (Previously, New York Stock Exchange Rule 390 forbade an NYSE member firm from trading an NYSE-listed stock in another U.S. market during NYSE trading hours.) The above "quote" rule further provides that market makers engaging in over-the-counter trading in "Rule 19c–3 securities" are similarly subject to the compulsory quote rule.[33]

The competition that has emerged to date among the exchanges seems considerably different from the type of price competition that the SEC envisioned when it championed the national market system. Instead of competing for the customer's business through tighter spreads between their bid and asked prices, regional exchanges have competed instead to reduce their costs, or offer inducements in the form of rebates, to win the customer's broker's

33. Securities Exchange Act Rel. No. 18482 (Feb. 11, 1982).

business. This competition benefits customers only if (and to the extent that) their brokers pass their cost savings through in the form of lower commissions.[34] Also, major broker-dealers are increasingly seeking to "internalize order flow" by acquiring specialist seats on regional exchanges, in order to be able to direct customer orders to a regional exchange where its affiliate serves as a specialist. When a broker so directs the customer's order, the customer may lose, even though the bid/asked spread on the regional exchange is the same as that on the primary exchange, because there is a greater possibility of "price improvement" (namely, an execution between the bid and asked spread) on the primary exchange.[35]

Execution Systems Based Upon Order Size: Small Orders. Competition between primary and derivative markets in multiply-traded stocks has resulted in the reduction of transaction costs in processing small orders. Since a high percentage of transactions entail orders between 100 and 500 shares, the regional exchanges and Nasdaq have developed small order automated execution systems which are faster and less expensive than that available on the NYSE or AMEX. Under some of these systems, a broker or trading department can electronically route an order to the specialist on the floor of the exchange. The specialist must accept the order at the best price quotation available at any of the market centers reporting on the Consolidated Quotation System. If the specialist does not respond, after a specified number of seconds, the specialist is required to execute the order at a price equal to the best quotation in the consolidated quotation system.

The NASD has the Small Order Execution System, SOES, providing for rapid, automatic execution of trades up to specified limits (generally, 1000 shares). Customer orders can be entered into SOES through a Nasdaq terminal. The order is executed and confirmed automatically, by computer, in seconds, at the best quotation available. The system then automatically reports the trade to Nasdaq and sends the transaction details to the clearing corporation.

Although SOES is probably the fastest order execution system (because it wholly eliminates any need for telephone contact between the broker and the market maker), it encountered substantial problems during the 1987 crash. The chief problem was the tendency of many market makers to withdraw not only from SOES but from Nasdaq stocks entirely during conditions of high market stress.[36] At the time, a market maker who withdrew from making a market in a stock was banned from re-entering that market for only two business days. During October 19–21, 1987, Nasdaq market makers withdrew from 5,257 market making positions, resulting in what some termed a "total breakdown of the over-the-counter market."[37] In the aftermath of the crash,

---

34. Although there seems little doubt that in a competitive market, some customers benefit from these rebates paid by dealers and exchanges to brokers, it is not clear that the retail customer is a principal beneficiary (as opposed to institutional investors, who have greater sophistication and leverage).

35. For example, if both exchanges quote a bid price of 10 and an asked price of 10¼, it remains possible that the customer's buy order will be more likely to be executed at 10⅛ on the primary exchange either be-

cause of the larger "crowd" of traders surrounding the specialist's post on the primary exchange or because it will cross with an incoming public sell order.

36. See 5 L. Loss and J. Seligman, Securities Regulation 2588–90 (3rd ed. 1990).

37. An unexcused withdrawal now results in a 20 business day suspension. Id., at 2590. A new SOES "tiered" system assigns each security a maximum order size between 200 and 1,000 shares based on its trading characteristics.

the NASD has required market makers in NMS securities to participate in SOES on a mandatory basis.[38] The result is a firm quotation system for NMS securities up to the SOES order limits.[39]

The rival NYSE and the AMEX systems differ from these other systems in several respects. The NYSE Designated Order Turnaround System, known as SUPERDOT, is an electronic order-routing system through which member firms transmit market and limit orders directly to the post where the security is traded, thereby dispensing with the messenger services of a floor broker. Member firms can enter market or limit orders into SUPERDOT in amounts up to three million shares;[40] this very high capacity has enabled the NYSE to compete effectively for institutional and other large orders (and may partially explain the lesser inroads that ECNs have made against the NYSE). The specialist exposes market orders to the "crowd" of floor brokers in front of the specialist's post, and the order will be executed either by a floor broker or the specialist. The limit order system electronically files orders which are then executed if a specific price is reached. SUPERDOT has the advantage of exposing orders to the auction system. This can result in better prices to the customer, but as a result it is slower and its transaction costs exceed that of the competing systems of the regional exchanges and Nasdaq.

Block Transactions. The tremendous growth of institutional trading has put a severe strain upon the mechanism of the exchanges' auction market system. Special methods have been devised to handle block transactions. The SEC defines these as transactions of 10,000 shares or more or involving securities having a market value of $200,000 or more.[41] In recent years, block trading has accounted for roughly 50% of NYSE reported volume, indicating the high level of institutional investor activity on the NYSE.[42] Although most block transactions require special handling, several institutional computerized communication systems have been developed to facilitate block trading. These systems essentially evolved into the fourth market, but at the outset they were simply computerized communication systems that permitted brokers and dealers to advertise their interest as a buyer or seller of a block of securities at or near the current market price. Transactions were then consummated by direct communication. From the outset, the Instinet system has been more sophisticated; it permits financial intermediary subscribers to transact anonymous block trades directly through the Instinet computer facility without the interposition of a broker or dealer, thereby facilitating the fourth market. Moreover, each Instinet terminal now provides direct access to a marketplace of broker-dealers, exchange specialists, market makers and all types of institutional investors.

Market Linkage. A comprehensive market linkage system has been developed which permits orders for the purchase and sale of multiply-traded securi-

38. NASD market makers have complained that "professional traders" (known as "SOES bandits" in the industry) are exploiting them by breaking up large orders into smaller orders that fit within SOES's limits. Many in the industry refused to honor the orders of SOES bandits, resulting in so-called "backing away" violations. In part, it was the NASD's failure to enforce these rules that lead to the 1995–1996 NASD scandals and SEC censure.

39. NYSE Fact Book 1991 at 21.

40. See Securities Exchange Act Release No. 44399 (2001).

41. SEC Exchange Act Release No. 19372 (Dec. 23, 1982) [1982–83 Transfer Binder] (CCH) Fed.Sec.L.Rep. ¶ 83,307 at 85,-677.

42. NYSE Fact Book 1991 at 15.

ties to be routed between market centers for execution. The first phase was that of linking the various exchange markets where stocks are multiply-traded. The Intermarket Trading System (ITS) is an electronic communication network that now links the trading floors of all the stock exchanges and the Nasdaq system. It enables any broker or market maker in any of these markets to shop all participating markets and route an order to another market center for execution whenever the nationwide Composite Quotation System shows a better price is available.

The next significant development involved the linking of the exchange markets and the over-the-counter dealer markets where the same securities were traded. The reason for the separation of these markets is historical. Until 1979, NYSE Rule 390 prohibited NYSE members from engaging in off-board trading in NYSE-listed securities off the floor of the NYSE or the floor of a regional exchange where the stock had a multiple listing. Then, SEC Rule 19c–3 abrogated off-board trading rules with respect to stocks which were listed on an exchange after April 26, 1979. This linkage of the exchange markets and the Nasdaq system permits orders in so-called "Rule 19c–3 securities" to be efficiently routed between exchange and over-the-counter markets where multiple trading exists. This development has also given NYSE members an incentive to acquire specialist firms on regional exchanges so that they can route orders to their own specialist (rather than using the NYSE specialist) in order to "internalize" their order flow and capture the entire trading profit.

E.   HOW MARKETS WORK: REPRESENTATIVE TRANSACTIONS

The foregoing discussion of markets may seem dense and forbidding to the student with little familiarity with markets and their operation. Thus, this section will provide greater institutional detail (and hopefully a fuller sense of the reality of market transactions) by walking through some standard transactions, explaining who does what and what the objectives of the participants are. Initially, retail trades by small individual customers on the NYSE and Nasdaq will be outlined, and then institutional transactions will be described in which the professional trader searches a variety of markets.

1.   A Retail Trade on the NYSE

Assume that Samantha would like to buy 200 shares of IBM as an investment. She is a young associate at a law firm and has just received a year end bonus. She knows that if she puts the money in a bank or buys debt securities, she will be taxed at a high rate on the interest. The major alternative investment option for her is real estate, but her relationship with her boyfriend, Bill, is just "not ready" for her to buy a coop apartment with him. Hence, Samantha calls her existing retail broker (although she could also enter the order herself on her brokers's Internet-based order entry system). Samantha's brokerage firm could be a full service brokerage firm, of which the largest is Merrill Lynch, or a national discount brokerage, such as Charles Schwab, or perhaps a local deep discount brokerage firm.[43] Samantha knows that she pays higher commissions with a full service broker, but she likes having someone to talk to about investment decisions.

---

43. Samantha has a broad and diverse range of brokerage firms from which she can choose, which compete in a highly competitive industry. As of late 2001, Yahoo! listed 268 full-service brokerage firms, 141 discount firms, 70 day trading firms, and 116 Internet trading firms (some of these firms are listed in multiple categories).

Samantha asks her broker for the current quotes for IBM's common stock. The broker checks a screen on her desk that displays the best bids and offers for IBM that traders display in the Consolidated Quotation System. These quotes come from the specialist at the New York Stock Exchange, from dealers at several regional exchanges that also quote IBM, from some "Third Market" dealers (i.e., independent NASD dealers who quote NYSE-listed stocks), and from some electronic communications networks (ECNs) that display "limit orders" that their clients have placed with them. Having checked, the broker responds that the best (highest) bid for IBM is at $78.00 and the best (lowest) offer is at $78.10. The broker also tells Samantha that the last trade in IBM was at $78.05. Having heard the quotes on both sides, Samantha now reveals that she wants to purchase, and she gives her broker instructions to buy 200 shares.

Samantha can give her broker either a market order or a limit order. A market order instructs the broker to buy at the best price available in the market. A limit order instructs the broker to buy at the best price possible, but in no event pay more then a ceiling price that Samantha specifies. If Samantha uses a limit order, she must specify when she wants the order to expire (for example, a day order will expire when that day's trading session ends).

Samantha likes to shop for bargains, both as an investor and a consumer. She knows that if she submits a day limit order for no more than $78.00 per share, this leaves open the possibility that her order might never be executed (if the "asked" price did not fall to this level). Nonetheless, Samantha instructs her broker to do so, because she wants "to gain an edge." Her broker reads back her order to ensure that her instructions have been correctly understood. (This conversation is taped by the brokerage firm in case a dispute arises about what was said). After Samantha confirms the order, the broker enters it into the firm's order entry system, which directs it to an exchange or to a dealer.

While IBM primarily trades on the New York Stock Exchange, Samantha's broker might not send her order there. Her brokerage firm might send the order to a regional exchange or to a NASD dealer, both of which pay the broker a rebate (equal typically to one cent per share) for order flow directed to them (provided that Samantha's brokerage firm must send them a minimum of one million shares a year). This rebate is not unlawful and will not be passed on to Samantha (the brokerage firm argues that this practice is desirable because it allows it to charge Samantha a lower brokerage commission).

In fact, the brokerage's order entry system sends Samantha's order to the NYSE through the NYSE's SuperDot order routing system. Within seconds, SuperDot presents the order to the specialist who handles all IBM trading on the floor of the NYSE. Who is this specialist? Essentially, the specialist is an auctioneer through whom all orders must run. The NYSE gives the specialist certain privileges in return for his accepting some special responsibilities. Although the specialist receives all of the SuperDot order flow in IBM, it is required correspondingly to administer the trading in IBM to ensure that trading is orderly and proceeds without any sharp price discontinuities. For the privilege of receiving all public orders that come to the NYSE for execution, the NYSE requires that the specialist trade for its own account to fill customer market orders, buying or selling, as the buyer or seller of last resort. In practice, the specialist will be involved, as buyer or seller, in about a quarter of all transactions in the stock it handles, but this percentage will be much lower in the case of a very actively traded stock like IBM.

Because Samantha's order is a limit order, the specialist first checks to see if anyone is interested in filling it immediately. No sellers are presently interested because other traders are bidding higher than $78.00. The specialist then places her order in its electronic limit order book. Samantha's order will stand in the book until the specialist can match it with someone who wants to sell at or below her $78.00 limit price, or until the order expires, or until Samantha tells her broker to cancel it.

Assume instead that Samantha had submitted a market order instead of a limit order. Now, the specialist would conduct an auction to find the trader willing to sell at the lowest price. The party whose order crosses with Samantha's might be a trader on the floor, a standing limit order in the order book, an incoming market order to sell, or the specialist itself. If no one wants to fill the market order, the specialist would be required to fill the order itself by selling Samantha 200 of its own shares in IBM. Actually, if the specialist senses that IBM's stock price is rising, it may be willing to buy sell limit orders at a price above the market in order to increase its inventory.

As it happens, a large seller sends a market order through Superdot only minutes after Samantha entered her order. This order is large enough to exhaust all market orders and all limit orders to buy at prices above $18.00 per share, and thus it moves the market price downward. The specialist uses his computer to match this order with several orders including Samantha's limit order. The orders all trade at $78.00. The NYSE's trading system then reports the trade to the Consolidated Trade Reporting System, which reports trade prices and sizes to various data vendors, who in turn distribute the trade reports throughout the world.

Superdot also reports the trade to Samantha's broker in a process called confirming the trade. Samantha's broker then reports the confirmation to her. If this order had been a market order, the total time between the order entry and the final confirmation might have been as quick as twenty seconds. Possibly, Samantha might even receive her trade confirmation on the same telephone call on which she placed her order. Instead, because Samantha's limit order took a while to trade, the broker phones Samantha with the confirmation.

Samantha must, of course, pay for her purchase. Possibly, she has sufficient funds already in her brokerage account. That day, the brokerage house mails her a written confirmation of the trade. The confirmation instructs her to pay the purchase price times 200 shares plus the brokerage commission. Depending on the type of brokerage account used, her commission may be as low as $20 dollars (at a deep discount firm) or as high as $150 (approximately 1% of her total $15,600 purchase price) at a full service brokerage firm. Even lower commissions are available if she traded over the Internet.

Three business days later ("T+3" in the vernacular), the trade must settle. (Beginning in the near future, settlements will be required to occur on "T+1"). Samantha's broker pays for the stock, and the seller delivers it to her broker. If Samantha has not yet paid for the stock, her broker will collect money from any cash she holds in her account. If no cash is available and if Samantha has executed a margin agreement, the brokerage will lend her up to half the purchase price, but charge her high interest on the remaining amount due. The broker will hold Samantha's newly acquired IBM stock and other securities in her account as collateral for such a loan. If Samantha does not maintain adequate collateral to support this loan, the broker will sell the stock and charge her for the commission and for any losses incurred.

Samantha can ask to have a stock certificate issued in her name (at least once she has fully paid for the share). If she requests this, her broker will transfer the shares to IBM's transfer agent, who will issue a new certificate and mail it to her. Being a smart lawyer, Samantha places the certificate in a safety deposit box or deposits it in another brokerage account for safekeeping. More likely, however, Samantha will keep the shares registered in the broker's name (this is referred to as "street name" ownership, but she will be the beneficial holder, and her broker will solicit and follow any voting instructions that she gives).

2. A Retail Trade on NASDAQ

Samantha's relationship with Bill has hit the rocks, and she plans to take herself to the Caribbean for a vacation to forget him. To do so, she needs to sell some Intel stock that she owns. Unlike IBM, Intel does not trade on the NYSE, but is instead quoted by between thirty and forty independent dealers who disseminate their quotes on Nasdaq's National Market System. On average, stocks listed on Nasdaq's National Market System have over fourteen dealers trading them at any time, although the number can range from as few as three to more than seventy. These dealers sit at their desks throughout the country and enter their quotes into Nasdaq Level III workstations that are linked together through a private data network.

Now, when Samantha asks her broker for a quote, the broker pulls up a montage on his screen that displays the bids and offers of the, hypothetically, 35 Nasdaq market makers and electronic communications networks who were providing quotes in Intel on this date. The bids are ranked from highest to lowest, and the offers (asks) are ranked from lowest to highest. Looking at this screen, the broker reports that Intel last traded at $26.64 down 12¢ from the previous close; the market is currently at $26.62 bid; $26.65 asked.

Samantha tells her broker to sell 100 shares of Intel at the market. The broker knows that this instruction means that she wants the order filled quickly at the best price available. Alternatively, Samantha could use a limit order, in which case she would be more likely to send it to an ECN, which now account for over 40 percent of all Nasdaq transactions. Samantha's motivation to use an ECN might be either her desire to obtain an above market price (as almost all orders placed with ECNs are limit orders) or, more likely in this case, a desire to economize on transaction costs, as ECNs do not typically charge brokerage commissions, but only a much more modest access fee (which may be only 1% of the cost of using a "full service" brokerage firm). On the other hand, Samantha may want to talk to a "real person" who she knows, which is only possible at some (and not all) broker-dealers. The largest and best known ECNs are Instinet and Island, which together account for over 20% of the trading on Nasdaq.[44] If Samantha decides to use a limit order, she might enter a sell limit order at a significant amount above the market price (say $27.00). Still, because she is only selling 100 shares and wants the proceeds promptly for her planned trip, she decides to use a market order.

---

44. In June, 2002, these two firms announced a plan to merger. Their merger would create a strong competitor for Nasdaq, which has itself been recently privatized.

The broker sees from her records that Samantha owns 200 shares of Intel. If the broker did not see this on the firm's records, he would inquire how Samantha intended to settle this trade. If Samantha did not own the shares, she would be selling the stock "short." To settle such a trade, Samantha would have to borrow the shares from the broker. All order tickets must be marked by the broker as either "long" or "short."

Again, the broker enters Samantha's order into the firm's order entry system and reads it back to her. If the brokerage firm does not itself deal in Intel, its order entry system will send the order to the Nasdaq Small Order Execution System (SOES). If the brokerage does trade Intel, it will more likely handle the transaction itself, buying from Samantha at the highest price offered by any dealer in the market (even if this broker's own "bid" price was below this level). This is because Samantha's broker is under a legal duty of "best execution." It must find the best available price in the market. Thus, even though it receives rebates for its order flow, it can only give Samantha's order to a dealer who will match the highest bid or lowest sale price in the market for that quantity of shares (this interior spread of the highest bid and lowest sale price is known as the "National Best Bid and Offer"—or "NBBO"). Note, however, that if the dealer matching this NBBO price also pays a rebate to Samantha's brokerage firm, it might logically have been willing to pay a still superior price to Samantha (and no rebate to her broker). If Samantha's broker does trade Intel, it will likely buy from her itself at the NBBO (this practice is called "internalization" as the order does not interact with other orders in a central marketplace). Some worry that internalization will fragment the market or impede the price discovery process, but none of these concerns are on Samantha's mind.

Assume that Samantha's broker does not make a market in Intel. SOES then routes the order to one of the Nasdaq dealers. Typically, Samantha's broker will still select the dealer to which SOES sends her order. If the brokerage did not specify a dealer, SOES would have sent the sell order to one of the dealers who are displaying the best (highest) bid. Samantha's broker selects a particular dealer because that dealer has arrange to give the brokerage a cash rebate (again probably one cent a share or less) to obtain its order flow at the NBBO price.

The dealer who receives Samantha's order executes it by buying the stock for his own account. Many dealers have computer systems that automatically execute such small market orders when they arrive. The trade price will be at least $26.62 (assuming that the bid has not changed).

Once the dealer fills the order, it is required to report the transaction to Nasdaq within 90 seconds. Samantha's broker then confirms the transaction to Samantha by phone and by mail. Nasdaq forwards the trade report to various data vendors who report it to the public.

Again, the trade settles three business days later ("T + 3" again). At that time, Samantha's brokerage delivers the 100 shares of Intel to the dealer, and the dealer pays for them. The brokerage credits Samantha's account with the proceeds of the sale, less any brokerage commission charged and a small fee that the Securities and Exchange Commission collects from sellers of securities.

3.   An Institutional Trade in NYSE Stock

Now, let's consider trading on a much larger scale. Assume that Jack, who is not a licensed broker, is responsible for executions and trading at Portfolio

Investments General, Inc. ("PIG"), which is an investment management firm that manages money for several university endowments and some corporate pension funds. These funds have given PIG discretionary authority to trade on their behalf. PIG manages a total of 5 billion dollars invested primarily in US and European equities.

At 1:00 PM Eastern Time, Sally, a portfolio manager, instructs Jack to buy 500,000 shares of Citigroup Inc. for their clients. Because the current price of Citigroup is near $42.50, the principal value of this trade is around $21.25 million. This makes it a sizable trade, but not an especially large one in term of Citigroup's market capitalization. On the date of this order, this trade represents less than 0.01 percent of the total number of shares outstanding in Citigroup, less than one half of one percent of the PIG's portfolio, and only 5.5 percent of the average daily volume (about 9,000,000 shares) in Citigroup. Jack's responsibility is to get this order filled at the lowest possible cost.

Jack knows that it is important to determine what PIG's real needs are. If PIG believes it has important information that Citigroup's stock will shortly increase with some positive announcement, Jack must act quickly. Of course, this might also suggest that PIG has "inside" information, and Jack neither wants to make such an indelicate suggestion; nor to learn such information and thereby become a potential aider and abettor in the SEC's eyes. On the other hand, if PIG wants Citigroup stock only because it believes that Citigroup is fundamentally undervalued, Jack can proceed more patiently. In the latter case, Jack can employ whatever combination of means will best economize on transaction costs. In a cautious discussion with PIG's portfolio managers, Jack gets the impression that there is no short-term urgency and that he has "time to trade." Now, Jack's leading concern becomes confidentiality. If other market participants (including even people in his own firm) realize that he is working a 500,000 share buy order in Citigroup and will be quietly making purchases over the trading day, they may advise their own clients to buy Citigroup fast, because Jack's purchases should send the market price up. Such "frontrunning" of Jack's order is unlawful under some circumstances, but, to maintain confidentiality and minimize any increase in Citigroup's price while he completes filling his order, Jack may still decide to trade on an ECN, where his client's identity and trading intentions can better be kept secret.

Jack next evaluates the recent price and trade history for Citigroup, using several on-line services. In particular, he searches to see if any other large traders are actively selling. If any large seller were seeking to execute a significant order, Jack might "luck out" and be able to cross his order with its, thereby avoiding the likelihood of having to pay a premium over the prior market price in order to fill his large buy order. However, if Jack must compete with another large buyer, things will be tougher. Declining recent prices usually mean that large buy orders will be easier to execute than large sell orders. To the extent that Citigroup's stock tends to move with the market as a whole, Jack may need to compare Citigroup's recent price history with movements in the S&P 500.

Jack's first goal is to find any large trader interest in Citigroup. Jack searches several electronic information systems that collect information about trader interests. Autex, Bridge and Instinet are among the best-known such systems. Although these systems show that several traders have expressed interest in Citigroup stock, Jack cannot tell from them how serious traders may be (or even whether they have already filled their orders). He must approach them directly.

To assure confidentiality, Jack seeks out a broker with whom PIG has done considerable business. He selects Scott, a floor broker on the NYSE known for his discretion, who Jack trusts to keep quiet because Jack does not want it known that PIG is in the market for Citigroup stock. Without revealing his specific interest, Jack asks Scott what the market conditions are in Citigroup's stock. Scott knows that Jack works large orders, and he goes out of his way to inquire. Scott goes to the specialist who trades Citigroup on the NYSE floor and tries to gather any useful information. Scott watches the trading for ten minutes and asks the specialist and other nearby traders who has expressed interest in trading. Predictably, he gets guarded answers and knows that they be holding back information. Nonetheless, Scott calls back Jack to advise him that no large trader interest is currently evident in the stock, but notes that a Merrill Lynch broker was actively selling earlier in the day. Jack knows that he could ask Scott to intercept all incoming sell orders that come to the specialist's post and buy them at or just above the prevailing bid price. Although this tactic will preserve Jack's anonymity (at least for a while), it also will signal substantial buying interest and possibly drive prices up.

Given the currently tepid selling interest on the NYSE, Jack instead enters an order to buy 500,000 shares in Citigroup in POSIT. POSIT (Portfolio System for Institutional Trading) is an electronic trading system that runs an automated auction at periodic intervals. Technically, POSIT is not an ECN (because it does not match orders on a continuing basis), but it is an ATS or "Alternative Trading System." POSIT has other competitors at this technique (the Arizona Stock Exchange uses a similar methodology), but Jack has had good experience with POSIT and is loyal to it. POSIT collects buy and sell orders, primarily from institutional traders and attempts to match them. Its special attraction is that its service has a good reputation for confidentiality. Jack enters his order on POSIT using software provided by POSIT.

Several times a day, POSIT automatically matches buyers with sellers. When the total POSIT buy order volume exceeds the total POSIT sell order volume, all sell orders will be filled completely, and the buy orders will be prorated. Correspondingly, when sell orders exceed buy orders, all buy orders will be filled, and sell orders will be prorated.

POSIT determines the trade price by computing the average of the bid and ask in the primary market on which the stock trades (here, the NYSE) at a random time within seven minutes prior to each scheduled auction. Effectively, this means that both buyers and sellers get the midpoint of the spread at that moment and thus do better than if they traded at the bid or asked price. Once the cross is completed, POSIT reports the trades to its clients and to the NASD.

Ten minutes after the 2:00 pm auction, Jack learns that 100,000 shares of his 500,000 share order have been filled at a price of $42.10. From this information, Jack can estimate that POSIT's buy order volume greatly exceeded its sell order volume. As a practical matter, he can estimate the size of the unfilled POSIT buy order volume from the total size of the cross, which he can read off the Consolidated Tape. If the cross is for 100,000 shares, Jack would know that he was the only buyer. If the cross was for 200,000 shares, he could roughly infer that the total POSIT buy order volume was around 2.5 million shares because the 100,000 share partial fill on his 500,000 share order represented one fifth of his order. From this, Jack knows that there must be some other large buyers out there with whom he will be in competition.

Jack then calls Rodger, a trader at Merrill, Lynch, with whom Jack's firm has an account, to inquire about the posted indication he had seen earlier. This broker sits at Merrill, Lynch's equity trading desk. Although Rodger says that he has already filled his client's sell order, he hints that his client may be willing to sell more. Jack expresses some interest, and Rodger calls his other client while holding Jack on line. A negotiation takes place through Rodger's intermediation. In the end, the Rodger arranges a trade for 200,000 Citigroup shares at $42.25.

Rodger then telephones Merrill, Lynch floor broker at the NYSE and asks him to "print the trade." This floor trader then goes to the Citigroup post and tells the specialist that he would like to cross a block of 200,000 shares at $42.25. This price is inside the current bid/asked spread of $42.23 bid and $42.26 asked (the market has already moved up over the last five minutes since the block price was negotiated). Although the specialist approves this print, he would not be able to do so if instead the trade price were higher than the asked price (i.e., if the negotiated block price were $42.30). Then, the specialist would be required to ask the floor broker to allow the sell orders standing in the limit order book below that price to participate in the trade. The specialist reports the trade to an exchange computer, which forwards it to the Consolidated Trade Reporting System.

Other traders standing at the post ask Rodger, the Merrill, Lynch broker, whether there is more interest on either side of the trade. Rodger says that he will call to find out. Rodger calls his trading desk, and the sales trader calls Jack.

Immediately prior to Jack's receipt of this call, Jack hears again from Scott, the floor broker to whom he had earlier spoken. The broker reports that Merrill, Lynch just crossed 200,000 shares. Jack acknowledges that he was the buyer, but Jack then gives Scott a market buy order for 100,000 shares. The specific instruction tells the floor broker to buy shares at his discretion. When Jack gets the later call from Rodger, he says that he is no longer actively interested in Citigroup stock, hoping this will dampen interest in the stock.

Scott now stands in the crowd in front of the specialist's position where Citigroup is traded on the NYSE and waits for sell orders to appear there. Unlike a public customer, this floor broker can step in front of incoming sell orders and buy them at just above the bid price, because he is entitled to precedence over the specialist who can only be the buyer of last resort. In the next hour, he buys 25,000 at $42.25, 30,000 shares at $42.30 and 20,000 shares at $42.40. He calls Jack back with these confirmations.

Not wanting to continue public buying in this manner, which appears to be driving the price up, Jake now gives Rodger a market order to buy the remaining 125,000 shares that he needs to complete his 500,000 share order. He deliberately uses Rodger instead of Scott in order not to appear to be the same buyer. Meanwhile, the Citigroup price is rising, with bid price now at $42.40, good for 200 round lots of 100 shares (or 200,000 shares). Also, the S&P average is generally rising, which suggests that Citigroup's price may continue rising. Rodger therefore turns to the Citigroup specialist and immediately asks to buy 125,000 shares for $42.40. The specialist, acting as broker for several traders whose sell limit orders are also on the book at $42.40 or less, sells him the shares and reports the trades. The specialist then raises his bid and offer, and Rodger calls Jack to report his trades.

Jack has now filled his 500,000 share order. The average cost of his trades was around $42.30 per share, not counting commissions, and Jack feels that he has been successful for his clients in a difficult market. Jack reports the trades to his firm's back office, which will arrange settlement. He also reports the trades to the portfolio manager.

Jack's firm, PIG, will not actually own or purchase the shares that Jack brought. Instead, PIG's pension fund client will purchase and hold the shares. The back office must now tell the custodians of these funds that PIG made purchases on their behalf. PIG divides the 500,000 shares among the various endowment pension funds in proportion to the money that they have placed under management at PIG. Three days later ("T + 3" again), the various pension fund custodians will pay for and receive their Citigroup shares. Each will pay the same price per share.

Although Jack feels successful in his buying program, there was an alternative technique available to him that he did not use: the block trading desks of major investment banking firms. Seeking 500,000 shares, he might have, for example, gone to the block trading desk at Goldman Sachs, Morgan, Stanley or Salomon (all major players in this field) and asked one of them to quietly assemble such a block. This is called sending the transaction "upstairs," as no broker would now buy or solicit in the general retail market (or "downstairs"). Instead, major institutional investors known to hold Citigroup stock would be solicited quietly (very large institutional holders are required to file reports on their holdings under § 13F of the Securities Exchange Act and thus they can usually be identified). Typically, some premium above the market will have to be paid (and persons with sell limit orders below that price may have to be permitted to participate in the block transaction). In general, the costs associated with block positioning are likely to be higher than those incurred by Jack in the foregoing example, but if the block he sought were, for example, significantly larger than the average daily trading volume in that stock, Jack might be compelled to use this technique.

F.   THE FUTURE DIRECTION OF THE NATIONAL MARKET SYSTEM

The rapid appearance of new substitutes for exchanges—ECN's and Alternative Trading Systems—has raised concerns about market fragmentation. When in late 1999 the NYSE finally agreed, under pressure, to rescind its Rule 390, which long had barred NYSE brokers from trading NYSE-listed securities off the NYSE,[45] this long awaited development still raised fears that there would be a rush to internalization by brokers, who would all siphon off order flow from any central market because it was more profitable to trade directly with one's customer than to send the order flow to a specialist on an exchange. If this diversion of order flow occurred, an externality could result: the price discovery capacity of the central market might be impaired. Concerned about this danger, the SEC promulgated a Concept Release in early 2000 on this

---

45. In truth, Rule 390 did not prevent the NYSE member firm from taking a transaction to another market, as agent for its customer, but only precluded the member firm as principal from competing with the NYSE by trading as a principal off the NYSE while it was open.

market fragmentation issue that outlined various approaches for dealing with it.[46]

In particular, this Concept Release raised again a proposal that the SEC had seriously considered at the time of the 1975 amendments to the Securities Exchange Act that created the National Market System: namely, a central limit order book—or "CLOB." Essentially, a central limit order book would assemble all limit orders, wherever entered, in one centralized book and establish comprehensive price and time priority for all "displayed trading interest." Other investors would submit market orders to be executed against this book. Thus, the sale would always go to the highest bidder (or the lowest seller), even if the buy and sell orders were entered in different markets. Also, time priority would always be given to the first order entered at the same price, again regardless of where it was entered. But to protect time and price priority, virtually all trades outside this system would need to be prohibited.

The CLOB reform has its zealous proponents—and its equally adamant critics. The proponents point to its efficiency enhancing properties, as a deep liquid central market would result and the same stock could not trade at different prices at the same time (as now could potentially happen on multiple ECNs). Critics reply that to create such a unified market, the government would have to effectively take control of all existing exchanges; in effect, the SEC, they argue, would run the market as an administrator, not simply as a regulator. Others object that the creation of one unified market precludes competition and innovation (the post office, they observe, once had a similar monopoly). Still others suggest that the problem with a CLOB is that not all investors want the same thing: some investors want the best possible price (and will wait for it if some delay is required); others want the quickest possible execution; and still others want confidentiality and anonymity because their expression of any trading interest is likely to move the market. In this light, critics argue that a CLOB is a "one size fits all" solution that overlooks the diversity of desires among investors.[47] Given this level of controversy, SEC action on fundamental issues of market structure seems unlikely over the short to intermediate run. But these issues continue to overhang the market.

SECTION 4. THE FORCES RESHAPING THE SECURITIES MARKETS

While the preceding section has described the contemporary equity markets, dynamic forces are at work reshaping those markets. Some technological innovations, such as the Internet, have only begun to effect these markets, but could facilitate direct trading among investors and reduce the traditional role of financial intermediaries, such as dealers and underwriters.[1] But if the impact of technological change is still difficult to estimate, the four forces discussed in this section have had a more visible and certain impact—but one that has also greatly complicated the challenges facing securities regulators. Those four are: (1) the rise of the institutional investor and the consequent "institutionalization" of the market; (2) the appearance of new financial products and new

46. See Securities Exchange Act Release No. 43450 (February 23, 2000).

47. For this view see Marshall Blume, supra note 11.

1. See John C. Coffee, Jr., Brave New World?: The Impact(s) of the Internet on Securities Regulation, 52 Bus.Law 1195 (1997).

portfolio trading strategies; (3) the internationalization of the securities markets (with the accompanying prospect that both capital and entrepreneurs may flee what they perceive as an excessively restrictive legal regime); and (4) the convergence of the banking and securities industries into a unified financial services industry.

A.   THE RISE OF INSTITUTIONAL INVESTORS

The last half-century has witnessed a quiet revolution in terms of the ownership of equity securities. From a time at mid-century when ownership and control were clearly separated and stock ownership was broadly dispersed, the pendulum has swung back towards a reconcentration of stock ownership.

Chart 2 below from the New York Stock Exchange's 1991 Institutional Investor Fact Book shows that institutions owned about 43.5% of the total equities outstanding in the United States as of the end of 1989, up from only 8.1% at the end of 1950. Some later sources put the level of institutional ownership at around 53%.[2]

Chart 2
Holdings of U.S. Corporate Equities, 1950 and 1989

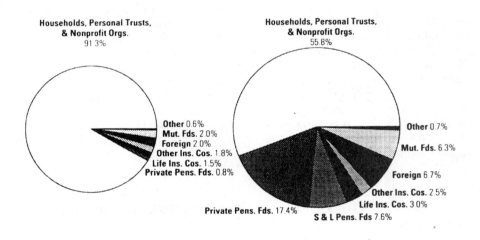

Households, Personal Trusts, & Nonprofit Orgs. 91.3%	Households, Personal Trusts, & Nonprofit Orgs. 55.8%
Other 0.6%	Other 0.7%
Mut. Fds. 2.0%	Mut. Fds. 6.3%
Foreign 2.0%	Foreign 6.7%
Other Ins. Cos. 1.8%	Other Ins. Cos. 2.5%
Life Ins. Cos. 1.5%	Life Ins. Cos. 3.0%
Private Pens. Fds. 0.8%	S & L Pens. Fds 7.6%
	Private Pens. Fds. 17.4%

1950
Total: $142.7 Billion

1989
Total: $3,827.0 Billion

Source: Board of Governors, Federal Reserve System *Flow of Funds*   [G8403]

2. The Columbia University Institutional Investor Project put the figure at 45% in 1987. See Brancato, The Pivotal Role of Institutional Investors in Capital Markets, in Institutional Investing: The Challenges and Responsibilities of the 21st Century (A. Sametz, ed. 1991) at 3, 13. A 1991 update of this study now places that figure at slightly above 53%. However, the 1996 NYSE Fact Book places the level of institutional ownership at 45.6%, proving that different studies use different definitions of institutional ownership. *Id.* at 59.

Looking at institutional investors as a class, one finds the following breakdown in terms of their relative asset ownership, which has remained relatively constant.

Pension Funds	42.9%
Investment Companies	15.6%
Insurance Companies	24.1%
Foundations/Endowments	2.5%
Bank Trust Departments	14.8%

This focus on the aggregate level of institutional ownership may understate the significance of institutional ownership for at least two reasons. First, among major public corporations (where institutions tend to concentrate their holdings), the level is much higher. If one looks at the largest 1000 U.S. corporations, the level of institutional ownership had risen to 57.2 percent by year-end 1995.[3] Some of these corporations (over 4 percent) had institutional ownership levels in excess of 90 percent.[4] Second, if one looks not to ownership, but to trading, institutional activity dominates the market to an even greater extent, accounting for around 70 percent of trading volume.[5] Third, other data, which includes unlisted equities, suggests that individuals held only 38 percent of the total value of equities held by U.S. investors, thus implying that institutions held the balance.[6]

However the data is counted, institutional investors would appear to be in a position to dominate American corporate managements, dictating financial and business strategies to them. But clearly, institutional investors do not behave this way (although they have become increasingly active over the last twenty years). Recently, several commentators have argued that the leading reason that institutions do not play a greater role in corporate governance is that they have been overregulated by the federal securities laws (and also by state law) in a way that deliberately denies them the ability to hold a controlling block of stock in any public corporation.[7] In this view, the same populist tradition in American politics that underlay the passage of the federal securities laws feared the concentration of financial power (and in particular the dominance of Eastern financial interests). Responding to these pressures, Congress (and state legislatures) separated investment from commercial banking and otherwise sought to fragment the principal American financial institutions (banks, insurance companies, mutual funds, and, more recently, pension funds) or at least deny them the ability to actively control corporate managements.

Others have criticized this view that American law has forced investors into passivity by pointing to other factors that may have had greater causal responsibility for the historic reluctance of institutional investors to become

3. See The Conference Board, The Brancato Report on Institutional Investment (Sept. 1996) at p. 4.

4. Id.

5. See Weiss and Beckerman, Let the Money Do the Monitoring: How Institutional Investors Can Reduce Agency Costs in Securities Class Actions, 104 Yale L.J. 2053, 2056 n. 10 (1995).

6. This estimate was made by Wharton Professor Marshall Blume based on U.S. Flow of Funds data as of September, 2001. See Blume, The Structure of the U.S. Equity Markets (Working Paper January 2002). Because this estimate looks to market value, not share ownership, it uses a different frame of reference than most other analyses.

7. The leading work expressing this view is Mark Roe, Strong Managers, Weak Owners: The Political Roots of American Corporate Finance (1994).

actively involved in corporate governance. They cite factors such as a preference for liquidity (which is often inconsistent with holding a control block) or the lack of any payoff to institutional money managers from such involvement.[8] Increasingly also, institutional investors have followed an investment strategy known as "indexing" under which they cease to pick individual stocks, but hold the market as a whole (or at least hold a representative index thereof, such as the "S&P 500").[9] But, such indexing invites passivity, largely because there is decreased incentive to monitor individual corporations in your portfolio closely once the size of that stock portfolio expands to the 500 securities in the S&P 500 index.[10] Still, both sides in this debate agree that the impact of some SEC rules—most notably, the rules governing the solicitation of proxies, the regulation of takeover contests, and the rules under § 16(b) of the Securities Exchange Act—had made communications among institutional investors legally risky and hence chilled institutional activism, at least as of the early 1990's.[11] In particular, the proxy rules seemed to inhibit the formation of groups of institutional investors who might act to monitor corporate managements.[12] Group formation requires communication, and this process is slowed and made more costly if inter-institutional communications are deemed either to be proxy solicitations (requiring the filing of a proxy statement)[13] or to require disclosure under the Williams Act once the "group" collectively owns more than 5% of the issuer's stock.[14] In 1992, the SEC acknowledged this danger of overregulation of investor communications and amended its proxy rules in order to facilitate inter-shareholder communications when the shareholder was "disinterested" and did not seek to obtain proxy authority.[15] Thus, institutional investors can today freely exchange views on management proposals or performance, provided that the party making the communication is not seeking to obtain proxies.

8. See Coffee, Liquidity Versus Control: The Institutional Investors As Corporate Monitor, 91 Colum.L.Rev. 1277 (1991); Rock, The Logic and (Uncertain) Significance of Institutional Shareholder Activism, 79 Geo. L.J. 445 (1991). Both these writers stress that collective action problems may make institutional investors "rationally apathetic."

9. As an investment strategy, indexing largely reflects the acceptance by these institutions of the "efficient capital market hypothesis", which theory implies that the search for undervalued stocks in a liquid public market is futile. This thesis (and recent criticisms of it) are discussed in Chapter 3 infra.

10. Some institutional investors hold several thousand stocks in their portfolio. Also, institutional investors are investing increasingly in derivative securities products and stock index futures, including international stock indices, thus further weakening their focus on individual corporations. See Coffee, supra note 8, at 1340–42.

11. See Coffee, The SEC and the Institutional Investor: A Half–Time Report, 15 Cardozo L.Rev. 837 (1994) (surveying impact of Williams Act rules and other obstacles).

12. For the fullest statement of this view, see Black, Shareholder Passivity Reexamined, 89 Mich.L.Rev. 520 (1990); see also Conard, Beyond Managerialism: Investor Capitalism? 22 U.Mich.J.L.Ref. 117 (1988); Grundfest, The Subordination of American Capital, 27 J.Fin.Econ. 89 (1991).

13. Under Rule 14a–1(*l*), under the 1934 Act, any solicitation that is "reasonably calculated to result in the procurement, withholding or revocation of a proxy" normally requires the filing of a detailed proxy statement, unless the solicitation is directed to ten or fewer persons. See Rule 14a–2(b)(2).

14. The Williams Act added several sections to the Securities Exchange Act of 1934 (chiefly, §§ 13(d) and (e) and §§ 14(d) and (e)). These sections regulate tender offers and the process of acquiring control of a public corporation. Under Rule 13d–1 of the 1934 Act, a disclosure document, known as a Schedule 13D, must be filed once a "group" owns more than 5% of any class of certain issuers. For a fuller consideration of the meaning of "group," see infra Chapter 12, Section 2.

15. See Rule 14a–2(b)(2).

Other rules continue to pose obstacles, and the debate about whether the SEC chills institutional investors from becoming active shareholders continues.

At the same time, it has become increasingly clear that all institutional investors are not alike. While public pension funds have become increasingly active in the 1990's, mutual funds and insurance companies have remained relatively passive, content largely to follow the traditional "Wall Street rule" of selling stocks when they disapproved of their managements, but seldom challenging them openly.

B. NEW FINANCIAL PRODUCTS

During the 1980s, financial engineering emerged as a special field of investment banking. Entire new categories of financial instruments appeared: "mortgage-backed" or "asset-backed" securities, swap transactions, equity derivatives, and even more exotic attempts to "unbundle" a share of stock into its component parts (each then to be separately marketed). There is general agreement that the rate of innovation was unprecedented, and its scale is revealed by the following statistics: in 1990, issuers raised $4.6 billion in initial public offerings of stock, but raised $177.3 billion in "mortgage-backed" and "asset-backed" securities; in addition, during simply the first six months of 1990, $656 billion in "swaps" were entered into.[16] While the business of designing new securities has been driven by often abstruse mathematical applications of economic theory, lawyers ultimately have a central role to play in this design process.[17]

What forces cause financial innovation? A partial answer is taxes and regulation. If an issuer can avoid either by designing a new instrument, it has a rational incentive to do so. Another answer is that corporate issuers attempt to reduce their aggregate cost of capital by exploiting any special taste that a particular clientele has for some combination of risk and return. Often, the new security is some hybrid of debt and equity that gives the investors features of both.[18] Or the investment may permit the investor to hedge as well as receive an interest rate return. For example, the issuer may key its interest rate not to the prime rate (or some other standard benchmark) but to the performance of some index of securities or foreign currencies. Ultimately, this process of innovation widens investor choice, affording investors new and competing

---

16. See, Hu, New Financial Products, the Modern Process of Financial Innovation, and the Puzzle of Shareholder Welfare, 69 Tex.L.Rev. 1273 (1991).

17. If further incentive is necessary, law students should understand that a recent "biography" of one of the nation's leading law firms reported that one of the four ways to make partner there was to "[i]nvent a new securities instrument." See N. Lisagor & F. Lipsius, A Law Unto Itself: The Untold Story of The Law Firm of Sullivan & Cromwell (1988) at 277–78.

18. Some new products have elicited disapproval from the SEC's staff. An example is the inverse floating rate bond (or "inverse floater"), whose interest rate varies inversely with the prevailing rate on short-term debt. Thus, its yield is high when short-term rates

are low, but it can drop precipitously when prevailing rates rise. In 1991, the SEC's staff warned money market funds that it considered such a risky security "highly inappropriate" for them to hold. See Jasen, Some Funds Drop "Inverse Floaters" After SEC Warning, Wall St.J., Dec. 27, 1991 at C–1.

An example of a less controversial hybrid is convertible exchangeable preferred stock, which was first introduced in 1982. It gives the holder a right to convert it into common stock, but also gives the issuer the right to exchange the preferred stock for the issuer's convertible debentures. See, Hu, supra note 16, at 1294. Increasingly, debt securities now come with novel warrant provisions, sometimes involving detachable warrants that can be separately traded.

products that both provide them an economic return and partially hedge them against interest and currency fluctuations.

Despite the flurry of new products, some common denominators in this process of transition stand out and merit brief emphasis:

1. *Equity Derivatives.* An equity derivative is a security or private contract whose cash value rises or falls based on some stock or market index to which it is tied.[19] It can take the form of an option, a warrant, a swap, a bond, or some other hybrid. While some corporations issue such products, securities dealers do so more frequently in the form of put and call options on any of a number of domestic and foreign stock indices (such as, for example, the Nikkei 225 stock index for those wishing to bet for or against the Japanese stock market).

2. *Securitization.* While definitions vary, "securitization" refers to a process by which an illiquid financial asset that has no secondary market is converted into a tradeable security with an active secondary market.[20] The process first developed through the efforts of banks and other lenders to repackage their mortgage loans into a pool in which they could sell collateralized interests to investors. To do this, banks would transfer a large number of such loans to a trustee or other special purpose entity (who would administer and service the pool) and then would sell debt securities in the pool. By pooling their loans and selling interests in them, banks improved their capital ratios and escaped regulatory requirements that otherwise forced them to maintain reserves on their own balance sheets equal to some proportion of the transferred loans.

There are usually two key steps in the process of securitization: First, there typically must be some "credit enhancer"—another bank, surety company, insurer, or possibly a federal agency, who provides credit support, either through a letter of credit, guarantee, or other assurance that the cash flow from the pooled financial assets will be sufficient to meet the principal and interest payments due on the securities. Second, the financial asset being securitized must be segregated from the sponsor's other assets in order to insulate the securitized asset from any financial risks associated with the sponsor's possible insolvency. This second step is achieved by transferring the assets to a trust or some "special purpose vehicle" that is restricted from engaging in any other activity.

The variety of securitized loans has proliferated. After mortgage-backed loans, financial institutions next repackaged car loans, credit card loans, computer leases, and insurance premium loans. Even "securitized" third world loans are now being marketed. By the end of 1989, roughly $900 billion in mortgage-backed securities was outstanding, and General Motors Acceptance Corporation alone had securitized over $7 billion worth of its car loans.[21]

3. *"Unbundling."* Another development in securities design has been the attempt to subdivide a common stock share into its different economic compo-

19. Hansell, Is The World Ready For Synthetic Equity? Institutional Investor, Aug.1990, at 54, 55; for a broader overview, see Kleinbard, Equity Derivative Products: Financial Innovation's Newest Challenge to the Tax System, 69 Texas L.Rev. 1319 (1991).

20. See T. Frankel, Securitization: Structured Financing, Financial Asset Pools, and Asset–Backed Securities (1991); Shenker & Coletta, Asset Securitization: Evolution, Current Issues, and New Frontiers, 69 Tex. L.Rev. 1369 (1991).

21. See Frankel, supra note 20, at 8.

nents, which are then separately marketed to different groups of investors. For example, one investment banking house proposed to subdivide the shares of several of its major corporate clients into three component units: (1) one unit representing the current dividend stream; (2) another unit reflecting any dividend increase in the future; and (3) a final unit holding the right to any equity appreciation.[22]

As contemplated, the firm's clients would offer their shareholders an opportunity to exchange their common shares for a package of these three units, which would thereafter trade separately. Although this particular plan was eventually dropped,[23] third parties have put similar unbundling plans into operation, even without the consent of the issuer. Under a device known as an "Americus Trust," shares of a corporation are placed in a trust, which then issues a "Prime" security, reflecting the dividend and voting rights of the stock, and a "Score" security, reflecting capital appreciation above a stated price.[24] Underlying these marketing efforts is again the search for investors with special tastes and preferences (either for more or less risk or for special tax treatment).

4. *Exchange Traded Funds ("ETFs").* The newest and most dramatically successful product are exchange traded funds. ETFs are derivatives or baskets of securities that generally track a well-known index or industry sector, but at the same time trade like a share of stock. For example, an ETF could replicate the "S&P 500," the "Nasdaq 100," or the "Dow Jones Index." A mutual fund could also do this, but open-ended mutual funds can only be traded as of the end of the day through redemptions and closed-end mutual funds usually are subject to substantial discounts below their net asset value. In contrast, an ETF owns a fixed basket of stocks, and the investor buys or sells this basket, instead of a proportionate interest in a larger mutual fund. Typically, the EFT's market value does not deviate more than one-half percentage point from the net value of its underlying assets. Also, while trades in even closed-end mutual funds will be valued as of the closing price at 4 p.m., ETFs permit the investor who wants immediacy to buy at the 10:00 a.m. price of the ETF and sell at its 2:00 p.m. price, realizing any intra-day gain or loss. Some ETFs are now well known: "Spiders" track the Standard & Poor's 500–stock index, while "Diamonds" mimic the Dow Jones Industrial Average. In the nine years since ETFs were invented in 1993,[25] their assets have grown to $81 billion, and some 117 ETFs are now traded.[26]

In short, the success of ETFs seems to show how competition spurs innovation—and also how much investors want to trade not individual stocks, but baskets of securities, as next discussed.

22. See Anders & Salwen, Package Deal: Firms Seeking to Raise Value of Shares, Plan to Restructure Stock, Wall St. J., Dec. 6, 1988, at A–1; see also Hu, supra note 16, at 1299–1300.

23. Eventually, the plan failed because of special accounting problems. See Anders & Winkler, Shearson to Withdraw Unbundled Stock Plan, Wall St. J., Mar. 29, 1989, at C1. Certain of Shearson's major corporate clients had, however, bought the idea and begun to implement it.

24. See Hu, supra note 16, at 1300.

25. The first ETFs were Spiders (or "SPDRs" for S&P Depositary Receipts) which began trading on the AMEX in 1993. See Walter Updegrave, "Index Mania: Is the Flood of New Index funds too much of a good thing?" MONEY, p. 75 (June, 2002).

26. See Jeffrey Kosnett, "Who's Afraid of Spiders," Kiplinger's Personal Finance Magazine, at p. 38 (June 2002).

C.   NEW TRADING STRATEGIES

The October 1987 stock market crash raised the danger that developments in one market could impact adversely on another. Some even assigned partial causal responsibility for the crash to excessive reliance on new trading strategies known as "portfolio insurance" and dynamic hedging.

"Portfolio insurance" refers to a variety of dynamic hedging strategies used by investors to control market risk in both equity and fixed income portfolios.[27] These strategies are designed to provide protection against loss at the cost of some limitation on the opportunities for appreciation. The core of these strategies is disciplined buying or selling triggered by pre-set parameters relating to substantial market movements. A small market decline may trigger pre-determined selling by indexed investors in order to mitigate exposure. In this manner, portfolio insurance strategies are roughly analogous to the use of "stop-loss" orders in individual securities where a sell order is created if the market price of the security falls to the "stop" price. Traditional "stop-loss" orders, however, generally are placed with an exchange specialist, providing the specialist, and indirectly the market as a whole, an indication of potential selling activity. Portfolio insurance, on the other hand, is handled by an upstairs firm and does not provide any prior warning of the amount of potential selling activity it represents—either to the specialist or other market participants.

Portfolio insurance for equity portfolios initially employed the purchase and sale of stocks, but today it is usually implemented through the purchase and sale of stock index futures. As stock prices fluctuate, the portfolio is continually rebalanced between a risky component (stocks) and a riskless component (Treasury bills) so that, in theory, the total portfolio value cannot fall below a specified minimum value. By selling stock index futures while holding a portfolio of the stocks comprising the index, a totally hedged position is created. The stock index future is used in this manner to replicate a riskless security. This hedged position (often called "synthetic cash") provides a return similar to Treasury bills. The "insurance" protection comes through a hedging strategy which involves selling futures, and thus increasing the weighting of synthetic cash relative to stocks, as stock values decline. Conversely, as the value of the stock portfolio increases, stock index futures are purchased, increasing the weighting of stocks relative to synthetic cash. Futures are used instead of stocks because of the increased speed and reduced transaction costs in trading a single product in the futures markets.

Typically, portfolio insurance seeks to assure a minimum value for the portfolio over a specified time period. For example, a typical insurance program might attempt to assure the maintenance of a minimum of 95% of the current portfolio value. The cost of this protection was estimated to be potentially under performing a rising market by two to four percent.

Two things are required to achieve the goal of maintaining a minimum value of the portfolio: the disciplined selling in a declining market (or buying in a rising market) of a set amount of futures at various trigger points and the presence of a presumed level of liquidity in the futures markets. In this regard,

---

27. Because of frequent adjustment of the hedge over time and of changes in the value of the portfolio, this strategy also is called "dynamic hedging."

the insurance program is intended to be similar to a long-term index put option with a strike price equal to the ending minimum portfolio value.

As early as 1986, the SEC noted concern by some commentators that index-related trading strategies could fuel a market decline severe and rapid enough to cause a stock market collapse through the following "cascade scenario:" the scenario begins with index futures prices moving to a sufficient discount (because of fundamentals and other factors) to trigger short side index arbitrage; this in turn necessitated block sales of stocks, which further depress the equity market to levels that trigger portfolio insurance programs; these programs, which involve futures sales, further depress futures prices and cause the cycle to repeat itself; the resultant plunge in stock prices triggers stop-loss sell orders in individual stocks, and forces additional liquidations to meet margin calls and broker-dealer capital requirements, finally leading to a market collapse.[28]

Did these passive trading strategies actually cause the market collapse in 1987? Could they do so again? The Presidential Task Force on Market Mechanisms (the "Brady Commission") appointed by President Bush to identify the causes of the October 1987 crash saw one central lesson emerging from that crash: namely that the stock and futures markets are interdependent and thus their regulation must be coordinated. Its principal findings are summarized below:

Excerpt from:

Report of the Presidential Task Force on Market Mechanisms
January, 1988.

Chapter Six

ONE MARKET: STOCKS, STOCK INDEX FUTURES, AND STOCK OPTIONS

Analysis of market behavior during the crucial days in mid-October makes clear an important conclusion. From an economic viewpoint, what have been traditionally seen as separate markets—the markets for stocks, stock index futures, and stock options—are in fact one market. Under ordinary circumstances these marketplaces move sympathetically, linked by a number of forces. The pathology which resulted when the linkages among these market segments failed underlay the market break of October.

Many mechanisms link these marketplaces. The instruments—stocks, stock index futures and stock options—are fundamentally driven by the same economic forces. The same major investment banks dominate the trading among all three segments, both in executing orders for others and for their own accounts. In addition, many of the same institutions are responsible for a large amount of the trading in all three instruments, and particularly in stocks and index futures.

Many of the trading strategies discussed in this Report also serve to link these marketplaces. Index arbitrage provides a direct linkage between the stock

---

28.   The fullest statement of the "Cascade Scenario" can be found in Report by the Division of Market Regulation, U.S. Securities and Exchange Commission, THE OCTOBER 1987 MARKET BREAK (February, 1988).

and index futures markets. Faced with increasingly chaotic markets in October, portfolio insurers, to the extent possible, abandoned their reliance on the futures markets to execute their strategies and switched to selling stocks directly, underlining the commonality among market functions. Another link is the routine use of the futures markets by institutions investing in index funds as a fast and low-cost entry and exit vehicle to the stock market. And, of course, a host of hedging strategies for individual stock positions employ counterbalancing purchases and sales by market makers in these marketplaces.

Market makers in these markets routinely hedge their positions by trading in two markets. For example, market makers in the S&P 100 option hedge by using the S&P 500 futures contract, and some NYSE specialists also hedge their market making activities with futures contracts. Specialists and market makers in futures and options constantly monitor up-to-the-minute prices in other markets on electronic screens. Market makers tend to carry minimal positions from day-to-day, providing liquidity for normal market moves but not for the kind of abnormally large swings experienced in October 1987.

Clearing procedures in the several market segments produce further intertwining. While it is not yet possible to cross-margin positions, proceeds from sales in one market segment may provide funds needed to pay for purchases in another. Fears that a clearinghouse in one market segment might be unable to deliver funds owed to investors can ignite concern throughout the system, as it did in October.

In sum, what may appear superficially to be three separate markets—for stocks, stock options, and stock index futures—in fact behaves as one market.

As the data in Chapter Four make clear, the market's break was exacerbated by the failure of institutions employing portfolio insurance strategies to understand that the markets in which the various instruments trade are economically linked into one equity market. Portfolio insurance theory assumes that it would be infeasible to sell huge volumes of stock on the exchange in short periods of time with only a small price impact. These institutions came to believe that the futures market offered a separate haven of liquidity sufficient to allow them to liquidate huge positions over short periods of time with minimal price displacement.

In October, this belief proved to be unrealistic. The futures market simply could not absorb such selling pressure without dramatic price declines. Moreover, reflecting the natural linkages among markets, the selling, pressure washed across to the stock market, both through index arbitrage and direct portfolio insurance stock sales. Large amounts of selling, and the demand for liquidity associated with it, cannot be contained in a single market segment. It necessarily overflows into the other market segments, which are naturally linked. There are, however, natural limits to intermarket liquidity which were made evident on October 19 and 20.

Just as the failure of sellers to understand that they were trading in a single equity market exacerbated the market break, so, too, did the breakdown of certain structural mechanisms linking these separate market segments. Unopened stocks inhibited trading in the derivative instruments. The CME's [Chicago Mercantile Exchange] temporary closing, and the difficulties the CBOE [Chicago Board Options Exchange] had in opening options trading, interfered with intermarket transactions. Transaction delays through the

NYSE's DOT system, and the subsequent decision to prohibit proprietary index arbitrage through the system, also disconnected the market segments.

Under normal circumstances, index arbitrage acts as one of the primary bridges between stock and futures markets. By midday October 19, this arbitrage became difficult. First, transactions backed up in the DOT system, and then, on subsequent days, access to the system was denied to these traders. However, had the system functioned more effectively, this linkage would have been incapable of transmitting the full weight of the estimated $25 billion of selling dictated by portfolio insurance strategies.

Even as direct arbitrage between stocks and futures failed, portfolio insurers provided some indirect arbitrage when they switched from selling futures to selling stocks. The amount of such indirect arbitrage was limited by, among other things, structural and regulatory rigidities. Many insurers were authorized to sell only futures, not stocks, for their clients, and so they continued to sell futures despite the large discount which confronted them. Many institutional stock investors are not authorized to purchase futures contracts, and therefore they could not supply buying support to the market despite the discount.

Differences in margin and clearinghouse mechanisms contributed further to the failure of linkages within the single equity market. Many investors, not fully understanding margin and clearing mechanisms in futures, responded to rumors of payment failures, and the reality of late payments, by the CME clearinghouse, by refusing to buy in the futures market.

The decisions of lenders were also influenced by concerns over inconsistencies among the several markets. The complexity of clearing massive volumes of stocks, options, and futures through separate clearinghouses caused some lenders to hesitate in extending credit. The consequent threat of financial gridlock posed the prospect of major financial system breakdown on October 20, prompting the Federal Reserve to boost investor confidence by promising to inject liquidity into the market.

A number of factors ultimately contributed to the failure of the stock and futures markets to function as one market. As the markets became disengaged, a near freefall developed in both markets. Sellers put direct downward pressure on both markets. As large discounts developed between futures and stocks, those investors who could, switched from selling futures to selling stocks. Those unable to switch continued to sell futures, driving these prices down further. Stock investors not authorized to purchase futures, or fearful of buying them, provided no offsetting buying support in the futures market.

The enormous futures discounts signalled to prospective stock buyers that further declines were imminent. At one point on October 20, for example, the stock index futures price was "forecasting" a Dow of 1,400. This "billboard effect" inhibited some stock purchases. Moreover, the futures discount made stocks appear expensive, inhibiting buying support for the market.

The pathology of disconnected markets fed on itself. Faced with a surfeit of sellers and a scarcity of buyers, both markets—futures and stock—were at times on October 19 and 20 nearly in freefall.

The ability of the equity market to absorb the huge selling pressure to which it was subjected in mid-October depended on its liquidity. During periods of normal volume, the liquidity provided by market makers and specialists in the separate market segments is sufficient. When abnormal demands confront the equity market, the liquidity in each marketplace is unimportant. Specialists in the stock market and market makers in the futures market go home at the end of each day with, at most, relatively small positions. Investors must depend on the liquidity supplied by participants in the entire equity market. The ability to sell futures is linked to stock market liquidity and vice versa.

The liquidity apparent during periods of normal volume provided by the activities of market makers and active traders on both sides of the market is something of an illusion. Liquidity sufficient to absorb the selling demands of a limited number of investors becomes an illusion of liquidity when confronted by massive selling, as everyone shows up on the same side of the market at once. As with people in a theatre when someone yells "Fire!", these sellers all ran for the exit in October, but it was large enough to accommodate only a few. For these sellers, it takes time to find buyers on the other side of the market. Potential buyers, such as value investors, do not operate by formula and must have adequate time to assemble data and make evaluations before they will commit to buy.

Certain important conclusions should be drawn from the behavior of the markets for stocks, stock index futures, and options in mid-October. First and foremost, these apparently separate markets are in an economic sense one market. They are linked by instruments, participants, trading strategies and clearing flows. Nonetheless, institutional and regulatory structures interfere with the linkages among them and hinder their smooth and efficient operation.

The illusion of liquidity in the futures, options and stock markets contrasts with the reality of the overall equity market's liquidity—the finite capacity of this single, inextricably fused system of markets to absorb major selling or buying demands. Ironically, it was this illusion of liquidity which led some similarly motivated investors, such as portfolio insurers, to adopt strategies which call for liquidity far in excess of what the market could supply.

A number of failures of the one market system contributed to the violent break of the separate market segments in October and pushed the country to the brink of the financial system's limits. It is not possible to prevent investors from being misinformed about the capabilities of markets or to prevent markets from adjusting to the demands put upon them. But it is only prudent to design mechanisms to protect investors, the market's infrastructures, the financial system and the economy from the destructive consequence of violent market breaks.

* * *

———————

Responses to Market Volatility. The growth in market volatility has many explanations and few easy answers on the policy level. Clearly, the growth in institutional trading, the development of parallel markets in equity derivatives, and the appearance of new inter-market trading strategies (both index arbitrage and portfolio insurance) contribute to the explanation of the 1987 crash and subsequent smaller market breaks. Most, but not all, commentators believe that the market mechanisms failed during the 1987 crash.[29] Among the

29. For the most notable dissenter from this view, see Roll, The International Crash of 1987, in Black Monday and the Future of the Financial Markets 35, 36–39

structural failures that much commentary has pointed to, the following usually are cited: (1) the overwhelming of the capacity of stock exchange specialists and Nasdaq dealers to handle the selling pressure that was generated, first by portfolio trading strategies and later by panic; (2) the breakdown of linkages between the stock and futures markets; and (3) the misperception by institutional investors of the market's liquidity and their ability to trade ahead of market adjustments through the use of portfolio insurance.

In the wake of the crash, a host of regulatory proposals were made, including (1) to designate one regulatory agency to coordinate and supervise inter-market trading in equity products; (2) to transfer the CFTC's jurisdiction over stock index futures to the SEC; (3) to raise margin levels on financial futures; (4) to adopt "circuit breakers," such as price or volume-triggered trading halts, to prevent panic; (5) to prohibit index arbitrage and program trading (and possibly equity derivatives as well); (6) to develop a stock market "basket" product that would trade on the New York Stock Exchange and replace stock index futures and options; and (7) to increase the capital requirements for specialists and dealers.[30] Today, nearly five years later, it seems clear that the forces of inertia have proven generally more powerful than the forces for change. No constituency exists for significant structural reform of the securities and futures markets.

Some more modest reforms have, however, been implemented:

Restrictions on Index Arbitrage. Although the Brady Commission argued that any restrictions on program trading or index arbitrage needed to be imposed on a market-wide basis (lest they otherwise exacerbate inter-market disparities), the growing friction between the stock and futures exchanges resulted in localized, single-market reforms that seemingly violate its "one market" concept. Alarmed by growing evidence of market volatility, the New York Stock Exchange ("NYSE") sought by various means to limit the use of index arbitrage during periods of market instability. In 1990, the NYSE secured SEC approval on a one-year pilot basis for an NYSE rule that restricts index arbitrage trading whenever the Dow Jones Industrial Average moves 50 points or more (up or down) from the previous day's close. Under NYSE Rule 80A (known popularly as the "Collar Rule"), index arbitrage orders in the component stocks of the S&P 500 index are then subjected to a "tick test." That is, if the market falls 50 points or more, arbitrage sell orders may only be executed on a "plus or zero-plus tick" (meaning that the last price movement in the stock must have been upward). Conversely, if the market rises 50 points or more, buy orders for arbitrage purposes may only be executed on a "minus" or "zero-minus" tick.[31]

Implemented by the NYSE at the same time as tensions escalated in the Persian Gulf in late 1990, Rule 80A was triggered 23 times in 22 days between August 1, 1990 and December 31, 1990.[32] Studying the impact of Rule 80A, the

(R. Kamphuis, R. Kormendi & J. Watson eds. 1989). Professor Roll, a distinguished financial economist, points out that the major stock indices of most industrialized countries around the world declined during October 1987, which, he asserts, "debunks the notion that an institutional defect in the U.S." caused the crash.

30. These proposals are reviewed in detail in 5 L. Loss & J. Seligman, Securities Regulation (3rd ed. 1990), at 2494–2506. See also M. Mayer, Markets (1988).

31. Thus, the "tick test" parallels similar restrictions imposed by the stock exchanges on short selling.

32. See New York Stock Exchange, Inc., The Rule 80A Index Arbitrage Tick

NYSE reported that it significantly dampened index arbitrage activity, while also reducing volatility in the stock markets. Still, although a milder restriction than a trading halt, the NYSE approach does protect the stock market by attempting to shelter it from volatility emanating from the futures exchanges— seemingly the type of piecemeal reform against which the Brady Commission had warned.

After an extended consideration of the NYSE's report on Rule 80A, the SEC concluded in late 1991 that the rule had not adversely impacted on the equity derivatives market and approved it as a permanent rule.[33]

Circuit Breakers. In contrast to the each-exchange-for-itself philosophy underlying Rule 80A's limitations on index arbitrage, a more coordinated, system-wide approach has been taken with regard to "circuit breakers." Under NYSE Rule 80B, if the Dow Jones Industrial Average falls by 250 points or more below its previous day's close, trading in all stocks will halt for one hour. If, thereafter, the decline continues to 400 points or more, a trading delay of an additional hour will be imposed.[34] Similar rules or policies have been adopted by the principal other stock and futures exchanges.

At the time of their adoption, the NYSE's circuit breaker rule required a 12% and 19% one day price drop before its two trading halts were triggered. With the tremendous appreciation in the stock market during the 1990s, however, a 250 point decline became a much smaller percentage decline (roughly 3.7% in mid–1997). As a result, the NYSE proposed, and the SEC agreed, in 1997 to move the circuit breaker levels to 350 and 550 points, respectively, with the first decline triggering only a half-hour trading halt and the second an additional hour.[35] This change may also support the widely held belief that the primary purpose of this rule was symbolic: to maintain investor confidence by assuring them that rules exist to present the market from nose-diving into a free fall.

Large Traders and Emergency Trading Suspensions. The principal legislative response to the 1987 crash (and the subsequent increase in stock volatility) was the Market Reform Act of 1990 which added Sections 12(k) and 13(h) to the 1934 Act. Under Section 12(k), the SEC can now order a trading suspension or, in language that is potentially very broad, enter an emergency order "to alter, supplement, suspend, or impose requirements or restrictions * * * to maintain or restore fair and orderly securities markets." Section 13(h) is more limited in its focus. In order to enable the SEC to reconstruct the trading activity of large traders during periods of market stress, Section 13(h) instructs the SEC to develop a "large trader" reporting system. Under Rule 13h–1,

Test: Interim Report to the U.S. Securities & Exchange Commission (January 31, 1991). The report also found no "statistically significant evidence that Rule 80A produces a 'magnet effect.' " Some have worried that "circuit breakers" and similar rules restricting trade would encourage prices to move with greater momentum as the threshold at which trading would stop was neared.

33. See Securities Exch. Act Rel. No. 34–29854 (Oct. 24, 1991).

34. See Securities Exch. Act Rel. No. 34–26198 (Oct. 19, 1988) (adopting initial circuit breaker rule); Securities Exch. Act Rel. No. 34–29768 (Sept. 30, 1991) (proposed extension of circuit breaker rules to late 1992).

35. See Securities Exchange Act Rel. No. 34–38221, 1997 SEC LEXIS 234, 1997 WL 39720 (January 31, 1997).

broker-dealers are required to maintain and preserve aggregated data on the trading activity of such traders.[36]

Steps Not Taken. Despite efforts by the Brady Commission and the SEC to harmonize the margin rules applicable to stocks and stock index futures, Congress has declined to move in this direction. Indeed, Congress has instead moved in a deregulatory direction, and the National Securities Markets Improvement Act of 1997 largely deregulated broker dealers that are members of a national securities exchange, both in extending credit and in arranging for the extension of credit by others.[37] Increasingly, there is a sense that the original purposes underlying the margin rules (namely, to limit the credit available for securities purchases in order to inhibit boom-and-bust stock market cycles and to prevent the drying up of credit to other sectors of the economy) have become outdated.[38]

While program trading volume declined briefly after the 1987 crash, it has rebounded sharply and according to recent estimates now accounts for approximately 12% of the volume on the New York Stock Exchange.[39] Indeed, some argue that the virtue of program trading is that it today provides a level of liquidity to the New York Stock Exchange that renders the traditional specialist system effectively obsolete.[40]

D. INTERNATIONALIZATION: CAUSES AND CONSEQUENCES

Twenty years ago, it would have been meaningless to talk about the worldwide securities market or global trading. Back then, local securities markets were protected by barriers to cross-border capital flow, currency differences, and the sheer improbability that technological changes could create functional equivalents to securities exchanges that were beyond the effective reach of any single regulator. Local securities exchanges were usually considered quasi-public entities and were protected by paternalistic governments from competitive pressure. All this changed dramatically during the 1990's.

Change came from two different directions at the same time. First, institutional investors, particularly in the U.S., recognized the need to diversify their portfolios to escape country-specific risk. They were attracted both by the high rates of return in some emerging markets and also by the prospect that one national economy could decline, while others surged; international portfolio diversification was the best protection against this risk. As a result, institutional investors began to invest significant portions of their portfolios in offshore investments. Second, as the formerly Socialist world transformed itself, foreign governments began to undertake massive privatization programs by which formerly nationalized industries were sold to the public. The scale of these programs dwarfed local equity markets and required that at least a portion of

---

36. See Securities Exch. Act Rel. No. 34–29593 (August 22, 1991). Large traders are required by this rule to file a Form 13H in order that they can be given a standardized identification number so that their trades through different brokers can be aggregated.

37. See § 8(c)(2) of the Securities Exchange Act of 1934.

38. Critics of margin regulation generally deny that there is any close linkage be-

tween margin regulation and stock market volatility. See e.g., Hsieh and Miller, Margin Regulation and Stock Market Volatility, 45 J. Finance 3 (March, 1990).

39. See Booth, The Uncertain Case for Regulating Program Trading, 1994 Col.Bus. L.Rev. 1, 6 (1994).

40. See Booth, supra note 39 (reviewing arguments on both sides).

the offering be sold in the U.S. These offerings started a broader migration by which foreign corporations came to list their securities in the U.S. market, in particular on the NYSE. Between 1985 and 2002, the number of foreign issuer listings on the NYSE rose from 3.5% of its listings to over 16%. As of early 2001, over 970 non-U.S. firms were listed on the NYSE, Nasdaq or the AMEX,[41] and over 1,951 "active" depository receipt programs involving 1,525 firms from 80 countries had been created in the U.S. by which foreign issuers made it possible for U.S. investors to trade their shares.[42]

Why did these issuers migrate to the U.S. to cross-list on U.S. exchanges? Reasons vary. Many emerging market companies cross-listed on U.S. exchanges in order to do equity offerings that would not be feasible in their own country. Adopting the higher disclosure and accounting standards that U.S. law requires may have also helped them assure minority investors that they would not be overreached.[43] European companies have often cross-listed their shares in the U.S. in order to convert their shares into an attractive currency for purposes of stock-for-stock acquisitions of U.S. companies. In the case of emerging markets, particularly those in Latin America, trading in the stock has followed in the wake of the cross-listing, and often the majority of the trading in major Mexican and Brazilian stocks now occurs on the NYSE, with the consequence that liquidity has been drained from local markets.

Competition among exchanges has not always worked to the U.S.'s advantage. For example, trading in the financial futures markets has predominantly moved to London and Europe, where once the U.S. had a virtual monopoly as the inventor of financial futures.[44] Both the improved technology employed by European exchanges and the lesser degree of regulation to which they are subject may explain this migration. Also, in the competition among market centers, liquidity attracts liquidity. Once any market becomes appreciably deeper than its rivals, it will naturally drain liquidity from them.

As U.S. investors have gone abroad, a scenario has arisen under which the SEC could lose much of its power to regulate transactions that might effectively move beyond its reach. For example, if an offshore Internet exchange were to appear and begin to trade U.S. companies, U.S. investors might be able to trade on it in ways that would not be permitted in the U.S. (selling short when they could not do so in the U.S., employing more margin than U.S. law permits, and engaging in insider trading). Some academic commentators believe such a state of affairs would be desirable because it would create a "regulatory competition"

41. See Michael Gruson, Global Shares of German Corporations and their Dual Listings on the Frankfurt and New York Stock Exchanges, 22 U. Pa. J. Int'l Econ. L. 185 (2001).

42. Claessens, Djankov and Klingebeil, Stock Markets in Transition Economies, World Bank Financial Sector Discussion Paper No. 5 (Sept. 2000).

43. The entry of foreign issuers into the U.S. market may represent a form of "bonding." That is, by voluntarily subjecting themselves to public and private enforcement (by the SEC and by class action plaintiffs) and by agreeing to reconcile their financial statements to U.S. generally accepted accounting principles (U.S. GAAP), foreign issuers credibly commit to make fuller and fairer disclosure—and thereby reduce their cost of capital. See John Coffee, The Future As History: The Prospects for Global Convergence in Corporate Governance and Its Implications, 93 Nw. U. L. Rev. 641 (explaining this "bonding" thesis).

44. See Merton Miller, International Competitiveness of U.S. Futures Exchanges, 4 J. of Fin. Services Research 387 (Dec. 1990).

that would prune inefficient or out-of-date regulation.[45] Thus, they have argued that the SEC should anticipate these developments by allowing all firms to choose the disclosure and securities law applicable to them (even if they are U.S. based firms). In other words, U.S. issuers listed on the NYSE could choose to be governed by Taiwan or Chile's securities law. Others have disagreed, arguing that such an "issuer choice" system would produce sub-optimal disclosure, because issuers, as private entities, will not incur the costs necessary to assure the socially optimal level of disclosure.[46]

Meanwhile, securities regulators around the world have sought to resist any such regulatory competition and instead have focused on harmonizing their disclosure requirements to accommodate the growing global market. The International Organization of Securities Commissions ("IOSCO") has led this effort and essentially reached international consensus on securities disclosure standards. Before full harmonization is possible, however, similar agreement must be reached on accounting standards. Here, the SEC and the International Accounting Standards Committee ("IASC") appear to be resolving their differences, but consensus has not yet been reached.

Globalization has caused the SEC to relax some standards. Rule 144A, adopted in 1991, permits foreign issuers and nonpublic U.S. companies to do private offerings with very sophisticated U.S. institutions and then allows these investors to trade these securities freely among themselves. This exemption from the SEC's normal registration requirements was motivated at least in part by the perception that U.S. institutions would have otherwise gone abroad to effect these same transactions with foreign issuers, with one result being that U.S. investment banking firms would have been left out of these transactions.

Another continuing development spurred by globalization has been the growth of multi-national securities exchanges. Nasdaq now has branches in Europe, Japan and Hong Kong, and several foreign exchanges have merged (Euronext, a union of the Paris, Belgium and Netherlands markets, being the largest of these); others are rapidly forming international alliances. Simultaneously, Nasdaq and most European exchanges have privatized themselves and are now operated as profit-making entities. As such, they are eager to do a more global business, either by crossing borders themselves or attracting foreign issuers to cross-list on them.

Will globalization produce a regulatory "race to the bottom" as issuers cross-list on the exchanges with the least regulation? The current evidence is that the reverse is happening, as firms appear to be migrating to exchanges with the highest listing and disclosure standards in order to reduce their cost of capital and achieve other goals.[47]

Other factors that need to be evaluated in any discussion of globalization include the following:

45. See Roberta Romano, Empowering Investors: A Market Approach to Securities Regulation, 107 Yale L. J. 2359 (1998); Stephen Choi & Andrew Guzman, Portable Reciprocity: Rethinking the International Reach of Securities Regulation, 71 S. Cal. L. Rev. 903 (1998).

46. See Merritt B. Fox, Retaining Mandatory Securities Disclosure: Why Issue Choice Is Not Investor Empowerment, 85 Va. L. Rev. 1335 (1999).

47. See Howell Jackson and Eric Pan, Regulatory Competition in International Securities Markets: Evidence from Europe in 1999—Part I, 56 Bus. Law. 653 (2001).

Market interconnections. When the Dow Jones Industrial Average fell over 22% on one day in October, 1987, a ripple went around the world. The Tokyo Stock market declined 15 percent the next day, and the London market similarly fell 12.2 percent. Developments on one market clearly impact others.

Capital Market Imbalances. Because of international differences in savings rates, trade imbalances and investment opportunities, some nations are capital exporters; others, capital importers. Early in the 1980s, the OPEC nations were the principal capital exporters; later, Japan with its high savings rate assumed that role. Consistently, the U.S. has been an importer, creating worldwide shifts in capital flows.

Technology. Advances in computer and telecommunications technology have reduced the cost of trading in all markets, and made the worldwide communication of financial information on a current basis feasible. Armed with computers, traders anywhere in the world can analyze complex data quickly and retrieve market prices from any of the world's capital markets on their computer screens.

Finance Theory. Modern finance theory stresses the necessity of portfolio diversification and teaches techniques for arbitraging between markets to reduce risk. Diversification across national markets is simply an obvious application of this theory in order to reduce risks from any one national economy.

Derivative Markets. The growth of markets in equity derivatives has greatly reduced the cost of diversification, so that investors can quickly and cheaply invest in, or hedge through, stock indices covering a particular national economy. A U.S. investor can buy futures or options contracts covering market indices broadly reflecting the Japanese, British, Canadian or Asian economies.

Deregulation. With the deregulation of the London stock exchanges in 1987 (as part of their "Big Bang"[48]), a competition has begun among markets on an international scale to determine which can offer higher liquidity, lower transaction costs, and less unnecessary regulation. The threat of foreign competition and capital flight has increasingly become a lobbying tool and political weapon in U.S. regulatory debates.

E.   RESTRUCTURING OF THE FINANCIAL SERVICES INDUSTRY

For decades, banks, securities firms, and insurance companies have been legislatively separated, legally unable to own, or to engage in the core activities of, the others. Two principal statutes enforced this separation: the 1933 Glass–Steagall Act, which denied banks the ability to underwrite securities, and the 1956 Bank Holding Act, which effectively separated banks from insurance companies. Although the Federal Reserve Board had gradually relaxed many of the prohibitions of both statutes over the last decade, full convergence between these three types of financial institutions was not possible without legislative action. On at least ten occasions over the last twenty years, Congress had considered legislation that would have removed or modified these restrictions, but for a variety of different reasons each attempt failed—until 1999.

The Repeal of Glass–Steagall. In late 1999, the Gramm–Leach–Bliley Financial Modernization Act ("GLB") passed Congress with overwhelming

---

48. For an overview, see Poser, Big Bang and The Financial Services Act Seen Through American Eyes, 14 Brooklyn J. of Int'l. L. 317 (1988).

support and was signed into law. Despite earlier failures, the passage of GLB in 1999 reflected both a sense that market developments had already outflanked many of the legislative restrictions, which now seemed antiquated, and a newly dominant view that financial convergence was desirable. The Glass–Steagall Act had been a product of the Great Depression and the then prevalent belief that the involvement of banks in securities transactions had contributed to the massive bank insolvencies during the Depression and also the severity of the 1929 stock market crash. Although revisionist economic historians have increasingly challenged these assumptions, GLB incorporates a number of safeguards and procedures that show continuing Congressional concern about banks straying too far from their traditional activities.

Essentially, GLB does the following:

1. It repeals the restrictions on banks affiliating with securities firms that were formerly contained in sections 20 and 32 of the Glass–Steagall Act, which sections had prohibited commercial banks from being affiliated with companies that were "principally engaged" in securities underwriting;

2. It authorizes a new entity—a "financial holding company"—which is permitted to engage in a statutorily provided list of financial activities, including insurance and securities underwriting;

3. It specifically permits financial holding companies to engage in "merchant banking" and thereby hold equity stakes, including controlling positions, in non-financial corporations (in effect, a Citicorp could now in theory own a controlling stake in IBM or General Motors);

4. It preserves the existing system of "functional regulation" by mandating that most securities activities undertaken by a financial institution will be overseen by the SEC, most insurance activities by state insurance commissions, and most banking activities by the Comptroller of the Currency, the Federal Reserve or state banking agencies; and

5. It preempts inconsistent state laws and potentially creates a federal self-regulatory body to regulate insurance, which body would have authority to adopt uniform standards—unless at least a majority of the states adopt uniform or reciprocal laws meeting defined minimum standards, which are intended to assure that states do not discriminate against insurance companies affiliated with a bank, by November 2002.

Limitations. This new freedom conferred on financial holding companies to diversify broadly came, however, subject to several important limitations:

First, to qualify as a "financial holding company," all "depository institutions" owned or controlled by a bank holding company must be found to be "well capitalized" and "well managed;" in addition, each "insured depository institution" must have at least a "satisfactory" rating under the Community Reinvestment Act.

Second, in order to maintain a degree of organizational separation between traditional banking and other activities, the holding company must conduct its riskier activities through affiliates or subsidiaries that do not conduct banking activities. Thus, banks themselves still many only underwrite securities to a limited degree, which activity will generally be conducted by some other subsidiary of the financial holding company.

Third, the broad exemption that banks had enjoyed from broker-dealer registration with the SEC has been replaced by narrower exemptions, which were intended to permit banks to continue their current activities and develop new products, but to require that most securities activities by banks be conducted through a separate securities affiliate, which would be required to register as a broker-dealer with the SEC. In particular, banks that advise mutual funds will be required to register under the Investment Advisers Act.

Fourth, although financial holding companies may now hold controlling stakes in non-financial companies, they may not directly manage the day-to-day activities of such firms—a restriction that seems to reflect a Congressional concern about banks (or their parent companies) becoming too deeply involved in non-financial activities.

Finally, apprehensive that massive new financial conglomerates that combined insurance, banking, and securities activities could infringe the consumer's rights to privacy, GLB enacts special privacy restrictions that require all financial institutions to disclose their privacy policy regarding the sharing of non-public personal information and mandate a notice to customers and an opportunity to "opt-out" of sharing of such information with non-affiliated third parties (subject to limited exceptions).

The new financial holding structure created by GLB was designed in part to create a "two-way street," one in which securities firms or insurance companies could also establish a financial holding company and then acquire a bank. Although bank acquisitions of securities firms have been more common than the reverse form of acquisition (probably because of the typically larger size of bank), securities firm acquisitions of banks have also occurred since the passage of GLB.

Early experience. As of early 2001, slightly more than five hundred financial holding companies had been formed in response to GLB's invitation. Most were modestly capitalized, and appear to have been intended to conduct insurance or merchant banking activities, and not to make acquisitions or engage in underwriting. One large acquisition of a bank (U.S. Trust Corporation) by a broker-dealer (Charles Schwab) occurred in 2000, and the acquirer (Schwab) formed a financial holding company to avail itself of the GLB's permission for cross-sector financial acquisitions.

Controversy has, however, surrounded rules proposed by the SEC to define the activities that banks may conduct without direct SEC oversight. In late June, 2001, the Federal Reserve Board, the Treasury Department, and the Federal Deposit Insurance Corp. jointly criticized the SEC's proposed rules on the grounds that they would force banks to transfer most existing securities activities to a securities affiliate and would thereby "significantly disrupt and may force discontinuation of major lines of business for banks."[49] Such interagency frictions seem likely to continue (on a perhaps less visible level), as the SEC tends to regard banking agencies as "soft" on consumer protection issues, while the latter agencies see the SEC as overly "aggressive."

Commodity Futures Modernization Act of 2000 ("CFMA"). Although less sweeping in scope than GLB, this statute significantly overhauled the regulation of derivatives in three deregulatory respects:

(1) it authorizes the trading of futures on individual securities and narrow-based stock indexes;

---

49. See M. Schroeder, "Federal Regulators Decry 'Critical Flaws' in SEC Rules for Banks' Securities Work," Wall St. J., July 3, 2001 at C–16.

(2) it clarifies the legal status of swaps and other over-the-counter derivatives by exempting derivative contracts entered into by qualifying parties from the oversight of the Commodities Futures Trading Commission ("CFTC"); and

(3) it creates a three-tier structure of derivatives markets and permits the lower two-tier to operate largely outside the oversight of CFTC because they will trade only lower risk products or only between sophisticated parties.

Futures on Individual Securities. The CFMA removed an 18 year-old ban on single-stock futures and narrow-based security indexes, collectively known as "securities futures products."[50] The regulation of such hybrid security and futures products had created a long-standing jurisdictional quandary. When both the Securities and Exchange Commission ("SEC") and the CFTC could not resolve their differences, Congress, in 1982, passed the Shad–Johnson Accord (which was an agreement reached by the then Chairmen of the SEC and CFTC to define their respective jurisdictions), which prohibited the trading of futures contracts on individual nonexempt securities and narrow-based indexes of securities. The rationale for this prohibition was that the CFTC could not as effectively as the SEC police insider trading and market manipulation, and single stock futures and narrow indexes seemingly invited both. However, when foreign exchanges began to trade single-stock futures, futures exchanges objected that their market was moving offshore because U.S. firms were legally disabled from trading products that other markets were happy to trade.

Under the CFMA, the CFTC and the SEC share jurisdiction over security futures products. Consequently, security futures must be traded on markets and through brokers subject to either SEC or CFTC regulation. Although registration with both agencies is necessary for trading in security futures, an interested exchange or broker registered with the SEC, for instance, can obtain parallel registration with the CFTC through an immediately effective notice filling. Moreover, the CFMA amends both the Commodity Exchange Act ("CEA") and the federal securities laws to exempt eligible entities from the otherwise applicable requirements through this notice filing process. In this way, a futures exchange trading single-stock futures can register with the SEC without becoming subject to many requirements applicable to national securities exchanges.

Exclusions for Swaps and OTC derivatives. Ending the legal uncertainty surrounding the $80 trillion market for swaps and OTC derivatives was an important goal of the CFMA. The Act provides exemptions from regulation for those derivative contracts, including swaps, that are entered into by qualifying parties, called "eligible contract participants" ("ECPs"). Eligibility criteria for this designation is limited to individuals and institutions that possess substantial assets ($5,000,000 in the case of a natural person, who even then may only trade in true hedging transactions). Transactions involving "excluded commodities" that are not executed on a trading facility are now outside of the CFTC's jurisdiction, but certain other newer futures products (known as "exempt commodities") remain subject to that agency's anti-fraud, anti-manipulation, and clearing organization provisions.

Swaps on all commodities, not including agricultural commodities, are generally outside of the CEA if, as with "excluded" commodities, the agreement

---

50. Trading in single stock futures should begin in the near future, but awaits registration of the National Futures Associa- tion as a national securities association with the SEC.

is (i) entered into between ECPs, and (ii) not executed or traded on a trading facility. Additionally, swaps qualifying for regulatory immunity must involve individual negotiation between the contract participants.

Regulating exchanges. The CFMA significantly altered the CEA and established three categories of markets: (1) "designated contract markets" (which was the term previously used by the CEA to describe basically the futures exchanges); (2) "derivatives transaction execution facilities" ("DTEFs"); and (3) "exempt" markets.

Only "designated contract markets" can offer products to retail customers on an unrestricted basis—that is, without regard to the type of commodity to be traded or the sophistication of investors. Those exchanges that were already compliant under the old legislative regime automatically qualified for designation as a "designated contract market" after passage of the CFMA. Still, it is possible that some existing futures exchanges (and most new entrants) will prefer to be regulated as DTEFs, at least for some products. DTEFs are subject to an intermediate level of regulation, but can only trade derivatives on specified types of commodities that are perceived as having a low susceptibility to market manipulation. Alternatively, a DTEF can limit trading to ECPs, in which event it can trade any derivatives product, other than a limited number of agricultural products.

The last type of market, an exempt market, is exempted from all provisions of the CEA, other than the CFTC's anti-fraud and anti-manipulation regulations. These entities are envisioned as primarily a forum for "business to business" trading and must therefore satisfy certain restrictive criteria, just as a DTEF must also, concerning the types of market participants (i.e., ECPs) and the characteristics of the underlying commodities traded (in order, for example, to minimize the possibility of manipulation or price fixing). Exempt boards of trade are specifically prohibited from trading futures on securities, including security futures products, exempt securities, and security indexes. The CFMA recognizes, however, that even an exempt market generates some information that should be publicly available. Thus, if the CFTC determines that an exempt board of trade fulfills an important price-discovery function for the underlying commodity, the Act requires that the board daily publish data on trading volume, price, and other information "as appropriate to the market."

Post–Enron reconsiderations. No sooner was Glass–Steagall repealed than a scandal broke which has caused some to reconsider the wisdom of its repeal. Both in the case of Enron and several other recent financial debacles, large financial institutions, acting as both investment banks and commercial banks, have played prominent roles in structuring and financing off-balance sheet transactions by their clients that either have appeared to be fraudulent or that at least denied full disclosure to public investors. Some critics have viewed these questionable transactions as the product of conflicts of interest that the repeal of Glass–Steagall made possible.

In this light, what were the policies underlying Glass–Steagall? The legislative history of the Act was reviewed by Mr. Justice Stewart in *Investment Co. Institute v. Camp*, 401 U.S. 617, 629–34 (1971). Congress foresaw three categories of hazards which might arise through the mixing of commercial and investment banking. First, the involvement of the bank in investment banking and securities activities might lead to the making of unsound loans and investments. Such loans might be made to companies of dubious credit standing in whose stock the securities affiliate had invested, in order to make the stock more attractive. Loans might be made to customers to facilitate the purchase of securities, thereby encouraging speculation. And loans might be made to securities affiliates that had become overextended. The Senate investigation of stock market practices had disclosed that the securities affiliates had become overextended by investing and trading in speculative securities in the rising stock market of the 1920's, only to be wiped out by the disastrous losses incurred in the ensuing bear market.[51] Second, there was thought to be a danger of loss of public confidence in the commercial bank because of its association with an entity that was engaged in the high-risk activity of investment banking. The Court noted that "pressures are created because the bank and the affiliate are closely associated in the public mind, and should the affiliate fare badly, public confidence in the bank might be impaired." Finally, the conflict between the promotional interests of the investment banker and the "obligation of the commercial banker to render disinterested investment advice" might lead to the bank's violation of its fiduciary responsibilities. Mr. Justice Stewart pointed out: "Congress had before it evidence that security affiliates might be driven to unload excessive holdings through the trust department of the sponsor bank."[52] Such fear of "unloading" was justified by the exposure of conflicts of interest and self-dealing which had been engaged in by the banks, the banks' securities affiliates and by the banks' officers and directors.

Academics have been more skeptical about the purposes underlying the Glass–Steagall Act. Some believe that it was intended to redirect the banking industry back to its traditional role as the supplier of commercial credit, while others argue that it was purely the product of a clash of interest groups.[53] In any event, the impact of the Act was clear: national banks that had previously engaged both in commercial and deposit banking on the one hand and investment banking on the other were compelled to choose between commercial banking and investment banking. This completely eliminated the commercial

---

51. Apparently most banks had decided to curtail their investment banking activities even prior to the adoption of the Glass–Steagall Act, although it is not altogether clear whether they simply were making a strategic retreat or whether their withdrawal resulted from seeing the handwriting on the wall. Thus in April, 1933, two months before the passage of the Glass–Steagall Act, the Chase National Bank and the Chase Securities Corporation jointly notified their shareholders (who held the same number of shares in each corporation) that "the experience of the past 10 years had clearly indicated the advisability of separating commercial banking from the general business of investment banking." The proposal was stated to be "in the best interests of the bank and in accord not only with sound banking policy but responsive to enlightened public opinion." Since it appeared impossible to sell the securities business to outside interests, the governing boards recommended that the securities business be terminated and that the securities

affiliate undergo an orderly liquidation. See Senate Hearings on Stock Exchange Practices, supra note 69, at 2296–2297.

52. Investment Co. Institute v. Camp, 401 U.S. at 633, citing Hearings Before a Subcomm. of the Senate Comm. on Banking and Currency, 71st Cong., 3d Sess., on the Operation of National and Federal Reserve banking systems, pursuant to S.Res. 71, at 237.

53. Compare Langevoort, Statutory Obsolescence and the Judicial Process: The Revisionist Role of the Courts in Federal Banking Regulation, 85 Mich.L.Rev. 672, 716–17 (1987) (intent was to return banks to "historic role as provider of commercial credit") with Macey, Special Interest Groups Legislation and the Judicial Function: The Dilemma of Glass–Steagall, 33 Emory L.J. 1, 4 (1984). See also, Comment, Securities Activities Under the Glass–Steagall Act, 35 Emory L.J. 463 (1986).

banks and trust companies from this sector of the investment banking business, and the various bank affiliates were dissolved and liquidated.

SECTION 5.   THE REGULATORY FRAMEWORK

Introduction. Authority for the regulation and oversight of the securities markets in the United States is shared among three levels of regulators; (1) the Securities and Exchange Commission, a federal administrative agency established by the Securities Exchange Act of 1934, (2) a level of self-regulatory organizations, including the stock exchanges, the National Association of Securities Dealers (NASD) (to which virtually all broker-dealers are required by law to belong), and several specialized bodies (such as, for example, the Municipal Securities Rulemaking Board), and (3) state securities commissioners or other state officials who enforce state securities statutes popularly known as the "Blue Sky laws." In addition, the Commodities Futures Trading Commission is an independent federal administrative agency with exclusive authority over the regulation of futures (including most derivatives). The line between where the SEC's authority ends and the CFTC's authority begins has been hazy in the past and is by any standard unrationalized. This brief note will survey each of these organizations and the shifting relationships between them.

The Securities Exchange Commission. An independent non-partisan agency, the SEC administers and enforces the federal securities laws. Above all, the SEC's primary responsibilities are to ensure that the securities markets are fair and honest and to provide investors with adequate disclosure. Organizationally, the Commission is composed of five members: a Chairman and four Commissioners. Commission members are appointed by the President, with the advice and consent of the Senate, for five-year terms. The Chairman is designated by the President. Terms are staggered; one expires on June 5th of every year. Not more than three members may be of the same political party.

Although the foregoing nutshell description covers the basics, it leaves out the SEC's essential role: it is the tough cop of Wall Street. Both in terms of the publicity it receives and the enemies it makes, these disproportionately result from its law enforcement activities. Particularly in this area, the SEC has acquired a reputation for zeal, integrity, and imagination that distinguishes it from most other federal regulatory agencies. Although there is no way to establish which agency is the "best" of the federal agencies, it is fair to assume that the SEC and its staff believe that it has long held that title. More recently, however, the SEC has been chronically underfunded (as the size of the market and its enforcement obligations have expanded while its staff has remained relatively constant). This has created some morale problems.

Organizational Structure. Internally, the SEC is organized into four principal divisions and several important advisory offices:

The Division of Corporate Finance has the overall responsibility of ensuring that disclosure requirements are met by issuers registered with the Commission. Much of its work involves the review of registration statements for public offerings, quarterly and annual reports from publicly held companies, proxy statements, tender offer documents, and related filings in mergers and acquisitions. It also has the primary responsibility for rendering administrative interpretations of the Securities Act of 1933.

The Division of Market Regulation oversees the secondary trading markets, including the registration and performance of stock exchanges, broker-dealers, and other participants in these markets (such as transfer agents and clearing organizations).

The Division of Investment Management has special responsibility for mutual funds and investment advisers (and also, more recently, public utilities). It reviews the financial responsibility, sales practices, advertising and compliance with SEC rules of these entities.

The Division of Enforcement is charged with investigating possible violations of the federal securities laws and, when authorized by the Commission, with undertaking enforcement actions, either by way of administrative proceedings or by seeking injunctions and/or civil penalties in federal court. Although it may cooperate with the Department of Justice and various U.S. Attorney's Offices, the SEC itself does not have authority to commence criminal prosecutions.

The Office of General Counsel provides legal advice and represents the Commission in appellate litigation. Often, it plays a particularly significant role in the formulation of new policies within the Commission, serving sometimes as a "think tank" for the SEC. Accounting policies and most other matters relating to the form and content of financial information filed with the SEC are the responsibility of the Office of Chief Accountant. Through Regulation S–X and its Accounting Series Releases and Financial Reporting Releases, this office establishes the financial reporting requirements applicable to the federal securities laws.[1] Finally, the Office of Economic Analysis performs a data collection and advisory role, which has waxed and waned over recent years depending on the willingness of individual Commissioners to rely on economic analysis.

The SEC administers six statutes that comprise the federal securities laws:

- Securities Act of 1933;

- Securities Act of 1934;

- Public Utility Holding Act of 1935;

- Trust Indenture Act of 1939;

- Investment Company Act of 1940; and

- Investment Advisers Act of 1940.

In addition, a seventh statute, "The Public Company Accounting Reform and Investor Protection Act of 2002" (better known as the "Sarbanes–Oxley Act"), was enacted in 2002 in the wake of recent corporate scandals and significantly expanded the scope and orientation of the Securities Exchange Act of 1934. Therefore, it is also discussed below.

1. Although the SEC has authority under the 1934 Act to promulgate its own accounting standards, it has long deferred to the "generally accepted accounting standards" (GAAP) of the accounting profession (which are today set by the Financial Accounting Standards Board (FASB)). "Generally accepted auditing standards" (GAAS) are in turn set by the American Institute of Certified Public Accountants (AICPA). This practice of deference to the accounting profession was formally acknowledged in Accounting Series Release No. 150 (1973). See also Arthur Andersen & Co. v. SEC, [1978 Transfer Binder]   Fed.Sec.L.Rep.   (CCH),   ¶ 96,374 (N.D.Ill.1978) (deference to industry found not to represent unlawful delegation to private body).

The 1933 Act. Chapters 2 and 3 of this Casebook focus on the Securities Act of 1933. Essentially, it prohibits the offer or sale of a security (except in certain exempt transactions) unless the security has been registered with the SEC; it also requires the delivery of a prospectus to a purchaser and to other persons to whom a written offer is made. Very favorable causes of action are given to purchasers of securities if the registration statement contains a materially misleading statement or omits to disclose material information (see § 11 of the '33 Act) or if other material misstatements or omissions, including oral ones, are made by a seller (§ 12(2) of the '33 Act).

The 1934 Act. The Securities Exchange Act of 1934 has a far broader coverage than that of the '33 Act. Publicly held companies must enter its continuous disclosure system and file annual and quarterly reports with the SEC, and also must preclear proxy statements with the SEC before soliciting shareholder proxies or votes. The 1934 Act also sets up a self-regulatory system for the supervision of the trading markets and gives the SEC oversight jurisdiction over both the stock exchanges and the NASD, which is the principal self-regulatory body for broker-dealers. Under § 15 of the 1934 Act, virtually all broker-dealers must register with the SEC, which has very broad rulemaking powers to define and proscribe practices of broker-dealers that it considers to be "manipulative, deceptive or otherwise fraudulent." Also, under Sections 7 and 8, the '34 Act regulates the credit available for securities purchases—known as margin—by authorizing the Federal Reserve to establish limits on the amount of credit that can be extended in connection with a securities purchase.

The '34 Act has been frequently amended; indeed, it has become the Christmas tree on which Congress almost annually hangs a new ornament in the form of new amendments. Among the most important amendments have been: (1) the Williams Act, passed in 1968, which amended Sections 13 and 14 to regulate tender offers and the control acquisition process; (2) the Securities Investor Protection Corporation, which was created by virtue of a 1970 amendment in order to establish an analogue to the Federal Deposit Insurance Corporation and thereby protect investors from the risk that their brokerage firms would become insolvent; (3) the 1975 Securities Acts Amendments, discussed earlier, that sought to establish a "national market system" and foster competition over commissions; (4) Section 15B, passed in 1975, which created the Municipal Securities Rulemaking Board and established minimal disclosure standards for municipal securities; (5) Section 30A, added in 1977 by the Foreign Corrupt Practices Act, which mandates that publicly held firms satisfy and maintain internal accounting controls and which prohibits bribery, both foreign and domestic; (6) Section 15C, passed in 1986, which brings government securities brokers under the limited oversight of the SEC; (7) the Insider Trading Sanctions Act of 1984 and the Insider Trading and Securities Fraud Enforcement Act of 1988, which amended § 21A of the '34 Act to establish civil penalties and related sanctions for insider trading; (8) the Securities Law Enforcement Remedies Act of 1990, which gave the Commission civil penalties, including a "cease and desist" power, that it could impose administratively; (9) the Private Securities Litigation Reform Act of 1995, which, based upon the perception that much private securities litigation was abusive or frivolous, created a safe harbor for forward-looking information for certain corporate issuers, and heightened the pleading standards, and erected other procedural barriers that a private plaintiff must satisfy in order to state a cause of action; and (10) the National Securities Markets Improvements Act of

1996, which partially preempted state securities law (thereby significantly revising the allocation of authority between federal and state regulators) and also vastly increased the scope of the SEC's exemptive authority (thereby conferring broad authority on the SEC to scale back its own requirements in cases or categories where it believes regulation is unwarranted). To date, the SEC has been cautious about using this new exemptive authority, but attitudes could change with each new Administration.

The Public Company Accounting Reform and Investor Protection Act of 2002. Passed in 2002 in the wake of the Enron, WorldCom and other recent corporate scandals that highlighted accounting and financial reporting irregularities by major public corporation, this statute (popularly known as the Sarbanes–Oxley Act) broadly amends the '34 Act in a far-reaching effort to improve financial reporting by public companies, impose tighter oversight over the accounting profession, and regulate some areas of corporate governance that were formerly left to the states. Toward this end, the Act does the following:

1.   creates a self-regulatory body, the "Public Company Accounting Oversight Board," to regulate the accounting profession, establish auditing standards, and impose appropriate discipline in a manner that parallels the National Association of Securities Dealers' ("NASD") oversight of, and authority over, the brokerage industry;

2.   restricts the consulting and other services that an audit firm can provide to an audit client in the belief that such other services create a conflict of interest that may permit the client to induce the auditor to acquiesce in dubious accounting policies by offering lucrative consulting services to a "cooperative" auditing firm;

3.   mandates that a public company's audit committee be composed exclusively of independent directors (as defined by the Act) and strengthens the powers and responsibilities of the audit committee, requiring that it (and not management or the full board) "be directly responsible for the appointment, compensation, and oversight of the work" of the outside auditors;

4.   instructs the SEC to develop a new disclosure document to be known as the "internal control report" which will assess the adequacy of the company's "internal control structure;"

5.   seeks to increase auditor independence by (i) requiring the mandatory rotation of the lead audit partner at the audit firm at least every five years and (ii) disqualifying any former employee of the audit firm from serving as a senior financial executive of a former client for at least one year after leaving the audit firm;

6.   instructs the SEC to promulgate rules of practice that require attorneys appearing before it to report "evidence" of material securities law violations, fiduciary breaches or similar misconduct to a "reporting" company's chief legal counsel or CEO and, if those officers fail to act "appropriately," to the company's audit committee, its independent directors, or the board of directors as a whole;

7.   requires the chief executive officer ("CEOs") and chief financial officers ("CFOs") of "reporting companies" to provide on a continuing basis a prescribed certification of their company's financial statements and imposes greatly enhanced criminal sanctions for certifications that are knowingly false;

8. requires "reporting" companies to make more current, "real time" disclosure of material changes in their financial condition and to report all material off-balance sheet transactions, arrangements, and other relationships that might have a material effect on the current or future financial health of the company;

9. amends § 16(b) of the Exchange Act to obligate corporate directors, principal stockholders and officers to disclose transactions in their company's securities within two business days;

10. instructs the SEC to promulgate rules governing the independence and objectivity of securities analysts and protecting analysts from retaliation by their firms because of negative research or ratings;

11. bars public companies from making "personal loans" to directors or senior executives and forbids from trading in the company's stock during "blackout periods" when holders of individual retirement accounts are barred from trading;

12. extends the statute of limitations for securities fraud suits;

13. protects "whistleblowers" through new criminal penalties and a private right of action for compensatory damages; and

14. creates a forfeiture penalty under which the chief executive officer and chief financial officer must disgorge to the company all incentive, bonus or equity compensation received, or any trading profits made, during a period in which the company's earnings were overstated.

Virtually all these provisions appear traceable to specific abuses at Enron, WorldCom or Tyco. Although the full impact of these provisions cannot yet be judged, they reveal a deep skepticism about contemporary corporate governance practices and hence an unprecedented willingness to override state corporate law.

The Public Utility Holding Company Act of 1935. Although no longer an important statute because the SEC has largely deregulated the field, this statute requires public utility holding companies (as defined) to secure approval from the Commission before issuing securities or otherwise changing their financial structures. The Act chiefly applies to interstate holding companies engaged, through subsidiaries, in the electric utility industry or in the retail distribution of natural or manufactured gas. Detailed reporting and SEC approvals were formerly required for most significant corporate action by such holding companies.

The Trust Indenture Act. The Trust Indenture Act of 1939 ("TIA") has a limited but important focus. It applies to public offerings of debt securities in excess of $1 million and essentially specifies the form of indenture which must be used, including many of the substantive terms that must be set forth in the indenture. The trust indenture is the contract establishing the duties of the trustee who monitors and enforces the contractual rights of the bondholders. Basically the TIA attempts to prohibit the selection of a trustee with a disabling conflict of interest and establishes standards of conduct and responsibility for the trustee.

The Investment Company Act of 1940. Investment companies—which term includes both "open end" and "closed end" mutual funds and money market funds—are companies that hold and manage a portfolio of securities for investment. Increasingly, middle class Americans buy shares in mutual funds, rather than attempting to pick stocks directly themselves. The Investment Company Act specifies substantive corporate governance standards for the operation of such investment companies, including maintaining an independent board, providing for an annual review of the management contract between the investment company and its investment adviser, subjecting certain transactions between the investment company and its officers and directors to SEC approval, and regulating the investment company's capital structure.

The Investment Advisers Act of 1940. An investment adviser engages in the business of giving investment advice to others for compensation. This Act requires such persons to register with the SEC, prohibits fraud and deceptive practices, regulates aspects of their compensation, and specifies some related requirements intended to ensure fair dealing. In essence, it does for investment advisers on a lesser scale what the 1934 Act does for broker-dealers.

Administrative Procedure. The SEC is subject to the Administrative Procedure Act ("APA"). The APA establishes the standards for judicial review of SEC administrative decisions and specifies procedures to be followed when the SEC is engaged in rulemaking. Normally, the SEC will give advance notice of rule proposals and will afford interested parties an opportunity to comment. Typically, it acts at open meetings, and the discussions among the Commissioners or between them and their staff at these meetings can be candid, sharp and often revealing.

However, the Commission does not act only through formal rulemaking. For example, it has never defined by rule what constitutes "insider trading," and indeed it has resisted efforts aimed at legislative codification of this critical concept. Instead, it has made law on a case by case basis by pursuing an enforcement strategy. This "I-know-it-when-I-see-it" approach has been criticized on the grounds that it places a bureaucracy's interest in maximizing its discretionary power ahead of the industry's interest in bright-line standards and fair notice.[2]

The Commission staff also has developed a unique system of lawmaking by responding to inquiries from the bar about how it interprets (or will enforce) various provisions of the federal securities laws. If the staff agrees with an interpretation proposed by an attorney with respect to a specific set of facts, it will state in its response that it will not recommend any enforcement action to the Commission if the attorney's client proceeds along the lines indicated in the letter (and the factual statements in the letter are accurate and complete).[3] These "no-action" letters are made publicly available by the Commission and afford an important source of guidance for the bar. However, no-action letters are not binding on the Commission, which from time to time does overrule the staff and takes a position inconsistent with the staff's interpretation.[4] The staff may also change its views prospectively and cease to follow a position taken in an earlier no-action letter. In either case, controversy usually follows because practitioners understandably believe that the publication of no-action letters is intended to provide them with guidance which they cannot safely ignore but

---

2. The Commission has been sharply criticized by one former Commissioner precisely on this grounds for relying excessively on litigation and enforcement proceedings to make law. See Roberta Karmel, Government by Prosecution (1981).

3. See Securities Act Rel. No. 4553 (Nov. 6, 1962).

4. See 17 C.F.R. § 202.1(d).

the Commission can. When, in 1991, the Commission reversed a long-standing staff no-action position, Commissioner Fleischman dissented sharply:

> "No matter how often the Commission repeats the mantra that no-action letters 'only purport to represent the views of the officials who give them' or 'set forth staff positions only' that 'are not rulings of the Commission or its staff on questions of law or fact,' the Commission's own contrary actions, not to speak of the contrary actions of the Commission's staff, belie that message to the practicing securities bar."[5]

Since the SEC first made no-action letters publicly available in 1971, they increasingly have come (as Commissioner Fleischman also noted) to state more general principles of law and to offer guidance relevant to persons beyond the immediate addressee.

On several occasions in the 1990s, issues have arisen about the legal status of no-action letters. Repeatedly, courts have held that they are not judicially reviewable, finding that they amount to neither agency adjudication nor rulemaking.[6]

Criticism. Although the SEC enjoys a enviable reputation with the public, the press and most of the bar, it has received criticism. Some academic critics have suggested that the SEC inefficiently and paternalistically over-regulates, placing investor protection on a special pedastel and never balancing it against other policy goals. Much of this criticism comes from "law and economics" scholars who subscribe to "public choice" theory.[7] Public choice theory assumes that regulators do not simply pursue the public interest, but seek to maximize their own political support and accordingly favor the interests of powerful interest groups.[8] From this perspective, agencies typically are captured by "rent-seeking" interest groups, and regulation usually amounts to the allocation of subsidies to allies and the imposition of restraints on their competitors.

The bar has largely disdained this critique for another one. Practitioners frequently accuse the SEC of avoiding "bright-line" rules in favor of vague or subjective tests that maximize agency discretion. Professor Homer Kripke once argued that, in part because the SEC is dominated by attorneys, it has developed a regulatory "theology" that is part law and part lore but cannot be confidently understood by non-specialists.[9] Its role, he suggests, is again to maximize the agency's discretion to do what it wants under the circumstances.

---

5. See Securities Exchange Act Release No. 34–28990 (March 20, 1991). For another critique of the uncertainty created by the Commission's refusal to treat no-action letters as a more formal source of law, see Loss, Summary Remarks, 30 Bus.Law. 163, 164–65 (1975).

6. See New York City Employees' Retirement System v. SEC, 45 F.3d 7 (2d Cir. 1995) (SEC not required to follow notice and comment procedures of Administrative Procedure Act in issuing no-action letter that reverses long-established prior policy); Roosevelt v. E.I. Du Pont de Nemours & Co., 958 F.2d 416, 427 n. 19 (D.C.Cir.1992) (no-action letter neither an adjudication nor rulemaking); Board of Trade of the City of Chicago v. SEC, 883 F.2d 525, 529–31 (7th Cir.

1989) (no-action letters not judicially reviewable because not orders of the Commission).

7. George Stigler, a Nobel Prize winning economist who taught at Columbia University and the University of Chicago, is usually seen as the father of this school.

8. For "public choice" critiques of the SEC, see S.M. Phillips & J.R. Zecher, The SEC and the Public Interest (1981); Jonathan Macey, Administrative Agency Obsolescence and Interest Group Formation: A Case Study of the SEC at Sixty, 15 Cardozo L. Rev. 909 (1994); Greg Jarrell, Change at the Exchange: The Causes and Effects of Deregulation, 27 J. L. & Econ. 373 (1984).

9. See Homer Kripke, The SEC and Corporate Disclosure: Regulation In Search of a Purpose (1979).

To note these criticisms is not to endorse them, but to suggest perspectives that may from time to time be applied to specific SEC decisions and policies that will be considered later in this casebook.

Self–Regulatory Organizations. The Securities Exchange Act of 1934 prescribes a concurrent and cooperative structure of regulation by and among the SEC and several specialized "self-regulatory organizations" (or SROs). Justice William O. Douglas, an early SEC Chairman, described the strategy underlying this approach as that of giving the frontline enforcement responsibilities to the SROs, while the SEC "would keep the shotgun, so to speak, behind the door, well-oiled, cleaned and ready for use."[10]

Several different justifications underlie this approach. First, the SROs do receive a considerable degree of cooperation from the industry, because they are heavily populated with industry personnel. Second, because the SROs finance their activities by essentially taxing the industry for dues, they increase the effective total enforcement budget for industry surveillance and monitoring, as the SEC could not count on Congress allocating equivalent funds to it if the SROs did not exist. Finally, this two-tier structure was probably a historical inevitability, because some of these self-regulatory organizations predated the SEC (the New York Stock Exchange dates back to 1792). Although the Securities Exchange Act granted the SEC significant authority over the stock exchanges, this two-tier structure of regulation represented an important political accommodation. Specifically, § 5 of the Act requires all stock exchanges to register as "national securities exchanges." To register, a national securities exchange must satisfy § 6, which requires that the rules of the exchange meet specified governance and law compliance objectives, including that they are "designed to prevent fraudulent and manipulative acts and practices, to promote just and equitable principles of trade, . . . to remove impediments to and perfect the mechanism of a free and open market and a national market system, and, in general to protect investors and the public interest." Today, under § 19(c) of the Act, the SEC has authority to amend or revise the rules of a stock exchange (or any SRO) as it deems appropriate to maintain a national market system.

Unlike the stock exchanges, the National Association of Securities Dealers (or "NASD") was a creation of the federal securities law. In 1938, the Maloney Act added § 15A to the Securities Exchange Act of 1934, which section authorizes the registration of an association of brokers and dealers as a "national securities association". Again, under § 15A, the rules of such an association must be designed to meet the same standards as those under § 6, including the same broad reference to "just and equitable principles of trade."[11] To date, only one such "national securities association" has ever been established: the National Association of Securities Dealers. Essentially, the NASD was jointly sponsored by the industry and the SEC as a means of self-regulation in order to forestall the possibility of more intrusive direct regulation. Under § 15(b)(8)–(9) a broker-dealer may not effect securities transaction unless it is a member of a registered securities association (i.e., the NASD), unless it limits its activities to a stock exchange of which it is a member. This effectively ensures that virtually every broker-dealer must join the NASD and comply with its rules; suspension or expulsion by the NASD as a practical matter means disbarment from the industry.

---

10. See William O. Douglas, DEMOCRACY AND FINANCE, 82 (1940).

11. See § 15A(b)(6) of the Securities Exchange Act of 1934.

SROs have broad disciplinary authority, which is, in turn, subject to SEC review. The concept of "just and equitable principles of trade" was deliberately elastic. The idea behind self-regulation is that professionals in the marketplace "know it when they see it" and can recognize and discipline misconduct even when greater specificity would be required of a governmental agency. Thus, the NASD's Rules of Fair Practice (which provides the basis for most NASD disciplinary actions) open with the requirement that members must "observe high standards of commercial honor and just and equitable principles of trade" (Article III, Section 1). This would presumably be too vague a standard for criminal enforcement, but it can be enforced, much like the rules of a private club, by the NASD.

NASD discipline can take a variety of forms: fines, censure, suspension from supervisory positions, or suspension from the industry (either permanently or temporarily). Both firms and individual employees are subject to discipline. Also, the NASD can enforce both its own rules, SEC rules and statutes, and other statutes. Typically, NASD discipline begins at a district level (there are some 14 district offices), where committees composed of industry members hold hearings, reach decisions, and impose sanctions. Appeals can be taken to a National Business Conduct Committee (and further appeals to the NASD's board of directors and the SEC).[12]

Obviously, procedural issues surround this self-regulatory structure which delegates enormous discretion to an essentially private body. A policy question also surrounds the desirability of allowing competitors to discipline their business rivals. Still, courts have largely accepted NASD discipline against claims of procedural irregularity.[13] In part, they have relied on the requirement in § 15A that SRO disciplinary rules provide a "fair procedure."[14]

Problems of a different sort with industry self-regulation surfaced in the 1990s. With the creation of the Nasdaq market in 1971, the NASD became not only a self-regulatory body, but also the sponsor of its own electronic stock market. The explosive growth of Nasdaq brought these roles into conflict. After the disappointing experience during the 1987 stock market crash, when Nasdaq market makers essentially shut down (rather than buy stock from customers during a time of rapid market decline), the NASD in response improved and automated the Nasdaq Small Order Execution System (SOES) in order to assure small investors that they would always have access to the Nasdaq market, even in times of market stress. Some active traders (the so-called "SOES bandits") began to use SOES as a way of entering into automated trades with market makers whose prices lagged momentarily behind the market. In retaliation, some market makers refused to deal with such traders, despite an obligation to honor their price quotations. In turn, the SOES bandits filed charges alleging "backing away" violations against these market makers with the NASD. But NASD's disciplinary panels were heavily staffed with industry personnel who had similar reasons to disfavor the SOES bandits, and the impartiality of the disciplinary process was thought by some to be seriously compromised. Simultaneously, the mysterious tendency of Nasdaq market

---

12. Under § 19(e) of the Securities Exchange Act of 1934, the SEC can modify or overturn an NASD-imposed sanction, but not increase it.

13. See First Jersey Sec., Inc. v. Bergen, 605 F.2d 690 (3d Cir.1979); Merrill Lynch, Pierce, Fenner & Smith v. NASD, 616 F.2d 1363 (5th Cir.1980).

14. See § 15A(b)(8) of the Securities Exchange Act of 1934.

makers to trade only in even eighths (and not odd eighths) came to public attention and suggested tacit collusion among Nasdaq market makers.

Dissatisfied with NASD's ability to police itself, the SEC pressed for changes. In particular, a select committee headed by former Senator Warren Rudman recommended,[15] and the NASD agreed in 1996, to transfer regulatory and supervisory authority over broker-dealers to a newly created subsidiary, NASD Regulation, Inc., thus insulating it from possible pressures or influences from the Nasdaq market. Also, the NASD agreed to revise its governance structure, expanding the public members on its governing board to 60% (from 19% in 1995). Culminating this rehabilitation process, the SEC brought, and settled in 1996, a disciplinary action against the NASD, which charged that the NASD had inadequately supervised Nasdaq market makers in a manner that fostered anticompetitive practices.[16] At the same time, the SEC introduced new order handling rules[17] and compelled a change in the executive leadership of the NASD.

While the SEC's disciplining of the NASD in 1996 resembled an elaborately negotiated plea bargain, the SEC can act in more formal ways with regard to any SRO. Section 19(c) of the Securities Exchange Act of 1934 authorizes the SEC to "abrogate, add to, or delete from ... the rules of a self-regulatory organization as the Commission deems necessary or appropriate to insure the fair administration of the self-regulatory organization ... or otherwise in furtherance of the purposes of this title." Broad as this authority to amend SRO rules is, it is not unlimited. In the late 1980's, the SEC ordered the New York Stock Exchange to adopt rules that denied listed companies the ability to issue supervoting stock that deviated from the traditional norm of "one share, one vote." (Such stock was usually issued as a takeover defense). The D.C. Circuit, however, invalidated these rules, finding that the SEC's authority under § 19(c) was essentially limited to rules that sought to create a national market system, not to rules that regulated basic corporate governance.[18]

Other SROs exist in addition to the NASD and the stock exchanges. The newest example is the Public Company Accounting Oversight Board (the "Accounting Board"), which was created by the Sarbanes–Oxley Act of 2002. The Accounting Board is a private body, established as a non-profit corporation, but is subject to SEC oversight in much the same manner as is the NASD. The five members of the Accounting Board are appointed by the SEC (after consultation with the Chairman of the Board of Governors of the Federal Reserve System and the Secretary of the Treasury) for five-year terms.[19] Two (but only two) of the Accounting Board's five members must be certified public accountants.[20] These restrictions are obviously intended to prevent the "capture" of the Accounting Board by the accounting profession.

---

15. See Report of the NASD Select Committee on Structure and Governance, [1995 Transfer Binder] Fed.Sec.L.Rep. (CCH) Para. 85,660 (Sept. 15, 1995).

16. See Report Pursuant to Section 21(a) of the Securities Exchange Act of 1934. Regarding the NASD and the Nasdaq Market, [1996 Transfer Binder] Fed.Sec.L.Rep. (CCH) Para. 85,824 (August 8, 1996).

17. See Exchange Act Rel. No. 37,619A [1996 Transfer Binder] Fed.Sec.L.Rep. (CCH) Para. 85,837 (August 29, 1996).

18. See Business Roundtable v. SEC, 905 F.2d 406 (D.C.Cir.1990).

19. See Section 101(e)(5)(A) of the Sarbanes–Oxley Act.

20. See Section 101(e)(2) of the Sarbanes–Oxley Act. The chairperson may not, however, have been a practicing accountant for at least five years prior to his or her appointment to the Board.

All accounting firms that prepare audit reports for public companies must register with the Accounting Board and maintain their registration. The Act further directs the Accounting Board to:

a) "establish or adopt ... auditing, quality control, ethics, independence and other standards relating to the preparation of audit reports for issuers;"

b) "conduct investigations and disciplinary proceedings concerning, and impose appropriate sanctions where justified upon, registered public accounting firms and associated persons of such firms;" and

c) enforce compliance with the Act, the rules of the Board, professional standards, and the federal securities laws relating to the preparation and issuance of audit reports and the obligations and liabilities of accountants.

The Accounting Board is given broad rulemaking authority with respect to auditing, attestation, quality control and ethical standards, but the actual formulation of "generally accepted accounting" standards remains the responsibility of a different private body, the Financial Accounting Standards Board (or "FASB"). The Accounting Board is further instructed by the Sarbanes–Oxley Act to conduct compliance inspection investigations of registered audit firms, which must be conducted annually for firms auditing more than 100 clients and not less than every three years for other firms.[21] The Accounting Board may impose sanctions ranging from censure to revocation of a firm's accounting license (or that of any associated person) and may levy fines of up to $15 million in the case of intentional misconduct by a firm.[22]

Still another important SRO is the Municipal Securities Rulemaking Board (MSRB), which regulates not only disclosure in the municipal securities market, but, as noted earlier in this Chapter, has sought to end the practice of "pay to play" political contributions by municipal securities underwriters. Registered clearing agencies constitute a last type of SRO.[23]

In the last analysis, self regulation will always continue to be a debatable issue in the current structure of securities regulation. Critics fear that self-regulation allows the industry to capture the regulatory process and even to focus its discipline on outsiders and new entrants. Conversely, proponents argue that the industry invariably understands its own problems better than distant bureaucrats in a government agency. The debate will continue.

Blue Sky Regulation. Every American state has a statute regulating the offering of securities. Typically, these statutes—known as "blue sky laws"—effect a comprehensive system of regulation, requiring either registration of the securities with a state agency or the satisfaction of an applicable exemption,

21. See Section 104(a) and (b) the Sarbanes–Oxley Act.

22. See Section 105(c)(4) of the Sarbanes–Oxley Act.

23. Section 17A ("National System for Clearance and Settlement of Securities Transactions") of the Securities Exchange Act of 1934 requires the registration of clearing agencies and similarly specifies standards for the rules of such an agency in § 17A(b)(3).

imposing registration and supervision requirements on securities professionals (i.e. broker dealers and investment advisers), and creating civil and criminal liabilities that broadly parallel the liabilities under the federal securities laws.

The term "blue sky" requires a special word of explanation. The first comprehensive state statute regulating offerings and broker dealers was adopted by Kansas in 1911 in reaction to fraudulent promoters who were believed to be luring gullible citizens into buying into highly "speculative schemes which have no more basis than so many feet of 'blue sky'."[24] In general, the perception underlying these early statutes was that questionable Eastern promoters were swindling the honest local citizens by syndicating insubstantial offerings of "blue sky". Some more recent commentators have offered the more skeptical view that the enactment of the blue sky laws was an attempt by state banking regulators to expand "their regulatory turf" and advance "the financial interests of the banks under their supervision".[25] Clearly, the Blue Sky laws were part of the broad Progressive-era attempt to bring suspect forms of business activity under closer governmental supervision, and financial syndications to the public were at this time viewed as highly suspect (possibly in part as a result of a general populist distrust of Eastern financial interests).

With the later passage of the federal securities laws, corporate issuers and securities professionals had to comply with dual and overlapping systems of regulation. Even more bothersome to corporate issuers were the different regulatory styles underlying these two legal regimes. As originally enacted, Blue Sky laws attempted to regulate the substantive fairness of the transaction and banned securities issuances within the state that the local blue sky administrator deemed excessively risky, or unfair, or overly generous to the promoters. Often, these statutes authorized the state blue sky administrator to preclude any offering in the state that the administrator found not to be "fair, just and equitable"; others authorized a ban if the terms of the offering were deemed "grossly unfair." Obviously, some subjectivity surrounds these judgments. In any event, this form of "merit regulation" (which continues in a minority of the states today) contrasted sharply with the disclosure philosophy of the federal securities laws, which expects investors to protect their own interests once full disclosure is made.

Another common criticism of merit regulation was that its costs were borne by investors. As an ABA Committee has observed, when a securities offering is banned from one jurisdiction, the practical effect may be only that investors in that jurisdiction buy the stock in the secondary market (which is not covered by blue sky laws) at the higher post-offering price.[26] From this perspective, merit regulation may both paternalistically deny investors the opportunity to make high risk, high return investments and cost them the chance to buy at the often lower offering price. In response to these criticisms, a number of states dropped merit regulation, and moved to a full disclosure philosophy during the 1980s and early 1990s.[27] In addition, the National

24. See Hall v. Geiger–Jones Co., 242 U.S. 539, 550 (1917) (upholding Ohio "Blue Sky Law" and discussing statutory purposes).

25. See Jonathan Macey & Geoffrey Miller, Origin of the Blue Sky Laws, 70 Tex. L.Rev. 347, 351 (1991).

26. See Report on State Merit Regulation of Securities Offerings, 41 Bus.Law. 785 (1986).

27. For a discussion of these legislative battles and the basically mixed outcomes, see Sargent, The Challenge to Merit Regulation—Part I, 12 Sec.Reg.L.J. 276 (1984), and

Conference of Commissioners on Uniform State Laws adopted a Revised Uniform Securities Act ("RUSA") in 1985, which, while not rejecting merit regulation, attempted to limit the blue sky administrators' authority over more "seasoned" issuers.[28]

The adoption of RUSA by the National Conference of Commissioners on Uniform State Laws ("NCCUSL") in 1985 touched off a political battle. The North American Securities Administrators Association ("NASAA"), an organization of U.S., Canadian, and Mexican blue sky administrators, opposed the adoption of RUSA, seeing it as excessively deregulatory and in particular overly restrictive of their enforcement ability to deal with new and novel abuses. Given the opposition of NASAA, RUSA has received relatively few adoptions, and the dominant statutory model remains the Uniform Securities Act, which was promulgated by the NCCUSL in 1956 and which some 37 states continue to follow. The majority of states have "adapted" the Uniform Securities Act, adding or deleting their own pet provisions; a few states have adopted RUSA, and New York and California (the two most important states for purposes of securities offerings) have long had their own distinctive statutes, based on neither model. California has been a strong "merit regulation" jurisdiction (along with Texas and Massachusetts), while New York basically administers an antifraud statute (but does apply merit regulation to a narrow spectrum of real estate and theatrical syndications). Not only do state blue sky statutes differ significantly (with some jurisdictions exempting the vast majority of offerings), but enforcement practices vary at least as much. Both because of budget constraints and the shifting philosophies of individual blue sky administrators, a state may move from an aggressive to a passive posture (and back again) over the course of a decade. The principal force for uniformity has been NASAA, which does seek to coordinate the actions of its members when common interests exist.

For the future, it is likely that Uniform Securities Act will retain its dominant position, as a new version of that Act was approved by NCCUSL in 2002 (with Dean Joel Seligman serving as the Reporter). While its provisions are discussed in Chapter 17, its overarching aims are to encourage uniformity and cooperation both among state regulators and among state, federal and self-regulatory regulators.

The need for revisions to the Uniform Securities Act was necessitated in part by the passage of the National Securities Markets Improvement Act of 1996. Section 18 of the Securities Act of 1933 had expressly saved blue sky laws from preemption. But, in 1996, Congress amended Section 18 to preempt state blue sky laws—*partially*. Under amended Section 18(a), securities listed (or to be listed on the completion of the offering) on the New York Stock Exchange, the American Stock Exchange, or Nasdaq's National Market System are exempted from the registration procedures (but not the antifraud rules) of the states. In addition, the SEC is authorized to exempt securities listed on regional stock exchanges or sold to "qualified purchasers" (a term referring to sophisticated purchasers that the SEC is authorized to define by rule). Securities of

Sargent, Blue Sky Law—The Challenge to Merit Regulation—Part II, 12 Sec.Reg.L.J. 367 (1985).

28. RUSA adopted a narrow exclusion from merit review for seasoned companies and placed certain restrictions on blue sky administrators' ability to require escrow of "cheap" stock held by promoters. See Hensley, The Development of a Revised Uniform Securities Act, 40 Bus.Law 721 (1985); Sargent, Some Thoughts on the Revised Uniform Securities Act, 14 Sec.Reg.L.J. 62 (1986).

registered investment companies (i.e., mutual funds) were also expressly exempted from state regulation. Finally, securities issued in transactions exempt from federal registration requirements were also protected from state regulation (other than for certain minimal notice filing requirements). The upshot is that state blue sky law registration requirements (but not the state's antifraud enforcement or investigatory authority) is confined to relatively small offerings (and then only if not sold to sophisticated or otherwise "qualified" investors).

Similarly, the National Securities Markets Improvement Act also cut back on state broker-dealer registration requirements by adding § 15(h)(1) to the Securities Exchange Act of 1934. This provision effectively preempts most substantive state regulation of broker-dealers, including any rules establishing capital, custody, margin, financial responsibility, record-keeping and reporting requirements to the extent that such requirements differed from, or were in addition to, the rules and requirements under the Securities Exchange Act of 1934. In effect, the state can enforce and monitor the SEC's requirements, but no more.

Finally, Title III of the National Securities Markets Improvement Act divided regulation of investment advisers between state and federal regulators, assigning to state regulation those advisers having assets under management of $25 million or less.

The rationale for this major re-allocation of federal and state responsibilities was expressed in the Act's Conference Report:[29]

"[T]he system of dual Federal and state securities regulation has resulted in a degree of duplicative and unnecessary regulation. Securities offerings and the brokers and dealers engaged in securities transactions are all currently subject to a dual system of regulation that, in many instances, is redundant, costly, and ineffective.

During the course of consideration of this legislation, the Congress received testimony indicating that this duplicative regulation tends to raise the cost of capital to American issuers of securities without providing commensurate protection to investors or to our markets. Testimony also indicated that technological change has transformed the capital raising process, necessitating changes in the regulatory scheme to facilitate the flow of information to potential investors and reduce the marginal costs of capital to firms. The managers have sought to eliminate duplicative and unnecessary regulatory burdens while preserving important investor protections by reallocating responsibility over the regulation of the nation's securities markets in a more logical fashion between the Federal government and the states.

With respect to securities offerings, the [Act's] Managers have allocated regulatory responsibility between the Federal and state governments based on the nature of the securities offering. Some securities offerings, such as those made by investment companies, and certain private placements are inherently national in nature, and are therefore subject to only Federal regulation. Smaller, regional, and intrastate securities offerings remain subject to state regulation. The Managers have preserved the authority of the states to protect investors through application of state antifraud laws.

---

29. See Conference Report on National Securities Markets Improvement Act of 1996, H.R. 104–864, 104th Cong., 2d Sess., 1996– 1997 Fed.Sec.L.Rep. (CCH) Para. 85,847 at p. 88,650.

This preservation of authority is intended to permit state securities regulators to continue to exercise their police power to prevent fraud and broker-dealer sales practice abuses, such as churning accounts or misleading customers. It does not preserve the authority of state securities regulators to regulate the securities registration and offering process through commenting on and/or imposing requirements on the contents of prospectuses or other offering documents."

Although many of these concerns are addressed in the 2002 revision of the Uniform Securities Act, a new jurisdictional issue has recently surfaced. The aggressive enforcement of the New York blue sky statute (the Martin Act) by the New York Attorney General against Merrill Lynch in 2002, as a result of seemingly overstated "buy" recommendations made by the latter's securities analysts, has caused the securities industry to fear and protest the possible "Balkanization" of securities regulation because of variant, or even idiosyncratic, interpretations by individual state regulators.[30] Lobbying efforts that sought to cut back on even the antifraud authority of state regulators proved unsuccessful,[31] but the issue of the degree to which a single state should be able to force an industry-wide restructuring remains alive and may be compelling the SEC to take a more activist stand on issues, such as securities analysts' conflicts. Despite these new issues, the primary enforcement role of state blue sky administrators remains the prosecution of local frauds. Typically, smaller and local scandals (often those involving so-called "penny stocks," "boiler shops," Ponzi schemes, or dubious limited partnership syndications) are detected first and prosecuted most successfully by blue sky authorities, because such smaller offerings tend to pass below the SEC's national radar screen.

30. This episode is discussed in more detail in the Introductory Note that precedes Chapter 2. Essentially, what prompted the industry's alarm was the New York Attorney General's proposal for prophylactic structural reform that would separate securities research from investment banking. See Susanne Craig, "State Regulators See Clout Increase with Recent Victories on Wall Street," The Wall Street Journal, June 21, 2002 at C–1.

31. See Charles Gasparino, "Morgan Stanley Goes to Washington," The Wall Street Journal, June 21, 2002 at C–1.

PART II

REGULATION OF THE DISTRIBUTION OF SECURITIES

SUBDIVISION A. THE REGISTRATION AND DISTRIBUTION PROCESS UNDER THE SECURITIES ACT OF 1933

The Underlying Process: An Overview

Perhaps the first point to be made about the role of underwriters is that use of an underwriter is not legally required, but tends to be a marketing necessity. Companies can "self-underwrite" and market their own securities to the public.[1] But they rarely do. Instead, corporate issuers go to investment banking firms to help them market their securities to investors for several reasons. First, of course, is the obvious fact that investment banking firms have large inventories of clients who wish to purchase securities, whereas a young, start-up firm will typically have few such contacts. Often, investors purchase a portfolio of offerings from the same underwriter, relying on it to generate attractive returns for them across this portfolio, in effect conceding that the individual investor cannot itself tell a good deal from a bad one. Second, the underwriter plays a special role as a "reputational intermediary" who in effect pledges its reputational capital in order to assure investors that the issuer is reliable and honest. Such implicit assurances by the underwriter are credible for at least two reasons: first, the underwriter has little to gain from fraud, because it receives a relatively modest underwriting fee (typically around 7% of the proceeds of an initial public offering) and typically does not share in any equity appreciation (even if the stock price rises during the offering, each underwriter will sell its entire allotment at the original offering price). Second,

---

1. Such transactions do occur. However, if a corporate issuer markets its securities itself to investors, it will probably have to register as a broker-dealer under the Securities Exchange Act of 1934 and possibly under various state laws because it will have come within the definition of a "dealer" in Section 3(a)(5) of the Securities Exchange Act of 1934. Nonetheless, with the advent of the Internet, the prospect of such direct offerings, made by an issuer without an underwriter, is again surfacing.

if the offering does prove to have involved material misstatements or omissions that the underwriter could have detected, the underwriter will face both reputational loss and a high potential legal liability. Because major underwriters have strong reputations developed over decades of working for many clients, they should logically be disinclined to sacrifice their reputations for a single client in a transaction that will make only a modest contribution to the underwriter's annual revenues. The Securities Act of 1933 reinforces this natural tendency by basically holding the underwriter liable to purchasers in the offering for any material misstatement made by the issuer, *unless* the underwriter can affirmatively establish a "due diligence" defense which requires it to have conducted a reasonable investigation into the statements made in the issuer's registration statement. The policy rationale for placing this affirmative obligation on the underwriter to prove in effect its non-negligence is that it should convert the underwriter into a vigilant gatekeeper who will therefore protect the public investor. Nonetheless, despite the existence of both these legal and market incentives that encourage the underwriter to monitor its client the issuer, securities fraud does regularly occur, and sometimes underwriters appear to treat their legal exposure as simply a cost of business, which they can insure.

A second basic point about underwriters is that few brokerage firms engage in this activity. It is a specialization, and a capital intensive one. Historically, many of the most famous underwriting houses (e.g., Goldman, Sachs or Lazard Freres) did not engage in retail brokerage operations, preferring to specialize in financing offerings that were chiefly sold to investor clients of other brokerage firms. More recently, there has been a trend towards vertical integration, as traditional "financial" underwriters have merged with retail brokerage firms (for example, Morgan Stanley & Co. and Dean Witter merged during the 1990's). Smaller retail firms still are deterred from underwriting activities by the significant capital requirements needed to engage in this business;[2] however, they may participate in underwritten offerings in a secondary role as marketers, but not as underwriters, as later discussed. Given the different specializations of different investment banking firms (some primarily financial institutions with little marketing presence and some primarily retail brokerage firms without the financial capacity to underwrite), the managing underwriter performs a delicate balancing act in many offerings by combining the financial strength of some firms with the marketing ability of others so that shares "underwritten" by the former are actually sold to clients of the latter.

A. *Varieties of Offerings.* A number of different techniques for selling securities by an issuer to the public can be used, some involving underwriters and some not. Each deserves a brief discussion.

Direct Offerings. Securities may be sold, without the use of an underwriter or marketing syndicate, in a direct offering by the issuer. There are five types of direct offerings: (a) a direct public offering; (b) a direct offering limited to existing shareholders, usually in the form of a "rights offering"; (c) an offer for sale by tender (or "Dutch auction"); (d) an "all or none" offering; or (e) a direct private placement.

---

2. The SEC imposes "net capital" rules on all brokers, but these rules are particularly demanding in the capital that they require firms to have that underwriter securities. See Rule 15c3–1 ("Net Capital Requirements for Brokers and Dealers").

(a) *Direct Public Offering.* In a direct public offering, the issuer of a new security gambles upon its ability to sell the entire issue without the intervention of an underwriter or marketing syndicate. The issuer thus assumes the entire risk of failure to acquire the needed capital. Accordingly, the success of the offering depends greatly upon prevailing market conditions; the method is used rarely, except by an issuer with a strong credit rating and existing demand for its securities, or by a start-up company or speculative business operation either going public for the first time, or seeking to raise capital from a circle of investors with prior knowledge of the particular business enterprise. With the advent of the Internet, however, some start-up issuers have begun to consider use of this technique without an underwriter.

(b) *Rights Offerings.* Another type of direct offering is that made to existing shareholders. Although shareholders may be solicited without the allocation of rights, the usual procedure is to make a "rights offering". In a rights offering, existing shareholders are offered warrants or rights to subscribe to securities of the issuer, usually at some small discount off the market price. Rights are allocated in proportion to the size of existing holdings of the issuer's securities. Shareholders are an obvious source of capital for a seasoned public company. Often, underwriters will be asked to make a "standby" commitment to buy remaining shares that the shareholders do not buy at a slightly lower price. The advantage to the issuer from this approach is that the discount offered to existing shareholders may be less than the standard underwriter's discount.

(c) *Dutch Auction.* The "offer for sale by tender" (or "Dutch auction") is used by issuers more frequently in the United Kingdom than in the United States. In the United Kingdom, the Dutch auction has often been used to maximize initial returns to issuers, especially those companies going public for the first time. The securities are offered at a stated minimum price, subject to specified conditions. One condition is that each buyer has the option of bidding for any number of shares. The final offering price is fixed at the maximum price at which all shares can be sold pursuant to the bids. All shares will be sold at that final, maximum price. In practice, however, the offer by tender may require the investment advice of an experienced underwriter, and some kind of underwriting commitment.

In the United States, the offer by tender is a rare form of direct offering, and it has yet to be used in this country for any initial public offering of equity securities. In other contexts, however, the offer by tender is becoming an accepted form of direct offer. The United States Treasury Department now uses the Dutch auction as a method of marketing federal government securities. Regulated issuers, such as public utilities, are required by law in some instances to use competitive, public bids among underwriters to sell their debt offerings. Also, Exxon Corporation has sometimes used the Dutch auction to sell various forms of debt securities, with or without the use of underwriters.[3] The Dutch auction has enabled Exxon to maximize its returns, eliminate or reduce underwriting commissions, and lower interest rates on new issues.

---

3. Wall St.J., Oct. 29, 1976, p. 25, ed. 5; N.Y. Times, Nov. 17, 1976, at 61, col. 2. For the mechanics of Dutch auctions, see Exxon Corporation (Avail. April 7, 1977), Fed.Sec. L.Rep. (CCH) ¶ 81,198; Note, Auctioning New Issues of Corporate Securities, 71 Va.L.Rev. 1381 (1985).

(d) *"All or None" Offerings.* In some situations where a minimum amount of funds are needed for a special purpose, securities may be offered by the issuer on an "all or none" basis. Thus, unless a designated number of shares are sold and paid for in full within a specified period, the offering will be terminated and all funds returned, with interest, to the subscribers. The subscribers' funds are placed "in escrow" with a designated depositary and do not become available for disposition until the terms of the offering are met. Some state securities administrators may require the use of an "all or none" offering under certain circumstances.[4]

(e) *Private Placements.* The last form of direct offering is a private placement. A private placement allows an issuer to sell securities to a legally restricted number of institutional and other sophisticated investors. The most important factors indicating a private placement of securities, either by the issuer directly or with the assistance of an underwriter, are necessity, secrecy, speed and cost.

Necessity dictates use of a private placement for some issuers. A private offering is frequently used by issuers to place new debt securities with institutional investors such as private pension plans and insurance companies. This route may be necessary where the public market may absorb only high-quality issues of well-known issuers in amounts of $50 million or more. More recently, the private placement has been used to market high-yield, high-risk "junk bonds." In addition, confidential matters such as sources of raw materials, executive compensation, and secret manufacturing processes may be hidden from public view. In a private placement, the small number of sophisticated investors purchasing the issue are less likely to disclose any such material, non-public information.

A private placement is far quicker than an initial public offering. The most important factor reducing the time required for a private placement is that a registration statement need not be filed with, and approved by, the SEC. In a private placement, the issuer or underwriter contacts a restricted number of highly sophisticated purchasers to whom much of the detail required in a registration statement or statutory prospectus is unimportant. Although institutional and other sophisticated purchasers will want material investment information, it is made available to them in a different form. If an offering prospectus is necessary, frequently it will be less difficult to prepare. In addition, any written information can be supplemented by direct meetings between company officials and the prospective buyers. In dealing with sophisticated investors, the issuer (or its investment banker) can explain a highly speculative financing, or a highly technical offering, to a class of investors more likely to understand its terms than others, and to commit the funds necessary to consummate the financing.

A private offering is also far less costly than a public offering. Several factors increase the costs of a public offering, including legal fees, accounting costs, registration expenses, underwriters' fees and printing bills. In a private placement, it may be possible to avoid a fresh audit, and legal expenses will be substantially less. If an offering circular is required, there will be no prospectus

---

4. See SEC v. Manor Nursing Centers, Inc., 458 F.2d 1082 (2d Cir.1972); SEC Securities Exchange Act Rules 10b–9, 15c2–4; Robbins, All-or-None Offerings, 19 Rev. of Sec. & Commodities Reg. 59 (1986); Robbins, All-or-None Offerings: An Update, 19 Rev. of Sec. & Commodities Reg. 181 (1986).

to print. And, the transaction may be exempt from "blue sky" registration and regulatory requirements at the state level.

Although securities sold in private placements that are exempt from the registration requirements of the 1933 Act may not be resold to public investors (at least without a substantial holding period), institutional investors may resell such "restricted" securities to each other (and thus enjoy some liquidity to this degree). In 1990, the SEC approved an NASD proposal to create a secondary market to trade privately placed securities.[5] This electronic trading system—known as the PORTAL market—got off to a rocky start, and by the end of 1990 only 27 issues were quoted in the system (25 of which were foreign issues).[6] Since then, however, its use has grown, and some rival systems for trading privately placed securities have also appeared.[7]

Underwriting. The term "underwriter" was borrowed from the field of insurance. It was originally used to describe those individuals or firms that insured the issuer against any loss in connection with an offering of securities if the public investors failed to subscribe fully to the issue. This arrangement is known as a "strict underwriting." The term "underwriting," however, has long since lost this meaning, and strict underwriting is rarely, if ever, used today. The term "underwriter" now signifies a firm that specializes in the marketing of new issues of securities or secondary offerings of securities by selling shareholders. Section 2(11) of the Securities Act of 1933 broadly defines an "underwriter" to mean any person who has purchased from the issuer (or controlling persons) (1) with a view to, or (2) offers or sells for an issuer in connection with, the distribution of any security, or (3) participates in any such undertaking.

Underwriters may be used in all forms of public offerings of securities, including all-or-none offerings, as well as in private placements; they render financial advice with respect to the method of financing, the type of security to be offered, the market to be reached, the manner of offering and serve as managers of the offering.

Types of Underwritings. The most common types of underwritings are three: (a) a firm commitment underwriting; (b) a "stand-by" underwriting and (c) a "best-efforts" underwriting. In a firm commitment underwriting, the underwriter (or syndicate) agrees to purchase all or specific amounts of the offering for cash, subject to certain "market-outs."[8] A "stand-by" underwriting

5. See Securities Exchange Act Rel. No. 34–27956 (April 27, 1990); Lewis, PORTAL Opens for Business, Institutional Investor, August, 1990. PORTAL is designed to trade securities issued under Rule 144A, which is discussed in more detail infra in Chapter 9, Section 5.

6. See NASD, Building Markets for a New Era, 1990 Annual Report, at 8; Gillen, NASD System for Private Placements Draws Yawns from Market Participants, The Bond Buyer, Dec. 14, 1990, at 3. For a discussion at PORTAL's lack of early success, see Chu, Private Markets for Foreign Securities, Bankers Mag., Jan./Feb. 1991, at p. 55.

7. See e.g., Angel Capital Electronic Networks SEC No Action Letter, 1996 WL

636094 (Oct. 25, 1996); Lamp Technologies, Inc. SEC No Action Letter, 1997 WL 282988 (May 29, 1997); Niphix Investments, Inc. SEC No Action Letter, 1997 WL 209335 (April 18, 1997); see also Mehta, "Angel Investors to Get On–Line Service," Wall Street Journal, Oct. 28, 1996 at B–2. These systems would provide only a matching service, and not an automated market or dealer intermediaries.

8. In general, "market-out" clauses in firm commitment underwriting agreements are triggered only upon the occurrence of "a material, adverse event affecting the issuer that materially impairs the investment quality of the offered securities." Such a clause has generally been strictly read to refer only

is one in which a new issue is offered only to existing shareholders. The underwriters agree to "stand by" and purchase any shares not purchased by existing shareholders, at the expiration of a specified period. In a "best efforts" underwriting, the underwriter neither purchases the securities from the issuer nor resells them to the investing public; the underwriter agrees only to act as an agent of the issuer in marketing the issue to investors.[9]

In smaller issues, the investment banker may market the issue solely by the use of its own organization; in larger issues, a syndicate of other dealers of securities is organized to facilitate the distribution. In these cases, the so-called managing underwriter receives a special commission for managing the offering, and the other members of the syndicate receive a concession off the public offering price as compensation for assuming part of the underwriting risk and for services.[10] As indicated, in some cases the underwriting syndicate may make a firm commitment to the issuing company to take and pay for the securities directly and assume the risk of any wholesaler and retailer in merchandising a product. In the case of "rights offerings" to existing shareholders, the underwriting group may merely agree to act as agent in reselling the securities, but nevertheless "underwrite" the issue by agreeing to take up and pay for any securities not subscribed for by the public. It is customary to add a selling group of retailers of securities who purchase a portion of the offering at a concession off the offering price, but assume no part of the underwriting risk. Finally, the banking firm may merely agree to use its best efforts to sell the securities for the issuer, without making a firm commitment.

In actual practice, however, the members of the underwriting syndicate usually purchase the securities outright and resell them to the public. In such purchase transactions, each underwriter commits itself only for a specified portion of the offering, rather than assuming a joint liability, because under Section 11 of the Securities Act of 1933, an underwriter's overall civil liability is limited to the total public offering price of the securities underwritten by it.

In a firm commitment underwriting, the issuer will discuss its proposed offering with one or more investment banking firms which it selects to be the lead underwriter or underwriters. When the parties reach an understanding as to the type, nature and form of offering, this is usually reduced to writing, in a "letter of intent," which is usually expressly not binding on either party.[11] The

to an unforeseeable and extraordinary decline in the securities markets. See Walk–In Medical Centers, Inc. v. Breuer Capital Corp., 818 F.2d 260, 264 (2d Cir.1987). See also SEC No–Action Letter, First Boston Corporation (Available Sept. 2, 1985), Fed.Sec.L.Rep. (CCH) ¶ 78,152.

9. On distribution techniques in general, see 1 Securities Law Techniques ch. 18 (A.A. Sommer, Jr. ed. 1986); 1 Loss, Securities Regulation 159–172 (2d ed. 1961), (Supp. 1969); Merrett, Howe & Newbould, Equity Issues and the London Capital Market 511 (1967); United States v. Morgan, 118 F.Supp. 621, 635–655 (S.D.N.Y.1953).

10. For sample forms of underwriting agreements, agreements among underwriters and selling-group forms, see R. Shapiro, A. Sachs and C. Olander, Securities Regulation Forms (1983 rev., Loose-leaf); Weiss, The Underwriting Agreement—Form and Commentary, 26 Bus.Law. 647 (1971).

11. Several decisions have held that such a letter is not enforceable and creates no duty to negotiate further. See Dunhill Securities Corporation v. Microthermal Applications, Inc., 308 F.Supp. 195 (S.D.N.Y. 1969); Beaumont v. American Can Co., 621 F.Supp. 484, 493 (S.D.N.Y.1985), aff'd, 797 F.2d 79 (2d Cir.1986). Where, however, there is no language expressly making the letter of intent nonbinding, courts have divided over its enforceability. See Newharbor Partners v. F.D. Rich Co., 961 F.2d 294 (1st Cir.1992) (collecting cases).

underwriter and issuer will arrive at a maximum public offering price for SEC filing fee purposes. The day before the registration statement becomes effective, the issuer and the lead underwriter will get together and reach the final terms as to price and related matters. The final terms will be based upon such factors as general market conditions and trends, and the reaction to the marketing efforts of the underwriting syndicate in receiving indications of buyer interest. At this point, the underwriters bid is firm for the entire issue, subject almost always to a "market out" if conditions change prior to effectiveness of the registration statement or an unconditional "out" prior to that time.

At an early stage of the underwriting process, the lead underwriter will prepare a syndicate list and discuss it with the issuer. The issuer will be asked whether there are other security dealers who have shown an interest in the issuer and should be brought into the syndicate. News of the impending underwriting may have become a matter of general knowledge and other underwriters may contact either the lead underwriter or the issuer and request that they be made members of the syndicate. In a registered offering, during the period between the filing of the registration statement and its effectiveness (the so-called waiting period) the preliminary prospectus will be available and other underwriters will be asked to become members of the syndicate. At the same time as the signing of the underwriting agreement, the members of the syndicate will enter into an "agreement among underwriters." This agreement will designate the underwriter or underwriters who will manage the offering and fix the various terms and agreements among the members of the syndicate. The underwriting agreement is executed by the issuer and the lead underwriter, acting as agent for the other underwriters in the syndicate, who thereby also become parties to the underwriting agreement.

When the underwriting agreement is signed, the underwriters are committed for the entire issue, subject to "market outs" on certain contingencies, and it is only at this point that the issuer is assured of receiving the proceeds when the offering is completed.

If the pre-sale interest is so disappointing as to indicate that the proposed amount of the issue cannot all be sold, the underwriters will advise either that the size of the offering be cut back or that the contemplated price be reduced or that the offering be deferred until market conditions improve. If, however, the issuer and underwriters arrive at the price and related terms, the issuer will have a firm commitment from the group to purchase its securities.

A registered public offering is more complicated and time consuming than a private placement. It can take as long as two to four months to arrange the financing, allow for the underwriters to make the investigation, and to prepare the documentation for a registration statement. Depending upon the complexity of the company, and the workload of the SEC staff, it may take from three weeks to three months for the registration statement to become effective and the offering to take place. By contrast, a private placement might be completed in as little as one month. A major factor in this time differential is the nature of the documents required.

Syndication. The managing underwriter will have completed the formation of the underwriting syndicate sometime after the registration statement is filed with the Securities and Exchange Commission. During the waiting period members of the syndicate will have tested the market by distributing the preliminary prospectus among securities dealers, and received written indications of interest by prospective down the line purchasers. On the basis of this accumulation of buyer interest, the allocation of the amount of securities to be purchased by each member of the syndicate will be made, thereby separating members of the syndicates into groups based upon the size of their purchase commitments.

In the formation of the underwriting syndicate, the lead underwriter will organize a syndicate designed to give the widest possible distribution to the issue. In a large issue, the syndicate will comprise several groups of underwriters based upon the size of an underwriter's commitment. The first level will consist of "major-bracket underwriters"—a relatively small group of large investment banking firms, who bring substantial capital and prestige to the offering, in addition to their most important asset, that of distributing capability. These first-level firms will constitute the "major" group in the syndicate. A second-tier or "mezzanine" group will normally consist of a combination of New York Stock Exchange member firms having branch offices outside of New York (called "wire houses" because, at least historically, the main office was connected with branch offices and correspondent brokers by private, leased telephone wires), and leading regional investment banking firms around the nation. Depending upon the size of the issue, the syndicate may also include other firms located throughout the United States and, in some cases, in financial centers throughout the world. Anywhere from ten to a hundred firms could be members of the underwriting group in any given issue. A combination of large institutionally-oriented firms, large wire houses, and locally based retailers has proven to be the most effective combination for achieving a good nationwide distribution and a reasonably satisfactory pricing of the offering from the standpoint both of the issuer and the underwriter.

Over the years, there has been a definite pecking order among investment banking firms. In any syndicate, the choice spot is that of managing underwriter. A syndicate manager of an attractive issue would be subject to considerable pressure by second-tier underwriters to be elevated to a first-tier position. On the "tombstone ad" (see infra, at pp. 129 to 130), the managing underwriter or underwriters will receive top billing. The first level underwriters would then be listed from left to right in alphabetical order, followed by a similar listing within the various subgroups. This pecking order established a ranking of underwriters within and without the industry, and the name of the game was to be in the first level if possible, or as near the top as possible. On occasion, an underwriter would withdraw from a syndicate if its allotment was less than it felt it was entitled to, or if it felt that it had been assigned to a rank below that to which it was entitled. In recent mergers among investment banking firms, the merging parties sometimes played games with the new firm name so as to move closer to the head of the alphabet for the purpose of ranking within any particular group.

Much diplomacy surrounds the listing of the underwriters on the cover page of the prospectus or on the "tombstone ad." Some of the biggest underwriting firms (e.g., Goldman, Sachs & Co., Merrill Lynch Capital Markets, Morgan Stanley & Co., Salomon Brothers Inc., and Lehman Brothers Inc.) have created a special or "bulge" bracket for themselves above the major bracket. In debt offerings, and less frequently in equity offerings, the "bulge" bracket is followed by a "mezzanine" bracket, a sub-major bracket and a bracket for the regional firms. Some major bracket firms have refused to accept a lesser status and will not participate without "star" billing. Nevertheless, institutional investors have become such a dominant factor in the new issue market that many new issues may be distributed by the "bulge" bracket underwriters, by forming a small syndicate, or even by a single underwriter.[12]

After the registration statement is filed, the syndicate manager as well as the syndicate members will test the market for the offering by making oral offers and, as we shall see later, by means of the use of the preliminary prospectus and the "tombstone ad". If the offer is in demand, other broker-dealers may seek to become members of the syndicate or become members of the "selling group." Those firms that are not included in the syndicate can be invited to become members of the "selling group," and thus will not be excluded from participating in the offering. Members of the selling group serve as retailers of the securities. Only members of the National Association of Securities Dealers, Inc., are eligible to become members of the underwriting syndicate or the selling group or to receive a concession off of the offering price.[13]

Members of the syndicate may themselves deal directly with the public, or they may sell a portion of their shares to members of the "selling group." In actual practice, however, the "syndicate manager" or the lead underwriter will notify each underwriter of the amount of stock which it is to retain for sale. For example, a firm which has committed itself to take 10,000 shares may be told by the syndicate manager that it will have 5,000 shares only of the 10,000 shares for sale to its own clients. The remainder of the securities go into the syndicate account, the "pot," which is under the direct control of the syndicate manager. These securities are used to satisfy the demand of those firms which are members of the selling group, as distinguished from the underwriting group. Members of the selling group are liable solely for the amount of stock they have agreed to purchase. Securities dealers outside of the underwriting syndicate who have received indications of interest from their clients with respect to the offering will contact the syndicate manager asking to become a member of the selling group and obtain an allotment of stock. A selling group member gets compensated in the form of a selling concession, which typically amounts to 50–60% of the gross spread between the public offering price and the net amount received by the issuer.

This "gross spread" is the difference between the price to the issuer and the public offering price. It represents the compensation which is distributed among the managing underwriter, members of the underwriting syndicate and the members of the selling group—the "underwriting discounts and commissions" shown on the cover page of the prospectus or offering circular. The issuer sells the securities to the underwriting syndicate at a discount from the public offering price. In an initial public offering, this discount has long been in the range of 7% to 7 ½%; indeed, there is so little variation that the Antitrust Division commenced an investigation into these pricing arrangements in the late 1990's, but later dropped it without taking action. The discount is considerably less for seasoned equity offerings by already public corporations and even less for debt offerings. Simply to illustrate the allocation of this discount within the underwriting group, let us assume that the issue is to be sold to the public

---

12. Just Like Film Stars, Wall Streeters Battle to Get Top Billing, Wall St. J., Jan. 15, 1986, p. 1, col. 4.

13. In 1938 the Maloney Act added Section 15A to the Securities Exchange Act of 1934 and authorized the organization of na-

tional securities associations under the supervision of the SEC. The National Association of Securities Dealers, Inc. ("NASD") is the only organization so registered and is discussed in Chapter One. See supra at pp. 73 to 75.

for $10, with $9 going to the issuer. On this basis, the compensation might be sliced up as follows. First, the lead underwriter will receive a management fee of 20 cents per share for finding and packaging the issue, and to compensate it for managing the offering and in "running the books." The next slice would be a fee of about 30 cents per share which is called the "gross underwriting fee." This fee provides compensation to the underwriting group for their expenses, such as underwriters' counsel, "tombstone" advertising and stabilizing expenses. The rest of this 30 cents represents compensation for the use of capital and for assuming the risk of the underwriting. The remaining 50 cents of the spread goes to the underwriting firm or the selling group member that actually sells the stock at retail.

Pricing. In the context of an initial public offering (or "IPO"), the pricing of the issue is the most sensitive matter to be negotiated between the underwriters and the issuer. As discussed below, there is considerable evidence that underwriters try to "underprice" a new issue so that the investors who purchase in the initial offering will receive an immediate return over the first day or two of trading. This run-up in price is intended to compensate the IPO investors for the riskiness of new offerings, but it tends to create a very volatile new issue aftermarket (because if the offering does not appreciate quickly, many investors who are expecting an immediate return will dump their shares, creating price pressure). In these price negotiations, both sides will come armed with data about other recent public offerings of similar companies and about the price/earnings ratios of comparable companies in the industry. The issuer will point to the fact that some of its rivals in the industry are trading at, say, 20:1 price/earnings multiples, and the underwriters will reply that the issuer's examples are all "seasoned" companies, while the untested character of the issuer's projected earnings stream requires application of a discount. The outcome of these negotiations is indeterminate, but relatively few deals fall apart at the last moment over price (unless market conditions suddenly turn sour).

In the case of a seasoned issuer, the price of the offering will have to be closely related to the existing market price. Still, there is an earlier problem management must face in deciding to issue equity. The announcement of a public offering has a seemingly paradoxical impact on the market price for the issuer's stock: it goes down! A considerable body of research shows that the securities market responds negatively to an announcement of a common stock offering by a seasoned issuer.[14] There are two explanations for this phenomenon: First, corporate managers who have non-public access to material information about the firm's future cash flows may be more likely to issue equity securities when they perceive the firm to be overvalued by the market than when they perceive it to be undervalued.[15] In contrast, when they believe the firm is undervalued, they will prefer to issue debt securities. Aware of this incentive, investors may reduce the firm's value upon the announcement of a common stock issue, viewing the announcement as a signal of overvaluation.

14.   See Asquith and Mullins, Equity Issues and Offering Dilution, 15 J.Fin.Econ. 61 (1986); Barclay and Litzenberger, Announcement Effects of New Equity Issues and the Use of Intraday Price Data, 21 J.Fin.Econ. 71 (1988); Mikkelson and Partch, Valuation Effects of Security Offerings and the Issuance Process, 15 J.Fin.Econ. 31 (1986).

15.   For this explanation, see Myers and Majluf, Corporate Financing and Investment Decisions When Firms Have Information That Investors Do Not Have, 13 J.Fin.Econ. 187 (1984).

Second, an alternative explanation is that the demand for an issuer's stock is not perfectly elastic and thus any increase in supply will result in a new supply and demand equilibrium. Early research suggested that new issuances or the sale of large blocks created very little price pressure on common stock (unless the market viewed the sale or issuance as a signal of reduced earnings),[16] but more recent research has challenged this conclusion, suggesting that management must therefore incorporate an expectation of some share discount into its corporate financing decisions.[17]

This perceived market penalty for equity offerings by seasoned issuers may contribute to an explanation of another puzzling phenomenon: seasoned corporations make very little use of equity public offerings to obtain capital. Instead, they rely almost exclusively on retained earnings and debt.[18] For example, only $85 billion in stock was sold to the public in new issuances between 1980 and 1984, compared to the over $5.2 trillion in outstanding stock that was traded on registered exchanges between 1978 and 1985.[19]

B. *The New Issues Market.* The new issues market is at once extremely important, extremely volatile, and extremely "thin." The number of initial public offerings varies dramatically from year to year, following a seeming boom-or-bust cycle. The following chart indicates how cyclical it can be:

Number of Offerings and Gross Proceeds of IPOs 1980–2001[20]

Year	Number of Offerings	Gross Proceeds $ Millions
1980	70	$2,020
1981	191	$4,613
1982	77	$1,839
1983	442	$15,348
1984	172	$3,543
1985	179	$6,963
1986	378	$19,653
1987	271	$16,299
1988	97	$5,324
1989	105	$6,773
1990	104	$5,611
1991	273	$15,923
1992	385	$26,373
1993	483	$34,422

16. See Scholes, The Market for Securities: Substitution Versus Price Pressure and the Effects of Information on Share Prices, 45 J.Bus. 179 (1972).

17. See Loderer, Cooney and Van Drunen, The Price Elasticity of Demand for Common Stock, 46 J.Fin. 621 (1991); Asquith and Mullins, supra note 18; Masulis and Korwar, Seasoned Equity Offerings: An Empirical Investigation, 15 J.Fin.Econ. 91 (1986).

18. See Stout, The Unimportance of Being Efficient: An Economic Analysis of Stock Market Pricing and Securities Regulation, 87 Mich.L.Rev. 613, 645 and n. 179 ("During the 1980s, new issues of common stock averaged only about 1 percent of total stock outstanding...."); see also Smith, Investment Banking and The Capital Acquisition Process, 15 J.Fin.Econ. 3 (1986).

19. See Smith supra note 18. Comment, Equity Financing for Public Corporations: Reasons and Methods to Encourage It, 138 U.Pa.L.Rev. 1411, 1419 n. 32 (1990).

20. See Jay R. Ritter and Ivo Welch, A Review of IPO Activity, Pricing and Allocations, 57 J.Fin.1795 (2002). For another study, see Seligman, The Merits Do Matter: A Comment on Professor Grundfest's "Disimplying Private Rights of Action Under the Federal Securities Laws": The Commission's Authority, 108 Harv.L.Rev. 438, 457 (1994) (relying on SEC Ann.Rep. at 51 (1993)).

Year	Number of Offerings	Gross Proceeds $ Millions
1994	387	$19,323
1995	432	$28,347
1996	621	$45,940
1997	432	$31,701
1998	267	$34,628
1999	457	$66,770
2000	346	$62,593
2001	80	$34,344

Not only did the number of IPOs and the aggregate proceeds fluctuate significantly, but also the average first day returns were equally volatile, ranging from a low of 3.6% in 1984 to a high of 71.7% in 1999 (and then back down to 14.0% in 2001). This pattern of an alternating "boom and bust" cycle in IPOs has been with us for some time.[21] After several lean years following the 1987 stock crash, the IPO market roared back in the mid–1990s, repeatedly hitting records throughout the late 1990's. Then, in 2000, the Nasdaq "high tech" bubble seemingly burst, and IPOs dried up in both 2000 and 2001.

Some argue that the thinness of the new issue market renders it much less efficient than the much deeper secondary market. One survey shows that 2,800 companies went public between January 1975 and June 1985, selling $27.5 billion worth of common shares.[22] This averages out to nearly $3 billion per year in IPOs, while over this same period the annual trading volume on the NYSE ranged between $1 trillion and $2 trillion. In fact, the disparity is so great that the aggregate annual commissions paid on trading on the principal stock exchanges easily exceed the total primary market offerings made each year. The typical initial public offering is also relatively small.[23] The consequence may be that little incentive exists for securities analysts or other independent market professionals to attempt to evaluate the merits of the offering or its pricing. Other factors also suggest the likelihood of mispricing. First, sales commissions on IPOs are typically several times those on secondary market transactions.[24] Second, the price/earnings ratios on new public offerings can vary significantly from year to year. Initial public offerings that in 1980 sold at 16 times estimated earnings were a few years later snapped up at price/earnings ratios in the high 30s and low 40s. Premiums of such a magnitude encouraged issuers and underwriters to rush new issues to the market, possibly before product lines were adequately tested or developed. Predictably, the bubble burst in the early 1980's, and again in 2000.

The economic evidence on initial public offerings is even more puzzling. Numerous studies have found that IPOs tend to be underpriced over the short-run; for example, measured from the initial offering price to the market price at the end of the first day of trading, IPOs in the 1980's yielded an average initial return of 16.4%.[25] However this phenomenon of underpricing has been highly

21. For data for earlier years, see Lowenstein, Shareholder Voting Rights: A Response to SEC Rule 19c–4 and to Professor Gilson, 89 Colum.L.Rev. 979, 994 (1989).

22. Why New Issues Are Lousy Investments, Forbes, Dec. 2, 1985 at 152–54 (estimating average initial public offering to them be for $13 million); see also Lowenstein, supra note 21, at 994–95.

23. Lowenstein, supra note 21, at 995 (citing Jay R. Ritter, The Long–Run Performance of Initial Public Offerings, 46 J.Fin. 3 (1991)).

24. Id. at 998.

25. See Ibbotson, Sindelar and Ritter, Initial Public Offerings, J.App.Corp.Fin. 37 (1988) (sample of 8,668 IPOs going public in 1960–87); Tinic, Anatomy of Initial Public Offerings of Common Stock, 43 J.Fin. 789 (1988); Miller and Reilly, An Examination of Mispricing, Returns and Uncertainty for Ini-

cyclical, with very high initial returns being reported across the new issue market for some months and then flat returns for other periods.[26] Over the years, financial economists have tried to explain this data in a variety of ways: (1) underpricing could represent an insurance premium for the higher legal liability underwriters face in IPOs;[27] (2) it may reflect monopsony power held by investment banking firms vis-a-vis small issuers; or (3) it may be the result of investors' inability to judge IPOs on an individual basis so that they decide to invest on a portfolio basis at an average price, leading to the underpricing of higher quality offerings.[28]

None of these explanations, however, could explain the extraordinary underpricing that occurred in the late 1990's during the Nasdaq "high tech" boom. During this era, IPOs frequently rose 400%, 500%, and on occasion even higher simply on their first day of trading. One recent study finds that the average first day return was 44% for IPOs between 1997 and 1999; that is, the first day closing price was 44% above the initial offering price at which IPO allocations were sold to favored investors.[29] If a stock is sold at an initial offering price of $10 per share and yet the very first trade in the secondary market is at $20 and the first day's closing price is $50 (as happened regularly in 1999 and 2000), this extraordinary undepricing would seemingly offend the issuer—on the ground that the underwriter had knowingly underpriced it and caused it to receive only 20% of the value that the market quickly placed on this stock. The underwriter would presumably know that the stock was underpriced because it (and usually it alone) knows the ratio between the "indications of interest" it has received from potential purchasers and the number of shares to be sold (for example, if this ratio were as high as ten to one, the underwriter would know that it had a very hot offering). Yet, few such complaints were heard from issuers during this period. Instead, an intense competition developed among investors for allocation of stock in IPOs, as everyone anticipated that such an allocation amounted to "free money" because the IPO stock would predictably rise sharply in the secondary market.

What explains the puzzling phenomenon? There are multiple theories, but most incorporate two additional factors: First, investment banking firms have close and multiple relationships with institutional investors. Conferring underpriced stock (or, in effect, free money) on institutions that buy in IPOs (most typically, mutual funds) may be a way of obtaining an institution's brokerage business or other advisory business from it. While unproven, it is widely believed that underwriters allocate stock in the "hottest" (or most oversubscribed) offerings to those institutions that have given them the most business,

---

tial Public Offerings, 16 Financial Management 33 (1987).

26. Ibbotson and Jaffe, "Hot Issue" Markets, 30 J.Fin. 1027 (1975); Jay Ritter, The "Hot Issue" Market of 1980, 32 J.Bus. 215 (1984).

27. Under Section 11 of the Securities Act of 1933, the underwriter can only be held liable for the difference between the initial offering price and the lower price on the date of any lawsuit's filing. Hence, underpricing the initial offering price reduces the potential damages to the underwriter.

28. For a survey of these theories and the most recent evidence, see Loderer, Sheehan and Kadlec, The Pricing of Equity Offerings, 29 J.Fin.Econ. 35 (1991). No similar pattern of underpricing is associated with seasoned offerings.

29. See Norman Garfinkle, Burton Malkiel and Costin Bontas, Effect of Underpricing and Lock–Up Provisions in IPOs, 28 J. of Portfolio Management 50, 52 (2002). According to the Ritter and Welch study set forth in the chart at footnote 20, the average first day returns in 1999 were over 71%.

and informal formulas that relate brokerage commissions received to IPO allocations given probably exist. But, even if such favoritism for institutional investors understandably exists, it still does not explain the issuer's passivity in tolerating IPO underpricing.

Here, the second factor comes into play. Insiders in most IPOs—i.e., officers, directors, and venture capitalists—own most of the existing stock in the firm. The underwriters almost invariably require them to enter into "lock-up" agreements, which contractually bar these insiders from selling their shares in the secondary market until the expiration of a specified period after the effectiveness of the registration statement (usually, six months). This is done to assure investors that the insiders will not "bail out" and sell immediately after the offering. Underwriters insist on this because otherwise it would be difficult to market the stock to investors, but lock-up agreements have two consequences. First, they cause the insiders to focus less on the price of the stock at the end of the offering (which is when the underpricing occurs) and more on its likely price on the expiration of their lock-up (at which point they will typically sell a substantial portion of their shares to diversify their wealth). One scenario for why underpricing was tolerated by issuers is that the insiders whose stock is subject to "lock-ups" believe that a sharp first day price spike creates favorable publicity and attention for their company and maximizes the possibility that the stock price will remain high at the point when they become able to sell. Possibly too, the underwriters have quietly agreed to have one of their "star" securities analysts recommend the stock in a published report issued just before the lock-up expiration date is reached (this practice is called a "booster shot" in the parlance). Such services may convince the firm's controlling shareholders to accept considerable underpricing in return for services that maximize the stock price at this later lock-up expiration point, which may be more important to them.

A second interpretation is that lock-ups by their very nature create an imbalance in supply and demand that results in sharp price spikes on the offering day. For example, assume that 10 million shares are to be sold by the company, but 40 million shares are already held by the firm's founding shareholders, but the latter shares will be locked up for six months. Thus, only 10 million shares are in the public float in secondary market. Arguably as a result, there is a supply and demand imbalance that produces a price spike until the lock-up expires. Supporting this interpretation is the fact that the typical IPO issuer's stock price usually does decline (and significantly) just before the lock-up expires.[30] (Of course, this could also be explained by the market anticipating that the stock is about to come under heavy selling pressure, both from insiders and from short-sellers, who tend to exploit this known tendency). This supply and demand imbalance is further aggravated by the practice of many underwriters in imposing "anti-flipping" rules on their retail customers (but seldom on their institutional customers, who have more leverage). These rules tell the retail customer that if it sells (or "flips") its IPO allocation during the period immediately after the offering (for example, the first month), it will receive no further IPO allocations (or at least not for a defined period).[31]

30. Id. at 54–56.

31. Restrictions on "flipping" by retail purchasers imposed by multiple underwriters have been attacked on antitrust grounds as a restraint of trade. However, in a recent decision, "anti-flipping" restrictions have been

Still, a third explanation is that the apparent underpricing is, at least in part, a product of market manipulation. Because initial allocations of IPO stock are valuable, numerous recent class action lawsuits have charged that underwriters have required institutions who desire to receive such allocations to agree, as a condition of their receipt, to buy additional stock at progressively higher prices on the first day of trading. This practice—known as "laddering"—creates an artificial demand for the stock and so results in a distorted price which is not the true product of the "real" supply and demand for the stock. It is also illegal, and the SEC is currently conducting a much publicized investigation into whether IPO prices were manipulated by arrangements between underwriters and institutions. Any such manipulation would give rise to the appearance (although not necessarily the reality) of underpricing.

Of course, all three explanations could be true and complementary. While the debate over the cause of underpricing will continue, one loser is obvious: the evidence is clear that those who buy IPO stocks in the secondary market during the interval between the end of the first trading day and the expiration of the lock-up period systematically lose.[32] Some believe that this evidence justifies regulatory restrictions on lock-ups as themselves an interference with natural market forces.

One further puzzle is associated with IPO pricing. IPOs tend to systematically underperform the market in the first year after the offering. Indeed, some studies show that, over a three year period following the IPO, issuing firms appear to underperform the market significantly, doing far worse than a sample of similar firms over the same period.[33] While there is substantial variation from year to year and across industries in this rate of underperformance, companies that went public in high volume years appear to fare the worst, so that, despite initial underpricing, no gains in excess of the market average remain after three years. This data seems to support three generalizations: (1) the IPO market may not approach the informational efficiency of the deeper secondary markets (i.e., the exchanges and the Nasdaq); (2) investors are cyclically over optimistic about the earnings potential of emerging high growth companies; and (3) some investors who buy in the IPO secondary market are systematically prejudiced by current practices.

C. *The Fixed Price Offering and Resale Price Maintenance.* The typical underwriting agreement requires all the underwriters and selling group members to adhere to the public offering price as stated in the prospectus. Such a fixed price offering eliminates the prospect of competition among the underwriting group (particularly for the same institutional customers), but it essentially amounts to a price-fixing agreement. Early on, both the SEC and the courts held that such agreements did not violate the antitrust laws, although they could violate certain provisions of the securities laws.[34]

upheld on the ground that such restrictions were consistent with the SEC's regulatory scheme and so had implied immunity from the antitrust laws. See Friedman v. Salomon/Smith Barney, Inc., CCH Fed. Sec. L. Rep. Para. 93, 275 (S.D.N.Y. Dec. 8, 2000). The impact of these restrictions is that only institutional investors may be able to sell during the period in which the price spike typically occurs.

32. See Garfinkle, Malkiel, and Bontas, supra note at 29.

33. Jay R. Ritter, The Long–Run Performance of Initial Public Offerings, 46 J.Fin. 3 (1991); see also Garfinkle, Malkiel, and Bontas, supra note 28.

34. One early SEC decision, In the Matter of National Association of Securities Dealers, 19 S.E.C. 424 (1945), found that an agreement to make an offering at a fixed

A practical problem arises under the Securities Act of 1933 because the offering price must be stated in the Prospectus (on the front cover), and any sales by underwriters below that price make the Prospectus false and misleading (unless it is amended or supplemented) and subjects all of the underwriters to liability under Section 11 of the Act. Therefore, it is arguably impossible to carry out a fixed-price distribution without some sort of agreement, formal or informal, among all of the underwriters that they will adhere to the stated public offering price. Clearly, Congress did not think that fixed-price distributions were illegal when it enacted that statute.

Although resale price maintenance may be lawful in this field, it is difficult to enforce. Institutions have persistently searched for ways of evading the fixed-price structure of IPOs, and they appear to obtain volume discounts. A number of low-visibility techniques for paying discounts to large institutional buyers have been devised. The SEC described these practices in Securities Exchange Act Release No. 15807 (1979):

"The growth of institutional participation in the securities markets has exerted increasing pressure on the fixed price offering system. In connection with distributions, a number of practices have developed which may have the economic effect of granting to institutional and other large purchasers a rebate of some portion of the gross spread in fixed price offerings. Such practices include both direct discounting techniques, such as 'overtrading' in swap transactions and certain types of fee recapture, and indirect compensation arrangements, such as the provision of goods and services in return for so-called 'syndicate soft dollars.'

In swap transactions, securities are taken in trade for a customer, in lieu of cash, in exchange for the offered securities. A discount from the fixed offered price may be granted to the purchaser of the offered securities where the syndicate member purchases the securities taken in trade at a price exceeding their market value. This "overtrade" is economically equivalent to paying less than the stated offering price for the securities being distributed.

A customer may seek to recapture underwriting fees by designating a broker-dealer affiliate to be included in the selling group. The customer may then purchase the offered securities through its affiliate, thereby recapturing the selling commission. Such concession payments to an affiliate enable the customer to obtain direct discounts from the fixed offering price.

A broker-dealer providing research or other services to the customer may be compensated for those services, at least in part, through purchase by the customer at the fixed offering price. The customer can either purchase the securities directly through the broker-dealer or can contact the managing underwriter and "designate" the dealer to receive credit for the order. In these instances, the dealer is compensated indirectly by

price did not violate the Sherman Antitrust Act, but did violate what is now § 15A(b)(6) of the 1934 Act, which forbids the rules of the NASD "to fix minimum profits, to impose any schedule of prices, or to impose any schedule or fix minimum rates of commission, allowances, discounts or other charges." See also United States v. Morgan, 118 F.Supp. 621, 699 (S.D.N.Y.1953) (resale price maintenance did not violate Sherman Act).

receiving "soft dollars' concessions for the research or other services it has provided."[35]

Although easy to evade, the fixed offering price system remains politically popular with small investors, who do not like the idea of large institutions receiving a discount that they did not also get. As a result, in 1980, the SEC reversed its prior position and permitted the NASD to adopt rules enforcing resale price maintenance and thereby enforce fixed-price offerings. It reasoned that because the underwriting discount and selling group concessions were separately negotiated with respect to each new public issue, the NASD was not attempting to impose discounts and commissions in violation of § 15A(b)(6) of the 1934 Act.[36] Rather, the SEC said it was simply enforcing the voluntary agreement of the underwriters and selling group members to adhere to the offering price, until the managing underwriter released the group from those restrictions.

This may seem a strained interpretation, but the real message of the above quoted language from Release 15807 is that the large institutional purchaser who wants a volume discount on the securities it purchases can often find a way to both receive it and disguise its receipt. Thus, the NASD may have its rule, but institutional purchasers still, to some degree, have their discounts. The result is a continuing tension between the NASD and some of its members over these practices, and recurring NASD disciplinary proceedings.

D. *The Role of the Security Analyst.* A last player in the public offering process who needs to be introduced at this stage is the securities analyst. Analysts work both for brokerage firms (the so-called "sell side") and institutional investors and money managers (the so-called "buy side"). The research done by analysts on the buy side is usually kept confidential as proprietary information, but "sell side" research, including ratings and recommendations, is widely disseminated in order to encourage brokerage transactions by investors (as brokerage firms chiefly earn their revenues from brokerage commissions). Not surprisingly, buy recommendations usually outnumber sell recommendations (in part because "buy" recommendations address all investors, while "sell" recommendations address only the much smaller population of investors who already own the stock or who are willing to sell it "short").

Securities analysts are chartered by a professional organization (the Association for Investment Management and Research (or "AIMR")), which administers a continuing education program and conducts a rigorous examination for analysts who wish to become "chartered financial analysts" (or "CFAs"). AIMR also has adopted certain "best practice" standards in keeping with the industry's view that the securities analyst is a professional, much like an attorney or an auditor. This view of the analyst as an objective professional conflicts, however, with the analyst's involvement in sales and marketing activities. During the 1990's, analysts became major participants in the IPO

---

35. For a fuller discussion of "soft dollars," see Jorden, "Paying Up" for Research: A Regulatory and Legislative Analysis, 1975 Duke L.J. 1103; Burgunder & Hartmann, Soft Dollars and Section 28(e) of the Securities Exchange Act of 1934: A 1985 Perspective, 24 Am.Bus.L.J. 139 (1986).

36. See Securities Exchange Act Rel. No. 17371 (Dec. 31, 1980). Section 15A(b) of the 1934 Act is discussed supra at note 1. See generally, Price Maintenance in the Distribution of Securities, 56 Yale L.J. 333 (1947); Jennings, Self–Regulation in the Securities Industry: The Role of the Securities and Exchange Commission, 29 Law & Contemp.Pub. 663 (1964); Pickard & Djinis, NASD Disciplinary Proceedings: Practice and Procedure, 37 Bus.Law. 1213 (1982).

marketing process. At least in part, this was attributable to the fact that some analysts during this period acquired a celebrity status (often being featured on T.V. shows and quoted in newspaper stories), and investment bankers recognized that analyst support could sell a particular initial public offering. With this recognition came a sudden competition to hire "star" analysts, and well-recognized analysts increasingly migrated from small, boutique brokerage firms that specialized in research to large, integrated brokerage firms that specialized in underwriting (with this migration "star" analysts' salaries soared from relatively modest levels to the multi-million dollar range). Once hired by investment banking firms, analysts were regularly assigned to the "road shows" at which prospective IPO's were sold to institutional investors.

But as the competition for analysts became more heated, conflicts of interest began to surface. Allegedly, some investment banking firms competed for IPO's by promising (implicitly or even explicitly) that their "star" analysts in the IPO firm's industry would issue a "strong buy" recommendation on the stock shortly after secondary trading began. At this point, an obvious conflict arises between the analyst's professional role as a neutral umpire, evaluating securities for investors, and the analyst's role as a salesman for the investment banking division of the analyst's firm.

After the collapse of the Nasdaq "high tech" market in 2000, pointed questions were raised in the media about the reasons for the persistence of many analysts in maintaining "buy" recommendations on stocks that fell 80% or more during this crash. Similarly, seventeen out of the eighteen analysts who followed Enron maintained buy recommendations on its stock up until shortly before its bankruptcy filing in 2001 (with the lone dissenting analyst working for a brokerage firm that did not have an investment banking department).

Discontent with the seeming conflicts surrounding analysts led to Congressional hearings in 2001, to rule-making by the NASD and the NYSE that was initiated in 2001, and, most importantly, to a civil action brought by the New York State Attorney General in 2002 against Merrill, Lynch & Co. The last action, brought by New York Attorney General Eliot Spitzer, had particularly explosive consequences because the Attorney General filed a public affidavit which quoted excerpts from emails sent by Merrill Lynch securities analysts to their colleagues contemporaneously with buy recommendations issued by the firm, which emails seemingly trashed the stocks so recommended, describing the stocks in some cases as "pieces of junk" (and worse). The affidavit further quoted some analysts warning their superiors that several of the stocks recommended would cost small investors their retirement savings and implying that the buy recommendations were based only on the investment banking fees that they would generate for the firm. Over the following weeks, the market capitalization of Merrill Lynch sank by 20%, seemingly in response to this controversy. Meanwhile, the New York Attorney General announced an intent to achieve structural reforms that would separate securities research from investment banking (much as the Glass–Steagall Act had once separated commercial and investment banking), and the securities industry in turn objected to a single state's Attorney General attempting to restructure the securities industry in ways never suggested nor favored by the SEC.

In May 2002, Merrill Lynch and the New York Attorney General reached a compromise settlement whose most notable provision was that Merrill Lynch agreed to "separate completely the evaluation and determination of compensation for U.S.-based equity research analysts from Merrill Lynch's investment banking business."[37] This settlement left Merrill's investment banking division still able to subsidize securities research (if it chose to do so) but not to determine or influence the allocation of this subsidy among analysts (or otherwise to communicate regarding analyst compensation). The premise here was that such a prophylactic rule would leave securities analysts free to pursue their own individual desires to develop personal reputations for accurate and objective research, unconstrained by the threat of reduced compensation for negative research. The Merrill Lynch settlement has now been adopted voluntarily by several other brokerage firms and is being demanded by some institutional investors as a precondition for their brokerage business.

The Merrill Lynch settlement came hard on the heels of the SEC's approval in 2002 of new rules by both the NASD and the NYSE that similarly restrict investment banking influence and control over securities analysts.[38] These rules (NASD Rule 2711 and NYSE Rule 473) addressed analyst conflicts of interest in connection with the preparation and publication of research reports on equity securities and imposed the following restrictions:

1. No research analysts may be supervised or controlled by a firm's investment banking department;

2. Investment banking personnel may not discuss pending research reports with research analysts prior to their distribution (with certain limited exceptions);

3. Promise of favorable research in return for investment banking business are forbidden as is compensation to analysts tied to specific investment banking transactions;

4. Restrictions are placed on an analyst's personal trading, including in particular a prohibition on purchases by an analysts of an issuer's securities prior to an IPO;

5. Disclosures are mandated both about the brokerage firm's economic relationships with an issuer and about the percentage breakdown of its securities recommendations (i.e., the relative percentages of buy, sell and hold recommendations); and

6. No analyst research report may be disseminated by an underwriter in an IPO during the 40 day period following the effectiveness of the registration statement (this "blackout period" is intended to eliminate any conflict of interest that might tempt the underwriter to promote the IPO stock during this critical period).

These regulations still stop short of restricting the analyst to the role of an objective professional. Under them, an analyst may still participate in the "road show" marketing process by which IPOs are sold to institutions, and the compensation of the investment research department as a whole may still depend on the services it provides to the investment banking division, because investment research is not an independent profit center for most integrated broker-dealer firms.

---

37. See Agreement Between the Attorney General of the State of New York and Merrill Lynch, Pierce, Fenner & Smith, Inc., dated May 21, 2002, at Paragraph 7.

38. See Securities Exchange Act Release No. 34–45908 (May 16, 2002).

Still, the regulatory picture remains in flux. The Sarbanes–Oxley Act of 2002 mandates that the SEC (or any SROs the which it delegates the issue) must adopt rules by late 2003 to address analyst conflicts of interests. These rules must not only prohibit investment banking involvement in the compensatory evaluation of analysts (as the existing SRO rules discussed above have begun to do), but must protect analysts from retaliation or threats of retaliation for "adverse, negative, or otherwise unfavorable research reports" and "establish structural and institutional safeguards within registered brokers or dealers to assure that securities analysts are separated by appropriate informational partitions within the firm from the review, pressure, or oversight of those whose involvement in investment banking activities might potentially bias their judgment or supervision."[39]

At present, the likely impact of these prospective rules is necessarily uncertain. On the one hand, "sell side" securities research seems likely to remain dependent upon an economic subsidy from investment banking, because the "buy side" remains unwilling to pay for such research. On the other hand, "sell side" analysts do have their own incentives to develop personal reputations for accurate and useful research, which they are now freer to pursue. How these opposing forces will play out remains an open question. There is evidence, however, that the market increasingly discounts the recommendations of "sell side" analysts who are connected with an underwriter of the issuer,[40] preferring to rely on independent analyst firms, who are unconnected to underwriters, or on "buy side" analysts.

The objectivity and independence of the securities analyst has also been significantly enhanced by another SEC reform, which aimed at a different problem. Regulation FD, adopted in 2000,[41] now prohibits selective disclosure by corporate managements of material information to analysts, institutional investors, and shareholders likely to trade based on such information. Although aimed at selective disclosure, a variety of insider trading that had not been clearly prohibited by law, Regulation FD has restricted the ability of corporate managers to retaliate against, or threaten, analysts who published negative research about their companies. Prior to Regulation FD, the analyst could be cut off from the flow of sensitive information about the company and so had to be careful not to offend management with critical research or ratings. For the future, management's ability to discipline the analyst has been constrained by Regulation FD, but only time can tell whether analysts will become more independent and critical as a result.

---

39. The Sarbanes–Oxley Act added new Section 15D to the '34 Act to authorize the SEC to promulgate these rules.

40. See Roni Michaely and Kent Womack, Conflict of Interest and the Credibility of Underwriter Analyst Recommendations, 12 Review of Financial Studies 653 (1999).

41. See Securities Act Release No. 33–7881 (August 15, 2000). For the debate over the rule compare Merritt B. Fox, Regulation FD and Foreign Issuers: Globalization's Strains and Opportunities, 41 Va. J. Int'l L. 653 (2001) with William K.S. Wang, Selective Disclosure by Issuers, Its Legality and Ex Ante Harm: Some Observations In Response to Professor Fox, 42 Va. J. Int'l L. 869 (2002).

CHAPTER 2

THE BASIC STRUCTURE AND PROHIBITIONS OF THE SECURITIES ACT

SECTION 1.   THE STATUTORY FRAMEWORK

Statute

Securities Act, §§ 5, 17, 2, 3, 4, 6, 7, 8, 10 (and Schedule A), 11, 12, 13, 19, 20, 24, 9, 22.

Introductory Note

The Securities Act of 1933 has two basic objectives: (1) to provide investors with material financial and other information concerning new issues of securities offered for sale to the public; and (2) to prohibit fraudulent sales of securities. Its scope, however, is strictly limited, for jurisdiction is always tied to some use of the mails or of interstate facilities to accomplish a forbidden transaction; however, the use of the "jurisdictional means" can almost always be found. We commence our study of the 1933 Act with a guided tour through the various sections of the statute.

The basic prohibitions are found in two substantive provisions: Section 5 which prescribes the rules for compelling full disclosure and §§ 17 and 12(2) which relate to fraud or misrepresentation in interstate sales of securities. Section 17 and § 12(a)(2) may appear to overlap to some extent, but the former provides criminal sanctions and the latter exclusively civil sanctions. Section 17 also provides a basis for enforcement by the Securities and Exchange Commission through disciplinary proceedings or by way of an injunction. The Supreme Court has yet to decide whether a private right of action will be implied under Section 17(a).[1]

The key provision is § 5 around which most of the rest of the Act revolves. Its overall purpose is to require that new issues of securities offered by the use of the mails or other instrumentalities of interstate commerce shall be registered with the Commission, and that a prospectus (filed as a part of the registration statement) shall be furnished to the purchaser prior to the sale or, in some cases, at the time of the delivery of the security after sale. Section 5 can only be understood, however, by taking § 2 into account, for that section defines a number of the technical terms used in Section 5. Section 3 exempts from the operation of the Act (except for the antifraud provisions of §§ 17 and 12(a)(2)) a laundry list of different types of securities and thus further limits § 5. In addition, § 4 specifically provides that § 5 shall not apply to certain specified transactions (most notably, private placements) and thus further restricts the section. Finally, although § 5 seemingly applies to "any person," we learn in § 4(1) that the section does not apply to transactions by

---

1. Reversing an earlier trend, the Courts of Appeal are uniformly concluding that there is no private cause of action under § 17(a). See Zink v. Merrill Lynch Pierce Fenner & Smith, 13 F.3d 330 (10th Cir.1993); Finkel v. The Stratton Corporation, 962 F.2d 169 (2d Cir.1992); Newcome v. Esrey, 862 F.2d 1099, 1107 (4th Cir.1988) (en banc).

anyone unless the person is "an issuer, underwriter, or dealer"—something quite different. Again, these terms are words of art which are defined in § 2.

The "registration statement" referred to in § 5 is defined in § 2(a)(8). Sections 6 through 8 set forth the procedures for registering securities from the filing of the registration statement with the SEC until it becomes effective. Section 5 also regulates the use of the "prospectus." That term is defined in § 2(10). The information required to be set forth in the registration statement is specified in § 7 (and in Schedule A) and § 10 prescribes the contents of a prospectus.

Other sections of the Act are concerned with enforcement procedures. Sections 11 and 12 give private remedies to buyers of securities. The scope of these remedies are the subject of Part IV on Civil Liabilities. The private remedy sector is rounded out by § 13 which fixes a short statute of limitations for Sections 11 and 12 actions; by § 14 which invalidates any contractual provision that attempts a waiver of remedies; and by § 15 which imposes a joint and several liability upon persons in a control relationship with any person liable under §§ 11 or 12.[2]

To complete the overall picture, reference needs to be made to a number of miscellaneous sections. Section 18 partially preempts state laws regulating the issuance and sale of securities.[3] However, Section 19(c)(1) authorizes the SEC to cooperate with the states in securities matters for the purpose of promoting uniformity and reducing the burdens of raising capital, particularly by small business. Section 19(a) gives the Commission rule making powers, including the power to define accounting, technical and trade terms used in the Act. It also contains the important good faith provision which immunizes from any liability persons who rely upon a rule of the Commission in good faith, even though the rule is later determined to be invalid.

The government may compel compliance in various ways. Sections 19(b) and 20(a) give the SEC investigative powers. Section 20 also authorizes the Commission to seek the judicial remedies of injunction and mandamus. Moreover, the Securities Enforcement Remedies Act of 1990 authorizes the federal courts to issue cease and desist orders for violation of the securities laws, order the payment of penalties in addition to disgorgement, and prohibit persons from serving as officers and directors of public companies (see infra at Chapter 21). However, the power to institute criminal proceedings is vested in the Attorney General. Criminal penalties are specified in § 24.[4]

---

2. This, for example, would include the promoters in the case of Old Dominion Copper Mining & Smelting Co. v. Lewisohn, 210 U.S. 206 (1908), even though the securities are sold by the corporation, rather than the promoters.

3. This topic and the impact of the National Securities Markets Improvement Act of 1996 was discussed in Chapter 1, supra at pp. 78 to 80. To the extent that it is not preempted, a state may require merit review of out-of-state offerings of securities to be made within the state, even though the offering has met the disclosure requirements of the 1933 Act. North Star Intern. v. Arizona Corporation Commission, 720 F.2d 578 (9th Cir.1983).

4. The SEC is authorized to conduct investigations which may result in the institution "of administrative proceedings looking to the imposition of remedial sanctions, initiation of injunctive proceedings in the courts, and, in the case of willful violation, reference of the matter to the Department of Justice for criminal prosecution." 17 C.F.R. § 202.5(b). The process is described in McLucas, Hammill, Shea & Dubow, An Overview of Various Procedural Considerations Associated With the Securities and Exchange Commission's Investigative Process, 45 Bus.Law. 625 (1990).

Congress and the courts have noted the "close working relationship" between the two agencies in their investigative capacities. SEC v. Dresser Industries, Inc., 628 F.2d 1368, 1386 (D.C.Cir.1980) (en banc), cert. denied, 449 U.S. 993 (1980). For the scope of the SEC's enforcement efforts, see infra at Chapter 21.

Court procedures are prescribed in §§ 9 and 22. Under § 9, a person aggrieved by an order of the Commission may have it reviewed in the United States Court of Appeals. Jurisdiction of "offenses and violations" is vested in the United States district courts by virtue of § 22(a), although the state and territorial courts have concurrent jurisdiction with respect to civil actions under the statute. In suits in the federal courts, venue may be laid in the district where the defendant is found, is an inhabitant, transacts business or where the offer or sale of the security occurred. Process runs throughout the world,[5] and the Court may order security for costs under § 11(e).

With this preview of the overall structure of the 1933 act, § 5 should be examined more closely. It is to be noted that the section states the ground rules for making offers and sales of securities during three distinct periods of time: (1) the pre-filing period; (2) the period between the filing of the registration statement and the effective date (the so-called waiting period); and (3) the post-effective period.

Section 5 states the rules and preconditions for making offers, sales, and the manner of sales of securities in registered public offerings. Section 5(a) requires an "effective" registration statement as a precondition to the sale of a security; § 5(b) states the prospectus delivery requirements; and § 5(c) governs activities in the pre-filing period. However, in order to understand what issuers, underwriters and dealers may or may not do in any period—pre-filing, waiting, or post-effective—one must read the entire section. None of the subsections standing alone states all the rules governing any one time period.

Problem on the Prohibitions of Section 5

Impel, Inc., incorporated in Delaware, is engaged in the business of waste management. Its principal executive offices are located in Peoria, Illinois. There are 3,000,000 shares of common stock and 2,000,000 shares of nonconvertible, nonparticipating 8% preferred stock outstanding. The common stock is listed on the New York Stock Exchange and is selling at about $60 a share; the preferred is unlisted and is traded over the counter. The company had net income of $3,000,000 in each of the last five fiscal years.

Impel has decided to expand into the business of radioactive waste disposal in order to meet a pressing public need in this area. The waste is to be gathered and ultimately stored in airtight containers to be stored in an underground desert location owned by Impel. Impel proposes to amend its certificate of incorporation: (1) to split the common stock six-for-one in order to provide an offering price of $10.00 a share and to increase the size of the offering to provide a broader market;

---

5. Under Section 22(a), process may be served "wherever the defendant may be found." Similar language appears in Section 27 of the 1934 Act. In Fitzsimmons v. Barton, 589 F.2d 330 (7th Cir.1979), nationwide service under Section 27 and F.R.C.P.Rule 4(e) withstood a constitutional attack on the basis of the Due Process Clause of the Fourteenth Amendment. In Bersch v. Drexel Firestone, Inc., 389 F.Supp. 446 (S.D.N.Y.1974), rev'd in part on other grounds, 519 F.2d 974 (2d Cir.1975), cert. denied, 423 U.S. 1018 (1975), service of process on a British corporation by mailing a copy of the summons and complaint pursuant to F.R.C.P.Rule 4(i)(1)(D), return receipt requested, to its office outside the United States was held sufficient, even though the envelope containing the summons and complaint was returned to the sender, marked "delivery refused". The court held defendant was "found" at its head office, despite its effort to avoid service of process merely by returning the papers. In SEC v. Unifund SAL, 910 F.2d 1028 (2d Cir.1990), the district court ordered service of process to be made by sending all relevant papers to the defendant in care of defendant's New York broker with instructions to forward the papers by overnight carrier to the defendant in Beirut. Service was held proper under § 27 of the Securities Exchange Act and Fed.R.Civ.P. 4(e) and 4(i). And see SEC v. International Swiss Invs. Corp., 895 F.2d 1272 (9th Cir. 1990).

and (2) to make a public offering of 10,000,000 shares of common stock at a proposed price of $10.00 per share.

The problem deals with activities occurring in three time frames: (a) the pre-filing period, (b) the waiting period, and (c) the post-effective period. Part (a) (problems 1–17) should be read and answered only after reading the material in section 2; part (b) (problems 18–26) only after reading the material in section 3; and parts (c) and (d) (problems 27–38) only after reading the material in section 4. The problem as posed assumes that Impel is a reporting company under the 1934 Act; as to each problem, where relevant, consider whether your answer would be different, if Impel were a non-reporting company.

(a) Assume that the securities will have to be registered under the Securities Act of 1933, but no registration statement has yet been filed. Determine the application of § 5 to the following transactions:

1. Able, the President of Impel, makes a telephone call from Peoria, Illinois to the Chicago office of Hazard & Co., investment bankers, and opens negotiations to have Hazard & Co. serve as principal underwriter of the issue.

2. Able is referred to the buying department of Hazard & Co. which is located in New York and pursues the matter further by telephoning the New York Office.

3. After further investigation by the head of the buying department of Hazard & Co. (including a tour of the plant) the corporation and Hazard & Co. reach an informal agreement that Hazard & Co. will serve as the principal underwriter of the issue and this agreement is embodied in a "letter of intent" signed by Hazard & Co. in New York and mailed to Peoria, Illinois where Able signs an acceptance on behalf of Impel and returns it to Hazard & Co. by mail. Did any of the foregoing activities result in Impel's common stock being "in registration"?

4. Impel publishes a notice announcing that it proposes to register 10,000,000 shares of common stock under the Securities Act of 1933 and make a public offering of the shares for cash at a price to be determined by market conditions at the time of the offering; that the proceeds are to be used for the purpose stated above; and that Hazard & Co. will serve as principal underwriter of the issue.

5. Assume that instead of Impel taking the action stated in question 4, Hazard & Co. distributes a press release to the New York papers and to the principal wire services announcing the forthcoming offering of 10,000,000 common shares by Impel to be distributed through a nationwide investment banking group that it will head as managing underwriter. The release also describes the use of the proceeds, the plans of management and indicates that the offering will be at or near the market price, as adjusted for the stock-split, when a registration statement with respect to the securities has become effective.

6. Hazard & Co. telephones or writes other underwriters throughout the nation and forms an underwriting group to purchase the Impel common stock. The members then sign an "Agreement among Underwriters" in which they agree to purchase the stock on specified terms and conditions and authorize Hazard & Co. to execute the underwriting agreement with Impel on their behalf. Hazard & Co. does so and mails each underwriter a duplicate original of the underwriting agreement.

7. Hazard & Co., as managing underwriter, uses the mails and interstate facilities to contact members of the NASD and invite them to become members of the retail selling group as participants in the sale of the stock.

8. Impel mails a proxy statement to its shareholders soliciting proxies on behalf of management to be voted in favor of an amendment of the certificate of incorporation splitting the common stock and increasing the authorized common stock at a forthcoming meeting of the stockholders.

9. Assume that the common stock will first be offered to existing shareholders and the underwriters have committed themselves to "stand by" until the subscription period has expired, at which time they must take and pay for the shares not subscribed. Impel mails a notice to its common stockholders on April 1, advising them that it proposes to offer to stockholders of record on May 15 the right to subscribe to common stock on a basis of one share for each ten shares held, by means of 30–day warrants at a price of about $9.00 per share, and that the offering will be made only by means of a prospectus.

10. On his way from Peoria to New York, Able stops off at Philadelphia, Pa. and has lunch with Barton, one of Impel's largest shareholders. During lunch, Able asks Barton whether she intends to exercise her warrants in order to give Hazard & Co. some indication as to the extent of the underwriters' standby commitment.

11. A dealer in Chicago, having heard of the proposed offering, mails a letter to Hazard & Co. in New York offering to buy some of the common stock when issued.

12. A customer in Wisconsin telephones a dealer in Chicago and offers to buy some of the common stock on a when-issued basis. The dealer rejects the offer.

13. A shareholder of Impel, having been notified of the proposed rights offering, writes a dealer and offers to sell it some of the stock on a when-issued basis. The dealer accepts and mails a written confirmation of the transaction.

14. Impel's President, Able, meets in Peoria with a group of 20 security analysts and discusses the state of Impel's business and competitive conditions in the industry. The meeting was set up by Impel after the signing of the "letter of intent" referred to in question 3. Suppose also that Able reveals material non-public information to these analysts.

15. Impel mails an Annual Report to Shareholders as it customarily does at this time of year, which report contains its usual amount of financial and other information concerning the company's products and activities during the past year.

16. Able is invited to appear on CNBC's evening talk show, "Market Update," which does a regular weekly segment on upcoming IPOs. He tentatively accepts and then calls you for legal advice. What do you advise?

17. Suppose Impel during this period decides to open a website (having never done so before). Although Impel's website says nothing about the offering or its future prospects, it does hyperlink to a securities analyst's research report, which report discusses Impel's impressive new business plan.

(b) Assume that Impel has filed a registration statement under the Securities Act of 1933 with respect to the 10,000,000 shares of common stock but that it has not yet become effective. Determine the application of § 5 to the following transactions:

18. Marjen Co., a securities dealer in Chicago, which is aware of the proposed public offering but does not intend to become a member of the underwriting syndicate or dealer group, discusses the prospects of Impel in its weekly market letter distributed to its clientele and recommends Impel common stock as a long-term investment.

19. Armitage Co., a securities dealer in Cleveland, Ohio, that intends to accept an invitation to become a member of the underwriting syndicate, in its regularly issued market letter publishes information regarding the Impel preferred stock with a recommendation of its purchase by prudent investors.

20. Armitage Co. also continues to list the Impel common stock in its monthly comprehensive list of securities currently being recommended by it as it has done

for the past four years, but changes its previous "hold" recommendation to a "buy" recommendation.

21. A sales representative of Hazard & Co. in New York telephones a dealer in Chicago and offers to reserve some of the common stock for its account with a view to having it purchase the shares at a discount and reoffer them to the public as soon as the registration statement has become effective.

22. Hazard & Co. publishes a "tombstone ad" with respect to the forthcoming issue in the Wall Street Journal.

23. Hazard & Co. mails the preliminary prospectus to selected dealers throughout the nation, enclosing a card inviting them to indicate to what extent they are interested in purchasing some of the common stock from the underwriting group at a discount and reoffering it to the public as soon as the registration statement becomes effective. What, if any, restrictions are imposed upon the solicitation of indications of interest from dealers?

24. A dealer writes a letter to one of his customers, offering her Impel common stock on a when-issued basis, but does not enclose a preliminary prospectus because it knows that its customer has already received one from another source.

25. As soon as the price amendment has been filed, a dealer in Chicago telephones its customer in Wisconsin and offers to sell 100 shares of Impel common stock at the proposed offering price as set forth in the final prospectus. The customer accepts the offer. When the registration statement becomes effective, the dealer mails a confirmation to its customer who never received a preliminary or final prospectus.

26. Able is again invited onto CNBC's "Market Watch" show. Can he appear? What guidelines should he be careful to observe?

(c) Assume that the Impel registration statement has become effective. Determine the application of § 5 to these transactions:

27. A dealer who is a member of the selling group writes a letter to one of its customers offering her Impel common stock. Must the dealer send a statutory prospectus with his letter or may a Rule 431 summary prospectus be used?

28. In question 25, assume that the dealer had been told by another broker-dealer that it had previously sent a statutory prospectus to the customer, so omitted to enclose any prospectus. Although the dealer is able to prove that a prospectus was mailed to the customer, the customer can establish that she never received it.

29. In question 25, instead of writing a letter, the dealer makes an interstate telephone call to its customer and offers her the stock which the customer accepts. The dealer then mails a confirmation of the sale. Must it enclose a statutory prospectus?

30. In question 27, after the customer accepts the offer, the dealer does not mail a confirmation but puts the stock certificates in an envelope and mails them directly to the customer. Must it enclose a statutory prospectus?

31. A dealer who is a member of the selling group mails a statutory prospectus to one of his customers and also encloses a brochure, prepared by Impel's public relations department, which paints a picture of the company's future, far more optimistic than the prospectus. Copies of this sales literature were never filed with the SEC.

32. Impel, having met the conditions of Rule 431, prepared and filed a summary prospectus as a part of the registration statement that has become

effective. A dealer who is a member of the selling group mails this summary prospectus to one of its customers. Is this permissible?

33.   Shortly after the public offering is made, Marjen Co., which was not a member of the selling group, solicits one of its customers to buy Impel common stock on the New York Stock Exchange, and executes a buy order for the customer. The securities are delivered to the customer. Must Marjen Co. enclose a statutory prospectus?

34.   Armitage & Co. failed to honor written requests from institutional investors for an Impel preliminary prospectus during the waiting period and a statutory prospectus after the effective date. What sanctions may the SEC impose against Armitage under these circumstances?

(d) Assume that Impel, as a reporting issuer, does the following to utilize electronic communications to reach its investor audience:

35.   During the waiting period, Impels posts its preliminary prospectus on its Web site on the World Wide Web.

36.   Similarly, during the waiting period, may Impel post an unrelated securities analyst's favorable evaluation of its securities on its web site? What result if it alternatively "hyperlinks" to such a report? Would any problem arise if Impel compensated the analyst?

37.   Immediately following effectiveness, Impel, as a Form S–3 issuer, electronically sends a copy of its "abbreviated term sheet" to investors who have earlier consented to electronic delivery. What must such an "abbreviated term sheet" disclose? May a broker electronically deliver by e-mail its confirmation of sale? Under what circumstances?

38.   Assume that Impel's "abbreviated term sheet" does not disclose the offering price (nor the underwriter's discount nor the final proceeds to the issuer), but the confirmation of sale does contain such information. Any problem?

(e) Assume that the outstanding shares of Impel are not listed on any securities exchange and that the corporation was not subject, immediately prior to the time of the filing of the registration statement, to the reporting requirements of Section 13 or 15(d) of the Securities Exchange Act of 1934. What, if any, difference would this make in your answers to the foregoing questions? List those questions as to which your answer would be affected and indicate what your answer would be in each such case.

SECTION 2.   THE PRE-FILING PERIOD ("GUN JUMPING")

Statutes and Regulations

Securities Act, §§ 23, 5(c), 2(a)(10), 2(a)(11), 2(a)(12), 2(a)(3), 2(a)(4), 4(1), 7, 10, 12(a)(1), 6; Rules 135, 135a, 137, 138, 139, 153a.[1]

1.   Some explanation should be made as to the SEC's system of rule numbering. Since about 1940 the rules have been published in the Code of Federal Regulations, Title 17, Chapter II. The general rules and regulations under each act administered by the SEC appear as the following parts of Chapter II: Securities Act of 1933, part 230; Securities Exchange Act of 1934, part 240; Public Utili- ty Holding Company Act of 1935, part 250; Trust Indenture Act of 1939, part 260; Investment Company Act of 1940, part 270; and the Investment Advisers Act of 1940, part 275. Until 1956, however, the SEC also maintained its own system of numbering. Rules under the Securities Act were not preceded by a letter, but rules under the other acts were preceded by the following letters: the

PRELIMINARY NEGOTIATIONS BETWEEN ISSUER AND UNDERWRITER

Section 5(c) makes it unlawful for *any person* to make use of interstate facilities or the mails to offer to sell or to offer to buy any security, before a registration statement with respect to the security has been filed with the SEC. Section 2(a)(3) defines the terms "sell" and "offer to sell" very broadly to embrace every attempt or offer to dispose of a security, for value. Even oral interstate telephone offers are proscribed for it is immaterial whether the offer is made by means of a prospectus or otherwise. (See § 2(a)(10)). Unless section 5(c) were further qualified, it would literally prohibit normal trading transactions in outstanding securities, either on the stock exchanges or in the over-the-counter market, if the mails or interstate facilities were used. The limiting language is found in § 4(1), which excludes from § 5, transactions "by any person other than an issuer, underwriter, or dealer."

Section 4(1) is significant in two respects. On the one hand, the ordinary investor who is not engaged in the securities business, but who buys and sells securities for his or her own account, is free of any restrictions, so long as he or she does not engage in a transaction which would result in the person becoming an issuer, underwriter or dealer.[2] (See §§ 2(a)(4), 2(a)(11), 2(a)(12)). On the other hand, standing alone, § 5(c) and § 4(1) would prohibit an issuer, or a controlling person, proposing to offer securities from using the mails or interstate facilities to contact a managing or lead underwriter with a view to a public issue, and preclude an underwriter from similarly approaching the issuer or controlling person, until a registration statement had been filed. Clearly, however, negotiations at this level should take place in the pre-filing period. And to prevent this cart before the horse approach, § 2(3) excludes from the definition of the terms "sell" and "offer" and the term "offer to buy" as used in § 5(c) "preliminary negotiations and agreements" between an issuer or any controlling person proposing to offer securities and any underwriter.

Activities in the Pre-filing Period. If as a result of negotiations between an issuer and underwriter they reach a tentative understanding that the underwriter will sponsor the issue, their mutual intention will sometimes be embodied in a "memorandum of understanding" or "letter of intent" which sets forth the amount of the issue, calls for preparation of a registration statement, and the formation of an underwriting group of which this underwriter will serve as manager, and determines how the various expenses of the offering will be allocated. The memorandum or letter may also indicate a proposed maximum and minimum offering price and a maximum percentage for underwriting discounts and dealer allowances, all subject, however, to market conditions. Finally, the memorandum will state that it is not intended to be a binding

Securities Exchange Act of 1934 by the letter "X"; the Public Utility Holding Company Act by the letter "U"; the Trust Indenture Act by the letter "T"; the Investment Company Act by the letter "N"; and the Investment Advisers Act by the letter "R". Thus, Rule X–10B–5 was the fifth rule adopted under § 10(b) of the Exchange Act. This system of numbering persisted within the Commission until about 1956. See SEC Ann.Rep. for the fiscal year ended June 30, 1957, p. 20. At that time the SEC began to change over to the CFR system of numbering. Thus Rule 135 of the Securities Act may sometimes be cited as Rule 230.135, or as Rule 230.135 (17 C.F.R. § 230.135) or simply as Rule 135 where identification of the particular statute (such as the Securities Act) is obvious.

2. 1 L.Loss & J. Seligman, Securities Regulation 433 (3d ed. 1989). But see Morgan, Offers to Buy Under the Securities Act of 1933, 1982 Ariz.St.L.J. 809 (1982).

commitment on either party, except as to any agreement regarding the assumption of expenses should the underwriting not materialize.[3]

A great deal of activity occurs in the pre-filing period. A team must be organized to prepare the registration statement. The players will normally include the chief executive officer and the chief financial officer of the issuer, the lead underwriter and any co-manager, counsel for the issuer and for the underwriter, and accountants. Some fifteen or more people may be involved in preparing the registration statement, and the average waiting period may last anywhere from thirty to more than sixty days, depending both on the SEC's case load at the time and how contentious are the negotiations between the issuer and the SEC's staff. Of course, the registrant chooses the filing date, but the SEC determines the effective date of the registration statement. It is important that no offer, not even an oral offer nor any attempt to offer a security, occur during the pre-filing period. Any announcement which tends to arouse interest in the offering may be deemed gun jumping. And gun jumping is a serious matter. The SEC may order a delay in the offering and delay may be fatal (if market conditions change). Accordingly, during the waiting period counsel for the issuer must review all press releases or other communications emanating from the issuer to determine whether an offer to sell a security may be entailed.

Unless the underwriter is willing to take the full commitment (which is unusual), it will spread the risk by inducing other underwriters to join in an underwriting group in which each member will purchase a part of the offering directly from the issuer. The agreement among underwriters is the basic document which appoints the managing underwriter as the representative of the other underwriters to conclude negotiations with the issuer and defines their relationships with the manager and with each other. Typical matters covered by the agreement among underwriters are the number of shares to be purchased by each underwriter; the public offering price, the underwriting spread and the price to the issuer; and the discounts or concessions to be allowed to members of the selling group. The agreement also usually vests in the manager broad discretion to reserve from each underwriter's participation a certain number of shares to be offered to institutional investors and to selling group members and otherwise to allocate the shares so as to balance supply with demand.

The Price Amendment and Rule 430A. Before the adoption of Rule 430A and the related amendments to Items 512 and 601 of Regulation S–K, and even now with respect to non-cash offerings, the issuer and underwriter did not arrive at a final agreement as to price until the registration statement had been filed with the SEC and had been completely processed so as to meet any deficiencies, except for the filing of the final price amendment. Having reached

---

3. Where a letter of intent stated that no liability was intended to be created, a prospective underwriter was denied recovery, in quantum meruit, for services performed and expenses incurred in implementation of the letter. Dunhill Securities Corp. v. Microthermal Applications, Inc., 308 F.Supp. 195 (S.D.N.Y.1969); Newharbor Partners v. F.D. Rich Co., 961 F.2d 294 (1st Cir.1992) (collecting cases). More ambiguity exists when there is no language expressly making the letter non–binding. See also M.L. Lee & Co. v. American Cardboard & Packaging Corp., 424 F.2d 532 (3d Cir.1970); 1 Securities Law Techniques § 18.04, app. 18C (A. Sommer ed. 1985) (sample letter of intent). Letters of intent pose special problems when used in corporate acquisition negotiations. See Comment, Devil's Advocate: Salvaging the Letter of Intent, 37 Emory L.J. 139 (1988).

this stage, the agreement among underwriters is executed by all underwriters; and the managing underwriter on their behalf then executes the underwriting agreement with the issuer. In the meantime the price amendment is prepared and filed with the SEC together with a request that the registration statement be made effective. Thus, only when the formal underwriting agreement is signed do the underwriters become firmly committed, subject even then to any "market out" clauses contained in the contract.[4]

Since 1987, however, Rule 430A permits a registration statement to be declared effective, even though it contains a prospectus that omits information on the public offering price, the underwriting syndicate, and certain other information which need not be disclosed in a pre-effective preliminary prospectus under Rule 430. Instead, the pricing and other "Rule 430A information" is now disclosed in a post-effective prospectus filed pursuant to Rules 424(b)(1) or (4) or 497. To obtain this Rule 430A privilege, the registration statement must contain an undertaking specified in Item 512(i) of Regulation S–K stating that for the purpose of determining liability under the Act, the information included in any post-effective prospectus shall be deemed to be a part of the registration statement at the time it became effective. As a practical matter, this change just simplifies life for the participants allowing them to get the registration statement "effective" before they price the offering and then filing that information on a post-effective basis.

The exception from the term "sell" in § 2(3) extends not only to the preliminary negotiations between issuer and underwriter but also to the final underwriting agreement as well. Furthermore, the 1954 amendments made clear that the exception also extends to negotiations and agreements between a controlling person proposing to offer securities and any underwriter. The language was also enlarged to encompass negotiations and agreements among underwriters who are to be in privity of contract with an issuer or controlling person. As the Report of the Senate Committee put it: "The sole purpose of this [language] is to make clear that the usual agreement among underwriters as well as the agreement between the underwriters and the issuer (or controlling person, as the case may be) may be made before the registration statement has been filed."[5]

On the other hand, apart from these activities between the issuer or its controlling persons and the underwriters, § 5(c) forbids any further selling effort downstream before the registration statement has been filed. This would include sales activity by the use of the mails or interstate facilities directed at dealers or any other prospective customers. A similar ban is placed upon dealers making offers to buy from the underwriters in the pre-filing period. However, as soon as a public offering is in the wind, the issuer may be inclined to shape its public relations program so as to release corporate information designed to awaken the interest of investors in the issuer and its securities. And once negotiations with the lead underwriter have commenced, news of the forthcoming offering travels fast in the financial world and issuers, underwriters and dealers are not easily kept under leash, despite these restraints on pre-filing selling activity.

When may the dissemination of information be regarded as a part of the normal flow of corporate information to security holders and the public,

---

4. Sec. Act Rel. 6714, 38 SEC Dock. 506, 517 (1987).

5. S.Rep.No. 1036, 83 Cong., 2d Sess. 11 (1954).

unrelated to selling effort, and when is it of a character calculated to arouse and stimulate investor and dealer interest and thus set in motion the processes of distribution? The following material sets forth the position of the Securities and Exchange Commission on the problem of "gun jumping."

THE DIVIDING LINE BETWEEN PRE–FILING SALES PUBLICITY AND TIMELY DISCLOSURES OF CORPORATE INFORMATION

Section 5(c) of the Securities Act prohibits offers to sell a security prior to the filing of a registration statement. At the same time, issuers subject to the reporting requirements of Section 13 or 15(d) of the 1934 Act and other publicly-held companies are under a duty to make prompt disclosure under the anti-fraud provisions of the securities acts or the timely disclosure policies of self-regulatory organizations.[1] A question of fact may arise as to whether an issuer is engaged in disseminating pre-filing sales publicity or is merely complying with its obligations of timely disclosure.

In the Matter of Carl M. Loeb, Rhoades & Co. and Dominick & Dominick, 38 S.E.C. 843 (1959), Davis, the owner of extensive real estate holdings, formed Arvida Corporation, transferred his real estate to the corporation, and sought additional capital through an offering of stock to the public. When the financing proposals reached final form, a press release, issued on the letterhead of Loeb, Rhoades, a registered broker-dealer, was distributed to the New York press and to the principal wire services. The release stated that Arvida would have assets of over one hundred million dollars, representing Mr. Davis' investment, and some $25 to $30 million of additional capital would be raised through an offering of stock to the public. The release further stated that a public offering was scheduled to be made within 60 days through a nationwide investment banking group headed by Loeb, Rhoades, and Dominick & Dominick, and that Davis would transfer to Arvida over 100,000 acres "in the area of the Gold Coast" in Florida. The release identified the principal officers of Arvida and stated that the corporation proposed to undertake a "comprehensive program of orderly development", under which some of the land would be developed immediately into residential communities and other portions would be held for investment and future development. The release attracted such buying interest from security dealers that over 100 firms contacted the proposed underwriters for inclusion in the underwriting syndicate. As a result of this pre-filing publicity, the SEC obtained a permanent injunction for violations of Section 5(c) by the proposed underwriters.[2]

Arvida subsequently filed a registration statement with respect to the proposed offering. The final prospectus disclosed that the properties were heavily mortgaged and that a substantial part of the proceeds from the financing might be required to meet mortgage indebtedness and would be unavailable to develop the property. The Commission thereupon instituted proceedings under Sections 15 and 15A of the 1934 Act to determine whether to revoke the registrations of Loeb, Rhoades, and of Dominick & Dominick, and to suspend or expel them from membership in the NASD. The Commission found

---

1. These comprise: (a) issuers with a class of securities listed or traded on an exchange; (b) issuers having both total assets exceeding $5 million and a class of equity securities held of record by 500 or more persons, (§ 12(g)(1) and Rule 12(g)(1)) and (c) issuers with outstanding securities sold pursuant to 1933 Act registration statement (§ 15(d) companies).

2. SEC v. Arvida Corp., 169 F.Supp. 211 (S.D.N.Y.1958).

willful violations of Section 5(c) of the Securities Act. However, since the Commission had taken steps to dispel the effect of the unlawful release of information and there were other mitigating factors, it concluded that public interest and protection of investors did not require the drastic action of revocation, suspension, or expulsion from membership in the NASD.

In the course of its opinion the Commission had this to say:[3]

"In permitting, but limiting the manner in which pre-effective written offers might be made, the Congress was concerned lest inadequate or misleading information be used in connection with the distribution of securities. We were directed to pursue a vigorous enforcement policy to prevent this from happening. In obedience to this mandate, we have made clear our position that the statute prohibits issuers, underwriters and dealers from initiating a public sales campaign prior to the filing of a registration statement by means of publicity efforts which, even though not couched in terms of an express offer, condition the public mind or arouse public interest in the particular securities. * * *

"[W]e find that the September 19, 1958, press release and resultant publicity concerning Arvida and its securities emanated from managing underwriters contemplating a distribution of such securities in the near future as to which a registration statement had not yet been filed * * *. We further find that such release and publicity was of a character calculated, by arousing and stimulating investor and dealer interest in Arvida securities and by eliciting indications of interest from customers to dealers and from dealer to underwriters, to set in motion the processes of distribution. In fact it had such an effect * * *.

"The principal justification advanced for the September 19 release and publicity was the claim that the activities of Mr. Davis, and specifically his interests in Florida real estate, are 'news' and that accordingly Section 5(c) should not be construed to restrict the freedom of the managing underwriters to release such publicity. We reject this contention. Section 5(c) is equally applicable whether or not the issuer or the surrounding circumstances have, or by astute public relations activities may be made to appear to have, news value.[b]

* * *

3. Carl M. Loeb, Rhoades & Co., 38 S.E.C. 843, 850–853 (1959).

b. For fifty years it was thought that the first amendment of the United States Constitution was inapplicable to the 1933 Act restrictions on advertising in the sale of securities. Thus, in SEC v. Starmont, 31 F.Supp. 264, 268 (E.D.Wash.1939), the use of a publication, "Mining Truth" to sell securities was enjoined despite the claim of interference with "the rights of free press." Recently, however, doubts have been voiced as to whether the restrictions on the general advertising of securities are excluded from the first amendment protections for commercial speech. See Virginia State Bd. of Pharmacy v. Virginia Citizens Consumer Council, Inc., 425 U.S. 748 (1976); Lowe v. SEC, 472 U.S. 181 (1985), rev'g, 725 F.2d 892 (2d Cir.1984), rev'g, 556 F.Supp. 1359 (E.D.N.Y.1983). Numerous articles have appeared discussing whether the restrictions on advertising under the Securities Act registration process, the regulation of advisers under the Investment Advisers Act of 1940, the regulation of proxy communications, and the antifraud and insider trading prohibitions under the Exchange Act unreasonably infringe on first amendment freedoms. See, e.g., Estreicher, Securities Regulation and the First Amendment, 24 Geo.L.Rev. 223 (1990); Neuborne, The First Amendment and Government Regulation of the Capital Markets, 55 Brooklyn L.Rev. 65 (1989); Winter, A First Amendment Overview, 55 Brooklyn L.Rev. 71, 74 (1988); Symposium—The First Amendment and Federal Securities Regulation, 20 Conn.L.Rev. 261

"Difficult and close questions of fact may arise as to whether a particular item of publicity by an issuer is part of a selling effort or whether it is an item of legitimate disclosure to investors unrelated to such an effort. Some of these problems are illustrated in Securities Act Release No. 3844. * * * This case, however, does not present such difficulties. Arvida was a new venture having, at the date of the September publicity, only 1 stockholder—Davis. There was no occasion to inform existing stockholders or investors in the trading markets concerning developments in its affairs in order that they might protect their interests or trade intelligently. We see no basis for concluding that the purpose of the release was different from its effect—the stimulation of investor and dealer interest as the first step in a selling effort."

It could hardly be said that a one-person company was subject to any timely disclosure obligations. A somewhat different problem was presented in Chris–Craft Industries, Inc. v. Bangor Punta Corp., 426 F.2d 569 (2d Cir.1970). The case involved a bitter contest for the control of Piper Aircraft Corporation between Chris–Craft Industries and Bangor Punta Corporation. Chris–Craft had made a cash tender offer for Piper stock. The Piper family thereupon negotiated a competing exchange offer of a package of securities from Bangor Punta Corporation under which all Piper shareholders would be entitled to exchange each share of Piper common stock held by them for Bangor Punta securities and cash "having a value in the written opinion of The First Boston Corporation, of $80 or more."

Since the Bangor Punta exchange offer entailed a public offering of securities to the Piper Aircraft shareholders, Bangor Punta prepared to file a registration statement under the 1933 Act covering the proposed exchange offer. Upon the conclusion of the agreement between them, Bangor Punta and the Piper management simultaneously issued a press release stating that Bangor Punta had "agreed to file a registration statement with the SEC covering the proposed exchange offer for any or all of the remaining outstanding shares of Piper Aircraft for a package of Bangor Punta securities to be valued in the judgment of The First Boston Corporation at not less than $80 per Piper share."

Chris–Craft sought a preliminary injunction to restrain Bangor Punta from making the exchange offer claiming that the press release violated Section 5(c) of the 1933 Act and Rule 135 promulgated thereunder. The contention was that Rule 135 exempts certain disclosures of pre-filing publicity from the definition of an "offer to sell" prohibited by Section 5(c); that the categories of information privileged under the Rule are exclusive and do not permit a disclosure of the value of the securities to be offered; and that the announcement that the package of securities to be offered by Bangor Punta would have a value of $80 overstepped the exemption and made the press release an offer to sell.

Reversing the district court's conclusion that the press release did not violate Section 5(c), the Court of Appeals for the Second Circuit stated:

"We agree with this contention. When it is announced that securities will be sold at some date in the future and, in addition, an attractive description of

(1988); Schoeman, The First Amendment and Restrictions on Advertising Under the Securities Act of 1933, 41 Bus.Law. 377 (1986). If the Supreme Court should accept an expansive view of first amendment freedoms in this area, a large part of the federal system of securities regulation might be disrupted or even dismantled. Such a development, however, still seems remote.

these securities and of the issuer is furnished, it seems clear that such an announcement provides much the same kind of information as that contained in a prospectus. See SEC v. Arvida Corp., 169 F.Supp. 211 (S.D.N.Y.1958). Doubtless the line drawn between an announcement containing sufficient information to constitute an offer and one which does not must be to some extent arbitrary. A checklist of features that may be included in an announcement which does not also constitute an offer to sell serves to guide the financial community and the courts far better than any judicially formulated 'rule of reason' as to what is or is not an offer. Rule 135 provides just such a checklist, and if the Rule is not construed as setting forth an exclusive list, then much of its value as a guide is lost.

"Moreover, it is reasonable to conclude that the assigning of a value to offered shares constitutes an offer to sell. One of the evils of a premature offer is its tendency to encourage the formation by the offeree of an opinion of the value of the securities before a registration statement and prospectus are filed. There is then no information on file at the SEC by which the Commission can check the accuracy of the information which forms the basis of the offeror's estimate of value, and any offeree, such as the reader of a press release, is encouraged to form a premature opinion of value without benefit of the full set of facts contained in a prospectus.

"Here a statement of the value of the securities Bangor Punta offered was made directly in the announcement. It is true that the value which the reader of the May 8 press releases could be expected to accept is a value based upon the opinion of a reputable financial corporation and not upon general and necessarily speculative facts about the nature of the offeror's business, as in *Arvida*, supra. However, the true significance of the $80 value which Bangor Punta claimed for its securities package was nonetheless unclear. Chris–Craft charges that the figure constituted an outright misrepresentation inasmuch as most readers would construe the figure as representing the market value of the package. In fact, Chris–Craft charges, some of the securities in the package had not previously been sold on the market at all, and the market value of Piper shares never reached $80 in response to the Bangor Punta exchange offer, so that the Bangor Punta securities did not have an $80 market value and could not honestly have been thought to have such a value. * * *

"Bangor Punta and Piper argue that even prior to the filing of a registration statement an immediate disclosure of market value is compelled in cases such as this both by SEC v. Texas Gulf Sulphur Co., 401 F.2d 833 (2 Cir.1968), cert. denied as to issues not pertinent here, sub nom. Coates v. SEC, Kline v. SEC, 394 U.S. 976 * * * (1969), and by the rules of the New York Stock Exchange. We do not agree. The only material fact in this case within the meaning of *Texas Gulf Sulphur* was Bangor Punta's commitment, to offer its securities for Piper Aircraft shares. Rule 135 provides adequately for the announcement of a material fact such as this; further disclosure would, as stated above, thwart other policies of the securities laws. Had Bangor Punta observed Rule 135 by revealing immediately its intention to make an exchange offer and by later revealing the titles of the securities it proposed to offer and the basis or ratio on which the exchange was proposed to be made as soon as these matters were decided, adequate information concerning the proposed transaction would have been placed before the public and the potentially misleading estimate of value would have been avoided. Even if we assume that knowledge of the value figure involved here might conceivably have conferred some benefit on insiders had it not been revealed, we feel that this risk of unfair advantage is outweighed by the danger that substantial numbers of investors were misled by the figure's publication. The fact that a few additional sophisticated investors could have discovered the $80 value guarantee in the description of the transaction which Bangor Punta filed with the SEC pursuant to Section 13(d) of the 1934 Act is of no moment. Such investors would almost certainly be small in number, and any arguable danger of permitting them an unfair advantage is outweighed by the stronger probability that the press release misled a large number of unsophisticated investors."

"The same principles apply to the New York Stock Exchange's requirement that insiders disclose information likely to affect the market unless such information can be restricted to a small group of top management officials. In any event, a policy of the New York Stock Exchange, although entitled to considerable respect, cannot bind the Commission or the courts. Silver v. New York Stock Exchange, 373 U.S. 341, 357 (1963). To hold that disclosure would be privileged here because the $80 value could not be kept secret and might affect the market would mean that many other companies could offer to sell securities before their registration by claiming that the terms of the proposed offer could not be kept totally secret and must therefore be disclosed in full."[4]

Securities Act Release No. 5009

Securities and Exchange Commission.
October 7, 1969.

PUBLICATION OF INFORMATION PRIOR TO OR AFTER THE FILING AND EFFECTIVE DATE OF A REGISTRATION STATEMENT UNDER THE SECURITIES ACT OF 1933

The Securities and Exchange Commission and its staff frequently receive inquiries concerning the impact of the registration and prospectus requirements of Section 5 of the Securities Act of 1933 ("Act") on publication of information concerning an issuer and its affairs by the issuer, its management, and by underwriters and securities dealers. Some of the more common prob-

---

4. Compare Sheinberg v. Fluor Corp., 514 F.Supp. 133 (S.D.N.Y.1981), where a shareholder of a target corporation charged the defendant bidder corporation with "gun jumping." The bidder corporation had filed a SEC Schedule 14D–9 tender offer statement in connection with a cash tender offer for 45 percent of the target's common stock at $60 a share. The tender offer statement also stated that if the tender offer was successful, the bidder and target corporations had agreed to a merger in which 1.2 shares of common stock of the bidder would be exchanged for each outstanding common share of the target. The proposal was also publicized in press releases and in communications sent to the target shareholders. The court distinguished Bangor Punta and held that disclosure of the merger terms not only was permitted by Rules 145(b)(1) and 135(a)(4) of the 1933 Act,

but was simply designed to inform the shareholders of the merger agreement between the bidder and target.

See Chiappinelli, Gun Jumping: The Problem of Extraneous Offers of Securities, 50 U.Pitt.L.Rev. 457 (1989); Note, Preregistration Publicity in an Exchange Offer, 119 U.Pa.L.Rev. 174 (1970); Pierce, Current and Recurrent Section 5 Gun Jumping Problems, 26 Case W.Res.L.Rev. 370 (1976); Note, Prereorganization Negotiations and Securities Act Section 5(c): A Proposed Solution to the Gunjumping Problem, 24 Case W.Res.L.Rev. 731 (1973); Lovejoy, Initial Public Offerings: Prefiling and Preeffective Publicity, PLI, 13 Ann. Inst. on Sec.Reg. 359 (1982); Mann, Initial Public Offerings: Problems in the Course of Distribution, PLI, 13 Ann.Inst. on Sec.Reg. 351 (1982).

lems which have arisen in this connection are discussed in Securities Act of 1933 Release No. 3844 (October 8, 1957).

Since the publication of that release there have been a number of developments relevant to this subject, including the broader reach of the reporting and proxy disclosure requirements through the 1964 amendments to the Securities Exchange Act of 1934 and the increased awareness of various self-regulatory organizations, corporate managements and others of the importance of timely disclosure. Moreover, in recent years the Commission and its staff also have become increasingly aware of the need for more clearly defined standards in this area. Concurrently with the publication of this release the Commission is proposing to adopt various rules which would accomplish this objective in certain respects * * *. The Commission believes that a discussion of certain factors to be considered in dealing with other aspects of this subject may be of help to issuers, their advisers and professionals in the securities business.

There has been an ever increasing tendency to publicize through many media information concerning corporate affairs which goes beyond statutory requirements. This practice reflects the commendable recognition on the part of business and the investment community of the importance of informing investors and the public with respect to important business and financial developments. It has been reinforced by the policies of various self-regulatory organizations regarding timely disclosure of information which might materially affect the market for an issuer's securities.[2]

As the Commission has stated:

"We realize, of course, that corporations regularly release various types of information and that a corporation in which there is wide interest may be called upon to release more information more frequently about its activities than would be expected of lesser known or privately held enterprises. In the normal conduct of its business a corporation may continue to advertise its products and services without interruption, it may send out its customary quarterly, annual and other periodic reports to security holders, and it may publish its proxy statements, send out its dividend notices and make routine announcements to the press. This flow of normal corporate news, unrelated to a selling effort for an issue of securities is natural, desirable and entirely consistent with the objectives of disclosure to the public which underlies the federal securities laws."[3]

However, the increasing obligations and incentives of corporations to make timely disclosures concerning their offerings raise a question as to a possible conflict between the obligation to make timely disclosure and the restriction on publication of information concerning an issuer which may have securities "in registration."[4] The Commission believes that such a conflict may be more

---

2. See, e.g., New York Stock Exchange Company Manual, pages [2–1 through 2–6, revised Feb., 1990, reprinted in 3 Fed.Sec. L.Rep. (CCH) ¶ 23,514]; American Stock Exchange Guide, [§§ 401–405, reprinted in 3 Fed.Sec.L.Rep. (CCH) ¶ 23,124A; Brown, Corporate Communications and the Federal Securities laws, 53 Geo.Wash.L.Rev. 741, 772–82 (1985).]

3. Carl M. Loeb, Rhoades & Co., 38 S.E.C. 843, 853 (1959).

4. "In registration" is used herein to mean the entire process of registration, at least from the time an issuer reaches an understanding with the broker-dealer which is to act as managing underwriter until the completion of the offering and the period of 40 or 90 days during which dealers must deliver a prospectus.

apparent than real. Events resulting in a duty to make prompt disclosure under the anti-fraud provisions of the securities laws or timely disclosure policies of self-regulatory organizations at a time when a registered offering of securities is contemplated are relatively infrequent and normally may be effected in a manner which will not unduly influence the proposed offering. Disclosure of a material event would ordinarily not be subject to restrictions under Section 5 of the Securities Act if it is purely factual and does not include predictions or opinions.

The Commission recognizes that difficult and close questions will inevitably arise with respect to whether particular items of publicity are subject to restriction, and encourages issuers and their counsel to seek informal consultation with the Commission's staff which is accustomed to dealing with such questions and is usually able to give rapid and definite responses.

A number of more specific questions have been raised concerning the restrictions on circulation of information by broker-dealers, particularly during the "pre-filing" period. There appears to be some confusion as to when the restrictions on publication activities commence. Ordinarily a broker-dealer becomes subject to restrictions at any time when he commences to participate in the preparation of a registration statement or otherwise reaches an understanding with the person on whose behalf a distribution is to be made that the firm will become a managing underwriter, whether or not the terms and conditions of the underwriting have been agreed upon. Other brokers become subject to restrictions at such time as they are invited by a managing underwriter or a person on whose behalf a distribution is to be made, to participate or seeks to participate. Persons who choose to forego such underwriting in order to be free to distribute such publications should not thereafter participate in the distribution as a dealer or otherwise.

Distribution of communications containing recommendations with respect to securities which have been registered for sale from time to time at prices prevailing in the market pose difficult questions. Usually no broker-dealer group has made arrangements with the selling shareholders for distribution of the securities. It does not appear that restrictions on the dissemination of such material are necessary until such time as a broker-dealer has reached an understanding that he will offer securities on behalf of the selling shareholder, whether or not he has technically accepted an order to sell the security.

After a particular security is "in registration," broker-dealers often do not know the extent to which they may follow up recommendations concerning the security made before the security was "in registration." If a broker-dealer is a participant in a proposed underwriting and material events occur during the "pre-filing" period, the broker should be able to make a brief, strictly factual report of these events to his customers.

After the registration statement is filed and until it becomes effective, written communications furnished to customers or others should be restricted to the preliminary prospectus ("red herring"), the summary prospectus described in Section 10(b), or the so-called "tombstone" announcements permitted under Section 2(a)(10) of the Act or Rule 134 thereunder. Also, Rule 135 permits certain announcements of offerings before and after a registration statement is filed.

It should be recognized that the foregoing discussion is intended to be only a general guide for brokers in disseminating information concerning an issuer which has securities "in registration." Particular fact situations may result in different conclusions. In such situations, a broker may find consultation with the staff of the Commission helpful.

* * *

Securities Act Release No. 5180

Securities and Exchange Commission.
August 16, 1971.

GUIDELINES FOR THE RELEASE OF INFORMATION BY ISSUERS WHOSE SECURITIES ARE IN REGISTRATION

The Commission today took note of situations when issuers whose securities are "in registration"[1] may have refused to answer legitimate inquiries from stockholders, financial analysts, the press or other persons concerning the company or some aspect of its business. The Commission hereby emphasizes that there is no basis in the securities acts or in any policy of the Commission which would justify the practice of non-disclosure of *factual* information by a publicly held company on the grounds that it has securities in registration under the Securities Act of 1933 ("Act"). Neither a company in registration nor its representatives should instigate publicity for the purpose of facilitating the sale of securities in a proposed offering. Further, any publication of information by a company in registration other than by means of a statutory prospectus should be limited to factual information and should not include such things as predictions, projections, forecasts or opinions with respect to value.[a]

* * * It has been asserted that the increasing obligations and incentives of corporations to make timely disclosures concerning their affairs creates a possible conflict with statutory restrictions on publication of information concerning a company which has securities in registration. As the Commission has stated in previously issued releases this conflict may be more apparent than real. Disclosure of factual information in response to inquiries or resulting from a duty to make prompt disclosure under the antifraud provisions of the securities acts or the timely disclosure policies of self-regulatory organizations, at a time when a registered offering of securities is contemplated or in process, can and should be effected in a manner which will not unduly influence the proposed offering.

* * *

Guidelines

The Commission strongly suggests that all issuers establish internal procedures designed to avoid problems relating to the release of corporate information when in registration. As stated above, issuers and their representatives

---

1. "In registration" is used herein to refer to the entire process of registration, at least from the time an issuer reaches an understanding with the broker-dealer which is to act as managing underwriter prior to the filing of a registration statement and the period of 40 to 90 days during which dealers must deliver a prospectus.

a. This statement expresses the SEC's former policy forbidding projections and other forms of forward-looking statements. The Commission now encourages issuers of securities to publish certain types of forward-looking and analytical information in documents filed with the Commission and otherwise, under controlled conditions. See Rule 175 and infra, at pages 231–233.

should not initiate publicity when in registration, but should nevertheless respond to legitimate inquiries for factual information about the company's financial condition and business operations. Further, care should be exercised so that, for example, predictions, projections, forecasts, estimates and opinions concerning value are not given with respect to such things, among others, as sales and earnings and value of the issuer's securities.[b]

It has been suggested that the Commission promulgate an all inclusive list of permissible and prohibited activities in this area. This is not feasible for the reason that determinations are based upon the particular facts of each case. However, the Commission as a matter of policy encourages the flow of factual information to shareholders and the investing public. Issuers in this regard should:

1.   Continue to advertise products and services.

2.   Continue to send out customary quarterly, annual and other periodic reports to stockholders.[c]

3.   Continue to publish proxy statements and send out dividend notices.

4.   Continue to make announcements to the press with respect to factual business and financial developments; i.e., receipt of a contract, the settlement of a strike, the opening of a plant, or similar events of interest to the community in which the business operates.

5.   Answer unsolicited telephone inquiries from stockholders, financial analysts, the press and others concerning factual information.

6.   Observe an "open door" policy in responding to unsolicited inquiries concerning factual matters from securities analysts, financial analysts, security holders, and participants in the communications field who have a legitimate interest in the corporation's affairs.

7.   Continue to hold stockholder meetings as scheduled and to answer shareholders' inquiries at stockholder meetings relating to factual matters.

In order to curtail problems in this area, issuers in this regard should avoid:

b.   Ibid.

c.   In the Harper Group (Avail. June 3, 1976), [1976–1977 Transfer Binder] (CCH) Fed.Sec.L.Rep. ¶ 80,631, the SEC Staff took a no-action posture when an issuer, a closely-held international freight company, proposed to distribute its annual report to shareholders, to customers and prospective customers, and to other persons who were closely related to the conduct of its business, including shareholders, agents, employees, air and ocean carriers and certain financial institutions as had been its custom in previous years. The annual report was of a character and content customarily published by the company and did not contain material designed to stimulate the proposed offering.

We shall see that under the present regime of integrated disclosure, annual reports are now required to contain "Management's discussion and analysis" of the audited financial statements and the company's financial condition and changes therein. Moreover, issuers are encouraged, but not required, to provide financial forecasts and other forward-looking data. The line between pre-filing sales publicity and timely disclosure has now become so blurred that the SEC should reconsider its policy on "gun-jumping."

For a proposal to permit all extraneous offers, oral or written, to be disseminated to the public, unless false and misleading, see Chiappinelli, Gun Jumping: The Problem of Extraneous Offers of Securities, 50 U.Pitt.L.Rev. 457, 492–96 (1989). Cf. Appel, Advertising of Securities Products in the United States and Europe, 24 Sec. & Commodities Reg. 187 (1991).

1.   Issuance of forecasts, projections, or predictions relating but not limited to revenues, income, or earnings per share.[d]

2.   Publishing opinions concerning values.[e]

In the event a company publicly releases material information concerning new corporate developments during the period that a registration statement is pending, the registration statement should be amended at or prior to the time the information is released. If this is not done and such information is publicly released through inadvertence, the pending registration statement should be promptly amended to reflect such information.

The determination of whether an item of information or publicity could be deemed to constitute an offer—a step in the selling effort—in violation of Section 5 must be made by the issuer in the light of all the facts and circumstances surrounding each case. The Commission recognizes that questions may arise from time to time with respect to the release of information by companies in registration and, while the statutory obligation always rests with the company and can never be shifted to the staff, the staff will be available for consultation concerning such questions. It is not the function of the staff to draft corporate press releases. If a company, however, desires to consult with the staff as to the application of the statutory requirements to a particular case, the staff will continue to be available, and in this regard the pertinent facts should be set forth in written form and submitted in sufficient time to allow due consideration.[f]

* * *

REAPPRAISAL OF THE "GUN–JUMPING DOCTRINE": THE ESTABLISHMENT OF GUIDELINES FOR SEPARATING PRE–FILING SALES PUBLICITY FROM TIMELY DISCLOSURE OF CORPORATE INFORMATION

The preceding material reveals that Sections 2(a)(3), 2(a)(10) and 5(c) furnished limited guidance to issuers and broker-dealers for distinguishing legitimate news about the issuer from publicity designed to "condition" the market during the registration process. Despite SEC releases and pronouncements and a certain amount of litigation, "gun jumping" remained a murky concept. An initial effort to make greater policy sense of the gun-jumping doctrine came in 1969 in an SEC policy study on disclosure to investors, popularly known as the "Wheat Report," after its Chairman, Commissioner Francis M. Wheat.[1] This report recommended that more clearly defined policies be adopted to deal with the publication of information during the time a company was "in registration."[2] The Commission responded by adopting a series of rules relating to publication of information by issuers and broker-

---

d. See note a supra.

e. See note a supra.

f. Brown, Corporate Communications and the Federal Securities Laws, 53 Geo. Wash.L.Rev. 741, 809–17 (1985).

1. SEC Disclosure to Investors (Wheat Report) ch. v (1969).

2. "In registration" was defined in Securities Act Release No. 5009 (Oct. 7, 1969). See page 128 supra, at n. 4.

dealers about a prospective public offering of securities either prior to or after the filing of a registration statement under the Securities Act.[3]

Rule 135, as amended, permits an issuer to publish a notice that it proposes to make a public offering of registered securities if the notice states that the offering will be made only by means of a prospectus and contains only certain additional information. Such information includes the title, amount and basic terms of the securities proposed to be offered, and a brief statement of the manner and purpose of the offering, without naming the underwriters. If a rights offering, an exchange offering, or an offering to employees is contemplated, further details with respect to the offering may be included. The notice may take the form of a news release, a published statement, or a written communication directed to prospective offerees.

Broker–Dealer Activities. We have seen that broker-dealers are subject to the provisions of Sections 2(a)(10) and 5 by virtue of Section 4(1) of the Act. In addition to Rule 135, applicable to issuers, Rules 137, 138 and 139 clarify the restrictions on broker-dealers in the advertising and sale of securities during the registration process.

Rule 137 relaxes the rules as to the dissemination of information with respect to issuers in registration under certain conditions. If the registrant is required to file reports pursuant to Sections 13 or 15(d) of the 1934 Act and the dealer does not propose to be a member of the underwriting syndicate, the dealer may continue to publish and distribute information, opinions or recommendations in the regular course of its business. The privilege is destroyed, however, if any consideration is received from the issuer in connection with the publication or distribution of such information.

Moreover, some restraints have been removed with respect to a dealer, even if it becomes a member of the underwriting syndicate or dealer group. Under Rule 138, if the registrant meets the requirements permitting the use of Forms S–2 or F–2,[4] and is registering a nonconvertible debt security or a nonconvertible, nonparticipating preferred stock, a participating underwriter or dealer may publish and distribute information, opinions or recommendations relating solely to common stock or to debt or preferred stock convertible into common stock of the registrant. Again, if the registrant is eligible to use Forms S–2 or F–2 and is registering common stock or debt or preferred stock convertible into common stock, a participating underwriter or dealer may publish or distribute information, opinions or recommendations relating solely to a nonconvertible debt security or to a nonconvertible nonparticipating preferred stock of the registrant.

Finally, under Rule 139, where a 1934 Act reporting company files a registration statement relating to its securities, an underwriter or dealer participating in the offering may continue to publish or distribute information, opinions or recommendations with respect to the registrant or its securities during the registration process if either (a) the registrant meets the registration requirements of Form S–3 or F–3 and the minimum float or investment grade securities provisions in the respective form, and such information is

---

3. Securities Act Release No. 5101 (Nov. 19, 1970).

4. Form S–2 is available to issuers incorporated and having their principal business in the United States if they have been reporting companies for a period of at least thirty-six months and meet certain other conditions. Form F–2 is a parallel form which is available to foreign private issuers meeting somewhat similar criteria.

contained in a publication which is regularly distributed in the normal course of business; or (b) such information, opinion or recommendation is contained in a publication which (1) is distributed with reasonable regularity in the normal course of business; (2) includes similar information with respect to a substantial number of companies in the registrant's industry or contains a comprehensive list of securities currently recommended by such broker or dealer; (3) the information is given no greater space or prominence in the publication than that given to other securities; and (4) an opinion as favorable or more favorable was published in the last publication addressing the subject prior to the commencement of participation in the distribution. Under this last condition, the dealer may not ride the security up, but may follow it down.

It should be emphasized that Rules 137, 138 and 139 are applicable only to 1934 Act reporting companies where presumably there is an efficient existing market for the registrant's outstanding securities. The rules are designed to permit broker-dealers to continue to advise the market in order to enhance market liquidity without over-conditioning the market during the registration process.

Media Fascination. Beginning in the late 1990's, increased public interest in the stock market (and IPOs specifically) led cable T.V. shows (particularly those on CNBC and CNN) and news magazines to focus on forthcoming IPOs as a matter of general news interest. This raised the question of whether a CEO or other corporate officer could appear on such a T.V. show, or give an interview to a magazine, about its upcoming offering. Cautious securities lawyers usually recommend against such publicity, particularly during the "quiet period" and even afterwards, noting that the SEC has said that the "quiet period" applies not only prior to the filing of the initial registration statement (at which point Section 5(c) of the Act ceases to apply), but during the entire time span through the end of the post-effective prospectus delivery period. Still, sometimes the brash, young entrepreneurs behind Internet companies resisted this advice. In several highly publicized cases in 1999 and 2000, the SEC delayed offerings and refused to accelerate them where there had been "excess publicity." In 1999, Webvan Group, Inc., an online supermarket, held an investor-only conference call during the "waiting period," whose substance was reported by journalists, whose stories contained specific information not in Webvan's prospectus. The SEC required a "cooling-off period," which delayed the issuer's ultimately successful offering for several weeks. In mid 2000, a similar incident involving Divine Interventures, Inc., an Internet funding company occurred, when the company's CEO gave interviews containing more optimistic financial predictions than had been set forth in its prospectus. The SEC required a recirculation of the prospectus in order to cause the issuer to expressly disclaim the earlier oral predictions.[5] The SEC's principal concern in these cases, which came after the filing of the registration statement, may have been less with the infringement of the quiet period than with the disparity that results between the information that institutional investors receive and that available to retail investors.

Is the Quiet Period Obsolete? The American Bar Association has suggested to the SEC that the "quiet period" is an out-of-date concept for seasoned public companies and should be cut back even in the case of IPOs. In an August 2001

5. See Stewart, "Criticism of the 'Quiet Period' Gets Louder," Chicago Tribune, July 8, 2000 at p. B1.

letter to the SEC's Division of Corporation Finance, the ABA's Committee on Federal Regulation of Securities has urged the Commission to recognize that, in the case of seasoned issuers, the goals of the "quiet period" are now infeasible, because a multitude of analysts and others will typically be following and commenting on pending developments at such a company. In the case of IPOs, the Committee recommended that the quiet period be limited to a period not more than 30 days prior to the filing of the registration statement. Even during this period, a broadened Rule 134 should authorize, they argued, ordinary course "factual business communications." Similar positions have earlier been taken by SEC Advisory Committees and in SEC staff studies. It seems only a matter of time until some version of these proposals are implemented in SEC rule proposals.

SECTION 3.   THE WAITING PERIOD

Statutes and Regulations

Securities Act, §§ 5(a), 5(b), 2(a)(10)(b), 10(a), 10(b); Rules 134, 135, 135a; Regulation C, Rules 418, 424, 430, 430A, 431, 432, 460, 461; Regulation S–K, Items 512(i) and 601, Instruction (1).

RESTRICTIONS ON OFFERS BY ISSUERS, UNDERWRITERS AND DEALERS

Issuers and Underwriters. When a registration statement is filed with respect to a security it will contain a prospectus in incomplete form, which will set forth most of the essential information about the company and its finances that will appear in the final prospectus. However, the final prospectus, complete with the offering price, underwriting discounts and commissions, discounts and commissions to dealers, and related data, is ordinarily not placed on file until the Commission has concluded its examination of the registration statement in this preliminary form. Then when the Commission has indicated to the registrant that the information on file is adequate to meet the full disclosure standard, except for the offering price and other missing data, the underwriting agreement is signed and a so-called price amendment is filed together with a request that the Commission accelerate the effective date of the registration statement and declare it to be effective at the date and time requested.[1]

The final or complete prospectus, the contents of which are specified in § 10(a), is commonly called the "statutory" prospectus so as to distinguish it from the "red herring" or "preliminary" prospectus which is on file during the waiting period, before the registration statement has become effective. Once the registration statement becomes effective, however, the statutory or § 10(a) prospectus becomes available for use as a selling document and eliminates the need for the preliminary prospectus.

a. The Preliminary or "Red–Herring" Prospectus. Prior to the 1954 amendments, the theory was that during the waiting period information contained in the registration statement on file with the Commission could be disseminated among potential investors, and, indeed, should be made available at least to interested dealers. The Act, however, specifically prohibited the

---

1.   See § 8(a) and Rules 460, 461.

issuer or underwriters from using the interstate facilities or mails to solicit buyers by making offers to sell, as such. The "red herring" prospectus was devised by the Commission for the purpose of preserving the subtle distinction between "solicitation" and "dissemination," for through it material information then on file with the Commission could be distributed to potential investors in a document which specifically stated that it was not to be treated as an offer to sell.[2]

After the 1954 amendments, the "red herring" prospectus (renamed the "preliminary prospectus") was given legitimacy and a number of other avenues were opened so that issuers and underwriters can now start their sales campaign as soon as the registration statement is placed on file without having to wait for it to become effective. Thus, offers to sell by the use of the mails or interstate facilities are no longer prohibited during the waiting period but the methods for making such offers are strictly regulated. Furthermore, although offers to sell can now be made during the waiting or cooling-off period, § 5(a)(1) makes it unlawful to "sell" the securities until the registration statement has become effective, thus forbidding any acceptance of the offer until after the effective date.

Section 5(b)(1) does not prohibit *oral* offers to sell by means of interstate facilities, for example, by making an interstate telephone call. The section is aimed solely at the use of a "prospectus," a term broadly defined in § 2(a)(10) to include any communication, written or by radio or television, which offers a security for sale or confirms the sale. Under § 5(b)(1), a prospectus which meets the requirements of § 10 may be used to make offers to sell during the waiting period. We have seen that the statutory prospectus referred to in § 10(a) is not yet available, since the registration statement has not become effective. But § 10(b) authorizes the Commission to issue rules allowing the use for § 5(b)(1) purposes of a prospectus which summarizes or omits a part of the information in the statutory prospectus specified in § 10(a).

Rule 430 provides that a form of prospectus filed as a part of the registration statement shall be deemed to meet the requirements of § 10 for the purpose of 5(b)(1) prior to the effective date of the registration statement, if it contains substantially the information required to meet the requirements of § 10(a), except for the omission of information "with respect to the offering price, underwriting discounts or commissions, discounts or commissions to dealers, amounts of proceeds, conversion rates, call prices, or other matters dependent upon the offering price." This document may be referred to as a § 10(b) prospectus to distinguish it from a § 10(a) prospectus. The red-herring tradition is carried forward in Regulation S–K, Item 501(8); that Item requires that any preliminary prospectus to be used before the effective date of the registration statement (or, any post-effective prospectus that omits information permitted by Rule 430A) contain, in red ink, the caption "Subject to Completion" and a specifically prescribed legend which disclaims any intention to make an offer to sell or solicit an offer to buy the securities proposed to be offered.

---

2. See Securities Act Release No. 464 (Aug. 19, 1935). The name originated from the red ink legend disclaiming any intent to solicit offers to buy or make an offer to sell which appeared on each page of the "red herring prospectus." Lobell, Revision of the Securities Act, 48 Colum.L.Rev. 324 (1948); Dean, Twenty–Five Years of Federal Regulation by the Securities and Exchange Commission, 59 Colum.L.Rev. 697, 714–15 (1959).

For many years, the normal practice among underwriters and issuers was to "price" the offering the evening before the SEC was expected to declare the offering effective and then to file a "pricing amendment" the next morning, which would contain all price-related information. Once the Commission then declared this amended registration statement effective (after the dawn filing of the pricing amendment), sales could then be consummated. This procedure protected the underwriters from last minute adverse market movements, but required a somewhat frenzied ritual of printing the price amendment and flying copies of it to Washington for a morning filing when the SEC opened for business.

As a part of a general deregulatory program in the 1990s, the Commission adopted Rule 430A, which permits a registration statement to be declared effective without the inclusion of price-related information (e.g., the public offering price, the underwriting discount, the use of proceeds, the identity of the underwriting syndicate, and other price-dependent factors, such as conversion rates and call dates, etc.). Under Rule 430A, this information could be disclosed to the Commission in a revised form of prospectus filed within fifteen business days thereafter. If such a delayed filing was not made, however, a formal post-effective amendment would have to be filed (which is a step that the issuer and underwriters wish to avoid, because, as will be seen, it restarts the running of the statute of limitations and creates a new date on which the accuracy of the registration statement is tested for purposes of liability under Section 11 of the 1933 Act). Although the idea of a prospectus that lacks the price of the security and other essential marketing terms may seem anomalous, the net impact of Rule 430A is to permit the registration statement to be declared effective prior to the final pricing negotiations between the issuer and the underwriters (or between both and the institutional investors who are often the principal buyers). For the issuer, this means that it will not be necessarily engaged in simultaneous negotiations with both the SEC and the underwriters.

Rule 430A does contain one meaningful limitation on its permission to withhold information: although it is possible to cut back the size of the offering if marketing problems are encountered, the reductions in price and volume may not represent more than a 20% reduction in the maximum aggregate offering price (as stated in the registration statement when declared effective). Any greater cutback would instead require a post-effective amendment.

A post-effective prospectus that omits the Rule 430A information may be used after effectiveness and prior to pricing. (See Rule 430A(c)). Presumably, a Preliminary Prospectus which meets these conditions may continue to be used in the interval between effectiveness and pricing. However, this prospectus may be used only for informational purposes; it may not be used to satisfy the requirements of § 10(a), or § 5(b)(2) in connection with delivery of a security for sale or delivery after sale by the use of the mails or interstate facilities, or to satisfy the requirements of § 2(a)(10)(a) in connection with the delivery of a confirmation or other written communications to investors.

b. The Summary Prospectus. Under Rule 431, a summary prospectus (or a Preliminary Summary Prospectus) may be prepared and filed as a part of the registration statement. This type of prospectus is available, however, only if the registration form to be used to register the securities provides for its use. The conditions for use are prescribed by Rule 431 and by the authorizing Form. In general, a summary prospectus may be used (1) by domestic issuers that have their principal business operations in the United States; (2) are "reporting companies," that is, are issuers registered pursuant to § 12(b) of the Securities Exchange Act of 1934 or have a class of equity securities registered pursuant to § 12(g) or are required to file reports pursuant to § 15(d) of that Act; and (3) have filed in a timely manner all reports under sections 13, 14, or 15(d) of the 1934 Act for three years prior to the filing of the 1933 Act registration statement. There are other criteria, including the absence of defaults in dividend or sinking fund obligations on preferred stock or on debt obligations.

A number of forms authorize the use of summary prospectuses. These include Forms S–1 and S–2, applicable to certain reporting companies, and Form N–1A, applicable to open-end management investment companies. A registrant that is a foreign private issuer eligible to use Form F–2 may also avail itself of a summary prospectus.

The summary prospectus (as well as the preliminary prospectus) is authorized pursuant to § 10(b) of the Act. That subsection provides that a § 10(b) prospectus filed as a part of the registration statement shall not be deemed a part of the registration statement for the purposes of § 11 which imposes civil liability upon issuers, underwriters and others for defective registration statements. The summary prospectus is to be used for informational purposes only and, like the preliminary prospectus, may not be used to satisfy the prospectus requirements of § 10(a) of the Act.

c.   *The "Tombstone Ad"*. The Act also envisages one other way for reaching potential customers—the "tombstone ad" which derives its quaint name from the starkness of its contents. Even before 1954, there was excluded from the general definition of a prospectus contained in § 2(a)(10)—a term which must be distinguished from the § 10(a) and 10(b) prospectuses—any communication in respect of a security "if it states from whom a written prospectus meeting the requirements of § 10 [before the 1954 amendments] may be obtained and, in addition, does no more than identify the security, state the price thereof, and state by whom orders will be executed." The use of this "tombstone ad" was not permitted until after the registration statement had become effective. In 1954, however, § 2(a)(10) was amended to permit the use of the statutory "tombstone ad" during both the waiting period and the post-effective period, but not in the pre-filing period. Although § 2(a)(10)(b) states that a statutory tombstone ad is not a "prospectus," it does not say it is not an "offer." Accordingly, § 5(c) prohibits its use in the pre-filing period.

d.   *The Identifying Statement*. Section 2(a)(10)(b) was also amended to permit the Commission to issue rules authorizing an expanded "tombstone ad" or "identifying statement" containing such additional information as it deems appropriate. The Commission has responded by the issuance of Rule 134 which permits the use of an enlarged statement, provided the conditions of the rule are met.

Rule 134 enumerates fourteen items of information which may be included in the statement. In addition to such matters as name of issuer, title of the security, its price, a statement of the source of a § 10 prospectus, and the identity of persons by whom orders will be executed—all of which are permitted by a tombstone ad—Rule 134 permits the communication to include a brief indication of the general type of business, and specific information generally relating to senior securities, that is, debt securities, convertible securities, and preferred stock. In connection with rights offerings, there is also some overlap with Rule 135 which permits certain communications even in the pre-filing period.

The "tombstone ad" and "identifying statement" are not intended to serve as selling documents but serve "purely as a screening device to ascertain what persons [are] * * * sufficiently interested to warrant delivery to them of the statutory prospectus."[3] Certain mandatory provisions are designed to accomplish this objective. If the registration statement has not become effective, the identifying statement (1) must contain a "red-herring" like legend stating that it does not contain an offer to sell a security; (2) a statement as to whether the offering is a new issue or a secondary offering by security holders, or both; and (3) the name and address of persons from whom a § 10(a) prospectus may be obtained. Finally, if the communication is accompanied or preceded by a prospectus which satisfies the requirements of § 10 at that time, the communication may solicit an offer to buy or an indication of interest in the security, but only if the communication contains a specified legend stating that no offer to buy can be accepted and that an indication of interest entails no commitment to purchase a security.

It should also be noted that Rule 134 grants a special dispensation for investment companies that permits an expanded text to include attention-getting headlines and pictorial illustrations. Most investment companies issue redeemable securities and their securities are the subject of a continuous offering, unlike that of other issuers. The investment company exception regarding publicity reflects the fact that the distribution of investment company shares differs markedly from that of other offerings and that investment companies are subject to comprehensive regulation under the Investment Company Act of 1940. There is additional language in Rule 134 which suggests that other types of issuers may take advantage of these advertising practices. However, when real estate syndicators began to use some of the same kind of information in their advertisements as investment companies, the Commission took the position that only registered investment companies are eligible to use these special provisions.[4]

Furthermore, Rule 135a permits underwriters or sponsors of investment company securities to engage in *generic* or *institutional* advertising of investment company products. Generic advertising must be restricted to explanatory information relating to investment companies generally, the different types of funds, products and services offered, and an invitation to inquire for further information.[5] The communication must contain the name of the broker or dealer or other person sponsoring the communication, but may not refer by name to the securities of a particular company or to the investment company itself. This device for contacting the public is infrequently used, however, since issuers and underwriters may use newspapers to publish a much more attractive Rule 134 identifying statement inviting the public to telephone toll-free or write for a statutory prospectus of a particular fund in the investment fund complex.

When trading in standardized options commenced in the early 1970's, the SEC adopted Rule 9b–1 of the 1934 Act prescribing the form and content of an "Options disclosure document." At the same time the Commission issued Rule

---

3. SEC Securities Act Release No. 3224, June 6, 1947, Memorandum of the Statutory Revision Committee addressed to the Commission, p. 2.

4. Securities Act Release No. 6518 (Mar. 22, 1984) at n. 2; Romeo, Advertising of Real Estate Offerings, 18 Rev. of Sec. & Commodities Reg. 17 (Jan. 23, 1985).

5. Securities Act Release No. 5248 (May 9, 1972).

134a which provides that certain written materials, including advertising, shall not be deemed to be a prospectus for the purposes of section 2(a)(10) provided the conditions of the rule are met.[6]

Having said all this, the fact is that, in practice, it is not customary to publish a "tombstone ad" during the waiting period and the expanded "identifying statement" is rarely used in the waiting period or post-effective period, even by nonreporting issuers to whom the summary prospectus is not available. Apparently, institutional and other sophisticated investors prefer to receive the preliminary prospectus.

However, an identifying statement may be used during the waiting period to test the market for the securities and attain a wider dissemination of the preliminary prospectus. There is set forth below an identifying statement for a proposed offering of common shares of Owens–Illinois Inc., which appeared in various metropolitan newspapers during the waiting period. After testing the market, the proposed offering was reduced from 2 million to 1.4 million shares. The tombstone ad which was used in the post-effective period is also set forth, to show the changes occurring in the composition of the underwriting syndicate.

6. See 1 L. Loss & J. Seligman 476 (3d ed. 1989).

IDENTIFYING STATEMENT USED IN THE WAITING PERIOD

A registration statement relating to these securities has been filed with the Securities and Exchange Commission but has not yet become effective. These securities may not be sold nor may offers to buy be accepted prior to the time the registration statement becomes effective. This advertisement shall not constitute an offer to sell or the solicitation of an offer to buy nor shall there be any sale of these securities in any State in which such offer, solicitation or sale would be unlawful prior to registration or qualification under the securities laws of any such State.

Proposed New Issue   February 22, 1976

2,000,000
Common Shares

OWENS-ILLINOIS, INC.

($3.125 par value)

Owens-Illinois is one of the world's leading and most diversified manufacturers of packaging products. It is the world's largest manufacturer of glass containers. In addition to glass containers its products include semi-rigid plastic containers, metal and plastic closures for such containers, corrugated and solid fiber shipping containers and containerboard for such containers, metal cans, composite cans, paper and plastic bag and film products, disposable paper and plastic cups, tubs, lids and plates, and plywood. In addition, an important part of Owens-Illinois' business consists of specialized glass products, such as glass television bulbs (for color and black-and-white picture tubes), scientific and laboratory glassware, and glass tumblers and stemware for household and institutional use.

Lazard Frères & Co.	**Goldman, Sachs & Co.**

Bache Halsey Stuart Inc.	**The First Boston Corporation**	**Blyth Eastman Dillon & Co.** Incorporated
Dillon, Read & Co. Inc.	**Drexel Burnham & Co.** Incorporated	**Hornblower & Weeks-Hemphill, Noyes** Incorporated
E. F. Hutton & Company Inc.	**Kidder, Peabody & Co.** Incorporated	**Kuhn, Loeb & Co.** **Lehman Brothers** Incorporated
Loeb, Rhoades & Co.	**Merrill Lynch, Pierce, Fenner & Smith** Incorporated	**Paine, Webber, Jackson & Curtis** Incorporated
Reynolds Securities Inc.	**Salomon Brothers**	**Smith Barney, Harris Upham & Co.** Incorporated
Wertheim & Co., Inc.	**White, Weld & Co.** Incorporated	**Dean Witter & Co.** Incorporated
Mitchell, Hutchins Inc.		**Shearson Hayden Stone Inc.**

ABD Securities Corporation	**Basle Securities Corporation**	**Alex. Brown & Sons**
F. Eberstadt & Co., Inc.	**EuroPartners Securities Corporation**	**Robert Fleming** Incorporated
Kleinwort, Benson Incorporated	**Moseley, Hallgarten & Estabrook Inc.**	**New Court Securities Corporation**
Oppenheimer & Co., Inc.		**Piper, Jaffray & Hopwood** Incorporated
R. W. Pressprich & Co. Incorporated	**Shields Model Roland Securities** Incorporated	**SoGen-Swiss International Corporation**
Thomson & McKinnon Auchincloss Kohlmeyer Inc.		**Spencer Trask & Co.** Incorporated
Tucker, Anthony & R. L. Day, Inc.	**UBS-DB Corporation**	**Warburg Paribas Becker Inc.**
Weeden & Co. Incorporated	**William D. Witter, Inc.**	**Wood, Struthers & Winthrop Inc.**
Shuman, Agnew & Co., Inc.	**Sutro & Co.** Incorporated	**Birr, Wilson & Co., Inc.**
Robertson, Colman, Siebel & Weisel		**Stone & Youngberg**

- -

Please send me a free copy of the Preliminary Prospectus of Owens-Illinois, Inc.

Name_____

Street_____City_____State_____Zip____

Telephone_____
       (business)   (residence)

A copy of the Preliminary Prospectus may be obtained by mailing or delivering this coupon to any of the above firms or to Lazard Frères & Co., One Rockefeller Plaza, New York, N.Y. 10020 or Goldman, Sachs & Co., 55 Broad Street, New York, N.Y. 10004.

TOMBSTONE AD USED IN THE POST–EFFECTIVE PERIOD

This announcement is neither an offer to sell nor a solicitation of an offer to buy any of these securities.
The offer is made only by the Prospectus.

NEW ISSUE

1,400,000
Common Shares
OWENS-ILLINOIS, INC.

($3.125 par value)

Price $57.50 Per Share

Copies of the Prospectus may be obtained only from such of the underwriters,
including the undersigned, as may lawfully offer these securities in this State.

Lazard Frères & Co.   Goldman, Sachs & Co.

Bache Halsey Stuart Inc.	The First Boston Corporation	Blyth Eastman Dillon & Co. Incorporated
Dillon, Read & Co. Inc.	Drexel Burnham & Co. Incorporated	Hornblower & Weeks-Hemphill, Noyes Incorporated
E. F. Hutton & Company Inc.	Kidder, Peabody & Co. Incorporated	Kuhn, Loeb & Co. Lehman Brothers Incorporated
Loeb, Rhoades & Co.	Merrill Lynch, Pierce, Fenner & Smith Incorporated	Paine, Webber, Jackson & Curtis Incorporated
Reynolds Securities Inc.	Salomon Brothers	Smith Barney, Harris Upham & Co. Incorporated
Wertheim & Co., Inc.	White, Weld & Co. Incorporated	Dean Witter & Co. Incorporated
Mitchell, Hutchins Inc.		Shearson Hayden Stone Inc.

ABD Securities Corporation	Basle Securities Corporation	Alex. Brown & Sons
F. Eberstadt & Co., Inc.	EuroPartners Securities Corporation	Robert Fleming Incorporated
Kleinwort, Benson Incorporated	Moseley, Hallgarten & Estabrook Inc.	New Court Securities Corporation
Oppenheimer & Co., Inc.	Piper, Jaffray & Hopwood Incorporated	Prescott, Ball & Turben
R. W. Pressprich & Co. Incorporated	Shields Model Roland Securities Incorporated	SoGen-Swiss International Corporation
Thomson & McKinnon Auchincloss Kohlmeyer Inc.		Spencer Trask & Co. Incorporated
Tucker, Anthony & R. L. Day, Inc.	UBS-DB Corporation	Weeden & Co. Incorporated
William D. Witter, Inc.		Wood, Struthers & Winthrop Inc.

Bateman Eichler, Hill Richards Incorporated	Crowell, Weedon & Co.	Shuman, Agnew & Co., Inc.
Sutro & Co. Birr, Wilson & Co., Inc. Incorporated	Boettcher & Company	Bosworth, Sullivan & Company Incorporated
Foster & Marshall Inc.	Robertson, Colman, Siebel & Weisel	Stern, Frank, Meyer & Fox Incorporated
Stone & Youngberg		Jefferies & Company, Inc.

March 4, 1976

In summary, therefore, the 1933 Act and rules now permit issuers, underwriters and dealers to use the following methods for reaching prospective purchasers during the waiting period: (1) oral offers to sell, whether face-to-face, or by interstate telephone, although offers to buy cannot be accepted until after the effective date; (2) publication of a "tombstone" advertisement pursuant to § 2(a)(10)(b) or an "identifying statement" pursuant to Rule 134; (3) a preliminary prospectus which meets the conditions of Rule 430 or 430A; and (4) a preliminary summary prospectus prepared by the issuer and complying with Rule 431 and the applicable Form.

The Commission has described the limitations on the sales activities of underwriters and dealers during the waiting period in these terms:[7]

> During the period after the filing of a registration statement, the freedom of an underwriter or dealer expecting to participate in the distribution to communicate with his customers is limited only by the antifraud provisions of the Securities Act and the Securities Exchange Act, and by the fact that written offering material other than a statutory[a] prospectus or tombstone advertisement may not be used. In other words, during this period "free writing" is illegal. The dealer, therefore, can orally solicit indications of interest or offers to buy and may discuss the securities with his customers and advise them whether or not in his opinion the securities are desirable or suitable for them. In this connection a dealer proposing to discuss an issue of securities with his customers should obtain copies of the preliminary prospectus in order to have a reliable source of information. This is particularly important where he proposes to recommend the securities, or where information concerning them has not been generally available. The corollary of the dealer's obligation to secure the copy is the obligation of the issuer and managing underwriters to make it readily available. Rule 460 provides that as a condition to acceleration of the effective date of a registration statement, the Commission will consider whether the persons making the offering have taken reasonable steps to make the information contained in the registration statement available to dealers who may participate in the distribution.

> It is a principal purpose of the so-called "waiting period" between the filing date and the effective date to enable dealers and, through them, investors to become acquainted with the information contained in the registration statement and to arrive at an unhurried decision concerning the merits of the securities. Consistently with this purpose, no contracts of sale can be made during this period, the purchase price may not be paid or received and offers to buy may be cancelled.

e. *Delivery During The Waiting Period.* In 1969, in response to a recommendation of the "Wheat Report," the Commission adopted Rule 15c2–8 under the Exchange Act relating to the distribution of preliminary and final prospectuses.[8] In the case of a seasoned issuer that is a reporting company, Rule 15c2–8 simply requires the broker or dealer to respond to written requests for the preliminary prospectus. But in the case of an issuer that is not yet filing periodic reports under the Securities Exchange Act of 1934 (i.e., chiefly IPO issuers), Rule 15c2–8(b) requires the broker or dealer to "deliver a copy of the prospectus to any person who is expected to receive a confirmation of sale at least 48 hours prior to the sending of such confirmation." This mandatory delivery requirement for new issues closed a hole in the Act because otherwise

7. Securities Act Release No. 4697 (May 24, 1964).

a. For the purpose of this release, a "statutory" prospectus was defined to include the preliminary prospectus authorized in Rule 433, the predecessor of Rule 430, as well as the summary prospectuses provided for in Rules 434 and 434A, the predecessors of Rule 431. This terminology confuses the statutory prospectus specified in § 10(a) with the preliminary and summary prospectuses which the Commission may prescribe by rule pursuant to § 10(b).

8. Securities Act Release No. 5101 (Nov. 19, 1970).

the key disclosure document was only required to be delivered with the confirmation of sale—well after the investment decision had been made. In effect, the 48 hour rule gives the customer a "cooling off" period to reconsider before the customer is called after the registration statement goes effective and a binding commitment can be made.

f. Testing the Market. During the waiting period the managing underwriter will test the market for the securities. The firm may prepare a "book" listing the entities that are expected to purchase the securities. The underwriters may stage "road shows" in which meetings are held with securities firms and institutional investors in the leading financial centers at home and abroad. This provides an opportunity to publicize the offering through the preliminary prospectus and by answering questions. Originally, the "roadshow" developed as a means by which participating underwriters in the offering could demonstrate their "due diligence" in order to satisfy the statutory standard of a "reasonable investigation" under § 11 of the 1933 Act. In theory, regional underwriters did so by interviewing senior management in a series of conferences held in various cities across the country. Over time, this "due diligence" function gave way to a marketing function, as securities analysts for institutional buyers came to use the occasion to interview senior management (and seek projections—explicit or implicit—of future earnings and performance). As a result, issues arose as to the written materials that can be used at this stage. Typically, the issuer's executives will make a presentation that may use charts, slides, or other aids, but no written materials (other than the preliminary prospectus) will be distributed; also, the press and public investors will usually be excluded.

Because the issuer's executives will predictably be asked probing questions as to future results or projections at roadshows, the issuer's attorneys may advise them not to answer these questions or may prepare a script of proposed answers. Indeed, if the issuer's executives answer questions involving future projections, they run a risk of "adopting" the third party's projections. As a result, issuer's counsel may seek to safeguard such projections by preparing and filing a "meaningful cautionary statement" with the SEC in order to obtain the protection of a special safe harbor for "forward looking information" that was enacted as part of the Private Securities Litigation Reform Act of 1995.[9] Potentially, statements made at a roadshow could constitute material, nonpublic information that the broader market does not possess. However, a curious exemption in Regulation FD exempts any disclosure made "in connection with a securities offering registered under the securities Act ..."[10] Nonetheless, even though these statements are exempt from Regulation FD, they could amount to insider trading if the fiduciary breach requirements for insider trading liability can be established.

Another protective technique used at road shows has been for the issuer to present its own securities analyst at these sessions (known as a "sell-side analyst") to present its own predictions as to future corporate results for the issuer. These projections are presumed by the audience to reflect management's

9. See Section 27A of the Securities Act of 1933 and Section 21E of the Securities Exchange Act of 1934. It should be emphasized that this safe harbor applies only to "reporting" issuers that file periodic reports under the 1934 Act and not to an initial public offering. See § 21E(b)(2)(D).

10. See Rule 100(b)(2)(14).

own projections (and they probably have been clearer by the issuer), but responsibility for them is disclaimed by the issuer.

Increasingly, roadshows are being videotaped and disseminated by private networks, on either a live or delayed time basis, to institutional buyers across the country (including via the Internet). This practice raises both issues about whether such videotapes amount to a prospectus under § 2(a)(10) of the 1933 Act and whether such selective disclosure to institutions only is appropriate.

The managing underwriter need not postpone organization of the selling group until after the registration statement has become effective, as was the case before the 1954 amendments. Indeed, the managing underwriter is expected to contact prospective members of the selling group both orally and by use of preliminary prospectuses, and get indications of interest, or even offers to buy, during the waiting period.

Information regarding issues "in registration" with the SEC is broadcast in other ways. There is a financial publication, the Investment Dealers Digest, which collects current information on issues in registration. As soon as the registration statement is filed, this publication sends a card to its subscribers describing the proposed offering. A brief notice is also published in a special section of the magazine which generally includes such information as the original SEC filing date, type of securities, proposed use of the proceeds, approximate offering price, the target date for the offering, and the name of the managing underwriter. Interested dealers may then contact the lead underwriter directly if they wish to be included in the selling group. Furthermore, following recommendations contained in the Wheat Report[11] the Commission issued Rule 15c2–8 under the 1934 Act to assure that issuers and managing underwriters distributed the preliminary prospectus to prospective underwriters and dealers during the waiting period.[12]

g. Electronic Communications: Of Web Sites, Electronic Roadshows, and E-mail. Although oral selling is allowed during the waiting period, the use of "free writing" (that is, written offering material not authorized by any specific rule) is not. This categorical distinction between oral and written communications created some uncertainty with the advent of the Internet and the increasing use by issuers (and underwriters) of Web sites. The Commission has raised no objection to the posting of a prospectus on a Web site (where typically it will be downloadable), but other offering-related written material used during the waiting period must fall within Rule 134 (or it would otherwise be deemed a non-complying prospectus under § 2(a)(10)).[13] The Commission has also made it clear that an issuer may not "hyperlink" its preliminary prospectus to research reports prepared by another firm, as such linking will be viewed the same as if the issuer itself mailed the report to the investor.[14] Clearly, such a mailing during the waiting period would normally constitute impermissible free writing.

---

11. SEC, Disclosure to Investors (Wheat Report), Ch. iv (1969).

12. Supra, at 122.

13. In Securities Act Release No. 7233 ("Use of Electronic Media for Delivery Pur-

poses") (October 13, 1995), the SEC gives several examples of when written material may be posted on a Web site. See infra at pp. 142 to 149.

14. *Id.* at Example 16 (see infra at p. 149).

E-mail raises still other issues because it permits a continuum of possible types of communication. At one end of the continuum, e-mail is analogous to oral communication because it enables an interactive and more convenient information flow between, for example, the broker and the client. But, if e-mail were to be used to transmit a twenty page offer document (which document was not otherwise authorized by some exemptive rule), the prohibition on "free writing" could be effectively flouted. In a 1996 release, the Commission indicated that the legal status of an e-mail communication under the Securities Act of 1933 was not inherently fixed, but would likely depend on whether it "replaces or substitutes for telephone conversations".[15] In short, brief interactive exchanges are probably "oral" in nature and permitted during the waiting period, but dissemination of an offering document by e-mail to a broader audience is not.

A final issue involving electronic communications involves the recent emergence of the electronic roadshow. Roadshows long ago became a feature of the marketing process during the waiting period. Often, senior management and the underwriters will make a series of oral presentations, followed by question and answer sessions, in several major cities during the waiting period. Because of the all important distinction between oral selling and written materials, management may present a slide show or a "PowerPoint" demonstration at the road show, but may not hand out copies of its slides or notes (which would be impermissible "free writing"). *Query*: Does this difference really matter on the policy level? Attendance at these sessions will be limited to broker-dealers, institutional investors and other major buyers in the particular type of offering (that is, public investors and the press are excluded). Typically, securities analysts seek at these sessions to elicit forward-looking information (earnings projections or product development estimates) that may not be included in the prospectus (thus raising sensitive issues about selective disclosure of material information).

Institutions not able to attend such meetings began to request videotapes of the exchanges between management and the securities analysts. Although issuers were willling to comply (and could easily place such videotapes on CD-ROMS), a legal issue posed an obstacle. Section 2(a)(10) of the 1933 Act defines the term "prospectus" to include "any . . . communication, written or by radio or television, which offers a security for sale. . . ." Nonetheless, in 1997, the Commission's staff granted a no-action letter to the Private Financial Network, a subsidiary of MSNBC Interactive LLC (a joint venture of NBC and Microsoft Corporation) permitting it to broadcast issuer roadshows, either on a live or delayed basis, to its subscribers over its private network.[16] The rationale for this position was that the term "prospectus" in § 2(a)(10) was "intended to reach to those documents or communications that are widely disseminated to an undifferentiated public" rather than to a discreet, "invited audience."[17] (PFF had at the time only 100 or less subscribers). Typically, a password

15. See Securities Act Release No. 7288 ("use of Electronic Media by Broker–Dealers, Transfer Agents and Investment Advisors for Delivery of Information"), (May 9, 1996).

16. See Private Financial Network, 1997 SEC No–Act. LEXIS 406 (March 12, 1997).

17. *Id.* In part, this interpretation of § 2(a)(10) was based on a controversial Supreme Court decision that construed § 2(a)(10). See Gustafson v. Alloyd Co. Inc., 513 U.S. 561 (1995) (discussed infra at pp. 938–952).

protection system has been used to control access and limit the viewers to sophisticated investors.

While this "limited audience" rationale could be squared with the language of § 2(a)(10), it heightened the problem of selective disclosure of potentially material information only to institutional investors. Later in 1997, the SEC announced that it would authorize another firm (Net Roadshow Inc.) to transmit roadshows directly over the Internet, but again only to an audience of money managers and institutional investors.[18] They would be given special access codes and would agree by contract not to download the video roadshow. Effectively, this approach ensures that only sophisticated investors would have access to the projections (explicit or implicit) made at roadshows. On occasion, however, the SEC has insisted that any explicit projections which it detected being made at the roadshow be included in the prospectus, and the staff regularly asks for copies of any script used at a roadshow.

Why is the SEC resistant to opening the roadshow to public investors? Probably, it fears that the roadshow would quickly come to contain salesmanship and "hype" that might confuse retail investors. Possibly, it also fears that the electronic roadshow would become more popular with investors than the traditional (and somewhat stodgy) prospectus and thereby trivialize its significance. But, is this concern overly paternalistic? The unhappy alternative is to continue to permit the roadshow to communicate often sensitive and material information to institutional investors, which seems a clear form of selective disclosure (even if it is expressly permitted by Regulation FD).

Commentators have suggested that the SEC should open the roadshow to public investors by permitting their general dissemination over the Internet.[19] Although the broad statutory definition of prospectus in § 2(a)(10) presents a doctrinal obstacle, the SEC now has general exemptive authority under the National Securities Markets Improvements Act of 1996, which would permit it to override § 2(a)(10) and grant a broader exemption in order to equalize the informational advantages that institutional investors now possess over public investors.

Securities Act Release No. 4968

Securities and Exchange Commission.
April 24, 1969.

PRIOR DELIVERY OF PRELIMINARY PROSPECTUS

The Commission again called attention to the continued high volume of registration statements filed under the Securities Act of 1933, and noted that the number of companies filing registration statements for the first time continues to mount, so that well over half of the filings now being made are by such companies. The Commission emphasized that the investing public should be aware that many such offerings of securities are of a highly speculative character and that the prospectus should be carefully examined before an

---

18. See Net Roadshow, Inc., 1997 SEC No–Act LEXIS 864 (Sept. 8, 1997); see also Beckett, SEC Gives Nod to Roadshows Over the Internet, The Wall Street Journal, Septmeber 9, 1997 at B–4.

19. See Quinn, The Road Less Traveled: The Advent of Electronic Roadshows, 11 Insights 3 (July 1997); see also McLaughlin, "Booting" the Federal Securities Laws Into the 21st Century, 11 Insights 21 (July 1997).

investment decision is reached. It is characteristic of such speculative issues that the company has been recently organized, that the promoters and other selected persons have obtained a disproportionately large number of shares for a nominal price with the consequent dilution in the assets to be contributed by the investing public, and that the underwriters receive fees and other benefits which are high in relation to the proceeds to the issuer and which further dilute the investment values being offered.

The Commission has declared its policy in Rule 460 that it will not accelerate the effective date of a registration statement unless the preliminary prospectus contained in the registration statement is distributed to underwriters and dealers who it is reasonably anticipated will be invited to participate in the distribution of the security to be offered or sold. The purpose of this requirement is to afford all persons effecting the distribution a means of being informed with respect to the offering so that they can advise their customers of the investment merits of the security. Particularly in the case of a first offering by a nonreporting company, salesmen should obtain and read the current preliminary or final prospectus before offering the security to their clients.

The Commission also announced, in the exercise of its responsibilities in accelerating the effective date of a registration statement under Section 8(a) of the Securities Act of 1933, and particularly the statutory requirement that it have due regard to the adequacy of the information respecting the issuer theretofore available to the public, that it will consider whether the persons making an offering of securities of an issuer which is not subject to the reporting requirements of Section 13 or 15(d) of the Securities Exchange Act of 1934, have taken reasonable steps to furnish preliminary prospectuses to those persons who may reasonably be expected to be purchasers of the securities. The Commission will ordinarily be satisfied by a written statement from the managing underwriter to the effect that it has been informed by participating underwriters and dealers that copies of the preliminary prospectus complying with Rule 433(a) [the predecessor of Rule 430] have been or are being distributed to all persons to whom it is then expected to mail confirmations of sale not less than 48 hours prior to the time it is expected to mail such confirmations. Such distribution should be by air mail if the confirmations will be sent by air mail, or a longer period to compensate for the difference in the method of mailing the prospectus should be provided. Of course, if the form of preliminary prospectus so distributed was inadequate or inaccurate in material respects, acceleration will be deferred until the Commission has received satisfactory assurances that appropriate correcting material (including a memorandum of changes) has been so distributed.

In view of the situation above discussed, the Commission proposes to invoke this acceleration policy immediately. When the Commission gains sufficient experience under this policy, it anticipates proposing appropriate revision of its rules.

SECTION 4. THE POST-EFFECTIVE PERIOD

Statutes and Regulations

Securities Act, §§ 4, 5, 2(3), 2(a)(10), 10.

Rules 153, 153a, 174; Exchange Act Rule 15c2–8; Regulation C, Rules 424, 427, 430A, 431, 434, 463; Form SR; Regulation S–K, Items 501 and 502, particularly Item 502(e).

Uniform Commercial Code § 8–319.

PROSPECTUS REQUIREMENTS IN THE POST–EFFECTIVE PERIOD

Section 5(a) concerns the "sale" of a security; it is both prohibitive and permissive. In its prohibitive aspect, § 5(a)(1) forbids the use of interstate facilities or the mails to "sell" a security by means of a prospectus or otherwise in the pre-effective period, which embraces both the pre-filing and waiting periods. Once the registration statement in respect of a security has become effective, however, the permissive aspect of § 5(a)(1) comes into play. It is no longer illegal to make use of the mails or interstate facilities to "sell" such security, a "sale" being defined in § 2(a)(3) to include "every contract of sale or disposition of a security * * * for value."

Section 5(b) concerns prospectuses; it must be read in conjunction with § 2(a)(10). Section 5(b)(1) prohibits the use of the mails or interstate facilities to transmit any prospectus relating to a security with respect to which a registration statement has been filed, unless such prospectus meets the requirements of § 10. A "prospectus" is defined in § 2(a)(10) to include every written communication which "offers any security for sale or confirms the sale of any security." The "confirmation" referred to is the slip of paper which the broker or dealer sends to the buyer to confirm the transaction and thus comply with the statute of frauds and SEC regulations.[1]

We have seen that during the waiting period only those prospectuses meeting the requirements of § 10(b) may be used for § 5(b)(1) purposes. But § 5(b)(1) is so framed as to reach past the waiting period into the post-effective period, for it encompasses the entire post-filing period. Thus, after the registration statement has become effective, a § 10(a) prospectus may then be used for § 5(b)(1) purposes, but a § 10(b) summary prospectus may also be used pursuant to Rule 431 for informational and screening purposes. However, under § 5(b)(2), the delivery of the security pursuant to the sale must be accompanied or preceded by a § 10(a) prospectus.

There remains one further qualification to the prohibitions of § 5(b)(1). It will be recalled that § 2(a)(10) defines a "prospectus" to include any written communication which "offers any security for sale or confirms the sale of any security." There is then excluded from this definition any communication sent or given after the effective date (other than a § 10(b) prospectus) if it is proved that prior to or at the same time a written prospectus meeting the requirements of § 10(a) was sent or given to the person to whom the communication was directed. Section 2(a)(10) has the effect of eliminating duplication in the furnishing of a statutory prospectus, whether given by the same or by different persons, for there is no requirement that the § 10(a) prospectus and the later communication be sent by the same person. It should be noted, however, that this exception does not apply to the use of a § 10(b) prospectus which is sent or given prior to the effective date; in this case the offeror must itself send the § 10(b) prospectus. Moreover, where such a written communication offering a security is sent, even if it is accompanied or preceded by a § 10(b) prospectus,

---

1.   U.C.C. § 8–319; Rule 10b–10; NASD Manual (CCH) ¶ 3509; M. Mendelson & S. Robbins, Investment Analysis and Securities Markets 25–86 (1976).

there is a violation; such offers during the waiting period may be made only by use of the preliminary prospectus. Finally, § 2(a)(10) permits other selling literature to be sent to a prospective buyer *after the effective date*, so long as this communication has been preceded or is accompanied by a statutory prospectus. This "free-writing" privilege is only allowed in the post-effective period.

At present, supplementary sales material need not be filed with the SEC—with one exception. Section 24(b) of the Investment Company Act requires all investment company sales literature directed at prospective investors to be filed with the Commission. In addition, the NASD imposes substantive standards on sales literature used by its members in certain high-risk, tax-sheltered "direct participation programs," providing for flow-through tax consequences. All such advertising must be filed with the NASD and is subject to review by any NASD District Business Conduct Committee.[2]

As previously indicated, § 5(a) concerns sales of a security; § 5(b) concerns prospectuses. The delivery of a security for the purpose of sale or delivery after sale is dealt with in §§ 5(a)(2) and 5(b)(2). Section 5(a)(2) provides that it is unlawful to use the mails or interstate facilities to transport a security for the purpose of sale or for delivery after sale, unless a registration statement is in effect as to such security. The result is to prohibit such deliveries in both the pre-filing period and during the waiting period. Since oral interstate offers to sell may be made during the waiting period, so long as no actual sale is made, § 5(a)(2) forestalls the possibility of using interstate facilities or the mails to transport a security either for the purpose of sale or for delivery after sale in the pre-effective period. Furthermore, even in the case of face-to-face transactions or intrastate sales made without the use of the mails or interstate facilities, § 5(a)(2) forbids use of these media to deliver the security following the sale.

Section 5(b)(2) provides that it is unlawful to use the mails or interstate facilities to transport a security for sale or delivery after sale, unless accompanied or preceded by a § 10(a) prospectus. Thus, even if the contract of sale has been negotiated by means of an *oral* interstate telephone call made during the post-filing period, once the registration statement has become effective, the seller may not mail a written "confirmation" of the transaction, thereby closing the deal, unless the confirmation is accompanied or preceded by a statutory prospectus. Indeed, if the negotiations are conducted face-to-face, or by intrastate or interstate telephone and no written confirmation is transmitted by the use of the mails or interstate facilities, then the security may not be mailed to the buyer unless it is accompanied (or preceded) by a statutory prospectus.[3] In that event, as Lobell has put it: "the buyer in these transactions gets his prospectus more as a memento than as a vehicle of information."[4]

---

2. NASD Manual (CCH) Rules of Practice, Secs. 34, 35, ¶ 2191, ¶ 2192.

The SEC has adopted Reg. § 270.24b–3 under the Investment Company Act which specifies that any investment company sales literature shall be deemed filed with the Commission for § 24(d) purposes upon filing with a national securities association registered under § 15A of the 1934 Act and which has adopted standards relating to investment company advertising practices and procedures to review such advertising. Only the NASD qualifies. See SEC Securities Act Release No. 6753 (Feb. 2, 1988).

3. A telegraphic "offer to sell" or "confirmation of the sale," standing alone, collides with § 5(b)(1) for a telegram is a written communication and thus a "prospectus" as defined in § 2(a)(10). See Harper v. United States, 143 F.2d 795, 801 (8th Cir.1944).

4. Lobell, Revision of the Securities Act, 48 Colum.L.Rev. 313, 323 (1948).

This anomaly that the statutory prospectus comes after the time of the investment decision was heightened by the adoption of earlier-noted Rule 430A, which allows the omission of most price-related information from the statutory prospectus. While § 5 may not be violated by the use of such an incomplete statutory prospectus, both Rule 10b–5 and § 12(a)(2) of the 1933 Act (the two principal antifraud remedies available to buyers) could well deem such an omission material and give the buyer the right to damages (if, for example, the market price were to decline after the sale). Hence, price-related information needs to be communicated to investors in some document.

Just how then is delivery effected? Years ago, the pricing amendment would incorporate all material information into the final prospectus, and this document would be printed on the eve of effectiveness and so could be mailed out with the confirmation of sale shortly after the moment of effectiveness. But Rule 430A eliminated the need to prepare such a last minute and costly document (to the industry's great relief). More importantly, a new and unrelated development arose which aggravated the timing problem. In 1995, the SEC (in conjunction with the Federal Reserve Board) shortened the settlement time for a securities transaction from five business days to (in most cases) the third business following the trade date (or, in the industry's parlance, "T+3").[5] This was a change that the industry wanted (as it meant that underwriters and other sellers of securities get paid more quickly), but it complicated the problem of mailing out a statutory prospectus (with the confirmation of sale) in this telescoped time period. In light of this change, the securities industry convinced the SEC to adopt what became known as its T+3 Prospectus Delivery Rules.[6] Specifically, new Rule 434 was promulgated to allow the information traditionally required to be included in the final prospectus to be delivered instead to investors in piecemeal fashion in multiple documents (at least in the case of firm commitment, all-cash offerings and certain offerings of investment grade securities). Within these confines (which describe the mainstream business of the traditional Wall Street investment banks), Rule 434 has essentially put to rest the original concept of a complete, self-contained disclosure document (which the traditional statutory prospectus was).

Operationally, Rule 434 distinguishes between issuers who qualify to use Form S–3 and those that do not. For issuers eligible to use Form S–3, the issuer need only deliver the normal preliminary prospectus plus an "abbreviated term sheet" along with the confirmation of sale.[7] The abbreviated term sheet sets forth a general description of the securities (for example, any redemption, call, or conversion features not previously disclosed in the preliminary prospectus) and any material changes affecting the issuer since its last filing under the Securities Exchange Act's periodic disclosure system. Some pricing information (i.e., offering price and underwriters' discount) will typically be simply set forth on the confirmation of sale. Information that is offering-specific (such as the use of proceeds and the plan of distribution) need not be sent or given to investors if it is filed with the SEC pursuant to Rule 424 on or prior to the date the confirmations of sale are sent or given.

For issuers that do not qualify for Form S–3 (including, of course, initial public offerings), Rule 434 requires the issuer to provide: (1) a "prospectus

---

5. See Securities Exchange Act Rule 15c6–1. It is contemplated that settlement date will be advanced to "T + 1" in the near future.

6. Securities Act Release No. 7168 (May 11, 1995).

7. See Rule 434(c).

subject to completion'' (which term is defined by Rule 434(g) to mean either a preliminary prospectus or a final prospectus minus the pricing information which Rule 430A permits the issuer to omit), and (2) a term sheet that sets "forth all information material to investors with respect to the offering that is not disclosed in the prospectus subject to completion or the confirmation."[8] If new material information has arisen or if the terms of the offering have been materially changed from those disclosed in the registration statement at the time of effectiveness, Rule 434 requires the non-Form S–3 issuer to file a post-effective amendment to the registration statement.

In general, however, all issuers are permitted to use a new document—the "term sheet" or, for Form S–3 issuers, the "abbreviated term sheet"—as a practical substitute for the statutory prospectus. That is, in the typical case, the mailing prior to effectiveness of a preliminary prospectus (or a Rule 430A prospectus after effectiveness) plus a term sheet containing the basic price-dependent information is deemed to constitute a statutory prospectus. Given such delivery, brokers can mail the confirmation of sale, or make delivery of the shares, or send out additional written offering material. Effectively, this procedure economizes on printing and mailing costs as two different prospectuses (preliminary and final) will not need to be printed or mailed. These costs can be still further reduced (as discussed later) if delivery can be effected electronically via the Internet.

One final statutory issue under § 5(b) involves the duration of its restrictions. For how long must an issuer, underwriter or dealer deliver a statutory prospectus (even if today delivering the statutory prospectus simply means following the preliminary prospectus with a term sheet)? In theory, the obligation to deliver continues only during the period when the securities are being distributed, as the 1933 Act is concerned with the distribution process and not with trading transactions as such. The cut-off dates when issuers, underwriters and dealers are no longer subject to § 5(b) are prescribed by § 4(3). The prospectus requirements apply to the issuer so long as it is offering any of the securities to the public. § 4(3). Under § 4(3)(C) any underwriter or dealer participating in the distribution is subject to the prospectus requirements so long as it is offering an unsold allotment. Furthermore, under § 4(3)(B), all underwriters and dealers must comply with the prospectus requirements during a 40–day period following the effective date of the registration statement or the commencement of the public offering, whichever occurs later, whether or not they are then engaged in a distributive transaction. Under the 1964 amendment program, however, if securities of the issuer have not previously been sold pursuant to an effective registration statement under the 1933 Act, the applicable period is extended to 90 days. § 4(3)(C).

At the same time, the Commission was given the power, by rule or order, to prescribe a shorter period than the 40 or 90 day periods prescribed in § 4(3) for the delivery of prospectuses by dealers. Under this authority, the Commission has issued Rule 174. Irrespective of whether the 40 or 90 day period would otherwise be applicable, dealers (including an underwriter who is no longer acting as such with respect to the security) need not deliver a prospectus to the purchaser, if the issuer was subject, prior to the filing of the registration statement, to the reporting requirements of §§ 13 or 15(d) of the 1934 Act. Moreover, the obligation of a dealer to deliver a prospectus is entirely dispensed

---

8. See Rule 434(b)(3).

with if the registration statement is on Form F–6 (for registration of American Depositary Receipts issued against securities of foreign issuers to be deposited with an American depositary). Where a registration statement relates to offerings to be made from time to time (the so-called shelf-registration to be considered at page 239) the prospectus delivery requirements are dispensed with upon the expiration of the initial prospectus delivery period specified in § 4(3) following the first bona fide offering of the securities. Regulation S–K, Item 502(e) requires that the inside front cover page or the back cover page of the prospectus contain a legend in bold-face type alerting dealers as to their prospectus delivery obligations and the date when such obligations terminate. The dealers' exemption after such 40–day or 90–day period, as well as the brokers' exemption provision (§ 4(4)), will be considered along with other exemptions in Chapter 9.

Further complications arise in the prospectus requirements when the transaction is effected on a stock exchange or in the over-the-counter market. Is it sufficient for the seller or his or her broker to deliver a prospectus to the buyer's broker, even though the buyer never sees it? And is the buyer's broker bound by the prospectus requirements when he or she confirms or delivers the securities to the buyer by use of the channels of interstate commerce or the mails? If the buyer's broker is acting as an agent rather than as a principal, delivery of a prospectus to the broker should be regarded as a delivery to the principal. On the other hand, the buyer's broker may be under an independent duty to comply with the prospectus requirements if he or she has solicited the buyer to purchase the security. See Section 4(4).

Rule 153 relaxes the requirements for delivery of a statutory prospectus to stock exchange members where a sale is made on a national securities exchange by permitting the delivery to the Exchange upon its request of a sufficient number of copies to comply with the requests of members; it does not apply to NASDAQ or other over-the-counter transactions.[9]

Finally, although the registration statement speaks only as of the effective date, registrants, underwriters and dealers must take care to see that the statutory prospectus and any supplemental sales literature is at the time of use not false and misleading under the anti-fraud provisions of the 1933 and 1934 Acts, as may be seen from the following cases. And if the offering continues over an extended period, the prospectus should be kept current under the standards of § 10(a)(3).

SECTION 5.   ELECTRONIC COMMUNICATIONS AND THE '33 ACT

Statutes and Regulations

Securities Act, §§ 2(a)(10), 5(a), 5(b)

Rule 134 and 434 and Exchange Act Rule 15c2–8

The advent of the Internet represented a major conceptual challenge for the federal securities laws, both because they are rooted in a paper-based technology and because the Securities Act of 1933 in particular draws a fundamental distinction between oral and written communications (permitting

---

9. National securities exchanges register under § 6 of the Exchange Act; the NASD is the only registered securities association which has qualified under § 15A of that Act.

the former during the waiting period, while largely prohibiting the latter). In 1995, the SEC began the process of updating the securities laws to reflect the ubiquity of electronic communications and to realize the significant cost savings available to issuers and underwriters from use of electronic communications.

Securities Act Release No. 7233

Securities and Exchange Commission.
October 13, 1995.

Use of Electronic Media for Delivery Purposes

I. Introduction

The Commission today is publishing its views with respect to using electronic media as a means of delivering information required under the Securities Act of 1933 ("Securities Act"), the Securities Exchange Act of 1934 ("Exchange Act"), and the Investment Company Act of 1940 ("Investment Company Act"). Advances in computers and electronic media technology are enabling companies to disseminate information to more people at a faster and more cost-effective rate than traditional distribution methods, which have been largely paper-based. The Commission appreciates the promise of electronic distribution of information in enhancing investors' ability to access, research, and analyze information, and in facilitating the provision of information by issuers and others. The Commission believes that, given the numerous benefits of electronic distribution of information and the fact that in many respects it may be more useful to investors than paper, its use should not be disfavored.

Until recently, on-line use of corporate information was generally limited to large corporations and institutional investors. The dramatic growth in personal computer ownership, however, is enabling many small investors to access on-line corporate information just as readily as institutions. Access to information through electronic means permits small investors to communicate quickly and efficiently with companies as well as with each other.

Use of electronic media also enhances the efficiency of the securities markets by allowing for the rapid dissemination of information to investors and financial markets in a more cost-efficient, widespread, and equitable manner than traditional paper-based methods. Recognizing the multiple benefits of electronic technology, the Commission initiated its Electronic Data Gathering, Analysis, and Retrieval ("EDGAR") system in 1984 to automate the receipt, processing and dissemination of disclosure documents filed with the Commission under the Securities Act, Exchange Act and Investment Company Act. As a result of this automation, filings made with the Commission through EDGAR are available promptly to the public and financial markets. Today, more than 70% of all domestic public companies file electronically through EDGAR, and by May 1996, all domestic registrants will be required to file electronically through EDGAR.

In February 1995, the Commission's Division of Corporation Finance issued an interpretive letter intending to address certain legal issues relating to electronic delivery of prospectuses ("Brown & Wood letter"). The Brown & Wood letter established a number of conditions in order for a prospectus to be considered "delivered" electronically. The intention at the time of the release of the Brown & Wood letter was that the Commission would review this area in greater detail after the issuance of the letter with a view toward, through an appropriate release, providing further interpretive advice or proposed rulemaking. Because of these developments, along with the fact that none of the federal securities statutes exclusively require paper delivery of information, the Commission believes that interpretive guidance on the use of electronic media is appropriate. While the Commission anticipates that issuers and others will rely upon the guidance of this release, continued reliance on the generally more stringent requirements of the Brown & Wood letter is no longer required, but would be permissible.

　　* * *

The liability provisions of the federal securities laws apply equally to electronic and paper-based media. For instance, the antifraud provisions of the federal securities laws as set forth in Section 10(b) of the Exchange Act and Rule 10b–5 thereunder would apply to any information delivered electronically, as it does to information delivered in paper. As another example, Section 17(b) of the Securities Act would apply to any report circulated on the Internet just as if the report were provided in paper.

Given the numerous benefits of electronic media, the Commission encourages further technological research, development and application. The Commission believes that the use of electronic media should be at least an equal alternative to the use of paper-based media. Accordingly, issuer or third party information that can be delivered in paper under the federal securities laws may be delivered in electronic format. The Commission also expects that paper delivery of information will continue to be made available by issuers and others until such time as electronic media become more universally accessible and accepted, although the Commission recognizes that, for example, various offerings may now be made exclusively through electronic means.

II.   Use of Electronic Media

A.   General

The federal securities statutes do not prescribe the medium to be used for providing information by or on behalf of issuers, or by or on behalf of third parties with respect to issuers. The Commission believes that delivery of information through an electronic medium generally could satisfy delivery or transmission obligations under the federal securities laws.

The Commission believes that the question of whether delivery through electronic media has been achieved is most easily examined by analogy to paper delivery procedures. The Commission would view information distributed through electronic means as satisfying the delivery or transmission requirements of the federal securities laws if such distribution results in the delivery to the intended recipients of substantially equivalent information as these recipients would have had if the information were delivered to them in paper form.[22] As is the case with paper delivery, there should be an opportunity to retain a permanent record of the information.

---

22. Issuers and other persons required to satisfy delivery requirements should consider establishing record-keeping or other procedures to evidence satisfaction of applicable requirements through electronic means. Presumably, such procedures would be analogous to comparable procedures followed when a paper document is delivered.

B. Guidance Regarding Electronic Delivery

The Commission believes that the analysis of whether an electronic communication is delivered or transmitted for purposes of the federal securities laws should be determined in accordance with the preceding discussion. In making such determinations with respect to information communicated, in particular, over the Internet, through on-line services, or through analogous computer networks, the Commission believes that the following concepts discussed in this section reflect issues that should be considered in determining whether applicable statutory requirements have been satisfied.

This release is intended to provide guidance and a degree of certainty regarding the manner in which electronic delivery can be achieved. An issuer or other party that structures its delivery in accordance with the principles and examples set forth below can be assured that it is satisfying its delivery obligations under the federal securities laws. The Commission wishes to emphasize, however, that the factors discussed below are not the only factors relevant to determining whether the legal requirements pertaining to delivery or transmission of documents have been satisfied. If an issuer or third party develops a method of electronic delivery that differs from those discussed below, but provides assurance comparable to paper delivery that the required information will be delivered, that method may satisfy delivery or transmission obligations. The ultimate responsibility for satisfying the applicable statutory requirements remains with the issuer or other party to whom the law assigns the responsibility.

Notice. When an issuer delivers a paper document through the postal mail, the investor will most likely be made aware that new information exists and that the investor might have to take some action within a certain period of time. The Commission believes that those providing electronic information should consider the extent to which the electronic communication provides timely and adequate notice to investors that information for them is available and, if necessary, consider supplementing the electronic communication with another communication that would provide notice similar to that provided by delivery in paper. If an electronic document itself is provided—for example, on computer disk, CD–ROM, audio tape, videotape, or e-mail—that communication itself should generally be sufficient notice. If the document is provided on an Internet Web site, however, separate notice would be necessary to satisfy the delivery requirements unless the issuer can otherwise evidence that delivery to the investor has been satisfied or the document is not required to be delivered under the federal securities laws.

Access. When a document is delivered through the postal mail, a recipient generally is provided with access to the required disclosure. The Commission believes that recipients who are provided information through electronic delivery should have comparable access; consequently, the use of a particular medium should not be so burdensome that intended recipients cannot effectively access the information provided.[24] Moreover, as is the case with a paper

24. For example, if an investor must proceed through a confusing series of ever-changing menus to access a required document so that it is not reasonable to expect that access would generally occur, this procedure would likely be viewed as unduly burdensome. In that case, delivery would be deemed not to have occurred unless delivery otherwise could be shown.

document, a recipient should have the opportunity to retain the information or have ongoing access equivalent to personal retention.[25]

    * * *

Finally, because of possible system failures, computer incompatibilities, and those cases, for example, where consents are used in connection with the delivery of information electronically and the person providing the consent revokes it, a necessary precaution given the current state and use of communications technology is that issuers must be able to make available paper versions of documents delivered in an electronic medium. Specifically, the Commission believes that, as a matter of policy, where a person has a right to receive a document under the federal securities laws and chooses to receive it electronically, that person should be provided with a paper version of the document if any consent to receive documents electronically were revoked or the person specifically requests a paper copy (regardless of whether any previously provided consent was revoked).[26]

    * * *

C. Evidence to Show Delivery

Providing information through postal mail provides reasonable assurance that the delivery requirement is satisfied. The Commission believes that issuers and others providing electronic delivery of information should similarly have reason to believe that any electronic means so selected will result in the satisfaction of the delivery requirements. Examples of procedures evidencing satisfaction of the delivery requirements include: (1) obtaining an informed consent from an investor to receive the information through a particular electronic medium coupled with assuring appropriate notice and access, as discussed above; (2) obtaining evidence that an investor actually received the information, for example, by electronic mail return-receipt or confirmation of accessing, downloading, or printing * * *; (3) disseminating information through certain facsimile methods * * *; (4) an investor's accessing a document with hyper linking to a required document * * *; and (5) using forms or other material available only by accessing the information * * *.

Moreover, an issuer could rely on consents provided to an underwriter, a brokerage firm or other service provider. Similarly, an underwriter or brokerage firm could rely on a consent that its customer provided to the issuer, and deliver that issuer's document through the same electronic medium.

D. Examples

A series of examples is provided below to illustrate various applications of the above concepts and to provide guidance in applying them to specific facts and circumstances. The analysis required to determine compliance with the delivery requirements is fact-specific, and any different or additional facts might require a different conclusion. Although this interpretation is effective

---

25. In many cases, the investor will be able to download the document from the electronic medium, which is sufficient to satisfy this need.

26. This policy would not preclude an issuer from structuring its offering as one that will be made only through electronic documents. However, companies conducting initial public offerings must consider prospectus delivery requirements for secondary market trading under Securities Act Rule 174.

immediately, the Commission requests comment on whether other examples might be appropriate for publication in a subsequent release.

Securities Act

(1) Company XYZ places its final prospectus on its Internet Web site. Company XYZ then confirms by mail the sale of securities to investors with a note stating that the final prospectus is available on its Web site and giving the Internet location of the Web site.

Unlike paper delivery of a final prospectus where access to the document can be presumed with delivery, not all investors purchasing securities could be presumed to have the ability to access the final prospectus via an Internet Web site. Therefore, absent other factors such as express consent from the investor or an investor's actually accessing the document on the Web site, the procedures described above by themselves would not satisfy the delivery requirements under the Securities Act.

(2) Company XYZ places its final prospectus on its Internet Web site. Company XYZ then confirms by mail the sale of securities to those investors who have consented to electronic delivery via the Company's Internet Web site. A note on the bottom of the confirmation states that the final prospectus is available on its Web site and the Internet location of the Web site.

This would satisfy delivery obligations, as it is reasonable to presume that investors who have consented to delivery of the final prospectus via an Internet Web site have the ability to access the final prospectus once such investors are supplied with notice of the Internet location of the Web site.

(3) While reviewing Company XYZ's preliminary prospectus on its Internet Web site, Investor John Doe consented to delivery of all future documents only through electronic mail, not by Web site access. Company XYZ subsequently places its final prospectus on its Internet Web site. Company XYZ then confirms by mail the sale of securities to John Doe. A note on the bottom of the confirmation states that the final prospectus is available on its Internet Web site and the location of that Web site.

Again, absent other factors such as John Doe's actually accessing the final prospectus on the Web site, the above-stated procedure of Company XYZ would not by itself satisfy the obligations to deliver the final prospectus to John Doe, as John Doe consented to delivery only by electronic mail, not via an Internet Web site. If consent is to be relied upon, the consent should indicate the specific electronic medium or media that may be used for delivery.

* * *

(5) Investor John Doe consents to delivery of all documents electronically via Company XYZ's Web site. Two days after consenting, John Doe realizes that the online service he subscribes to does not allow Internet access. John Doe notifies Company XYZ that he is revoking his consent for any electronic delivery as he is not able to access the Company's Internet Web site. Three weeks later, John Doe receives in the mail a confirmation of his purchase of Company XYZ's securities stating the Internet location of the Company's Web site where the final prospectus can be obtained.

Since John Doe revoked his consent for electronic delivery, the Company's notice to John Doe is insufficient because the Company knows that its attempted delivery through the Internet will not satisfy the statutory requirements for

John Doe. A final paper prospectus would have to be delivered to John Doe instead. Although a consent is revocable at any time, revocation would have to be given to the company or its agent a reasonable time before electronic delivery has commenced for the company to be on notice that electronic delivery will not satisfy the statutory requirements.

(6) Company LMN, a non-reporting issuer, commences an initial public offering. Company LMN agrees with its underwriter, Brokers Firm DFG, to place its preliminary prospectus on the Company's Internet Web site at least 48 hours prior to confirmations being sent. Investors John and Jane Doe are both expected to purchase securities in the Company's initial public offering. Both John and Jane Doe previously provided Company LMN with consents for electronic delivery through the Company's Internet Web site. Brokerage Firm DFG, pursuant to its prospectus delivery obligation under Exchange Act Rule 15c2–8(b), provides notice to John and Jane Doe at least 48 hours prior to sending them confirmations.

The underwriter may satisfy its obligation under Rule 15c2–8(b) to John and Jane Doe by this means since both have consented to electronic delivery through the Company's Internet Web site. Although consent was not provided directly to the underwriter, the underwriter can rely on the consent supplied to the Company. Similarly, had the consent been provided to the underwriter, the Company could rely on it as well.

* * *

(8) Company XYZ sends the final prospectus via electronic mail to those investors that previously had requested delivery by electronic mail.

The Company would meet its delivery obligation with this procedure.

(9) Company XYZ places a preliminary prospectus on its Internet Web site. After a material amendment to the registration statement, it is determined that recirculation of an updated prospectus will be required prior to effectiveness. Company XYZ updates the preliminary prospectus on its Web site.

The Company need only send notice of the update to those investors who are expected to purchase securities in the offering (or take other measures to deliver the information to those investors). There is no need to send notice to individuals who are not expected to purchase securities in the offering.

(10) Company XYZ places its final prospectus on its Internet Web site. Its underwriters mail confirmations of sales to all purchasers. At the same time the confirmations are mailed, the underwriters send via electronic mail notice of the location of the Internet Web site where the final prospectus is available. Notice is sent to all investors who had consented to electronic delivery via an Internet Web site and who provided their electronic mail addresses for purposes of being notified. To those investors that did not provide an electronic mail address but did consent to electronic delivery of the final prospectus, the underwriters mailed the notice of the location of the Internet Web site with the confirmation.

As the notice made investors aware of the availability and location of the electronic document, the delivery requirement would be satisfied.

(11) Company XYZ posts its final prospectus for sale of its common stock on its Internet Web site. Company XYZ's stock is traded on the New York Stock Exchange (NYSE). The NYSE requests 300 paper copies of Company XYZ's final prospectus pursuant to Securities Act Rule 153. Rather than

sending 300 copies of its final prospectus to the NYSE, Company XYZ provides the NYSE with notice of its Internet Web site, where the final prospectus can be accessed and downloaded.

This would be insufficient delivery under Securities Act Rule 153. Company XYZ must supply the 300 paper copies to the NYSE. The NYSE must be in the position to provide paper copies of Company XYZ's final prospectus because there is no reasonable expectation that delivery would otherwise be satisfied with regard to investors who do not use any electronic means to receive information. The NYSE would, however, satisfy its delivery obligations with respect to any investor who received delivery of the information through electronic means.

(12) Company XYZ places its preliminary prospectus on its Internet Web site. Upon effectiveness of its registration statement, the Company decides to deliver a term sheet pursuant to Securities Act Rule 434. The term sheet, however, will not be placed on the Company's Web site, but will be delivered in paper format with confirmation of the sale to all investors.

Delivery of a mixed medium final prospectus would satisfy delivery obligations. Generally, if investors received the preliminary prospectus electronically, issuers are encouraged to deliver all documents that constitute the final prospectus in electronic format.

(13) Company XYZ wants to deliver investors a CD–ROM version of its prospectus. The CD–ROM version includes within the prospectus a movie illustrating the Company's operations. Investors viewing the CD–ROM prospectus would not have to exit the prospectus in order to view the movie, as the movie is actually a part of the prospectus.

While Company XYZ may include the movie as part of the prospectus, it would need to file with the Commission as an appendix to the prospectus the script of the movie and a fair and accurate narrative description of the graphic or image material just as it would have to supplementally provide to the Commission scripts and descriptions of such material in sales material.

(14) Company XYZ places a copy of its final prospectus on its Internet Web site. The electronic final prospectus will remain there throughout the period for which delivery is required. Company XYZ also places supplemental sales literature on its Internet Web site. Both the sales literature and the prospectus can be accessed from the same menu, are clearly identified on, and appear in close proximity to each other; the supplemental sales literature may be accessed before viewing or downloading the prospectus.

Sales literature, whether in paper or electronic form, is required to be preceded or accompanied by a final prospectus. In this example, the prospectus would accompany the sales literature since investors can access both the prospectus and sales literature from the same menu. The sales literature and final prospectus should appear in close proximity to each other on the menu. For example, the sales literature should not be presented on the first page of a menu while the final prospectus is buried within the menu.

(15) Company XYZ places its sales literature in a discussion forum located on the Internet World Wide Web. The sales literature contains a hyperlink to the Company's final prospectus. While viewing the literature the individual can click on a box marked "final prospectus," and almost instantly the person will be linked directly to the Company's Web site and the final prospectus will appear on the person's computer screen.

Sales literature, whether in paper or electronic form, is required to be preceded or accompanied by a final prospectus. The hyperlink function enables the final prospectus to be viewed directly as if it were packaged in the same envelope as the sales literature. Therefore, the final prospectus would be considered to have accompanied the sales literature. Consequently, the placing of sales literature in a discussion forum on a Web site would satisfy delivery obligations provided that a hyperlink that provides direct access to the final prospectus is included.

(16) Company XYZ places a preliminary prospectus on its Internet Web site and provides direct access via a hyperlink to a research report on the Company written by ABC Corporation, a registered brokerage firm. The investor reviewing the preliminary prospectus can click on a box marked "ABC's research report" and the investor will be linked to the brokerage firm's Web site where the research report is available.

The hyperlink function provides the ability to access information located on another Web site almost instantaneously. This direct and quick access to ABC's research report would be similar to the Company including the paper version of the research report in the same envelope that it is using to mail the paper version of the preliminary prospectus to potential investors. During the waiting period, the Company may make offers only through the use of a preliminary prospectus, whether in paper or electronic format; therefore, its use of the research report under these circumstances would not be permissible.

(17) Company XYZ places its final prospectus on its Internet Web site. The Company then mails sales literature to individuals for whom delivery through the Internet Web site was effective (regardless of whether the individuals consented to delivery). Similarly, Brokerage Firm ABC mails Company XYZ sales literature to its customers for whom delivery through the Internet Web site was effective (regardless of whether the individuals consented to delivery). In the forepart of Company XYZ's sales literature is notice of the availability and Internet Web site location of its final prospectus.

The mailing of sales literature to these individuals is permissible, provided that notice of the availability of the final prospectus and its Internet Web site location accompanies or precedes the sales literature. When notice is included within sales literature, it should be in the forepart of the literature and clearly highlighted to make investors aware of the availability and location of the final prospectus.

(18) Company XYZ places a tombstone advertisement complying with Securities Act Rule 134 on its Internet Web site.

This would be permissible, provided that the advertisement otherwise complies with Rule 134.

(19) Company XYZ files a registration statement with the Commission. The Company then places a "tombstone" advertisement in accordance with Securities Act Rule 134 in the Wall Street Journal. In the advertisement the Company includes the name and address of the underwriter from whom a paper prospectus can be obtained as well as the location of its Internet Web site where an electronic prospectus can be obtained.

This inclusion of an electronic address for obtaining the materials in this "tombstone" advertisement would be permissible under Rule 134 * * *.

In 1996, the Commission extended the principles set forth in Securities Act Rel. No. 7233 to the delivery obligations of broker-dealers, transfer agents, and investment advisers.[1] This extension meant that confirmations of sale could be sent electronically (subject, of course, to the same basic notice, access, consent and record-keeping requirements as under Release 7233). The latest and most important statement by the SEC on electronic media came in 2000 in Securities Act Release No. 33–7856:

Use of Electronic Media

Releases Nos. 33–7856, 34–42728, IC–24426.
(April 28, 2000).

I. Introduction

By facilitating rapid and widespread information dissemination, the Internet has had a significant impact on capital-raising techniques and, more broadly, on the structure of the securities industry. Today, almost seven million people invest in the U.S. securities markets through online brokerage accounts. To serve this increasing interest in online trading, there has been a surge in online brokerage firms offering an array of financial services. Additionally, many publicly traded companies are incorporating Internet-based technology into their routine business operations, including setting up their own Web sites to furnish company and industry information. Some provide information about their securities and the markets in which their securities trade. Investment companies use the Internet to provide investors with fund-related information, as well as shareholder services and educational materials. Issuers of municipal securities also are beginning to use the Internet to provide information about themselves and their outstanding bonds, as well as new offerings of their securities. The increased availability of information through the Internet has helped to promote transparency, liquidity and efficiency in our capital markets.

This release is designed to provide guidance to issuers of all types, including operating companies, investment companies and municipal securities issuers as well as market intermediaries, on several issues involving the application of the federal securities laws to electronic media. In developing this guidance, we considered the significant benefits that investors can gain from the increased use of electronic media. We also considered the potential for electronic media, as instruments of inexpensive, mass communication, to be used to defraud the investing public. We believe that the guidance advances our central statutory goals: ensuring full and fair disclosure to investors; promoting the public interest, including investor protection, efficiency, competition and capital formation; and maintaining fair and orderly markets.

* * *

Today's interpretive guidance will do the following:

● Facilitate electronic delivery of communications by clarifying that

● investors may consent to electronic delivery telephonically;

● intermediaries may request consent to electronic delivery on a "global," multiple-issuer basis;

1. See Securities Act Release No. 33–7288 (May 9, 1996).

- issuers and intermediaries may deliver documents in portable document format, or PDF, with appropriate measures to assure that investors can easily access the documents; an embedded hyperlink within a Section 10 prospectus or any other document required to be filed or delivered under the federal securities laws causes the hyperlinked information to be a part of that document;

- the close proximity of information on a Web site to a Section 10 prospectus does not, by itself, make that information an ''offer to sell,'' ''offer for sale'' or ''offer'' within the meaning of Section 2(a)(3) of the Securities Act; and

- municipal securities underwriters may rely on a municipal securities issuer to identify the documents on the issuer's web site that comprise the preliminary, deemed final and final official statements. Reduce uncertainty regarding permissible web site content to encourage more widespread information dissemination to all investors by clarifying some of the facts and circumstances that may result in an issuer having adopted information on a third-party web site to which the issuer has established a hyperlink for purposes of the anti-fraud provisions of the federal securities laws; and

- general legal principles that govern permissible web site communications by issuers when in registration.

- Facilitate online offerings by clarifying

- general legal principles that broker-dealers should consider when developing and implementing procedures for online public offerings; and

- circumstances under which a third-party service provider may establish a web site to facilitate online private offerings.

II.   Interpretive Guidance

A.   Electronic Delivery

We first published our views on the use of electronic media to deliver information to investors in 1995. The 1995 Release focused on electronic delivery of prospectuses, annual reports to security holders and proxy solicitation materials under the Securities Act of 1933, the Securities Exchange Act of 1934 and the Investment Company Act of 1940. Our 1996 electronic media release focused on electronic delivery of required information by broker-dealers (including municipal securities dealers) and transfer agents under the Exchange Act and investment advisers under the Investment Advisers Act of 1940.

We believe that the framework for electronic delivery established in these releases continues to work well in today's technological environment. Issuers and market intermediaries therefore must continue to assess their compliance with legal requirements in terms of the three areas identified in the releases—notice, access and evidence of delivery. Although we believe that this framework continues to be appropriate, we provide below guidance that will clarify some regulatory issues relating to electronic delivery.

1.   Telephonic Consent

As noted above, one of the three elements of satisfactory electronic delivery is obtaining evidence of delivery. The 1995 Release provided that one method for satisfying the evidence-of-delivery element is to obtain an informed consent from an investor to receive information through a particular electronic medium. The 1996 Release stated that informed consent should be made by written or electronic means. Some securities lawyers have concluded that, based on the 1996 Release, telephonic consent generally is not permitted. Others have opined that telephonic consent may be permissible if an issuer or intermediary retains a record of the consent.

In today's markets, where speed is a priority, significant matters often are communicated telephonically. It is common (and increasingly popular), for instance, for security holders to vote proxies and even transfer assets over the telephone where permitted under applicable state law. In addition investors can place orders to trade securities over the telephone. We believe these practices have developed because business can be transacted as effectively over the telephone today as it can in paper. We are of the view, therefore, that an issuer or market intermediary may obtain an informed consent telephonically, as long as a record of that consent is retained. As with written or electronic consent, telephonic consent must be obtained in a manner that assures its authenticity.

2.   Global Consent

The 1995 Release stated that consent to electronic delivery could relate to all documents to be delivered by or on behalf of a single issuer. The 1995 Release also stated that an issuer could rely on consent obtained by a broker-dealer or other market intermediary. Some securities lawyers have questioned the permissible scope of consents that are obtained by brokerdealers or banks (or their agents) from investors who hold securities of multiple issuers in their brokerage, trust or other accounts. Specifically, they have asked whether an investor can consent to electronic delivery of all documents of any issuer in which that investor buys or owns securities through a particular intermediary.

We believe that an investor may give a global consent to electronic delivery—relating to all documents of any issuer—so long as the consent is informed. Given the broad scope of a global consent and its effect on an investor's ability to receive important documents, we believe intermediaries should take particular care to ensure that the investor understands that he or she is providing a global consent to electronic delivery. For example, a global consent that is merely a provision of an agreement that an investor is required to execute to receive other services may not fully inform the investor. To best inform investors, broker-dealers could obtain consent from a new customer through an account-opening agreement that contains a separate section with a separate electronic delivery authorization, or through a separate document altogether. We believe that a global consent to electronic delivery would not be an informed consent if the opening of a brokerage account were conditioned upon providing the consent. Therefore, absent other evidence of delivery, we believe that if the opening of an account were conditioned upon providing a global consent, evidence of delivery would not be established.

Similarly, because of the broad scope of a global consent, an investor should be advised of his or her right to revoke the consent at any time and receive all covered documents in paper format. We recognize that a system allowing an investor to revoke consent to electronic delivery with respect to some issuers' documents, but not others, may be difficult to administer. An intermediary might be uncertain about whether or not it has complied with its delivery obligations. Thus, intermediaries, if they wish, may require revocation on an "all-or-none" basis, provided that this policy is adequately disclosed when the consent is obtained.

As noted in the 1995 Release, an informed consent must specify the type of electronic media to be used (for example, a limited proprietary system or an Internet web site). This is particularly true for global consents where multiple documents may be delivered through different media. An investor should not be disadvantaged by inadvertently consenting to electronic delivery through a medium that is not compatible with the investor's computer hardware and software.

3.   Use of Portable Document Format

The 1995 Release stated that "the use of a particular medium should not be so burdensome that intended recipients cannot effectively access the information provided." Many issuers have interpreted this statement to preclude delivery of PDF documents which cannot be accessed without special software. Instead, those issuers use hypertext markup language, or HTML, which may be viewed without the need for additional software. We believe that issuers and market intermediaries delivering documents electronically may use PDF if it is not so burdensome as effectively to prevent access. For example, PDF could be used if issuers and intermediaries inform investors of the requirements necessary to download PDF when obtaining consent to electronic delivery; and provide investors with any necessary software and technical assistance at no cost.

4.   Clarification of the "Envelope Theory"

The 1995 Release provided a number of examples designed to assist issuers and market intermediaries in meeting their delivery obligations through electronic media. One example provided that documents in close proximity on the same web site menu are considered delivered together. Other examples confirmed the proposition that documents hyperlinked to each other are considered delivered together as if they were in the same paper envelope. The premise underling these examples has come to be called the "envelope theory."

The purpose of these examples was to provide assurance to issuers and intermediaries that they are delivering multiple documents simultaneously to investors when so required by the federal securities laws. For example, in a registered offering, sales literature cannot be delivered to an investor unless the registration statement has been declared effective and a final prospectus accompanies or precedes the sales literature. It is easy to establish concurrent delivery when multiple documents are included in one paper envelope that is delivered by U.S. postal mail or a private delivery service. When electronic delivery is used, however, it is somewhat more difficult to establish whether multiple documents may be considered delivered together. The guidance provided in the 1995 Release about the use of "virtual" envelopes was intended to alleviate this difficulty.

Nevertheless, some issuers and intermediaries believe that the envelope theory has created ambiguities as to appropriate web site content when an issuer is in registration. Some securities lawyers have expressed concern that if a Section 10 prospectus is posted on a web site, the operation of the envelope theory causes everything on the web site to become part of that prospectus. They also have raised concerns that information on a web site that is outside of the four corners of the Section 10 prospectus, but in close proximity to it, would be considered free writing.

Information on a web site would be part of a Section 10 prospectus only if an issuer (or person acting on behalf of the issuer, including an intermediary with delivery obligations) acts to make it part of the prospectus. For example, if an issuer includes a hyperlink within a Section 10 prospectus, the hyperlinked information would become a part of that prospectus. When embedded hyperlinks are used, the hyperlinked information must be filed as part of the prospectus in the effective registration statement and will be subject to liability under Section 11 of the Securities Act. In contrast, a hyperlink from an external document to a Section 10 prospectus would result in both documents being delivered together, but would not result in the non-prospectus document being deemed part of the prospectus. Issuers nevertheless may be subject to liability under Section 12 of the Securities Act for the external document depending on whether the external document is itself a prospectus or part of one.

With respect to the free writing concern, the focus on the location of the posted prospectus is misplaced. Regardless of whether or where the Section 10 prospectus is posted, the web site content must be reviewed in its entirety to determine whether it contains impermissible free writing. The Commission staff will continue to raise questions about information on an issuer s web site that is either inconsistent with the issuer's Section 10 prospectus or that would constitute an "offer to sell," "offer for sale" or "offer" under Section 2(a)(3) of the Securities Act.

B.   Web Site Content

Issuers have raised a number of questions about their responsibility for the content of their web sites, both when they are in registration and when they are not. It is important for issuers, including municipal securities issuers, to keep in mind that the federal securities laws apply in the same manner to the content of their web sites as to any other statements made by or attributable to them. While many of these questions may be resolved by reference to current law, we recognize that further guidance would be helpful on two fundamental issues affecting web site content. We first consider issuer responsibility for hyperlinked information under the anti-fraud provisions of the federal securities laws. We then discuss the regulation of issuers' web site communications during registered offerings.

1.   Issuer Responsibility for Hyperlinked Information

Issuers are responsible for the accuracy of their statements that reasonably can be expected to reach investors or the securities markets regardless of the medium through which the statements are made, including the Internet. Some issuers have asked whether they can be held liable under Section 10(b) of the Exchange Act and Rule 10b–5 for third-party information to which they have hyperlinked from their web sites. This concern stems largely from case law and our findings in the 1997 settlement of an enforcement action. These questions focus on the consequences of issuer hyperlinks to analyst research reports, although issuers also have expressed concern about their potential liability for hyperlinks to other information as well.

Whether third-party information is attributable to an issuer depends upon whether the issuer has involved itself in the preparation of the information or explicitly or implicitly endorsed or approved the information. In the case of issuer liability for statements by third parties such as analysts, the courts and we have referred to the first line of inquiry as the "entanglement" theory and the second as the "adoption" theory.

In the case of hyperlinked information, liability under the "entanglement" theory would depend upon an issuer's level of pre-publication involvement in the preparation of the information. In contrast, liability under the "adoption" theory would depend upon whether, after its publication, an issuer, explicitly or implicitly, endorses or approves the hyperlinked information.

Below we discuss factors that we believe are relevant in deciding whether an issuer has adopted information on a third-party web site to which it has established a hyperlink. While the factors we discuss below form a useful framework of analysis, we caution that they are neither exclusive nor exhaustive. We are not establishing a "bright line" mechanical test. We do not mean to suggest that any single factor, standing alone, would or would not dictate the outcome of the analysis.

a. Context of the Hyperlink

Whether third-party information to which an issuer has established a hyperlink is attributable to the issuer is likely to be influenced by what the issuer says about the hyperlink or what is implied by the context in which the issuer places the hyperlink. An issuer might explicitly endorse the hyperlinked information. For example, a hyperlink might be incorporated in or accompany a statement such as "XYZ's web site contains the best description of our business that is currently available." Likewise, a hyperlink might be used to suggest that the hyperlinked information supports a particular assertion on an issuer's web site. For example, the hyperlink may be incorporated in or accompany a statement such as, "As reported in Today's Widget, our company is the leading producer of widgets worldwide." Moreover, even when an issuer remains silent about the hyperlink, the context nevertheless may imply that the hyperlinked information is attributable to the issuer.

In the context of a document required to be filed or delivered under the federal securities laws, we believe that when an issuer embeds a hyperlink to a web site within the document, the issuer should always be deemed to be adopting the hyperlinked information. In addition, when an issuer is in registration, if the issuer establishes a hyperlink (that is not embedded within a disclosure document) from its web site to information that meets the definition of an "offer to sell," "offer for sale" or "offer" under Section 2(a)(3) of the Securities Act, a strong inference arises that the issuer has adopted that information for purposes of Section 10(b) of the Exchange Act and Rule 10b–5.

b. Risk of Confusion

Another factor we would consider in determining whether an issuer has adopted hyperlinked information is the presence or absence of precautions against investor confusion about the source of the information. Hyperlinked information on a third-party web site may be less likely to be attributed to an issuer if the issuer makes the information accessible only after a visitor to its web site has been presented with an intermediate screen that clearly and prominently indicates that the visitor is leaving the issuer's web site and that the information subsequently viewed is not the issuer's. Similarly, there may be less likelihood of confusion about whether an issuer has adopted hyperlinked information if the issuer ensures that access to the information is preceded or accompanied by a clear and prominent statement from the issuer disclaiming responsibility for, or endorsement of, the information. In contrast, the risk of investor confusion is higher when information on a third-party web site is framed or inclined. We are not suggesting, however, that statements and disclaimers will insulate an issuer from liability for hyperlinked information when the relevant facts and circumstances otherwise indicate that the issuer has adopted the information.

c.   Presentation of the Hyperlinked Information

The presentation of the hyperlinked information by an issuer is relevant in determining whether the issuer has adopted the information. For example, an issuer's efforts to direct an investor's attention to particular information by selectively providing hyperlinks is a relevant consideration in determining whether the information so hyperlinked has been adopted by the issuer. Where a wealth of information as to a particular matter is available, and where the information accessed by the hyperlink is not representative of the available information, an issuer's creation and maintenance of the hyperlink could be an endorsement of the selected information. Similarly, an issuer that selectively establishes and terminates hyperlinks to third-party web sites depending upon the nature of the information about the issuer on a particular site or sites may be viewed as attempting to control the flow of information to investors. Again, this suggests that the issuer has adopted the information during the periods that the hyperlink is operative.

Finally, the layout of the screen containing a hyperlink is relevant in determining whether an issuer will be deemed to have adopted hyperlinked information. Any action to differentiate a particular hyperlink from other hyperlinks on an issuer's web site, through its prominence, size or location, or to draw an investor's attention to the hyperlink, may suggest that the issuer favors the hyperlinked information over other information available to the investor on or through the site. For example, a particular hyperlink might be presented in a different color, type font or size from other hyperlinks on an issuer's web site. Where the method of presenting the hyperlink influences disproportionately an investor's decision to view third-party information, the hyperlinked information is more likely attributable to an issuer.

2.   Issuer Communications During a Registered Offering

Because of the increasing use by issuers of web sites to communicate in the ordinary course of business with their security holders, customers, suppliers and others, issuers have asked us for guidance on the permissible content of their Internet communications when they are in registration An issuer in registration must consider the application of Section 5 of the Securities Act to all of its communications with the public, in our view, this includes information on an issuer's web site as well as information on a third-party web site to which the issuer has established a hyperlink The Securities Act and accompanying regulations currently limit information about an offering that issuers and persons acting on their behalf may provide to investors to the content of the Section 10 prospectus and any permissible communications under available Securities Act safe harbors. Thus, information on a third-party web site to which an issuer has established a hyperlink that meets the definition of an "offer to sell," "offer for sale" or "offer" under Section 2(a)(3) of the Securities Act raises a strong inference that the hyperlinked information is attributable to the issuer for purposes of a Section 5 analysis. To ensure compliance with Section 5, an issuer in registration should carefully review its Web site and any information on third-party Web sites to which it hyperlinks.

An issuer that is in registration should maintain communications with the public as long as the subject matter of the communications is limited to ordinary-course business and financial information, which may include the following:

- advertisements concerning the issuer's products and services;
- Exchange Act reports required to be filed with the Commission;
- proxy statements, annual reports to security holders and dividend notices;
- press announcements concerning business and financial developments;
- answers to unsolicited telephone inquiries concerning business matters from securities analysts, financial analysts, security holders and participants in the communications field who have a legitimate interest in the issuer's affairs; and
- security holders' meetings and responses to security holder inquiries relating to these matters.

Statements containing information falling within any of the foregoing categories, or an available Securities Act safe harbor, may be posted on an issuer's Web site when in registration, either directly or indirectly through a hyperlink to a third-party Web site, including the Web site of a broker-dealer that is participating in the registered offering.

Although our original guidance was directed at communications by reporting issuers when in registration, it also should be observed by non-reporting issuers preparing to offer securities to the public for the first time. A non-reporting issuer that has established a history of ordinary course business communications through its Web site should be able to continue to provide business and financial information on its site consistent with our original guidance. A non-reporting issuer preparing for its first registered public offering that contemporaneously establishes a Web site, however, may need to apply this guidance more strictly when evaluating its web site content because it may not have established a history of ordinary-course business communications with the marketplace. Thus, its web site content may condition the market for the offering and, due to the unfamiliarity of the marketplace with the issuer or its business, investors may be unable to view the issuer's communications in an appropriate context while the issuer is in registration. In other words, investors may be less able to distinguish offers to sell an issuer's securities in a registered offering from product or service promotional activities or other business or financial information.

C. Online Offerings

1. Online Public Offerings

Increasingly, issuers and broker-dealers are conducting public securities offerings online, using the Internet, electronic mail and other electronic media to solicit prospective investors. Examples of these electronic communications include investor questionnaires on investment qualifications, broker-dealer account-opening procedures and directives on how to submit indications of interest or offers to buy in the context of a specific public offering. These developments present both potential benefits and dangers to investors. On the positive side, numerous "online brokers" appear to have begun to give individual investors more access to public offerings, including initial public offerings, or IPOs. Still, dangers accompany these expanded online investment opportunities. Retail investors often are unfamiliar with the public offering process generally, and, in particular, with new marketing practices that have evolved in connection with online public offerings. We are concerned that there may be insufficient information available to investors to enable them to understand fully the online public offering process. We also are concerned that investors are being solicited to make hasty, and perhaps uninformed, investment decisions.

Two fundamental legal principles should guide issuers, underwriters and other offering participants in online public offerings. First, offering participants can neither sell, nor make contracts to sell, a security before effectiveness of the related Securities Act registration statement. A corollary to this principle dictates that "[n]o offer to buy . . . can be accepted and no part of the purchase price can be received until the registration statement has become effective."

Second, until delivery of the final prospectus has been completed, written offers and offers transmitted by radio and television cannot be made outside of a Section 10 prospectus except in connection with business combinations. After filing the registration statement, two limited exceptions provide some flexibility to offering participants to publish notices of the offering. Following effectiveness, offering participants may disseminate sales literature and other writings so long as these materials are accompanied or preceded by a final prospectus. Oral offers, in contrast, are permissible as soon as the registration statement has been filed. Offering participants may use any combination of electronic and more traditional media, such as paper or the telephone, to communicate with prospective investors, provided that use of these media is in compliance with the Securities Act.

These key legal principles must underpin the development of appropriate procedures for online offerings. To date, the Division of Corporation Finance has reviewed numerous procedures in connection with online distributions of IPOs. The Division also has issued a no-action letter regarding permissible procedures for the use of the Internet in IPOs. We understand, however, that a number of online brokers have urged that we make additional regulatory accommodations to facilitate online offerings. We appreciate the benefits that technology brings to the offering process and fully support the need to craft a regulatory system that maximizes these benefits. We also are mindful of our investor protection mandate and the fundamental principles established by the Securities Act for the offer and sale of securities. Many of the procedures urged upon us by online brokers may be properly the subject of regulatory action. Accordingly, in this release, we do not prescribe any specific procedures that must be followed. Instead, we will continue to analyze this area as practice, procedures and technology evolve, with a view to possible regulatory action in the future. Additionally, the Commission staff will continue to review procedures submitted in connection with online offerings.

2. Online Private Offerings under Regulation D

Broad use of the Internet for exempt securities offerings under Regulation D is problematic because of the requirement that these offerings not involve a general solicitation or advertising. When we first considered whether exempt offerings could be conducted over the Internet, we concluded that an issuer's unrestricted, and therefore publicly available, Internet web site would not be consistent with the restriction on general solicitation and advertising. Specifically, the 1995 Release included an example indicating that an issuer's use of an Internet web site in connection with a purported private offering would constitute a "general solicitation" and therefore disqualify the offering as "private."

Subsequently, the Divisions of Corporation Finance and Market Regulation issued interpretive guidance to a registered broker-dealer and its affiliate, IPONET, that planned to invite previously unknown prospective investors to complete a questionnaire posted on the affiliate's Internet web site "as a means of building a customer base and database of accredited and sophisticated investors" for the broker-dealer. A password-restricted web page permitting access to private offerings would become available to a prospective investor only after the affiliated broker-dealer determined that the investor was "accredited" or "sophisticated" within the meaning of Regulation D. Additionally, a prospective investor could purchase securities only in offerings that were posted on the restricted web site after the investor had been qualified by the affiliated broker-dealer as an accredited or sophisticated investor and had opened an account with the broker-dealer. The Divisions' interpretive letter was based on an important and well-known principle established over a decade ago: a general solicitation is not present when there is a pre-existing, substantive relationship between an issuer, or its broker-dealer, and the offerees.

We understand that some entities have engaged in practices that deviate substantially from the facts in the IPONET interpretive letter. Specifically, third-party service providers who are neither registered broker-dealers nor affiliated with registered broker-dealers have established web sites that generally invite prospective investors to qualify as accredited or sophisticated as a prelude to participation, on an access-restricted basis, in limited or private offerings transmitted on those web sites. Moreover, some non-broker-dealer web site operators are not even requiring prospective investors to complete questionnaires providing information needed to form a reasonable belief regarding their accreditation or sophistication. Instead, these web sites permit interested persons to certify themselves as accredited or sophisticated merely by checking a box.

These web sites, particularly those allowing for self-accreditation, raise significant concerns as to whether the offerings that they facilitate involve general solicitations. In these instances, one method of ensuring that a general solicitation is not involved is to establish the existence of a "preexisting, substantive relationship." Generally, staff interpretations of whether a "preexisting, substantive relationship" exists have been limited to procedures established by broker-dealers in connection with their customers. This is because traditional broker-dealer relationships require that a broker-dealer deal fairly with, and make suitable recommendations to, customers, and, thus, implies that a substantive relationship exists between the broker-dealer and its customers. We have long stated, however, that the presence or absence of a general solicitation is always dependent on the facts and circumstances of each particular case. Thus, there may be facts and circumstances in which a third party, other than a registered broker-dealer, could establish a "pre-existing, substantive relationship" sufficient to avoid a "general solicitation."

Notwithstanding the analysis for purposes of Section 5 of the Securities Act, web site operators need to consider whether the activities that they are undertaking require them to register as broker-dealers. Section 15 of the Exchange Act essentially makes it unlawful for a broker or dealer "to effect any transactions in, or to induce or attempt to induce the purchase or sale of, any security (other than an exempted security or commercial paper, bankers' acceptances, or commercial bills)" unless the broker or dealer is registered with the Commission. The "exempted securities" for which broker-dealer registration is not required under Section 15 are strictly limited. They do not include, for example, securities issued under Regulations A, D or S or privately placed securities that would be "restricted" securities under Securities Act Rule 144. Thus, broker-dealer registration generally is required to effect transactions in securities that are exempt from registration under the Securities Act. In other words, third-party service providers that act as brokers in connection with securities offerings are required to register as broker-dealers, even when the securities are exempt from registration under the Securities Act. . . .

D. Technology Concepts

Each technological advance brings changes to the structure of the capital markets and the securities industry. While we believe that the guidance provided in this release will be useful in the near term, we also recognize that we will need to reexamine our regulatory system and interpretive guidance as technology evolves. We will continue to examine and consider the removal of regulations that pose unnecessary barriers to electronic commerce and maintain those regulations that are essential to protect investors. In that regard, we request comment below on specific issues that may arise in the future in several areas. We also solicit comment on whether there are issues involving electronic media under the federal securities laws that we have not identified.

1. Access Equals Delivery

Various commentators have suggested that additional regulatory changes may be warranted in the use of electronic media for delivery purposes. The 1995 Release stated that issuers and market intermediaries with delivery obligations would need to continue to make information available in paper form until such time as electronic media became more universally accessible and accepted. Some believe that this time has come and, therefore, that we should shift from the present delivery model to an "access-equals-delivery" model. Under the latter model, investors would be assumed to have access to the Internet, thereby allowing delivery to be accomplished solely by an issuer posting a document on the issuer's or a third-party's web site.

We believe that the time for an "access-equals-delivery" model has not arrived yet. Internet access is more prevalent than in 1995, but many people in this country still do not enjoy the benefits of ready access to electronic media. Moreover, even investors who are online are unlikely to rely on the Internet as their sole means of obtaining information from issuers or intermediaries with delivery obligations. Some investors decline electronic delivery because they do not wish to review a large document on their computer screens. Others decline electronic delivery because of the time that it takes to download and print a document.

We request comment, however, as to whether there are circumstances in which, consistent with investor protection, an "access-equals-delivery" model might be appropriate. How many U.S. households currently have Internet access? Is there data supporting the conclusion that most investors have access to the Internet? Similarly, is there data supporting the belief that investors who are online will rely on the Internet as their sole means of obtaining information from issuers or intermediaries? Assuming that this data exists, how will investors know when disclosure information has been posted on an issuer's web site? If we were to adopt an ''access-equals-delivery'' model, would we be creating a system that requires ownership of a late-model, sophisticated computer to participate in the securities markets?

E. Examples

A series of examples is provided below to illustrate various applications of the interpretations outlined in this release and to provide guidance in applying them to specific facts and circumstances. We note, however, that these examples are non-exclusive methods of ways to comply with the above interpretations. Additionally, the analysis required to determine compliance with the federal securities laws is fact-specific, and any different or additional facts might require a different conclusion. We request comment on whether other examples might be appropriate for publication.

(1) Investor John Doe gives XYZ Delivery Service his informed consent over the telephone using automated touch tone instructions (after accessing the service using a personal identification number). The automated instructions informed John Doe of the manner, costs and risks of electronic delivery. The consent related to electronic delivery of documents. Before delivering any electronic documents to Investor John Doe, XYZ Delivery Service sends Investor John Doe a letter confirming that he had consented to electronic delivery.

The confirming letter sent by XYZ Delivery Service provides assurance that John Doe consented to the same extent as if he had provided a written or electronic consent. Thus, XYZ Delivery Service's procedures would evidence satisfaction of delivery. We also note that XYZ Delivery Service has reason to be assured of the authenticity of John Doe's telephonic consent because of his use of a personal identification number.

(2) In speaking with Broker DEF over the telephone, Investor Jane Doe (a long-term customer of Broker DEF) consents to electronic delivery to all future documents of Company XYZ on Company XYZ's Internet web site. Broker DEF agrees to notify Jane Doe by electronic mail (or other acceptable means of notification) that Company XYZ has posted the documents on its web site when the posting occurs. Before obtaining Jane Doe's consent, Broker DEF advises Jane Doe that she may incur certain costs associated with delivery in this manner (for example, online time and printing) and possible risks (for example, system outages). Broker DEF also advises Jane Doe that the term of the consent is indefinite but that the consent can be revoked at any time. Broker DEF maintains a signed and dated memorandum in its files regarding the details of the conversation.

In this situation, Jane Doe's consent would be informed regarding the manner, costs and risks of electronic delivery. We also note that Broker DEF has reason to be assured of the authenticity of Jane Doe's telephonic consent because Jane Doe is well known to Broker DEF.

(3) In seeking a global consent to electronic delivery from Investor John Doe, Broker DEF specifies that the electronic media that may be used to deliver documents will be CD–ROM, an Internet web site, electronic mail or facsimile

transmission, and further advises John Doe that if he does not have access to all of these media he should not consent to electronic delivery. John Doe consents to electronic delivery from Broker DEF.

In this situation, John Doe's consent would be informed regarding the manner of electronic delivery. The consent need not specify which form of media a specific issuer may use.

(4) Investor Jane Doe consents to delivery via a third-party delivery service's Internet web site of all future documents of Company ABC, Company XYZ and any additional companies in which she invests in the future. Jane Doe subsequently purchases securities of Company DEF. Thereafter, Company XYZ and Company DEF post their final prospectuses on the third-party web site and notify Jane Doe by electronic mail (or other acceptable means of notification) of the availability of the prospectuses. Company ABC does not post its prospectus on the third-party web site but delivers a CD–ROM version of its prospectus.

Company XYZ has satisfied its delivery obligations. Additionally, although not specifically identified in the consent, Company DEF has satisfied its delivery obligations because the consent covered delivery by companies added at a later date. Absent other factors indicating that Jane Doe actually accessed Company ABC's CD–ROM prospectus, however, Company ABC's procedure would not satisfy its delivery obligations because Jane Doe consented to delivery only by an Internet web site. If consent is to be relied upon, the consent must cover the specific electronic medium or media that may be used for delivery.

(5) Investor John Doe consents to delivery of all future documents of Company XYZ electronically via Company *XYZ's* Internet web site, including documents delivered in PDF. The form of consent advises John Doe of the system requirements necessary for receipt of documents in PDF and cautions that downloading time may be slow. Company XYZ places its proxy soliciting materials and annual report to security holders in PDF on its Internet web site, with a hyperlink on the same screen enabling users to download a free copy of Adobe Acrobat (software permitting PDF viewing) and a toll-free telephone number that investors can use to contact someone during Company XYZ's business hours for technical assistance or to request a paper copy of a document.

Company XYZ has satisfied its delivery obligations. Under these circumstances, John Doe can effectively access the information provided.

(6) Company XYZ, which is engaged in a public offering of its securities, places its preliminary prospectus on its Internet web site. In the Business section of the prospectus, Company XYZ has placed a hyperlink to a report by a marketing research firm located on a third-party web site regarding Company XYZ's industry.

Because the hyperlink is embedded within the prospectus, the report becomes a part of the prospectus and must be filed with the Commission. In addition, Company XYZ must obtain a written consent from the person preparing the report in accordance with Securities Act Rule 436, 17 CFR 230.436. This consent also must be filed with the Commission. Moreover, the report will be subject to liability under Section 11 of the Securities Act, as well as other anti-fraud provisions of the federal securities laws.

(7) Company XYZ, which is engaged in a public offering of its securities, places its preliminary prospectus on its Internet web site. Each of the topics in

the Table of Contents is a hyperlink, allowing investors to pick a topic and immediately be hyperlinked to the section in the prospectus relating to that topic.

The hyperlinks present no federal securities law issues. The hyperlinks do no more than allow investors to turn electronically to a specific page in the prospectus.

(8) Company XYZ, which is engaged in a public offering of its securities, places its preliminary prospectus on its Internet web site. Immediately following the button for the prospectus on the web site, Company XYZ offers investors the ability to download its financial statements in spreadsheet format. This financial information is not modified in any way from that contained in the filed document.

The provision of financial statements in spreadsheet format would be permissible when the download results only in a mere difference in format without any difference in text. The completeness of the financial statements must not be compromised by any difference in the electronic version from the paper version. . . .

––––––––

1. *Online Offerings.* The market is also responding to the revolution in electronic communications by restructuring the offering process. The change has been most evident in firms struggling to reach the elusive retail investor. Currently, it is likely that 80% or more of the stock in a hot IPO is initially sold to institutional investors. There multiple reasons that explain why underwriters prefer the institutional investor to retail investors (including that the institutions may direct their lucrative brokerage commissions to the underwriters in return for allocations of "hot" IPO offerings). But at least one reason for this pattern is the difficulty that underwriters face in confirming a sale to an individual customer on the effective date. Logistically, it is difficult to telephone hundreds (and possibly thousands) of retail customers within a limited time period and secure their final post-effective consent to accept shares earlier reserved for them out of the particular underwriter's allocation. Particularly as the size of the typical IPO grew during the late 1990's, this need to secure post-effective date consent proved to he a practical obstacle for the online brokerage industry, most of whose customers are retail investors.

In response, one online broker, Wit Capital Corporation, secured the SEC's consent in 1999 to a significant revision in the procedures by which shares are sold to investors in a public offering. Under the no-action letter that Wit Capital received, it was permitted to solicit revocable offers to buy from investors during the waiting period, which it could accept after the effective date of the registration statement. Thus, instead of the customer accepting the underwriter's offer to sell after the effective date, the underwriter confirmed by email or fax to the customer its acceptance of the customer's offer to buy. Formal as this distinction may sound, its practical significance was that it eliminated any need to contact the customer on the morning of effectiveness. The SEC, however conditioned use of this procedure on several important conditions.[2] First, customers who made a conditional offer to buy prior to the effective date could withdraw the offer at any time prior to Wit Capital's

2. Wit Capital Corporation, 1999 SEC No–Act. LEXIS 620 (July 14, 1999).

acceptance of it. Second, Wit Capital would have to obtain a re-confirmation email from each customer of the customer's conditional offer to buy after the time of pricing, and such reconfirmation would have to come from the customer after the time of pricing and within two business days of the expected date of effectiveness; such a re-confirmation from the customer would also remain valid for only five business days (thus ensuring that in the event that the effective date was significantly delayed, the customer's consent would have to be again secured). In effect, this procedure precluded long-term advance offers to buy from the customer, and required Wit Capital to contact the customer and obtain the customer's consent just prior to effectiveness (and after pricing).

The Wit Capital procedure still leaves questions open that the SEC has not yet addressed about the possible misuse of conditional offers to buy in sticky or delayed offerings. One reason that the SEC may have been willing to accept Wit Capital procedure is that Wit Capital agreed to offer all its allotted shares in such an offering on a first-come, first-served basis, with no preference given to institutions.

2. *"Free Stock."* To increase their subscriber base, some Internet companies in the late 1990's devised a series of "stock giveaway" or "free stock" programs under which persons who registered with their website (or who simply visited it) received free stock of the issuer. Because a larger subscriber base enable the issuer to charge more to advertisers (and to appear a more significant presence in its field, as it approached its IPO), this arrangement made sense to issuers, who in turn sought to convince the SEC that no sale had been made to the recipient of these shares, because the recipient had paid nothing and made no commitment to the issuer. In a series of "no action" letters, the SEC rejected these requests, finding that the issuance of securities in consideration of a person's registration on, or visit to, an issuer's Internet site would be an event of sale within the meaning of Section 2(a)(3) of the 1933 Act.[3] Indeed, even when the recipient needed only to send a self-addressed envelope to the issuer, the SEC has taken a similar position, finding that such a "registration" with the issuer by the recipient conferred "value" on the issuer and so came within Section 2(a)(3).[4]

SECTION 6.   JUDICIAL TREATMENT OF THE "PROSPECTUS" CONCEPT

Diskin v. Lomasney & Co.

United States Court of Appeals, Second Circuit, 1971.
452 F.2d 871.

[Plaintiff Diskin and defendant Lomasney had conversations with respect to the securities of two companies, Ski Park City West S. I. and Continental Travel Ltd. Lomasney had agreed to sell up to 60,000 common shares of the former on a "best efforts" basis and was the principal underwriter for the sale of 350,000 common shares of the latter. A registration statement with respect

---

3. Simplystocks.com, 1999 SEC No–Act. LEXIS 131 (February 4, 1999); *Vanderkam & Sanders,* 1999 SEC No–Act. LEXIS 96 (January 27, 1999).

4. Jones and Rutten, 1999 SEC No–Act. LEXIS 555 (June 8, 1999).

to the shares of Continental had been filed with the SEC, but did not become effective until February 11, 1969. In the meantime, however, on September 17, 1968, Lomasney sent Diskin a final prospectus for Ski Park City West, as to which a registration statement had become effective, together with a letter as follows:

"I am enclosing herewith, a copy of the Prospectus on SKI PARK CITY WEST. This letter will also assure you that if you take 1,000 shares of SKI PARK CITY WEST at the issue price, we will commit to you the sale at the public offering price when, as and if issued, 5,000 shares of CONTINENTAL TRAVEL, LTD."

Diskin thereupon placed an order for the 1,000 shares of Ski Park City West, received a written confirmation, and later paid for the shares.

On February 12, 1969, after the Continental Travel registration statement had become effective, Lomasney sent Diskin a confirmation of the sale of 5,000 shares of Continental Travel at $12 per share, without any further communication. Subsequently, Diskin received from Lomasney a final prospectus for these shares. Diskin thereupon paid for the shares, and received delivery. Later, he demanded rescission, and upon refusal, he brought this action under § 12(1), claiming that the letter, insofar as it related to the shares of Continental Travel, was a violation of § 5(b)(1) of the 1933 Act.

The district judge dismissed the complaint on the ground that the letter relating to the Continental Travel shares came within the exclusion set forth in the last sentence of § 2(3) of the 1933 Act.]

■ FRIENDLY, CHIEF JUDGE: * * *

We have considered whether, despite the error in dismissing the complaint on this ground, the judgment could be affirmed on the basis that a registration statement concerning the Continental Travel shares had been filed prior to September 17, 1968, although it had not yet become effective. See § 5(c). However, the mere filing of a registration statement does not ensure the legality of *any* written offer made during the post-filing, pre-effective period; to be lawful, such written offers must be made by way of a "prospectus" which meets the requirements of § 10. See § 5(b)(1). * * * We perceive no basis for disagreeing with Professor Loss' summary of the law in this respect:

> In sum there are five legal ways in which offers may be made during the waiting period even if the mails or interstate facilities are used: by means of (1) oral communication, (2) the "tombstone ad," whether the old-fashioned variety under § 2(10)(b) or the expanded type under Rule 134 (successor to the old "identifying statement"), (3) the preliminary prospectus under Rule 433 [issued pursuant to § 10(b)] (successor to the "red herring prospectus"), (4) the "buff card" type of summary prospectus independently prepared under § 10(b) and Rule 434, and (5) the summary prospectus filed as part of the registration statement under § 10(b) and Rule 434a (successor to the old "newspaper prospectus" but not limited to newspapers).[a]

I Loss, Securities Regulation 243 (2d ed. 1961). See also Jennings & Marsh, Securities Regulation 89–92 (2d ed. 1968). The letter of September 17, 1968,

---

a. The bracketed material was inserted by the Court. In the 1982 program integrating disclosure obligations, former Rule 433 was redesignated as Rule 430 and Rule 434 was consolidated with Rule 434a and redesignated as Rule 431.

was none of these. Indeed, the confirmation of February 12, 1969, was a further violation unless a prospectus had been furnished, see §§ 2(10) and 5(b)(1), which the agreed statement does not say.

We pass therefore to the arguments which defendants made in their memorandum, which the district court did not reach. These were (1) that the letter was not an "offer" but was a mere expression of willingness to sell; (2) that the violation was cured by Diskin's receipt of a prospectus prior to the actual purchase; and (3) that the action was brought more than one year after the violation and was thus untimely under § 13 of the Securities Act.

Although there is a paucity of authority on these issues, we think none constituted a valid defense. The statutory language defining "offer" in § 2(3) "goes well beyond the common law concept of an offer." I Loss, supra, at 181; cf. Carl M. Loeb, Rhoades & Co., Securities Exch. Act Release No. 5870, at 7–8 (1959) * * *. Consequently, we entertain no doubt that the portion of the letter of September 17 dealing with the Continental Travel shares constituted an "offer" within § 2(3). Moreover, whether or not a dealer can lawfully "make a conditional and revocable offer to sell [without employing any of the five established procedures] if it is made clear that the offer cannot be accepted until the effective date," see I Loss, supra, at 224, the offer of September 17 did not measure up to that standard since it was not revocable. This case, where Lomasney apparently confirmed the sale without any further word from Diskin, would be a peculiarly unattractive one for endeavoring to carve out an exception to the statutory words. Indeed, as previously indicated, the confirmation, if unaccompanied by a prospectus, was itself a violation of § 5(b)(1).

On the second point, we again agree with Professor Loss that "[w]hatever doubt there may once have been as to the applicability of § 12(1) to illegal offers [followed by legal sales] was resolved when the original definition of sale was split into separate definitions of 'sale' and 'offer' in 1954, with the incidental amendment of § 12(1) to refer to any person 'who offers or sells a security in violation of section 5' so as 'to preserve the effect of the present law' by not excluding the newly permissible pre-effective offers from liabilities under § 12." III Loss, supra, at 1695–96. With respect to the one-year period of limitation, although § 13 dates this from the "violation" in cases of claims under § 12(1), it would be unreasonable to read § 13 as starting the short period for an action at a date before the action could have been brought—a construction which might lead in some extreme cases to a running of the statute of limitations before the claim had even arisen. Furthermore, the limitation argument would be wholly drained of force if, as seems likely, the confirmation of February 12, 1968, was itself a violation.

The result here reached may appear to be harsh, since Diskin had an opportunity to read the final prospectus before he paid for the shares. But the 1954 Congress quite obviously meant to allow rescission or damages in the case of illegal offers as well as of illegal sales. Very likely Congress thought that, when it had done so much to broaden the methods for making legal offers during the "waiting period" between the filing and the taking effect of a registration statement, it should make sure that still other methods were not attempted. Here all Lomasney needed to have done was to accompany the September 17, 1968 letter with any one of the three types of prospectus for the Continental shares mentioned in the extract we have quoted from Professor Loss' treatise. Very likely Congress thought a better time for meaningful prospectus reading was at the time of the offer rather than in the context of confirmation and demand for payment. In any event, it made altogether clear that an offeror of a security who had failed to follow one of the allowed paths could not achieve absolution simply by returning to the road of virtue before receiving payment.

The judgment dismissing the complaint is reversed, with instructions to enter judgment for the plaintiff that, upon delivery of 5,000 shares of Continental Travel, Ltd., he shall receive $60,000 with interest from February 28, 1969, and costs.[b]

Byrnes v. Faulkner, Dawkins and Sullivan

United States Court of Appeals, Second Circuit, 1977.
550 F.2d 1303.

■ Before MEDINA, HAYS* and OAKES, CIRCUIT JUDGES.

■ OAKES, CIRCUIT JUDGE:

These appeals are by would-be sellers of stock from decisions granting one buyer judgment on its * * * [defense] to the sellers' suit for breach of contract. * * * The principal issue on appeal is whether the * * * District Court * * * correctly upheld the affirmative defense of the appellee-buyer, a broker-dealer, that the contract for sale of stock was unenforceable because the written "comparison" sent to it by appellant sellers' agent constituted a prospectus as defined in Section 2(10) of the Securities Act * * *, did not contain the information required of a prospectus by Section 10 of that Act, and was therefore unlawful under Section 5(b)(1) * * *. We affirm the judgments.

Facts

Insofar as here relevant, the facts * * * are not in dispute. Byrnes, Santangelo, and their associates (hereinafter sellers or appellants) were the owners of 148,000 shares of stock of White Shield Corp. on and after September 6, 1968. This stock had been acquired from certain officers or directors of White Shield. It was not registered under the 1933 Act and therefore could not readily be sold, but appellants had acquired the right to include the stock in a registration statement filed at some future time under the Act.

In 1971 White Shield filed several registration statements under the Act. Appellants' stock was included in one that was a so-called "shelf registration" or "shelf secondary," that is, a registration statement filed on behalf of certain named owners of theretofore unregistered shares who, the statement indicates, could then sell the stock in the open market "from time to time," generally through member firms of the National Association of Securities Dealers, Inc. (NASD). The prospectus offering for sale appellants' shares and those of some 25 other selling shareholders bears the same date that the registration statement * * * "became effective": June 7, 1971. Just before June 7, appellants arranged with Tobey & Kirk, a securities broker-dealer registered with the SEC and a member firm of the NASD, to sell their stock when the registration

---

b. Note, A Critique of the Delayed Offer Concept of Section 2(3) of the Securities Act of 1933 in the Light of Diskin v. Lomasney & Co., 21 J.Pub.L. 433 (1972).

* Judge Hays, owing to illness, has not formally concurred in this opinion, but we believe him to agree with the result reached.

statement became effective, and appellants delivered to Tobey & Kirk copies of a preliminary or "red herring" prospectus.

On June 7, 1971, Tobey & Kirk agreed to sell to Faulkner, Dawkins & Sullivan (hereinafter Faulkner, buyer, or appellee), at a price of $14 per share, 44,000 shares of the White Shield stock owned by appellants and included in the White Shield registration statement. At that time Faulkner was a "market-maker"[1] in White Shield stock and regularly entered bid and asked quotations in the "Pink Sheets" of the National Quotation Bureau, Inc., and in NASDAQ, the automated quotation system of the NASD. On or about June 7, 1971, Faulkner sent a written "comparison" or confirmation of the purchase to Tobey & Kirk, showing that Faulkner was a market-maker in White Shield stock, and Tobey & Kirk on the same day sent a written comparison of the sale to Faulkner. This latter comparison did not show that the stock was part of a registered distribution, and it was not preceded or accompanied by a prospectus.

Only with delivery of the stock certificates themselves on June 15, 1971, did Tobey & Kirk deliver a prospectus to Faulkner. At that time Faulkner rejected the securities and informed Tobey & Kirk that the transaction was illegal.[2] The prospectus identified the selling shareholders and said that both they and the participating members of the NASD who rendered assistance to them in connection with the sale "may be deemed to be underwriters as that term is defined in the [1933 Act]."

* * *

Appellants subsequently resold the rejected White Shield stock in the open market for considerably less than the $14 per share purchase price of the June 7, 1971, agreement. They then brought suit * * * in federal court. The action was then heard by Judge Werker, who issued the substantive judgment appealed from here, following upon an agreed statement of certain facts and affidavits supporting cross motions for summary judgment.

The Affirmative Defense

Faulkner's * * * [affirmative defense] on which it prevailed by summary judgment below, was that its contract with appellants should not be enforced because Section 5(b)(1) of the 1933 Act was violated. The violation was a result, the defense runs, of Tobey & Kirk's omission to disclose the information that the Act requires to be in a prospectus when Tobey & Kirk sent its "comparison" to Faulkner. Section 5(b)(1) makes it "unlawful for any person, directly or indirectly to make use of any means * * * of * * * communication in interstate commerce * * * to carry or transmit any prospectus relating to any security

---

1. The term "market-maker" refers to a broker-dealer who, with respect to a particular security that is not traded on a national securities exchange (an "over-the-counter" security), "report[s] for quotation 'bid' and 'asked' prices to indicate, respectively, amounts for which it propose[s] to buy or sell the stock." * * *

2. The apparent reason for Faulkner's refusal was that it was only when the prospectus information was received that Faulkner found out that the stock it had just agreed to purchase was part of a registered secondary distribution. Because Faulkner made a market in White Shield, such a purchase was of doubtful legality. Compare In re Jaffee & Co., [1969–1970 Transfer Binder] Fed.Sec.L.Rep. (CCH) ¶ 77,805 (SEC 1970), with In re Collins Securities Corp., [1975–1976 Transfer Binder] Fed.Sec.L.Rep. (CCH) ¶ 80,327 (SEC 1975); see H. Bloomenthal, Securities and Federal Corporate Law § 6.17 (1975).

with respect to which a registration statement has been filed * * * unless such prospectus meets the requirements of [Section 10 of the Act].'' Section 10 essentially requires the prospectus, or selling circular, to contain or be accompanied by a document that includes the information found in the registration statement itself. It is conceded that Tobey & Kirk's comparison did not satisfy the requirements of Section 10.

Appellants' first response is based upon their reading of Section 2(10) of the 1933 Act which states, however, that ''unless the context otherwise requires * * * [t]he term 'prospectus' means any prospectus, notice, circular, advertisement, letter, or communication * * * which offers any security for sale *or confirms the sale of any security * * * *''(emphasis added). Appellants admit, as they must, that their comparison falls within the literal terms of Section 2(10), but they argue, relying on the caveat ''unless the context otherwise requires,'' that a comparison should not be deemed a prospectus in the context of an interbroker confirmation. They do recognize, however, that the party seeking to avoid the explicit language of the statute has the burden of proof. * * *

Appellants direct us to the history of Section 2(10), pointing out that its original language did not specifically mention confirmations. In 1941, however, the SEC's general counsel issued an opinion to the effect that the term ''prospectus'' included ''within its meaning an ordinary confirmation,'' as well as ''every kind of written communication * * * which constitutes a contract of sale or disposition of a security for value.'' Securities Act Release No. 2623 (1941), * * * (1946). A 1954 statutory amendment incorporated this opinion in substance into the language of Section 2(10) of the 1933 Act as quoted above * * *.

Appellants attempt to avoid this consistent and straightforward history with an elaborate argument, set out in the margin,[4] directed at showing,

---

4. Appellants argue that each of the general counsel's answers to the eleven hypothetical questions making up the bulk of his 1941 opinion, Securities Act Release No. 2623 (1941) can be explained by reference to specific provisions of the 1933 Act exempting transactions from the prospectus-delivery requirements of Section 5. * * * Question and Answer 6, which state that prospectus requirements do not apply to purchase transactions executed by a broker upon the unsolicited instructions of his customer, are explained, appellants say, by Section 4(4) of the Act which exempts unsolicited brokers' transactions from Section 5's provisions. Similarly, in Question and Answer 7, involving an unsolicited sell order given by the customer to his broker, it is stated that the broker need not send a prospectus along with the confirmation of the sale.

Question and Answer 8, on which appellants most heavily rely, we reprint in full:

Question 8. Pursuant to the sell order received in Question 7, John Doe [the broker] sells [his customer] Richard Roe's warrants to Henry Hoe, another dealer, who purchases for his own account. Must John Doe, in confirming the sale to Henry Hoe, or in delivering the warrants to him, send him a copy of the prospectus?

Answer. No. John Doe, in making the sale, is completing the execution of an unsolicited brokerage order, and therefore is exempt from the prospectus requirements. * * *

Question 9 in the 1941 opinion assumes that a broker solicits a sell order from his customer, and the answer holds that no prospectus need be delivered to the customer with the solicitation, since the broker is offering to sell for, not to, the customer. Question 10 assumes the facts of Question 9 and that the customer gives the sell order to his broker, who in turn sells the rights to a purchasing dealer. The answer to Question 10 was that the transaction, although on a brokerage basis, results from a solicitation, and consequently the prospectus requirements are ap-

through the language of the general counsel's 1941 opinion, that since a prospectus was not meant to be delivered in an inter-broker comparison situation, the confirmation is not a prospectus. To a degree, this argument confuses the definition of a prospectus with the exemptions from the prospectus delivery requirement, which will be discussed infra. On the definition of a prospectus, however, the general counsel's opinion is quite explicit. It states that *any* confirmation is a prospectus, a conclusion adopted in the 1954 statutory amendment. The general counsel's opinion, in discussing situations in which the 1933 Act provides exemptions from the prospectus delivery requirements, does have its opaque moments, see note 4 supra, but none are sufficient to help appellants meet their burden of overcoming the statutory language.

Nor is In re Collins Securities Corp., [1975–76 Transfer Binder] Fed.Sec. L.Rep. (CCH) ¶ 80,327 (SEC 1975), of any help to appellants. The SEC there held only that the Pink Sheets themselves are not prospectuses under Section 2(10) and hence do not have to contain all the information required of a prospectus to avoid a violation of Section 5, *Collins* holds, and we agree, that Section 2(10) need not literally apply if reason indicates otherwise. There the Commission was faced with the practical difficulties that would ensue if Pink Sheets were treated as prospectuses.[a] It was the perfect illustration of a situation in which "the context" required Section 2(10) not to be read literally. A sale by an underwriter through a broker to a broker-dealer is quite different. Here, the only consequence of our decision will be that the selling broker will have to accompany his first written communication to the purchasing broker with a Section 10(a) prospectus. This requirement accords with the congressional vision of the prospectus as a document to be read by the would-be purchaser before the sale becomes legally binding. See Diskin v. Lomasney & Co., 452 F.2d 871, 876 (2d Cir.1971). Since sellers' confirmations can meet statute of frauds requirements if the purchaser does not send written objections within ten days after receipt, U.C.C. § 8–319(c), the time of delivery of the confirmation is the logical time for delivery of the prospectus.

While we therefore hold that a comparison is a prospectus for purposes of the 1933 Act, this holding is not the end of our inquiry. Section 4 of the Act provides exemptions from the prospectus delivery requirements for specified types of transactions, and appellants assert that the transaction at issue here was exempt. * * * [H]owever, we find that none of the Section 4 exemptions is applicable here.

Section 4(1) exempts "transactions by any person other than an issuer, underwriter, or dealer." While appellants argue that Tobey & Kirk was not one of these, Tobey & Kirk concededly was registered as a securities broker-dealer with the Securities and Exchange Commission and was a member firm of the NASD. "Dealer" is defined in Section 2(12) to include "any person who engages either for all or part of his time, directly or indirectly, as agent, broker, or

plicable to the broker-to-dealer sale. Appellants conclude that Answer No. 10 is wrong.

a. The "Pink Sheets" are a national daily quotation service published by the National Quotation Bureau, Inc., a subsidiary of Commerce Clearing House, Inc., and disseminated among broker-dealers. It was widely used prior to the advent of NASDAQ. The sheets list certain stocks traded over counter, set forth the names of the broker-dealers making markets in the stock and their wholesale or "inside" quotations. These are only available to other broker-dealers. See SEC, Report of Special Study of Securities Markets, pt. 2, at 595–610 (1963); 5 L. Loss & J. Seligman, Securities Regulation 2579 (3d ed. 1989).

principal, in the business of offering, buying, selling, or otherwise dealing or trading in securities issued by another person." Clearly Tobey & Kirk was a dealer, * * * if not also an underwriter. * * *

Section 4(2) is inapplicable on its face; it exempts "transactions by an issuer not involving any public offering." Section 4(3) exempts the usual transaction by a dealer, but not, *inter alia*, those which take place prior to the expiration of 40 days from the date the relevant registration statement becomes effective. Here, because the transaction occurred within that 40–day period, Section 4(3) does not provide an exemption.

Appellants might draw most comfort from Section 4(4), which exempts "brokers' transactions executed upon customers' orders on any exchange or in the over-the-counter market but not the solicitation of such orders," but we hold that it too is inapplicable to this sale. Appellants were themselves distributing stock in a registered offering, which makes their position quite different from that of the broker in Question No. 8 of the 1941 general counsel's opinion, on which appellants rely, see note 4 supra. As distributors of newly registered stock, appellants were subject to the requirements of Section 5 of the Securities Act, regardless whether their broker was an underwriter. See United States v. Wolfson, 405 F.2d 779, 782–83 (2d Cir.1968), cert. denied, 394 U.S. 946 (1969). The definition of underwriter in Section 2(11) includes one who "participates or has a direct or indirect participation in any [distribution of any security by an issuer], or participates or has a participation in the direct or indirect underwriting of any such undertaking." Appellants and their associates arranged to have their stock included in one of the White Shield registration statements and were identified as putative underwriters in the White Shield prospectus. Appellants therefore became participants in the White Shield distribution and accordingly became underwriters. * * * As underwriters, appellants have no basis for arguing that they should be relieved of the consequences of Tobey & Kirk's failure to deliver a prospectus.

* * *

Appellants further suggest that a market-maker who is publishing his offers to purchase may be presumed to have a prospectus. * * * While this argument might be persuasive with regard to shares as to which a registration statement had previously become effective, or as to shares sold on an exchange where SEC Rule 153 would require that an adequate number of copies of the prospectus be available, * * * rather than over the counter as here, it does not persuade us in the instant case. Here a registration statement was filed and became effective only on the date of the over-the-counter sale. * * *

* * *

Finally, appellants argue that, even if there has been a violation of the 1933 Act, their contract with Faulkner is still enforceable. While a contract that violates the Act may not be voided if to do so would hinder the purposes of the Act, A. C. Frost & Co. v. Coeur D'Alene Mines Corp., 312 U.S. 38, 43 (1941), it is certainly voidable when the purposes of the Act are thereby furthered, Kaiser–Frazer Corp. v. Otis & Co., 195 F.2d 838, 843–44 (2d Cir.) (A. Hand, J.) (in sale by issuer to underwriters as initial step in public offering of securities, contract voided because of misleading statement in the prospectus), cert. denied, 344 U.S. 856 (1952). * * * Since Section 12(1) of the 1933 Act, gives an absolute right of rescission to an innocent purchaser of securities offered or sold in violation of the prospectus requirements, it would be anomalous to require that a buyer pay on a contract that violated those requirements and then sue under Section 12(1) to have his money returned. 3 L. Loss, supra at 1797–98 (1961); Note, Enforceability of Underwriting Contracts Illegal Under the Securities Act of 1933, 73 Harv.L.Rev. 1345, 1354 (1960). Since a violation of the prospectus requirements by Tobey & Kirk has been made out, therefore, Faulkner's contract with appellants is unenforceable.

* * *

Judgments affirmed.

Securities and Exchange Commission v. Manor Nursing Centers, Inc.

United States Court of Appeals, Second Circuit, 1972.
458 F.2d 1082.

[The SEC brought this action pursuant to § 22(a) of the 1933 Act, and § 27 of the 1934 Act. The complaint alleged violations of § 17(a) of the 1933 Act, and of § 10(b) and Rule 10b–5 of the 1934 Act; it also alleged violation of the prospectus-delivery requirement of § 5(b)(2) of the 1933 Act.

The case stemmed from a primary offering of 350,000 shares and a secondary offering of 100,000 shares of Manor Nursing Centers, which were to be offered and sold by the underwriter on an "all or nothing" basis. This meant, according to the prospectus, that unless all of the 450,000 shares were sold and paid for within 60 days the offering would terminate and all funds would be returned, with interest, to the subscribers. The subscribers' funds were to be held "in escrow" by a designated bank and were not to be available for other use until the terms of the offering were met.

The district judge, after trial, concluded that the defendants had violated the antifraud provisions of the 1933 and 1934 Acts and the prospectus-delivery requirement of the 1933 Act. The Court permanently enjoined certain of the defendants; ordered them to disgorge any proceeds, profits and income received in connection with the sale of the common stock of Manor Nursing Centers; appointed a trustee to receive these funds and to reimburse the defrauded public investors; and ordered a freeze on the assets of all defendants until they had transferred to the trustee the proceeds received from the sale. Defendants appealed.]

■ TIMBERS, CIRCUIT JUDGE: * * *

The conduct of appellants in connection with the public offering of Manor shares, upon analysis, demonstrates beyond a peradventure of a doubt that they violated the antifraud provisions of the federal securities laws—§ 17(a) of the 1933 Act and § 10(b) of the 1934 Act.

The gravamen of this case is that each of the appellants participated in a continuing course of conduct whereby public investors were fraudulently induced to part with their money in the expectation that Manor and the selling stockholders would return the money if all Manor shares were not sold and all the proceeds from the sale were not received by March 8, 1970. It is undisputed that, as of March 8, Manor and the selling stockholders had not sold all the 450,000 shares and that all the proceeds expected from the sale had not been received. Moreover, it is clear that all appellants knew, or should have known, that the preconditions for their retaining the proceeds of the offering had not been satisfied. Nevertheless, rather than complying with the terms of the offering by returning the funds of public investors, appellants retained these funds for their own financial benefit. * * *

All appellants also violated § 10(b) of the 1934 Act and Rule 10b–9 promulgated thereunder by making a misrepresentation with respect to the terms of an "all or nothing" offering. Recognizing the great potential for fraudulent conduct on the part of persons in connection with public offerings of securities on an "all or nothing" basis, the SEC in 1962 adopted Rule 10b–9, which provides in relevant part:

"It shall constitute a 'manipulative or deceptive device or contrivance,' * * * to make any representation:

"(1) to the effect that the security is being offered or sold on an 'all-or-none' basis, unless the security is part of an offering or distribution being made on the condition that all or a specified amount of the consideration paid for such security will be promptly refunded to the purchaser unless (A) all of the securities being offered are sold at a specified price within a specified time, and (B) the total amount due to the seller is received by him by a specified date. * * * *"

Here, it is clear, that all appellants knew that the offering was presented on an "all or nothing" basis. Moreover, the evidence established that appellants knew, or should have known, that all of the shares had not been sold and that all of the proceeds had not been received by March 8, 1970. Under the circumstances, there can be no doubt that representing that the offering would be on an "all or nothing" basis violated Rule 10b–9.

It also is clear that appellants violated the antifraud provisions of the federal securities laws by offering Manor shares when they knew, or should have known, that the Manor prospectus was misleading in several material respects. After the registration statement became effective on December 8, 1969, at least four developments occurred which made the prospectus misleading: the public's funds were not returned even though the issue was not fully subscribed; an escrow account for the proceeds of the offering was not established; shares were issued for consideration other than cash; and certain individuals received extra compensation for agreeing to participate in the offering. These developments were not disclosed to the public investors. That these developments occurred after the effective date of the registration statement did not provide a license to appellants to ignore them. Post-effective developments which materially alter the picture presented in the registration statement must be brought to the attention of public investors.[14] "The effect of the antifraud provisions of the Securities Act (§ 17(a)) and of the Exchange Act (§ 10(b) and Rule 10b–5) is to require the prospectus to reflect any post-effective changes necessary to keep the prospectus from being misleading in any material respect * * *."

III. *Violations of Prospectus—Delivery Requirement of 1933 Act*

In addition to concluding that appellants had violated the antifraud provisions of the federal securities laws, the district court also correctly held that

14. "The way the new facts * * * are brought to the attention of offerees as a matter of mechanics is by putting a sticker on the prospectus or supplementing it otherwise, not by amending the registration statement." 1 Loss, Securities Regulation 293 (2d ed. 1961, Supp.1969). See 17 C.F.R. § 230.424(c) (1971).

they had violated the prospectus-delivery requirement of § 5(b)(2) of the 1933 Act.

Section 5(b)(2) prohibits the delivery of a security for the purpose of sale unless the security is accompanied or preceded by a prospectus which meets the requirements of § 10(a) of the 1933 Act * * *. To meet the requirements of § 10(a), a prospectus must contain, with specified exceptions, all "the information contained in the registration statement * * *." In turn, the registration statement, pursuant to § 7 of the 1933 Act must set forth certain information specified in Schedule A of the 1933 Act. Among the items of information which Schedule A requires the registration statement, and therefore the prospectus, to contain are the use of proceeds (item 13), the estimated net proceeds (item 15), the price at which the security will be offered to the public and any variation therefrom (item 16), and all commissions or discounts paid to underwriters, directly or indirectly (item 17).

The Manor prospectus purported to disclose the information required by the above items of Schedule A. The evidence adduced at trial showed, however, that developments subsequent to the effective date of the registration statement made this information false and misleading. Moreover, Manor and its principals did not amend or supplement the prospectus to reflect the changes which had made inaccurate the information which § 10(a) required the prospectus to disclose. We hold that implicit in the statutory provision that the prospectus contain certain information is the requirement that such information be true and correct. * * *. A prospectus does not meet the requirements of § 10(a), therefore, if information required to be disclosed is materially false or misleading. Appellants violated § 5(b)(2) by delivering Manor securities for sale accompanied by a prospectus which did not meet the requirements of § 10(a) in that the prospectus contained materially false and misleading statements with respect to information required by § 10(a) to be disclosed.

Manor contends, however, that § 5(b)(2) does not require that a prospectus be amended to reflect material developments which occur subsequent to the effective date of the registration statement. This contention is premised on the assumptions that the prospectus spoke only as of the effective date of the registration statement and that the prospectus contained no false or misleading statements as of the effective date—December 8, 1969. Assuming the Manor prospectus was accurate as of December 8, 1969, appellants' claim is without merit.

In support of their argument that the prospectus need not be amended or supplemented to reflect post-effective developments, appellants cite an administrative decision in which the SEC held that it will not issue a stop order with respect to a registration statement which becomes misleading subsequent to its effective date because of material post-effective events. Funeral Directors Manufacturing and Supply Co., 39 S.E.C. 33, 34 (1959). * * * Under this line of SEC decisions, a registration statement need not be amended after its effective date to reflect post-effective developments.[23] These decisions, however, are not apposite here. Assuming that the registration statement does speak as of its

---

23. The SEC has held that in some situations it may be necessary to amend the registration statement to reflect post-effective changes. As noted in * * * note 14, post-effective developments generally are brought to the attention of offerees by putting a sticker on the prospectus or otherwise supplementing it. * * * We do not reach the question whether merely supplementing the prospectus would have been adequate in the instant case.

effective date and that Manor did not have to amend its registration statement,[24] appellants were obliged to reflect the post-effective developments referred to above in the prospectus. Even those SEC decisions holding that the registration statement need not be amended to reflect post-effective developments recognize that the prospectus must be amended or supplemented in some manner to reflect such changes. * * *. In addition, as noted above * * *, the effect of the antifraud provisions of the 1933 and 1934 Acts is to require that the prospectus reflect post-effective developments which make the prospectus misleading in any material respect. There is no authority for the proposition that a prospectus speaks always as of the effective date of the registration statement.

We hold that appellants were under a duty to amend or supplement the Manor prospectus to reflect post-effective developments; that their failure to do so stripped the Manor prospectus of compliance with § 10(a); and that appellants therefore violated § 5(b)(2).[a]

[The judgment of the district court was affirmed except that portion ordering disgorgement of the profits and income earned on the proceeds of the offering; as to this, the Court reversed and remanded for modification in accordance with its opinion.]

24. As to what date the registration statement speaks, there appears to be some ambiguity in the statute. Section 11 of the 1933 Act imposes civil liability on the issuer and other persons "[i]n case any part of the registration statement, when such part became effective, contained an untrue statement * * *". On the other hand, Section 8(d) of the 1933 Act authorizes a stop order "[i]f it appears to the Commission *at any time* that the registration statement includes any untrue statement * * *." (Emphasis added). The House Report supports the view that the SEC can require the issuer to amend the registration statement to reflect post-effective developments:

"In determining whether a stop order should issue, the Commission will naturally have regard to the facts as they then exist and will stop the further sale of securities, even though the registration statement was true when made, [and] it has become untrue or misleading by reason of subsequent developments." H.R.Rep.No.85, 73d Cong., 1st Sess. 20 (1933).

* * *

a. Note, Prospectus Must Reflect Developments Subsequent to Effective Date of Registration Statement to Meet Requirements of Section 10(a) of Securities Act of 1933, 71 Mich.L.Rev. 591 (1973); Note, Truth up to the Date of Use as a Requirement for a Section 10(a) Prospectus: The Implications of SEC v. Manor Nursing Centers, Inc., 24 Case W.Res.L.Rev. 771 (1973); Note, Prospectus Liability for Failure to Disclose Post–Effective Developments: A New Duty and its Implications, 48 Ind.L.J. 464 (1973).

Was the court in Manor Nursing Centers correct in holding that a defective prospectus that did not meet the requirements of § 10 violated § 5(b)(2)? In a civil action for damages under §§ 11 or 12, should defendant be deprived of his or her defenses relating to plaintiff's knowledge or defendant's conduct? In SEC v. Blazon Corp., 609 F.2d 960, 968–69 (9th Cir.1979), the court held that the filing of defective Regulation A materials did not result in an "automatic loss of the Reg. A exemption" and thus constitute a violation of § 5. Accord, SEC v. Southwest Coal & Energy Co., 624 F.2d 1312 (5th Cir.1980). On the other hand, in Jefferies & Co. v. Arkus–Duntov, 357 F.Supp. 1206, 1214–15 (S.D.N.Y. 1973), the court held that a defective prospectus that did not meet the requirements of § 5 would give rise to a § 12(1) action based upon a violation of § 5, thereby depriving the defendant of its defenses under § 11 and § 12(2). A.L.I. Fed.Sec.Code § 1702(f) specifically rejects the novel result reached in Jefferies, which Professor Loss, the Reporter, views as "erroneously" decided.

CHAPTER 3

THE REGISTRATION PROCESS

Statutes and Regulations

Exchange Act Registration and Reporting Requirements

A. Registration: 12(a), 12(b), 12(g), Rule 12g–1, Form 10, Regulation S–K, Items 303, 401, 404, 702, 510, 512(i).

B. Reports: 13, 14, 15(d), Regulation 12B, Rules 14a–3, 14c–3.

SECTION 1. THE SEC's INTEGRATED DISCLOSURE SYSTEM

DISCLOSURE OBLIGATIONS UNDER THE EXCHANGE ACT AND SECURITIES ACT

a. Exchange Act Registration and Reporting Requirements. Originally two separate and distinct disclosure systems were established under the federal securities laws, one applicable to the Securities Act of 1933, the other to the Securities Exchange Act of 1934. The reasons for this dual disclosure system were rooted in the fact that the two statutes were supposedly designed to fulfill different needs. The Securities Act regulates public offerings of securities under a regime of full disclosure. However, the 1933 Act disclosure obligations were never triggered except when an issuer resorted to the public markets to sell its securities. The 1934 Act regulated the trading markets for securities. Disclosure obligations depended upon the issuer's status; disclosure was triggered only with respect to (1) issuers with a class of securities listed and traded on an exchange (Section 12(b) companies); (2) issuers having total assets exceeding $1 million and a class of equity securities held of record by 500 or more persons (Section 12(g)(1) companies);[1] and (3) issuers with outstanding securities sold pursuant to a 1933 Act registration (Section 15(d) companies). The disclosure obligations of companies caught by these tests were then mandated under the periodic reporting requirements of Sections 12 and 13, the proxy rules of Section 14, and the special requirement of Rule 14a–3 that an annual report be sent to shareholders.

This dual system spawned separate sets of registration statements, periodic reports, and proxy rules, each with its own set of instructions. The 1933 Act disclosure documents were designed primarily for companies going public for the first time. They were comprehensive documents, disclosing all material financial and non-financial information. This approach could be justified in the case of first-time 1933 Act registrants, since material information was disclosed which was not previously available. However, 1934 Act reporting companies were required to repeat company specific information already on file with the Commission or publicly available through the distribution of annual reports or proxy statements. Thus, the same financial or other information would find its

---

1. Exemptive rules have raised the "total assets" test of Section 12(g)(1) up to its current level of $10 million (see Rule 12g–1), but "total assets" means assets without consideration of the firm's liabilities.

way into a 1933 Act registration statement, a 1934 Act filed document (e.g. a Form 10–K Annual Report) or in a Rule 14a–3 annual report to shareholders.

Not only was the material duplicative; it was different in form and content. The financial statements included in an annual report to shareholders needed only to conform to generally accepted accounting principles (GAAP). The financials in 1933 Act registration statements and in Form 10–K's and other Exchange Act filed documents had to conform to the more stringent standards of Regulation S–X, mandating the form and content of financial statements. Again, the same type of non-financial information might be mandated in a 1933 Act or 1934 Act filed document or under the proxy rules, but a different set of instructions was applicable, frequently containing inconsistencies in form and content.

b. Integrated Disclosure under the 1933 and 1934 Acts. The Commission instituted the integration program in order to achieve a more uniform, simplified and integrated disclosure system under the 1933 and 1934 Acts "so that investors and the marketplace are provided meaningful, non-duplicative information periodically, and when securities are sold to the public, while the costs of compliance for public companies are decreased."[2]

A first step was taken in 1977, by the adoption of Regulation S–K prescribing a single standard set of instructions for filing forms under the Securities Act and the Exchange Act. Thus, when the same type of information is mandated in the various forms under either Act, a single set of instructions applies.

More drastic surgery was performed in January, 1980 with the adoption of sweeping revisions of Form 10–K (the annual report which updates Form 10), Rule 14a–3 (prescribing the annual report to shareholders under the proxy rules), Regulation S–X, and the revision of Regulation S–K (prescribing instructions for filings under the 1933 and 1934 Acts). The effect of these amendments is to prescribe uniform financial disclosure requirements for virtually all documents required to be filed under either the 1933 or 1934 Acts. This has been accomplished by mandating that the audited financial statements that must be included in annual reports to shareholders of 1934 Act reporting companies must now comply with the requirements of Regulation S–X. Moreover, Regulation S–X was amended to eliminate most of the differences between the requirements of generally accepted accounting principles and those of Regulation S–X. Under the new regime, financial disclosures need only include the basic disclosures required under GAAP (as prescribed by the pronouncements of the Financial Accounting Standards Board, and the pronouncements of predecessor bodies) and a few additional disclosures not required under GAAP that the Commission regards as essential.

The Commission explained this phase in the establishment of the SEC integrated disclosure system in the release announcing these changes.[3]

* * *

The Commission today is adopting and proposing major changes in the Securities Act and Exchange Act disclosure systems. These changes are designed to improve the disclosure made to investors and other users of financial information, to facilitate the integration of the two disclosure

2. Securities Act Release No. 6235 (Sept. 2, 1980), 20 SEC Dock. 1175, at 1177.

3. Securities Act Release No. 6231 (Sept. 2, 1980).

systems into the single disclosure system long advocated by many commentators,[4] and to reduce current impediments to combining informal security holder communications, such as annual reports to security holders, with official Commission filings.

* * *

The Commission's review of the purpose and utility of the Form 10–K led it to believe that there is a basic information package which most, if not all, investors expect to be furnished. Further, it has become apparent that this basic information package, which in the context of Form 10–K developed to support the current information requirements of an active trading market, is virtually identical to the similar information package independently developed in connection with the registration and sale of newly issued shares under the Securities Act. The essential content of these Form 10–K and registration statement information packages includes audited financial statements, a summary of selected financial data appropriate for trend analysis, and a meaningful description of the registrant's business and financial condition.

The restructured Form 10–K which the Commission is adopting today is specifically designed to segregate the basic information package contained in that Form from proxy related or supplemental information. In this regard, the new Form 10–K is structured in four parts. The first part retains the detailed disclosure requirements relating to business, properties, legal proceedings and beneficial ownership. Much of this information, which in the past has been required primarily in Securities Act filings and not in annual reports to security holders, has been placed in a supplemental role. The second part consists of the basic disclosure package which is common to both Securities Act and Exchange Act filings. The third part consists of the traditional proxy disclosure information relating to directors and executive officers and management remuneration. Finally, the fourth part contains requirements for financial statement schedules and * * * scaled-down requirements for exhibits.

* * *

[The] Commission [has also] amended Rules 14a–3 and 14c–3 to require that annual reports to security holders contain a variety of information, including certified financial statements, a summary of operations, a management analysis, a brief description of the issuer's business, a line of business breakdown, an identification of the issuer's directors and executive officers, and an identification of the principal market in which the securities entitled to vote were traded. * * *

————

The next phase in the evolution of integrated disclosure entailed the SEC's effort to simplify and streamline the disclosure requirements under the 1933 Act. As a part of the integrated disclosure package the Commission undertook a

4. See generally Cohen, "Truth in Securities" Revisited, 79 Harv.L.Rev. 1340 (1968); SEC, Disclosure to Investors (Wheat Report) (1969); Report of the Advisory Committee on Corporate Disclosure to the Securities and Exchange Commission, Committee Print 95–29, House Committee on Interstate and Foreign Commerce 95th Cong., 1st Sess., November 3, 1977 ("Advisory Committee").

drastic revision of the major registration forms then in use under the 1933 Act. Forms S–1, S–2 and S–3, as adopted, established a new three-tier system for the registration of securities under the Securities Act, other than certain specialized types of offerings.[1] Regulation S–K was revised and expanded to set forth standard instructions for both registration statements and 1934 Act periodic filings, and the prior Guides for the Preparation and Filing of Registration Statements and Reports were largely rescinded. The general tenor of these and other integrally related proposals are summarized in the following release, which also contains a discussion of the theoretical foundations of the integration concept and the background leading to the final adoption of the integration package:

Proposed Rulemaking to Implement the Integrated Disclosure System

Securities and Exchange Commission.
Executive Summary of Securities Act Release Nos. 6331–6338 (Aug. 6, 1981).

The Commission today is publishing a group of eight releases which represent its most significant effort to date to implement an integrated corporate disclosure system, which will affect the over 9,000 public companies subject to reporting obligations under the federal securities laws. The disclosure systems under the federal securities laws are of great importance to capital raising and investor protection in the securities markets. Last year, over $600 billion in equity securities were traded on exchanges and in the over-the-counter market. There were public offerings of over $100 billion in equity and in debt securities. The continuous reporting system imposed by the Securities Exchange Act of 1934 (the "Exchange Act") and the registration system mandated by the Securities Act of 1933 (the "Securities Act") facilitate this trading activity and capital formation by assuring that investors and the market place are given the information necessary for investment decisions.

The integrated disclosure system harmonizes the two disclosure systems— which have grown up independently and on a largely piece-meal basis for the more than forty years since the statutes were enacted—into a single comprehensive disclosure system. It will perform the roles envisioned by both statutes but, at the same time, will eliminate or reduce the overlapping or duplicative corporate reporting, which was the product of two distinct systems, and will streamline corporate reporting generally.

Today's action is part of an ongoing process to integrate the disclosure systems. The foundation was laid by rulemaking actions taken over a period of more than ten years, but the most critical steps have been taken in the past two years. The Commission is publishing all eight releases as proposed rule-making actions rather than taking any final action at this time. While this means the republication of some proposals which have already been the subject of public comment, the Commission believes that publication of the eight releases together will allow the public to see the complete system before it is adopted. This will give the Commission the benefit of public comment not only on the individual components of the system, but also on their interaction * * *.

---

1. These include Form S–8 (for securities offered to employees), Form S–4 (for securities issued in business combinations) and Form S–18 designed to meet the special needs of small businesses.

Overview

The integrated disclosure system simplifies corporate reporting in three ways: (1) disclosure requirements are made uniform under the Securities Act and the Exchange Act; (2) Exchange Act periodic reporting is used to satisfy much of the disclosure necessary in Securities Act registration statements; and (3) the use of informal shareholder communications is encouraged, but not required, to satisfy formal statutory requirements under both Acts. The Commission adopted the first components of the integrated disclosure system in 1980 and early 1981. In addition, other components were proposed for comment. These outstanding proposals and the five newly developed coordinating projects being published today are as follows:

(1) Proposed Forms S–1, S–2 and S–3 to establish a new three tier system for the registration of securities under the Securities Act.

(2) Revision and expansion of Regulation S–K and rescission of the Guides for the Preparation and Filing of Registration Statements and Reports (the "Guides"), other than the Guides relating to specific industries.

(3) General revision and "sunset" review of the procedural requirements of Regulation C under the Securities Act and Regulation 12B under the Exchange Act.

(4) New Rule [415] under the Securities Act governing the registration of securities to be sold in delayed or continuous offerings. This rule was originally published as part of the general revision of Regulation S–K and the Guides in the Guides Release.

(5) New Rule 176 under the Securities Act relating to the responsibility in an integrated disclosure system of persons subject to Section 11 of the Securities Act and reproposed provisions relating to the effective date and modifying and superseding statement aspects of documents incorporated by reference. The latter provisions were previously published for comment in Securities Act Release No. 5988 (November 17, 1978) and the ABC Release.

(6) New Rule 436(g) and amendment to Rule 134(a) under the Securities Act to facilitate the Commission's decision to permit the voluntary disclosure of security ratings.

(7) Amendments to existing Securities Act registration forms to coordinate those forms with revised Regulation S–K and other aspects of the integrated disclosure system.

(8) Amendments to Exchange Act rules, forms and schedules to coordinate with revised Regulation S–K and other aspects of the integrated disclosure system; amendments to Rule [176] under the Securities Act and the corresponding safe harbor rules relating to projections under the other federal securities laws to broaden and clarify the scope of protection provided thereunder; and amendments (reproposed without change) to Schedule 14A relating to business and other relationships between a director and an issuer and the vote required for the election of directors.

Each of these releases is integrally related to the others and to the rulemaking actions taken in 1980. In the integrated disclosure system, a Securities Act registrant looks (1) to the available form for a determination of the type and amount of disclosure which must be delivered to investors, (2) to Regulation S–K for substantive disclosure requirements and (3) to Regulation C for procedural regulations. Separate releases address the role in the integrated system of security ratings, delayed or continuous offerings and Securities Act liabilities in connection with Exchange Act periodic reports incorporated by reference into Securities Act registration statements. Finally, the Commission's integration of the two existing corporate disclosure systems includes a wide ranging "sunset" review, resulting in revisions to Regulation C and in the proposed coordinating changes to rules and forms under the two systems.

The eight releases contain comprehensive discussions of the proposed actions as well as texts of the proposed rule and form provisions. * * *

Proposed Forms S–1, S–2 and S–3

The proposed Securities Act framework would establish three categories of registration statements. Proposed Form S–3 relies on the efficient market theory and thus allows maximum use of incorporation by reference of Exchange Act reports and requires minimal disclosure in the prospectus. In addition to being available for equity offerings by companies widely followed in the marketplace, Form S–3 could be used by most reporting companies to register investment grade debt offerings, securities offered under dividend and interest reinvestment plans and rights offerings, conversions and warrants. Companies which have been subject to the periodic reporting system of the Exchange Act for three or more years, but which are not as widely followed, would be eligible for Form S–2, which combines reliance on incorporation by reference of Exchange Act reports and presentation of streamlined information in the prospectus or in an annual report to shareholders delivered with the prospectus. Companies which have been in the Exchange Act reporting system for less than three years, and any others who choose to do so, would use Form S–1, which requires complete disclosure in the prospectus and permits no incorporation by reference.

A critical issue in Forms S–1, S–2 and S–3 has been developing criteria for determining when and by whom the abbreviated forms may be used to register securities. Since the use of abbreviated disclosure is based, to a large degree, on the theory of an efficient market, the criteria for the use of Forms S–2 and S–3 are designed to be indicative of following in the market place. The Commission believes that the standards of Exchange Act reporting experience and a minimum value of voting stock held by non-affiliates (the "float") are indicative of market place following, and thus it has moved away from registrant quality criteria (such as net income). The Commission is proposing a $150 million float test for Form S–3, which results in approximately 30% of NYSE, Amex and Nasdaq companies being eligible to use the Form, and is also considering an alternative test involving two market factors, a $100 million float and 3 million share annual trading volume, which would address regionally followed companies.[a]

Revision of Regulation S–K

The revision of Regulation S–K represents the evolution of that regulation into the repository of uniform disclosure provisions relating to substantially all of the information to be set forth in registration statements under the Securities Act and in annual and other periodic reports required pursuant to the Exchange Act. Disclosure requirements are centralized in Regulation S–K in

---

a. After experience with Form S–3, the Commission lowered the float test to $75 million. See General Instruction IB.1 to Form S–3.

order to avoid the need to refer to multiple sources for document content requirements. Thus, certain disclosure requirements currently included in the Guides, in proposed Form A, in Regulation C and in various Securities Act registration forms and Exchange Act forms will now be moved to Regulation S–K.

The Regulation S–K release also represents the completion of the "sunset" review of the Guides. In addition to including certain substantive Guide provisions in Regulation S–K, the "sunset" review of the Guides has resulted in including certain procedural provisions in Regulation C and deleting 50% of the Guides as obsolete. The only remaining Guides will be those relating to specific industries, where greater flexibility is essential. * * *

Delayed or Continuous Offerings

Proposed Rule [415] would facilitate new methods of financing. For the first time, the Commission would specify by rulemaking the conditions under which registrants could register securities to be offered on a delayed or continuous basis on the market (so called "shelf registration"). * * *

Liability Issues

Some members of the financial community have expressed concerns about the integrated disclosure system because it relies on Exchange Act periodic reports to satisfy Securities Act registration disclosure requirements and allows rapid financings. These persons believe that underwriters may have diminished opportunity to conduct what would be deemed a reasonable investigation of the information incorporated by reference from Exchange Act reports into a Securities Act registration statement so as to discharge their obligations under Section 11(b) of the Securities Act. In light of these concerns, the Commission is publishing for comment several proposals addressing the questions of liability which arise in the context of the integrated disclosure system. While the proposed rules would not derogate from Section 11 with respect to the responsibilities of underwriters, they would set forth certain factors which bear on issues of liability.

First, proposed Rule 176 would codify Section 1704(g) of the draft Federal Securities Code, as modified and approved by the Commission in 1980. The proposed rule identifies certain circumstances, including incorporation by reference, which may bear upon the determination of what constitutes reasonable investigation and reasonable ground for belief as those terms are used in Section 11.

Second, the Commission is proposing to codify in Regulation C the previously proposed provisions regarding the effective date of documents incorporated by reference and the making of modifying or superseding statements. * * *

The above proposals were implemented, with some modifications, in Securities Act Release No. 6383 (March 3, 1982). In this release, the Commission introduced an important distinction between "registrant-specific" information and "transaction-specific" information and used it to explain the relationship between the registration forms under the Securities Act and the periodic reporting forms under the Exchange Act.

Securities Act Release No. 6383

Securities and Exchange Commission.
March 3, 1982.

ADOPTION OF INTEGRATED DISCLOSURE SYSTEM

New Forms S–1, S–2 and S–3 provide the basic framework for the registration of securities under the Securities Act. These Forms establish three categories for registration statements. The same information will be required to be part of Securities Act registration statements in all categories, either presented in, or delivered with, the prospectus or incorporated by reference from another document. Differences among the three Forms reflect the Commission's determination as to (1) when this required information must be presented in full in the prospectus delivered to investors, (2) when certain of the delivered information may be presented on a streamlined basis and supplemented by documents incorporated by reference, and (3) when certain information may be incorporated by reference from documents in the Exchange Act continuous reporting system without delivery to investors.

Generally, it is the registrant-oriented portion of the information relating to a public offering, as opposed to the transaction-specific information, which sometimes may be satisfied otherwise than through full prospectus presentation. Much of this registrant-oriented information is the same as that which is required to be presented in annual reports to the Commission on Form 10–K and in annual reports to security holders, as well as in quarterly and current reports on Forms 10–Q and 8–K, respectively. Information about the offering, however, will not have been reported on in any other disclosure document or otherwise have been publicly disseminated and thus will be required to be presented in the prospectus in all cases.

The registration statement for the first category is Form S–1. It requires complete disclosure to be set forth in the prospectus and permits no incorporation by reference. Form S–1 is to be used by registrants in the Exchange Act reporting system for less than three years and also may be used by any registrants who choose to do so or for whom no other form is available.

The second category of registration statement is Form S–2, which combines reliance on incorporating Exchange Act reports by reference with delivery to investors of streamlined information. Registrants in the Exchange Act reporting system for three years may use this Form, which allows them to choose to either: (1) Deliver a copy of their annual report to security holders along with the prospectus describing the offering or (2) present registrant-oriented information comparable to that of the annual report in the prospectus along with the description of the offering. In either case, the more complete information in the Form 10–K is incorporated by reference into the prospectus.

Form S–3, in reliance on the efficient market theory, allows maximum use of incorporation by reference of Exchange Act reports and requires the least disclosure to be presented in the prospectus and delivered to investors. Generally, the Form S–3 prospectus will present the same transaction-specific information as will be presented in a Form S–1 or S–2 prospectus. Information concerning the registrant will be incorporated by reference from Exchange Act reports. The prospectus will not be required to present any information concerning the registrant unless there has been a material change in the registrant's affairs which has not been reported in an Exchange Act filing or the Exchange Act reports incorporated by reference do not reflect certain restated financial statements or other financial information.

* * *

———

1. *Integrated Disclosure: Was Efficient Market Theory the Rationale or a Makeweight?* Although Release 6383 states its "reliance on the efficient market theory," skeptics have doubted that it really explains the SEC's motivation for integrating the 1933 Act's and 1934 Act's disclosure systems.[1] They suggest that the costs of maintaining two distinct systems of disclosure simply outweighed their benefits. Also, they point out that some 1,600 companies were originally eligible to use Form S–3 (or about one third of the companies then trading on the NYSE, Amex and Nasdaq National Market System),[2] but an SEC study a few years earlier in 1977 had found only about 1,000 issuers to be closely followed by securities analysts.[3] Further, the fact that Form S–3 can be used for any investment grade debt security may represent a sensible cost/benefit judgment (given the lower risk of such securities), but such securities hardly trade in an efficient market (rather, they trade in relatively thin and nontransparent secondary markets).

Since the adoption of Form S–3 in 1982, the SEC has further liberalized eligibility for its use. The current eligibility rules require the aggregate market value for the voting stock held by non-affiliates to be $75 million or more (for a primary offering of stock for cash);[4] this is down by half from the original $150 million level in 1982.

While the SEC's judgment underlying Form S–3 that investors in both primary and secondary markets need the same information for informed decisions seems sound, one critical difference between these two markets should be underscored: the issuer has a far greater incentive to deceive when it is selling stock (and will receive the proceeds) in a primary offering than when the only trading is between investors in the secondary market. For this reason, the Securities Act of 1933 places liability without proof of fault on third parties (underwriters, experts, directors, and accountants) in order to give them a strong incentive to test the adequacy of the issuer's disclosures. As will be seen later in this Chapter, much of the current debate surrounding 1933 Act disclosure has centered on the continued ability of these third parties to play this "gatekeeping" role as verifiers of the adequacy of the issuer's disclosures within the very time-constrained limits of shelf registration. In fairness to the SEC's decision to relax the 1933 Act's requirements for seasoned issuers, it should be noted that in the fifteen years since the advent of shelf registration

———

1. See Langevoort, Theories, Assumptions and Securities Regulation: Market Efficiency Revisited, 140 U.Pa.L.Rev. 851 (1992).

2. See Sec.Act.Rel. No. 6331 (1981).

3. See Report of the Advisory Committee on Corporate Disclosure to the Securities Exchange Commission, H.R.Rep. No. 29, 95th Cong., 1st Sess. 41–42 (1977) (noting that most institutional investors followed and invested only in companies with a market capi-

talization of $500 million or above). Although the boundaries of the efficient market could certainly expand over time, the current market capitalization required for Form S–3 is only $75 million—thus perhaps doubling the number of eligible issuers from the number in 1982.

4. See Form S–3, General Instructions, Instruction B1.

in 1982 there has been no major scandal involving the disclosures of such an eligible Form S–3 issuer.

2. *Small Business Issuers.* The next significant relaxation of the 1933 Act's requirements came in 1992 when the SEC introduced streamlined registration procedures for "small business issuers." Such an issuer is defined as a U.S. or Canadian issuer with revenues of less than $25 million during its last fiscal year and with an aggregate market value for its voting stock held by non-affiliates of less than $25 million. Obviously, such tiny companies rarely trade in an efficient market.

Qualifying small business issuers are eligible to use two simplified registration forms: Form SB–1 for the sale of up to $10 million in securities and Form SB–2, which has no dollar limit for securities offered for cash. Not only are these forms considerably less detailed and burdensome than Form S–1 (which most issuers in initial public offerings must use), but a modified Form 10–K (known as Form 10KSB) and a modified Form 10–Q (known as Form 10–QSB) also relax the requirements of the 1934 Act's continuous disclosure system for such issuers. Also, in the case of such issuers, Regulation S–B supersedes Regulation S–K, which contains the requirements for the non-financial sections of registration statements on other forms (including Forms S–1, S–2, and S–3). Lastly, the requirements of Regulation S–X, which governs the financial statements included in any other report or registration statement filed with the SEC, are simply waived (although the "small business issuer" must still comply with generally accepted accounting principles).

3. *Management's Discussion and Analysis.* It would be misleading to suggest that all revisions to the disclosure requirements of the federal securities laws during the last twenty years have been deregulatory. The most important counterexample has been the Commission's steady enhancement of the disclosure requirements under the Management Discussion and Analysis of Financial Condition and Results of Operations (the "MDA"). Item 303 of Regulation S–K sets forth the required MDA disclosures and calls for a narrative discussion, written from management's perspective, of the company's current financial position and future prospects. Essentially, the registrant must disclose and assess future "trends, demands, commitments or events" that it considers "reasonably likely" to have a material impact on its financial condition or earnings. In a series of releases during the 1980's, the Commission tightened these requirements and increased the quantification of future possibilities that a registrant must undertake. The specific requirements and philosophy of the MDA are discussed *infra* in Section 3 of this Chapter, but a key point here is the tradeoff between the enhancement of the MDA and the advent of integrated disclosure. That is, the Commission sought to upgrade the reporting requirements under the 1934 Act (in particular, by focusing on the quality of the issuer's earnings) at the same time that it integrated the 1933 Act's and 1934 Act's two disclosure systems and allowed seasoned issuers to incorporate by reference 1934 Act filings to satisfy the bulk of their 1933 Act disclosure requirements.

4. *EDGAR.* The Electronic Data Gathering, Analysis, and Retrieval System ("EDGAR") was the next step by which the SEC has moved from a paper-based technology to the world of electronic communications. Although introduced first with respect to 1934 Act filings, EDGAR today requires that domestic registrants file both their periodic filings under the 1934 Act and their registration statements by either e-mail transmissions to the SEC or the

physical delivery of diskettes or magnetic tapes to the SEC. One advantage of EDGAR is that information is usually available within a half-hour of filing at the SEC at the SEC's World Wide Web site.[5]

5. *Post Enron–Developments.* The bankruptcy of Enron in late 2001 has proven a traumatic event both for the markets and the SEC. In particular, as the SEC has recognized, Enron's failure seems to have demonstrated significant shortcomings in the SEC's existing disclosure system, particularly as it relates to the ability of issuers to (1) hide off-balance sheet liabilities that significantly reduced the issuer's liquidity and capital resources; (2) engage in trading activities involving non-exchange traded derivatives, where the issuer could inflate its earnings depending upon the "fair value" it assigned to these contracts; and (3) conceal relationships and transactions with related parties. Because the SEC does not determine "generally accepted accounting principles" (rather the Financial Accounting Standards Board (or "FASB") does), the SEC could not respond to Enron by itself tightening "GAAP." Instead, the Commission turned to its own invention, the MD&A, and suggested that the impact of off-balance sheet and derivatives transactions must be better disclosed in it.[6] In addition, the Commission decided that the current disclosure system had become "antiquated" and needs to be strengthened by a more immediate obligation to disclose material information on a "real time" basis. To this end, the Commission proposed a drastic overhaul of Form 8–K, which calls for accelerated disclosure of a significantly increased number of transactions, in many cases within two business days after the transaction.[7] Responding to the delayed disclosures in Enron, the Commission proposed that new Form 8–K would be required to disclose on an expedited basis directors' and executive officers transactions in company equity securities, transactions outside the ordinary course of the issuer's business, and changes in critical accounting policies.[8] Similarly, the due dates for Form 10–K and Form 10–Q would be accelerated, depending on the market capitalization of the issuer, to 60 days after the end of the fiscal year (in the case of Form 10–K) and 30 days after the end of the first three quarters (in the case of Form 10–Q). Lastly, the Commission required that a company's chief executive officer and its chief financial officer certify that, to the best of their knowledge, the information contained in each annual and quarterly report is true in all important respects and contains all information about the company of which they are aware that they believe is important to a reasonable investor.[9]

Congress, however, did not wait for the SEC to adopt its own proposed rules. Instead, it legislated them in substance, in some cases going considerably further than the SEC had proposed. Specifically, the Sarbanes–Oxley Act of 2002 (the "Act") did the following to require increased disclosures in response to specific abuses that came to light during the course of the Enron scandal:

a. *Executive Certifications.* Section 302 of the Act directed the SEC to adopt rules within 30 days requiring the chief executive officer and the chief

5. The SEC's Internet address is http://www.sec.gov.

6. Securities Act Release No. 33–8056 ("Commission Statement About Management's Discussion and Analysis of Financial Condition and Results of Operations") (January 25, 2002).

7. Securities Act Release No. 33–8089 (April 23, 2002).

8. See SEC Press Release No. 2002–22 (Feb. 13, 2002) and Release No. 33–8089 (April 23, 2002).

9. Securities Exchange Act Release No. 34–46079 (June 14, 2002).

financial officer to certify that they have reviewed each annual and quarterly report and concluded that "based on the officer's knowledge, the report does not contain any untrue statement of a material fact … [and] the financial statements, and other financial information included in the reports fairly present in all material respects the financial condition and results of operations of the issuer as of, and for, the periods presented."[10] In addition, these officers must further certify as to the adequacy of the issuer's internal controls.[11] Adding suspenders to Section 302's belt, Section 906 of the Act amends the federal criminal code to require an additional certification by the same two executive officers and makes it a felony to make knowingly false statements therein.[12] The Section 302 and Section 906 certifications differ marginally in their content, thus adding to the transitional confusion.

b. *"Real Time" Issuer Disclosures.* Section 409 of the Act mandates that reporting companies "shall disclose to the public on a rapid and current basis concerning material changes in the financial condition or operations of the issuer, in plain English, which may include trend and qualitative information and graphic presentations, as the Commission determines … is necessary or useful for the protection of investors and in the public interest."[13] The Act does not itself prescribe time periods, nor specify whether such disclosure should be made by press release of Form 8–K, but the Commission has already read it to justify its proposals for expedited filing dates for the Form 10–K and Form 10–Q.[14]

c. *Section 16b Reports.* Section 403 of the Act amends Section 16 of the '34 Act to require reports of changes in beneficial ownership (i.e., the standard Form 4) to be filed by covered officers, directors, and shareholders with the SEC by the end of the second business day after the day of the execution of the transaction. Beginning one year after enactment, a electronic filing must also be made with the SEC.

d. *Off Balance Sheet Items and Pro Forma Figures.* Section 401 of the Act adds a new Section 13(j) to the '34 Act requiring the SEC to adopt rules requiring that Form 10–K's and Form 10–Q's "disclose all material off-balance sheet transactions, arrangements, obligations (including contingent obligations), and other relationships of the issuer with unconsolidated entities or other persons, that may have a material current or future effect on financial condition, changes in financial condition, results of operations, liquidity, capital expenditures, capital resources, or significant components of revenues or expenses." Similarly, the Act requires the SEC to adopt rules requiring that pro forma financial information in SEC reports or press releases be presented so as to (1) not contain an untrue statement of a material fact or be otherwise materially misleading, and (2) reconcile such pro forma information "with the financial condition and results of operations of the company under generally accepted accounting principles."[15]

---

10. See Section 302(a)(2) and (3) of the Act.

11. See Section 302(a)(4) and (5) of the Act.

12. See 18 U.S.C. § 1350. This section specifies a fine of up to $1 million and a criminal sentence of up to ten years to knowingly provide a false certification and elevates the penalty to a $5 million fine and a 20 year sentence for a "willfully" false certification.

13. This provision is codified as Section 13(*l*) of the Securities Exchange Act of 1934.

14. See Securities Exchange Act Release No. 46421 (August 27, 2002).

15. See Section 401(b) of the Act.

e. *Internal Controls Report.* Section 404 of the Act mandates that the Commission develop a new "internal control report" which must be included in each Form 10–K and must assess the effectiveness of management's internal controls and procedures. The company's outside auditor must "attest to and report on" this assessment.

f. *SEC Review of Public Companies.* Section 408 of the Act requires the Commission to review disclosures made by reporting companies "on a regular and systematic basis," at least once every three years. This appears to have been a response to published reports that the financially-pressed SEC had not been able to review Enron's filings for a number of years.

g. *Code of Ethics.* Section 406 of the Act requires a reporting company to disclose "whether or not, and if not, the reasons therefor, such issuer has adopted a code of ethics for senior financial officers." Any change or waiver of this code must be disclosed immediately on Form 8–K or by electronic means.

SECTION 2.   PREPARATION OF THE REGISTRATION STATEMENT

Statutes and Regulations

Securities Act, §§ 6–7.

Regulation C.

Forms S–1, S–2, S–3, S–18.

Regulation S–K.

Introductory Note

The preparation of a 1933 Act registration statement, especially that of an issuer going public, is a demanding and intricate undertaking which can challenge the imagination and ingenuity of the corporation lawyer. A great deal of expertise must be acquired in practice preferably by working with competent and experienced securities lawyers.

A study of the mechanics of preparing a registration statement should begin with an examination of the 1933 Act (particularly §§ 6–7 and Schedule A), and Regulation C, which contains the general rules governing the registration process.

The Commission has prescribed a number of registration forms for use based upon the type of issuer, whether it is a reporting or non-reporting company, the form of transaction, and the extent to which the Commission believes that previously disseminated information need not be repeated in the prospectus, but may simply be incorporated therein by reference.

Regulation S–K contains standard instructions applicable to the non-financial portion of registration forms filed under the 1933 Act and registration statements, periodic reports and proxy statements filed under the 1934 Act; it was issued as a part of the Commission's integrated disclosure program.

A substantial amount of "know how" may be gained by first studying the statute and Regulation C, then moving to Form S–1 and thereafter analyzing a well-drafted prospectus in light of the statute, rules, and form.[1] It is also helpful to prepare a cross reference sheet of the type specified in Rule 404(d) showing the

---

1. See also 2 CCH Fed.Sec.L.Rep. under the tab guide "How to Answer Form S–1," ¶ 8001 et seq.

location in the prospectus of the information which must be included in the prospectus in response to the various items of Form S–1. This might be followed by studying a complete registration file, including Part II relating to information not contained in the prospectus, the various amendments, and the exhibits.

There also are a few books devoted to "going public," and the mechanics of preparing a 1933 Act registration statement, written from the lawyer's point of view.[2]

The decision to "go public" is important to the future of an issuer, and should be taken only after weighing the advantages and disadvantages of becoming a public company.

In a period of rising stock prices and business expansion, the managers of private companies may be dazzled by the supposed advantages of going public, with the opportunity to cash in on the increased net worth of the company. Once into a recession, however, these perceived advantages may quickly fade. Thus, business people who took their companies public in the 1960's suddenly wished to have it both ways by "going private" at the rock bottom stock prices of 1974–75.[3]

Carl W. Schneider, Joseph M. Manko, and Robert S. Kant, members of the Philadelphia bar, have enumerated a number of advantages and disadvantages of going public.[4] In summary, the motivations for going public include: 1. To raise funds for such corporate purposes as increasing working capital, expanding plant and equipment, research and development, retiring existing debt, or for diversification of operations. 2. If a secondary offering is included, the selling shareholders may cash in on a part of their investment under favorable market conditions. 3. By going public the company may gain prestige, become better known, and obtain a wider market for its products or services, particularly if the company is engaged in distributing consumer goods or services to the public. 4. A company with publicly traded stock is in a better position to acquire other businesses through the issuance of stock, instead of cash. 5. An existing public market for the securities permits the adoption of stock option and other employee purchase plans as a means of attracting and retaining personnel. 6. A public offering of stock will improve net worth thereby enabling the company to raise funds on more favorable terms, either in the equity markets, or privately from institutional investors. 7. The establishment of a public market may give the owners a sense of financial success and self-fulfillment as well as providing liquidity for their personal estates.

The disadvantages, which are frequently overlooked during periods of business expansion, only to be suddenly perceived at the bottom of a business cycle include: 1. The relatively high expense of maintaining a public company. 2. The full disclosure obligations of reporting companies with respect to salaries, transactions with management, conflicts-of-interest, information as to sales, profits and competitive position, all of which become available to shareholders and competitors. 3. The loss of flexibility in management arising from practical, if not legal, limitations on salaries and fringe benefits, the placing of relatives on the payroll and the necessity of acting only after approval of outside directors or shareholders. 4. Increased costs of administration, and legal, accounting and other fees associated with operating as a company subject to the reporting requirements of the Securities Exchange Act of

2. See particularly, D. Goldwasser, The Underwritten Offering; L. Sonsini, Preparing the Registration Statement, 1 Securities Law Techniques ch. 18, 19 (A.A. Sommer, Jr. ed., 1985 Looseleaf); H. Bloomenthal, C. Harvey & S. Wing, 1986 Going Public Handbook; A. Jacobs, Manual of Corporate Forms for Securities Practice (1985 rev.).

3. On the "going private" phenomenon, see infra at pages 853–869.

4. See Schneider, Manko and Kant, Going Public—Practice, Procedure and Consequences, 27 Vill.L.Rev. 1 (1981).

1934. 5. Possible loss of control over dividend policy, although frequently the company reserves the right to pay no dividends for the foreseeable future. 6. The business decisions of a public company may become affected by short-term considerations arising from management's preoccupation with day-to-day stock market price fluctuations rather than a consideration of long-term benefits. 7. If a sufficiently large proportion of the company's shares are sold to the public, the company may later become a candidate for a takeover bid, with a loss of control by the insiders. 8. Finally, the supposed advantages of an active public market for the company's shares may not develop, and the shares may actually sell at a discount substantially below the price anticipated on the basis of earnings and book values.

There are two different basic perspectives on the process by which a registration statement is prepared by the issuer (and the underwriters) and reviewed by the SEC: (1) the issuer's, and (2) the SEC's. This section attempts to view the process from both perspectives in excerpts from two well-known articles, the first describing events through the issuer's eyes and the second through the SEC's:

Excerpt from: Carl W. Schneider, Joseph M. Manko, and Robert S. Kant.

Going Public: Practice, Procedure and Consequences

27 Villanova L.Rev. 1, 1–50 (1981).[a]

Introduction

WHEN A COMPANY WISHES TO "GO PUBLIC" it faces a complex and challenging process. It is the purpose of this article to focus on the sections of the Securities Act of 1933 (the '33 Act) dealing with registration as it applies to companies selling securities to the public for the first time—"going public." The authors' aim is to cover the practice and procedure, as well as certain important consequences, of going public. In a nutshell, the '33 Act is designed to prohibit the public distribution of securities without disclosure of relevant information to the investor. In this context, distribution refers to a public offering by the company itself—a "primary offering." The '33 Act also covers certain offerings by existing security holders, who may or may not be those persons who control the company—"secondary offerings" or, more opprobriously, "bailouts."

SELECTION OF AN UNDERWRITER

Once the decision has been made to go public, the parties immediately face perhaps the most important decision to be made—selecting the managing underwriter. Investment banking firms vary widely in prestige, financial strength and ability to provide the various services which the company can expect. Some underwriters are not ordinarily interested in first offerings, while others specialize in them. Some underwriters have particular stature and experience in specific industries. Underwriters may have pre-existing relationships with customers, suppliers, or competitors of a prospective company going public, which can be both an advantage and a disadvantage from varying points

a. Reprinted with permission from Villanova Law Review and the Authors. Copyright 1981 by the Authors. This printing reflects revisions made by the authors through May, 1988. The article covers the practice and procedure, as well as various consequences of going public. Although only a portion is reprinted here, the entire article is recommended. Copies are available from Packard Press, Philadelphia, Pa. And see the companion article, Schneider and Shargel, "Now That You Are Publicly Owned * * *", 36 Bus.Law. 1631 (1981).

of view. In short, a managing underwriter appropriate for one company may be wholly inappropriate for another.

In selecting the underwriters, advice should be obtained from experienced advisers who have a background in the area of public offerings. The company's attorneys, auditors and bankers may be helpful in making the selection. Some advisers, particularly underwriters themselves, warn of dire consequences from "shopping" an offering, and suggest dealing with a single underwriter at a time. Opinions on the subject vary. There are some small and speculative offerings where the trick is to find any underwriter, and there may be little chance for selection. Additionally, among smaller underwriters, there may be a reluctance to evaluate, negotiate and otherwise develop an underwriting prospect unless the company is dealing exclusively with the particular firm at that time.

On the other hand, if the proposed offering is good enough to appeal to the larger underwriters, management may be best advised to select a few firms, possibly three to five, with which to begin preliminary discussions more or less simultaneously. If the offering has merit, the larger underwriters normally are most willing to spend time investigating the company to decide whether or not they wish to proceed, and thereafter to sell themselves and their proposal if they do wish to handle the transaction. It is important to deal in candor. Each prospective underwriter should be told that other underwriters are being considered. For offerings of genuine merit, this element of competition may well whet the appetite and stand the company in good stead. This is not to suggest, however, that a company should put itself in an auction, trying to get each bidder to top the others.

Finally, it must be stressed that price is not the sole element of comparison, nor is it necessarily advantageous for the stock to be sold for the very top dollar which any prospective underwriter will offer. If the initial offering price is set too high, the issue may have a poor reception and a weak after-market for some time to follow. Some underwriters will frankly advise the company to set the initial offering price slightly under the projected after-market price, perhaps 5 percent to 10 percent below, simply to assure a good reception for the stock. For companies with a good history and earnings record, the proper pricing of the issue often must be determined by the market conditions prevailing on the offering date. Therefore, many underwriters will indicate during the preliminary negotiations the price, or price range, at which the offering could be made if it were being made at that time, with the express reservation that final pricing will be determined by prevailing conditions on the offering date, which is normally at least a few months in the future. Thus, the managing underwriter is often selected at a time when the parties have not yet fixed the specific offering price.

* * *

Several services can be expected from the underwriters. Initially, the managing underwriter will take the lead in forming the underwriting syndicate. The underwriters are also expected to provide after-market support for the security being sold. They may serve as over-the-counter market makers which stand ready to purchase or sell the stock in the inter-dealer market; they may purchase the stock for their own account; and they may take the initiative in bringing the stock to the attention of analysts and investors, including their own customers. Ideally, the company should seek a managing underwriter which customarily makes a continuous inter-dealer market for the issues it manages, although there are some managing underwriters that do not perform this function themselves.

In addition, managing underwriters traditionally supply other investment banking services to the company following the offering. They will assist in obtaining additional financing from public or private sources as the need arises, advise the company concerning possible acquisitions and generally make available their expertise as financial institutions. In some cases, they will recommend or furnish experienced persons to become members of the company's board of directors, or to serve as officers or key employees.

* * *

STRUCTURE OF THE OFFERING

Once a company has decided to make a public offering, it must determine, in consultation with its managing underwriter, what class of securities should be offered. Most first offerings include common stock. Some first offerings consist of a package including other securities such as debentures, which may or may not be convertible into common stock, or warrants to purchase common stock. It is normally not practicable to have a publicly-traded security convertible into common stock or a publicly-traded warrant to purchase common stock unless a public market exists for the underlying common stock.

There are two other interrelated variables to consider: the number of shares offered and the offering price for the shares. It is generally felt that a minimum of 300,000 to 350,000 shares, and preferably 400,000 shares or even slightly more, is desirable in the public "float" to constitute a broad national distribution and to support an active trading market thereafter. As to price level, many of the larger investment banking firms and many investors are not particularly interested in dealing with securities offered at less than $10. The $5 level is often another psychological breakpoint below which many investment bankers and investors lose interest. * * *

For an offering of $5,000,000, 500,000 shares at $10 per share would be considered in the optimum range. If the offering is below $4,000,000, a decrease in the offering price per share is recommended, rather than a reduction in the number of shares offered below 400,000. These are matters of judgment, however, which should be reviewed carefully with the underwriters in each situation. * * *

In determining the amount of public investment which can be profitably employed in the business, the underwriters will normally evaluate the company's needs for funds and the dilution in earnings per share to result from the issuance of additional stock. If the optimum level of proceeds to the company would constitute too small an offering, it may be desirable for existing shareholders to sell some of their own shares as part of the offering in order to increase its size. Sometimes the underwriters will suggest, or even insist on, a partial secondary offering with some shares to be sold by existing shareholders even though the shareholders would prefer to retain all their shares.

* * *

PREPARING THE REGISTRATION STATEMENT

The "quarterback" in preparing the registration statement is normally the attorney for the company. Company counsel is principally responsible for preparing the non-financial parts of the registration statement. Drafts are circulated to all concerned. There are normally several major revisions before sending the job to the printer and at least a few more printed drafts before the final filing. Close cooperation is required among counsel for the company, the underwriters' counsel, the accountants and the printer. Unless each knows exactly what the others expect, additional delay, expense and irritation are predictable.

It is essential for the issuer and all others involved in the financing to perceive correctly the role of company counsel. Counsel normally assists the company and its management in preparing the document and in performing their "due diligence" investigation to verify all disclosures for accuracy and completeness. Counsel often serves as the principal draftsman of the registration statement. Counsel typically solicits information both orally and in writing from a great many people and exercises his best judgment in evaluating the information received for accuracy and consistency. Experience indicates that executives often overestimate their ability to give accurate information from their recollections without verification. It shows no disrespect, but merely the professionally required degree of healthy skepticism, when the lawyer insists on backup documentation and asks for essentially the same information in different ways and from different sources.

A lawyer would be derelict in the discharge of his or her professional obligations if the lawyer allowed his client's registration statement to include information which the lawyer knew or believed to be inaccurate, or if the lawyer failed to pursue an investigation further in the face of factors arousing suspicions about the accuracy of the information received. On the other hand, it should be understood that a lawyer generally is not an expert in the business or financial aspects of a company's affairs. The normal scope of a professional engagement does not contemplate that the lawyer will act as the ultimate source to investigate or verify all disclosures in the registration statement or to assure that the document is accurate and complete in all respects. Indeed, in many cases the lawyer would lack the expertise to assume that responsibility. In some instances, the lawyer may lack the technical background even to frame the proper questions and must depend upon the client for education about the nature of the business. Counsel does not routinely check information received against books of original entry or source documents, as auditors do, nor does counsel generally undertake to consult sources external to the client to obtain or verify information supplied by the client.

In the last analysis, the company and its management must assume the final responsibility to determine that the information in the registration statement is accurate and complete. Management cannot properly take a passive role and rely entirely upon counsel to identify the information to be assembled, verify the information and prepare the registration statement properly.

Clients may have, quite appropriately, a different expectation of the lawyer's role relating to those parts of the prospectus which deal with primarily "legal" matters such as descriptions of litigation, legal proceedings, tax consequences of various transactions, interpretation of contracts and descriptions of governmental requirements. To the extent that such matters are discussed, it is fair and reasonable that the company rely primarily on its counsel for the accuracy and completeness of the descriptive material in the registration statement, assuming proper disclosure of factual matters has been made to counsel. In addition, company counsel normally renders a formal opinion on the legality of the securities being registered, which is filed as an exhibit to the registration statement. In connection with a common stock offering, the opinion would state that the shares being offered are legally issued, fully paid and non-assessable.

It is typical for counsel to the company, as well as counsel to the underwriters, to be named in a prospectus, usually under a caption heading such as "Legal Opinions" or "Legal Matters." Since the naming of counsel under such a broad heading may tend to lead public investors to misconceive the lawyer's role and responsibility in the offering, it may be more appropriate for the name of the counsel to be inserted under the caption heading dealing with the description of the securities offered, along with a statement of the substance of the opinion being rendered. Such presentation would emphasize that the legal opinion being rendered relates only to these formal legal matters except to the extent that the prospectus otherwise indicates in appropriate sections regarding other specific matters such as litigation or tax consequences. An engagement letter with the client, setting forth the specific terms of counsel's responsibility, also may be a helpful practice. Such a letter can contribute materially to a better understanding between lawyer and client as to their respective responsibilities.

The authors consider it essential for the lawyers, accountants and executives to be in close coordination while the prospectus is being written. It frequently occurs that the lawyers and the accountants initially have different understandings as to the structure of a transaction, or the proper characterization or effect of an event. These differences may not be apparent readily, even from a careful reading of the registration statement's narrative text together with the financial statements. Lawyers sometimes miss the full financial implication of some important matter unless the accountants are readily available to amplify upon the draft statements and supply background information. The text is often written by counsel before the financial statements are available, based upon counsel's incorrect assumptions regarding the as yet unseen financial statement treatment of a transaction.

Experience indicates that the best and sometimes only way to flush out financial disclosure problems as well as inconsistencies between the narrative text and the financial statements is through the give and take of discussion as the structure of the offering is being determined and the draft registration statement is being reviewed. The accountant's participation in this process is often essential.

On the other hand, the authors are mindful of the expense involved when accounting representatives attend long and sometimes tedious meetings. An acceptable compromise is to request their attendance on a selective basis, and to focus only on the matters requiring their participation during the period of their presence. For example, it would be wasteful to have a page by page review of a draft with accountants present, and to have them sit through the discussions of management biographies or other details having no bearing on the financial presentation.

* * *

THE UNDERWRITING AGREEMENT

The company often signs a "letter of intent" with its managing underwriter once the selection of the underwriter has been made. If used, the letter outlines the proposed terms of the offering and the underwriting compensation.

However, it expressly states that it is not intended to bind either party, except with respect to specific matters. One typical exception is a binding provision dealing with payment of one party's expenses by the other under certain conditions if the offering aborts before the letter of intent is superceded by the formal underwriting agreement.

In a "firm commitment" underwriting agreement, the underwriters agree that they will purchase the shares being offered for the purpose of resale to the public. The underwriters must pay for and hold the shares for their own account if they are not successful in finding public purchasers. This form of underwriting is almost always used by the larger underwriters and provides the greater assurance of raising the desired funds. In the other common type of underwriting arrangement, the underwriters agree to use their "best efforts" to sell the issue as the company's agent. To the extent that purchasers cannot be found, the issue is not sold. Some best efforts agreements provide that no shares will be sold unless buyers can be found for all, while others set a lower minimum such as fifty percent. For certain special types of securities, such as tax shelter limited partnership offerings, even the major underwriters normally use the best efforts or agency underwriting relationship.

In either form of underwriting, the underwriters' obligations are usually subject to many conditions: various "outs," such as the right not to close (even if the company is not otherwise in default) in the event of certain specified adverse developments prior to the closing date; and compliance by the company with its numerous representations and warranties.[30] The underwriters also condition their obligations upon the receipt of certain opinions of counsel and representations, sometimes called a "cold comfort letter," from the company's auditors.

The binding firm underwriting agreement normally is not signed until within twenty-four hours of the expected effective date of the registration statement—often on the morning of effectiveness. Thus, throughout the process of preparing the registration statement and during the waiting period, the company has incurred very substantial expenses with no assurance that the offering will take place. Once preparation of the registration statement has begun, however, reputable underwriters rarely refuse to complete the offering, although this can occur with some frequency, especially for small and highly speculative offerings, if there is a sharp market drop during the waiting period. However, as indicated above, the underwriters must price the offering and organize the underwriting syndicate in relationship to market conditions prevailing at the time of the offering. Thus, if market conditions have worsened materially after the letter of intent stage, the issue must either come to the market at a price below that originally contemplated, or it must be postponed until conditions improve. Furthermore, it is not uncommon for underwriters to suggest a reduction in the size of the offering if the market conditions are unfavorable. The company may find itself in a position of accepting a less than

---

30. Liability has been imposed on an underwriter that breached its firm commitment underwriting agreement by unjustifiably exercising the "market-out clause." See Walk–In Medical Centers, Inc. v. Breuer Capital Corp., 818 F.2d 260 (2d Cir.1987). The court held, however, that the decision to cancel the agreement did not result from general adverse market conditions but rather from a decline in the stock's after-market. Therefore, the court found that the underwriter was not justified in terminating the agreement and upheld the trial court's judgment for the issuing company in the amount of $2.160 million, the agreed price of the securities.

satisfactory final proposal, regarding size and pricing of the offering, as a preferable alternative to postponement or complete abandonment of the offering. On the other hand, sharply improved market conditions may result in a higher offering price than the parties originally anticipated.

Final settlement with the underwriters usually takes place seven to ten days after the registration statement has become effective, so as to allow the underwriters time to obtain the funds from their customers. At that time, the company receives the proceeds of the sale, net of the underwriting compensation.

SEC rules permit underwriters to offer and sell to the public more shares than the underwriters are obligated to purchase under the underwriting agreement—a practice known as "over-allotment." If the underwriters over-allot, they will have a "short" position, which may help to establish a better after-market for the shares following the offering, since any shares resold by original purchasers will have been placed effectively in advance through the over-allotment sales. The underwriting agreement often gives the underwriters an option to purchase additional shares from the issuer, or possibly from selling shareholders, solely for the purpose of covering over-allotments. The shares covered by the over-allotment option are purchasable on the same price terms that apply to the shares which are part of the basic offering. This option of the underwriters, often referred to as a "Green Shoe option" (based on the offering of its initial use), typically covers under present practice up to a maximum of 15% of the number of shares included in the basic offering and can only be exercised within thirty days of the offering date. To illustrate, if the basic offering is 500,000 shares, the firm commitment will obligate the underwriters to purchase and pay for 500,000 shares; the over-allotment option will entitle them to purchase up to 75,000 additional shares solely to cover over-allotments.

The NASD also reviews the underwriting arrangements in accordance with guidelines which are not fully spelled out in detail to the public. The NASD will disapprove underwriting arrangements if it considers the underwriters' compensation to be excessive under these guidelines. Occasionally an underwriter who bargains hard for a very attractive compensation package from an issuer finds that the regulatory agency will disapprove the arrangement unless some aspect of the underwriters' benefits are decreased.

PRELIMINARY PREPARATION

For the average first offering, a very substantial amount of preliminary work is required which does not relate directly to preparing the registration statement as such. To have a vehicle for the offering, the business going public normally must be conducted by a single corporation or a parent corporation with subsidiaries. In most cases, the business is not already in such a neat package when the offering project commences. It is often conducted by a number of corporations under common ownership, by partnerships or by combinations of business entities. Considerable work must be done in order to reorganize the various entities by mergers, liquidations and capital contributions. Even when there is a single corporation, a recapitalization is almost always required so that the company will have an appropriate capital structure for the public offering. A decision must be made regarding the proportion of the stock to be sold to the public. Any applicable blue sky limitations on insiders' "cheap stock" should be considered in this context, especially if the company has been organized in the relatively recent past.

Among other common projects in preparing to go public, it is often necessary to enter into, revise, or terminate employment agreements, adopt stock option plans and grant options thereunder, transfer real estate, revise leases, rewrite the corporate charter and by-laws, prepare new stock certificates, engage a transfer agent and registrar, rearrange stockholdings of insiders, draw, revise or cancel agreements among shareholders, revamp financing arrangements, prepare and order stock certificates, obtain a CUSIP number and secure a tentative ticker symbol.[b]

An increasing number of companies consider adoption of defenses against hostile takeover attempts as part of the pre-offering revision of charter, by-laws and employment arrangements. So-called "shark repellent" (or "porcupine") devices, which help to deter or defeat unwelcome tender offers, include provisions for staggered multi-year terms for directors and "supermajority" voting provisions applicable to certain types of corporate transactions (to assure that a relatively small minority can veto certain proposals which may be sponsored by the holder of a majority of the stock). Various employment devices, often referred to as "golden parachutes," may protect the status and employment benefits, or may provide very favorable severance arrangements, for executives and key employees whose positions may be adversely affected by a takeover or other abrupt change of control.

On the other hand, some underwriters may resist adoption of such devices on the ground that they appear too defensive or unattractive to investors, since investors may profit handsomely from the premium paid in a hostile tender. Furthermore, adoption of some of the more effective shark repellent devices may disqualify the offering from compliance with the blue sky laws of key states. Accordingly, many issuers omit the shark repellent provisions at the time of the initial public offering. Such issuers are free, of course, to adopt shark repellent provisions at a later date, which would normally require a majority vote of all shareholders, including the public ones. If the issuer had a fixed, preconceived plan at the time of the public offering to propose such provisions at a future date, it should consider the need to disclose such plans in the prospectus.

In preparing the registration statement, there are occasionally important threshold or interpretive problems which can have a major effect on the preparation process or, indeed, on the feasibility of the offering. It is often possible to discuss such problems with the SEC staff in a pre-filing conference, although some pre-filing conference requests are denied by the staff. However, decisions to request a pre-filing conference should be made with caution. Among other considerations, once a question has been asked in advance of a filing, there may be no practical alternative other than to wait for the staff's answer, which may delay a filing considerably. Frequently, the decision is made simply to proceed with the filing, resolving the threshold issue on the basis which the company considers most appropriate, in the hope that a satisfactory resolution of the problem (either the issuer's initial solution or some other) will be achieved during the review process.

---

b. The acronym CUSIP signifies the Committee on Uniform Security Identification Procedures which was established by the American Bankers Association. The CUSIP number is an eight-digit number which is imprinted on the certificate; it is used by transfer agents to identify each issue for the purpose of identifying the issue, insuring authenticity and permitting rapid identification.

TIMETABLE

Although laymen find it difficult to believe, the average first public offering normally requires two to three months of intensive work before the registration statement can be filed. One reason so much time is required is the need to accomplish the preparatory steps just referred to at the same time the registration statement is being prepared. There are many important and often interrelated business decisions to be made and implemented and rarely are all of these questions decided definitively at the outset. Some answers must await final figures, or negotiations with underwriters, and must be held open until the last minute. In many instances, a businessman first exposed to these considerations will change his mind several times in the interim. Furthermore, drafting of the prospectus normally begins before the financial statements are available. Almost inevitably, some rewriting must be done in the non-financial parts after the financial statements are distributed in order to blend the financial and non-financial sections together. Laymen frequently have the frustrating feeling as the deadline approaches that everything is hopelessly confused. They are quite surprised to see that everything falls into place at the eleventh hour.

After the registration statement is filed with the Commission, the waiting period begins. It is during this interval that red herrings are distributed. The Commission reviews the registration statement and finally issues its letter of comments. There is a wide variation in the time required for the SEC to process a registration statement. Relevant factors include the level of the Commission's backlog of filings and the time of year. There is normally a considerable rush of filings at the end of each calendar quarter, and particularly at the end of March for filings with financial statements as of December 31.

The SEC's current policy calls for the issuance of an initial letter of comments within thirty days of the filing of a registration statement, but the delay is often longer and at times has exceeded one hundred days. * * *.

The overall time lapse between the beginning of preparation of a company's first registration statement and the final effective date may well exceed six months. Rarely will it be less than three months.

The SEC's requirements for unaudited financial statements for periods after the end of a company's last fiscal year represent another important ingredient in the timetable. In the case of a registration statement for a company going public for the first time, a company filing within forty-five days after its fiscal year end must include interim financial statements at least as current as the end of the third fiscal quarter of its most recently completed fiscal year as well as the required fiscal year end audited financial statements for the prior years; a company filing after forty-five days but within 134 days of the end of the company's most recent fiscal year end must include audited financial statements for its most recently completed fiscal year; and a company filing more than 134 days subsequent to the end of its most recent fiscal year must include interim financial statements within 135 days of the date of the filing as well as the required fiscal year end audited financial statements. The financial statement for the interim periods need not be audited, however, and the statements required are not as complete as those required for the audited periods. Of course, audited financial statements must be substituted once available in lieu of unaudited financial statements.

At the time the registration statement becomes effective, the unaudited interim financial statements must be as of a date within 135 days of the effective date, except that such financial statements may be as of the end of the third fiscal quarter of the most recently completed fiscal year if the registration statement becomes effective within forty-five days after the end of the most recent fiscal year. Audited financial statements for the most recently completed fiscal year must be included if the registration statement becomes effective between forty-five and ninety days after the end of such fiscal year.

EXPENSES

A major expense in going public is usually the underwriters' compensation. The underwriting cash discount or cash commission on a new issue generally ranges from 7% to 10% of the public offering price. The maximum amount of direct and indirect underwriting compensation is regulated by the National Association of Securities Dealers, Inc. (NASD), a self-regulatory agency which regulates broker-dealers. Normally, the three largest additional expenses are legal fees, accounting fees and printing costs. The following are general estimates of the expenses for a typical medium size offering on Form S–1.

Legal fees for a first offering can vary over a wide range depending on the complexity of the offering, the ease with which information can be assembled and verified, the extent of risk factors or other difficult disclosures and other factors. Fees in the range of $125,000 to $150,000 would be typical. This amount includes not only the preparation of the registration statement itself, but also all of the corporate work, house cleaning and other detail which is occasioned by the public offering process. Fees for smaller offerings tend to be somewhat lower. In part, this may reflect the fact that offerings for start-up companies, which tend to be smaller in size, typically require less legal work in investigating business operations, since there are none. However, start-up offerings can be more difficult in other respects—for example, risk factors are more prevalent and minor matters may require disclosure on points which would be immaterial to an established company with a history of operations. Therefore, start-up offerings occasionally are even more demanding than offerings of larger seasoned companies. * * *

For a normal first public stock offering of several million dollars, total expenses in the $225,000 to $500,000 range would be typical, exclusive of the underwriting discount or commission but inclusive of any expense allowance (whether or not accountable) payable to the underwriters. However, it should be emphasized that there are wide variations among offerings. The estimates for aggregate as well as individual expenses given above can be too low if unusual problems or complications develop in a particular offering. * * *

In addition to cash disbursements, there are other costs of going public to consider. As part of the arrangement underwriters sometimes bargain for "cheap stock"—securities which they purchase at less than the public offering price and often at a nominal price as low as a mill a share. They may insist upon receiving options or warrants exercisable over a number of years to purchase the securities being offered at a price usually equal to or above the offering price. These benefits, most typical of the smaller offerings done by the smaller underwriters, introduce an element of dilution of the security. Here again the NASD imposes limitations on the amount of cheap stock and warrants which underwriters may receive.

* * *

CONCLUSION

The process of going public is a major development in the business life of any company. It is a step which should be taken only after a thorough analysis of the advantages, disadvantages, consequences and alternative means of financing. Going public is a relatively time consuming and expensive means of raising capital, although the commensurate benefits may more than outweigh these disadvantages in the appropriate situation. * * *

———

1. *What Does It Cost?* The above article by Schneider, Manko, & Kent is from 1981, and, with the inevitable impact of inflation, costs have risen since then. A recent estimate places legal expenses at between $150,000 and $300,000, audit expenses at $100,000 to $150,000, and printing costs at $50,000 to $100,000;[1] in addition, the issuer may bear some of the underwriters' expenses. On a percentage basis, a recent SEC survey found that the total costs of an initial public offering (i.e., underwriting discount plus direct out-of-pocket costs) came to 9.3% of the offering for initial offerings registered on Form S–1 between 1993 and 1995.[2]

Perhaps more important are the imputed costs of the executive time. One estimate is that during registration, the chief financial officer will spend 75 percent of his or her time on the offering; and the chief executive officer, 40 percent.[3]

———

Excerpt from: William W. Barker

SEC Registration of Public Offerings Under the Securities Act of 1933

52 Bus.Law. 65 (1996).[a]

INTRODUCTION

The staff of the Division of Corporation Finance (Division) at the Securities and Exchange Commission (Commission) knows public offerings. More than 8800 regis-

———

1. See Loeb & Whalen, IPOs in the 1990s: Company Counsel's Role, PLI Advanced Securities Law Workshop 309, 312–313 (1995).

2. See Report of the Advisory Committee on the Capital Formation and Regulatory Processes, App. A, tbl I (SEC 1996).

3. See Loeb & Whalen, supra note 1, 313.

a. Reprinted with permission of the author. Mr. Barker is Senior Counsel to the Division of Corporation Finance at the SEC.

tration statements were filed with the Commission during fiscal year 1995 under the Securities Act of 1933 (Securities Act), registering more than $823 billion of securities. Of these 8800 registration statements, 1520 statements were selected for full review by the staff, including all of the 1000 initial public offerings that were filed. This was in addition to the staff's examination of other securities filings.[2]

* * *

The time that an issuer spends "in registration" varies.[3] Over the past few years, a first-time issuer could expect to spend seventy days in registration, on average, with some first-time issuers spending as little as forty-five days, or as many as ninety days or more, in registration.[4] At the upper end of this range, the time spent in registration must seem interminable, prompting issuers to wonder what could be done to speed the process along. Even at the lower end of the range, it is always desirable for the registration process to run more smoothly.

The comment process is predictable, which should work to an issuer's advantage. Most disclosure and other problems are recurring and can be avoided, resulting in a shorter and smoother registration process for any issuer. The primary constant in the review process is the time allotted for the staff to review filings and provide comments, which runs about thirty days from the date a registration statement is filed initially with the Commission to the date of the first round of

2. The breakdown of registration statements assigned a "full review" for fiscal years 1993 through 1995, and dollar amounts registered, is as follows:

	Total	Billion $	Full Review	Billion $	IPOs	Billion $
1995	8832	$823	1520	$265	1000	$123
1994	8651	$815	1730	$226	1382	$117
1993	7815	$868	1670	$261	989	$113

In 1995, the staff review of 1520 registration statements was in addition to the full review of 455 merger and other proxies with full financial statements, the full review of 3080 Form 10–Ks, and the legal review of 840 confidential treatment requests. In 1994, the staff review of 1730 registration statements was in addition to the full review of 343 merger and other proxies, the full review of 2473 Form 10–Ks, and 751 confidential treatment requests. In 1993, the staff review of 1670 registration statements was in addition to the full review of 300 merger and other proxies, the full review of 2703 Form 10–Ks, and 661 confidential treatment requests. *See* U.S. Sec. & Exch. Comm'n, Report of the SEC Advisory Committee on the Capital Formation and Regulatory Process, app. A, tbl. 1, at 5 . . . [hereinafter Wallman Report]. In 1996, almost 12,000 registration statements were filed, of which approximately 2000 were fully reviewed by the staff, including 1298 initial public offerings. The Division staff is not large, consisting of approximately 319 persons, including roughly 75 staff attorneys, 14 financial analysts, and 80 staff accountants at the examination level.

3. "In registration" means the total number of days between the date that a registration statement is first filed with the Commission and the date it is declared effective.

4. Of the 70 days referred to in the text, 37 days are attributed to the staff; that is, 30 days for the initial review of the registration statement and seven days for amendments. The remaining 33 days are attributed to the time taken by the issuer to respond to staff comments. In comparison, the total elapsed time in registration for repeat issuers is about 77 days, with the additional seven days attributed to the issuer. Registration statements not resolved within this time frame are generally those with significant problems or are complex filings that simply require more response time.

202 PART TWO REGULATION OF THE DISTRIBUTION OF SECURITIES

comments, and five calendar days for each amendment. There are fewer variables in the review process than issuers may imagine.

The purposes of this Article are: (i) to illustrate that the length of time an issuer spends in registration depends on factors largely within an issuer's control, (ii) to describe the most common pitfalls to be avoided, and (iii) to explain what can be done by issuers to speed along the registration process. Registration statements that are declared effective within the more expeditious time range are drafted by counsel who understand the staff's role in the registration process, avoid likely comments, and work with the staff to resolve problems quickly.

THE DIVISION OF CORPORATION FINANCE

GENERAL

The Division is staffed with lawyers, financial analysts, and accountants who provide a broad range of services in connection with the examination of public offerings filed under the Securities Act, proxy solicitations and reports filed under the Securities Exchange Act of 1934 (Exchange Act), and filings made under the Trust Indenture Act of 1939. Most Division lawyers have two or three years of previous law firm experience, and many also hold an M.B.A. or LL.M. degree. All Division financial analysts hold M.B.A. degrees. All Division accountants are certified public accountants, each person having a minimum of three years of prior public accounting experience, usually with a "Big Six" accounting firm or the equivalent. . . .

CHAIN OF COMMAND

There are nine Division offices that examine registration statements and other filings, including one office devoted to small business issuers. Each of the nine examining offices is responsible for approximately 1550 active reporting companies (a total of approximately 14,000 Division-wide). Issuers are assigned to a particular examining office on the basis of the standard industrial code (SIC) activity which generates the most significant portion of the issuer's revenues.

Each of the nine examining offices is administered by an Assistant Director, who directs a legal and accounting staff of twenty-five to thirty persons engaged in work pertaining to the Securities Act and other filings that require an Assistant Director's signature on a Commission order. Assistant Directors are involved more closely with public offerings and enforcement referrals than with other filings. Each Assistant Director is responsible for implementing the policies and practices of the Division at the examining staff level and developing his or her own policies and practices when the Division has taken no formal position, both of which are important mechanisms for achieving consistency in the review of filings.

Excepting instances when persons at the Associate Director level or higher become involved in the review of a registration statement, the Assistant Director generally provides the highest level of review and approval necessary for a registration statement to be declared effective.[11] By necessity, some of the Assistant Director's review responsibilities in connection with Securities Act

---

11. Above the Assistant Director in the chain of command are the Chief Counsel, Associate Director of Legal Operations, Associate Director of Disclosure Operations, Associate Director of Accounting Operations, Senior Associate Director, Deputy Director, and Director.

filings are delegated to senior staff members. In the early stages of staff review, the Assistant Director is likely to work more closely with the staff attorney or financial analyst on nonaccounting aspects of the registration statement. The Assistant Director, however, is involved actively with all aspects of the offering after the legal and accounting staff have completed their review and have no further comments. The registration statement is placed on the Assistant Director's calendar for final review within approximately forty-eight hours of the scheduled effective date.

Working under each Assistant Director is a Special Counsel who supervises staff attorneys in connection with discrete legal issues, such as registration and integration problems, and other matters, such as confidential treatment requests and enforcement referrals. In addition, each Assistant Director also supervises three Assistant Chief Accountants who are responsible directly for reviewing the accounting staff's primary examination of filings.

At the bottom of the chain of command is the remainder of the staff, which consists of approximately fifteen accountants, ten staff attorneys, two financial analysts, and the clerical staff. Decisions concerning the registration statement, comments, and timing of the staff's schedule begin with an individual examiner or accountant, but final disposition on most matters requires some degree of consultation with supervisory staff. * * *

FILING DOCUMENTS ON EDGAR

Registration statements are filed on the Commission's Electronic Data Gathering, Analysis, and Retrieval (EDGAR) system, the computer system for the receipt, acceptance, review, and dissemination of documents filed in electronic format. Documents that are filed on EDGAR are available to the staff immediately upon acceptance. Registration statements are routed electronically to the appropriate examining office, screened, and distributed to the examination team. Registration statements and amendments also are available immediately to the public via computer terminals in the Commission's Public Reference Room. The statements and amendments become available for inspection and copying twenty-four hours after filing through private document services for a fee. As a result of the efforts of Chairman Arthur Levitt, registration statements and other filings are available to the public without additional charge on the Internet through the Commission's World Wide Web site.[14]

TEAM APPROACH

Registration statements are examined by a team consisting of a staff attorney or financial analyst (commonly called "examiners") and a staff accountant. The examination team changes from registration statement to registration statement. The examiner's work is reviewed by the Assistant Director or a senior staff member, usually a lawyer. The accountant's work is reviewed by an Assistant Chief Accountant.

After receiving the registration statement, the examiner will make any necessary referrals, including referrals to support offices or other divisions within the Commission, state regulators, or other federal agencies. Such referrals may lead to further or more accurate disclosure. Except for interna-

---

14. As of the date of this publication, the Commission's Internet address is: <http:/ /www.sec.gov>.

tional offerings, initial public offerings usually do not require support offices of the Division to become involved in the review of a registration statement.

The staff examines the registration statement carefully. Examiners first review the registration statement for major structural defects, sometimes called "show stoppers," which would prevent the transaction from going forward until resolved. Examiners then scrutinize the prospectus and Part II information, including exhibits, for compliance with other applicable federal securities laws. . . .

The preliminary results of the staff review of an initial filing and amendments are described in written internal memoranda, or "examination reports." The examination reports are the Commission's nonpublic written records of the analyses, thoughts, and impressions of the respective members of the examination team, whether or not expressed in the comment letter to the issuer that follows. Pursuant to * * * the rules of the Freedom of Information Act (FOIA),[23] staff examination reports are not required to be produced in response to a FOIA request by an outside party.

The accounting and nonaccounting portion of the examination and review of registration statements proceed separately. The accounting portion of the staff review passes from the staff accountant to an Assistant Chief Accountant. The nonaccounting portion of the staff review passes from the examiner to a senior staff member. Throughout the examination process, however, the examiners and accountants exchange ideas and work together to develop comments. This is particularly true of accounting or financial issues that need to be drawn out in the text of the prospectus. Both portions of the staff review come together in the hands of the examiner shortly before comments are communicated to the issuer. Comments will not be communicated to an issuer until both portions have been reviewed by supervisory staff. Sending accounting and nonaccounting comments out to issuers as they become available invariably causes more problems and delays than are avoided.

The examiner is the "point person" responsible for monitoring the involvement of other examining offices and divisions, the status of the accounting staff review, coordinating and compiling the comment letter, and communicating staff views to the issuer. The legal and accounting staff remain autonomous in most matters because neither group has authority to direct the activities or pace of the other.

THE SELECTIVE REVIEW PROCESS

Rule 202.3 of the Commission's Rules of Practice and Investigation provides that registration statements, proxy statements, periodic reports, trust indenture filings, and similar documents filed with the Commission are routed to the Division. The Division initially passes upon the adequacy of disclosure and recommends initial action to be taken. The Division does not have the resources necessary to examine all registration statements and other documents filed with the Commission each year. As a result, the selective review process was implemented in 1980.

Registration statements are "screened" in the appropriate examining office, according to predetermined criteria, to select which of four levels of review

---

23. *See* 17 C.F.R. § 200.80(b)(4) (1996); *see also* 5 U.S.C. § 552(a)–(d) (1994). An overview of the subject is found in Robert G. Belair, *SEC FOIA Practice,* REV. OF SEC. & COMM. REG., Jan. 24, 1990, at 11.

is appropriate: (i) deferred review, (ii) monitor, (iii) no review, or (iv) full review.[26] While the Division's detailed screening procedures are nonpublic, as most practitioners probably are aware from personal experience, the selective review process is financially oriented and very practical. Registration statements filed by first-time issuers will be assigned a full and thorough review.[27] Subsequently, issuers are selected for review on an "as needed" basis.[28] In the selective review system, it is important nothing be left to chance so that no filing that should be reviewed "slips by" unnoticed. Consequently, it is to an issuer's advantage to communicate with the staff regarding any prefiling, filing, or disclosure issues, or other questions an issuer may have.

Filings that are deficient materially or incomplete when filed may receive a deferred review. Common examples of materially deficient filings are registration statements filed with financial statements that are stale or registration statements filed with incomplete financial or other information. Materially deficient filings are summarily rejected from the review process by the staff issuance of a "bed-bug letter" outlining the material deficiencies which prevent further review. Bed-bugged filings will not proceed any further in the review process and the thirty-day review period will not begin again until an amendment is filed that does not contain comparable deficiencies. The staff usually is unwilling to expedite the thirty-day review period when an amendment correcting the deficiencies is filed, for to do so would delay unfairly more conscientious filers. For the same reason, the staff will not consider reviewing portions of the registration statement that are not deficient while the deficient portions are being corrected. The issuer may lose the number of days between the date the deficient filing was made and the date upon which the issuer was notified that the filing was bed-bugged.

Repeat issuers often receive a "no review" when there is little or no practical purpose served by subjecting an issuer, or the staff, to another full review. The most common example of no reviews are offerings filed by issuers who very recently had another registration statement fully reviewed, are current and timely in their reporting obligations under the Exchange Act, have not had financial difficulties, and do not raise any enforcement issues. There are no published criteria describing the type of financial difficulties that will trigger review, but, "like pornography, a lawyer should know what financial difficulties are when he or she sees them."

There also are less rigorous types of reviews. Specific aspects of a registration statement may be targeted by the staff for review or monitoring. An issuer that may otherwise qualify for a "no review" may be monitored for aspects of the offering that are of special interest to the staff or that are different from the last fully reviewed registration statement filed. Issues that commonly result

---

26. *See* Expediting Registration Statements Filed Under the Securities Act of 1933, Securities Act Release No. 4934, [1967–1969 Transfer Binder] Fed.Sec.L.Rep. (CCH) ¶ 77,-677, at 83,345 (Nov. 21, 1968); Division of Corporation Finance's Procedures to Curtail Time in Registration Under the Securities Act, Securities Act Release No. 5231, [1971–1972 Transfer Binder] Fed.Sec.L.Rep. (CCH) ¶ 78,509, at 81,103 (Feb. 3, 1972).

27. *See* Richard H. Rowe, *SEC Review Practices: A Primer,* INSIGHTS, Jan. 1990, at 22.

28. Issuers also may receive a full review based upon the nature of the transaction (e.g., exchange offers and merger proxies filed on Form S–4), special industry concerns, outstanding comments on reports filed under the Exchange Act, or simply because it has been two or three years since the issuer's last full review.

in monitoring include outstanding comments on Exchange Act reports, unusual securities or plans of distribution, and enforcement interest in the issuer. Similarly, reports filed under the Exchange Act may be selected for "financial statement only" review by the accounting staff, which targets the issuer's financial statements and the Management's Discussion and Analysis (MD&A) section of the report. Often, the purpose of monitoring a filing is to examine only one or two issues of interest to the staff and to ensure that those issues are in compliance with the federal securities laws. Where an offering is monitored, as opposed to being reviewed fully, comments tend to be fewer and more focused, and available in less than thirty days. Depending on the issues, it may be possible for the staff to review proposed changes in draft form rather than by amendment.

PREFILING CONSIDERATIONS

The hard work is completed before the registration statement is filed with the Commission. Avoiding disclosure and other registration problems begins early by addressing any transactional, disclosure, or accounting obstacles an issuer may have, considering the documents to be filed, and planning in order to avoid delays.

PRELIMINARY ISSUES

* * *

An issuer should conduct as much industry research as possible. Many staff comments, particularly those made with respect to the Business and MD&A sections, will be drawn from recent newspapers, magazines, trade publications, electronic data bases, and industry, market, or investment reports. These sources provide valuable insight into sales, trends, competition, and other facets of the issuer's business. The staff catches most "gun jumping" issues as a result of research through comprehensive news and industry data bases.[47]

"MODEL" PROSPECTUSES

The best advice to an issuer is to shop carefully. One of the problems with selecting a model is that only approximately fifteen to twenty percent of all registration statements filed with the Commission are reviewed fully in the selective review process. Consequently, many of the remaining registration statements not reviewed fully contain errors, making them poor models. There also are subjective elements in the review process to consider. A good model will reflect the types of comments likely to be raised in connection with the issuer's registration statement. At a minimum, registration statements used as models should be those that were given a full review by the staff, have the same SIC as the issuer, and were reviewed in the same Assistant Director group that will review the issuer's registration statement. If necessary, select a second model covering the accounting presentation. Select models that are straightforward, balanced, and fairly representative of good disclosure practices throughout the issuer's industry.

* * *

---

47. Potentially offending news articles or other material that may condition the market prior to the effective date of the registration statement should be drawn to the staff's attention rather than waiting to see whether the staff will notice. . . .

PRESENTATION OF THE REGISTRATION STATEMENT

Present the disclosure in a clear, concise, and understandable fashion as required by Rule 421. Write short, simple sentences in plain English. Grammar and writing software are available to aid in this task. Gratuitous or repetitive information should be deleted because it obscures material information and makes the prospectus more difficult to read. Superior registration statements contain almost no repetition.

The prospectus should be informative. Try to anticipate the types of questions a reader might raise concerning how the issuer makes money, the market for the issuer's products, marketing and distribution, and which products and product lines generate material revenues. Questions not answered easily within the four corners of the prospectus by a casual reading probably will result in comments. * * *

PREFILING AND OTHER CONFERENCES

The Commission has an established policy of making its staff available to issuers in advance of filing a registration statement, a service that is probably under-utilized.[56] Face-to-face meetings are rare because of the time involved. Although meetings usually are unnecessary, the staff will take the time to meet with anyone who requests a meeting. Informal conference calls are much more common and can be arranged with the staff reviewing the registration statement. A conference call can be used to discuss unusual problems that the issuer must overcome to accomplish registration or simply to discuss a novel or unique accounting or legal issue likely to become the subject of comment. In addition, because the staff reviews so many registration statements, issues unfamiliar in counsel's experience may be fairly common to the staff. The staff enjoys participating in conference calls with other professionals, particularly when it believes that its time has been well-spent.

In preparing for conference calls, it is helpful to study the treatment of the same or similar issues in other offerings, particularly accounting issues, which tend to be more concrete than others.[57] While not required, the issuer should

---

56. *See* Guides for Preparation and Filing of Registration Statements, Securities Act Release No. 4936, [1967–1969 Transfer Binder] Fed.Sec.L.Rep. (CCH) ¶ 77,636, at 83,370 (Dec. 9, 1968); *see also* Commission's Rules of Practice and Investigation, Pre-filing Assistance and Interpretative Advice, 17 C.F.R. § 202.2 (1996). Rule 202.2 directs the staff to provide assistance to prospective issuers and the general public. This assistance may concern the availability of an exemption, the application of a statute or rule, preparation of registration statements, and the scope of the items contained in the forms. No-action letters are examples of interpretive advice. Novel or unique plans of distribution are sometimes submitted to the Division's Office of Chief Counsel and/or the Assistant Director for pre-review to ensure legal compliance. One example of pre-review occurred when a firm commitment underwriting of common stock was proposed to take place concurrently with a self-underwritten offering to customers through coupons attached to products. *See* Boston Beer Co. (SEC File No. 33–96162) (Rule 424(b)(4) prospectus, filed Nov. 22, 1995) (consumer offering) (on file with *The Business Lawyer,* University of Maryland School of Law); Boston Beer Co. (SEC File No. 33–96164) (Rule 424(c) prospectus, filed Nov. 29, 1995) (firm commitment) (on file with *The Business Lawyer,* University of Maryland School of Law).

57. Disclosure in prior registration statements may be more or less authoritative depending upon: (i) whether a particular model was given a full review, (ii) whether the issue in question was raised by the staff, (iii) if any factual differences impacted materiality, (iv) the staff's level of experience, and (v) if the disclosure in question represents the views of the Division at the Chief Counsel or Chief Accountant level or higher.

address any concerns to be covered in the conference call in an advance letter to the staff. The letter should outline the facts and issues to be discussed, the treatment of the issues in similar filings, and the issuer's rationale and proposed solutions. It is helpful to memorialize the results of the meeting in a letter back to the staff after the conference call.

CONFIDENTIAL TREATMENT REQUESTS UNDER RULE 406[58]

A confidential treatment request filed with the Office of the Secretary of the Commission under Rule 406 in connection with a registration statement invariably creates a risk of delay. Confidential treatment requests are routed promptly from the Office of the Secretary of the Commission to the appropriate examining office, through the Special Counsel, and into the examiner's hands. * * *

Confidential treatment requests filed under Rule 406 in connection with registration statements receive close attention. The registration statement disclosure relating to the confidential treatment request will be scrutinized carefully not only by the examiner and Special Counsel, but also by the Assistant Director, who must sign a separate order granting confidential treatment under Rule 406. To avoid the most common problems, the issuer should ensure that the confidential treatment request is drawn narrowly (key words, dollar amounts, quantities) and supported amply, as required by Rule 406. In particular, the nonconfidential portions of each exhibit must be disclosed fully and explained in the registration statement. This is done sometimes on a contract-by-contract basis for clarity. Material terms usually include the names of parties to the contract, term and termination provisions, and any material minimum or aggregate dollar amounts. Issuers also often overlook the fact that confidential treatment is not available for information that is financially or otherwise material. * * *

THE STAFF'S ROLE IN THE REGISTRATION PROCESS

THE DISCLOSURE SYSTEM

* * * When choosing among investment opportunities, investors primarily are interested in an issuer's earnings potential. Recognizing this, the staff directs its comments and encourages issuers to provide full disclosure of those factors that have had a material effect upon historical earnings or may have a material effect upon future earnings.

To facilitate disclosure of material information, Regulation S-K, which evolved in part from the old self-contained forms and numerous Guides on the Preparation and Filing of Registration Statements and Reports (Guides), was developed to codify existing informal disclosure requirements. The Guides were developed as a broad-based effort to cover recurring disclosure issues and general types of information that may be material to an investor in evaluating the business and earnings of an issuer and an investment in an issuer's securities, and to prevent fraud. While the adoption of the integrated disclosure system rescinded whatever authority the Guides had, the Guides continue to be valuable for their historical perspective, generality, and accompanying rationale, all of which were lost in the drafting of the current rules. Regulation C

---

58. For further information that may be helpful in preparing confidential treatment applications, see Spencer G. Feldman, *Withholding Confidential Information From Required Filings,* REV. OF SEC. & COMM. REG., May 20, 1992, at 1.

evolved similarly, codifying the procedures applicable to the registration process. In adopting Regulation S–K, the Commission believed that compliance with the Securities Act and the Exchange Act would be aided by the development of a uniform disclosure regulation.

ROLE OF THE STAFF IN EXAMINING FILINGS

The Commission does not have the authority to approve or disapprove offerings for lack of merit. The only standard that must be met in the registration of securities is adequate and accurate disclosure of the material facts concerning the issuer's business, finances, securities, proposed offering, and risks. * * *

THE STAFF'S COMMENT LETTER

Much of the exchange between staff and issuers previously occurred informally over the telephone and without documentation. Now these exchanges more appropriately take place through detailed written correspondence intended to document the comment process. Rule 202.3 of the Commission's Rules of Practice and Investigation establishes the basis for the review process and, indirectly, the basis for the current comment process. For example, if the registration statement appears to afford inadequate disclosure through omission of material information or noncompliance with generally accepted accounting principles, the usual practice is to bring the deficiencies to the attention of the issuer through a letter. * * *

Today's comment letter is more extensive than the original "deficiency letter" sent out by the staff in the early days of the registration process to stave off stop order proceedings. Though sent out over the signature of an Assistant Director or senior staff member, a comment letter is a collection of questions and perceived deficiencies raised by staff attorneys, accountants, and analysts. These individuals possess differing levels of experience, are located in different examining offices or divisions, and are positioned at various levels of staff or management.

The comment letter fulfills two purposes. It documents staff concerns regarding the adequacy and accuracy of the information contained in the registration statement and reflects the staff's consideration of different facets of the offering, such as legal compliance of underwriting arrangements and the plan of distribution. As a result of comments, the staff receives issuer revisions or, where there is disagreement, information supporting and documenting the issuer's belief that it has a reasonable basis for its actions.

Comment letters are surrounded by a unique internal protocol that results from the type of integrated examination registration statements receive. Because comment letters are an integrated effort among the legal, financial, and accounting disciplines, a cursory reading of a comment letter may indicate that four or more staff members contributed comments to the letter. Additional comments may be contributed by staff members in support offices or other divisions depending upon the issues involved in the offering. To avoid altering the substance of the various staff members' concerns, and to assure comments are given to issuers in a timely manner, comments provided to the examiner by these persons are included in the comment letter without any editorial changes.

In reviewing the registration statement to ensure the adequacy and accuracy of the disclosure, the staff issues two types of comments: (i) comments requesting supplemental information as provided in Rule 418; and (ii) comments requesting revision to the registration statement, including requests for clarification as provided in Rule 421. The disclosure in the registration statement is the responsibility of the issuer and the issuer's representatives. Over the years, the staff's shorthand instruction—"advise or revise"—has conveyed the notion that comments may be addressed either in the issuer's response letter or by revision to the registration statement, so long as the staff's underlying concern regarding the adequacy or accuracy of the proposed disclosure is resolved. * * *

COMMON DISCLOSURE PITFALLS

* * * Because most disclosure and other problems that result in comments are recurring, avoiding these pitfalls should result in fewer comments and a shorter and smoother registration process for any issuer.

* * *

COVER PAGE OF THE PROSPECTUS

Because the Cover Page and Summary are an investor's first, and possibly last, glimpse at the offering, the trend in recent years has been toward an abbreviated "at a glance" format of terms and the elimination of boilerplate language. This trend is likely to continue. Item 501(c) of Regulation S–K calls for a concise sketch of the terms of the offering, including title and amount of securities offered, price or price range, shares offered by selling security holders, and cross-reference to material risks.

* * *

Registration statements that omit pricing information in reliance on Rule 430A must include the price range on the Cover Page or, when appropriate, the formula by which the price is to be determined. Issuers frequently fail to include this information, prompting the staff to request that the price range or formula be included.

SUMMARY INFORMATION

The length and complexity of prospectuses usually result in a Summary being provided under Item 503(a) of Regulation S–K. The most common problem in the Summary is the failure to provide the information in a concise, balanced manner that fairly summarizes the salient features of the offering and other information in the prospectus. Summary financial information, key financial ratios, total shares offered and outstanding, intended trading symbol and market information, amount of dilution, shares eligible for future sale, and similar abbreviated information are helpful to a reader.

A "balanced presentation" contemplates that equal prominence will be given to both favorable information and unfavorable information. Where only favorable information is presented in the Summary, the staff may request the favorable information be balanced against less favorable information contained in other parts of the prospectus, such as disappointing operating results, the absence of material sales, or negative shareholder equity. Where there is more unfavorable information regarding an issuer than favorable information, however, a very brief summary limited to a short statement of the issuer's business and terms of the offering may suffice as a balanced presentation.

RISK FACTORS

Item 503(c) of Regulation S–K, captioned "Risk Factors," calls for a discussion of the principal factors that make the offering speculative or one of high risk. The placement and title of this section are important. Because of the importance of risk disclosure to investors and the lack of any requirement that risk factors be summarized in the Summary, the item specifically requires that this section shall immediately follow the Summary. If no Summary is included, the Risk Factors section should immediately follow the Cover Page. This section is to be captioned "Risk Factors," not "Certain Considerations," "Certain Factors," "Investment Consideration," or similar titles. To ensure material risks are not obscured, all material risks should be set out in full in the Risk Factor section of the prospectus and not incorporated by reference from other filings or portions of the document. The latter point is particularly true in the case of initial public offerings, but is becoming increasingly important in all offerings.

The regulations do not require specifically that risk factors be prioritized, but the disclosure of the risks should be stated fairly and not obscured. Where important risks are buried in the back of the Risk Factor section, or the disclosures are too lengthy or cumbersome for the average investor to appreciate, the issuer may draw comments requesting that one or more risk factors be moved to a more prominent position and be made clear, concise, and understandable. Immaterial risks should not be included.

Common risks covered in this section include: (i) absence of operating history or profitable operations in recent periods; (ii) financial condition of the issuer (including leverage); (iii) business, product, life-cycle, and competitive risks; (iv) adverse sales trends; (v) dependence on material suppliers and customers; and (vi) concentration of credit risk. Special risk-factor disclosure is also required for low priced stocks quoted on the National Association of Securities Dealers' Automated Quotation (NASDAQ) system. This disclosure often is requested by the staff when the possible loss of NASDAQ system quotation in the future may have a material adverse effect.

＊ ＊ ＊

MANAGEMENT'S DISCUSSION AND ANALYSIS

The MD&A section is intended to give investors an opportunity to look at the issuer through the eyes of management by providing both short-and long-term analyses of the business of the issuer and to examine the financial information of the issuer.[132] In addition to an explanation in plain English of year-to-year changes in the issuer's financial statements, the MD&A section should address general economic conditions, industry concerns, and developments regarding the issuer's business or products as sources of potential trends, events, or uncertainties (collectively "uncertainties") that may impact an investment in the issuer. The legal and accounting staff both will focus closely on the disclosure required in the MD&A section by Item 303 of Regulation S–K.

Issuers usually do well calling uncertainties to the attention of investors in the Risk Factor section, but less so in elaborating upon the likelihood that an

---

132. *See* Management's Discussion and Analysis of Financial Condition and Results of Operations; Certain Investment Company Disclosures, Securities Act Release No. 6835, 43 S.E.C. Docket (CCH) 1330 (May 18, 1989).

uncertainty will have a material effect on the issuer in the MD&A section. A common problem is that issuers sometimes do not discuss potential effects of uncertainties, based upon the argument that management does not have a "crystal ball" and is not accurately able to foresee or predict whether the uncertainty will occur or its materiality. . . .

Item 303 of Regulation S–K adopts disclosure criteria intentionally more inclusive than the *Basic* test. The MD&A Release makes clear that the type of limited disclosure resulting from application of the "crystal ball" theory is not adequate.[136] Under the standard set out in Item 303, further disclosure of uncertainties is required where an issuer cannot conclude that: (i) the uncertainty is not reasonably likely to occur, or (ii) that the uncertainty is not material.[137] If the issuer cannot pass these tests, then the uncertainty should be disclosed on the assumption that it will occur and will be material.[138] This is true whether an uncertainty is identified in a news article, in an analyst's report, or by the staff in a comment letter.

The trend of administrative proceedings brought by the SEC's Division of Enforcement supports this view.[139] Where an issuer has determined the uncertainty is likely to occur but cannot make a determination on the issue of materiality, or has concluded that the impact is likely to be material but cannot assess *how* material, the better disclosure practice is to acknowledge the uncertainty, disclose that the issuer cannot make a determination regarding the impact of the uncertainty, explain the reasons, and provide a helpful explanation of the factors that may affect the outcome. * * *

136. Under the test set out in Item 303, "probability" is not balanced against "magnitude" to determine whether disclosure is required. If an uncertainty is reasonably likely to occur, disclosure is required unless the uncertainty is not material. Therefore, the disclosure required by Item 303 is in addition to any disclosure that may be required by the *Basic* test. *See* Paul N. Edwards, *The Limits of Forward–Looking Information in MD&A,* J. Corp. Acct. & Fin., Summer 1991, at 425–36 . . .; *see also* Justin P. Klein & Gerald J. Guarcini, *Through the Eyes of Management,* Rev. of Sec. & Comm. Reg., Sept. 23, 1992, at 177–82.

137. Klein & Guarcini, *supra* note 136, at 181.

138. Edwards, *supra* note 136, at 426.

139. The administrative trend has been to view the reasonableness of management's conclusions in this regard with the benefit of common sense and hindsight, which punctuates the limited usefulness of the crystal ball argument. In *SEC v. Bank of New England Corp.,* Litigation Release No. 12742, 47 S.E.C. Docket (CCH) 1327 (Dec. 21, 1990), the uncertainty was whether the effects of the recession in New England would continue to result in increased loan loss reserves and lower net income. Because the issuer could not conclude that the effects of the recession would not continue, the potential continued effect on loan loss reserves and net income should have been disclosed. *Id.* at 1328. In *In re Caterpillar, Inc.,* Exchange Act Release No. 30532, 51 S.E.C. Docket (CCH) 147 (Mar. 31, 1992), the uncertainty was whether Brazilian economic reforms would effect Brazilian operations materially, which accounted for 23% of consolidated net income previously (because of hyperinflation in Brazil). Because the issuer could not conclude that economic reforms were not likely to occur, the potential material impact should have been disclosed. *Id.* at 153. Finally, in *In re Presidential Life Corp.,* Exchange Act Release No. 31934, 53 S.E.C. Docket (CCH) 1563 (Mar. 1, 1993), the uncertainty was whether investments in high-yield securities comprising 80% of the bond portfolio presented a material risk to the issuer's investment portfolio. Declines in the issuer's high-yield securities portfolio were classified as "temporary," on the hope that the market value would again rise and, therefore, had not been reflected in the carrying value of the securities portfolio. Because many of the high-yield issuers were in or near default, or in bankruptcy, the Commission found that the issuer could not conclude that uncertainty was unlikely to occur. *Id.* at 1572.

BUSINESS

Item 101 of Regulation S–K requires disclosure of the general development of the issuer's business, the business done and intended to be done by the issuer and its subsidiaries, segment information,[142] and foreign operations. Issuers are permitted significant latitude in the Business section to "showcase" their operations, provided the disclosure is presented in a balanced manner that is fair to investors. Most of the staff comments on the Business section are directed at ensuring: (i) the line item requirements of Item 101 Regulation S–K are present; (ii) the disclosure is clear, concise, and understandable in its explanation of the issuer's business, products, and markets; and (iii) the statements made in the Business section can be supported. * * *

Item 101(c)(1)(i) of Regulation S–K requires disclosure of an issuer's principal products and services as well as the markets for and methods of distributing products and services. The word "principal" is interpreted by the staff to mean "material." A common disclosure error is lumping disclosure of revenues into one overbroad class of products or services (e.g., "computer software"), without further disclosure of material products or services within a class of similar products or services. Without more specific disclosure of material products or services, investors will not be able to determine which products or services account for material revenues. Further, investors will be less able to make themselves aware of shifts or declines in revenues that may adversely impact their investment. Competitive concerns are outweighed by the material nature of the information. Therefore, where any single product or service, or logical group of similar products or services, generates material revenues, disclosure of this information must be provided on a product-by-product, service-by-service, and group-by-group basis. Revenues attributed to products or services that do not account for material revenues, individually or in the aggregate, need not be disclosed separately.

Item 101(c)(1)(vii) of Regulation S–K requires disclosure of material customers, which generally are considered those customers that account for approximately ten percent or more of revenues, but only if the loss of such a customer would have a material adverse effect on the issuer. The words, "if the loss of such a customer would have a material adverse effect," assume that the issuer's continuing revenue stream depends upon "repeat," as opposed to "new," business. For example, semiconductor and computer companies tend to rely upon ongoing customer relationships, while the customer base of home construction companies tends to change from year to year. As a result, the staff usually does not insist on disclosure of material customers where the issuer can represent accurately that repeat business is not a material factor in the issuer's business. * * *

Item 101(c)(1)(viii) of Regulation S–K requires disclosure of product order backlog believed to be firm, as of a recent date and as of a comparable date in the preceding fiscal year, together with the portion of backlog not reasonably expected to be filled within the current portion of the fiscal year, and seasonal or other material aspects of backlog. The disclosure of backlog required by Item 101(c)(1)(viii) is a frequent topic of comment by the staff, in part because a

---

142. There are no Commission rules defining a business "segment." FASB defines a segment as "a component of an enterprise engaged in providing a product or service or group of related product or services * * * to unaffiliated customers." FIN. ACCOUNTING STANDARDS BD., STATEMENT OF FINANCIAL ACCOUNTING STANDARDS NO. 14, FINANCIAL REPORTING FOR SEGMENTS OF A BUSINESS ENTERPRISE ¶ 10(a) (1976)....

decrease in backlog often signals a downturn in the fortunes of an issuer and may impact the disclosure that is required in the MD&A section. Disclosure of backlog is material to an understanding of the issuer's business taken as a whole, rather than based upon a percentage of revenues, and therefore should be included in every case. Issuers who do not believe that backlog is a meaningful indicator of their future business prospects may include an additional qualifying disclosure in the prospectus explaining their views. * * *

MATERIAL LEGAL PROCEEDINGS

Item 103 of Regulation S–K requires disclosure of "material pending legal proceedings, other than ordinary routine litigation incidental to the business." The wording of this item sometimes results in disagreements concerning whether disclosure of material legal proceedings may be omitted on the basis that the proceedings are "ordinary and routine" in nature or "incidental" to the business of the issuer. Neither basis for omitting discussion of material litigation appears to be the intention of Item 103. Accordingly, the staff is likely to request disclosure of legal proceedings where legal proceedings are or may be material. Where an issuer is involved in litigation arising in the ordinary course of its business, none of which is believed to be material, a simple statement to that effect should suffice. Most other comments result when issuers do not include a complete description of the name of the court or agency in which the proceedings are pending, case number, date instituted, brief description of the factual basis for the action, and the relief sought.

EXECUTIVE COMPENSATION

Item 402 of Regulation S–K contemplates a highly specialized format for disclosing executive compensation, with disclosure issues covered exhaustively in Securities Act Release No. 6940[153] and Securities Act Release No. 6962.[154] Most of the staff comments result from issuers not following the specialized format required by the item. Where disclosure of inapplicable items is omitted, as permitted by the rules, it may not be clear to the examiner whether the disclosure was omitted due to inapplicability or oversight. The better registration statements avoid comments by carefully indicating the basis for the inapplicability of key item requirements in the text, rather than omitting any mention of inapplicable items altogether.

* * *

AFFILIATED TRANSACTIONS

Item 404 of Regulation S–K requires disclosure of certain transactions between the issuer, its affiliates, and their family members when the transaction exceeds a specified dollar amount (currently $60,000), during the last fiscal year. Disclosure of the issuer's belief concerning the fairness of the terms of affiliated transactions is material to investors. As to each transaction required to be disclosed, the issuer also should state whether the terms of these transactions are at least as fair to the issuer as could have been obtained from unaffiliated third parties. Affiliated transactions are scrutinized closely by the staff to ensure that all material terms of these transactions are explained

153. *See* Executive Compensation Disclosure, Securities Act Release No. 6940, [1992 Transfer Binder] Fed.Sec.L.Rep. (CCH) ¶ 85,003, at 82,852 (June 23, 1992).

154. *See* Executive Compensation Disclosure, Securities Act Release No. 6962, [1992 Transfer Binder] Fed.Sec.L.Rep. (CCH) ¶ 85,056, at 83,414 (Oct. 16, 1992).

clearly so that investors can appreciate any benefits derived from the relationship, or that the issuer at least believes that there were no special benefits. Companies that may go public in the future should consider cleaning up these transactions sufficiently far in advance of the public offering so that disclosure in a registration statement is not required.

    * * *

PLAN OF DISTRIBUTION

Item 508 of Regulation S–K calls for a description of the plan of distribution of securities to the public and the terms on which the distribution is to be made. Where common equity is being registered for the first time and there is no established trading market (including initial public offerings or securities for which quotations are limited or sporadic), or where there is a material disparity between the offering and market prices, Item 505 of Regulation S–K requires that the issuer describe the various factors considered in determining the offering price. Unfortunately, the item invites boilerplate responses. For example, statements that the "initial public offering price has been arbitrarily determined" or "the offering price has been established by negotiations between the underwriter and representative" do not by themselves provide meaningful disclosure. These statements should be accompanied with the basis for that conclusion, which may include the basis for concluding that companies used for comparison are comparable and, if true, that the initial public offering price bears little or no relationship to the issuer's assets, earnings, or other criteria of value. Where the staff perceives a great disparity in the offering price of the issuer's securities and the market price of securities of "comparable companies," the staff may request additional information concerning the identities, recent market prices, and price earnings data of the comparable companies. In some cases, the staff may request the identities of the comparable companies be disclosed so investors can make their own determination whether the comparable companies are truly comparable or if the securities of the issuer simply are overpriced. * * *

THE ISSUER'S RESPONSE LETTER

The issuer's response letter sets the tone for the remainder of the review process. Well-written response letters will result in a smoother and more efficient review process because the staff will work first on amendments that can be completed quickly. Avoiding a few simple mistakes can increase the success rate of responses to staff comments and will result in fewer rounds of comments.

Choose battles carefully. Giving the staff all information and revisions requested in the comment letter is the fastest route to "going effective." . . .

It usually is unproductive to dispute whether a comment should have been included in the comment letter; one should instead focus on the response. A well-reasoned response often can persuade the staff quickly not to pursue a comment that will not lead to meaningful disclosure. . . . Because comments can be waived only by supervisory staff, which may require additional time, focusing upon the adequacy and accuracy of the existing disclosure in the response letter usually is the most expedient approach to resolving comments.[176]

176. A 10% test often is employed as a general rule of thumb to gauge materiality, particularly with respect to financial matters. This is not intended, however, to be a bright-

Issuers frequently fail to provide the staff with data and other information necessary for the staff to determine whether the issue has complied with the comments. Each response should briefly indicate *how* the issuer has complied with the comment. Responses also should state the page numbers where disclosure in response to each comment is located. The language used in the comment will often indicate the disclosure the staff is seeking or the approach suggested by the staff. Making the staff search the amended registration statement for disclosure in response to each of the staff comments slows the process.

When a comment is not complied with, the most common shortcoming in response letters is the failure to provide sufficient factual information for the staff to either agree or disagree with the issuer's position. Thus, the comment will be reissued. To avoid this, detail the factual basis for disagreement in the response letter and focus the analysis on the *reasons* the disclosure is believed to be adequate. * * *

A question frequently arises whether staff comments should be addressed by letter, in a draft, or by amendment. The staff prefers revisions be provided by pre-effective amendment, which is available immediately to the public, rather than in a response letter or in draft form, which is not available publicly. To a lesser extent, the staff would also like to avoid issuers treating the staff's informal review of draft changes as an opportunity to take a "free bite at the apple." Requests for the staff to review draft responses therefore are more likely to be accepted in response to later rounds of comments when there are only a few issues left outstanding. Comments impacting Part II of the registration statement, including the undertakings required by Item 512 of Regulation S–K, disclosure of recent sales of unregistered securities that is required by Item 701 of Regulation S–K, and exhibits required by Item 601 of Regulation S–K must be made by pre-effective amendment.

Most issuers receive at least two rounds of comment and will file at least two amendments, assuming that no additional "voluntary" amendments are filed. Where the last changes agreed to by the issuer are minor, changes may be made in the final prospectus filed under Rule 424(b) after the effective date at the discretion of the Assistant Director.[182] Issuers should be aware this is the exception, not the rule, and the practice varies throughout the Division.

line test. As explained in Comment of Proposed Guides, Securities Act Release No. 5622, [1975–1976 Transfer Binder] Fed.Sec. L.Rep. (CCH) ¶ 80,305, at 85,690 (Oct. 1, 1975), the determination of materiality depends on particular facts and is not subject to objective rules. In some cases, such as bank holding companies and insurance companies, where the figures may be large, the staff has not accepted the argument that a certain figure is not material because it is less than a certain percentage of, for example, a loan portfolio or total assets. Some dollar amounts simply may be too large not to be considered qualitatively material. There also may be other more relevant reference points to be taken into consideration. The test for materiality, as enunciated by the Supreme Court, is whether a reasonable investor would consider the particular fact important in making an investment decision. *See* Basic Inc. v. Levinson, 485 U.S. 224, 238–40 (1988). * * *

182. Whether a change may be made by pre-effective amendment or in the 424(b) final prospectus often depends on how significant the change is and the impact of the change upon the issuer's liability. The liability provisions of Section 11 of the Securities Act apply to a "registration statement," composed of the prospectus and the Part II information. *See* 15 U.S.C. § 77k (1994). The liability provisions of section 12 of the Securities Act apply only to the "prospectus" portion of the registration statement. *Id.* § 77*l*. Because section 11 liability does not attach

"GOING EFFECTIVE"

The process of submitting acceleration requests and going effective is much more troublesome and misunderstood than it should be. Section 8(a) provides that a registration statement will become effective, automatically, twenty days after filing with the Commission, or on such earlier date as the Commission may determine. The twenty-day statutory delay in the effective date of the registration statement prescribed by section 8(a) may be delayed indefinitely by affixing the delaying amendment proscribed by Rule 473(a).

The procedure for requesting acceleration is straightforward and has been made easier by changes to the rules. Requests for the acceleration of the effective date must be submitted under Rule 461 at least forty-eight hours before the desired effective date. The acceleration request may be made by letter, facsimile, or orally.

The staff will make every effort to meet reasonable requests and work with issuers to resolve any outstanding concerns. Issuers should appreciate, however, that concerns which persist until this point in the review process are likely to be important. Before the registration statement can be declared effective, all staff comments must be resolved. The issuer should also plan on filing a pre-effective amendment containing any material agreed upon changes that have not been previously filed. This is made easier by EDGAR. Any necessary clearances from the NASD should also be provided to the staff before requesting acceleration. Additionally, the Assistant Director needs approximately two days at the end of the staff review to work the filing into his or her schedule, and to work out any remaining disclosure issues in order to ensure the disclosure is complete and accurate.

The forty-eight hour period provided in Rule 461 normally is sufficient to accomplish all of these tasks, provided the acceleration request is not submitted prematurely. This sometimes occurs when an acceleration request is submitted with an amendment that will draw additional comments. Acceleration requests submitted prematurely may be met with a telephone call requesting a written withdrawal of the request. Removing the delaying amendment as provided in Rule 473(b) and causing the registration statement to become effective under section 8(a) of the Securities Act is not practical for most issuers.[188]

One of the staff's objectives is to facilitate efficient and timely access to the capital markets. The staff does not exercise the kind of broad discretion to delay issuers sometimes described by commentators and, at the Division level, does not have authority to deny acceleration. Having due regard for the adequacy of information available to the public regarding the issuer, and the ease with which information regarding the issuer, its capital structure, and securities can be understood, Rule 461(b) states, "it is the general policy of the Commission * * * to permit acceleration of the effective date of the registration statement as soon as possible after the filing of appropriate amendments, if any." The staff is mindful that a refusal to accelerate the effective date of a

---

to changes filed in a final Rule 424(b) prospectus, the staff prefers that all revisions be made to the registration statement on a pre-effective basis. *See* 17 C.F.R. § 230.424(b) (1996).

188. [See 17 C.F.R. § 230.461] The delaying amendment must not only be removed, but it must also be replaced by language required by Rule 473(b) announcing: "This registration statement shall hereafter become effective in accordance with the provisions of section 8(a) of the Securities Act of 1933." *Id.* § 230.473(b).

registration statement would pass the matter to the Commission and require the type of substantial support for a stop order that is set out in Rule 461(b)(1) through (b)(7), which would principally require that the prospectus is not reasonably concise and understandable, is incomplete or misleading in a material respect, that the Commission is making an investigation of the issuer or underwriters, or that there is market manipulation involved. Whether or not a stop order could be supported, a misstep at this point can derail an offering. * * *

THE INFORMAL APPEAL PROCESS

There is opportunity for frustration in the comment process. Honest disagreements about the application of statutes, regulations, or accounting principles are common. The staff comments, passing as they do from hand to hand, are not always models of clarity or direction. It may not always be clear what change in the filing or what additional information is being requested by the staff. The basis for a comment may not be clear. Additional information or disclosure called for by a comment may seem burdensome. Positions on legal and accounting issues change and the rationale for positions are not always publicized. Interpretation of Division policy may differ somewhat between various Assistant Director groups. * * *

It is important that issuers have confidence in the registration process and believe they are being treated fairly, particularly when the staff's objectives are not perfectly aligned with the issuer or counsel's objectives. Issuers are entitled and encouraged to seek any necessary clarification or explanation of the staff's actions, including whether a position taken by the staff represents the views of the Division, is particular to that examining office, or is the view of the examiner or accountant. It is for exactly this reason that the telephone numbers of the Division's supervisory staff are included at the end of each comment letter.

Most concerns can be resolved over the telephone. * * *

When a problem or question cannot be resolved between the examiner or staff accountant and the issuer, or the issuer believes it is not receiving prompt attention, is being treated unfairly, requires an explanation, or has some other concern, the issuer has several means by which to obtain satisfaction. It is perfectly acceptable for the issuer to request the matter be raised with supervisory staff immediately above the examiner and accountant. The examiner or accountant will arrange a conference call. The issuer also may contact the supervisory staff, including the Assistant Director, directly by telephone. The supervisory staff are often able to provide a more satisfying explanation than the examiner or staff accountant has provided, or may modify or waive a comment if that is the appropriate solution. Some issuers simply find it comforting to hear the same answer at a higher level.

The line of informal appeal to be followed depends upon the nature of the problem. Legal and financial problems that cannot be resolved between the issuer and the Assistant Director may be appealed to the Chief Counsel, one of the Associate Directors, the Deputy Director, or Director of the Division. Accounting problems that cannot be resolved between the issuer and the Assistant Chief Accountant may be appealed to the Deputy Chief Accountant or Chief Accountant. Informal appeal is used to determine whether or not there is a general agreement with the position that is being taken by the staff, or simply where the issuer continues to believe the staff position is in error. The process need not take long because telephone calls usually are sufficient to provide for a complete exchange of views.

CONCLUSION

* * *

The duration of the registration process seems to depend more upon the issuer and counsel, rather than upon the staff. Experience indicates that avoiding recurring disclosure problems at the drafting stage of the registration statement, before it is filed with the Commission, will result in a much shorter and smoother registration for any issuer. Issuers who file registration statements that are declared effective at the short end of the range are always those issuers who begin with the end in mind—by ensuring that their registration statements contain the disclosure that the staff will look for and by avoiding disclosure pitfalls that will trigger comments. These registration statements are those that always provide an investor with all the information suggested by the regulations, in addition to other information necessary to evaluate intelligently the business of the issuer, market for its products, revenues, and risks. * * *

SECTION 3. QUALITATIVE DISCLOSURE

Statutes and Regulations

Securities Act, § 7.

Regulation C, Rules 400–418, 421, 425, 425A, 426.

In the Matter of Franchard Corporation

Securities and Exchange Commission, 1964.
42 S.E.C. 163.

■ CARY, CHAIRMAN: These are consolidated proceedings pursuant to Sections 8(c) and 8(d) of the Securities Act of 1933 ("Securities Act") to determine whether a stop order should issue suspending the effectiveness of three registration statements filed by Franchard Corporation, formerly Glickman Corporation ("registrant"), and whether certain post-effective amendments filed by the registrant should be declared effective. * * *

I. FACTS

A. *Background*

Louis J. Glickman ("Glickman") has for many years been a large-scale real estate developer, operator and investor. From 1954 to 1960 he acquired control of real estate in this country and in Canada by means of "syndication" arrangements. * * * Glickman conducted some of these syndication activities and certain other phases of his real estate business through a number of wholly owned corporations, the most important of which was Glickman Corporation of Nevada, now known as Venada Corporation ("Venada").

In May of 1960, Glickman caused registrant to be formed in order to group under one entity most of the publicly owned corporations and limited partnerships under his control. Registrant was to operate on a so-called "cash flow" basis, i.e., the amount available for distribution to its stockholders was to be gauged by the excess of cash receipts over cash disbursements, without reference to such non-cash deductions from gross receipts as depreciation and leasehold amortization. Registrant's stock was divided into two classes, Class A common and Class B common, with the B stockholders given the right to elect ⅔ of registrant's directors until 1971, when all outstanding B shares become A shares. Glickman established control of registrant by acquiring 450,000 of its 660,000 authorized B shares for $1 per share. He exercised a dominant role in the management of registrant's affairs as president at the time of its formation and later as its first chairman of the board.

The first of the three registration statements here involved ("1960 filing") became effective on October 12, 1960. * * *

The second of the three registration statements ("first 1961 filing") became effective on October 2, 1961 * * *. All of the A shares offered to the public for cash under the 1960 filing and the first 1961 filing were sold as were the A shares offered under the second 1961 filing, and the exchange offer in the 1960 filing was accepted by most of the offerees.

B.   Glickman's Withdrawals and Pledges

Registrant's 1960 prospectus stated that Glickman had from time to time advanced substantial sums to the partnerships and corporations that were about to become subsidiaries of the registrant. It also said that he had advanced $211,000 to the registrant for the purpose of defraying its organization and registration costs and that this advance would be repaid without interest out of the proceeds of the public offering. On October 14, 1960—two days after the effective date of registrant's 1960 filing—Glickman began secretly to transfer funds from the registrant to Venada, his wholly owned corporation. Within two months the aggregate amount of these transfers amounted to $296,329. By October 2, 1961, the effective date of registrant's first 1961 filing, Glickman had made 45 withdrawals which amounted in the aggregate to $2,372,511. Neither the 1961 prospectuses nor any of the effective amendments to the 1960 filing referred to these transactions.

All of registrant's prospectuses stated that Glickman owned most of its B as well as a substantial block of it's a stock. On the effective date of the 1960 filing Glickman's shares were unencumbered. In the following month, however, he began to pledge his shares to finance his personal real estate ventures. By August 31, 1961, all of Glickman's B and much of his A stock had been pledged to banks, finance companies, and private individuals. On the effective dates of the two 1961 filings the loans secured by these pledges aggregated about $4,250,000. The effective interest rates on these loans ran as high as 24% annually. Glickman retained the right to vote the pledged shares in the absence of a default on the loans. The two 1961 filings made no mention of Glickman's pledges or the loans they secured.

C.   Action of the Board of Directors

In May 1962 the accountants who had audited the financial statements in registrant's 1960 and 1961 filings informed its directors that Glickman had from time to time diverted funds from the registrant's treasury to Venada. The directors then met with Glickman, who assured them that the withdrawals had been without wrongful intent and would not recur. Glickman agreed to repay all of the then known unauthorized withdrawals with the interest at the rate of 6%. Registrant's directors soon discovered that Glickman had made other withdrawals, and they retained former United States District Court Judge Simon H. Rifkind to determine Glickman's liability to registrant. Glickman agreed to be bound by Judge Rifkind's determination and was continued in office.

In a report submitted on August 20, 1962, Judge Rifkind found that Glickman had on many occasions withdrawn substantial sums from registrant; that Bernard Mann, who was registrant's as well as Venada's treasurer but not a member of registrant's board of directors, was the only one of registrant's officers who had known of the withdrawals and had collaborated with Glickman in effecting them; that registrant's inadequate administrative procedures had to some extent facilitated Glickman's wrongdoing; and that all of the withdrawals had been made good with 6% interest. Judge Rifkind also found that 6% was an inadequate interest rate because Glickman and Venada had been borrowing at appreciably higher interest rates from commercial finance companies and others. Accordingly, he concluded that registrant was entitled to additional interest from Glickman and from Venada in the amount of $145,279. Registrant has not thus far been able to collect any part of this sum.[10]

On November 30, 1962, registrant's directors learned that Glickman had continued to make unauthorized withdrawals after he had promised to desist from so doing and after the issuance of the Rifkind report, that Glickman and his wife had pledged all of their shares of the registrant's stock, and that Glickman and Venada were in financial straits. Glickman and Mann thereupon resigned from all of their posts with the registrant, and Glickman sold all his B stock and some of his Class A stock to a small group of investors. Monthly cash distributions to A stockholders, which registrant had made every month since its inception, were discontinued in January 1963, and registrant changed its name from Glickman Corporation to Franchard Corporation.

II. ALLEGED DEFICIENCIES—ACTIVITIES OF MANAGEMENT

A. Glickman's Withdrawals of Registrant's Funds and Pledges of His Shares

Of cardinal importance in any business is the quality of its management. Disclosures relevant to an evaluation of management are particularly pertinent where, as in this case, securities are sold largely on the personal reputation of a company's controlling person. The disclosures in these respects were materially deficient. The 1960 prospectus failed to reveal that Glickman intended to use substantial amounts of registrant's funds for the benefit of Venada, and the 1961 prospectuses made no reference to Glickman's continual diversion of substantial sums from the registrant. Glickman's pledges were not discussed in either the effective amendments to the 1960 filings or in the two 1961 filings.

In our view, these disclosures were highly material to an evaluation of the competence and reliability of registrant's management—in large measure, Glickman. In many respects, the development of disclosure standards adequate for informed appraisal of management's ability and integrity is a difficult task. How do you tell a "good" business manager from a "bad" one in a piece of paper? Managerial talent consists of personal attributes, essentially subjective in nature, that frequently defy meaningful analysis through the impersonal medium of a prospectus. Direct statements of opinion as to management's

---

10. In February 1963 Glickman and Venada filed petitions in the United States District Court * * * seeking arrangements with their creditors pursuant to Chapter XI of the Bankruptcy Act. * * *

ability, which are not susceptible to objective verification, may well create an unwarranted appearance of reliability if placed in a prospectus. The integrity of management—its willingness to place its duty to public shareholders over personal interest—is an equally elusive factor for the application of disclosure standards.[a]

Evaluation of the quality of management—to whatever extent it is possible—is an essential ingredient of informed investment decision. * * * Appraisals of competency begin with information concerning management's past business experience, which is elicited by requirements that a prospectus state the offices and positions held with the issuer by each executive officer within the last five years. With respect to established companies, management's past performance, as shown by comprehensive financial and other disclosures concerning the issuer's operations, furnish a guide to its future business performance. To permit judgments whether the corporation's affairs are likely to be conducted in the interest of public shareholders, the registration requirements elicit information as to the interests of insiders which may conflict with their duty of loyalty to the corporation. Disclosures are also required with respect to the remuneration and other benefits paid or proposed to be paid to management as well as material transactions between the corporation and its officers, directors, holders of more than 10 percent [now 5%—Eds.] of its stock, and their associates.

Glickman's withdrawals were material transactions between registrant and its management, and the registration forms on which registrant's filings were made called for their disclosure. Registrant's argument that the withdrawals were not material because Glickman's undisclosed indebtedness to registrant never exceeded 1.5% of the gross book value of registrant's assets not only minimizes the substantial amounts of the withdrawals in relation to the stockholders' equity and the company's cash flow, but ignores the significance to prospective investors of information concerning Glickman's managerial ability and personal integrity. * * *

A description of Glickman's activities was important on several grounds. First, publication of the facts pertaining to Glickman's withdrawals of substantial funds and of his pledges of his control stock would have clearly indicated his strained financial position and his urgent need for cash in his personal real estate ventures. * * *

Second, disclosure of Glickman's continual diversion of registrant's funds to the use of Venada, his wholly owned corporation, was also germane to an evaluation of the integrity of his management. This quality is always a material factor. * * *

Third, Glickman's need for cash * * * gave him a powerful and direct motive to cause registrant to pursue policies which would permit high distribution rates and maintain a high price for registrant's A shares. * * * Investors were entitled to be apprised of these facts and such potential conflicts of interest.

a. How realistic is it to expect that there can or will be meaningful disclosure regarding the quality of management in the prospectus? Nonetheless, the SEC's forms focus on this issue. Cf. Form S–1, Item 11(j) and Reg. S–K, Item 401. This problem is also raised in an acute form in A. Solmssen, The Comfort Letter (1975), a novel centering on the preparation of a registration statement for a rising young tycoon who is gradually losing touch with reality.

Finally, the possibility of a change of control was also important to prospective investors. As we have noted, registrant's public offerings were largely predicated on Glickman's reputation as a successful real estate investor and operator. Disclosure of Glickman's secured loans, the relatively high interest rates that they bore, the secondary sources from which many of the loans were obtained, and the conditions under which lenders could declare defaults would have alerted investors to the possibility of a change in the control and management of registrant * * *.

* * *

With respect to disclosure of pledged shares, registrant is not aided by pointing out that our registration forms under the Securities Act and the reports required under the Securities Exchange Act do not call for disclosure of encumbrances on a controlling stockholder's shares, and that proposals to require such disclosures in reports filed with us under the Securities Exchange Act have not been adopted. The fact that such disclosures are not required of all issuers and their controlling persons in all cases does not negate their materiality in specific cases. The registration forms promulgated by us are guides intended to assist registrants in discharging their statutory duty of full disclosure. They are not and cannot possibly be exhaustive enumerations of each and every item material to investors in the particular circumstances relevant to a specific offering. The kaleidoscopic variety of economic life precludes any attempt at such an enumeration. The preparation of a registration statement is not satisfied, as registrant's position suggests, by a mechanical process of responding narrowly to the specific items of the applicable registration form. On the contrary, Rule 408 under the Securities Act makes clear to prospective registrants that: "In addition to the information expressly required to be included in a registration statement, there shall be added such further material information, if any, as may be necessary to make the required statements in the light of the circumstances under which they were made, not misleading."

B.   Activities of Registrant's Directors

Another issue raised in these proceedings concerns the disclosure to be required in a prospectus regarding the adequacy of performance of managerial functions by registrant's board of directors. The Division urges that the prospectuses, by identifying the members of the board of directors, impliedly represented that they would provide oversight and direction to registrant's officers. * * *

It was obvious * * * that Glickman would exercise the dominant role in managing registrant's operations and the prospectuses contained no affirmative representations concerning the participation of the directors in registrant's affairs. Moreover, the board met regularly and received information as to registrant's affairs from Glickman and in connection with the preparation of registrant's registration statements, post-effective amendments, and periodic reports filed with us. It is clear we are not presented with a picture of total abdication of directorial responsibilities. Thus, the question posed by the Division must be whether the prospectuses were deficient in not disclosing that the directors, in overseeing the operations of the company, failed to exercise the degree of diligence which the Division believes was required of them under the circumstances in the context of the day-to-day operations of the company. We find no deficiencies in this area.

This is an issue raising fundamental considerations as to the functions of the disclosure requirements of the Securities Act. The civil liability provisions of Section 11 do establish for directors a standard of due diligence in the preparation of a registration statement—a federal rule of directors' responsibility with respect to the completeness and accuracy of the document used in the public distribution of securities. The Act does not purport, however, to define federal standards of directors' responsibility in the ordinary operations of business enterprises and nowhere empowers us to formulate administratively such regulatory standards. The diligence required of registrant's directors in overseeing its affairs is to be evaluated in the light of the standards established by state statutory and common law.

In our view, the application of these standards on a routine basis in the processing of registration statements would be basically incompatible with the philosophy and administration of the disclosure requirements of the Securities Act. Outright fraud or reckless indifference by directors might be readily identifiable and universally condemned. But activity short of that, which may give rise to legal restraints and liabilities, invokes significant uncertainty. * * * To generally require information in Securities Act prospectuses as to whether directors have performed their duties in accordance with the standards of responsibility required of them under state law would stretch disclosure beyond the limitations contemplated by the statutory scheme and necessitated by considerations of administrative practicality. * * * [T]he disclosures sought here by the staff would require evaluation of the entire conduct of a board of directors in the context of the whole business operations of a company in the light of diverse and uncertain standards. In our view, this is a function which the disclosure requirements of the Securities Act cannot effectively discharge. It would either result in self-serving generalities of little value to investors or grave uncertainties both on the part of those who must enforce and those who must comply with that Act.

* * *

V. CONCLUSIONS

The deficiencies we have found in registrant's effective filings are serious. * * * Omissions of so material a character would normally require the issuance of a stop order.

Here, however, several factors taken together lead us to conclude that the distribution of copies of this opinion to all of registrant's past and present stockholders, as registrant has proposed, will give adequate public notice of the deficiencies in registrant's effective filings, and that neither the public interest nor the protection of investors requires the issuance of a stop order. Among those factors are Glickman's departure, the transfer of his controlling B shares to a management which has made a substantial financial commitment in registrant's securities, and registrant's voluntary disclosures to our staff prior to the initiation of these proceedings. Registrant also filed post-effective amendments to its 1960 filings which, though admittedly inadequate, represented a bona fide effort to remedy the deficiencies in its effective filings. In addition, * * * unusually extensive publicity was given to the true facts affecting registrant's affairs and to the resulting deficiencies in its effective filings.

Any new post-effective amendment should conform to the views expressed in this opinion. After the Division has reviewed such amendment, it will communicate its views with respect to it to the registrant, and thereafter the matter will be submitted to us for appropriate action.

    * * *

---

    a. Integrity Disclosures. The Commission's concern in *Franchard* that investors be provided with qualitative information enabling them to appraise the character, integrity and ability of their management has today been codified in a series of provisions in Subpart 400 of Regulation S–K, which focus on managerial experience, compensation, stock ownership and conflicts of interest. Item 401(f) requires registrants to disclose "certain legal proceedings" that "occurred during the last five years and that are material to an evaluation of the ability or integrity of any director, person nominated to be a director or executive officer of the registrant." Listed under this heading are: (1) bankruptcy or reorganization petitions; (2) criminal convictions and "pending criminal proceedings" (other than traffic offenses and similar "minor offenses"); (3) orders, judgments or decrees enjoining or otherwise limiting the individual from engaging in the securities business, or "engaging in any type of business practice"; and (4) any finding in a civil action that the individual "violated any federal or state securities law." Except in the case of criminal proceedings, Regulation S–K focuses only on adjudications within the past five years and does not require disclosure of pending litigation. Nonetheless, the courts have sometimes found both pending civil litigation[1] and securities law adjudications that were more than five years old to have been material on specific facts.[2] The Commission maintains that its five-year rule is only a "guide to disclosure" and "events occurring outside this period may be material and should be disclosed."[3]

    In *Franchard,* the Commission focused at length on the possibility that Glickman's strained financial position would affect his management style and give him "a powerful and direct motive to cause registrant to pursue policies" that favored current dividends over future growth. Also, the SEC noted the increased possibility of a sudden change in control if Glickman were forced to

---

1. In Zell v. InterCapital Income Securities, Inc., 675 F.2d 1041 (9th Cir.1982), the failure to disclose pending securities litigation against the investment adviser of a mutual fund was found material where the proxy statement related to the management contract between the adviser and the fund. See also SEC v. Pace, 173 F.Supp.2d 30 (D.D.C.2001) (embezzlement of any amount of money from corporation by officer would be material). However, in the City of Philadelphia v. Fleming Companies, 264 F.3d 1245, 1256–57 (10th Cir.2001), the failure to disclose pending litigation was not found to be material. Similarly, in GAF Corp. v. Heyman, 724 F.2d 727 (2d Cir.1983), the Second Circuit did not find allegations of fraud brought against a contestant in a proxy fight by his own sister to be material where the

case had resulted in only a settlement, and not an adjudication.

2. See Bertoglio v. Texas Intern. Co., 488 F.Supp. 630 (D.Del.1980) (the failure to disclose in a proxy statement a fifteen year old adjudication of securities law violations was material where there was also pending civil litigation alleging securities law violations); but see, Securities and Exchange Commission v. Goldfield Deep Mines Co. of Nevada, 758 F.2d 459 (9th Cir.1985) (failure to disclose 17 year old conviction for embezzlement was not material, even though defendant had also violated state securities laws just over five years ago). See also United States v. Matthews, 787 F.2d 38 (2d Cir.1986) (discussed infra at note 12).

3. Securities Act Release No. 5758 (Nov. 2, 1976).

sell his interest. Today, Item 402 of Regulation S–K requires detailed disclosure of executive officers' compensation, including stock options, for the five most highly compensated officers whose cash compensation exceeds $60,000 and for all executive offices as a group. In addition, disclosure must be made under Item 403 of management's beneficial securities ownership, including any "arrangements, known to the registrant, including any pledge by any person of securities of the registrant * * *, the operation of which may at a subsequent date result in a change of control of the registrant."[4] This drafting seems to reflect the Commission's concerns in *Franchard.*

The most important provision in Subpart 404 of Regulation S–K is Item 404, which covers conflict of interest transactions. Basically, it requires disclosure of any transaction exceeding $60,000 between the registrant and any executive officer, director, director nominee, owner of more than 5%, or an immediate family member of any of the foregoing. Item 404(c) focuses on loans to management, and Item 404(b) requires disclosure of transactions between the registrant and any business entity in which the director has a significant business interest (for example, if the director is a lawyer and the registrant uses the law firm in which the director is a partner, the fees paid to the law firm may have to be disclosed).[5]

b. Case Law. Given the breadth of the disclosure obligation, it makes sense to examine with particular care those cases in which the courts have found immaterial (or have otherwise excused) the failure to disclose unlawful acts or other conduct seemingly bearing on management's integrity. A representative case is Gaines v. Haughton,[6] in which plaintiffs alleged that Lockheed's failure to disclose extensive payments to foreign governments and officials in its proxy statement constituted a material omission. Upholding summary judgment for the defendants, the Ninth Circuit offered the following standard for when unlawful or questionable conduct was material to shareholders:

> "We draw a sharp distinction * * * between allegations of director misconduct involving a breach of trust or self-dealing—the nondisclosure of which is presumptively material—and allegations of simple breach of fiduciary duty/waste of corporate management—the nondisclosure of which is never material for '14(a) purposes * * *. The distinction between 'mere' bribes and bribes coupled with kickbacks to the directors makes a great deal of sense, indeed it is fundamental to a meaningful concept of materiality under § 14(a) and the preservation of state corporate law."[7]

Where directors received a personal benefit from an unlawful transaction, courts have generally found its nondisclosure to constitute a material omission.[8] Where, however, the illegality is on behalf of the corporation and does

---

4.   See Regulation S–K, Item 403(c).

5.   The test for disclosure in the case of a director who is a partner in a law firm is whether the payments to the law firm exceeded 5% of the law firm's consolidated gross revenue for its last full year. See Regulation S–K, Item 404(b)(4).

6.   645 F.2d 761 (9th Cir.1981).

7.   Id. at 776–778. See also, In re Tenneco Securities Litigation, 449 F.Supp. 528 (S.D.Tex.1978).

8.   See Weisberg v. Coastal States Gas Corp., 609 F.2d 650 (2d Cir.1979); United States v. Fields, 592 F.2d 638 (2d Cir.1978); Shields v. Erikson, [1989–1990 Transfer Binder] Fed.Sec.L.Rep. (CCH) ¶ 94,723 (N.D.Ill.1989). For a recent holding that embezzlement of even a modest amount by an

not involve a personal benefit to the officer, courts have employed a variety of theories to shield the defendants from liability. Sometimes, as in *Gaines,* they have found the omission to be immaterial; other times, they have relied on a doctrine known as "transaction causation" to justify dismissal: namely, because the alleged loss from the unlawful payment preceded the proxy statement or other disclosure document, the omission to disclose it did not cause the loss.[9] More recent cases have relied on Basic Inc. v. Levinson[10] to find that even though the illegal bribe was material, there was no affirmative duty to disclose it.[11]

c. Unadjudicated Charges. Suppose an individual knows that he or she is being investigated by law enforcement authorities for criminal law violations, but maintains his or her innocence. In such circumstances, must the individual disclose in a proxy statement or registration statement that an investigation is ongoing or that such person has received a "target" letter from the U.S. Attorney indicating that he or she is a potential (or even likely) defendant? United States v. Matthews[12] holds that there is no such obligation to disclose, but its holding may be limited to criminal prosecutions for failure to make this disclosure. The defendant in *Matthews* was the general counsel of Southland Corporation (the owner of the 7–Eleven convenience store chain), who was eventually indicted for aiding and abetting a scheme to bribe members of the New York State Tax Commission and also for failing to disclose such scheme in the proxy statement pursuant to which he was elected to the Southland board. The jury acquitted Matthews of the bribery charge, but convicted him of securities fraud. At the time of the proxy statement's preparation, Matthews had been informed that he was the "subject" of the grand jury investigation that eventually resulted in his indictment.

Read literally, Item 401(f) of Regulation S–K only expressly requires disclosure of convictions within five years and pending legal proceedings.[13] Fearing that a criminal prosecution on these grounds raised due process problems and might require individuals to accuse themselves of wrongdoing under fear of a future criminal prosecution, the Second Circuit said:

> "[S]o long as uncharged criminal conduct is not required to be disclosed by any rule lawfully promulgated by the SEC, nondisclosure of such conduct cannot be the basis of a criminal prosecution. Our unwillingness to permit Section 14(a) to be used as expansively as the Government has done here rests not only on the history of the Commission's approach to the problem of qualitative disclosures and the case law that has developed on this subject, but on the obvious due process implications that would arise from permitting a conviction to stand in the absence of clearer notice as to what disclosures are required in this uncertain area."[14]

officer from his corporation was material, see SEC v. Pace, 173 F.Supp.2d 30 (D.D.C.2001).

9. See Abbey v. Control Data Corp., 603 F.2d 724, 732 (8th Cir.1979); Rosengarten v. ITT Corp., 466 F.Supp. 817, 827–828 (S.D.N.Y.1979).

10. 485 U.S. 224 (1988). See infra at pages 998–1005.

11. See Roeder v. Alpha Industries, Inc., 814 F.2d 22 (1st Cir.1987).

12. 787 F.2d 38 (2d Cir.1986).

13. Id. at 43–44.

14. Id. at 49. One court has even held that the receipt of a "target letter" from a prosecutor indicating that prosecution is under consideration need not be disclosed, because the criminal conduct remains uncharged. In re Browning–Ferris Indus., Inc. Shareholder Derivative Litig., 830 F.Supp. 361, 369 (S.D.Tex.1993), aff'd, 20 F.3d 465 (5th Cir.1994); see also United States v. Crop

Matthews should not be overread. It is entirely possible that a civil enforcement proceeding brought by the SEC on the same facts would be upheld; also, the facts of *Matthews* are rarely duplicated: defendants are seldom acquitted of the substantive tax fraud charge, but convicted of nondisclosure. *Matthews* was also a proxy statement case, and not a case where a promoter was seeking to sell stock without disclosure of his forthcoming indictment. Could a CEO who knew he would be indicted next week go effective with a registration statement today without disclosure of this fact?

d. *Private litigation.* Most private cases have rejected attempts by private plaintiffs to use the failure to make integrity disclosures about management's conduct or character in order to establish liability for private damages. A few cases have granted injunctive relief and ordered a new proxy solicitation before a shareholders' meeting could be held. Sometimes, as in *Gaines v. Haughton,* supra, the successful defense has been based on causation theories; other times, the court has found that there was no duty to disclose at the particular time in question under *Basic v. Levinson,* supra, because the corporation was neither trading nor soliciting proxies.[15]

e. *Law Violations Not Involving Senior Management.* Item 404 applies by its terms only when senior management is involved in a violation of law or a pending legal proceeding. Assume instead that lower-echelon officials have been involved in under the table payments to bribe potential customers and the amounts involved were not by themselves material to the corporation based on financial criteria alone. While the involvement of senior management may be *per se* material (at least in a civil proceeding),[16] other theories must be relied upon when senior officials are not implicated. The SEC has advanced at least two theories with some success: (1) unlawful practices are material when they constitute the corporation's basic method of competition; and (2) illegality is material when it exposes the corporation to economically material sanctions (either in the form of fines or other financial penalties or disqualifications from doing business in a jurisdiction or line of business upon conviction).[17]

f. *Antisocial Conduct Not Involving Violations of Law.* While most private cases have declined to find material forms of misbehavior that did not involve actual violations of law or conflicts of interest between management and its shareholders, there have been noteworthy exceptions to this generalization. The easiest case is where the magnitude of the corporation's potential liabilities are themselves material. Thus, in Grossman v. Waste Management, Inc.,[18] the

Growers Corp., 954 F.Supp. 335 (D.D.C.1997) (analyzing case law under *Matthews*).

15. See, e.g., Roeder v. Alpha Industries, Inc., supra note 11. For a general discussion of the law, see Ferrara, Starr & Steinberg, Disclosure of Information Bearing on Management Integrity and Competence, 76 Nw.U.L.Rev. 555 (1981).

16. See SEC v. Kalvex Inc., 425 F.Supp. 310, 315 (S.D.N.Y.1975); Cooke v. Teleprompter Corp., 334 F.Supp. 467 (S.D.N.Y. 1971).

17. See SEC v. Jos. Schlitz Brewing Co., 452 F.Supp. 824 (E.D.Wis.1978) (where licenses to sell beer at risk because of unlaw-

ful payments to tavern owners, such practices were material although amounts paid were immaterial). See also Note, Disclosure of Corporate Payments and Practices: Conduct Regulation through the Federal Securities Laws, 43 Brooklyn L.Rev. 681 (1977); Note, Disclosure of Payments to Foreign Government Officials under the Securities Acts, 89 Harv. L.Rev. 1848 (1976).

18. [1983–1984 Transfer Binder] Fed. Sec.L.Rep. (CCH) Para. 99,530 (N.D.Ill.1983). See also, Bagby, Murray & Andrews, How Green Was My Balance Sheet?: Corporate Liability and Environmental Disclosure, 14 Va.Envtl.L.J. 225 (1995). But see, In re Browning–Ferris Industries, Inc. Shareholder

Court held it a material omission to fail to disclose the registrant's potential liabilities for the required cleanup of toxic waste under environmental laws. Such a standard is entirely consistent with Basic v. Levinson's traditional probability/magnitude tradeoff for determining materiality. Beyond this point, however, courts have seldom gone. In Natural Resources Defense Council v. SEC,[19] the D.C. Circuit refused to expand the definition of materiality to include the special interests of the "ethical investor". Similarly, allegations that all directors were willfully involved in a campaign to engage in anti-union activities in violation of the federal labor laws were found not to be material where no allegation of self-dealing or personal benefit was made.[20] Note, however, that statements that the corporation is not involved in such conduct or that the corporation's activities in a specified field were in compliance with law may constitute material affirmative misrepresentations.[21] In addition, even if environmental liabilities are not yet material or do not involve misconduct by senior managements, there remains the distinct possibility that such liabilities constitute a future trend, uncertainty, or commitment that may become material in the future and so may have to be disclosed in the MDA section of the registration statement or periodic report.[22]

g. *The Special Case of Environmental Liabilities.* Environmental liabilities receive special attention in Item 103 of Regulation S–K. On its face, Item 103 simply requires disclosure of "any material pending legal proceedings, other than ordinary routine litigation incidental to the business." The instructions to this item then explain that litigation involving a claim for damages under ten percent of the registrants' current assets can generally be ignored. However, a special instruction says that administrative and judicial proceedings arising under Federal, state or local laws "regulating the discharge of materials into the environment or primarily for the purpose of protecting the environment shall not be deemed 'ordinary routine litigation incidental to the business'" and shall be disclosed when a governmental authority is a party to the proceeding unless the registrant "reasonably believes that such proceeding will result in * * * monetary sanctions * * * of less than $100,000."[23] Although the Commission has thus given environmental liabilities a marginally preferred status under its disclosure rules, it has nonetheless resisted attempts of environmental groups to use the federal securities laws as a lever by which to promote social goals unrelated to investor interests. In Natural Resources Defense Council, Inc. v. SEC,[24] the D.C. Circuit upheld the Commission's determination that the focus of its disclosure policy should remain on economically significant information and rejected the claim that a special priority should be given to environmental concerns under the National Environmental Policy Act ("NEPA"). Still, despite the SEC's victory, plaintiffs have sometimes

---

Derivative Litig., 830 F.Supp. 361 (S.D.Tex. 1993).

19. 606 F.2d 1031, 1051 (D.C.Cir.1979); see also Sec.Act.Rel. No. 5627 (Oct. 14, 1975).

20. See Amalgamated Clothing & Textile Workers v. J.P. Stevens & Co., 475 F.Supp. 328 (S.D.N.Y.1979), vacated as moot per curiam, 638 F.2d 7 (2d Cir.1980).

21. See In re Copley Pharmaceutical, Inc. Securities Litigation, [1995 Transfer Binder] Fed.Sec.L.Rep. (CCH) Para. 98,695 (D.Mass.1995); In re AES Corp. Sec. Litig., 825 F.Supp. 578 (S.D.N.Y.1993); Ballan v. Upjohn Co., 814 F.Supp. 1375 (W.D.Mich. 1992).

22. See infra at pp. 233–239.

23. See Instruction 5 to Item 103 of Regulation S–K.

24. 606 F.2d 1031 (D.C.Cir.1979).

been successful in convincing courts that the issuer's failure to disclose uncharged violations of the environmental laws was material under circumstances where a failure to disclose other liabilities might have been upheld.[25] In the most recent decision dealing with environmental liabilities, Levine v. NL Industries, Inc., the Second Circuit specifically focused on Item 101(c)(xii) of Regulation S–K, which provides in part that:

> "Appropriate disclosure" shall be made as to the material effects that compliance with Federal, state and local provisions ... regulating the environment ... may have upon the capital expenditures, earnings and competitive position of the registrant and its subsidiaries.

Construing this provision in a case where the registrant had carelessly operated a uranium processing plant, the Second Circuit gave a considerably broader interpretation to the disclosure obligation than had the district court:

> "The district court's decision might be read as interpreting this section to require disclosure only of the cost of complying with environmental regulations, but not the cost of failing to comply with them * * * Such an inference would be incorrect. Disclosure of potential costs for violations of environmental laws, if material, is ordinarily required."[26]

Thus, while the district court in *Levine* had ruled that unasserted claims did not need to be disclosed in the registrant's Form 10–K filing, the Second Circuit's decision seems to suggest that an estimate of future liabilities must be made by an issuer that has (in the SEC's words) "a policy or approach toward compliance with environmental regulations which is reasonably likely to result in substantial fines, penalties or other significant effects on the corporation."[27] In effect, although Item 103 ("Legal Proceedings") does not require disclosure of unasserted claims, Item 101 ("Description of Business") may require such disclosure where those claims are likely to be asserted based on a management "policy or approach toward compliance with environmental regulations." *Query:* Can environmental liabilities be distinguished in this regard from other regulatory schemes that similarly provide for substantial penalties? Should a managerial policy of "flouting the law" now require disclosure without any claim having been asserted? Or, is the Second Circuit just especially sensitive to environmental concerns?

25. Compare Grossman v. Waste Management, Inc., 589 F.Supp. 395, 407–08 (N.D.Ill.1984) (omissions of disclosures of environmental liabilities were actionable) and Levine v. NL Industries, Inc., 717 F.Supp. 252 (S.D.N.Y.1989), aff'd, 926 F.2d 199 (2d Cir.1991). (failure to disclose potential environmental liability for serious penalties in Form 10–K not material where Items 101 and 103 of Regulation S–K do not require disclosure of contingent liabilities not yet asserted by any party). See Caron, SEC Disclosure Requirements for Contingent Environmental Liability, 14 B.C. Environmental Affairs L.Rev. 729 (1987). Outside the environmental context, no similar rule seems to require disclosure of violations of other federal regulatory statutes or rules. See Anderson v. Abbott Laboratories, 140 F.Supp.2d 894 (N.D.Ill.2001) (distinguishing *Grossman*).

26. Levine v. NL Industries, Inc., 926 F.2d 199 (2d Cir.1991). The Second Circuit affirmed summary judgment for defendants because they were indemnified by the U.S. Department of Energy and thus faced no economic exposure to loss.

27. Id. (citing In re United States Steel Corp., Securities Exchange Act Release No. 16,233 (Sept. 27, 1979)).

SECTION 4. NEW APPROACHES TO DISCLOSURE

SOFT INFORMATION: FROM FORBIDDEN TO REQUIRED

Historically, the SEC took a "just the facts, ma'am" approach to disclosure and discouraged the inclusion of forward-looking information or projections. Indeed, in 1956, the SEC listed "predictions as to specific future market values, earnings, or dividends" as types of information that, because of their potential to mislead, should generally not be included in proxy statements.[1] There was a latent paternalism in this policy, which many commentators began to criticize during the 1970s on the ground that it denied the market precisely the forms of information that the market considered most valuable. Some suggested that the SEC was overly preoccupied with making disclosures fully comprehensible to a hypothetical layman who did not in fact read disclosure documents and who had in any event little impact on price determination;[2] others saw the SEC's policy as defensive, protecting it from potentially embarrassing charges that it had failed to detect fraud in filings made with it. A number of commentators suggested that the SEC's hostility to projections and other soft information rendered disclosure documents sterile—both unreadable and unread.[3] In response to these critics, the SEC organized a study of corporate disclosure during the mid–1970s, which recommended a significant change in policy, including a greater receptivity to projections and estimates.[4] The slow, painful process by which the SEC gradually accepted the legitimacy of "soft information"—that is, information about an issuer that inherently involves some subjective analysis or extrapolation, such as projections or estimates—reached an important milestone in 1979, when the SEC adopted Rule 175 under the 1933 Act and Rule 3b–6 under the 1934 Act to encourage the use of such information in SEC filings.[5] Both rules created safe harbors for certain defined types of "forward-looking statements" by specifying that a qualifying statement "shall be deemed not to be a fraudulent statement . . . unless it is shown that such statement was made or reaffirmed without a reasonable basis or was disclosed other than in good faith."[6]

---

1. See Walker v. Action Industries, Inc., 802 F.2d 703, 707 (4th Cir.1986). (discussing Securities Exchange Act Rel. No. 5276). This footnote to Rule 14a–9 precluding the use of such projections was eliminated in 1976.

2. The most influential critic in this debate was Professor Homer Kripke. See Kripke, The Myth of the Informed Layman, 28 Bus.Law. 631 (1973); Kripke, The SEC, the Accountants, Some Myths and Some Realities, 45 N.Y.U.L.Rev. 1151 (1970); Kripke, A Search for a Meaningful Securities Disclosure Policy, 31 Bus.Law. 293 (1975).

3. Mann, Prospectuses: Unreadable or Just Unread?—A Proposal to Reexamine Policy Against Permitting Projections, 40 Geo.

Wash.L.Rev. 222 (1971); Schneider, Nits, Grits and Soft Information in SEC Filings, 121 U.Pa.L.Rev. 254 (1972).

4. See Report of the Advisory Committee on Corporate Disclosure to the Securities and Exchange Commission. For an excellent overview of this debate and the gradual transition in SEC philosophy, see H. Kripke, The SEC and Corporate Disclosure: Regulation in Search of a Purpose (1979).

5. See Securities Act Rel. No. 33–6084 (June 25, 1979).

6. See Rule 175(a) and Rule 3b–6(a). The term "forward-looking statement" is defined in Rule 175(c) and Rule 3b–6(c).

a. *The Contemporary Use of Projections.*

Issuers remained hesitant, however, about including projections in prospectuses, both out of anxiety about the high liability created by § 11 of the 1933 Act and a more specific fear that courts might conclude, with perfect hindsight, that a specific projection lacked a reasonable basis. In fact, however, judicial decisions construing Rule 175 have been extremely protective to date. For example, in Wielgos v. Commonwealth Edison Co.,[7] the Seventh Circuit upheld summary judgment for defendants based on Rule 175, even though the estimates made in the prospectus as to the completion costs of several nuclear reactors owned by the public utility were "erroneous—not only in the sense that they turned out to be inaccurate, but also in the sense that * * * when it sold the stock, Commonwealth Edison's internal cost estimates exceeded those in the documents in its file."[8] Why then did the district court grant summary judgment for defendants and the Seventh Circuit affirm (in a decision written by Judge Easterbrook)? Because the estimates qualified as "forward-looking statements" under Rule 175(c)(1), the Seventh Circuit found that, by implication from Rule 175(a), the burden shifted to the plaintiff to show the lack of a "reasonable basis" or the absence of "good faith."[9] Because the plaintiff had not tried to establish bad faith, the *Wielgos* decision focused only on whether there was a reasonable basis for the estimates. It said:

> "Commonwealth Edison made point estimates: [the reactors] will cost $3.34 billion and start in 1984 and 1985. Everyone understands that point estimates are almost certainly wrong. Things will not go exactly as predicted * * *. Inevitable inaccuracy of a projection does not eliminate the safe harbor, however. Rule 175 does not say that projections qualify only if firms give ranges and identify the variables that will lead to departure. * * * Rule 175 assumes that readers are sophisticated, can understand the limits of a projection—and that if any given reader does not appreciate its limits, the reactions of the many professional investors and analysts will lead to prices that reflect the limits of the information."[10]

The language in *Wielgos* that investors must understand that projections are necessarily speculative has been echoed by other decisions.[11] But *Wielgos* went on to say that Rule 175 does not require the disclosure of "data, assumptions or methods" upon which the projections were based, even though "Commonwealth Edison was estimating the costs it would experience *if nothing* went wrong and nothing unexpected happened" and "[t]hese were poor assumptions."[12] Indeed, the Seventh Circuit opinion described these assumptions as not only wrong, but "biased in the sense of having a predictable kind of inaccuracy."[13] Even the fact that Commonwealth Edison had different tentative internal estimates at the time it used the "stale" projection in its prospectus did not render the use of the old projection unreasonable:

> "Issuers need not reveal all projections. Any firm generates a range of estimates internally or through consultants. It may reveal the projection it

7.   892 F.2d 509 (7th Cir.1989).

8.   Id. at 512.

9.   Id. at 513.

10.   Id. at 514.

11.   See, e.g., Decker v. Massey–Ferguson, Ltd., 681 F.2d 111, 117–18 (2d Cir.1982); In re RAC Mortgage Investment Corporation

Securities Litigation, 765 F.Supp. 860 (D.Md. 1991); Halye v. Lamson & Sessions Co., 752 F.Supp. 822, 827 (N.D.Ohio 1990); Boley v. Pineloch Assoc., Ltd., 700 F.Supp. 673, 679 (S.D.N.Y.1988).

12.   Id. at 515.

13.   Id.

thinks best while withholding others, so long as the one revealed has a 'reasonable basis.' "[14]

The conclusion that an issuer may have multiple estimates or projections and may use the most favorable, without disclosing the others, seems unlikely to be accepted by other Circuits.[15] Although a strong judicial consensus exists that projections cannot be easily attacked by plaintiffs,[16] other decisions have recognized that projections and predictions can sometimes be actionable.[17] However, these latter cases have restricted liability to instances where defendants "recklessly expressed opinions which they had good reason to believe were baseless."[18]

   b.   *When Are Projections Mandatory: The Case of the MD&A.*

During the late 1980s, the SEC's most important initiative that enhanced disclosure standards was to strengthen the Management's Discussion and Analysis ("MD&A") of Financial Condition and Results of Operations. Two important SEC releases effected this expansion, which are both excerpted below:

Securities Act Release No. 6711

Securities and Exchange Commission.
April 21, 1987.

CONCEPT RELEASE ON MANAGEMENT'S DISCUSSION AND ANALYSIS OF FINANCIAL CONDITION AND OPERATIONS

* * *

II.   The Purpose of MD&A and Current Requirements

The Commission has long recognized the need for a narrative explanation of the financial statements, because a numerical presentation and brief accompanying footnotes alone may be insufficient for an investor to judge the quality of earnings and the likelihood that past performance is indicative of future performance. MD&A is intended to give the investor an opportunity to look at the company through the eyes of management by providing both a short and long-term analysis of the business of the company. The Item [303 of Regulation

---

14. Id. at 516.

15. See Starkman v. Marathon Oil Co., 772 F.2d 231 (6th Cir.1985) (projections and soft information may be used "provided that the assumptions and hypotheses underlying predicted values are also disclosed.")

16. See Luce v. Edelstein, 802 F.2d 49, 56 (2d Cir.1986) ("We are not inclined to impose liability on the basis of statements that clearly 'bespeak caution.' ") See also cases at note 11 supra.

17. See, e.g., EP Medsystems, Inc. v. EchoCath, Inc., 235 F.3d 865, 879 (3d Cir. 2000); Isquith v. Middle South Utilities, Inc.,

847 F.2d 186, 203–04 (5th Cir.1988); Eisenberg v. Gagnon, 766 F.2d 770, 775–78 (3d Cir.1985); Goldman v. Belden, 754 F.2d 1059, 1068–69 (2d Cir.1985); Polin v. Conductron Corp., 552 F.2d 797, 804–07 (8th Cir.1977).

18. Eisenberg v. Gagnon, supra note 17, at 778. *Query:* Under this standard is there not at least a jury question as to recklessness on the facts of *Wielgos*? For a case seemingly reaching this result and refusing to dismiss based on the "bespeaks caution" doctrine, see In re NationsMart Corporation Sec. Litig., 130 F.3d 309 (8th Cir.1997).

S–K] asks management to discuss the dynamics of the business and to analyze the financials. . . .

A wide range of corporate events and changes may warrant MD&A disclosure. The examples provided by the Commission in 1974 are still useful illustrations:

1. Material changes in product mix or in the relative profitability of lines of business;

2. Material changes in advertising, research, development, product introduction or other discretionary costs;

3. The acquisition or disposition of a material asset other than in the ordinary course of business;

4. Material and unusual charges or gains, including credits or charges associated with discontinuation of operations;

5. Material changes in assumptions underlying deferred costs and the plan for amortization of such costs;

6. Material changes in assumed investment return and in actuarial assumptions used to calculate contributions to pension funds; and

7. The closing of a material facility or material interruption of business or completion of a material contract.

Perhaps the most misunderstood aspect of MD&A is its relationship to statements of a prospective nature. MD&A requires disclosure of "known trends or any known demands, commitments, events or uncertainties that will result in or that are reasonably likely to result in the registrant's liquidity increasing or decreasing in any material way."[14] Additionally, the Item calls for a description of any known material trends in the registrant's capital resources and any expected changes in the mix or cost of such resources. Elsewhere, the Item requires disclosure of known trends or uncertainties that are reasonably expected to have a material impact on net sales, revenues, or income from continuing operations. The Instructions add that MD&A "shall focus specifically on material events and uncertainties known to management that would cause reported financial information not to be necessarily indicative of future operating results or of future financial condition."

Conversely, Instruction 7 of Item 303(a) states that registrants are encouraged, but not required, to supply "forward-looking" [*10] information. The Instruction was not intended to detract from the requirements noted above but instead to make clear that "forward-looking information" (as that term is used in the Instruction) should be distinguished from presently known data that is reasonably expected to have a material impact on future results.

"Both required disclosure regarding the future impact of presently known trends, events or uncertainties and optional forward-looking information may involve some prediction or projection. The distinction between the two rests with the nature of the prediction required. Required disclosure is based on currently known trends, events, and uncertainties that are reasonably expected to have material effects, such as: a reduction in the registrant's product prices; erosion in the registrant's market share; changes in insurance coverage; or likely non-renewal of a material contract. In contrast, optional forward-looking

14. 17 CFR 229.303(a)(1).

disclosure involves anticipating a future trend or event or anticipating a less predictable impact of a known event, trend, or uncertainty * * *."

————

Securities Act Release No. 6835

Securities and Exchange Commission.
May 18, 1989.

INTERPRETIVE RELEASE: MANAGEMENT'S DISCUSSION AND ANALYSIS OF FINANCIAL CONDITION AND RESULTS OF OPERATIONS

* * *

The Commission has determined that interpretive guidance is needed regarding the following matters: prospective information required in MD&A * * *.

B.   Prospective Information

Several specific provisions in Item 303 require disclosure of forward-looking information. MD&A requires discussions of "known trends or any known demands, commitments, events or uncertainties that will result in or that are reasonably likely to result in the registrant's liquidity increasing or decreasing in any material way." Further, descriptions of known material trends in the registrant's capital resources and expected changes in the mix and cost of such resources are required. Disclosure of known trends or uncertainties that the registrant reasonably expects will have a material impact on net sales, revenues, or income from continuing operations is also required. Finally, the Instructions to Item 303 state that MD&A "shall focus specifically on material events and uncertainties known to management that would cause reported financial information not to be necessarily indicative of future operating results or of future financial condition."

* * *

A disclosure duty exists where a trend, demand, commitment, event or uncertainty is both presently known to management and reasonably likely to have material effects on the registrant's financial condition or results of operations. Registrants preparing their MD&A disclosure should determine and carefully review what trends, demands, commitments, events or uncertainties are known to management. In the following example, the registrant discloses the reasonably likely material effects on operating results of a known trend in the form of an expected further decline in unit sales of mature products:

> While market conditions in general remained relatively unchanged in 1987, unit volumes declined 10% as the Company's older products, representing 40% of overall revenues, continue to approach the end of their life cycle. Unit volumes of the older products are expected to continue to decrease at an accelerated pace in the future and materially adversely affect revenues and operating profits.

In preparing the MD&A disclosure, registrants should focus on each of the specific categories of known data. For example, Item 303(a)(2)(I) requires a description of the registrant's material "commitments" for capital expenditures as of the end of the latest fiscal period. However, even where no legal commitments, contractual or otherwise, have been made, disclosure is required if material planned capital expenditures result from a known demand, as where the expenditures are necessary to a continuation of the registrant's current growth trend. Similarly, if the same registrant determines not to incur such expenditures, a known uncertainty would exist regarding continuation of the current growth trend. If the adverse effect on the registrant from discontinuation of the growth trend is reasonably likely to be material, disclosure is required. Disclosure of planned material expenditures is also required, for example, when such expenditures are necessary to support a new publicly announced product or line of business.

In the following example, the registrant discusses planned capital expenditures, and related financing sources, necessary to maintain sales growth:

> The Company plans to open 20 to 25 new stores in fiscal 1988. As a result, the Company expects the trend of higher sales in fiscal 1988 to continue at approximately the same rate as in recent years. Management estimates that approximately $50 to $60 million will be required to finance the company's cost of opening such stores. In addition, the Company's expansion program will require increases in inventory of about $1 million per store, which are anticipated to be financed principally by trade credit. Funds required to finance the Company's store expansion program are expected to come primarily from new credit facilities with the remainder provided by funds generated from operations and increased lease financing. The Company recently entered into a new borrowing agreement with its primary bank, which provides for additional borrowings of up to $50 million for future expansion. The Company intends to seek additional credit facilities during fiscal 1988.

Events that have already occurred or are anticipated often give rise to known uncertainties. For example, a registrant may know that a material government contract is about to expire. The registrant may be uncertain as to whether the contract will be renewed, but nevertheless would be able to assess facts relating to whether it will be renewed. More particularly, the registrant may know that a competitor has found a way to provide the same service or product at a price less than that charged by the registrant, or may have been advised by the government that the contract may not be renewed. The registrant also would have factual information relevant to the financial impact of non-renewal upon the registrant. In situations such as these, a registrant would have identified a known uncertainty reasonably likely to have material future effects on its financial condition or results of operations, and disclosure would be required.

In the following example, the registrant discloses the reasonably likely material effect of a known uncertainty regarding implementation of recently adopted legislation:

> The Company had no firm cash commitments as of December 31, 1987 for capital expenditures. However, in 1987, legislation was enacted which may require that certain vehicles used in the Company's business be equipped with specified safety equipment by the end of 1991. Pursuant to this legislation, regulations have been proposed which, if promulgated, would require the expenditure by the company of approximately $30 million over a three-year period.

Where a trend, demand, commitment, event or uncertainty is known, management must make two assessments:

(1) Is the known trend, demand, commitment, event or uncertainty likely to come to fruition? If management determines that is not reasonably likely to occur, no disclosure is required.

(2) If management cannot make that determination, it must evaluate objectively the consequences of the known trend, demand, commitment, event or uncertainty, on the assumption that it will come to fruition. Disclosure is then required unless management determines that a material effect on the registrant's financial condition or results of operations is not reasonably likely to occur.[15]

Each final determination resulting from the assessments made by management must be objectively reasonable, viewed as of the time the determination is made * * *

---

1. *Significance.* The MD&A is required to be included in registration statements, the registrant's Annual Report on Form 10–K, and its Quarterly Report on Form 10–Q. Thus, the process of estimating the impact of those trends, events, and uncertainties that the registrant is unable to conclude will not have a material effect on its financial condition or results of operations is a constant and continuing one for publicly held companies. Moreover when MD&A disclosure is required, the SEC has said that the disclosures must be "quantified to the extent reasonably practicable."[1]

2. *Recent SEC Expansion of the MD&A's Role.* Responding to Enron and the wave of accounting irregularity cases, the SEC proposed in May 2002 to require disclosure in the MD&A of the application of a firm's "critical accounting policies."[2] Specifically, firms would be required to disclose (1) accounting estimates that the firm made in applying its accounting policies, and (2) the initial adoption of an accounting policy that had a material impact on its financial presentation. A company would be required to identify and justify in its MD&A those accounting estimates reflected in its financial statements that it considers to have been highly uncertain as of the time of estimation. When a company chooses a new accounting policy that has a material impact on its financial presentation, Securities Act Release No. 8098 further instructs the company to disclose information about the circumstances that gave rise to the initial adoption, its impact, and the choices that existed among accounting policies. Further, companies are required to update this information and disclose any material changes in estimates and their impact in their quarterly reports on Form 10–Q. Although this proposed change is far from revolutionary, it illustrates the impact of corporate scandals on disclosure policy and

---

15. MD&A mandates disclosure of specified forward-looking information, and specifies its own standard for disclosure—i.e., reasonably likely to have a material effect. This specific standard governs the circumstances in which Item 303 requires disclosure. The probability/magnitude test for materiality approved by the Supreme Court in Basic, Inc., v. Levinson, 485 U.S. 224 (1988), is inapposite to Item 303 disclosure.

1. See In the Matter of Caterpillar Inc., SEC Exch.Act Rel. No. 30532 (Mar. 31, 1992).

2. See Securities Act Release No. 8098 (May 10, 2002).

suggests that a continuing accordion-like expansion of the MD&A seems predictable.

3. *Private Litigation.* Because the MD&A uses its own unique test of materiality that departs from the probability/magnitude formula of Basic v. Levinson[3], most courts have found that material departures from the requirements of Item 303 are not enough to support a private antifraud action.[4] That is, even if management is aware of known adverse trends or uncertainties and fails to disclose them, this omission is not actionable under Rule 10b–5—at least unless the trend or uncertainty would have been material under the Basic v. Levinson standard. More broadly, some courts have also said that the failure to disclose a forecast of future events is not actionable under the federal securities laws. More modestly, others have simply held that the failure to reveal inconsistent internal forecasts is insufficient to demonstrate scienter.[5]

4. *SEC Enforcement.* Nonetheless, the SEC can enforce its MD&A requirement, in particular by administrative enforcement proceedings. In the Matter of Caterpillar Inc.,[6] the SEC brought an administrative proceeding against Caterpillar under § 21C of the Securities Exchange Act of 1934 for failure to comply with § 13(a) of the 1934 Act, and Rules 13a–1 and 13a–13 thereunder, based on the following facts: In its Form 10–K for 1989, Caterpillar failed to disclose that 23% of its net profits were attributable to its Brazilian subsidiary ("CBSA"). This contribution by CBSA to Caterpillar's overall earnings was hidden by the consolidated accounting system used by Caterpillar; also, several nonoperating items of income (involving mainly currency translations and tax loss carryforwards) substantially increased CBSA's earnings for 1989. At the same time, hyperinflation in Brazil was leading to dramatic political changes which made CBSA's future ability to contribute to Caterpillar's 1990 earnings highly uncertain. By June, 1990, a new Brazilian austerity program indicated to Caterpillar's management that CBSA would suffer substantial losses. When this was publicly announced to the market, Caterpillar's stock immediately dropped 9%. The Commission found that Caterpillar had failed to comply with Item 303 both by failing to disclose the nature and extent of CBSA's contribution to Caterpillar's earnings and, In its Form 10–Q for the first quarter of 1990, by failing to indicate the known uncertainty surrounding CBSA's ability to continue to make its past contribution (which uncertainty had been clearly recognized by Caterpillar's management).

While securities analysts have largely welcomed the SEC's new insistence on disclosure (and quantification) of known trends and uncertainties, some academic commentators are skeptical. Professor Edward Kitch has argued that these heightened standards deprive the issuer of proprietary information and permit its business rivals to gain significant competitive advantages over it. He claims that:

> It is impossible for a management to prepare a "good" MD&A—that is, a disclosure that truly achieves the objectives of the MD&A required disclosure—without revealing a good deal of what it thinks about its businesses,

3.   485 U.S. 224 (1988).

4.   See In re VeriFone Securities Litigation, 11 F.3d 865, 869 (9th Cir.1993).

5.   See Stack v. Lobo, 903 F.Supp. 1361, 1370 (N.D.Cal.1995); In re Syntex Corp. Securities Litigation, 855 F.Supp. 1086, 1095 (N.D.Cal.1994), aff'd, 95 F.3d 922 (9th Cir. 1996).

6.   Sec.Exch.Act.Rel. No. 30532 (Mar. 31, 1992).

the markets In which its businesses operates, and how those markets will evolve.[7]

How great was the competitive advantage that competitors could have gained if Caterpillar had complied with Item 303? Still, Professor Kitch's broader point is worthy of attention: a public disclosure system, particularly one that requires mandatory projections as to future profitability, informs not only investors, but also competitors.

c. *The Statutory Safe Harbor for Forward–Looking Information.*

The Private Securities Litigation Reform Act of 1995 added new § 27A to the 1933 Act and new § 21E to the 1934 Act In order to encourage issuers and registrants to make forward-looking statements as to earnings, product development and related matters. Both safe harbors require the issuer or registrant to accompany its forward-looking statement with a "meaningful cautionary statement." This topic of what constitutes such a "meaningful" statement is examined infra at Chapter 14, along with the general standard of liability for projections. However, it needs to be emphasized here that this safe harbor is not available to all issuers, and specifically not to non-reporting companies and to initial public offerings.

d. *Note on "Plain English Disclosure."*

In Securities Act Release No. 7497 (January 28, 1998), the SEC revised rules 421, 461, and 481 of Regulation C to require registrants to employ "plain English" in writing certain sections of the registration statement and prospectus. These new rules followed a several year pilot project that convinced the SEC that simpler, more readable prospectuses were feasible. Technically, only the cover pages, summary and risk factors sections are covered by the new "plain English" rule (Rule 421(d)), but the new communications philosophy is now strongly encouraged by the SEC's staff. And revisions to Rule 421(b) empower the staff to reject any registration statement whose style or contents flunk the Commission's new standards.

In explaining its new rule in Release 7497, the Commission was, itself, concise and blunt about the change it expected:

"Full and fair disclosure is one of the cornerstones of investor protection under the federal securities laws. If a prospectus fails to communicate information clearly, investors do not receive that basic protection. Yet, prospectuses today often use complex, legalistic language that is foreign to all but financial or legal experts. The proliferation of complex transactions and securities magnifies this problem. A major challenge facing the securities industry and its regulators is assuring that financial and business information reaches investors in a form they can read and understand."

In response to this challenge, we undertake today a sweeping revision of how issuers must disclose information to investors. This new package of rules will change the face of every prospectus used in registered public offerings of securities. Prospectuses will be simpler, clearer, more useful, and we hope, more widely read.

---

7. Kitch, The Theory and Practice of   (1995).
Securities Disclosure, 61 Va.L.Rev. 763, 859

First, the new rules require issuers to write and design the cover page, summary, and risk factors section of their prospectuses in plain English. Specifically, in these sections, issuers will have to use: short sentences; definite, concrete, everyday language; active voice; tabular presentation of complex information; no legal or business jargon; and no multiple negatives. Issuers will also have to design these sanctions to make them inviting to the reader. In response to comments, the new rules will not require issuers to limit the length of the summary, limit the number of risk factors, or prioritize risk factors.

Second, we are giving guidance to issuers on how to comply with the current rule that requires the entire prospectus to be clear, concise, and understandable. Our goal is to purge the entire document of legalese and repetition that blur important information investors need to know.

III. *Rules on How to Prepare Prospectuses*

A.   Plain English Rule—Rule 421(d)

Rule 421(d), the plain English rule, requires you to prepare the front portion of the prospectus in plain English. You must use plain English principles in the organization, language, and design of the front and back cover pages, the summary, and the risk factors section. Also, when drafting the language in these front parts of the prospectus, you must comply substantially with six basic principles:

- Short sentences;
- Definite, concrete, everyday language;
- Active voice;
- Tabular presentation or bullet lists for complex material, whenever possible;
- no legal jargon or highly technical business terms; and
- no multiple negatives.

A number of comment letters noted that our rule dictates how to write the front of the prospectus. They are correct. We have seen marked improvement in the clarity of disclosure when pilot participants have used these widely recognized, basic principles of clear writing. We believe the benefits to investors support mandating the use of these writing principles for the front of the prospectus.

In addition, you must design the cover page, summary, and risk factors section to make them easy to read. You must format the text and design the document to highlight important information for investors. The rule permits you to use pictures, charts, graphics, and other design features to make the prospectus easier to understand.

B.   Clear, Concise, and Understandable Prospectuses—Rule 421(b)

Rule 421(b) currently requires that the entire prospectus be clear, concise, and understandable. This requirement is in addition to the plain English rule we are adopting, which applies only to the front of the prospectus.

We are adopting, as proposed, amendments to Rule 421(b). These amendments provide guidance on how to prepare a prospectus that is clear, concise, and understandable. The amendments set out four general writing techniques that you must follow and list four conventions to avoid when drafting the prospectus. As several comment letters noted, these amendments codify our earlier interpretive advice.

Amended Rule 421(b) requires you to use the following techniques when writing the entire prospectus:

- Present information in clear, concise sections, paragraphs, and sentences. Whenever possible, use short explanatory sentences and bullet lists;

- Use descriptive headings and subheadings;

- Avoid frequent reliance on glossaries or defined terms as the primary means of explaining information in the prospectus. Define terms in a glossary or other section of the document only if the meaning is unclear from the context. Use a glossary only if it facilitates understanding of the disclosure; and

- Avoid legal and highly technical business terminology.

The new note to Rule 421(b) provides guidance on how to comply with the rule's general requirements. The note lists the following drafting conventions to avoid because they make your document harder to read:

- Legalistic or overly complex presentations that make the substance of the disclosure difficult to understand;

- Vague boilerplate explanations that are readily subject to differing interpretations;

- Complex information copied directly from legal documents without any clear and concise explanation of the provision(s); and

- Repetitive disclosure that increases the size of the document, but does not enhance the quality of the information.

C. Comments on Proposed Amendments to Rule 421(b) and Rule 421(d)

Several comment letters stated that we should permit public companies to use legal and technical business terminology. The letters noted, for example, that high technology companies must use technical terms to distinguish their products or services from others in the industry. We recognize that certain business terms may be necessary to describe your operations properly. But, you should avoid using excessive technical jargon that only your competitors or an industry specialist can understand.

You should write the disclosure in your prospectus for investors. When you use many highly technical terms, the investor must learn your dictionary of terms to understand your disclosure. If technical terms are unavoidable, you should make every effort to explain their meaning the "first time you use them."

SECTION 5. DISCLOSURE POLICY AND THE DEBATE OVER THE EFFICIENT MARKET

Both the SEC[1] and the Supreme Court[2] have at times characterized the market for publicly traded securities as "efficient." In so doing, they are

---

1. In adopting its integrated disclosure system, the Commission acknowledged that

its deregulatory policy was premised on the assumptions that "investors are protected by

alluding to a fundamental concept known as the Efficient Capital Market Hypothesis (or "ECMH"). The central and least disputed claim of the ECMH is that available information about securities traded in the principal securities markets is impounded into stock prices with sufficient speed that even sophisticated investors cannot systematically profit by trading on newly available information. Thus, the most common definition of an efficient market is that prices in such a market "fully reflect" all "available" information.[3] But what do "fully reflect" and "available" mean? A clearer definition is that a market is efficient with respect to specific information "if prices act *as if* everyone knows the information."[4]

Not even the strongest proponent of the ECMH argues that the market's judgment will always (or even usually) prove correct in the long-run. Too much uncertainty is inherent in economic life for this assertion to be true. Rather, the central claim of the ECMH is that consensus valuation of an efficient market will be the best possible, least biased measure of value at any given time. The ECMH developed historically from the empirical observation that traders cannot exploit "available information" to develop profitable trading or arbitrage strategies. Still, we know that some traders—i.e., those using "inside" information—do profit, and thus some forms of non-public information can be successfully exploited. Accordingly, one must specify carefully what one means by "available information." In a much cited article, Professor Eugene Fama distinguished three different versions or ways of interpreting the ECMH: "weak," "semi-strong," and "strong."[5] The "weak" form of the theory claims only that the history of securities prices provides no useful information to the investor; that is, knowing that a stock has risen three points in the last hour or day will not tell the investor whether the next price movement will be positive or negative. The "semi-strong" theory makes the same assessment about publicly released information (such as the information contained in SEC filings). Finally, the "strong" form of the theory hypothesizes that even non-public information is reflected in price. As Fama demonstrated, some empirical studies support each of these interpretations, but the weight of the evidence underlying the "semi-strong" version has accumulated to the point that there is no serious challenge today to its claim that the market absorbs and reflects new information with great speed.

But, if so, so what? The policy implications of the ECMH to securities regulation and disclosure policy are important, but far more controversial. A

the market's analysis of information about certain companies which is widely available * * * and that such analysis is reflected in the price of the securities offered." See also, Securities Act Release No. 6383 (1982). For an analysis of the differences between the standard ECMH and the SEC's more qualified acceptance of it, see Pickholz & Horahan, The SEC's Version of the Efficient Market Theory and Its Impact on Securities Law Liabilities, 39 Wash. & Lee L.Rev. 943 (1982).

2. See Basic Inc. v. Levinson, 485 U.S. 224 (1988), infra p. 998 (explaining that its fraud on the market theory is a natural extension of the ECMH).

3. See Gilson & Kraakman, The Mechanisms of Market Efficiency, 70 Va.L.Rev. 549, 554 (1989).

4. See Beaver, Market Efficiency, 56 Acct.Rev. 23, 35 (1981). For an even more precise definition—that the market is efficient with respect to a specific information set if revealing that information to all traders would not alter stock prices or the composition of stock portfolios—see Latham, Informational Efficiency and Information Subsets, 41 J.Fin. 39, 40 (1986).

5. Fama, Efficient Capital Markets: A Review of the Theory and Empirical Work, 25 J.Fin. 383 (1970).

first implication of the ECMH is that stock prices will move unpredictably—or, in the jargon, will follow a "random walk." This implication follows because if stock prices incorporate all available information, then they will move only when truly new (i.e., unforeseen) information becomes available. This tendency for stock prices to move unpredictably was observed early in this century,[6] and the formal theory of market efficiency is essentially an attempt to explain such random movements.

The next implication is far more debatable. Many read the ECMH to imply that in an efficient market "every security's price equals its investment value at all times."[7] This claim that because securities prices incorporate all available information there can be no divergence between the corporation's "intrinsic" or "investment value" and its market price is premised on additional assumptions that are not always carefully specified: (1) that all investors are equally rational; (2) that they have relatively costless access to the available information; and (3) that arbitrage opportunities will be exploited until any evident disparity between "investment value" and market price is eliminated.[8] These assumptions are challenged by many who believe that the market is "speculatively efficient" (in the sense that its movements cannot be predicted) but not "allocatively efficient" (in the sense that there is no divergence between "investment" and "market" value).[9] In principle, when all the preconditions of the formal model are satisfied, there should be an identity between asset and securities values,[10] but few believe that the theoretical conditions for such an identity between market value and investment value actually exist.

Indeed, a powerful argument can be made that these conditions cannot exist. Financial economists use the term "efficiency paradox" to refer to a fundamental conflict between the need of securities analysts and other market professionals for an acceptable return on their investment in acquiring and verifying securities information and the impossibility of such a return if the securities market were perfectly efficient. Inevitably, information collection is costly, and such activities will be reduced or suspended if a positive return is not obtainable; at that point, the market becomes less efficient. As a result, Professors Grossman and Stigilitz, both noted economists, have argued that a perfectly efficient market is impossible.[11] Rather, the market may experience oscillating cycles of near perfect efficiency followed by relative inefficiency, as traders suspend the costly pursuit of new information as returns from such activity fade, but then later resume their search for new information once the market becomes less efficient and so offers positive returns from the acquisition of new information. Ultimately, they argue, some "equilibrium level of disequilibrium" will be attained—meaning that the market will absorb information quickly, but not so quickly as to deny professionals a "normal" profit.

6. See Bachlier, Theory of Speculation (1900), reprinted in P. Cootner, The Random Character of Stock Prices 17 (1964). For a general history of the efficient markets literature, see LeRoy, Efficient Capital Markets and Martingales, 27 J.Econ.Lit. 1583 (1989).

7. See G. Alexander & W. Sharpe, Fundamentals of Investments 67 (1989).

8. Id.

9. See Gordon & Kornhauser, Efficient Markets, Costly Information, and Securities Research, 60 N.Y.U.L.Rev. 761 (1985); see also Wang, Some Arguments That the Stock Market Is Not Efficient, 19 U.C. Davis L.Rev. 341 (1986).

10. Gilson & Kraakman, supra note 3, at 558.

11. See Grossman & Stiglitz, On the Impossibility of Informationally Efficient Markets, 70 Am.Econ.Rev. 393 (1980).

Courts, however, have sometimes bordered on reading the ECMH to imply that stocks will trade at their investment value. The leading example is Wielgos v. Commonwealth Edison Co.,[12] in which an investor brought a class action on behalf of the purchasers of the stock of Commonwealth Edison issued under a shelf registration statement on Form S–3. The plaintiff alleged that projections made by the issuer as to when certain nuclear generators would be operational and approved by the Nuclear Regulatory Commission were materially misleading. Writing for the Seventh Circuit, Judge Easterbrook acknowledged that the projections were based on plainly unrealistic assumptions, but still affirmed the grant of a summary judgment for the defendants because, he concluded, market professionals must have known that the projections were wrong. The opinion opens with an observation that suggests the market can seldom be fooled:

> "The Securities and Exchange Commission believes that markets correctly value the securities of well-followed firms, so that new sales may rely on information that has been digested and expressed in the security's price."[13]

It is doubtful that the Commission believes this (it probably accepts only the more modest conclusion that the costs of requiring additional disclosure by publicly held firms already subject to the 1934 Act's continuous disclosure system would outweigh the benefits). More importantly, economic theory does not necessarily make this strong a claim. Fischer Black, a prominent financial economist, has argued that a reasonable definition of an efficient market is "one in which the price is within a factor of 2 of value, i.e., the price is more than half of value and less than twice value."[14] If this test defines "efficiency," then misleading predictions and statements about events or matters where it is difficult or costly for the market to verify the information provided it may also be impounded into stock prices; in short, the market may quickly reflect misinformation as well as accurate information. As a result, it is important to focus in more detail in this section on:

(1) the forces or mechanisms that make the market efficient—and how the law can facilitate or retard them;

(2) the critiques of market efficiency—are there other explanations that can explain the same phenomena of seemingly random price movements?; and

(3) does the theory really dictate policy consequences? Are there realistic policy options that truly hinge on its validity?

A. WHAT MAKES THE MARKET EFFICIENT?: THE ROLE OF UNDERWRITERS

While economists have concentrated on measuring the market's efficiency in responding to new information, legal scholars have focused more on understanding the forces that increase or retard market efficiency. In one well-known article, Professors Ronald Gilson and Reinier Kraakman argue that the level of market efficiency is essentially determined by two factors: (1) the relative cost

---

12. 892 F.2d 509 (7th Cir.1989). For a similar view that an efficient market will see through misleading projections, see In re Apple Computer Securities Litigation, 886 F.2d 1109, 1116 (9th Cir.1989); In re Convergent Technologies Securities Litigation, 721 F.Supp. 1133 (N.D.Cal.1988), aff'd, 948 F.2d 507 (9th Cir.1991).

13. Id. at 510.

14. Black, Noise, 41 J.Fin. 529, 533 (1986).

of acquiring, processing, and verifying different types of information, and (2) the initial distribution of the information among traders in the market. Thus, some types of information that are more costly to acquire or difficult to verify may not be impounded by the market into price as quickly as, for example, the financial information in SEC filings, which not only comes partially verified by the issuer's public accountants but is also distributed widely to the entire market. Moreover, cost also determines the distribution of a particular type of information among traders. The lower the cost of acquiring it, the wider will be its distribution in the market, and, ultimately, the more effective will be the capital market at impounding it into price. Based on this starting point, they then examine how the information market attempts to economize on the costs of information acquisition and verification. In particular, they propose a different way of understanding the role of the investment banker:

Excerpt from: Ronald J. Gilson and Reinier H. Kraakman

The Mechanisms of Market Efficiency
70 Virginia Law Review 549, 612–621 (1984).

The core of our analysis, then, is that the cost of information critically determines market efficiency because it dictates not only the amount of information attending a particular security but also the distribution of that information among traders, which in turn determines the operative capital market mechanism. This focus on information costs also identifies the invisible hand that moves the market toward greater informational efficiency. Information market incentives lead to economizing on information costs and thus to the availability of more effective capital market mechanisms. The result is an integrated understanding of the mechanisms of market efficiency that we believe provides both theoretical insights and new opportunities for employing the market efficiency concept to inform regulatory policy.

In this section we apply our synthesis of the operation of the capital and information markets to * * * explain the investment banker's role in increasing the efficiency of the market's response. * * *

A.   *Role of the Investment Banker*

* * *

Investment bankers are typically seen as having two principal functions in the distribution of securities. First, investment bankers serve as distributors for the issuer, providing the sales force and facilities necessary to sell the securities to the public. Second, they provide a form of risk sharing or insurance, at least in connection with "firm commitment underwriting," that relieves the issuer of some of the risks inherent in the offering of a security. But even taken together, these two functions do not entirely explain the modern underwriter's role. While distribution is obviously an important function, a sizable percentage of the total underwriting compensation goes to participants who do not actually engage in selling the security. Nor does risk sharing account for the remainder of the modern underwriting function, since the underwriter need bear little risk even in a firm commitment underwriting. In a typical firm commitment underwriting, the price that the underwriter pays to the issuer is not set, and the underwriter is not committed to purchase the securities, until approximately twenty-four hours before the registration statement is declared effective and the public sale of the securities commences. The issuer thus bears virtually all risk of changed market conditions prior to the commencement of sale. Moreover, the practice of soliciting "indications of interest"—non-binding statements of intent to buy the securities—from prospective purchasers during the period between the filing of the registration statement and the commencement of sales further reduces the risk that the securities will be priced too high.

The only risk that then remains for the underwriter to "share" is that of a change in market conditions during the short period, typically no more than a week, required by the underwriter to complete the sale. But even here the underwriter need bear little risk; the futures and options markets permit it to hedge the risk of market changes during the offering period. For example, if the underwriter fears that interest rates may rise while it is trying to sell a fixed rate bond, it can eliminate all risk by selling treasury bills for future delivery. Similar hedging of overall market conditions is possible in equity offerings through the use of futures markets in various stock composites.

If distribution and risk sharing do not adequately account for the investment banker's function, some additional factor must be at work. Our analysis suggests that investment bankers play a third role, that of an information and reputational intermediary, which is particularly important in the context of new issues and other innovations.

Recall the problem facing an innovative issuer. Buyers find it too expensive to determine for themselves whether the issuer's new form of security warrants a higher price; and even if the issuer could educate them individually, the verification problem remains. Buyers still must be convinced of the accuracy of the information the issuer provides. A reputable investment banker may be able to solve both problems. Processing costs are obviously lower for a single investment banker than for a disparate group of individual buyers. This fact reflects the savings that accrue both from collectivization and from the potential for scale and scope economies in information processing.

From our perspective, however, the investment banker's role in reducing verification costs is even more critical. The difficulty confronting the issuer and prospective buyers is that determining the quality of the issuer's information is expensive ex ante, but not ex post. Before the sale, prospective buyers must incur verification costs to assess the issuer's good faith; after the sale, the issuer's behavior will reveal the quality of the information at virtually no cost. In this setting, a common technique for economizing on information costs is for sellers to make capital investments in brand name or reputation as a means of signaling the quality of the information. By making the investment in reputation, the seller signals its belief that when the purchaser learns the truth ex post, the quality of the information provided by the seller ex ante will be proved high. If the original information proves to be of low quality, the value of the seller's investment in reputation will diminish. Thus, the seller's investment in reputation demonstrates that it is not in his interest to misrepresent the accuracy of its information; and the buyer can rely upon that signal in lieu of engaging in costly verification itself.

The disadvantage of this economizing technique, however, is that in many cases it may not be available to an information seller. First, the seller may lack the capital to invest in a reputation.[194] Second, it may lack the time to build a

---

194. Even if the seller has the capital to invest in reputation, it still may be cheaper to "rent" a reputation depending on the size and frequency of anticipated offerings. There

reputation prior to the contemplated sale. Third, even if the seller is willing to invest the necessary time and resources, prospective buyers may still harbor doubts about its good faith—an investment in reputation cannot wholly eliminate the incentive to behave opportunistically. Suppose, for example, that an issuer contemplates going to the capital market only once, and thereafter intends to finance its growth internally. In that case, an investment in reputation may be not a bond but bait, willingly lost in order to catch a more valuable fish. The gains from opportunism may well exceed the costs of lost reputation. Finally, each of these three difficulties—of money, time, and lingering suspicion—are particularly acute when an issuer makes its first offering.

It is in this setting that the critical role of the investment banker as a reputational intermediary becomes clear. In essence, the investment banker rents the issuer its reputation. The investment banker represents to the market (to whom *it,* and not the issuer, sells the security) that it has evaluated the issuer's product and good faith and that it is prepared to stake its reputation on the value of the innovation. Moreover, because the investment banker, unlike the issuer, is certain to be a "repeat player" in the capital markets, there are no final period problems to dampen the signal of value.[195]

The investment banker's role as an informational and reputational intermediary can dramatically affect the efficiency of the market's response to an innovative security. As the cost of information about the security is reduced, information is more widely distributed and, therefore, more effectively reflected in market price.[196] Of course, the market never becomes *completely* efficient with respect to the innovative security. Information costs are always greater than zero: information concerning the innovation will not be perfectly processed, and the investment banker's signal, itself costly, will not be perfectly credible. The market price of the innovative security will therefore still be lower than it would be if information costs were zero. Nonetheless, the investment banker helps make the market *more* efficient than it otherwise

are economies of scale in the creation and use of reputations.

195. Baron, A Model of the Demand for Investment Banking Advising and Distribution Services for New Issues, 37 J.Fin. 955 (1982), and Baron & Holmstrom, The Investment Banking Contract for New Issues Under Asymmetric Information: Delegation and the Incentive Problem, 35 J.Fin. 1115 (1980), focus on a different, but related, informational role for investment bankers. They argue that the investment banker has much better information concerning what the issuer's securities are worth than the issuer, and the resulting asymmetry is between the banker and the issuer rather than between the issuer and the buyer. Our focus here is on the latter asymmetry, which Baron notes but does not pursue. Baron, supra, at 956.

196. The role of investment bankers in reducing information costs is also apparent from an examination of their historical development. For example, Goldman Sachs & Co. had its origin in Marcus Goldman's commercial paper business, in which he would purchase short-term notes from small manufacturers for resale to banks. V. Carosso, Investment Banking in America 19 (1970). The early development of investment banking, during periods when more primitive communication capability—in terms of both technology and a common accounting language—served to ensure very high barriers to verification, may best be understood from the perspective of information costs. Cf. F. Allen, The Great Pierpont Morgan 70–71 (1965) (Morgan firm's unprecedented reorganization and underwriting fees justified in large part by the enormous value of the Morgan reputation; Morgan firm's efforts to tie up further control of reorganized railroads in voting trust was necessary to safeguard its reputation).

would be. And from our perspective, a more complete picture of the role of this critical actor in the capital markets demonstrates the value of understanding the relationship between information costs and market efficiency.[197]

197. An understanding of the investment banker's cost-economizing role as a reputational intermediary may also help unravel what Brealey & Myers have described as one of "the ten unsolved problems in finance." * * * Ibbotson, Price Performance of Common Stock New Issues, 2 J.Fin.Econ. 235 (1975), found that initial public offerings are significantly underpriced. An investor purchasing a portfolio of such securities in their initial offering would earn an abnormal return of 11.4% over the first month. The puzzle is to explain this phenomenon. Of course, the strength of the underwriter's bargaining position may reduce the prices that issuers receive for their securities. Cf. Baron, supra note 195, at 972–74 (unseasoned issuers that are less informed about market demand for their securities are more likely to accept too low a price from investment bankers). But the question remains as to why the investment bankers would pass the benefit on to the public.

Our approach to the puzzle begins by recognizing that underwriters, as reputational intermediaries, reduce verification costs, and so increase the value of offered securities. * * *

In part, how the issuer and the underwriter split the increase in value arising from verification depends on competitive conditions in the market for underwriters, information asymmetries, and the costs of contracting. Baron, supra note 195. The underwriter's portion of the increase represents a deduction from the price the issuer would receive if information were costless and verification unnecessary. The problem, however, is that abnormal returns to investors also represent such a deduction. Why do investment bankers content themselves with half a loaf, when they are apparently in a position to claim the public's share as well?

The answer, we think, lies in the fact that the investment banker provides verification by pledging its investment in reputation as a bond that the information offered by the issuer is correct. But characterizing the banker's reputation as an investment raises the issue of what form that investment takes. We argue that passing on to the customer a portion of the return the underwriter receives for pledging its reputation is best understood as a capital investment in reputation, a way of ensuring that the customer's ex post experience will be consistent with the issuer's and investment banker's ex ante representations. And, like corporate image advertising, an investment in reputation is a wasting asset that requires ongoing replenishment. A reputation for accurate pricing in the past does not eliminate the need for continued investment in the future. This analysis is consistent with competitive conditions in both the market for supplying investment banking services to issuers and the market for selling new securities to the public. It merely suggests an additional capital cost associated with successfully operating in such markets.

That underwriters may underprice an issue in order to dispose customers favorably toward future issues is not original to us. Indeed, Ibbotson considered and rejected just such an explanation for his empirical results: "Although this explanation is prevalent on Wall Street, it clearly violates an efficient market framework." Ibbotson, supra, at 264. Our information cost analysis of market efficiency, however, alters the framework to which Ibbotson refers. Positive verification costs, in the form of payments from issuers to underwriters for acting as reputational intermediaries and payments by underwriters to customers as investments in reputation, are entirely consistent with an efficient market framework in anything other than the frictionless world of perfect markets. Our explanation might be tested in part by investigating whether the extent of underpricing depends on the magnitude of the investment banker's reputation.

B. NEW CRITIQUES OF THE EFFICIENT MARKET HYPOTHESIS

Andrei Shleifer and Lawrence H. Summers

The Noise Trader Approach to Finance

4 Journal of Economic Perspectives 19–33 (1990).

If the efficient markets hypothesis was a publicly traded security, its price would be enormously volatile. Following Samuelson's (1965) proof that stock prices should follow a random walk if rational competitive investors require a fixed rate of return and Fama's (1965) demonstration that stock prices are indeed close to a random walk, stock in the efficient markets hypothesis rallied. Michael Jensen was able to write in 1978 that "the efficient markets hypothesis is the best established fact in all of social sciences."

Such strong statements portend reversals, the efficient markets hypothesis itself notwithstanding. Stock in the efficient markets hypothesis lost ground rapidly following the publication of Shiller's (1981) and Leroy and Porter's (1981) volatility tests, both of which found stock market volatility to be far greater than could be justified by changes in dividends.[1] The stock snapped back following the papers of Kleidon (1986) and Marsh and Merton (1986) which challenged the statistical validity of volatility tests. A choppy period then ensued, where conflicting econometric studies induced few of the changes in opinion that are necessary to move prices. But the stock in the efficient markets hypothesis—at least as it has traditionally been formulated—crashed along with the rest of the market on October 19, 1987. Its recovery has been less dramatic than that of the rest of the market.

This paper reviews an alternative to the efficient markets approach that we and others have recently pursued. Our approach rests on two assumptions. First, some investors are not fully rational and their demand for risky assets is affected by their beliefs or sentiments that are not fully justified by fundamental news. Second, arbitrage—defined as trading by fully rational investors not subject to such sentiment—is risky and therefore limited. The two assumptions together imply that changes in investor sentiment are not fully countered by arbitrageurs and so affect security returns. We argue that this approach to financial markets is in many ways superior to the efficient markets paradigm.

Our case for the noise trader approach is threefold. First, theoretical models with limited arbitrage are both tractable and more plausible than models with perfect arbitrage. The efficient markets hypothesis obtains only as an extreme case of perfect riskless arbitrage that is unlikely to apply in practice. Second, the investor sentiment/limited arbitrage approach yields a more accurate description of financial markets than the efficient markets paradigm. The approach not only explains the available anomalies, but also readily explains broad features of financial markets such as trading volume and actual investment strategies. Third, and most importantly, this approach yields new and testable implications about asset prices, some of which have been proved to be consistent with the data. It is absolutely *not true* that introducing

---

1. See Shiller, Do Stock Prices Move Too Much to be Justified by Subsequent Changes in Dividends?, 71 American Economic Review 421 (1981); Leroy and Porter, Stock Price Volatility: Tests Based on Implied Variance Bounds, 49 Econometrica 97 (1981)—Eds.

a degree of irrationality of *some* investors into models of financial markets "eliminates all discipline and can explain anything."

The Limits of Arbitrage

We think of the market as consisting of two types of investors: "arbitrageurs"—also called "smart money" and "rational speculators"—and other investors. Arbitrageurs are defined as investors who form fully rational expectations about security returns. In contrast, the opinions and trading patterns of other investors—also known as "noise traders" and "liquidity traders"—may be subject to systematic biases. In practice, the line between arbitrageurs and other investors may be blurred, but for our argument it helps to draw a sharp distinction between them, since the arbitrageurs do the work of bringing prices toward fundamentals.

Arbitrageurs play a central role in standard finance. They trade to ensure that if a security has a perfect substitute—a portfolio of other securities that yields the same returns—then the price of the security equals the price of that substitute portfolio. If the price of the security falls below that of the substitute portfolio, arbitrageurs sell the portfolio and buy the security until the prices are equalized, and vice versa if the price of a security rises above that of the substitute portfolio. When the substitute is indeed perfect, this arbitrage is riskless. As a result, arbitrageurs have perfectly elastic demand for the security at the price of its substitute portfolio. Arbitrage thus assures that relative prices of securities must be in line for there to be no riskless arbitrage opportunities. Such riskless arbitrage is very effective for derivative securities, such as futures and options, but also for individual stocks and bonds where reasonably close substitutes are usually available.

Although riskless arbitrage ensures that relative prices are in line, it does not help to pin down price levels of, say, stocks or bonds as a whole. These classes of securities do not have close substitute portfolios, and therefore if for some reason they are mispriced, there is no riskless hedge for the arbitrageur. For example, an arbitrageur who thinks that stocks are underpriced cannot buy stocks and sell the substitute portfolio, since such a portfolio does not exist. The arbitrageur can instead simply buy stocks in hopes of an above-normal return, but this arbitrage is no longer riskless. If the arbitrageur is risk-averse, his demand for underpriced stocks will be limited. With a finite number of arbitrageurs, their combined demand curve is no longer perfectly elastic.

Two types of risk limit arbitrage. The first is fundamental risk. Suppose that stocks are selling above the expected value of future dividends and an arbitrageur is selling them short. The arbitrageur then bears the risk that the realization of dividends—or of the news about dividends—is better than expected, in which case he loses on his trade. Selling "overvalued" stocks is risky because there is always a chance that the market will do very well. Fear of such a loss limits the arbitrageur's original position, and keeps his short-selling from driving prices all the way down to fundamentals.

The second source of risk that limits arbitrage comes from unpredictability of the future resale price * * *. Suppose again that stocks are overpriced and an arbitrageur is selling them short. As long as the arbitrageur is thinking of liquidating his position in the future, he must bear the risk that at that time stocks will be *even more* overpriced than they are today. If future mispricing is more extreme than when the arbitrage trade is put on, the arbitrageur suffers a loss on his position. Again, fear of this loss limits the size of the arbitrageur's initial position, and so keeps him from driving the price all the way down to fundamentals.

Clearly, this resale price risk depends on the arbitrageur having a finite horizon. If the arbitrageur's horizon is infinite, he simply sells the stock short and pays dividends on it in all the future periods, recognizing that the present value of those is lower than his proceeds from the short sale. But there are several reasons that it makes sense to assume that arbitrageurs have short horizons. Most importantly, arbitrageurs have to borrow cash or securities to implement their trades, and as a result must pay the lenders *per period* fees. These fees cumulate over the period that the position remains open, and can add up to large amounts for long term arbitrage. The structure of transaction costs thus induces a strong bias toward short horizons. In addition, the performance of most money managers is evaluated at least once a year and usually once every few months, also limiting the horizon of arbitrage. As a result of these problems, resources dedicated to long-term arbitrage against fundamental mispricing are very scarce.

Japanese equities in the 1980s illustrate the limits of arbitrage. During this period, Japanese equities have sold at the price earning multiples of between 20 and 60, and have continued to climb. Expected growth rates of dividends and risk premia required to justify such multiples seem unrealistic. Nonetheless, an investor who believes that Japanese equities are overvalued and wants to sell them short, must confront two types of risk. First, what if Japan actually does perform so well that these prices are justified? Second, how much more out of line can prices get, and for how long, before Japanese equities return to more realistic prices? Any investor who sold Japanese stocks short in 1985, when the price earnings multiple was 30, would have lost his shirt as the multiples rose to 60 in 1986.

These arguments that risk makes arbitrage ineffective actually understate the limits of arbitrage. After all, they presume that the arbitrageur knows the fundamental value of the security. In fact, the arbitrageur might not exactly know what this value is, or be able to detect price changes that reflect deviations from fundamentals. In this case, arbitrage is even riskier than before. Summers * * * shows that a time series of share prices which deviate from fundamentals in a highly persistent way looks a lot like a random walk.[2] Arbitrageurs would have as hard a time as econometricians in detecting such a deviation, even if it were large. An arbitrageur is then handicapped by the difficulty of identifying the mispricing as well as by the risk of betting against it. Are economists certain that Japanese stocks are overpriced at a price earnings ratio of 50?

Substantial evidence shows that, contrary to the efficient markets hypothesis, arbitrage does not completely counter responses of prices to fluctuations in uninformed demand. Of course, identifying such fluctuations in demand is tricky, since price changes may reflect new market information which changes the equilibrium price at which arbitrageurs trade. Several recent studies do, however, avoid this objection by looking at responses of prices to changes in demand that do not plausibly reflect any new fundamental information because they have institutional or tax motives.

2. Summers, Does the Stock Market Rationally Reflect Fundamental Values?, 41   Journal of Finance 591 (1986)—Eds.

For example, Harris and Gurel[3] and Shleifer[4] examine stock price reactions to inclusions of new stocks into the Standard & Poor 500 stock index. Being added to the S&P 500 is not a plausible example of new information about the stock, since stocks are picked for their representativeness and not for performance potential. However, a stock added to the S&P 500 is subsequently acquired in large quantities by the so-called "index funds," whose holdings just represent the index. Both Harris and Gurel and Shleifer find that announcements of inclusions into the index are accompanied by share price increases of 2 to 3 percent. Moreover, the magnitude of these increases over time has risen, paralleling the growth of assets in index funds. Clearly, the arbitrage trade in which rational speculators sell the new stock and buy back close substitutes is not working here. And simply selling short the newly included stock on the theory that it is now overpriced must be too risky.

Further evidence on price pressure when no news is transmitted comes from Ritter's[5] work on the January effect. The January effect is the name for the fact that small stocks have outperformed market indices by a significant percentage each January over the last 50 or so years. Ritter finds that small stocks are typically sold by individual investors in December—often to realize capital losses—and then bought back in January. These share shifts explain the January effect as long as arbitrage by institutions and market insiders is ineffective, since aggressive arbitrage should eliminate the price effects of temporary trading patterns by individual investors. Either risk or borrowing constraints keep arbitrageurs from eliminating the price consequences of year-end trading.

Less direct evidence also shows that news is not the only force driving asset prices, suggesting that arbitrage is not successful in eliminating the effects of uninformed trading on prices. For example, French and Roll[6] look at a period when the U.S. stock market was closed on Wednesdays and find that the market is less volatile on these days than on Wednesdays when it is open. By focusing on Wednesdays, they control for the intensity of release of public information. This result may reflect incorporation of private information into prices during open hours, but it may also reflect the failure of arbitrage to accommodate intraday demand shifts. Roll[7] demonstrates that most idiosyncratic price moves in individual stocks cannot be accounted for by public news. He finds that individual stocks exhibit significant price movements unrelated to the market on days when there are no public news about these stocks. A similar and more dramatic result is obtained for the aggregate stock market by Cutler, Poterba, and Summers,[8] who find that the days of the largest aggregate market movements are not the days of most important fundamental news and vice

3.   Harris and Gurel, Price and Volume Effects Associated with Changes in the S&P 500: New Evidence for the Existence of Price Pressure, 41 Journal of Finance 851 (1986)—Eds.

4.   Shleifer, Do Demand Curves for Stocks Slope Down?, 41 Journal of Finance 579 (1986)—Eds.

5.   Ritter, The Buying and Selling Behavior of Individual Investors at the Turn of the Year, 43 Journal of Finance 701 (1988)—Eds.

6.   French and Roll, Stock Return Variances: The Arrival of Information and the Reaction of Traders, 17 Journal of Financial Economics 5 (1986)—Eds.

7.   Roll, R-squared, 43 Journal of Finance 541 (1988)—Eds.

8.   Cutler, Poterba and Summers, What Moves Stock Prices?, 15 Journal of Portfolio Management 4 (1989)—Eds.

versa. The common conclusion of these studies is that news alone does not move stock prices; uninformed changes in demand move them too.

Investor Sentiment

Some shifts in investor demand for securities are completely rational. Such changes could reflect, for example, reactions to public announcements that affect future growth rate of dividends, risk, or risk aversion. Rational demand changes can also reflect adjustment to news conveyed through the trading process itself. Finally, rational demand changes can reflect tax trading or trading done for institutional reasons of the types discussed above.

But not all demand changes appear to be so rational; some seem to be a response to changes in expectations or sentiment that are not fully justified by information. Such changes can be a response to pseudo-signals that investors believe convey information about future returns but that would not convey such information in a fully rational model. An example of such pseudo-signals is advice of brokers or financial gurus. We use the term "noise traders" to describe such investors * * *. Changes in demand can also reflect investors' use of inflexible trading strategies or of "popular models" that Shiller describes in this journal. One such strategy is trend chasing. Although these changes in demand are unwarranted by fundamentals, they can be related to fundamentals, as in the case of overreaction to news.

These demand shifts will only matter if they are correlated across noise traders. If all investors trade randomly, their trades cancel out and there are no aggregate shifts in demand. Undoubtedly, some trading in the market brings together noise traders with different models who cancel each other out. However, many trading strategies based on pseudo-signals, noise, and popular models are correlated, leading to aggregate demand shifts. The reason for this is that judgment biases afflicting investors in processing information tend to be the same. Subjects in psychological experiments tend to make the same mistake; they do not make random mistakes.

Many of these persistent mistakes are relevant for financial markets. For example, experimental subjects tend to be overconfident,[9] which makes them take on more risk. Experimental subjects also tend to extrapolate past time series, which can lead them to chase trends. Finally, in making inferences experimental subjects put too little weight on base rates and too much weight on new information,[10] which might lead them to overreact to news.

The experimental evidence on judgment biases is corroborated by survey and other evidence on how investors behave. For example, extrapolation is a key feature of the popular models discovered by the surveys Shiller describes in this journal.[11] He finds that home buyers as well as investors in the crash of 1987 seem to extrapolate past price trends. Similar results have been found by Frankel and Froot (1986) in their analysis of exchange rate forecasts during the

---

9. See Kahneman, Slovic and Tversky, Judgment Under Uncertainty: Heuristics and Biases (1982)—Eds.

10. Tversky and Kahneman, "Evidential Impact of Base Rates" in Kahneman, Slovic and Tversky, supra note 9—Eds.

11. Shiller, Speculative Prices and Popular Models, 4 Journal of Economic Perspectives 55 (1990)—Eds.

mid–1980s: over the short horizon, professional forecasters expect a price trend to continue even when they expect a long run reversion to fundamentals.

* * *

So-called "technical analysis" is another example of demand shifts without a fundamental rationalization. Technical analysis typically calls for buying more stocks when stocks have risen (broke through a barrier), and selling stocks when they fall through a floor. "Adam Smith" refers to the informal theorem of chartism that classifies phases of price movements in terms of categories—accumulation, distribution and liquidation. The suggested trading strategies then respond to the phase of the cycle the security is supposed to be in. These trading strategies are based on noise or "popular models" and not on information.

There can be little doubt that these sorts of factors influence demand for securities, but can they be big enough to make a difference? The standard economist's reason for doubting the size of these effects has been to posit that investors trading on noise might lose their money to arbitrageurs, leading to a diminution of their wealth and effect on demand.[12] Noise traders might also learn the error of their ways and reform into rational arbitrageurs.

However, the argument that noise traders lose money and eventually disappear is not self-evident. First, noise traders might be on average more aggressive than the arbitrageurs—either because they are overoptimistic or because they are overconfident—and so bear more risk. If risk-taking is rewarded in the market, noise traders can earn higher expected returns even despite buying high and selling low on average. The risk rewarded by the market need not even be fundamental; it can be the resale price risk arising from the unpredictability of future noise traders' opinions. With higher expected returns, noise traders as a group do not disappear from the market rapidly, if at all.

Of course, higher expected returns because of higher risk come together with a greater variance of returns. Noise traders might end up very rich with a trivial probability, and poor almost for sure. Almost for sure, then, they fail to affect demand in the long run. But in principle, either the expected return or the variance effect can dominate.

Learning and imitation may not adversely affect noise traders either. When noise traders earn high average returns, many other investors might imitate them, ignoring the fact that they took more risk and just got lucky. Such imitation brings more money to follow noise trader strategies. Noise traders themselves might become even more cocky, attributing their investment success to skill rather than luck. As noise traders who do well become more aggressive, their effect on demand increases.

The case against the importance of noise traders also ignores the fact that new investors enter the market all the time, and old investors who have lost money come back. These investors are subject to the same judgment biases as the current survivors in the market, and so add to the effect of judgment biases on demand.

12. Friedman, "The Case for Flexible Exchange Rates," in Friedman, Essays in   Positive Economics (1953)—Eds.

These arguments suggest that the case for long run unimportance of noise traders is at best premature. In other words, shifts in the demand for stocks that do not depend on news or fundamental factors are likely to affect prices even in the long run.

Explaining the Puzzles

When arbitrage is limited, and investor demand for securities responds to noise and to predictions of popular models, security prices move in response to these changes in demand as well as to changes in fundamentals. Arbitrageurs counter the shifts in demand prompted by changes in investor sentiment, but do not eliminate the effects of such shifts on the price completely.

In this market, prices vary more than is warranted by changes in fundamentals, since they respond to shifts in investor sentiment as well as to news.[13] Stock returns are predictably mean-reverting, meaning that high stock returns lead to lower expected stock returns. This prediction has in fact been documented for the United States as well as the foreign stock prices by Fama and French (1988)[14] and Poterba and Summers (1988).[15]

The effects of demand shifts on prices are larger when most investors follow the finance textbooks and passively hold the market portfolio. In this case, a switch in the sentiment of some investors is not countered by a change of position of all the market participants, but only of a few arbitrageurs. The smaller the risk bearing capacity of arbitrageurs, the bigger the effect of a sentiment shift on the price. A simple example highlights this point. Suppose that all investors are sure that the market is efficient and hold the market portfolio. Now suppose that one investor decides to hold additional shares of a particular security. Its price is driven to infinity.

This approach fits very neatly with the conventional nonacademic view of financial markets. On that view, the key to investment success is not just predicting future fundamentals, but also predicting the movement of other active investors. Market professionals spend considerable resources tracking price trends, volume, short interest, odd lot volume, investor sentiment indexes and numerous other gauges of demand for equities. Tracking these possible indicators of demand makes no sense if prices responded only to fundamental news and not to investor demand. They make perfect sense, in contrast, in a world where investor sentiment moves prices and so predicting changes in this sentiment pays. The prevalence of investment strategies based on indicators of demand in financial markets suggests the recognition by arbitrageurs of the role of demand.

Not only do arbitrageurs spend time and money to predict noise trader moves, they also make active attempts to take advantage of these moves. When noise traders are optimistic about particular securities, it pays arbitrageurs to create more of them. These securities might be mutual funds, new share issues,

---

13. Shiller, supra note 1; Shiller, Stock Prices and Social Dynamics, Brookings Papers on Economic Activity 457 (1984)—Eds.

14. Fama and French, Permanent and Temporary Components of Stock Market Prices, 96 Journal of Political Economy 246 (1988)—Eds.

15. Poterba and Summers, Mean Reversion in Stock Prices: Evidence and Implications, 22 Journal of Financial Economics 27 (1988)—Eds.

penny oil stocks, or junk bonds: anything that is overpriced at the moment.
* * *

When they bet against noise traders, arbitrageurs begin to look like noise traders themselves. They pick stocks instead of diversifying, because that is what betting against noise traders requires. They time the market to take advantage of noise trader mood swings. If these swings are temporary, arbitrageurs who cannot predict noise trader moves simply follow contrarian strategies. It becomes hard to tell the noise traders from the arbitrageurs.

But saying that a market affected by investor sentiment looks realistic is hardly a rigorous test. To pursue this line of thought, we must derive and test implications that are not obvious and perhaps that are new. We consider first the implications of unpredictability or randomness of changes in investor sentiment. Second, we look at implications of strategies followed by investors who buy when prices rise and sell when prices fall, possibly because their expectations are simple extrapolations.

Implications of Unpredictability of Investor Sentiment

Even without taking a position on how investor sentiment moves, we can learn something from the observation that it moves in part unpredictably. Even if arbitrageurs know that noise traders are pessimistic today and hence will on average become less pessimistic in the future, they cannot be sure when this will happen. There is always a chance that noise traders become even more pessimistic first. This unpredictability contributes to resale price risk, since the resale price of an asset depends on the state of noise trader sentiment. If investor sentiment affects a broad range of assets in the same way, this risk from its unpredictability becomes systematic. Systematic risk has a price in equilibrium. Consequently, assets subject to whims of investor sentiment should yield higher average returns than similar assets not subject to such whims. Put differently, assets subject to unpredictable swings in investor sentiment must be underpriced in the market relative to their fundamental values.

* * * [Commentators cite two forms of evidence to support this argument:] First, stocks are probably subject to larger fluctuations of investor sentiment than bonds. In this case, equilibrium returns on stocks must be higher than warranted by their fundamentals—the latter being given by dividends and by covariation of dividends with consumption. In particular, the difference between average returns on stocks and on bonds—the risk premium—must be higher than is warranted by fundamentals. Such excess returns on stocks are in fact observed in the U.S. economy....

The second application we examined involves the pricing of closed-end mutual funds. These funds, like open-end funds, hold portfolios of other securities, but unlike open-end funds, have a fixed number of shares outstanding. As a result, an investor who wants to liquidate his holdings of a closed-end fund must sell his shares to other investors; he cannot just redeem his shares as with an open-end fund. Closed-end funds present one of the most interesting puzzles in finance, because their fundamental value—the value of the assets in their portfolios—is observed, and tends to be systematically higher than the price at which these funds trade. The pervasiveness of discounts on closed-end funds is a problem for the efficient markets hypothesis: in the one case where value is observed, it is not equal to the price.

De Long, Shleifer, Summers and Waldmann argue that investor sentiment about closed-end funds changes, and that this sentiment also affects other securities. When investors are bullish about closed-end funds, they drive up their prices relative to fundamental values, and discounts narrow or turn into premiums. When investors in contrast are bearish about closed-end funds, they drive down their prices and discounts widen. Any investor holding a closed-end fund bears two kinds of risk. The first is the risk from holding the fund's portfolio. The second is the resale price risk: at the time the investor needs to sell the fund the discount might widen. If investor sentiment about closed-end funds affects many other securities as well, bearing the resale price risk should be rewarded. That is, closed-end funds should on average sell at a discount. Put differently, the reason there are discounts *on average* is that discounts fluctuate, and investors require an extra return for bearing the risk of fluctuating discounts.

This theory explains why arbitrage does not effectively eliminate discounts on closed-end funds. An arbitrageur who buys a discounted fund and sells short its portfolio runs the risk that at the time he liquidates his position the discount widens and so his arbitrage results in a loss. An arbitrageur with an infinite horizon need not worry about this risk. But if the arbitrageur faces some probability of needing to liquidate his position in finite time, the risk from unpredictability of investor sentiment at the time he liquidates prevents him from aggressive betting that would eliminate discounts.

* * *

Implications of Positive Feedback Trading

One of the strongest investor tendencies documented in both experimental and survey evidence is the tendency to extrapolate or to chase the trend. Trend chasers buy stocks after they rise and sell stocks after they fall: they follow positive feedback strategies. Other strategies that depend on extrapolative expectations are "stop loss" orders, which prescribe selling after a certain level of losses, regardless of future prospects, and portfolio insurance, which involves buying more stocks (to raise exposure to risk) when prices rise and selling stocks (to cut exposure to risk) when prices fall.

When some investors follow positive feedback strategies—buy when prices rise and sell when prices fall—it need no longer be optimal for arbitrageurs to counter shifts in the demand of these investors. Instead, it may pay arbitrageurs to jump on the bandwagon themselves. Arbitrageurs then optimally buy the stocks that positive feedback investors get interested in when their prices rise. When price increases feed the buying of other investors, arbitrageurs sell out near the top and take their profits. The effect of arbitrage is to stimulate the interest of other investors and so to contribute to the movement of prices away from fundamentals. Although eventually arbitrageurs sell out and help prices return to fundamentals, in the short run they feed the bubble rather than help it to dissolve.

Some speculators indeed believe that jumping on the bandwagon with the noise traders is the way to beat them. George Soros, the successful investor and author of Alchemy of Finance (1987), describes his strategy during the conglomerate boom in the 1960s and the Real Estate Investment Trust boom in the 1970s precisely in these terms. The key to success, says Soros, was not to counter the irrational wave of enthusiasm about conglomerates, but rather to ride this wave for a while and sell out much later. Rational buying by speculators of already overvalued conglomerate stocks brought further buying by the noise traders, and enabled the speculators to make more money selling out at the top. Soros is not alone in trading this way; John Train (1987), in his book on successful U.S. investors, calls the strategy of one of his protagonists "Pumping Up the Tulips."

Trading between rational arbitrageurs and positive feedback traders gives rise to bubble-like price patterns. Positive feedback trading reinforced by arbitrageurs' jumping on the bandwagon leads to a positive autocorrelation of returns at short horizons. Eventual return of prices to fundamentals, accelerated as well by arbitrage, entails a negative autocorrelation of returns at longer horizons. Since news results in price changes that are reinforced by positive feedback trading, stock prices overreact to news.

These predictions have been documented in a number of empirical studies. Cutler, Poterba and Summers find evidence of a positive correlation of returns at horizons of a few weeks or months and a negative one at horizons of a few years for several stock, bond, foreign exchange, and gold markets. They report the average first order monthly serial correlation of more than .07 for 13 stock markets, and positive in every case. Evidence on overreaction of stock prices to changes in fundamentals is presented for individual securities by DeBondt and Thaler (1985)[16] and Lehmann (1990),[17] and for the aggregate stock market by Campbell and Kyle (1988). The last paper, for example, decomposes stock returns into the fundamental and noise components and finds that the two are strongly positively correlated, meaning that prices overreact to news.

The finding of a positive serial correlation at short horizons implies that a substantial number of positive feedback traders must be present in the market, and that arbitrage does not eliminate the effects of their trades on prices.

The presence of positive feedback traders in financial markets also makes it easier to interpret historical episodes, such as the sharp market increase and the crash of 1987. According to standard finance, the market crash of October 1987 reflected either a large increase in risk premiums because the economy became a lot riskier, or a large decrease in expected future growth rate of dividends. These theories have the obvious problem that they do not explain what news prompted a 22 percent devaluation of the American corporate sector on October 19. Another problem is that there is no evidence that risk increased tremendously—volatility indeed jumped up but came back rapidly as it usually does—or that expected dividend growth has been revised sharply down. An examination of OECD long-term forecasts shows no downward revision in forecasts of long run growth rates after the crash, even though the crash itself could have adversely affected expectations. Perhaps most strikingly, Seyhun (1989) finds that corporate insiders bought stocks in record numbers during and after the crash, and moreover bought more of the stocks that later had a greater rebound. Insiders did not share the view that growth of dividends will slow or that risk will increase and *they were right!* Fully rational theories have a clear problem with the crash.

The crash is much easier to understand in a market with significant positive feedback trading. Positive feedback trading can rationalize the dramatic price increase during 1987, as more and more investors chase the trend.

16. DeBondt and Thaler, Does the Stock Market Overreact?, 40 Journal of Finance 793 (1985).

17. Lehmann, Fads, Martingales and Market Efficiency, Quarterly Journal of Economics (1990).

Positive feedback trading, exacerbated by possible front-running by investment banks, can also explain the depth of the crash once it has started. One still needs a theory of what broke the market on October 19, but the bad news during the previous week might have initiated the process, albeit with some lag. A full theory of the crash remains to be developed: prospects for such a theory look a lot brighter, however, if it incorporates positive feedback trading.

Conclusion

This paper has described an alternative to the efficient markets paradigm that stresses the roles of investor sentiment and limited arbitrage in determining asset prices. We have shown that the assumption of limited arbitrage is more general and plausible as a description of markets for risky assets than the assumption of perfect arbitrage which market efficiency relies on. With limited arbitrage, movements in investor sentiment are an important determinant of prices. We have also shown that this approach yields a large number of implications about the behavior of both investors and speculative prices which are consistent with the evidence. Perhaps most importantly, we have shown that this approach yields some new testable implications about security returns. Some of these implications, such as the ones on closed-end funds, have been tested and confirmed. It is thus not the case that the investor sentiment approach deprives finance of the discipline to which it is accustomed.

Assuming that our approach has some explanatory power and therefore intellectual merit, what are its implications for welfare and for policy? There are two normative issues relevant to the evaluation of noise trading. First, should something be done to prevent noise traders from suffering from their errors? Second, do noise traders impose a cost on the rest of market participants and, if so, how can this cost be reduced? Although answers to these questions ultimately turn on open empirical problems, both theory and empirical work permit some tentative remarks.

Investors who trade on noise or on popular models are worse off than they would be if their expectations were rational (if welfare is computed with respect to the correct distribution of returns). They need not lose money on average, as the simplest logic might suggest. But even if they earn higher average returns, it is because they bear more risk than they think. And even if they get rich over time, it is only because they underestimate the risk and get lucky. If investors had perfect foresight and rationality, they would know that noise trading always hurts them.

Whether the government should do anything to save noise traders from themselves depends on the social welfare function. People are allowed to participate in state lotteries, to lose fortunes in casinos, or to bet on the racetrack even though benevolent observers know that they are being taken to the cleaners. The case for making it costly for investors to bet on the stock market to protect them from their own utility losses is in principle identical to the case for prohibiting casinos, horse races, and state lotteries.

Noise trading, however, can also affect the welfare of the rest of the community. One effect is to benefit arbitrageurs who take advantage of noise traders. These benefits accrue both to those who bet against noise traders and those who feed their demand by providing financial services. Interestingly, the combined receipts of the NYSE member firms amounted to a sixth of the total U.S. corporate income in 1987. Of course, some of these benefits to arbitrageurs are also a social *opportunity* cost as valuable human and other resources are allocated to separating noise traders from their money.

But noise trading also has a private cost, as it makes returns on assets more risky, and so can reduce physical investment. The overall impact of noise trading on the rest of the market participants and society can be negative. Some have also argued that noise trading in foreign exchange markets distorts the flow of goods between countries and leads to inefficient choice of production. Others have argued that noise trading forces managers to focus on the short term, and to bias the choice of investments against long-term projects. The policy reaction to noise trading can be dangerous as well; for example, sharp contractions of money supply by the Federal Reserve have often been justified as responses to excessive speculation. In this case, the consequences of such policies are more costly than the speculation itself.

Awareness of these costs of noise trading raises the question of what (if anything) should be done about it. Some businessmen and economists have proposed short term capital gains taxes as a way to cripple noise trading, while others * * * have advocated transaction taxes to the same end. It is not our goal in this paper to evaluate these proposals. We note, however, that one benefit of the research on markets where investor sentiment matters is to allow a more systematic evaluation of these proposals.

———

1. *Behavioral Theories.* The foregoing noise trading critique by Sheifler and Summers (the latter author later became Secretary of the Treasury under President Clinton and then President of Harvard) stays essentially within the domain of financial economics and asserts that markets can remain inefficient because it is too costly and risky for arbitrageurs to correct them. Other critics, however, suggest that there are systematic psychological and cognitive biases at work that distort markets from time to time. One leading behavioral finance theorist, Yale Economics Professor Robert Shiller, argues that contagions can dominant valuation because investors are heavily influenced by each other, and not just by market fundamentals.[1] Moreover, with improvements in information technology, the vulnerability of the market to fads, rumors, and misinformation increases (for example, misinformed investors on online "chat rooms" can convince each other through repetition of widely inaccurate information).

This view of the market dates back at least to a famous metaphor coined by John Maynard Keynes in the 1930's. Like Shiller, he believed that the market reflected investors strategically attempting to assess what other investors were likely to do (e.g., how would they react to a new announcement or world development). Keynes suggested that this process was not unlike the "beautiful baby" contests then popular in the London newspapers in which contestants competed to select the most beautiful child from a number of pictures, with the winner being determined by which baby received the most votes. Hence, he concluded the best strategy was not to choose the child's inherent characteristics (i.e., market fundamentals), but rather to predict which child the other entrants would consider most beautiful (i.e., guess what the noise traders would do).[2]

---

1. Robert J. Shiller, Market Volatility 379–400 (1989).

2. See John Maynard Keynes, The General Theory of Employment, Interest and

Recent research can be read to support this view of the market because it seems to show that investors routinely overreact or underreact to corporate announcements—a persistent phenomenon that some attribute to the psychological tendency of investors to be overconfident about the accuracy of the information they possess.[3] Investor overreaction can be partially attributed to institutional forces (such as the extraordinary ratio of buy recommendations to sell recommendations, which around 2000 reached the level of 100 to 1) or on innate investor psychology. Whatever the explanation, it is today clear that a growing body of opinion believes that finance theory must be supplemental by reference to social and psychological theories and forces to adequately understand market behavior.[4]

2. *Noise Theory.* The new popularity of noise trading as an explanation for market inefficiency may owe a good deal to the euphemistic character of this phrase. Essentially, noise theory posits that factors unrelated to fundamental news or rational expectations about market values can cause stock prices to deviate for non-trivial periods of time from their consensus values if all traders possessed the same information. Some have suggested that financial economists have been able to accept this phrase—but not the nearly equivalent idea that "irrational" forces could move the market.[5]

C. POLICY IMPLICATIONS

Suppose securities prices are "noisy" and a substantial element of irrationality and faddishness is reflected in the securities market. What implications follow from that conclusion? At a minimum, the premise of a "noisy" stock market implies that earlier discussed decisions such as *Wielgos* and *Apple Computer* that doubt that the market can be fooled by misleading predictions or estimates may need to be reconsidered. Going much further, however, Professor Lynn Stout argues that market efficiency should be abandoned as a goal of securities regulation:

> "Careful analysis indicates that the connection between prices in the public trading market for stocks and the allocation of real resources is a weak one, and that stock markets may have far less allocative importance than has generally been assumed. That finding in turn suggests a need to reexamine the existing consensus that we should spend resources and sacrifice other goals of securities regulation (such as investor protection or fair and honest markets) to further market efficiency."[6]

Her argument is largely based on evidence of mispricings in initial public offerings, on the limited influence of secondary market prices on the proceeds received by corporations making equity issues, and the general "unimportance

Money 156 (1936).

3. See Barber and Odean, Trading Is Hazardous to Your Wealth: The Common Stock Investment Performance of Individual Investors, 55 J. Fin. 773 (2000) (finding overreaction and excessive trading). Daniel, Hirschleiver and Subrahmanyam, Investor Psychology and Security Markets Under-and-Overreacting, 53 J. Fin. 1839.

4. See Lawrence Cunningham, From Random Walk to Chaotic Crashes: The Linear Genealogy of the Efficient Capital Market

Hypothesis, 62 Geo. Wash. L. Rev. 546 (1994).

5. Leroy, Efficient Capital Market Theory and Martingales, 27 J. Econ. Lit. 1583, 1612 (1989) (asserting that the phrase "noise trading" "sanitized irrationality" and rendered it "palatable" to many financial economists).

6. Stout, The Unimportance of Being Efficient: An Economic Analysis of Stock Market Pricing and Securities Regulation, 87 Mich.L.Rev. 613 (1988).

of equity as a source of capital."[7] Given this, she suggests that the costs of informational efficiency may be excessive, and both private and public "expenditures on stock information and trading may outweigh any resulting private or public benefit."[8] In her view, the securities markets resemble race tracks: investors, like the bettors at the track, care intensely about the outcome, but nothing else hinges on these outcomes other than their personal wealth. If the consequences are only distributive and not allocative, society, she concludes, should not tax itself to subsidize such an activity.

There is, however, an alternative perspective: the stock market does have an effect on allocational efficiency,[9] and the SEC's system of mandatory disclosure can be viewed as a means of economizing on information costs. By collectivizing the acquisition of securities information, the securities laws reduce potentially duplicative and socially wasteful investments by private parties.[10] In addition, even if the securities market is as inefficient as Professor Stout contends, it is by no means clear that it is inevitably inefficient or that society should give up on the pursuit of greater efficiency (both to protect investors and to promote allocative efficiency). A rival view to Professor Stout's claim that the pursuit of market efficiency is an illusory quest for a Holy Grail is the view discussed below that the SEC's mandatory disclosure system represents the lowest cost means of correcting the market's failure to provide adequate securities research and verification:

Excerpt from: John C. Coffee, Jr.

Market Failure and the Economic Case for a Mandatory Disclosure System

70 Virginia Law Review, 717, 725–733 (1984).

* * *

I.   A PUBLIC GOODS PERSPECTIVE

Easy as it is today to criticize the original premise of the federal securities laws—i.e., that mandatory disclosure would enable the small investor to identify and invest in higher quality and lower risk securities—such criticism does not take us very far because its target has shifted. The securities markets have evolved significantly since the 1930's, and one of the most important developments is the appearance of the professional securities analyst.[19] Little known in 1934 and common today, the analyst seems likely to become the critical mechanism of market efficiency because on-line computerization of SEC-filed

---

7.   Id. at 644–645.

8.   Id. at 704.

9.   For the standard view that securities markets do affect the allocation of capital resources, see Fama & Laffler, Information and Capital Markets, 44 J.Bus. 289 (1971).

10.   See Coffee, Market Failure and the Economic Case for a Mandatory Disclosure System, 70 Va.L.Rev. 717, 734 (1984).

19.   The SEC's Advisory Committee on Corporate Disclosure found that there were some 14,646 professional securities analysts

employed by financial institutions, brokerage firms, and consulting services as of 1977. * * * Presumably, this profession has survived because it performs a useful service. Typically, the chief source of firm-specific data used by the analyst appears to come from personal conversations with managers. Id. at 66–68. That managers do divulge information in this fashion to analysts provides some support for the theory of voluntary disclosure discussed below. * * *

data makes access to such information both immediate and relatively costless to the analyst.[20]

The work of the securities analyst can be subdivided into two basic functions. First, the analyst searches for information obtainable from non-issuer sources bearing on the value of a corporate security. Often, this information is critical because the issuer's performance may be substantially dependent on exogenous factors—e.g., interest rates, the behavior of competitors, governmental actions, consumer attitudes, and demographic trends—about which the issuer has no special knowledge or the analyst has superior access. Second, the analyst verifies, tests, and compares the issuer's disclosures, both to prevent deliberate fraud and to remove the unconscious bias that usually affects all forms of information transfer.

Although individual investors could also perform these search and verification functions, the professional securities analyst typically can do so at a lower cost because there appear to be significant economies of scale and specialization associated with these tasks. As a result, most accounts explaining the stock market's efficiency assign a substantial responsibility to the competition among analysts for securities information.[22]

In principle, the information volume developed by securities analysts is determined by the usual market forces and should result in the usual equilibrium: analysts should invest in verifying and obtaining material information about corporate securities until the marginal cost of this information to them equals their marginal return. Ordinarily, this private equilibrium should also result in allocative efficiency: social resources would be devoted to information verification until the social costs rose to meet the social benefits. There is a basic flaw, however, in this simple neoclassical analysis, and it involves a recurring problem that arises whenever a public good is produced.

A.   Market Failure as a Cause of Insufficient Securities Research

Public goods are a well-known economic concept. What has not been adequately recognized, however, is the degree to which information about corporate securities from non-issuer sources resembles (albeit imperfectly) a public good. The key characteristic of a public good is the non-excludability of users who have not paid for it; people benefit whether or not they contribute to the costs of acquiring the good, in part because consumption of the good by one

20. For this view of the future, see Sanger, S.E.C.'s Computer Revolution: Benefits Seen for Investors, N.Y. Times, Apr. 3, 1984, at D1, col. 3. As contemplated, issuers would both file and update their reports electronically. Although the individual investor could also obtain access, the analyst and the broker would have significant economies of scale, operating in their favor.

22. The view that the competition among analysts to "ferret out and analyze information" maintains market efficiency has now received the imprimatur of the Supreme Court in Dirks v. SEC, 463 U.S. 646 (1983): "Imposing a duty to disclose or abstain solely because a person knowingly receives material nonpublic information from an insider and trades on it could have an inhibiting influence on the role of market analysts, *which the SEC itself recognizes is necessary to the preservation of a healthy market."* Id. at 3263 (emphasis added). It needs to be emphasized that the ECMH does not imply that securities research is without value, although it does call into question the price that is often paid. See Fama, Random Walks in Stock Market Prices, Fin.Anal.J., Sept.–Oct. 1965, at 55–59; Pozen, Money Managers and Securities Research, 51 N.Y.U.L.Rev. 923, 950–53 (1976).

user does not diminish its availability to others. The net result is that public goods tend to be underprovided.[24]

Securities information displays this key characteristic of non-excludability. It seldom can be confined to a single user because many people have a motive to leak it. When the corporate insider tips a friend of a material impending development, the information does not stop with the tippee, but tends to be passed on. In fact, it is generally in the tippee's interest, once he has traded, to inform others to create excitement and induce a market upswing. Otherwise, the tippee achieves only the dubious victory of owning an undervalued security, and as the Wall Street Traders' credo says: "A bargain that remains a bargain is no bargain." Subsequent users thus gain a largely gratuitous benefit from material information leaked to them, although the value of the benefit quickly diminishes because of the market's rapid adjustment.[25]

As applied to the securities analyst, the public goods-like character of securities research implies that the analyst cannot obtain the full economic value of his discovery, and this in turn means that he will engage in less search or verification behavior than investors collectively desire. The public goods character of securities research is illustrated by the well-known commercial: "When E.F. Hutton talks, people listen." Indeed, people do listen, but the eavesdroppers do not pay for what they receive; they are, in the parlance, "free riders." Typically, securities research is reduced to an analyst's report that is circulated among prominent institutional investors in return for expected future commissions or other investment banking business. Contracting for research in this fashion is presumably more efficient than each institutional investor employing its own analysts (which also happens) because of the economies of scale and specialization.[27] Once securities research is initially disseminated in this fashion (or any similar fashion), however, free riding is predictable: news leaks out almost immediately because the confidentiality of a circulated report cannot be protected for long and because institutional investors have an incentive (after they trade) to make the analyst's report a self-fulfilling prophecy by encouraging others to trade. Either way, those in the

---

24. Judge Easterbrook and Professor Fischel have elsewhere utilized this analysis to explain why shareholders will not resist management. See Easterbrook & Fischel, The Proper Role of a Target's Management in Responding to a Tender Offer, 94 Harv. L.Rev. 1161, 1171 (1981). Because the benefit of any resistance undertaken by a single shareholder or a group of shareholders must be shared with all shareholders, "each shareholder finds it in his self-interest to be passive." Id. This free-riding problem also applies to the analyst as well as to the shareholder, because the securities analyst cannot obtain the full economic value that his efforts created. * * *

25. The rapidity of the market's response depends, however, on whether the information is truly publicly available information (e.g., earnings reports or projections or dividend announcements) or semi-public data that is slowly being leaked from an

inside source. The facts of Dirks v. SEC, 463 U.S. 646 (1983), illustrate this. In *Dirks*, Ronald Secrist, a former officer of Equity Funding, sought without success to alert regulatory authorities and others to the existence of a classic fraud. Between March 7, 1973, when Secrist alerted both Dirks and insurance authorities and March 28th, when the SEC suspended trading, the critical information was in the hands of numerous individuals. Their reaction time was relatively slow (for a number of understandable reasons). Dirks' clients were thus able to liquidate their positions in the stock and avoid serious loss, even though the details of the fraud had been described to public authorities two weeks earlier. * * *

27. See supra text accompanying note 22. If it were not more efficient, such an institutional structure would presumably not have survived.

tippee chain do not compensate the analyst. As a result, securities research is likely to be undercompensated. This undercompensation implies that there is underinvestment in securities research in terms of the aggregate wealth it creates or preserves. Thus, we are back to the classic public goods problem: so long as the free riders do not have to pay, the commodity will be underprovided.

A related problem with securities research involves the difficulties inherent in contracting for it. Normally, compensation for such research is on an ex post basis because the investor cannot know its value in advance. * * * The only objective test of the advice's value is the ultimate occurrence of the predicted market reaction. Although the buyer of valuable information should be willing to compensate the provider (at least to the extent that the buyer wishes to obtain such information from him in the future), the ex post and unilateral character of the payment results in less compensation being paid than if the negotiation were on a bilateral basis.

This problem is further complicated because payment typically is not made in cash. Rather, the user directs some of its brokerage business to the firm whose analyst supplied the information. In effect, the institutional investor pays above market price for brokerage services to obtain valuable research; the investor purchases advice with nothing more than the promise of future brokerage commissions at a premium rate. This premium is evidenced by the recent appearance of discount brokers, who offer only clearing services and provide no investment advice. The cost of such brokerage is estimated to be fifty percent below that of full service brokerage firms.[30] Thus, the customer has his choice of financial services—a simple clearing service or a clearing service plus advice.

This curious institutional structure has two important implications, which the neoclassical critics of mandatory disclosure have simply ignored. First, there is clearly an incentive for the buyer to cheat on the implicit deal; he can use the investment advice provided by the full service firm and then steer the majority of his brokerage business to the discount firm. Second, the persistence of full service firms and the very survival of the securities analyst as a profession in the face of this price competition suggest that consumers do want securities advice and research, both on the individual client and institutional investor levels. Otherwise, brokerage firms would fire their analysts to cut costs. Moreover, one cannot dismiss this evident demand for securities research as an irrational preference because the consumers include the most sophisticated of institutional investors.

These contractual problems, in combination with the public goods nature of securities research, help explain how a mandatory disclosure system benefits investors. Put simply, if market forces are inadequate to produce the socially optimal supply of research, then a regulatory response may be justified. Although securities advisers are regulated only in the most minimal way by the federal securities laws,[31] they are in effect heavily subsidized by these statutes.

---

30. See Vartan, Those Discount Stockbrokers, N.Y. Times, Jan. 19, 1984, at D10, col. 3. * * *

31. Securities analysts may be required to register as investment advisers under the Investment Advisers Act of 1940, 15 U.S.C. § 80b–1 (1982), which contains reporting and anti-fraud provisions. No educational or other qualifications, however, are required to be an investment adviser, and the regulatory strictures appear to be relatively looser than those that apply to broker dealers. For an overview, see L. Loss, Fundamentals of Securities Regulation 733–48 (1983).

Thus, the contemporary impact of the '34 Act may lie less in providing usable information to the ultimate investor than it does in reducing costs for the securities analyst.[32] Indeed, the detailed periodic reports that "reporting" companies file under the '34 Act are chiefly useful only to the professional analyst and not the individual trader. It is therefore no surprise that the professional investment community has long supported the continuous disclosure system of the '34 Act: to them the system implies cost savings.[34]

What do these cost savings imply for the structure and efficiency of the securities market? To the extent that mandated disclosure reduces the market professional's marginal cost of acquiring and verifying information, it increases the aggregate amount of securities research and verification provided. That is, because the analyst as a rational entrepreneur will increase his output until his marginal cost equals his marginal return, it follows axiomatically that the collectivization of securities information will produce more information. Over time, excess returns to securities analysts will induce new competitors to enter the market, which will increase the competitiveness of the industry. Casual empiricism suggests that both these predictions can be observed in the post–1934 experience of the securities industry. Certainly, the volume of securities research is much higher today than in 1934, and the very title "securities analyst" would not have been understood back then.[35]

The unresolved question is why these cost savings were not clearly reflected in stock price increases or any other observable impact immediately following the '34 Act's passage?[36] Although the one existing study of the

32. For a similar analysis of the impact of the '34 Act, see Gilson & Kraakman, The Mechanisms of Market Efficiency, 70 Va. L.Rev. 559, 637–42 (1983). Although they see the '34 Act as "a form of special-interest relief legislation" to aid the securities industries, id., this evaluation appears to give too little attention to the benefits that flow to ordinary investors in the form of more publicly available research and a greater number of companies being closely followed by securities analysts. * * * Although this data will not enable them to "beat the market," it should benefit investors in at least two distinct ways: (1) it better enables the investor to assess the risk level of individual securities, to avoid investing in securities whose risk level exceeds his personal level of risk aversion, and (2) it should reduce the variance in returns applicable to those securities not traded on major exchanges, which otherwise analysts would not closely watch.

34. See J. Seligman, supra note 9, at 311–12, 630 n. 50 (1982) (industry welcomed 1964 amendments expanding scope of '34 Act to corporations having over 500 shareholders and defined level of assets). The industry did, however, oppose the Securities Act of 1933 bitterly and conducted what Professor Seligman has termed a "capital strike." Id. at 71–115.

35. The term "security analysis" was popularized by Benjamin Graham and David Dodd, whose immensely influential statement of the fundamental principles of financial analysis was published, interestingly enough, in 1934. See B. Graham & D. Dodd, Security Analysis: Principles and Techniques (1st ed. 1934). Although this book had its precursors, it is as difficult to conceive of the securities analyst developing in recognizable form before its publication as it is to imagine the job description of psychoanalyst arising before Freud. For example, the New York Society of Security Analysts, the largest professional organization in this field, was not founded until the late 1930's. Telephone interview with staff official, New York Society of Security Analysts (Apr.1984). Admittedly, publications such as Moody's were published in the 19th century, and a prototype of the securities analyst can be traced back well before 1934, but the real development of the modern securities analyst had to await both the development of the theory that Graham and Dodd codified and the rise of the institutional investor, which essentially occurred in the 1960's. * * *

36. Only one study has been conducted on the effect of the '34 Act on stock prices. See Benston, An Evaluation of the Securities Exchange Act of 1934, supra note 2. Profes-

market's reaction to the '34 Act's adoption may have been too methodologically flawed to capture any changes that occurred, another possible answer is that all the gains were captured by informed traders and other market professionals in the form of cost reductions. Arguably, these traders received the same approximate volume of information both before and after 1934, but simply obtained this data at a lower price after the '34 Act.[37] Yet this answer seems incomplete; it ignores that the securities analyst—or his predecessor in that era—should produce more information if he has a lower marginal cost.

This argument that lower costs for the securities analyst should result in more information production takes us only so far. As Professors Easterbrook and Fischel correctly observe, it is theoretically possible that too much information is already produced, particularly because not all, or even most, investors need to be well informed for the market to be efficient.[38] Yet they stop at this point, which seems to be the threshold where close analysis should begin.

According to the SEC Advisory Committee on disclosure, only about 1,000 of the 10,000 odd "reporting" companies registered under the '34 Act are regularly followed by securities analysts.[39] In the absence of analyst monitoring and in the presence of erratic trading, there is considerable reason to doubt that the market for the other 9,000 firms is "efficient," even in some cases in the "weak" sense of that term. Although other mechanisms exist by which to

---

sor Benston isolated two groups of companies for comparison: one that disclosed their sales figures prior to the '34 Act and the other that did not. Neither group showed significant changes in its aggregate rate of return after the Act's passage. In theory, one might expect the non-disclosing companies to experience abnormal negative returns as investors learned of adverse information that had previously been withheld by management. Nevertheless, Professor Benston concluded that the Act had no effect. Professor Benston's methodology, however, has been recurrently challenged, in part because his "non-disclosure" group appears to have consisted of companies that did in fact disclose net income, the most important variable for investors. See Friend & Westerfield, supra note 5, at 468–70; Seligman, supra note 5, at 17. Professors Friend and Westerfield also found that both the disclosing and non-disclosing firms performed better in the post–1934 period. See Friend & Westerfield, supra note 5, at 468–70. But see Benston, Required Disclosure and the Stock Market: Rejoinder, 65 Am.Econ.Rev. 473 (1975). Although it is commonplace for scholars to rely on Benston's findings without pointing out the serious methodological flaws in his approach (or the variable interpretations that can be placed on his data), the issue still seems to be unresolved as to whether the '34 Act had an immediate impact on stock prices or investors.

37. This is the thesis that Professors Gilson and Kraakman advance. See Gilson & Kraakman, supra note 32, at 636–38.

38. "The more sophisticated version of the public goods explanation is that although investors produce information, they produce both too much and too little." Easterbrook & Fischel, supra note 13, at 681. Although their statement appears to be correct, it only frames the problem, and does not assess the impact of the '34 Act, which encourages the analyst to produce more information, while also eliminating the need for wasteful duplication of efforts by rival analysts or rival investors. Professors Easterbrook and Fischel instead rely on the Coase Theorem, which by its own terms is inapplicable when transaction costs are high, as is likely the case for widely dispersed small shareholders.

39. Advisory Committee Report, supra note 6, at xviii-xix. Professor Kripke has challenged this number as too low. H. Kripke, supra note 6, at 126–28. This challenge appears to be correct, but only in terms of degree. Even if the number of closely watched companies were twice as high, this figure would leave 8,000 corporations with over 500 shareholders and no following within the professional financial analyst community.

achieve efficiency, their efficacy is unproven and highly debatable.[40] The desirability of expending social resources to improve the efficiency of the trading in these smaller issues can also be reasonably disputed. What seems to be beyond argument, however, is the consequence of increasing the securities analysts' marginal costs for obtaining or verifying information. If we repealed the '34 Act, and thereby increased analysts' marginal costs, the number of companies regularly followed by analysts would likely decline below this 1,000 figure.[41] In short, cost reductions for analysts imply broader coverage of firms, and cost increases imply the converse. This conclusion, in turn, leads to the bottom line: the more firms that are closely followed by analysts, the greater assurance both that capital markets will be allocatively efficient and that the game will be fair with respect to such companies.

* * *

In 1934, institutional investors represented only a small fraction of equity securities trading; the dominant figure was still the professional trader, who relied more on rumors, tips, and personal contacts than on hard data. Only with the later appearance (probably in the 1960's) of the institutional investor—and in particular, a nationwide population of institutional investors—did the institutional structure arise that could support the modern securities analyst.[43] In this light, the '34 Act becomes the logical, if premature, answer to a problem that had yet to emerge: how to increase the volume of securities research, which then was not even in demand. In 1934, any gains that the Act created may well have been fully captured by a small coterie of professional traders, but with the subsequent expansion of the industry, the cost savings that the '34 Act engendered helped to create the securities analyst as a distinct profession. That this result was serendipitous does not make it any less desirable.

40. Of course, some will argue that market forces are adequate to induce disclosure even if monitoring by analysts is not occurring. This theory of self-induced disclosure is examined in section II of this article, which finds it a partial truth.

41. At the margin, the securities analyst can be expected as his marginal cost increases to reduce his operations (and either follow fewer companies or investigate the same number less thoroughly). One test of this thesis might be to compare the number of companies that were closely followed prior to 1934. There is, however, no simple measure of this variable, partly because there were fewer securities analysts in this era and their techniques were more rudimentary. A cursory survey reveals that as of 1941, there were 1,210 issuers listed on the New York Stock Exchange. See 7 SEC Ann.Rep. 305 (1941). Assuming that this number constitutes the upper boundary of closely followed stocks, it still does not contrast sharply with the estimated number of closely followed stocks today. * * * This figure of 1,210, however, probably overstates the number of firms that were closely monitored; Professor Seligman has informed this author that in his view few firms prior to 1934 released enough data to be closely watched to the degree presumed by the SEC Advisory Committee in its estimate that currently analysts closely follow 1,000 firms. Another test of this thesis would be to contrast the number of full time securities analysts before and after 1934. Although the 14,646 figure given by the SEC Advisory Committee in 1977, see supra note 19, probably is greatly in excess of the pre-1934 figure, this is an illegitimate comparison because the securities analysis profession was then only in its infancy.

43. The volume of institutional trading on the New York Stock Exchange rose during the 1960's from a low of 17% to a high of 52% in 1969. See J. Seligman, supra note 9, at 351–52.

B. Social Waste and the Problem of Excess Research

This hypothesis that a mandatory disclosure system reduces the costs incurred by market professionals has another important corollary: aggregate social wealth is arguably increased because the partial collectivization of securities information that the '34 Act mandates in effect economizes on the total amounts expended in pursuing trading gains. From a social welfare perspective, trading gains do not create additional wealth; one party's gain comes at the other party's loss, whereas the process of researching and verifying securities information consumes real resources.[44] Although securities research sometimes creates social wealth (both by perfecting the allocative efficiency of the capital markets and by facilitating the entrepreneur's ability to raise capital for wealth-creating projects), the '34 Act chiefly addresses the secondary trading market. Here, one can view the participants as engaged in pursuing trading gains that do not affect aggregate shareholder wealth. Their expenditures in pursuit of such gains therefore represent social waste, as Professor Hirschleifer long ago pointed out in a classic article.[45] In this light, a major significance of a mandatory disclosure system is that it can reduce these costs. Rival firms do not need to incur expenses to produce essentially duplicative data banks when a central securities data bank is in effect created at the SEC. Thus, rather than the '34 Act producing too much information (as Professors Easterbrook and Fischel suggest),[46] it probably reduces wasteful duplication by establishing a central information repository.

This claim that wasteful duplication is eliminated by a mandatory disclosure system may sound inconsistent with the earlier assertion that inadequate securities research occurs because of the public goods-like character of securities information. Yet there is no contradiction. Financial professionals may simultaneously expend both too little and too much resources on verifying and obtaining information. The first problem arises because too few companies are followed or are researched inadequately; the second, because investigations by one analyst are duplicated by another. Still, the existence of a central information repository in the form of the SEC is at least a partial answer to both problems.

C. Allocative Efficiency: The Public Interest in Adequate Securities Research

Which of the last two problems discussed—too much research or too little—is more serious? This question is important because the design of an optimal disclosure system depends in large part on how one answers it. Two very different perspectives are possible on the securities market. If we see it as simply a "fair game" in which securities prices are "unbiased" (that is, prices are as likely to move in the buyer's favor as the seller's), there is little cause for regulatory intervention (except possibly to prevent insider trading). Moreover, because in this light the securities market is essentially a "zero-sum game"—that is, one side's gain in every transaction is the other side's loss—society has no reason to encourage the parties to invest their resources in this nonproduc-

---

44. See Fama & Laffer, Information and Capital Markets, 44 J.Bus. 289 (1971); Hirshleifer, The Private and Social Value of Information and the Reward to Inventive Activity, 61 Am.Econ.Rev. 561 (1971).

45. See Hirshleifer, supra note 44. Indeed, society might rationally decide to pay analysts not to engage in rival research efforts where the resources so utilized would only affect the distribution of trading gains and not increase market efficiency.

46. See Easterbrook & Fischel, supra note 13, at 693–95.

tive attempt to obtain wealth at the other's expense. So viewed, a mandatory disclosure system would be justifiable principally as a means of minimizing the wasted resources devoted to the pursuit of trading gains.

Conversely, if we view the securities market as the principal allocative mechanism for investment capital, the behavior of securities prices is important not so much because of their distributive consequences on investors but more because of their effect on allocative efficiency. In this light, it is important not only that the game be fair, but that it be accurate—that is, that capital be correctly priced. Depending on a firm's share price, its cost for obtaining capital will be either too high or low as compared to the cost that would prevail in a perfectly efficient market. In either case, society's mechanism for allocating scarce investment capital among competing users becomes distorted, even though the game remains equally fair to buyers and sellers. From this perspective, the critical empirical question shifts from whether the federal securities laws improved the mean return to investors to whether they reduced the variance associated with these returns. That is, if the federal securities laws reduced the dispersion associated with the returns on new issues, it can reasonably be inferred that they made the market for new issues more allocatively efficient. Professor Stigler appears to acknowledge this point: "Price dispersion," he writes, "is a manifestation—and, indeed, it is a measure—of ignorance in the market."[47] The greater this variance associated with securities returns, the greater the uncertainty and heterogeneity of investor expectations, and the less the likelihood that our capital allocation mechanism is working efficiently. Yet the stock market may still appear efficient to the extent that prices move randomly and mandatory public disclosures appear not to cause price adjustments.

Once the focus is shifted to the degree of dispersion associated with securities prices in the presence or absence of a mandatory disclosure system, the empirical issue is narrowed. Every scholar who has investigated the impact of the federal securities laws—including Stigler, Bentson, Jarrell, and Friend—appears to agree that price dispersion declined after the passage of the Securities Act of 1933.[48] The most logical conclusion to draw from this evidence is that allocative efficiency was enhanced and that investors thereby benefited.

---

47. See Stigler, The Economics of Information, 69 J.Pol.Econ. 213, 214 (1961).

48. Professor Stigler's initial study found that the variance associated with the returns on new securities issues declined after the passage of the '33 Act. See Stigler, Comment, 37 J.Bus. 414, 418–19 (1964); Stigler, supra note 1, at 122. Cf. Seligman, supra note 5, at 10–11 (criticizing Stigler's conclusion that a decline in the variance of new securities' prices was not meaningful). Similar findings were reported by Friend and Herman. See Friend & Herman, The SEC Through a Glass Darkly, supra note 5. In response, Professor Benston has not contested that there was a reduction in the standard deviations associated with security issues after 1933, but has disputed this reduction's relevance. See Benston, Required Disclosure and the Stock Market: Rejoinder, 65 Am. Econ.Rev. 473 (1974). For the latest round in this debate, see Friend, supra note 5, at 8–12. Finally, in a recent study Professor Jarrell has also found a decline in the variance in returns associated with new stock issues after 1933. See Jarrell, supra note 7. Like Benston, he also doubts that this reduction in variance is a meaningful achievement and suggests that it instead signifies excessive paternalism on the SEC's part. Their position is that because this variance reduction was not associated with an increase in the mean returns, it did not benefit investors; rather, it implies to them that the SEC discouraged attractive high risk offerings at the same rate that it discouraged fraudulent ones. Even if this were true, it is curious to interpret it as a dubious achievement. If we assume that investors are risk averse, any reduction in the variance (or risk associated with a return) that does not reduce the mean return is desirable. * * *

The key point then is that the social benefit of the federal securities laws may exceed their benefit to investors. The beneficiaries of increased allocative efficiency include virtually all members of society, not just investors. In this light, it is myopic to view the '34 Act as simply a subsidy for investors or to denigrate its benefits as merely trading gains.

This focus on allocative efficiency should also frame future research efforts. Rather than debate endlessly the effect that the federal securities laws had a half century ago, it is time to turn to issues of greater contemporary significance. For example, has the recent trend toward deregulation in connection with the administration of the '34 Act been associated with any increase in price dispersions or market volatility? To ask this question is not to answer it. Testable hypotheses, however, can be framed: for example, one could inquire whether price dispersion has increased following the adoption of the integrated disclosure system in 1982[50] and the expanded use of shelf registration statements.[51] If not, the cost reductions to corporate issuers associated with these regulatory reforms would seem justified.[52] Clearly, however, this question cannot be safely answered by looking only at the market's immediate reaction to these developments or only at the change, if any, in mean returns to investors. Once we recognize that there is a social interest associated with an allocatively efficient capital market, then it is an overly narrow form of social cost accounting to calculate only the costs to issuers and benefits to investors.

SECTION 6.   LOWERING THE BARRIERS TO SHELF REGISTRATION

A.   "SHELF REGISTRATION"

In preparing a registration statement, a decision must be reached as to how many securities are to be registered. It would be convenient to register all

---

50. For an overview, see SEC Securities Act Release No. 6383, 47 Fed.Reg. 11,380 (1982), reprinted in [1937–1982 Accounting Series Releases Transfer Binder] Fed.Sec. L.Rep. (CCH) ¶ 72,328 (Mar. 3, 1982). Under integrated disclosure, some issuers may use a prospectus consisting almost exclusively of references to previously filed '34 Act reports. Compare Banoff, Regulatory Subsidies, Efficient Market, and Shelf Registration: An Analysis of Rule 415, 70 Va.L.Rev. 135 (1984), with Fox, Shelf Registration, Integrated Disclosure, And Underwriter Due Diligence: An Economic Analysis 70 Va.L.Rev. 1005 (1984).

51. See SEC Rule 415 * * *. For an overview, see Ferrara & Sweeney, Shelf Registration Under SEC Temporary Rule 415, 5 Corp.L.Rev. 308 (1982).

52. A substantial debate is continuing as to whether integrated disclosure and shelf registration statements will erode the due diligence efforts of underwriters and their counsel. Because Rule 176 * * * reduces the potential liability of underwriters for data that is incorporated by reference into a prospectus, it is arguable that underwriters and their counsel have less incentive today to verify the accuracy of information under an integrated disclosure system. * * * On the positive side of the ledger, it is clear that Rule 415 has reduced underwriters' commissions by encouraging greater competition among underwriters. See Ehrbar, Upheaval in Investment Banking, Fortune, Aug. 23, 1982, at 90. The suggestion made here is that any significant decline in socially desirable "due diligence" efforts would be observable in higher stock volatility (net of overall market movement) and increased price dispersion. Until efforts are made to test this thesis, the debate is indeterminable.

of the securities which an issuer might conceivably intend to distribute at any time in the future, that is, to allow registration for the "shelf." However, Securities Act § 6(a) states: "A registration statement shall be deemed effective only as to the securities specified therein as proposed to be offered." Initially, the SEC took the view that, by reason of this language, the registration of more securities than are presently intended to be offered would be misleading.[1] The SEC's obvious concern was that if the registration statement went effective and the offering were delayed, information in it would become stale.

This situation placed the SEC in a dilemma. Section 11 imposes civil liability on the registrant and other named persons with respect to misstatements and omissions in the registration statement *when it became effective.* Section 12(a)(2) gives buyers a private action against their seller for misstatements and omissions in connection with interstate sales of securities, whether registered or not. Since the registration speaks as of the effective date, the proper procedure to correct a misstatement of fact in the registration statement is to file a post-effective amendment curing the defect in an attempt to minimize § 11 liability. On the other hand, if a statement was accurate when made, but developments after the effective date render it false, § 12(a)(2) becomes implicated. Thus, any correction should be made by placing a sticker on the cover page of the prospectus correcting the defect. See Registration C, Rules 423, 424(c).

In spite of these apparent impediments to shelf registration, the Commission found it desirable in some instances to permit or require such offerings. These permissible offerings, now dubbed "traditional shelf offerings," evolved over the years and are described in the Shelf Registration Release which follows. The administrative device used to overcome the statutory barriers to shelf registration was simply to add a requirement that the registrant file an "undertaking" in the initial registration statement. This undertaking, in effect, constituted a commitment, by the registrant to file a post-effective amendment to the statement to reflect in the prospectus any material changes in information. This gave the Staff an opportunity to review the revised prospectus prior to its use and postponed the commencement of the limitation period prescribed in § 13 of the Securities Act with respect to § 11 actions.

When introducing the integrated disclosure system it will be recalled that registrants were divided into three categories: (1) companies which are widely followed by professional analysts; (2) companies which have been subject to the Exchange Act periodic reporting requirements for at least three years, but are not widely followed by the analysts; and (3) companies which have been subject to the Exchange Act reporting requirements for less than three years. The first category is eligible to use a short form registration statement (Form S–3) which relies upon incorporation by reference of Exchange Act reports (see Rules 411 and 412) and permits minimal disclosure in the prospectus. The second category is eligible to use Form S–2, which combines incorporation by reference of Exchange Act reports with supplemental information contained in the prospectus or in annual reports to security holders. The third category is required to use Form S–1 which requires full disclosure.

In the integration process the Commission also considered whether the option of shelf registration should be extended to firms whose shares traded under efficient market conditions. After a period of experimentation, the

---

1. Shawnee Chiles Syndicate, 10 S.E.C. 109, 113 (1941).

Commission expanded the use of shelf-registration by the adoption of Rule 415. At the same time, the Commission added Regulation S–K, Item 512(a) (relating to the undertaking applicable to Rule 415 offerings), Rule 176 (identifying the factors bearing on the issue of due diligence under § 11 of the Securities Act) and Rule 412 (relating to the effective date of documents incorporated by reference and the use of modified or superseded statements).

Rule 415 provides procedural flexibility in timing periodic offerings of registered securities so as to take advantage of favorable "market windows." The Rule also applies to other types of "traditional shelf registrations." These will be considered in connection with various types of secondary distributions infra in Chapter 9.

Securities Act Release No. 6499

Securities and Exchange Commission.
November 17, 1983.

Shelf Registration

SUMMARY: The Commission today announced the adoption of a revised shelf registration rule. Rule 415 relates to the registration of securities to be offered or sold on a delayed or continuous basis in the future. As revised, the Rule is available for offerings qualified to use short form registration statements and for traditional shelf offerings. These modifications reflect experience with the Rule and the views that have been expressed, particularly those relating to disclosure and due diligence.

* * *

I.　Executive Summary

In the eighteen months since its adoption on a temporary basis, Rule 415 has operated efficiently and has provided registrants with important benefits in their financings, most notably cost savings. The cost savings are attributable to a number of factors, including flexibility to respond to rapidly changing markets, reduced legal, accounting, printing and other expenses and increased competition among underwriters. At the same time, however, concerns have been raised, including institutionalization of the securities markets, impact on retail distribution, increased concentration in the securities industry, effects on the secondary markets, adequacy of disclosure and due diligence.

The Commission has considered the concerns that have been expressed about Rule 415. Some relate to economic factors, such as volatile interest rates and other market forces, which exist apart from Rule 415 and thus are not appropriate bases on which to take action on the Rule. The Commission believes that the concerns about disclosure and due diligence, however, should be addressed because they may be affected by the manner in which offerings under the Rule may proceed. Accordingly, the Commission has determined to modify the Rule to limit its availability to those offerings where the benefits of shelf registration are most significant and where the disclosure and due diligence concerns are mitigated by other factors. The Commission believes that limiting the Rule to primary offerings of securities qualified to be registered on Form S–3 or F–3 and to traditional shelf offerings strikes the appropriate balance.

The integrated disclosure system recognizes that, for companies in the top tier, there is a steady stream of high quality corporate information continually furnished to the market and broadly digested, synthesized and disseminated. In addition, procedures for conducting due diligence investigations of such registrants, including continuous due diligence by means such as designated underwriters' counsel, are being adapted to the integrated disclosure system and shelf registration. The Commission believes that the widespread market following of such companies and the due diligence procedures being developed serve to address the concerns about the adequacy of disclosure and due diligence and, thus, ensure the protection of investors.

With respect to traditional shelf offerings, the Commission believes that continued use of Rule 415 also is appropriate. First, concerns have not been expressed about these offerings. Second, these offerings may not be feasible on other than a delayed or continuous offering basis.

As to other offerings by non-S–3 or F–3 registrants, however, disclosure and due diligence concerns need to be addressed. Accordingly, the Commission has determined not to allow the Rule to be used for such offerings.

As revised, Rule 415 enumerates the securities which are allowed to be offered on a continuous or delayed basis. Unless the securities fall within one of the provisions spelling out the various traditional shelf offerings, they must qualify for registration on Form S–3 or F–3. If they do not, they may not be registered for delayed or continuous offerings.

II. Background

Securities have been registered for continuous and delayed offerings for many years. Some of the instances in which shelf registration was allowed were set forth in Guide 4, which was promulgated in 1968. These included securities to be issued in continuing acquisition programs or those underlying exercisable options, warrants or rights. Administrative practice, however, accommodated traditional shelf offerings beyond those specified in the Guide. Shelf registration was permitted for such diverse offerings as limited partnership tax shelters, employee benefit plans, pools of mortgage backed pass through certificates offered from time to time, and customer purchase plans.

Rule 415 arose in connection with the development of the integrated disclosure system. As part of that effort, the Commission comprehensively reviewed all of the Guides for the Preparation and Filing of Registration Statements and Reports and reorganized them to separate the substantive disclosure and procedural provisions. The shelf rule was the procedural rule which resulted from the reevaluation of Guide 4 and reflected current administrative practice as well as the provisions of the Guide.

The Rule was published for comment twice before being adopted on a temporary basis in March 1982. * * *

Two dominant themes emerged from these comments on Rule 415. The majority of commentators, mostly registrants, have been pleased with the Rule and favor its adoption on a permanent basis. Members of the securities industry, on the other hand, have expressed a wide spectrum of views and have reiterated several concerns. In the most recent comment solicitation, they emphasize concerns over the adequacy of disclosure and due diligence. While these commentators voice concerns, only a few of them believe that there should be no shelf registration rule at all. Others with concerns about the Rule recommend that it be retained, either in its present form or in modified form.

The suggested modifications of Rule 415 include: (1) Restricting eligibility for use of the Rule to (a) investment grade debt securities, (b) a combination of investment grade debt securities and limited types of equity securities or (c) registrants that are widely followed in the marketplace; (2) requiring advance notice to the marketplace of forthcoming offerings; and (3) imposing some form of "cooling off period" between the announcement and sale of securities. Some commentators also suggest providing underwriters relief from liability under the Securities Act.

III. Experience

The Commission, registrants, the securities industry, and others have had over eighteen months of experience with the shelf registration rule. During this time, the Commission has monitored the operation and impact of the Rule, has been provided information concerning actual experience with the Rule and has considered empirical data and studies related to the Rule.

  *   *   *

Over 85% of the shelf registrations have been traditional shelf filings. Filings for employee benefit plans and dividend or interest reinvestment plans alone account for 55% of the shelf filings and represent 26% of the $181 billion in shelf registered securities.

Most of the balance have been filings for investment grade debt securities offered and sold from time to time on a delayed basis. These 369 debt filings (registering almost $70 billion) represent 53% of the $133 billion of total debt issues filed from March 1982 through September 1983. Approximately 94% of the 369 delayed debt filings were on Form S–3. Over 35% of the filings were made by companies in the financial industry and over 20% were made by utilities.

The remaining shelf filings related to 195 delayed equity filings (registering $12.5 billion). These filings amounted to about 3% of the over 7,700 equity registration statements and 6% of the $212 billion in equity securities registered. Over half were fixed price syndicated offerings which were filed under Rule 415 largely for the procedural convenience afforded by the Rule. Of the remaining delayed equity filings, 90% were on Form S–3. Approximately 70% were for common stock and 30% were for preferred stock. Fifteen percent listed an "at the market" distribution as one of the potential distribution methods described. Eleven of these filings were for so-called "dribble-outs" by utility companies, in which common stock is offered through an underwriter into an existing trading market on a regular basis.

IV. Discussion

A. *Benefits of Shelf Registration*

Virtually all commentators state that shelf registration provides substantial benefits for corporate financings. The principal benefit cited by commentators is that of cost savings. Empirical studies on shelf registration also suggest that securities sold under Rule 415 have lower issuance costs than securities not sold under the Rule.

Cost savings and other benefits are attributed to a number of factors. Flexibility is the Rule's most frequently cited benefit, because it is the source of the greatest cost savings and provides other advantages as well. Commentators stress that flexibility is important in today's volatile markets; that the procedural flexibility afforded by the Rule enables a registrant to time its offering to avail itself of the most advantageous market conditions; that by being able to meet "market windows," registrants are able to obtain lower interest rates on debt and lower dividend rates on preferred stock, thereby benefiting their existing shareholders. The flexibility provided by the Rule also permits variation in the structure and terms of securities on short notice, enabling registrants to match securities with the current demands of the marketplace. Some commentators attributed the success of their offerings to the flexibility provided by the Rule. Empirical studies also support the importance of enhanced financing flexibility in new issue design, market timing and choice of distribution technique. While most discussion of flexibility is in the context of debt offerings, some commentators also assert that flexibility is necessary in the equity markets.

Simplification of the securities registration process also is cited as reducing costs. Legal, accounting, printing and other costs are stated to have been reduced, because only a single registration statement need be filed for a series of offerings, rather than a separate registration statement each time an offering is made. Some commentators also state that simplification of the registration process has given them more flexibility in planning their financing schedules.

Finally, some commentators stress that increased competition among underwriters has resulted in lower underwriting spreads and offering yields, which produce cost savings for registrants and their shareholders. Empirical studies of debt and equity offerings under Rule 415 found lower issuance costs and attributed this primarily to increased competition among investment bankers. Some commentators note that increased competition has spurred the innovation of new financing products.

On the basis of the benefits cited, many commentators, especially registrants, support permanent adoption of Rule 415 as proposed.

B.   *Concerns*

1.   *Adequacy of Disclosure.* A number of commentators, especially those from the securities industry, express concerns relating to the adequacy of disclosure. While Rule 415 has been the focal point of these concerns, these commentators question aspects of the Commission's integrated disclosure system, such as short form registration and incorporation by reference. They question the amount and quality of information available, as well as whether investors receive it in time to make investment decisions. These commentators express concern that the Rule contributes to deficiencies in the disclosure provided to investors caused, in great part, by short form registration statements.

The Commission believes that the integrated disclosure system has enhanced the level of disclosure to investors. The basis for the system was the upgrading of the continuous reporting requirements under the Securities Exchange Act of 1934 (the "Exchange Act"). This upgrading was designed to ensure that complete and current information is available to all investors on a continuous basis, not only when a registrant makes a public offering of its securities, but for the trading markets as well. This focus recognized that the secondary trading market volume dwarfs the volume of Securities Act offerings.

For Securities Act registration, the integrated disclosure system builds upon the existence of timely and accurate corporate reporting. Thus, registrants that are widely followed in the marketplace may use Forms S–3 and F–3, which allow maximum use of incorporation by reference of Exchange Act reports and generally do not require information contained in those reports to be reiterated in the prospectus and delivered to investors. Forms S–3 and F–3 recognize the applicability of the efficient market theory to those companies which provide a steady stream of high quality corporate information to the marketplace and whose corporate information is broadly disseminated. Information about these companies is constantly digested and synthesized by financial analysts, who act as essential conduits in the continuous flow of information to investors, and is broadly disseminated on a timely basis by the financial press and other participants in the marketplace. Accordingly, at the time S–3/F–3 registrants determine to make an offering of securities, a large amount of information already has been disseminated to and digested by the marketplace.

2. *Due Diligence.* Concerns expressed about the quality of disclosure also relate to underwriters' ability to conduct due diligence investigations. Commentators attribute concerns about due diligence largely to fast time schedules. Under the Rule, any underwriter may be selected to handle a particular offering. Some commentators suggest that no underwriter can afford to devote the time and expense necessary to conduct a due diligence review before knowing whether it will handle an offering and that there may not be sufficient time to do so once it is selected. These commentators also indicate that they may not have the opportunity to apply their independent scrutiny and judgment to documents prepared by registrants many months before an offering.

On the other hand, registrants using the Rule indicate that procedures for conducting due diligence investigations have developed and are developing to enable underwriters to adapt to the integrated disclosure system and the shelf registration environment. They note the use of continuous due diligence programs, which employ a number of procedures, including designated underwriters' counsel. These registrants believe that underwriters' ability to conduct adequate due diligence investigations in this environment has not been impaired and, in some cases, has been enhanced.

The Commission recognizes that procedures for conducting due diligence investigations of large, widely followed registrants have changed and are continuing to change. Registrants and the other parties involved in their public offerings—attorneys, accountants, and underwriters—are developing procedures which allow due diligence obligations under Section 11(b) to be met in the most effective and efficient manner possible. The anticipatory and continuous due diligence programs being implemented combine a number of procedures designed both to protect investors by assuring timely and accurate disclosure of corporate information and to recognize the separate legal status of underwriters by providing them the opportunity to perform due diligence.

The trend toward appointment of a single law firm to act as underwriters' counsel is a particularly significant development. Of course, this procedure is not new. Appointing a single law firm to act as underwriters' counsel has been done traditionally by public utility holding companies and their subsidiaries subject to the competitive bid underwriting requirements of Rule 50 under the Public Utility Holding Company Act of 1935. This technique is now being followed more broadly in the shelf registration environment and represents what the Commission believes to be a sound practice because it provides for due diligence investigations to be performed continually throughout the effectiveness of the shelf registration statement. Designation of underwriters' counsel facilitates continuous due diligence by ensuring on-going access to the registrant on the underwriters' behalf. Recognizing the independent statutory basis on which underwriters perform due diligence, registrants cooperate with underwriters and designated counsel in making accommodations necessary for them to perform their due diligence investigation.

Other procedures registrants have developed complement the use of underwriters' counsel by presenting various opportunities for continuous due diligence throughout the shelf process. A number of registrants indicate that they hold Exchange Act report "drafting sessions." This affords prospective underwriters and their counsel an opportunity to participate in the drafting and review of periodic disclosure documents before they are filed.

Another practice is to hold so-called periodic due diligence sessions. Some registrants hold sessions shortly after the release of quarterly earnings to provide prospective underwriters and their counsel an opportunity to discuss with management the most recent financial results and other events of that quarter. Periodic due diligence sessions also include annual meetings with management to review financial trends and business developments. In addition, some registrants indicate that prospective underwriters and underwriters' counsel are able to schedule individual meetings with management at any time.

The Commission believes that the development of anticipatory and continuous due diligence techniques is consistent with the integrated disclosure system and will permit underwriters to perform due diligence in an orderly, efficient manner. Indeed, in adopting Rule 176 as part of that system, the Commission recognized that, just as different registration forms are appropriate for different companies, the method of due diligence investigation may not be the same for all registrants. Rule 176 sets forth a non-exclusive list of circumstances which the Commission believes bear upon the reasonableness of the investigation and the determination of what constitutes reasonable grounds for belief under Section 11(b) of the Securities Act. Circumstances which may be particularly relevant to an underwriter's due diligence investigation of registrants qualified to use short form registration include the type of registrant, reasonable reliance on management, the type of underwriting arrangement and the underwriter's role, and whether the underwriter participated in the preparation or review of documents incorporated by reference into the registration statement. The Commission expects that the techniques of conducting due diligence investigations of registrants qualified to use short form registration, where documents are incorporated by reference, would differ from due diligence investigations under other circumstances.

3. *Other Concerns.* Securities industry commentators also raise concerns relating to institutionalization of the securities markets, the impact on retail distribution, increased concentration in the securities industry and effects on the secondary markets. Specifically, these commentators believe that Rule 415 is accelerating the trends toward institutionalization of the securities markets and concentration in the securities industry. In their view, the Rule is decreasing the number of syndicated offerings in which regional securities firms participate and excluding individual investors from the new issues market.

While the Commission recognizes the existence of these trends, it believes that they reflect economic and other factors apart from shelf registration. These factors include volatile interest rates and markets, the growth of mutual and pension funds which act as intermediaries for individual investors, and the homogenization of the financial services industry. These factors are not necessarily affected by Rule 415. Rule 415 is a procedural rule which presents an optional filing technique. It does not mandate any particular method of distribution. Indeed, many offerings of debt and equity securities registered under the Rule have been sold in traditional syndicated offerings. The Commission therefore believes that these concerns transcend Rule 415.

V. Commission Action

The Commission has considered all views and suggestions with respect to Rule 415. There are several reasons why it may be appropriate to adopt the shelf registration rule in substantially its present form. During the eighteen months the Rule has been in effect, it has worked well and has provided registrants with substantial benefits in their financings. Also, most of the concerns raised transcend shelf registration. On the other hand, the Commission believes that concerns raised about the quality and timing of disclosure and due diligence are important to address because they relate to the adequacy of disclosure investors receive in connection with public offerings. Having weighed all considerations, the Commission is modifying Rule 415 to strike an appropriate balance by making it available for offerings eligible to be registered on Form S–3 or F–3 and for traditional shelf offerings.

* * *

For registrants not eligible to use short form registration, however, the Commission believes that concerns about disclosure and due diligence outweigh the benefits of Rule 415. The Commission also notes that shelf registration may not be as advantageous for such registrants because they cannot rely on subsequently filed Exchange Act reports for certain updating of the information in the shelf registration statement. Such updating requires the filing of post-effective amendments. Indeed, few non-S–3 or F–3 registrants have used Rule 415 for other than traditional shelf offerings.

VI. Operation of Revised Rule 415

* * *

A. *Offerings Permitted Under Revised Rule*

1. *Traditional Shelf Offerings.* A number of traditional shelf offerings were enumerated in former paragraphs (a)(1)(ii) through (vii). These provisions have been retained and redesignated as paragraphs (a)(1)(i) through (vi).

Other traditional shelf offerings came within former paragraph (a)(1)(i). Because the primary offerings which may be made under Rule 415 are now limited, paragraph (a)(1)(i) has been deleted. That paragraph provided that any securities not falling within one of the categories specifically enumerated in the balance of paragraph (a)(1) could be registered under the Rule, but were limited to an amount reasonably expected to be offered and sold within two years. Those traditional offerings covered by former paragraph (a)(1)(i) are now set forth in paragraphs (a)(1)(vii) through (ix).

Mortgage related securities, such as mortgage backed debt and mortgage participation or pass through certificates, are listed in paragraph (a)(1)(vii). Generally, the securities are registered and then offered from time to time as series of mortgage backed debt are established or pools of mortgages are formed. Shelf registration is essential to sale of these securities. Together with the formation of blind pools, shelf registration allows registrants to match capital demands with portfolio holdings. They can form pools of mortgages as sales of securities backed by those mortgages take place. It is not necessary for the mortgages to be purchased before the securities are priced and sold. With an effective shelf registration statement, pricing and sales can occur contemporaneously with mortgage acquisition.

Paragraph (a)(1)(viii) relates to securities to be issued in connection with business combination transactions. All other traditional shelf offerings are covered by paragraph (a)(1)(ix), which permits offerings that (1) will be commenced promptly, (2) will be made on a continuous basis and (3) may continue for a period in excess of 30 days from the date of initial effectiveness.

Examples of the traditional shelf offerings which come within paragraph (a)(1)(ix) are: customer purchaser plans; exchange, rights, subscription and rescission offers; offers to employees, consultants or independent agents; offerings on a best efforts basis; tax shelter and other limited partnership interests; commodity funds; condominium rental pools; time sharing agreements; real estate investment trusts; farmers' cooperative organizations or others making distributions on a membership basis; and continuous debt sales by finance companies to their customers.

2. *Short Form Registration Shelf Offerings.* New paragraph (a)(1)(x) relates to primary delayed or continuous offerings of securities registered, or qualified to be registered, on Form S–3 or F–3. Unless an offering falls within one of the categories of offerings specified in paragraphs (a)(1)(i) through (a)(1)(ix), it must come within paragraph (a)(1)(x) or it cannot be registered pursuant to Rule 415. Thus, only traditional shelf offerings and primary shelf offerings that qualify for short form registration may be offered or sold under the Rule.

* * *

Commissioner Thomas, Concurring in Part and Dissenting in Part:

I respectfully dissent from that portion of the Commission's decision today to adopt Rule 415 for offerings qualified to be registered on Forms S–3 and F–3 insofar as it relates to equity securities only. Although I am gratified at the compromise adopted by the Commission and sincerely believe that such a compromise was only reached because of the strong opposition to the Rule voiced by many during the experimental period, I must continue to express my reservations about the Rule on the basis of principle.

* * *

After studying the comment letters and conferring with issuers, representatives of the securities industry, and institutional and individual investors, I continue to believe that the Rule as applied to equity offerings (1) reduces the quality and timeliness of disclosure available to investors when making their investment decisions, and (2) jeopardizes the liquidity and stability of both our primary and secondary securities markets by encouraging greater concentration of underwriters, market-makers, and other financial intermediaries and by discouraging individual investor participation in the capital market, thereby furthering the trend toward institutionalization of securities holders.

Although I do not believe that it is possible at this time to quantify the various elements of these risks due to the exceptionally strong market we have been experiencing during most of the experimental period and the inactive market experienced at the beginning of the experimental period, I am convinced that many of these risks are real. Incurring these risks is antithetical to the statutory duty of the Commission to protect investors and to maintain the integrity of our capital markets.[a]

---

1. *Impact of Rule 415.* While much controversy surrounded the adoption of shelf registration, one impact of Rule 415 is fairly certain: it has introduced a heightened degree of competition into the market for underwriting services. This is particularly evident in the differential between the average underwriting discount on non-shelf offerings and those on shelf offerings. The SEC's Advisory Committee on the Capital Formation and Regulatory Process reported that from 1993 to 1995 the median underwriting commission for a public offering of common stock was 7.0% on Form S–1, 6.0% on Form S–2, 5.0% on non-shelf offerings on Form S–3, and only 4.6% for shelf offerings on Form S–3.[1] The reason for this differential probably lies, at least in part, in the practical leverage that shelf registration affords corporate financial officers to seek competing bids, in effect calling up rival underwriters and asking for a bid for an offering later that same week. In contrast, the classic Form S–1 involves an extended process of collaboration between the underwriter and the issuer in preparing the registration statement—before the critical pricing moment was reached. To a considerable degree, this delay locked the issuer into its choice of underwriter and reduced its leverage in pricing negotiations. At the outset of this extended period, it was clearly too early to expect the underwriter to commit to a price for the still distant offering. But, at the end of this process, calling off the offering (because of a pricing dispute) would result in greater harm for the issuer than for the underwriting group. After all, the issuer had invested time and money, which would not be recouped if the offering were canceled; it might desperately need the funds; and it might suffer a serious reputational loss, particularly if the market suspected that the offering had been canceled because the underwriters had discovered an undisclosed problem.

Note, however, that while underwriting discounts have been sharply reduced by Rule 415, the rule does require that the issuer use an underwriter in an equity offering "at the market." See Rule 415(a)(4)(iii) and (iv) (requiring that "the securities must be sold through an underwriter" and that "the underwriter or underwriters be named in the prospectus which is part of the registration statement"). This provision of Rule 415 effectively responded to the investment banking industry's fear that large corporations would directly market offerings to institutional investors, for example, by calling up a half dozen mutual funds to sell a small equity offering without underwriters. But should the SEC protect the industry in this fashion if issuers really believed

---

a. One study comparing shelf and traditional equity offerings found that a negative price reaction was observed both for traditional and shelf registrations; however, no statistically significant differences were observed between these types of offerings. See Moore, Peterson & Peterson, Shelf Registrations and Shareholder Wealth: A Comparison of Shelf and Traditional Equity Offerings, 41 J. Finance 451 (1986).

1. See Report of the Advisory Committee on the Capital Formation and Regulatory Process, App. A, at tbl. 4 (SEC 1996); see also Kidwell, Marr & Thompson, Shelf Registration: Competition and Market Efficiency, 30 J.L. & Econ. 181 (1987).

that they did not need the services of underwriters? Why shouldn't costly financial intermediaries (such as underwriters) wither away if they are not needed? One possible response might be that the underwriter is the best positioned party to test the accuracy of the issuer's statements. In the absence of underwriters, sophisticated institutional buyers might quickly resell the "untested" securities purchased in shelf registered offerings to less sophisticated public investors. But, on the other hand, these same public investors might just as easily buy equity securities of the same issuer in the secondary market without any effort being made by anyone to test the issuer's disclosures.

2. *Equity Offerings.* A curious fact about Rule 415 is that it was initially little used for equity offerings (whereas it was immediately exploited for debt offerings).[2] The most likely explanation for this phenomenon involves the earlier noted fact that an issuer's stock price normally declines on an announcement of an equity offering, probably as a result of the market's sense that management believes that its stock's price has peaked. After all, if management believed on the basis of nonpublic information that the stock price would soon rise further, they would logically delay the offering. Whether for this reason or the alternative explanation that a large supply of new stock depresses the market price because it creates an imbalance between supply and demand, the phenomenon of an adverse market reaction to news of an impending equity offering by a seasoned issuer is well established.[3] This same negative market reaction occurred when an equity shelf registration was filed, and sometimes it was severe.[4] As a result, management was reluctant to file a shelf registration statement for an equity offering and incur an immediate stock price penalty for a still distant offering. From their perspective, the transaction cost savings were more than offset by the market penalty.

In response to this problem, the SEC in 1993 amended shelf registration procedures to eliminate the need to specify the number of shares that were being registered for potential future sale. Under this new "universal registration statement," the issuer need identify only the classes of securities being registered (debt and equity) and the aggregate expected proceeds from all sales. Because most shelf registration statements are for debt securities and the listing of additional equity classes does not mean that common stock will actually be sold, this procedure apparently reduced the penalty for registering equity securities (in effect by masking the intended equity sales). But, while favorable to issuers, did this action benefit investors (the SEC's traditional constituency)? In any event, the use of shelf registration statements for equity offerings has picked up markedly since 1993.[5]

2. See Denis, Shelf Registration and the Market for Seasoned Equity Offerings, 64 J.Bus. 189 (1991).

3. See Barclay and Litzenberger, Announcement Effects of New Equity Issuers and the Use of Intraday Price Data, 21 J.Fin. Econ. 71 (1988).

4. For one study finding no significant differences in market reaction to announcements of the filing of shelf registration statements versus traditional equity offerings, see Moore, Peterson & Peterson, Shelf Registrations and Shareholder Wealth: A Comparison of Shelf and Traditional Equity Offerings, 41 J.Fin. 451 (1986).

5. Between January, 1994 and December 1995, a review of all registration statements covering common stock shows that issuers filed 486 such shelf registration statements on Form S–3 covering common stock as opposed to 416 such non-shelf registration statements on Form S–3, 310 such registration statements on Form S–1 and 79 such registration statements on Form S–2 or S–11. See Report of Advisory Committee on the Capital Formation and Regulatory Processes, App. table 2. (SEC 1996). In short, the "uni-

3. *The Due Diligence Debate.* Academics have vigorously debated the impact of Rule 415 on the underwriters' ability to perform due diligence. Professor Barbara Banoff concluded that Rule 415 "clearly benefits issuers, investors and the economy as a whole." Moreover, she believes that some S–2 issuers should also be allowed to use shelf registration, and that the restrictions imposed on "at-the-market" equity offerings should be lifted. Banoff, Regulatory Subsidies, Efficient Markets, and Shelf Registration: An Analysis of Rule 415, 70 Va.L.Rev. 135 (1984). Feeney, The Saga of Rule 415: Registration for the Shelf, 9 Corp.L.Rev. 41 (1986), is in general agreement.

On the other hand, Professor Merritt B. Fox questioned some of the assumptions underlying Professor Banoff's conclusions. He projects a broader view of the economic role which the securities market plays in the national economy. In addition to viewing the securities market in terms of its impact upon participants, he believes that the market also "monitors and structures the allocation of scarce resources in the economy." He concludes: "The improvement in the quality of information about an issuer that results from underwriter due diligence enhances efficient allocation of resources of the economy. Short form and shelf registration—the heart of the integrated disclosure program—can be expected to reduce the amount of due diligence underwriters perform, and therefore reduce the benefits to the economy that flow from that activity." Accordingly, "benefits of the traditional level of underwriter due diligence are worth their accompanying costs." Fox, Shelf Registration, Integrated Disclosure, and Underwriter Due Diligence: An Economic Analysis, 70 Va.L.Rev. 1005 (1984).

4. *The SEC's Compromise on Due Diligence: Rule 176.* At the time of adoption of shelf registration, many underwriters complained that their inability to conduct due diligence under the time constraints it created exposed them to unfair liability under § 11 of the Securities Act of 1933. To alleviate these concerns the Commission adopted Rule 176 which codified Section 1704(g) of the American Law Institute's proposed Federal Securities Code. The Commission stated that Rule 176 "is intended to make explicit what circumstances may bear upon the determination of what constitutes a reasonable investigation and reasonable ground for belief as these terms are used in Section 11(b) of the Securities Act."[6]

In discussing due diligence in an integrated disclosure system, the Commission had this to say:[7]

"[T]he Securities Act imposes a high standard of conduct on specific persons, including underwriters and directors, associated with a registered public offering of securities. * * *

"The principal goal of integration is to simplify disclosure and reduce unnecessary repetition and redelivery of information which has already been provided, not to alter the roles of participants in the securities distribution process as originally contemplated by the Securities Act. The integrated disclosure system, past and proposed, is thus not designed to modify the responsibility of underwriters and others to make a reasonable investigation. Information presented in the registration statement, wheth-

---

versal shelf" seems to have succeeded in extending shelf registration to equity securities.

6. SEC Securities Act Release No. 6335 (Aug. 6, 1981), Fed.Sec.L.Rep. (CCH) No.

926, Special Rep., 2d Extra Ed. (Aug. 13, 1981), at 65.

7. Id. at 88–91.

er or not incorporated by reference, must be true and complete in all material respects and verified where appropriate. Likewise, nothing in the Commission's integrated disclosure system precludes conducting adequate due diligence. This point can be demonstrated by addressing the two principal concerns which have been raised.

"First, * * * commentators have expressed concern about the short time involved in document preparation. There also may be a substantial reduction in the time taken for pre-effective review at the Commission. As to the latter point, however, commentators * * * themselves noted that due diligence generally is performed prior to filing with the Commission, rendering the time in registration largely irrelevant. As to the former point, there is nothing which compels an underwriter to proceed prematurely with an offering. Although, as discussed below, he may wish to arrange his due diligence procedures over time for the purpose of avoiding last minute delays in an offering environment characterized by rapid market changes, in the final analysis the underwriter is never compelled to proceed with an offering until he has accomplished his due diligence.

"The second major concern relates to the fact that documents, prepared by others, often at a much earlier date, are incorporated by reference into the registration statement.[52] Again, it must be emphasized that due diligence requires a reasonable investigation of all the information presented therein and any information incorporated by reference. If such material contains a material misstatement, or omits a material fact, then, in order to avoid liability, a subsequent document must be filed to correct the earlier one, or the information must be restated correctly in the registration statement. Nothing in the integrated disclosure system precludes such action.

"The Commission specifically rejects the suggestion that the underwriter needs only to read the incorporated materials and discuss them with representatives of the registrant and named experts. Because the registrant would be the sole source of virtually all information, this approach would not, in and of itself, include the element of verification required by the case law and contemplated by the statute.

"Thus, verification in appropriate circumstances is still required, and if a material misstatement or omission has been made, correction by amendment or restatement must be made. For example, a major supply contract on which the registrant is substantially dependent should be reviewed to avoid the possibility of inaccurate references to it in the prospectus. On the other hand, if the alleged misstatement in issue turns on an ambiguity or nuance in the drafted language of an incorporated document making it a close question as to whether a violation even has been committed, then the fact that a particular defendant did not participate in preparing the incorporated document, when combined with judgmental difficulties and practical concerns in making changes in prepared documents, would seem to be an appropriate factor in deciding whether

52. It should be noted that Item 11 of proposed Form S–2 gives preparers the choice of either incorporating by reference specified information about the registrant from the annual report to security holders and its latest Form 10–Q or of setting forth such information directly in the registration statement.

"reasonable belief" in the accuracy of statements existed and thus in deciding whether to attach liability to a particular defendant's conduct.

"In sum, the Commission strongly affirms the need for due diligence and its attendant vigilance and verification. The Commission's efforts towards integration of the Securities Act and the Exchange Act relate solely to elimination of unnecessary repetition of disclosure, not to the requirements of due diligence which must accompany any offering. Yet, in view of the fact that court decisions to date have construed due diligence under factual circumstances not involving an integrated system, and in order to encourage a focus on a flexible approach to due diligence rather than a rigid adherence to past practice, the Commission believes that it would be helpful to codify its prior statements so that courts and others may fully understand the new system."

B. BEYOND SHELF REGISTRATION: COMPANY REGISTRATION AND OTHER DEREGULATORY OPTIONS—THE POLICY ISSUES FOR THE FUTURE

Securities Act Concepts and Their Effects on Capital Formation

Securities and Exchange Commission, Sec.Act.Rel. No. 7314.
(July 25, 1996).

I. INTRODUCTION

The Securities Act of 1933 (the "Securities Act") and the rules and regulations thereunder have long provided the foundation for a capital formation system whose integrity, fairness and liquidity are unparalleled. Because U.S. capital formation methods and markets are characterized by innovation, the Commission vigilantly seeks to identify ways to improve its regulatory framework governing that system.[3] Two studies presented to the Commission

---

3. The current reexamination of the Securities Act registration system is the most recent step in the modern reevaluation of the regulatory framework that many date back to the publication of the 1966 article by Milton Cohen which first suggested the integration of the Securities Act and the Securities Exchange Act of 1934 (the "Exchange Act") (15 U.S.C. §§ 78a et seq.) disclosure systems. See M. Cohen, "Truth in Securities" Revisited, 79 Harv.L.Rev. 1340 (1966). Since the publication of that article, the Commission has conducted or arranged several studies related to the disclosure system, including those completed by the Commission's Disclosure Policy Study Group in 1969 and the Commission's Advisory Committee on Corporate Disclosure in 1977. See Disclosure to Investors—A Reappraisal of Administrative Policies under the '33 and '34 Acts (Mar. 1969) (commonly referred to as the

"Wheat Report"); Report of the Advisory Committee on Corporate Disclosure to the Securities and Exchange Commission (Nov. 1977). Those efforts paved the way for significant integration of the Securities Act and Exchange Act disclosure systems by the Commission in 1982. See Securities Act Release No. 6383 (Mar. 3, 1982). Further refinement of the Securities Act registration system included, for example, the development of the short-form shelf registration system, which has enabled "seasoned issuers" to conduct a primary offering on a delayed or continuous basis if certain requirements are met. Shelf registration has afforded an eligible registrant a certain degree of flexibility by enabling it to time its offering when market conditions are most advantageous. The Commission's subsequent adoption of a "universal" shelf registration system in 1992 increased this flexibility even further by per-

this year are assisting the Commission with its most recent efforts to reexamine that regulatory framework.

The first report delivered to the Commission was the Report of the Task Force on Disclosure Simplification (the "Task Force") of March 1996 (the "Task Force Report"). Among many other recommendations, the Task Force identified a number of areas in which modernization and simplification of the registration and disclosure processes could be accomplished.

Today, the second report is being presented to the Commission by the Advisory Committee, chaired by Commissioner Steven M.H. Wallman.[9] The Advisory Committee has been studying the securities offering process and the Commission's rules regulating it since February 1995. The objective of the Advisory Committee has been to assist the Commission in evaluating the efficacy of the regulatory process relating to the public offering of securities, securities market trading, and corporate reporting. The Advisory Committee Report is being published contemporaneously with this release and reflects 18 months of extensive study and analysis of the regulatory framework * * *.

The Advisory Committee Report's primary recommendation is that the Commission further its integrated disclosure system by implementing a system based on a "company registration" concept first envisioned by the American Law Institute's Federal Securities Code.[10] As formulated by the Advisory Committee, a company registration system generally would be accomplished through the following steps:

- on a one-time basis, the issuer[11] files a registration statement (deemed effective immediately) that includes information similar to that currently provided in an initial short-form shelf registration statement. This registration statement could then be used for all types of securities and all offerings (including those offered in furtherance of business acquisitions) and all offerings could be subject to Section 11 strict liability;

- current and future Exchange Act reports are incorporated by reference into that registration statement;

- around the time of the offering, transactional and updating disclosures are filed with the Commission, usually in a Form 8–K that is incorporat-

mitting an eligible company to register debt, equity, and other securities on a single shelf registration statement, without having to specify the amount of each class of securities to be offered. See Securities Act Release Nos. 6499 (Nov. 17, 1983) and 6964 (Oct. 22, 1992).

9. Report of the Advisory Committee on the Capital Formation and Regulatory Processes (July 24, 1996).

10. The American Law Institute's Federal Securities Code was developed, after many years of effort, under the direction of Professor Louis Loss. See American Law Institute, Federal Securities Code (1980). See also L. Loss, "The American Law Institute's Federal Securities Code Project," 25 Bus.Law 27 (1969).

11. The Advisory Committee recommends that eligibility for an initial pilot be limited to issuers that: have registered at least one public offering under the Securities Act; have been reporting under the Exchange Act for two years; have a public float of at least $75 million; and have securities listed on the New York Stock Exchange, the American Stock Exchange or NASDAQ NMS. Foreign issuers would be eligible if they file annual, quarterly and other periodic reports with the Commission on forms designed for domestic issuers, although the Advisory Committee specifically requests the Commission to consider whether current foreign issuer eligibility requirements for Form F–3 primary offerings should be sufficient for eligibility in the pilot. Most foreign countries (other than Canada) do not require their issuers to prepare quarterly reports.

ed by reference into the registration statement and subject to Section 11 strict liability, but in certain cases, at the option of the issuer, through a prospectus supplement like those traditionally filed in shelf takedowns;

- other than a nominal fee paid at the initial filing, registration fees would be paid at the time of sale rather than prior to making any offers (the "pay as you go" feature);

- issuers would be required to adopt some disclosure enhancements (and encouraged to adopt others) that seek to improve the quality and timeliness of disclosure provided to investors and the markets; and

- formal prospectuses would be required to be physically delivered only in non-routine transactions and, when so required to be delivered, they would have to be delivered in time to be considered in connection with the investment decision. In almost all instances, an issuer could incorporate by reference filed information into selling materials or the confirmation of sale to satisfy the legal obligation to deliver a prospectus (which, under the statute, must precede or accompany a confirmation of sale) * * *.

II.   SECURITIES ACT CONCEPTS

The Securities Act and the issuer disclosure provisions of the Exchange Act are premised on the view that investors are best protected in making investment decisions if they are presented with full and fair disclosure of all material information about the investments. The continuing challenge for the Commission lies in adapting the statutory disclosure framework to developments in the capital markets while ensuring that investors receive full and fair disclosure in a manner and at a time that allows such informed decision-making.

Faced with the following developments, among others: increasing institutionalization of the markets; advances in technology and communication media; continuing globalization of securities markets; and the erosion of distinctions between private and public transactions, the Commission is examining whether the existing investor protection mechanisms, such as registration of both offers and sales of physical delivery of final prospectuses to investors around the time of sale, remain the best methods for accomplishing this full disclosure objective. The Commission is considering as well whether specific aspects of the integration of the registration requirements under the Securities Act and the periodic reporting requirements under the Exchange Act, if adjusted, could better serve investors' needs for distinctions between public and private offerings of public companies remain necessary and how the increasingly institutional nature of investors should be reflected in the regulatory framework.

A.   Request for Comments on Securities Act Concepts

In this release, the Commission seeks comment on the best methods for eliminating unnecessary obstacles to capital formulation while improving the quality and timing of disclosure and, therefore, investor protection. To assist the Commission in its deliberations, certain concepts that are central to the current capital-raising process and transcend any one approach to reform are highlighted below. Comment is solicited regarding the best approach is one or more of the approaches mentioned herein, a combination thereof, or any approach not described in this release * * *.

1. Quality of Ongoing Disclosure

Investors in primary offerings for repeat issuers and investors in the secondary markets generally rely on periodic disclosure prepared pursuant to the Exchange Act. The existing Securities Act registration system for larger, seasoned issuers is heavily dependent upon incorporation of disclosure from such reports into the registration statement. Some observers have suggested that, while issuers undertaking registration of public offerings often devote significant resources to developing disclosure of the quality required under the Securities Act, equivalent resources are not necessarily devoted to preparing disclosure in Exchange Act periodic reports.

Given the importance of investor protection, both with respect to investors in primary offerings and investors in the secondary trading markets, the Commission solicits comment regarding whether, in fact, a significant difference exists in the quality of disclosure between Securities Act and Exchange Act documents. If such a difference exists, what Commission action should be taken to address this concern? Should enhancement of current safeguards (such as the application of liability provisions) or the adoption of newly devised safeguards, or both, be used to ensure that disclosure in Exchange Act documents is equal in quality to that in Securities Act documents?

Are there particular aspects of Exchange Act disclosure that are in need of improvement, and thus require specific Commission focus? Is there information in Securities Act disclosure that should be mandated in Exchange Act reports? To enhance disclosure quality, should further participation of persons independent of the issuer, such as independent accountants, be required in the preparation of Exchange Act reports?

If various reforms would result in disclosure less often being prepared specifically in connection with the offering process, or would allow issuers quicker, more frequent (potentially continuous) access to the capital markets, would any concern about existing Exchange Act disclosure quality be exacerbated? Are improvements needed to ensure that Exchange Act reports provide a more current stream of information to investors? For example, should consideration be given to adopting a requirement, similar to certain self-regulatory organizations' requirements, that information that could materially affect the market for an issuer's securities be disclosed promptly in a public filing with the Commission? Should the filing dates for Exchange Act reports (e.g. Form 8–K) be accelerated or should the events that trigger such reports be broadened? Should the disclosure of particular events be accelerated? * * *

2. Informing Investors

b. Timing of Delivery

One key element of the full disclosure objective is ensuring that investors are given sufficient time to consider material information in making investment decisions. Under current rules, prospectus delivery is required prior to or at the same time with the confirmation in primary offerings. In practice, therefore, Section 10(a) prospectuses may be unlikely to be sent to investors in advance of the decisions to purchase. In some cases, preliminary prospectuses are delivered, but they generally are not required to be delivered if the issuer is reporting under the Exchange Act. For reporting issuers, material company information for the most part will have been widely available at the time of any offering, but information regarding the offering transaction and any information that reflects material developments since the last Exchange Act report was filed would not have been. Comment is requested with regard to whether investors in primary offerings by reporting companies receive transactional and material developments information in the traditional physical form in sufficient time to make informed investment decisions. If not, what Commission action would be appropriate to ensure that result?

c. Limitations on Written Communications Other than the Statutory Prospectuses

The drafters of the Securities Act intended that the statutory prospectuses be the written selling document for securities. "Free writing" outside the statutory prospectus is not generally permitted except in the post-effective period when the Section 10(a) prospectus has been delivered to investors. Comment is solicited with respect to whether more flexibility to inform investors by use of written vehicles other than the traditional prospectus should be permitted. For example, should simplified profile prospectuses be permitted or required? With respect to offerings by seasoned issuers, if significant ongoing information is and has been available to investors with respect to such issuers, is the potential for harm from allowing or encouraging non-prospectus information delivery minimized? Would investor protection be likely to improve to the extent that issuers are encouraged to provide written, rather than oral, information about the basic terms of the transaction? Alternatively, would more flexibility be likely to result in use of selling materials driven by marketing needs that (in the distributed form) significantly differ from the prospectus envisioned by the Securities Act? If so, would investors' focus shift to the marketing language instead of the mandated prospectus disclosure, particularly if the latter is constructively rather than physically delivered? What standard of liability should attach to such other selling materials?

Would a system allowing incorporation by reference of the required prospectus disclosure from a registration statement previously filed with the Commission facilitate the use of simplified term sheets or other types of "free writing?" Would that system facilitate free-writing if such selling materials had to be filed and subject to liability under Section 12(a)(2)? Would sufficient investor protection exist where Section 12(a)(2) liability is applied?

To what extent would issuers be more inclined to provide selling materials under that sort of system? Would the requirement to have a Section 10(a) prospectus (and the selling materials) on file by the time of use of the selling materials present any difficulty as a practical matter, even though statutory disclosure may be wholly incorporated by reference rather than delivered physically?

3. Timeliness of Disclosure—Informing the Market

Under the current shelf system, information concerning shelf takedowns (contained in a prospectus supplement) is not required to be filed until the second business day following the earlier of: the date of determination of the offering price, or the date of first use in connection with the offering. Some have expressed concern that the current structure of the shelf registration system does not require timely disclosure to the secondary markets of all material information that is being disclosed to investors in the primary offering.

Does the post-takedown filing of prospectus supplements strike an appropriate balance between quick access to capital and timely disclosure to investors in the secondary markets for such securities? Is this balance appropriate if the prospectus supplement is available earlier? Are the secondary markets having difficulty assimilating such information during the period before it is filed with the Commission because of limited access to such information?

Does it matter if transaction-specific disclosure that does not amount to a material development is not assimilated until some time after the offering? Should a special requirement apply in cases where the offering involves a type of security never before sold by the issuer? Should there be certain events (e.g. a percentage of equity being offered) that will always be deemed material developments?

In addition, comment is requested with regard to whether takedown information should be filed in an Exchange Act report that is incorporated by reference into the registration statement. Should all Securities Act Rule 424(b) prospectus supplements be deemed to be a part of the effective registration statement, as in the case with prospectus supplements filed in connection with Rule 430A?

4.   The Role of "Gatekeepers" in Maintaining Quality of Disclosure

The civil liability provisions of the Securities Act registration system provide strong incentives for certain parties independent of the issuer (such as underwriters, accounting professionals, and others) to take steps to ensure the quality of disclosure. Given the interest of issuers in quick access to the capital markets, some commenters and reports have argued that these "gatekeepers" may not currently be given the amount of time they wish or need in which to perform their traditional "due diligence" role, particularly in connection with delayed shelf offerings. Comment and specific data are solicited with respect to the nature and prevalence of such difficulties. Comment is requested on whether there is tension between the traditional role of "gatekeepers" and the issuer's desire to have quick access to the capital markets.

Can the independent "gatekeepers" role be reconfigured in order to facilitate the issuer's ability to access the capital markets quickly while maintaining or enhancing investor protection? If not, should reliance on such "gatekeepers" continue if a collateral effect may be to slow down access to the capital markets? Is the increasing ability of issuers to access the securities markets directly by themselves affecting the role of underwriters as "gatekeepers," particularly in light of advances in technology and communications? Has there been a change in the role other parties play, such as analysts and rating agencies, that should be considered in evaluating the role of traditional "gatekeepers?" In what ways has the "due diligence" process changed to reflect these changes?

Are there mechanisms that could be adopted to allow such "gatekeepers" to operate effectively? Have advances in technology and communications and the existence, in some cases, of auditors engaging in interim reviews, and analysts and rating agencies made performance of the "gatekeeper" function possible on a continuous basis, or with little notice, due to the dissemination of information about issuers on a continuing basis?

Would requiring a separate filing that is subject to Section 11 liability (such as an Exchange Act filing incorporated by reference into the registration statement) focus the issuer and other parties on the quality of disclosure and the need to undertake due diligence? If so, should the timing thereof be dependent upon the type of security involved and the size of the offering? Should there be a different or supplemental mechanism (for example, a requirement that independent "gatekeepers" be notified of (or engaged for, as applicable) an offering at least several days in advance, or a requirement that a certificate be filed by independent "gatekeepers" prior to the offering that they have performed due diligence)? Would these mechanisms be consistent with today's demands for quick access to capital?

Would a "disclosure committee" of an issuer's board of directors operate as an effective "gatekeeper?"[37] Would such a "disclosure committee" likely improve the monitoring of disclosure by directors or improve the accuracy of disclosure? Would it result in a diminished oversight role for the rest of the board? What effect would it have on the liability of the directors serving on the committee? What effect would it have on the liability of the other directors on the board? Would board members be willing to serve on such a committee if there were no Commission guidance on liability?[38] How would it operate differently from the audit committee?

5.   Staff Review

The Advisory Committee Report states that the uncertainty surrounding whether there will be staff review of registration statement disclosure, in cases other than initial public offerings and major restructurings, results in delays and uncertainties that may not be justified in terms of public interest and investor protection benefits. The Advisory Committee Report suggests that, for those issuers in a company registration system, under certain circumstances, staff review be eliminated with respect to pre-transaction filings in favor of enhanced reviews of Exchange Act filings that could provide a similar deterrent effect.

Only a small percentage of the Commission's current reviews of Securities Act registration statements focus on issuers that are neither making their initial public offering nor offering securities in connection with major restructurings. Many of those reviews involve issuers that are either financially troubled or are offering a new type of security to the public. Comment is requested with respect to whether the Commission staff should shift its review of repeat issuers from Securities Act registration statements to the review of Exchange Act reports. If so, under what circumstances? Should the Commission instead consider: making public its criteria used to determine whether to review repeat issuers' registration statements; limiting its review of repeat issuers' registration statements to those issuers that are financially troubled or are engaging in an extraordinary transaction; or allowing repeat issuers to request review of their Exchange reports well in advance of a public offering? . . . .

----

37. See the full description of this concept at pp. 31–34 of the Advisory Committee Report. This concept is recommended by the Advisory Committee, although it is not identified as an essential element of company registration.

38. Although the Advisory Committee Report stops short of recommending a particular change in the application of liability to "gatekeepers," three members of the Advisory Committee, in a separate statement, expressed doubt that practitioners would recommend, or that corporations would adopt, some of the reforms proposed by the Advisory Committee, and particularly the disclosure committee concept, unless the Commission accompanied it with a transition in liability rules. See "Separate Statement of John C. Coffee, Jr., Edward F. Greene, and Lawrence W. Sonsini" in the Advisory Committee Report at Section IV., p. 38.

1. *The SEC's New Exemptive Power.* The SEC Advisory Committee sought to identify revisions in the traditional disclosure system that could be achieved without legislation. At that time, the SEC lacked a broad exemptive power. But in 1996, § 28 of the Securities Act was enacted, which broadly authorizes the Commission to exempt "any class of persons, securities, or transactions, from any provision or provisions of this title, to the extent that such exemption is . . . consistent with the protection of investors." In light of this provision, a number of commentators have recently recommended a variety of deregulatory initiatives, including: (1) a relaxation of provision § 5(b)'s "free writing" restrictions, (2) a shortening of the "quiet period" under '5(c), or (3) complete deregulation of offers in the case of seasoned issuers. Under the last approach, which the Commission continues to consider, seasoned issuers could offer securities, but not sell them in the absence of an effective registration statement.

2. *The Aircraft Carrier Release.* In Securities Act Release No. 7606A (November 3, 1998), the SEC followed up on the Advisory Committee's report by proposing extensive, indeed sweeping, changes in the rules regulating the public offering process. So ambitious and comprehensive was this release, that it has come to be known as the "Aircraft Carrier Release". In overview, the Aircraft Carrier Release was a curious mixture of deregulatory proposals coupled with an attempt to take back some earlier deregulatory steps. Because of the latter effort, the Release became controversial and has received a largely skeptical reception from underwriters and much of the securities bar. Still, the Release is a guide both to those areas where the SEC is most prepared to deregulate and abandon some of the traditional restrictions of the 1933 Act and those where it is not.

The Aircraft Carrier Release would eliminate many of the traditional features of the 1933 Act's registration procedure and would generally simplify and expedite the registration process, as follows:

a. *Incorporation by Reference.* Issuers who had been a reporting company for 24 months could incorporate by reference 1934 Act reports into their registration statement. Today, Form S–1 does not permit such incorporation.

b. *"Gun-Jumping" and the Quiet Period.* The Release would effectively supercede § 5(c) of the 1933 Act by broadly permitting communications during the period before a registration statement is filed. In the case of a seasoned issuer, the Release would not impose any quiet period; in the case of new registrants, a safe harbor would immunize all communications made more than 30 days before the filing of the registration statement.

c. *Free Writing.* Although "free writing" (that is, sales literature or sales-oriented written communications to potential investors) is today barred before the registration statement becomes effective, the Release would remove this prohibition, but would require the filing of such sales material with the SEC and would subject it to liability under § 12(a)(2) of the 1933 Act (but not § 11).

d. *Research Reports.* A revised Rule 139 would remove all restrictions on research reports by broker dealers for seasoned offerings. In the case of initial or other unseasoned offerings, any research report issued by broker dealer more than 30 days prior to the filing of the registration statement would similarly be exempt, and even within this 30 day window the SEC would exempt research reports on seasoned issuers.

e. *Timing and Filing.* In a major change, the Release would permit seasoned issuers to obtain immediate market access by having their registration statements declared effective on demand. In addition, such issuers would not be required to file a registration statement until the first sale of a security. Thus, selling efforts could precede the filing of the registration statement. In effect, the SEC comment letter and subsequent negotiations with the staff over the contents of the prospectus would occur only in case of IPOs and offerings by unseasoned issuers.

f. *"Pay-as-You-Go" Filing Fees.* Whereas an issuer using shelf registration today pays a filing fee at the outset based on the amount of securities registered by it, the Aircraft Carrier Release contemplated a "pay-as-you-go" system under which filing fees are paid only if and when the securities are sold.

g. *Due Diligence Procedures.* The Aircraft Release proposed to expand Rule 176 to include a general reference to practices that courts would be invited to view as demonstrating satisfaction of the underwriter's due diligence defense. However, the SEC was unwilling to establish a rebut table presumption that such practices satisfied the underwriter's obligation (as underwriters has urged the SEC to do).

SECTION 7. POST-FILING REVIEW AND RESTRICTIONS

Statutes and Regulations

Securities Act, § 8.

Regulation C, Rules 459–463, 470–479; Form SR.

POST-FILING PROCESSING

If a security is required to be registered under the Securities Act of 1933, sales of the security are prohibited unless a registration statement as to such security[1] is "in effect." The registration statement becomes effective on "the twentieth day after the filing thereof,"[2] unless it is the subject of a refusal order[3] or stop order[4] by the Commission or unless it is made effective sooner (i.e., "accelerated") by the Commission.[5]

This statutory scheme originally contemplated that in the usual case the registration statement would be filed; it would be reviewed by the Commission and information about the issue disseminated during the 20–day "waiting period"; and the Statement would become effective at the end of 20 days and the offering then commenced. This is not the way that it has worked out at all, for several reasons.

Delaying Amendments. During the early history of the Commission, it was possible for issues as to which there were no unusual problems to become effective in the basic 20 day period or even earlier. By an amendment to the statute in 1940, the Commission was given power not only to consent to the filing of all amendments "as of" the original filing, but also to shorten this basic period.[6] During this early era, many registrants statements were made effective in 15 to 18 days after the original filing.

---

1. Securities Act § 5(a).

2. Id. § 8(a).

3. Id. § 8(b).

4. Id. § 8(d).

5. Id. § 8(a).

6. 54 Stat. 857 (1940).

In the event that there were deficiencies in the registration statement which had not been corrected by amendment, and the 20 day period was about to expire, the Commission would generally suggest to the issuer that it file a "delaying amendment" to prevent the Statement "from becoming effective in deficient form," unless the Commission thought that the deficiencies were so serious as to warrant stop-order proceedings. Since any amendment, no matter how trivial, starts a new 20–day period running, such a delaying amendment consists merely of changing one word on the front cover of the Statement. The approximate date of the proposed public offering is required to be stated on the cover, and it is generally expressed in some such language as this: "As soon as practicable after the effective date of the Registration Statement." A delaying amendment consists, for example, of changing the word "practicable" to "possible." A second delaying amendment, if one is required, could consist of changing the word "possible" back to "practicable." Such an amendment can be filed under Rule 473 by telegram and later confirmed in writing.

The sort of timetable discussed above has become obsolete. Since the late 1950's, instead of getting the Commission's letter of comment within about 10 days after filing, there has been a delay of from one to three months before the letter was forthcoming. This delay has been due to a tremendous increase in the number of filings together with the failure of Congress to provide an adequate staff to the Commission to handle the work load. Consequently the possibility of becoming effective in the basic 20–day period originally set by Congress became practically nonexistent.

If the original filing is complete, an issuer could theoretically force a review by the Commission within the 20–day period by refusing to file a delaying amendment. The Commission will suggest that such an amendment be filed to "prevent the Statement from becoming effective in deficient form," even though no one at the Commission has yet looked at it or knows whether it is in deficient form or not. In order to eliminate the necessity of the issuer filing several of such amendments while waiting for the Commission to get around to reviewing the Statement, the Commission has adopted a rule (Rule 473) permitting what is in effect a permanent delaying amendment to be filed along with the original Statement.[7] Few issuers have been willing to confront the Commission by omitting this amendment.

Nonetheless, in Las Vegas Hawaiian Development Co. v. Securities and Exchange Commission,[8] a registrant did refuse to file a further delaying amendment after the SEC failed to declare a registration statement to be effective. Predictably, shortly before the registration would have become effective, the Commission responded by issuing an order authorizing its staff to conduct a '8(e) examination to determine whether a stop order proceeding under § 8(d) was necessary with respect to the proposed public offering. The registrant then filed a complaint in federal court for a declaratory judgment asserting that § 8(e) could not be used by the Commission "to delay indefinitely the sale of securities under an effective registration statement."

The practical effect of the Commission's order to conduct an examination pursuant to § 8(e) was to bring into operation § 5(c) of the 1933 Act which prohibits the use of interstate facilities to offer to sell securities "while the registration is the subject of * * * [prior to the effective date of the registra-

---

7. Securities Act Release No. 4329 (Feb. 21, 1961), amending Rule 473.

8. 466 F.Supp. 928 (D.Hawai'i 1979).

tion] any public proceeding or examination under § 8(e)." Accordingly, any sales activity concerning the registered securities was foreclosed by virtue of § 5(c).

The Commission contended that a § 8(e) examination was within the Commission's discretionary powers, that plaintiffs had not shown an abuse of discretion and that the authorization of a § 8(e) examination was not a final Commission action which was reviewable. However, the district court was unwilling to back the Commission this far. It wrote:

"While the SEC is given broad powers and wide discretion, provision is made for time limits, notices, hearings, appeals, and judicial reviews of actions that affect the issuance and sale of securities. It is not a sufficient answer to say that authorizing a section 8(e) examination is not a final Commission action, or to say that no one has a right to register securities for public sale. A registrant does have a right to have the Commission follow the applicable statutes and regulations, and attempts by the Commission to circumvent statutorily imposed time limits may be attacked in a judicial proceeding. See SEC v. Sloan, 436 U.S. 103 (1978)."

Yet Congress has not placed any time limitation on the duration of a section 8(e) examination. Nor is an order authorizing such an examination reviewable under section 9 of the Act. See Stardust, Inc. v. SEC, 225 F.2d 255 (9th Cir.1955). This leaves the registrant with whatever remedy may be had pursuant to the Administrative Procedure Act (APA).

In my opinion, a district court may, upon the petition of a registrant under the Securities Act of 1933, compel the SEC to make a determination within a reasonable time whether to notice a hearing on the issuance of a stop order under section 8(d), where the Commission has ordered an examination under section 8(e) prior to the effective date of a registration statement and the determination whether a stop order should issue has been unreasonably delayed.

The court may not compel the Commission to institute a section 8(d) proceeding. Crooker v. SEC, 161 F.2d 944 (1st Cir.1947). But the clear import of 5 U.S.C. § 706 is that the court may compel the SEC to either terminate a section 8(e) examination or institute a section 8(d) proceeding in a situation where the SEC's inaction has the effect of prohibiting the sale of registered securities, and when this determination has been unreasonably withheld.[9]

Nonetheless, the complaint was dismissed since it was not alleged that the Commission's determination whether to institute a § 8(d) proceeding had been unreasonably delayed within the intendment of § 706 of the Administrative Procedure Act. The Court also refused to place a limit on the § 8(e) examination which would have forestalled any inquiry into the circumstances surrounding the earlier land sales; the scope of such examinations was deemed to be a matter within the discretion of the Commission.

Although the case has not generated an attack upon the Commission's authority with respect to delaying amendments or acceleration of the effectiveness of registration statements, it does suggest that judicial review is available.

Entry Into the Exchange Act. After an initial public offering, company counsel should educate the corporate officers as to their ongoing responsibilities

---

9. 466 F.Supp. 928, 932.

as a public company under the federal securities laws, particularly the Exchange Act.

As a result of going public, an issuer becomes subject to the periodic reporting requirements of § 13 by virtue of § 15(d) of the Exchange Act. In all probability, the Company will also have to comply with the registration provisions of § 12. A registrant under the 1934 Act must comply with numerous provisions: the proxy rules (§ 14); recapture of short-swing profits (§ 16(b)); the beneficial ownership reporting requirements (§ 16(a)); restrictions on short sales (§ 16(c)); the tender offer and reporting provisions of the Williams Act (§§ 14(d) and (e) and §§ 13(d) and (e)); the Foreign Corrupt Practices Act (§ 13(b)(2)); and the obligation to furnish annual reports to shareholders (§ 14 and Rules 14a–6 and 14c–3). See Schneider and Shargel, "Now That You Are Publicly Owned * * * ", 36 Bus.Law. 1631 (1981).

Use of Proceeds. Under Rule 463, an issuer filing its first registration statement under the 1933 Act must file a report on Form SR, within ten days after the end of the first three-month period following the effective date of the registration statement, and at six month intervals thereafter, which report must set forth detailed information concerning the use and application of the proceeds of the offering. This filing obligation, which applies only to first-time registrants, continues until the later of the time at which the proceeds of the offering are fully applied or the offering is terminated. Essentially, Rule 463 is an anti-fraud protection, which allows the Commission to monitor whether proceeds have been applied in accordance with the prospectus.

Acceleration. The decision whether to grant the request for acceleration is actually made by the Director of the Division of Corporation Finance, to whom the Commission has delegated this power. Requests for acceleration must be made in writing by the registrant, the managing underwriters of the offering, and the selling security holders, if any, in compliance with other conditions specified in Rule 461. The conditions governing the granting of the acceleration are set forth in Rules 460 and 461.

To qualify for acceleration, the underwriter must make an adequate distribution of the preliminary prospectus to all dealers who are expected to participate in the proposed offering reasonably in advance of the anticipated effective date of the statement. Rule 15c2–8 requires that all brokers or dealers participating in the distribution take reasonable steps to furnish preliminary prospectuses to those who make a written request for copies. Copies must also be made available to each associated person who is expected to solicit customers' orders during the waiting period. Rule 460 specifies the information which the registrant must furnish to the Division of Corporation Finance in order to satisfy these requirements.

Refusal and Stop Orders. A refusal order under Section 8(b) is not generally employed by the Commission, since such an order requires the Commission to act within 10 days after the filing of the Registration Statement. At least in recent years, such quick action is not possible. Furthermore, the requirement in the case of a refusal order that the deficiencies be apparent "on the face" of the Statement might raise difficulties if the proceedings show that there are deficiencies, but there is an argument over whether they are so apparent. Since under Red Bank Oil Co., 20 S.E.C. 863 (1945), the stop order is equally available whenever a refusal order might be issued and it is not subject to either of these limitations, this is the type of proceeding normally instituted by the Commission. Instances in which the Commission has found it necessary to institute stop order proceedings have been relatively few in comparison to the large number of registration statements filed.[1]

Withdrawal of Registration Statement. A controversy long surrounded the asserted right of a registrant voluntarily to withdraw a registration statement prior to effectiveness, despite the opposition of the Securities and Exchange Commission based upon public interest considerations. SEC Rule 477 used to provide that a registration statement or any amendment or exhibit thereto could be withdrawn upon application of the registrant only if the Commission found such withdrawal consistent with the public interest and the protection of investors and consented thereto. This rule seemingly reversed the result in Jones v. SEC, 298 U.S. 1 (1936), in which the Supreme Court, in a sharply divided decision, sustained the right of a registrant to withdraw the registration statement prior to the effective date despite objections by the SEC. Because the registrant had not commenced business and there were no securities outstanding in the hands of the public, the Court saw no public interest issue involved in that case.

The validity of Rule 477 has been sustained in a number of cases, particularly when securities of the registrant are outstanding in the hands of the public at the time of the proposal to withdraw the registration statement.[2] Why did the SEC care if the registrant wished to call off the offering? The SEC's concern seemingly was that it would remain possible for the registrant to resort to Regulation A or some other exemption and capitalize upon its prior sales effort, thereby defeating the investor's right to public disclosure from a registration statement.

Nonetheless, in early 2001, the SEC revised Rule 477 so that an issuer's application to withdraw a pre-effective registration statement becomes effective upon filing, unless the Commission objects within 15 days after such filing.[3] This revision still permits the Commission to halt what it suspects is an attempt to substitute a fraudulent exempt offering for a public offering, but it also enables the issuer to control timing in most cases. The importance of this change for the issuer is that it thereby reduces the prospect that a later offering will be "integrated" with the prior public offering (and thereby forfeit its exempt status). This problem of the "integration" of offerings is considered further in Chapter 8 in connection with the discussion of the SEC's new Rule 155.

SECTION 8.   REGULATION OF UNDERWRITERS AND THE DISTRIBUTION PROCESS

Statutes and Regulations

Securities Act, § 8.

Regulation M, Rules 460, 461.

1. But see McLucas, Stop Order Proceedings Under the Securities Act of 1933: A Current Assessment, 40 Bus. Law. 515 (1985) (indicating an increasing use of this device).

2. See Columbia General Investment Corp. v. SEC, 265 F.2d 559 (5th Cir.1959);

Wolf Corp. v. SEC, 115 U.S.App.D.C. 75, 317 F.2d 139 (1963).

3. Securities Act Release No. 7943 (January 26, 2001).

To this point, this Chapter has focused primarily on the issuer. But underwriters are also closely regulated during the distribution process by both the SEC and NASD (as well as state blue sky commissioners—to the extent that their jurisdiction is not preempted).

A. *NASD Review of Underwriters' Compensation*

The National Association of Securities Dealers (and also some state securities administrators) review and limit the amount of compensation which underwriters may receive in connection with a public offering. The NASD's review is premised on its Rules of Fair Practice, which require its members to comply with the "high standards of commercial honor and just and equitable principles of trade."[4] Based on these principles, the NASD has promulgated NASD Conduct Rule 2710, which elaborately specifies the information that the NASD will consider in reviewing underwriter compensation.[5] The NASD reads its rule to entitle it to reject any offering in which "unfair or unreasonable compensation" will be paid to any of its members. But what's unfair or unreasonable about compensation that the issuer and the underwriter are able to negotiate between themselves? As a practical matter, abuses have chiefly arisen in the case of unseasoned companies that find it difficult to enter the public market and are willing to pay high compensation to any underwriter willing to handle their securities. In such cases, some underwriting firms seek additional compensation in the form of "cheap stock" (i.e., stock purchased below the market or offering price) or warrants to purchase its stock in the future. The fear may be that an overcompensated underwriter (particularly in a best efforts offering) will overreach its customers in order to obtain the excessive compensation. Given this fear, it becomes understandable that certain high-quality offerings, such as shelf-registered offerings on Form S–3 and certain debt offerings, are exempt from NASD review.

Procedurally, the managing underwriter files the underwriting documents and the prospectus with NASD, where a Committee on Corporate Financing (whose membership is kept secret) reviews it.[6] Although few clear guidelines exist as to what constitutes "unreasonable" compensation in the NASD's eyes, an underwriter may not (1) purchase securities of the issuer at a price significantly below the offering price within a twelve-month period before the offering; (2) receive warrants to purchase issuer securities in excess of ten percent of the securities to be offered or warrants having an exercise price below the offering price or a maturity in excess of five years; (3) obtain an over-allotment option exceeding fifteen percent of the offering; or (4) sell warrants or stock received from the issuer as compensation until one year after the offering is completed.

The guidelines on overall compensation are vaguer, but commentators suspect that the NASD has long used a rule of thumb that compensation should not exceed fifteen percent of the offering amount in a "best efforts" offering of under $15 million, and that this ceiling on underwriter compensation declines as the size of the offering increases and in the case of a "fixed price" offering. Empirically, for offerings in the $10 million range, underwriter compensation

---

4. See NASD Rules of Fair Practice, Article III, Section 1.

5. See Securities Exchange Act Release No. 34–42619 (April 4, 2000) (containing latest revisions to rule).

6. For a discussion of this process, see Current Problems of Securities Underwriters and Dealers, 18 Bus.Law. 27, at 45–48 (1962).

averages eleven percent of the offering amount.[7] Violations of the NASD's rules on compensation can result in disciplinary sanctions.[8]

B. *Hot Issues: Oversubscription and the Problem of Asymmetric Information.*

During the waiting period, the underwriters will often learn that demand for the offering far outstrips supply. At the contemplated offering price, they may be able to sell not 5,000,000 shares, but 8,000,000. The practical implication of this information is that the secondary market price should rise, because the allocation to many of those who wished to purchase in the offering will be cut back and this unsatisfied demand will likely cause the secondary market price to jump from the outset of the offering. Of course, the underwriters could raise the offering price—until supply and demand balance. But this would make it more difficult for them to market the stock and would deny their investor clients the expected first day appreciation.

An alternative course is for the underwriters (or some of them) to exploit this information that demand exceeds the supply by themselves subscribing for a significant portion of their own allotment—in effect, jumping in front of their clients based on their possession of non-public information that the offering is oversubscribed. In turn, this further reduction of the supply available to public investors will aggravate the supply/demand imbalance and make it even more likely that the secondary market price will immediately rise. Alternatively, an underwriter in possession of this knowledge may sell portions of its allotment to its partners, officers, employees or friendly parties with whom it engages in reciprocal business transactions.

Both the SEC and the NASD have long objected to such practices. In the SEC's view, the statement in the registration statement that the securities will be offered to the public at the public offering price amounts to a representation, which would become materially false if most shares were withheld for underwriters, insider, or their affiliates.[9] Thus, the issuer needs to make a bona fide offering to the public in order to avoid a material misrepresentation.

The NASD views the underwriter as a conduit through whom securities in an underwritten offering should freely pass in their transmission from the issuer to the public. Under its fair practices rules, the NASD insists that the underwriter not siphon off securities intended for the public to itself, its affiliates, or other allies, based on its knowledge that the offering is oversubscribed.[10] The NASD's rules apply not only to withholding of securities by underwriters but also by their employees for themselves or their families.[11] Based on this view of the underwriter as performing a service as a fiduciary, the NASD also does not permit the underwriter to raise the primary offering price if during the course of the distribution the secondary market price rises

---

7. See H. Bloomenthal, 3A Securities and Federal Corporate Law § 6.20; Frome, Proposed NASD Curbs on Underwriters Compensation, N.Y.L.J. at 3 (Jan. 31, 1989).

8. See, e.g., In the Matter of Application of May & Co., Inc., Fed.Sec.L.Rep. (CCH) Para. 77,904 (Sept. 8, 1970).

9. See Sec. Act Rel. No. 4150 (Oct. 23, 1959).

10. See Free–Riding and Withholding, NASD Interpretations of the Board of Governors, NASD Manual (IM–2110–1); see also NASD Conduct Rule 2110.

11. See also, *In re First Philadelphia Corp.* [1991 Transfer Binder] Fed.Sec.L.Rep. (CCH) Para. 84,841 (1990) (sale of shares in oversubscribed offering to family member to hold in custodial account for broker's son violates NASD fair practice rule).

above that price. In effect, this built-in profit must go to the subscribing investors. Although there is no private cause of action available to plaintiffs for violation of NASD or NYSE rules, arbitration panels have awarded punitive damages and substantial compensatory damages where stock in a hot IPO offering has been allocated to affiliates of the underwriter in violation of these rules.[12]

Other issues and potential abuses surround the allocation of an oversubscribed "hot issue." Some customers may place an order with an underwriter for stock in an IPO, intending to purchase only if the stock price rises in the immediate aftermarket. If the price does not rise, they will decline to purchase the stock allocated to them (as they are legally entitled to do given that a binding sale cannot be consummated under § 5(a) prior to the time of effectiveness). This practice (known as "free riding") can, however, be seen as a violation of Rule 10b–5 if the prospective purchaser represented that it intended to buy; nonetheless, it is seldom prosecuted (even civilly) in the case of investors.

When an offering is oversubscribed, powerful institutional buyers (e.g. mutual funds and pension funds) may also insist that their desired allocation not be cut back (but instead that public investors bear the brunt of the rationing). These institutions may threaten not to participate in future offerings of the lead underwriter for a defined period (the so-called "penalty box") if they do not receive their full allocation. Although the SEC would like to ensure that some stock is distributed to public investors in any public offering, SEC rules still permit the underwriters great discretion in allocating stock in oversubscribed offering. Predictably, this means that those with the least leverage get cut back the most. However, the SEC and the NASD have imposed stiff penalties when underwriters seek to charge higher brokerage commissions to those willing to pay a premium in order to receive scarce allocations in hot IPOs. In early 2002, the SEC and NASD settled charges against Credit Suisse First Boston Corporation, a major underwriter, relating to latter's IPO allocation practices for total fines plus disgorgement of $100 million.[13] The central charge in this litigation was that the defendant underwriter exploited its privileged position by allocating shares in very hot IPOs to institutional customers willing to pay "excessive" brokerage commissions, thereby "extracting" from these customers between one third and two thirds of their trading gains from these IPOs.[14]

Another abuse has been "spinning": the deliberate allocation by an underwriter of "hot issue" shares in the offering of one issuer to the officers and directors of another issuer to obtain their future business.[15] This practice may also violate the NASD's Free–Riding and Withholding Interpretation, but no definitive decision has yet been reached.

---

12. See *Sanders v. Gardner*, 7 F.Supp.2d 151 (E.D.N.Y.1998) (upholding arbitration panel award of punitive damages for violation of "free-riding" rule).

13. See SEC Litigation Release No. 17327 (January 22, 2002), 2002 SEC LEXIS 147.

14. The SEC NASD asserted that these practices violated NASD conduct Rules 2110 and 2330 and also Section 17(a)(1) of the Securities Act.

15. See NASD Sends Members Warning Concerning Allocation of Hot IPOs, (BNA) Sec. Reg. & Law Rep., Vol. 29, no. 47, at p. 1667 (1998).

D. *The SEC's Trading Rules.*

When the issuer has had prior offerings and its stock is traded in the secondary market, the offering price in a primary offering will normally be its trading price in the secondary market. This price could be inflated, however, if the underwriters were to undertake significant purchases of the issuer's stock in the period immediately prior to the offering. Even in the case of an initial public offering, the offering's success would be greatly assisted if the issuer or underwriters (or agents of either) were to buy the stock in the secondary market after the primary offering commenced in order to cause the secondary market price to rise about the fixed price in the offering. Purchases in both contexts are inherently suspicious, because the buyer's intent may be to manipulate the price of the stock to assure the success of the offering. For this reason, the SEC has long restricted the ability of issuers and underwriters to buy what they are selling during a distribution. For many years, this restriction was embodied in Rule 10b–6, but in 1997, the SEC codified a series of trading rules in new Regulation M.

Rule 101 of Regulation M focuses on (i) underwriters, (ii) brokers or dealers who have agreed to participate or who are participating in a distribution of securities, and (iii) "affiliated purchasers," which term includes those acting in concert with the above persons or who control of any participant in the distribution.[16] Such persons are prohibited from making purchases or bids during a "distribution" until they have completed their participation in the distribution. Rule 101's prohibition applies during a "restricted period" which depends on the trading volume associated with the security. When a security has an average daily trading volume ("ADTV") of $100,000 or more and its issuer has a public float of $20 million or more,[17] Rule 100 specifies that the restricted period begins one business day prior to the determination of the offering price (or such later time when the person becomes a distribution participant). Otherwise, the restricted period begins on the later of five business days prior to the determination of the offering price or the date on which the person becomes a distribution participant. Rule 101 grants an exemption from these restrictions for certain "excepted securities", including securities having an ADTV of at least $1 million and a public float of $150 million. In these "excepted" cases, although Regulation M does not bar a broker-dealer from purchasing or bidding for the security during the distribution, it is still open to the Commission or a private party to seek to prove a manipulative intent in violation of Rule 10b–5.

Rule 102 applies similar prohibitions to the issuer, selling shareholders, and their affiliates, and Rule 103 provides an exception for "passive" market making on NASDAQ. This permits an underwriter to make a secondary market in the stock so long as it does not bid for or purchase the stock at a price that exceeds the highest independent bid.

It is important to understand that Regulation M applies broadly to any "distribution," which term is defined by Rule 100 to cover "an offering of securities, whether or not subject to regulation under the Securities Act, that is distinguished from ordinary trading transactions by the magnitude of the offering and the presence of special selling efforts and selling methods."

---

16. See 17 C.F.R. 242.101 ("Activities by distribution participants").

17. "Float" refers to the value of the stock held by public investors (i.e. non-insiders or "affiliates").

Conceivably, an attempt by a large, but non-controlling, shareholder to liquidate its substantial stake (say 15%) could amount to a "distribution" and thus make Regulation M applicable, even though registration of the securities was not required.

E.   *Stabilization.*

The underwriters' great fear during a distribution is that the secondary market price will fall below the offering price. This could be the result of (1) exogenous changes in the outside world (i.e., some surprise announcement of unexpected news), (2) a loss of confidence in the offering by short-term oriented investors ("flippers") who hoped for immediate stock appreciation in the first hours of the offering and were disappointed, or (3) the activities of short sellers (who want the aftermarket price to fall once they have made substantial short sales). To guard principally against the latter two possibilities, the underwriting group typically attempts to place a floor under the secondary market price during the period of the distribution by placing a standing offer to buy all stock offered in the market at below the offering price. This is called "stabilizing" the stock (i.e., the fixing of a security market's price through purchases or bids at the offering price in order to preclude or retard any decline in the price during the distribution). Stabilization had long been permitted within certain defined boundaries by a special rule (Rule 10b–7), which has now been codified in Regulation M as Rule 104.

Rule 104 is both an exception to Rule 101 (which broadly forbids purchases and bids during a distribution) and a safe harbor that protects the underwriter from any claim that it has "manipulated" the stock's price. Section 9(a)(6) of the Exchange Act prohibits "pegging, fixing, or stabilizing the price" of a security in contravention of the SEC's rules. Thus, by complying with Rule 104, the underwriter avoids liability under § 9(a)(6) and Rule 10b–5. Under Rule 104, underwriters can bid for the stock so long as they do not exceed the lower of the offering price or "last independent transaction price for the security in the principal market."[18] Thus, if the offering price is $100 and the secondary market price rises to $102, the underwriters may not stabilize (i.e. peg the price) at this level. Stabilizing is also forbidden in an "at-the-market offering."[19]

Stabilizing activities can be suspended at any time and will typically be halted once the distribution is completed (i.e., once all allotments have been sold by the underwriters). In effect, this means that the floor placed under the stock's price can suddenly be removed, and the stock's price, which had seemed stable, can suddenly nose dive at the end of the offering day. For this reason, sophisticated investors may be leery of the offering if the price does not immediately rise in the aftermarket, because a stable aftermarket price is often illusory (as it is being artificially and temporarily maintained by the underwriters).

F.   *Short Selling.*

Public offerings have proven an inviting target for short sellers. Sometimes acting in concert, they sell the stock in large quantities on or before the offering

---

18.   See Rule 104(f)(2).

19.   See Rule 104(e). "At-the-market" offerings have no fixed offering price and simply sell to investors at the then current secondary market price.

date in order to drive the price down and cover at the lower price. Although stabilizing purchases by the underwriters may offset these short sales, the underwriters will usually cease "stabilizing" the market once they have sold their allotments. Thus, the price may decline immediately thereafter as the market maker responds to the imbalance of sales and purchases.

What makes a public offering a special target for short selling? A possible answer is that short sellers can uniquely protect themselves in this context from the normal risk that the stock price may rise in the aftermarket, which would force them to cover at a loss. They can do so by subscribing to shares in the offering at the offering price. Of course, this is another example of "free riding" because they may intend to purchase the offered shares only if the aftermarket price rises. (If it falls, they will either renege or buy them at a depressed price below the offering price). As a result, short sellers could view primary offerings as presenting them with a "can't lose" opportunity. In response, underwriters lobbied the SEC for protection, and in the 1990s, the Commission adopted Rule 10b–22, which has now been codified in Regulation M as Rule 105. Rule 105 does not forbid short selling in connection with a public offering, but rather prohibits any person from covering "a short sale with offered securities purchased from an underwriter or broker or dealer participating in the offering" if the short sale occurred within a prescribed period that will normally begin five business days before the pricing of the offered security and end with the pricing of the security. This rule does not apply to shelf registrations (where the market is believed to be too deep for short selling to have much effect) or best efforts underwritings (where there tends not to be any fixed offering price). Although Rule 105 chills short selling on the eve of a public offering, it has proven difficult to enforce because of the difficulty of detection, and some public offerings remain plagued by short selling campaigns.

SECTION 9.   PENNY STOCKS AND BLANK CHECK OFFERINGS

Although the federal securities laws are based on a disclosure philosophy that assumes that informed investors can protect themselves and thus do not authorize the SEC to engage in the same "merits review" of the offering that many state securities regulators conduct,[1] a clear exception to this pattern was passed by Congress in 1990 to deal with what are termed "blank check" offerings. In the Securities Enforcement Remedies and Penny Stock Reform Act of 1990,[2] Congress found that "blank check" registration had "been used extensively for abusive and fraudulent practices in the penny stock market."[3]

---

1. Thirty-six states use "merit review" powers to protect investors from abusive practices in "blank check" offerings. See National Association of Securities Administrators' Report on Fraud and Abuse in the Penny Stock Market (1989). Some states wholly preclude such offerings, while others mandate the use of escrow funds and special reporting procedures as to the use of proceeds of the offering.

2. P.L. 101–429, 104 Stat. 931, Tit. V. (1990). This legislation also amended the 1934 Act for the purpose of "curbing the pervasive fraud and manipulation in the penny stock market." House Comm. on Energy and Commerce, Penny Stock Reform Act of 1990, H.R.Rep. 101–617, 101st Cong., 2d Sess., at 7 (1990). The 1934 Act provisions regarding secondary market trading in penny stocks are considered infra in Chapter 8 at pages 513–514.

3. Id. at 22.

As the name implies, "blank check" offerings involved newly formed companies without a preexisting history or assets; the investor is thus asked to trust the promoter (i.e., to write it a blank check) to use the offering proceeds to acquire virtually any kind of assets that the promoter considers attractive. Indeed, because the promoter often has no specific business plans, there is relatively little to disclose (other than the promoter's prior history and the obvious risks in such an offering). Not infrequently, the secondary market in such stocks was manipulated by the promoter to give the impression of a rising stock price, even though the proceeds of the offering were not re-invested or were actually diverted into the promoter's own pockets.

In response, the 1990 legislation directed the SEC to prescribe specific rules applicable to such "blank check" offerings. Under new Section 7(b) of the 1933 Act, the Commission may require such issuers to (1) provide additional disclosures, both before and after the registration statement is declared effective, (2) place limitations on the use of the proceeds obtained in such an offering and on the distribution of the securities sold, and (3) provide a right of rescission to shareholders.

Section 7(b) applies only to registration statements filed by issuers that are "blank check companies," which term is defined by § 7(b)(3) to mean "any development stage company that is issuing a penny stock * * * and that * * * (A) has no specific business plan or purpose; or (B) has indicated that its business plan is to merge with an unidentified company or companies." The term "penny stock" is then defined by new § 3(a)(51) of the Exchange Act to include any equity security other than a security registered on a national securities exchange or authorized for quotation on NASDAQ. In order to prevent evasion, subsection (B) of § 3(a)(51) also grants to the Commission the authority to designate as a penny stock any security that is registered on an exchange or quoted on NASDAQ, if trading in the security also occurs outside the exchanges or in the non-NASDAQ over-the-counter market. The fear is that once registered on an exchange, or quoted on NASDAQ "most of the trading activity may be directed to the non-NASDAQ over-the-counter market, where a lack of trading or quotation information, higher spreads and markups, and other factors may operate to the disadvantage of public investors."[4] Aside from exchange and NASDAQ traded securities, the section excludes from the definition of a penny stock the securities of investment companies registered under the Investment Company Act of 1940 and any security which the Commission excludes on the basis of exceeding a minimum price, net tangible assets of the issuer, or other relevant criteria.[5]

An important distinction is intended by § 7(b) between what are known as "blind pool" offerings and "blank check" offerings, and § 7(b) does not reach the former. A "blind pool" offering may raise funds to acquire still unidentified

4. H.R.Rep. 101–617, supra note 2, at 15.

5. The SEC has issued proposed 1934 Act regulations for penny stocks. See Securities Exchange Act Release No. 29093 (Apr. 17, 1991) [1990–1991 Transfer Binder] Fed. Sec.L.Rep. (CCH) ¶ 84,727, at 81,449. Rule 3a51–1 defines penny stock to exclude securities that are priced at five dollars or more. The five dollar figure is derived from 1934 Act Rule 15c2–6 and is intended to include as penny stocks "only those low-priced securities that * * * are the most susceptible to fraudulent sales practices." Id. at 81,461. The five dollar number is also the figure used in the Uniform Limited Offering Registration ("ULOR"), which provides a short-form registration procedure at the state level for offerings of less than $1,000,000 exempt from registration under Rule 504 of Regulation D.

assets (for example, real estate investments in a specific market), but so long as there is a "specific business plan" (i.e. to operate motels or suburban garden apartments according to some operating criteria), the issuer is exempt from the "blank check" designation under § 7(b)(3)(A).

What is most distinctive about § 7(b) is the substantive authority it confers upon the Commission to regulate the use of proceeds and to provide investors with a continuing right of rescission (on terms to be specified by the SEC). This authority closely resembles the merit authority exercised by state blue sky commissioners. To date, the Commission has given every indication that it means to use this authority aggressively. In 1991, the Commission proposed for comment Rule 419 to govern 1933 Act registration statements relating to an offering by a blank check company.[6] The Commission summarized the proposed rule this way:[7]

> "[P]roposed new Securities Act Rule 419 would require funds received and securities issued in an offering of penny stock by a blank check company to be placed in an escrow or trust account ('Rule 419 Account') until specified conditions have been met. These conditions would include the filing of a post-effective amendment upon the consummation of an acquisition if the business or assets being acquired met specified criteria. Purchasers would have the opportunity to have their deposited funds (less certain withdrawals) returned upon receipt of the prospectus describing the acquisition. If these conditions had not been met within 18 months, the funds would be required to be returned to the purchaser.
>
> To further achieve the purposes of the legislation, the Commission also proposes for comment new Exchange Act Rule 15g–8, which would prevent trading of securities of a blank check company held in the Rule 419 Account. Finally, Securities Act Rule 174 would be amended to provide that the statutory prospectus delivery period would not terminate until 90 days following the release of the blank check company's securities from the Rule 419 Account."

In addition, the proposed Exchange Act rules (Rules 15g–1 through 15g–7 and Schedule 15G) provide for a risk disclosure document, require monthly customer account statements with respect to penny stocks held for customers, and mandate special continuing disclosures as to compensation, market quotations, and whether the broker-dealer is acting as the sole market maker in the security. If the experience of this type of aggressive regulation at the state level is indicative, it is likely that the number of blank check offerings coming to market will be greatly diminished.[8]

---

6. Securities Act Release No. 6891 (Apr. 17, 1991) [1990–1991 Transfer Binder] Fed. Sec.L.Rep. (CCH) ¶ 84,728.

7. Id. at 81,503.

8. See House Comm. on Energy and Commerce, Penny Stock Reform Act of 1990, H.R.Rep. 101–617, 101st Cong., 2d Sess., at 19.

CHAPTER 4

DEFINITIONS OF "SECURITY" AND "EXEMPTED SECURITIES"

SECTION 1.   WHAT IS A "SECURITY"?

Statute

Securities Act, § 2(a)(1).

A.   "INVESTMENT CONTRACT"

DEFINITION OF A "SECURITY": A STUDY IN STATUTORY INTERPRETATION

Securities Act § 2(a)(1) and Exchange Act § 3(a)(10) each define a "security" in both specific and more general terms. Thus, there is not a single test for determining what constitutes a security; there is first a specific test, followed by a more general test. The purpose of the two-part test was "to include within the definition the many types of instruments that in our commercial world fall within the ordinary concept of a security."[1]

The list of specific instruments include any "note," "stock," "bond," and "debenture."

The general catch-all phrases include within the statutory definition instruments of a more variable character such as any "evidence of indebtedness," "certificate of interest or participation in any profit-sharing agreement," "investment contract" and any "instrument commonly known as a 'security.'"

Both the specific and the general definitions in the Securities Acts apply "unless the context otherwise requires." Thus, although an instrument may be presumed to fall into any of the statutory definitions of a security, it nevertheless may not be held to be a security under the federal securities laws if the context otherwise requires.

In Securities and Exchange Commission v. C.M. Joiner Leasing Corporation,[2] the Supreme Court for the first time considered the application of the

---

1.   H.R.Rep. No. 85, 73 Cong., 1st Sess.   11 (1933).

2.   320 U.S. 344 (1943).

statute to the sale of interests in oil and gas leases coupled with the promise by the seller to drill test wells so located as to discover the oil-producing possibilities of the surrounding land. Justice Jackson noted that the definition was similar to that found in many state "Blue Sky" laws and considered what rules of statutory construction might serve to ascertain the legislative intent. In rejecting the argument that the Act should be strictly construed, he stated:[3]

> In the Securities Act the term "security" was defined to include by name or description many documents in which there is common trading for speculation or investment. Some, such as notes, bonds, and stocks, are pretty much standardized and the name alone carries well-settled meaning. Others are of more variable character and were necessarily designated by more descriptive terms, such as "transferable share," "investment contract," and "in general any interest or instrument commonly known as a security." We cannot read out of the statute these general descriptive designations merely because more specific ones have been used to reach some kinds of documents. Instruments may be included within any of these definitions, as a matter of law, if on their face they answer to the name or description. However, the reach of the Act does not stop with the obvious and commonplace. Novel, uncommon, or irregular devices, whatever they appear to be, are also reached if it be proved as [a] matter of fact that they were widely offered or dealt in under terms or courses of dealing which established their character in commerce as "investment contracts," or as "any interest or instrument commonly known as a 'security.'"

In applying the two tests for the security under § 2(a)(1) to the facts, Justice Jackson first applied the specific instruments test to determine whether the oil leasehold interests were included within the specifically designated instruments. Obviously, the list of specific instruments did not include divided interests in oil and gas. He therefore proceeded to the second test by considering the terms of a more variable character, specifically "investment contract." Noting that the leasehold interests were sold on the condition that the purchasers would share in any appreciation in value of their lease interests if oil were discovered on adjacent land, Justice Jackson concluded that these leaseholds constituted "investment contracts," and therefore were "securities."

In recent years, some federal courts, engaging in an extreme form of judicial activism, reversed this process and began to apply the test for "investment contracts" declared by the Supreme Court in SEC v. W.J. Howey Co.,[4] to specific instruments expressly enumerated in the statutory definition of a security. These courts found that the "context otherwise requires" that certain specifically enumerated instruments should be deemed to be non-securities, thereby placing such securities outside the purview of the statute. Furthermore, these courts seized upon the "economic reality" test, a test formulated to "afford the investing public a full measure of protection," and converted it into an exception to the definition of a security, thereby narrowing the scope of the statute.[5] The result was to stand the statute on its head and deprive investors of the registration, disclosure and antifraud provisions of the Securities Acts.

---

3. Id. 350–51.

4. 328 U.S. 293 (1946), infra at page 308.

5. See e.g. Judge Posner's opinion in Sutter v. Groen, 687 F.2d 197 (7th Cir.1982).

For a criticism, see Cohen, Posnerian Jurisprudence and Economic Analysis of Law: The View from the Bench, 133 U.Pa.L.Rev. 1117, 1133–34 (1985). Compare Judge Friendly's opinion in The Exchange Nat. Bank of Chicago v. Touche Ross & Co., 544 F.2d 1126 (2d

This novel doctrine of statutory construction produced a flood of cases holding that "notes" and "stock" were non-securities in the particular context on the basis that "economic realities" justified reinterpreting the scope of the statute. As Judge Cardamone remarked, "Like modern day beachcombers with 'finders' rods seeking treasure beneath the sand, circuit courts cull through Supreme Court decisions in search of a phrase to fortify their view of how 'security' is defined under the acts."[6] And after surveying the law in this area, Judge Hill concluded that "in the end one is left with the impression that he is dealing with an area of the law subject to wide variations, serious anomalies, and judicial disagreement, if not confusion. In short, the wealth of judicial writings on the subject has produced few discernible principles of decision."[7]

The following cases provide an interesting study in statutory interpretation.

Securities & Exchange Commission v. W. J. Howey Co.

Supreme Court of the United States, 1946.
328 U.S. 293, 66 S.Ct. 1100, 90 L.Ed. 1244.

■ MR. JUSTICE MURPHY delivered the opinion of the Court.

This case involves the application of § 2(a)(1) of the Securities Act of 1933 to an offering of units of a citrus grove development coupled with a contract for cultivating, marketing and remitting the net proceeds to the investor.

The Securities and Exchange Commission instituted this action to restrain the respondents from using the mails and instrumentalities of interstate commerce in the offer and sale of unregistered and non-exempt securities in violation of § 5(a) of the Act. The District Court denied the injunction, * * * and the Fifth Circuit Court of Appeals affirmed the judgment * * *. We granted certiorari * * *.

* * * The respondents, W. J. Howey Company and Howey-in-the-Hills Service, Inc., are Florida corporations under direct common control and management. The Howey Company owns large tracts of citrus acreage in Lake County, Florida. During the past several years it has planted about 500 acres annually, keeping half of the groves itself and offering the other half to the public "to help us finance additional development." Howey-in-the-Hills Service, Inc., is a service company engaged in cultivating and developing many of these groves, including the harvesting and marketing of the crops.

Each prospective customer is offered both a land sales contract and a service contract, after having been told that it is not feasible to invest in a grove unless service arrangements are made. While the purchaser is free to make arrangements with other service companies, the superiority of Howey-in-the-Hills Service, Inc., is stressed. Indeed, 85% of the acreage sold during the 3–year period ending May 31, 1943, was covered by service contracts with Howey-in-the-Hills Service, Inc.

Cir.1976), and Judge Gibbons opinion in Ruefenacht v. O'Halloran, 737 F.2d 320 (3d Cir. 1984), aff'd 471 U.S. 701 (1985).

6. Seagrave Corp. v. Vista Resources, 696 F.2d 227, 229 (2d Cir.1982), cert. dismissed by consent, 468 U.S. 1226 (1984); Arnold, "When is a Car a Bicycle?" and Oth-er Riddles: The Definition of a Security Under the Federal Securities Laws, 33 Clev. St.L.Rev. 448, 483 (1984–85).

7. Van Huss v. Associated Milk Producers, Inc., 415 F.Supp. 356 (N.D.Tex.1976).

The land sales contract with the Howey Company provides for a uniform purchase price per acre or fraction thereof, varying in amount only in accordance with the number of years the particular plot has been planted with citrus trees. Upon full payment of the purchase price the land is conveyed to the purchaser by warranty deed. Purchases are usually made in narrow strips of land arranged so that an acre consists of a row of 48 trees. During the period between February 1, 1941, and May 31, 1943, 31 of the 42 persons making purchases bought less than 5 acres each. The average holding of these 31 persons was 1.33 acres and sales of as little as 0.65, 0.7 and 0.73 of an acre were made. These tracts are not separately fenced and the sole indication of several ownership is found in small land marks intelligible only through a plat book record.

The service contract, generally of a 10–year duration without option of cancellation, gives Howey-in-the-Hills Service, Inc., a leasehold interest and "full and complete" possession of the acreage. For a specified fee plus the cost of labor and materials, the company is given full discretion and authority over the cultivation of the groves and the harvest and marketing of the crops. The company is well established in the citrus business and maintains a large force of skilled personnel and a great deal of equipment, including 75 tractors, sprayer wagons, fertilizer trucks and the like. Without the consent of the company, the land owner or purchaser has no right of entry to market the crop; thus there is ordinarily no right to specific fruit. The company is accountable only for an allocation of the net profits based upon a check made at the time of picking. All the produce is pooled by the respondent companies, which do business under their own names.

The purchasers for the most part are non-residents of Florida. They are predominantly business and professional people who lack the knowledge, skill and equipment necessary for the care and cultivation of citrus trees. They are attracted by the expectation of substantial profits. * * * Many of these purchasers are patrons of a resort hotel owned and operated by the Howey Company in a scenic section adjacent to the groves. The hotel's advertising mentions the fine groves in the vicinity and the attention of the patrons is drawn to the groves as they are being escorted about the surrounding countryside. They are told that the groves are for sale; if they indicate an interest in the matter they are then given a sales talk.

It is admitted that the mails and instrumentalities of interstate commerce are used in the sale of the land and service contracts and that no registration statement or letter of notification has ever been filed with the Commission in accordance with the Securities Act of 1933 and the rules and regulations thereunder.

Section 2(a)(1) of the Act defines the term "security" to include the commonly known documents traded for speculation or investment. This definition also includes "securities" of a more variable character, designated by such descriptive terms as "certificate of interest or participation in any profit-sharing agreement," "investment contract" and "in general, any interest or instrument commonly known as a 'security.'" The legal issue in this case turns upon a determination of whether, under the circumstances, the land sales contract, the warranty deed and the service contract together constitute an "investment contract" within the meaning of § 2(a)(1) * * *.

The term "investment contract" is undefined by the Securities Act or by relevant legislative reports. But the term was common in many state "blue sky" laws in existence prior to the adoption of the federal statute and, although the term was also undefined by the state laws, it had been broadly construed by state courts so as to afford the investing public a full measure of protection. Form was disregarded for substance and emphasis was placed upon economic reality. An investment contract thus came to mean a contract or scheme for "the placing of capital or laying out of money in a way intended to secure income or profit from its employment." State v. Gopher Tire & Rubber Co., 146 Minn. 52, 56, 177 N.W. 937, 938. This definition was uniformly applied by state courts to a variety of situations where individuals were led to invest money in a common enterprise with the expectation that they would earn a profit solely through the efforts of the promoter or of some one other than themselves.

By including an investment contract within the scope of § 2(a)(1) of the Securities Act, Congress was using a term the meaning of which had been crystallized by this prior judicial interpretation. It is therefore reasonable to attach that meaning to the term as used by Congress, especially since such a definition is consistent with the statutory aims. In other words, an investment contract for purposes of the Securities Act means a contract, transaction or scheme whereby a person invests his money in a common enterprise and is led to expect profits solely from the efforts of the promoter or a third party, it being immaterial whether the shares in the enterprise are evidenced by formal certificates or by nominal interests in the physical assets employed in the enterprise. Such a definition necessarily underlies this Court's decision in S.E.C. v. Joiner Corp., 320 U.S. 344, and has been enunciated and applied many times by lower federal courts. It permits the fulfillment of the statutory purpose of compelling full and fair disclosure relative to the issuance of "the many types of instruments that in our commercial world fall within the ordinary concept of a security." H.Rep. No. 85, 73d Cong., 1st Sess., p. 11. It embodies a flexible rather than a static principle, one that is capable of adaptation to meet the countless and variable schemes devised by those who seek the use of the money of others on the promise of profits.

The transactions in this case clearly involve investment contracts as so defined. The respondent companies are offering something more than fee simple interests in land, something different from a farm or orchard coupled with management services. They are offering an opportunity to contribute money and to share in the profits of a large citrus fruit enterprise managed and partly owned by respondents. They are offering this opportunity to persons who reside in distant localities and who lack the equipment and experience requisite to the cultivation, harvesting and marketing of the citrus products. Such persons have no desire to occupy the land or to develop it themselves; they are attracted solely by the prospects of a return on their investment. Indeed, individual development of the plots of land that are offered and sold would seldom be economically feasible due to their small size. Such tracts gain utility as citrus groves only when cultivated and developed as component parts of a larger area. A common enterprise managed by respondents or third parties with adequate personnel and equipment is therefore essential if the investors are to achieve their paramount aim of a return on their investments. Their respective shares in this enterprise are evidenced by land sales contracts and warranty deeds, which serve as a convenient method of determining the investors' allocable shares of the profits. The resulting transfer of rights in land is purely incidental.

Thus all the elements of a profit-seeking business venture are present here. The investors provide the capital and share in the earnings and profits; the promoters manage, control and operate the enterprise. It follows that the arrangements whereby the investors' interests are made manifest involve investment contracts, regardless of the legal terminology in which such contracts are clothed. The investment contracts in this instance take the form of land sales contracts, warranty deeds and service contracts which respondents offer to prospective investors. And respondents' failure to abide by the statutory and administrative rules in making such offerings, even though the failure result from a bona fide mistake as to the law, cannot be sanctioned under the Act.

This conclusion is unaffected by the fact that some purchasers choose not to accept the full offer of an investment contract by declining to enter into a service contract with the respondents. The Securities Act prohibits the offer as well as the sale of unregistered, non-exempt securities. Hence it is enough that the respondents merely offer the essential ingredients of an investment contract.

* * *

Reversed.

———

Securities and Exchange Commission v. Life Partners, Inc.

United States Court of Appeals for the District of Columbia Circuit, 1996.
87 F.3d 536.

■ Before WALD, GINSBURG and HENDERSON.

■ GINSBURG, CIRCUIT JUDGE: A viatical settlement is an investment contract pursuant to which an investor acquires an interest in the life insurance policy of a terminally ill person—typically an AIDS victim—at a discount of 20 to 40 percent, depending upon the insured's life expectancy. The investor's profit is the difference between the discounted purchase price paid to the insured and the death benefit collected from the insurer, less transaction costs, premiums paid, and other administrative expenses.

Life Partners, Inc. ("LPI") arranges these transactions and performs certain post-transaction administrative services. The SEC contends that the fractional interests marketed by LPI are securities, and that LPI violated the [federal securities laws] by selling them without first complying with the registration and other requirements of those Acts. The district court agreed and preliminarily enjoined LPI from making further sales. . . .

We agree with the district court that viatical settlements are not exempt from the securities laws because they are insurance contracts. Contrary to the district court, however, we conclude that LPI's contracts are not securities subject to the federal securities laws because the profits from their purchase do not derive predominantly from the efforts of a party or parties other than the investors. . . .

I. BACKGROUND

Although some promoters of viatical settlements do register them as securities under the federal securities laws, LPI observes that registration under the federal securities laws means higher costs for investors and correspondingly lower prices for terminally ill policy holders and objects that any significant administrative delay . . . might be fatal in this context. . . .

. . . LPI sells fractional interests in insurance policies to retail investors, who may pay as little as $650 and buy as little as 3% of the benefits of a policy. In order to reach its customers, LPI uses some 500 commissioned "licensees," mostly independent financial planners. For its efforts, LPI's net compensation is roughly 10% of the purchase price after payment or referral and other fees. . . .

[The structure of LPI's transactions have] gone through three iterations during the course of this litigation. In each, LPI performed or performs a number of pre-purchase functions: Specifically, even before assembling the investors, LPI evaluates the insured's medical condition, reviews his insurance policy, negotiates the purchase price, and prepares the legal documents. The difference among the three versions is that LPI performs ever fewer (and ultimately no) post-purchase functions.

[In the original Version, LPI or an agent, were the record owners of the insurance policies. An independent escrow agent performed most of the post-purchase administrative functions, holding the policy, disbursing all funds, and filing the death claim. Under Version II, the investors were the owners of record and thus were in privity with the insurance company. Although investors were told that they did not need to use the escrow agent's post-purchase services, these services were offered to them on an optional basis, which most took. Under Version III, LPI ceased to provide any post-purchase services to purchasers either directly or through any agent. All such services became the sole responsibility of the investor; however, an escrow agent was still available to provide services as the agent of the investor.]

II. ANALYSIS

[The Court first rejected LPI's argument that the viatical settlements were insurance contracts exempted under Section 3(a)(8) of the Securities Act, relying on the SEC's argument that the seller of a viatical settlement was actually "giving up the protection of an insurance policy," not acquiring protection against future risks.] . . . We turn next to the question whether the contracts are properly characterized as securities . . . That determination is controlled by the Supreme Court's decision in *Howey* which . . . holds that an investment contract is a security subject to the Act if investors purchase with (1) an expectation of profits arising from (2) a common enterprise that (3) depend upon the efforts of others . . .

1. Expectation of Profits

. . . LPI maintains that under *United Housing Foundation, Inc. v. Forman, 421 U.S. 837(1975)*, profits must be derived from "either capital appreciation resulting from the development of the initial investment or a participation in earnings resulting from the use of the investors' funds," neither of which obtains with respect to viatical contracts . . .

The Court's general principle we think, is only that the expected profits must, in conformity with ordinary usage, be in the form of a financial return on the investment, not in the form of consumption. This principle distinguishes between buying a note secured by a car and buying the car itself.

The asset acquired by an LPI investor is a claim on future death benefits. The buyer is obviously purchasing not for consumption—unmatured claims cannot be currently consumed—but rather for the prospect of a return on his investment. As we read the *Forman* gloss on *Howey,* that is enough to satisfy the requirement that the investment be made in the expectation of profits.

2. Common Enterprise

The second element of the *Howey* test for a security is that there be a "common enterprise." So-called horizontal commonality—defined by the pooling of investment funds, shared profits, and shared losses—is ordinarily sufficient to satisfy the common enterprise requirement ... Here, LPI brings together multiple investors and aggregates their funds to purchase the death benefits of an insurance policy. If the insured dies in a relatively short time, then the investors realize profits; if the insured lives a relatively long time, then the investors may lose money or at best fail to realize the return they had envisioned; i.e., they experience a loss of the return they could otherwise have realized in some alternative investment of equivalent risk. Any profits or losses from an LPI contract accrue to all of the investors in that contract; i.e., it is not possible for one investor to realize a gain or loss without each other investor gaining or losing proportionately, based upon the amount that he invested. In that sense, the outcomes are shared among the investors; the sum that each receives is a predetermined portion of the aggregate death benefit.

LPI claims, however, that there is no pooling and therefore no shared profits or losses because each investor acquires his own interest in the policy.... It seems to us that the pooling issue reduces to the question whether there is a threshold percentage of a policy that must be sold before an investor can be assured that his purchase of a smaller percentage interest will be consummated. If not, then each investor's acquisition is independent of all the other investors' acquisitions and LPI is correct in asserting that there is no pooling. On the other hand, if LPI must have investors ready to buy some minimum percentage of the policy before the transaction will occur, then the investment is contingent upon a pooling of capital.

When we raised this point at oral argument, the SEC contended that interdependency among investors was not necessary to a determination that their funds are pooled; the test, according to the Commission, is whether the funds are "commingled." In this context, however, commingling in itself is but an administrative detail; it is the interdependency of the investors that transforms the transaction substantively into a pooled investment.... Many of the postpurchase administrative functions (e.g., monitoring the insured's health, collecting the death benefit) involve costs that are seemingly invariant to the number of investors or the percentage of a policy that has been sold. Neither LPI nor the investors would be anxious to spread these costs over contracts representing much less than the full value of a policy.

Therefore, we think that pooling is in practice an essential ingredient of the LPI program; that is, any individual investor would find that the profitability if not the completion of his or her purchase depends upon completion of the larger deal. Because LPI's viatical settlements entail this implicit form of pooling, and because any profits or losses accrue to all investors (in proportion to the amount invested), we conclude that all three elements of horizontal commonality—pooling, profit sharing, and loss sharing—attend the purchase of a fractional interest through LPI . . .

3.   Profits Derived Predominantly from the Efforts of Others

The final requirement of the *Howey* test for an investment to be deemed a security is that the profits expected by the investor be derived from the efforts of others. In this connection, the SEC suggests that investors in LPI's viatical settlements are essentially passive; their profits, the Commission argues, depend predominantly upon the efforts of LPI, which provides pre-purchase expertise in identifying existing policyholders and, together with Sterling, provides post-purchase management of the investment. Meanwhile, LPI argues that its pre-purchase functions are wholly irrelevant and that the post-purchase functions, by whomever performed, should not count because they are only ministerial. On this view, once the transaction closes, the investors do not look to the efforts of others for their profits because the only variable affecting profits is the timing of the insured's death, which is outside of LPI's and Sterling's control. By its terms *Howey* requires that profits be generated "solely" from the efforts of others. Although the lower courts have given the Supreme Court's definition of a security broader sweep by requiring that profits be generated only "predominantly" from the efforts of others, . . . they have never suggested that purely ministerial or clerical functions are by themselves sufficient; indeed, quite the opposite is true. . . . Because post-purchase entrepreneurial activities are the "efforts of others" most obviously relevant to the question whether a promoter is selling a "security," we turn first to the distinction between those post-purchase functions that are entrepreneurial and those that are ministerial; thereafter, we consider the relevance of pre-purchase entrepreneurial services.

Ministerial versus entrepreneurial functions, post purchase. In Version I of its program, LPI and not the investor could appear as the owner of record of the insurance policy. LPI's ownership gave it the ability, post-purchase, to change the party designated as the beneficiary of the policy, indeed to substitute itself as beneficiary. That ability tied the fortunes of the investors more closely to those of LPI in the sense that it made the investors dependent upon LPI's continuing to

deal honestly with them, at least to the extent of not wrongfully dropping them as beneficiaries. This does not, however, establish an association between the profits of the investors and the "efforts" of LPI. Nothing that LPI could do by virtue of its record ownership had any effect whatsoever upon the near exclusive determinant of the investors' rate of return, namely how long the insured survives. . . . The promoter's "efforts" not to engage in criminal or tortious behavior, or not to breach its contract are not the sort of entrepreneurial exertions that the Howey Court had in mind when it referred to profits arising from "the efforts of others."

In Version II LPI no longer appeared as the record owner of a policy, but LPI and Sterling continued to offer the following post-purchase services: holding the policy, monitoring the insured's health, paying premiums, converting a group policy into an individual policy where required, filing the death claim, collecting and distributing the death benefit (if requested), and assisting an investor who might wish to resell his interest. LPI characterizes these functions as clerical and routine in nature, not managerial or entrepreneurial, and therefore unimportant to the source of investor expectations. The district court seemed to agree with LPI about the character if not the significance of most post-purchase services, for it described them as "often ministerial in nature."

The Commission disputes the district court's characterization of post-purchase services as ministerial, but attempt to portray only one service in particular as entrepreneurial: we refer to the secondary market that LPI purportedly makes. By establishing a resale market, according to the SEC, LPI links the profitability of the investments it sells to the success of its own efforts. We find this argument unconvincing for several reasons. First, there is no evidence in the record before us that investors actually seek to liquidate their investments prior to the receipt of death benefits. Second, there is no evidence that LPI's potential as that appears, get the same help with resale (if any is needed) through assistance adds value to the investment contract; an investor could, for all any one of the many firms that sell viatical settlements. Third, LPI is quite specific in warning its clients that viatical transactions are not liquid assets ... LPI's promise of help in arranging for the resale of a policy is not an adequate basis upon which to conclude that the fortunes of the investors are tied to the efforts of the company, much less that their profits derive "predominantly" from those efforts.

In Version III LPI provides no post-purchase services. All such services are the sole responsibility of the investors, who may purchase them from Sterling or not, as they choose. The district court minimized the significance of this choice, stating that "it is neither realistic nor feasible for multiple investors, who are strangers to each other, to perform post-purchase tasks without relying on the knowledge and expertise of a third party ..." As we have seen, none of Sterling's post-purchase services can meaningfully affect the profitability of the investment. It is therefore of no moment whether Sterling performs those services usually or always, or whether it does so as the agent of LPI or as the agent of the investor.

In sum, the SEC has not identified any significant non-ministerial service that LPI or Sterling performs for investors once they have purchased their fractional interests in a viatical settlement. Nor do we find that any of the ministerial functions have a material impact upon the profits of the investors. Therefore, we turn to the question whether LPI's prepurchase services count as "the efforts of others" under the Howey test.

Entrepreneurial functions, pre-purchase. LPI's assertion that its pre-purchase efforts are irrelevant receives strong, albeit implicit, support from the Ninth Circuit decision in *Noa v. Key Futures, Inc., 638 F2d 77(1980)* (per curiam). In that case, which involved investments in silver bars, the court observed that the promoter made pre-purchase efforts to identify the investment and to locate prospective investors; offered to store the silver bars at no charge for a year after purchase and to repurchase them at the published spot price at any time without charging a brokerage fee. The court concluded, however, that these services were only minimally related to the profitability of the investment: "Once the purchase ... was made, the profits to the investor depended upon the fluctuations of the silver market, not the managerial efforts of [the promoter]." Id. at 79–80. ...

In [these cases], the courts of appeals regarded the promoter's pre-purchase efforts as insignificant to the question whether the investments—in silver bars and parcels of land, respectively—were securities. The different outcomes trace wholly to the promoters' commitment to perform meaningful post-purchase functions in [one case but not the other].

Even if [LPI's investor played a significant prepurchase role in setting their own purchase criteria], the district court appropriately characterized LPI's pre-purchase efforts as "undeniably essential to the overall success of the investment." The investors rely heavily, if not exclusively, upon LPI to locate insureds and to evaluate them and their policies, as well as to negotiate an attractive purchase price.

The SEC urges us to go even further than did the district court, however, in appraising the significance of LPI's pre-purchase activities insofar as they count toward "the efforts of others." The Commission reminds us that the Supreme Court did not draw a bright line distinction in *Howey* between pre-and post-purchase efforts, and notes that LPI may continue to perform some functions, such as preparing the preliminary agreement and evaluating the insured's policy and medical file, right up to the closing of the transaction. . . .

Absent compelling legal support for the Commission's theory—and the Commission actually furnishes no support at all—we cannot agree that the time of sale is an artificial dividing line. It is a legal construct but a significant one. If the investor's profits depend thereafter predominantly upon the promoter's efforts, then the investor may benefit from the disclosure and other requirements of the federal securities laws. But if the value of the promoter's efforts has already been impounded into the promoter's fees or into the purchase price of the investment, and if neither the promoter nor anyone else is expected to make further efforts that will affect the outcome of the investment, then the need for federal securities regulation is greatly diminished. . . .

While we doubt that pre-purchase services should ever count for much, for present purposes we need only agree with the district court that pre-purchase services cannot by themselves suffice to make the profits of an investment arise predominantly from the efforts of others, and that ministerial functions should receive a good deal less weight than entrepreneurial activities . . .

In this case it is the length of the insured's life that is of overwhelming importance to the value of the viatical settlements marketed by LPI. As a result, the SEC is unable to show that the promoter's efforts have a predominant influence upon investors' profits; and because all three elements of the *Howey* test must be satisfied before an investment is characterized as a security, we must conclude that the viatical settlements marketed by LPI are not securities. . . .

■ WALD, CIRCUIT JUDGE, dissenting.

. . . I part company with the majority . . . because I believe that the third requirement of the *Howey* test, that (3) the expected profits be generated solely from the efforts of other, is also met here . . . Rather, I would distinguish between investments that satisfy the *Howey* third prong and those which do not by focusing on the kind and degree of dependence between the investors' profits and the promoter's activities. I believe that the third prong of the *Howey* test can be met by prepurchase managerial activities of a promoter when it is the success of these activities, either entirely or predominantly, that determines whether profits are eventually realized. . . .

When profits depend on the intervention of market forces, there will be public information available to an investor by which the investor could assess the likelihood of the investment's success. Thus, for example, a purchaser of silver bars has access to information on the trends in silver prices, an investor in paintings can get a sense, at least generally, of how the market for artwork is faring, and a purchaser of an undeveloped lot has access to information on growth trends in the area. . . .

Where profits depend on the success of the promoter's activities, however, there is less access to protective information and the type of in-formation that is needed is more specific to the promoter. . . . This need for information holds true in regard to investors prior to purchase as much as to investors who have committed their funds—indeed, more so, if they are to avoid over-risky invest-ments. . . .

I believe that the majority's position, precluding any pre-purchase manage-rial activities of a promoter from ever satisfying the third prong of the *Howey* test, is unwarranted and will serve to undercut the necessary flexibility of our securities laws . . . Therefore, I respectfully dissent.

---

1. *Managerial Efforts: When and By Whom.* The *Howey* test for the existence of an investment contract is now read by all courts to require the showing of three elements: (1) an expectation of profits arising from (2) a common enterprise that (3) depends predominantly for its success on the efforts of others. Although the *Howey* decision seems to say that an investment contract could be found only if profits are to be derived "solely" from the managerial efforts of the promoter or third parties, subsequent courts have re-interpreted "solely" to mean "predominantly", recognizing that otherwise promoters could circumvent the federal securities laws by simply assigning investors some nominal role in the enterprise.[1]

Most of the interpretive issues under the *Howey* test have involved either the meaning of commonality (which is discussed in the next note) or the nature of the managerial or entrepreneurial efforts that the promoter can provide without giving rise to a security. A number of colorful cases have involved animal breeding programs in which the promoter sells the breeding stock to investors and promises to repurchase the offspring they raise.[2] Sometimes in these cases, substantial efforts are required of the investors simply to obtain any offspring. Thus, in Miller v. Central Chinchilla Group, Inc.,[3] the investors had to expend considerable efforts to raise chinchillas (which have a high mortality rate) in order to be able to resell them to the promoters at the agreed above-market price. The Eighth Circuit focused, however, on the promoters' representation that only minimal care was required. Finding that the invest-ment could only yield a profit if the promoters could continue their pyramid selling scheme by finding new investors to buy the offspring raised by earlier

---

1. See SEC v. International Loan Net-work, Inc., 968 F.2d 1304, 1308 (D.C.Cir. 1992) (profits must be "expected to accrue, if not solely, at least predominantly from the efforts of others").

2. See Smith v. Gross, 604 F.2d 639 (9th Cir.1979) (earthworms); Continental Mktg. Corp. v. SEC, 387 F.2d 466 (10th Cir. 1967) (beavers); SEC v. Payne, 35 F.Supp. 873 (S.D.N.Y.1940) (a pre-*Howey* case involv-ing silver foxes).

3. 494 F.2d 414 (8th Cir.1974).

investors, the Eighth Circuit concluded that the promoters had the critical role and hence the breeding program amounted to an investment contract.

Subtract the feature of a pyramid selling scheme, however, and most franchise/franchisee relationships will not be found to constitute investment contracts under *Howey* because the efforts required of the franchisee/investor are too significant.[4] Where, however, the franchisee is used not simply as a sales agent, but as a source of capital for the production of the product (as the next case illustrates), the uncertain line between legitimate franchise and unregistered investment contract can be crossed.[5]

Life Partners draws a new distinction between pre-and post-purchase services. A number of commentators have doubted the wisdom of drawing this distinction.[6] The SEC has also resisted the majority's decision, although it succeeded in a later case largely by showing that the defendant's post-purchase activities were more substantial than in *Life Partners*. In Securities and Exchange Commission v. Larry W. Tyler & Advanced Fin. Servs., Inc.,[7] the SEC prevailed by emphasizing the secondary market that the defendant created in order to provide liquidity for the fractional viatical shares that it sold.[8] But for this fact, however, the court added that it would be inclined to follow *Life Partners*.

Securities and Exchange Commission v. Koscot Interplanetary, Inc.

United States Court of Appeals, Fifth Circuit, 1974.
497 F.2d 473.

■ Before Rives, Gewin and Roney, Circuit Judges.

■ Gewin, Circuit Judge: This appeal emanates from a district court order denying an injunction sought by the Securities & Exchange Commission (SEC) against Koscot Interplanetary, Inc., (Koscot) for allegedly violating the federal securities laws. Specifically, the SEC maintained that the pyramid promotion enterprise operated by Koscot was within the ambit of the term security, as employed by the Securities Act of 1933 and the Securities Exchange Act of 1934, that as such it had to be registered with the SEC pursuant to the '33 Act, and that the manner in which Koscot purveyed its enterprise to potential investors contravened the anti-fraud provisions of the '34 Act. In a comprehensive opinion, * * *, the district court denied the injunction holding that the

---

4. See Crowley v. Montgomery Ward & Co., 570 F.2d 875 (10th Cir.1975).

5. See SEC v. Aqua–Sonic Products Corp., 687 F.2d 577 (2d Cir.1982) (franchise agreement was an investment contract where circumstances made it clear that franchisee was neither able nor expected to sell firm's product to customers).

6. See Albert, The Future of Death Futures: Why Viatical Settlements Must Be Classified As Securities, 19 Pace L. Rev. 345 (1999); Lann, Viatical Settlements: An Explanation of the Process, An Analysis of State Regulations, and An Examination of Viatical Settlements As Securities, 46 Drake L. Rev. 923 (1998).

7. 2002 WL 257645 (N.D.Tex.2002).

8. The district court relied heavily on Gary Plastic Packaging Corp. v. Merrill Lynch, 756 F.2d 230 (2d Cir.1985), in which the Second Circuit found that the heavily advertised provision of such a secondary market by the seller could convert certificates of deposits, which are ordinarily not securities, into an investment package that constituted a security.

Koscot Scheme did not involve the sale of a security. Because of our disagreement with the district court's reasoning, we reverse.

I

A. *The Koscot Scheme*

The procedure followed by Koscot in the promotion of its enterprise can be synoptically chronicled. A subsidiary of Glenn W. Turner Enterprises, Koscot thrives by enticing prospective investors to participate in its enterprise, holding out as a lure the expectation of galactic profits. All too often, the beguiled investors are disappointed by paltry returns.

The vehicle for the lure is a multi-level network of independent distributors, purportedly engaged in the business of selling a line of cosmetics. At the lowest level is a "beauty advisor" whose income is derived solely from retail sales of Koscot products made available at a discount, customarily of 45%. Those desirous of ascending the ladder of the Koscot enterprise may also participate on a second level, that of supervisor or retail manager. For an investment of $1,000, a supervisor receives cosmetics at a greater discount from retail price, typically 55%, to be sold either directly to the public or to be held for wholesale distribution to the beauty advisors. In addition, a supervisor who introduces a prospect to the Koscot program with whom a sale is ultimately consummated receives $600 of the $1,000 paid to Koscot. The loftiest position in the multi-level scheme is that of distributor. An investment of $5,000 with Koscot entitles a distributor to purchase cosmetics at an even greater discount, typically 65%, for distribution to supervisors and retailers. Moreover, fruitful sponsorship of either a supervisor or distributor brings $600 or $3,000 respectively to the sponsor.

The SEC does not contend that the distribution of cosmetics is amenable to regulation under the federal securities laws. Rather, it maintains that the marketing of cosmetics and the recruitment aspects of Koscot's enterprise are separable and that only the latter are within the definition of a security. * * *

The modus operandi of Koscot and its investors is as follows. Investors solicit prospects to attend Opportunity Meetings at which the latter are introduced to the Koscot scheme. Significantly, the investor is admonished not to mention the details of the business before bringing the prospect to the meeting, a technique euphemistically denominated the "curiosity approach." * * *

Thus, in the initial stage, an investor's sole task is to attract individuals to the meeting.

Once a prospect's attendance at a meeting is secured, Koscot employees, frequently in conjunction with investors, undertake to apprise prospects of the "virtues" of enlisting in the Koscot plan. The meeting is conducted in conformity with scripts prepared by Koscot. * * * The principal design of the meetings is to foster an illusion of affluence. Investors and Koscot employees are instructed to drive to meetings in expensive cars, preferably Cadillacs, to dress expensively, and to flaunt large amounts of money. It is intended that prospects will be galvanized into signing a contract by these ostentations displayed in the evangelical atmosphere of the meetings. * * *

The final stage in the promotional scheme is the consummation of the sale. If a prospect capitulates at * * * an Opportunity Meeting * * *, an investor will not be required to expend any additional effort. Less fortuitous investors whose prospects are not as quickly enticed to invest do have to devote additional effort to consummate a sale, the amount of which is contingent upon the degree of reluctance of the prospect.

* * *

The district court rebuffed the SEC's effort to subject Koscot's promotional scheme to the federal securities laws. * * *

Of * * * immediate concern is the reasoning employed by the district court in rejecting the SEC's contention that Koscot sold "investment contracts," for it is our disagreement with this conclusion that prompts us to reverse. The district court correctly cited * * * language from SEC v. W. J. Howey Co., * * * as the standard controlling its disposition of the case.

* * *

This test subsumes within it three elements: first, that there is an investment of money; second, that the scheme in which an investment is made functions as a common enterprise; and third, that under the scheme, profits are derived solely from the efforts of individuals other than the investors. * * *. The district court pretermitted a consideration of the first two elements in finding that the third component of the test was not satisfied because Koscot investors expended effort in soliciting recruits to meetings, in participating in the conduct of meetings, and in attempting to consummate the sale of distributorships and subdistributorships. * * *

II

Thus, we are called upon to address that which the court below did not consider—whether the Koscot scheme satisfies the first two elements of the *Howey* test—and that which the district court did consider—whether the scheme satisfies the third component of the test. The latter inquiry entails, in the first instance, a determination of whether the "solely from the efforts of others" standard is to be literally or functionally applied. We address these issues seriatim.

A. *The First Two Elements*

Since it cannot be disputed that purchasers of supervisorships and distributorships made an investment of money, * * * our initial concern is whether the Koscot scheme functions as a common enterprise. As defined by the Ninth Circuit, "[a] common enterprise is one in which the fortunes of the investor are interwoven with and dependent upon the efforts and success of those seeking the investment or of third parties." SEC v. Glenn W. Turner Enterprises, Inc., supra at 482 n. 7. The critical factor is not the similitude or coincidence of investor input, but rather the uniformity of impact of the promoter's efforts.

[T]his definition comports with the standard applied by the Supreme Court * * * in *Howey*, supra. * * *

Similarly, here, the fact that an investor's return is independent of that of other investors in the scheme is not decisive. Rather, the requisite commonality is evidenced by the fact that the fortunes of all investors are inextricably tied to the efficacy of the Koscot meetings and guidelines on recruiting prospects and consummating a sale. * * *

B. *The Third Element—Solely from the Efforts of Others*

As was noted earlier, the critical issue in this case is whether a literal or functional approach to the "solely from the efforts of others" test should be adopted, i.e., whether the exertion of some effort by an investor is inimical to the holding that a promotional scheme falls within the definition of an investment contract. We measure the viability of the SEC's advocacy of a functional approach by its compatibility with the remedial purposes of the federal securities acts, the language employed and the derivation of the test utilized in *Howey*, and the decisions in this circuit and other federal courts.

1. The Legal Standard

* * *

A literal application of the *Howey* test would frustrate the remedial purposes of the Act. As the Ninth Circuit noted in SEC v. Turner Enterprises, Inc., supra at 482, "[i]t would be easy to evade [the *Howey* test] by adding a requirement that the buyer contribute a modicum of effort." The admitted salutary purposes of the Acts can only be safeguarded by a functional approach to the *Howey* test.

Moreover, a close reading of the language employed in *Howey* and the authority upon which the Court relied suggests that, contrary to the view of the district court, we need not feel compelled to follow the "solely from the efforts of others" test literally. Nowhere in the opinion does the Supreme Court characterize the nature of the "efforts" that would render a promotional scheme beyond the pale of the definition of an investment contract. Clearly the facts presented no issue of how to assess a scheme in which an investor performed mere perfunctory tasks. Indeed, * * * the Court observed that "the promoters *manage, control* and *operate* the enterprise." 328 U.S. at 300 (emphasis added).

* * *

In view of * * * our analysis of the import of the language in and the derivation of the *Howey* test, we hold that the proper standard in determining whether a scheme constitutes an investment contract is that explicated by the Ninth Circuit in SEC v. Glenn W. Turner Enterprises, Inc., supra. In that case, the court announced that the critical inquiry is "whether the efforts made by those other than the investor are the undeniably significant ones, those essential managerial efforts which affect the failure or success of the enterprise." Id. at 482.

* * *

2. Application of the Test to the Instant Facts

Having concluded that the district court misperceived the controlling standard, it becomes incumbent upon us to determine whether Koscot's scheme falls with[in] the standard adopted.

Our task is greatly simplified by the Ninth Circuit's decision in SEC v. Glenn W. Turner Enterprises, Inc., supra. The promotional scheme confronting the Ninth Circuit is largely paralleled by that exposed before this court. * * *

As in the Koscot scheme, the initial task of a purchaser of a Dare plan was to lure prospects to meetings, denominated Adventure Meetings. These were characterized by the same overzealous and emotionally charged atmosphere at which the illusion of affluence fostered in Opportunity Meetings was created and relied upon in securing sales. The Adventure Meetings were run according to script but, as the Ninth Circuit noted, "The Dare People, not the purchaser—'salesmen', run the meetings and do the selling." 474 F.2d at 479. * * *

The recruitment role played by investors in Koscot coincides with that played by investors in Dare to be Great. That investors in the latter did not participate in Adventure Meetings while they do in the Koscot scheme is insignificant. Since Koscot's Opportunity Meetings are run according to preordained script, the deviation from which would occasion disapprobation or perhaps exclusion from the meetings, the role of investors at these meetings can be characterized as little more than a perfunctory one. Nor does the fact that Koscot investors may have devoted more time than did Dare investors to closing sales transmute the essential congruity between the two schemes. The act of consummating a sale is essentially a ministerial not managerial one, * * * one which does not alter the fact that the critical determinant of the success of the Koscot Enterprise lies with the luring effect of the opportunity meetings. As was noted earlier, investors are cautioned to employ the "curiosity approach" in attracting prospects. Once attendance is secured, the sales format devised by Koscot is thrust upon the prospect. An investor's sole contribution in following the script is a nominal one. Without the scenario created by the Opportunity Meetings and Go–Tours, an investor would invariably be powerless to realize any return on his investment.

III

We confine our holding to those schemes in which promoters retain immediate control over the essential managerial conduct of an enterprise and where the investor's realization of profits is inextricably tied to the success of the promotional scheme. Thus, we acknowledge that a conventional franchise arrangement, wherein the promoter exercises merely remote control over an enterprise and the investor operates largely unfettered by promoter mandates presents a different question than the one posed herein. But the Koscot scheme does not qualify as a conventional franchising arrangement.

> * * *

Accordingly, this cause is reversed and remanded for further proceedings consistent with this opinion.

------

1. *"Vertical" versus "Horizontal" Commonality.* In finding a common enterprise, the *Koscot* court focused on the vertical commonality between the investors and the promoters. Under this approach, a common enterprise may be found when the activities of the promoter are the dominant factor in the investment's success—even though there is no pooling of funds or interests by multiple investors.[1] Some courts apply this approach more restrictively and insist upon a direct relationship between the promoters' financial success and that of its investors.[2] This latter view—known as "strict vertical commonality"

1. See also SEC v. Continental Commodities Corp., 497 F.2d 516 (5th Cir.1974); Villeneuve v. Advanced Business Concepts Corp., 698 F.2d 1121, 1124 (11th Cir.1983), aff'd en banc 730 F.2d 1403 (11th Cir.1984).

2. See Mordaunt v. Incomco, 686 F.2d 815 (9th Cir.1982).

as opposed to "broad vertical commonality"—"requires that the fortunes of investors be tied to the fortune of the promoter" (as opposed to the investors' fortunes being "linked only to the *efforts* of the promoter"[3]).

Other circuits appear, however, to insist upon horizontal commonality—in short, that there be a pooling of investor funds.[4] Usually, there will also be a pro rata distribution of profits among the investors. A leading case is Wals v. Fox Hills Development Corporation,[5] in which the plaintiff bought a time sharing interest (for one week) in a golf course condominium and simultaneously entered into an annually renewable agreement with the developer under which the developer would rent the unit during that week on behalf of the plaintiff (with the rental being split on a 70/30 basis between the plaintiff and the developer). Rejecting the argument that this agreement created a common enterprise between the developer of the condominium and the owner of this one week time-sharing interest, Judge Posner wrote for the Seventh Circuit:

> "The [1993] Act is a disclosure statute. It requires promoters and issuers to make uniform disclosure to all investors, and this requirement makes sense only if the investors are obtaining the same thing, namely an undivided share in the same pool of assets and profits. This is not what the plaintiffs in this case received * * *. Their investment was in a specific time slice of a specific apartment, the physical and temporal characteristics of which (including price) differed from those of other apartments."[6]

Nonetheless, a year later in SEC v. Lauer,[7] Judge Posner authored another opinion for the Seventh Circuit in which he found that an investment in specially designed package of high-yield securities was, itself, a security, even though this investment package was sold by the broker only to a single investor. Although defendants predictably argued, based on *Wals,* that no "horizontal commonality" was present, Judge Posner answered their arguments, thusly:

> "[I]t is the character of the investment vehicle, not the presence of multiple investors, that determines whether there is an investment contract. Otherwise, a defrauder who was content to defraud a single investor * * * would have immunity from the federal securities laws. That would not make any sense, and is not contemplated by any of the cases that require horizontal commonality."[8]

Apparently then, an intention to involve multiple investors can result in horizontal commonality.

Some commentators argue that the requirement of horizontal commonality is formalistic and lacks any relationship to the policy goals of the 1933 Act.[9] Nonetheless, there is at least one context in which most courts seem inclined to

3.   See Revak v. SEC Realty Corp., 18 F.3d 81, 88 (2d Cir.1994).

4.   See, e.g., SEC v. Banner Fund International, 211 F.3d 602 (D.C.Cir.2000) (pooling of funds so that small investors could participate in deals requiring large capital outlays created horizontal commonality, even though each investor had a separate account); Hart v. Pulte Homes of Michigan, 735 F.2d 1001, 1004 (6th Cir.1984); Salcer v. Merrill, Lynch, Pierce, Fenner & Smith, Inc., 682 F.2d 459, 460 (3d Cir.1982) (investment must be "part of a pooled group of funds").

5.   24 F.3d 1016 (7th Cir.1994).

6.   Id. at 1019.

7.   52 F.3d 667 (7th Cir.1995).

8.   Id. at 670.

9.   See Gordon, *Common Enterprise and Multiple Investors,* 3 Colum.Bus.L.Rev. 635, 660–62 (1988).

require it: discretionary trading accounts managed by securities and commodities traders. Suppose, for example, a broker contracts with a customer to receive a specified percentage of the gains from his discretionary trading in the account for the customer. If horizontal commonality is required, this relationship cannot give rise to a common enterprise or a security (because there is no pooling of investor funds).[10] Note that even if vertical commonality is deemed sufficient, the "strict vertical commonality" approach would find a common enterprise only if the broker is compensated out of the profits from its trading for the customer.[11] Conversely, if the broker does not share the financial risks of the discretionary trading account (for example, if it is compensated on a commission basis), then only the "broad vertical commonality" approach would deem their relationship to amount to a common enterprise.[12]

Some commentators argue that both the horizontal and vertical approaches to commonality are overinclusive.[13] Why, they argue, should it make a difference whether a single investor, or two brothers, open a discretionary commodities trading account with a commodities broker? In the latter case, horizontal commonality seems present, but unimportant. Correspondingly, when an investor and a broker share the profits from a discretionary trading account, their interests are aligned. Although this pattern would satisfy a vertical commonality approach, it is unclear why a federal remedy is needed in this context (where the conflicts of interest are minimal), but not in the case where the broker is paid by a single investor on a pure commission basis (which relationship creates an incentive to churn the account and hence a greater conflict of interests, but fails the "strict vertical commonality" standard). Also, if the discretionary account is trading commodities subject to the jurisdiction of the Commodities Futures Trading Commission, is it wise to overlay SEC jurisdiction on top of the CFTC's simply because the broker has discretionary authority? Does this create an unwise potential for regulatory turf battles?

2. *Commonality and the Internet.* In SEC v. SG Ltd.,[14] the First Circuit reversed the district court and held that the "virtual shares" generated by an Internet game were securities. The defendant operated a website under the name of "StockGeneration," where visitors could buy "virtual shares" of "virtual companies" on a "virtual stock exchange." One such company was known as the "privileged company," and the website indicated that its shares would constantly rise by ten percent a month (that is, the computer—not any market—was programmed to do this). Participants had to invest real money to buy shares, and if participants referred new players to the site, they would receive a percentage of the new player's payments. Finding this to be a game or a lottery, not a common enterprise, the district court dismissed the SEC's complaint, which alleged a *Howey*-style investment contract. The First Circuit, however, agreed with the SEC and in particular found the requisite "horizontal commonality" to be present because the defendant pooled the investors' funds in a single account which was used to pay the appreciation on the "privileged company." In addition, the SEC alleged that the only way that the defendant

10. See Milnarik v. M–S Commodities, Inc., 457 F.2d 274 (7th Cir.1972), cert. denied, 409 U.S. 887 (1972); see also, Prendergast, Discretionary Trading Accounts—Revisited, 16 Rev.Sec.Reg. 854 (1983).

11. See Meyer v. Dans un Jardin, S.A., 816 F.2d 533 (10th Cir.1987).

12. See SEC v. Continental Commodities, supra note 1.

13. See Karjala, Federalism, Full Disclosure, and the National Markets in the Interpretation of Federal Securities Laws, 80 NW.U.L.Rev. 1473, 1508 (1986).

14. 265 F.3d 42 (1st Cir.2001).

could pay a guaranteed increased price on such shares was through the new infusion of new money through a "Ponzi" or pyramid type scheme. Similarly, the SEC argued that the payments made to contestants for referring new players also came from this pooled fund, as the defendant had no other source of funds. Finally, because the contestants themselves could do nothing to increase the value of the stocks in the game, the third (or "predominantly dependent upon others") prong of *Howey* was found to be satisfied.

Query: What if the defendant had designed the game so that contestants only received payments from the contestants that they referred to the website? Would this be more like *Koscot*? Would circuits that required horizontal commonality dismiss the SEC's complaint?

B. THE "ECONOMIC REALITIES" TEST: DOWNSIZING THE DEFINITION OF SECURITY

United Housing Foundation, Inc. v. Forman

Supreme Court of the United States, 1975.
421 U.S. 837, 95 S.Ct. 2051, 44 L.Ed.2d 621.

■ MR. JUSTICE POWELL delivered the opinion of the Court.

The issue in these cases is whether shares of stock entitling a purchaser to lease an apartment in Co-op City, a state subsidized and supervised nonprofit housing cooperative, are "securities" within the purview of the Securities Act of 1933 and the Securities Exchange Act of 1934.

In May 1965, subsequent to the completion of the initial planning, Riverbay circulated an Information Bulletin seeking to attract tenants for what would someday be apartments in Co-op City. After describing the nature and advantages of cooperative housing generally and of Co-op City in particular, the Bulletin informed prospective tenants that the total estimated cost of the project, based largely on an anticipated construction contract with CSI, was $283,695,550. Only a fraction of this sum, $32,795,550, was to be raised by the sale of shares to tenants. The remaining $250,900,000 was to be financed by a 40–year low-interest mortgage loan from the New York Private Housing Finance Agency. After construction of the project the mortgage payments and current operating expenses would be met by monthly rental charges paid by the tenants. While these rental charges were to vary, depending on the size, nature, and location of an apartment, the 1965 Bulletin estimated that the "average" monthly cost would be $23.02 per room, or $92.08 for a four-room apartment.

Several times during the construction of Co-op City, Riverbay, with the approval of the State Housing Commissioner, revised its contract with CSI to allow for increased construction costs. In addition, Riverbay incurred other expenses that had not been reflected in the 1965 Bulletin. To meet these increased expenditures, Riverbay, with the Commissioner's approval, repeatedly secured increased mortgage loans from the State Housing Agency. Ultimately the construction loan was $125 million more than the figure estimated in the 1965 Bulletin. As a result, while the initial purchasing price remained at $450 per room, the average monthly rental charges increased periodically, reaching a figure of $39.68 per room as of July 1974.

These increases in the rental charges precipitated the present lawsuit. Respondents, 57 residents of Co-op City, sued in federal court on behalf of all

15,372 apartment owners, and derivatively on behalf of Riverbay, seeking upwards of $30 million in damages, forced rental reductions, and other "appropriate" relief. Named as defendants (petitioners herein) were UHF, CSI, Riverbay, several individual directors of these organizations, the State of New York, and the State Private Housing Finance Agency. The heart of respondents' claim was that the 1965 Co-op City Information Bulletin falsely represented that CSI would bear all subsequent cost increases due to factors such as inflation. Respondents further alleged that they were misled in their purchases of shares since the Information Bulletin failed to disclose several critical facts. On these bases, respondents asserted two claims under the fraud provisions of the federal Securities Act of 1933, as amended, § 17(a) * * * and the Securities Exchange Act of 1934, as amended, § 10(b), * * * and * * * 10b–5. * * *

Petitioners, while denying the substance of these allegations, moved to dismiss the complaint on the ground that federal jurisdiction was lacking. They maintained that shares of stock in Riverbay were not "securities" within the definitional sections of the federal Securities Acts. * * *

The District Court granted the motion to dismiss. * * *

The Court of Appeals for the Second Circuit reversed * * *.

I

Co-op City is a massive housing cooperative in New York City. Built between 1965 and 1971, it presently houses approximately 50,000 people on a 200–acre site containing 35 high-rise buildings and 236 town houses. The project was organized, financed, and constructed under the New York State Private Housing Finance Law, commonly known as the Mitchell–Lama Act, enacted to ameliorate a perceived crisis in the availability of decent low-income urban housing. In order to encourage private developers to build low-cost cooperative housing, New York provides them with large long-term, low-interest mortgage loans and substantial tax exemptions. Receipt of such benefits is conditioned on a willingness to have the State review virtually every step in the development of the cooperative. See N.Y.Priv.Hous.Fin.Law §§ 11–37, as amended (1962 and Supp.1974–1975). The developer also must agree to operate the facility "on a nonprofit basis," § 11–a(2a), and he may lease apartments only to people whose incomes fall below a certain level and who have been approved by the State.

The United Housing Foundation (UHF), a nonprofit membership corporation established for the purpose of "aiding and encouraging" the creation of "adequate, safe and sanitary housing accommodations for wage earners and other persons of low or moderate income," * * * was responsible for initiating and sponsoring the development of Co-op City. Acting under the Mitchell–Lama Act, UHF organized the Riverbay Corporation (Riverbay) to own and operate the land and buildings constituting Co-op City. Riverbay, a nonprofit cooperative housing corporation, issued the stock that is the subject of this litigation. UHF also contracted with Community Services, Inc. (CSI), its wholly owned subsidiary, to serve as the general contractor and sales agent for the project. As required by the Mitchell–Lama Act, these decisions were approved by the State Housing Commissioner.

To acquire an apartment in Co-op City an eligible prospective purchaser must buy 18 shares of stock in Riverbay for each room desired. The cost per share is $25, making the total cost $450 per room, or $1,800 for a four-room apartment. The sole purpose of acquiring these shares is to enable the purchaser to occupy an apartment in Co-op City; in effect, their purchase is a recoverable deposit on an apartment. The shares are explicitly tied to the apartment: they cannot be transferred to a nontenant; nor can they be pledged or encumbered; and they descend, along with the apartment, only to a surviving spouse. No voting rights attach to the shares as such: participation in the affairs of the cooperative appertains to the apartment, with the residents of each apartment being entitled to one vote irrespective of the number of shares owned.

Any tenant who wants to terminate his occupancy, or who is forced to move out, must offer his stock to Riverbay at its initial selling price of $25 per share. In the extremely unlikely event that Riverbay declines to repurchase the stock, the tenant cannot sell it for more than the initial purchase price plus a fraction of the portion of the mortgage that he has paid off, and then only to a prospective tenant satisfying the statutory income eligibility requirements. * * *

In view of the importance of the issues presented we granted certiorari. * * * As we conclude that the disputed transactions are not purchases of securities within the contemplation of the federal statutes, we reverse.

II

* * *

A

We reject at the outset any suggestion that the present transaction, evidenced by the sale of shares called "stock," must be considered a security transaction simply because the statutory definition of a security includes the words "any * * * stock." Rather we adhere to the basic principle that has guided all of the Court's decisions in this area:

"[I]n searching for the meaning and scope of the word 'security' in the Act[s], form should be disregarded for substance and the emphasis should be on economic reality." Tcherepnin v. Knight, 389 U.S. 332, 336 (1967).

See also *Howey,* supra, at 298.

The primary purpose of the Acts of 1933 and 1934 was to eliminate serious abuses in a largely unregulated securities market. The focus of the Acts is on the capital market of the enterprise system: the sale of securities to raise capital for profit-making purposes, the exchanges on which securities are traded, and the need for regulation to prevent fraud and to protect the interest of investors. Because securities transactions are economic in character Congress intended the application of these statutes to turn on the economic realities underlying a transaction, and not on the name appended thereto. Thus, in construing these Acts against the background of their purpose, we are guided by a traditional canon of statutory construction:

"[A] thing may be within the letter of the statute and yet not within the statute, because not within its spirit, nor within the intention of its makers." Church of the Holy Trinity v. United States, 143 U.S. 457, 459 (1892).

* * *

Respondents' reliance on *Joiner* as support for a "literal approach" to defining a security is misplaced. The issue in *Joiner* was whether assignments of interests in oil leases, coupled with the promoters' offer to drill an exploratory well, were securities. Looking to the economic inducement provided by the proposed exploratory well, the Court concluded that these leases were securities even though "leases" as such were not included in the list of instruments mentioned in the statutory definition. In dictum the Court noted that "[i]nstruments *may* be included within [the definition of a security], as [a] matter of law, if on their face they answer to the name or description." 320 U.S., at 351 (emphasis supplied). And later, again in dictum, the Court stated that a security *"might"* be shown "by proving the document itself, which on its face would be a note, a bond, or a share of stock." Id., at 355 (emphasis supplied). By using the conditional words "may" and "might" in these dicta the Court made clear that it was not establishing an inflexible rule barring inquiry into the economic realities underlying a transaction. On the contrary, the Court intended only to make the rather obvious point that, in contrast to the instrument before it which was not included within the explicit statutory terms, most instruments bearing these traditional titles are likely to be covered by the statutes.

In holding that the name given to an instrument is not dispositive, we do not suggest that the name is wholly irrelevant to the decision whether it is a security. There may be occasions when the use of a traditional name such as "stocks" or "bonds" will lead a purchaser justifiably to assume that the federal securities laws apply. This would clearly be the case when the underlying transaction embodies some of the significant characteristics typically associated with the named instrument.

In the present case respondents do not contend, nor could they, that they were misled by use of the word "stock" into believing that the federal securities laws governed their purchase. Common sense suggests that people who intend to acquire only a residential apartment in a state-subsidized cooperative, for their personal use, are not likely to believe that in reality they are purchasing investment securities simply because the transaction is evidenced by something called a share of stock. These shares have none of the characteristics "that in our commercial world fall within the ordinary concept of a security." H.R.Rep. No. 85, supra, at 11. Despite their name, they lack what the Court in *Tcherepnin* deemed the most common feature of stock: the right to receive "dividends contingent upon an apportionment of profits." 389 U.S., at 339. Nor do they possess the other characteristics traditionally associated with stock: they are not negotiable; they cannot be pledged or hypothecated; they confer no voting rights in proportion to the number of shares owned; and they cannot appreciate in value. In short, the inducement to purchase was solely to acquire subsidized low-cost living space; it was not to invest for profit.

B

The Court of Appeals, as an alternative ground for its decision, concluded that a share in Riverbay was also an "investment contract" as defined by the Securities Acts. Respondents further argue that in any event what they agreed to purchase is "commonly known as a 'security'" within the meaning of these laws. In considering these claims we again must examine the substance—the economic realities of the transaction—rather than the names that may have been employed by the parties. We perceive no distinction, for present purposes, between an "investment contract" and an "instrument commonly known as a 'security.'" In either case, the basic test for distinguishing the transaction from other commercial dealings is "whether the scheme involves an investment of money in a common enterprise with profits to come solely from the efforts of others." *Howey,* 328 U.S., at 301.[16]

This test, in shorthand form, embodies the essential attributes that run through all of the Court's decisions defining a security. The touchstone is the presence of an investment in a common venture premised on a reasonable expectation of profits to be derived from the entrepreneurial or managerial efforts of others. By profits, the Court has meant either capital appreciation resulting from the development of the initial investment, as in *Joiner,* supra (sale of oil leases conditioned on promoters' agreement to drill exploratory well), or a participation in earnings resulting from the use of investors' funds, as in Tcherepnin v. Knight, supra (dividends on the investment based on savings and loan association's profits). In such cases the investor is "attracted solely by the prospects of a return" on his investment. *Howey,* supra, at 300. By contrast, when a purchaser is motivated by a desire to use or consume the item purchased—"to occupy the land or to develop it themselves," as the *Howey* Court put it, ibid.—the securities laws do not apply. See also *Joiner,* supra.

In the present case there can be no doubt that investors were attracted solely by the prospect of acquiring a place to live, and not by financial returns on their investments. The Information Bulletin distributed to prospective residents emphasized the fundamental nature and purpose of the undertaking * * *.

Nowhere does the Bulletin seek to attract investors by the prospect of profits resulting from the efforts of the promoters or third parties. On the contrary, the Bulletin repeatedly emphasizes the "non-profit" nature of the endeavor. It explains that if rental charges exceed expenses the difference will be returned as a rebate, not invested for profit. It also informs purchasers that they will be unable to resell their apartments at a profit since the apartment must first be offered back to Riverbay "at the price * * * paid for it." Id., at 163a. In short, neither of the kinds of profits traditionally associated with securities was offered to respondents.

* * *

There is no doubt that purchasers in this housing cooperative sought to obtain a decent home at an attractive price. But that type of economic interest characterizes every form of commercial dealing. What distinguishes a security transaction—and what is absent here—is an investment where one parts with his money in the hope of receiving profits from the efforts of others, and not where he purchases a commodity for personal consumption or living quarters for personal use.

* * *

Since respondents' claims are not cognizable in federal court, the District Court properly dismissed their complaint. The judgment below is therefore

16. This test speaks in terms of "profits to come *solely* from the efforts of others." (Emphasis supplied.) Although the issue is not presented in this case, we note that the Court of Appeals for the Ninth Circuit has held that "the word 'solely' should not be read as a strict or literal limitation on the definition of an investment contract, but rather must be construed realistically, so as to include within the definition those schemes which involve in substance, if not form, securities." SEC v. Glenn W. Turner Enterprises, 474 F.2d 476, 482, cert. denied, 414 U.S. 821 (1973). We express no view, however, as to the holding of this case.

Reversed.

* * *

———

1. Although Co-op City was a subsidized, non-profit cooperative as to which both the Supreme Court and the Second Circuit agreed that there was no "possible profit on a resale," was its non-profit status central to the Supreme Court's reasoning? What result in the case of a non-subsidized, private cooperative or condominium, which permits its shareholders to sell their stock for a profit to new tenants? See Grenader v. Spitz, 537 F.2d 612 (2d Cir.1976) (where profit motive "purely incidental" to purchase of residential housing, shares in cooperative did not constitute securities).

International Brotherhood of Teamsters, Chauffeurs, Warehousemen and Helpers of America v. Daniel

Supreme Court of the United States, 1979.
439 U.S. 551, 99 S.Ct. 790, 58 L.Ed.2d 808.

■ MR. JUSTICE POWELL delivered the opinion of the Court.

This case presents the question whether a noncontributory, compulsory pension plan constitutes a "security" within the meaning of the Securities Act of 1933 and the Securities Exchange Act of 1934 (Securities Acts).

I

In 1954 multiemployer collective bargaining between Local 705 of the International Brotherhood of Teamsters, Chauffeurs, Warehousemen, and Helpers of American and Chicago trucking firms produced a pension plan for employees represented by the Local. The plan was compulsory and noncontributory. Employees had no choice as to participation in the plan, and did not have the option of demanding that the employer's contribution be paid directly to them as a substitute for pension eligibility. The employees paid nothing to the plan themselves.

The collective-bargaining agreement initially set employer contributions to the Pension Trust Fund at $2 a week for each man-week of covered employment. The Board of Trustees of the Fund, a body composed of an equal number of employer and union representatives, was given sole authority to set the level of benefits but had no control over the amount of required employer contributions. Initially, eligible employees received $75 a month in benefits upon retirement. Subsequent collective-bargaining agreements called for greater employer contributions, which in turn led to higher benefit payments for retirees. At the time respondent brought suit, employers contributed $21.50 per employee man-week and pension payments ranged from $425 to $525 a month depending on age at retirement.[3] In order to receive a pension an employee was

3. Because the Fund made the same payments to each employee who qualified for a pension and retired at the same age, rather than establishing an individual account for each employee tied to the amount of employer contributions attributable to his period of service, the plan provided a "defined benefit." * * *

required to have 20 years of continuous service, including time worked before the start of the plan.

The meaning of "continuous service" is at the center of this dispute. Respondent began working as a truck driver in the Chicago area in 1950, and joined Local 705 the following year. When the plan first went into effect, respondent automatically received 5 years credit toward the 20–year service requirement because of his earlier work experience. He retired in 1973 and applied to the plan's administrator for a pension. The administrator determined that respondent was ineligible because of a break in service between December 1960, and July 1961.[4] Respondent appealed the decision to the trustees, who affirmed. Respondent then asked the trustees to waive the continuous service rule as it applied to him. After the trustees refused to waive the rule, respondent brought suit in federal court against the International Union (Teamsters), Local 705 (Local), and Louis Peick, a trustee of the fund.

Respondent's complaint alleged that the Teamsters, the Local, and Peick misrepresented and omitted to state material facts with respect to the value of a covered employee's interest in the pension plan. Count I of the complaint charged that these misstatements and omissions constituted a fraud in connection with the sale of a security in violation of § 10(b) of the Securities Exchange Act of 1934, and the Securities and Exchange Commission's Rule 10b–5. Count II charged that the same conduct amounted to a violation of § 17(a) of the Securities Act of 1933. * * * Respondent sought to proceed on behalf of all prospective beneficiaries of Teamsters pension plans and against all Teamsters pension funds.

The petitioners moved to dismiss the first two counts of the complaint on the ground that respondent had no cause of action under the Securities or Securities Exchange Acts. The District Court denied the motion. * * * It held that respondent's interest in the Pension Fund constituted a security within the meaning of § 2(a)(1) of the Securities Act and § 3(a)(10) of the Securities Exchange Act because the plan created an "investment contract" as that term had been interpreted in SEC v. W.J. Howey Co. * * *. It also determined that there had been a "sale" of this interest to respondent within the meaning of § 2(3) of the Securities Act and § 3(a)(14) of the Securities Exchange Act. It believed respondent voluntarily gave value for his interest in the plan, because he had voted on collective-bargaining agreements that chose employer contributions to the Fund instead of other wages or benefits.

[T]he Court of Appeals for the Seventh Circuit affirmed. * * * We granted certiorari and now reverse.

II

"The starting point in every case involving the construction of a statute is the language itself." Blue Chip Stamps v. Manor Drug Stores, 421 U.S. 723, 756 (1975) (Powell, J., concurring); * * *. In spite of the substantial use of employee pension plans at the time they were enacted, neither § 2(a)(1) of the Securities Act nor § 3(a)(10) of the Securities Exchange Act, which define the term "security" in considerable detail and with numerous examples, refers to

---

4. Respondent was laid off from December 1960, until April, 1961. In addition, no contributions were paid on his behalf between April and July 1961, because of embezzlement by his employer's bookkeeper. During this seven-month period respondent could have preserved his eligibility by making the contributions himself, but he failed to do so.

pension plans of any type. Acknowledging this omission in the statutes, respondent contends that an employee's interest in a pension plan is an "investment contract," an instrument which is included in the statutory definitions of a security.

To determine whether a particular financial relationship constitutes an investment contract, "[t]he test is whether the scheme involves an investment of money in a common enterprise with profits to come solely from the efforts of others." *Howey, supra,* * * *. This test is to be applied in light of "the substance—the economic realities of the transaction—rather than the names that may have been employed by the parties." United Housing Foundation, Inc. v. Forman, 421 U.S. 837, 851–852 (1975). * * * Looking separately at each element of the *Howey* test, it is apparent that an employee's participation in a noncontributory, compulsory pension plan such as the Teamsters' does not comport with the commonly held understanding of an investment contract.

A. *Investment of Money*

An employee who participates in a noncontributory, compulsory pension plan by definition makes no payment into the pension fund. He only accepts employment, one of the conditions of which is eligibility for a possible benefit on retirement. Respondent contends, however, that he has "invested" in the Pension Fund by permitting part of his compensation from his employer to take the form of a deferred pension benefit. By allowing his employer to pay money into the Fund, and by contributing his labor to his employer in return for these payments, Respondent asserts he has made the kind of investment which the Securities Acts were intended to regulate.

In order to determine whether respondent invested in the Fund by accepting and remaining in covered employment, it is necessary to look at the entire transaction through which he obtained a chance to receive pension benefits. In every decision of this Court recognizing the presence of a "security" under the Securities Acts, the person found to have been an investor chose to give up a specific consideration in return for a separable financial interest with the characteristics of a security. See * * * *Howey, supra* (money paid for purchase, maintenance, and harvesting of orange grove); SEC v. C.M. Joiner Leasing Corp., 320 U.S. 344 (1943) (money paid for land and oil exploration). * * * In every case the purchaser gave up some tangible and definable consideration in return for an interest that had substantially the characteristics of a security.

In a pension plan such as this one, by contrast, the purported investment is a relatively insignificant part of an employee's total and indivisible compensation package. No portion of an employee's compensation other than the potential pension benefits has any of the characteristics of a security, yet these noninvestment interests cannot be segregated from the possible pension benefits. Only in the most abstract sense may it be said that an employee "exchanges" some portion of his labor in return for these possible benefits.[12] He surrenders his labor as a whole, and in return receives a compensation package that is substantially devoid of aspects resembling a security. His decision to accept and retain covered employment may have only an attenuated relationship, if any, to perceived investment possibilities of a future pension. Looking at the economic realities, it seems clear that an employee is selling his labor primarily to obtain a livelihood, not making an investment.

---

12. This is not to say that a person's "investment," in order to meet the definition of an investment contract, must take the form of cash only rather than of goods and services. See *Forman, supra,* 421 U.S., at 852 n. 16.

Respondent also argues that employer contributions on his behalf constituted his investment into the Fund. But it is inaccurate to describe these payments as having been "on behalf" of any employee. The trust agreement used employee man-weeks as a convenient way to measure an employer's overall obligation to the Fund, not as a means of measuring the employer's obligation to any particular employee. Indeed, there was no fixed relationship between contributions to the Fund and an employee's potential benefits. A pension plan with "defined benefits," such as the Local's, does not tie a qualifying employee's benefits to the time he has worked. * * * One who has engaged in covered employment for 20 years will receive the same benefits as a person who has worked for 40, even though the latter has worked twice as long and induced a substantially larger employer contribution. Again, it ignores the economic realities to equate employer contributions with an investment by the employee.

B. *Expectation of Profits From A Common Enterprise*

As we observed in *Forman*, the "touchstone" of the *Howey* test "is the presence of an investment in a common venture premised on a reasonable expectation of profits to be derived from the entrepreneurial or managerial efforts of others." 421 U.S., at 852. The Court of Appeals believed that Daniel's expectation of profit derived from the Fund's successful management and investment of its assets. To the extent pension benefits exceeded employer contributions and depended on earnings from the assets, it was thought they contained a profit element. The Fund's trustees provided the managerial efforts which produced this profit element.

As in other parts of its analysis, the court below found an expectation of profit in the pension plan only by focusing on one of its less important aspects to the exclusion of its more significant elements. It is true that the Fund, like other holders of large assets, depends to some extent on earnings from its assets. In the case of a pension fund, however, a far larger portion of its income comes from employer contributions, a source in no way dependent on the efforts of the Fund's managers. The Local 705 Fund, for example, earned a total of $31 million through investment of its assets between February 1955, and January 1977. During this same period employer contributions totaled $153 million. Not only does the greater share of a pension plan's income ordinarily come from new contributions, but unlike most entrepreneurs who manage other people's money, a plan usually can count on increased employer contributions, over which the plan itself has no control, to cover shortfalls in earnings.

The importance of asset earnings in relation to the other benefits received from employment is diminished further by the fact that where a plan has substantial preconditions to vesting, the principal barrier to an individual employee's realization of pension benefits is not the financial health of the Fund. Rather, it is his own ability to meet the Fund's eligibility requirements. Thus, even if it were proper to describe the benefits as a "profit" returned on some hypothetical investment by the employee, this profit would depend primarily on the employee's efforts to meet the vesting requirements, rather than the Fund's investment success. When viewed in light of the total compensation package an employee must receive in order to be eligible for pension benefits, it becomes clear that the possibility of participating in a plan's asset earnings "is far too speculative and insubstantial to bring the entire transaction within the Securities Acts," *Forman*, supra, at 856.

III

The court below believed that its construction of the term "security" was compelled not only by the perceived resemblance of a pension plan to an investment contract, but by various actions of Congress and the SEC with regard to the Securities Acts. In reaching this conclusion, the court gave great weight to the SEC's explanation of these events, an explanation which for the most part the SEC repeats here. Our own review of the record leads us to believe that this reliance on the SEC's interpretation of these legislative and administrative actions was not justified.

A.   Actions of Congress

The SEC in its *amicus curiae* brief refers to several actions of Congress said to evidence an understanding that pension plans are securities. A close look at each instance, however, reveals only that Congress might have believed certain kinds of pension plans, radically different from the one at issue here, came within the coverage of the Securities Acts. There is no evidence that Congress at any time thought noncontributory plans similar to the one before us were subject to federal regulation as securities.

The first action cited was the rejection by Congress in 1934 of an amendment to the Securities Act that would have exempted employee stock investment and stock option plans from the Act's registration requirements. The amendment passed the Senate but was eliminated in conference. The legislative history of the defeated proposal indicates it was intended to cover plans under which employees contributed their own funds to a segregated investment account on which a return was realized. * * * In rejecting the amendment, Congress revealed a concern that certain interests having the characteristics of a security not be excluded from Securities Act protection simply because investors realized their return in the form of retirement benefits. At no time however, did Congress indicate that pension benefits in and of themselves gave a transaction the characteristics of a security.

The SEC also relies on a 1970 amendment of the Securities Act which extended § 3's exemption from registration to include "any interest or participation in a single or collective trust fund maintained by a bank * * * which interest or participation is issued in connection with (A) a stock bonus, pension, or profit-sharing plan which meets the requirements for qualification under section 401 of Title 26, * * * " § 3(a)(2) of the Securities Act, as amended. It argues that in creating a registration exemption, the amendment manifested Congress' understanding that the interests covered by the amendment otherwise were subject to the Securities Acts. It interprets "interest or participation in a single * * * trust fund * * * issued in connection with * * * a stock bonus, pension, or profit-sharing plan" as referring to a prospective beneficiary's interest in a pension fund. But this construction of the 1970 amendment ignores that measure's central purpose, which was to relieve banks and insurance companies of certain registration obligations. The amendment recognized only that a pension plan had "an interest or participation" in the fund in which its assets were held, not that prospective beneficiaries of a plan had any interest in either the plan's bank-maintained assets or the plan itself.

B.   SEC Interpretation

The court below believed, and it now is argued to us, that almost from its inception the SEC has regarded pension plans as falling within the scope of the

Securities Acts. We are asked to defer to what is seen as a longstanding interpretation of these statutes by the agency responsible for their administration. But there are limits, grounded in the language, purpose and history of the particular statute, on how far an agency properly may go in its interpretative role. Although these limits are not always easy to discern, it is clear here that the SEC's position is neither longstanding nor even arguably within the outer limits of its authority to interpret these Acts.[20]

As we have demonstrated above, the type of pension plan at issue in this case bears no resemblance to the kind of financial interests the Securities Acts were designed to regulate. Further, the SEC's present position is flatly contradicted by its past actions. Until the instant litigation arose, the public record reveals no evidence that the SEC had ever considered the Securities Acts to be applicable to noncontributory pension plans. In 1941, the SEC first articulated the position that voluntary, contributory plans had investment characteristics that rendered them "securities" under the Acts. At the same time, however, the SEC recognized that noncontributory plans were not covered by the Securities Acts because such plans did not involve a "sale" within the meaning of the statutes. * * *

In an attempt to reconcile these interpretations of the Securities Acts with its present stand, the SEC now augments its past position with two additional propositions. First, it is argued, noncontributory plans are "securities" even where a "sale" is not involved. Second, the previous concession that noncontributory plans do not involve a "sale" was meant to apply only to the registration and reporting requirements of the Securities Acts; for purposes of the antifraud provisions, a "sale" is involved. As for the first proposition, we observe that none of the SEC opinions, reports, or testimony cited to us address the question. As for the second, the record is unambiguously to the contrary. Both in its 1941 statements and repeatedly since then, the SEC has declared that its "no sale" position applied to the Securities Acts as a whole. * * * Congress acted on this understanding when it proceeded to develop the legislation that became ERISA. [Employee Retirement Income Security Act of 1976, 88 Stat. 829, 29 U.S.C. § 1001 (1988)] * * * As far as we are aware, at no time before this case arose did the SEC intimate that the antifraud provisions of the Securities Acts nevertheless applied to noncontributory pension plans.

IV

If any further evidence were needed to demonstrate that pension plans of the type involved are not subject to the Securities Acts, the enactment of ERISA in 1974 would put the matter to rest. Unlike the Securities Acts, ERISA deals expressly and in detail with pension plans. ERISA requires pension plans to disclose specified information to employees in a specified manner, * * * in contrast to the indefinite and uncertain disclosure obligations imposed by the antifraud provisions of the Securities Acts * * *. Further, ERISA regulates the substantive terms of pension plans, setting standards for plan funding and

---

20. It is commonplace in our jurisprudence that an administrative agency's consistent, longstanding interpretation of the statute under which it operates is entitled to considerable weight. This deference is a product both of an awareness of the practical expertise which an agency normally develops, and of a willingness to accord some measure of flexibility to such an agency as it encounters new and unforeseen problems over time. But this deference is constrained by our obligation to honor the clear meaning of a statute, as revealed by its language, purpose and history. On a number of occasions in recent years this Court has found it necessary to reject the SEC's interpretation of various provisions of the Securities Acts. [Citations omitted.]

limits on the eligibility requirements an employee must meet. For example, with respect to the underlying issue in this case—whether respondent served long enough to receive a pension—§ 203(a) of ERISA now sets the minimum level of benefits an employee must receive after accruing specified years of service, and § 203(b) governs continuous service requirements. Thus if Daniel had retired after § 1053 took effect, the Fund would have been required to pay him at least a partial pension. The Securities Acts, on the other hand, do not purport to set the substantive terms of financial transactions.

The existence of this comprehensive legislation governing the use and terms of employee pension plans severely undercuts all arguments for extending the Securities Acts to noncontributory, compulsory pension plans. Congress believed that it was filling a regulatory void when it enacted ERISA, a belief which the SEC actively encouraged. Not only is the extension of the Securities Acts by the court below unsupported by the language and history of those Acts, but in light of ERISA it serves no general purpose. * * * Whatever benefits employees might derive from the effect of the Securities Acts are now provided in more definite form through ERISA.

V

We hold that the Securities Acts do not apply to a noncontributory, compulsory pension plan. Because the first two counts of respondent's complaint do not provide grounds for relief in federal court, the District Court should have granted the motion to dismiss them. The judgment below is therefore

Reversed.

* * *

---

1.   After *Daniel,* in which the SEC had unsuccessfully argued as an amicus curiae that the federal securities laws applied to even noncontributory pension plans, the SEC issued Securities Act Release No. 6188 (Feb. 1, 1980), which announced that it would thereafter deem only those pension plans that were both voluntary and contributory to constitute securities. See also Uselton v. Commercial Lovelace Motor Freight, Inc., 940 F.2d 564 (10th Cir.1991) (reading *Daniel* as limited to compulsory, noncontributing plans). Is this the critical distinction in the Supreme Court's analysis in *Daniel?* Or, is it the existence of ERISA, an alternative regulatory regime, which also applies to voluntary, contributory plans?

1.   CONDOMINIUMS AND REAL ESTATE DEVELOPMENTS

Securities Act Release No. 5347

Securities and Exchange Commission.
January 4, 1973.

GUIDELINES AS TO THE APPLICABILITY OF THE FEDERAL SE-CURITIES LAWS TO OFFERS AND SALES OF CONDOMINI-UMS OR UNITS IN A REAL ESTATE DEVELOPMENT

The Securities and Exchange Commission today called attention to the applicability of the federal securities laws to the offer and sale of condominium units, or other units in a real estate development, coupled with an offer or agreement to perform or arrange certain rental or other services for the purchaser. The Commission noted that such offerings may involve the offering of a security in the form of an investment contract or a participation in a profit sharing arrangement within the meaning of the Securities Act of 1933 and the Securities Exchange Act of 1934.[1] Where this is the case any offering of any such securities must comply with the registration and prospectus delivery requirements of the Securities Act, unless an exemption therefrom is available, and must comply with the anti-fraud provisions of the Securities Act and the Securities Exchange Act and the regulations thereunder. In addition, persons engaged in the business of buying or selling investment contracts or participations in profit sharing agreements of this type as agents for others, or as principal for their own account, may be brokers or dealers within the meaning of the Securities Exchange Act, and therefore may be required to be registered as such with the Commission under the provisions of Section 15 of that Act.

The Commission is aware that there is uncertainty about when offerings of condominiums and other types of similar units may be considered to be offerings of securities that should be registered pursuant to the Securities Act. The purpose of this release is to alert persons engaged in the business of building and selling condominiums and similar types of real estate developments to their responsibilities under the Securities Act and to provide guidelines for a determination of when an offering of condominiums or other units may be viewed as an offering of securities. Resort condominiums are one of the more common interests in real estate the offer of which may involve an offering of securities. However, other types of units that are part of a development or project present analogous questions under the federal securities laws. Although this release speaks in terms of condominiums, it applies to offerings of all types of units in real estate developments which have characteristics similar to those described herein.

The offer of real estate as such, without any collateral arrangements with the seller or others, does not involve the offer of a security. When the real estate is offered in conjunction with certain services, a security, in the form of an investment contract, may be present. The Supreme Court in Securities and Exchange Commission v. W. J. Howey Co., 328 U.S. 293 (1946) set forth what has become a generally accepted definition of an investment contract * * *.

The *Howey* case involved the sale and operation of orange groves. The reasoning, however, is applicable to condominiums.

* * *

The existence of various kinds of collateral arrangements may cause an offering of condominium units to involve an offering of investment contracts or interests in a profit sharing agreement. The presence of such arrangements indicates that the offeror is offering an opportunity through which the purchaser may earn a return on his investment through the managerial efforts of the promoters or a third party in their operation of the enterprise.

For example, some public offerings of condominium units involve rental pool arrangements. Typically, the rental pool is a device whereby the promoter or a third party undertakes to rent the unit on behalf of the actual owner during that period of time when the unit is not in use by the owner. The rents

---

1. It should be noted that where an investment contract is present, it consists of the agreement offered and the condominium itself.

received and the expenses attributable to rental of all the units in the project are combined and the individual owner receives a ratable share of the rental proceeds regardless of whether his individual unit was actually rented. The offer of the unit together with the offer of an opportunity to participate in such a rental pool involves the offer of investment contracts which must be registered unless an exemption is available.

Also, the condominium units may be offered with a contract or agreement that places restrictions, such as required use of an exclusive rental agent or limitations on the period of time the owner may occupy the unit, on the purchaser's occupancy or rental of the property purchased. Such restrictions suggest that the purchaser is in fact investing in a business enterprise, the return from which will be substantially dependent on the success of the managerial efforts of other persons. In such cases, registration of the resulting investment contract would be required.

In any situation where collateral arrangements are coupled with the offering of condominiums, whether or not specifically of the types discussed above, the manner of offering and economic inducements held out to the prospective purchaser play an important role in determining whether the offerings involve securities. In other words, condominiums, coupled with a rental arrangement, will be deemed to be securities if they are offered and sold through advertising, sales literature, promotional schemes or oral representations which emphasize the economic benefits to the purchaser to be derived from the managerial efforts of the promoter, or a third party designated or arranged for by the promoter, in renting the units.

In summary, the offering of condominium units in conjunction with any one of the following will cause the offering to be viewed as an offering of securities in the form of investment contracts:

1. The condominiums, with any rental arrangement or other similar service, are offered and sold with emphasis on the economic benefits to the purchaser to be derived from the managerial efforts of the promoter, or a third party designated or arranged for by the promoter, from rental of the units.

2. The offering of participation in a rental pool arrangement; and

3. The offering of a rental or similar arrangement whereby the purchaser must hold his unit available for rental for any part of the year, must use an exclusive rental agent or is otherwise materially restricted in his occupancy or rental of his unit.

In all of the above situations, investor protection requires the application of the federal securities laws.

If the condominiums are not offered and sold with emphasis on the economic benefits to the purchaser to be derived from the managerial efforts of others, and assuming that no plan to avoid the registration requirements of the Securities Act is involved, an owner of a condominium unit may, after purchasing his unit, enter into a non-pooled rental arrangement with an agent not designated or required to be used as a condition to the purchase, whether or not such agent is affiliated with the offeror, without causing a sale of a security to be involved in the sale of the unit. Further a continuing affiliation between

the developers or promoters of a project and the project by reason of maintenance arrangements does not make the unit a security.

* * *

* * * Whether an offering of securities is involved necessarily depends on
the facts and circumstances of each particular case. The staff of the Commission will be available to respond to written inquiries on such matters.

* * *

———

Re-assessment. Confident as the SEC's words are in the foregoing release,
they were written in 1973, well before the Circuits came to split over the
question of "vertical" versus "horizontal" commonality. In those Circuits that
agree with Judge Posner's analysis in Wals v. Fox Hills Development Corporation (Casebook supra p. 323), what facts would the SEC have to show before a
purchaser of a condominium unit in a ski lodge could be said to have purchased
a security? For example, suppose the rental proceeds of the unit are not pooled
with those of other investors, but are instead simply split on a 70/30 basis
between the owner of the individual unit and the developer of the condominium?

2.   PARTNERSHIPS LIMITED PARTNERSHIPS, AND LIMITED LIABILITY COMPANIES

Steinhardt Group Inc. v. Citicorp

United States Court of Appeals, Third Circuit, 1997.
126 F.3d 144.

■ Before: Becker and Mansmann, Circuit Judges, and Hoevoler, District Judge.

■ Mansmann, Circuit Judge.

In this appeal, we are asked to decide whether a highly structured
securitization transaction negotiated between Citicorp and an investor in a
limited partnership constitutes an "investment contract" as that term is
defined by the Supreme Court in *SEC* v. *W.J. Howey Co.* Examining the
economic reality of the transaction as a whole, we conclude that the limited
partner retained pervasive control over its investment in the limited partnership Such that it cannot be deemed a passive investor under *Howey* and its
progeny. Accordingly, we find the securitization transaction here does not
constitute an investment contract. We will, therefore, affirm the judgment of
the district court.

I.

* * *

A.

The controversy here arises out of alleged violations of Sections 10(b) and
20(a) of the Securities Exchange Act of 1934, and Rule 10b–5 involving the
"securitization" of a pool of delinquent residential mortgage loans ("Mortgage
Loans") and real estate owned by Citicorp as a result of foreclosed loans

("REO") The plaintiffs are The Steinhardt Group Inc. ("Steinhardt" Group) and C.B. Mtge., L.P. ("C.B.Mtge."). . . .

The fraudulent conduct alleged in the amended complaint arises out of a severe financial crisis faced by Citicorp during the early 1990's. With bad loans and illiquid assets threatening the very existence of the nation's then-largest banking institution, Citicorp was looking for a way to extricate itself from its financial problems. The securitization transaction was thus conceived by Citicorp to remove the nonperforming assets from its financial books and replace them with cash.

In essence, the securitization required Citicorp to create an investment vehicle limited partnership ultimately named Bristol Oaks, L.P. that would issue both debt securities, in the form of nonrecourse bonds, and equity securities, in the form of partnership interests, to investors. Bristol would acquire title to the nonperforming Mortgage Loans and REO properties and would retain Ontra, Inc. to manage and liquidate the assets. Then Bristol would obtain bridge financing from Citibank and CNAI; shortly thereafter, CSI would securitize and underwrite a public offering of bonds and other debt securities to pay off the bridge financing. All of the investors' money was to be paid to Bristol and become the capital of that investment vehicle. The return on these investments was to come from the same pool of assets.

During late 1993 and the first half of 1994, representatives of CSI made a series of written and oral presentations to the Steinhardt Group in which they described returns of 18% or more annually by investing in Bristol. Throughout these presentations and in other meetings and telephone discussions, Citicorp explained how it had created the proprietary "Citicorp Non–Performing Loan Model" (the "Pricing Model"), based on its own past experience, intimate knowledge of the assets at issue, and the valuation of such assets. Citicorp represented the Pricing Model to be an accurate means of pricing the Mortgage Loans and REO properties in the portfolio and of providing the Steinhardt Group with the promised 18% or greater returns. In particular, Citicorp represented to the Steinhardt Group that no institution in America had more experience in single-family residential mortgages, or more knowledge about the process of collecting on defaulted mortgage loans. Moreover, Citicorp touted not only its longstanding reputation in the banking industry, but also how the assumptions in the Pricing Model were firmly grounded upon Citicorp's own unparalleled experience and expertise.

A series of factual assumptions lies at the core of the Pricing Model. First, Citicorp assumed that the most accurate "proxy" for the values of the REO and the properties mortgaged for the Mortgage Loans would be Broker's Price Opinions ("BPOs"). These BPOs would be obtained from independent real estate brokers reflecting collateral value as well as the proceeds that would be obtained within six months if the properties were listed for sale. In addition, these BPOs were to provide "as is" values indicating what the properties were worth in light of their overall exterior and interior physical condition. Finally, an integral component of Citicorp's valuation methodology was obtaining BPOs for all of the assets, rather than just a sampling, thereby resulting in a more accurate valuation of the portfolio and significantly reducing the investment risk.

Under the Pricing Model, Citicorp represented the BPOs would be used to calculate a current Loan-to-Value ("LTV") ratio for each of the properties. The LTV ratio was used to project the probability of possible outcomes with respect to each of the Mortgage Loans, as well as the ultimate cash proceeds that would flow from each of the possible resolutions. The Pricing Model further assumed that each of the existing and to-be-foreclosed REO properties could be sold for 98% of the BPO, which Citicorp represented to be conservative and designed to assure realization of its promised 18% return on the portfolio. . . .

According to the amended complaint, Citicorp knew at the time it made these representations that several of the assumptions underlying the Pricing Model were false. Steinhardt claims that Citicorp obtained inflated valuations by promising the brokers they would later be hired to list the properties for sale if the BPOs were satisfactory to Citicorp. The inflated valuations, in turn, caused the assets to be overpriced, which resulted in the overstatement of future cash flow. Steinhardt further contends that [Citicorp] failed to follow its own internal controls for insuring unbiased appraisals, that it employed brokers not on Citicorp's approved list, and that it required brokers to provide large numbers of valuations within grossly inadequate periods of time, which further undermined their accuracy. Although Citicorp was allegedly warned repeatedly by one of its own officers that the assets were overpriced, these warnings were never revealed to Steinhardt. Rather, Steinhardt contends these warnings were actively concealed in order to induce it to invest in Bristol.

According to the amended complaint, Citicorp concealed other information from Steinhardt, including the true cost of repairs and maintenance, low-end BPOs and other appraisals, recent appraisals which reflected the decline in the real estate market, the true cost and time for foreclosures, the true likelihood of delays caused by bankruptcy proceedings, and Citicorp's intention not to provide a conduit for the sale of reinstated loans. Steinhardt claims that "[t]he cumulative effect of all these misrepresentations by Citicorp was to fraudulently inflate the purchase price for the entire portfolio."

Based on Citicorp's representations, Steinhardt entered into a letter agreement dated May 26, 1994, with . . . Citicorp (the "Letter Agreement"), in which it committed to make an equity contribution of between $40 and $45 million in Bristol. According to the Letter Agreement, a portfolio of approximately $540 million to $660 million in Mortgage Loans and REO properties was to be sold by [Citicorp] to a newly formed limited partnership, Bristol. To fund the acquisition of the properties, [Citicorp] agreed to lend the newly formed partnership no less than 90% of the total purchase price; the remaining 10% was to be provided by the Partnership in the form of a cash payment representing the Partnership's total equity. Subsequently, debt securities were to be issued by the Partnership and underwritten by CSI to repay the [Citicorp] loans.

The Letter Agreement further provided that "[t]he Partnership will contract with Ontra, Inc. . . ., an independent third party who is experienced in loan servicing, loan workouts, REO sales, and oversight of these asset types", to service the properties. An affiliate of Ontra, BGO, was named the general partner of the new limited partnership in exchange for a 1% equity contribution. . . .

The first step of the securitization transaction was completed in the early part of July, 1994, in accordance with two Sale Agreements dated June 30, 1994. Pursuant to the Sale Agreements, Bristol and BHT purchased approximately 3,100 Mortgage Loans and 900 REO properties from Citibank and CNAI for close to $415 million. Bristol purchased all of the assets except the New

York REOs which were acquired by BHT. C.B. Mtge. invested $42 million in Bristol and acquired a 98.79% limited partner interest....

On December 14, 1994, the second step of securitization transaction was completed with the issuance of the debt securities. According to Steinhardt, Citicorp controlled every aspect of the securitization by: structuring all aspects of the securitization; drafting the prospectus; leading all material discussions with the rating agencies; acting as the sole underwriter for the issuance of the debt securities; separately indemnifying Bristol and its affiliates; purchasing an interest rate cap to minimize the risk of any changes in the Variable interest rates; arranging for credit enhancement; paying for all of the expenses of securitization; in lieu of customary underwriter's fees, applying the proceeds of the securitization to pay off the bridge loans; and reimbursing Bristol for additional operating expenses resulting from the securitization.

According to the amended complaint, Steinhardt first learned of Citicorp's allegedly fraudulent scheme in 1995 through conversations with a former officer of CMI, which ultimately led to an investigation and the discovery of the alleged fraud. On December 1, 1995, Bristol and BHT (collectively the "Partnerships"), sent Citibank and CNAI a repurchase notice for more than 2,300 assets; however, Citibank and CNAI refused to honor their obligations to repurchase these assets....

II.

The outcome of this dispute hinges upon whether, under the circumstances, the securitization transaction constitutes an investment contract within the meaning of section 2(1) of the Securities Act of 1933. In order to invoke the protections of the federal securities laws, an investor must show, as a threshold matter, that the instrument in question is a security. Section 2(1) of the Act sets forth the definition of the term "security." Included in this definition are several catch-all categories which were designed to cover other securities interests not specifically enumerated in the statute.... One such category is the "investment contract."

The term investment contract has not been defined by Congress, nor does the legislative history to the 1933 and 1934 Acts illuminate what Congress intended by the term investment contract. The interpretation of this term has thus been left to the judiciary. In 1946, the Supreme Court took up the task of defining the parameters of an investment contract in the seminal case of *SEC v. W.J. Howey*. The Court stated:

> an investment contract for purposes of the Securities Act means a contract, transaction or scheme whereby a person invests his money in a common enterprise and is led to expect profits solely from the efforts of the promoter or a third party ...

Clearly Steinhardt has alleged sufficient facts to meet the first prong of *Howey*. The Steinhardt Group, through its affiliate, C.B. Mtge., has invested $42 million dollars in Bristol with the expectation of receiving a return on its investment of approximately 18%. Thus the facts alleged show that Steinhardt has undertaken some degree of economic risk....

Regarding the second prong, commonality, we have previously applied a horizontal commonality approach in determining whether a particular investment constitutes a security. *See, Salcer v. Merrill Lynch, Pierce, Fenner and Smith,* 682 F.2d 459, 460 (3d Cir.1982).... In the case before us, Steinhardt maintains that the district court erred in concluding that horizontal commonality was not adequately pleaded. In the alternative, Steinhardt argues that vertical commonality exists here and urges us to find that vertical commonality can satisfy the *Howey* common enterprise prong. On the other hand, the Citicorp Defendants agree with the district court's finding as to the common enterprise element but disagree with the court's ruling insofar as it found that the third element of the Howey test was adequately pleaded—the "solely from the efforts of others" element. The Citicorp Defendants entreat us to find that Steinhardt negotiated such pervasive control over its investment in Bristol Oaks that it cannot meet the third element of *Howey*.

The district court found that only vertical commonality, and not horizontal commonality, was successfully pleaded in this case. Stating that the court of appeals has not adopted vertical commonality, the district court held that the common enterprise prong of the *Howey* test had not been adequately pleaded in the complaint. We have addressed horizontal commonality only once previously in *Salcer, supra,* where we summarily held the investment was not part of a pooled group of funds. We do not need to consider whether vertical commonality should be adopted here, or whether horizontal community was adequately pleaded, because we believe the third element of *Howey* is dispositive.

The third prong of the Supreme Court's test in *Howey* test requires that the purchaser be attracted to the investment by the prospect of a profit on the investment rather than a desire to use or consume the item purchased. *United Housing Foundation, Inc. v. Forman,* 421 U.S. 837, 853–54, 95 S.Ct. 2051, 2060–61, 44 L.Ed.2d 621 (1975) (court concluded that sale of shares in a housing cooperative did not give rise to a securities transaction where none of the promotional materials emphasized profit and there was a low probability the shares would actually produce a profit). In analyzing this element, the courts have also looked at whether the investor has meaningfully participated in the management of the partnership in which it has invested such that it has more than minimal control over the investment's performance.

In *SEC v. Glenn W. Turner Enterprises, Inc.,* 474 F.2d 476, 482 (9th Cir.1973), the court of appeals stated that the critical inquiry is "whether the efforts made by those other than the investor are the undeniably significant ones, those essential managerial efforts which affect the failure or success of the enterprise." . . . .

We cited with approval the test set forth in *Glenn W. Turner Enterprises, supra,* for determining whether the third prong of Howey had been met in *Lino v. City Investing* Co., 487 F.2d 689, 692–93 (3d Cir.1973), where we concluded that franchise licensing agreements did not constitute investment contracts because of the significant efforts of th? licensee in promoting the franchise. . . . We held that ""an investment contract can exist where the investor is required to perform some duties, as long as they are nominal or limited and would have "little direct effect upon receipt by the participant of the benefits promised by the promoters." *Id.* (quoting Securities Act Release No. 5211, supra). Thus, we refused to read literally the term "solely," as used in the *Howey* test, when evaluating the efforts of the investor. *Id.* . . .

To resolve the issue of whether Steinhardt's involvement in the Bristol Oaks Limited Partnership was limited to that of a passive investor, we must look at the transaction as a whole, considering the arrangements the parties made for the operation of the investment vehicle in order to determine who exercised control in generating profits for the vehicle. The Limited Partnership

Agreement ("LPA"), which establishes the relative powers of the partners in running the enterprise, therefore governs our inquiry.

Section 3.1(f) of the LPA, as amended, requires that "the Managing Partner" shall not have the right to take any of the following actions ("Material Actions") without the consent of . . . a Majority of the Partners (or pursuant to an approved Business Plan). . . ." The "Material Actions", set forth in section 3.1(f) of the LPA, include most tasks that are crucial to turning the mortgages and REO into profit, which is the basic purpose of Bristol Oaks, e.g., entering into any written or verbal material agreement or transaction with any borrower outside of the Loan Documents; giving any material consent required to be obtained by any borrower under the Loan Documents; modifying or amending any of the Loan Documents; exercising any rights under the Loan Documents; selling, exchanging, securitizing, conveying, or otherwise voluntarily disposing of, or placing any encumbrance on, the Properties. Under the LPA, a "Majority of the Partners" is defined as "those Partners holding greater than fifty percent (50%) of the Percentage Interests . . .", meaning that Steinhardt alone constitutes a "Majority of the Partners."

Steinhardt approved the interim business plan and although Citicorp drafted that plan, Steinhardt retains the power to amend that plan as it wishes in one of two ways: (1) in its capacity as "Majority of the Partners," Steinhardt can propose and approve a new business plan; and (2) if the general partner proposes a new business plan, Steinhardt retains veto power, which it can exercise merely by declining to approve the proposed change within fifteen business days. Thus, we agree with the Citicorp Defendants that "Steinhardt's consent is required for the taking of any 'Material Action,' whether through its control over the business plan, or through its veto power over 'Material Actions' that fall outside the parameters of the business plan."

The LPA further provides that where a Majority of the Partners proposes a Material Action, the general partner "shall use best efforts to implement such Material Action at the Partnership's expense on the terms proposed by such Majority of the Partners," i.e., Steinhardt. If the general partner refuses to act, with such best efforts in pursuit of Steinhardt's proposals, Steinhardt can remove and replace the general partner without notice.

As the above provisions demonstrate, the LPA gives Steinhardt pervasive control over the management of the Partnership. Indeed, these quite significant powers are far afield of the typical limited partnership agreement whereby a limited partner leaves the control of the business to the general partners. We find the agreement altogether consistent with the arrangement before us: Steinhardt, a sophisticated investor, made a $42 million capital contribution in Bristol Oaks, thereby becoming a 98.79% partner through a highly negotiated transaction.

Moreover, it appears the parties have carefully constructed the LPA to give Steinhardt significant control without possibly running afoul of the Delaware Revised Uniform Limited Partnership Act, 6 Del. C. § 17–101, et seq. Indeed, Steinhardt has proposal and approval rights rather than more affirmative responsibilities. We also find unpersuasive Steinhardt's contention that its powers were limited under the LPA. First, Steinhardt points out language in the LPA that:

[e]xcept for specific rights to propose and approve or disapprove certain Partnership matters as set forth in the Agreement, the Limited Partners

shall not take any part whatsoever in, or have any control over, the business or affairs of the Partnership, nor shall the Limited Partners have any right or authority to act for or bind the Partnership.

Section 3.1(g) of the LPA. Given the extensive proposal and approval rights retained by Steinhardt under the LPA, the "except" clause swallows the general rule of nonparticipation. Second, Steinhardt points out that if a business plan was in place, as it was as soon as Steinhardt approved the interim agreement, Steinhardt's approval was not required for the general partner to take Material Actions. Steinhardt's argument lacks substance, however, since Steinhardt could amend the business plan at any time, and the general partner needed Steinhardt's approval to take any Material Action not provided for under the business plan.

At oral argument, counsel for Steinhardt made a corollary argument that since the interim agreement was in place, the general partner could operate the partnership without Steinhardt exercising the authority given to it under the LPA. Accordingly, counsel argued, Steinhardt's amended complaint could survive a 12(b)(6) motion. However, ... the issue does not turn on whether the investor actually exercised its rights, but rather, on what *"legal* rights and powers [were] enjoyed by the investor." Moreover, on a 12(b)(6) motion, we must consider the commercial realities of the transaction and, in doing so, we conclude that without Steinhardt's involvement, the Partnership could only operate in a static, inflexible way that is unrealistic and impractical in today's business climate.

Steinhardt further argues that the Delaware Revised Uniform Limited Partnership Act supports its position that it was a passive investor. The Act enumerates those actions of the limited partners that do not equate to controlling the management of the partnership and includes many of the approval rights given to Steinhardt. Steinhardt submits that since under the Act it would not be deemed to have exercised control, it must be a passive investor for *Howey* purposes.

We find that the Act is not controlling here. The LPA states "[e]xcept as otherwise expressly provided in this Agreement, the rights and duties of the Partners and the administration and termination of the Partnership shall be governed by the Act." The Act defines control, however solely for the purpose of limiting the liability of the limited partners to third parties—a situation not present here. 6 Del. C. § 17–303(b). This does not necessarily equate to the threshold for finding a passive investor under federal securities laws. The Delaware Act puts third parties on notice that just because limited partners undertake certain responsibilities with regard to the management of the partnership, that does not make them liable for the obligations of the partnership. Here, Steinhardt is not trying to shield itself from liability, but rather, is seeking relief for alleged violations of federal securities laws. Federal law therefore determines whether the investor's involvement is significant enough to place it outside the role of a passive investor.

Thus, accepting, as we must, the facts as alleged in the amended complaint, we do not find Steinhardt is entitled to relief under *Howey* and its progeny.

III.

We find that the rights and powers assigned to Steinhardt under the LPA were not nominal, but rather, were significant and, thus, directly affected the profits it received from the Partnership. Accordingly, we hold Steinhardt's investment in the Bristol Oaks Limited Partnership does not constitute an investment contract.

Because we find that Steinhardt was not a passive investor, we need not consider whether the securitization here constituted a common enterprise. We will, therefore, affirm the judgment of the district court.

Great Lakes Chemical Corporation v. Monsanto Company

United States District Court for the District of Delaware, 2000.
96 F.Supp.2d 376.

■ McKELVIE, DISTRICT JUDGE.

... On May 3, 1999, Great Lakes purchased NSC Technologies Company, LLC ("NSC"), from Monsanto and STI. NSC is a Delaware limited liability company with its principal place of business in Mount Prospect, Illinois.

On January 4, 2000, Great Lakes filed the complaint in this action, alleging that Monsanto and STI violated § 10(b) of the Securities Exchange Act of 1934, and Rule 10b–5 promulgated thereunder, by failing to disclose material information in conjunction with the sale of NSC. ...

On March 9, 2000, Monsanto and STI moved to dismiss the complaint pursuant to Fed. R. Civ. P. 9(b) and 12(b)(6), for failure to plead fraud with specificity and for failure to state a claim upon which relief may be granted. Among their assertions, Monsanto and STI argue that the interests sold to Great Lakes were not "securities," as defined by § 2(a)(1) of the Securities Act of 1933, and that Great Lakes has failed to plead adequate facts in support of its claim for securities fraud.

* * *

II.   DISCUSSION

A.   What Is an LLC?

In Delaware, LLCs are formed pursuant to the Delaware Limited Liability Company Act, 6 Del. C. §§ 18–101 et seq. LLCs are hybrid entities that combine desirable characteristics of corporations, limited partnerships, and general partnerships. LLCs are entitled to partnership status for federal income tax purposes under certain circumstances, which permits LLC members to avoid double taxation, i.e., taxation of the entity as well as taxation of the members' incomes. See Treas. Reg. §§ 301.7701–1 et seq. Moreover, LLCs members, unlike partners in general partnerships, may have limited liability, such that LLC members who are involved in managing the LLC may avoid becoming personally liable for its debts and obligations. See 6 Del. C. §§ 18–303. In addition, LLCs have greater flexibility than corporations in terms of organizational structure. The Delaware Limited Liability Company Act, for example, establishes the default rule that management of an LLC shall be vested in its members, but permits members to establish other forms of governance in their LLC agreements. See 6 Del. C. §§ 18–402.

* * *

B.   Are the Interests in NSC That Were Transferred Pursuant to the Purchase Agreement "Securities" Under Federal Law?

To prevail in its claim that defendants engaged in securities fraud under § 10(b) of the Securities Exchange Act of 1934, Great Lakes must demonstrate that: (i) defendants made a misstatement or omission; (ii) of a material fact; (iii) with scienter; (iv) in connection with the purchase or sale of securities; (v) upon which plaintiffs relied; and (vi) that reliance proximately caused plaintiffs' losses. See In re Westinghouse Securities Litigation, 90 F.3d 696, 710 (3d Cir.1996). A threshold question in this matter is whether defendants' alleged misconduct involved a purchase or sale of securities. Defendants contend that plaintiff's claim fails as a matter of law because the Interests in NSC do not constitute securities. [The court then quotes the definition of "security" in Section 2(a)(1) of the Securities Act of 1933.]

* * *

1.   Key Cases Governing the Characterization of Novel Instruments

It is helpful, before determining whether the Interests in NSC constitute "stock," an "investment contract," or "any interest or instrument commonly known as a security," to review a series of cases that provide guidance as to how to characterize novel financial instruments.

a.   SEC v. W.J. Howey

The Supreme Court defined the parameters of an "investment contract" for the purposes of federal securities law in the case of SEC v. W.J. Howey Co., 328 U.S. 293, 298, (1946). Howey concerned a Florida corporation, the Howey Company, that sold small tracts of land in a citrus grove to forty-two purchasers, many of whom were patrons of a resort hotel. See id. at 296. For the most part, the purchasers lacked the knowledge, skill, and equipment necessary for the care and cultivation of citrus trees. They invested in the enterprise for profit. The purchasers were free to contract with a number of companies to service the tracts, but the sales contract stressed the superiority of Howey-in-the-Hills Service, Inc., which the purchasers chose to service 85% of the acreage sold. The service contracts granted Howey-in-the-Hills full and complete possession of the acreage, and the individual purchasers had no right of entry to market the crop. Purchasers of tracts shared in the profits of the enterprise, which amounted to 20% in the 1943–44 growing season. The Howey Company did not register the interests in the enterprise as securities.

The Securities and Exchange Commission ("SEC") brought an action pursuant to § 5(a) of the Securities Act seeking to enjoin the Howey Company from using interstate mail to offer and sell interests in the enterprise. Because the interests at issue did not constitute any of the traditional kinds of securities enumerated in § 2(a)(1) of the Securities Act, the SEC argued that the interests were "investment contracts." Noting that the term "investment contract" was not defined by Congress, but that the term was widely used in state securities laws, the Court largely adopted the definition used at the time by state courts. The Court stated that "an investment contract for purposes of the Securities Act means a contract, transaction or scheme whereby a person invests his money in a common enterprise and is led to expect profits solely from the efforts of the promoter or a third party." Howey, 328 U.S. at 298–99. Thus, the three requirements for establishing an investment contract are: (1) "an investment of money," (2) "in a common enterprise," (3) "with profits to come solely from the efforts of others." Id. at 301. In articulating this test, the Supreme Court stated that this definition "embodies a flexible rather than a static principle, one that is capable of adaptation to meet the countless and variable schemes devised by those who seek the use of the money of others on the promise of profits." Id. at 299.

b.   United Housing Foundation, Inc. v. Forman

The Supreme Court established guidelines for whether non-traditional instruments labeled "stock" constitute securities in United Housing Foundation, Inc. v. Forman, 421 U.S. 837, (1975). Forman concerned a nonprofit housing cooperative that sold shares of "stock" to prospective tenants. The sole purpose of acquiring the shares was to enable the purchaser to occupy an apartment in the cooperative. The shares essentially represented a recoverable deposit on the apartment. The shares were explicitly tied to the apartment, as they could not be transferred to a non-tenant. Nor could they be pledged or encumbered. No voting rights attached to the shares.

After the housing cooperative raised rental charges, the residents sued the cooperative under § 17(a) of the Securities Act, asserting that the cooperative falsely represented that it would bear all subsequent cost increases due to factors such as inflation. The Supreme Court held that the "stock" issued by the cooperative did not constitute a security. The shares, the Court found, lacked the five most common features of stock: (1) the right to receive dividends contingent upon an apportionment of profits; (2) negotiability; (3) the ability to be pledged or hypothecated; (4) voting rights in proportion to the number of shares owned; and (5) the ability to appreciate in value. Id. at 851. Finding that the purchasers obtained the shares in order to acquire subsidized low-cost living space, not to invest for profit, the Court ruled that the "stock" issued by the cooperative was not a security. See id. at 852.

c.   Landreth Timber Co. v. Landreth

Following the issuance of Forman, a number of lower courts began to apply the Howey test to distinguish between investment transactions, which were covered by the securities laws, and commercial transactions, which were not. See, e.g., Landreth Timber Co. v. Landreth, 731 F.2d 1348, 1352 (9th Cir.1984) (citing cases). In Landreth, the Ninth Circuit addressed whether a single individual who purchased 100% of the stock in a lumber corporation, and who had the power to actively manage the acquired business, could state a claim under the securities laws for alleged fraud in the sale of the business. The Ninth Circuit found that the purchaser bought full control of the corporation, and that the economic reality of the transaction was the purchase of a business, and not an investment in a security. See id. at 1353. The court held that the sale of 100% of the stock of a closely held corporation was not a transaction involving a "security."

Reversing the Ninth Circuit, the Supreme Court reasoned that it would be burdensome to apply the Howey test to transactions involving traditional stock. See Landreth Timber Co. v. Landreth, 471 U.S. 681, 686–88, (1985). The Court held that, insofar as a transaction involves the sale of an instrument called "stock," and the stock bears the five common attributes of stock enumerated in Forman, the transaction is governed by the securities laws. The Court noted that stock is specifically enumerated in § 2(a)(1) of the Securities Act as a security, and that stock is so "quintessentially a security" that it is unnecessary to apply the Howey test to determine if it is a security. Id. at 693. The financial instrument involved in the case, the Court reasoned, "is traditional stock, plainly within the statutory definition." Id. at 690. "There is no need here," the Court continued, "to look beyond the characteristics of the instrument to determine whether the [Securities] Acts apply." Id. The Court stated that the Howey test should only be applied to determine whether an instrument is an "investment contract," and should not be applied in the context of other instruments enumerated in §§ 2(1) of the Securities Act. See id. at 691–92.

* * *

2. Prior Cases Concerning Whether Interests in LLCs are Securities

The present case raises novel issues regarding the regulation of transactions involving interests in LLCs. The court has identified three cases in which other courts have determined whether interests in LLCs constitute securities.

a. Keith v. Black Diamond Advisors, Inc.

In Keith v. Black Diamond Advisors, Inc., 48 F.Supp.2d 326 (S.D.N.Y. 1999), the plaintiff, Keith, founded a sub-prime mortgage lending firm, Eagle Corp., and brought it to profitability. Milton was an original investor in Eagle. Black Diamond, a venture capital firm, proposed a joint venture in which it would contribute $150,000 in cash, and Keith and Milton would each contribute their interests in Eagle, to form a New York limited liability company, Pace LLC. Through this transaction, Black Diamond acquired 50% of the interests in Pace, and Keith and Milton each received a 25% stake. Keith alleged that Black Diamond subsequently used its majority position to strip him of control of Pace. Keith sued Black Diamond for federal securities fraud.

The court applied the Howey test, and found that Keith had invested money in a common enterprise. The court, however, found that Keith had retained substantial control over the enterprise, such that he did not have an expectation of profits "solely from the efforts of others." As such, the court concluded that the LLC interests were not investment contracts. The court dismissed the case for lack of jurisdiction.

b. SEC v. Parkersburg Wireless LLC

SEC v. Parkersburg Wireless LLC, 991 F.Supp. 6 (D.D.C.1997), involves a LLC that was established to provide wireless cable services. The promoters of the company sold "memberships" in the company to over 700 individuals in 43 states. The promoters targeted prospective investors who had Individual Retirement Accounts, and encouraged them to divert funds from their IRAs to buy membership units of the company.

The SEC sought to enjoin the sale of the membership interests. The court found that the interests sold in the LLC "easily satisfy" the Howey test for investment contracts. The investors' $10,000 minimum contribution constituted an "investment of money." Because the 700 individuals were to receive a pro rata share of the company's revenues, the court found there was a common enterprise. Moreover, the investors had little, if any, input into the company, so their profits were to come solely from the efforts of others.

c. SEC v. Shreveport Wireless Cable Television Partnership

SEC v. Shreveport Wireless Cable Television Partnership, 1998 WL 892948 (D.D.C.1998), involves three entities: Reading Partnership and Shreveport Partnership, which are both general partnerships, and Baton Rouge LLC. All three entities were established to provide wireless cable services. Each entity engaged the services of a corporation to develop the telecommunications services and to solicit public investment in the enterprises. The promoters sold memberships in the three entities to approximately 2000 investors.

The SEC sought to enjoin the sale of interests in the ventures. In ruling upon defendants' motion for summary judgment that the interests were not securities, the court applied the Howey test to determine whether the interests were investment contracts. The court found that the purchasers of the interests had invested money in a common enterprise. The court found, however, that there was a question of fact as to whether the investors exercised significant control over the management of the corporation, and denied defendants' motion for summary judgment.

Having reviewed these other cases in which courts have considered whether LLC interests might constitute securities, the court will determine whether the Interests in NSC constitute "stock," an "investment contract," or "any interest or instrument commonly known as a security."

3.   Are the Interests In NSC "Stock"?

Great Lakes contends that NSC is the functional equivalent of a corporation, and that the Interests in NSC should be treated as stock. Great Lakes notes that the LLC Agreement refers to the Interests as "equity securities," and that the LLC Agreement prohibits the transfer of the Interests in such a way as would "violate the provisions of any federal or state securities laws."

* * *

As discussed above, the Supreme Court has described the five most common characteristics of stock as follows: (1) the right to receive dividends contingent upon an apportionment of profit; (2) negotiability; (3) the ability to be pledged or hypothecated; (4) the conferring of voting rights in proportion to the number of shares owned; and (5) the capacity to appreciate in value. See Landreth, 471 U.S. at 686; Forman, 421 U.S. at 851.

As noted by plaintiffs, these attributes of stock also characterize, at least to some degree, the Interests in NSC. NSC's Members are entitled to share, pro rata, in distributions of Net Cash Flow, contingent upon its distribution by the Board of Managers. The Interests are negotiable and may be pledged or hypothecated, subject to approval by the Board of Managers. See Sulkow v. Crosstown Apparel Inc., 807 F.2d 33, 37 (2d Cir.1986) (stating that some limitations on a stock's negotiability and pledgeability are insufficient to negate the character of the stock as a security). Members in NSC have voting rights in proportion to their Percentage Interest in the company. And, the Interests in NSC have the capacity to appreciate in value. The Interests in NSC are undoubtedly stock-like in character, but the question remains if the Interests can be characterized as "stock" for the purposes of the federal securities laws.

The primary goal of the securities laws is to regulate investments, and not commercial ventures. See Howey, 328 U.S. at 298 (restricting scope of "investment contracts" to those enterprises with passive investors); Reves v. Ernst & Young, 494 U.S. 56, 64–65 (1989) (articulating "family resemblance test" to distinguish between notes that are used in the investment market from those having commercial character). In transactions involving traditional stock, lower courts had attempted to distinguish between investment transactions and commercial transactions. See Landreth, 731 F.2d at 1352. The Supreme Court, as discussed above, held that it is unnecessary to attempt to distinguish between commercial and investment transactions when the financial instrument in question is traditional stock. See Landreth, 471 U.S. at 690. Because stock is listed in § 2(a)(1) of the Securities Act as a security, and because people trading in traditional stock are likely to have a high expectation that their activities are governed by the securities laws, the Court ruled that all transactions involving traditional stock are covered by the securities laws, regardless if the transaction is of an investment or commercial character. See id. The Court expressly limited this rule to transactions involving traditional stock. See id. at 694.

The Supreme Court suggested, prior to the issuance of Landreth, that certain stock-like instruments might be construed as "stock" for the purposes of the federal securities laws. In Tcherepnin v. Knight, 389 U.S. 332 (1967), the Court considered whether purchasers of withdrawable capital shares in a savings and loan association could state a claim under the federal securities laws for allegedly misleading statements made in solicitation materials. Holders of the withdrawable capital shares were entitled to be members of the association and were granted voting rights in proportion to the number of shares they owned. The holders were entitled to dividends declared by the association's board of directors and based on the association's profits. Certain restrictions applied to the transferability of the instruments. The Court rejected the lower court's finding that the restrictions on negotiability precluded a finding that the shares were securities. The Court ruled that the instruments constituted "investment contracts" under Howey. See id. at 339. The Court continued, stating that the instruments could also be characterized as "certificates of interest or participation in any profit-sharing agreement," as "transferable shares," or as "stock." Id. at 339–40. The Court held that the holders of withdrawable capital shares were entitled to the protections afforded by the securities laws.

In Marine Bank v. Weaver, 455 U.S. 551, 557 (1982), the Court reaffirmed its holding in Tcherepnin that the withdrawable capital shares in that case were "like ordinary shares of stock." This statement arose in the context of a suit brought by holders of certificates of deposit who were allegedly defrauded into pledging their certificates to guaranty a third party loan. The lower court held that the certificates of deposit were securities, as they were deemed to be the functional equivalent of the withdrawable capital shares at issue in Tcherepnin. The Court found that the certificates of deposit had different characteristics than withdrawable capital shares, as they conferred upon their holders the right to a fixed rate of interest and did not entitle holders to voting rights. The Court found that the certificates of deposit were not securities. . . .

In the present case, the LLC Interests, although they are "stock-like" in nature, are not traditional stock. Landreth, thus, is inapplicable to this case, and the court must determine whether the sale of NSC was essentially an investment transaction, in which case the securities laws apply, or whether it was a commercial transaction, in which case they do not. To make this determination, the court will apply the Howey test for investment contracts. See Landreth, 471 U.S. at 691–92; see also Keith v. Black Diamond Advisors, Inc., 48 F.Supp.2d 326 (S.D.N.Y.1999) (dismissing securities fraud complaint after applying only the Howey test to determine whether interests in an LLC were securities). The court will also consider whether the Interests can be characterized as "any interest or instrument commonly known as a security."

4.   Are the Interests in NSC an "Investment Contract"?

As stated above, to constitute an "investment contract," the instruments purchased by Great Lakes must involve: (1) "an investment of money," (2) "in a common enterprise," (3) "with profits to come solely from the efforts of others." Howey, 328 U.S. at 301. The parties do not dispute that the first prong of the Howey test—an investment of money—is satisfied by the facts of this case. The court will now consider whether Great Lakes invested in a "common enterprise," and whether Great Lakes' profits in NSC were to come "solely from the efforts of others."

a.   Did Great Lakes invest in a "common enterprise"?

Monsanto and STI argue that Great Lakes' purchase of the Interests in NSC fails the second prong of the Howey test, which requires that an investor invest its money in a "common enterprise." According to defendants, Great Lakes bought the entirety of NSC without pooling its contributions with those of other investors.

Great Lakes, on the other hand, contends that when Monsanto and STI created NSC, they pooled their resources and established NSC as a common enterprise. At the time of sale of the membership Interests, Great Lakes contends, the Interests were securities, and they did not cease to be securities when they were transferred to Great Lakes.

To determine whether a party has invested funds in a common enterprise, courts look to whether there is horizontal commonality between investors, or vertical commonality between a promoter and an investor. Horizontal commonality requires a pooling of investors' contributions and distribution of profits and losses on a pro-rata basis among investors. Steinhardt Group Inc. v. Citicorp., 126 F.3d 144, 151 (3d Cir.1997). The vertical commonality test is less stringent, and requires that an investor and promoter be engaged in a common enterprise, with the "fortunes of the investors linked with those of the promoters." Securities and Exchange Commission v. R.G. Reynolds Enterprises, Inc., 952 F.2d 1125, 1130 (9th Cir.1991); Securities and Exchange Commission v. Professional Associates, 731 F.2d 349, 354 (6th Cir.1984). The Third Circuit has applied the horizontal commonality approach, see Salcer v. Merrill Lynch, Pierce, Fenner and Smith Inc., 682 F.2d 459, 460 (3d Cir.1982), but has subsequently indicated that the vertical commonality test might be applicable in other cases, see Steinhardt, 126 F.3d at 152.

In this case, Great Lakes bought 100% of the Interests of NSC from Monsanto and STI. Great Lakes, accordingly, did not pool its contributions with those of other investors, as is required for horizontal commonality. After the sale, Monsanto and STI retained no interest in NSC, so it cannot be said that the fortunes of Great Lakes were linked to those of defendants, as is required for vertical commonality.

Great Lakes urges that when the Interests in NSC were created, Monsanto and STI pooled their contributions in a common enterprise. Great Lakes contends that Monsanto's and STI's Interests were securities when they were created, and that they did not cease to be securities when conveyed to Great Lakes. In support of this proposition, Great Lakes relies on Great Western Bank & Trust v. Kotz, 532 F.2d 1252 (9th Cir.1976).

Great Western involves a company, Artko, that obtained a line of credit from a bank and executed an interest-bearing, unsecured promissory note to the bank. The bank allegedly relied on considerable financial data prepared by Artko before extending the line of credit. After the bank did not receive payment on the note, it sought recovery from Artko's president under §§ 17(a) of the Securities Act ... The question before the court was whether the promissory note constituted a security. Although "notes" are included in the statutory definition of a security, the court recognized that not all notes are securities. See Great Western, 532 F.2d at 1256 (citing cases). The court inquired whether the bank had contributed "risk capital" subject to the "entrepreneurial or managerial efforts" of Artko, as would support a finding that the note was a security. See id. at 1257. The court stated that the circumstances of issuance of the note, rather than how the proceeds of the line of credit were used, were determinative of the character of the note. See Great Western, 532 F.2d at 1258. Great Western reaffirms the principle that the character of a financial instrument is determined by the terms of its offer, the plan of its distribution, and the economic inducements held out to potential purchasers. See SEC v. C.M. Joiner Leasing Corp., 320 U.S. 344, 352–53, (1943). Great Western does not draw into question the principle that courts are to look at the specific transaction at issue to determine whether the interests being transferred are securities. See Steinhardt, 126 F.3d at 153.

In this case, the challenged transaction is the sale of NSC by defendants to Great Lakes, and not the formation of NSC. Thus, the fact that Monsanto and STI pooled their contributions in the formation of NSC does not change the character of the sale of NSC to Great Lakes. The court concludes that Great Lakes did not invest in a common enterprise.

b. Were Great Lakes' Profits in NSC To Come "Solely from the Efforts of Others"?

Monsanto and STI argue that the profits in NSC did not come solely from the efforts of others, as would support a finding that the Interests in NSC were securities. Howey, 328 U.S. at 298–99. Rather, defendants contend that Great Lakes had the power to control NSC through its authority to remove managers with or without cause, and to dissolve the entity.

Great Lakes argues, on the other hand, that it depended solely on the efforts of others to profit from NSC, as the LLC Agreement provides that the Members would retain no authority, right, or power to manage or control the operations of the company. In the alternative, Great Lakes contends that the Howey test does not apply to the sale of 100% of a business over which the purchaser intended to exercise control.

i. profits solely from the efforts of others

There is little caselaw establishing guidelines for determining whether a member in an LLC is sufficiently passive that he is dependent solely on the efforts of others for profits. In the context of general partnerships and limited partnerships, by contrast, there has been extensive litigation on whether partnership interests may qualify as securities. An analogy to partnership law is convenient for analyzing interests in LLCs, but there are important differences between general partnerships, limited partnerships, and LLCs.

General partnerships in Delaware are formed pursuant to the Delaware Revised Uniform Partnership Act, 6 Del. C. §§ 15–101 et seq. Each partner has equal rights in the management and conduct of the partnership business and affairs. 6 Del. C. §§ 15–401(f). In general, all partners are liable jointly and severally for all obligations of the partnership. 6 Del. C. §§ 15–306(a). Because partners have equal rights in the management of general partnerships, and because they are not protected by limited liability, courts consistently state that partners in general partnerships are unlikely to be passive investors who profit solely on the efforts of others. Some courts have adopted per se rules that partnership interests are not securities. See, e.g., Goodwin v. Elkins & Co., 730 F.2d 99, 107 (3d Cir.1983). Other courts have adopted a presumption that partnership interests are not securities, but permit a finding that partnership interests are securities when a partner has so little control over the management as to be a passive investor. See Williamson v. Tucker, 645 F.2d 404, 424 (5th Cir.1981).

Limited partnerships in Delaware are formed pursuant to 6 Del. C. §§ 17–101 et seq. Limited partnerships are comprised of general partners and limited partners. General partners in limited partnerships have all the powers and duties of general partners in general partnerships, and are liable for the debts of the partnership. 6 Del. C. §§ 17–403(b). Limited partners have limited liability, but become liable as general partners if they take part in the control of the business. See 6 Del. [**49] C. §§ 17–303(a); Unif. Ltd. Partnership Act (1916) §§ 7, 6A U.L.A. 336 (1995). A limited partner may advise a general partner with respect to the business of the limited partnership, or cause a general partner to take action by voting or otherwise, without losing his limited liability. See 6 Del. C. §§ 17–303(b)(2). In cases involving transactions of interests in limited partnerships, wherein the limited partners exercised no managerial role in the partnership's affairs, courts treat the limited partners as passive investors, and find that the membership interests of limited partners constitute securities under federal law. See, e.g., Mayer v. Oil Field Systems Corp., 721 F.2d 59, 65 (2d Cir.1983). Where, however, a limited partner is found to have exercised substantial control over the management of the partnership, courts find that the limited partner has not profited solely from the efforts of others, and rule that the interest in the partnership is not a security. See, e.g., Steinhardt, 126 F.3d at 153.

Membership interests in LLCs are distinct from interests in general partnerships and limited partnerships. The primary differences between LLCs and general partnerships are that members of LLCs are entitled to limited liability, and, depending on the terms of the operating agreement giving rise to the particular LLC at issue, the members of the LLC may be less involved in the management of the enterprise than partners in a general partnership. As such, the grounds for creating a per se rule, or at least a presumption, that interests in general partnerships are not securities are lacking in the context of LLCs.

In comparison with limited partnerships, the Delaware Limited Liability Company Act permits a member in an LLC to be an active participant in management and still to retain limited liability. 6 Del. C. §§ 18–303. Thus, there is no statutory basis, as with limited partnerships, to presume that LLC members are passive investors entitled to protection under the federal securities laws.

The Delaware Limited Liability Company Act grants parties substantial flexibility in determining the character of an LLC. Accordingly, the terms of the operating agreement of each LLC will determine whether its membership interests constitute securities. The presumptions that courts have articulated with respect to general partnerships and limited partnerships do not apply to

LLCs. Rather, to determine whether a member's profits are to come solely from the efforts of others, it is necessary to consider the structure of the particular LLC at issue, as provided in its operating agreement.

In the present case, the Members of NSC had no authority to directly manage NSC's business and affairs. Section 5.1(a) of the LLC Agreement states:

Except as otherwise expressly set forth in this Agreement, the Members shall not have any authority, right or power to bind the Company, or to manage or control, or to participate in the management or control of, the business and affairs of the Company in any manner whatsoever. Such management shall in every respect be the full and complete responsibility of the Board alone as provided in this Agreement.

The Members, however, had the power to remove any Manager with or without cause, and to dissolve the company. Great Lakes exercised this authority on October 5, 1999, when it filed a Certificate of Cancellation with the State of Delaware, dissolving NSC as a separate entity. Moreover, Great Lakes' complaint avers that, prior to selling NSC, Monsanto and STI had the power to control the actions of the Managers, insofar as defendants allegedly prohibited NSC's management from speaking directly with Great Lakes regarding sales, sales forecasts, and customer orders.

The powers held by Great Lakes in NSC are comparable to those discussed in Steinhardt, 126 F.3d at 154, wherein the Third Circuit considered whether a limited partner in a limited partnership could state a claim under the securities laws. The limited partner, Steinhardt, purchased a 98.8% interest in the limited partnership, which acquired title to non-performing mortgage loans. The court noted that limited partners generally are passive investors entitled to protection under federal securities law. Upon analyzing the governance of the limited partnership at issue, however, the court found that Steinhardt alone constituted a "Majority of the Partners," and that Steinhardt was free to remove and replace the general partner without notice if the general partner refused to carry out Steinhardt's proposals. See id. at 154. In light of this factor and others, the court found that the limited partnership agreement at issue gave Steinhardt significant powers that directly affected the profits it received from the partnership. Accordingly, the court concluded that Steinhardt was not a passive investor, and that Steinhardt's membership in the partnership did not qualify as an investment contract.

The powers held by Great Lakes were comparable to those of Steinhardt, in that Great Lakes had the authority to remove NSC's managers without cause. Because Great Lakes was the sole owner of NSC, its power to remove managers was not diluted by the presence of other ownership interests. See Williamson, 645 F.2d at 423 (noting that a partner in a general partnership might be deemed to be a passive investor if there were a sufficient number of other partners to dilute the partner's voting rights). Great Lakes' authority to remove managers gave it the power to directly affect the profits it received from NSC. Thus, the court finds that Great Lakes' profits from NSC did not come solely from the efforts of others. See Howey, 328 U.S. at 299.

ii.   sale of 100% of a business

Alternatively, Great Lakes argues that, even if it did exercise substantial control over NSC, the transfer of Interests in NSC is nonetheless covered by the securities laws, because it bought 100% of the Interests in NSC and intended to operate the business. Great Lakes relies on Landreth, 471 U.S. at 681, in support of this proposition.

Under Landreth, as discussed above, a stock transaction is covered by the securities laws even though the purchaser exercises control over the acquired corporation. See id. at 690. Landreth, however, is applicable only to those cases involving stock, or other financial instruments which are listed in § 2(a)(1) of the Securities Act. See id. When the financial instrument in question is a less traditional instrument that is not enumerated in the statute, but that might qualify as an "investment contract," then the complainant must demonstrate that the instrument satisfies the Howey test. As discussed above, the Interests in NSC do not constitute stock, and so Landreth is inapplicable.

The court finds that Great Lakes did not invest in a common enterprise, and did not have an expectation of profits "solely from the efforts of others," as is required by Howey. The Interests in NSC, thus, are not investment contracts.

5. Are the Interests in NSC "Any Interest or Instrument Commonly Known as a Security"?

Great Lakes argues that, even if the Interests in NSC do not otherwise satisfy the Howey test for investment contracts, they should be deemed to be "any interest or instrument commonly known as a security," as provided for in § 2(a)(1) of the Securities Act. Great Lakes notes that the LLC Agreement refers to the Interests at issue as "equity securities," and that the LLC Agreement prohibits the transfer of the Interests in such a way as would "violate the provisions of any federal or state securities laws." Moreover, Great Lakes contends, ten states have defined interests in LLCs as securities, including Indiana, where NSC has its principal place of business.

Monsanto and STI contend that the Interests cannot be an "interest or instrument commonly known as a security," because the Interests in NSC do not satisfy the Howey test.

The Supreme Court has indicated that the term "any interest or instrument commonly known as a security" covers the same financial instruments as referred to by the term "investment contract." In United Housing Foundation, Inc. v. Forman, 421 U.S. 837, (1975), the Court stated that "we perceive no distinction, for present purposes, between an 'investment contract' and an 'instrument commonly known as a "security." In either case, the basic test for distinguishing the transaction from other commercial dealings is 'whether the scheme involves an investment of money in a common enterprise with profits to come solely from the efforts of others.'" Id. at 852 (quoting Howey, 328 U.S. at 301); see also Landreth, 471 U.S. at 692 n.5 (same). The Howey test, the Court explained, "embodies the essential attributes that run through all of the Court's decisions defining a security." Forman, 421 U.S. at 852.

When confronted with novel financial instruments, numerous courts have considered whether to distinguish between an "investment contract" and "any interest or instrument commonly known as a security," and have declined to do so. See, e.g., Procter & Gamble Co. v. Bankers Trust Co., 925 F. Supp. 1270, 1282 (S.D.Ohio 1996) (declining to find that swaps constitute an "interest or instrument commonly known as a security"); Crabtree Investments, Inc. v. Aztec Enterprises, Inc., 483 F. Supp. 211, 215 (M.D.La.1980) (declining to find that a continuing guaranty to secure loans was an "interest or instrument commonly known as a security"). In this case, too, the court finds that it would be improper to extend the definition of a security by reinterpreting the term "any interest or instrument commonly known as a security."

In sum, the court finds that the Interests in NSC constitute neither "stock," nor an "investment contract," nor "any interest or instrument commonly known as a security." The court will grant defendants' motion to dismiss Count I of Great Lakes' complaint.

———

1. *Partnerships.* General partnerships have rarely been deemed securities, even when most partners in the partnership remain passive.[1] Still, in Williamson v. Tucker,[2] the Fifth Circuit offered the following much cited formula for determining when a general partnership interest could constitute a security:

> "A general partnership or joint venture interest can be designated a security if the investor can establish, for example, that (1) an agreement among the parties leaves so little power in the hands of the partner or venturer that the arrangement in fact distributes power as would a limited partnership; or (2) the partner or venturer is so inexperienced and unknowledgeable in business affairs that he is incapable of intelligently exercising his partnership or venture powers; or (3) the partner or venturer is so dependent on some unique entrepreneurial or managerial ability of the promoter or manager that he cannot replace the manager of the enterprise or otherwise exercise meaningful partnership or venture powers."[3]

Although *Williamson* indicates that the mere form of the organization (general partnership vs. limited partnership) is not necessarily dispositive, most subsequent cases have indicated that a general partner who seeks to characterize his partnership interest as a security faces a high barrier. Few such plaintiffs have been successful.[4] A few cases have, however, found partnership interests to constitute securities, but generally these have been enforcement actions brought by the SEC.[5]

2. *Limited Partnerships.* Most decisions do find limited partnerships interests to constitute securities.[6] Thus, *Steinhardt* represents the exceptional case. Still, according to Judge Easterbrook, writing for the Seventh Circuit, the test for an exemption will be whether the limited partnership interests "carried more control than normal investment units."[7] The degree of control is critical,

---

1. See Rivanna Trawlers Unlimited v. Thompson Trawlers, Inc., 840 F.2d 236 (4th Cir.1988); Matek v. Murat, 862 F.2d 720 (9th Cir.1988); Goodwin v. Elkins & Co., 730 F.2d 99 (3d Cir.1984).

2. 645 F.2d 404 (5th Cir.1981). Williamson's criteria appear to have been accepted by the Ninth Circuit in an *en banc* decision. See Hocking v. Dubois, 885 F.2d 1449 (9th Cir. 1989), *cert. denied*, 494 U.S. 1078 (1990).

3. Id. at 424.

4. See, e.g., Rivanna Trawlers Unlimited v. Thompson Trawlers, Inc., 840 F.2d 236 (4th Cir.1988).

5. See SEC v. Professional Assocs., 731 F.2d 349, 357 (6th Cir.1984) (noting that at least some investors were "entirely passive"); SEC v. Telecom Marketing, Inc., 888 F.Supp. 1160, 1166 (N.D.Ga.1995) ("investors were targeted for their ignorance of law, accounting, and the * * * industry").

6. See, e.g., SEC v. Murphy, 626 F.2d 633 (9th Cir.1980); L & B Hospital Ventures, Inc. v. Healthcare International, Inc., 894 F.2d 150 (5th Cir.), *cert. denied*, 498 U.S. 815 (1990).

7. See National Tax Credit Partners L.P. v. Havlik, 20 F.3d 705, 709 (7th Cir. 1994).

he found, under the Supreme Court's decision in Marine Bank v. Weaver.[8]

3. *Limited Liability Companies.* Relatively few decisions have to date considered the case of the LLC, but several have followed the *Steinhardt* and *Monsanto* line of analysis.[9] Other cases continue to find that interests in LLCs are "investment contracts" under *Howey* and hence securities.[10] Absent an authoritative appellate decision, division in the case law seems likely to persist on this issue. One distinctive issue that has surfaced in this context involves whether investors in an LLC should be permitted to opt out of the securities laws, by a provision in the LLC agreement. For an argument in favor of such a position, see Park McGinty, The Limited Liability Company: Opportunity for Selective Securities Law Deregulation, 64 U. Cin. L. Rev. 369 (1996). For the opposing view, see Welle, Freedom of Contract and the Securities Laws: Opting Out of Securities Regulation by Private Agreement, 56 Wash. & Lee L. Rev. 519 (1999). Professor Ribstein has argued for the view that the securities laws should inherently not apply to general partnerships and LLC's, but should presumptively apply to corporations and limited partnerships, on the grounds that this would give investors a "bright line" choice through their selection of the organizational form. See Larry Ribstein, Form and Substance in the Definition of a "Security": The Case of Limited Liability Companies, 51 Wash. & Lee L. Rev. 807 (1994).

C. "STOCK"

Landreth Timber Company v. Landreth

Supreme Court of the United States, 1985.
471 U.S. 681, 105 S.Ct. 2297, 85 L.Ed.2d 692.

■ JUSTICE POWELL delivered the opinion of the Court.

This case presents the question whether the sale of all of the stock of a company is a securities transaction subject to the antifraud provisions of the federal securities laws (the Acts).

I

Respondents Ivan K. Landreth and his sons owned all of the outstanding stock of a lumber business they operated in Tonasket, Washington. The Landreth family offered their stock for sale through both Washington and out-of-state brokers. Before a purchaser was found, the company's sawmill was heavily damaged by fire. Despite the fire, the brokers continued to offer the stock for sale. Potential purchasers were advised of the damage, but were told that the mill would be completely rebuilt and modernized.

Samuel Dennis, a Massachusetts tax attorney, received a letter offering the stock for sale. On the basis of the letter's representations concerning the

---

8. 455 U.S. 551 (1982). See Casebook infra at p. 378.

9. See, e.g., Nelson v. Stahl, 173 F.Supp.2d 153 (S.D.N.Y.2001); Keith v. Black Diamond Advisors, Inc., 48 F.Supp.2d 326, 354 (S.D.N.Y.1999). For overviews, see Michael Garrison and Terry Kneopfle, Limited Liability Company Interests As Securities: A Proposed Framework for Analysis, 33 Am.

Bus. L.J. 577 (1996); Mark Sargent, Are Limited Liability Company Interests Securities?, 19 Pepp. L. Rev. 1069 (1992).

10. See Ak's Dak's Communications, Inc. v. Securities Division, 138 Md.App. 314, 771 A.2d 487 (2001)(applying Maryland law but following *Howey*); Tschetter v. Berven, 621 N.W.2d 372 (S.D.2001)(applying South Dakota law).

rebuilding plans, the predicted productivity of the mill, existing contracts, and expected profits, Dennis became interested in acquiring the stock. He talked to John Bolten, a former client who had retired to Florida, about joining him in investigating the offer. After having an audit and an inspection of the mill conducted, a stock purchase agreement was negotiated, with Dennis the purchaser of all of the common stock in the lumber company. Ivan Landreth agreed to stay on as a consultant for some time to help with the daily operations of the mill. Pursuant to the terms of the stock purchase agreement, Dennis assigned the stock he purchased to B&D Co., a corporation formed for the sole purpose of acquiring the lumber company stock. B&D then merged with the lumber company, forming petitioner Landreth Timber Co. Dennis and Bolten then acquired all of petitioner's Class A stock, representing 85% of the equity, and six other investors together owned the Class B stock, representing the remaining 15% of the equity.

After the acquisition was completed, the mill did not live up to the purchasers' expectations. Rebuilding costs exceeded earlier estimates, and new components turned out to be incompatible with existing equipment. Eventually, petitioner sold the mill at a loss and went into receivership. Petitioner then filed this suit seeking rescission of the sale of stock and $2,500,000 in damages, alleging that respondents had widely offered and then sold their stock without registering it as required by the Securities Act of 1933 (the 1933 Act). Petitioner also alleged that respondents had negligently or intentionally made misrepresentations and had failed to state material facts as to the worth and prospects of the lumber company, all in violation of the Securities Exchange Act of 1934 (the 1934 Act).

Respondents moved for summary judgment on the ground that the transaction was not covered by the Acts because under the so-called "sale of business" doctrine, petitioner had not purchased a "security" within the meaning of those Acts. The District Court granted respondents' motion and dismissed the complaint for want of federal jurisdiction. It acknowledged that the federal statutes include "stock" as one of the instruments constituting a "security," and that the stock at issue possessed all of the characteristics of conventional stock. Nonetheless, it joined what it termed the "growing majority" of courts that had held that the federal securities laws do not apply to the sale of 100% of the stock of a closely held corporation. * * * Relying on United Housing Foundation, Inc. v. Forman, 421 U.S. 837 (1975), and SEC v. W.J. Howey Co., 328 U.S. 293 (1946), the District Court ruled that the stock could not be considered a "security" unless the purchaser had entered into the transaction with the anticipation of earning profits derived from the efforts of others. Finding that managerial control of the business had passed into the hands of the purchasers, and thus, that the transaction was a commercial venture rather than a typical investment, the District Court dismissed the complaint.

The United States Court of Appeals for the Ninth Circuit affirmed the District Court's application of the sale of business doctrine. [W]e granted certiorari. We now reverse.

II

It is axiomatic that "[t]he starting point in every case involving construction of a statute is the language itself." Blue Chip Stamps v. Manor Drug Stores, 421 U.S. 723, 756 (1975) (POWELL, J., concurring); accord, Teamsters v.

Daniel, 439 U.S. 551, 558 (1979). Section 2(a)(1) of the 1933 Act * * * defines a "security" * * *.

    * * *

As we have observed in the past, this definition is quite broad, Marine Bank v. Weaver, 455 U.S. 551, 556 (1982), and includes both instruments whose names alone carry well-settled meaning, as well as instruments of "more variable character [that] were necessarily designated by more descriptive terms," such as "investment contract" and "instrument commonly known as a 'security.'" SEC v. C.M. Joiner Leasing Corp., 320 U.S. 344, 351 (1943). The face of the definition shows that "stock" is considered to be a "security" within the meaning of the Acts. As we observed in United Housing Foundation, Inc. v. Forman, 421 U.S. 837 (1975), most instruments bearing such a traditional title are likely to be covered by the definition. * * *

As we also recognized in *Forman,* the fact that instruments bear the label "stock" is not of itself sufficient to invoke the coverage of the Acts. Rather, we concluded that we must also determine whether those instruments possess "some of the significant characteristics typically associated with" stock, * * * recognizing that when an instrument is both called "stock" and bears stock's usual characteristics, "a purchaser justifiably [may] assume that the federal securities laws apply," * * * We identified those characteristics usually associated with common stock as (i) the right to receive dividends contingent upon an apportionment of profits; (ii) negotiability; (iii) the ability to be pledged or hypothecated; (iv) the conferring of voting rights in proportion to the number of shares owned; and (v) the capacity to appreciate in value.[2] * * *

Under the facts of *Forman,* we concluded that the instruments at issue there were not "securities" within the meaning of the Acts. That case involved the sale of shares of stock entitling the purchaser to lease an apartment in a housing cooperative. The stock bore none of the characteristics listed above that are usually associated with traditional stock. Moreover, we concluded that under the circumstances, there was no likelihood that the purchasers had been misled by use of the word "stock" into thinking that the federal securities laws governed their purchases. The purchasers had intended to acquire low-cost subsidized living space for their personal use; no one was likely to have believed that he was purchasing investment securities. Ibid.

In contrast, it is undisputed that the stock involved here possesses all of the characteristics we identified in *Forman* as traditionally associated with common stock. Indeed, the District Court so found. * * * Moreover, unlike in *Forman,* the context of the transaction involved here—the sale of stock in a corporation—is typical of the kind of context to which the Acts normally apply. It is thus much more likely here than in *Forman* that an investor would believe he was covered by the federal securities laws. Under the circumstances of this case, the plain meaning of the statutory definition mandates that the stock be treated as "securities" subject to the coverage of the Acts.

Reading the securities laws to apply to the sale of stock at issue here comports with Congress' remedial purpose in enacting the legislation to protect investors by "compelling full and fair disclosure relative to the issuance of 'the

---

2. Although we did not so specify in *Forman,* we wish to make clear here that these characteristics are those usually associated with common stock, the kind of stock often at issue in cases involving the sale of a business. Various types of preferred stock may have different characteristics and still be covered by the Acts.

many types of instruments that in our commercial world fall within the ordinary concept of a security.'" SEC v. W.J. Howey Co., 328 U.S., at 299 (quoting H.R.Rep. No. 85, 73d Cong., 1st Sess., 11 (1933)). Although we recognize that Congress did not intend to provide a comprehensive federal remedy for all fraud, Marine Bank v. Weaver, 455 U.S. 551, 556 (1982), we think it would improperly narrow Congress' broad definition of "security" to hold that the traditional stock at issue here falls outside the Acts' coverage.

III

Under other circumstances, we might consider the statutory analysis outlined above to be a sufficient answer compelling judgment for petitioner.[3] Respondents urge, however, that language in our previous opinions, including *Forman,* requires that we look beyond the label "stock" and the characteristics of the instruments involved to determine whether application of the Acts is mandated by the economic substance of the transaction. Moreover, the Court of Appeals rejected the view that the plain meaning of the definition would be sufficient to hold this stock covered, because it saw "no principled way," 731 F.2d, at 1353, to justify treating notes, bonds, and other of the definitional categories differently. We address these concerns in turn.

A

It is fair to say that our cases have not been entirely clear on the proper method of analysis for determining when an instrument is a "security." This Court has decided a number of cases in which it looked to the economic substance of the transaction, rather than just to its form, to determine whether the Acts applied. In SEC v. C.M. Joiner Leasing Corp., for example, the Court considered whether the 1933 Act applied to the sale of leasehold interests in land near a proposed oil well drilling. In holding that the leasehold interests were "securities," the Court noted that "the reach of the Act does not stop with the obvious and commonplace." 320 U.S., at 351. Rather, it ruled that unusual devices such as the leaseholds would also be covered "if it be proved as matter of fact that they were widely offered or dealt in under terms or courses of dealing which established their character in commerce as 'investment contracts,' or as any interest or instrument commonly known as a 'security.'" Ibid.

SEC v. W.J. Howey Co., supra, further elucidated the *Joiner* Court's suggestion that an unusual instrument could be considered a "security" if the circumstances of the transaction so dictated. At issue in that case was an offering of units of a citrus grove development coupled with a contract for cultivating and marketing the fruit and remitting the proceeds to the investors. The Court held that the offering constituted an "investment contract" within the meaning of the 1933 Act because, looking at the economic realities, the transaction "involve[d] an investment of money in a common enterprise with profits to come solely from the efforts of others." 328 U.S., at 301.

This so-called "*Howey* test" formed the basis for the second part of our decision in *Forman,* on which respondents primarily rely. As discussed above, see Part II, supra, the first part of our decision in Forman concluded that the instruments at issue, while they bore the traditional label "stock," were not "securities" because they possessed none of the usual characteristics of stock.

---

3. Professor Loss suggests that the statutory analysis is sufficient. L. Loss, Fun- damentals of Securities Regulation 212 (1983).

We then went on to address the argument that the instruments were "invest-ment contracts." Applying the *Howey* test, we concluded that the instruments likewise were not "securities" by virtue of being "investment contracts" because the economic realities of the transaction showed that the purchasers had parted with their money not for the purpose of reaping profits from the efforts of others, but for the purpose of purchasing a commodity for personal consumption. 421 U.S., at 858.

Respondents contend that *Forman* and the cases on which it was based[4] require us to reject the view that the shares of stock at issue here may be considered "securities" because of their name and characteristics. Instead, they argue that our cases require us in every instance to look to the economic substance of the transaction to determine whether the *Howey* test has been met. According to respondents, it is clear that petitioner sought not to earn profits from the efforts of others, but to buy a company that it could manage and control. Petitioner was not a passive investor of the kind Congress intended the Acts to protect, but an active entrepreneur, who sought to "use or consume" the business purchased just as the purchasers in *Forman* sought to use the apartments they acquired after purchasing shares of stock. Thus, respondents urge that the Acts do not apply.

We disagree with respondents' interpretation of our cases. First, it is important to understand the contexts within which these cases were decided. All of the cases on which respondents rely involved unusual instruments not easily characterized as "securities." * * * Thus, if the Acts were to apply in those cases at all, it would have to have been because the economic reality underlying the transactions indicated that the instruments were actually of a type that falls within the usual concept of a security. In the case at bar, in contrast, the instrument involved is traditional stock, plainly within the statu-tory definition. There is no need here, as there was in the prior cases, to look beyond the characteristics of the instrument to determine whether the Acts apply.

Contrary to respondents' implication, the Court has never foreclosed the possibility that stock could be found to be a "security" simply because it is what it purports to be. In SEC v. C.M. Joiner Leasing Corp., 320 U.S. 344 (1943), the Court noted that "we do nothing to the words of the Act; we merely accept them. * * * In some cases, [proving that the documents were securities] might be done by proving the document itself, which on its face would be a note, a bond, or a share of stock." Id., at 355. Nor does *Forman* require a different result. Respondents are correct that in *Forman* we eschewed a "literal" approach that would invoke the Acts' coverage simply because the instrument carried the label "stock." *Forman* does not, however, eliminate the

---

4. Respondents also rely on Tcherepnin v. Knight, 389 U.S. 332 (1967), and Marine Bank v. Weaver, 455 U.S. 551 (1982), as support for their argument that we have mandated in every case a determination of whether the economic realities of a transac-tion call for the application of the Acts. It is sufficient to note here that these cases, like the other cases on which respondents rely, involved unusual instruments that did not fit squarely within one of the enumerated specif-ic kinds of securities listed in the definition. *Tcherepnin* involved withdrawable capital shares in a state savings and loan association, and *Weaver* involved a certificate of deposit and a privately negotiated profit sharing agreement. See Marine Bank v. Weaver, su-pra, at 557, n. 5, for an explanation of why the certificate of deposit involved there did not fit within the definition's category "cer-tificate of deposit, for a security."

Court's ability to hold that an instrument is covered when its characteristics bear out the label. See supra, at 686–687.

Second, we would note that the *Howey* economic reality test was designed to determine whether a particular instrument is an "investment contract," not whether it fits within *any* of the examples listed in the statutory definition of "security." Our cases are consistent with this view.[5] Teamsters v. Daniel, 439 U.S., at 558 (appropriate to turn to the *Howey* test to "determine whether a particular financial relationship constitutes an investment contract"); United Housing Foundation, Inc. v. Forman, 421 U.S. 837 (1975); see supra, at 689. Moreover, applying the *Howey* test to traditional stock and all other types of instruments listed in the statutory definition would make the Acts' enumeration of many types of instruments superfluous. Golden v. Garafalo, 678 F.2d 1139, 1144 (C.A.2 1982). See Tcherepnin v. Knight, 389 U.S. 332, 343 (1967).

Finally, we cannot agree with respondents that the Acts were intended to cover only "passive investors" and not privately negotiated transactions involving the transfer of control to "entrepreneurs." The 1934 Act contains several provisions specifically governing tender offers, disclosure of transactions by corporate officers and principal stockholders, and the recovery of short-swing profits gained by such persons. See, e.g., 1934 Act, §§ 14, 16. Eliminating from the definition of "security" instruments involved in transactions where control passed to the purchaser would contravene the purposes of these provisions. Accord, Daily v. Morgan, 701 F.2d 496, 503 (C.A.5 1983). Furthermore, although § 4(2) of the 1933 Act exempts transactions not involving any public offering from the Act's registration provisions, there is no comparable exemption from the antifraud provisions. Thus, the structure and language of the Acts refute respondents' position.[6]

B

We now turn to the Court of Appeals' concern that treating stock as a specific category of "security" provable by its characteristics means that other

5. In support of their contention that the Court has mandated use of the *Howey* test whenever it determines whether an instrument is a "security," respondents quote our statement in Teamsters v. Daniel, 439 U.S. 551, 558, n. 11 (1979) that the *Howey* test " 'embodies the essential attributes that run through all of the Court's decisions defining a security' " (quoting *Forman,* 421 U.S., at 852). We do not read this bit of dicta as broadly as respondents do. We made the statement in *Forman* in reference to the purchasers' argument that if the instruments at issue were not "stock" and were not "investment contracts," at least they were "instrument[s] commonly known as a 'security' " within the statutory definition. We stated, as part of our analysis of whether the instruments were "investment contracts," that we perceived "no distinction, *for present purposes,* between an 'investment contract' and an 'instrument commonly known as a "security." ' " 421 U.S., at 852 (emphasis added). This was not to say that the *Howey* test

applied to any case in which an instrument was alleged to be a security, but only that once the label "stock" did not hold true, we perceived no reason to analyze the case differently whether we viewed the instruments as "investment contracts" or as falling within another similarly general category of the definition—an "instrument commonly known as a 'security.' " Under either of these general categories, the *Howey* test would apply.

6. In criticizing the sale of business doctrine, Professor Loss agrees. He considers that the doctrine "comes dangerously close to the heresy of saying that the fraud provisions do not apply to private transactions; for nobody, apparently, has had the temerity to argue that the sale of a *publicly* owned business for stock of the acquiring corporation that is distributed to the shareholders of the selling corporation as a liquidating dividend does not involve a security." L. Loss, Fundamentals of Securities Regulation 212 (1983) (emphasis in original) (footnote omitted).

categories listed in the statutory definition, such as notes, must be treated the same way. Although we do not decide whether coverage of notes or other instruments may be provable by their name and characteristics, we do point out several reasons why we think stock may be distinguishable from most if not all of the other categories listed in the Acts' definition.

Instruments that bear both the name and all of the usual characteristics of stock seem to us to be the clearest case for coverage by the plain language of the definition. First, traditional stock "represents to many people, both trained and untrained in business matters, the paradigm of a security." Daily v. Morgan, supra, at 500. Thus persons trading in traditional stock likely have a high expectation that their activities are governed by the Acts. Second, as we made clear in *Forman,* "stock" is relatively easy to identify because it lends itself to consistent definition. See supra, at 686. Unlike some instruments, therefore, traditional stock is more susceptible of a plain meaning approach.

Professor Loss has agreed that stock is different from the other categories of instruments. He observes that it "goes against the grain" to apply the *Howey* test for determining whether an instrument is an "investment contract" to traditional stock. L. Loss, Fundamentals of Securities Regulation 211–212 (1983). As Professor Loss explains,

> "It is one thing to say that the typical cooperative apartment dweller has bought a home, not a security; or that not every installment purchase 'note' is a security; or that a person who charges a restaurant meal by signing his credit card slip is not selling a security even though his signature is an 'evidence of indebtedness.' But *stock* (except for the residential wrinkle) is so quintessentially a security as to foreclose further analysis." Id., at 212 (emphasis in original).

We recognize that in SEC v. C.M. Joiner Leasing Corp., 320 U.S. 344 (1943), the Court equated "notes" and "bonds" with "stock" as categories listed in the statutory definition that were standardized enough to rest on their names. Id., at 355. Nonetheless, in *Forman,* we characterized *Joiner's* language as dictum. 421 U.S., at 850. As we recently suggested in a different context in Securities Industry Association v. Board of Governors, 468 U.S. 137 (1984), "note" may now be viewed as a relatively broad term that encompasses instruments with widely varying characteristics, depending on whether issued in a consumer context, as commercial paper, or in some other investment context. See id., at 150. We here expressly leave until another day the question whether "notes" or "bonds" or some other category of instrument listed in the definition might be shown "by proving [only] the document itself." SEC v. C.M. Joiner Leasing Corp., supra, at 355. We hold only that "stock" may be viewed as being in a category by itself for purposes of interpreting the scope of the Acts' definition of "security."

IV

We also perceive strong policy reasons for not employing the sale of business doctrine under the circumstances of this case.[7] By respondents' own

---

7. JUSTICE STEVENS dissents on the ground that Congress did not intend the anti-fraud provisions of the federal securities laws to apply to "the private sale of a substantial ownership interest in [a business] simply be-cause the transaction[ ] w[as] structured as [a] sale[ ] of stock instead of assets." * * * Justice Stevens, of course, is correct in saying that it is clear from the legislative history of the Securities Acts of 1933 and 1934 that

admission, application of the doctrine depends in each case on whether control has passed to the purchaser. It may be argued that on the facts of this case, the doctrine is easily applied, since the transfer of 100% of a corporation's stock normally transfers control. We think even that assertion is open to some question, however, as Dennis and Bolten had no intention of running the sawmill themselves. Ivan Landreth apparently stayed on to manage the daily affairs of the business. Some commentators who support the sale of business doctrine believe that a purchaser who has the ability to exert control but chooses not to do so may deserve the Acts' protection if he is simply a passive investor not engaged in the daily management of the business. Easley, Recent Developments in the Sale-of-Business Doctrine: Toward a Transactional Context–Based Analysis for Federal Securities Jurisdiction, 39 Bus.Law. 929, 971–972 (1984); Seldin, When Stock is Not a Security: The "Sale of Business" Doctrine Under the Federal Securities Laws; 37 Bus.Law. 637, 679 (1982). In this case, the District Court was required to undertake extensive fact-finding, and even requested supplemental facts and memoranda on the issue of control, before it was able to decide the case. * * *

More importantly, however, if applied to this case, the sale of business doctrine would also have to be applied to cases in which less than 100% of a company's stock was sold. This inevitably would lead to difficult questions of line-drawing. The Acts' coverage would in every case depend not only on the percentage of stock transferred, but also on such factors as the number of purchasers and what provisions for voting and veto rights were agreed upon by the parties. As we explain more fully in Gould v. Ruefenacht, post, at 701, decided today as a companion to this case, coverage by the Acts would in most cases be unknown and unknowable to the parties at the time the stock was

---

Congress was concerned primarily with transactions "in securities * * * traded in a public market." United Housing Foundation, Inc. v. Forman, 421 U.S. 837, 849 (1975). It also is true that there is no indication in the legislative history that Congress considered the type of transactions involved in this case and in Gould v. Ruefenacht, infra.

The history is simply silent—as it is with respect to other transactions to which these Acts have been applied by the Commission and judicial interpretation over the half century since this legislation was adopted. One only need mention the expansive interpretation of § 10(b) of the 1934 Act and Rule 10b–5 adopted by the Commission. What the Court said in Blue Chip Stamps v. Manor Drug Stores, 421 U.S. 723 (1975), is relevant:

"When we deal with private actions under Rule 10b–5, we deal with a judicial oak which has grown from little more than a legislative acorn. Such growth may be quite consistent with the congressional enactment and with the role of the federal judiciary in interpreting it, see J.I. Case Co. v. Borak, [377 U.S. 426 (1964)], but it would be disingenuous to

suggest that either Congress in 1934 or the Securities and Exchange Commission in 1942 foreordained the present state of the law with respect to Rule 10b–5. It is therefore proper that we consider, in addition to the factors already discussed, what may be described as policy considerations when we come to flesh out the portions of the law with respect to which neither the congressional enactment nor the administrative regulations offer conclusive guidance." Id., at 737.

See also Ernst & Ernst v. Hochfelder, 425 U.S. 185, 196–197 (1976).

In this case, unlike with respect to the interpretation of § 10(b) in Blue Chip Stamps, we have the plain language of § 2(a)(1) of the 1933 Act in support of our interpretation. In Forman, supra, we recognized that the term "stock" is to be read in accordance with the common understanding of its meaning, including the characteristics identified in Forman. See supra, at 280–281. In addition, as stated in Blue Chip Stamps, supra, it is proper for a court to consider—as we do today—policy considerations in construing terms in these Acts.

sold.[a] These uncertainties attending the applicability of the Acts would hardly be in the best interests of either party to a transaction. Cf. Marine Bank v. Weaver, 455 U.S., at 559 n. 9 (rejecting the argument that the certificate of deposit at issue there was transformed, chameleon-like, into a "security" once it was pledged). Respondents argue that adopting petitioner's approach will increase the workload of the federal courts by converting state and common law fraud claims into federal claims. We find more daunting, however, the prospect that parties to a transaction may never know whether they are covered by the Acts until they engage in extended discovery and litigation over a concept as often elusive as the passage of control. Accord, Golden v. Garafalo, 678 F.2d 1145–1146.

V

In sum, we conclude that the stock at issue here is a "security" within the definition of the Acts, and that the sale of business doctrine does not apply. The judgment of the United States Court of Appeals for the Ninth Circuit is therefore

Reversed.[b]

■ JUSTICE STEVENS, dissenting. [The opinion is omitted.]

D. "NOTE"

Reves v. Ernst & Young

Supreme Court of the United States, 1990.
494 U.S. 56, 110 S.Ct. 945, 108 L.Ed.2d 47.

■ JUSTICE MARSHALL delivered the opinion of the Court.

This case presents the question whether certain demand notes issued by the Farmer's Cooperative of Arkansas and Oklahoma are "securities" within the meaning of § 3(a)(10) of the Securities Exchange Act of 1934. We conclude that they are.

I

The Co–Op is an agricultural cooperative that, at the time relevant here, had approximately 23,000 members. In order to raise money to support its general business operations, the Co–Op sold promissory notes payable on demand by the holder. Although the notes were uncollateralized and uninsured, they paid a variable rate of interest that was adjusted monthly to keep it higher than the rate paid by local financial institutions. The Co–Op offered the notes to both members and nonmembers, marketing the scheme as an "Investment Program." Advertisements for the notes, which appeared in each Co–Op newsletter, read in part: "YOUR CO–OP has more than $11,000,000 in assets to stand behind your investments. The Investment is not Federal [sic] insured but it is * * * Safe * * * Secure * * * and available when you need it." App. 5

---

a. In Gould v. Ruefenacht, 471 U.S. 701 (1985), the Court held that the sale of 50 percent of the stock of a business corporation entailed the sale of a security.

b. See Hazen, Taking Stock of Stock and the Sale of Closely Held Corporations: When is Stock Not a Security?, 61 N.C.L.Rev. 393 (1983); Rosin, Functional Exclusions from the Definition of a Security, (pts. 1–2) 28 So.Tex.L.Rev. 333, 575 (1986–1987).

(ellipses in original). Despite these assurances, the Co–Op filed for bankruptcy in 1984. At the time of the filing, over 1,600 people held notes worth a total of $10 million.

After the Co–Op filed for bankruptcy, petitioners, a class of holders of the notes, filed suit against Arthur Young & Co., the firm that had audited the Co–Op's financial statements (and the predecessor to respondent Ernst & Young). Petitioners alleged, *inter alia,* that Arthur Young had intentionally failed to follow generally accepted accounting principles in its audit, specifically with respect to the valuation of one of the Co–Op's major assets, a gasohol plant. Petitioners claimed that Arthur Young violated these principles in an effort to inflate the assets and net worth of the Co–Op. Petitioners maintained that, had Arthur Young properly treated the plant in its audits, they would not have purchased demand notes because the Co–Op's insolvency would have been apparent. On the basis of these allegations, petitioners claimed that Arthur Young had violated the antifraud provisions of the 1934 Act as well as Arkansas' securities laws.

Petitioners prevailed at trial on both their federal and state claims, receiving a $6.1 million judgment. Arthur Young appealed, claiming that the demand notes were not "securities" under either the 1934 Act or Arkansas law, and that the statutes' antifraud provisions therefore did not apply. A panel of the Eighth Circuit, agreeing with Arthur Young on both the state and federal issues, reversed. Arthur Young & Co. v. Reves, 856 F.2d 52 (1988). We granted certiorari to address the federal issue * * * and now reverse the judgment of the Court of Appeals.

II

A

This case requires us to decide whether the note issued by the Co–Op is a "security" within the meaning of the 1934 Act. Section 3(a)(10) of that Act is our starting point.

* * *

The fundamental purpose undergirding the Securities Acts is "to eliminate serious abuses in a largely unregulated securities market." United Housing Foundation, Inc. v. Forman, 421 U.S. 837, 849 (1975). In defining the scope of the market that it wished to regulate, Congress painted with a broad brush. It recognized the virtually limitless scope of human ingenuity, especially in the creation of "countless and variable schemes devised by those who seek the use of the money of others on the promise of profits," SEC v. W.J. Howey Co., 328 U.S. 293, 299 (1946), and determined that the best way to achieve its goal of protecting investors was "to define 'the term "security" in sufficiently broad and general terms so as to include within that definition the many types of instruments that in our commercial world fall within the ordinary concept of a security.' " *Forman,* supra, at 847–848 (quoting H.R.Rep. No. 85, 73d Cong., 1st Sess., 11 (1933)). Congress therefore did not attempt precisely to cabin the scope of the Securities Acts.[1] Rather, it enacted a definition of "security"

---

1. We have consistently held that "[t]he definition of a security in § 3(a)(10) of the 1934 Act, is virtually identical [to the 1933 Act's definition] and, for present purposes, the coverage of the two Acts may be considered the same." United Housing Foundation, Inc. v. Forman, 421 U.S. 837, 847, n. 12 (1975) (citations omitted). We reaffirm that principle here.

sufficiently broad to encompass virtually any instrument that might be sold as an investment.

Congress did not, however, "intend to provide a broad federal remedy for all fraud." Marine Bank v. Weaver, 455 U.S. 551, 556 (1982). Accordingly, "[t]he task has fallen to the Securities and Exchange Commission (SEC), the body charged with administering the Securities Acts, and ultimately to the federal courts to decide which of the myriad financial transactions in our society come within the coverage of these statutes." *Forman,* supra, at 848. In discharging our duty, we are not bound by legal formalisms, but instead take account of the economics of the transaction under investigation. See, e.g., Tcherepnin v. Knight, 389 U.S. 332, 336 (1967) (in interpreting the term "security," "form should be disregarded for substance and the emphasis should be on economic reality"). Congress' purpose in enacting the securities laws was to regulate *investments,* in whatever form they are made and by whatever name they are called.

A commitment to an examination of the economic realities of a transaction does not necessarily entail a case-by-case analysis of every instrument, however. Some instruments are obviously within the class Congress intended to regulate because they are by their nature investments. In Landreth Timber Co. v. Landreth, 471 U.S. 681 (1985), we held that an instrument bearing the name "stock" that, among other things, is negotiable, offers the possibility of capital appreciation, and carries the right to dividends contingent on the profits of a business enterprise is plainly within the class of instruments Congress intended the securities laws to cover. *Landreth Timber* does not signify a lack of concern with economic reality; rather, it signals a recognition that stock is, as a practical matter, always an investment if it has the economic characteristics traditionally associated with stock. Even if sparse exceptions to this generalization can be found, the public perception of common stock as the paradigm of a security suggests that stock, in whatever context it is sold, should be treated as within the ambit of the Acts. Id., at 687, 693.

We made clear in *Landreth Timber* that stock was a special case, explicitly limiting our holding to that sort of instrument. Id., at 694. Although we refused finally to rule out a similar *per se* rule for notes, we intimated that such a rule would be unjustified. Unlike "stock," we said, " 'note' may now be viewed as a relatively broad term that encompasses instruments with widely varying characteristics, depending on whether issued in a consumer context, as commercial paper, or in some other investment context." Ibid. (citing Securities Industry Assn. v. Board of Governors, FRS, 468 U.S. 137, 149–153 (1984)). While common stock is the quintessence of a security, *Landreth Timber,* supra, at 693, and investors therefore justifiably assume that a sale of stock is covered by the Securities Acts, the same simply cannot be said of notes, which are used in a variety of settings, not all of which involve investments. Thus, the phrase "any note" should not be interpreted to mean literally "any note," but must be understood against the backdrop of what Congress was attempting to accomplish in enacting the Securities Acts.

Because the Landreth Timber formula cannot sensibly be applied to notes, some other principle must be developed to define the term "note." A majority of the Courts of Appeals that have considered the issue have adopted, in varying forms, "investment versus commercial" approaches that distinguish, on the basis of all of the circumstances surrounding the transactions, notes issued in an investment context (which are "securities") from notes issued in a commercial or consumer context (which are not). See, e.g., McClure v. First Nat. Bank of Lubbock, Texas, 497 F.2d 490, 492–494 (C.A.5 1974); Holloway v. Peat, Marwick, Mitchell & Co., 879 F.2d 772, 778–779 (C.A.10 1989), cert. pending sub nom. Peat, Marwick Main & Co., No. 89–532.

The Second Circuit's "family resemblance" approach begins with a presumption that *any* note with a term of more than nine months is a "security." See, e.g., Exchange Nat'l Bank of Chicago v. Touche Ross & Co., 544 F.2d 1126, 1137 (C.A.2 1976). Recognizing that not all notes are securities, however, the Second Circuit has also devised a list of notes that it has decided are obviously not securities. Accordingly, the "family resemblance" test permits an issuer to rebut the presumption that a note is a security if it can show that the note in question "bear[s] a strong family resemblance" to an item on the judicially crafted list of exceptions, id., at 1137–1138, or convinces the court to add a new instrument to the list. See, e.g., Chemical Bank v. Arthur Andersen & Co., 726 F.2d 930, 939 (C.A.2 1984).

In contrast, the Eighth and District of Columbia Circuits apply the test we created in SEC v. W.J. Howey Co., 328 U.S. 293 (1946), to determine whether an instrument is an "investment contract" to the determination whether an instrument is a "note." Under this test, a note is a security only if it evidences "(1) an investment; (2) in a common enterprise; (3) with a reasonable expectation of profits; (4) to be derived from the entrepreneurial or managerial efforts of others." Arthur Young & Co. v. Reves, 856 F.2d, at 54. Accord Baurer v. Planning Group, Inc., 215 U.S.App.D.C. 384, 391–393, 669 F.2d 770, 777–779 (1981). See also Underhill v. Royal, 769 F.2d 1426, 1431 (C.A.9 1985) (setting forth what it terms a "risk capital" approach that is virtually identical to the *Howey* test).

We reject the approaches of those courts that have applied the *Howey* test to notes; *Howey* provides a mechanism for determining whether an instrument is an "investment contract." The demand notes here may well not be "investment contracts," but that does not mean they are not "notes." To hold that a "note" is not a "security" unless it meets a test designed for an entirely different variety of instrument "would make the Acts' enumeration of many types of instruments superfluous," Landreth Timber, 471 U.S., at 692, and would be inconsistent with Congress' intent to regulate the entire body of instruments sold as investments, see supra, at 3–5.

The other two contenders—the "family resemblance" and "investment versus commercial" tests—are really two ways of formulating the same general approach. Because we think the "family resemblance" test provides a more promising framework for analysis, however, we adopt it. The test begins with the language of the statute; because the Securities Acts define "security" to include "any note," we begin with a presumption that every note is a security.[3]

3. The Second Circuit's version of the family resemblance test provided that only notes *with a term of more than nine months* are presumed to be "securities." See supra, at 6. No presumption of any kind attached to notes of less than nine months duration. The Second Circuit's refusal to extend the presumption to *all* notes was apparently founded on its interpretation of the statutory exception for notes with a maturity of nine months or less. Because we do not reach the question of how to interpret that exception, see infra, at 13, we likewise express no view on how that exception might affect the presumption that a note is a "security."

We nonetheless recognize that this presumption cannot be irrebutable. As we have said, supra, at 3–4, Congress was concerned with regulating the investment market, not with creating a general federal cause of action for fraud. In an attempt to give more content to that dividing line, the Second Circuit has identified a list of instruments commonly denominated "notes" that nonetheless fall without the "security" category. See *Exchange Nat. Bank,* supra, at 1138 (types of notes that are not "securities" include "the note delivered in consumer financing, the note secured by a mortgage on a home, the short-term note secured by a lien on a small business or some of its assets, the note evidencing a 'character' loan to a bank customer, short-term notes secured by an assignment of accounts receivable, or a note which simply formalizes an open-account debt incurred in the ordinary course of business (particularly if, as in the case of the customer of a broker, it is collateralized)"); *Chemical Bank,* supra, at 939 (adding to list "notes evidencing loans by commercial banks for current operations").

We agree that the items identified by the Second Circuit are not properly viewed as "securities." More guidance, though, is needed. It is impossible to make any meaningful inquiry into whether an instrument bears a "resemblance" to one of the instruments identified by the Second Circuit without specifying what it is about *those* instruments that makes *them* non-"securities." Moreover, as the Second Circuit itself has noted, its list is "not graven in stone," ibid., and is therefore capable of expansion. Thus, some standards must be developed for determining when an item should be added to the list.

An examination of the list itself makes clear what those standards should be. In creating its list, the Second Circuit was applying the same factors that this Court has held apply in deciding whether a transaction involves a "security." First, we examine the transaction to assess the motivations that would prompt a reasonable seller and buyer to enter into it. If the seller's purpose is to raise money for the general use of a business enterprise or to finance substantial investments and the buyer is interested primarily in the profit the note is expected to generate, the instrument is likely to be a "security." If the note is exchanged to facilitate the purchase and sale of a minor asset or consumer good, to correct for the seller's cash-flow difficulties, or to advance some other commercial or consumer purpose, on the other hand, the note is less sensibly described as a "security." See, e.g., Forman, 421 U.S., at 851 (share of "stock" carrying a right to subsidized housing not a security because "the inducement to purchase was solely to acquire subsidized low-cost living space; it was not to invest for profit"). Second, we examine the "plan of distribution" of the instrument, SEC v. C.M. Joiner Leasing Corp., 320 U.S. 344, 353 (1943), to determine whether it is an instrument in which there is "common trading for speculation or investment," id., at 351. Third, we examine the reasonable expectations of the investing public: The Court will consider instruments to be "securities" on the basis of such public expectations, even where an economic analysis of the circumstances of the particular transaction might suggest that the instruments are not "securities" as used in that transaction. Compare Landreth Timber, 471 U.S., at 687, 693 (relying on public expectations in holding that common stock is always a security) with id., at 697–700 (Stevens, J., dissenting) (arguing that sale of business to single informed purchaser through stock is not within the purview of the Acts under the economic reality test). See also *Forman,* supra, at 851. Finally, we examine whether some factor such as the existence of another regulatory scheme significantly reduces the risk of the instrument, thereby rendering application of the Securities Acts unnecessary. See, e.g., Marine Bank, 455 U.S., at 557–559, and n. 7.

We conclude, then, that in determining whether an instrument denominated a "note" is a "security," courts are to apply the version of the "family resemblance" test that we have articulated here: a note is presumed to be a "security," and that presumption may be rebutted only by a showing that the note bears a strong resemblance (in terms of the four factors we have identified) to one of the enumerated categories of instrument. If an instrument is not sufficiently similar to an item on the list, the decision whether another category should be added is to be made by examining the same factors.

B

Applying the family resemblance approach to this case, we have little difficulty in concluding that the notes at issue here are "securities." Ernst & Young admits that "a demand note does not closely resemble any of the Second Circuit's family resemblance examples." Brief for Respondent 43. Nor does an examination of the four factors we have identified as being relevant to our inquiry suggest that the demand notes here are not "securities" despite their lack of similarity to any of the enumerated categories. The Co–Op sold the notes in an effort to raise capital for its general business operations, and purchasers bought them in order to earn a profit in the form of interest.[4] Indeed, one of the primary inducements offered purchasers was an interest rate constantly revised to keep it slightly above the rate paid by local banks and savings and loans. From both sides, then, the transaction is most naturally conceived as an investment in a business enterprise rather than as a purely commercial or consumer transaction.

As to the plan of distribution, the Co–Op offered the notes over an extended period to its 23,000 members, as well as to nonmembers, and more than 1,600 people held notes when the Co–Op filed for bankruptcy. To be sure, the notes were not traded on an exchange. They were, however, offered and sold to a broad segment of the public, and that is all we have held to be necessary to establish the requisite "common trading" in an instrument. See, e.g., *Landreth Timber,* supra (stock of closely held corporation not traded on any exchange held to be a "security"); Tcherepnin, 389 U.S., at 337 (nonnegotiable but transferable "withdrawable capital shares" in savings and loan association held to be a "security"); Howey, 328 U.S., at 295 (units of citrus grove and maintenance contract "securities" although not traded on exchange).

The third factor—the public's reasonable perceptions—also supports a finding that the notes in this case are "securities". We have consistently identified the fundamental essence of a "security" to be its character as an "investment." See supra, at 4, 7–8. The advertisements for the notes here

4. We emphasize that by "profit" in the context of notes, we mean "a valuable return on an investment," which undoubtedly includes interest. We have, of course, defined "profit" more restrictively in applying the *Howey* test to what are claimed to be "investment contracts." See, e.g., Forman, 421 U.S., at 852 ("[P]rofit" under the *Howey* test means either "capital appreciation" or "a participation in earnings"). To apply this restrictive definition to the determination whether an instrument is a "note" would be to suggest that notes paying a rate of interest not keyed to the earning of the enterprise are not "notes" within the meaning of the Securities Acts. Because the *Howey* test is irrelevant to the issue before us today, see supra, at 7, we decline to extend its definition of "profit" beyond the realm in which that definition applies.

characterized them as "investments," see supra, at 1, and there were no countervailing factors that would have led a reasonable person to question this characterization. In these circumstances, it would be reasonable for a prospective purchaser to take the Co–Op at its word.

Finally, we find no risk-reducing factor to suggest that these instruments are not in fact securities. The notes are uncollateralized and uninsured. Moreover, unlike the certificates of deposit in *Marine Bank,* supra, at 557–558, which were insured by the Federal Deposit Insurance Corporation and subject to substantial regulation under the federal banking laws, and unlike the pension plan in Teamsters v. Daniel, 439 U.S. 551, 569–570 (1979), which was comprehensively regulated under the Employee Retirement Income Security Act of 1974, 88 Stat. 829, 29 U.S.C. § 1001 *et seq.,* the notes here would escape federal regulation entirely if the Acts were held not to apply.

The court below found that "[t]he demand nature of the notes is very uncharacteristic of a security," 856 F.2d, at 54, on the theory that the virtually instant liquidity associated with demand notes is inconsistent with the risk ordinarily associated with "securities." This argument is unpersuasive. Common stock traded on a national exchange is the paradigm of a security, and it is as readily convertible into cash as is a demand note. The same is true of publicly traded corporate bonds, debentures, and any number of other instruments that are plainly within the purview of the Acts. The demand feature of a note does permit a holder to eliminate risk quickly by making a demand, but just as with publicly traded stock, the liquidity of the instrument does not eliminate risk all together. Indeed, publicly traded stock is even more readily liquid than are demand notes, in that a demand only eliminates risk when and if payment is made, whereas the sale of a share of stock through a national exchange and the receipt of the proceeds usually occur simultaneously.

We therefore hold that the notes at issue here are within the term "note" in § 3(a)(10).

III

Relying on the exception in the statute for "any note * * * which has a maturity at the time of issuance of not exceeding nine months," [Section 3(a)(10)], respondent contends that the notes here are not "securities," even if they would otherwise qualify. Respondent cites Arkansas cases standing for the proposition that, in the context of the state statute of limitations, "[a] note payable on demand is due immediately." See, e.g., McMahon v. O'Keefe, 213 Ark. 105, 106, 209 S.W.2d 449, 450 (1948) (statute of limitations is triggered by the date of issuance rather than by date of first demand). Respondent concludes from this rule that the "maturity" of a demand note within the meaning of § 3(a)(10) is immediate, which is, of course, less than nine months. Respondent therefore contends that the notes fall within the plain words of the exclusion and are thus not "securities."

Petitioners counter that the "plain words" of the exclusion should not govern. Petitioners cite legislative history of a similar provision of the 1933 Act, [§ 3(a)(3)], for the proposition that the purpose of the exclusion is to except from the coverage of the Acts only commercial paper—short-term, high quality instruments issued to fund current operations and sold only to highly sophisticated investors. See S.Rep. No. 47, 73d Cong., 1st Sess., 3–4 (1933); H.R.Rep. No. 85, 73d Cong., 1st Sess., 15 (1933). Petitioner also emphasizes that this Court has repeatedly held (see supra, at 3–6) that the plain words of the definition of a "security" are not dispositive, and that we consider the economic reality of the transaction to determine whether Congress intended the Securities Acts to apply. Petitioner therefore argues, with some force, that reading the exception for short-term notes to exclude from the Acts' coverage investment notes of less than nine months duration would be inconsistent with Congress' evident desire to permit the SEC and the courts flexibility to ensure that the Acts are not manipulated to investors' detriment. If petitioners are correct that the exclusion is intended to cover only commercial paper, these notes, which were sold in a large scale offering to unsophisticated members of the public, plainly should not fall within the exclusion.

We need not decide, however, whether petitioners' interpretation of the exception is correct, for we conclude that even if we give literal effect to the exception, the notes do not fall within its terms.

Respondent's contention that the demand notes fall within the "plain words" of the statute rests entirely upon the premise that Arkansas' statute of limitations for suits to collect demand notes is determinative of the "maturity" of the notes, as that term is used in the *federal* Securities Acts. The "maturity" of the notes, however, is a question of federal law. To regard States' statutes of limitations law as controlling the scope of the Securities Acts would be to hold that a particular instrument is a "security" under the 1934 Act in some States, but that the same instrument is not a "security" in others. Compare *McMahon,* supra, at 106 (statute runs from date of note) with 42 Pa.Cons.Stat. § 5525(7) (1988) (statute runs "from the later of either demand or any payment of principal of or interest on the instrument"). We are unpersuaded that Congress intended the Securities Acts to apply differently to the same transactions depending on the accident of which State's law happens to apply.

The Chief Justice's argument in partial dissent is but a more artful statement of respondent's contention, and it suffers from the same defect. The Chief Justice begins by defining "maturity" to mean the time when a note becomes due. Post, at 2 (quoting Black's Law Dictionary 1170 (3d ed. 1933)). Because a demand note is "immediately 'due' such that an action could be brought at any time without any other demand than the suit," post, at 2, the Chief Justice concludes that a demand note is due immediately for purposes of the federal securities laws. Even if the Chief Justice is correct that the "maturity" of a note corresponds to the time at which it "becomes due," the authority he cites for the proposition that, as a matter of federal law, a demand note "becomes due" immediately (as opposed to when demand is made or expected to be made) is no more dispositive than is Arkansas case law. The Chief Justice's primary source of authority is a treatise regarding the *state* law of negotiable instruments, particularly the Uniform Negotiable Instruments Law. See M. Bigelow, The Law of Bills, Notes, and Checks v–vii (W. Lile rev. 1928). The quotation upon which the Chief Justice relies is concerned with articulating the general *state* law rule regarding when suit may be filed. The only other authority the Chief Justice cites makes plain that state-law rules governing when a demand note becomes due are significant only in that they control the date on which statutes of limitation begin to run and whether demand must precede suit. See 8 C.J. Bills and Notes § 602, p. 406 (1916). Indeed, the treatise suggests that States were no more unanimous on those questions in 1933 than they are now. Ibid. In short, the dissent adds nothing to respondent's argument other than additional authority for what "maturity" means in certain state-law contexts. The dissent provides no argument for its implicit, but essential, premise that state rules concerning the proper method of collecting a debt control the resolution of the federal question before us.

Neither the law of Arkansas nor that of any other State provides an answer to the federal question, and as a matter of federal law, the words of the statute are far from "plain" with regard to whether demand notes fall within the exclusion. If it is plausible to regard a demand note as having an immediate maturity because demand *could* be made immediately, it is also plausible to regard the maturity of a demand note as being in excess of nine months because demand *could* be made many years or decades into the future. Given this ambiguity, the exclusion must be interpreted in accordance with its purpose. As we have said, we will assume for argument's sake that petitioners are incorrect in their view that the exclusion is intended to exempt only commercial paper. Respondent presents no competing view to explain why Congress would have enacted respondent's version of the exclusion, however, and the only theory that we can imagine that would support respondent's interpretation is that Congress intended to create a bright-line rule exempting from the 1934 Act's coverage *all* notes of less than nine months' duration, because short-term notes are, as a general rule, sufficiently safe that the Securities Acts need not apply. As we have said, however, demand notes do not necessarily have short terms. In light of Congress' broader purpose in the Acts of ensuring that investments of all descriptions be regulated to prevent fraud and abuse, we interpret the exception not to cover the demand notes at issue here. Although the result might be different if the design of the transaction suggested that both parties contemplated that demand would be made within the statutory period, that is not the case before us.

IV

For the foregoing reasons, we conclude that the demand notes at issue here fall under the "note" category of instruments that are "securities" under the 1933 and 1934 Acts. We also conclude that, even under a respondent's preferred approach to § 3(a)(10)'s exclusion for short-term notes, these demand notes do not fall within the exclusion. Accordingly, we reverse the judgment of the Court of Appeals and remand the case for further proceedings consistent with this opinion.

So ordered.

■ Justice Stevens, concurring.

While I join the Court's opinion, an important additional consideration supports my conclusion that these notes are securities notwithstanding the statute's exclusion for currency and commercial paper that has a maturity of no more than nine months. See § 3(a)(10) of the Securities Exchange Act of 1934. The Courts of Appeals have been unanimous in rejecting a literal reading of that exclusion. They have instead concluded that "when Congress spoke of notes with a maturity not exceeding nine months, it meant commercial paper, not investment securities." * * *

In my view such a settled construction of an important federal statute should not be disturbed unless and until Congress so decides. * * *

* * * Perhaps because the restriction of the exclusion to commercial paper is so well established, respondents admit that they did not even argue before the Court of Appeals that their notes were covered by the exclusion. A

departure from this reliable consensus would upset the justified expectations of both the legal and investment communities.

* * *

■ CHIEF JUSTICE REHNQUIST, with whom JUSTICE WHITE, JUSTICE O'CONNOR, and JUSTICE SCALIA join, concurring in part and dissenting in part.

I join part II of the Court's opinion, but dissent from part III and the statements of the Court's judgment in parts I and IV. In Part III, the court holds that these notes were not covered by the statutory exemption for "any note * * * which has a maturity at the time of issuance of not exceeding nine months." * * *

* * *

In construing any terms whose meanings are less than plain, we depend on the common understanding of those terms at the time of the statute's creation. * * *

* * *

To be sure, demand instruments were considered to have "the peculiar quality of having two maturity dates—one for the purpose of holding to his obligation the party primarily liable (e.g. maker), and the other for enforcing the contracts of parties secondarily liable (e.g. drawer and indorsers)." M. Bigelow, supra, § 350, p. 266. But only the rule of immediate maturity respecting makers of demand notes has any bearing on our examination of the exemption; the language in the Act makes clear that it is the "maturity at time of issuance" with which we are concerned. [§ 3(a)(10)] Accordingly, in the absence of some compelling indication to the contrary, the maturity date exemption must encompass demand notes because they possess "maturity at the time of issuance of not exceeding nine months."

Petitioners and the lower court decisions cited by Justice Stevens rely, virtually exclusively, on the legislative history of § 3(a)(3) of the *1933* Act for the proposition that the terms "any note" in the exemption in § 3(a)(10) of the 1934 Act encompass only notes having the character of short-term "commercial paper" exchanged among sophisticated traders. I am not altogether convinced that the legislative history of § 3(a)(3) supports that interpretation even with respect to the terms "any note" in the exemption in § 3(a)(3), and to bodily transpose that legislative history to another statute has little to commend it as a method of statutory construction.

The legislative history of the 1934 Act—under which this case arises—contains nothing which would support a restrictive reading of the exemption in question. Nor does the legislative history of § 3(a)(3) of the 1933 Act support the asserted limited construction of the exemption in § 3(a)(10) of the 1934 Act. Though the two most pertinent sources of congressional commentary on § 3(a)(3)—H.R.Rep. No. 85, 73d Cong., 1st Sess. 15 (1933) and S.Rep. No. 47, 73d Cong., 1st Sess. 3–4 (1933)—do suggest an intent to limit § 3(a)(3)'s exemption to short-term commercial paper, the references in those reports to commercial paper simply did not survive in the language of the enactment. Indeed, the Senate report stated "[n]otes, drafts, bills of exchange, and bankers' acceptances *which are commercial paper* and arise out of current *commercial, agricultural, or industrial* transactions, *and which are not intended to be marketed to the public,* are exempted. * * *" S.Rep. No. 47, supra (emphasis added). Yet the provision enacted in § 3(a)(3) of the 1933 Act exempts "*[a]ny* note, draft, bill of exchange, or banker's acceptance which arises out of a current transaction or the proceeds of which have been or are to be used for current transaction, and which has a maturity at the time of issuance of not exceeding nine months, * * * '' [Section 3(a)(3)] (emphasis added).

Such broadening of the language in the enacted version of § 3(a)(3), relative to the prototype from which it sprang, cannot easily be dismissed in interpreting § 3(a)(3). *A fortiori,* the legislative history's restrictive meaning cannot be imputed to the facially broader language in a different provision of another act. Although I do not doubt that both the 1933 and 1934 Act exemptions encompass short-term commercial paper, the expansive language in the statutory provisions is strong evidence that, in the end, Congress meant for commercial paper merely to be a subset of a larger class of exempted short-term instruments.[a]

NOTES, COMMERCIAL PAPER AND CERTIFICATES OF DEPOSIT

Notes. In the *Reves* case, the Supreme Court recognized that conventional "stock" is different from other categories of instruments. Traditional stock is the "quintessence" of a security. In contrast, an instrument bearing the label "note" encompasses instruments with widely varying characteristics depending on whether the instrument was issued in an investment context and therefore a security or was issued in a commercial or consumer context and thus constitutes a nonsecurity.[1]

At the same time, the Court rejected the use of the *Howey* test in the case of "notes" and indicated that the application of *Howey* is to be confined to determining whether an instrument is an "investment contract" and perhaps to other instruments of a more variable character. As the Court put it:[2] "To hold that a 'note' is not a 'security' unless it meets a test designed for an entirely different variety of instrument would make the Act's enumeration of many types of instruments superfluous. * * * (quoting *Landreth Timber*) and would be inconsistent with Congress' intent to regulate the entire body of instruments sold as investments. * * * ''

The Court adopted the "family resemblance" test formulated by Judge Friendly as a framework for analysis rather than the investment/commercial test theretofore used by some Circuits. Because the statute defines a security to include "any note," there is a presumption that every note is a security. The Court then adopted the list of securities identified by Judge Friendly as constituting nonsecurities: (1) a note delivered in consumer financing; (2) a note secured by a home mortgage; (3) a short-term note secured by a lien on a small business or some of its assets; (4) a note evidencing a "character" loan to a bank customer; (5) short-term notes secured by an assignment of accounts receivable; (6) a note formalizing an open-account debt incurred in the ordinary

---

a. See Schneider & Cohen, Reves v. Ernst & Young: A Note–Worthy Departure in Defining "Security," 23 Rev.Sec. & Comm. Reg. 191 (1990).

1. 494 U.S. at 62, 110 S.Ct. at 950. On the legislative history concerning the extent to which "notes" and other debt instruments should be deemed to be "securities," see Rosin, Historical Perspectives on the Definition of a Security, 28 S.Tex.L.Rev. (pt. 2) 575 (1987).

2. 494 U.S. at 64, 110 S.Ct. at 951.

course of business; and (7) notes evidencing loans by commercial banks for current operations.

The Court then suggested some standards to be applied for separating "note" instruments which were securities from those which were nonsecurities: (1) what motivations normally would prompt a reasonable buyer and seller to enter into such a transaction; (2) what was the issuer's "plan of distribution" in offering the instrument; (3) what were the reasonable expectations of the investing public; and (4) was there another regulatory regime in existence which significantly reduced the risk of the instrument, thereby rendering application of the Securities Acts unnecessary.

Commercial Paper. Although these guidelines may be helpful in some borderline situations, they do not take into account the vast changes in commercial banking practices since 1933. For example, when Congress was considering Section 3(a)(3) of the 1933 Act which exempts short-term notes issued to evidence a loan for current operations, the Senate Report described the difference between commercial banking and investment banking this way:[3]

> The primary function of commercial banking is to furnish short-term credits for financing production and distribution of consumable goods. By their nature, such loans should be self-liquidating. A sharp line of demarcation should exist between the function of the commercial banker and the investment banker. Long-term capital financing * * * is the proper field of the investment banker, since such loans are not self-liquidating within the prescribed limits of short-term commercial banking operations.

We have already seen that this sharp line of demarcation between commercial banking and investment banking thought to be imposed by the Glass–Steagall Act has now been breached by administrative action and the courts.[4] Although the Supreme Court at first held that commercial paper is included within the category of "notes and other securities" under Section 16 of the Glass–Steagall Act,[5] it remanded the case for a determination whether the "placement" of commercial paper, as agent, constituted "underwriting" of securities under section 21 of Glass–Steagall. On remand, the D.C. Circuit held that a state chartered member bank of the Federal Reserve system may place commercial paper issued by corporate issuers, as agent, without engaging in "underwriting" and crossing the line into investment banking under Glass–Steagall.[6]

Following this breach in the wall separating commercial and investment banking, the wall soon crumbled. The final blow was struck by the Second Circuit when it sustained the authority of the Federal Reserve Board under the

---

3.   Sen.Banking & Currency Comm., Stock Exchange Practices, S.Rep. No. 1455, 73d Cong., 2d Sess. 155 (1934), reprinted in 3 Legislative History of the Securities Act of 1933 and Securities Exchange Act of 1934, at Item 21 (J. Ellenberger & E. Mahar eds. 1973). The quotation is also reprinted and discussed in Rosin, Historical Perspectives on the Definition of a Security, 28 S.Tex.L.Rev. 57, at 587 (1987). This is the second part of a two-part article. For part I, see Rosin, Functional Exclusions From the Definition of a Security, 28 S.Tex.L.Rev. 331 (1986). These

articles trace the origins and legislative history of the definition of a "security" under the 1933 and 1934 Acts.

4.   See supra, at 77–86.

5.   Securities Industry Ass'n v. Board of Governors of Federal Reserve System, 468 U.S. 137 (1984).

6.   Securities Industry Ass'n v. Board of Governors of Federal Reserve System, 807 F.2d 1052 (D.C.Cir.1986), cert. denied, 483 U.S. 1005 (1987).

Bank Holding Company Act presently to permit affiliates of bank holding companies to underwrite commercial paper, certain other debt securities, and eventually equity securities, subject to limitations, without violation of section 20 of the Glass–Steagall Act.[7]

In *Reves,* the Court left open the question whether commercial paper and certificates of deposit having a stated maturity of less than nine months were within the short-term "note" exclusion of the Exchange Act. The Court found it unnecessary to resolve this question because demand notes may not necessarily mature in less than nine months.

Of course, many transactions in which a "note" is issued may be exempt from the 1933 Act registration provisions, but if a "security" transaction occurs, the antifraud provisions of the 1933 and 1934 Acts will still apply. Commercial banks are now engaged in many creative lending activities which go far beyond traditional commercial banking practices. In these situations, when will the "note" be regarded as being utilized in a commercial context rather than an investment context?

Certificates of Deposit. In Marine Bank v. Weaver,[8] discussed in *Landreth Timber* and *Reves,* the Court held that a certificate of deposit issued by a bank that was regulated by the federal government and insured by the Federal Deposit Insurance Corporation is a "security" under the Securities Acts. Sam and Alice Weaver had purchased a $50,000 certificate of deposit from the Marine Bank. The instrument had a six year maturity and was insured by the FDIC. The Weavers subsequently pledged the certificate to the Bank to guarantee a $65,000 loan made by the Bank to Columbus Packing Company as a part of a business transaction between the Weavers and Columbus. Columbus owed the Bank $33,000 at the time for prior loans and was also substantially overdrawn on its checking account with the Bank. The Weavers claimed that Bank officers told them that Columbus would use the $65,000 loan as working capital in its business but instead the Bank applied the loan to pay Columbus' overdue obligations to it as well as debts owed to third persons. Columbus became bankrupt four months later.

The Weavers brought a Rule 10b–5 action for fraud asserting that had they known of Columbus' precarious financial condition and the Bank's plans, they would not have guaranteed the loan. The Court, relying on the Daniel case,[9] held that a government insured certificate of deposit was unique and differed from other long-term obligations and was not a "security". The reason:[10] "This certificate of deposit was issued by a federally regulated bank which is subject to the comprehensive set of regulations governing the banking industry. * * * The * * * purchaser of a certificate of deposit is virtually guaranteed payment in full, whereas the holder of an ordinary long-term debt obligation assumes

---

7. Securities Industry Ass'n v. Board of Governors of Federal Reserve System, 839 F.2d 47 (2d Cir.1988), cert. denied, 486 U.S. 1059 (1988). And see, Securities Industries Ass'n v. Board of Governors of Federal Reserve System, 900 F.2d 360 (D.C.Cir.1990) (Securities Industry Association is precluded from challenging authority of the Federal Reserve Board and relitigating issues determined by Second Circuit). The story is told in Litt, Macey, Miller & Rubin, Politics, Bureaucracies, and Financial Markets: Bank Entry

Into Commercial Paper Underwriting in the United States and Japan, 139 U.Pa.L.Rev. 369, 375–79, 383–403 (1990). And see Kuruza, Ballen & Diana, Securities and Investment Activities of Banks—Recent Developments, 46 Bus.Law. 325 (1990).

8. 455 U.S. 551 (1982).

9. Supra at 324.

10. 455 U.S. at 557–59.

the risk of the borrower's insolvency. The definition of security in the 1934 Act provides that an instrument which seems to fall within the broad sweep of the Act is not considered a security if the context otherwise requires. It is unnecessary to subject issuers of bank certificates of deposit to liability under the antifraud provisions of the federal securities laws since the holders of bank certificates of deposit are abundantly protected under the federal banking laws. We therefore hold that the certificate of deposit purchased by the Weavers is not a security."

The "comparable protection" rationale applied in *Daniel* and *Marine Bank* has come under severe criticism.[11] In the first place, the idea that it is impossible to lose your money if you put it in a bank (or in a pension plan regulated under ERISA) has turned out in retrospect to be demonstrably false. Secondly, Federal deposit insurance only protects against bank insolvency, not against bank fraud against customers. Indeed, Chief Justice Burger admitted that not all certificates of deposit are nonsecurities. In famous footnote 11, he had this to say: "It does not follow that a certificate of deposit * * * invariably falls outside the definition of a security as defined by the federal statutes. Each transaction must be analyzed and evaluated on the basis of the content of the instruments in question, the purposes intended to be served, and the factual setting as a whole."[12] Third, federal bank regulation may be more intended to protect the solvency and stability of banks than the interests of investors.[13]

Risk Reduction: How Far Does this Rationale Extend? Although *Marine Bank* and *Daniel* applied only to federal regulatory systems, several courts of appeal have applied the comparable regulation rationale to cover issuers that are not federally regulated and even in one case to foreign issuers subject only to foreign regulation.[14] *Reves* did not address whether federal courts may

---

11. Bloomenthal, 1982 Securities Law Handbook xlix, xiviii, ("The Court's rationale for its holding, if an answer to a law examination including the identical question would probably have been graded F by 97% of the securities regulation professors in the United States."); Arnold, "When is a Car a Bicycle?" and Other Riddles: The Definition of a Security Under the Federal Securities Laws, 33 Cleve.St.L.Rev. 448, 474 (1984–85) ("The *Weaver* decision immediately preceded the collapse of Penn Square Bank. In that failure and several failures since then, it appears as if uninsured depositors stand to lose a significant portion of their principal."); Steinberg & Kaulbach, The Supreme Court and the Definition of "Security": The "Context" Clause, "Investment Contract" Analysis, and Their Ramifications, 40 Vand.L.Rev. 489, 492 (1987) ("not only is *Weaver* riddled with ambiguity, the decision is simplistic, and its understanding of securities law is weak"); Note, Curbing Preemption of Securities Act Coverage in Absence of Clear Congressional Direction, 72 Va.L.Rev. 195, 196 (1988). ("[T]he context clause * * * does not justify an examination of statutes offering compara-

ble protections * * * [and that] approach fails to implement congressional intent.").

12. See Jones, Footnote 11 of Marine Bank v. Weaver: Will Unconventional Certificates of Deposit Be Held Securities, 24 Hous. L.Rev. 492 (1987); Quinn, After *Reves v. Ernst & Young*, When Are Certificates of Deposit "Notes" Subject to Rule 10b–5 of the Securities Exchange Act?, 46 Bus.Law. 173, 179 (1990).

13. See Kornegay, Bank Loans As Securities: A Legal and Financial Economic Analysis of the Treatment of Marketable Bank Assets Under the Securities Acts, 40 UCLA L. Rev. 799 (1993).

14. Dubach v. Weitzel, 135 F.3d 590 (8th Cir.1998); Wolf v. Banamex, 739 F.2d 1458 (9th Cir.1984), cert. denied, 469 U.S. 1108 (1985) (certificate of deposit for pesos issued by a Mexican Bank to U.S. resident); West v. Multibanco Comermex, S.A., 807 F.2d 820 (9th Cir.), cert. denied, 482 U.S. 906 (1987) (same); Tafflin v. Levitt, 865 F.2d 595 (4th Cir.1989), aff'd as to unrelated issue, 493 U.S. 455 (1990); Contra, Holloway v. Peat, Marwick, Mitchell & Co., 879 F.2d 772 (10th Cir.1989), aff'd after remand, 900 F.2d

consider state (or foreign) regulation of a note when considering whether a note is a security. When applying the fourth factor on risk reduction, however, the Court emphasized that the instruments considered in *Marine Bank* and *Daniel* were subject to comprehensive regulation under federal law and that the notes in Reves "would escape federal regulation entirely if the [federal securities laws] were held not to apply."[15]

Curiously enough, the question of whether state banking regulation would preempt the federal securities laws was then pending before the Court in Holloway v. Peat, Marwick, Mitchell & Co.[16] Rather than deciding *Holloway,* the Court remanded the case for further consideration in the light of *Reves.* On remand, the Holloway court adhered to its decision that pass book savings certificates and thrift certificates issued by a state bank and a trust company were securities within the meaning of the federal securities laws.

The Court of Appeals in *Holloway* noted that the *Reves* Court stressed the fact that *Marine Bank* and *Daniel* emphasized federal regulation and that the notes in *Reves* would "escape federal regulation entirely" if the federal securities laws did not apply. Moreover, the Court pointed out that *Reves* rejected the resort to state law to determine when a demand note matures in favor of federal law. Accordingly, the court reaffirmed its holding "that under the supremacy clause, U.S. Const., art. VI, cl. 2, our focus must be on *federal* regulation; state regulatory schemes cannot displace the [Securities] Acts."[17] Yet, more Circuits have held the reverse, finding that state regulation exempts and one has even found that foreign regulation is sufficient.[18]

The significance of this issue comes into clearer focus when one realizes that whether certificates of deposit are "notes" and thus securities under the Exchange Act "has particular importance today in light of the increasing number of failed lending institutions and widespread allegations that many of these lenders committed fraud. Although depositors with federally insured lenders will be able to recover their deposits, many certificates of deposit are not adequately insured, or are uninsured. Because Exchange Act Rule 10b–5 probably provides the most attractive remedy for depositors who can allege fraud, litigation over its applicability to certificates of deposit is likely to increase."[19] There is no private right of action under the federal banking laws.[20]

Most courts have focused only on regulation as a risk-reducing factor, but at least one has considered the existence of collateral as a significant risk-reduction factor. In *Bass v. Janney Montgomery Scott Inc.,*[21] the Sixth Circuit found that notes should not be deemed securities where they were secured by assets of the borrower and stock in a subsidiary of the borrower. How far can

1485 (10th Cir.1990), cert. denied sub nom. KPMG Peat, Marwick v. Holloway, 498 U.S. 958 (1990) (savings certificates and passbook accounts issued by financial institutions regulated by the state were securities).

15.   494 U.S. at 69, 110 S.Ct. at 953.

16.   879 F.2d 772 (10th Cir.1989), aff'd after remand, 900 F.2d 1485 (10th Cir.1990), cert. denied sub nom. KPMG Peat, Marwick v. Holloway, 498 U.S. 958 (1990).

17.   900 F.2d 1485, 1488.

18.   See *Wolf v. Banamex,* supra note 14.

19.   After *Reves v. Ernst & Young,* When Are Certificates of Deposit "Notes" Subject to Rule 10b–5 of the Securities Exchange Act, 46 Bus.Law. 173 (1990).

20.   Id.

21.   210 F.3d 577 (6th Cir.2000).

this approach be pushed? The defendant in *Stoiber v. SEC*[22] argued that contractual provisions in a loan agreement sufficiently reduced risk to affect the note/security determination. The D.C. Circuit refused to buy this argument, however, finding that contractual provisions, which were in essence early acceleration clauses, "are significantly less valuable than collateral or insurance and not by our thinking an adequate substitute for the protection of the federal securities laws."[23]

Overlap With "Investment Contract" and the Howey Test. Many ambiguous instruments can be analyzed under either the *Reves* test or the *Howey* test. For example, viatical settlements may be assessed under both standards.[24] What happens, however, if the instrument is deemed to be a security under one test, but not the other? Presumably, the definition of "security" in Section 2(a)(1) is disjunctive, but *Reves* can be read to mean that there are instruments Congress did not want classified as securities. To the extent that courts have given primary weight to the *Reves* test, and considered *Howey* only secondarily, they have seemed inclined to classify ambiguous instruments as non-securities. For example, in *Great Rivers Cooperative of Southeastern Iowa v. Farmland Industries, Inc.,*[25] "capital credits" issued by an agricultural cooperative to its members were found not to constitute securities, even though the credits (1) were transferable (but only with the consent of the defendant's board); (2) represented retained equity in the firm that was issued by the defendant in an attempt to raise capital; (3) were purchased by the members in return for shares in the cooperative that they surrendered; (4) entitled their members to receive distributions of the defendant's earnings; and (5) were dependent for their economic value upon the managerial efforts of the defendant's officers.[26] Essentially, a majority of the holders of the credits received them as a result of the conversion of their common stock into "capital credits." Yet, overshadowing all these factors in the Eighth Circuit's opinion was the fact that the holders had entered into a commercial relationship with the cooperative and viewed the credits as "patronage refunds or equity interests reflecting a membership or former membership in that cooperative...."[27] *Query*: At this point, is *Reves* beginning to overshadow *Howey* by creating a new commercial/investment dichotomy?

Problems

(1) Suppose Apex Software Co. wants to raise funds for plant expansion and working capital? It issues preferred stock in a private or public offering and negotiates a bank loan with a commercial bank for $3 million evidenced by a 3–year note bearing interest at 1% above the prime rate. The bank also takes a warrant giving it an option to purchase stock in the company? Is the note a "security?"

(2) Suppose a business corporation finds itself in financial difficulties. It owes its suppliers for goods sold on open-account. To avoid bankruptcy, the company issues term notes to 45 of its trade creditors evidencing the debts. Is this a commercial or investment transaction?

22. 161 F.3d 745 (D.C.Cir.1998).

23. *Id.* at 751–52.

24. In SEC v. Larry W. Tyler & Advanced Fin. Servs., Inc., 2002 WL 257645 (S.E.C.2002), the district court found the viatical settlements there at issue to constitute securities under both tests.

25. 198 F.3d 685 (8th Cir.1999).

26. *Id.* at 796–98.

27. Id. at 700.

(3) In Gary Plastic Packaging Corp. v. Merrill Lynch, Pierce, Fenner & Smith, Inc.,[28] defendant investment firm offered to the public federally insured $100,000 certificates of deposit of savings banks and agreed to maintain a secondary market in the certificates. In addition, Merrill Lynch offered a variety of other services, which included screening banks to determine which offered the most competitive yields, monitoring the creditworthiness of the banks, and negotiating for the best terms with these banks. The plaintiff alleged that the defendant failed to disclose that the rates of interest on their CDs were lower than the interest rates paid by the banks on direct sales of CDs and that defendants pocketed the difference between the rates as an undisclosed commission. Were the CDs sold through the CD program securities? The Second Circuit said yes, but would the D.C. Circuit majority in the *Life Partners* case (Casebook supra p. 311) agree? Or would they classify these services as "pre-purchase" services? Should this distinction matter in this context where we are applying the *Reves* criteria rather than the *Howey* criteria?

LOAN PARTICIPATIONS

Increasingly, commercial banks syndicate the loans they make to corporate borrowers to institutional investors (in particular, foreign banks, insurance companies and mutual funds). The bank may charge for its services in making the loan by retaining the spread between the actual interest rate on the loan (say, 10.25%) and the lower rate at which these institutional loan participants agree to purchase their participation (say, 10.10%). So long as the latter rate exceeds the money market rate on comparable instruments of a similar risk levels, the institutional purchasers may not object to this retention by the bank. But what is the legal status of these loan participations?

In Banco Espanol de Credito v. Security Pacific National Bank,[1] Security Pacific made short-term loans, ranging in duration from overnight to one year (with most being for less than one month), to Integrated Resources, a large financial services conglomerate, to finance the latter's current business operations. Security Pacific sold participation interests in its Integrated loan portfolio to some eleven financial institutions, each of which agreed to buy without recourse against Security Pacific and to conduct its own credit analysis of the borrower. These institutions had previously purchased other "loan notes" from Security Pacific, which specialized in this form of syndication, and had signed a Master Participation Agreement with Security Pacific, covering the basis and terms on which Security Pacific would offer it loan participations in short-term loans to many of its corporate borrowers. When Integrated Resources defaulted and went into bankruptcy in 1989, several of these loans participants sued Security Pacific, asserting both that the instruments were securities and that they had been sold to them while Security Pacific was in possession of material, non-public information about Integrated's declining financial condition.

Applying the four *Reves* factors, a divided Second Circuit panel affirmed the district court's dismissal of the complaint on the ground that Security Pacific's "loan notes" were not securities:

"In addressing the first *Reves* factor, the district court found that Security Pacific was motivated by a desire to increase lines of credit to Integrated while diversifying Security Pacific's risk, that Integrated was motivated by

---

28.   756 F.2d 230 (2d Cir.1985).   **1.**   973 F.2d 51 (2d Cir.1992).

a need for short-term credit at competitive rates to finance its current operations, and that the purchasers of the loan participations sought a short-term return on excess cash. Based on these findings, the district court concluded that 'the overall motivation of the parties was the promotion of commercial purposes' rather than an investment in a business enterprise.

Weighing the second *Reves* factor—the plan of distribution of the instrument—the district court observed that only institutional and corporate entities were solicited and that detailed individualized presentations were made by Security Pacific's sales personnel. The district court therefore concluded that the plan of distribution was "a limited solicitation to sophisticated financial or commercial institutions and not to the general public." We agree.

The plan of distribution specifically prohibited resales of the loan participation without the express written permission of Security Pacific. This limitation worked to prevent the loan participation from being sold to the general public, thus limiting eligible buyers to those with the capacity to acquire information about the debtor * * *.

With regard to the third factor—the reasonable perception of the instrument by the investing public—the district court considered the expectations of the sophisticated purchasers who signed MPA's [Master Participation Agreements] and determined that these institutions were given ample notice that the instruments were participations in loans and not investments in a business enterprise.

Finally, the district court noted that the Office of the Comptroller of the Currency has issued specific policy guidelines addressing the sale of loan participation. Thus, the fourth factor—the existence of another regulatory scheme—indicated that application of the securities laws was unnecessary.

Thus, under the *Reves* family resemblance analysis, as properly applied by the district court, we hold that the loan participations in the instant case are analogous to the enumerated category of loans issued by banks for commercial purposes and therefore do not satisfy the statutory definition of "notes" which are "securities" * * *[2]

In dissent, Judge Oakes saw Security Pacific's loan participation program in an entirely different light and concluded that the majority decision "makes bad banking law and bad securities law, and stands on its head the law of this Circuit and of the Supreme Court in *Reves* * * *":

" * * * [T]he loan note program engaged in by Security Pacific, while bearing a superficial resemblance to traditional loan participations, differs from those traditional participations in several important respects, including (1) who the participants are; (2) what the purposes of the purchasers or participants are; and (3) what the promotional basis used in marketing the loan notes is. The participants, rather than being commercial lenders who engage in traditional loan participations, were instead in many cases non-financial entities not acting as commercial lenders but making an investment, and even though there were some banks that purchased the so-called loan notes, they generally did so not through their lending departments but through their investment and trading departments * * *. The pro-

---

2. Id. at 55–56.

motional literature put out by Security Pacific advertised the so-called loan notes as competitive with commercial paper, a well-recognized security under the Security Act * * *.

Beyond that, . . . these loan notes differ from traditional loan participations in the scope of information available to the purchasers. In the traditional loan participation, participants generally engage in one-to-one negotiation with the lead lender, and at times with the borrower, and can inspect all information, public and non-public, that is relevant, and consequently are able to do their own credit analysis. Here, Security Pacific did not provide the participants with non-public information it had, provided only publicly-available documents or ratings, and the purchasers were not in a position to approach the hundred or more possible borrowers in the program and conduct their own examinations * * *."[3]

Accordingly, Judge Oakes concluded that the loan participants did not have the opportunity to verify information that "normal" loan participants had in those forms of bank syndications that were traditionally beyond the scope of the federal securities laws.

When certiorari was applied for, the Supreme Court requested the views of the Solicitor General, which characterized the Second Circuit's decision as "flawed", but advised against granting certiorari (possibly because the federal banking agencies were concerned that a contrary ruling would expose banks to significantly heightened liabilities). On this basis, the Supreme Court declined to grant certiorari.

While the result in *Banco Espanol* is debatable, the controversy was inevitable. With increased competition in the financial services industry, a convergence of banking and brokerage firms has resulted, and traditional distinctions between how banks and brokerage firms behave no longer provides very useful guideposts for the future. Indeed, had the Second Circuit found that the short term loans that Security Pacific was syndicating (which typically were between ten days and one month in duration) were securities, would it have been feasible for Security Pacific to market them? Although Security Pacific could have made a private placement of such notes, the preparation of a private placement brochure for each such offering (particularly those where the loan would be outstanding for less than ten days) seems disproportionate.

In 1994, the Second Circuit returned to the topic of loan participations in Pollack v. Laidlaw Holdings, Inc.[4] This time the instruments were uncollateralized participations in mortgages, which had been sold in many cases by brokers and investment advisers to unsophisticated investors. The Second Circuit reversed the district court, which had found that the instruments not to be securities, based in part on *Banco Espanol,* and distinguished *Banco Espanol* on the ground that it did not apply to "broad-based, unrestricted sales to the general investing public."[5]

---

3.   Id. at 56–57. For another criticism of the majority's reasoning, see Roberts & Quinn, Leveling the Playing Field: The Need For Investor Protection for Bank Sales of Loans Participation Agreements, 63 Fordham L. Rev. 2115 (1995).

4.   27 F.3d 808 (2d Cir.1994). For a similar result, also emphasizing that those solicited were individuals, not institutions, see *Stoiber v. SEC,* 161 F.3d 745 (D.C.Cir.1998).

5.   Id. at 814.

SWAPS

Derivatives are financial instruments, chiefly used for hedging, whose value derives from that of another asset (such as a stock, a stock index, a government bond, etc.) to which they are pegged. One particularly important form of derivative is the swap. A swap is a contract between two parties (usually called the counterparties) under which they agree to exchange a series of cash flows over time. Why? Usually, the goal is to protect one side from interest rate or currency fluctuations, for which protection the other side gains some *expected* profit. For example, the simplest swap agreement is a fixed for floating interest rate swap.[1] Under this form of agreement, one counterparty agrees to make fixed-rate payments to the other, while the second party agrees to make payments whose amounts "float" with prevailing interest rates. If prevailing interest rates rise above the fixed rate, the second party (who pays the floating rate) will lose on the contract; if prevailing rates fall below the fixed rate, it will win. Typically, the motivation for the party paying the fixed rate is to protect itself against an interest rate rise on its own outstanding floating debt, because the payments it receives under the swap contract will to that extent offset any increase it incurs in its own interest rate expense. Correspondingly, the party making the floating rate payments may fear a decline in interest rates (because, for example, it may hold a portfolio of floating rate securities) and so it protects itself under the swap contract against the danger that floating rates will fall below the fixed rate.

Typically, swaps are not traded on exchanges, but are customized contracts written for a particular corporate debtor or financial institution by a swaps dealer (usually, a commercial bank). Also, in most swaps, the two sides do not in actual practice make the two reciprocal streams of payments; rather, the losing side simply pays the winner the differential between the two payments on each payment date.

Do such swap contracts amount to "securities" under the *Reves* criteria? For a time, considerable uncertainty surrounded this issue, and the SEC asserted in some enforcement actions that certain swaps amounted in effect to options and thus constituted securities.[2] In this light of the continuing uncertainty about the legal status of swaps (and the explosive growth in the swaps market), the President's Working Group recommended in 1999 that over-the-counter swaps be deregulated and removed from both the SEC's jurisdiction and also from the CFTC's jurisdiction (except that certain antifraud and antimanipulation provisions of the CFTC's statute would continue to apply). Its principal rationale for deregulation was that financial derivatives were less subject to manipulation than derivatives based on physical commodities, because the market in physical commodities has a finite supply and thus can be cornered or squeezed. In response to this recommendation and enormous lobbying pressure from the banking industry, Congress adopted amendments to

---

1. For a fuller discussion of swaps, see Romano, A Thumbnail Sketch of Derivative Securities and Their Regulation, 55 Md. L.Rev. 1 (1996).

2. However, in Procter & Gamble Co. v. Bankers Trust Co., 925 F.Supp. 1270 (S.D.Ohio 1996), the district court found that interest rate swaps were not securities under the *Reves* test. It emphasized that the defen-

dants bank's motive was "to generate a fee and commission, while P&G's expressed motive was, in substantial part, to reduce its funding costs." It also emphasized that the swaps would not be distributed to the market in the manner of securities and hence failed to meet *Reves*'s second prong in its test for a security.

both the Securities Act of 1933 and the Securities Act of 1934, which exempt both "security-based swap agreements" and "non-security based swap agreements" from the definition of security.[3] Effectively, these two terms cover the waterfront and exempt all swap agreements.

SECTION 2.   EXEMPTED SECURITIES: SECTIONS 3(A)(2) THROUGH 3(A)(8)

Sections 3 and 4 of the Securities Act provide certain specific exemptions from the broad registration and prospectus requirements of § 5, although the antifraud provisions of both the 1933 and 1934 Acts remain applicable. Read literally, section 3 seems to exempt the securities themselves from the operation of the Act, unless the Act elsewhere provides otherwise. On the other hand, the various clauses of § 4 clearly are transaction exemptions, rather than securities exemptions.

Section 3(a)(1), repealed in 1987, was a transition section. It exempted from the registration requirements of the Act securities which were offered to the public prior to or shortly after adoption of the Act. After fifty years, § 3(a)(1) was regarded as obsolete. The amendment reserved paragraph (1) for future use and retained the numbering of the remaining subsections.[1]

The securities covered by §§ 3(a)(2) through 3(a)(8), inclusive, are such that they were thought to be inappropriate subjects of regulation in this Act either because already subject to regulation by another governmental authority or because of the intrinsic nature of the securities themselves. Thus, broadly speaking, these comprise: (1) any security issued or guaranteed by any federal, state or territorial governmental entity or by a national or state bank [§ 3(a)(2)][2]; (2) short term notes or bills of exchange which arise out of a current transaction [§ 3(a)(3)]; (3) securities of nonprofit, religious, educational, fraternal or charitable institutions [§ 3(a)(4)]; (4) securities of certain savings and loan associations and farmers' cooperatives [§ 3(a)(5)]; (5) interests in railroad equipment trusts [§ 3(a)(6)]; (6) certificates of a receiver, or trustee or debtor in possession in a bankruptcy proceeding, when issued with court approval [§ 3(a)(7)]; and (7) insurance policies or annuity contracts, issued subject to the supervision of a domestic governmental authority [§ 3(a)(8)]. However, § 24(d) of the Investment Company Act makes the § 3(a)(8) exemption inapplicable to any security of which an investment company is the issuer.

1.   Section 3(a)(2)

In recent years a series of amendments have been made to § 3(a)(2) expanding this exemption to include: (1) certain types of industrial develop-

3.   See Section 2A of the Securities Act of 1933 and Section 3A of the Securities Act of 1934. The terms "security-based swap agreement" and "non-security based swap agreement" are defined in Sections 206B and 206C of the Gramm–Leach–Bliley Act.

1.   S.Rep. No. 100–105, 100th Cong., 1st Sess. 15–16 (1987).

2.   This subsection is interpreted by the Commission also to include securities issued or guaranteed by United States branches or agencies of foreign banks located in the United States if federal or state regulation of the particular branch or agency is substantially equivalent to that applicable to domestic banks doing business in the same jurisdiction. Securities Act Release 6661 (Sept. 29, 1986).

ment bonds, the interest on which is excludable from gross income under § 103(a)(1) of the Internal Revenue Code; (2) interests and participations in the traditional forms of common trust funds maintained by banks as investment vehicles in which the bank holds the assets in a bona fide fiduciary capacity; (3) interests and participations in collective trust funds maintained by banks for funding certain stock bonus, pension or profit-sharing plans which meet the requirements for qualification under § 401(a) of the Internal Revenue Code; and (4) any interest or participation in a "separate account" maintained by an insurance company for funding certain stock bonus, pension or profit-sharing plans which meet the requirements for qualification under IRC § 401(a) and certain annuity plans under IRC § 404(a)(2).

a. *Municipal Securities.* The municipal securities market was surveyed earlier in Chapter 1, along with the SEC's efforts to improve disclosure in it by regulating the brokers and dealers active in this market through Rule 15c2–12. Effectively, Rule 15c2–12 requires a disclosure document (known as the "official statement") for municipal securities offerings above a minimal floor (i.e., those over $1,000,000), even through an exemption from § 5 of the 1933 Act is available under § 3(a)(2). Adopted in 1989 and later significantly amended in 1994,[3] Rule 15c2–12 was a response to the default on the bonds issued by the Washington Public Power System (WPPSS) and the near-default on New York City's bonds in the mid-to-late 1970s. Both episodes disrupted the municipal securities market and gave rise to calls for reform and increased regulation.

Another amendment extended § 3(a)(2) to exempt certain industrial development bonds (IDBs) not previously exempted.[4] IDBs are a form of revenue bond used by a municipality or other governmental subdivision to attract industry, provide housing or for other commercial purposes. Typically, the municipality issues revenue bonds to finance the construction of an industrial facility for a private corporation. The corporation rents the facility on a long-term basis for an amount which covers principal and interest on the bonds. The bonds are secured solely by a pledge of the revenues and a mortgage on the facilities, so that payment of the bonds is dependent upon the credit of the private corporation, rather than the municipal issuer. Thus, IDBs actually are "private activity" bonds which are funded by an industrial or commercial enterprise and conceptually are "indistinguishable from other corporate debt securities" that are subject to the registration requirements of the 1933 Act.[5]

---

3. See SEC Exch.Act Rel. No. 26,985 (June 28, 1989) and Sec.Exch.Act Rel. No. 34,961 (Nov. 10, 1994). To the extent applicable, Rule 15c2–12 requires participating underwriters in a municipal securities offering to obtain and review a copy of the issuer's official statement and provide it to requesting customers, thus establishing on a modest level a registration-like requirement.

4. See Securities Act Release No. 5103 (Nov. 6, 1970) with respect to the exemption of industrial development bonds under § 3(a)(2) where the proceeds were to be used to provide a narrow range of specified facilities. The exemption applied only to issues that did not exceed five million dollars, which was later increased to $10 million. Rule 131 of the 1933 Act and Rule 3b–5 of the 1934

Act deny the exemption to these governmental obligations if they are funded by payments received from an industrial or commercial enterprise for use of such facilities. In that event, the obligations are deemed to be a separate "security" issued by the private entity and the exemption is not available. However, these rules do not apply to revenue bonds or other evidences of indebtedness issued by a governmental entity to finance a revenue producing public project to be operated by that entity.

5. The SEC sponsored the Industrial Development Bond Act of 1978 which would have subjected these bonds to the registration requirements of the 1933 Act. S. 3323, 95th Cong., 2d Sess. (1978). The bill died for lack of support. For the history of industrial

They have been widely used by retail chain stores and other private entrepreneurs because they provided tax advantages for the bondholder, a bonanza for the industrial enterprise as compared to competitors, and an exemption from the disclosure obligations of the 1933 Act. The Tax Equity and Fiscal Responsibility Act of 1982 (TEFRA) placed restrictions on the type of facilities financed with small issue IDBs and otherwise curtailed their use.[6] And the Tax Reform Act of 1986 has further curbed the abuses of this tax bonanza for certain private sector beneficiaries.

b. *Securities Issued or Guaranteed by a Bank.* The application of § 3(a)(2) to banks is more complicated than initially appears from a first reading of this section. Of course, § 3(a)(2) exempts stock or bonds issued by a bank, but it does not apply to securities issued by a bank holding company.[7] The § 3(a)(2) exemption is available, however, for financial institutions (known as "industrial loan companies") that function as the economic equivalent of a commercial bank (i.e., taking deposits and making loans), but that are not actually regulated as a bank under state law.[8] These financial institutions will typically have FDIC insurance and be subject to very similar regulation under state law. The U.S. branches of foreign banks are also permitted to use the § 3(a)(2) exemption, but on a special non-discriminatory condition that the foreign branches of U.S. banks in the foreign banks home jurisdiction receive parity of treatment.[9]

The significance of § 3(a)(2) has been much enhanced in recent years by the surge in popularity of structured financings and asset-backed securitizations. Typically, in these transactions, a bank guarantees that a pool of assets (usually, mortgages or accounts receivable) will be sufficient to pay the principal and interest on debt securities issued by a nominal corporate debtor set up to acquire and hold this pool of assets. Almost any form of income-product instrument with standardized terms can be pooled, thereby permitting the corporation that had held these instruments to free up its capital for other uses. For example, if the sales financing subsidiary of General Motors or Ford sells its accounts receivable (i.e., auto loans) from automobile purchasers to such a nominal debtor, which pays for them by issuing bonds in the public market, the addition of a major bank's guarantee that the auto loans in the

development bonds and a discussion of abuses arising from their use, see Seligman, supra note 2; Hellige, Industrial Development Bonds: The Disclosure Dilemma, 6 J. of Corp.L. 291 (1981). And see Note, Municipal Bonds and the Federal Securities Laws: The Results of Forty Years of Indirect Regulations, 28 Vand.L.Rev. 561, 605–11 (1975); Comment, Federal Regulation of Municipal Securities: A Constitutional and Statutory Analysis, 1976 Duke L.J. 1261, 1278–81 (1976); Note, Industrial Development Bonds, A Proposal for Reform, 65 Minn.L.Rev. 961 (1981); Note, Municipal Bonds: Is There a Need for Mandatory Disclosure?, 58 U.Det.J.U.L. 255 (1981); Shores v. Sklar, 647 F.2d 462 (5th Cir.1981).

6.   McGee, The Impact of TEFRA and the 1984 Act on Small Issue Industrial Development Bonds, 33 Emory L.J. 779 (1984);

Note, Bedtime for [Industrial Development] Bonds?: Municipal Bond Tax Legislation of the First Reagan Administration, 48 L. & Contemp.Prob. 212 (Autumn 1985); Leifer & Plump, Uses of Industrial Development Bonds, 42 N.Y.U.Ann.Inst. on Fed.Tax. 7–1 (1984).

7.   See Bankers Trust Co., SEC No–Action Letter, [1971–72 Transfer Binder] Fed. Sec.L.Rep. (CCH) Para. 78,474 (Sept. 22, 1971).

8.   See Morris Plan Co. of California, SEC No–Action Letter, 1990 SEC No–Act. LEXIS 797 (May 7, 1990).

9.   See SEC Act.Rel. No. 6661 (Sept. 29, 1986). Nondiscriminatory treatment of foreign banks was required by the 1978 International Banking Act (IBA).

pool will be sufficient to pay principal and interest on these bonds will both satisfy the bond purchasers and the requirements of § 3(a)(2), thereby eliminating the need for SEC registration.[10]

The success of commercial banks in providing this service has led to a clamor from their principal rival (insurance companies) that the § 3(a)(2) exemption should be expanded to cover securities guaranteed by them as well. Predictably, banks have not wanted to let their competitors in on this business. The SEC has also resisted pressure to expand § 3(a)(2) to cover insurers, fearing in part that the adequacy of state insurance regulation was questionable. Instead, the SEC suggested that § 3(a)(2) be repealed as an overbroad exemption and be replaced by a grant of authority to the SEC to exempt those securities or transactions where registration was not necessary.[11] Neither the banking nor insurance industries liked this idea, and Congress has not acted on it for over a decade.

c. *Keoghs and IRAs.* Keogh plans are tax-deferred retirement plans established by self-employed individuals for the benefit of themselves and for their employees. The plans enable these taxpayers to obtain some of the tax advantages previously available only to employees under corporate plans. The House Committee Report explained that § 3(a)(2) "does not exempt interests or participations issued by either bank collective trust funds or insurance company separate accounts in connection with 'H.R. 10 plans,' because of their fairly complex nature as an equity investment and because of the likelihood that they could be sold to self-employed persons, unsophisticated in the securities field."[12]

It should also be noted that the provisions of § 3(a)(2) relating to interests in certain investment vehicles maintained by banks and insurance companies do not extend an exemption from registration to: (1) either bank collective trust funds or insurance company "separate accounts" in connection with Keogh (H.R. 10) plans complying with the Self–Employed Individuals Tax Retirement Act of 1962, and (2) interests or participations in connection with qualified corporate pension or profit-sharing plans which constitute H.R. 10 plans covering employees, some or all of whom are employees within the meaning of IRC § 401(c)(1).

The Employee Retirement Security Act of 1974 (ERISA) established IRAs (Individual Retirement Accounts) which permit employees who are not covered under a corporate or Keogh plan to obtain tax benefits similar to those provided under such plans. And the Revenue Act of 1978 created "Simplified Employee Pensions" which provide for simplified reports to the IRS and to employees. Congress did not extend the § 3(a)(2) exemption to these plans and they have the same status as IRAs under the securities laws.[13]

Although the 1970 amendment to section 3(a)(2) grants the Commission authority to exempt these security interests from the registration provisions of the 1933 Act, the Commission did not use this power until 1976, when an exemptive order was issued with respect to participation interests in connection

---

10. See Report by the United States Securities and Exchange Commission on the Financial Guarantee Market: The Use of the Exemption in Section 3(a)(2) of the Securities Act of 1933 by Banks and the Use of Insurance Policies to Guarantee Debt Securities (Aug. 28, 1987).

11. Id. at 95.

12. H.R.Rep. No. 91–1382, 91st Cong., 2d Sess. 44 (1970).

13. Securities Act Release No. 6246 (Oct. 9, 1980).

with the establishment of a Keogh plan by a large law partnership. For some years thereafter, the Commission proceeded to issue *ad hoc* exemptive orders to groups of professionals where the employer was organized as a partnership, rather than a corporation.[14] In 1981, however, the Commission codified this practice by adopting Rule 180 which exempts from registration Keogh tax-qualified retirement plans established by a single employer or by interrelated partnerships; however, the exemption is confined to law firms, accounting firms, investment banking firms, and firms that have secured independent expert investment advice in connection with their plans.[15] Parallel amendments have been added to § 3(a)(12) and § 12(h) of the Securities Exchange Act of 1934. Thus these non-corporate employers maintaining tax-qualified retirement plans can obtain tax benefits similar to those previously available to corporate taxpayers and their employees.

2. Sections 3(a)(4) to 3(a)(8)

Under the section 3(a)(4) exemption, the securities must be issued by an entity which is organized and operated *exclusively* for charitable purposes. In SEC v. Children's Hospital, 214 F.Supp. 883 (D.Ariz.1963), the court enjoined the issuing institution from using the exemption where ten percent of the net proceeds were to be paid to the promoters as compensation for their services in planning and supervising the construction of the facility.[16] And the exemption granted to securities of savings and loan associations by section 3(a)(5) was denied to a Maryland association where the vast majority of the shares were sold to the public not to provide loans for members but to use the proceeds to acquire slow-moving, dubious assets from the control group or their associates. Thus, although operating in the guise of a savings and loan association, the company failed to meet the test that substantially all of its business must be confined to making loans to members.[17]

Another issue which for a time was the subject of hot dispute between two segments of the insurance industry and the regulatory authorities was the place of the so-called "variable annuity" in the scheme of insurance and securities regulation. Section 3(a)(8) exempts "insurance" and "annuity" contracts when "subject to the supervision of the insurance commissioner * * * of any State. * * *" This clearly covers the fixed annuities which insurance companies have traditionally issued under which the annuitant is offered a specified and definite amount beginning at a certain time in the future.

On the other hand, the variable annuity was invented to provide a hedge against inflation. Under these contracts, a greater portion of the premiums collected are invested in common stocks; and the periodic benefits payable to the annuitant depend on the success of the insurance company's investment policy. In a sense the annuitant's interest in the portfolio of securities is something like that of an investor in a mutual fund. Because the variable

14. Securities Act Release No. 6188 (Feb. 1, 1980), 19 SEC Docket 465, 492–93 (Feb. 19, 1980).

15. Securities Act Release 6363 (Nov. 24, 1981).

16. The California Corporations Code § 25100(J) codifies this principle by denying its analogous charitable exemption "if any promoter thereof expects or intends to make a profit directly or indirectly from any business or activity associated with the organization or operation of such nonprofit organization or from remuneration received from such nonprofit organization."

17. SEC v. American International Savings & Loan Association, 199 F.Supp. 341 (D.Md.1961).

annuity "places all the investment risks on the annuitant, none on the company" and "the concept of 'insurance' involves some investment risk-taking on the part of the company," the Supreme Court held that it was not an "annuity" for purposes of the § 3(a)(8) exemption.[18]

More recently, the insurance industry has created a modified type of annuity which provides certain guarantees of principal and interest, regardless of investment results. The SEC has now accepted this investment vehicle, generally known as a "guaranteed investment contract," as entitled to an exemption from registration under § 3(a)(8), if it is issued and marketed under certain conditions.

These conditions are specified in new Rule 151 which establishes a "safe harbor" under the § 3(a)(8) exemption. To qualify, the annuity contract must (1) be issued by a corporation (the insurer) that is subject to the supervision of a state insurance commissioner or an agency performing like functions; (2) provide guarantees of principal and interest sufficient for the insurer to be deemed to assume the investment risk; and (3) not be marketed primarily as an investment. The rule thus includes single premium deferred annuities.[19]

It should be noted also that there is no exemption for insurance company stocks and securities as such; only the "insurance" and "annuity" contracts written by them are exempt. Most of the problems relating to insurance company securities activities have arisen under the Investment Company Act of 1940.

Apart from §§ 3(a)(2) to 3(a)(8) the securities falling in the other paragraphs of Section 3(a) possess no inherent characteristics which should make them the subjects of a permanent exemption from federal regulation. They are in fact transaction exemptions. In addition, § 3(b) gives the SEC statutory authority by rule to exempt certain securities transactions if not necessary in the public interest. The maximum amount of any such issue may not exceed $5,000,000. Section 3(c) grants the Commission an exemptive authority with respect to securities issued by a small business investment company under the Small Business Investment Act of 1958. The consideration of these exemptions will be delayed until Chapter 6.

---

18. SEC v. Variable Annuity Life Ins. Co., 359 U.S. 65 (1959). And see SEC v. United Benefit Life Insurance Co., 387 U.S. 202 (1967), holding that a "flexible fund annuity" contract did not come within the § 3(a)(8) insurance exemption of the Securities Act of 1933. On "Insurance Products," see 2 L. Loss & J. Seligman, Securities Regulation 1000–20 (3d ed. 1989).

19. See Securities Act Release No. 6645 (May 29, 1986).

SUBDIVISION C. TRANSACTION EXEMPTIONS AVAILABLE TO ISSUERS OF SECURITIES

CHAPTER 5

THE PRIVATE OFFERING EXEMPTIONS: SECTIONS 4(2) AND 4(6)

Statutes and Regulations

Securities Act, §§ 2(a)(4), 2(a)(2), 4(1), 4(2).

Introductory Note

We have been using the words "issuer" and "underwriter" without paying very much attention to what they mean in terms of the Securities Act. Although § 5 broadly prohibits the use of the channels of interstate commerce or the mails to sell a security unless a registration statement is in effect, § 4(1) specifically exempts transactions "by any person other than an issuer, underwriter, or dealer * * *." These terms thus serve to separate those persons who are subject to the registration or prospectus requirements from those who may ignore them. In this Chapter we explore the concept of "issuer" and the transaction exemptions that are applicable to issuers in connection with the sale of securities. In Chapter 9, we will consider the meaning of the terms "underwriter" and "dealer" and their obligation to comply with the registration and prospectus provisions of the Act.

1. *Who is an "Issuer"?* An "issuer" is defined in § 2(a)(4). In many cases there is not much difficulty in identifying the issuer of a security, although it need not be a corporation. Indeed, the issuer may be almost any juridical "person," since that term is defined in § 2(a)(2) to include an individual, a partnership, a trust or other unincorporated association, and a foreign or domestic government or its political subdivisions.[1]

It is to be noted further that an "issuer" includes persons who propose to issue a security as well as those who actually follow through and complete the transaction. The act of issuing a security arises from the creation of a right in some other person in the form of an investment contract, whether or not evidenced by a written

---

1. The Exchange Act has similar, but not identical definitions of "issuer" and "person." See §§ 3(a)(8) (issuer) and 3(a)(9) (person). It is to be noted that municipal issuers are subject to the 1933 and 1934 Acts, including antifraud provisions. But see §§ 12(a)(2) and 17(c) of the 1933 Act.

instrument, such as a share of stock. Thus, when a promoter proposes to take a preincorporation subscription for shares in a corporation not yet formed, he intends to issue a security in the form of a "preorganization certificate or subscription." Obviously, the corporation cannot be the issuer for it is not in existence. The contract is to be made with the promoter and he has already become an issuer although this might come as a surprise to him.

If no exemption from registration is available, an added burden arises in having to register preincorporation subscriptions, because the underlying security will also be subject to registration. In actual practice, therefore, the promoter will usually dispense with the use of preorganization subscriptions. Instead, the corporation will be formed and the securities proposed to be issued will be registered without going through the extra motions. When this procedure is not followed, however, any preorganization selling activity, except preliminary negotiations between the issuer and an underwriter, is forbidden, unless some exemption from registration is available.

In *SEC v. Murphy*, 626 F.2d 633 (9th Cir.1980), the court engaged in a search to determine the "issuer" in connection with a complex promotion entailing the sale of limited partnership interests. Murphy was a founder, director and officer of Intertie, a corporation engaged in financing, construction and management of cable television systems. Intertie would promote limited partnerships to which it sold newly packaged cable TV systems. Intertie would purchase an existing television system on credit. It would then sell the system to a newly organized partnership, and lease back the system from the partnership. ISC, a brokerage firm, unaffiliated with Intertie or Murphy, sold the limited partnership interests. An ISC representative was usually the general partner of the partnership, but neither Murphy nor Intertie were partners. Murphy was the architect of this promotion by which Intertie took approximately $7.5 million from 400 investors in 30 partnerships. He participated actively in the offerings. In an SEC injunction proceeding alleging violation of the registration and antifraud provisions of the securities acts, the court held Murphy to be an issuer of the securities: "[W]hen a person organizes or sponsors the organization of limited partnerships and is primarily responsible for the success or failure of the venture for which the partnership is formed, he will be considered an issuer for purposes of determining the availability of the private offering exemption."[2]

There are a number of anomalous types of securities where the "issuer" is not readily identifiable. These include certificates of deposit; voting trust certificates; certificates of interest in unincorporated associations, investment trusts and business trusts; equipment trust certificates; and fractional undivided interests in oil, gas and other mineral rights. As to these securities, § 2(a)(4) describes in some detail the persons who shall be treated as issuer for the purposes of the Securities Act. Thus, in the case of oil, gas and mineral rights generally, the issuer is any owner of such right (whether whole or fractional) who splits up his right into fractions for the purpose of making a public offering of those interests. Designation of the issuer has a bearing on who shall sign the registration statement as well as determining possible liability under Section 11.

2. *The Private Offering Exemptions.* There are a number of transaction exemptions which enable an issuer to avoid the registration and prospectus requirements of the 1933 Act. It is important to remember, however, that issuers who avail themselves of these exemptions remain subject to the antifraud provisions of the

---

2. 626 F.2d 633, 644. Accord, *SEC v. Holschuh*, 694 F.2d 130 (7th Cir.1982). The court noted that § 4(1) is a transaction exemption and that one who participates in or is a "substantial factor" in the unlawful sales transaction satisfies the test for primary liability in an enforcement action for injunctive relief.

1933 and 1934 Acts, including Rule 10b–5. Indeed, the disclosure obligations under these civil remedies go a long way toward filling the void left by the absence of the protection afforded by registration.

One set of these exemptions is available where the transaction by the issuer does not involve any public offering of securities. Two of the private offering exemptions are statutory: § 4(2) and § 4(6). Section 4(2), which is commonly referred to as the "private offering" exemption, excludes from registration "transactions by an issuer not involving any public offering." Such an exemption is absolutely essential for there to be a workable system of federal securities regulation. It would be unreasonable to require that when any business is formed and capital is obtained from anyone outside of the entrepreneurial group, federal registration would be required, unless some other exemption were available, such as Regulation A (the small issue exemption) or the intrastate offering g3 exemption.

At one end of the private placement spectrum is the case in which business people about to start up a new business or expand a small, closely held business, need additional capital. Frequently, the most immediate sources of capital for such "start-up" companies are members of the family, or friends, or business, professional or social acquaintances. So long as offerings were confined to a limited number of these persons who presumably knew the principals and were willing to make an investment in the projected enterprise, it had generally been assumed that the nonpublic offering exemption was available. The purchase, however, must be for "investment" and not with a view to resale. Frequently the "seed capital" to launch the business would be raised from these immediate sources. The result was the saving of enormous costs entailed in registration such as legal and accounting fees, underwriting expenses, printing costs and the like.

At the other end of the spectrum, well established companies are in a position to make a private placement of institutional grade securities with insurance companies, pension funds, foundations and other institutional investors. Underwriters and some banks have specialized in making these private placements, and again, it was generally assumed that the private offering exemption was available because of the sophistication of the offerees of the securities. The number of participants was not thought to be significant.

In between these types of financing, there developed a grey area as to which it was difficult for lawyers to give opinions with any confidence. Moreover, beginning in the 1950's, start-up, growth companies were organized in which more remote sources of capital were tapped, such as wealthy individuals, venture capital firms, small business investment companies, and institutional investors, including mutual funds. Sometimes a group of investors would provide the "seed capital" for the first round of financing with a view toward further participation in later rounds of financing as the business expanded.

During the 1980's, spurred both by academic criticism and congressional pressure, the SEC used its exemptive powers to broaden expansively the opportunities for an issuer to offer and sell substantial amounts of securities without registration under the 1933 Act. Indeed, it is now possible for a start-up company to save time and money, undergo less regulation, and raise as much or more investment capital through one or private placements than by resorting to registered public offerings. Yet, that was not always the case. The present regime is the result of an evolutionary process extending over a number of years. Initially, the Section 4(2) exemption embodied a very vague and imprecise concept—what constitutes a nonpublic offering. With the adoption of Regulation D in 1982, new "bright-line" standards facilitated substantial offerings of securities without 1933 Act registration, because they eliminated most legal uncertainty. Partly in consequence, the venture capital industry burgeoned in the 1980's. In addition to Regulation D, Rule

701 similarly permits offers and sales of securities to employees, consultants and business advisers under various forms of stock incentive and compensatory benefit plans without 1933 Act registration. This Chapter will trace the transformation of the early, largely amorphous concepts of a nonpublic offering into the present specific conditions which now allow offers and sales of securities without having to incur enormous registration expenditures or to accept the legal uncertainty that formerly surrounded use of the private placement exemption. In overview, it should be understood that this is a context in which increased legal clarity contributed greatly to the growth of a distinctive industry: the venture capital business, which in turn fueled the growth of Silicon Valley.

The Statutory Standard. Section 4(2) exempts "transactions by an issuer, not involving any public offering" from the registration requirements of the 1933 Act. The exemption is self-determining with the burden of proof being placed on the issuer and others relying upon the exemption. However, the statute and legislative history throw very little light on its scope. The House Committee Report contained the cryptic statement that these transactions were exempted "so as to permit an issuer to make a specific or an isolated sale of its securities to a particular person, but if a sale * * * should be made generally to the public that transaction would come within the purview of the Act." The Committee further emphasized that the bill "carefully exempts from its application transactions where there is no practical need for its application or where the public benefits are too remote."[3]

Administrative Interpretations. In the early years of the administration of the Act, a number of criteria were suggested for determining what constitutes a nonpublic offering.

(1) *Number of Offerees.* At the lower end of the spectrum, the General Counsel early on expressed the view that an offering to not more than approximately twenty-five persons is not an offering to a substantial number of persons and presumably does not involve a public offering.[4] In fact, however, sales were made of large blocks of investment quality securities to institutional investors. In some cases the number approached 100, but the Commission did not raise any question as the availability of the private offering exemption if all were institutional investors such as insurance companies and pension trusts. As to these persons, numbers seemed less important. The policy of treating institutional investors differently for both issuer transactions and resales in the secondary market was legitimized in 1990 by the adoption of Rule 144A regulating private resales of securities by institutions. See infra at 581.

(2) *The Availability of Information.* The availability of information to the offerees is a key factor in establishing the exemption—some argue it is essentially the only factor that should be considered. They stress that this appears "to be the proper approach, since disclosure is in fact all that the registration process provides by way of investor protection (apart from the antifraud provisions)".[5]

(3) *Access to Information.* The access test may be met in two ways: (1) by actually furnishing such information directly to the offeror; or (2) by the offeree having access to such information either as an employee, by virtue of a family relationship or through economic bargaining power. Cf. SEC v. Ralston Purina Co., infra at 397.

(4) *Nature of the Offerees.* It is clear that the Commission and courts also took into account the financial sophistication of the investor. For a time, the investor's

---

3. H.R. No. 85, 73d Cong., 1st Sess. 16 (1933).

4. General Counsel's Opinion, Securities Act Release No. 285, Jan. 24, 1935.

5. Schneider, Section 4(2) in 12th Ann. Inst. on Sec.Reg. 295, 296 (PLI 1981).

ability to bear the economic risk of the investment was also a factor (and it may still influence some judicial decisions), but it has more recently been rejected as an improperly paternalistic standard that distinguishes between investors based on their wealth, rather than their sophistication.

(5) *Manner of Offering.* The concept of a private offering precludes general advertising or general solicitation through which offers are made.

(6) *Limitation on Resales.* The purchase must be for investment, not with a view to resale. This factor is based in part on the notion that if there are resales, the numbers limitation could be exceeded. It is also based on § 4(1) which exempts from the provisions of § 5 "transactions by any person *other than* and issuer, underwriter, or dealer." Furthermore, § 2(a)(11) defines an underwriter as "any person who has purchased from an issuer *with a view to* * * * the distribution of any security." A "distribution" is tantamount to a public offering which would destroy the exemption.

In actual practice, however, application of the § 4(2) exemption proved to be extremely difficult, so that it became a source of uncertainty and controversy among the securities bar. In 1974, the Commission sought to provide "more objective standards" under the private offering exemption by adopting former Rule 146. The Rule provided that transactions by an issuer shall not be deemed to involve any public offering within the meaning of § 4(2) if they were part of an offering that met all of the conditions of the rule.

The adoption of former Rule 146 did not stem the tide of criticism of the stringent criteria imposed by § 4(2) as interpreted by the courts. (See particularly *Doran v. Petroleum Management Corp.*, infra at page 402. Although Rule 146 was described by the Commission as a "safe harbor" from the pitfalls of § 4(2), it imposed even more stringent and subjective standards upon issuers and their representatives regarding the qualifications of an offeree with respect to his or her knowledge and experience in financial matters and ability to evaluate and bear the risks of a prospective investment.

In 1980, the Commission issued Rule 242 in response to complaints voiced by various commentators concerning compliance with the strictures of Rule 146.[6] Although Rule 242 was promulgated pursuant to the Commission's authority under Section 3(b), the small issues exemption, it was essentially a private offering exemption in that it prohibited public solicitation and general advertising and limited offers and sales only to specified types of persons and to a maximum number of purchasers. The rule introduced the concept of an "accredited investor," defined to include various types of institutional investors, corresponding to the list later enumerated in § 2(a)(15) of the 1933 Act, but adding persons who purchased $100,000 or more of the issue, and directors and executive officers. Individuals within this category presumably were assumed to be "sophisticated." Sales could be made of restricted securities up to $2 million within any six months period to an unlimited number of accredited investors plus thirty-five other qualified persons. Rule 242 was superseded by Rule 505 of Regulation D.

In the meantime, Congress had become concerned that American business, and particularly small business, had experienced difficulty in raising investment capital

---

6. See Summary of Comments Relating to Small Business Hearings and Proposed Form S–18, Division of Corporation Finance, Securities and Exchange Commission, File No. S 7–734 at 148; Securities Act Release No. 6180 (Feb. 25, 1980); Marsh, Who Killed the Private Offering Exemption? A Legal Whodunit, 71 Nw.U.L.Rev. 470 (1976); Campbell, The Plight of Small Issuers Under the Securities Act of 1933: Practical Foreclosure From the Capital Markets, 1977 Duke L.J. 1139; Heumann, Is Rule 146 Too Subjective to Provide the Needed Predictability in Private Offerings?, 55 Neb.L.Rev. 1 (1975).

and that part of the problem arose from difficulties in complying with the stringent criteria imposed by Section 4(2) and former Rule 146, now superseded by Rule 506 of Regulation D.[7] Although the Commission had alleviated some of these concerns by the adoption of Rule 242, Congress took further action to aid small business through the enactment of the Small Business Incentive Act of 1980.[8] A new Section 4(6) was added to the 1933 Act that provides an additional statutory exemption for offers and sales by an issuer to "accredited investors," if the offer and sale does not exceed the dollar limit allowed under Section 3(b), and where there is no advertising or public solicitation entailed in the offer. Section 4(6) thus adopts the "accredited investor" concept used in former Rule 242 and that term is defined in new Section 2(a)(15). Furthermore, the Commission is granted the authority to enlarge the definition to include additional purchasers as "accredited investors" based upon "such factors as financial sophistication, net worth, knowledge and experience in financial matters, or amount of assets under management." It is to be noted that under § 4(6), offers or sales may be made to an unlimited number of "accredited investors". Thus, here numbers become irrelevant. Rule 501(a) of Regulation D essentially tracks §§ 4(6) and 2(15), but there are significant differences that should be checked out. For example, § 2(a)(15) omits savings and loan associations from its list of accredited investors while Rule 501(a)(1) permits those entities to act as fiduciaries of employee benefit plans subject to ERISA. And there are a number of categories of accredited investors enumerated in Rule 501(a)(1) that are not found in § 2(15).

Section 4(2), Rule 506, Rule 505 and Section 4(6) are interrelated, although they contain differing conditions for their use. Persons who acquire securities from issuers in a transaction complying with any of these exemptions receive securities that are unregistered; they are thus deemed to be "restricted securities" and can only be reoffered or resold if registered, or pursuant to an exemption from the registration provisions of the Act. The restrictions on resales of such securities are explored in Chapter 9. In this Chapter, our focus is on Section 4(2) and the evolution of the judicial interpretation of this provision.

Statutes and Regulations

Securities Act §§ 4(2), 4(6), 2(15), Form 4(6).

Securities and Exchange Commission v. Ralston Purina Co.

Supreme Court of the United States, 1953.
346 U.S. 119, 73 S.Ct. 981, 97 L.Ed. 1494.

■ Mr. Justice Clark delivered the opinion of the Court. Section 4(1)[a] of the Securities Act of 1933 exempts "transactions by an issuer not involving any public offering" from the registration requirements of § 5. We must decide whether Ralston Purina's offerings of treasury stock to its "key employees" are

---

7. Hearings on Small Business Access to Equity and Venture Capital Before the Subcomm. on Capital Investment and Business Opportunities of the House Comm. on Small Business, 95th Cong., 1st Sess. (1977): Hearings on the Economic Problems of Small Business Before the Subcomm. on Energy and Environment of the House Comm. on Small Business, 94th Cong. 2d Sess. (1977); Hearings on the Overregulation of Small Business Before the Subcomm. on Government Regulation of the Senate Select Comm. on Small Business, 94th Cong., 1st Sess. (1977).

8. Pub. Law 96–477, § 602.

a. In 1964, the second clause of former paragraph (1) was redesignated as Section 4(2). Act of Aug. 20, 1964, § 12, 78 Stat. 580.

within this exemption. On a complaint brought by the Commission under § 20(b) of the Act seeking to enjoin respondent's unregistered offerings, the District Court held the exemption applicable and dismissed the suit. The Court of Appeals affirmed. The question has arisen many times since the Act was passed; an apparent need to define the scope of the private offering exemption prompted certiorari. * * *

Ralston Purina manufactures and distributes various feed and cereal products. Its processing and distribution facilities are scattered throughout the United States and Canada, staffed by some 7,000 employees. At least since 1911 the company has had a policy of encouraging stock ownership among its employees; more particularly, since 1942 it has made authorized but unissued common shares available to some of them. Between 1947 and 1951 * * * Ralston Purina sold nearly $2,000,000 of stock to employees without registration and in so doing made use of the mails.

In each of these years, a corporate resolution authorized the sale of common stock "to employees * * * who shall, without any solicitation by the Company or its officers or employees, inquire of any of them as to how to purchase common stock of Ralston Purina Company." A memorandum sent to branch and store managers after the resolution was adopted, advised that "The only employees to whom this stock will be available will be those who take the initiative and are interested in buying stock at present market prices." Among those responding to these offers were employees with the duties of artist, bakeshop foreman, chow loading foreman, clerical assistant, copywriter, electrician, stock clerk, mill office clerk, order credit trainee, production trainee, stenographer, and veterinarian. The buyers lived in over fifty widely separated communities scattered from Garland, Texas to Nashua, New Hampshire and Visalia, California. The lowest salary bracket of those purchasing was $2,700 in 1949, $2,435 in 1950 and $3,107 in 1951. The record shows that in 1947, 243 employees bought stock, 20 in 1948, 414 in 1949, 411 in 1950, and the 1951 offer, interrupted by this litigation, produced 165 applications to purchase. No records were kept of those to whom the offers were made; the estimated number in 1951 was 500.

The company bottoms its exemption claim on the classification of all offerees as "key employees" in its organization. Its position on trial was that "A key employee * * * is not confined to an organization chart. It would include an individual who is eligible for promotion, an individual who especially influences others or who advises others, a person whom the employees look to in some special way, an individual, of course, who carries some special responsibility, who is sympathetic to management and who is ambitious and who the management feels is likely to be promoted to a greater responsibility." That an offering to all of its employees would be public is conceded.

The Securities Act nowhere defines the scope of § 4(1)'s private offering exemption. Nor is the legislative history of much help in staking out its boundaries. The problem was first dealt with in § 4(1) of the House Bill, H.R. 5480, 73d Cong., 1st Sess., which exempted "transactions by an issuer not with or through an underwriter; * * *." The bill, as reported by the House Committee, added "and not involving any public offering." H.R.Rep. No. 85, 73d Cong., 1st Sess. 1. This was thought to be one of those transactions "where there is no practical need for * * * [the bill's] application or where the public benefits are too remote." Id., at 5. The exemption as thus delimited became law. It assumed its present shape with the deletion of "not with or through an underwriter" by

§ 203(a) of the Securities Exchange Act of 1934, * * * a change regarded as the elimination of superfluous language. H.R.Rep. No. 1838, 73d Cong., 2d Sess. 41.

Decisions under comparable exemptions in the English Companies Acts and state "blue sky" laws, the statutory antecedents of federal securities legislation have made one thing clear—to be public, an offer need not be open to the whole world. In Securities and Exchange Comm. v. Sunbeam Gold Mines Co., 9 Cir., 1938, 95 F.2d 699, 701, this point was made in dealing with an offering to the stockholders of two corporations about to be merged. Judge Denman observed that:

"In its broadest meaning the term 'public' distinguishes the populace at large from groups of individual members of the public segregated because of some common interest or characteristic. Yet such a distinction is inadequate for practical purposes; manifestly, an offering of securities to all red-headed men, to all residents of Chicago or San Francisco, to all existing stockholders of the General Motors Corporation or the American Telephone & Telegraph Company, is no less 'public' in every realistic sense of the word, than an unrestricted offering to the world at large. Such an offering, though not open to everyone who may choose to apply, is none the less 'public' in character, for the means used to select the particular individuals to whom the offering is to be made bear no sensible relation to the purposes for which the selection is made. * * * To determine the distinction between 'public' and 'private' in any particular context, it is essential to examine the circumstances under which the distinction is sought to be established and to consider the purposes sought to be achieved by such distinction."

The courts below purported to apply this test. * * *

Exemption from the registration requirements of the Securities Act is the question. The design of the statute is to protect investors by promoting full disclosure of information thought necessary to informed investment decisions. The natural way to interpret the private offering exemption is in light of the statutory purpose. Since exempt transactions are those as to which "there is no practical need for [the bill's] application," the applicability of § 4(1) should turn on whether the particular class of persons affected need the protection of the Act. An offering to those who are shown to be able to fend for themselves is a transaction "not involving any public offering."

The Commission would have us go one step further and hold that "an offering to a substantial number of the public" is not exempt under § 4(1). We are advised that "whatever the special circumstances, the Commission has consistently interpreted the exemption as being inapplicable when a large number of offerees is involved." But the statute would seem to apply to a "public offering" whether to few or many. It may well be that offerings to a substantial number of persons would rarely be exempt. Indeed nothing prevents the commission, in enforcing the statute, from using some kind of numerical test in deciding when to investigate particular exemption claims. But there is no warrant for superimposing a quantity limit on private offerings as a matter of statutory interpretation.

The exemption, as we construe it, does not deprive corporate employees, as a class, of the safeguards of the Act. We agree that some employee offerings may come within § 4(1), e.g., one made to executive personnel who because of their position have access to the same kind of information that the act would make available in the form of a registration statement. Absent such a showing of special circumstances, employees are just as much members of the investing "public" as any of their neighbors in the community. Although we do not rely on it, the rejection in 1934 of an amendment which would have specifically exempted employee stock offerings supports this conclusion. The House Managers, commenting on the Conference Report said that "the participants in employees' stock-investment plans may be in as great need of the protection afforded by availability of information concerning the issuer for which they work as are most other members of the public." H.R.Rep. No. 1838, 73d Cong., 2d Sess. 41.

Keeping in mind the broadly remedial purposes of federal securities legislation, imposition of the burden of proof on an issuer who would plead the exemption seems to us fair and reasonable. * * * Agreeing, the court below thought the burden met primarily because of the respondent's purpose in singling out its key employees for stock offerings. But once it is seen that the exemption question turns on the knowledge of the offerees, the issuer's motives, laudable though they may be, fade into irrelevance. The focus of inquiry should be on the need of the offerees for the protections afforded by registration. The employees here were not shown to have access to the kind of information which registration would disclose. The obvious opportunities for pressure and imposition make it advisable that they be entitled to compliance with § 5.

Reversed.

■ The CHIEF JUSTICE and MR. JUSTICE BURTON dissent.[b]

SCOPE OF THE PRIVATE OFFERING EXEMPTION: JUDICIAL INTERPRETATIONS IN THE PRE–RULE 146 PERIOD

After the *Ralston Purina* case in 1953, there were a number of cases interpreting the private offering exemption. In many of those cases the defendant foundered on the inability to meet the burden of proof as to the number of offers actually made. Then, beginning in 1971 and often at the urging of the SEC, the federal courts began to impose extremely strict standards in applying the *Ralston Purina* tests for establishing a private offering. Thus in Lively v. Hirschfeld,[1] the defendants sought to establish a private offering on the basis that the offeree "had such information and capabilities that the registration statements and disclosures were not needed by them or would not add anything to what they had available." One of the plaintiffs was an airline pilot possessing "considerable business experience" who had purchased stocks from time to time. He was given information as to the number of outstanding shares, the stock structure and the names of the officers. He sought no further information and none was withheld.

In applying the *Ralston Purina* standard, the Tenth Circuit said: "The 'need' requirement is strict. The Supreme Court in its description of a possible 'private' group in Ralston Purina includes only persons of exceptional business experience, and [in] 'a position where they have regular access to all the information and records which would show the potential for the corporation.'" The court concluded that the offerees did not possess "unusual business experience and skill" nor have "the degree of access to the type of data as

---

b. Notes, 48 Nw.U.L.Rev. 771 (1954); 21 U.Chi.L.Rev. 113 (1953). The opinions of the lower courts evoked comments in 66

Harv.L.Rev. 1144 (1953); 39 Va.L.Rev. 376 (1953).

1. 440 F.2d 631, 632 (10th Cir.1971).

would meet the standard."[2] It was this kind of language that aroused forebodings among securities lawyers.

In the same year, the Fifth Circuit decided Hill York Corp. v. American International Franchises, Inc.[3] Thirteen persons had paid $5,000 each for stock in a fast-food franchising corporation. All of the purchasers were sophisticated businessmen and attorneys who planned to do business with the issuer, not the average man on the street. The record, however, contained no evidence of the total number of offerees. The plaintiffs brought an action to rescind the transaction and, in a jury trial, were awarded rescission of the stock sale and damages on the basis of violations of Sections 5 and 12(2) of the 1933 Act. In affirming the judgment, the court approved the trial court's jury charge "that every offeree had to have information equivalent to that which a registration statement would disclose." The court also rejected the contention that a high degree of business or legal sophistication on the part of the offerees would be enough to establish the exemption. Even if the offerees were lawyers and businessmen, if they did not possess the information required to be contained in a registration statement, "they could not bring their sophisticated knowledge of business affairs to bear in deciding whether or not to invest. * * * "[4]

Hill York was followed in the Fifth Circuit by the *Continental Tobacco* bombshell, SEC v. Continental Tobacco Co., 463 F.2d 137 (5th Cir.1972). In *Continental Tobacco*, a written prospectus, including unaudited financial statements prepared by a Certified Public Accountant was used in the offering. Moreover, the offerees who purchased signed "investment letters" acknowledging receipt of the prospectus, which was designed to give them all the information registration would have afforded. Nevertheless, the court held that even if the prospectus sent to the purchasers contained all the information that a registration would have disclosed, "that fact alone would not justify the exemption." The court emphasized that the purchasers did not have the opportunity to inspect the corporation's records or to verify the statements made in the prospectus, and that at least some of the purchasers had never met any officers of the company prior to acquiring the stock, thereby denying them "access." In sum, in *Hill York* and *Continental Tobacco*, the court seemed to lay down a test that the exemption was lost unless: (1) the offer was made to a limited number of offerees; (2) who must be sophisticated purchasers having a relation to each other and to the issuer; (3) with access to all the information a registration would disclose; and (4) with an actual opportunity to inspect the company's records or otherwise verify for themselves the statements made to them as inducements for the purchase.

On the same day that *Continental Tobacco* was decided, in Henderson v. Hayden, Stone Inc.,[5] the Fifth Circuit allowed a wealthy investor who had invested $180,000 in a speculative "start-up" company to rescind the transaction and get his money back, even though he was aware at the time of the transaction that the stock was not registered. The plaintiff managed his own investment portfolio of several million dollars, had some six brokerage accounts, read the leading financial publications, and, admittedly, could only be described as a sophisticated investor. Although the evidence showed that sales had actually been made only to seven other individuals, the Fifth Circuit

---

2. *Id.* at 633.

3. 448 F.2d 680 (5th Cir.1971).

4. *Id.* at 690.

5. 461 F.2d 1069 (5th Cir.1972).

reversed the district court because defendants failed to establish how many other offers may have been made by those engaged in the selling effort.

On the basis of these decisions, some commentators contended that the private offering exemption had been destroyed for all practical purposes.[9] It is important to note, however, that in each of these cases, the defendants had failed to meet the burden of proof placed upon persons claiming entitlement to the exemption. Two years later, the Commission adopted Rule 146 to provide "more objective standards" for determining when sales by an issuer would be deemed to be a transaction not involving a public offering within the meaning of Section 4(2).

In Woolf v. S. D. Cohn & Co.[10] and Doran v. Petroleum Management Corp.,[11] the Fifth Circuit sought to explain, if not to limit, *Continental Tobacco*. As you read *Doran*, which follows, what are your answers to the following questions: (1) How, if at all, does *Doran* limit *Continental Tobacco*? (2) What factors are relevant in determining whether an offering qualifies for the § 4(2) exemption? (3) What factors are essential to establish the exemption, even if not alone sufficient? (4) What various combinations of factors are together sufficient to establish the exemption? (5) In your opinion, are the factors (and combinations of factors) given in response to questions (3) and (4) appropriate for determining whether a transaction should qualify for the exemption? (6) When does an offeree have access? How is the existence of access to be determined? What is the relationship between access and offeree sophistication? (7) In *Doran*, the issuer was not a 1934 Act reporting company. Would access to information exist whenever the issuer is a 1934 Act reporting company? To what extent are the SB1 registration disclosures duplicated in the Form 10–K and Form 10–Q reports that are filed under the 1934 Act? To what extent would (should) these 1934 Act reports be deemed accessible to offerees?

Doran v. Petroleum Management Corp.

United States Court of Appeals, Fifth Circuit, 1977.
545 F.2d 893.

■ Before GOLDBERG, DYER and SIMPSON, CIRCUIT JUDGES.

■ GOLDBERG, CIRCUIT JUDGE:

In this case a sophisticated investor who purchased a limited partnership interest in an oil drilling venture seeks to rescind. The question raised is whether the sale was part of a private offering exempted by § 4(2) of the Securities Act of 1933, from the registration requirements of that Act. * * *[1]

9. See Kripke, Wrap-up, in Revolution in Securities Regulation, 29 Bus.Law. 185, 187 (Special Issue, Mar. 1974); Kripke, SEC Rule 146: A "Major Blunder," N.Y.L.J., July 5, 1974; S. Goldberg, Private Placements and Restricted Securities § 2.16[a] (rev. ed. 1975); Marsh, Who Killed the Private Offering Exemption?, A Legal Whodunit, 71 Nw. U.L.Rev. 470 (1977).

10. 515 F.2d 591 (5th Cir.1975), reh. denied 521 F.2d 225, on remand 546 F.2d 1252 (5th Cir.1977), cert. denied 434 U.S. 831.

11. 545 F.2d 893 (5th Cir.1977).

1. * * * The SEC's adoption of Rule 146 * * * which establishes a sufficient set of conditions for coming within the exemption, does not bear directly on the case at bar. The transaction at issue began in 1970, and the plaintiff filed suit in 1972. Rule 146 was not adopted until 1974. It applies to offers commencing on or after June 10, 1974.

I. Facts

Prior to July 1970, Petroleum Management Corporation (PMC) organized a California limited partnership for the purpose of drilling and operating four wells in Wyoming. The limited partnership agreement provided for both "participants," whose capital contributions were to be used first to pay all intangible expenses incurred by the partnership, and "special participants," whose capital contributions were to be applied first to pay tangible drilling expenses.

PMC and Inter–Tech Resources, Inc., were initially the only "special participants" in the limited partnership. They were joined by four "participants." As found by the district court, PMC contacted only four other persons with respect to possible participation in the partnership. All but the plaintiff declined.

During the late summer of 1970, plaintiff William H. Doran, Jr., received a telephone call from a California securities broker previously known to him. The broker, Phillip Kendrick, advised Doran of the opportunity to become a "special participant" in the partnership. PMC then sent Doran the drilling logs and technical maps of the proposed drilling area. PMC informed Doran that two of the proposed four wells had already been completed. Doran agreed to become a "special participant" in the Wyoming drilling program. In consideration for his partnership share, Doran agreed to contribute $125,000 toward the partnership. Doran was to discharge this obligation by paying PMC $25,000 down and in addition assuming responsibility for the payment of a $113,643 note owed by PMC to Mid–Continent Supply Co. Doran's share in the production payments from the wells was to be used to make the installment payments on the Mid–Continent note.

Pursuant to this arrangement, on September 16, 1970, Doran executed a promissory note, already signed by the President and Vice President of PMC in their individual capacities, for $113,643 payable to Mid–Continent. On October 5, 1970, Doran mailed PMC a check for $25,000. He thereby became a "special participant" in the Wyoming drilling program.

        * * *

Following the cessation of production payments between November 1971 and August 1972 and the decreased yields thereafter, the Mid–Continent note upon which Doran was primarily liable went into default. Mid–Continent subsequently obtained a state court judgment against Doran, PMC, and the two signatory officers of PMC for $50,815.50 plus interest and attorney's fees.

On October 16, 1972, Doran filed this suit in federal district court seeking damages for breach of contract, rescission of the contract based on violations of the Securities Acts of 1933 and 1934, and a judgment declaring the defendants liable for payment of the state judgment obtained by Mid–Continent.

The court below found that the offer and sale of the "special participant" interest was a private offering because Doran was a sophisticated investor who did not need the protection of the Securities Acts. * * * Doran filed this appeal.

II. The Private Offering Exemption

No registration statement was filed with any federal or state regulatory body in connection with the defendants' offering of securities. Along with two other factors that we may take as established—that the defendants sold or offered to sell these securities, and that the defendants used interstate transportation or communication in connection with the sale or offer of sale—the plaintiff thus states a prima facie case for a violation of the federal securities laws. * * *

The defendants do not contest the existence of the elements of plaintiff's prima facie case but raise an affirmative defense that the relevant transactions came within the exemption from registration found in § 4(2). Specifically, they contend that the offering of securities was not a public offering. The defendants, who of course bear the burden of proving this affirmative defense, must therefore show that the offering was private. * * *

This court has in the past identified four factors relevant to whether an offering qualifies for the exemption. The consideration of these factors, along with the policies embodied in the 1933 Act, structure the inquiry. * * * The relevant factors include the number of offerees and their relationship to each other and the issuer, the number of units offered, the size of the offering, and the manner of the offering. Consideration of these factors need not exhaust the inquiry, nor is one factor's weighing heavily in favor of the private status of the offering sufficient to ensure the availability of the exemption. Rather, these factors serve as guideposts to the court in attempting to determine whether subjecting the offering to registration requirements would further the purposes of the 1933 Act.

* * *

In the case at bar, the defendants may have demonstrated the presence of the latter three factors. A small number of units offered, relatively modest financial stakes, and an offering characterized by personal contact between the issuer and offerees free of public advertising or intermediaries such as investment bankers or securities exchanges—these aspects of the instant transaction aid the defendants' search for a § 4(2) exemption.

Nevertheless, with respect to the first, most critical, and conceptually most problematic factor, the record does not permit us to agree that the defendants have proved that they are entitled to the limited sanctuary afforded by § 4(2). We must examine more closely the importance of demonstrating both the number of offerees and their relationship to the issuer in order to see why the defendants have not yet gained the § 4(2) exemption.

A. *The Number of Offerees*

Establishing the number of persons involved in an offering is important both in order to ascertain the magnitude of the offering and in order to determine the characteristics and knowledge of the persons thus identified.

The number of offerees, not the number of purchasers, is the relevant figure in considering the number of persons involved in an offering. Hill York Corp. v. American International Franchises, Inc. * * * [448 F.2d 680, at 691 (5th Cir.1971)]. A private placement claimant's failure to adduce any evidence regarding the number of offerees will be fatal to the claim. SEC v. Continental Tobacco Co. * * * [463 F.2d 137 at 161 (5th Cir.1972)]. The number of offerees is not itself a decisive factor in determining the availability of the private offering exemption. Just as an offering to few may be public, so an offering to many may be private. * * * Nevertheless, "the more offerees, the more likelihood that the offering is public." Hill York Corp. v. American International Franchises, Inc., supra, 448 F.2d at 688. In the case at bar, the record indicates that eight investors were offered limited partnership shares in the drilling program—a total that would be entirely consistent with a finding that the offering was private.

The defendants attempt to limit the number of offerees even further, however. They argue that Doran was the sole offeree because all others contacted by PMC were offered "participant" rather than "special participant" interests. The district court, which did not issue a finding of fact or conclusion of law with respect to this argument, appears to have assumed that there were eight offerees.

The argument is, in any event, unsupported by the record. * * * We must therefore reject the argument that Doran was the sole offeree.

In considering the number of offerees solely as indicative of the magnitude or scope of an offering, the difference between one and eight offerees is relatively unimportant. Rejecting the argument that Doran was the sole offeree is significant, however, because it means that in considering the need of the offerees for the protection that registration would have afforded we must look beyond Doran's interests to those of all his fellow offerees. Even the offeree-plaintiff's 20–20 vision with respect to the facts underlying the security would not save the exemption if any one of his fellow offerees was blind.

B. *The Offerees' Relationship to the Issuer*

Since SEC v. Ralston, supra, courts have sought to determine the need of offerees for the protections afforded by registration by focusing on the relationship between offerees and issuer and more particularly on the information available to the offerees by virtue of that relationship. * * * Once the offerees have been identified, it is possible to investigate their relationship to the issuer.

The district court concluded that the offer of a "special participant" interest to Doran was a private offering because Doran was a sophisticated investor who did not need the protections afforded by registration. It is important, in light of our rejection of the argument that Doran was the sole offeree, that the district court also found that all four "participants" and all three declining offerees were sophisticated investors with regard to oil ventures.

The need of the offerees for the protection afforded by registration is, to be sure, a question of fact dependent upon the circumstances of each case. * * * Nevertheless, the trial court's conclusion with respect to the availability of the private offering exemption may be set aside if induced by an erroneous view of the law. * * *

1. *The role of investment sophistication*

The lower court's finding that Doran was a sophisticated investor is amply supported by the record, as is the sophistication of the other offerees. Doran holds a petroleum engineering degree from Texas A&M University. His net worth is in excess of $1,000,000. His holdings of approximately twenty-six oil and gas properties are valued at $850,000.

Nevertheless, evidence of a high degree of business or legal sophistication on the part of all offerees does not suffice to bring the offering within the private placement exemption. We clearly established that proposition in Hill York Corp. v. American International Franchises, Inc., supra, 448 F.2d at 690. We reasoned that "if the plaintiffs did not possess the information requisite for a registration statement, they could not bring their sophisticated knowledge of business affairs to bear in deciding whether or not to invest * * *." Sophistication is not a substitute for access to the information that registration would disclose. * * * As we said in *Hill York*, although the evidence of the offerees' expertise "is certainly favorable to the defendants, the level of sophistication will not carry the point. In this context, the relationship between the promoters and the purchasers and the 'access to the kind of information which registration would disclose' become highly relevant factors." 448 F.2d at 690.

In short, there must be sufficient basis of accurate information upon which the sophisticated investor may exercise his skills. Just as a scientist cannot be without his specimens, so the shrewdest investor's acuity will be blunted without specifications about the issuer. For an investor to be invested with exemptive status he must have the required data for judgment.

2. *The requirement of available information*
* * *

The requirement that all offerees have available the information registration would provide has been firmly established by this court as a necessary condition of gaining the private offering exemption. * * *

More specifically, we shall require on remand that the defendants demonstrate that all offerees, whatever their expertise, had available the information a registration statement would have afforded a prospective investor in a public offering. Such a showing is not independently sufficient to establish that the offering qualified for the private placement exemption, but it is necessary to gain the exemption and is to be weighed along with the sophistication and number of the offerees, the number of units offered, and the size and manner of the offering. * * * Because in this case these latter factors weigh heavily in favor of the private offering exemption, satisfaction of the necessary condition regarding the availability of relevant information to the offerees would compel the conclusion that this offering fell within the exemption.

C. *On Remand: The Issuer–Offeree Relationship*

In determining on remand the extent of the information available to the offerees, the district court must keep in mind that the "availability" of information means either disclosure of or effective access to the relevant information. The relationship between issuer and offeree is most critical when the issuer relies on the latter route.

To begin with, if the defendants could prove that all offerees were actually furnished the information a registration statement would have provided, whether the offerees occupied a position of access pre-existing such disclosure would not be dispositive of the status of the offering. If disclosure were proved and if, as here, the remaining factors such as the manner of the offering and the investment sophistication of the offerees weigh heavily in favor of the private status of the offering, the absence of a privileged relationship between offeree and issuer would not preclude a finding that the offering was private.
* * *

Alternatively it might be shown that the offeree had access to the files and record of the company that contained the relevant information. Such access might be afforded merely by the position of the offeree or by the issuer's promise to open appropriate files and records to the offeree as well as to answer inquiries regarding material information. In either case, the relationship between offeree and issuer now becomes critical, for it must be shown that the offeree could realistically have been expected to take advantage of his access to ascertain the relevant information.[12] Similarly the investment sophistication of the offeree assumes added importance, for it is important that he could have been expected to ask the right questions and seek out the relevant information.

* * *

1.   *Disclosure or access: a disjunctive requirement*

That our cases sometimes fail clearly to differentiate between "access" and "disclosure" as alternative means of coming within the private offering exemption is, perhaps, not surprising. Although the *Ralston Purina* decision focused on whether the offerees had "access" to the required information, * * * the holding that "the exemption question turns on the knowledge of the offerees," could be construed to include possession as well as access. Such an interpretation would require disclosure as a necessary condition of obtaining a private offering notwithstanding the offerees' access to the information that registration would have provided.

Both the Second and the Fourth Circuits, however, have interpreted *Ralston Purina* as embodying a disjunctive requirement. * * *

The cases in this circuit are not inconsistent with this view. * * *

* * *

Although Rule 146 cannot directly control the case at bar, we think its disjunctive requirement that the private offering claimant may show either "access" or "disclosure" expresses a sound view that this court has in fact implicitly accepted. * * *

2.   *The role of insider status*

Once the alternative means of coming within the private placement exemption are clearly separated, we can appreciate the proper role to be accorded the requirement that the offerees occupy a privileged or "insider" status relative to the issuer. That is to say, when the issuer relies on "access" absent actual disclosure, he must show that the offerees occupied a privileged position relative to the issuer that afforded them an opportunity for effective access to the information registration would otherwise provide.[18] When the issuer relies on actual disclosure to come within the exemption, he need not demonstrate that the offerees held such a privileged position. Although mere disclosure is not a sufficient condition for establishing the availability of the private offering exemption, and a court will weigh other factors such as the manner of the

---

12.   For example, the offeree's ability to compel the issuer to make good his promise may depend on the offeree's bargaining power or on his family or employment relationship to the issuer.

18.   That all offerees are in certain respects "insiders" does not ensure that the issuer will gain the private placement exemption. An insider may be an insider with respect to fiscal matters of the company, but an outsider with respect to a particular issue of securities. He may know much about the financial structure of the company but his position may nonetheless not allow him access to a few vital facts pertaining to the transaction at issue. If Doran had effective access to all information that registration would provide, he would be a transactional insider. That is all we require regarding the availability of information. If, on the other hand, his inside knowledge was incomplete or his access ineffective, he would be a transactional outsider despite the fact that we might consider him an "insider" for other purposes.

offering and the investment sophistication of the offerees, the "insider" status of the offerees is not a necessary condition of obtaining the exemption.

Because the line between access and disclosure has sometimes been obscured, some have interpreted this court's decision in *Continental* [supra at page 401] as limiting the § 4(2) exemption to insider transactions.[19] As we pointed out in our recent decision in *Woolf,* however, such fears are unfounded. 515 F.2d at 610.

The language from *Continental* that gave rise to those fears consists in the court's findings that "Continental did not affirmatively prove that all offerees of its securities had received both written and oral information concerning Continental, that all offerees of its securities had access to any additional information which they might have required or requested, and that all offerees of its securities had personal contacts with the officers of Continental." 463 F.2d at 160. It is possible to read this as a list of the necessary conditions for coming within the § 4(2) exemption, and therefore to infer that a private placement claimant must show the "insider" status of the offerees. Properly viewed in context, however, these statements were not clearly intended to establish necessary conditions, but only to point to the manifold weaknesses of the defendant's claim which, taken together, precluded private offering status.

In *Continental,* the court admittedly agreed with the SEC's position that even if the prospectus that Continental had sent to purchasers contained all the information registration would disclose, that fact alone would not justify the exemption. 463 F.2d at 160. That is doubtless true, since even if all the purchasers of Continental's securities had received full disclosure, the defendant would not have established that all offerees had received full disclosure. Because Continental had failed to sustain its burden of demonstrating the number of offerees, moreover, even the fact that all known offerees might have received disclosure would still have been insufficient to ensure the availability of the exemption. But the court's language in *Continental* should not be read as requiring in addition to full disclosure to all offerees a demonstration of the offerees' insider status.

Rather, the court's language regarding Continental's failure to show that all offerees had access to the requisite information and that all offerees had personal contacts with Continental's officers may be read as foreclosing the possible alternative route to the § 4(2) exemption. Because the prospectus did not contain all the information registration would provide and because it was not established that all offerees received the prospectus, it was clear that Continental could not rely upon actual disclosure. The additional language in *Continental,* though admittedly subject to other interpretations, may be read as making clear that there was in that case no privileged relationship between the offerees and the issuer that might have compensated for the defendant's palpable failure to disclose.

Although the disjunctive nature of the requirement is, to be sure, not made explicit in *Continental,* it is important that the pertinent conclusion of fact held

---

19. For example, one commentator has written that "if Continental Tobacco represents the current state of the law regarding private placement exemption in non-Rule 146 transactions (highly doubtful), its availability is limited to insider transaction." 2 S. Goldberg, Private Placements and Restricted Securities § 2.16[e] (1975). See also Schwartz, The Private Offering Exemption—Recent Developments, 37 Ohio St.L.J. 1, 19 (1976), and cases cited therein; Rediker, The Fifth Circuit Cracks Down on Not–So Private Offerings, 25 Ala.L.Rev. 289, 311–17 (1973).

clearly erroneous in that case was that "the offerees * * * were furnished and/or provided access to the same type of information that would have been provided in a registration statement * * *." 463 F.2d at 159. In order to hold this conclusion clearly erroneous, it was thus necessary to show that the defendant had failed to prove either disclosure or access.

In any event, absent a clear and unambiguous indication to the contrary, we do not read *Continental* as requiring insider status. We think that any such requirement would inhibit the ability of business to raise capital without the expense and delay of registration under circumstances in which the offerees did not need the protection of registration. * * *

Rule 146 offers some rays of sunlight into the limbos and uncertain depths of § 4(2). The cases cast at best a faint beacon toward the horizon of decision. While we appreciate full well that the test we have fashioned remains too fluid to enable the would-be private offering issuer to feel entirely secure, we are confident that, at long last, the safe harbor of Rule 146 will provide that security and that few private placement claimants will stray far from that harbor. * * *

* * *

IV. Conclusion

An examination of the record and the district court's opinion in this case leaves unanswered the central question in all cases that turn on the availability of the § 4(2) exemption. Did the offerees know or have a realistic opportunity to learn facts essential to an investment judgment? We remand so that the trial court can answer that question.[a]

* * *

1. *Subsequent Cases.* In *Securities and Exchange Commission v. Kenton Capital, Ltd.,*[1] defendant was a Cayman Islands corporation that through a sales agent in the United States sought to raise capital to finance a "trading program" in securities and other instruments. Apparently on his own initiative, the sales agent projected returns of 3850% per week, which the defendant later conceded were not achievable. Over 40 investors agreed to invest some $1,700,000 in the defendant's trading program—at which point the SEC learned of the scheme and brought an injunctive action in federal court. The SEC conceded that the number of offerees was limited and that no general solicitation had occurred, but it challenged both the investors' sophistication and their access to relevant information. The court found as follows:

"Defendants support their allegations that their offerees were sophisticated by evidence that they screened their offerees. Wallace [the defendant's President] testified that he developed a checklist of information that was required of all investors, which was included in the material that Kenyon sent to investors. Closer examination of this list, however, reveals that the information requested therein consisted of a photocopy of the investor's passport, a copy of the investors's driver license or social security card, and a bank reference showing the investor to be in good standing with a bank.

a. The defendant had initially also pleaded the one year statute of limitations under § 13 for violation of § 12(a)(1). On remand, it prevailed on this ground and the judgment was affirmed. Doran v. Petroleum Management Corp., 576 F.2d 91 (5th Cir. 1978).

1. 69 F.Supp.2d 1 (D.D.C.1998).

This information is wholly irrelevant to the sophistication of the offerees. The Court is equally unimpressed by Wallace's contention that Kenton's minimum investment requirement provided any safeguard of investor sophistication."[2]

The court added that even if sophistication were established, it would still not be a substitute for access to the information that registration would disclose, citing *Doran v. Petroleum Management Corp.*

Although a minimum investment requirement did not work in *Kenton*, cases upholding the private placement exemption have often looked to the size of the investment made by the plaintiff, particularly as a proportion of the total offering or of all outstanding shares. See *Lewis v. Fresne*, 252 F.3d 352, 358 (5th Cir.2001) (purchase of 29% of outstanding shares is consistent with private character of offering); *Koehler v. Pulvers*, 614 F.Supp. 829, 842 (S.D.Cal.1985).

2. *Pre-Screening Procedures.* Although the screening procedures employed in *Kenton Capital* were deemed insufficient, more elaborate procedures, typically involving a substantial "investor questionnaire," are used today by most broker dealers to determine whether an offeree is qualified, and courts have given these some weight.[3] Still, courts often found problems elsewhere in the offering. In *Weprin v. Peterson*,[4] the "due diligence" procedures were approved by the court, but it still found non-compliance with the requirements of Regulation D on another basis, and ruled that "strict compliance" was necessary. What happens if an investor misrepresents and overstates his or her qualifications? Can the investor still assert that the investor was insufficiently sophisticated? Or, alternatively, what if a simple "due diligence" investigation by the broker dealer or the issuer would have turned up discrepancies and demonstrated the investor's lack of qualifications? In *Wright v. National Warranty Co.*,[5] the Sixth Circuit refused to permit husband and wife investors to disavow statements and representations made to the issuer in which these investors represented that they had sufficient business experience to invest in the proposed private placement. But how far should this principle of estoppel be carried? Should it be sufficient that the investor makes a conclusory representation that it is a qualified offeree with substantial business and investing experience?

3. *The Meaning of Sophistication.* How sophisticated must an offeree be in order for the private placement exemption to be available? Does the answer depend to some degree on the character of the disclosures made or the degree of access the offeree receives to information about the issuer?

Obviously, "sophistication" is not an either/or issue, and degrees of sophistication exist. An experienced, successful businessman may have had considerable success, have founded his own company, negotiated many complex transactions, and yet be uninformed with regard to a technical area of finance

---

2. Id. at 11. Accord: *Securities and Exchange Commission v. Current Fin. Servs.*, 100 F.Supp.2d 1 (D.D.C.2000).

3. See in particular Mary S. Krech Trust v. Lakes Apartments, 642 F.2d 98 (5th Cir.1981) (approving use of "formidable" due diligence investigation).

4. 736 F.Supp. 1124 (N.D.Ga.1988).

5. 953 F.2d 256 (6th Cir.1992). In *Wright*, the plaintiffs were the company's incoming chief financial officer and his wife (who purchased at the time that he was hired). Although they had access to all corporate information, they sought to assert that the wife was insufficiently experienced. It is not surprising that the court was unsympathetic to this claim on these facts, and thus the decision may not apply broadly.

(such as derivatives). Thus, an ABA position paper on the scope of the § 4(2) exemption concluded:

"The relevant inquiry should be whether the investor can understand and evaluate the nature of the risk based upon the information supplied to him. The relevant inquiry should not be whether the investor is *au courant* in all of the latest nuances and techniques of corporate finance.[6]

Nonetheless, courts have sometimes seemingly required a higher standard. In Lively v. Hirschfield,[7] the Tenth Circuit indicated that only "persons of exceptional business experience" would satisfy the standard for an offeree under § 4(2). *Doran* seemed instead to focus more on the quality of the disclosure provided by the issuer. The Eighth Circuit has gone further than other Circuits and seemingly subordinated sophistication to the access to information requirement, emphasizing the economic bargaining power of the offerees.[8] Another Eighth Circuit decision assumed that a buyer of restricted securities was sophisticated because his net income exceeded $200,000, his net worth was over $1 million, and his trading account had an approximately $500,000 balance.[9] But many professional athletes (some of whom did not graduate from college) can meet this standard.

Special problems exist when an issuer seeks to obtain summary judgment on the availability of the § 4(2) exemption. In Hedden v. Marinelli,[10] one investor held a bachelor's degree in economics from Stanford, a law degree from Hastings, and was the founding director of a bank; the other investor was a former CEO of the company whose stock he was purchasing. Still, the court refused to grant summary judgment on the issue of sophistication.

One commentator has found that courts examine the issue of sophistication in a variety of different contexts under the federal securities law and, across this continuum, tend to place primary emphasis on the professional status and investment experience of the investor, including exposure to and prior consultation with investment professionals.[11] This would make sense, but the case law under § 4(2) continues to show courts looking to talismanic factors, such as personal wealth or apparent bargaining power.

Courts have also continued to place the burden on the issuer of identifying and establishing the requisite qualifications of all offerees where the claimed exemption is based on § 4(2).[12] As will next be seen, this contrasts sharply with the current standards under Regulation D.

6. See Section 4(2) and Statutory Law: A Position Paper of the Federal Regulation of Securities Committee, Section of Corporation, Banking and Business law of the American Bar Association, 31 Bus.Law. 485 (1975).

7. 440 F.2d 631 (10th Cir.1971). But see Cowles v. Dow Keith Oil & Gas, Inc., 752 F.2d 508 (10th Cir.1985).

8. See Van Dyke v. Coburn Enters., Inc., 873 F.2d 1094, 1098 (8th Cir.1989) (conditions of § 4(2) satisfied where offerees "had the economic bargaining power to demand any information necessary to make an informed investment decision").

9. See Ackerberg v. Johnson, 892 F.2d 1328 (8th Cir.1989).

10. 796 F.Supp. 432 (N.D.Cal.1992).

11. See Fletcher, Sophisticated Investors Under the Federal Securities Laws, 1988 Duke L.J. 1081.

12. See SEC v. Life Partners, Inc., 912 F.Supp. 4 (D.D.C.1996) (defendants "have the burden of identifying all offerees, and because [they] cannot provide this information, defendants' offerings do not qualify for exemption under Section 4(2)."), rev'd on other grounds, 87 F.3d 536 (D.C.Cir.1996).

CHAPTER 6

THE LIMITED OFFERING EXEMPTIONS: SECTION 3(b), REGULATION D AND REGULATION A

This Chapter will consider several different registration exemptions, which in common are relied upon by small business issuers who wish to avoid the costs and/or liabilities of SEC registration: Regulation A, which provides for a form of "mini-registration;" Regulation D, which codifies the private placement safe harbor but also relies upon the § 3(b) small issue exemption; Rule 701, which exempts offers and sales of securities by non-reporting issuers pursuant to compensatory employee benefit plans; Regulation CE, which applies only to limited offerings in California, but may be generalized to other states in the future; and, lastly, § 4(6), which is little used. For most small businesses, the principal alternatives will be Regulation A or Regulation D (although the latter is much used by larger companies as well, particularly for offerings of debt securities).

The Commission is authorized under § 3(b) of the 1933 Act to exempt from the registration provisions other securities if it finds that registration of these securities is not necessary in the public interest and for the protection of investors by reason of the small amount involved or the limited character of the public offering. The section specifies a maximum aggregate offering amount which initially was $100,000. The ceiling has been repeatedly increased to counteract the ravages of inflation, and is now set at $5,000,000. Acting under this authority, the Commission has issued a number of rules and regulations, the most important of which from the standpoint of capital formation by small businesses are Regulation D and Regulation A.

Regulation D was adopted by the Commission in March, 1982, and relies on both § 3(b) and § 4(2), which exempts "transactions not involving any public offering." Regulation D is designed to coordinate the various limited offering exemptions previously contained in Rules 146, 240 and 242, to streamline the requirements applicable to private offerings and sales of securities, and to provide a safe harbor for issuers if all of the conditions of the rule are met. The regulation represents an effort to remove the impediments to capital formation by small businesses to the extent that the lifting of the existing burdens are deemed consistent with the public interest and the protection of investors.

Regulation D also impacts on state securities registration requirements. Under § 18 of the 1933 Act (added by the National Securities Markets Improvement Act of 1996), state securities registration requirements are preempted if a security qualifies as a "covered security" under § 18(b). Section 18(b)(4)(D) deems any security exempted pursuant to "commission rules or regulations under Section 4(2)" to be such a "covered security." Thus, to the extent that certain of the rules collected in Regulation D rely on § 4(2) of the

1933 Act, § 18 thereby preempts state registration requirements with respect to such a security. Section 18(b)(4)(D) does, however, permit a state to require a "notice filing" to the extent that such a requirement was "in effect on September 1, 1996."

To the extent that a security is not exempted from state registration requirements by § 18, the SEC and the North American Securities Administrators Association, Inc. ("NASAA")[1] have established special procedures for coordinating state securities regulation with federal regulation.

In September, 1983, NASAA adopted a Uniform Limited Offering Exemption (ULOE) for enactment at the state level.[2] ULOE would exempt from state registration any offering if it complies with Rules 501, 502, 503, 505 and 506 of Regulation D, so long as certain additional conditions are also complied with. As of 1992, virtually every state has adopted some form of nonpublic limited offering exemption or simply dispenses with securities qualification. About 30 or 60% of the states have adopted ULOE with or without variations or dispense with securities qualification altogether, thereby eliminating duplicative regulation of small issues at the state level.[3]

A principal alternative to Regulation D is Regulation A, which was significantly expanded in 1992 to permit an issuer to sell securities in an unregistered offering up to an aggregate amount of $5 million in an 12–month period (the prior ceiling had been $1.5 million). Regulation A (Rules 251 to 263) relies for its authority on § 3(b) of the 1933 Act, the "small offering" exemption. In contrast to Regulation D, compliance with Regulation A results in the issuance of unrestricted securities, which may be freely resold by the purchaser. Also, an offering under Regulation A may be conducted as a public offering without restrictions on the manner of offering or the eligibility of offerees or purchasers. As will be seen, this is generally not true under Regulation D. The relative advantages of these two alternatives are discussed later, but the countervailing advantage of Regulation D is that its Rule 506 has no ceiling on the amount of securities that can be issued in reliance on it. Thus, Rule 506 may be used both by relatively small issuers and giant public corporations, while Regulation A is mainly attractive to the small business issuer. In common, both Regulation A and Regulation D have the advantage (from the issuer's perspective) that the issuer and its officers, directors, and underwriters do not become subject to the liabilities created by § 11 (which applies only to registration statements).

---

1. NASAA is a voluntary organization composed of securities regulatory agencies of 49 states, the Commonwealth of Puerto Rico and Guam, Mexico and 13 provinces of Canada.

2. Section 19(c) of the 1933 Act authorized the SEC to "cooperate" with the NASAA to achieve "greater uniformity in Federal–State securities matters." The ULOE was an outgrowth of that cooperation. Nonetheless, in 1996, Congress decided to largely preempt state registration requirements by adding § 18 to the 1933 Act.

3. See Maynard, the Uniform Limited Offering Exemption: How Uniform is Uniform?, 36 Emory L.J. 357 (1987); Hainsfurther, Summary of Blue Sky Exemptions Corresponding to Regulation D, 38 Sw.L.J. 989 (1984) (containing a chart summarizing the law in all states as of August 1, 1984); T. Loo & K. Berke, 1 Securities Law Techniques, ch. 2 (A.A. Sommer, Jr. ed. 1985, Supp. 1990) (containing chart of state adoptions of Regulation D); MacEwan, Blue Sky Regulation of Regulation D Offerings, 18 Rev. of Sec. & Commodities Reg. 103 (1985); NASAA Rep. (CCH) ¶ 6401 (1990).

SECTION 1.   REGULATION D: COORDINATION OF FORMER RULES 146, 240 AND 242

Statutes and Regulations

Securities Act § 3(b).

Regulation D.

Securities Act Release No. 6389

Securities and Exchange Commission.
March 8, 1982.

REGULATION D—REVISION OF CERTAIN EXEMPTIONS FROM REGISTRATION UNDER THE SECURITIES ACT OF 1933 FOR TRANSACTIONS INVOLVING LIMITED OFFERS AND SALES

The Commission announces the adoption of a new regulation governing certain offers and sales of securities without registration under the Securities Act of 1933 and a uniform notice of sales form to be used for all offerings under the regulation. The regulation replaces three exemptions and four forms, all of which are being rescinded. The new regulation is designed to simplify and clarify existing exemptions, to expand their availability, and to achieve uniformity between federal and state exemptions in order to facilitate capital formation consistent with the protection of investors.

* * *

I. Background

Regulation D is the product of the Commission's evaluation of the impact of its rules and regulations on the ability of small businesses to raise capital. This study has revealed a particular concern that the registration requirements and the exemptive scheme of the Securities Act impose disproportionate restraints on small issuers. In response to this concern, the Commission has taken a number of actions, including a relaxation of certain aspects of Regulation A * * * and the introduction of Form S–18, a simplified registration statement for certain first time issuers.

Coincident with the Commission's small business program, Congress enacted the Small Business Investment Incentive Act of 1980 (the "Incentive Act") [94 Stat. 2275 (codified in scattered sections of 15 U.S.C.)]. The Incentive Act included three changes to the Securities Act: the addition of an exemption in Section 4(6) for offers and sales solely to accredited investors,[3] the increase in the ceiling of Section 3(b) from $2,000,000 to $5,000,000, and the addition of Section 19(c) which, among other things, authorized "the development of a uniform exemption from registration for small issuers which can be agreed upon among several States or between the States and the Federal Government."

---

3. The Incentive Act also added Section 2(a)(15) to the Securities Act which defined   "accredited investor" * * *.

As a result of the Commission's reevaluation of the impact that its rules and regulations have on small businesses and the provisions of the Incentive Act, the Commission undertook a general examination of the exemptive scheme under the Securities Act. * * *

II. Discussion

A. *Overview*

Regulation D is a series of six rules, designated Rules 501–506, that establishes three exemptions from the registration requirements of the Securities Act and replaces exemptions that currently exist under Rules 146, 240, and 242. The regulation is designed to simplify existing rules and regulations, to eliminate any unnecessary restrictions that those rules and regulations place on issuers, particularly small businesses, and to achieve uniformity between state and federal exemptions in order to facilitate capital formation consistent with the protection of investors.

Rules 501–503 set forth definitions, terms, and conditions that apply generally throughout the regulation. The exemptions of Regulation D are contained in Rules 504–506. Rules 504 and 505 * * * provide exemptions from registration under Section 3(b) of the Securities Act. Rule 506 succeeds Rule 146 and relates to transactions that are deemed to be exempt from registration under Section 4(2) of the Securities Act.

Rule 504 generally expands Rule 240 by increasing the amount of securities sold in a 12 month period from $100,000 to [$1,000,000], eliminating the ceiling on the number of investors, and removing the prohibition on payment of commissions or similar remuneration. Rule 504 also removes restrictions on the manner of offering and on resale if an offering is conducted exclusively in states where it is registered and where a disclosure document is delivered under the applicable state law. * * * Rule 504 does not prescribe specific disclosure requirements. Rule 504 is an effort by the Commission to set aside a clear and workable exemption for small offerings by small issuers to be regulated by state "Blue Sky" requirements and to be subject to federal antifraud provisions and civil liability provisions such as Section 12(2). Therefore, the exemption is not available to issuers that are subject to the reporting obligations of the Securities Exchange Act of 1934 * * * or are investment companies as defined under the Investment Company Act of 1940 * * *.

Rule 505 replaces Rule 242. Its offering limit is $5,000,000 in a 12–month period, an increase from the $2,000,000 in six months ceiling in Rule 242. Like its predecessor, Rule 505 permits sales to 35 purchasers that are not accredited investors and to an unlimited number of accredited investors. However, the class of accredited investors has now been expanded. The exemption is available to all non-investment company issuers,[8] an expansion of the restriction in Rule 242 that limited the exemption's availability to certain corporate entities. An issuer under Rule 505 may not use any general solicitation or general advertising. * * *

Rule 506 takes the place of Rule 146. As under its predecessor, Rule 506 is available to all issuers for offerings sold to not more than 35 purchasers.

---

8. * * * Rule 505 is not available to issuers that are subject to the disqualifica- tions of Regulation A.

Accredited investors, however, do not count towards that limit. Rule 506 requires an issuer to make a subjective determination that each purchaser meets certain sophistication standards, a provision that narrows a similar requirement as to all offerees under Rule 146. The new exemption retains the concept of the purchaser representative so that unsophisticated purchasers may participate in the offering if a purchaser representative is present. Like Rule 146, Rule 506 prohibits any general solicitation or general advertising.

* * *

III. Synopsis

The following section-by-section discussion of the provisions of Regulation D, the significant commentary on the proposals, and the revisions made to the proposed regulation are included to assist in understanding the regulation as adopted. Attention is directed to the text of Regulation D for a more complete understanding. Attention is also directed to the chart following the synopsis which compares the provisions of Regulation D exemptions to those of predecessor exemptions.

A. *Preliminary Notes*

Regulation D contains [seven] preliminary notes. The first preliminary note reminds issuers that Regulation D offerings, although exempt from Section 5 of the Securities Act, are not exempt from antifraud or civil liability provisions of the federal securities laws. The note also reminds issuers conducting Regulation D offerings of their obligation to furnish whatever material information may be needed to make the required disclosure not misleading.

Note 2 underscores an issuer's obligation to comply with applicable state law and highlights certain areas of anticipated differences between Regulation D at the federal and state levels. * * *

Note 3 makes clear that reliance on any particular exemption in Regulation D does not act as an election. An issuer may always claim the availability of any other applicable exemption. Several commentators believed this note should address specifically the availability of an exemption under Section 4(2) of the Securities Act. The Commission has reworded the note by including language that appeared in proposed Rule 506(a) and clarified the specific availability of Section 4(2).

The fourth note specifies that Regulation D is available only to the issuer of the securities and not to its affiliates or others for resales of the issuer's securities. The note further provides that Regulation D exemptions are only transactional. * * *

Preliminary Note 5, which confirms the availability of Regulation D for business combinations, clarifies a question raised by commentators.

The sixth note provides that the regulation is not available for use in a plan or scheme to evade the registration requirements of the Securities Act.

[Preliminary Note 7 was added in 1990 when Regulation S was promulgated. Securities offered and sold outside the United States in conformity with Regulation S may be conducted simultaneously with offers and sales within the United States in accordance with Regulation D without causing the two transactions to be integrated, unless the issuer elects to rely on Regulation D for offers and sales made to persons outside the United States. It has been estimated that about 25% of private offerings are sold offshore.]

B. *Rule 501—Definitions and Terms Used in Regulation D*

Rule 501 sets forth, alphabetically, definitions that apply to the entire regulation. The definitions generally represent distillations of concepts in Rules 146, 240, and 242. The definition of "accredited investor," however, is an expansion of the term "accredited person" in Rule 242.

* * *

1. *Accredited investor.* * * *

The following subsections review the eight categories of accredited investor in Rule 501(a).

a. Rule 501(a)(1)—Institutional Investors. Rule 501(a)(1) repeats the listing of institutional investors included in Section 2(15)(i) of the Securities Act. One such investor is an employee benefit plan within the meaning of Title I of the Employee Retirement Income Security Act of 1974 ("ERISA") [codified in scattered sections of 26, 29 U.S.C.], the investment decisions for which are made by a bank, insurance company, or registered investment adviser. The Commission recognizes, and several commentators noted, that many plans, have internalized the function of the plan fiduciary and thus could not qualify under the proposed category. For this reason the Commission believes it is appropriate to extend accredited investor status to any ERISA plan with total assets in excess of $5,000,000.

b. Rule 501(a)(2)—Private Business Development Companies. This category applies to private business development companies as defined in Section 202(a)(22) of the Investment Advisers Act of 1940. As proposed, the category referred to Sections 55(a)(1) through (3) and 2(a)(47) of the Investment Company Act. The proposal was intended to include business development companies that had not made an election under Section 2(a)(48)(C) of the Investment Company Act. Several commentators noted, however, that the intent of the category could be more accurately accomplished by referring to the definition of private business development company in Section 202(a)(22) of the Advisers Act. Although the new reference expands the class of private business development companies that may be qualified as accredited investors, it still delimits the class by the obligation of its members to provide "significant managerial assistance" as defined in Section 2(a)(47) of the Investment Company Act.[12]

c. Rule 501(a)(3)—Tax Exempt Organizations. Proposed Rule 501(a)(3) created a category of accredited investor for college or university endowment funds with assets in excess of $25 million. Upon further consideration and based on commentary the Commission has determined that this category can be expanded to all organizations that are described as exempt organizations in Section 501(c)(3) of the Internal Revenue Code. Additionally, the Commission has lowered the asset level to $5 million.

d. Rule 501(a)(4)—Directors, Executive Officers and General Partners. Rule 501(a)(4) provides that certain insiders of the issuer are accredited investors. As proposed, the category pertained only to directors and executive

---

12. Section 202(a)(22) of the Advisers Act refers to Section 2(a)(48) of the Investment Company Act for the core of its meaning. Section 2(a)(48) defines a business development company as a company that, among other things, "makes available significant managerial assistance," a phrase that is defined in Section 2(a)(47) of the Investment Company Act.

officers. A number of comment letters recommended that the provision be modified to cover general partners of limited partnerships. The category thus has been revised to include general partners of issuers, as well as directors, executive officers and general partners of those general partners.

e. Rule 501(a)(5)—$150,000 Purchasers. [Initially, former Rule 501(a)(5) provided that any "person" became an accredited investor upon the purchase of at least $150,000 of securities if the total purchase price did not exceed 20% of the person's net worth at the time of sale, with some exceptions. In 1988, that paragraph was deleted and replaced by former Rule 501(a)(6).] * * *

f. Rule 501(a)[(5)]—$1,000,000 Net Worth Test. This category extends accredited investor status to any natural person whose net worth at the time of purchase is $1,000,000. Net worth may be either the individual worth of the investor or the joint net worth of the investor and the investor's spouse. * * *

g. Rule 501(a)[(6)]—$200,000 Income Test. A natural person who has an income in excess of $200,000 in each of the last two years [or joint income with that person's spouse in excess of $300,000 in each of those years] and who reasonably expects [his or her income to reach the same level] in the current year is an accredited investor.

* * *

[h.] [Rule 501(a)(7)—Trusts With Assets Exceeding $5,000,000. Any such trust, not formed for the specific purpose of acquiring the securities offered and whose purchase is directed by a "sophisticated person", is an accredited investor. That term is defined in Rule 501(b)(2)(ii) to be a person who possesses "such knowledge and experience in financial and business matters that he [or she] is capable of evaluating the merits and risks of the prospective investment."]

[i.] Rule 501(a)(8)—Entities Made up of Certain Accredited Investors. The proposed definition of accredited investor did not take into account an entity owned entirely by accredited investors. Rule 501(a)(8) of the final regulation extends accredited investor status to entities in which all the equity owners are accredited investors * * *.

2. *Affiliate.* The definition of affiliate in Rule 501(b) is the same as that contained in Rule 405 of Regulation C.

3. *Aggregate Offering Price.* Rule 501(c) defines the method for calculating the aggregate offering price. * * *

4. *Business Combination.* The definition of business combination in Rule 501(d) has undergone only technical revision.

5. *Calculation of Number of Purchasers.* Rule 501(e) sets forth principles that govern the calculation of the number of purchasers in offerings under Rules 505 and 506. * * *

6. *Executive Officer.* The definition of executive officer in Rule 501(f) has been modified to conform with the definition of that term set forth in Rule 405 of Regulation C.

7. *Issuer.* The term "issuer", as set forth in Rule 501(g), has been revised to conform with the terminology in the Federal Bankruptcy Code [11 U.S.C. 101 et seq.].

8. *Purchaser Representative.* In response to comments, the definition of purchaser representative in Rule 501(h) has been revised in three respects.

First, the introductory language to the paragraph has been reformulated. As adopted, the definition includes any person who satisfies the conditions of the term in fact, as well as any person the issuer reasonably believes falls within the category. A second change incorporated the categories set forth in Rule 501(e)(1)(ii) and (iii) into subparagraphs (ii) and (iii). Thirdly, paragraph (2) was revised to permit the purchaser representative to make the requisite evaluation of the prospective investment "with the purchaser."

C.   *Rule 502—General Conditions to be Met*

Rule 502 sets forth general conditions that relate to all offerings under Rules 504 through 506. These cover guidelines for determining whether separate offers and sales constitute part of the same offering under principles of integration, requirements as to specific disclosure requirements in Regulation D offerings, and limitations on the manner of conducting the offering and on the resale of securities acquired in the offering.

* * *

1.   *Integration.* Rule 502(a) provides that all sales that are part of the same Regulation D offering must be integrated. The rule provides a safe harbor for all offers and sales that take place at least six months before the start of or six months after the termination of the Regulation D offering, so long as there are no offers and sales, excluding those to employee benefit plans, of the same securities within either of these six-month periods.

Along with several technical revisions, the Commission changed the word "issue" to "offering" throughout the provision. This change makes the language of the rule consistent with the principle of integration.

[Offers and sales of securities within the United States that are made in compliance with Regulation D will not be integrated with a simultaneous transaction made in accordance with Regulation S.]

2.   *Information Requirements.* Rule 502(b) provides when and what type of disclosure must be furnished in Regulation D offerings. If an issuer sells securities under Rule 504 or only to accredited investors, then Regulation D does not mandate any specific disclosure. If securities are sold under Rule 505 or 506 to any investors that are not accredited, then Rule 502(b)(1) requires delivery of the information specified in Rule 502(b)(2) to all purchasers. The type of information to be furnished varies depending on the size of the offering and the nature of the issuer.

* * *

The specific disclosure requirements are as follows:

a.   Non-reporting companies. Disclosure requirements for companies that are not subject to the reporting obligations of the Exchange Act are set forth in Rule 502(b)(2)(i). These requirements are keyed to the size of the offering.

* * *

[The disclosure requirements of Regulation D were substantially revised in 1993. If the issuer is a non-reporting company, its obligation to disclose non-financial information depends principally on the size of the offering. For offerings over $5 million, it must disclose the same information that would be required in a registration statement; but for offerings under $5 million, it need only provide the information that would be required in a Regulation A offering. The financial information that must be disclosed varies even more significantly with the size of the offering, with different requirements becoming applicable depending on whether the offering is below $2 million, between $2 million and $7.5 million, or above $7.5 million. Even in the category of offerings below $2 million, however, an audited balance sheet, dated within 120 days of the commencement of the offering, must be provided at a minimum, and more extensive audited financial statements are required for the larger categories of offerings. For non-reporting companies, the obligation to provide this information is, however, subject to an ambiguous clause in Rule 502(b)(i), which mandates the foregoing disclosures "to the extent material to an understanding of the issuer, its business, and the securities being offered." *Query*: When is such information not material?

If the issuer is a reporting company, Rule 502(b)(2)(ii) governs and specifies the filings under the 1934 Act's continuous disclosure system that must be provided to a purchaser.]

* * *

b. Reporting companies. Companies that are subject to Exchange Act reporting obligations must furnish the same kind of disclosure regardless of the size of the offering. These issuers, however, have an option as to the form that this disclosure may take. Under Rule 502(b)(2)(ii)(A), a reporting company may provide its most recent annual report to shareholders, assuming it is in accordance with Rule 14a–3 or 14c–3 under the Exchange Act, the definitive proxy statement filed in connection with that annual report, and, if requested in writing, the most recent Form 10–K. Alternatively, those issuers may elect under Rule 502(b)(2)(ii)(B) to provide the information contained in the most recent of its Form 10–K or a Form S–1 registration statement under the Securities Act or a Form 10 registration statement under the Exchange Act. Although the requirement under subparagraph (B) refers to specific forms, it does not mandate delivery of the actual reference documents. An issuer, for instance, may choose to prepare and deliver a separate document that contains the necessary information.

Regardless of the issuer's choice of disclosure in subparagraph (A) or (B), Rule 502(b)(2)(ii)(C) requires the basic information to be supplemented by information contained in certain Exchange Act reports filed after the distribution or filing of the report or registration statement in question. Further, the issuer must provide certain information regarding the offering and any material changes in the issuer's affairs that are not disclosed in the basic documents.

* * *

c. Other information requirements. The balance of Rule 502(b)(2) provides for the treatment of exhibits, the right of purchasers that are not accredited to receive information which was furnished to accredited investors, and, in offerings involving nonaccredited investors, the right of all purchasers to ask questions of the issuer concerning the offering, and a specific obligation by the issuer to disclose all material differences in terms or arrangements as between security holders in a business combination or exchange offer. * * *

3. *Manner of Offering.* Rule 502(c) prohibits the use of general solicitation or general advertising in connection with Regulation D offerings, except in certain cases under Rule 504. * * *

4. *Limitations on Resale.* Securities acquired in a Regulation D offering, with the exception of certain offerings under Rule 504, have the status of securities acquired in a transaction under Section 4(2) of the Securities Act. As

further provided in Rule 502(d), the issuer shall exercise reasonable care to assure that purchasers of securities are not underwriters, which reasonable care will include certain inquiry as to investment purpose, disclosure of resale limitations and placement of a legend on the certificate. [Moreover, written disclosure must be made to each purchaser prior to sale that the securities have not been registered and, therefore, cannot be resold unless they are registered or an exemption from registration is available.] * * *

D.   *Rule 503—Filings of Notice of Sales*

The Commission is adopting a uniform notice of sales form for use in offerings under both Regulation D and Section 4(6) of the Securities Act. The form is an adaptation of Form 242 and Form 4(6) to the Regulation D context. As with the predecessor forms, issuers will furnish information on Form D mainly by checking appropriate boxes. The form requires an indication of the exemptions being claimed.

Rule 503 sets forth the filing requirements for Form D. The notice is due 15 days after the first sale of securities in an offering under Regulation D.[27] Subsequent notices are due every six months after first sale and 30 days after the last sale. One copy of each notice must be manually signed by a person duly authorized by the issuer.

Rule 503(d) requires an undertaking in Form D to furnish the staff, upon its written request, with the information provided to purchasers that are not accredited in a Rule 505 offering. * * *

E.   *Rule 504—Exemption for Offers and Sales Not Exceeding $1,000,000*

Rule 504, which replaces Rule 240, provides an exemption under Section 3(b) of the Securities Act for certain offers and sales not exceeding an aggregate offering price of $1,000,000. * * * Proceeds from securities sold within the preceding 12 months in all transactions exempt under Section 3(b) or in violation of Section 5(a) of the Securities Act must be included in computing the aggregate offering price under Rule 504. The exemption is not available to investment companies or issuers subject to Exchange Act reporting obligations. Commissions or similar transaction related remuneration may be paid.

As under Rule 240, the exemption under Rule 504 does not mandate specific disclosure requirements. However, the issuer remains subject to the antifraud and civil liability provisions of the federal securities laws and must also comply with state requirements.

Offers and sales under Rule 504 must be made in accordance with all the general terms and conditions in Rules 501 through 503. However, if the entire offering is made exclusively in states that require registration and the delivery of a disclosure document, and if the offering is in compliance with those requirements, then the general limitations on the manner of offering and on resale will not apply. [Moreover, if the securities have been registered and offered for sale in at least one state that provides for registration and delivery of a disclosure document before sale, such securities may also be offered and

---

27. In response to commentators, the Commission notes that generally the acceptance of subscription funds into an escrow account pending receipt of minimum subscriptions would trigger the filing requirements. [The significance of Rule 503 was greatly reduced in 1989 when the availability of the exemption under Regulation D was no longer conditioned on its filing. See also Rule 507, which is discussed infra at p. 443—Eds.].

sold in states that do not require registration if such document is delivered to all purchasers of the securities.]

* * *

F. *Rule 505—Exemption for Offers and Sales Not Exceeding $5,000,000*

Rule 505 replaces Rule 242. The rule provides an exemption under Section 3(b) of the Securities Act for offers and sales to no more than 35 purchasers that are not accredited where the aggregate offering price over 12 months does not exceed $5,000,000. As with Rule 504, the aggregate offering price includes proceeds from offers and sales under Section 3(b) or in violation of Section 5(a) of the Securities Act.[31] * * *

Rule 505 is available to any issuer that is not an investment company. * * *

Finally, Rule 505 is not available to issuers that are subject to any of the disqualification provisions contained in Rule 252(c), (d), (e) or (f) of Regulation A. * * *

G. *Rule 506—Exemption for Offers and Sales Without Regard to Dollar Amount*

Rule 506 relates to transactions that are deemed to be exempt under Section 4(2) of the Securities Act. It modifies and replaces Rule 146. Like its predecessor, Rule 506 exempts offers and sales to no more than 35 purchasers. Whereas Rule 146 excludes certain purchasers from the count, Rule 506 excludes accredited investors in computing the number of purchasers. More significantly, Rule 506 modifies the offeree qualification principles of Rule 146 in two ways. First, Rule 506 requires that only purchasers meet the sophistication standard. Second, the rule eliminates the economic risk test. Commentators endorsed both modifications.[33]

31. Based on its experience with Rule 242, the Commission is aware that in computing the aggregate offering price issuers frequently misunderstand the interaction of the concepts of aggregation and integration as applicable under Rule 504(b)(2)(i) and 505(b)(2)(i). Aggregation is the principle by which an issuer determines the dollar worth of exempt sales available directly under Section 3(b) of the Securities Act. Integration is a principle under which an issuer determines overall characteristics of its offering. The following examples illustrate the application of these concepts. An issuer that has conducted an offering under Rule 505 in May 1982 must aggregate the proceeds from that offering with the proceeds of a Rule 505 offering conducted in December 1982. If the May offering had been under Rule 506, however, it would not need to be aggregated with the December offering. In either case, the May offering should be exempt from principles of integration by virtue of the safe harbor provision in Rule 502(a). If a Rule 506 offering had been conducted in July 1982, the integration

safe harbor would not be available as to a subsequent Rule 505 offering in December. Although the proceeds from the July 506 offering would not be added to the December 505 aggregate offering price under aggregation principles, they would have to be included if the two offerings could be integrated. Assuming the two offerings were integrated, then the issuer would have to evaluate all characteristics of the combined transactions, e.g., number of investors, aggregate offering price, etc., when determining the availability of an exemption.

33. Commentators expressed concern that this exemption was not clearly designated as a safe harbor rule under Section 4(2) of the Securities Act. Such a connection is important, they noted, for purposes of exemption from Regulation T (12 CFR 220.1–220.8) of the Federal Reserve Board, exemption from the definition of "investment company" under Section 3(c)(1) of the Investment Company Act, and exemption from registration under certain state laws. The final language of Rule 506 responds to this concern. In

H. *Rule 507—Disqualification Relating to Exemptions Under Rules 504, 505 and 506*

Rule 507, adopted in 1989, disqualifies issuers from using Regulation D, if the issuer, any predecessor or affiliate has been found by a court to have violated the Form D filing requirements specified in Rule 503.

I. *Rule 508—Insignificant Deviations From a Requirement of Regulation D*

Rule 508, adopted in 1989, provides that isolated failures to comply with Regulation D will not necessarily cause the loss of an exemption. Although Form D is still required to be filed, it is no longer a condition to an exemption under Regulation D. Rule 508 responds to the criticism that the limited offering rules are too complex and impose intolerable risks for inadvertent violations. See supra at page 410, for the discussion of Weprin v. Peterson.[b]

IV. Effective Date and Operation of Regulation D

* * *

The staff will issue interpretive letters to assist persons in complying with Regulation D, but the staff will not issue no-action letters as to whether a transaction satisfies the requirements of the regulation. With respect to resales of securities, the staff will continue its present policy of not expressing an opinion on inquiries regarding the following: (1) hypothetical situations; (2) the removal of restrictive legends from securities; (3) whether a person is an affiliate; or (4) requests for no-action positions regarding securities acquired on or after April 15, 1972, as set forth in Release No. 33–6099 (August 2, 1979).

addition, the Commission's Division of Corporation Finance has conferred with and has been assured by the staff of the Federal Reserve Board that transactions under Rule 506 will be exempt from the operation of Regulation T. Finally, the Commission regards Rule 506 transactions as non-public offerings for purposes of the definition of "investment company" in Section 3(c)(1) of the Investment Company Act and as Section 4 transactions for purposes of Section 304(b) of the Trust Indenture Act of 1939 [15 U.S.C. 77aaa et seq., as amended].

b. See also Schneider, A Substantial Compliance ("I&I") Defense and Other Changes are Added to SEC Regulation D, 44 Bus.Law. 1207 (1989).

Comparative Chart of Securities Act Limited Offering Exemptions and Alternatives [a]

Comparison Item	Rule 504	Rule 505	Rule 506	Rule 701	Sec. 4(6)	Reg. A
Dollar Ceiling	$1,000,000 (12 mos.)	$5,000,000 (12 mos.)	Unlimited	$5,000,000 (12 mo.) aggregate but not subject to aggregation with other § 3(b) offerings. However, aggregate offering price of securities subject to outstanding offers may not exceed greater of (1) $1,000,000 or (2) greater of (i) 15% of total assets as of end of last fiscal year or (ii) 15% of outstanding securities of that class. (Outstanding securities of class includes securities of that class issuable pursuant to outstanding options, warrants or conversion rights, unless such options, warrants or conversion rights were issued under Rule 701). Rule 701 offerings are not subject to integration with offerings outside of Rule 701.	$5,000,000	$5,000,000 (12 mos.)
Number of Investors	Unlimited	35 plus unlimited accredited investors	35 plus unlimited accredited investors	Unlimited	Unlimited accredited only	Unlimited
Investor Qualification	None required	Accredited or none required	Purchaser must be sophisticated (alone or with representative). Accredited presumed to be qualified	Directors, officers, employees; general partners, trustees of business trusts, consultants or advisers if they render bona fide services and offering to them is not part of a capital-raising transaction.	Accredited	None required
Commissions	Permitted	Permitted	Permitted	Permitted	Permitted	Permitted
Limitations on Manner of Offering	General solicitation permitted if shares are issued pursuant to Rule 504(b) (i) in one or more states that provide for the registration of securities and require the distribution of a substantive disclosure document before sale, (ii) in states not so providing for registration or public filing if a substantive disclosure document meeting standards of a state requiring registration is provided to each purchaser before sale; or (iii) exclusively to accredited investors pursuant to state law exemptions that permit general solicitation and advertising.	No general solicitation permitted	No general solicitation permitted	Offering must be made under (a) a written compensatory benefit plan of issuer, its parent or majority-owned subsidiaries or (b) a written compensatory contract with issuer.	Unlimited accredited only	Unlimited

a. This chart prepared by the SEC has been updated to reflect later developments

Comparative Chart of Securities Act Limited Offering Exemptions and Alternatives—Continued

Comparison Item	Rule 504	Rule 505	Rule 506	Rule 701	Sec. 4(6)	Reg. A
Limitations on Resale	Restricted, unless sales made pursuant to Rule 504(b), as described above	Restricted	Restricted	Restricted as defined in Rule 144(a)(3). Ninety days after issuer becomes a reporting company (1) nonaffiliates of issuer may resell securities without compliance with paragraphs (c), (d), (e) and (h) and (2) affiliates may resell without compliance with paragraph (d).	Restricted	No restrictions
Issuer Qualification	Not available for reporting companies, investment companies or "development stage companies" lacking "specific business or purpose" or having only a plan to engage in a merger or mergers.	No investment companies or issuers disqualified under Reg. A	None	No reporting or investment companies	Accredited investors (Rule 215) including investment companies	Only U.S. and Canadian issuers. No investment companies or oil and gas rights. No issuers or underwriters disqualified under Reg. A.
Notice of Sale	Form D required—5 copies filed with SEC 15 days after first sale.	Same as Rule 504	Same as Rule 504	Form 701 required as condition of exemption—6 copies filed with SEC within 30 days after first sale that brings aggregate sales above $100,000 and thereafter within 30 days of end of issuer's fiscal year.	Same as Rule 504	Form 1-A: 5 copies to Regional Office 10 days before offering. Sales material—4 copies filed 5 days before use.
Information Requirements	No information specified	1. If purchased solely by accredited, no information specified		None other than requirement to furnish a copy of a compensatory benefit plan to each participant in the plan and a copy of any written compensatory contract to the counterparty.	No information specified	Offering Circular—See Rule 256

Comparative Chart of Securities Act Limited Offering Exemptions and Alternatives—Continued

Comparison Item	Rule 504	Rule 505	Rule 506	Rule 701	Sec. 4(6)	Reg. A
		2. If purchased by non-accredited: a. Non-reporting issuers must furnish i. Offerings up to $2 million—(A) *Non-financial information:* If the issuer is eligible to use Regulation A, then the same kind of information as is required in Part II of Form 1-A. If not eligible to use Regulation A, then the same kind of information as is required in Part I of a registration statement for which the issuer is eligible; (B) *Financial information:* (1) offerings up to $2 million: the financial statements required by Item 310 of Regulation S–B, except that if undue effort or expense would be required, in the case of issuers other than limited partnerships, only the issuer's balance sheet must be audited, which must be as of a date within 120 days of the offering's start. ii. Offerings up to $7.5 million—Information required in Form SB–2, except that if undue effort or expense would be required, in the case of issuers other than limited partnerships, only the issuer's balance sheet must be audited, which shall be dated within 120 days of offering's start.				

Comparative Chart of Securities Act Limited Offering Exemptions and Alternatives—Continued

Comparison Item	Rule 504	Rule 505	Rule 506	Rule 701	Sec. 4(6)	Reg. A

		iii. Offerings over $7.5 million—Information in Part I of available registration statement—if undue effort or expense, issuers other than limited partnerships only balance sheet as of 120 days before offering must be audited—if limited partnership and undue effort or expense, financials may be tax basis
		b. Reporting issuers must furnish
		  i. Rule 14a-3 or 14c-3 annual report to shareholders, def. proxy statement and 10-K, if requested, plus subsequent reports and other updating information, or
		  ii. information in more recent Form S-1 or Form 10-K plus subsequent reports and other updating information
		c. Issuers must make available prior to sale
		  i. exhibits
		  ii. written information given accredited investors
		  iii. opportunity to ask questions and receive answers				

Comparative Chart of Securities Act Limited Offering Exemptions and Alternatives—Continued

Comparison Item	Section 3(a)(11)	Rule 147
Dollar Ceiling	Unlimited	Unlimited
Number of Investors	All offerees and purchasers must be "residents" of state of issuer; no maximum number	Same as § 3(a)(11)
Investor Qualification	No qualifications or numerical limits other than "residence"	Same as § 3(a)(11)
Commissions	Permitted	Permitted
Limitations on Manner of Offering	Advertising and general solicitation within offering state permitted	Same as § 3(a)(11)
Limitation on Resale	Resales permitted to in-state residents; resales by nonaffiliates to out-of-state residents permitted 12 mo. after last offer or sale	Resales permitted to in-state residents; No resales by nonaffiliates to out-of-state residents until 9 mo. after last offer or sale
Issuer Qualification	Issuer must be organized and doing business in state where securities sold	Issuers only (no resales); issuer must be organized and doing business in state where securities sold (at least 80% of assets, sales, etc.) and 80% of proceeds expended
Notice of Sale	None required	None required
Information Requirements	None required	None required

Securities Act Release No. 6455ª

Securities and Exchange Commission.
March 3, 1983.

Interpretive Release on Regulation D

* * *

1. General

The definition of "accredited investor" includes any person who comes within or "who the issuer reasonably believes" comes within one of the enumerated categories "at the time of the sale of the securities to that person." What constitutes "reasonable" belief will depend on the facts of each particular case. For this reason, the staff generally will not be in a position to express views or otherwise endorse any one method for ascertaining whether an investor is accredited.

(1) *Question:* A director of a corporate issuer purchases securities offered under Rule 505. Two weeks after the purchase, and prior to completion of the offering, the director resigns due to a sudden illness. Is the former director an accredited investor?

Answer: Yes. The preliminary language to Rule 501(a) provides that an investor is accredited if he falls into one of the enumerated categories "at the time of the sale of securities to that person." One such category includes directors of the issuer. *See* Rule 501(a)(4). The investor in this case had that status at the time of the sale to him.

2. Certain Institutional Investors—Rules 501(a)(1)–(3)

(2) *Question:* A national bank purchases $100,000 of securities from a Regulation D issuer and distributes the securities equally among ten trust accounts for which it acts as trustee. Is the bank an accredited investor?

Answer: Yes. Rule 501(a)(1) accredits a bank acting in a fiduciary capacity.

(3) *Question:* An ERISA employee benefit plan will purchase $200,000 of the securities being offered. The plan has less than $5,000,000 in total assets and its investment decisions are made by a plan trustee who is not a bank, insurance company, or registered investment adviser. Does the plan qualify as an accredited investor?

Answer: Not under Rule 501(a)(1). Rule 501(a)(1) accredits an ERISA plan that has a plan fiduciary which is a bank, insurance company, or registered investment adviser or that has total assets in excess of $5,000,000. [Nor can the plan qualify as an accredited investor under Rules 501(a)(5) or (6). They apply only to natural persons, not juristic persons.] * * *

(4) *Question:* A state run, not-for-profit hospital has total assets in excess of $5,000,000. Because it is a state agency, the hospital is exempt from federal income taxation. Rule 501(a)(3) accredits any organization described in section 501(c)(3) of the Internal Revenue Code that has total assets in excess of $5,000,000. Is the hospital accredited under Rule 501(a)(3)?

a. This Release has been updated to reflect additions and amendments to Regulation D after March 3, 1983.

Answer: Yes. This category does not require that the investor have received a ruling on tax status under section 501(c)(3) of the Internal Revenue Code. Rather, Rule 501(a)(3) accredits an investor that falls within the substantive description in that section.

(5) *Question:* A not-for-profit, tax exempt hospital with total assets of $3,000,000 is purchasing $100,000 of securities in a Regulation D offering. The hospital controls a subsidiary with total assets of $3,000,000. Under generally accepted accounting principles, the hospital may combine its financial statements with that of its subsidiary. Is the hospital accredited?

Answer: Yes, under Rule 501(a)(3). Where the financial statements of the subsidiary may be combined with those of the investor, the assets of the subsidiary may be added to those of the investor in computing total assets for purposes of Rule 501(a)(3).

3. Insiders—Rule 501(a)(4)

(6) *Question:* The executive officer of a parent of the corporate general partner of the issuer is investing in the Regulation D offering. Is that individual an accredited investor?

Answer: Rule 501(a)(4) accredits only the directors and executive officers of the general partner itself. Unless the executive officer of the parent can be deemed an executive officer of the subsidiary, that individual is not an accredited investor.

* * *

5. Natural Persons—Rules 501(a)(5)–(6)

Rules 501(a)(5) and (6) apply only to natural persons. Paragraph (5) accredits any natural person with a net worth at the time of purchase in excess of $1,000,000. If the investor is married, the rule permits the use of joint net worth of the couple. Paragraph (6) accredits any natural person whose income has exceeded $200,000 [or joint income with the person's spouse in excess of $300,000] in each of the two most recent years and is reasonably expected to [reach the same income level in the current year.]

(20) *Question:* A corporation with a net worth of $2,000,000 purchases securities in a Regulation D offering. Is the corporation an accredited investor under Rule 501(a)(5)?

Answer: No. Rule 501(a)(5) is limited to "natural" persons.

(21) *Question:* In calculating net worth for purposes of Rule 501(a)(5), may the investor include the estimated fair market value of his principal residence as an asset?

Answer: Yes. Rule 501(a)(5) does not exclude any of the purchaser's assets from the net worth needed to qualify as an accredited investor.

(22) *Question:* May a purchaser take into account income of a spouse in determining possible accreditation under Rule 501(a)(6)?

[*Answer:* Yes. An individual who had net income in excess of $200,000 in each of the most recent years *or* joint income with that person's spouse in excess of $300,000 in each of those years and has reasonable expectation of reaching the same income level in the current year qualifies as an accredited investor.]

(23) *Question:* May a purchaser include unrealized capital appreciation in calculating income for purposes of Rule 501(a)(6)?

Answer: Generally, no.

6. Entities Owned By Accredited Investors—Rule 501(a)(8)

Any entity in which all equity owners are accredited investors under any of the qualifying categories is accredited under Rule 501(a)(8).

(24) *Question:* All but one of the shareholders of a corporation are accredited investors by virtue of net worth or income. The unaccredited shareholder is a director who bought one share of stock in order to comply with a requirement that all directors be shareholders of the corporation. Is the corporation an accredited investor under Rule 501(a)(8)?

Answer: No. Rule 501(a)(8) requires "all of the equity owners" to be accredited investors. The director is an equity owner and is not accredited. Note that the director cannot be accredited under Rule 501(a)(4). That provision extends accreditation to a director of the issuer, not of the investor.

(25) *Question:* Who are the equity owners of a limited partnership?

Answer: The limited partners.

7. Trusts as Accredited Investors

(26) *Question:* May a trust qualify as an accredited investor under Rule 501(a)(1)?

Answer: Only indirectly. Although a trust standing alone cannot be accredited under Rule 501(a)(1), if a bank is its trustee and makes the investment on behalf of the trust, the trust will in effect be accredited by virtue of the provision in Rule 501(a)(1) that accredits a bank acting in a fiduciary capacity.

(27) *Question:* May a trust qualify as an accredited investor under Rule 501(a)(7)?

Answer: Yes [, but only if it has total assets in excess of $5,000,000, and is not formed for the specific purpose of acquiring the securities offered, whose purchase is directed by a sophisticated person, as described in Rule 506(b)(2)(ii).]

* * *

(29) *Question:* A trustee of a trust has a net worth of $1,500,000. Is the trustee's purchase of securities for the trust that of an accredited investor under Rule 501(a)(5)?

Answer: No. Except where a bank is a trustee, the trust is deemed the purchaser, not the trustee. The trust is not a "natural" person.

(30) *Question:* May a trust be accredited under Rule 501(a)(8) if all of its beneficiaries are accredited investors?

Answer: Generally, no. Rule 501(a)(8) accredits any entity if all of its "equity owners" are accredited investors. The staff does not interpret this provision to apply to the beneficiaries of a conventional trust. The result may be different, however, in the case of certain non-conventional trusts where, as a result of powers retained by the grantors, a trust as a legal entity would be deemed not to exist. Thus, where the grantors of a revocable trust are accredited investors under Rule 501(a)(5) (*i.e.* net worth exceeds $1,000,000) and the trust may be amended or revoked at any time by the grantors, the trust is accredited because the grantors will be deemed the equity owners of the trust's assets. Similarly, where the purchase of Regulation D securities is made by an Individual

Retirement Account and the participant is an accredited investor, the account would be accredited under Rule 501(a)(8).

B. Aggregate Offering Price—Rule 501(c)

The "aggregate offering price," defined in Rule 501(c), is the sum of all proceeds received by the issuer for issuance of its securities. The term is important to the operation of Rules 504 and 505, both of which impose a limitation on the aggregate offering price as a specific condition to the availability of the exemption.

(31) *Question:* The sole general partner of a real estate limited partnership contributes property to the program. Must that property be valued and included in the overall proceeds of the offering as part of the aggregate offering price?

Answer: No, assuming the property is contributed in exchange for a general partnership interest.

    * * *

(33) *Question:* Where the investors pay for their securities in installments and these payments include an interest component, must the issuer include interest payments in the "aggregate offering price?"

Answer: No. The interest payments are not deemed to be consideration for the issuance of the securities.

(34) *Question:* An offering of interests in an oil and gas limited partnership provides for additional voluntary assessments. These assessments, undetermined at the time of the offering, may be called at the general partner's discretion for developmental drilling activities. Must the assessments be included in the aggregate offering price, and if so, in what amount?

Answer: Because it is unclear that the assessments will ever be called, and because if they are called, it is unclear at what level, the issuer is not required to include the assessments in the aggregate offering price. In fact, the assessments will be consideration received for the issuance of additional securities in the limited partnership. This issuance will need to be considered along with the original issuance for possible integration, or, if not integrated, must find its own exemption from registration.

(35) *Question:* In purchasing interests in an oil and gas partnership, investors agree to pay mandatory assessments. The assessments, essentially installment payments, are non-contingent and investors will be personally liable for their payment. Must the issuer include the assessments in the aggregate offering price?

    * * *

Answer: Yes.

C. Executive Officer—Rule 501(f)

The definition of executive officer in Rule 501(f) is the same as that in Rule 405 of Regulation C.

(37) *Question:* The executive officer of the parent of the Regulation D issuer performs a policy making function for its subsidiary. May that individual be deemed an "executive officer" of the subsidiary?

Answer: Yes.

D.   Purchaser Representative—Rule 501(h)

A purchaser representative is any person who satisfies, or who the issuer reasonably believes satisfies, four conditions enumerated in Rule 501(h). Beyond the obligations imposed by that rule, any person acting as a purchaser representative must consider whether or not he is required to register as a broker-dealer under section 15 of the Securities Exchange Act of 1934 or as an investment adviser under section 203 of the Investment Advisers Act of 1940.

(38) *Question:* May the officer of a corporate general partner of the issuer qualify as a purchaser representative under Rule 501(h)?

Answer: Rule 501(h) provides that "an affiliate, director, officer or other employee of the issuer" may not be a purchaser representative unless the purchaser has one of three enumerated relationships with the representative. The staff is of the view that an officer or director of a corporate general partner comes within the scope of "affiliate, director, officer or other employee of the issuer."

(39) *Question:* May the issuer in a Regulation D offering pay the fees of the purchaser representative?

Answer: Yes. Nothing in Regulation D prohibits the payment by the issuer of the purchaser representative's fees. Rule 501(h)(4), however, requires disclosure of this fact.

II.   *Disclosure Requirements—Rule 502(b)*

A.   When Required

Rule 502(b)(1) sets forth the circumstances when disclosure of the kind specified in the regulation must be delivered to investors. The regulation requires the delivery of certain information [to the purchaser "at a reasonable time] prior to sale" if the offering is conducted in reliance on Rule 505 or 506 and if there are unaccredited investors. If the offering is conducted in compliance with Rule 504 or if securities are sold only to accredited investors, Regulation D does not specify the information that must be disclosed to investors.

(40) *Question:* An issuer furnishes potential investors a short form offering memorandum in anticipation of actual selling activities and the delivery of an expanded disclosure document. Does Regulation D permit the delivery of disclosure in two installments?

Answer: So long as all the information is delivered prior to sale, the use of a fair and adequate summary followed by a complete disclosure document is not prohibited under Regulation D. Disclosure in such a manner, however, should not obscure material information.

(41) *Question:* An issuer commences an offering in reliance on Rule 505 in which the issuer intends to make sales only to accredited investors. The issuer delivers those investors an abbreviated disclosure document. Before the completion of the offering, the issuer changes its intentions and proposes to make sales to non-accredited investors. Would the requirement that the issuer deliver the specified information to all purchasers prior to sale if any sales are made to non-accredited investors preclude application of Rule 505 to the earlier sales to the accredited investors?

Answer: No. If the issuer delivers a complete disclosure document to the accredited investors and agrees to return their funds promptly unless they should elect to remain in the program, the issuer would not be precluded from relying on Rule 505.

B.   What Required

Regulation D divides disclosure into two categories: that to be furnished by non-reporting companies and that required for reporting companies. In either case, the specified disclosure is required to the extent material to an understanding of the issuer, its business and the securities being offered.

* * *

2.   Reporting Issuers—Rule 502(b)(2)(ii)

If the issuer is subject to the reporting requirements of section 13 or 15(d) of the Exchange Act, Regulation D sets forth two alternatives for disclosure: the issuer may deliver certain recent Exchange Act reports (the annual report, the definitive proxy statement, and, if requested, the Form 10–K) or it may provide a document containing the same information as in the Form 10–K or Form 10 under the Exchange Act or in a registration statement under the Securities Act. In either case the rule also calls for the delivery of certain supplemental information.

(50) *Question:* Rule 502(b)(2)(ii)(B) refers to the information contained "in a registration statement on Form S–1." Does this requirement envision delivery of Parts I and II of the Form S–1?

Answer: No. Rule 502(b)(2)(ii)(B) should be construed to mean Part I of Form S–1.

(51) *Question:* A reporting company with a fiscal year ending on December 31 is making a Regulation D offering in February. It does not have an annual report to shareholders, an associated definitive proxy statement, or a Form 10–K for its most recently completed fiscal year. The issuer's last registration statement was filed more than two years ago. What is the appropriate disclosure under Regulation D?

Answer: The issuer may base its disclosure on the most recently completed fiscal year for which an annual report to shareholders or Form 10–K was timely distributed or filed. The issuer should supplement the information in the report used with the information contained in any reports or documents required to be filed under sections 13(a), 14(a), 14(c) and 15(d) of the Exchange Act since the distribution or filing of that report and with a brief description of the securities being offered, the use of the proceeds from the offering, and any material changes in the issuer's affairs that are not disclosed in the documents furnished.

* * *

III.   *Operational Conditions*

A.   Integration—Rule 502(a)

* * *

(53) *Question:* An issuer conducts offering (A) under Rule 504 of Regulation D that concludes in January. Seven months later the issuer commences offering (B) under Rule 506. During that seven month period the issuer's only offers or sales of securities are under an employee benefit plan (C). Must the issuer integrate (A) and (B)?

Answer: No. Rule 502(a) specifically provides that (A) and (B) will not be integrated. [See also Rule 701(b)(6).]

B.   Calculation of the Number of Purchasers—Rule 501(e)

Rule 501(e) governs the calculation of the number of purchasers in offerings that rely either on Rule 505 or 506. Both of these rules limit the number of non-accredited investors to 35. Rule 501(e) has [three] parts. The first excludes certain purchasers from the calculation. The second establishes basic principles for counting of corporations, partnerships, or other entities. [The third concerns non-contributory employee benefit plans within the meaning of ERISA. Such plans are to be counted as one purchaser where the trustee makes all investment decisions for the plan.]

(54) *Question:* One purchaser in a Rule 506 offering is an accredited investor. Another is a first cousin of that investor sharing the same principal residence. Each purchaser is making his own investment decision. How must the issuer count these purchasers for purposes of meeting the 35 purchaser limitation?

Answer: The issuer is not required to count either investor. The accredited investor may be excluded under Rule 501(e)(1)(iv), and the first cousin may then be excluded under Rule 501(e)(1)(i).

(55) *Question:* An accredited investor in a Rule 506 offering will have the securities she acquires placed in her name and that of her spouse. The spouse will not make an investment decision with respect to the acquisition. How many purchasers will be involved?

Answer: The accredited investor may be excluded from the count under Rule 501(e)(1)(iv) and the spouse may be excluded under Rule 501(e)(1)(i). The issuer may also take the position, however, that the spouse should not be deemed a purchaser at all because he did not make any investment decision, and because the placement of the securities in joint name may simply be a tax or estate planning technique.

(56) *Question:* An offering is conducted in the United States under Rule 505. At the same time certain sales are made overseas. Must the foreign investors be included in calculating the number of purchasers?

Answer: Offers and sales of securities to foreign persons made outside the United States in such a way that the securities come to rest abroad generally do not need to be registered under the Act. This basis for non-registration is separate from Regulation D and offers and sales relying on this interpretation are not required to be integrated with a coincident domestic offering. Thus, assuming the sales in this question rely on this interpretation, foreign investors would not be counted. [See also, Regulation D, preliminary Note 7 and Regulation S.]

(57) *Question:* An investor in a Rule 506 offering is a general partnership that was not organized for the specific purpose of acquiring the securities offered. The partnership has ten partners, five of whom do not qualify as accredited investors. The partnership will make an investment of $100,000. How is the partnership counted and must the issuer make any findings as to the sophistication of the individual partners?

Answer: Rule 501(e)(2) provides that the partnership shall be counted as one purchaser. The issuer is not obligated to consider the sophistication of each individual partner.

* * *

(59) *Question:* An investor in a Rule 506 offering is an investment partnership that is not accredited under Rule 501(a)(8). Although the partnership was organized two years earlier and has made investments in a number of offerings, not all the partners have participated in each investment. With each proposed investment by the partnership, individual partners have received a copy of the disclosure document and have made a decision whether or not to participate. How do the provisions of Regulation D apply to the partnership as an investor?

Answer: The partnership may not be treated as a single purchaser. Rule 501(e)(2) provides that if the partnership is organized for the specific purpose of acquiring the securities offered, then each beneficial owner of equity interests should be counted as a separate purchaser. Because the individual partners elect whether or not to participate in each investment, the partnership is deemed to be reorganized for the specific purpose of acquiring the securities in each investment. Thus, the issuer must look through the partnership to the partners participating in the investment. The issuer must satisfy the conditions of Rule 506 as to each partner.

C. Manner of Offering—Rule 502(c)

  * * *

In analyzing what constitutes a general solicitation, the staff considered a solicitation by the general partner of a limited partnership to limited partners in other active programs sponsored by the same general partner. In determining that this did not constitute a general solicitation the Division underscored the existence and substance of the pre-existing business relationship between the general partner and those being solicited. The general partner represented that it believed each of the solicitees had such knowledge and experience in financial and business matters that he or she was capable of evaluating the merits and risks of the prospective investment. * * *

In analyzing whether or not an issuer was using a general advertisement to offer or sell securities, the staff declined to express an opinion on a proposed tombstone advertisement that would announce the completion of an offering. *See* letter re *Alma Securities Corporation* dated July 2, 1982. Because the requesting letter did not describe the proposed use of the tombstone announcement and because the announcement of the completion of one offering could be an indirect solicitation for a new offering, the staff did not express a view. In a letter re *Tax Investment Information Corporation* dated January 7, 1983, the staff considered whether the publication of a circular analyzing private placement offerings, where the publisher was independent from the issuers and the offerings being analyzed, would violate Rule 502(c). Although Regulation D does not directly prohibit such a third party publication, the staff refused to agree that such a publication would be permitted under Regulation D because of its susceptibility to use by participants in an offering. Finally, in the letter re *Aspen Grove* dated November 8, 1982 the staff expressed the view that the proposed distribution of a promotional brochure to the members of the "Thoroughbred Owners and Breeders Association" and at an annual sale for horse owners and the proposed use of a magazine advertisement for an offering of interests in a limited partnership would not comply with Rule 502(c).

(60) *Question:* If a solicitation were limited to accredited investors, would it be deemed in compliance with Rule 502(c)?

Answer: The mere fact that a solicitation is directed only to accredited investors will not mean that the solicitation is in compliance with Rule 502(c). Rule 502(c) relates to the nature of the offering not the nature of the offerees.

D.   Limitations on Resale—Rule 502(d)

Rule 502(d) makes it clear that Regulation D securities have limitations on transferability and requires that the issuer take certain precautions to restrict the transferability of the securities.

(61) *Question:* An investor in a Regulation D offering wishes to resell his securities within a year after the offering. The issuer has agreed to register the securities for resale. Will the proposed resale under the registration statement violate Rule 502(d)?

Answer: No. The function of Rule 502(d) is to restrict the unregistered resale of securities. Where the resale will be registered, however, such restrictions are unnecessary.

IV.   *Exemptions*

A.   Rule 504

Rule 504 is an exemption under section 3(b) of the Securities Act available to non-reporting and non-investment companies for offerings not in excess of $1,000,000.

(62) *Question:* A foreign issuer proposes to use Rule 504. The issuer is not subject to section 15(d) and its securities are exempt from registration under Rule 12g3–2. May this issuer use Rule 504?

Answer: Yes.

(63) *Question:* An issuer proposes to make an offering under Rule 504 in two states. The offering will be registered in one state and the issuer will deliver a disclosure document pursuant to the state's requirements. The offering will be made pursuant to an exemption from registration in the second state. Must the offering satisfy the limitations on the manner of offering and on resale in paragraphs (c) and (d) of Rule 502?

Answer: Yes. An offering under Rule 504 is exempted from the manner of sale and resale limitations only if it is registered in *each* state in which it is conducted and only if a disclosure document is required by state law.

(64) *Question:* The state in which the offering will take place provides for "qualification" of any offer or sale of securities. The state statute also provides that the securities commissioner may condition qualification of an offering on the delivery of a disclosure document prior to sale. Would the issuer be making its offering in a state that "provides for registration of the securities and requires the delivery of a disclosure document before sale" if its offering were qualified in this state on the condition that it deliver a disclosure document before sale to each investor?

Answer: Yes.

(65) *Question:* If an issuer is registering securities at the state level, are there any specific requirements as to resales outside of that state if the issuer is attempting to come within the provision in Rule 504 that waives the limitations on the manner of offering and on resale in Rules 502(c) and (d)?

Answer: No. The issuer, however, must intend to use Rule 504 to make bona fide sales in that state and not to evade the policy of Rule 504 by using sales in one state as a conduit for sales into another state. *See* Preliminary Note 6 to Regulation D.

B.   Rule 505

Rule 505 provides an exemption under section 3(b) of the Securities Act for non-investment companies for offerings not in excess of $5,000,000.

(66) *Question:* An issuer is a broker that was censured pursuant to a Commission order. Does the censure bar the issuer from using Rule 505?

Answer: No. Rule 505 is not available to any issuer who falls within the disqualifications for the use of Regulation A. *See* Rule 505(b)(2)(iii). One such disqualification occurs when the issuer is subject to a Commission order under section 15(b) of the Exchange Act. A censure has no continuing force and thus the issuer is not subject to an order of the Commission.

C.   Questions Relating to Rules 504 and 505

Both Rules 504(b)(2)(i) and 505(b)(2)(i) require that the offering not exceed a specified aggregate offering price. The allowed aggregate offering price, however, is reduced by the aggregate offering price for all securities sold within the last twelve months in reliance on section 3(b) or in violation of section 5(a) of the Securities Act.

(67) *Question:* An issuer preparing to conduct an offering of equity securities under Rule 505 raised $2,000,000 from the sale of debt instruments under Rule 505 eight months earlier. How much may the issuer raise in the proposed equity offering?

Answer: $3,000,000. A specific condition to the availability of Rule 505 for the proposed offering is that its aggregate offering price not exceed $5,000,000 less the proceeds for *all* securities sold under section 3(b) within the last 12 months.

(68) *Question:* An issuer is planning a Rule 505 offering. Ten months earlier the issuer conducted a Rule 506 offering. Must the issuer consider the previous Rule 506 offering when calculating the allowable aggregate offering price for the proposed Rule 505 offering?

Answer: No. The Commission issued Rule 506 under section 4(2), and Rule 505(b)(2)(i) requires that the aggregate offering price be reduced by previous sales under section 3(b).

(69) *Question:* Seven months before a proposed Rule 504 offering the issuer conducted a rescission offer under Rule 504. The rescission offer was for securities that were sold in violation of section 5 more than 12 months before the proposed Rule 504 offering. Must the aggregate offering price for the proposed Rule 504 offering be reduced either by the amount of the rescission offer or the earlier offering in violation of section 5?

Answer: No. The offering in violation of section 5 took place more than 12 months earlier and thus is not required to be included when satisfying the limitation in Rule 504(b)(2)(i). The staff is of the view that the rescission offer relates back to the earlier offering and therefore should not be included as an adjustment to the aggregate offering price for the proposed Rule 504 offering.

(70) *Question:* Rules 504 and 505 contain examples as to the calculation of the allowed aggregate offering price for a particular offering. Do these examples contemplate integration of the offerings described?

Answer: No. The examples have been provided to demonstrate the operation of the limitation on the aggregate offering price in the absence of any integration questions.

(71) *Question:* Note 2 to Rule 504 is not restated in Rule 505. Does the principle of the note apply to Rule 505?

Answer: Yes. Note 2 to Rule 504 sets forth a general principle to the operation of the rule on limiting the aggregate offering price which is the same for both Rules 504 and 505. It provides that if, as a result of one offering, an issuer exceeds the allowed aggregate offering price in a subsequent unintegrated offering, the exemption for the first offering will not be affected.

* * *

INTERPRETATIONS OF "GENERAL SOLICITATION" UNDER REGULATION D

Section 502(c) limits the manner in which securities may be offered or sold pursuant to Regulation D. First, there must be a determination as to whether a communication constitutes a form of general solicitation or general advertising. Second, it must be determined whether the communication is being used by the issuer, or any person acting on its behalf, to offer to sell securities.

The Division of Corporation Finance has issued a number of interpretive letters addressing these questions. In E.F. Hutton & Company, avail. in LEXIS (Dec. 3, 1985), Hutton established procedures under which Regulation D offerings would be made only (1) to persons who have within the last three years invested in limited partnerships sponsored or sold by them, and (2) to persons who had satisfactorily responded to a suitability questionnaire and a new account form. A suitability questionnaire and new account form dated within 12 months of the offer which indicated that the person was presently qualified to purchase in a private placement also was required of prior customers. Offering materials were to be then sent only to a small percentage of eligible individuals.

The Division stated that the avoidance of a general solicitation depends upon the substance of prior relationships between the issuer and its agents and those persons being solicited. Although there is no requirement of a preexisting relationship, it is an important factor in showing that there is no public solicitation. On the facts presented, the Division concurred in the view that substantive relationships had been created between Hutton and the previous public and private investors, even though some offerees had not previously invested in securities offered by Hutton.

When the solicitation has been broader, and with only a general economic or professional status being used to filter out the general public, the Commission's attitude has been to find a general solicitation. For example, in In the Matter of Kenman Corp.,[1] a broker dealer solicited investors for a limited partnership offering, in part by using (1) a list of officers at 50 Fortune 500 companies, (2) a list of physicians in the State of California, and (3) a list of persons who had previously invested $10,000 or more in real estate offerings syndicated by other broker-dealers, (4) a list of managerial employees at Hughes Aircraft Company, and (5) a list of company presidents of firms based in Morris County, New Jersey. On this basis, where neither the issuer nor the

---

1. See Sec.Exch.Act Rel. No. 21962 (Apr. 19, 1985).

broker had any prior relationship with the potential investors, and little, if anything, connected the persons on these lists, the Commission concluded that a general solicitation had occurred.

Courts have had little difficulty in finding a mass mailing of a "confidential memorandum" to 2,500 persons to constitute a general solicitation.[2] Grayer issues emerge when a communication describing an offering is sent to a smaller and more targeted audience. The SEC's staff attempts to distinguish "limited" from "general" communications in terms of whether the issuer or its agent had some preexisting relationship with the recipient of the communication. The importance of such a relationship in the Staff's mind is that it enables the issuer or broker-dealer "to be aware of the financial circumstances or sophistication of the persons with whom the relationship exists . . ."[3]

Read literally, Rule 502(c) prohibits only general solicitation activities by the issuer or any person acting on its behalf. But what if a third party publishes a newsletter that describes and discusses all forthcoming private placements? One SEC no-action letter has addressed such a case and found a general solicitation to have occurred, but the critical fact may have been that the issuers prepared the materials that were used in this newsletter and paid for their publication.[4] A different result has been reached in the case of matching services, which are paid by both the investor and the entrepreneur to advise each of transactions or investors who meet their stated criteria. In a 1994 no-action letter, the staff found that a general solicitation had not occurred where a nonprofit corporation maintained a computerized data base that sought to match investors with investment opportunities that satisfied their stated criteria.[5] This system, however, did not inform the issuers of the names of potential investors, but only notified the investors of the forthcoming offerings that seemed of interest to them. Also, all investors were required to represent that they were accredited investors or otherwise experienced in financial matters.

Logically, it is but a small leap from such a computerized databank to the Internet. Initially, however, the SEC seemed skeptical about any use of the Internet to reach investors. In an important 1995 release, it said:

> "The placing of [offering] materials on the Internet would not be consistent with the prohibitions against general solicitation in Rule 502(c) of Regulation D."[6]

More recently, and after some prodding, the SEC's Staff has become more Internet-friendly. The critical step in this accommodation has been the develop-

---

2. See Johnston v. Bumba, 764 F.Supp. 1263 (N.D.Ill.1991).

3. See Mineral Lands Research & Marketing Corp., SEC No–Action Letter (Nov. 4, 1985). In this no-action request, an issuer proposed to offer securities to 600 persons who were clients of an insurance broker, who was an officer of the issuer. Because this prior relationship did not permit the insurance broker to evaluate the financial experience or sophistication of its clients, the staff concluded that it had an insufficient basis and record upon which to grant the requested no-action letter.

4. See J.D. Manning, Inc. SEC No–Action Letter (Jan. 29, 1986).

5. See Texas Capital Network, Inc., SEC No–Action Letter (Feb. 23, 1994); see also The Colorado Capital Alliance, Inc., SEC No–Action Letter, 1995 SEC No–Act. LEXIS 503 (May 4, 1995); Michigan Growth Capital Symposium, SEC No–Action Letter, 1995 SEC No–Act. LEXIS 499 (May 4, 1995) (University of Michigan annual symposium to match investors and entrepreneurs did not amount to a general solicitation).

6. See Sec.Act Rel. No. 7233, at example 20 (Oct. 13, 1995).

ment of a password protected procedure to qualify the potential offeree as an accredited investor before an offer is made.[7] Typically, a broker dealer or other agent of the issuer will place an investor questionnaire on its home page on the World Wide Web. Investors who complete this questionnaire will be evaluated to determine if they qualify as an accredited investor. If they do, they will be given a password that will enable them to review any current and future private placement offering materials which the broker dealer has prepared or is using. In effect, this new methodology permits a solicitation of accredited investors who volunteer to be solicited.

Some commentators have argued that the SEC's continued insistence in determining whether a general solicitation has occurred is inconsistent with Regulation D's primary emphasis on the sophistication of the actual purchasers.[8] To a degree, the SEC has listened. In 1987, it requested comment on whether it should narrow the scope of its prohibition on general solicitation,[9] and in 1992, it amended Regulation D to remove Rule 502(c)'s application to Rule 504 offerings. In 1995, the SEC indicated that it was thinking of removing or amending Rule 502(c) entirely. Instead, it adopted Regulation CE (Rule 1001), which applies only to California offerings. Still, more deregulatory action may be in the offing.[10]

RECENT DEVELOPMENTS UNDER REGULATION D

1. *The Sophistication Test.* Regulation D relaxed the standards applicable to the purchaser's qualifications by permitting the issuer to "reasonably believe immediately prior to making any sale that such purchaser" meets Rule 506's standard. What does this require? In Mark v. FSC Securities Corp.[1] the defendant broker dealer circulated a subscription letter to investors in which they were asked to represent that they had "sufficient knowledge in business affairs to enable ... [them] ... to evaluate the risks of the investment" and provided them with an offeree questionnaire in which they were to set forth their investment background. Although the Sixth Circuit acknowledged that a review of each executed subscription agreement could have provided the issuer with a "reasonable belief" sufficient to satisfy Rule 506, it found that simply a general awareness of these procedures and the investors' representations was insufficient. In short, evidence as to "the circumstances under which those sales were intended to have been made" was not enough.[2] Having shown nothing more, the issuer failed its burden of proving the exemption's availability.

2. *Rule 135c.* Rule 502(c) was amended in 1994 to provide "that publication by an issuer of a notice in accordance with Rule 135c shall not be deemed to constitute general advertising for purposes of this section." While this rule has very little relevance to the small business issuer, the public corporation

---

7. See IPONET SEC No–Action Letter, 1996 SEC No–Act. LEXIS 642 (July 26, 1996); see also Lamp Technologies, Inc. SEC No–Action Letter, 1997 SEC No–Act. LEXIS 638 (May 29, 1997).

8. See Daughterty, Rethinking the Ban on General Solicitation, 38 Emory L.J. 67, 127 (1989).

9. See Sec.Act.Rel. No. 6683 (Jan. 16, 1987).

10. See Sec.Act.Rel. No. 7285 (May 1, 1994) (Commission determined to defer "action on the general solicitation question"); Sec.Act.Rel. No. 7314 (July 25, 1994) (Commission requests comments on whether the general solicitation prohibitions should be scaled back).

1. 870 F.2d 331 (6th Cir.1989).

2. Id. at 337.

that intends to make an unregistered offering may now disclose its plans in approximately the same manner as it may disclose an intention to make a public offering under Rule 135.

3. *"Bad Boy" Disqualifiers.* If an issuer, including any predecessor or affiliate, or a director, general partner, or 10% shareholder of the issuer, or any underwriter has engaged in certain specified conduct that violates the federal securities laws, Rule 262 of Regulation A prohibits the issuer from utilizing Regulation A for a five year period thereafter (unless the SEC grants an exemption). Rule 505(b)(2)(iii) carries this same standard over to Rule 505, but there is no corresponding prohibition in the case of Rule 504 or 506. Why not? Is it because Rule 505 is the most logical alternative to Regulation A for those denied its availability under Rule 262?[3]

4. *Fraud and Rule 504.* Rule 504 has long been thought to invite fraud because uniquely it (1) permits issuers to sell freely tradeable securities, (2) to an unlimited number of purchasers, (3) through a general solicitation of investors. Hence, small, non-reporting "penny stock" issuers could market their offerings to the world under Rule 504 (up to a $1 million aggregate annual ceiling) and not experience the same liquidity discount that investors would impose on "restricted securities" sold under Rule 506 because in the latter case the securities could not be freely resold. After a series of fraudulent transactions involving "microcap companies" in the late 1990's, the SEC cracked down and in 1999 amended Rule 504 by conditioning the availability of Rule 504 for public offerings on the existence of state regulation over the offering.[4] Rule 504(b) now permits the issuer to escape the general solicitation prohibition of Rule 502(c) and the limitations on resale of Rule 502(d) only if the offering is made (i) exclusively in one or more states that provide for the registration of the securities under state law and require the public filing and delivery of a prospectus; (ii) in one or more states that do not provide for the registration of securities or the public filing and delivery of a prospectus, if the securities were registered in a state that did provide for such registration before sale and its disclosure document is delivered before sale to all purchasers (including those in states that have no such procedures); or (iii) exclusively pursuant to a state law exemption that permits general solicitation so long as sales are made only to "accredited investors" (as defined in Rule 501(a)). In so doing, the Commission backed off an earlier proposal that it had considered to make Rule 504 securities "restricted securities"—and thus not freely tradeable. It justified its compromise as "an effective way to combat the abuses we have described and at the same time preserve the ability of legitimate small businesses to raise capital."[5] Had the Commission restricted resales under Rule 504, it feared (and many smaller firms protested) that their securities could only be marketed at a significant discount below the prices that could be obtained if the securities were freely tradeable. If the Rule 504 issuer does not register its securities in a qualifying state,[6] it can still use Rule 504, but may not make a general solicitation and must advise purchasers that they are purchasing "restricted securities."

3. See Sec.Act.Rel. No. 6683 (Jan. 16, 1987).

4. See Securities Act Release 7644 (February 25, 1999).

5. *Id.*

6. The vast majority of states require registration of Rule 504 offerings. However, New York and the District of Columbia do not. *Id.* at n. 12.

5. *Rule 503.* Initially, Regulation D's availability was expressly conditioned upon the filing of a Form D within fifteen days after the first sale of securities under Regulation D. In 1989, the commission adopted Rule 507 and simultaneously changed the language of Rule 503. The net effect is that Regulation D's availability is now denied by Rule 507 for a failure to file Form D only if there has been an injunction enjoining the issuer (or a predecessor or affiliate) "for failure to comply with Rule 503." Even then, the issuer can seek relief from the Commission "upon a showing of good cause" that the exemption should not be denied.

Was it the purpose of this amendment to protect the issuer simply from an arbitrary penalty if its filing of Form D was a day or two late? Or, is the filing today effectively optional, unless the SEC decides that the issuer's conduct was egregious? Note that the SEC has proposed eliminating the filing requirement under Form D.[7] Suppose an issuer resists filing Form D because it does not wish to alert the SEC to its unregistered offering? What would you advise? Is the issuer's conduct unlawful or merely inadvisable? Remember that Regulation D is only a safe harbor, and the issuer can still rely on § 4(2) if it is willing to accept the burden of proving that all offerees were qualified.

6. *Rule 508.* Should your answer to the preceding question be influenced by Rule 508, which codifies an "innocent and immaterial" defense to asserted violations of Regulation D? This defense had long been resisted by the SEC's Staff, before it was finally adopted in 1989.[8] Note that the conditions in Regulation D relating to dollar ceilings, numerical purchaser limits, and general solicitation are expressly placed beyond the scope of this defense. As a result, such errors or misjudgments can seemingly never be deemed immaterial. Does this imply that other conditions are secondary in importance?

SECTION 2.   REGULATION A OFFERINGS

Statutes and Regulations

Securities Act § 3(b).

Regulation A and Forms.

In 1992, as part of a program to facilitate capital formation by small businesses, the Commission amended Regulation A (Rules 251 to 263) to increase the aggregate offering price ceiling under Regulation A from $1.5 million to $5 million. Overnight, this made Regulation A a highly competitive alternative to Rule 505 under Regulation D. One advantage of Regulation A over Regulation D is that securities issued under Regulation A are not "restricted securities" and thus can be freely resold. In addition, Regulation A can be used for secondary offerings by existing security holders, up to a maximum of $1.5 million in any 12 month period.[1] However, affiliate resales are not

---

7. See Sec.Act.Rel. No. 7301 (May 31, 1996).

8. See Sec.Act.Rel. No. 6825 (March 14, 1989).

1. See Rule 251(b).

permitted "if the issuer has not had income from continuing operations in at least one of the last two fiscal years."[2]

Regulation A is not available to reporting companies, "blank check" development companies, investment companies, and certain issuers who have been enjoined, convicted, or disciplined for certain specified offenses within the past five years.[3] In contrast, Rule 505 is available to some of these companies, and Rule 506 is available to all of them.

Among practitioners, Regulation A is commonly viewed as a form of "mini-registration," closer to Form SB–1 for small business issuers than to a private placement brochure. Rule 252 requires the issuer to file a scaled-down disclosure document (known as an offering statement (Form 1–A)) with the SEC, which can comment upon and effectively require revisions before the document can be used. However, Form 1–A is not a registration statement for purposes of § 11 of the 1933 Act. Although its format resembles that of a registration statement, the offering statement need not contain audited financial statements (unless the issuer has audited financial statements). Just as the registration statement contains a prospectus, so does the offering statement contain a component, known as the offering circular, which must be provided to prospective purchasers.[4] The same procedure for delaying amendments (or a 20 day waiting period if no delaying notation is placed on the offering statement) is built into Regulation A offerings, as is followed in registered offerings as a result of § 8(a) of the 1933 Act.[5] The major procedural difference is largely semantic: an offering statement does not become "effective"; rather, it is deemed to have been "qualified". Nonetheless, the same "red herring" legend must appear on the cover page of the offering circular as appears on the prospectus.[6]

In 1992, the Commission did introduce one new procedure applicable to date only to Regulation A offerings. Under Rule 254, prior to the filing of any offering statement, an issuer may "test the waters" by publishing or disseminating to prospective investors a written document (or T.V. or radio script) "to determine whether there is any interest in a contemplated securities offering."[7] Thereafter, oral communications with investors are also permitted (otherwise, offers can only be made once the offering statement is filed). Offers cannot be accepted, and any money received must be returned, until the offering statement has been qualified.[8] The rationale for this "testing the waters" procedure was that the preparation of a formal disclosure document (such as the offering statement) was costly and arguably inadvisable to incur "without knowing whether there will be any investor interest in the company."[9] To guard against § 12(a)(2) liability, Rule 254(e) provides that such a "testing the waters" soliciting document cannot be deemed a prospectus under § 2(a)(10) of the 1933 Act.

Although this feasibility-testing rationale is understandable, it has received some criticism. For example, once an investor reads the "testing the waters"

---

2. Id.

3. See Rule 251(a). The so-called "bad boy" disqualifiers are set forth in Rule 262. These disqualifiers also apply to offerings under Rule 505. See Rule 505(b)(2)(iii).

4. See Rule 253 ("Offering Circular").

5. See Rule 252(g).

6. See Rule 253(d).

7. See Rule 254(a).

8. See Rule 254(b)(2)(i).

9. See Sec. Act.Rel. No. 6949 (July 30, 1992).

disclosure document and becomes interested, is this investor as likely to read the offering statement? Or, will the latter document become simply a memento of the transaction, drafted in abstruse lawyer-like detail to disclose all risks because it is no longer the principal marketing document?

Despite this concern that the "testing the waters" document may trivialize the later, more formal disclosure document, the Commission proposed in 1995 to adopt a similar procedure with regard to registered public offerings.[10] To date, no action has been taken on this proposal, but it may imply that the Commission is prepared to consider relaxing substantially the "quiet period" and "free writing" prohibitions of § 5.

Regulation A has a special integration rule. Rule 251(c) precludes the integration of a Regulation A offering with either (1) *any* prior offerings, or (2) later offerings that are registered, made in compliance with Rule 701 or Regulation S (which covers extraterritorial offerings outside the United States), or made more than six months after the Regulation A offering. Thus, an offering done pursuant to Regulation D that ended one month before the Regulation A offering began will presumably not destroy the Regulation A offering. Commentators have suggested that the language of Rule 251(c) provides a "two-sided" protection from integration which assures the issuer both that the Regulation A exemption will not be lost *and* that the exemption for the prior or subsequent offering (if done pursuant to an exemption) will be secure also.[11] Although Rule 251(c) clearly provides greater protection than does Rule 502(a) for an immediately preceding offering, its other principal practical difference with Rule 502(a) is less obvious: Rule 251(c) does not require that its six-month window period be "clean" (that is, without any offers being made in that interval). A "dirty" six month interval following a Regulation D offering will not preclude integration with subsequent sales, but apparently will preclude integration following a Regulation A offering.

SECTION 3. OTHER EXEMPTIONS: RULE 701, REGULATION CE, AND SECTION 4(6)

Statutes and Regulations

Securities Act § 3(b), 4(2) and 4(6).

RULE 701

Venture capital companies attract and hold key employees by offering them incentive compensation in the form of stock options, profit sharing and stock purchase plans. Thus, the employee shares in any appreciation in the firm's value, and the employee's self-interest is arguably better aligned with the firm's than if the employee received strictly cash compensation. For the public corporation, it is comparatively simple to register its continuing offer of stock to its employees through stock options and warrants by filing and keeping current a Form S-8 registration statement, which was the traditional form of shelf registration. But for a non-reporting company, which has probably not yet

10. See Sec. Act.Rel. No. 7188 (June 27, 1995), (proposing Rule 135(d) which would generalize Rule 254 "testing the waters" solicitation for all offerings).

11. Bradford, Regulation A and the Integration Doctrine, The New Safe Harbor, 55 Ohio St.L.J. 255 (1994).

made an initial public offering, the problem is more difficult. Of course, *Ralston Purina,* supra, requires registration of the stock so offered to employees, unless an exemption is available, but the costs of registration can be disproportionate for a small, non-reporting company.

Rule 701 is a response to this problem, tailored to meet the needs of the non-reporting company. Adopted in 1988, it provides an exemption under § 3(b) for offers and sales of securities by non-reporting issuers where such offers and sales are pursuant to compensatory employee benefit plans or are included in employment contracts. The premise of Rule 701 is that such compensatory benefit plans are not an attempt to raise capital by the issuer, but rather to use stock options and related compensation to bind the employee to the firm. Thus, Preliminary Note 5 to the Rule states:

> "[T]he rule is not available for plans or schemes to circumvent this [compensatory] purpose, such as to raise capital. In such cases, registration or some other exemption from registration under the Act is required."[1]

In part to enforce this restriction on capital-raising, Rule 701 limits the amount of securities that can be issued in reliance on it in any 12–month period. The total amount so issued may not exceed the greater of $1,000,000 or the amounts determined under two different formulae. The first formula limits this amount to 15% of the issuer's total assets as of the end of its last fiscal year, while the second restricts the amount to no more than 15% of the outstanding securities in the class. In any case, the aggregate offering price of securities subject to outstanding offers and sold in the preceding 12 months may not exceed $5 million.

Rule 701 offerings are deemed to be part of a single discrete offering and are not subject to integration with other offerings.[2] Similarly, given the assumed compensatory nature of a Rule 701 offering, aggregation is limited to offerings under Rule 701 within the prior 12 months, and thus the ceiling for other offerings made pursuant to § 3(b) is not affected by the Rule 701 offering.

Rule 701 does not require affirmative disclosures about the issuer (other than that the issuer provide plan participants with a copy of the plan and any written contract relating to compensation). Is this consistent with the approach taken under Rule 505? Could there be liability under Rule 10b–5?

Rule 701 can be used to offer securities not only to employees but also to "consultants and advisers, provided that bona fide services shall be rendered by consultants and advisers and such services must not be in connection with the offer and sale of securities in a capital raising transaction."[3] This language seemingly excludes underwriters and the issuer's corporate lawyers who worked on an offering. On the other hand, this permission to compensate consultants and advisers might be stretched to allow the issuer to designate potential investors as nominal advisers or consultants. In such a case, the SEC could turn to its above quoted Preliminary Note 5.

When stock is sold to a consultant or adviser, the value of services performed by the adviser must be counted against the aggregate offering price

---

1.   See Sec.Act.Rel. No. 6768 (April 14, 1988).

2.   See Rule 701(b)(6).

3.   See Rule 701(b)(1). See also Herff Jones, Inc., SEC No–Action Letter, 1990 SEC No–Act. LEXIS 1026 (Nov. 13, 1990) (stock plan that covered sales representatives who were not employees complied with Rule 701).

ceilings under Rule 701(b)(4)(i). However, the value of services performed by an employee in the regular course of his or her employment is not so counted.[4]

REGULATION CE

In 1996, the SEC adopted a new form of exemption in Rule 1001.[5] Essentially, it combines features of both the intrastate exemption (§ 3(a)(11)) and the small issue exemption (§ 3(b)). Rule 1001 provides an exemption that tracks a California state law exemption set forth in § 25102(n) of the California Corporation Code, which permits California corporations and certain foreign business entities (namely, those that (i) can attribute more than 50 percent of property, payroll and sales to California, and (ii) have more than 50 percent of their outstanding voting securities held of record by California shareholders) to sell up to $5 million of their securities to certain qualified purchasers who meet criteria similar to, but more liberal than, those set forth in the definition of "accredited investor" in Rule 501(a). For example, the California definition of qualified purchaser includes any person purchasing more than $150,000 of securities in the offering, any natural person with a net worth in excess of $500,000, or any natural person whose net worth exceeds $250,000 if that person's annual income exceeds $100,000 (and certain other conditions are satisfied). In addition, the California exemption, which Rule 1001 tracks, permits a form of general solicitation using a "test the waters" concept that parallels Regulation A.

Rule 1001 is not conditioned on any aggregation concept; rather, its $5 million ceiling is applied on an offering by offering basis. Standard integration concepts, however, do apply, thus meaning that a Rule 1001 offering can be integrated with other roughly contemporaneous offerings so that exemptions are forfeited for some or all of them.[6]

Most importantly, in the Release adopting Rule 1001, the Commission indicated its willingness "to provide the same exemption for each state that enacts a transaction exemption incorporating the same standards used by California."[7] On this basis, the Commission captioned Rule 1001 "Regulation CE" for "Coordinated Exemptions" in the anticipation that other states would soon enact "similar" statutory exemptions. The New York State Bar Association's Securities Committee has, however, voiced concern that this approach may create a "confusing patchwork of similar, but not identical approaches" that undercut the uniformity of the federal securities laws.[8]

In the same release, the Commission again indicated that it was considering dropping the general solicitation prohibition in Rule 502(c).

---

4. This distinction, which is not obvious on the face of the rule, was made in Sec.Act. Rel. No. 6768. Contrast this inclusion of non-cash consideration with the very different approach taken in Rule 501(c), which excludes such consideration.

5. See Sec.Act.Rel. No. 7285 (May 1, 1996).

6. Sec.Act.Rel. No. 7285, at n. 31, 61 Federal Register 21356, 21357.

7. Id. at 21358.

8. See "N.Y. Lawyers Voice Concerns Over California Registration Exemptions," Sec.Reg. & L.Rep. (BNA) (Sept. 15, 1995). For a sharp criticism of Regulation CE as an unwise delegation of federal power to state authorities, see Bradford, The SEC's New Regulation CE Exemption: Federal–State Coordination Run Rampant, 52 U.Miami L.Rev. 429 (1998).

Securities issued under Regulation CE are "restricted securities" and subject to the same resale limitations that apply under Regulation D.[9]

SECTION 4(6)

Section 4(6) exempts offers or sales by an issuer "solely to one or more accredited investors", subject to whatever aggregate ceiling is provided from time to time in § 3(b). Section 2(a)(15) defines the term "accredited investor," which concept is further spelled out in Rule 215.

As a practical matter, § 4(6) has been largely subsumed by Regulation D. Not only is Rule 506 under Regulation D unlimited in the aggregate amount that can be offered under it, but Regulation D has clearer, bright line standards on such issues as aggregation, integration, and solicitation. Although § 4(6) does not seem to require that any disclosure document be provided, Rule 502(b) requires such a disclosure document only in the case of non-accredited investors (and thus again supplies a broader exemption with more specific standards).

PROBLEM ON EXEMPTIONS FROM SECTION 5 OF THE SECURITIES ACT OF 1933*

On January 15, 1996, three individuals, A, B and C (the "Founders") organized a Nevada corporation (the "Company") to develop, manufacture and market network computer systems. All of the Founders resided in Nevada except for C, who resided in Boston, Massachusetts, to operate the Company's east coast sales activities. On January 20, 1996, the Company issued and sold 800,000 shares of Common Stock (a total of 2,400,000 shares) at a price of $.10 per share, to each of the Founders, for the total purchase price of $240,000. A and B purchased their shares for cash. C purchased his shares for a promissory note (the "Note"). The Note was a full recourse note, unsecured, maturing on January 20, 1999. The shares were not registered under the Securities Act of 1933. Each Founder's shares were subject to repurchase by the Company, at cost, in the event a Founder's employment with the Company was terminated. This repurchase right terminated as to ¹⁄₆₀ of the shares for each month of the Founder's continuous employment.

Each of A, B and C were officers and members of the Board of Directors of the Company.

The following transactions then occurred. All offers and sales of securities were accomplished by the use of mails or interstate facilities.

(1) On February 15, 1996, the Company sold and issued 750,000 shares of Series A Preferred Stock, at a price of $1.00 per share, cash (a total of $750,000), to 40 individual investors. All of the purchasers of the securities resided in California at the time of the purchase. The proceeds from the sale of these securities were to be used principally to commence development of the Company's first system. Each purchaser executed a subscription agreement and represented that the shares were being acquired for investment and not with a view towards distribution. No further written material or written information

---

9. See Rule 1001(c).

* This problem was prepared by Larry W. Sonsini, Esq., a member of the law firm of Wilson, Sonsini, Goodrich & Rosati, Palo Alto, California, and Lecturer in Law at the University of California School of Law, Berkeley. The Authors are indebted to Mr. Sonsini for granting us permission to publish it.

was provided to the purchasers. The offer and sale of the shares was conducted by the Founders, each one being given the task to contact potential purchasers for the offering. The Founders did not keep records as to the number of persons contacted; however, most of the investors were friends and acquaintances of one or more of the Founders. The Founders believed that the investors were generally familiar with financial and business matters. The Series A Preferred Stock was convertible into Common Stock (initially 1–forB1) and had dividend, liquidation and voting preferences over the Common Stock.

(2) Over the next several months, the Company made significant progress in completing the initial design and development of its network computer system. It was now ready to move into final development and early production. Accordingly, in order to raise additional capital for this next phase, the Company offered and sold on September 30, 1996, 3,000,000 shares of a Series B Preferred Stock, at a cash price of $1.50 per share (a total of $4,500,000) to 38 investors residing in the States of California, Nevada and Massachusetts. Of these investors, 35 were individuals and three were limited partnerships. Of the 35 individual investors, three had a net worth in excess of $1,000,000 and five had an individual net income in excess of $200,000 and all were generally knowledgeable of the computer industry and were frequent investors in the stock markets. Of the three partnerships, two were well known, established venture capital funds (the partners of which each had a net worth in excess of $1,000,000), and the third was a recently organized Massachusetts limited partnership which had yet to make any investment. This latter partnership had 10 limited partners, four of whom were accredited (within the meaning of Regulation D), but all of whom had general experience in investing in "restricted" securities from time to time. Each purchaser of the securities received a copy of a private placement memorandum which was prepared by the Company and the Founders containing a description of the offering, a description of the Company's business and financial information (the "Series B Placement Memorandum").

The rights, preferences, privileges and restrictions of the Series B Preferred Stock were substantially similar to the provisions of the Series A Preferred Stock, except as to the difference in price.

(3) As a condition to the Series B Preferred Stock financing, the venture capital firms required, as a condition to their investment, that the Series A Preferred Stock be converted into Common Stock, so as to eliminate any liquidation preference senior to the Series B Preferred, or that, alternatively, each 1.50 shares of Series A Preferred Stock be exchanged for one share of Series B Preferred Stock of the type being purchased by the investors. This was accomplished when (i) holders of 400,000 shares of Series A Preferred Stock converted their shares into 400,000 shares of Common Stock, (ii) holders of 300,000 of Series A Preferred Stock exchanged their shares for 200,000 shares of Series B Preferred Stock, and (iii) a holder of 50,000 shares of Series A Preferred Stock, who has refused to convert or exchange, had his shares repurchased by the Company at $1.50 per share cash.

(4) In order to create incentive for key employees, the Company, upon its organization in January 1996, adopted an employee stock option plan under which it had reserved 500,000 shares of Common Stock. During the period from February 15 through December 1996, the Company had granted options to purchase a total of 400,000 shares of Common Stock to 72 employees under the plan (such options were granted every other month by the Board of Directors).

The options were granted at prices ranging from $.10 to $.50 per share. Each option had a term of five years and was exercisable to the extent of 20% of the shares per year, based upon continued employment of the optionee. Each employee received a summary of the stock option plan, but no further information with respect to the Company's business. Several of the optionees were located at the site of the Company's sales office in Boston, Massachusetts. The Company intends to continue to grant options under the plan.

(5) In order to gain broader distribution of its products, the Company decided to acquire a marketing and distribution firm, Computer Marketing Inc. ("CMI"), a Delaware corporation, located in Boston, Massachusetts. CMI was a privately held corporation with 2,000,000 outstanding shares of Common Stock held by 85 shareholders. The acquisition was consummated on November 5, 1996 through the merger of CMI with and into the Company, pursuant to which each issued and outstanding share of CMI Common Stock was converted into .5 shares of Series B Preferred Stock of the Company (a total of 1,000,000 shares of the Company's Series B Preferred Stock issued in the merger). The Series B Preferred Stock was valued at $1.50 per share. The merger was accomplished through a majority vote of the issued and outstanding CMI shares. Of the outstanding CMI shares, 500,000 shares (25%) were owned beneficially by D (which he purchased from CMI in 1994), who was also the President and Chairman of the Board of Directors of CMI. The Company delivered to each CMI stockholder an updated version of the Series B Placement Memorandum together with a summary of the Merger Transaction.

(6) On August 15, 1997, F, one of the original purchasers of the Company's Series A Preferred Stock, decided to sell 85,000 shares of the Series B Preferred Stock which he received in exchange for the Series A Preferred Stock in the conversion and exchange offering which is referred to in transaction (3) above. The 85,000 shares represented approximately 1% of the then outstanding shares. F needed to sell the shares in order to obtain cash because of his failing business. To sell his shares, he contacted one of the Founders who gave him the names of 12 individuals who were not shareholders of the Company, but who were familiar with the Company in that each of them, from time to time, had performed consulting services for the Company in the field of product design and product marketing. Although none of these individuals were known to F, he approached each one and finally concluded the sale on September 10, 1997, with 10 of the individuals contacted. All of the purchasers signed a purchase agreement representing that they were acquiring the shares for investment and not with a view to distribution. None of the purchasers received any information regarding the affairs of the Company.

(7) Following a period of rapid growth, the Board of Directors of the Company decided in February 1998 to effect an initial public offering of the Company's Common Stock. Accordingly, pursuant to a registration statement filed by the Company with the Securities and Exchange Commission, the Company effected an underwritten public offering of 5,000,000 shares of Common Stock, at a price of $8 per share, on May 5, 1998, the effective date of the registration statement. As a result of the offering, the Company had issued and outstanding 12,400,000 shares of Common Stock (all Preferred had then been converted into Common Stock prior to the public offering) and unexercised options to purchase an additional 550,000 shares. Shortly after the registered offering, the Company registered as a reporting company under

§ 12(g) of the Securities Exchange Act of 1934. At 120 days after the effective date of the registration statement, the following transactions occurred:

(a) One of the Founders, C, paid his Note in full on August 5, 1997, which he gave in payment for his Founder's shares upon the Company's formation (see above), and sold 100,000 shares of the Company's Common Stock through a broker in the over-the-counter market.

(b) D, who was the President of CMI, sold all of his shares of the Company's Common Stock which he acquired in the merger of CMI and the Company, also in the over-the-counter market in a normal brokerage transaction.

(c) G, who was a purchaser of Series A Preferred from F, in Transaction (6), sold all of his shares of Common Stock (received upon conversion of the Preferred on the effective date of the registration statement) in the over-the-counter market.

With respect to each of the above transactions (1) through (7), please explain what exemption if any from § 5 of the Securities Act of 1933 you would recommend as most appropriate with respect to the securities offered and sold and the basis for such exemption. In selecting the most appropriate exemption, keep in mind all transactions (including the initial issuance of shares by the Company to the Founders) and their effect, if any, upon your decision and analysis. Assume that all of today's law (statutes, rules and cases) was in effect and available at all relevant times.

For the solution of transactions (1) through (4), see Chapters 5–7; for transaction (5), see Chapter 8; and for transactions (6) and (7), see Chapter 9.

CHAPTER 7

INTRASTATE OFFERINGS: SECTION 3(a)(11) AND RULE 147

SECTION 1. THE SECTION 3(A)(11) EXEMPTION

Statutes

Securities Act § 3(a)(11). Rule 147.

Securities Act Release No. 4434

Securities and Exchange Commission.
December 6, 1961.

SECTION 3(a)(11) EXEMPTION FOR LOCAL OFFERINGS

The meaning and application of the exemption from registration provided by Section 3(a)(11) * * * have been the subject of court opinions, releases of the Securities and Exchange Commission * * * and opinions and interpretations expressed by the staff of the Commission in response to specific inquiries. This release is published to provide in convenient and up-to-date form a restatement of the principles underlying Section 3(a)(11) as so expressed over the years and to facilitate an understanding of the meaning and application of the exemption.[1]

General Nature of Exemption

Section 3(a)(11), as amended in 1954, exempts from the registration and prospectus requirements of the Act:

> "Any security which is a part of an issue offered and sold only to persons resident within a single State or Territory, where the issuer of such security is a person resident and doing business within, or, if a corporation, incorporated by and doing business within, such State or Territory."

The legislative history of the Securities Act clearly shows that this exemption was designed to apply only to local financing that may practicably be consummated in its entirety within the State or Territory in which the issuer is both incorporated and doing business. As appears from the legislative history, by amendment to the Act in 1934, this exemption was removed from Section 5(c) and inserted in Section 3, relating to "Exempted Securities", in order to relieve dealers of an unintended restriction on trading activity. This amend-

---

1. Since publication of the 1937 release, the Investment Company Act of 1940 was enacted, and under Section 24(d) thereof, the Section 3(a)(11) exemption for an intrastate offering is not available for an investment company registered or required to be registered under the Investment Company Act.

ment was not intended to detract from its essential character as a transaction exemption.[3]

"Issue" Concept

A basic condition of the exemption is that the *entire issue* of securities be offered and sold exclusively to residents of the state in question. Consequently, an offer to a non-resident which is considered a part of the intrastate issue will render the exemption unavailable to the entire offering.

Whether an offering is "a part of an issue", that is, whether it is an integrated part of an offering previously made or proposed to be made, is a question of fact and depends essentially upon whether the offerings are a related part of a plan or program. * * * Thus, the exemption should not be relied upon in combination with another exemption for the different parts of a single issue where a part is offered or sold to non-residents.

The determination of what constitutes an "issue" is not governed by state law. Shaw v. U. S., 131 F.2d 476, 480 (C.A.9, 1942). Any one or more of the following factors may be determinative of the question of integration: (1) are the offerings part of a single plan of financing; (2) do the offerings involve issuance of the same class of security; (3) are the offerings made at or about the same time; (4) is the same type of consideration to be received, and (5) are the offerings made for the same general purpose.

Moreover, since the exemption is designed to cover only those security distributions, which, as a whole, are essentially local in character, it is clear that the phrase "sold only to persons resident" as used in Section 3(a)(11) cannot refer merely to the initial sales by the issuing corporation to its underwriters, or even the subsequent resales by the underwriters to distributing dealers. To give effect to the fundamental purpose of the exemption, it is necessary that the entire issue of securities shall be offered and sold to, and come to rest only in the hands of residents within the state. If any part of the issue is offered or sold to a non-resident, the exemption is unavailable not only for the securities so sold, but for all securities forming a part of the issue, including those sold to residents. Securities Act Release No. 201 (1934); Brooklyn Manhattan Transit Corporation; 1 S.E.C. 147 (1935); S.E.C. v. Hillsborough Investment Corp., 173 F.Supp. 86 (D.N.H.1958); Hillsborough Investment Corp. v. S.E.C., 276 F.2d 665 (C.A.1, 1960); S.E.C. v. Los Angeles Trust Deed & Mortgage Exchange, et al., 186 F.Supp. 830, 871 (S.D.Cal., 1960), aff'd 285 F.2d 162 (C.A.9, 1960). It is incumbent upon the issuer, underwriter, dealers and other persons connected with the offering to make sure that it does not become an interstate distribution through resales. It is understood to be customary for such persons to obtain assurances that purchases are not made with a view to resale to non-residents.

Doing Business Within the State

In view of the local character of the Section 3(a)(11) exemption, the requirement that the issuer be doing business in the state can only be satisfied

---

3. See Report of the Securities and Exchange Commission to the Committee on Interstate and Foreign Commerce, dated August 7, 1941, on Proposals for Amendments to the Securities Act of 1933 and the Securities Exchange Act of 1934 where in referring to Sections 3(a)(1), 3(a)(9), 3(a)(10), 3(a)(11) and 3(b) of the Securities Act of 1933, it was said: " * * * Since these are in reality transaction exemptions, the Commission proposes and representatives of the securities' industry agree that they should be redesignated as transaction exemptions and transferred to Section 4. * * * " (p. 24).

by the performance of substantial operational activities in the state of incorporation. The doing business requirement is not met by functions in the particular state such as bookkeeping, stock record and similar activities or by offering securities in the state. Thus, the exemption would be unavailable to an offering by a company made in the state of its incorporation of undivided fractional oil and gas interests located in other states even though the company conducted other business in the state of its incorporation. While the person creating the fractional interests is technically the "issuer" as defined in Section 2(4) of the Act, the purchaser of such security obtains no interest in the issuer's separate business within the state. Similarly, an intrastate exemption would not be available to a "local" mortgage company offering interests in out-of-state mortgages which are sold under circumstances to constitute them investment contracts. Also, the same position has been taken of a sale of an interest, by a real estate syndicate organized in one state to the residents of that state, in property acquired under a sale and leaseback arrangement with another corporation organized and engaged in business in another state.

If the proceeds of the offering are to be used primarily for the purpose of a new business conducted outside of the state of incorporation and unrelated to some incidental business locally conducted, the exemption should not be relied upon. S.E.C. v. Truckee Showboat, Inc., 157 F.Supp. 824 (S.D.Cal.1957). So also, a Section 3(a)(11) exemption should not be relied upon for each of a series of corporations organized in different states where there is in fact and purpose a single business enterprise or financial venture whether or not it is planned to merge or consolidate the various corporations at a later date. S.E.C. v. Los Angeles Trust Deed & Mortgage Exchange et al., 186 F.Supp. 830, 871 (S.D.Cal.1960), aff'd 285 F.2d 162 (C.A.9, 1960).

Residence Within the State

Section 3(a)(11) requires that the entire issue be confined to a single state in which the issuer, the offerees and the purchasers are residents. Mere presence in the state is not sufficient to constitute residence as in the case of military personnel at a military post. * * * The mere obtaining of formal representations of residence and agreements not to resell to non-residents or agreements that sales are void if the purchaser is a non-resident should not be relied upon without more as establishing the availability of the exemption.

An offering may be so large that its success as a local offering appears doubtful from the outset. Also, reliance should not be placed on the exemption for an issue which includes warrants for the purchase of another security unless there can be assurance that the warrants will be exercised only by residents. With respect to convertible securities, a Section 3(a)(9) exemption may be available for the conversion.

A secondary offering by a controlling person in the issuer's state of incorporation may be made in reliance on a Section 3(a)(11) exemption provided the exemption would be available to the issuer for a primary offering in that state. It is not essential that the controlling person be a resident of the issuer's state of incorporation.

Resales

From these general principles it follows that if during the course of distribution any underwriter, any distributing dealer (whether or not a member of the formal selling or distributing group), or any dealer or other person purchasing securities from a distributing dealer for resale were to offer or sell such securities to a non-resident, the exemption would be defeated. In other words, Section 3(a)(11) contemplates that the exemption is applicable only if the entire issue is distributed pursuant to the statutory conditions. Consequently, any offers or sales to a non-resident in connection with the distribution of the issue would destroy the exemption as to all securities which are a part of that issue, including those sold to residents regardless of whether such sales are made directly to non-residents or indirectly through residents who as part of the distribution thereafter sell to non-residents. It would furthermore be immaterial that sales to non-residents are made without use of the mails or instruments of interstate commerce. Any such sales of part of the issue to non-residents, however few, would not be in compliance with the conditions of Section 3(a)(11), and would render the exemption unavailable for the entire offering including the sales to residents.

This is not to suggest, however, that securities which have actually come to rest in the hands of resident investors, such as persons purchasing without a view to further distribution or resale to non-residents, may not in due course be resold by such persons, whether directly or through dealers or brokers, to non-residents without in any way affecting the exemption. The relevance of any such resales consists only of the evidentiary light which they might cast upon the factual question whether the securities had in fact come to rest in the hands of resident investors. If the securities are resold but a short time after their acquisition to a non-resident this fact, although not conclusive, might support an inference that the original offering had not come to rest in the state, and that the resale therefore constituted a part of the process of primary distribution; a stronger inference would arise if the purchaser involved were a security dealer. It may be noted that the non-residence of the underwriter or dealer is not pertinent so long as the ultimate distribution is solely to residents of the state.

Use of the Mails and Facilities of Interstate Commerce

The intrastate exemption is not dependent upon non-use of the mails or instruments of interstate commerce in the distribution. Securities issued in a transaction properly exempt under this provision may be offered and sold without registration through the mails or by use of any instruments of transportation or communication in interstate commerce, may be made the subject of general newspaper advertisement (provided the advertisement is appropriately limited to indicate that offers to purchase are solicited only from, and sales will be made only to residents of the particular state involved), and may even be delivered by means of transportation and communication used in interstate commerce, to the purchasers. Similarly, securities issued in a transaction exempt under Section 3(a)(11) may be offered without compliance with the formal prospectus requirements applicable to registered securities. Exemption under Section 3(a)(11), if in fact available, removes the distribution from the operation of the registration and prospectus requirements of Section 5 of the Act. It should be emphasized, however, that the civil liability and anti-fraud provisions of Sections 12(2) and 17 of the Act nevertheless apply and may give rise to civil liabilities and to other sanctions applicable to violations of the statute.

Conclusion

In conclusion, the fact should be stressed that Section 3(a)(11) is designed to apply only to distributions genuinely local in character. From a practical point of view, the provisions of that section can exempt only issues which in reality represent local financing by local industries, carried out through local investment. Any distribution not of this type raises a serious question as to the availability of Section 3(a)(11). Consequently, any dealer proposing to participate in the distribution of an issue claimed to be exempt under Section 3(a)(11) should examine the character of the transaction and the proposed or actual manner of its execution by all persons concerned with it with the greatest care to satisfy himself that the distribution will not, or did not, exceed the limitations of the exemption. Otherwise the dealer, even though his own sales may be carefully confined to resident purchasers, may subject himself to serious risk of civil liability under Section 12(1) of the Act for selling without prior registration a security not in fact entitled to exemption from registration. In Release No. 4386, we noted that the quick commencement of trading and prompt resale of portions of the issue to non-residents raises a serious question whether the entire issue has, in fact, come to rest in the hands of investors resident in the state of the initial offering.

The Securities Act is a remedial statute, and the terms of an exemption must be strictly construed against one seeking to rely on it. * * * The courts have held that he has the burden of proving its availability. * * *

Securities and Exchange Commission v. McDonald Investment Co.

United States District Court, D. Minn., 1972.
343 F.Supp. 343.

MEMORANDUM OPINION

■ NEVILLE, DISTRICT JUDGE: The question presented to the court is whether the sale exclusively to Minnesota residents of securities, consisting of unsecured installment promissory notes of the defendant, a Minnesota corporation, whose only business office is situate in Minnesota, is exempt from the filing of a registration statement under § 3(a)(11) of the 1933 Securities Act, when the proceeds from the sale of such notes are to be used principally, if not entirely, to make loans to land developers outside of Minnesota. Though this is a close question, the court holds that such registration is required and the defendants have not satisfied their burden of proving the availability of an exemption under the Act; this despite the fact that the securities have heretofore been duly registered with the Securities Commissioner of the State of Minnesota for whom this court has proper respect.

Plaintiff, the Securities and Exchange Commission, instituted this lawsuit pursuant to § 20(b) of the 1933 Securities Act. The defendants are McDonald Investment Company, a Minnesota corporation, and H. J. McDonald, the company's president, treasurer, and owner of all the company's outstanding common stock. Plaintiff requests that the defendants be permanently enjoined from offering for sale and selling securities without having complied with the registration requirements of Section 5 of the Act.

Plaintiff and defendants have stipulated to the following pertinent facts: The defendant company was organized and incorporated in the State of Minnesota on November 6, 1968. The principal and only business office from which the defendants conduct their operations is located in Rush City, Minnesota, and all books, correspondence, and other records of the company are kept there.

Prior to October 19, 1971, the defendants registered an offering for $4,000,000 of its own installment notes with the Securities Division of the State of Minnesota pursuant to Minnesota law. The prospectus offering these installment notes became effective on October 19, 1971 by a written order of the Minnesota Commissioner of Securities making the registration and prospectus effective following examination and review by the Securities Division. Sales of the installment notes, according to the amended prospectus of January 18, 1972, are to be made to Minnesota residents only. Prior to the institution of this action, the defendants were enjoined from their past practices of selling, without Securities and Exchange Commission registration, notes secured by lien land contracts and first mortgages on unimproved land located at various places in the United States, principally Arizona. The defendant company is said to have sold $12,000,000 of such to some 2,000 investors. The present plan contemplates that those purchasing defendant company's securities henceforth will have only the general unsecured debt obligation of the company, though the proceeds from the installment notes will be lent to land developers with security taken from them in the form of mortgages or other liens running to the defendant corporation. The individual installment note purchasers will not, however, have any direct ownership or participation in the mortgages or other lien security, nor in the businesses of the borrowers.

No registration statement as to the installment notes described in McDonald Investment Company's amended prospectus is in effect with the United States Securities and Exchange Commission, nor has a registration statement been filed with the Commission. Furthermore, the defendants will make use of the means and instruments of transportation and communication in interstate commerce and of the mails to sell and offer to sell the installment notes though only to residents of Minnesota.

* * *

The plaintiff predicates its claim for a permanent injunction on the ground that the defendants will be engaged in a business where the income producing operations are located outside the state in which the securities are to be offered and sold and therefore not available for the 3(a)(11) exemption. Securities and Exchange Commission v. Truckee Showboat, 157 F.Supp. 824 (S.D.Cal.1957); Chapman v. Dunn, 414 F.2d 153 (6th Cir.1969). While neither of these cases is precisely in point on their facts, the rationale of both is clear and apposite to the case at bar.

In *Truckee* the exemption was not allowed because the proceeds of the offering were to be used primarily for the purpose of a new unrelated business in another state, i.e., a California corporation acquiring and refurbishing a hotel in Las Vegas, Nevada. Likewise, in *Dunn* the 3(a)(11) exemption was unavailable to an offering by a company in one state, Michigan, of undivided fractional oil and gas interests located in another state, Ohio. The *Dunn* court specifically stated at page 159:

"* * * in order to qualify for the exemption of § 3(a)(11), the issuer must offer and sell his securities only to persons resident within a single State and the issuer must be a resident of that same State. *In addition to this, the issuer must conduct a predominant amount of his business within this same State.* This business which the issuer must conduct within the same

State refers to the income producing operations of the business in which the issuer is selling the securities * * *." [Emphasis added]

This language would seem to fit the instant case where the income producing operations of the defendant, after completion of the offering, are to consist entirely of earning interest on its loans and receivables invested outside the state of Minnesota. While the defendant will not participate in any of the land developer's operations, nor will it own or control any of the operations, the fact is that the strength of the installment notes depends perhaps not legally, but practically, to a large degree on the success or failure of land developments located outside Minnesota, such land not being subject to the jurisdiction of the Minnesota court. The investor obtains no direct interest in any business activity outside of Minnesota, but legally holds only an interest as a creditor of a Minnesota corporation, which of course would be a prior claim on the defendant's assets over the shareholder's equity, now stated to be approximately a quarter of a million dollars.

This case does not evidence the deliberate attempt to evade the Act as in the example posed by plaintiff of a national organization or syndicate which incorporates in several or many states, opens an office in each and sells securities only to residents of the particular state, intending nevertheless to use all the proceeds whenever realized in a venture beyond the boundaries of all, or at best all but one of the states. See Securities & Exchange Commission v. Los Angeles Trust Deed & Mortgage Exchange, 186 F.Supp. 830, 871 (S.D.Cal. 1960), aff'd 285 F.2d 162 (9th Cir.1960). Defendant corporation on the contrary has been in business in Minnesota for some period of time, is not a "Johnny come lately" and is not part of any syndicate or similar enterprise; yet to relieve it of the federal registration requirements where none or very little of the money realized is to be invested in Minnesota, would seem to violate the spirit if not the letter of the Act.

Persuasive language is found in the Securities and Exchange Commission Release No. 4434, December 6, 1961, relating to exemptions for local offerings:

[The court quotes that portion of the Release, supra at page 391, under the heading: "Doing Business Within the State".]

Exemptions under the Act are strictly construed, with the burden of proof on the one seeking to establish the same. Securities and Exchange Commission v. Culpepper, 270 F.2d 241, 246 (2d Cir.1959); Securities and Exchange Commission v. Ralston Purina Co., 346 U.S. 119, 126 (1954) * * *.

Defendant notes that agreements with land developers will by their terms be construed under Minnesota law; that the income producing activities will be the earning of interest which occurs in Minnesota; that the Minnesota registration provides at close proximity all the information and protection that any investor might desire; that whether or not registered with the Securities and Exchange Commission, a securities purchaser has the protection of [Section 12] which attaches liability to the issuer whether or not registration of the securities are exempted for fraudulent or untrue statements in a prospectus or made by oral communications; that plaintiff blurs the distinction between sale of securities across state lines and the operation of an intrastate business; and that if injunction issues in this case it could issue in any case where a local corporation owns an investment out of the particular state in which it has its principal offices and does business such as accounts receivable from its customers out of state. While these arguments are worthy and perhaps somewhat more applicable to the facts of this case than to the facts of *Truckee* and *Chapman*, supra, on balance and in carrying out the spirit and intent of the Securities Act of 1933, plaintiff's request for a permanent injunction should be granted.

––––––––

Busch v. Carpenter[1] arose out of an offer and sale of shares in the amount of $500,000 by Sonic Petroleum, Inc., a Utah corporation, solely to residents of Utah in reliance on the § 3(a)(11) intrastate exemption. Following the offering, Sonic did not engage in any business activity, but did maintain its corporate office, books and records in Utah.

Seven months after the intrastate offering Carpenter, the President of Sonic, was contacted by Mason, an Illinois oil and gas promoter, about a merger of Sonic with Mason's operations in Illinois. As a result of these negotiations, Sonic issued a controlling block of stock to Mason and acquired an Illinois drilling corporation privately owned by Mason and his family. Upon becoming president of the new company, renamed Mason Oil, Mason withdrew $350,000 of the net proceeds of $435,000 which remained from the intrastate offering and transferred it to Illinois.

Upon joining forces, Mason and Carpenter set up Norbil Investments, a brokerage account in Utah, so that Mason and his friends could buy shares of Sonic. Plaintiffs were residents of California who bought shares in the open market through Norbil within seven months after the initial offering. They brought a § 12(1) action against the officers and directors of Sonic at the time of the intrastate offering, including Carpenter, its then president, to recover the purchase price of their shares.

Plaintiffs claimed that the exemption was lost because: (1) the securities had not "come to rest" in the hands of the residents of Utah who resold their stock within seven months of the offering; and (2) the issuer did not meet the "doing business within" condition of § 3(a)(11). Liability was sought to be imposed upon defendants as controlling persons under § 15 of the 1933 Act. The district court rejected these contentions and granted summary judgment to defendant. On appeal to the Tenth Circuit, the SEC appeared as *Amicus* on behalf of the plaintiffs. The Commission argued that because the defendants had the burden of showing their right to the exemption, they were required to present evidence at the trial that the original buyers bought with investment intent. In the absence of such a showing, the grant of summary judgment was improper. The court of appeals responded by affirming the judgment on the first issue but reversing and remanding as to the second.

With respect to the "coming to rest" requirement, the court of appeals had this to say:

> We reject Amicus' argument. The intrastate offering exemption requires that the issue be "offered and sold only to persons resident within a single state." * * * In our view, a seller seeking summary judgment makes a prima facie showing that the offering was consummated within a state by showing that the stock was sold only to residents of that state. We disagree with Amicus that, in order to be entitled to summary judgment, the issuer

––––––––

1.   827 F.2d 653 (10th Cir.1987).

should be required to disprove all the possible circumstances that might establish the stock has not come to rest. It seems more logical to us to impose on the other party the burden of producing some contrary evidence on this issue when the seller claiming the exemption has satisfied the facial requirement of the statute. In the face of defendants' undisputed showing that all of the original buyers were Utah residents, plaintiffs were therefore required to produce evidence that the stock had not come to rest but had been sold to people who intended to resell it out of state.

    * * * [T]he interstate purchases by Mason and others of freely traded shares several months after the completion of the intrastate offering do not, without more, impugn the investment intent of the original buyers or otherwise imply an effort to evade the federal securities laws. Norbil served as a conduit for over-the-counter purchases made by Olsen & Company [a brokerage firm] on behalf of Mason and various acquaintances. Although Carpenter did collect from buyers, pay Olsen, and transfer the stock certificates to their new owners, there is simply no indication that those who sold through Norbil had not originally purchased their stock for investment purposes.

With respect to the "doing business in" requirement, the Court added:

    Although neither the statute nor its legislative history defines the doing business requirement, courts have uniformly held that it refers to activity that actually generates revenue within an issuer's home state. * * * [The court then discussed Chapman v. Dunn, 414 F.2d 153 (6th Cir.1969); SEC v. Truckee Showboat, Inc., 157 F.Supp. 824 (S.D.Cal.1957); and SEC v. McDonald Investment Co., supra at page 456.]

    These cases make clear that an issuer cannot claim the exemption simply by opening an office in a particular state. Conducting substantially all income-producing operations elsewhere defeats the exemption * * *. Doing business under the 1933 Act means more than maintaining an office, books, and records in one state. * * *

    Viewing the evidence and drawing reasonable inferences most favorably to plaintiffs, a fact issue exists regarding whether Sonic's plans for the use of proceeds are distinguishable from the issuer's plans in Truckee * * *. Here the corporation never did more than maintain its office, books, and records in Utah. This was not sufficient to make a prima facie showing of compliance with the intrastate offering exemption. While its prospectus stated that no more than twenty percent of all proceeds would be used outside of Utah, Sonic nonetheless transferred essentially all of its assets to Mason in Illinois. The record contains no evidence, moreover, of any prior efforts whatever at locating investment opportunities within Utah. These considerations support a reasonable inference that Sonic may have intended all along to invest its assets outside the state. * * *

    * * *

    * * * Accordingly, we conclude that a genuine issue of material fact exists precluding summary judgment in favor of all defendants.

On the issue of defendants' liability, the court ruled that none of the defendants, other than Carpenter, could be said to have participated in the resales to nonresidents and thereby became "sellers" within the meaning of section 12. As for Carpenter, however, the court held that the record raised fact issues as to the extent of his participation. Accordingly, summary judgment on this issue was improper.

SECTION 2.   RULE 147

Securities Act Release No. 5450

Securities and Exchange Commission.
January 7, 1974.

NOTICE OF ADOPTION OF RULE 147 UNDER
THE SECURITIES ACT OF 1933

* * *

The Securities and Exchange Commission today adopted Rule 147 which defines certain terms in, and clarifies certain conditions of, Section 3(a)(11) of the Securities Act of 1933 ("the Act"). Section 3(a)(11) (the "intrastate offering exemption") exempts from the registration requirements of Section 5 of the Act, securities that are part of an issue offered and sold only to persons resident within a single state or territory, if the issuer is a person resident and doing business within that state or territory. * * *

In developing the definitions in, and conditions of, Rule 147 the Commission has considered the legislative history and judicial interpretations of Section 3(a)(11) as well as its own administrative interpretations. The Commission believes that adoption of the rule, which codifies certain of these interpretations, is in the public interest, since it will be consistent with the protection of investors and provide, to the extent feasible, more certainty in determining when the exemption provided by that Section of the Act is available. Moreover, the Commission believes that local businesses seeking financing solely from local sources should have objective standards to facilitate compliance with Section 3(a)(11) and the registration provisions of the Act, and that the rule will enable such businesses to determine with more certainty whether they may use the exemption in offering their securities. The rule also will give more assurance that the intrastate offering exemption is used only for the purpose that Congress intended, i.e., local financing of companies primarily intrastate in character. Neither Section 3(a)(11) nor Rule 147 provides an exemption from the civil liability provisions of Section 12(2) of the Act, the anti-fraud provisions of the Act or of the Securities Exchange Act of 1934 ("Exchange Act"), the registration and periodic reporting provisions of Sections 12(g) and 13 of the Exchange Act, or any applicable state laws.

Rule 147 is another step in the Commission's continuing efforts to provide protection to investors and, where consistent with that objective, to add certainty, to the extent feasible, to the determination of when the registration provisions of the Act apply. * * *

This notice contains a general discussion of the background, purpose and general effect of the rule. A brief analysis of each section of the rule is also included. However, attention is directed to the attached text of the rule for a more complete understanding of its provisions.

Background and Purpose

Congress, in enacting the federal securities laws, created a continuous disclosure system designed to protect investors and to assure the maintenance of fair and honest securities markets. The Commission, in administering and implementing these laws, has sought to coordinate and integrate the disclosure system with the exemptive provisions provided by the laws. Rule 147 is a further effort in this direction.

Section 3(a)(11) was intended to allow issuers with localized operations to sell securities as part of a plan of local financing. Congress apparently believed that a company whose operations are restricted to one area should be able to raise money from investors in the immediate vicinity without having to register the securities with a federal agency. In theory, the investors would be protected both by their proximity to the issuer and by state regulation. Rule 147 reflects this Congressional intent and is limited in its application to transactions where state regulation will be most effective. The Commission has consistently taken the position that the exemption applies only to local financing provided by local investors for local companies.[2] To satisfy the exemption, the entire issue must be offered and sold exclusively to residents of the state in which the issuer is resident and doing business. An offer or sale of part of the issue to a single non-resident will destroy the exemption for the entire issue.

Certain basic questions have arisen in connection with interpreting Section 3(a)(11). They are:

1.   what transactions does the Section cover;

2.   what is "part of an issue" for purposes of the Section;

3.   when is a person "resident within" a state or territory for purposes of the Section; and

4.   what does "doing business within" mean in the context of the Section?

The courts and the Commission have addressed themselves to these questions in the context of different fact situations, and some general guidelines have been developed. Certain guidelines were set forth by the Commission in Securities Act Release No. 4434 and, in part, are reflected in Rule 147. However, in certain respects, as pointed out below, the rule differs from past interpretations.

The Transaction Concept

Although the intrastate offering exemption is contained in Section 3 of the Act, which Section is phrased in terms of exempt "securities" rather than "transactions", the legislative history and Commission and judicial interpretations indicate that the exemption covers only specific transactions and not the securities themselves. Rule 147 reflects this interpretation.

The "Part of an Issue" Concept

The determination of what constitutes "part of an issue" for purposes of the exemption, i.e. what should be "integrated", has traditionally been dependent on the facts involved in each case. The Commission noted in Securities Act Release 4434 that "any one or more of the following factors may be determinative of the question of integration:

---

2.   See e.g., Securities Act of 1933 Release No. 4434 (December 6, 1961).

"1. are the offerings part of a single plan of financing;

"2. do the offerings involve issuance of the same class of security;

"3. are the offerings made at or about the same time;

"4. is the same type of consideration to be received; and

"5. are the offerings made for the same general purpose."

In this connection, the Commission generally has deemed intrastate offerings to be "integrated" with those registered or private offerings of the same class of securities made by the issuer at or about the same time.

The rule as initially proposed would have done away with the necessity for such case-by-case determination of what offerings should be integrated by providing that all securities offered or sold by the issuer, its predecessor, and its affiliates, within any consecutive six month period, would be integrated. As adopted, the rule provides in Subparagraph (b)(2) that, for purposes of the rule only, certain offers and sales of securities, discussed below, will be deemed not to be part of an issue and therefore not be integrated, but the rule does not otherwise define "part of an issue." Accordingly, as to offers and sales not within (b)(2), issuers who want to rely on Rule 147 will have to determine whether their offers and sales are part of an issue by applying the five factors cited above.

The "Person Resident Within" Concept

The object of the Section 3(a)(11) exemption, i.e., to restrict the offering to persons within the same locality as the issuer who are, by reason of their proximity, likely to be familiar with the issuer and protected by the state law governing the issuer, is best served by interpreting the residence requirement narrowly. In addition, the determination of whether all parts of the issue have been sold only to residents can be made only after the securities have "come to rest" within the state or territory. Rule 147 retains these concepts, but provides more objective standards for determining when a person is considered a resident within a state for purposes of the rule and when securities have come to rest within a state.

The "Doing Business Within" Requirement

Because the primary purpose of the intrastate exemption was to allow an essentially local business to raise money within the state where the investors would be likely to be familiar with the business and with the management, the doing business requirement has traditionally been viewed strictly. First, not only should the business be located within the state, but the principal or predominant business must be carried on there.[4] Second, substantially all of the proceeds of the offering must be put to use within the local area.[5]

Rule 147 reinforces these requirements by providing specific percentage amounts of business that must be conducted within the state, and of proceeds from the offering that must be spent in connection with such business. In addition, the rule requires that the principal office of the issuer be within the state.

4. Chapman v. Dunn, 414 F.2d 153 (C.A.6, 1969).

5. SEC v. Truckee Showboat, Inc., 157 F.Supp. 824 (S.D.Cal., 1957).

Synopsis of Rule 147

1.   Preliminary Notes

The first preliminary note to the rule indicates that the rule does not raise any presumption that the Section 3(a)(11) exemption would not be available for transactions which do not satisfy all of the provisions of the rule. The second note reminds issuers that the rule does not affect compliance with state law. The third preliminary note to the rule briefly explains the rule's purpose and provisions.

As initially proposed, the rule was intended not to be available for secondary transactions. In order to make this clear, the fourth preliminary note indicates that the rule is available only for transactions by an issuer and that the rule is not available for secondary transactions. However, in accordance with long standing administrative interpretations of Section 3(a)(11), the intrastate offering exemption may be available for secondary offers and sales by controlling persons of the issuer, if the exemption would have been available to the issuer.[6]

2.   Transactions Covered—Rule 147(a)

Paragraph (a) of the rule provides that offers, offers to sell, offers for sale and sales of securities that meet all the conditions of the rule will be deemed to come within the exemption provided by Section 3(a)(11). Those conditions are: (1) the issuer must be resident and doing business within the state or territory in which the securities are offered and sold (Rule 147(c)); (2) the *offerees* and purchasers must be resident within such state or territory (Rule 147(d)); (3) resales for a period of 9 months after the last sale which is part of an issue must be limited as provided (Rule 147(e) and (f)). In addition, the revised rule provides that certain offers and sales of securities by or for the issuers will be deemed not "part of an issue" for purposes of the rule only (Rule 147(b)).

3.   "Part of an Issue"—Rule 147(b)

Subparagraph (b)(1) of the rule provides that all securities of the issuer which are part of an issue must be offered, offered for sale or sold only in accordance with all of the terms of the rule. For the purposes of the rule only, subparagraph (b)(2) provides that all securities of the issuer offered, offered for sale or sold pursuant to the exemptions provided under Section 3 or 4(2) of the Act or registered pursuant to the Act, prior to or subsequent to the six month period immediately preceding or subsequent to any offer, offer to sell, offer for sale or sale pursuant to Rule 147 will be deemed not part of an issue provided that there are no offers, offers to sell or sales of securities of the same or similar class by or for the issuer during either of these six month periods. If there have been offers or sales during the six months, then in order to determine what constitutes part of an issue, reference should be made to the five traditional integration factors discussed above.

As initially proposed the rule would have deemed all securities of the issuer, its predecessors and affiliates offered or sold by the issuer, its predecessors and affiliates within any consecutive six month period to be part of the same issue. On reconsideration, the Commission believes this would be too restrictive and has revised the rule as discussed above. Since subparagraph

---

6.   Sec. Act Rel. No. 4434 (December 6, 1961).

(b)(2) does not define "part of an issue", a note has been added to paragraph (b) which refers to the discussion of the five factors to be considered in determining whether a transaction is part of an issue. These factors are discussed in the third preliminary note to the rule, and should be considered in determining whether any offers and sales falling outside the scope of subparagraph (b)(2) and offers and sales made in reliance on the rule must be integrated. Neither Section 3(a)(11) nor Rule 147 can be relied upon in combination with another exemption for different parts of a single issue where a part is offered or sold to non-residents.

As initially proposed for comment the rule provided that securities offered or sold by a person which was a business separate and distinct from the issuer and which was affiliated with the issuer solely by reason of the existence of a common general partner would be deemed not to be part of the same issue. Since paragraph (b) has been revised to no longer automatically integrate offerings of affiliates, this proviso is no longer necessary and has been deleted.

Paragraph (b), as revised, is intended to create greater certainty and to obviate in certain situations the need for a case-by-case determination of when certain intrastate offerings should be integrated with other offerings, such as those registered under the Act or made pursuant to the exemption provided by Section 3 or 4(2) of the Act.

4. Nature of the Issuer—Rule 147(c)—"Person Resident Within"—Rule 147(c)(1)

Subparagraph (c)(1) of the rule defines the situations in which issuers would be deemed to be "resident within" a state or territory. A corporation, limited partnership or business trust must be incorporated or organized pursuant to the laws of such state or territory. Section 3(a)(11) provides specifically that a corporate issuer must be incorporated in the state. A general partnership or other form of business entity that is not formed under a specific state or territorial law must have its principal office within the state or territory. The rule also provides that an individual who is deemed an issuer, e.g., a promoter issuing preincorporation certificates, will be deemed a resident if his principal residence is in the state or territory. As initially proposed, the rule provided that in a partnership, *all* the general partners must be resident within such state or territory. The Commission has reconsidered this provision in light of the provisions applicable to corporations and determined to treat all business entities in a similar manner.

5. Nature of the Issuer—Rule 147(c)—Doing Business Within—Rule 147(c)(2)

Subparagraph (c)(2) of the rule provides that the issuer will be deemed to be "doing business within" a state or territory in which the offers and sales are to be made if: (1) at least 80 percent of its gross revenues and those of its subsidiaries on a consolidated basis (a) for its most recent fiscal year (if the first offer of any part of the issue is made during the first six months of the issuer's current fiscal year) or (b) for the subsequent six month period, or for the twelve months ended with that period (if the first offer of any part of the issue is made during the last six months of the issuer's current fiscal year) were derived from the operation of a business or property located in or rendering of services within the state or territory; (2) at least 80 percent of the issuer's assets and those of its subsidiaries on a consolidated basis at the end of the most recent fiscal semi-annual period prior to the first offer of any part of the issue are located within such state or territory; (3) at least 80 percent of the net proceeds to the issuer from the sales made pursuant to the rule are intended to be and are used in connection with the operation of a business or property or the rendering of services within such state or territory; and (4) the issuer's principal office is located in the state or territory.

* * *

Finally, subparagraph (c)(2) of the rule provides that an issuer which has not had gross revenues from the operation of its business in excess of $5,000 during its most recent twelve month period need not satisfy the revenue test of subsection (c)(2)(i).

The provisions of paragraph (c) are intended to assure that the issuer is primarily a local business. Many comments were received requesting more elaboration with respect to the above standards. The following examples demonstrate the manner in which these standards would be interpreted:

Example 1. X corporation is incorporated in State A and has its only warehouse, only manufacturing plant and only office in that state. X's only business is selling products throughout the United States and Canada through mail order catalogs. X annually mails catalogs and order forms from its office to residents of most states and several provinces of Canada. All orders are filled at and products shipped from X's warehouse to customers throughout the United States and Canada. All the products shipped are manufactured by X at its plant in State A. These activities are X's sole source of revenues.

Question. Is X deriving more than 80 percent of its gross revenues from the "operation of a business or * * * rendering of services" within State A?

Interpretive Response. Yes, this aspect of the "doing business within" standard is satisfied.

Example 2. Assume the same facts as Example 1, except that X has no manufacturing plant and purchases the products it sells from corporations located in other states.

Question. Is X deriving more than 80 percent of its gross revenues from the "operation of a business or * * * rendering of services" within State A?

Interpretive Response. Yes, this aspect of the "doing business within" standard is satisfied.

Example 3. Y Corporation is incorporated in State B and has its only office in that state. Y's only business is selling undeveloped land located in State C and State D by means of brochures mailed from its office throughout the United States.

Question. Is Y deriving more than 80 percent of its gross revenues from the "operation of a business or of property or rendering of services" within State B?

Interpretive Response. There are not sufficient facts to respond. If Y owns an interest in the developed land, it might not satisfy the "80 percent of assets" standard as well as the "80 percent of gross revenues" standard. Moreover, Y could not use more than 20 percent of the proceeds of any offerings made pursuant to the rule in connection with the acquisition of the undeveloped land.

Example 4. Z company is a firm of engineering consultants organized under the laws of State E with its only office in that state. During any year, Z will provide consulting services for projects in other states. 75 percent of Z's work in terms of man hours will be performed at Z's offices where it employs some 50 professional and clerical personnel. Z has no employees located outside of State E. However, professional personnel visit project sites and clients' offices in other states. Approximately 50 percent of Z's revenue is derived from clients located in states other than State E.

Question. Is Z deriving more than 80 percent of its gross revenues from "rendering services" within State E?

Interpretive Response. Yes, this aspect of the "doing business within" standard is satisfied.

Example 5. The facts are the same as in Example 4. In addition, at the end of Z's most recent fiscal quarter 25 percent of its assets are represented by accounts receivable from clients in other states.

Question. Does Z satisfy the "assets" standard?

Interpretive Response. Yes, Z satisfies the "assets" standard. For purposes of the rule, accounts receivable arising from a business conducted in the state would generally be considered to be located at the principal office of the issuer.

6. Offerees and Purchasers: Persons Resident—Rule 147(d)

Paragraph (d) of the rule provides that offers and sales may be made only to persons resident within the state or territory. An individual offeree or purchaser of any part of an issue would be deemed to be a person resident within the state or territory if such person has his principal residence in the state or territory. Temporary residence, such as that of many persons in the military service, would not satisfy the provisions of paragraph (d). In addition, if a person purchases securities on behalf of other persons, the residence of those persons must satisfy paragraph (d). If the offeree or purchaser is a business organization its residence will be deemed the state or territory in which it has its principal office, unless it is an entity organized for the specific purpose of acquiring securities in the offering, in which case it will be deemed to be a resident of a state only if all of the beneficial owners of interests in such entity are residents of the state.

As initially proposed, subparagraph (d)(2) provided that an individual, in order to be deemed a resident, must have his principal residence in the state and must not have any present intention of moving his principal residence to another state. The Commission believes that it would be difficult to determine a person's intentions, and accordingly, has deleted the latter requirement. In addition, as initially proposed, the rule would have deemed the residence of a business organization to be the state in which it was incorporated or otherwise organized. The Commission believes that the location of a company's principal office is more of an indication of its local character for purposes of the offeree residence provision of the rule than is its state of incorporation. Section 3(a)(11) requires that an issuer corporation be incorporated within the state, but there is no similar requirement in the statute for a corporation that is an offeree or purchaser.

7. Limitations on Resales—Rule 147(e)

Paragraph (e) of the rule provides that during the period in which securities that are part of an issue are being offered and sold and for a period of nine months from the date of the last sale by the issuer of any part of the issue, resales of any part of the issue by any person shall be made only to persons resident within the same state or territory. This provides objective standards for determining when an issue "comes to rest." The rule as initially proposed limited both *reoffers* and resales during a twelve month period after the last sale by the issuer of any part of the issue. However, the Commission believes that it would be difficult for an issuer to prohibit or even learn of reoffers. Thus, the limitation on reoffers would be impractical because, if any purchaser made a reoffer outside of such state or territory, the issuer would lose the exemption provided by the rule. In addition, the Commission determined that a shorter period would satisfy the coming to rest test for purposes of the rule. Thus, the twelve month period has been reduced to nine months.

Persons who acquire securities from issuers in transactions complying with the rule would acquire unregistered securities that could only be reoffered and resold pursuant to an exemption from the registration provisions of the Act.

The Commission, as it indicated in Rel. 33–5349, considered alternatives to the twelve month period. The Commission has determined that it is in the public interest to adopt a specific time period, but such period has been reduced to nine months and applied to resales only, which provides the necessary protections to investors against interstate trading markets springing up before the securities have come to rest within the state. As an additional precaution, a note to paragraph (e) reminds dealers that they must satisfy the requirements of Rule 15c2–11 under the Securities Exchange Act of 1934 prior to publishing any quotation for a security, or submitting any quotation for publication in any quotation medium.

A note to the rule indicates that where convertible securities are sold pursuant to the rule, resales of either the convertible security, or if it is converted, of the underlying security, could be made during the period specified in paragraph (e) only to residents of the state. However, the conversion itself, if pursuant to Section 3(a)(9) of the Act, would not begin a new period. In the case of warrants and options, sales upon exercise, if done in reliance on the rule, would begin a new period.

8.   Precautions Against Interstate Offers and Sales—Rule 147(f)

Paragraph (f) of the rule requires issuers to take steps to preserve the exemption provided by the rule, since any resale of any part of the issue before it comes to rest within the state to persons resident in another state or territory will, under the Act, be in violation of Section 5. The required steps are: (i) placing a legend on the certificate or other document evidencing the security stating that the securities have not been registered under the Act and setting forth the limitations on resale contained in paragraph (e); (ii) issuing stop transfer instructions to the issuer's transfer agent, if any, with respect to the securities, or, if the issuer transfers its own securities, making a notation in the appropriate records of the issuer; and (iii) obtaining a written representation from each purchaser as to his residence. Where persons other than the issuer are reselling securities of the issuer during the time period specified in paragraph (e) of the rule, the issuer would, if the securities are presented for transfer, be required to take steps (i) and (ii). In addition, the rule requires that the issuer disclose in writing the limitations on resale imposed by paragraph (e) and the provisions of subsections (f)(1)(i) and (ii) and subparagraph (f)(2).

Operation of Rule 147

Rule 147 will operate prospectively only. The staff will issue interpretative letters to assist persons in complying with the rule, but will consider requests for "no action" letters on transactions in reliance on Section 3(a)(11) outside the rule only on an infrequent basis and in the most compelling circumstances.

The rule is a nonexclusive rule. However, persons who choose to rely on Section 3(a)(11) without complying with all the conditions of the rule would have the burden of establishing that they have complied with the judicial and administrative interpretations of Section 3(a)(11) in effect at the time of the offering. The Commission also emphasizes that the exemption provided by Section 3(a)(11) is not an exemption from the civil liability provisions of Section 12(2) or the anti-fraud provisions of Section 17 of the Act or of Section 10(b) of the Securities Exchange Act of 1934. The Commission further emphasizes that Rule 147 is available only for transactions by issuers and is not available for secondary offerings.

In view of the objectives and policies underlying the Act, the rule would not be available to any person with respect to any offering which, although in technical compliance with the provisions of the rule, is part of a plan or scheme by such person to make interstate offers or sales of securities. In such cases, registration would be required. In addition, any plan or scheme that involves a series of offerings by affiliated organizations in various states, even if in technical compliance with the rule, may be outside the parameters of the rule and of Section 3(a)(11) if what is being financed is in effect a single business enterprise.[a]

* * *

DEVELOPMENTS UNDER RULE 147

1. *"Doing Business Within"*. In a series of no-action letters, the SEC's staff has maintained the same strict attitude (some would call it "intransigent") under Rule 147 that SEC v. McDonald Investment Co., supra page 456, reflects toward the "doing business within requirement" under § 3(a)(11). In a 1991 no-action letter request,[1] an issuer sought clarification under Rule 147(c)(2) where it proposed to acquire and service the loan portfolios of several insolvent out-of-state financial institutions from the Federal Deposit Insurance Corporation and another receiver. The purchased loan portfolios would have been serviced exclusively from offices within the state, but most of the loans had been made by the original lenders to out-of-state entities. The SEC declined to issue the requested ruling, noting "that more than 20% of the net proceeds to be received from the proposed offering may be used in connection with services to be performed outside of the state * * *." Sensible result? One commentator has described the result as "hopelessly confused."[2]

2. *Policy Considerations*. A premise of § 3(a)(11) is that the state regulation is adequate to protect investors in legitimately "local" offerings. But is this true? Remember that under either § 3(a)(11) or Rule 147 there is neither a requirement of investor sophistication nor of a disclosure document; similarly, no limitation is placed on the number of purchasers, the aggregate offering size, or the use of general solicitation techniques. In these regards, Rule 147 is far more open-ended than exemptions based on either § 3(b) or § 4(2). Of course,

---

a. See Note, SEC Rule 147: Ten Years of SEC Interpretation, 38 Okla.L.Rev. 507 (1985).

1. See First Commerce of America, Inc., 1991 SEC No–Act. LEXIS 1121 (Sept. 30, 1991); [1991–1992 Transfer Binder] Fed.Sec. L.Rep. (CCH) Para. 76,029.

2. See Haft, Analysis of Key SEC No–Action Letters (1995–1996 ed.).

neither § 3(a)(11) nor Rule 147 contains any exemption from the application of the anti-fraud rules, including Rule 10b–5. Possibly because of the lack of constraints on a Rule 147 offering, the SEC has never adopted the same "innocent and immaterial" defense that it has accepted under Regulation D and Regulation A, which permit the issuer to show that it substantially complied with the exemption's terms even if there was an insubstantial departure. Compare Rules 508 under Regulation D and 260 under Regulation A. Some, however, have suggested that such an "innocent and immaterial" defense should be added to Rule 147.[3]

3. *The Relevance of Offerees.* Should Rule 147 focus simply on purchasers, and ignore offerees (as, for the most part, Regulation D does)? Note, however, that § 3(a)(11) originally exempted securities "sold only to persons resident within a single state," but it was amended to cover only securities "offered and sold" to residents of a single state. Can the SEC ignore this suggestion of legislative intent and adopt a more exemptive rule? Consider the SEC's new and very broad exemptive power under § 28 of the 1933 Act.

4. *Secondary Transactions.* Both Release 5450 (which adopted Rule 147) and Release 4434 (which contains the fullest SEC statement on § 3(a)(11)) indicate that the intrastate offering exemption may be available for secondary offers and sales by controlling persons of the issuer, if the exemption would have been available to the issuer itself. See also Preliminary Note 4 to Rule 147. Nonetheless, some decisions have disagreed. In SEC v. Tuchinsky,[4] the court said that "the exemption created by this section is limited to the original issue of the securities and does not exempt secondary distribution" (citing Vol. III L. Loss & J. Seligman, SECURITIES REGULATION 1142–44 and nn. 5–6 (3d. ed. 1989)). Even if an exemption were not available in the past, should the SEC use its new exemptive power under § 28 of the 1933 Act to create such an exemption? Or is § 3(a)(11) already too overbroad?

5. *The Impact of NSMIA.* In 1996, Congress enacted the National Securities Market Improvement Act of 1996 ("NSMIA") in order to reduce the costs incident to a "dual system of regulation" that required many issuers to register their securities both at the federal and state levels. Although NSMIA has eliminated state "blue sky" review in the case of registered offerings, it has had, by most accounts, "virtually no effect on an issuer making instate offerings."[5] Some critics hold state regulators responsible for persisting in maintaining state-specific compliance regulations that increase compliance costs: "[S]tates had the power to neutralize any of the federal rules that improve access to capital by small (or large) issuers. By enacting or letting stand more restrictive state rules, state regulators were able to exercise hegemony over the SEC, thus effectively neutralizing the new balance struck at the federal level between capital formation and investor protection."[6]

But is this a fair criticism when applied to state rules that apply to offerings covered by Rule 147 or Section 3(a)(11)? After all, the premise of these

3. See Morrissey, Think Globally, Act Locally: It's Time to Reform the Intrastate Exemption, 20 Sec.Reg.L.J. 59 (1992).

4. See [1992 Transfer Binder] Fed.Sec. L.Rep. (CCH) Para. 96,917 (S.D.Fla.June 29, 1992), 1992 WL 226302, at *11–12.

5. See Douglas J. Dorch, National Securities Market Improvement Act: How Improved is the Securities Market?, 36 Duq. L. Rev. 365, 377 (1998).

6. See Rutherford B. Campbell, Jr., The Impact of NSMIA on Small Issuers, 53 Bus. Law. 575, 580 (1998).

rules is that federal regulation is unnecessary because there will be an offering only in one jurisdiction, which will regulate that offering. Hence, the danger of multiple states imposing inconsistent and/or overlapping standards here seems minimal.

6. *Possible Reforms.* In its 1996 report, the SEC's Task Force on Disclosure Simplification discussed several ways in which the § 3(a)(11) intrastate offering exemption could be broadened. These included adopting a more liberalized version of Rule 147 under § 3(b) to cover essentially local offerings (an approach that the SEC had earlier followed in the case of Rule 505, which reads like a private placement exemption, but primarily relies on § 3(b)). Additional ideas recommended by the Task Force included:

a. focusing on purchasers, rather than offerees;

b. permitting the offering to be made to persons who spend substantial time in the jurisdiction, even if they legally reside elsewhere;

c. reducing the "triple 80 percent" test in Rule 147(b)(2) to some lower percentage (possibly 50%) or substituting for the existing test a looser, more qualitative standard, such as "substantial operational activities" or "predominant amount of business". It was also suggested that the use of proceeds test (which was critical in the *McDonald* case) could be deleted.

d. lowering the nine-months resale requirement in Rule 147 to a six month period or even 90 days (the SEC has also considered limiting the definition of an "offering" under § 3(b) to a six month time frame, thereby permitting $10 million to be sold under § 3(b) in any twelve month time period);

e. permitting an offering to cross state lines to a contiguous state or area (i.e., the New York City metropolitan area). This approach would again be most easily implemented by adopting a new exemption paralleling Rule 147 under § 3(b).

f. adopting an "innocent and immaterial" defense under Rule 147 that parallels Rule 508.

CHAPTER 8

REORGANIZATIONS AND RECAPITALIZATIONS

SECTION 1. SECTION 2(A)(3) AND THE THEORY OF "SALE"

Statutes and Regulations

Securities Act, §§ 2(a)(3), 5.

Introductory Note

For § 5 to become operative there must be a "sale" or "offer" of a security. Section 2(a)(3) defines the term "sale" to include "every contract of sale or disposition of a security * * *, for value." There are various types of corporate transactions involving the issue of securities in which the question of whether there must be registration will hinge upon the finding of a "sale" as that term is used in the Securities Act.

(a) *Warrants, Options and Conversion Privileges.* A warrant or right to subscribe to a security is itself a security by the express terms of § 2(a)(1). And the fact that a restricted stock option is non-transferable will not in and of itself remove it from this category.[1] Nevertheless, a warrant, option or right to subscribe need not be registered unless it is to be offered or disposed of for value. Thus, in the ordinary rights offering in which transferable warrants are issued to shareholders without any consideration, the warrants themselves need not be registered. A warrant, however, if immediately exercisable, constitutes an offer to sell the security called for in the warrant and thus makes the registration requirements applicable to that security.[2] This conclusion is consistent with the implication of the last sentence of § 2(a)(3) relating to conversion and subscription rights which are not exercisable until a future date. It also follows that the offer of a security which by its terms is immediately convertible into another security of the same issuer or another entity entails an offer both of the convertible security and of the security into which it may be converted. In practice, therefore, the Commission requires the registration of the securities issuable upon conversion along with registration of the convertible securities.

On the other hand, warrants are frequently sold to underwriters in connection with a public offering of stock of the same class. If these warrants are transferable and may be exercised immediately, the SEC staff takes the view that both the warrants and the stock subject thereto must be registered along with the stock being offered to the general public, even though, for tax or other reasons, exercise of the warrants will in fact not occur for some time after the registration statement becomes effective. Where distribution of the securities subject to the warrants is to be thus postponed, the registration statement must include an undertaking to file a

---

1. See Middle South Utilities, Inc., SEC Holding Co. Act Release No. 14,367 (Feb. 7, 1961); see also Collins v. Rukin, 342 F.Supp. 1282 (D.Mass.1972) (stock option granted to employee held to constitute a security).

2. Securities Act Release No. 3210 (April 9, 1947).

post-effective amendment which shall set forth the manner and terms of the offering and shall become effective prior to any such distribution.[3]

So far we have dealt with warrants and options which are immediately exercisable. Section 2(a)(3) provides that the issue or transfer of a right of conversion or a warrant to subscribe to another security "which * * * cannot be exercised until some future date, shall not be deemed to be an offer or sale of such other security; but the issue or transfer of such other security upon the exercise of such right * * * shall be deemed a sale of such other security." According to the House Report:[4]

> This makes it unnecessary to register such a security prior to the time that it is to be offered to the public, although the conversion right or the right to subscribe must be registered. When the actual securities to which these rights appertain are offered to the public, the bill requires registration as of that time. This permits the holder of any such right of conversion or warrant to subscribe to judge whether upon all the facts it is advisable for him to exercise his rights.

The Report is ambiguous as to when a warrant or conversion right must be registered where the right to exercise is postponed to a future date. Apparently, both the warrant and the underlying security must be registered prior to the exercise date of the warrant, rather than its date of issue.

(b) *Stock Dividends.* Conventional stock dividends "are exempt without express provision as they do not constitute a sale, not being given for value."[5] And while the waiver of a right would constitute "value" under § 2(a)(3), the General Counsel opined that where a corporation declares a dividend payable at the election of the shareholder in cash or securities, "neither the declaration of the dividend, nor the distribution of securities to stockholders who elect to take the dividend in that form, would * * * constitute a sale within the meaning of the Securities Act, and no registration of the securities so distributed would be required by that Act." If, however, the board of directors is so ill-advised as to declare a cash dividend payable to shareholders, and thereafter shareholders are permitted to waive their right to payment of the dividend in cash and to receive the dividend in stock, it was the General Counsel's opinion that a "sale of securities" might be entailed. This conclusion is based upon the prevailing view that upon the public declaration of a cash dividend the holders of the securities with respect to which the dividend is declared thereby become creditors of the corporation and cannot be divested of these rights by subsequent action of the board. It is also another example of the importance of heeding the admonition to "think like a lawyer"![6]

(c) *"Free Stock."* To increase their subscriber base, some Internet companies in the late 1990's devised a series of "stock giveaway" or "free stock" programs under which persons who registered with their website (or who simply visited it) received free stock of the issuer. Because a larger subscriber base enabled the issuer to charge more to advertisers (and to appear a more significant presence in its field, as it approached its IPO), this arrangement made sense to issuers, who in turn sought to convince the SEC that no sale had been made to the recipient of these shares, because the recipient had paid nothing and made no commitment to the issuer. In a series of "no action" letters, the SEC rejected those requests, finding that the issuance of securities in consideration of a person's registration on, or visit to, an issuer's Internet site would be an event of sale within the meaning of Section

3. See Rule 415, Regulation S–K, Item 512(c); 1 L. Loss & J. Seligman, supra note 1, at 567–572 (Rev. ed. 1998).

4. H.R.Rep. No. 85, 73d Cong., 1st Sess. 11 (1933).

5. H.R.Rep. No. 152, 73d Cong., 1st Sess. 25 (1933).

6. SEC Securities Act Release No. 929 (1936).

2(a)(3) of the 1933 Act.[7] Indeed, even when the recipient needed only to send a self-addressed envelope to the issuer, the SEC has taken a similar position, finding that such a "registration" with the issuer by the recipient conferred "value" on the issuer and so came within Section 2(a)(3).[8]

Query: Suppose a beer manufacturer offers one free share of its stock to every purchaser of one case of its beer, and it can demonstrate that there is no discount or bargain thereby conferred because the price of its product is set by local state law and has in any event remained constant for some time. Has a sale occurred? Note in this regard that Section 2(a)(3) of the Securities Act reads in part that "[a]ny security given or delivered with, or as a bonus on account of, any purchase of securities or any other thing, shall be conclusively presumed to constitute a part of the subject of such purchase and to have been offered and sold for value."[9]

(d) *Pledge of Securities.* The Courts of Appeal were divided as to whether a pledge of securities as collateral for a loan entails a sale or disposition of a security or an interest in a security, for value, within the meaning of § 2(a)(3) and § 17(a) of the 1933 Act. Some circuits, relying on the "context" clause prefacing Section 2, concluded that although the securities laws appear literally to apply, the economic reality of the transaction consisted merely of a transfer of possession of securities to the creditor to secure a loan and that no sale or disposition takes place until foreclosure following default on the loan. The Second Circuit reached a contrary result.[10] In Rubin v. United States,[11] the Supreme Court settled the matter and affirmed a criminal conviction for fraud under § 17(a) of the 1933 Act perpetrated by defendant who pledged worthless stock to a bank as collateral for a commercial loan. The Court found the terms of the statute "unambiguous" in determining that a pledge entailed a "disposition of * * * [an] interest in a security, for value." Justice Blackmun concurred, but concluded that a pledge of stock as collateral simply constituted a "disposition" within the meaning of § 2(a)(3), also noting the parallel provision of § 3(a)(14) of the 1934 Act. Accordingly, the transaction may also be subject to the antifraud provisions of Rule 10b–5, although the proscribed act must be committed with respect to the pledged securities.[12]

(e) *Exchanges of Securities.* Although the definition of "sale" does not in terms include an exchange, the courts have had no difficulty in finding an exchange of securities to be a sale. As one court put it: "[O]ne may sell a security and be paid therefor in cash, or in another security, or in any other object of value such as a house. * * * "[13] Congress obviously took this view in enacting §§ 3(a)(9) and 3(a)(10) which exempt certain types of exchanges of securities from the operation of the act. The matter seems quite clear when the security holder voluntarily surrenders the document evidencing the security and receives an entirely different security. But an exchange proposal may result in a substantial change in the rights of an outstanding security without a physical exchange of securities. Thus, in SEC

---

7. See Simplystocks.com, 1999 WL 51836 (S.E.C. No–Action Letter), 1999 SEC No–Act. LEXIS 131 (February 4, 1999); Vanderkam & Sanders, 1999 SEC No–Act. LEXIS 96 (January 27 1999).

8. See Jones and Rutten, 1999 S.E.C. No–Act. LEXIS 555 (June 8, 1999).

9. For the SEC's position, see American Brewing Company, 1999 WL 38280 (S.E.C. No–Action Letter) (January 27, 1999).

10. Mallis v. FDIC, 568 F.2d 824 (2d Cir.1977), cert. dismissed sub nom. Bankers Trust Co. v. Mallis, 435 U.S. 381 (1978).

11. 449 U.S. 424 (1981); Note, New Protection for Defrauded Pledges of Securities Under the Federal Securities Laws, 23 B.C.L.Rev. 821 (1982).

12. Chemical Bank v. Arthur Andersen & Co., 726 F.2d 930 (2d Cir.1984); Head v. Head, 759 F.2d 1172 (4th Cir.1985); United States v. Kendrick, 692 F.2d 1262 (9th Cir. 1982), cert. denied 461 U.S. 914 (1983).

13. United States v. Riedel, 126 F.2d 81 (7th Cir.1942); United States v. Wernes, 157 F.2d 797 (7th Cir.1946).

v. Associated Gas & Electric Co.,[14] extension of the maturity date on a bond by stamping the outstanding certificates with a legend was held to be a new issue and sale of a security under the Public Utility Holding Company Act of 1935. The modification of the original obligation by negotiation between the holders and issuer was deemed to be equivalent to an exchange of the new security for the old. Moreover, a material change in the rights of outstanding securities by way of a charter amendment or otherwise, even though authorized by the law of the state of incorporation, may entail the issue and sale of a new security.[15]

Another common form of exchange arises in a corporate acquisition in which one corporation makes an offer to the shareholders of another corporation to exchange its securities for the securities of the other corporation. In all of the exchanges discussed so far each offeree is free to accept or reject the offer as an individual matter. It is this element of individual consent which differentiates these voluntary exchanges from the corporate reorganizations and recapitalizations entailing a "cram-down," in which the non-consenting security holders are bound by the vote of a majority, subject to any right of appraisal.

SECTION 2.   EXEMPTED EXCHANGES OF SECURITIES BETWEEN AN ISSUER AND ITS SECURITY HOLDERS: SECTION 3(A)(9)

Statutes and Regulations

Securities Act § 3(a)(9).

Rules 149, 150.

Securities Act Release No. 646

Securities and Exchange Commission.
February 3, 1936.

[In 1936, the General Counsel issued two interpretive letters relating to Section 3(a)(9) of the 1933 Act. The first letter concerned a proposed exchange of bonds with three noteholders. In responding to this query, the General Counsel had this to say:]

* * *

"I believe Section 3(a)(9) is applicable only to exchanges which are bona fide, in the sense that they are not effected merely as a step in a plan to evade the registration requirements of the Act. For example, Corporation A, as part of such a plan, might issue a large block of its securities to Corporation B, and might then issue new securities to Corporation B in exchange for the first-issued securities, with the understanding that such new securities are to be offered to the public by Corporation B. In my opinion, the mere fact that the exchange in such case might comply with the literal conditions of Section 3(a)(9) would not avail to defeat the necessity for registration of the securities issued in such exchange. Cf. Gregory v. Helvering, 293 U.S. 465.

14. 99 F.2d 795 (2d Cir.1938).

15. United States v. New York, New Haven & Hartford Railroad Co., 276 F.2d 525 (2d Cir.1960), cert. denied 362 U.S. 961 (1960); Western Air Lines, Inc. v. Sobieski, 191 Cal.App.2d 399, 12 Cal.Rptr. 719 (1961); McGuigan & Aiken, Amendment of Securities, 9 Rev. of Sec.Reg. 935 (1976).

"In determining whether a particular exchange had been effected merely as a step in a plan to evade the registration requirements of the Act, I believe that a court would take into account various factors such as the length of time during which the securities received by the issuer were outstanding prior to their surrender in exchange, the number of holders of the securities originally outstanding, the marketability of such securities, and also the question whether the exchange is one which was dictated by financial considerations of the issuer and not primarily in order to enable one or a few security holders to distribute their holdings to the public. * * *

The second opinion of the General Counsel was in reply to an inquiry whether securities previously received by a controlling stockholder in a bona fide exchange exempt under Section 3(a)(9) should be registered before being offered to the public through an underwriter. The relevant portion of the opinion follows:

"In order to make clear my position on this question, I must briefly review the legislative histories of the present Section 3(a)(9) and of Section 2(11) of the Securities Act of 1933.

"The last sentence of Section 2(11) * * * by defining an underwriter to include a person purchasing from one in a control relation with the issuer, makes the exemption afforded by Section 4(1) inapplicable to transactions by such a person and thus necessitates registration before distribution to the public of securities acquired from a person in a control relation. The report of the House Committee, which considered the identical language in the bill then before the Committee (H.R. 5480), leaves no doubt as to the reason for this requirement * * *.

    * * *

"Section 2(11) thus gives expression to the clear intent of Congress to subject to the registration requirements of the Act any redistribution of securities purchased from persons in a control relation with the issuer.[a]

"Turning to the present Section 3(a)(9), I call your attention to the fact that, although this Section in terms excepts *securities* issued in certain transactions of exchange, its predecessor, Section 4(3) exempted only such *transactions* of exchange. Consequently, before the 1934 amendments, distribution by a controlling person through an underwriter of stock previously issued in a transaction exempt under form Section 4(3), was subject to the registration requirements. The reasons for the relevant amendment therefore become important.

"The question early arose whether dealers' transactions in securities exchanged in a Section 4(3) transaction were exempt from the registration requirements of the Securities Act. Section 4(1) specifically excepts from the dealers' exemption

    " 'transactions within one year after the first date upon which a security was bona fide offered to the public';

but in order to effectuate the evident purpose of the Act, the Federal Trade Commission took the position that dealers' transactions in securities originally issued in a transaction exempt under Section 4(3) were exempt, even though

---

    a. See H.R. 85, 73d Cong., 1st Sess., pp. 13–14.

such dealers' transactions were effected within a year of the first offering of such securities.

"[T]he purpose of the amendment changing Section 4(3) to Sections 3(a)(9) and 3(a)(10) was to incorporate in the Act this opinion of the Commission[. This] appears from the * * * report of the Conference Committee which considered these amendments.[b]

* * *

"This language clearly evidences that the Congressional intent was merely to offer a more adequate statutory basis for the Commission's previous interpretation, and not to alter the fundamental requirement of Section 2(11).

"Moreover, the fact that the securities in question fall within Section 3(a) does not necessarily preclude consideration of the necessity of their registration before certain transactions therein can be effected. Sections 3(a)(2) to 3(a)(8) inclusive describe classes of securities which are of such an intrinsic nature that it is evident that Congress felt that, regardless of the character of the transaction in which they have been or are to be issued or publicly offered, their registration was not necessary for the protection of investors. * * * In the language of House Report No. 85, quoted supra, a large public offering of such securities possesses all the dangers attendant upon a new offering by their issuer.

* * *

"In view of the Congressional purpose in enacting the last sentence of Section 2(11), the legislative history of the present Section 3(a)(9), and the lack of any rational basis for the continuance of the exemption provided by Section 3(a)(9) to a later offering of securities by an underwriter, it is my opinion that securities received in a Section 3(a)(9) exchange should be registered before their public distribution through an underwriter by a person in control of their issuer."

Securities Act Release No. 2029

Securities and Exchange Commission.
August 8, 1939.

[Letter of General Counsel Relating to Sections 3(a)(9) and 4(1).]

* * *

You have requested an opinion as to the applicability of Section 3(a)(9) and the second clause of Section 4(1) of the Securities Act of 1933 in the following circumstances:

The subject company has an "open end" mortgage upon its properties, the only issue of bonds now outstanding thereunder being denoted as Series A bonds. It is proposed to create two new series of bonds under the mortgage, to be called Series B and Series C bonds respectively, for the purpose of refunding the outstanding bonds. The Series B and Series C bonds will differ substantially from each other in respect of maturity date, interest rate, redemption prices and default provisions.

b. The statement of the report of the Conference Committee in H.R. 1838, 73d Cong., 2d Sess., p. 40 is omitted.

The Series B bonds will be offered in exchange to the holders of the outstanding Series A bonds on the basis of an equal principal amount of Series B bonds for those of Series A, with interest adjustment. No commission or other remuneration will be paid or given, directly or indirectly, for soliciting such exchange.

The necessary funds to redeem any unexchanged Series A bonds will be raised by the sale for cash of Series C bonds. The Series C bonds will be offered and sold to not more than twelve insurance companies, which will agree to purchase for investment and without a view to distribution.

If the proposed exchange offer and the proposed cash offer were isolated transactions, it would be clear that no registration under the Securities Act would be required. The Series B bonds would be exempted as securities "exchanged by the issuer with its existing security holders exclusively where no commission or other remuneration is paid or given directly or indirectly for soliciting such exchange;" and the offering and sale of the Series C bonds would be exempted by the second clause of Section 4(1), as "transactions by an issuer not involving any public offering." The interdependence of the two offerings, however, requires a more comprehensive analysis of the Act.

Section 3(a)(9) contains no language expressly limiting the exemption to securities forming part of an issue the whole of which is sold as specified in the exempting provision. At first reading, therefore, Section 3(a)(9) appears to confer exemption upon any security exchanged with the issuer's existing security holders, even though other securities of the same class, as a part of the same plan of financing, are sold to others than existing security holders, or to existing security holders otherwise than by way of exchange. Such a construction, however, gives insufficient weight to the use of the word "exclusively," as employed both in Section 3(a)(9) and in its predecessor, former Section 4(3). In neither section is the grammatical function of the word entirely clear; but in order to avoid an interpretation which would reject the word as pure surplusage, it is necessary to adopt the view that the exemption is available only to securities constituting part of an issue which, as a whole, is exchanged in conformity with the requirements of the section.

This conclusion appears to be supported by the legislative history of Section 3(a)(9). * * * [T]he changes in the proposed Section 3(a)(9) made in conference were "intended only to clarify its meaning" (H.R. (Conf.) Rep. No. 1838, 73rd Cong., 2nd Sess., p. 40).

Interpretation of the so-called "private offering" exemption provided by the second clause of Section 4(1) [the predecessor of § 4(2)] presents similar considerations. You will note that the clause in question does not exempt every transaction which is not itself a public offering, but only transactions "not involving any public offering." Accordingly, I am of the opinion that the exemption is not available to securities privately offered if any other securities comprised within the same issue are made the subject of a public offering.

It appears, therefore, that both with respect to Section 3(a)(9) and with respect to Section 4(1) the necessity of registering the Series B and Series C bonds depends upon whether they should be deemed separate issues or merely parts of a single issue. I believe it unnecessary at this time to enter into any extended discussion of what constitutes an "issue" for the purposes of the Act. The opinion of the Commission in In the Matter of Unity Gold Corporation (Securities Act Release No. 1776) discusses this question as it arises under

Section 3(b) of the Act. The point is also touched upon, at least inferentially, in the discussion of Section 3(a)(11) contained in Securities Act Release No. 1459. Whatever may be the precise limits of the concept of "issue" when all securities involved are of the same class, I do not believe that securities of different classes can fairly be deemed parts of a single "issue." Since on the facts submitted the Series B and Series C bonds appear to be securities of different classes, they constitute separate "issues," and may be offered and sold in the manner above described without being registered under the Securities Act.[a]

In expressing this opinion I do not mean to imply that any difference in the incidents of two blocks of securities, however trivial, renders the blocks separate classes and consequently separate "issues" for the purposes of the Act. In this case, however, the differences between the Series B and Series C bonds are, I believe, sufficiently substantial to warrant treating them as separate classes even though they will be issued under the same mortgage indenture.

THE STATUS OF SECTION 3(a)(9) EXCHANGES

Like § 3(b) (the small issue exemption), § 3(a)(9) is a transaction exemption tucked away in § 3 amidst other exemptions that apply to classes of securities. Its existence is largely attributable to the economic exigencies of the early Depression era when many financially-strained corporations were forced to attempt voluntary reorganizations in which they exchanged equity securities (or some package of equity and debt securities) for senior securities on which they could no longer pay the interest or principal on maturity.[1]

Although today § 3(a)(9) is frequently used by issuers that are not in any financial peril, the most common transaction under it remains an offer by an issuer to swap a new security for an outstanding senior security (often one whose principal is approaching maturity). However, an exchange transaction can also be used today to take a company private in a leveraged buyout (with the company's shareholders receiving debt securities plus cash for their common shares) or to issue special "superweighted" voting stock as a defensive measure in order to "protect" a company from a hostile takeover. Although most exchanges under § 3(a)(9) are voluntary, an involuntary exchange can be compelled under many state laws if there is a shareholder approved amendment of the articles of incorporation (or if state law otherwise permits a mandatory exchange). In such cases, a proxy solicitation will be used if the company is a reporting company, but the exemption under the 1933 Act will come from either § 3(a)(9) or Rules 144 or 145, which are discussed later.

1. *Convertible Securities.* Section 3(a)(9) applies to the conversion of convertible stock (such as a preferred stock that is convertible into common shares). The interrelationship of § 3(a)(9) and § 2(a)(3) merits special attention here. As noted earlier in this Chapter, § 2(a)(3) provides that "[t]he issue or transfer of a right or privilege . . . giving the holder of such security the right to convert such security into another security of the same issuer" is not an offer or sale of the underlying security if the right cannot be exercised until some

----

a. In 1939, the integration doctrine was at an early stage in its development. This opinion discusses its application in the context of §§ 4(2), 3(b) and 3(a)(11). See the section on "Integration of Exemptions", infra, at page 514.

1. See H.R.Rep. No. 152, 73rd Cong., 1st Sess. 25 (1933).

future date. Thus, if in 1998 a company issues convertible preferred stock which cannot be transferred into common stock until 1999, there is no obligation to register the common stock today. Section 2(a)(3) provides that the subsequent conversion is a sale, but § 3(a)(9) is then available to exempt this exchange transaction from registration. There still remains the question of whether a continuing offer is being made once the conversion feature becomes exercisable, even though the actual exchange of the convertible preferred for the common will be exempt under § 3(a)(9). Here, the Commission's position has wavered over the years, but currently it agrees that § 3(a)(9) exempts the continuing offer of the common stock from §§ 5(b) and (c), as well as the sale from § 5(a).

2. *The Dual Meanings of "Exclusively".* Securities Act Release No. 2029 indicates that the word "exclusively" in § 3(a)(9) is read by the SEC to have two consequences: (1) the issuer must offer the exchange exclusively for a class of securities held by its securityholders and not ask them to contribute cash as well, and (2) the offering must be exclusively with an existing class of security-holders; that is, shares of the same class (or a similar class) may not be contemporaneously offered to other investors for other consideration. If they are, the two offerings may be integrated into a single offering, and the § 3(a)(9) exemption will be lost. Note, however, that there is no barrier to the issuer offering cash plus a new class of securities for an outstanding class of securities. Indeed, Rule 150 expressly permits such payments by the issuer. Rather, the prohibition under § 3(a)(9) is on the investor being asked to make a further cash or property investment. Even this barrier has been relaxed slightly. Rule 149 permits the issuer to request securityholders to pay cash to the extent "necessary to effect an equitable adjustment" in the dividends or interest for the exchanged security.

Suppose an issuer has cumulative accrued dividends of $30 per share outstanding on its preferred stock, and offers to exchange three shares of common stock for each share of the cumulative preferred (with the result that the cumulative dividends of $30 per share will be lost). Does this exchange which requires the surrender of a likely future cash payment by the shareholder meet the "exclusively" test? The Commission interprets § 3(a)(9) to bar only the investment of new consideration by the investor, and thus it has not objected to such an exchange under § 3(a)(9). Indeed, the Commission has even permitted an exchange under § 3(a)(9) where the shareholders were required to release claims underlying a securities fraud lawsuit as a condition of the exchange.[2]

3. *Solicitation Expenses.* One of the practical barriers to the use of § 3(a)(9) is that the issuer cannot hire an underwriter or other agent to solicit the class of securityholders because of the final clause of § 3(a)(9) which prohibits payment of any "commission or other renumeration ... directly or indirectly for soliciting such exchange." Although the issuer can use its own employees, this may not be practical; nor may sophisticated investors place much weight on their analyses. The Commission has, however, relaxed this prohibition in recent no-action letters. In one important no-action letter, a financially imperilled issuer won permission to use an investment banking firm, which was the company's financial adviser, to meet with a committee of institutional investors to discuss and answer questions regarding the issuer's proposed restructuring through an exchange offer.[3] To obtain the requested no-

---

2. See First Pennsylvania Mortgage Trust, SEC No-Action Letter, 1997 WL 13863 (Feb. 4, 1977); See also Seaman Furniture Co., 1989 SEC No-Act. LEXIS 1014, *13–*14.

action letter, the issuer represented that its investment banking firm would only play an informational role and would not express its views or recommendations on the proposed exchange. Can this fuzzy line between providing information and making recommendations be effectively monitored? More generally, should the SEC liberalize § 3(a)(9) where it (like § 3(a)(11)) requires no disclosure statement and contains no restrictions on the nature of the investors to whom the offer can be made? For the view that § 3(a)(9) represents an overbroad exemption in its present form, see Hicks, Recapitalizations Under Section 3(a)(9) of the Securities Act of 1933, 61 Va.L.Rev. 1057 (1995).

4. *Resales.* Section 3(a)(9) exempts only the exchange transaction, not the subsequent resale by the investor who makes the exchange. For most investors, the exemption that will permit them to resell immediately the exchanged securities is § 4(1). That is, if the securities surrendered were not "restricted securities" (a term that is defined in Rule 144), those received in return will also not be "restricted" and can be sold immediately. But controlling persons remain controlling persons, and should they seek to resell the exchanged security, the resulting transaction may involve an underwriter under the last sentence of § 2(a)(11). Hence, they will typically need to comply with the "trickle" provisions of Rule 144 or make a private sale, both of which options are discussed later in Chapter 9. Even noncontrolling shareholders may have to find another exemption (other than § 4(1)) if the securities surrendered by them in the exchange were issued under an exemption, such as § 3(a)(11) or § 4(2). Remember that under Rule 147 there is a nine month wait before securities issued in an exempt intrastate offering can be sold out of state, and an exchange under § 3(a)(9) does not shorten that period. Under § 4(2), "restricted securities" remain restricted securities, and a § 3(a)(9) exchange does not free them for immediate sale.[4] Instead, the holder will typically wait out the holding period under Rule 144 or make a private sale pursuant to the so-called § 4(1½) exemption, as discussed later in Chapter 9.

SECTION 3.   REORGANIZATIONS AND RECLASSIFICATIONS: THE "NO-SALE" RULE AND ITS ABOLITION

A.   THE ORIGINAL DOGMA: RULE 133 AND THE "NO-SALE" THEORY

Excerpt from:

"Disclosure to Investors"—Report and Recommendations to the Securities and Exchange Commission from the Disclosure Policy Study

"The Wheat Report", pp. 251–278 (1969).[a]

* * *

BUSINESS COMBINATIONS

Business combinations in which payment by the acquiring corporation is made in its own securities are effected in three standard ways: (1) a voluntary

---

3. See Seaman Furniture Co., supra note 2.

4. For a fuller discussion, see Campbell, Resales of Securities Under the Securities Act of 1933, 52 Wash. & Lee L.Rev. 1333, 1356–59 (1995).

a. The Chairman of this policy study was Francis M. Wheat, an SEC Commissioner.

exchange of securities, (2) a statutory merger or consolidation, and (3) a sale of the assets of the acquired company in exchange for securities of the acquiring company, which are thereupon transferred to the seller's shareholders on its dissolution.

Where method (1) is used, an offer of securities of the acquiring corporation is made directly to the shareholders of the acquired corporation. In methods (2) and (3), the shareholders of the corporation to be acquired are asked to cast their individual votes for or against approval of the acquisition, or, in realistic terms, for or against a legal procedure by which their present shareholdings are exchanged for shares in another company.

Employment of method (1) subjects the transaction to the disclosure requirements of the '33 Act. Employment of methods (2) or (3) does not [at the time of this report]. The reason for this lies in the existence of a longstanding Commission rule (Rule 133) under which the submission of the acquisition transactions to the vote of shareholders is not deemed to involve a "sale" or "offer to sell" the shares of the acquiring company so far as those shareholders are concerned.

Rule 133 has led a controversial life. It seems clear to the Study that its theoretical basis—the notion that the change in the stockholdings of the shareholders of the acquired corporation occurs exclusively through "corporate action"—is, in the words of Professor Loss, "unforgivably formalistic."

* * *

A renewed attempt must be made to solve the problems associated with business combinations. The following guideposts are suggested:

(a) Commission policy should recognize the fact that when a shareholder is asked to vote on the question whether or not his company should be acquired by another and, accordingly, whether or not he wishes to exchange his shares for the securities of the acquired company, an offer of a security within the meaning of the '33 Act is made to him;

(b) When the offering to such shareholders constitutes a "public offering" within the meaning of the '33 Act, Commission policy should be to give the shareholders of the company to be acquired a disclosure document containing the information essential to an intelligent choice;

(c) When the offering to such shareholders constitutes a nonpublic offering under the '33 Act, Commission policy should be to provide the shareholders of the company to be acquired with clear and appropriate guidelines as to where and how they can resell the new shares which they have received. Such guidelines should eliminate the unwarranted distinctions which presently exist between a business combination accomplished by a voluntary exchange of shares on the one hand, and one which takes the form of a statutory merger or sale of assets on the other.

* * *

Three years later the Commission followed the recommendations of the Disclosure Policy Study "The Wheat Report" with respect to disclosure in business combinations. Despite considerable opposition, the Commission abolished the "no-sale" theory embodied in Rule 133 in 1972 and adopted Rule 145 imposing registration in certain business combinations.

B. THE NEW REVISIONISM: BUSINESS COMBINATIONS UNDER RULE 145 AND FORM S–4

Statutes and Regulations

Securities Act: Rules 145, 153A and Form S–4.

Exchange Act Rules: 14a–2, 14a–6, 14a–9, 14c–5.

Securities Act Release No. 5316

Securities and Exchange Commission.
October 6, 1972.

NOTICE OF ADOPTION OF RULES 145, AND 153A, PROSPECTIVE RESCISSION OF RULE 133, AMENDMENT OF FORM S–14[a] UNDER THE SECURITIES ACT OF 1933 AND AMENDMENT OF RULES 14a–2, 14a–6 AND 14c–5 UNDER THE SECURITIES EXCHANGE ACT OF 1934

The Securities and Exchange Commission today announced the adoption of Rule 145 under the Securities Act of 1933 ("Act") and several related proposals and the prospective rescission of Rule 133 under that Act. The effect of this action will be to subject transactions involving business combinations of types described in the new rule to the registration requirements of the Act. * * *

* * *

BACKGROUND AND PURPOSE

Congress, in enacting the federal securities statutes, created a continuous disclosure system designed to protect investors and to assure the maintenance of fair and honest securities markets. The Commission in administering and implementing the objectives of these statutes has sought to coordinate and integrate this disclosure system, and the rescission of Rule 133 and adoption of Rule 145 and related matters are further steps in this direction.

* * *

Rule 145 is * * * intended to inhibit the creation of public markets in securities of issuers about which adequate current information is not available to the public. This approach is consistent with the philosophy underlying the Act, that a disclosure law provides the best protection for investors. If a security holder who is offered a new security in a Rule 145 business combination transaction has available to him the material facts about the transaction, he will be in a position to make an informed investment judgment. In order to provide such information in connection with public offerings of these securities, Rule 145 will require the filing of a registration statement with the Commission and the delivery to security holders of a prospectus containing accurate and current information concerning the proposed business combination transaction.

a. Form S–14 has been replaced by Form S–4, effective July 1, 1985. Securities Act Release No. 6578 (Apr. 23, 1985). Form F–4 is available to foreign private issuers.

EXPLANATION AND ANALYSIS

I. *Rescission of Rule 133. Definition for Purposes of Section 5 of "Sale,"*
   "Offer to Sell," and "Offer for Sale."

Rule 133 provides that for purposes only of Section 5 of the Act, the submission to a vote of stockholders of a corporation of a proposal for certain mergers, consolidations, reclassifications of securities or transfers of assets is not deemed to involve a "sale", "offer", "offer to sell", or "offer for sale" of the securities of the new or surviving corporation to the security holders of the disappearing corporation. That rule further provides that persons who are affiliates of the constituent corporation are deemed to be underwriters within the meaning of the Section 2(11) of the Act, and except for certain limited amounts cannot sell their securities in the surviving corporation without registration.

The "no-sale" theory embodied in Rule 133 is based on the rationale that the types of transactions specified in the rule are essentially corporate acts, and the volitional act on the part of the individual stockholder required for a "sale" was absent. The basis of this theory was that the exchange or alteration of the stockholder's security occurred not because he consented thereto, but because the corporate action, authorized by a specified majority of the interests affected, converted his security into a different security.

* * *

Transactions of the type described in Rule 133 do not, in the Commission's opinion, occur solely by operation of law without the element of individual stockholder volition. A stockholder faced with a Rule 133 proposal must decide on his own volition whether or not the proposal is one in his own best interest. The basis on which the "no-sale" theory is predicated, namely, that the exchange or alteration of the stockholder's security occurs not because he consents thereto but because the corporation by authorized corporate action converts his securities, in the Commission's opinion, is at best only correct in a formalistic sense and overlooks the reality of the transaction. The corporate action, on which such great emphasis is placed, is derived from the individual consent given by each stockholder in voting on a proposal to merge or consolidate a business or reclassify a security. In voting, each consenting stockholder is expressing his voluntary and individual acceptance of the new security, and generally the disapproving stockholder is deferring his decision as to whether to accept the new security or, if he exercises his dissenter's rights, a cash payment. The corporate action in these circumstances, therefore, is not some type of independent fiat, but is only the aggregate effect of the voluntary decisions made by the individual stockholders to accept or reject the exchange. Formalism should no longer deprive investors of the disclosure to which they are entitled.

* * *

In addition, the Commission has difficulty in reconciling Rule 133 with certain exemptive provisions of the Act. For example, Section 3(a)(9) of the Act exempts from the registration provisions of the Act the issuance of securities in a reclassification only where no commission or other remuneration is paid or given directly or indirectly for solicitation. Notwithstanding, Rule 133 in effect provides an exemption from registration for the issuance of securities in a reclassification even though a commission or other remuneration is paid for solicitation. Further, Section 3(a)(10) exempts from the registration provisions of the Act securities issued only in court or administratively supervised reorganizations. Yet Rule 133 in effect provides that securities issued in reorganizations of the type described therein are not subject to the registration provisions of the Act even though there is no judicial or administrative supervision.

Furthermore, the Commission is aware of situations in which companies have utilized the Rule to avoid or evade the registration provisions of the Act. This has resulted in large quantities of unregistered securities being distributed to the public and has not been in the public interest or for the protection of investors.

* * *

In view of the above, the Commission is of the opinion that transactions covered by Rule 133 involve a "sale", "offer", "offer to sell", or "offer for sale" as those terms are defined in Section 2(3) of the Act. The Commission no longer sees any persuasive reason why, as a matter of statutory construction or policy, in light of the broad remedial purposes of the Act and of public policy which strongly supports registration, this should not be the interpretative meaning.

II. *Adoption of Rule 145. Reclassifications of Securities, Mergers, Consolidations and Acquisitions of Assets.*

* * *

B. Rule 145(a). Transactions Within the Rule

Paragraph (a) of Rule 145 provides that the submission to a vote of security holders of a proposal for certain reclassifications of securities, mergers, consolidations, or transfers of assets, is deemed to involve an "offer", "offer to sell", "offer for sale", or "sale" of the securities to be issued in the transaction. The effect of the Rule is to require registration of the securities to be issued in connection with such transactions, unless an exemption from registration is available. * * *

In response to comments received from the public, several textual changes have been made in Rule 145(a) as proposed. * * * [T]he rule has been revised to read "corporation or other person" in order to make clear that it applies to all issuers, without distinction as to the form of business organization. Also, the phrase "certificate of incorporation" has been revised to read "certificate of incorporation or similar controlling instruments."

A number of comments focused upon the question of whether foreign issuers should be included within the scope of Rule 145. * * * The United States securities statutes were intended to protect United States investors who buy securities of foreign issuers, and the need for the protections afforded by registration is not diminished because the issuer has a foreign domicile. Accordingly, Rule 145 will apply to foreign issuers making offers or sales of securities to United States investors, unless an exemption is available under the Securities Act. * * * To clarify the applicability of Rule 145 to foreign issuers, the phrase "state of incorporation" has been changed to read "jurisdiction".

Also in response to public comments, Rule 145 has been revised to make clear that it covers transactions involving action taken upon security holder approval. The words "or consent" have been added to the word "vote" wherever it appears.

1. Rule 145(a)(1). Reclassifications.

Rule 145(a), as proposed, covered any reclassification "other than a stock split or reverse stock split which involves the substitution of a security for another security." The rule has been revised to also exclude any reclassification which involves only a change in par value.

2. Rule 145(a)(2). Mergers or Consolidations.

Rule 145(a)(2) has been revised in three respects. The first revision adds the phrase "or similar plan of acquisition" after the words "merger or consolidation" because a number of similar transactions do not fit precisely within the terms "merger or consolidation". The second revision adds the phrase "held by such security holders" to describe those securities which will become or be exchanged for other securities. This revision is designed to clarify that in a transaction of the character described in Rule 145(a), an offer occurs under the rule only as to security holders who are entitled to vote or consent to the matter, and who hold securities which become or will be exchanged for new securities. The third revision adds an exception to indicate that registration is not required where a merger or consolidation is effected solely to change an issuer's domicile.[b]

Several commentators suggested that the applicability of Rule 145 to short-form mergers should be clarified. In certain instances, state law allows a merger of a parent and its 85 to 90 percent owned subsidiary to be consummated without shareholder approval. Because Rule 145(a) is couched in terms of offers arising in connection with a submission for the vote or consent of security holders, short-form mergers not requiring such vote or consent are not within the scope of the Rule. However, if a security is to be issued in such short-form mergers, the Commission is of the opinion that the transaction involves an "offer", "offer to sell", "offer for sale" or "sale", within the meaning of Section 2(3) of the Act, and accordingly such transactions are subject to the registration provisions of the Act unless an exemption is available.

3. Rule 145(a)(3). Transfers of Assets.

Rule 145(a)(3) has been revised to clarify those conditions under which Rule 145 is applicable to a stock for assets transaction. As revised, the rule applies only if: (1) the matter voted upon provides for dissolution of the corporation receiving the securities; (2) the matter voted upon provides for a pro rata distribution by the corporation receiving the securities; (3) the directors of the corporation receiving the securities adopt resolutions relative to (1) or (2) within one year after the vote; or (4) a subsequent dissolution or distribution is part of a pre-existing plan for distribution. However, if the securities acquired in the transaction are distributed after one year, notwithstanding the absence of a plan, such securities must be registered unless a statutory exemption from registration is then available.

With regard to the third condition above, if the vote of the stockholders of the selling corporation is taken to authorize the sale, and the selling corporation thereafter decides to dissolve or distribute the securities within one year

b. Rule 145(a)(2) has been amended to make clear that the change of domicile exception does not apply when a change in nation-al jurisdiction is involved. Securities Act Release No. 6579 (Apr. 23, 1985).

after the transaction, the sale of assets and the dissolution or distribution by the selling corporation are deemed to be portions of the same transaction and to involve a sale for value of the purchasing corporation's stock to the shareholders of the selling corporation. Accordingly, the transaction should be registered on Form [S–4] at the time the plan or agreement for the sale of assets is submitted to shareholders for their vote or consent if it is contemplated that the corporation receiving the securities will adopt resolutions within one year for dissolution or distribution of the securities received. If the transaction is not registered at the time of submission of the plan or agreement for the vote or consent of security holders, but a resolution for dissolution or distribution of the securities received is adopted within one year, the issuer should file a registration statement covering the dissolution or distribution of securities on the appropriate form other than Form [S–4], unless an exemption is available.

C. Rule 145(b). Communications Not Deemed to Be a "Prospectus" or "Offer to Sell"

Notice of a proposed action or of a meeting of security holders for voting on transactions of the character specified in Rule 145 is generally sent or furnished to security holders. Because the Rule will make the registration provisions of the Act applicable to these transactions, questions have been raised as to whether such notices will constitute statutory prospectuses or involve an offer for sale of a security. Paragraph (b) of Rule 145 is designed to resolve these questions by providing that any written communication which contains no more than the information specified in paragraph (b) of the Rule shall not be deemed a prospectus for purposes of Section 2(10) of the Act and shall not be deemed an "offer for sale" of the security involved for the purposes of Section 5 of the Act.

Rule 145(b) has been revised to expand the permissible information that may be included in the announcement. The revised Rule permits the identification of all parties to the transaction; a brief description of their business; a description of the basis upon which the transaction will be made; and any legend or similar statement required by federal law or state or administrative authority. Also, paragraph (b) of the Rule has been revised to indicate that the notice may take the form of a written communication "or other published statement."[c]

D. Rule 145(c). Persons and Parties Deemed to Be Underwriters

Rule 145(c), as proposed, contained specific criteria designed to clarify the underwriter status of persons who acquire substantial amounts of securities in a business combination registered on Form [S–4], and who desire to resell such securities. The public comments on the proposal noted legal and policy arguments against any interpretation that imposes statutory underwriter status on persons solely by virtue of their receiving more than a certain amount of securities in a business combination. * * * Because the question of the underwriter status of persons taking substantial portions of registered offerings arises in connection with all registered offerings, the Commission believes that

---

c. Cf. Rule 145(b) with Rule 135 permitting tombstone ads in the waiting period of the registration process and Rule 14a–12 allowing advance solicitations in proxy contests and tender offers. All are designed to protect against the charge of gun-jumping.

the matter should be dealt with in a more comprehensive manner after further study, and not just in the limited context of business combinations.

Accordingly, Rule 145(c) has been revised by deleting the quantitative standards contained in the proposal. * * * Revised paragraph (c) of the Rule provides that any party to any transaction specified in Rule 145(a), other than the issuer, or any person who is an affiliate of such party at the time any such transaction is submitted for vote or consent, who [publicly] offers or sells securities acquired in such transaction, shall be deemed to be engaged in a distribution and therefore an underwriter, except with respect to the limited resales permitted pursuant to paragraph (d) of Rule 145. Moreover, from a practical standpoint, because such persons usually are in a position to verify the accuracy of information set forth in the registration statement, and usually are in a position to influence the transaction, the Commission believes that this provision is not unreasonably burdensome.

Rule 145(c) includes a definition of the term "party" with respect to the phrase "any party to any transaction specified in paragraph (a) * * * "The term is defined to mean the corporations, business entities, or other persons, other than the issuer, whose assets or capital structure are affected by the transaction specified in paragraph (a).

The securities received in a Rule 145 transaction by persons who are neither affiliates of the acquired company nor of the acquiring company are registered securities without restriction on resale.

E.   Rule 145(d).   Resale Provisions For Persons and Parties Deemed Underwriters

Rule 145(d) provides that a person or party specified in paragraph (c) shall not be deemed to be engaged in a distribution if he sells in accordance with certain provisions of Rule 144: paragraph (c) (Current Public Information); (e) (Limitation on Amount of Securities Sold); (f) (Manner of Sale); and (g) (Brokers' Transactions). This provision is designed to permit public sale by such persons or parties in ordinary trading transactions of limited quantities of securities. Such resales are permissible within successive [three]-month periods, but no accumulation is permitted, i.e., the person cannot skip [three] months and then sell an accumulated amount in the following [three] months.[d]

The volume limitations of Rule 144(e) for resales of securities [within the three-months measuring period for both listed and unlisted securities may not exceed the *greater* of (1) one percent of the outstanding securities of a class, or (2) the average weekly trading volume of the four calendar weeks preceding the sale. The trading volume of listed securities is measured by all national securities exchange trading volume, of unlisted securities traded on NASDAQ by NASDAQ trading volume, and of National Market System securities by national securities exchange and NASDAQ trading volume.] It should be noted that the holding period requirement of Rule 144(d), and the requirement to file a Form 144 pursuant to Rule 144(h) are not applicable. In addition to resales

---

d. Rule 145(d) has been amended to permit a non-affiliate of the issuer who has held such securities for at least two years, where the issuer meets the reporting requirements of Rule 144(c), to make resales of the securities without restriction. A non-affiliate who has held the securities for at least three years is free to make resales without any restrictions. Securities Act Release No. 6508 (Feb. 10, 1984).

permitted by Rule 145(d), Form [S–4] may be used for the registration under the Act of distributions by persons or parties who are deemed underwriters.

F. Rule 145(e). Definition of "Person"

Paragraph (e) of Rule 145 provides that the term "person" in paragraphs (c) and (d) of the rule when used with reference to a person for whose account securities are to be sold, shall have the same meaning as the definition of that term in paragraph (a)(2) of Rule 144 under the Act.

III. *Rule 153A. Definition of "Preceded by a Prospectus" as used in Section 5(b)(2) of the Act, in Relation to Certain Transactions Requiring Approval of Security Holders.*

Rule 153A defines the phrase "preceded by a prospectus" in connection with transactions of the type subject to Rule 145. The rule has been revised in two respects. First, the word "delivery" has been substituted for the word "sending" to conform the Rule to the General Instructions in [Form S–4]. Second, the Rule has been revised to apply the delivery requirement when action is taken by consent.

The persons entitled to vote on or consent to a Rule 145 transaction will usually be determined either: (1) by the fixing of a record date for shareholders so entitled or, (2) by the closing of the stock transfer records of the acquired company. The group of persons thus determined may, because of interim transfers, vary somewhat from the group of persons ultimately entitled to receive the securities issued in the transaction. Thus, Rule 153A provides that the delivery of the final prospectus to security holders entitled to vote on or consent to the transaction shall be deemed to satisfy the prospectus delivery requirements of Section 5(b)(2) of the Act.

* * *

Securities Act Release No. 5463

Securities and Exchange Commission.
February 28, 1974.

DIVISION OF CORPORATION FINANCE'S INTERPRETATIONS OF RULE 145 AND RELATED MATTERS

* * *

The following illustrations, which are intended to supplement the explanation and analysis of Rule 145 set forth in Securities Act Release No. 5316, reflect the views of the Division of Corporation Finance as of the date of this release notwithstanding any previous interpretations expressed to the contrary by the Division orally or in writing: It should be assumed in each of the following illustrations that the use of the means and instruments of interstate commerce or of the mails is involved and that no statutory exemption is applicable unless so stated.

I. *Relationship of Rule 145 to Exemptions Set Forth in Sections 3 and 4 of the Act (See generally Preliminary Note to Rule 145).*

Illustration A

Facts: X Company proposes to issue common stock in exchange for the assets of Y Company after Y Company obtains the approval of its several stockholders, as required by state law, with respect to an agreement setting forth the terms and conditions of the exchange and providing for a distribution of the X Company common stock to the Y Company stockholders. X Company has determined that the private offering exemption afforded by Section 4(2) of the Act would be available for the transaction.

Question: In light of Rule 145, may X Company choose between relying upon the private offering exemption available under Section 4(2) and registering the securities to be issued in the transaction on Form [S–4]?

Interpretative Response: Yes, X Company may choose between relying upon the private offering exemption available under Section 4(2) and registering the securities to be issued in the transaction on Form [S–4]. Rule 145 does not affect statutory exemptions which are otherwise available. However, by virtue of Rule 145(a)(3)(B), X Company may register the securities to be issued in the transaction on Form [S–4] so that an affiliate of Y Company would be able to resell immediately his securities pursuant to the registration statement, if such resales are so disclosed in the registration statement, or subject to the limitations referred to in Rule 145(d).

Illustration B

Facts: X Company, an insurance company organized and regulated under the laws of State A, intends to establish Y Company, a corporation organized under the laws of State A, and to effect a Rule 145 type transaction which would result in Y Company becoming a statutory insurance holding company and the stockholders of X Company receiving securities of Y Company in return for their holdings. Among other things, the laws of State A, in this type of situation, expressly authorize its Commissioner of Insurance to hold a hearing and to make a finding on the fairness to the stockholders of X Company of the terms and the conditions of the transaction. The Commissioner is required to give appropriate notice of the hearing, and of their right to appear, to all stockholders of X Company prior to the hearing.

Question: Assuming that the Commissioner holds such a hearing and makes the appropriate findings, may Y Company rely upon the exemption afforded by Section 3(a)(10) of the Act notwithstanding that the transaction comes within Rule 145?

Interpretative Response: Yes. Rule 145 does not affect the availability of any exemption which is otherwise available so that an issuer may rely upon the exemption afforded by Section 3(a)(10) of the Act if all of the conditions of that exemption are met. Inasmuch as Section 3(a)(10) provides an exemption for the initial issuance of securities but not for the resale of such securities, it should be noted that an issuer may choose to register the securities to be issued in the transaction on Form [S–4] or S–1 in order to be more certain of the status under the Act of public resales by underwriters of securities received in the transaction.

Illustration C

Facts: X Company, a corporation organized and existing under the laws of State A, has a class of preferred stock and a class of common stock outstanding. X Company is now considering a plan of reclassification which, if approved by the requisite majority of each class, would result in X Company having only one class of equity securities outstanding. X Company has determined that it will not utilize the services of a proxy soliciting firm.

Question: May X Company rely upon the exemption afforded by Section 3(a)(9) of the Act notwithstanding that the transaction comes within Rule 145?

Interpretative Response: Yes. Assuming that all the requirements of that exemption are met, then X Company may rely upon the exemption afforded by Section 3(a)(9) of the Act because Rule 145 does not affect the availability of any statutory exemption which is otherwise available.

* * *

II. *Application of Rule 145 to Various Types of Reclassifications and Business Combination Transactions (See Paragraph (a) of Rule 145).*

Illustration A

Facts: X Company has a class of preferred stock and a class of common stock outstanding. As required by the laws of its state of incorporation, X Company intends to submit to both classes of its stockholders a plan of recapitalization, which, if approved by the requisite majority of each class, would provide, among other things, for a three-for-one stock split with respect to the common stock and for a simultaneous exchange of eight shares of common stock for each share of preferred stock. In order to assure adoption of the plan, X Company has retained the services of P Company, a proxy soliciting firm which will actively solicit proxies for approval of the plan.

Question: Inasmuch as P Company is receiving remuneration for its services and the exemption afforded by Section 3(a)(9) of the Act is, accordingly, not available, does Rule 145 require registration of the securities to be issued in connection with the stock split and preferred stock exchange?

Interpretative Response: Yes. Because this single plan of recapitalization involves a reclassification of one class of securities in addition to a stock split of the other class of securities (which in and of itself would not have to be registered under these circumstances because of the exception set forth in Rule 145(a)(1)), the entire transaction would be considered to be a reclassification within the meaning of Rule 145(a)(1) and the securities to be issued in the transaction would have to be registered on Form [S–4] or S–1.

Illustration B

Facts: In order to change its domicile, X Company, a corporation organized and existing under the laws of State A with its only class of outstanding securities registered under the Securities Exchange Act of 1934 ("the Exchange Act"), proposes to effect a statutory merger with Y Company, its newly-created wholly-owned subsidiary which was organized under the laws of State B. Y Company's Articles of Incorporation are similar to X Company's Articles of Incorporation except that Y Company's charter contains a substantially broader corporate purpose provision and authorizes a class of preferred stock. As a result of this proposed transaction, which is subject to stockholder approval, stockholders' pre-emptive rights and cumulative voting rights would be eliminated.

Question: Does Rule 145 require the registration of the securities to be issued in this transaction?

Interpretative Response: No. While a statutory merger is deemed to involve a "sale" within the meaning of Section 2(3) of the Act, Rule 145(a)(2) provides a specific exception "where the sole purpose of the transaction is to change an issuer's domicile [solely within the United States]." Notwithstanding the inclusion of a broader corporate purpose provision and the authorization of another class of securities in the charter and notwithstanding the effects on the preemptive and cumulative voting rights of X Company's stockholders, the exception would be applicable. It should be noted that since X Company is a reporting company under the Exchange Act, any changes in stockholders' rights should be disclosed pursuant to the applicable proxy rules.

* * *

Illustration D

Facts: X Bank, chartered under the laws of State A, proposes to enter into an agreement and plan of reorganization which, if approved by its stockholders, will result in X Bank becoming a wholly-owned subsidiary (except for directors' qualifying shares) of a newly-formed holding company, X Bancshares, organized under the laws of State B. Following the reorganization, the former stockholders of X Bank will have the same relative equity interest in X Bancshares; the directors of X Bank will be the directors of X Bancshares; and initially the sole asset of X Bancshares will be the stock of X Bank.

Question: May this transaction be effected without registration under the Act on the basis of the change-in-domicile exception set forth in Rule 145(a)(2)?

Interpretative Response: No. Inasmuch as the transaction involves significant changes in the issuer's basic organizational structure, the exception set forth in Rule 145(a)(2) is not applicable. Accordingly, absent an applicable statutory exemption, the securities issued in the transaction are required to be registered under the Act.[a]

Illustration E

Facts: X Company proposes to acquire at least 80% of the outstanding common stock of Y Company by offering its common stock to the stockholders of Y Company in exchange for their Y Company common stock in a transaction intended to qualify as a taxfree reorganization pursuant to Section 368(a)(1)(B) of the Internal Revenue Code of 1954, as amended.

Question: Is Rule 145 applicable to such an exchange offer so that X Company can utilize Form S–14?

Interpretative Response: No. Rule 145 and Form S–14 are not applicable to "B" type reorganizations. Absent a statutory exemption, the securities issued in the transaction would have to be registered under the Act on Form S–1 or on another form if applicable.[b]

a. Illustration B shows that the Staff is willing to except a merger under Rule 145(a)(2) which goes beyond a change in domicile and affects significant rights of shareholders, including cumulative voting and preemptive rights. However, a more rigid posture would simply force the issuer to engage in a two-step transaction entailing a migration into another state followed by a charter amendment with the associated additional costs.

On the other hand, Illustration D indicates that where the transaction involves significant changes in the issuer's organizational structure, the exception to the rule is inapplicable. See 3 L. Loss & J. Seligman, Securities Regulation 1255–57 (3d ed. 1989).

b. The answer to this question will now be different in light of the replacement of Form S–14 by S–4. Although Rule 145 is not applicable to such exchange offers, Form S–4 is available not only for the registration of securities in connection with Rule 145 trans-

Illustration F

Facts: The board of directors of X Company is considering an offer by Y Company whereby a significant portion (but not substantially all) of X Company's assets will be transferred to Y Company in return for shares of Y Company common stock which would be distributed to the stockholders of X Company on a pro-rata basis. Although not required to do so by state law or by X Company's certificate of incorporation or by-laws, X Company's board of directors will submit the matter to the stockholders of X Company for their authorization.

Question: Assuming that no statutory exemption is available, is Rule 145 applicable to this proposed transaction?

Interpretative Response: Yes. Rule 145(a)(3) states that:

(a) "sale" shall be deemed to be involved, within the meaning of Section 2(3) of the Act, so far as the security holders of a corporation * * * are concerned where, pursuant to statutory provisions * * * or similar controlling instruments, *or otherwise*, there is submitted for the vote or consent of such security holders a plan or agreement for * * * transfers of assets. (emphasis added)

Accordingly, inasmuch as the board of directors in its discretion determined to submit the matter to stockholders, Rule 145 is applicable and the transaction may be registered on Form [S–4] or S–1.

* * *

V. *Related Matters.*

　　* * *

Illustration B

Facts: X Company has been utilizing a Form S–1 "shelf registration" for the issuance of its securities, and for certain resales thereof, in connection with a series of acquisitions, each of which, in and of itself, might have been effected without registration under the Act by virtue of the intrastate or private offering exemptions afforded by Sections 3(a)(11) and 4(2) of the Act. X Company now intends to make an acquisition by means of a statutory merger subject to Rule 145 for which no other statutory exemption is available.

Question B–1: May X Company utilize the Form S–1 shelf registration for the proposed Rule 145 transaction?

Interpretative Response: Yes. Although X Company could file a new registration statement on Form [S–4] or S–1 for the Rule 145 transaction, it can utilize the existing Form S–1 shelf registration statement if sufficient shares are registered and the financial statements and other disclosures are current.

Question B–2: If X Company elects to utilize its shelf registration for the merger, is additional information required to be included in its shelf registration statement?

actions but may also be availed of in connection with other mergers such as short form mergers, exchange offers and resales of securities registered on the Form. See General Instructions, paragraph A.

Interpretative Response: Yes. The information required by Form [S–4] should be set forth in a post-effective amendment to X Company's shelf registration statement.

* * *

BUSINESS COMBINATIONS UNDER RULE 145

1.   Form S–4. Although Rule 145 by its terms is not available for "B" type reorganizations or short-form mergers, Form S–4 extends the principles underlying the integrated disclosure system to all business combination transactions, not just those enumerated in Rule 145. The philosophical underpinnings of Form S–4 are stated in the release adopting that registration form:[1]

> Form S–4 provides simplified and streamlined disclosure in prospectuses for business combinations whether the transactions are effected by merger or exchange offer.

> The integrated disclosure system, on which Form S–4 is based, proceeds from the premise that investors in the primary market need much the same information as investors in the trading market. Integration also specifies the manner in which information should be delivered to investors. Under Forms S–1, S–2 and S–3, transaction oriented information must be presented in the prospectus. Company oriented information, however, may be presented in, delivered with, or incorporated by reference into the prospectus, depending on the extent to which Exchange Act reports containing the information have been disseminated and assimilated in the market. Thus, for registrants qualified to use Form S–3, the most widely followed companies, company specific information that has been included in Exchange Act reports need not be reiterated in the prospectus, but may be incorporated by reference. Registrants qualified to use Form S–2, reporting companies which are less widely followed, must present certain company information, but may do so either by delivering the annual report to security holders or reiterating that level of company information in the prospectus. Finally, S–1 registrants must present all company information in the prospectus.

> The prospectus requirements of Form S–4 are divided into four sections. The first section calls for information about the transaction, which will be presented in the prospectus in all cases, and which is designed to make the presentation of the complex transactions that typify business combinations more easily understood by investors. The next two sections specify the information about the businesses involved and prescribe different levels of prospectus presentation and incorporation by reference depending upon which form under the Securities Act the company could use in making a primary offering of its securities not involving a business combination. The last section sets forth the requirements as to voting and management information. All voting information must be presented in the prospectus, while the amount of prospectus presentation for management information, like company information, depends on which form could be used in a primary offering not involving a business combination.

> The use of the S–1–2–3 approach in Form S–4 reflects the premise that decisions made in the context of business combination transactions and those made otherwise in the purchase of a security in the primary or

---

1.   Securities Act Release No. 6578 (Apr. 23, 1985).

trading market are substantially similar. At the same time, the Commission recognizes that there are significant differences. In particular, business combination decisions are not of the same volitional nature as other investment decisions. Moreover, typically mergers may give rise to a change in security ownership as a consequence of inaction.

To address the differences in the nature of the investment decision, special provisions have been included in the Form. First, a specifically tailored item covering risk factors, ratio of earnings to fixed charges, certain per share data and other information must be presented in the prospectus regardless of the level of disclosure available to the companies involved. This item, as adopted, has been expanded to reflect commentators' suggestions that the item include: (1) certain additional financial data; and (2) information about regulatory approvals.

2. *Rule 14a–6.* A special advantage of Rule 145 is that it permits a registration statement on Form S–4 or F–4 (for foreign issuers) to also serve as the proxy statement when shareholder approval is sought in the case of a reporting company.[2] However, if the issuer does not qualify for Form S–3 (which means that it cannot use Form S–4), then a separate proxy statement must be prepared.

3. *Exclusivity and Other Exemptions.* The SEC views Rule 145 as exclusive as it applies to public resales of registered securities received in a Rule 145 transaction.[3] This is in marked contrast to Rule 144, Rule 147 or Regulation D. But what if the acquisition transaction is effected through a private placement because the target corporation has only a few shareholders? Then, the securityholder who receives securities in such a transaction can apparently make a private resale under the § 4(1½) exemption.[4] Presumably, in any transaction effected under § 4(2) or § 3(11), if the securityholder surrenders "restricted securities," the new securities it acquires will be similarly restricted.[5] This means that the recipient can either sell under the holding period (and "tacking") provisions of Rule 144, make a private sale under § 4(1½), or, possibly, claim that it did not take with a view to distribution, but rather resold based on a change of circumstances. Thus, even though Rule 145(c) may exclude an individual from the definition of an underwriter, such an individual can nonetheless be deemed an underwriter if the Rule 145 transaction is structured as a private placement and the individual sells the privately placed shares publicly before the expiration of the requisite holding period.

4. *Holding Period.* In 1997, Rule 145 was amended to shorten its applicable holding periods.[6] Rule 145(d) now permits resale of securities acquired in a Rule 145 transaction by a person who is not an affiliate of the issuer after one year (with the one year period being determined in accordance with Rule 144(d)) if the issuer meets the "current public information requirements" of

---

2. See Rule 14a–6(j).

3. See Sec.Act.Rel. No. 5932 (May 15, 1978).

4. Sidney Stahl, 1981 SEC No-Act. LEXIS 3465 (April 23, 1981).

5. A long line of no-action letters has, however, taken the position that stock acquired pursuant to a § 3(a)(10) reorganization is treated as Rule 145 stock for pur-

poses of resale and may be publicly resold in compliance with Rule 145. See Control and Restricted Securities: Ground Rules for the Resale of Stock Acquired in Corporate Reorganizations—the Section 3(a)(10) Exemption, 16 Sec.L.J. (Summer 1988); see also Staff Legal Bulletin No. 3 (July 25, 1997).

6. See Sec.Act.Rel. No. 7390 (Feb. 20, 1997).

Rule 144(c). Similarly, if the issuer is not a reporting company and does not otherwise meet the "current public information" requirements of Rule 144(c), then the holding period is two years. This change from the former two and three periods, respectively, followed and corresponded with similar 1997 revisions in the holding periods under Rule 144.

5. *Regulation M–A.* In 1999, the Commission adopted Regulation M–A, which has significantly changed the timing and procedures incident to business combinations, tender offers, and proxy solicitations.[7] Regulation M–A is discussed in more detail in Chapter 12, but its interface with Rule 145 needs to be understood here. Regulation M–A's two critical rules—Rules 165 and 166— apply only to transactions that fall under Rule 145 or that involve an exchange offer of securities of the acquirer for securities of the target. As a result, the definitions in Rule 145(a) control who is eligible to receive the more relaxed regulatory treatment afforded by Rules 165 and 166. Prior to these two rules, it was necessary to file a registration statement before the acquirer could release deal-related information in an acquisition in which it was issuing securities. Otherwise, there would be a classic "gun-jumping" problem, as discussed in Chapter 2. Today, as more fully discussed in Chapter 12, immediate release of the critical deal information may precede the filing of a registration statement. Effectively, this enables tender offers or mergers utilizing equity as consideration to compete more effectively with cash deals (which do not require registration under the Securities Act of 1933).

6. *Rule 153A and Prospectus Delivery in Business Combinations.* The real significance of Rule 153A may not be understood the first time one reads it. By defining the statutory term "preceded by a prospectus" in Section 5(b)(2) of the 1933 Act to mean delivery to securities holders of record prior to the vote on a business combination, Rule 153A solves the problem that would otherwise arise because of the high likelihood that the shareholders who vote on, or consent to, the merger or other combination will be different than those who ultimately receive securities under the merger or other combination.[8] Consider the case of the shareholder in the target firm who sells his or her shares after voting (or not voting) on the transaction. The incoming purchaser of these shares in the target later receives shares in the acquiring firm, but has received no disclosure document of any kind. Absent Rule 153A, Section 5(b)(2) would inevitably be violated.

––––––––

For a fuller analysis, of Rule 145, see 3 L. Loss & J. Seligman, Securities Regulation 1253–60 (3d ed. 1989); Campbell, Resales of Securities Under the Securities Act of 1933, 52 Wash. & Lee L. Rev. 13333, 1362–76 (1995); Campbell, Rule 145; Mergers, Acquisitions and Recapitalizations Under the Securities Act of 1933, 46 Fordham L.Rev. 277 (1987); Schneider & Manko, Rule 145, 5 Rev.Sec.Reg. 811 (1972), 6 Rev.Sec.Reg. 1 (1973); Schneider & Manko, Rule 145 Updated, 6 Rev.Sec.Reg. 878 (1973); Halligan, Shareholders after Merger: What They Can and Cannot Do under SEC Rules 144 and 145, 15 B.C.Ind. & Com.L.Rev. 70 (1973); Heyman, Implications of Rule 145 under the

7. See Securities Act Release No. 7760 (October 26, 1999).

8. For an explanation of the purpose and impact of Rule 153A, see Securities Act Release No. 5316 (Oct. 6, 1972).

Securities Act of 1933, 53 B.U.L.Rev. 785 (1973); Cohen, Some Practical and Impractical Aspects of a "Rule 145" Transaction, 30 Bus.Law. 51 (1974).

SECTION 4.   COURT AND AGENCY APPROVED REORGANIZATIONS AND OTHER EXCHANGES

Statutes

Securities Act, § 3(a)(10).

Securities Act Release No. 312

Securities and Exchange Commission.
March 15, 1935.

[The following is an excerpt from an interpretive letter of the SEC General Counsel with respect to exchange transactions under Section 3(a)(10).]

* * *

"I shall take up in order the three questions you have raised as to the interpretation of [Section 3(a)(10)].

"1. Is adequate notice to all persons to whom it is proposed to issue securities of the hearing on the fairness of their issuance necessary for an exemption under Section 3(a)(10)?

"Although the wording of Section 3(a)(10) does not demand such notice, in my opinion this requirement is to be implied from the necessity for a 'hearing * * * at which all persons to whom it is proposed to issue securities * * * shall have the right to appear'. To give substance to this express requirement, some adequate form of notice seems necessary. The usual practice of giving notice to persons who will receive securities in reorganizations, mergers and consolidations supports this view. Of course, the question of what mode of notice is adequate cannot be answered in the abstract but may vary with the facts and circumstances in each case.

"2. Is a grant of 'express authorization of law' to a state governmental authority to approve the fairness of the terms and conditions of the issuance and exchange of securities necessary for an exemption under Section 3(a)(10), or is express authorization merely to approve the terms and conditions sufficient?

"The punctuation and grammatical construction of the last clause of Section 3(a)(10) indicate that the words 'expressly authorized * * * by law' were not intended to modify 'courts or officials or agencies of the United States'. In my opinion a State governmental authority (with the possible exception of a banking or insurance commission) must possess express authority of law to approve the *fairness* of the terms and conditions of the issuance and exchange of the securities in question. This interpretation seems necessary to give meaning to the express requirement of a hearing upon the fairness of such terms and conditions, which must subsume authority in the supervisory body to pass upon the fairness from the standpoint of the investor, as well as the issuer and consumer, and to disapprove terms and conditions because unfair either to those who are to receive the securities or to other security holders of the issuer, or to the public. This requirement seems the more essential in that the whole justification for the exemption afforded by Section 3(a)(10) in that the examination and approval by the body in question of the fairness of the issue in question is a substitute for the protection afforded to the investor by the information which would otherwise be made available to him through registration. The requisite express authorization of law to approve the fairness of such terms and conditions, however, probably need not necessarily be in haec verba but, to give effect to the words 'express' and 'by law', must be granted clearly and explicitly.

"3. Does a hearing by an authority expressly authorized by law to hold such a hearing satisfy the requirement of a hearing in Section 3(a)(10), if the state law does not require a hearing?

"I believe that, as a corollary to the view expressed in my answer to the second question, supra, and in order that a hearing have legal sanction, the approving authority must be expressly authorized by law to hold the hearing; but in my opinion it is unnecessary that the hearing be mandatory under applicable state law. Therefore, if state law expressly authorizes the approving authority to hold a hearing on the fairness of the terms and conditions of the issuance and exchange of securities, and such a hearing is in fact held, this requirement of Section 3(a)(10) is satisfied. * * * "

REORGANIZATIONS AND OTHER EXCHANGES UNDER SECTION 3(a)(10)

Section 3(a)(10) provides an exemption from the registration and prospectus delivery requirements of Section 5 for securities issued in certain exchange transactions. Although the history is sparse, apparently the section was designed to exempt judicially or administratively approved reorganizations or recapitalizations on the theory that if the plans were approved as to "fairness," after a hearing at which all security holders affected could appear, there would be no need for additional regulation. The "fairness" hearing before a court or administrative agency was assumed to be "a substitute for the protection afforded * * * to the investor by the information which would otherwise be made available * * * through registration."[1]

Non-judicially Supervised Exchanges. For the exemption to be available for non-judicially supervised exchanges, implementing legislation is necessary expressly to confer upon a federal or state agency the authority to grant approval, subject to the prescribed conditions.

At the state level, only California, Idaho, Ohio, Oregon and North Carolina, have state securities legislation tracking the section and authorizing the securities administrator to hold a fairness hearing in conformity with the conditions of the Section.[2] As regards regulated industries, a number of states have

1. Securities Act Release No. 312 (Mar. 15, 1933). And see H.R.Rep. No. 85, 73d Cong., 1st Sess. 16 (1933): "Reorganizations carried out without such judicial supervision possess all the dangers implicit in the issuance of new securities and are, therefore, not exempt from the act. For the same reason the provision [Section 3(a)(10)] is not broad enough to include mergers or consolidations of corporation entered into without judicial supervision."

2. Ohio Rev.Code Ann. § 1707.4 (Banks–Baldwin 1994); Cal.Corp.Code § 25142 (West 1997); N.C.Gen.Stat. § 78A–30(a) (Supp.1994); Ore.Rev.Stat. § 59.095 (1983); Idaho Code § 30–1435A (1996). In Plaine v. McCabe, 797 F.2d 713, 718–21 (9th Cir.1986), involving a collateral attack on an administrative finding that a merger price was fair, the court gave preclusive effect to a final adjudication in the prior administrative proceeding.

comparable legislation relating to insurance, public utilities, banking and other financial institutions.[3]

At the federal level, facilitating legislation sufficient to permit the use of § 3(a)(10) exists under the Public Utility Holding Company Act,[4] and the Investment Company Act of 1940.[5]

Reorganization of Financially Distressed Entities. The applicability of the § 3(a)(10) exemption in connection with the reorganization of distressed corporations was unclear prior to the adoption of the Bankruptcy Reform Act of 1978.[6] That uncertainty was eliminated by the adoption of the 1978 legislation which amended § 3(a)(10) and also §§ 3(a)(7) and 3(a)(9) to exclude from the operation of these exemptions, the issuance of securities in a bankruptcy context.[7] The securities regulation aspects of the issuance of securities of financially distressed firms under the Bankruptcy Act is the subject of a separate Section, infra at page 506. We shall see that securities issued under a plan of corporate reorganization are issued subject to supervision of the bankruptcy court. Unlike § 3(a)(10), however, solicitation of approval of a plan of corporate reorganization must be accompanied by a disclosure statement approved by the bankruptcy court as to its adequacy.[8] The court is authorized to hold a hearing on the plan and confirmation is conditioned on a finding that the plan "does not discriminate unfairly, and is fair and equitable, with respect to each class of claims that is impaired under, and has not accepted the plan."[9] The Bankruptcy Code thus represents a significant departure from the § 3(a)(10) model.

Judicially-Supervised Exchanges Pursuant to Settlement of Litigation. With the demise of the equity receivership for the organization of financially embarrassed corporations[10] and the recent bankruptcy legislation, there would seem to be little or no role for court supervised exchanges of securities pursuant to § 3(a)(10). However, the publication since December 1, 1970 of the Commission's no-action letters issued in response to inquiries concerning the application of the federal securities laws to proposed transactions has disclosed the use of § 3(a)(10) in connection with the issuance of securities by defendants and other litigants in negotiated settlements of litigation subject to court supervision.[11] Unlike state governmental agencies, courts of the United States need not be granted express authority to approve the fairness of the terms of such securities exchanges.[12]

---

3. For a survey of state statutes, see Ash, Reorganizations and Other Exchanges Under Section 3(a)(10) of the Securities Act of 1933, 75 Nw.U.L.Rev. 1, 45–60 (1980).

4. 15 U.S.C. §§ 79, 79k(e) (1976 & Supp. III, 1979).

5. 15 U.S.C. §§ 80a–17(b) and 17(d) (1976 & Supp. III, 1979).

6. 11 U.S.C. §§ 364, 1125, 1145 (1976 & Supp. III, 1979).

7. Sec. 306, 92 Stat. 2674 (1978).

8. See supra note 6, at § 1125.

9. Id., §§ 1128, 1129.

10. See Jennings, Mr. Justice Douglas: His Influence on Corporate and Securities

Regulation, 73 Yale L.J. 920, 931, 935–941 (1964).

11. An important function of no-action letters has been to flush out the SEC Staff's views as to the application of the federal securities laws to proposed transactions. These letters have produced an enormous amount of information which had not theretofore been available and has aided to the understanding of SEC practice. See, for example, Hicks, Recapitalizations Under Section 3(a)(9) of the Securities Act of 1933, 61 Va.L.Rev. 1020 (1975); Deaktor, Integration of Securities Offerings, 31 U.Fla.L.Rev. 465 (1979); Ash, supra note 3.

12. Securities Act Release No. 312 (Mar. 15, 1935), supra at p. 498 n. 1.

Professor Barbara A. Ash, after reviewing approximately sixty publicly available no-action letters relating to the use of the § 3(a)(10) exemption in the settlement of litigation, has concluded that the "staff has consistently taken a no-action position based on counsel's opinion as to the availability of section 3(a)(10) irrespective of whether the issuer was one of the defendants or a corporation, a substantial number of whose securities happened to be held by one or more of the defendants."[13]

As to the usefulness of § 3(a)(10) for the settlement of litigation, Professor Ash found that:[14]

> Since section § 3(a)(10) may be relied on in connection with the settlement of litigation of almost any nature, it is of widespread utility. As noted above, the amount of litigation under the federal securities laws has become rather substantial and often lends itself to a settlement agreement involving the issuance of securities. In more than a majority of the approximately sixty no-action letters referred to above, the underlying litigation was pursuant to the Federal securities laws, frequently the antifraud provisions of the Act or the Exchange Act or the federal proxy rules, and in one case interestingly enough section 3(a)(10) itself. In addition, the no-action letters indicate that section 3(a)(10) is quite often useful to the settlement of litigation arising from various provisions of the state corporation codes and to court-supervised liquidations, distributions for the benefit of creditors, and various other insolvency-related issuances of securities not pursuant to the Federal Bankruptcy Act. Despite the seeming inconsistency between the Commission's longstanding position that section 3(a)(10) was unavailable to reorganizations under the Bankruptcy Act and its unquestioned allowance of reliance on the Exchange Exemption in the case of substantively similar court-supervised issuances of securities, there appears to be no limitation, even in the Commission's view, on the availability of the Exchange Exemption because of the nature of the litigation proposed to be settled.

In the typical non-judicially supervised reorganization before an administrative agency, the agency passes upon the "fairness" of the exchange, including the valuation of issuer's business and the value of the securities being exchanged as compared with the value of the claims of loss.

In *Securities and Exchange Commission v. Blinder Robinson & Co., Inc.*, 511 F.Supp. 799 (D.Colo.1981), a court used § 3(a)(10) to exempt securities issued pursuant to a settlement of an enforcement action brought by the SEC. The Commission had sought injunctive and ancillary equitable relief for Securities Act violations in connection with a public offering of securities of the issuer and sought rescission of the transaction. In order to avoid the prospect of costly litigation and possible liquidation, the defendants entered into a settlement agreement with the Commission that involved the offer of common stock and promissory notes to shareholders and former shareholders of the issuer in exchange for the release of all claims by those accepting the offer.

---

13. Ash, supra note 3, at 38 (footnotes omitted). For an example of the use of § 3(a)(10) in settling litigation, see Brucker v. Thyssen–Bornemisza Europe N.V., 424 F.Supp. 679, 690–91 (S.D.N.Y.1976).

14. Ash, supra note 3, at 38–39 (footnotes omitted).

In passing on the fairness of the settlement, the *Blinder, Robinson* court articulated a standard to be applied in this type of non-class action case which seemingly lowered the standard of judicial review from that used in non-judicially supervised reorganizations or under former Chapter X of the Bankruptcy Act, which contexts require a finding that the reorganization plan is fair, equitable and feasible. In contrast, the district court saw the fairness hearing as "the functional equivalent of the full disclosure which would be provided in an appropriate prospectus and registration statement."

The factors considered by the court in determining the "fairness" of the offer included: (1) the recommendations of counsel; (2) the scope of the discovery record as an indicator of the adequacy of the investigation into the facts; (3) the apparent alternatives to settlement; (4) the nature and volume of responses from those receiving notice of the hearing; and (5) the opportunity for direct participation in the process of attaining full disclosure. The court noted that persons who did not wish to accept the offer were not foreclosed from pursuing private claims of relief. It also emphasized that the SEC had initiated the enforcement proceeding and had specifically accepted the settlement agreement. Because the standard differs from that applied in class action settlements where approval may be given under Rule 23 of the Federal Rules of Civil Procedure only if the settlement offered is fair, reasonable and adequate, it is unclear that the lesser standard enunciated by the *Blinder, Robinson* court would apply in other contexts or be followed by other courts.[15]

Foreign Proceedings. In Staff Legal Bulletin No. 3R (October 20, 1999), the SEC's Division of Corporation Finance has indicated that it will permit the Section 3(a)(10) exemption to apply to court approvals given by foreign courts, provided that the reviewing court (a) approves the fairness of the terms and conditions of the exchange, (b) holds a hearing open to all affected persons to whom securities will be issued, and (c) provides adequate notice of the hearing to all such persons.[16] Query: Is there any obvious limit on this procedure? To date, the Commission has only extended Section 3(a)(10) to settlements approved by courts following traditional common law principles. Suppose a tribal court in an emerging market country approves the issuance of shares after duly holding a hearing and providing notice? Or is it too ethnocentric (or even possibly racist) to restrict Section 3(a)(10) to the traditional common law process?

Advantages to the Issuer. From the issuer's perspective, § 3(a)(10) has some distinct advantages over the use of a § 3(a)(9) exchange (either to settle litigation or to effect a restructuring of a financially strained company). First,

15. See 7 J. Hicks, Exempted Transactions Under the Securities Act of 1933 § 3.02[4][c] (1990 rev.); Glazer, Schiffman & Packman, Settlement of Securities Litigation Through the Issuance of Securities Without Registration: The Use of Section 3(a)(10) in SEC Enforcement Proceedings, 50 Fordham L.Rev. 533 (1982) (criticizing the procedure used in *Blinder Robinson & Co.*); Note, Fairness Requirement in Section 3(a)(10) of the Securities Act of 1933, 23 Wm. & Mary L.Rev. 549 (1982); Note, Section 3(a)(10) of the Securities Act of 1933—SEC v. Blinder Robinson & Co.,—Proposed Standards for Fairness Hearings, 17 New Eng.L.Rev. 1397 (1982).

16. The Division has granted no-action letters on this basis for judicially approved amalgamations under English, Australian, Singaporean and Indian procedures. See ICI-CI Bank Limited, 2001 WL 161753 (S.E.C. No–Action Letter, December 13, 2001). In Ashanti Goldfields Company Limited, 2002 WL 1359408 (S.E.C. No–Action Letter, June 19, 2002), the staff similarly gave its no-action approval to a "Scheme of Arrangement" approved by the Grand Court of the Cayman Islands.

there is no barrier under § 3(a)(10) to offering securities for cash and simultaneously exchanging them for outstanding securities (in contrast, the "exclusively" limitation under § 3(a)(9) would bar this). Second, unlike under § 3(a)(9), the securities need not be of the same issuer; thus, a reorganization involving multiple companies can be more easily effected under § 3(a)(10). Third, there is no limitation on commissions or other remuneration paid to solicitors (as there is under the final clause of § 3(a)(9)); this enables the issuer to use a broker dealer to solicit its securityholders.

On the other hand, there are some doctrinal problems. For example, when the court or agency mails the notice of the hearing to all affected securityholders, no exemption clearly protects this notice, which arguably could violate § 5(c).[17] Also, an agency that lacks statutory authority to approve the fairness of the exchange may not qualify under § 3(a)(10), even if the agency is authorized to consider the effect of the proposed transaction on, hypothetically, consumers or the public interest. As with any other transaction exemption, resales are also not protected by § 3(a)(10), and the typical securityholder will need to rely on either § 4(1) of the 1933 Act or Rule 144 thereunder.

Impact of NSMIA. The National Securities Markets Improvements Act of 1996 ("NSMIA") broadly preempts state blue sky laws with respect to "covered securities" (which definition includes securities listed on a national securities exchange or NASDAQ). Commentators are uncertain as to whether NSMIA closes down the § 3(a)(10) exemption for companies listed on such exchanges or NASDAQ (although it would clearly remain applicable for securities traded over the counter or listed on NASDAQ's "small cap" or bulletin board markets).[18] The issue is whether state blue sky regulators still have authority to review the fairness of certain transactions, even though their permission for the issuance of securities is not required. In response to the passage of NSMIA, the California Commissioner of Corporations issued a memorandum stating its intention to continue to hold fairness hearings, even in the case of "covered securities", in the belief that NSMIA did not intend to affect § 3(a)(10). As of mid–1997, the SEC had taken no position on the question.

Public Policy. The premise of § 3(a)(10) is that the fairness hearing it requires will protect the affected securityholders. Even if this debatable premise is accurate (and the various agencies and tribunals, state and federal, that are authorized to approve the fairness of a transaction clearly differ in terms of the scrutiny they will give a transaction, ranging from excellent to dubious), this hearing may do little to inform the secondary market. As a result, § 3(a)(10) can permit a massive distribution of unregistered securities to reach the public market without sufficient disclosure to inform that market. Some commentators have suggested that this objection (which applies also to § 3(a)(9)) has led the SEC to give a deliberately narrow construction to § 3(a)(10) and to attempt to limit its availability to reporting companies.[19]

---

17. Clearly, this notice does not fall within Rule 135 (as there is no registration statement). Practitioners believe that so long as the notice strictly conforms to judicial or agency rules, the SEC will raise no objection. See Mann, The Section 3(a)(10) Exemption: Recent Interpretations, 22 UCLA L.Rev. 1247 (1975).

18. See Davidson, Section 3(a)(10) of the Securities Act of 1933: The Use of State Fairness Hearings in Mergers and Acquisitions After the National Securities Markets Improvements Act of 1996, in PLI Private Placements 1997 (B4–7184 May 1997).

19. See Ash, supra note 3, 75–76.

INTERPLAY BETWEEN RULE 145, THE SECTIONS 3 AND 4 TRANSACTION EXEMPTIONS AVAILABLE TO ISSUERS, AND FORM S–4

a. Rule 145 Transactions. In effecting a business combination or in other corporate reorganizations and reclassifications, there may be a choice between the use of Rule 145 or one of the transaction exemptions from registration available under §§ 3 or 4. Rule 145 applies when security holders of a corporation or other legal entity, pursuant to statutory provisions, controlling instruments, or otherwise, are asked to vote or consent to a plan or agreement for: (1) a reclassification of securities, other than stock splits, reverse stock splits, and changes in par value; (2) a merger or similar plan of acquisition, except where the sole purpose of the transaction is to change an issuer's domicile solely within the United States; and (3) certain transfers of assets for securities when followed by a subsequent distribution of such securities to those voting on the transfer of the assets.

Under state law, a reclassification of outstanding securities may sometimes be effected by the issuer making a voluntary exchange offer with its existing security holders; in that event no vote would be required and, if none is taken, the transaction would not come within Rule 145. On the other hand, an involuntary reclassification may sometimes be effected by a direct charter amendment that requires a vote of shareholders in a "cram-down" situation. This would include an amendment of the articles of incorporation to change the right to vote cumulatively for directors to a system of straight voting,[1] to reclassify preferred shares into common shares, or to eliminate preferred dividend arrearages where the charter and state law permit such action.[2] It would also embrace similar action accomplished through the device of a merger.[3]

In the case of a business combination, Rule 145 specifically applies to fusions brought about through a merger, consolidation, and, with some exceptions, a sale of substantially all the assets for stock or other securities, all of which require a vote of shareholders of the acquired corporation. These forms of business combination include "A" and "C" reorganizations under § 368(a)(1) of the Internal Revenue Code. On the other hand, in a "B" type reorganization, the acquiring company makes an independent offer to the shareholders of the company proposed to be acquired to exchange their shares for shares of the acquiring company—an offer which the shareholders are free to accept or reject without any stockholder vote. Accordingly, Rule 145 is not available for "B" type reorganizations and former registration Form S–14 also was unavailable.

b. Availability of Form S–4. We have seen, however, that Form S–4 is now available for use in "B" type exchange reorganizations. Furthermore, Form S–4 standardizes the treatment of transactions requiring filings under the Securities Act and Exchange Act, e.g. merger reorganizations, sale-of-assets reorganizations and tender offers. Thus, in situations where shareholder approval of the

---

1. See Maddock v. Vorclone Corp., 17 Del.Ch. 39, 147 A. 255 (1929).

2. See McNulty v. W. & J. Sloane, 184 Misc. 835, 54 N.Y.S.2d 253 (Sup.Ct.1945); Sherman v. Pepin Pickling Co., 230 Minn. 87, 41 N.W.2d 571 (1950).

3. See Federal United Corp. v. Havender, 24 Del.Ch. 318, 11 A.2d 331 (Sup.Ct. 1940); Langfelder v. Universal Laboratories, Inc., 163 F.2d 804 (3d Cir.1947).

transaction is required, Form S–4 may also serve as a proxy statement, thereby enabling the acquiring company and the company being acquired to file a combined registration statement/proxy statement and deliver to shareholders a single prospectus/proxy statement.

If the proxy or information material to be sent to security holders is subject to Regulation 14A or 14C under the Exchange Act, then the provisions of these regulations apply; the "wrap-around" prospectus may be in the form of a proxy or information statement, but may contain the information specified in Form S–4 in lieu of that required by Schedule 14A or 14C of Regulation 14A or 14C under the Exchange Act.[4]

If the proxy or information material to be sent to security holders is not subject to Regulation 14A or 14C, such material must nevertheless be filed as part of the Form S–4 registration statement.

If the issuer has a class of equity securities registered pursuant to § 12 of the Exchange Act and the transaction in which the securities are being registered are to be issued subject to §§ 13(e), 14(d) or 14(e) (basically tender offers, or self-tenders), the provisions of those sections apply to the transaction in addition to those of Form S–4. Accordingly, Form S–4 may also be used to satisfy the Schedule 14D–1 (Tender Offer Statement) and the Schedule 14D–9 (target company's Tender Offer Solicitation/Recommendation Statement) filing requirements, if the parties exercise this option.

c.   Alternatives to Use of Rule 145 and Form S–4. When a relatively closely held corporation is being acquired in a "B" or exchange reorganization, the private offering exemption may be available either under Rule 506 or § 4(2) of the Act. Moreover, the issuer should consider the availability of Regulation A under the 3(b) (small issue) exemption, *supra* at page 443, as well as the intrastate exemption, if all of the requirements of Rule 147 or the § 3(a)(11) statutory exemption can be met.

In a "C" or transfer of assets reorganization in which Rule 145 is applicable, the private offering exemption may also be available under Rule 506, or § 4(2) of the Act. The issuer then has a choice between using the private offering exemption or Rule 145. Although Rule 145 does not affect statutory exemptions which are otherwise available, under Rule 145(a)(3), the acquiring company may wish to register the securities to be issued in the transaction on Form S–4, in order that affiliates of the acquired company may make resales either pursuant to the registration statement, subject to proper disclosure, or subject to the resale provisions of Rule 145(d).[5] In one case, a company acquiring the assets of a corporation with a single shareholder was permitted to use Rule 145, and the sole shareholder was thus enabled to make resales under Rule 145(d) without being subject to the two-year holding period of Rule 144.[6]

---

4. Form S–4 consists of the facing page of the Form, the prospectus containing the information specified in part I, and the information contained in part II. Where shareholder approval of the transaction is required, a Form S–4 facing sheet is simply wrapped around the prospectus/proxy statement, hence the term "wrap-around" prospectus.

5. Securities Act Release No. 5463 (Feb. 28, 1974), pt. I, Illustration A.

6. Open Road Industries, Inc. (available Feb. 5, 1973); Eppler, Rule 145 in Practice, 5 PLI Institute on Securities Regulation 326 (1974).

If an issuer proposes to effect a corporate acquisition in a Rule 145 type transaction and the private offering exemption is not available, consideration should be given to the availability of Regulation A under § 3(b) of the Act. If Regulation A is available, the Form 1–A there prescribed must be modified so that the offering circular also discloses the type of information required by Form S–4. It must be noted, however, that the resale provisions of Rule 145(d) are only applicable to "registered securities acquired" in a Rule 145 transaction. A Regulation A offering under § 3(b) is not a registered offering; it is an exempt offering. Resales within twelve months by affiliates would therefore be subject to the limitations of § 3(b) and Rule 254.[7]

In certain exchanges and reclassifications of securities, the § 3(a)(9) exemption may be available. However, that section is restricted to exchanges of securities between a single corporation and its existing security holders exclusively where no remuneration is paid for solicitation of the exchange. As discussed earlier in this Chapter, the latter restriction may bar the issuer from engaging an underwriter to solicit its securityholders.

Section 3(a)(10) was especially designed to exempt judicially or administratively approved reorganizations or recapitalizations on the theory that if the plans were approved as to "fairness," after a hearing at which all security holders affected could appear, there is no need for additional regulation. The section applies both to "voluntary exchanges" and to "cram downs," so long as the other conditions are met.[9]

Rule 145(a)(1) includes any reclassification of securities of an issuer, other than a stock split, reverse stock split, or change in par value, which involves the substitution of a security for another security. Thus, apparently, voluntary as well as compulsory reclassifications are made subject to the rule, if the plan is submitted to a vote of shareholders. According to interpretations of the Division of Corporation Finance, however, § 3(a)(9) remains available to all reclassifications of securities, assuming that all the requirements of that exemption are met. Thus, if an issuer has a class of preferred and a class of common stock outstanding, and proposes a plan of reclassification by charter amendment which, if approved by the requisite majority of each class, would result in the issuer having only one class of common shares outstanding, Rule 145 will apply if the reclassification is submitted for the vote or consent of the security holders. If the issuer proposes to utilize the services of a proxy soliciting firm, § 3(a)(9) will be unavailable, because of the prohibition against payments for soliciting security holders to make the exchange. If, however, the company determines that it will not utilize the services of a proxy soliciting firm, Section 3(a)(9) will be available provided that all the requirements of that section are met, even though the transaction also comes within Rule 145.[10]

The § 3(a)(10) exemption is free of several of the restrictions limiting the usefulness of the § 3(a)(9) exemption; it may also be available to avoid the

---

7. Supra note 5, at pt. I, Illustration D.

9. See Comment, Effect of Section 3(a)(10) of the Securities Act as a Source of Exemption for Securities Issued in Reorganizations, 45 Yale L.J. 1050, 1051 (1936); Ash, Reorganizations and Other Exchanges Under Section 3(a)(10) of the Securities Act of 1933, 75 Nw.U.L.Rev. 1, 42–44 (1980). As to the efficacy of court or agency supervision, see

Note, Protection for Shareholder Interests in Recapitalizations of Publicly Held Corporations, 58 Colum.L.Rev. 1030 (1958).

10. Release No. 5463, supra note 5, pt. I, Illustration C; Pt. II, Illustration A; 7 J. Hicks, Exempted Transactions Under the Securities Act of 1933, § 2.07[2][a] (1990 rev. ed.).

burdens of registration following the repeal of Rule 133 and the adoption of Rule 145. Accordingly, every proposed transaction must be analyzed to determine which of the available alternatives is the most advantageous. In fact, since the repeal of Rule 133 and the adoption of Rule 145, the § 3(a)(10) exemption takes on an added significance, for as one knowledgeable securities lawyer puts it, the exemption fulfills a "need to find a new exemption for mergers and acquisitions in situations where either the time or expense of registration is not justifiable."[11] This situation may arise in connection with mergers and acquisitions, where the availability of the Rule 506 or § 4(2) statutory private offering exemption is uncertain. The § 3(a)(10) exemption may also be useful "when a large listed corporation intends to acquire a relatively small corporation too closely held to be subject to the proxy rules, yet too large to fit within the parameters of Rule [506], in a transaction which need not be approved by the shareholders of the acquiring corporation."[12] It may also prove advantageous in a "B" reorganization under I.R.C. § 368(a)(1) where the shareholders of the corporation to be acquired are invited to exchange their stock in the acquired corporation for stock in the acquiring corporation. In all mergers and corporate acquisitions § 3(a)(9) is unavailable, for the reason that the exchange is not with the issuer's security holders. In such event, the § 3(a)(10) exemption may provide an alternative to a 1933 Act registration.

SECTION 5.   THE BANKRUPTCY EXEMPTIONS

REORGANIZATIONS UNDER THE FEDERAL BANKRUPTCY CODE: CHAPTER 11

Chapter 11. The Bankruptcy Reform Act of 1978[1] made significant substantive changes in the reorganization of financially distressed companies and in the application of the federal securities laws to the issuance of securities during reorganization and the resale of such securities. The result has been some conflict and some confusion, because the Bankruptcy Reform Act fundamentally seeks to reduce costs and so authorizes somewhat scaled-down disclosure. The goal of reform was a faster, more efficient reorganization process. Under the prior Bankruptcy Act, reorganizations could be effected under Chapter X, arrangements under Chapter XI, and real property arrangements by persons other than corporations under Chapter XII. As originally enacted, it had been contemplated that Chapter X would be used for pervasive reorganizations of publicly-owned corporations and Chapter XI would be utilized for the judicial enforcement of an arrangement in which the owners of a business, whether or not incorporated, would enter into an extension or composition of unsecured debts of the firm. As a result of the cumbersome and time-consuming procedures under Chapter X, debtor corporations (and their creditors) tended to resort to Chapter XI even though the reorganization effectuated material modifications in the rights of public investors. Critics of this dual system of

11. Mann, The Section 3(a)(10) Exemption: Recent Interpretations, 22 UCLA L.Rev. 1247, at 1248 (1975).

12. Id. at 1252.

1. The bankruptcy laws were revised generally by the 1978 Act and enacted as Title 11, Bankruptcy, of the United States Code by Pub.L. 96–598, Nov. 6, 1978, 92 Stat. 2549. There is no official "Bankruptcy Code." Nevertheless, the Courts and the Bankruptcy Bar refer to Title 11 of the Code as the Bankruptcy Code to distinguish the 1978 Act from the prior Bankruptcy Act.

reorganization argued that there were no objective standards for determining whether a reorganization belonged under Chapter X or Chapter XI.[2] The upshot was that a consolidated approach to the reorganization of distressed companies was taken in the enactment of Chapter 11.

Disclosure Requirements in Exchanges of Securities. An integral feature of a corporate reorganization is the restructuring of the debtor's capital and debt. That process necessarily involves the exchange of new debt or equity securities for outstanding claims or interests. In principle, some of these exchanges could have often been handled under § 3(a)(9), at least in cases where the claimants in bankruptcy held a security, but registration would have been required when claimants were owed money or held property claims. Without some exemption for these transactions and for persons who wish to resell securities received in an exchange, funds needed to revitalize the business would have been absorbed by 1933 Act registration expenses. Yet, all agreed that if a plan of reorganization entails the issuance of securities in exchange for outstanding claims or interests, some disclosure obligations should be imposed upon the debtor-issuer of the securities. This problem is solved by § 1125 of the Bankruptcy Act, which supplants the disclosure obligations which otherwise would be applicable under the 1933 Act with a regime run under the supervision of the bankruptcy court.

The resulting tradeoff is that Section 1125 requires "adequate information," but carefully avoids using the securities laws' fundamental concept of "materiality." The adequacy of disclosure is to be determined not simply based on the informational needs of investors, but also based on the debtor's ability to make the desired disclosures (for example, what condition its books and records are in becomes a relevant consideration). A broad safe harbor is also provided that exempts from liability for misleading statements under the federal securities laws those who in good faith solicit sales or approvals pursuant to the reorganization plan.[3]

The operation of these these disclosure requirements has been explained in these terms:[4]

> * * * This section is new. It is the heart of the consolidation of the various reorganization chapters found in current law. It requires disclosure before solicitation of acceptances of a plan of reorganization.
>
> Subsection (a) contains two definitions. First, "adequate information" is defined to mean information of a kind, and in sufficient detail, as far as is reasonably practical in light of the nature and history of the debtor and the condition of the debtor's books and records, that would enable a hypothetical reasonable investor typical of holders of claims or interests of the relevant class to make an informed judgment about the plan. Second, "investor typical of holders of claims or interests of the relevant class" is

2. Comments of Homer Kripke on Summary of Comments of the SEC Staff on H.R. 6, H.R.Rep. No. 95–595, 95th Cong., 1st Sess., App. II, 261 (1977).

3. See 11 U.S.C. § 1125(4). It is still largely unresolved whether this immunity from liability applies to transactions that are not exempted under the Bankruptcy Act, but that instead seek fresh capital and thus must comply with the federal securities laws.

4. Report of the Committee on the Judiciary, H.R.Rep. No. 95–595, 95th Cong., 1st Sess. 408–10 (1977). And see Epling & Thompson, Securities Disclosures in Bankruptcy, 39 Bus.Law. 855 (1984); Phelan & Cheatham, Would I Lie to You?—Disclosure in Bankruptcy Reorganizations, 9 Sec. Reg. L.J. 140 (1981).

defined to mean an investor having a claim or interest of the relevant class, having such a relationship with the debtor as the holders of other claims or interests of the relevant class have, and having such ability to obtain information from sources other than the disclosure statement as holders of claims or interests of the relevant class have. That is, the hypothetical investor against which the disclosure is measured must not be an insider if other members of the class are not insiders, and so on. In other words, the adequacy of disclosure is measured against the typical investor, not an extraordinary one.

* * * Precisely what constitutes adequate information in any particular instance will develop on a case-by-case basis. Courts will take a practical approach as to what is necessary under the circumstances of each case, such as the cost of preparation of the statements, the need for relative speed in solicitation and confirmation, and, of course, the need for investor protection.

Subsection (b) is the operative subsection. It prohibits solicitation of acceptances or rejections of a plan after the commencement of the case unless, at the time of the solicitation or before, there is transmitted to the solicitee the plan or a summary of the plan, and a written disclosure statement approved by the court as containing adequate information. * * *

Subsection (d) excepts the disclosure statements from the requirements of the securities laws (such as section 14 of the 1934 Act and section 5 of the 1933 Act), and from similar State securities laws (blue sky laws, for example). The subsection permits an agency or official whose duty is to administer or enforce such laws (such as the Securities and Exchange Commission or State Corporation Commissioners) to appear and be heard on the issue of whether a disclosure statement contains adequate information, but the agencies and officials are not granted the right of appeal from an adverse determination in any capacity. They may join in an appeal by a true party in interest, however.

Subsection (e) is a safe harbor provision, and is necessary to make the exemption provided by subsection (d) effective. Without it, a creditor that solicited an acceptance or rejection in reliance on the court's approval of a disclosure statement would be potentially liable under antifraud sections designed to enforce the very sections of the securities laws from which subsection (d) excuses compliance. The subsection protects only persons that solicit in good faith and in compliance with the applicable provisions of the reorganization chapter. It provides protection from legal liability as well as from equitable liability based on an injunctive action by the SEC or other agency or official.

In substance, this language overrules the federal securities laws' traditional materiality standard (which focuses on the informational needs of the investor) and replaces that standard with a balancing test that must factor into the equation the debtor's capacity to make disclosures (as determined by the court on a case-by-case basis). Even if the disclosure document is materially misleading under this relaxed standard, defendants who solicit sales or approvals on the basis of such disclosures in good faith will apparently enjoy the protections of the safe harbor in § 1125(e).

Exemptions From the Securities Laws. Although the 1933 Act's standard exemptions from registration still are applicable in theory to a debtor undertaking a reorganization under Chapter 11, they are overshadowed by Section 1145 of the Bankruptcy Act, which exempts from registration any securities issued under a Chapter 11 reorganization plan if they are issued "principally" in exchange for the debtor's existing debts and securities. Thus, the debtor's creditors can be asked to contribute some cash for the securities to be issued to them, but their consideration must consist principally of their claims against, or interest in, the debtor. The Bankruptcy Act does not grant any exemption if equity securities are sold to other investors to raise fresh capital. However, Section 3(a)(7) of the Securities Act of 1933 exempts the issuance of trustee or receiver certificates issued with the court's approval. Indeed, Section 364(f) of the Bankruptcy Act goes even further than this provision by exempting the issuance of debt securities from Section 5, regardless of whether the approval of the bankruptcy court is obtained.[5]

Sales by a Debtor in Possession or Trustee of Portfolio Securities. The debtor in possession or trustee in Chapter 11 may own securities which it may wish to sell to raise cash in order to facilitate the reorganization; these are known as "portfolio securities." Section 1145(a)(3) permits the debtor or trustee to make such sales free from the registration and prospectus provisions of § 5 of the Securities Act of 1933, subject to certain conditions. This exemption is not needed if there is in the 1933 Act itself an exemption for such sales. For example, if the debtor is not in a control relationship with the issuer and acquired the securities in the public market, the debtor in possession or the trustee may sell such securities like any similar holder without registration under the 1933 Act. The bankruptcy "portfolio exemption" has been explained this way:

Legislative Statement of Rep. Don Edwards. * * *

* * * Section 1145(a)(3) grants a debtor in possession or trustee in Chapter 11 an extremely narrow portfolio security exemption from section 5 of the Securities Act of 1933 * * * or any comparable State law. The provision was considered by Congress and adopted after much study. * * *

The Commission rule [148] would permit a trustee or debtor in possession to distribute securities at the rate of 1 percent every 6 months. [Rule 148 was subsequently rescinded—*Eds.*] Section 1145(a)(3) permits the trustee to distribute 4 percent of the securities during the 2–year period immediately following the date of the filing of the petition [and thereafter one percent of the securities outstanding during any 180–day period following such two-year period]. In addition, the security must be of a reporting company under section 13 [or § 15(d)] of the Securities and Exchange Act of 1934 * * *, and must be in compliance with all applicable requirements for the continuing of trading in the security on the date that the trustee offers or sells the security. [Thus within a three year period following the date of the petition, a debtor or trustee may distribute

---

5. Some uncertainty exists as to whether convertible securities can be issued under § 364(f). Section 364(f) seems to indicate that the term equity security was to have the meaning specified in § 101(15) of the Code. Since convertible debentures do not come within the Code definition of equity security, they would seem to qualify to be issued without registration under § 364(f). Nevertheless, the legislative history accompanying § 1145 and quoted below makes reference to § 364(f) as exempting "any security that is not an equity security or convertible into an equity security." H.R.Rep. No. 95–595, 95th Cong., 1st Sess. 419 (1977). And see ALI Federal Securities Code § 302(13), Comments (1) and (2).

portfolio securities held by it in an amount not exceeding 6 percent of the securities of the class outstanding, provided that no more than 4 percent is sold during the two year period and no more than 1 percent is sold in each of the two successive 180–day periods thereafter.].

With these safeguards the trustee or debtor in possession should be able to distribute [6] percent of the securities of a class at any time during the [3]-year period immediately following the date of the filing of the petition in the interests of expediting bankruptcy administration. The same rationale that applies in expeditiously terminating decedents' estates applies no less to an estate under title 11.[6]

Resales of § 1145(a) Exchange Securities. The value of securities received on an exchange pursuant to § 1145(a)(1) and (2) depends to some extent upon the ease with which they may be resold in the public markets. Under § 4(1) of the Securities Act of 1933, secondary sales are exempt from registration, unless the seller is an issuer, underwriter or dealer.

Most creditors will accept § 1145(a) exchange securities in satisfaction of their claims with a view to reselling them for cash as soon as feasible. If the creditors are deemed to be underwriters engaged in a distribution, however, 1933 Act registration would be required. If a holder of securities received on a Section 1145(a) exchange is not an affiliate of the issuer of the securities, he or she may resell the securities under Section 4(1) of the 1933 Act unless deemed to be an underwriter under Section 2(11) of the 1933 Act. If the securities are acquired directly from the debtor, or an affiliate of the debtor, in a transaction not involving any public offering, such securities are "restricted securities" and are subject to the resale limitations imposed by Rule 144 (see infra at page 562).

If the holder is an affiliate of the issuer, under Section 2(11) of the Securities Act, any person purchasing from the affiliate with a view to resale of the securities would be deemed to be an underwriter, thereby triggering the 1933 Act registration requirements. Moreover, under the presumptive underwriter doctrine (infra at page 529), the Commission had taken the position that the purchaser of 10% or more of the issuer's securities in a reorganization is presumptively an underwriter of the securities and thereby subject to the 1933 Act registration requirements in connection with resales. To avoid restrictions on resale of Section 1145(a) exchange securities, Congress provided a statutory exemption for sales of portfolio securities of the debtor (§ 1145(a)(3)) and resales by a person of exchange securities free of the restrictions of section 5 of the 1933 Act or the state securities acts.

Section 1145(b) establishes the conditions under which exchange securities may be resold. If the holder of securities received on an exchange under § 1145(a) is not an affiliate of the issuer of such securities, he or she may freely resell the securities unless deemed to be an underwriter within the meaning of § 1145(b). The application of the section was explained this way:[7]

Subsection (b) * * * specifies the standards under which a creditor, equity security holder, or other entity acquiring securities under the plan may resell them. The Securities Act places limitations on sales by underwriters. This subsection defines who is an underwriter, and thus restricted,

---

6. 124 Cong.Rec. H 11105 (Sept. 28, 1978) (Remarks of Rep. Don Edwards).

7. Committee on the Judiciary, Sen. Rep. No. 95–989, 95th Cong., 2d Sess. 131–132 (1978).

and who is free to resell. Paragraph (1) enumerates real underwriters that participate in a classical underwriting. A person is an underwriter if he purchases a claim against, interest in, or claim for an administrative expense in the case concerning the debtor, with a view to distribution [of the] * * * interest. This provision covers the purchase of a certificate of indebtedness issued under proposed 11 U.S.C. 364 and purchased from the debtor, if the purchase of the certificate was with a view to distribution.

A person is also an underwriter if he offers to sell securities offered or sold under the plan for the holders of such securities, or offers to buy securities offered or sold under the plan from the holders of such securities, if the offer to buy is with a view to distribution of the securities and under an agreement made in connection with the plan, with the consummation of the plan or with the offer or sale of securities under the plan. Finally, a person is an underwriter if he is an issuer, as used in section 2(11) of the Securities Act of 1933.

* * *

Paragraph (3) specifies that if an entity is not an underwriter under the provisions of paragraph (1), as limited by paragraph (2), then the entity is not an underwriter for the purposes of the Securities Act of 1933 with respect to the covered securities, that is, those offered or sold in an exempt transaction specified in subsection (a)(2). This makes clear that the current definition of underwriter in section 2(11) of the Securities Act of 1933 does not apply to such a creditor. The definition in that section technically applies to any person that purchases securities with "a view to distribution." If literally applied, it would prevent any creditor in a bankruptcy case from selling securities received without filing a registration statement or finding another exemption.

* * *

Subsection (c) makes an offer or sale of securities under the plan in an exempt transaction (as specified in subsection (a)(2)) a public offering, in order to prevent characterization of the distribution as a "private placement" which would result in restrictions, under rule 144 of the SEC * * * on the resale of the securities.

Sales by Controlling Persons and Affiliates. The exemptions from the registration provisions of federal and state law under § 1145(a) do not apply to offers or sales by an underwriter. (§ 1145(b)(1)) A controlling person of the debtor-issuer is deemed to be an issuer as that term is used in § 2(a)(11) of the 1933 Act, and § 1145(b)(1)(D) specifies that such persons are underwriters with respect to exchange securities. The test of what constitutes a controlling interest is not spelled out. Although § 101(2) of the Bankruptcy Code defines an affiliate as a person or entity with 20% ownership of the voting securities of another entity, § 1145(b)(1)(D) by reference to § 2(a)(11) of the Securities Act would seem to envisage that the concept of control should be determined by 1933 Act standards. The House Judiciary Committee Report states that any creditor with 10% of the debtor's securities is a controlling person.[8] The 10% test may stem from the SEC's presumptive underwriter doctrine, infra at page 529, but it would seem that the 10% test would not be the exclusive method for determining whether the person is in control. Indeed, an affiliate under

---

8. H.R.Rep. No. 95–595, 95th Cong., 1st Sess. 238 (1977).

§ 2(a)(11) might include any officer, director or ten percent shareholder, or any affiliate of the foregoing, of the debtor and thus prohibit resales by affiliates without registration.[9]

Despite the seeming inconsistencies between § 1145 and SEC Rule 144, there is nothing in the legislative history to indicate that Congress intended to preclude the use of Rule 144 by enacting Section 1145. Indeed, the major purpose of enacting § 1145 was to override the more restrictive provisions applicable to resales by entities receiving securities under a plan of reorganization, particularly the presumptive underwriter doctrine. Accordingly, there is no indication in the legislative history that Congress intended by the enactment of Section 1145 to withdraw any authority of the SEC to issue a broader exemption than contained in that section or to exempt transactions which are not exempted by that section.

We have seen that Section 1145(c) states that "an offer or sale of securities of the kind and in the manner specified under subsection (a)(1) of this Section is deemed to be a public offering." The purpose of this provision was to preclude the characterization of a transaction as a private placement which would result in restrictions under Rule 144 on the resale of the securities.

With this background, an analysis of the relation of Section 1145(b) to Rule 144 leads to the following conclusions.

Resales by Real Underwriters. Section 1145(b)(1) deems certain holders of § 1145(a)(1) exchange securities to be underwriters under § 2(a)(11) of the Securities Act. These persons may not resell such securities without finding an independent exemption under the 1933 Act or complying with the registration and prospectus requirements of that Act.

Resales by Non–Affiliates. The effect of §§ 1145(b)(3) and (c) is to permit persons who are not underwriters under paragraph (b)(1) or under § 2(a)(11) of the 1933 Act to resell § 1145(a)(1) exchange securities without volume limitations. Since offers and sales of § 1145(a)(1) securities are deemed to be public offerings, resales of such securities are not subject to the volume and holding period limitations of Rule 144 and therefore they may be sold immediately.

On the other hand, since §§ 1145(b)(3) and (c) apply only to securities issued pursuant to § 1145(a)(1), persons holding portfolio securities sold to them in a § 1145(a)(3) transaction must search elsewhere for an exemption when reselling securities. One possibility is the Section 4(1) exemption under the Securities Act. If the portfolio securities are acquired from the debtor or an affiliate in brokers' transactions under the leakage provisions of § 1145(a)(3)(C), the purchaser would hold unrestricted securities. If the securities were restricted securities in the hands of the debtor and were acquired in a private sale they would be restricted securities within the meaning of Rule 144(a)(3). Persons acquiring such portfolio securities in a private sale would be subject to the holding-period requirements of Rule 144(d) and the volume limitation of Rule 144(e).

Resales by Affiliates. The problem of resales of 1145(a) exchange securities is complicated by the drafting of Sections 1145(a)(1) and 1145(b)(3). Section 1145(a) exempts from section 5 of the 1933 Act the issuance of exchange

---

9. See Sommer, Who's "in Control?" 475 S.E.C., 21 Bus.Law. 559 (1966), infra, at 545.

securities by the debtor, except with respect to an entity that is an underwriter under § 1145(b). Section 1145(b)(1)(D) defines an underwriter to include an entity that is an issuer, as used in section 2(a)(11) of the 1933 Act with respect to the securities. The purpose of subsection (d) was to exclude an issuer or controlling person from the exemption granted in § 1145(b)(3). There is nothing in the legislative history, however, to indicate that other exemptions might not be available, including the exemption in Rule 144 for sales of controlling persons within the parameters of that rule. Otherwise, Section 1145 would restrict resales beyond the restrictions previously imposed by the SEC, preclude the availability of the Section 4(1) exemption and thus prohibit any resales by affiliates without registration. Moreover, such an interpretation would discriminate against affiliates of debtor-issuers in favor of affiliates of other public companies who own unrestricted control shares. Under Rule 144, affiliates of issuers that are subject to the 1934 Act reporting requirements who hold control shares may resell such securities by complying with Rule 144, without the holding period of Rule 144(d). In Calstar, Inc.,[10] the Staff recognized the ambiguity in § 1145 and allowed affiliates to resell reorganization securities issued under § 1145(a)(1) and (2) in compliance with Rule 144, without the holding period of Rule 144(d).

Stockbrokers' Exemption. Section 1145(a)(4) provides an exemption for resales of securities received in a transaction under § 1145(a)(1) or (2) through a stockbroker provided certain conditions are met. The sale must occur before the expiration of 40 days after the first date on which the security was bona fide offered to the public by the issuer or by or through an underwriter; and the issuer must furnish a disclosure statement approved under § 1125, and supplementary information, if the court so orders. The exemption is patterned on § 4(3)(A) of the Securities Act. Since § 1145(a)(4) is limited to § 1145(a)(1) or (2) securities, it has no application to resales of portfolio securities received in a § 1145(a)(3) transaction.

Relation of § 3(a)(7) of the Securities Act to § 364 of the Bankruptcy Code. Section 364(a) of the Bankruptcy Code permits a trustee who is authorized to operate the business of a debtor to issue securities in the ordinary course of business, without obtaining prior approval of the court. Under subsections (b) and (c), the trustee may issue securities not in the ordinary course of business, with approval of the court. Section 364(f) exempts from the registration provisions of Section 5 of the 1933 Act, the Trust Indenture Act, and State securities laws, offers and sales of these securities, except as to a person that is an underwriter as defined in § 1145(b). Although § 364(f) is a necessary exemption from registration for securities issued in the ordinary course of business under § 364(a), it seems redundant as applied to court authorized securities which are also exempt from Section 5 registration by virtue of § 3(a)(7) of the Securities Act. With respect to any debt security issued by a trustee or the debtor in possession, § 3(a)(7) continues to apply and provide an express exemption from the § 5 registration and prospectus provisions under that Act for certificates of indebtedness issued to finance post-petition operations, with approval of the court.

---

10. Calstar, Inc. [1985–86 Transfer Binder] Fed.Sec.L.Rep. (CCH) ¶ 78,137 at 76,-619 (avail. Sept. 26, 1985); 3 L. Loss & J. Seligman, Securities Regulation 1274 (3d ed. 1989); Morgan, Application of the Securities Laws in Chapter 11 Reorganizations under the Bankruptcy Reform Act of 1978, 1983 U. Ill.L.Rev. 861, 881–901; 5 Collier on Bankruptcy §§ 1145.01–1145.03 (15th ed., 1990 rev.).

The conventional view has been that § 3(a)(7) of the Securities Act is a security exemption which grants a permanent exemption from registration, rather than a transaction exemption.[11] Curiously enough, the legislative history indicates that the House Committee on the Judiciary understood § 364, § 3(a)(7), and § 3(a)(10) to be transaction exemptions, not perpetual exemptions for the security.[12] Moreover, the "underwriter" limitation in § 364(f) supports the view that § 364(f) is a transaction exemption. Nevertheless, the accepted view is that § 3(a)(7), unlike § 3(a)(10), is a security exemption permitting resales without restriction. This view has been accepted in ALI Federal Securities Code § 302(13), codifying § 3(a)(7) on the ground that the need for limitations against resales by a § 1145(b) underwriter "is not apparent with respect to securities issued under court approval in order to finance the receivership, bankruptcy or reorganization proceedings, and in view of the absence of similar restrictions in [§ 3(a)(7) of the Securities Act] as amended by the Reform Act, § 302(13) here follows the § 3(a)(7) rather than the 11 U.S.C. § 364(f) model."[13] If, however, a claim for administrative expense, represented by a certificate of indebtedness, issued pursuant to a § 3(a)(7) exemption, is exchanged for plan securities under § 1145(a)(1), the securities so received would not be exempt securities.

For discussions of the securities regulation aspects of Chapter 11 of the Bankruptcy Reform Act of 1978, see Epling & Thompson, Securities Disclosures in Bankruptcy, 39 Bus.Law. 855 (1984); Morgan, Application of the Securities Laws in Chapter 11 Reorganizations Under the Bankruptcy Reform Act of 1978, 1983 U.Ill.L.Rev. 861; Phelan & Cheatham, Would I Lie to You?— Disclosure in Bankruptcy Reorganizations, 9 Sec. Reg. L.J. 140 (1981); 7 Hicks, Exempted Transactions Under the Securities Act of 1933, Ch. 3 (1991 rev.); Corotto & Picard, Business Reorganizations and the Bankruptcy Reform Act of 1978—A New Approach to Investor Protection and the Role of the SEC, 28 DePaul L.Rev. 961 (1979); King, Chapter 11 of the 1978 Bankruptcy Code, 53 Am.Bankr.L.J. 107 (1979); Mitchell, Securities Regulation in Bankruptcy Reorganization, 54 Am.Bankr.L.J. 99 (1980); Orlanski, The Resale of Securities Issued in Reorganization Proceedings and the Bankruptcy Reform Act of 1978, 53 Am.Bankr.L.J. 327 (1979); Trost, Business Reorganizations Under Chapter 11 of the New Bankruptcy Code, 34 Bus.Law. 1309 (1979); Note, 53 So.Cal. L.Rev. 1527 (1980).

SECTION 6.   INTEGRATION OF EXEMPTIONS

INTEGRATED OFFERINGS

The Securities Act contains a number of discrete transaction exemptions from the registration and prospectus delivery requirements of § 5 which are available to issuers of securities. Among these are the private offering exemptions (§ 4(2), § 4(6) and Regulation D, Rule 506); the limited offering exemp-

---

11. Thompson Ross Securities Co., 6 S.E.C. 1111, 1118 (1940); 7 Hicks, Exempted Transactions Under the Securities Act of 1933 § 1.01 [3] (1991 rev.); 2 Collier, Bankruptcy & 364.07 (15th ed. 1980); Orlanski, Resale of Securities, 53 Am. Bankr.L.J. 327, 348 (1979). Contra, Mitchell, Securities Regu-lation in Bankruptcy Reorganizations, 54 Am.Bankr. L.J. 99, 108, 137 (1980).

12. H.R.Rep. No. 95–595, supra note 2, at 236–38.

13. ALI, Federal Securities Code § 302(13), Comment (3).

tions under § 3(b) (Rules 504, 505, 701 and Regulation A); the intrastate exemption (§ 3(a)(11) and Rule 147); and the §§ 3(a)(9) and 3(a)(10) exemptions for certain exchange transactions.

As these sections are construed, for an exemption to be available, each transaction must satisfy all of the conditions of a single exemption. Moreover, where there are a series of offerings, every proposed unregistered (or registered) offering may be linked with a prior or subsequent offering; if such linkage occurs, two or more ostensibly discrete offerings may be deemed to comprise a single transaction.

The doctrine of integration entails the process of combining multiple offerings into a single offering, and the effect of such combination may be to destroy one or more of the exemptions. For example, A, B and C form X corporation in State Y and issue shares to themselves at $10 a share. A is a resident of State Z; B and C are residents of State Y. So far, there is no problem. Immediately thereafter, however, the corporation makes a public offering of shares at the same price utilizing the § 3(a)(11) intrastate exemption, the offers and sales being restricted solely to residents of State Y. If these two offerings were integrated into a single transaction, the § 4(2) private offering exemption would be nullified by backward integration and the § 3(a)(11) exemption would be unavailable as a result of forward integration. Again, suppose that two years later X corporation makes another intrastate offering of common stock in strict compliance with § 3(a)(11) which is followed by a 1933 Act registered offering of common stock in which sales are made to nonresidents of State Y. If the two later offerings are integrated, the § 3(a)(11) exemption would be nullified, although the registered offering might remain unaffected. In that case, the concept would result only in one-way integration. The underlying policy behind the doctrine is that issuers should not be permitted to avoid registration, by splitting what is essentially a single financing into two or more ostensibly separate and distinct transactions, each of which, if regarded as a discrete transaction, would qualify under one of the exemptions. We have encountered the integration doctrine in a number of contexts. It may be helpful at this point to bring these threads together.

Genesis of the Doctrine. The principle first emerged in connection with § 3(a)(11) which makes the intrastate exemption hinge upon the *entire issue* being offered and sold only to residents of the state in question.[1] Although the Commission has stated that whether an offering will be regarded as a part of a larger offering, and thus be integrated is a question of fact, it added:[2]

> "Any one or more of the following factors may be determinative of the question of integration: (1) are the offerings part of a single plan of financing; (2) do the offerings involve issuance of the same class of security; (3) are the offerings made at or about the same time; (4) is the

1. Securities Act Release No. 97 (Dec. 28, 1933), 11 Fed.Reg. 10,949 (1946).

2. Securities Act Release No. 4434 (Dec. 6, 1961) supra at page 452. And see In re Unity Gold Corp., 3 S.E.C. 618 (1938) (considering whether offerings constituted separate issues). For an analysis of the SEC Staff's treatment of these five components in no-action letters, during the period 1971–1979, see Deaktor, Integration of Securities Offerings, 31 U.Fla.L.Rev. 465, 525–538 (1979). The Staff ceased to render no-action letters respecting integration in 1979 but reversed itself and resumed the practice in 1985. See Clover Financial Corporation (avail. Apr. 5, 1979); 17 BNA Sec.Reg. & L.Rep. 403 (1985).

same type of consideration to be received, and (5) are the offerings made for the same general purpose."

According to this formulation, it is possible that the presence of a single factor may cause two offerings to be parts of a single issue. The same linguistic formulation of the doctrine appears in Rule 147.[3] At the same time, Rule 147(b)(2) provides a safe harbor against the application of the doctrine to Rule 147 offerings of the issuer pursuant to the exemptions provided by § 3 or § 4(2) of the Act or pursuant to a 1933 Act registration statement which occurs, outside of six month "window-periods" immediately preceding or immediately following offerings made pursuant to the rule. However, offerings by the issuer of the same or similar class of securities as that offered pursuant to Rule 147 during a "window-period" causes a loss of this safe-harbor. In that event, to determine whether offerings should be integrated, one should apply the foregoing five-factor test as set forth in Securities Act Release No. 4434.

The "issue" concept is read into the § 4(2) private offering exemption, since that exemption, with some exceptions hereafter noted, is available only to "transactions by an issuer *not involving any* public offering." In Securities Act Release No. 4552 (Nov. 6, 1962), the Commission again stated that with respect to the § 4(2) exemption the determination of whether offerings should be integrated "depends on the particular facts or circumstances," but that the five integration factors set forth above *"should be considered."*[4] Nothing was said as to what weight should be given to the various factors, whether a single factor might be determinative, or why the formulation differs from that under § 3(a)(11) and Rule 147. This same difference in language has been repeated in Rule 502, raising the theoretical possibility that a § 3(a)(11) transaction which is followed by a § 4(2) transaction might result in backward integration so as to destroy the § 3(a)(11) exemption, although the § 4(2) transaction might remain intact.[5] Rule 502(a) contains a safe-harbor provision against integration of offerings identical with that provided in Securities Act Release No. 4552 and former Rule 146.

The safe-harbor provisions of Rule 502(a) and Rule 147(b)(2) provide a shield for a Regulation D or Rule 147 offering as the case may be, but neither of those provisions provides a safe-harbor for the other exempt offering. Thus, if an issuer were to make a Rule 506 offering separated by more than six months from a § 3(a)(9), § 3(a)(11) or a § 4(2) offering, the latter offering could lose its exemption, if the conditions for integration under the five-factor test were applicable. The integration would be only one way, however, and the Rule 506 transaction would not be affected. Accordingly, it would be advisable to arrange the transactions so that they constitute different plans of financing and achieve different general purposes using different classes of securities whenever feasible.

The "issue" concept is also imported into § 3(a)(9). This is accomplished by reading the word "exclusively" as modifying both "exchanged" and "security holders." Accordingly, an exchange of securities with existing security holders cannot be combined with a § 4(2) private offering of the same class of securities to institutional investors.[6] Indeed, if the exchange with the share-

---

3. Preliminary Note 3 to Rule 147.

4. Securities Act Release No. 4552 (Nov. 6, 1962).

5. Preliminary Note 3 to Rule 147; see Deaktor, supra note 2, at 503.

6. See SEC Securities Act Release No. 2029 (Aug. 8, 1939).

holders is itself a public offering,[7] the private offering exemption would also be lost. If, however, the offerings entail different "issues" of securities, the exemption is not destroyed.[8]

Section 3(b) authorizing the Commission by rule to add any class of securities to those exempted in § 3, specifies that no such issue shall be exempted "where the aggregate amount at which such issue is offered to the public exceeds $5,000,000."

The Commission has made exceptions to the doctrine of integration as applied to the § 4(2) private offering exemption and to Regulation A and Regulation E exempting offerings of up to $100,000 of Small Business Investment Companies,[9] presumably under the authority granted in § 19(a) to define technical terms.

Rule 152. In an effort to protect issuers from technical traps that could deny them access to the public capital market, the Commission adopted Rule 152, which states: "The phrase 'transactions by an issuer not involving any public offering' in section 4(2) shall be deemed to apply to transactions not involving any public offering at the time of said transactions although subsequently thereto the issuer decides to make a public offering and/or files a registration statement."

Absent such a rule, an issuer that made a private placement and found it needed still more capital to achieve its objective could be denied access to the public market for a time, because otherwise the subsequent public offering could be integrated with the earlier private placement. Yet, no one is protected by this doctrinal formalism and the issuer is arguably restricted for little reason. Still, despite its efficient purpose, Rule 152 presents a number of ambiguities. First, the antecedent of "thereto" is not self-evident. Must the decision to make a public offering and/or file a registration statement be subsequent to the abandonment or completion of the § 4(2) offering? Will the issuer escape the integration pitfall simply because it later files a registration statement? The ambiguous "and/or" in Rule 152 literally applies to "any public offering", whether registered or unregistered.

Despite all this, the SEC has ruled that the § 3(a)(11) exemption will be destroyed if the issuer "is unsuccessful in selling the entire issue to residents of the state and offers the rest of the issue, even after registration, to residents of other states * * *."[10] On the other hand, we have seen that SEC staff has taken the position that Regulation A and Regulation E, even though promulgated under § 3(b), qualify under Rule 152.[11] And a number of the § 3(b) exemptions provide for safe-harbors precluding integration.

Originally, the purpose of Rule 152 was to allow "those who have contemplated or begun to undertake a private offering to register securities without incurring any risk of liability as a consequence of having first contemplated or

---

7. Cf. SEC v. Ralston Purina Co., 346 U.S. 119 (1953) supra at page 397.

8. See supra note 6.

9. Vintage Group, Inc., SEC No–Action Letter, [1988 Transfer Binder] Fed.Sec. L.Rep. (CCH) ¶ 78,700 at 77,978 (Apr. 11, 1988). And see Johnson & Patterson, The Reincarnation of Rule 152: False Hope on the Integration Front, 46 Wash. & Lee L.Rev. 539, 560 (1989).

10. Texas Glass Manufacturing Corp., 38 S.E.C. 630 (1958). Although Rule 147(b)(2) contains a safe-harbor, that does not preclude integration under the § 3(a)(11) statutory exemption.

11. See supra note 9.

begun to undertake a private offering."[12] Thus, if a private offering failed, it could be converted into a public offering. If, however, a private offering and/or a registered offering were planned at the same time, the rule literally seemed to offer no protection. In reality, most "high-tech" firms were probably contemplating an eventual public offering from the day they were formed.

Despite the ambiguities of the rule, the SEC Staff issued several no-action letters which in effect accepted the idea of an initial "seed round venture financing" of a start-up company, notwithstanding the issuer's "contemplation" of an eventual registered public offering at the time of the placement.[13] These rulings permitted planning activities for the second phase public offering to commence while the first private offering was still in progress. But what if work on the public offering began before all the privately placed securities in the initial private offering were sold and taken down by investors? In a much discussed 1990 no-action letter to Black Box, Inc.,[14] the staff concluded that the critical date was the filing of the registration statement for the second offering. So long as the purchasers in the first offering were unconditionally bound by this date, even though the closing had not yet occurred, the second offering would meet the "subsequently thereto" requirement in Rule 152. However, if there was any renegotiation of the first private offering after that filing date for the second offering, then Rule 152 could not be satisfied, and the two offerings would be presumably integrated.

Rule 155. Eventually, the Commission recognized the need for a clearer safe harbor than Rule 152 could afford and adopted Rule 155 in 2001.[15] Rule 155 is two sided; it applies to both (a) a public offering following abandonment of a prior private offering, and (b) a private offering following abandonment of a prior public offering.[16] The preconditions to Rule 155's application require a clean break between the private and public offering, and they are also intended to assure that investors understand the differences between their legal protections in the two types of offerings. Unlike Rule 152, Rule 155 does not require that the future public offering not have been contemplated or foreseen at the time of the private placement. When the public offering follows the abandoned private offering, Rule 155(b) requires that (i) all offering activity in the private offering have terminated, and (ii) the issuer files its registration statement at

---

12. Securities Act Release No. 305 (Mar. 2, 1935), quoted in Deaktor, supra note 2, at 497 n. 206 (1979).

13. See Verticom, Inc., 1986 SEC No–Act. LEXIS 1751 (Feb. 12, 1986); BBI Assocs., 1986 SEC No–Act. LEXIS 3036 (Dec. 29, 1986). The scenario of multiround high-tech start-up financing set forth above is more fully described in Counsel's request for a no-action letter in Verticom, Inc. See also Stevenson, Integration and Private Placements, 19 Rev. of Sec. & Commodities Reg. 49–55 (1986).

What is the difference between "contemplating" and "planning" an IPO? At some stage of the financing the documents may contain extensive provisions granting piggyback and demand registration rights to the venture investors. One would hope that these arrangements were still only contemplative.

14. See Black Box, Inc., 1990 SEC No-Act. LEXIS 926 (June 26, 1990). A later no-action letter further fleshed out the details of this position. See Squadron, Ellenoff, Pleasant & Lehrer, 1992 S.E.C. No–Act. LEXIS 363 (February 28, 1992). See also Glover, The Offerings that Precede An Initial Public Offerings—How to Preserve Exemptions And Avoid Integration, 24 Sec.Reg.L.J. 3 (1996).

15. See Securities Act Release No. 7943 ("Integration of Abandoned Offerings") (February 5, 2001).

16. Why is the latter safe harbor necessary when there were no sales in the abandoned public offering? Because a public offering involves an inherent general solicitation, Rules 505 and 506 cannot be satisfied if they are integrated with even an abandoned earlier public offering.

least 30 calendar days after termination of all offering activity in the private offering, unless securities in the private offering were offered only to either accredited or sophisticated investors. In the reverse, case where the private offering follows the abandonment of the public offering, Rule 155(c) again conditions the safe harbor on a thirty day period elapsing after the withdrawal of the registration statement. In order to expedite this process, Rule 477 was amended to permit an issuer to withdraw its registration statement prior to its effectiveness, unless the SEC objects within 15 calendar days after the issuer applies to withdraw it.

Rule 155 is still limited in some important respects. First, Rule 155(a) defines a private offering as an offering that is exempt from registration under Section 4(a) or 4(b) or Rule 506 of Regulation D. Hence, Rule 155 does not apply to Rule 504 or 505 offerings; nor would it seemingly have any application to a Section 3(a)(11) intrastate offering, a Section 3(a)(10) reorganization, or a Section 3(a)(9) exchange offering. Even more basic is the fact that Rule 155 applies only when the initial offering (private or public) was abandoned and no securities were sold pursuant to it.

Query: Suppose an issuer sells to two persons in a private offering and then abandons the private offering. If the two sales are rescinded, can Rule 155 be relied upon.

Finally, it should be underscored that Rule 155 is only a safe harbor. Transactions that do not quite come within its four corners might still be exempt under traditional integration criteria. Or the issuer could sometimes fall back on Rule 152.

Foreign Offerings. The Commission has also taken the position that the registration provisions of Securities Act § 5 "are primarily intended to protect American investors." Accordingly, sales of securities that "come to rest" abroad will generally not be integrated with contemporaneous sales in the United States, provided that precautions are taken to ensure that securities that come to rest abroad will not flow back into the hands of American investors. These principles have been formalized by the adoption of Regulation S governing off-shore offerings by domestic issuers and by the safe-harbor provision now found in preliminary note 7 of Regulation D.[17]

SECTION 7. THE NARROWING BOUNDARIES BETWEEN PUBLIC AND PRIVATE TRANSACTIONS

Private transactions have certain advantages over public ones. They are low cost; the issuer can control the time schedule (while it may not be able to control the timing of SEC review of a registration statement), and expedition is possible. Conversely, private transactions do not result in freely tradeable shares and are subject to a liquidity discount. Nonetheless, the line between the public transaction and the private one has recently narrowed, as the following now standard transactions illustrate:

1. *PIPEs Transaction.* This acronym stands for a "private investment in public equities"—in short, a private placement by an issuer who is already a

---

17. Regulation S is discussed in Chapter 9 infra at p. 585.

reporting company. These transactions were most commonly used by biotech or other technology firms facing high demands for additional capital, "but with market capitalizations too small to comfortably allow for follow-on offerings large enough to provide the needed capital."[1] The buyers, who are often leveraged buyout firms, can also come into the corporation's headquarters, negotiate contractual protections, and perform detailed due diligence reviews to assure themselves that their investment is sound.

2. *"Exxon Capital" or "A/B" Exchange Offerings.* Suppose a company with a risky credit rating (i.e., below "investment grade") needs capital. If it undertakes a debt offering, it will not qualify for Form S–3 (which requires an "investment grade" rating), and thus it cannot be certain as to when the SEC will declare its registration statement effective. This may be a problem if it needs capital fast. One solution that works in this context is to make a private placement to institutional investors with the promise that the issuer will later exchange registered bonds that are identical for these privately placed bonds held by the purchasers within a defined period (typically, within nine months to a year). Thus, the issuer gets its capital fast, and the purchaser eventually gets freely tradeable, registered bonds. Enforcing this arrangement is a provision in the original bonds that increases their interest rate by a penalty amount (say 2 of 1%) if the exchange offering is not effected within the promised period. Although the SEC permits such pre-arranged exchange offers with regard to nonconvertible debt offerings, it adamantly resists the use of this procedure with regard to equity private placements. How can it draw or enforce a distinction? If such an exchange of registered common stock for unregistered common stock were to be attempted, the SEC would insist that the exchanging security holders be named in the registration statement as selling shareholders or underwriters, and thus they would have Section 11 and Section 12(a)(2) liability, subject to their affirmative due diligence defenses. This would not be attractive to institutional investors. In the case of debt and certain types of preferred stock offerings, the SEC has granted no action letters that permit the exchanging shareholders to escape underwriter status.[2] This type of exchange is increasingly used in Rule 144A offerings, which are discussed in Chapter 9. Note also that the investment banking firm that structures the initial private placement also escapes underwriter status when the exchange offer is used, because it deliberately avoids any role in the subsequent public offering; hence, only the issuer faces Section 11 liability when this exchange procedure is utilized.

At a minimum, these exchange offerings, which remain popular, show the high price that some issuers will pay to avoid the costs and delay sometimes incident to 1933 Act registration.

1. For a brief discussion of PIPEs, see Joseph A. Grundfest, The Ambiguous Boundaries Between Public and Private Securities Markets, 51 Case Wes. Res. L. Rev. 483 (2001).

2. For no-action letters approving this technique for debt securities, see Morgan Stanley & Co. Inc., S.E.C. No–Action Letter, 1991 S.E.C. No–Act. LEXIS 762 (June 5, 1991); Exxon Capital Holdings Corp., S.E.C. No–Act. LEXIS 682 (May 13, 1998). The Aircraft Carrier Release, which is discussed in Chapter 3, proposed to restrict this technique once "company registration" was achieved, but this proposal elicited a storm of opposition. See Securities Act Release No. 7606A (November 17, 1998) ("The Regulation of Securities Offerings") at * 52.

SECTION 8. GOING PUBLIC BY THE BACK DOOR

Securities and Exchange Commission v. Datronics Engineers, Inc.[a]

United States Court of Appeals, Fourth Circuit, 1973.
490 F.2d 250, cert. denied 416 U.S. 937.

■ Before BRYAN, SENIOR CIRCUIT JUDGE, and FIELD and WIDENER, CIRCUIT JUDGES.

■ ALBERT A. BRYAN, SENIOR CIRCUIT JUDGE: The Securities and Exchange Commission in enforcement of the Securities Act of 1933, § 20(b), and the Securities Exchange Act of 1934, § 21(e), sought a preliminary injunction to restrain Datronics Engineers, Inc., its officers and agents, as well as related corporations, from continuing in alleged violation of the registration and antifraud provisions of the Acts. The breaches are said to have been committed in the sale of unregistered securities, § 5 of the 1933 Act, and by the employment of false representations in their sale, § 10(b) of the 1934 Act, and Rule 10b–5 of the Commission.

Summary judgment went for the defendants, and the Commission appeals. We reverse.

Specifically, the complaint charged transgressions of the statutes by Datronics, assisted by the individual defendants, in declaring, and effectuating through the use of the mails, "spin-offs" to and among its stockholders of the unregistered shares of stock owned by Datronics in other corporations. With exceptions to be noted, and since the decision on appeal rests on a motion for summary judgment, there is no substantial dispute on the facts. Datronics was engaged in the construction of communications towers. Its capital stock was held by 1000 shareholders and was actively traded on the market. All of the spin-offs occurred within a period of 13 months * * * and the spun-off stock was that of nine corporations, three of which were wholly owned subsidiaries of Datronics and six were independent corporations.

The pattern of the spin-offs in each instance was this: Without any business purpose of its own, Datronics would enter into an agreement with the principals of a private company. The agreement provided for the organization by Datronics of a new corporation, or the utilization of one of Datronics' subsidiaries, and the merger of the private company into the new or subsidiary corporation. It stipulated that the principals of the private company would receive the majority interest in the merger-corporation. The remainder of the stock of the corporation would be delivered to, or retained by, Datronics for a nominal sum per share. Part of it would be applied to the payment of the services of Datronics in the organization and administration of the proposed spin-off, and to Datronics' counsel for legal services in the transaction. Datronics was bound by each of the nine agreements to distribute among its shareholders the rest of the stock.

---

a. As modified on denial of rehearing and rehearing en banc. Cert. denied 416 U.S. 937 (1974).

Before such distribution, however, Datronics reserved for itself approximately one-third of the shares. Admittedly, none of the newly acquired stock was ever registered; its distribution and the dissemination of the false representations were accomplished by use of the mails.

I.   Primarily, in our judgment each of these spin-offs violated § 5 of the Securities Act in that Datronics caused to be carried through the mails an unregistered security "for the purpose of sale or for delivery after sale". Datronics was actually an issuer, or at least a coissuer, and not exempted from § 5 by § 4(1) of the Act, as "any person other than an issuer".

Datronics and the other appellees contend, and the District Court concluded, that this type of transaction was not a sale. The argument is that it was no more than a dividend parceled out to stockholders from its portfolio of investments. A noteworthy difference here, however, is that each distribution was an obligation. Their contention also loses sight of the definition of "sale" contained in § 2 of the 1933 Act. As pertinent here that definition is as follows:

"When used in this subchapter, unless the context otherwise requires—

* * *

"(3) The term 'sale' or 'sell' shall include every contract of sale or *disposition* of a security or interest in a security, *for value.* The term 'offer to sell', 'offer for sale', or 'offer' shall include every attempt or offer to dispose of, or solicitation of an offer to buy, a security or interest in a security, *for value.* * * * " (Accent added.)

As the term "sale" includes a "disposition of a security", the dissemination of a new stock among Datronics' stockholders was a sale. However, the appellees urged, and the District Court held, that this disposition was not a statutory sale because it was not "for value", as demanded by the definition. Here, again, we find error. Cf. Securities and Exchange Commission v. Harwyn Industries Corp., 326 F.Supp. 943, 954 (S.D.N.Y.1971). Value accrued to Datronics in several ways. First, a market for the stock was created by its transfer to so many new assignees—at least 1000, some of whom were stockbroker-dealers, residing in various States. Sales by them followed at once—the District Judge noting that "[i]n each instance dealing promptly began in the spun-off shares". This result redounded to the benefit not only of Datronics but, as well, to its officers and agents who had received some of the spun-off stock as compensation for legal or other services to the spin-off corporations. Likewise, the stock retained by Datronics was thereby given an added increment of value. The record discloses that in fact the stock, both that disseminated and that kept by Datronics, did appreciate substantially after the distributions.

This spurious creation of a market whether intentional or incidental constituted a breach of the securities statutes. Each of the issuers by this wide spread of its stock became a publicly held corporation. In this process and in subsequent sales the investing public was not afforded the protection intended by the statutes. Further, the market and the public character of the spun-off stock were fired and fanned by the issuance of shareholder letters announcing future spin-offs, and by information statements sent out to the shareholders.

Moreover, we think that Datronics was an underwriter within the meaning of the 1933 Act. Hence its transactions were covered by the prohibitions, and were not within the exemptions, of the Act. §§ 3(a)(1) and 4(1) of the 1933 Act. By definition, the term underwriter "means any person who has purchased from an issuer with a view to, or offers or sells for an issuer in connection with, the distribution of any security, or participates or has a direct or indirect participation in any such undertaking. * * * " § 2(11) of the 1933 Act. Clearly, in these transactions the merger-corporation was an issuer; Datronics was a purchaser as well as a co-issuer; and the purchase was made with a view to the distribution of the stock, as commanded by Datronics' preacquisition agreements. By this underwriter distribution Datronics violated § 5 of the 1933 Act—sale of unregistered securities.

II.   The Commission charged a violation by Datronics and its officers of § 10(b) of the 1934 Act and of Rule 10b–5. The breach occurred through untrue factual statements incident to the spin-offs. The District Court quite justifiably found that "in certain instances misleading statements were made by" Datronics and the individual defendants. This finding was reiterated by the District Court in discussing the announcements which were made to Datronics' stockholders with each spin-off.

A common explanation of the distribution to its stockholders was that it was "impractical" for Datronics itself to run the merger-corporations. Of course, as the minority stockholder, Datronics could not do so. The District Court termed the explanation false and a "pure subterfuge".

Since, however, the District Court was of the opinion that the distribution of the stock among Datronics' shareholders was not a sale, it held that the "misleading statements" were not outlawed by § 10(b) or by Commission Rule 10b–5. These provisions condemn such misrepresentations only when they are used "in connection with the purchase or sale of any security". Inasmuch as we believe there was a sale in each spin-off, we cannot agree with the District Court's determination. * * *

This was one of the trial court's reasons for not granting an injunction. Other grounds were that there was no indication that in the future the defendants might violate the statutes in suit; that the officers and agents who formulated and executed the spin-offs were no longer connected with Datronics; and that the present officers and agents assured the District Court that no more spin-offs of this kind would be indulged in. Moreover, the Court felt that by its interpretative releases the Commission had led Datronics and its codefendants to believe that spin-offs were not proscribed by these statutes. The Court was also persuaded by the failure of the Commission to act more vigilantly. While the issuance of an injunction is discretionary, it seems to us that overall, notwithstanding these considerations, the facts in this case warranted the grant of an injunction. * * *

Finally, a summary of the activities of Datronics is conclusively convincing that they violated the statutes in question, and should now be restrained to prevent recurrences. To begin with, it is noteworthy that they were not isolated or minimal transgressions. There were, to repeat, nine sales and distributions of unregistered stocks in little more than a year. They were huge in volume, ranging from 75,000 to 900,000 shares. The distribution was not confined to a small number of recipients; nor was it incidental to Datronics' corporate functions. Concededly, none of the several distributions had a business purpose. In short, the spin-offs seemingly constituted the major operation of Datronics at the time.

We cannot read the releases or letters of the Commission or its abstention from earlier suits as evincing express or implied approval of the repeated and large-scale violations as are here. The releases do not approve or condone a campaign, such as Datronics engaged in, to develop means and opportunities to promote spin-offs. Indeed, one of Datronics' agents was a "finder" of opportunities for spin-offs.

The dismissal order of the District Court will be vacated, and the cause remanded for the entry of a judgment sustaining the appellant's motion for the preliminary injunction sought in its complaint.

■ WIDENER, CIRCUIT JUDGE (concurring):

I concur in the issuance of the temporary injunction * * *.

I note that the opinion of the court may not be broadly enough read to cast doubt upon the legitimate business acquisition of one company by another, or the legitimate business merger of two companies, although a market for securities spun off as a consequence of the transfer may be thereby created; for, as the opinion of the court recites, the market created by Datronics' spin-offs was spurious, doubtless meaning illegitimate, however actual it might have been, and Datronics caused the consummation of the transactions complained of without any business purpose of its own.

In my own opinion, the root of this case is the pre-existing agreement between Datronics and the various companies whose stocks it spun off with no apparent purpose other than the incidental benefits of creation of a public market for the stock. If the transactions were with a view to creating a public market for the stock which the various companies could not otherwise do absent compliance with the statute, then I think Datronics may be held to be an underwriter. The value requirement of a sale, for the issuer did receive value, I think, may be satisfied by the exchange of stock of the various companies with Datronics or by the exchange of stock of the various companies for services of Datronics. See also 58 Va.L.Rev. 1451.[b]

                              * * *

SPIN OFFS AND THE SHELL GAME

a. *Restricting Back Door Entry to the Market.* The *Datronics* case may seem like slightly strained reasoning in support of the correct policy result. The policy problem is that the trading of securities of inactive or shell corporations can easily be manipulated, and spin offs were regularly used to effect "pump and dump" schemes. In the 1960's, a technique came into use by which it was thought that a private company could achieve the status of a public company without a 1933 Act registration, in effect going public through the back door. A variety of patterns were used, but the overall objective remained the same. The most popular of these devices was that employed in the *Datronics* case—a privately-held company wishing to "go public" would issue additional stock to a second publicly-held company (usually a shell corporation with no asset other than its stockholder list), which would then distribute most of the stock to its public shareholders as a dividend, keeping a portion as its "fee" for acting as the conduit in this operation. It would then repeat the operation again and

b. On motions to reconsider, the defendants represented to the Court that no more spin offs would be undertaken. On that basis, the Court rescinded that part of the opinion which required the trial court to award a preliminary injunction, and remanded for a determination by the District Court, consistently with the remainder of the opinion, of whether an injunction should or should not be issued restraining Datronics in respect to such transactions as the opinion of the Court declares to be impermissible. Datronics' request for a rehearing in banc was denied.

again for different companies desiring a public market for their stocks without any of the disclosures required by the 1933 Act or 1934 Act.

In SEC v. Harwyn Industries Corp.,[1] the SEC sought to plug this possible loophole in the 1933 Act by seeking to enjoin various forms of spin offs of a subsidiary corporation's shares to the parent's stockholders without registration, thereby converting the subsidiary into a public corporation whose unregistered shares would then be actively traded on the market. The court held that the *Harwyn* spin offs "violated the spirit and purpose of the registration requirements of '5 of the 1933 Act". Nevertheless, the court concluded that defendants' interpretation of § 2(3) and 5 was "neither frivolous nor wholly unreasonable," and was made in good faith and on the advice of counsel. The court was moved by the somewhat ambivalent attitude of the Commission both before and after the Commission's Interpretative Release No. 4982.[2] That Release emphasized that the appropriate test for when a spin off required registration was whether it had a proper business purpose. Upon assurance by counsel for defendants in *Harwyn* that their clients would no longer engage in further distributions of the type in question without registration (because the Commission had now set forth its views), the court denied the Commission's motion for a preliminary injunction.

The *Datronics* case delivered the coup de grace to the more blatant forms of the spin off and shell game, while still permitting conventional spin offs. Indeed, in United States v. Rubinson,[3] defendants who persisted in engaging in spin-offs followed by the resale of worthless securities to the unsuspecting public were convicted for violation of the registration and anti-fraud provisions of the federal securities laws. In addition, the Commission recognized that the definition of "sale" in Section 3(a)(14) of the Securities Exchange Act of 1934 does not have the same "for value" requirement, and thus it did need to engage in the same elaborate (and possibly strained) analysis of the spin off's benefits to the issuer as was necessary in *Datronics*.[4]

In any event, the Commission's thinking about spin offs changed changed over subsequent years. Deemphasizing its early focus in Release 4982 on the existence of a "proper business purpose," the Commission shifted to an emphasis on whether adequate disclosures had been made at the time of the spin off. Later decisions have also held that spin offs that receive adequate disclosure are not sales or purchases of securities.[5] After issuing a multitude of no-action letters on the line between those spin offs that require registration and those that do not, the staff of the Division of Corporation Finance codified them in Staff Legal Bulletin No. 4 in 1997.[6] In this bulletin, the staff took the position that a spin-off will not be required to be registered if each of the following five conditions are satisfied:

1. 326 F.Supp. 943 (S.D.N.Y.1971).

2. Securities Act Release No. 4982 (July 2, 1969).

3. 543 F.2d 951 (2d Cir.1976), cert. denied 429 U.S. 850.

4. Thus, in *International Controls Corp. v. Vesco*, 490 F.2d 1334 (2d Cir.), *cert.denied*, 417 U.S. 932 (1974), a much simpler analysis was used to find that a spin off amounted to a sale of securities.

5. See *Isquith v. Caremark International, Inc.*, 136 F.3d 531 (7th Cir.1998); *Rathborne v. Rathborne*, 683 F.2d 914, 919–20 (5th Cir.1982) (sale results if transactions produces "fundamental change in the nature" of the investment).

6. See 1997 SEC No–Act. LEXIS 869 (Sept. 16, 1997).

1. *No consideration.* The parent corporation's shareholders must provide no consideration for the spin-off shares (otherwise, obviously there is a sale).

2. *Pro-rata distribution of shares.* The spin-off must be pro-rata to the parent corporation's shareholders with no surrender of rights or value required by those who receive the spun-off shares.

3. *Adequate information.* The parent corporation must provide adequate information to both its shareholders and to the market. If the subsidiary to be spun off is not a reporting company, the staff indicated that the parent corporation must (1) provide an information statement by the date of the spin-off that describes the transaction and complies with Regulation 14A or 14C under the 1934 Act, and (2) cause the subsidiary to promptly register as a reporting company under the 1934 Act. Where the subsidiary is a reporting company, it must have been subject to the 1934 Act's reporting requirements for at least 90 days, be current in its 1934 Act reports, and provide certain specific disclosures about the transaction.

4. *Valid Business Purpose.* Where there is a valid business purpose for the transaction, the staff indicated its view that the spin-off transaction is less likely to amount to a sale. What constitutes an invalid purpose? The bulletin gave several examples, such as creating a public market for a development stage subsidiary that had no specific business plan or objective (other than to seek a merger). The common premise underlying these examples was that an attempt to market a company through the back door without adequate information is an invalid purpose.

5. *Restricted Securities.* Where a parent corporation spins off "restricted securities," the staff indicated that the parent corporation may be deemed an underwriter of those securities for at least two years. If, however, the parent has held the subsidiary's stock for at least two years prior to the spin-off, the parent will not be deemed an underwriter. (This interpretation apparently applies only to stock acquired by the parent and not subsidiaries that it created itself).

b. *Rule 15c2–11.* In addition, the staff advised that affiliates of the parent that acquire shares in a spin off may be required to hold such shares as restricted securities and sell them only pursuant to Rule 144 or some other exemption.

In an entirely different and earlier approach to end the spin-off game, the Commission has sought to regulate the broker dealers who trade such securities. In 1971, the Commission adopted Rule 15c2–11 under the 1934 Act for the purpose of preventing a broker or dealer from initiating or resuming quotations respecting a security in the absence of adequate information concerning the security and the issuer.[7] In adopting the rule, the Commission emphasized that the rule was particularly applicable in connection with the distribution of securities of "shell" corporations by means of the "spin off" device. The Commission noted, however, that a fraudulent and manipulative potential also existed whenever a broker or dealer submitted quotations concerning any infrequently-traded security in the absence of adequate information. Rule 15c2–11 illustrates the Commission's use of the anti-fraud provisions of the 1934 Act to buttress the disclosure provisions of the 1933 Act.

7. Securities Exchange Act Release No. 9310 (Sept. 13, 1971).

Nonetheless, the efficacy of Rule 15c2–11 is open to debate. Although it clearly creates a disincentive for the broker-dealer who has no information about a non-reporting issuer from beginning to trade that stock, this disincentive is undercut in several ways. Under subsection (f)(3) of the Rule, a dealer may make a market in the stock of a non-reporting company, even though it lacks the requisite information otherwise required by Rule 15c2–11, if the security has been quoted by another broker dealer for at least 12 days within the previous 30 calendar days. This "piggyback" exemption means that only the first market-maker needs to possess the requisite information (and it may later suspend its quotations, with the result that no broker dealer necessarily has the information). In addition, under Rule 15c2–11(f)(3)(iii), a dealer may "self piggyback" on its own initial compliance with the rule after the first month and need not maintain current information about the issuer so long as quotations continue to be continuously quoted with respect to the security. These exceptions may well overwhelm the rule.

Although the Securities Enforcement Remedies and Penny Stock Reform Act of 1990 (the "Penny Stock Act") gave the SEC additional authority to deal with fraud and abuse in penny stocks, the definition of a "penny stock" is somewhat arbitrarily limited in most cases to stocks priced at five dollars or less.[8] Promoters quickly learned that they could escape the more onerous provisions of the Penny Stock Act if they priced the security above $5 per share.

Thus, the 1990s witnessed a major resurgence of trading in low-priced, illiquid stocks that trade in non-transparent markets. Indeed, of the 55,000 publicly traded companies in the U.S., less than 10,000 trade on an organized stock exchange or NASDAQ.[9] The balance trade in over-the counter markets, including the NASDAQ bulletin board. Probably most of the issuers at the lower end of this market are not reporting companies. Hence, the problem of back door listings has resurfaced as a major problem, largely because new technological innovations have made the Internet and OTC electronic bulletin boards an effective substitute for a stock exchange listing. Faced with endemic problems in its bulletin board market, the NASD responded in 1997 by purging most non-reporting companies from that market (with the result that these firms could trade only in the over-the-counter "pink sheets").[10] Although concerned about the loss of liquidity, the SEC supported this proposal, and in 1998, it proposed amendments to tighten Rule 15c2–11 to deal with "microcap" fraud by requiring all brokers to possess and review more current information about an issuer when they publish price quotations for the issuer's securities.[11] The effect of these amendments might be to chill the willingness of brokers to publish quotations for non-reporting issuers; possibly for this reason and possibly because of lobbying pressure, the Commission had not acted on its proposals as of mid–2002.

8. See Rule 3a51–1. To escape the definition of a "penny stock", not only must the stock be priced above $5 per share, but the issuer must also meet certain fairly modest financial criteria (e.g., net tangible assets in excess of $2 million or certain other levels, etc.).

9. Hernandez, Broker–Dealer Regulation Under the New Penny Stock Disclosure Rules: An Appraisal, 1993 Colum.Bus.L.Rev. 27, 29.

10. Knight, "NASD Tries to Reduce the Risk of OTC Trading," Wash. Post, Dec. 15, 1997, at F 23.

11. See Sec.Exch.Act Rel. No. 39670 (Feb. 17, 1998).

c. *The Continuing Use of the Backdoor.* The dimensions of the "micro-cap" market continue to grow. As of January 2002, the SEC estimated that there were approximately 1,876 securities quoted exclusively in the OTC Bulletin Board, 3,942 quoted exclusively in the Pink Sheets, and 1,889 quoted on both—for a total of 7,707 OTC securities.[12]

Enforcement cases continue to detect sales of "public" shell corporations to persons owning non-public operating companies who are eager to go public by the backdoor.[13] Often, the shell corporation purports to comply with Rule 15c2–11 in order to qualify for over-the-counter trading, but the company is "sold" to the operating company's management solely for its existing status as a publicly traded company. Sometimes, the sellers of the shell corporation will sell part of the stock to the purchasers of the operating business in "matched" trades that are reported to the NASD in order to manipulating the market by creating the illusion of a rising market place.[14]

---

12. See SEC, Comment Request, 67 FR 15424 (April 1, 2002).

13. See *SEC v. Lybrand*, 200 F.Supp.2d 384 (S.D.N.Y.2002) (finding violations of both Section 5 and Rule 10b–5 where promoters made repetitive sales of shell corporations); *SEC v. Cavanagh*, 1 F.Supp.2d 337 (S.D.N.Y. 1998).

14. Such conduct will violate the anti-fraud rules as well as Section 5 of the 1933 Act. "Matched trades" are pre-arranged buys and sells that have not been exposed to the market and hence often represent inflated or otherwise fictitious prices.

SUBDIVISION D.   THE OBLIGATION TO REGISTER RESALES OF SECURITIES BY PERSONS OTHER THAN THE ISSUER

CHAPTER 9

OFFERINGS BY UNDERWRITERS, AFFILIATES AND DEALERS

SECTION 1.   THE CONCEPT OF "UNDERWRITER"

Statutes and Regulations

Securities Act, §§ 2(a)(2), 2(a)(11), 4(1).

Rules 140–143, 152a, 405.

Statutory and Presumptive Underwriters

Statutory Underwriters. Section 5 prohibits the use of interstate facilities or the mails to sell a security unless a registration statement has become effective. However, § 4(1) specifically exempts transactions "by any person other than an issuer, underwriter or dealer * * *." Thus, only issuers, underwriters and dealers are subject to the registration and prospectus requirements of the 1933 Act. We have already explored the meaning of the term "issuer" as used in the Securities Act. We now consider the concept of "underwriter."

The definition of "underwriter" is found in § 2(a)(11). The term means "any person who": [1] "has purchased from an issuer [or controlling person] with a view to, or [2] offers or sells for an issuer [or a controlling person] in connection with, the distribution of any security, or [3] participates or has a direct or indirect participation in any such undertaking, or [4] participates or has a participation in the direct or indirect underwriting of any such undertaking."

The addition of the bracketed material takes account of the last sentence of the paragraph which defines the term "issuer" as used therein to include, in addition to an issuer, any person in a control relationship with the issuer.

The House Committee Report described the meaning of the term "underwriter" this way:[1]

1. Report of Committee on Interstate and Foreign Commerce, H.R.Rep.No.85, 73d Cong., 1st Sess., 13–14 (1933).

The term [underwriter] is defined broadly enough to include not only the ordinary underwriter, who for a commission promises to see that an issue is disposed of at a certain price, but also includes as an underwriter the person who purchases an issue outright with the idea of then selling that issue to the public. The definition of underwriter is also broad enough to include two other groups of persons who perform functions, similar in character, in the distribution of a large issue. The first of these groups may be designated as the underwriters of the underwriter, a group who, for a commission, agree to take over pro rata the underwriting risk assumed by the first underwriter. The second group may be termed participants in the underwriting or outright purchase, who may or may not be formal parties to the underwriting contract, but who are given a certain share or interest therein.

The term "underwriter," however, is interpreted to exclude the dealer who receives only the usual distributor's or seller's commission. This limitation, however, has been so phrased as to prevent any genuine underwriter passing under the mark of a distributor or dealer. The last sentence of this definition, defining "issuer" to include not only the issuer but also affiliates or subsidiaries of the issuer and persons controlling the issuer, has two functions. The first function is to require the disclosure of any underwriting commission which, instead of being paid directly to the underwriter by the issuer, may be paid in an indirect fashion by a subsidiary or affiliate of the issuer to the underwriter. Its second function is to bring within the provisions of the bill redistribution whether of outstanding issues or issues sold subsequently to the enactment of the bill. All the outstanding stock of a particular corporation may be owned by one individual or a select group of individuals. At some future date they may wish to dispose of their holdings and to make an offer of this stock to the public. Such a public offering may possess all the dangers attendant upon a new offering of securities. Wherever such a redistribution reaches significant proportions, the distributor would be in the position of controlling the issuer and thus able to furnish the information demanded by the bill. This being so, the distributor is treated as equivalent to the original issuer and, if he seeks to dispose of the issue through a public offering, he becomes subject to the act. The concept of control herein involved is not a narrow one, depending upon a mathematical formula of 51 percent of voting power, but is broadly defined to permit the provisions of the act to become effective wherever the fact of control actually exists.

The somewhat nebulous question of who is an underwriter is addressed by two important SEC rules. First, Rule 141 makes clear that the dealer's "commission" referred to in § 2(a)(11) is the usual "spread" between the underwriter's offering price to dealers and the public offering price, provided the profit margin is usual and customary for the type and size of the offering. The rule applies whether the dealer buys outright and resells the security or whether it is acting merely as a broker. Note that there is a second implication to Rule 141: if you are not an "underwriter" under this rule, then you cannot engage in preliminary negotiations with the issuer prior to the filing of the registration statement, because Section 2(a)(3) exempts only "underwriters" (and only those who are to be in privity with the issuer).

Second, Rule 142 permits persons who are not affiliated with the issuer or underwriter to make a commitment with the underwriter to purchase all or a part of any unsold portion of the offering after the passage of a specified period of time following the commencement of the offering, if the securities are acquired for investment rather than for distribution. According to the General Counsel of the SEC, this rule was adopted "in recognition of the value of secondary capital in facilitating the flow of investment funds into industry, and of the fact that the owners of such secondary capital cannot practicably perform the duty of thorough analysis imposed by the Act on the underwriter proper."[2] The rule thus makes clear "that a person who does no more than agree with an underwriter to take over some or all of the undistributed portion of the issue, and who purchases for investment any securities which his commitment thus obliges him to take up, does not thereby subject himself to liability as an underwriter of the securities of the issue actually distributed to the public."[3] As a practical matter, the rule opens the way for institutional investors, such as insurance and investment companies or pension funds, to make an advance commitment to purchase stock on a "standby" basis at a discount off the initial offering price if the public will not purchase all the offering—without incurring the liabilities of an underwriter. However, Rule 142 requires that (i) the securities must be purchased "for investment and not with a view to distribution," and (ii) the agreement not be directly with the issuer. Thus, under Rule 142, these institutional investors cannot perform a distributive function; nor can they have control relationship with the issuer or a principal underwriter.

Presumptive Underwriters. In recent years, during periods of a strong new issues market, there have been instances where a wealthy investor or an institution purchased a large block of a registered offering, presumably for investment, and thereafter resold the securities to the public without the use of a statutory prospectus. To cope with this situation, the Commission and Staff have developed the "presumptive underwriter" doctrine. The doctrine as first formulated established an administrative rule-of-thumb that any person who purchased ten percent or more of a registered offering was presumed to be an underwriter within the meaning of § 2(a)(11) of the 1933 Act. The rule was first enunciated and applied in business combination transactions under Rule 145, see supra at page 483. The doctrine, though never officially adopted by formal action of the Commission, nevertheless is applied in practice by the Staff. A definition of the doctrine as consistent with Commission practice has been formulated in these terms:

> A person may be deemed to be an underwriter, within the meaning of § 2(11) of the Securities Act, if such person purchases or acquires a significant percentage of the securities offered pursuant to a registered distribution, except that such purchaser is not deemed to be an underwriter if he resells such securities in limited quantities.[4]

The Staff applies the presumptive underwriter doctrine in individual cases so as to prevent unrestricted resales by purchasers of large blocks of registered offerings free of the disclosure requirements generally applicable to registered offerings. Under the doctrine, such purchases followed by a resale creates a

---

2.   Opinion of General Counsel, SEC Securities Act Release No. 1862, Dec. 13, 1938.

3.   Ibid.

4.   Ahrenholz and Van Valkenberg, The Presumptive Underwriter Doctrine: Statuto- ry Underwriter Status for Investors Purchasing a Specified Portion of a Registered Offering, 1973 Utah L.Rev. 773, 775–776.

presumption that the seller is a statutory underwriter unless the burden is rebutted through showing of a change of circumstance or other justifiable cause. The Commission's practice is gleaned from no-action letters responding to interpretive requests. In practice, the Commission generally advises that such resales will not violate the Securities Act if such resales do not exceed the quantity limitations of Rule 144 or Rule 145 to be considered later in this Chapter.

The doctrine, however, should not be applied woodenly where a person or entity is not engaging in a distributive activity. Thus, the Staff gave a no-action opinion that an insurance company would not be considered an underwriter in connection with recurrent purchases of large amounts of registered securities for investment so long as the securities were acquired from the issuer or underwriter in the ordinary course of the company's business, and no arrangement existed between the insurance company and others to participate in the distribution of securities. Insurance companies and pension funds must make investments which are sufficiently liquid to meet foreseeable obligations as well as unforeseen demands. This need for portfolio liquidity requires that such institutional investors be certain when purchasing securities that they will be able to resell the securities if the need arises without being tagged as a "presumptive underwriter."[5]

For an analysis and critique of the presumptive underwriter doctrine as an instrument in securities law enforcement, see 2 L. Loss & J. Seligman, Securities Regulation 1114–15 (3d ed. 1989); Ahrenholz and Van Valkenberg, The Presumptive Underwriter Doctrine: Statutory Underwriter Status for Investors Purchasing a Specified Portion of a Registered Offering, 1973 Utah L.Rev. 773; Nathan, Presumptive Underwriters, 8 The Review of Securities Regulation 881 (1975).

Securities and Exchange Commission v. Chinese Consolidated Benevolent Association, Inc.[a]

United States Circuit Court of Appeals, Second Circuit, 1941.
120 F.2d 738.

■ AUGUSTUS N. HAND, CIRCUIT JUDGE. The Securities and Exchange Commission seeks to enjoin the defendant from the use of any instruments of interstate commerce or of the mails in disposing, or attempting to dispose, of Chinese Government bonds for which no registration statement has ever been made.

The defendant is a New York corporation organized for benevolent purposes having a membership of 25,000 Chinese. On September 1, 1937, the Republic of China authorized the issuance of $500,000,000 in 4% Liberty Bonds, and on May 1, 1938 authorized a further issue of $50,000,000 in 5% bonds. In October, 1937, the defendant set up a committee which has had no official or contractual relation with the Chinese government for the purpose of:

(a) Uniting the Chinese in aiding the Chinese people and government in their difficulties.

---

5. American Council of Life Insurance (Avail. June 10, 1983), Fed.Sec.L.Rep. (CCH) [1983–84 Transfer Binder] ¶ 77,526.

a. Cert. denied, 314 U.S. 618 (1941).

(b) Soliciting and receiving funds from members of Chinese communities in New York, New Jersey and Connecticut, as well as from the general public in those states, for transmission to China for general relief.

All the members of the committee were Chinese and resided in New York City. Through mass meetings, advertising in newspapers distributed through the mails, and personal appeals, the committee urged the members of Chinese communities in New York, New Jersey and Connecticut to purchase the Chinese government bonds referred to and offered to accept funds from prospective purchasers for delivery to the Bank of China in New York as agent for the purchasers. At the request of individual purchasers and for their convenience the committee received some $600,000 to be used for acquiring the bonds, and delivered the moneys to the New York agency of the Bank of China, together with written applications by the respective purchasers for the bonds which they desired to buy. The New York agency transmitted the funds to its branch in Hong Kong with instructions to make the purchases for the account of the various customers. The Hong Kong bank returned the bonds by mail to the New York branch which in turn forwarded them by mail to the purchasers at their mailing addresses, which, in some cases, were in care of the defendant at its headquarters in New York. Neither the committee, nor any of its members, has ever made a charge for their activities or received any compensation from any source. The Bank of China has acted as an agent in the transactions and has not solicited the purchase of bonds or the business involved in transmitting the funds for that purpose.

No registration statement under the Securities Act has ever been made covering any of the Chinese bonds advertised for sale. Nevertheless the defendant has been a medium through which over $600,000 has been collected from would-be purchasers and through which bonds in that amount have been sold to residents of New York, New Jersey and Connecticut.

Motions for judgment were made by both parties upon pleadings setting forth the foregoing facts. As a result the court below entered a decree denying complainant's motion, granting defendant's motion and dismissing the complaint. The Commission has taken an appeal from the decree, which, in our opinion, ought to be reversed.

It should be observed at the outset that the Commission is not engaged in preventing the solicitation of contributions to the Chinese government, or its citizens. Its effort is only to prevent the sale of Chinese securities through the mails without registry. * * *

Section 5 of the Act provides as follows. [The court quotes §§ 5(a)(1) and (2) imposing the registration and prospectus requirements in connection with sales of securities by the use of interstate facilities or the mails.]

Section 4 provides the following exemptions from the requirements of Section 5 supra:

"Sec. 4. The provisions of section 5 shall not apply to any of the following transactions:

"(1) Transactions by any person other than an issuer, underwriter, or dealer; * * *."

Under Section 2(11) an "underwriter" is defined as: "any person who has purchased from an issuer with a view to, or sells for an issuer in connection with, the distribution of any security, or participates or has a direct or indirect participation in any such undertaking; * * * ''.

We think that the defendant has violated Section 5(a) of the Securities Act when read in connection with Section 2(3) because it engaged in selling unregistered securities issued by the Chinese government when it solicited offers to buy the securities "for value". The solicitation of offers to buy the unregistered bonds, either with or without compensation, brought defendant's activities literally within the prohibition of the statute. Whether the Chinese government as issuer authorized the solicitation, or merely availed itself of gratuitous and even unknown acts on the part of the defendant whereby written offers to buy, and the funds collected for payment, were transmitted to the Chinese banks does not affect the meaning of the statutory provisions which are quite explicit. In either case the solicitation was equally for the benefit of the Chinese government and broadly speaking was for the issuer in connection with the distribution of the bonds.

* * *

Under Section 4(1) the defendant is not exempt from registration requirements if it is "an underwriter". The court below reasons that it is not to be regarded as an underwriter since it does not sell or solicit offers to buy "for an issuer in connection with, the distribution" of securities. In other words, it seems to have been held that only solicitation authorized by the issuer in connection with the distribution of the Chinese bonds would satisfy the definition of underwriter contained in Section 2(11) and that defendant's activities were never for the Chinese government but only for the purchasers of the bonds. Though the defendant solicited the orders, obtained the cash from the purchasers and caused both to be forwarded so as to procure the bonds, it is nevertheless contended that its acts could not have been for the Chinese government because it had no contractual arrangement or even understanding with the latter. But the aim of the Securities Act is to have information available for investors. This objective will be defeated if buying orders can be solicited which result in uninformed and improvident purchases. It can make no difference as regards the policy of the act whether an issuer has solicited orders through an agent, or has merely taken advantage of the services of a person interested for patriotic reasons in securing offers to buy. The aim of the issuer is to promote the distribution of the securities, and of the Securities Act is to protect the public by requiring that it be furnished with adequate information upon which to make investments. Accordingly the words "[sell] for an issuer in connection with the distribution of any security" ought to be read as covering continual solicitations, such as the defendant was engaged in, which normally would result in a distribution of issues of unregistered securities within the United States. Here a series of events were set in motion by the solicitation of offers to buy which culminated in a distribution that was initiated by the defendant. We hold that the defendant acted as an underwriter.

There is a further reason for holding that Section 5(a)(1) forbids the defendant's activities in soliciting offers to buy the Chinese bonds. Section 4(1) was intended to exempt only trading transactions between individual investors with relation to securities already issued and not to exempt distributions by issuers. The words of the exemption in Section 4(1) are: "Transactions by any person other than an issuer, underwriter, or dealer; * * * ''. The issuer in this case was the Republic of China. The complete transaction included not only solicitation by the defendant of offers to buy, but the offers themselves, the transmission of the offers and the purchase money through the banks to the Chinese government, the acceptance by that government of the offers and the delivery of the bonds to the purchaser or the defendant as his agent. Even if the defendant is not itself "an issuer, underwriter, or dealer" it was participating in a transaction with an issuer, to wit, the Chinese Government. The argument on behalf of the defendant incorrectly assumes that Section 4(1) applies to the component parts of the entire transaction we have mentioned and thus exempts defendant unless it is an underwriter for the Chinese Republic. Section 5(a)(1), however, broadly prohibits sales of securities irrespective of the character of the person making them. The exemption is limited to "transactions" by persons other than "issuers, underwriters or dealers". It does not in terms or by fair implication protect those who are engaged in steps necessary to the distribution of security issues. To give Section 4(1) the construction urged by the defendant would afford a ready method of thwarting the policy of the law and evading its provisions.

It is argued that an injunction ought not to be granted because the interests of a foreign state are involved. But the provisions for registration statements apply to issues of securities by a foreign government. (See Section 2(a)(2) and Section 7.) Section 6(a), moreover, permits a registration relating to securities issued by a foreign government to be signed by the underwriter, which we have held the defendant to be.

* * *

The decree is reversed with directions to the District Court to deny the defendant's motion to dismiss and to issue the injunction as prayed for in the bill of complaint. * * *

———

1. *Promoters.* Based on the *Chinese Consolidated Benevolent Association* case, it is fairly easy to see how those who promote the sale of unregistered securities can be classified as underwriters. If a person arranges for research reports or other promotional efforts designed to stimulate trading or if that person causes over-the-counter trading to occur, they may fall within the definition of an "underwriter" as one who "participates . . . in such undertaking."[6] But as next seen, this same broad statutory language can also ensnare creditors and institutional investors.

Securities and Exchange Commission v. Guild Films Co.[1]

United States Court of Appeals, Second Circuit, 1960.
279 F.2d 485.

■ MOORE, CIRCUIT JUDGE. This is an appeal * * * from an order by the district court * * * granting a preliminary injunction to restrain the sale of 50,000 shares of Guild Films Company, Inc. common stock by two of the appellants, the Santa Monica Bank and The Southwest Bank of Inglewood. Pending a final

---

6. See Securities and Exchange Commission v. Allison, [1982 Transfer Binder] Fed. Sec. L. Rep. (CCH) Para. 98,774 (N.D. Cal. 1982).

1. Cert. denied, 364 U.S. 819 (1960).

determination of this action, the preliminary injunction was issued "unless and until" a registration statement should be filed under the Securities Act of 1933.

Section 5 of the Act makes it unlawful for anyone, by any interstate communication or use of the mails, to sell or deliver any security unless a registration statement is in effect. Section 4 provides, however, that "the provisions of section 5 * * * shall not apply to * * * (1) Transactions by any person other than an issuer, underwriter, or dealer." The banks claim that they come within this exemption to the registration requirements. The district court rejected this claim, holding that the banks were "underwriters" within the meaning of the Act. While the issue involved can be simply stated, a rather complete discussion of the facts is necessary.

The Original Loans by the Banks and the Security Therefor

On September 17, 1958, the Santa Monica Bank and The Southwest Bank of Inglewood jointly agreed to loan Hal Roach, Jr., $120,000 represented by two notes. * * *

The loans were * * * secured * * * by 30,000 shares of [F.L.Jacobs Co.] stock. Roach had used a large part of the proceeds of the loans to purchase a substantial number of the 30,000 Jacobs shares put up as collateral.

The Jacobs Stock and the Renewal Notes

Roach was an officer, director, and the controlling shareholder of F. L. Jacobs Co. * * * This company controlled the Scranton Corp. which owned Hal Roach Studios, which in turn owned both W–R Corp. and Rabco T.V. Production, Inc.

W–R Corp. and Guild Films, Inc. had made an agreement on January 23, 1959, under which W–R Corp. was to obtain 400,000 shares of Guild Films common stock (the registration of 50,000 shares of this stock is here in dispute) and a number of promissory notes in exchange for certain film properties. The stock was not registered with the S.E.C., but Guild Films agreed to use its best efforts to obtain registration. However, seeking to come within an exemption provided in section 4 of the Securities Act, the parties provided the following in their agreement:

"Stock Taken for Investment: W–R warrants, represents and agrees that all of the said 400,000 shares of Guild's common stock being contemporaneously issued hereunder, whether registered in the name of W–R or in accordance with the instructions of W–R, are being acquired for investment only and not for the purpose or with the intention of distributing or reselling the same to others. Guild is relying on said warranty and representation in the issuance of said stock."

On February 5, 1959, for reasons discussed below, Roach directed that 100,000 shares of the Guild Films stock be issued in the name of W–R Corp. and 100,000 shares (represented by two 50,000 share certificates) in the name of Rabco. Meacham, the treasurer of Guild Films, directed that the transfer agent stamp this restriction on the stock certificates:

"The shares represented by this certificate have not been registered under the Securities Act of 1933. The shares have been acquired for investment and may not be sold, transferred, pledged or hypothecated in the absence of an effective registration statement for the shares under the Securities Act of 1933 or an opinion of counsel to the company that registration is not required under said Act." The remaining 200,000 shares were not issued as the promised film properties were never transferred.

Although the Guild Films stock was issued "for investment only," the district court found that Roach "unquestionably" purchased it in order to have it resold. * * * These findings are uncontested.

* * *

[In December, 1958, the lending banks learned that the Jacobs stock had been suspended from trading on the New York Stock Exchange. The Santa Monica Bank asked Roach to liquidate the loan because the Jacobs stock, which was then being traded over-the-counter, had dropped to $5 a share and was not deemed by the bank to be acceptable collateral. Roach asked the banks for more time to deposit acceptable collateral and make a cash payment on the note. As negotiations continued the banks agreed to defer action until February 10, 1959.]

* * *

On that date Roach wired The Southwest Bank that he had sent 50,000 shares of Guild Films stock to the Santa Monica Bank. By a divided vote the Loan Committee of The Southwest Bank decided to renew the note, making it payable "On 'Demand' if 'No Demand' then all due March 18, 1959." On February 12th, one of the 50,000 share Guild Films certificates in the name of Rabco T.V. Productions was received by the Santa Monica Bank. The restrictive legend quoted above was stamped on the face of the certificate. * * *

* * *

On February 12th, the Santa Monica Bank and The Southwest Bank learned that the Jacobs stock had been suspended from all trading by the S.E.C. The Santa Monica Bank immediately telegraphed Roach demanding payment by February 16th, and stating that otherwise the stock would be sold to liquidate the loan. Roach failed to pay and the banks attempted to sell the securities through brokers on the American Stock Exchange.

The Guild Films transfer agent refused to transfer the stock to the banks because of the stamped restriction. The Santa Monica Bank then wired Guild Films that unless the stock was released or exchanged for unrestricted securities, the matter would be taken to the American Stock Exchange and the S.E.C. "for their assistance and release." Guild Films refused to act; it also refused an offer to exchange the 50,000 shares for 25,000 shares of unrestricted stock; and no application for registration was made to the S.E.C.

In August, 1959, the Santa Monica Bank brought an action against Guild Films in the New York Supreme Court to compel the transfer of the stock. On September 18, 1959, that court ordered the transfer of the stock to the bank. The court based its order on a referee's report which found that the stock was exempt from the Securities Act of 1933. The Santa Monica Bank thereupon ordered 9,500 shares of the Guild Films stock sold. The S.E.C. learned of the sale and notified the bank and Guild Films that the stock could not be sold without registration. The bank then sought a Commission ruling that the stock was exempt. Despite an adverse opinion by the Commission, the bank sold an additional 10,500 shares on September 24, 1959. At that point, the Commission filed this suit to restrain the delivery of these shares and the sale of the remainder of the stock. The district court granted a preliminary injunction against delivery and further sale.

The Securities Act of 1933 was primarily intended to "protect investors by requiring registration with the Commission of certain information concerning securities offered for sale." Gilligan, Will & Co. v. S.E.C., 2 Cir., 1959, 267 F.2d 461, 463. An exemption from the provisions of § 5 of the Act was provided by § 4(1) for "transactions by any person other than an issuer, underwriter or dealer" because it was felt that no protection was necessary in these situations. * * * The primary question involved in this case is: were appellants issuers, underwriters or dealers within this exemption?

An "underwriter" is defined in § 2(11) as "any person who has purchased from an issuer with a view to, or sells for an issuer in connection with, the distribution of any security, * * * or participates or has a participation in the direct or indirect underwriting of any such undertaking * * *." The burden of proof is on the one seeking an exemption. * * *

The banks cannot be exempted on the ground that they did not "purchase" within the meaning of § 2(11). The term, although not defined in the Act, should be interpreted in a manner complementary to "sale" which is defined in § 2(3) as including "every * * * disposition of * * * a security or interest in a security, for value * * *." In fact, a proposed provision of the Act which expressly exempted sales "by or for the account of a pledge holder or mortgagee selling or offering for sale or delivery in the ordinary course of business and not for the purpose of avoiding the provisions of the Act, to liquidate a bona fide debt, a security pledged in good faith as collateral for such debt," was not accepted by Congress.

* * *

Nor is it a defense that the banks did not deal directly with Guild Films. This court has recently stated that "the underlying policy of the Act, that of protecting the investing public through the disclosure of adequate information, would be seriously impaired if we held that a dealer must have conventional or contractual privity with the issuer in order to be an 'underwriter'." S.E.C. v. Culpepper, 2 Cir., 1959, 270 F.2d 241, 246, following S.E.C. v. Chinese Consol. Benev. Ass'n, 2 Cir., 1941, 120 F.2d 738 * * *. It was held in these two cases that § 4(1) "does not in terms or by fair implication protect those who are engaged in steps necessary to the distribution of a security issue. To give Section 4(1) the construction urged by the defendant would afford a ready method of thwarting the policy of the law and evading its provisions." S.E.C. v. Chinese Consol. Benev. Ass'n, supra * * *.

The banks have contended that they were "bona fide pledgees" and therefore "entitled upon default to sell the stock free of restrictions." They assume that "good faith" in accepting the stock is a sufficient defense. See Loss, Securities Regulation, 346 (1951). But the statute does not impose such a "good faith" criterion. The exemption in § 4(1) was intended to permit private sales of unregistered securities to investors who are likely to have, or who are likely to obtain, such information as is ordinarily disclosed in registration statements. * * * The "good faith" of the banks is irrelevant to this purpose. It would be of little solace to purchasers of worthless stock to learn that the sellers had acted "in good faith." Regardless of good faith, the banks engaged in steps necessary to this public sale, and cannot be exempted.

Without imputing to the banks any participation in a preconceived scheme to use the pledge of these securities as a device for unlawful distribution, it may be noted that when the 50,000 shares of Guild Films stock were received on

February 12, 1959, the banks knew that they had been given unregistered stock and that the issuer had specifically forbidden that the stock "be sold, transferred, pledged or hypothecated in the absence of an effective registration statement for the shares under the Securities Act of 1933 or an opinion of counsel to the company that registration is not required under said Act." Furthermore, from Roach's prior unfulfilled promises, the banks should have known that immediate sale was almost inevitable if they were to recoup their loans from the security received. On February 11, 1959, the day before the stock was received, the S.E.C. suspended trading in the Jacobs stock. And on the very day that the stock was received, appellants wired Roach that they would call the loan unless payment were made. For months the banks had threatened action but declined to act; circumstances finally required action. The banks cannot now claim that this possibility was unforeseeable. The district court properly enjoined the threatened violation.

Affirmed.

––––––

1. *How Little Does It Take?* Section 2(a)(11) states that anyone who "participates or has a direct or indirect participation in any such undertaking" is a statutory underwriter. This "participation" standard is obviously intended to be broad. But how broad? In Harden v. Raffensperger, Hughes & Co., Inc.,[1] the issuer was itself a broker-dealer which wished to underwrite an offering by its subsidiary. Under NASD rules, such "self underwriting" required that it employ a "qualified independent underwriter" to review the pricing of the offering (given the issuer's conflict of interest) and to perform due diligence with regard to the registration statement. The defendant, Raffensperger, Hughes & Co., Inc., was hired to perform these functions, but it did not offer or sell the securities. Nonetheless, it was found liable under § 11. The Seventh Circuit reached this conclusion on two grounds. First, it said that the words "participates" or "takes part" in an underwriting were "broad enough to encompass all persons who engage in steps necessary to the distribution of securities."[2] Second and more important, it noted that the NASD had determined that "qualified independent underwriters were subject to § 11 liability."[3] *Query:* Would "independent" underwriters have sufficient incentive to perform due diligence (to the degree that the 1933 Act intended) if they were immune from liability under that Act?

In Byrnes v. Faulkner, Dawkins & Sullivan,[4] the owners of unregistered shares exercised a "piggyback" right to include shares they owned in a registration statement filed by the company. The registration statement indicated that they might be deemed statutory underwriters. When the registration statement became effective, they sold their shares through a broker, but failed to include a statutory prospectus with the confirmation of sale. Their purchasers argued that the sale violated § 5. Because the sellers "arranged to have their stock included in * * * [the issuer's] registration statements and were identified as putative underwriters," the court concluded that they "therefore

---

1.   65 F.3d 1392 (7th Cir.1995).

2.   Id. at 1400. *Query:* Would this standard make the engraver of debentures liable?

3.   Id. at 1401.

4.   550 F.2d 1303 (2d Cir.1977).

became participants in the * * * distribution and accordingly became underwriters."[5]

This is not the only possible standard. Other cases have read the word "participates" in § 2(a)(11) to focus on whether the defendant has furnished assistance that facilitated the issuer's distribution.[6] *Byrnes* does seem to expose venture capitalists and institutional investors to liability when they exercise contractual rights to include unregistered stock earlier acquired in a private placement in an initial public offering. In contrast, other courts have ruled that such investors should not be deemed underwriters, at least where they neither contribute professional services nor share in the economic risks of the offering.[7]

2. *Rule 142.* Institutional investors do receive some relief under Rule 142 under circumstances where they might otherwise be deemed to have participated in a distribution. This rule defines the term "participates" and "participation" for purposes of § 2(a)(11) to exempt a person who agrees to purchase shares that cannot be sold in the offering. The Rule 142 exemption applies only where the person entering such a contingent or "standby" purchase commitment acquires the securities for investment and does not reach an agreement directly with the issuer. For example, a pension fund could agree contingently with an underwriter to purchase shares at a discount which the latter was unable to sell and thereby avoid being deemed an underwriter, itself (if it acquired the securities for investment purposes).

SECTION 2. STATUTORY RESTRICTIONS ON DISTRIBUTIONS OF SECURITIES BY CONTROLLING PERSONS OR AFFILIATES

Statutes and Regulations

Securities Act, § 2(a)(11).

Regulation C, Rule 405 (Definition of "Control").

In the Matter of Ira Haupt & Co.

Securities and Exchange Commission, 1946.
23 S.E.C. 589.

FINDINGS AND OPINION OF THE COMMISSION

This proceeding was instituted under Sections 15(b) and 15A(*l*)(2) of the Securities Exchange Act of 1934 to determine whether Ira Haupt & Co. ("Respondent") willfully violated Section 5(a) of the Securities Act of 1933 and, if so, whether the revocation of its registration as a broker-dealer and its expulsion or suspension from membership in the National Association of Securities Dealers, Inc. ("NASD"), a registered securities association, would be in the public interest.

---

5. Id. at 1312.

6. See, e.g., SEC v. North Am. Research & Dev. Corp., 424 F.2d 63 (2d Cir.1970).

7. See McFarland v. Memorex Corp., 493 F.Supp. 631, 644–46 (N.D.Cal.1980) modified on other grounds, 581 F.Supp. 878 (N.D.Cal.1984); see also, O'Hare, Institutional Investors, Registration Rights and the Spectre of Liability Under Section 11 of the Securities Act of 1933, 1996 Wisc.L.Rev. 217.

The alleged violation of Section 5(a) is based on respondent's sale, for the accounts of David A. Schulte, a controlled corporation of Schulte's, and the David A. Schulte Trust (sometimes hereinafter referred to collectively as the "Schulte interests"), of approximately 93,000 shares of the common stock of Park & Tilford, Inc., during the period November 1, 1943, to June 1, 1944. It is conceded that the Schulte interests were in control of Park & Tilford during this period, that the sales were effected by use of the mails and instrumentalities of interstate commerce, and that the stock was not covered by a registration statement under the Securities Act.

After appropriate notice a hearing was held before a trial examiner. At the hearing a stipulation of facts was submitted in lieu of testimony. A trial examiner's report was waived, briefs and reply briefs were filed, and we heard argument.

* * *

[David A. Schulte was the president and director of Park & Tilford, Inc. The company had 243,731 shares of common stock outstanding, of which the Schulte interests owned 225,482 shares or 92 per cent, and the public 18,249 shares or 8 per cent. Schulte had been a long time customer of respondent brokerage firm. In December 1943, during the period of wartime shortages, Schulte announced that Park & Tilford was issuing a dividend in whiskey to its shareholders at cost. Ira Haupt, the senior partner of respondent, testified that Schulte called him, explained that, with the announcement of the liquor plan, it was likely that the market would become "terribly active" and placed a standing order to sell from one to three hundred shares at every quarter or half point so as "to create an orderly market." As anticipated, the trading became extremely active and in a rising market Haupt was able to dispose of some 90,000 shares at prices ranging from 58 to 96. The market was further stimulated when Park & Tilford offered to sell stockholders up to six cases of whiskey for each share of stock. At this point the wartime Office of Price Administration stepped in and limited resale prices of both the purchase rights and the whiskey, and the stock fell to 30. All told, during a six months period, respondent disposed of some 93,000 shares of stock for the Schulte interests, by use of the facilities of the New York Stock Exchange, the public's holdings thereby increasing to 115,344 shares or 46 per cent.]

* * *

It is conceded that respondent's transactions in Park & Tilford stock for the account of the Schulte interests constitute a violation of Section 5(a) unless an exemption was applicable to such transactions. Respondent contends that * * * the following [exemption] was applicable: * * *

Section 4(2)[a] which exempts

Brokers' transactions, executed upon customers' orders on any exchange or in the open or counter market, but not the solicitation of such orders.

The applicability of the foregoing [exemption] involves the following subissues:

---

a. The Securities Acts Amendments of 1964, 78 Stat. 565, recast Section 4 so that   former § 4(2) is now § 4(4).

(1) Was Respondent an "underwriter" as that term is defined in Section 2(11)?

* * *

(3) Is the brokerage exemption of Section 4(2) [the predecessor of § 4(4)] available to an underwriter who effects a distribution of an issue for the account of a controlling stockholder through the mechanism of a stock exchange?

If the violation of Section 5(a) is established, there are the further questions whether the violation was "willful" and, if so, whether it is in the public interest to revoke respondent's registration, or to expel or suspend it from the NASD.

1.   WAS RESPONDENT AN "UNDERWRITER"?

Section 2(11) defines an "underwriter" as

any person who * * * sells for an issuer in connection with, the distribution of any security * * * As used in this paragraph the term "issuer" shall include * * * any person * * * controlling * * * the issuer * * *

The purpose of the last sentence of this definition is to require registration in connection with secondary distributions through underwriters by controlling stockholders. This purpose clearly appears in the House Report on the Bill which states that it was intended:

to bring within the provisions of the bill redistribution whether of outstanding issues or issues sold subsequently to the enactment of the bill. All the outstanding stock of a particular corporation may be owned by one individual or a select group of individuals. At some future date they may wish to dispose of their holdings and to make an offer of this stock to the public. Such a public offering may possess all the dangers attendant upon a new offering of securities. Wherever such a redistribution reaches significant proportions, the distributor would be in the position of controlling the issuer and thus able to furnish the information demanded by the bill. This being so, the distributor is treated as equivalent to the original issuer and, if he seeks to dispose of the issue through a public offering, he becomes subject to the act.

It is conceded that the Schulte interests controlled Park & Tilford and the respondent was, therefore, "selling for" a person in control of the issuer. However, respondent denies that these sales were effected "in connection with the distribution of any security." It asserts that at no time did it intend, nor was it aware that Schulte intended, a distribution of a large block of stock. It emphasizes that, in connection with the sales by which Schulte disposed of approximately 52,000 shares over a period of 6 months, each order was entered by Schulte to maintain an orderly market and was limited to 200 to 300 shares at a specific price; that the authority to sell 73,000 shares for the Trust was dependent upon a market price of at least 80; that the total amount which would be sold was never fixed or ascertained, and that consequently it did not intend to sell in connection with a distribution.

"Distribution" is not defined in the Act. It has been held, however, to comprise "the entire process by which in the course of a public offering the block of securities is dispersed and ultimately comes to rest in the hands of the investing public." In this case, the stipulated facts show that Schulte, owning in excess of 50,000 shares, had formulated a plan to sell his stock over the exchange in 200 share blocks "at 59 and every quarter up" and that the trust, holding 165,000 shares, specifically authorized the sale over the exchange of 73,000 shares "at $80 per share or better." A total of 93,000 shares was in fact sold by respondent for the account of the Schulte interests pursuant to these authorizations. We think these facts clearly fall within the above quoted definition and constitute a "distribution." We find no validity in the argument that a predetermination of the precise number of shares which are to be publicly dispersed is an essential element of a distribution. Nor do we think that a "distribution" loses its character as such merely because the extent of the offering may depend on certain conditions such as the market price. Indeed, in the usual case of an offering at a price, there is never any certainty that all or any specified part of the issue will be sold. And where part of an issue is outstanding, the extent of a new offering is almost always directly related to variations in the market price. Such offerings are not any less a "distribution" merely because their precise extent cannot be predetermined.

Nor can we accept respondent's claim that it was not aware of the distribution intended by the Schulte interests. * * *

    * * *

We conclude from the foregoing facts that respondent was selling for the Schulte interests, controlling stockholders of Park & Tilford, in connection with the distribution of their holdings in the stock and was, therefore, an "underwriter" within the meaning of the Act.

    * * *

3.   IS THE BROKERAGE EXEMPTION OF SECTION 4(2) AVAILABLE TO AN UNDERWRITER WHO EFFECTS A DISTRIBUTION OF AN ISSUE FOR THE ACCOUNT OF A CONTROLLING STOCKHOLDER THROUGH THE MECHANISM OF A STOCK EXCHANGE?

Respondent's final argument on this phase of the case is that, notwithstanding the inapplicability of * * * [Section] 4(1) and even though respondent may be found to be an underwriter, its transactions fall within Section 4(2) which exempts "brokers' transactions, executed upon customers' orders on any exchange * * * but not the solicitation of such orders." * * *

    * * *

It is clear from Section 4(1), read in conjunction with Section 2(11), that public distributions by controlling persons, through underwriters, are intended generally to be subject to the registration and prospectus requirements of the Act. Section 4(1) exempts transactions "by any person other than an issuer, underwriter, or dealer," "transactions by an issuer not involving a public offering" and "transactions by a dealer" other than those "within one year after the first date upon which the security was bona fide offered to the public * * * by or through an underwriter * * * "" This shows a specific intention to subject to the registration and prospectus requirements public offerings by issuers or by or through "underwriters." And, as we have seen, Section 2(11) defines "underwriter" to include any person who sells for the issuer or a person controlling the issuer in connection with the distribution of a security.

These sections, by their terms, provide that whenever anyone controlling an issuer makes a public distribution of his holdings in the controlled corporation by selling through another person acting for him in connection with the distribution, the sales by which the distribution is accomplished are transactions by an underwriter which are subject to the registration requirements. Applied to such transactions by which substantial quantities of securities are disposed of to the public, the registration requirement is consistent with and calculated to further the general purpose of the Act to provide investors with pertinent information as a means of self-protection. The legislative history of the Act strongly sustains this conclusion.

We find nothing in the language or legislative history of Section 4(2) to compel the exemption of this type of secondary distribution and the consequent overriding of the general objectives and policy of the Act. On the contrary, there are affirmative indications that Section 4(2) was meant to preserve the distinction between the "trading" and "distribution" of securities which separates the exempt and non-exempt transactions under Section 4(1). This conclusion becomes apparent on examination of the legislative comments on Sections 4(1) and 4(2).

* * *

* * * [I]n discussing the limited exemption for dealers in the third clause of Section 4(1),[b] the House Report again emphasized the distinction between "trading" and "distribution":

> * * * Recognizing that a dealer is often concerned not only with the *distribution* of securities but also with *trading* in securities, the dealer is exempted as to *trading* when such *trading* occurs a year after the public offering of the securities. Since before that year the dealer might easily evade the provisions of the act by a claim that the securities he was offering for sale were not acquired by him in the process of *distribution* but were acquired after such process had ended, transactions during that year are not exempted. The period of a year is arbitrarily taken because, generally speaking, the average public offering has been distributed within a year and the imposition of requirements upon the dealer so far as that year is concerned is not burdensome. (Emphasis added.)

From the foregoing, it is apparent that transactions by an issuer or underwriter and transactions by a dealer during the period of *distribution* (which period for purposes of administrative practicality is arbitrarily set at one year) must be preceded by registration and the use of a prospectus. It is likewise apparent that Congress intended that, during this period, persons other than an issuer, underwriter, or dealer should be able to *trade* in the security without use of a prospectus. Since such persons would carry on their trading largely through the use of brokers (who are included in the general definition of dealers), such trading through brokers without the use of a prospectus could be permitted during the first year after the initial offering only if there were a special exemption for dealers acting as brokers. * * * That this was the specific purpose of Section 4(2) is clearly seen from the comment on this provision by the House Committee which considered the legislation:

> Paragraph (2) exempts the ordinary brokerage transaction. *Individuals may thus dispose of their securities according to the method which is now customary without any restrictions imposed either upon the individual or the broker. This exemption also assures an open market for securities at all times, even though a stop order against further distribution of such*

---

b. Originally, the dealers' exemption appeared in § 4(1). In the 1954 amendment program, the exemption was moved to § 4(3) and the one year period was reduced to 40 days. See infra at page 551.

securities may have been entered. Purchasers, provided they are not dealers, may thus in the event that a stop order has been entered, cut their losses immediately, if there are losses, by disposing of the securities. *On the other hand, the entry of a stop order prevents any further distribution of the security.* (Emphasis added.)

To summarize: Section 4(2) permits individuals to sell their securities through a broker in an ordinary brokerage transaction, during the period of distribution or while a stop order is in effect, without regard to the registration and prospectus requirements of Section 5. But the process of distribution itself, however carried out, is subject to Section 5.

* * *

We conclude that Section 4(2) cannot exempt transactions by an underwriter executed over the Exchange in connection with a distribution for a controlling stockholder. * * *

WILLFULNESS

* * * We find that Respondent knew that it was effecting a distribution for a controlling person and that no registration statement was in effect for the securities being distributed. Since Respondent was fully aware of what it was doing, its violation was willful within the meaning of the Act.

PUBLIC INTEREST

Even though Respondent willfully violated the Securities Act, its registration as a broker-dealer may not be revoked, and it may not be suspended or expelled from the NASD, unless such action is found to be in the public interest.

* * *

[W]e cannot overlook the fact that respondent, in the course of a public distribution of securities, engaged in a willful violation of the Securities Act—a violation which, the evidence indicates, would have been regarded as such even under previous interpretations of Section 4(2)—and, by its failure to insist on registration and the attendant disclosure of information, made it possible for the distribution to be effected to an uninformed public which suffered heavy losses. Accordingly, we find it appropriate in the public interest and for the protection of investors to suspend Respondent from membership in the NASD for a period of 20 days.

An appropriate order will issue.[c]

Excerpt from: A. A. SOMMER, JR.

Who's "In Control"?—S.E.C.

21 Business Lawyer 559, 559–583 (1966).*

A basic concept running through all of the statutes administered by the Securities and Exchange Commission is that of "control". * * * Some of the

---

c. Note, 14 U.Chi.L.Rev. 307 (1943); Flanagin, The Federal Securities Act and the Locked–In Stockholder, 63 Mich.L.Rev. 1139 (1965); Note, The Controlling Persons Provisions: Conduits of Secondary Liability Under Federal Securities Laws, 19 Vill.L.Rev. 621 (1974).

statutes administered by the Securities and Exchange Commission contain definitions of "control"; the Securities Act of 1933 and the Securities Exchange Act of 1934, however, the two statutes of most significance for most businesses, and the statutes which are discussed in this paper, do not include such definitions. The absence of a definition, however, has not prevented the Commission by rule, ruling and releases from limning the outlines of a definition and it has not mitigated the vital importance of determining the meaning of "control".

* * *

Who Is A Controlling Person?

* * * [T]he situation of a "controlling person" may be perilous—and expensive. When so much attaches to the identification of a person within that category it would be most desirable if the identification could be done with certainty and precision, as, for instance, can often be done under the Internal Revenue Code. Alas, such is rarely the case with key concepts in the structure of federal securities law, and this is particularly true in the case of the concept of "control". Like so many key notions the imprecise limits of the term have been limned through the painstaking process of rule, interpretation, judicial decision and ad hoc determinations in "no action letters". Out of these there has come no mathematical standard, no slide rule computation, no certain rule which can infallibly guide counsel and client in making this most important determination—a determination which can be costly if wrongly made. Often, of course, the answer is easily arrived at; for instance, concluding that a holder of 90% of the voting power of a corporation whose stock is unencumbered and who personally runs the affairs of the corporation is a controlling person demands no subtlety. Often, however, the problem is more complex. In those situations it has become axiomatic that in deciding who is a "controlling person" the entire situation within the corporation at the time of determination, together with some of the history of the corporation, must be considered; single factors—shareholdings, offices held, titles, conduct—are rarely determinative, at least not in the close cases (clearly that ninety percent shareholder will rarely, if ever, enjoy the luxury of being found not to be in control even if every other conceivable pointer in the direction of control is lacking).

The Securities Act itself is of little help in determining who is a controlling person. * * * The Commission through Rule 405 under the Securities Act has sought to clarify the meaning of the concept of "control":

> The term "control" (including the terms "controlling," "controlled by" and "under common control with") means the possession, direct or indirect, of the power to direct or cause the direction of the management and policies of a person, whether through the ownership of voting securities, by contract, or otherwise.

This definition introduces some new notions in addition to those intimated by Section 15 of the Securities Act: control is a "power" (Section 15 speaks of one who "controls," which implies exercise of the power), it may be possessed directly or indirectly, it may exist by reason of ownership of voting securities, contract or "otherwise," and the power is the power to direct or "cause the direction of management and policies" of another person (almost always a corporation). With Section 15 of the Securities Act and Rule 405 as starters, we must look principally to reported determinations, Commission and court, supplemented by logical analysis of the concept, for further delineation of this elusive notion. The administrative and judicial determinations arise in a variety of contexts; in some cases the issue is whether a person is a controlling person, thus establishing a purchaser of his stock for distribution as an underwriter; in others the question is whether a person was a "parent" of a registrant under the 1933 or 1934 Act and hence should have been identified as such in filings with the Commission; and in some few instances the question has been the derivative liability of an alleged controlling person under Section 15 of the Securities Act or Section 20 of the Securities Exchange Act.

Some basic notions should preliminarily be recognized. The *power* to control, even if unexercised, may constitute a person a controlling person. In the Walston and Co.[16] case the principal creditor of the registrant, who was the principal source of its business, had options to acquire the interests of others in the company, and received 90% of profits, had nevertheless not actively participated in the direction of the business; the Commission nonetheless held that it had the *power* to control if it so wished and hence was a controlling person of Walston and should have been so disclosed.

Correlatively, those who exercise control by the sufferance of those with the power to control may also be controlling persons. In North Country Uranium and Minerals Ltd.,[17] the holder of only a nominal amount of stock was held to be a controlling person of the defendant company because he actively managed the enterprise, which he had been instrumental in organizing, without interference from the clearly dominant shareholder who would apparently be also considered a controlling person because of his *power* to control. Similarly, in SEC v. Franklin Atlas Corp.,[18] the president and person who actually ran the corporation was not a shareholder, but because of the actuality of his control—even though subject to termination at the whim of those who controlled the stock—he was held to be a controlling person.

Thus either *the power to control* or *the actual exercise of control*, even though by sufferance of another who possesses the ultimate power to control, is sufficient to make a person a controlling person. This duality is in a sense reducible to the single notion of power to control: the person who actually controls with the acquiescence of the one having the ultimate power is realistically exercising, one might say by terminable default, the power of the other person.

Chairman Cohen of the Commission once suggested a very practical criterion for determining the person or group in control: what individual or group has the power to cause a registration statement under the Securities Act to be signed? At least one court has also used this standard for determining the identity of controlling persons. Registration statements can only be filed by an issuer and must be signed by the registrant, a majority of the board of directors, the chief executive officer, the chief financial officer, and the chief accounting officer. Obviously the statement can only be signed by the registrant under authority from the board of directors. So it would appear that control is in the hands of whoever or whatever group can cause a majority of the board to authorize the registrant's signature on the statement. At first blush it would appear this criterion offered a simple escape from their problems for purported

---

16.   7 S.E.C. 937 (1940).

17.   37 S.E.C. 608 (1957).

18.   154 F.Supp. 395 (S.D.N.Y.1957).

controlling persons: simply arrange for the board to be presented with a proposal that a registration statement be signed and filed for the shares of the ostensible controlling person and have the board refuse to permit the registrant to sign and file the statement—presto, the purported controlling person has flunked the test: he could not produce a majority vote to sign the statement and he may therefore sell without the expense and bother of a registration statement. Needless to say, any board refusal other than a simon-pure bona fide refusal could be of no avail. Furthermore, for a refusal to be of any significance, the person proposing that the corporation file a registration statement with respect to his shares must agree to indemnify the registrant for its expenses in connection with the registration; otherwise, the board might well refuse—and probably should refuse—to authorize signing and filing on the legitimate ground that the corporation could not properly incur expenses for the benefit of a shareholder.

With these propositions as starters, it is possible to discern some further guides in Commission and court cases and logical analysis of the concept of control.

* * *

* * * The initial source of power of necessity must be ownership of voting securities, not only because of the specific mention of this in Rule 405, but because under modern corporation law the power of management is *ultimately*—in theory and law, if not in practice—in the hands of the holders of voting securities. * * *

* * *

How little stock may a person own or have the power to vote and still be considered a controlling person? This depends upon many circumstances. Principal among these are the distribution of the other shares and the other relationships the shareholder has with the corporation and with other shareholders. Initially, record or beneficial ownership of (or right to vote) 10% or more of the voting stock of a corporation has become something of a benchmark and when this is encountered a red warning flag should run up. Schedule A to the Securities Act of 1933, the proxy statement rules, and many of the registration forms promulgated by the Commission require disclosure of all persons who own of record or beneficially more than 10% of any class of stock of the issuer, and the reporting and penalty provisions of Section 16 of the Securities Exchange Act (the so-called "insider trading" provisions) apply to the beneficial owners of more than 10% of a class of equity security registered pursuant to Section 12 of that Act. While there is nothing in the statutes or the regulations or rulings by the Commission which says such a holder is *ipso facto* a controlling person, generally such degree of ownership should create caution and might be regarded as creating a rebuttable presumption of control, especially if such holdings are combined with executive office, membership on the board, or wide dispersion of the remainder of the stock.

That such a percentage of ownership or right to vote is not *conclusive* evidence of control, however, is almost self-evident. In a situation in which one person owned 89% of the voting stock and the other 11% was owned by an antagonist, it is evident the owner of the 11% is not a controlling person (barring the improbable situation where unanimous shareholder action is required): he could not cause the company to file a registration statement and he could not elect a majority of the board; in fact, unless the size of the board and cumulative voting combine to afford him board representation, he is powerless save for the rights which belong to any shareholder regardless of holdings, e.g. right to inspect books, to bring a derivative suit, to secure the fair value of his shares in certain circumstances. On the other hand, ownership of less than 10% of the voting power of a corporation does not automatically spell non-control. Apart from the circumstance that a holder of less than 10% may be a member of a group which controls, a person with less than 10% may alone be a controlling person; generally to be such his ownership would have to be combined with dominant executive office and fairly wide dispersion of the remainder of the voting power. It has been suggested that ownership of as little as 5% of a corporation's stock by an officer or director may give rise to a presumption that such a person is a member of a control group.

    * * *

When—and why—a person who owns or has the right to vote a minority of the outstanding stock of a corporation may be considered in control is not easily answered. The holder of twenty or twenty-five percent of stock of a widely and publicly held company could be defeated in a proxy contest; if he asserts control based upon his acquisition of a substantial interest the majority of the board and the officers might defy him and deny him any board representation until the next shareholders' meeting, or accord him only representation proportionate to his holdings. Victor Muscat and his associates suffered this fate in 1962 when they purchased 29 percent of the shares of B.S.F. Co. Upon demanding control of the Board of Directors, they were rebuffed. * * * One thus rebuffed could hardly be called a controlling person. Thus in many instances more than a substantial minority stockholding, even in a corporation with widely held stock, is the prerequisite to the establishment of control; such a holding may really constitute control only when it has actually resulted in the yielding of control by those who have previously possessed it. Thus, while unencumbered ownership of more than fifty percent of the outstanding voting power of a corporation will usually constitute control even though unexercised simply because the power to control is there, ownership of substantially less than 50% of the stock may be indicative of control only if the power inherent in the voting power has in some fashion been manifested through the exercise of control, usually through the election of a favorably inclined majority of the board of directors.

    * * *

The Controlling Group

    There are innumerable instances in which a single person does not appear to have actual operating control or the power to control. Then the problem is to identify the *group* which is in control and those who constitute the group. The search for the group commences when the search for the individual in control or having the power to control fails. Is there always a controlling person or a controlling group in every corporation? I would suggest that there is: someone runs the show or some group runs the show, some person has the power to run the show or some group has that power. As a beginning, it may be safely suggested that simply being a member of the board of directors, or an officer of the company, does not automatically constitute one a member of the controlling group. At least as far as the directors are concerned, this is self-evident: if the corporation is subject to cumulative voting requirements some, and perhaps one short of a majority, of the directors may be quite hostile to management and to the majority of the board; it would obviously be wrong to call them members of the controlling group. It is less obvious that principal executive officers are not *ipso facto* members of the controlling group, since they serve at the will of the board and hence it may be fairly implied they would be compliant with the will of whoever controls the board; however, even then a situation is conceivable where an officer with an employment contract may be out of step with the controlling group, but perhaps the fact of his contract alone may be sufficient to cause him to be considered a controlling person if his prerogatives are broad enough. In some instances it may be pertinent to distinguish "inside" directors (i.e. directors who are officers and involved in the active management of the corporation) from "outside" directors (i.e. those *not* a part of active management); obviously "inside" directors would be more likely to be found to be in control, but this would stem from roles and positions over and above that of being a director. In general, however, unless a person or identifiable group clearly is in control by reason of possession *and* use of voting power, all directors and policy-making officers are presumptively members of the controlling group and only compelling evidence to the contrary should remove them from the group. Generally there must be some homogeneity among individuals if they are to be regarded as members of the controlling group, some significant business characteristic or relationship or course of conduct that affords an element of unity. It is clear from the legislative history of the Securities Act, judicial decisions and releases of the Commission that some "cement", other than mere association on a board, or the circumstance that adding up the holdings of a number of people yields an actual or working majority of the voting power of the corporation, is necessary to constitute individuals a controlling group. * * *

* * *

The question of control is subtle and difficult in many instances. Often, to be sure, the focus of control is simply determined. Just as often, and perhaps oftener particularly in corporations in which there is substantial public participation in ownership, the answer is clouded. Ultimately the test is briefly stated: taking into account history, family, business affiliations, shareholdings, position and all the other circumstances, what person or what group calls the day-to-day shots? The shots in major matters? What person or what group could, if it wished, call those shots? When these are identified the controlling persons and the controlling group are identified. * * *

* * *

TRANSACTIONS BY DEALERS AND BROKERS

The registration and prospectus requirements of § 5 are always applicable to issuers and to underwriters who, by definition, are engaged in the process of distribution of a block of securities to the public. This is not so as to dealers despite § 4(1).

(a) *The Dealer's Exemption.* Section 4(3) exempts transactions by a dealer (including an underwriter who is no longer acting as such in respect of the security involved in such transaction) with three exceptions. These exceptions in effect fix periods during which dealers are subject to the registration and prospectus requirements of § 5. The statutory language now excludes from the exemption:

(A) transactions taking place prior to the expiration of forty days after the first date upon which the security was bona fide offered to the public by the issuer or by or through an underwriter,

(B) transactions in a security, as to which a registration statement has been filed, taking place prior to the expiration of forty days after the effective date of such registration statement or prior to the expiration of forty days after the first date upon which the security was bona fide offered to the public by the issuer or by or through an underwriter after such effective date, whichever is later (excluding in the computation of such forty days any time during which a stop order issued under section 8 is in effect as to the security), or such shorter period as the Commission may specify by rules and regulations or order, and

(C) transactions as to securities constituting the whole or a part of an unsold allotment to or subscription by such dealer as a participant in the distribution of such securities by the issuer or by or through an underwriter.

The term "dealer" is defined in § 2(a)(12) to mean "any person who engages either for all or part of his time, directly or indirectly, as agent, broker, or principal, in the business of offering, buying, selling, or otherwise dealing or trading in securities issued by another person." It is to be noted that the definition includes a broker as well as a principal trading for his or her own account. According to the House Report, the sole object of this definition was "to subject brokers to the same advertising restrictions [prospectus provisions] that are imposed upon dealers, so as to prevent the broker from being used as a cloak for the sale of securities."[1] At the same time, under § 2(a)(11), a dealer is excluded from the definition of "underwriter" even though he or she purchases securities from an underwriter at a price below the public offering price and resells the securities to the public so long as the "commission" or "spread" is not in excess of the usual and customary dealer's commission.

In its original form, the Securities Act imposed a period of one year during which dealers not participating in the distribution of a new issue were required to deliver prospectuses in connection with trading transactions. In the 1954 amendment program, this period was reduced to 40 days. In supporting the change the Commission had this to say: "The 1–year provision has long been recognized as unrealistic, since dealers trading in a security publicly offered within 1 year find themselves unable to obtain prospectuses. This fact has rendered compliance by dealers and enforcement by the Commission difficult."[2]

At the same time § 24(d) was added to the Investment Company Act making the exemption provided in § 4(3) of the Securities Act inapplicable to transactions in the securities of investment companies that are offered to the public on a continuous basis because of the special characteristics of these offerings. Although the largest group affected are the open-end mutual funds that offer redeemable securities on a continuous basis, face-amount certificate companies and unit investment trusts also engage in continuous offering practices and are similarly affected. In place of the then existing 1 year period, § 24(d) provides that dealers not participating in the distribution must never-

1. H.R.Rep. No. 85, 73d Cong., 1st Sess. 14 (1933).

2. Hearings on S. 2846 Before a Subcommittee of the Senate Committee on Banking and Currency, 83d Cong., 2d Sess. 6 (1954).

theless use the prospectus in offering any such security so long as the issuer is offering any securities of the same class. This requirement imposes an added burden on independent dealers in investment company securities as compared to dealers executing trades in other kinds of securities. The burden is mitigated, however, by the practice of investment companies to make copies of their prospectuses readily available to all dealers who request them.[3]

The Senate Report explained the dealer's exemption as amended this way:[4]

Apart from the change to a 40–day period, the amendment is not designed to affect the nature or extent of the dealer's exemption in section 4(1). For example, in the case of an unlawful offering of unregistered securities, a dealer would not be able to trade lawfully in such securities within 40 days * * * after the date on which the unlawful distribution of such securities to the public in fact commenced. And if the dealer is a participant in any such unlawful distribution he cannot lawfully effect transactions in the unregistered securities so long as he is engaged in the distribution even though the 40–day period has expired. It is unlawful for a dealer to effect transactions in unregistered securities which are about to be registered, but he may ordinarily trade in other outstanding securities of the same class which are not being registered or involved in a registrable distribution or public offering. The amendment does not change these effects of the present provisions of the Securities Act.

In the case of registered securities the dealer's exemption will not be available to any dealer participating in the distribution so long as he has an unsold allotment or subscription, but dealers who are merely trading and are not participants in the distribution will be subject to the provisions of section 5 of the Securities Act only during the 40–day period. Under the revision of section 5, the offering of a registered security may commence as soon as the registration statement has been filed, but it will continue to be within the power of the registrant or the underwriters to delay the offering until some later date in the waiting period or even to some date after the registration statement has become effective. The amendment, therefore is so worded as to make dealers subject to the provisions of section 5 for 40 days after whichever is the later of the two events; i.e., the effective date of the registration statement or the date the public offering in fact commences.

A question may arise as to when a bona fide offering of an unregistered security actually commences for § 4(3) purposes. In Kubik v. Goldfield,[5] the court held that a bona fide offer to the public dated from the time when another dealer entered quotations in the National Daily Quotations Service "pink sheets" even though there was no relationship or collaboration between the dealers.[6]

In the case of registered securities, the offering date is readily ascertainable, but the issuance of a stop order under § 8 extends the period beyond the

3. S.Rep. No. 1036, 83d Cong., 2d Sess. 14 (1954).

4. Id. at 14.

5. 479 F.2d 472 (3d Cir.1973). Cf. Slagell v. Bontrager, 616 F.Supp. 634 (W.D.Pa. 1985) interpreting § 13 of the 1933 Act and holding that the limitation period began when the purchaser was first offered the security.

6. Cf. SEC v. North American Research & Development Corp., 280 F.Supp. 106 (S.D.N.Y.1968), aff'd in part, 424 F.2d 63 (2d Cir.1970).

40 days by the length of time during which the order is in effect as to the security.

The Securities Acts Amendments of 1964[7] extended the 40 day period prescribed in § 4(3)(B) to 90 days, if the securities of the issuer have not previously been sold pursuant to an earlier effective registration statement; however, the Commission was empowered by rule or order to fix a shorter period. The Commission has since issued Rule 174 dispensing with the prospectus delivery requirements for dealers (including an underwriter no longer acting as such in respect of the security) if the issuer is subject, immediately prior to the time of filing the registration statement, to the reporting requirements of §§ 13 or 15(d) of the 1934 Act. Even where the issuer is not a reporting company, Rule 174(d) shortens the prospectus delivery period for dealers to twenty–five calendar days if the issuer is listed on a stock exchange or authorized for quotation on NASDAQ as of the offering date. And where securities are registered under the 1933 Act for an offering to be made from time to time (such as a shelf-registration), no prospectus need be delivered after the expiration of the initial prospectus delivery period specified in § 4(3) following the first bona fide offering of the registered securities. Moreover, in certain other types of registered issues, the dealer's obligation to deliver a prospectus is dispensed with altogether.

(b) *The Broker's Exemption.* This exemption now contained in § 4(4) is discussed at length in the *Haupt* case, supra at page 540. Its purpose is to permit the ordinary investor to sell his or her securities during the period of distribution or while a stop order is in effect as to a security without being subject to the prospectus requirements of § 5. Of course, the customer's part of the transaction is exempt under § 4(1). But such sales will almost always be made by the use of a broker. And since brokers are included within the definition of dealer in § 2(a)(12), the dealer's exemption may not be available to the broker. For example, a stop order, by suspending the effectiveness of the registration statement, closes the mails and channels of interstate commerce to further sales of the security by issuers and underwriters and by dealers selling for their own account. It was to keep the securities markets open to the investing public that § 4 exempted ''brokers' transactions, executed upon customers' orders on any exchange or in the over-the-counter market, but not the solicitation of such orders.''

The narrow purpose of the exemption was explained by the Federal Trade Commission, which administered the Securities Act for about a year before the Securities and Exchange Commission was established: ''The exemption * * * applies only to the broker's part of a brokerage transaction. It does not extend to the customer. Whether the customer is excused from complying with the registration requirements of Section 5 depends upon his own status or upon the character of the particular transaction. Thus, an issuer selling through a broker on the stock exchange is subject to the registration requirements of this Act.''[8] This statement, although accurate as far as it goes, can be misunderstood. For the *Haupt* case teaches that a broker who sells for a controlling person in *connection with the distribution* of a security becomes an underwriter and

---

7. Pub.L. 88–467, 78 Stat. 565. See Patterson, Delivery of Prospectuses in Exempted Dealer Transactions and the Securities Amendments of 1964, 20 Bus. Law. 303 (1965).

8. FTC Securities Act Release No. 131, March 13, 1934.

thereby loses his broker's exemption. Of course, the brokers' exemption is never available to issuers.[9]

Section 4(4) is far from clear as to the meaning of the phrase "solicitation of such orders." In a brokerage transaction, the broker may solicit the seller's order or the buyer's order. Furthermore, is it only the solicitation that is prohibited, so that if interstate facilities or the mails are not used for this part of the transaction, the exemption is not thereby destroyed? Rule 154 as adopted in 1951 provided that the "term solicitation of such orders * * * shall be deemed to include the solicitation of an order to buy a security, but shall not be deemed to include the solicitation of an order to sell a security." By way of further amplification, the Commission said:[10]

[I]f the broker solicits the purchaser to buy the security, Section 4(2) [now § 4(4)] does not provide an exemption *either for the solicitation itself or for the resulting transaction.* On the other hand, if the broker does not solicit the purchaser to buy, the mere fact that he may solicit the seller to sell will not destroy any exemption otherwise available to him under Section 4(2); this construction is based on the fact that the statute is designed primarily for the protection of buyers rather than for the protection of sellers. [Emphasis supplied.]

It should also be noted that the prospectus delivery requirements are not restricted to transactions between brokers and public customers; they have been held also to be applicable between two broker-dealers.[11]

United States v. Wolfson

United States Court of Appeals, Second Circuit, 1968.
405 F.2d 779, certiorari denied 394 U.S. 946 (1969).

■ Before Moore, Woodbury* and Smith, Circuit Judges.

■ Woodbury, Senior Circuit Judge:

It was stipulated at the trial that at all relevant times there were 2,510,000 shares of Continental Enterprises, Inc., issued and outstanding. The evidence is clear, indeed is not disputed, that of these the appellant Louis E. Wolfson himself with members of his immediate family and his right hand man and first lieutenant, the appellant Elkin B. Gerbert, owned 1,149,775 or in excess of 40%. The balance of the stock was in the hands of approximately 5,000 outside shareholders. The government's undisputed evidence at the trial was that

9. Stadia Oil & Uranium Co. v. Wheelis, 251 F.2d 269 (10th Cir.1957). But Rule 144, considered later, also was thought to provide protection to the controlling shareholder if all of the conditions of the respective rule were met. "Although the Rule was expressly directed at § 4(4), it was obviously contemplated that the seller's part of the transaction would be considered to be exempt under § 4(1) whenever the broker's part came within the Rule." 3 L. Loss & J. Seligman, Securities Regulation 1476 n. 642 (3d Ed. Rev. 1999); When Corporations Go Public 30–31 (Israels and Duff ed. 1962); S.E.C. Problems of Controlling Stockholders and in

Underwritings 44 (Israels ed. 1962). The *Wolfson* case, infra at page 554, however, rejects this view if the controlling person deceives his broker.

10. SEC Securities Act Release No. 3421 Aug. 2, 1951. On the broker's exemption, see 3 L. Loss & J. Seligman, Securities Regulation 1467–1477 (3d Ed. Rev. 1999).

11. Byrnes v. Faulkner, Dawkins & Sullivan, 550 F.2d 1303 (2d Cir.1977), supra at page 539.

* Of the First Circuit sitting by designation.

between August 1, 1960, and January 31, 1962, Wolfson himself sold 404,150 shares of Continental through six brokerage houses, that Gerbert sold 53,000 shares through three brokerage houses and that members of the Wolfson family, including Wolfson's wife, two brothers, a sister, the Wolfson Family Foundation and four trusts for Wolfson's children sold 176,675 shares through six brokerage houses.

Gerbert was a director of Continental. Wolfson was not, nor was he an officer, but there was ample evidence that nevertheless as the largest individual shareholder he was Continental's guiding spirit in that the officers of the corporation were subject to his direction and control and that no corporate policy decisions were made without his knowledge and consent. Indeed Wolfson admitted as much on the stand. No registration statement was in effect as to Continental; its stock was traded over-the-counter.

The appellants do not dispute the foregoing basic facts. They took the position at the trial that they had no idea during the period of the alleged conspiracy, stipulated to be from January 1, 1960, to January 31, 1962, that there was any provision of law requiring registration of a security before its distribution by a controlling person to the public. On the stand in their defense they took the position that they operated at a level of corporate finance far above such "details" as the securities laws; as to whether a particular stock must be registered. They asserted and their counsel argued to the jury that they were much too busy with large affairs to concern themselves with such minor matters and attributed the fault of failure to register to subordinates in the Wolfson organization and to failure of the brokers to give notice of the need. Obviously in finding the appellants guilty the jury rejected this defense, if indeed, it is any defense at all.

The appellants assert numerous claims of error. We shall dispose of the claims more or less in the order of their importance.

Section 5 of the Act in pertinent part provides: "(a) Unless a registration statement is in effect as to a security, it shall be unlawful for any person, directly or indirectly—

"(1) to make use of any means or instruments of transportation or communication in interstate commerce or of the mails to sell or offer to buy such security through the use or medium of any prospectus or otherwise; * * *."

However, § 4 of the Act exempts certain transactions from the provisions of § 5 including:

"(1) Transactions by any person other than an issuer, underwriter, or dealer."

The appellants argue that they come within this exemption for they are not issuers, underwriters or dealers. At first blush there would appear to be some merit in this argument. The immediate difficulty with it, however, is that § 4(1) by its terms exempts only "transactions," not classes of persons * * * and ignores § 2(11) of the Act which defines an "underwriter" to mean any person who has purchased from an issuer with a view to the distribution of any security, or participates directly or indirectly in such undertaking unless that person's participation is limited to the usual and customary seller's commission, and then goes on to provide:

"As used in this paragraph the term 'issuer' shall include, in addition to an issuer, any person directly or indirectly *controlling* or controlled by *the issuer*, or any person under direct or indirect common control with the 'issuer.' " (Italics supplied.)

In short, the brokers provided outlets for the stock of issuers and thus were underwriters. * * * Wherefore the stock was sold in "transactions by underwriters" which are not within the exemption of § 4(1), supra.

But the appellants contend that the brokers in this case cannot be classified as underwriters because their part in the sales transactions came within § 4(4) which exempts "brokers' transactions executed upon customers' orders on any exchange or in the over-the-counter market but not the solicitation of such orders." The answer to this contention is that § 4(4) was designed only to exempt the brokers' part in security transactions. * * * Control persons must find their own exemptions.

There is nothing inherently unreasonable for a broker to claim the exemption of § 4(4), supra, when he is unaware that his customer's part in the transaction is not exempt. Indeed, this is indicated by the definition of "brokers' transaction" in * * * Rule 154 [the predecessor of Rule 144, infra at page 562] which provides:

"(a) The term 'brokers' transaction' in Section 4(4) of the act shall be deemed to include transactions by a broker acting as agent for the account of any person controlling, controlled by, or under common control with, the issuer of the securities which are the subject of the transaction where:

"(4) The broker is *not aware* of circumstances indicating * * * that the transactions are part of a distribution of securities on behalf of his principal."

And there can be no doubt that appellants' sale of over 633,000 shares (25% of the outstanding shares of Continental and more than 55% of their own holdings), was a distribution rather than an ordinary brokerage transaction. See Rule 154(6) which defines "distribution" for the purpose of paragraph (a) generally as "substantial" in relation to the number of shares outstanding and specifically as a sale of 1% of the stock within six months preceding the sale if the shares are traded on a stock exchange.

Certainly if the appellants' sales, which clearly amounted to a distribution under the above definitions had been made through a broker or brokers with knowledge of the circumstances, the brokers would not be entitled to the exemption. It will hardly do for the appellants to say that because they kept the true facts from the brokers they can take advantage of the exemption the brokers gained thereby.

* * *

In conclusion it will suffice to say that full consideration of the voluminous record in this rather technical case discloses no reversible error.

Affirmed.

REGISTERED SECONDARY SHELF OFFERINGS

We have already explored Rule 415 which allows certain kinds of registered offerings for the shelf. It may be worthwhile to review the textual note on "Shelf Registrations", supra at page 268 as well as Rule 415 and Regulation S–K, Item 512(a). It is to be noted that Rule 415 is not confined to issuer transactions, but extends to secondary offerings as well: (1) Rule 415(a)(1)(i) permits the registration of securities held by persons other than the registrant or the registrant's affiliates. (2) Rule 415(a)(1)(viii) allows the registration of securities which are to be issued in connection with a business combination, including restricted securities held by affiliates. Rule 415(a)(2) provides, however, that securities to be issued in business combinations may be shelf registered only if it is reasonably expected that the securities will be offered and sold within two years from the initial effective date of the registration. (3) In the case of "at the market" offerings of equity securities, the offering is limited to an amount of securities not exceeding 10% of the aggregate market value of the registrant's outstanding voting securities. Furthermore, in such offerings, the manner of offering is prescribed.

We have seen that in certain mergers or sale-of-assets reorganizations, a controlling person of a constituent corporation who receives securities in a Rule 145 transaction may not make a public sale of the securities without registration, even though this person is not in a control relationship with the surviving corporation after the reorganization is completed. See supra at page 495. Under some circumstances, Form S–4 is available for registration of securities acquired in such Rule 145 transactions. At the same time, these persons may not have any present intention of selling the securities on a stock exchange or in the over-the-counter market, but the situation may change at some later date, so that they will wish to protect themselves by making a "shelf registration" of their securities. As to securities registered under Form S–4, Item 22 specifies that for the purposes of any subsequent public offering the registrant must file the undertaking required by Item 512 of Regulation S–K to file post-effective amendments so as to bring the registration statement up-to-date. And aside from any question of resales by controlling persons of the acquired company, if an issuer is engaged in a program of acquiring other companies on a more or less continuous basis, the Commission may take the position that the acquiring company is making a continuous offering of its stock, that all transactions should be integrated into a single public offering, and that the securities should be registered for the "shelf."

Another example of the usefulness of the shelf-registration device arose after the decision in SEC v. Guild Films Co., supra at page 535, which dealt with the question whether a pledgee of control shares is to be regarded as an "underwriter" under § 2(a)(11) so that a public sale of the securities may not be made in satisfaction of the pledge without a prior registration. At the same time, however, it is probable or at least possible that the sale may never occur. Under Rule 415 a "shelf registration" may be made, possibly as a part of the normal financing operations of the issuer, with an undertaking to file a post-effective amendment so as to keep the registration statement up-to-date in the event of the later offering.

FROM IRA HAUPT TO RULE 144

(a) *Sales by Controlling Persons.* Before the *Haupt* case, there was great uncertainty as to the rules governing sales of securities by controlling persons. That case entailed a massive distribution of equity securities through the facilities of the stock exchange by control persons relying upon the exemption provided in § 4(4) for broker's transactions. The *Haupt* case also cast doubt as to the quantity of shares which a controlling person might sell in brokerage transactions without thereby engaging in a "distribution" of securities. Although the sale of a few hundred shares by a controlling person over the stock exchange clearly would not amount to a distribution of securities, it was impossible to determine when additional sales might be regarded as sufficient to destroy the exemption; also, it was not clear as to what holding period would suffice to establish that the purchase was made with an investment intent in determining whether a distribution was intended at the time of the purchase.

When the 1954 amendment program was underway, the securities industry recommended an amendment to the 1933 Act to "Restore the 'broker's exemption' * * * so as to give relief from the popular interpretation" of the *Haupt* opinion.[1] The Commission recommended instead that the matter be handled by a rule, and Congress acquiesced, the Senate Committee expressing the hope that the SEC "will give favorable consideration to a rule that will deal effectively with the problem."[2] The upshot was that in 1954 the Commission revised Rule 154, the predecessor of Rule 144, to clarify and limit the scope of the brokers' exemption embodied in § 4(4) with respect to secondary sales by controlling persons in reliance on the exemption.

Rule 154 defined the term "brokers" transactions in § 4(4) of the Act to include transactions by a broker acting as an agent for a control person, provided: (1) the buy order was not solicited from purchasers; (2) the broker performed no more than the usual brokerage functions; and (3) the broker was not aware of circumstances indicating that the transaction was a part of the distribution or that the broker's principal was an underwriter. The amount of securities that could be sold within a specified period was prescribed by defining "distribution" in the negative; no "distribution" would be entailed if a transaction or series of transactions did not involve an amount of sales "substantial in relation to the number of shares of the security outstanding and the aggregate volume of trading in such security." More specifically, the rules defined the term "distribution" as not including a sale or series of sales of securities, which, together with all other sales of the same person within the preceding six months, in the case of a security traded over-the-counter, did not exceed 1% of the outstanding shares, and in the case of stock exchange transactions, did not exceed the lesser of either 1% of the outstanding shares of the class, or the largest reported volume of trading on securities exchanges during any one week within the four calendar weeks preceding the receipt of the sell order. Under these "leakage" provisions, controlling persons were permitted to make limited sales of control shares, under conditions which would not disrupt the trading market for the securities and where only normal brokerage functions were performed. However, the rule provided no avenue for the sale of securities which the control person otherwise would be unable to sell without registration, such as investment securities acquired pursuant to the private offering exemption. Resales of such securities would constitute the controlling person an underwriter, irrespective of Rule 154.

Moreover, Rule 154, like § 4(4), exempted only the broker's part of the transaction; it provided no protection to the controlling person who might have violated the Act. And through a curious method of drafting, the Securities Act does not subject controlling persons to the registration and prospectus requirements of § 5 in specific terms. A controlling person is not an issuer as that term is used in § 4(1); and such person is defined as an issuer under § 2(a)(11) solely for the purpose of determining who is an "underwriter." Accordingly, it

---

1. Hearings on S. 2846 before a Subcommittee of the Senate Committee on Banking and Currency, 83d Cong., 2d Sess. 4 (1954).

2. S.Rep. No. 1036, 83d Cong., 2d Sess. 14 (1954).

could be argued that the broker who sold for the controlling person with knowledge that it was participating in a distribution would be subject to criminal penalties, whereas no specific substantive provision of the Act in terms imposes liability upon the controlling person. On the other hand, if the broker, after a reasonable investigation, reasonably believed that it was not participating in a distribution by a controlling person so that it would be exempt from liability by virtue of Rule 154, would the controlling person still be exempt from liability by virtue of the lacunae in the regulatory scheme? The *Wolfson* case, supra at page 554, gave a negative answer to this question; since Rule 154 and § 4(4) are transaction exemptions, the exemption is not available to anyone participating in the forbidden transaction.

(b) *Resales of Securities Purchased in "Private Offerings."* Alongside the problem of sales of securities by controlling persons, other than investment securities, a similar problem existed with respect to the conditions under which the holder of investment securities (whether or not a controlling person) could make resales of such securities. Persons purchasing securities in a nonpublic offering pursuant to the § 4(2) exemption must purchase for investment and not with a view to distribution of the securities, otherwise they will be deemed to be an "underwriter" as defined in § 2(a)(11). To prove an investment intent, the practice developed of having the purchaser sign an "investment letter" asserting that he or she was taking the securities for investment, and not with a view to their later distribution. Clearly, such an investment letter was worthless, if the purchaser disproved the assertion by turning around and reselling the securities shortly after their purchase. This presented the question of how long the purchaser had to hold the securities to establish an "investment intent." Was he or she ever to be relieved of the disability against resale of the securities? This was the question in United States v. Sherwood.[3] Sherwood owned 8 percent of the shares in a Canadian corporation which he had acquired in a private purchase from one Doyle, a control person of the issuer. This was a criminal contempt proceeding against Sherwood for violation of an injunction prohibiting sales of these securities in violation of the registration provisions of the 1933 Act or the availability of an exemption from registration. The court ruled that Sherwood was not a control person, had not purchased the shares with a view to distribution and therefore was not an underwriter. The evidence established that Sherwood had held the securities for two years prior to any resales. The court therefore concluded that the evidence was sufficient to establish an intention to purchase for investment and not with a view to distribution.

The "two-year rule" declared in *Sherwood* to be sufficient to establish a presumption of investment intent was relied on by some securities lawyers in counseling clients, but other more cautious (or conscientious) lawyers recommended a waiting period of from three to five years before making resales.[4] And in the pre-Rule 144 period, on occasion, the SEC Staff would issue no-action letters advising investors that it would not look with disfavor on a resale after five years.[5]

(c) *The Doctrine of "Change of Circumstances."* If the length of holding of the securities did not itself furnish sufficient evidence of an original "invest-

---

3.   175 F.Supp. 480 (S.D.N.Y.1959).

4.   For the history of this period and the origin of the "Cohen two-year rule" named after Commissioner Manuel F. Cohen, later Chairman of the Commission, see 3 L. Loss &

J. Seligman, Securities Regulation 1478–1504 (3rd Ed. Rev. 1999).

5.   The Commission often receives letters from Counsel, on behalf of a client, setting forth facts concerning a proposed sale of

ment intent," then the doctrine evolved that one must demonstrate that the resale was made solely as a result of a "change in circumstances" between the original purchase and the subsequent resale. The Staff and holders of investment securities frequently disagreed as to whether the investor had suffered a "change in circumstances" which would negate an original intent to purchase with a view to distribution rather than for investment.

In Gilligan, Will & Co. v. SEC,[6] an enforcement proceeding was brought by the SEC against the Gilligan firm, a registered broker-dealer, and Gilligan and Will, the firm partners, asserting that the defendants had engaged as underwriters in a distribution of securities without registration in violation of § 5 of the 1933 Act. The securities were part of a private placement of Crowell–Collier Publishing Company convertible debentures sold to four specific purchasers, including Gilligan. Although these purchasers had represented that they purchased the debentures for investment, they had converted the securities and resold the stock received on conversion on the stock exchange at a profit.

The defendants denied that the resales of the securities amounted to a distribution, and that they were "underwriters" within the meaning of § 4(1) of the 1933 Act. They argued that § 4(2), applicable to issuer transactions, was not involved; that whether there was a distribution should be judged solely by their acts and intentions; and that their purchases and resales were exempt under § 4(1) because their resales did not amount to a "public offering" and hence they were not underwriters.

On appeal, the Second Circuit, relying on the Ralston Purina test under § 4(2), held that the resales by the defendants amounted to a "public offering" and a "distribution" and that defendants were underwriters and their transactions were not exempt under § 4(1).

The defendants contended that the conversion and sales of the stock occurred more than ten months after the purchase of the debentures, thereby establishing a presumption of investment intent. Moreover, they asserted that

securities with an opinion of counsel to the effect that registration under the Securities Act is not required on the basis of a claimed exemption and a request that the Commission advise whether they concur in the opinion. The Commission may or may not give a no-action letter in reply to these requests. If it does so, an authorized member of the Staff will sign the letter which in substance states that, on the basis of the facts set forth in the letter, no action will be recommended to the Commission, if the proposed sales are made, in the manner described, without registration under the act, in reliance on Counsel's opinion that registration is not required. Common subjects for no-action letters in the Pre–Rule 144 period were requests concerning the question of availability of the private offering exemption or the existence of "control." Thus, a person who could be thought to be in a control relationship with an issuer but who disclaimed control might be asked by a broker to get a no-action letter prior to selling unregistered securities in a brokers' transac-

tion. As to their utility one knowledgeable Securities lawyer put it this way: "The sad truth seems to be that you get 'no-action' letters in the clear cases but have an awful time getting them—or don't even ask—in the cases where you really need them." SEC Problems of Controlling Stockholders and in Underwritings 19 (Israels ed.1962).

Beginning in 1970, the Commission commenced to make available to public inspection requests for interpretative advice and no-action letters and written responses thereto with respect to all six Acts administered by it. Securities Act Release No. 5098 (Oct. 29, 1970), adopting 17 CFR 200.80. For the procedures applicable to requests for no-action and interpretive letters, see Securities Act Release No. 6253 (Oct. 28, 1980); Securities Act Release No. 6269 (Dec. 5, 1980). See generally, 1 L. Loss & J. Seligman, Securities Regulation 533–536 (Rev.3d ed.1998).

6. 267 F.2d 461 (2d Cir.1959).

in any event the failure of *Crowell–Collier* to continue to operate profitably resulted in a change of circumstances which would have led a prudent investor to sell. The court rejected this argument as a means of demonstrating an investment intent. The court concluded that an intention to retain the securities only if *Crowell–Collier* operated at a profit was "equivalent to a 'purchase * * * with a view to * * * distribution' within the statutory definition of underwriters in § 2(11)." The holding period requirement and the "change of circumstance" doctrine emerged from efforts of the Commission and staff to stem the flow of securities from issuers to the public without compliance with the registration and prospectus requirements of the Act.

(d) *The Fungibility Concept.* This doctrine was also developed to preserve the integrity of the holding period concept. Suppose A buys 10,000 shares of an issuer's stock in the trading markets. One month later, A buys an additional 10,000 shares of the issuer's stock in a private placement pursuant to the § 4(2) exemption. May A now sell 5,000 shares of the unrestricted stock previously purchased without destroying the § 4(2) exemption? Under the fungibility concept as applied by the Commission's staff, A could not; the entire 20,000 shares is now locked-up and cannot be resold until the expiration of the holding period for the shares purchased in the private placement. If, however, the transactions were reversed, and A made a purchase of an issuer's shares in a private placement, followed by a purchase of the issuer's shares in the trading markets, it was uncertain whether the doctrine of fungibility applied so as to restrict the sale of the after-acquired securities. Moreover, uncertainty existed when there was a series of purchases of shares from the issuer pursuant to the § 4(2) exemption. Even though the holding period may have expired with respect to an earlier purchase, it was by no means certain whether those shares were locked-in as a result of the subsequent purchases of securities or whether resales of those securities could be made without thereby destroying the § 4(2) exemption.

The "Wheat Report" identified these problems and concluded that the doctrines governing the resale of securities purchased pursuant to the § 4(2) exemption were "of uncertain application, created serious administrative burdens and produce[d] results incompatible with the policy objectives of the Act."[7] The Commission thereupon rescinded Rule 154 and adopted Rule 144 to solve these problems as they related to controlling and non-controlling persons. The new rule built upon Rule 154 and regulates resales of securities held by controlling persons pursuant to the § 4(4) brokerage exemption. Unlike Rule 154, however, Rule 144 also applies to resales of investment securities held by controlling persons. In addition, Rule 144 also regulates resales by non-controlling person of securities acquired in a private placement by permitting limited resales of these securities in brokerage transactions after they have been held at risk for a two-year period and unlimited resales after three years.

SECTION 3. RESTRICTIONS ON RESALES OF CONTROL SHARES AND RESTRICTED SECURITIES UNDER RULE 144

Statutes and Rules

Securities Act § 2 (a)(11), Rule 144 and Form 144

7. SEC, "Disclosure to Investors"—Report and Recommendations to the Securities and Exchange Commission From the Disclosure Policy Study, "The Wheat Report", 160–77 (1969).

Rule 144—A Summary Review

By James H. Fogelson.[*]

Rule 144 under the Securities Act of 1933, as amended (the "1933 Act") has been in effect for 1972. Most of the interpretive problems have been addressed. Rule 144 has eliminated much of the previous uncertainty with respect to public sales by control persons ("affiliates") and holders of privately placed securities ("restricted securities"[1]). While there are still some annoying procedural problems in the day-to-day operations of Rule 144, there is general agreement that it has been a major success in administrative rule making. The following reviews in summary form the principal provisions and interpretations of Rule 144 as set forth in Release No. 5223[2] which promulgated Rule 144, Release No. 5306[3] which was the first general interpretative release by the SEC, Release No. 6099,[4] Release No. 6862 (April 23, 1990), Release No. 7390 (February 20, 1997) and the numerous interpretative letters and no-action letters that have been issued by the SEC.

Rule 144 applies to the sale of "control" securities or restricted securities if the following basic conditions are met:

(1) Adequate current public information with respect to the issuer is available.

(2) If the securities are restricted securities, a one-year holding period has been satisfied.[5]

(3) The amount of securities sold by an affiliate in each three-month period does not exceed the greater of (i) 1% of the outstanding securities of that class or (ii) the average weekly reported exchange volume of trading and/or reported through NASDAQ during the four-week period prior to the date of the notice referred to in (5) below or (iii) the average weekly volume of trading in that class reported through the consolidated transaction reporting system during such

[*] Deceased Member of the law firm of Wachtell, Lipton, Rosen & Katz, New York City. This article was prepared with the assistance of Pamela S. Seymon, a third-year law student at New York University. This article updates an article earlier appearing at 29 Bus. Law. 1183–1203 (1974) and reflects the current state of the law. The article has been updated for the purposes of this Edition of this book by Jesse M. Brill, Publisher/Editor of The *Corporate Counsel* and Securities Counsel for Morgan Stanley, and by Robert A. Barron, Esq., Sr. Vice President, Salomon Smith Barney Inc. (Retired). Copyright 1974, 1982 by The American Bar Association. Professors Coffee and Seligman wish to acknowledge their appreciation of the efforts of Messrs. Bill and Barrow in updating and thus preserving Mr. Fogelson's much respected article.

1. "Restricted securities" are defined as securities that are acquired directly or indirectly from the issuer, or from an affiliate of the issuer, in a transaction or chain of transactions not involving any public offering, or securities acquired from the issuer that are subject to the resale limitations of Rule 502(d) of Regulation D or Rule 701(c), or securities acquired under Rule 144A, Regulation CE, Rules 901 or 903 under Regulation S, Rule 801 and Rule 802. 17 C.F.R. § 240.144(a)(3), as amended (effective April 15, 1982).

2. Securities Act Release No. 5223 (Jan. 11, 1972), [1971–72 Transfer Binder] Fed. Sec. L. Rep. (CCH) ¶ 78,487.

3. Securities Act Release No. 5306 (Sept. 26, 1972), [1972–73 Transfer Binder] Fed. Sec. L. Rep. (CCH) ¶ 79,000.

4. Securities Act Release No. 6099 (Aug. 2, 1979).

5. It bears emphasis that affiliates' sales of nonrestricted securities are subject to the Rule; however, compliance with the one-year holding period is not required under such circumstances.

period. The same limitation applies with respect to sales of restricted securities by non-affiliates unless the two-year cutoff under Rule 144(k) discussed below is available, in which case there is no limit as to amount.

(4) The sales are made in either ordinary brokerage transactions or directly with a market maker.

(5) Except for small sales (not more than 500 shares or $10,000 aggregate sales price in the three-month period), the seller files a notice of sale on Form 144 with the SEC and, in the case of listed securities, the principal stock exchange, concurrently with either placing the order to sell with a broker or executing the sale directly with a market maker.[6]

Availability of Rule 144

Rule 144 may be utilized notwithstanding the fact that the holder of restricted securities (1) has contractual registration rights, (2) is discussing with the issuer registration of his/her restricted securities, (3) has restricted securities which were included in a pending registration statement, but which securities were withdrawn voluntarily from registration before the registration statement became effective, or (4) has restricted securities which were effectively registered, but which are withdrawn from registration when the registration statement is withdrawn or are included in a registration statement which can no longer be used because it no longer is current, whether or not the registration statement included an undertaking to file a post-effective amendment and update the prospectus prior to any offering during the "stale" period. In addition, Rule 144 is available for shares which are covered by an effective registration statement even if the registration statement does not expressly provide that the shares so offered may be sold either by means of the registration statement or by means of Rule 144, and even if the shares are not withdrawn from the registration statement.[7]

Concurrent sales of registered securities pursuant to an effective registration statement or pursuant to exemptions provided by Regulation A or Section 4 of the 1933 Act and securities of the same class not included in the registration statement or within any applicable exemption pursuant to Rule 144 are permitted. This is consistent with the abandonment of fungibility for Rule 144 purposes.

While the general rule is that unregistered securities received pursuant to an employee benefit plan can be resold only if such securities subsequently are registered or sold in compliance with an applicable exemption, the SEC has provided an exception to that rule for stock bonus and similar plans that are not registered.[8] A plan participant desiring to effect resales of securities may do so without compliance with Rule 144 provided the following three conditions are satisfied: (1) the issuer of the securities is subject to the periodic reporting requirements of Section 13 or 15(d) of the Securities Exchange Act of 1934 (the "1934 Act"); (2) the stock being distributed is actively traded in the open

---

6. Id. § 230.144(h), as amended (effective March 16, 1981). But see the discussion of the Rule 144(k) two-year cutoff, below.

7. See Dean Witter Reynolds Inc., (avail. Jan. 17, 1986) and The Corporate Counsel, Vol. X, No. 6, at p. 7.

8. Securities Act Release No. 6188 (Feb. 1, 1980), SEC Docket, Vol. 19, No. 7, pp. 465–500. Generally, the SEC does not require registration of stock bonus plans. Such plans include ESOPs (employee stock ownership plans) and SARs (stock appreciation rights).

market; and (3) the number of shares being distributed is relatively small in relation to the number of shares of that class issued and outstanding.[9] Where employee stock plans are registered, Rule 144 is not applicable for resales by non-affiliates of securities received under such plans since such securities are acquired in a registered offering and therefore are not "restricted securities."[10] In the case of stock option plans registered on Form S–8, affiliates cannot rely on the Form S–8 Prospectus to resell the securities received pursuant thereto.[11]

The SEC has permitted utilization of Rule 144 by security holders whose shares were purchased in purported private placements that do not comply with the private offering exemption and therefore were sold illegally. Moreover, the illegal issuance of stock (which would entitle the holder to a put back to the company) will not toll the holding period.[12]

Current Public Information

The current public information requirement is met if the issuer has (1) securities registered under either the 1933 Act or the 1934 Act, and (2) been subject to the periodic reporting requirements for a period of at least 90 days prior to the sale and (3) filed all 1934 Act reports required to be filed during the 12 months (or such shorter period that the issuer was subject to the reporting requirements) preceding the sale.

Where an issuer registers securities under the 1933 Act for the first time, the 90–day waiting period applies even though no 1934 Act reports are required to be filed during that period. The SEC generally requires prospectus disclosure of the future availability of Rule 144 sales of securities of certain registrants, especially first-time registrants, and the present intention of insiders with respect thereto. Where an issuer registers securities under the 1934 Act for the first time, the 90–day waiting period commences on the effective date of the 1934 Act registration statement which is normally 60 days after filing; therefore, in such cases Rule 144 will become available 150 days after the date on which the 1934 Act registration statement was filed.

The 1934 Act report forms require issuers to state whether they have been subject to the reporting requirements for the past 90 days and have met the reporting requirements for the past 12 months (or such shorter period to which the issuer has been subject thereto). Unless he/she knows or has reason to believe that the issuer has not complied with the reporting requirements, the Rule 144 seller is entitled to rely on the issuer's statement in the latest of such reports or on a written statement from the issuer that the reports have been filed. An issuer that has received an extension of time to file a 1934 Act report has not filed all required reports for Rule 144 purposes, but will be deemed current when the filing is made.

9. Securities Act Release No. 6188 (Feb. 11, 1980).

10. Id. Thus, non-affiliates who receive securities in such a manner may freely sell the securities. However, affiliates who receive bonus securities-although registered-can only resell such securities pursuant to an effective registration statement or pursuant to Rule 144.

11. Affiliates, however, may effect resales of Form S–8 securities under Rule 144 (without a holding period) or pursuant to a separate S–3 prospectus filed with the S–8 registration statement provided the issuer satisfies the requirements set forth in Form S–8, General Instruction C.

12. Hadron, Inc., (letter available July 31, 1981), [1981–82 Transfer Binder] Fed. Sec. L. Rep. (CCH) ¶ 77,041.

Small companies that are not subject to the Section 12(g) registration requirements of the 1934 Act (fewer than 500 shareholders or $10 million or less in assets) may voluntarily register, and, thus, make Rule 144 available to their shareholders. Accordingly, in addition to the usual 1934 Act registration covenants, purchasers in private placements, in order to assure the availability of Rule 144, should consider obtaining the covenant of the issuer to register and maintain registration under the 1934 Act and file timely the requisite periodic reports.[13] Rule 144 is available for sales of securities of an issuer which has been required under Section 15(d) of the 1934 Act to file reports but is no longer so obligated (because it has fewer than 300 shareholders of record ; or fewer than 500, where the total assets of the issuer have not exceeded $10 million on the last day of each of the issuer's three most recent fiscal years) if the issuer voluntarily continues to make periodic filings under the 1934 Act.

Under Rule 144(c)(2), the information requirement can be met by nonreporting companies if the information required by Rule 15c2–11 to permit a broker to quote an over-the-counter security is available publicly. This provision does not apply to a reporting company; therefore, it does not enable Rule 144 sales of securities of a delinquent reporting company. If a 1933 Act registration statement is filed by a 15c2–11 issuer, the availability of 15c2–11 information can no longer be relied on and Rule 144 is not available until 90 days after the registration statement has become effective.

Compliance with the publicly available information provision is a factual question to be decided on a case by case basis. The SEC has taken the position that information about nonreporting company is publicly available for Rule 144 purposes if th company has distributed reports containing the 15c2–11 information to its shareholders, brokers, market makes and any other interested persons and information about the company is published in a recognized financial reporting service.[14] It is not sufficient that the company has furnished the 15c2–11 information to the broker through which the Rule 144 sale is to be made.[15] The SEC staff no longer issues interpretive responses to inquiries concerning satisfaction of the Rule 144(c)(2) information requirement.[16]

Holding Period

A major policy predicate of Rule 144 is that the acquirer of restricted securities must take the full economic risk of a one-year holding period. Thus, restricted securities must have been fully paid for and held for one year before they can b sold under Rule 144. In Release No. 7390 (Feb. 20, 1997) the SEC reduced the Rule 144(e) holding period from two years to one year and the Rule 144 (k) holding period from three years to two years.

If securities are purchased from the issuer with notes or other obligations, they are not considered fully paid unless (1) the notes or other obligations are with full recourse, (2) the note or obligation is paid in full before the sale and (3) there is adequate collateral, other than the purchased securities, the fair market value of which is throughout the one-year period equal to the unpaid portion of the purchase price. The holding period is tolled for any periods

---

13. See Miller, Venture Capital: Techniques for Increasing Liquidity with a View Toward Rule 144, 29 Bus. Law. 461 (Jan. 1974).

14. Securities Act Release No. 6099, supra note 4, at Question 20.

15. Id. at Illustration to Question 20.

16. See Anadac, Inc. (avail. Mar. 15, 1990).

during which the fair market value of the collateral falls below the unpaid portion of the purchase price. Excess collateral may be withdrawn without affecting the holding period.

Shares of stock issuable upon exercise of options at a stated price are not fully paid until the option has been exercised and the exercise price has been fully paid.

If restricted securities are purchased on an installment basis, the holding period commences on a staggered basis. The holding period is tolled only as to those securities which do not meet the full-recourse or collateralization requirements.

The staff of the SEC has taken the position that where money is borrowed from a third party non-affiliate lender (e.g., a bank) to purchase restricted securities, the loan is not guaranteed, directly or indirectly, by the issuer and the restricted securities are pledged as the only collateral for a normal full-recourse loan, the restricted securities are considered fully paid and the holding period is deemed to have commenced upon purchase of the restricted securities.

Fungibility does not apply to Rule 144 situations. The acquisition of restricted securities will not restart the holding period on previously acquired restricted securities. * * * Likewise, fungibility does not apply in non-Rule 144 situations. The acquisition of restricted securities does not taint unrestricted securities previously acquired.[17] The holder merely must be able to trace the securities to their purchase dates.

A private sale of restricted or control securities pursuant to the "Section 4(1 ½) exemption" will start a new one-year holding period if the seller is an affiliate of the issuer. The holding of the previous private placee cannot be tacked to the holding of the subsequent placee where the seller is an affiliate of the issuer. If the seller is a non-affiliate of the issuer, such tacking is permitted. See SEC Release No. 6862 (April 23, 1990).

Partners who receive restricted securities as distributions by their partnership may tack their holding periods to that of the partnership,[18] but all of the partners receiving such securities must aggregate their sales for the purpose of the amount limitation discussed below if they tack the holding periods. However, if the unlimited resale provision of paragraph (k) applies by reason of the partner not being an affiliate of the issuing corporation and the combined holding period exceeds two years, aggregation is inapplicable. During any period the partners are unable to utilize the unlimited resale provisions (and up to one year after the distribution), the partners are required to aggregate. In the case of a closely-held corporation, the same analysis applies.

Tacking is permitted for stock dividends and stock splits, recapitalizations (including recapitalizations resulting in changes in par values), reincorporations that do not result in changes in the business or management, conversions of convertible securities (provided the security is convertible into securities of the same issuer), warrants (provided that the only consideration surrendered

---

17. See Borden and Fleischman, The Continuing Development of Rule 144: Significant SEC Staff Interpretations, Eighth Annual Institute on Securities Regulation 91, 126–27 (1977) (hereinafter "The Continuing Development of Rule 144").

18. It should be noted that tacking is permitted only if the distribution does not require the distributee to furnish additional consideration as, for example, when his/her partnership interest is being redeemed. Securities Act Release No. 6099, supra note 4, at Question 34 n.11.

upon exercise of the warrant consists of other securities of the same issuer) and securities acquired as contingent payments in business combinations. In each of these situations, for Rule 144 purposes, the subsequently acquired securities are deemed to have been acquired at the time the related restricted securities were acquired.

Stock dividends on restricted securities are restricted securities for Rule 144 purposes; however, the holding period for securities acquired as a dividend is deemed to have commenced as of the date the securities on which the dividend was paid were acquired.

Tacking is permitted for bona fide pledgees, donees of gifts and trusts. However, if an affiliate settlor of a trust sells rather than donates the restricted securities to the trust, tacking is not permitted. Restricted securities are deemed to have been acquired when they were acquired by the pledgor, donor or settlor. The SEC has taken the position that multiple donees or beneficiaries need not aggregate horizontally provided that they do not otherwise act in concert.

Where an estate is an affiliate, tacking is permitted, and the amount limitations apply. Moreover, where a beneficiary who is an affiliate receives restricted securities from the estate, tacking is permitted of both the decedent and the estate holding periods. If the affiliated beneficiary is trustee or executor under the instrument as well, the trust or estate is deemed to be an affiliate and thus the amount limitations apply. Where the estate is not an affiliate or the securities are sold by a beneficiary who is not an affiliate, no holding period is required, and the amount limitations and the manner of sale requirement do not apply even if one or more beneficiaries (other than the trustee as discussed immediately above) are affiliates, but the other conditions of Rule 144 as to current information and notice of sale do apply. However, where the trustee or executor is an affiliate (even though the securities are non-restricted securities in the hands of the non-affiliated trust or estate), the trustee or executor must aggregate his/her personal sales with those of the trust or estate. Conversely, the non-affiliated trust or estate need not aggregate its sales with those of the trustee or executor for purposes of the volume limitation. The special provisions for an estate apply only to restricted securities acquired by the estate from the decedent, not to restricted securities acquired otherwise, such as by exchange of securities owned by the decedent, to which Rule 144 applies fully.

Tacking of holding periods that have been broken by transfers of restricted securities from one entity to another within a "person", as defined in Rule 144, is not permitted unless the transferor is a non-affiliate or the transfer is of a type included in the Rule 144(d)(3) tacking provisions for pledges, gifts, trusts and estates.

Limitation on Amount of Securities Sold

The limitation on the amount of securities which may be sold pursuant to the Rule in any three-month period is the greater of 1% of the outstanding securities of the class being sold or the average weekly volume of that class on all exchanges or reported through the consolidated transaction reporting system for the four calendar weeks prior to the filing of the notice of sale. Sales pursuant to registered offerings and pursuant to exemptions provided by Regulation A and Section 4 of the 1933 Act are not aggregated with Rule 144 sales in determining the amount permitted to be sold under the Rule. See Rule 144(e)(3)(vii). It should be noted that a Rule 144 seller utilizing Form 144 is required to set forth in Table II certain information concerning any securities of the issuer which the seller has sold in the prior three months. According to the SEC staff, this includes securities, which pursuant to Rule 144(e)(3)(vii) are not required to be counted in computing permissible volume under Rule 144(d). *Sue Ann Inc.* (avail. Sept. 6, 1977). Where a security is traded on a national securities exchange and NASDAQ, the NASDAQ volume may be used in lieu of the national securities exchange volume or the two may be combined. Where securities are unlisted, the NASDAQ volume alone may be used.

There is no prohibition on sales in successive three-month periods, but carry-forward and accumulation are not permitted.

Both restricted and unrestricted securities are aggregated for determining the amount limitation for sales by affiliates. Only restricted securities are considered in determining the limitation on sales by non-affiliates.

Sales by persons acting in concert are aggregated. The mere fact that several affiliates sell at the same time will not in and of itself be considered acting in concert, but it does give rise to a situation which must be considered carefully. Where investors have agreed not to sell more than a specified percentage of their securities during a specified period, the SEC staff in the past has taken the position that this constitutes an agreement to act in concert. The treatment for aggregation purposes of several funds or other accounts under the same investment management is not covered specifically in the Rule. The SEC staff has indicated that in the case of two trusts managed by the same bank it would treat each trust as a separate person, notwithstanding common trustees so long as the trusts are not administered in a manner that results in their acting in concert. But the SEC has stated that aggregation would be required if the bank made a common decision to sell securities for more than one trust—even where such decision was required due to its fiduciary duty. However, the bank must aggregate its own sales with the various trusts or estates it administers.

"Person" is defined in Rule 144 to include relatives of the seller who share a permanent home with the seller, trusts and estates in which the seller and such relatives collectively own a 10% or greater beneficial interest or which any of them serves as trustee or executor, and corporations or other entities in which the seller, such relatives and such trusts and estates together have a 10% equity interest or own 10% of a class of equity securities. Generally, sales by all those included in the definition of person are aggregated for the purpose of Rule 144. But aggregation is not required by a non-affiliated trust or estate that wishes to dispose of nonrestricted securities—even though the trustee, executor or beneficiary is an affiliate. The trustee or executor, however, would be required to aggregate his/her personal sales with those of the trust or estate under such circumstances. An institutional investor or other person who owns 10% or more of any class of equity securities of a company is considered one person with such company for the purpose of Rule 144, and, therefore, the institutional investor would have to inquire of all companies in which it holds a 10% interest to determine if any of them had or planned transactions in a restricted security the institution wishes to sell under Rule 144. Directors of charitable foundations are not deemed to act in a capacity similar to that of a trustee or executor for the purpose of Rule 144; thus, aggregation is not required. In the pledge, gift and trust contexts there is aggregation with sales by the pledgor, donor or settlor. Such aggregation terminates one year after the original transfer to the pledgee, donee or trust, or upon completion of the Rule

144(k) two-year holding period, whichever occurs first. Pledgees should therefore consider restricting the pledgor by contract or escrow in order to ensure the availability of Rule 144 in the event of default. There is no amount limitation for estates and beneficiaries which are not affiliates even though the beneficiary (other than a beneficiary who is also a trustee) is an affiliate.

Section (e)(3)(i) of the Rule is a rather confusingly drafted provision which provides that where both a convertible and the underlying security are being sold, the amount of the underlying security for which the convertible being sold may be converted is aggregated with sales of the underlying security in determining the aggregate amount of both securities allowed to be sold. Thus, the amount limitations of Paragraph (e) cannot be circumvented by selling an amount of the underlying security in compliance with those limits, while at the same time selling an amount of the convertible security which would meet amount limitations for the convertible if it were looked at separately, but which would have resulted in an excessive sale of the underlying security if the convertible had first been converted and the sale of both blocks of securities had taken place.

Where an over-the-counter company subsequently lists on an exchange, the listed security volume limitation becomes applicable four weeks after listing and all sales in the preceding three months are considered in determining the volume limitation.

The number of shares to be sold under Rule 144 may be adjusted for stock splits or stock dividends paid after the Form 144 has been filed. Form 144 can be amended to change the designation of the broker who has been given the sale order. No notice on Form 144 is required if the amount of securities to be sold during any three months does not exceed 500 shares or units and the aggregate sales price does not exceed $10,000. The SEC may soon increase these amounts to 1000 shares and $40,000. See Securities Regulation Law Journal Summer 2002, A Heads Up For Rule 144 Practitioners.

Manner of Sale

Sales under the Rule can be made in either brokers' transactions within the meaning of Section 4(4) of the 1933 Act or transactions directly with ''a market maker'' as defined in the 1934 Act. The seller cannot solicit or arrange for the solicitation of buy orders or make any payment in connection with the sale other than usual commissions to the broker who executes the order.

A ''market maker'' is defined in Section 3(a)(38)of the l934Act as, either (1) a specialist who is permitted to act as a dealer, (2) a dealer who acts as a block positioner or (3) a dealer who holds himself out as willing to buy and sell a particular security for his own account on a regular or continuous basis.

A market maker is precluded from specifically soliciting buy orders for securities the market maker wishes to buy in a Rule 144 transaction. However, a solicitation will not be implied from the fact that the market maker continues to engage in normal market making activities. All that is required is that the market maker not engage in a special campaign to solicit buyers for the shares it proposes to purchase pursuant to Rule 144. However, once the market maker consummates a purchase of securities in a Rule 144 transaction, the securities are freed of their restrictive character. The market maker may then solicit buy orders for such shares.

The staff has recognized that the Rule's prohibition of prior solicitations may impose particular hardships, on block positioners. Due to the risks incident to block positioning, the block positioner often will attempt to cover his block in part by soliciting buyers prior to committing himself to purchase the block. Because the exchanges limit the ability of member block positioners to trade off-board securities which are listed or admitted to unlisted trading privileges on an exchange, the block positioner's purchase will not be consummated until its execution on the exchange. According to the Rule, the block positioner technically cannot solicit buy orders until this time. However, in recognition of the fact that the block positioner will have made a firm commitment to purchase the block prior in time to the execution on the exchange (at the time of accepting an order from a seller), the staff has indicated that under such circumstances the block positioner can solicit buy orders prior to the consummation of the purchase on the exchange but subsequent to the acceptance of the order.

Brokers' transactions are defined as those in which the broker (1) does no more than execute a sell order as agent for the usual commission and (2) does not solicit buy orders. The broker may inquire of other brokers who have indicated an interest within the preceding 60 days. Such inquiry may also be made of clients, institutional and non-institutional, who are bona fide and unsolicited and indicate an interest, in the preceding 10 days. Brokers should maintain written records of such indications in order to substantiate the bona fide nature thereof.

Brokers can continue to make a two-way market in a security for which they have a Rule 144 sale order, if prior to receipt of the order they were making such market and published quotes 12 out of the preceding 30 calendar days with no more than four business days in succession without such two-way quotations.

Where a broker effects a cross of securities sold in a Rule 144 transaction, the broker may collect commissions from both buyer and seller provided such commissions are usual and customary. Where negotiated commissions are applicable they are permitted under Rule 144 if "negotiated in the usual and customary manner."

Rule 144 provides that the broker should obtain and retain a copy of the notice of sale and make a reasonable inquiry to ascertain whether the seller is engaged in a distribution. Reasonable inquiry should include the following:

(1) The length of time the securities have been held by the person for whose account they are to be sold. If practicable, the inquiry should include physical inspection of the securities;

(2) The nature of the transaction in which the securities were acquired by such person;

(3) The amount of securities of the same class sold during the past three months by all persons whose sales are required to be aggregated;

(4) Whether such person intends to sell additional securities of the same class through any other means;

(5) Whether such person has solicited or made any arrangement for the solicitation of buy orders in connection with the proposed sale of securities;

(6) Whether such person has made any payment to any other person in connection with the proposed sale of the securities; and

(7) The number of shares or other units of the class outstanding, or the relevant trading volume.

In addition to the foregoing, the broker should also obtain and retain a copy of the 1934 Act filing or the written statement of the issuer on which the Rule 144 seller is predicating satisfaction of the current information requirement and a representation letter from the seller.

Short sales may be effected under Rule 144, provided that (i) the specific securities to be used to cover the short sale are eligible for sale under Rule 144 at the time of the short sale, (ii) the seller delivers such securities to the broker at the time of the short sale, and (iii) those specific securities are eventually used to cover the short sale. All of the requirements of the Rule, including the filing of Form 144, must be met at the time of the short sale, not when the short position is covered.

Rule 144 is available for short sales against the box as well provided all conditions of the Rule are satisfied. The sale is deemed to involve a broker's transaction on the date the short sale is executed rather than the date the seller's securities are replaced for the borrowed securities. To assure the availability of Rule 144 for short sales against the box, the non-affiliate initially must place his/her restricted securities in the box—he/she cannot sell securities short and then use the restricted securities to cover the short position. [Note: Section 16(c) effectively prevents officers, directors, and ten-percent owners from engaging in short sales.]

Listed call options may be written by both affiliates and non-affiliates. To utilize Rule 144, the affiliate must comply with the Rule's requirements at the time of writing the options; the non-affiliate, on the other hand, may not become subject to Rule 144 by the mere writing of options. It is only when the non-affiliate either (1) covers his/her option position with restricted securities, (2) uses restricted securities to meet margin obligations, or (3) uses restricted securities for delivery upon exercise of an option that all the Rule 144 conditions must be met. See SEC Release No. 6099, at 69–79 (Aug. 2, 1979) for the basic ground rules on writing covered listed call options on control and restricted stock. As option transactions are fraught with potential § 16(b) and Rule 10b–5 exposure, officers, directors and ten-percent shareholders should generally be counseled against engaging in such transactions.[19]

The securityholder who files the Form 144 must have a bona fide intention to sell the securities referred to therein within a reasonable time after filing.[20]

Rule 144(k)—No Restrictions After Two Years

Rule 144(k) provides that restricted securities that have been held for at least two years may be sold without complying with any of the requirements of Rule 144, provided the holder is not an affiliate and has not been an affiliate for three months prior to the sale. Thus there is now a complete cutoff from the requirements of Rule 144 once a non-affiliate has held restricted securities for

---

19. See The Corporate Counsel, Vol. XXVI, No. 5, at p. 4.

20. For a discussion of the interaction between the Rule 144(i) requirement (bona fide intention to sell) with SEC Rule 10b5–1 sale plans, see "SEC Rule 105–1 and Rule 10b5–1 Trading Plans (Revisited)" Securities Regulation Law Journal (Fall 2001) pp. 298 et seq.

two years. At that time all legends and transfer restrictions should be removed from the securities.[21]

A holder who sells restricted securities pursuant to the Rule 144(k) unlimited resale provision may concurrently sell other restricted securities to which the amount limitation applies. The former securities are stripped of all volume restrictions and thus are not aggregated with restricted securities which must be sold in compliance with the amount limitation.

Tacking is permitted to satisfy the two-year holding period. A shareholder of a close corporation or a partner who receives restricted securities of another issuer as a distribution from a corporation or partnership can immediately sell the securities so received pursuant to the unlimited resale provision—even if the partnership or corporation is an affiliate of the issuer—if the seller is not and has not been an affiliate of the issuer for three months preceding the sale and the combined holding periods of the corporation or partnership and the distributee equal two years. During the time in which the distributee is subject to the amount limitation (up to a maximum of one rear from the date he or she acquired the restricted securities), sales must be aggregated.

The above analysis also applies to the pledge, gift and trust situations. Even where the donor (pledgor) is an affiliate and the securities involved are non-restricted securities, donees (pledgees) may rely on Rule 14(k) and sell without restriction, even though the affiliate donor (pledgor) would have to sell under Rule 144. Availability of the Rule 144(k) unlimited resale provision will depend upon the satisfaction of two elements—namely the donee (pledgee) must not be an affiliate at the time of the sale and (2) the donor (pledgor) and donee (pledgee) must have a combined holding period of two years.[22] Moreover, the Staff is no longer taking the position that the donor must aggregate his or her sales with the donee for two years subsequent to the gift where the donee sells under Rule 144(k).[23]

Where two or more individuals share the same household and are deemed to be a "person" within the meaning of the Rule, the unlimited n provision is unavailable to any of them if one of them is an affiliate.

Exclusivity and Operation of Rule 144

The SEC by amendment in 1979 inserted new paragraph (j) to Rule 144. This paragraph provides that Rule 144 is not exclusive with respect to non-affiliates' sales of restricted stock nor with respect to affiliates' sales, whether they are selling restricted or unrestricted securities. The affiliate or non-affiliate may also effect such sales pursuant to (1) a registration statement, (2) an exempt transaction or (3) Regulation A. However, the affiliate who desires to effect sales pursuant to the individual exemption provide Section 4(1) of the 1933 Act can only sell in reliance on Rule 144. In other words, reliance on Section 4(1) by an affiliate can only be predicated on Rule 144. On the other hand, Rule 144 is purely a nonexclusive safe harbor for non-affiliates' sales of restricted securities.

---

21. See The Corporate Counsel Vol. XIII, No. 5. See also the Smith Barney Harris Upham & Co. Inc. interpretive letter (avail. Sept. 16, 1988).

22. See David D. Wexler, avail. July 23, l981,and Morgan Stanley & Co., avail. Oct. 30, 1984, and see The Corporate Counsel, Vol. VI, No. 4, at p 7.

23. See *Jesse M Brill,* avail. Sept. 26, 1986.

Now that Rule 144(k) provides a complete cutoff after two years, the need for legal opinions in reliance on Section 4(1) has been greatly reduced. Such opinions are, however, commonly rendered to avoid the Rule 144(k) three month wait for former affiliates who have held restricted securities for two years.[24]

Rule 144 is not available where there is technical compliance, but the Rule 144 sales are part of a plan to effect a distribution.[25] Rule 144 does not exempt sales from the antifraud, civil liability or short-swing profits provisions of the securities laws. The SEC position is that the Rule is to be strictly construed and persons selling under the Rule have the burden of proving its availability.

———

Developments in the administration of Rule 144 are reported in The Corporate Counsel Newsletter, Jesse M. Brill, Editor. And see 3 L. Loss & J. Seligman, Securities Regulation 1502–75 (3d ed. 1989); 7B J. Hicks, Exempted Transactions Under the Securities Act of 1933, ch. 10 (1990 rev.).

SECTION 4.   THE SECTION "4(1½)" EXEMPTION

Excerpt from: Carl W. Schneider

The Section "4(1½)" Phenomenon: Private Resales of "Restricted" Securities*

34 Business Lawyer 1961–1978 (1979).[a]

INTRODUCTION

The purpose of this Report is to consider the available methods by which a person may resell privately securities initially issued in a private placement ("restricted securities") without registration under the Securities Act of 1933. This variety of sale has become popularly known as "section 4(1½)" transactions, primarily because the SEC, in no-action letters and other pronouncements, frequently has required that such resales meet at least some of the established criteria for exemptions under both section 4(1) and section 4(2).[3] In this Report the term "Holder" is used to refer to a person who holds restricted

---

24. See The Corporate Counsel, Vol. XV, No. 3, at p. 5.

25. Securities Act Release No. 5223, supra note 2, at 81,061. The SEC staff, however, has indicated that Rule 144 provides a safe harbor for sale of restricted securities even where sales pursuant to the Rule would seriously impact the trading market for the issuing company's shares. WCS Int'l. (letter available Jan. 12, 1979).

* A Report to the Committee on Federal Regulation of Securities from the Study Group on Section "4(1½)" of the Subcommittee on 1933 Act * * *.

a. Copyright 1979 by the American Bar Association. All rights reserved. Reproduced with the permission of the American Bar Association and its Section of Corporation, Banking and Business Law.

3. In this Report, the phrases "4(1½) transaction" or "4(1½) Sale", are used generically to describe resales of restricted securities otherwise than through holders in public markets.

securities and the term "Purchaser" to refer to a person who purchases restricted securities from a Holder.

* * *

OVERVIEW OF THE 4(1½) PHENOMENON

* * *

Our initial inquiry in analyzing the scope of permissible sales of Restricted Securities is to determine what subsection within section 4 is applicable. Sections 4(3), 4(4) and 4(5) may be ruled out summarily. Because section 4(2) exempts only "transactions *by an issuer*" and a sale by a Holder is not a sale "by an issuer", a literal reading of this section makes it inapplicable as the basis for an exemption. Of necessity, one then must turn to section 4(1), which exempts "transactions by any person other than an issuer, underwriter, or dealer." Recognizing that the Holder, by hypothesis, is not an "issuer" (as defined in section 2(4)) and assuming that he is not a "dealer", the critical inquiry is whether he or his Purchaser may be deemed an "underwriter", as defined in section 2(11) of the 1933 Act. To avoid "underwriter" status, the Holder (i) must not have purchased the shares from the issuer "with a view to" their "distribution" and (ii) must not offer or sell the shares "for an issuer in connection with, the distribution".

The term "distribution", although central to the "underwriter" analysis, is not defined in the 1933 Act, and it is at this point that section 4(2) concepts are typically introduced and the "underwriter" analysis becomes confusing. Because a "distribution", in the context of section 4(1), is generally considered to be functionally equivalent to a "public offering" as used in section 4(2), it seems reasonable in defining "distribution" to borrow by analogy from judicial and administrative interpretations of the term "public offering". Moreover, in considering a resale of Restricted Securities soon after the Holder has acquired them from the issuer, the application of section 4(2) standards to the resale may be necessary to assure that the issuer's original section 4(2) exemption is not vitiated by the resale.

Separate from the line of decisions and SEC staff positions that apply section 4(2) standards in determining whether a "distribution" is involved is the theory that section 4(2) may independently provide an exemption for sales by a Holder.

Against this general background of inconsistent application of various criteria and the lack of any clear agreement on even the applicable theory of exemption, we turn first to an analysis of the legislative history of section 4.

LEGISLATIVE HISTORY

The legislative history of the 1933 Act sheds little light on any of the questions posed above. * * *

* * * James Landis, a principal draftsman of H.R. 5480, commented upon the general scope of the 1933 Act as follows:

"Public offerings" as distinguished from "private offerings" proved to be the answer [to the question what scope the 1933 Act was to have]. The sale of an issue of securities to insurance companies or to a limited group of experienced investors was certainly not a matter of concern to the federal government. That bureaucracy, untrained in these matters as it was, could hardly equal these investors for sophistication, provided only it was their own money that they were spending. And so the conception of an exemption for all sales, other than by an issuer, underwriter, or dealer came into being, replacing the concept of "isolated transactions" theretofore traditional to blue sky legislation.[14]

The precise process by which the desire to exempt a sale by an issuer to a small group of sophisticated investors as described by Landis led to an exemption for sales by a person other than an "issuer, underwriter, or dealer" is unclear. The first part of the quoted language seems more appropriately directed to validating the private offering exemption of section 4(2) than the exemption of section 4(1). * * *

        * * *

There is some support for the theory that section 4(1) was designed to cover resales in much the same fashion as section 4(2) was aimed at delineating the scope of the exemption for sales by an issuer. One House Report on this legislation reflects a primary intention to distinguish between regular trading and distributions (whether made by the issuer, affiliates or nonaffiliates).[19]

        * * *

The Report also indicates that the regulation of sales of control securities was intended to be effected by shaping the definition of "underwriter" in section 2(11) and incorporating that term in the section 4(1) exemption:

        * * *

From this [Report] one may draw some support for the notions that section 4(2) is properly addressed solely to issuers and that section 4(1) above should govern all resales, including sales of both Restricted Securities and securities held by controlling persons. * * *

JUDICIAL INTERPRETATIONS

Judicial efforts to identify the statutory provision to be applied to sales of restricted securities and to define the parameters of the appropriate exemption have been far more successful than legislative endeavors and generally support the view that section 4(1) is the provision to be applied.

The earliest such cases were United States v. Sherwood[22] and Gilligan, Will & Co. v. SEC.[23] In *Sherwood*, criminal contempt proceedings were brought against Sherwood, the holder of 8 percent of a company's stock, for violating an injunction prohibiting sales of the company's stock absent registration or the availability of an exemption. The stock in question had been acquired by Sherwood from one Doyle, who had received the stock from the issuer. The court found that Sherwood was not a control person, had not acquired the stock with a view to distribution, and therefore was not an "underwriter". The fact that Sherwood had held the shares two years persuaded the court of Sherwood's investment intent. Sherwood's sales of the stock were found to be exempt under section 4(1).

---

14. Landis, The Legislative History of the Securities Act of 1933, 28 Geo. Wash.L.Rev. 29, 37 (1959).

19. House of Representatives Report No. 85, at 5 (May 4, 1933) (hereinafter cited as "H.Rep. 85").

22. 175 F.Supp. 480 (S.D.N.Y.1959). [Supra at page 559.]

23. 267 F.2d 461 (2d Cir.1959). [Supra at page 560.]

In *Gilligan, Will* two registered dealers had participated in the placement of $3,000,000 of convertible debentures of Crowell–Collier Publishing Co. Gilligan, a partner of Gilligan, Will & Co., purchased $100,000 of the debentures for his own account and made representations that he purchased for investment. Notwithstanding these representations, Gilligan quickly sold $45,000 of the debentures to one Louis Alter, and Gilligan also made offers to two other potential purchasers, selling $5,000 of debentures to one of them. Ten months after these sales, Gilligan, Will & Co., Gilligan and Alter converted their debentures into common stock and sold the stock at a profit on the American Stock Exchange.

Gilligan and Alter later subscribed to an additional $200,000 of debentures which they similarly converted to common stock. Gilligan, Will & Co. also was active in selling $200,000 of the debentures to a mutual fund, and as a result of this transaction, other parties received warrants to purchase Crowell–Collier stock.

In a subsequent SEC enforcement action, Gilligan, Will attempted to have its own acts viewed in isolation, claiming that they were not "underwriters" because the transactions effected by them, viewed alone, did not constitute a "public offering." Similar transactions had been effected by another dealer contemporaneously with Gilligan, Will's transactions. Taken together, however, the total number of offerees was quite small. In addition to Gilligan and Alter, only two other offerees were involved. The defendants stipulated that none of the four offerees had access to the kind of information made available by registration. The court found that, even though the number of offerees was small, the offering could not be viewed as a "private" one, under the criteria established for the section 4(2) exemption, in the *Ralston Purina* case. Accordingly, Gilligan, Will was held to be an "underwriter", having purchased with a view to public distribution.

Although the result in *Gilligan, Will* is not surprising, the court's analysis of the defendants' claims of exemption is instructive. The court focused on the section 4(1) exemption, and determined that the initial inquiry was whether a "distribution" was involved. In determining the existence of a "distribution" the court noted that the term was equivalent to "public offering"[24] and turned to the *Ralston Purina* decision for instruction on that point. Finding that the Ralston "access" requirement had not been met, the court held that a "distribution" had occurred.

The court also recognized that a person could rely on the section 4(1) exemption even if a "distribution" had occurred, provided that person's acquisition of the shares had not been with a "view" to the subsequent distribution. In this part of its analysis, the court (i) rejected the particular "change of circumstances" asserted by the defendants (without rejecting the concept) and (ii) held that a ten-month holding period was not sufficient to establish that the defendants had not acquired the stock with a "view" to distribution.[26]

* * *

A clearer analysis of the statutory exemptions is present in Value Line Income Fund, Inc. v. Marcus.[34] This case involved an attempted rescission of an

24. Id. at 466 (citing H.R. Rep.No. 1838, 73d Cong., 2d Sess. (1934) at 41).

26. 267 F.2d at 466.

34. [1964–1966 Transfer Binder] Fed. Sec.L.Rep. (CCH) Para. 91,523, 94,953 (S.D.N.Y.1965).

agreement between a mutual fund and Marcus, the principal shareholder and president of a machinery company, in which the mutual fund agreed to purchase one-half of Marcus' shares in the company. The transaction was completed as planned, but when the stock declined drastically in price within a year, Value Line sought to rescind the agreement on the ground that Marcus had made fraudulent representations and the shares had not been registered.

The two major defendants in *Value Line* were Marcus, the "Holder", and Van Alstyne, Noel & Co. ("Vanco"), the party through whom Marcus sold his shares to Value Line. Vanco was unaware of any misrepresentations made by Marcus, and more importantly, the court found that Vanco was neither an issuer, underwriter, or dealer, and therefore the transaction was considered exempt under section 4(1). Marcus, as a control person, was an "issuer" for purposes of determining whether Vanco was an "underwriter."[35] The only offerings of Marcus' stock made by Vanco were to mutual funds, which were recognized as highly sophisticated investors with sufficient "access" for private offering purposes. The court found there was no "distribution" or "view to distribution" by Vanco, with the result that Vanco was not an "underwriter" under section 2(11) and was entitled to rely upon the section 4(1) exemption. On the same analysis, the section 4(1) exemption was found to be available to Marcus.

Like * * * *Gilligan, Will, * * * Value Line* recognizes that private resales may be made in reliance on section 4(1). Moreover, *Value Line* is particularly significant in its recognition that such resales may be made immediately after the shares are acquired, provided the ultimate purchasers are persons to whom the issuer could have made a valid direct sale under section 4(2).

* * *

In summary, our review of the cases dealing with the section 4(1½) phenomenon indicates the following:

1. The appropriate exemptive provision is section 4(1) and not 4(2).

2. No particular holding period is required.

3. The Purchasers' sophistication and access to information appear to have been viewed as essential in * * * the * * * decisions.

4. The number of purchasers, viewed alone, is not dispositive of the availability of an exemption.

5. Restrictions on resales by a Purchaser generally have not been required.

6. No decision has articulated an affirmative duty on a Holder to provide registration-type information to a Purchaser.

SEC INTERPRETATIONS

The Staff No–Action Letters

General

The SEC Staff has never enunciated the statutory basis on which it has permitted private resales of Restricted Securities, and the staff letters are relatively few in number and show little consistency. On a number of occasions,

---

35. Id. at p. 94,969.

the staff has implied that the section 4(2) exemption would be applicable. Yet in one letter the Staff expressly repudiated the notion that the section 4(2) exemption is available to any party other than the issuer and suggested that section 4(1) might be the appropriate theory on which to base private resales. Similarly, the most recent step in the evolution of paragraph (e)(3)(G) of rule 144 further supports the section 4(1) basis for section 4(1½) sales by indicating that private resales can be made in reliance upon the section 4(1) exemption if the sale is one "not involving any public offering." * * *

* * *

Qualification of Purchasers

The staff letters are mixed with respect to the necessity that the purchaser be a sophisticated investor. Most staff letters make no reference to this requirement. A few, however, grant no-action requests upon the express condition that the purchaser be somewhat sophisticated. * * * In two letters the staff went even further, requiring the purchaser to be able "to afford the risk of the highly speculative investment."

Access to or Furnishing of Information

The staff has grappled somewhat unsuccessfully with the question whether the Purchaser must have access to registration-type information or be supplied such information by the Holder. In one letter the staff required that "prospective purchasers * * * be limited to persons who have access to the same information about [the issuer's] stock that a registration statement would provide." In others, the staff has required that the seller advise all offerees where information regarding the issuer might be obtained, and in one letter the staff merely required the seller to disclose all information regarding the issuer that was known to the seller.

Restrictions on Purchaser's Resales

The staff letters tend uniformly to provide that Purchasers of restricted securities are deemed to have received restricted shares and may not resell them *publicly* without compliance with the registration provisions of the Act. In a few letters the staff also has required that restrictive legends and stop-transfer orders be placed upon the shares. In a number of other letters, however, the staff has denied that it has any power to require the placement or removal of restrictive legends.

GENERAL GUIDELINES: THEORY AND PRACTICE

Basis of Exemption

Initially, we conclude that the only proper statutory basis for section 4(1½) sales is section 4(1). We consider that the limiting phrase "by an issuer" in section 4(2) poses an insurmountable barrier to reliance on that exemption as an affirmative basis for the exemption of section 4(1½) sales. As discussed below, however, we consider it appropriate to apply certain section 4(2) criteria to limit the manner in which some varieties of section 4(1½) transactions may otherwise be effected.

Sales of Restricted Securities

Where a nonaffiliate proposes to sell Restricted Securities, the critical inquiries in determining his status as an "underwriter" are whether his acquisition was made "with a view to * * * distribution" and whether his sale is to be made "for an issuer in connection with" a "distribution". Because these phrases appear in the disjunctive in section 2(11), strict statutory analysis indicates that if either question is answered in the affirmative, the Holder would not be entitled to rely upon section 4(1). As discussed below, however, even a purchase made subjectively "with a view to * * * distribution" may under certain conditions be made under section 4(1). Each of these phrases in section 2(11) focuses, first, on the status of the shares in the hands of the Holder (specifically, have they "come to rest") and second, whether his sales constitute a "distribution".

Under the traditional (pre-rule 144) approach, the prevailing view of securities law practitioners was that once restricted securities had "come to rest" (in the sense that the resales would not be a further step in the issuer's distributive process), there should be no restriction on the manner of resale. Analytically, such resales by definition would not vitiate the issuer's 4(2) exemption and would be sufficiently removed from the original placement that (i) the Holder's resale would not be deemed "for" the issuer and (ii) the Holder's original purchase would not be deemed to have been made with the proscribed "view". We think that this traditional approach has continuing validity and that the section 4(1) exemption should be available if the Holder can demonstrate (i) that he did not acquire the restricted securities from the issuer or an affiliate "with a view to" distribution *and* (ii) that the resale is not being made "for an issuer" (or in the case of the resale of restricted securities acquired from an affiliate, for the affiliate). The best objective evidence on these questions will be the length of time the Holder has owned the securities. If he has established a sufficiently long holding period,[69] this alone should demonstrate conclusively that (i) his original acquisition was not "with a view" to distribution and (ii) that the resale is not being made "for the issuer". With respect to each of these standards, the mere length of the holding period should be sufficient. In this regard, we suggest that a Holder who subjectively intended when he acquired the Restricted Securities, to "distribute" them, may nevertheless thereafter resell them in reliance on section 4(1) if his actual retention of them has been consistent with the opposite intent.

In the case of restricted securities that have not "come to rest", the Holder may nevertheless sell them if the sale does not constitute a "distribution" (unless, as discussed below, the sale may be considered part of the original placement). In determining whether a "distribution" will result from the Holder's sale, we consider the better view to be that only the manner of sale and the number of purchasers are relevant. In short, only the quantitative aspects of the term "distribution" should be considered. We find no basis in the language or legislative history of the 1933 Act to impose the requirements that the Purchaser be sophisticated or have access to registration-type information.

69. Although any particular specification of a minimum holding period would be arbitrary, we agree with Professor Loss that a three-year holding period is "well-nigh conclusive" evidence of both the Holder's nondistribution intent and the lack of any connection between his original acquisition and his resale. 1 Loss, Securities Regulation 672 (1961). In many situations, counsel may consider a holding period of less than three years to be sufficient. By comparison, we note the SEC has approved holding periods of [one year] and of nine months under rules 144 and 147, respectively, for the limited resales that may be made under those rules, and recently has [removed the limitations on rule 144 sales by nonaffiliates after at least three years has elapsed since the later of the date the securities were acquired from the issuer or from an affiliate.]

Accordingly, a Holder should be able to dispose of restricted securities provided there are few purchasers and the securities are not offered by means of mass communications. Nor, analytically, should there be any particular limit on the amount that may be sold. Obviously, some reasonable limitations must be observed on these points but there are no hard and fast rules. Similarly, the use of a broker to locate a few purchasers should not be ruled out, provided reasonable restrictions are placed on the breadth of the broker's solicitation efforts. Thus, even if the restricted securities have not "come to rest" at the time of resale, if under this second step of the "underwriter" analysis, one determines that no "distribution" will result, section 4(1) will be available.

If the restricted securities have been acquired from the issuer under circumstances in which it cannot be concluded that the shares have come to rest after their sale in the section 4(2) transaction, it is appropriate for section 4(2) requirements of offeree sophistication and access to be applied to the Holder resales. But this is appropriate only for the purpose of assuring that the issuer's original section 4(2) exemption for its sale to the Holder is not lost.

Status of Securities in the Purchaser's Hands

As a theoretical matter, a Purchaser of restricted securities can resell immediately so long as he adheres to the standards discussed above for the Holder's sale (*i.e.*, "privately") and his resales (and all others occurring around the same time) do not result in a "distribution" or otherwise vitiate the issuer's original section 4(2) exemption. The Purchaser thus is essentially in the same position as the Holder and should be able to make resales in the same fashion described herein for Holders.

* * *

———

1. *Purchaser Sophistication.* The foregoing interpretation of the § 4(1½) exemption focuses primarily on whether the distribution has "come to rest"—a mode of analysis that gives little weight to the sophistication of the buyer but instead focuses on quantitative criteria about the number of purchasers and the manner of sale. Yet, continuing uncertainty surrounds the legitimacy of this approach. If the scope of the § 4(1½) exemption is to be determined at least in part by reference to the criteria applicable to an issuer private placement under § 4(2), buyer sophistication may be at the heart of the inquiry. In Gilligan, Will & Co. v. SEC,[1] the Second Circuit seemed to say precisely this: that the term "distribution" in § 2(a)(11) is to be read in light of the criteria applicable to an issuer exemption under § 4(2). Still, most courts to date have been able to duck the issue of whether full compliance is necessary with the standards announced in SEC v. Ralston Purina Co.[2] in order to satisfy the § 4(1½) exemption. In Value Line Fund, Inc. v. Marcus,[3] discussed in the preceding excerpt, all five offerees were obviously sophisticated mutual funds. Similarly, in Ackerberg v. Johnson,[4] the plaintiff had a net worth over $1,000,000, had read a ninety-nine page private placement memorandum prepared by the broker for the seller, and was found by the court to be a "sophisticated investor." Thus, the Eighth

1. 267 F.2d 461 (2d.Cir.1959).

2. 346 U.S. 119 (1953) (supra at p. 397).

3. [1964–1965 Transfer Binder] Fed. Sec.L.Rep. (CCH), Para. 91,523 (S.D.N.Y. 1965).

4. 892 F.2d 1328 (8th Cir.1989).

Circuit had no difficulty in upholding the availability of the § 4(1½) exemption both on the ground that the seller had held the privately placed securities for at least four years prior to the sale (which implied to the court that the distribution had come to rest) and on the ground that the purchaser could fend for himself (thus satisfying *Ralston Purina*). Conversely, in SEC v. Manus,[5] the defendant, who was a controlling person, held the stock for four years and then sold to relatively unsophisticated buyers (a junior high school teacher and several other individuals who had not invested before). Not surprisingly, the defendant lost.

In contrast, Rule 144 ignores the sophistication of the buyer and basically permits resale to anyone if the securities have been held for a requisite holding period and are resold in small quantities (i.e. normally 1% or less) that are unlikely to impact the market. The policy issue then is: Should the § 4(1½) exemption be interpreted more in keeping with Rule 144's quantitative criteria or instead according to *Ralston Purina*?

2. *Other Criteria.* A consensus exists that a general solicitation will destroy the availability of the § 4(1½) exemption. Still, some no-action letters have permitted the holders of large blocks to publicly advertise their availability, at least when the entire block was to be sold to one purchaser.[6] Sellers often prepare a private placement memorandum when seeking to rely on the § 4(1½) exemption (although this could equally be based on a controlling person's fear of antifraud liability under Rule 10b–5). In contrast, no information furnishing obligation exists under Regulation D in the case of "accredited investors." Should the § 4(1½) exemption require more information than Regulation D?

3. *The Future of the § 4(1½) Exemption.* In the wake of the 1997 reduction of the holding periods under Rule 144 and the development of an active resale market under Rule 144A, does the § 4(1½) exemption still matter? Its availability is probably most important in the case of affiliates of the issuer who wish to sell large blocks. Equity securities of public domestic issuers will generally not qualify for Rule 144A (because of the fungibility exemption), and such affiliates can also not use Rule 144(k). But for the non-affiliate, Rule 144 today probably provides a much simpler and less uncertain exit vehicle.[7]

SECTION 5. RULE 144A AND THE PRIVATE RESALE MARKET

Resale of Restricted Securities

Securities Act Release No. 6862.
(April 23, 1990).

A. GENERAL

* * *

5. [1981–1982 Transfer Binder] Fed. Sec.L.Rep. (CCH), Para. 98,307 (S.D.N.Y. 1981). See also McDaniel v. Compania Minera Mar de Cortes, 528 F.Supp. 152 (D.Ariz. 1981).

6. See Schneider, Section 4(1½)—Private Resales of Restricted or Control Securities, 49 Ohio St.L.J. 501, 507 (1988).

7. For a case in which no information was provided (and the purchasers were unsophisticated), see United States v. Lindo, 18 F.3d 353 (6th Cir.1994).

Rule 144A sets forth a non-exclusive safe harbor from the registration requirements of Section 5 of the Securities Act for the resale of restricted securities to specified institutions by persons other than the issuer of such securities. The transactions covered by the safe harbor are private transactions that, on the basis of a few objective standards, can be defined as outside the purview of Section 5, without the necessity of undertaking the more usual analysis under Sections 4(1) and 4(3) of the Securities Act. Each transaction will be assessed under the Rule individually. The exemption for an offer and sale complying with the Rule will be unaffected by ... transactions by other sellers. The Commission wishes to emphasize that Rule 144A is not intended to preclude reliance on traditional facts-and-circumstances analysis to prove the availability of an exemption outside the safe harbor it provides.

* * *

In the case of securities originally offered and sold under Regulation D of the Securities Act, a person that purchases securities from an issuer and immediately offers and sells such securities in accordance with the Rule is not an "underwriter" within the meaning of Rule 502(d) of Regulation D. Issuers making a Regulation D offering, who generally must exercise reasonable care to assure that purchasers are not underwriters, therefore would not be required to preclude resales under Rule 144A. Similarly, the fact that purchasers of securities from the issuer may purchase such securities with a view to reselling such securities pursuant to the Rule will not affect the availability to such issuer of an exemption under Section 4(2) of the Securities Act from the registration requirements of the Securities Act.

B.   ELIGIBLE SECURITIES

Rule 144A would not extend to the offer or sale of securities that, when issued, were of the same class as securities listed on a national securities exchange registered under Section 6 of the Exchange Act or quoted in an automated inter-dealer quotation system. Accordingly, privately-placed securities that, at the time of their issuance, were fungible with securities trading on a U.S. exchange or quoted in NASDAQ would not be eligible for resale under the Rule.

Where American Depositary Shares ("ADSs") are listed on a U.S. exchange or quoted in NASDAQ, the deposited securities underlying the ADSs also would be considered publicly traded, and thus securities of the same class as the deposited securities could not be sold in reliance on the Rule * * *. Under the Rule, a convertible security is to be treated as both the convertible and the underlying security unless, at issuance, it is subject to an effective conversion premium of at least 10 percent.

C.   ELIGIBLE PURCHASERS

1.   TYPES OF INSTITUTIONS COVERED

As discussed above, except for registered broker-dealers, to be a "qualified institutional buyer" an institution must in the aggregate own and invest on a discretionary basis at least $100 million in securities of issuers that are not affiliated with the institution.

a.   Banks and Savings and Loan Associations

Banks, as defined in Section 3(a)(2) of the Securities Act, and savings and loan associations as referenced in Section 3(a)(5)(A) of the Act, must, in addition to owning and investing on a discretionary basis at least $100 million in securities, have an audited net worth of at least $25 million, as demonstrated in their latest published annual financial statements * * *. As federally-insured depository institutions, domestic banks and savings and loans are able to purchase securities with funds representing deposits of their customers. These deposits are backed by federal insurance funds administered by the Federal Deposit Insurance Corporation ("FDIC"). In light of this government support, these financial institutions are able to purchase securities without placing themselves at risk to the same extent as other types of institutions. In this respect, banks and savings and loans effectively are able to purchase securities using public funds. Therefore, the amount of securities owned by a bank or savings and loan institutions may not, on its own, be a sufficient measure of such institution's size and investment sophistication * * *. A combined securities ownership and net worth test [was therefore adopted] * * *.

b. Registered Broker–Dealers

* * *

Commenters stated that the definition of qualified institutional buyer, as reproposed, would exclude a number of registered broker dealers from acting as intermediaries in the Rule 144A resale market. They also stated that if the $100 million test was retained for registered broker-dealers in all situations, significant segments of the registered broker-dealer community, whose participation was important to the efficient functioning of the market, would be excluded from participation in the market as principals.

In response to these comments, the Rule as adopted provides that a broker-dealer registered under the Exchange Act which in the aggregate owns and invests on a discretionary basis at least $10 million in securities of issuers that are not affiliated with the broker-dealer is a qualified institutional buyer. Additionally, the Rule provides that registered broker-dealers acting as riskless principals for identified qualified institutional buyers would themselves be deemed to be qualified institutional buyers * * *.

D. INFORMATION REQUIREMENT

* * *

As adopted, availability of the Rule is conditioned upon the holder and a prospective purchaser designated by the holder having the right to obtain from the issuer, upon the holder's request to the issuer, certain basic financial information, and upon such prospective purchaser having received such information at or prior to the time of sale, upon such purchaser's request to the holder or the issuer. This information is required only where the issuer does not file periodic reports under the Exchange Act, and does not furnish home country information to the Commission pursuant to Rule 12g3–2(b). Additionally, the Rule has been revised to exempt from the information requirement securities issued by a foreign government * * *. The holder must be able to obtain, upon request, and the prospective purchaser must be able to obtain and must receive if it so requests, the following information (which shall be reasonably current in relation to the date of resale under Rule 144A): a very brief statement of the nature of the issuer's business and of its products and services offered, comparable to that information required by subparagraphs (viii) and (ix) of Exchange Act Rule 15c2–11(a)(5); and its most recent balance sheet and profit and loss and retained earnings statements, and similar financial statements for such part of the two preceding fiscal years as it has been in operation. The financial information required is the same as that required by subparagraphs (xii) and (xiii) of Rule 15c2–11(a)(5). The financial statements should be audited to the extent audited financial statements are reasonably available.

The Commission does not believe that the limited information requirement should impose a significant burden on those issuers subject to the requirement. Many foreign issuers that will be subject to the requirement, which were the focus of the commenters' concern, will have securities traded in established offshore markets, and already will have made the required information publicly available in such markets. Even for domestic issuers, the required information presents only a portion of that which would be necessary before a U.S. broker or dealer could submit for publication a quotation for the securities of such an issuer in a quotation medium in the United States * * *. Financial statements meeting the timing requirements of the issuer's home country or principal trading markets would be considered sufficiently current for purposes of the information requirement of the Rule * * *.

The Rule does not specify the means by which the right to obtain information would arise. The obligation could be, inter alia, imposed in the terms of the security, by contract, by corporate law, by regulatory law, or by rules of applicable self-regulatory organizations.

E.   OTHER REQUIREMENTS

Although the Rule imposes no resale restrictions, a seller or any persons acting on its behalf must take reasonable steps to ensure that the buyer is aware that the seller may rely on the exemption from the Securities Act's registration requirements afforded by Rule 144A.

---

1. *PORTAL.* Contemporaneously with the adoption of Rule 144A, the SEC also in 1990 approved the creation by the NASD of an electronic market to trade Rule 144A securities.[1] Known as PORTAL (for "The Private Offering, Resale and Trading Through Automated Linkages System"), this market trades only securities that qualify under Rule 144A and only permits investors who qualify as "qualified institutional buyers" (or "QIBS") to trade. Prior approval of the investor as a QIB by PORTAL is necessary before it can trade, and this requirement is further enforced by a clearance and settlement system which the Depository Trust Company ("DTC") administers to prevent the leakage of Rule 144A securities into public markets.

While PORTAL got off to an initially shaky start,[2] it has become a major success and has added a unique level of liquidity to the private placement process. It made Rule 144A attractive to foreign issuers, who could have done

---

1. See Sec. Act Rel. No. 6864 (April 30, 1990).

2. In its first two years, PORTAL attracted only 75 subscribers out of an estimated universe of over 3300 QIBs. See Bostwick, The SEC Response to Internationalization and Institutionalization Rule 144A: Merit Regulation of Investors, 27 Law & Policy In

International Business 423, n. 75 (1996). Subsequently, it has grown to become a significant market center for the trading of equity securities of foreign issuers, but less so for debt securities. In 1997, it was estimated that some 3000 QIBs traded on PORTAL. See Levels of Access to the U.S. Investor, Corporate Finance at p. 28 (June 1997).

offshore offerings, but were instead attracted by the prospects of a liquid secondary market (which did not exist in their home country). As a result, roughly 30% of Rule 144A offerings are made by foreign issuers, and many of these later become "reporting companies" and graduate to a listing on Nasdaq or the New York Stock Exchange.[3]

2. *Documentation and Form.* Although envisioned as a form of private placement, Rule 144A offerings have come to look more and more like public offerings. Typically, they involve a disclosure document that more or less parallels a Form S–1 prospectus, with similar financial statements, risk factors, and often a Management's Discussion and Analysis of Financial Condition. Typically, the offering will be of convertible securities (particularly in the case of U.S. issuers) with a premium sufficient to satisfy Rule 144A's "fungibility test." Unlike a typical private placement, where the investment banker functions only as an agent of the issuer, the major investment banks in a Rule 144A offering will purchase the securities from the issuer as the "initial purchasers" and then resell to the QIB purchasers, thus functionally paralleling the role of underwriters.

3. *The Information Requirement.* Some controversy has surrounded Rule 144A's information requirement in subsection (d)(4) of the rule. Under Regulation D, no information need normally be provided to an accredited investor; nor must information be provided under the statutory exemption in § 4(6). On average, these investors are less sophisticated and have less bargaining power than QIBs. If information need not be provided to such investors in the primary offering, why should it be required at the time of the secondary market transaction? Perhaps, the answer was that the SEC's attention was focused in Rule 144A on foreign issuers who would conduct their primary offerings abroad (under the protective auspices of Regulation S), and the SEC wanted to ensure that securities of such issuers could not reach the U.S. secondary markets (such as PORTAL) without some commitment by the issuer to provide continuing information.

4. *Impact.* In 1994, the annual dollar volume of securities sold through Rule 144A transactions was estimated to be approximately 5% of the dollar volume of all securities annually registered under § 5 of the 1933 Act.[4] Consider what the percentage would be if the SEC eliminated the "fungibility" exclusion which effectively precludes most domestic public corporations from using Rule 144A for equity securities. Does this explain why the New York Stock Exchange and other U.S. stock markets insisted on the fungibility exclusion before they would support Rule 144A? Today, Rule 144A securities still seem to trade at a discount off the price of equivalent stocks in public markets, suggesting that the illiquidity discount has been reduced, but only marginally.

SECTION 6. REGULATION S: AN EXEMPTION FOR OFFERINGS OUTSIDE THE UNITED STATES

For the issuer seeking to avoid the costs, delay and potential liability associated with the registration of securities, an obvious tactic is to issue the

---

3. See James D. Cox, Regulatory Duopoly in U.S. Securities Markets, 99 Colum. L. Rev. 1200, 1227 (1999).

4. See Staff Report on Rule 144A, [1994–1995 Transfer Binder] Fed.Sec.L.Rep. (CCH), Para. 85,428 (August 18, 1994).

securities abroad. The problem with this technique is that the Securities Act of 1933 does not on its face exempt extraterritorial offerings from its reach. To the contrary, § 5 of the 1933 Act applies to any offering or sale in "interstate commerce," and § 2(a)(7) defines "interstate commerce" to include "trade or commerce in securities or any transportation or communication relating thereto * * * between any foreign country and any State, Territory, or the District of Columbia." Section 5's worldwide reach results in considerable overbreadth that potentially subjects to the registration requirements of § 5 both U.S. issuers who sought to sell securities abroad (for example, by making phone calls from the United States) and foreign issuers whose securities entered the United States through resales.

Such a literal interpretation of § 5's scope would produce dismay from foreign issuers and U.S. issuers with foreign operations and might result in confrontations with regulators in other countries. Not surprisingly, the SEC has never attempted to extend § 5 to its fullest conceivable reach. The problems inherent in extraterritorial offerings first became apparent in the 1960s with the development of the Eurobond market. Essentially, because of persistent U.S. balance of payments deficits (caused in large part by the Cold War and the stationing of U.S. troops in Europe), European financial institutions held large reserves of dollar deposits, which they were prepared to lend at lower rates of interest than were domestic U.S. financial institutions. To tap this attractive financial market, U.S. issuers wanted to make bond offerings in Europe. But they could foresee that some of the securities so issued would re-enter the United States—with the possible result that the SEC would consider them to have made a public offering in violation of § 5. To enable U.S. issuers to access this market, the SEC issued Release No. 4708 in 1964, which stated that the U.S. securities laws were "primarily intended to protect American investors * * *" and concluded that debt securities could be sold by U.S. issuers without need for registration under the 1933 Act if "the offering is made under circumstances reasonably designed to preclude distribution or redistribution of the securities within, or to nationals of, the United States." Over the next twenty-five years, the SEC interpreted and re-interpreted Release 4708 in a voluminous series of no-action letters, which still left some continuing uncertainties. Cautious counsel developed an elaborate set of contractual provisions to satisfy this Release. Typically, these procedures required (1) a "lock-up" of the securities and their release to buyers in definitive form at a delayed point (usually 90 days after the closing) that was sufficiently after the completion of the distribution to ensure that the offering had ended and the securities had come to rest; and (2) an express agreement by the underwriters that they would not sell to U.S. nationals or residents. The obvious difficulty with this approach was that it denied U.S. institutional investors the ability to participate in foreign offerings. As U.S. institutional investors increasingly desired to diversify their portfolios on an international basis, pressure developed to reconsider Release No. 4708.

Regulation S, which was adopted in 1990, essentially reflects a shift from a "national" approach focused on protecting U.S. nationals (wherever located) to a "territorial" approach (which permits U.S. and foreign issuers to sell unregistered securities in foreign markets, even to U.S. nationals). Structurally, Regulation S consists of a general statement (in Rule 901) and two specific safe harbors (in Rules 903 and 904). Rule 903 provides a safe harbor for participants in a distribution (referred to as "distributors"), including issuers, underwriters and selling group members. In turn, Rule 904 sets forth a safe harbor for resales by others, including investors who acquire securities in a U.S. private placement or in a transaction exempt from registration under Rule 144A.

Rule 903 focuses on the relative likelihood that securities of the issuer will enter U.S. markets. As a result, it subdivides issuers into three categories: (1) foreign issuers without "substantial U.S. market interest" for their securities (see Rule 903(c)(1)); (2) foreign or U.S. issuers that are "reporting" companies under the 1934 Act and foreign issuers of debt securities (see Rule 903(c)(2)); and (3) all other issuers (see Rule 903(c)(3)). In the case of a foreign issuer that falls into the first category because it lacks a "substantial U.S. market interest," Rule 903's safe harbor is available so long as the securities are offered and sold in an "offshore transaction" and no "directed selling efforts" are made in the United States. The buyer in such a case may be a U.S. national and the entire transaction can be planned and preparatory activities undertaken in the United States, because the transaction will be deemed an "offshore transaction" under Rule 902(i) so long as the buyer is outside the United States at the time the "buy offer is originated" or the transaction is executed on the "physical trading floor" of a foreign securities exchange. In the case of the second category ("reporting" companies and foreign issuers of debt securities), there are additional requirements: a 40–day "restricted period" is required during which offers or sales may not be made to U.S. persons; "offering restrictions" must be implemented; and a notice requirement becomes applicable. In the case of the third category (all other issuers),[1] more elaborate procedural requirements are specified, including certification and lock-up requirements for debt securities and a one-year restricted period, coupled with a stop-transfer restriction, for equity securities. These restrictions parallel the former standards under Release No. 4708. The rationale for this tripartite classification is explained below in the adopting release.

Offshore Offers and Sales

Securities Act Release No. 6863.
(April 24, 1990).

* * * Regulation S as adopted includes two safe harbors. One safe harbor applies to offers and sales by issuers, securities professionals involved in the distribution process pursuant to contract, their respective affiliates, and persons acting on behalf of any of the foregoing (the "issuer safe harbor"), and the other applies to resales by persons other than the issuer, securities professionals involved in the distribution process pursuant to contract, their respective affiliates (except certain officers and directors), and persons acting on behalf of any of the foregoing (the "resale safe harbor"). An offer, sale or resale of securities that satisfies all conditions of the applicable safe harbor is deemed to be outside the United States within the meaning of the General Statement and thus not subject to the registration requirements of Section 5.

Two general conditions apply to the safe harbors. First, any offer or sale of securities must be made in an "offshore transaction," which requires that no offers be made to persons in the United States and that either: (i) the buyer is (or the seller reasonably believes that the buyer is) offshore at the time of the origination of the buy order, or (ii) for purposes of the issuer safe harbor, the

---

1. Although described broadly as "all other issuers," this third category is likely to be very small and will chiefly consist of U.S. issuers that are not reporting companies and a few foreign issuers that have a "substantial U.S. market interest."

sale is made in, on or through a physical trading floor of an established foreign securities exchange, or (iii) for purposes of the resale safe harbor, the sale is made in, on or through the facilities of a designated offshore securities market, and the transaction is not pre-arranged with a buyer in the United States. Second, in no event could "directed selling efforts" be made in the United States in connection with an offer or sale of securities made under a safe harbor. "Directed selling efforts" are activities undertaken for the purpose of, or that could reasonably be expected to result in, conditioning of the market in the United States for the securities being offered. Exceptions to the general conditions are made with respect to offers and sales to specified institutions not deemed U.S. persons, notwithstanding their presence in the United States.

The issuer safe harbor distinguishes three categories of securities offerings, based upon factors such as the nationality and reporting status of the issuer and the degree of U.S. market interest in the issuer's securities. The first category of offerings has been expanded from the Proposals and includes: securities offered in "overseas directed offerings," securities of foreign issuers in which there is no substantial U.S. market interest, securities backed by the full faith and credit of a foreign government, and securities issued pursuant to certain employee benefit plans. The term "overseas directed offerings" includes an offering of a foreign issuer's securities directed to any one foreign country, whether or not the issuer's home country, if such offering is conducted in accordance with local laws, offering practices and documentation. It also includes certain offerings of a domestic issuer's non-convertible debt securities, specified preferred stock and asset-backed securities denominated in the currency of a foreign country, which are directed to a single foreign country, and conducted in accordance with local laws, offering practices and documentation. The second category has been revised to include offerings of securities of U.S. reporting issuers and offerings of debt securities, asset-backed securities and specified preferred stock of foreign issuers with a substantial U.S. market interest. * * *

The issuer safe harbor requires implementation of procedural safeguards, which differ for each of the three categories, to ensure that the securities offered come to rest offshore. Offerings under the first category may be made offshore under the issuer safe harbor without any restrictions beyond the general conditions. Offerings made in reliance on the other two categories are subject to additional safeguards, such as restrictions on offer and sale to or for the account or benefit of U.S. persons.

The resale safe harbor has been expanded from the Proposals to allow reliance thereon by certain officers and directors of the issuer or distributors. In such a transaction, no remuneration other than customary broker's commissions may be paid. Otherwise, the resale safe harbor is adopted substantially as reproposed. Under the resale safe harbor, dealers and others receiving selling concessions, fees or other remuneration in connection with the offering (such as sub-underwriters) must comply with requirements designed to reinforce the applicable restriction on directed selling efforts in the United States and the offshore transaction requirement. * * *

The safe harbors are not exclusive and are not intended to create a presumption that any transaction failing to meet their terms is subject to Section 5. Reliance on one of the safe harbors does not affect the availability of any exemption from the Securities Act registration requirements upon which a person may be able to rely.

Regulation S relates solely to the applicability of the registration requirements of Section 5 of the Securities Act. The Regulation does not limit in any way the scope or applicability of the antifraud or other provisions of the federal securities laws or provisions of state law relating to the offer and sale of securities.

* * *

At or around the time of adoption of this Regulation, the Department of the Treasury is adopting regulations establishing new procedures applicable to foreign-targeted offerings of bearer debt obligations. Persons contemplating issuance of such obligations in reliance on this Regulation are advised to direct their attention also to the Treasury regulations. See Treas.Reg. § 1.163–5(c).

II. *BACKGROUND AND INTRODUCTION*

The registration requirements of the Securities Act literally apply to any offer or sale of a security involving interstate commerce or use of the mails, unless an exemption is available. The term "interstate commerce" includes "trade or commerce in securities or any transaction or communication relating thereto * * * between any foreign country and any State, Territory or the District of Columbia. * * * " The Commission, however, historically has recognized that registration of offerings with only incidental jurisdictional contacts should not be required. In Release 4708, the Commission stated that it would not take any enforcement action for failure to register securities of U.S. corporations distributed abroad solely to foreign nationals, even though the means of interstate commerce were used, if the distribution was effected in a manner that would result in the securities coming to rest abroad.

* * *

The development of active international trading markets and the significant increase in offshore offerings of securities, as well as the significant participation by U.S. investors in foreign markets, present numerous questions under the U.S. securities laws. For companies raising capital abroad, a principal issue under the federal securities laws is the reach across national boundaries of the registration requirements under Section 5 of the Securities Act.

The Regulation adopted today is based on a territorial approach to Section 5 of the Securities Act. The registration of securities is intended to protect the U.S. capital markets and investors purchasing in the U.S. market, whether U.S. or foreign nationals. Principles of comity and the reasonable expectations of participants in the global markets justify reliance on laws applicable in jurisdictions outside the United States to define requirements for transactions effected offshore. The territorial approach recognizes the primacy of the laws in which a market is located. As investors choose their markets, they choose the laws and regulations applicable in such markets.

* * *

Regulation S relates solely to the applicability of the registration requirements of Section 5 of the Securities Act, and does not limit the scope or extraterritorial application of the antifraud or other provisions of the federal securities laws or provisions of state law relating to the offer and sale of securities. The antifraud provisions have been broadly applied by the courts to protect U.S. investors and investors in U.S. markets where either significant conduct occurs within the United States (the "conduct" test) or the conduct occurs outside the United States but has a significant effect within the United

States or on the interests of U.S. investors (the "effects" test). It is generally accepted that different considerations apply to the extraterritorial application of the antifraud provisions than to the registration provisions of the Securities Act. While it may not be necessary for securities sold in a transaction that occurs outside the United States, but touching this country through conduct or effects, to be registered under United States securities laws, such conduct or effects have been held to provide a basis for jurisdiction under the antifraud provisions of the United States securities laws.

III. *DISCUSSION OF REGULATIONS*

A. *General Statement*

Rule 901(a) is a general statement of the applicability of the registration provisions of the Securities Act. The General Statement provides that any offer, offer to sell, sale, or offer to buy that occurs within the United States is subject to Section 5 of the Securities Act, while any such offer or sale that occurs outside the United States is not subject to Section 5. The determination as to whether a transaction is outside the United States will be based on the facts and circumstances of each case. If it can be demonstrated that an offer or sale of securities occurs "outside the United States," the registration provisions of the Securities Act will not apply, regardless of whether the conditions of the safe harbor are met. For a transaction to qualify under the General Statement, both the sale and the offer pursuant to which it was made must be outside the United States. * * *

B. *Safe Harbors*

Rules 903 and 904 set forth non-exclusive safe harbors for extraterritorial offers, sales and resales of securities. The safe harbors include conditions to protect against indirect, unregistered, non-exempt offerings into the U.S. capital markets.

An offer or sale by an issuer, a distributor, an affiliate of either, or any person acting on behalf of any of the foregoing, that meets the applicable conditions of the issuer safe harbor (Rule 903) is outside the United States for the purposes of Rule 901. For purposes of the Regulation, the term "distributor" includes all underwriters, dealers, and other persons who are participating in a distribution of securities pursuant to contractual arrangements, such as sub-underwriters, but does not include persons participating pursuant to contract only in ancillary positions, such as fiscal agents or persons hired to perform clearing services.

Distributors and their affiliates are not prevented by the Regulation from engaging in secondary transactions in securities of the same class being distributed, provided the securities are not borrowed or replaced with shares from the offering. Once the distribution has ended and any applicable restricted period specified in Rule 903 has expired, distributors that have sold their allotments will no longer have distributor status and therefore will be able to use Rule 904's resale safe harbor. So long as a distributor still holds some portion of its allotment, it will continue to be unable to rely on Rule 904 with respect to the offer and sale of the unsold allotment.

The resale safe harbor is available for offers and sales by all persons except an issuer, a distributor, an affiliate of either (other than specified officers and directors), and any person acting on behalf of any of the foregoing. An offer or sale that meets the applicable conditions of Rule 904 is outside the United

States for the purposes of Rule 901. Unlike the reproposal, resales of securities by officers and directors who may be affiliates of the issuer or distributor, and thus would have been ineligible to use the resale safe harbor, may be made in reliance upon that safe harbor provided specified conditions are met. Of course, the resale safe harbor is not available for such officers and directors if they are being used as conduits to sell securities for persons ineligible to rely upon the resale safe harbor.

1. *General Conditions*

Two general conditions apply to all offers, sales and resales made in reliance on the safe harbors. First, such an offer or sale must be made in an "offshore transaction." Second, no "directed selling efforts" may be made in the United States in connection with an offer or sale of securities in reliance on such safe harbors.

a. *Requirement of Offshore Transaction*

An "offshore transaction" is a transaction in which no offer is made to a person in the United States and either of two additional sets of requirements is met. The first alternative requires at the time the buy order is originated, that the buyer be outside the United States (or the seller and any person acting on its behalf reasonably believe that the buyer is outside the United States). The second alternative covers certain transactions executed in, on or through the facilities of a designated offshore securities market (unless the seller or a person acting on its behalf knows that the transaction was prearranged with a buyer in the United States) and certain transactions executed in, on or through the physical trading floor of an established foreign securities exchange located outside the United States.

The first alternative focuses on the location of the buyer for two reasons. First, the location of the buyer overseas clearly and objectively provides evidence of the offshore nature of the transaction. The requirement that the buyer itself, rather than its agent, be outside the United States reduces evidentiary difficulties and problems in administering the Regulation, both for regulators and private parties attempting to ensure compliance with the conditions of the safe harbor. Second, the buyer's location outside the United States supports the expectation that the buyer is or should be aware that the transaction is not subject to registration under the Securities Act.

When the buyer is a corporation or partnership, if an authorized employee places the buy order while abroad, the requirement that the buyer be outside the United States will be satisfied. When the buyer is an investment company, if an authorized person employed by either such company or its investment adviser places the buy order outside the United States, the requirement that the buyer be outside the United States will be satisfied.

The second alternative definition of "offshore transaction" provides that certain transactions executed in, on or through certain offshore securities markets are offshore transactions, without regard to the location of the person originating the buy order. In order to be considered a sale of securities in, on or through the facilities of an offshore securities market, the sale must be effected outside the United States under the auspices and supervision of such a securities market, by or through a member of such market or any other person authorized to effect such sales thereon. Such execution of a transaction in a foreign marketplace provides objective evidence of the foreign locus of the transaction. Moreover, buyers in such markets may be presumed to rely on the regulatory protections afforded by local law and not U.S. registration requirements. * * *

b.   *Directed Selling Efforts*

A person making an offer or sale otherwise in accordance with the conditions of the issuer safe harbor will be unable to rely on the provisions of the safe harbor if any directed selling efforts are being made in the United States by an issuer, a distributor, any of their respective affiliates, or any person acting on behalf of any of the foregoing. With respect to resales under Rule 904, a directed selling effort by the seller, any of its affiliates, or any person acting on behalf of either, will preclude reliance on the resale safe harbor by that seller; directed selling efforts by any other person will not affect the seller's ability to rely on the resale safe harbor.

Under the issuer safe harbor, directed selling efforts in the United States may not be made during the period the issuer, the distributors, their respective affiliates or persons acting on behalf of any of the foregoing, are offering and selling the securities and, for offerings under the second and third safe harbor categories, during the restricted period as well.

"Directed selling efforts" are those activities that could reasonably be expected, or are intended, to condition the market with respect to the securities being offered in reliance upon the Regulation. This provision precludes, *inter alia,* marketing efforts in the United States designed to induce the purchase of the securities purportedly being distributed abroad. Activities such as mailing printed material to U.S. investors, conducting promotional seminars in the United States, or placing advertisements with radio or television stations broadcasting into the United States or in publications with a general circulation in the United States, which discuss the offering or are otherwise intended to condition, or could reasonably be expected to condition, the market for the securities purportedly being offered abroad, constitute directed selling efforts in the United States.

Publications with a general circulation in the United States, as defined in the Regulation, include all publications printed primarily for distribution in the United States, and all publications that, on average during the preceding 12 months, have had a circulation in the United States of 15,000 copies or more per issue.

The definition of directed selling efforts specifically excludes several forms of advertisements. First, an advertisement will not be deemed a directed selling effort under the Regulation if publication of the advertisement is required by foreign or U.S. law or the rules or regulations of a U.S. or foreign regulatory or self-regulatory authority, such as a stock exchange, provided that the advertisement contains no more information than legally required and includes a statement to the effect that the securities have not been registered under the Securities Act and may not be offered or sold in the United States (or to a U.S. person, if the advertisement relates to an offering under the second or third issuer safe harbor categories) absent registration or an applicable exemption from the registration requirements. * * *

Distribution or publication in the United States of information, opinions or recommendations concerning the issuer or any class of its securities could constitute directed selling efforts, depending upon the facts and circumstances. Directed selling efforts will not be deemed to exist, however, if the information, opinion or recommendation of a distributor or its affiliate with respect to a reporting issuer: (i) is contained in a publication that is distributed with reasonable regularity in its normal course of business, and includes similar information, opinions or recommendations in that issue with respect to a substantial number of companies in the issuer's industry or sub-industry, or contains a comprehensive list of securities recommended by such entity; (ii) is given no materially greater space or prominence in such publication than that given to securities of other issuers; and (iii) with respect to an opinion or recommendation, is no more favorable to the issuer than the opinion or recommendation published by the entity in its last issue addressing the issuer or its securities. When the issuer is not a reporting issuer, the effect on the market of publication or distribution of information, opinions or recommendations about the issuer or its securities can be expected to be more significant due to the possible absence of other publicly available information about the issuer. Distributors and their affiliates should exercise even greater caution in publication or distribution of information, opinions or recommendations concerning non-reporting issuers or their securities.

An isolated, limited contact with the United States generally will not constitute directed selling efforts that result in a loss of the safe harbor for the entire offering. The Regulation likewise is not intended to inhibit routine activities conducted in the United States for purposes other than inducing the purchase or sale of the securities being distributed abroad, such as routine advertising and corporate communications. The dissemination of routine information of the character and content normally published by a company, and unrelated to a securities selling effort, generally would not be directed selling efforts under the Regulation. For example, press releases regarding the financial results of the issuer or the occurrence of material events with respect to the issuer generally will not be deemed to be "directed selling efforts."

* * *

Legitimate selling activities carried out in the United States in connection with an offering of securities registered under the Securities Act or exempt from registration pursuant to the provisions of Section 3 or 4 of the Securities Act will not constitute directed selling efforts with respect to offers and sales made under Regulation S.

* * *

2.   *Issuer Safe Harbor*

The issuer safe harbor is available for issuers, distributors, their respective affiliates, and persons acting on behalf of any of the foregoing. The issuer safe harbor distinguishes among three classes of securities, with varying procedural safeguards imposed to have the securities offered come to rest offshore. The criteria used to divide securities into three groups, such as nationality and reporting status of the issuer and the degree of U.S. market interest in the issuer's securities, were chosen because they reflect the likelihood of flowback into the United States and the degree of information available to U.S. investors regarding such securities.

* * *

a.   *Category 1: Foreign Issuers With No Substantial U.S. Market Interest;*
        Overseas Directed Offerings; Securities Backed by the Full Faith and
        Credit of a Foreign Government; Employee Benefit Plans

The first issuer safe harbor category is available for offers and sales of securities of foreign issuers with no "substantial U.S. market interest" for their securities, securities offered and sold in "overseas directed offerings," securities backed by the full faith and credit of a foreign government, and securities offered and sold pursuant to certain employee benefit plans. Securities issued by foreign entities that do not have a substantial U.S. interest in their securities may be expected to flow back or remain in their major or home market, and are not likely to flow into the United States following an offshore offering. Flowback concerns also are limited where securities of a foreign issuer, even with a substantial U.S. market, are offered and sold in an offering directed at residents of a single foreign jurisdiction and conducted in accordance with local laws, and customary local practices and documentation. Flowback concerns are reduced where a U.S. issuer's non-convertible debt securities, asset-backed securities and non-participating preferred stock denominated in a currency other than U.S. dollars are offered and sold in an offering directed at residents of a single foreign jurisdiction, and the offering is conducted in accordance with local laws, and customary local practices and documentation. Securities offered and sold pursuant to employee benefit plans established and administered under foreign law are less likely to flow back into the United States where steps are taken to preclude sales to U.S. residents (other than employees on temporary assignment in the United States) and other conditions specified in the Regulation are met.

Offers and sales of securities included in this category may be made in reliance on the safe harbor without any limitations or restrictions other than the general conditions that the transaction be offshore and that no directed selling efforts be made in the United States. Offers and sales of securities to U.S. investors who are overseas at such time will not preclude reliance on the safe harbor for securities in this category. Of course, trading of a substantial amount of such securities in the United States shortly after they had been offered offshore may indicate a plan or scheme to evade the registration provisions; where a transaction is part of such a plan or scheme, Regulation S is not available.

(1) *"Substantial U.S. Market Interest"*

      * * *

A "substantial U.S. market interest" in a class of a foreign issuer's equity securities is defined to exist where at the commencement of the offering (a) the securities exchanges and inter-dealer quotation systems in the United States in the aggregate constitute the single largest market for such securities in the shorter of the issuer's prior fiscal year or the period since the issuer's incorporation or (b) 20 percent or more of the trading in the class of securities took place in, on or through the facilities of securities exchanges and inter-dealer quotation systems in the United States and less than 55 percent of such trading took place in, on or through the facilities of securities markets of a single foreign country in the shorter of the issuer's prior fiscal year or the period since the issuer's incorporation.

Commenters on the Reproposing Release expressed concern that defining substantial U.S. market interest by use of percentage and numerical tests would present difficulties because records of trading in an issuer's equity securities may be inaccessible or incomplete. In response to those concerns, the Regulation as adopted permits an issuer to rely upon its reasonable belief as to the existence of a substantial U.S. market interest. Where a foreign or domestic market does not record all trading in a security, only the trading that is recorded (to the extent such information is available to the issuer), is otherwise known to the issuer, or can be reasonably measured or approximated need be considered. Where a substantial market for the issuer's equity securities does not record trading volume, the issuer may reasonably believe there is not a substantial U.S. market interest in that class of securities where less than 20 percent of the class is held of record by persons for whom a U.S. address appears on the records of the issuer, its transfer agent, voting trustee, depositary or person performing similar functions.

A "substantial U.S. market interest" in an issuer's debt securities is dependent upon the aggregation of three types of securities. In addition to traditional debt securities, outstanding non-convertible capital stock, the holders of which are entitled to a preference in payment of dividends and in distribution of assets on liquidation, dissolution or winding up of the issuer, but are not entitled to participate in residual earnings or assets of the issuer (referred to hereinafter as "non-participating preferred stock"), is now included in the measurement of U.S. market interest in debt. * * *

With respect to debt securities, substantial U.S. market interest is measured at the commencement of the offering and is defined as: (A) the issuer's debt securities, its non-participating preferred stock and its asset-backed securities, in the aggregate, being held of record by 300 or more U.S. persons; (B) $1 billion or more of the principal amount outstanding of its debt securities, the greater of liquidation preference or par value of its non-participating preferred stock, and the principal amount or principal balance of its asset-backed securities, in the aggregate, being held of record by U.S. persons; and (C) 20 percent or more of the principal amount outstanding of its debt securities, the greater of liquidation preference or par value of its non-participating preferred stock, and the principal amount or principal balance of its asset-backed securities, in the aggregate, being held of record by U.S. persons.

Substantial U.S. market interest in warrants is measured by the level of market interest in the securities to be purchased upon exercise of the warrants. Substantial U.S. market interest in non-participating preferred stock and asset-backed securities is measured by use of the debt securities test in the definition.

Foreign issuers with no "substantial U.S. market interest" are eligible to rely on the first category of the issuer safe harbor, whether or not they are reporting under the Exchange Act, have securities listed on a U.S. exchange or quoted on NASDAQ, or sponsor an American depositary receipt ("ADR") facility.

    * * *

(2) "Overseas Directed Offerings"

* * * "Overseas directed offering" includes two classes of securities offerings. The first class involves offerings of securities of foreign issuers directed to residents of a single country other than the United States made in accordance with local laws, and customary practices and documentation of that country. The second class involves offerings of nonconvertible debt securities, asset-backed securities and non-participating preferred stock of domestic issuers directed to residents of a single foreign country in accordance with local laws, and customary practices and documentation of that country, provided that the principal and interest of the securities are denominated in a currency other than U.S. dollars and the securities are neither convertible into U.S. dollar-denominated securities nor linked to U.S. dollars in a manner that has the

effect of converting the securities into U.S. dollar-denominated securities. Related currency or interest rate swap transactions that are commercial in nature will not cause securities denominated in a currency other than the U.S. dollar to be treated as if they were denominated in U.S. dollars.

Of particular importance in the concept of "overseas directed offering" is the requirement that such offerings be "directed" at a single country. Where the foreign issuer, a distributor, any of their respective affiliates, or a person acting on behalf of any of the foregoing, knows or is reckless in not knowing that a substantial portion of the offering will be sold or resold outside that country, the offering will not qualify as an overseas directed offering.

* * *

b. *Category 2: Reporting Issuers; Non–Reporting Foreign Issuers' Debt Securities; Non–Reporting Foreign Issuers' Non–Participating Preferred Stock and Asset–Backed Securities*

Securities of all domestic issuers that file reports under the Exchange Act are subject, under the second safe harbor category, both to the general conditions that an offer or sale be an offshore transaction and that no directed selling efforts may be made in the United States, and to specified selling restrictions. Securities of foreign reporting issuers with substantial U.S. market interest are subject to the same restrictions. The selling restrictions applicable to the second category are designed to protect against an indirect unregistered public offering in the United States during the period the market is most likely to be affected by selling efforts offshore. In the event flowback of reporting issuers' securities does occur after the restricted period, the information relating to such securities publicly available under the Exchange Act generally should be sufficient to ensure investor protection.

The second category also applies to offerings of debt securities of any non-reporting foreign issuer. The inclusion of those offerings in this category reflects the view that offering restrictions applicable to the category provide adequate protection against an indirect U.S. distribution because of the generally institutional nature of the debt market and the trading characteristics of debt securities. Moreover, because debt securities are usually issued in separate classes or series, debt securities can be tracked more easily to detect use of offshore transactions to evade the registration obligation for distributions into the United States.

Reflecting public comment, certain equity securities of non-reporting foreign issuers have been moved to this category from the more restrictive third issuer safe harbor category because of the similarity of the market for these securities to the debt market. Non-participating preferred stock and asset-backed securities of non-reporting foreign issuers are now included in the second category.

Two types of selling restrictions exist for securities in the second category—"transactional restrictions" and "offering restrictions."

(1) *Transactional Restrictions*

Transactional restrictions require that the securities sold under the safe harbor prior to the expiration of a 40–day restricted period not be offered or sold to or for the benefit or account of a U.S. person. Persons relying on the second issuer safe harbor category are required to ensure (by whatever means they choose) that any non-distributor to whom they sell securities is a non-U.S. person and is not purchasing for the account or benefit of a U.S. person. Transactional restrictions also require a distributor selling securities to certain securities professionals to send a confirmation or notice to such purchasers advising that the purchaser is subject to the same restrictions on offers and sales that apply to a distributor.

(a) *U.S. Person*

Rule 902(*o*) contains a definition of the term "U.S. person." Unlike no-action letters pursuant to Release 4708, U.S. residency rather than U.S. citizenship is the principal factor in the test of a natural person's status as a U.S. person under Regulation S. Thus, for example, a French citizen resident in the United States is a U.S. person.

Trusts and estates generally are U.S. persons for purposes of the Regulation if any trustee, executor or administrator is a U.S. person. In response to commenters' concerns with respect to the competitive effects on U.S. professional fiduciaries, the definition of U.S. person has been revised so that an estate with a U.S. professional fiduciary acting as executor or administrator is not deemed a U.S. person if: an executor or administrator who is not a U.S. person has sole or shared investment discretion with respect to the estate assets, and the estate is governed by foreign law. An exclusion from the definition of U.S. person is provided for a trust with a U.S. professional fiduciary acting as trustee, provided a trustee who is not a U.S. person has sole or shared investment discretion with respect to the trust assets, and no beneficiary (and no settlor if the trust is revocable) is a U.S. person.

With respect to forms of business organization, such as corporations and partnerships, the definition codifies and elaborates on positions set forth in no-action letters. With regard to such entities, the place of incorporation or organization generally controls. The status of subsidiaries and affiliated companies, which generally have separate legal identities, is determined according to the place of incorporation or organization. An entity organized under foreign law by a U.S. person principally for the purpose of investing in unregistered securities is a U.S. person unless organized and owned by accredited investors (as defined in Regulation D) who are not natural persons, estates or trusts.

A branch or agency of a foreign entity is treated as a U.S. person if it is located in the United States. Branches and agencies of U.S. banks and insurance companies located outside the United States are not treated as U.S. persons, if they: (i) operate for valid business reasons; (ii) are engaged in the banking or insurance business; and (iii) are subject to substantive local banking or insurance regulation.

With respect to fiduciary accounts (other than trusts and estates), the definition generally treats the person with the investment discretion as the buyer; therefore the status of that person governs. Thus, where a U.S. person has discretion to make investment decisions for the account of a non-U.S. person, the account is treated as a U.S. person. Conversely, where a non-U.S. person makes investment decisions for the account of a U.S. person, that account is not treated as a U.S. person. Several exceptions from that general principle, however, are established in the definition.

* * *

(b) *Measurement of the Restricted Period*

The 40–day restricted period begins to run on the later of the date of the closing of the offering or the date the first offer of the securities to persons other than distributors is made.

(2) *Offering Restrictions*

"Offering restrictions" are procedures that must be adopted with regard to the entire offering by the issuer, distributors, their respective affiliates, and all persons acting on behalf of any of the foregoing, in order for a transaction to be in compliance with the second or third categories of the issuer safe harbor. Failure to implement the offering restrictions precludes the availability of the issuer safe harbor for all parties. In effect, offering restrictions are procedures set up by such persons to ensure compliance with the transactional restrictions, particularly the restrictions on offer or sale of the securities to or for the account or benefit of U.S. persons. When the issuer, a distributor, an affiliate of either, or a person acting on behalf of any of the foregoing, is the seller of securities, that person is in a position to ensure, and should ensure, that procedures designed to discourage flowback are used with respect to the entire offering.

* * *

The offering restrictions require distributors, who by definition are participating in the distribution pursuant to a contractual arrangement, to contract that all their offers and sales of the securities will be made in accordance with the safe harbor (or pursuant to registration under the Securities Act or an exemption therefrom).

The issuer, distributors, their respective affiliates, and persons acting on behalf of any of the foregoing, must ensure that certain materials disclose that the securities have not been registered and may not be offered or sold in the United States or to a U.S. person (other than a distributor), unless registered or an exemption from registration is available. Disclosure of the restrictions must appear in any prospectus, offering circular or other document (other than a press release) used in connection with the distribution prior to the expiration of the restricted period. All advertisements relating to the securities are subject to that requirement. The disclosure may appear in summary form on prospectus cover pages and in advertisements.

c. *Category 3: Non–Reporting U.S. Issuers; Equity Offerings by Non–Reporting Foreign Issuers With Substantial U.S. Market Interest*

All securities not covered by the prior two categories fall into this residual category, which is subject to procedures intended to protect against an unregistered U.S. distribution where there is little (if any) information available to the marketplace about the issuer and its securities and there is a significant likelihood of flowback. This category includes securities of non-reporting U.S. issuers and equity securities of non-reporting foreign issuers with substantial U.S. market interest in their equity securities.

As in the case of securities of reporting issuers, offerings of securities in this category are subject to the two general conditions and to offering and transactional restrictions. Offering restrictions that must be adopted for offerings of these securities are the same as for offerings of securities of reporting issuers. In contrast to offerings in the second category, more restrictive transactional restrictions to prevent flowback are applicable.

In essence, the restrictive procedures are similar to those that evolved under the no-action letters involving Release 4708. * * * These distinguish between debt and equity securities, recognizing that debt securities are generally sold in institutional markets and that the likelihood of flowback is less than in the case of common equity. The category includes a restricted period of one year for equity securities and forty days for debt securities. Two types of a non-reporting U.S. issuers' securities, which would include non-convertible, nonparticipating preferred stock and asset-backed securities, will be subject to the same restrictions as debt securities in the third category, including a 40–day restricted period rather than a one-year restricted period. Offerings of securities of a non-reporting foreign issuer of those two types have been added to the second issuer safe harbor category.

* * * Prior to the expiration of the one-year restricted period, the securities may not be sold to U.S. persons or for the account or benefit of U.S. persons (other than distributors). Purchasers of the securities (other than distributors) are required to certify that they are not U.S. persons and are not acquiring the securities for the account or benefit of a U.S. person other than persons who purchased securities in transactions exempt from the registration requirements of the Securities Act. Such purchasers are also required to agree only to sell the securities in accordance with the registration provisions of the Securities Act or an exemption therefrom, or in accordance with the provisions of the Regulation.

With respect to equity securities of domestic issuers, the safe harbor requires that a legend be placed on the shares stating that transfer is prohibited other than in accordance with the Regulation. The safe harbor further requires that any issuer, by contract or a provision in its bylaws, articles, charter or comparable document, refuse to register any transfer of equity securities not made in accordance with the provisions of the Regulation. Where bearer securities are being sold, or foreign law prevents an issuer from refusing to register securities transfers, use of reasonable procedures, such as a legend, will suffice to satisfy the requirement designed to prevent transfer of equity securities other than in accordance with the Regulation.

Purchasers of debt securities offered under the third issuer safe harbor category (other than distributors) are subject to different restrictions than equity purchasers under this category. Prior to the expiration of the forty day restricted period, the securities may not be sold to U.S. persons or for the account or benefit of U.S. persons (other than distributors). The debt securities must be represented by temporary global securities not exchangeable for definitive securities until expiration of the restricted period. Upon expiration, persons exchanging their temporary global security for the definitive security are required to certify beneficial ownership by: a non-U.S. person or a U.S. person who purchased securities in a transaction that did not require registration under the Securities Act.

Distributors selling equity or debt securities prior to the expiration of the restricted period are required to send a confirmation or other notice to purchasers who are distributors, dealers or persons receiving remuneration in connection with the sale. The notice must state that the purchaser is subject to the same restrictions on offers and sales as the distributor. Non-distributors are not required to send such a confirmation or notice.

3. *Resale Safe Harbor*

* * *

Persons other than: (1) dealers and persons receiving a selling concession, fee or other remuneration in respect of the securities offered or sold, which may include sub-underwriters (all referred to herein as "securities professionals"), and (2) affiliated officers and directors eligible to rely upon the resale safe harbor, may resell any securities in reliance on this safe harbor, with no restrictions other than the general conditions that the offer and sale be made in an offshore transaction (including offers and sales in a designated offshore securities market not prearranged with a buyer in the United States) and without directed selling efforts within the United States.

Resales by securities professionals also are subject to the offshore transaction requirement and the prohibition on directed selling efforts (and the conditions applying to affiliated officers and directors, as applicable). In addition, if the securities being resold are not in the first issuer safe harbor category and the resale is made prior to the expiration of any applicable restricted period, neither the securities professional nor any person acting on its behalf may knowingly offer or sell to a U.S. person. Further, if the selling securities professional or a person acting on its behalf knows the purchaser of the securities is a securities professional, the seller is required to send a confirmation or other notice of the applicable restrictions to the purchaser.

The resale safe harbor is available for the resale offshore of any securities, whether or not acquired in an offshore transaction under Regulation S. Resales pursuant to Rule 904 of securities originally placed privately will not affect the validity of the private placement exemption relied upon by the issuer.

4. *Safe Harbor Protections*

If an issuer, distributor, any of their respective affiliates (other than officers and directors relying on the resale safe harbor), or any person acting on behalf of any of the foregoing: (1) fails to comply with the offering restrictions; or (2) engages in a directed selling effort in the United States, the Rule 903 safe harbor is unavailable to any person in connection with the offering of securities. If the issuer, a distributor, any of such respective affiliates, or any person acting on behalf of any of the foregoing, fails to comply with any other requirement of the issuer safe harbor, the safe harbor is not available for any offer or sale in reliance thereon made by the person failing to comply, its affiliates or persons acting on their behalf. The availability of Rule 903 for other persons' offers and sales of securities is unaffected.

Under the reproposal, the failure to comply with the conditions, other than the offering restrictions and the restrictions on directed selling efforts in the United States, would have precluded reliance upon the safe harbor only for non-complying offers and sales. Under Rule 903 as adopted, reliance upon the safe harbor for all offers and sales made by a non-complying person and its affiliates is precluded as an appropriate incentive to comply fully with the conditions of the safe harbor.

The availability of the Rule 904 resale safe harbor generally is unaffected by the actions of the issuer, distributor, their respective affiliates (other than certain officers and directors relying upon Rule 904), or persons acting on behalf of any of the foregoing. An offer or sale of securities made in compliance with the provisions of Rule 904 is within the safe harbor, notwithstanding non-complying offers or resales by other unaffiliated persons not acting on behalf of the seller.

As Preliminary Note 2 states, the Regulation is not available to any transaction or series of transactions that, although in technical compliance with the rules, is part of a plan or scheme to evade the registration provisions of the Securities Act. Thus, for example, a participant in a distribution, regardless of whether it literally takes all steps required for reliance upon the protection of the Regulation, does not have the protection of the Regulation if it knows or is reckless in not knowing that a person to whom it sells securities in reliance upon the Regulation will not comply with the requirements. Clearly, if an underwriter were told by a dealer to whom it intended to sell securities in reliance upon Rule 903 that the dealer had a customer in New York waiting for the securities, that underwriter would not be able to rely upon the protection of the Rule in connection with its sale to that dealer, even if the underwriter complied with all the Regulation's requirements. The same would be true if the underwriter knew or was reckless in not knowing that the dealer to whom it intended to sell had consistently sold to U.S. residents in violation of resale restrictions in other offerings made pursuant to the safe harbor provisions of the Regulation. If, on the other hand, an underwriter sold to a dealer and the dealer sold to a customer in the United States, and the underwriter did not know and was not reckless in failing to know that the non-conforming sale would occur, the underwriter would not lose the protection of the safe harbor.

C. *Interaction with Other Securities Act Provisions*

1. *Contemporaneous U.S. and Offshore Offerings*

Offshore transactions made in compliance with Regulation S will not be integrated with registered domestic offerings or domestic offerings that satisfy the requirements for an exemption from registration under the Securities Act, even if undertaken contemporaneously. Resales of securities offered and sold in offshore transactions pursuant to Rule 144A are consistent with Rule 904. Of course, the securities sold pursuant to Rule 144A would be restricted securities.

* * *

Offshore Offers and Sales

Securities Act Release No. 7392.
(February 20, 1997).

* * *

Since the adoption of Regulation S in 1990, the Commission has become aware of uses of Regulation S that the rule not only did not contemplate, but in fact expressly prohibited. Some issuers, affiliates and others involved in the distribution process are using Regulation S as a guise for distributing securities into the U.S. markets without the protections of registration under Section 5 of the Securities Act. In June 1995, the Commission issued an interpretive release that listed certain problematic practices under Regulation S and requested comment on whether the Regulation should be amended to limit its vulnerability to abuse.[8]

8. Securities Act Release No. 7190 (June 27, 1995) (the "Interpretive Release").

As a result of the continuation of certain of these abusive practices and in response to the comment letters received on the Interpretive Release, the Commission is proposing to stop these abusive practices by amending Regulation S for placements of equity securities by domestic companies. In addition, although abusive practices involving the equity securities of foreign issuers are not as evident as with domestic issuers, there is equal potential for abuse where the principal trading market for those securities is in the United States. Therefore, the Commission also is proposing to amend the safe harbor procedures for placements of equity securities of foreign issuers where the principal market for those securities is in the United States. In general, the "principal market" would be in the United States if more than half of the trading in that security takes place in the United States.

These Regulation S proposals would:

• classify these equity securities placed offshore under Regulation S as "restricted securities" within the meaning of Rule 144;

• align the Regulation S restricted period for these equity securities with the Rule 144 holding periods by lengthening from 40 days (currently applicable to reporting issuers) or one year (currently applicable to non-reporting issuers) to two years the period during which persons relying on the Regulation S safe harbor may not sell these equity securities to U.S. persons (unless pursuant to registration or an exemption);

• impose certification, legending and other requirements now only applicable to sales of equity securities by non-reporting issuers;

• require purchasers of these securities to agree not to engage in hedging transactions with regard to such securities unless such transactions are in compliance with the Securities Act;

• prohibit the use of promissory notes as payment for these securities;

• make clear that offshore resales under Rule 901 or 904 of equity securities of these issuers that are "restricted securities," as defined in Rule 144, will not affect the restricted status of those securities.

The combination of these proposed amendments should prevent the sale of equity securities offshore under Regulation S in transactions that effectively result in unregistered distributions of the securities into the U.S. markets

* * *

1. *The Structure of Regulation S.* Although it adopts a broad "territorial" approach to the registration requirement, Regulation S essentially does so by the narrow definitional tactic of defining the terms "offer," "offer to sell," "sell" and "offer to buy." This definitional approach was taken because, at the time Regulation S was adopted the 1933 Act did not then authorize the SEC to adopt broader exemptions based on policy considerations. Today, § 28 of the 1933 Act seemingly would authorize exemptions on such a basis.

2. *Abuse of Regulation S.* As originally adopted, Regulation S represented an immediate liberalization over prior Release 4708, which required a 90 day "seasoning" period. Under Regulation S, foreign issuers without a "substantial U.S. market interest" had no "restricted" or seasoning period, and reporting issuers had only a 40 day period. But Release 7392 shows one consequence of

this liberalization: financial intermediaries could buy stocks at a substantial discount in Regulation S offerings and dump them 40 days later in the U.S. market. Moreover, they could seemingly hedge their holdings over this period by selling the same security short (if it was traded in a U.S. market) at or before the time they bought in the U.S. market. Alternatively, they could purchase their investment with promissory notes (possibly even on a non-recourse basis), so that they were not obligated to pay before they sold. Or, they would use even more sophisticated hedging strategies involving options futures, equity swaps, or other derivatives. To combat this, the SEC suggested in 1995 in Release 7190 that purchasers who sold short at or about the same time they sold were in effect reselling the securities in the U.S. that they had purchased abroad under Regulation S. *Query:* Did this assertion involve an exhumation of the long dead fungibility doctrine that the SEC had long ago abandoned under Rule 144?

3. *The 1998 Reforms.* Following up quickly on its 1997 criticisms of the misuse of Regulation S, the Commission in 1998 amended Rule 903 to increase the period (now described as the "distribution compliance period") from forty days to one year during which an offer or sale of equity securities of a U.S. issuer (or certain foreign issuers) could not be made to a U.S. person (other than a distributor).[1] See Rule 903(b)(3). Effectively, this ended the incentive to use Regulation S as an alternative to a Regulation D private placement. In addition, to achieve full equivalence, equity securities of U.S. issuers that are acquired from the issuer, a distributor, or an affiliate of either, were made "restricted securities" so that they could only be sold in compliance with the volume limitation of Rule 144 (or pursuant to some other exemption—for example, Rule 144A). See Rule 905.

The 1998 reforms also required that purchasers (other than distributors) of equity securities of U.S. issuers must certify that they are not U.S. persons and are not acquiring the securities for the benefit of U.S. persons. In addition, all U.S. issuers of equity securities in Regulation S transactions must (i) place into effect a stop transfer instruction to prevent resales not in accordance with Regulation S, and (ii) include a restrictive legend on the share certificates forbidding resales in violation of the 1933 Act. Previously, such restrictions were required only of non-reporting U.S. issuers.

U.S. issuers are also now obligated to report Regulation S sales of equity securities on a quarterly basis on Form 10–Q (thereby alerting the SEC's staff).

4. *Criticisms.* In adopting its 1998 reforms, the SEC was motivated by evidence that U.S. issuers were selling securities at large discounts abroad, which securities would then flow back to the U.S. after the expiration of the then forty day parking period. To the SEC, this suggested that these securities were overvalued and were sold abroad to escape the SEC's scrutiny. Professor Stephen Choi has disagreed. His empirical study finds that foreign investors are unable to resell foreign-issued U.S. securities ahead of the market's negative reaction to the news of a foreign offering pursuant to Regulation S.[2] Thus, he concludes that it is unlikely that the purchasers of U.S. securities in Regulation S offerings are overreaching domestic investors in the U.S. Still, do the deep

---

1. See Securities Act Release 7505 (February 17, 1998).

2. Stephen J. Choi, The Unfounded Fear of Regulation S: Empirical Evidence on Offshore Securities Offerings, 50 Duke L. J. 663 (2000).

discounts at which Regulation S offerings are often made and/or the adverse market reaction to their public announcement suggest that these issuers have made inadequate disclosure to U.S. investors and hence fear registration? In any event, Professor Choi finds the 1998 reforms to be an "untailored response to opportunism" and that they "unnecessarily raise the cost of mitigating the separate overvaluation risk."[3]

5. *Rule 901*. Rule 901 states very generally that "the terms 'offer,' 'offer to sell,' 'sell,' 'sale,'and 'offer to buy' shall be deemed ... not to include offers and sales that occur outside the United States." It had been thought that this broad statement would have little impact, with the real work of Regulation S being performed by the much more complicated Rule 903 and the two resale rules, Rule 904 and 905. However, in *Europe & Overseas Commodity Traders v. Banque Paribas*,[4] the Second Circuit upheld the dismissal of a complaint based on Rule 901 that alleged that a securities transaction occurred within the United States, even though it was unable to conclude that there were no "directed selling efforts" in the U.S. or that the offer was made in an "offshore transaction"—the two critical prerequisites for the application of Rule 903. Essentially, a French investment bank was syndicating the securities of a foreign issuer to foreign institutional investors, and in connection therewith called a foreign agent of a foreign institution who was then working in Florida. This agent faxed back his purchase order from Florida. Finding these contacts with the U.S. to be *de minimis*, the Second Circuit upheld dismissal, based on Rule 901, even though it acknowledged that the plaintiffs had adequately plead that "directed selling efforts" had reached into the U.S. Hence, Rule 901 may work for defendants, even when the safe harbor of Rule 903 is unavailable.

6. *TEFRA D*. A long-standing federal tax policy disfavors the use of bearer bonds because experience has convinced the IRS that many holders of bearer bonds will fail to report interest earned on them. Thus, Section 163(f) of the Internal Revenue Code disallows the issuer an interest deduction on such bonds, and Section 4701 also imposes an excise tax on the issuer. Because bearer bonds are standard in European markets, however, a compromise was necessary between competing IRS and SEC policies. Shortly after the adoption of Regulation S, the Treasury Department adopted new regulations, known as "TEFRA D" that partially shield the issuer from these penalties if during the 40–day restricted period the bearer bonds are sold only abroad "under arrangements reasonably designed to insure that the obligation will be sold * * * only to a person who is not a U.S. person." See Treas.Reg. § 1.163–5(c)(2)(i)(D). The impact of TEFRA D is generally to preclude underwriters or selling group members from selling debt securities in bearer form to U.S. investors.

7. *Business Implications*. As discussed below, a principal significance of Regulation S may lie in its interface with Rule 144A. Together with Rule 144A, Regulation S permits U.S. investment banks to participate as underwriters in an unregistered offshore offering that normally would be closed to U.S. investors and to market a portion of the offering to qualified institutional buyers within the United States. In effect, Regulation S provides a safe harbor for sales of securities outside the U.S., and Rule 144A provides a safe harbor for resales of those securities to institutions in the United States. See American Bar Association, Subcommittee on Annual Review, Survey: Federal Securities Regulation, 44 Bus.Law. 839 (1989). Furthermore, the Regulation S resale safe

3. Id. at 745.   **4.** 147 F.3d 118 (2d Cir. 1998).

harbor (Rule 904) can provide a critical exit from the Rule 144A market to offshore markets, where liquidity for some securities might be substantially greater than in the U.S.

Among the other practical implications of Regulation S are the following:

(1) It shortens the restrictions on continuous offerings. Many issuers in the Eurobond market make continuous offerings of their debt securities and were subject to resale restrictions because these individual offerings could be integrated. Regulation S provides that each identifiable tranche of securities will be subject to a separate seasoning requirement, thus ending the likelihood of integration.

(2) Under Regulation S, underwriters can offer and sell unseasoned securities in some circumstances to (i) discretionary accounts of U.S. investors where the account is managed or co-managed by a fiduciary located outside the United States, and (ii) U.S. fiduciaries who have discretionary authority over the accounts of foreign investors.

(3) Under the resale safe harbor of Rule 904, securities that were privately placed in the United States or sold there under Rule 144A can be resold abroad immediately, including on foreign securities exchanges.

Relationship With Rule 144A. Regulation S's interrelationship with Rule 144A merits special attention and is discussed in the following excerpt:

Excerpt from: Edward A. Perell, James A. Kiernan III and Andrew L. Sommer*

Regulation S and Rule 144A: A Non–US Issuer's Perspective

Welcome to America Foreign Investors, Special Supp. to Sept. 1990 Issues of Corp. Fin. and Int'l Fin.L.Rev. 13–21.**

* * *

Foreign issuers, however, have generally not made wide use of the private placement market because they could get a better deal in foreign markets. In theory, this disparity was at least partially the result of an illiquidity premium required for sales into the private placement market, since resale is restricted for privately placed securities. In the absence of a liquid resale market, buyers required better terms before they would purchase restricted securities.

The SEC hoped that the adoption of Rule 144A, with its streamlined rules for resales of privately placed securities, would fuel the ultimate elimination of the illiquidity premium. PORTAL, a new NASD sponsored automated system for trading of Rule 144A securities by institutional investors that was approved by the SEC on the same day as it adopted Rule 144A, would be an engine that would pump liquidity into the new market. While making the private placement market more attractive for foreign issuers, the interaction of Rule 144A with

* Members of Debevoise & Plimpton's London and Paris offices.

** Reprinted with permission from Issues of Corp. Fin. and Int'l Fin.L.Rev. and the authors. © Copyright 1990 by Euromoney Publications plc.

Regulation S would provide foreign issuers with a new basis for selling their securities into the US during the course of a non-US distribution.

* * *

RELATIONSHIP BETWEEN RULE 144A AND REGULATION S

Perhaps the most significant feature of the new rules from the perspective of foreign issuers is that they will open up new avenues for securities sold outside the US, even securities sold in an offshore public offering, to be resold in the United States without delay or traditional private placement offering restrictions.

In such circumstances the underwriter for the offshore foreign offering (conducted in compliance with Regulation S) or another investment banker would purchase the securities and sell them into the US in a private placement under Rule 144A. Such a resale would generally be subject to a 40–day seasoning period under Regulation S (for issuers under categories two or three)[5] or Section 4(3) of the Securities Act, which provides an exemption from registration for sales by a dealer who is not acting as an underwriter, unless the sale occurs 40 days after the security was first *bona fide* offered to the public or is part of the dealer's unsold allotment as a participant in the distribution of such securities.

Regulation S excepts, however, sales to distributors from the 40–day lock-up requirement, and permits the distributor to resell the securities pursuant to a transaction which is otherwise exempt from registration under the Securities Act, such as a Rule 144A transaction.

Moreover, Regulation S and Rule 144A permit a dealer who has acted as underwriter for the foreign offering under Regulation S to resell its unsold allotment to a QIB under Rule 144A and a dealer who acquires the securities in the secondary market to resell the securities without regard to the 40–day seasoning period. No *bona fide* offering to the public is deemed to have occurred for purposes of Section 4(3)(A) either in connection with the offshore offering or the private placement, since offerings made pursuant to Regulation S and Rule 144A are not public offerings under the Securities Act, and the dealer is not an underwriter.

Similarly, neither the offshore offering nor the private placement constitutes a "distribution" for purposes of Section 4(3)(C), which in this context is synonymous with a US public offering.

DIRECTED SELLING EFFORTS

Would sales into the institutional market in the US be "directed selling efforts" under Regulation S, vitiating the protection afforded by the safe harbour? The question is specifically and helpfully addressed in the adopting release for the Regulation, which provides that "legitimate selling activities carried out in the United States in connection with an offering of securities registered under the Securities Act or exempt from registration pursuant to Section 3 or 4 of the Securities Act would not constitute directed selling efforts with respect to offers and sales made under Regulation S * * *. For example, legitimate US selling activities made in connection with the sale of securities in

---

5. [Eds.—This statement was made prior to the 1998 reforms that extended the lockup period to one year for equity securities of U.S. issuers. It remains accurate, however, for debt securities.]

compliance with Rule 144A * * * generally will not result in directed selling efforts''.

* * *

The registration requirements of Section 12(g) of the Exchange Act will be applicable to foreign private issuers who sell securities pursuant to Rule 144A. An issuer is required to register with the SEC and to satisfy the periodic reporting requirements of the Exchange Act if it has over 500 holders of equity securities and assets totalling at least US$1m. Under Rule 12g3–2(a), equity securities of any class of a foreign issuer are exempt from these requirements if the class has fewer than 300 holders resident in the US. Rule 12g3–2(b) provides a further exemption if the issuer furnishes to the SEC whatever information the issuer, since the beginning of its last fiscal year (a) has made or is required to make public pursuant to the law of the country of its domicile or in which it is incorporated or organized, (b) has filed or is required to file with a stock exchange on which its securities are traded and which was made public by such exchange, or (c) has distributed to its security holders.

If a liquid market for resale of restricted securities does indeed develop as a result of the adoption of Rule 144A, it is reasonable to expect that increasing numbers of foreign issuers will find themselves with in excess of 300 US security holders. The availability of the Rule 12g3–2(b) exemption will, however, enable such foreign issuers to avoid the burdens of Exchange Act reporting, which would require many of the same disclosures that foreign issuers find objectionable in the Securities Act context, by filing their home country reports with the SEC. The information contained in such filings would then become subject to the antifraud provisions of the US securities laws described above.

* * *

The adoption of Rule 144A and Regulation S represents a major step by the SEC in its effort to adapt US securities regulation to the realities of an emerging global securities market. Foreign issuers will derive significant benefits under the liberalized regime created by the rules. Although the regulatory barriers which historically have discouraged foreign issuers from entering the US public markets will remain intact, the adoption of the rules will provide foreign issuers with increased access to the US private capital market. Enhanced liquidity resulting from the streamlined resale procedures of Rule 144A should allow for far more favourable pricing of issues than has been true in the past, increasing the allure of the private placement market for foreign issuers. At the same time, moreover, the safe harbour of Regulation S will provide foreign issuers with increased protection from the complex registration requirements of the Securities Act in connection with their offshore offerings.[a]

SECTION 7. RESTRICTIONS ON RESALES OF SECURITIES ISSUED IN REORGANIZATIONS AND RECAPITALIZATIONS AND UNDER THE BANKRUPTCY REFORM ACT OF 1978

The Section 3 Transaction Exemptions: Sections 3(a)(9) through 3(a)(11). Section 3 purports to exempt from the registration and prospectus require-

a. And see E. Greene, A. Beller, G. Cohen, M. Hudson, Jr., & E. Rosen, U.S. Regulation of the International Securities Markets—A Guide for Domestic and Foreign Issuers and Intermediaries Ch. 4 (1992).

ments of Section 5 various classes of securities. However, only the securities falling under §§ 3(a)(2) through 3(a)(8) possess inherent characteristics which make them appropriate subjects of a permanent exemption from federal regulation.

In Securities Act Release No. 646, supra page 475, the SEC General Counsel took the position that § 3(a)(9) merely exempts the transaction of exchange and not the securities themselves. Otherwise, § 3(a)(9) literally would allow a group in control of a corporation to engineer a voluntary recapitalization for the purpose of liberating the control shares from the registration and prospectus requirements of § 5.

The General Counsel's position has been adopted by the Commission. In Thompson Ross Securities Co.[1], the Commission spiked an attempt to use a stock split to secure for control shares a permanent immunity from registration, by reading Section 3 this way:[2]

> Unlike securities which fall within Sections 3(a)(2) to 3(a)(8), inclusive, of the Act, there is nothing in the intrinsic nature of the securities falling within Section 3(a)(9) which justifies their permanent exemption from registration. The basis of the exemption under Section 3(a)(9) is merely the circumstances surrounding the issuance of securities.

> The sale to the public of a large block of securities previously exempted from registration when they were exchanged for other securities possesses all the dangers attendant upon a new offering of securities to the public by the issuer. Section 3(a)(9) does not, therefore, permanently exempt securities offered in a transaction of exchange. This view is confirmed by the legislative history of the Act.

On this basis, the same principles are regarded as applicable to securities issued in a judicially or administratively approved exchange under § 3(a)(10); to securities issued under the intrastate exemption of § 3(a)(11); and to securities exempted from registration by Commission rule issued under §§ 3(b) and (c). Indeed, since these exemptions are regarded as transaction exemptions, from the standpoint of good drafting, they properly belong in § 4. In the abortive 1941 amendment program, which was interrupted by World War II, the House Committee Print of a SEC Report on proposals for amendments of the Securities Act had this to say:[3]

> The act exempts certain securities not because of their inherent attributes but because of the circumstances surrounding their issuance. These exemptions are contained in sections * * * 3(a)(9), 3(a)(10), 3(a)(11), and 3(b) of the act. Since these are in reality transaction exemptions rather than security exemptions, the Commission proposes and representatives of the securities industry agree that they should be redesignated as transaction exemptions and transferred to section 4.

This remains the generally accepted view both within and without the Commission, even though the transfer has never occurred.

---

1. 6 S.E.C. 1111 (1940).

2. Id. at 1118.

3. SEC, Report on Proposals for Amendments to the Securities Act of 1933 and the Securities Exchange Act of 1934, submitted by the SEC on August 7, 1941 during the Hearings Before the Committee on Interstate and Foreign Commerce of the House of Representatives, 77th Cong., 1st Sess. 24 (Comm.Print 1941).

Resales of Section 3(a)(9) Securities. Since § 3(a)(9) is a transaction exemption, the normal rules for the sale of unregistered securities should be applicable. Nonaffiliates of the issuer who exchange unrestricted stock for securities in a § 3(a)(9) exchange may rely upon the § 4(1) exemption on the basis that the transaction is by a person other than an issuer, underwriter, or dealer. If, however, a nonaffiliated person exchanges restricted securities as defined in Rule 144(a)(3), resales may be made only pursuant to registration or in accordance with Rules 144 or 144A. However, the tacking provisions of 144(d)(3)(i), (ii) or (iii) will apply. These sections provide that securities acquired in stock splits, recapitalizations or conversions shall be deemed to have been acquired at the same time as the securities surrendered on the exchange or, in the case of the contingent issuance of securities, at the time of sale.

If an affiliated person surrenders restricted securities in a § 3(a)(9) exchange, whether public or private, the securities received are restricted. Under Rule 144(d)(3), tacking will be allowed to reduce the holding period as in the case of nonaffiliates. No tacking, however, is permitted where the affiliate resells the securities as the purchase from an affiliate triggers the commencement of a new holding period for the new owner.[4] Presumably, an affiliated person who engages in a § 3(a)(9) transaction would retain that status after the exchange, although that would not necessarily be the case in, for example, a preferred stock bail-out. In that event, would the recipient still be locked-in and be subject to the registration provisions or Rules 144 or 144A in connection with subsequent resales?

Even though an exchange of securities would seem to qualify for an exemption under both § 3(a)(9) and § 4(2), the Commission has sometimes sought to deny the § 3(a)(9) exemption and assert that since the exchange resembles a private placement, the securities so received in the exchange are restricted securities, and subject to the holding period of Rule 144(d) or that the transaction is a "negotiated" exchange, rather than a "recapitalization" within the meaning of Rule 144(d)(3)(i).[5] This position does not seem to have been tested in the courts and appears extremely doubtful, provided all of the conditions of § 3(a)(9) have been met. Indeed, the Staff apparently no longer insists on this narrow interpretation of § 3(a)(9). This switch is consistent with the abandonment of the former requirement that restricted securities be held for the full holding period by each successive owner before permitting Rule 144 sales.[6]

Resales of Registered Securities Issued Pursuant to Rule 145. Rule 145 provides that certain transactions involving reclassifications, mergers and sale-of-assets reorganizations are subject to the registration requirements of the 1933 Act. Furthermore, in paragraphs (c) and (d), the rule states that persons who are affiliates of target companies which are acquired in a Rule 145 transaction in the event of resale shall be deemed to be engaged in a distribution and therefore underwriters of the securities received by them in such

---

4. See Rule 144(d)(1). Cf. Rule 144(d)(3).

5. See generally, 7 J.W. Hicks, Exempted Transactions Under the Securities Act of 1933, § 2.08[2][b] (1991 rev.). There is some disagreement among commentators on this point. Others maintain, and the bar generally asserts, that securities received in a Section 3(a)(9) exchange are restricted only if the securities surrendered were restricted. See Campbell, Resales of Securities Under the Securities Act of 1933, 52 Wash. & Lee L. Rev. 1333, 1356–69 (1995).

6. Id.

transactions. Resales of the 145 securities outside of registration may only be made in accordance with the conditions, other than the holding period and notice requirements, of Rule 144, or in accordance with Rule 144A. Thus, in a mini-acquisition, a person who controlled a target corporation, but was not in a control relationship with the acquiring company, would be subject to the information, volume and manner of sale provisions of Rule 144, even though the person received an insubstantial amount of securities in the acquirer. Because Rule 145 is an exclusive rule, unlike Rule 144, it forecloses reliance on the § 4(1) exemption for the resale of securities.[7] On the other hand, if the transaction is structured as a registered stock-for-stock exchange reorganization with an S-4 registration, nonaffiliates of the acquiring corporation may resell their securities without restrictions, unless they propose to make resales in sufficient quantities to trigger the presumptive underwriter doctrine.[8]

The Commission ultimately recognized that, in a Rule 145 transaction, to stigmatize such nonaffiliated persons as underwriters for an indefinite period was unduly burdensome and unnecessary for the protection of investors. Rule 145, as amended, now provides that a recipient of Rule 145 securities from the issuer may resell such securities without any limitations after they have been held for one year, provided that the holder is not affiliated with the issuer and that certain other conditions relating to the issuer are met. These conditions require that the issuer of the Rule 145 securities meets the information requirements of Rule 144(c).

Moreover, an affiliate of the issuer who is no longer affiliated, and has not been affiliated for at least three months, may resell such securities without any limitations if a period of two years has elapsed since the date the securities were acquired from the issuer in the transaction. The one or two year holding periods are computed under Rules 144(d) or (k).

Rule 144(d)(3)(viii) provides that the holding period for securities acquired in a Rule 145(a) transaction shall commence on the date the securities were acquired by the purchaser. That provision, however, does not apply to a transaction effected solely for the purpose of forming a holding company. Tacking is permitted in such a transaction only if four conditions are met: (1) the holding company shares are issued solely in exchange for shares of the operating company; (2) security holders receive securities of the same class and in the same proportions as securities exchanged; (3) the holding company is formed to serve as a vehicle to effect the transaction, possesses no significant assets except operating company securities after the transaction, and, following the exchange, has substantially the same assets and liabilities, on a consolidated basis, as those possessed by the operating company immediately prior to the exchange; and (4) the interests of the common shareholders in the holding company are substantially the same as those previously possessed as common shareholders in the operating company.[9]

Persons who were not affiliates of either the target corporation or the acquiring corporation are not deemed to be underwriters as defined in paragraph (c) of Rule 145. Accordingly, they may resell their Rule 145 securities,

7. Securities Act Release No. 5932 (May 15, 1978).

8. See supra, at page 495.

9. Securities Act Release No. 6862, Fed. Sec.L.Rep. (CCH) No. 1390, Extra Edition (Apr. 27, 1990) at 54. And see Morgan, Olmstead, Kennedy & Gardner Capital Corp. no action letter [1987–1988 Transfer Binder] Fed.Sec.L.Rep. (CCH) ¶ 78,672 (avail. Dec. 8, 1987).

based on the exemption afforded by § 4(1). And, apparently, the Staff does not apply the presumptive underwriter doctrine in this context, as is done in traditional registered offerings.[10] Finally, even though restricted stock is exchanged for Rule 145 securities, a nonaffiliated person would be immediately free to resell publicly all of the securities which were acquired in the transaction.[11]

Securities Act Release No. 5463

Securities and Exchange Commission.
February 28, 1974.

DIVISION OF CORPORATION FINANCE'S INTERPRETATIONS OF RULE 145 AND RELATED MATTERS

* * *

IV.   *Resales of Securities Acquired in Rule 145 Transactions (See Paragraphs (c), (d) and (e) of Rule 145).*

Illustration A

Facts: X Company filed a registration statement on Form S–1 covering the proposed issuance of its common stock (but not covering the resale thereof) in connection with a proposed acquisition of Y Company in a Rule 145 type statutory merger which, if approved by Y Company's stockholders, would result in Y Company's stockholders receiving common stock of X Company. X Company's registration statement indicates that, for accounting purposes, the acquisition will be treated as a purchase.

Question A–1: Assuming for the purposes of this question only that A is a controlling person of X Company and also owns common stock of Y Company, would his resales of the X Company common stock which he receives in this transaction be subject to the limitations of Rule 145(d)?

Interpretative Response: No. Inasmuch as A controls X Company, he is already deemed to be an affiliate of X Company and is subject to the provisions of Rule 144. Accordingly, the resale of any additional shares of X Company common stock, which he acquires in a Rule 145 transaction or otherwise, is subject to the provisions of Rule 144.

Question A–2: Assuming for the purposes of this question only that B does not own any common stock of X Company but is a controlling person of Y Company and that after the merger he will become a controlling person of X Company, would his resales of the X Company common stock which he receives in this transaction be subject to the limitations of Rule 145(d).

Interpretative Response: No. Inasmuch as B will become a controlling person of X Company, he would be deemed to be an affiliate of X Company. By virtue of his becoming an affiliate of X Company, B would become subject to

---

10. Cyprus Mines Corp., 1978 SEC No–Act. LEXIS 701 (Mar. 2, 1978); Ash, Reorganizations and Other Exchanges Under Section 3(a)(10) of the Securities Act of 1933, 75 Sw.U.L.Rev. 1, 81 at note 423 (1980).

11. Securities Act Release 5463 (Feb. 28, 1974), at IV, Illus. A, Q. A–4, infra at page 612.

Rule 144 and the resale of all of his X Company common stock would be subject to the provisions of Rule 144.

Question A–3: Assuming for the purposes of this question only that C is an affiliate of Y Company but not of X Company; what restrictions are imposed by Rule 145(d) on C's public resale of the X Company common stock which he receives in the Rule 145 transaction?

[Under Rule 145(d)(2), C may resell such Rule 145 securities without any limitation after they have been held for one year provided that the issuer meets the qualifications of 145(d)(2).]

* * *

Question A–4: Assuming for the purposes of this question only that D is not an affiliate of X Company or of Y Company and that his only relationship to the transaction is that he owns Y Company common stock, some of which was purchased previously in a private offering, would D be immediately free to resell publicly all of the X Company common stock which he receives in the transaction?

Interpretative Response: Yes. Since D is not an affiliate of X Company or Y Company then he is not deemed to be an underwriter with respect to the securities he receives in the Rule 145 transaction. Accordingly, D is immediately free to resell publicly all of the X Company common stock which he receives in the transaction regardless of whether some of his Y Company common stock was restricted.

RESALES OF SECTION 3(a)(10) SECURITIES

Since Section 3(a)(10) is a transaction exemption, affiliates of the acquiring corporation are subject to the usual restrictions applicable to persons in a control relationship with the issuer of the securities. In the absence of registration, they may resell in a private sale pursuant to the Section "4(1½)" exemption or in accordance with all of the conditions of Rule 144, except for the one-year holding period, or Rule 144A. If the securities exchanged for the § 3(a)(10) securities had been acquired in a private placement and qualified as restricted securities under Rule 144(a)(3), the one-year holding period would be applicable; however the holder may tack his or her holding period of the exchanged securities in computing the one-year holding period under Rule 144(d).

In *NWS Enterprises, Inc.*,[1] the Staff issued a no-action letter which laid down rules with respect to resales of securities in transactions governed by Rule 145 of the 1933 Act, but where registration is not required because of compliance with the § 3(a)(10) exemption. These rules, as announced, however, apply only where: (1) all of the parties to the transaction are registered under § 12 of the 1934 Act and are required to comply with the proxy solicitation requirements of § 14 of that Act; and (2) the issuer will be subject to the § 13 or § 15(d) reporting requirements after the transaction is consummated.

First, securities of an issuer received in a business combination exempt from registration under § 3(a)(10) are not deemed to be "restricted" if issued in exchange for securities that are not restricted.

Second, as previously stated, securities acquired in exchange for "restricted securities" in a Section 3(a)(10) transaction continue to be "restricted," but the

---

1. 1980 SEC No–Act. LEXIS 3877 (Oct. 30, 1980).

holder may tack the holding period of the exchanged securities in computing the one-year holding requirement of Rule 144(d).

Third, persons who are not affiliates of any party to the business combination and who are not affiliates of the surviving issuer may freely resell securities received on a § 3(a)(10) transaction in exchange for their unrestricted securities pursuant to the exemption from registration specified in § 4(1) of the 1933 Act, provided that the issuer meets the information and reporting requirements of Rule 144(c).

Since all parties to the reorganization are subject to the periodic reporting requirements of § 13(d) and the proxy solicitation requirements of § 14 of the 1934 Act, there would generally be available adequate information both at the time of issuance of the securities as well as after the transaction. Accordingly, in this situation, the Staff waived the condition generally imposed in § 3(a)(10) transactions that if a nonaffiliate receives an amount of securities in the transaction that are "substantial" in amount as compared to the total amount of securities issued in the transaction, resales must be made in compliance with paragraphs (c), (e), (f) and (g) of Rule 144. The staff appears to regard an amount which exceeds one percent of the total amount of securities issued in the transaction as being substantial for this purpose. This condition represents an application of the "presumptive underwriter" doctrine. See supra at page 531.

Fourth, by analogy to Rule 145, affiliates of an acquired company, who are not affiliates of the acquiring company, will be deemed to be engaged in a distribution and therefore underwriters of the securities received by them in the transaction. However, resales may be made pursuant to the leakage provisions of Rule 145(d) and such persons are given the benefit of the one-year cutoff provision of Rule 145(d)(2).

Fifth, persons who become affiliates of the issuer in connection with a § 3(a)(10) transaction may sell securities acquired in such transactions pursuant to Rule 144 or Rule 144A, except that the one-year holding period is applicable only to the extent that it applied to the securities exchanged in the transaction.[2]

---

2. See generally, 1 Securities Law Techniques § 6.05 (A.A. Sommer, Jr. ed. 1990 rev.); 7 J. Hicks, Exempted Transactions Under the Securities Act of 1933, § 3.06 (1991 rev.); 3 L. Loss & J. Seligman, Securities Regulation 1588 (3d ed. 1989).

*

PART III

REGULATION OF TRADING IN SECURITIES

THE SECURITIES EXCHANGE ACT OF 1934: AN OVERVIEW

The Securities Act of 1933 is a more or less coherent and unified statute directed almost entirely at two fundamental objectives: full disclosure in connection with the distribution of securities and the prevention of fraud in the sale of securities. The Securities Exchange Act of 1934 (the "1934 Act"), on the other hand, is something of a hodge-podge of different provisions, some of which are largely unrelated to others. Over time, whenever there has been a crisis or a new challenge, Congress's typical response has been to amend the 1934 Act to deal with the new issue or problem. The 2001–2002 corporate governance and accounting scandals, which began with the Enron bankruptcy, have proven no exception to this generalization and have resulted in major new legislation: "The Public Company Accounting Reform and Investor Protection Act of 2002" (the "2002 Act"), which once again materially amends the 1934 Act.

Unlike the 1933 Act, the 1934 Act's primary focus is not on the issuance of securities, but on the secondary markets in which securities trade and on the provision of adequate and continuing disclosure to those trading in these markets. In order to ensure full and fair disclosure in these markets, the 1934 Act took a number of interrelated steps:

1. *The SEC.* The 1934 Act created the Securities and Exchange Commission to replace the less specialized Federal Trade Commission (which had originally been given jurisdiction over the Securities Act of 1933). Possibly, the intent of some was to substitute a more industry-friendly regulator, but the history of the SEC during the 1930's shows this hope to have been ill-founded.

2. *The Stock Exchanges.* The 1934 Act adopted a comprehensive system of federal regulation over the stock exchanges, including the specialists and broker-dealers who worked on them. Section 5 of the 1934 Act subjected all exchanges to an SEC registration requirement, and § 6 dictated that their rules, regulations, system of governance, and operating procedures meet certain public interest standards. These provisions of the 1934 Act have recently had unintended consequences with the evolution of new electronic trading systems (known as "ECNs") that functionally compete with traditional exchanges but

that would have substantial difficulty in complying with many of the standards and conditions specified in § 6.

Because there was substantial concern in the 1930's about excessive speculation in the securities markets, §§ 7 and 8 established a system of margin regulation which placed controls over the amount of credit that could be extended to finance the purchase of securities. Similarly, § 9 authorized the SEC to prohibit manipulation and to restrict options trading, and § 10(a) gave the SEC power to regulate and restrict short-selling. Both options trading and short-selling were regarded in that Depression era as risky speculative practices that required close regulation in order not to destabilize the markets.[1]

3. *Self–Regulatory Organizations.* A third major focus of the 1934 Act involved conferring on the SEC jurisdiction over broker-dealers. Section 15 ("Registration and Regulation of Brokers and Dealers") of the 1934 Act was the first step in this direction, and it continues to serve as the SEC's authority for broad rules regulating broker-dealer conduct, operations, and financial condition (many of which are prophylactic rules that require no showing of fraud—such as the "net capital" rule). In 1938, a further and, to some extent, duplicative step was taken with the passage of the Maloney Act, which added § 15A to the 1934 Act. This provision established a system of self-regulation for broker-dealers paralleling that earlier created for the exchanges under §§ 5 and 6. Formally, § 15A provided for the registration of an association of broker-dealers that would act as a self-regulatory body. Only one such organization— the National Association of Securities Dealers ("NASD")—has ever been created under § 15A. Today (although not originally), virtually all brokers and dealers must become members of the NASD, because § 15(b)(8) of the 1934 Act makes it "unlawful for any registered broker or dealer to effect any transaction in * * * any security * * * unless such broker or dealer is a member of a securities association registered pursuant to Section 15A of this title * * *."[2] The NASD is not the only self-regulatory organization. The exchanges also enforce rules and administer disciplinary sanction. In 1975, two other SROs were created, one to monitor registered clearing agencies,[3] and the other—the Municipal Securities Rulemaking Board ("MSRB")—to establish rules regulating the conduct of municipal securities brokers and dealers with respect to transactions in such securities.[4] The net result is that all broker-dealers are as a practical matter subject to the active and overlapping oversight of at least two administrative systems (the SEC's and that of at least one SRO), each or both of which can take disciplinary action for violations of their rules. In 1975, Congress enhanced the authority of the SEC over its SROs by amending § 19(b) and (c) of the 1934 Act so that (i) any rule change proposed by an SRO

---

1. This concern about excessive speculation in the securities markets may no longer rank high on the SEC's agenda, but it continues to be stressed by some commentators. See Stout, Are Stock Markets Costly Casinos? Market Failure and Securities Regulation, 81 Va. L. Rev. 611 (1995). For a rejoinder, see Mahoney, Is There a Cure for "Excessive" Trading, 81 Va. L. Rev. 713 (1995).

2. There are some modest exceptions to this requirement, including one for a broker or dealer who effects transactions exclusively on a securities exchange of which it is a member.

3. See § 17A of the 1934 Act. Clearing agencies handle the clearance and settlement of securities transactions and the safeguarding of investors' funds and securities in their custody.

4. See § 15B of the 1934 Act. All municipal securities dealers, including banks, must register with the SEC. The MSRB is composed of fifteen members appointed by the SEC.

must today be approved by the SEC in order to become effective, and (ii) the SEC may in its discretion "abrogate, add to, and delete from" the SRO's rules "as the Commission deems necessary or appropriate to insure the fair administration of the self-regulatory organization * * * [or] otherwise in furtherance of the purposes of this title * * * " Despite this enhanced power, the SROs are far from pawns of the SEC, and the relationship between the SEC and the exchanges or the NASD has at times been relatively adversarial.[5] This topic of self regulation is addressed in more detail in Chapters 10 and 11.

The newest SRO is the Public Company Accounting Oversight Board, which was created by Congress in 2002 in the wake of a series of accounting scandals to supervise the standard setting process for auditing standards and to assume the disciplinary and investigative functions formerly handled by the accounting profession internally. The provisions of the 2002 Act are discussed below.

4. *The Continuous Disclosure System.* A fourth major focus of the 1934 Act was the creation of a continuous disclosure system for publicly held companies. Several different provisions of the 1934 Act combine to produce this continuous disclosure system. Section 12 requires the registration of "listed" or "reporting" companies. Section 13 requires certain periodic reports to keep current the information supplied in the initial registration. Section 14 and Regulation 14A, which implements it, regulate the solicitation of proxies by registered corporations. Section 16 provides for the recapture of certain short-swing profits made in the securities of their companies by officers, directors and 10% stockholders of registered corporations.

Prior to 1964, these various regulations applied only to corporations with securities listed on a national securities exchange. The Securities Acts Amendments of 1964 extended their application to certain publicly-held corporations whose securities were traded in the over-the-counter markets. Today, a company must register a class of equity securities with the SEC if, as of the last day of its fiscal year, that class is held of record by 500 or more holders *and* the issuer has more than $10 million in total assets.[6] Note, however, two aspects of this threshold that may not be self-evident: (1) § 12(g)'s focus on the last day of the fiscal year encourages some gaming behavior by issuers who may issue stock during the year and then repurchase at the close of the fiscal year to avoid the 500 record shareholder level;[7] and (2) both § 12(g) and Rule 12(g)–1 focus on "total assets," not net assets. Thus, if an issuer had $100 million in assets, subject to $99 million (or even, in principle, $105 million in liabilities), it

5. In 1996, the SEC brought a disciplinary action against the NASD, which chiefly charged the NASD with inadequate supervision over dealers in the Nasdaq market who regularly "backed away" from filling orders placed by certain disfavored customers. This proceeding was related to more general allegations of collusive price-fixing by Nasdaq market makers that produced several large antitrust settlements. For the SEC's findings, see Report Pursuant to Section 21(a) of the Securities Exchange Act of 1934 Regarding the NASD and the NASDAQ Market [1996 Transfer Binder], Fed. Sec. L. Rep. (CCH), Para. 85,824 (Aug. 8, 1996).

6. See Rule 12g–1. This rule has been frequently amended to raise the level of "total assets" that triggers the registration requirement. Section 12(g) of the 1934 Act refers to a $1,000,000 total assets requirement, and for a number of years (until 1997), Rule 12g–1 used a $5,000,000 requirement.

7. Rule 12g5–1(b)(3) addresses this problem, however, by providing that if an issuer "has reason to know that the form of holding securities is used to circumvent the provisions of section 12(g) or 15(d) of the Act, the beneficial holders shall be deemed to be the record owners thereof."

would still fall within § 12(g) and be required to become a reporting company. Foreign private issuers are also permitted to avoid becoming reporting companies (if they are neither listed on an exchange nor Nasdaq) if they comply with the provisions of Rule 12g3–2, which requires them to provide the same information to the SEC as they file with their home country or home stock exchange or otherwise distribute (or are required to distribute) to their security holders.[8]

Issuers may subsequently delist as reporting companies pursuant to Rule 12g–4 if the class of registered equity securities (i) is held of record by less than 300 persons, or (ii) is held by less than 500 persons and its total assets have not exceeded $10,000,000 on the last day of the issuer's three most recent fiscal years.

Section 15(d) of the 1934 Act, enacted in 1936, closes down one possible escape hatch from the 1934 Act's reporting requirements. It provides that an issuer that files a registration statement under the 1933 Act must also comply with the periodic reporting requirements of § 13 of the 1934 Act, even if it does not have 500 shareholders. Foreign issuers (whether covered by § 12(g) or § 15(d)) do not, however, become subject to the 1934 Act's proxy rules or its "short-swing" trading provisions in § 16.[9]

Except in the case of certain highly regulated issuers (e.g., banks, insurance companies, savings and loan associations, and investment companies) who are exempted from § 12's reporting requirements, the basic effect of § 12 is to subject those companies trading in public secondary markets to a continuing disclosure requirement. Such issuers are required to file an initial registration form (either on Form 8–A or Form 10) and thereafter to file annual and quarterly reports on Forms 10–K and 10–Q, respectively. Until recently, the 1934's continuous disclosure system contemplated annual and quarterly filings, supplemental by only occasional "current reports" on Form 8–K. In response to the Enron scandal and related instances in which highly material information reached the market only belatedly, the Commission in 2002 announced a series of proposed changes intended to shift this continuous disclosure system to a more current, "real time" basis. These changes would both accelerate the filing deadlines for annual and quarterly reports and, more importantly, would require many more events to be disclosed on Form 8–K, which would be required to be filed within two business days after the event.[10] The premise underlying these proposals is that additional and more timely disclosure by companies of significant events will diminish the opportunities for deception and earnings manipulation. Some of the proposals are clearly driven by recent instances (Enron, WorldCom, and others) in which the impact of fundamental and questionable accounting policies has been hidden from investors.[11] Their

---

8. Subject to a grandfather clause for companies listed on Nasdaq prior to 1983, foreign private issuers listed on Nasdaq today must become "reporting companies," and foreign private issuers listed on an exchange are in any event subject to § 12(b) (to which Rule 12g3–2 does not apply).

9. See Rule 3a12–3 (exempting "foreign private issuer," as defined in Rule 3b–4, from proxy rules and § 16).

10. See Securities Exchange Act Release No. 46084 (June 25, 2002); Securities Exchange Act Release No. 45742 (April 12, 2002); Securities Exchange Act Release No. 45471 (April 23, 2002).

11. Hence, in May, 2002, the Commission proposed new rules requiring enhanced disclosure of "critical accounting policies." See Securities Act Release No. 8098 (May 10, 2002). These disclosures would be required in the "Management Discussion and Analysis"

impact will be, however, to increase significantly the responsibilities of counsel—both in-house and outside counsel—to monitor, detect and report a broad series of events on a rapid and continuing basis. For example, the proposed expansions of Form 8–K would require the prompt disclosure within two business days of any agreement "that is material to the registrant's business and not made in the ordinary course of the registrant's business" or any transaction or agreement that creates a material direct or contingent financial obligation for the registrant.[12] Taken together, these proposals show that the Commission seems intent on recasting its system of continuous disclosure, shifting from periodic reports to constant "real time" reports. Although it is not clear that there would be any litigation remedy or liability consequence that would necessarily follow from a delinquent filing, the Commission has indicated that it intends to condition eligibility for short-form registration and possibly other exemptions on compliance with its new reporting requirements. The 2002 Act, enacted in the wake of the Enron, WorldCom, and related scandals, endorses and codifies this SEC initiative, requiring reporting companies to disclose "on a rapid and current basis such additional information concerning material changes in the financial condition or operations of the issuer, in plain English, which may include trend or qualitative information . . ., as the Commission determines . . . is necessary or useful for the protection of investors and in the public interest."[13] In particular, the foregoing "plain English" requirement may necessitate changes in the style of financial reporting, especially in the footnotes to financial statements.

5. *Criminal Enforcement of the Continuous Disclosure System.* As an apparent exercise in shock therapy, Congress required in 2002 that the chief executive and chief financial officer of every reporting company certify under oath with respect to periodic reports containing financial statements that are filed pursuant to Section 13(a) or 15(d) of the 1934 Act that "the information contained in the periodic report fairly presents, in all material respects, the financial condition and results of operations of the issuer." Although criminal penalties already existed for knowingly filing false information with the Commission, this new provision—18 U.S.C. § 1350—deliberately adds to the formality of the process and requires the senior officers to accept personal responsibility. However, liability attaches only to knowing or willful violations, and hence corporate officials can continue to defend on the grounds that they were deceived by subordinates. The developing practice seems to be that the certifying senior officials will demand parallel certifications from line officials beneath them with responsibility for divisional financial statements. Note that the mandated certification makes no reference to "generally accepted accounting principles" (or "GAAP"), thus strongly suggesting that financial statements prepared in accordance with GAAP could still be found not to "fairly present" the issuer's financial condition or results of operations.

6. *The National Market System.* In 1975, in the most comprehensive revision of the 1934 Act to date, the Securities Acts Amendments of 1975 sought to integrate and encourage competition among the various market systems that were then rapidly evolving. Some of the impetus for this legisla-

---

section of both a registration statement and annual and quarterly reports.

12. See Proposed Items 1.01 and 1.02 of Proposed Form 8–K in Securities Exchange Act Release No. 46084 (June 25, 2002).

13. Section 409 ("Real Time Issuer Disclosures") adds a new Section 13(*l*) to the 1934 Act containing this language.

tion was technological, as new trading systems (Nasdaq, Instinet and the Third Market) had only recently appeared; also, institutional investors had just arrived on the scene as a major force and were clamoring for changes. More fundamental, however, was Congress's desire to encourage competition and end the long prevailing system under which brokerage commissions were set by the regulatory fiat of the exchanges and not by market forces. To most, this looked suspiciously like price fixing in the guise of regulation; § 6(e) of the 1934 Act effectively ended fixed commissions as of May 1, 1975, and under competition, brokerage rates declined radically almost overnight. In addition, § 11A of the 1934 Act, adopted as part of these 1975 amendments, specified criteria by which the SEC was instructed to oversee the national market system. Fundamentally, § 11A endorses a philosophy of multiple competing (but linked) markets in preference to a single centralized marketplace (which might have otherwise evolved from the starting point of the New York Stock Exchange).

In the late 1990's, following disclosures that Nasdaq dealers had failed to compete, but rather had seemingly developed collusive customs and procedures that maintained artificially wide spreads in the secondary market for Nasdaq-traded securities, the Commission adopted new "Order Handling Rules" under § 11A in an attempt to encourage competition. As discussed in Chapter 10, these rules had the impact of encouraging the appearance and growth of electronic communications networks (or "ECNs") that now dominate trading in Nasdaq securities and that have contributed to a major reduction in the spreads quoted in secondary markets and hence to the cost of trading. The SEC's efforts to implement its vision of a national market system in a world now populated by these ECNs and other alternative trading systems remain the subject of continuing debate and controversy, which is reviewed next in Chapter 10.

7. *Accounting Reform.* The 2002 Act significantly restructures the regulation of the accounting profession. First, Title I of the 2002 Act creates the Public Company Accounting Oversight Board (the "Board") under the aegis of the SEC, to oversee the audit of public companies. Accounting firms that audit publicly held companies are required to register with it, and the board is authorized to establish auditing, quality control, ethics, independence and related standards that will be binding on such firms. The lead audit partner for every client must be rotated every five years in an effort to preclude "clubby" relationships between the client and auditor, but the 2002 Act stopped short of requiring mandatory rotation of the audit firm (although a further study of this possible reform was required). The Board is given investigative and disciplinary powers over both accounting firms and their associated persons that are roughly comparable to those given the NASD over the brokerage industry. In particular, the Board is instructed to conduct a continuing program of inspections to assess the degree of compliance by each registered public accounting firm with the rules of the Board and the SEC. This is intended as a substitute for the accounting profession's long-standing system of "peer review," under which selected audits of each accounting firm were periodically reviewed by a comparable firm for compliance with professional standards. The 2002 Act also prohibits public accounting firms from providing nine specified types of consulting services to audit clients in the belief that the pursuit of such revenues compromises the firm's independence.[14] It further requires that the audit

14. The prohibited services include: (i) bookkeeping services related to accounting records or financial statements of the client; (ii) financial information systems design

committee of a public corporation's board of directors be "directly responsible for the appointment, compensation, and oversight" of the auditor (including the resolution of any disagreements between management and the auditor regarding financial reporting). The auditor must report directly to the audit committee, and the 2002 Act mandates that the audit committee approve any other services that the audit firm is to provide to the corporation. In short, the 2002 Act seems to vest sole responsibility for the choice, compensation, dismissal, and oversight of the audit firm in the audit committee, to the exclusion of the management and possibly the full board and the shareholders.

8. *Other Professionals.* The 2002 Act was potentially as sweeping in its treatment of lawyers. The 2002 Act requires the SEC to promulgate rules governing the professional responsibilities of attorneys practicing before it. In particular, Section 307 of the Act mandates the SEC to adopt rules that require an attorney to "report evidence of a material violation of securities laws or breach of fiduciary duty or similar violation by the company or any agent" to the corporation's chief legal officer or chief executive officer. If those persons do not take appropriate action, the rules similarly require that the evidence be reported to the audit committee or some similar committee of independent directors. This provision, added late in the statute's passage by a floor amendment, appears to have been a response to a rejection of similar rules proposed by an ABA Task Force by the American Bar Association's House of Delegates in 2001.

The 2002 Act also requires the promulgation of SEC rules restricting analyst conflicts of interest and protecting analysts from internal retaliation because of negative research reports or ratings. Independently, the SEC proposed Regulation AC ("analyst certification") in July 2002, to require analysts to certify that the views they express are their own and not the product of pressure from investment banking personnel or clients.[15]

9. *The Williams Act.* In 1968, the Williams Act (named after its sponsor, Senator Harrison A. Williams) was enacted to add Subsections (d) and (e) to Section 13 and Subsections (d), (e) and (f) to Section 14 of the 1934 Act. These provisions regulate tender offers and certain other corporate control transactions by requiring the offeror to prepare and file a disclosure document prior to making a tender offer and to disclose acquisitions above the 5% level of any class of the equity security of any "reporting" company registered under §§ 12(b) or (g). Most (but not all of its provisions) are limited to tender offers for, or acquisitions of, equity securities of "reporting" companies. Recurrent litigation has surrounded the definition of "tender offer," which the Act does not define, and the scope of the "best price" rule which requires the bidder to

and implementation; (iii) appraisal or valuation services, including fairness opinions; (iv) actuarial services; (v) internal audit outsourcing services; (vi) management or human resources services; (vii) broker-dealer or investment banking services; (viii) legal or expert services related to the audit; (ix) any other service that the Board deems impermissible. Notably not covered was tax advice, which audit firms have long provided to their audit clients.

15. As proposed by the Commission, Regulation AC would require analysts to certify the truthfulness of their views in research reports and public appearances and to disclose whether they have received any compensation related to the specific recommendation provided in those reports or appearances. See SEC News Digest Issue 2002–144 (July 26, 2002).

pay the same price to any holder that it pays to some holders. Chapter 12 reviews the Williams Act's requirements in detail.

10.   *Other Provisions.* Even prior to the 2002 Act, the 1934 Act was the subject of significant revisions in 1986, 1995, and 1996. The Government Securities Act of 1986 eliminated the exemption for government securities brokers and dealers, which chiefly applied to commercial banks. A new § 15C of the Exchange Act provides for their registration and regulation. Registered securities brokers and dealers under § 15 and municipal securities dealers under § 15B that also act as government securities brokers and dealers must notify their appropriate regulatory government agencies that they are a government securities broker or dealer. The Federal Reserve Board, the Secretary of the Treasury and the SEC now share regulatory authority over government securities brokers and dealers. In 1995, Congress passed the Private Securities Litigation Reform Act of 1995, chiefly to curb perceived abuses in the securities class action field. It added § 21D ("Private Securities Litigation") and § 21E ("Application of Safe Harbor for Forward–Looking Statements"), whose still uncertain impact are reviewed in later chapters. Most recently, as described earlier in Chapter 1, the National Securities Markets Improvements Act of 1996 has significantly changed the balance of power between state and federal regulators by curtailing the authority of state regulators, both with regard to public offerings and brokers and investment advisers. It also added § 36 to the 1934 Act, which grants the SEC broad exemptive authority, permitting it to override express provisions of the 1934 Act to the extent it finds such an "exemption is necessary or appropriate in the public interest, and is consistent with the protection of investors."

CHAPTER 10

REGULATION OF THE SECURITIES MARKETS

Introduction: Change in the Markets. Once, the world of securities markets was settled and stable. Around the globe, exchanges had de facto monopolies, protected by national boundaries from international competition, and were largely run as not-for-profit, club-like enterprises in the interests of the various constituencies—brokers, specialists, and traded firms—that ran them. Today, the two dominant forces reshaping the modern world—globalization and technological change—are also reshaping the securities markets. Globalization has created international competition among markets, with the result that nearly 17% of the issuers listed on the New York Stock Exchange ("NYSE") as of mid–2002 were incorporated in foreign jurisdictions. Technology has in turn given rise to new electronic trading markets: the electronic communications networks (or "ECNs") that now handle an estimated thirty percent of the trading in Nasdaq-traded securities. The factors giving rise to the appearance and sudden growth of these new competitors and their impact on established exchanges are assessed in this Chapter.

Increased competitive pressure has had one other impact on the world of exchanges: the old "clubby" world of exchanges organized as not-for-profit entities has given way to a more entrepreneurial environment in which exchanges have been privatized (or "demutualized" in the industry's preferred term) so that they are now owned by shareholders. In Europe, the major exchanges have all been privatized, and shareholder control seems likely to simplify the internal decision-making process, thereby making these exchanges more effective competitors, able to respond more quickly to competitive pressures, because no longer do a variety of constituencies hold veto powers. Along with privatization has come a wave of consolidating mergers (and even attempted takeovers) by exchanges.[1] Within the United States, Nasdaq is now majority owned by institutional investors and anticipates making an initial public offering; the two largest ECNs—Instinet and Island—have announced a proposed merger, and another ECN (Archipelago) has essentially acquired the Pacific Coast Stock Exchange. Only the NYSE has remained relatively unchanged.

The internal structure of markets has also changed. In discussing market structure, it is conventional to distinguish "quote-driven markets" from "order-driven markets." In the former, securities dealers, known as market-makers, compete for transactions by making rival bids and offers, that is, indicating their willingness to buy and sell at specified prices. Brokers representing customers take their customers' order to the dealer offering the highest bid price or the lowest offer price available at the time (for that quantity of stock); thus transactions between an investor who wishes to buy and one who wishes to sell must go through a professional dealer, who buys from one and

---

1. For succinct reviews of these developments, see Norman S. Poser, The Stock Exchange of the United States and Europe: Automation, Globalization and Consolidation, 22 U. Pa. J. Int'l Eco. L. 497 (2001); Reena Aggarwal, Demutualization and Corporate Governance of Stock Exchanges, 15 J. App. Corp. Fin. 105 (2002).

sells to the other and who is compensated for assuming the risk of holding the security over this interval by the spread (i.e., the price difference between the bid and offer prices). In contrast, in an "order driven" market, brokers direct their customers' orders to a central location, where these orders can be executed against each other, without the necessary intervention of a dealer. The NYSE is such a market, and the specialist at each security's trading post effectively administers an auction, matching buying and selling interest. Yet, even the NYSE is not entirely order driven, because in the absence of buyer or seller on the other side of a transaction, the specialist is required to buy or sell the public customer's stock, and thus it too will profit on the spread. The originally sharp differences between "order driven" and "quote driven" markets begin to blur in the late 1990's when, for reasons hereafter discussed, the SEC adopted "Order Handling Rules" that sometimes permit persons other than dealers to transact with public customers in the Nasdaq market.

Still, the most dramatic change from these developments has been the significant reduction in the size of the average spreads in the equity markets. Once, an eighth of a point was the minimum increment in which securities were quoted, and spreads of a quarter to a half point were normal, even in the case of widely traded stocks. Since April 9, 2001, all U.S. equity markets have been quoting stocks in decimals. Today, spreads are often as narrow as one cent and have tended to average approximately 1.9 cents in the more actively traded stocks.[2] Approximately, 4% to 6% of trades in Nasdaq securities now even occur in subpenny increments.[3] This dramatic reduction in trading costs seems to have been the result of highly successful SEC policy initiatives.

The new competition among market centers has also forced exchanges, dealers, and ECNs to reconsider what it is that they essentially do. Clearly, they operate secondary trading markets, but they also generate and sell information (price quotations and transaction reports) to vendors who disseminate such information to the market. This production of price and trade information accounts for a significant proportion of the revenues of exchanges, and the entitlement to such information is increasingly producing conflicts and political jockeying for position among market participants. It is also creating a powerful incentive leading some ECNs to seek to register as securities exchanges in order to share in this revenue stream.

SECTION 1.   WHAT IS AN EXCHANGE?: A BRIEF SURVEY FROM THE 1934 ACT TO REGULATION ATS

Statutes and Regulations

Securities Exchange Act of 1934, §§ 3(a) 1, 5, 6, 11A, 15(c), and 17A.

————

2. See Securities Exchange Act Release No. 44568 (July 18, 2001) at *3 n. 3 (citing Nasdaq Decimalization Impact Study at 15–16.

3. Id. at *4. This practice, however, has raised concerns at the Commission, because it can result in confusing and rapidly changing quote montages on the Nasdaq screen (i.e., "flickering quotes").

The term "exchange" is broadly defined by § 3(a)(1) of the 1934 Act to mean

> "any organization, association, or group of persons, * * * which constitutes, maintains, or provides a market place or facilities for bringing together purchasers and sellers of securities or for performing with respect to securities the functions commonly performed by a stock exchange as that term is generally understood, and includes the market place and the market facilities maintained by such exchange."

For many years, this definition posed no problem for securities regulators because the concept of an exchange was in fact "generally understood" (as § 3(a)(1) assumed). However, the combination of the technological capacity afforded by the computer plus the growth in institutional trading eventually resulted in the appearance of proprietary trading systems.[4] The initial alternative trading such system, Instinet, which began operations in 1969, essentially functioned as a clearinghouse in which large institutions interested in trading large quantities of securities could trade directly with each other.[5] Instinet operates without any specialist or market maker and does not itself quote a bid/asked spread in the manner of a dealer; rather, its subscribers furnish all quotes and orders to it. Subscribers could either execute transactions automatically based on the then price of a security on its primary exchange (i.e., the NYSE or the American Stock Exchange) or simply advertise their purchasing and selling interest and then engage in direct negotiations with each other. In other, newer trading systems, large institutions can trade whole portfolios of exchange-listed securities with each other.[6] For the most part, institutions did not use these trading systems on a large scale as a cheaper substitute for the market, but rather employed them to trade either after the primary market had closed or when they wished to pursue trading strategies without attracting the market's attention.[7]

4. Originally, these trading systems were sometimes called the "fourth market" to distinguish them from (1) the exchanges, (2) the over-the-counter dealer market, and (3) the "third market," which consists of market makers trading exchange-listed securities on NASDAQ in competition with the exchange's specialist. For a fuller description, see 6 L. Loss & J. Seligman, Securities Regulation, at 2577, 2662–2663 (3d ed. 1990). Prior to the mid–1990's, these systems primarily serviced institutional investors seeking to trade sizable blocks. Some eleven different proprietary trading systems had received no-action letters from the SEC's staff as of April 1989, indicating that the staff would not object to their commencing trading operations without registering as an exchange. Id. at 2659.

5. Instinet provides last sale and quotation information on exchange-listed and over-the-counter securities, but also permits its subscribers (chiefly, bank trust departments, mutual and pension funds, and other institutional investors) to execute transactions through its computer facility.

6. The POSIT (Portfolio System for Institutional Trading) system permits the trading of equity portfolios by customers such as mutual funds. The system permits its subscribers to post an indication of interest to be matched on a confidential basis against other orders in the system. POSIT specializes in facilitating program trading for indexed investors. Some estimate that its transactions in combination with those on Instinet account for up to 50% of the volume in program trading. See Stern, "A Dwindling Monopoly," Forbes, May 13, 1991, at 64. Other systems specialize in debt or government securities.

7. Because large institutional traders can pursue portfolio trading strategies on Instinet or similar systems without attracting the market's attention, they may use the "fourth market" to avoid signaling their trading intentions to the broader market as a whole.

On the policy level, the SEC seems to have accepted the appearance of proprietary trading systems as a natural evolutionary development. While it required that those operating a trading system register as a broker-dealer, it distinguished these systems from exchanges on the following grounds:

> "The Commission believes that the proprietary trading systems that have developed to date are distinguishable in function from exchange markets. These proprietary systems offer to participants the capacity to execute automatically transactions based on derivative pricing.... These systems have not, however, evolved into interdealer quotation or transaction mechanisms in which participants enter two-sided quotations on a regular or continuous basis, thus ensuring a liquid marketplace."[8]

Eventually, existing exchanges challenged the willingness of the Commission's staff to grant no-action letters to proprietary trading systems. In Board of Trade of City of Chicago v. Securities and Exchange Commission,[9] the Seventh Circuit found the particular proprietary trading system there at issue to be

> "neither fish nor fowl, neither an exchange after the pattern of the Board of Trade and the New York Stock Exchange nor an over-the-counter market after the fashion of the NASDAQ. Developments in automation and communication are bound to produce more of these hard-to-classify entities. Section 3(a)(1) is a product of the '30s, [the proprietary trading system] a product of the 80's."[10]

The Seventh Circuit remanded the case to the SEC for a formal determination of whether the particular proprietary trading system was an "exchange."

On remand, the SEC stuck to its guns and insisted that the Delta trading system (which three firms had collectively developed to trade options on federal government securities) did not amount to an exchange. In part, the SEC clearly based its determination on its fear that a strict interpretation of § 3(a)(1) would result in a "straitjacket" on the evolution of new forms of trading systems. It concluded:

> In summary, employing an expansive interpretation of Section 3(a)(1) results in potential conflicts with other central regulatory definitions under the Act as well as adverse effects on innovation and competition. Rather, each system must be analyzed in light of the statutory objectives and the particular facts and circumstances of that system. In conducting such an analysis, the central focus of the Commission's inquiry should be whether the system is designed, whether through trading rules, operational procedures or business incentives, to centralize trading and provide buy and sell quotations on a regular or continuous basis so that purchasers and sellers have a reasonable expectation that they can regularly execute their orders at those price quotations. The means employed may be varied, ranging from a physical floor or trading system (where orders can be centralized and executed) to other means of intermediation (such as a formal market

---

8. See Securities Exchange Act Release No. 26708 (Apr. 11, 1989), 43 S.E.C. Dock. 979, 984.

9. 883 F.2d 525 (7th Cir.1989).

10. Id. at 535. Writing for the Seventh Circuit panel, Judge Easterbrook added: "We could not find a single case under § 3(a)(1) discussing which attributes (if any) are necessary, and which are sufficient, for sorting a trading apparatus into the 'exchange bin.'" Id.

making system or systemic procedures such as a consolidated order book or regular single price auction).[11]

The Commission also relied on the "absence of complete * * * standardization" in the terms of the options quoted by Delta and the fact that the lack of "regulatory requirements to ensure two-sided quotations make the development of regular or continuous trading unlikely." Although the Commission noted that an embryonic trading system might well grow into a "continuous or regular auction market," it concluded that the Delta trading system was still at too early and formative a stage to make that prediction.

In overview, the principal criteria stressed by Release 27611 for defining an exchange were centralized trading, continuous two-sided quotations, the expectation of liquidity, and the standardization of terms. However, as a practical matter, the Commission's decision not to deem the Delta system an exchange chiefly served to protect those emerging trading systems that did not provide continuous trading (but which were either passive systems which adopted prices derived from another system or systems that functioned as electronic bulletin boards through which potential trading partners could negotiate price and others terms). Even before the Seventh Circuit's decision, the Commission had proposed a special rule—proposed Rule 15c2–10—to govern proprietary trading systems by requiring that they be sponsored by a broker-dealer (which thus made them effectively subject to Commission oversight).[12] The proposed rule defined the term "trading system" to include "any system providing for the dissemination outside the sponsor and its affiliates of indications of interest, quotations, or orders to purchase or sell securities, and providing procedures for executing or settling transactions in such securities."[13] Although Rule 15c2–10 was never adopted, the Commission continued to resist the mandatory classification of new trading systems as exchanges, preferring to allow them to opt for the less restrictive alternative of broker-dealer registration.

Meanwhile, with the stage thus set, the case went back to the Seventh Circuit the next year:

Board of Trade of the City of Chicago v. Securities and Exchange Commission

United States Court of Appeals, Seventh Circuit, 1991.
923 F.2d 1270.

■ POSNER, CIRCUIT JUDGE. This case is before us for the second time * * * The question we must answer this time is whether a system for trading options on

---

11. See Securities Exchange Act Release No. 27611 (January 12, 1990), 1990 SEC LEXIS 100, at *49.

12. The earliest forerunner of proposed Rule 15c2–10 was originally proposed in 1969 when Instinet began operations. See Securities Exchange Act Release No. 8661 (1969). This rule was withdrawn in 1975 following the adoption of the 1975 amendments to the 1934 Act, which required the registration of "securities information processors." In 1989, the Commission again proposed a new Rule 15c2–10 to govern proprietary trading systems. See Securities Exchange Act Release No. 26,708 (Apr. 11, 1989). One concern mo-

tivating the Commission in adopting this release was that foreign entities might participate in the trading system who were not financially responsible; their financial collapse, it was feared, might have an adverse domino effect on the particular trading system (and other institutions as a whole).

13. See Proposed Rule 15c2–10(b)(1). The proposed Rule, which was never adopted, required each operator of a proprietary trading system to submit a plan to the S.E.C., specifying 15 items of information. See Proposed Rule 15c2–10(c)(i).

federal government securities that has been put together by RMJ, a broker; Delta, a clearing agency; and SPNTCO, a bank (the last playing an essentially custodial role unnecessary to discuss further) is an "exchange" within the meaning of section 3(a)(1) of the Securities Exchange Act of 1934, in which event it must register with the Securities Exchange Commission. The Commission, faced as it was merely with an application by Delta to register as a clearing agency under section 17A(b) of the Act, thought it unnecessary to decide whether the Delta system—as we shall call the trading system put together by the three firms—is an exchange. We disagreed in our first opinion. We held that the Commission could not, as it had done, approve Delta's application without deciding whether the system whose trades it intended to clear could lawfully operate without registering as an exchange. We therefore remanded the case to the Commission for a determination of the system's status. The Commission held that it was not an exchange, and therefore adhered to its decision to register Delta as a clearing house. The Board of Trade and the Chicago Mercantile Exchange again petition for review. They are concerned about competition from the Delta system. We held in our first opinion that this concern gives them standing to challenge the Commission's decision to allow Delta to become a registered clearing house.

An ingenious device for facilitating the purchase and sale of securities, the Delta system works roughly as follows. * * * The system specifies the form of option contract that shall be the security traded. Some of the terms of the contract are fixed, such as the maximum term of the option and the day of the month on which it expires. Others are left open to be negotiated by the parties, such as the premium, the exercise price, and the month of expiration. The traders, who consist not only of securities dealers but also of banks, pension funds, and other institutional investors, communicate their buy or sell offers to RMJ, which enters the offers in the system's computer. Delta, the clearing agency, monitors the computer and when it sees a matching buy and sell offer it notifies the traders that they have a deal (but doesn't tell them with whom) and it takes the necessary steps to effectuate the completed transaction. The interposition of Delta between the traders protects the anonymity of each from the other as well as guaranteeing to each that the other will honor the terms of the option traded.

The fixing of some standardized terms so that one trader is not offering to buy apples and the other offering to sell oranges; the guarantees of anonymity and performance; the pooling of buy and sell offers in a single (electronic) place—these essential features of the Delta system are methods for creating a market that will bring together enough buy and sell offers to enable transacting at prices that will approximate the true market values of the things traded. Does this make the Delta system an exchange, that is, "any organization, association, or group of persons * * * which constitutes, maintains, or provides a market place or facilities for bringing together purchasers and sellers of securities or for otherwise performing with respect to securities the functions commonly performed by a stock exchange as that term is generally understood"? There is no doubt that the Delta system creates an electronic marketplace for securities traders, and the petitioners say that no more is required to establish that the system must register as an exchange. The Commission's reply emphasizes the words "generally understood." The Delta system is not— not quite, anyway—what is generally understood by the term "stock exchange." It lacks a trading floor. It lacks specialists, who enhance the liquidity of an exchange by using their own capital to trade against the market when the trading is light, in order to buffer price swings due to the fewness of offers rather than to changes in underlying market values. Not all conventional exchanges have specialists, but those that do not have brokers who trade for their own account as well as for their customers' accounts, and the additional trading enhances the market's liquidity. It is fitting that such brokers are called "market makers." Securities Exchange Act of 1934, § 3(a)(38). RMJ does not trade for its own account in the Delta system.

The petitioners reply that the words "generally understood" apply only to functions other than the central one of "provid[ing] a market place or facilities for bringing together purchasers and sellers of securities." In other words they want us to put a comma after "sellers of securities." This done, they argue as follows: the statute defines exchange as any entity that provides a facility for bringing together purchasers and sellers of securities, whether or not in providing that facility it is performing an exchange function as the term exchange is generally understood; the Delta system provides a facility for bringing together purchasers and sellers of securities; therefore Delta is an exchange.

Unless the petitioners can be permitted to add their own punctuation to the statute, we do not think that their reading is any more persuasive, even at the literal level, than the Commission's reading, which places the provision of a market place or of other facilities for bringing securities traders together among those functions performed by a stock exchange as the term is generally understood, and thus subjects "provid[ing] a market place or facilities" to the qualifying force of "generally understood." Moreover, if the petitioners are to be consistent in advancing a "literal" reading of the statute, they should read "bring together" literally too. But even an admitted exchange does not literally "bring together" purchasers and sellers of securities, except when the floor brokers are trading for their own account. It does not bring them into physical propinquity. And a broker's waiting room, which does bring purchasers and sellers of securities into physical propinquity, is not an exchange. We therefore question whether the petitioners have a coherent approach to the interpretation of the statute.

The consequence of their interpretation must also give us pause. The Delta system cannot register as an exchange, because the statute requires that an exchange be controlled by its participants, who must in turn be registered brokers or individuals associated with such brokers. Securities and Exchange Act of 1934, §§ 6(b)(3), (c)(1); Securities Exchange Act Release No. 21439, 49 Fed.Reg. 44577, 44578 (Oct. 31, 1984). So all the financial institutions that trade through the Delta system would have to register as brokers, and RMJ, Delta, and the bank would have to turn over the ownership and control of the system to the institutions. The system would be *kaput*. One must question an interpretation of the definitional provision that would automatically prevent competition for the exchanges from an entity that the exchanges are unable to show poses a threat to the safety of investors by virtue of not being forced to register and assume the prescribed exchange format. As the Commission stresses, each of the three firms that constitute the Delta system is comprehensively regulated; no regulatory gaps are created by declining to place the system itself in the exchange pigeonhole; the only thing that such classification would do would be to destroy the system.

What is true is that the Delta system differs only in degree and detail from an exchange. Its trading floor is a computer's memory. Its structure is designed to encourage liquidity, though not to the same extent as the structure of an exchange is. Section 3(a)(1) is broadly worded. No doubt (considering the time when and circumstances in which it was enacted) this was to give the Securities and Exchange Commission maximum control over the securities industry. So the Commission could have interpreted the section to embrace the Delta system. But we do not think it was compelled to do so. The statute is not crystal clear; on the contrary, even when read literally, which is to say without regard to context and consequence, it does not support the petitioners' argument without repunctuation of the statute and without overlooking the impossibility of a consistently literal reading. An administrative agency has discretion to interpret a statute that is not crystal clear. Chevron v. Natural Resources Defense Council, 467 U.S. 837, 844–45, 104 S.Ct. 2778, 2782–83, 81 L.Ed.2d 694 (1984). The Securities and Exchange Commission can determine better than we generalist judges whether the protection of investor and other interests within the range of the statute is advanced, or retarded, by placing the Delta system in a classification that will destroy a promising competitive innovation in the trading of securities. Of course, if the statute were unambiguous, the Commission would have to bow. Board of Governors v. Dimension Financial Corp., 474 U.S. 361, 106 S.Ct. 681, 88 L.Ed.2d 691 (1986); American Bankers Ass'n v. SEC, 804 F.2d 739, 744 (D.C.Cir.1986). It has not been given the power of statutory revision. But in this case there is enough play in the statutory joints that its decision must be affirmed.

■ FLAUM, CIRCUIT JUDGE, dissenting.

No doubt there is some ambiguity in the statutory definition of "exchange." The ambiguity lies in the broad formula Congress adopted: "as that term is generally understood." On one point, however, the statute is not ambiguous. An organization that "constitutes, maintains, or provides a market place or facilities for bringing together purchasers and sellers of securities" is an exchange. The statute makes it unnecessary to speculate whether bringing together buyers and sellers is one of the "generally understood" functions of an exchange; it makes *that* function a determinative characteristic, sufficient unto itself to confer exchange status. Entities that *"otherwise"* perform the functions of a stock exchange—whatever those may be—may also constitute exchanges, but the statute leaves no doubt that bringing together buyers and sellers is the principal function of an exchange. Since—as the majority acknowledges—we cannot ignore an unequivocal statutory mandate, I respectfully dissent from the court's decision to defer to an SEC interpretation that does.

* * *

----

1. *Square Pegs and Round Holes.* The immediate problem for an alternative trading system, if it were deemed to be an exchange, is that the 1934 Act mandates a governance structure for exchanges based on a conception of them as not-for-profit organizations run for the benefit of participating dealers. Proprietary systems are, of course, run for their own benefit (or that of their owners). Section 6(b) of the 1934 Act contemplates that an exchange will be essentially a membership organization, administered on a not-for-profit basis. Thus § 6(b)(3) requires "fair representation" of its members in the selection of the directors, and § 6(b)(4) contemplates that the rules of the exchange will provide for "the equitable allocation" of costs among members and other users

of its facilities. Neither of these sections contemplate a privately owned "exchange," such as the Delta System. In 1934, Congress was obviously looking to the existing structure of exchanges as more-or-less private clubs organized for trading purposes and did not contemplate that anyone could "own" the technological equivalent of a trading floor. This was, of course, an anomaly that the SEC could today correct through exemptive rulemaking under § 36 ("General Exemptive Authority") of the 1934 Act. But § 36 did not exist at the time of the Delta System case, and any exemptive rulemaking proceeding would then have been both lengthy and subject to legal challenge.

2. *The Varieties of Alternative Trading Systems.* New trading systems continue to be developed, and any taxonomy of them is likely to become dated quickly. Still, some basic distinctions should be understood:

a. *Matching Systems.* These allow participants to display firm, priced orders to other participants and to execute automatically against other orders in the system. Examples of such systems are the Real–Time Trading Service, operated by Instinet Corporation ("Instinet"), The Island System, operated by Datek Securities Corp., and Tradebook, operated by Bloomberg Tradebook, L.L.C. Market participants often enter superior prices on such a system than they display on Nasdaq (where they are primarily dealing with retail customers).

b. *Crossing Systems.* These allow participants to enter unpriced orders, which are then executed with matching interest on the other side at a single price, usually derived from the primary public market for each crossed security. The attraction of these systems is that they allow institutional investors to split the bid/asked spread. That is, if two pension funds see a spread of $18 bid and $18½ asked, they would each prefer to execute a transaction between them at $18¼ than to accept an inferior price from dealers. The leading example of such a "passive" system is POSIT (Portfolio System for Institutional Trading). These systems are, however, not "active" in the sense that a large market participant will offer a superior price on them to what is available in the public market in order to liquidate (or acquire) a sizable block of securities in an issuer.

c. *Single–Price Auction Systems.* These systems allow participants to enter priced orders, which a computer then compares to determine the single price at which the largest volume of orders can be executed. All orders are then matched and executed at that price. The best known example of this type of system is the Arizona Stock Exchange.[1] For example, if the "auction price" that best equalizes supply and demand is 42⅜, then all orders to buy at 42½ and higher would be filled at 42⅜, and all orders to sell at 42¼ or less would be filled at 42⅜.[2] A special attraction of this system is the ability of each customer to see at all times (on its own computer terminal) the bids and offers made by all other users. In effect, the computer gives each investor direct access to the specialist's book (and then replaces the specialist with a computer procedure for determining the market-clearing price). For some, this "open book" procedure

---

1. Securities Exchange Act Release No. 28,899 (Feb. 28, 1991); see also Wunsch Auction Systems, Inc., 1991 WL 178593 (S.E.C.) (Feb. 28, 1991).

2. Buy orders set below 42⅜ and sell orders set above 42⅜ will go unfilled, and orders exactly at 42⅜ will be filled on a first come, first served basis. For a fuller explanation, see Stern, "A Dwindling Monopoly," Forbes, May 13, 1991, at 64.

is a desirable improvement on existing auction procedures because it eliminates the role of the specialist, who can sometimes act in a self-interested fashion.

3. *The Arizona Aftermath.* Interestingly, the Arizona Stock Exchange, which is a single-price auction system, did not ask the Commission to rule that it was not an exchange. Instead, it asked for and received an exemption under the last clause of § 5 of the 1934 Act based on the "limited volume of transactions effected on such exchange." Only time will tell if computers can begin to replace specialists, but to the extent that they were successful, the one certainty would be that they would begin to execute far more than a "limited volume of transactions." Thus, as new trading systems grew, the problem of identifying the defining criteria of an "exchange" was becoming more central and had to be faced by the Commission.

Securities Exchange Act Release No. 38672

Securities and Exchange Commission.
May 23, 1997.

REGULATION OF EXCHANGES

Stock markets play a critical role in the economic life of the United States. The phenomenal growth of the U.S. markets over the past 60 years is a direct result of investor confidence in those markets. Technological trends over the past two decades have also contributed greatly to this success. In particular, technology has provided a vastly greater number of investment and execution choices, increased market efficiency, and reduced trading costs. These developments have enhanced the ability of U.S. exchanges to implement efficient market linkages and advanced the goals of the national market system ("NMS").

At the same time, however, technological changes have posed significant challenges for the existing regulatory framework, which is ill-equipped to respond to innovations in U.S. and cross-border trading. Specifically, two key developments highlight the need for a more forward-looking, flexible regulatory framework: (1) the exponential growth of trading systems that present comparable alternatives to traditional exchange trading; and (2) the development of automated mechanisms that facilitate access to foreign markets from the United States.

The Commission estimates that alternative trading systems[1] currently handle almost 20 percent of the orders[2] in over-the-counter ("OTC") stocks and almost 4 percent of orders in securities listed on the New York Stock ("NYSE"). The explosive growth of alternative trading systems over the past

---

1. Trading systems not registered as exchanges have been referred to in previous Commission releases as "proprietary trading systems," "broker-dealer trading systems," and "electronic communications networks." The latter two terms are defined in Rule 17a–23 and 11Ac1–1 under the Securities Exchanges Act of 1934 ("Exchange Act"), 17 CFR 240.17a–23 and 240.11Ac1–1, respectively. The term "alternative trading systems" will be used throughout this release to refer generally to automated systems that centralize, display, match, cross, or otherwise execute trading interest, but that are not currently registered with the Commission as national securities exchanges or operated by a registered securities association.

2. For purposes of this release, the term "order" generally means any firm trading interest, including both limit orders and market maker quotations.

several years has significant implications for public secondary market regulation. Even though many of these systems provide essentially the same services as traditional markets, most alternative trading systems are regulated as broker-dealers. As a result, they have been subject to regulations designed primarily to address traditional brokerage, rather than market, activities. For example, these systems are typically subject to oversight by self-regulatory organizations ("SROs") that themselves operate exchanges or quotation systems, which raises inherent competitive concerns.

At the same time, alternative trading systems are not fully integrated into the national market system. As a result, activity on alternative trading systems is not fully disclosed to, or accessible by, public investors. The trading activity on these systems may not be adequately surveilled for market manipulation and fraud. Moreover, these trading systems have no obligation to provide investors a fair opportunity to participate in their systems or to treat their participants fairly, nor do they have an obligation to ensure that they have sufficient capacity to handle trading demand. These concerns together with the increasingly important role of alternative trading systems, call into question the fairness of current regulatory requirements, the effectiveness of existing NMS mechanisms, and the quality of public secondary markets.

* * *

B. **Alternatives for Revising Domestic Market Regulation**

The questions raised by technological developments in the U.S. markets could be addressed in a variety of ways. As an initial matter, the Commission is soliciting comment on whether the current statutory and regulatory framework remains appropriate in light of the myriad new means of trading securities made possible by emerging and evolving technologies. The Commission is also soliciting comment on alternative ways of addressing these issues within the existing securities law framework. The release discusses two alternatives in particular that would integrate alternative trading systems more fully into mechanisms that promote market-wide transparency, investor protection, and fairness.

First, the Commission could continue to regulate alternative trading systems as broker-dealers and develop rules applicable to these systems, and their supervising SROs, that would more actively integrate these systems into NMS mechanisms. The Commission could, for example, require alternative trading systems to provide additional audit trail information to SROs, to assist SROs in their surveillance functions, and to adopt standard procedures for ensuring adequate system capacity and the integrity of their system operations. The Commission could then require SROs to integrate trading on alternative trading systems into their ongoing, real-time surveillance for market manipulation and fraud, and to develop surveillance and examination procedures specifically targeted to alternative trading systems they supervise. In addition, the Commission could require alternative trading systems to make all orders in their systems available to their supervising SROs, and require such SROs to incorporate those orders into the public quotation system. The Commission could also require that alternative trading systems provide the public with access to these orders on a substantially equivalent basis as provided to system participants.

Alternatively, the Commission could integrate alternative trading systems into the national market system as securities exchanges, by adopting a tiered approach to exchange regulation. The first tier, under this type of approach, could consist of the majority of alternative trading systems, those that have limited volume or do not establish trading prices, which could be exempt from traditional exchange requirements. For example, exempt exchanges could be required to file an application and system description with the Commission, report trade, maintain an audit trail, develop systems capacity and other operational standards, and cooperate with SROs that inspect their regulated participants. Most alternative trading systems currently regulated as broker-dealers would be exempt exchanges.

The second tier of exchanges under this approach could consist of alternative trading systems that resemble traditional exchanges because of their significant volume of trading and active price discovery. These systems could be regulated as national securities exchanges. The Commission could then use its exemptive authority to eliminate barriers that would make it difficult for these non-traditional markets to register as exchanges, by exempting such systems from any exchange registration requirements that are not appropriate or necessary in light of their business structure or other characteristics. For example, the Commission could exempt alternative trading systems that register as exchanges from requirements that exchanges have a traditional membership structure, and from requirements that limit exchange participation to registered broker-dealers. The Commission could also use its exemptive authority to reduce or eliminate those exchange requirements that are incompatible with the operation of for-profit, non-membership alternative trading systems.

This approach could integrate those alternative trading systems more fully into NMS mechanisms and the plans governing those systems, potentially by requiring these systems to become members of those plans. Because alternative trading systems differ in several key respects from currently registered exchanges, this could require revision of those plans in order to accommodate diverse and evolving trading systems.

Finally, a third tier of exchanges, consisting of traditional membership exchanges, could continue to be regulated as national securities exchanges. The Commission could then use its exemptive authority to reduce overall exchange requirements. In this regard, the Commission is considering ways to reduce unnecessary regulatory requirements that make it difficult for currently registered exchanges to remain competitive in a changing business environment. The Commission, for example, could further accelerate rule filing and approval procedures for national securities exchanges and securities associations, and allow fully automated exchanges to meet their regulatory requirements in non-traditional ways.

One way for the Commission to implement this tiered approach would be to expand its interpretation of the definition of "exchange." For example, the Commission could reinterpret the term "exchange" to include any organization that both: (1) consolidates orders of multiple parties; and (2) provides a facility through which, or sets material conditions under which, participants entering such orders may agree to the terms of a trade.

* * *

1. *The SEC's Concerns.* The SEC's historic attitude of benign neglect toward alternative trading systems was largely a product of their low volume plus the fear that close regulation would retard their evolution as competitive alternatives to the traditional markets.[1] By the time of the foregoing Concept Release in 1997, the growth of alternative trading systems (then amounting to 20% of Nasdaq volume, but now exceeding 40%) had convinced the SEC that such systems could no longer be treated as infants to be sheltered in a protective legal nursery, but rather that hard issues about their operation and regulation had to be faced. Among these issues, the following stood out:

a. *Market Access.* Small investors may not have access to the principal alternative trading systems (such as Instinet), which primarily serve institutional investors and other large traders. Thus, if there are superior prices available on such systems, small investors may not benefit from them. On the other hand, the access issue is not easy to resolve because alternative trading systems may not be willing to guarantee execution if one of the trading parties defaults. This risk of default is greatest in the case of the individual investor, and is eliminated in the national securities markets by the market's own guarantee that the trade will be executed at the agreed price. An alternative trading system may not be willing to assume this cost and may therefore wish to exclude smaller traders in order to minimize counterparty trading risk (i.e., the risk that the other party to a trade will default).

b. *Market Transparency.* As the foregoing Concept Release noted, the SEC's 1996 investigation of Nasdaq trading found that the majority of the bids and offers displayed by Instinet and SelectNet (the two most significant alternative trading systems for Nasdaq securities) were better than those posted publicly on Nasdaq. The SEC believed this lack of transparency was harmful to investors in several ways. Because Nasdaq dealers could trade with each other through non-public trading systems, they have reduced economic incentive to reduce their price spreads and compete based on price. The resulting wider public spreads, of course, increased the transaction costs for public investors and indirectly the cost of capital to corporate issuers. In response to these findings, the Commission introduced new order handling rules in 1996, which required a market maker or specialist to make publicly available any superior prices that it privately offers through certain types of alternative trading systems (known as electronic communications networks or "ECNs"). These order handling rules permit an ECN to satisfy this obligation on behalf of market makers using its system by submitting its best market maker bid/ask quotation to the exchange or Nasdaq for inclusion into the public quotation displays (the so-called "ECN Display Alternative"). Although these reforms served to integrate orders submitted by broker-dealers to private trading systems into the broader public quotation system, they were subject to a significant limitation: institutional orders placed with alternative trading systems are not similarly required to be publicly displayed. The Concept Release thus noted:

1. In 1994, the SEC did adopt Rule 17a–23, which is a recordkeeping and reporting rule for broker-dealers that operate alternative trading systems. The rule requires a broker-dealer to report quarterly the trading volume on such system and to provide a description of the trading system. See Securities Exchange Act Release No. 35124 (Dec. 20, 1994).

Because a majority of trading interest on alternative trading systems is not integrated into the national market system, price transparency is impaired and dissemination of quotation information is incomplete.[2]

The reason for this lack of transparency is largely that some market participants (such as large institutional traders) desire anonymity. For example, a large trader seeking to sell 100,000 shares may offer it privately on an anonymous basis at a superior (i.e. cheaper) price than is reflected in the public quotation. Because it is known to hold a large block, it does not wish to disclose its willingness to sell for fear that this will drive the market price down. Some alternative trading systems (such as Instinet) were thought to attract institutional customers principally because of their ability to afford such anonymity. Nonetheless, the SEC wants the superior price quotations submitted by such market participants integrated into the public quotation market. In turn, alternative trading systems feared that this would make them less attractive to their customers.

c. *Market Surveillance.* Although alternative trading systems are operated by broker dealers which are, themselves, subject to the oversight of the NASD and the exchanges, the capacity of these self-regulatory organizations (or "SROs") to monitor their own markets for fraud or other violations of the federal securities laws does not extend as a practical matter to observing quote activity on alternative trading systems. For example, a market participant who wished to manipulate the market in a thinly traded stock might bid it up in a public market, while quietly selling it off contemporaneously in an alternative trading system that was beyond the effective surveillance of any SRO. At the same time, the SEC is also concerned that surveillance activities by an SRO might be in fact motivated by a desire to impede or injure an alternative trading system that was a competitor to an exchange or to Nasdaq. In particular, Instinet has become a significant competitor to Nasdaq and may in the future similarly take business from the New York Stock Exchange. From this perspective, SRO oversight could be biased or even driven by competitive, rather than regulatory, concerns.

For all these and other reasons, the Concept Release concluded that "the current regulation of alternative trading systems does not address the market activities performed by such systems."[3]

2. *The SEC's Response: Regulation ATS.* In 1998, the Commission adopted Regulation ATS to address its concern that ECNs were becoming "private markets" that offered superior prices to institutional investors, but excluded public investors.[4] The essential goal of Regulation ATS is to allow developing systems with low volume to operate under minimal regulatory burdens, while requiring systems with larger volumes to comply with more extensive regulation of their quotation dissemination and access standards. To accomplish this, the Commission adopted Rule 3a1–1, which exempts from the definition of "exchange" those systems that comply with Regulation ATS and do not exercise self-regulatory responsibilities. At the same time the Commission also adopted Rule 13b–16 to clarify the definition of "exchange." It provides that an entity will generally not be considered an exchange if it operates only as a "crossing" or "matching" system, or simply routes orders to a market for execution. It adds that an entity will generally be considered an

---

2. *Id*. at *52.

3. *Id*. at *58.

4. See Securities Exchange Act Release No. 40760 (Dec. 8, 1998).

exchange if it brings together buyers and sellers and establishes rules for executing their orders. Once a trading system exceeds certain volume levels, it provided that the Commission could, after giving notice and an opportunity to comment, withdraw the exemption and classify the system as an exchange.

Trading systems that are subject to Regulation ATS must register as broker-dealers. In order to integrate the prices on alternative trading systems with those in the principal markets, Regulation ATS mandates that for securities for which the trading system displays orders and has a trading volume of at least five percent of the total average daily volume in that security, the trading system must supply its best prices to a national securities exchange or to Nasdaq for public dissemination, and it provide registered broker-dealers with an ability to execute against such orders.[5] Although a sound conceptual solution, this guarantee of fair access has lead to a further practical problem: ECNs generate their revenues by charging access fees to their subscribes. But Regulation ATS requires alternative trading systems to open their systems to broker-dealers acting on behalf of retail customers, and these broker-dealers will often not be subscribers who have agreed to pay an access fee. Can an alternative trading system charge non-subscribers who are simply trying to access the best bid or offer price available in the market (as their duty of best execution requires them to do)? Rule 301(b)(4) provides somewhat cryptically that an alternative trading system may not charge a fee that is "inconsistent with [the] equivalent access to the system" require by Rule 301(b)(3). At present, access fees are being charged in these cases, but disputes have frequently arisen in arbitration cases about their legitimacy and reasonableness. Unavoidably, the SEC has been drawn into the rate regulation business, reviewing the reasonableness of ECN's access charges (without conceding that it is doing so).

It needs to be underscored that Regulation ATS does not integrate all orders into the national market system. Rather, its fair access rules create an exclusion for systems that match customers orders without displaying them or that execute orders pursuant to an automated quotation system.[6]

SECTION 2.   THE STRUGGLE FOR COMPETITIVE RATES

Statutes and Regulations

Securities and Exchange Act of 1934, §§ 6(e) and 28(e).

Gordon v. New York Stock Exchange

United States Supreme Court, 1975.
422 U.S. 659, 95 S.Ct. 2598, 45 L.Ed.2d 463.

■ MR. JUSTICE BLACKMUN delivered the opinion of the Court.

This case presents the problem of reconciliation of the antitrust laws with a federal regulatory scheme in the particular context of the practice of the

---

5. See Rule 301(b)(3), 17 C.F.R. § 242.301(b)(3).

6. For example, some alternative trading systems match orders received overnight at the market's opening price, or they match unpriced orders at the midpoint of the bid and offer spread. Such systems are not subject to the fair access rules. See Rule 301(b)5(iii).

securities exchanges and their members of using fixed rates of commission. The United States District Court for the Southern District of New York and the United States Court of Appeals for the Second Circuit concluded that fixed commission rates were immunized from antitrust attack because of the Securities and Exchange Commission's authority to approve or disapprove exchange commission rates and its exercise of that power.

I

In early 1971 petitioner Richard A. Gordon, individually and on behalf of an asserted class of small investors, filed this suit against the New York Stock Exchange, Inc. (NYSE), the American Stock Exchange, Inc. (Amex), and two member firms of the exchanges. The complaint challenged a variety of exchange rules and practices and, in particular, claimed that the system of fixed commission rates, utilized by the exchanges at that time for transactions less than $500,000, violated §§ 1 and 2 of the Sherman Act, 15 U.S.C.A. §§ 1 and 2. Other challenges in the complaint focused on (1) the volume discount on trades over 1,000 shares, and the presence of negotiated rather than fixed rates for transactions in excess of $500,000; (2) the rules limiting the number of exchange memberships; and (3) the rules denying discounted commission rates to nonmembers using exchange facilities.

Respondents moved for summary judgment on the ground that the challenged actions were subject to the overriding supervision of the Securities and Exchange Commission (SEC) under § 19(b) of the Securities Exchange Act of 1934, and, therefore, were not subject to the strictures of the antitrust laws. The District Court granted respondents' motion as to all claims * * *. Dismissing the exchange membership limitation and the Robinson–Patman Act contentions as without merit, the court focused on the relationship between the fixed commission rates and the Sherman Act mandates. It utilized the framework for analysis of antitrust immunity in the regulated securities area that was established a decade ago in Silver v. New York Stock Exchange, 373 U.S. 341 (1963). Since § 19(b)(9) of the Exchange Act authorized the SEC to supervise the exchanges "in respect of such matters as * * * the fixing of reasonable rates of commission," the court held applicable the antitrust immunity reserved in *Silver* for those cases where "review of exchange self-regulation [is] provided through a vehicle other than the antitrust laws." 373 U.S., at 360. It further noted that the practice of fixed commission rates had continued without substantial challenge after the enactment of the 1934 Act, and that the SEC had been engaged in detailed study of the rate structure for a decade, culminating in the requirement for abolition of fixed rates as of May 1, 1975.

On appeal, the Second Circuit affirmed. Characterizing petitioner's other challenges as frivolous, the appellate court devoted its opinion to the problem of antitrust immunity. It, too, used *Silver* as a basis for its analysis. Because the SEC, by § 19(b)(9), was given specific review power over the fixing of commission rates, because of the language, legislative history, and policy of the Exchange Act, and because of the SEC's actual exercise of its supervisory power, the Court of Appeals determined that this case differed from *Silver*, and that antitrust immunity was proper.

By his petition for certiorari, petitioner sought review only of the determination that fixed commission rates are beyond the reach of the antitrust laws.

Because of the vital importance of the question, and at the urging of all the parties, we granted certiorari.

II

Resolution of the issue of antitrust immunity for fixed commission rates may be made adequately only upon a thorough investigation of the practice in the light of statutory restrictions and decided cases. We begin with a brief review of the history of commission rates in the securities industry.

Commission rates for transactions on the stock exchanges have been set by agreement since the establishment of the first exchange in this country. The New York Stock Exchange was formed with the Buttonwood Tree Agreement of 1792, and from the beginning minimum fees were set and observed by the members. That Agreement itself stated:

"We the Subscribers, Brokers for the Purchase and Sale of Public Stock, do hereby solemnly promise and pledge ourselves to each other, that we will not buy or sell from this day for any person whatsoever, any kind of Public Stock at a less rate than one-quarter percent Commission on the Specie value, and that we will give a preference to each other in our negotiations." F. Eames, The New York Stock Exchange 14 (1968 ed.).

See generally, R. Doede, The Monopoly Power of the New York Stock Exchange, reprinted in Hearings on S. 3169 before the Subcomm. on Securities of the Senate Comm. on Banking, Housing and Urban Affairs, 92d Cong., 2d Sess., 405, 412–427 (1972). Successive constitutions of the NYSE have carried forward this basic provision. Similarly, when Amex emerged in 1908–1910, a pattern of fixed commission rates was adopted there.

* * *

Despite the monopoly power of the few exchanges, exhibited not only in the area of commission rates but in a wide variety of other aspects, the exchanges remained essentially self-regulating and without significant supervision until the adoption of the Securities Exchange Act of 1934. At the lengthy hearings before adoption of that Act, some attention was given to the fixed commission rate practice and to its anticompetitive features. * * *

Perhaps the most pertinent testimony in the hearings preparatory to enactment of the Exchange Act was proffered by Samuel Untermyer formerly Chief Counsel to the committee that drafted the Pujo Report. In commenting on proposed S. 2693, Mr. Untermyer noted that although the bill would provide the federal supervisory commission with

"the right to prescribe uniform rates of commission, it does not otherwise authorize the Commission to fix rates, which it seems to me it should do and would do by striking out the word 'uniform.' That would permit the Commission to fix rates.

"The volume of the business transacted on the exchange has increased manyfold. Great fortunes have been made by brokers through this monopoly. The public has no access to the exchange by way of membership except by buying a seat and paying a very large sum for it. Therefore it is a monopoly. Probably it has to be something of a monopoly. But after all it is essentially a public institution. It is the greatest financial agency in the world, and should be not only controlled by the public but it seems to me its membership and the commissions charged should either be fixed by some governmental authority or be supervised by such authority. As matters now stand, the exchange can charge all that the traffic will bear, and that is a burden upon commerce." Senate Hearings 7705.

As finally enacted, the Exchange Act apparently reflected the Untermyer suggestion for it gave the SEC the power to fix and insure "reasonable" rates. Section 19(b) provided:

"(b) *The Commission is further authorized, if* after making appropriate request in writing to a national securities exchange that such exchange effect on its own behalf specified changes in its rules and practices, and after appropriate notice and opportunity for hearing, *the Commission determines* that such exchange has not made the changes so requested, and that *such changes are necessary or appropriate for the protection of investors or to insure fair dealing in securities traded in* upon such exchange or to insure fair administration of such exchange, by rules or regulations or by order *to alter or supplement the rules of such exchange* (insofar as necessary or appropriate to effect such changes) *in respect of such matters as * * * (9) the fixing of reasonable rates of commission,* interest, listing, and other charges." (Emphasis added.)

This provision conformed to the Act's general policy of self-regulation by the exchanges coupled with oversight by the SEC. It is to be noted that the ninth category is one of 12 specifically enumerated. In Merrill Lynch, Pierce, Fenner & Smith v. Ware, 414 U.S. 117, 127–128 (1973), we observed:

"Two types of regulation are reflected in the Act. Some provisions impose direct requirements and prohibitions. Among these are mandatory exchange registration, restrictions on broker and dealer borrowing, and the prohibition of manipulative or deceptive practices. Other provisions are flexible and rely on the technique of self-regulation to achieve their objectives. * * * Supervised self-regulation, although consonant with the traditional private governance of exchanges, allows the Government to monitor exchange business in the public interest."

The congressional reports confirm that while the development of rules for the governing of exchanges, as enumerated in § 19(b), was left to the exchanges themselves in the first instance, the SEC could compel adoption of those changes it felt were necessary to insure fair dealing and protection of the public. See H.R.Rep. No. 1383, 73d Cong., 2d Sess., 15 (1934); S.Rep. No. 792, 73d Cong., 2d Sess., 13 (1934). The latter report, at 15, noted that registered exchanges were required to provide the SEC with "complete information" regarding its rules.

III

With this legislative history in mind, we turn to the actual post–1934 experience of commission rates on the NYSE and Amex. After these two exchanges had registered in 1934 under § 6 of the Exchange Act, both proceeded to prescribe minimum commission rates just as they had prior to the Act. * * * These rates were changed periodically by the exchanges, after their submission to the SEC pursuant to § 6(a)(4) and SEC Rule 17a–8. Although several rate changes appear to have been effectuated without comment by the SEC, in other instances the SEC thoroughly exercised its supervisory powers. Thus, for example, as early as 1958 a study of the NYSE commission rates to determine whether the rates were "reasonable and in accordance with the standards contemplated by applicable provisions of the Securities Exchange Act of 1934," was announced by the SEC. SEC Exchange Act Release No. 5678, April 14, 1958. * * * This study resulted in an agreement by the NYSE to reduce commission rates in certain transactions, to engage in further study of the rate structure by the NYSE in collaboration with the SEC, and to provide the SEC with greater advance notice of proposed rate changes. SEC Exchange Act Release No. 5889, February 20, 1959. * * * The SEC specifically stated that it had undertaken the study "in view of the responsibilities and duties imposed upon the Commission by Section 19(b) * * * with respect to the rules of national securities exchanges, including rules relating to the fixing of commission rates." Ibid.

Under subsection (d) of § 19 of the Act (which subsection was added in 1961) * * * the SEC was directed to investigate the adequacy of exchange rules for the protection of investors. Accordingly, the SEC began a detailed study of exchange rules in that year. In 1963 it released its conclusions in a six-volume study. SEC Report of Special Study of Securities Markets, H.Doc. No. 95, 88th Cong., 1st Sess. The Study, among other things, focused on problems of the structure of commission rates and procedures, and standards for setting and reviewing rate levels. Id., pt. 5, at 102. The SEC found that the rigid commission rate structure based on value of the round lot was causing a variety of "questionable consequences," such as "give-ups" and the providing of special services for certain large, usually institutional, customers. These attempts indirectly to achieve rate alterations made more difficult the administration of the rate structure and clouded the cost data used as the basis for determination of rates. These effects were believed by the SEC to necessitate a complete study of the structure. Moreover, the SEC concluded that methods for determining the reasonableness of rates were in need of overhaul. Not only was there a need for more complete information about the economics of the securities business and commission rates in particular, but also for a determination and articulation of the criteria important in arriving at a reasonable rate structure. Hence, while the Study did not produce any major immediate changes in commission rate structure or levels, it did constitute a careful articulation of the problems in the structure and of the need for further studies that would be essential as a basis for future changes. * * *

In 1968, the SEC, while continuing the study started earlier in the decade, began to submit a series of specific proposals for change and to require their implementation by the exchanges. Through its Exchange Act Release No. 8324, May 28, 1968, the SEC requested the NYSE to revise its commission rate schedule, including a reduction of rates for orders for round lots in excess of 400 shares or, alternatively, the elimination of minimum rate requirements for orders in excess of $50,000. These changes were viewed by the SEC as interim measures, to be pending further consideration "in the context of the Commission's responsibilities to consider the national policies embodied both in the securities laws and in the antitrust laws." Letter of May 28, 1968, from SEC Chairman Cohen to NYSE President Haack. App. A284, A285. In response to these communications, the NYSE (and Amex) eventually adopted a volume discount for orders exceeding 1,000 shares, as well as other alterations in rates, all approved by the SEC. * * *

In 1971 the SEC concluded its hearings begun in 1968. Finding that "minimum commissions on institutional size orders are neither necessary nor appropriate," the SEC announced that it would not object to competitive rates on portions of orders above a stated level. Letter of February 3, 1971, from SEC

Commissioner Smith to President Haack. App. A353. See also SEC Exchange Act Release No. 9007, October 22, 1970. Although at first supporting a $100,000 order as the cutoff below which fixed rates would be allowed, ibid., the SEC later decided to permit use of $500,000 as the breakpoint. After a year's use of this figure, the SEC required the exchanges to reduce the cutoff point to $300,000 in April 1972. Statement of the SEC on the Future Structure of the Securities Markets, February 2, 1972. * * * (Policy Study).

The 1972 Policy Study emphasized the problems of the securities markets, and attributed as a major cause of those problems the prevailing commission rate structure. The Policy Study noted:

"Our concern with the fixed minimum commission * * * is not only with the level of the rate structure but with its side effects as well. Of these, perhaps the most important are the following:

"(a) Dispersion of trading in listed securities.

"(b) Reciprocal practices of various kinds.

"(c) Increasing pressure for exchange membership by institutions."
Id., at A385.

Since commission rates had been fixed for a long period of time, however, and since it was possible that revenue would decline if hasty changes were made, the SEC believed that there should be no rush to impose competitive rates. Rather, the effect of switching to competition should be gauged on a step-by-step basis, and changes should be made "at a measured, deliberate pace." Id., at A387. The result of the introduction of competitive rates for orders exceeding $500,000 was found to be a substantial reduction in commissions, with the rate depending on the size of the order. In view of this result, the SEC determined to institute competition in the $300,000–$500,000 range as well.

Further reduction followed relatively quickly. * * * In June, the SEC began hearings on the rate schedules, stimulated in part by a request by the NYSE to permit an increase of 15% of the current rate on all orders from $5,000 to $300,000, and to permit a minimum commission on small orders (below $5,000) as well. * * * Three months later, after completion of the hearings, the SEC determined that it would allow the increases. * * * The SEC also announced, however: "It will act promptly to terminate the fixing of commission rates by stock exchanges after April 30, 1975, if the stock exchanges do not adopt rule changes achieving that result." Id., at 28.

Elaboration of the SEC's rationale for this phasing out of fixed commission rates was soon forthcoming. * * * Although not purporting to elucidate fully its reasons for abolishing fixed rates, the SEC did suggest several considerations basic to its decision: the heterogeneous nature of the brokerage industry; the desirability of insuring trading on, rather than off, the exchanges; doubt that small investors are subsidized by large institutional investors under the fixed rate system; and doubt that small firms would be forced out of business if competitive rates were required. * * *

The SEC formally requested the exchanges to make the appropriate changes in their rules. When negative responses were received from the NYSE and others, the SEC released for public comment proposed Securities Exchange Act Rules 19b–3 and 10b–22. Proposed Rule 19b–3, applicable to intra-and nonmember rates effective May 1, 1975, would prohibit the exchanges from using or compelling their members to use fixed rates of commission. It also would require the exchanges to provide explicitly in their rules that nothing therein requires or permits arrangements or agreements to fix rates. Proposed Rule 10b–22 would prohibit agreements with respect to the fixing of commission rates by brokers, dealers, or members of the exchanges. See SEC Exchange Act Release No. 11073, October 24, 1974. * * *.

Upon the conclusion of hearings on the proposed rules, the SEC determined to adopt Rule 19b–3, but not Rule 10b–22. SEC Exchange Act Release No. 11203, January 23, 1975. * * * Effective May 1, 1975 competitive rates were to be utilized by exchange members in transactions of all sizes for persons other than members of the exchanges. Effective May 1, 1976, competitive rates were to be mandatory in transactions for members as well, i.e., floor brokerage rates. Competition in floor brokerage rates was so deferred until 1976 in order to permit an orderly transition. * * *

In 1975 both Houses of the Congress did in fact enact legislation dealing directly with commission rates. Although the bills initially passed by each chamber differed somewhat, the Conference Committee compromised the differences. Compare H.R. 4111, § 6(p), as discussed in H.R.Rep.No.94–123, 94th Cong., 1st Sess., 51–53, 67–68 (1975), with S.249, § 6(e), as discussed in S.Rep.No.94–75, 94th Cong., 1st Sess., 71–72, 98 (1975). The measure, as so compromised, was signed by the President on June 5, 1975.

The new legislation amends § 19(b) of the Securities Exchange Act to substitute for the heretofore existing provision a scheme for SEC review of proposed rules and rule changes of the various self-regulatory organizations. Reference to commission rates is now found in the new § 6(e), generally providing that after the date of enactment "no national securities exchange may impose any schedule or fix rates of commissions, allowances, discounts, or other fees to be charged by its members." An exception is made for floor brokerage rates which may be fixed by the exchanges until May 1, 1976. Further exceptions from the ban against fixed commissions are provided if approved by the SEC after certain findings: prior to November 1, 1976, the Commission may allow the exchanges to fix commissions if it finds this to be "in the public interest," § 6(e)(1)(A); after November 1, 1976, the exchanges may be permitted by the SEC to fix rates of commission if the SEC finds (1) the rates are reasonable in relation to costs of service (to be determined pursuant to standards of reasonableness published by the SEC), and (2) if the rates "do not impose any burden on competition not necessary or appropriate in furtherance of the purposes of this title, taking into consideration the competitive effects of permitting such schedule or fixed rates weighed against the competitive effects of other lawful actions which the Commission is authorized to take under this title." § 6(e)(1)(B)(ii). The statute specifically provides that even if the SEC does permit the fixing of rates pursuant to one of these exceptions, the SEC by rule may abrogate such practice if it finds that the fixed rates "are no longer reasonable, in the public interest, or necessary to accomplish the purposes of this title." § 6(e)(2).

* * *

As of May 1, 1975, pursuant to order of the SEC, fixed commission rates were eliminated and competitive rates effectuated. Although it is still too soon to determine the total effect of this alteration, there have been no reports of disastrous effects for the public, investors, the industry, or the markets.

* * *

IV

This Court has considered the issue of implied repeal of the antitrust laws in the context of a variety of regulatory schemes and procedures. Certain axioms of construction are now clearly established. Repeal of the antitrust laws by implication is not favored and not casually to be allowed. Only where there is a "plain repugnancy between the antitrust and regulatory provisions" will repeal be implied. * * *

The starting point for our consideration of the particular issue presented by this case, viz., whether the antitrust laws are impliedly repealed or replaced as a result of the statutory provisions and administrative and congressional experience concerning fixed commission rates, of course, is our decision in *Silver*. There the Court considered the relationship between the antitrust laws and the Securities Exchange Act, and did so specifically with respect to the action of an exchange in ordering its members to remove private direct telephone connections with the offices of a nonmember. Such action, absent any immunity derived from the regulatory laws, would be a *per se* violation of § 1 of the Sherman Act. 373 U.S., at 347. Concluding that the proper approach to the problem was to reconcile the operation of the antitrust laws with a regulatory scheme, the Court established a "guiding principle" for the achievement of this reconciliation. Under this principle, "[r]epeal is to be regarded as implied only if necessary to make the Securities Exchange Act work, and even then only to the minimum extent necessary." Id., at 357.

In *Silver*, the Court concluded that there was no implied repeal of the antitrust laws in that factual context because the Exchange Act did not provide for SEC jurisdiction or review of particular applications of rules enacted by the exchanges. It noted:

"Although the Act gives to the Securities and Exchange Commission the power to request exchanges to make changes in their rules, '19(b), and impliedly, therefore, to disapprove any rules adopted by an exchange, see also § 6(a)(4), it does not give the Commission jurisdiction to review particular instances of enforcement of exchange rules." Ibid.

At the time *Silver* was decided, both the rules and constitution of the NYSE provided that the exchange could require discontinuance of wire service between the office of a member and a nonmember at any time. There was no provision for notice or statement of reasons. While these rules were permissible under the general power of the exchanges to adopt rules regulating relationships between members and nonmembers, and the SEC could disapprove the rules, the SEC could not forbid or regulate any particular application of the rules. Hence, the regulatory agency could not prevent application of the rules that would have undesirable anticompetitive effects; there was no governmental oversight of the exchange's self-regulatory action, and no method of insuring that some attention at least was given to the public interest in competition.

The Court, therefore, concluded that the absence in *Silver* of regulatory supervision over the application of the exchange rules prevented any conflict arising between the regulatory scheme and the antitrust laws. * * * The Court in *Silver* cautioned, however, that "[s]hould review of exchange self-regulation be provided through a vehicle other than the antitrust laws, a different case as to antitrust exemption would be presented." 373 U.S., at 360. It amplified this statement in a footnote:

"Were there Commission jurisdiction and ensuing judicial review for scrutiny of a particular exchange ruling * * * a different case would arise concerning exemption from the operation of laws designed to prevent anticompetitive activity, an issue we do not decide today." 373 U.S., at 358 n. 12.

It is patent that the case presently at bar is, indeed, that "different case" to which the Court in *Silver* referred. In contrast to the circumstances of *Silver*, § 19(b) gave the SEC direct regulatory power over exchange rules and practices with respect to "the fixing of reasonable rates of commission." Not only was the SEC authorized to disapprove rules and practices concerning commission rates, but the agency also was permitted to require alteration or supplementation of the rules and practices when "necessary or appropriate for the protection of investors or to insure fair dealings in securities traded in upon such exchange." Since 1934 all rate changes have been brought to the attention of the SEC, and it has taken an active role in review of proposed rate changes during the last 15 years.[a] Thus, rather than presenting a case of SEC impotence to affect application of exchange rules in particular circumstances, this case involves explicit statutory authorization for SEC review of all exchange rules and practices dealing with rates of commission and resultant SEC continuing activity.

Having determined that this case is, in fact, the "different case," we must then make inquiry as to the proper reconciliation of the regulatory and antitrust statutes involved here, keeping in mind the principle that repeal of the antitrust laws will be "implied only if necessary to make the Securities Exchange Act work, and even then only to the minimum extent necessary." Id., at 357. We hold that these requirements for implied repeal are clearly satisfied here. To permit operation of the antitrust laws with respect to commission rates, as urged by petitioner Gordon and the United States as *amicus curiae*, would unduly interfere, in our view, with the operation of the Securities Exchange Act.

    * * *

Our disposition of this case differs from that of the Seventh Circuit in Thill Securities Corp. v. New York Stock Exchange, 433 F.2d 264 (1970), cert. denied, 401 U.S. 994 (1971), where antitrust immunity for the NYSE's antirebate rule was claimed and denied. The Court of Appeals reversed a grant of summary judgment in favor of the NYSE, and remanded for further evidence regarding the effects of the anti-rebate rule on competition, the degree of actual review by the SEC, and the extent to which the rule was necessary to make the Exchange Act work. 433 F.2d, at 270. This ruling is persuasively distinguishable on at least two grounds from the case at bar: First, there was no evidence presented regarding the extent of SEC review of the challenged rule. Second, the antirebate practice differs from fixed commission rates in that (1) it was not among the items specifically listed in § 19b, although the practice might reasonably be thought to be related to the fixing of commission rates, and (2) it does not necessarily apply uniformly, and may be applied in a discriminatory manner. We do not believe it necessary, in the circumstances of this case, to take further evidence concerning the competitive effects of fixed rates, or the

---

a. For a different reading of history relating to SEC exercise of its § 19(b)(9) authority over commission rates, see Werner, Adventure in Social Control of Finance: The National Market System for Securities, 75 Colum. L. Rev. 1233, 1289–1292 (1975).

necessity of fixed rates as a keystone of the operation of exchanges under the Exchange Act. To the extent that the Court of Appeals in *Thill* viewed the question of implied repeal as a question of fact, concerning whether the particular rule itself is necessary to make the Act work, we decline to follow that lead.

* * *

In sum, the statutory provision authorizing regulation, § 19(b)(9), the long regulatory practice, and the continued congressional approval illustrated by the new legislation, point to one, and only one, conclusion. The Securities Exchange Act was intended by the Congress to leave the supervision of the fixing of reasonable rates of commission to the SEC. Interposition of the antitrust laws, which would bar fixed commission rates as *per se* violations of the Sherman Act, in the face of positive SEC action, would preclude and prevent the operation of the Exchange Act as intended by Congress and as effectuated through SEC regulatory activity. Implied repeal of the antitrust laws is, in fact, necessary to make the Exchange Act work as it was intended; failure to imply repeal would render nugatory the legislative provision for regulatory agency supervision of exchange commission rates.

Affirmed.

■ [JUSTICES DOUGLAS and STEWART each wrote concurring opinions.]

––––––––

1. *Primary Jurisdiction.* The primary jurisdiction doctrine, relied upon in *Gordon,* is "specifically applicable to claims properly cognizable in court that contain some issue within the special competence of an administrative agency."[1] When properly invoked, this doctrine "permits the court to make a 'referral' to the agency, staying further proceedings so as to give the parties reasonable opportunity to seek an administrative ruling." Until recently, attempts to invoke this doctrine in other areas involving the SEC's special competence had met with less success.[2] However, in *Friedman v. Salomon/Smith Barney, Inc.,*[3] a federal district court in late 2000 dismissed an antitrust class action alleging that the major U.S. underwriting firms had conspired to restrict the ability of investors to sell shares in initial public offerings by imposing "anti-flipping" restrictions, based on the *Gordon* doctrine of implied antitrust immunity. Although the court indicated that claims of implied immunity are not favored, it found the following factors relevant: (1) statutory language authorized the SEC to regulate the conduct at issue; (2) the evidence showed that Congress was aware of the practices involved at the time it legislated; (3) the SEC had considered the possibility of regulation of the challenged conduct; and (4) permitting the antitrust action would subject defendants to conflicting standards. Still, because the SEC had never authorized the anti-flipping rules or penalties that the underwriters had imposed, *Friedman* appears to go beyond the prior case law.

1. See Reiter v. Cooper, 507 U.S. 258, 268 (1993).

2. See In re NASDAQ Market–Makers Antitrust Litig., 169 F.R.D. 493 (S.D.N.Y. 1996); In re Prudential Ins. Co. of America Sales Practices Litig., 962 F.Supp. 450 (D.N.J.1997).

3. 2000 WL 1804719, Fed. Sec. L. Rep. (CCH) Para. 91,273 (S.D.N.Y.2000).

2. *Repeal of Fixed Commissions.* That the New York Stock Exchange imposed a schedule of commissions that amounted in substance to a lawful price-fixing agreement among NYSE member brokers proved highly objectionable to Congress (even if it did not to the Supreme Court). As a result, § 6(e) of the 1934 Act was enacted as part of the Securities Act Amendments of 1975 to prohibit fixed commission rates as of May 1, 1975, unless the SEC made specific findings and utilized special exemptions set forth in the legislation.[4] Reading the writing on the wall, the Commission declined to utilize its special exemptive power to uphold fixed commissions and instead adopted Rule 19b–3, which precluded fixed commission rates after May 1, 1975 (long known as "May Day" in the industry). Immediately, there was a dramatic drop in average commissions (with the decline exceeding 50% in the case of the commissions charged to large institutional customers).[5] Trading volume surged, and brokerage profits actually increased. Today, it is estimated that a retail trade that cost $200 in brokerage costs in 1974 may cost as little as $10 (or even less) from a deep discount broker.[6] None of the adverse consequences long predicted by the NYSE if fixed commissions were ended (i.e., failures of brokerage houses, loss of market liquidity, and higher prices to small customers) came to pass. One unexpected crisis did, however, result: many firms were logistically unable to handle the increase in trading that followed, sometimes with serious financial consequences.

Overall, May Day was less a revolution than an evolution, because the fixed rate system had been breaking down for a decade. Moreover, some of the means by which institutions avoided fixed commission rates have survived and continue to complicate any more thoroughgoing attempt at institutionalizing active price competition within the national market system. In particular, the existence of fixed brokerage commissions probably explains the appearance of the following special practices within the industry:

3. *The Third Market.* If the costs of executing transactions on the NYSE were artificially high during this era of fixed commissions, an obvious alternative was to take the transaction to another market. The difficulty with the alternative was that a long-standing NYSE rule (known as Rule 390) prohibited NYSE members from executing a trade in an NYSE–listed security off the floor of the NYSE. This "off-board" trading restriction effectively meant that only broker-dealers who were not members of the NYSE could make an alternative market in NYSE–listed securities in order to reduce transaction costs. With the growth in institutional trading and block trading, such a "third market" did develop in the late 1950s.[7] This over-the-counter market traded exchange-listed

---

4. For the suggestion that the consistency for fixed commissions had dissipated as NYSE specialists saw business being diverted to other markets, and so did not resist the abolition of fixed rates aggressively, see Jarrell, Change at the Exchange, The Causes and Effects of Deregulation, 27 J.L. & Econ. 273 (1984).

5. The SEC has estimated that investor savings simply for the year 1976 from ending fixed rates amounted to $485.3 million. See 6 L. Loss & J. Seligman, Securities Regulation (3d ed.1990) at 2883. Commission rates declined by 57% for institutional investors and

20% for individual investors. *Id.* at 2882. In addition, profitability of the securities industry increased significantly, and share volume more than tripled between 1974 and 1980. *Id.* at 2883.

6. See Mark Borrelli, Market Making in the Electronic Age, 32 Loy. U. Chi. L. J. 815 (2001).

7. The term "third market" assumes that the exchanges are the "first market" and that the over-the-counter market is the second market. The "third market" is then the over-the-counter market in exchange-list-

securities and explicitly offered volume discounts. For a time, it became a serious threat to the exchanges, as institutions directed their business there.

4. *The Winners and Losers Under Deregulation.* The abolition of fixed commissions in 1975 produced a number of immediate changes in market structure. First, the "third market" largely disappeared for a time; third market volume shrank from 7.87% of the total volume of exchange-listed securities in 1972 to less than 3% in 1978.[8] Second, a new institution appeared: the discount broker, who charged commissions from 50% to 90% lower than those charged by full service brokerage firms.[9] Regional exchanges also lost business, as the need for reciprocity vanished once competitive rates were mandated. Still, the industry as a whole thrived as trading volume increased dramatically.

5. *"Soft Dollars" and § 28(e).* Fixed commissions had given rise to an evasionary tactic known as "give-ups," under which institutional customers with economic leverage would demand that their broker share its fixed commission with another broker who provided the institutional client with some free service (such as securities research or computer services). In this way, they negotiated a hidden discount that partially (and, ultimately, largely) undercut the fixed commission system. As a result, numerous "research boutique" brokerage firms grew up, supported by the "give-up" system with its hidden discounts. Although the competitive need to utilize give-ups as a way of outflanking fixed commissions ended in 1975, the practice survived. First, money managers secured legislative protection for paying above-market brokerage commissions. Fearing that in the absence of legislative authorization they would be forced to use the lowest priced broker or otherwise would be liable to their clients for breach of fiduciary duty, institutional money managers successfully lobbied Congress for the addition of § 28(e) to the 1934 Act. Essentially, § 28(e) creates a "safe harbor" that allows money managers to pay above-market commission rates in return for special services that the broker either provides or arranges for. These special services—known in the trade as "soft dollars"—chiefly consist of research and advisory services or computer facilities made available to the money manager. Obviously, there is a potential for a substantial conflict of interest, because such services may not necessarily benefit the clients that the money manager serves as a fiduciary. Suppose, for example, that the special research is presented to the money manager's leading employees at a seminar held at a ski lodge in Vail, Colorado during the January season? Is this research or employee compensation—or both?

By its terms, § 28(e) applies to protect the money manager from being found to have breached its fiduciary responsibilities because it paid an above-market commission only when it "determined in good faith that such amount of commission was reasonable in relation to the value of the brokerage and research services provided by such member broker or dealer, viewed in terms of either that particular transaction or [its] * * * overall responsibilities with respect to the account for which [it] * * * exercises investment discretion." As a result, the degree to which § 28(e) covers "give-ups" remains uncertain, even fifteen years after its adoption.[10] Clearly, it was intended to preempt common

---

ed securities, and the "fourth market" is represented by proprietary trading systems.

8. See 6 L. Loss & J. Seligman, supra note 5, at 2882.

9. Between 1976 and 1980, the market share of discount brokers increased from less than 0.4% to 6.0%. See 6 Loss and Seligman, supra note 5 at 2883.

10. For overviews, see Blanc, "Soft Dol-

law principles or any other state or federal law interpretations that would expose fiduciaries to liability solely because they failed to obtain the lowest brokerage commission available. But it does not absolve fiduciaries from all liability. The House Report accompanying the legislation made the following distinction:

> "[A] challenge to fiduciary conduct must be premised on the basis that a fiduciary has failed to use reasonable business judgment in selecting his broker and valuing the services rendered. It is, of course, expected that money managers paying brokers an amount which is based on the quality and reliability of the broker's services including the availability and value of the research would stand ready and be required to demonstrate that such expenditures were bona fide."[11]

For the SEC, the major question in interpreting the scope of 28(e) has been that of allocating between true "research" costs and other costs. In a 1986 release, it drew the following distinction:

> "[T]he controlling principle to be used to determine whether something qualifies as research is whether it provides lawful and appropriate assistance to the money manager in the performance of his investment decision-making responsibilities. In making this determination, the fact that a product or service is readily and customarily available and offered to the general public on a commercial basis does not dictate that the product or service is not research * * *.
>
> In many cases, a product or service termed "research" may serve other functions that are not related to the making of investment decisions. For example, management information systems may integrate such diverse functions as trading, execution, accounting, recordkeeping and other administrative matters, such as measuring the performance of accounts. Where a product obtained with soft dollars has a mixed use, a money manager faces a conflict of interest in obtaining that product by causing his clients to pay more than competitive brokerage commission rates. Therefore, the Commission believes that where a product has a mixed use, a money manager should make a reasonable allocation of the cost of the product according to its use. The percentage of the service or specific component that provides assistance to a money manager in the investment decision-making process may be paid in commission dollars, while those services that provide administrative or non-research assistance are outside the section 28(e) safe harbor and must be paid for by the money manager using his own funds. The money manager must keep adequate books and records concerning allocations so as to be able to make the required allocations."[12]

In this same Release, the Commission restated its prior position that a money manager could pay "soft dollars" to a broker for research produced by third parties. Research may even be delivered directly by the third party to the money manager (and not routed through the broker for redelivery to the money

---

lars," 18 Rev. Sec. & Comm. Reg. 51 (1985); Myers, Directed Brokerage and "Soft Dollars" Under ERISA: New Concerns for Plan Fiduciaries, 42 Bus. Law. 553 (Feb.1987); Herzel, Paying Up On Stock Brokerage Commissions Under Section 28(e) of the Securities Exchange Act, 31 Bus. Law. 1479 (1976).

11. H.R.Rep. No. 94–123, 94th Cong., 1st Sess. 95 (1975); see also 6 Loss and Seligman, supra note 5, at 2886–87.

12. Securities Exchange Act Release No. 23,170, 35 SEC Dock. 703, 705–06 (1986).

manager) so long as the broker/money manager contract specifies that the "research" is to be "provided by" the broker. As practices have evolved, the Commission will not object to a money manager paying "reasonable" soft dollar commissions to a broker for "third party" research so long as the manager does not commit itself to performing a minimum number of transactions in return for the research. However, the manager may, with the beneficiaries' consent, obligate itself to pay directly for the cost of research if a minimum number of transactions does not occur.[13] At this point, however, there seems to be little to distinguish "third party" research paid for with "soft dollars" from the old-fashioned customer directed "give-up."

One last point must be understood about § 28(e): by its own terms, it can never be violated. It is simply a "safe harbor," and when transactions fall outside that safe harbor, it is still necessary to look to the statutory or common law defining the relevant fiduciary obligation.

SECTION 3. UNCERTAIN PROGRESS TOWARDS A NATIONAL MARKET SYSTEM

Statutes and Regulations

Securities Exchange Act of 1934 §§ 11, 11A, 12(f)(2), 19.

Exchange Act Rules 11a–1; 11a1–1(T); 11a1–2; 11b–1; 11Aa3–1; 11Aa3–2; 11Ac1–1; 11Ac1–2; 11Ac1–4; 11Ac1–5; 11Ac1–6; 11Ac1–7.

———

The 1975 Securities Acts Amendments contemplated much greater changes than simply the abolition of fixed commission rates; rather, they envisioned a national market system that would ensure investors competitive markets and "best execution" of their trades. Section 11A, which was the centerpiece of the 1975 Securities Acts Amendments, specified five basic goals that the SEC was to pursue through rulemaking in implementing the national market system:

1. Economically efficient execution of transactions;

2. Fair competition among broker-dealers; among exchanges, and between exchanges and other markets;

3. Ready availability of quotation and transaction information to broker-dealers and investors;

4. The ability of broker-dealers to execute orders in the best market; and

5. An opportunity, consistent with other goals, for investors to executive orders without the participation of a dealer.

In theory, the competition among markets would prevent specialists on the primary exchanges (NYSE or AMEX) from charging monopolistic prices for trading in listed securities. Bid and asked spreads in listed securities would thus tighten in the face of competitive pressure. From a viewpoint more than twenty-five years later, it is apparent that active price competition did not

13. See 6 Loss and Seligman, supra note 5, at 2892–93; see also Securities Ex- change Act Rel. No. 16,679 (1980).

develop between market centers (at least to the extent the Commission hoped). Instead, a different form of competition developed between market centers: namely, competition for stock listings (particularly among high technology stocks that became the subject of continuing battles between Nasdaq and the NYSE).

What explains the initially limited progress toward price competition? Some believe that the five goals listed above in § 11A were in tension; for example, as discussed below, new market centers sometimes arose because they reduced transparency by allowing broker-dealers to execute "hidden" orders different from their public orders. Others point to collusive practices and related anti-competitive practices, such as payments for order flow, by which new market centers (such as the Third Market) competed for the broker's business by offering rebates to the broker, instead of reduced commissions to the customer.[1] Others fault the SEC for a lack of will and energy, suggesting that in this area the Commission has been captured by the industry.[2] In all likelihood, however, the SEC was probably more constrained in implementing the national market system by a fear of market fragmentation: namely, the concern that as new market centers sprang up, securities could come to trade at different prices in different markets at the same time, with an overall loss in market efficiency.

In evaluating the SEC's overall progress, it is necessary to focus on the different goals of the national market system and recognize that some goals were easier to achieve than others:

1. *Transaction and Quotation Information.* On this front, the 1975 Securities Act Amendments did effect an informational revolution. Market transparency requires that investors be able to see the quotations being offered and the transactions being executed across markets on a close to real time basis. As a practical matter, this requires that transaction and quotation information from different markets be consolidated into a single stream of data that is available to all market participants and investors. This is today done by the Consolidated Tape Association ("CTA"),[3] which collects transaction information on listed securities and the Consolidated Quotation System ("CQS"),[4] which aggregates quotation data for listed securities, and Nasdaq, which disseminates both for Nasdaq securities.[5]

During the early 1980s, the Commission extended last-sale transaction reporting to a broad number of over-the-counter stocks (such securities being known today as the National Market System).[6] In addition, the Commission

---

1. For a description of these practices, see Note, The Perils of Payment for Order Flow, 107 Harv. L. Rev. 1675 (1994).

2. See Macey & Haddock, Shirking at the SEC: The Failure of the National Market System, 1985 U.Ill.L.Rev. 315; Seligman, Another Unspecial Study: The SEC's Market 2000 Report and Competitive Developments in the U.S. Capital Markets, 50 Bus. Law. 485 (1995).

3. The CTA provides "last sale" information for all listed stocks in all markets. It was created pursuant to Rule 17a–15, which required all exchanges and Nasdaq to agree to a transaction reporting plan.

4. Rule 11Ac1–1 resulted in the creation of the Consolidated Quotation Plan, which was filed with the SEC on July 25, 1978. See Securities Exchange Act Release No. 16,410 (Dec. 7, 1979).

5. All three systems—CTA, CQSm and Nasdaq—disseminate their data pursuant to their filed plans for fees that are paid by various vendors (for example, Bloomberg and Reuters), who in turn charge subscriber fees to broker-dealers and other end users.

6. See Rules 11Aa3–1 and 11Aa3–2. In 1987, the Commission largely ceded to the stock exchanges and the NASD the responsibility for determining the standards for eligi-

imposed an obligation on market makers and specialists in exchange-listed or National Market System ("NMS") securities to report immediately all changes in their bid and asked quotations and to execute at their quoted prices subject to Commission guidelines.[7] These changes brought a wave of sunlight to the over-the-counter market, which had historically been characterized by uncertainty as to the then prevailing price and illusory price quotations. As a result, the transition to a National Market System has been largely achieved on the *informational* level: market participants today have easy access to current and reliable information about most securities in which there is active trading. Yet, as noted at the end of this Chapter, the system created to collect and transmit this information—chiefly, the CTA and the CQS—was a governmentally created monopoly, which some believe resulted in excessive costs and discriminated against new entrants. Hence, one of the newest issues in securities regulation, discussed below, is how to determine these charges and allocate the revenues.

2. *"Off–Board" Trading Restrictions.* Since early in its existence, the New York Stock Exchange ("NYSE") prohibited members from trading NYSE-listed securities away from the NYSE. Although such a prohibition, which was long embodied in NYSE Rule 390, obviously restricted competition, the SEC moved cautiously and slowly to repeal it, gradually chipping away at it (although it had clear authority under the 1975 Securities Acts Amendments to order its immediate repeal). The SEC's principal concern was that market fragmentation might result if broker-dealers could "internalize" order flow (that is, trade themselves with their own customers in off-exchange transactions at the then prevailing spread) if Rule 390 were eliminated. Initially, the SEC adopted Rule 19c–1 in 1975, which made off-board trading restrictions imposed by stock exchange rules inapplicable to agency transactions; that is, an NYSE-member broker could take a client's trade to the Third Market, another exchange, or Nasdaq, but it could not itself buy or sell as a principal in NYSE-listed stocks in those markets. In 1980, the SEC went further and, in Rule 19c–3, it limited the reach of Rule 390 to stocks listed on the NYSE before April 26, 1979. Over time, this meant that the majority of NYSE stocks were no longer subject to Rule 390 because they had been listed after that date, but the most heavily traded stocks were still subject to Rule 390. Finally, in 2000, the NYSE itself sought and received SEC approval for the repeal of Rule 390.[8] The restriction had ultimately become an embarrassment for the NYSE that it could not easily defend.

3. *Quotation and Order Handling Rules.* Since 1975, the SEC has increasingly focused on the improvement of order execution. Prior to 1978, the quotes disseminated on Nasdaq did not specify size (or the number of shares to which the quote applied). Market makers also did not always honor their quotes and might refuse to trade at the specified price in any volume. Also, some market makers might simply suspend operations for the day if market conditions soured or they feared excessive volatility. In 1978, the SEC adopted the "Firm Quote Rule," Rule 111Ac1–1, to deal with problems.[9] The rule requires broker-dealers who maintain quotes for a security to promptly disseminate these

---

bility for inclusion in the NMS. See Securities Exchange Act Release No. 24635 (June 23, 1987).

7. This obligation to report bid and asked prices gave rise to the "consolidated quotation system." See Rules 11Ac1–1 and

11Ac1–2. Securities Act Release No. 18482 (1982).

8. See Securities Exchange Act Release No. 42,758 (May 5, 2000).

9. See Securities Exchange Act Release No. 14415 (Jan. 26, 1978).

quotations and to honor them by executing transactions at the quoted prices and sizes. In 1996, the SEC extended this rule to apply to Nasdaq market makers who issued quotations on exchange-listed securities, at least if the market maker is responsible for more than one percent of the volume in the security.[10] As a result, a significant number of NASD enforcement and arbitration disputes came to focus on "backing away" complaints in which the assertion is made that a market maker had failed to honor its quotation.

Even more important than the Firm Quote Rule in the evolution of the National Market System were the SEC's Order Handling Rules, which were adopted in 1996. The backdrop to these rules is critical to understanding their intent. In the mid–1990's, a major controversy erupted when it was discovered that a "pricing convention" had developed among Nasdaq market-makers, under which they quoted stocks only in even-eighth prices, thus effectively maintaining the minimum price spread at a seemingly artificially inflated quarter of a point. Although this controversy led to SEC discipline, reform of the NASD's governance structure, and to a class action settlement of over $1 billion, the policy problem facing the SEC was how to reduce the seemingly artificial price spreads in Nasdaq quotations if Nasdaq dealers were inclined to collude. The SEC's innovative answer was to utilize limit orders that customers could introduce into the Nasdaq quotation display at prices between the bid and asked spread. A limit order is an order to buy or sell at a specific price (as opposed to a "market order," which is an order to buy or sell at the best price then available in the market). Thus, if the prices quoted by market makers left an artificially wide spread, a new source of competition could be introduced in the form of public customers by allowing them to introduce price quotations that would narrow the bid/asked spread. Once these limit orders narrowed the displayed spread, then brokers holding market orders from their clients would be required by their duty of best execution to execute their trades against these limit orders.

Essentially, this is what the SEC's Order Handling Rules, introduced in 1996, attempt to do.[11] Under Rule 11Ac1–4 (the "Display Rule"), dealers who accept limit orders and specialists must display any customer's limit order, including their full size, when the order is placed at a price superior to the market maker or specialist's own quotation. To illustrate, if the market maker's quotation were $18 bid and $19 asked, a customer might place a limit order with this market-maker to buy at $18.50, and this would improve the market-maker's bid quotation to $18.50 bid and $19 asked.[12] If $18.50 were the highest bid price of all bid quotations submitted to Nasdaq and if $18.75 were the lowest asked quotation, then the National Best Bid and Offer ("NBBO") would become $18.50 to $18.75, and all transactions would have to be at this price until the orders were exhausted or a still superior price was quoted.

The Order Handling Rules gave one basic alternative to the market-maker that did not want to improve its quotation upon receipt of a customer's superior limit order: it could send the quotation to an ECN or a market-maker that would comply with the Display Rule.[13] This exemption, however, necessi-

---

10. See Securities Exchange Act Release No. 37619A (Sept. 6, 1996) at *42.

11. See Securities Exchange Act Release No. 37619A (Sept. 12, 1996).

12. Nasdaq's rules only permit a market maker to submit one quotation at a time for display. Hence, to comply with the Display Rule, the market maker must improve its own quotation.

13. See Rule 11Ac1–4(b).

tated an amendment of the Firm Quote Rule to assure that any superior prices displayed on an ECN were available to the public (and not just to the ECN's subscribers). Thus, under an amendment to the Firm Quote Rule, known as the "ECN Amendment," specialists and market-makers who place orders on an ECN at a price superior to their own public quotation must make that price publicly available.[14] This obligation is deemed satisfied if the ECN on which the order is placed displays the superior quotation and allows broker-dealers to execute against it.[15]

The impact of the Order Handling Rules was dramatic. According to some studies, the spreads on Nasdaq tightened by over one-third within just a few years. Another impact, next discussed, was equally important.

4. *The Rise of the ECNs.* While some ECNs predated the Order Handling Rules, their explosive growth in the late 1990's, seems primarily attributable to those rules. Not only could public customers seek matching transactions on an ECN, but now they were assured that, if their limit order was or became superior to other orders on the ECN, it would be displayed on the Nasdaq screen, and all brokers would be required to execute against their limit order if it became part of the inside spread (the NBBO). This was important because the inherent problem with matching systems (which most ECNs are) is that a user can encounter only limited liquidity within them and thus can be left behind if the broader market moves adversely. The Order Handling Rules addressed this problem by integrating orders within the ECN with those in broader market.[16]

A second major advantage of ECNs was their lower execution costs. Because customer orders can interact with each other without the intervention of a market-maker, retail customers flocked to ECNs to avoid paying a spread. Although ECNS charge their subscribers access fees, these fees were no more than $.015 per share as of late 2001[17] and may be even lower if the subscriber qualifies for a volume discount.

A final advantage of ECNs is that market-makers can use it to trade anonymously. If a market-maker or specialist wishes to display a quotation on an ECN that it is different than its publicly offered spread, it may do so under Order Handling Rules (so long as the superior price is accessible to the public generally). Thus, if a market-maker on Nasdaq was offering an aggressively high "offer" price (the price at which it will sell) but wishes to reduce its inventory of that stock for liquidity reasons, it could offer a lower offer price on an ECN. If that lower offer price were the best offer price on that ECN, it would be displayed on the Nasdaq screen—but under the ECN's name, not the market maker's name. This ability to trade on an anonymous basis is important to market-makers who want to signal their belief above future price directions in stocks, but cannot afford to hold a large inventory of the stock.

---

14. See Rule 11Ac–1–1.

15. See Securities Exchange Act Release No. 37619A (Sept. 12, 1996) at *2.

16. A technical qualification is necessary here. Regulation ATS requires that the orders of any subscriber, including a retail customer, must be displayed on Nasdaq if they represent the ECN's best bid or offer price—but only if the ECN is large enough to account for a minimum percentage of trading in the specific security. Hence, some smaller ECNs do not need to display their orders on Nasdaq.

17. See Borrelli, Market Making in the Electronic Age, 32 Loy. U. Chi. L. J. 815, 859 (2001).

ECN's have been less successful in trading NYSE stocks. Initially, the barrier was that they were not entitled to participate in the Consolidated Quotation System ("CQS") because they were not exchanges. In 2000, the SEC partially resolved this problem by approving a Nasdaq rule under which ECNs could place quotations in the CQS in the name of Nasdaq (which is a CQS member).[18] But to qualify, the ECNs are required to register as market-makers with Nasdaq, and many of them have been reluctant to do so. Still, by late 2000, some were trading NYSE-listed stocks through Nasdaq's system.

5. *Exchange Trading of OTC Stocks.* The flip-side of the coin to ECNs trading exchange-listed stocks is the exchange specialist making a market in Nasdaq or other over-the-counter stocks. Such a competition could be created by granting "unlisted trading privileges" to Nasdaq securities on the exchanges.[19] Congress envisioned such a possibility in the 1975 Securities Acts Amendments by enacting § 12(f)(2) of the 1934 Act, which permits exchange specialists to compete directly with market makers in the trading of unlisted stocks. However, § 12(f)(2) requires the SEC to conclude that "unlisted trading" by an exchange specialist in an OTC stock "is consistent with the maintenance of fair and orderly markets and the protection of investors" before granting unlisted trading privileges. The legislative history to this section makes clear that Congress intended that exchanges should ultimately trade "any unlisted security with suitable characteristics."[20] Nonetheless, the SEC has moved very tentatively in this area. In 1985, the SEC adopted a policy under which exchanges could apply to commence unlisted trading in up to 25 Nasdaq National Market System securities, provided certain conditions were satisfied to ensure fuller coordination between Nasdaq and the exchanges.[21] The NYSE declined to participate in this system, and to date only a few regional exchanges have satisfied all the SEC's conditions.[22] As a result, unlisted trading on the exchanges has failed to emerge as a source of serious price competition for Nasdaq dealers.

6. *Decimalization.* Although the Order Handling Rules reduced the price spreads in the equity markets, their impact was in turn overshadowed by decimalization. Since the founding of the NYSE, U.S. securities markets had quoted securities in minimum increments of eighths of a dollar. This tradition dated back to the days when Spanish doubloons, which could be broker physically into "pieces of eight," were the principal currency of exchange, but it was increasingly anachronistic in an era when computerization had reduce trading cost and the volume of trading had increased exponentially. To many, the convention of quoting in terms of minimum increments of one eighths represented the last lawful price-fixing agreement.

Believing that the convention produce excess profits for traders, Congressional leaders of both parties introduced in March 1997 the "Common Cents

---

18. See Securities Exchange Act Release No. 42536 (March 16, 2000).

19. Unlisted trading privileges do not require that the issuer apply to the exchange to list its securities. Thus, an exchange can commence unlisted trading even over the issuer's objections. For an overview, see Simon & Colby, The National Market System for Over–the–Counter Stocks, 55 Geo.Wash. L. Rev. 17, 68–71 (1986).

20. See S.Rep. No. 75, 94th Cong., 1st Sess. 19–20 (1975); see also Parker & Becker, Unlisted Trading Privileges, 14 Rev. Sec. Reg. 853 (1981) (discussing § 12(f)); 5 L. Loss & J. Seligman, Securities Regulation (3d ed. 1990) at 2600.

21. Securities Exchange Act Release No. 22,412 (1987).

22. Securities Exchange Act Release No. 24,407 (1987).

Stock Pricing Act of 1997," which would have required the quotation of equity securities in decimals within one year. Although the bill was opposed by each of the NYSE, the Amex, and the NASD, each yielded to Congressional pressure and voted within months to begin trading stocks in decimals, rather than fractions. Full scale conversion to decimals came in 2000 in the case of the NYSE and 2001 in the case of Nasdaq.[23] Despite predictions by the industry of adverse consequences, the conversion occurred smoothly and spreads fell to a few cents. Institutional investors have complained, however, that the shift to trading in pennies allows the specialists to profit at their expense by stepping in front of large ordes by raising their bid or offer price by a nominal amount.[24]

7. *Remaining Issues in the National Market System.* Although the advent of limit orders, ECNs, and decimalization have narrowed spreads, the competitive struggle between the established market centers and the new entrants has continued, and new issues have surfaced.

SuperMontage. Responding to the fact that ECNs have captured 40% or more of the trading in Nasdaq securities, Nasdaq in 2002 introduced a new trading platform that many saw as a retaliatory blow to the ECNs. It permits market participants to display their trading interest anonymously, as can be done today on ECNs, thus eliminating one motivation for a market maker to send a transaction to an ECN. In addition, the system's display montage will show not only on the best bids and offers at the "top of the market," but trading interest two price levels away; again, this was a response to the competitive challenge of the ECNs, which similarly show trading interest several levels away from the top of the market. The ECNs opposed the adoption of the SuperMontage system, because, at least in its initial versions, it gave the ECNs a low trading priority (i.e., incoming trades would be assigned to Nasdaq market-makers first). Although this procedure was ultimately scrapped, the impact of SuperMontage on ECNs remains a matter of uncertainty and could affect the level of competition in the industry.

"Internalization." The repeal of off-board restrictions (chiefly NYSE Rule 390, discussed earlier) has made it possible for a broker-dealer when it receives an order from a client to "internalize" the order, either trading with the client, itself, as a principal or effecting an "in-home cross" by crossing another client's shares as the counterparty, without in either case exposing the transaction to the market. The Commission has concerns about the "internalization" of order flow, a practice that, it notes, leads to "the withholding of retail orders from other market centers for the purpose of executing them 'in house' as principal, without exposing those orders to buying and selling interest in those other market centers...."[25] What are the SEC's fears if this transaction must occur at the NBBO (i.e., the best price then available in the market)? Essentially, it

---

23. In June, 2000, the SEC ordered the NASD and each of the exchanges to develop decimal conversion places and begin such trading by April, 2001. See Securities Exchange Act Release No. 42914 (June 8, 2000).

24. For example, suppose the bid price in a stock is today $20 and the asked price is $20.05 and a large institution is seeking to acquire a substantial number of shares without moving the market price substantially upward by using limit orders. Sensing that the institution is seeking to buy a substantial

block, the specialist may raise the price above $20 to $20.01 in order to step in front of a limit order at $20, knowing that it can resell to the institution at a higher price. While institutions find this practice unfair, it should be noted that the seller in this example does receive a small incremental profit when the specialist improves the price paid to it.

25. See Securities Exchange Act Release No. 16888 (June 11, 1980).

has two concerns: (1) the dealer may not search for price improvement by exposing the order to others, but will prefer to trade at the existing price because it is the counterparty; and (2) the withdrawal of a large volume of trading from the principal market results in market fragmentation and the possibility that price determination in the principal market will be less accurate.

Although it is clear that the SEC is not prepared to ban internalization, possible compromises include requiring the dealer who internalizes order flow to grant price improvement.[26]

ECN Access to The CQS. Today, ECNs can only trade NYSE-listed stocks by sending their orders through Nasdaq. This is because they do not qualify for membership in the Central Quotation System, because they are neither an exchange nor a registered association. This technological barrier has apparently slowed the ability of ECNs to compete with the NYSE (as of 2000, ECNs accounted for only around 5% of NYSE trading, as opposed to 30% of Nasdaq). Progress toward a truer National Market System will require still fuller integration of ECNs into the trading system.

8. *Best Execution: The "Missing" Duty.* Suppose a security is traded on multiple exchanges or both on an exchange and in the Third Market. Perhaps the exchange specialist's "bid" price is $10 and its "asked" price is $10¼ (thus, the specialist stands ready to buy at $10 and sell at $10.25). But another dealer in the Third Market or on a regional exchange is quoting a "bid" price of $10 and an "asked" price of $10⅜. Can a retail broker buy stock for its client at $10⅜ when it is available at $10.25? Doing so may violate the broker's duty of "best execution," but there is no SEC rule codifying this doctrine.[27] Rather, the duty of best execution derives from agency law and a legal doctrine, known as "shingle theory," which is discussed in Chapter 11, but which holds that a broker-dealer assume a special duty to deal fairly with its customers when it "hangs out its shingle." Conceivably, justifications can be given for taking a transaction to a market that is charging a higher price: for example, it may have greater liquidity and be able to absorb a large order without changing its price; or, it may be faster at executing the transaction (which can be important in a volatile market).

Much more subtle ambiguities also surrounded the duty of best execution. For example, does the broker have a duty to search for price improvement? Should it have to pass through to the customer any inducement paid i to direct a transaction to a particular market? Two developments aggravate this prob-

---

26. This was the NYSE's proposal at the time it repealed Rule 390. See Securities Exchange Act Release No. 42450 (Feb. 23, 2000) at *5.

27. For a critique of this omission, see Lipton, Best Execution: The National Market System's Missing Ingredient, 57 Notre Dame L. Rev. 449 (1982). In 1963, the SEC's Special Study of the Securities Markets recommended that the SEC adopt a "best execution" rule requiring broker-dealers to ascertain the best inter-dealer quotation and provide in all retail transactions an execution as "favorable as may reasonably be ob-

tained." See Simon & Colby, supra note 19, at 27. No such rule has been adopted, although in 1967 the NASD Manual was revised to clarify the duty of best execution:

> "In any transaction for or with a customer, a member * * * shall use reasonable diligence to ascertain the best inter-dealer market for the subject security and buy or sell in the market so that the resulting price to the customer is as favorable as possible under prevailing market conditions."

See NASD Manual (CCH), ¶ 2151 at 2035–36.

lem: (1) large brokerage firms often rely heavily on high speed automatic order routing systems that route the customer's order to a particular market for execution (for example, the NYSE's DOT, the AMEX's PER, the NASD's SOES, and the Pacific Coast's SCOREX, or the Midwest Stock Exchange's MAX);[28] and (2) market-makers pay a small commission to retail brokers for "order flow."[29] Such payments for "directed order flow," which are typically one cent to two cents per share, create an obvious conflict of interest between the broker's desire to maximize its commission revenue and the customer's interest in best execution. Usually, the dealer will charge the same bid/asked spread as the primary exchange, but the exchanges claim that there is a higher possibility that the trade will be effected at a price between the bid and asked quotation (for example, $10\frac{1}{8}$ if the bid is $10 and the asked $10\frac{1}{4}$) when done over an exchange. The exchange's claim is based on the possibility that the specialist will "stop" the customer's buy order, guaranteeing its execution at no worse than the then prevailing best bid or asked price, but delaying it to see if it can cross with an incoming sell order. If, for example, buy and sell orders are matched and crossed at $10\frac{1}{8}$ when the specialist's quotation is $10 bid and $10\frac{1}{4}$ asked, both participants make out better. Although there is evidence that transactions on the primary exchanges are more likely to be between the quotes than those in the same securities executed by NASD Third Market dealers, the dealers respond that customers receive faster execution at guaranteed prices through its facilities. The industry's basic position is that the duty of best execution should require no more than that the customer's broker execute the transaction at the best current displayed bid or offer—thus permitting the broker to internalize the trade, or receive payment for order flow, or use an automatic order routing system.[30] An NASD Committee that studied the problem concluded that the benefits to the customer of receiving low-cost, fast execution, at an assured price, probably exceeded the benefits of an execution between the quotation spread on a primary exchange.

Other commentators have faulted the Commission for not incorporating a duty of best execution as a centerpiece of its national market system.[31]

The SEC's response to the growth during the 1980s of the practice of paying for order flow was highly equivocal. In 1990, in part to legitimize the controversial practice, the NASD proposed a revision in its disclosure policy to require that certain disclosures be made on the customer confirmation when firms receive payments for order flow for customer orders.[32] The Midwest Stock Exchange objected to this proposal, suggesting that it did not go far enough. They asked the SEC to adopt a rule requiring brokers to pass through to their

28. For a description of these automatic order routing and execution systems, see 5 L. Loss & J. Seligman, supra note 20, at 2560–2562. While most (but not all) these systems provide for exposing the order to the market for a brief period (usually fifteen seconds) to improve the execution price, the possibility of such a "between the quotes" execution is seemingly diminished when an order is routed automatically. Also, the NASD's SOES system executes trades automatically at the "inside" market price without order exposure. Id. at 2587.

29. See Simon & Colby, supra note 19, at 96–98 (criticizing the practice); see also Note, supra note 1.

30. See N.A.S.D., Inducements for Order Flow: A Report to the Board of Governors (July 1991). The Report concluded that inducements for order flow did not impair best execution on small orders.

31. See Lipton, supra note 27.

32. See Becker, Sakach & Herring, "Broker–Dealer Order Execution Duties" in PLI, Trading Practices, The Portfolio Execution Process and Soft Dollar Practices (Pickard, ed. 1990) at 453, 473–74.

customers any payment received from a dealer for order flow. Their premise is that a broker's fiduciary obligation to its customer requires it to credit to the customer any undisclosed rebate it received on the customer's business.[33] The SEC declined to adopt the reform proposed by the Midwest Stock Exchange and instead pursued an enhanced disclosure route. In 1994, it adopted Rule 11Ac1–3 and amended Rule 10b–10.[34] Rule 11Ac1–3 requires broker-dealers to disclose, on their annual account statements that they send customers and on new account forms, their policies regarding the receipt of payment for order flow and to provide a detailed description of the nature of the compensation received. Rule 10b–10 was amended to require broker-dealers to state on confirmations whether they receive payments for order flow and that the source and nature of the compensation will be provided to the customer upon written request. The resulting disclosures were largely of a boilerplate nature, and few customers request more specific descriptions. Even if these rules might cause a mild degree of embarrassment to a broker-dealer forced to disclose its practice of receiving rebates for in effecting selling its customer's orders to a market center, the greater impact of these rules was to cut off and preempt any claim that such practices violated state law or breached common law fiduciary duties. In a series of cases, state and federal courts have read these new rules to preempt such attacks.[35]

As a practical matter, the debate over payment for order flow may have been largely superceded by the movement to decimal pricing. Although the significance of payments for order flow has declined, the Commission has nonetheless recently updated and revised its approach to best execution. Its concern is that market fragmentation, caused in part by the success of the ECNs, may impair the quality of order execution. Always uncomfortable with direct regulation of market structure, the Commission in November, 2000, adopted rules that require enhanced disclosure about order routing and execution practices, but do not mandate or bar specific conduct by broker-dealers.[36] Their premise is that such disclosure will allow broker-dealers and investors to make more informed comparisons among market centers when deciding where to route customer dealers. New Rule 11Ac–5 requires "market centers" to disclose on a monthly basis information about the execution of exchange-listed and Nasdaq National Market Securities, including speed of execution, "average realized spread," "average effective spread," and degree of price improvement.[37] The goal of this disclosure is to enable investors and their agents to engage in effective comparison shopping.

As a companion to this rule covering "market centers," the Commission also adopted new Rule 11Ac1–6, which requires disclosure of the material facts relating to a broker-dealer's relationship with each market center to which it routes orders. Beyond disclosure of any inducements paid to the broker for its order flow this Rule also requires disclosure of the broker's "objectives" in routing its order flow.

---

33. Id. at 475.

34. See Securities Exchange Act Release No. 34902 (Oct. 27, 1994).

35. See Gilman v. BHC Secs., Inc., Fed. Sec. L. Rep. (CCH), Para. 99,051 (S.D.N.Y. 1995); Dahl v. Charles Schwab & Co., 545 N.W.2d 918 (Minn.1996).

36. See Securities Exchange Act Release No. 43590 (Nov. 17, 2000).

37. The "effective spread" is intended as a measure of the market center's willingness to grant price improvement.

9. *Is the NBBO Enough?* For many years, market-makers on Nasdaq had assumed that they satisfied their duty of best execution if they executed customers' orders on the inside spread, as shown on their Nasdaq computer screen. This inside spread is known as the "National Best Bid and Offer" (or "NBBO"). But in the 1990's, technological advances made it possible for market-makers to execute orders at prices quoted on private on-line services, such as Instinet and SelectNet (a Nasdaq "wholesale" market chiefly used by dealers themselves), at often superior prices. Was it necessary for market-makers to canvass this market to satisfy their duty of best execution? Must they do so even for a small order that could be automatically executed through the SOES system? Nasdaq market-makers assumed that there was no such duty to look beyond the NBBO, arguing that further inquiry would impose undue costs on them and slow down the process of executing small orders. They also claimed that the SEC had long recognized that NBBO executions satisfied the duty. In *Newton v. Merrill Lynch Pierce Fenner & Smith Inc.,*[38] however, a class action was brought against several large market makers, alleging that the failure to consider this alternative market, which was known to offer superior prices much of the time, breached the defendants' duty of best execution. Although the district court granted summary judgement for defendants, an *en banc* Third Circuit reversed, finding that a trial was necessary to determine the feasibility of using these alternative markets on a large scale to execute retail orders. The duty of best execution, according to the Third Circuit, requires that a market-maker seek to obtain for its customer orders the most favorable terms reasonably available under the circumstances. If prices superior to the NBBO "were reasonably available and the defendants, at the time of accepting plaintiffs' orders, intended to accept solely by reference to the NBBO, they made a material misrepresentation in connection with the purchase and sale of the securities involved."[39] What was "reasonably available," however, required, it said, a trial on the merits.

For the future, this issue may have been overtaken by the SEC's Order Handling Rules, which were issued after the class period in *Newton,* because they effectively integrate the alternative market centers that plaintiffs in *Newton* said should be considered into the National Market System.

SECTION 4. SPECIALISTS AND MARKET MAKERS

Statutes and Regulations

Securities Exchange Act of 1934 §§ 11(b) and 15A.

Exchange Act Rules 10b–10, 11b–1, 11Aa3–1, 11Ac1–1.

———

In all markets, buyers and sellers do not arrive at the same time. Thus, to preserve trading continuity and prevent excessive intra-day price volatility, there must be an intermediary who will bridge the order imbalances that result from these timing differences. On the exchanges, the intermediary who performs this role of the economic lubricant is the specialist; in dealer markets,

---

38. 135 F.3d 266 (3d Cir. 1998) (en banc).

39. Id. at 270.

such as NASDAQ, it is the market-maker. Each is subject to special rules and duties, discussed below.

A. *The Specialist System.* The specialist has been the heart of the exchange system. To maintain a continuous auction market, the exchanges were required to solve two problems: (1) how to provide a mechanism for handling "away from the market" orders (known as "limit orders") by persons who wish to buy or sell only if the stock rises or falls to a different level than its current price, and (2) how to provide continuity and liquidity in the market and reduce random price fluctuations. According to legend, the first specialist was a stockbroker on the NYSE who broke his leg back in the 1870s, after which he took up a position where Western Union stock was traded and handled orders there for other members.[1] By 1987, there were 55 specialist firms and approximately 420 individual registered specialists operating on the NYSE, making a market in 1,625 common stocks.[2]

The role of the specialist has three elements: First, as brokers, they handle orders for others; typically, these orders are limit orders, forwarded to the specialist by an exchange member for a customer, which orders will be executed only in the event that the market price rises or falls to the specified price. Second, as dealers, specialists are charged with a legal obligation to buy or sell securities for their own account to the extent necessary to maintain a "fair and orderly market." Third, as auctioneers, specialists set the opening price and establish the bid and asked spread within which others trade.

To a limited extent, the specialist is a monopolist, since no one else on the exchange floor may make a market in the same stock. In return for this privilege (and the high rate of profit that it historically assured), specialists are subject to three basic legal obligations: (1) to trade against the market's trend in order to maintain a "fair and orderly market" (the affirmative trading obligation); (2) to restrict the specialist's own trading activities "so far as practicable to those reasonably necessary to permit him to maintain a fair and orderly market";[3] and (3) to observe exchange rules specifying minimum net capital obligations.

The specialist system has been controversial over the years, in part because of its seemingly monopolistic position. When the 1934 Act was debated in Congress, early drafts would have abolished the specialist by prohibiting the combination of broker and dealer. As passed, the 1934 Act merely instructed the SEC to study the "feasibility and advisability" of a complete segregation of such functions. In 1936, the Commission reported that the proposed reform seemed inadvisable, and the issue remained dormant thereafter.[4]

In 1934 and for some years thereafter, there were actually competing specialists in the same stocks on the New York Stock Exchange, but by 1967 all such competition among NYSE specialists had ended. This raised the prospect of monopolistic profits. One recent survey estimates that in 1999 (a very good year for the market and possibly unrepresentative), NYSE specialists earned an

---

1. See 5 L. Loss & J. Seligman, Securities Regulation (3d ed.1990) at 2513.

2. Id.

3. See Rule 11b–1; see also Securities Exchange Act Releases 7465 (1964) and 17,-574 (1981).

4. Report on the Feasibility and Advisability of the Complete Segregation of the Functions of Dealer and Broker, at 109 (SEC 1936).

average return on equity of 30%.[5] A second and independent concern about the specialists involves the misuse of nonpublic proprietary information that they possess.[6] In 1963, the Commission published its *Special Study of the Securities Markets,* which found that many specialists were engaged in excessive trading for their own accounts, without such trading being related to the goal of market stabilization. By the early 1960s, specialists trading for their own accounts exceeded 29% of total trading in the market.[7] Because the specialist has a unique form of "inside" information (namely, knowledge of its limit order book and the likely trend of future trading), extensive trading by specialists seemed an unfair use of such information. Hence, in 1965, the Commission adopted Rule 11b–1. It directs the stock exchanges to require by their own rules that a specialist both (1) "assist in the maintenance, so far as practicable, of a fair and orderly market," and (2) desist from trading by limiting its dealings to "those reasonably necessary to permit him to maintain a fair and orderly market." In effect, the rule sets forth both an affirmative and a negative obligation: "don't participate in the market too much, but also don't do it too little." The enforcement of these duties was, however, principally entrusted to the exchanges, themselves.

This concept that a specialist should be a "buyer of last resort" (but in these instances must be a buyer) has been implemented by New York Stock Exchange Rule 104, which provides in part:

The function of a member acting as regular specialist on the Floor of the Exchange includes * * * the maintenance, in so far as reasonably practicable, of a fair and orderly market on the Exchange in the stocks in which he is so acting. This is more specifically set forth in the following:

(1) The maintenance of a fair and orderly market implies the maintenance of price continuity with reasonable depth, and the minimizing of the effects of temporary disparity between supply and demand.

(2) In connection with the maintenance of a fair and orderly market, it is commonly desirable that a member acting as specialist engage to a reasonable degree under existing circumstances in dealings for his own account when lack of price continuity, lack of depth, or disparity between supply and demand exists or is reasonably to be anticipated.

(3) Transactions on the Exchange for his own account effected by a member acting as specialist must constitute a course of dealings reasonably calculated to contribute to the maintenance of price continuity with reasonable depth, and to the minimizing of the effects of temporary disparity between supply and demand, immediate or reasonably to be anticipated. Transactions not part of such a course of dealings * * * are not to be effected[8] (emphasis added).

---

5. See "Smart Gamble," U.S. Banker (Sept. 2001) at 12; see also Carol Vinzant, "Do We Need a Stock Exchange?" Fortune (Nov. 22, 1999) at 259 (average operating margin for specialists in 1999 was 55%).

6. One study found that specialist transactions for their own accounts were profitable over 80% of the time. See Neider-hoffer & Osborne, Market Making and Reversal on the Stock Exchange, 61 J.Am.Stat. Ass'n 897 (1966).

7. 5 Loss & Seligman, supra note 1, at 2519.

8. NYSE Rule 104.10, N.Y. Stock Exch. Guide (CCH) ¶ 2104.

The phrase "so far as reasonably practicable" makes this a somewhat subjective standard. The NYSE employs several objective standards, however, to measure specialist performance:[9]

Price Continuity: In 1987, 89% of transactions occurred with variations of ⅛ point, or less.

Quotation Spread. In 1987, the quotation spread—the difference between the bid and asked prices—was ¼ point or less in 67.5% of NYSE quotations.

Market Depth. This is a measure of liquidity: how much may be bought or sold before the price changes. The NYSE computer determines the net price change over each 1,000 shares in a specific stock. On average, stocks showed price changes of ⅛ point or less 87.2% of the time in 1987.

Stabilization Rates. This test measures the degree to which a specialist leans against the market to stabilize it. In 1987, 90.7% of specialist transactions were against the market's last movement.

Ultimately, the specialists' high rate of return is only excessive if it is not risk justified. Here, there is some room for debate. In the October 1987 market crash, specialists made approximately $485 million in net purchases on October 19th, and then on October 20th, when the market rose by nearly 16%, they made net sales of $450 million.[10] The Brady Report and the SEC found that most specialists had behaved in compliance with their obligations and had sought to stabilize the market. Indeed, on October 19th, specialists bought 19% of all stocks sold, despite record volume.

However, the performance of individual specialists was uneven. Thus, one criticism did emerge from the SEC's and other post-crash studies: The NYSE seemed very reluctant to use its reallocative powers to discipline those specialists who failed to live up to their responsibilities.[11] Under SEC pressure, the NYSE adopted a revised Rule 103A in 1988, requiring for the first time that specialist performance be measured by objective criteria and quarterly floor broker evaluations.[12]

The October 1987 crash also forced a revaluation of the minimum net capital rules for specialists. By the end of October 19th, the SEC found that 13 out of 55 specialist firms on the NYSE had exhausted their buying power.[13] Since 1988, specialists must now meet stiffer net capital requirements that require them to be able to assume a position of 150 trading units (15,000 shares) in each common stock in which they are the registered specialist; in addition, they must have net liquid assets equal to $1 million. This is an increase from the prior rules that required only an ability to assume 50 trading units (5,000 shares) plus net liquid assets of $100,000. In consequence, many smaller firms have sold out or been acquired by major broker-dealers.

For the future, the traditional concerns about the excessive profits earned by specialists may have been rendered moot by decimalization and the shrinking of spreads. Competition from ECNs, which is only beginning to develop,

---

9. 5 L. Loss & J. Seligman, *supra* note 1, at 2525.

10. Id. at 2527.

11. See SEC, Div. of Mkt.Reg., The October 1987 Market Break 4–28 to 4–29 (1988) (criticizing the NYSE's unwillingness to use its reallocative or disciplinary powers).

12. See Securities Exchange Act Release No. 25,681 (1988).

13. See SEC, Div. of Mkt. Reg., *supra* note 11, at 4–58.

may shrink profits further. Decimalization has, however, raised concerns over a new issue: the ability of the specialist to step in front of large institutional trades by improving the price by only a nominal amount. The specialist then sells to the original institution at a slightly enhanced price. While the specialist would be required to grant priority to a public customer if its purchase were at the same price,[14] it can, for example, improve the price by a penny and thereby obtain priority. This practice has so angered institutional investors that they have demanded (and obtained) greater automation of NYSE-trading to reduce such self-interested intervention by the specialist.

B. *Market Makers.* Trading in the over-the-counter market is different from an exchange in two obvious respects: (1) there is no exchange floor or specialist's post; (2) there are multiple market makers, often a dozen or more. For securities traded in the National Market System, the Firm Quote rule requires dealers to supply firm quotes to Nasdaq,[15] and last sale reports must be reported by dealers within 90 seconds of execution.[16] With such data, investors can ascertain the best bid and asked prices and can rely on these prices more or less as confidently as they can on the quotations on an exchange. However, many over-the-counter securities do not meet the issuer qualification standards for the NMS. In such cases, last-sale prices are not reported and current information on the bid/asked prices available from all dealers may be lacking. In such an environment, a customer wishing to purchase or sell such a security becomes more dependent on the dealer to learn what the current price is and more vulnerable to exploitation.

Lehl v. Securities and Exchange Commission

United States Court of Appeals, Tenth Circuit, 1996.
90 F.3d 1483.

■ Before Anderson, McWilliams, and Engel, Circuit Judges.

■ Anderson, Circuit Judge.

Daniel R. Lehl petitions for review of a final order by the Securities and Exchange Commission ("SEC") sustaining disciplinary action taken against him by a registered securities association, the National Association of Securities Dealers, Inc. ("NASD"). Based on our review of the record, we affirm the SEC's order.

In 1990, Lehl was a securities salesman associated with First Choice Securities in Denver. First Choice was a registered member of the NASD and Lehl was a registered representative. Between July 17 and August 3, 1990, Lehl sold 285,000 shares of stock in Champions Sports, Inc., to retail customers in eleven separate transactions. Lehl charged his customers 6.5 cents per share, the "execution price" established by his firm. The Denver branch of First Choice obtained the stock from the firm at a "strike price" of 5 cents per share. Each of these prices was posted daily on a board in the front of the Denver office. The difference between the strike price and the execution price constituted the firm's "gross commission" on each transaction, from which Lehl's individual commissions were paid. Lehl knew these facts. He did not know,

---

14. See Rule 11a1–1(T) (requiring members to yield priority to orders of non-members).

15. See Rule 11Ac1–1.

16. See Rule 11Aa3–1.

however, and never inquired into, the price per share the firm had paid for its Champions stock, which was in fact 3.125 cents in nine of the transactions and 3.5 cents in the other two.

In 1991, the NASD commenced disciplinary proceedings against First Choice and various individuals associated with the firm, including Lehl, for their actions in marketing Champions stock. The NASD District Business Conduct Committee found Lehl had violated the NASD Rules of Fair Practice by charging unfair and excessive prices without proper disclosure to his customers. The Committee censured Lehl and ordered him to requalify by examination as a registered representative. On appeal, the NASD National Business Conduct Committee affirmed and added a $5000 fine, plus costs. On de novo review, the SEC affirmed in pertinent part and sustained the NASD's sanctions. Lehl seeks review of the SEC's adverse decision.

Our jurisdiction to review final SEC orders comes from Section 25(a)(1) of the Securities Exchange Act of 1934, 15 U.S.C. § 78y(a)(1). The SEC's factual findings are conclusive if supported by substantial evidence.[2] *Id.* § 78y(a)(4); *see General Bond & Share Co. v. SEC*, 39 F.3d 1451, 1453 (10th Cir.1994). We review de novo the SEC's legal conclusions in this case. *See Kapcia v. INS*, 944 F.2d 702, 705 (10th Cir.1991); Orkin v. SEC, 31 F.3d 1056, 1063 (11th Cir.1994).

The SEC found Lehl violated Sections 1 and 4 of the NASD Rules of Fair Practice, Article III. Section 1 reads: "A member, in the conduct of his business, shall observe high standards of commercial honor and just and equitable principles of trade." Section 4 reads:

> In "over-the-counter" transactions, whether in "listed" or "unlisted" securities, if a member ... sells for his own account to his customer, he shall ... sell at a price which is fair, taking into consideration all relevant circumstances, including market conditions with respect to such security at the time of the transaction, the expense involved, and the fact that he is entitled to a profit....

See also NASD Rules of Fair Practice, art. I, § 5 ("Persons associated with a member shall have the same duties and obligations as a member under these Rules of Fair Practice."), *reprinted* in Resp't Br., Statutory Addendum at 2A.

In his petition, Lehl advances five reasons why he should not be held accountable for selling Champions stock at unfair markups: (1) the SEC's findings of misconduct varied from the misconduct charged against him; (2) the NASD never properly adopted its markup policy; (3) SEC enforcement of the NASD markup policy is an improper regulation of securities prices; (4) the SEC improperly calculated the markups; and (5) the record contains insufficient evidence to support the SEC's finding that Lehl was personally culpable. We will address each of these contentions in turn.

* * *

2. "Substantial evidence" in this context refers to a minimum quantity of relevant evidence objectively adequate to support the findings when viewed in light of the record as a whole. See Steadman v. SEC, 450 U.S. 91, 98, 100, 101 S.Ct. 999, 1007, 67 L.Ed.2d 69 (1981); Universal Camera Corp. v. NLRB, 340 U.S. 474, 477, 488, 71 S.Ct. 456, 459, 464–65, 95 L.Ed. 456 (1951); Wall Street West, Inc. v. SEC, 718 F.2d 973, 974 (10th Cir.1983); Buchman v. SEC, 553 F.2d 816, 820 (2d Cir.1977); Archer v. SEC, 133 F.2d 795, 799 (8th Cir.), cert. denied, 319 U.S. 767, 63 S.Ct. 1330, 87 L.Ed. 1717 (1943).

2. *The NASD Markup Policy.* Lehl next argues that the SEC never formally approved the NASD markup policy, as required for any changes in registered association rules. See 15 U.S.C. § 78s(b)(1). The NASD policy, which interprets Sections 1 and 4 as they relate to markups, prohibits registered representatives from entering into "any transaction with a customer in any security at any price not reasonably related to the current market price of the security." NASD Mark–Up Policy, Interpretation of the Board of Governors, *reprinted* in Resp't Br., Statutory Addendum at 4A. We have previously acknowledged the SEC's conclusion that this interpretation does no more than express what was already clearly implied in Section 1 and expressly set forth in Section 4; it does not establish a "new standard of conduct" and therefore is not a "rule change" requiring formal SEC approval. *General Bond & Share Co. v. SEC*, 39 F.3d 1451, 1459 (10th Cir.1994) (citing *In re NASD*, Exchange Act Release No. 3623, 17 S.E.C. 459, 1944 WL 976 (Nov. 25, 1944)). That principle applies here.

Lehl nevertheless focuses his argument specifically on a guideline within that interpretation, the so-called "5% policy."[4] He argues that the SEC employed the 5% policy as a substantive rule in this case, sanctioning him for selling Champions stock at prices exceeding 5% of the market price—even though the NASD never formally adopted the policy as a rule. We disagree with the premise of this argument. "[T]here is no hard and fast '5 percent rule' as complained of by petitioner. The Commission did not discipline him merely because his commissions were in excess of 5 per cent." *Samuel B. Franklin & Co. v. SEC*, 290 F.2d 719, 725 (9th Cir.), *cert. denied*, 368 U.S. 889, 82 S.Ct. 142, 7 L.Ed.2d 88 (1961). Rather it found, without reference to the 5% policy, that markups of 86% and 100% over market price were unfair. A substantial body of established case law supports this determination, independent of the 5% policy. *E.g., Duker & Duker*, Exchange Act Release No. 2350, 6 S.E.C. 386, 1939 WL 1332, at *3 (Dec. 19, 1939) ("Judged by any standards," markup of 44% was "plainly excessive and unreasonable.") (pre–5% policy); *Charles Hughes & Co. v. SEC*, 139 F.2d 434, 435 (2d Cir.1943) (prices marked up 40% were "very substantially over those prevailing in the . . . market"), *cert. denied*, 321 U.S. 786, 64 S.Ct. 781, 88 L.Ed. 1077 (1944); *Samuel B. Franklin & Co.*, 290 F.2d at 725 (markups greater than 20% were clearly excessive and not reasonably related to market prices); *Costello, Russotto & Co.*, Exchange Act Release No. 7729, 42 S.E.C. 798, 1965 WL 6611, at *3 (Oct. 22, 1965) ("We have repeatedly held that mark-ups of more than 10 percent are unfair even in the sale of low priced securities. . . ."); *cf. Robert B. Orkin*, Exchange Act Release No. 32,035, 53 S.E.C. Docket 1963, 1993 WL 89023, at *4 n. 30 (Mar. 23, 1993) (markups ranging from 16% to 100% make challenge to 5% policy "largely academic"), *aff'd*, 31 F.3d 1056 (11th Cir.1994). Lehl's attack on the 5% policy in this case fails.

---

4. To guide its members in determining when a price is "reasonably related to the current market price," the NASD surveyed industry pricing practices, concluding that the vast majority of transactions occurred at markups of 5% or less. It then issued guidelines setting 5% as a benchmark of reasonableness, to be considered with other relevant factors. The NASD cautioned, however, that the 5% policy "is a guide—not a rule"; that a "mark-up pattern of 5% or even less may be considered unfair or unreasonable"; and that "[i]n the case of certain low-priced securities, such as those selling below $10.00, a somewhat higher percentage may sometimes be justified." See Handley Inv. Co. v. SEC, 354 F.2d 64, 65 (10th Cir.1965); Samuel B. Franklin & Co. v. SEC, 290 F.2d 719, 725 (9th Cir.), cert. denied, 368 U.S. 889, 82 S.Ct. 142, 7 L.Ed.2d 88 (1961); NASD Mark–Up Policy, reprinted in Resp't Br., Statutory Addendum at 4A.

3. *NASD Regulatory Authority*. Lehl next argues that the SEC's enforcement of the "NASD markup rules" is an improper regulation of securities prices. See 15 U.S.C. § 78o–3(b)(6) (rules of registered securities association may not fix rates of commissions). We disagree. As the SEC has observed in rejecting a similar contention, "[t]he NASD does not set prices, but merely requires that whatever prices its members set be fair to retail customers. As Congress has noted, this policy serves 'to protect investors against "gouging" and promotes just and equitable principles of trade." *Richard R. Perkins*, Exchange Act Release No. 32,188, 53 S.E.C. Docket 2442, 1993 WL 128738, at *3 (Apr. 21, 1993) (quoting S.Rep. No. 75, 94th Cong., 1st Sess. 28, *reprinted in* 1975 U.S.C.C.A.N. 179, 206) (citation corrected) (and noting further that the SEC has "rejected similar arguments before"); *see also* R. Vol. 3 at 2261 n.22 (same). In this case, the SEC did not sanction Lehl for selling securities above a certain price or for receiving commissions in excess of a fixed rate, but rather for selling securities to his customers at prices that were blatantly unfair. Lehl's attack on the NASD's regulatory authority fails.

4. *The Champions Markups*. Lehl argues next that the SEC improperly calculated the Champions markups. The parties agree that the starting point for determining the markups is the "prevailing market price" of the stock, *see, e.g., Orkin*, 31 F.3d at 1063, but disagree as to what that price was in this case. "The general rule is that in the absence of countervailing evidence, the best evidence of prevailing market price is the dealer's contemporaneous cost...." *Id.; accord Associated Sec. Corp. v. SEC*, 293 F.2d 738, 741 (10th Cir.1961). "A dealer charged with markup violations may prevent application of th[is] general rule[ ] by presenting countervailing evidence that another measure is better evidence of prevailing market price." *Orkin*, 31 F.3d at 1064.

Lehl suggests that his firm bought Champions stock at an inter-dealer concession, making cost an inappropriate indicator of market price. *See, e.g., A. Bennett Johnson*, Exchange Act Release No. 10,258, 45 S.E.C. 278, 1973 WL 12517, at *2 (June 29, 1973). To support this argument, Lehl points out that First Choice purchased Champions stock in large blocks. This evidence is wholly insufficient. Large stock purchases may indeed involve a price concession, *see id.*, but no other evidence points to one in this case, distinguishing the relevant decisions. See id. (inferring price concession when firm obtained stock with no active market by competitive bid in bankruptcy sale); *Strathmore Sec., Inc.*, Exchange Act Release No. 7864, 42 S.E.C. 993, 1966 WL 3112, at *2 (Apr. 8, 1966) (finding price concession in isolated transaction when seller had previously failed to move stock and firm purchased smaller blocks at nearly double the price); *Langley–Howard, Inc.*, Exchange Act Release No. 7986, 43 S.E.C. 155, 1966 WL 3140, at *5 (Oct. 26, 1966) ($2.30 per share substantially lower than $5 per share other dealers were paying in the market). The SEC refused to draw the inference that First Choice bought Champions stock at a below market price, and based on the evidence, we think properly so.[6]

Lehl also argues that the price other dealers were quoting for Champions stock is a proper measure of market price. We disagree. "[T]he use of quotations to establish the prevailing market price ... is widely recognized as problematic." *Orkin*, 31 F.3d at 1064 (citing *LSCO Sec., Inc.*, Exchange Act

---

6. Lehl's related attempt to rely on the testimony of an NASD examiner to prove a price concession yields nothing, as she testified conclusively that she did not know and did not investigate the specific arrangement between First Choice and its Champions supplier. *See* R. Vol. 1 at 298–300.

Release No. 28,994, 48 S.E.C. Docket 681, 1991 WL 296502, at *3 (Mar. 21, 1991); *Alstead, Dempsey & Co.*, Exchange Act Release No. 20,825, 30 S.E.C. Docket 208, 1984 WL 50800, at *2 (Apr. 5, 1984)); *see also Merritt, Vickers, Inc. v. SEC*, 353 F.2d 293, 296–97 (2d Cir.1965) (quotations appropriate as prima facie evidence of market price only absent evidence of contemporaneous cost). The SEC has "frequently pointed out" that "quotations merely propose a transaction. They do not reflect the actual result of a completed sale." *LSCO Sec., Inc.*, 48 S.E.C. Docket 681, 1991 WL 296502, at *3. The test of their reliability comes "by comparing them with actual inter-dealer transactions during the period in question." *Alstead, Dempsey & Co.*, 30 S.E.C. Docket 208, 1984 WL 50800, at *2. Lehl has submitted no evidence of this nature. Consequently, we find no error in the SEC's markup calculations.

5. *Lehl's Personal Accountability.* Finally, Lehl argues there is insufficient evidence in the record to demonstrate that he should be held personally responsible for any markup violation that may have occurred. Lehl's liability in this case turns on whether he had reason to know that the markups he charged were excessive. *See, e.g., Amato v. SEC*, 18 F.3d 1281, 1284 (5th Cir.), cert. denied, 513 U.S. 928, 115 S.Ct. 316, 130 L.Ed.2d 278 (1994); *Orkin*, 31 F.3d at 1065.

The record is clear that Lehl did not know the actual price First Choice paid for the stock. However, the record is equally clear that Lehl knew the firm's "strike" and "execution" prices, which differed by 30%; that he knew the 5% policy; and that he knew the firm grossed a commission on each transaction equal to 23% of each customer's investment. See R. Vol. 1 at 374, 376–77, 382–83.[7] This information was sufficient to put Lehl on notice that the firm was charging unfair and excessive prices. *See, e.g., Langley–Howard, Inc.*, 43 S.E.C. 155, 1966 WL 3140, at *5 (markups exceeding 10% were "clearly excessive," violating Sections 1 and 4), *cited in Amato*, 18 F.3d at 1284 ("Implicit in the [*Langley–Howard*] holding is that a registered representative could incur liability if he was on notice that the markup he was charging was excessive."); *Handley Inv. Co. v. SEC*, 354 F.2d 64, 66 (10th Cir.1965) (5% policy adequate to put NASD members on notice of obligations under Sections 1 and 4); *John G. Harmann*, Exchange Act Release No. 32,932, 55 S.E.C. Docket 58, 1993 WL 380029, at *2, *4 (Sept. 21, 1993) (gross commissions ranging upward from 16% "were clear indications to the salespeople that they needed to inquire about the propriety of the prices"); *Robert A. Amato*, Exchange Act Release No. 31,974, 53 S.E.C. Docket 1686, 1993 WL 71123, at *2 (Mar. 10, 1993) (size of commissions should have led sales representatives to question markup, regardless of whether they knew firm's contemporaneous cost), aff'd, 18 F.3d 1281 (5th Cir.), cert. denied, 513 U.S. 928, 115 S.Ct. 316, 130 L.Ed.2d 278 (1994). Lehl's decision to ignore those warning signs makes NASD sanctions against him appropriate.

7. Additionally, Lehl testified that the Denver office posted the price that dealers were bidding for Champions stock—slightly more than 3 cents in this case—and that he believed his firm kept at least "a good portion" of the difference between that bid price and the strike price, which in fact it did. See R. Vol. 1 at 376, 378–79; R. Vol. 3 at 2255 n.7 (firm kept difference between bid and strike prices); cf. John G. Harmann, Exchange Act Release No. 32,932, 55 S.E.C. Docket 58, 1993 WL 380029, at *2 n. 14 (Sept. 21, 1993) ("[T]he salespeople could not reasonably have believed that the firm's cost exceeded the strike price.").

We are unimpressed with Lehl's attempt to minimize his involvement in the Champions affair to the point of no responsibility. The SEC gave Lehl the benefit of the doubt for his inexperience by dismissing fraud charges against him, despite markups large enough to support a fraud finding. See *James E. Ryan*, Exchange Act Release No. 18,617, 24 S.E.C. Docket 1716, 1982 WL 32453, at *3 (Apr. 5, 1982) ("We have repeatedly held that, generally, markups of more than 10% are fraudulent, even in the sale of low priced securities.") (footnote omitted). Lehl's position as a registered securities representative required him to understand the basis for the prices he was charging the public and to assure himself those prices were fair. This he failed to do.

For the foregoing reasons, we AFFIRM the order of the SEC.

MARK–UP POLICY: NASD AND SEC INTERPRETATIONS

Possibly the most controversial of the rules and interpretations of the NASD has been its so-called "5% mark-up philosophy." Since 1943, the NASD has enforced an interpretation of its Rules of Fair Practice that deems it inconsistent with "just and equitable" principles of trade for a member to enter into any transaction with a customer at a price not reasonably related to the current market price of the security.[1] In 1943, the NASD surveyed its members and determined that 47% of transactions by its members were made at mark-ups of 3% or less and 71% of the transactions were affected at mark-ups of 5% or less. Based on this evidence, the NASD adopted a 5% guideline to determine when mark-ups became excessive.[2]

A guideline is by no means a prophylactic rule, and the NASD has identified a variety of factors that need to be considered in determining the fairness of a mark-up in an individual case. These include:

1. *The type of security involved.* Generally, mark-ups on equity securities may be larger than mark-ups on debt securities.[3]

2. *The availability of the security.* When the market in a stock is inactive, the dealer will usually spend more time and effort obtaining the security, thus justifying a higher mark-up. When there is an active market, and less effort is needed to obtain the stock, the same mark-up is not justified.[4]

3. *The price of the security.* Although there is no direct correlation, the percentage of mark-up or rate of commission generally increases as the price of the security decreases. Handling costs tend to be the same for both high and low priced securities, and thus justify a commission that is higher on a percentage basis in the case of the low priced securities. However, where the size of the transaction is large, even though the security's price is low, higher mark-ups may not be justified.[5]

1. See Interpretation of the Board of Governors, NASD Mark-Up Policy, CCH NASD Manual, ¶ 2154 at 2054–61.

2. See In re Thill Securities Corp., 42 S.E.C. 89, 91 n. 4 (1964).

3. See In re Staten Securities Corp., 47 S.E.C. 766, 768 (1982).

4. See In re NASD, 17 S.E.C. 459, 466–67 (1944).

5. See In re Maryland Securities Co., 40 S.E.C. 443, 446 (1960).

4. *The amount of money involved in the transaction.* A transaction that involves a small amount of money may warrant a higher percentage of mark-up to cover handling costs.[6]

5. *Disclosure to the customer.* Any disclosure made to the customer before the transaction about the mark-up will be considered, but is not alone a justification for a commission otherwise "unfair or excessive in light of all the other relevant circumstances."[7]

6. *The pattern of mark-ups.* The NASD will look beyond the individual transaction to the overall pattern of the member's mark-ups to determine if they are generally excessive.

7. *The nature of the member's business.* A dealer that provides other services, such as research, advice or financial planning, may be justified in charging a higher mark-up.

The NASD has vigorously enforced its mark-up policy over recent years and has brought a number of disciplinary proceedings for charging excessive mark-ups.[8] At the same time, it has also revised its policy to require more detailed procedures to establish what the prevailing price is. In the case of securities not traded over Nasdaq, determining the prevailing price (to which the mark-up is then added) is often the principal issue in the case. In 1988, the SEC approved an amendment to the NASD Rules of Fair Practice requiring the member to mark customer order tickets for each transaction in a non–Nasdaq stock to indicate the dealers contacted and the price quotations received in order to determine the prevailing price.[9] Also in 1988, the NASD issued an interpretation restating its "5% Policy" that set forth the following rules for determining the "prevailing market price."

1. When there is a competitive market for the securities, the prices paid by other dealers to the market maker under review are to be considered the most accurate reflection of the prevailing market price.

2. Market makers who engage in principal transactions with their retail clients are normally entitled to the "inside" spread, and the best available price (i.e., the "inside" asked price) would be used to calculate the mark-up. Where the dealer does not make a market in the security, it may use its contemporaneous cost as the primary basis from which to compute a mark-up.

3. Where there is no independent market or where the market maker dominates the market, the contemporaneous prices paid by the market maker for the stock are the best available evidence of the prevailing market price, and such cost should be used as the basis for the mark-up.

4. A dominant market maker may not use its own quoted spread as the basis for a mark-up (as it would be entitled to if there was a competitive market in the stock), but should use its cost.[10]

6. See In re Greenberg, 40 S.E.C. 133, 136 (1960).

7. CCH NASD Manual, ¶ 2154.

8. For representative cases, see, e.g., In re Nicholas Codispoti, Securities Exchange Act Release No. 24946 (Sept. 29, 1987); In re Voss & Co., Inc., Securities Exchange Act Release No. 21301 (Sept. 10, 1984).

9. See NASD Notice to Members 88–83 (discussed in Mathews & Citera, "Markups" in PLI, Trading Practices, the Portfolio Execution Process), and Soft–Dollar Arrangements (L. Pickard, ed., 1989) at 195.

10. See Mathews & Citera, supra note 9, at 196.

Independently, the SEC has also enforced its own mark-up policy under the antifraud provisions of the federal securities laws. In 1943, the Second Circuit accepted the SEC's position that the duty of fair dealing included an implied representation that the price a dealer charges bears a "reasonable relationship" to the prevailing market price.[11] Absent disclosure, the dealer thus violates Rule 10b–5 if its price is "substantially different" from the prevailing market price.[12] When the mark-up exceeds ten percent of the "prevailing market price," the SEC has repeatedly held in administrative proceedings that such a mark-up is fraudulent per se.[13] Unlike the NASD, the SEC has consistently disfavored the use of offer quotations from other market makers in determining the "prevailing market price," believing them to be unreliable for this purpose and preferring to use instead the market maker's actual contemporaneous purchase price.[14] The SEC applies its mark-up policy not only to corporate equities, but to government and municipal securities as well, and in this latter context, a recent release sharply criticized the practice of charging mark-ups based on the face amount of bonds that are sold at a steep discount.[15]

Rule 10b–10 partially implements the SEC's policy on mark-ups by specifying what must be disclosed on the confirmation of sale sent to the customer. In some circumstances, it requires specific disclosure of the mark-up.[16] Generally, Rule 10b–10 requires disclosure of the net price to the customer, but does not require disclosure of mark-ups. Compliance with Rule 10b–10 does not, however, create a safe harbor that absolves the dealer from liability for excessive mark-ups.[17]

SECTION 5. MARKET DATA

Statutes and Regulations

Securities Exchange Act of 1934 § 11A.

Exchange Act Rules 11Aa3–1; 11Ac1–1.

Securities exchanges and Nasdaq basically support themselves through three sources of revenue: (1) listing fees charged to listed companies; (2) fees and expenses charged to member firms; and (3) market data fees, which are

11. Charles Hughes & Co. v. SEC, 139 F.2d 434 (2d Cir.1943).

12. See, e.g., Ettinger v. Merrill Lynch, Pierce, Fenner & Smith, Inc., 835 F.2d 1031 (3d Cir.1987); In re James E. Ryan, 47 S.E.C. 759 (1982).

13. See Alstead, Dempsey & Co., Securities Exchange Act Release No. 20825 (April 5, 1984); In re Peter J. Kisch, Securities Exchange Act Release No. 19005 (Aug. 24, 1982).

14. See Alstead Dempsey & Co., supra note 13; In re Rooney, Pace Inc., Securities Exchange Act Release No. 25125 (Nov. 13, 1987).

15. Notice to Broker-Dealers Concerning Disclosure Requirements for Mark-ups on Zero-Coupon Securities, Securities Exchange Act Release No. 24368 (April 21, 1987).

16. See Rule 10b–10(2)(8)(A) and (B). For equity securities in the National Market System, the rule requires disclosures based on which an intelligent customer can calculate the mark-up.

17. Ettinger v. Merrill Lynch, Pierce, Fenner & Smith, 835 F.2d 1031 (3d Cir. 1987); Krome v. Merrill Lynch & Co., 637 F.Supp. 910, 916 (S.D.N.Y.1986).

paid for transaction and quotation information. Only the last is controversial, in part because there is some dispute as to who should own this information. The exchanges believe they have an ownership interest in market data generated on their exchange (and have long sold it). Broker dealers, led by Charles Schwab & Co., have challenged this claim, believing that the broker-dealers generate the information. Also, the discount brokers claim that the exchanges' fees are excessive and exceed the reasonable costs of gathering the information. The conflict is at bottom between the owners of the property right and its users, because the market data fees typically are borne by the broker-dealer. That is, while the exchange sells its data to a vendor (for example, Bloomberg), the vendor charges a fee to its subscribers, who are mostly broker dealers, and the latter typically do not pass on these costs (at least directly) to their customers. In 1998, as this controversy came to a head, the exchanges received $414 million in market data fees, while Schwab paid in that year a total of $20 million for access to NYSE data alone.[1]

The positions of the antagonists diverge dramatically.[2] Some discount brokers want market data fees to be closely tied to the costs actually incurred in generating this data. Inevitably, this would involve the SEC in rate regulation, much like a public utility commission, and the SEC's competence at such a task is open to doubt. Conversely, the NYSE would like to dissolve the Consolidated Tape Association, which allocates the revenues among exchanges, in favor or a system in which each exchange would sell its own data to vendors. Others fear that the NYSE still has a sufficiently dominant position that it would largely monopolize these fees today.

Seeking to develop a consensus, the SEC appointed an advisory committee in 2000 to develop recommendations, which was chaired by Dean Joel Seligman of Washington University Law School. The Advisory Committee on Market Information reported in 2001 and recommended that the institutional structure for the collection of market data be revised to provide for multiple consolidators of market data.[3] This would seemingly mean that, in place of the CTA, competitors might bid for market data in order to consolidate it and sell it to vendors. The Committee did not favor either the SEC's earlier suggestion that a "flexible cost-plus" pricing system be established (under SEC oversight) or the suggestion that the existing market data fee formulas be revised. Its preference for a competitive solution does, however, suggest some Committee members had a degree of sympathy for the original Schwab critique that a governmentally mandated monopoly (such as the CTA) tended to favor the interests of exchanges over those of online brokers. The SEC has not yet acted on the Committee's recommendations, and some political lobbying is likely over these financially important issues.

Meanwhile, market data revenues are affecting the decisions of ECNs. They have recognized that so long as they remain broker-dealers they will not share in this revenue, but as exchanges they are entitled to share. Hence, some have filed applications with the SEC to register as exchanges.[4]

---

1. See David Ignatius, "Putting a Meter on the Flow of Information," Washington Post, June 30, 1999, at A–31.

2. For an overview of the issues, see Securities Exchange Act Release No. 42208.

3. See Report of the Advisory Committee on Market Information (Sept. 8, 2001);

see also Schroeder, "Market Data Report Backs Multiple Consolidators," Securities Industry News, October 1, 2001.

4. To date, only one ECN, Archipelago, has had its application granted. Exchanges also must accept surveillance and self-regulatory responsibilities, and the SEC has thus

---

SECTION 6.   SELF REGULATION IN THE SECURITIES INDUSTRY

Statutes and Regulations

Securities Exchange Act § 6; 15A; 15B; 15C; 19.

Because the NYSE and other exchanges existed for well over a century before the SEC was created, a system of self-regulation was already in place at the time the federal securities laws were enacted, which they largely adopted. In effect, SEC regulation was overlaid on top of exchange regulation, rather than substituted for it. Still, because the Congress was dissatisfied with the performance of the exchanges during the late 1920's, when it believed that "pools" and other conspiracies manipulated securities prices, the 1934 Act required the registration of all securities exchanges with the SEC and gave the Commission strong enforcement powers over them.[1] Later in 1938, Congress passed the Maloney Act, which authorized the creation of a similar self-regulatory body to regulate broker-dealers (many of whom were not NYSE members).[2] Although Section 15A authorized the formation of multiple such self-regulatory associations, only one—the National Association of Securities Dealers ("NASD"), founded in 1939—was ever formed.[3]

The merits of self-regulation have long been debated, but at least in theory, two important advantages of such a two-tiered structure of regulation, with the SEC and "self-regulatory organizations" (or "SROs") sharing overlapping authority, can be imagined. First, SROs have the ability to tax the relevant industry to fund their monitoring and enforcement costs; this is in contrast to the SEC, which depends on a sometimes parsimonious Congress for its annual appropriation, and thus this two-tier structure implies some level of assured financing. "Taxing the industry" is simple to achieve because the ability to practice in the industry or profession can be conditioned on registration and payment of membership fees. Second, while the SEC is primarily an anti-fraud enforcement agency, SROs can be authorized to employ a lower threshold of regulatory attention and discipline negligence or unprofessional conduct that falls short of fraud. The NASD has long promulgated and enforced Rules of Fair Practice, which, for example, require a member broker to have "reasonable grounds for believing that [a securities] recommendation is suitable" for the specific customer to whom the recommendation is made.[4] In theory, the NASD's Roles of Fair Practice obligate its members to "observe high standards of commercial honor and just and equitable principles of trade"[5]—in short, the rules that honest merchants would naturally observe. In practice, these rules authorize enforcement and sanctions in cases that anti-fraud rules would often have difficulty reaching. In addition, because the rules of private bodies (as both the NYSE and NASD are in the eyes of the court) do not give rise to

---

been cautious about approving such application.

1. See Section 6 of the Securities Exchange Act of 1934.

2. See Section 15A of the Securities Exchange Act of 1934.

3. It was actually a successor to an earlier body, the Code Committee, created in 1933 as part of the National Recovery Act, which Act was later held unconstitutional by the Supreme Court.

4. This is the basis for the suitability doctrine discusses later in Chapter 11. Similarly, the NYSE Rule 405—"Know Your Customer Rule" performs a similar function.

5. NASD Rules of Fair Practice, Article III (1992).

implied causes of action, SRO regulations authorize only public enforcement and not private enforcement, which may arguably make it possible for SRO rules to establish more aspirational standards.

1.   *Governance.* Both the NYSE and the NASD are non-profit organizations owned by their members. The NASD is administered by a Board of Governors, a majority of whom under its by-laws must be "non-industry" governors (in essence, the equivalent of independent, outside directors). The NYSE has a twenty-four member board of directors, all of whom are elected by exchange members, but half of whom are "public" directors and half are "industry" directors.

2.   *Rule-making.* Rules of all self-regulatory organizations must be approved by the SEC.[6] In addition, under Section 19(c) of the 1934 Act, the SEC "may abrogate, add to, and delete from . . . the rules of self-regulatory organization." This seemingly broad power to impose rules on SROs is, however, subject to judicial limitations. The SEC cannot use this power to impose its preferred rules of corporate governance on listed companies, but must show that the purposes of any such SEC amendment are to advance the goals of the National Market System.[7]

3.   *Enforcement.* SROs have an obligation to enforce compliance with both their own rules and the federal securities laws. Correspondingly, the SEC can enforce SRO rules, and it can bring its own overlapping charges without regard to considerations of double jeopardy or res judicata.[8] Procedurally, § 15A(b)(8) of the 1934 Act requires that the rules of the NASD must "provide a fair procedure." But the NYSE and the NASD in disciplining their members are regarded as private actors and hence are not subject to the Fifth Amendment's privilege against self-incrimination. This means that they can suspend and/or expel any member or associated person who refuses to testify before it or who pleads the Fifth Amendment before it—at least so long as the SRO acts independently of government influence and not as an agent of the state.[9]

4.   *SEC Jurisdiction.* Section 15(a) of the 1934 Act prohibits any person from acting as a broker or a dealer in securities unless registered with the SEC or otherwise exempted from registration. Both the terms "broker" and "dealer" are broadly defined in §§ 3(a)(4) and (5), respectively, of the 1934 Act. A broker is defined as a person "engaged in the business of effecting transactions in securities for the accounts of others," while a dealer is a person who engages "in the business of buying and selling securities for his own account." Note the emphasis in both definitions on the phrase "in the business;" it is intended to distinguish professionals who act for others or make markets as a profession from very active personal investors.[10]

---

6.   See Section 19(b) of the Securities Exchange Act of 1934.

7.   See *Business Roundtable v. SEC*, 905 F.2d 406 (D.C.Cir.1990) (invalidating SEC-imposed "one share, one vote" rule as a listing condition for NYSE and Nasdaq traded companies because it exceeded SEC's authority under Section 19(c)).

8.   See *Jones v. SEC*, 115 F.3d 1173 (4th Cir.1997).

9.   See *D.L. Cromwell Invs., Inc. v. NASD Regulation, Inc.*, 279 F.3d 155 (2d Cir.2002).

10.   See *SEC v. Ridenour*, 913 F.2d 515 (8th Cir.1990); see also Lipton, A Primer on Broker–Dealer Registration, 36 Cath. U. L. Rev. 899 (1987).

Under § 15(b)(1) of the 1934 Act, the SEC has authority to deny (or to revoke) a broker-dealer registration—after "notice of the grounds ... and opportunity for hearing." Also, under § 15(b)(7), the SEC is empowered to set "standards of operational capability," both for the broker-dealer and "all natural persons associated with such broker or dealer." These standards may specify such minimum "standards or training, experience, competence and such other qualifications as the Commission finds necessary or appropriate in the public interest or for the protection of investors." Accordingly, in conjunction with the NASD, the Commission can (and has) established a testing program for entry into the broker-dealer industry that is the functional equivalent of the Bar exam for lawyers.[11]

5. *The Pros and Cons of Self Regulation.* The usual argument against self regulation emphasizes the dangers of regulatory capture: the process will be dominated by the industry and will primarily serve to insulate it from new entrants and increased competition. Another claim is that it adds "a layer of arguably redundant regulation" on the existing system of SEC regulation, which raises costs in return for little added benefit.[12] Proponents of self-regulation typically reply that industry rule-making is (or at least can be) more detailed, more responsive, and is able to deal with ethical and moral issuers that a governmental agency cannot as legitimately regulate. Also, self-regulation invites the participation of the regulated, thereby increasing the prospect of law compliance. To some degree, a measure of self-regulation seems inevitable; the SEC could not feasibly regulate floor activities on the stock exchanges, where decisions must be made, or disputes resolved between market participants, within hours (or even minutes) of the moment at which they arise. This debate over the degree of reliance that should be placed on self-regulation will predictably continue. The terms of the debate have, however, been changed by substantial structural reforms undertaken within the NASD in 1996 to introduce public members onto the NASD board (and onto various committees). Also, the NASD sought to insulate its regulatory functions by placing them in a separate subsidiary (NASD Regulation, Inc.), where they would be less exposed to any conflicts or pressures arising from the NASD's proprietary interest in its Nasdaq market.[13]

11. See Securities Exchange Act Release No. 13629 (1977).

12. For a skeptical assessment of self-regulation from an industry participant, see Miller, Self–Regulation of the Securities Markets: A Critical Examination; 42 Wash. & Lee L. Rev. 853 (1985); see also Smythe, Government Supervised Self–Regulation in the Securities Industry and the Antitrust Laws: Some Suggestions for an Accommodation, 62 N. C. L. Rev. 475 (1984).

13. These reforms were recommended by a special blue ribbon committee chaired by former Senator Warren Rudman. In response, the NASD expanded the public membership on its board and placed its regulatory operations in a separate subsidiary with its own board (NASD Regulation, Inc.).

CHAPTER 11

REGULATION OF BROKER–DEALERS

Statutes and Regulations

> Securities Exchange Act, §§ 3(a)(4), 3(a)(5), 3(a)(51), 9, 10, 15(b)(1), 15(b)(4), 15(b)(6), 15(b)(7), 15(c), 15(g), 29(b).

> Rules 2b–3; 10a–1; 10a–2; 10b–3; 10b–5; 10b–10; 10b–16; 15c1–1 through 15c1–9.

Introduction

As with other financial service industries (but probably even more so), the broker-dealer industry is closely regulated. The SEC, multiple SROs, and state "blue sky" authorities share oversight responsibilities, as described below. In addition, broker-dealers may be liable to their customers, either in court or in arbitration proceedings, for asserted breaches of fiduciary duties owed to the customer or for breach of SRO rules.[1]

1. *SEC Authority Over Broker—Dealers.* Section 15(a) of the 1934 Act prohibits any person from acting as a broker or a dealer unless registered with the SEC or expressly exempted. But registration is not automatic. Section 15(b)(1) of the 1934 Act authorizes the SEC to deny registration for certain specified reasons, and § 15(b)(4) empowers it to "censure, place limitations on the activities, functions, or operations of, suspend for a period not exceeding twelve months, or revoke the registration of any broker or dealer if it finds ... [that such action] ... is in the public interest and that such broker or dealer" has engaged in certain specified forms of misconduct (including, in both cases, making false statements in any application or report required to be filed with the SEC). In short, broker-dealers can be thrown out of the industry, or otherwise disciplined to a less drastic extent, if at any time they run afoul of the SEC. Similarly, under § 15(b)(6), the SEC has equivalent authority over any person "associated" with a broker-dealer, meaning that the Commission can enter a lifetime disbarment order barring an individual from any employment or other association with a broker-dealer. Section 15(b)(7) also gives the Commission important additional authority by prohibiting any broker or dealer from effecting any transaction in, or inducing the purchase or sale of any security, "unless such broker or dealer meets such standards of operational capability and such broker or dealer and all natural persons associated with it meet such standards of training, experience, competence, and such other qualifications as the Commission finds necessary or appropriate in the public interest or for the protection of investors." Effectively, this provision authorizes the Commission to establish tests and training standards to regulate entry into the profession. Finally, § 15(c) contains several broad antifraud provisions specifically directed at broker-dealers

---

1. The vast majority of decisions do not recognize an implied cause of action for breach of a stock exchange or NASD rule. See Colonial Realty Corp. v. Bache & Co., 358 F.2d 178 (2d Cir.1966). Some courts do, however, view the violation of such a rule as evidence of negligence. See Piper, Jaffray & Hopwood, Inc. v. Ladin, 399 F.Supp. 292, 298 (S.D.Iowa 1975). In any event, even if there is no private cause of action that may be asserted in court, arbitration panels often take a broader view of their responsibilities and award damages based on equitable principles, as discussed later in this introduction.

which authorize the Commission to adopt rules and regulations to define practices that are "manipulative, deceptive or otherwise fraudulent."[2]

Beyond these antifraud rules, the 1934 Act also focuses on regulating the financial soundness of broker-dealers. Thus, § 15(c)(3) empowers the Commission to prescribe rules and regulations "to provide safeguards with respect to the financial responsibility and related practices of brokers and dealers, including ... the acceptance of custody and use of customers' securities and the carrying and use of customers' deposits or credit balances." Here, the concern is with the solvency of a broker-dealer as a financial institution (much like a bank or a savings and loan) that holds "other people's money." Pursuant to this authority, the SEC has adopted elaborate and detailed rules regulating the capital structure of broker-dealers.[3]

The broad scope of SEC authority over broker-dealers is further enhanced by an expansive definition of the terms "broker" and "dealer" and the limited scope of the exemptions from § 15's registration requirement. Section 3(a)(4) of the 1934 Act defines "broker" as "any person engaged in the business of effecting transactions in securities for the account of others," and § 3(a)(5) defines "dealer" as "any person engaged in the business of buying and selling securities for his own account." The phrase "in the business" in both definitions is intended to distinguish the professional market maker from simply an "active investor" who trades frequently. Sometimes, however, the line can be close between these two. In SEC v. Ridenour,[4] a bond account executive at a broker-dealer was found, himself, to be a broker-dealer subject to § 15(a)'s registration requirement, where he actively traded bonds for his own account with a regular clientele of institutional clients. The court found that "his level of activity ... made him more than an active investor,"[5] but perhaps the key factor was his attempt to develop his own clientele of trading partners who relied on his services.

Employees of an issuer could in theory also be deemed a "broker" because of their work, for example, in a shareholder relations department, seeking to induce purchase of the firm's shares. Here, however, the SEC has provided a protective safe harbor in the form of Rule 3a4—1, which indicates that participation in certain specified activities (which do not involve oral solicitations of public investors) does not require registration as a broker.

Relatively few exemptions exist from § 15(a). The most important exemptions are for (1) banks,[6] (2) firms that deal exclusively in exempt securities,[7] (3) persons who do business "exclusively intrastate" and who do "not make use of any facility of a national securities exchange,"[8] and (4) foreign brokers who have only "indirect" contacts with U.S. investors.[9]

2. *SRO Authority.* As noted in Chapter 10, the NASD's Conduct Rules rest on the broad expectation that members are expected to "observe high standards of commercial honor and just and equitable principles of trade."[10] Previously, it was seen that these rules could invalidate mark-ups that seemed unreasonable or

2. See § 15(c)(1)(D) of the 1934 Act.

3. See Rules 15c3—1 to 15c3—3.

4. 913 F.2d 515 (8th Cir.1990).

5. Id. at 517.

6. See §§ 3(a)(4), 3(a)(5).

7. Section 15(a)(1) specifically exempts transactions in "an exempted security, or commercial paper, bankers' acceptances, or commercial bills." Many of these dealers will, however, be subject to § 15B ("Municipal Securities") or § 15C ("Government Securities Brokers and Dealers") of the 1934 Act.

8. See § 15(a)(1).

9. See Rule 15a—6 (exempting certain limited activities, such as execution of unsolicited transactions and the provision of research to institutional investors).

10. NASD Manual, Conduct Rules, Rule 2110 ("Standards of Commercial Honor and Principles of Trade") (1996).

underwriters' compensation that was deemed "excessive." Both the NYSE's and the NASD's rules can also be used, however, to impose affirmative obligations on broker-dealers to advise customers that certain securities are excessively risky (or "unsuitable" in the industry parlance) for their economic position or needs. This doctrine—known as the "suitability doctrine"—rests on the premise that brokers have an obligation to know their customer and make only recommendations that are "suitable" to their customer's needs and financial position. The development and uncertain status of "suitability" theory is reviewed later in this chapter.

Although it is unlikely that customers can sue their brokers in private actions based on the NYSE or NASD's "Know Your Customer" rules, commentators report that arbitration panels do regularly enforce these norms by requiring broker-dealers to share in the losses experienced by customers who are advised to buy "unsuitable" or high risk securities.[11] Indeed, the Arbitrator's Manual that governs these proceedings advises arbitrators that they are to do equity and may "go beyond the written law."[12] Also, arbitrators may award punitive damages on state law theories (which the federal securities laws preclude).

3. *State Authority.* The Uniform Securities Act requires the annual registration of broker-dealers doing business in the jurisdiction and provides for broad disciplinary powers in the state agency. However, the National Securities Markets Improvements Act of 1996 added § 15(h) to the 1934 Act, which imposes substantial limitations on the authority of state blue sky regulators over broker-dealers. Basically, § 15(h) restricts state blue sky regulation of broker-dealers by precluding capital, operational, or record-keeping rules which are in addition to those established by the SEC. It also permits associated persons of a broker-dealer not registered in the particular jurisdiction to engage in certain limited transactions in that jurisdiction on behalf of a broker-dealer that is so registered.[13] Although this restriction limits state oversight, no restriction was placed by the Act on state antifraud rules relating to broker-dealers or on state enforcement powers.

4. *Common Law Duties.* A broker is an agent to the customer and thus owes the duties established by the law of agency. But is the broker also a "fiduciary," who arguably owes a duty to warn the customer of risks or to disclose adverse information about the issuer that is in the broker's possession? Here, the prevailing rule is that where the account is "non-discretionary," meaning that the customer makes the investment decisions and the stock broker merely receives and executes the customer's orders, the relationship does not give rise to general fiduciary duties.[14] In *Independent Order of Foresters v. Donald, Lufkin & Jenrette,*[15] the Second Circuit announced this rule, which relied on New York law,[16] in a case involving a seemingly sophisticated institutional investor who complained that its investment banker had not warned it about the dangers inherent in certain derivative securities.[17] The logic of these cases is essentially that the fiduciary relationship requires that there be two critical elements that are not present in the

11. See Lewis Lowenfels and Alan Bromberg, Beyond Precedent: Arbitral Extensions of Securities Law, 56 Bus. Law. 999 (2002).

12. Id. at 1001 (citing Secs. Industry Conference on Arbitration, THE ARBITRATOR'S MANUAL 2 (2001)).

13. See § 15(h)(2).

14. See Independent Order of Foresters v. Donald, Lufkin, & Jenrette, 157 F.3d 933, 940 (2d Cir.1998).

15. *Id.*

16. See Yang v. Witter, 282 A.D.2d 271, 724 N.Y.S.2d 149 (1st Dept. 2001); Perl v. Smith Barney Inc., 230 A.D.2d 664, 646 N.Y.S.2d 678, 680 (1st Dept.1996).

17. However, the Second Circuit declined to dismiss and reinstated claims that the defendant broker-dealer had caused an employee of the plaintiff institutional investor to breach his fiduciary duties to the plaintiff by authorizing the purchase of the risky securities in return for kickbacks.

case of a simple non-discretionary brokerage account: (1) reliance by the customer on the broker, and (2) domination and control by the broker.[18] Thus, the majority rule deems the broker to owe at most a fiduciary duty that is bounded by the scope of the relationship with the client and that requires the broker only to perform diligently the instructions given to it by the client. In contrast, in the case of a discretionary account, where the broker does exercise trading authority, a fuller fiduciary relationship would arise, and the broker would be under a duty for example, to warn the customer as to adverse information or risks known to the broker.

This summary is, however, deceptively simple, in several respects. First, even in the case of a non-discretionary account, some duties are owed. For example, at a minimum, the broker has a duty to execute requested trades and seek their best execution.[19] And, if the terms of the account require the customer's specific authorization, it violates the broker's duty to execute unauthorized trades.[20] More importantly, some decisions find that, even in the case of the non-discretionary account, the broker has "the duty to recommend a stock only after studying it sufficiently to become informed as to its nature, price and financial prognosis."[21] Second, the existence of a fiduciary relationship is a question of state law, and some states have a more liberal attitude than does New York. In *Patsos v. First Albany Corp.*,[22] the Massachusetts Supreme Court found that a fiduciary relationship existed where the broker-dealer's registered representative had assured his customer-plaintiffs that if they followed his investment advice, they could make "a great deal of money."[23] Following his advice, they bought $8 million of the stock of a single small bank, approximately one-half of which was purchased on a margin account. Later, the broker induced his clients to use even greater margin, thereby increasing their leverage and potential exposure. Although the Massachusetts Supreme Court agreed that a simple brokerage relationship is not fiduciary in character, it found that special facts could show that a sufficient "degree of discretion" had been entrusted to the broker to create a full fiduciary relationship.[24] A customer's "lack of investment acumen" could also be an important factor, it said, in determining whether a full fiduciary relationship existed.[25] Although they probably constitute only a minority rule, other decisions have taken a similarly liberal stance.[26] Some others waffle on this issue by finding that the scope of the fiduciary relationship is a factual question for the jury to resolve.

One of the more controversial recent decisions on the scope of the fiduciary relationship is *De Kwiatkowski v. Bear Stearns*.[27] There, in a case involving an extremely experienced and wealthy private investor (to whom the jury awarded a recovery of $111.5 million plus interest based on the broker's negligence), the district court ruled that the broker owed even this sophisticated, nondiscretionary account customer a duty to investigate issuers whose securities were under consideration, to refrain from self-dealing, and to report any conflicting or personal

18. See United States v. Chestman, 947 F.2d 551, 568—69 (2d Cir.1991) (en banc) (defining when a fiduciary relationship arises for purposes of insider trading law).

19. See Shearson Lehman Hutton, Inc. v. Wagoner, 944 F.2d 114, 120 (2d Cir.1991).

20. See Conway v. Icahn & Co., 16 F.3d 504, 510 (2d Cir.1994).

21. See Leib v. Merrill Lynch, Pierce, Fenner & Smith, Inc., 461 F.Supp. 951, 952 (E.D.Mich.1978).

22. 433 Mass. 323, 741 N.E.2d 841 (2001).

23. Id. at 844.

24. Id. at 849—50.

25. Id. at 850—51.

26. See, e.g., Banca Cremi, S.A. v. Alex. Brown & Sons, 132 F.3d 1017, 1038 (4th Cir.1997); Romano v. Merrill Lynch, Pierce Fenner & Smith, 834 F.2d 523, 530 (5th Cir.1987).

27. 126 F.Supp.2d 672 (S.D.N.Y.2000).

interest that the broker may have had in the transaction. As a result, it upheld the jury's apparent finding that the defendant's failure to provide its customer with certain information that it possessed breached the broker's duty of reasonable care. The basis for this unusual result seems to have been the court's finding that, over the course of dealing with this very large account, the defendant undertook in fact the role of investment adviser and was relied upon by the plaintiff to provide him with the information that the defendant omitted to provide. On appeal, the Second Circuit reversed, finding that, although the broker owes a duty of reasonable care to the client, this duty "begins and ends with each transaction" and does not comprehend any ongoing or open-ended duty to warn the client or monitor the client's account.[28] The broker cannot be held liable for a failure to warn a nondiscretionary client, it said, in the absence of clear evidence that it had contractually agreed to undertake a substantial advisory role. Even though the broker may volunteer advice, this does not create an ongoing duty to continue to do so.

Criminal law also defines and enforces the fiduciary duties owed by brokers to their customers, and criminal liability has not depended on whether a full fiduciary relationship exists between the broker and the customer. Where exorbitant commissioners were not disclosed, it has been held sufficient, in order to uphold a conviction for breaching the duty of "honest services" under 18 U.S.C. § 1346 (one of the federal mail and wire fraud statutes), that simply a relationship of trust and confidence existed between the broker and the customer. In *United States v. Szur*,[29] the Second Circuit recently upheld criminal convictions of brokers who agreed to market the controlling stake of a majority holder in a small corporation to their retail customers in return for commissions that were agreed in advance to be fifty percent of any proceeds received from these sales. Although defendants protested that they owed no fiduciary duty (and the Second Circuit agreed), it still found a relationship of trust and confidence to accompany any broker-customer relationship, with the result that the failure to disclose excessive commissions was a material omission that amounted to fraud.

5. *Nature of the Governmental Interests.* Both federal and state regulation of broker-dealers serve multiple interests and goals. One obvious interest is the prevention of market manipulation; another is protection of the financial solvency of broker-dealers because they are essentially financial institutions, holding customers' funds and securities. Still another interest is the protection of customers from certain abusive practices that may not amount to classic fraud, but involve an arguable breach of fiduciary duty. This chapter considers these distinct regulatory goals in succession focusing first on the prevention of fraud and manipulation, then on protection of the customer from high risk and insolvency, and finally on the fiduciary duties of a broker-dealer.

SECTION 1. REGULATION AIMED AT FRAUD AND MANIPULATION

A. *Regulation of Short Sales.* Whether to regulate short sales and, if so, how to do it have been controversial topics for at least three centuries.[1] A Senate investigation of stock market practices in 1934 described short selling this way: "Short selling is a device whereby the speculator sells stock which he does not own, anticipating that the price will decline and that he will thereby

---

28. De Kwiatkowski v. Bear Stearns & Co., 2002 U.S. App. LEXIS 19274, at *33 (2d Cir. September 19, 2002).

29. 289 F.3d 200 (2d Cir.2002).

1. For a brief history, see L. Loss and J. Seligman, Fundamentals of Securities Regulation 699–703 (3d ed. 1995).

be enabled to 'cover,' or make delivery of the stock sold by purchasing it at the lesser price. If the decline materializes, the short seller realizes as a profit the differential between the sales price and the lower purchase or covering price."[2]

Daniel Drew, a nineteenth century stock market operator, characterized the consequences of a failure to "cover" a short-sale in his oft quoted jingle:

> He that sells what isn't his'n,
> Must buy it back or go to prison.[3]

It was a commonly held view that during the stock market crash of 1929, professional speculators conducted "bear raids" through short sales thereby deriving enormous profits while accelerating the stock market decline and postponing recovery.[4]

When the 1934 Act was before Congress, it was recognized that previous attempts in other countries to outlaw short sales had ended in failure and that most such laws were later repealed. Thus, rather than adopting an inflexible statute, Section 10(a) simply delegates to the SEC the authority to regulate short sales of any security registered on a national securities exchange. The section is applicable whether the short sale is effected on an exchange or in the over-the-counter market, and it applies to all persons, not just broker-dealers.

The SEC has promulgated four rules that together regulate short selling. Their purpose is to prevent speculative raids on securities (bear raids), which force prices down. Rule 3b–3 defines a short sale. Rule 10a–1 prohibits short selling in a falling market. Rule 10a–2 prescribes the methods to be used in covering a short sale; it also prohibits a broker or dealer from facilitating the making of a short sale by another person. Regulation M, which is discussed below, contains Rule 105, which is designed to prevent manipulative short selling of securities in anticipation of a public offering of those same securities.

Rule 3b–3 defines a short sale as any sale of a security which the seller does not own or any sale which is consummated by the delivery of a security borrowed by, or for the account of, the seller. The rule also identifies various legal arrangements that will meet the ownership requirement other than the holding of legal title directly or through an agent.

Rule 10a–1 prohibits any person from effecting a short sale of any exchange traded security, wherever traded: (1) below the last reported price at which such security was sold, regular way; or (2) at the same price, unless that price is above the next preceding price at which a sale of such security, regular

2. Stock Exchange Practices, Report of Com. on Banking & Currency, S.Rep. No. 1455, 73d Cong., 2d Sess. (1934) 50.

3. See B. White, The Book of Daniel Drew 180 (1910). John Steele Gordon in his history of early Wall Street also attributes this quotation to Daniel Drew, without the citation of any source except "Wall Street tradition." Gordon, *The Scarlet Woman of Wall Street* 73 (1988). We have followed these authors in crediting him with its authorship, although it seems highly unlikely that "Uncle Daniel" (also known as the "Great Bear" because of his bear raids) in fact originated this *bon mot* since he was the most notorious short-seller in the entire history of Wall Street. See Gordon, *op. cit., passim.* Mr. Gordon at another point quotes Commodore Vanderbilt as saying in response to a reporter's badgering him for a statement regarding a "corner" he had engineered in a particular stock and the squeeze he was putting on the short-sellers: "Don't you never buy anything you don't want, nor sell anything you hain't got." (Id. at p. 85) Possibly this vernacular response was later transformed by some unknown literary artist into the traditional, more elegant, couplet quoted above.

4. See L. Loss and J. Seligman, supra note 1, at 699–700.

way, was reported.[5] In stock market jargon, short sales on a *minus-tick* or a *zero-minus* tick are prohibited. Short sales, however, may be made on a *plus tick* or a *zero-plus* tick. A plus tick occurs when the last previous sale price is lower than the price at which the short sale is effected. A zero-plus tick occurs when a short sale is effected at the same price as the last previous price, provided that price is higher than the preceding different sale price of the security. In other words, the short seller may not ride the market down but may make purchases on an uptick even in a down market.

For example, if the last sale of X stock on Exchange A was at 48¾, regular way, a sale at 48½ (minus tick) in the over-the-counter market is prohibited; however, a sale of X stock, regular way, at 48⅞ on any exchange or in the over-the-counter market may be made (plus tick) or at 48¾ so long as that price is higher than the preceding different sale price of the security. Rule 10a–1(2) permits an exchange to adopt the tick test and the New York Stock Exchange and the other exchanges have done so.[6]

Rule 10a–1(c) requires that sell orders for exchange reported securities, or admitted to unlisted trading privileges, be marked either "long" or "short." Under Rule 10a–1(d) brokers and dealers must inform themselves that the customer is in a position to consummate a "long" or "short" order as marked. Rule 10a–1(e) exempts a variety of transactions from the strictures of these rules, including transactions by odd-lot dealers, specialists on exchanges, stabilizing transactions subject to Rule 10b–7, and certain arbitrage and hedge activities of block positioners.[7]

Finally, Rule 105 of Regulation M is designed to prevent manipulative short selling of securities in anticipation of a public offering. Originally, the rule was adopted under § 10(b), as Rule 10(b)–21, at the request of the National Association of Securities Dealers (NASD) based on concerns by issuers that short selling prior to a public offering "can and does have the effect of driving down the price of the securities to be distributed."[8] In this context, the short selling may result in either a lowering of the public offering price or the cancellation of the proposed offering. Today, the content of former Rule 10b–21 has been moved to Rule 105 of Regulation M, which was adopted in 1997 as part of a general codification of the Commission's rules on trading practices during a distribution.[9] The scope of Rule 105 has also been marginally narrowed. It now applies only to short sales during the five business days prior to the pricing of the offering. As to these covered short sales, Rule 105 makes it unlawful to cover short sales of equity securities of the same class as securities offered for cash pursuant to a 1933 Act registration statement or a notification on Form 1–A under Regulation A with any securities purchased from an underwriter or broker or dealer participating in the offering. Rule 105 only applies to firm commitment underwritings; it does not apply to shelf-offerings under Rule 415.

5. NYSE Rule 64 defines a sale of stock, "regular way," to be in units of 100 shares, with settlement of the transaction to occur within five business days following the sale. See 2 N.Y.S.E. Guide (CCH) ¶ 2064 (1989).

6. See Worley, The Regulation of Short Sales: The Long and Short of It, 55 Fordham L. Rev. 1255 (1990).

7. Rule 10a–2 sets forth the requirements for covering of short sales.

8. See Securities Act Release No. 6789 (Aug. 25, 1988) [1988–1989 Transfer Binder] Fed.Sec.L.Rep. (CCH) ¶ 84,315, at 89,384.

9. See Securities Act Release No. 7375 (January 3, 1997).

Under Rule 105(c), the Commission can grant exemptions from this prohibition on covering short sales out of the securities in the offering, and typically it will do so based on special terms and conditions. It must be emphasized that Rule 105 does not prohibit short sales in connection with a distribution; such "bear raids" by those who believe the offering price is unrealistically high (particularly in the aftermarket of an IPO) remain relatively common. Rather, Rule 105 precludes the short seller using securities it has reserved in the offering to cover its sales, because this makes the transaction essentially riskless to the short seller.

It should be noted that under the Securities Enforcement Act of 1990 the Commission may impose monetary fines for short selling on a downtick.

It is generally conceded that the uptick rule does not prevent abusive short-sale activities; it is only a deterrent and short sales may still be made on the uptick. Moreover, Rule 10a–1 does not apply to derivative trading which accentuates volatility to a much greater degree than does short selling. This loophole has enabled stock market traders to develop strategies to circumvent the uptick rule and conduct bear raids which some firms regard as manipulative.[10]

The present solution to the problem of market volatility is to rely on Rule 10a–1 as a device to deter manipulative and abusive short selling activities and rely upon various circuit breaker mechanisms involving trading halts which are designed to cushion the impact of broad market declines during periods of abnormal market volatility.

B. *Manipulation During a Distribution: Regulation M and the Trading Practice Rules.* An issuer and the underwriters assisting it in a distribution have an obvious incentive to attempt to raise the issuer's stock price just prior to the time of the offering. By buying the stock (even in fairly modest amounts) in the period immediately preceding the offering, they may be able to inflate the issuer's stock price in order to obtain a higher price in the offering (or simply give the false impression that there is widespread demand for the stock). Of course, this is the essence of manipulation: that is, purchases intended to artificially peg the security's price, and not based on any investment decision as to the security's inherent value.

Relying on its authority under § 10(b) of the 1934 Act to proscribe "manipulative or deceptive devices or contrivances," the SEC since 1955 has prohibited the issuer and other participants in a distribution from bidding for or purchasing securities that were the subject of a current or contemplated distribution. For many years, these prohibitions were contained in Rules 10b–6, 10b–7 and 10b–8. These rules were extremely technical and were subject to numerous exceptions that sometimes seemed to overwhelm the principal prohibitions.

Accordingly, in 1997, in a deregulatory effort long sought by the industry, the SEC reorganized these trading rules, collecting them under a new Regula-

---

10. See Torres, Are "Slam Dunks" on Troubled Stocks a Foul? Wall St. J., Feb. 1, 1991, at C1, col. 3, describing the mechanics of a "slam dunk" in which the trader buys a few thousand shares of stock of a troubled company together with several dozen deep-in-the-money put options on the same stock. This strategy, known as the "married put" is unwound by selling the shares and put options simultaneously. Speculators using options-related strategies have thus found a way to sell into a market decline and circumvent the constraints of the uptick rule.

tion M, simplifying their prohibitions and narrowing their scope. Rule 101 now applies to underwriters (including prospective underwriters) and any broker, dealer "or other person who has agreed to participate or is participating in the distribution" (all such persons being defined by Rule 100 as "distribution participants"). Rule 102 reaches the issuer or any other person (such as a selling shareholder) on whose behalf the distribution is being conducted. "Distribution" is for this purpose broadly defined by Rule 100 to mean:

> "an offering of securities, whether or not subject to registration by the Securities Act, that is distinguished from ordinary trading transactions by the magnitude of the offering and the presence of special selling efforts and selling methods."

Thus, Regulation M could easily apply to an exempt intrastate offering under § 3(a)(11), or to a § 3(a)(9) or § 3(a)(10) offering. Regulation M's prohibition against buying what you are selling applies only for a relatively brief "restricted period", which varies depending upon the average daily trading volume ("ADTV") in the stock and the nature of the transaction. For issuers with an average daily trading volume of $100,000 or more and that also have a "public float value" (i.e., the value of stock held by public shareholders and not affiliates) of $25 million or more, the restricted period begins on the later of one business day prior to the pricing of the offering or such time as the broker-dealer or other person becomes a distribution participant; the restricted period continues until such person completes its participation in the distribution. For issuers that do not satisfy this high trading volume standard, the "restricted period" begins on the later of five business days prior to the pricing of the stock or such later point on which the person becomes a distribution participant, and it continues similarly until the person completes its participation in the distribution. (These time periods are shorter than the prior time periods of two or nine business days, depending upon trading volume, under former Rule 10b–6). In the case of mergers, acquisitions and exchange offers, the restricted period is typically longer and begins on the day that proxy solicitations or other offering materials are first disseminated to security holders and continues until the completion of the distribution.

Regulation M is subject to a number of important exceptions. Under Rule 101(c)(1), such "actively-traded securities" are exempted on the apparent premise that such securities cannot be feasibly manipulated. For this exemption to become applicable, the securities must have an ADTV of $1 million and be issued by a company with a public float of at least $150 million. As of 1995, it was estimated that some 1,900 companies would qualify for this exemption. Although dealers and underwriters are thus no longer subject to trading restrictions on actively traded securities, issuers and selling shareholders remain subject to such restrictions during a distribution, even if the security is "actively traded." The apparent rationale is that broker-dealers have legitimate reasons for wanting to buy stock during a distribution, but issuers have less justification. Also, it needs to be understood that Regulation M is not a safe harbor. If intent to manipulate can be shown, a dealer, underwriter or any other person would presumably violate Rule 10b–5, even if it had complied with the applicable rules under Regulation M.

Regulation M also accords special significance to the existence of "information barriers" (sometimes called "Chinese Walls"). Under Rule 100, the term "affiliated purchaser" is defined so as to exclude affiliates of underwriters, selling shareholders, or issuers so long as the underwriter or issuer maintains and enforces written "information barriers" and obtains an annual independent assessment of the operation of such barrier.

Rules 101 and 102 generally exempt transactions in securities eligible for Rule 144A when sold in the U.S. to "qualified institutional buyers" in transactions complying with Rule 144A, Regulation D, or § 4(2), or sold under Regulation S. Note, however, that proof of an actual intent to manipulate the market in the case of such an exempted transaction would still presumably violate Rule 10b–5.

Rules 101 and 102 apply not only to the security being distributed, but also to any "reference security." This term is defined by Rule 100 to mean "a security into which a security that is the subject of a distribution ('subject security') may be converted, exchanged or exercised or which, under the terms of the subject security being distributed, may in whole or in significant part determine the value of the security being distributed." On this basis, if common stock were being distributed, trading in a convertible debt security convertible into that common stock would not be affected by Regulation M, but if the same convertible debt were being distributed, trading in the underlying common stock would be restricted. Trading in options and other derivative securities are thus also outside the scope of Rules 101 and 102 (whereas they were formerly covered by Rule 10b–6).

C. *"Laddering."* Suppose in an oversubscribed or "hot" offering the underwriter tells a prospective customer that it can receive an allocation of 5,000 shares but only if it agrees to purchase another 5,000 shares (or perhaps 10,000 or even more shares) in the aftermarket on the first day of the offering. Sometimes, the arrangement allegedly calls for the customer to make its required aftermarket purchases only after the market price in the secondary market reaches a specified level (hence the term "laddering" as the secondary market purchases are pre-arranged on a "ladder" of ascending prices).[1] The impact of any such "tie-in" arrangement is to create an artificial demand for the shares, which should increase the first day price spike seen in many "hot" offerings. Who is the victim? Not the customer who agrees to this "tie-in" (as this customer willingly agreed to buy additional shares at a possibly inflated price in order to obtain an initial allocation that this customer probably regards as "free money"). The truer victim is the customer who buys in the aftermarket, not knowing that the price of the security has been artificially inflated. In Staff Legal Bulletin No. 10,[2] the SEC's Division of Market Regulation announced its view in 2000 that any "tie-in" arrangement that requires the customer to buy additional shares in the aftermarket as a condition of receiving an allocation in the offering violated Rules 101 and 102 of Regulation M. See Rule 101(a). Staff Legal Bulletin No. 10 also warned that the anti-manipulation provisions of Section 17(a) of the 1933 Act and Section 10(b) of the 1934 Act would also be violated by such conduct.

A large number of class actions alleging laddering are pending in the Southern District of New York as of mid–2002. Some also allege that the underwriter reached an agreement whereby the purchaser who received the allocation in a "hot" IPO was required to split its profits with the underwriter

---

1. See Peter Beshar, "The New Wave of Securities Litigation—the Laddering Cases" in How to Prepare an Initial Public Offering 2001, 343 (PLI Corporate Law and Practice Course Handbook Series No. BO–01BW, 2001).

2. See 2000 SEC No–Act LEXIS 820 (August 25, 2000).

(thereby possibly defrauding the issuer as well as the secondary market issuer, because such a profit-sharing agreement gives the underwriter a strong incentive to underprice the stock).[3]

D. *Stabilization.* One major exception to the prohibitions in Regulation M is recognized by the SEC for certain activities conducted by underwriters during a distribution in order to "stabilize" the security's price (or, more accurately, to prevent or retard the decline of the security's price below the offering price). Such activities could also in theory be deemed "manipulative" (because they seek to "peg" the price of the distributed security), but a long history of SEC interpretations has largely carved them out of the SEC's trading rules in order to facilitate distributions.

In principle, § 9(a)(6) of the 1934 Act prohibits transactions for the purpose of "pegging, fixing, or stabilizing" the price of a security only when they are "in contravention of such rules and regulations as the Commission may prescribe as necessary or appropriate in the public interest or for the protection of investors." In 1940 in its Statement of Policy on the Pegging, Fixing and Stabilizing of Security Prices,[4] the majority of the Commission, over the dissent of Commissioner Healy, interpreted this provision as a mandate to the Commission to *regulate* rather than *prohibit* stabilizing transactions by an underwriting syndicate to facilitate a distribution of securities. It decided at that time to experiment with rules designed to eliminate the "vicious and unsocial aspects" of stabilization and issued a rule regulating initially only offerings "at the market."

The present rules developed as a result of this experimentation consist of a general prohibition in Rules 101 and 102 against any "distribution participant" from bidding for or purchasing the security being distributed or any security of the same class, with exceptions for, among other things, any stabilizing transactions carried out in conformity with Rule 104. Although Commissioner Healy lost the war, he eventually won the battle, since the present rules completely prohibit stabilizing in connection with an offering "at the market,"[5] to which he particularly objected.

E. *"Offering" Versus "Distribution".* New Rule 104, which replaced old Rule 10b–7 at the time that Regulation M was codified, has a broader scope than its predecessor. Under Rule 104(a), all stabilizing activities are covered in connection with any securities "offering" (a term which the adopting release indicates is deliberately broader than the conventional term "distribution").[6] Otherwise, Rule 104 largely continues the prior practices with regard to stabilizing, which (1) require any person entering the stabilizing bid to grant priority to independent bids (see Rule 104(c)), (2) permit only one stabilizing bid to be made at a time in any market (see Rule 104(d)), and (3) require disclosure to the market of the stabilizing bid (Rule 104(h)). However, Rule 104 does give the underwriters greater freedom and discretion in stabilizing because it enables the underwriter to initiate and change its stabilizing bid based

---

3. See MDCM Holdings, Inc. v. Credit Suisse First Boston, 2002 U.S. Dist. LEXIS 11237, 2002 WL 1377408 (S.D.N.Y. June 25, 2002) (declining to dismiss complaint containing such allegations).

4. Securities Exchange Act Release No. 2446 (SEC 1940).

5. Rule 104(e). An offering "at the market" is defined as "an offering of securities at other than a fixed price." See Rule 100.

6. See Securities Exchange Act Release No. 7375 ("Anti-manipulation Rules Concerning Securities Offerings") (January 3, 1997).

upon the current independent price in the market, provided that their bid does not exceed the offering price.[7] Also, in recognition of the global nature of securities markets and the increasing prevalence of international offerings, Rule 104 permits stabilizing bids to be made with reference to independent prices in the principal market for the security. Thus, if the principal market were in London and the offering were being conducted in both the U.S. and the U.K., a U.S. underwriter would enter a stabilizing bid at the highest independent U.K. market price, even if this were above the U.S. price, so long as it did not exceed the offering price.

F. *Passive Market Making.* Rule 103 ("Nasdaq Passive Market Making") permits an underwriter or dealer to continue to make a market on Nasdaq in a security during a distribution. However, the market maker must remain "passive"; this means that its bid or purchase cannot exceed the highest independent bid for, or purchase of, a covered security at the time of the transaction. In other words, if an independent market maker that is not participating in the distribution advances the bid from, say, $16 to $16⅛, a distribution participant may similarly increase its bid to match this bid, but it might not increase its bid otherwise. In addition, if the independent market maker's bid is subsequently lowered to $16, the distribution participant must follow it back down and cannot maintain its bid at $16⅛ (see Rule 103(b)(3)). Also, passive market making must be suspended if a stabilizing bid is made pursuant to Rule 104 or if the offering is an "at the market offering." Finally, Rule 103 places restrictions on the aggregate amount that can be purchased in a day (i.e., 30% of average daily trading volume—Rule 103(b)(2)) and on the displayed size of the bid (the passive market maker's bid size may not exceed the minimum quotation size for the covered security—Rule 103(b)(4)).

Rule 103 is limited to transactions on Nasdaq and does not apply to other over-the-counter securities.

G. *Shelf Registration and Trading Practices.* Over the long history of Rule 10b–6, the fact pattern that caused the greatest difficulty was the shelf registration by selling shareholders of a substantial quantity of stock for a continuous offering. Suppose one shareholder buys during a period when it is not selling, but other shareholders in the same group are selling? Could this be a reciprocal agreement? In the *Jaffee & Company* case,[8] the SEC took the position in a case where thirty-four selling shareholders had registered shares that each holder had to coordinate its individual purchases with the sales of the other thirty-three shareholders so as to assure that purchases and sales did not overlap within any restricted period. In 1986, the SEC relaxed this relatively strict position, requiring the selling shareholder thereafter to observe the requisite restricted period only with respect to its own sales transactions.[9]

H. *Scienter.* Originally, courts did not require the SEC to prove that a defendant intentionally violated the SEC's trading practices rules, but only that the challenged practice could "distort the ... market."[10] But this pro-enforcement attitude may not survive Ernst & Ernst v. Hochfelder[11], which today

7. See Rule 104(f)(2) and (4).

8. See 44 SEC 285 (1970), affirmed in part and vacated in part, Jaffee & Co. v. SEC, 446 F.2d 387 (2d Cir.1971).

9. See Securities Exchange Act Release No. 23,611 (September 11, 1986).

10. See Jaffee & Co. v. SEC, 446 F.2d 387, 391 (2d Cir.1971).

11. 425 U.S. 185 (1976); see also Aaron v. SEC, 446 U.S. 680 (1980) (*Hochfelder's* standard applies to SEC as well as to private plaintiffs).

requires all plaintiffs, including the SEC, to demonstrate scienter in order to make out a violation of Rule 10b–5b. The case law strongly suggests that scienter will be required, at least as a pleading matter.[12] The Commission, however, has continued to maintain that it can adopt prophylactic rules to regulate the distribution process. This issue may be litigated again in the wake of the adoption of Regulation M, but Regulation M is also phrased as an anti-manipulation rule.

I. *"Hot Issues," "Free Riding" and "Withholding": SEC and NASD Interpretations.* Attempts to support the price of a security occur in weak or declining markets, where "sticky" offerings (or extended ones) are common. In contrast, the reverse pattern is typical in the "bull markets" that often typify the IPO marketplace. In this world, the issuer and its underwriters do not necessarily want to sell to the "mere" public, but may wish to reserve shares for the affiliates of underwriters and for insiders at favored clients. The SEC and the NASD have fought this pattern for decades. In one of its first releases on this topic, "Preliminary Report on Practices in Distributions of 'Hot Issues',"[1] the SEC said in 1959:

"The practices in question involve a combination of some or all of the following elements:

"1. In addition to allotments of the offered securities to his own customers and to selling group dealers, if any, the underwriter may allot a portion of the offering at the public offering price to trading firms active in the over-the-counter market. These firms are expected to commence making a market in such securities at or immediately after the start of the public offering. Some of these firms sell their allotments at prices substantially in excess of the public offering price stated in the prospectus, and in some cases bid for and purchase the security while they are distributing their allotments. The inquiry also discloses that such distributions may be made by these firms without any use of a prospectus.

"In one recent offering, which almost doubled in price on the first day of trading, over thirteen percent of the entire offering was sold by the underwriters at the public offering price to four broker-dealers and one of these broker-dealers sold out its entire allotment in the course of trading activities within three weeks of the offering date at substantially higher prices. In another 'hot issue' offering the principal underwriter sold substantial amounts of its participation at the public offering price of $3 per share to several broker-dealers and on the first day of trading, six of these firms appeared in the 'sheets' of the National Daily Quotation Service with bids and offers ranging from 5¾ to 7¼.

"2. Underwriters and selling group dealers may allot a substantial portion of the securities acquired by them to partners, officers, employees or relatives of such persons ('insiders'), to other broker-dealers with whom they may have reciprocal arrangements or to 'insiders' of such other broker-dealers. Such allotments are made notwithstanding the fact that customers of such firms are unable to obtain a part of the original distribution and therefore could only purchase the securities in the market at the higher price.

---

12. See SEC v. Burns, 614 F.Supp. 1360, 1362–63, aff'd, 816 F.2d 471 (9th Cir. 1987).

1. See "Preliminary Report on Practices in Distribution of Hot Issues," Securities Act Release No. 4150 (Oct. 23, 1959).

"In one recent offering, which more than doubled in price on the offering date, the selling group allotted over twenty-eight percent of its total participation to 'insiders'. One member of that selling group diverted to 'insiders' over seventy-five percent of its 3,000 share allotment of the 100,000 share offering, and another sold almost fifty percent of its 5,000 share allotment to 'insiders'. Underwriters have indulged in the same practice. The underwriters in a recent offering of an electronics stock diverted almost twenty-two percent of the entire offering to 'insider' accounts. In another offering one of the underwriters diverted over eighty-seven percent of its participation to 'insider' accounts and another sold forty-seven percent to such accounts."

Following this SEC Release in 1959, the NASD issued an Interpretation with respect to "Free–Riding and Withholding." That Interpretation, as amended, concluded:[2]

FREE–RIDING AND WITHHOLDING

Introduction

"(1) This Interpretation is based upon the premise that members have an obligation to make a bona fide public distribution at the public offering price of securities of a public offering which trade at a premium in the secondary market whenever such secondary market begins (a 'hot issue') regardless of whether such securities are acquired by the member as an underwriter, as a selling group member, or from a member participating in the distribution as an underwriter or a selling group member, or otherwise. The failure to make a bona fide public distribution when there is a demand for an issue can be a factor in artificially raising the price. Thus, the failure to do so, especially when the member may have information relating to the demand for the securities or other factors not generally known to the public, is inconsistent with high standards of commercial honor and just and equitable principles of trade and leads to an impairment of public confidence in the fairness of the investment banking and securities business. Such conduct is, therefore, in violation of Article III, Section 1 of the Association's Rules of Fair Practice [today Rule 2110—eds.] and this Interpretation thereof which establishes guidelines in respect to such activity.

  * * *

Interpretation

"Except as provided herein, it shall be inconsistent with high standards of commercial honor and just and equitable principles of trade and a violation of Article III, Section 1 of the Association's Rules of Fair Practice for a member, or a person associated with a member, to fail to make a bona fide public distribution at the public offering price of securities of a public offering which trade at a premium in the secondary market whenever such secondary market begins regardless of whether such securities are acquired by the member as an underwriter, a selling group member or from a member participating in the distribution as an underwriter or selling group member, or otherwise. Therefore, it shall be a violation of Article III, Section 1 for a member, or a person associated with a member, to:

2. For the current and nearly identical text of this rule, see NASD Manual, Conduct Rules, Rule 2110, IM–2110–1 ("Free–Riding and Withholding") (1996).

"1. Continue to hold any of the securities so acquired in any of the member's accounts;

"2. Sell any of the securities to any officer, director, general partner, employee or agent of the member or of any other broker/dealer, or to a person associated with the member or with any other broker/dealer, or to a member of the immediate family of any such person;

"3. Sell any of the securities to a person who is a finder in respect to the public offering or to any person acting in a fiduciary capacity to the managing underwriter, including, among others, attorneys, accountants and financial consultants, or to a member of the immediate family of any such person;

"4. Sell any securities to any senior officer of a bank, savings and loan institution, insurance company, registered investment company, registered investment advisory firm or any other institutional type account, domestic or foreign, or to any person in the securities department of, or to any employee or any other person who may influence or whose activities directly or indirectly involve or are related to the function of buying or selling securities for any bank, savings and loan institution, insurance company, registered investment company, registered investment advisory firm, or other institutional type account, domestic or foreign, or to a member of the immediate family of any such person;

"5. Sell any securities to any account in which any person specified under paragraphs (1), (2), (3) or (4) hereof has a beneficial interest;

"Provided, however, a member may sell part of its securities acquired as described above to:

(a) persons enumerated in paragraphs (3) or (4) hereof; and

(b) members of the immediate family of persons enumerated in paragraph (2) hereof provided that such person enumerated in paragraph (2) does not contribute directly or indirectly to the support of such member of the immediate family; and

(c) any account in which any person specified under paragraph (3) or (4) or subparagraph (b) of this paragraph has a beneficial interest;

if the member is prepared to demonstrate that the securities were sold to such persons in accordance with their normal investment practice with the member, that the aggregate of the securities so sold is insubstantial and not disproportionate in amount as compared to sales to members of the public and that the amount sold to any one of such persons is insubstantial in amount.

"6. Sell any of the securities, at or above the public offering price, to any other broker/dealer; provided, however, a member may sell all or part of the securities acquired as described above to another member broker/dealer upon receipt from the latter in writing assurance that such purchase would be made to fill orders for bona fide public customers, other than those enumerated in paragraphs (1), (2), (3), (4) or (5) above, at the public offering price as an accommodation to them and without compensation for such.

"7. Sell any of the securities to any domestic bank, domestic branch of a foreign bank, trust company or other conduit for an undisclosed principal unless:

(a) An affirmative inquiry is made of such bank, trust company or other conduit as to whether the ultimate purchasers would be persons enumerated in paragraphs (1) through (5) hereof and receives satisfactory assurance that the ultimate purchasers would not be such persons, and that the securities would not be sold in a manner inconsistent with the provisions of paragraph (6) hereof; otherwise, there shall be a rebuttable presumption that the ultimate purchasers were persons enumerated in paragraphs (1) through (5) hereof or that the securities were sold in a manner inconsistent with the provisions of paragraph (6) hereof;

(b) A recording is made on the order ticket, or its equivalent, or on some other supporting document, of the name of the person to whom the inquiry was made at the bank, trust company or other conduit as well as the substance of what was said by that person and what was done as a result thereof;

(c) The order ticket, or its equivalent, is initialed by a registered principal of the member; and

(d) Normal supervisory procedures of the member provide for a close follow-up and review of all transactions entered into with the referred to domestic bank, trust companies or other conduits for undisclosed principals to assure that the ultimate recipients of securities so sold are not persons enumerated in paragraphs (1) through (6) hereof. * * *

---

1. *Spinning.* The principal target of the foregoing NASD rule is the underwriter who allocates some of its stock in a "hot" offering to its own officers or directors or to personnel at another underwriter (even if the latter is not participating in the offering, because of the fear that reciprocal understandings would develop under which "hot" allocations were exchanged). But can the underwriter give an allocation in a "hot" offering to a prospective client (or, more likely, the CEO of such a prospective client)? Now, the underwriter's goal is to use allocations in hot offerings to win future business, and this practice is known as "spinning." Although "spinning" is inconsistent with the idea in the foregoing release that NASD members "have an obligation to make a bona fide public distribution at the public offering price," spinning did not violate any of the actual prohibitions in the release or in NASD Conduct Rule 2110. Thus, underwriters had a strong incentive to allocate IPO stock to venture capital firms (or their insiders) in the hope that such firms would steer their next IPO to the underwriter.

In the wake of a wave of lawsuits in 2000 to 2001 challenging IPO practices, the NASD decided to reform the IPO allocation process. In mid–2002, it announced proposed rules that would expressly curb both "spinning" and "laddering." The NASD's Chairman has said that shares could not be distributed under the proposed rule "in a manner that puts an investment bank's interests above those of its clients."[3] But is this goal really attainable? Institu-

---

3. See Healy, "The Other Side of IPOs," The Boston Globe, July 30, 2002 (quoting Robert Glauber).

tional investors direct their brokerage business to major underwriting firms and expect to receive IPO allocations in return. When shares are allocated to institutions instead of to retail customers, the underwriter's motivation is probably to obtain or hold future brokerage business. This practice will not change under the new rule, as it is deeply embedded in the structure of multi-service investment banking firms. Should there instead be a broader "equal opportunity" rule that gives all customers an equal entitlement to IPO allocations? Or, should the underwriter's preference for the large institution that may want 10% of the offering be justifiable because the institution is in reality a wholesale purchaser, who in most markets receives a priority over retail customers?

2. *"Normal Investment Practice"*. The foregoing NASD Interpretation made an exception for securities sold "in accordance with the normal investment practice with the [NASD] member," provided that the aggregate amount so sold was "insubstantial" and not "disproportionate" in amount compared to the sales to the public. "Normal investment practice" was interpreted to mean the "history of investment of a restricted person in an account or accounts maintained by the restricted person," subject to a general guideline that a sale was not disproportionate if it did not exceed ten percent of the member firm's underwriting allocation. Note also that the rule does not preclude the issuer from, itself, directing that shares be issued to its "family and friends" because these persons do not work for the underwriters. In a "hot" offering, the "family and friends" category may come to 10 percent of the offering.

3. *"Free Riding"* and *"Flipping"*. As a practical matter, a customer is legally free to reject any allocation of shares that have been committed to his account until after the effective date. This invites an abuse—known as "free riding"—in which the customer orally commits to buy the shares, subject to the secret and unexpressed intention not to honor the non-binding commitment unless the aftermarket price rises. This intention of buying only if the aftermarket price rises is arguably "deceptive and manipulative" in violation of Rule 10b–5 by the SEC. Nonetheless, many underwriters find such practices both common and difficult to deter.

J. *Manipulation: The General Issues.* Section 9 of the Securities Exchange Act of 1934 is designed to prohibit manipulation of the securities markets. It has been termed by the SEC the "very heart of the act."[1] Section 9 itself applies only to listed securities, but the prohibitions in that section have been held to be incorporated into Sections 10(b) and 15(c)(1), which prohibit "manipulative" devices with respect to over-the-counter securities also.[2] In addition to various specific provisions aimed at the more notorious practices of the "pools" of the 1920's, such as wash sales, matched orders, tipster sheets, etc., Section 9(a)(2) contains a general prohibition against effecting "a series of transactions * * * creating actual or apparent active trading in * * * or raising or depressing the price of" a security *"for the purpose of inducing the purchase or sale of such security by others."* The first part of the requirement of this section would be met by almost any conceivable market activity, other than a single purchase or sale. *Any* series of transactions would almost inevitably create actual or apparent trading or raise or depress the price of the security dealt in. The crucial question is the *purpose* for which the transactions are effected. If the

1. See 3 Loss, Securities Regulation 1549 (2d ed. 1961).

2. Securities and Exchange Commission v. Resch–Cassin & Co., Inc., 362 F.Supp. 964 (S.D.N.Y.1973).

activity is engaged in for the purpose of inducing the purchase or sale of such security by others, then it is unlawful. However, as the Commission stated in the *Halsey, Stuart*[3] case: "There is not here (as indeed there rarely is) any subjective evidence of such a purpose. If found, it must, as in most cases, be inferred from the circumstances of the case."

In *Crane Company v. Westinghouse Air Brake Company*[4] the Second Circuit had no difficulty in determining that the purchases by American Standard of the Westinghouse Air Brake stock were made for the purpose of manipulating the market in that stock and defeating the Crane tender offer. Although it was true that that was a particularly aggravated case (because the purchases on the floor of the exchange were accompanied by off-board sales at a loss), the Court nonetheless stated that: "When a person who has a 'substantial, direct pecuniary interest in the success of a proposed offering takes active steps to effect a rise in the market' in the security, we think that a finding of manipulative purpose is prima facie established."[5]

In *Securities and Exchange Commission v. Resch–Cassin & Co., Inc.*[6] a brokerage firm, which was the principal market maker in a security following a public offering, ran the price up in thirty-four minutes on one day from $11 to $16 and in another 20 day period from $13 to $17 ½; but in less than two months after the issue came out at $10, the price was down to $4. The court said:

"Of course, once it is established that a price rise occurred, it becomes necessary to show that defendants caused it. There are various factors which characterize attempts by manipulators to raise the price of an over-the-counter security: (a) price leadership by the manipulator; (b) dominion and control of the market for the security; (c) reduction in the floating supply of the security; and (d) the collapse of the market for the security when the manipulator ceases his activity. As already discussed herein, the tactic of inserting successively higher bids in the pink sheets has the effect of giving an appearance of activity. However, it also has the effect of causing a price rise. Similarly, the use of actual purchases and sales at successively higher prices not only has the effect of giving an appearance of activity, it raises the price of the over-the-counter security. * * *

"It is true, of course, that § 9(a)(2) of the Exchange Act requires that any manipulation be 'for the purpose of inducing the purchase or sale of such security by others'. Although defendants claim they were engaged in 'normal trading', it seems clear that their transactions in Africa stock were designed to induce others to purchase the security. Here they were engaged in the distribution of the stock and obviously had the purpose of inducing the purchase of the security by others. They had an obvious incentive to artificially influence the market price of the security in order to facilitate its distribution or increase its profitability. Here the defendants used the manipulated after-market to sell the Africa stock to the public."[7]

The use of manipulative techniques prohibited by §§ 9(a)(1) and 9(a)(2) is especially inviting "in contemporary markets which feature derivative instruments, option exchanges, future markets, intermarket trading, and hedging."[8]

---

3. In the Matter of Halsey, Stuart & Co., Inc., 30 S.E.C. 106, 123–24 (1949).

4. 419 F.2d 787 (2d Cir.1969).

5. 419 F.2d at 795.

6. 362 F.Supp. 964 (S.D.N.Y.1973).

7. 362 F. Supp. at 976–77.

K. *The General Fraud Sections as Applied to Broker–Dealers:* Section 17(a) of the Securities Act of 1933, Section 10(b) (as implemented by Rule 10b–5) of the Securities Exchange Act and Section 15(c)(1) of the Securities Exchange Act all prohibit manipulative, deceptive and fraudulent actions in the securities markets. Section 17(a) outlaws (1) any device, scheme, or artifice to defraud, (2) any untrue statement of a material fact or any omission to state a material fact necessary to make the statements made not misleading, and (3) any transaction, practice, or course of business which operates or would operate as a fraud or deceit. Section 10(b) itself refers only to "any manipulative or deceptive device or contrivance," but Rule 10b–5 has copied the language of the three subdivisions of Section 17(a). Section 15(c)(1) refers to "any manipulative, deceptive, *or other fraudulent* device or contrivance." But again Rule 15c1–2 has incorporated into this section the substance of the three subdivisions of Section 17(a).

The major differences between these three sections and the rules implementing them are that Section 17(a) applies only to *sales,* whereas Sections 10(b) and 15(c)(1) apply to both purchases and sales and that Section 15(c)(1) applies only to a "broker or dealer," whereas Sections 17(a) and 10(b) apply to "any person." There are other minor variations in language, which are not too significant. In connection with a revocation proceeding against a broker-dealer involving allegedly fraudulent sales of securities, the Commission uniformly cites all three sections (and their related rules).

1. *The "Shingle Theory."* The "shingle theory" was developed by the Commission as a basis for a liberalized finding of statutory fraud under these sections in cases where no intentional misstatement or omission on the part of the broker-dealer could be established. In brief, the theory is that when a broker-dealer goes into business (hangs out his "shingle") he impliedly represents that he will deal fairly and competently with his customers and that he will have an adequate basis for any statements or recommendations which he makes concerning securities. In *Kahn v. Securities and Exchange Commission,*[1] Judge Clark, in a concurring opinion, stated that under this theory the broker-dealer "implicitly *warrants* the soundness of statements of stock value." This statement unquestionably goes much too far. Certainly the broker-dealer is not liable for *unavoidable* errors of fact, much less of analysis and opinion, and today proof of scienter will be required in any action based on Rule 10b–5. The *Hughes* case[2] was the initial judicial opinion upholding this theory of the Commission. The charge in that case, as in most of the early cases involving shingle theory, was that the broker-dealer sold securities to his customers at prices greatly in excess of their market value and without disclosure of the market value, thus making false his implied representation that he would deal

8. See L. Lowenfels, Sections 9(a)(1) and 9(a)(2) of the Securities Exchange Act of 1934: An Analysis of Two Important Anti–Manipulation Provisions Under the Federal Securities Laws, 85 Nw. U. L.Rev. 698, at 702–705 (1991), discussing Michael Betterman, Ragnar Option Corp., Victor Sperandeo, Exchange Act Release No. 12,278, 9 SEC Dock. 307 (Mar. 29, 1976, amended, Nov. 2, 1976).

And see Poser, Stock Market Manipulations and Corporate Control Transactions, 40 U. Miami L. Rev. 671 (1986) (discussing § 14(e) of the 1934 Act prohibiting manipulative activity in connection with tender offers).

1. 297 F.2d 112 (2d Cir.1961).

2. Charles Hughes & Co. v. SEC, 139 F.2d 434 (2d Cir.1943), cert. denied, 321 U.S. 786 (1944).

with them fairly and at prices reasonably related to market value. Today, the survival of "shingle theory" is open to debate,[3] but it is clear that if a broker-dealer makes optimistic statements to its customers about a security without any factual basis, this will be seen by the SEC as violating its implied representation that he will have a reasonably adequate basis for any such statements.[4]

2. *Boiler Rooms.* A "boiler room" operation is a high-pressure selling campaign for a particular block of securities of a single issuer (frequently intrinsically worthless[5]), usually carried out by long-distance telephone. The name comes from the fact that sometimes 10 to 20 telephones will be connected in a single room, at each of which a salesman will sit telephoning prospective buyers whose names have been obtained from a "sucker list."

In *Kahn v. Securities and Exchange Commission*[6] and *Berko v. Securities and Exchange Commission*,[7] which both involved an appeal from orders of the Commission disciplining salesmen who were allegedly involved in a "boiler room" operation, the Second Circuit worried that the Commission was attempting to fashion a *"per se* rule" to the effect that any such telephone solicitation of purchasers was illegal, and the court remanded the cases to the Commission for further findings. When the Commission reaffirmed its former action and a second appeal was taken to the Second Circuit in *Berko v. Securities and Exchange Commission*,[8] the Court then upheld the action of the Commission and stated that the Commission was "fully justified * * * in holding Berko, a 'boiler-room' salesman, chargeable with knowledge of the contents of the brochures [furnished to him by the broker-dealer relating to the company whose stock was being sold] and with responsibility for allowing customers to rely upon them. * * * The Commission acted well within its mandate in concluding that the 'public interest' requires that a salesman working out of a 'boiler-room' be held to a higher duty to prospective customers than a salesman working out of a legitimate sales operation, and in concluding that a 'boiler-room' salesman does not meet his obligation when he has no knowledge other than opinions and brochures furnished by the broker, 'without any checking, investigation, or determination of the correctness of the same before putting them out to the public.' " The court also stated in a footnote that the Commission's second opinion had made it clear that it was "not attempting to fashion a *per se* rule to be applied indiscriminately in all 'boiler-room' cases."

---

3. See Roberta Karmel, Is the Shingle Theory Dead?, 52 Wash. & Lee L. Rev. 1371 (1995).

4. See In re BT Alex Brown Inc., Securities Exchange Act Release No. 42145 (Nov. 17, 1999); In re Alexander Reid & Co., Inc., Securities Exchange Act Release No. 6727 (1962).

5. This was not true of the stock of Sports Arenas (Delaware) Inc. which was being sold by Kahn and Berko in the cases referred to in the next paragraph. In the fiscal year ended June 30, 1961, the corporation had in operation 29 bowling arenas with a total of 936 lanes, it grossed $5,159,458, and it had a net profit of $287,158 equal to 27.8 cents per share. Securities Exchange Act Release Rel. No. 6846 n. 36 (1962). While these accomplishments are far short of Kahn's prediction to customers that earnings would reach a level of $1.18 per share by the end of the calendar year 1958, they do show that this was a substantial business operation. On the other hand, the typical corporation whose stock is being promoted in a "boiler room" operation is a uranium company which has no mine or an electronics company which has no plant.

6. 297 F.2d 112 (2d Cir.1961).

7. 297 F.2d 116 (2d Cir.1961).

8. 316 F.2d 137 (2d Cir.1963).

3. *Scienter.* There remains, however, the question of whether the principles in these early cases can be broadly enforced by the SEC (or even the NASD), or whether the enforcing agency or private litigant must today plead and prove a fraudulent intent on the part of the defendant.[9] Scienter is, of course, universally required in any cause of action that relies on Rule 10b–5, but its existence may be more easily inferred in an enforcement action. Thus, the practical answer to this question may depend largely on whether the proceeding is brought (1) by a private plaintiff in a federal court action, (2) by an agency in an enforcement proceeding, or (3) in an arbitration proceeding pursuant to a pre-dispute arbitration clause between the individual customer and the broker-dealer.

SECTION 2. REGULATION AIMED AT PROTECTION FROM HIGH RISK AND INSOLVENCY

As in the case of other financial institutions, federal regulatory policy toward broker-dealers seeks to ensure their financial soundness.[1] The regulatory objective is not only protection of the customers of the individual firm, but, in light of the interdependence of firms, protection of the system from a domino-like cascade of failing firms. As discussed below, this is achieved both through direct regulation, financial controls, segregation of customer funds, and a governmentally administered insurance system. Some rules also indirectly reduce the overall financial risk to the system. For example, in 1998, the SEC mandated that every contract for the purchase or sale of a security (with some exceptions for exempted and governmental securities and commercial paper) settle within three business days.[2] By requiring a short settlement cycle (now known as "t + 3"), the Commission reduced the overall risk to the system from longer-term extensions of credit.

Beyond seeking to reduce aggregate risk, federal policy, since the inception of the 1934 Act, has paternalistically sought to discourage the individual investor from pursuing heavily leveraged investment strategies in securities. Toward this end, § 7 of the 1934 Act subjects broker-dealers and other lenders and borrowers to margin controls that are intended to prevent "excessive" use of credit for the purpose of purchasing or carrying securities.

A. *Broker–Dealer Record–Keeping.* Section 17(a) of the 1934 Act requires broker-dealers to keep extensive records. Under Rule 17a–5, every broker-dealer who clears transactions or carries customer accounts must file both monthly and quarterly reports (known as FOCUS reports) with the SEC on its financial condition. The same rule also requires the broker-dealer to send periodically to its customers specified information about its financial position.[3] A broker-dealer that overstates its income or assets is subject to SEC discipline and sanctions, because necessarily the FOCUS reports it files with the Commis-

---

9. Where the litigation is brought as a class action, this question has been specifically addressed by the Private Securities Litigation Reform Act, which mandates special heightened pleading standards. See § 21D(b)(2) of the 1934 Act.

1. For an overview of federal policy toward financial institutions, see Clark, The Soundness of Financial Intermediaries, 86 Yale L.J. 1 (1976).

2. See Rule 15c6–1, 17 C.F.R. § 240.15c6–1.

3. See Rule 17a–5(c).

sion will be overstated.[4] Thus, Rule 17a–5 provides a jurisdictional hook for cases involving a variety of forms of misconduct that wrongfully transfer customer funds to the broker-dealer.

Other rules under § 17 require broker-dealers to keep specified records (blotters containing daily itemized records of all purchases and sales of securities, ledgers of the firm's income and expense and capital accounts, ledger accounts as to each customer account, a memorandum of each brokerage order, etc.)[5] and to preserve these records for specified periods.[6] These records are subject to periodic inspections by government regulators (state and federal), and the net result is not unlike the standard examination procedures that a bank or savings and loan undergoes.

Section 17(a) does not give a defrauded creditor any private right of action (either against the broker-dealer or its auditors).[7] Rather, the Supreme Court viewed it as a tool to aid regulators, not as a grant of rights to investors.

B. *The Net Capital Rules.* Based on authority granted it by § 15(b)(7) of the 1934 Act, the SEC directly regulates the capital of broker-dealers, requiring high liquidity in order to protect customers and creditors of broker-dealers from financial exposure in the event of broker insolvency. The key rule—Rule 15c3–1—"requires broker-dealers to maintain sufficient liquid assets to enable firms that fall below the minimum net capital requirements to liquidate in an orderly fashion without the need for a formal proceeding."[8] Setting a liquidation threshold equal to the aggregate of customer accounts promotes orderly self-liquidations of financially distressed broker-dealers and reduces the costs incurred in bankruptcy proceedings. Still, the cost of such a policy is considerable: necessarily some broker-dealers are forced into liquidation that are not insolvent and that would not become insolvent (but that have crossed the early warning thresholds imposed by Rule 15c3–1). Also, the rule impacts heavily on the behavior of broker-dealers: they cannot easily hold investments in securities, because the rule writes down such investments to a fraction of their market value. In the industry, this is referred to as "taking a haircut," and it induces broker-dealers to maintain high cash reserves. The rule also restricts entry into the broker-dealer industry by imposing high minimum capital requirements.

Nonetheless, the Commission justifies Rule 15c3–1 (which has been in force since 1965) on three grounds:

> "First, firms handling customer funds and securities should have sufficient capital so that they are not dependent upon customer assets to make up the principal working capital of the firm. Second, firms should have adequate capital, resources, and equipment so that the securities markets function smoothly and efficiently and market participants have the resulting confidence to carry out business responsibly. Finally, if the liability of a broker-dealer to its customers from violations of state and federal law is to

---

4. See Securities Exchange Act Release No. 7279 ("In the Matter of Gruntal & Co. Inc.") (April 9, 1996) (broker-dealer subjected to cease and desist order under § 21C of the 1934 Act and other sanctions under § 15b(4) for overstating earnings on its FOCUS report by diverting customer funds to broker-dealer's own account).

5. See Rule 17a–3.

6. See Rule 17a–4 (six year preservation required).

7. See Touche Ross & Co. v. Redington, 442 U.S. 560, 569 (1979).

8. See Securities Exchange Act Release No. 27, 249 (Sept. 15, 1990).

be a deterrent to improper conduct, a firm should be required to maintain a reasonable financial stake in its business."[9]

In 1992, the SEC significantly revised its net capital standards to make them more responsive to the specific activities engaged in by a broker-dealer, but it also raised the capital normally required to conduct business.[10]

Rule 15c3–1 uses a dual measuring standard for a broker-dealer's capital requirements. Two types of financial ratio computations are specified: (1) an "aggregate indebtedness standard" which generally prohibits the broker or dealer from permitting its aggregate indebtedness to exceed 1500 percent of its net capital, and (2) an "alternative standard" which requires that a broker not permit its net capital to be less then the greater of $250,000 or two percent of aggregate debit items as computed under the rule.[11] A broker-dealer who carries customer accounts must also maintain net capital of not less than $250,000.[12] This requirement often induces smaller brokers to use larger clearing brokers to hold and service their customers' accounts.

Another aspect of the net capital rule is the requirement that broker-dealers maintain fully-paid customer securities in a "segregated" account with the brokerage firm or a bank.[13] Often, this is arranged between the brokerage firm and the Depositary Trust Company ("DTC").[14] These rules also restrict the "hypothecation" of customer securities: that is, their use by the broker-dealer as collateral for its own borrowings or short sales.

C. *Securities Investor Protection Corporation.* The SIPC was established in 1970, and registered broker-dealers are required to become members. Essentially, the SIPC insures the accounts of customers with brokerage firms in much the same manner as the Federal Deposit Insurance Corporation ("FDIC") does for the banking industry.[15] As with the FDIC, there are ceilings on this insurance (securities in customer accounts are covered by the SIPC up to $500,000 in the event of a broker-dealer's insolvency). Another advantage of this insurance system is that it spares the customer the delay involved in bankruptcy and insolvency reorganizations.

D. *Credit Regulation: The Margin Requirements.* Section 7 of the 1934 Act subjects broker-dealers, most other lenders, and borrowers to margin controls that are intended to prevent "excessive" use of credit for the purpose of purchasing or carrying securities. Congress's intent was to chill speculation in securities trading (which from the vantage point of 1934 seemed a major cause of the 1929 stock market crash).

Section 7(a) requires the Federal Reserve Board ("FRB") to prescribe regulations with respect to the amount of credit that may be initially extended

---

9. *Id.*

10. See Securities Exchange Act Release No. 31,511 (November 24, 1992). For an overview of the rule's operation, see Jamroz, The Net Capital Rule, 47 Bus. Law. 863 (1992).

11. See Rule 15c3–1(a)(1)(i) and (ii).

12. See Rule 15c3–1(a)(2)(i).

13. See Rule 15c3–3(c); see also Rule 8c–1.

14. See Securities Exchange Act Release No. 26,250 (November 3, 1998) (detailing procedures for "memo segregation" by DTC).

15. See 15 U.S.C. § 78aaa (authorizing SIPC). The broker membership requirement is codified at 15 U.S.C. § 78ccc(a)(2)(A) for a review of the SIPC's performance, see Bloomenthal & Salcito, Customer Protection from Brokerage Failure: The Securities Investor Protection Corporation and the SEC, 54 U. Colo. L. Rev. 161 (1983).

and subsequently maintained on any security, other than an exempt security. Although the FRB has the authority to promulgate the regulations and to fix from time to time the minimum margin level (currently 50%), the SEC and the securities regulatory agencies (SROs) are charged with the responsibility of enforcing the margin rules with respect to broker-dealers. The current regulation governing lending on securities by broker-dealers is designated Regulation T. There is a similar, but by no means identical, regulation governing loans by banks secured directly or indirectly by margin stock "for the purpose * * * of buying or carrying margin stock,"[1] which is designated Regulation U, and relatively new regulations governing lending by persons other than broker-dealers and banks, who engage in the business of making loans for the purpose of buying or carrying margin securities (Regulation G)[2] and governing borrowing by persons in the United States from either domestic or foreign lenders (Regulation X).[3]

Regulation T formerly prohibited a broker-dealer from lending for the purpose of purchasing or carrying any securities other than those which are either registered on a national securities exchange or are widely traded over-the-counter stocks on a list of "OTC Margin Stocks" issued by the FRB or are "exempted securities" as defined in the Securities Exchange Act (primarily governments). By an amendment to Regulation T adopted on June 30, 1984, however, this prohibition was eliminated, but the required margin for a purchase of other over-the-counter securities is 100%;[4] therefore, such a loan does not substantially assist the customer in the purchase of such securities

1. For a discussion of the differences between the regulation of lending on securities by broker-dealers, on the one hand, and by banks, on the other, prior to 1968, see Report of Special Study of the Securities Markets, H.Doc.No.95, 88th Cong., 1st Sess., Pt. 4 at 15–25 (1963).

The primary difference prior to that time was that broker-dealers could not lend at all on over-the-counter securities, whereas lending by banks on such securities was completely unregulated. By Act of July 29, 1968, 82 Stat. 452, Section 7 of the Securities Exchange Act was amended to give the FRB the authority to regulate credit on OTC securities and to eliminate the prohibition against broker-dealers lending on such securities. While the current Regulation T permits lending by broker-dealers on any securities, the required margin is 100% with respect to over-the-counter securities which are neither exempted securities nor on the list of "OTC Margin Stocks" issued by the FRB. On the other hand, a bank may lend on any such securities without regard to the margin requirement, and may assign a loan value to such collateral of any amount (not exceeding 100% of current market) upon the basis of which "a bank, exercising sound banking judgment, would lend, without regard to the customer's other assets held as collateral in connection with unrelated transactions." 12

C.F.R. §§ 220.4(b), 220.18(a), 221.2(f), 221.3(a), 221.8(b).

2. 12 C.F.R. Part 207 (§ 207.0 et seq.) effective March 11, 1968. This regulation in general conforms to Regulation U applicable to banks.

3. 12 C.F.R. Part 224 (§ 224.1 et seq.). This regulation was authorized by Act of October 26, 1970, P.L. 91–508, 84 Stat. 1124, adding subsection (f) to Section 7 of the Securities Exchange Act. While primarily intended to stop the practice of United States persons borrowing from foreign lenders in order to evade the margin requirements, the statute and Regulation X originally applied to any borrowing, whether domestic or foreign, and thus for the first time made the borrower as well as the lender guilty of an offense when there is a violation of the margin rules. On January 23, 1984, Regulation X was revised to apply to a domestic borrowing *only* if "the borrower willfully causes the credit to be extended in contravention of Regulations G, T, or U." Basically, Regulation X simply says that the borrower is prohibited from borrowing if the lender is prohibited from lending by Regulation T, U, or G or, in the case of a foreign lender, if he or she would have been prohibited from lending by Regulation G had the person been subject to it.

4. 12 C.F.R. § 220.18(e).

since he must deposit (or already have on deposit) in his margin account the entire purchase price of the securities. Such securities held in a margin account do, however, have a loan value in the margin account and may assist in avoiding a margin call if the market value has increased to an amount in excess of the initial purchase price (i.e., the amount of the original loan), and, conversely, will increase the chances of a margin call in connection with future transactions if they have declined in value.[5]

Basically, Regulation T provides for two types of accounts which may be maintained for a customer by a broker-dealer: a "margin account" and a "cash account" (i.e., an account which is not subject to the margin requirements).

In a margin account, the loan value of the account must be maintained at the current required level, i.e., under the currently required 50% "margin" the debit balance of an account cannot be permitted to exceed 50% of the current market value of the securities held as collateral in the account in connection with any additional purchase of securities.[6] (Although the FRB has authority to require maintenance levels of margin as well as initial levels, it has never done so; therefore, Regulation T never requires "margin calls" if no new securities are purchased.[7] This is a matter regulated entirely by the rules of the stock exchanges and the contract between the customer and the broker-dealer.)[8] For example, Rule 431 of the New York Stock Exchange requires (with some exceptions) that an account maintain a margin level of not less than twenty-five percent with respect to the securities "long" in the account. Thus, if an investor purchased securities using fifty percent margin from the broker dealer, and the value of the securities so purchased falls, the broker must make a "margin call" (i.e. a demand for additional cash or collateral) once this "maintenance" margin level is reached. Or, the broker will be required to liquidate the securities in the account to pay off the customer's indebtedness to it. Such "margin calls" often occur in rapidly falling markets and were thought by Congress to accelerate the market's decline. In addition, brokers often specify "house maintenance margin" limits in their brokerage agreements with customers, which are stricter than the levels specified by the stock exchanges. These agreements may entitle the broker-dealer to make a margin call with virtually no notice or grace period or simply to liquidate the customer's securities if the house maintenance margin level is exceeded.[9] In contrast, federal law, which applies only to the initial margin requirement on a purchase, gives the customer five business days to satisfy any margin call.[10]

---

5. For the different provisions relating to banks, see Note 1, supra.

6. 12 C.F.R. §§ 220.4, 220.18.

7. The withdrawal of cash or securities from a margin account is not permitted, however, even though no new securities are being purchased, if thereafter the adjusted debit balance of the account would exceed the maximum loan value of the securities remaining, with certain exceptions. 12 C.F.R. § 220.4(e).

8. Report of Special Study of the Securities Markets, H.Doc.No.95, 88th Cong., 1st Sess. Pt. 4, pp. 5–6 (1963); 12 C.F.R. § 220.3(c).

9. Such agreements are enforceable, even when no notice is given. See First Union

Discount Brokerage Services, Inc. v. Milos, 997 F.2d 835 (11th Cir.1993).

10. 12 C.F.R. § 220.4(c)(3). This provision of Regulation T, adopted in 1998, works off on an SEC rule, Rule 15c6–1. Section 220.(4)(c)(3) requires that a margin call be satisfied "within one payment period after the margin deficiency was created." Section 220.2 then defines "payment period" to mean "the number of business days in the standard settlement cycle in the United States, as defined in paragraph (a) of SEC Rule 15c6–1 ... plus two business days." Rule 15c6–1 requires all contracts for the purchase or sale of securities to settle within three business days—i.e., "t + 3" (subject to several excep-

On the other hand, a broker-dealer may in fact extend short-term credit on any securities in any amount in a "cash account" if he accepts "in good faith the customer's agreement that the customer will promptly make full cash payment for the security and does not contemplate selling it prior to making such payment."[11] If the customer "has not made full cash payment" for the security within "one payment period" (or five business days) after the date on which the security is so purchased, the "creditor shall promptly cancel or otherwise liquidate" the transaction or the unsettled portion thereof.[12] If the customer sells a security within the five business day period without previously having paid for it, then a 90-day "freeze" is put on the account during which time the broker-dealer may not purchase any securities for that customer without having cash deposited in advance to cover the full purchase price.[13] This led to what were called "clearance loans" whereby an "unregulated lender"[14] would make a 1-day loan to the customer of the purchase price so that he could deposit it with the broker-dealer prior to making the sale and thereby avoid the 90-day freeze.[15] Effective March 11, 1968, the FRB's Regulation G brought such previously unregulated lenders under the margin rules and both banks and Regulation G lenders are now prohibited from making "clearance loans" except in compliance with the margin rules applicable to those lenders.[16]

In addition to the FRB margin rules, in 1970, the SEC adopted Rule 10b-16 which requires a broker-dealer extending credit to a customer in a margin transaction to disclose the credit terms to the customer. Following the "Truth in Lending" paradigm, the rule provides, among other things, that at the opening of the account, the customer shall be furnished a written statement of the conditions under which the interest charge will be imposed, the method of computing the interest, and the conditions under which additional collateral can be required.

During the merger mania of the 1980s, junk bonds were used to finance corporate acquisitions and the question arose whether certain financing arrangements constituted an extension of credit that was secured indirectly by margin stock under Regulation G. Such deals were structured by having the bidder company form a shell corporation that would make a tender offer for a controlling block of the voting stock of the target company. The shell corporation had essentially no assets or function other than to acquire and hold the stock of the target. To finance the tender offer, the shell corporation would issue and sell debt securities to "sophisticated" investors. If the tender offer was successful, the bidder corporation then acquired the stock of the target company through a long-form merger of the shell corporation into the bidder corporation. When the matter came before the FRB, the board ruled that the

---

tions). Hence, Section 220.2 defines "payment period" to mean five business days.

11. 12 C.F.R. § 220.8(a)(1).

12. 12 C.F.R. § 220.8(b)(4).

13. 12 C.F.R. § 220.8(c).

14. Prior to March 11, 1968, only broker-dealers and banks had been subjected to the lending restrictions of the FRB's margin rules. For a discussion of the unregulated lenders, sometimes called "factors", see Re-

port of Special Study of the Securities Markets, H.Doc.No.95, 88th Cong., 1st Sess., Pt. 4, pp. 25–35 (1963).

15. The customer was sometimes charged a minimum of 1 month's interest for such a loan, at a rate which was already 12% to 24% per annum. Report of Special Study of the Securities Markets, H.Doc.No.95, 88th Cong., 1st Sess., Pt. 4, at 27 (1963).

16. 12 C.F.R. §§ 221.3, 207.3.

"arrangement constituted an extension of credit that [was] secured indirectly by margin stock."[17]

The National Securities Market Improvements Act of 1996 effected some significant deregulation in the scope of the margin rules and the FRB's authority. First, it repealed former § 8(a) and amended § 7 of the 1934 Act, which together had authorized the FRB to regulate the sources of credit for broker-dealers, and substituted a weaker requirement under which the FRB could regulate loans to broker dealers only if it found that such rules were necessary or appropriate in the public interest or for the protection of investors. The FRB has expressly declined to make any such finding.[18] Hence, broker-dealers are not restricted today in their own pursuit of credit by the margin-setting authority of the FRB.

Also, in 1996, the FRB amended its own Regulation T to relax substantially the former restrictions on the "arranging for" credit by broker-dealers. Today, a broker-dealer may effectively arrange for credit that it, itself, could not advance.[19] That is, the broker-dealer may arrange for credit that does not otherwise violate the lending provisions of the FRB's margin regulations (such as from an unregulated or foreign lender), but it may not arrange for credit from a lender that would itself violate Regulations G, T or U. Part of the rationale for this significant change was the increasingly global character of the market in which broker-dealers operated and the prospect that U.S. broker-dealers would be at a competitive disadvantage to foreign broker-dealers who could arrange for credit without restriction.

SECTION 3. REGULATION AIMED AT ESTABLISHING THE DUTIES OF BROKERS TO THEIR CUSTOMERS

The relationship between a broker-dealer and its customer may or may not be a fiduciary one. Courts seem regularly to disagree. In addition, although the "just and equitable" rules of the SROs may seem to imply such a duty, courts are reluctant to enforce such rules in private litigation or to imply any private cause of action based on them. Thus, private plaintiffs usually are forced to rely on Rule 10b–5 when they wish to litigate allegations of broker misconduct.

Under these circumstances, plaintiffs have effectively two options. First, they can seek to establish that their relationship with the broker was a fiduciary one under the traditional common law standards. This will depend upon evidence showing that a relationship of trust and confidence was recognized by both sides. Some courts have found such a relationship to exist even when the client is sophisticated,[1] but the more recent tendency has been to find a fiduciary relationship only when the client is dependent upon the broker (as in the case of a discretionary trading account) or the relationship has otherwise

---

17. 12 C.F.R. § 207.112 (Jan. 15, 1986).

18. See Federal Reserve System, "Securities Credit Transactions; Borrowings by Brokers and Dealers," 61 F.R. 60166 (November 26, 1996).

19. See Federal Reserve System, "Securities Credit Transactions; Review of Regulation T," 61 F.R. 20386 (May 6, 1996). Section 7 of the 1934 Act forbids a broker-dealer

from "arranging" credit on terms forbidden by the FRB, but it does not restrict the FRB's ability to permit broker-dealers to arrange credit on terms they cannot themselves advance.

1. See Romano v. Merrill Lynch, Pierce, Fenner & Smith, 834 F.2d 523 (5th Cir.1987).

called for the broker to perform special duties or provide special warnings.[2] Because these cases are so fact sensitive, the law on this question of fiduciary relationship has little certainty. Often, the cases involve detailed examinations of the individual relationship between broker and client with little general criteria emerging, other than that evidence that one side dominated the relationship tends to be persuasive in establishing a fiduciary relationship.

An alternative route by which to impose legal duties on the broker-dealer is to rely on a doctrine known as "shingle theory," which holds that a broker-dealer impliedly represents that it is a professional (much like a lawyer or doctor who similarly hangs out a shingle with their name on it) and will therefore deal both fairly and competently in the manner of a true professional with their clients. This doctrine derives from an early Second Circuit case, *Charles Hughes & Co. v. SEC*,[3] which found that a broker-dealer impliedly represented that it would deal fairly with customers and not charge unreasonable mark-ups. The attraction of this theory is that if a fiduciary relationship exists (by reason of the broker-dealer's implied representation that it is a professional who will deal fairly with its customers), then any failure to disclose material facts constitutes an actionable omission under Rule 10b–5. The doctrinal problem with this theory is that it seems to create a fiduciary relationship as a matter of federal law without regard to state law. This conflicts with the trend of the recent cases that have held that the existence of a fiduciary relationship to be a matter of state law.[4] Arguably, shingle theory may be a throwback to an earlier era when the Supreme Court did not agonize over these federalism-related issues, and it may not survive in some Circuits. Still, it clearly survives in SEC enforcement cases where the Commission recurrently assumes that fiduciary relationship between broker and client is the norm.

A. THE DUTY OF BEST EXECUTION

Chapter 10 has already covered this duty as an element of the national market system, where it serves to integrate markets that otherwise might simultaneously trade the same security at different prices. Although there is no SEC rule requiring best execution, the SROs do have rules. NASD Conduct Rule 2320 ("Best Execution Rule") requires a NASD member firm and persons associated with it, in any transaction for a customer, to:

> "use reasonable diligence to ascertain the best inter-dealer market for the subject security and to buy or sell in such market so that the resultant price to the customer is as favorable as possible under prevailing market conditions."

In determining whether the "reasonable diligence" test has been satisfied, the Rule 2320 considers four factors:

> "(1) the character of the market for the security, e.g., price volatility, relative liquidity, and pressure on available communications; (2) the size and type of the transaction; (3) the number of primary markets checked;

2. Compare Independent Order of Foresters v. Donald, Lufkin & Jenrette, 157 F.3d 933 (2d Cir.1998) (no fiduciary duty owed to non-discretionary account) with de Kwiatkowski v. Bear Stearns, 126 F.Supp.2d 672 (S.D.N.Y.2000) (duty to warn existed where such obligation assumed by broker during course of relationship).

3. 139 F.2d 434 (2d Cir.1943).

4. See Santa Fe Industries, Inc. v. Green, 430 U.S. 462 (1977).

[and] (4) location and accessibility to the customer's broker-dealer of primary markets and quotation sources."[5]

In the case of a stock listed on Nasdaq's National Market System, this standard generally does not present difficult problems,[6] but in a stock traded over-the-counter and not quoted on Nasdaq, issues can frequently arise, because the lowest price quoted may not be "firm" or current or may be for a much smaller quantity than a seemingly less attractive quote. Issues can also arise, even with regard to Nasdaq-listed stocks, as to when a broker is subject to the duty of best execution. For example, suppose one broker refers its customer's order for execution to another broker-dealer. Is the latter executing broker also subject to the duty of best execution?[7]

Although Rule 10b–5 can be used to enforce the duty of best execution (if its elements, including the requirement of scienter are satisfied),[8] the duty's contours will more likely be adjudicated in arbitration proceedings brought by customers against their broker-dealer.

B. THE DUTY TO PROTECT LIMIT ORDERS

Assume that a customer gives a broker dealer a limit order to sell 5,000 shares of XYZ Corp. at $17½ at a time when the inside quotation (the "NBBO") is $17 bid and $17⅛ asked. Later, the NBBO widens to $17 bid and $17½ asked. At this point, the broker-dealer sells 5,000 of its own shares at $17½. It never executes its customer's limit order because the market price of XYZ thereafter declines, and it defends its own trading on the grounds that the bid price (the price at which it would buy) never rose to $17½. Yet, in an important 1988 case, the SEC found that a broker-dealer who traded in this fashion had "traded ahead" of its customer's limit order in breach of its fiduciary duty to the customer for whom it held the limit order.[9] The majority of a divided SEC found that the broker's selling its own stock from its inventory at $17½, when it could have instead executed its customer's limit order, gave an unlawful priority to the broker's own interests over that of the customer to whom it owed a fiduciary duty (the minority replied that the existence of a fiduciary duty depended on state law and could not be assumed in this fashion). Although this decision was controversial at the time, it has since been codified in an NASD rule, which requires a market-maker not to trade ahead of a customer's limit order at a price equal to or better than the limit order price.[10] However, broker-dealers have no obligation to accept limit orders (although most do) and may charge a higher commission for doing so.

---

5. See NASD Conduct Rule 2320(a).

6. Some issues do arise even in this context because of the uncertain trade-off between the customer's desire for speed of execution and the customer's desire for price improvement, which two goals tend to be inversely related. See Jonathan Macey and Maureen O'Hara, The Law and Economics of Best Execution, 6 J. of Fin. Intermediation 188 (1997).

7. In July, 2002, the NASD sent a notice to members indicating its view that the duty did normally apply to the executing broker under these circumstances, at least if the order ultimately came from a customer of the routing broker. See NASD Notice to Members 02–40 (July, 2002).

8. See Newton v. Merrill Lynch, 135 F.3d 266 (3d Cir.1998) (failure to disclose that broker has not traded at best available price can violate Rule 10b–5).

9. See In re E.F. Hutton and Company, Inc., Securities Exchange Act Release No. 25887 (July 6, 1988). This case is widely known as the "Manning" decision, after the name of the plaintiff, William Manning.

10. See Securities Exchange Act Release No. 35751 ("Limit Order Protection on Nasdaq") (May 22, 1995).

C.   THE DUTY TO INVESTIGATE

Hanly v. Securities and Exchange Commission

United States Court of Appeals, Second Circuit, 1969.
415 F.2d 589.

■ Before: LUMBARD, FEINBERG AND TIMBERS.

■ TIMBERS, DISTRICT JUDGE:

Five securities salesmen petition to review an order of the Securities and Exchange Commission which barred them from further association with any broker or dealer. The Commission found that petitioners, in the offer and sale of the stock of U.S. Sonics Corporation (Sonics) between September 1962 and August 1963, willfully violated the antifraud provisions of Section 17(a) of the Securities Act of 1933, ... Sections 10(b) and 15(c)(1) of the Securities and Exchange Act of 1934, ... and Rule 10b–5.... Specifically, the Commission held that "the fraud in this case consisted of the optimistic representations or the recommendations ... without disclosure of known or reasonably ascertainable adverse information which rendered them materially misleading.... It is clear that a salesman must not merely avoid affirmative misstatements when he recommends the stock to a customer; he must also disclose material adverse facts of which he is or should be aware." Petitioners individually argue that their violations of the federal securities laws were not willful but involved at most good faith optimistic predictions concerning a speculative security, and that the sanctions imposed by the Commission exceeded legally permissible limits. The Commission, upon an independent review of the record before the hearing examiner, affirmed his findings as to individual violations, rejected his finding of concerted action, and increased the sanctions he had imposed. We affirm in all respects the order of the Commission as to each of the five petitioners.

VIOLATIONS

The primary witnesses before the hearing examiner were customers of each of petitioners and the former president of Sonics. Since the Commission rejected the conclusion of the hearing examiner that petitioners had acted in concert in the conduct of their fraudulent activities, we have considered separately the evidence against each petitioner and have considered the sanctions against each in the light of his specific alleged violations....

U.S. Sonics Corporation

Sonics was organized in 1958. It engaged in the production and sale of various electronic devices. From its inception the company operated at a deficit. During the period of the sales of its stock here involved, the company was insolvent.

By 1962 the company had developed a ceramic filter which was said to be far superior to conventional wire filters used in radio circuits. Sonics' inability to raise the capital necessary to produce these filters led it to negotiate with foreign and domestic companies to whom Sonics hoped to grant production licenses on a royalty basis. Licenses were granted to a Japanese and to a West German company, each of which made initial payments of $25,000, and to an Argentine company, which made an initial payment of $50,000. License negotiations with domestic companies continued into 1963 without success; negotiations terminated with General Instrument Corporation on March 20, 1963 and with Texas Instruments, Incorporated, on June 29, 1963. In addition, testing of the filter by prospective customers provided unsatisfactory results.

Merger negotiations with General Instrument and Texas Instruments likewise proved unsuccessful. Sonics' financial condition continued to deteriorate with the cancellation by the Navy of anticipated orders for hydrophones. On December 6, 1963 bankruptcy proceedings were instituted against Sonics, and on December 27, 1963 it was adjudicated a bankrupt.

During most of the relevant period petitioners were employed in Richard J. Buck & Co., a partnership registered as a broker-dealer. Gladstone and Fehr were co-managers of the firm's Forest Hills, N.Y., branch office. Hanly was the manager of its Hempstead, N.Y., office. Stutzmann and Paras were salesmen in the Hempstead office.

Gladstone.

Gladstone (along with Paras) first heard of Sonics in September 1962 during a conversation with one Roach who had been a sales manager for his prior employer, Edwards and Hanly. Roach compared Sonics to Ilikon, whose stock he had previously recommended and which had been lightly successful. Sonic was praised for its good management, large research and development expenses and, most important, its development of a ceramic filter. In January 1963 Roach told Gladstone of the possibility of a domestic license and furnished him with a copy of an allegedly confidential 14 page report which predicted a bright future for the company. In February Gladstone met with Eric Kolm, Sonics' president, who confirmed most of the statements in the report. During the spring of 1963 Gladstone learned of the licensing and merger negotiations mentioned above.

On the basis of this information and knowing that Sonics had never shown a year end profit since its inception, that it was still sustaining losses, and that the 14 page report was not identified as to source and did not contain financial statements, Gladstone told Hanly, Stutzmann, and Paras about the company and made certain representations to his customers.

Evidence of affirmative misrepresentations by Gladstone to his customers regarding Sonics stock included the following: Sonics was a winner and would make money. It had a fabulous potential and would double or triple. It would make Xerox look like a standstill and would revolutionize the space age industry. Gladstone himself had purchased the stock for his own account and he would be able to retire and get rich on it. It had possibilities of sky-rocketing and would probably double in price within six months to a year. Although it had not earned money in the past, prospects were good for earnings of $1 in a year. Sonics had signed a contract with General Instrument. The stock would go from 6 to 12 in two weeks and to 15 in the near future. The 14 page report had been written by Value Line. The company was not going bankrupt. Its products were perfected and it was already earning $1 per share. It was about to have a breakthrough on a new product that was fantastic and would revolutionize automobile and home radios.

In addition to these affirmative misrepresentations, the testimony disclosed that adverse information about Sonics' financial difficulties was not disclosed by Gladstone; that some customers had received confirmation for orders they had not placed; and that literature about the company was not provided. Most of the customer-witnesses testified that they had purchased in reliance upon the recommendations of Gladstone.

Paras

Paras learned of Sonics during the same September 1962 conversation between Roach, Gladstone and Paras referenced to above.

Evidence of affirmative misrepresentations by Paras to his customers regarding Sonics stock included the following: Sonics had a good growth possibility. It should double after three or four weeks (to one customer); it could double, i.e. increase 8 to 10 points, within four to six months (to another customer); and it would rise 10 to 15 points (to still another customer). Paras had bought the stock himself. The company was about to enter into a favorable contract for its filters with Texas Instruments and Texas Instruments might acquire Sonics.

In addition to these affirmative misrepresentations, Paras never mentioned Sonics' adverse financial condition; he never provided any literature about the company; and in at least one instance he sent a confirmation to a customer who claims not to have ordered the stock.

When asked by the hearing examiner why he recommended a stock like Sonics when the commissions he would receive would be negligible, Paras replied that on the basis of his reliable information he hoped that Sonics would make money for his customers who would refer others to him. "[I]t would be a feather in my cap to buy a stock at $8 and sell it at $29 or $30." . . .

* * *

Law Applicable to Violations

In its opinion the Commission quoted from the record in attributing the representations discussed above respectively to each of the petitioners. It concluded that their optimistic representations or recommendations were materially false and misleading. Fraud was found both in affirmative falsehoods and in recommendations made without disclosure of known or reasonably ascertainable adverse information, such as Sonics' deteriorating financial condition, its inability to manufacture the filter, the lack of knowledge regarding the filter's commercial feasibility, and the negative results of pending negotiations.

The Commission found that the sophistication of the customers or prior relationships which many of them had enjoyed with the respective petitioners were irrelevant. It held that the absence of a boiler room did not justify affirmative misrepresentations or a failure to disclose adverse financial information. The relevance of a customer's nonloss of money or a salesman's speculation in the stock likewise was discounted.

The sensitivity of operations in the securities field and the availability of opportunities where those in a position of trust can manipulate others to their own advantage led Congress to pass the antifraud provisions of the statutes with which the instant proceedings are concerned. Congress committed to the Commission the responsibility of supervising the activity of broker-dealers and registered representatives.

When a securities salesmen fraudulently violates the high standards with which he is charged, he subjects himself to variety of punitive, compensatory and remedial sanctions. In the instant proceedings petitioners have not been criminally charged, nor have they been sued for damages by their customers arising from the alleged misrepresentations. Instead, in private proceedings initiated by the Commission, each petitioner's privilege of being employed in the securities industry has been revoked. It is in this context that the issues before the Court must be considered. More particularly, we are here concerned with the expertise of the Commission in its assessment of how the public interest best may be protected from various kinds of intentional fraud and reckless misconduct which often threaten securities transactions, especially, as here, in the over the counter market.

Brokers and salesmen are "under a duty to investigate, and their violation of that duty brings them within the term 'willful' in the Exchange Act." Thus, a salesman cannot deliberately ignore that which he has a duty to know and recklessly state facts about matters of which he is ignorant. He must analyze sales literature and must not blindly accept recommendations made therein. The fact that his customers may be sophisticated and knowledgeable does not warrant a less stringent standard. Even where the purchaser follow the market activity of the stock and does not rely upon the salesman's statements, remedial sanctions may be imposed since reliance is not an element of fraudulent misrepresentation in this context.

Just as proof of specific intent to defraud is irrelevant for insider violations of Rule 10b–5, it is irrelevant in private proceedings such as these:

"In an enforcement proceeding for equitable or prophylactic relief, the common law standard of deceptive conduct has been modified in the interests of broader protection for the investing public so that negligent insider conduct has become unlawful * * * Absent any clear indication of a legislative intention to require a showing of specific fraudulent intent * * * the securities laws should be interpreted as an expansion of the common law both to effectuate the broad remedial design of Congress * * * and to insure uniformity of enforcement * * *[10]

A securities dealer occupies a special relationship to a buyer of securities[11] in that by his position he implicitly represents he has an adequate basis for the opinions he renders. While this implied warranty may not be as rigidly enforced in a civil action where an investor seeks damages for losses allegedly caused by reliance upon his unfounded representations, its applicability in the instant proceedings cannot be questioned.[12]

---

10. SEC v. Texas Gulf Sulphur Co., 401 F.2d 833, 854–55 (2d Cir. 1968) (en banc), cert. denied, sub. nom. Kline v. SEC, 394 U.S. 976 (1969). The applicability of the above quoted language to misrepresentation such as that before the Court in the instant case would appear self-evident.

11. SEC v. Great American Industries, Inc., 407 F.2d 453 (2d Cir. 1968) (paralleling the affirmative duty of disclosure imposed upon insiders with that imposed upon broker-dealers).

12. Petitioners argue that their activities are to be distinguished from those of a "boiler room" and that, absent a finding of boiler room operations here, the Commission's strict standards should not be applied against petitioners.

A boiler room usually is a temporary operation established to sell a specific speculative security. Solicitation is by telephone to new customers, the salesman cohering favorable earnings projections, predictions of price rises and other optimistic prospects without a factual basis. The prospective buyer is not informed of known or readily ascertainable adverse information; he is not cautioned about the risks inherent in purchasing a speculative security; and he is left with a deliberately created expectation of gain without risk. Berko v. SEC, 316 F.2d 137, 139 n. 3 (2 Cir.1963). See also R.A. Holman & Co., Inc. v. SEC, 366 F.2d 446 (2 Cir.1966), modified on other grounds, 377 F.2d 665 (2d Cir.) (per curiam), cert. denied, 389 U.S. 991 (1967); Harold Grill, 41 S.E.C. 321 (1963).

Sonics was an over the counter stock. Those who purchased through petitioners could not readily confirm the information given them. In Charles Hughes & Co., Inc. v. SEC, 139 F.2d 434 (2 Cir.1943), cert. § denied, 321 U.S. 786 (1944), this Court recognized the difficulties involved in over the counter stocks and the special duty imposed upon those who sell such stocks not to take advantage of customers in whom confidence has been instilled.

In summary, the standards by which the actions of each petitioner must be judged are strict. He cannot recommend a security unless there is an adequate and reasonable basis for such recommendation. He must disclose facts which he knows and those which are reasonably ascertainable. By his recommendation he implies that a reasonable investigation has been made and that his recommendation rests on conclusions based on such investigation. Where the salesman lacks essential information about a security, he should disclose this as well as the risks which arise from his lack of information.

A salesman may not rely blindly upon the issuer for information concerning a company, although the degree of independent investigation which must be made by a securities dealer all vary in each case. Securities issued by smaller companies of recent origin obviously require more through investigation.

SANCTIONS

The Commission is authorized by Section 15(b)(7) of the Securities Exchange Act, 15 U.S.C. § 78o(b)(7), to bar any person from association with a broker or dealer "if the Commission finds that such * * * barring * * * is in the public interest * * *," and that such person has willfully violated the Securities Act or the Securities Exchange Act.

Acting pursuant to this statutory authority and upon a finding that it was in the public interest to do so, the Commission, having found that each petitioner had violated the antifraud provisions of the securities law, ordered that each be barred from further association with any broker or dealer, except that Fehr was barred for only 60 days, after which he may return to the securities business in a non-supervisory capacity and upon an appropriate showing that he will be adequately supervised.

The courts, including ours, uniformly have recognized the fundamental principle that imposition of sanctions necessarily must be entrusted to the expertise of a regulatory commission such as the SEC; and only upon a showing of abuse of discretion—such as the imposition of a sanction unwarranted in law or without justification in fact—will a reviewing court intervene in the matter of sanctions. * * * [The court upheld the sanctions imposed by the SEC].

----

1. *Scienter and the Duty to Investigate.* Why is it that a failure to investigate a stock is fraudulent, rather than simply negligent? Later cases

Salesmen in a boiler room are held to a high duty of truthfulness which is not met by a claim of lack of knowledge. The Commission has previously refused to condone misrepresentation in the absence of a boiler room. See Charles P. Lawrence, Securities Exchange Act Release No. 8213, p. 3 (December 19, 1967), aff'd, 398 F.2d 176 (1 Cir. 1968), cited in Armstrong Jones and Co., Securities Exchange Act Release No. 8420, p. 9 (October 3, 1968). We specifically reject petitioners' argument that absence of boiler room operations here is a defense to a charge of misrepresentation.

after *Hanly* have seen this as a significant doctrinal problem.[1] The SEC's standard answer was most fully articulated in a 1977 administrative proceeding involving Merrill, Lynch where it said:[2]

> "A recommendation by a broker-dealer is perceived by a customer as (and it in fact should be) the product of independent and objective analysis [which] can only be achieved when the scope of the investigation is extended beyond the company's management ... The fact that ... management disseminated inaccurate and misleading information to ... [the Merrill Lynch employees] will not excuse [their] failure to conduct a reasonable investigation."[3]

2. *The Clearing Broker.* Smaller brokers often use a clearing broker who executes trades for them, holds the customer's funds and securities, and otherwise handles all paperwork. This system both allows the "introducing" broker to economize on costs and to reduce the minimum capital it must have before the SEC will permit it to register as a broker-dealer. Also, it may give the customer greater confidence because the customer's funds are being held by a large established "clearing" broker. Still, what duties does the clearing broker owe to the "introducing" broker's customer, whose account it services? The traditional answer was that the clearing broker did not owe a duty to the introducing broker's customers and did not aid and abet its fraud by performing only normal services.[4]

Then, in 1999, the SEC faced a case in which substantial evidence suggested that the clearing broker knew that the introducing broker had made numerous unauthorized trades, had engaged in serious sales practices violations, and was at least technically insolvent and in violation of the SEC's net capital rules. Indeed, many customers had complained to the clearing broker that the trades for which they were being charged were unauthorized. The SEC imposed a $30 million penalty on Bear Stearns, the clearing broker,[5] and in response to this scandal, both the NYSE and Nasdaq have tightened their rules. Essentially, the new rules require the clearing broker to establish standards for the monitoring and disposition of customer complaints about the introducing broker.[6] Yet, the new rules do not make the clearing broker a fiduciary or clearly impose any direct duty on it owed to the introducing broker's clients. The scope of the Commission's theory in the *Bear Stearns* case thus remains open to dispute, but seems to depend on at least reckless awareness by the clearing broker of the introducing broker's misconduct plus passivity by the clearing broker. A few judicial decisions, probably still a minority, have,

1. See McDonald v. Alan Bush Brokerage Co., 863 F.2d 809 (11th Cir.1989) (Inadequate investigation is insufficient to violate Rule 10b–5 unless there was also an awareness of lack of knowledge and likelihood that recommendation would mislead).

2. In the Matter of Merrill Lynch, Pierce Fenner & Smith, Securities Exchange Act Release No. 14149, 1977 SEC LEXIS 412 (November 9, 1977).

3. 1977 SEC LEXIS 412, at *18.

4. See Carlson v. Bear, Stearns & Co., 906 F.2d 315 (7th Cir.1990); Mars v. Wedbush Morgan Securities, Inc., 231 Cal.App.3d 1608, 283 Cal.Rptr. 238 (1991); Connolly v. Havens, 763 F.Supp. 6, 10–11 (S.D.N.Y.1991) (clearing broker owes no fiduciary duty to such client and does not aid and abet introducing broker's fraud by performing normal services).

5. See In the Matter of Bear, Stearns Securities Corp., Securities Act Release No. 7718 (August 5, 1999), 1999 WL 569554.

6. Both NASD Conduct Rule 3230 and NYSE Rule 382 were amended in light of the Bear Stearns case. See also Securities Exchange Act Release No. 41468 (June 9, 1999).

however, found that clearing brokers can be held liable for the actions of the introducing broker (more typically, on the theory that they aided and abetted such violation).[7]

3. *Investment Advisers.* A broker who executes a transaction initiated by an independent investment adviser, including an investment adviser who has discretionary authority over the account, may still be under an obligation to investigate.[8] The standard here appears to be that when the broker knows that the transactions are inconsistent with the customer's finances and investment objectives, the broker cannot remain passive.

D. UNSUITABILITY

O'Connor v. R.F. Lafferty & Co., Inc.

United States Court of Appeals, Tenth Circuit, 1992.
965 F.2d 893.

■ Before: BRORBY, McWILLIAMS, CIRCUIT JUDGES, and ALLEN, DISTRICT JUDGE

■ BRORBY, CIRCUIT JUDGE.

Plaintiff appeals the district court's grant of summary judgement disposing of her federal and state securities law claims. She also appeals the district court's decision to submit her remaining state law tort claims to arbitration. We affirm in part, and reverse in part.

I. FACTS

In 1975, Carol M. O'Connor received a $200,000 property settlement from her divorce. She deposited this entire sum into an account with the investment firm of R.F. Lafferty & Company, Inc., to be handled by Roy Foulke. Ms. O'Connor's brother recommended Mr. Foulke who was a family friend and who had previously handled accounts for other members of Ms. O'Connor's family.

Ms. O'Connor gave Mr. Foulke and Lafferty complete discretion to handle her account. Mr. Foulke knew Ms. O'Connor was not an experienced investor. In fact, prior to her association with Lafferty she had only invested in a savings account. Her husband or her father had always handled her finances. Ms. O'Connor informed Mr. Foulke the money she deposited represented virtually all of her assets. Ms. O'Connor also instructed Mr. Foulke she would need to rely on the $700 income generated from her deposit and the $800 maintenance payments from her ex-husband to met her monthly living expenses. Ms. O'Connor also expected her account to generate sufficient income to cover the taxes on her alimony and on the account, the fees of her accountant and the servicing fees for her account. Mr. Foulke knew Ms. O'Connor relied on him to make all decisions concerning her securities account. Consequently, Mr. Foulke traded on Ms. O'Connor's account and notified her of the trading activity by sending a trade ticket within thirty-six hours and again at the end of the month in their statement.

7. See Hirata Corp. v. J.B. Oxford and Co., 193 F.R.D. 589 (S.D.Ind.2000) (holding clearing broker liable under Indiana law).

8. See Ahluwalia/Shetty v. Kidder, Peabody & Co., 1998 U.S. Dist. LEXIS 3286, 1998 WL 122592 (S.D.N.Y. March 17, 1998); Rolf v. Blyth, Eastman, Dillon & Co., 570 F.2d 38, 48 (2d Cir.1978).

In 1985, because of the success in Ms. O'Connor's investment account, her husband was relieved of his alimony obligation. Understandably, this event changed the nature of her financial plan. From that point, Ms. O'Connor's account would have to generate $2,100 a month. Ms. O'Connor first became concerned about the value of her account in February 1987. Ms. O'Connor contends that from 1982 through 1987 Mr. Foulke and Lafferty purchased several securities unsuitable for her investment objectives. Specifically, Ms. O'Connor objects to investments in oil and gas limited partnerships; units of stock and warrants in Patient Medical Systems Corporation; units of International Surgical and Pharmaceutical Corporation securities; units in Job Stores, Inc. securities; units in R.T. Acquisition Corporation securities; and units of Kerkoff Industries, Inc. securities. Ms. O'Connor requested a judgment for actual damages of $329,000 plus a reasonable rate of return on amounts unsuitably invested that earned no income.

In 1988, Ms. O'Connor directed Mr. Foulke to stop all trading on her account. She brought suit against Mr. Foulke and against Lafferty for the acts of Mr. Foulke as a controlling person and under the doctrine of respondent superior asserting seven claims: (1) violation of § 10(b) of the 1934 Securities Exchange Act and Rule 10b–5 promulgated thereunder; (2) breach of fiduciary duty; (3) negligent failure to supervise; (4) professional negligence; (5) common law fraud; (6) intentional infliction of emotional distress; and (7) violations of Colo.Rev.Stat. §§ 11–51–123 and 11–51–125(2), (3) and (5).

The district court granted Defendant's motion for summary judgment as to count one and subsequently dismissed counts five and seven. The court submitted the remaining state law claims to arbitration. The court later adopted the arbitrator's award of $30,000 in favor of Ms. O'Connor.

Ms. O'Connor appeals all the district court's rulings. She asserts the district court erred in (1) granting summary judgment on her § 10(b) and Rule 10b–5 claim; (2) dismissing her claim for common law fraud; (3) dismissing her state securities claims; (4) compelling arbitration of her remaining state law claims; and (5) failing to award her attorney's fees.

II. ANALYSIS

A. Unsuitability

The district granted Defendants' motion for summary judgment against Ms. O'Connor's § 10(b) and Rule 10b–5 claim. The court found the Defendants did not possess the requisite scienter or intent to defraud to sustain such a claim. The court also found that although the Defendants did invest in securities unsuitable for Ms. O'Connor's investment objectives, Ms. O'Connor could not demonstrate her justifiable reliance on the purchases where she had information that the securities may be unsuitable and acted recklessly by failing to investigate. The court found persuasive deposition testimony by Ms. O'Connor where she admitted Mr. Foulke did not intend to defraud or hurt her. She further testified he did not willfully withhold information or lie to her * * *.

Ms. O'Connor claims Defendants bought securities which were unsuitable for her investment needs. Federal courts recognize such a claim as a violation of § 10(b) and Rule 10b–5. Clark v. John Lamula Investors, Inc., 583 F.2d 594, 599–600 (2d Cir.1978).

The unsuitability doctrine is premised on New York Stock Exchange Rule 405—Know Your Customer Rule[3] and the National Association of Securities Dealers Rules of Fair Practice.[4] In Re Trujillo, 1987 SEC LEXIS 1978, at *60–61 (April 23, 1987); Mark C. Jensen, Abuse of Discretion Claims Under Rule 10b–5: Churning, Unsuitability, and Unauthorized Transaction, 18 Sec.Reg.L.J. 374, 380 (1991).[5] Unsuitability claims can be analyzed as omission cases or fraudulent practices cases. See City of San Jose v. Paine, Webber, Jackson & Curtis Inc., No. C. 84–20601 RFP, 1991 WL 352485, *1, 1991 U.S.Dist. LEXIS 8318, at *1 (N.D.Ca. June 6, 1991); Trujillo, at *61.

Some courts examining a § 10(b), Rule 10b–5 unsuitability claim have analyzed it simply as a misrepresentation or failure to disclose a material fact. See, e.g., Lefkowitz v. Smith Barney, Harris Upham & Co., Inc., 804 F.2d 154, 155 (1st Cir.1986). In such a case, the broker has omitted telling the investor the recommendation is unsuitable for the investor's interests. The court may then use traditional laws concerning omission to examine the claim.

Under a misrepresentation or omission theory, a plaintiff can establish § 10(b), Rule 10b–5 liability by showing that in connection with the purchase or sale of a security the broker made an untrue statement of a material fact, or failed to state a material fact, that in so doing, the broker acted knowingly with intent to deceive or defraud, and that plaintiff relied on the misrepresentations, and sustained damages as a proximate result of the misrepresentations. Farlow v. Peat, Marwick, Mitchell & Co., 956 F.2d 982, 986 (10th Cir.1992).

In contrast, Ms. O'Connor asserts an unsuitability claim based on fraud by conduct. She does not assert Mr. Foulke omitted to tell her stocks he purchased were unsuitable for her investment needs. Rather, she claims that his purchase of the stocks for her account acted as fraud upon her.

Fraud by conduct is a violation of Rule 10b–5(a) and (c) and is analogous to a churning claim. Trujillo, at *61; Woodruff v. Merrill Lynch, Pierce, Fenner, & Smith, Inc., Fed.Sec.L.Rep. (CCH) 95,386, 1989 WL 224581 at *3 1989 U.S.Dist. Lexis 17196 at *9 (D.Neb. July 14, 1989). Churning is excessive trading on an account by a broker in light of the investor's objectives. Hotmar v. Lowell H. Listrom & Co., 808 F.2d 1384, 1385–86 (10th Cir.1987). This circuit has also recognized a violation of the NYSE Know Your Customer rule and the NASD Suitability Rule can be used to determine whether an account had been churned. Id. at 1386–87. See also Miley v. Oppenheimer & Co., Inc., 637 F.2d 318, 333 (5th Cir.1981). The *Miley* court acknowledged these rules are excellent tools to assess the "reasonableness or excessiveness of a broker's handling of an

---

3. This rule provides: "Every member organization is required * * * to (1) Use due diligence to learn the essential facts relative to every customer, every order, every cash or margin account accepted or carried by such organization."

4. Article 3, § 2 of these rules states: In recommending to a customer the purchase, sale or exchange of any security, a member shall have reasonable grounds for believing that the recommendation is suitable for such customer upon the basis of the facts, if any, disclosed by such customer as to his other securities holdings and as to his financial situation and need.

5. This circuit has not decided whether a violation of these rules gives rise to a private cause of action. See Utah State Univ. of Agric. & Applied Science v. Bear, Stearns & Co., 549 F.2d 164, 168–69 (10th Cir.), cert. denied, 434 U.S. 890, 98 S.Ct. 264, 54 L.Ed.2d 176 (1977). We need not decide the issue today whether actions which violate the NASD Rules may give rise to a violation of § 10(b) of the Securities Exchange Act. *Lamula*, 583 F.2d at 599–600.

investor's account." 637 F.2d at 333 (emphasis added). Thus, the rules are used to assess the quantity and quality of the broker's trading activity.

As noted above, churning deals with the quantity of securities purchased for an account, while unsuitability concerns the quality of the purchased securities. Federal courts have used the NYSE and NASD rules to analyze both forms of broker misconduct. Thus, we will examine the elements of a churning claim to aid our analysis of unsuitability elements.

While the elements of a churning claim are well established, the elements of an unsuitability claim based on fraud are not. To sustain a churning claim, the plaintiff must prove: (1) trading in the account is excessive in light of the investor's objectives; (2) the broker exercised control over trading in the account; and (3) the broker acted with an intent to defraud or with willful disregard for the investor's interests. Hotmar, 808 F.2d at 1385.

Because an unsuitability claim is so similar to a churning claim, we are persuaded the established "churning" elements can aid in our determination of the appropriate elements for an unsuitability cause of action. Today we adopt three elements to establish unsuitability based on fraud by conduct: The plaintiff must prove (1) the broker recommended (or in the case of a discretionary account purchased) securities which are unsuitable in light of the investor's objectives; (2) the broker recommended or purchased the securities with an intent to defraud or with reckless disregard for the investor's interests; and (3) the broker exercised control over the investor's account.[6]

Whether the control element of a churning claim applies to its cousin the unsuitability claim has been an open question. We believe the control element is essential to satisfy the causation/reliance requirement of a § 10(b), Rule 10b–5 violation.

In this case, we conclude the scienter element is dispositive. Based on our review of the record we hold Ms. O'Connor has failed, as a matter of law, to establish the scienter requirement of an unsuitability claim and affirm the district court's summary judgment against Ms. Connor's § 10(b), Rule 10b–5 claim.

A cause of action under § 10(b) and Rule 10b–5 requires scienter. Ernst & Ernst v. Hochfelder, 425 U.S. 185, 193, 96 S.Ct. 1375, 1381, 47 L.Ed.2d 668 (1976); Utah State Univ., 549 F.2d at 169. We have held that recklessness satisfies the scienter requirement for a § 10(b), Rule 10b–5 violation. Hackbart v. Holmes, 675 F.2d 1114, 1117 (10th Cir.1982). Therefore, in our test for unsuitability a plaintiff must show the broker purchased the securities with an intent to defraud or with reckless disregard for the investor's interests. Recklessness is defined as "conduct that is 'an extreme departure from the standards of ordinary care, and which presents a danger of misleading buyers or

---

6. In establishing these elements we incorporate the Second Circuit's test for unsuitability and add the element of control. The Second Circuit has developed elements for an unsuitability claim not based on misrepresentations or omissions. The plaintiff must merely prove a recommendation of unsuitable securities and scienter. Lamula, 583 F.2d at 600. Unsuitability can be found where the investor proves the broker knew or reasonably believed the recommended securities were unsuitable but recommended them anyway. We acknowledge the unsuitability cases do not always distinguish between fraud by conduct and fraud by misrepresentation or omission. In fact, the Lamula court uses omission language in its discussion of fraud by conduct. Essentially, the court examined the alleged omission as probative of the defendant's scienter. No separate fraud by omission claim existed.

sellers that is either known to the defendant or is so obvious that the actor must have been aware of it'." Id. at 1118 (quoting Sundstrand Corp. v. Sun Chemical Corp., 553 F.2d 1033, 1045, cert. denied, 434 U.S. 875, 98 S.Ct. 225, 54 L.Ed.2d 155 (1977)).

Ms. O'Connor alleges facts exist sufficient to prove Defendants' scienter. She asserts this proof consists of evidence of self-dealing including an increase in fees, and misrepresentations and omissions concerning (1) the commissions; (2) Mr. Foulke's lack of qualifications as an investment advisor; (3) the unsuitable nature of the purchased securities; (4) the depletion of principal due to monthly withdrawals; and (5) the promise that she would receive $20,000 a year in income from the oil and gas investment.

The parties do not dispute the basic facts of this case. Ms. O'Connor presented the fact that Mr. Foulke charged a one percent fee per year for financial services. In addition, he received a fifty percent commission split with Lafferty. However, the record reflects Ms. O'Connor was aware of the fees and commissions she paid to Mr. Foulke because they were reported in the monthly statements she received concerning her account.

Ms. O'Connor also presented deposition testimony that Lafferty was the underwriter for R.T. Corporation and Patient Medical Systems. Additional evidence established that Mr. Foulke was himself a director of Kerkoff. Yet, when deposed, Ms. O'Connor testified that she considered an investment less risky if Mr. Foulke were involved with the company. Furthermore, the prospectuses Ms. O'Connor received properly disclosed the fact Lafferty was the underwriter for several of the issues in which Mr. Foulke invested.

Next, Ms. O'Connor contends Mr. Foulke omitted to tell her he was not qualified as an investment advisor. In support, Ms. O'Connor presented deposition testimony that Mr. Foulke is not an investment advisor and has never been registered with the Securities Exchange Commission. But Mr. Foulke's deposition also revealed he never held himself out to be an investment advisor.

To prove the unsuitable nature of securities purchased by Mr. Foulke, Ms. O'Connor presented evidence that her investment objectives were conservative. She then presented evidence tending to show the securities in which Mr. Foulke invested were risky. For example, Ms. O'Connor demonstrated that the prospectus for Patient Medical Systems said it involved a high degree of risk and the investor should be prepared to lose her entire investment. However, in his deposition, Mr. Foulke testified he believed that Patient Medical Systems was only modestly risky and that risk was mitigated because Lafferty was the underwriter.

Ms. O'Connor testified in her deposition a geologist friend told her the oil and gas partnerships which Mr. Foulke purchased for her account were a bad investment and she should get out of them. But, Ms. O'Connor knew that Mr. Foulke had investigated the oil and gas operation before investing in it. In fact, he personally investigated all investment opportunities before he purchased any securities for Ms. O'Connor's account.

Furthermore, Mr. Foulke was able to give his reasons for purchasing each of the units of stock to which Ms. O'Connor objects. For example, Mr. Foulke testified the purchase of units in R.T. Acquisition Corporation was appropriate for Ms. O'Connor's account because he believed only low risk was involved because each shareholder would get back dollar for dollar invested with no dilution. He also felt the purchase of units in Kerkoff was appropriate based on the company's long-standing reputation and his own conversations with the owners of the company. He was also very impressed with the fact that the first day Kerkoff stock was listed it listed on the American Stock Exchange.

Additionally, Ms. O'Connor claimed Mr. Foulke omitted to tell her that her principal was being depleted by monthly withdrawals. She then presented Mr. Foulke's deposition testimony wherein Mr. Foulke stated he never expressly informed Ms. O'Connor that her monthly withdrawals were depleting her principal. Further testimony revealed that Mr. Foulke knew the $200,000 with which Ms. O'Connor opened her account comprised nearly all of her assets. Testimony also established Mr. Foulke knew Ms. O'Connor was unemployed, so if the account lost money she had no way to replace it other than through the account itself. Yet, Ms. O'Connor was notified of the activity in her account by trade tickets and monthly statements. These statements clearly reflect the fact that the monthly withdrawals did deplete her principal.

We conclude the facts presented fail to rise to the level of recklessness necessary to sustain a section § 10(b), Rule 10b–5 claim. No indication appears in the record that Mr. Foulke intentionally or recklessly defrauded Ms. O'Connor. Instead, the record reflects Mr. Foulke successfully handled Ms. O'Connor's account for many years. Therefore, we affirm the district court's summary judgment order against Ms. O'Connor's § 10(b), Rule 10b–5 claim....

---

1. *Varieties of Unsuitability.* When articulated under Rule 10b–5, an unsuitability cause of action must be framed in one of two ways: (1) as a misrepresentation or omission of a material fact (i.e., the unsuitability of the securities to the investor), or (2) as fraud by conduct. *O'Connor* seems a rare example of this latter type of case, and it is not surprising that its facts also involved churning, which is another type of "fraud by conduct." When unsuitability cases are instead brought in arbitration, considerably more expansive claims can be raised, which come close to holding the broker liable for either a negligent recommendation or a negligent failure to investigate.[1] The SEC has consistently taken the position that the suitability doctrine applies not only to the choice of securities, but also to the pattern of trading that the broker recommends. For example, if the broker recommends the use of borrowed funds (i.e., margin trading) or day trading over the Internet, this recommendation may also be unsuitable for the customer because of the high risks involved.[2]

2. *Written Disclaimers.* Suppose oral recommendations are made that the securities have low risk and are suitable for the investor, but an offering brochure or prospectus clearly warns the investor to the contrary that the securities are risky. Which statements control? Is the investor under a duty to read? Recent cases suggest that investors do have such a duty and cannot rely upon oral statements by the broker which the written documents rebut. In Brown v. E.F. Hutton Group, Inc.,[3] some 400 "presumably unsophisticated" investors in a limited partnership that became worthless were assumed, for purposes of summary judgment, to have informed their brokers that their

---

1. See Lowenfels and Bromberg, Beyond Precedent: Arbitral Extensions of Securities Law, 57 Bus. Law. 999 (2002).

2. See In re Application of Rangen, SEC Admin. Proc. File No. 3–8994, 1997 SEC LEXIS 762 at *9 (April 8, 1997).

3. 991 F.2d 1020 (2d Cir.1993).

investment objectives were essentially low risk oriented and were informed in turn by the broker that the limited partnerships had "either no risk or low risk." Nonetheless, they lost both their investments and on summary judgment their unsuitability claims under Rule 10b–5 where the prospectus clearly disclosed the high risk nature of the investments. The Second Circuit said:

> "We find that the Limited Partners' reliance on the oral statements presumptively made by Hutton as to the low risk, conservative character of the investment is not justified as a matter of law ... No reasonable investor reviewing the disclosure documents could fail to appreciate that the partnership could result in a total loss."[4]

3. *Implied Causes of Action and SRO Rules.* Although some early decisions recognized an implied cause of action for breach of SRO rules regarding suitability,[5] the modern cases have tended to go in the opposite direction.[6] Some courts, however, have regarded the violation of an SRO rule as relevant to the scienter issuer under Rule 10b–5.[7]

4. *Institutional Investors.* Although institutional investors clearly do not resemble the widows, orphans and retirees in classic suitability cases, they also are legally entitled to the benefits of the rule—at least according to the NASD.[8] In a 1996 interpretation, the NASD indicated its view that the obligation to make only suitable recommendations applies to institutional customers as well—unless the broker determines that the customer is capable of making an "independent assessment of the opportunities and risks presented by a potential investment, market factors and other investment considerations."[9] This inquiry by the broker requires that it determine both that (1) these factors will be evaluated, and (2) that the persons making the decision have the experience, capacity, and access to information to conduct such a suitability analysis. Recent experience with investments in derivatives by certain institutional investors (most notably Orange County and Procter and Gamble[10]) suggests that even the most experienced institutions may lack capacity in some areas. Consider also the case of a small college in the boondocks or a regional school board with some investment funds. Is it similar or different from an individual investor? Still, in practice, arbitration panels appear less willing to apply the essentially paternalistic suitability doctrine to justify recoveries for even small institutions.

5. *Do the SRO Rules Differ?* The NASD and the New York Stock Exchange have somewhat different suitability rules. The NASD's rule requires that the broker-dealer in recommending to a customer the purchase or sale of a security must have "reasonable grounds for believing that the recommendation is suitable for such customer upon the basis of the facts, if any, disclosed by such customer as to his other security holdings and as to his financial situation

---

4. Id. at 1031–1033.

5. See, e.g., Buttrey v. Merrill Lynch, Pierce, Fenner & Smith, 410 F.2d 135 (7th Cir.1969).

6. See, e.g., Jablon v. Dean Witter & Co., 614 F.2d 677 (9th Cir.1980).

7. See Miley v. Oppenheimer & Co., 637 F.2d 318, 327–28 (5th Cir.1981).

8. For a strong defense of this position, see Norman Poser, Liability of Broker-Dealers for Unsuitable Recommendations to Institutional Investors, 2001 B.Y.U. L. Rev. 1493 (2001).

9. See Securities Exchange Act Release No. 36,921 (March 14, 1996).

10. See In the Matter of BT Securities Corp., [1994–1995 Transfer Binder] Fed.Sec. L.Rep. (CCH) Para. 85,477 (December 22, 1994).

and needs."[11] While this rule does not by its express terms impose any duty of inquiry upon the broker-dealer, a policy statement of the Board of Governors of the NASD prohibits the broker-dealer from:[12]

"1. Recommending speculative low-priced securities to customers without knowledge of or attempt to obtain information concerning the customers' other securities holdings, their financial situation and other necessary data. The principle here is that this practice, by its very nature, involves a high probability that the recommendation will not be suitable for at least some of the persons solicited. This has particular application to high pressure telephonic sales campaigns.

* * *

"3. Trading in mutual fund shares, particularly on a short-term basis. It is clear that normally these securities are not proper trading vehicles and such activity on its face may raise the question of rule violation.

* * *

"5. Recommending the purchase of securities or the continuing purchase of securities in amounts which are consistent with the reasonable expectation that the customer has the financial ability to meet such a commitment."

The New York Stock Exchange rule, on the other hand, is phrased in terms of a duty of inquiry without any express prescription of what action is supposed to follow on the basis of the facts discovered. It requires that a member broker use "due diligence to learn the essential facts relative to every customer"[13] (sometimes known as the "Know Thy Customer Rule"). Obviously implicit in this injunction, though, is the requirement that the broker's recommendations be responsibly related to the investment objectives and financial situation of the customer discovered by the investigation.

6. *Suitability and the Internet.* By 2000, it was estimated that nearly six million investors were trading online, meaning that they had direct access to the market (often through broker-provided software). Hence, their broker did not stand between them and the market in a position to give useful advice or cautions. To the extent that the suitability doctrine requires that the broker make an actual recommendation, is the doctrine still relevant to this world where the broker is not interposed between the customer and the market? Or should our idea of what constitutes a recommendation be updated? One possibility is that the broker may be making "recommendations" that are sufficient to result in liability under the suitability doctrine when it provides customized information to the investor. This position focuses on the new

---

11. NASD Manual, Conduct Rules, Rule 2310(a) (1996); see also In the Matter of Boren & Co., Securities Exchange Act Release No. 6851, July 17, 1962, which deals with the so-called "equity funding" of the purchase of mutual fund shares, i.e., the purchase of such shares together with a policy of life insurance, the premiums on which are paid by money borrowed on the shares. The Rule provides that it is a fraudulent practice for a broker-dealer to sell a customer such a "package" unless, among other things, the broker-dealer "obtains from such person information concerning his financial situation and needs, reasonably determines that the entire transaction, including the loan arrangement, is suitable for such person, and delivers to such person a written statement setting forth the basis upon which the broker or dealer made such determination."

12. Id.

13. NYSE Rule 405, CCH New York Stock Exchange Manual Para. 2405.

technology of "data mining" used by brokerage firms to study and record their customers' online trading behavior. For example, assume that a broker-dealer has discovered that a particular customer regularly buys "blue chip" stocks after they have fallen in a market dip. Next, assume that the broker-dealer emails the customer to notify him or her that a particular "blue chip" stock fell yesterday by 15%. Is this customized information, which is seemingly intended to cause the customer to buy the stock, a "recommendation" for purposes of the suitability rule? In a report done for the Commission in 2000, Commissioner Laura Unger suggested that customized information provided through "data mining" could, and sometimes should, be so construed.[14]

E.   CHURNING

Nesbit v. McNeil

United States Court of Appeals, Ninth Circuit, 1990.
896 F.2d 380.

■ Before WRIGHT, TANG and FERNANDEZ, CIRCUIT JUDGES.

■ FERNANDEZ, CIRCUIT JUDGE:

Virginia H. Nesbit and the W. Wallace Nesbit Trust ("plaintiffs") brought this action against Steve McNeil and Black & Company, Inc. ("defendants") and alleged that the defendants had churned the plaintiffs' investment accounts. Among other things, plaintiffs sought to recover for violations of the Securities and Exchange Act of 1934 § 10(b) and Rule 10b–5, and under the State of Oregon securities laws [Or.Rev.Stat. § 59.135 (1987)]. The district court directed a verdict against the plaintiffs on the Oregon securities law claim, and submitted the federal securities claim to the jury. The jury brought in a verdict against defendants, and awarded damages in the amount of the excess commissions generated by the churning of the plaintiffs' accounts. The district court denied a motion for judgment notwithstanding the verdict, and entered judgment accordingly.

Defendants now appeal and claim that the district court erred because it did not permit the offset of trading gains against the excess commissions, because the evidence of churning was insufficient to support the verdict, and because the plaintiffs' claims were barred by the statute of limitations in whole or in part. Defendants also claim that they should not have been required to disgorge the full amount of excess commissions, but only their net gain on those commissions.

In their cross-appeal, plaintiffs assert that the district court should not have granted a directed verdict on the Oregon securities law claim, since plaintiffs should be able to recover attorney's fees, even if they were unable to prove any other damages under Oregon law.

We affirm the district court on each of these issues.

BACKGROUND FACTS

Virginia H. Nesbit was a retired school teacher and the widow of W. Wallace Nesbit, a businessman. Upon his death, Mr. Nesbit left a portfolio of

---

14. See Laura Unger, On–Line Brokerage: Keeping Apace of Cyberspace (2000) (available at www.sec.gov/news/studies/cyberspace.htm).

securities that were rather conservative although not necessarily highly successful. Those, as well as other assets, were divided between Mrs. Nesbit and the W. Wallace Nesbit Trust ("the Trust"). Mrs. Nesbit was the trustee of the Trust. From then until 1974, the investments remained conservative and did not do very well. By 1974, there had been a significant loss of value. Mrs. Nesbit then opened accounts for herself and the Trust at Black & Company, Inc. They were opened through Steve McNeil, who was the son of a friend of Mrs. Nesbit. The equity in Mrs. Nesbit's account was then $167,463, and the equity in the Trust's account was $44,177. Mrs. Nesbit, who was not knowledgeable in these matters, told the defendants that her investment objectives for herself and the Trust were stability, income and growth. Defendants claim that she told them she wanted to recoup the losses that had been suffered previously.

Defendants then embarked on a course of conduct that extended over a period of eleven and one half years. By the time the accounts were closed out in October of 1985, the equity in Mrs. Nesbit's account was $301,711, and the equity in the Trust's account was $92,844. There can be little dispute that this was a substantial increase in value. However, the activities of defendants during those eleven and one half years are called into question in this case.

Plaintiffs have pointed out that defendants first liquidated some of the securities in plaintiffs' portfolio. Mr. McNeil then embarked on a course of trading that involved 150 issues, one thousand trades, and an overall transaction value of $4,400,000. While the plaintiffs' account values did grow by $182,915 during the period in question, the defendants' commissions came to $250,000. Moreover, the investments chosen by defendants were not the kind of investments that one would purchase if one sought a stable, income-producing portfolio. Rather, they were often speculative in nature and were not income-producing. By the time the accounts terminated, many of the investments had accrued losses.

By 1984, Mrs. Nesbit became concerned about the level of activity in the accounts. She kept in closer contact with Mr. McNeil, and the level of trading decreased, but did not end entirely. She became even more concerned in 1985. At that time she discovered losses in the portfolio when calls were made upon her by lenders to whom she had pledged certain of the securities. Her concerns increased when the handling of the accounts was questioned by Ronald Linn, an analyst at Titan Capital, and were not particularly allayed when visits with Mr. McNeil brought forth an apology and an expression of embarrassment at the list of losing stocks. All of this ultimately led to the closing of the accounts in October of 1985. Over one year later, plaintiffs filed this action.

* * *

DISCUSSION

Although the principal question before us is whether plaintiffs can recover damages for churning when they have had an increase in portfolio values that exceeds the amount of commissions they were charged, the defendants have also claimed that there was insufficient evidence to support the verdict, and that the action is barred by the statute of limitations. If defendants were to prevail on either of the latter issues, there would be no need to consider the damage issue. Therefore, we will address them first.

A. *Sufficiency of the Evidence.*

The detection and proof of churning is not a simple matter. Churning can only be identified when one considers the whole history of an account, and even then expert testimony is virtually essential. Shad v. Dean Witter Reynolds, Inc., 799 F.2d 525, 530 (9th Cir.1986). As we explained in Mihara v. Dean Witter & Co., Inc., 619 F.2d 814, 820–21 (9th Cir.1980):

> When a securities broker engages in excessive trading in disregard of his customer's investment objectives for the purpose of generating commission business, the customer may hold the broker liable for churning in violation of Rule 10b–5. * * * In order to establish a claim of churning, a plaintiff must show (1) that the trading in his account was excessive in light of his investment objectives; (2) that the broker in question exercised control over the trading in the account; and (3) that the broker acted with the intent to defraud or with the wilful and reckless disregard for the interests of his client. [citations omitted]

Plaintiffs presented substantial evidence on each of these elements, as our statement of background facts has shown. This case involves a relatively unsophisticated investor, who relied upon a person in whom she had confidence—the son of a family friend—to handle her portfolio in a safe and income-generating manner. There can be little doubt that Mr. McNeil did exercise a great deal of de facto control over that account, and the mere fact that he told his client what was being done does not change that situation. This case is quite unlike Brophy v. Redivo, 725 F.2d 1218 (9th Cir.1984), where the only real claim was that certain transactions had been executed without plaintiff's permission and even against her directions. Here the gravamen of the complaint is that the defendants used their position to overtrade in the account and to do so in a way that they knew did not meet the client's true investment desires and objectives. See Follansbee v. Davis, Skaggs & Co., Inc., 681 F.2d 673, 676 (9th Cir.1982); Mihara v. Dean Witter & Co., 619 F.2d at 821; Hecht v. Harris, Upham & Co., 430 F.2d 1202, 1209 (9th Cir.1970). In other words, there was a good deal of evidence about the relationship between the parties and Mr. McNeil's control over the account. That is underscored by Mr. McNeil's embarrassment when he was confronted with the condition of certain securities toward the end of the period. His apology showed that he had something to be embarrassed about; he was not simply executing orders at the direction of Mrs. Nesbit. In addition, the testimony of plaintiffs' expert showed that one could infer the necessary degree of scienter arising out of the handling of this account, and demonstrated that there was excessive trading.

Defendants contend that there was insufficient evidence of excessive trading in the account. Relying on this circuit's comments that expert testimony is virtually essential, see *Shad,* 799 F.2d at 530, defendants argue that Nesbit's expert did not present objective statistical evidence of excessive trading. In particular, they complain that the expert did not testify about a turnover ratio for the account as a whole or for an annualized period[3] and that the commission ratio[4] indicated there was no churning.

---

3. The turnover ratio is the ratio of the total cost of the purchases made for the account during a given period of time to the amount invested. 2 A. Bromberg & L. Lowenfels, *Securities Fraud and Commodities Fraud* § 5.7(322) (1988).

4. The commission ratio is "the ratio of the broker's commissions generated by the account to the size of the customer's invest-

Although courts often rely on the turnover ratio and commission ratio to indicate excessive trading, no single factor or test identifies excessive trading. See 2 A. Bromberg & L. Lowenfels, *Securities Fraud and Commodities Fraud* § 5.7(310) & (322) (1988). Certainly these ratios can make the presence of excessive trading fairly obvious. Id. However, that does not mean that lower ratios will preclude a finding of excessive trading.

Here, Mr. Olson testified that in his expert opinion the 1,000 trades, the high amount of commission compared to the value of the account, the volume of trading, and the presence of losing stock that had been held for some time all pointed toward an improper handling of this account, considering the investment objectives of the client. While defendants have presented evidence and arguments to the contrary, we are in no position to say that the jury improperly found against them on this record. We will not second guess the jury's determination of the facts, where, as here, the evidence is in conflict and there is substantial evidence to support the jury's decision.

B.   Statute of Limitations

Defendants claim that the federal securities claims were barred by the statute of limitations. [The court rejected this contention.]

* * *

C.   *The Measurement of Damages.*

As we have already noted, defendants obtained commissions of $250,000 from the plaintiffs. The jury found that $134,000 of that constituted excess commissions. At the same time, the value of plaintiffs' accounts increased in the sum of $182,915. Defendants claimed below, and continue to claim, that the plaintiffs' portfolio gain should be offset against the plaintiffs' commission loss, as a result of which plaintiffs can recover no damages whatever. The district court disagreed, and gave the following instruction to the jury: "If you find that the plaintiffs have proven their claims for churning, excessive trading, plaintiffs may recover as damages any commissions they paid as a result of the churning in excess of commissions that would have been reasonable on transactions during the pertinent time period." The district court did not go on to instruct the jury that it could then offset the trading gains against those commission losses. We agree with the district court.

We begin with the rather straightforward principle announced in Mihara v. Dean Witter & Co., Inc., 619 F.2d at 826, where we said that, "While damage for churning are limited to commissions and interest, plaintiff's claim as to the suitability of the securities purchased would also encompass trading losses." As the Fifth Circuit Court of Appeals explained in Miley v. Oppenheimer & Co., Inc., 637 F.2d at 326, there are two separate and distinct possible harms when an account has been churned, and those are:

> First, and perhaps foremost, the investor is harmed by having had to pay the excessive commissions to the broker. * * * Second, the investor is harmed by the decline in the value of his portfolio * * * as a result of the broker's having intentionally and deceptively concluded transactions, aimed at generating fees, which were unsuitable for the investor. The

ment in that account." 2 A. Bromberg & L. Lowenfels, *Securities Fraud and Commodi-*   *ties Fraud* § 5.7(322) (1988).

intentional and deceptive mismanagement of a client's account, resulting in a decline in the value of that portfolio, constitutes a compensable violation of both the federal securities laws and the broker's common law fiduciary duty, regardless of the amount of the commissions paid to the broker.

In the case at hand, the plaintiffs only suffered one of those harms, but there is no reason to find that they should be denied a recovery because their portfolio increased in value, either because of or in spite of the activities of the defendants.

We are mindful of our decision in Hatrock v. Edward D. Jones & Co., 750 F.2d 767 (9th Cir.1984). In that case we pointed out that the investor could recover both the "excessive commissions charged by the broker, and the decline in value of the investor's portfolio resulting from the broker's fraudulent transactions." Id. at 774. However, the investor had in fact suffered both of those losses, and nothing in that opinion suggested that we intended to declare that an investor must suffer both harms before he can recover from the broker. It is not surprising that a broker who is guilty of churning—an element of which is the making of unsuitable investment decisions—may also have purchased unsuitable investments. That does not mean that the two concepts should be conflated, and we have never said that they must be. Rather, our decisions are properly harmonized to reach an unremarkable result which ultimately makes the plaintiff whole in any event—a plaintiff may separately recover either or both types of damages, but gains in portfolio will not offset losses in commissions. That is a result that prevents the broker from escaping with improper commissions. Defendants would have us say that a broker who, for example, engages in unsuitable management of the account but actually buys suitable or successful investments cannot be held responsible for his actions. One can easily envision a single successful security which is bought and sold an unreasonable number of times, thereby relieving the client of gains and improperly enriching the broker. We would be remiss if we were to find no redress within the securities law for that kind of wrongdoing. Finally, it would be a poor rule indeed that unnecessarily forced courts and juries to enter into the complex determinations needed to determine whether any gain on a portfolio was due to the improper activities of a broker. Once the trier of fact finds that the trading was excessive it has determined that the trading should not have taken place. It should not be forced to decide whether gains or losses are a result of market forces, luck, good times, or intrinsically good stock. Nor should the trier of fact have to decide what part of the loss or gain should be allocated to any given factor. That is one reason we have said that proof of causation is not a necessary element of a plaintiff's case. See Hatrock v. Edward D. Jones & Co., 750 F.2d at 773. The broker will have made trades that should not have been made, and he should not retain his ill gotten gain. This salutory rule also informs the brokerage community that churning is a fraud that will violate the securities laws, regardless of the ultimate condition of the client's portfolio. It therefore serves to forward the deterrent policies which underlie the federal securities laws. Randall v. Loftsgaarden, 478 U.S. 647, 664, 106 S.Ct. 3143, 3153, 92 L.Ed.2d 525 (1986).

As a final attack on damages, the defendants rely on a portion of the Supreme Court's decision in *Randall v. Loftsgaarden,* id., for the proposition that the plaintiff must lean upon the concept of unjust enrichment in order to recover. Reasoning from that proposition, defendants ask that the brokers' expenses be deducted from the commissions and that plaintiffs recover, at most, the difference. It is true that *Randall* addresses the question of unjust enrichment at 478 U.S. 661–64, 106 S.Ct. 3152–53, but it does not mandate the theory suggested by defendants. The core of the defendants' position must be that if a broker defrauds a client of a commission, the broker ought to be able to deduct the expenses he incurred in perpetrating the fraud and then return the rest to the client. We believe that the very statement of the proposition refutes it, and not a shard of judicial precedent supports it. *Randall,* on the other hand, merely offers the possibility that even if a plaintiff has not lost as much as a defendant has gained, the plaintiff should recover that gain from the defendant. To apply that to a situation where defendant has not netted as much as he has taken from the plaintiff would stand *Randall* on its head. It takes no hierophant to discover that.

Therefore, we must reject defendants' assault on the damage award in this case.

[Plaintiffs' claim under the Oregon Securities Law was rejected.]

CONCLUSION

We have been presented with the rather unusual case of plaintiffs whose portfolios increased while under the guidance and control of the defendants, and who still chose to bring an action to recover commissions that they had paid to those same defendants.

The jury before which this case was tried could have decided that defendants were perfectly honest brokers, who were being victimized by rather greedy clients. The jury did not do so. Instead, it found that plaintiffs were indeed wronged by the defendants' churning of the accounts. That determination was supported by substantial evidence. As we have noted, the jury's determination that the statute of limitations had not run in this case was also properly supported.

As a result, the defendants were properly required to disgorge the inappropriate portion of their commissions, even if the portfolio itself increased in value, since, as we have shown, issues regarding the performance of the portfolio are separate from issues related to excess commissions. Just as there can be gains or losses when trading is appropriate, there can be gains or losses when it is inappropriate. The propriety of the trading determines the right to a commission. The same evidence may also influence the right to recover for losses, but that does not mean that gains should undermine the plaintiffs' right to recover improper commissions. The wrongs are separate, and the result of each should be analyzed separately.

* * *

AFFIRMED.

———

1. *Churning Litigation.* Rule 15c1–7 prohibits what is generally known as "churning," i.e., excessive trading by a broker for an account in which he or she holds discretionary powers, for the purpose of collecting commissions. In In

the Matter of Norris & Hirshberg, Inc., 21 S.E.C. 865 (1949),[1] the Commission stated that while the Rule itself specifically applies only to cases where the broker or dealer has been "vested" with discretionary powers, either orally or in writing, "the handling of a customer's account may become fraudulent whenever the broker or dealer is in a position to determine the volume and frequency of transactions by reason of the customer's willingness to follow the suggestions of the broker or dealer and he abuses the customer's confidence by overtrading."[2] Judicial decisions have placed even greater emphasis on the existence of "control" on the part of the broker over the account. Thus, in Arceneaux v. Merrill, Lynch, Pierce, Fenner & Smith, the Eleventh Circuit required the plaintiff to "prove three elements in order to establish a cause of action for churning: (1) the trading in his account was excessive in light of the customer's investment objectives; (2) the broker in question exercised control over the trading in the account; and (3) the broker acted with the intent to defraud or with willful and reckless disregard for the investor's interest."[3] But what shows control? Even if the client retains investment discretion, the fact that the client automatically follows the broker's recommendations may constitute sufficient evidence to sustain a jury verdict (as the *Arceneaux* case seemingly held).[4] Other cases have in contrast focused on the intelligence and experience of the client and framed the test in terms of whether the customer "has sufficient intelligence and understanding to evaluate the broker's recommendations and reject one when he finds it unsuitable."[5] One commentator has suggested that the test should focus on whether the broker has invited the customer's trust and then breached that trust.[6] Finally, "churning" and unsuitability cases tend to overlap. Thus, even when there is insufficient control by the broker over the account to establish a churning case, it might still be argued that the broker made unsuitable recommendations in order to maximize its commissions.[7]

The Nesbit case is thus typical. Mrs. Nesbit was not knowledgeable in investment matters. She told her broker that the investment objectives for herself and the trust were stability, income and growth. Although her broker was vested with discretionary powers, Mrs. Nesbit regularly received written confirmations of each transaction over a period of eleven years without raising any objections either to a failure to meet her investment objectives or as to the excessive commissions. Only then did she become concerned about the level of activity in the accounts.

1. Aff'd, 177 F.2d 228 (D.C.Cir.1949). For a general overview of the development of this doctrine, see Note, Churning by Securities Dealers, 80 Harv. L. Rev. 869 (1967).

2. 21 S.E.C. at 890.

3. 767 F.2d 1498, 1501 (11th Cir.1985); for a more recent statement of this formula, see Rizek v. SEC, 215 F.3d 157, 162 (1st Cir.2000). Other decisions stress that the heart of a churning case is the use of the broker's authority over an account to generate excessive commissions, while at the same time leading the customer to believe that the broker is attempting to fulfill the customer's objectives. See Manela v. Garantia Banking Ltd., 5 F.Supp.2d 165 (S.D.N.Y.1998). This verbal formula seemingly gives a greater role to evidence of deception.

4. See also Mihara v. Dean Witter & Co., 619 F.2d 814 (9th Cir.1980).

5. See Follansbee v. Davis, Skaggs & Co., 681 F.2d 673, 677 (9th Cir.1982).

6. See O'Hara, The Elusive Concept of Control in Churning Claims under the Federal Securities and Commodities Law, 75 Geo. L.J. 1875 (1987).

7. O'Connor v. R.F. Lafferty & Co., supra p. 711, represents exactly such a case in which these overlapping allegations were raised.

2. *Excessive Trading.* Courts typically look to the "turnover ratio" in determining if trading is excessive. That ratio compares the total cost of purchases made for an account (typically over a one year period) to the total amount invested in the account. Several decisions have suggested that a turnover ratio in excess of six reflects excessive trading.[8] Of course, trading can only be excessive in terms of the customer's investment objectives, and the aggressive customer may want "excessive" trading. Courts also sometimes look to the commissions earned on the account, either as a percentage of the individual broker's income or the branch office's commission revenues.[9] Trading patterns are also relevant: "in and out" day trading in which securities are bought and sold on the same day is particularly suspicious. From an economic perspective, there is a view that the best standard for comparison would be to match the account with a mutual fund having a similar risk preference and determine if the account traded significantly more frequently than the fund over the same period.[10]

3. *Damages.* What damages should the victim receive: the excessive commissions or the decline in portfolio value? In Hecht v. Harris, Upham & Co.,[11] the Ninth Circuit allowed only the former and denied any decline in market value. This result was partly based on a specific factual issue involving waiver and estoppel issue in that case. Although the plaintiff customer had regularly received confirmations and was thus deemed by the Ninth Circuit to have been estopped to deny knowledge of the transactions in her account, the Ninth Circuit still permitted her to claim lack of knowledge that her account was excessively traded. But as a result, it limited the damages to the excessive commissions.

Later cases have generally rejected the result reached in Hecht with respect to portfolio damages.[12] As the Nesbit court makes clear the investor may recover *both* the excessive commission charged by the broker, and the decline in value of the investor's portfolio resulting from the "churning" of the account. Furthermore, if the portfolio increases in value, the gain will not be offset against the excessive commissions charged by the broker to reduce the damages.

Davis v. Merrill Lynch, Pierce, Fenner & Smith, Inc.,[13] was a rather egregious churning case brought on behalf of an eighty-seven year old widow. The account had a value of about $144,000 at the beginning and a value of $197,000 at the end of the trading period, so that the account realized a cumulative net profit of $53,000 during the period it was churned. If the account had not been churned, however, the portfolio would have had a further

---

8. See, e.g., Arceneaux v. Merrill Lynch, Pierce, Fenner & Smith, supra note 3; Mihara v. Dean Witter & Co., 619 F.2d 814, 821 (9th Cir.1980); Costello v. Oppenheimer & Co., 711 F.2d 1361, 1369 (7th Cir.1983).

9. See Hecht v. Harris Upham & Co., 283 F.Supp. 417 (N.D.Cal.1968), aff'd in part, 430 F.2d 1202 (9th Cir.1970).

10. See Winslow and Anderson, A Model for Determining the Excessive Trading Element in Churning Claims, 68 N.C. L. Rev. 327 (1990).

11. 430 F.2d 1202 (9th Cir.1970).

12. Rolf v. Blyth, Eastman Dillon & Co., 570 F.2d 38 (2d Cir.1978), cert. denied, 439 U.S. 1039 (1978); Miley v. Oppenheimer & Co., 637 F.2d 318 (5th Cir.1981); Davis v. Merrill Lynch, Pierce, Fenner & Smith, Inc., 906 F.2d 1206 (8th Cir.1990); Hatrock v. Edward D. Jones & Co., 750 F.2d 767 (9th Cir.1984).

13. 906 F.2d 1206 (8th Cir.1990). The Nesbit and Davis cases are discussed in Booth, New Churning Cases Add Twist to Claims for Portfolio Damages, Nat'l L.J., June 24, 1991, at 34.

increase in value of about $56,000. The Eighth Circuit, following the Nesbit case, upheld an award of $44,000 in damages for excessive trading despite the increase in the value of the portfolio. Adding a new twist, however, the court upheld an additional award of $56,000 for the loss in portfolio value arising from churning, plus punitive damages of $2,000,000.

The Court stated: "Churning is a species of fraud prohibited by Section 10(b) and Rule 10b–5 regardless of whether the account's profits or its principal is misappropriated. Under the law of this circuit, if an account earned $50,000 but would have earned $100,000 if it was not churned, the customer has sustained actual damages in the amount of $50,000 plus excess commissions paid. * * * Because Mrs. Davis paid over $40,000 in commissions and would have earned over $50,000 more than she did had her account not been churned, it is nonsensical to argue that she did not suffer actual damages as a result of the churning."[14]

In some situations, an award of portfolio damages may require the comparison of profit or loss in the portfolio during the trading period with the performance of a comparable well-recognized index such as the Dow Jones Industrials or the Standard and Poor's Index, or a specialized index or a combination of indexes.[15] Thus in Miley v. Oppenheimer & Co.,[16] both the market and the value of the portfolio had declined. The court held that compensatory damages for portfolio losses should be measured by the decline in the value of the portfolio in excess of the average decline in the stock market during the time in which the broker handled the account. Moreover, in the absence of either a specialized portfolio or the availability of a more accurate measure, the actual portfolio loss should be reduced by the average percentage decline in value of the Dow Jones Industrials or the Standard and Poor's Index during the relevant period. This method was said to prevent the award of windfall profits arising from the ordinary hazards of the stock market.[17]

Options are an entirely different game. They are far more complex than stocks. This complexity, coupled with the various options' strategies available with variable degrees of risk, calls for an entirely different approach to the measurement of churning. It has been said that instead of using mathematical measurements, "federal courts have abandoned the traditional measurements of churning. Instead the inquiry as to whether the broker's conduct toward his customer was fraudulent tends to focus on the riskiness of the particular strategy used and the ability and willingness of the customer to assume the risks."[18]

4. *Unauthorized Transactions, Churning, and the "In Connection With" Requirement.* Suppose a broker trades securities in a nondiscretionary account without the customer's permission. Of course, this is actionable, but does it violate Rule 10b–5? Some courts have said that the broker's failure to disclose the transaction to the client is a material omission of the fact that it is not dealing fairly with the customer,[19] but others have found that it is no more

14. 906 F.2d at 1218–19.

15. On the economic aspects, see J. Lorie, P. Dodd & M. Kimpton, The Stock Market: Theories and Evidence Ch. 3 (2d ed. 1985).

16. 637 F.2d 318 (5th Cir.1981).

17. Miley v. Oppenheimer & Co., Inc., 637 F.2d 318, 327 (5th Cir.1981).

18. Poser, Options Account Fraud: Securities Churning in a New Context, 39 Bus. Law. 571 (1984).

19. See Mansbach v. Prescott, Ball & Turben, 598 F.2d 1017, 1026–27 (6th Cir.

than a contractual breach.[20] These more conservative courts have expressed doubt that there was a sufficient connection between the trade and any implied misrepresentation to satisfy the "in connection with" standard under Rule 10b–5.

The "in connection with" requirement is less of a problem in churning cases, because the court can view the churning trades as themselves fraudulent or deceptive acts which violate Rule 10b–5 without the need for any material misrepresentation or omission.[21] Still, it remains debatable whether such conduct more resembles the type of fiduciary breach that must be established under state law standards under Sante Fe Industries, Inc. v. Green.[22]

F. *The Penny Stock Reform Act of 1990*

The Securities Enforcement and Penny Stock Reform Act of 1990 has been called "the most significant attack on securities fraud and white collar crime in many years."[1] The first four titles of the Act deal with civil enforcement remedies. The Remedies Act authorizes the Commission to impose fines for myriad violations including manipulation in penny stocks. That legislation is considered in Chapter 21 dealing with SEC Enforcement. Title V is the Penny Stock Reform Act; it mandates and authorizes the SEC to provide greater protection to investors in those low priced securities known as "penny stocks."

The House Committee Report explained the purpose and scope of this legislation in this way:[2]

This legislation amends both the Securities Exchange Act of 1934 (Exchange Act) and the Securities Act of 1933 (Securities Act) and issues legislative directives with the intention of curbing the pervasive fraud and manipulation in the penny stock market. The bill adds a new paragraph (51) to Section 3(a) of the Exchange Act to define the term "penny stock" and determine the scope of securities covered under this Act; amends Section 15(b)(6) of the Exchange Act to expand the scope of the Securities and Exchange Commission's (Commission) authority to bar individuals from the securities business; adds a new paragraph (g) to Section 15 of the Exchange Act to establish a system for more comprehensive disclosure in the penny stock market; mandates that the Commission, at the earliest feasible time, facilitate the establishment and continued use of an automated quotation system to collect and provide information regarding all penny stocks; instructs the Commission to conduct a broad review of the enforcement and oversight activities of the self-regulatory organizations which monitor the penny stock market and to present its findings and concurrent recommendations to the Congress within one year; amends Section 29(b) of the Exchange Act to make voidable securities contracts made in violation of the Commission's penny stock cold calling rule and all

1979); see also Nye v. Blyth, Eastman, Dillon & Co., 588 F.2d 1189 (8th Cir.1978).

20. See, e.g., Brophy v. Redivo, 725 F.2d 1218, 1220 (9th Cir.1984); Forkin v. Rooney, Pace, Inc., 804 F.2d 1047, 1049–50 (8th Cir.1986) (unauthorized rescission of trade not actionable deception).

21. See Clark v. Kidder Peabody & Co., 636 F.Supp. 195, 198 (S.D.N.Y.1986).

22. 430 U.S. 462 (1977). On these themes, see Langevoort, Fraud and Deception

by Securities Professionals, 61 Tex. L. Rev. 1247, 1279–83 (1983).

1. Legislative statement of Rep. Edward Markey, 136 Cong. Rec. H8532 (daily ed. Oct. 1, 1990).

2. House Comm. on Energy and Commerce, Penny Stock Reform Act of 1990, H.R. Rep. 101–617, 101st Cong., 2d Sess. 7–35 (1990).

other rules adopted pursuant to Section 15(c)(2) of the Exchange Act; amends Section 7 of the Securities Act by mandating that the Commission adopt rules to place restrictions on blank check company registrations, which have been prevalent in fraud in the penny stock market; and amends Section 15A of the Exchange Act to mandate that the National Association of Securities Dealers (NASD) and other registered securities associations establish a toll-free telephone listing to receive customer inquiries concerning the disciplinary history of its members and associated persons.

* * *

The Penny Stock Reform Act of 1990 represents the response of this Committee to reports over the past several years of rampant fraud and manipulation of investors by participants in the penny stock market. Former Commission Chairman David Ruder called penny stock fraud "one of the most menacing problems facing investors, regulators, and the legitimate securities industry." According to the testimony of Dee Benson, United States Attorney for the District of Utah, speaking on behalf of the Department of Justice, "the penny stock industry lends itself to a brand of theft that is particularly difficult for the casual investor to perceive and for the criminal investigator to prove." In September 1989, the North American Securities Administrators Association (NASAA) submitted a report, *The NASAA Report on Fraud and Abuse in the Penny Stock Industry,* which concluded, based on a 50–state survey, that: "Penny stock swindles are now the No. 1 threat of fraud and abuse facing small investors in the United States." It is the view of this Committee that the present regulations and enforcement mechanisms under which the penny stock market operates need to be strengthened to curtail further abusive activity. This legislation contains a series of statutory changes and additional legislative directives which the Committee views as necessary to protect the innocent and unwary investor and restore confidence in the lower end of the securities market.

Penny stocks are low-priced, highly speculative stocks generally sold in the over-the-counter (OTC) market and generally not listed on an exchange. Often, they do not qualify for listing on the National Association of Securities Dealers Automated Quotation system (NASDAQ). According to the NASD, out of an estimated 55,000 publicly traded corporations in the United States, approximately 3,350 are listed on the New York or American Stock Exchanges. An additional 4,970 are quoted on the NASDAQ system. Approximately half of those NASDAQ securities qualify for the NASDAQ/National Market System, which has last sale reporting. The remaining 47,000 securities fall entirely outside exchange or NASDAQ listings. Although these stocks have been used in the past to finance small, innovative companies, some of which have developed into successful corporations, recently the issuance and subsequent trading of such securities has been increasingly used as means for defrauding investors.

* * *

The history of the U.S. penny stock market can be traced back to the speculation surrounding the Colorado gold mining boom of the 1880's. The issuance and trading of penny stocks was also prevalent during the Cold War years of the 1950's, when the U.S. Atomic Energy Commission announced that it was seeking to purchase all available quantities of uranium. Thousands of investors lost millions of dollars in worthless, low-priced uranium mining stocks sold over the counter of coffee shops in Salt Lake City, Utah. From that point until roughly 1983, the penny stock industry was primarily regional in nature with most firms headquartered in Denver, Salt Lake City, and Spokane. During that period, abuses in the market were regarded by most regulators as a "mountain state" problem worthy of little national concern. Though a small amount of telemarketing of penny stocks was made to investors in other states, most of the trading was done by those investors residing close to those regional markets.

Until recent years, regulators' concerns in the penny stock market have focused on abuses related to "hot issues," initial public offerings of small, new companies with supposed bright and profitable features ahead of them, such as energy and mining, high tech and health-related breakthroughs, and other topical areas. As long as the brokerages dealing in these low priced securities remained beholden to the cyclical and unpredictable nature of these "hot issues," there would be little chance of developing the large and diverse investor base needed as a first step to the emergence as a large, national penny stock brokerage firm. * * * The fundamental nature of the penny stock marketplace changed dramatically in the mid–1980's, however, as a substantial number of brokerage firms ceased their traditional dependence on the initial public offering of "hot issues" as the forum for stock market manipulation, and instead intensified their efforts on the secondary market, where the initial offerings are subsequently traded. Technology has also played a role. With the growth of computers, telefax machines, inexpensive long-distance access through toll-free long distance phone numbers, and the ability to buy telephone lists, manipulators of penny stocks are now operating nationwide and, in increasing instances, globally.[a]

* * *

One component of the penny stock market is that of "blank check" offerings. * * * [B]lank checks are securities offerings in which the issuer discloses no specific business plan or purpose. There is little material information included in such registration statements, since there is no business to describe, no history of operations, and only minimal assets and liabilities to include in the financial statements. According to NASAA, nearly 70 percent of all penny stock issues offered in 1988 and through the third quarter of 1989 were blank checks; money raised with no purpose stated for its use. * * *

The stated purpose of the blank check company is to merge with an operating business after the securities being registered are sold. In some cases, manipulative activity may take place without any merger. False rumors are put out about a possible merger and the profitability of the alleged target and the price of the blank check company's stock increases on the basis of such rumors. In other cases, the merger is accomplished by issuing additional securities in the blank check company for the assets of the private company. These types of mergers are often reverse mergers, that is a merger where the shareholders of the company being acquired own a majority of the shares of the surviving company after the merger is consummated. A private firm which goes public through a merger with a blank check company generally escapes the scrutiny to which it would be subject if it were forced to go through the routine process involved in Commission and state registration.[b]

a. See The "King of Penny Stocks" Wants to Rule From Asia, Bus. Week, Apr. 8, 1991, at 74, recounting how Meyer Blinder, dubbed the "King of Penny Stocks" is push-ing new stock from Hong Kong after being put out of business in the United States.

b. See Spin Offs and the Shell Game, supra, at 511.

Once the stock in the blank check company is distributed, often in large part to the underwriting broker, his business associates, relatives and friends, the occurrence of the sudden merger or rumors of possible merger provides the basis for engineering an upward manipulation in the price of the stock as brokers, in calls to potential investors, fervently depict the blank check as having just merged with an emerging growth company with tremendous prospects. The price then continues skyward until the broker decides to unload his own and his friends' shares upon the public, sending the price plummeting.

The Committee has been impressed with the success of states such as Utah, which have engaged in aggressive attempts to increase regulation of blank check offerings. According to the testimony of U.S. Attorney Benson, in 1983, Utah had 212 blank check blind pool offerings which raised a total of $19.6 million. After Utah enacted its blank check restrictions in 1986, the number of such offerings fell to nine in 1987 and to two in 1988. In this legislation, the Committee seeks results similar to those in states such as Utah. The bill thus mandates that the Commission adopt new blank check rules which the Committee expects will contain at least three critical elements: (1) information regarding the company to be acquired by the blank check company prior to or after the date the registration becomes effective; (2) limitations on the use of proceeds of blank check offerings and the distribution of the securities of the issuer until such time as adequate disclosure has been made; and (3) a right of rescission for shareholders who disapprove of the disclosed acquisition.

* * *

In the view of the Committee, the need for additional reform is clear. Any contribution that the penny stock market, as it presently operates, makes to the economy, must be weighed against the significant economic consequences of the penny stock market's diversion of $2 billion which would otherwise be invested in the creation and expansion of legitimate small businesses. Equally distressing is the loss of investor confidence in the marketplace. * * *

Section-by-Section Analysis

* * *

Section 3.   Definition of a Penny Stock

Subsection (a) of Section 3 of the bill adds a new paragraph (51), defining the term "penny stock," to Section 3(a) of the Exchange Act. Subparagraph (51)(A) would define as penny stocks equity securities that do not fall within one of several excluded categories. Subparagraph (51)(A)(i) would exclude securities registered or approved for registration and traded on a national securities exchange so long as that exchange meets criteria the Commission shall prescribe. Subparagraph (51)(A)(ii) would exclude securities authorized for quotation on an automated quotation system sponsored by a registered securities association that was established before January 1, 1990. The only quotation system meeting this requirement is the NASDAQ system.

* * *

The Committee is aware that certain securities that should properly be categorized as penny stocks may be able to gain registration on regional exchanges. Once registered on an exchange, most of the trading activity in these securities may be directed to the non–NASDAQ over-the-counter market, where a lack of trading or quotation information, higher spreads and markups, and other factors may operate to the disadvantage of public investors. * * *

The Committee believes that transactions in securities that (1) are traded in the non–NASDAQ over-the-counter market and (2) would fall within the definition of the term "penny stock" absent their registration on an exchange or authorization on NASDAQ involve investor protection concerns of the type the Act is meant to address. Subparagraph (51)(B) will provide the Commission with the necessary flexibility to ensure that the scope of securities covered by the Act is consistent with its intent and that the exemptions provided by subparagraphs 51(A)(i) and (ii) do not serve to shield unscrupulous practices involving penny stocks. Given the flexibility provided the Commission under this section, the Committee expects that the Commission will exercise this authority consistent with the findings in this Act.

* * *

In addition, the Commission would be expected to exempt from the definition of "penny stock" equity securities whose price exceeds a certain dollar amount, as it did in promulgating Rule 15c2–6(c)(1). Thus the Commission would have to identify those transactions which are not likely to be the subject of manipulation.

* * *

Section 4. Exclusion of Sanctioned Persons From Participating In Distributions of Penny Stocks

Section 4 amends Section 15(b)(6) of the Exchange Act. The new subparagraph (6)(A) would extend the Commission's existing authority in Section 15(b)(6) of the Exchange Act, which allows it to limit or prohibit association of certain persons with a broker-dealer. Subparagraph (6)(A) would grant to the Commission authority to ensure, suspend, bar, or place limitations on the activities or functions of any person associated or seeking to become associated with a broker or dealer or to bar such person from participating in the distribution of any penny stock, provided such action is in the public interest and the person has committed or omitted certain acts, or been convicted of or enjoined from certain activities specified in section 15(b)(4) of the Exchange Act. Furthermore, subparagraph (6)(A) would make it unlawful for any person subject to a Commission order that bars or suspends such person from participation in a distribution of any penny stock from associating or seeking to become associated with a broker or dealer, or participating in the distribution of penny stock without the consent of the Commission. Finally, this provision would make it unlawful for any broker or dealer to participate in a distribution of any penny stock, without the consent of the Commission, if in the exercise of reasonable care the broker-dealer is aware of, or should have been aware of, the participation of a barred person, regardless of whether such person is an associated person of such broker or dealer. Subparagraph (6)(A) is designed to enable the Commission to prohibit persons from participating in penny stock activities through remote affiliations with broker-dealers or issuers.

Currently, Section 15(b)(6), together with self-regulatory membership requirements, serve as the primary barriers to prevent barred persons from entering the securities industry. The Committee is aware, however, that numerous persons have participated in securities activities through a variety of arrangements with broker-dealers and penny stock issuers. These persons present serious customer protection concerns for the securities industry with respect to the promotion and sale of penny stocks. Therefore, such affiliations entered into by barred persons provide a potential avenue for circumventing the protections provided in the Exchange Act.

The Committee believes that the Commission needs broader proscriptive authority to address patterns of reentry and recidivism in penny stock distributions. Subparagraph (6)(A) will provide the Commission with the necessary flexibility to prevent the participation of barred persons in the penny stock distribution process by means of affiliations with broker-dealers and penny stock issuers.

  * * *

Section 5.   Requirements for Brokers and Dealers of Penny Stocks

Subsection (a) of Section 5 adds a new paragraph (g) to section 15 of the Exchange Act to establish a system for more comprehensive disclosure and regulatory oversight for the operation of the penny stock market, from the initiation of broker-customer contact through the confirmation of trading of these stocks and the maintenance of customer accounts in such stocks. The subsection mandates that the Commission adopt rules to impose additional broker and dealer disclosure obligations prior to transactions, at the time of confirmation, and through monthly account statements.

Subparagraph (g)(2) requires the Commission to adopt rules within one year to mandate that, prior to effecting any penny stock transactions, a broker or dealer must provide customers with a specific "risk disclosure" document. This document must contain a description of the nature and level of risk involved in the penny stock market; a full description of the broker's or dealer's duties to the customer and of the rights and remedies available in the event of any violation of such duties or other legal requirements; the nature of "bid" and "ask" prices, in that market; identification of means to receive information on broker-dealer disciplinary histories through a new toll-free telephone number, and a description of all significant terms used in the risk disclosure document which would assist customers in their understanding of the penny stock market. The Act directs the Commission to require by rule or regulation the appropriate form for the document (including language, type size and format) which will insure it is the most meaningful possible document for the customer. The Commission may also require for inclusion in this document any additional language it deems appropriate.

Subparagraph (g)(3)(A) adds a requirement that the Commission adopt a rule or regulation to require brokers and dealers to disclose to each customer, prior to effecting any transaction in, and at the time of confirming any transaction with respect to, any penny stock, among other things, the bid and ask prices for the penny stock, or comparably accurate and reliable pricing information if bid and ask prices are not available. While the Committee believes that the disclosure of bid and ask quotations to customers will provide an additional source of useful information for customers to assess the relative merits of a particular investment, the Committee notes that quotations for such securities frequently are the subject of negotiation and may not accurately reflect the actual price a customer would pay or receive for the securities; in other words, they may not reflect accurately the "prevailing market price."

The Committee believes that it is important to note that, because of the questions on the reliability of quotations on penny stocks, the requirement to disclose quotations to customers before and after a transaction does not necessarily sanction the use of quotations for other purposes. In particular, such quotations are not, absent a further showing of their probative value, the appropriate basis for computing penny stock markups. This is clearly established in the well-developed body of law on how to calculate excessive markups and the Committee wishes to emphasize that this provision is not intended to supersede that law.

The leading case in this area, Alstead, Strangis & Dempsey, Inc., 47 S.E.C. 1034 (1984), clearly established the standards to be used to evaluate whether a customer was charged excessive markups by a dealer that both makes a market in the security and sells the security to retail customers. *Alstead* held that, in competitive markets where no one firm dominates or controls the market for the security, the dealer's own inter-dealer sales or, if they can be validated by comparison with actual inter-dealer sales, the lowest independent offer quotation may be used as the best evidence of the prevailing market price for purposes of calculating markups. *Alstead* also recognized, however, that where the market for a security is dominated and controlled by a single dealer, which is very often the case for penny stocks, quotations generally do not provide reliable evidence of the prevailing market price. Thus, *Alstead* held, the dealer's contemporaneous purchase price, and not quotations, may be used as the best evidence of the prevailing market price and, as such, should be used as the basis for computing markups in such cases. The Committee believes that disclosure of quotations to customers will not relieve brokers and dealers of liability for excessive markups.

Subparagraph (g)(3)(B) requires all brokers and dealers to provide each customer whose account contains penny stocks with a monthly statement indicating the market value of the penny stocks in that account or indicating that the market value cannot be determined because of the unavailability of firm quotes. The Committee intends that, in the Commission's rule, this market value is to be calculated according to the prevailing bid price per share of the penny stock, if any, at the time that the monthly statement is sent out. The Committee views these mandatory monthly statements as crucial for providing investors more accurate, up-to-date information regarding all of their holdings of penny stocks.

Subparagraph (g)(4) grants the Commission the authority to exempt any person or class of persons or transaction or class of transactions from the requirements of this subsection, provided the Commission determines that any exemption would be consistent with the public interest and the protection of investors. * * *

Subparagraph (g)(5) grants general rulemaking authority to the Commission with regard to the implementation of the new subsection 15(g) of the Exchange Act or penny stocks in general. * * *

　　　* * *

Section 6.   Development of Automated Quotation Systems for Penny Stocks

This section adds a new Section 17B to the Exchange Act mandating the development of automated quotation systems for penny stocks. The Committee notes that through the adoption of Section 11A of the Exchange Act in 1975, Congress sought an electronic national market system for equity securities qualified for trading in that market. Penny stocks have not been included in this evolving national market system. Thus, the Committee adopted section 6 in order to enhance both the availability and quality of information available to investors and regulators regarding the penny stock market.

* * *

Section 8 amends Section 29(b) of the Exchange Act to make voidable those contracts in violation of rules adopted under Section 15(c)(2) of the Exchange Act. Section 29(b) gives customers the ability to protect themselves from abusive conduct in the securities markets by voiding trades that violate the securities laws and rules thereunder. * * *

[New Section 7(b) of the Securities Act mandating that the Commission prescribe special rules to restrict the use of blank check registration statements is discussed supra at page 261.]

Section 10.   Broker/Dealer Disciplinary History

* * * Section 15A of the Exchange Act [is amended] by adding a new subsection (i), which mandates that the NASD and any other registered securities association establish a toll-free telephone listing to receive customer inquiries concerning the disciplinary history of its members and associated persons. The association must respond to such inquiries promptly and in writing. This section also provides immunity from liability regarding actions taken or omitted in good faith pursuant to this section.

The Committee notes that under current practices, the NASD notifies brokers when customers make written inquiries concerning the disciplinary histories of NASD members and associated persons. Given the likelihood of far more customer inquiries with this toll-free number, the Committee expects that both the NASD and the Commission will review current policy and seek the adoption of new rules to assure that customer confidentiality is maintained, and thus that customers are protected from potential retaliation by their brokers and dealers.

* * *

---

1. *New SEC Rules.* Pursuant to the Penny Stock Reform Act of 1990, the SEC has adopted Rules 15g–1 through 15g–9. Rule 3a51–1 also defines penny stocks as basically stocks trading below $5 per share (but with numerous qualifications). Although some of these rules are traditional disclosure rules, requiring generic disclosure of risks inherent to the Penny Stock Market (Rule 15g–2) or disclosures about broker compensation (Rules 15g–4 and 15g–5), Rule 15g–9 imposes a direct affirmative suitability obligation on the broker or dealer that must be satisfied prior to the transaction being effected. In addition, Rule 15g–9 also requires delivery of a document (Schedule 15G) that seeks to discourage the investor from entering the transaction. Finally, Rule 15g–9 effectively chills high pressure "cold call" telephone selling tactics by requiring that the investor's account first be approved by the broker, that the broker then deliver certain elaborately mandated written disclosures, and finally that the customer give written instructions before a penny stock transaction can be effected. This is the use of disclosure less to provide sunlight than to disrupt certain abusive marketing practices.[1]

1. For a fuller description of practices in this market, see Goldstein, Ramshaw and   Ackerson, An Investment Masquerade: A Descriptive Overview of Penny Stock Fraud and

2. *Rule 15c2–11.* Many "penny stocks" are not reporting companies under § 12(g) of the 1934 Act. In such cases Rule 15c2–11 basically prohibits the broker-dealer from quoting an over-the-counter security that is not quoted on NASDAQ unless it has on hand specified information about the security and the issuer.

The information to be accumulated depends on the classification of the issuer. In the case of 1933 Act and 1934 Act reporting companies, the broker-dealer must have on hand the most recent 1933 Act prospectus, the annual, quarterly and current reports filed pursuant to sections 13 or 15(d) of the 1934 Act, and a copy of the Offering Circular used in any Regulation A offering. Similar documented financial and other available information must be obtained with respect to insurance companies exempt from reporting requirements under Section 12(g) of the 1934 Act, foreign private issuers, and American Depository Receipts (ADRs) that represent deposited shares of such foreign issuers. In addition, the broker-dealer is required to have on hand any other material information (including adverse information) which comes to its attention or possession before the submission of a quotation with respect to such securities.

Having collected and retained this information, the broker-dealer is prohibited from quoting any such over-the-counter security unless it first determines that, based on such documents and information, it has "a reasonable basis under the circumstances for believing that the * * * information is accurate in all material respects, and that the sources of [such] information is reliable." (Rule 15c2–11(a)).

But this is not all. There are sixteen other items of current information with respect to issuers and their securities that are required to be collected and preserved by the broker-dealer and which it shall make reasonably available upon request to any person expressing an interest in a proposed transaction in any such security. These items list information about the issuer, its securities, the nature of its business, the products or services offered, its facilities, its most recent balance sheet and income statement and similar financial information for the two preceding fiscal years.

If a broker-dealer makes such information available to others upon request, it "shall not constitute a representation by the broker or dealer that such information is accurate, but shall constitute a representation * * * that the information is reasonably current in relation to the day the quotation is submitted, that the broker or dealer has a reasonable basis under the circumstances for believing the information is accurate in all material respects, and that the information was obtained from sources which the broker or dealer has a reasonable basis for believing are reliable."[2]

While this does not make the broker-dealer a guarantor of the accuracy of the information, and at least literally does not impose upon the broker any duty of investigation or "due diligence" beyond going to what the broker reasonably believes are reliable sources, the possible exposure to civil liability of a broker-dealer quoting a non-registered security is obvious. The Rule was adopted primarily for the purpose of attempting to stop the "shell game" (see Chapter

the Federal Securities Law, 47 Bus.Law. 773 (1992).

2. Exchange Act Release No. 21470 (Nov. 8, 1984), 31 SEC Dock. 797, 798 (1984).

8, supra at p. 524), but it was also designed "to prohibit broker-dealers from establishing arbitrary quotations for infrequently traded over-the-counter securities."[3]

The effectiveness of Rule 15c2–11 is, however, subject to some potentially crippling limitations on the rule's application. Under subparagraph (f)(3), a "piggyback" exception exempts securities that have been quoted in an inter-dealer quotation system (such as the OTC Bulletin Board) where they have been quoted on "at least 12 days within the previous 30 calendar days, with no more than 4 business days in succession without a quotation." Effectively, this means that once one dealer quotes the stock (presumably based on compliance with the Rule), others can piggyback on its efforts and need not have current information in their possession. In addition, under Rule 15c2–11(f)(3)(iii), even the original dealer is freed from this obligation to have current information once the stock has been quoted for this requisite period. This is known as "self piggybacking", and it implies that no dealer may actually possess at any given time the information described in Rule 15c2–11(b).

As a result of this curious state of affairs, the NASD has estimated that as many as 50% of the companies traded on its Bulletin Board (which has no listing or eligibility standards) may not be reporting companies.[4] It has asked the SEC for permission to delist such non-reporting companies, which it believes taint the Bulletin Board Market In response, the SEC proposed in 1998 to amend Rule 15c2–11 to tighten its exceptions and largely eliminate the "piggyback" exception[5].

G. *Market Domination: The Problem of the Captive or Controlled Market*

Both the Penny Stock Market and certain other thinly traded equity markets are capable of being dominated by one or more dealers or underwriters, acting collectively. Although the SEC and the NASD seek to restrict and regulate the mark-ups on the securities traded in such markets to a "reasonable" level (see Chapter 10 supra), the mark-up rules do not adequately address all the problems in this market. In particular, it may often be difficult to establish the market price if there is no true market, but only a few transactions carefully orchestrated by the dominant market makers acting collusively.

The SEC has responded in several different ways to this problem. First, Rule 15c1–8 makes it unlawful for a broker-dealer participating in a distribution of securities to represent that such security is being offered "at the market" unless he knows or has reasonable grounds to believe that a market exists "other than that made, created, or controlled by him, or by any person for whom he is acting or with whom he is associated in such distribution." However, this principle is not limited, as the rule is by its terms, to "distributions." As the Commission stated in In the Matter of Norris & Hirshberg, Inc.: "As to sales made on the express representation that they are 'at market' we have repeatedly held that such a representation is false where in fact the 'market' has been subject to artificial influences or where no true market existed."[6] And under the "shingle theory" every sale by a broker-dealer carries

---

3. Ibid.

4. See Knight, NASD Tries to Reduce the Risk of OTC Trading, Washington Post, December 15, 1997, at p. F23.

5. NASD Manual, Conduct Rules, Rule 2310(a) (1996); see also In the Matter of Boren & Co., Securities Exchange Act Release No. 34–39670 (Feb. 17, 1998).

6. 21 S.E.C. at 882 (1946), aff'd, 177 F.2d 228 (D.C.Cir.1949).

with it the implied representation that the price is "reasonably related to that prevailing in an open market." For an excellent analysis of the problems which these principles pose to a dealer making an over-the-counter market, see Bloomenthal, The Case of the Subtle Motive and the Delicate Art—Control and Domination in Over–The–Counter Securities Markets, 1960 Duke L.J. 196.

In Chasins v. Smith, Barney & Co., Inc.,[2] the plaintiff brought a Rule 10b–5 action against his broker-dealer for selling over-the-counter securities without disclosing in the confirmation that it was acting as a principal for its own account and also was "making a market" in the securities sold to him. At the time of the transactions in question, Chasins was the musical director of a radio station in New York City and was the commentator sponsored by Smith Barney. He claimed that he opened the brokerage account as a result of this relationship with defendant. Smith Barney recommended that Chasins sell certain stocks and purchase stocks in which defendant was dealing as a market maker. The defense was "that all brokerage firms had followed the same practice and had never thought such disclosure was required." Indeed, Rule 15c1–4, the predecessor of Rule 10b–10, only required a broker or dealer to furnish the customer "written notification disclosing: (1) whether he is acting as a broker for such customer, as a dealer for his own account, as a broker for some other person, or as a broker for both such customer and some other person * * *."

The district court ruled that Smith Barney had violated Rule 10b–5 in not disclosing to Chasins that it was making a market in the securities it sold Chasins in the over-the-counter market. Damages were awarded to Chasins of $18,616, with interest, which constituted the difference between the price at which Chasins purchased the securities and the price at which he later sold them, prior to discovering Smith Barney's market making activities in the securities.

The principle embodied in Rule 15c1–8 prohibiting a broker-dealer participating in a distribution of securities to represent that such security is being offered "at the market" under certain circumstances, has always presented a perhaps insoluble problem of disclosure to any broker-dealer who is the only one "in the sheets" with respect to a particular over-the-counter stock. On any realistic test, such a broker-dealer "controls" or "dominates" the market in that stock, although it is doubtful if very many take steps to make effective disclosure to their customers of this fact. However, until the bombshell exploded by the District Court opinion in the *Chasins* case that defendant had violated Rule 10b–5, no one thought that a broker-dealer who was one of several making a market in a stock and who did not execute a predominant portion of the trades in that stock had to make any disclosure to his customer other than to confirm the transaction as "principal."

The scope of the *Chasins* case has long been debated, but the practical answer may have been supplied by the SEC's adoption of Rule 10b–10. It requires a broker-dealer to disclose to the customer in a written confirmation of each transaction "Whether he is acting as agent for such customer, as agent for some other person, as agent for both such customer and some other person, or as principal for his own account" and, if he is acting as agent for such customer or for some other person or both, to disclose, among other things, "The amount of any remuneration received or to be received by him from such customer in

2.   438 F.2d 1167 (2d Cir.1970).

connection with the transaction." If he is acting as principal for his own account, in that case he must disclose the amount of any mark-up or mark-down with respect to a simultaneous or "riskless" transaction and, with respect to a transaction in an equity security, "whether he is a market maker in that security." With the proliferation of the amount of information which must be included on the confirmation slip, and the necessity for having them printed by computer in order to manage the "back office" problems of the brokerage industry, the practice has developed of having code numbers printed on the front of the confirmation slip to refer to certain statements contained on the back of the form, including the fact, if it is true, that the broker-dealer was acting as principal in the transaction.

In Shivangi v. Dean Witter Reynolds, Inc.,[3] a retail customer brought a Rule 10b–5 action against Dean Witter, a broker-dealer acting as a market-maker, on the ground that it failed to disclose that its account executives received higher compensation for principal trades of over-the-counter stocks in which it acted as a market maker than for agency transactions. Rule 10b–10 does not require a market maker acting as a principal to disclose the account executive's commission in this situation nor did the plaintiff introduce evidence that the compensation to sales personnel is ordinarily disclosed in the securities industry. The district court held that although the failure to disclose the compensation distinction between an agency and a principal transaction was a material omission, there was no actual intent to deceive on the part of Dean Witter and thus there was a failure to establish scienter under Rule 10b–5. The Court of Appeal affirmed, noting that compliance with SEC requirements manifests a "lack of severe recklessness."

The difficult problems under Rule 10b–10 arise in connection with deter-mining when the broker-dealer *must* act as an agent for the customer because he has acquired a fiduciary status and cannot deal with him as principal without his informed consent in advance. In In the Matter of Norris & Hirshberg, Inc.,[4] the Commission held that the broker-dealer violated his fiduciary duty in purporting to trade with his customers as principal, under the following circumstances:

"Norris and Hirshberg maintained personal friendly relations with many customers and were highly successful in procuring the trust and confidence of their customers. Because of the great reliance of many customers on respon-dent it had an unusual amount of control over their trading, its power ranging from formal written and oral discretion specifically vested in it by certain customers to an ability to initiate and suggest trading with almost complete assurance of the acceptance of the trades. Notwithstanding the nature of its relations with customers, the precise terms of its discretionary powers, or the legal character of customers' orders, respondent without sufficient disclosure, purported to deal with these customers almost universally as a dealer at a profit. Its power over accounts was augmented by the fact that many of them were margin accounts. Consequently, respondent had physical possession and the powers of a creditor and pledgee over the securities in margin accounts. Margin trading also permitted respondent to effect a larger volume of business with customers than would have been possible on the basis of cash trading alone.

---

3. 825 F.2d 885 (5th Cir.1987).

4. 21 S.E.C. 865 (1946), aff'd, 177 F.2d 228 (D.C.Cir.1949).

"As a result of this combination of factors, respondent was able to acquire large portions of the available trading supplies of the securities in which it specialized, sell those securities to customers, buy them back, sell them again to the same and to other customers, turn over its inventories again and again at kited prices unilaterally fixed by respondent in a market consisting almost wholly of itself and its customers, to a great degree unaffected by normal bargaining influences."[5]

The result in the *Chasins* case, it would seem, might have been based upon the doctrine that the broker-dealer, having solicited the trust and confidence of the customer, could not, as in *Norris & Hirshberg*, deal with the customer as a principal without his informed consent in advance. The principles expressed in *Norris & Hirschberg* have been recently followed and extended by the Commission in an important enforcement action. In SEC v. First Jersey Securities, Inc.,[6] the Commission was faced with a leading penny stock underwriter and dealer that it found had totally controlled and manipulated the market in the stocks it underwrote, maintaining in effect a captive market in which it handled all transactions internally within its own offices. The SEC found that "the firm's manner of trading allowed it to fix the prices of the securities in a market largely unaffected by competition and that the noncompetitive nature of the market in which the securities were traded was a material fact that the firm had an obligation to reveal to its clients."[7] Relying on *Norris & Hirschberg,* the Second Circuit upheld the SEC, quoting the language in that case which said:

"Each of [its] sales carried with it the clear—though implied—representation that the price was reasonably related to that prevailing in an open market.... Without disclosure fully revealing that the 'market' was an internal system created, controlled and dominated by the [defendant] that representation was materially false and misleading."[8]

Noting that First Jersey "received the vast majority of its revenues from trading securities for its own accounts, including securities that it had underwritten,"[9] the Second Circuit upheld the District Court's finding that "First Jersey dominated and controlled the markets for the ... securities at issue because the vast majority of the transactions in those securities were conducted by First Jersey."[10] This is a common pattern in penny stock frauds.

---

5. 21 S.E.C. 865, at 867.

6. 101 F.3d 1450 (2d Cir.1996).

7. Id. at 1468.

8. Id.

9. Id. at 1457.

10. Id. at 1460.

CHAPTER 12

TENDER OFFERS, MANAGEMENT BUYOUTS, AND TAKEOVER CONTESTS

Statutes and Regulations

Securities Exchange Act, §§ 13(d) and (e), 14(d), (e) and (f).

Rules 10b–4; 10b–18; Regulation 13D–G; Rules 13e–1 to 13e–4; Regulation 14D; Regulation 14E; Schedule TO.

Introduction

Over the last three decades, no area of corporate and securities law has produced equivalent controversy, resulted in more legislation, or yielded as many academic theories, as has the topic of hostile takeovers. Over this period, the tide of the battle has regularly shifted. Prior to the Williams Act's passage in 1968, bidders could make very short tender offers, lasting only several days. At least in theory, shareholders of the target could be coerced by such offers, because if they spurned the bidder's premium and the offer succeeded, they might be left holding a minority interest in an illiquid stock controlled by the bidder. Fear of the unknown bidder and its potential plans for their corporation might also stampede shareholders into tendering because widely dispersed public shareholders could not easily unite to take collective action in response to a hostile bid, even if they perceived it to be inadequate. In response, Congress passed the Williams Act in 1968 to fill a perceived gap in the disclosure received by target shareholders and to authorize the SEC to adopt rules regulating certain substantive aspects of tender offers. As the Senate Committee that drafted the bill explained:

* * * Under this bill, the material facts concerning the identity, background, and plans of the person or group making a tender offer or acquiring a substantial amount of securities would be disclosed.

Any person or group acquiring more than 10 percent [later reduced to 5 percent] of any class of equity security registered under the Securities Exchange Act would be required to disclose the size of the holdings of the person or group involved, the source of the funds used or to be used to acquire the shares, any contracts or arrangements relating to the shares, and, if the purpose of the acquisition is to acquire control of the company, any plans to liquidate the company, sell its assets, merge it with another company, or make major changes in its business or corporate structure.

As initially introduced, the bill would have required the disclosure statement to be filed with the Securities and Exchange Commission 5 days before the tender offer was made to allow the staff of the Securities and Exchange Commission an opportunity to review the material for compliance with the applicable requirements. At the hearings it was urged that this prior review was not necessary and in some cases might delay the offer when time was of the essence. In view of the authority and responsibility of the Securities and Exchange Commission to take appropriate action in the event that inadequate or misleading information is disseminated to the public to solicit acceptance of a tender offer, the bill as approved by the committee requires only that the statement be on file with the Securities and Exchange Commission at the time the tender offer is first made to the public.[1]

Although the passage of the Williams Act initially slowed the growth of the takeover movement, bidders quickly discovered techniques by which to regain the advantage. During the 1970s and early 1980s, the bidder would typically employ a three stage attack: (1) quietly buying up to 5% of the class (at which point § 13(d) of the Williams Act required it to file within ten days thereafter a disclosure document known as a Schedule 13D), (2) launching a hostile tender offer for control, and (3) merging out shortly thereafter any remaining minority interest that had failed to tender. As an additional tactic to pressure shareholders, bidders might also structure their offer as a "two-tier" partial bid in which they offered an above-market tender offer premium for 50% of the stock, but announced a plan to merge out the remaining minority shareholders at a lower price once they obtained control (thus, the tender offer was said to be "front-loaded").

In response to these coercive tactics, target managements resorted to rough-and-tumble defensive tactics of their own: (1) a target might seek a friendly acquisition partner (a "white knight") or an institutional investor (a "white squire") who would acquire a blocking position so that the bidder could not safely acquire a controlling position or effect a squeeze-out merger; (2) it might grant a "lock-up" to some third party, either of its stock or of certain "crown jewel" assets, (usually, this would involve giving the third party an option to buy assets or stock at a below-market price, possibly in return for its agreement to make a counter-offer at a higher price); (3) it might repurchase its own shares in order to drive their price above the tender offer; (4) conceivably, it might launch a counter-tender offer for the bidder (the so-called "Pac–Man" defense, but only rarely used); or (5) most likely, it would adopt (or utilize a previously adopted) "poison pill" shareholder rights plan (typically, this involves a distribution of options or warrants that, in order to dilute the bidder's holdings in the target, entitles all target shareholders, other than the bidder, to purchase the target's stock at an extremely attractive below-market price under specified circumstances, such as if the bidder crossed a specified threshold—say 20%—of the target's stock). Almost invariably, the bidder would go to court to enjoin these defensive measures ("scorched earth" tactics in its view) as a breach of target management's fiduciary duties to its shareholders. More recently, the target's defense would also rely on whatever antitakeover statute its jurisdiction of incorporation had adopted; these statutes might require a statutorily defined "fair price" or a supermajority vote, disenfranchise the bidder's shares, grant special compensation to employees, authorize the target to recapture gains from certain large shareholders, or simply preclude a follow-up merger for a designated "moratorium" period.

While these tactics are discussed in more detail in this chapter, they obviously spawned epic legal battles. But, for the most part, the legal issues involved were those of state corporate law and the common law of fiduciary duties. This chapter will principally focus on takeovers from a federal securities law perspective. From that perspective, it is far from clear that target shareholders need much protection from bidders, for two reasons. First, the indisputable fact about takeovers is that the target shareholders profit significantly from them.[2] Although greater ambiguity

---

1. S.Rep. No. 500 (Committee on Banking and Currency), 90th Cong., 1st Sess., pp. 4–5 (1967).

2. For a summary of the statistical evidence from "event studies" of takeover

stocks, see Jarrell, Brickley and Netter, The Market for Corporate Control: The Empirical Evidence Since 1980, 2 Journal of Economic Perspectives 49 (1988) (on average, 30% ab-

surrounds the impact of takeovers on bidder shareholders,[3] on bondholders,[4] and on employees,[5] the measurable losses suffered by these other constituencies, even when aggregated, clearly do not begin to approach the stock price gains to target shareholders. Second, target shareholders have a very effective armory of self-help weapons against "unfair" hostile bids, which target managements are more than ready to employ.

From this starting point that shareholders are "net gainers" from takeovers, it sensibly can be asked: why should takeovers be subject to special federal regulation (other than the general antifraud rules that apply to all securities transactions)? After all, federal regulation may only give self-interested target managements another weapon with which to ward off lucrative bids that their own shareholders desire. Arguably, if the intended beneficiaries of the Williams Act (i.e. shareholders) need little protection, the statute might sensibly be given a minimalist interpretation in order to prevent it from interfering with the market's healthy functioning. During the late 1980s and early 1990s, the force of this argument has been underscored by an unmistakable and probably long-term shift in the tide of battle toward the target. As a result of a variety of factors—especially potent defensive tactics (most notably, the poison pill), state anti-takeover statutes, and the decline in junk bond financing—fewer takeovers have been launched, and fewer of those launched have been successful.

The standard answer to the claim that takeovers are overregulated involves the special problem of coercion: dispersed shareholders are incapable of collective action in a takeover, and various offensive tactics, such as the two-tier partial bid,[6] may coerce them into selling at prices well below that at which a single owner of all the target stock would be willing to sell.[7] So viewed, the Williams Act's disclosure and timing provisions may make sense primarily as a means by which to reduce coercion

normal gain on announcement of tender offer).

3. Different studies show bidder shareholders experiencing small gains, no gains, or small losses on the announcement of a takeover. Some commentators believe that the market's reaction understates the expected loss to the bidder's shareholders from overpayment because the market already anticipated the loss. See Black, Bidder Overpayment in Takeovers, 41 Stan.L.Rev. 597 (1985).

4. See Asquith & Wizman, Event Risk, Wealth Redistribution and the Return to Existing Bondholders in Corporate Buyouts, 27 J.Fin.Econ. 195 (1990).

5. Coffee, Shareholders Versus Managers: The Strain in The Corporate Web, 85 Mich.L.Rev. 1 (1986).

6. In a "two-tier" bid, the acquirer offers a high price for that percentage of the shares necessary to give it majority control (which, for example, may be only 35% if it already owns 15%) and then indicates that it plans to merge out the remaining shareholders at a lower price. Even if it offers the same price for the "back end," this amount may only be received much later, possibly in the form of debt securities that will trade below

their face value, and without interest to cover the intervening period. As a result, this approach increases the pressure to tender into the front-end.

7. The shareholders' problem can be explained as a variant of the standard "prisoner's dilemma." If shareholders believe the offer is inadequate, they could in theory hold out, but in a world where the second-step merger may be at a lower price (or may be a delayed payment of the same price, given the time value of money), a shareholder who holds out will be in a worse-off position if other shareholders tender and the offer is successful. Then the holdouts will become minority shareholders in a thinly traded or untraded firm. The "front-loaded" tender offer exacerbates this problem by offering a special advantage to those who defect from any implicit agreement not to tender. In short, in a setting where shareholders would be best off from not tendering, it is likely that shareholders who cannot organize will be forced to tender. See Carney, Shareholder Coordination Costs, Shark Repellents and Takeout Mergers: The Case Against Fiduciary Duties, 1983 A.B.F.Res.J. 341.

and facilitate an auction market in which bidders compete on an equal footing to acquire control so that shareholders will receive higher takeover premiums. From this perspective, the Williams Act should serve mainly to ensure a level playing field on which the contestants do battle. But, the actual impact of the Williams Act has been to increase takeover premiums[8] and hence possibly reduce the number of bids made.[9] Even the desirability of a competitive auction market for takeovers has been the subject of much academic debate.[10] Thus, while it can be debated whether the Williams Act has made shareholders as a class better off, it almost certainly has protected smaller shareholders from coercive tactics that might have forced them to tender at lower prices.

The legislative history of the Williams Act does reveal a Congressional desire to preserve a fair balance in takeover contests so that managerial defensive tactics could only be used up to the point where they were likely to increase value for target shareholders. Indeed, the chief draftsman of the Williams Act (Senator Harrison Williams of New Jersey) observed that "extreme care" had been taken in writing the legislation to avoid "tipping the balance of regulation either in favor of management or in favor of the person making the takeover bid."[11] Still, any notion that the Williams Act places substantive limitations on the defensive tactics available to management (other than those that directly contravene the Act's few regulatory provisions) was forcefully rejected by the Supreme Court in Schreiber v. Burlington Northern, Inc.[12] As a result, the Williams Act necessarily constrains bidders much more than target managements.

Different justifications for federal regulation of takeovers have been advanced by others. Some believe that shareholders need protection because takeover premiums are not "true" premiums as the market price of the target's stock arguably trades at a substantial discount from its asset value.[13] Alternatively, another goal of the Williams Act may be ensuring equal treatment within the target shareholder class through an equitable allocation of the takeover premium. In particular, Rule 14d–10 seeks to ensure that the "best price" paid to any shareholder must be paid to all shareholders. Absent this rule, large shareholders might receive a higher premium than small shareholders; or, tender offers might be made only to a limited class of shareholders. Yet, as will be seen, Rule 14d–10 has spawned unanticipated

---

8. Studies have found that in the wake of the Williams Act's passage, the average premium over the pre-offer price in a cash tender offer rose from 32% to nearly 53%. See Jarrell and Bradley, The Economic Effects of Federal and State Regulation of Cash Tender Offers, 23 J.L. & Econ. 371 (1980).

9. For example, some takeover contests have been stretched out over a year through the use of "poison pills" and other techniques that allow the target to seek a higher bid.

10. Those who favor auctions believe that they direct the target's assets to the most efficient user (i.e., the firm that will realize the greatest synergy from the combination). See Gilson, Seeking Competitive Bids Versus Pure Passivity in Tender Offer Defense, 35 Stan.L.Rev. 51 (1982). Those who oppose auctions believe that, unless the first bidder's search costs are rewarded, bidders will be deterred from making takeover bids, and the number of bids will decline. See

Easterbrook & Fischel, Auctions and Sunk Costs in Tender Offers, 35 Stan.L.Rev. 1 (1982). Proponents of auctions doubt that search costs play a large role in takeovers. Another critique of auctions is that, absent unique synergies, auctions waste social resources. See Schwartz, The Fairness of Tender Offer Prices in Utilitarian Theory, 17 J. Legal Stud. 165 (1988).

11. 113 Cong.Rec. 24664; see also U.S.Code Cong. & Admin.News 1968, at 2813; H.R.Rep. No. 1711, 90th Cong., 2d Sess., 4 (1968).

12. 472 U.S. 1 (1985).

13. See Kraakman, Taking Discounts Seriously: The Implications of Discounted Share Prices As An Acquisition Motive, 88 Colum.L.Rev. 891 (1988); see also, Stout, Are Takeover Premiums Really Premiums? Market Price, Fair Value and Corporate Law, 99 Yale L.J. 1235 (1990).

litigation in cases where payments made by the bidder to officer/shareholders were seemingly for other and legitimate purposes (such as to retain employees). Finally, there are the classic arguments for disclosure: control of major institutions arguably should not shift virtually overnight without the "sunlight" of disclosure focusing on the new owners. Whether shareholders actually benefit from this disclosure process may not have been the principal concern of Congress, which instead may have been accommodating a clash of interest groups.

Still, however one understands the political motives underlying the Williams Act, a regulatory dilemma remains: the party most likely to seek to enforce the Williams Act and its associated rules is target management. To set high disclosure standards or to impose substantive obligations on the bidder may be to arm the target's management with a potent weapon to their shareholders' disadvantage. Thus, some have urged that target management be denied standing to enforce the Williams Act.[14] In most instances, however, no other private enforcer is available, and other studies contend, based on some empirical evidence, that target-initiated litigation actually enhances shareholder wealth by furthering the auction process.[15] The debate over the desirability of defensive tactics will predictably continue, but the claim that they succeed in raising premiums is always open to the rejoinder that if takeover premiums were raised to the point that the expected gains to the bidder disappear, there would be fewer, and eventually no, takeovers.

Another way to frame the regulatory problem is to ask: to what degree should the law regard target management as the negotiating agent of the target shareholders? Some commentators believe that because target shareholders cannot negotiate for themselves, their management should be given substantial discretion to do so on their behalf.[16] Others believe that target management has too substantial a conflict of interest to be accorded much discretion. Moreover, it can be argued that the Williams Act provides a superior means by which to promote auctions and raise premiums.[17] Even if it were not Congress's intent to promote auctions when it passed the Williams Act, the evidence seems to show that the chief effect of the Act has been to enable target shareholders to capture the vast majority of the gains from takeovers, with bidders receiving only statistically insignificant gains on average.

This chapter examines the current regulatory balance that has been struck between underregulation and overregulation, recognizing that the only constant about takeovers has been constant and often sudden change.

SECTION 1.   AN OVERVIEW OF THE WILLIAMS ACT

Enacted in 1968 and amended in 1970, the Williams Act was a product of both a Congressional sense that "something had to be done" about corporate takeovers and a Congressional irresolution about what precisely should be done. Although the original force behind the introduction of the Williams Act was probably the desire of target managements to obtain protection from takeover bids made by brash, young entrepreneurs who were the beneficiaries

---

14. Rosenzweig, Target Litigation, 85 Mich.L.Rev. 110 (1986).

15. Jarrell, The Wealth Effects of Litigation by Targets: Do Interests Diverge in a Merger?, 28 J.L. & Econ. 151 (1985).

16. See, e.g., Leebron, Games Corporations Play: A Theory of Tender Offers, 61

N.Y.U.L.Rev. 153 (1987); Haddock, Macey & McChesney, Property Rights in Assets and Resistance to Tender Offers, 73 Va.L.Rev. 701 (1987).

17. This assumes that auctions are desirable. But see note 10 supra.

of the 1960s "bull market" (which enabled firms with high price/earnings ratios to exchange their securities for the lower valued securities of target firms), the draft legislation was substantially modified during the Congressional hearings on the advice of the SEC.[1] Because of the concerns of a number of academic critics that a "strong" statute would entrench incumbent (and perhaps inefficient) management, the legislative history to the Williams Act displays a strong desire to "avoid tipping the balance of regulation in favor of management or in favor of the person making the takeover bid."[2] As a result, the Williams Act is avowedly neutral, but seeks to assist shareholder decision-making through a potpourri of disclosure provisions, antifraud rules, substantive regulations governing the conduct of tender offers, and a substantial grant of rulemaking authority to the SEC.

Organizationally, the Williams Act added Section 13(d) and (e) and Section 14(d)–(f) to the 1934 Act. Its principal provisions are briefly summarized below.

A. THE SECTION 13(d) TRIP WIRE

Essentially, § 13(d) mandates that a person or "group" who becomes the beneficial owner of more than 5 percent of a class of an equity security of a publicly held company must file a disclosure document (either a Schedule 13D or shorter document, known as a Schedule 13G, depending on the circumstances). In most cases, the person or group will be required to use a Schedule 13D, which must be filed within ten days after the purchase or act that crosses the 5 percent threshold. However, certain institutional investors who acquire "such securities in the ordinary course of [their] business and not with a purpose nor with the effect of changing or influencing the control of the issuer" may instead use a short-form statement, known as Schedule 13G, which need not be filed until within 45 days after the end of the calendar year (and only then if the investor or group continues to own 5% at year end).[3] Copies of either Schedule must also be transmitted to the relevant stock exchanges and the target company.

The instructions to Schedule 13D require the reporting person or group to disclose information approximating that which would have to be disclosed in a contested proxy fight: the identity and background of the party or group making the filing, the source of funding, the number of shares owned by them, any contracts or arrangements with respect to the shares and, most importantly, the purpose of the transaction (including whether it is to acquire control). If any "material" changes occur in any of the information so disclosed in Schedule 13D, Rule 13d–2 requires that the information be "promptly" updated. As a practical matter, the SEC usually interprets "promptly" in this context to mean within two business days.[4] Rule 13d–2 further indicates that an acquisition or disposition of 1% or more of the class will be deemed "material," and lesser acquisitions or dispositions may also be material depending on their

1. For a review of the legislative history of the Williams Act, see L. Loss & J. Seligman, 5 Securities Regulation (3rd ed. 1990) at 2163–2168.

2. S.Rep. No. 550, 90th Cong., 1st Session 3 (1967); see also Rondeau v. Mosinee Paper Corp., 422 U.S. 49, 58–59 (1975) (reviewing legislative history).

3. See Rule 13d–1(b)(1)(i).

4. In Securities Exchange Act Release No. 34–22171 (June 26, 1985), the Commission declined to specify a precise rule for determining whether an amendment was "prompt," but indicated that in the case of Schedule 13D "promptness" must be "judged * * * by the market's sensitivity to a particular change of fact triggering the obligation to amend * * *."

facts. In consequence, once a potential acquirer crosses the 5% threshold of a publicly held company subject to § 14(d), it must anticipate that it is entering a fishbowl of public disclosure in which its every action and possible motive will be subject to the close scrutiny not only by the target, but also by market professionals (the arbitrageurs or "arbs") who invest or speculate in takeover stocks.

Although technical issues abound under § 13(d), two policy issues stand out: First, do shareholders really benefit from the "distant early warning" system that § 13(d) establishes? Critics of the Williams Act argue that its true beneficiary is target management, which gains time to put takeover defenses in place or to find a white knight. Specifically, they argue that § 13(d) increases both the cost and risk of takeovers, and by lowering the bidder's expected return it may decrease the likelihood of a takeover bid being made in the first instance.[5] Conversely, others reply that, but for § 13(d), most of the gains from a takeover would be captured by the bidder, which could assemble a controlling position (without actually making a tender offer) by effecting slow, steady "creeping control" purchases in the open market that do not alert market professionals or potential other bidders. Thus, § 13(d) arguably achieves a "fairer" allocation of the gains between the bidder and the target's shareholders. However, there is also some evidence that the competitive character of the takeover market erodes away all gains for the bidder once it loses the benefit of secrecy.[6]

A second and independent criticism of the regulations underlying § 13(d) is their tendency to inhibit institutional investors from joining together to take collective action to resist corporate management. Suppose a half dozen institutions, each of whom owns 1%–2% of the common stock of a corporation subject to the Williams Act, wish to oppose a proposal by the corporation's management to adopt a "shark repellent" charter amendment or to award themselves lucrative "golden parachute" contracts. Collectively, these institutions (typically public pension funds) have no desire to lead a takeover or to oust management, but in the aggregate they may own well over 5% of a class. Must they file a Schedule 13D as a "group"? Under Rule 13d–5, when "two or more persons agree to act together for the purpose of acquiring, holding, *voting,* or disposing of equity securities of an issuer, the group formed thereby shall be deemed to have acquired beneficial ownership, for purposes of Sections 13(d) and 13(g) of the Act, as of the date of such agreement, of all equity securities of that issuer beneficially owned by any such persons" (emphasis added).[7] Recently, several commentators have suggested that § 13(d) contributes to the overregulation of institutional investors and deters them from greater involvement in corporate governance.[8]

B.   DISCLOSURE UNDER THE WILLIAMS ACT

Above all, the Williams Act is a disclosure statute, and § 14(d)(1) implements this purpose by requiring the bidder to prepare and file a disclosure

---

5. For a forceful statement of this perspective, see Macey & Netter, Regulation 13D and the Regulatory Process, 65 Wash.U.L.Q. 131 (1987).

6. See Black, Bidder Overpayment in Takeovers, 41 Stan.L.Rev. 597 (1989).

7. Interestingly, § 13(d)(3) does not refer to "voting," but only to a group formed "for the purpose of acquiring, holding, or

disposing." Do the SEC's rules overregulate here?

8. See Gilson & Kraakman, Reinventing the Outside Director: An Agenda for Institutional Investors, 43 Stan.L.Rev. 863 (1991); Black, Shareholder Passivity Reexamined, 89 Mich.L.Rev. 520 (1990).

statement with the SEC. Today, the document filed with the SEC is the Schedule TO, and it will include all prior communications sent by the bidder to security holders. The actual tender offer itself will be set forth in a separate document, incorporated within the Schedule TO, which will typically have earlier been summarized in a newspaper advertisement and mailed or sent to security holders who request it. Increasingly, it is a lengthy document, because most bidders believe it necessary to include their own financial statements in these documents. Although the case law provides few clear guidelines, it has indicated that such financial information may be material to a target shareholder in determining whether to tender (in part because the shareholder might decide that it was more attractive to remain as a minority shareholder under a new, more efficient management).[9] In 1977, the SEC amended Regulation 14D to state that financial information had to be included when it was "material."[10] This tautological advice hardly resolved the ambiguities, but the Release did point to several nonexclusive factors that the bidder should evaluate.[11]

Why should the bidder be required to make detailed disclosures about its own financial condition? Arguably, given the usual premium over the prior market price in a takeover, the investment decision for the target shareholder is as simple as deciding whether to exchange a $5 bill for a $10 bill. One answer to this claim may be that a tender offer can be only a partial bid, thus ensuring that most shareholders will continue to own some shares in the target after the tender offer is consummated. Another is that some shareholders may believe (or wish to determine) whether the offer is inadequate. Or perhaps, they believe that they will gain more from becoming minority investors in the target company under the bidder's new, presumably more efficient management. These theories are subject to powerful rejoinders: an efficient market should imply that it is desirable to accept a premium over the market, and target shareholders seldom have the opportunity to remain as minority shareholders under the new management, because the bidder usually merges out the nontendering shareholders through a squeeze-out merger within a year or two after the tender offer. Still, courts have reasoned that if all the shareholders were fully informed and knew the bidder's estimates of the value of the target's assets, they might reject the offer.

9. See Corenco Corp. v. Schiavone & Sons, Inc., 362 F.Supp. 939 (S.D.N.Y.1973), aff'd, 488 F.2d 207 (2d Cir.1973); Alaska Interstate Co. v. McMillian, 402 F.Supp. 532 (D.Del.1975); Copperweld Corp. v. Imetal, 403 F.Supp. 579 (W.D.Pa.1975).

10. Securities Exchange Act Release No. 5844 (July 21, 1977).

11. These included, without limitation: "(1) the terms of the tender offer, particularly those terms concerning the amount of securities being sought, such as any or all, a fixed minimum with a right to accept additional shares tendered, all or none, and a fixed percentage of the outstanding; (2) whether the purpose of the offer is for control of the subject company; (3) the plans or proposals of the bidder described in Item 5 of the Schedule; and (4) the ability of the bidder to pay for the securities bought in the tender offer and/or to repay any loans made to the bidder * * *." Id. For an intriguing case applying these criteria, see Prudent Real Estate Trust v. Johncamp Realty, Inc., 599 F.2d 1140, 1147 (2d Cir.1979) (noting differences between an "any and all" offer and a partial bid). *Johncamp Realty* reasoned that target shareholders might have a reason to be interested in the bidder's poor financial condition even in an "any and all" bid for fear that "control of the company might otherwise pass into irresponsible hands." *Query:* Would not disclosure of this information increase the pressure?

On this basis, some courts have held that "tender offer materials must disclose soft information, such as * * * asset appraisals based upon predictions regarding economic and corporate events," but they have limited this obligation to disclose projections and appraisals to circumstances where "the predictions underlying the appraisal are substantially certain to hold."[12] For bidders, this can be a substantial disclosure burden, particularly when their source of information may be speculative or out of date. Moreover, how far does this obligation to disclose the bidder's estimate of the target's potential value go? For example, could a court require a bidder to disclose its reservation or "walk away" price at which it would abandon its efforts to acquire control? This seems unlikely, but if this disclosure is not material, why should the law require disclosure of the projections and asset appraisals based upon which this bottom line price has been determined? Perhaps, the answer is that such disclosure will encourage new bidders to enter the fray, but is it appropriate to compel disclosure of proprietary information when the bidder owes no fiduciary duty to the target shareholders?

Another much debated disclosure issue arises when a bidder commences a tender offer without first obtaining firm financing for the funds necessary to pay for the shares. Although it is obviously necessary for the bidder to disclose its source and amounts of funds,[13] suppose the bidder discloses only that it has received a letter from its investment banker that the banker is "highly confident" that it can secure the financing before the time of acceptance.[14] In addition, suppose the tender offer is made conditional on the bidder's obtaining adequate financing by the end of the tender offer period. Courts have accepted such conditional offers on the theory that the Williams Act, as primarily a disclosure statute, only requires the bidder to disclose the information it knows and does not impose substantive restrictions, except those expressly set forth in the statute or the SEC's rules thereunder. On the other hand, an attempt by the bidder to withdraw its offer because it did not consider the financing terms available to it to be attractive might not fare as well, even if the bidder disclosed clearly that it was reserving the right to do so "in its sole discretion."[15]

Although some early takeover bids were enjoined on disclosure grounds, most federal courts have since heeded Judge Henry Friendly's admonition that courts should not "impose an unrealistic requirement of laboratory conditions that might make the * * * [Williams Act] a potent tool for incumbent management to protect its own interests against the desires and welfare of the stockholders."[16] As a result, courts today will rarely grant the target corpora-

---

12. Radol v. Thomas, 772 F.2d 244, 252–53 (6th Cir.1985); see also Flynn v. Bass Bros. Enterprises, Inc., 744 F.2d 978 (3d Cir. 1984).

13. Disclosure of this information is required by Item 7 of Schedule TO.

14. See Newmont Mining Corp. v. Pickens, 831 F.2d 1448 (9th Cir.1987), (permitting offer to proceed based on Drexel Burnham's "highly confident" letter). *Query*: What is the investment banker's liability if it proves to have been "overconfident" and cannot finance the offer?

15. Both the SEC and standard contract law tend to view "sole discretion" clauses as actually imposing an objective standard of reasonableness. The SEC's staff has informed bidders that any attempt to use a subjective "sole discretion" standard may be viewed as a material amendment of the offer, requiring its extension.

16. See Electronic Specialty Co. v. International Controls Corp., 409 F.2d 937, 938 (2d Cir.1969). See also, Susquehanna Corp. v. Pan American Sulphur Co., 423 F.2d 1075 (5th Cir.1970); Seaboard World Airlines, Inc.

tion more than a temporary injunction, halting the tender offer pending corrective disclosure, and almost never require the bidder to divest itself of shares already acquired (or to cease to vote them).[17]

Procedurally, the bidder has a choice as to how to disclose under the Williams Act. Under Rule 14d–4, it may choose either "long-form publication" or "summary publication." The former involves publication in a newspaper or newspapers of general circulation of the bidder's offer, which publication must set forth the full terms of its offer. The alternative of summary publication permits the publication of a "summary advertisement of the tender offer" plus a mailing of the full terms to each security holder who requests the full terms in response to the summary advertisement. This second approach is generally the more practical and less costly option. Under Rule 14d–6, summary publication can be quite concise and basically resembles a "tombstone" ad.

The target corporation is also subject to a disclosure obligation under the Williams Act. Rule 14d–9 provides that any person who solicits or makes a recommendation to shareholders in respect of a tender offer must file a Schedule 14D–9, which must basically disclose any conflicts of interest and also requires the target to disclose any recent or pending negotiations and transactions relating to the takeover bid in which the target company is engaged.[18] The obligation to file a Schedule 14D–9 cannot be avoided by the target management, because under Rule 14e–2, the target is required, no later than 10 business days from the date the tender offer is first published or sent, to give its security holders a statement disclosing its position on the offer (i.e., whether it recommends acceptance, rejection, or is unable to take a position). This statement must "also include the reasons for the position * * *." Because this mandatory Rule 14e–2 statement requires a recommendation, it in turn triggers the obligation to file a Schedule 14D–9.[19]

C. SUBSTANTIVE RULES

The Williams Act sets forth a rudimentary framework within which takeover contests must be conducted. For example, Section 14(d)(5) states that shareholders may withdraw their tendered shares either within the first seven days of the offer or after sixty days from its commencement. Similarly, Section 14(d)(6) requires bidders to prorate shares received during the first ten days of the offer if the offer is oversubscribed; for example, if the bidder tenders for 50% and all shares are tendered, then each tendering shareholder will have 50% of its shares accepted and 50% of its shares returned. Clearly, the purpose of these provisions is to reduce the pressure to tender on the shareholder.

---

v. Tiger International, Inc., 600 F.2d 355 (2d Cir.1979).

17. For decisions limiting the relief to corrective disclosure or refusing to grant damages (even to shareholders) for misstatements under § 13(d) or § 14(d), see Rondeau v. Mosinee Paper Corp., 422 U.S. 49 (1975); Dan River, Inc. v. Icahn, 701 F.2d 278 (4th Cir.1983) (reversing "sterilization" order); Florida Commercial Banks v. Culverhouse, 772 F.2d 1513 (11th Cir.1985) (appropriate remedy is corrective disclosure); Portsmouth Square Inc. v. Shareholders Protective Committee, 770 F.2d 866 (9th Cir.1985).

18. So long as an "agreement in principle" has not been reached, the target need not disclose the parties or terms if it believes this would "jeopardize" the negotiations. See Instructions to Item 7 to Schedule 14D–9. The failure of Allied Stores Corp., a target corporation, to disclose such defensive negotiations resulted in an important case, discussed infra, on an attorney's responsibilities under the federal securities laws. See In the Matter of George C. Kern, Jr., Securities Act Release No. 29356 (June 21, 1991).

19. Rule 14d–9(f) states this explicitly.

Absent a proration rule, bidders might announce a "first-come, first-served" policy on acceptance so that in a partial bid those who tendered after the first few days would likely have all their shares returned.

Although both §§ 14(d)(5) and 14(d)(6) of the Williams Act state "bright line" standards, their significance has been largely eclipsed by subsequent SEC rules that extend both the length of the tender offer and the period during which proration and withdrawal rights continue. Today, Rule 14e–1 requires a 20 business day duration for a tender offer, and Rule 14d–8 continues proration rights for the life of the tender offer. This raises an obvious question about the SEC's authority. If the Williams Act specifies a seven day withdrawal period and a ten day proration period, what authority does the SEC have to adopt rules requiring a longer duration or longer withdrawal or proration periods? The SEC's answer is that § 14(e) of the Williams Act authorizes the Commission to adopt rules "reasonably designed to prevent such acts and practices as are fraudulent, deceptive, or manipulative." Thus, although a seven day tender offer may not be inherently fraudulent, a rule requiring a 20–day period is still "reasonably designed" to prevent fraud and deception. The scope of the SEC's power in this area remains debatable and has never reached the Supreme Court. However, in Schreiber v. Burlington Northern, Inc.,[20] the Supreme Court held that § 14(e) does not prohibit manipulation unless there has been some element of deception through a material misrepresentation or omission. If so, where is the requisite deception in an openly disclosed seven day tender offer?

Before examining the SEC's rules in more detail, one other important consequence should be noted that follows from the SEC's decision to utilize § 14(e) as a basis for rulemaking. While § 14(d) applies only to equity securities registered pursuant to § 12 of the 1934 Act (and some miscellaneous exempt issuers), § 14(e) applies more broadly to all tender offers. Thus, tender offers for debt securities or for the equity securities of a privately held company are subject to the rules promulgated under § 14(e), but not those under § 14(d).

1. *Timing and Duration Rules.* Rule 14e–1(a) mandates that a tender offer be held open for at least 20 business days from the date the offer is first published, sent, or given to security holders. In addition, Rule 14e–1(b) requires that a tender offer be held open for an additional ten business days in the event of an "increase or decrease in the percentage of the class being sought or the consideration offered" (and also in the event of a change in the dealer's soliciting fee). Obviously, both rules are intended to reduce the pressure on shareholders to tender, and they also have the effect (whether or not intended) of giving the target additional time to find a "white knight" or to make its own counter-proposal.

Interpretive issues can arise under Rule 14e–1 as to whether clause (a) or clause (b) applies to a given transaction. For example, suppose a bidder announces a change from a 100% bid (usually referred to as an "any and all" tender offer) to a partial two-tier bid (which, it announces, will be followed by a squeeze-out merger at a lower cash price). Is this an amendment under Rule

20. 472 U.S. 1 (1985). But see Polaroid Corp. v. Disney, 862 F.2d 987 (3d Cir.1988) (upholding SEC's authority to promulgate Rule 14d–10, known as the "All Holders Rule," even though it was only tangentially related to ensuring complete disclosure).

14e–1(b) requiring only a ten business day extension, or a new offer requiring a twenty business day minimum period under Rule 14e–1(a)?[21]

In addition to these rules, the Commission has followed a policy of requiring that a minimum period of time remain in the offering period following any material change in the information received by investors.[22] Where the new information is disseminated by a press release that reaches the market generally, the Commission will typically deem five business days to be an adequate remaining period during which investors can evaluate the new information; otherwise, if the information is only mailed to shareholders, it may require ten business days. In one representative case, the SEC found that the waiver by the bidder of a minimum share condition in its offer was such a material change in information to require a five business day extension after dissemination of the information, even though the bidder did not increase or decrease the shares it sought so as to come within Rule 14e–1(b).[23]

An important timing rule governs the commencement of a tender offer: Under Rule 14d–1(a), a tender offer commences "on the date when the bidder has first published, sent or given the means to tender to security holders." Under prior rules, a pre-commencement announcement of an intent to commence a tender offer could actually start the statutory period running, but the SEC ultimately decided that this created too much of a trap for the unwary and now allows pre-commencement communications so long as the communication does not include a means for tendering the shares and such communication is eventually filed under cover of the Schedule TO.[24]

2. *Withdrawal and Proration.* Although § 14(d)(5) provides that shares tendered in a tender offer may be withdrawn during the first seven days of the offer, Rule 14d–7 overshadows this statutory provision by extending withdrawal rights for the life of the offer.[25] Similarly, § 14(d)(6) requires the bidder to prorate shares received during the first ten days if the offer is oversubscribed, but Rule 14d–8 extends the proration period throughout the life of the offer. One justification for these rules, which obviously rest on an uncertain jurisdictional foundation, is that without them the purpose of the twenty business day rule (Rule 14e–1(a)) would be frustrated, because in a partial bid if bidders could limit proration rights to the first ten days of the offer, then target shareholders would be under substantial pressure to tender within that time

---

21. See CRTF Corp. v. Federated Dept. Stores, Inc., 683 F.Supp. 422 (S.D.N.Y.1988) (finding ten day extension sufficient). *Query:* Would the result be the same if the offered consideration changed from cash to debentures? The SEC's staff has suggested that the 20 day period would be necessary in this case.

22. See Securities Exchange Act Release No. 34–23421 (July 17, 1986) and Securities Exchange Release No. 34–24296 (April 3, 1987).

23. See Securities Exchange Act Release No. 34–24296 (April 13, 1987).

24. See Rule 14d–2(b).

25. Rule 14d–7 does permit a bidder to curtail withdrawal rights during a "subsequent offering period," which it is permitted

to add onto its tender offer in order to receive additional shares. See Rule 14d–7(a)(2). For example, if a bidder obtains a majority of the shares in its tender offer, it may wish to add such an additional period to encourage shareholders who initially resisted its offer to now tender into this subsequent offering period at the same price. This both helps those shareholders who initially resisted and who may now wish to tender (rather than hold stock in a controlled and possibly illiquid company), and it allows the bidder to cross the threshold specified under state law (typically, 80%) at which it can do a short-form merger without a shareholder vote. The subsequent offering period may be from three business days to twenty business days and is governed by Rule 14d–11.

period (particularly if the bidder announced that it intended to follow up its partial bid with a squeeze-out merger at a lower price). To date, courts have upheld the validity of these rules.[26]

3. *Anti–Discrimination Rules.* Section 14(d)(7) sets forth the Williams Act's "best price" rule: each security holder is entitled to the best price paid to any other security holder pursuant to the tender offer. Thus, a shareholder who tenders into the initial offer at, for example, $23.50 per share must receive the higher price if the bidder subsequently increases its offer to $25. But what happens if the bidder accepts all shares at $23.50 and then, after the apparent conclusion of the tender offer, pays $25 per share to the largest shareholder who had held out and not tendered? A variant on this fact pattern arose in Field v. Trump,[27] where the bidder "withdrew" its offer at $22.50 per share, purchased at $25 per share the shares of a shareholder group that owned 18.4% of the target's stock and also held two seats on the target's board, and then reinstated its tender offer at a price of $23.50 per share. The Second Circuit found that the original tender offer at $22.50 and the later tender offer at $23.50 could be "integrated" into a continuous offer, because otherwise "successive tender offers interrupted by withdrawals * * * [could render] the 'best-price rule' * * * meaningless." Therefore, the bidder was required to purchase plaintiff's shares at the higher price. Still, the question remains: at what point should a bidder's post-tender purchase of target securities of the same class be sufficiently distant to escape integration?[28]

Two SEC rules protect the flanks of § 14(d)(7)'s "best price" rule. Rule 14d–10 (the "All Holders Rule") requires that a tender offer be open to all holders of the class. Thus, a bidder cannot limit its tender offer to a limited group (for example, institutional shareholders or target management). Of course, if the group is small enough and private purchases are individually negotiated, such a limited purchasing program will probably not amount to a "tender offer." Interestingly, Rule 14d–10 appears to have been adopted not in response to any abusive tactic by bidders, but to trump a defensive tactics by targets. In response to a hostile bid from Mesa Petroleum (which was controlled by Boone Pickens), Unocal Corp. made a discriminatory self-tender offer for its own shares at a price well above Mesa's offer, which self-tender was open to all shareholders, except Mesa Petroleum. This tactic was upheld by the Delaware Supreme Court,[29] but, although losing the battle, the SEC won the war by adopting Rules 14d–10 and 13e–4(f)(8).[30] In their wake, a discriminatory self-tender by a target is today unlawful, as federal securities law has effectively preempted a tactic that was permissible under state corporate law.

---

26. See Pryor v. United States Steel Corp., 794 F.2d 52 (2d Cir.1986) (proration rule valid and shareholders have private right of action to enforce it); Field v. Trump, 850 F.2d 938 (2d Cir.1988); Polaroid Corp. v. Disney, 862 F.2d 987 (3d Cir.1988) ("All Holders Rule" upheld).

27. 850 F.2d 938 (2d Cir.1988).

28. Should a court look to the six month safe harbor in Rule 502(a) of Regulation D with respect to the integration of successive sales of unregistered securities? Is this too long given the pace of takeovers? Or, does the obviously egalitarian purpose underlying § 14(d)(7) justify requiring such a time

frame before the parties can safely pay insiders more than other shareholders?

29. See Unocal Corp. v. Mesa Petroleum Co., 493 A.2d 946 (Del.1985).

30. Rule 13e–4 applies to issuer self-tenders, whereas Rule 14d–10 applies to tender offers by third parties. In Polaroid Corp. v. Disney, 862 F.2d 987 (3d Cir.1988), the SEC's authority to adopt Rule 14d–10 was upheld, but the Third Circuit found that the target corporation lacked standing to raise a violation of the rule on behalf of its shareholders.

Rule 14e–5 also enforces this same norm of equal treatment of target shareholders. Subsequent to some limited exceptions, Rule 14e–5 prohibits a bidder (or its affiliates or agents) from purchasing (or making arrangements to purchase) equity securities that are the subject of the tender offer otherwise than pursuant to the tender offer during the pendency of the offer. Once the offer commences, no private purchase can be arranged or consummated by the bidder with any shareholder.[31]

Issues have arisen about the William Act's "best price" and antidiscrimination rules in a variety of settings. For example, a bidder may make a tender offer, call it off, purchase shares in the open market at a price below the tender price, and then reinstate its tender offer. Can those who sold in the open market at a price below the tender offer price claim that these various steps should be integrated and that therefore they should get the higher tender offer price?[32] Even trickier problems arise when a target officer or a controlling shareholder receives some additional or different consideration that the other shareholders do not receive. What if this consideration was paid by the bidder in the form of an employment contract ostensibly intended to secure the officer's continued employment after the bidder took control of the target? Here, as the next case shows, the critical language in Rule 14d–10 that must be construed is its requirement that "the consideration paid to any security holder *pursuant to the tender offer* is the highest paid to any other security holder *during such tender offer*" (emphasis added).

Epstein v. MCA, Inc.

United States Court of Appeals, Ninth Circuit, 1995.
50 F.3d 644.

■ Before: Norris, Wiggins and O'Scannlain, Circuit Judges.

■ Norris, Circuit Judge:

In 1990, Matsushita Electrical Co., Ltd, ("Matsushita") acquired MCA, Inc. ("MCA") for $6.1 billion. The acquisition was accomplished through a tender offer of $71 per share of MCA common stock.

Lew Wasserman, MCA's chairman and chief executive officer at the time, owned 4,953,927 shares of MCA common stock worth $351,728,817 at the tender price of $71 per share. His cost basis was 3per share. Rather than tender his shares at the tender offer price, Wasserman entered into a separate agreement with Matsushita, known as the "Capital Contribution and Loan Agreement," pursuant to which Wasserman exchanged his shares for preferred stock in a wholly-owned Matsushita subsidiary called "MEA Holdings." Matsushita agreed to fund MEA Holdings by contributing 106% of the tender price multiplied by the number of MCA shares Wasserman exchanged. The MEA Holdings preferred stock Wasserman received pays a dividend of 8.75% annual-

---

31. Rule 14e–5 is a successor to a long-standing former rule, Rule 10b–13. A complicated question, which has never been fully resolved, involves who has standing to sue under that rule (besides the SEC). Compare Beaumont v. American Can Co., 797 F.2d 79 (2d Cir.1986) (non-tendering shareholder may not sue) and Warren v. Bokum Resources Corp., 433 F.Supp. 1360 (D.N.M. 1977) (tendering shareholders have cause of action). Rule 14e–5 does not bar purchases outside the tender offer during the subsequent offering period. See Rule 14e–5(a).

32. For the answer that they can indeed integrate these transactions, see Field v. Trump, 850 F.2d 938 (2d Cir.1988).

ly, is secured by letters of credit, and is redeemable upon the death of Wasserman or his wife, but in no event earlier than five years from the date of the exchange. Wasserman was 77 at the time. It is not disputed that the transaction was designed to be a tax-free exchange of Wasserman's MCA stock under Internal Revenue Code § 351(a) * * *. [Plaintiffs sued claiming that this transaction violated Rule 14d–10, the all holders/best-price rule. The Ninth Circuit first held that a private cause of action could be maintained for a violation of this rule and then turned to the facts of the Wasserman transaction.]

II. THE WASSERMAN TRANSACTION

Captioned the "Equal treatment of securities holders," Rule 14d–10 prohibits a bidder from making a tender offer that is not open to all shareholders or that is made to shareholders at varying prices. The gist of plaintiffs' claims is that Matsushita violated the antidiscrimination requirements of the Rule by paying Wasserman and Sheinberg [MCA's President—eds.] premiums pursuant to the tender offer.

Negotiations between Matsushita and MCA began in August 1990. When a representative of Matsushita telephoned MCA's financial advisor to express interest in acquiring MCA. During the course of the talks, Matsushita stressed that it wanted Wasserman and Sheinberg to commit their shares to Matsushita in advance of the friendly takeover and to remain in MCA's employment for five years. On the morning of November 26, 1990, Matsushita and Wasserman entered into the Capital Contribution and Loan Agreement, pursuant to which Wasserman agreed to exchange his MCA shares for preferred stock in a subsidiary Matsushita would create called "MEA Holdings."

Performance of the Capital Contribution and Loan Agreement was conditioned on the tender offer in several respects. First, neither Matsushita nor Wasserman was obligated to perform the Agreement if any of the conditions of the tender offer were not satisfied. *See* Capital Contribution and Loan Agreement § 7(c). If, for example, Matsushita did not acquire 50% of MCA's common stock as a result of the tender offer, the Wasserman deal would be off. Second, the timing of performance was tied to the tender offer. The Wasserman exchange was scheduled to take place "immediately following the time at which shares of MCA Common Stock are accepted for payment pursuant to and in accordance with the terms of the offer * * *." Id. § 2(a). Third, the amount of cash Matsushita was required to contribute in order to fund MEA Holdings was dependent upon the tender price, with Matsushita agreeing to contribute to MEA Holdings 106% of the "highest price paid * * * for any shares of MCA Common Stock, pursuant to the [tender] offer." Id. at § 1(c). Finally, the redemption value of Wasserman's preferred stock was set as the tender price. Id. Thus if Matsushita increased the tender price at the last minute in response to a competitive bid for MCA, Matsushita would have been required to increase both its funding of MEA Holdings and the amount paid upon the redemption of the Wasserman preferred stock.

Moments after signing the Capital Contribution and Loan agreement, Matsushita and MCA announced the $71 per share tender offer. Shareholders were given from the time of the announcement until 12:01 A.M. on December 29, 1990 to tender their shares. The owners of 91% of MCA's common stock did so, and at 12:05 A.M., Matsushita accepted all tendered shares for payment. At 1:25 A.M., Matsushita exchanged Wasserman's shares for MEA Holdings preferred stock pursuant to the Capital Contribution and Loan Agreement. MCA was merged into Matsushita as a wholly owned subsidiary on January 3, 1991.

Whether the Wasserman transaction violated rule 14d–10 depends upon whether Wasserman received greater consideration than other MCA shareholders "during such tender offer," Rule 14d–10(a)(2), or whether he received a type of consideration not offered to other MCA shareholders "in a tender offer." Rule 14d–10(c).

Matsushita argues that the Wasserman transaction falls outside the Rule's ambit because it closed *after* the tender offer period expired. The tender offer period, Matsushita contends, ended when it accepted the tendered MCA shares for payment—at 12:05 A.M. on December 29, 1990, one hour and 20 minutes before Wasserman's shares were exchanged. In Matsushita's view, liability under Rule 14d–10 boils down to a pure question of timing: the Rule is simply a "mechanical provision" concerned with "payments to shareholders of a target corporation only *during a specifically-defined tender offer period.*" Brief of Matsushita at 23 (emphasis in original). Outside that period, Matsushita insists, "Rule 14d–10 is without effect" because the Rule "is engaged (or not engaged) depending upon *when payment is made.*" Id. at 23, 35 (emphasis in original).

Although Matsushita argues that Rule 14d–10 is designed to operate only during a "specifically-defined tender offer period," neither the phrase "tender offer period" nor a specific time frame is to be found in the Rule's text. To be sure, section (a)(2) of the Rule prohibits paying one security holder more than another "during such tender offer." But the term "tender offer," as used in the federal securities laws, has never been interpreted to denote a rigid period of time. On the contrary, in order to prevent bidders from circumventing the Williams Act's requirements, Congress, the SEC, and the courts have steadfastly refused to give the term a fixed definition. Instead, we have held that "[t]o serve the purposes of the Williams Act, there is a need for flexibility in fashioning a definition of a tender offer." SEC v. Carter Hawley Hale Stores, Inc., 760 F.2d 945 (9th Cir.1985) * * *.

An inquiry more in keeping with the language and purposes of Rule 14d–10 focuses not on when Wasserman was paid, but on whether the Wasserman transaction was an integral part of Matsushita's tender offer. If it was, Matsushita violated Rule 14d–10 because it paid him, pursuant to the tender offer, different, and perhaps more valuable consideration than it offered to other shareholders.

Matsushita contends that the Wasserman transaction cannot be deemed a part of the tender offer because it was merely a private exchange of stock, structured to take place after the tender offer finished. But Matsushita's assumption that the Wasserman transaction was private, rather than a part of the tender offer, begs the question. In Field v. Trump, 850 F.2d at 944, the Second Circuit held that "[w]hether [an] acquisition of shares in a corporation is part of the tender offer for purposes of the Act cannot be determined by rubber-stamping the label used by the acquiror." To hold otherwise, the court stated, would render "virtually all of the provisions of the Williams Act, including its filing and disclosure requirements," subject to evasion "simply by an offeror's announcement that offers to purchase * * * stock were private purchases." Id. Thus, the court observed that because the Williams Act and its implementing regulations do not define the term "tender offer," "[c]ourts faced with the question of whether purchases of a corporation's shares are privately negotiated or are part of a tender offer have applied a functional test that scrutinizes such purchases in the context of various salient characteristics of tender offers and the purposes of the Williams Act." Id. at 943–44. *See also* SEC Release No. 34–22198, 1985 WL 61507, 1985 SEC LEXIS 1175, at *7 (July 1, 1985) ("'[T]he fact that * * * different consideration is offered to different holders of the same class of securities, does not mean that a tender offer has not been made under the Williams Act. Rather, if such a transaction is found to be a tender offer, then the tender offer would not have been made in compliance with the all-holders requirement'").

Because the terms of the Wasserman Capital Contribution and Loan Agreement were in several material respects conditioned on the terms of the public tender offer, we can only conclude that the Wasserman transaction was an integral part of the offer and subject to Rule 14d–10's requirements. Two facts compel this conclusion: first, the redemption value of Wasserman's preferred stock incorporated the tender offer price by reference, and second, the Capital Contribution and Loan Agreement was conditioned on the tender offer's success. If the tender offer failed, Wasserman would have remained the owner of his MCA stock. This is precisely the arrangement Matsushita made with its shareholders through its public tender offer: if an insufficient number of shares were tendered, each shareholder too would have retained ownership of her MCA stock. The deal Matsushita made with Wasserman thus differed from the tender offer in only one material respect—the type (and possibly the value) of consideration provided. Rule 14d–10(c)(1) forbids just such a transaction.

To be sure, the fact that a private purchase of stock and a public tender offer are both part of a single plan of acquisition does not, by itself, render the purchase a part of a tender offer for purposes of Rule 14d–10. Rule 14d–10 does not prohibit transactions entered into or effected before, or after, a tender offer—provided that all material terms of the transaction stand independent of the tender offer. Thus a bidder who purchases shares from a particular shareholder before a tender offer begins does not violate Rule 14d–10. See, e.g., Kahn v. Virginia Retirement System, 13 F.3d 110 (4th Cir.1993) (bidder's *unconditional* private purchase of target's shares two days before tender offer was formally announced did not violate section 14(d)(7) and rule 14d–10), *cert. denied,* 114 S.Ct. 1834, 128 L.Ed.2d 462 (1994).

If, in advance of the tender offer, Wasserman had become unconditionally obligated to exchange his MCA shares, the transaction would not have violated Rule 14d–10, even if Matsushita believed that acquiring Wasserman's shares was a first step in acquiring MCA. In such a case, both Wasserman and Matsushita would have assumed the burdens of their agreement despite the risk that an anticipated tender offer should fail, or command a different price. But such a course was not followed. Matsushita sought to acquire MCA *without* purchasing the holdings of individual shareholders block by block and accordingly subjecting itself to the risk that it would end up with a huge investment in MCA stock, but without control. The tender offer device is designed to avoid this risk, but only if holders of the same security are offered precisely the same consideration * * *.

Accordingly, we reverse the summary judgment in favor of Matsushita * * *, reverse the district court's order denying summary judgment that the Wasserman transaction did violate Rule 14d–10, and remand for further proceedings on the question whether the consideration Wasserman received in exchange for his MCA stock had a greater value than what plaintiffs received and, if so, how much greater * * *.

———

1. *MCA Distinguished.* The MCA case was reversed by the Supreme Court on unrelated grounds (a prior class action in Delaware Chancery Court was found to preclude it[1]). Even though the Supreme Court did not reach the issues of scope and standing under Rule 14d–10, at least one other appellate court has disagreed with the approach of the Ninth Circuit in its *MCA* decision and suggested a much narrower, more formalist reading of Rule 14d–10. In Lerro v. Quaker Oats Co.,[2] the Quaker Oats Company ("Quaker") offered $14 in cash for all the shares of Snapple Beverage Corporation (for a total of $1.7 billion). At least thirty-five percent of Snapple was owned by a single investor (Thomas H. Lee), and Quaker entered into a separate Distributor Agreement with a company controlled by him, which granted this company the exclusive right to distribute in certain Midwestern states certain Snapple and Gatorade products. Focusing on the expected profits under this agreement, plaintiffs contended that the agreement provided Mr. Lee with extra compensation in violation of Rule 14d–10 and § 14(d)(7) of the 1934 Act. Hence, a similar amount had to be paid, plaintiffs asserted, to every other security holder who tendered shares pursuant to the tender offer.

The district court dismissed this claim on the ground that because the distributorship agreement had been signed prior to the commencement of the tender offer, it fell outside Rule 14d–10, which applies only to "consideration paid to any other security holder during such tender offer."[3] The Seventh Circuit agreed, but did not limit its holding to this factual setting alone. Plaintiffs also contended that the tender offer and the merger were a single integrated transaction, and hence because the Distributor Agreement was conditioned on the merger's approval, it should be seen, they argued, as having been negotiated and closed as part of that integrated transaction. Such a rule, the Seventh Circuit responded, would "imperil countless ordinary transactions, * * * [including] simple employment agreements under which the surviving entity promises to employ managers for stated terms or give severance pay."[4] However, the Seventh Circuit opinion conceded that if an investor, such as Mr. Lee, were paid $14 during the tender offer along with other shareholders, but an additional $6 one month later, this "boot" could be treated as having been paid during the tender offer.[5]

Although the *Lerro v. Quaker Oats* decision thus acknowledges that a "boot" transaction (which it did not define) would fall within the proscription of Rule 14d–10, its basic approach is formalistic; under it, the key question is: did the shareholder sell shares in the period between the public announcement of the tender offer and its expiration or withdrawal? This approach may be criticized as underinclusive. For example, suppose a bidder pays the same

1. See Matsushita Electric Industrial Co. v. Epstein, 516 U.S. 367 (1996).

2. 84 F.3d 239 (7th Cir.1996).

3. See Lerro v. Quaker Oats Co., 897 F.Supp. 1131 (N.D.Ill.1995). Other courts have reached a similar result. See, e.g., Kramer v. Time Warner Inc., 937 F.2d 767, 778–79 (2d Cir.1991); Kahn v. Virginia Retirement System, 783 F.Supp. 266, 269–70 (E.D.Va.1992), aff'd on other grounds, 13 F.3d 110 (4th Cir.1993).

4. 84 F.3d 239, 244.

5. Id. at 245.

amount to all shareholders, but also pays the target CEO $5 million in cash for signing a noncompete agreement. These are the facts of *Gerber v. Computer Associates International, Inc.,*[6] but there the district court refused to dismiss the complaint, finding that the plaintiff had adequately alleged that the cash payment and the tender offer were "integral parts of a single plan."[7] While the *Gerber* district court thus followed the more liberal "integral part" test of the Second Circuit in *Field v. Trump* and the Ninth Circuit in *MCA*, this same case might have to be dismissed in the Seventh Circuit (unless its ambiguous "boot" exception applied). Before concluding that the Seventh Circuit's "bright line" standard is underinclusive, one needs to consider the problems that lurk in the more expansive, "integral part" tests of the Second and Ninth Circuits, as next examined.

2. *Overinclusion and Employment Agreements.* The "integral part" test may sweep very broadly if the bidder seeks to negotiate to retain target employees, even though these employees are incapable of meaningful resistance to the tender offer. In *Pererz v. Chiron Corp.,*[8] the bidder granted "put" options at the tender offer price to non-tendering, option-holding employees, thereby insulating them from any future decline in the target's stock price. Under *MCA*, this was, however, viewed as an "integral part" of the tender offer, and hence the action could not be dismissed. In *Gerber v. Computer Associates Int'l, Inc.,*[9] a payment made to the target's chief executive officer for signing a noncompete agreement was found by a jury to constitute additional compensation for his shares. While Gerber involved a chief executive officer whose 25% ownership seemingly controlled the company, the share ownership held by the officers in *Katt v. Titan Acquisitions*[10] was under 2%, and yet the district court still rejected a motion to dismiss a complaint that alleged that the acquirer's willingness to honor the target executives' employment agreements violated Rule 14d–10, even though the employment agreements had been adopted or amended by the target, itself, months before the tender offer when the target decided to put itself up for sale. Again, in *Millionerrors Investment Club v. General Electric Co.,*[11] the plaintiffs alleged that stock option awards to target executives by the target company were a bonus to be attributed to the bidder. Although plaintiffs seek to characterize such payments as bribes to induce the target executives not to oppose the offer, acquirers reply that effective resistance was not possible in many of these cases (because, for example, the target board had already decided to sell) and the bonuses or employment agreements were intended instead to retain critical executives without whom the acquirer would have difficulty running the company. Other decisions have accepted defendants' arguments, finding after fact-intensive analyses that the intent of the challenged payment was to compensate the employee for services, and not to provide a bonus for tendering,[12] but the legal uncertainty that has resulted has chilled the use of employment agreements in this context.

---

6. 812 F.Supp. 361 (E.D.N.Y.1993).

7. Id. at 364–66, 368.

8. 1996 U.S. Dist. LEXIS 22503 (N.D.Cal. May 8, 1996).

9. 303 F.3d 126 (2d Cir.2002). A key, but unstated, distinction between those cases that have imposed liability and those that have not appears to be the percentage of ownership held by the defendants. Obviously, persons holding only a 1% block cannot de-

termine the success of the tender offer, while those with a control block can and so may be able to command a premium.

10. 133 F.Supp.2d 632 (M.D.Tenn. 2000).

11. 2000 U.S. Dist. LEXIS 4778 (W.D. Pa. Feb. 8, 2000).

12. See, e.g., Harris v. Intel Corp., 2002 U.S. Dist. LEXIS 13796, 2002 WL 1758817 (N.D.Cal.2002) (finding deal bonuses, non-

The stakes in these cases are often enormous because of the "best price" rule. Given the damages inherent in Rule 14d–10, one commentator has recently observed that:

> "A claim that a 0.1% holder of a twenty billion dollar company received an extra five million dollars in compensation would carry damages of five billion dollars."[13]

As a result, some acquirers may be deterred from offering employment compensation and may even feel compelled to challenge option grants or agreements reached by the target board.

What compromises are possible that are neither overinclusive nor underinclusive? Payments made by the target company can be disregarded under a formalist approach on the grounds that such payments are neither "pursuant to the tender offer" or "paid . . . during the tender offer" within the language of Rule 14d–10(a)(2). (Typically, the plaintiffs reply that the bidder conspired with the target to divert the takeover premium to target shareholders or otherwise ratified the payment "during the tender offer.") A more economically sophisticated approach might be to assume that the rational bidder would only pay a bonus to the target executives or to other shareholders if it needed their shares (or their support) to make its tender offer successful. This was probably true in *MCA* (where the payments were to the CEO and the President of the target, who were also large shareholders), but in many other cases the executives who received employment agreements or stock options may have owned only 1% or less of the target's stock. Thus, one recent commentator has suggested the use of the following presumption: if the target executives own less than five percent of the target's stock, the bidder has no reason to divert the takeover premium to them in order to make its offer succeed, and hence such employment payments should be presumed to have been paid for legitimate employee retention motives and not "pursuant to the tender offer."[14]

3. *When does the Offer Commence?* Although there is some tension between the *Quaker Oats* and *MCA* decisions, their combined effect is to place great weight on Rule 14d–2(a), which defines when a tender offer commences. Because the Distributor Agreement and the Merger Agreement in *Quaker Oats* were signed on November 1, 1994 and the tender offer was announced on November 4th, defendants believed that they were in the clear. Plaintiffs contended that because the terms of the offer had already been communicated to Mr. Lee as of the time that he caused the Distributor Agreement to be signed, the offer had been commenced as of that earlier moment under Rule 14d–2(a)(5), which looks to the time "the tender offer is first published or sent or given to security holders by the bidder by any means not otherwise referred to in paragraphs (a)(1) through (a)(4) of this rule." The Seventh Circuit rejected this expansive theory, saying that under 14d–2(a)(5), one looked to the "definitive announcement, not negotiations looking toward an offer."[15] This result seems clearly correct, but it still underlines the enormous damages that could flow from the inadvertent or premature announcement of a tender offer, as it could trigger the application of Rule 14d–10 to agreements or payments

compete payments and severance payments not to have been intended to induce recipient executives of target to tender their shares).

13. See Note, Employment Agreements and Tender Offers: Reforming the Problematic Treatment of Severance Plans Under Rule 14d–10, 102 Colum. L. Rev. 774, 808 (2002).

14. Id. at 807.

15. Id.

that were intended to have been completed or paid prior to the offer's commencement.

4. *A Query.* Suppose, after announcing a tender offer, a bidder reaches a new deal with a corporation's leading shareholder to acquire its shares, and then follows this up by negotiating a merger with the board of the target at the same price. An agreement in principle is reached with the target's board, but the target board then accepts a better deal offered by a new bidder. The first bidder sues the second bidder for tortious interference with its contract rights, but the second bidder defends on the grounds that the first bidder's original agreement was unlawful because it violated Rule 10b–13. These are the facts of *Texaco, Inc. v. Pennzoil, Co.,*[16] in which the largest civil judgment in U.S. history (originally over $10 billion) was entered against Texaco (and largely upheld), despite Texaco's claim that Pennzoil had violated Rule 10b–13. Query: Should Texaco, as a rival bidder, have standing to assert a violation of Rule 10b–13?

D.   LITIGATION ISSUES

Litigation in takeover battles has gained a somewhat disreputable reputation, because the litigants often are seeking not a judicial victory, but one or more of several ulterior purposes: to harass their adversary, to gain a discovery "window" into their opponent's planning, or, at best, to require corrective disclosure that will delay the consummation of the offer.[1] In general, courts have recognized this tendency and tend to resist allowing courtroom battles to decide the outcome of a fundamentally economic contest.

Possibly as a result of a skeptical view of takeover litigation, courts have sometimes imposed significant obstacles on the private plaintiff seeking to enforce the Williams Act. First, as a matter of standing, the Supreme Court made clear in *Chris–Craft* that a bidder does not have a private right of action to sue for damages because it is not among those for whose "especial benefit" the statute was enacted.[2] Still, almost all courts have held that target shareholders have standing to assert violations and seek damages under § 14(d)(6) and 14(d)(7) of the Williams Act[3] and have similar standing to seek injunctive relief under § 13(d).[4] But they have resisted shareholder standing to seek damages or divestment under § 13(d).[5]

In the case of § 14(e), it is clear that the statute intentionally abolished the purchaser/seller requirement of *Blue Chip Stamps v. Manor Drug Stores.*[6] However, courts have disagreed on whether the plaintiff must still have relied

---

16.   729 S.W.2d 768 (Tex.App.1987).

1.   For a candid statement of these ulterior purposes by a leading takeover practitioner, see Wachtell, Special Tender Offer Litigation Tactics, 32 Bus.Law. 1433 (1977).

2.   Piper v. Chris–Craft Industries, Inc., 430 U.S. 1, 35 (1977).

3.   Polaroid Corp. v. Disney, 862 F.2d 987, 996–97 (3d Cir.1988); Field v. Trump, 850 F.2d 938, 946 (2d Cir.1988); Pryor v. United States Steel Corp., 794 F.2d 52, 57–58 (2d Cir.1986).

4.   Compare Florida Commercial Banks v. Culverhouse, 772 F.2d 1513 (11th Cir. 1985) (suit for equitable relief) and Liberty Nat. Ins. Holding Co. v. Charter Co., 734 F.2d 545 (11th Cir.1984).

5.   See Kamerman v. Steinberg, 891 F.2d 424 (2d Cir.1989); Sanders v. Thrall Car Mfg. Co., 582 F.Supp. 945 (S.D.N.Y.1983), aff'd, 730 F.2d 910 (2d Cir.1984). Shareholders who purchased at a relevant time period may, however, have a suit under Rule 10b–5 against a bidder who files a materially false Schedule 13D or Schedule 14D–1.

6.   421 U.S. 723 (1975).

on a misrepresentation or omission.[7] The more recent tendency is to permit a shareholder to recover based on a showing of causal injury, and not to require individual reliance; thus, proof that sufficient other shareholders were misled to approve the transaction suffices to show causation.[8] Another unique causation issue in the tender offer context arises when the bidder withdraws, or fails to commence, a tender offer because of allegedly false statements or deceptive conduct by the target or a rival bidder. Can shareholders sue the party whose misstatement caused the bidder to withdraw, claiming to have relied on its misstatement, even though they never had the chance to have their shares accepted? In *Panter v. Marshall Field & Co.*,[9] the Seventh Circuit found that a withdrawal by the bidder precludes reliance by the individual shareholder. Sound result?

Must the plaintiff prove scienter to establish a prima facie case under § 14(e)? On its face, § 14(e) so closely resembles § 17 of the 1933 Act as to suggest that scienter need not be proven with respect to alleged material misrepresentations or omissions. Nonetheless, most cases have read § 14(e) in pari materia with Rule 10b–5 and required scienter in damage actions.[10]

SECTION 2.   DEFINITIONAL ISSUES: GROUP, TENDER OFFER, AND BIDDER

A.   "GROUP" THERAPY

GAF Corp. v. Milstein

United States Court of Appeals, Second Circuit, 1971.
453 F.2d 709.

■ Before KAUFMAN and MANSFIELD, CIRCUIT JUDGES, and LEVET, DISTRICT JUDGE.

■ KAUFMAN, CIRCUIT JUDGE. This appeal involves the interpretation of section 13(d) of the Securities Exchange Act, hitherto a largely unnoticed provision[2] added in 1968 by the Williams Act. We write, therefore, on a relatively *tabula rasa,* despite the burgeoning field of securities law. Essentially, section 13(d) requires any person, after acquiring more than 10% (now 5%[4]) of a class of

---

7. Compare Lewis v. McGraw, 619 F.2d 192, 195 (2d Cir.1980) with Plaine v. McCabe, 797 F.2d 713 (9th Cir.1986).

8. See Plaine v. McCabe, supra note 7.

9. 646 F.2d 271 (7th Cir.1981). Prior to *Panter,* the Second Circuit held in Lewis v. McGraw, 619 F.2d 192 (2d Cir.1980) that fraud by the target company would not support an action under § 14(e) where its effect was to cause the bid never to have been made. *Panter* extends this holding to the case of an announced, but withdrawn, offer.

10. See Connecticut Nat. Bank v. Fluor Corp., 808 F.2d 957 (2d Cir.1987); see also Lowenstein, Section 14(e) of the Williams Act and Rule 10b–5 Comparisons, 71 Geo.L.J. 1311 (1983).

2. We are aware of only four other cases which considered the section. Bath Industries, Inc. v. Blot, 305 F.Supp. 526 (E.D.Wis.1969), aff'd, 427 F.2d 97 (7th Cir. 1970); Ozark Air Lines, Inc. v. Cox, 326 F.Supp. 1113 (E.D.Mo.1971); Sisak v. Wings and Wheels Express, Inc., CCH Fed.Sec. L.Rep. ¶ 92,991 (S.D.N.Y. Sept. 9, 1970); Grow Chemical Corp. v. Uran, 316 F.Supp. 891 (S.D.N.Y.1970). See generally Comment, Section 13(d) and Disclosure of Corporate Equity Ownership, 119 U.Pa.L.Rev. 853 (1971).

4. As of December 22, 1970, section 13(d)(1) was amended to require filing after the acquisition of 5%. Act of December 22, 1970, Pub.L. No. 91–567, § 1, 84 Stat. 1497, amending Securities Exchange Act § 13(d)(1), 15 U.S.C. § 78m(d)(1).

registered equity security, to send to the issuer and the exchanges on which the security is traded and file with the Commission the statement required by the Act. Although the section has not attracted as much comment as section 14(d), also added by the Williams Act and requiring disclosure by persons engaging in tender offers, the section has potential for marked impact on holders, sellers and purchasers of securities.

GAF Corporation filed its complaint in the United States District Court for the Southern District of New York alleging that Morris Milstein, his two sons, Seymour and Paul, and his daughter, Gloria Milstein Flanzer, violated section 13(d) of the Securities Exchange Act first by failing to file the required statements and then by filing false ones. The complaint also alleged violation of section 10(b) based on the same false statements and, in addition, market manipulation of GAF stock. The Milsteins moved for dismissal under Rule 12(b)(6), F.R.Civ.P., on the ground that the complaint failed to state a claim on which relief could be granted or, in the alternative, for summary judgment under Rule 56. Judge Pollack aptly framed the issues involved:

> The ultimate issue presented by the defendants' motion to dismiss the first count is whether, organizing a group of stockholders owning more than 10% of a class of equity securities with a view to seeking control is, without more, a reportable event under Section 13(d) of the Exchange Act; and as to the second count, whether in the absence of a connected purchase or sale of securities, the target corporation claiming violation of Section 10 and Rule 10b(5), has standing to seek an injunction against a control contestant for falsity in a Schedule 13D filing. (Footnote omitted.)

324 F.Supp. 1062, 1064–1065 (S.D.N.Y.1971). Judge Pollack granted the Milsteins' motion to dismiss under Rule 12(b)(6), and GAF has appealed. We disagree with Judge Pollack's determination that GAF failed to state a claim under section 13(d) and Rule 13d–1 promulgated thereunder, and thus reverse his order in this respect, but we affirm the dismissal of the second claim of the complaint on the ground that GAF, as an issuer, has no standing under section 10(b).

Before considering the merits of the issues involved on appeal, a statement of the facts as presented in the complaint and the briefs is in order. We note also that in this posture of the proceeding we must accept as true all well pleaded allegations in the complaint.

The four Milsteins received 324,166 shares of GAF convertible preferred stock, approximately 10.25% of the preferred shares outstanding, when The Ruberoid Company, in which they had substantial holdings, was merged into GAF in May, 1967. They have not acquired any additional preferred shares since the merger.

The complaint informs us that at some time after July 29, 1968, the effective date of the Williams Act, the Milsteins "formed a conspiracy among themselves and other persons to act as a syndicate or group for the purpose of acquiring, holding, or disposing of securities of GAF with the ultimate aim of seizing control of GAF for their own personal and private purposes." It is necessary for our purposes to examine only a few of the nine overt acts GAF alleged were taken in furtherance of this conspiracy.

The complaint alleged that initially the Milsteins sought senior management and board positions for Seymour Milstein with GAF. When this sinecure was not forthcoming, the Milsteins allegedly caused Circle Floor Co., Inc., a company in their control, to reduce its otherwise substantial purchases from GAF. It also charged that the Milsteins thereafter undertook a concerted effort to disparage its management and depress the price of GAF common and preferred stock in order to facilitate the acquisition of additional shares. On May 27, 1970, the Milsteins filed a derivative action in the district court, charging the directors, *inter alia,* with waste and spoliation of corporation assets. A companion action was filed in the New York courts. GAF further alleged that these actions were filed only to disparage management, to depress the price of GAF stock and to use discovery devices to gain valuable information for their takeover conspiracy.

In the meantime, the complaint tells us, Paul and Seymour Milstein purchased respectively 62,000 and 64,000 shares of GAF common stock. When GAF contended that the Milsteins were in violation of section 13(d) because they had not filed a Schedule 13D as required by Rule 13d–1, the Milsteins, although disclaiming any legal obligation under section 13(d), filed such a schedule on September 24, 1970. In their 13D statement (appended to the complaint), the Milsteins disclosed their preferred and common holdings and stated they "at some future time [might] determine to attempt to acquire control of GAF. * * * " They also stated that they had "no present intention as to whether or not any additional securities of GAF [might] be acquired by them in the future. * * * " Indeed, within the next two months, commencing with October 2, Paul and Seymour each purchased an additional 41,650 shares of common. The Milsteins thereafter filed a Restated and Amended Schedule 13D on November 10 to reflect these new purchases.

Then, on January 27, 1971, the Milsteins filed a third Schedule 13D, disclosing their intention to wage a proxy contest at the 1971 annual meeting. Although the statement again disclaimed any present intention to acquire additional shares, Paul purchased 28,300 shares of common stock during February, 1971. These last purchases, which brought the Milsteins' total common holdings to 237,600 shares having a value in excess of $2 million and constituting 1.7% of the common shares outstanding, were reflected in a February 23 amendment to the January 27 Schedule 13D.

The last essential datum for our purposes is the proxy contest. On May 10, 1971, it was announced that GAF management had prevailed at the April 16 meeting by a margin of some 2 to 1.

GAF's complaint in this action filed on December 16, 1970, requested that the Milsteins be preliminarily and permanently enjoined from (1) acquiring or attempting to acquire additional GAF stock; (2) soliciting any proxy from a GAF shareholder to vote GAF stock; (3) voting any shares of GAF stock held or acquired during the conspiracy; and (4) otherwise acting in furtherance of the conspiracy. It asks for this relief "until the effects of the conspiracy have been fully dissipated and the unlawful acts committed pursuant to the conspiracy fully corrected. * * * "

I.

At the time the conspiracy allegedly was formed, section 13(d)(1) in relevant part provided:

Any person who, after acquiring directly or indirectly the beneficial owner-ship of any equity security of a class which is registered pursuant to section 12 of this title * * *, is directly or indirectly the beneficial owner of more than 10 per centum of such class shall, within ten days after such acquisition, send to the issuer of the security at its principal executive office, by registered or certified mail, send to each exchange where the security is traded, and file with the Commission, a statement. * * *

This section, however, exempts from its filing requirements any acquisition which, "together with all other acquisitions by the same person of securities of the same class during the preceding twelve months, does not exceed 2 per centum of that class." Section 13(d)(6)(B). Section 13(d)(3), which is crucial to GAF's claim, further provides that "[w]hen two or more persons act as a partnership, limited partnership, syndicate, or other group for the purpose of acquiring, holding, or disposing of securities of an issue, such syndicate or group shall be deemed a 'person' for the purposes of [section 13(d)]." On the assumption that the facts alleged in the complaint are true, we cannot conclude other than that the four Milsteins constituted a "group" and thus, as a "person," were subject to the provisions of section 13(d). We also are aware of the charge that the Milsteins agreed after July 29, 1968, to hold their GAF preferred shares for the common purpose of acquiring control of GAF. Further-more, the individuals collectively or as a "group" held more than 10% of the outstanding preferred shares—a registered class of securities. Since the section requires a "person" to file only if he acquires more than 2% of the class of stock in a 12–month period after July 29, 1968,[12] the principal question presented to us is whether the complaint alleges as a matter of law that the Milstein *group* "acquired" the 324,166 shares of preferred stock owned by its members after that date. We conclude that it does and thus that it states a claim under section 13(d).

The statute refers to "acquiring directly or indirectly the beneficial owner-ship of securities." Thus, at the outset, we are not confronted with the relatively simple concept of legal title, but rather with the amorphous and occasionally obfuscated concepts of indirect and beneficial ownership which pervade the securities acts.

The Act nowhere explicitly defines the concept of "acquisition" as used in section 13(d). Although we are aware of Learned Hand's warning "not to make a fortress out of the dictionary," Cabell v. Markham, 148 F.2d 737, 739 (2d Cir.), aff'd, 326 U.S. 404 (1945), some light, although dim, is shed by Webster's Third International Dictionary. It tells us that "to acquire" means "to come into possession [or] control." If the allegations in the complaint are true, then the group, which must be treated as an entity separate and distinct from its members, could have gained "beneficial control" of the voting rights of the preferred stock[13] only after its formation, which we must assume occurred after the effective date of the Williams Act. Manifestly, according to the complaint, the group when formed acquired a beneficial interest in the individual holdings

---

12. The Milsteins concede that their group would have been required to file if the individual members had acquired additional preferred shares after the effective date of the Williams Act and within a 12–month peri-od which amounted to more than 2% of the outstanding shares.

13. The convertible preferred stock votes share-for-share with the common stock. Each share of preferred is convertible into 1.25 shares of common stock.

of its members. We find ourselves in agreement with the statement of the Court of Appeals for the Seventh Circuit in Bath Industries, Inc. v. Blot, 427 F.2d 97, 112 (7th Cir.1970), that in the context of the Williams Act, where the principal concern is focused on the battle for corporate control, "voting control of stock is the only relevant element of beneficial ownership." Thus, we hardly can agree with Judge Pollack that the language of the statute compels the conclusion that individual members must acquire shares before the group can be required to file.

We are well aware of the first catechism of statutory construction which teaches that we should begin the process of interpretation with "the language of the statute itself," see Jones v. Alfred H. Mayer Co., 392 U.S. 409, 420 (1968); that, however, is *toto caelo* from saying that the process must end there or that we are required to blind ourselves to other relevant aids to construction, particularly when dealing with a statute as complex as the one before us. The wisdom of Learned Hand guides us again: "it is one of the surest indexes of a mature and developed jurisprudence * * * to remember that statutes always have some purpose or object to accomplish, whose sympathetic and imaginative discovery is the surest guide to their meaning." Cabell v. Markham, supra, 148 F.2d at 739. See also United States v. Dickerson, 310 U.S. 554, 562 (1940). We are, therefore, totally puzzled by the experienced trial judge's conclusion that "the legislative reports should not be resorted to here since the specific statutory language is clear. * * * " 324 F.Supp. at 1067. Indeed, the statute before us is anything but a model of clarity[14] and the ritualistic approach to statutory interpretation which the district judge suggests would close off the only light available to illumine the statute.

The legislative history, as well as the purpose behind section 13(d), bear out our interpretation. Any residual doubt over its soundness is obviated by the following clear statement appearing in both the House and Senate reports accompanying the Williams Act:

> "[Section 13(d)(3)] would prevent a group of persons who seek to pool their voting or other interests in the securities of any issuer from evading the provisions of the statute because no one individual owns more than 10 per cent of the securities. *The group would be deemed to have become the beneficial owner, directly or indirectly, of more than 10 percent of a class of securities at the time they agreed to act in concert. Consequently, the group would be required to file the information called for in section 13(d)(1) within 10 days after they agree to act together, whether or not any member of the group had acquired any securities at that time.*" S.Rep. No. 550, 90th Cong., 1st Sess. 8 (1967); H.R.Rep. No. 1711, 90th Cong., 2d Sess. 8–9 (1968), U.S.Code Cong. & Admin.News p. 2818 (Emphasis added).

Indeed, Professor Loss, one of the foremost scholars of securities law, reached the same interpretation in his treatise, citing this passage. 6 L. Loss, Securities Regulation 3664 (Supp.1969).

---

14. The meaning of "acquiring" hardly could be considered plain when two district court judges recently failed to agree on whether an inheritance of stock was an "acquisition." Compare Sisak v. Wings and Wheels Express, Inc., CCH Fed.Sec.L.Rep. ¶ 92,991 (S.D.N.Y.1970), with Ozark Air Lines, Inc. v. Cox, 326 F.Supp. 1113 (E.D.Mo. 1971).

The Senate and House reports and the Act as finally enacted, contrary to appellees' contention,[15] are entirely consistent in our view. This conclusion is buttressed by a consideration of the purpose of the Act. The 1960's on Wall Street may best be remembered for the pyrotechnics of corporate takeovers and the phenomenon of conglomeration. Although individuals seeking control through a proxy contest were required to comply with section 14(a) of the Securities Exchange Act and the proxy rules promulgated by the SEC, and those making stock tender offers were required to comply with the applicable provisions of the Securities Act, before the enactment of the Williams Act there were no provisions regulating cash tender offers or other techniques of securing corporate control. According to the committee reports:

"The [Williams Act] would correct the current gap in our securities laws by amending the Securities Exchange Act of 1934 to provide for full disclosure in connection with cash tender offers and other techniques for accumulating large blocks of equity securities of publicly held companies." S.Rep. No. 550 at 4; H.R.Rep. No. 1711 at 4, U.S.Code Cong. & Admin.News p. 2814.

Specifically, we were told, "the purpose of section 13(d) is to require disclosure of information by persons who have acquired a substantial interest, or increased their interest in the equity securities of a company by a substantial amount, within a relatively short period of time." S.Rep. No. 550 at 7; H.R.Rep. No. 1711 at 8, U.S.Code Cong. & Admin.News p. 2818. Otherwise, investors cannot assess the potential for changes in corporate control and adequately evaluate the company's worth. See generally Comment, Section 13(d) and Disclosure of Corporate Equity Ownership, 119 U.Pa.L.Rev. 853, 854–55, 858, 865–66 (1971).

That the purpose of section 13(d) is to alert the marketplace to every large, rapid aggregation or accumulation of securities, regardless of [the] technique employed, which might represent a potential shift in corporate control is amply reflected in the enacted provisions. Section 13(d)(1)(C) requires the person filing to disclose any intention to acquire control. If he has such an intention, he must disclose any plans for liquidating the issuer, selling its assets, merging it with another company or changing substantially its business or corporate structure. It is of some interest, moreover, that section 13(d)(6)(D) empowers the Commission to exempt from the filing requirements "any acquisition * * * as not entered into for the purpose of, and not having the effect of, changing or influencing the control of the issuer *or otherwise* as not comprehended within the purpose of [section 13(d)]." (Emphasis added.)

The alleged conspiracy on the part of the Milsteins is one clearly intended to be encompassed within the reach of section 13(d). We have before us four shareholders who together own 10.25% of an outstanding class of securities and allegedly agreed to pool their holdings to effect a takeover of GAF. This certainly posed as great a threat to the stability of the corporate structure as the individual shareholder who buys 10.25% of the equity security in one transaction. A shift in the *loci* of corporate power and influence is hardly dependent on an actual transfer of legal title to shares, and the statute and history are clear on this.

---

15. Appellees in their brief "concede" that the 1968 committee reports are "against" them. Professor Loss, co-counsel for the Milsteins both in this and the lower court, informed us at the argument that the view set forth in his treatise was "a mistake" and that this passage is "diametrically opposed to the text of the statute" and the purpose and intent of the Williams Act.

In light of the statutory purpose as we view it, we find ourselves in disagreement with the interpretation of *Bath Industries,* supra, that the group owning more than 10%, despite its agreement to seize control, in addition, must agree to acquire more shares before the filing requirement of section 13(d) is triggered. The history and language of section 13(d) make it clear that the statute was primarily concerned with disclosure of *potential changes* in control resulting from new aggregations of stockholdings and was not intended to be restricted to only individual stockholders who made future purchases and whose actions were, therefore, more apparent.[18] See Comment, Section 13(d) and Disclosure of Corporate Equity Ownership, 119 U.Pa.L.Rev. 853, 869–72 (1971). It hardly can be questioned that a group holding sufficient shares can effect a takeover without purchasing a single additional share of stock.

Two "policy" considerations have been advanced against our interpretation. First, the district judge warned that "[t]he inherent difficulty of ascertaining when a group was formed is akin to an attempt to grasp quicksilver." 324 F.Supp. at 1068. This supposed difficulty, however, would not be dissipated even under his view—that individual members must acquire more than 2% after July 29, 1968, before the group can be compelled to file. The court still would be required to determine whether the individuals indeed constituted a "group." But, we hardly envision this as an insuperable obstacle to stating a claim in a complaint. GAF, in order to succeed on the merits, will have to carry its burden of proof by a fair preponderance of the evidence. It will have to produce evidence establishing that the conspiracy came into being after July 29, 1968, with the purpose of seizing control. If GAF should succeed on the merits, any difficulty in pinpointing the precise date, as distinguished from an approximate time, when the conspiracy was formed and the group became subject to section 13(d) can be one of the elements considered by the district judge in fashioning appropriate equitable relief.

The Milsteins also caution us against throwing our hook into the water and catching too many fish—namely, hundreds of families and other management groups which control companies with registered securities and whose members collectively own more than 5% of a class of the company's stock. Although this problem is not part of the narrow issue we must decide, we cannot close our eyes to the implications of our decision. Upon examination, however, the argument while superficially appealing proves to be totally without substance. Management groups *per se* are not customarily formed for the purpose of "acquiring, holding, or disposing of securities of [the] issuer" and would not be required to file unless the members conspired to pool their securities interests for one of the stated purposes.[20]

It is not sufficient that we merely conclude that the allegations of the complaint state a violation of section 13(d). We also must determine whether

---

18. Section 13(d)(3) refers to groups formed "for the purpose of acquiring, holding, *or* disposing of securities." Bath Industries would read out "holding" and "disposing."

20. The more difficult question, and a question we need not decide on this appeal, is whether management groups which expressly agree to pool their interests to fight a poten-

tial takeover are subject to section 13(d). Nor do we intimate any view on whether an insurgent group which has filed under section 13(d) and subsequently is successful in its takeover bid remains subject to the section. In any event, as we have already indicated, the Commission can forestall any untoward effects under the exemptive power conferred upon it by section 13(d)(6)(D).

GAF has standing to assert those violations. Here, unlike in our prior discussion we write with the aid of substantial precedent.

The Milsteins do not contend, with good reason, that there is no private right of action under section 13(d). The teachings of J.I. Case Co. v. Borak, 377 U.S. 426 (1964), are part of the ABC's of securities law. Nor do the Milsteins challenge the standing of GAF as an issuer.[21]

* * *

III.

The more difficult question is whether GAF has standing under section 13(d) to seek an injunction against allegedly false and misleading filings. The Milsteins in their brief argue that "the short answer" is that false filing does not violate the section that requires the filing—i.e., section 13(d)—but rather the penal provision on false filings, section 32(a), or one of the antifraud provisions, for example, section 10(b). This response, deceptively pleasing in its simple, compartmental approach to the Securities Exchange Act, immediately brings to mind the Supreme Court's instruction that the securities acts should not be construed technically and restrictively, but "flexibly to effectuate [their] remedial purposes." S.E.C. v. Capital Gains Research Bureau, Inc., 375 U.S. 180, 195 (1963). With this teaching in mind, we conclude that the obligation to file *truthful* statements is implicit in the obligation to file with the issuer, and *a fortiori,* the issuer has standing under section 13(d) to seek relief in the event of a false filing.

The Williams Act was entitled "An Act Providing for full disclosure of corporate equity ownership of securities under the Securities Exchange Act of 1934." In particular, section 13(d) was intended to alert investors to potential changes in corporate control so that they could properly evaluate the company in which they had invested or were investing. Disclosure which is false or misleading subverts this purpose. In some instances, a false filing may be more detrimental to the informed operation of the securities markets than no filing at all. We also find support for our conclusion in section 13(d)(2) which places a continuing obligation on the person filing to amend his statements "[i]f any material change occurs in the facts set forth." Indeed, it is an argument not without force to urge that false statements immediately place those required to file in violation of Rule 13d–2 which requires "prompt" amendment.[23]

* * *

In reversing that part of Judge Pollack's order which dismissed Claim I of GAF's complaint on the ground that it failed to state a claim on which relief could be granted, we emphasize that we are not yet called upon to determine whether the Milsteins have in fact violated section 13(d), or, if they have, what relief would be appropriate. That part of Judge Pollack's order dismissing

21. Clearly, a shareholder has standing. See Grow Chemical Corp. v. Uran, 316 F.Supp. 891 (S.D.N.Y.1970).

23. GAF informs us that the Milsteins' first Schedule 13D, dated September 24, 1970, was false because it disclaimed any present intention to acquire additional stock, whereas Paul and Seymour Milstein purchased 83,800 shares of GAF common stock within the next two months. The Milsteins, however, did not amend their Schedule 13D until after these purchases were completed. Thus, even assuming that the statement filed on September 24 accurately and truthfully reflected their intentions, clearly those intentions changed when the Milsteins decided to make the additional purchases and before those purchases were actually completed.

Claim II of the complaint under section 10(b) is affirmed. Costs to the appellant.

What Makes a Group? Today, Rule 13d–5 goes beyond the statutory language in § 13(d)(3) quoted in *GAF* to state that a "group" arises "[w]hen two or more persons agree to act together for the purpose of acquiring, holding, *voting*, or disposing of equity securities" (emphasis added). No reference to "voting" appears in § 13(d)(3), which speaks only of "acquiring, holding or disposing." Should voting together be treated the same as acquiring or holding together? Does this chill, for example, the willingness of mutual and pension funds to join together to vote against a management proxy proposal that they consider ill-advised? Of course, the impact of Rule 13d–5 depends on the sanctions available for its violation. In that light, see *SEC v. First City Financial Corp., Ltd.*, infra, p. 771.

In *Wellman v. Dickinson*,[1] the Second Circuit focused on the word "disposing" in § 13(d)(3) and held that five target company shareholders became a "group" when they reached an understanding under which they agreed to sell their stock if a third party could be found to make a takeover proposal for their company. Their unsuccessful defense was that there had been no understanding or agreement on any specific set of terms or any specific takeover proposal, but only a collective willingness to "go with the deal." Is the desire to find a lucrative bidder the same as a purpose to dispose?

In *Portsmouth Square Inc. v. Shareholders Protective Committee*,[2] a committee of shareholders, who solicited funds from other shareholders by requesting an assignment of their dividends in order to fund litigation to challenge the conduct of insiders who had just effected a change in control of the corporation, were found not to be a "group" under § 13(d). Although their "grouphood" was clear in terms of their level of organization, they lacked the requisite purpose of "acquiring, holding, voting or disposing" in common, as their goal was instead to sue in common. The court stated that their agreement to act together "invoked neither voting power nor investment power" (referring to the twin tests under Rule 13d–3(a)).

Purpose. Suppose a "group" says that it is holding securities "for investment purposes," but it is in fact considering and evaluating a range of options. Item 4 to Schedule 13D requires the reporting person to state the "purpose of the acquisition of securities" and then lists a variety of specific transactions (sales, changes in dividend policy, or changes in board composition, etc.) that must be disclosed if the reporting person has "plans or proposals * * * which relate to" them. In *K–N Energy, Inc. v. Gulf Interstate Corp.*,[3] the court held the claim that a group was holding "for investment purposes" to be materially false when the evidence indicated that it was in fact seeking to influence corporate affairs. Again, does this doctrine provide management with a weapon by which to threaten and silence dissident or activist shareholders who seek to persuade management to change corporate policy?

Conversely, in *SEC v. Amster & Co.*,[4] the district court granted summary judgment against the SEC where it had brought an injunctive action against

---

1. 682 F.2d 355 (2d Cir.1982).   **3.** 607 F.Supp. 756 (D.Colo.1983).

2. 770 F.2d 866, 874 (9th Cir.1985).   **4.** 762 F.Supp. 604 (S.D.N.Y.1991).

arbitrageurs who took a position in Graphic Scanning Corp. and characterized their investment in their Schedule 13D as being "for the purpose of making an investment in the Company and not with the present intention of acquiring control. * * *" The SEC charged that defendants later abandoned their investment intent, but failed to amend Item 4 of their Schedule 13D promptly to reflect their new intent to acquire control. Rejecting the SEC's claim that "§ 13(d) requires disclosure whenever 'the securities purchaser has a perceptible desire to influence substantially the issuer's operations' " the court concluded that such a "desire" does rise to level of a "control" purpose that must be disclosed by an amendment to the Schedule 13D. A mere "desire" to influence operations was insufficient, it said, adding: "If the hot air balloon of desire is separated from the ballast of control purpose or intent, it is free to soar wherever an advocate's winds may blow. * * * [T]he reporting of desires not yet transformed into purpose or intent could mislead investors in manners contrary to the statute's purpose. To change the metaphor, the SEC argues for a 13(d) *Streetcar Named Desire*. I do not think that streetcar runs." Although the *Amster* decision may (or may not) signal a shift in the winds of judicial opinion, earlier decisions do seem to have required disclosure of a control purpose whenever the reporting person took any significant step to influence the issuer (or began to prepare to launch a proxy fight or tender offer). See *Chromalloy American Corp. v. Sun Chemical Corp.*, 611 F.2d 240, 246–47 (8th Cir.1979); *Dan River, Inc. v. Unitex Ltd.*, 624 F.2d 1216, 1226 n. 9 (4th Cir.1980). Should the SEC's proposed "perceptible desire to influence substantially the issuer's operations" be the test of "grouphood"? Note that Item 4 to Schedule 13D also requires reporting persons to disclose any plans or proposals which "relate to or would result in" a change of control, apparently regardless of whether the reporting person has a control purpose. Focusing on this language, the SEC's staff has suggested that even contingent plans may have to be disclosed. Is this a practicable standard for disclosure policy? Would the *Amster* court buy it?

Securities and Exchange Commission v. First City Financial Corp., Ltd.

United States Court of Appeals, District of Columbia Circuit, 1989.
890 F.2d 1215.

■ Before EDWARDS, GINSBURG and SILBERMAN, CIRCUIT JUDGES.

■ SILBERMAN, CIRCUIT JUDGE.

Section 13(d) of the Securities Exchange Act of 1934, 15 U.S.C. § 78m(d), requires any person who has directly or indirectly obtained the beneficial ownership of more than 5 percent of any registered equity security to disclose within 10 days certain information to the issuer, the exchanges on which the security trades, and to the Securities and Exchange Commission ("SEC"). The SEC charged appellants, First City Financial Corporation, Ltd. ("First City") and Marc Belzberg, with deliberately evading section 13(d) and its accompanying regulations in their attempted hostile takeover of Ashland Oil Company ("Ashland") by filing the required disclosure statement after the 10 day period. The district court concluded that appellants had violated the statute; it then enjoined them from further violations of section 13(d) and ordered them to disgorge all profits derived from the violation. See *SEC v. First City Financial Corp., et al.* 688 F.Supp. 705 (D.D.C.1988). * * *

I.

The SEC's case is based on its contention that on March 4, 1986 Marc Belzberg, a vice-president of First City, telephoned Alan ("Ace") Greenberg, the Chief Executive Officer of Bear Stearns, a large Wall Street brokerage firm, and asked Greenberg to buy substantial shares of Ashland for First City's account. Appellants claim that Greenberg "misunderstood" Belzberg: the latter intended only to recommend that Bear Stearns buy Ashland for its own account.

* * *

[O]n March 4, Marc Belzberg telephoned Greenberg and engaged him in a short conversation that would be the centerpiece of this litigation. At his deposition, Greenberg described the conversation in the following manner:

> [Marc Belzberg] called me and said something to the effect that—something like, "It wouldn't be a bad idea if you bought Ashland Oil here," or something like that. And I took that to mean that we were going to do another put and call arrangement that we had done in the past. * * * I was absolutely under the impression I was buying at their risk and I was going to do a put and call.[4]

While Greenberg interpreted Marc Belzberg's call as an order to purchase Ashland stock on behalf of First City, Marc Belzberg later claimed that he intended only to recommend that Greenberg buy stock for himself, that is, for Bear Stearns, and that Greenberg apparently misunderstood Belzberg. Immediately after the phone call, Greenberg purchased 20,500 Ashland shares. If purchased for First City, those shares would have pushed First City's Ashland holdings above 5 percent and triggered the beginning of the 10 day filing period of section 13(d). In that event, First City would have been obliged to file a Schedule 13D disclosure statement on March 14 with the SEC.

Between March 4 and 14, Greenberg purchased an additional 330,700 shares of Ashland stock for First City costing more than $14 million. Greenberg called Marc Belzberg periodically during those ten days to discuss various securities, including Ashland. In these conversations, Greenberg reported to Marc Belzberg the increasing number of Ashland shares Greenberg had accumulated. According to Greenberg, Belzberg replied to these reports by saying, " 'Fine, keep going,' or something to that effect." Greenberg also characterized Belzberg's response as "grunt[ing]" approvingly. Belzberg did not squarely deny that testimony; he testified that he, Belzberg, said "uh-huh, I think it's cheap." Over the March 15–16 weekend, Marc Belzberg met with his father and uncles in Los Angeles to discuss Ashland. On Sunday, March 16, Samuel Belzberg decided that First City should continue to buy Ashland stock. Marc Belzberg then advised his father that Greenberg had accumulated a block of Ashland shares that "First City could acquire quickly." Samuel Belzberg later testified that he had no prior knowledge of the Greenberg purchases.

---

4. Large investors sometimes purchase stock through "put and call agreements." Under these agreements, a broker such as Bear Stearns would purchase the stock subject to the agreement and place it in its own account. The agreement entitles the investor to "call" or purchase the shares from the broker for an agreed upon period at an agreed upon price, the cost to the broker plus interest and a small commission. At the same time, the broker has the right to "put" or sell the shares to the investor at the same price. As a result, the investor rather than the broker bears all of the market risks in buying the stock. The put and call agreements were developed apparently in response to the pre-merger notification requirements of the Hart–Scott–Rodino Act.

Returning to New York the next morning, March 17, Marc Belzberg called Greenberg and arranged a written put and call agreement for the 330,700 shares Bear Stearns had accumulated. During that conversation, Marc Belzberg did not mention a price to Greenberg. Several days later, Marc Belzberg received the written agreement with a "strike price," or the price Bear Stearns was charging First City, of $43.96 per share. This price was well below the then market price of $45.37; thus, the total March 17 put and call price was almost $500,000 below market. Marc Belzberg apparently expressed no surprise that Bear Stearns was charging almost half a million dollars less than market value. He later testified that he believed that Bear Stearns was acting as a "Santa Claus" and that Greenberg was giving him "a bit of a break" to gain more business from First City in the future.

When Blumenstein, the officer responsible for ensuring First City's compliance with the federal securities laws, noticed the strike price, he immediately met with Marc Belzberg. Blumenstein recognized that the computation of the price reflected only the cost to Bear Stearns of acquiring the stock over the two week period before the written agreement (plus interest and commission), thus creating an inference that First City was the beneficial owner of the securities before March 17. After Blumenstein outlined the problem to Belzberg, the two men called Greenberg on a speakerphone. Belzberg later testified, "I informed Mr. Greenberg [during that conversation] that the letter [the written agreement] was incorrect, that I didn't care what the price of the stock was that he bought for himself, I didn't care what day he made the trades for himself, that I was buying stock from him as of today." Belzberg then testified that Greenberg said, "[Y]ou're right, the letter's wrong, I didn't read it before it went out, throw it out and I will send you a corrected copy." Greenberg, however, testified that Belzberg referred only to an error in the calculation of interest and not to the date on which First City acquired the stock. At the end of the conversation, Belzberg suggested he pay $44.00 per share, 4 cents per share higher than the original strike price but still $1.36, or a total of nearly $450,000, below the market price. At trial, Belzberg admitted to picking the $44 figure "out of the air" and that he "did not want the price [he] was paying to relate to [Greenberg's] cost." Between March 17 and 25, on Marc Belzberg's instructions, Greenberg bought another 890,100 Ashland shares on behalf of First City using several put and call agreements.

After these purchases, Samuel Belzberg sent a letter to Ashland's management, informing them of First City's holdings in their stock and proposing a friendly takeover of the company. Ashland rejected the offer, and on the morning of March 25 the company issued a press release disclosing that First City held between 8 and 9 percent of Ashland's stock. Almost immediately, the price of Ashland stock rose 10 percent to $52.25. The next day, on March 26, First City filed the Schedule 13D disclosure statement required by section 13(d). The statement indicated that First City had accumulated 9 percent of Ashland stock and intended to launch a tender offer for the remaining shares at $60 per share. The market price of Ashland stock then rose to $55, peaking at $55.75 per share the next day. * * *

The district court found that Marc Belzberg and First City entered into an informal put and call agreement on March 4 and then deliberately violated the 10 day filing requirement of section 13(d). The district court, in an extensive opinion, relied primarily on First City's acknowledged ultimate purpose to take over Ashland, Greenberg's understanding of his March 4 telephone conversation with Marc Belzberg, the subsequent conversations between Belzberg and Greenberg, and the suspicious price of the March 17 written agreement. The court discounted Marc Belzberg's "misunderstanding" explanation as "self-serving, inconsistent with his later actions and [not] squar[ing] with the objective evidence." 688 F.Supp. at 712. Belzberg, to put it bluntly, was not credited. The court also refused to consider Greenberg's later testimony that there might have been an "honest misunderstanding" since Greenberg reached that conclusion based only on Belzberg's suggestions and statements. See id. at 720.

The district court permanently enjoined appellants from future violations of section 13(d) because they violated the statute deliberately, showed no "remorse," and were engaged in a business which presented opportunities to violate the statute in the future. See id. at 725–26. The court also ordered appellants to disgorge approximately $2.7 million, representing their profits on the 890,000 shares of Ashland stock acquired between March 14 and 25. The court reasoned that appellants were able to purchase these shares at an artificially low price due to their failure to make the section 13(d) disclosure on March 14. See id. at 726–28. Appellants appeal the district court's finding of violation as unsupported by the evidence and a product of judicial bias. They further contend that the district court abused its discretion in ordering the injunction and disgorgement remedies.

II.

A shareholder must comply with the section 13(d) disclosure law if he beneficially owns 5 percent of a public company's equity securities. Under Commission Rule 13d–3(a), whenever a person possesses investment or voting power through any agreement or understanding, he enjoys beneficial ownership. Rule 13d–3 is crafted broadly enough to sweep within its purview informal, oral arrangements that confer upon a person voting or investment power. See SEC v. Savoy Indus., Inc., 587 F.2d 1149, 1163 (D.C.Cir.1978), cert. denied, 440 U.S. 913, 99 S.Ct. 1227, 59 L.Ed.2d 462 (1979); see also Wellman v. Dickinson, 682 F.2d 355, 363–67 (2d Cir.1982), cert. denied, 460 U.S. 1069, 103 S.Ct. 1522, 75 L.Ed.2d 946 (1983). Appellants concede that a put and call agreement, even if informal, constitutes beneficial ownership to the investor of the stock subject to the agreement.

The case before the district court turned on the question whether the put and call agreement between First City and Bear Stearns was entered into on March 4, as the SEC claims, or not until March 17 as First City argues. That issue, of course, is a question of fact (or of mixed fact and law), the district court's answer to which normally may not be overturned on appeal unless clearly erroneous. * * *

IV.

The district court directed disgorgement of profits, and appellants' challenge to this aspect of the order presents an issue of first impression—whether federal courts have the authority to employ that remedy with respect to section 13(d) violations and whether it is appropriate in this sort of case. Appellants also claim that the amount ordered disgorged is excessive. We reject both arguments and affirm the district court's order on these issues as well.

Appellants, by claiming that Congress did not explicitly authorize a monetary remedy for section 13(d) violations, misapprehend the source of the court's authority. Disgorgement is an equitable remedy designed to deprive a wrong-doer of his unjust enrichment and to deter others from violating the securities laws. See SEC v. Tome, 833 F.2d 1086, 1096 (2d Cir.1987), cert. denied, 486 U.S. 1014, 108 S.Ct. 1751, 100 L.Ed.2d 213 (1988); SEC v. Blavin, 760 F.2d 706, 713 (6th Cir.1985); SEC v. Texas Gulf Sulphur Co., 446 F.2d 1301, 1307 (2d Cir.), cert. denied, 404 U.S. 1005, 92 S.Ct. 561, 30 L.Ed.2d 558 (1971). "Unless otherwise provided by statute, all the inherent equitable powers of the District Court are available for the proper and complete exercise of that jurisdiction." Porter v. Warner Holding Co., 328 U.S. 395, 398, 66 S.Ct. 1086, 1089, 90 L.Ed. 1332 (1946); see also Mitchell v. Robert DeMario Jewelry, Inc., 361 U.S. 288, 291–92, 80 S.Ct. 332, 334–35, 4 L.Ed.2d 323 (1960). We see no indication in the language or the legislative history of the 1934 Act that even implies a restriction on the equitable remedies of the district courts. See Mills v. Electric Auto–Lite Co., 396 U.S. 375, 391, 90 S.Ct. 616, 625, 24 L.Ed.2d 593 (1970). Disgorgement, then, is available simply because the relevant provisions of the Securities Exchange Act of 1934, sections 21(d) and (e), 15 U.S.C. §§ 78u(d) and (e), vest jurisdiction in the federal courts.

Indeed, appellants concede that disgorgement is rather routinely ordered for insider trading violations despite a similar lack of specific authorizations for that remedy under the securities law. See, e.g., SEC v. Tome, 833 F.2d at 1096; SEC v. Materia, 745 F.2d 197, 201 (2d Cir.1984); see generally L. Loss, Fundamentals of Securities Regulation 1004–11 (1988). But they seek to distinguish section 13(d) violations as a "technical" transgression of reporting rules that really do not cause injury. In contrast, they argue, insider trading under modern theory is tantamount to theft; an actual injury is inflicted on the individual or institution entitled to confidentiality. Section 13(d), however, is the pivot of the entire Williams Act regulation of tender offers. To be sure, some may doubt the usefulness of that statute generally or the section 13(d) requirement specifically, but it is hardly up to the judiciary to second-guess the wisdom of Congress' approach to regulating takeovers. Suffice it for us to note that section 13(d) is a crucial requirement in the congressional scheme, and a violator, it is legislatively assumed, improperly benefits by purchasing stocks at an artificially low price because of a breach of the duty Congress imposed to disclose his investment position. The disclosure of that position—a holding in excess of 5 percent of another company's stock—suggests to the rest of the market a likely takeover and therefore may increase the price of the stock. Appellants circumvented that scheme, and the theory of the statute, by which we are bound, is that the circumventions caused injury to other market participants who sold stock without knowledge of First City's holdings. We therefore see no relevant distinction between disgorgement of inside trading profits and disgorgement of post-section 13(d) violation profits.

There remains, of course, the question of how the court measures those illegal profits. Appellants vigorously dispute the $2.7 million figure that the district court arrived at by simply calculating all of the profits First City realized (in its eventual sale back to Ashland) on the 890,000 shares First City purchased between March 14 and 25. See 688 F.Supp. at 728 n. 24. The SEC's claim to disgorgement, which the district court accepted, is predicated on the assumption that had First City made its section 13(d) disclosure on March 14, at the end of the statutory 10 day period, the stock it purchased during the March 14–25 period would have been purchased in a quite different and presumably more expensive market. That hypothetical market would have been affected by the disclosure that the Belzbergs had taken a greater than 5 percent stake in Ashland and would soon propose a tender offer.

Since disgorgement primarily serves to prevent unjust enrichment, the court may exercise its equitable power only over property causally related to the wrongdoing. The remedy may well be a key to the SEC's efforts to deter others from violating the securities laws, but disgorgement may not be used punitively. See SEC v. Blatt, 583 F.2d 1325, 1335 (5th Cir.1978); SEC v. Manor Nursing Centers, Inc., 458 F.2d 1082, 1104 (2d Cir.1972). Therefore, the SEC generally must distinguish between legally and illegally obtained profits. See CFTC v. British Am. Commodity Options Corp., 788 F.2d 92, 93 (2d Cir.), cert. denied, 479 U.S. 853, 107 S.Ct. 186, 93 L.Ed.2d 120 (1986). Appellants assert that the hypothetical market between March 14–25 that the SEC urged and the district court accepted was simplistic, quite unrealistic, and so *de facto* punitive. It did not take into account other variables—besides the section 13(d) disclosure—which caused the post-March 25 price of the stock to rise above that which prevailed during the March 14–25 period. At trial appellants' expert witness testified that four independent factors combined to increase the stock price to the level it reached on March 25 and that these factors were not present on March 14, when the defendants should have disclosed. He identified these factors as: (1) the Belzbergs by the 25th held between 8 and 9 percent of Ashland, (2) the Belzbergs had prior to the 25th communicated to Ashland the size of their holdings, (3) Ashland publicly disclosed the Belzbergs' position on the 25th before the 13(d) disclosure, and (4) by the 25th, rumors swirled of an imminent takeover bid at $55 per share. In an attempt to hypothesize how the Belzbergs would have acted—had they disclosed on March 14—and how the market would have responded to those actions, the witness presented three alternative scenarios that in his view more accurately measured the impact of the nondisclosure and which yielded disgorgement figures of zero, $496,050, and $864,588. Perhaps not surprisingly, appellants' witness testified that the most realistic scenario required no disgorgement at all.[23]

If exact information were obtainable at negligible cost, we would not hesitate to impose upon the government a strict burden to produce that data to measure the precise amount of the ill-gotten gains. Unfortunately, we encounter imprecision and imperfect information. Despite sophisticated econometric modelling, predicting stock market responses to alternative variables is, as the district court found, at best speculative. Rules for calculating disgorgement must recognize that separating legal from illegal profits exactly may at times be a near-impossible task. See, e.g., Elkind v. Liggett & Myers, Inc., 635 F.2d 156, 171 (2d Cir.1980).

Accordingly, disgorgement need only be a reasonable approximation of profits causally connected to the violation. In the insider trading context, courts typically require the violator to return all profits made on the illegal trades,

---

23. The expert witness concluded that disgorgement was unnecessary because if First City had disclosed on March 14, as the SEC claims it should have, we should assume that the 890,000 shares actually bought in the March 17–25 period (the 10-day window in Belzberg's view) would have been purchased in the lawful March 4–14 10-day window. Since Ashland prices were lower in the March 4–14 period than during March 17–25, the witness believed that no disgorgement was appropriate. This analysis, however, does not consider the impact of buying these 890,000 shares within this 10-day period—in addition to the 330,000 shares the Belzbergs actually purchased then—which presumably would have itself pushed up the price.

see, e.g., SEC v. Texas Gulf Sulphur Co., 446 F.2d 1301, 1307 (2d Cir.), cert. denied, 404 U.S. 1005, 92 S.Ct. 561, 30 L.Ed.2d 558 (1971), and have rejected calls to restrict the disgorgement to the precise impact of the illegal trading on the market price. See Elkind, 635 F.2d at 171; cf. CFTC v. British Am. Commodity Options Corp., 788 F.2d 92 (2d Cir.) (concluding that a nexus between the unlawful conduct and the disgorgement figure need not be shown because of the pervasiveness of the fraud), cert. denied, 479 U.S. 853, 107 S.Ct. 186, 93 L.Ed.2d 120 (1986).

Although the SEC bears the ultimate burden of persuasion that its disgorgement figure reasonably approximates the amount of unjust enrichment, we believe the government's showing of appellants' actual profits on the tainted transactions at least presumptively satisfied that burden. Appellants, to whom the burden of going forward shifted, were then obliged clearly to demonstrate that the disgorgement figure was not a reasonable approximation. Defendants in such cases may make such a showing, for instance, by pointing to intervening events from the time of the violation. In SEC v. MacDonald, 699 F.2d 47 (1st Cir.1983) (en banc), the First Circuit reversed a district court order requiring the defendant to disgorge all profits from an illegal insider trade when the defendant had held on to the stock for more than a year. The court restricted the amount to a figure based on the price of the stock "a reasonable time after public dissemination of the inside information." Id. at 55. Similarly, the Second Circuit in SEC v. Manor Nursing Centers, Inc., 458 F.2d 1082 (2d Cir.1972), refused to extend the disgorgement remedy to income subsequently earned on the initial illegal profits. In those cases, the defendant demonstrated a clear break in or considerable attenuation of the causal connection between the illegality and the ultimate profits.

Here, appellants took a different approach using a sophisticated expert witness. As we noted, they maintained that the post-March 25 price was influenced by four other independent factors besides the belated section 13(d) disclosure, so even if First City had disclosed on March 14, the price would not have run up then to the extent it did after March 25. The difficulty we see with appellants' argument is that none of the four factors are independent of the section 13(d) disclosure determination. Thus, although by March 25 First City had accumulated 8–9 percent of Ashland, whereas on March 14 it had slightly over 5 percent (and although the market might react more strongly to the higher figure), we do not see why we should not assume that First City would have acquired 8–9 percent before March 14—if they knew they had to disclose on the earlier date. Second, it seems likely that First City would have notified Ashland's management on March 13 if they had planned to disclose on the next day, just as they did on March 25. Third, Ashland's premature disclosure of First City's holdings (prior to the section 13(d) notice) would likely have also occurred. And finally, the March 25 market takeover rumors were probably associated with all of the above activity, which is inextricably linked with the impending section 13(d) notice. We therefore agree with the district court that appellants' efforts to hypothesize both the takeover efforts of a First City that complied with section 13(d) and the market reaction to that are impossibly speculative.

Placing the burden on the defendants of rebutting the SEC's showing of actual profits, we recognize, may result, as it has in the insider trader context, in actual profits becoming the typical disgorgement measure. But the line between restitution and penalty is unfortunately blurred, and the risk of uncertainty should fall on the wrongdoer whose illegal conduct created that uncertainty. See SEC v. MacDonald, 699 F.2d 47, 55 (1st Cir.1983) (*en banc*); Elkind v. Liggett & Myers, Inc., 635 F.2d 156, 171 (2d Cir.1980); cf. Bigelow v. RKO Radio Pictures, 327 U.S. 251, 265, 66 S.Ct. 574, 580, 90 L.Ed. 652 (1946) (placing the risk of uncertainty on the wrongdoer in the antitrust context).

* * *

———

New Teeth for § 13(d). With the decision in *First City Financial Corp.,* the SEC acquired a powerful new weapon to combat stock parking. Note, however, that use of the "put and call" agreements discussed in footnote 4 of the court's opinion have also been criminally prosecuted.[1] *Query:* would disgorgement be equally appropriate if the defendants had filed a timely Schedule 13D but instead of disclosing a control purpose had simply claimed an "investment" purpose? Does the market really believe such claims about purpose when the parties are well-known takeover raiders? Should they justify the very heavy financial penalties imposed in First City Financial?

Consider again the position of defendant's expert witness described in footnote 23 of the court's opinion. Isn't it correct that, whenever the group was formed and the initial obligation to file a Schedule 13D was triggered, the defendants would still have had ten days thereafter to purchase stock before they had to file their Schedule 13D? If so, can it be fairly said that the defendants' delay in filing the Schedule 13D "caused" their profits when they could have legally assembled at least most of the same substantial block in an uninformed market? In part for this reason, the SEC has proposed to Congress that the 10 day window be shortened and further purchases over 5% be barred until it has been filed.

Private Remedies. Although the SEC can now sue for disgorgement (and indeed may seek it in an administrative proceeding under new Section 21B(e) of the 1934 Act), private plaintiffs have less remedies available to them. Most federal courts have recognized an implied right of action in the target to seek equitable relief for violations of § 13(d).[2] However, the Supreme Court's decision in *Rondeau v. Mosinee Paper Corp.,*[3] which overruled an injunction "sterilizing" the shares held by a defendant who failed to file a Schedule 13D (apparently out of simple ignorance), has been read by most lower federal courts as a virtual bar to the use of divestment or sterilization as remedies in § 13(d) cases.[4] Typically, courts will grant only a temporary injunction pending corrective disclosure.[5]

1. See United States v. Bilzerian, 926 F.2d 1285 (2d Cir.1991).

2. See Florida Commercial Banks v. Culverhouse, 772 F.2d 1513 (11th Cir.1985); Gearhart Industries Inc. v. Smith Intern. Inc., 741 F.2d 707 (5th Cir.1984). However, in Liberty Nat. Ins. Holding Co. v. Charter Co., 734 F.2d 545 (11th Cir.1984), the Eleventh Circuit found that there was no implied right in the target to seek divestment.

3. 422 U.S. 49 (1975).

4. See Dan River Inc. v. Icahn, 701 F.2d 278 (4th Cir.1983).

5. A few decisions have granted a short "cooling-off" period for the revised disclosures to reach and be digested by the market. See Kirsch v. Bliss & Laughlin Indus. Inc., 495 F.Supp. 488 (W.D.Mich.1980) (30 day cooling off period). But see, Chromalloy American Corp. v. Sun Chemical Corp., 611 F.2d 240 (8th Cir.1979).

When shareholders (rather than the target company) sue, standing is again recognized, but courts have not read § 13(d) as authorizing an award of damages.[6] On the other hand, shareholders may have a valid claim under Rule 10b–5 if they purchased shares during an interval in which a materially inaccurate Schedule 13D filed by a defendant was misinforming the market.[7]

B. THE DEFINITION OF ''TENDER OFFER''

Securities and Exchange Commission v. Carter Hawley Hale Stores, Inc.

United States Court of Appeals, Ninth Circuit, 1985.
760 F.2d 945.

■ Before: GOODWIN, SNEED, and SKOPIL, CIRCUIT JUDGES.

■ SKOPIL, CIRCUIT JUDGE.

The issue in this case arises out of an attempt by The Limited (''Limited''), an Ohio corporation, to take over Carter Hawley Hale Stores, Inc. (''CHH''), a publicly-held Los Angeles corporation. The SEC commenced the present action for injunctive relief to restrain CHH from repurchasing its own stock in an attempt to defeat the Limited takeover attempt without complying with the tender offer regulations. The district court concluded CHH's repurchase program was not a tender offer. The SEC appeals from the district court's denial of its motion for a preliminary injunction. We affirm.

FACTS AND PROCEEDINGS BELOW

On April 4, 1984 Limited commenced a cash tender offer for 20.3 million shares of CHH common stock, representing approximately 55% of the total shares outstanding, at $30 per share. Prior to the announced offer, CHH stock was trading at approximately $23.78 per share (pre-tender offer price). Limited disclosed that if its offer succeeded, it would exchange the remaining CHH shares for a fixed amount of Limited shares in a second-step merger.

In compliance with section 14(d) of the Securities Exchange Act of 1934 (''Exchange Act''), Limited filed a Schedule 14D–1 disclosing all pertinent information about its offer. The schedule stated that (1) the offer would remain open for 20 days, (2) the tendered shares could be withdrawn until April 19, 1984, and (3) in the event the offer was oversubscribed, shares would be subject to purchase on a pro rata basis.

While CHH initially took no public position on the offer, it filed an action to enjoin Limited's attempted takeover. Carter Hawley Hale Stores, Inc. v. The Limited, Inc., 587 F.Supp. 246 (C.D.Cal.1984). CHH's motion for an injunction was denied. Id. From April 4, 1984 until April 16, 1984 CHH's incumbent management discussed a response to Limited's offer. During that time 14 million shares, about 40% of CHH's common stock, were traded. The price of CHH stock increased to approximately $29.25 per share. CHH shares became concentrated in the hands of risk arbitrageurs.

---

6. See Kamerman v. Steinberg, 891 F.2d 424 (2d Cir.1989); Sanders v. Thrall Car Mfg. Co., 582 F.Supp. 945 (S.D.N.Y.1983), aff'd, 730 F.2d 910 (2d Cir.1984).

7. In re Phillips Petroleum Securities Litigation, 881 F.2d 1236 (3d Cir.1989).

On April 16, 1984 CHH responded to Limited's offer. CHH issued a press release announcing its opposition to the offer because it was "inadequate and not in the best interests of CHH or its shareholders." CHH also publicly announced an agreement with General Cinema Corporation ("General Cinema"). CHH sold one million shares of convertible preferred stock to General Cinema for $300 million. The preferred shares possessed a vote equivalent to 22% of voting shares outstanding. General Cinema's shares were to be voted pursuant to CHH's Board of Directors recommendations. General Cinema was also granted an option to purchase Walden Book Company, Inc. a profitable CHH subsidiary, for approximately $285 million. Finally, CHH announced a plan to repurchase up to 15 million shares of its own common stock for an amount not to exceed $500 million. If all 15 million shares were purchased, General Cinema's shares would represent 33% of CHH's outstanding voting shares.

CHH's public announcement stated the actions taken were "to defeat the attempt by Limited to gain voting control of the company and to afford shareholders who wished to sell shares at this time an opportunity to do so." CHH's actions were revealed by press release, a letter from CHH's Chairman to shareholders, and by documents filed with the Securities and Exchange Commission ("SEC")—a Schedule 14D–9 and Rule 13e–1 transaction statement. These disclosures were reported by wire services, national financial newspapers, and newspapers of general circulation. Limited sought a temporary restraining order against CHH's repurchase of its shares. The application was denied. Limited withdrew its motion for a preliminary injunction.

CHH began to repurchase its shares on April 16, 1984. In a one-hour period CHH purchased approximately 244,000 shares at an average price of $25.25 per share. On April 17, 1984 CHH purchased approximately 6.5 million shares in a two-hour trading period at an average price of $25.88 per share. By April 22, 1984 CHH had purchased a total of 15 million shares. It then announced an increase in the number of shares authorized for purchase to 18.5 million.

On April 24, 1984, the same day Limited was permitted to close its offer and start purchasing, CHH terminated its repurchase program having purchased approximately 17.5 million shares, over 50% of the common shares outstanding. On April 25, 1984 Limited revised its offer increasing the offering price to $35.00 per share and eliminating the second-step merger. The market price for CHH then reached a high of $32.00 per share. On May 21, 1984 Limited withdrew its offer. The market price of CHH promptly fell to $20.62 per share, a price below the pre-tender offer price.

On May 2, 1984, two and one-half weeks after the repurchase program was announced and one week after its apparent completion,[1] the SEC filed this action for injunctive relief. The SEC alleged that CHH's repurchase program constituted a tender offer conducted in violation of section 13(e) of the Exchange Act, and Rule 13e–4. On May 5, 1984 a temporary restraining order was granted. CHH was temporarily enjoined from further stock repurchases. The district court denied the SEC's motion for a preliminary injunction, finding the

---

1. In addition to seeking to enjoin further stock purchases, the SEC sought preliminary injunctive relief requiring CHH to issue 17.9 million shares of its common stock to trustees who, pending a trial on the merits, would be required to vote such shares in the same proportion as the votes of unaffiliated shareholders. This matter therefore is not moot.

SEC failed to carry its burden of establishing "the reasonable likelihood of future violations * * * [or] * * * a 'fair chance of success on the merits' * * *." SEC v. Carter Hawley Hale Stores, Inc., 587 F.Supp. 1248, 1257 (C.D.Cal.1984) (citations omitted). The court found CHH's repurchase program was not a tender offer because the eight-factor test proposed by the SEC and adopted in Wellman v. Dickinson, 475 F.Supp. 783 (S.D.N.Y.1979), aff'd on other grounds, 682 F.2d 355 (2d Cir.1982), cert. denied, 460 U.S. 1069 (1983), had not been satisfied. SEC v. Carter Hawley Hale Stores, Inc., 587 F.Supp. at 1255. The court also refused to adopt, at the urging of the SEC, the alternative test of what constitutes a tender offer as enunciated in S–G Securities, Inc. v. Fuqua Investment Co., 466 F.Supp. 1114 (D.Mass.1978). 587 F.Supp. at 1256– 57. On May 9, 1984 the SEC filed an emergency application for an injunction pending appeal to this court. That application was denied.

DISCUSSION

The grant or denial of a preliminary injunction is reviewed to determine if the district court abused its discretion. Lopez v. Heckler, 725 F.2d 1489, 1497 (9th Cir.), rev'd on other grounds, 104 S.Ct. 10 (1983). A district court abuses its discretion if it rests its conclusion on clearly erroneous factual findings or an incorrect legal standard. Id.; Apple Computer, Inc. v. Formula International, Inc., 725 F.2d 521, 523 (9th Cir.1984).

The SEC urges two principal arguments on appeal: (1) the district court erred in concluding that CHH's repurchase program was not a tender offer under the eight-factor *Wellman* test, and (2) the district court erred in declining to apply the definition of a tender offer enunciated in *S–G Securities*, 466 F.Supp. at 1126–27. Resolution of these issues on appeal presents the difficult task of determining whether CHH's repurchase of shares during a third-party tender offer itself constituted a tender offer.

1. *The Williams Act.*

A. *Congressional Purposes*

The Williams Act amendments to the Exchange Act were enacted in response to the growing use of tender offers to achieve corporate control. Edgar v. MITE Corp., 457 U.S. 624, 632 (1982) (citing Piper v. Chris–Craft Industries, 430 U.S. 1, 22 (1977)). Prior to the passage of the Act, shareholders of target companies were often forced to act hastily on offers without the benefit of full disclosure. See H.R.Rep. No. 1711, 90th Cong., 2d Sess. (1968), reprinted in 1968 U.S.Code, Cong. & Admin.News 2811 ("House Report 1711").[2] The Williams Act was intended to ensure that investors responding to tender offers received full and fair disclosure, analogous to that received in proxy contests. The Act was also designed to provide shareholders an opportunity to examine all relevant facts in an effort to reach a decision without being subject to unwarranted pressure. House Report 1711.

---

2. For additional discussion of the concerns giving rise to the Williams Act amendments, see Full Disclosure of Corporate Equity Ownership and in Corporate Takeover Bids: Hearing on S. 510 Before the Subcommittee on Securities of the Senate Committee on Banking and Currency, 90th Cong., 1st Sess. (1967) ("Senate Hearings"); Takeover Bids: Hearing on H.R. 14475, and S. 510 Before the Subcommittee on Commerce and Finance of the House Committee on Interstate and Foreign Commerce, 90th Cong., 2d Sess. (1968) ("House Hearings").

This policy is reflected in section 14(d), which governs third-party tender offers, and which prohibits a tender offer unless shareholders are provided with certain procedural and substantive protections including: full disclosure; time in which to make an investment decision; withdrawal rights; and pro rata purchase of shares accepted in the event the offer is oversubscribed.

There are additional congressional concerns underlying the Williams Act. In its effort to protect investors, Congress recognized the need to "avoid favoring either management or the takeover bidder." *Edgar,* 456 U.S. at 633; see also Financial General Bank Shares, Inc. v. Lance, [1978] Fed.Sec.L.Rptr. (CCH) ¶ 96,403 at 93,424–25 (D.D.C.1978) (quoting Rondeau v. Mosinee Paper Corp., 422 U.S. 49, 58 (1975)). The Supreme Court has recognized that to serve this policy it is necessary to withhold "from management or the bidder any undue advantage that could frustrate the exercise of informed choice." *Edgar,* 456 U.S. at 634. Congress was also concerned about avoiding undue interference with the free and open market in securities. City Investing Co. v. Simcox, 633 F.2d 56, 62 n. 14 (7th Cir.1980) (noting less burdensome regulations in cases involving certain open market purchases); see also 113 Cong.Rec. 856 (1968). Each of these congressional concerns is implicated in the determination of whether CHH's issuer repurchase program constituted a tender offer.

B. *Issuer Repurchases Under Section 13(e)*

Issuer repurchases and tender offers are governed in relevant part by section 13(e) of the Williams Act and Rules 13e–1 and 13e–4 promulgated thereunder.

The SEC argues that the district court erred in concluding that issuer repurchases, which had the intent and effect of defeating a third-party tender offer, are authorized by the tender offer rules and regulations. The legislative history of these provisions is unclear. Congress apparently was aware of an intent by the SEC to regulate issuer tender offers to the same extent as third-party offers. Senate Hearings 214–16, 248; Exchange Act Release No. 16,112 [1979] Fed.Sec.L.Rptr. (CCH) ¶ 82,182 at 82,205 (Aug. 16, 1979) (proposed amendments to tender offer rules). At the same time, Congress recognized issuers might engage in "substantial repurchase programs * * * inevitably affect[ing] market performance and price levels." House Hearings at 14–15; see also House Report 1711 at 2814–15. Such repurchase programs might be undertaken for any number of legitimate purposes, including with the intent "to preserve or strengthen * * * control by counteracting tender offer or other takeover attempts. * * * " House Report 1711 at 2814; House Hearings at 15. Congress neither explicitly banned nor authorized such a practice. Congress did grant the SEC authority to adopt appropriate regulations to carry out congressional intent with respect to issuer repurchases. The legislative history of section 13(e) is not helpful in resolving the issues.

There is also little guidance in the SEC Rules promulgated in response to the legislative grant of authority. Rule 13e–1 prohibits an issuer from repurchasing its own stock during a third-party tender offer unless it discloses certain minimal information. The language of Rule 13e–1 is prohibitory rather than permissive. It nonetheless evidences a recognition that not all issuer repurchases during a third-party tender offer are tender offers. Id. In contrast, Rule 13e–4 recognizes that issuers, like third parties, may engage in repurchase activity amounting to a tender offer and subject to the same procedural and substantive safeguards as a third-party tender offer. The regulations do not specify when a repurchase by an issuer amounts to a tender offer governed by Rule 13e–4 rather than 13e–1.[3]

We decline to adopt either the broadest construction of Rule 13e–4, to define issuer tender offers as virtually all substantial repurchases during a third-party tender offer, or the broadest construction of Rule 13e–1, to create an exception from the tender offer requirements for issuer repurchases made during a third-party tender offer. Like the district court, we resolve the question of whether CHH's repurchase program was a tender offer by considering the eight-factor test established in *Wellman,* 587 F.Supp. at 1256–57.[4]

To serve the purposes of the Williams Act, there is a need for flexibility in fashioning a definition of a tender offer. See Smallwood v. Pearl Brewing Co., 489 F.2d 579 (5th Cir.), cert. denied 419 U.S. 873 (1974). The *Wellman* factors seem particularly well suited in determining when an issuer repurchase program during a third-party tender offer will itself constitute a tender offer. *Wellman* focuses, *inter alia,* on the manner in which the offer is conducted and whether the offer has the overall effect of pressuring shareholders into selling their stock. *Wellman,* 475 F.Supp. at 823–24. Application of the *Wellman* factors to the unique facts and circumstances surrounding issuer repurchases should serve to effect congressional concern for the needs of the shareholder, the need to avoid giving either the target or the offeror any advantage, and the need to maintain a free and open market for securities.

2. *Application of the Wellman Factors.*

Under the *Wellman* test, the existence of a tender offer is determined by examining the following factors:

(1) Active and widespread solicitation of public shareholders for the shares of an issuer; (2) solicitation made for a substantial percentage of the issuer's stock; (3) offer to purchase made at a premium over the prevailing market price; (4) terms of the offer are firm rather than negotiable; (5) offer contingent on the tender of a fixed number of shares, often subject to a fixed maximum number to be purchased; (6) offer open only for a limited period of time; (7) offeree subjected to pressure to sell his stock; [and (8)] public announcements of a purchasing program concerning the target company precede or accompany rapid accumulation of a large amount of target company's securities.

475 F.Supp. at 823–24.

3. The procedural and substantive requirements that must be complied with under Rule 13e–4 differ from those under Rule 13e–1. An issuer engaged in a repurchase under Rule 13e–1 is required to file a brief statement with the SEC setting forth the amount of shares purchased; the purpose for which the purchase is made; and the source and amount of funds used in making the repurchase. CHH complied with the requirements of Rule 13e–1.

An issuer engaged in a tender offer under Rule 13e–4 must comply with more burdensome regulations. All the substantive and procedural protections for shareholders come into play under Rule 13e–4 including: full disclosure; time in which to make investment decisions; withdrawal rights; and requirements for pro rata purchase of shares. CHH did not comply with Rule 13e–4.

4. We have followed the *Wellman* test in another context, see Polinsky v. MCA, Inc., 680 F.2d 1286, 1290–91 (9th Cir.1982) (open market purchases made in anticipation of a tender offer met none of the *Wellman* indicia), but have not addressed the question of the applicability of the *Wellman* factors to issuer repurchase programs during third-party tender offers.

Not all factors need be present to find a tender offer; rather, they provide some guidance as to the traditional indicia of a tender offer. Id. at 824; see also Zuckerman v. Franz, 573 F.Supp. 351, 358 (S.D.Fla.1983).

The district court concluded CHH's repurchase program was not a tender offer under *Wellman* because only "two of the eight indicia" were present. 587 F.Supp. at 1255. The SEC claims the district court erred in applying *Wellman* because it gave insufficient weight to the pressure exerted on shareholders; it ignored the existence of a competitive tender offer; and it failed to consider that CHH's offer at the market price was in essence a premium because the price had already risen above pre-tender offer levels.

A. *Active and Widespread Solicitation*

The evidence was uncontroverted that there was "no direct solicitation of shareholders." 587 F.Supp. 1253. No active and widespread solicitation occurred. See Brascan Ltd. v. Edper Equities Ltd., 477 F.Supp. 773, 789 (S.D.N.Y. 1979) (no tender offer where defendant "scrupulously avoided any solicitation upon the advice of his lawyers"). Nor did the publicity surrounding CHH's repurchase program result in a solicitation. 587 F.Supp. 1253–54. The only public announcements by CHH were those mandated by SEC or Exchange rules. See Ludlow Corp. v. Tyco Laboratories, 529 F.Supp. 62, 68–69 (D.Mass. 1981) (schedule 13d filed by purchaser could not be characterized as forbidden publicity); Crane Co. v. Harsco Corp., 511 F.Supp. 294, 303 (D.Dela.1981) (Rule 13e–1 transaction statement and required press releases do not constitute a solicitation); but cf. S–G Securities, Inc., 466 F.Supp. at 1119–21 (tender offer present where numerous press releases publicized terms of offer).

B. *Solicitation for a Substantial Percentage of Issuer's Shares*

Because there was no active and widespread solicitation, the district court found the repurchase could not have involved a solicitation for a substantial percentage of CHH's shares. 587 F.Supp. 1253–54. It is unclear whether the proper focus of this factor is the solicitation or the percentage of stock solicited. The district court probably erred in concluding that, absent a solicitation under the first *Wellman* factor, the second factor cannot be satisfied, see Hoover Co. v. Fuqua Industries, [1979–80] Fed.Sec.L.Rptr. (CCH) ¶ 97,107 at 96,148 n. 4 (N.D.Ohio 1979) (second *Wellman* factor did not incorporate the type of solicitation described in factor one), but we need not decide that here. The solicitation and percentage of stock elements of the second factor often will be addressed adequately in an evaluation of the first *Wellman* factor, which is concerned with solicitation, and the eighth *Wellman* factor, which focuses on the amount of securities accumulated. In this case CHH did not engage in a solicitation under the first *Wellman* factor but did accumulate a large percentage of stock as defined under the eighth *Wellman* factor. An evaluation of the second *Wellman* factor does not alter the probability of finding a tender offer.

C. *Premium Over Prevailing Market Price*

The SEC contends the open market purchases made by CHH at market prices were in fact made at a premium not over market price but over the pre-tender offer price. At the time of CHH's repurchases, the market price for CHH's shares (ranging from $24.00 to $26.00 per share) had risen above the pre-tender offer price (approximately $22.00 per share). Given ordinary market dynamics, the price of a target company's stock will rise following an announced tender offer. Under the SEC's definition of a premium as a price greater than the pre-tender offer price, a premium will always exist when a target company makes open market purchases in response to a tender offer even though the increase in market price is attributable to the action of the third-party offeror and not the target company. See LTV Corp. v. Grumman Corp., 526 F.Supp. 106, 109 & n. 7 (E.D.N.Y.1981) (an increase in price due to increased demand during a tender offer does not represent a premium). The SEC definition not only eliminates consideration of this *Wellman* factor in the context of issuer repurchases during a tender offer, but also underestimates congressional concern for preserving the free and open market. The district court did not err in concluding a premium is determined not by reference to pre-tender offer price, but rather by reference to market price. This is the definition previously urged by the SEC, Exchange Act Release No. 16,385 [1979–80] Fed.Sec.L.Rptr. (CCH) ¶ 82,374 at 82,605 (Nov. 29, 1979) (footnotes omitted) (proposed amendments to tender offer rules) (premium defined as price "in excess of * * * the current market price * * * "), and is the definition we now apply. See LTV Corp., 526 F.Supp. at 109 & n. 7.

D.   *Terms of Offer Not Firm*

There is no dispute that CHH engaged in a number of transactions or purchases at many different market prices. 587 F.Supp. at 1254.

E.   *Offer Not Contingent on Tender of Fixed Minimum Number of Shares*

Similarly, while CHH indicated it would purchase up to 15 million shares, CHH's purchases were not contingent on the tender of a fixed minimum number of shares. 587 F.Supp. at 1254.

F.   *Not Open for Only a Limited Time*

CHH's offer to repurchase was not open for only a limited period of time but rather was open "during the pendency of the tender offer of The Limited." 587 F.Supp. at 1255. The SEC argues that the offer was in fact open for only a limited time, because CHH would only repurchase stock until 15 million shares were acquired. The fact that 15 million shares were acquired in a short period of time does not translate into an issuer-imposed time limitation. The time within which the repurchases were made was a product of ordinary market forces, not the terms of CHH's repurchase program.

G–H.   *Shareholder Pressure and Public Announcements Accompanying a Large Accumulation of Stock*

With regard to the seventh *Wellman* factor, following a public announcement, CHH repurchased over the period of seven trading days more than 50% of its outstanding shares. 587 F.Supp. at 1255. The eighth *Wellman* factor was met.

The district court found that while many shareholders may have felt pressured or compelled to sell their shares, CHH itself did not exert on shareholders the kind of pressure the Williams Act proscribes. Id.

While there certainly was shareholder pressure in this case, it was largely the pressure of the marketplace and not the type of untoward pressure the tender offer regulations were designed to prohibit. See Panter v. Marshall Field & Co., 646 F.2d 271, 286 (7th Cir.) (where no deadline and no premium, shareholders "were simply not subjected to the proscribed pressures the

Williams Act was designed to alleviate"), cert. denied, 454 U.S. 1092 (1981); Brascan Ltd. v. Edper Equities, 477 F.Supp. at 789–92 (without high premium and threat that the offer will disappear, large purchases in short time do not represent the kind of pressure the Williams Act was designed to prevent); Kennecott Copper Corp. v. Curtiss–Wright Corp., 449 F.Supp. 951, 961 (S.D.N.Y.), aff'd in relevant part, rev'd in part, 584 F.2d 1195, 1207 (2d Cir.1978) (where no deadline and no premium, no pressure, other than normal pressure of the marketplace, exerted on shareholders).

CHH's purchases were made in the open market, at market and not premium prices, without fixed terms and were not contingent upon the tender of a fixed minimum number of shares. CHH's repurchase program had none of the traditional indicia of a tender offer. See, e.g., Energy Ventures, Inc. v. Appalachian Co., 587 F.Supp. 734, 739 (D.Del.1984) (major acquisition program involving open market purchases not subject to tender offer regulation); Ludlow Corp. v. Tyco Laboratories, Inc., 529 F.Supp. at 68 (no tender offer where shareholders not pressured into making hasty ill-advised decision due to premium, fixed terms, or active solicitation); LTV Corp. v. Grumman, 526 F.Supp. at 109 (massive buying program, with attendant publicity, made with intent to defeat third-party tender offer, not itself a tender offer); Brascan Ltd. v. Edper Equities, 477 F.Supp. at 792 (the pressure the Williams Act attempts to eliminate is that caused by "a high premium with a threat that the offer will disappear within a certain time").

The shareholder pressure in this case did not result from any untoward action on the part of CHH. Rather, it resulted from market forces, the third-party offer, and the fear that at the expiration of the offer the price of CHH shares would decrease.

The district court did not abuse its discretion in concluding that under the *Wellman* eight factor test, CHH's repurchase program did not constitute a tender offer.

3. *Alternative S–G Securities Test.*

The SEC finally urges that even if the CHH repurchase program did not constitute a tender offer under the *Wellman* test, the district court erred in refusing to apply the test in *S–G Securities*, 466 F.Supp. at 1114.[5] Under the more liberal *S–G Securities* test, a tender offer is present if there are

> (1) A publicly announced intention by the purchaser to acquire a block of the stock of the target company for purposes of acquiring control thereof,

---

5. Some courts have opted for the broader *S–G Securities* definition of a tender offer, see, e.g., Panter v. Marshall Field & Co., 646 F.2d at 286 (also citing *Wellman*); Hoover Co. v. Fuqua Industries, [1979–80] Fed.Sec.L.Rptr. (CCH) ¶ 97,107 at 96,146–149 (also citing *Wellman*); Nachman Corp. v. Halfred, Inc., [1973–74] Fed.Sec.L.Rptr. (CCH) ¶ 94,455 at 95,590 (N.D.Ill.1973); Cattlemen's Investment Co. v. Fears, 343 F.Supp. 1248, 1251 (W.D.Okla.1972), vacated per stipulation, No. 75–152 (W.D.Okla. May 8, 1972), while other courts have rejected this broad test in favor of the eight-factor *Wellman* test. See, e.g., Kennecott Copper Corp. v. Curtiss–Wright Corp., 584 F.2d at 1207; LTV Corp. v. Grumman Corp., 527 F.Supp. at 109; Brascan Ltd. v. Edper Equities Ltd., 477 F.Supp. at 791; D–Z Investment Co. v. Holloway, [1974–75] Fed.Sec.L.Rep. (CCH) ¶ 94,-771 at 96,562–63 (S.D.N.Y.1974). There is no one factor other than the result which distinguishes these cases although the greater weight of authority seems to have accepted the *Wellman* test.

and (2) a subsequent rapid acquisition by the purchaser of large blocks of stock through open market and privately negotiated purchases.

Id. at 1126–27.

There are a number of sound reasons for rejecting the *S–G Securities* test. The test is vague and difficult to apply. It offers little guidance to the issuer as to when his conduct will come within the ambit of Rule 13e–4 as opposed to Rule 13e–1. SEC v. Carter Hawley Hale Stores, 587 F.Supp. at 1256–57. A determination of the existence of a tender offer under *S–G Securities* is largely subjective and made in hindsight based on an *ex post facto* evaluation of the response in the marketplace to the repurchase program. Id. at 1257. The SEC's contention that these concerns are irrelevant when the issuer's repurchases are made with the intent to defeat a third-party offer is without merit. See, e.g., LTV Corp. v. Grumman Corp., 526 F.Supp. at 109–10 (Rule 13e–1 may apply to open market purchases even when made to thwart a tender offer); Crane Co. v. Harsco Corp., 511 F.Supp. 294, 300–301 (D.Dela.1981) (same).

The SEC finds further support for its application of the two-pronged *S–G Securities* test in the overriding legislative intent "to ensure that shareholders * * * are adequately protected from pressure tactics * * * [forcing them to make] * * * ill-considered investment decisions." The *S–G Securities* test does reflect congressional concern for shareholders; however, the same can be said of the *Wellman* test. The legislative intent in the context of open market repurchases during third-party tender offers is, at best, unclear. 587 F.Supp. 1256; see pages 8–11, supra. The *S–G Securities* test, unlike the *Wellman* test, does little to reflect objectively the multiple congressional concerns underlying the Williams Act, including due regard for the free and open market in securities. * * *

We decline to abandon the *Wellman* test in favor of the vague standard enunciated in *S–G Securities*. The district court did not err in declining to apply the *S–G Securities* test or in finding CHH's repurchases were not a tender offer under *Wellman*.

Affirmed.

Hanson Trust PLC v. SCM Corporation

United States Court of Appeals, Second Circuit, 1985.
774 F.2d 47.

■ Before MANSFIELD, PIERCE and PRATT, CIRCUIT JUDGES.

■ MANSFIELD, CIRCUIT JUDGE.

Hanson Trust PLC, HSCM Industries, Inc., and Hanson Holdings Netherlands B.V. (hereinafter sometimes referred to collectively as "Hanson") appeal from an order of the Southern District of New York, 617 F.Supp. 832 (1985), Shirley Wohl Kram, Judge, granting SCM Corporation's motion for a preliminary injunction restraining them, their officers, agents, employees and any persons acting in concert with them, from acquiring any shares of SCM and from exercising any voting rights with respect to 3.1 million SCM shares acquired by them on September 11, 1985. The injunction was granted on the ground that Hanson's September 11 acquisition of the SCM stock through five private and one open market purchases amounted to a "tender offer" for more than 5% of SCM's outstanding shares, which violated §§ 14(d)(1) and (6) of the

Williams Act and rules promulgated by the Securities and Exchange Commission (SEC) thereunder. See 17 C.F.R. §§ 240.14(e)(1) and 240.14d–7. We reverse.

The setting is the familiar one of a fast-moving bidding contest for control of a large public corporation: first, a cash tender offer of $60 per share by Hanson, an outsider, addressed to SCM stockholders; next, a counterproposal by an "insider" group consisting of certain SCM managers and their "White Knight," Merrill Lynch Capital Markets (Merrill), for a "leveraged buyout" at a higher price ($70 per share); then an increase by Hanson of its cash offer to $72 per share, followed by a revised SCM–Merrill leveraged buyout offer of $74 per share with a "crown jewel" irrevocable lock-up option to Merrill designed to discourage Hanson from seeking control by providing that if any other party (in this case Hanson) should acquire more than one-third of SCM's outstanding shares (66⅔% being needed under N.Y.Bus.L. § 903(a)(2) to effectuate a merger), Merrill would have the right to buy SCM's two most profitable businesses (consumer foods and pigments) at prices characterized by some as "bargain basement." The final act in this scenario was the decision of Hanson, having been deterred by the SCM–Merrill option (colloquially described in the market as a "poison pill"), to terminate its cash tender offer and then to make private purchases, amounting to 25% of SCM's outstanding shares, leading SCM to seek and obtain the preliminary injunction from which this appeal is taken. A more detailed history of relevant events follows.

SCM is a New York corporation with its principal place of business in New York City. Its shares, of which at all relevant times at least 9.9 million were outstanding and 2.3 million were subject to issuance upon conversion of other outstanding securities, are traded on the New York Stock Exchange (NYSE) and Pacific Stock Exchange. Hanson Trust PLC is an English company with its principal place of business in London. HSCM, a Delaware corporation, and Hanson Holdings Netherlands B.V., a Netherlands limited liability company, are indirect wholly-owned subsidiaries of Hanson Trust PLC.

On August 21, 1985, Hanson publicly announced its intention to make a cash tender offer of $60 per share for any and all outstanding SCM shares. Five days later it filed the tender offer documents required by § 14(d)(1) of the Williams Act and regulations issued thereunder. The offer provided that it would remain open until September 23, unless extended, that no shares would be accepted until September 10, and that

> "Whether or not the Purchasers [Hanson] purchase Shares pursuant to the Offer, the Purchasers may thereafter determine, subject to the availability of Shares at favorable prices and the availability of financing, to purchase additional Shares in the open market, in privately negotiated transactions, through another tender offer or otherwise. Any such purchases of additional Shares might be on terms which are the same as, or more or less favorable than, those of this Offer. The Purchasers also reserve the right to dispose of any or all Shares acquired by them." *Offer to Purchase For Cash Any and All Outstanding Shares of Common Stock of SCM Corporation* (Aug. 26, 1985) at 21.

On August 30, 1985, SCM, having recommended to SCM's stockholders that they not accept Hanson's tender offer, announced a preliminary agreement with Merrill under which a new entity, formed by SCM and Merrill, would acquire all SCM shares at $70 per share in a leveraged buyout sponsored by Merrill. Under the agreement, which was executed on September 3, the new entity would make a $70 per share cash tender offer for approximately 85% of SCM's shares. If more than two-thirds of SCM's shares were acquired under the offer the remaining SCM shares would be acquired in exchange for debentures in a new corporation to be formed as a result of the merger. On the same date, September 3, Hanson increased its tender offer from $60 to $72 cash per share. However, it expressly reserved the right to terminate its offer if SCM granted to anyone any option to purchase SCM assets on terms that Hanson believed to constitute a "lock-up" device. *Supplement Dated September 5, 1985, to Offer to Purchase*, at 4.

The next development in the escalating bidding contest for control of SCM occurred on September 10, 1985, when SCM entered into a new leveraged buyout agreement with its "White Knight," Merrill. The agreement provided for a two-step acquisition of SCM stock by Merrill at $74 per share. The first proposed step was to be the acquisition of approximately 82% of SCM's outstanding stock for cash. Following a merger (which required acquisition of at least 66⅔%), debentures would be issued for the remaining SCM shares. If any investor or group other than Merrill acquired more than one-third of SCM's outstanding shares, Merrill would have the option to buy SCM's two most profitable businesses, pigments and consumer foods, for $350 and $80 million respectively, prices which Hanson believed to be below their market value.

Hanson, faced with what it considered to be a "poison pill," concluded that even if it increased its cash tender offer to $74 per share it would end up with control of a substantially depleted and damaged company. Accordingly, it announced on the Dow Jones Broad Tape at 12:38 P.M. on September 11 that it was terminating its cash tender offer. A few minutes later, Hanson issued a press release, carried on the Broad Tape, to the effect that "all SCM shares tendered will be promptly returned to the tendering shareholders."

At some time in the late forenoon or early afternoon of September 11 Hanson decided to make cash purchases of a substantial percentage of SCM stock in the open market or through privately negotiated transactions. Under British law Hanson could not acquire more than 49% of SCM's shares in this fashion without obtaining certain clearances, but acquisition of such a large percentage was not necessary to stymie the SCM–Merrill merger proposal. If Hanson could acquire slightly less than one-third of SCM's outstanding shares it would be able to block the $74 per share SCM–Merrill offer of a leveraged buyout. This might induce the latter to work out an agreement with Hanson, something Hanson had unsuccessfully sought on several occasions since its first cash tender offer.

Within a period of two hours on the afternoon of September 11 Hanson made five privately-negotiated cash purchases of SCM stock and one open-market purchase, acquiring 3.1 million shares or 25% of SCM's outstanding stock. The price of SCM stock on the NYSE on September 11 ranged from a high of $73.50 per share to a low of $72.50 per share. Hanson's initial private purchase, 387,700 shares from Mutual Shares, was not solicited by Hanson but by a Mutual Shares official, Michael Price, who, in a conversation with Robert Pirie of Rothschild, Inc., Hanson's financial advisor, on the morning of September 11 (before Hanson had decided to make any private cash purchases), had stated that he was interested in selling Mutual's Shares' SCM stock to Hanson. Once Hanson's decision to buy privately had been made, Pirie took Price up on his offer. The parties negotiated a sale at $73.50 per share after Pirie refused

Price's asking prices, first of $75 per share and, later, of $74.50 per share. This transaction, but not the identity of the parties, was automatically reported pursuant to NYSE rules on the NYSE ticker at 3:11 P.M. and reported on the Dow Jones Broad Tape at 3:29 P.M.

Pirie then telephoned Ivan Boesky, an arbitrageur who had a few weeks earlier disclosed in a Schedule 13D statement filed with the SEC that he owned approximately 12.7% of SCM's outstanding shares. Pirie negotiated a Hanson purchase of these shares at $73.50 per share after rejecting Boesky's initial demand of $74 per share. At the same time Rothschild purchased for Hanson's account 600,000 SCM shares in the open market at $73.50 per share. An attempt by Pirie next to negotiate the cash purchase of another large block of SCM stock (some 780,000 shares) from Slifka & Company fell through because of the latter's inability to make delivery of the shares on September 12.

Following the NYSE ticker and Broad Tape reports of the first two large anonymous transactions in SCM stock, some professional investors surmised that the buyer might be Hanson. Rothschild then received telephone calls from (1) Mr. Mulhearn of Jamie & Co. offering to sell between 200,000 and 350,000 shares at $73.50 per share, (2) David Gottesman, an arbitrageur at Oppenheimer & Co. offering 89,000 shares at $73.50, and (3) Boyd Jeffries of Jeffries & Co., offering approximately 700,000 to 800,000 shares at $74.00. Pirie purchased the three blocks for Hanson at $73.50 per share. The last of Hanson's cash purchases was completed by 4:35 P.M. on September 11, 1985.

In the early evening of September 11 SCM successfully applied to Judge Kram in the present lawsuit for a restraining order barring Hanson from acquiring more SCM stock for 24 hours. On September 12 and 13 the TRO was extended by consent pending the district court's decision on SCM's application for a preliminary injunction. Judge Kram held an evidentiary hearing on September 12–13, at which various witnesses testified, including Sir Gordon White, Hanson's United States Chairman, two Rothschild representatives (Pirie and Gerald Goldsmith) and stock market risk-arbitrage professionals (Robert Freeman of Goldman, Sachs & Co., Kenneth Miller of Merrill Lynch, and Danial Burch of D.F. King & Co.). Sir Gordon White testified that on September 11, 1985, after learning of the $74 per share SCM–Merrill leveraged buyout tender offer with its "crown jewel" irrevocable "lock-up" option to Merrill, he instructed Pirie to terminate Hanson's $72 per share tender offer, and that only thereafter did he discuss the possibility of Hanson making market purchases of SCM stock. Pirie testified that the question of buying stock may have been discussed in the late forenoon of September 11 and that he had told White that he was having Hanson's New York counsel look into whether such cash purchases were legally permissible.

SCM argued before Judge Kram (and argues here) that Hanson's cash purchases immediately following its termination of its $72 per share tender offer amounted to a *de facto* continuation of Hanson's tender offer, designed to avoid the strictures of § 14(d) of the Williams Act, and that unless a preliminary injunction issued SCM and its shareholders would be irreparably injured because Hanson would acquire enough shares to defeat the SCM–Merrill offer. Judge Kram found that the relevant underlying facts (which we have outlined) were not in dispute * * * and concluded that "[W]ithout deciding what test should ultimately be applied to determine whether Hanson's conduct constitutes a 'tender offer' within the meaning of the Williams Act * * * SCM has demonstrated a likelihood of success on the merits of its contention that

Hanson has engaged in a tender offer which violates Section 14(d) of the Williams Act." * * * The district court, characterizing Hanson's stock purchases as "a deliberate attempt to do an 'end run' around the requirements of the Williams Act," * * * made no finding on the question of whether Hanson had decided to make the purchases of SCM before or after it dropped its tender offer but concluded that even if the decision had been made after it terminated its offer preliminary injunctive relief should issue. From this decision Hanson appeals.

DISCUSSION

A preliminary injunction will be overturned only when the district court abuses its discretion. * * *

Since, as the district court correctly noted, the material relevant facts in the present case are not in dispute, this appeal turns on whether the district court erred as a matter of law in holding that when Hanson terminated its offer and immediately thereafter made private purchases of a substantial share of the target company's outstanding stock, the purchases became a "tender offer" within the meaning of § 14(d) of the Williams Act. Absent any express definition of "tender offer" in the Act, the answer requires a brief review of the background and purposes of § 14(d).

* * *

The typical tender offer, as described in the Congressional debates, hearings and reports on the Williams Act, consisted of a general, publicized bid by an individual or group to buy shares of a publicly-owned company, the shares of which were traded on a national securities exchange, at a price substantially above the current market price. * * * The offer was usually accompanied by newspaper and other publicity, a time limit for tender of shares in response to it, and a provision fixing a quantity limit on the total number of shares of the target company that would be purchased.

Prior to the Williams Act a tender offeror had no obligation to disclose any information to shareholders when making a bid. The Report of the Senate Committee on Banking and Currency aptly described the situation: "by using a cash tender offer the person seeking control can operate in almost complete secrecy. At present, the law does not even require that he disclose his identity, the source of his funds, who his associates are, or what he intends to do if he gains control of the corporation."

* * *

The purpose of the Williams Act was, accordingly, to protect the shareholders from that dilemma by insuring "that public shareholders who are confronted by a cash tender offer for their stock will not be required to respond without adequate information." Piper v. Chris–Craft Industries, 430 U.S. 1, 35 (1977); Rondeau v. Mosinee Paper Corp., 422 U.S. 49, 58 (1975).

Congress took "extreme care," 113 Cong.Rec. 24664 (Senator Williams); id. at 854 (Senator Williams), however, when protecting shareholders, to avoid "tipping the balance of regulation either in favor of management or in favor of the person making the takeover bid." * * *

Congress finally settled upon a statute requiring a tender offer solicitor seeking beneficial ownership of more than 5% of the outstanding shares of any class of any equity security registered on a national securities exchange first to file with the SEC a statement containing certain information specified in § 13(d)(1) of the Act, as amplified by SEC rules and regulations. Congress' failure to define "tender offer" was deliberate. Aware of "the almost infinite variety in the terms of most tender offers" and concerned that a rigid definition would be evaded, Congress left to the court and the SEC the flexibility to define the term. * * *

Although § 14(d)(1) clearly applies to "classic" tender offers of the type described above * * *, courts soon recognized that in the case of privately negotiated transactions or solicitations for private purchases of stock many of the conditions leading to the enactment of § 14(d) for the most part do not exist. The number and percentage of stockholders are usually far less than those involved in public offers. The solicitation involves less publicity than a public tender offer or none. The solicitees, who are frequently directors, officers or substantial stockholders of the target, are more apt to be sophisticated, inquiring or knowledgeable concerning the target's business, the solicitor's objectives, and the impact of the solicitation on the target's business prospects. In short, the solicitee in the private transaction is less likely to be pressured, confused, or ill-informed regarding the businesses and decisions at stake than solicitees who are the subjects of a public tender offer.

These differences between public and private securities transactions have led most courts to rule that private transactions or open market purchases do not qualify as a "tender offer" requiring the purchaser to meet the pre-filing strictures of § 14(d). Kennecott Copper Corp. v. Curtiss–Wright Corp., 449 F.Supp. 951, 961 (S.D.N.Y.), aff'd in relevant part, 584 F.2d 1195, 1206–07 (2d Cir.1978); Stromfeld v. Great Atlantic & Pac. Tea Co., Inc., 496 F.Supp. 1084, 1088–89 (S.D.N.Y.), aff'd mem., 646 F.2d 563 (2d Cir.1980); SEC v. Carter Hawley Hale Stores, Inc., 760 F.2d 945, 950–53 (9th Cir.1985); Brascan Ltd. v. Edper Equities, Ltd., 477 F.Supp. 773, 791–92 (S.D.N.Y.1979); Astronics Corp. v. Protective Closures Co., 561 F.Supp. 329, 334 (W.D.N.Y.1983); LTV Corp. v. Grumman Corp., 526 F.Supp. 106, 109 (E.D.N.Y.1981); Energy Ventures, Inc. v. Appalachian Co., 587 F.Supp. 734, 739–41 (D.Del.1984); Ludlow v. Tyco Laboratories, Inc., 529 F.Supp. 62, 67 (D.Mass.1981); Chromalloy American Corp. v. Sun Chemical Corp., 474 F.Supp. 1341, 1346–47 (E.D.Mo.), aff'd, 611 F.2d 240 (8th Cir.1979). The borderline between public solicitations and privately negotiated stock purchases is not bright and it is frequently difficult to determine whether transactions falling close to the line or in a type of "no man's land" are "tender offers" or private deals. This has led some to advocate a broader interpretation of the term "tender offer" than that followed by us in Kennecott Copper Corp. v. Curtiss–Wright Corp., supra, 584 F.2d at 1207, and to adopt the eight-factor "test" of what is a tender offer, which was recommended by the SEC and applied by the district court in Wellman v. Dickinson, 475 F.Supp. 783, 823–24 (S.D.N.Y.1979), aff'd on other grounds, 682 F.2d 355 (2d Cir.1982), cert. denied, 460 U.S. 1069 (1983), and by the Ninth Circuit in SEC v. Carter Hawley Hale Stores, Inc., supra. The eight factors are:

"(1) active and widespread solicitation of public shareholders for the shares of an issuer;

(2) solicitation made for a substantial percentage of the issuer's stock;

(3) offer to purchase made at a premium over the prevailing market price;

(4) terms of the offer are firm rather than negotiable;

    (5) offer contingent on the tender of a fixed number of shares, often subject to a fixed maximum number to be purchased;

    (6) offer open only for a limited period of time;

    (7) offeree subjected to pressure to sell his stock;

* * *

    [(8)] public announcements of a purchasing program concerning the target company precede or accompany rapid accumulation of large amounts of the target company's securities." (475 F.Supp. at 823–24).

Although many of the above-listed factors are relevant for purposes of determining whether a given solicitation amounts to a tender offer, the elevation of such a list to a mandatory "litmus test" appears to be both unwise and unnecessary. As even the advocates of the proposed test recognize, in any given case a solicitation may constitute a tender offer even though some of the eight factors are absent or, when many factors are present, the solicitation may nevertheless not amount to a tender offer because the missing factors outweigh those present. Id., at 824; *Carter,* supra, at 950.

We prefer to be guided by the principle followed by the Supreme Court in deciding what transactions fall within the private offering exemption provided by § 4(1) of the Securities Act of 1933, and by ourselves in *Kennecott Copper* in determining whether the Williams Act applies to private transactions. That principle is simply to look to the statutory purpose. In S.E.C. v. Ralston Purina Co., 346 U.S. 119 (1953), the Court stated, "the applicability of § 4(1) should turn on whether the particular class of persons affected need the protection of the Act. An offering to those who are shown to be able to fend for themselves is a transaction 'not involving any public offering.' " Id., at 125. Similarly, since the purpose of § 14(d) is to protect the ill-informed solicitee, the question of whether a solicitation constitutes a "tender offer" within the meaning of § 14(d) turns on whether, viewing the transaction in the light of the totality of circumstances, there appears to be a likelihood that unless the pre-acquisition filing strictures of that statute are followed there will be a substantial risk that solicitees will lack information needed to make a carefully considered appraisal of the proposal put before them.

Applying this standard, we are persuaded on the undisputed facts that Hanson's September 11 negotiation of five private purchases and one open market purchase of SCM shares, totalling 25% of SCM's outstanding stock, did not under the circumstances constitute a "tender offer" within the meaning of the Williams Act. Putting aside for the moment the events preceding the purchases, there can be little doubt that the privately negotiated purchases would not, standing alone, qualify as a tender offer, for the following reasons:

    (1) In a market of 22,800 SCM shareholders the number of SCM sellers here involved, six in all, was miniscule compared with the numbers involved in public solicitations of the type against which the Act was directed.

    (2) At least five of the sellers were highly sophisticated professionals, knowledgeable in the market place and well aware of the essential facts needed to exercise their professional skills and to appraise Hanson's offer, including its financial condition as well as that of SCM, the likelihood that the purchases might block the SCM–Merrill bid, and the risk that if Hanson acquired more than 33⅓% of SCM's stock the SCM–Merrill lockup

of the "crown jewel" might be triggered. Indeed, by September 11 they had all had access to (1) Hanson's 27–page detailed disclosure of facts, filed on August 26, 1985, in accordance with § 14(d)(1) with respect to its $60 tender offer, (2) Hanson's 4–page amendment of that offer, dated September 5, 1985, increasing the price to $72 per share, and (3) press releases regarding the basic terms of the SCM–Merrill proposed leveraged buyout at $74 per share and of the SCM–Merrill asset option agreement under which SCM granted to Merrill the irrevocable right under certain conditions to buy SCM's consumer food business for $80 million and its pigment business for $350 million.

(3) The sellers were not "pressured" to sell their shares by any conduct that the Williams Act was designed to alleviate but by the forces of the market place. Indeed, in the case of Mutual Shares there was no initial solicitation by Hanson; the offer to sell was initiated by Mr. Price of Mutual Shares. Although each of the Hanson purchases was made for $73.50 per share, in most instances this price was the result of private negotiations after the sellers sought higher prices and in one case price protection, demands which were refused. The $73.50 price was not fixed in advance by Hanson. Moreover, the sellers remained free to accept the $74 per share tender offer made by the SCM–Merrill group.

(4) There was no active or widespread advance publicity or public solicitation, which is one of the earmarks of a conventional tender offer. Arbitrageurs might conclude from ticker tape reports of two large anonymous transactions that Hanson must be the buyer. However, liability for solicitation may not be predicated upon disclosures mandated by Stock Exchange Rules. See S.E.C. v. Carter Hawley Hale Stores, Inc., supra, 760 F.2d at 950.

(5) The price received by the six sellers, $73.50 per share, unlike that appearing in most tender offers, can scarcely be dignified with the label "premium." The stock market price on September 11 ranged from $72.50 to $73.50 per share. Although risk arbitrageurs sitting on large holdings might reap sizeable profits from sales to Hanson at $73.50, depending on their own purchase costs, they stood to gain even more if the SCM–Merrill offer of $74 should succeed, as it apparently would if they tendered their shares to it. Indeed, the $73.50 price, being at most $1 over market or 1.4% higher than the market price, did not meet the SEC's proposed definition of a premium, which is $2.00 per share or 5% above market price, whichever is greater. SEC Exchange Act Release No. 16,385 (11/29/79) [1979–80] Fed.Sec.L.Rep. ¶ 82,374.

(6) Unlike most tender offers, the purchases were not made contingent upon Hanson's acquiring a fixed minimum number or percentage of SCM's outstanding shares. Once an agreement with each individual seller was reached, Hanson was obligated to buy, regardless what total percentage of stock it might acquire. Indeed, it does not appear that Hanson had fixed in its mind a firm limit on the amount of SCM shares it was willing to buy.

(7) Unlike most tender offers, there was no general time limit within which Hanson would make purchases of SCM stock. Concededly, cash transactions are normally immediate but, assuming an inability on the part of a seller and Hanson to agree at once on a price, nothing prevented a resumption of negotiations by each of the parties except the arbitrageurs'

speculation that once Hanson acquired 33⅓% or an amount just short of that figure it would stop buying.

In short, the totality of circumstances that existed on September 11 did not evidence any likelihood that unless Hanson was required to comply with § 14(d)(1)'s pre-acquisition filing and waiting-period requirements there would be a substantial risk of ill-considered sales of SCM stock by ill-informed shareholders.

There remains the question whether Hanson's private purchases take on a different hue, requiring them to be treated as a *"de facto"* continuation of its earlier tender offer, when considered in the context of Hanson's earlier acknowledged tender offer, the competing offer of SCM–Merrill and Hanson's termination of its tender offer. After reviewing all of the undisputed facts we conclude that the district court erred in so holding.

In the first place, we find no record support for the contention by SCM that Hanson's September 11 termination of its outstanding tender offer was false, fraudulent or ineffective. Hanson's termination notice was clear, unequivocal and straight-forward. Directions were given, and presumably are being followed, to return all of the tendered shares to the SCM shareholders who tendered them. Hanson also filed with the SEC a statement pursuant to § 14(d)(1) of the Williams Act terminating its tender offer. As a result, at the time when Hanson made its September 11 private purchases of SCM stock it owned no SCM stock other than those shares revealed in its § 14(d) pre-acquisition report filed with the SEC on August 26, 1985.

The reason for Hanson's termination of its tender offer is not disputed: in view of SCM's grant of what Hanson conceived to be a "poison pill" lockup option to Merrill, Hanson, if it acquired control of SCM, would have a company denuded as the result of its sale of its consumer food and pigment businesses to Merrill at what Hanson believed to be bargain prices. Thus, Hanson's termination of its tender offer was final; there was no tender offer to be "continued." Hanson was unlikely to "shoot itself in the foot" by triggering what it believed to be a "poison pill," and it could not acquire more than 49% of SCM's shares without violating the rules of the London Stock Exchange.

Nor does the record support SCM's contention that Hanson had decided, before terminating its tender offer, to engage in cash purchases. Judge Kram referred only to evidence that "Hanson had *considered* open market purchases before it announced that the tender offer was dropped" (emphasis added) but made no finding to that effect. Absent evidence or a finding that Hanson had decided to seek control of SCM through purchases of its stock, no duty of disclosure existed under the federal securities laws.

Second, Hanson had expressly reserved the right in its August 26, 1985, pre-acquisition tender offer filing papers, whether or not tendered shares were purchased, *"thereafter * * * to purchase additional Shares in the open market, in privately negotiated transactions, through another tender offer or otherwise."* (Emphasis added). * * * Thus, Hanson's privately negotiated purchases could hardly have taken the market by surprise. Indeed, professional arbitrageurs and market experts rapidly concluded that it was Hanson which was making the post-termination purchases.

Last, Hanson's prior disclosures of essential facts about itself and SCM in the pre-acquisition papers it filed on August 26, 1985, with the SEC pursuant to § 14(d)(1), are wholly inconsistent with the district court's characterization of Hanson's later private purchases as "a deliberate attempt to do an 'end run' around the requirements of the Williams Act." * * *

In the present case we conclude that since the district court erred in ruling as a matter of law that SCM had demonstrated a likelihood of success on the merits, based on the theory that Hanson's post-tender offer private purchases of SCM constituted a *de facto* tender offer, it was an abuse of discretion to issue a preliminary injunction. Indeed, we do not believe that Hanson's transactions raise serious questions going to the merits that would provide a fair ground for litigation. In view of this holding it becomes unnecessary to rule upon the district court's determination that the balance of hardships tip in favor of SCM and that absent preliminary relief it would suffer irreparable injury. However, our decision is not to be construed as an affirmance of the district court's resolution of these issues.

* * *

The order of the district court is reversed, the preliminary injunction against Hanson is vacated, and the case is remanded for further proceedings in accordance with this opinion. The mandate shall issue forthwith.

———

Unconventional offers. Both *Hanson Trust* and *Carter Hawley Hale* deal with open market purchasing (or "street sweeps"). More often litigated have been privately negotiated purchases from a limited group of purchasers. In *Hoover Co. v. Fuqua Industries, Inc.*,[1] the court held that an offer made to over one hundred members of the family of the founder of the company amounted to a tender offer. Although earlier decisions had found offers to a limited group of sophisticated purchasers not to be a tender offer,[2] the *Hoover* court found that the family shareholders who were there solicited had little in common, had not worked for the company, and owned widely varying shareholdings. Thus, it found the solicitation of the family to be "the equivalent of a solicitation of all the public shareholders." *Query:* should an offer limited to fifty to one hundred of the senior officers of a target corporation be deemed a tender offer? Note that if the answer is yes, Rule 14d–10 requires that the offer be made to all shareholders.

In *Wellman v. Dickinson*,[3] the court found that a solicitation to sell stock in a target company made to thirty large institutional holders and nine individuals was a tender offer, applying the eight "factors" which are discussed in the *Carter Hawley Hale* case. The solicitation was carried out like a military operation with thirty different representatives of the brokerage firm, each sitting with a lawyer, telephoning the solicitees at 4 p.m. New York time after the close of the New York Stock Exchange and giving them only one hour to decide whether or not to accept the offer, which was at a substantial premium over market. By this operation, the offeror acquired approximately thirty-four percent of the outstanding stock of the target company. The solicitees had been alerted earlier to expect a phone call at 4 p.m. New York time, but were not given the exact price that was going to be offered until those phone calls were made after the close of the market. Judge Carter indicated that in his opinion

1. Fed.Sec.L.Rep. (CCH), Para. 97,107 (N.D.Ohio 1979). For a case involving a widespread telephone solicitation of shareholders, see Cattlemen's Investment Co. v. Fears, 343 F.Supp. 1248 (W.D.Okl.1972).

2. See Kennecott Copper Corp. v. Curtiss–Wright Corp., 584 F.2d 1195, 1206 (2d Cir.1978); D–Z Investment Co. v. Holloway, Fed.Sec.L.Rptr. (CCH), Para. 94,771 (S.D. N.Y. 1974).

3. 475 F.Supp. 783 (S.D.N.Y.1979), aff'd on other grounds, 682 F.2d 355 (2d Cir.1982).

all the "factors" were satisfied except one, the widespread publication of the offer to the general body of shareholders. It would not appear that the *Hanson Trust* case has overruled that decision, although the court did not approve the automatic use of these "factors."

Street Sweeps. In 1979, the SEC proposed, but never adopted, a definition of tender offer that would have included many street sweeps.[4] Under Proposed Rule 14d–1(b)(1), the term "tender offer" would have had four elements: (1) one or more offers to purchase, or solicitations of offers to sell, securities of a single class; (2) during any 45 day period; (3) directed to more than 10 persons; and (4) seeking the acquisition of more than 5% of the class. However, an exception was also proposed for open market purchases by a broker or its customer at the then current market price on a national securities exchange or in the over-the-counter market if three conditions were present: (1) the open market purchases were unsolicited; (2) the broker or dealer performed only the customary functions of a broker or dealer; and (3) the broker or dealer received no more than the customary commission or markup for executing the trade. Does this deal adequately with the "street sweep"? Note that the transaction in *Carter Hawley Hale* would probably not have been a tender offer under the proposed rule, as the purchases were at the then current market price and the other criteria of the open market exemption were also seemingly satisfied.

In 1987, the SEC again proposed, but never adopted, a special rule to deal with street sweeps.[5] Proposed Rule 14a–11 would provide that after the termination of a tender offer a bidder could not for 30 days increase its beneficial ownership in the target by 10 percent or more (except by means of another tender offer). Also, any other person (such as arbitrageurs) would be similarly precluded for ten days. The proposed rule seems to have been a direct response to the *Hanson Trust* case and the problem of the confused aftermarket following the termination of a tender offer.

Obviously, there was an egalitarian dimension to Proposed Rule 14d–11, because the chief beneficiaries of street sweeps are professional investors, who have easy access to the market within the short time frames during which street sweeps occur, while "little" investors typically miss out. An expansive definition of tender offer (without any exclusion for open market purchasing at the market price) might be defended on the ground that it promotes equality of treatment among stockholders. From such a policy perspective, one may well ask a broader question: should not the tender offer be the preferred and indeed mandatory technique for the hostile acquisition (as it is in effect in Great Britain)?

C.   WHO'S THE BIDDER?

MAI Basic Four, Inc. v. Prime Computer, Inc.

United States Court of Appeals, First Circuit, 1989.
871 F.2d 212.

■ Before CAMPBELL, Chief Judge, COFFIN, SENIOR CIRCUIT JUDGE, and BOWNES, CIRCUIT JUDGE.

■ COFFIN, SENIOR CIRCUIT JUDGE.

---

4. Securities Exchange Act Release No. 16385 (Nov. 29, 1979).

5. Securities Exchange Act Release No. 24976. For an overview, see Osterle, The Rise and Fall of Street Sweep Takeovers, 1989 Duke L.J. 202. An equivalent to proposed Rule 14a–11 has, however, been adopted for issuer self-tenders. See Rule 13e–4(f)(6) (ten business day cooling off period).

This expedited appeal arises out of the efforts of a group of companies in the computer industry, MAI Basic Four, Choice Corporation, and Brooke Partners, L.P. (collectively Basic), to take over control of Prime Computer, Inc. (Prime). Although Basic filed the first complaint, attacking Massachusetts anti-takeover statutes in connection with its November 15, 1988, tender offer, the present issues flow from the district court's action on Prime's counterclaim. In this counterclaim Prime alleged, principally, that Basic had violated the Williams Act Amendments to the Securities Exchange Act (the Act), by failing to disclose in its Offer to Purchase sufficient information concerning the involvement, interests, and condition of its investment advisor, investor, and underwriter, Drexel Burnham Lambert, Inc. (Drexel). It contended that Drexel fell under the Act's disclosure requirements because it was in reality a "bidder." SEC Rule 14d–1(b)(1), 17 C.F.R. § 240.14d–1(b)(1); Rule 14d–6, 17 C.F.R. § 14d–6; SEC Schedule 14D–1, 17 C.F.R. § 240.14d–100.

Prime sought a preliminary injunction against consummation of the tender offer, which was granted on December 9, 1988. The injunction has survived several subsequent proceedings in which supplemental disclosures made by Basic were considered. The inquiry on this appeal is whether the district court committed either an error of law or abuse of discretion in continuing to enjoin the consummation of the offer pending receipt of further information from Basic regarding Drexel.

THE TENDER OFFER

The elements of the tender offer are as follows. Basic is offering $20 a share in cash for all shares of Prime, a price that exceeds the pre-offer market price. As of the date of oral argument, March 2, 1989, approximately 61 percent of Prime stock had been tendered, 46 percent on a fully diluted basis.[1] The offer is conditioned upon there being tendered, prior to its expiration, 67 percent of the shares on a fully diluted basis. * * * The financing consists of $20 million in cash, supplied by Brooke Partners, L.P.; $650 million in bank financing; and $875 million in high yield, interest bearing, increasing rate notes (*i.e.,* "junk bonds"), placement to be arranged by Drexel. Upon consummation of the offer, Basic intends to merge itself and Prime and cash out any remaining Prime stockholders at $20 a share.

DREXEL'S INVOLVEMENT

Drexel's past, present, and contemplated roles in connection with the offer lie at the heart of this appeal. Since 1986 Drexel has been associated in arranging financing for Basic's principal stockholders, Bennett S. LeBow and William Weksel, in several other acquisitions (of Liggett Group, Inc. and of Western Union Corp.) in which Drexel has obtained both substantial fees and equity positions. In the spring of 1988, Drexel tried unsuccessfully to interest Prime in buying MAI Basic Four. Subsequently, Basic decided to be the acquirer. Drexel's undertaking, as financial advisor for this transaction, is to "include, but not be limited to * * * advising and assisting [Basic] in determining the possible alternative ways in which the Transaction might be structured, and advising and assisting [Basic] with respect to the completion of the Transaction."

---

1. That is, after taking into account additional shares projected to be issued in connection with (or in response to) the tender offer.

Drexel has an equity interest in MAI Basic Four, Inc., which will be 5 percent on a diluted basis, with a right to purchase at half price another 9 percent. In addition to this 14 percent of direct interest, it possesses, through two intermediary partnership entities, a one-third equity interest in LeBow, Inc., and, through another entity, a 17 percent equity interest in Brooke Partners. LeBow, Inc., is the sole owner of L. Holdings, which is Brooke's sole general partner. As of the date of the offer, Drexel also, through a stockholders agreement, had the right to name one of the three directors of LeBow, Inc., with veto power over some corporate actions. During this litigation, the agreement was changed to remove Drexel's right to a board member, but Drexel continues to have the right to attend board meetings and is guaranteed first refusal in future underwriting and placement.

Drexel's role in placing $875 million in junk bonds will entitle it to $65 million in fees, if the placement is successful. At the moment, the record indicates that none of these notes have been sold. Even if the offer fails, Drexel will be entitled to 15 percent of any profit Basic realizes from selling Prime stock now held. There is some ambiguity with regard to a further role Drexel may have in relation to the notes. The offer to Purchase merely reflects Drexel's view that it is "highly confident" that it can place the $875 million of notes and its agreement "to use its best efforts to arrange the financing."

CONTENTIONS OF THE PARTIES

The positions taken by the parties could not be farther apart. Basic * * * challenges the court's finding that Drexel is a bidder. Finally it argues that even if Drexel could be considered a bidder, no additional disclosure is required by the Act. When asked why Basic could not readily furnish the kind of information concerning Drexel that was provided in *Interco*, counsel's response was that other questions would be asked and that "no amount of disclosure is ever going to be enough."

Prime, on the other hand, maintains that Drexel should, as a bidder, furnish all items of information required for compliance with Schedule 14D-1. In oral argument counsel stated, without citing any authority, that even if Drexel is not a bidder, it is still such a key participant that its financial condition was material information which must be more thoroughly disclosed under the Williams Act.

　　　* * *

The facts in this case bear some similarity to those in Koppers Co. v. American Express Co., 689 F.Supp. 1371 (W.D.Pa.1988), where an investment bank was held to be a bidder for purposes of Rule 14d. In Koppers, two Shearson entities, Shearson Holdings and its subsidiary Shearson Lehman, and their indirect subsidiary, SL–Merger, Inc., were found collectively to have become aggressively involved in a takeover plan at an early stage; to have contributed $23.05 million for purchasing shares of the target; to own 46 percent of the Class B common stock in the target; to have committed themselves to a contribution of $570 million for notes or preferred stock; and to have earned large brokerage fees. The court accepted, as criteria for a bidder, "those who are central to the offer," 689 F.Supp. at 1388 (citation omitted), "playing a central participatory role," being "a motivating force," "one of the principal planners and players." Id. at 1390. It acknowledged the multiple roles of the Shearson entities—advisor, underwriter, equity partner, financier, broker-dealer—deeming these roles as far surpassing that of an investment banker. The court labelled Shearson "a major equity participant," "one of the entities on whose behalf the tender offer is made." Id.

In the case at bar, Drexel has equity interests in various affiliates associated with LeBow. It has a background of association with Basic and other LeBow interests. Like Shearson in Koppers, Drexel participated in the planning of the Prime tender offer very early, well before the offer. It had a director with veto power in LeBow, Inc., the sole owner of the general partner of Brooke Partners. Brooke in turn supplied the entire $20 million of equity for this highly leveraged deal, which funds Drexel was instrumental in raising through earlier tender offers. Drexel has relinquished this directorship, but only after commencement of the tender offer and without explication. Of course the projected equity position of Drexel is far less than Shearson's 46 percent interest in Koppers. Finally, Drexel will enjoy substantial fees, perhaps in excess of $65 million, for its heavy participation in the offer.

In a similar vein, the present case is at least somewhat distinguishable from City Capital Assocs. Ltd. Partnership v. Interco, Inc., 860 F.2d 60 (3d Cir.1988). In *Interco,* the court of appeals pointed out that Drexel was not engaged by the acquirer until after the tender offer was made. The court distinguished *Koppers* on the basis that Drexel was to have no representation on the board of the surviving entity, id. at 63 n. 5., and emphasized that there was no indication that Drexel had any control over the offer or that it would have any other role than that of investor. Id. at 63. The court chose not to determine the significance of a recent development, that (apparently due to its inability to secure outside financing) Drexel had committed itself to purchase $609 million of preferred securities, implying that on this basis the district court might properly reach a different result on the bidder issue.

Given Drexel's early and pervasive role in the planning and execution of the present offer, its erstwhile board representation in the corporation controlling the sole equity participant in the bidder group, and record evidence sufficient to reasonably suggest an expectation, though not a contractual obligation, that Drexel would itself provide additional financing if it could not place the $875 in junk bonds elsewhere, we might accept the approach of the Third Circuit while distinguishing *Interco* on its facts. Such a decision on our part would be consistent with one of the formulations of the test in *Interco,* that if a stockholder in an acquirer "is in a position to have a significant impact on the future of that corporation, information about the stockholder may well be material to a decision of stockholders of the target whether to take the offer or hang on with the hope of a greater return." Id. at 65.

But we recognize that in the end the court in *Interco* concluded that financial statements are not required from an entity that will wind up as a minority stockholder. It reached this result based on the perceived need for a bright-line test in the takeover context, requiring a narrow construction of Rule 14d–1(b)(1), and a strict application of Schedule 14D–1, General Instruction G, Item 9, 17 C.F.R. § 240.14d–100, reading the latter to indicate that "bidder" under the SEC regulations means an entity formally making a tender offer and those who *control* it. Because the traditional indicia of control were lacking, ipso facto Drexel was deemed not to be a bidder. We think the more realistic prescription is that of *Interco's* dissenter, who wrote:

> [I]n the event of doubt on a particular disclosure question, courts should exercise liberality in order to carry out the remedial purposes of the

[Williams Act]. Excess information may well be harmless, but inadequate disclosure could be disastrous to the shareholder.

860 F.2d at 68 (Weis, J., dissenting). The more flexible, fact-based approach advocated by Judge Weis is consistent with our reading of the Williams Act.[5]

The purpose of the Williams Act was explained by an often quoted report of the House Interstate and Foreign Commerce Committee as follows:

> The persons seeking control * * * have information about themselves and about their plans which, if known to investors, might substantially change the assumptions on which the market price is based. This bill is designed to make the relevant facts known so that shareholders have a fair opportunity to make their decision.

H.R.Rep. No. 1711, 90th Cong., 2d Sess. 2, reprinted in 1968 U.S.Code Cong. & Admin.News 2811, 2813.

Section 14(d) of the Act governs the disclosures required of those initiating tender offers. Section 14(d)(1) bars an offer by

> any person, directly or indirectly * * * if, after consummation thereof, such person would, directly or indirectly, be the beneficial owner of more than 5 per centum of such class, unless * * * such person has filed with the Commission a statement containing such of the information specified in section 78m(d) of this title, and such additional information as the Commission may by rules and regulations prescribe as necessary or appropriate in the public interest or for the protection of investors.

15 U.S.C. § 78n(d)(1). The statute then defines "person":

> When two or more persons act as a partnership, limited partnership, syndicate, or other group for the purpose of acquiring, holding, or disposing of securities of an issuer, such syndicate or group shall be deemed a "person" for purposes of this subsection.

Williams Act § 14(d)(2), 15 U.S.C. § 78n(d)(2).

The SEC Rule, 14d–1(b)(1) * * * uses the word "bidder" in place of "person" in the statute. It defines a bidder as "any person who makes a tender offer or on whose behalf a tender offer is made." Id. The SEC, in a 1979 Release, stated that bidder was a "shorthand reference[ ] to [a] principal participant[ ] in a tender offer." Exchange Act Release No. 15,548 [1979 Transfer Binder] Fed.Sec.L.Rep. (CCH) ¶ 81,935, at 81,216 (Feb. 5, 1979). We read the "on whose behalf" language of Rule 14d–1(b)(1) to incorporate the "group" concept of sections 13(d) and 14(d) of the Williams Act. As pointed out by Judge Weis in *Interco*, the statute authorizes the SEC to require "additional information," but does not appear to grant the Commission discretion to narrow the definition of "person" explicitly defined in the Act.

Our interpretation of bidder under Rule 14d–1(b)(1) is consistent with the statute. Section 14(d) of the Act, as quoted supra, by explicit cross-reference incorporates the scope of the disclosure requirements of § 13(d), 15 U.S.C. § 78m(d). The definition of "person" in § 14(d)(2) is identical to the formulation found in § 13(d)(3). The legislative history of the latter section contradicts

---

5. The appellant in *Interco* disavowed that Drexel was part of a "group," and the majority therefore declined to reach this issue. 860 F.2d at 65 n. 6. In view of our interpretation and application of the group concept, infra, our analysis may not ultimately contradict that of the Third Circuit.

an exclusive focus on control, a factor provisionally raised in Schedule 14D–1, General Instruction G, Item 9, in determining who is a bidder under the regulation. * * *

We distill from these guides, which use the words "directly or indirectly," "on whose behalf," "principal participant[ ]," and "any contract, understanding, relationship, agreement or other arrangement" that there is no bright, hard-line test for bidder under the regulation. We empathize with the Third Circuit when it said in *Interco,* "[t]his is an area of law in which predictability is of crucial importance." 860 F.2d at 64. But we are skeptical. We suspect that any bright-line test, separating those who are subject to the Williams Act from those who are not, would merely invite the ingenuity of resourceful counsel to place their client formally on the desired side of the line, whatever the underlying reality may be.

In this case we cannot say that, as a matter of law, an active advisor-broker-financier-participant who owns less than a majority interest in the surviving entity is not a bidder where, as here, there has been a history of close association, equity sharing, board representation and involvement from the beginning of the present offer, and where there is the possibility of the advisor-broker being the indispensable key to the offer's success. Nor can we say that while a 46 percent stockholder qualifies as a bidder, a 14 percent direct stockholder with other indirect equity interests cannot qualify.[9] At a minimum it is evident that Drexel has "act[ed] as a partnership, limited partnership, * * * or other group for the purpose of acquiring, holding, or disposing of securities of an issuer." 15 U.S.C. § 78n(d)(2). We are not convinced that the district court erred in determining that Prime demonstrated a likelihood of success on the merits, and therefore affirm the court's ruling that Drexel is a bidder.

This does not end our inquiry. We must determine whether the information still required by the court is "material."

An omitted fact is material if there is a substantial likelihood that a reasonable shareholder would consider it important in deciding how to vote. * * * [This standard] does not require proof of a substantial likelihood that disclosure of the omitted fact would have caused the reasonable investor to change his vote. What the standard does contemplate is a showing of a substantial likelihood that, under all the circumstances, the omitted fact would have assumed actual significance in the deliberations of the reasonable shareholder.

TSC Indus., Inc. v. Northway, Inc., 426 U.S. 438, 449, 96 S.Ct. 2126, 2132, 48 L.Ed.2d 757 (1976).[10] In pointing out that materiality under Item 9 depends on the facts and circumstance of a given case, the SEC has explained:

9. We recognize, too, the possibility that the prospect of Drexel becoming a major creditor by itself purchasing the junk bonds might, in light of all the circumstances, make its financial condition material for purposes of § 14(e) irrespective of the bidder issue. Prime has not pressed this argument, and we decline to reach it.

10. While in *TSC Industries* the Court dealt with materiality under Rule 14a–9 concerning proxy contests, this formulation has since been adopted for purposes of § 14(d), see, e.g., Prudent Real Estate Trust v. Johncamp Realty, Inc., 599 F.2d 1140, 1146–47 (2d Cir.1979); Koppers Co. v. American Express Co., 689 F.Supp. 1371, 1384 (W.D.Pa. 1988)., and § 14(e), Staffin v. Greenberg, 672 F.2d 1196 (3d Cir.1982).

These may include, but are not limited to * * * (4) the ability of the bidder to pay for the securities sought in the tender offer and/or to repay any loans made by the bidder or its affiliates in connection with the tender offer or otherwise. It should be noted that the factors described above are not exclusive nor is it necessary that any or all such factors be present in order to trigger the materiality test.

Filing and Disclosure Relating to Tender Offers, Exchange Act Release No. 13,787, 42 Fed.Reg. at 38,346 (July 21, 1977).

It is not clear to us that the financial strength or vulnerability of Drexel, including the adverse impact of Drexel's plea bargain and other legal difficulties, is immaterial to Prime shareholders' deliberations. As opposed to the "highly confident" opinion of Drexel and the conclusory report that Drexel has over $2 billion of capital, and despite the argument that Drexel has recently financed far larger deals, the *Interco* submission indicated an equity of $1.4 billion as of June 24, 1988, *before* the $650 million plea bargain. As Judge Friendly put it:

> In applying [the materiality] test to a cash tender offer, it is necessary to appreciate the problem faced by a stockholder of the target company in deciding whether to tender, to sell or to hold part or all of his securities. It is true that, in the case of an "any and all" offer such as that here at issue, a stockholder who has firmly decided to tender has no interest in the financial position of the offeror *other than its ability to pay * * ** since he will have severed all financial connections with the target.

Prudent Real Estate Trust v. Johncamp Realty, Inc., 599 F.2d 1140, 1147 (2d Cir.1979) (emphasis added). Even assuming the professed ability to pay the offered price,

> [T]he shareholder of the target company faces a hard problem in determining the most advantageous course of action, a problem whose difficulty is enhanced by his usual ignorance of the course other shareholders are adopting. If the bidder is in a flourishing financial condition, the stockholder might decide to hold his shares in the hope that, if the offer was only partially successful, the bidder might raise his bid after termination of the offer. * * * *Per contra,* a poor financial condition of the bidder might cause the shareholder to accept for fear that control of the company would pass into irresponsible hands.

Id. That shareholders might reasonably hold out for a higher offer is supported by the determination of the Delaware Chancery Court, rejecting Basic's challenge to the institution of takeover defenses by Prime directors, that the directors reasonably relied on independent investment bankers' valuation of Prime stock between $23 and $28 per share. In turn, whether Drexel be seen as weak or strong is a legitimate datum for Prime stockholders.

Nor can we discount the possible impact of Drexel's plea bargain and other legal difficulties as immaterial. This area of corporate cannibalism is not a neat and tidy one. We must rely to a large extent on the judgment of the trial judge who lives with the case. * * *

This leads us to the issue of remedy. We see no reason, even though we have upheld the district court's decision that Drexel is to be considered a bidder, to require a full Schedule 14D–1 disclosure in the exercise of the court's equitable power. We agree with the court in Pacific Realty Trust v. APC Investments, Inc., 685 F.2d 1083, 1086 (9th Cir.1982), that a curative disclosure is sufficient. See also *Riggs Nat'l Bank v. Allbritton*, 516 F.Supp. 164, 182 (D.D.C.1981).

We affirm the order of the district court. We further direct that if Basic files with the SEC 1) current financial statements of Drexel, 2) identification of all Drexel-affiliated officers and directors, and 3) disclosure of recent trading in shares by Drexel, then the district court, upon determining that these disclosures appear accurate and reasonably equivalent to the information voluntarily disclosed in *Interco* (but brought up to date), shall vacate the injunction insofar as it is based on nondisclosure. * * *

————

Materiality Revisited. Why is financial information about a minority shareholder of the bidder material to the shareholders of the target? The First Circuit panel relied on Judge Friendly's statement in *Johncamp Realty, Inc.* that the poor financial condition of the bidder might cause shareholders to accept "for fear that control of the company would pass into irresponsible hands." But if such information will tend to stampede the shareholders into tendering, should disclosure policy force the bidder to disclose it? Suppose to the contrary that Drexel were in strong financial shape. Would it then be a realistic scenario for the target shareholders to fail to tender "in the hope that * * * the bidder might raise his bid after the termination of the offer?" Isn't it more likely that the bidder will simply use a squeeze-out merger to eliminate holdout shareholders at the same price or at an even lower price?

As a policy matter, an expansive definition of materiality can be defended on the ground that it fosters an auction market and drives up the premiums in takeovers. But the counter-argument is that if the bidder can be delayed interminably in disclosure litigation and forced to pay a higher premium, such a legal policy will reduce the incentive to make a takeover bid and hence eventually reduce the number of takeovers.[a] In light of this debate, what balance does the SEC strike in its instructions to Schedules 13D and 14D–1?

SECTION 3.   REFORMING THE TENDER OFFER PROCESS

In late 1999, after much debate, the SEC revised takeover procedures significantly with its adoption of Regulation M–A, whose principal goal, as next describes, was to achieve greater transactional parity between cash offers and equity offers. This required significant deregulation and relaxing of the normal rules surrounding the issuance of equity securities (which were analyzed in Chapter 2).

Securities Act Release No. 7760

Securities and Exchange Commission.
October 22, 1999.

* * *

---

a. Compare Rosenzweig, Target Litigation, 85 Mich.L.Rev. 110 (1986) (target litigation should be discouraged as contrary to shareholder interests) with Jarrell, The Wealth Effects of Litigation by Targets: Do Interests Diverge in a Merger?, 28 J.L. & Econ. 151 (1985) (target litigation drives up takeover premiums).

Last fall, we proposed comprehensive changes to the various regulatory schemes applicable to issuer and third-party tender offers, mergers, going-private transactions and security holder communications. The proposed changes were prompted by an increase in the number of transactions where securities are offered as consideration; an increase in the number of hostile transactions involving proxy or consent solicitations; and significant technological advances that have resulted in more and faster communications with security holders and the markets. Because these trends have continued since we issued the Proposing Release and commenters, for the most part, viewed the proposals as favorable, we are adopting the proposals, with some modification.

As we noted in the Proposing Release, the existing regulatory framework imposes a number of restrictions on communications with security holders and the marketplace. In addition, the disparate regulatory treatment of cash and stock tender offers may unduly influence a bidder's choice of offering cash or securities in a takeover transaction. We also noted unnecessary differences in regulatory requirements between tender offers and other types of extraordinary transactions, such as mergers. Finally, we noted that the multiple regulatory schemes that can apply to a transaction may impose additional compliance costs without necessarily providing a sufficient marginal benefit to security holders. Our goals in proposing and adopting these changes are to promote communications with security holders and the markets, minimize selective disclosure, harmonize inconsistent disclosure requirements and alleviate unnecessary burdens associated with the compliance process, without a reduction in investor protection.

* * *

We believe these new rules and revisions should provide participants in the securities markets sufficient flexibility to accommodate changes in deal structure and advances in technology that continue to occur in today's markets. Briefly, the new rules and amendments adopted today will:

* * *

● balance the treatment of stock and cash tender offers by permitting both issuer and third-party stock tender offers to commence as early as the filing of a registration statement;

● simplify and integrate the various disclosure requirements for tender offers, going-private transactions, and other extraordinary transactions in a new series of rules within Regulation S–K, called "Regulation M–A";

* * *

F.   Disclosure Requirements for Tender Offers and Mergers

1.   Schedules Combined and Disclosure Requirements Moved to Subpart 1000 of Regulation S–K ("Regulation M–A")

Currently, there are different disclosure schedules for issuer tender offers, third-party tender offers and going-private transactions. Since a given transaction may involve more than one of these regulatory schemes, a company may be required to file a separate disclosure document to satisfy each applicable disclosure regime. In addition, the disclosure requirements appearing in the rules and schedules can often lead to duplicative, and sometimes inconsistent, requirements. In light of the increased pressure to announce a business combination transaction soon after it is entered into and the attendant requirement to file mandated disclosure documents quickly, we proposed to integrate, simplify and update the disclosure requirements currently in the rules and schedules. Our basic approach was to combine all the disclosure requirements in one central location in a subpart of Regulation S–K, called Regulation M–A. The specific disclosure requirements in schedules were keyed to items under Regulation M–A in a manner consistent with the integrated disclosure system previously adopted for proxy and registration statements.

All commenters addressing the proposed changes in this area believed that it was time to update and simplify the disclosure requirements for business combination transactions. We are adopting Regulation M–A substantially as proposed. This series of disclosure items incorporates all the current disclosure requirements for issuer and third-party tender offers, tender offer recommendation statements and going-private transactions. The new regulation includes some disclosure items for cash merger proxy statements as well. We have made slight modifications, where necessary, to harmonize and clarify the requirements, as well as a few substantive changes that are discussed below in more detail. In some cases the disclosure requirements may appear different, but that is because we have made an effort to draft the items in Regulation M–A using clear, plain language. In the future, we expect to expand this new regulation to cover additional disclosure items as necessary.

We are combining current Schedules 13E–4 and 14D–1 (the schedules now used for issuer and third-party tender offers, respectively), into new Schedule TO, as proposed. In addition, we are changing the rules to allow one filing to satisfy both the tender offer and going-private disclosure requirements. As a result, the information required by Schedules 14D–1, 13E–4 and 13E–3 can be disclosed in one combined filing. We believe that these revisions will reduce the need to file two or more schedules for what is essentially the same transaction.

We have included an instruction in new Schedule TO, as proposed, listing the specific line items that must be complied with for different types of transactions. In addition, we have revised the current instruction requiring information that is incorporated by reference to be filed as an exhibit. As revised, filers can incorporate information included in documents previously filed electronically on EDGAR without refiling that information as an exhibit to the schedule. To the extent that the existing schedules permit filers to include negative answers in the schedule, but not in the disclosure document sent to security holders, filers will continue to have the ability to omit that information from documents sent to security holders.

At this time we are not extending the one filing satisfies all approach to encompass transactions involving the Securities Act and proxy rules as well as the tender offer and going-private rules. In the future, we may consider integrating the requirements further, to permit the satisfaction of the disclosure required under all four regulatory schemes with one filing.

We also are revising the rules that require filing persons to include a fair and adequate summary of the information required by the schedules in the disclosure document sent to security holders. Instead of specifying some items and excluding others, as the current rules do, the revised rules simply require that the document given to security holders summarize all items in the schedule (except for exhibits). As noted in the Proposing Release, this change is not intended to increase the amount of information that is given to security holders. Instead, it is intended to simplify the requirements. We expect filers to exercise their judgment in determining the specific information that must be included in the disclosure document sent to security holders to provide a fair and adequate summary. We are not, however, changing the current requirement that certain disclosure required in a going-private transaction be set forth in full in the disclosure document delivered to security holders.

---

1. *The Goal of Transaction Parity.* The basic thrust of Regulation M–A is to deregulate shareholder communications incident to most forms of business combinations and takeovers in order to ensure that acquirers offering equity securities do not operate at a substantial disadvantage to those offering cash. Prior to these rules, a prospective acquirer who proposed to exchange its securities for securities of the target (either in a friendly merger or a less frequent hostile exchange offer) operated at a substantial disadvantage to a bidder (either friendly or hostile) who offered cash. The acquirer who offered stock had to register its securities and could not commence its exchange offer until the SEC had reviewed the registration statement covering these securities and declared it effective. Even if the SEC expedited its review, this factor added an element of uncertainty. In contrast, a cash bidder could consummate a cash tender offer, which only has to remain open for 20 business days (or, typically, about a month), much more quickly. The upshot was an incentive for a bidder to use cash instead of stock because the longer the period before the offer could be consummated, the more vulnerable the bidder was to a "disruptive" higher bid by a hostile, third party.

New Rule 162 seeks to reduce this incentive to prefer cash over stock by permitting an offeror to solicit tenders of securities in an exchange offer "before a registration statement is effective as to the security offered, so long as no securities are purchased until the registration statement is effective and the tender offer has expired in accordance with the tender offer rules." Of course, such an exchange bidder would have to distribute a preliminary prospectus to target shareholders, but in effect cash and exchange offers can now be commenced at the same point and consummated equivalently—at least so long as the SEC's staff quickly reviews and declares effective the exchange offer's registration statement within the 20 business day period mandated by the tender offer rules. To date, the SEC's staff has been able to meet this goal of processing registration statements in exchange offers within this period.

Publicity and Gun-jumping. Prior to the new rules, any announcement of an exchange offer by the bidder could be seen as a "gun-jumping" violation under Section 5(c) of the Securities Act, unless a registration statement covering the offered securities had already been filed. This meant that an issuer had to file its registration statement before it could safely announce an exchange offer; also, written materials might violate the prohibition on the use of "free writing" under Section 5(b) of the 1933 Act. These problems effectively chilled the exchange bidder and created another unintended legal advantage for the cash bidder. The new rules end (or at least reduce substantially) this disparity. Under Rule 165(a), an offeror of securities to be issued in a business combination may make an offer to sell, or may solicit an offer to buy, those securities beginning with the first public announcement of the transaction, so long as any written communication made in connection with, or relating to, the transaction is filed under new Rule 425 and such "prospectus" contains a prescribed legend. Further, once the registration statement is filed relating to the proposed business combination, Rule 165(b) provides that any written communication made in connection with, or relating to, the transaction will not constitute a "Section 10" prospectus or other form of unlawful "free writing" (and thus need not comply with the disclosure requirements of Section 10 of the 1933 Act), so long as the written communication is filed under Rule 424 or Rule 425 with the SEC and contains a prescribed legend. Anti-fraud liability under Section 12(a)(2) of the 1933 Act will, however, attach to these communications.

Proxy rule reform. A similar exemptive rule was adopted under the proxy rules, so that the offeror could begin at once to solicit proxies prior to filing a proxy statement. Under Rule 14a–12, a proxy solicitation may now be made before shareholders are given a proxy statement if, basically, (1) all proxy soliciting material is given to the SEC, and (ii) a definitive proxy statement is sent to shareholder at or before the time that they are given proxy or consent cards or forms.

Commencement of the Offer. Prior to the new rules, a bidder who disclosed its intention to make a cash tender offer was required to formally commence (or withdraw) the offer within five business days. The point of this rule was to minimize market uncertainty and preclude deceptive stock manipulation tactics. This rule has now been repealed. Bidders and targets may now communicate freely with shareholders undeterred by the threat that a statement may inadvertently trigger a tender offer (or force an embarrassing withdrawal of one that was never truly commenced). The only restriction is that a letter of transmittal (or similar instructions on how to tender) may not be sent prior to commencement (this parallels the equivalent restriction under the proxy rules barring a proxy card being distributed ahead of the proxy statement).

To discourage attempts to manipulate the market by misleading announcements of intended tender offers, the SEC has adopted a new Rule 14e–8, which makes it fraudulent for a person to announce a plan to make a tender offer if the person does not have a bona fide intent to launch the offer within a reasonable time period or lacks a reasonable belief that it will have the means to purchase the securities for which it has tendered.

Because Rule 165's exemption from the 1933 Act's gun-jumping rules is conditioned on an obligation to file all written communications with the SEC after the first public announcement of the transaction, it is still possible that an issuer could blunder and violate the 1933 Act. The term "public announcement" is broadly defined in Rule 165(f)(3), and an issuer who casually indicated its intention to make a tender or exchange offer could thus violate the 1933 Act if it failed to file written communications released after this point.

Subsequent Offering Period. Under the new rules, a bidder may (but need not) tender for shares during a "subsequent offering period" that would follow the date all conditions to its offer were satisfied and the bidder accepted the tendered shares. Shares would have to be purchased as they are tendered during this period, and corresponding tendering shareholders would not have withdrawal rights. The subsequent offer period could be as short as three business days and could be extended by the bidder up to a maximum period of 20 business days.

The purpose of this new period seems to be to permit the bidder to tender for the remaining shares once it has clearly acquired control in the initial tender offer. This would either allow the bidder to clean up the transaction, acquiring all remaining shares without the typical back-end merger, or to raise its level of ownership to the percentage level under state law (typically, 90%) that enabled it to effect a short-form merger without a shareholder vote.

Rule 14e–5. Replacing old Rule 10b–13, new Rule 14e–5 similarly precludes (subject to a list of exceptions) any purchase by a bidder, its affiliates, or advisors of the securities subject to a tender offer (or securities convertible or exchangeable into the same) other than pursuant to the offer. The rule applies from the time the tender offer is announced until the offer expires. During any subsequent offering period, however, purchases outside the offer are permitted, so long as the form and amount of consideration are the same as that offered in the tender offer.

Disclosure Forms. Consolidating the forms and specific disclosure requirements for different types of business combinations, the SEC has adopted "Regulation M–A" as a new subpart of Regulation S–K. It now sets forth the disclosure requirements for issuer tender offers, third-party tender offers and going private transactions. Former Schedule 13E–4 (used in "going private" transactions) and Schedule 14D–1 (used in third party tender offers) have been merged into new Schedule TO. Schedule 13E–3 will still be used when a "going private" transaction is to be effected by a means other than a tender offer. Offers to purchase in cash tender offers and proxy statements in cash mergers are now required to include a "plain English" summary term sheet that highlights in bullet point fashion the principal terms of the transaction.

Impact. The SEC did not grant all the requests of the "M & A" bar for regulatory relief. Despite urging from the bar, the SEC did not provide that registration statements in the case of business combinations would become effective on filing (although it has promised rapid review), and it refused to extend the safe harbor for forward-looking information to tender and exchange offers. Still, the new rules appear to make it possible to effect an exchange offer as quickly as a cash tender offer. Given that there are also tax advantages to the use of equity securities as the currency for business combinations and that exchange offers do not require the bidder to negotiate with a bank or other financial institution over financing terms, exchange offers are becoming more popular and may come to rival the cash tender offers in frequency.

SECTION 4.   DEFENSIVE TACTICS: THE TARGET STRIKES BACK

A fundamental fact about the regulation of takeovers in the United States is that the bidder and target are chiefly regulated by different bodies of law: the bidder by federal law; and the target by state corporate law. The result is an asymmetry that many see as producing inconsistent and even contradictory bodies of law.[1] At a minimum, there has clearly been a tension between federal and state regulation with the SEC at times seeking to preempt some state statutes and also to preclude defensive tactics that state courts have expressly upheld. (One example was the adoption of the "All Holders" Rule to preclude a discriminatory self-tender by the target corporation—a result expressly upheld in Unocal Corp. v. Mesa Petroleum Co.,[2] the leading Delaware decision on takeover defenses).

---

1. For such a critique, see Fiflis, Of Lollipops and Law—A Proposal for a National Policy Concerning Tender Offer Defenses, 19 U.C. Davis L.Rev. 303 (1986).

2.   493 A.2d 946 (Del.1985).

A.   THE WILLIAMS ACT'S APPLICATION TO THE TARGET

The Williams Act applies to the target as well as to the bidder. Schedule 14D–9 must be filed by any person who makes a solicitation or recommendation to target shareholders, and this clearly covers the target company and its management, because Rule 14e–2 requires the target to notify its shareholders of its position with respect to the offer not later than 10 business days from the commencement of the tender offer. This mandatory recommendation in turn triggers the filing of a Schedule 14D–9, which in turn must be updated in the event of a material change. Thus, if midway through a tender offer the target enters into serious negotiations with a third party that wishes to buy a material portion of the target's assets, an amendment of the Schedule 14D–9 may be necessary in order to respond to Item 7 of that Schedule, which requires disclosure of "Certain Negotiations and Transactions by the Subject Company."[3] The instructions to Item 7 may, however, provide an escape clause for the target: disclosure is not required "if no agreement in principle has been reached" and disclosure would "in the opinion of the Board of Directors * * * jeopardize continuation of such negotiations." Even then, a statement that preliminary discussions or negotiations are under way (without naming the target) is required.[4]

Rule 14d–5 also applies to the target and is a corollary to a similar provision in the proxy rules. Under it, the target must choose whether to give the bidder a shareholder list or to mail its tender materials for it. (Predictably, it chooses the latter).

Any misstatement by the target can produce litigation brought by the bidder against the target under § 14(e) of the Williams Act. Under § 14(e), the target need not have purchased or sold securities to bring suit. Although the Supreme Court's decision in Piper v. Chris–Craft Indus., Inc.[5] implies that the bidder lacks standing to sue the target for damages (on the theory that only the target shareholders were the intended beneficiaries of the Williams Act), most courts do permit the bidder to seek injunctive relief for corrective disclosure.[6] Nontendering shareholders other than the bidder can sue the target under § 14(e) for monetary damages where they can allege that but for a fraudulent statement or omission they would have tendered.[7] Of course, the target is also subject to Rule 10b–5 liability to those shareholders who purchased or sold its stock during a period when the market was affected by any material misstatement made by it.

Potentially, § 14(e) could have severely constrained target management's ability to engage in self-interested defensive tactics. However, to employ § 14(e) in this way, courts would have had to read the term "manipulative" in § 14(e) to cover fully disclosed conduct that was in breach of the target management's

---

3. This was essentially the fact pattern in In the Matter of George C. Kern, Jr., see infra at p. 1494.

4. If the Schedule 14D–9 states that negotiations are not under way but that such discussions are possible, a prompt amendment is required when negotiations commence. See In the Matter of Revlon, Inc., Securities Exchange Act Rel. No. 34–23320 (June 16, 1986).

5. 430 U.S. 1 (1977).

6. See Humana, Inc. v. American Medicorp, Inc., 445 F.Supp. 613 (S.D.N.Y.1977).

7. See Plaine v. McCabe, 797 F.2d 713 (9th Cir.1986). Even when the bidder is a target shareholder, it may not seek monetary damages under § 14(e). See Kalmanovitz v. G. Heileman Brewing Co., 769 F.2d 152 (3d Cir.1985).

fiduciary duties to its shareholders. Exactly such a construction was considered and decisively rejected by the Supreme Court in Schreiber v. Burlington Northern, Inc., 472 U.S. 1 (1985). Instead, the Court ruled:

> "We hold that the term 'manipulative' as used in § 14(e) requires misrepresentation or nondisclosure. It connotes 'conduct designed to deceive or defraud investors by controlling or artificially affecting the price of securities.' Ernst & Ernst v. Hochfelder, 425 U.S. 185 at 199. Without misrepresentation or nondisclosure, § 14(e) has not been violated."

Subsequent decisions have assumed that a fully disclosed defensive tactic, however, egregious, is thus immune from attack under § 14(e).[8]

B. DEFENSIVE TACTICS: THE TARGET'S REPERTOIRE

A basic ambiguity surrounds defensive tactics: from one perspective they are self-interested attempts by the target's management to entrench itself; from another, the target's management is serving as a negotiator (and possibly auctioneer) for its shareholders and attempting to get a higher premium. The truth may lie somewhere in between and depend on the status of the legal rules in the target's jurisdiction of incorporation. A complete review of these legal rules is beyond the scope of this chapter, because it essentially involves issues of state corporation law. However, many defensive tactics—particularly, dual class voting, share repurchases, management buyouts, poison pills, and "shark repellent" charter amendments—also involve federal securities law issues. This section will examine the interrelationships between federal and state law as they apply to defensive tactics.

1. *Fiduciary Duties and Defensive Tactics.* Under the recent Delaware decisions, management defensive actions will be reviewed under an intermediate standard of review, somewhere between the traditional business judgment rule and the rule of intrinsic fairness applicable to self-dealing transactions. In Unocal Corporation v. Mesa Petroleum Co.,[9] the Delaware Supreme Court announced a standard under which a defensive tactic "must be reasonable in relation to the threat posed." Months later in Revlon, Inc. v. MacAndrews & Forbes Holdings, Inc.,[10] the Delaware Supreme Court added a supplementary rule: once the sale of the company becomes "inevitable," defensive tactics must cease, and the board's role becomes that of a "fair auctioneer," who must focus on maximizing value for shareholders.

The emergence of a proportionality standard of review in *Unocal* superseded the prior test under the Delaware case law, which looked to the "primary" or "sole" purpose of the defensive action (i.e., did it have other justifications besides seeking to perpetuate management in control?)[11] Still, it was very uncertain what the new test meant: for example, what qualified as a "threat" under it, and how closely would courts monitor the reasonableness of a defensive response to a threat? Although the threat from a coercive tender offer (such as a two-tier or partial bid) may have been obvious, it was uncertain

8. See Data Probe Acquisition Corp. v. Datatab Inc., 722 F.2d 1 (2d Cir.1983). See Panter v. Marshall Field & Co., 646 F.2d 271 (7th Cir.1981).

9. 493 A.2d 946 (Del.1985); see also, Moran v. Household International, Inc., 500 A.2d 1346 (Del.1985). Earlier cases often (but not always) accorded target management the full protection of the business judgment rule.

10. 506 A.2d 173 (Del.1985).

11. See Cheff v. Mathes, 41 Del.Ch. 494, 199 A.2d 548 (1964).

whether target management's good faith belief that its company was undervalued (and thus that the tender offer was inadequate, notwithstanding the premium offered) passed muster under the *Unocal* analysis. Some decisions of the Delaware Chancery Court in this period did read *Unocal* expansively and invalidated defensive tactics as disproportionate to any realistic threat.[12] These decisions seemed to imply that the target board's perception of the tender offer as inadequate would not justify preclusive defensive measures (although it would justify delay and an attempt to find or propose alternative transactions).

Then came Paramount Communication's 1989 tender offer for Time Incorporated, which followed in the wake of a proposed merger between Time and Warner Communications. In response to Paramount's bid, Time made a friendly tender offer for Warner Communications, Inc. Refusing Paramount's request that it enjoin Time's bid for Warner under either the *Unocal* or *Revlon* standards, the Delaware Supreme Court restated its prior decisions on takeover defensive tactics in a way that revived the possibility that a target company "could just say no." Its decision in Paramount Communications, Inc. v. Time Incorporated,[13] addressed both the *Unocal* and *Revlon* line of cases and significantly reshaped each. First, under *Unocal,* the initial question confronting the court was whether the Paramount offer for Time amounted to a "threat." Here, the Delaware Supreme Court seemed to return to a business judgment mode of analysis, finding that there would be a "threat" to the corporation even from an offer that was not inadequate:

> "The open-ended analysis mandated by *Unocal* is not intended to lead to a simple mathematical exercise: that is, of comparing the discounted value of Time–Warner's expected trading price at some future date with Paramount's offer and determining which is higher. Indeed, in our view, precepts underlying the business judgment rule mitigate against a court's engaging in the process of merits of a long-term versus a short-term investment goal for shareholders. To engage in such an exercise is a distortion of the *Unocal* process. * * * "[14]

What then was the "threat"? The decision suggested a danger of shareholder confusion: "Time shareholders might elect to tender into Paramount's cash offer in ignorance or a mistaken belief of the strategic benefit which a business combination with Warner might produce."[15] Still, the broader message of the decision seems to be that the target's board has business judgment discretion in defining what constitutes a threat, unless the evidence shows it to be "lacking in good faith or dominated by motives of either entrenchment or self-interest."[16] Proceeding to the second step of the *Unocal* analysis (i.e., was the defensive measure reasonably proportionate to the threat), the court found the Time board's actions passed this test because its tender for Warner did not

12. See AC Acquisitions Corp. v. Anderson, Clayton & Co., 519 A.2d 103 (Del. Ch.1986); Grand Metropolitan Public Ltd. Co. v. Pillsbury Company, 558 A.2d 1049 (Del.Ch.1988); City Capital Associates v. Interco, Inc., 551 A.2d 787 (Del.Ch.1988). In *Pillsbury* and *Interco,* the Chancery Court required redemption of a poison pill, and in *Anderson, Clayton* it enjoined a coercive self-tender by the target.

13. 571 A.2d 1140 (Del.1989).

14. Id. at 1153.

15. Id. For whatever, if anything, that it proves, as of late 1991, Time–Warner has generally traded in the range of $80 to $90 (in contrast to the $200 bid by Paramount). Who then was more confused?

16. Id. at 1153. In essence, this seems to have been the prior standard under Cheff v. Mathes, supra note 11, which also looked at the board's motives.

wholly foreclose Paramount from pursuing its tender offer (the Chancery Court had reached a similar finding).

Turning to *Revlon,* the Delaware Supreme Court rejected Paramount's claim that Time was already up for sale by virtue of its proposed merger with Warner. The Chancery Court had found the *Revlon* auction to be triggered only by a shift of control, which, it said, was not occurring even though Time shareholders would own less than half of a merged Time–Warner. That seemed sensible, because the dispersed Warner shareholders could not control Time's management. However, the Delaware Supreme Court declined to adopt this bright line test and instead ruled that *Revlon* is triggered only if the board "initiates an active bidding process seeking to sell" the company or takes other action that makes "the dissolution or breakup of the company inevitable. * * * "17

Depending on how it was read, the *Time* decision seemed to uphold most defensive tactics (including the so-called "just say no" defense, which is implemented by a board that simply refuses to redeem its poison pill) so long as the target's board was prepared to assert that the company's long term value was above the tender offer price. Any stock merger (or possibly any merger with a majority stock component) could be similarly effected by the board, even in the face of a higher tender offer, so long as the board could place a higher long-term value on the new entity and could convince shareholders to vote for, or tender into, the lower-priced offer. From this perspective, the *Unocal* enhanced scrutiny test seemed to have been eclipsed.

But Delaware case law took two more surprising turns in the 1990s. First in Paramount Communications Inc. v. QVC Network Inc.,18 the Delaware Supreme Court was again faced with a strategic merger (as in *Time*) that a hostile bidder wished to upset by offering a higher bid. This time, Paramount was the target; Viacom, Inc. was the friendly bidder; and QVC Network Inc. was the hostile bidder. But there was one critical factual difference from the *Time* case: one shareholder (Sumner Redstone) owned 85% of Viacom's voting Class A stock. In the view of the Delaware Supreme Court, this changed matters significantly, based on the following rationale:

> "When a majority of a corporation's voting shares are acquired by a single person or entity, or by a cohesive group acting together, there is a significant diminution in the voting power of those who thereby become minority stockholders. Under the statutory framework of the General Corporation Law, many of the most fundamental corporate changes can be implemented only if they are approved by a majority vote of the stockholders. * * * Because of the overriding importance of voting rights, this Court and the Court of Chancery have consistently acted to protect stockholders from unwarranted interference with such rights.

> In the absence of devices protecting the minority stockholders, stockholder votes are likely to become mere formalities where there is a majority stockholder. For example, minority stockholders can be deprived of a continuing *equity* interest in their corporation by means of a cash-out merger. *Weinberger.* 457 A.2d at 703. Absent effective protective provisions, minority stockholders must rely for protection solely on the fiduciary duties owed to them by the directors and the majority stockholder, since

---

17. Id. at 1150.

18. 637 A.2d 34 (Del.1994).

the minority stockholders have lost the power to influence corporate direction through the ballot. The acquisition of majority status and the consequent privilege of exerting the powers of majority ownership come at a price. That price is usually a control premium which recognizes not only the value of a control block of shares, but also compensates the minority stockholder for their resulting loss of voting power.

In the case before us, the public stockholders (in the aggregate) currently own a majority of Paramount's voting stock. Control of the corporation is not vested in a single person, entity, or group, but vested in the fluid aggregation of unaffiliated stockholders. In the event the Paramount–Viacom transaction is consummated, the public stockholders will receive cash and a minority equity voting position in the surviving corporation. Following such consummation, there will be a controlling stockholder who will have the voting power to: (a) elect directors; (b) cause a break-up of the corporation; (c) merge it with another company; (d) cash-out the public stockholders; (e) amend the certificate of incorporation; (f) sell all or substantially all of the corporate assets, or (g) otherwise alter materially the nature of the corporation and the public stockholders' interests. Irrespective of the present Paramount Board's vision of a long-term strategic alliance with Viacom, the proposed sale of control would provide the new controlling stockholder with the power to alter that vision.

Because of the intended sale of control, the Paramount–Viacom transaction has economic consequences of considerable significance to the Paramount stockholders. Once control has shifted, the current Paramount stockholders will have no leverage in the future to demand another control premium. As a result, the Paramount stockholders are entitled to receive, and should receive, a control premium and/or protective devices of significant value. There being no such protective provisions in the Viacom–Paramount transaction, the Paramount directors had an obligation to take the maximum advantage of the current opportunity to realize for the stockholders the best value reasonably available."[19]

Accordingly, the Delaware Supreme Court ruled that a sale of control imposed "the obligation of acting reasonably to seek the transaction offering the best value reasonably available to stockholders,"[20] and it found that the Paramount board had breached its fiduciary duties by not doing so.

Did this shift away from the deferential attitude in *Time* signal a major change in the Delaware jurisprudence? One year later, in perhaps its most important decision since *Time,* the Delaware Supreme Court reversed a Chancery Court decision that had enjoined a target corporation from repurchasing its own stock as part of an effort to deter a hostile bidder and again rephrased its critical *Unocal* standard in *Unitrin v. American General Corp.*[21] The Chancery Court had barred Unitrin from repurchasing up to ten million of its shares because this would raise the percentage of ownership held by its board from 23% to 28%. Given a supermajority voting provision in Unitrin's certificate of incorporation that required a 75% shareholder vote to approve any business combination with a more-than–15% shareholder, the Unitrin board could thus itself vote to block any merger with American General, even if the latter's tender offer succeeded. This tactic struck the Chancery Court as

---

19. Id. at 42–43.

20. Id. at 43.

21. 651 A.2d 1361 (Del.1995).

disproportionate to any threat (in part because Unitrin already had a valid poison pill in place). Nonetheless, the Delaware Supreme Court reversed because, it said, the Chancery Court had misapplied *Unocal:*

> "The Court of Chancery applied an incorrect legal standard when it ruled that the Unitrin decision to authorize the Repurchase Program was disproportionate because it was 'unnecessary'. The Court of Chancery stated: Given that the Board had already implemented the poison pill and the advance notice provision, the repurchase program was unnecessary to protect Unitrin from an inadequate bid."[22]

In view of the Delaware Supreme Court, the Chancery Court might only substitute its judgment for the target board's if it first found that the defensive measures were "draconian." What makes a defensive tactic "draconian"? Here, the Delaware Supreme Court reviewed its *Unocal* precedents:

> "As common law applications of *Unocal's* proportionality standard have evolved, at least two characteristics of draconian defensive measures taken by a board of directors in responding to a threat have been brought into focus through enhanced judicial scrutiny. In the modern takeover lexicon, it is now clear that since Unocal, this Court has consistently recognized that defensive measures which are either preclusive or coercive are included within the common law definition of draconian.
>
> If a defensive measure is not draconian, however, because it is not either coercive or preclusive, the *Unocal* proportionality test requires the focus of enhanced judicial scrutiny to shift to "the range of reasonableness." Paramount Communications Inc. v. QVC Network Inc., Del.Supr., 637 A.2d 34, 45–46 (1994). Proper and proportionate defensive responses are intended and permitted to thwart perceived threats. When a corporation is not for sale, the board of directors is the defender of the metaphorical medieval corporate bastion and the protector of the corporation's shareholders. The fact that a defensive action must not be coercive or preclusive does not prevent a board from responding defensively before a bidder is at the corporate bastion's gate.
>
> The ratio decidendi for the "range of reasonableness" standard is a need of the board of directors for latitude in discharging its fiduciary duties to the corporation and its shareholders when defending against perceived threats. The concomitant requirement is for judicial restraint. Consequently, if the board of directors' defensive response is not draconian (preclusive or coercive) and is within a "range of reasonableness," a court must not substitute its judgment for the board's. Paramount Communications Inc. v. QVC Network Inc., 637 A.2d at 45–46."[23]

Ultimately, the Delaware Supreme Court left the door part way open for the Chancery Court on remand:

> "The adoption of the poison pill and the limited Repurchase Program was not coercive and the repurchase may not be preclusive. Although each make a takeover more difficult, individually and collectively, if they were not coercive or preclusive the Court of Chancery must determine whether they were within the range of reasonable defensive measures available to the Board."[24]

22. Id. at 1385.   **24.** Id. at 1390.
23. Id. at 1387–88.

With the *Unocal* standard so revised, subsequent federal court decisions construing Delaware law have decided that Delaware courts would respect the so-called "just say no" defense.[25] Will they in fact do this? Past experience suggests that the course of Delaware takeover jurisprudence may zig and zag once again.

2. *Supervoting Stock and the One–Share/One–Vote Controversy.* The takeover defensive tactic that probably most implicates the interests of the federal securities laws is the dual class recapitalization. Clearly, the one insurmountable deterrent to a hostile takeover is for target management to obtain majority control of the company. There are two basic ways target management can gain such voting control: (1) it can buy the company (or most of it)—a process typically called a "leveraged buyout" and specifically regulated by § 13(e) of the Williams Act; or (2) it can effect a recapitalization under which one class of voting stock (held by it) gains much greater voting power relative to the other class (held by the public shareholder).

Various techniques can be used to effect such a recapitalization. One approach is to authorize a new class of supervoting common (for example, one having 10 votes per share) but with lower dividend rights; some "recap" plans also provide that the supervoting stock loses its enhanced voting power on any transfer. Then, if all shareholders are given the right to exchange their existing common shares for this newly authorized class with high voting but low dividend rights, it is likely that only those interested in holding on to control (at the price of some reduction in dividends) will make the exchange. Another technique is to use a special stock dividend, instead of an exchange offer, under which the same new class of supervoting stock is distributed to all shareholders. Predictably, public shareholders will transfer their shares, given the high turnover rates of most stocks, and, on transfer, their supervoting rights will lapse. Alternatively, a charter amendment can provide that supervoting rights accrue only to shares that have been held for a requisite period. The impact of all these techniques is the same: using a 10:1 voting differential, the new class of supervoting stock can give a group owning less than 10% of the original common stock absolute voting control.

Critics of these techniques object that insider groups use them to achieve the same end result (acquisition of control) as in a leveraged buyout, but without paying other shareholders an equivalent premium.[1] Although a shareholder vote would ordinarily be necessary to authorize any new class of supervoting stock, they argue that management can skew voting decisions by offering "sweeteners" (such as special large cash dividends) or by threatening to reduce payouts to shareholders if shareholder approval is not received.[2]

One major obstacle existed to the use of dual class recapitalizations. Since 1926, the New York Stock Exchange (NYSE) had required listed companies to afford shareholders equal voting rights on a per share basis. This policy—known as the "one-share, one-vote" rule—precluded the largest U.S. corporations from adopting dual class recapitalizations. Yet, because neither the American Stock Exchange (AMEX) or the National Association of Securities

---

25. See Moore Corp. v. Wallace Computer Servs., 907 F.Supp. 1545 (D.Del.1995).

1. See Gilson, Evaluating Dual Class Common Stock: The Relevance of Substitutes, 73 Va.L.Rev. 807 (1987).

2. See Gordon, Ties That Bond: Dual Class Common Stock and the Problem of Shareholder Choice, 76 Calif.L.Rev. 1 (1988).

Dealers Automatic Quotation System (NASDAQ) had a similar policy against unequal voting rights, the NYSE was exposed to the competitive threat that issuers would delist from it and move to either of them. Faced with this threat, the NYSE proposed in 1986 to amend its rules to permit dual class recapitalizations, so long as any modification of existing shareholders' voting rights was approved by a majority of both the independent directors and the disinterested shareholders.[3]

Under § 19 of the 1934 Act, proposed changes in the rules of a national securities exchange are subject to SEC approval before they can become effective. During 1986 and the first half of 1987, the SEC sought to negotiate a compromise among the NYSE, AMEX and NASDAQ under which each would agree to some form of a "one-share, one-vote" policy. When these efforts proved unsuccessful, the SEC proposed a new Rule 19c–4, which would prohibit the listing of the securities of an issuer if, after May 15, 1987, the issuer "issues any class of security or takes any other corporate action that would have the effect of nullifying, restricting or disparately reducing the per share voting rights of holders of an outstanding class" of common stock.[4] Note that this Rule did not preclude the issuance of low voting or nonvoting stock, but only supervoting stock that could reduce the voting power of existing stockholders. Its premise was that investors dealing at arms' length with the corporation could decide to buy lower voting stock without the need for special SEC protection, but that existing shareholders were exposed to coercion and seduction through the use of "sweeteners" and related techniques.[5]

Rule 19c–4 was formally adopted in 1988,[6] and was quickly challenged in court by the Business Roundtable on the ground that the SEC had exceeded its jurisdiction under § 19(c) to impose rules on the exchanges. In Business Roundtable v. SEC,[7] the D.C. Circuit agreed with the Business Roundtable and invalidated the Rule. The D.C. Circuit's decision did not, however, affect the status of the various exchanges' own rules (each of the NYSE, the AMEX, and NASDAQ had in the interim adopted a rule to comply with Rule 19c–4). After much negotiation, assisted by some SEC prodding, the three principal markets worked out a common "one share, one vote" standard.[8] This new standard expressly grandfathered, however, those companies that had been listed with dual class voting structures under the prior rules, and even permits them to issue additional shares under those classes. But it does preclude them from creating new classes of supervoting stock in the future that further reduced the voting rights of common shareholders. In addition, foreign issuers were exempted from these voting rights standards in deference to their often very different systems of corporate governance.

---

3. For the text of the NYSE's proposal, see 18 Sec.Reg. & L.Rep. (BNA), No. 37, at 1389–92 (Sept. 19, 1986).

4. Securities Exchange Act Release No. 34–24623 ("Voting Rights Listing Standards—Proposed Disenfranchisement Rule") (June 22, 1987).

5. The SEC appears to have adopted an approach recommended by Professor Gilson in this regard. See Gilson, supra note 1.

6. Securities Exchange Act Release No. 34–25891 (July 7, 1988).

7. 905 F.2d 406 (D.C.Cir.1990).

8. See Securities Exchange Act Release No. 35121 (December 19, 1994) (approving joint shareholder voting rights policy of NYSE, AMEX, and NASDAQ). Essentially, this policy forbids listing on the NYSE or AMEX or inclusion in the Nasdaq system of "companies that disenfranchise shareholders of public common stock." See 1994 SEC LEXIS 4072 at *4.

3. *Issuer Repurchases.* One response by a target to a hostile bid is to outbid the bidder by purchasing its own shares (either in the open market or by means of a self-tender). The goal in either case is to make the market price rise above the hostile bidder's tender price so shareholders will not tender. In addition, by depleting itself of cash, the target reduces its own value and may make the bidder either reconsider or lower its offer.

A debate exists over whether target self-tenders are in the best interests of target shareholders. Some believe that self-tenders create an auction and represent a valid means by which target shareholders can negotiate for a higher premium;[1] others disagree, arguing that it allows the target an unfair advantage.[2] Still, agreement exists on one point: as Professors Bradley and Rosenzweig have shown,[3] any repurchase by a target of less than the number of shares sought by the hostile bidder is potentially coercive. In essence, such a partial bid is the equivalent of a two-tier front-loaded bid (in part, because the remaining—or "stub"—value of the target's shares after a significant repurchase should be substantially lower). In addition, if the shareholder tenders into the hostile bidder's offer (because it is for more shares and thus will involve less proration), the shareholder incurs the risk that this offer may be withdrawn or revised because of the success (or potential success) of the target's bid, thus leaving the shareholder holding only the "stub value" for all of its shares. In part for these reasons, the Delaware Chancery Court has enjoined a target's partial bid for its shares where it sought fewer shares than the bidder and its offer would expire first.[4] However, in light of the earlier discussed *Unitrin* decision, issuer repurchases are unlikely to be enjoined as a fiduciary breach by a Delaware court, unless the court can be convinced that the repurchases are either preclusive or coercive.[5]

Open market share repurchasing presents even greater possibilities for confusion, coercion and market uncertainty than do self-tenders. Thus, proponents of self-tenders have argued that self-tenders (as opposed to open market purchases) should be the exclusive means by which a target purchases its shares in a takeover contest.[6]

Issuer repurchases are regulated by the federal securities laws in several respects: First, when any third party commences a tender offer for a publicly held target (i.e., one subject to § 13(e) of the 1934 Act), Rule 13e-1 states that the target may not purchase its own shares until it has disclosed certain factual information (including the amount to be purchased, the source of funds, and the markets it is entering). Essentially, the purpose of this rule is to prevent

---

1. Bradley & Rosenzweig, Defensive Stock Repurchases, 99 Harv.L.Rev. 1378 (1966).

2. Gordon & Kornhauser, Takeover Defense Tactics: A Comment on Two Models, 96 Yale L.J. 295 (1986).

3. See Bradley & Rosenzweig, supra note 1.

4. AC Acquisitions Corp. v. Anderson, Clayton & Co., 519 A.2d 103 (Del.Ch.1986). Today, the target's bid will typically not expire first as the same time periods apply to self-tenders under Rule 13e-4 as to third

party tenders under Rule 14e-1. However, if the hostile bidder were to amend its offer and thereby become subject to Rule 14e-1(b)'s 10 day extension, such a timing disparity could again result.

5. See Unitrin v. American General Corp., 651 A.2d 1361 (Del.1995). The repurchases were in fact found coercive in AC Acquisitions Corp. v. Anderson, supra note 4.

6. See Bradley & Rosenzweig, supra note 1.

manipulation and deception, as shareholders might otherwise attribute the market rise to the prospect of a rival third party bid.[7]

Second, if the purchasing program amounts to a tender offer, then Rule 13e–4 must be complied with. Although the target corporation is exempt from § 14(d) of the Williams Act by virtue of § 14(d)(8)(B), the SEC has adopted virtually equivalent rules under § 13(e). As a result, the same disclosure statement must be prepared, and Rule 13e–4(f)(8) parallels Rule 14d–10 by requiring that the offer be open to all holders. Hence, the target could not make a discriminatory offer that excluded the bidder from participating (as it did in *Unocal*). Also, in response to the *Hanson Trust* case, the SEC adopted a "cooling off" period that prevents the issuer or an affiliate from purchasing shares that were the subject of its offer until the expiration of at least ten business days after the termination of the offer.[8] The target is also partially exempt from Rule 10b–13, which prohibits persons from buying outside their own tender offer.[9]

Suppose even before a takeover bid is made, a potential target corporation suspects that it is about to be put "in play," and it begins an open-market purchasing campaign for its own stock in order to boost its stock price. This program will not violate Rule 13e–1 because no tender offer has yet been announced. However, it can violate § 9(a)(2) of the 1934 Act or Rule 10b–5 as being "manipulative" in its intent, *unless* the purchasing program complies with Rule 10b–18. Rule 10b–18 is a "safe harbor" rule, and noncompliance with its restrictions does not create any presumption of unlawful conduct.[10] Essentially, the Rule establishes restrictions on the timing, price, volume and manner of purchase, which, if complied with by the issuer, protect it from the claim that it has manipulated the market for its stock. These restrictions basically require that:

(i) the issuer purchase through only one broker or dealer on a single day (in order to prevent any appearance of a broad market interest in the stock if multiple dealers were used);

(ii) the issuer's purchases do not constitute the opening transaction or come during the last half hour of trading;

(iii) the issuer may not purchase at a price above the market price (i.e., it may not cause the price to increase); and

(iv) the volume of its purchases may not exceed 25% of the average daily trading volume (as determined over the four prior calendar weeks) in the case of a publicly traded security or, in the case of other securities, the volume over a several day period may not exceed $\frac{1}{20}$ of 1% of the outstanding shares of the security (exclusive of shares held by affiliates).

---

7. Undisclosed open-market purchasing of the target stock could violate not only Rule 13e–1, but in addition might be found "manipulative" and therefore in violation of both § 9(a)(2) of the 1934 Act and Rule 10b–5 if their purpose were to drive the target's stock price above the tender price. See Crane Co. v. Westinghouse Air Brake Co., 419 F.2d 787 (2d Cir.1969). However, the Supreme Court's *Piper* decision may bar one bidder from suing another for damages in such a case. See

Crane Co. v. American Standard, Inc., 603 F.2d 244 (2d Cir.1979).

8. See Rule 13e–4(f)(6). No similar "cooling off" period has been adopted for third party tender offers, although the SEC did propose such a general rule.

9. See Rule 10b–13(c).

10. See Rule 10b–18(c).

These basic restrictions are subject to numerous exceptions and qualifications (for example, block trades and purchases pursuant to Rule 13e–1 are exempt). Still, Rule 10b–18 has an importance that transcends the takeover context because as a practical matter it establishes "bright line" limitations on issuer repurchases. Its adoption was motivated by the practices of acquisition-minded companies that used their shares as their preferred currency for acquisitions; supporting their stock price by buying their shares thus enabled them to use an inflated currency for their acquisitions. During the 1960s the SEC brought several injunctive actions against such practices,[11] and in 1970 it proposed Rule 13e–2.[12] This rule was never adopted, although it long supplied the governing criteria used by the SEC in manipulation cases. Rule 10b–18 was adopted in 1982 and generally followed the standards contained in Proposed Rule 13e–2.[13] Although Rule 13e–2 was proposed to be mandatory, so that any purchases above its limits were unlawful, Rule 10b–18 is only a safe harbor.

One final rule that an issuer must consider in repurchasing its own securities is Rule 102 of Regulation M, which precludes the issuer from buying stock that is the subject of a distribution. If, for example, the issuer has outstanding warrants or a class of convertible securities, it is technically engaged in a distribution of securities and thus must secure an exemption from Rule 102. The issuer can, however, apply for a specific exemption from the SEC.

4. *Poison Pills.* The "poison pill" became an accepted takeover defensive tactic with a 1985 decision of the Delaware Supreme Court.[1] Since that time, some decisions have invalidated the poison pill on the state law ground that it impermissibly discriminated among shareholders of the same class,[2] but even in these states, curative legislation has generally restored the pill to the target's arsenal of weapons.[3] Today, the poison pill has become the principal defensive weapon of the target company, and thousands of publicly held corporations have adopted it. Put simply, the great attraction of the poison pill in compari-

---

11. See Securities and Exchange Commission v. Georgia–Pacific Corp., Fed.Sec. L.Rep. (CCH) Para. 91,680 (1966).

12. Sec.Exch. Act Rel. No. 34–8930 (July 13, 1970).

13. Sec.Exch. Act Rel. No. 34–19244 (Nov. 17, 1982). Rule 13e–2 limited issuer purchases to 15% of the daily trading volume, whereas Rule 10b–18 relaxes this test to 25%.

1. Moran v. Household International, Inc., 500 A.2d 1346 n. 1 (Del.1985). The SEC split 3–2 in deciding to file an amicus curiae brief asking the Delaware Supreme Court to invalidate the pill.

2. Many state corporation statutes require that shares of the same class have equal rights. This provision was used by some courts to find impermissible discrimination, because "flip in" poison pill plans do not allow the hostile bidder to purchase shares under them at the same discount price that other shareholders receive. See, e.g., Minstar Acquiring Corp. v. AMF Inc., 621 F.Supp. 1252 (S.D.N.Y.1985) (poison pill un-

fairly discriminates under New Jersey law against shareholders who acquire their shares after the issuance of the pill); Amalgamated Sugar Co. v. NL Industries, Inc., 644 F.Supp. 1229 (S.D.N.Y.1986); Asarco, Inc. v. Court, 611 F.Supp. 468 (D.N.J.1985) (supervoting preferred stock plan invalid); The Bank of New York Co. v. Irving Bank Corp., 139 Misc.2d 665, 528 N.Y.S.2d 482 (1988), aff'd, 143 A.D.2d 1070, 533 N.Y.S.2d 411 (1st Dept.1988) (restriction on power of directors in poison pill plan was invalid because not set forth in the charter).

3. New Jersey amended its corporation law in response to *Minstar,* supra note 2, to authorize rights or options that were discriminatory. See N.J.Bus.Corp. Act § 14D: 7–7(3). New York similarly responded to the *Irving Bank* case, supra note 2. See N.Y.Bus.Corp. Law §§ 912(a)(10), 4603(a). See also Fla.Gen. Corp. Act § 607.058; Ohio Rev.Code § 1701.01.

son to "shark repellent" is that the pill does not require a favorable shareholder vote.

Over recent years, "shareholder rights plans" (as their proponents call them) have evolved considerably. Today, the two principal types of rights plans are (1) the "call" plan, and (2) the "put" plan.[4] Under the former, the holder receives a right to buy securities of the target at a discount under certain circumstances; under the latter (also known as a "back-end" plan), the holder can require the issuer of the right, or the acquiring company, to purchase its securities at a premium under certain circumstances. Call plans evolved first and were chiefly intended to force the acquirer to negotiate with the target, by increasing the cost to the acquirer of effecting a post-tender merger. Often, the plan would simply provide that a target shareholder could buy stock from either the target or any surviving company resulting from a merger involving the target at half price. This provision that the right became exercisable against the acquirer was known as a "flip-over" provision (because it "flipped over" to apply against the acquirer). Later, other triggering conditions were added (such as self-dealing transactions between the target and an acquirer). Of particular importance was a later modification known as a "flip-in" provision, which is typically triggered by the acquirer crossing some threshold (such as purchasing 20% of the target's stock). At this point, the plan usually provides that the holder of the right can acquire shares of the target at a discount that prohibitively dilutes the bidder's share ownership. This difference is important because the early "flip-over" pills were designed to protect against two-tier, front-loaded takeovers, while the "flip-in" pills are designed to limit creeping control acquisitions. Both force the potential acquirer to deal with the target's board because it can redeem the shareholder rights and thus permit a friendly merger.

Put plans are less common, but allow the target shareholder to sell its shares (i.e., "put" them) to the issuer for a specified amount of cash, debt securities or both. This may be an advantage for smaller shareholders less able to buy securities, even at a discount. Still, the "put" plan is subject to some potential legal difficulties; because under it the shareholders are selling their shares to the target, this transaction can arguably be called a tender offer. In addition, if the bidder is excluded by a provision limiting the "put's" exercise to holders owning below a specified threshold, this may represent a discriminatory tender offer in violation of the SEC's "All Holders" rule.[5]

During the late 1980s, the principal role of the "poison pill" seemed to be that it forced the bidder to negotiate with the target—in effect, it gave the board a gavel with which to run an auction.[6] If the target board refused to negotiate or held out even after the auction had clearly been resolved, then courts on occasion would order the redemption of the poison pill.[7] More recently, following the *Time* and *Unitrin* decisions, a few courts have upheld the "just say no" defense, under which the company refuses to negotiate with a bidder and does not redeem its poison pill.[8] In addition, as target managements

4. For a fuller discussion of poison pill plans, see R. Ferrara, M. Brown & J. Hall, Takeovers, 337–356 (1987).

5. See Rule 13e–4(f)(8).

6. See CRTF Corp. v. Federated Dept. Stores, Inc., 683 F.Supp. 422 (S.D.N.Y.1988).

7. See, e.g., Grand Metropolitan Public Ltd. Co. v. Pillsbury Co., 558 A.2d 1049 (Del. Ch.1988).

8. See Moore Corp. v. Wallace Computer Servs., 907 F.Supp. 1545 (D.Del.1995); Invacare Corporation v. Healthdyne Technologies, Inc. 968 F.Supp. 1578 (N.D.Ga.1997).

have grown bolder in their use of the pill, they have also broadened its triggering criteria to become applicable if any person or group solicits proxies or forms a "group" with other shareholders to seek election to the corporation's board of directors (at least if the "group" owns or holds proxies for a specified percentage of the firm's shares). Effectively, such a provision uses SEC Rule 13d–5 on beneficial ownership as a triggering concept for a "flip-in" pill. The larger issue here is whether the poison pill may be used to chill the shareholder's traditional right of franchise.[9]

In recent years, the most important issue concerning the poison pill has surrounded the validity of what is known as the "deadhand" or "continuing director" poison pill. Typically, such a pill contains a provision to the effect that it may be redeemed only by the directors in office prior to the commencement of the tender offer or the start of any proxy contest, or other directors nominated or approved by them. Thus, it effectively nullifies the utility of a proxy contest as a means of ousting the incumbent board, because by winning such a proxy contest, the bidder unseats the only persons who could redeem the pill. Delaware has rejected the use of such a "deadhand" pill on statutory grounds[10] (as has one New York decision[11]). Nonetheless, at least one federal court construing non-Delaware law has upheld the "deadhand" poison pill.[12] As a result, some practitioners still insert such provisions into poison pills, possibly on a "what-do-we-have-to-lose" rationale.

Meanwhile, the empirical evidence from stock price studies continues to show that adoption of a poison pill results in a statistically significant stock price decline for the target shareholders.[13] The negative effect is small for most companies, but higher for those who are the subject of takeover speculation. Ultimately, there are arguments for and against the poison pill. But the case for it rests on the board serving as the agent of the target shareholders and seeking higher bids or alternative transactions. This seems most likely to occur when the board's behavior is subject to at least some substantive judicial review.

5. *Greenmail.* The tactic known as "greenmail" consists of buying off the putative bidder by the target repurchasing its shares from the bidder, either at a premium over the market or at the market price in a market inflated by takeover rumors, and then requiring the bidder to sign a "standstill agreement" whereby the bidder agrees not to acquire additional shares in the target for a defined period (usually five to ten years). The problem with this defensive tactic is that it often simply attracts a second bidder who also wants the same largesse (this is referred to as "double dipping"). Once a takeover target is identified in the market's eye, it often cannot escape just by in effect bribing the first bidder on the scene to go away.

Legal challenges to greenmail must principally be framed in terms of state law issues of the fiduciary responsibilities of target directors and officers. Only

9. For a Delaware decision upholding such a shareholder rights plan, see Stahl v. Apple Bancorp., Inc., Fed.Sec.L.Rep. (CCH), Para. 95,412 (Del.Ch.1990).

10. See Quickturn Design Sys. v. Shapiro, 721 A.2d 1281 (1998).

11. See Bank of New York v. Irving Bank Corporation, 139 Misc.2d 665, 528 N.Y.S.2d 482 (N.Y.Sup.Ct.1988).

12. See Invacare Corp. v. Healthdyne Technologies, Inc., 968 F.Supp. 1578 (N.D.Ga.1997).

13. For the most recent study, see Ryngaert, The Effect of Poison Pill Securities on Shareholder Wealth, 20 J.Fin.Econ. 377 (1988).

one decision appears to have enjoined greenmail payments,[1] and Delaware law has been especially tolerant of such payments.[2] Under federal law, the open and disclosed payment of greenmail does not amount to deception or manipulation.[3] Indeed, this result seems a necessary consequence of Schreiber v. Burlington Northern, Inc.,[4] which held that "manipulation" under § 14(e) requires a showing of deception. Still, misstatements about either the putative bidder's intent or about the target's conduct might support an action under Rule 10b–5 if plaintiffs purchased during the period that such statement affected the market.[5]

On the policy level, an academic debate has long surrounded greenmail. Although the dominant view has been that such practices serve to entrench management, others believe that the putative bidder provides a service for other shareholders by identifying an undervalued target and stimulating an auction.[6] This argument is premised on the fact that the average stock price gains on the announcement of a Schedule 13D filing by the putative bidder usually exceed the average loss on the announcement of a greenmail repurchase. Still, at least one problem with this argument is that net gains remaining after the greenmail repurchase tend to gradually disappear unless there is a subsequent successful offer.[7] Another problem with the optimistic thesis that greenmail benefits shareholders by initiating a gradual auction is that much of it is invisible: bidders may contact target management and arrange a sale at a premium without crossing the 5% threshold in order to avoid publicity, litigation and subsequent bidder "double dipping."[8]

The prevalence of greenmail transactions has been chilled to a degree by I.R.C. § 5881, enacted in 1987, which imposes a 50% nondeductible excise tax on the profit realized from the receipt of greenmail (this results in an overall 84% effective rate of taxation on such profits). The definition of "greenmail" in this statute is, however, seriously underinclusive, as it applies only to corporate payments to a stockholder (1) who has held the stock for less than 2 years, and (2) who has made or threatened to make a tender offer for the stock. Obviously, a sophisticated "greenmailer" will avoid making or threatening a tender offer or will at least keep its threat implicit.

6. *Nullifying the Proxy Contest: The New Defensive Tactics.* Since the advent of the poison pill, it has become increasingly apparent to any sophisticated bidder that it will probably have to win a proxy fight to unseat the incumbent board in order to redeem the target's poison pill and thus eliminate

---

1. See Heckmann v. Ahmanson, 168 Cal.App.3d 119, 214 Cal.Rptr. 177 (1985).

2. See Polk v. Good, 507 A.2d 531 (Del. 1986) (transaction valid unless sole or primary purpose was to perpetuate management in control).

3. Pin v. Texaco, Inc., 793 F.2d 1448 (5th Cir.1986); see also Kamerman v. Steinberg, 891 F.2d 424 (2d Cir.1989) (shareholder who did not purchase or sell may not sue derivatively to seek damages for greenmail absent proof that issuer was deceived).

4. 472 U.S. 1 (1985).

5. See In re Phillips Petroleum Securities Litigation, 881 F.2d 1236 (3d Cir.1989).

6. Compare Macey & McChesney, A Theoretical Analysis of Corporate Greenmail, 95 Yale L.J. 13 (1985) with Gordon & Kornhauser, Takeover Defense Tactics: A Comment on Two Models, 96 Yale L.J. 295 (1986).

7. See Ang & Tucker, The Shareholder Wealth Effects of Corporate Greenmail, 11 J.Fin.Res. 265 (1988) (gains from first bidder's appearance vanish if greenmail is not followed by a subsequent, successful bid).

8. For a discussion of other forms of disguised greenmail, see Gilson, Drafting an Effective Greenmail Prohibition, 88 Colum.L.Rev. 329 (1988).

it as a takeover obstacle. Of course, one anticipatory response to the use of the proxy fight in this fashion by the bidder is to adopt a "continuing director" poison pill, which cannot be redeemed by the newly-elected directors. But this tactic has been rejected by Delaware courts and has not been clearly upheld by the highest court in state.[9]

Thus, two other tactics are more likely to be relied on by the target. The first is the use of a staggered board, which by typically creating three classes of directors requires the bidder to win two annual shareholder elections to unseat a majority of the board. This is an effective defense and widely used,[10] as few bidders will take on such a two year contest,[11] but it is virtually impossible today to adopt a staggered board because institutional shareholders will not vote to so amend the corporate charter. Hence, unless the staggered board was specified in the original certificate of incorporation, it is not a feasible defense option. The second technique is in effect to "stuff the ballot box" by issuing a large block of shares to a perceived ally, such as an Employee Stock Ownership Plan (or "ESOP"), which is next discussed.

7. *Stuffing the Ballot Box.* Often, shares are issued by the target to parties it perceives to be friendly allies. Sometimes, this tactic can backfire, as it did in *NCR Corp. v. American Telephone and Telegraph Co.*[12] There, in response to AT&T's hostile tender offer and proxy contest, NCR created an Employee Stock Ownership Plan ("ESOP") and issued it at 5.5 million preferred shares, or approximately 8% of NCR's total voting power. AT&T sought and obtained an injunction against the voting of the ESOP shares on the grounds that the primary purpose of the ESOP's creation was not to create an employee benefit plan, but to perpetuate management in control. While other cases have upheld the use of such an ESOP,[13] NCR attempted to add too many features to its plan that both allowed employees to purchase its shares at little or no cost to themselves and made them indifferent to the tender offer premium. For example, under a "reset" provision, if the price of NCR stock dropped (as it was likely to if AT&T withdrew or lost its tender offer), the conversion feature for the NCR preferred stock would be "reset" so as to compensate NCR employees for the decline in the common stock's value. These and other extreme features convinced the court that the stock issuance flunked the "primary purpose" test and could not be justified as a compensation system. The message of this decision may then be that shares can be issued to employees and other allies so as to influence a proxy contest—but only if the target's management is fairly circumspect and does not stretch the legal rubber band too far.

8. *The NYSE's 20% Rule.* Even when the target corporation's issuance of shares to an ESOP or other ally does not constitute a fiduciary breach, it may violate a New York Stock Exchange Rule that requires shareholder approval of

9. See Quickturn Design Sys. v. Shapiro, 721 A.2d 1281 (1998).

10. See Michael Useem, Investor Capitalism: How Money Managers Are Changing the Face of Corporate America (1996) at 160 (noting rise from 55% to 59% of companies with staggered boards between 1989 and 1992).

11. Empirical research suggests that a poison pill alone is not a significant deterrent to a takeover contest, but a staggered board plus a poison pill is a serious deterrent that few hostile bidders will take on. See John C. Coates, IV, Empirical Evidence on Structural Takeover Defenses: Where Do We Stand?, 54 U. Miami L. Rev. 783 (2000).

12. 761 F.Supp. 475 (S.D.Ohio 1991).

13. See Shamrock Holdings, Inc. v. Polaroid Corp., 559 A.2d 257 (Del.Ch.1989).

certain transactions, including any issuance of stock exceeding 20% of the corporation's common stock (either in a single transaction or in an integrated series of transactions).[14] In *Norlin Corporation v. Rooney, Pace Inc.*,[15] Norlin issued shares amounting to approximately 49% of its outstanding stock to a wholly-owned Panamanian subsidiary, in order to ward off a threatened hostile takeover. Norlin claimed that the law of Panama permitted its subsidiary to vote its shares in Norlin. While the Second Circuit rejected this argument, it rested its injunction invalidating the stock issuance on an alternative ground as well: the prospect of delisting from the New York Stock Exchange for violation of its listing standard threatened shareholders with irreparable injury and thus justified an injunction. In particular, both the District Court and the Second Circuit focused on the likely loss of liquidity to investors if the NYSE delisted Norlin.[16] *Query:* would delisting from the NYSE constitute a significant injury today if the corporation could list on another exchange or on NASDAQ (where some substantial corporations eligible for the NYSE prefer to list)? Note, however, that NASDAQ today has the same shareholder approval rule as the NYSE. Finally, if the target corporation is the subject of competitive bidding between two corporate bidders and it acts to prefer one by granting a stock lockup in excess of 20%, how can the threat of delisting injure its shareholders when it is about to disappear anyway?

9. *Stock Lockups.* Faced with a bidder seeking control, a target may decide to issue shares to a "white knight" or a friendly ally for a variety of reasons:

(1) Such an issuance at a below-market price may supply the incentive necessary to induce the white knight to make a tender offer at a higher price than the first bidder's; the rationale here is that the first bidder had an opportunity to buy shares at a lower price in the open market before it announced its bid and this issuance (or option) simply "levels the playing field";

(2) Such an issuance, particularly if made to another company in return for its assets, may increase the size of the target to a level where the hostile bidder has difficulty in financing the acquisition; this was the apparent strategy in Time's defensive acquisition of Warner to defeat Paramount,[17] and it had been used in earlier battles as well.[18]

(3) In an extreme case, a stock lockup can simply shift control. In *Data Probe Acquisition Corp. v. Datatab, Inc.*,[19] the target granted its preferred merger partner an option to buy 1,407,674 authorized, but unissued,

---

14. Originally, the ceiling on stock issuances without shareholder approval was 18½%, but in 1989 the NYSE raised it to 20% and the NASD adopted a similar limit for NASDAQ-listed stocks. See Sec.Exch. Act Rel. No. 34–27035 (NYSE rule) (July 14, 1989) and Sec.Exch. Act Rel. No. 34–27489 (NASDAQ rule) (Nov. 30, 1989). See also NYSE Listed Company Manual at § 312.03.

15. 744 F.2d 255 (2d Cir.1984).

16. Id. at 268.

17. Paramount Communications, Inc. v. Time Inc., 571 A.2d 1140 (Del.1989).

18. See Treadway Companies, Inc. v. Care Corp., 638 F.2d 357 (2d Cir.1980); Panter v. Marshall Field & Co., 646 F.2d 271 (7th Cir.1981); Chris–Craft Industries, Inc. v. Piper Aircraft Corp., 480 F.2d 341 (2d Cir.1973). But see, Royal Industries, Inc. v. Monogram Industries, Inc., Fed.Sec.L.Rep. (CCH), Para. 95,863 (C.D.Cal.1976).

19. 722 F.2d 1 (2d Cir.1983). The District Court had enjoined such a lockup as "manipulative," but in this pre-*Schreiber* decision, the Second Circuit anticipated the result in that case by finding that adequately disclosed actions could not be manipulative.

shares when there were only 703,836 shares outstanding. Thus, even if the bidder bought all outstanding shares, it would still hold less than one third of the outstanding stock (and thus could not block a merger, which required two thirds approval under New York law).

(4) Increasingly, the motive behind a lockup is to achieve blocking position. Originally, blocking position meant precluding the hostile bidder from obtaining the two thirds majority necessary to effect a second-step merger under the laws of those states that require such a supermajority vote. More recently, the goal has been to prevent the bidder from evading state antitakeover statutes or obtaining the vote necessary to oust the incumbent board in a proxy fight. For example, under the Delaware antitakeover statute (Del.Gen.Corp.Law § 203), a bidder who acquires 85% or more of the stock is not subject to the restrictions of that statute that impose a three year moratorium on follow-up mergers between the bidder and the target. In *Shamrock Holdings, Inc. v. Polaroid Corp.*,[20] the target issued 14% of its stock to a newly created ESOP, thus leaving the bidder with only a 1% margin for error that it could not meet. Although the Delaware Chancery Court placed the burden on Polaroid's board to demonstrate that the transaction was "entirely fair," it found that the creation of the ESOP was fair to shareholders, because they did not fund it. Rather, it was funded by employees, who took a voluntary salary cut in return for the ESOP. *Query:* Is this answer satisfactory?

Because the trustees of an Employee Stock Ownership Plan (or ESOP) are customarily members of management, it might seem a fairly simple procedure to rely on their loyalty and expect that they will not tender shares in the plan under their control. However, ERISA largely precludes such a straightforward tactic, as trustees who fail to tender may incur fiduciary liability for lost profits.[21] Thus, most ESOPs "pass through" the decision to tender to the employees, who, it anticipates, will prefer to remain independent. However, most shares held by an ESOP do not belong to any individual employee; rather, the ESOP's stock is held in a suspense account and released for allocation to employees' accounts as the acquisition loan incurred by the ESOP to buy the stock is repaid. Normally, the ESOP's trustees have discretionary control over these unallocated shares and are thus subject to ERISA fiduciary liability if they act to protect target management.[22] As a result, many ESOPs have adopted a "mirrored voting" provision under which the trustees bind themselves in advance to vote or tender the shares in the same proportion as the employees vote or tender their allocated shares. It remains unresolved whether the Department of Labor will accede to the use of such a contractual formula, or will insist that the fiduciary use its own judgment and prudence with respect to the decision to tender. In the *NCR* case, supra, the consequence of a mirrored voting provision was extreme: NCR employees could not yet elect to

---

20.   559 A.2d 257 (Del.Ch.1989).

21.   See Donovan v. Bierwirth, 680 F.2d 263 (2d Cir.1982) (trustees of corporate pension plan violated their fiduciary duties by failing to tender and by buying additional shares of their company at a price inflated by the pendency of the takeover bid).

22.   Sections 404(a)(1)(A) and (B) of ERISA impose the following overlapping

duties on a fiduciary: the fiduciary must discharge its duties "solely in the interests of the participants and beneficiaries," must act "for the exclusive purpose" of providing benefits to them, and must perform its duties "with the care, skill, prudence, and diligence under the circumstances then prevailing" of a prudent person.

join the NCR ESOP, but because NCR gave all 24,000 of its employees one share each of its stock and adopted "mirrored voting" to vote the remaining shares in the ESOP, each NCR employee controlled the voting of 229 shares, without investing a penny. In enjoining NCR's issuance of shares to its ESOP, the district court distinguished *Shamrock Holdings Inc. v. Polaroid,* because in that case the employees had correspondingly agreed to accept salary reductions to finance the ESOP's purchase of the Polaroid shares. Thus, the *Shamrock Holdings* court had concluded that Polaroid's plan was "shareholder neutral" and thereby passed the standard of "entire fairness."

During the 1980s, ESOPs seem to have been utilized primarily to capture tax benefits that Congress made specially applicable to them. However, the Revenue Reconciliation Act of 1989 has substantially curtailed these tax advantages. Whereas formerly a lender received a 50% interest exclusion on a loan to an ESOP, this tax incentive for financing ESOPs will today apply only if the ESOP holds over 50% of the firm's stock—thereby effectively ending the availability of this tax subsidy in the case of most large, publicly held corporations.

10. *Asset lockups.* The most common form of lockup is an option to purchase a "crown jewel" asset granted by the target to a preferred corporate suitor. Sometimes, the motive is to tip the balance in favor of that bidder, and sometimes it is to remain independent by chilling the willingness of the first bidder to continue (in such a case the option would be exercisable only if the first bidder engaged in some defined act, such as making a tender offer). Courts have frequently invalidated asset lockups, most commonly when they are given to aid a management group in effecting a leveraged buyout.[23] Where the lockup is instead granted to a third party in return for a higher bid, courts have been more tolerant.[24]

One irony about asset lockups was recognized by the *Hanson Trust* court: "[T]he very purpose of an asset lockup in a takeover contest is to give the optionee a bargain as an incentive to bid and an assured benefit should its bid fail."[25] In short, a fair asset lockup option simply does not achieve the target's purpose. What then should a court look to? Should it compare the benefit to shareholders from its increased bid versus the value of the lockup option? Or is this for the target board to consider in its business judgment? Perhaps this is why asset lockups have been chiefly invalidated in the leveraged buyout context where the recipient is a management group and hence a hint of self-dealing may be detectable.

SECTION 5.   STATE ANTITAKEOVER LEGISLATION

Although the Williams Act is avowedly neutral between bidder and target, the states have not been neutral, but have sided consistently with the target.

23.   See, e.g., Hanson Trust PLC v. ML SCM Acquisition, Inc., 781 F.2d 264 (2d Cir. 1986); Revlon, Inc. v. MacAndrews & Forbes Holdings, Inc., 506 A.2d 173 (Del.1985).

24.   See, e.g., Crouse–Hinds Co. v. Inter-North, Inc., 634 F.2d 690 (2d Cir.1980); Treadway Companies, Inc. v. Care Corp., 638 F.2d 357 (2d Cir.1980).

25.   781 F.2d at 276. See also, Note, Lock–Up Options: Towards a State Law Standard, 96 Harv.L.Rev. 1068 (1983); Fraidin & Franco, Lock–Up Arrangements, 14 Rev. Sec.Reg. 821 (1981).

Commentators disagree about the motivation for such legislation. Some see state antitakeover statutes as simply the product of individual target companies overreaching a compliant state legislature (in which out-of-state shareholders have little voice or influence),[1] while others believe an antitakeover political consensus has developed among a broad coalition of groups that is driven by the latent (and sometimes explicit) desire to protect non-shareholder constituencies from risk.[2] Clearly, whether as the result of ignorance or distaste for what they have seen, the public at large, as revealed by public opinion polls, is skeptical and suspicious of hostile takeovers.[3] This section will examine, first, the case law and, second, the newer forms of antitakeover statutes.

A.   THE CASE LAW

CTS Corporation v. Dynamics Corporation of America

Supreme Court of the United States, 1987.
481 U.S. 69, 107 S.Ct. 1637, 95 L.Ed.2d 67.

■ JUSTICE POWELL delivered the opinion of the Court.

This case presents the questions whether the Control Share Acquisitions Chapter of the Indiana Business Corporation Law, Ind.Code § 23–1–42–1 et seq. (Supp.1986), is preempted by the Williams Act or violates the Commerce Clause of the Federal Constitution, Art. I, § 8, cl. 3.

I

A

On March 4, 1986, the Governor of Indiana signed a revised Indiana Business Corporation Law. That law included the Control Share Acquisitions Chapter. Beginning on August 1, 1987, the Act will apply to any corporation incorporated in Indiana, unless the corporation amends its articles of incorporation or bylaws to opt out of the Act. Before that date, any Indiana corporation can opt into the Act by resolution of its board of directors. The Act applies only to "issuing public corporations." The term "corporation" includes only businesses incorporated in Indiana. An "issuing public corporation" is defined as:

> "a corporation that has:
>
> > "(1) one hundred (100) or more shareholders;
> >
> > "(2) its principal place of business, its principal office, or substantial assets within Indiana; and
> >
> > "(3) either:
> >
> > > "(A) more than ten percent (10%) of its shareholders resident in Indiana;
> > >
> > > "(B) more than ten percent (10%) of its shares owned by Indiana residents; or

1. Romano, The Political Economy of Takeover Statutes, 73 Virginia L. Rev. 111 (1987) (describing enactment of takeover statutes).

2. See, e.g., Johnson & Millon, Missing the Point About State Takeover Statutes, 87 Mich.L.Rev. 846 (1989).

3. Romano, The Future of Hostile Takeovers: Legislation and Public Opinion, 57 Cinn.L.Rev. 457 (1988) (noting negative public perception of hostile takeovers).

"(C) ten thousand (10,000) shareholders resident in Indiana."
§ 23-1-42-4(a).

The Act focuses on the acquisition of "control shares" in an issuing public corporation. Under the Act, an entity acquires "control shares" whenever it acquires shares that, but for the operation of the Act, would bring its voting power in the corporation to or above any of three thresholds: 20%, 33⅓%, or 50%. An entity that acquires control shares does not necessarily acquire voting rights. Rather, it gains those rights only "to the extent granted by resolution approved by the shareholders of the issuing public corporation." Section 9 requires a majority vote of all disinterested[2] shareholders holding each class of stock for passage of such a resolution. The practical effect of this requirement is to condition acquisition of control of a corporation on approval of a majority of the pre-existing disinterested shareholders.[3]

The shareholders decide whether to confer rights on the control shares at the next regularly scheduled meeting of the shareholders, or at a specially scheduled meeting. The acquiror can require management of the corporation to hold such a special meeting within 50 days if it files an "acquiring person

---

2. "Interested shares" are shares with respect to which the acquiror, an officer or an inside director of the corporation "may exercise or direct the exercise of the voting power of the corporation in the election of directors." § 23-1-42-3. If the record date passes before the acquiror purchases shares pursuant to the tender offer, the purchased shares will not be "interested shares" within the meaning of the Act; although the acquiror may own the shares on the date of the meeting, it will not "exercise * * * the voting power" of the shares.

As a practical matter, the record date usually will pass before shares change hands. Under SEC regulations, the shares cannot be purchased until 20 business days after the offer commences. 17 CFR § 240.14e-1(a) (1986). If the acquiror seeks an early resolution of the issue—as most acquirors will—the meeting required by the Act must be held no more than 50 calendar days after the offer commences, about three weeks after the earliest date on which the shares could be purchased. See § 23-1-42-7. The Act requires management to give notice of the meeting "as promptly as reasonably practicable * * * to all shareholders of record as of the record date set for the meeting." § 23-1-42-8(a). It seems likely that management of the target corporation would violate this obligation if it delayed setting the record date and sending notice until after 20 business days had passed. Thus, we assume that the record date usually will be set before the date on which federal law first permits purchase of the shares.

3. The United States and appellee Dynamics Corporation suggest that § 23-42-9(b)(1) requires a second vote by *all* shareholders of record. Brief for Securities and Exchange Commission and United States as *Amici Curiae* 5, and n. 6; Brief for Appellee Dynamics Corp. of America 2-3, and n. 5. Indiana disputes this interpretation of its Act. Brief for Intervenor-Appellant Indiana 29, n. Section 23-1-42-9(b)(1) provides:

"[T]he resolution must be approved by:

"(1) each voting group entitled to vote separately on the proposal by a majority of all the votes entitled to be cast by that voting group, with the holders of the outstanding shares of a class being entitled to vote as a separate voting group if the proposed control share acquisition would, if fully carried out, result in any of the changes described in [Indiana Code § 23-1-38-4(a) (describing fundamental changes in corporate organization)]."

The United States contends that this section always requires a separate vote by all shareholders and that the last clause merely specifies that the vote shall be taken by separate groups if the acquisition would result in one of the listed transactions. Indiana argues that this section requires a separate vote only if the acquisition would result in one of the listed transactions. Because it is unnecessary to our decision, we express no opinion as to the appropriate interpretation of this section.

statement,"[4] requests the meeting, and agrees to pay the expenses of the meeting. See § 23–1–42–7. If the shareholders do not vote to restore voting rights to the shares, the corporation may redeem the control shares from the acquiror at fair market value, but it is not required to do so. § 23–1–42–10(b). Similarly, if the acquiror does not file an acquiring person statement with the corporation, the corporation may, if its bylaws or articles of incorporation so provide, redeem the shares at any time after 60 days after the acquiror's last acquisition. § 23–1–42–10(a).

B

On March 10, 1986, appellee Dynamics Corporation of America (Dynamics) owned 9.6% of the common stock of appellant CTS Corporation, an Indiana corporation. On that day, six days after the Act went into effect, Dynamics announced a tender offer for another million shares in CTS; purchase of those shares would have brought Dynamics' ownership interest in CTS to 27.5%. Also on March 10, Dynamics filed suit in the United States District Court for the Northern District of Illinois, alleging that CTS had violated the federal securities laws in a number of respects no longer relevant to these proceedings. On March 27, the Board of Directors of CTS, an Indiana corporation, elected to be governed by the provisions of the Act, see § 23–1–17–3.

Four days later, on March 31, Dynamics moved for leave to amend its complaint to allege that the Act is pre-empted by the Williams Act and violates the Commerce Clause, Art. I, § 8, cl. 3. Dynamics sought a temporary restraining order, a preliminary injunction, and declaratory relief against CTS's use of the Act. On April 9, the District Court ruled that the Williams Act pre-empts the Indiana Act and granted Dynamics' motion for declaratory relief. * * * Relying on JUSTICE WHITE's plurality opinion in Edgar v. MITE Corp., 457 U.S. 624 (1982), the court concluded that the Act "wholly frustrates the purpose and objective of Congress in striking a balance between the investor, management, and the takeover bidder in takeover contests." * * * A week later, on April 17, the District Court issued an opinion accepting Dynamics' claim that the Act violates the Commerce Clause. This holding rested on the court's conclusion that "the substantial interference with interstate commerce created by the [Act] outweighs the articulated local benefits so as to create an impermissible indirect burden on interstate commerce." Id., at 406. The District Court certified its decisions on the Williams Act and Commerce Clause claims as final under Fed.Rule Civ.Proc. 54(b). Ibid.

CTS appealed the District Court's holdings on these claims to the Court of Appeals for the Seventh Circuit. Because of the imminence of CTS's annual meeting, the Court of Appeals consolidated and expedited the two appeals. On April 23—23 days after Dynamics first contested application of the Act in the District Court—the Court of Appeals issued an order affirming the judgment of the District Court. The opinion followed on May 28. 794 F.2d 250 (1986).

* * *

II

The first question in this case is whether the Williams Act pre-empts the Indiana Act. As we have stated frequently, absent an explicit indication by Congress of an intent to pre-empt state law, a state statute is pre-empted only

---

4. An "acquiring person statement" is an information statement describing, inter alia, the identity of the acquiring person and the terms and extent of the proposed acquisition. See § 23–1–42–6.

" 'where compliance with both federal and state regulations is a physical impossibility * * *,' Florida Lime & Avocado Growers, Inc. v. Paul, 373 U.S. 132, 142–143 (1963), or where the state 'law stands as an obstacle to the accomplishment and execution of the full purposes and objectives of Congress.' Hines v. Davidowitz, 312 U.S. 52, 67 (1941) * * *." Ray v. Atlantic Richfield Co., 435 U.S. 151, 158 (1978).

Because it is entirely possible for entities to comply with both the Williams Act and the Indiana Act, the state statute can be pre-empted only if it frustrates the purposes of the federal law.

> * * *

B

The Indiana Act differs in major respects from the Illinois statute that the Court considered in Edgar v. MITE Corp., 457 U.S. 624 (1982). After reviewing the legislative history of the Williams Act, Justice White, joined by Chief Justice Burger and Justice Blackmun (the plurality), concluded that the Williams Act struck a careful balance between the interests of offerors and target companies, and that any state statute that "upset" this balance was pre-empted. Id., at 632–634.

The plurality then identified three offending features of the Illinois statute. Justice White's opinion first noted that the Illinois statute provided for a 20–day precommencement period. During this time, management could disseminate its views on the upcoming offer to shareholders, but offerors could not publish their offers. The plurality found that this provision gave management "a powerful tool to combat tender offers." Id., at 635. This contrasted dramatically with the Williams Act: Congress had deleted express precommencement notice provisions from the Williams Act. According to the plurality, Congress had determined that the potentially adverse consequences of such a provision on shareholders should be avoided. Thus, the plurality concluded that the Illinois provision "frustrate[d] the objectives of the Williams Act." Ibid. The second criticized feature of the Illinois statute was a provision for a hearing on a tender offer that, because it set no deadline, allowed management " 'to stymie indefinitely a takeover,' " id., at 637 (quoting MITE Corp. v. Dixon, 633 F.2d 486, 494 (C.A.7 1980)). The plurality noted that " 'delay can seriously impede a tender offer,' " 457 U.S. at 637 (quoting Great Western United Corp. v. Kidwell, 577 F.2d 1256, 1277 (C.A.5 1978) (per Wisdom, J.)), and that "Congress anticipated that investors and the takeover offeror would be free to go forward without unreasonable delay," 457 U.S., at 639. Accordingly, the plurality concluded that this provision conflicted with the Williams Act. The third troublesome feature of the Illinois statute was its requirement that the fairness of tender offers would be reviewed by the Illinois Secretary of State. Noting that "Congress intended for investors to be free to make their own decisions," the plurality concluded that " '[t]he state thus offers investor protection at the expense of investor autonomy—an approach quite in conflict with that adopted by Congress.' " Id., at 639–640 (quoting *MITE Corp. v. Dixon*, supra, at 494).

C

As the plurality opinion in *MITE* did not represent the views of a majority of the Court,[6] we are not bound by its reasoning. We need not question that

---

6. Justice White's opinion on the preemption issue, 457 U.S. at 630–640, was joined only by Chief Justice Burger and by Justice Blackmun. Two Justices disagreed

reasoning, however, because we believe the Indiana Act passes muster even under the broad interpretation of the Williams Act articulated by Justice White in *MITE*. As is apparent from our summary of its reasoning, the overriding concern of the *MITE* plurality was that the Illinois statute considered in that case operated to favor management against offerors, to the detriment of shareholders. By contrast, the statute now before the Court protects the independent shareholder against both of the contending parties. Thus, the Act furthers a basic purpose of the Williams Act, " 'plac[ing] investors on an equal footing with the takeover bidder,' " Piper v. Chris–Craft Industries, 430 U.S., at 30 (quoting the Senate Report accompanying the Williams Act, S.Rep. No. 550, 90th Cong., 1st Sess., 4 (1967)).

The Indiana Act operates on the assumption, implicit in the Williams Act, that independent shareholders faced with tender offers often are at a disadvantage. By allowing such shareholders to vote as a group, the Act protects them from the coercive aspects of some tender offers. If, for example, shareholders believe that a successful tender offer will be followed by a purchase of nontendering shares at a depressed price, individual shareholders may tender their shares—even if they doubt the tender offer is in the corporation's best interest—to protect themselves from being forced to sell their shares at a depressed price. As the SEC explains: "The alternative of not accepting the tender offer is virtual assurance that, if the offer is successful, the shares will have to be sold in the lower priced, second step." Two–Tier Tender Offer Pricing and Non–Tender Offer Purchase Programs, SEC Exchange Act Rel. No. 21079 (June 21, 1984), [1984 Transfer Binder] CCH Fed.Sec.L.Rep. ¶ 83,637, p. 86,916 (footnote omitted) (hereinafter SEC Release No. 21079). See Lowenstein, Pruning Deadwood in Hostile Takeovers: A Proposal for Legislation, 83 Colum.L.Rev. 249, 307–309 (1983). In such a situation under the Indiana Act, the shareholders as a group, acting in the corporation's best interest, could reject the offer, although individual shareholders might be inclined to accept it. The desire of the Indiana Legislature to protect shareholders of Indiana corporations from this type of coercive offer does not conflict with the Williams Act. Rather, it furthers the federal policy of investor protection.

In implementing its goal, the Indiana Act avoids the problems the plurality discussed in *MITE*. Unlike the *MITE* statute, the Indiana Act does not give either management or the offeror an advantage in communicating with the shareholders about the impending offer. The Act also does not impose an indefinite delay on tender offers. Nothing in the Act prohibits an offeror from consummating an offer on the 20th business day, the earliest day permitted under applicable federal regulations, see 17 CFR § 240.14e–1(a) (1986). Nor does the Act allow the state government to interpose its views of fairness between willing buyers and sellers of shares of the target company. Rather, the Act allows *shareholders* to evaluate the fairness of the offer collectively.

D

The Court of Appeals based its finding of pre-emption on its view that the practical effect of the Indiana Act is to delay consummation of tender offers

with Justice White's conclusion. See id., at 646–647 (Powell, J., concurring in part); id., at 655 (Stevens, J. concurring in part and concurring in judgment). Four Justices did not address the question. See id., at 655 (O'Connor, J., concurring in part); id., at 664 (Marshall, J., with whom Brennan, J. joined, dissenting); id., at 667 (Rehnquist, J., dissenting).

until 50 days after the commencement of the offer. 794 F.2d, at 263. As did the Court of Appeals, Dynamics reasons that no rational offeror will purchase shares until it gains assurance that those shares will carry voting rights. Because it is possible that voting rights will not be conferred until a shareholder meeting 50 days after commencement of the offer, Dynamics concludes that the Act imposes a 50–day delay. This, it argues, conflicts with the shorter 20–business–day period established by the SEC as the minimum period for which a tender offer may be held open. 17 CFR § 240.14e–1 (1986). We find the alleged conflict illusory.

The Act does not impose an absolute 50–day delay on tender offers, nor does it preclude an offeror from purchasing shares as soon as federal law permits. If the offeror fears an adverse shareholder vote under the Act, it can make a conditional tender offer, offering to accept shares on the condition that the shares receive voting rights within a certain period of time. The Williams Act permits tender offers to be conditioned on the offeror's subsequently obtaining regulatory approval. E.g., Interpretive Release Relating to Tender Offer Rules, SEC Exchange Act Rel. No. 34–16623 (Mar. 5, 1980), 3 CCH Fed.Sec.L.Rep. ¶ 24,284I, p. 17,758, quoted in Macfadden Holdings, Inc. v. JB Acquisition Corp., 802 F.2d 62, 70 (C.A.2 1986). There is no reason to doubt that this type of conditional tender offer would be legitimate as well.[9]

Even assuming that the Indiana Act imposes some additional delay, nothing in *MITE* suggested that *any* delay imposed by state regulation, however short, would create a conflict with the Williams Act. The plurality argued only that the offeror should "be free to go forward without *unreasonable* delay." 457 U.S., at 639 (emphasis added). In that case, the Court was confronted with the potential for indefinite delay and presented with no persuasive reason why some deadline could not be established. By contrast, the Indiana Act provides that full voting rights will be vested—if this eventually is to occur—within 50 days after commencement of the offer. This period is within the 60–day maximum period Congress established for tender offers in [Exchange Act § 14(d)(5)]. We cannot say that a delay within that congressionally determined period is unreasonable.

Finally, we note that the Williams Act would pre-empt a variety of state corporate laws of hitherto unquestioned validity if it were construed to pre-empt any state statute that may limit or delay the free exercise of power after a successful tender offer. State corporate laws commonly permit corporations to stagger the terms of their directors. See Model Business Corp. Act § 37 (1969 draft) in 3 Model Business Corp. Act Ann. (2d ed. 1971) (hereinafter MBCA); American Bar Foundation, Revised Model Business Corp. Act § 8.06 (1984 draft) (1985) (hereinafter RMBCA). By staggering the terms of directors, and thus having annual elections for only one class of directors each year, corporations may delay the time when a successful offeror gains control of the board of

---

9. Dynamics argues that conditional tender offers are not an adequate alternative because they leave management in place for three extra weeks, with "free rein to take other defensive steps that will diminish the value of tendered shares." Brief for Appellee Dynamics Corp. of America 37. We reject this contention. In the unlikely event that management were to take actions designed to diminish the value of the corporation's shares, it may incur liability under state law. But this problem does not control our pre-emption analysis. Neither the Act nor any other federal statute can assure that shareholders do not suffer from the mismanagement of corporate officers and directors. Cf. Cort v. Ash, 422 U.S. 66, 84 (1975).

directors. Similarly, state corporation laws commonly provide for cumulative voting. See MBCA § 33, par. 4; RMBCA § 7.28. By enabling minority shareholders to assure themselves of representation in each class of directors, cumulative voting provisions can delay further the ability of offerors to gain untrammeled authority over the affairs of the target corporation. See Hochman & Folger, Deflecting Takeovers: Charter and By–Law Techniques, 34 Bus.Law. 537, 538–539 (1979).

In our view, the possibility that the Indiana Act will delay some tender offers is insufficient to require a conclusion that the Williams Act pre-empts the Act. The longstanding prevalence of state regulation in this area suggests that, if Congress had intended to pre-empt all state laws that delay the acquisition of voting control following a tender offer, it would have said so explicitly. The regulatory conditions that the Act places on tender offers are consistent with the text and the purposes of the Williams Act. Accordingly, we hold that the Williams Act does not pre-empt the Indiana Act.

III

As an alternative basis for its decision, the Court of Appeals held that the Act violates the Commerce Clause of the Federal Constitution. We now address this holding. On its face, the Commerce Clause is nothing more than a grant to Congress of the power "[t]o regulate Commerce * * * among the several States * * *," Art. I, § 8, cl. 3. But it has been settled for more than a century that the Clause prohibits States from taking certain actions respecting interstate commerce even absent congressional action. See, e.g., Cooley v. Board of Wardens, 12 How. 299 (1852). The Court's interpretation of "these great silences of the Constitution," H.P. Hood & Sons, Inc. v. Du Mond, 336 U.S. 525, 535 (1949), has not always been easy to follow. Rather, as the volume and complexity of commerce and regulation has grown in this country, the Court has articulated a variety of tests in an attempt to describe the difference between those regulations that the Commerce Clause permits and those regulations that it prohibits. See, e.g., Raymond Motor Transportation, Inc. v. Rice, 434 U.S. 429, 441, n. 15 (1978).

A

The principal objects of dormant Commerce Clause scrutiny are statutes that discriminate against interstate commerce. See, e.g., Lewis v. BT Investment Managers, Inc., 447 U.S. 27, 36–37 (1980); Philadelphia v. New Jersey, 437 U.S. 617, 624 (1978). See generally Regan, The Supreme Court and State Protectionism: Making Sense of the Dormant Commerce Clause, 84 Mich. L.Rev. 1091 (1986). The Indiana Act is not such a statute. It has the same effects on tender offers whether or not the offeror is a domiciliary or resident of Indiana. Thus, it "visits its effects equally upon both interstate and local business," *Lewis v. BT Investment Managers, Inc.,* supra, at 36.

Dynamics nevertheless contends that the statute is discriminatory because it will apply most often to out-of-state entities. This argument rests on the contention that, as a practical matter, most hostile tender offers are launched by offerors outside Indiana. But this argument avails Dynamics little. "The fact that the burden of a state regulation falls on some interstate companies does not, by itself, establish a claim of discrimination against interstate commerce." Exxon Corp. v. Governor of Maryland, 437 U.S. 117, 126 (1978). See Minnesota v. Clover Leaf Creamery Co., 449 U.S. 456, 471–472 (1981) (rejecting a claim of discrimination because the challenged statute "regulate[d] evenhandedly * * * without regard to whether the [commerce came] from outside the State"); Commonwealth Edison Co. v. Montana, 453 U.S. 609, 619 (1981) (rejecting a claim of discrimination because the "tax burden [was] borne according to the amount * * * consumed and not according to any distinction between in-state and out-of-state consumers"). Because nothing in the Indiana Act imposes a greater burden on out-of-state offerors than it does on similarly situated Indiana offerors, we reject the contention that the Act discriminates against interstate commerce.

B

This Court's recent Commerce Clause cases also have invalidated statutes that adversely may affect interstate commerce by subjecting activities to inconsistent regulations. E.g., Brown–Forman Distillers Corp. v. New York State Liquor Authority, 476 U.S. 573 (1986); Edgar v. MITE Corp., 457 U.S., at 642 (plurality opinion of White, J.); Kassel v. Consolidated Freightways Corp., 450 U.S. 662, 671 (1981) (plurality opinion of Powell, J.). See Southern Pacific Co. v. Arizona, 325 U.S. 761, 774 (1945) (noting the "confusion and difficulty" that would attend the "unsatisfied need for uniformity" in setting maximum limits on train lengths); *Cooley v. Board of Wardens,* supra, at 319 (stating that the Commerce Clause prohibits States from regulating subjects that "are in their nature national, or admit only of one uniform system, or plan of regulation"). The Indiana Act poses no such problem. So long as each State regulates voting rights only in the corporations it has created, each corporation will be subject to the law of only one State. No principle of corporation law and practice is more firmly established than a State's authority to regulate domestic corporations, including the authority to define the voting rights of shareholders. See Restatement (Second) of Conflict of Laws § 304 (1971) (concluding that the law of the incorporating State generally should "determine the right of a shareholder to participate in the administration of the affairs of the corporation"). Accordingly, we conclude that the Indiana Act does not create an impermissible risk of inconsistent regulation by different States.

C

The Court of Appeals did not find the Act unconstitutional for either of these threshold reasons. Rather, its decision rested on its view of the Act's potential to hinder tender offers. We think the Court of Appeals failed to appreciate the significance for Commerce Clause analysis of the fact that state regulation of corporate governance is regulation of entities whose very existence and attributes are a product of state law. As Chief Justice Marshall explained:

> "A corporation is an artificial being, invisible, intangible, and existing only in contemplation of law. Being the mere creature of law, it possesses only those properties which the charter of its creation confers upon it, either expressly, or as incidental to its very existence. These are such as are supposed best calculated to effect the object for which it was created." Trustees of Dartmouth College v. Woodward, 4 Wheat. 518, 636 (1819).

See First National Bank of Boston v. Bellotti, 435 U.S. 765, 822–824 (1978) (Rehnquist, J., dissenting). Every State in this country has enacted laws regulating corporate governance. By prohibiting certain transactions, and regulating others, such laws necessarily affect certain aspects of interstate commerce. This necessarily is true with respect to corporations with shareholders in States other than the State of incorporation. Large corporations that are listed on national exchanges, or even regional exchanges, will have shareholders in many States and shares that are traded frequently. The markets that facilitate this national and international participation in ownership of corporations are essential for providing capital not only for new enterprises but also for established companies that need to expand their businesses. This beneficial free market system depends at its core upon the fact that a corporation—except in the rarest situations—is organized under, and governed by, the law of a single jurisdiction, traditionally the corporate law of the State of its incorporation.

These regulatory laws may affect directly a variety of corporate transactions. Mergers are a typical example. In view of the substantial effect that a merger may have on the shareholders' interests in a corporation, many States require supermajority votes to approve mergers. See, e.g., MBCA § 73 (requiring approval of a merger by a majority of all shares, rather than simply a majority of votes cast); RMBCA § 11.03 (same). By requiring a greater vote for mergers than is required for other transactions, these laws make it more difficult for corporations to merge. State laws also may provide for "dissenters' rights" under which minority shareholders who disagree with corporate decisions to take particular actions are entitled to sell their shares to the corporation at fair market value. See, e.g., MBCA §§ 80–81; RMBCA § 13.02. By requiring the corporation to purchase the shares of dissenting shareholders, these laws may inhibit a corporation from engaging in the specified transactions.[12]

It thus is an accepted part of the business landscape in this country for States to create corporations, to prescribe their powers, and to define the rights that are acquired by purchasing their shares. A State has an interest in promoting stable relationships among parties involved in the corporations it charters, as well as in ensuring that investors in such corporations have an effective voice in corporate affairs.

There can be no doubt that the Act reflects these concerns. The primary purpose of the Act is to protect the shareholders of Indiana corporations. It

---

12. Numerous other common regulations may affect both nonresident and resident shareholders of a corporation. Specified votes may be required for the sale of all of the corporation's assets. See MBCA § 79; RMBCA § 12.02. The election of directors may be staggered over a period of years to prevent abrupt changes in management. See MBCA § 37; RMBCA § 8.06. Various classes of stock may be created with differences in voting rights as to dividends and on liquidation. See MBCA § 15; RMBCA § 6.01(c). Provisions may be made for cumulative voting. See MBCA § 33, par. 4; RMBCA § 7.28; n. 9, supra. Corporations may adopt restrictions on payment of dividends to ensure that specified ratios of assets to liabilities are maintained for the benefit of the holders of corporate bonds or notes. See MBCA § 45 (noting that a corporation's articles of incorporation can restrict payment of dividends);

RMBCA § 6.40 (same). Where the shares of a corporation are held in States other than that of incorporation, actions taken pursuant to these and similar provisions of state law will affect all shareholders alike wherever they reside or are domiciled.

Nor is it unusual for partnership law to restrict certain transactions. For example, a purchaser of a partnership interest generally can gain a right to control the business only with the consent of other owners. See Uniform Partnership Act § 27, 6 U.L.A. 353 (1969); Uniform Limited Partnership Act § 19 (1916 draft), 6 U.L.A. 603 (1969); Revised Uniform Limited Partnership Act §§ 702, 704 (1976 draft), 6 U.L.A. 259, 261 (Supp.1986). These provisions—in force in the great majority of the States—bear a striking resemblance to the Act at issue in this case.

does this by affording shareholders, when a takeover offer is made, an opportunity to decide collectively whether the resulting change in voting control of the corporation, as they perceive it, would be desirable. A change of management may have important effects on the shareholders' interests; it is well within the State's role as overseer of corporate governance to offer this opportunity. The autonomy provided by allowing shareholders collectively to determine whether the takeover is advantageous to their interests may be especially beneficial where a hostile tender offer may coerce shareholders into tendering their shares.

Appellee Dynamics responds to this concern by arguing that the prospect of coercive tender offers is illusory, and that tender offers generally should be favored because they reallocate corporate assets into the hands of management who can use them most effectively. See generally Easterbrook and Fischel, The Proper Role of a Target's Management in Responding to a Tender Offer. 94 Harv.L.Rev. 1161 (1981). As indicated supra, at 12, Indiana's concern with tender offers is not groundless. Indeed, the potentially coercive aspects of tender offers have been recognized by the Securities and Exchange Commission, see SEC Release No. 21079, p. 86,916, and by a number of scholarly commentators, see, e.g., Bradley & Rosenzweig, Defensive Stock Repurchases, 99 Harv.L.Rev. 1377, 1412–1413 (1986); Macey & McChesney, A Theoretical Analysis of Corporate Greenmail, 95 Yale L.J. 13, 20–22 (1985); Lowenstein, 83 Colum.L.Rev., at 307–309. The Constitution does not require the States to subscribe to any particular economic theory. We are not inclined "to second-guess the empirical judgments of lawmakers concerning the utility of legislation," Kassel v. Consolidated Freightways Corp., 450 U.S., at 679 (Brennan, J., concurring in judgment). In our view, the possibility of coercion in some takeover bids offers additional justification for Indiana's decision to promote the autonomy of independent shareholders.

Dynamics argues in any event that the State has " 'no legitimate interest in protecting the nonresident shareholders.' " Brief for Appellee Dynamics Corp. of America 21 (quoting Edgar v. MITE Corp., 457 U.S., at 644). Dynamics relies heavily on the statement by the *MITE* Court that "[i]nsofar as the * * * law burdens out-of-state transactions, there is nothing to be weighed in the balance to sustain the law." 457 U.S., at 644. But that comment was made in reference to an Illinois law that applied as well to out-of-state corporations as to in-state corporations. We agree that Indiana has no interest in protecting nonresident shareholders *of nonresident corporations*. But this Act applies only to corporations incorporated in Indiana. We reject the contention that Indiana has no interest in providing for the shareholders of its corporations the voting autonomy granted by the Act. Indiana has a substantial interest in preventing the corporate form from becoming a shield for unfair business dealing. Moreover, unlike the Illinois statute invalidated in *MITE*, the Indiana Act applies only to corporations that have a substantial number of shareholders in Indiana. See Ind.Code § 23–1–42–4(a)(3) (Supp.1986). Thus, every application of the Indiana Act will affect a substantial number of Indiana residents, whom Indiana indisputably has an interest in protecting.

D

Dynamics' argument that the Act is unconstitutional ultimately rests on its contention that the Act will limit the number of successful tender offers. There is little evidence that this will occur. But even if true, this result would not substantially affect our Commerce Clause analysis. We reiterate that this Act does not prohibit any entity—resident or nonresident—from offering to purchase, or from purchasing, shares in Indiana corporations, or from attempting thereby to gain control. It only provides regulatory procedures designed for the better protection of the corporations' shareholders. We have rejected the "notion that the Commerce Clause protects the particular structure or methods of operation in a * * * market." Exxon Corp. v. Governor of Maryland, 437 U.S., at 127. The very commodity that is traded in the securities market is one whose characteristics are defined by state law. Similarly, the very commodity that is traded in the "market for corporate control"—the corporation—is one that owes its existence and attributes to state law. Indiana need not define these commodities as other States do; it need only provide that residents and nonresidents have equal access to them. This Indiana has done. Accordingly, even if the Act should decrease the number of successful tender offers for Indiana corporations, this would not offend the Commerce Clause.

IV

On its face, the Indiana Control Share Acquisitions Chapter even-handedly determines the voting rights of shares of Indiana corporations. The Act does not conflict with the provisions or purposes of the Williams Act. To the limited extent that the Act affects interstate commerce, this is justified by the State's interests in defining the attributes of shares in its corporations and in protecting shareholders. Congress has never questioned the need for state regulation of these matters. Nor do we think such regulation offends the Constitution. Accordingly, we reverse the judgment of the Court of Appeals.

It is so ordered.

■ JUSTICE SCALIA, concurring in part and concurring in the judgment.

I join Parts I, III–A, and III–B of the Court's opinion. However, having found, as those Parts do, that the Indiana Control Share Acquisitions Chapter neither "discriminates against interstate commerce," ante, at 88, nor "create[s] an impermissible risk of inconsistent regulation by different States," ante, at 89, I would conclude without further analysis that it is not invalid under the dormant Commerce Clause. While it has become standard practice at least since Pike v. Bruce Church, Inc., 397 U.S. 137 (1970), to consider, in addition to these factors, whether the burden on commerce imposed by a state statute "is clearly excessive in relation to the putative local benefits," id., at 142, such an inquiry is ill suited to the judicial function and should be undertaken rarely if at all. This case is a good illustration of the point. Whether the control shares statute "protects shareholders of Indiana corporations," Brief for Appellant in No. 86–97, p. 88, or protects incumbent management seems to me a highly debatable question, but it is extraordinary to think that the constitutionality of the Act should depend on the answer. Nothing in the Constitution says that the protection of entrenched management is any less important a "putative local benefit" than the protection of entrenched shareholders, and I do not know what qualifies us to make that judgment—or the related judgment as to how effective the present statute is in achieving one or the other objective—or the ultimate (and most ineffable) judgment as to whether, given importance-level x, and effectiveness-level y, the worth of the statute is "outweighed" by impact-on-commerce z.

One commentator has suggested that, at least much of the time, we do not in fact mean what we say when we declare that statutes which neither discriminate against commerce nor present a threat of multiple and inconsistent burdens might nonetheless be unconstitutional under a "balancing" test. See Regan, The Supreme Court and State Protectionism: Making Sense of the Dormant Commerce Clause, 84 Mich.L.Rev. 1091 (1986). If he is not correct, he ought to be. As long as a State's corporation law governs only its own corporations and does not discriminate against out-of-state interests, it should survive this Court's scrutiny under the Commerce Clause, whether it promotes shareholder welfare or industrial stagnation. Beyond that, it is for Congress to prescribe its invalidity.

I also agree with the Court that the Indiana Control Shares Act is not preempted by the Williams Act, but I reach that conclusion without entering into the debate over the purposes of the two statutes. The Williams Act is governed by the antipre-emption provision of the Securities Exchange Act of 1934, [§ 28(a)], which provides that nothing it contains "shall affect the jurisdiction of the securities commission (or any agency or officer performing like functions) of any State over any security or any person insofar as it does not conflict with the provisions of this chapter or the rules and regulations thereunder." Unless it serves no function, that language forecloses pre-emption on the basis of conflicting "purpose" as opposed to conflicting "provision." Even if it does not have literal application to the present case (because, perhaps, the Indiana agency responsible for securities matters has no enforcement responsibility with regard to this legislation), it nonetheless refutes the proposition that Congress meant the Williams Act to displace *all* state laws with conflicting purpose. And if any are to survive, surely the States' corporation codes are among them. It would be peculiar to hold that Indiana could have pursued the purpose at issue here through its blue-sky laws, but cannot pursue it through the State's even more sacrosanct authority over the structure of domestic corporations. Prescribing voting rights for the governance of state-chartered companies is a traditional state function with which the Federal Congress has never, to my knowledge, intentionally interfered. I would require far more evidence than is available here to find implicit pre-emption of that function by a federal statute whose provisions concededly do not conflict with the state law.

I do not share the Court's apparent high estimation of the beneficence of the state statute at issue here. But a law can be both economic folly and constitutional. The Indiana Control Shares Acquisition Chapter is at least the latter. I therefore concur in the judgment of the Court.

———

■ JUSTICE WHITE, with whom JUSTICE BLACKMUN and JUSTICE STEVENS join as to Part II, dissenting.

The majority today upholds Indiana's Control Share Acquisitions Chapter, a statute which will predictably foreclose completely some tender offers for stock in Indiana corporations. I disagree with the conclusion that the Chapter is neither pre-empted by the Williams Act nor in conflict with the Commerce Clause. The Chapter undermines the policy of the Williams Act by effectively preventing minority shareholders, in some circumstances, from acting in their own best interests by selling their stock. In addition, the Chapter will substantially burden the interstate market in corporate ownership, particularly if other

States follow Indiana's lead as many already have done. The Chapter, therefore, directly inhibits interstate commerce, the very economic consequences the Commerce Clause was intended to prevent. The opinion of the Court of Appeals is far more persuasive than that of the majority today, and the judgment of that court should be affirmed.

I.

The Williams Act expressed Congress' concern that individual investors be given sufficient information so that they could make an informed choice on whether to tender their stock in response to a tender offer. The problem with the approach the majority adopts today is that it equates protection of individual investors, the focus of the Williams Act, with the protection of shareholders as a group. Indiana's Control Share Acquisitions Chapter undoubtedly helps protect the interests of a majority of the shareholders in any corporation subject to its terms, but in many instances, it will effectively prevent an individual investor from selling his stock at a premium. Indiana's statute, therefore, does not "furthe[r] the federal policy of *investor* protection," ante, at 1646 (emphasis added), as the majority claims.

* * *

The majority claims that if the Williams Act pre-empts Indiana's Control Share Acquisitions Chapter, it also pre-empts a number of other corporate-control provisions such as cumulative voting or staggering the terms of directors. But this view ignores the fundamental distinction between these other corporate-control provisions and the Chapter: unlike those other provisions, the Chapter is designed to prevent certain tender offers from ever taking place. It is transactional in nature, although it is characterized by the State as involving only the voting rights of certain shares. "[T]his Court is not bound by '[t]he name, description or characterization given [a challenged statute] by the legislature or the courts of the State,' but will determine for itself the practical impact of the law." Hughes v. Oklahoma, 441 U.S. 322, 336 (1979). The Control Share Acquisitions Chapter will effectively prevent minority shareholders in some circumstances from selling their stock to a willing tender offeror. It is the practical impact of the Chapter that leads to the conclusion that it is pre-empted by the Williams Act.

II.

Given the impact of the Control Share Acquisitions Chapter, it is clear that Indiana is directly regulating the purchase and sale of shares of stock in interstate commerce. Appellant CTS's stock is traded on the New York Stock Exchange, and people from all over the country buy and sell CTS's shares daily. Yet, under Indiana's scheme, any prospective purchaser will be effectively precluded from purchasing CTS's shares if the purchaser crosses one of the Chapter's threshold ownership levels and a majority of CTS's shareholders refuse to give the purchaser voting rights. This Court should not countenance such a restraint on interstate trade.

The United States, as *amicus curiae,* argues that Indiana's Control Share Acquisitions Chapter "is written as a restraint on the *transferability* of voting rights in specified transactions, and it could not be written in any other way without changing its meaning. Since the restraint on the transfer of voting rights is a restraint on the transfer of shares, the Indiana Chapter, like the Illinois Act [in *MITE*], restrains 'transfers of stock by stockholders to a third party.'" Brief for Securities and Exchange Commission and United States as *Amici Curiae* 26. I agree. The majority ignores the practical impact of the Chapter in concluding that the Chapter does not violate the Commerce Clause. The Chapter is characterized as merely defining "the attributes of shares in its corporations," ante, at 94. The majority sees the trees but not the forest.

* * *

With all due respect, I dissent.

———

1. *Was the Indiana Statute Truly Preclusive?* Some commentators believe that the Indiana "control share acquisition" statute at issue in *CTS* could not block a determined bidder and may actually assist it. Contrasting Indiana's statute with "fair price" and "redemption" statutes, Professor Roberta Romano predicted that "shareholders may tender more frequently under a control share statute than a fair price provision."[4] Ordinarily, antitakeover defenses seek to prevent the shareholders from voting, but the Indiana statute actually entitled them to vote on the offer. Although the Indiana statute effectively also mandated a 50–day delay before the bidder can obtain a vote and pursue its offer, today a target board could probably secure approximately the same delay through the use of a poison pill. Thus, to believe that the bidder is really disadvantaged by the vote requirement, one must believe that the target shareholders who hold its shares prior to the commencement of a takeover would vote differently on its mandated referendum than would the shareholders who thereafter acquire those shares. Proponents of this statutory approach evidently believe that the "true" shareholders will vote down an offer that the "arbs" and "speculators" who acquire takeover stocks would approve. This is a questionable premise, as the "true" shareholders have arguably "voted with their feet" by tendering to the arbitrageurs.

2. *Delaware's Response.* Within days after the Supreme Court's decision in *CTS*, Delaware began to draft an antitakeover statute. After considering and rejecting an Indiana-style control share acquisition statute, the Corporate Law Section of the Delaware State Bar Association turned instead to New York State for a precedent and largely borrowed N.Y.Bus.Corp.L. § 912. This form of statute—known as a "moratorium" or "business combination" statute—imposes no obstacle to a tender offer, but delays any second-step merger for several years (5 years in New York; 3 years in Delaware). As adopted, Delaware Gen.Corp.Law § 203 (see Statutory Supplement) bars an acquirer of more than 15% of the voting stock of a Delaware corporation from effecting a "business combination" (as defined) between it and the target for three years. The practical impact of such an antitakeover statute is to bar the financing of "bust-up" takeovers. Because the bidder cannot get access to the target's assets for the moratorium period, it cannot issue junk bonds based largely on the target's liquidation value. Thus, a moratorium statute may not preclude a well-financed Whale Co. from a takeover of Minnow Inc., but it does largely deter Minnow from tendering for Whale.

4. Romano, The Political Economy of   (1987).
Takeover Statutes, 73 Va.L.Rev. 111, 169

3. *The Post–CTS Case Law.* The first decisions after *CTS* involved the new Delaware statute.[5] Each found that the Delaware statute left hostile bidders "a meaningful opportunity for success" while also concluding that a statute that wholly insulated targets from bidders would not pass constitutional muster under a Commerce Clause analysis, even after CTS. At least implicitly, these decisions seemed to continue to use a balancing mode of analysis: that is, a state could pursue legitimate corporate governance objectives in a way that chilled takeovers, so long as it did not wholly preclude them. But, as the next case illustrates, the tide turned quickly.[6]

Amanda Acquisition Corp. v. Universal Foods Corp.

United States Court of Appeals, Seventh Circuit, 1989.
877 F.2d 496.

■ Before BAUER, CHIEF JUDGE, EASTERBROOK, CIRCUIT JUDGE, and WILL, SENIOR DISTRICT JUDGE.

■ EASTERBROOK, CIRCUIT JUDGE.

States have enacted three generations of takeover statutes in the last 20 years. Illinois enacted a first-generation statute, which forbade acquisitions of any firm with substantial assets in Illinois unless a public official approved. We concluded that such a statute injures investors, is preempted by the Williams Act, and is unconstitutional under the dormant Commerce Clause. MITE Corp. v. Dixon, 633 F.2d 486 (7th Cir.1980). The Supreme Court affirmed the judgment under the Commerce Clause, Edgar v. MITE Corp., 457 U.S. 624, 643–46, (1982). * * *

Indiana enacted a second-generation statute, applicable only to firms incorporated there and eliminating governmental veto power. Indiana's law provides that the acquiring firm's shares lose their voting power unless the target's directors approve the acquisition or the shareholders not affiliated with either bidder or management authorize restoration of votes. We concluded that this statute, too, is inimical to investors' interests, preempted by the Williams Act, and unconstitutional under the Commerce Clause. Dynamics Corp. of America v. CTS Corp., 794 F.2d 250 (7th Cir.1986). This time the Supreme Court did not agree. It thought the Indiana statute consistent with both [the] Williams Act and Commerce Clause. CTS Corp. v. Dynamics Corp. of America, 481 U.S. 69, 107 S.Ct. 1637, 95 L.Ed.2d 67 (1987). Adopting Justice White's view of preemption for the sake of argument, id. at 81, 107 S.Ct. at 1645, the Court found no inconsistency between state and federal law because Indiana allowed the bidder to *acquire* the shares without hindrance. Such a law makes the shares less attractive, but it does not regulate the process of bidding. As for the Commerce Clause, the Court took Indiana's law to be regulation of internal corporate affairs, potentially beneficial because it would allow investors to avoid the "coercion" of two-tier bids and other tactics. * * *

5. See BNS, Inc. v. Koppers Co., Inc., 683 F.Supp. 458 (D.Del.1988); RP Acquisition Corp. v. Staley Continental, Inc., 686 F.Supp. 476 (D.Del.1988); City Capital Associates Ltd. v. Interco, Inc., 696 F.Supp. 1551 (D.Del. 1988).

6. For another decision rejecting the "meaningful opportunity for success" standard, see WLR Foods, Inc. v. Tyson Foods, Inc., 65 F.3d 1172 (4th Cir.1995).

Wisconsin has a third-generation takeover statute. Enacted after *CTS*, it postpones the kinds of transactions that often follow tender offers (and often are the reason for making the offers in the first place). Unless the target's board agrees to the transaction in advance, the bidder must wait three years after buying the shares to merge with the target or acquire more than 5% of its assets. We must decide whether this is consistent with the Williams Act and Commerce Clause.

I

* * *

No firm incorporated in Wisconsin and having its headquarters, substantial operations, or 10% of its shares or shareholders there may "engage in a business combination with an interested stockholder ... for 3 years after the interested stockholder's stock acquisition date unless the board of directors of the [Wisconsin] corporation has approved, before the interested stockholder's stock acquisition date, that business combination or the purchase of stock", Wis.Stat. § 180.726(2). An "interested stockholder" is one owning 10% of the voting stock, directly or through associates (anyone acting in concert with it), § 180.726(1)(j). A "business combination" is a merger with the bidder or any of its affiliates, sale of more than 5% of the assets to bidder or affiliate, liquidation of the target, or a transaction by which the target guarantees the bidder's or affiliates debts or passes tax benefits to the bidder or affiliate, § 180.726(1)(e). The law, in other words, provides for almost hermetic separation of bidder and target for three years after the bidder obtains 10% of the stock—unless the target's board consented before then. No matter how popular the offer, the ban applies: obtaining 85% (even 100%) of the stock held by non-management shareholders won't allow the bidder to engage in a business combination, as it would under Delaware law. See BNS, Inc. v. Koppers Co., 683 F.Supp. 458 (D.Del.1988); RP Acquisition Corp. v. Staley Continental, Inc., 686 F.Supp. 476 (D.Del.1988); City Capital Associates L.P. v. Interco, Inc., 696 F.Supp. 1551 (D.Del.), affirmed, 860 F.2d 60 (3d Cir.1988). Wisconsin firms cannot opt out of the law, as may corporations subject to almost all other state takeover statutes. In Wisconsin it is management's approval in advance, or wait three years. Even when the time is up, the bidder needs the approval of a majority of the remaining investors, without any provision disqualifying shares still held by the managers who resisted the transaction, § 180.726(3)(b). The district court found that this statute "effectively eliminates hostile leveraged buyouts". As a practical matter, Wisconsin prohibits any offer contingent on a merger between bidder and target, a condition attached to about 90% of contemporary tender offers.

* * *

II

Courts try to avoid constitutional adjudication. There is no escape for us today, however. * * *

A

If our views of the wisdom of state law mattered, Wisconsin's takeover statute would not survive. Like our colleagues who decided *MITE* and *CTS*, we believe that antitakeover legislation injures shareholders.[5] Managers frequently realize gains for investors via voluntary combinations (mergers). If gains are to be had, but managers balk, tender offers are investors' way to go over managers' heads. If managers are not maximizing the firm's value—perhaps because they have missed the possibility of a synergistic combination, perhaps because they are clinging to divisions that could be better run in other hands, perhaps because they are just not the best persons for the job—a bidder that believes it can realize more of the firm's value will make investors a higher offer. Investors tender; the bidder gets control and changes things. Michael Bradley, Anand Desai & E. Han Kim, Synergistic Gains from Corporate Acquisitions and Their Division Between the Stockholders of Target and Acquiring Firms, 21 J.Fin.Econ. 3 (1988). The prospect of monitoring by would-be bidders, and an occasional bid at a premium, induces managers to run corporations more efficiently and replaces them if they will not.

Premium bids reflect the benefits for investors. The price of a firm's stock represents investors' consensus estimate of the value of the shares under current and anticipated conditions. Stock is worth the present value of anticipated future returns—dividends and other distributions. Tender offers succeed when bidders offer more. Only when the bid exceeds the value of the stock (however investors compute value) will it succeed. A statute that precludes investors from receiving or accepting a premium offer makes them worse off. It makes the economy worse off too, because the higher bid reflects the better use to which the bidder can put the target's assets. (If the bidder can't improve the use of the assets, it injures itself by paying a premium.)

Universal, making an argument common among supporters of anti-takeover laws, contends that its investors do not appreciate the worth of its business plans, that its stock is trading for too little, and that if investors tender reflexively they injure themselves. If only they would wait, Universal submits, they would do better under current management. A variant of the argument has it that although smart investors know that the stock is underpriced, many investors are passive and will tender; even the smart investors then must tender to avoid doing worse on the "back end" of the deal. State laws giving management the power to block an offer enable the managers to protect the investors from themselves.

Both versions of this price-is-wrong argument imply: (a) that the stock of firms defeating offers later appreciates in price, topping the bid, thus revealing the wisdom of waiting till the market wises up; and (b) that investors in firms

---

5. Because both the district court and the parties—like the Williams Act—examine tender offers from the perspective of equity investors, we employ the same approach. States could choose to protect "constituencies" other than stockholders. Creditors, managers, and workers invest human rather than financial capital. But the limitation of our inquiry to equity investors does not affect the analysis, because no evidence of which we are aware suggests that bidders confiscate workers' and other participants' investments to any greater degree than do incumbents—who may (and frequently do) close or move plants to follow the prospect of profit. Joseph A. Grundfest, a Commissioner of the SEC, showed in Job Loss and Takeovers, address to University of Toledo College of Law, Mar. 11, 1988, that acquisitions have no logical (or demonstrable) effect on employment. See also Brown & Medoff, The Impact of Firm Acquisitions on Labor, in Corporate Takeovers: Causes and Consequences 9 (A. Auerbach ed. 1988); Roberta Romano, The Future of Hostile Takeovers: Legislation and Public Opinion, 57 U.Cin.L.Rev. 457 (1988); C. Steven Bradford, Protecting Shareholders from Themselves? A Policy and Constitutional Review of a State Takeover Statute, 67 Neb. L.Rev. 459, 529–34 (1988).

for which no offer is outstanding gain when they adopt devices so that managers may fend off unwanted offers (or states adopt laws with the same consequence). Efforts to verify these implications have failed. The best available data show that if a firm fends off a bid, its profits decline, and its stock price (adjusted for inflation and market-wide changes) never tops the initial bid, even if it is later acquired by another firm. Stock of firms adopting poison pills falls in price, as does the stock of firms that adopt most kinds of anti-takeover amendments to their articles of incorporation. Studies of laws similar to Wisconsin's produce the same conclusion: share prices of firms incorporated in the state drop when the legislation is enacted.

Although a takeover-*proof* firm leaves investors at the mercy of incumbent managers (who may be mistaken about the wisdom of their business plan even when they act in the best of faith), a takeover-*resistant* firm may be able to assist its investors. An auction may run up the price, and delay may be essential to an auction. Auctions transfer money from bidders to targets, and diversified investors would not gain from them (their left pocket loses what the right pocket gains); diversified investors would lose from auctions if the lower returns to bidders discourage future bids. But from targets' perspectives, once a bid is on the table an auction may be the best strategy. The full effects of auctions are hard to unravel, sparking scholarly debate. Devices giving managers some ability to orchestrate investors' responses, in order to avoid panic tenders in response to front-end-loaded offers, also could be beneficial, as the Supreme Court emphasized in *CTS*, 481 U.S. at 92–93, 107 S.Ct. at 1651–52. ("Could be" is an important qualifier; even from a perspective limited to targets' shareholders given a bid on the table, it is important to know whether managers use this power to augment bids or to stifle them, and whether courts can tell the two apart.)

State anti-takeover laws do not serve these ends well, however. Investors who prefer to give managers the discretion to orchestrate responses to bids may do so through "fair-price" clauses in the articles of incorporation and other consensual devices. Other firms may choose different strategies. A law such as Wisconsin's does not add options to firms that would like to give more discretion to their managers; instead it destroys the possibility of divergent choices. Wisconsin's law applies even when the investors prefer to leave their managers under the gun, to allow the market full sway. Karpoff and Malatesta found that state anti-takeover laws have little or no effect on the price of shares if the firm already has poison pills (or related devices) in place, but strongly negative effects on price when firms have no such contractual devices. To put this differently, state laws have bite only when investors, given the choice, would deny managers the power to interfere with tender offers (maybe already *have* denied managers that power).

B

Skepticism about the wisdom of a state's law does not lead to the conclusion that the law is beyond the state's power, however. We have not been elected custodians of investors' wealth. States need not treat investors' welfare as their summum bonum. Perhaps they choose to protect managers' welfare instead, or believe that the current economic literature reaches an incorrect conclusion and that despite appearances takeovers injure investors in the long run. Unless a federal statute or the Constitution bars the way, Wisconsin's choice must be respected.

Amanda relies on the Williams Act of 1968, incorporated into §§ 13(d), (e) and 14(d)–(f) of the Securities Exchange Act of 1934, 15 U.S.C. §§ 78m(d), (e), 78n(d)–(f). The Williams Act regulates the conduct of tender offers. Amanda believes that Congress created an entitlement for investors to receive the benefit of tender offers, and that because Wisconsin's law makes tender offers unattractive to many potential bidders, it is preempted. See *MITE*, 633 F.2d at 490–99, and Justice White's views, 457 U.S. at 630–40, 102 S.Ct. at 2634–40.

Preemption has not won easy acceptance among the Justices for several reasons. First there is § 28(a) of the '34 Act, 15 U.S.C. § 78bb(a), which provides that "[n]othing in this chapter shall affect the jurisdiction of the securities commission * * * of any State over any security or any person insofar as it does not conflict with the provisions of this chapter or the rules and regulations thereunder." Although some of the SEC's regulations (particularly the one defining the commencement of an offer) conflict with some state takeover laws, the SEC has not drafted regulations concerning mergers with controlling shareholders, and the Act itself does not address the subject. States have used the leeway afforded by § 28(a) to carry out "merit regulation" of securities—"blue sky" laws that allow securities commissioners to forbid sales altogether, in contrast with the federal regimen emphasizing disclosure. So § 28(a) allows states to stop some transactions federal law would permit, in pursuit of an approach at odds with a system emphasizing disclosure and investors' choice. Then there is the traditional reluctance of federal courts to infer preemption of "state law in areas traditionally regulated by the States". States have regulated corporate affairs, including mergers and sales of assets, since before the beginning of the nation.

Because Justice White's views of the Williams Act did not garner the support of a majority of the Court in *MITE*, we reexamined that subject in *CTS* and observed that the best argument for preemption is the Williams Act's "neutrality" between bidder and management, a balance designed to leave investors free to choose. * * *

There is a big difference between what Congress *enacts* and what it *supposes* will ensue. Expectations about the consequences of a law are not themselves law. To say that Congress wanted to be neutral between bidder and target—a conclusion reached in many of the Court's opinions, e.g., Piper v. Chris–Craft Industries, Inc., 430 U.S. 1, 97 S.Ct. 926, 51 L.Ed.2d 124 (1977)—is not to say that it also forbade the states to favor one of these sides. Every law has a stopping point, likely one selected because of a belief that it would be unwise (for now, maybe forever) to do more. Nothing in the Williams Act says that the federal compromise among bidders, targets' managers, and investors is the only permissible one. * * *

The Williams Act regulates the *process* of tender offers: timing, disclosure, proration if tenders exceed what the bidder is willing to buy, best-price rules. It slows things down, allowing investors to evaluate the offer and management's response. Best-price, proration, and short-tender rules ensure that investors who decide at the end of the offer get the same treatment as those who decide immediately, reducing pressure to leap before looking. After complying with the disclosure and delay requirements, the bidder is free to take the shares. *MITE* held invalid a state law that increased the delay and, by authorizing a regulator to nix the offer, created a distinct possibility that the bidder would be unable to buy the stock (and the holders to sell it) despite compliance with federal law. Illinois tried to regulate the process of tender offers, contradicting in some respects the federal rules. Indiana, by contrast, allowed the tender offer to take its course as the Williams Act specified but "sterilized" the acquired shares until the remaining investors restored their voting rights. Congress said nothing about the voting power of shares acquired in tender offers. Indiana's law reduced the benefits the bidder anticipated from the acquisition but left the process alone. So the Court, although accepting Justice White's views for the purpose of argument, held that Indiana's rules do not conflict with the federal norms.

CTS observed that laws affecting the voting power of acquired shares do not differ in principle from many other rules governing the internal affairs of corporations. Laws requiring staggered or classified boards of directors delay the transfer of control to the bidder; laws requiring supermajority vote for a merger may make a transaction less attractive or impossible. 481 U.S. at 85–86, 107 S.Ct. at 1647–48. Yet these are not preempted by the Williams Act, any more than state laws concerning the *effect* of investors' votes are preempted by the portions of the Exchange Act, 15 U.S.C. § 78n(a)–(c), regulating the process of soliciting proxies. Federal securities laws frequently regulate process while state corporate law regulates substance. Federal proxy rules demand that firms disclose many things, in order to promote informed voting. Yet states may permit or compel a supermajority rule (even a unanimity rule) rendering it all but impossible for a particular side to prevail in the voting. Are the state laws therefore preempted? How about state laws that allow many firms to organize without traded shares? Universities, hospitals, and other charities have self-perpetuating boards and cannot be acquired by tender offer. Insurance companies may be organized as mutuals, without traded shares; retailers often organize as co-operatives, without traded stock; some decently large companies (large enough to be "reporting companies" under the '34 Act) issue stock subject to buy-sell agreements under which the investors cannot sell to strangers without offering stock to the firm at a formula price; Ford Motor Co. issued non-voting stock to outside investors while reserving voting stock for the family, thus preventing outsiders from gaining control (dual-class stock is becoming more common); firms issue and state law enforces poison pills. All of these devices make tender offers unattractive (even impossible) and greatly diminish the power of proxy fights, success in which often depends on buying votes by acquiring the equity to which the vote is attached. None of these devices could be thought preempted by the Williams Act or the proxy rules. If they are not preempted, neither is Wis.Stat. § 180.726.

Any bidder complying with federal law is free to acquire shares of Wisconsin firms on schedule. Delay in completing a second-stage merger may make the target less attractive, and thus depress the price offered or even lead to an absence of bids; it does not, however, alter any of the procedures governed by federal regulation. Indeed Wisconsin's law does not depend in any way on how the acquiring firm came by its stock: open-market purchases, private acquisitions of blocs, and acquisitions via tender offers are treated identically. Wisconsin's law is no different in effect from one saying that for the three years after a person acquires 10% of a firm's stock, a unanimous vote is required to merge. Corporate law once had a generally-applicable unanimity rule in major transactions, a rule discarded because giving every investor the power to block every reorganization stopped many desirable changes. (Many investors could use their "hold-up" power to try to engross a larger portion of the gains, creating a complex bargaining problem that often could not be solved.) Wisconsin's more restrained version of unanimity also may block beneficial transactions, but not by tinkering with any of the procedures established in federal law.

Only if the Williams Act gives investors a right to be the beneficiary of offers could Wisconsin's law run afoul of the federal rule. No such entitlement can be mined out of the Williams Act, however. Schreiber v. Burlington Northern, Inc., 472 U.S. 1, 105 S.Ct. 2458, 86 L.Ed.2d 1 (1985), holds that the cancellation of a pending offer because of machinations between bidder and target does not deprive investors of their due under the Williams Act. The Court treated § 14(e) as a disclosure law, so that investors could make informed decisions; it follows that events leading bidders to cease their quest do not conflict with the Williams Act any more than a state law leading a firm not to issue new securities could conflict with the Securities Act of 1933. * * * Investors have no right to receive tender offers. More to the point—since Amanda sues as bidder rather than as investor seeking to sell—the Williams Act does not create a right to profit from the business of making tender offers. It is not attractive to put bids on the table for Wisconsin corporations, but because Wisconsin leaves the process alone once a bidder appears, its law may co-exist with the Williams Act.

C

The Commerce Clause, Art. I, § 8 cl. 3 of the Constitution, grants Congress the power "[t]o regulate Commerce * * * among the several States". * * *

When state law discriminates against interstate commerce expressly—for example, when Wisconsin closes its border to butter from Minnesota—the negative Commerce Clause steps in. The law before us is not of this type: it is neutral between inter-state and intra-state commerce. Amanda therefore presses on us the broader, all-weather, be-reasonable vision of the Constitution. Wisconsin has passed a law that unreasonably injures investors, most of whom live outside of Wisconsin, and therefore it *has* to be unconstitutional, as Amanda sees things. Although Pike v. Bruce Church, Inc., 397 U.S. 137, 90 S.Ct. 844, 25 L.Ed.2d 174 (1970), sometimes is understood to authorize such general-purpose balancing, a closer examination of the cases may support the conclusion that the Court has looked for discrimination rather than for baleful effects. * * * At all events, although *MITE* employed the balancing process described in *Pike* to deal with a statute that regulated all firms having "contacts" with the state, *CTS* did not even cite that case when dealing with a statute regulating only the affairs of a firm incorporated in the state, and Justice Scalia's concurring opinion questioned its application. * * * Although the scholars whose writings we cited in Part II.A conclude that laws such as Wisconsin's injure investors, Wisconsin is entitled to give a different answer to this empirical question—or to decide that investors' interests should be sacrificed to protect managers' interests or promote the stability of corporate arrangements.

Illinois's law, held invalid in *MITE,* regulated sales of stock elsewhere. Illinois tried to tell a Texas owner of stock in a Delaware corporation that he could not sell to a buyer in California. By contrast, Wisconsin's law, like the Indiana statute sustained by *CTS,* regulates the internal affairs of firms incorporated there. Investors may buy or sell stock as they please. Wisconsin's law differs in this respect not only from that of Illinois but also from that of Massachusetts, which forbade any transfer of shares for one year after the failure to disclose any material fact, a flaw that led the First Circuit to condemn it. Hyde Park Partners, L.P. v. Connolly, 839 F.2d 837, 847–48 (1st Cir.1988).

Buyers of stock in Wisconsin firms may exercise full rights as investors, taking immediate control. No interstate transaction is regulated or forbidden. True, Wisconsin's law makes a potential buyer less willing to buy (or depresses the bid), but this is equally true of Indiana's rule. Many other rules of corporate law—supermajority voting requirements, staggered and classified boards, and so on—have similar or greater effects on some persons' willingness to purchase stock. States could ban mergers outright, with even more powerful consequences. Wisconsin did not allow mergers among firms chartered there until 1947. We doubt that it was violating the Commerce Clause all those years. Every rule of corporate law affects investors who live outside the state of incorporation, yet this has never been thought sufficient to authorize a form of cost-benefit inquiry through the medium of the Commerce Clause.

Wisconsin, like Indiana, is indifferent to the domicile of the bidder. A putative bidder located in Wisconsin enjoys no privilege over a firm located in New York. So too with investors: all are treated identically, regardless of residence. Doubtless most bidders (and investors) are located outside Wisconsin, but unless the law discriminates according to residence this alone does not matter. * * *

Wisconsin could exceed its powers by subjecting firms to inconsistent regulation. Because § 180.726 applies only to a subset of firms incorporated in Wisconsin, however, there is no possibility of inconsistent regulation. Here, too, the Wisconsin law is materially identical to Indiana's. This leaves only the argument that Wisconsin's law hinders the flow of interstate trade "too much". *CTS* dispatched this concern by declaring it inapplicable to laws that apply only to the internal affairs of firms incorporated in the regulating state. States may regulate corporate transactions as they choose without having to demonstrate under an unfocused balancing test that the benefits are "enough" to justify the consequences.

To say that states have the power to enact laws whose costs exceed their benefits is not to say that investors should kiss their wallets goodbye. States compete to offer corporate codes attractive to firms. Managers who want to raise money incorporate their firms in the states that offer the combination of rules investors prefer. Laws that in the short run injure investors and protect managers will in the longer run make the state less attractive to firms that need to raise new capital. If the law is "protectionist", the protected class is the existing body of managers (and other workers), suppliers, and so on, which bears no necessary relation to state boundaries. States regulating the affairs of domestic corporations cannot in the long run injure anyone but themselves. * * *

　　　* * *

The long run takes time to arrive, and it is tempting to suppose that courts could contribute to investors' welfare by eliminating laws that impose costs in the short run. The price of such warfare, however, is a reduction in the power of competition among states. Courts seeking to impose "good" rules on the states diminish the differences among corporate codes and dampen competitive forces. Too, courts may fail in their quest. How do judges know which rules are best? Often only the slow forces of competition reveal that information. Early economic studies may mislead, or judges (not trained as social scientists) may misinterpret the available data or act precipitously. Our Constitution allows the states to act as laboratories; slow migration (or national law on the authority of the Commerce Clause) grinds the failures under. No such process weeds out judicial errors, or decisions that, although astute when rendered, have become anachronistic in light of changes in the economy. Judges must hesitate for these practical reasons—and not only because of limits on their constitutional competence—before trying to "perfect" corporate codes.

The three district judges who have considered and sustained Delaware's law delaying mergers did so in large measure because they believed that the law left hostile offers "a meaningful opportunity for success". BNS, Inc. v. Koppers Co., 683 F.Supp. at 469. See also RP Acquisition Corp., 686 F.Supp. at 482–84, 488; City Capital Associates, 696 F.Supp. at 1555. Delaware allows a merger to occur forthwith if the bidder obtains 85% of the shares other than those held by management and employee stock plans. If the bid is attractive to the bulk of the unaffiliated investors, it succeeds. Wisconsin offers no such opportunity, which Amanda believes is fatal.

Even in Wisconsin, though, options remain. Defenses impenetrable to the naked eye may have cracks. Poison pills are less fatal in practice than in name (some have been swallowed willingly), and corporate law contains self-defense mechanisms. Investors concerned about stock-watering often arranged for firms to issue pre-emptive rights, entitlements for existing investors to buy stock at the same price offered to newcomers (often before the newcomers had a chance to buy in). Poison pills are dilution devices, and so pre-emptive rights ought to be handy countermeasures.[11] So too there are countermeasures to statutes deferring mergers. The cheapest is to lower the bid to reflect the costs of delay. Because every potential bidder labors under the same drawback, the firm placing the highest value on the target still should win. Or a bidder might take down the stock and pledge it (or its dividends) as security for any loans. That is, the bidder could operate the target as a subsidiary for three years. The corporate world is full of partially owned subsidiaries. If there is gain to be had from changing the debt-equity ratio of the target, that can be done consistent with Wisconsin law. The prospect of being locked into place as holders of illiquid minority positions would cause many persons to sell out, and the threat of being locked in would cause many managers to give assent in advance, as Wisconsin allows. (Or bidders might demand that directors waive the protections of state law, just as Amanda believes that the directors' fiduciary duties compel them to redeem the poison pill rights.) Many bidders would find lock-in unattractive because of the potential for litigation by minority investors, and the need to operate the firm as a subsidiary might foreclose savings or synergies from merger. So none of these options is a perfect substitute for immediate merger, but each is a crack in the defensive wall allowing some value-increasing bids to proceed.

At the end of the day, however, it does not matter whether these countermeasures are "enough". The Commerce Clause does not demand that states

---

11. Imagine a series of Antidote rights, issued by would-be bidding firms, that detach if anyone exercises flip-over rights to purchase the bidder's stock at a discount. Antidote rights would entitle the bidder's investors, *other than those who exercise flip-over rights,* to purchase the bidder's stock at the same discount available to investors exercising flip-over rights. Antidotes for flip-in rights also could be issued. In general, whenever one firm can issue rights allowing the purchase of cheap stock, another firm can issue the equivalent series of contingent preemptive rights that offsets the dilution.

leave bidders a "meaningful opportunity for success". Maryland enacted a law that absolutely banned vertical integration in the oil business. No opportunities, "meaningful" or otherwise, remained to firms wanting to own retail outlets. *Exxon Corp. v. Governor of Maryland* held that the law is consistent with the Commerce Clause, even on the assumption that it injures consumers and investors alike. A state with the power to forbid mergers has the power to defer them for three years. Investors can turn to firms incorporated in states committed to the dominance of market forces, or they can turn on legislators who enact unwise laws. The Constitution has room for many economic policies. "[A] law can be both economic folly and constitutional." *CTS*, 481 U.S. at 96–97, 107 S.Ct. at 1653–54 (Scalia, J., concurring). Wisconsin's law may well be folly; we are confident that it is constitutional.

––––––––

1. *Was It Overwritten? Amanda Acquisition* gives *CTS* its broadest possible interpretation: First, the negative impact of the Commerce Clause simply precludes discriminatory legislation and does not require "that states leave bidders 'a meaningful opportunity for success'" (as the earlier decisions involving the Delaware statute had required). Second, the preemption claim is dismissed because the Williams Act is said not to mandate a neutral balance between bidder and target, but only to regulate "the process of tender offers." Because "investors have no right to receive tender offers," *Amanda Acquisition* declares that state law may prevent a bidder from launching a takeover bid; provided that it not interfere with the process of the tender offer should a bidder proceed. *Query:* Is this a sensible interpretation of Congressional intent? Would Congress have wanted to insist on neutrality between bidder and target at the federal level, but then allow the Williams Act to be rendered an empty formality by state legislation?

More importantly, is such a view of preemption consistent with the Court's analysis in *CTS?* A plausible reading of the *CTS* decision is that it permits a state to protect shareholders from coercion so long as it does not unduly favor management. Arguably, the Indiana statute maximized shareholder power and so promoted the Williams Act's goals. In contrast, the Wisconsin statute presents a far clearer case of undue favoritism: the statute contains none of the escape clauses in the Delaware statute (such as the provision making the statute inapplicable if 85% in interest tender), employs a lower threshold (5% of the target's shares as opposed to Delaware's 15%), and has no opt-out provision.

B.   STATE ANTITAKEOVER LEGISLATION AFTER *CTS*: CONSTITUENCY AND DISGORGEMENT STATUTES

At least nominally, state takeover legislation before *CTS* (and even the Delaware and Wisconsin statutes after it) sought to protect shareholders from the allegedly coercive character of hostile takeovers. More recently, however, the focus has shifted from protecting shareholders to protecting "stakeholders": employees, bondholders, local communities and other constituencies. Perhaps their protection was always a motivating force behind state antitakeover laws, but traditionally the negative impact of the Commerce Clause posed a formidable barrier to legislation restricting plant closings or worker terminations. After *CTS*, this barrier seemed less formidable, and legislatures became more explicit about their intended beneficiaries. Initially, these statutes authorized directors to consider the "long-term" interests of the corporation (in contrast, it seemed, to the "short-term" interests of shareholders).[1] Next, statutes began to permit the board to consider the interests of non-shareholder constituencies. At least 26 states have adopted some form of constituency legislation, although in most every case these statutes permit, but do not require, the board to consider the interests of non-shareholder constituencies.[2] Some, however, expressly authorize the board to subordinate shareholder interests to those of other constituencies.[3]

This statutory reformulation of the duties of directors raises numerous questions. In the case where the statute provides that the board may consider non-shareholder interests, but does not expressly authorize subordination of shareholder interests, should such legislation be read as changing the board's responsibilities or as simply codifying the common law (which clearly permitted some consideration of other interests if consistent with long-term shareholder welfare)? Consider the views on this topic of the American Bar Association's Committee on Corporate Laws (which has declined to add a constituency provision to the ABA's Revised Model Business Corporations Act):

> The Committee has concluded that permitting—much less requiring—directors to consider [non-shareholder] interests without relating such consideration in an appropriate fashion to shareholder welfare (as the Delaware courts have done) would conflict with directors' responsibility to shareholders and could undermine the effectiveness of the system that has made the corporation an efficient device for the creation of jobs and wealth.
>
> The Committee believes that the better interpretation of these statutes, and one that avoids such consequences, is that they confirm what the common law has been: directors may take into account the interests of other constituencies but only as and to the extent that the directors are acting in the best interests, long as well as short term, of the shareholders and the corporation.[4]

The latest form of antitakeover legislation (and the most controversial statute to date) is the Pennsylvania "disgorgement" statute.[5] Section 2572 of this legislation announces that its purposes are to prevent greenmail, "promote a stable relationship among the various parties involved" in public corporations, and "ensure that speculators who put * * * corporations 'in play' do not misappropriate corporate values for themselves at the expense of the corporation and groups affected by corporate actions." Section 2575 then announces its unique enforcement strategy: investors who join a control group that acquires 20% of a Pennsylvania corporation's voting power are made liable to the corporation for profits on shares acquired within two years prior to the point at

---

1. New York's statute, passed in 1988, authorized the board to consider whether a poison pill (or "shareholder rights plan") should be "deployed, enforced or waived in the best long-term and short-term interests of the corporation and its shareholders considering, without limitation, the prospects for potential growth, development, productivity and profitability of the corporation." See N.Y.Bus.Corp.Law § 505(a)(2)(ii).

2. For a survey of these statutes, see Committee on Corporate Laws, Other Con-

stituencies Statutes: Potential for Confusion, 45 Bus.Law. 2253 (1990).

3. See 15 Pa. Cons. Stat. § 1721(e) (1990).

4. Committee on Corporate Laws, supra note 2, at 2268–9.

5. Sections 2571–2576 of Title 15 of the Pennsylvania Consolidated Statutes are included in the Statutory Supplement.

which the person or group became a "controlling person" if they are disposed of within 18 months after that point. In effect, Pennsylvania has enlarged the "short swing" liability provisions of § 16(b) of the 1934 Act, and effectively mandated a period of illiquidity of at least 18 months after the investor becomes a member of a control group. Moreover, the definition of "control" and "control group" is largely borrowed from § 13(d) of the 1934 Act and thus has sufficient breadth to reach institutional investors who might join together in a proxy contest or similar effort to oppose takeover defenses.

Many institutional investors perceived the Pennsylvania statute as an attempt at intimidation directed at them. They lobbied Pennsylvania chartered corporations to exercise their statutory right to opt out of the Pennsylvania statute. During a three month opt-out period that ended in July 1990, 67 out of approximately 300 public corporations subject to the Pennsylvania statute (including 11 of the 16 Fortune 500 companies chartered in Pennsylvania) did exercise their right to opt out.[6] Does this send a message to other states considering such a statute? Or is it more relevant that well over 200 firms remained subject to the statute?

Is the Pennsylvania statute constitutional, even after *CTS* and *Amanda Acquisition?* Suppose your client is a public pension fund in Arizona that has no contacts with the state of Pennsylvania. It buys a 1% block in a Pennsylvania chartered corporation and allegedly cooperates with a group of other investors who organize a proxy contest to oust the incumbent management. The proxy fight is unsuccessful, but there is a general market rise across the securities markets anyway; it sells its stock 15 months later over the New York Stock Exchange, and the corporation sues to recapture the profits. Is this an out of state market transaction that Pennsylvania cannot regulate under *Edgar v. MITE* or is it an aspect of corporate governance that *CTS* would say Pennsylvania law can control?

SECTION 6.   GOING PRIVATE AND MANAGEMENT BUYOUTS

Excerpt from: Louis Lowenstein

Management Buyouts

85 Colum.L.Rev. 730 (1985).

The first management buyouts appeared about ten years ago [i.e., around 1975—Eds.]. Then called "going private," most of those transactions involved small firms that had gone public in the hot new issue market of the late 1960s and early 1970s. By 1974 the stock market had declined considerably, and while the founders or managers of these new issue companies still owned controlling interests, the benefits of being a public company had paled. A number of them turned to their public shareholders and announced that, by one device or another, the publicly owned shares would be bought back. The hue and cry was immediate. The decision to go private had been made at a time picked by management, the fragmented public investors had no mechanism for collective bargaining, and there was no opportunity for others to bid. Even though said to be fair, the price was suspect.

---

6.   See 22 Sec.Reg. & Law Rptr. 1177 (August 10, 1990).

Though the supply of these small, "inadvertent" public companies has dried up since the early 1970s, management buyouts are still with us. But while the basic conflict of interest remains, management buyouts have in other respects changed considerably. Not until 1979 did the first management buyout much above $100 million take place, but now a transaction of $1 billion or even $2 billion is not remarkable. In these larger firms, the managers do not own controlling interests, so bidding contests have appeared. The announcement of a buyout is often the beginning of a rather lively auction. For one group of these larger buyouts, the median premium over the previous market price was 58%.

How can managers and their buying consortia pay so much?

---

1. *Going Private versus Management Buyouts.* These two terms are over-lapping, but need to be distinguished. "Going private" transactions typically involve a transaction in which there is a preexisting controlling shareholder or shareholder group, who took the company public in a bull market and now wishes to buy out the minority public shareholders in a depressed market. In contrast, management buyouts (or "MBOs") typically involve a much larger public corporation in which the management group owns only a small percent-age of the shares (but with the help of an investment banking firm and the use of junk bonds it is able to finance an offer for all the firm's shares). In both cases, the public shareholder who holds out takes the risk of illiquidity because, after the transaction, the firm will probably cease to be publicly traded and may become a highly leveraged and much more risky investment.

Both contexts also involve the prospect of a unique, but massive, kind of insider trading: inherently, management has access to material, non-public information that other shareholders lack; instead of buying stock, management simply buys the company in a MBO. Further enhancing the popularity of this explanation is the difficulty most commentators have in explaining why man-agement can afford to pay a large premium to its own shareholders. Unlike hostile takeovers, buyouts seemingly do not involve the replacement of ineffi-cient management or synergy gains from combining related businesses or financial gains from diversification.

Although there are thus sinister explanations for MBOs, a more sanguine story is also possible. Repeated studies have found that the public shareholders in LBOs receive substantial gains, roughly equivalent to the gains received by shareholders in third party takeover bids.[1] Some organizational studies of MBOs report that because of the pressure of a heavy debt load incurred to finance the buyout and the incentive effects of giving management a substan-tial equity stake in the firm, buyouts do lead to increased efficiency and improved operating performance.[2] Perhaps the explanation is that a manage-

---

1. See DeAngelo, DeAngelo & Rice, Go-ing Private: Minority Freezeouts and Stock-holder Wealth, 27 J.L. & Econ. 367 (1984) (study of 81 buyout proposals finds positive abnormal returns of 30.4% on average over the 40 day period prior to the buyout an-nouncement); Marais, Schipper & Smith, Wealth Effects of Going Private for Senior Securities, 23 J.Fin.Econ. 155 (1988). See also, Gilson, Evaluating Dual Class Common Stock: The Relevance of Substitutes, 73 Va. L.Rev. 807, 816–832 (1987).

2. Kaplan, The Effects of Management Buyouts on Operations and Value, 24 J.Fin. Econ. 217 (1988); Baker & Wruck, Organiza-

ment group that lacks a significant equity stake in the firm has little incentive to take the kind of risks that with an equity incentive it will accept.[3]

2. *The SEC's Response: Rule 13e–3.* A controversial "going private" transaction in 1974 involving a well-known advertising firm, Wells, Rich, Greene, Inc. ("WRG"), brought matters to a head. A respected SEC Commissioner, A.A. Sommer, Jr., criticized the transaction as unfair. He pointed out that if the offer were unsuccessful and all the public shareholders tendered, the firm's CEO, Mary Wells Lawrence, would go from a 7% interest to a 43% interest "without a single dime of additional investment from her."[4] In addition, shareholders who might wish not to tender were chilled by the fact, carefully pointed out in the prospectus used in the transaction, that after the exchange offer, the company would be delisted from the New York Stock Exchange and deregistered under the 1934 Act and would have little liquidity. To some, this disclosure of illiquidity seemed a coercive threat.

Nonetheless, when plaintiffs sued WRG, charging violations of §§ 10(b) and 14(e) of the 1934 Act, the court found that all material facts had been fully disclosed. It added:

> "There is nothing immoral *per se* in a corporate effort to free itself from federal regulation, provided that the means and the methods used to effectuate that objective are allowable under law. Nor has the federal securities law placed profit-making or shrewd business tactics designed to benefit insiders, without more, beyond the pale. Those laws * * * are satisfied if full and fair disclosure is made * * *."[5]

In response, the SEC issued for comment, first in 1975 and later in 1977, proposed rules under § 13(e) at the Williams Act to regulate "going private" transactions, but after the *Santa Fe* case[6] in 1977, the SEC realized that such an aggressive assertion of jurisdiction might be invalidated by the courts as an unauthorized interference with state corporate governance. Hence, the Commission backed off, and the final version of the Rule 13e–3 purported only to require disclosure with respect to the transaction, including the reasons why management thought it was fair. But, does this fairness disclosure requirement convert any transaction that seems substantively unfair to the court into a disclosure violation? Also, is such a statement material to shareholders? If all material facts are disclosed, why does the majority group's state of mind or assessment matter? Courts continue to wrestle with these problems, as the next case shows:

Howing Co. v. Nationwide Corp.

United States Court of Appeals, Sixth Circuit, 1987.
826 F.2d 1470.

■ Before MERRITT, GUY and NORRIS, CIRCUIT JUDGES.

■ MERRITT, CIRCUIT JUDGE.

Under § 13(e) of the Securities Exchange Act of 1934, a Williams Act provision enacted in 1968, a company that has issued publicly traded stock is

---

tional Changes and Value Creation in Leveraged Buyouts: The Case of O.M. Scott & Sons Company, 25 J.Fin.Econ. 163 (1989).

3. For an elaboration of this hypothesis, see Osterle & Norberg, Management Buyouts: Creating or Appropriating Shareholder Wealth, 41 Vand.L.Rev. 207 (1988).

4. Sommer, "Going Private: A Lesson in Corporate Responsibility" Fed.Sec.L.Rep. (CCH) Para. 80,010 (1974).

5. Kaufmann v. Lawrence, 386 F.Supp. 12 17 (S.D.N.Y.1974).

6. Santa Fe Industries Inc. v. Green, 430 U.S. 462 (1977).

prohibited from buying it back unless the issuer complies with rules promulgated by the SEC. This appeal raises issues concerning the existence of a private right of action under § 13e–3, the nature of the disclosure duty imposed by Rule 13e–3, and the interrelationship of this provision with other antifraud rules.

Pursuant to its authority under § 13e–3, the SEC has issued Rule 13e–3 and Schedule 13e–3, a long and detailed set of disclosure requirements governing such "going private" transactions. Schedule 13e–3 accompanying the Rule requires that numerous items of information about the transaction be filed with the Commission, including three items pertinent to this case, i.e., Items 7, 8 and 9. Item 7 covers the "reasons" for the transaction; Item 8 requires a statement concerning the fairness of the transaction; and Item 9 requires disclosure of appraisals and other information concerning the value of the stock. The Rule also provides that this same information be disclosed to the selling shareholders.

The basic questions presented in this case are: (1) whether the plaintiffs have a private right of action under § 13e–3 to police non-compliance with Rule 13e–3; (2) and if so, whether the disclosure requirements of Rule 13e–3 have been met; and (3) if those requirements have not been met, whether defendant's conduct in violating Rule 13e–3 also gives rise to liability under the antifraud provisions of Rules 10b–5 and 14a–9.

Parties and Summary of Disposition Below

Defendant Nationwide Corporation is one of the largest life insurance holding companies in the United States. Originally incorporated in 1947 as Service Insurance Agency, the company has enjoyed steady growth since its affiliation with the Nationwide group of insurance companies in September 1955. As a result of this affiliation, the company adopted its present name and issued a special class of common stock (Class B common) which was held entirely by two Nationwide companies: Nationwide Mutual Insurance Company and Nationwide Mutual Fire Insurance Company. The Class A common stock continued in the hands of individual shareholders.

Because of the way voting rights were allocated between the Class A and Class B stock, complete ownership of the Class B shares gave Nationwide Mutual and Nationwide Mutual Fire effective control of the corporation. The Class B shares were entitled as a class to one-half of the voting power of the corporation as long as the percentage of Class B shares outstanding relative to outstanding shares of all classes combined did not fall below forty percent. Since it appears that the amount of outstanding Class B common was at all times sufficient to meet this threshold, Nationwide Mutual and Nationwide Mutual Fire held the same voting power as all the Class A shares combined. Under these circumstances, it is clear that these companies controlled the corporation despite wide public ownership of the Class A shares.

Nationwide Mutual and Nationwide Mutual Fire began to eliminate public ownership of Nationwide Corporation in December 1978 when these companies made a tender offer to buy the Class A shares for $20.00 per share net in cash. By January 1979, Nationwide Mutual and Nationwide Mutual Fire had purchased 4,074,695 Class A shares through this offer. After the tender offer,

Nationwide Mutual and Nationwide Mutual Fire continued to purchase shares in the open market at prices ranging between $22.50 and $24.62 per share. These transactions ultimately gave Nationwide Mutual and Nationwide Mutual Fire ownership of 85.6% of the Class A common stock formerly held by the public.

In November 1982, the Board of Directors of Nationwide Corporation approved a transaction in which Nationwide Mutual and Nationwide Mutual Fire would acquire the remaining Class A shares at $42.50 per share. As a result, Nationwide Corporation would become a wholly-owned subsidiary of the two mutuals, and would have no public ownership. This transaction was approved by 94.7% of the Class A shares. Plaintiffs in the present litigation abstained from voting their shares respecting the merger or seeking their appraisal remedy under state law.

The present class action began with an action by Belle Efros, a Nationwide shareholder, seeking a preliminary injunction with respect to a vote on the proposed merger. Following the denial of the Efros motion for a preliminary injunction, the merger was approved by 94.7% of the voted public shares. * * *

The defendants moved for summary judgment and plaintiffs filed a cross-motion for partial summary judgment. The District Court granted defendants' motion, denied plaintiffs' cross-motion, and dismissed the amended complaint, 625 F.Supp. 146 (D.Ohio 1985).

The District Court identified compliance with Rule 13e–3 as the principal issue in the case. The District Court framed its scope of review as follows:

> We therefore will review the proxy material of Nationwide Corporation to see if it meets the standards of disclosure required by Rule 13e–3. If in any instance there has been a failure to meet the standard, we will then examine whether such failure constitutes a material breach, and if we conclude that there is a jury question concerning the materiality of the breach, then, of course, there would be a genuine issue of fact to be determined.

625 F.Supp. at 151.

In reviewing the proxy statement's compliance with Rule 13e–3, the District Court begins with Item 7 of the Rule which essentially covers the "reasons" for the transaction. The District Court concluded that the proxy statement adequately disclosed the purposes of the transaction as well as its benefits and detriments. The District Court stated that "[w]e decline to second guess the directors of Nationwide as to the stated purpose for the merger," 625 F.Supp. at 152, and stated further that "[w]e conclude that the detriments and benefits were adequately discussed in the proxy statement and that the gravamen of plaintiffs' argument on this issue is actually that the merger price itself was not fair to the public stockholders." Id. at 153.

With respect to the proxy statement's compliance with the Item 8 fairness disclosure, the District Court considered three contentions by plaintiffs: (1) the proxy statement did not sufficiently discuss the net book value, liquidation value, and going concern values of Nationwide shares; (2) the proxy statement did not explicitly state that Nationwide stock was "thinly traded"; and (3) the proxy statement did not sufficiently discuss the basis for the First Boston opinion letter.

On the question of valuation, the District Court noted that "the proxy statement contained extensive financial information necessary to compute the net book, liquidation, and going concern values of Nationwide shares." 625 F.Supp. at 155. The District Court found that the proxy statement met the requirements of Rule 13e–3 in this regard:

> Rule 13e–3 "merely requires that an opinion be given and the material factors on which it is based be disclosed." We conclude that defendants satisfied this requirement of Rule 13e–3 by listing the factors considered by the Evaluation Committee and by candidly stating that no specific weight was given to any one factor, but of particular importance in the consideration was First Boston's opinion and the fact that the merger price represented a premium over the market price of the stock.

Id.

The District Court concluded overall that the proxy statement satisfied the requirements of Rule 13e–3. The District Court stated:

> Most important, there was sufficient information disclosed in the proxy statement to enable the stockholders to make an informed decision on what to do. It is the conclusion of the Court, therefore, that there is no genuine issue of material fact concerning the adequacy of the proxy statement when measured against the standards set forth in Rule 13e–3, and that any omissions pointed out by plaintiffs were not material as defined by the Court in *TSC Industries, Inc. [Northway Inc.]*, 426 U.S. [438] at 449, 96 S.Ct. [2126] at 2132 [48 L.Ed.2d 757 (1976)].

Id.

Private Right of Action Under § 13(e)

In the present case, we must decide a question of first impression in the federal courts of appeals: Does § 13(e) of the Securities and Exchange Act of 1934 allow a private right of action for damages? The District Court assumed that a private right of action exists, and we agree. Based upon our review of the statute, the legislative history, and the Supreme Court's decisions respecting private rights of action, we conclude that such a right of action does exist under § 13(e).

The law relating to judicially-implied private rights of action under federal statutes has undergone a process of evolution over the past seventy years. When federal lawmaking was a less detailed and comprehensive endeavor, a private remedy was ordinarily presumed in favor of the class for whose benefit the statute was enacted. *See* Merrill Lynch, Pierce, Fenner & Smith v. Curran, 456 U.S. 353, 374–75, 102 S.Ct. 1825, 1837–38, 72 L.Ed.2d 182 (1982) (citing Texas & Pacific Ry. Co. v. Rigsby, 241 U.S. 33, 36 S.Ct. 482, 60 L.Ed. 874 (1916)). As the complexity of federal legislation and volume of litigation increased, the liberal *Rigsby* rule became unworkable. A unanimous Supreme Court responded by modifying the law on implied private rights of action. The result, announced in Cort v. Ash, 422 U.S. 66, 95 S.Ct. 2080, 45 L.Ed.2d 26 (1975), was a four-part test that focused primarily on congressional intent. Under *Cort,* a private right of action exists where: (1) the plaintiff is a member of the class for whose especial benefit the statute was enacted; (2) there is any indication, explicit or implicit, of legislative intent to support such a remedy; (3) an implied private right of action is consistent with the purposes of the legislative scheme; and (4) the cause of action is not "one traditionally relegated to state law, in an area basically the concern of the states, so that it would be inappropriate to infer a cause of action based solely on federal law." *Id.* at 78, 95 S.Ct. at 2088 (citations omitted).

This decision and those following it, such as Cannon v. University of Chicago, 441 U.S. 677, 99 S.Ct. 1946, 60 L.Ed.2d 560 (1979), were intended to suggest that Congress be more explicit about private remedies in future legislation. However, because the rule announced by *Cort* was such a departure from existing law, there has been some reluctance to apply it to legislation enacted prior to that decision. According to *Cannon,* Congress is entitled to rely on the "contemporary legal context" in which it acts, 441 U.S. at 698–99, 99 S.Ct. at 1958. When Congress passed legislation prior to *Cort,* that context would presume a private remedy if the statute and its history were otherwise silent. *See Curran,* 456 U.S. at 374–75, 382 n. 66, 102 S.Ct. at 1837–38, 1841 n. 66.

The decision in *Cannon v. University of Chicago* is particularly instructive. In that case, the Supreme Court held that Congress indicated its intent to allow a private right of action to enforce Title IX of the Education Amendments of 1972 when it patterned that law on another statute—Title VI of the Civil Rights Act of 1964—which had been interpreted to support private suits. Although the *Cort* test was still applied, this adoption theory satisfied the crucial legislative intent test contained in the second *Cort* factor. Given a contemporary legal context in which Title VI had been construed to support a private cause of action, Congress' choice to pattern Title IX after that previous statute made it "not only appropriate but also realistic to presume that Congress was familiar with these unusually important precedents * * * and that it expected its enactment to be interpreted in conformity with them." *Cannon,* 441 U.S. at 699, 99 S.Ct. at 1958.

In order to determine the existence of a private right of action under § 13(e), therefore, we must apply the criteria established by *Cort v. Ash* with consideration for the "contemporary legal context" in which the legislation was passed. Such an undertaking requires that we understand the history and the structure of the statute in question.

Section 13(e)(1) of the Securities Exchange Act was not part of the original statute but was added by the Williams Act in 1968. The stated purpose of the Williams Act was to protect investors from potential manipulation of tender offers and corporate repurchases of stock. *See* Piper v. Chris–Craft Indus., 430 U.S. 1, 26–35, 97 S.Ct. 926, 941–46, 51 L.Ed.2d 124 (1977). The legislation was explicitly patterned after the statutes and regulations then governing proxy solicitations. *See* 113 *Cong.Rec.* 24,665 (1967) (statement of Senator Williams). As a result, the language of § 13(e) and other Williams Act provisions parallel that used in § 14(a) of the Securities Exchange Act of 1934.

From this legislative history, it is clear that the first three *Cort* factors are satisfied with respect to § 13(e). The first *Cort* factor applies the old *Rigsby* test and asks if the plaintiff is one for whose especial benefit the statute was enacted. Since the Supreme Court established in *Piper* that the Williams Act was intended "for the protection of investors," 430 U.S. at 35, 97 S.Ct. at 946, it cannot be gainsaid that the investors such as the current plaintiffs fall within the benefitted class. Thus, the first *Cort* factor is met.

The second *Cort* factor—whether there is evidence of a legislative intent to allow or deny a private remedy—favors a private cause of action for two distinct reasons. First, since the Williams Act was explicitly patterned on the proxy rules, the analysis employed by the Supreme Court in *Cannon v. University of Chicago* applies here. When § 13(e) was adopted in 1967, the Supreme Court had already recognized an implied private right of action under § 14(a) in J.I. Case v. Borak, 377 U.S. 426, 84 S.Ct. 1555, 12 L.Ed.2d 423 (1964). In support of the private action upheld in *Borak,* Justice Clark, speaking for the Court, placed special emphasis on the power granted to the SEC "to protect investors." *Id.* at 432, 84 S.Ct. at 1559. Under the rationale of *Cannon,* therefore, Congress indicated its desire to allow a private right of action under § 13(e) when it chose language that was identical to the crucial language supporting a private right of action under § 14(a). *See also* Lorillard v. Pons, 434 U.S. 575, 580–81, 98 S.Ct. 866, 870, 55 L.Ed.2d 40 (1978) (Congress presumed to incorporate interpretations of prior law when it incorporates text into new law).

Aside from Congress' choice of § 14(a) as a model, there is a second aspect of the "contemporary legal context" which supports a private right of action for § 13(e). At the time the Williams Act was passed, implied rights of action were in a heyday of sorts. *See Cannon,* 441 U.S. at 718, 99 S.Ct. at 1968 (Rehnquist, J., concurring); Leist v. Simplot, 638 F.2d 283, 316–17 (2d Cir.1980). Congress could have justifiably presumed that its silence with regard to private actions would be interpreted to indicate authorization. Silence, in the contemporary legal context of the Williams Act, did not constitute disapproval of an implied private action. Since there is no evidence of legislative intent to deny a private remedy, Congress' choice to incorporate the proxy rules without additional comment is an indication of legislative intent sufficient to satisfy the second *Cort* test. *See Cannon,* 441 U.S. at 698–99, 99 S.Ct. at 1958–59; *Cort,* 422 U.S. at 82, 95 S.Ct. at 2089.

The third element of the *Cort* test—whether an implied private action is consistent with the legislative scheme—is also satisfied by § 13(e). Although the statute is designed for the protection of investors, no mechanism is provided by which these investors can vindicate their interests. As noted by Justice Clark in *Borak* with respect to the proxy rules, private enforcement may be the *only* way to achieve the purposes of § 13(e) given limited resources under the SEC's command. *Borak,* 377 U.S. at 433, 84 S.Ct. at 1560. Under these circumstances, "it is the duty of the courts to be alert to provide such remedies as are necessary to make effective * * * congressional purpose." *Id.* Since a private right of action would fill a void in enforcement, it is entirely consistent with the legislative scheme established by § 13(e).

The fourth *Cort* factor concerns whether the cause of action is one traditionally relegated to state law. Since 1933, the obligations of an issuer to the public and its stockholders have been a matter of federal law. The specific disclosure duty at issue here is a federal law. In light of the inherently federal nature of this claim, it is clear that a private right of action would not interfere with the regulatory prerogatives of the various states. It is also clear that the plaintiffs in this case meet the requirements set forth by *Cort v. Ash* and its progeny, and are therefore entitled to maintain a private action against Nationwide for violations of § 13(e).

Rule 13e–3 Compliance

Going private transactions raise unique problems because of their inherently coercive nature: minority shareholders are forced to exchange their shares for cash or other consideration. The coercive effect of these transactions is reinforced by the fact that the majority shareholders control the timing and terms of the transaction.

In promulgating Rule 13e–3 pursuant to § 13(e), 17 C.F.R. § 240.13e–3, the SEC recognized the potential for overreaching in going private transactions:

> The nature of and methods utilized in effecting going private transactions present an opportunity for overreaching of unaffiliated security holders by an issuer or its affiliates. This is due, in part, to the lack of arms-length bargaining and the inability of unaffiliated security holders to influence corporate decisions to enter into such transactions. Additionally, such transactions have a coercive effect in that security holders confronted by a going private transaction are faced with the prospects of an illiquid market, termination of the protections under the federal securities laws and further efforts by the proponent to eliminate their equity interest.

Exchange Act Release No. 34–17719, *reprinted in* 3 Fed.Sec.L.Rep. (CCH) ¶ 23,709, at 17, 245–28 (April 13, 1981).

Rule 13e–3 serves as the primary and most direct vehicle under the federal securities laws for mandating this disclosure in going private transactions. Subsection (e) of Rule 13e–3 prescribes which information from the issuer's Schedule 13e–3 filing with the Commission shall be provided to shareholders as well as the form and content of this public disclosure. *See* 17 C.F.R. § 240.13e–3(e). Subsection (e) mandates, for example, that where a going private transaction requires the use of a proxy statement, the Rule 13e–3 disclosure be presented in a "Special Factors" section of the proxy statement. 17 C.F.R. § 240.–13e–3(e)(1), (3)(i).

Rule 13e–3 does not require that the issuer's Schedule 13e–3 filing with the Commission be reproduced in its entirety in the communication with shareholders. Most items from that Schedule may be summarized. However, Items 7, 8 and 9 must be disclosed verbatim. The rationale behind complete disclosure of these items is that they go to the essence of the transaction. Item 7 requires full disclosure of the purposes, alternatives, reasons, and effects of the transaction; Item 8 requires a statement as to the fairness of the transaction and the factors upon which such belief is based; and Item 9 requires disclosure of reports, opinions, appraisals and certain negotiations.

A.   Item 7 Disclosure

Item 7 of Schedule 13e–3 requires that the issuer (1) state the purpose for the transaction, (2) discuss any alternative means considered, (3) state the reasons for the structure of the transaction and for its timing, and (4) describe the effects of the transaction on the issuer, its affiliates and unaffiliated security holders. Instruction 2 to Item 7 contains the following guidance: "The description required by Item 7(d) should include a reasonably detailed discussion of the benefits and *detriments* of the Rule 13e–3 transaction to the issuer, its affiliates and unaffiliated security holders. The benefits and detriments of the Rule 13e–3 transaction should be quantified to the extent practicable." (emphasis added).

In the proxy statement, defendants enumerated four reasons for undertaking the transaction: first, eliminating potential conflict of interest problems; second, increasing management flexibility in the insurance and financial markets; third, simplifying the management structure of the Nationwide companies as a whole; and fourth, eliminating the substantial costs of servicing its public shareholders. The proxy statement indicates that the Company considered the possibility of a further tender offer, but rejected this option since the Company did not believe it compared favorably with the going private route in achieving the Company's overall objectives. The proxy statement indicates further that the Company proposed the transaction when it did in order to "maintain their competitive position in the industry." The proxy statement also states that the "[i]nitial out-of-pocket savings to Nationwide Corporation are estimated to be $300,000 per year."

The gravamen of plaintiffs' case on Item 7 compliance appears to be that the proxy statement failed to disclose adequately the "detriment" to Nationwide Mutual of the transaction and thereby concealed the true purpose of the transaction. Plaintiffs argue that a "company does not sacrifice $3,000,000 of annual income in order to save $300,000 and to achieve other non-quantifiable benefits. Having determined that the stated benefits were not genuine, a shareholder would search for the true purpose of the transaction: to acquire the minority interest at a bargain price." Brief of Appellants at p. 37.

In reviewing defendants' Item 7 disclosure, we find as did the District Court that defendants have complied with this part of Rule 13e–3. Plaintiffs do not suggest specific reasons not enumerated by defendants for undertaking the transaction; their challenge on this point reduces to an attack on the substantive fairness of the transaction. Defendants have specified legitimate reasons for the transaction, and since plaintiffs bear the burden of proof on this issue, plaintiffs' Item 7 challenge must fail.

B.   Item 8 Disclosure

The instructions accompanying Schedule 13e–3 are quite definite in the level of specificity required in certain disclosures.[5] The Instruction to Item 8 states that "[c]onclusory statements, such as 'The Rule 13e–3 transaction is fair to unaffiliated security holders in relation to net book value, going concern value and future prospects of the issuer' *will not be considered sufficient disclosure in response to Item 8(a)*." (emphasis added.)

The Commission has expressed special concern with disclosures under Item 8(b) of Schedule 13e–3, the Item concerning the factors underlying a belief as to the fairness of the transaction. The Commission has issued the following guidance to prospective issuers:

5. The Instructions to Item 8(b) of the Schedule identify the following factors to be discussed in the disclosure:

Instructions. (1) The factors which are important in determining the fairness of a transaction to unaffiliated security holders and the weight, if any, which should be given to them in a particular context will vary. Normally such factors will include, among others, those referred to in paragraphs (c), (d) and (e) of this Item and whether the consideration offered to unaffiliated security holders constitutes fair value in relation to:

(i) Current market prices,

(ii) Historical market prices,

(iii) Net book value,

(iv) Going concern value,

(v) Liquidation value,

(vi) The purchase price paid in previous purchases disclosed in Item 1(f) of Schedule 13e–3,

(vii) Any report, opinion, or appraisal described in Item 9 and

(viii) Firm offers of which the issuer or affiliate is aware made by any unaffiliated person, other than the person filing this statement, during the preceding eighteen months . . .

The Division is concerned that in many instances the Item 8(b) disclosure being made to security holders is vague and non-specific and is therefore of limited utility to security holders.... Each such factor which is material to the transaction should be discussed and, in particular, if any of the sources of value indicate a value higher than the value of the consideration offered to unaffiliated security holders, the discussion should specifically address such difference and should include a statement of the bases for the belief as to fairness in light of the difference.

Exchange Act Release No. 34–17719, at 17, 245–42.

The most serious problem in defendants' proxy statement concerns Item 8(b) compliance. Our review of the proxy statement indicates that defendants have made precisely the kind of conclusory statements prohibited by the Rule. In describing the fairness of the transaction as required by Item 8(b), defendants have done nothing more than provide a laundry list of factors considered by their investment banker.

This kind of non-specific disclosure runs counter not only to the SEC's position taken in the Commission release discussed above but also to the Instruction to Item 8(b) of Schedule 13e–3. The Instruction states that the issuer shall "[d]iscuss in reasonable detail the material factors upon which the belief stated in Item 8(a) is based and, to the extent practicable, *the weight assigned to each factor.*" (emphasis added). Thus, the proxy statement is incomplete in that we are not provided with any indication of the weights given the various factors as required by Rule 13e–3, incorporating Schedule 13e–3. Moreover, we therefore have no indication as to whether any of the "sources of value indicate a value higher than the value of the consideration offered to unaffiliated security holders." Exchange Act Release No. 34–17719, at 17, 245–42.

Instead of providing this itemized disclosure called for by Rule 13e–3, defendants rely heavily on the First Boston opinion letter to discharge their disclosure obligations. Indeed, the proxy materials state specifically, "Although the Evaluation Committee did not give specific weight to each of the various factors considered in evaluating the fairness of the proposed merger, particular emphasis was placed upon the receipt of the opinion of First Boston."

While the Commission has stated that an issuer in a going private transaction can rely on an investment banker's opinion to meet its disclosure obligations, such opinion itself must fully analyze the factors enumerated in Item 8(b) as well as be "expressly adopted" by the issuer. Exchange Act Release No. 34–17719, at 17, 245–42. The issuer in this case did not conduct its own investigation but chose to rely on the expertise of First Boston. The problem with defendants adopting the First Boston opinion letter as their disclosure to shareholders is that this one-page letter is itself woefully inadequate when measured against the specific disclosure requirements of the Rule. An issuer cannot insulate itself from 13e–3 liability by relying on an investment banker's opinion letter which itself does not comply with the specific disclosure requirements of the Rule. Therefore, defendants' conclusory statements are not cured by conclusory statements made by First Boston in its opinion letter.

Somewhere in the proxy materials the Nationwide shareholders should have received a reasonably detailed analysis of the various financial valuation methods discussed by the Rule and the weights attached thereto. Even if certain valuation methods were not particularly relevant, this should itself have been noted and explained. *See* Exchange Act Release No. 34–17719, at 17,245–42. Without this disclosure, Nationwide shareholders did not possess the information necessary to make an informed decision concerning the going private transaction.

C. Item 9 Disclosure

Item 9 requires disclosure of various factors relating to appraisals by an outside party. For example, the issuer must disclose the identity of the outside party; the qualification of the outside party; the method of selection of the outside party; the relationship between the outside party and the issuer over the past two years or any relationship which is contemplated, and any compensation received or to be received; whether the issuer or outside party recommended the amount of consideration to be paid; and a summary of the appraisal.

In the section of the proxy statement entitled "Opinion of the First Boston Corporation," defendants appear to have covered all the elements required in Item 9 disclosure. The proxy statement, for example, reveals the following: First Boston had served as a financial advisor to the Nationwide companies on several matters in the recent past; First Boston recommended the cash-out price of $42.50; and Nationwide Mutual agreed to pay First Boston a fee of $175,000 in connection with the proposed merger as well as all reasonable out-of-pocket expenses, including counsel's fees. The proxy statement also reviewed the information reviewed and relied upon by First Boston.

Plaintiffs main argument on Item 9 compliance centers on one factor considered by First Boston and cited in defendants' proxy statement—"present value of projected future cash flows of the Corporation." Plaintiffs contend that "[s]ince the actual projection of increased revenue and earnings was the most important single basis for First Boston's recommendation, disclosure was required."

Plaintiff reads more into Item 9 than is actually required: the challenge to Item 9 compliance seems to constitute an Item 8 claim if anything. As the above discussion indicates, Item 9 requires the disclosure of procedural matters. Accordingly, since defendants appear to have complied with this Item, we find no problem in Item 9 compliance.

D. Rule 13e–3 Liability

The basic problem with the disposition below is that the District Court did not engage in the detailed analysis required by Rule 13e–3, particularly with respect to Item 8(b) of Schedule 13e–3. The District Court's error in this regard may stem from its reliance on the following language from this Court's decision in Starkman v. Marathon, 772 F.2d 231, 240 (6th Cir.1985): "[w]e have rejected the position that SEC rules regarding freezeout mergers and proxies should determine the disclosure obligations of target management in the first stage of a two-tier tender offer." *Starkman* is inapposite to the present case because this is not the first stage of a two-tier tender offer, but rather the second and final step in this process.

Subsection (b)(2) of Rule 13e–3 states that "it shall be unlawful for an issuer * * * to engage, directly or indirectly, in a Rule 13e–3 transaction unless [the] issuer" * * * complies with the filing, disclosure, and dissemination requirements of the Rule. As discussed above, defendants did not comply with the disclosure obligation imposed by the Rule—a failure declared unlawful by subsection (b)(2) of the Rule. Accordingly, since plaintiffs have a private right of action under § 13(e) to police such unlawful behavior, the District Court erred in its disposition of plaintiffs' Rule 13e–3 claims.

The Antifraud Claims

In addition to liability under subsection (b)(2) of Rule 13e–3, plaintiffs also contend that the defendants breached the antifraud provisions of Rules 10b–5, 13e–3(b)(1), and 14a–9. In essence, plaintiffs contend that a failure to disclose information required by Rule 13e–3 *ipso facto* constitutes an "omission" actionable under the anti-fraud provisions. They argue that Rules 10b–5 and 14a–9 incorporate Rule 13e–3 by reference in the going private context.

The three antifraud provisions at issue here spring from distinct statutes which have unique texts and histories. All three, however, parallel the common law of fraud and deceit. Absent special circumstances, an action for deceit would lie at common law for both falsehoods and half-truths, but not for a complete failure to disclose. *See* III L. Loss, *Securities Regulation* at 1433–35. As was noted by this circuit almost fifty years ago with regard to a similarly worded antifraud provision in the Securities Act of 1933:

> The statute did not require appellant to state every fact about stock offered that a prospective purchaser might like to know or that might, if known, tend to influence his decision, but it did require appellant not "to obtain money or property by means of any untrue statement of a material fact *or any omission to state a material fact necessary in order to make the statements made, in the light of the circumstances under which they were made, not misleading*."

Otis & Co. v. SEC, 106 F.2d 579, 582 (6th Cir.1939) (emphasis in original) (construing § 17(a)(2) of the Securities Act of 1933).

The second clauses of Rules 10b–5 and 13e–3(b)(1), and similar language in Rule 14a–9, adopt the common law rule and prohibit silence only where the omitted information is necessary to prevent inaccuracy in existing disclosure. As a result, these provisions have been considered by commentators and the courts alike to be concerned with half-truth rather than omissions *per se. See* Myzel v. Fields, 386 F.2d 718, 733 n. 6 (8th Cir.1967); Trussell v. United Underwriters, Ltd., 228 F.Supp. 757, 767 (D.Col.1964); Cochran v. Channing Corp., 211 F.Supp. 239, 243 (S.D.N.Y.1962); *see also* III L. Loss, *Securities Regulation* at 1439; A. Bromberg & L. Lowenfels, *Securities Fraud & Commodities Fraud* § 2.6(2).

The essence of plaintiff's claim is that a failure to provide items of disclosure required by Rule 13e–3(e) always constitutes a material omission under the antifraud rules. This is tantamount to incorporating the disclosure provisions of the securities laws into the antifraud provisions. No longer would omissions be actionable only where a half-truth resulted. Instead, any failure to comply with SEC disclosure obligations would be actionable by private litigants under the antifraud provisions.

Although the antifraud rules are the "catch-all" provisions of the securities laws, the Supreme Court has emphasized in the Rule 10b–5 context that they apply only where some fraud has been committed. *See* Chiarella v. United States, 445 U.S. 222, 234–35, 100 S.Ct. 1108, 1117–18, 63 L.Ed.2d 348 (1980). Congress did not enact sections 10(b), 13(e), or 14(a) to give private litigants the same enforcement powers granted to the Commissioner of the SEC.

Allowing private suits based on any non-disclosure, without regard to the "half-truth" limitation, would contravene the congressional intent behind these statutes. Therefore, we hold that omission of disclosure required by Rule 13e–3(e) will constitute a violation of the antifraud provisions of sections 10(b), 13(e), and 14(a) only where the information is necessary to prevent half-truth. The violations of Rule 13e–3, Item 8, itemized above, do not constitute "fraud" under sections 10(b) and 14(a) but should be considered as violations only of the specific rule in question.[11]

* * *

_____

1. _Subsequent History._ On remand, the district court found that the alleged omissions were immaterial and granted summary judgment for defendants.[1] This was reversed again by the Sixth Circuit.[2] The Sixth Circuit also faced two new problems on this remand: how could it find causation after _Virginia Bankshares_[3] when the shareholder defendants held a voting majority? It reasoned that the nondisclosures were actionable because they caused the minority to waive their state law remedies, including appraisal.

2. _Impact. Howing_ shows that Rule 13e–3 can apparently reach cases that Rules 10b–5 and 14a–9 do not. But does the 1934 Act intend or support this distinction? Would the Supreme Court agree? Also, should scienter be required under Rule 13e–3?[4]

3. _The Going Private Debate After 25 Years._ A legion of commentators joined Commissioner Sommer in expressing concern about the conflicts of interest inherent in going private transactions.[5] Their concern was not simply the fairness of the price, but rather the possibility that management would take the company public again in the next "bull market." As Professors O'Neal and Thompson observe in their treatise:

> "Management can pick the time for the transaction and set the price with no input from the public shareholders. The price may include a substantial premium over the current market price but the offer may come at a time when the market for the particular company or its industry is depressed and outsiders do not yet see the favorable signs of an upturn that are known to the insiders."[6]

11. Under certain circumstances, violations of Rule 13e–3 may be indicative of a "scheme or artifice to defraud" which would violate the antifraud provisions. Such is not the case here, however, where non-disclosure is claimed to be a violation standing alone.

1. See Howing Co. v. Nationwide Corp., [1989–1990 Transfer Binder] Fed.Sec.L.Rep. (CCH) Para. 94,858 (S.D.Ohio 1989).

2. 927 F.2d 263 (6th Cir.1991).

3. Virginia Bankshares Inc. v. Sandberg, 501 U.S. 1083 (1991).

4. A number of decisions have required proof of scienter under § 14(e) of the Williams Act. See Lowenschuss v. Kane, 520 F.2d 255, 268 n. 10 (2d Cir.1975); Connecticut Nat'l Bank v. Fluor Corp., 808 F.2d 957, 961 (2d Cir.1987). Presumably, the same rule would apply to § 13(e).

5. See, e.g., Brudney and Chirelstein, A Restatement of Corporate Freezeouts, 87 Yale L.J. 1354; Greene, Corporate Freezeout Mergers: A Proposed Analysis, 28 Stan.L.Rev. 487 (1976).

6. F.H. O'Neal and R. Thompson, Oppression of Minority Shareholders, at 163 (1986).

Recent evidence adds a new dimension to this debate. In fact, companies that are taken private in leveraged buyouts do typically return to the public—but only after a substantial period of private ownership. One study of 183 large leveraged buyouts completed between 1979 and 1986 found that as of August 1990, 63% were still privately owned, 14% were independent public companies, and 23% were owned by other public companies. The median time that LBOs in this study remained private was 6.7 years.[7] Its author concluded that "LBO organizations are neither short-lived nor permanent." Other studies have found that LBO organizations hold only a small portion of the acquired assets two to three years later, with the majority of the assets moving to corporate buyers in the same industry.[8] From this perspective, the LBO functions more as a broker or asset arbitrageur than as an operator, and the takeover gains may reflect the ultimate buyer's willingness to pay a premium for market power. Such evidence suggests less that the LBO organization is efficient than that the corporate conglomerate taken private was inefficient.

But does an eventual return to public ownership prove or imply unfairness to the former shareholders? Here, new evidence also exists and suggests that the former shareholders fare much better in the 1980s than they did in the 1970s, when Commissioner Sommer expressed concern. In the 1970s, the typical "going private" transaction involved a company having a mean market value of only $3 million.[9] By the late 1980s, the scale had increased by several orders of magnitude to the point that RJR Nabisco was taken private in a leveraged buyout for $25 billion (which transaction started as a management buyout until management was outbid by a rival LBO bidder headed by Kohlberg Kravis & Roberts). The RJR Nabisco deal supplies a paradigm of the 1980s transaction: the "going private" proposal triggered an auction and eventually the highest bidder (more or less) won. A study of 1980s buyouts by Professor Lowenstein found the median premium paid to be 58% over the market price thirty days before the first announcement of the offer (and a staggering 76% above that price in cases where there were three or more bidders)[10] In consequence, shareholders stopped fearing MBOs and began to welcome them.

Are the original critics convinced that MBOs are today fair and efficient and should be viewed sanguinely by the law? In a word, no! In 1991, Commissioner Sommer, whose objections started the debate in 1975, reviewed the evidence and acknowledged the substantial gains to shareholders, but still expressed reservations:

> "All the while the *process* of going private has become relatively routine. The SEC and the courts have sufficiently articulated the ground rules so that attorneys may advise clients with confidence about how to take a company private. And while the recession, the retrenching of banks, the departure of Michael Milken and Drexel Burnham from the economic scene have slowed the pace of such transactions, they continue to be done.
>
> But * * * the more things change, the more they are the same. The same questions of overall fairness and fiduciary responsibilities hang like a

---

7. Kaplan, The Staying Power of Leveraged Buyouts, NBER Working Paper No. 3653 (March 1991).

8. Bhagat, Shleifer, and Vishny, Hostile Takeovers in the 1980s: The Return to Corporate Specialization, Brookings Papers on Economic Activity: Microeconomics, 1 (1990).

9. See Lowenstein, Management Buyouts, 85 Colum.L.Rev. 730, 735 (1985) (citing study of 45 companies listed on the New York or American Stock Exchange).

10. Id. at 738.

shadow over the process. The courts in effect sanction the transactions if the proper disclosures are made and the conventional procedures—investment banker opinion, approval by disinterested directors, satisfaction of the minimal restraints of the business judgment rule—are followed. But there continue to be doubters that the legal analysis has been rigorous enough."[11]

4. *State Responses to Going Private.* In 1977, the Delaware Supreme Court, overruling prior cases, found in Singer v. Magnavox Co.[12] that a squeeze-out transaction could be enjoined where it lacked a "valid business purpose." This raised the almost metaphysical question of what the corporate purpose underlying "going private" is. Is it to economize on the costs of filing documents and reports under the 1934 Act? Possibly in part, but these costs simply do not explain the 25% to 30% abnormal gains paid to shareholders in such buyouts. While these questions taxed the imagination of corporate lawyers seeking to justify such transactions for several years, the Delaware Supreme Court retreated from this position in 1983 in Weinberger v. UOP, Inc.,[13] which overruled *Singer.* Still, the Delaware Supreme Court did not simply relegate the minority shareholders in a squeeze-out merger to an appraisal remedy. Rather, the court acknowledged that appraisal "may not be adequate in certain cases, particularly where fraud, misrepresentation, self-dealing, deliberate waste of corporate assets, or gross and palpable overreaching are involved."[14] In some states (including New York), however, the requirement of an "independent corporate purpose" remains alive and well and continues to confound those who deal with these cases. In 1984, the New York Court of Appeals supplied the following criteria:

"In the context of a freeze-out merger, variant treatment of the minority shareholder * * * will be justified when related to the advancement of a general corporate interest. The benefit need not be great, but it must be for the corporation. For example, if the sole purpose of the merger is reduction of the number of profit sharers—in contrast to increasing the corporation's capital or profits, or improving its management structure—there will exist no 'independent corporate interest'. * * * All of these purposes ultimately seek to increase the individual wealth of the remaining shareholders. What distinguishes a proper corporate purpose from an improper one is that, with the former, removal of the minority shareholders furthers the objective of conferring some general gain upon the corporation. Only then will the fiduciary duty of good and prudent management of the corporation serve to override the concurrent duty to treat all shareholders fairly. * * * We further note that a finding that there was an independent corporate purpose for the action taken by the majority will not be defeated merely by the fact that the corporate objective could have been accomplished in another way, or by the fact that the action chosen was not the best way to achieve the bona fide business objective."[15]

5. *Exemptions.* Rule 13e–3 contains several important exemptions: First, Rule 13e–3(g)(1) exempts second-step, clean-up transactions that occur within

---

11. Sommer, "Going Private" Half A Generation Later (Address at Washington University Law School, November, 1991).

12. 380 A.2d 969 (Del.1977).

13. 457 A.2d 701 (Del.1983).

14. Id. at 714.

15. Alpert v. 28 Williams Street Corp., 63 N.Y.2d 557, 483 N.Y.S.2d 667, 473 N.E.2d 19 (1984); see also, Coggins v. New England Patriots Football Club, Inc., 397 Mass. 525, 492 N.E.2d 1112 (1986).

one year of a tender offer by or on behalf of a bidder who, as a result of the transaction, became an affiliate, provided that the bidder pays at least equal consideration in the second-step merger (and certain other elements of the rule are met). In essence, such a two step sequence of tender offer and follow-up merger is regarded as a unitary transaction and, because the bidder was not subject to Rule 13e–3 at the outset (as a non-affiliate), it remains outside the rule for the second step. The motive for this exemption is presumably to induce the bidder to pay the same consideration at both ends (i.e., not to make a "front-loaded" and arguably coercive bid). Second, transactions, including recapitalizations, are exempted under Rule 13e–3(g)(2) if security holders are offered only an equity security that is a common stock or has essentially the same attributes of the equity security that is the subject of the transaction. Thus, an offer to exchange "new" preferred shares for "old" preferred could fall outside Rule 13e–3. Redemptions, calls, or similar purchases of an equity security pursuant to the specific terms of the instrument creating it are exempted by Rule 13e–3(g)(4).

6. *Affiliates.* Rule 13e–3 applies not only to the issuer, but any affiliate of the issuer that makes a tender offer for the issuer's stock. Close questions can arise as to when the participation of one or more present or former corporate officers in the bidder entity (which is typically set up by an investment banking firm to make a tender offer for the corporation) makes the bidder an affiliate for purposes of Rule 13e–3.

7. *Disclosure Under Rule 13e–3.* In 1988, the Commission brought an administrative proceeding against an issuer that was seeking shareholder approval of a merger under which it would become a privately held company.[16] In its Schedule 13E–3 disclosure statement, the company simply provided a boilerplate list of possible motives for, and effects of, the transaction. The SEC found that the issuer had thereby failed to disclose adequately the purposes, benefits, and detriments of the transaction (Item 7), the basis for the board's belief that the merger price was fair (Item 8), the circumstances surrounding previous inquiries made to purchase the company's stock (Item 3), and certain appraisals of its assets which were used by an investment banking firm to support its fairness review (Item 9). In particular, the SEC insists that the management group defend a transaction's fairness in terms of the premiums paid in similar recent transactions. Item 9 of Schedule 13E–3 also requires the issuer to file all valuation reports and appraisals. To ensure that these reports are not cosmetically edited, the SEC's staff now requires that all preliminary drafts be provided to it, along with offering circulars and loan syndication memoranda provided to the institutions financing the transaction. Any projections or nonpublic financial data provided to an affiliate must also be given to the staff.

SECTION 7. NEW DEVELOPMENTS

A. CROSS–BORDER TENDER OFFERS

The increasingly international character of the world's securities markets can create a special problem for U.S. investors. Suppose they hold a small

---

16. In the Matter of Meyers Parking System, Inc., Sec. Exch. Act Rel. No. 26069 (Sept. 12, 1988). For recent commentary on Rule 13e–3, see Repetti, Management Buy-outs, Efficient Markets, Fair Value and Soft Information, 67 N.C.L.Rev. 121 (1988); Shaw, Resolving the Conflict of Interest in Management Buyouts, 19 Hofstra L.Rev. 143 (1990).

percentage of the stock of an English or European company that becomes the subject of a tender offer. Faced with the complexity of the U.S. securities laws, a foreign bidder might well decide to exclude them from its offer rather than undertake the costs of compliance or face the prospect of litigation in the United States. In addition, express regulatory conflicts can arise between the Williams Act and, for example, the City Code on Takeovers that regulates British takeovers. While the SEC had dealt with these problems on an administrative basis in several instances (usually by allowing bidders to make dual offers, one under British law and one to American securityholders under the Williams Act), it initially proposed in 1991 to formalize an exemption when the percentage of U.S. shareholdings in the target were under ten percent.[1]

Yet, given the large holdings of U.S. institutional investors, this ten percent ceiling did relatively little. As a consequence, European acquirers increasingly tended to exclude U.S. citizens from European tender offers in order to avoid any need to comply with the Williams Act. In response, the SEC adopted a two-tier exemptive structure, which became effective in 2000.[2] Tender offers for the securities of foreign private issuers are now exempt from most of the provisions of the Williams Act and the registration provisions of 1934 Act when U.S. investors hold ten percent or less of the class sought in the tender offer; this is known as a "Tier I" exemption. When U.S. investors hold forty percent or less of the foreign private issuer's securities, a more limited exemption provides relief from the Williams Act (but not from securities registration requirements); this is known as a "Tier II" exemption.[3] Typically, the Tier II acquirer will make separate (but equal) offers to U.S. and foreign holders, which may have slightly different terms and procedures. At the same time, the SEC adopted Rule 802, which exempts the foreign private issuer engaged in a business combination or exchange offer from any obligation to comply with Section 5 of the Securities Act of 1933 if U.S. investors (i) hold ten percent or less of the subject securities, and (ii) are permitted "to participate in the exchange offer or business combination on terms at least as favorable as those offered any other holder of the subject securities."[4] Query: although the intent here is to assure equal treatment, does this create the same problems as the "best price" provisions of Rule 14d–10? That is, what happens if one European shareholder receives a special bonus in the form of an ostensible employment contract or non-compete agreement? New Rule 801 also affords a similar exemption for rights offerings.

While these rules provide exemptions from the Williams Act and, to a lesser extent, the 1933 Act's registration requirements, the antifraud and anti-manipulation provisions of the federal securities laws continue to apply to cross-border transactions, as seemingly do the civil liability provisions of the federal securities laws.

B. DEBT TENDER OFFERS

Firms that issued junk bonds in the eighties are facing the prospect of insolvency in the nineties. One tactic that a highly leveraged firm may exploit is

---

1. See Sec. Act Rel. No. 33–6897 (June 5, 1991).

2. See Securities Act Release No. 7759 (October 22, 1999); see also Securities Act Release No. 7760 (November 10, 1999).

3. The scope of the Tier I exemption is set forth in Rule 14d–1(c), and the scope of the Tier II exemption is set forth in Rule 14d–1(d).

4. See Rule 802(a)(2).

to seek to make an exchange or cash tender offer under which it buys back its debt securities, usually for a package of debt or equity securities (possibly with a cash component also), at a substantial discount off their face value but at a premium over their then trading price in the market. Suppose Thin Equity Inc. issued $1 billion in junk bonds in 1988 and they are now trading in the market at 30% of their face value. If Thin Equity can offer new debentures, equity securities, cash (or some package of all three) worth $400 for bonds having a par value of $1,000, it can avert insolvency, and the bondholders may get a premium over the market price ($400 for bonds trading at $300 or a 33⅓% premium).

However, a new player in these negotiations—the vulture fund—complicates matters for the issuer. Typically, vulture funds buy the debt securities of financially distressed issuers at a discount and hold out. Ideally, their hope is that if all other bondholders tender, the issuer will be sufficiently financially relieved that it can pay off their bonds in full on maturity (in order to avert bankruptcy). This entirely lawful tactic destroys the value of the exchange offer for the issuer. Indeed, if as many as 10% of its bondholders refuse to accept the exchange offer, their holding out will typically frustrate the issuer's plans.

Debtor corporations respond to this problem in two ways: First, they use a high minimum tender condition so that 90% or 95% in principal amount of the bonds must tender pursuant to their offer or they are not obligated to purchase. Sometimes other bondholders insist on this condition because they fear the bidder corporation will reach a side deal at a premium with the vulture fund. Second, issuers will conduct an "exit consent solicitation" pursuant to which they ask tendering bondholders to vote to amend the indenture under which the bonds were issued to waive most financial covenants (and possibly even to subordinate the bonds to newly issued debt securities issued in exchange for them). Granting such an "exit consent" is made a condition of a valid tender of the debt securities. This tactic is intended to coerce the vulture funds (and others) into tendering, because if they fail to tender they will now hold debt securities stripped of their covenants. Also, the bidder may offer a cash payment for votes from bondholders to amend the indenture.[5]

Suppose in a debt tender offer the issuer corporation ignores the "best price," proration, and withdrawal rules and makes a "first come, first served" partial tender offer. Can it do this? Do the rules under § 14(d) apply to a tender offer for debt securities? Can the bidder also ignore the rule requiring a 20 business day duration?[6] Why not?

Possibly as a deterrent to excesses in this area,[7] the SEC's staff has taken the position that when the financial covenants are stripped from bonds or other material changes are made, it is equivalent to the issuance of "new" securities for old securities. As a result, the "new," covenant-less bonds have to be registered under the 1933 Act or an exemption from registration must be

---

5. This would be unlawful "vote buying" in the case of common stock, but it has been upheld in this context. See Katz v. Oak Industries, Inc., 508 A.2d 873 (Del.Ch.1986).

6. If the bidder is the issuer, this rule is set forth in Rule 13e–4(f)(1)(i); otherwise, it is in Rule 14e–1.

7. For the view that new rules are not needed see Note, Debt Tender Offer Techniques and the Problem of Coercion, 91 Colum.L.Rev. 846 (1991). For a counter-view, see Coffee & Klein, Bondholder Coercion: The Problem of Constrained Choice in Debt Tender Offers and Recapitalizations, 58 U.Chi.L.Rev. 1207 (1991).

found. Still, what about the exemption under § 3(a)(9) of the 1933 Act for an exchange of securities? Are any of its limitations relevant?

Note finally that although "exit consent" solicitations can waive or amend most provisions in the indenture, the Trust Indenture Act prohibits (in the case of publicly held debt) the modification of the principal amount, the interest rate, or the maturity date. But, does this provision matter if everything else can be amended and the old bonds can be subordinated to other securities?

C.   "Mini-Tenders"

A tender offer that results in the bidder owning less than 5 percent of any class of the target's stock is exempt from Section 14(d)—but not from Section 14(e).[1] The SEC recently reported that it has "observed an increase in tender offers that would result in the bidder holding not more than five percent of a company's securities."[2] The SEC was concerned that these offers were not accompanied by adequate disclosures, were structured as "first-come, first served" offers without proration or withdrawal rights in order to maximize the pressure on shareholders, and in some cases were even made below the stock market price of the target. One ploy reported by the SEC was for the bidder in such a "mini-tender" to tender at or just above the then market price but deny any withdrawal rights. Then, if the market price rose, the issuer could buy at a now below market price by denying shareholders the right to withdraw. In some other cases, issuers were found not to have made prompt payment in violation of Rule 14e–1(c). Similar problems were reported in connection with tender offers for limited partnership interests.

Although Securities Exchange Act Release No. 43069, which was issued by the SEC in mid–2000, did not adopt any new substantive rules, it warned bidders that certain of the foregoing practices could be found to be fraudulent or manipulative on their facts, specified "recommended" minimum disclosures for such mini-tender offers, and strongly advised bidders in mini-tenders to use a pro-rata acceptance procedure to avoid excessive pressure on shareholders to tender.

---

1. In contrast, issuer self-tenders are governed by Rule 13e–4, which applies to all tender offers by an issuer for any class of its securities and in any amount, at least if the issuer has at least one class registered under the 1934 Act.

2. See Securities Exchange Act Release No. 43069 (July 24, 2000).

PART IV

CIVIL LIABILITIES UNDER THE FEDERAL SECURITIES LAWS

CHAPTER 13

CIVIL LIABILITY UNDER THE SECURITIES ACT OF 1933

A. SECTION 11

Introductory Note

Section 11 of the Securities Act of 1933 is among the more prolix of the federal securities provisions. But at its core is a relatively simple concept. The issuer and a list of statutorily defined potential defendants (including the underwriter and outside experts such as the accountant) can be held liable if the registration statement, when it became effective, contains a material misrepresentation or omission. Primarily because § 11 could reach underwriters, it proved to be the *bête noir* of the 1933 Act and prompted amendments as early as 1934.[1] Ironically the Section did not produce a substantial recovery for 30 years. In the past few years,

---

1. On the history of the 1933 Act, *see* Joel Seligman, The Transformation of Wall Street: A History of the Securities and Exchange Commission and Modern Corporate Finance chs. 2, 3 (rev. ed. 1995); James M. Landis, The Legislative History of the Securities Act of 1933, 28 Geo. Wash. L. Rev. 29 (1959).

however, § 11 has been used more frequently. As a result it is worth parsing the provision with care.

A suit may be brought under § 11 by any person who acquired a registered security whether in the registration process or in the secondary market.[2]

All that the plaintiff must prove, according to § 11(a), is that "any part of the registration statement, when such part became effective, contained an untrue statement of a material fact or omitted to state a material fact required to be stated therein or necessary to make the statements therein not misleading." In Chapter 14 we will examine how a plaintiff proves material misrepresentations or omissions. Materiality, on the one hand, and misrepresentations or omissions, on the other hand, are separate concepts. Nonetheless proof of materiality and of misrepresentations or omissions is identical or virtually identical under each of the antifraud remedies addressed in detail in this book (§§ 11 and 12 of the 1933 Act; §§ 10(b), 14(a), 14(d), and 14(e) of the 1934 Act). The lessons of Chapter 14 with respect to materiality and misrepresentations or omissions are equally applicable here.

Normally the plaintiff need not prove reliance unless the plaintiff bought after the issuer had made generally available to its security holders an earnings statement covering a period of at least a year beginning after the effective date; but even then "reliance may be established without proof of the reading of the registration statement by such person."[3]

The plaintiff need not prove causation, but damages are reduced to the extent that the defendant proves that the damages did not result from his or her misconduct.[4]

The text of § 11(a) itself sets forth with specificity the persons who can be made defendants in an action under the Section. These persons are: (1) the registrant (i.e., the issuing corporation which is included as a "person who signed the registration statement" since all registration statements must be signed by the issuer even when they relate to a secondary offering); (2) all directors of the issuer (including all persons who are named as "about to become" directors); (3) all other persons who sign the registration statement (i.e., the principal executive officer, the principal financial officer and the principal accounting officer of the issuer, who must sign whether or not they are also directors); (4) all underwriters of the offering; and (5) any "expert" who is named as having prepared or certified any part of the registration statement (this would always include the independent accountants who certify the financial statements and occasionally other persons who "expertise" particular statements in the registration statement, such as geologists who give opinions on mineral reserves or lawyers who give title opinions on real property or other legal matters). In addition § 15 can reach anyone whom the plaintiff can show to be in control of any of these persons. Liability of such control persons is analyzed in Chapter 15.

Under § 11 an issuer's liability is absolute with but one exception: The issuer has the defense available to all defendants of showing that the plaintiff knew of the untruth or omission at the time the plaintiff acquired the security.[5] For other defendants an elaborate series of reasonable care or due diligence defenses are available.

---

2. When shares are bought in the open or secondary market, they must be "traced" to the registered offering.

3. § 11(a), last par.; cf. Haralson v. E. F. Hutton Group, Inc., 919 F.2d 1014, 1032 (5th Cir.1990).

4. § 11(e).

5. § 11(a)

(A) A defendant might establish that before the effective date of the part of the registration statement, or upon becoming aware of its effectiveness, the defendant had taken appropriate steps to sever all described connections with the issuer, and had advised the issuer and the Commission in writing that he or she had taken such action and would not be responsible for that part of the statement, or the defendant had given reasonable public notice that part of the statement had become effective without his or her knowledge and the defendant subsequently had severed all connections with the issuer and given notice to the issuer and Commission.[6]

(B) A nonexpert defendant (often a director, officer, or underwriter), sued on a "nonexpertized" portion of a registration statement as well as an expert sued on an "expertized" portion must establish that "he had, after reasonable investigation, reasonable ground to believe and did believe, at the time such part of the registration statement became effective," that it was true and complete.[7] The standard of reasonableness is defined in § 11(c) to be "that required of a prudent man in the management of his own property."

(C) A nonexpert defendant sued on an "expertized" portion of the registration statement has a double negative defense: that "he had no reasonable ground to believe and did not believe, at the time such part of the registration statement became effective, that the statements therein were untrue or that there was an omission to state a material fact required to be stated therein or necessary to make the statements therein not misleading."[8]

1.   THE DUE DILIGENCE DEFENSE

Escott v. BarChris Construction Corp.

United States District Court, S.D., New York, 1968.
283 F.Supp. 643.

■ McLean, District Judge. This is an action by purchasers of 5½ per cent convertible subordinated fifteen year debentures of BarChris Construction Corporation (BarChris). Plaintiffs purport to sue on their own behalf and "on behalf of all other and present and former holders" of the debentures. When the action was begun on October 25, 1962, there were nine plaintiffs. Others were subsequently permitted to intervene. At the time of the trial, there were over sixty.

The action is brought under Section 11 of the Securities Act of 1933. Plaintiffs allege that the registration statement with respect to these debentures filed with the Securities and Exchange Commission, which became effective on May 16, 1961, contained material false statements and material omissions.

Defendants fall into three categories: (1) the persons who signed the registration statement; (2) the underwriters, consisting of eight investment banking firms, led by Drexel & Co. (Drexel); and (3) BarChris's auditors, Peat, Marwick, Mitchell & Co. (Peat, Marwick).

The signers, in addition to BarChris itself, were the nine directors of BarChris, plus its controller, defendant Trilling, who was not a director. Of the

---

6.   §§ 11(b)(1)–(2).

7.   §§ 11(b)(3)(A)–(B).

8.   Section 11(b)(3)(C). In 1995, as part of the Private Securities Litigation Reform Act, the Commission was authorized by amended § 11(f) to limit by rule the liability of outside directors.

nine directors, five were officers of BarChris, i.e., defendants Vitolo, president; Russo, executive vice president; Pugliese, vice president; Kircher, treasurer; and Birnbaum, secretary. Of the remaining four, defendant Grant was a member of the firm of Perkins, Daniels, McCormack & Collins, BarChris's attorneys. He became a director in October 1960. Defendant Coleman, a partner in Drexel, became a director on April 17, 1961, as did the other two, Auslander and Rose, who were not otherwise connected with BarChris.

Defendants, in addition to denying that the registration statement was false, have pleaded the defenses open to them under Section 11 of the Act, plus certain additional defenses, including the statute of limitations. Defendants have also asserted cross-claims against each other, seeking to hold one another liable for any sums for which the respective defendants may be held liable to plaintiffs.

This opinion will not concern itself with the cross-claims or with issues peculiar to any particular plaintiff. These matters are reserved for later decision. On the main issue of liability, the questions to be decided are (1) did the registration statement contain false statements of fact, or did it omit to state facts which should have been stated in order to prevent it from being misleading; (2) if so, were the facts which were falsely stated or omitted "material" within the meaning of the Act; (3) if so, have defendants established their affirmative defenses?

* * *

In general, BarChris's method of operation was to enter into a contract with a customer, receive from him at that time a comparatively small down payment on the purchase price, and proceed to construct and equip the bowling alley. When the work was finished and the building delivered, the customer paid the balance of the contract price in notes, payable in installments over a period of years. BarChris discounted these notes with a factor and received part of their face amount in cash. The factor held back part as a reserve.

In 1960 BarChris began a practice which has been referred to throughout this case as the "alternative method of financing." In substance this was a sale and leaseback arrangement. It involved a distinction between the "interior" of a building and the building itself, i.e., the outer shell. In instances in which this method applied, BarChris would build and install what it referred to as the "interior package." Actually this amounted to constructing and installing the equipment in a building. When it was completed, it would sell the interior to a factor, James Talcott Inc. (Talcott), who would pay BarChris the full contract price therefor. The factor then proceeded to lease the interior either directly to BarChris's customer or back to a subsidiary of BarChris. In the latter case, the subsidiary in turn would lease it to the customer.

Under either financing method, BarChris was compelled to expend considerable sums in defraying the cost of construction before it received reimbursement.[4] As a consequence, BarChris was in constant need of cash to finance its operations, a need which grew more pressing as operations expanded.

---

4. Under the sale and leaseback arrangement, Talcott paid part of the price to   BarChris as the work progressed.

In December 1959, BarChris sold 560,000 shares of common stock to the public at $3.00 per share. This issue was underwritten by Peter Morgan & Company, one of the present defendants.

By early 1961, BarChris needed additional working capital. The proceeds of the sale of the debentures involved in this action were to be devoted, in part at least, to fill that need.

The registration statement of the debentures, in preliminary form, was filed with the Securities and Exchange Commission on March 30, 1961. A first amendment was filed on May 11 and a second on May 16. The registration statement became effective on May 16. The closing of the financing took place on May 24. On that day BarChris received the net proceeds of the financing.

By that time BarChris was experiencing difficulties in collecting amounts due from some of its customers. Some of them were in arrears in payments due to factors on their discounted notes. As time went on those difficulties increased. Although BarChris continued to build alleys in 1961 and 1962, it became increasingly apparent that the industry was overbuilt. Operators of alleys, often inadequately financed, began to fail. Precisely when the tide turned is a matter of dispute, but at any rate, it was painfully apparent in 1962.

In May of that year BarChris made an abortive attempt to raise more money by the sale of common stock. It filed with the Securities and Exchange Commission a registration statement for the stock issue which it later withdrew. In October 1962 BarChris came to the end of the road. On October 29, 1962, it filed in this court a petition for an arrangement under Chapter XI of the Bankruptcy Act. BarChris defaulted in the payment of the interest due on November 1, 1962 on the debentures.

* * *

Summary

For convenience, the various falsities and omissions which I have discussed in the preceding pages are recapitulated here. They were as follows:

1. *1960 Earnings*
   (a) *Sales*

As per prospectus	$9,165,320
Correct figure	8,511,420
Overstatement	$ 653,900

   (b) *Net Operating Income*

As per prospectus	$1,742,801
Correct figure	1,496,196
Overstatement	$ 246,605

   (c) *Earnings per Share*

As per prospectus	$ .75
Correct figure	.65

5. *Earnings Figures for Quarter ending March 31, 1961*
   (a) *Sales*

As per prospectus	$2,138,455
Correct figure	1,618,645
Overstatement	$ 519,810

   (b) *Gross Profit*

As per prospectus	$ 483,121
Correct figure	252,366
Overstatement	$ 230,755

6.	*Backlog as of March 31, 1961*	
	As per prospectus	$6,905,000
	Correct figure	2,415,000
	Overstatement	$4,490,000
7.	*Failure to Disclose Officers' Loans Outstanding and Unpaid on May 16, 1961*	$ 386,615
8.	*Failure to Disclose Use of Proceeds in Manner not Revealed in Prospectus*	
	Approximately	$1,160,000
9.	*Failure to Disclose Customers' Delinquencies in May 1961 and BarChris's Potential Liability with Respect Thereto*	
	Over	$1,350,000
10.	*Failure to Disclose the Fact that BarChris was Already Engaged, and was about to be More Heavily Engaged, in the Operation of Bowling Alleys*	

* * *

[The contingent liabilities as of December 31, 1960 arose from BarChris's selling practices. Under the first method, the corporation accepted customers' installment notes with maturities up to seven years as part payment for products sold or services performed. The notes were generally discounted to financial institutions. Under the alternative method of financing, the corporation sold the product directly to financial institutions. Under Type A contracts used under the alternative method, BarChris sold the bowling alley to a factor, James Talcott Inc., and Talcott leased the property directly to a BarChris customer. BarChris guaranteed the customer's performance in an amount equal to 25% of the customer's total obligation under the lease. In Type B contracts, also used under the alternative method, BarChris sold the bowling alley to Talcott, who leased back the property to a BarChris subsidiary, BarChris Leasing Corporation, who in turn leased the property to the customer. In Type B arrangements, BarChris was liable to the extent of 100% for the performance by its subsidiary of its obligations under the leases.]

[With respect to the contingent liabilities for 1960, the prospectus stated that under the second method of financing, the Company was contingently liable in an amount equal to 25% of the customers' aggregate unexpired rental payments under the leases. Although this was correct as to the Type A contracts, the contingent liabilities on Type B contracts were understated to the extent of 75% of unpaid balances under the leases.]

The "Due Diligence" Defenses

Section 11(b) of the Act provides that:

" * * * no person, other than the issuer, shall be liable * * * who shall sustain the burden of proof—

* * *

"(3) that (A) as regards any part of the registration statement not purporting to be made on the authority of an expert * * * he had, after reasonable investigation, reasonable ground to believe and did believe, at the time such part of the registration statement became effective, that the statements therein were true and that there was no omission to state a material fact required to be stated therein or necessary to make the statements therein not misleading; * * * and *(C) as regards any part of the registration statement purporting to be made on the authority of an expert (other than himself) * * * he had no reasonable ground to believe and did not believe, at the time such part of the registration statement became effective, that the statements therein were untrue or that there was an omission to state a material fact required to be stated therein or necessary to make the statements therein not misleading. * * *"

Section 11(C) defines "reasonable investigation" as follows:

"In determining, for the purpose of paragraph (3) of subsection (b) of this section, what constitutes reasonable investigation and reasonable ground for belief, the standard of reasonableness shall be that required of a prudent man in the management of his own property."

Every defendant, except BarChris itself, to whom, as the issuer, these defenses are not available, and except Peat, Marwick, whose position rests on a different statutory provision, has pleaded these affirmative defenses. Each claims that (1) as to the part of the registration statement purporting to be made on the authority of an expert (which, for convenience, I shall refer to as the "expertised portion"), he had no reasonable ground to believe and did not believe that there were any untrue statements or material omissions, and (2) as to the other parts of the registration statement, he made a reasonable investigation, as a result of which he had reasonable ground to believe and did believe that the registration statement was true and that no material fact was omitted. As to each defendant, the question is whether he has sustained the burden of proving these defenses. Surprising enough, there is little or no judicial authority on this question. No decisions directly in point under Section 11 have been found.

Before considering the evidence, a preliminary matter should be disposed of. The defendants do not agree among themselves as to who the "experts" were or as to the parts of the registration statement which were expertised. Some defendants say that Peat, Marwick was the expert, others say that BarChris's attorneys, Perkins, Daniels, McCormack & Collins, and the underwriters' attorneys, Drinker, Biddle & Reath, were also the experts. On the first view, only those portions of the registration statement purporting to be made on Peat, Marwick's authority were expertised portions. On the other view everything in the registration statement was within this category, because the two law firms were responsible for the entire document.

The first view is the correct one. To say that the entire registration statement is expertised because some lawyer prepared it would be an unreasonable construction of the statute. Neither the lawyer for the company nor the lawyer for the underwriters is an expert within the meaning of Section 11. The only expert, in the statutory sense, was Peat, Marwick, and the only parts of the registration statement which purported to be made upon the authority of an expert were the portions which purported to be made on Peat, Marwick's authority.

The parties also disagree as to what those portions were. Some defendants say that it was only the 1960 figures (and the figures for prior years, which are not in controversy here). Others say in substance that it was every figure in the prospectus. The plaintiffs take a somewhat intermediate view. They do not claim that Peat, Marwick expertised every figure, but they do maintain that Peat, Marwick is responsible for a portion of the text of the prospectus, i.e., that pertaining to "Methods of Operation," because a reference to it was made in footnote 9 to the balance sheet.

Here again, the more narrow view is the correct one. The registration statement contains a report of Peat, Marwick as independent public accountants dated February 23, 1961. This relates only to the consolidated balance sheet of BarChris and consolidated subsidiaries as of December 31, 1960, and the related statement of earnings and retained earnings for the five years then ended. This is all that Peat, Marwick purported to certify. It is perfectly clear that it did not purport to certify the 1961 figures, some of which are expressly stated in the prospectus to have been unaudited.

Moreover, plaintiffs' intermediate view is also incorrect. The cross reference in footnote 9 to the "Methods of Operation" passage in the prospectus was inserted merely for the convenience of the reader. It is not a fair construction to say that it thereby imported into the balance sheet everything in that portion of the text, much of which had nothing to do with the figures in the balance sheet.

I turn now to the question of whether defendants have proved their due diligence defenses. The position of each defendant will be separately considered.

* * *

Kircher

Kircher was treasurer of BarChris and its chief financial officer. He is a certified public accountant and an intelligent man. He was thoroughly familiar with BarChris's financial affairs. He knew the terms of BarChris's agreements with Talcott. He knew of the customers' delinquency problem. He participated actively with Russo in May 1961 in the successful effort to hold Talcott off until the financing proceeds came in. He knew how the financing proceeds were to be applied and he saw to it that they were so applied. He arranged the officers' loans and he knew all the facts concerning them.

Moreover, as a member of the executive committee, Kircher was kept informed as to those branches of the business of which he did not have direct charge. He knew about the operation of alleys, present and prospective. He knew that Capitol was included in 1960 sales and that Bridge and Yonkers were included in first quarter 1961 sales despite the fact that they were not sold. Kircher knew of the infirmities in customers' contracts included in the backlog figure. Indeed, at a later date, he specifically criticized Russo's handling of the T–Bowl situation. In brief, Kircher knew all the relevant facts.

Kircher worked on the preparation of the registration statement. He conferred with Grant and on occasion with Ballard. He supplied information to them about the company's business. He had the prospectus and understood it. He knew what it said and what it did not say.

Kircher's contention is that he had never before dealt with a registration statement, that he did not know what it should contain, and that he relied wholly on Grant, Ballard and Peat, Marwick to guide him. He claims that it was their fault, not his, if there was anything wrong with it. He says that all the facts were recorded in BarChris's books where these "experts" could have seen them if they had looked. He says that he truthfully answered all their questions. In effect, he says that if they did not know enough to ask the right questions and to give him the proper instructions, that is not his responsibility.

There is an issue of credibility here. In fact, Kircher was not frank in dealing with Grant and Ballard. He withheld information from them. But even if he had told them all the facts, this would not have constituted the due diligence contemplated by the statute. Knowing the facts, Kircher had reason to believe that the expertised portion of the prospectus, i.e., the 1960 figures, was in part incorrect. He could not shut his eyes to the facts and rely on Peat, Marwick for that portion.

As to the rest of the prospectus, knowing the facts, he did not have a reasonable ground to believe it to be true. On the contrary, he must have known that in part it was untrue. Under these circumstances, he was not entitled to sit back and place the blame on the lawyers for not advising him about it.

Kircher has not proved his due diligence defenses.

* * *

Birnbaum

Birnbaum was a young lawyer, admitted to the bar in 1957, who, after brief periods of employment by two different law firms and an equally brief period of practicing in his own firm, was employed by BarChris as house counsel and assistant secretary in October 1960. Unfortunately for him, he became secretary and a director of BarChris on April 17, 1961, after the first version of the registration statement had been filed with the Securities and Exchange Commission. He signed the later amendments, thereby becoming responsible for the accuracy of the prospectus in its final form.

Although the prospectus, in its description of "management," lists Birnbaum among the "executive officers" and devotes several sentences to a recital of his career, the fact seems to be that he was not an executive officer in any real sense. He did not participate in the management of the company. As house counsel, he attended to legal matters of a routine nature. Among other things, he incorporated subsidiaries, with which BarChris was plentifully supplied. Among the subsidiaries which he incorporated were Capitol Lanes, Inc. which operated Capitol, Yonkers Lanes, Inc. which eventually operated Yonkers, and Parkway Lanes, Inc. which eventually operated Bridge. He was thus aware of that aspect of the business.

Birnbaum examined contracts. In that connection he advised BarChris that the T-Bowl contracts were not legally enforceable. He was thus aware of that fact.

One of Birnbaum's more important duties, first as assistant secretary and later as full-fledged secretary, was to keep the corporate minutes of BarChris and its subsidiaries. This necessarily informed him to a considerable extent about the company's affairs. Birnbaum was not initially a member of the executive committee, however, and did not keep its minutes at the outset. According to the minutes, the first meeting which he attended, "upon invitation of the Committee," was on March 22, 1961. He became a member shortly thereafter and kept the minutes beginning with the meeting of April 24, 1961.

It seems probable that Birnbaum did not know of many of the inaccuracies in the prospectus. He must, however, have appreciated some of them. In any case, he made no investigation and relied on the others to get it right. Unlike Trilling, he was entitled to rely upon Peat, Marwick for the 1960 figures, for as far as appears, he had no personal knowledge of the company's books of account or financial transactions. But he was not entitled to rely upon Kircher, Grant and Ballard for the other portions of the prospectus. As a lawyer, he should have known his obligations under the statute. He should have known that he was required to make a reasonable investigation of the truth of all the statements in the unexpertised portion of the document which he signed. Having failed to make such an investigation, he did not have reasonable ground to believe that all these statements were true. Birnbaum has not established his due diligence defenses except as to the audited 1960 figures.

Auslander

Auslander was an "outside" director, i.e., one who was not an officer of BarChris. He was chairman of the board of Valley Stream National Bank in Valley Stream, Long Island. In February, 1961, Vitolo asked him to become a director of BarChris. Vitolo gave him an enthusiastic account of BarChris's progress and prospects. As an inducement, Vitolo said that when BarChris received the proceeds of a forthcoming issue of securities, it would deposit $1,000,000 in Auslander's bank.

In February and early March 1961, before accepting Vitolo's invitation, Auslander made some investigation of BarChris. He obtained Dun & Bradstreet reports which contained sales and earnings figures for periods earlier than December 31, 1960. He caused inquiry to be made of certain of BarChris's banks and was advised that they regarded BarChris favorably. He was informed that inquiry of Talcott had also produced a favorable response.

On March 3, 1961, Auslander indicated his willingness to accept a place on the board. Shortly thereafter, on March 14, Kircher sent him a copy of BarChris's annual report for 1960. Auslander observed that BarChris's auditors were Peat, Marwick. They were also the auditors for the Valley Stream National Bank. He thought well of them.

Auslander was elected a director on April 17, 1961. The registration statement in its original form had already been filed, of course without his signature. On May 10, 1961, he signed a signature page for the first amendment to the registration statement which was filed on May 11, 1961. This was a separate sheet without any document attached. Auslander did not know that it was a signature page for a registration statement. He vaguely understood that it was something "for the SEC."

Auslander attended a meeting of BarChris's directors on May 15, 1961. At that meeting he, along with the other directors, signed the signature sheet for the second amendment which constituted the registration statement in its final form. Again, this was only a separate sheet without any document attached. Auslander never saw a copy of the registration statement in its final form.

At the May 15 directors' meeting, however, Auslander did realize that what he was signing was a signature sheet to a registration statement. This was the first time that he had appreciated that fact. A copy of the registration statement in its earlier form as amended on May 11, 1961, was passed around at the meeting. Auslander glanced at it briefly. He did not read it thoroughly.

At the May 15 meeting, Russo and Vitolo stated that everything was in order and that the prospectus was correct. Auslander believed this statement.

In considering Auslander's due diligence defenses, a distinction is to be drawn between the expertised and non-expertised portions of the prospectus. As to the former, Auslander knew that Peat, Marwick had audited the 1960 figures. He believed them to be correct because he had confidence in Peat, Marwick. He had no reasonable ground to believe otherwise.

As to the non-expertised portions, however, Auslander is in a different position. He seems to have been under the impression that Peat, Marwick was responsible for all the figures. This impression was not correct, as he would have realized if he had read the prospectus carefully. Auslander made no investigation of the accuracy of the prospectus. He relied on the assurance of Vitolo and Russo, and upon the information he had received in answer to his inquiries back in February and early March. These inquiries were general ones, in the nature of a credit check. The information which he received in answer to them was also general, without specific reference to the statements in the prospectus, which was not prepared until some time thereafter.

It is true that Auslander became a director on the eve of the financing. He had little opportunity to familiarize himself with the company's affairs. The question is whether, under such circumstances, Auslander did enough to establish his due diligence defense with respect to the non-expertised portions of the prospectus.

Although there is a dearth of authority under Section 11 on this point, an English case under the analogous Companies Act is of some value. In Adams v. Thrift [1915] 1 Ch. 557, aff'd [1915] 2 Ch. 21, it was held that a director who knew nothing about the prospectus and did not even read it, but who relied on the statement of the company's managing director that it was "all right," was liable for its untrue statements.

* * *

Section 11 imposes liability in the first instance upon a director, no matter how new he is. He is presumed to know his responsibility when he becomes a director. He can escape liability only by using that reasonable care to investigate the facts which a prudent man would employ in the management of his own property. In my opinion, a prudent man would not act in an important matter without any knowledge of the relevant facts, in sole reliance upon representations of persons who are comparative strangers and upon general information which does not purport to cover the particular case. To say that such minimal conduct measures up to the statutory standard would to all intents and purposes, absolve new directors from responsibility merely because they are new. This is not a sensible construction of Section 11, when one bears in mind its fundamental purpose of requiring full and truthful disclosure for the protection of investors.

I find and conclude that Auslander has not established his due diligence defense with respect to the misstatements and omissions in those portions of the prospectus other than the audited 1960 figures.

* * *

Grant

Grant became a director of BarChris in October 1960. His law firm was counsel to BarChris in matters pertaining to the registration of securities. Grant drafted the registration statement for the stock issue in 1959 and for the warrants in January 1961. He also drafted the registration statement for the debentures. In the preliminary division of work between him and Ballard, the underwriters' counsel, Grant took initial responsibility for preparing the registration statement, while Ballard devoted his efforts in the first instance to preparing the indenture.

Grant is sued as a director and as a signer of the registration statement. This is not an action against him for malpractice in his capacity as a lawyer. Nevertheless, in considering Grant's due diligence defenses, the unique position which he occupied cannot be disregarded. As the director most directly concerned with writing the registration statement and assuring its accuracy, more was required of him in the way of reasonable investigation than could fairly be expected of a director who had no connection with this work.

There is no valid basis for plaintiffs' accusation that Grant knew that the prospectus was false in some respects and incomplete and misleading in others. Having seen him testify at length, I am satisfied as to his integrity. I find that Grant honestly believed that the registration statement was true and that no material facts had been omitted from it.

In this belief he was mistaken, and the fact is that for all his work, he never discovered any of the errors or omissions which have been recounted at length in this opinion, with the single exception of Capitol Lanes. He knew that BarChris had not sold this alley and intended to operate it, but he appears to have been under the erroneous impression that Peat, Marwick had knowingly sanctioned its inclusion in sales because of the allegedly temporary nature of the operation.

Grant contends that a finding that he did not make a reasonable investigation would be equivalent to holding that a lawyer for an issuing company, in order to show due diligence, must make an independent audit of the figures supplied to him by his client. I do not consider this to be a realistic statement of the issue. There were errors and omissions here which could have been detected without an audit. The question is whether, despite his failure to detect them, Grant made a reasonable effort to that end.

Much of this registration statement is a scissors and paste-pot job. Grant lifted large portions from the earlier prospectuses, modifying them in some instances to the extent that he considered necessary. But BarChris's affairs had changed for the worse by May 1961. Statements that were accurate in January were no longer accurate in May. Grant never discovered this. He accepted the assurances of Kircher and Russo that any change which might have occurred had been for the better, rather than the contrary.

It is claimed that a lawyer is entitled to rely on the statements of his client and that to require him to verify their accuracy would set an unreasonably high standard. This is too broad a generalization. It is all a matter of degree. To require an audit would obviously be unreasonable. On the other hand, to require a check of matters easily verifiable is not unreasonable. Even honest clients can make mistakes. The statute imposes liability for untrue statements regardless of whether they are intentionally untrue. The way to prevent mistakes is to test oral information by examining the original written record.

There were things which Grant could readily have checked which he did not check. For example, he was unaware of the provisions of the agreements between BarChris and Talcott. He never read them. Thus, he did not know, although he readily could have ascertained, that BarChris's contingent liability on Type B leaseback arrangements was 100 per cent, not 25 per cent. He did not appreciate that if BarChris defaulted in repurchasing delinquent customers' notes upon Talcott's demand, Talcott could accelerate all the customer paper in its hands, which amounted to over $3,000,000.

As to the backlog figure, Grant appreciated that scheduled unfilled orders on the company's books meant firm commitments, but he never asked to see the contracts which, according to the prospectus, added up to $6,905,000. Thus, he did not know that this figure was overstated by some $4,490,000.

Grant was unaware of the fact that BarChris was about to operate Bridge and Yonkers. He did not read the minutes of those subsidiaries which would have revealed that fact to him. On the subject of minutes, Grant knew that minutes of certain meetings of the BarChris executive committee held in 1961 had not been written up. Kircher, who had acted as secretary at those meetings, had complete notes of them. Kircher told Grant that there was no point in writing up the minutes because the matters discussed at those meetings were purely routine. Grant did not insist that the minutes be written up, nor did he look at Kircher's notes. If he had, he would have learned that on February 27, 1961, there was an extended discussion in the executive committee meeting about customers' delinquencies, that on March 8, 1961 the committee had discussed the pros and cons of alley operation by BarChris, that on March 18, 1961 the committee was informed that BarChris was constructing or about to begin constructing twelve alleys for which it had no contracts, and that on May 13, 1961 Dreyfuss, one of the worst delinquents, had filed a petition in Chapter X.

Grant knew that there had been loans from officers to BarChris in the past because that subject had been mentioned in the 1959 and January 1961 prospectuses. In March Grant prepared a questionnaire to be answered by officers and directors for the purpose of obtaining information to be used in the prospectus. The questionnaire did not inquire expressly about the existence of officers' loans. At approximately the same time, Grant prepared another questionnaire in order to obtain information on proxy statements for the annual stockholders' meeting. This questionnaire asked each officer to state whether he was indebted to BarChris, but it did not ask whether BarChris was indebted to him.

Despite the inadequacy of these written questionnaires, Grant did, on March 16, 1961, orally inquire as to whether any officers' loans were outstanding. He was assured by Russo, Vitolo and Pugliese that all such loans had been repaid. Grant did not ask again. He was unaware of the new loans in April. He did know, however, that, at Kircher's request, a provision was inserted in the indenture which gave loans from individuals priority over the debentures. Kircher's insistence on this clause did not arouse his suspicions.

It is only fair to say that Grant was given to understand by Kircher that there were no new officers' loans and that there would not be any before May 16. It is still a close question, however, whether, under all the circumstances, Grant should have investigated further, perhaps by asking Peat, Marwick, in the course of its S–1 review, to look at the books on this particular point. I believe that a careful man would have checked.

There is more to the subject of due diligence than this, particularly with respect to the application of proceeds and customers' delinquencies.

The application of proceeds language in the prospectus was drafted by Kircher back in January. It may well have expressed his intent at that time, but his intent, and that of the other principal officers of BarChris, was very different in May. Grant did not appreciate that the earlier language was no longer appropriate. He never learned of the situation which the company faced in May. He knew that BarChris was short of cash, but he had no idea how short. He did not know that BarChris was withholding delivery of checks already drawn and signed because there was not enough money in the bank to pay them. He did not know that the officers of the company intended to use immediately approximately one-third of the financing proceeds in a manner not disclosed in the prospectus, including approximately $1,000,000 in paying old debts.

In this connection, mention should be made of a fact which has previously been referred to only in passing. The "negative cash balance" in BarChris's Lafayette National Bank account in May 1961, included a check dated April 10, 1961 to the order of Grant's firm, Perkins, Daniels, McCormack & Collins, in the amount of $8,711. This check was not deposited by Perkins, Daniels until June 1, after the financing proceeds had been received by BarChris. Of course, if Grant had knowingly withheld deposit of this check, until that time, he would be in a position similar to Russo, Vitolo and Pugliese. I do not believe, however, that that was the case. I find that the check was not delivered by BarChris to Perkins, Daniels until shortly before June 1.

This incident is worthy of mention, however, for another reason. The prospectus stated on page 10 that Perkins, Daniels had "received fees aggregating $13,000" from BarChris. This check for $8,711 was one of those fees. It had not been received by Perkins, Daniels prior to May 16. Grant was unaware of this. In approving this erroneous statement in the prospectus, he did not consult his own bookkeeper to ascertain whether it was correct. Kircher told him that the bill had been paid and Grant took his word for it. If he had inquired and had found that this representation was untrue, this discovery might well have led him to a realization of the true state of BarChris's finances in May 1961.

As far as customers' delinquencies are concerned, although Grant discussed this with Kircher, he again accepted the assurances of Kircher and Russo that no serious problem existed. He did not examine the records as to delinquencies, although BarChris maintained such a record. Any inquiry on his part of Talcott or an examination of BarChris's correspondence with Talcott in April and May 1961 would have apprised him of the true facts. It would have led him to appreciate that the statement in this prospectus, carried over from earlier prospectuses, to the effect that since 1955 BarChris had been required to repurchase less than one-half of one per cent of discounted customers' notes could no longer properly be made without further explanation.

Grant was entitled to rely on Peat, Marwick for the 1960 figures. He had no reasonable ground to believe them to be inaccurate. But the matters which I have mentioned were not within the expertised portion of the prospectus. As to this, Grant was obliged to make a reasonable investigation. I am forced to find that he did not make one. After making all due allowances for the fact that BarChris's officers misled him, there are too many instances in which Grant failed to make an inquiry which he could easily have made which, if pursued, would have put him on his guard. In my opinion, this finding on the evidence in this case does not establish an unreasonably high standard in other cases for company counsel who are also directors. Each case must rest on its own facts. I conclude that Grant has not established his due diligence defenses except as to the audited 1960 figures.

The Underwriters and Coleman

The underwriters other than Drexel made no investigation of the accuracy of the prospectus. One of them, Peter Morgan, had underwritten the 1959 stock issue and had been a director of BarChris. He thus had some general familiarity with its affairs, but he knew no more than the other underwriters about the debenture prospectus. They all relied upon Drexel as the "lead" underwriter.

Drexel did make an investigation. The work was in charge of Coleman, a partner of the firm, assisted by Casperson, an associate. Drexel's attorneys acted as attorneys for the entire group of underwriters. Ballard did the work, assisted by Stanton.

On April 17, 1961 Coleman became a director of BarChris. He signed the first amendment to the registration statement filed on May 11 and the second amendment constituting the registration statement in its final form, filed on May 16. He thereby assumed a responsibility as a director and signer in addition to his responsibility as an underwriter.

The facts as to the extent of the investigation that Coleman made may be briefly summarized. He was first introduced to BarChris on September 15, 1960. Thereafter he familiarized himself with general conditions in the industry, primarily by reading reports and prospectuses of the two leading bowling alley builders, American Machine & Foundry Company and Brunswick. These indicated that the industry was still growing. He also acquired general information on BarChris by reading the 1959 stock prospectus, annual reports for prior years, and an unaudited statement for the first half of 1960. He inquired about BarChris of certain of its banks and of Talcott and received favorable replies.

The purpose of this preliminary investigation was to enable Coleman to decide whether Drexel would undertake the financing. It did not have direct reference to any specific registration statement for at that time, of course, none had been prepared. Coleman was sufficiently optimistic about BarChris's prospects to buy 1,000 shares of its stock, which he did in December 1960.

On January 24, 1961, Coleman held a meeting with Ballard, Grant and Kircher, among others. By that time Coleman had about decided to go ahead with the financing, although Drexel's formal letter of intent was not delivered until February 9, 1961 (subsequently revised on March 7, 1961). At this meeting Coleman asked Kircher how BarChris intended to use the proceeds of the financing. In reply to this inquiry, Kircher wrote a letter to Coleman dated January 30, 1961 outlining BarChris's plans. This eventually formed the basis of the application of proceeds section in the prospectus.

Coleman continued his general investigation. He obtained a Dun & Bradstreet report on BarChris on March 16, 1961. He read BarChris's annual report for 1960 which was available in March.

By mid-March, Coleman was in a position to make more specific inquiries. By that time Grant had prepared a first draft of the prospectus, consisting of a marked-up copy of the January 1961 warrant prospectus. Coleman attended the meetings to discuss the prospectus with BarChris's representatives. The meetings were held at Perkins, Daniels' office on March 20, March 23 and March 24, 1961. Those present included Grant or his partner McCormack and Kircher for the company,[22] and Coleman, Casperson and Ballard for the underwriters.

---

22. Grant was in charge of this work for his firm, but he was out of town on March 20 and March 23, and McCormack substituted for him on those days.

Logan, Peat, Marwick's manager of the 1960 audit, was present at one of the meetings.

At these discussions, which were extensive, successive proofs of the prospectus were considered and revised. At this point the 1961 figures were not available. They were put in the prospectus in May.

Coleman and Ballard asked pertinent questions and received answers which satisfied them. Among other things, the following transpired.

Logan explained some of the 1960 figures, including the reserve for bad debts, which he considered adequate.

There was a discussion of the application of proceeds section. It was not changed in any respect material here.

As to the backlog of orders on hand, Ballard said that the figure, not then available, must be "hard and fast," not "puffy." Grant and Kircher "concurred."

There was talk about the 15 to 25 per cent down payment figure. Kircher said that this was accurate.

More important for our purposes, there was a discussion of the one-half of one percent figure with respect to BarChris's past experience in repurchasing discounted customers' notes. Kircher said that this figure was "conservative." Ballard inquired whether, regardless of what past experience had been, there was "any real chance that you see of being forced to take any [alleys] back in the future?" Kircher's answer was "negative."

The alternative method of financing was explained. Kircher said that BarChris's contingent liability was only 25 percent.

There was talk about operating alleys. Kircher said that BarChris did not operate any. Coleman and Ballard inquired whether BarChris built alleys on speculation, i.e., without any customer's contract for them. Kircher said BarChris did not.

There was discussion of officers' loans. Kircher said that the $155,000 had been repaid and that no further officers' loans were contemplated. Coleman said that this was wise, for loans from officers "indicated financial instability of the company."

Coleman did not participate personally in any further meetings of this sort. Casperson attended some and reported to Coleman. Ballard advised Coleman as to what he was doing.

After Coleman was elected a director on April 17, 1961, he made no further independent investigation of the accuracy of the prospectus. He assumed that Ballard was taking care of this on his behalf as well as on behalf of the underwriters.

In April 1961 Ballard instructed Stanton to examine BarChris's minutes for the past five years and also to look at "the major contracts of the company."[23] Stanton went to BarChris's office for that purpose on April 24. He asked Birnbaum for the minute books. He read the minutes of the board of

---

23. Stanton was a very junior associate. He had been admitted to the bar in January 1961, some three months before. This was the first registration statement he had ever worked on.

directors and discovered interleaved in them a few minutes of executive committee meetings in 1960. He asked Kircher if there were any others. Kircher said that there had been other executive committee meetings but that the minutes had not been written up.

Stanton read the minutes of a few BarChris subsidiaries. His testimony was vague as to which ones. He had no recollection of seeing the minutes of Capitol Lanes, Inc. or Biel or Parkway Lanes, Inc. He did not discover that BarChris was operating Capitol or that it planned to operate Bridge and Yonkers.

As to the "major contracts," all that Stanton could remember seeing was an insurance policy. Birnbaum told him that there was no file of major contracts. Stanton did not examine the agreements with Talcott. He did not examine the contracts with customers. He did not look to see what contracts comprised the backlog figure. Stanton examined no accounting records of BarChris. His visit, which lasted one day, was devoted primarily to reading the directors' minutes.

On April 25 Ballard wrote to Grant about certain matters which Stanton had noted on his visit to BarChris the day before, none of which Ballard considered "very earth shaking." As far as relevant here, these were (1) Russo's remark as recorded in the executive committee minutes of November 3, 1960 to the effect that because of customers' defaults, BarChris might find itself in the business of operating alleys; (2) the fact that the minutes of Sanpark Realty Corporation were incomplete; and (3) the fact that minutes of the executive committee were missing.

On May 9, 1961, Ballard came to New York and conferred with Grant and Kircher. They discussed the Securities and Exchange Commission's deficiency letter of May 4, 1961 which required the inclusion in the prospectus of certain additional information, notably net sales, gross profits and net earnings figures for the first quarter of 1961. They also discussed the points raised in Ballard's letter to Grant of April 25. As to the latter, most of the conversation related to what Russo had meant by his remark on November 3, 1960. Kircher said that the delinquency problem was less severe now than it had been back in November 1960, that no alleys had been repossessed, and that although he was "worried about one alley in Harlem" (Dreyfuss), that was a "special situation." Grant reported that Russo had told him that his statement on November 3, 1960 was "merely hypothetical." On the strength of this conversation, Ballard was satisfied that the one-half of one percent figure in the prospectus did not need qualification or elaboration.

As to the missing minutes, Kircher said that those of Sanpark were not significant and that the executive committee meetings for which there were no written minutes were concerned only with "routine matters."

It must be remembered that this conference took place only one week before the registration statement became effective. Ballard did nothing else in the way of checking during that intervening week.

Ballard did not insist that the executive committee minutes be written up so that he could inspect them, although he testified that he knew from experience that executive committee minutes may be extremely important. If he had insisted, he would have found the minutes highly informative, as has previously been pointed out * * *. Ballard did not ask to see BarChris's schedule of delinquencies or Talcott's notices of delinquencies, or BarChris's correspondence with Talcott.

Ballard did not examine BarChris's contracts with Talcott. He did not appreciate what Talcott's rights were under those financing agreements or how serious the effect would be upon BarChris of any exercise of those rights.

Ballard did not investigate the composition of the backlog figure to be sure that it was not "puffy." He made no inquiry after March about any new officers' loans, although he knew that Kircher had insisted on a provision in the indenture which gave loans from individuals priority over the debentures. He was unaware of the seriousness of BarChris's cash position and of how BarChris's officers intended to use a large part of the proceeds. He did not know that BarChris was operating Capitol Lanes.[24]

Like Grant, Ballard, without checking, relied on the information which he got from Kircher. He also relied on Grant who, as company counsel, presumably was familiar with its affairs.

The formal opinion which Ballard's firm rendered to the underwriters at the closing on May 24, 1961 made clear that this is what he had done. The opinion stated (italics supplied):

> In the course of the preparation of the Registration Statement and Prospectus by the Company, we have had numerous conferences with representatives of and counsel for the Company and with its auditors and we have raised many questions regarding the business of the Company. Satisfactory answers to such questions were in each case given us, and all other information and documents we requested have been supplied. We are of the opinion that the *data presented* to us are accurately reflected in the Registration Statement and Prospectus and that there has been omitted from the Registration Statement no material facts *included in such data*. Although *we have not otherwise verified* the completeness or accuracy of the information furnished to us, on the basis of the foregoing and with the exception of the financial statements and schedules (which this opinion does not pass upon), we have no reason to believe that the Registration Statement or Prospectus contains any untrue statement of any material fact or omits to state a material fact required to be stated therein or necessary in order to make the statements therein not misleading.

Coleman testified that Drexel had an understanding with its attorneys that "we expect them to inspect on our behalf the corporate records of the company including, but not limited to, the minutes of the corporation, the stockholders and the committees of the board authorized to act for the board." Ballard manifested his awareness of this understanding by sending Stanton to read the minutes and the major contracts. It is difficult to square this understanding with the formal opinion of Ballard's firm which expressly disclaimed any attempt to verify information supplied by the company and its counsel.

In any event, it is clear that no effectual attempt at verification was made. The question is whether due diligence required that it be made. Stated another way, is it sufficient to ask questions, to obtain answers which, if true, would be

---

24. Stanton was also unaware of this, although there was a reference to it in the minutes of the board of directors' meeting of November 22, 1960, which he presumably read.

thought satisfactory, and to let it go at that, without seeking to ascertain from the records whether the answers in fact are true and complete?

I have already held that this procedure is not sufficient in Grant's case. Are underwriters in a different position, as far as due diligence is concerned?

The underwriters say that the prospectus is the company's prospectus, not theirs. Doubtless this is the way they customarily regard it. But the Securities Act makes no such distinction. The underwriters are just as responsible as the company if the prospectus is false. And prospective investors rely upon the reputation of the underwriters in deciding whether to purchase the securities.

There is no direct authority on this question, no judicial decision defining the degree of diligence which underwriters must exercise to establish their defense under Section 11.[25]

There is some authority in New York for the proposition that a director of a corporation may rely upon information furnished him by the officers without independently verifying it.

See Litwin v. Allen, 25 N.Y.S.2d 667 (Sup.Ct.1940).

In support of that principle, the court in Litwin, (25 N.Y.S.2d at 719) quoted from the opinion of Lord Halsbury in Dovey v. Cory, [1901] App.Cas. 447, 486, in which he said:

"The business of life could not go on if people could not trust those who are put into a position of trust for the express purpose of attending to details of management."

Of course, New York law does not govern this case. The construction of the Securities Act is a matter of federal law. But the underwriters argue that *Litwin* is still in point, for they say that it establishes a standard of reasonableness for the reasonably prudent director which should be the same as the standard for the reasonably prudent underwriter under the Securities Act.

In my opinion the two situations are not analogous. An underwriter has not put the company's officers "into a position of trust for the express purpose of attending to details of management." The underwriters did not select them. In a sense, the positions of the underwriter and the company's officers are adverse. It is not unlikely that statements made by company officers to an underwriter to induce him to underwrite may be self-serving. They may be unduly enthusiastic. As in this case, they may, on occasion, be deliberately false.

The purpose of Section 11 is to protect investors. To that end the underwriters are made responsible for the truth of the prospectus. If they may escape that responsibility by taking at face value representations made to them by the company's management, then the inclusion of underwriters among those liable under Section 11 affords the investors no additional protection. To effectuate the statute's purpose, the phrase "reasonable investigation" must be construed to require more effort on the part of the underwriters than the mere accurate reporting in the prospectus of "data presented" to them by the company. It should make no difference that this data is elicited by questions

---

25.   There are at least two decisions of the Securities and Exchange Commission which indicate that it is the Commission's view that an underwriter must go beyond and behind the representations of management. Matter of Richmond Corp., [1962–1964 Decisions] CCH Sec.L.Rep. ¶ 76,904 (1963); Matter of Charles E. Bailey & Co., 35 S.E.C. 33 (1953).

addressed to the company officers by the underwriters, or that the underwriters at the time believe that the company's officers are truthful and reliable. In order to make the underwriters' participation in this enterprise of any value to the investors, the underwriters must make some reasonable attempt to verify the data submitted to them. They may not rely solely on the company's officers or on the company's counsel. A prudent man in the management of his own property would not rely on them.

It is impossible to lay down a rigid rule suitable for every case defining the extent to which such verification must go. It is a question of degree, a matter of judgment in each case. In the present case, the underwriters' counsel made almost no attempt to verify management's representations. I hold that that was insufficient.

On the evidence in this case, I find that the underwriters' counsel did not make a reasonable investigation of the truth of those portions of the prospectus which were not made on the authority of Peat, Marwick as an expert. Drexel is bound by their failure. It is not a matter of relying upon counsel for legal advice. Here the attorneys were dealing with matters of fact. Drexel delegated to them, as its agent the business of examining the corporate minutes and contracts. It must bear the consequences of their failure to make an adequate examination.

The other underwriters, who did nothing and relied solely on Drexel and on the lawyers, are also bound by it. It follows that although Drexel and the other underwriters believed that those portions of the prospectus were true, they had no reasonable ground for that belief, within the meaning of the statute. Hence, they have not established their due diligence defense, except as to the 1960 audited figures.[26]

The same conclusions must apply to Coleman. Although he participated quite actively in the earlier stages of the preparation of the prospectus, and contributed questions and warnings of his own, in addition to the questions of counsel, the fact is that he stopped his participation toward the end of March 1961. He made no investigation after he became a director. When it came to verification, he relied upon his counsel to do it for him. Since counsel failed to do it, Coleman is bound by that failure. Consequently in his case also, he has not established his due diligence defense except as to the audited 1960 figures.

Peat, Marwick

Section 11(b) provides:

"Notwithstanding the provisions of subsection (a) no person * * * shall be liable as provided therein who shall sustain the burden of proof—

* * *

"(3) that * * * (B) as regards any part of the registration statement purporting to be made upon his authority as an expert * * * (I) he had, after reasonable investigation, reasonable ground to believe and did believe, at the time such part of the registration statement became effective, that the statements therein were true and that there was no omission to

---

26. In view of this conclusion, it becomes unnecessary to decide whether the underwriters other than Drexel would have been protected if Drexel had established that as lead underwriter, it made a reasonable investigation.

state a material fact required to be stated therein or necessary to make the statements therein not misleading * * *."

This defines the due diligence defense for an expert. Peat, Marwick has pleaded it.

The part of the registration statement purporting to be made upon the authority of Peat, Marwick as an expert was, as we have seen, the 1960 figures. But because the statute requires the court to determine Peat, Marwick's belief, and the grounds thereof, "at the time such part of the registration statement became effective," for the purposes of this affirmative defense the matter must be viewed as of May 16, 1961, and the question is whether at that time Peat, Marwick, after reasonable investigation, had reasonable ground to believe and did believe that the 1960 figures were true and that no material fact had been omitted from the registration statement which should have been included in order to make the 1960 figures not misleading. In deciding this issue, the court must consider not only what Peat, Marwick did in its 1960 audit, but also what it did in its subsequent "S–1 review." The proper scope of that review must also be determined.

It may be noted that we are concerned at this point only with the question of Peat, Marwick's liability to plaintiffs. At the closing on May 24, 1961, Peat, Marwick delivered a so-called "comfort letter" to the underwriters. This letter stated:

"It is understood that this letter is for the information of the underwriters and is not to be quoted or referred to, in whole or in part, in the Registration Statement or Prospectus or in any literature used in connection with the sale of securities."

Plaintiffs may not take advantage of any undertakings or representations in this letter. If they exceeded the normal scope of an S–1 review (a question which I do not now decide) that is a matter which relates only to the crossclaims which defendants have asserted against each other and which I have postponed for determination at a later date.

The 1960 Audit

Peat, Marwick's work was in general charge of a member of the firm, Cummings, and more immediately in charge of Peat, Marwick's manager, Logan. Most of the actual work was performed by a senior accountant, Berardi, who had junior assistants, one of whom was Kennedy.

Berardi was then about thirty years old. He was not yet a C.P.A. He had had no previous experience with the bowling industry. This was his first job as a senior accountant. He could hardly have been given a more difficult assignment.

After obtaining a little background information on BarChris by talking to Logan and reviewing Peat, Marwick's work papers on its 1959 audit, Berardi examined the results of test checks of BarChris's accounting procedures which one of the junior accountants had made, and he prepared an "internal control questionnaire" and an "audit program." Thereafter, for a few days subsequent to December 30, 1960, he inspected BarChris's inventories and examined certain alley construction. Finally, on January 13, 1961, he began his auditing work which he carried on substantially continuously until it was completed on

February 24, 1961. Toward the close of the work, Logan reviewed it and made various comments and suggestions to Berardi.

It is unnecessary to recount everything that Berardi did in the course of the audit. We are concerned only with the evidence relating to what Berardi did or did not do with respect to those items which I have found to have been incorrectly reported in the 1960 figures in the prospectus. More narrowly, we are directly concerned only with such of those items as I have found to be material.

Capitol Lanes

First and foremost is Berardi's failure to discover that Capitol Lanes had not been sold. This error affected both the sales figure and the liability side of the balance sheet. Fundamentally, the error stemmed from the fact that Berardi never realized that Heavenly Lanes and Capitol were two different names for the same alley. In the course of his audit, Berardi was shown BarChris's contract file. He examined the contracts in the file and made a list of them. The file must have included a contract with an outside purchaser for Heavenly Lanes, although no such contract was ever produced at the trial, for Berardi included Heavenly on his list. Apparently there was no contract in the file for a lane named Capitol because that name did not appear on Berardi's list.

Kircher also made a list of jobs. Heavenly was on his list. Capitol was not. Berardi compared the two lists and satisfied himself that he had the proper jobs to be taken into account. Berardi assumed that Heavenly was to be treated like any other completed job. He included it in all his computations.

The evidence is conflicting as to whether BarChris's officers expressly informed Berardi that Heavenly and Capitol were the same thing and that BarChris was operating Capitol and had not sold it. I find that they did not so inform him.

Berardi did become aware that there were references here and there in BarChris's records to something called Capitol Lanes. He also knew that there were indications that at some time BarChris might operate an alley of that name. He read the minutes of the board of directors' meeting of November 22, 1960 which recited that:

> " * * * the Chairman recommended that the Corporation operate Capitol Lanes, 271 Main Street, East Haven, Connecticut, through a corporation which would be a subsidiary of Sanpark Realty Corp."

The minutes further recorded that:

> " * * * it was unanimously agreed that the officers of the Corporation exercise their discretion as to operating Capitol Lanes through the aforesaid subsidiary on an experimental basis."

The junior accountant Kennedy, read the minute book of Capitol Lanes, Inc., a Connecticut corporation organized in December 1960. The book contained a certificate of incorporation which empowered the corporation, among many other things, to own and manage bowling alleys. There was no minute in the book, however, that indicated that the corporation actually did own or manage one.

Berardi knew from various BarChris records that Capitol Lanes, Inc., was paying rentals to Talcott. Also, a Peat, Marwick work paper bearing Kennedy's initials recorded that Capitol Lanes, Inc. held certain insurance policies, including a fire insurance policy on "contents," a workman's compensation and a public liability policy. Another Peat, Marwick work paper also bearing Kennedy's initials recorded that Capitol Lanes, Inc. had $1,000 in a fund in Connecticut. A note on this paper read:

"Traced to disbursements book—advanced for operation of alley—not expensed at 12/31/60."

Logan's written comments upon the audit contained an entry reading as follows:

"When talking to Ted Kircher in latter part of '60 he indicated one subsidiary is leasing alley built by BarChris—the profit on this job should be eliminated as its ownership is within the affiliated group."

Opposite this note is an entry by Berardi reading as follows:

"Properties sold to others by affiliates. Capitol Lanes is paying currently lease rentals which amount to a lease purchase plan."

This note is somewhat ambiguous. If by "others" Berardi meant outside buyers, then it would seem that he should have accounted in some way for this sale, which he did not do. Presumably, by "others" he meant "other affiliates." Hence, he regarded the transaction, whatever he thought it to have been, as an intercompany one. Apparently Logan so understood Berardi's explanation.

Berardi testified that he inquired of Russo about Capitol Lanes and that Russo told him that Capitol Lanes, Inc. was going to operate an alley some day but as yet it had no alley. Berardi testified that he understood that the alley had not been built and that he believed that the rental payments were on vacant land.

I am not satisfied with this testimony. If Berardi did hold this belief, he should not have held it. The entries as to insurance and as to "operation of alley" should have alerted him to the fact that an alley existed. He should have made further inquiry on the subject. It is apparent that Berardi did not understand this transaction.

In any case, he never identified this mysterious Capitol with the Heavenly Lanes which he had included in his sales and profit figures. The vital question is whether he failed to make a reasonable investigation which, if he had made it, would have revealed the truth.

Certain accounting records of BarChris, which Berardi testified he did not see, would have put him on inquiry. One was a job cost ledger card for job no. 6036, the job number which Berardi put on his own sheet for Heavenly Lanes. This card read "Capitol Theatre (Heavenly)." In addition, two accounts receivable cards each showed both names on the same card, Capitol and Heavenly. Berardi testified that he looked at the accounts receivable records but that he did not see these particular cards. He testified that he did not look on the job cost ledger cards because he took the costs from another record, the costs register.

The burden of proof on this issue is on Peat, Marwick. Although the question is a rather close one, I find that Peat, Marwick has not sustained that burden. Peat, Marwick has not proved that Berardi made a reasonable investigation as far as Capitol Lanes was concerned and that his ignorance of the true facts was justified.

Howard Lanes Annex

Berardi also failed to discover that this alley was not sold. Here the evidence is much scantier. Berardi saw a contract for this alley in the contract file. No one told him that it was to be leased rather than sold. There is no evidence to indicate that any record existed which would have put him on notice. I find that his investigation was reasonable as to this item.

* * *

This disposes of the inaccuracies in the 1960 sales figures. I turn now to the errors in the current assets which involve four items: cash, reserve for Federal Lanes, factors' reserves and Howard Lanes Annex, which latter I have already covered.

As to cash, Berardi properly obtained a confirmation from the bank as to BarChris's cash balance on December 31, 1960. He did not know that part of this balance had been temporarily increased by the deposit of reserves returned by Talcott to BarChris conditionally for a limited time. I do not believe that Berardi reasonably should have known this. Although Peat, Marwick's work papers record the fact that these reserves were returned, there was nothing to indicate that the payment was conditional. Russo obviously did not reveal this fact. It would not be reasonable to require Berardi to examine all of BarChris's correspondence files when he had no reason to suspect any irregularity.

* * *

As to factors' reserves, it is hard to understand how Berardi could have treated this item as entirely a current asset when it was obvious that most of the reserves would not be released within one year. If Berardi was unaware of that fact, he should have been aware of it.

The net result, as far as current assets are concerned, is that Peat, Marwick is responsible for the errors as to reserves but not for those involving the cash item and the receivable from Howard Lanes Annex.

* * *

The S–1 Review

The purpose of reviewing events subsequent to the date of a certified balance sheet (referred to as an S–1 review when made with reference to a registration statement) is to ascertain whether any material change has occurred in the company's financial position which should be disclosed in order to prevent the balance sheet figures from being misleading. The scope of such a review, under generally accepted auditing standards, is limited. It does not amount to a complete audit.

Peat, Marwick prepared a written program for such a review. I find that this program conformed to generally accepted auditing standards. Among other things, it required the following:

"1. Review minutes of stockholders, directors and committees * * *.

"2. Review latest interim financial statements and compare with corresponding statements of preceding year. Inquire regarding significant variations and changes.

* * *

"4. Review the more important financial records and inquire regarding material transactions not in the ordinary course of business and any other significant items.

* * *

"6. Inquire as to changes in material contracts * * *.

* * *

"10. Inquire as to any significant bad debts or accounts in dispute for which provisions has not been made.

* * *

"14. Inquire as to * * * newly discovered liabilities, direct or contingent * * *."

Berardi made the S–1 review in May 1961. He devoted a little over two days to it, a total of 20½ hours. He did not discover any of the errors or omissions pertaining to the state of affairs in 1961 which I have previously discussed at length, all of which were material. The question is whether, despite his failure to find out anything, his investigation was reasonable within the meaning of the statute.

What Berardi did was to look at a consolidating trial balance as of March 31, 1961 which had been prepared by BarChris, compare it with the audited December 31, 1960 figures, discuss with Trilling certain unfavorable developments which the comparison disclosed, and read certain minutes. He did not examine any "important financial records" other than the trial balance. As to minutes, he read only what minutes Birnbaum gave him, which consisted only of the board of directors' minutes of BarChris. He did not read such minutes as there were of the executive committee. He did not know that there was an executive committee, hence he did not discover that Kircher had notes of executive committee minutes which had not been written up. He did not read the minutes of any subsidiary.

In substance, what Berardi did is similar to what Grant and Ballard did. He asked questions, he got answers which he considered satisfactory, and he did nothing to verify them. For example, he obtained from Trilling a list of contracts. The list included Yonkers and Bridge. Since Berardi did not read the minutes of subsidiaries, he did not learn that Yonkers and Bridge were intercompany sales. The list also included Woonsocket and the six T–Bowl jobs, Moravia Road, Milford, Groton, North Attleboro, Odenton and Severna Park. Since Berardi did not look at any contract documents, and since he was unaware of the executive committee minutes of March 18, 1961 (at that time embodied only in Kircher's notes), he did not learn that BarChris had no contracts for these jobs. Trilling's list did not set forth contract prices for them, although it did for Yonkers, Bridge and certain others. This did not arouse Berardi's suspicion.

Berardi noticed that there had been an increase in notes payable by BarChris. Trilling admitted to him that BarChris was "a bit slow" in paying its bills. Berardi recorded in his notes of his review that BarChris was in a "tight cash position." Trilling's explanation was that BarChris was experiencing "some temporary difficulty."

Berardi had no conception of how tight the cash position was. He did not discover that BarChris was holding up checks in substantial amounts because there was no money in the bank to cover them.[27] He did not know of the loan from Manufacturers Trust Company or of the officers' loans. Since he never read the prospectus, he was not even aware that there had ever been any problem about loans from officers.

During the 1960 audit Berardi had obtained some information from factors, not sufficiently detailed even then, as to delinquent notes. He made no inquiry of factors about this in his S–1 review. Since he knew nothing about Kircher's notes of the executive committee meetings, he did not learn that the delinquency situation had grown worse. He was content with Trilling's assurance that no liability theretofore contingent had become direct.

Apparently the only BarChris officer with whom Berardi communicated was Trilling. He could not recall making any inquiries of Russo, Vitolo or Pugliese. As to Kircher, Berardi's testimony was self-contradictory. At one point he said that he had inquired of Kircher and at another he said that he could not recall making any such inquiry.

There had been a material change for the worse in BarChris's financial position. That change was sufficiently serious so that the failure to disclose it made the 1960 figures misleading. Berardi did not discover it. As far as results were concerned, his S–1 review was useless.

Accountants should not be held to a standard higher than that recognized in their profession. I do not do so here. Berardi's review did not come up to that standard. He did not take some of the steps which Peat, Marwick's written program prescribed. He did not spend an adequate amount of time on a task of this magnitude. Most important of all, he was too easily satisfied with glib answers to his inquiries.

This is not to say that he should have made a complete audit. But there were enough danger signals in the materials which he did examine to require some further investigation on his part. Generally accepted accounting standards required such further investigation under these circumstances. It is not always sufficient merely to ask questions.

Here again, the burden of proof is on Peat, Marwick. I find that that burden has not been satisfied. I conclude that Peat, Marwick has not established its due diligence defense.

* * *

Defendants' motions to dismiss this action, upon which decision was reserved at the trial, are denied. Motions made at various times during the trial to strike certain testimony are also denied, except in so far as such motions pertain to evidence relating to the issues still undecided.

Pursuant to Rule 52(a), this opinion constitutes the court's findings of fact and conclusions of law with respect to the issues determined herein.

So ordered.

---

27. One of these checks was a check to the order of Peat, Marwick in the amount of $3,000. It was dated April 4, 1961. It was deposited by Peat, Marwick on May 29, 1961.

In re Software Toolworks Inc.

United States Court of Appeals, Ninth Circuit, 1994.
50 F.3d 615.

OPINION

■ CYNTHIA HOLCOMB HALL, CIRCUIT JUDGE.

In July 1990, Software Toolworks, Inc., a producer of software for personal computers and Nintendo game systems, conducted a secondary public offering of common stock at $18.50 a share, raising more than $71 million. After the offering, the market price of Toolworks' shares declined steadily until, on October 11, 1990, the stock was trading at $5.40 a share. At that time, Toolworks issued a press release announcing substantial losses and the share price dropped another fifty-six percent to $2.375.

The next day, several investors ("the plaintiffs") filed a class action alleging that Toolworks, auditor Deloitte & Touche ("Deloitte"), and underwriters Montgomery Securities and PaineWebber, Inc. ("the Underwriters") had issued a false and misleading prospectus and registration statement in violation of sections 11 and 12(2) of the Securities Act of 1933 ("the 1933 Act") and had knowingly defrauded and assisted in defrauding investors in violation of section 10(b) and Rule 10b–5 of the Securities Exchange Act of 1934 ("the 1934 Act"). Specifically, the plaintiffs claimed that the defendants had (1) falsified audited financial statements for fiscal 1990 by reporting as revenue sales to original equipment manufacturers ("OEMs") with whom Toolworks had no binding agreements, (2) fabricated large consignment sales in order for Toolworks to meet financial projections for the first quarter of fiscal 1991 ("the June quarter"), and (3) lied to the Securities Exchange Commission ("SEC") in response to inquiries made before the registration statement became effective.

Toolworks and its officers quickly settled with the plaintiffs for $26.5 million. After the completion of discovery, the district court granted summary judgment in favor of the Underwriters on all claims and in favor of Deloitte on all claims other than one cause of action under section 11. *See In re Software Toolworks, Inc. Sec. Litig.*, 789 F.Supp. 1489 (N.D.Cal.1992) [*Toolworks I*]. The district court held that (1) the Underwriters had established a "due diligence" defense under sections 11 and 12(2) as a matter of law, *id.* at 1494–98. (2) Deloitte had made no material misrepresentations or omissions, other than the OEM revenue statements, on which liability under sections 11 and 12(2) could attach, *id.* at 1510–11, and (3) the plaintiffs had failed to establish that any defendant acted with scienter, a necessary element of liability under section 10(b), *id.* at 1498–1510.

Because section 11's "reasonable investigation" standard is similar, if not identical, to section 12(2)'s "reasonable care" standard, *see Sanders v. John Nuveen & Co.*, 619 F.2d 1222, 1228 (7th Cir.1980), *cert. denied,* 450 U.S. 1005, 101 S.Ct. 1719, 68 L.Ed.2d 210 (1981), the analysis of each on summary judgment is the same, *see Weinberger v. Jackson,* [1990–91] Fed.Sec.L.Rep. (CCH) ¶ 95,693 at 98,255, 1990 WL 260676 (N.D.Cal.1990). In determining whether an underwriter meets the due diligence test under either provision, "the standard of reasonableness shall be that required of a prudent man in the management of his own property." 15 U.S.C. § 77k(c): *see* 17 C.F.R. § 230.176 (factors affecting the reasonableness of an investigation under section 11). Thus, due diligence is, "[i]n effect, * * * a negligence standard." *Ernst & Ernst v. Hochfelder,* 425 U.S. 185, 208, 96 S.Ct. 1375, 1388, 47 L.Ed.2d 668 (1976).

The district court held that the Underwriters had established due diligence as a matter of law and, accordingly, issued summary judgment against the plaintiffs on the section 11 and 12(2) claims. On appeal, the plaintiffs contend that due diligence is so fact-intensive that summary judgment is inappropriate even where underlying historical facts are undisputed. The plaintiffs further contend that, in any event, the district court erred by ignoring disputed issues of material fact in this case. We hold that, in appropriate cases, summary judgment may resolve due diligence issues but that, in this case, the district court erred by granting summary judgment in favor of the Underwriters on several claims.

The plaintiffs first argue that "due diligence * * * [and] the reasonableness of the defendants' investigation * * * is a question for the jury, even on undisputed facts." We agree, of course, that summary judgment is generally an inappropriate way to decide questions of reasonableness because "the jury's unique competence in applying the 'reasonable man' standard is thought ordinarily to preclude summary judgment." TSC Indus. v. Northway, Inc., 426 U.S. 438, 450 n. 12, 96 S.Ct. 2126, 2133 n. 12, 48 L.Ed.2d 757 (1976). We have, however, squarely rejected the contention that "reasonableness is *always* a question of fact which precludes summary judgment." West v. State Farm Fire & Casualty Co., 868 F.2d 348, 350 (9th Cir.1989) (emphasis added). Rather, reasonableness "becomes a question of law and loses its triable character if the undisputed facts leave no room for a reasonable difference of opinion." *Id.* Accordingly, "reasonableness [is] appropriate for determination on [a] motion for summary judgment when only one conclusion about the conduct's reasonableness is possible." *Id.* at 351. *See TSC Indus.*, 426 U.S. at 450, 96 S.Ct. at 2133 (summary judgment proper where "reasonable minds cannot differ") (internal quotation omitted).

Courts therefore may resolve questions of due diligence in those cases where no rational jury could conclude that the defendant had not acted reasonably. Several courts have, in fact, done just that. *See Weinberger,* ¶ 95.693 at 98,255 (summary judgment in favor of underwriters); *In re Avant–Garde Computing, Inc. Sec. Litig.,* No. 85–4149 (AET), 1989 WL 103625 at *7–*9 (D.N.J. Sept.5, 1989) (summary judgment in favor of outside director); *Laven v. Flanagan,* 695 F.Supp. 800, 811–12 (D.N.J.1988) (summary judgment in favor of outside directors); cf. *Bamco 15 v. Buchanan Residential Real Estate Ltd. Partnership,* [1986–87] Fed.Sec.L.Rep. (CCH) ¶ 93,062 at 95.285–86, 1986 WL 15333 (S.D.N.Y.1986) (summary judgment in favor of *plaintiff* where defendant produced no evidence of due diligence).

The district court, therefore, properly held that "the adequacy of due diligence may be decided on summary judgment when the underlying historical facts are undisputed." *Toolworks I,* 789 F.Supp. at 1496.

The plaintiffs next assert that a material issue of fact exists regarding whether the Underwriters diligently investigated, or needed to investigate, Toolworks' recognition of OEM revenue on its financial statements. The plaintiffs claim that the Underwriters "blindly rel[ied]" on Deloitte in spite of numerous "red flags" indicating that the OEM entries were incorrect and that, as a result, the district court erred in granting summary judgment.

An underwriter need not conduct due diligence into the "expertised" parts of a prospectus, such as certified financial statements. Rather, the underwriter need only show that it "had no reasonable ground to believe, and did not believe * * * that the statements therein were untrue or that there was an omission to state a material fact required to be stated therein or necessary to make the statements therein not misleading." 15 U.S.C. § 77k(b)(3)(c); *see WOW II*, 35 F.3d at 1421. The issue on appeal, therefore, is whether the Underwriters' reliance on the expertised financial statements was reasonable as a matter of law.

As the first "red flag," the plaintiffs point to Toolworks' "backdated" contract with Hyosung, a Korean manufacturer. During the fourth quarter of fiscal 1990, Toolworks recognized $1.7 million in revenue from an OEM contract with Hyosung. In due diligence, the Underwriters discovered a memorandum from Hyosung to Toolworks stating that Hyosung had "backdated" the agreement to permit Toolworks to recognize revenue in fiscal 1990. [ER 283:11]. The plaintiffs claim that, after discovering this memorandum, the Underwriters could no longer rely on Deloitte because the accountants had approved revenue recognition for the transaction.

If the Underwriters had done nothing more, the plaintiffs' contention might be correct. The plaintiffs, however, ignore the significant steps taken by the Underwriters after discovery of the Hyosung memorandum to ensure the accuracy of Deloitte's revenue recognition. The Underwriters first confronted Deloitte, which explained that it was proper for Toolworks to book revenue in fiscal 1990 because the company had contracted with Hyosung in March, even though the firms did not document the agreement until April. [ER 283:12–13]. The Underwriters then insisted that Deloitte reconfirm, in writing, the Hyosung agreement and Toolworks' other OEM contracts. [ER 283:12–13]. Finally, the Underwriters contacted other accounting firms to verify Deloitte's OEM revenue accounting methods. [ER 278:13].

Thus, with regard to the Hyosung agreement, the Underwriters did not "blindly rely" on Deloitte. The district court correctly held that, as a matter of law, the Underwriters' "investigation of the OEM business was reasonable." *Toolworks I*, 789 F.Supp. at 1498.

The plaintiffs next assert that the Underwriters could not reasonably rely on Deloitte's financial statements because Toolworks' counsel, Riordan & McKinzie, refused to issue an opinion letter stating that the OEM agreements were binding contracts. This contention has no merit because, contrary to the plaintiffs' assertions, Toolworks had never requested the law firm to render such an opinion. [ER 317/Sylvester:36–42]. The plaintiffs attempt to infer wrongdoing in such circumstances is patently unreasonable. The district court correctly granted summary judgment in favor of the Underwriters on this issue.

Finally, the plaintiffs assert that, by reading the agreements, the Underwriters should have realized that Toolworks had improperly recognized revenue. Specifically, the plaintiffs claim that several of the contracts were contingent and that it was facially apparent that Toolworks might not receive any revenue under them. As the Underwriters explain, this contention misconstrues the nature of a due diligence investigation:

> [The Underwriters] reviewed the contracts to verify that there was a written agreement for each OEM contract mentioned in the Prospectus— not to analyze the propriety of revenue recognition, which was the responsibility of [Deloitte]. Given the complexity surrounding software licensing revenue recognition, it is absurd to suggest that, in perusing Toolworks' contracts, [the Underwriters] should have concluded that [Deloitte] w[as] wrong, particularly when the OEM's provided written confirmation.

We recently confirmed precisely this point in a case involving analogous facts: "[T]he defendants relied on Deloitte's *accounting decisions* (to recognize revenue) about the sales. Those expert decisions, which underlie the plaintiffs' attack on the financial statements, represent precisely the type of 'certified' information on which section 11 permits non-experts to rely." *WOW II,* 35 F.3d at 1421; [Citation omitted.]

Thus, because the Underwriters' reliance on Deloitte was reasonable under the circumstances, the district court correctly granted summary judgment on this issue. *See Toolworks I,* 789 F.Supp. at 1498 ("Given the complexity of the accounting issues, the Underwriters were entitled to rely on Deloitte's expertise.").

The plaintiffs next attack the Underwriters' due diligence efforts for the period after Toolworks filed a preliminary prospectus and before the effective date of the offering.[2] During this time, several significant events transpired. First, *Barron's* published a negative article about Toolworks that questioned the company's "aggressive accounting." [ER 289/22]. Second, in response to the *Barron's* article, the SEC initiated a review of Toolworks' prospectus. [ER 341/Weeks:32–33]. Third, Toolworks sent two letters responding to the SEC. And, fourth, Toolworks booked several consignment sales that made the company appear to have a prosperous quarter, thereby ensuring success of the offering.

The district court held that the Underwriters satisfied their due diligence obligations during this period primarily by relying on Toolworks' representations to the SEC. *Id.* at 1497–98. For the following reasons, we conclude that disputed issues of material fact exist regarding the Underwriters' efforts and, accordingly, we reverse and remand for a trial on the merits.

The plaintiffs first contend that the Underwriters should have done more to investigate the *Barron's* allegations of slumping sales and improper accounting. The Underwriters established, however, that they contacted a representative of Nintendo and several large retailers to confirm the strength of the market in response to the *Barron's* article. Moreover, as explained above, the Underwriters' reliance on Deloitte's accounting decisions was reasonable as a matter of law. Summary judgment was appropriate on this issue.

b.

Next, the plaintiffs raise the issue of Toolworks' July 4, 1990 letter to the SEC, which described the company's June quarter performance. [ER 316/2006]. In the letter, Toolworks represented that, although preliminary financial data was not available, Toolworks anticipated revenue for the quarter between $21 and $22 million. The plaintiffs claim that Toolworks deliberately falsified these estimates and that the Underwriters knew of this deceit.

The Underwriters claim that they were not involved in drafting the July 4 SEC letter and that, as a result, they have no responsibility for its contents. The plaintiffs presented evidence, however, that the letter was a joint effort of

---

2. The Underwriters' contention that the events of this period are inapplicable to sections 11 and 12(2) liability is clearly incorrect. Both statutory provisions require disclosure of information needed in order to make a prospectus truthful and not misleading. As the Underwriters' own experts testified, poor first quarter earnings prior to the effective date of the offering would definitely constitute material information and would have to be disclosed.

all professionals working on the offering, including the Underwriters. In fact, a Riordan & McKinzie partner specifically testified that, "[w]hen the letter finally went to the SEC, all parties had been involved in the process of creating it. There had been conference calls discussing it and comments and changes made by a lot of different members of the working group." [ER 317/Weeks:40–41]. Others similarly testified that the Underwriters were actively involved in discussions of how to respond to the SEC's inquiries regarding the June quarter. [*See* ER 317/Barker:23–24; ER 317/Sylvester:18–19].

The Underwriters argue that, even if they participated in initial discussions about the letter, they never knew that Toolworks' financial data actually was available and that, as a result, they could not have known that the letter (and the prospectus) were misleading. Given the Underwriters participation in drafting both documents, however, we think this is an unresolved issue of material fact. A reasonable factfinder could infer that, as members of the drafting group, the Underwriters had access to all information that was available and deliberately chose to conceal the truth. We therefore hold that summary judgment was inappropriate on this issue.

c.

After suffering lagging sales in the first two months of the June quarter, Toolworks booked several large consignment sales in late June, the quarter's final month, thereby enabling the company to meet its earning projections. [ER 299/300:MB10048–49; ER 289/33; ER 289/502; ER 289/505]. Toolworks later had to reverse more than $7 million of these sales in its final financial statements for the quarter. [ER 322:20–26]. The plaintiffs presented evidence that the Underwriters knew that Toolworks had performed poorly in April, that Toolworks had no orders for the month as of June 8, that the June quarter is traditionally the slowest of the year for Nintendo sales, and that the late June sales accounted for more revenue than the cumulative total of Toolworks' Nintendo sales for the prior two and a half months. For its due diligence investigation of these sales, however, the Underwriters did little more than rely on Toolworks' assurances that the transactions were legitimate. A reasonable inference from this evidence is that Toolworks fabricated the June sales to ensure that the offering would proceed and that the Underwriters knew, or should have known, of this fraud. As a result, we conclude that summary judgment regarding the Underwriters' diligence on this issue was also inappropriate. *See* Feit v. Leasco Data Processing Equip. Corp., 332 F.Supp. 544, 582 (E.D.N.Y.1971) ("Tacit reliance on management is unacceptable: the underwriters must play devil's advocate.").

Thus, we hold that the district court properly granted summary judgment in favor of the Underwriters on the section 11 and 12(2) issues regarding their due diligence investigation into Toolworks' Nintendo sales practices and description of OEM revenue. The district court erred, however, by granting summary judgment on the section 11 and 12(2) claims regarding the July 4 SEC letter and Toolworks' June quarter results. We remand for a trial on the merits of those claims.

THE "DUE DILIGENCE" DEFENSE UNDER § 11

How Much Diligence is Due?[1] So far as the issuer is concerned, the only defense available under § 11, if a material misstatement or omission is shown,

---

1. *See* 17 Kan. L. Rev. 651 (1969) from which this heading is borrowed.

is to prove that the plaintiff at the time of his acquisition of the security knew of the untruth or omission, a defense which is available to all defendants. Obviously, this theoretical defense is of no practical significance in this age of class actions, because the defense could never be proven as to more than a handful of the numerous plaintiffs, if it can be proven as to any. All defendants other than the issuer, however, have the defense that they had, "after reasonable investigation, reasonable grounds to believe and did believe" that the statements were true and complete, which is commonly referred to as the "due diligence defense." Under this requirement, mere passive ignorance is wholly insufficient. There must be an affirmative belief based upon reasonable grounds *and upon reasonable investigation*. It was stated by the Committee report at the time of the enactment of the 1933 Act that this casts a burden of "competence as well as innocence" upon the persons involved in an issue of securities.[2] While *Escott v. BarChris* has provided the foundation of much of the law of due diligence since 1968, several recent developments have amplified its basic lessons.

Outside Directors: This phrase refers to directors who are not employed by the issuer and who normally have other full time occupations. In *BarChris* the court held that while the outside director can delegate a duty of investigation, he or she is liable if the person to whom this duty was delegated does not perform it properly.

BarChris also held two outside directors (a lawyer and an investment banker) with relevant areas of expertise to a higher standard than that of a run-of-the-mill outside director. The court rejected the contention that the law firm by undertaking the preparation of the registration statement "expertised" the entire prospectus. The court also concluded that the investment banker was not liable individually as an underwriter but only in conjunction with his firm. But it was held that the attorney or underwriter by undertaking the laboring oar in the preparation of the registration statement the attorney or underwriter made themselves liable *as directors* when their performance fell short of what the court considered proper for an attorney or investment banker engaged in that task. In other words, they were apparently judged by the standards applicable to their professions, rather than those which might be applied to a director who had no expertise in the registration process and did not undertake to oversee compliance with the requirements.

Similarly in Feit v. Leasco Data Processing Equip. Corp.,[3] Judge Weinstein concluded that Hodes, a partner in a law firm that represented the issuer, was so intimately involved in the preparation of the registration statement "that to treat him as anything but an insider would involve a gross distortion of the realities of [the issuer's] management."

Subsequent cases have been more kind to outside directors. In Laven v. Flanagan,[4] for example, outside directors' reliance on representations of management could not be characterized as unreasonable, particularly when confirmed by investigations conducted by Price Waterhouse and Merrill Lynch. The court noted: "Their work was imperfect, to the regret of plaintiff and certainly, in light of its $57.3 million dollar loss, to Curtiss–Wright. But their

---

2. H.R. Rep. No. 85, 73d Cong., 1st Sess. 9 (1933).

3. 332 F. Supp. 544, 576 (E.D.N.Y. 1971).

4. 695 F. Supp. 800 (D.N.J.1988).

activities were a far cry from the passive and total reliance on company management that defeated the due diligence defense in *Escott v. BarChris* ... As such, we must deem it to have been a reasonable effort to seek verification of the truth of the registration statement."[5]

In Weinberger v. Jackson,[6] the court seemingly went further when it wrote:

> Since Valentine was an outside director, he was not obliged to conduct an independent investigation into the accuracy of all the statements contained in the registration statement. He could rely upon the reasonable representations of management, if his own conduct and level of inquiry were reasonable under the circumstances. He was reasonably familiar with the company's business and operations. He regularly attended board meetings at which the board discussed every aspect of the company's business. And he reviewed the company's financial statements. He was familiar with the company's development of its new product lines. He was involved with various company decisions. He reviewed six drafts of the registration statement and saw nothing suspicious or inconsistent with the knowledge that he had acquired as a director. And he discussed certain aspects of the registration statement with management.

> With respect to the alleged misrepresentations about shipment of the lines of products, he could not reasonably have noticed any ambiguity in the phrase "in quantity" in light of his understanding of the company's business and its practice of increasing production from the time a new model is first introduced. With respect to alleged misrepresentations regarding the availability of software, Valentine knew what the prospectus stated, that is, that software was provided by outside vendors, and that application software might not be available for new models when they are first introduced.

> Plaintiffs argue that Valentine did not make specific inquiries of the company's management with respect to the representations contained in the prospectus. But he had no duty to do so as long as the prospectus statements were consistent with the knowledge of the company which he had reasonably acquired in his position as director. He was also given comfort by the fact that the prospectus and the information in it were reviewed by underwriters, counsel and accountants. This met the standards of due diligence and reasonable inquiry.

Inside Directors and Officers: These defendants were held by the court in *BarChris* to a very high standard of diligence. The court in *Feit v. Leasco Data Processing* added:

> Inside directors with intimate knowledge of corporate affairs and of the particular transactions will be expected to make a more complete investigation and have more extensive knowledge of facts supporting or contradicting inclusions in the registration statements than outside directors.[7]

5. Id. at 812.

6. 1990–1991 Fed. Sec. L. Rep. (CCH) ¶ 95,693 at 98,256 (N.D. Cal. 1990).

7. 332 F. Supp. at 578.

This demanding due diligence standard for inside or employee directors and officers has endured because of their familiarity with corporate operations and records.[8]

Underwriters: The court in the *BarChris* case indicated that the underwriters will also be held to a very high standard of diligence, although perhaps not as great as that of the "inside" defendants, because the public looks to them for an independent, disinterested investigation of the business, and for advice regarding the issue.

The members of the underwriting syndicate other than the managing or so-called "lead" underwriter typically do not undertake an investigation of the issuer at all, but rely entirely upon the managing underwriter to do an investigations for them. There should be no doubt that the syndicate members are entitled to rely upon his investigation if it in fact complies with the statutory requirements.[9] Conversely, however, it is fairly inferable from the *BarChris* opinion that if the performance falls short, they are equally liable. Whether the underwriting syndicate might have some action over against the managing underwriter for this failure is debatable, although the typical "agreement among underwriters" attempts to negate any fiduciary relationship between the managing underwriter and the other syndicate members.

The lurking fear that perhaps the other members of the underwriting syndicate will not be permitted to rely upon the investigation by the managing underwriter has led to a ritual known as the "due diligence meeting." Shortly before the effective date of the registration statement, representatives of all of the underwriters gather in a room with officers of the issuer, ostensibly to question the officers about the company's affairs as disclosed in the registration statement. In fact, the questions are more likely to be about matters which are not disclosed in the registration statement, but which may be useful in selling the issue, such as: "What is the projection for next quarter's earnings?" It would seem that this meeting, which is frequently a pure formality, is not going to save the other underwriters if the managing underwriter has failed in his duty of investigation; on the other hand, if he had performed that duty, it would seem to be unnecessary.

In *Software Toolworks*, the court held that an underwriter need not conduct due diligence into the "expertised" parts of a prospectus such as certified financial statements if the underwriter had no reasonable grounds to believe the expertised statements were misleading.[10] In this case, the Ninth Circuit found a "red flag," a "backdated" agreement allegedly to permit Toolworks to recognize income in an earlier year. The underwriter defendant was entitled to summary judgment because the underwriter confronted the accountant on this issue, insisted that the accountant reconfirm that the income recognition was proper, and the underwriter contacted other accounting firms to verify the appropriateness of the Toolworks' accountant's revenue recognition methods.

The underwriter was *not* entitled to summary judgment, however, with regard to the period after a preliminary prospectus was filed until the effective

---

8. *See* Kitchens v. U.S. Shelter, 1988–1989 Fed. Sec. L. Rep. (CCH) ¶ 93,920 at 90,155 (D.S.C. 1988).

9. *See, e.g.,* Weinberger v. Jackson, 1990–1991 Fed. Sec. L. Rep. (CCH) ¶ 95,693 at 98,255 (N.D. Cal. 1990).

10. 50 F.3d at 623.

date when the underwriters did little more than rely on Toolworks' assurances that specified sales transactions were legitimate.[11]

Further guidance regarding an underwriters' due diligence was provided in International Rectifier Sec. Litig.,[12] where the court wrote:

[The] following are factors this court considered in determining the "reasonableness" of the Underwriters' diligence:

1. whether the Underwriters were familiar with IR's finances, management, and operations [citations omitted];

2. whether the Underwriters possessed knowledge of the industry in which IR is involved [citations omitted];

3. whether the Underwriters conducted interviews of IR's employees [citations omitted];

4. whether the Underwriters conducted interviews of and/or confirmed data with IR's customers or other third parties [citations omitted].

5. whether the Underwriters obtained written verification from IR and/or outside accountants that the information contained in the prospectus was accurate [citation omitted].

"Experts" and Liability With Respect to "Expertised Portions" of the Registration Statement: An expert is liable under § 11 only with respect to those portions of a registration statement which are expressly stated to be made on his or her authority as an expert. The court in the *BarChris* case properly rejected the contentions that the accountants were liable for all of the figures in the registration statement, even those that were uncertified, and that the lawyer was liable for the entire statement because he or she wrote it. The investigation required of such an expert with respect to that portion for which he or she is responsible would certainly have to conform to the standards generally considered appropriate in his or her profession. The court in *BarChris* did not have to go further than this, because the court found that the accountants neither met those standards, nor indeed even complied with their own written procedures for an S–1 review. However, the *Simon* case[13] in the Second Circuit held that compliance with the standards of his profession would not necessarily insulate an accountant from even criminal prosecution, if the court considered them too lax; it would seem *a fortiori* not to insulate him from liability under § 11.

Subsequently, in Monroe v. Hughes,[14] the Ninth Circuit significantly added:

We have held that an accountant's good faith compliance with Generally Accepted Accounting Principles and Generally Accepted Auditing Standards discharges the accountant's professional obligation to act with reasonable care. *See* SEC v. Arthur Young & Co., 590 F.2d 785, 788–789 (9th Cir.1979). A corollary rule, however, is that compliance with GAAP and

11. Id. at 625–626. *See also* Endo v. Albertine, 863 F. Supp. 708, 731–733 (N.D.Ill. 1994) (questions of fact whether an underwriter was entitled to due diligence defenses); Glosser v. Cellcor Inc., 1994–1995 Fed. Sec. L. Rep. (CCH) ¶ 98,424 at 90,914 (Del. Ch. 1994) (question of fact whether defendant could prove due diligence defense).

12. 1997 Fed. Sec. L. Rep. (CCH) ¶ 99,-469 at 97,140 (C.D. Cal. 1997).

13. United States v. Simon, 425 F.2d 796 (2d Cir.1969), *cert. denied*, 397 U.S. 1006 (1970).

14. 31 F.3d 772 (9th Cir.1994).

GAAS do not immunize an accountant who consciously chooses not to disclose on a registration statement a known material fact.[15]

In *Hughes* the court declined to hold an accountant liable when there was compliance with General Accepted Accounting Principles, but there was no disclosure of deficiencies in internal accounting controls.[16]

An attorney who provides a legal opinion used in connection with a registration statement is an expert within the meaning of § 11.[17] Attorneys, in contrast, who are not acting as experts in the preparation of a registration statement are not liable under § 11.[18]

In 1982, when the Commission permitted disclosure of security ratings for debt and preferred stocks by nationally recognized statistical rating organizations, it adopted Rule 436(g) to exclude such ratings from § 11(a)(4).[19]

Earlier the Commission had adopted Rules 436(c)–(d). Rule 436(c) excludes an independent accountant's report on unaudited interim financial information (as defined in Rule 436(d)) from consideration as part of a registration statement "prepared or certified by an accountant or a report prepared or certified by an accountant within the meanings of sections 7 and 11 of the Act."

An incidental impact of § 11 with unique effect for auditors is to continue the auditor's responsibility until the effective date rather than only the date of the audit opinion. It is always possible that information available to the auditor at the opinion date might justify one audit opinion although additional information available at or near the effective date might then *require* a different opinion.[20]

With respect to an "expertised portion" of the registration statement, the burden of defense of all of the other defendants, except the expert himself and the issuer, is considerably relaxed. No investigation need be shown, and the defendant must only prove that he "had no reasonable ground to believe, and did not believe," that the statements were false. Thus passive ignorance is sufficient with respect to these statements, unless the defendant had some

---

15. Id. at 774.

16. An accountant can be held liable for notes to the financial statement to the extent that they are prepared or certified by him or her. In Endo v. Arthur Andersen & Co., S.C., 163 F.3d 463 (7th Cir.1999), the court declined to hold an accountant liable for the republication of a note made by a former auditor. This result was based on two primary reasons: (1) the accountant did not purport to certify that footnote and (2) the former accountant could be held liable. Cf. Cashman v. Coopers & Lybrand, 877 F. Supp. 425, 434–435 (N.D.Ill.1995) (accountant can be held liable for expertised materials in registration statement even if they were prepared by others); Danis v. USN Communications, Inc., 121 F. Supp. 2d 1183 (N.D.Ill. 2000)(an auditor can be held liable under § 11 unless the auditor establishes a due diligence defense).

17. American Continental Corp. Sec. Litig., 794 F. Supp. 1424, 1453 (D.Ariz.1992).

18. Ahern v. Gaussoin, 611 F. Supp. 1465, 1482 (D.Or.1985) (citing cases).

19. Sec. Act Rel. 6383, 24 SEC Dock. 1262, 1282–1283 (1982).

20. *See* R. James Gormley, Accountants' Professional Liability—A Ten Year Review, 29 Bus. Law. 1205, 1217 (1974).

In Glassman v. Computervision Corp., 90 F.3d 617, 628 (1st Cir.1996), the court summarized two similar points:

First, a failure to continue to investigate the company up to the effective date of the offering is likely to be a failure to do due diligence. [Citations omitted.] Second, it also may be a failure of due diligence to rely solely on management representations as to the state of the company where those representations can reasonably be verified. [Citations omitted.]

reason to question them. All of the defendants in *BarChris* were absolved of liability for the errors in the certified financial statements, except the accountants who certified them and the insiders who knew or should have known that they were false; but this was probably of small comfort to them, because they were all held liable for misstatements in other portions of the same prospectus.

PROBLEM 13–1

In March 2001 AmericasBank sold $480 million of subordinated debt on a Form S–3 registration statement. Form S–3 incorporates by reference the registrant's latest annual report on Form 10–K and subsequent periodic reports on Forms 10–Q and 8–K. Annual and periodic reports were prepared by AmericasBank management. The underwriting firm of Bixwell Golden was hired to be lead underwriter in the preparation of the Form S–3 in January 2001.

At the time banks in the geographic region where AmericasBank was located were experiencing relatively high bankruptcy rates as a result of a spate of commercial loan failures. Bixwell Golden asked its law firm of Navis Jones & Ito to conduct due diligence. Partner Sarah Jones worked with three associates over a two week period to distribute questionnaires to management; review prior SEC filings; review AmericasBank's material contracts; and minutes. All minutes were provided in a timely fashion except AmericasBank Executive Committee meeting minutes for 2000 which had not been typed up yet. Upon inquiry from Jones to AmericasBank CEO Ralph Smith, Jones was informed "there were no problems in the minutes, just an overworked staff."

Shortly after the March 2001 offering a federal depository institution regulator announced it had initiated a formal investigation of AmericasBank's recordkeeping because of concerns that there had not been appropriate evaluation of the collateral for its commercial loans in its home region.

AmericasBank's subordinated debt, which had been sold at $100 per bond, slumped to $86, and in May 2001 a Section 11 lawsuit was filed against: (1) the board of directors of AmericasBank; (2) the underwriter Bixwell Golden; and (3) Navis Jones & Ito.

During discovery the Executive Committee meeting minutes for 2000 were typed up. They revealed ongoing discussions between the Executive Committee (which included three inside directors, Ralph Smith; principal financial officer Paula Larsen; and executive vice president Harriet Zahn) and the federal depository institution regulator. The federal depository institution regulator had proposed a consent settlement in February 2001, which had been rejected by the Executive Committee that month. The Executive Committee meetings were not attended by the three long time outside directors who were attorney Sarah Jones and business executives Peter Quirk and Hazel Choi.

How should a court rule in a Section 11 lawsuit with respect to each of the defendants?

IS THERE A DIFFERENCE BETWEEN THE § 11 DUE DILIGENCE DEFENSE AND THE § 12(a)(2) REASONABLE CARE DEFENSE?

In Sanders v. John Nuveen & Co., Inc.,[1] the Seventh Circuit found no difference in the reasonable investigation required by § 11 and the § 12(a)(2) defense of reasonable care. The court stated in part:

---

1. 619 F.2d 1222 (7th Cir.1980), *cert. denied*, 450 U.S. 1005 (1981).

It is not at all clear that Congress intended to impose a higher standard of care under § 12(2). The difference in language appeared in the House bill and was retained in the Act as agreed to by the Joint Conference Committee and as passed by both Houses. *See* H.R. 5480, 73d Cong., 1st Sess. §§ 11 & 12 (1933), reprinted at 1 Legislative History, *supra*, Item 1 (bill as passed by both Houses), and 3 id., Items 25 & 26 (bill as presented to the House by its Committee on Interstate and Foreign Commerce and as originally passed by House). The Conference Committee report, in its discussion of the standard of liability imposed for a misleading registration statement, describes the standard adopted not as one of "reasonable investigation," but one of "reasonable care." H.R. Rep. No. 152, 73d Cong., 1st Sess. 26 (1933) (Conference Report), reprinted at 2 Legislative History, *supra*, Item 19. More specifically, Congress does not appear to have intended that a different standard apply to underwriters. Thus, the House Report draws no distinction between an underwriter's burden in the case of misleading statements in a prospectus, for which it can be liable only under § 12(2) and its § 11 duty to conduct a "reasonable investigation." H.R. Rep. No. 85, 73d Cong., 1st Sess. 9 (1933), reprinted at 2 Legislative History, *supra*, Item 18. The difference in language can be explained not as an attempt to impose different duties of care under §§ 11 and 12, but by the fact that § 12(2) imposes the duty on all sellers of securities, while § 11 imposes liability only on specified groups of persons having such a close relationship with the registration statement that the 1933 Act, before it was amended the following year, treated them as fiduciaries. *See* Securities Act of 1933, ch. 38, § 11(c), 48 Stat. 74, 83 (1933); Securities Exchange Act of 1934, ch. 404, § 206(c), 48 Stat. 881, 907 (1934). Thus the general duty of reasonable care, the specific requirements of which are determined by the circumstances of the case, was to be applied in § 11 only to persons who had a stronger connection with a registration statement than a seller necessarily has to a prospectus, so a more stringent articulation of the standard was appropriate.

In the circumstances of this case, the reasonable care standard required the reasonable investigation described in *Sanders II*. Since what constitutes reasonable care under § 12(2) depends upon the circumstances, we, of course, do not intimate that the duty of a seller under § 12(2) is always the same as that of an underwriter in a registration offering under § 11.[2]

The Supreme Court denied *certiorari*, but Justice Powell, joined by Justice Rehnquist, dissented on the ground that the lower court failed to appropriately distinguish the standards of care applicable under § 11 and what is now § 12(a)(2) (then § 12(2)) in John Nuveen & Co., Inc. v. Sanders.[3] Justice Powell wrote in part:

Section 11(a) of the 1933 Act imposes liability on certain persons for selling securities in a registered public offering pursuant to a materially false or misleading registration statement. A registered offering is the class of financial transactions for which Congress prescribed the most stringent regulation. The standard of care imposed on an underwriter is that it must have "had, after *reasonable investigation*, reasonable ground to believe and

---

2. Id. at 1228.   **3.** 450 U.S. 1005 (1981).

did believe" that the registration statement was accurate. Section 11(b)(3)(A) of the Act (emphasis added).

Liability in this case was not imposed on petitioner under § 11, but under § 12(2). Under the latter section, it is necessary for sellers to show only that they "did not know, and in the exercise of *reasonable care* could not have known," that their statements were false or misleading. (Emphasis added).

In providing standards of care under the 1933 Act, Congress thus used different language for different situations. "Reasonable *investigation*" is required for registered offerings under § 11, but nothing more than "mer[e] * * * 'reasonable *care*'" is required by § 12(2). W.O. Douglas & G.E. Bates, The Federal Securities Act of 1933, 43 Yale L.J. 173, 208 (1933). The difference in language is significant, because in the securities acts Congress has used its words with precision. *See, e.g.,* Ernst & Ernst v. Hochfelder, 425 U.S. 185, 198–201 (1976); Blue Chip Stamps v. Manor Drug Stores, 421 U.S. 723, 755, 756 (1975) (Powell J., concurring). "Investigation" commands a greater undertaking than "care." See W.O. Douglas & G.E. Bates, *supra,* at 208, n. 205.

In a brief filed in this case with the Court of Appeals, the SEC expressly stated that the standard of care under § 12 (2) is less demanding than that prescribed by § 11:

"[It] would be inconsistent with the statutory scheme to apply precisely the same standards to the scope of an underwriter's duty under Section 12(2) as the case law appropriately has applied to underwriters under Section 11. Because of the vital role played by an underwriter in the distribution of securities, and because the registration process is integral and important to the statutory scheme, we are of the view that a higher standard of care should be imposed on those actors who are critical to its proper operations. Since Congress has determined that registration is not necessary in certain defined situations, we believe that it would undermine the Congressional intent—that issuers and other persons should be relieved of registration—if the same degree of investigation were to be required to avoid potential liability whether or not a registration statement is required." Brief for SEC, [at 69, *Sanders III,* 554 F.2d 790 (1977)].

The Court of Appeals' opinion may be read as holding that petitioner's duty of "reasonable care" under § 12(2) required it independently to *investigate* the accuracy and completeness of the certified financial statements. It was customary, however—and in my view entirely reasonable—for petitioner to rely on these statements as accurately reflecting W & H's financial condition. Even under § 11 of the Act, an underwriter is explicitly absolved of the duty to investigate with respect to "any part of the registration statement purporting to be made on the authority of an expert" such as a certified accountant if "he had no reasonable ground to believe, and did not believe" that the information therein was misleading. § 11(b)(3)(c) of the Act; see § 11(a)(4). This provision is in the Act because, almost by definition, it *is* reasonable to rely on financial statements certified by public accountants. Yet, in this case, the Court of Appeals nevertheless seems to have imposed the higher duty prescribed by § 11 to investigate, but denied petitioner the right to rely on "the authority of an expert" that also is provided by § 11.

As the court in *Software Toolworks*,[4] suggested, the law remains unsettled whether the § 11 reasonable investigation standard is identical, similar, or materially different than the § 12(a)(2) reasonable care standard.[5] Perhaps most significantly the court in *Software Toolworks* suggested that even if there are different standards under §§ 11 and 12(a)(2), the analysis of each on summary judgement may be identical.

DUE DILIGENCE: A WORK IN PROGRESS

While technically only a defense to a § 11 claim, due diligence or "doing due diligence" is currently used broadly in legal and popular speech. Underwriters, lawyers, accountants, and issuers today do their "due diligence" for securities offerings exempt from § 11,[1] or for annual or quarterly report filings that raise potential Rule 10b–5, not § 11, liability.

Due diligence has also proven to be a dynamic concept. As an American Bar Association Comm. on Fed. Reg. of Sec. stated in its 1993 Report of Task Force on Sellers' Due Diligence and Similar Defenses under the Federal Securities Laws:[2]

The last half century and more have seen developments that would have astounded the drafters of the 1933 and 1934 Acts. These developments, which have had a profound effect on the way securities are distributed, include the following:

- a great expansion of publicly held companies' periodic disclosure obligations under the 1934 Act;

- progress in technology and communications that has revolutionized the dissemination and retrieval of information about reporting companies;

- drastic changes in the SEC's administration of registration procedures under the 1933 Act, particularly in regard to the "integrated" disclosure system and shelf registration;

- unprecedented institutionalization and globalization of the securities markets; and

- radical changes in the techniques and economics of the distribution of securities.

The Commission has attempted to accommodate change. In 1982 the Commission adopted Rule 176 to delineate relevant circumstances to determine whether or not the conduct of a person constitutes a reasonable investigation or a reasonable ground for belief under § 11(c). These include:

(a) The type of issuer;

(b) The type of security;

(c) The type of person;

(d) The office held when the person is an officer;

---

4. 50 F.3d at 621.

5. Cf. Associated Randall Bank v. Griffin, Kubik, Stephens & Thompson, Inc., 3 F.3d 208, 213 (7th Cir.1993) (rejecting suggestion that there is no difference between the reasonable investigation standard in § 11 and reasonable care standard in § 12(a)(2)).

1. *See, e.g.,* Statement Regarding Disclosure Obligations of Municipal Securities Issuers and Others, Sec. Act Rel. 7049, 56 SEC Dock. 479 (1994).

2. 48 Bus. Law. 1185, 1185–1186 (1993).

(e) The presence or absence of another relationship to the issuer when the person is a director or proposed director;

(f) Reasonable reliance on officers, employees, and others whose duties should have given them knowledge of the particular facts (in the light of the functions and responsibilities of the particular person with respect to the issuer and the filing);

(g) When the person is an underwriter, the type of underwriting arrangement, the role of the particular person as an underwriter and the availability of information with respect to the registrant; and

(h) Whether, with respect to a fact or document incorporated by reference, the particular person had any responsibility for the fact or document at the time of the filing from which it was incorporated.

Rule 176(h), based on the American Law Institute, Federal Securities Code Section 1704(g)(6), intended to relax § 11 liability for underwriters, in particular, when abbreviated registration statement forms such as the Form S–3 and/or shelf registration are used.[3]

Rule 176 appears to have had little impact on § 11 litigation.[4] Ironically, in Shaw v. Digital Equip. Corp.,[5] which involved a shelf registration on a truncated Form S–3 registration statement, the court stressed instructions to that Form's Item 11(a) which required disclosure of "any and all material changes in the registrant's affairs" since the completion of the Form 10–K annual report and other forms incorporated by reference. The court denied the defendants summary judgment, focusing solely on the instructions to Items 11(a), and not on Rule 176, when it wrote:

> Defendants assert here that the disclosure requirements of the Securities Act and regulations, including Item 11(a) of Form S–3, should be interpreted so that they would *never* mandate the provision of current information about a company's performance in the quarter in progress at the time of a public offering, so long as the company satisfies its quarterly and annual periodic disclosure obligations under the Exchange Act. That argument cuts severely against the very reason the shelf registration rule was made available to issuers like DEC: that "S–3" companies would provide the market with a continuous stream of high quality corporate information. The rule permits offerings to be made on a "continuous" or "delayed" basis because it envisions "continuous" disclosure. It would be inconsistent with this rationale to permit an issuer to take refuge in its periodically-filed Forms 10–Q or 10–K to avoid the obligation to disclose current material facts in its shelf offering prospectus.[6]

In 1996, when the SEC's Advisory Committee on the Capital Formation and Regulatory Processes proposed a form of company registration, the Committee focused on due diligence in its relatively brief report, stating in part:

> As part of the adoption of company registration, the Committee recommends that the Commission provide interpretive guidance to gate-

---

3. *See generally* 2 Louis Loss & Joel Seligman, Securities Regulation 623 (3d ed. rev. 1999).

4. Cf. Kramer v. Time Warner Inc., 937 F.2d 767, 777 (2d Cir.1991) ("One thus might question whether the wholesale incorporation of the Joint Proxy Statement by reference in

Time's Offer to Purchase sufficed to meet the requisite standard of disclosure concerning management's conflict of interest").

5. 82 F.3d 1194 (1st Cir.1996).

6. Id. at 1209.

keepers as to more effective methods of satisfying the "reasonable investigation" and "reasonable care" standards, respectively, of Sections 11 and 12(a)(2) of the Securities Act. In this regard, the Committee recommends expanding the factors (currently enumerated in Securities Act Rule 176) that may be taken into account by gatekeepers or monitors in determining their appropriate due diligence investigation, to refer specifically to compliance with the mandatory and voluntary procedures outlined in the disclosure enhancements.[7]

In a separate statement, John C. Coffee, Jr., Edward Greene, and Lawrence W. Sonsini articulated their view that this may prove to be somewhat more difficult than the Committee believed:

> We share the view clearly stated in this Report that company registration has not made, and should not make, obsolete the efforts of the corporation's independent "gatekeepers" (i.e., its outside directors, accountants, and underwriters) to verify and monitor the accuracy of the corporation's disclosures. No less than our colleagues on the committee, we believe such due diligence efforts play a critical role in assuring the integrity of our disclosure system. * * *

> * * * To the extent that company registration is adopted (or that any significant step is taken toward simplifying the existing system of shelf registration), corporate issuers may come to make more frequent use of the debt and equity markets. Issuers seeking to make frequent use of company registration (or the existing shelf registration system) face a problem, because repetitive debt or equity offerings co-exist uneasily at best with the statutory structure of the Securities Act of 1933. By regularly tapping the capital markets through repetitive offerings, the corporation exposes its directors to an increased risk of § 11 liability under circumstances that make effective compliance with their statutory "due diligence" defenses infeasible. Although we have no doubt that the board should familiarize itself with the contents of the registration statement in the context of a major public offering, there is not the same opportunity for factual verification and searching questioning in the context of smaller, repetitive offerings. Nor is it necessarily efficient to consume the board's limited time in this fashion. The dilemma then is that either (1) board members are overexposed to liability because they cannot establish their due diligence defenses within these compressed time frames, or (2) the corporation must forgo repetitive offerings because of the legal risks to its directors. Neither option is attractive; nor is this choice necessary. * * *

> How might the liability provisions of the Securities Act of 1933 be modified? Lest we be misunderstood, we stress at the outset that we do not seek to abolish liability under § 11 or § 12. Although there are multiple forces that drive our disclosure system, the risk of liability is one of the most significant, and it motivates independent gatekeepers to test and, if necessary, challenge the issuer's proposed disclosure. The proposed Form 8–K requirement (which we support) at least technically increases the risk of § 11 liability for both board members and underwriters.

> In seeking to strike the proper balance, we believe the proper starting point is to define a realistic role for gatekeepers that is sensitive to both the time constraints imposed on issuers and underwriters by the market-

---

7. SEC Advisory Comm. on Capital Formation and Regulatory Processes 29 (1996).

place and the character of the modern board of directors. When the Securities Act of 1933 was drafted, both were very different. Corporate boards were then insider-dominated with few truly independent directors, and as a result it was natural to assume that board members would be familiar with all material pending corporate developments. The modern board is now predominantly composed of outside directors, who are not necessarily familiar on a daily basis with all material information concerning their corporation and who have other commitments and business obligations that preclude them from devoting unlimited time to the corporations they serve as outside directors. Correspondingly, where once a public offering of debt or equity securities was a long, drawn-out process which permitted ample time for conducting a due diligence review, it can now occur from conception to consummation under shelf registration within the space of a single day. As a result, the full board of directors, dispersed in the typical case across the country and subject to their own time constraints, often cannot undertake a meaningful due diligence review, at least not within the compressed time frames that the equity marketplace imposes.[8]

In 2001 members of the American Bar Association Committee on Federal Regulation of Securities proposed a system of universal shelf registration and proposed reducing the liability burden of one "gatekeeper," underwriters:

> For nearly 20 years, the SEC has taken steps to enable issuers to obtain "on demand financing," *i.e.*, the ability to access the securities markets immediately whenever capital needs arise or market opportunities present themselves. However, the benefits of "on demand financing" (subject, of course, to the potential registration delays described above when a new shelf is filed) are undermined by continuing to impose on financial intermediaries and other "gatekeepers" the responsibility to take the time necessary to do a sufficient due diligence investigation to assure quality disclosure without recognizing and making allowances for their difficulty or even inability to do so. It is not possible for underwriters and others to meet this standard in the current financing environment.

> In theory, the liabilities of § 11 are imposed on those "gatekeepers" best able to ensure that the investor receives full and fair disclosure. In reality, most frequent issuers act as their own gatekeepers. Underwriters have little ability—because of integrated disclosure and shelf registration— to influence the issuer's disclosure. They nevertheless remain subject to § 11 liabilities, having only the defense that they conducted a reasonable investigation.

> It is also anomalous that an underwriter's liability under § 11 in respect of a shelf registration statement is measured on the state of the facts at the time the underwriter becomes an underwriter, while the liability of the issuer, signing officers and directors is measured on the state of facts at the time the registration statement becomes effective or the filing of the last annual report, which may be months earlier.[9]

---

8. Id. at 39–43.

9. Letter to David B.H. Martin, Director, SEC Div. of Corp. Fin. from Stanley

Keller, Chair, ABA Comm. on Fed. Reg. of Sec. 9 (Aug. 22, 2001).

2. CAUSATION AND DAMAGES

The plaintiff does not have the affirmative burden to prove either reliance or causation in a § 11 case,[1] but the defendant can advance causation as a defense to the plaintiff's damages claim under the proviso in § 11(e), which states:

> *Provided, that* if the defendant proves that any portion or all of such damages represents other than the depreciation in value of such security resulting from such part of the registration statement, with respect to which his liability is asserted, not being true or omitting to state a material fact required to be stated therein or necessary to make the statements therein not misleading, such portion of or all such damages shall not be recoverable.

Section 11(e) thus creates a type of "negative causation" or, more grandly, "comparative causation with a reverse twist."[2]

Akerman v. Oryx Communications, Inc.

United States Court of Appeals, Second Circuit, 1987.
810 F.2d 336.

This case arises out of a June 30, 1981, initial public offering of securities by Oryx, a company planning to enter the business of manufacturing and marketing abroad video cassettes and video discs of feature films for home entertainment. Oryx filed a registration statement and an accompanying prospectus dated June 30, 1981, with the Securities and Exchange Commission (SEC) for a firm commitment offering of 700,000 units. Each unit sold for $4.75 and consisted of one share of common stock and one warrant to purchase an additional share of stock for $5.75 at a later date.

The prospectus contained an erroneous *pro forma* unaudited financial statement relating to the eight month period ending March 31, 1981. It reported net sales of $931,301, net income of $211,815, and earnings of seven cents per share. Oryx, however, had incorrectly posted a substantial transaction by its subsidiary to March instead of April when Oryx actually received the subject sale's revenues. The prospectus, therefore, overstated earnings for the eight month period. Net sales in that period actually totaled $766,301, net income $94,529, and earnings per share three cents.

Oryx's price had declined to four dollars per unit by October 12, 1981, the day before Oryx revealed the prospectus misstatement to the SEC. J.App. at 154. The unit price had further declined to $3.25 by November 9, 1981, the day before Oryx disclosed the misstatement to the public. J. App. at 140. After public disclosure, the price of Oryx rose and reached $3.50 by November 25, 1981, the day this suit commenced. J. App. at 140.

Plaintiffs allege that the prospectus error rendered Oryx liable for the stock price decline pursuant to sections 11 and 12(2) of the Securities Act of 1933. In July 1982, Oryx moved for summary judgment on the grounds, *inter alia,* that the misstatement was not material for purposes of establishing liability under section 11 and that the misstatement had not actually caused the price decline for purposes of damages under section 11. * * *

---

1. *See, e.g.,* Lyne v. Arthur Andersen & Co., 772 F.Supp. 1064, 1067 (N.D.Ill.1991).

2. 9 Louis Loss & Joel Seligman, Securities Regulation 4251 (3d ed. 1992).

Plaintiffs in the Akermans' situation, if successful, would be entitled to recover the difference between the original purchase price and the value of the stock at the time of suit. 15 U.S.C. § 77k(e). A defendant may, under section 11(e), reduce his liability by proving that the depreciation in value resulted from factors other than the material misstatement in the registration statement. 15 U.S.C. § 77k(e); *Greenapple v. Detroit Edison Co.,* 618 F.2d 198, 203 n. 9 (2d Cir.1980). A defendant's burden in attempting to reduce his liability has been characterized as the burden of "negative causation." *Beecher v. Able,* 435 F.Supp. 397, 409 (S.D.N.Y.1975).

The district court determined that plaintiffs established a *prima facie* case under section 11(a) by demonstrating that the prospectus error was material "as a theoretical matter." *Akerman,* 609 F.Supp. at 366–68. The court, however, granted defendants' motion for summary judgment on damages under section 11(e), stating: "[Defendants] have carried their heavy burden of proving that the [Oryx stock price] decline was caused by factors other than the matters misstated in the registration statement." *Id.* at 372. The precise issue on appeal, therefore, is whether defendants carried their burden of negative causation under section 11(e).

Defendants' heavy burden reflects Congress' desire to allocate the risk of uncertainty to the defendants in these cases. [Citation omitted.] Defendants' burden, however, is not insurmountable; section 11(e) expressly creates an affirmative defense of disproving causation. [Citation omitted.]

The misstatement resulted from an innocent bookkeeping error whereby Oryx misposted a sale by its subsidiary to March instead of April. Oryx received the sale's proceeds less than one month after the reported date. The prospectus, moreover, expressly stated that Oryx "expect[ed] that [the subsidiary's] sales will decline." J.App. at 102. Indeed, Morris Akerman conceded that he understood this disclaimer to warn that Oryx expected the subsidiary's business to decline. J.App. at 33–34. [Citation omitted.]

Thus, although the misstatement may have been "theoretically material," *Akerman,* 609 F.Supp. at 366, when it is considered in the context of the prospectus' pessimistic forecast of the performance of Oryx's subsidiary, the misstatement was not likely to cause a stock price decline. [Citation omitted.]

Indeed, the public not only did not react adversely to disclosure of the misstatement, Oryx's price actually *rose* somewhat after public disclosure of the error.

The applicable section 11(e) formula for calculating damages is "the difference between the amount paid for the security (not exceeding the price at which the security was offered to the public) and . . . the value thereof as of the time such suit was brought." 15 U.S.C. § 77k(e). The relevant events and stock prices are:

Date	Event	Oryx Stock Price
June 30, 1981	Initial public offering	$4.75
October 15, 1981	Disclosure of error to SEC	$4.00
November 10, 1981	Disclosure of error to public	$3.25
November 25, 1981	Date of suit	$3.50

The price decline before disclosure may not be charged to defendants. *See Beecher v. Able,* 435 F.Supp. 397, 407 (S.D.N.Y.1975) (price decline before misstatement revealed not attributable to defendants under section 11(e)); *Fox v. Glickman Corp.,* 253 F.Supp. 1005, 1010 (S.D.N.Y.1966) (same). At first blush, damages would appear to be zero because there was no depreciation in Oryx's value between the time of public disclosure and the time of suit.

The Akermans contended at trial, however, that the relevant disclosure date was the date of disclosure to the SEC and not to the public. Under plaintiffs' theory, damages would equal the price decline subsequent to October 15, 1981, which amounted to fifty cents per share. Plaintiffs attempted to support this theory by alleging that insiders privy to the SEC disclosure—Oryx's officers, attorneys and accountants, and underwriters and SEC officials—sold Oryx shares and thereby deflated its price before public disclosure. *Akerman,* 609 F.Supp. at 370–71. The district court attributed "at least possible theoretical validity" to this argument. *Id.* at 370. After extensive discovery, however, plaintiffs produced absolutely no evidence of insider trading. *Id.* at 371. Plaintiffs' submissions and oral argument before us do not press this theory.

The Akermans first attempted to explain the public's failure to react adversely to disclosure by opining that defendant-underwriter Moore & Schley used its position as market maker to prop up the market price. This theory apparently complemented the Akermans' other theory that insiders acted on knowledge of the disclosure to the SEC to deflate the price before public disclosure. The Akermans failed after extensive discovery to produce any evidence of insider trading and have not pressed the theory on appeal.

The district court invited statistical studies from both sides to clarify the causation issue. Defendants produced a statistical analysis of the stocks of the one hundred companies that went public contemporaneously with Oryx. The study tracked the stocks' performances for the period between June 30, 1981 (initial public offering date) and November 25, 1981 (date of suit). The study indicated that Oryx performed at the exact statistical median of these stocks and that several issues suffered equal or greater losses than did Oryx during this period. *Akerman,* 609 F.Supp. at 372. Defendants produced an additional study which indicated that Oryx stock "behaved over the entire period * * * consistent[ly] with its own inherent variation." *Id.*

Plaintiffs offered the following rebuttal evidence. During the period between SEC disclosure and public disclosure, Oryx stock decreased nineteen percent while the over-the-counter (OTC) composite index rose five percent (the first study). During this period, therefore, the OTC composite index outperformed Oryx by twenty-four percentage points. Plaintiffs also produced a study indicating that for the time period between SEC disclosure and one week after public disclosure, eighty-two of the one hundred new issues analyzed in the defendants' study outperformed Oryx's stock. J.App. at 1120–22.

Plaintiffs' first study compared Oryx's performance to the performance of the OTC index in order to rebut a comparison offered by defendants to prove that Oryx's price decline resulted not from the misstatement but rather from an overall market decline. As previously stated, defendants' comparison indicated that the OTC index generally declined for the period between Oryx's offering date and the date of suit. *Akerman,* 609 F.Supp. at 371. The parties' conflicting comparisons, however, lack credibility because they fail to reflect any of the countless variables that might affect the stock price performance of a single company. [Citation omitted.] Statistical analyses must control for relevant variables to permit reliable inferences. *Id.; A. Koutsoyiannis, Theory of Econometrics*, chs. 2, 12 (2d ed.1977).

The studies comparing Oryx's performance to the other one hundred companies that went public in May and June of 1981 are similarly flawed. The studies do not evaluate the performance of Oryx stock in relation to the stock of companies possessing any characteristic in common with Oryx, *e.g.*, product, technology, profitability, assets or countless other variables which influence stock prices, except the contemporaneous initial offering dates.

Perhaps more important, the Akermans' study of the one hundred new issues focuses on a time frame which controverts one of their own theories explaining the public's failure to react adversely to disclosure. The Akermans argue that the thin market in Oryx stock prevented immediate public reaction to disclosure of the prospectus error. J.App. at 599–600. Their study, however, measures Oryx's performance from SEC disclosure to *one week* after public disclosure. A thin market, according to the Akermans' own explanation, would not reflect the impact of bad news in such a short time period (one week). This internal inconsistency seriously undercuts the probative value of the Akermans' study.

Finally, we note that this time period drew its relevance from the Akermans' theory that insider trading deflated Oryx's price during this period. As previously stated, this theory has no support even after extensive discovery and is not pressed on appeal.

Granting the Akermans every reasonable, favorable inference, the battle of the studies is at best equivocal; the studies do not meaningfully point in one direction or the other. * * *

Defendants met their burden, as set forth in section 11(e), by establishing that the misstatement was barely material and that the public failed to react adversely to its disclosure. With the case in this posture, the plaintiffs had to come forward with "specific facts showing that there is a genuine issue for trial." [Citation omitted.] Despite extensive discovery, plaintiffs completely failed to produce any evidence, other than unreliable and sometimes inconsistent statistical studies and theories, suggesting that Oryx's price decline actually resulted from the misstatement. [Citation omitted.]

NEGATIVE CAUSATION

In re Worlds of Wonder Sec. Litig.,[1] a court added about what it termed "loss" rather than "negative" causation:

To establish a "loss causation" defense under section 11(e). Deloitte needed to prove "that the depreciation in value [of the debentures] resulted from factors other than the [alleged] material misstatement in the [1987 financial] statement." *Akerman v. Oryx Communications, Inc.*, 810 F.2d 336, 340 (2d Cir.1987). *Accord, e.g., Fortune Sys.*, 680 F.Supp. at 1364. The district court concluded that Deloitte met this burden by showing that WOW never disclosed to the market the fact that the 1987 financial statements contained material errors. This analysis was, quite simply, far too narrow.

Loss causation exists where "the misrepresentation *touches upon the reasons* for the investment's decline in value." [Citations omitted.]

---

1.   35 F.3d 1407 (9th Cir.1994).

Under the correct inquiry, summary judgment was clearly inappropriate in this case. As Deloitte acknowledges, "the decline in the value of WOW's investment securities * * * corresponded precisely to a series of fiscal 1988 public disclosures." The plaintiffs introduced expert testimony that those disclosures *directly related* to the transactions for which Deloitte allegedly made erroneous accounting determinations, and that, as a result, Deloitte's alleged errors "touched upon" the reasons for the decline in the value of WOW's debentures. Several examples are illustrative:

> * The plaintiffs allege that Deloitte improperly recognized revenue on 1987 "sales" for which WOW offered price protection. WOW's subsequently announced losses for the second quarter of fiscal 1988 included a $13.2 million reserve for price protection in connection with the 1987 transactions. Following disclosure of those losses, the market price of the debentures declined.

> * The plaintiffs allege that Deloitte improperly recognized revenue on the 1987 "K–Mart Transaction," in which WOW offered the retailer extended payment terms, stock balancing, and guaranteed sales. When WOW subsequently announced losses for the second quarter of fiscal 1988, including a $9.9 million charge for K–Mart's cancellation of the "sales," the market price of the debentures declined.

> * The plaintiffs allege that Deloitte improperly failed to account for WOW's excess and obsolete inventory. When WOW subsequently announced losses for the second quarter of fiscal 1988, including the creation of a $12 million inventory reserve, the market price of the debentures declined.

In light of that evidence, the auditor clearly did not overcome, as matter of law, "Congress' desire to allocate to the defendants the risk of uncertainty in [section 11(e)] cases." *Akerman,* 810 F.2d at 341. We therefore reverse the district court's holding that Deloitte established a "loss causation" defense as a matter of law and remand for a trial on the merits of (1) whether the 1987 financial statements were in fact misleading (an issue not decided by the court) and (2) whether Deloitte can affirmatively establish a loss causation defense.

Given the damages formula in § 11(e), benefit of the bargain damages are not recoverable under that Section. McMahan & Co. v. Wherehouse Entertainment, Inc., 65 F.3d 1044 (2d Cir.1995), *cert. denied,* 517 U.S. 1190 (1996). See generally Paul Grier, A Methodology for the Calculation of Section 11 Damages, 5 Stan. J. L. Bus. & Fin. 99 (1999).

A CAP ON § 11 DAMAGES

Section 11(g) adds a further cap on § 11 damages by providing: "In no case shall the amount recoverable under this section exceed the price at which the security was offered to the public." This primarily limits the plaintiff who purchased in the open market rather than in the course of a distribution. When the security has been disposed of in the open market before suit, the measure of damages is purchase price less resale price (with no mention of interest or of deducting income received on the security as in § 12). If the market goes up *pending suit* and the security is disposed of before judgment, the defendant gets the benefit of the increase over the value at the time of suit; but if the market goes *down* and the security is disposed of pending suit the plaintiff still gets only the difference between the purchase price and the value at the time of suit. In other words it is to the plaintiff's advantage not to hold the security after filing suit if he or she wants to be sure of being made whole.

3.   SECTION 11 PLAINTIFFS

Hertzberg v. Dignity Partners, Inc.

United States Court of Appeals, Ninth Circuit, 1999.
191 F.3d 1076.

■ Before: THOMPSON and FLETCHER, CIRCUIT JUDGES, and LASNIK, DISTRICT JUDGE. W. Fletcher, Circuit Judge:

This case arises out of alleged misstatements and omissions contained in Appellee Dignity Partners, Inc.'s ("Dignity's") registration statement filed with the Securities and Exchange Commission for an initial public offering of Dignity common stock. Dignity was in the business of buying the rights to life insurance proceeds from people with AIDS, paying a lump sum up front, and taking over the responsibility for paying the premiums. Shortly after the offering, the fact that AIDS patients were living longer than expected because of new AIDS treatments became public knowledge. As a result of the longer lives of the insured, Dignity posted huge losses, and the stock plummeted.

Plaintiffs/appellants Hertzberg, Derosa, and Feinman ("Hertzberg") are investors who purchased Dignity stock on the open market more than 25 days after the initial offering but before the news of the longer life expectancy or large losses became public knowledge. They brought a class action for several violations of the securities laws by Dignity, including violation of Section 11 of the Securities Act of 1933 ("Securities Act"), ("Section 11"). Hertzberg claims that Dignity knew of the longer life expectancy but failed to disclose it in the registration statement. The district court dismissed the Section 11 causes of action on the ground that, because appellants had not bought their stock in the initial public offering, or within 25 days thereof, they did not have standing to bring the claim. * * *

We reverse the district court's holding that the original named plaintiffs lacked standing under Section 11. * * *

BACKGROUND

On February 14, 1996, Dignity filed a registration statement for an initial public offering of approximately 2.7 million shares of common stock. Hertzberg asserts, on behalf of a class of persons who purchased Dignity stock between February 14, 1996, and July 16, 1996, that the registration statement contained materially false and misleading statements and omitted material facts. He seeks damages under Section 11 as well as under other provisions of the federal securities laws.

Dignity was in the business of making "viatical settlements." It purchased the rights to the proceeds of life insurance policies from individuals with terminal illnesses, and in exchange, paid lump sums to the individuals and assumed responsibility for the payment of premiums. The amounts Dignity paid to the individuals were based on their estimated expectancies, and the profits Dignity received depended on the accuracy of those estimates. Nearly all of the individuals from whom Dignity purchased its right had AIDS.

By 1995, new drugs and treatments for AIDS became available, and many of the individuals with whom Dignity had contracted began to live longer than expected. Hertzberg alleges that, as a consequence, the value of Dignity's business was in jeopardy because it could not collect the life insurance proceeds as rapidly as expected, it had to pay premiums for longer periods than expected, and it could no longer estimate with accuracy the life expectancy of the persons with whom it contracted.

Hertzberg alleges that the owners of this privately held company saw the prospect of their entire investment disappearing and decided to liquidate much of their holding by taking the company public. According to Hertzberg, the financial statements in Dignity's registration statement were misleading because they misrepresented the true worth of the business. Hertzberg alleges that shortly before the offering Dignity adopted the accrual method of accounting, under which Dignity counted the potential rights, rather than when it actually received the proceeds. Hertzberg hid the facts that Dignity was taking longer to collect on those policies and that Dignity could no longer accurately estimate when individuals would die. Finally, Hertzberg alleges that Dignity violated Section 11 by failing to disclose its inability to make accurate estimations of life expectancies, the "adverse trends" experienced in 1995, and the fact that its accrual Dignity's accounting method did not comport with Generally Accepted Accounting Principles.

After the facts concerning the lengthened life expectancies for AIDS patients became public knowledge, Dignity's stock fell from the initial offering price of $12 a share to about $6. In June of 1995, less than five months after the beginning of the initial public offering, Dignity announced an anticipated quarterly loss of $10 million, and a month later announced that it would abandon the viatical settlement business. As a result of these announcements, the stock fell to $1 a share before settling at about $2 at the time the action was filed.

Dignity moved to dismiss Hertzberg's Section 11 claims because the named plaintiffs had not purchased their shares "in" the registered offering. The district court, ruling from the bench, held that because the named plaintiffs purchased their stock more than 25 days after the registration statement was filed, they did not have standing to bring an action under Section 11. It therefore dismissed their Section 11 claims. * * *

DISCUSSION

We review the district court's interpretation of Section 11 *de novo*. *See* In re Stac Elecs. Sec. Litig., 89 F.3d 1399, 1403 (9th Cir.1996). In determining the meaning of a statute, we look first to its text. *In re: Kelly,* 841 F.2d 908, 912 (9th Cir.1988). Section 11(a) provides that where a material fact is misstated or omitted from a registration statement accompanying a stock filing with the Securities and Exchange Commission, "any person acquiring such security" may bring an action for losses caused by the misstatement or omission, 15 U.S.C. § 77K(a). The district court read this phrase as if it had been written, "any person acquiring such security *on the first day of an initial public offering or in the twenty-five day period thereafter.*"[3] This reading adds a significant limitation not found in the original text.

---

3. The district court ruled from the bench and did not issue a written decision, so we are not certain where it got the 25-day period. Such a 25-day period was most likely

The term "any person" is quite broad, and we give words their ordinary meaning. United States v. Alvarez–Sanchez, 511 U.S. 350, 357, 114 S. Ct. 1599, 128 L.Ed.2d 319 (1994). According to *Webster's Third New Int'l Dictionary* (3d ed. 1986), "any" means "one, no matter what one"; "ALL"; "one or more discriminately from all those of a kind." This broad meaning of "any" has been recognized by this circuit. Madrid v. Gomez, 150 F.3d 1030, 1036 (9th Cir.1998) (the court must accept "the plain meaning of the word 'any.' In its conventional usage, 'any' means "ALL-used to indicate a maximum or whole." It certainly does not mean 'some.' ") (citations omitted).

The limitation on "any person" is that he or she must have purchased "such security." Clearly, this limitation only means that the person must have purchased a security issued under that, rather than some other, registration statement. *See* Barnes v. Osofsky, 373 F.2d 269 (2d Cir.1967). While it might present a problem of proof in a case in which stock was issued under more than one registration statement, the only Dignity stock ever sold to the public was pursuant to the allegedly misleading registration statement at issue in this case. Thus, as long as Hertzberg is suing regarding this security, he is "any person purchasing such security," regardless of whether he bought in the initial offering, a week later, or a month after that.

Further, paragraph (e) of Section 11 uses "the amount paid for the security (not exceeding the price at which the security was offered to the public)" as the baseline for measuring damages. 15 U.S.C. § 77k(e); *see also* 15 U.S.C. § 77k(g). Such a provision would be unnecessary if only a person who bought in the actual offering could recover, since, by definition, such a person would have paid "the price at which the security was offered to the public." We will "avoid a reading which renders some words altogether redundant." Gustafson v. Alloyd Co., Inc. 513 U.S. 561, 574, 115 St.Ct. 1061, 131 L.Ed.2d 1 (1995).

Finally, Dignity believes that its reading of Section 11 is supported by the Supreme Court's decision in *Gustafson*. We believe that Dignity is mistaken. In *Gustafson*, the Supreme Court interpreted Section 12 of the Security Act, 15 U.S.C. § 771, rather than Section 11, and limited its decision to determining what was a "prospectus" under Section 12. Dicta in *Gustafson* indicate that a suit under Section 12 may only be maintained by a person who purchased the stock in the offering under the prospectus, 513 U.S. at 571–72, 115 S.Ct. 1061, but the Court gave no indication that it intended this restriction to apply to Section 11.

Dignity relies on the Supreme Court's statements in *Gustafson* that Section 12 is a companion to Section 11 for its claim that Section 11 applies only to people who purchased their stock in the initial offering. However, while Section 11 and Section 12 are indeed parallel statutes, their wording is significantly different as to who can bring a suit. As already noted, Section 11 permits suit without restriction by "any person acquiring such security." Section 12, by contrast, permits suit against a seller of a security by prospectus only by "the person purchasing such security *from him*," thus specifying that a

borrowed from the 25–day after-market period of 17 C.F.R. § 230.174. However, this section pertains to false statements in prospectuses (a Section 12 violation), not registration statements (a Section 11 violation). We note that defendant does not seriously argue in support of the 25–day period. Rather, it argues that *any* after-market purchase is excluded from the protection of Section 11, whether made one day or 26 days after the initial public offering.

plaintiff must have purchased the security directly from the issuer of the prospectus. 15 U.S.C. § 771(a)(2) (emphasis added).

Congress's decision to use "from him" in Section 12 but not in Section 11 must mean that Congress intended a different meaning in the two sections. *See* Russello v. United States, 464 U.S. 16, 23, 104 S.Ct. 296, 78 L.Ed.2d 17 (1983) ("[W]here Congress includes particular language in one section of a statute but omits it in another section of the same Act, it is generally presumed that Congress acts intentionally and purposefully in the disparate inclusion or exclusion.") (citations and internal quotation marks omitted). Further, there is nothing in the reasoning or underlying logic of *Gustafson* that indicates that we should read into Section 11 the express privity requirement of Section 12.

Other circuits that have addressed this issue agree with our reading of the text and have uniformly allowed for recovery by purchasers in the aftermarket. Versyss Inc. v. Coopers and Lybrand, 982 F.2d 653, 657 (1st Cir.1992), *cert. denied,* 508 U.S. 974, 113 S.Ct. 2965, 125 L.Ed.2d 665 (1993) (Section 11 "is remarkably stringent where it applies, readily imposing liability on ancillary parties to the registration statement (like accountants) for the benefit *even of purchasers after the original offering")* (emphasis added); *Barnes, supra,* 373 F.2d 269 (2d Cir.1967); Columbia General Inv. Corp. v. SEC, 265 F.2d 559, 562 (5th Cir.1959) ("Persons other than those who purchase the new stock under the Registration may be affected in point of fact and may, under certain circumstances, have remedies in point of law for misrepresentations in a Registration"). We are unaware of any circuit that in light of *Gustafson* has either reconsidered its view or has disagreed with the circuits that have previously decided the question. Two district courts, in addition to the district court in this case, have read *Gustafson* in the manner suggested by Dignity, *see* Gould v. Harris, 929 F. Supp. 353, 358–59 (C.D.Cal.1996); Gannon v. Continental Insurance Co., 920 F. Supp. 566 (D.N.J.1996), but for the reasons given above, we believe they have misread both *Gustafson* and Section 11.

Where the meaning of a statute is clear from the text, we need look no further. *In re: Kelly, supra,* 841 F.2d at 912. However, we note that even if we were to find the wording of the statute ambiguous, the legislative history supports Hertzberg's reading of Section 11.

The House Report accompanying the version of the bill that ultimately became the Securities Act of 1933 provides:

> the civil remedies accorded by [Section 11] are given to all purchasers * * * regardless of whether they bought their securities at the time of the *original offer or at some later date,* provided, of course, that the remedy is prosecuted within the period of limitations provided by section 13.

H.R.Rep. No. 73–85, at 22 (emphasis added). By expressly referring to purchasers who bought their securities at "some later date" other than "at time of the original offer," the Report makes it clear that purchasers in the aftermarket are intended to have a cause of action under the Section. Similarly, when Congress amended Section 11 in 1934 to add a requirement of proof of reliance on the registration statement if there had been an intervening earning statement, the House Report stated:

> The basis of this provision is that in all likelihood the purchase and price of the security purchased after publication of such an earning statement will be predicated upon that statement rather than upon the information disclosed upon registration.

H.R.Rep. 73–1838 at 41. By referring to purchases after publication of an earning statement, the Report makes clear that purchasers in the aftermarket are within the group of purchasers provided a cause of action by Section 11.

Dignity does not effectively counter this legislative history. Rather, it points to comments made regarding an alternate bill which was never enacted, S. 875. This circuit relies on official committee reports when considering legislative history, not stray comments by individuals or other materials unrelated to the statutory language or the committee reports. *In re: Kelly, supra,* 841 F.2d at 912 n. 3; *see also* Garcia v. United States, 469 U.S. 70, 76, 105 S.Ct. 479, 83 L.Ed.2d 472 (1984). Dignity also cites pieces of the legislative history that show Congress meant Section 11 to deal with new offerings of securities. But that issue has never been in dispute. As discussed above, all the stock ever publicly issued by Dignity was sold in the single offering at issue in this case. The difficulties of tracing stock to a particular offering present in some cases are thus not present here.

REVERSED AND REMANDED

WHO MAY RECOVER UNDER § 11?

Section 11 liability is limited to material misrepresentations or omissions in the registration statement. Roadshow presentations, analysts' reports, and statements to investment publications do not establish a § 11 claim.[1]

A preliminary prospectus under Rule 430, will not give rise to § 11 liability if errors are corrected before the effective date. Section 11 liability also will not be created by a tombstone ad under Rule 134, since it is not filed as part of the registration statement, or a summary prospectus prepared under Rule 431, since § 11 liability is expressed excluded by § 10(b).

It is clear under the express terms of § 11 of the 1933 Act that the plaintiff must be a purchaser of a security ("any person acquiring such security"). Section 11 by its express terms eliminates any requirement of privity of contract between the plaintiff and the issuer as a defendant, as contrasted with § 12(a)(2). Obviously no privity of contract is required between the plaintiff and the collateral defendants made liable by § 11, such as directors and officers. Any purchaser in the market at any time before the statute of limitations has run may sue for a violation of that Section.

In the period before the United States Supreme Court decision in Gustafson v. Alloyd Co., 513 U.S. 561 (1995), the lower federal courts consistently had held that a § 11 suit could be brought by any investor who acquired a registered security, whether in the process of a securities distribution or in the open market. The open market purchaser, however, was required to trace his or her particular securities to securities sold in the registered offering.[2] This is a nonsensical but unavoidable result of a statutory scheme that registers *units*, not *classes*, of securities.[3]

---

1.   O'Sullivan v. Trident Microsystems, Inc., 1993–1994 Fed.Sec.L.Rep. (CCH) ¶ 98,116 at 98,907 (N.D.Cal.1994).

2.   See, e.g., Barnes v. Osofsky, 373 F.2d 269 (2d Cir.1967); Shapiro v. UJB Fin. Corp., 964 F.2d 272, 286 (3d Cir.1992), *cert. denied,* 506 U.S. 934 (1992).

3.   *See e.g.,* Klein v. Computer Devices, Inc., 591 F.Supp. 270, 273 n. 7 (S.D.N.Y. 1984), *reargument on other grounds,* 602 F.Supp. 837 (S.D.N.Y.1985); Guenther v. Cooper Life Sciences, Inc., 759 F.Supp. 1437, 1439 (N.D.Cal.1990) ("The burden of tracing shares to a particular public offering rests with plaintiffs"); Harden v. Raffensperger,

In the pre-*Gustafson* period these and other lower federal court cases consistently held that the plain language of § 11 provided a lawsuit for "any person acquiring such security." As Judge Friendly reasoned in Barnes v. Osofsky,[4] the most natural reading of this statutory language is to provide a remedy to both those who were original purchasers and those who could trace the lineage of their shares to the newly offered ones. Either a limitation of § 11 liability solely to those in direct privity with the initial sellers or a broader concept of liability extending to *all* holders of the same class of stock "would be inconsistent with the over-all statutory scheme."[5] Judge Friendly recognized that the House Report accompanying the Securities Act, H.R. Rep. No. 85, 73d Cong., 1st Sess. 5 (1933), provided further support for this construction when it stated that § 11 provided a remedy to purchasers "regardless of whether they bought their securities at the time of the original offer or at some later date."[6]

The Supreme Court majority in *Gustafson v. Alloyd Co., Inc.,*[7] does not address this issue. The case solely concerns which purchasers who brought suit under § 12(2) [now § 12(a)(2)] of the Securities Act have standing to sue. Since § 12(a)(2) limits liability to sellers who make misrepresentations or omissions "by means of a prospectus," the Supreme Court held that liability was limited to registered offerings by issuers and their controlling shareholders. The Court did not address whether § 11 provided standing to shareholders who could trace their purchases to a registration statement and, indeed, recognized that another section of the 1933 Act, § 17(a), applied both to a fraudulent scheme in an initial offer or sale of securities *and* in the course of open market trading.[8] The two inferences *Gustafson* most clearly supports are that each section of the 1933 Act deserves a separate analysis and that the Supreme Court in *Gustafson* did not address standing under § 11.

Most post-*Gustafson* cases have followed *Hertzberg v. Dignity Partners* and allowed tracing.[9]

Mechanically, how is tracing done? Statistical probability figured in an opinion by Judge Keeton in Elscint, Ltd. Sec. Litig.[10] On the one hand the tracing precedents do not require that a plaintiff "conclusively show, beyond question" that his or her shares were "new" shares. On the other hand the defendant's argument cannot be dismissed as no better than saying that the stock " 'might' have been issued pursuant to the challenged registration statement."[11] The plaintiff must simply prove by a preponderance of the evidence the purchase of some number of new shares, each at some particular price, so as to support determinations of both liability and amount of recovery.

Hughes & Co., Inc., 933 F.Supp. 763 (S.D.Ind.1996); Lilley v. Charren, 936 F.Supp. 708, 715 (N.D.Cal.1996).

4. 373 F.2d 269 (2d Cir.1967).

5. Id. at 272.

6. Id. at 273.

7. 513 U.S. 561 (1995).

8. Id. at 577.

9. See, e.g., Schwartz v. Celestial Seasonings, Inc., 178 F.R.D. 545, 555–556 (D.Colo.1998); Adair v. Bristol Tech. Sys., Inc., 179 F.R.D. 126, 132–133 (S.D.N.Y.1998); In re Number Nine Visual Tech. Corp. Sec. Litig., 51 F.Supp.2d 1, 25–26 (D.Mass.1999) (standing under § 11 for plaintiffs who purchased securities in aftermarket trading and can "trace" the purchase to a public offering); Feiner v. SS&C Tech., Inc., 47 F.Supp.2d 250, 251–252 (D.Conn.1999) (tracing permitted both under §§ 11 and 12(a)(2)); Milman v. Box Hill Sys. Corp., 192 F.R.D. 105 (S.D.N.Y.2000) (a class may be formed on the basis of secondary market purchasers who can trace their securities to a registered offering under § 11).

10. 674 F.Supp. 374 (D.Mass.1987).

11. Id. at 379.

"Also, ordinarily proof may be either direct or circumstantial, or both, and circumstantial evidence may include statistical evidence if it is based on data that are adequately authenticated and supportably interpreted."[12] But a statistical probability of more than 82 percent was not sufficient to support "an inference, reasoned from evidence, that any one of the plaintiffs, more probably than not, purchased at least some determinate number of 'new' shares."[13] Judge Keeton also declined to follow recent developments in the law of causation, especially in tort cases, to the effect that the defendant's negligence was a "substantial factor" in causing harm to a plaintiff on evidence "which might be characterized as 'statistical' or 'probabilistic.' "[14]

In Versyss Inc. v. Coopers & Lybrand,[15] the court wrestled with the phrase "acquiring a security." It was alleged that Northern Data System's (NDS) August 1984 registration statement contained materially false information certified by the accountant firm of Coopers & Lybrand. On May 17, 1985, Continental Telecom, Inc. (Contel), entered into a merger agreement with NDS under which NDS would be merged into a newly created subsidiary of Contel stock. The merger was effected on July 16, 1985, when the Contel subsidiary acquired effective ownership of the assets and liabilities of NDS and the separate corporate existence of NDS ceased to exist. "Thereafter, * * * the former NDS stockholders sent in their now defunct NDS stock certificates to Contel's exchange agent and received their Contel stock certificates."[16]

After the merger, Contel concluded that the NDS registration statement was fraudulent, and its assignee, Versyss, Inc., brought suit against Coopers & Lybrand.

Both the District Court and the First Circuit rejected the claim, holding that Contel did not qualify as a § 11 plaintiff because it had not acquired NDS securities, but rather the assets and liabilities of the former NDS.[17] "On the date of the merger, and before any NDS stock certificates were to be transferred to Contel's exchange agent, NDS ceased to exist as a corporation."[18] On the other hand the beneficial owner of a limited partnership interest exchanged for stock in a registered offering will have standing to sue under § 11(a).[19]

On § 11 law generally, see 9 Louis Loss & Joel Seligman, Securities Regulation 4246–4278 (3d ed. 1992); Jennifer O'Hare, Institutional Investors, Registration Rights, and the Specter of Liability under Section 11 of the Securities Act of 1933, 1996 Wis. L. Rev. 217; Barry D. Hunter, Liability of Issuer's Counsel in the Wake of *Central Bank of Denver*—To Whom Is the Lawyer's Due Diligence Due?, 86 Ky. L.J. 413 (1997–1998).

B.   SECTION 12

1.   SECTION 12(a)(1)

Section 12(a)(1), which until 1995 was denominated § 12(1), in essence provides that "[a]ny person who offers or sells a security in violation of Section

---

12. Id. at 380.

13. Ibid.

14. Ibid.

15. 982 F.2d 653 (1st Cir.1992).

16. Id. at 654.

17. Id. at 654.

18. Id. at 654–655.

19. 7547 Corp. v. Parker & Parsley Dev. Partners, L.P., 38 F.3d 211, 223 (5th Cir.1994).

5 shall be liable to the person purchasing such security from him." Liability is near absolute. The plaintiff need only prove that

(1) the defendant was a seller;

(2) the jurisdictional requirement of interstate commerce was satisfied;[1]

(3) the defendant failed to comply with the § 5 registration or prospectus requirement, typically by such means as an unregistered offer or sale or failure to timely deliver a prospectus or securities;[2]

(4) the action is not barred by the statute of limitations; and

(5) adequate tender is made when the plaintiff seeks the remedy of rescission (rather than damages).[3]

Unlike § 12(a)(2) which provides a defense of reasonable care, the only practical defense available to the defendant under § 12(a)(1) is to prove that the particular security or transaction was exempt from § 5. The defendant's culpability is irrelevant in a § 12(a)(1) action.[4]

Pinter v. Dahl

Supreme Court of the United States, 1988.
486 U.S. 622, 108 S.Ct. 2063, 100 L.Ed.2d 658.

■ JUSTICE BLACKMUN delivered the opinion of the court.

The questions presented by this case are * * * whether one must intend to confer a benefit on himself or on a third party in order to qualify as a "seller" within the meaning of § 12(1).

I

The controversy arises out of the sale prior to 1982 of unregistered securities (fractional undivided interests in oil and gas leases) by petitioner Billy J. "B.J." Pinter to respondents Maurice Dahl and Dahl's friends, family, and business associates. Pinter is an oil and gas producer in Texas and Oklahoma, and a registered securities dealer in Texas. Dahl is a California real estate broker and investor, who, at the time of his dealings with Pinter, was a veteran of two unsuccessful oil and gas ventures. In pursuit of further investment opportunities, Dahl employed an oil field expert to locate and acquire oil and gas leases. This expert introduced Dahl to Pinter. Dahl advanced $20,000 to Pinter to acquire leases, with the understanding that they would be held in the name of Pinter's Black Gold Oil Company and that Dahl would have a right of first refusal to drill certain wells on the leasehold properties. Pinter located leases in Oklahoma, and Dahl toured the properties, often without Pinter, in order to talk to others and "get a feel for the properties." App. to Pet. for Cert. 32. Upon examining the geology, drilling logs, and production history assembled by Pinter, Dahl concluded, in the words of the District Court, that "there was no way to lose." Ibid.

---

1. See 9 Louis Loss & Joel Seligman, Securities Regulation 4208–4211 (3d ed. 1992).

2. Id. at 4194–4197.

3. Section 12 requires "tender of such security" for rescission. See id. at 4241–4242.

4. See, e.g., Hill York Corp. v. American Int'l Franchises, Inc., 448 F.2d 680, 694 n. 19 (5th Cir.1971); SEC v. Holschuh, 694 F.2d 130, 137 n. 10 (7th Cir.1982).

After investing approximately $310,000 in the properties, Dahl told the other respondents about the venture. Except for Dahl and respondent Grantham, none of the respondents spoke to or met Pinter or toured the properties. Because of Dahl's involvement in the venture, each of the other respondents decided to invest about $7,500.[2]

Dahl assisted his fellow investors in completing the subscription-agreement form prepared by Pinter. Each letter-contract signed by the purchaser stated that the participating interests were being sold without the benefit of registration under the Securities Act, in reliance on Securities and Exchange Commission (SEC or Commission) Rule 146, 17 CFR § 230.146 (1982). In fact, the oil and gas interests involved in this suit were never registered with the Commission. Respondents' investment checks were made payable to Black Gold Oil Company. Dahl received no commission from Pinter in connection with the other respondents' purchases.

When the venture failed and their interests proved to be worthless, respondents brought suit against Pinter in the United States District Court for the Northern District of Texas, seeking rescission under § 12(1) of the Securities Act, 15 U.S.C. § 77l(1), for the unlawful sale of unregistered securities.

In a counterclaim, Pinter alleged that Dahl, by means of fraudulent misrepresentations and concealment of facts, induced Pinter to sell and deliver the securities. Pinter averred that Dahl falsely assured Pinter that he would provide other qualified, sophisticated, and knowledgeable investors with all the information necessary for evaluation of the investment. Dahl allegedly agreed to raise the funds for the venture from those investors, with the understanding that Pinter would simply be the "operator" of the wells. App. 69–73. Pinter also asserted, on the basis of the same factual allegations, that Dahl's suit was barred by the equitable defenses of estoppel and *in pari delicto*. Id., at 66–67.[6]

The District Court, after a bench trial, granted judgment for respondent-investors. Id., at 92. The court concluded that Pinter had not proved that the oil and gas interests were entitled to the private-offering exemption from registration. App. to Pet. for Cert. a–37. Accordingly, the court ruled that, because the securities were unregistered, respondents were entitled to rescission pursuant to § 12(1). Ibid.[7] The court also concluded that the evidence was insufficient to sustain Pinter's counterclaim against Dahl. The District Court made no mention of the equitable defenses asserted by Pinter, but it apparently rejected them. * * *

The Court of Appeals * * * considered whether Dahl was himself a "seller" of the oil and gas interests within the meaning of § 12(1), for if he was, the court assumed, he could be held liable in contribution for the other plaintiffs' claims against Pinter.[9] 787 F.2d, at 990, and n. 8. Citing Fifth Circuit

2. The venture included still others who were either interested in additional ventures organized by Pinter or were new investors who met Pinter through sources other than Dahl. Those investors are not parties to this litigation.

6. Pinter contended that all the respondents should be estopped from recovery because of Dahl's fraudulent conduct. He asserted his *in pari delicto* defense solely against Dahl.

7. Having reached this conclusion, the District Court found it unnecessary to consider respondents' § 12(2) claim. App. to Pet. for Cert. 37–38. The court rejected respondents' claim under § 10(b) and Rule 10b–5. App. to Pet. for Cert. a–37.

9. Because none of the other plaintiffs sought recovery from Dahl, Dahl's liability on their claims is at issue only if contribution is available to Pinter.

precedent, the court described a statutory seller as "(1) one who parts with title to securities in exchange for consideration or (2) one whose participation in the buy-sell transaction is a substantial factor in causing the transaction to take place." Id., at 990. While acknowledging that Dahl's conduct was a "substantial factor" in causing the other plaintiffs to purchase securities from Pinter, the court declined to hold that Dahl was a "seller" for purposes of § 12(1). Instead, the court went on to refine its test to include a threshold requirement that one who acts as a "promoter" be "motivated by a desire to confer a direct or indirect benefit on someone other than the person he has advised to purchase." 787 F.2d, at 991. The court reasoned that "a rule imposing liability (without fault or knowledge) on friends and family members who give one another gratuitous advice on investment matters unreasonably interferes with well-established patterns of social discourse." Ibid. Accordingly, since the court found no evidence that Dahl sought or received any financial benefit in return for his advice, it declined to impose liability on Dahl for "mere gregariousness." Ibid.

* * *

III

* * *

In determining whether Dahl may be deemed a "seller" for purposes of § 12(1), such that he may be held liable for the sale of unregistered securities to the other investor-respondents, we look first at the language of § 12(1). See Ernst & Ernst v. Hochfelder, 425 U.S. 185, 197, 96 S.Ct. 1375, 1382, 47 L.Ed.2d 668 (1976). That statute provides, in pertinent part: "Any person who * * * offers or sells a security" in violation of the registration requirement of the Securities Act "shall be liable to the person purchasing such security from him." 15 U.S.C. § 77l. This provision defines the class of defendants who may be subject to liability as those who offer or sell unregistered securities. But the Securities Act nowhere delineates who may be regarded as a statutory seller, and the sparse legislative history sheds no light on the issue. The courts, on their part, have not defined the term uniformly.

At the very least, however, the language of § 12(1) contemplates a buyer-seller relationship not unlike traditional contractual privity. Thus, it is settled that § 12(1) imposes liability on the owner who passed title, or other interest in

---

The Court of Appeals addressed Pinter's contention that Dahl was liable as a § 12(1) seller and thus should be accountable to Pinter in contribution for the amounts awarded to the other plaintiffs. 787 F.2d, at 987. It is not entirely clear how this claim was raised below. Pinter's pleadings do not state an explicit cause of action for contribution against Dahl, although Pinter did move, albeit unsuccessfully, to realign Dahl as a third-party defendant, based on Pinter's assertion that Dahl was a "seller" of the unregistered securities to the remaining plaintiffs and had made the allegedly actionable misrepresentations to them in connection with the sales. See 1 Record 164–165, 189. Presumably, the Court of Appeals construed Pinter's affirmative defense for contributory fault and his incorporation of this defense into his counterclaims, as effectively seeking contribution.

Unlike § 11 of the Securities Act, see 15 U.S.C. § 77k(f), § 12 does not expressly provide for contribution. The Court of Appeals did not reach the question whether Pinter is entitled to contribution under § 12(1) because it found that Dahl was not a seller for purposes of § 12(1), and therefore would not be the proper subject of a contribution claim. The parties have not raised or addressed the contribution issue before this Court, and we express no view as to whether a right of contribution exists under § 12(1) of the Securities Act.

the security, to the buyer for value. See Loss, at 1016. Dahl, of course, was not a seller in this conventional sense, and therefore may be held liable only if § 12(1) liability extends to persons other than the person who passes title.[20]

A

In common parlance, a person may offer or sell property without necessarily being the person who transfers title to, or other interest in, that property. We need not rely entirely on ordinary understanding of the statutory language, however, for the Securities Act defines the operative terms of § 12(1). Section 2(3) defines "sale" or "sell" to include "every contract of sale or disposition of a security or interest in a security, for value," and the terms "offer to sell," "offer for sale," or "offer" to include "every attempt or offer to dispose of, or solicitation of an offer to buy, a security or interest in a security, for value." 15 U.S.C. § 77b(3). Under these definitions, the range of persons potentially liable under § 12(1) is not limited to persons who pass title. The inclusion of the phrase "solicitation of an offer to buy" within the definition of "offer" brings an individual who engages in solicitation, an activity not inherently confined to the actual owner, within the scope of § 12. See Loss, at 1016; Douglas & Bates, The Federal Securities Act of 1933, 43 Yale L.J. 171, 206–207 (1933). Indeed, the Court has made clear, in the context of interpreting § 17(a) of the Securities Act, 15 U.S.C. § 77q(a), that transactions other than traditional sales of securities are within the scope of § 2(3) and passage of title is not important. See United States v. Naftalin, 441 U.S. 768, 773, 99 S.Ct. 2077, 2081, 60 L.Ed.2d 624 (1979). We there explained: "The statutory terms ['offer' and 'sell'], which Congress expressly intended to define broadly, * * * are expansive enough to encompass the entire selling process, including the seller/agent transaction." Ibid. See also Rubin v. United States, 449 U.S. 424, 430, 101 S.Ct. 698, 701, 66 L.Ed.2d 633 (1981) ("It is not essential under the terms of the Act that full title pass to a transferee for the transaction to be an 'offer' or a 'sale' ").

Determining that the activity in question falls within the definition of "offer" or "sell" in § 2(3), however, is only half of the analysis. The second clause of § 12(1), which provides that only a defendant "from" whom the plaintiff "purchased" securities may be liable, narrows the field of potential sellers.[21] Several courts and commentators have stated that the purchase

---

20. The "offers or sells" and the "purchasing such security from him" language that governs § 12(1) also governs § 12(2), which provides a securities purchaser with a similar rescissionary cause of action for misrepresentation. See 15 U.S.C. § 77l. Most courts and commentators have not defined the defendant class differently for purposes of the two provisions. See, e.g., Pharo v. Smith, 621 F.2d 656, 665–668, and nn. 6–8 (C.A.5 1980); Schneider, Section 12 of the Securities Act of 1933: The Privity Requirement in the Contemporary Securities Law Perspective, 51 Tenn.L.Rev. 235, 261, and nn. 144 and 145 (1983–1984). See also Schillner v. H. Vaughan Clarke & Co., 134 F.2d 875, 878 (C.A.2 1943) ("Clearly the word [sell] has the

same meaning in subdivision (2) as in subdivision (1) of section 12").

The question whether anyone beyond the transferor of title, or immediate vendor, may be deemed a seller for purposes of § 12 has been litigated in actions under both § 12(1) and § 12(2). Decisions under § 12(2) addressing the "seller" question are thus relevant to the issue presented to us in this case, and, to that extent, we discuss them here. Nevertheless, this case does not present, nor do we take a position on, the scope of a statutory seller for purposes of § 12(2).

21. One important consequence of this provision is that § 12(1) imposes liability on only the buyer's immediate seller; remote purchasers are precluded from bringing actions against remote sellers. Thus, a buyer requirement necessarily restricts § 12 primary liability to the owner of the security. E.g., Beck v. Cantor, Fitzgerald & Co., 621 F.Supp. 1547, 1560–1561 (N.D.Ill.1985); Abrams, The Scope of Liability Under Section 12 of the Securities Act of 1933: "Participation" and the Pertinent Legislative Materials, 15 Ford. Urban L.J. 877 (1987); see also Collins v. Signetics Corp., 605 F.2d 110, 113 (C.A.3 1979) (absent some "special relationship"—e.g., control—§ 12 requires privity between statutory seller and buyer). In effect, these authorities interpret the term "purchase" as complementary to only the term "sell" defined in § 2(3). Thus, an offeror, as defined by § 2(3), may incur § 12 liability only if the offeror also "sells" the security to the plaintiff, in the sense of transferring title for value. Abrams, 15 Ford. Urban L.J., at 922–923.

We do not read § 12(1) so restrictively. The purchase requirement clearly confines § 12 liability to those situations in which a sale has taken place. Thus, a prospective buyer has no recourse against a person who touts unregistered securities to him if he does not purchase the securities. Loss, at 884. The requirement, however, does not exclude solicitation from the category of activities that may render a person liable when a sale has taken place. A natural reading of the statutory language would include in the statutory seller status at least some persons who urged the buyer to purchase. For example, a securities vendor's agent who solicited the purchase would commonly be said, and would be thought by the buyer, to be among those "from" whom the buyer "purchased," even though the agent himself did not pass title. See Cady v. Murphy, 113 F.2d 988, 990 (CA1) (finding broker acting as agent of the owner liable as a statutory seller), *cert. denied*, 311 U.S. 705, 61 S.Ct. 175, 85 L.Ed. 58 (1940).

The Securities Act does not define the term "purchase." The soundest interpretation of the term, however, is as a correlative to both "sell" and "offer," at least to the extent that the latter entails active solicitation of an offer to buy. This interpretation is supported by the history of the phrase "offers or sells," as it is used in § 12(1). As enacted in 1933, § 12(1) imposed liability on "[a]ny person who ... sells a security." 48 Stat. 84. The statutory definition of "sell" included "offer" and the activities now encompassed by that term, including solicitation. Id., at 74. The words "offer or" were added to § 12(1) by the 1954 amendments to the Securities Act, when the original definition of "sell" in § 2(3) was split into separate definitions of "sell" and "offer" in order to accommodate changes in § 5. 68 Stat. 683, 686. Since "sells" and "purchases" have obvious correlative meanings, Congress' express definition of "sells" in the original Securities Act to include solicitation suggests that the class of those from whom the buyer "purchases" extended to persons who solicit him. The 1954 amendment to § 12(1) was intended to preserve existing law, including the liability provisions of the Act. H.R.Rep. No. 1542, 83d Cong., 2d Sess., 26 (1954), U.S.Code Cong. & Admin.News 1954, p. 2973; S.Rep. No. 1036, 83d Cong., 2d Sess., 18 (1954); Loss, at 884. Hence, there is no reason to think Congress intended to narrow the meaning of "purchased from" when it amended the statute to include "solicitation" in the statutory definition of "offer" alone.

The applicability of § 12 liability to brokers and others who solicit securities purchases has been recognized frequently since the passage of the Securi-

cannot recover against his seller's seller.   L.J., at 177.
Loss, at 1023–1024; Douglas & Bates, 43 Yale

ties Act. It long has been "quite clear," that when a broker acting as agent of one of the principals to the transaction successfully solicits a purchase, he is a person from whom the buyer purchases within the meaning of § 12 and is therefore liable as a statutory seller. See Loss, at 1016. Indeed, courts had found liability on this basis prior to the 1954 amendment of the statute. See, e.g., Wall v. Wagner, 125 F.Supp. 854, 858 (Neb.1954), aff'd sub nom. Whittaker v. Wall, 226 F.2d 868, 873 (C.A.8 1955) (principal and its agents); Schillner v. H. Vaughan Clarke & Co., 134 F.2d 875, 879 (C.A.2 1943) (seller's broker); Cady v. Murphy, *supra* (seller's broker); Boehm v. Granger, 181 Misc. 680, 42 N.Y.S.2d 246, 248 (Sup.1943), aff'd, 268 App.Div. 855, 50 N.Y.S.2d 845 (1944) (buyer's broker). Had Congress intended liability to be restricted to those who pass title, it could have effectuated its intent by not adding the phrase "offers or" when it split the definition of "sell" in § 2(3).

An interpretation of statutory seller that includes brokers and others who solicit offers to purchase securities furthers the purposes of the Securities Act—to promote full and fair disclosure of information to the public in the sales of securities. In order to effectuate Congress' intent that § 12(1) civil liability be *in terrorem*, see Douglas & Bates, 43 Yale L.J., at 173; Shulman, 43 Yale L.J., at 227, the risk of its invocation should be felt by solicitors of purchases. The solicitation of a buyer is perhaps the most critical stage of the selling transaction. It is the first stage of a traditional securities sale to involve the buyer, and it is directed at producing the sale. In addition, brokers and other solicitors are well positioned to control the flow of information to a potential purchaser, and, in fact, such persons are the participants in the selling transaction who most often disseminate material information to investors. Thus, solicitation is the stage at which an investor is most likely to be injured, that is, by being persuaded to purchase securities without full and fair information. Given Congress' overriding goal of preventing this injury, we may infer that Congress intended solicitation to fall under the mantle of § 12(1).

Although we conclude that Congress intended § 12(1) liability to extend to those who solicit securities purchases, we share the Court of Appeals' conclusion that Congress did not intend to impose rescission based on strict liability on a person who urges the purchase but whose motivation is solely to benefit the buyer. When a person who urges another to make a securities purchase acts merely to assist the buyer, not only is it uncommon to say that the buyer "purchased" from him, but it is also strained to describe the giving of gratuitous advice, even strongly or enthusiastically, as "soliciting." Section 2(3) defines an offer as a "solicitation of an offer to buy . . . for value." The person who gratuitously urges another to make a particular investment decision is not, in any meaningful sense, requesting value in exchange for his suggestion or seeking the value the titleholder will obtain in exchange for the ultimate sale. The language and purpose of § 12(1) suggest that liability extends only to the person who successfully solicits the purchase, motivated at least in part by a desire to serve his own financial interests or those of the securities owner. If he had such a motivation, it is fair to say that the buyer "purchased" the security from him and to align him with the owner in a rescission action.

B

Petitioner is not satisfied with extending § 12(1) primary liability to one who solicits securities sales for financial gain. Pinter assumes, without explication, that liability is not limited to the person who actually parts title with the securities, and urges us to validate, as the standard by which additional defendant-sellers are identified, that version of the "substantial factor" test utilized by the Fifth Circuit before the refinement espoused in this case. Under that approach, grounded in tort doctrine, a nontransferor § 12(1) seller is defined as one "whose participation in the buy-sell transaction is a substantial factor in causing the transaction to take place." Pharo v. Smith, 621 F.2d 656, 667 (C.A.5 1980). The Court of Appeals acknowledged that Dahl would be liable as a statutory seller under this test. 787 F.2d, at 990.

We do not agree that Congress contemplated imposing § 12(1) liability under the broad terms petitioners advocate. There is no support in the statutory language or legislative history for expansion of § 12(1) primary liability beyond persons who pass title and persons who "offer," including those who "solicit" offers. Indeed, § 12's failure to impose express liability for mere participation in unlawful sales transactions suggests that Congress did not intend that the section impose liability on participants' collateral to the offer or sale. When Congress wished to create such liability, it had little trouble doing so. Cf. Touche Ross & Co. v. Redington, 442 U.S. 560, 572, 99 S.Ct. 2479, 2487, 61 L.Ed.2d 82 (1979).[26]

The deficiency of the substantial-factor test is that it divorces the analysis of seller status from any reference to the applicable statutory language and from any examination of § 12 in the context of the total statutory scheme. Those courts that have adopted the approach have not attempted to ground their analysis in the statutory language. See n. 25, *supra*. Instead, they substitute the concept of substantial participation in the sales transaction, or proximate causation of the plaintiff's purchase, for the words "offers or sells" in § 12. The "purchase from" requirement of § 12 focuses on the defendant's relationship with the plaintiff-purchaser. The substantial-factor test, on the other hand, focuses on the defendant's degree of involvement in the securities transaction and its surrounding circumstances. Thus, although the substantial-factor test undoubtedly embraces persons who pass title and who solicit the purchase of unregistered securities as statutory sellers, the test also would extend § 12(1) liability to participants only remotely related to the relevant aspects of the sales transaction. Indeed, it might expose securities professionals, such as accountants and lawyers, whose involvement is only the performance of their professional services, to § 12(1) strict liability for rescission. The buyer

---

26. Congress knew of the collateral participation concept and employed it in the Securities Act and throughout its unified program of securities regulation. Liabilities and obligations expressly grounded in participation are found elsewhere in the Act, see, e.g., 15 U.S.C. § 77b(11) (defining "underwriter," who is liable under § 5, as including direct and indirect participants), and in the later Roosevelt administration securities Acts. For example, § 9 of the 1934 Act, passed by the same Congress that enacted the Securities Act, creates a private right of action that expressly imposes liability on participants. 15 U.S.C. § 78i(e). See Abrams, 15 Ford. Urban L.J., at 925–937.

Section 11 of the Securities Act, 15 U.S.C. § 77k, lends strong support to the conclusion that Congress did not intend to extend § 12 primary liability to collateral participants in the unlawful securities sales transaction. That section provides an express cause of action for damages to a person acquiring securities pursuant to a registration statement that misstates or omits a material fact. Section 11(a) explicitly enumerates the various categories of persons involved in the registration process who are subject to suit under that section, including many who are participants in the activities leading up to the sale. There are no similar provisions in § 12, and therefore we may conclude that Congress did not intend such persons to be defendants in § 12 actions.

does not, in any meaningful sense, "purchas[e] the security from" such a person.[27]

* * * The broad remedial goals of the Securities Act are insufficient justification for interpreting a specific provision " 'more broadly than its language and the statutory scheme reasonably permit.' " *Touche Ross*, 442 U.S., at 578, 99 S.Ct., at 2490, quoting SEC v. Sloan, 436 U.S. 103, 116, 98 S.Ct. 1702, 1711, 56 L.Ed.2d 148 (1978). We must assume that Congress meant what it said.

The substantial-factor test reaches participants in sales transactions who do not even arguably fit within the definitions set out in § 2(3); it "would add a gloss to the operative language of [§ 12(1)] quite different from its commonly accepted meaning." Ernst & Ernst v. Hochfelder, 425 U.S., at 199, 96 S.Ct., at 1983. We conclude that Congress did not intend such a gross departure from the statutory language. Accordingly, we need not entertain Petitioner's policy arguments. Being merely a "substantial factor" in causing the sale of unregistered securities is not sufficient in itself to render a defendant liable under § 12(1).

C

We are unable to determine whether Dahl may be held liable as a statutory seller under § 12(1). The District Court explicitly found that "Dahl solicited each of the other plaintiffs (save perhaps Grantham) in connection with the offer, purchase, and receipt of their oil and gas interests." App. to Pet. for Cert. a–34. We cannot conclude that this finding was clearly erroneous. It is not clear, however, that Dahl had the kind of interest in the sales that make him liable as a statutory seller. * * *

IV

The judgment of the Court of Appeals is vacated, and the case is remanded for further proceedings consistent with this opinion.

It is so ordered.

WHO IS A SELLER?

The lower courts have generally extended the Supreme Court's § 12(a)(1) analysis in *Pinter* to § 12(a)(2).[1]

---

27. For similar reasons, we reject the Commission's suggestion that persons who "participate in soliciting the purchase" may be liable as statutory sellers. Brief for SEC as Amicus Curiae 22. The Commission relies on Katz v. Amos Treat & Co., 411 F.2d 1046 (C.A.2 1969), where the court held that an attorney who had been "a party to the solicitation" of the plaintiff-purchaser was liable under § 12(1) because he had placed the brokerage firm for which he worked in a position "to tackle [the purchaser] for the money" owed on an investment he had made. Id., at 1053. Although in Katz the attorney spoke directly to the plaintiff prior to the delivery of money in plaintiff's investment, the "party

to a solicitation" concept could easily embrace those who merely assist in another's solicitation efforts. See Schneider, 51 Tenn. L.Rev., at 273 (suggesting that the Katz approach allows courts to interpret solicitation activities "rather broadly"). It is difficult to see more than a slight difference between this approach and the participation theory, which we have concluded does not comport with Congress' intent.

1. *See, e.g.,* Abell v. Potomac Ins. Co., 858 F.2d 1104, 1113–1115 (5th Cir.1988), *cert. denied sub nom.* Abell v. Wright, Lindsey & Jennings, 492 U.S. 918 (1989); Moore v. Kayport Package Express, Inc., 885 F.2d 531, 535–537 (9th Cir.1989); Royal Am. Man-

After *Pinter* the law is settled that brokers or other agents—persons who are not sellers in the mystical sense of passing title—may be held liable under § 12(a)(1) or 12(a)(2).[2]

If a broker may be liable under § 12, it is not inevitable that an officer or director or employee or other nonbroker agent of the seller who actively participates in the sale will be liable.[3] *Pinter* focused on solicitation of sales "motivated at least in part by a desire to serve his own financial interests or those of the securities owner." The Second Circuit, for example, followed *Pinter* in holding that two general partners in a coal mining venture were liable to the limited partners under § 12(a)(2) because they had prepared and circulated a prospectus to the plaintiffs. The "seller" status of a lawyer-promoter whose law firm drafted the prospectus and performed other legal work in connection with the venture did not preclude the general partners from being sellers since the lawyer's promotional efforts were "directly attributable" to the general partners.[4] In contrast the courts have had little difficulty exonerating attorneys, accountants, and board members who did not own the relevant security, initiate or participate in sales negotiations, or otherwise appear to solicit sales.[5]

Subject to exceptions involving statutory controlling persons, it seems quite clear that § 12 contemplates only an action by a buyer against *his or her immediate seller*.[6] That is to say, in the case of the typical firm commitment underwriting, the ultimate investor can recover only from the dealer who sold to him or her.[7] In effect, § 12 incorporates a privity requirement which does

---

agers, Inc. v. IRC Holding Corp., 885 F.2d 1011, 1016–1017 (2d Cir.1989); Craftmatic Sec. Litig. v. Kraftsow, 890 F.2d 628, 635–636 (3d Cir.1989); Ryder Int'l Corp. v. First Am. Nat'l Bank, 943 F.2d 1521, 1527–1529 (11th Cir.1991); Ackerman v. Schwartz, 947 F.2d 841, 844–845 (7th Cir.1991).

2. Pinter v. Dahl, 486 U.S. 622, 642–643 (1988). This result was reached frequently before *Pinter* on the logic that a broker for a seller is a "person who sells." *See* Cady v. Murphy, 113 F.2d 988 (1st Cir.1940), *cert. denied*, 311 U.S. 705 (1940); Lawler v. Gilliam, 569 F.2d 1283, 1287–1288 (4th Cir. 1978); Harelson v. Miller Fin. Corp., 854 F.2d 1141 (9th Cir.1988), *cert. denied sub nom.* Wilson v. Harelson, 488 U.S. 917 (1988).

3. *See* Smith v. American Nat'l Bank & Trust Co., 982 F.2d 936, 941–942 (6th Cir. 1992); SEC v. Tuchinsky, 1992 Fed.Sec. L.Rep. (CCH) ¶ 96,917 at 93,803 (S.D.Fla. 1992).

4. Capri v. Murphy, 856 F.2d 473, 478 (2d Cir.1988).

5. *See, e.g.*, Wilson v. Saintine Exploration & Drilling Corp., 872 F.2d 1124, 1126–1127 (2d Cir.1989) (attorney); Moore v. Kayport Package Express, Inc., 885 F.2d 531, 537 (9th Cir.1989) (attorney and accountant); Royal Am. Managers, Inc. v. IRC Holding

Corp., 885 F.2d 1011, 1017 (2d Cir.1989) (attorney and director); Ackerman v. Schwartz, 947 F.2d 841, 845 (7th Cir.1991) (attorney).

In Shaw v. Digital Equip. Corp., 82 F.3d 1194, 1215–1216 (1st Cir.1996) the court held:

> Because the issuer in a firm commitment underwriting does not pass title to the securities, DEC and its officers cannot be held liable as "sellers" under Section 12(2) [now § 12(a)(2)] unless they actively "solicited" the plaintiffs' purchase of securities to further their own financial motives, in the manner of a broker or vendor's agent. See Pinter 486 U.S. at 644–47, 108 S.Ct. at 2076–79. Absent such solicitation, DEC can be viewed as no more than a "seller's seller," whom plaintiffs would have no right to sue under Section 12(2).

6. *See, e.g.*, Cortec Indus. Inc. v. Sum Holding, L.P., 949 F.2d 42 (2d Cir.1991).

7. See, e.g., Lone Star Ladies Inv. Club v. Schlotzsky's Inc., 238 F.3d 363, 369–370 (5th Cir.2001).

Underwriters can be held liable if they sold directly to the plaintiffs. See Schaffer v. Evolving Sys., Inc., 29 F.Supp.2d 1213, 1222 (D.Colo.1998).

not exist under § 11.[8]

PROBLEM 13–2

Howard Ripple is an attorney who in June 2001 wrote a tax opinion that was circulated to investors in a limited partnership known as Organized Equipment Leasing (OEL). Ripple's letter described specific tax credits and deductions that would be available to investors. Several "facts" that Ripple described in his letter were fictions and the Internal Revenue Service subsequently disallowed each of the tax credits and deductions Ripple described.

Over 110 investors have now brought a § 12(a)(2) lawsuit against Ripple, among others. Will this suit succeed?

Would it make any difference if Ripple wrote personal notes to each investor bringing suit recommending that "you consider this investment seriously. It is a winner!"

Would it make any difference if Ripple's law firm was paid on a sliding sale basis depending on the dollar value of limited partnership units sold?

2.   SECTION 12(a)(2)

Section 12(a)(2) proscribes any person who offers or sells a security (including an exempt security other than a security exempted by § 3(a)(2) or (14)) by means of a prospectus or oral communication which includes a material misrepresentation or material omission. The offer or sale must satisfy a jurisdictional requirement of "use of any means of or instruments of transportation or communication in interstate commerce or of the mails." The *Pinter v. Dahl* definition of "seller" in the context of § 12(a)(1) is seemingly equally applicable to § 12(a)(2).

Defendants are provided two statutory defenses.

Section 12(a)(2) itself creates a "reasonable care" defense for a defendant who can sustain the burden of proof "that he did not know, and in the exercise of reasonable care could not have known" of a material misrepresentation or omission.

In 1995 Congress added a new § 12(b) to allow the defendant to reduce the amount recoverable under § 12(a)(2) by proving that the depreciation in value of the security was not caused by the material misrepresentation or omission. This "loss causation" or "negative causation" defense is similar, if not identical, to the § 11 causation defense.

Unlike the more frequently employed Rule 10b–5, § 12(a)(2) provides the plaintiff a mandatory right of rescission upon tender of the subject security. Alternatively plaintiffs may seek rescissory damages if they have sold the security and can not tender.

When the seller of a security is the issuer or an underwriter, a plaintiff may be able to bring a claim either under § 11 and 12(a)(2). When the ultimate seller is a dealer, § 12(a)(2) alone will be available.

---

8. See also William Fisher, *Parsing Pinter* Four Years Later: Defining a Statutory Seller under Section 12 of the Securities Act, 21 Sec. Reg. L.J. 46 (1993); Jack E. Karns, Edwin A. Doty & Steven S. Long, Accountant and Attorney Liability as "Sellers" of Securities under Section 12(2) of the Securities Act of 1933: Judicial Rejection of the Statutory, Collateral Participant Status Cause of Action, 74 Neb. L. Rev. 1 (1995).

As with the antifraud provisions generally concepts such as materiality, misrepresentation, omission, and fact have a generic meaning.

A plaintiff is not required under § 12(a)(2) to prove reliance, only that he or she did not know of the material misrepresentation or omission, normally a far easier matter.[1]

As with the antifraud remedies a plaintiff can sue the controlling person of a § 12(a) seller, as well as the seller. Until it was resolved in 1995, the most significant question under § 12(a)(2) was its scope: Was the Section limited to registered securities offerings "by means of a prospectus" or did the definition of prospectus in what was then § 2(10) (now § 2(a)(10)) extend to secondary marketing trading?

Gustafson v. Alloyd Company, Incorporated

Supreme Court of the United States, 1995.
513 U.S. 561, 115 S.Ct. 1061, 131 L.Ed.2d 1.

■ JUSTICE KENNEDY delivered the opinion of the Court.

Under § 12(2) of the Securities Act of 1933 buyers have an express cause of action for rescission against sellers who make material misstatements or omissions "by means of a prospectus." The question presented is whether this right of rescission extends to a private, secondary transaction, on the theory that recitations in the purchase agreement are part of a "prospectus."

I

Petitioners Gustafson, McLean, and Butler (collectively Gustafson) were in 1989 the sole shareholders of Alloyd, Inc., a manufacturer of plastic packaging and automatic heat sealing equipment. Alloyd was formed, and its stock was issued, in 1961. In 1989, Gustafson decided to sell Alloyd and engaged KPMG Peat Marwick to find a buyer. In response to information distributed by KPMG, Wind Point Partners II, L.P., agreed to buy substantially all of the issued and outstanding stock through Alloyd Holdings, Inc., a new corporation formed to effect the sale of Alloyd's stock. The shareholders of Alloyd Holdings were Wind Point and a number of individual investors.

In preparation for negotiating the contract with Gustafson, Wind Point undertook an extensive analysis of the company, relying in part on a formal business review prepared by KPMG. Alloyd's practice was to take inventory at year's end, so Wind Point and KPMG considered taking an earlier inventory to use in determining the purchase price. In the end they did not do so, relying instead on certain estimates and including provisions for adjustments after the transaction closed.

On December 20, 1989 Gustafson and Alloyd Holdings executed a contract of sale. Alloyd Holdings agreed to pay Gustafson and his coshareholders $18,709,000 for the sale of the stock plus a payment of $2,122,219, which reflected the estimated increase in Alloyd's net worth from the end of the previous year, the last period for which hard financial data were available. Article IV of the purchase agreement, entitled "Representations and Warran-

---

1. *See, e.g.*, Wright v. National Warranty Co., L.P., 953 F.2d 256, 262 (6th Cir.1992); Wamser v. J.E. Liss, Inc., 838 F.Supp. 393, 398 (E.D.Wis.1993). *See generally* 9 Louis Loss & Joel Seligman, Securities Regulation 4202–4205 (3d ed. 1992).

ties of the Sellers," included assurances that the company's financial statements "present fairly * * * the Company's financial condition" and that between the date of the latest balance sheet and the date the agreement was executed "there ha[d] been no material adverse change in * * * [Alloyd's] financial condition." App. 115, 117. The contract also provided that if the year-end audit and financial statements revealed a variance between estimated and actual increased value, the disappointed party would receive an adjustment.

The year-end audit of Alloyd revealed that Alloyd's actual earnings for 1989 were lower than the estimates relied upon by the parties in negotiating the adjustment amount of $2,122,219. Under the contract, the buyers had a right to recover an adjustment amount of $815,000, from the sellers. Nevertheless, on February 11, 1991, the newly formed company (now called Alloyd, Co., the same as the original company) and Wind Point brought suit in the United States District Court for the Northern District of Illinois, seeking outright rescission of the contract under § 12(2) of the Securities Act of 1933. Alloyd (the new company) claimed that statements made by Gustafson and his coshareholders regarding the financial data of their company were inaccurate, rendering untrue the representations and warranties contained in the contract. The buyers further alleged that the contract of sale was a "prospectus," so that any misstatements contained in the agreement gave rise to liability under § 12(2) of the 1933 Act. Pursuant to the adjustment clause, the defendants remitted to the purchasers $815,000 plus interest, but the adjustment did not cause the purchasers to drop the lawsuit.

Relying on the decision of the Court of Appeals for the Third Circuit in Ballay v. Legg Mason Wood Walker, Inc., 925 F.2d 682 (1991), the District Court granted Gustafson's motion for summary judgment, holding "that section 12(2) claims can only arise out of the initial stock offerings." App. 20. Although the sellers were the controlling shareholders of the original company, the District Court concluded that the private sale agreement "cannot be compared to an initial offering" because "the purchasers in this case had direct access to financial and other company documents, and had the opportunity to inspect the seller's property." Id., at 21.

On review, the Court of Appeals for the Seventh Circuit vacated the District Court's judgment and remanded for further consideration in light of that court's intervening decision in Pacific Dunlop Holdings Inc. v. Allen & Co. Inc., 993 F.2d 578 (1993). In Pacific Dunlop the court reasoned that the inclusion of the term "communication" in the Act's definition of prospectus meant that the term prospectus was defined "very broadly" to include all written communications that offered the sale of a security. Id., at 582. Rejecting the view of the Court of Appeals for the Third Circuit in Ballay, the Court of Appeals decided that § 12(2)'s right of action for rescission "applies to any communication which offers any security for sale * * * including the stock purchase agreement in the present case." 993 F.2d, at 595. We granted certiorari to resolve this Circuit conflict, 510 U.S. 1176, 114 S.Ct. 1215, 127 L.Ed.2d 562 (1994), and we now reverse.

II

The rescission claim against Gustafson is based upon § 12(2) of the 1993 Act, 48 Stat. 84, as amended, 15 U.S.C. § 771(2). * * * As this case reaches us, we must assume that the stock purchase agreement contained material misstatements of fact made by the sellers and that Gustafson would not sustain its burden of proving due care. On these assumptions, Alloyd would have a right to obtain rescission if those misstatements were made "by means of a prospectus or oral communication." The parties (and the courts of appeals) agree that the phrase "oral communication" is restricted to oral communications that relate to a prospectus. See Pacific Dunlop, *supra*, 993 F.2d, at 588; Ballay, *supra*, at 688. The determinative question, then, is whether the contract between Alloyd and Gustafson is a "prospectus" as the term is used in the 1933 Act.

Alloyd argues that "prospectus" is defined in a broad manner, broad enough to encompass the contract between the parties. This argument is echoed by the dissents. See post, at 1074 (Thomas, J., dissenting); post, at 1079 (Ginsburg, J., dissenting). Gustafson, by contrast, maintains that prospectus in the 1933 Act means a communication soliciting the public to purchase securities from the issuer. Brief for Petitioners 17–18.

Three sections of the 1933 Act are critical in resolving the definitional question on which the case turns: § 2(10), which defines a prospectus; § 10, which sets forth the information that must be contained in a prospectus; and § 12, which imposes liability based on misstatements in a prospectus. In seeking to interpret the term "prospectus," we adopt the premise that the term should be construed, if possible, to give it a consistent meaning throughout the Act. That principle follows from our duty to construe statutes, not isolated provisions. * * *

A

We begin with § 10. * * *

Although § 10 does not define what a prospectus is, it does instruct us what a prospectus cannot be if the Act is to be interpreted as a symmetrical and coherent regulatory scheme, one in which the operative words have a consistent meaning throughout. There is no dispute that the contract in this case was not required to contain the information contained in a registration statement and that no statutory exemption was required to take the document out of § 10's coverage. Cf. 15 U.S.C. § 77c. It follows that the contract is not a prospectus under § 10. That does not mean that a document ceases to be a prospectus whenever it omits a required piece of information. It does mean that a document is not a prospectus within the meaning of that section if, absent an exemption, it need not comply with § 10's requirements in the first place.

An examination of § 10 reveals that, whatever else "prospectus" may mean, the term is confined to a document that, absent an overriding exemption, must include the "information contained in the registration statement." By and large, only public offerings by an issuer of a security, or by controlling shareholders of an issuer, require the preparation and filing of registration statements. See 15 U.S.C. §§ 77d, 77e, 77b(11). It follows, we conclude, that a prospectus under § 10 is confined to documents related to public offerings by an issuer or its controlling shareholders.

This much (the meaning of prospectus in § 10) seems not to be in dispute. Where the courts are in disagreement is with the implications of this proposition for the entirety of the Act, and for § 12 in particular. Compare Ballay v. Legg Mason Wood Walker, Inc., 925 F.2d, at 688–689 (suggesting that the term prospectus is used in a consistent manner in both §§ 10 and 12), with Pacific Dunlop Holdings Inc. v. Allen & Co., 993 F.2d, at 584 (rejecting that view). We conclude that the term "prospectus" must have the same meaning under §§ 10 and 12. In so holding, we do not, as the dissent by Justice Ginsburg suggests, make the mistake of treating § 10 as a definitional section. See post at 1080–1081 (Ginsburg, J., dissenting). Instead, we find in § 10 guidance and instruction for giving the term a consistent meaning throughout the Act.

The Securities Act of 1933, like every Act of Congress, should not be read as a series of unrelated and isolated provisions. Only last term we adhered to the "normal rule of statutory construction" that "identical words used in different parts of the same act are intended to have the same meaning." * * * That principle applies here. If the contract before us is not a prospectus for purposes of § 10—as all must and do concede—it is not a prospectus for purposes of § 12 either.

The conclusion that prospectus has the same meaning, and refers to the same types of communications (public offers by an issuer or its controlling shareholders), in both §§ 10 and 12 is reinforced by an examination of the structure of the 1933 Act. Sections 4 and 5 of the Act together require a seller to file a registration statement and to issue a prospectus for certain defined types of sales (public offerings by an issuer, through an underwriter). See 15 U.S.C. §§ 77d, 77e. Sections 7 and 10 of the Act set forth the information required in the registration statement and the prospectus. See §§ 77g, 77j. Section 11 provides for liability on account of false registration statements; § 12(2) for liability based on misstatements in prospectuses. See 15 U.S.C. §§ 77k, 77l. Following the most natural and symmetrical reading, just as the liability imposed by § 11 flows from the requirements imposed by §§ 5 and 7 providing for the filing and content of registration statements, the liability imposed by § 12(2), cannot attach unless there is an obligation to distribute the prospectus in the first place (or unless there is an exemption).

Our interpretation is further confirmed by a reexamination of § 12 itself. The section contains an important guide to the correct resolution of the case. By its terms, § 12(2) exempts from its coverage prospectuses relating to the sales of government-issued securities. See 15 U.S.C. § 77l (excepting securities exempted by § 77c(a)(2)). If Congress intended § 12(2) to create liability for misstatements contained in any written communication relating to the sale of a security—including secondary market transactions—there is no ready explanation for exempting government-issued securities from the reach of the right to rescind granted by § 12(2). Why would Congress grant immunity to a private seller from liability in a rescission suit for no reason other than that the seller's misstatements happen to relate to securities issued by a governmental entity? No reason is apparent. The anomaly disappears, however, when the term "prospectus" relates only to documents that offer securities sold to the public by an issuer. The exemption for government-issued securities makes perfect sense on that view, for it then becomes a precise and appropriate means of giving immunity to governmental authorities.

The primary innovation of the 1933 Act was the creation of federal duties—for the most part, registration and disclosure obligations—in connection with public offerings. See, e.g., Ernst & Ernst v. Hochfelder, 425 U.S. 185, 195, 96 S.Ct. 1375, 1382, 47 L.Ed.2d 668 (1976) (the 1933 Act "was designed to provide investors with full disclosure of material information concerning public offerings"); Blue Chip Stamps v. Manor Drug Stores, 421 U.S. 723, 752, 95 S.Ct. 1917, 1933, 44 L.Ed.2d 539 (1975) ("The 1933 Act is a far narrower statute [than the Securities Exchange Act of 1934 (1934 Act)] chiefly concerned with disclosure and fraud in connection with offerings of securities—primarily, as here, initial distributions of newly issued stock from corporate issuers");

United States v. Naftalin, 441 U.S. 768, 777–778, 99 S.Ct. 2077, 2084, 60 L.Ed.2d 624 (1979) ("[T]he 1933 Act was primarily concerned with the regulation of new offerings"); SEC v. Ralston Purina Co., 346 U.S. 119, 122, n. 5, 73 S.Ct. 981, 983, n. 5, 97 L.Ed. 1494 (1953) (" '[T]he bill does not affect transactions beyond the need of public protection in order to prevent recurrences of demonstrated abuses' "), quoting H.R.Rep. No. 85, 73d Cong., 1st Sess., 7 (1933). We are reluctant to conclude that § 12(2) creates vast additional liabilities that are quite independent of the new substantive obligations the Act imposes. It is more reasonable to interpret the liability provisions of the 1933 Act as designed for the primary purpose of providing remedies for violations of the obligations it had created. Indeed, §§ 11 and 12(1)—the statutory neighbors of § 12(2)—afford remedies for violations of those obligations. See § 11, 15 U.S.C. § 77k (remedy for untrue statements in registration statements); § 12(1), 15 U.S.C. § 77l(1) (remedy for sales in violation of § 5, which prohibits the sale of unregistered securities). Under our interpretation of "prospectus," § 12(2) in similar manner is linked to the new duties created by the Act.

On the other hand, accepting Alloyd's argument that any written offer is a prospectus under § 12 would require us to hold that the word "prospectus" in § 12 refers to a broader set of communications than the same term in § 10. The Court of Appeals was candid in embracing that conclusion: "[T]he 1933 Act contemplates many definitions of a prospectus. Section 2(10) gives a single, broad definition; section 10(a) involves an isolated, distinct document—a prospectus within a prospectus; section 10(d) gives the Commission authority to classify many." Pacific Dunlop Holdings Inc. v. Allen & Co., 993 F.2d, at 584. The dissents take a similar tack. In the name of a plain meaning approach to statutory interpretation, the dissents discover in the Act two different species of prospectuses: formal (also called § 10) prospectuses, subject to both §§ 10 and 12, and informal prospectuses, subject only to § 12 but not to § 10. See post at 1080–1081 (Ginsburg, J., dissenting); see also post, at 1074–1075 (Thomas, J., dissenting). Nowhere in the statute, however, do the terms "formal prospectus" or "informal prospectus" appear. Instead, the Act uses one term—"prospectus"—throughout. In disagreement with the Court of Appeals and the dissenting opinions, we cannot accept the conclusion that this single operative word means one thing in one section of the Act and something quite different in another. The dissenting opinions' resort to terms not found in the Act belies the claim of fidelity to the text of the statute.

Alloyd, as well as Justice Thomas in his dissent, respond that if Congress had intended § 12(2) to govern only initial public offerings, it would have been simple for Congress to have referred to the § 4 exemptions in § 12(2). See Brief of Respondents 25–26; post, at 1077 (Thomas, J., dissenting). The argument gets the presumption backwards. Had Congress meant the term "prospectus" in § 12(2) to have a different meaning than the same term in § 10, that is when one would have expected Congress to have been explicit. Congressional silence cuts against, not in favor of, Alloyd's argument. The burden should be on the proponents of the view that the term "prospectus" means one thing in § 12 and another in § 10 to adduce strong textual support for that conclusion. And Alloyd adduces none.

B

Alloyd's contrary argument rests to a significant extent on § 2(10), or, to be more precise, on one word of that section. Section 2(10) provides that "[t]he term 'prospectus' means any prospectus, notice, circular, advertisement, letter, or communication, written or by radio or television, which offers any security for sale or confirms the sale of any security." 15 U.S.C. § 77b(10). Concentrating on the word "communication," Alloyd argues that any written communication that offers a security for sale is a "prospectus." Inserting its definition into § 12(2), Alloyd insists that a material misstatement in any communication offering a security for sale gives rise to an action for rescission, without proof of fraud by the seller or reliance by the purchaser. In Alloyd's view, § 2(10) gives the term "prospectus" a capacious definition that, although incompatible with § 10, nevertheless governs in § 12.

The flaw in Alloyd's argument, echoed in the dissenting opinions, post, at 1074–1075 (Thomas, J., dissenting); post, at 1080–1081 (Ginsburg, J., dissenting), is its reliance on one word of the definitional section in isolation. To be sure, § 2(10) defines a prospectus as, inter alia, a "communication, written or by radio or television, which offers any security for sale or confirms the sale of any security." 15 U.S.C. § 77b(10). The word "communication," however, on which Alloyd's entire argument rests, is but one word in a list, a word Alloyd reads altogether out of context.

The relevant phrase in the definitional part of the statute must be read in its entirety, a reading which yields the interpretation that the term prospectus refers to a document soliciting the public to acquire securities. We find that definition controlling. Alloyd's argument that the phrase "communication, written or by radio or television," transforms any written communication offering a security for sale into a prospectus cannot consist with at least two rather sensible rules of statutory construction. First, the Court will avoid a reading which renders some words altogether redundant. See United States v. Menasche, 348 U.S. 528, 538–39, 75 S.Ct. 513, 519–20, 99 L.Ed. 615 (1955). If "communication" included every written communication, it would render "notice, circular, advertisement, [and] letter" redundant, since each of these are forms of written communication as well. Congress with ease could have drafted § 2(10) to read: "The term 'prospectus' means any communication, written or by radio or television, that offers a security for sale or confirms the sale of a security." Congress did not write the statute that way, however, and we decline to say it included the words "notice, circular, advertisement, [and] letter" for no purpose.

The constructional problem is resolved by the second principle Alloyd overlooks, which is that a word is known by the company it keeps (the doctrine of noscitur a sociis). This rule we rely upon to avoid ascribing to one word a meaning so broad that it is inconsistent with its accompanying words, thus giving "unintended breadth to the Acts of Congress." Jarecki v. G.D. Searle & Co., 367 U.S. 303, 307, 81 S.Ct. 1579, 1582, 6 L.Ed.2d 859 (1961). The rule guided our earlier interpretation of the word "security" under the 1934 Act. The 1934 Act defines the term "security" to mean, inter alia, "any note." We concluded nevertheless that in context "the phrase 'any note' should not be interpreted to mean literally 'any note,' but must be understood against the background of what Congress was attempting to accomplish in enacting the Securities Acts." Reves v. Ernst & Young, 494 U.S. 56, 63, 110 S.Ct. 945, 950, 108 L.Ed.2d 47 (1990). These considerations convince us that Alloyd's suggested interpretation is not the correct one.

There is a better reading. From the terms "prospectus, notice, circular, advertisement, or letter," it is apparent that the list refers to documents of wide dissemination. In a similar manner, the list includes communications "by radio or television," but not face-to-face or telephonic conversations. Inclusion of the term "communication" in that list suggests that it too refers to a public communication.

When the 1933 Act was drawn and adopted, the term "prospectus" was well understood to refer to a document soliciting the public to acquire securities from the issuer. See Black's Law Dictionary 959 (2d ed. 1910) (defining "prospectus" as a "document published by a company * * * or by persons acting as its agents or assignees, setting forth the nature and objects of an issue of shares * * * and inviting the public to subscribe to the issue"). In this respect, the word prospectus is a term of art, which accounts for Congressional confidence in employing what might otherwise be regarded as a partial circularity in the formal, statutory definition. See 15 U.S.C. § 77b(10) ("The term 'prospectus' means any prospectus * * *."). The use of the term prospectus to refer to public solicitations explains as well Congress' decision in § 12(2) to grant buyers a right to rescind without proof of reliance. See H.R.Rep. No. 85, 73d Cong., 1st Sess., 10 (1933) ("The statements for which [liable persons] are responsible, although they may never actually have been seen by the prospective purchaser, because of their wide dissemination, determine the market price of the security * * *.").

The list of terms in § 2(10) prevents a seller of stock from avoiding liability by calling a soliciting document something other than a prospectus, but it does not compel the conclusion that Alloyd urges us to reach and that the dissenting opinions adopt. Instead, the term "written communication" must be read in context to refer to writings that, from a functional standpoint, are similar to the terms "notice, circular, [and] advertisement." The term includes communications held out to the public at large but that might have been thought to be outside the other words in the definitional section.

C

Our holding that the term "prospectus" relates to public offerings by issuers and their controlling shareholders draws support from our earlier decision interpreting the one provision of the Act that extends coverage beyond the regulation of public offerings, § 17(a) of the 1933 Act. See United States v. Naftalin, 441 U.S. 768, 99 S.Ct. 2077, 60 L.Ed.2d 624 (1979). In Naftalin, though noting that "the 1933 Act was primarily concerned with the regulation of new offerings," the Court held that § 17(a) was "intended to cover any fraudulent scheme in an offer or sale of securities, whether in the course of an initial distribution or in the course of ordinary market trading." The Court justified this holding—which it termed "a major departure from th[e] limitation [of the 1933 Act to new offerings]"—by reference to both the statutory language and the unambiguous legislative history. Id., at 777–778, 99 S.Ct. at 2084. The same considerations counsel in favor of our interpretation of § 12(2).

The Court noted in Naftalin that § 17(a) contained no language suggesting a limitation on the scope of liability under § 17(a). See id., at 778, 99 S.Ct. at 2084 ("the statutory language * * * makes no distinctions between the two kinds of transactions"). Most important for present purposes, § 17(a) does not contain the word "prospectus." In contrast, as we have noted, § 12(2) contains language, i.e., "by means of a prospectus or oral communication," that limits § 12(2) to public offerings. Just as the absence of limiting language in § 17(a) resulted in broad coverage, the presence of limiting language in § 12(2) requires a narrow construction.

Of equal importance, the legislative history relied upon in Naftalin showed that Congress decided upon a deliberate departure from the general scheme of the Act in this one instance, and "made abundantly clear" its intent that § 17(a) have broad coverage. See Naftalin, 441 U.S., at 778, 99 S.Ct. at 2084 (quoting legislative history stating that " 'fraud or deception in the sale of securities may be prosecuted regardless of whether * * * or not it is of the class of securities exempted under sections 11 or 12.' " S.Rep. No. 47, 73d Cong., 1st Sess., 4 (1933)). No comparable legislative history even hints that § 12(2) was intended to be a free-standing provision effecting expansion of the coverage of the entire statute. The intent of Congress and the design of the statute require that § 12(2) liability be limited to public offerings.

D

It is understandable that Congress would provide buyers with a right to rescind, without proof of fraud or reliance, as to misstatements contained in a document prepared with care, following well established procedures relating to investigations with due diligence and in the context of a public offering by an issuer or its controlling shareholders. It is not plausible to infer that Congress created this extensive liability for every casual communication between buyer and seller in the secondary market. It is often difficult, if not altogether impractical, for those engaged in casual communications not to omit some fact that would, if included, qualify the accuracy of a statement. Under Alloyd's view any casual communication between buyer and seller in the aftermarket could give rise to an action for rescission, with no evidence of fraud on the part of the seller or reliance on the part of the buyer. In many instances buyers in practical effect would have an option to rescind, impairing the stability of past transactions where neither fraud nor detrimental reliance on misstatements or omissions occurred. We find no basis for interpreting the statute to reach so far.

III

The SEC, as amicus, and Justice Ginsburg in dissent, rely on what they call the legislative background of the Act to support Alloyd's construction. With a few minor exceptions, however, their reliance is upon statements by commentators and judges written after the Act was passed, not while it was under consideration. See Brief for Securities and Exchange Commission as Amicus Curiae 19–23; post, at 1083 (Ginsburg, J., dissenting). Material not available to the lawmakers is not considered, in the normal course, to be legislative history. After-the-fact statements by proponents of a broad interpretation are not a reliable indicator of what Congress intended when it passed the law, assuming extratextual sources are to any extent reliable for this purpose.

The SEC does quote one contemporaneous memorandum prepared by Dean Landis. See id., at 1070 (citing James M. Landis, Reply to Investment Bankers Association Objections of May 5, 1933, p.5). The statement is quite consistent with our construction. Landis observed that, in contrast to the liabilities imposed by the Act " 'that flow from the fact of non-registration or registration,' " dealings may violate § 12(2) " 'even though they are not related to the fact of registration.' " See ibid. (emphasis added). This, of course, is true. The liability imposed by § 12(2) has nothing to do with the fact of registration, that is with the failure to file a registration statement that complies with §§ 7 and 11 of the Act. Instead, the liability imposed by § 12(2) turns on misstatements contained in the prospectus. And, one might point out, securities exempted by § 3 of the Act do not require registration, although they are covered by § 12. Landis' observation has nothing to do with the question presented here: whether a prospectus is a document soliciting the public to purchase securities from the issuer.

The SEC also relies on a number of writings, the most prominent a release by the FTC, stating that § 12(2) applied to securities outstanding on the effective date of the 1933 Act. See id., at 1072–1073. Again, this is an issue not in dispute. Although the Act as passed exempted securities from registration if sold by the issuer within sixty days of the passage of the Act, see 1933 Securities Act, § 3(a)(1), the limitation did not apply to § 12(2). See 15 U.S.C. § 771. Instead, actions brought under § 12(2) are subject to the limitation of actions provision in § 13. See 15 U.S.C. § 77m (one year from the date of discovery). A buyer who discovered a material omission in a prospectus after the passage of the Act could sue for rescission under § 12(2) even though the prospectus had been issued before enactment of the statute. This tells us nothing one way or the other, however, about whether the term "prospectus" is limited to a document soliciting the public to purchase securities from the issuer.

In large measure the writings on which both the SEC and Justice Ginsburg rely address a question on which there is no disagreement, that is, "to what securities does § 12(2) apply?" We agree with the SEC that § 12(2) applies to every class of security (except one issued or backed by a governmental entity), whether exempted from registration or not, and whether outstanding at the time of the passage of the Act or not. The question before us is the coverage of § 12(2), and the writings offered by the SEC are of little value on this point.

If legislative history is to be considered, it is preferable to consult the documents prepared by Congress when deliberating. The legislative history of the Act concerning the precise question presented supports our interpretation with much clarity and force. Congress contemplated that § 12(2) would apply only to public offerings by an issuer (or a controlling shareholder). The House Report stated: "[t]he bill affects only new offerings of securities * * *. It does not affect the ordinary redistribution of securities unless such redistribution takes on the characteristics of a new offering." H.R.Rep. No. 85, 73d Cong., 1st Sess., 5 (1933). The observation extended to § 12(2) as well. Part II, § 6 of the House Report is entitled "Civil Liabilities." See id., at 9. It begins: "Sections 11 and 12 create and define the civil liabilities imposed by the act * * *. Fundamentally, these sections entitle the buyer of securities sold upon a registration statement * * * to sue for recovery of his purchase price." Ibid. It will be recalled that as to private transactions, such as the Alloyd purchase, there will never have been a registration statement. If § 12(2) liability were imposed here, it would cover transactions not within the contemplated reach of the statute.

     * * *

Justice Ginsburg argues that the omission from the 1933 Act of the phrase "offering to the public" that appeared in the definition of "prospectus" in the British Companies Act of 1929 suggests that the drafters of the American bill intended to expand its coverage. See post, at 1081–1082 (Ginsburg, J., dissenting). We consider it more likely that the omission reflected instead the judgment that the words "offering to the public" were redundant in light of the understood meaning of "prospectus." Far from suggesting an intent to depart in a dramatic way from the balance struck in the British Companies Act, the legislative history suggests an intent to maintain it. In the context of justifying the "civil liabilities" provisions that hold "all those responsible for statements upon the face of which the public is solicited * * * to standards like those imposed by law upon a fiduciary," the House Report stated: "The demands of this bill call for the assumption of no impossible burden, nor do they involve any leap into the dark. Similar requirements have for years attended the business of issuing securities in other industrialized nations." H.R.Rep. No. 85, at 5. So, too, the Report provided: "The committee is fortified in these sections [that is, §§ 11 and 12] by similar safeguards in the English Companies Act of 1929. What is deemed necessary for sound financing in conservative England ought not to be unnecessary for the more feverish pace which American finance has developed." Id., at 9. These passages confirm that the civil liability provisions of the 1933 Act, §§ 11 and 12, impose obligations on those engaged in "the business of issuing securities," in conformance, not in contradiction to, the British example.

* * *

In sum, the word "prospectus" is a term of art referring to a document that describes a public offering of securities by an issuer or controlling shareholder. The contract of sale, and its recitations, were not held out to the public and were not a prospectus as the term is used in the 1933 Act.

The judgment of the Court of Appeals is reversed, and the case is remanded for further proceedings consistent with this opinion.

It is so ordered.

■ JUSTICE THOMAS, with whom JUSTICE SCALIA, JUSTICE GINSBURG, and JUSTICE BREYER join, dissenting.

From the majority's opinion, one would not realize that § 12(2) was involved in this case until one had read more than half-way through. In contrast to the majority's approach of interpreting the statute, I believe the proper method is to begin with the provision actually involved in this case, § 12(2), and then turn to the 1933 Act's definitional section, § 2(10), before consulting the structure of the Act as a whole. Because the result of this textual analysis shows that § 12(2) applies to secondary or private sales of a security as well as to initial public offerings, I dissent.

I

A

As we have emphasized in our recent decisions, " '[t]he starting point in every case involving construction of a statute is the language itself.' " Landreth Timber Co. v. Landreth, 471 U.S. 681, 685, 105 S.Ct. 2297, 2301, 85 L.Ed.2d 692 (1985) (quoting Blue Chip Stamps v. Manor Drug Stores, 421 U.S. 723, 756, 95 S.Ct. 1917, 1935, 44 L.Ed.2d 539 (1975) (Powell, J., concurring)). See also Central Bank of Denver, N.A. v. First Interstate Bank of Denver, N.A., 511 U.S. 164, 171–175, 114 S.Ct. 1439, 1445–47, 128 L.Ed.2d 119 (1994). Unfortunately, the majority has decided to interpret the word "prospectus" in § 12(2) by turning to sources outside the four corners of the statute, rather than by adopting the definition provided by Congress.

* * *

There is no reason to seek the meaning of "prospectus" outside of the 1933 Act, because Congress has supplied just such a definition in § 2(10). That definition is extraordinarily broad: "When used in this subchapter, unless the context otherwise requires—

* * *

"(10) The term 'prospectus' means any prospectus, notice, circular, advertisement, letter, or communication, written or by radio or television, which offers any security for sale or confirms the sale of any security." 15 U.S.C. § 77b(10). For me, the breadth of these terms forecloses the majority's position that "prospectus" applies only in the context of initial distributions of securities. Indeed, § 2(10)'s inclusion of a prospectus as only one of the many different documents that qualify as a "prospectus" for statutory purposes indicates that Congress intended "prospectus" to be more than a mere "term of art." Likewise, Congress' extension of prospectus to include documents that merely confirm the sale of a security underscores Congress' intent to depart from the term's ordinary meaning. Section 2(10)'s definition obviously concerns different types of communications rather than different types of transactions. Congress left the job of exempting certain classes of transactions to §§ 3 and 4, not to § 2(10). We should use § 2(10) to define "prospectus" for the 1933 Act, rather than, as the majority does, use the 1933 Act to define "prospectus" for § 2(10).

The majority seeks to avoid this reading by attempting to create ambiguities in § 2(10). According to the majority, the maxim noscitur a sociis (a word is known by the company it keeps) indicates that the circulars, advertisements, letters, or other communications referred to by § 2(10) are limited by the first word in the list: "prospectus." Thus, we are told that these words define the forms a prospectus may take, but the covered communications still must be "prospectus-like" in the sense that they must relate to an initial public offering. Noscitur a sociis, however, does not require us to construe every term in a series narrowly because of the meaning given to just one of the terms. See Russell Motor Car Co. v. United States, 261 U.S. 514, 519, 43 S.Ct. 428, 429–31, 67 L.Ed. 778 (1923); cf. Reves v. Ernst & Young, 494 U.S. 56, 64, 110 S.Ct. 945, 950–51, 108 L.Ed.2d 47 (1990).

The majority uses the canon in an effort to create doubt, not to reduce it. The canon applies only in cases of ambiguity, which I do not find in § 2(10). "Noscitur a sociis is a well-established and useful rule of construction where words are of obscure or doubtful meaning; and then, but only then, its aid may be sought to remove the obscurity or doubt by reference to the associated words." Russell, *supra*, 261 U.S. at 520, 43 S.Ct. at 430. There is obvious breadth in "notice, circular, advertisement, letter, or communication, written or by radio or television." To read one word in a long list as controlling the meaning of all the other words would defy common sense; doing so would prevent Congress from giving effect to expansive words in a list whenever they are combined with one word with a more restricted meaning. Section 2(10)'s very exhaustiveness suggests that "prospectus" is merely the first item in a long list of covered documents, rather than a brooding omnipresence whose meaning cabins that of all the following words. The majority also argues that a broad definition of prospectus makes much of § 2(10) redundant. See ante, at 1069. But the majority fails to see that "communication, written or by radio or television" is a catch-all. It operates as a safety net that Congress used to sweep up anything it had forgotten to include in its definition. * * *

The majority transforms § 10 into the tail that wags the 1933 Act dog. An analogy will illustrate the point. Suppose that the Act regulates cars, and that § 2(10) of the Act defines a "car" as any car, motorcycle, truck, or trailer. Section 10 of this hypothetical statute then declares that a car shall have seatbelts, and § 5 states that it is unlawful to sell cars without seatbelts. Section 12(2) of this Act then creates a cause of action for misrepresentations that occur during the sale of a car. It is reasonable to conclude that §§ 5 and 10 apply only to what we ordinarily refer to as "cars," because it would be absurd to require motorcycles and trailers to have seatbelts. But the majority's reasoning would lead to the further conclusion that § 12(2) does not cover sales of motorcycles, when it is clear that the Act includes such sales.

* * *

The majority argues that § 4's exemption suggests a contrary conclusion. Ante, at 1069. According to the majority, if Congress had intended § 12(2) to apply to private, secondary transactions, it would have said so explicitly. This reasoning goes too far, for it would render § 4 superfluous. After all, if the majority applied its approach to § 5 (which prohibits the sale of a security without first registering the security or without first sending a prospectus), then it would conclude—even in the absence of § 4—that § 5 refers only to initial offerings. But this would have precluded any need to include § 4 at all.

The majority claims that under my reading, "there is no ready explanation for exempting" government securities from § 12(2). Ante, at 1067. But Congress could have concluded that it was unnecessary to impose liability on the private or secondary sellers of a government security because information concerning government securities is already available either from the markets or from government entities. Or Congress could have chosen not to burden government securities with the costs that might accrue from additional liabilities on initial or secondary sales.

* * *

III

The majority's analysis of § 12(2) is motivated by its policy preferences. Underlying its reasoning is the assumption that Congress could never have intended to impose liability on sellers engaged in secondary transactions. Adopting a chiding tone, the majority states that "[w]e are reluctant to conclude that § 12(2) creates vast additional liabilities that are entirely independent of the new substantive obligations that the Act enumerates." Ante, at 1068. Yet, this is exactly what Congress did in § 17(a) of the 1933 Act as well as in § 10(b) of the 1934 Act. Later, the majority says: "[i]t is not plausible to infer that Congress created this extensive liability for every casual communication between buyer and seller in the secondary market." Ante, at 1071. It is not the usual practice of this Court to require Congress to explain why it has chosen to pursue a certain policy. Our job simply is to apply the policy, not to question it.

I share the majority's concern that extending § 12(2) to secondary and private transactions might result in an unwanted increase in securities litigation. But it is for Congress, and not for this Court, to determine the desired level of securities liability. As we said last Term in Central Bank of Denver, policy considerations " 'cannot override our interpretation of the text and structure of the Act, except to the extent that they may help to show that adherence to the text and structure would lead to a result 'so bizarre' that Congress could not have intended it.' " 511 U.S., at 188, 114 S.Ct., at 1442 (1994), quoting Demarest v. Manspeaker, 498 U.S. 184, 191, 111 S.Ct. 599, 604, 112 L.Ed.2d 608 (1991). The majority is concerned that a contrary reading would have a drastic impact on the thousands of private and secondary transactions by imposing new liabilities and new transaction costs. But the majority forgets that we are only enforcing Congress' decision to impose such standards of conduct and remedies upon sellers. If the majority believes that § 12(2)'s requirements are too burdensome for the securities markets, it must rely upon the other branches of government to limit the 1933 Act.

For the foregoing reasons, I respectfully dissent.

■ JUSTICE GINSBURG, with whom JUSTICE BREYER joins, dissenting.

A seller's misrepresentation made "by means of a prospectus or oral communication" is actionable under § 12(2) of the Securities Act of 1933, 15 U.S.C. § 77l(2). To limit the scope of this civil liability provision, the Court maintains that a communication qualifies as a prospectus only if made during a public offering.[1] Communications during either secondary trading or a private placement are not "prospectuses," the Court declares, and thus are not covered by § 12(2).

As Justice Thomas persuasively demonstrates, the statute's language does not support the Court's reading. Section 12(2) contains no terms expressly confining the provision to public offerings, and the statutory definition of "prospectus"—"any prospectus, notice, circular, advertisement, letter, or communication, written or by radio or television, which offers any security for sale or confirms the sale of any security," § 2(10), 15 U.S.C. § 77b(10)—is capacious.

The Court presents impressive policy reasons for its construction, but drafting history and the longstanding scholarly and judicial understanding of § 12(2) caution against judicial resistance to the statute's defining text. I would leave any alteration to Congress.

* * *

II

Most provisions of the Securities Act govern only public offerings, and the legislative history pertaining to the Act as a whole shares this orientation. See ante, at 1072 (citing H.R.Rep. No. 85, 73d Cong., 1st Sess. 1, 5 (1933)). Section § 17(a) of the Act, 15 U.S.C. § 77q(a), however, is not limited to public offerings; that enforcement provision, this Court has recognized, also covers secondary trading. See United States v. Naftalin, 441 U.S. 768, 99 S.Ct. 2077, 60 L.Ed.2d 624 (1979). The drafting history is at least consistent with the conclusion that § 12(2), like § 17(a), is not limited to public offerings.

The drafters of the Securities Act modeled this federal legislation on the British Companies Act, 19 & 20 Geo. 5, ch. 23 (1929). See Landis, The

---

1. I understand the Court's definition of a public offering to encompass both transactions that must be registered under § 5, 15 U.S.C. § 77e, and transactions that would have been registered had the securities involved not qualified for exemption under § 3, 15 U.S.C. § 77c.

Legislative History of the Securities Act of 1933, 28 Geo.Wash.L.Rev. 29, 34 (1959) (Landis and the other drafters "determined to take as the base of [their] work the English Companies Act"); see also SEC v. Ralston Purina Co., 346 U.S. 119, 123, 73 S.Ct. 981, 983–84, 97 L.Ed. 1494 (1953) (characterizing the Companies Act as a "statutory anteceden[t]" of federal securities laws). The Companies Act defined "prospectus" as "any prospectus, notice, circular, advertisement, or other invitation, offering to the public for subscription or purchase any shares or debentures of a company," 19 & 20 Geo. 5, ch. 23, § 380(1) (1929) (emphasis added). Though the drafters of the Securities Act borrowed the first four terms of this definition, they did not import from the British legislation the language limiting prospectuses to communications "offering [securities] to the public." This conspicuous omission suggests that the drafters intended the defined term "prospectus" to reach beyond communications used in public offerings.

    * * *

Commentators writing shortly after passage of the Act understood § 12(2) to cover resales and private sales, as well as public offerings. Felix Frankfurter, organizer of the team that drafted the statute, firmly stated this view. See Frankfurter, The Federal Securities Act: II, 8 Fortune 53, 108 (1933) (Act "seeks to terminate the facilities of the mails and of interstate commerce for dishonest or unfair dealings in the sale of all private or foreign government securities, new or old") (emphasis added). William O. Douglas expressed the same understanding. See Douglas & Bates, The Federal Securities Act of 1933, 43 Yale L.J. 171, 183 (1933) (noting that, except for transactions involving securities exempt under § 3(a)(2), 15 U.S.C. § 77c(a)(2), no securities or transactions are exempt from § 12(2)).

    * * *

In light of the text, drafting history, and longstanding scholarly and judicial understanding of § 12(2), I conclude that § 12(2) applies to a private resale of securities. If adjustment is in order, as the Court's opinion powerfully suggests it is,[8] Congress is equipped to undertake the alteration. Accordingly, I dissent from the Court's opinion and judgment.

THE SCOPE OF § 12 AFTER GUSTAFSON

Gustafson left unresolved a number of questions. Suppose, for example, a defendant violates § 5, fails to register a security, and sells the security by

---

8. Section 12(2) did not become prominent in Securities Act litigation until this Court held in Ernst & Ernst v. Hochfelder, 425 U.S. 185, 96 S.Ct. 1375, 47 L.Ed.2d 668 (1976), that an action for civil damages under § 10(b) of the Securities Exchange Act of 1934, 48 Stat. 891, 15 U.S.C. § 78j(b), and Securities and Exchange Commission Rule 10b–5, 17 CFR § 240.10b–5 (1975), requires proof of scienter. See Louis Loss, The Assault on Securities Act Section 12(2), 105 Harv. L. Rev. 908, 910 (1992). Though the Court of Appeals' reading of § 12(2) shows fidelity to the statute Congress passed, this Court's opinion makes noteworthy practical and poli-

cy points. As the Court observes, ante, at 1071, under the Court of Appeals' reading, § 12(2) would equip buyers with a rescission remedy for a negligent misstatement or omission even if the slip did not cause the buyer's disenchantment with the investment. And, in light of the "free writing" provision of § 2(10)(a), 15 U.S.C. § 77b(10)(a) (a communication will not be deemed a "prospectus" if its recipient was previously sent a prospectus meeting the requirements of § 10), the Court of Appeals' reading, ironically, would leave a seller more vulnerable in private transactions than in public ones.

means of a private placement offering circular. Will the plaintiff be deprived of § 12(a)(2) because the defendant violated the law and did not register? To date the lower courts have reached equivocal results. "[P]rivate placement memoranda, like those at issue are not 'prospectuses' for the purposes of a claim under [§ 12 (a)(2)]."[1] The court stated in JWP Inc. Sec. Litig.: "If the * * * plaintiffs wish to contend that the * * * offerings should have been registered, * * * the appropriate basis for that claim would be [§ 12(a)(1)], which provides for rescission of sales of securities improperly accomplished without registration."[2] Compare Sloane Overseas Fund, Ltd. v. Sapiens Int'l Corp., N.V.:[3] "Regulation S offerings are not exempted pursuant to § 3 or § 4 of the 1933 Act, 15 U.S.C. § 12(2) * * * if it is a public offering."

Section 12(a)(2) states that its scope includes exempt *securities* other than those exempted by § 3(a)(2) or 3(a)(14). Will an offering of commercial paper be subject to § 12(a)(2) even though these offerings are not made employing a § 10 prospectus? Section 3 is labeled "Exempted Securities." But it is generally recognized that the intrastate exemption in § 3(a)(11) is for an exempted transaction, not an exempted security.[4] If a private placement under § 4(2) is not subject to § 12(a)(2), should an intrastate exempt transaction under § 3(a)(11) also be outside the scope of § 12(a)(2)?[5]

THE REASONABLE CARE DEFENSE

Section 12(a)(2) provides a defense if a defendant sustains the burden of proof that "he did not know, and in the exercise of reasonable care could not have known," of the untruth or omission. The use of the phrase "could not have known" in the statute might suggest that the defendant has to prove that it would have been impossible for him to have discovered the truth through any amount of investigation. This is surely, however, not what Congress intended. This provision should be read as saying that the defendant may escape liability if he proves that, "*if* he [or she] had exercised reasonable care, he [or she]

---

1. In re JWP, 928 F.Supp. 1239, 1259 (S.D.N.Y.1996).

2. Ibid. Similarly in Maldonado v. Dominguez, 137 F.3d 1 (1st Cir.1998), the court unequivocally held, citing *Gustafson*, "the Supreme Court conclusively decided that section 12(2) applies exclusively to 'initial public offerings.'" Id. at 8.

But cf. Vannest v. Sage, Rutty & Co., Inc., 960 F.Supp. 651, 654 (W.D.N.Y.1997), where the court followed JWP, after citing authorities both ways and observed:

> The Supreme Court's simple conclusion that Section 12(2) applies only to public offerings does not make the process of determining what is and what is not a public offering any simpler. As one commentator has found [citing Janet E. Kerr, *Ralston Redux:* Determining which Section 3 Offerings Are Public under Section 12(2) after *Gustafson*, 50 SMU L. Rev. 175, 187–188 (1996)], the *Gustafson* court's attempt to equate public offerings with those that are registered ignores

the important fact that not all public offerings are registered.

3. 941 F.Supp. 1369, 1376 (S.D.N.Y. 1996).

4. See 3 Louis Loss & Joel Seligman, Securities Regulation 1142–1144 (3d ed. rev. 1999).

5. For a variety of views to these and related questions, see Elliot J. Weiss, Securities Act Section 12(2) after *Gustafson v. Alloyd Co.*: What Questions Remain?, 50 Bus. Law. 1209 (1995); Therese H. Maynard, The Impact of *Gustafson* and Its Methodology, 24 Sec. Reg. L.J. 61 (1996); Edmund Kitch, *Gustafson v. Alloyd Co.*: An Opinion that Did Not Write, 1995 Sup. Ct. Rev. 99; Peter Letsou, The Scope of Section 12(2) of the Securities Act of 1933: A Legal and Economic Analysis, 45 Emory L.J. 95 (1996); Therese H. Maynard, A Requiem: Reflections on *Gustafson*, 57 Ohio St. L.J. 1327 (1996); Elliot J.Weiss, Some Further Thoughts on *Gustafson v. Alloyd Co.*, 65 U. Cinn. L. Rev. 137 (1996).

would not have known." The Section thus imposes liability based on simple negligence and the defendant has the burden of establishing that he or she was free of negligence.

There is no defense under § 12(a)(2), as there is in § 11, based upon the "expertising" of certain statements. For example, if there is a misstatement in the financial statements which were "expertised" by independent accountants, a director of the issuer could defend under § 11 on the ground that he or she simply accepted their figures and "had no reasonable ground to believe" that they were erroneous, as in the *BarChris* case. On the other hand, in a suit under § 12(a)(2), the director is literally not given this defense. He or she must show that "in the exercise of reasonable care [he or she] could not have known" of the error.[1] Does reasonable care in this situation require any investigation by the director of the figures of the independent accounts? As we earlier discussed, the courts are divided whether the reasonable care standard in § 12(a)(2) is equivalent to the reasonable care standard in § 11 or imposes a lesser burden.

Until recently there was relatively little law addressing the meaning of reasonable care in § 12(a)(12) itself.[2]

In Franklin Savings Bank of New York v. Levy,[3] involving an action against Goldman, Sachs by a purchaser of Penn Central commercial paper, the court said:

> We have held that where a broker-dealer makes a representation as to the quality of the security he sells, he impliedly represents that he has an adequate basis in fact for the opinion he renders. Hanly v. Securities and Exchange Commission, 415 F.2d 589, 596–97 (2d Cir.1969). We see no reason why that theory is not at least equally appropriate in cases involving § 12(2) of the 1933 Act.

> Here Goldman, Sachs became an exclusive source of the Penn Central notes in issue. It was a professional vendor admittedly recommending this paper for sale to an institution authorized by statute only to invest in prime paper. Such an undertaking implies that Goldman, Sachs has conducted an ongoing investigation of Penn Central's financial condition. If Goldman, Sachs failed to exercise reasonable professional care in assembling and evaluating the financial data, particularly in view of the worsening condition of Penn Central, then its representation that the paper was credit worthy and high quality was untrue in fact and misleading no

---

1. *See* Gould v. Tricon, Inc., 272 F.Supp. 385 (S.D.N.Y.1967). *See generally* Comm. on Fed. Reg. of Sec., Report of Task Force on Sellers' Due Diligence and Similar Defenses under the Federal Securities Laws, 48 Bus. Law. 1185 (1993); Therese H. Maynard, The Affirmative Defense of Reasonable Care under Section 12(2) of the Securities Act of 1933, 69 Notre Dame L. Rev. 57 (1993).

2. The earliest decision is Murphy v. Cady, 30 F.Supp. 466, 468–469 (D.Me.1939), *aff'd on other grounds sub nom.* Cady v. Murphy, 113 F.2d 988 (1st Cir.1940), *cert. denied*, 311 U.S. 705 (1940). *See also* First Trust & Savings Bank of Zanesville, Ohio v. Fidelity–Philadelphia Trust Co., 214 F.2d 320 (3d Cir.1954), *cert. denied*, 348 U.S. 856 (1954); Jackson v. Oppenheim, 533 F.2d 826, 829 n. 7 (2d Cir.1976); Sanders v. John Nuveen & Co., 524 F.2d 1064 (7th Cir.1975), *vacated on other grounds sub nom.* John Nuveen & Co., Inc. v. Sanders, 425 U.S. 929 (1976), *on later appeal*, 619 F.2d 1222 (7th Cir.1980), *cert. denied sub nom.* John Nuveen & Co., Inc. v. Sanders, 450 U.S. 1005 (1981); Dennis v. General Imaging, Inc., 918 F.2d 496, 505 (5th Cir.1990).

3. 551 F.2d 521 (2d Cir.1977).

matter how honestly but mistakenly held. This view does not render Goldman, Sachs an insurer as appellants claim liable for some catastrophe beyond its control. Rather, it in fact makes the dealer responsible to Franklin if it is unable to shoulder the burden of establishing that it was not reasonable for it to have determined on March 16, 1970 that the quality of the paper it was purveying was less than that represented.[4]

We earlier addressed the § 11 "reasonable investigation" and § 12(a)(2) "reasonable care" standards and whether there are differences between the two standards.

Compare the following case.

Ambrosino v. Rodman & Renshaw, Inc.

United States Court of Appeals, Seventh Circuit, 1992.
972 F.2d 776.

■ Harlington Wood, Jr., Circuit Judge.

This case is about oil-and-gas investors in 1981 and 1982, the plaintiffs-appellants here, who are not satisfied with the tax benefits their investment of $2,340,000 procured; it is about alleged violations of federal and state securities laws; and it is about money. It is about a promoter, defendant Richard Berry, who, according to the district court, failed to reveal a material fact that a reasonable investor would consider important and, thus, was held liable for $1,840,000. It is also about a securities dealer, Rodman & Renshaw, Inc., and some of its employees (collectively, the "Rodman defendants") that, according to the district court, are free of liability because in selling three oil-and-gas, limited partnerships they either did not fail to disclose material facts, did not make material misrepresentations, or exercised due diligence although failing to discover a material fact. Because the district court did not misunderstand the applicable law, was not clearly erroneous in its findings of fact, and did not abuse its discretion, we affirm its judgment. * * *

FACTS

The plaintiffs-appellants here invested in up to three oil-and-gas drilling, limited partnerships sold by the Rodman defendants: the PEXCO 81–1 Drilling Program ("81–1"), the PEXCO 81–Year End Drilling Program ("81–Year End"), and the PEXCO 82–2 Drilling Program ("82–2"). The plaintiffs purchased interests in the programs either by paying 100% up front or by paying 10% down in cash and providing letters of credit against a loan for the balance. None of the drilling programs turned a profit; all lost money, and the letters of credit were drawn down. The Rodman defendants point out, however, that "the plaintiffs reduced their income taxes for the years in which they purchased their investments in multiples of their cash contributions ranging from 1.48 to 4.69."

The programs were not atypical: each described what the general partner, William J. Pitts Enterprises, Inc., "intended" or "expected" to do, the general nature of the proposed prospect or prospects, and what might or might not occur. The general partner expressly retained the right to make modifications and adjustments in the program. Each private placement memorandum, de-

---

4. Id. at 527.

nominated a "confidential memorandum" or "confidential private placement memorandum," clearly stated on its cover that the security was not registered and that it involved "A HIGH DEGREE OF RISK." All three memoranda also contained summary to extensive discussions under the following topic headings, among others: Summary of Offering; Definitions; Participation in Costs and Revenues; Terms of the Offering; Proposed Activities; Risk Factors; and Tax Aspects. These last two topic headings always captioned the lengthiest discussions.

Nine of the plaintiffs invested a total of $300,000 in the 81-1 program, which closed on June 1, 1981. The 81-1 memorandum described drilling prospects in Caldwell, Burleson, and Nolan Counties, Texas, and stated the general partner intended to drill only developmental, not exploratory wells. The Austin Chalk Formation and the Buda Limestone Formation were identified as intended objectives in Caldwell County. "Developmental acreage" was defined as "acreage on which a well is drilled to a known producing formation in a previously drilled field or adjacent to a previously drilled field." This definition is not the one published by the American Association of Petroleum Geologists ("AAPG") and was so noted in an amendment incorporated in the front of the memorandum.

The first hole drilled was in the Schuch prospect in Coke County, Texas, about thirty miles north of San Angelo. The prospect had not been identified in the 81-1 memorandum. The partnership expended one-third of the available drilling funds on the well, which was a dry hole. Eight wells were then drilled into the Austin Chalk Formation at a site in Caldwell County, east of San Antonio and south of Austin; they were on-line by December 1981. Although production dropped to a few barrels per day after six months or so and oil prices declined, these wells produced over $1,000,000 in revenue. Two dry holes were drilled in Kansas in January 1982, and the letters of credit were drawn down in July 1983.

All twenty-nine plaintiffs, including the nine who had participated in the 81-1 program, invested a total of $1,840,000 in the 81–Year End program, which was marketed as a year-end tax shelter and closed on December 28, 1981. This closing date did not leave the general partner time, under the circumstances, to secure a site and commence drilling, let alone complete a well in 1981; nonetheless, tax benefits accrued for the 1981 calendar year. The memorandum indicated the partnership intended to drill 80% developmental wells and 20% exploratory wells but did not identify any prospects, noting, instead, that its operations might "be conducted in any state. * * * *" It also indicated that three wells from a 1980 program, denominated 80–1, had been drilled but that no production data were available because division orders had not been published by the Texas Railroad Commission, the state agency that oversees oil and gas operations. This latter statement was erroneous on two counts: first, division orders are not the source of production data and, second, the data were available from the Railroad Commission. Richard Berry, a "geological consultant" doing business as Berry Petroleum Consultants in Dallas, Texas, actively participated in selecting the prospect and personally sold units of the 81–Year End program. The offering did not disclose, however, (1) where the partnership intended to drill, (2) that a waterflood project—secondary recovery via water injection—was contemplated, (3) that Berry had participated in selecting the site, or (4) that Berry had a leasehold interest in the prospect selected. The memorandum did disclose that affiliates of the operator might hold title to some leases, but it did not state that Berry was an affiliate of the operator, nor did it otherwise identify him.

In February 1982 the 81–Year End partnership started drilling to develop a waterflood project in the Ranger Sand of the Pritchard Field, Stevens County, Texas, about halfway between Abilene and Ft. Worth. This field first produced oil in the 1920s and was but one of many, similarly aged fields widely considered ripe for reactivation using secondary recovery techniques. Natural gas was detected in some of the zones encountered; thus, the waterflood project was deferred, and the holes were put on-line as gas wells. They produced about $100,000 in revenue before turning poisonous, producing sour, H_2S-bearing gas in September 1983. The purchaser refused further delivery of gas; thus, the wells were taken off-line and either shut-in completely or plugged with respect to the zones producing sour gas. Gas production, however, had declined significantly by late 1982; thus, the partnership started up the waterflood operation in January 1983. Waterflooding continued into September of that year when fresh water unexpectedly broke through the oil column in two low-productivity wells. It was then "discovered" that a waterflood operation had been conducted in the field in 1961. Berry resigned in December 1983, the status of the program was reported, and operations were terminated. The letters of credit were drawn down July 1984.

The district court found that defendant Berry "knew or should have known about the previous waterflood because it was his land and because he is a petroleum engineer." Ambrosino v. Rodman & Renshaw, Inc., No. 84 C 4586, memorandum opinion and order at 19, 1990 WL 129564 (N.D.Ill. Aug. 30, 1990, *amended* Nov. 13, 1990). The omission was material. Consequently, the court found Berry and Berry Petroleum Consultants liable under section 12(2) of the Securities Act of 1933 and awarded the plaintiffs $1,840,000 in damages. 15 U.S.C. § 77l(2). Conversely, the Rodman defendants were found not liable because, although they failed to discover and, thus, disclose the 1961 waterflood, they had exercised due diligence in investigating the 81–Year End program. * * *

[T]he plaintiffs argue the district court erred in finding the Rodman defendants had conducted a reasonable investigation of the 81–Year End program and, thus, had proven the defense of due diligence, although they failed to discover the previous waterflood operation in the Pritchard Field. * * *

Whether a defendant who failed to reveal a material fact exercised due diligence—that is, exercised reasonable care—depends on the circumstances of the case. *Sanders III,* 619 F.2d at 1228. One important circumstance is the nature of the securities at risk. For example, the court in *Sanders I,* 524 F.2d at 1071, took "into consideration the fact that the security was short term commercial paper rather than stock or long term indebtedness." Here, we take into consideration the fact that the 81–Year End memorandum did not expressly offer investors a waterflood program—in fact the plaintiffs complain because the offering memorandum did not state a waterflood was contemplated. It would be one thing if the plaintiffs had been sold a waterflood program or even a program expressly incorporating a waterflood project. *See, for example,* Varn v. Maloney, 516 P.2d 1328 (Okla.1973) (common-law fraud found based on materially false representations, both misstatements and omissions). But they were sold a very general, oil and gas program:

The General Partner presently estimates that not less than eighty percent (80%) of the Partnership subscriptions, less the Management Fee paid to the General Partner, will be expended on developmental wells. Operations may be conducted in any state if prospects considered attractive by the General Partner are presented to it.

81–Year End mem. at 25.

While it is a close call because of the extremely deleterious consequences a previous waterflood operation can cause, our review of the whole record indicates the district court did not abuse its discretion or clearly err in finding the Rodman defendants met their burden of proving due diligence. There was testimony by the Rodman defendant's expert witness, Louis G. Mosburg, Jr., an attorney with 30 years' experience in oil and gas law—both in investments and real estate—that Rodman & Renshaw's exercise of due diligence had been higher than the custom and practice of the industry at that time.[23] Defendant Rice, a CPA and registered representative of Rodman & Renshaw, testified that, upon learning in late 1983 that the Pritchard Field might have been previously waterflooded,[24] he contacted an organization in Austin, Texas, identified elsewhere as Records Research, Inc. The record of the prior waterflood was then discovered after a second, much more exhaustive search than Records Research had conducted earlier in 1983 for the general partner. The second search was also costlier, $200 versus $10. Thus, the trial court had testimony that a search had twice been undertaken to determine if a waterflood had been attempted in the field: once by the general partner before the operation got under way, and once by Rice of Rodman & Renshaw when a suspicion arose.

The plaintiffs also argue the trial court erred in finding the defendants adequately investigated the economic standing of prior PEXCO offerings and the Barringer process discussed in the 82–2 program. The record more than supports the court's finding on the former issue. For example, the Rodman defendants sought information about the general partner, the drilling contractor, and various prospects from the Texas Railroad Commission, Lewis Engineering, subsequently, McCord–Lewis Energy Services, and an engineer named Crutchfield, among other sources. On the latter issue, the court stated, "As to the Barringer Process used in 82–2, the defendants made no misrepresentations." *Ambrosino,* mem. op. at 20, 1990 WL 129564. Consequently, due diligence is not an issue.

Third, the plaintiffs argue the district court erred in finding the 81–1 investors' claim that the Rodman defendants "knowingly failed to disclose that the earlier programs would not be economically successful * * * is time-barred." The court went on to find that none of the alleged misstatements and omissions were material, except, as implied by the court's due-diligence holding, the prior waterflood.

23. But even conforming to industry standard may not shield one from liability. *See The T.J. Hooper,* 60 F.2d 737 (2d Cir.), *cert. denied,* 287 U.S. 662, 53 S.Ct. 220, 77 L.Ed. 571 (1932).

24. John J. Harte, a coprincipal of the general partner, testified that an employee of Stevens Engineering, a company hired to investigate the waterflood project, learned of the prior waterflood from an "old timer" he bumped into at the oilfield.

PROBLEM 13–3

Opus Mortgages sells mortgage related investments. Among other things it will provide individual mortgages to specific homeowners and sells portfolios of mortgages to investors.

To see these investments, Opus has a sales force that makes "cold" (unsolicited) telephone calls in which the mortgage brokers read from a script. The script states in part that "each mortgage is individually secured" and explains in detail the system of matching individual investments to individual mortgages.

Opus has twice been the subject of investigations by the State Attorney General. In 1999, the State Attorney General and Opus signed a consent order under which Opus agreed to have audited financial records. The consent order was negotiated for Opus by general counsel and vice president, Lawrence Haydn. In the next two years, Haydn on three occasions attempted to hire an accountant to audit the financial records of Opus. On each occasion the accountant was unable to give an unqualified opinion because, as the accountant put it, "the recordkeeping is a disaster area. I am unable to determine whether or not Opus is, in fact, matching mortgages." On several occasions Haydn reassured officials of the State Attorney General's office that he was making a good faith effort to comply with the consent order.

More recently, in 2001, after the State Attorney General had received several complaints from individuals about Opus, a second investigation began. This investigation discovered, among other things: (1) that the same "script" and offering circular had been used without change from 1997 to 1999; (2) that no audited financial records had ever been produced; (3) that the late chief executive officer of Opus, Koernke, had misappropriated (that is stolen) $7 million of Opus assets and (4) because no matching system had ever fully been in place, Opus was forced to liquidate. The $7 million stolen by Koernke was not recovered.

Haydn subsequently has been sued for federal securities law violations by a class of investors. Can Haydn be held liable under § 12(a)(2) of the Securities Act of 1933? If so, is he entitled to a reasonable care defense?

CHAPTER 14

Securities Exchange Act Civil Liability Provisions

A. Rule 14a–9: Proxy Fraud

Rule 14a–9 provides an antifraud remedy for false or misleading facts or omissions made in a proxy statement, form of proxy, notice of meeting, or other communication used in a proxy solicitation.[1] As we will read, the Rule itself has played a particularly consequential role in the development of implied causes of action under the federal securities laws and in the meaning of such generic terms as materiality.

1. IMPLIED CAUSE OF ACTION

J.I. Case Co. v. Borak

Supreme Court of the United States, 1964.
377 U.S. 426, 84 S.Ct. 1555, 12 L.Ed.2d 423.

■ Mr. Justice Clark delivered the opinion of the Court.

This is a civil action brought by respondent, a stockholder of petitioner J.I. Case Company, charging deprivation of the pre-emptive rights of respondent and other shareholders by reason of a merger between Case and the American Tractor Corporation. It is alleged that the merger was effected through the circulation of a false and misleading proxy statement by those proposing the merger. The complaint was in two counts, the first based on diversity and claiming a breach of the directors' fiduciary duty to the stockholders. The second count alleged a violation of § 14(a) of the Securities Exchange Act of 1934 with reference to the proxy solicitation material. The trial court held that as to this count it had no power to redress the alleged violations of the Act but was limited solely to the granting of declaratory relief thereon under § 27 of the Act. The court held Wis.Stat.1961, § 180.405(4), which requires posting security for expenses in derivative actions, applicable to both counts, except that portion of Count 2 requesting declaratory relief. It ordered the respondent to furnish a bond in the amount of $75,000 thereunder and, upon his failure to do so, dismissed the complaint, save that part of Count 2 seeking a declaratory judgment. On interlocutory appeal the Court of Appeals reversed on both counts, holding that the District Court had the power to grant remedial relief and that the Wisconsin statute was not applicable. 317 F.2d 838. We granted certiorari. 375 U.S. 901. We consider only the question of whether § 27 of the Act authorizes a federal cause of action for rescission or damages to a corporate stockholder with respect to a consummated merger which was authorized pursuant to the use of a proxy statement alleged to contain false and misleading statements violative of § 14(a) of the Act. This being the sole question raised by petitioners in their petition for certiorari, we will not consider other

---

1. On the proxy solicitation process generally, including the other proxy rules such as Rule 14a–8, see 4 Louis Loss & Joel Seligman ch. 6.C (3d ed. rev. 2000).

questions subsequently presented. See Supreme Court Rule 40(1)(d)(2); Local 1976, United Brotherhood of Carpenters v. Labor Board, 357 U.S. 93, 96 (1958); Irvine v. California, 347 U.S. 128, 129–130 (1954).

I.

Respondent, the owner of 2,000 shares of common stock of Case acquired prior to the merger, brought this suit based on diversity jurisdiction seeking to enjoin a proposed merger between Case and the American Tractor Corporation (ATC) on various grounds, including breach of the fiduciary duties of the Case directors, self-dealing among the management of Case and ATC and misrepresentations contained in the material circulated to obtain proxies. The injunction was denied and the merger was thereafter consummated. Subsequently successive amended complaints were filed and the case was heard on the aforesaid two-count complaint. The claims pertinent to the asserted violation of the Securities Exchange Act were predicated on diversity jurisdiction as well as on § 27 of the Act. They alleged: that petitioners, or their predecessors, solicited or permitted their names to be used in the solicitation of proxies of Case stockholders for use at a special stockholders' meeting at which the proposed merger with ATC was to be voted upon; that the proxy solicitation material so circulated was false and misleading in violation of § 14(a) of the Act and Rule 14a–9 which the Commission had promulgated thereunder; that the merger was approved at the meeting by a small margin of votes and was thereafter consummated; that the merger would not have been approved but for the false and misleading statements in the proxy solicitation material; and that Case stockholders were damaged thereby. The respondent sought judgment holding the merger void and damages for himself and all other stockholders similarly situated, as well as such further relief "as equity shall require." The District Court ruled that the Wisconsin security for expenses statute did not apply to Count 2 since it arose under federal law. However, the court found that its jurisdiction was limited to declaratory relief in a private, as opposed to a government, suit alleging violation of § 14(a) of the Act. Since the additional equitable relief and damages prayed for by the respondent would, therefore, be available only under state law, it ruled those claims subject to the security for expenses statute. After setting the amount of security at $75,000 and upon the representation of counsel that the security would not be posted, the court dismissed the complaint, save that portion of Count 2 seeking a declaration that the proxy solicitation material was false and misleading and that the proxies and, hence, the merger were void.

II.

It appears clear that private parties have a right under § 27 to bring suit for violation of § 14(a) of the Act. Indeed, this section specifically grants the appropriate District Courts jurisdiction over "all suits in equity and actions at law brought to enforce any liability or duty created" under the Act. The petitioners make no concessions, however, emphasizing that Congress made no specific reference to a private right of action in § 14(a); that, in any event, the right would not extend to derivative suits and should be limited to prospective relief only. In addition, some of the petitioners argue that the merger can be dissolved only if it was fraudulent or nonbeneficial, issues upon which the proxy material would not bear. But the causal relationship of the proxy material and the merger are questions of fact to be resolved at trial, not here. We therefore do not discuss this point further.

III.

While the respondent contends that his Count 2 claim is not a derivative one, we need not embrace that view, for we believe that a right of action exists as to both derivative and direct causes.

The purpose of § 14(a) is to prevent management or others from obtaining authorization for corporate action by means of deceptive or inadequate disclosure in proxy solicitation. The section stemmed from the congressional belief that "[f]air corporate suffrage is an important right that should attach to every equity security bought on a public exchange." H.R.Rep. No. 1383, 73d Cong., 2d Sess., 13. It was intended to "control the conditions under which proxies may be solicited with a view to preventing the recurrence of abuses which * * * [had] frustrated the free exercise of the voting rights of stockholders." Id., at 14. "Too often proxies are solicited without explanation to the stockholder of the real nature of the questions for which authority to cast his vote is sought." S.Rep. No. 792, 73d Cong., 2d Sess., 12. These broad remedial purposes are evidenced in the language of the section which makes it "unlawful for any person * * * to solicit or to permit the use of his name to solicit any proxy or consent or authorization in respect of any security * * * registered on any national securities exchange in contravention of such rules and regulations as the Commission may prescribe as necessary or appropriate in the public interest *or for the protection of investors.*" (Italics supplied.) While this language makes no specific reference to a private right of action, among its chief purposes is "the protection of investors," which certainly implies the availability of judicial relief where necessary to achieve that result.

The injury which a stockholder suffers from corporate action pursuant to a deceptive proxy solicitation ordinarily flows from the damage done the corporation, rather than from the damage inflicted directly upon the stockholder. The damage suffered results not from the deceit practiced on him alone but rather from the deceit practiced on the stockholders as a group. To hold that derivative actions are not within the sweep of the section would therefore be tantamount to a denial of private relief. Private enforcement of the proxy rules provides a necessary supplement to Commission action. As in anti-trust treble damage litigation, the possibility of civil damages or injunctive relief serves as a most effective weapon in the enforcement of the proxy requirements. The Commission advises that it examines over 2,000 proxy statements annually and each of them must necessarily be expedited. Time does not permit an independent examination of the facts set out in the proxy material and this results in the Commission acceptance of the representations contained therein at their face value, unless contrary to other material on file with it. Indeed, on the allegations of respondent's complaint, the proxy material failed to disclose alleged unlawful market manipulation of the stock of ATC, and this unlawful manipulation would not have been apparent to the Commission until after the merger.

We, therefore, believe that under the circumstances here it is the duty of the courts to be alert to provide such remedies as are necessary to make effective the congressional purpose. * * *

    * * *

Nor do we find merit in the contention that such remedies are limited to prospective relief. This was the position taken in Dann v. Studebaker–Packard Corp., 288 F.2d 201, where it was held that the "preponderance of questions of state law which would have to be interpreted and applied in order to grant the relief sought * * * is so great that the federal question involved * * * is really negligible in comparison." At 214. But we believe that the overriding federal law applicable here would, where the facts required, control the appropriateness of redress despite the provisions of state corporation law, for it "is not uncommon for federal courts to fashion federal law where federal rights are concerned." Textile Workers v. Lincoln Mills, 353 U.S. 448, 457 (1957). In addition, the fact that questions of state law must be decided does not change the character of the right; it remains federal. As Chief Justice Marshall said in Osborn v. Bank of the United States, 9 Wheat. 738 (1824):

"If this were sufficient to withdraw a case from the jurisdiction of the federal Courts, almost every case, although involving the construction of a law, would be withdrawn * * *." At 819–820, 6 L.Ed. 223, 224.

Moreover, if federal jurisdiction were limited to the granting of declaratory relief, victims of deceptive proxy statements would be obliged to go into state courts for remedial relief. And if the law of the State happened to attach no responsibility to the use of misleading proxy statements, the whole purpose of the section might be frustrated. Furthermore, the hurdles that the victim might face (such as separate suits, as contemplated by Dann v. Studebaker–Packard Corp. *supra*, security for expenses statutes, bringing in all parties necessary for complete relief, etc.) might well prove insuperable to effective relief.

IV.

Our finding that federal courts have the power to grant all necessary remedial relief is not to be construed as any indication of what we believe to be the necessary and appropriate relief in this case. We are concerned here only with a determination that federal jurisdiction for this purpose does exist. Whatever remedy is necessary must await the trial on the merits.

The other contentions of the petitioners are denied.

Affirmed.

THE DEVELOPMENT OF IMPLIED CAUSES OF ACTION

In 1946 a District Court in Kardon v. National Gypsum Co.,[1] held that there was a private right of action under Rule 10b–5, which is today the most frequently used antifraud remedy in the federal securities laws. The court based this result upon a general principle stated in the Restatement of Torts:

* * * "It is not, and cannot be, questioned that the complaint sets forth conduct on the part of the * * * [defendants] directly in violation of the provisions of Sec. 10(b) of the Act and of Rule X–10B–5 which implements it. It is also true that there is no provision in Sec. 10 or elsewhere expressly allowing civil suits by persons injured as a result of violation of Sec. 10 or of the Rule. However, 'The violation of a legislative enactment by doing a prohibited act, or by failing to do a required act, makes the actor liable for an invasion of an interest of another if; (a) the intent of the enactment is exclusively or in part to protect an interest of the other as an individual; and (b) the interest invaded is one which the enactment is intended to protect. * * *' Restatement, Torts, Vol. 2, Sec.

---

1. 69 F.Supp. 512, 513–514 (E.D.Pa. 1946).

286. This rule is more than merely a canon of statutory interpretation. The disregard of the command of a statute is a wrongful act and a tort."

Under this approach, of course, any violation of any section of the statutes or of any rule of the Commission would seem to create a cause of action in favor of any one injured by such violation, since the statutes were repeatedly stated in Congress and in the very text of the statutes themselves to be for the protection of investors and the rules of the Commission must be issued "for the protection of investors" in order for the Commission to have any authority to issue them. Therefore, all that a plaintiff need do was to identify himself as an "investor", which would presumably include every purchaser and every seller of securities—in the *Kardon* case itself, the plaintiff was a seller of securities rather than a purchaser, but the court said that he was an "investor" before he sold and that was good enough. The mere fact that the plaintiff was injured by the violation would seem to be sufficient to show that he was the type of investor which the statute or rule was intended to protect.

For a period of almost thirty years following the decision in the *Kardon* case, the courts routinely assumed that a private right of action for damages existed under whatever section of the statute or rule of the Commission was being invoked by the plaintiff as the basis for his law suit. The courts rarely even mentioned the existence of a private right of action as an issue to be resolved, presumably because the defendants did not seriously argue to the contrary, and were solely concerned with defining the requirements for and limitations upon such an action. These had, of course, been left totally undefined by Congress since it had not created any such cause of action other than by implication.

In 1975 the case of Cort v. Ash,[2] was decided by the Supreme Court. In that case, the court reversed this trend regarding the implication of causes of action generally (although that case dealt with the question of an implied right of action under the Hatch Act prohibiting corporate political contributions rather than under the securities laws) and stated that four "factors" should be considered in determining whether such a private right of action exists. The court said: "In determining whether a private remedy is implicit in a statute not expressly providing one, several factors are relevant. First, is the plaintiff 'one of the class for whose *especial* benefit the statute was enacted' * * *—that is, does the statute create a federal right in favor of the plaintiff? Second, is there any indication of legislative intent, explicit or implicit, either to create such a remedy or to deny one? * * * Third, is it consistent with the underlying purposes of the legislative scheme to imply such a remedy for the plaintiff? * * * And finally, is the cause of action one traditionally relegated to state law, in an area basically the concern of the States, so that it would be inappropriate to infer a cause of action based solely on federal law?"[3]

In 1979 the Supreme Court decided the case of Touche Ross & Co. v. Redington,[4] involving the question of whether there was an implied private right of action under Section 17(a) of the 1934 Act. That section requires the filing with the Commission of audited financial statements by registered broker-dealers. In an opinion by Mr. Justice Rehnquist, the Court held that there was no such private right of action (only Justice Marshall dissented). The Court said:

2.   422 U.S. 66 (1975).   **4.**   442 U.S. 560 (1979).

3.   Id. at 78.

"The question of the existence of a statutory cause of action is, of course, one of statutory construction. Cannon v. University of Chicago, 441 U.S. 677, 688 (1979); see National Railroad Passenger Corp. v. National Association of Railroad Passengers, 414 U.S. 453, 458 (1974) (hereinafter Amtrak). *SIPC's argument in favor of implication of a private right of action based on tort principles, therefore, is entirely misplaced.* [Italics added.] Brief for SIPC 22–23. As we recently have emphasized, 'the fact that a federal statute has been violated and some person harmed does not automatically give rise to a private cause of action in favor of that person.' Cannon v. University of Chicago, *supra*, at 688. Instead, our task is limited solely to determining whether Congress intended to create the private right of action asserted by SIPC and the Trustee. And as with any case involving the interpretation of a statute, our analysis must begin with the language of the statute itself. * * *

* * *

"In terms, § 17(a) simply requires broker-dealers and others to keep such records and file such reports as the Commission may prescribe. It does not, by its terms, purport to create a private cause of action in favor of anyone. It is true that in the past our cases have held that in certain circumstances a private right of action may be implied in a statute not expressly providing one. But in those cases finding such implied private remedies, the statute in question at least prohibited certain conduct or created federal rights in favor of private parties. * * * By contrast, § 17(a) neither confers rights on private parties nor proscribes any conduct as unlawful.

* * *

"The reliance of SIPC and the Trustee on § 27 is misplaced. Section 27 grants jurisdiction to the federal courts and provides for venue and service of process. It creates no cause of action of its own force and effect; it imposes no liabilities. The source of plaintiffs' rights must be found, if at all, in the substantive provisions of the 1934 Act which they seek to enforce, not in the jurisdictional provision. See Securities Investors Protection Corp. v. Barbour, 421 U.S., at 424. The Court in Borak found a private cause of action implicit in § 14(a). See Cannon v. University of Chicago, *supra*, at 690–693 n. 13; Piper v. Chris Craft Indus., Inc., 430 U.S. at 25; Allen v. State Bd. of Elections, 393 U.S. at 557. We do not now question the actual holding of that case, but we decline to read the opinion so broadly that virtually every provision of the securities acts gives rise to an implied private cause of action. E.g., Piper v. Chris–Craft Indus., Inc., *supra*.

"The invocation of the 'remedial purposes' of the 1934 Act is similarly unavailing. Only last Term, we emphasized that generalized references to the 'remedial purposes' of the 1934 Act will not justify reading a provision 'more broadly than its language and the statutory scheme reasonably permit.' Securities and Exchange Commission v. Sloan, 436 U.S. 103, 116 (1978); see Ernst & Ernst v. Hochfelder, 425 U.S., at 200."[5]

This approach is of course diametrically opposite to that of the *Kardon* case, which required affirmative evidence of an intent to *deny* a private right of action in order for one not to be implied under general principles of law. The *Redington* case was followed by that of Transamerica Mortgage Advisors, Inc. v.

---

5. Id. at 568–578.

Lewis.[6] In that case, the Supreme Court held that no private right of action for damages exists under Section 206 of the Investment Advisers Act of 1940, the general fraud section in that statute, the language of which parallels that of Rule 10b–5. However, the court held that a party to an investment advisory contract with an investment adviser could bring an action under Section 215 of the Act, declaring "void" any contract entered into in violation of the provisions of the Act, for rescission of the contract and the return of the consideration which he had paid (i.e., the advisory fees). The court relied upon the absence of any express provision in the Act for a private right of action for damages and the absence of any indication in the legislative history that Congress intended to create such a private right of action, as well as upon the provisions of Section 214 giving the Federal courts jurisdiction only over "suits in equity" as contrasted with the provision in other Federal securities statutes, which refer both to suits in equity and "actions at law."

The Court said: "Relying on the factors identified in Cort v. Ash, *supra*, the respondent and the Commission, as *amicus curiae,* argue that our inquiry in this case cannot stop with the intent of Congress, but must consider the utility of a private remedy, and the fact that it may be one not traditionally relegated to state law. We rejected the same contentions last Term in Touche Ross & Co. v. Redington, *supra*, where it was argued that these factors standing alone justified the implication of a private right of action under § 17(a) of the Securities Exchange Act of 1934." The four dissenters, in an opinion by Mr. Justice White, argued that all of the four "factors" set forth in Cort v. Ash pointed in this case to the implication of a private right of action for damages; that is, that the statute was enacted for the benefit of a special class of persons, the clients of investment advisers; that there was no evidence of any express or implicit legislative intent to negate a private right of action; that the existence of a private right of action was compatible with the legislative scheme and even essential to its achievement; and that the subject matter of the cause of action was not one which has traditionally been relegated to state law so as to make it inappropriate to infer a federal cause of action.

It was assumed by some as a result of the *Redington* case and the *Transamerica* case, listening as the Fifth Circuit says to the music if not the words, that no additional implied causes of action would be created in the securities law field and that those already recognized were in jeopardy. Some people even went so far as to predict that the Supreme Court would abolish any private right of action under Rule 10b–5. This euphoria of the defendants' Bar was short-lived.

In Merrill Lynch, Pierce, Fenner & Smith, Inc. v. Curran,[7] the Court by a 5–4 vote held that an investor could maintain an action against his broker in violation of the antifraud provision of the Commodity Exchange Act. Justice Stevens wrote in part:

* * * Our cases subsequent to Cort v. Ash have plainly stated that our focus must be on "the intent of Congress." Texas Industries, Inc. v. Radcliff Materials, Inc., 451 U.S. 630, 639 (1981). "The key to the inquiry is the intent of the Legislature." Middlesex County Sewerage Auth. v. National Sea Clammers Assn., 453 U.S. 1, 13 (1981). The key to these cases is our understanding of the intent of Congress in 1974 when it comprehensively reexamined and strengthened the federal regulation of futures trading. * * *

---

6.   444 U.S. 11 (1979).   **7.**   456 U.S. 353 (1982).

In determining whether a private cause of action is implicit in a federal statutory scheme when the statute by its terms is silent on that issue, the initial focus must be on the state of the law at the time the legislation was enacted. More precisely, we must examine Congress' perception of the law that it was shaping or reshaping. When Congress enacts new legislation, the question is whether Congress intended to create a private remedy as a supplement to the express enforcement provisions of the statute. When Congress acts in a statutory context in which an implied private remedy has already been recognized by the courts, however, the inquiry logically is different. Congress need not have intended to create a new remedy, since one already existed; the question is whether Congress intended to preserve the pre-existing remedy.[8]

The following year, by a 8–0 vote in Herman & MacLean v. Huddleston,[9] the court wrote in ringing terms:

* * * The Securities Act of 1933 and the Securities Exchange Act of 1934 "constitute interrelated components of the federal regulatory scheme governing transactions in securities." Ernst & Ernst v. Hochfelder, 425 U.S. 185, 206 (1976). The Acts created several express private rights of action, one of which is contained in § 11 of the 1933 Act. In addition to the private actions created explicitly by the 1933 and 1934 Acts, federal courts have implied private remedies under other provisions of the two laws. Most significantly for present purposes, a private right of action under § 10(b) of the 1934 Act and Rule 10b–5 has been consistently recognized for more than 35 years. The existence of this implied remedy is simply beyond peradventure.

The issue in this case is whether a party should be barred from invoking this established remedy for fraud because the allegedly fraudulent conduct would apparently also provide the basis for a damage action under § 11 of the 1933 Act. The resolution of this issue turns on the fact that the two provisions involve distinct causes of action and were intended to address different types of wrongdoing. * * *

Since § 11 and § 10(b) address different types of wrongdoing, we see no reason to carve out an exception to § 10(b) for fraud occurring in a registration statement just because the same conduct may also be actionable under § 11. Exempting such conduct from liability under § 10(b) would conflict with the basic purpose of the 1933 Act: to provide greater protection to purchasers of registered securities. It would be anomalous indeed if the special protection afforded to purchasers in a registered offering by the 1933 Act were deemed to deprive such purchasers of the protections against manipulation and deception that § 10(b) makes available to all persons who deal in securities.

While some conduct actionable under § 11 may also be actionable under § 10(b), it is hardly a novel proposition that the Securities Exchange Act and the Securities Act "prohibit some of the same conduct." United States v. Naftalin, 441 U.S. 768, 778 (1979) (applying § 17(a) of the 1933 Act to conduct also prohibited by § 10(b) of the 1934 Act in an action by the SEC). " 'The fact that there may well be some overlap is neither unusual nor unfortunate.' " Ibid., quoting SEC v. National Securities, Inc., 393 U.S. 453, 468 (1969). In savings clauses included in the 1933 and 1934 Acts, Congress rejected the notion that the express remedies of the securities laws would preempt all other rights of action. * * *

---

8. Id. at 377–380.   **9.** 459 U.S. 375 (1983).

* * * A cumulative construction of the securities laws also furthers their broad remedial purposes. * * *[10]

The enduring force of Cort v. Ash and Touche, Ross & Co. v. Redington when read with Merrill Lynch, Pierce, Fenner & Smith, Inc. v. Curran and Herman & MacLean has led the courts to quite variable results depending on which provision of the federal securities laws is being examined for a private cause of action.

Section 14(a): It has not been questioned since the *Borak* case that a private right of action exists under § 14(a) for a violation of the proxy rules. The reliance by the Court in *Borak* upon § 27 of the 1934 Act as a basis for implying a private right of action under any Section of the 1934 Act was repudiated, however, by the Supreme Court in the *Redington* case. Specifically § 27 confers upon the federal courts exclusive jurisdiction to entertain any suits "to enforce any liability or duty" created by that Act. However, in Franklin v. Gwinnett County Pub. Sch.,[11] the Court cited J.I. Case v. Borak with approval for "the general rule that all appropriate relief is available in an action brought to vindicate a federal right when Congress has given no indication of its purpose with respect to remedies."[12]

Rule 10b–5: All of the early cases dealing with Rule 10b–5 beginning with *Kardon* held that there was a private right of action under that Rule.[13] In 1971 the Supreme Court in Superintendent of Insurance of the State of New York v. Bankers Life and Casualty Co.[14] casually brushed aside this question in a one sentence footnote: "It is now established that a private right of action is implied under § 10(b)," and this question has now been conclusively resolved by the *Herman & MacLean* decision. It should be noted that this was a unanimous decision of the Supreme Court (although Justice Powell did not participate).

Section 10(b) by its terms applies to "any security registered [i.e., listed] on a national securities exchange or any security not so registered", which would seem to be all inclusive. However, on the basis of the expressed intention of Congress in the 1934 Act to regulate the exchanges and the over-the-counter markets, it was once argued that the Section and Rule do not apply to the purchase or sale of a security which is not traded in any organized market. The cases are in accord in rejecting this argument.[15] In fact, originally the great majority of private civil suits instituted under the Rule concerned closely held corporations whose securities were not actively traded in any market, although

---

10. Id. at 382–387.

11. 503 U.S. 60, 68 (1992).

12. *See also* Roosevelt v. E.I. Du Pont de Nemours & Co., 958 F.2d 416 (D.C.Cir. 1992) (Rule 14a–8 implies cause of action); United Paperworkers Int'l Union v. International Paper Co., 985 F.2d 1190 (2d Cir.1993) (either the proponent of a Rule 14a–8 proposal or another shareholder has standing to bring a Rule 14a–9 lawsuit); Koppel v. 4987 Corp., 167 F.3d 125 (2d Cir.1999) (implied causes of action under Rules 14a–4(a)(3) and 14a–4(b)(1)).

13. For early cases discussing the question, see Fischman v. Raytheon Mfg. Co., 188 F.2d 783 (2d Cir.1951); Fratt v. Robinson, 203 F.2d 627 (9th Cir.1953); Ellis v. Carter, 291 F.2d 270 (9th Cir.1961); Kardon v. National Gypsum Co., 69 F.Supp. 512 (E.D.Pa. 1946).

14. 404 U.S. 6 n. 9 (1971).

15. Fratt v. Robinson, 203 F.2d 627 (9th Cir.1953); Errion v. Connell, 236 F.2d 447 (9th Cir.1956); Ellis v. Carter, 291 F.2d 270 (9th Cir.1961); Stevens v. Vowell, 343 F.2d 374 (10th Cir.1965); but cf. Boone v. Baugh, 308 F.2d 711 (8th Cir.1962).

in recent years public corporations have been the primary target of these actions.

A subsequent reargued action which was fought against liability under Rule 10b–5 involved the contention that an action cannot be maintained under Rule 10b–5 where one of the express civil liability provisions of the 1933 Act or the 1934 Act is applicable. The unanimous decision in *Herman & MacLean* that a Rule 10b–5 lawsuit could be maintained concurrently with a § 11 claim presumably put to rest this argument not only for § 11, but also under § 12(a)(2) of the 1933 Act;[16] § 9 of the 1934 Act;[17] and § 18 of the 1934 Act.[18]

The 1975 amendment to the 1934 Act's definition of "person" in § 3(a)(9) to include governments, appeared to resolve also that Rule 10b–5 could be used in litigation against municipalities and other governments.[19] Section 3(a)(9), however, does not resolve whether the 11th Amendment may bar such lawsuits.[20]

Section 17(a) of the 1933 Act: Section 17(a) of the 1933 Act is identical to Rule 10b–5 so far as its substantive provisions are concerned, for the simple reason that the Commission copied § 17(a) when it adopted Rule 10b–5. However, the coverage of the two provisions is not identical because § 17(a) applies only to an "offer or sale", while Rule 10b–5 applies to a "purchase or sale." Section 17(a) applies to an *offer to sell* although Rule 10b–5 does not; and Rule 10b–5 applies to a purchase of security by the defendant although § 17(a)

---

16. *See* Ellis v. Carter, 291 F.2d 270 (9th Cir.1961) (upholding concurrent claims); Berger v. Bishop Inv. Corp., 695 F.2d 302, 308 (8th Cir.1982) (upholding concurrent claims).

17. In Chemetron Corp. v. Business Funds, Inc., 682 F.2d 1149 (5th Cir.1982), *cert. denied*, 460 U.S. 1013 (1983), the court initially held that an action could not be maintained under Rule 10b–5 where an action was available under § 9(e) of the 1934 Act, because § 9 only prohibited certain willful misconduct; therefore, the plaintiff was not assuming a greater burden of proof by suing under Rule 10b–5 and to recognize such a right of action would nullify the procedural restrictions applicable to an action under § 9. In fact, the court indicated that the plaintiff would have a *lesser* burden of proof under Rule 10b–5 because of the requirement that certain additional facts be proven under the express provisions of § 9(a)(1), (2) and (6). Judge Jerre Williams dissented from this decision.

The Supreme Court granted *certiorari* in this case and then vacated the judgment and remanded the case for "further consideration in the light of [the Supreme Court decision in] *Herman & MacLean v. Huddleston*." On remand, Judge Gee, who wrote the original majority opinion, adhered to his former opinion even "in the light of" the decision in the *Herman & MacLean* case, but Judge Reavley

changed his vote and Judge Williams wrote the new majority opinion upholding the Rule 10b–5 action despite the alleged conflict with § 9. Chemetron Corporation v. Business Funds, Inc., 718 F.2d 725 (5th Cir.1983). The Fifth Circuit then granted a hearing in the case *en banc*, but the lawsuit was settled before that *en banc* hearing.

18. *See* Ross v. A.H. Robins Co., Inc., 607 F.2d 545 (2d Cir.1979), *cert. denied*, 446 U.S. 946 (1980), *reh'g denied*, 448 U.S. 911 (1980) (upholding concurrent remedies).

19. *See, e.g.*, CitiSource, Inc. Sec. Litig., 694 F.Supp. 1069 (S.D.N.Y.1988).

20. Cf. Finkielstain v. Seidel, 857 F.2d 893 (2d Cir.1988), holding that it would not dismiss an action against the Maryland Deposit Insurance Corporation as barred by the 11th Amendment; Durning v. Citibank, N.A., 950 F.2d 1419 (9th Cir.1991) (11th Amendment did not bar an action against Wyoming Community Development Authority when offering circulars expressly disclaimed that state was liable for the bonds); Bair v. Krug, 853 F.2d 672 (9th Cir.1988) (11th Amendment barred federal securities law claims against state officials with regulatory oversight of state chartered thrift company); Mercer v. Jaffe, Snider, Raitt & Heuer, P.C., 730 F.Supp. 74, 78 (W.D.Mich.1990), *aff'd without op.*, 933 F.2d 1008 (6th Cir.1991) (11th Amendment barred securities claims against State of Michigan).

does not. On the other hand, the coverage of § 17(a) is almost identical to the coverage of the express civil liability provision in § 12(a)(2) of the 1933 Act, with the sole exception that § 17(a) covers all offers and sales which are exempt from registration by the provisions of § 3, while § 12(a)(2) does not cover transactions in two of the exempt securities, government and bank securities.

After a few early decisions upheld a private right of action under § 17(a),[21] more recent cases, with few exceptions,[22] have generally rejected the implication of a private cause of action under § 17(a).[23]

Sections 13(d), 14(d) and 14(e) of the 1934 Act: When litigation under the Williams Act came along, the initial Circuit Court decisions were in favor of the full implication of liability under § 14(e),[24] despite some initial misgivings expressed by a few district judges.[25] The holdings of these cases which held that a defeated tender offeror had an implied cause of action to collect damages damages from the target company and its directors and officers and other persons was, however, overruled by the Supreme Court decision in the *Piper* case.[26] The Supreme Court seemed to accept the idea, although it expressly does not rule on it since the issue was not before it, that a cause of action could be asserted under § 14(e) by the shareholders of the target company for whose "especial benefit" the Williams Act was enacted. But it is difficult to see how the shareholders of the target company could allege that they were injured in any way by having tendered as a result of false statements by the tender offeror, because the offer is usually at a substantial premium above market. As to those shareholders who fail to tender, this would hardly be the result of statements made by the tender offeror, which is attempting to induce them to accept, not reject, the offer. In any event, they are frequently cashed out at the same price as was paid in the tender offer.

In Kalmanovitz v. G. Heileman Brewing Co., Inc.,[27] the Third Circuit held that an unsuccessful tender offeror who was also a shareholder of the target company did not have standing under the *Piper* case to bring a suit for damages under § 14(e). The court stated that one who occupies those dual roles may be considered to be only an offeror for the purposes of judging his standing to bring claims under § 14(e). The court also said: "In *Piper*, the Supreme Court left open the questions whether a private right of action exists under § 14(e) and, if so, whether a shareholder has standing to assert such a claim. * * * Although plaintiff's contention [that a private right of action exists in favor of a shareholder of the target company in view of the Supreme Court's explicit

---

21. *See, e.g.*, Pfeffer v. Cressaty, 223 F.Supp. 756 (S.D.N.Y.1963); cf. Judge Friendly dictum in SEC v. Texas Gulf Sulphur Co., 401 F.2d 833, 867 (2d Cir.1968), *cert. denied sub nom.* Coates v. SEC, 394 U.S. 976 (1969): "Once it had been established, however, that an aggrieved buyer has a private action under § 10(b) of the 1934 Act, there seemed little practical point in denying the existence of such an action under § 17—with the important proviso that fraud, as distinct from mere negligence, must be alleged."

22. *See* Craighead v. E.F. Hutton & Co., Inc., 899 F.2d 485, 492–493 (6th Cir. 1990).

23. Finkel v. Stratton Corp., 962 F.2d 169, 174–175 (2d Cir.1992) (citing cases from seven other circuits); Maldonado v. Dominguez, 137 F.3d 1 (1st Cir.1998).

24. *See, e.g.*, H.K. Porter Co., Inc. v. Nicholson File Co., 482 F.2d 421 (1st Cir. 1973).

25. *See, e.g.*, Washburn v. Madison Square Garden Corp., 340 F.Supp. 504 (S.D.N.Y.1972).

26. Piper v. Chris–Craft Industries, Inc., 430 U.S. 1 (1977).

27. 769 F.2d 152 (3d Cir.1985).

statement that the act was passed to protect such shareholders] arguably may be correct, our disposition of this case does not require us to decide that issue."[28]

With respect to false statements by management and its allies in connection with such a takeover battle, in Panter v. Marshall Field & Co.[29] the Seventh Circuit held that the shareholders of the target company could not establish any cause of action under § 14(e) in a case where the tender offer was withdrawn, since they had not "relied" on the allegedly false statements in not tendering—they had never been given an opportunity to tender. If the *Panter* case is correct, then the holding would seem to leave only a situation where the tender offer is not withdrawn but is defeated by allegedly false statements of the management, and the price of the stock later declines, in which case the shareholders of the target company might be able to state a cause of action under § 14(e) by claiming that they had not tendered in reliance on the false statements of the management. This discussion, of course, relates to actions for damages and not for injunctive relief, which may be subject to different considerations.

The cases have generally held that an issuer has an implied private right of action under § 13(d) to seek injunctive relief, since Congress must have intended to confer a private remedy on the issuer as the only party with the capability and the incentive to pursue violations of the reporting statute. In Gearhart Industries, Inc. v. Smith International, Inc.,[30] the court stated: "[T]o conclude that such relief is available in no circumstances whatever—however flagrant—would be all but to license the filing of deliberately misleading 13(d) and 14(e) disclosure statements on pain of nothing more than a possible damage suit by sellers or intervention by the SEC—a body that assures us on amicus brief that its resources are inadequate to policy the myriad of 13(d) filings made each year so as to insure truthful disclosures."[31] The court held, however, reversing the district judge, that enjoining both the tender offer and the voting of the shares acquired was "too drastic" a remedy and that the injunction should only hold up the tender offer until corrective were filed.

Several circuits have now implied a private cause of action for target company stockholders under § 14(d)(7), "the Best Price" provision of the Williams Act.[32]

---

28. 769 F.2d at 158–159. For cases permitting injunctive relief by a tender offer bidder, target companies, or target shareholders, *see* 9 Louis Loss & Joel Seligman, Securities Regulation 4375–4380 (3d ed. 1992).

29. 646 F.2d 271 (7th Cir.1981), *cert. denied*, 454 U.S. 1092 (1981). *See also* Lewis v. McGraw, 619 F.2d 192 (2d Cir.1980), *cert. denied*, 449 U.S. 951 (1980).

30. 741 F.2d 707 (5th Cir.1984).

31. 741 F.2d at 714–715. Accord: Dan River, Inc. v. Unitex Ltd., 624 F.2d 1216 (4th Cir.1980), *cert. denied*, 449 U.S. 1101 (1981); Chromalloy American Corp. v. Sun Chemical Corp., 611 F.2d 240 (8th Cir.1979); Indiana Nat'l Corp. v. Rich, 712 F.2d 1180 (7th Cir. 1983); General Aircraft Corp. v. Lampert, 556 F.2d 90 (1st Cir.1977). But see Liberty Nat'l Ins. Holding Co. v. Charter Co., 734 F.2d 545 (11th Cir.1984) (no private cause of action for issuer under § 13(d) or § 14(d)); cf. Florida Commercial Banks v. Culverhouse, 772 F.2d 1513 (11th Cir.1985) (interpreting *Liberty National* as limited to a right of divestiture of the shares acquired by a tender offeror, nor injunctive relief).

32. *See, e.g.,* Field v. Trump, 850 F.2d 938, 946 (2d Cir.1988), *cert. denied*, 489 U.S. 1012 (1989); Polaroid Corp. v. Disney, 862 F.2d 987, 996 (3d Cir.1988); Epstein v. MCA, Inc., 50 F.3d 644, 652 (9th Cir.1995); *reversed on other grounds*, 516 U.S. 367 n. 1 (1996) (expressing no opinion whether an implied private cause of action exists under § 14(d)(6) or § 14(d)(7)).

Margin Rules: After earlier decisions had implied a private right of action under § 7 or Margin Regulation T,[33] later cases, some in reliance on 1970 amendments to the 1934 Act,[34] have followed *Cort v. Ash* and have declined to imply a private cause of action for violation of the 1934 Act's margin provisions or the margin rules today found Regulations in T or U.[35]

Violations of the Rules of the Stock Exchanges and the NASD: Under §§ 6 and 15A of the 1934 Act, the stock exchanges and the NASD (the self-regulatory agencies or "SROs") are required to adopt rules that among other things "are designed to prevent fraudulent and manipulative acts and practices, to promote just and equitable principles of trade, * * * and, in general, to protect investors and the public interest. * * * " Section 19(g) requires the SROs to enforce their own rules against their members and persons associated with such members. Section 21(d) authorizes the Commission to bring an injunctive action to prevent a violation of the rules of the exchanges and the NASD, as well as the provisions of the statute and the Commission's own rules. Section 27 of the 1934 Act, which confers exclusive jurisdiction on the federal courts of actions to enforce any liability or duty created by the 1934 Act refers only to such liabilities or duties created "by this title [i.e., the act itself] or the rules and regulations thereunder," and makes no mention of rules of SROs as do the other sections mentioned above.

Under this statutory scheme, is there any basis for implying a cause of action for a violation of one of the rules of the self regulatory organizations? Even if a cause of action is created by the statute and the rules of the SROs, would the federal courts have any jurisdiction to entertain it in view of the language in § 27?

In Colonial Realty Corp. v. Bache & Co.[36] the court, in an opinion by Judge Friendly, held that there was no cause of action for a violation of the requirement under the rules of the NYSE and the NASD that their members observe "just and equitable principles of trade." Judge Friendly refused, however, to say that there might never be an implied cause of action for violation of some of the rules of the SROs. He stated:

> What emerges is that whether the courts are to imply federal civil liability for violation of exchange or dealer association rules by a member cannot be determined on the simplistic all-or-nothing basis urged by the two parties; rather, the court must look to the nature of the particular rule and its place in the regulatory scheme, with the party urging the implication of a federal liability carrying a considerably heavier burden of persuasion than when the violation is of the statute or an SEC regulation. The case for implication would be strongest when the rule imposes an explicit duty unknown to the common law.[37]

33. *See, e.g.*, Pearlstein v. Scudder & German, 429 F.2d 1136 (2d Cir.1970), *cert. denied*, 401 U.S. 1013 (1971).

34. Pub. L. 91–508, 84 Stat. 1124.

35. *See, e.g.*, Stern v. Merrill Lynch, Pierce, Fenner, & Smith, Inc., 603 F.2d 1073 (4th Cir.1979); Bennett v. United States Trust Co. of N.Y., 770 F.2d 308 (2d Cir.1985), *cert. denied*, 474 U.S. 1058 (1986); Useden v. Acker, 947 F.2d 1563, 1582 (11th Cir.1991)

(no implied cause of action for Regulation U); Shearson Lehman Bros., Inc. v. M & L Inv., 10 F.3d 1510 (10th Cir.1993) (broker's violation of Regulation T was not an affirmative defense to his action for breach of contract).

36. 358 F.2d 178 (2d Cir.1966), *cert. denied*, 385 U.S. 817 (1966).

37. 358 F.2d at 182.

In Buttrey v. Merrill Lynch, Pierce, Fenner & Smith, Inc.[38] the Seventh Circuit in 1969 upheld a cause of action against a broker-dealer based upon his violation of Rule 405 of the New York Stock Exchange—the so-called "know your customer" rule.

Subsequently the pendulum swung decisively the other way. In 1980 the Ninth Circuit in Jablon v. Dean Witter & Co.[39] held that under the *Redington* case and the *Transamerica* case there could be no implication of a private right of action for a violation of any of the rules of the SROs, and indicated that its opinion in the *Buttrey* case had been overruled by those decisions of the Supreme Court. Virtually every subsequent appellate decision has agreed that there is no implied cause of action under the federal securities laws for violation of a stock exchange or NASD rule.[40]

The implication of private causes of action has given rise to occasional questions under several other provisions of the federal securities law, and has produced a substantial literature. For more detailed discussion and a bibliography of citations, see 9 Louis Loss & Joel Seligman 4312–4456 (3d ed. 1992).

2.   CAUSATION

Mills v. Electric Auto–Lite Co.

Supreme Court of the United States, 1970.
396 U.S. 375, 90 S.Ct. 616, 24 L.Ed.2d 593.

■ MR. JUSTICE HARLAN delivered the opinion of the Court.

This case requires us to consider a basic aspect of the implied private right of action for violation of § 14(a) of the Securities Exchange Act of 1934, recognized by this Court in J.I. Case Co. v. Borak, 377 U.S. 426 (1964). As in *Borak* the asserted wrong is that a corporate merger was accomplished through the use of a proxy statement that was materially false or misleading. The question with which we deal is what causal relationship must be shown between such a statement and the merger to establish a cause of action based on the violation of the Act.

I

Petitioners were shareholders of the Electric Auto–Lite Company until 1963, when it was merged into Mergenthaler Linotype Company. They brought

---

38.   410 F.2d 135 (7th Cir.1969), *cert. denied*, 396 U.S. 838 (1969).

39.   614 F.2d 677 (9th Cir.1980).

40.   *See, e.g.*, Spicer v. Chicago Bd. Options Exch., Inc., 977 F.2d 255 (7th Cir.1992) (§ 6(b) does not create private cause of action for investors who allege that marketmakers violated Chicago Board Options Exchange Rules); VeriFone Sec. Litig., 11 F.3d 865, 870 (9th Cir.1993) ("It is well established that violation of an exchange rule will not support a private claim"); Feins v. American Stock Exch., Inc., 81 F.3d 1215 (2d Cir.1996) (no private cause of action for monetary damages resulting from denial of application of membership in SRO); Desiderio v. NASD, Inc., 191 F.3d 198, 208 (2d Cir.1999), *cert. denied*, 531 U.S. 1069 (there is no private right of action available under the Securities Exchange Act to redress denials of membership in an exchange or to challenge an exchange's failure to follow its own rules). But see O'Connor v. R.F. Lafferty & Co., Inc., 965 F.2d 893, 897 (10th Cir.1992) (holding that unsuitability doctrine premised on NYSE and NASD rules is recognized as a violation of Rule 10b–5 and analyzed as either an omission case or a fraudulent practices case).

suit on the day before the shareholders' meeting at which the vote was to take place on the merger, against Auto–Lite, Mergenthaler, and a third company, American Manufacturing Company, Inc. The complaint sought an injunction against the voting by Auto–Lite's management of all proxies obtained by means of an allegedly misleading proxy solicitation; however, it did not seek a temporary restraining order, and the voting went ahead as scheduled the following day. Several months later petitioners filed an amended complaint, seeking to have the merger set aside and to obtain such other relief as might be proper.

In Count II of the amended complaint, which is the only count before us, petitioners predicated jurisdiction on § 27 of the 1934 Act, 15 U.S.C. § 78aa. They alleged that the proxy statement sent out by the Auto–Lite management to solicit shareholders' votes in favor of the merger was misleading, in violation of § 14(a) of the Act and SEC Rule 14a–9 thereunder. (17 CFR § 240.14a–9.) Petitioners recited that before the merger Mergenthaler owned over 50% of the outstanding shares of Auto–Lite common stock, and had been in control of Auto–Lite for two years. American Manufacturing in turn owned about one-third of the outstanding shares of Mergenthaler, and for two years had been in voting control of Mergenthaler and, through it, of Auto–Lite. Petitioners charged that in light of these circumstances the proxy statement was misleading in that it told Auto–Lite shareholders that their board of directors recommended approval of the merger without also informing them that all 11 of Auto–Lite's directors were nominees of Mergenthaler and were under the "control and domination of Mergenthaler." Petitioners asserted the right to complain of this alleged violation both derivatively on behalf of Auto–Lite and as representatives of the class of all its minority shareholders.

On petitioner's motion for summary judgment with respect to Count II, the District Court for the Northern District of Illinois ruled as a matter of law that the claimed defect in the proxy statement was, in light of the circumstances in which the statement was made, a material omission. The District Court concluded, from its reading of the *Borak* opinion, that it had to hold a hearing on the issue whether there was "a causal connection between the finding that there has been a violation of the disclosure requirements of § 14(a) and the alleged injury to the plaintiffs" before it could consider what remedies would be appropriate. (Unreported opinion dated February 14, 1966.)

After holding such a hearing, the court found that under the terms of the merger agreement, an affirmative vote of two-thirds of the Auto–Lite shares was required for approval of the merger, and that the respondent companies owned and controlled about 54% of the outstanding shares. Therefore, to obtain authorization of the merger, respondents had to secure the approval of a substantial number of the minority shareholders. At the stockholders' meeting, approximately 950,000 shares, out of 1,160,000 shares outstanding, were voted in favor of the merger. This included 317,000 votes obtained by proxy from the minority shareholders, votes that were "necessary and indispensable to the approval of the merger." The District Court concluded that a causal relationship had thus been shown, and it granted an interlocutory judgment in favor of petitioners on the issue of liability, referring the case to a master for consideration of appropriate relief. (Unreported findings and conclusions dated Sept. 26, 1967; opinion reported at 281 F.Supp. 826 (1967)).

The District Court made the certification required by 28 U.S.C. § 1292(b), and respondents took an interlocutory appeal to the Court of Appeals for the

Seventh Circuit. That court affirmed the District Court's conclusion that the proxy statement was materially deficient, but reversed on the question of causation. The court acknowledged that, if an injunction had been sought a sufficient time before the stockholders' meeting, "corrective measures would have been appropriate." 403 F.2d 429, 435 (1968). However, since this suit was brought too late for preventive action, the courts had to determine "whether the misleading statement and omission caused the submission of sufficient proxies," as a prerequisite to a determination of liability under the Act. If the respondents could show, "by a preponderance of probabilities, that the merger would have received a sufficient vote even if the proxy statement had not been misleading in the respect found," petitioners would be entitled to no relief of any kind. Id., at 436.

The Court of Appeals acknowledged that this test corresponds to the common-law fraud test of whether the injured party relied on the misrepresentation. However, rightly concluding that "[r]eliance by thousands of individuals, as here, can scarcely be inquired into" (id., at 436 n. 10), the court ruled that the issue was to be determined by proof of the fairness of the terms of the merger. If respondents could show that the merger had merit and was fair to the minority shareholders, the trial court would be justified in concluding that a sufficient number of shareholders would have approved the merger had there been no deficiency in the proxy statement. In that case respondents would be entitled to a judgment in their favor.

Claiming that the Court of Appeals has construed this Court's decision in *Borak* in a manner that frustrates the statute's policy of enforcement through private litigation, the petitioners then sought review in this Court. We granted certiorari, 394 U.S. 971 (1969), believing that resolution of this basic issue should be made at this stage of the litigation and not postponed until after a trial under the Court of Appeals' decision.

II

As we stressed in *Borak,* § 14(a) stemmed from a congressional belief that "[f]air corporate suffrage is an important right that should attach to every equity security brought on a public exchange." H.R.Rep. No. 1383, 73d Cong., 2d Sess., 13. The provision was intended to promote "the free exercise of the voting rights of stockholders" by ensuring that proxies would be solicited with "explanation to the stockholder of the real nature of the questions for which authority to cast his vote is sought." Id., at 14; S.Rep. No. 792, 73d Cong., 2d Sess., 12; see 377 U.S., at 431. The decision below, by permitting all liability to be foreclosed on the basis of a finding that the merger was fair, would allow the stockholders to be bypassed, at least where only legal challenge to the merger is a suit for retrospective relief after the meeting has been held. A judicial appraisal of the merger's merits could be substituted for the actual and informed vote of the stockholders.

The result would be to insulate from private redress an entire category of proxy—those relating to matters other than the terms of the merger. Even outrageous misrepresentations in a proxy solicitation, if they did not relate to the terms of the transaction, would give rise to no cause of action under § 14(a). Particularly if carried over to enforcement actions by the Securities and Exchange Commission itself, such a result would subvert the congressional purpose of ensuring full and fair disclosure to shareholders.

Further, recognition of the fairness of the merger as a complete defense would confront small shareholders with an additional obstacle to making a successful challenge to a proposal recommended through a defective proxy statement. The risk that they would be unable to rebut the corporation's evidence of the fairness of the proposal, and thus to establish their cause of action, would be bound to discourage such shareholders from the private enforcement of the proxy rules that "provides a necessary supplement to Commission action." J.I. Case Co. v. Borak, 377 U.S., at 432.

Such a frustration of the congressional policy is not required by anything in the wording of the statute or in our opinion in the *Borak* case. Section 14(a) declares it "unlawful" to solicit proxies in contravention of Commission rules, and SEC Rule 14a–9 prohibits solicitations "containing any statement which * * * is false or misleading with respect to any material fact, or which omits to state any material fact necessary in order to make the statements therein not false or misleading. * * * " Use of a solicitation that is materially misleading is itself a violation of law, as the Court of Appeals recognized in stating that injunctive relief would be available to remedy such a defect if sought prior to the stockholders' meeting. In *Borak,* which came to this Court on a dismissal of the complaint, the Court limited its inquiry to whether a violation of § 14(a) gives rise to "a federal cause of action for rescission or damages," 377 U.S., at 428. Referring to the argument made by petitioners there "that the merger can be dissolved only if it was fraudulent or non-beneficial, issues upon which the proxy material would not bear," the Court stated: "But the causal relationship of the proxy material and the merger are questions of fact to be resolved at trial, not here. We therefore do not discuss this point further." Id., at 431. In the present case there has been a hearing specifically directed to the causation problem. The question before the Court is whether the facts found on the basis of that hearing are sufficient in law to establish petitioners' cause of action, and we conclude that they are.

Where the misstatement or omission in a proxy statement has been shown to be "material," as it was found to be here, that determination itself indubitably embodies a conclusion that the defect was of such a character that it might have been considered important by a reasonable shareholder who was in the process of deciding how to vote. This requirement that the defect have a significant *propensity* to affect the voting process is found in the express terms of Rule 14a–9, and it adequately serves the purpose of ensuring that a cause of action cannot be established by proof of a defect so trivial, or so unrelated to the transaction for which approval is sought, that correction of the defect or imposition of liability would not further the interests protected by § 14(a).

There is no need to supplement this requirement, as did the Court of Appeals, with a requirement of proof of whether the defect actually had a decisive effect on the voting. Where there has been a finding of materiality, a shareholder has made a sufficient showing of causal relationship between the violation and the injury for which he seeks redress if, as here, he proves that the proxy solicitation itself, rather than the particular defect in the solicitation materials, was an essential link in the accomplishment of the transaction. This objective test will avoid the impracticalities of determining how many votes were affected, and, by resolving doubts in favor of those the statute is designed to protect, will effectuate the congressional policy of ensuring that the shareholders are able to make an informed choice when they are consulted on corporate transactions. Cf. Union Pac. R. Co. v. Chicago & N.W.R. Co., 226

F.Supp. 400, 411 (D.C.N.D.Ill.1964); 2 L. Loss, Securities Regulation 962 n. 411 (2d ed. 1961); 5 id., at 2929–2930 (Supp.1969).[7]

III

Our conclusion that petitioners have established their case by showing that proxies necessary to approval of the merger were obtained by means of a materially misleading solicitation implies nothing about the form of relief to which they may be entitled. We held in *Borak* that upon finding a violation the courts were "to be alert to provide such remedies as are necessary to make effective the congressional purpose," noting specifically that such remedies are not to be limited to prospective relief. 377 U.S., at 433, 434. In devising retrospective relief for violation of the proxy rules, the federal courts should consider the same factors that would govern the relief granted for any similar illegality or fraud. One important factor may be the fairness of the terms of the merger. Possible forms of relief will include setting aside the merger or granting other equitable relief, but, as the Court of Appeals below noted, nothing in the statutory policy "requires the court to unscramble a corporate transaction merely because a violation occurred." 403 F.2d, at 436. In selecting a remedy the lower courts should exercise " 'the sound discretion which guides the determinations of courts of equity,' " keeping in mind the role of equity as "the instrument for nice adjustment and reconciliation between the public interest and private needs as well as between competing private claims." Hecht Co. v. Bowles, 321 U.S. 321, 329–330 (1944), quoting from Meredith v. Winter Haven, 320 U.S. 228, 235 (1943). * * *

Monetary relief will, of course, also be a possibility. Where the defect in the proxy solicitation relates to the specific terms of the merger, the district court might appropriately order an accounting to ensure that the shareholders receive the value that was represented as coming to them. On the other hand, where, as here, the misleading aspect of the solicitation did not relate to terms of the merger, monetary relief might be afforded to the shareholders only if the merger resulted in a reduction of the earnings or earnings potential of their holdings. In short, damages should be recoverable only to the extent that they can be shown. If commingling of the assets and operations of the merged companies makes it impossible to establish direct injury from the merger, relief might be predicated on a determination of the fairness of the terms of the merger at the time it was approved. These questions, of course, are for decision in the first instance by the District Court on remand, and our singling out of some of the possibilities is not intended to exclude others. * * *

THE CAUSATION—MATERIALITY NEXUS

In Mills v. Electric Auto–Lite Co.,[1] the Supreme Court held that proof that a misstatement or omission was material normally did not need to be supple-

---

7. We need not decide in this case whether causation could be shown where the management controls a sufficient number of shares to approve the transaction without any votes from the minority. Even in that situation, if the management finds it necessary for legal or practical reasons to solicit proxies from minority shareholders, at least one court has held that the proxy solicitation might be sufficiently related to the merger to satisfy the causation requirement.

1. 396 U.S. 375 (1970).

mented "with a requirement of proof whether the defect actually had a decisive effect on the voting."[2]

In Footnote 7, the court allowed one possible exception:

> We need not decide in this case whether causation could be shown where the management controls a sufficient number of shares to approve the transaction without any votes from the minority. Even in that situation, if the management finds it necessary for legal or practical reasons to solicit proxies from minority shareholders, at least one court has held that the proxy solicitation might be sufficiently related to the merger to satisfy the causation requirement.[3]

In 1991 a 5–4 majority of the Supreme Court returned to this unresolved question in *Virginia Bankshares, Inc. v. Sandberg*,[4] and reasoned that where management possessed sufficient votes to approve a merger approval and plaintiffs could identify *no* remedy that was lost because of defendants alleged material misrepresentations or omissions, plaintiff would fail to demonstrate causation.

The majority decision on causation in *Virginia Bankshares* is quite narrow. Justice Souter specifically found that there was *no* link between the alleged misrepresentations to the minority stockholder and any lost state remedy. This left for another day the question whether minority shareholders could establish causation if they had been induced to forfeit a state law right to an appraisal remedy by voting to approve a transaction, or had been deterred from obtaining an order enjoining a damaging transaction by a proxy solicitation that misrepresented the facts on which an injunction could properly have been issued.

In Howing Co. v. Nationwide Corp.,[5] the court applied *Virginia Bankshares* to a claim under a different section of the Securities Exchange Act, and concluded that plaintiffs, there minority stockholders, could recover under a theory of loss of state law remedy.

3. MATERIALITY

Rule 14a–9(a) provides:

> No solicitation subject to this regulation shall be made by means of any proxy statement, form of proxy, notice of meeting, or other communication, written or oral, containing any statement which, at the time and in the light of the circumstances under which it is made, is false or misleading with respect to any material fact, or which omits to state any material fact necessary in order to make the statements therein not false or misleading or necessary to correct any statement in any earlier communication with respect to the solicitation of a proxy for the same meeting or subject matter which has become false or misleading.[1]

Under the basic federal securities law antifraud provisions the questions are whether a particular statement or omission is false and misleading and whether the statement or omission is material. These two questions tend to

2. Id. at 384–385.

3. Ibid.

4. 501 U.S. 1083, 1099–1108 (1991).

5. 972 F.2d 700, 709–710 (6th Cir. 1992), *cert. denied*, 507 U.S. 1004 (1993).

1. *See generally* 4 Louis Loss & Joel Seligman, Securities Regulation 2071–2105 (3d ed. rev. 2000).

merge here as they do in other fraud provisions both under the federal securities laws generally and at common law, but it is worth emphasizing that proof of (1) a false and misleading statement or omission, and (2) materiality are two separate elements.

A Note to Rule 14a–9 gives "some examples of what, depending upon particular facts and circumstances, may be misleading within the meaning of this rule":

(a) Prediction as to specific future market values.[2]

(b) Material which directly or indirectly impugns character, integrity of personal reputation, or directly or indirectly makes charges concerning improper, illegal or immoral conduct or associations, without factual foundation.

(c) Failure to so identify a proxy statement, form of proxy and other soliciting material as to clearly distinguish it from the soliciting material of any other person or persons soliciting for the same meeting or subject matter.

(d) Claims made prior to a meeting regarding the results of a solicitation.

In considering what is false or misleading there is some indication that a degree of freedom is permitted in proxy fights along the lines of the traditional concept of "puffing." In the analogous context of a contested tender offer Judge Friendly cautioned: "Courts should tread lightly in imposing a duty of self-flagellation on offerors with respect to matters that are known as well, or almost as well, to the target company; some issues concerning a contested tender offer can safely be left for the latter's riposte."[3]

There is no requirement that a material fact be expressed in certain words or in a certain form of language. "Fair accuracy, not perfection, is the appropriate standard."[4]

(a) The General Standard

The United States Supreme Court first addressed materiality in 1976.

TSC Industries, Inc. v. Northway, Inc.

Supreme Court of the United States, 1976.
426 U.S. 438, 96 S.Ct. 2126, 48 L.Ed.2d 757.

■ Mr. Justice Marshall delivered the opinion of the Court.

The proxy rules promulgated by the Securities and Exchange Commission under the Securities Exchange Act of 1934 bar the use of proxy statements that are false or misleading with respect to the presentation or omission of material facts. We are called upon to consider the definition of a material fact under

---

2. Until the 1979 adoption of Rule 3b–6, a "safe harbor" Rule for projections, Note (a) referred to "market value, earnings, or dividends." Regarding the revision of this Note, see Walker v. Action Indus., Inc., 802 F.2d 703, 707–710 (4th Cir.1986), *cert. denied*, 479 U.S. 1065 (1987).

3. Missouri Portland Cement Co. v. Cargill, Inc., 498 F.2d 851, 873 (2d Cir.1974), *cert. denied*, 419 U.S. 883 (1974).

4. *See, e.g.,* Kennecott Copper Corp. v. Curtiss–Wright Corp., 584 F.2d 1195, 1200 (2d Cir.1978).

those rules, and the appropriateness of resolving the question of materiality by summary judgment in this case.

I

The dispute in this case centers about the acquisition of petitioner TSC Industries, Inc. by petitioner National Industries, Inc. In February 1969 National acquired 34% of TSC's voting securities by purchase from Charles E. Schmidt and his family. Schmidt, who had been TSC's founder and principal shareholder, promptly resigned along with his son from TSC's board of directors. Thereafter, five National nominees were placed on TSC's board, Stanley R. Yarmuth, National's president and chief executive officer, became chairman of the TSC board, and Charles F. Simonelli, National's executive vice president, became chairman of the TSC executive committee. On October 16, 1969, the TSC board, with the attending National nominees abstaining, approved a proposal to liquidate and sell all of TSC's assets to National. The proposal in substance provided for the exchange of TSC Common and Series 1 Preferred Stock for National Series B Preferred Stock and Warrants. On November 12, 1969, TSC and National issued a joint proxy statement to their shareholders, recommending approval of the proposal. The proxy solicitation was successful, TSC was placed in liquidation and dissolution, and the exchange of shares was effected.

This is an action brought by respondent Northway, a TSC shareholder, against TSC and National, claiming that their joint proxy statement was incomplete and materially misleading in violation of § 14a of the Securities Exchange Act of 1934 and Rules 14a–3 and 14a–9 promulgated thereunder.

* * * The basis of Northway's claim under Rule 14a–3 is that TSC and National failed to state in the proxy statement that the transfer of the Schmidt interests in TSC to National had given National control of TSC. The Rule 14a–9 claim, insofar as it concerns us, is that TSC and National omitted from the proxy statement material facts relating to the degree of National's control over TSC and the favorability of the terms of the proposal to TSC shareholders.

Northway filed its complaint in the United States District Court for the Northern District of Illinois on December 4, 1969, the day before the shareholder meeting on the proposed transaction, but while it requested injunctive relief it never so moved. In 1972 Northway amended its complaint to seek money damages, restitution, and other equitable relief. Shortly thereafter, Northway moved for summary judgment on the issue of TSC's and National's liability. The District Court denied the motion, but granted leave to appeal pursuant to 28 U.S.C. § 1292(b). The Court of Appeals for the Seventh Circuit agreed with the District Court that there existed a genuine issue of fact as to whether National's acquisition of the Schmidt interests in TSC had resulted in a change of control, and that summary judgment was therefore inappropriate on the Rule 14a–3 claim. But the Court of Appeals reversed the District Court's denial of summary judgment to Northway on its 14a–9 claims, holding that certain omissions of fact were material as a matter of law. 512 F.2d 324 (C.A.7 1975).

We granted certiorari because the standard applied by the Court of Appeals in resolving the question of materiality appeared to conflict with the standard applied by other courts of appeals. 423 U.S. 820 (1975). We now hold that the Court of Appeals erred in ordering that partial summary judgment be granted to Northway.

II

A

As we have noted on more than one occasion, § 14a of the Exchange Act "was intended to promote 'the free exercise of the voting rights of stockholders' by ensuring that proxies would be solicited with 'explanation to the stockholder of the real nature of the questions for which authority to cast his vote is sought.'" Mills v. Electric Auto–Lite Co., 396 U.S. 375, 381 (1970), quoting H.R.Rep. No. 1383, 73d Cong., 2d Sess., 14; S.Rep. No. 792, 73d Cong., 2d Sess., 12. See also J.I. Case Co. v. Borak, 377 U.S. 426, 431 (1964). In *Borak,* the Court held that § 14a's broad remedial purposes required recognition under § 27 of the Exchange Act of an implied private right of action for violations of the provision. And in *Mills,* we attempted to clarify to some extent the elements of a private cause of action for violation of § 14a. In a suit challenging the sufficiency under § 14a and Rule 14a–9 of a proxy statement soliciting votes in favor of a merger, we held that there was no need to demonstrate that the alleged defect in the proxy statement actually had a decisive effect on the voting. So long as the misstatement or omission was material, the causal relation between violation and injury is sufficiently established, we concluded, if "the proxy solicitation itself * * * was an essential link in the accomplishment of the transaction." 396 U.S. at 385. After *Mills,* then, the content given to the notion of materiality assumes heightened significance.[7]

B

The question of materiality, it is universally agreed, is an objective one, involving the significance of an omitted or misrepresented fact to a reasonable investor. Variations in the formulation of a general test of materiality occur in the articulation of just how significant a fact must be or, put another way, how certain it must be that the fact would affect a reasonable investor's judgment.

The Court of Appeals in this case concluded that material facts include "all facts which a reasonable shareholder *might* consider important." 512 F.2d, at 330 (emphasis added). This formulation of the test of materiality has been explicitly rejected by at least two courts as setting too low a threshold for the imposition of liability under Rule 14a–9. Gerstle v. Gamble–Skogmo, Inc., 478 F.2d 1281, 1301–1302 (C.A.2 1973); Smallwood v. Pearl Brewing Co., 489 F.2d 579, 603–604 (C.A.5 1974). In these cases, panels of the Second and Fifth Circuits opted for the conventional tort test of materiality—whether a reasonable man *would* attach importance to the fact misrepresented or omitted in determining his course of action. See Restatement (Second) of Torts § 538(2)(a) (Tent.Draft No. 10, 1964). See also ALI Federal Securities Code § 256(a) (Tent.Draft No. 2, 1973). Gerstle v. Gamble–Skogmo, *supra,* at 1302, also approved the following standard, which had been formulated with reference to statements issued in a contested election: "whether, taking a properly realistic view, there is a substantial likelihood that the misstatement or omission may

---

7. Our cases have not considered, and we have no occasion in this case to consider, what showing of culpability is required to establish the liability under § 14(a) of a corporation issuing a materially misleading proxy statement, or of a person involved in the preparation of a materially misleading proxy statement. See Gerstle v. Gamble–Skogmo, Inc., 478 F.2d 1281, 1298–1301 (C.A.2 1973); Richland v. Crandall, 262 F.Supp. 538, 553 n. 12 (S.D.N.Y.1967); Jennings & Marsh, Securities Regulation: Cases and Materials 1358–1359 (3d ed. 1972). See also Ernst & Ernst v. Hochfelder, 425 U.S. 185 (slip op., at 23 n. 28) (Mar. 30, 1976).

have led a stockholder to grant a proxy to the solicitor or to withhold one from the other side, whereas in the absence of this he would have taken a contrary course." General Time Corp. v. Talley Industries, Inc., 403 F.2d 159, 162 (C.A.2 1968), cert. denied, 393 U.S. 1026 (1969).

In arriving at its broad definition of a material fact as one that a reasonable shareholder *might* consider important, the Court of Appeals in this case relied heavily upon language of this Court in Mills v. Electric Auto–Lite Co., *supra*. That reliance was misplaced. The *Mills* Court did characterize a determination of materiality as at least "embod[ying] a conclusion that the defect was of such a character that it might have been considered important by a reasonable shareholder who was in the process of deciding how to vote." 396 U.S., at 384. But if any language in *Mills* is to be read as suggesting a general notion of materiality, it can only be the opinion's subsequent reference to materiality as a "requirement that the defect have a significant *propensity* to affect the voting process." Ibid. (emphasis in original). For it was that require-ment that the Court said "adequately serves the purpose of ensuring that a cause of action cannot be established by proof of a defect so trivial, or so unrelated to the transaction for which approval is sought, that correction of the defect or imposition of liability would not further the interests protected by § 14(a)." Ibid. Even this language must be read, however, with appreciation that the Court specifically declined to consider the materiality of the omissions in *Mills*. Id., at 381 n. 4. The references to materiality were simply preliminary to our consideration of the sole question in the case—whether proof of the materiality of an omission from a proxy statement must be supplemented by a showing that the defect actually caused the outcome of the vote. It is clear, then, that *Mills* did not intend to foreclose further inquiry into the meaning of materiality under Rule 14a–9.

C

In formulating a standard of materiality under Rule 14a–9, we are guided, of course, by the recognition in *Borak* and *Mills* of the Rule's broad remedial purpose. That purpose is not merely to ensure by judicial means that the transaction, when judged by its real terms, is fair and otherwise adequate, but to ensure disclosures by corporate management in order to enable the share-holders to make an informed choice. See *Mills, supra*, at 381. As an abstract proposition, the most desirable role for a court in a suit of this sort, coming after the consummation of the proposed transaction, would perhaps be to determine whether in fact the proposal would have been favored by the shareholders and consummated in the absence of any misstatement or omis-sion. But as we recognized in *Mills, supra*, at 382 n. 5, such matters are not subject to determination with certainty. Doubts as to the critical nature of information misstated or omitted will be commonplace. And particularly in view of the prophylactic purpose of the Rule and the fact that the content of the proxy statement is within management's control, it is appropriate that these doubts be resolved in favor of those the statute is designed to protect. *Mills, supra*, at 385.

We are aware, however, that the disclosure policy embodied in the proxy regulations is not without limit. See id., at 384. Some information is of such dubious significance that insistence on its disclosure may accomplish more harm than good. The potential liability for a Rule 14a–9 violation can be great indeed, and if the standard of materiality is unnecessarily low, not only may the corporation and its management be subjected to liability for insignificant omissions or misstatements, but also management's fear of exposing itself to substantial liability may cause it simply to bury the shareholder in an avalanche of trivial information—a result that is hardly conducive to informed decisionmaking. Precisely these dangers are presented, we think, by the definition of a material fact adopted by the Court of Appeals in this case—a fact which a reasonable shareholder *might* consider important. We agree with Judge Friendly, speaking for the Court of Appeals in *Gerstle,* that the "might" formulation is "too suggestive of mere possibility, however unlikely." 478 F.2d, at 1302.

The general standard of materiality that we think best comports with the policies of Rule 14a–9 is as follows: an omitted fact is material if there is a substantial likelihood that a reasonable shareholder would consider it important in deciding how to vote. This standard is fully consistent with *Mills* general description of materiality as a requirement that "the defect have a significant *propensity* to affect the voting process." It does not require proof of a substantial likelihood that disclosure of the omitted fact would have caused the reasonable investor to change his vote. What the standard does contemplate is a showing of a substantial likelihood that, under all the circumstances, the omitted fact would have assumed actual significance in the deliberations of the reasonable shareholder. Put another way, there must be a substantial likelihood that the disclosure of the omitted fact would have been viewed by the reasonable investor as having significantly altered the "total mix" of information made available.

D

The issue of materiality may be characterized as a mixed question of law and fact, involving as it does the application of a legal standard to a particular set of facts. In considering whether summary judgment on the issue is appropriate, we must bear in mind that the underlying objective facts, which will often be free from dispute, are merely the starting point for the ultimate determination of materiality. The determination requires delicate assessments of the inferences a "reasonable shareholder" would draw from a given set of facts and the significance of those inferences to him, and these assessments are peculiarly ones for the trier of fact. Only if the established omissions are "so obviously important to an investor, that reasonable minds cannot differ on the question of materiality" is the ultimate issue of materiality appropriately resolved "as a matter of law" by summary judgment. John Hopkins University v. Hutton, 422 F.2d 1124, 1129 (C.A.4 1970). See Smallwood v. Pearl Brewing Co., 489 F.2d 579, 604 (C.A.5 1974); Rogen v. Ilikon Corp., 361 F.2d 260, 265–267 (C.A.1 1966).

III

The omissions found by the Court of Appeals to have been materially misleading as a matter of law involved two general issues—the degree of National's control over TSC at the time of the proxy solicitation, and the favorability of the terms of the proposed transaction to TSC shareholders.

A. *National's Control of TSC*

The Court of Appeals concluded that two omitted facts relating to National's potential influence, or control, over the management of TSC were material as a matter of law. First, the proxy statement failed to state that at the time the statement was issued, the chairman of the TSC board of directors was Stanley Yarmuth, National's president and chief executive officer, and the chairman of the TSC executive committee was Charles Simonelli, National's executive vice president. Second, the statement did not disclose that in filing reports required by the SEC, both TSC and National had indicated that National "may be deemed to be a 'parent' of TSC as that term is defined in the Rules and Regulations under the Securities Act of 1933." * * * App. 490, 512, 517. The Court of Appeals noted that TSC shareholders were relying on the TSC board of directors to negotiate on their behalf for the best possible rate of exchange with National. It then concluded that the omitted facts were material because they were "persuasive indicators that the TSC board was in fact under the control of National, and that National thus 'sat on both sides of the table' in setting the terms of the exchange." 512 F.2d at 333.

We do not agree that the omission of these facts, when viewed against the disclosures contained in the proxy statement, warrants the entry of summary judgment against TSC and National on this record. Our conclusion is the same whether the omissions are considered separately or together.

The proxy statement prominently displayed the facts that National owned 34% of the outstanding shares in TSC, and that no other person owned more than 10%. App. 262–263, 267. It also prominently revealed that five out of ten TSC directors were National nominees, and it recited the positions of those National nominees with National—indicating, among other things, that Stanley Yarmuth was president and a director of National, and that Charles Simonelli was executive vice president and a director of National. App. 267. These disclosures clearly revealed the nature of National's relationship with TSC and alerted the reasonable shareholder to the fact that National exercised a degree of influence over TSC. In view of these disclosures, we certainly cannot say that the additional facts that Yarmuth was chairman of the TSC board of directors and Simonelli chairman of its executive committee were, on this record, so obviously important that reasonable minds could not differ on their materiality.

Nor can we say that it was materially misleading as a matter of law for TSC and National to have omitted reference to SEC filings indicating that National "may be deemed to be a parent of TSC." As we have already noted, both the District Court and the Court of Appeals concluded, in denying summary judgment on the Rule 14a–3 claim, that there was a genuine issue of fact as to whether National actually controlled TSC at the time of the proxy solicitation. We must assume for present purposes, then, that National did not control TSC. On that assumption, TSC and National obviously had no duty to state without qualification that control did exist. If the proxy statements were to disclose the conclusory statements in the SEC filings that National "may be deemed to be a parent of TSC," then it would have been appropriate, if not necessary, for the statement to have included a disclaimer of National control over TSC or a disclaimer of knowledge as to whether National controlled TSC. The net contribution of including the contents of the SEC filings accompanied by such disclaimers is not of such obvious significance, in view of the other facts contained in the proxy statement, that their exclusion renders the statement materially misleading as a matter of law.[15]

15. We emphasize that we do not intend to imply that facts suggestive of control need be disclosed only if in fact there was control. If, for example, the proxy statement in this case had failed to reveal National's 34% stock interest in TSC and the presence

B. *Favorability of the Terms to TSC Shareholders*

The Court of Appeals also found that the failure to disclose two sets of facts rendered the proxy statement materially deficient in its presentation of the favorability of the terms of the proposed transaction to TSC shareholders. The first omission was of information, described by the Court of Appeals as "bad news" for TSC shareholders, contained in a letter from an investment banking firm whose earlier favorable opinion of the fairness of the proposed transaction was reported in the proxy statement. The second omission related to purchases of National common stock by National and by Madison Fund, Inc., a large mutual fund, during the two years prior to the issuance of the proxy statement.

1

The proxy statement revealed that the investment banking firm of Hornblower & Weeks–Hemphill, Noyes had rendered a favorable opinion on the fairness to TSC shareholders of the terms for the exchange of TSC shares for National securities. In that opinion, the proxy statement explained, the firm had considered, "among other things, the current market prices of the securities of both corporations, the high redemption price of the National Series B Preferred Stock, the dividend and debt service requirements of both corporations, the substantial premium over current market values represented by the securities being offered to TSC stockholders, and the increased dividend income." App. 267.

The Court of Appeals focused upon the reference to the "substantial premium over current market values represented by the securities being offered to TSC stockholders," and noted that any TSC shareholder could calculate the apparent premium by reference to the table of current market prices that appeared four pages later in the proxy statement. App. 271. On the basis of the recited closing prices for November 7, 1969, five days before the issuance of the proxy statement, the apparent premiums were as follows. Each share of TSC Series 1 Preferred, which closed at $12.00 would bring National Series B Preferred Stock and National Warrants worth $15.23—for a premium of $3.23, or 27% of the market value of the TSC Series 1 Preferred. Each share of TSC Common Stock, which closed at $13.25, would bring National Series B Preferred Stock and National Warrants worth $16.19—for a premium of $2.94, or 22% of the market value of TSC Common.

The closing price of the National Warrants on November 7, 1969, was, as indicated in the proxy statement, $5.25. The TSC shareholders were misled, the Court of Appeals concluded, by the proxy statement's failure to disclose that in a communication two weeks after its favorable opinion letter, the Hornblower firm revealed that its determination of the fairness of the offer to TSC was

of five National nominees on TSC's board, these omissions would have rendered the statement materially misleading as a matter of law, regardless of whether National can be said with certainty to have been in "control" of TSC. The reasons for this are twofold. First, to the extent that the existence of control was, at the time of the proxy statement's issuance, a matter of doubt to those responsible for preparing the statement, we would be unwilling to resolve that doubt against disclosure of facts so obviously suggestive of control. Second, and perhaps more to the point, even if National did not "control" TSC, its stock ownership and position on the TSC board make it quite clear that it enjoyed some influence over TSC, which would be of obvious importance to TSC shareholders.

based on the conclusion that the value of the Warrants involved in the transaction would not be their current market price, but approximately $3.50. If the Warrants were valued at $3.50 rather than $5.25, and the other securities valued at the November 7 closing price, the Court figured, the apparent premium would be substantially reduced—from $3.23 (27%) to $1.48 (12%) in the case of the TSC Preferred, and from $2.94 (22%) to $.31 (2%) in the case of TSC Common. "In simple terms," the Court concluded, "TSC and National had received some good news and some bad news from the Hornblower firm. They chose to publish the good news and omit the bad news." 512 F.2d at 335.

It would appear, however, that the subsequent communication from the Hornblower firm, which the Court of Appeals felt contained "bad news," contained nothing new at all. At the TSC board of directors meeting held on October 16, 1969, the date of the initial Hornblower opinion letter, Blancke Noyes, a TSC director and a partner in the Hornblower firm, had pointed out the likelihood of a decline in the market price of National Warrants with the issuance of the Additional Warrants involved in the exchange, and reaffirmed his conclusion that the exchange officer was a fair one nevertheless. The subsequent Hornblower letter, signed by Mr. Noyes, purported merely to explain the basis of the calculations underlying the favorable opinion rendered in the October 16th letter. "In advising TSC as to the fairness of the offer from [National]," Mr. Noyes wrote, "we concluded that the warrants in question had a value of approximately $3.50." On its face, then, the subsequent letter from Hornblower does not appear to have contained anything to alter the favorable opinion rendered in the October 16th letter—including the conclusion that the securities being offered to TSC shareholders represented a "substantial premium over current market values."

The real question, though, is not whether the subsequent Hornblower letter contained anything that altered the Hornblower opinion in any way. It is rather whether the advice given at the October 16th meeting, and reduced to more precise terms in the subsequent Hornblower letter—that there may be a decline in the market price of the National Warrants—had to be disclosed in order to clarify the import of the proxy statement's reference to "the substantial premium over current market values represented by the securities being offered to TSC stockholders." We note initially that the proxy statement referred to the substantial premium as but one of several factors considered by Hornblower in rendering its favorable opinion of the terms of exchange. Still, we cannot assume that a TSC shareholder would focus only on the "bottom line" of the opinion to the exclusion of the considerations that produced it.

TSC and National insist that the reference to a substantial premium required no clarification or supplementation, for the reason that there was a substantial premium even if the National Warrants are assumed to have been worth $3.50. In reaching the contrary conclusion, the Court of Appeals, they contend, ignored the rise in price of TSC securities between early October 1969, when the exchange ratio was set, and November 7, 1969—a rise in price that they suggest was a result of the favorable exchange ratio's becoming public knowledge. When the proxy statement was mailed, TSC and National contend, the market price of TSC securities already reflected a portion of the premium to which Hornblower had referred in rendering its favorable opinion of the terms of exchange. Thus, they note that Hornblower assessed the fairness of the proposed transaction by reference to early October market prices of TSC

Preferred, TSC Common, and National Preferred. On the basis of those prices and a $3.50 value for the National Warrants involved in the exchange, TSC and National contend that the premium was substantial. Each share of TSC Preferred, selling in early October at $11, would bring National Preferred Stock and Warrants worth $13.10—for a premium of $2.10, or 19%. And each share of TSC Common, selling in early October at $11.63, would bring National Preferred Stock and Warrants worth $13.25—for a premium of $1.62, or 14%. We certainly cannot say as a matter of law that these premiums were not substantial. And if, as we must assume in considering the appropriateness of summary judgment, the increase in price of TSC's securities from early October to November 7 reflected in large part the market's reaction to the terms of the proposed exchange, it was not materially misleading as a matter of law for the proxy statement to refer to the existence of a substantial premium.

There remains the possibility, however, that although TSC and National may be correct in urging the existence of a substantial premium based upon a $3.50 value for the National Warrants and the early October market prices of the other securities involved in the transaction, the proxy statement misled the TSC shareholder to calculate a premium substantially in excess of that premium. The premiums apparent from early October market prices and a $3.50 value for the National Warrants—19% on TSC Preferred and 14% on TSC Common—are certainly less than those that would be derived through use of the November 7 closing prices listed in the proxy statement—25% on TSC Preferred and 22% on TSC Common. But we are unwilling to sustain a grant of summary judgment to Northway on that basis. To do so we would have to conclude as a matter of law, first, that the proxy statement would have misled the TSC shareholder to calculate his premium on the basis of November 7 market prices, and second, that the difference between that premium and that which would be apparent from early October prices and a $3.50 value for the National Warrants was material. These are questions we think best left to the trier of fact.

2

The final omission that concerns us relates to purchases of National Common Stock by National and by Madison Fund, Inc., a mutual fund. Northway notes that National's board chairman was a director of Madison, and that Madison's president and chief executive, Edward Merkle, was employed by National pursuant to an agreement obligating him to provide at least one day per month for such duties as National might request. Northway contends that the proxy statement, having called the TSC shareholder's attention to the market prices of the securities involved in the proposed transaction, should have revealed substantial purchases of National Common Stock made by National and Madison during the two years prior to the issuance of the proxy statement. In particular, Northway contends that the TSC shareholders should, as a matter of law, have been informed that National and Madison purchases accounted for 8.5% of all reported transactions in National Common Stock during the period between National's acquisition of the Schmidt interests and the proxy solicitation. The theory behind Northway's contention is that disclosure of these purchases would have pointed to the existence, or at least the possible existence, of conspiratorial manipulation of the price of National Common Stock, which would have had an effect on the market price of the National Preferred Stock and Warrants involved in the proposed transaction.

Before the District Court, Northway attempted to demonstrate that the National and Madison purchases were coordinated. The District Court concluded, however, that there was a genuine issue of fact as to whether there was coordination. Finding that a showing of coordination was essential to Northway's theory, the District Court denied summary judgment.

The Court of Appeals agreed with the District Court that "collusion is not conclusively established." 512 F.2d, at 336. But observing that "it is certainly suggested," ibid., the Court concluded that the failure to disclose the purchases was materially misleading as a matter of law. The Court explained:

"Stockholders contemplating an offer involving preferred shares convertible to common stock and warrants for the purchase of common stock must be informed of circumstances which tend to indicate that the current selling price of the common stock involved may be affected by apparent market manipulations. It was for the shareholders to determine whether the market price of the common shares was relevant to their evaluation of the convertible preferred shares and warrants, or whether the activities of Madison and National actually amounted to manipulation at all." Ibid.

In short, while the Court of Appeals viewed the purchases as significant only insofar as they suggested manipulation of the price of National securities, and acknowledged the existence of a genuine issue of fact as to whether there was any manipulation, the Court nevertheless required disclosure to enable the shareholders to decide whether there was manipulation or not.

The Court of Appeals' approach would sanction the imposition of civil liability on a theory that undisclosed information may *suggest* the existence of market manipulation, even if the responsible corporate officials knew that there was in fact no market manipulation. We do not agree that Rule 14a–9 requires such a result. Rule 14a–9 is concerned only with whether a proxy statement is misleading with respect to its presentation of material facts. If, as we must assume on a motion for summary judgment, there was no collusion or manipulation whatsoever in the National and Madison purchases—that is, if the purchases were made wholly independently for proper corporate and investment purposes, then by Northway's implicit acknowledgment they had no bearing on the soundness and reliability of the market prices listed in the proxy statement, and it cannot have been materially misleading to fail to disclose them.

That is not to say, of course, that the SEC could not enact a rule specifically requiring the disclosure of purchases such as were involved in this case, without regard to whether the purchases can be shown to have been collusive or manipulative. We simply hold that if liability is to be imposed in this case upon a theory that it was misleading to fail to disclose purchases suggestive of market manipulation, there must be some showing that there was in fact market manipulation.

IV

In summary, none of the omissions claimed to have been in violation of Rule 14a–9 were, so far as the record reveals, materially misleading as a matter of law, and Northway was not entitled to partial summary judgment. The judgment of the Court of Appeals is reversed, and the case is remanded for further proceedings consistent with this opinion.

It is so ordered.

■ Mr. Justice Stevens took no part in the consideration or decision of this case.

WHAT FACTS ARE MATERIAL?

The standard of materiality in TSC Indus., Inc. v. Northway, Inc., is phrased at a high level of generalization: "An omitted fact is material if there is substantial likelihood that a reasonable shareholder would consider it important in deciding how to vote."[1] This definition of "materiality" has been applied, not only in actions under Section 14(a) of the 1934 Act, but also in actions brought under Rule 10b–5,[2] Section 11 of the 1933 Act,[3] Section 12(a)(2) of the 1933 Act,[4] Section 13(d) of the 1934 Act,[5] and Sections 14(d) and 14(e) of the 1934 Act.[6]

Cases after TSC Indus. Inc. v. Northway have substantially amplified this general definition of materiality.

1. In United Paperworkers Int'l Union v. International Paper Co.,[7] the court addressed the concept of the "total mix":

> The mere fact that a company has filed with a regulatory agency documents containing factual information material to a proposal as to which proxies are sought plainly does not mean that the company has made adequate disclosure to shareholders under Rule 14a–9. Corporate documents that have not been distributed to the shareholders entitled to vote on the proposal should rarely be considered part of the total mix of information reasonably available to those shareholders.

> The "total mix" of information may also include "information already in the public domain and facts known or reasonably available to the shareholders." Thus, when the subject of a proxy solicitation has been widely reported in readily available media, shareholders may be deemed to have constructive notice of the facts reported, and the court may take this into consideration in determining whether representations in or omissions from the proxy statement are materially misleading. [citations omitted.] However, the mere presence in the media of sporadic news reports does not give shareholders sufficient notice that proxy solicitation statements sent directly to them by the company may be misleading, and such reports should not be considered to be part of the total mix of information that would clarify or place in proper context the company's representations in its proxy materials.

> In the present case, the district court properly rejected Paper Co.'s contention that public press reports and its 10–K Report should be viewed as part of the total mix of information reasonably available to shareholders. Though the Company argued that news articles should be considered, the articles were few in number, narrow in focus, and remote in time.

1. 426 U.S. at 449.

2. Basic Inc. v. Levinson, 485 U.S. 224, 232 (1988).

3. Kronfeld v. Trans World Airlines, Inc., 832 F.2d 726 (2d Cir.1987), *cert. denied*, 485 U.S. 1007 (1988).

4. Simpson v. Southeastern Inv. Trust, 697 F.2d 1257 (5th Cir.1983).

5. SEC v. Savoy Indus., Inc., 587 F.2d 1149 (D.C.Cir.1978), *cert. denied*, 440 U.S. 913 (1979).

6. Seaboard World Airlines, Inc. v. Tiger Int'l, Inc., 600 F.2d 355 (2d Cir.1979); Macfadden Holdings, Inc. v. JB Acquisition Corp., 802 F.2d 62, 69 n. 3 (2d Cir.1986).

7. 985 F.2d 1190, 1199 (2d Cir.1993).

2. Information that is equally available to both parties, such as the effect of tight money on the mortgage market or current market quotations, need not be disclosed. See, for example, Seibert v. Sperry Rand Corp.,[8] where the registrant had had long and highly publicized labor troubles, about which the plaintiff alleged it had not been properly apprised, the court said that "there is no duty to disclose information to one who reasonably should already be aware of it," and that a party's "reasonable belief that the other party already has access to the facts should excuse him from new disclosures which reasonably appear to be repetitive." Similarly in Apple Computer Sec. Litig.,[9] the court held, "the defendant's failure to disclose material information may be excused where that information has been made credibly available to the market by other sources." Put another way, an omitted fact will not be material if it is already well known to the securities market.[10]

3. A case can be brought employing the "buried facts" doctrine:

Under the "buried facts" doctrine, a disclosure is deemed inadequate if it is presented in a way that conceals or obscures the information sought to be disclosed. The doctrine applies when the fact in question is hidden in a voluminous document or is disclosed in a piecemeal fashion which prevents a reasonable shareholder from realizing the "correlation and overall import of the various facts interspersed throughout" the document.[11]

4. The Supreme Court in *TSC Industries* was unwilling to require disclosure of information that might *suggest* the existence of market manipulation in the absence of some showing that there was in fact market manipulation.[12] Subsequently, the Second Circuit, in a criminal case, held that uncharged criminal conduct need not be disclosed under Rule 14a–9 unless it is required by an express Commission rule.[13] As one district court stated, "[n]o case [has] held that the proxy rules are violated because management has allegedly mismanaged the company and the proxy statement does not say so."[14] Nor must the registrant characterize or state conclusions about disclosed facts.[15]

5. Undisclosed conflicts of interest have frequently been held to be material. In *TSC Industries, Inc. v. Northway, Inc.,* the Court held that two omitted facts relating to another company's [National's] potential influence or

---

8. 586 F.2d 949, 952 (2d Cir.1978).

9. 886 F.2d 1109, 1115 (9th Cir.1989), *cert. denied sub. nom.* Schneider v. Apple Computer, Inc., 496 U.S. 943 (1990).

10. Longman v. Food Lion, Inc., 197 F.3d 675, 684 (4th Cir.1999). But see Judge Murnaghan's dissent on the ground that the information did not reach the market from a credible source. Id. at 686–688.

11. Werner v. Werner, 267 F.3d 288, 297 (3d Cir.2001), citing Kas v. Financial Gen. Bankshares, Inc., 796 F.2d 508, 516 (D.C.Cir.1986).

12. 426 U.S. at 460–463.

13. United States v. Matthews, 787 F.2d 38, 49 (2d Cir.1986); but see Roeder v. Alpha Indus., Inc. 814 F.2d 22, 25–26 (1st Cir.1987).

14. Markewich v. Adikes, 422 F.Supp. 1144, 1147 (E.D.N.Y.1976); *quoted in* Goldberger v. Baker, 442 F.Supp. 659, 667

(S.D.N.Y.1977); Bank & Trust Co. of Old York Road v. Hankin, 552 F.Supp. 1330, 1335–1336 (E.D.Pa.1982). Cf. Gaines v. Haughton, 645 F.2d 761, 776–777 (9th Cir. 1981), *cert. denied,* 454 U.S. 1145 (1982)

15. Gap Sec. Litig., 1989–1990 Fed.Sec. L.Rep. (CCH) ¶ 94,724 (N.D.Cal.1988) (defendants were not required to disclose the causes and trends ascribed to a buildup in inventory when they fully disclosed the dollar amounts by which the inventory had increased); New Am. High Income Fund Sec. Litig., 834 F.Supp. 501, 506 (D.Mass.1993), *aff'd in relevant part, rev'd on other grounds sub nom.* Lucia v. Prospect St. High Income Portfolio, 36 F.3d 170 (1st Cir.1994) ("There is, however, no obligation to disclose all securities information simply because the market would be interested, as long as the data that is disclosed is accurate and complete").

control over the management of TSC were not materials as a matter of law: (1) The chairman of the TSC board, Stanley Yarmuth, was National's president and chief executive officer, and the chairman of the TSC executive committee was Charles Simonelli, National's executive vice president; and (2) neither TSC nor National indicated that National "may be deemed to be a 'parent' of TSC as that term as defined in [SEC Rules and Regulations under the Securities Act of 1933]."[16]

In a footnote the Court, nonetheless, emphasized that the total omission of material information concerning a conflict of interest, *as a matter of law*, would have to be disclosed.[17]

The lower federal courts similarly have often required disclosure of conflicts of interest.[18] In Kronfeld v. Trans World Airlines, Inc.[19] the court held that the fact that a parent corporation was considering the possibility of a spinoff of its operating airline subsidiary (although no final decision had been made) was material to the purchasers of preferred stock of the subsidiary being offered in a registered offering because it would cut the "financial ties" between the parent and the subsidiary and therefore eliminate the possibility that the parent corporation would support the operations of the subsidiary even though it had no legal obligation to do so.

In McMahan & Co. v. Wherehouse Entertainment, Inc.,[20] in a registered offering of debentures, the debenture holders were given the right to tender the debentures to the corporation in the event of a hostile takeover bid and it was alleged that the independent directors (who could waive this right) were "tied to management" and would "inevitably" waive the right in any merger beneficial to management regardless of the debenture holders' interest. The court held that these allegations created an issue of fact in a suit by the debenture holders under Section 11 and Rule 10b–5, precluding a summary judgment in favor of the defendants. (The fact is, of course, that such a provision is usually inserted primarily for the protection of management against a hostile takeover, but the defendants could hardly argue that, since it might suggest that this right held out to the purchasers of the debentures was basically illusory from the beginning, which was the position taken by the plaintiffs.)

In Isquith v. Middle South Utilities, Inc.,[21] the court held that the district court had erred in concluding that disclosed predictions are never actionable,

---

16.   426 U.S. at 451–453.

17.   Id. at 453 n.15.

18.   See, e.g. Wilson v. Great Am. Indus., Inc., 855 F.2d 987, 993–994 (2d Cir. 1988) (in merger between corporations *A* and *B*, failure to disclose that general counsel of corporation *A* personally represented senior executives of corporation *B* and he and his firm served as counsel to several entities controlled by these executives); cf. Kas v. Financial Gen. Bankshares, Inc., 796 F.2d 508, 513 (D.C.Cir.1986) ("The violation arising from the failure to disclose such a potential conflict of interest does not turn on the failure to disclose a director's true motivations but rather stems from the failure to disclose a fact that puts the shareholder on notice of a

potential impairment of the director's judgment"); Cooperman v. Individual, Inc., 171 F.3d 43, 49 (1st Cir.1999) (a board level conflict over the future direction of a company can be material). See also Kramer v. Time Warner, Inc., 937 F.2d 767, 777 (2d Cir. 1991); "That inside directors stand to gain from a recommended transaction is material information that must be disclosed to shareholders considering a tender offer."

19.   832 F.2d 726 (2d Cir.1987), *cert. denied*, 485 U.S. 1007 (1988).

20.   900 F.2d 576 (2d Cir.1990), *cert. denied*, 501 U.S. 1249 (1991).

21.   847 F.2d 186 (5th Cir.1988), *cert. denied*, 488 U.S. 926 (1988).

since a "clear body of law" exists which recognizes those circumstances where liability can be imposed under the securities laws for disclosed predictions. (It might be questioned whether the indication in the *TSC Industries* case that the question of materiality is almost always a jury question furnishes any "clear body of law.")

In Howing Company v. Nationwide Corporation,[22] the Sixth Circuit agreed with the District Judge that the *TSC Industries* test of materiality applied in connection with the alleged omission of certain information required by Rule 13e–3 in a going-private transaction, but it ruled that the fact that this information was required by Rule 13e–3 created a "presumption" of materiality. The court said: "Although we agree with the District Court that the general TSC standard of materiality is applicable to transactions governed by Rule 13e–3, the clear and specific language of the instructions to Item 8 creates in effect a presumption that a discussion of book, going concern and liquidation value in the proxy statement would be material to a reasonable shareholder. The presumed fact—that the investor would likely find disclosure of such information significant—follows from Item 8's insistence that the information be stated." * * *

* * * The question of materiality has been discussed in general above, but arguably that issue takes on a different coloration where the complaint alleges a total non-disclosure than where the defendant is accused of a false statement or a misleading statement. Judge Waterman in the first decision in Securities and Exchange Commission v. Texas Gulf Sulphur Co.[23] adopts on the same page two wildly different tests of materiality. He first quotes Mr. Fleischer to the effect that a material fact is one which is "essentially *extraordinary in nature* and * * * [is] *reasonably certain* to have a substantial effect on the market price of the security * * *." He then states, quoting the same passage from Kohler v. Kohler Co. given above, but with an important italicization, that a material fact is "any fact ' * * * which in reasonable and objective contemplation *might* affect the value of the corporation's stock or securities * * *.' " (The italics in the first quotation are ours; those in the second are Judge Waterman's.) It seems obvious that reasonable certainty and any conceivable possibility (which the emphasis of the word "might" suggests) are not exactly the same thing.

(b) Quantitative and Qualitative Materiality

As a practical matter lawyers and accountants have long determined whether information is material by applying quantitative tests. It is often stated as part of the lore of securities law that there is a presumption that information that accounts for more than than a 10 percent stock price movement, an issuer or registrant's total assets, gross sales or net earnings is presumed to be material, while information that accounts for less than 5 percent is presumed not to be material, with a gray area between 5 and 10 percent. These 5 and 10 percent benchmarks are derived in part from such SEC rules as proxy Rule 14a–8(I)(5) which under certain circumstances does not require a registrant's management to circulate a shareholder proposal relating to operations if it accounts for less than 5 percent of an issuer's total assets and is less than 5 percent of its net earnings and gross sales for its most recent

---

22.   927 F.2d 263 (6th Cir.1991), *judgment vacated*, 502 U.S. 801 (1991).

23.   401 F.2d 833 (2d Cir.1968), *cert. denied*, 394 U.S. 976 (1969).

fiscal year. Similarly Instruction 2 to Regulation S–K Item 103 uses a 10 percent threshold to determine when certain pending legal proceedings must be disclosed. On occasion numerical benchmarks have also received the judiciary's imprimatur. In equity transactions the courts have affirmed SEC rulings that markups of more than 10 percent are fraudulent.[1]

Accountants and lawyers can safely assume also that required disclosure items may be presumed to be material.

Certain of the most difficult judgments concerning materiality have involved information that is not specifically required and not quantitatively material. Here there are residual concepts of materiality termed qualitative materiality, that on occasion are applicable.

In 1982 John Fedders, then the SEC's Director of Enforcement, offered an intriguing general statement with respect to qualitative materiality generally. Fedders spoke shortly after the SEC ended its questionable payments campaign. This campaign was inspired by the disclosure that certain corporations had made payments, typically to foreign political officials in an effort to secure various business advantages. Following a change in the membership of the Commission and of its Enforcement Division, this campaign was publicly abandoned in the Fall of 1982. On November 19, 1982, Fedders spoke to the Federal Regulation of Securities Committee of the American Bar Association relating to the SEC's enforcement policy in the questionable payment area. His speech stressed that the focus of the SEC would be upon disclosure of what he described as information which had economic or "quantitative" materiality to an investor or shareholder and indicated that the SEC would not insist upon the disclosure of information by a corporation solely on the basis that it might have a bearing on the integrity of the management of the corporation.

Fedders indicated in his speech that the Commission would continue to institute enforcement actions in cases (1) where illegal conduct by management may have material adverse economic consequences for the company, (2) where the actions in question involve self-dealing or conflict of interest transactions, (3) where there is a failure to disclose specific items mandated by the forms or rules for proxy statements, reports or registration statements, or (4) where the failure to disclose renders misleading specific statements contained in documents filed with the Commission. Absent any of these four circumstances, Fedders stated that "the Commission generally should not utilize the antifraud provisions of the securities law for law enforcement where there is a failure to disclose conduct which may be considered *qualitatively* material. The antifraud provisions of the securities laws work well in the area of *quantitative* materiality because disclosure and enforcement decisions can be related to the bench marks of earnings, assets or liabilities."

In 1999 Staff Accounting Bulletin (SAB) No. 99 discouraged exclusive reliance on quantitative assessments of materiality.[2] The Release stated in part:

1. *See, e.g.,* Alstead, Dempsey & Co., Inc., 47 SEC 1034, 1035 (1984). Cf. Adams v. Standard Knitting Mills, Inc., 623 F.2d 422, 433 (6th Cir.1980), *cert. denied,* 449 U.S. 1067 (1980), where the court characterized a 4 percent variance between an accountant's inventory count and that of the issuer as "insufficient to render the inventory figure a material misstatement of fact."

2. SAB 99, 70 SEC Dock. 785 (1999). See generally Kenneth C. Fang & Brad Jacobs, Clarifying and Protecting Materiality Standards in Financial Statements: A Review of SEC Staff Accounting Bulletin 99, 55 Bus. Law. 1039 (2000).

Evaluation of materiality requires a registrant and its auditor to consider *all* the relevant circumstances, and the staff believes that there are numerous circumstances in which misstatements below 5% could well be material. Qualitative factors may cause misstatements of quantitatively small amounts to be material; as stated in the auditing literature:

As a result of the interaction of quantitative and qualitative considerations in materiality judgments, misstatement of relatively small amounts that come to the auditor's attention could have a material effect on the financial statements.

Among the considerations that may well render material a quantitatively small misstatement of a financial statement item are—

- whether the misstatement arises from an item capable of precise measurement or whether it arises from an estimate and, if so, the degree of imprecision inherent in the estimate

- whether the misstatement makes a change in earnings or other trends

- whether the misstatement hides a failure to meet analysts' consensus expectations for the enterprise

- whether the misstatement changes a loss into income or vice versa

- whether the misstatement concerns a segment or other portion of the registrant's business that has been identified as playing a significant role in the registrant's operations or profitability

- whether the misstatements affects the registrant's compliance with regulatory requirements

- whether the misstatement affects the registrant's compliance with loan covenant or other contractual requirements

- whether the misstatement has the effect of increasing management's compensation—for example, by satisfying requirements for the award of bonuses or other forms of incentive compensation.

- whether the misstatement involves concealment of an unlawful transaction.

This is not an exhaustive list of the circumstances that may affect the materiality of a quantitatively small misstatement. Among other factors, the demonstrated volatility of the price of a registrant's securities in response to certain types of disclosures may provide guidance as to whether investors regard quantitatively small misstatements as material. Consideration of potential market reaction to disclosure of a misstatement is by itself "too blunt an instrument to be depended on" in considering whether a fact is material. When, however, management or the independent auditor expects (based, for example, on a pattern of market performance) that a known misstatement may result in a significant positive or negative market reaction. that expected reaction should be taken into account when considering whether a misstatement is material.

For the reasons noted above, the staff believes that a registrant and the auditors of its financial statements should not assume that even small intentional misstatements in financial statements, for example those pursuant to actions to "manage" earnings, are immaterial. While the intent of management does not render a misstatement material, it may provide significant evidence of materiality. The evidence may be particularly compelling where management has intentionally misstated items in the financial statements to "manage" reported earnings. In that instance, it presumably has done so believing that the resulting amounts and trends would be significant to users of the registrant's financial statements. The staff believes that investors generally would regard as significant a management practice to over or understate earnings up to an amount just short of a percentage threshold in order to "manage" earnings. Investors presumably also would regard as significant an accounting practice that, in essence, rendered all earnings figures subject to a management-directed margin of misstatement.

Ganino v. Citizens Util. Co.

United States Court of Appeals, Second Circuit, 2000.
228 F.3d 154.

I. Background

* * *

The plaintiffs in this action purchased or acquired the common stock of Citizens Utilities Company ("Citizens" or the "Company"), the corporate defendant, between May 7, 1996 and August 7, 1997 (the "Class Period"). * * * Citizens is a publicly traded communications and public services company. As of 1995, Citizens had reported over fifty consecutive years of increased revenue, earnings, and earnings per share, a fact which it emphasized in its public comments. In 1995, however, Citizens would not receive approximately $38 million in revenue from Pacific Bell. In order to continue to report increased earnings, the Company had to find another source of revenue.

That replacement source was Hungarian Telephone & Cable Corporation ("HTCC"), a U.S. company which provides telephone services in Hungary under telecommunications concessions from the Hungarian government. The concession contracts require HTCC to meet certain construction milestones. Failure to do so would subject HTCC to fines, reduction of its exclusivity period, or abrogation of the contracts. Unprofitable since its inception, HTCC by 1995 lacked the necessary funds to satisfy its contractual requirements and began looking for a source of financing. Beginning in May 1995, HTCC and Citizens (through a wholly owned subsidiary of Citizens) entered into a series of agreements under which Citizens agreed in 1995 to make and/or guarantee loans to HTCC. In consideration for these loans and guarantees, Citizens received substantial fees (the "Financial Support Fees" or the "Fees"), consisting primarily of HTCC stock and options. In addition, Citizens also provided management consulting services to HTCC.

1. *Allegations of Material Misrepresentations*

Although Citizens earned and received approximately $10.1 million in Financial Support Fees from HTCC in 1995, Citizens, according to the Complaint, fraudulently recognized this sum as 1996 first and second quarter income without proper disclosure. Because Citizens' 1995 annual financial statement ("1995 Form 10–K") filed with the Securities and Exchange Commission (the "SEC") stated that Citizens "ha[d] been compensated for . . . guarantees and financial support [to HTCC]," investors were allegedly misled into believing that the $10.1 million booked in 1996 was new income, unrelated to the 1995 HTCC loan and guarantee transactions. * * *

a. *May 7, 1996 Announcement of 1996 First Quarter Financial Results and First Quarter Form 10–Q.*

On May 7, 1996, Citizens publicly announced an after-tax net income of $38.9 million of the first quarter of 1996, up 15% from the corresponding period in 1995. These results were reflected in its 1996 first quarter financial statement ("First Quarter Form 10–Q"). The defendants did not disclose that "as much as $6.9 million of the $38.9 million * * * was HTCC related income which was deceptively 'stored' by Citizens" until the first quarter of 1996. According to the Complaint, the defendants also concealed the fact that this $6.9 million made up most if not all of the reported 15% increase during the first quarter of 1996.

b. *August 15, 1996 Press Release and 1996 Second Quarter form 10–Q*

On August 15, 1996, Citizens issued another press release announcing "record * * * profits for the three-and six-month periods ended June 30, 1996," with the second quarter's net income of $46.3 million representing a 10% increase over the comparable period in the preceding year. Citizens attributed this growth to "continuous above-average growth in volume and profitability in each of its sectors, particularly telecommunications." These results were reflected in its 1996 second quarter financial report ("Second Quarter Form 10–Q"). The Complaint charges that the August 15, 1996 press release and the 1996 Second Quarter Form 10–Q both failed to disclose that "approximately $10 million of the $85.1 million of reported income for the six months ended June 30, 1996 was HTCC related income" which should have been recognized in 1995. The Complaint states that the defendants also concealed the fact that this approximately $10 million accounted for the full 10% increase in income for the first six months of 1996 over the comparable period in 1995.

c. *Subsequent Financial Statements and Press Releases*

The $10.1 million of Financial Support Fees were also reported as part of the year-to-date earnings in Citizens' 1996 Third Quarter Form 10–Q, 1996 Form 10–K, and accompanying press releases. An additional $11.2 million of Fees were booked in the last quarter of 1996 and reflected in the 1996 year-end statement ("1996 Form 10–K"). In total, the Fees at issue added up to approximately $22 million, or 1.7% of Citizens' total revenue for 1996. As with the Form 10–Qs for the first two quarters of 1996, the defendants did not disclose in the Third Quarter Form 10–Q, 1996 Form 10–K, and accompanying press releases that the reported income included HTCC Fees earned and received in 1995.

On April 30, 1997, Citizens issued a press release announcing lower than expected earnings for the first quarter of 1997. These results were reflected in the Company's 1997 First Quarter Form 10–Q. Neither document attributed the drop in income to the decrease in HTCC Fees. Instead, according to the Complaint, the press release misleadingly focused on rising expenses. Beginning in or about May 1997, industry analysts began to report weaknesses in Citizens' earnings position. Their predictions were confirmed by Citizens in August 1997 with filing of its 1997 Second Quarter Form 10–Q, which also disclosed that the reported income for the first two quarters of 1996 included material income from HTCC. * * *

II. DISCUSSION

* * *

At the pleading stage, a plaintiff satisfies the materiality requirement of Rule 10b–5 by alleging a statement or omission that a reasonable investor would have considered significant in making investment decisions. *See Basic Inc. v. Levinson,* 485 U.S. 224, 231, 108 S.Ct. 978, 99 L.Ed.2d 194 (1988) (adopting the standard in *TSC Indus., Inc. v. Northway, Inc.,* 426 U.S. 438, 449, 96 S.Ct. 2126, 48 L.Ed.2d 757 (1976), for § 10(b) and Rule 10b–5 actions) * * *. It is not sufficient to allege that the investor might have considered the misrepresentation or omission important. On the other hand, it is not necessary to assert that the investor would have acted differently if an accurate disclosure was made. * * * An omitted fact may be immaterial if the information is trivial, *see Basic,* 485 U.S. at 231, * * *, or is "so basic that any investor could be expected to know it," *Levitin v. PaineWebber, Inc.,* 159 F.3d 698, 702 (2d Cir.1998) (internal quotation marks omitted), *cert. denied,* 525 U.S. 1144, 119 S.Ct. 1039, 143 L.Ed.2d 47 (1999). Therefore, whether an alleged misrepresentation or omission is material necessarily depends on all relevant circumstances of the particular case. * * *

a. Numerical Benchmark

The district court held that the alleged misrepresentations of the HTCC Fees as having been received in 1996 were immaterial as a matter of law because the Fees amounted to only 1.7% of Citizens' 1996 total revenue. The plaintiffs and the SEC, as amicus curiae, contend that the court's exclusive reliance on a single numerical or percentage benchmark to determine materiality was error. Their position is supported by amply authority. * * *

With respect to financial statements, the SEC has commented that various "[q]ualitative factors may cause misstatements of quantitatively small amounts to be material." SEC Staff Accounting Bulletin ("SAB") No. 99 * * *. Of particular relevance to this action are the following:

- whether the misstatement masks a change in earnings or other trends
- whether the misstatement hides a failure to meet analysts' consensus expectations for the enterprise[.] * * *

* * * SAB No. 99 is thoroughly reasoned and consistent with existing law—its non-exhaustive list of factors is simply an application of the well-established *Basic* analysis to misrepresentations of financial results—we find it persuasive guidance for evaluating the materiality of an alleged misrepresentation.

The two Court of Appeals cases cited by the district court support the approach we take here. In *Parnes v. Gateway 2000, Inc.,* 122 F.3d 539 (8th Cir.1997), the Eighth Circuit held that the alleged misrepresentations, which amounted to 2% of total assets, were immaterial as a matter of law *"[t]aken in context."* *Id.* at 547 (emphasis added). The court did not rely on the single numerical benchmark, but also took into consideration the fact that the case involved a high-risk/high-yield investment, and that the risk factors had been prominently disclosed in a prospectus. *Id.* at 542–43, 547. Similarly, in *Glassman v. Computervision Corp.,* 90 F.3d 617 (1st Cir.1996), the First Circuit

Court of Appeals considered whether a 3% or 9% drop in quarterly revenue was immaterial as a matter of law. It stated, in dicta, that "[w]here a variable, *although material*, is of only minor predictive value, disclosure of a rough estimate of that variable's value can obviate the need for more specific disclosure." *Id.* at 633 (emphasis added). The clear implication of this statement is that a 3% to 9% drop may be material depending on the circumstances. To the extent that the two district court decision also cited in the opinion below adopted a bright-line test for materiality, we disagree with their approach. * * *

Relevant Timeframes

We next consider the relevant timeframe. The plaintiffs, joined by the SEC, maintain that the court should have considered the impact of the alleged misrepresentations on all misstated items in the financial statement for all relevant periods, not only for the year as a whole. In this case, the Complaint alleged that substantial portions of the income reported during the first two quarters of 1996 were in fact the 1995 Fees. Accordingly, the plaintiffs and the SEC contend that the court should have assessed the impact of the Fees on Citizens' quarterly income. The defendants argue that the court correctly compared the Fees to the annual results only, because the plaintiffs theorized that the defendants deferred recognition of the Fees in order to maintain Citizens' annual growth trend.

We reject the defendants' contention. Materiality is determined in light of the circumstances existing at the time the alleged misstatement occurred. * * *

This Complaint

Applying the foregoing principles to this action, we conclude that the Complaint alleged material misrepresentations in the 1996 First and Second Quarter Form 10–Qs and corresponding press releases, namely, the alleged misrepresentation of $10.1 million of Fees received in 1995 as 1996 income. The $6.9 million of 1995 Fees booked during the first quarter of 1996 equaled 17.7% of Citizens' reported after-tax net income ($38.9 million), and 11.7% of its pre-tax net income ($58.78 million) for that quarter. The $10.1 million reflected in the 1996 Second Quarter Form 10–Q amounted to 11.9% of the after-tax net income ($85.15 million), and 8% of pre-tax net income ($126.62 million) for the first six months of 1996. We believe it is inappropriate to determine at this stage of the litigation that these substantial amounts, both in absolute terms and as percentages of total net income for the respective quarters, were immaterial as a matter of law.

Aside from the magnitude of the overstatements, the Complaint alleged that the defendants deceptively stored the Fees until 1996 in order the manage the Company's 1995 and 1996 income, and that they did so in order to conceal Citizens' failure to meet analysts' expectations and to sustain its 51–year earnings trend. The Complaint asserted that the $6.9 million of Fees reported in the First Quarter Form 10–Q accounted for "a substantial portion, if not all, of the increase in income for the first quarter 1996 compared to the first quarter of 1995[.]" Moreover, according to the Complaint, analysts' projections of Citizens' "income for the first six (6) months of 1996 were met and exceeded only as a result of th[e] additional HTCC-related income, and the increase in income for the first six months of 1996 compared to the first six months of 1995 was due *entirely* to the income recognized from HTCC." Viewed in this context, it cannot be said that no reasonable investor would have considered the misreporting of 1995 Fees as 1996 income to be significant or to have altered the total mix of information affecting their investment decisions. We therefore conclude that the Complaint alleged material misrepresentations.

PROBLEM 14–1

Humongous Mega Movies (HMM) earned over $100 million in net profits last year.

Would it be material to a reasonable investor that:

(1) Its CEO, Herman Humongous, who last year earned $12.5 million in executive compensation, embezzled $10,000 from petty cash last year?

(2) Its Co–CEO Marie Mega, has very high blood pressure and elevated cholesterol and has been ordered by her physician to take a one month vacation and try to relax? Last year Marie Mega was the executive producer of the most successful HMM film which alone was responsible for 50 percent of HMM's net profits.

(c) Forward Looking Statements

Basic Incorporated v. Levinson

Supreme Court of the United States, 1988.
485 U.S. 224, 108 S.Ct. 978, 99 L.Ed.2d 194.

■ BLACKMUN, J., delivered the opinion of the Court, in which BRENNAN, MARSHALL, and STEVENS, JJ., joined, and in Parts I, II, and III of which WHITE and O'CONNOR, JJ., joined. WHITE, J., filed an opinion concurring in part and dissenting in part, in which O'CONNOR, J., joined. REHNQUIST, C.J. and SCALIA and KENNEDY, JJ., took no part in the consideration or decision of the case.

■ JUSTICE BLACKMUN:

This case requires us to apply the materiality requirement of § 10(b) of the Securities Exchange Act of 1934 (1934 Act), and the Securities and Exchange Commission's Rule 10b–5, promulgated thereunder, in the context of preliminary corporate merger discussions. We must also determine whether a person who traded a corporation's shares on a securities exchange after the issuance of a materially misleading statement by the corporation may invoke a rebuttable presumption that, in trading, he relied on the integrity of the price set by the market.

I

Prior to December 20, 1978, Basic Incorporated was a publicly traded company primarily engaged in the business of manufacturing chemical refractories for the steel industry. As early as 1965 or 1966, Combustion Engineering, Inc., a company producing mostly alumina-based refractories, expressed some interest in acquiring Basic, but was deterred from pursuing this inclination seriously because of antitrust concerns it then entertained. See App. 81–83. In 1976, however, regulatory action opened the way to a renewal of Combustion's interest. The "Strategic Plan," dated October 25, 1976, for Combustion's Industrial Products Group included the objective: "Acquire Basic Inc. $30 million." App. 337.

Beginning in September 1976, Combustion representatives had meetings and telephone conversations with Basic officers and directors, including petitioners here,[2] concerning the possibility of a merger.[3] During 1977 and 1978, Basic made three public statements denying that it was engaged in merger negotiations.[4] On December 18, 1978, Basic asked the New York Stock Exchange to suspend trading in its shares and issued a release stating that it had been "approached" by another company concerning a merger. Id., at 413. On December 19, Basic's board endorsed Combustion's offer of $46 per share for its common stock, id., at 335, 414–416, and on the following day publicly announced its approval of Combustion's tender offer for all outstanding shares.

Respondents are former Basic shareholders who sold their stock after Basic's first public statement of October 21, 1977, and before the suspension of trading in December 1978. Respondents brought a class action against Basic and its directors, asserting that the defendants issued three false or misleading public statements and thereby were in violation of § 10(b) of the 1934 Act and of Rule 10b–5. Respondents alleged that they were injured by selling Basic shares at artificially depressed prices in a market affected by petitioners' misleading statements and in reliance thereon.

The District Court adopted a presumption of reliance by members of the plaintiff class upon petitioners' public statements that enabled the court to conclude that common questions of fact or law predominated over particular questions pertaining to individual plaintiffs. See Fed.Rule Civ.Proc. 23(b)(3). The District Court therefore certified respondents' class. On the merits, however, the District Court granted summary judgment for the defendants. It held that, as a matter of law, any misstatements were immaterial: there were no negotiations ongoing at the time of the first statement, and although negotiations were taking place when the second and third statements were issued, those negotiations were not "destined, with reasonable certainty, to become a merger agreement in principle." App. to Pet. for Cert. 103a.

2. In addition to Basic itself, petitioners are individuals who had been members of its board of directors prior to 1979: Anthony M. Caito, Samuel Eells, Jr., John A. Gelbach, Harley C. Lee, Max Muller, H. Chapman Rose, Edmund Q. Sylvester, and John C. Wilson, Jr. Another former director, Mathew J. Ludwig, was a party to the proceedings below but died on July 17, 1986, and is not a petitioner here. See Brief for Petitioners ii.

3. In light of our disposition of this case, any further characterization of these discussions must await application, on remand, of the materiality standard adopted today.

4. On October 21, 1977, after heavy trading and a new high in Basic stock, the following news item appeared in the Cleveland Plain Dealer:

"[Basic] President Max Muller said the company knew no reason for the stock's activity and that no negotiations were under way with any company for a merger. He said Flintkote recently de-

nied Wall Street rumors that it would make a tender offer of $25 a share for control of the Cleveland-based maker of refractories for the steel industry." App. 363.

On September 25, 1978, in reply to an inquiry from the New York Stock Exchange, Basic issued a release concerning increased activity in its stock and stated that "management is unaware of any present or pending company development that would result in the abnormally heavy trading activity and price fluctuation in company shares that have been experienced in the past few days." Id., at 401.

On November 6, 1978, Basic issued to its shareholders a "Nine Months Report 1978." This Report stated:

"With regard to the stock market activity in the Company's shares we remain unaware of any present or pending developments which would account for the high volume of trading and price fluctuations in recent months." Id., at 403.

The United States Court of Appeals for the Sixth Circuit affirmed the class certification, but reversed the District Court's summary judgment, and remanded the case. 786 F.2d 741 (1986). The court reasoned that while petitioners were under no general duty to disclose their discussions with Combustion, any statement the company voluntarily released could not be " 'so incomplete as to mislead.' " Id., at 746, quoting SEC v. Texas Gulf Sulphur Co., 401 F.2d 833, 862 (C.A.2 1968) (en banc), cert. denied sub nom. Coates v. SEC, 394 U.S. 976 (1969). In the Court of Appeals' view, Basic's statements that no negotiations were taking place, and that it knew of no corporate developments to account for the heavy trading activity, were misleading. With respect to materiality, the court rejected the argument that preliminary merger discussions are immaterial as a matter of law, and held that "once a statement is made denying the existence of any discussions, even discussions that might not have been material in absence of the denial are material because they make the statement made untrue." 786 F.2d at 749.

The Court of Appeals joined a number of other circuits in accepting the "fraud-on-the-market theory" to create a rebuttable presumption that respondents relied on petitioners' material misrepresentations, noting that without the presumption it would be impractical to certify a class under Fed. Rule Civ.Proc. 23(b)(3). See 786 F.2d at 750–751.

We granted certiorari, 484 U.S. 1083 (1987), to resolve the split, see Part III, *infra*, among the Courts of Appeals as to the standard of materiality applicable to preliminary merger discussions, and to determine whether the courts below properly applied a presumption of reliance in certifying the class, rather than requiring each class member to show direct reliance on Basic's statements.

II

* * *

The Court previously has addressed various positive and common-law requirements for a violation of § 10(b) or of Rule 10b–5. * * * The Court also explicitly has defined a standard of materiality under the securities laws, see TSC Industries, Inc. v. Northway, Inc., 426 U.S. 438 (1976), concluding in the proxy-solicitation context that "[a]n omitted fact is material if there is a substantial likelihood that a reasonable shareholder would consider it important in deciding how to vote." Id., at 449. Acknowledging that certain information concerning corporate developments could well be of "dubious significance," id., at 448, the Court was careful not to set too low a standard of materiality; it was concerned that a minimal standard might bring an overabundance of information within its reach, and lead management "simply to bury the shareholders in an avalanche of trivial information—a result that is hardly conducive to informed decisionmaking." Id., at 448–449. It further explained that to fulfill the materiality requirement "there must be a substantial likelihood that the disclosure of the omitted fact would have been viewed by the reasonable investor as having significantly altered the 'total mix' of information made available." Id., at 449. We now expressly adopt the *TSC Industries* standard of materiality for the § 10(b) and Rule 10b–5 context.

III

The application of this materiality standard to preliminary merger discussions is not self-evident. Where the impact of the corporate development on the target's fortune is certain and clear, the *TSC Industries* materiality definition admits straightforward application. Where, on the other hand, the event is contingent or speculative in nature, it is difficult to ascertain whether the "reasonable investor" would have considered the omitted information significant at the time. Merger negotiations, because of the ever-present possibility that the contemplated transaction will not be effectuated, fall into the latter category.[9]

A

Petitioners urge upon us a Third Circuit test for resolving this difficulty.[10] See Brief for Petitioners 20–22. Under this approach, preliminary merger discussions do not become material until "agreement-in-principle" as to the price and structure of the transaction has been reached between the would-be merger partners. See Greenfield v. Heublein, Inc., 742 F.2d 751, 757 (C.A.3 1984), cert. denied, 469 U.S. 1215 (1985). By definition, then, information concerning any negotiations not yet at the agreement-in-principle stage could be withheld or even misrepresented without a violation of Rule 10b–5.

Three rationales have been offered in support of the "agreement-in-principle" test. The first derives from the concern expressed in *TSC Industries* that an investor not be overwhelmed by excessively detailed and trivial information, and focuses on the substantial risk that preliminary merger discussions may collapse: because such discussions are inherently tentative, disclosure of their existence itself could mislead investors and foster false optimism. See Greenfield v. Heublein, Inc., 742 F.2d, at 756; Reiss v. Pan American World Airways, Inc., 711 F.2d 11, 14 (C.A.2 1983). The other two justifications for the agreement-in-principle standard are based on management concerns: because the requirement of "agreement-in-principle" limits the scope of disclosure obligations, it helps preserve the confidentiality of merger discussions where earlier disclosure might prejudice the negotiations; and the test also provides a usable, bright-line rule for determining when disclosure must be made. See Greenfield v. Heublein, Inc., 742 F.2d, at 757; Flamm v. Eberstadt, 814 F.2d 1169, 1176–1178 (CA7), cert. denied, 484 U.S. 853 (1987).

None of these policy-based rationales, however, purports to explain why drawing the line at agreement-in-principle reflects the significance of the information upon the investor's decision. The first rationale, and the only one

---

9. We do not address here any other kinds of contingent or speculative information, such as earnings forecasts or projections. See generally Hiler, The SEC and the Courts' Approach to Disclosure of Earnings Projections, Asset Appraisals, and Other Soft Information: Old Problems, Changing Views, 46 Md. L. Rev. 1114 (1987).

10. See Staffin v. Greenberg, 672 F.2d 1196, 1207 (C.A.3 1982) (defining duty to disclose existence of ongoing merger negotiations as triggered when agreement-in-principle is reached); Greenfield v. Heublein, Inc., 742 F.2d 751 (C.A.3 1984) (applying agreement-in-principle test to materiality inquiry), *cert. denied*, 469 U.S. 1215 (1985). Citing *Staffin,* the United States Court of Appeals for the Second Circuit has rejected a claim

that defendant was under an obligation to disclose various events related to merger negotiations. Reiss v. Pan American World Airways, Inc., 711 F.2d 11, 13–14 (C.A.2 1983). The Seventh Circuit recently endorsed the agreement-in-principle test of materiality. See Flamm v. Eberstadt, 814 F.2d 1169, 1174–1179 (C.A.7 [1987]) (describing agreement-in-principle as an agreement on price and structure), *cert. denied*, 484 U.S. 853 (1987). In some of these cases it is unclear whether the court based its decision on a finding that no duty arose to reveal the existence of negotiations, or whether it concluded that the negotiations were immaterial under an interpretation of the opinion in TSC Industries, Inc. v. Northway, Inc., [*supra*].

connected to the concerns expressed in *TSC Industries,* stands soundly rejected, even by a Court of Appeals that otherwise has accepted the wisdom of the agreement-in-principle test. "It assumes that investors are nitwits, unable to appreciate—even when told—that mergers are risky propositions up until the closing." Flamm v. Eberstadt, 814 F.2d, at 1175. Disclosure, and not paternalistic withholding of accurate information, is the policy chosen and expressed by Congress. We have recognized time and again, a "fundamental purpose" of the various securities acts, "was to substitute a philosophy of full disclosure for the philosophy of *caveat emptor* and thus to achieve a high standard of business ethics in the securities industry." SEC v. Capital Gains Research Bureau, Inc., 375 U.S. 180, 186 (1963). * * * The role of the materiality requirement is not to "attribute to investors a child-like simplicity, an inability to grasp the probabilistic significance of negotiations," Flamm v. Eberstadt, 814 F.2d, at 1175, but to filter out essentially useless information that a reasonable investor would not consider significant, even as part of a larger "mix" of factors to consider in making his investment decision. TSC Industries, Inc. v. Northway, Inc., 426 U.S., at 448–449.

The second rationale, the importance of secrecy during the early stages of merger discussions, also seems irrelevant to an assessment whether their existence is significant to the trading decision of a reasonable investor. To avoid a "bidding war" over its target, an acquiring firm often will insist that negotiations remain confidential, see, e.g., In re Carnation Co., Exchange Act Release No. 22214, 33 SEC Docket 1025 (1985), and at least one Court of Appeals has stated that "silence pending settlement of the price and structure of a deal is beneficial to most investors, most of the time." Flamm v. Eberstadt, 814 F.2d, at 1177.

We need not ascertain, however, whether secrecy necessarily maximizes shareholder wealth—although we note that the proposition is at least disputed as a matter of theory and empirical research[12]—for this case does not concern the *timing* of a disclosure; it concerns only its accuracy and completeness. We face here the narrow question whether information concerning the existence and status of preliminary merger discussions is significant to the reasonable investor's trading decision. Arguments based on the premise that some disclosure would be "premature" in a sense are more properly considered under the rubric of an issuer's duty to disclose. The "secrecy" rationale is simply inapposite to the definition of materiality.

The final justification offered in support of the agreement-in-principle test seems to be directed solely at the comfort of corporate managers. A bright-line rule indeed is easier to follow than a standard that requires the exercise of judgment in the light of all the circumstances. But ease of application alone is not an excuse for ignoring the purposes of the securities acts and Congress' policy decisions. Any approach that designates a single fact or occurrence as always determinative of an inherently fact-specific finding such as materiality,

12. See, e.g., Brown, Corporate Secrecy, the Federal Securities Laws, and the Disclosure of Ongoing Negotiations, 36 Cath. U. L. Rev. 93, 145–155 (1986); Bebchuk, The Case for Facilitating Competing Tender Offers, 95 Harv. L. Rev. 1028 (1982); Flamm v. Eberstadt, 814 F.2d, at 1177, n. 2 (citing scholarly debate). See also In re Carnation Co., Exchange Act Release No. 22214, 33 SEC Dock-et 1025, 1030 (1985) ("The importance of accurate and complete issuer disclosure to the integrity of the securities markets cannot be overemphasized. To the extent that investors cannot rely upon the accuracy and completeness of issuer statements, they will be less likely to invest, thereby reducing the liquidity of the securities markets to the detriment of investors and issuers alike").

must necessarily be over-or under-inclusive. In *TSC Industries* this Court explained: "The determination [of materiality] requires delicate assessments of the inferences a 'reasonable shareholder' would draw from a given set of facts and the significance of those inferences to him. * * * "426 U.S., at 450. After much study, the Advisory Committee on Corporate Disclosure cautioned the SEC against administratively confining materiality to a rigid formula.[14] Courts also would do well to heed this advice.

We therefore find no valid justification for artificially excluding from the definition of materiality information concerning merger discussions, which would otherwise be considered significant to the trading decision of a reasonable investor, merely because agreement-in-principle as to price and structure has not yet been reached by the parties or their representatives.

B

The Sixth Circuit explicitly rejected the agreement-in-principle test, as we do today, but in its place adopted a rule that, if taken literally, would be equally insensitive, in our view, to the distinction between materiality and the other elements of an action under Rule 10b–5:

> "When a company whose stock is publicly traded makes a statement, as Basic did, that 'no negotiations' are underway, and that the corporation knows of 'no reason for the stock's activity,' and that 'management is unaware of any present or pending corporate development that would result in the abnormally heavy trading activity,' information concerning ongoing acquisition discussions becomes material *by virtue of the statement denying their existence.*

> * * * * * * *

> "In analyzing whether information regarding merger discussions is material such that it must be affirmatively disclosed to avoid a violation of Rule 10b–5, the discussions and their progress are the primary considerations. However, once a statement is made denying the existence of any discussions, even discussions that might not have been material in absence of the denial are material because they make the statement made untrue." 786 F.2d, at 748–749 (emphasis in original).

This approach, however, fails to recognize that, in order to prevail on a Rule 10b–5 claim, a plaintiff must show that the statements were *misleading* as to a *material* fact. It is not enough that a statement is false or incomplete, if the misrepresented fact is otherwise insignificant.

C

Even before this Court's decision in *TSC Industries,* the Second Circuit had explained the role of the materiality requirement of Rule 10b–5, with

---

14. "Although the Committee believes that ideally it would be desirable to have absolute certainty in the application of the materiality concept, it is its view that such a goal is illusory and unrealistic. The materiality concept is judgmental in nature and it is not possible to translate this into a numerical formula. The Committee's advice to the [SEC] is to avoid this quest for certainty and to continue consideration of materiality on a case-by-case basis as problems are identified."

Report of the Advisory Committee on Corporate Disclosure to the Securities and Exchange Commission 327 (House Committee on Interstate and Foreign Commerce, 95th Cong., 1st Sess.) (Comm.Print) (1977).

respect to contingent or speculative information or events, in a manner that gave that term meaning that is independent of the other provisions of the Rule. Under such circumstances, materiality "will depend at any given time upon a balancing of both the indicated probability that the event will occur and the anticipated magnitude of the event in light of the totality of the company activity." SEC v. Texas Gulf Sulphur Co., 401 F.2d, at 849. Interestingly, neither the Third Circuit decision adopting the agreement-in-principle test nor petitioners here take issue with this general standard. Rather, they suggest that with respect to preliminary merger discussions, there are good reasons to draw a line at agreement on price and structure.

In a subsequent decision, the late Judge Friendly, writing for a Second Circuit panel, applied the *Texas Gulf Sulphur* probability/magnitude approach in the specific context of preliminary merger negotiations. After acknowledging that materiality is something to be determined on the basis of the particular facts of each case, he stated:

> "Since a merger in which it is bought out is the most important event that can occur in a small corporation's life, to wit, its death, we think that inside information, as regards a merger of this sort, can become material at an earlier stage than would be the case as regards lesser transactions—and this even though the mortality rate of mergers in such formative stages is doubtless high."

SEC v. Geon Industries, Inc., 531 F.2d 39, 47–48 (C.A.2 1976). We agree with that analysis.

Whether merger discussions in any particular case are material therefore depends on the facts. Generally, in order to assess the probability that the event will occur, a factfinder will need to look to indicia of interest in the transaction at the highest corporate levels. Without attempting to catalog all such possible factors, we note by way of example that board resolutions, instructions to investment bankers, and actual negotiations between principals or their intermediaries may serve as indicia of interest. To assess the magnitude of the transaction to the issuer of the securities allegedly manipulated, a factfinder will need to consider such facts as the size of the two corporate entities and of the potential premiums over market value. No particular event or factor short of closing the transaction need be either necessary or sufficient by itself to render merger discussions material.[17]

---

17. To be actionable, of course, a statement must also be misleading. Silence, absent a duty to disclose, is not misleading under Rule 10b–5. "No comment" statements are generally the functional equivalent of silence. See In Re Carnation Co., *supra*. See also New York Stock Exchange Listed Company Manual § 202.01, reprinted in 3 CCH Fed.Sec.L.Rep. ¶ 23,515 (premature public announcement may properly be delayed for valid business purpose and where adequate security can be maintained); American Stock Exchange Company Guide §§ 401–405, reprinted in 3 CCH Fed.Sec.L.Rep. ¶¶ 23,124A–23,124E (similar provisions).

It has been suggested that given current market practices, a "no comment" statement is tantamount to an admission that merger discussions are underway. See Flamm v. Eberstadt, 814 F.2d, at 1178. That may well hold true to the extent that issuers adopt a policy of truthfully denying merger rumors when no discussions are underway, and of issuing "no comment" statements when they are in the midst of negotiations. There are, of course, other statement policies firms could adopt; we need not now advise issuers as to what kind of practice to follow, within the range permitted by law. Perhaps more importantly, we think that creating an exception to a regulatory scheme founded on a predisclosure legislative philosophy, because complying with the regulation might be "bad for business," is a role for Congress, not this

As we clarify today, materiality depends on the significance the reasonable investor would place on the withheld or misrepresented information.[18] The fact-specific inquiry we endorse here is consistent with the approach a number of courts have taken in assessing the materiality of merger negotiations. Because the standard of materiality we have adopted differs from that used by both courts below, we remand the case for reconsideration of the question whether a grant of summary judgment is appropriate on this record.[20]

PROBLEM 14–2

Werner Gephardt, Chief Executive Officer of Weber, Inc., last night had dinner with his business school classmate, Frieda Durkheim, Chief Executive Officer of Lawrence Co. Both Weber and Lawrence are listed on the New York Stock Exchange (NYSE).

This morning average daily volume trebled on Weber, Inc. and its stock price was up 15 percent.

(1) If the appropriate NYSE representative telephones and asks if Weber, Inc. has any information about why the price and volume are up, can Weber's public relations officer state "absolutely none"?

(2) Suppose Durkheim had presented Gephardt with a two page proposed "merger of equals" and Gephardt had turned it down on September 7th. Could the public relations officer still state, "I know of absolutely nothing to allow for the stock price and volume increases"?

Court. See also id., at 1182 (opinion concurring in the judgment and concurring in part).

18. We find no authority in the statute, the legislative history, or our previous decisions, for varying the standard of materiality depending on who brings the action or whether insiders are alleged to have profited. See, e.g., Pavlidis v. New England Patriots Football Club, Inc., 737 F.2d 1227, 1231 (C.A.1 1984) ("A fact does not become more material to the shareholder's decision because it is withheld by an insider, or because the insider might profit by withholding it"); cf. Aaron v. SEC, 446 U.S. 680, 691 (1980) ("scienter is an element of a violation of § 10(b) and Rule 10b–5, regardless of the identity of the plaintiff or the nature of the relief sought").

We recognize that trading (and profit making) by insiders can serve as *an* indication of materiality, see SEC v. Texas Gulf Sulphur Co., 401 F.2d, at 851; General Portland, Inc. v. LaFarge Coppee S.A., CCH Fed. Sec.L.Rep. (1982–1983 Transfer Binder) ¶ 99,148, p. 95,544 (ND Tex.1981). We are not prepared to agree, however, that "[i]n cases of the disclosure of inside information to a favored few, determination of materiality has a different aspect than when the issue is, for example, an inaccuracy in a publicly disseminated press release." SEC v. Geon Industries, Inc., 531 F.2d 39, 48 (C.A.2 1976).

Devising two different standards of materiality, one for situations where insiders have traded in abrogation of their duty to disclose or abstain (or for that matter when any disclosure duty has been breached), and another covering affirmative misrepresentations by those under no duty to disclose (but under the ever-present duty not to mislead), would effectively collapse the materiality requirement into the analysis of defendant's disclosure duties.

20. The Sixth Circuit rejected the District Court's narrow reading of Basic's "no developments" statement, see n.4, *supra,* which focused on whether petitioners *knew* of any reason for the activity in Basic stock, that is, whether petitioners were aware of leaks concerning ongoing discussions. 786 F.2d, at 747. See also Comment, Disclosure of Preliminary Merger Negotiations Under Rule 10b–5, 62 Wash.L.Rev. 81, 82–84 (1987) (noting prevalence of leaks and studies demonstrating that substantial trading activity immediately preceding merger announcements is the "rule, not the exception"). We accept the Court of Appeals' reading of the statement as the more natural one, emphasizing management's knowledge of *developments* (as opposed to leaks) that would explain unusual trading activity. See id., at 92–93; see also SEC v. Texas Gulf Sulphur Co., 401 F.2d, at 862–863.

(3) Suppose Durkheim presented Gephardt with a two page proposed "merger of equals" and Gephardt said "I'll take it to my board for consideration next week." Could the public relations officer then state, "I know of nothing to account for the stock price and volume increases"?

FORWARD LOOKING STATEMENTS

While Basic v. Levinson was limited to premerger negotiations and did not generally address other forms of contingent or forward looking statements or prospectuses,[1] the holding of the case that materiality "will depend at any given time upon a balancing of both the indicated probability that the event will occur and the anticipated magnitude of the event in light of the totality of the company activity" provides a general approach to forward looking or soft information.[2]

In the ensuing decades there was some judicial expansion in required disclosure of forward looking statements. A few decisions required the disclosure of asset appraisals and similar soft information, at least in contexts where a bidder seeking to buy, or tender for, the target possessed such information.[3] Other circuits declined to require such disclosure.[4]

A different question is presented when the claim of the plaintiff is that liability arose from a failure to disclose internal projections of earnings in connection with a particular transaction. In Pavlidis v. New England Patriots Football Club,[5] it was claimed that the company should have disclosed, in a proxy statement for a going private merger transaction, certain projections of future earnings made by the management. The court rejected this contention. It stated: "The federal securities laws do not require corporate management to include speculations about future profitability in proxy statements; in fact, at the time the Patriots' proxy statement was issued, the Securities and Exchange Commission frowned on such disclosures. * * * Of course, stockholders may point to specific information in a financial projection as evidence that the management did not disclose all the material facts in its possession; but failure to disclose the projection itself does not establish a § 14(a) violation."[6]

In Herskowitz v. Nutri/System, Inc.,[7] the Third Circuit held that a jury question was presented as to whether it was reasonable for a bank to render a fairness opinion in connection with a leveraged buyout based on a cash flow projection that assumed a particular tax rate for a five year period. No mention was made of the safe harbor rules, presumably because the document was not filed with the Commission, although the rules do cover "an outside reviewer retained by the issuer" making such a forward looking statement which is filed.

In Lyondell Petrochemical Co. Sec. Litig.,[8] the court generalized about a company's responsibilities to disclose internal projections:

1. 485 U.S. at 232 n.9.

2. The lower courts have applied the *Basic-Texas Gulf Sulphur* test to other contingent events. *See, e.g.*, General Motors Class E Stock Buyout Sec. Litig., 694 F.Supp. 1119 (D.Del.1988).

3. *See, e.g.*, Flynn v. Bass Brothers Enter., Inc., 744 F.2d 978, 988 (3d Cir.1984); Starkman v. Marathon Oil Co., 772 F.2d 231, 241–242 (6th Cir.1985), *cert. denied*, 486 U.S.

1018 (1988) (projections must be disclosed if "substantially certain").

4. *See* Panter v. Marshall Field & Co., 646 F.2d 271, 292 (7th Cir.1981).

5. 737 F.2d 1227 (1st Cir.1984).

6. Id. at 1233.

7. 857 F.2d 179 (3d Cir.1988), *cert. denied*, 489 U.S. 1054 (1989).

8. 984 F.2d 1050 (9th Cir.1993).

This court recognizes that the Securities Exchange Commission (SEC) "does not require a company to disclose financial projections." Vaughn v. Teledyne, Inc., 628 F.2d 1214, 1221 (9th Cir.1980); accord In re Convergent Technologies Sec. Litig., 948 F.2d 507, 516 (9th Cir.1991) (as amended on denial of rehearing *en banc*). Plaintiffs argue that notwithstanding *Vaughn* and *Convergent*, once Lyondell opened the door by presenting forecasts to Morgan Guaranty, it was obligated to tell the whole truth to the public. We decline to adopt a "whole truth" exception in cases such as this where a corporation had disclosed internal projections outside the confines of the company, but not to the public generally. A corporation may be called upon to make confidential projections for a variety of sound purposes where public disclosure would be harmful. For example, a bank concerned about the security of its loan might require the corporation to provide a worst-case prediction which may or may not happen. A far-reaching disclosure requirement might not be in the best interests of the market, the corporation's legitimate business plans and, ultimately, investors such as Plaintiffs.[9]

The majority of the cases before the Supreme Court's opinion in the *Basic* case held that preliminary merger negotiations did not have to be disclosed before an agreement in principle on the "price and structure" of the proposed transaction.[10] These decisions were based upon two principal considerations: (1) Because of the "high mortality rate" of proposed mergers, the disclosure of such negotiations at a prior time was likely to be more misleading than informative to the traders in the market; (2) the disclosure of such preliminary discussions would likely cause many beneficial transactions to be aborted because the potential acquirer of the corporation did not want to negotiate in the public limelight. The Supreme Court held that neither of these considerations justified departing with respect to such merger negotiations from the general definition of materiality. Even before the *Basic* case, courts following the majority view relating to the "price and structure" test held that it did not apply where there was no public market for stock of the corporation, which was purchased by the corporation or an insider while negotiations regarding an acquisition of the corporation were being conducted. In Michaels v. Michaels,[11] the Seventh Circuit said that: "[T]he reasons for the 'price and structure' standard of materiality disappear when there is no public market for a shareholder's stock."[12] This decision is entirely consistent with a large number of early cases under Rule 10b–5 which dealt with the situation where the

---

9. Id. at 1052–1053.

10. Greenfield v. Heublein, Inc., 742 F.2d 751 (3d Cir.1984), *cert. denied*, 469 U.S. 1215 (1985); Flamm v. Eberstadt, 814 F.2d 1169 (7th Cir.1987), *cert. denied*, 484 U.S. 853 (1987).

Applying the *TSC Industries* and *Texas Gulf Sulphur* standards, the Commission, on the other hand, has viewed a pattern of one meeting and several telephone conversations discussing a potential merger as material. Carnation Co., Sec. Ex. Act Rel. 22,214, 33 SEC Dock. 874, 877–878 (1985).

In a different context, the Commission has interpreted Item 7(a) of Schedule 14D–9, which requires disclosure of control transaction "negotiations" by a subject company, as including "not only final price bargaining, but also * * * substantive discussions between the parties or their legal and financial advisers concerning a possible transaction." Revlon, Inc., Sec. Ex. Act Rel. 23,320, 35 SEC Dock. 1148, 1153 (1986).

11. 767 F.2d 1185, 1196 (7th Cir.1985), *cert. denied*, 474 U.S. 1057 (1986). This decision was reaffirmed in Jordan v. Duff & Phelps, Inc., 815 F.2d 429 (7th Cir.1987), *cert. dismissed*, 485 U.S. 901 (1988).

12. 767 F.2d at 1196.

majority shareholders were engaged in acquisition discussions at a time when they or the corporation purchased the shares of a minority shareholder at a price considerably less than that eventually realized when the acquisition in fact occurred.

The Courts of Appeals were cautious in their acceptance of the direction of the Supreme Court in the *Basic* case. In Taylor v. First Union Corporation of South Carolina,[13] the Fourth Circuit held that preliminary and tentative discussions between two banks regarding the possibility of a merger of the banks if interstate banking became legal were not required to be disclosed. The court said:

> In contrast to the circumstances of *Basic*, the evidence indicates that the discussions at issue here were preliminary, contingent, and speculative. At best, the merger discussions culminated in a vague "agreement" to establish a relationship. There was no agreement as to price or structure of the deal. While, after *Basic* this alone is not dispositive of the question of materiality, it is certainly not irrelevant to the totality of the circumstances test articulated in that case.[14]

The First Circuit in Jackvony v. RIHT Financial Corporation similarly stated: "The evidence shows no more than the type of concern about possible acquisition that many large companies frequently express; it reveals no concrete offers, specific discussions, or anything more than vague expressions of interest. It provides no reason to believe in the existence of any preliminary negotiations of the sort mentioned in *Basic*, a case in which the Supreme Court found that specific 'meetings and telephone conversations' among 'officers and directors' of the relevant firms 'concerning the possibility of a merger' might, or might not, prove material, depending upon the 'probability that the transaction will be consummated.' "[15]

More than case decisions, the most significant driving force for mandatory disclosure of forward looking statements was the SEC. Item 303(a) of Regulation S–K effectively requires management to disclose certain estimates and projections in its Management's Discussion and Analysis of Financial Condition and Results of Operations (the "MD & A"), which is a required item in both the Annual Report on Form 10–K and the Quarterly Report on Form10–Q. Specifically, the MD & A must contain a description of "known trends * * * demands, commitments, events or uncertainties that will result in or that are reasonably likely to result in the registrant's liquidity increasing or decreasing in any material way."[16] Similar disclosure is required of "any known trends or uncertainties that have had or that the registrant reasonably expects will have a material favorable or unfavorable impact on net sales or income from continuing operations."[17]

The SEC views the MD & A as its principal quarterly disclosure vehicle under which the issuer must both disclose "trends" or "uncertainties" that are "reasonably likely to have a material effect" on the issuer's financial condition or results of operations and update these estimates on a continuing basis. Clearly, the MD & A mandates some prospective information. But does this mean that projections are required in all prospectuses, as well as in Form 10–

---

13. 857 F.2d 240 (4th Cir.1988), *cert. denied*, 489 U.S. 1080 (1989).

14. 857 F.2d at 244.

15. 873 F.2d 411, 415 (1st Cir.1989).

16. Item 303(a)(1), Regulation S–K.

17. Item 303(a)(3), Regulation S–K.

Ks and Form 10–Qs? The SEC has drawn the following distinction between prospective information that is required to be disclosed and voluntary forward looking disclosure:

> Both required disclosure regarding the future impact of presently known trends, events or uncertainties and optional forward-looking information may involve some prediction or projection. The distinction between the two rests with the nature of the prediction required. Required disclosure is based on currently known trends, events and uncertainties that are reasonably expected to have material effects, such as a reduction in the registrant's product prices; erosion in the registrant's market share; changes in insurance coverage; or the likely non-renewal of a material contract. In contrast, optional forward-looking disclosure involves anticipating a future trend or event or anticipating a less predictable impact of a known event, trend or uncertainty.[18]

Is this distinction clear? Or, does it really imply that the registrant must make affirmative disclosure of all "trends" and "uncertainties" other than the most speculative? Conceptually, the issue posed by the SEC's position on the MD & A is that the registrant is subject to an affirmative disclosure obligation, after *Basic, Inc. v. Levinson* seemed to say that silence was not actionable with the absence of such a duty to speak.

When the Commission adopted its safe harbor rules for forward looking statements in 1979, it waffled on the significance of the disclosure of risk factors and assumptions to accompany a forward looking statement. The Commission generally requires the disclosure of risk factors in registration statements and prospectuses, but these requirements do not specifically address forward looking statements.

The absence of clear guidance from the Commission as to how assumption and risk factors should be disclosed in the context of various types of forward looking statements and whether disclosure of material assumptions and risks will reduce a firm's exposure to liability created a lacuna that the judiciary soon addressed.

In re Worlds of Wonder Securities Litigation

United States Court of Appeals, Ninth Circuit, 1994.
35 F.3d 1407.

■ Before: FLETCHER, HALL, and WIGGINS, CIRCUIT JUDGES.

■ CYNTHIA HOLCOMB HALL, CIRCUIT JUDGE:

In this appeal, we consider the saga of Worlds of Wonder, Inc. ("WOW"), a toy company that sold $80 million of "junk bonds" to the investing public in June 1987. When WOW defaulted on its very first interest payment and filed for bankruptcy just six months later, rendering the securities worthless, a class of disappointed investors filed this securities-fraud action, naming as defendants WOW's officers, directors, auditors, underwriters, and major shareholders. The district court granted summary judgment in favor of all defendants and the investors appealed. After considering a myriad of issues, we affirm in part and reverse in part.

---

18. Sec. Act Rel. 6711, 38 SEC Dock. 138, 140–141 (1987).

I.

In 1985, Donald Kingsborough formed WOW to manufacture and distribute "The World of Teddy Ruxpin," a product line featuring animated toy bears and accessories. Teddy Ruxpin was an immediate success, becoming a top seller for the 1985 Christmas season and generating net sales of $93 million in WOW's first fiscal year, which ended March 31, 1986. Shortly thereafter, WOW launched "Lazer Tag," a product line featuring *infra*red toy weapons. Lazer Tag became another instantaneous hit and, as Teddy Ruxpin continued to move briskly off the shelves, WOW posted two of the ten best-selling toys of the 1986 Christmas season. Ultimately, WOW recorded net sales of $327 million for fiscal 1987, which ended March 31, 1987.

Hoping to fund further expansion, WOW conducted a public offering of unsecured 9% convertible subordinated debentures on June 4, 1987 ("the Debenture Offering"), raising $80 million. (In common parlance, the debentures were "junk bonds" because they bore an above-market interest rate to compensate for the risk associated with their "below investment grade" rating). This additional infusion of capital, however, proved inadequate to sustain the corporation's uncontrolled growth and, almost immediately, WOW commenced a series of public disclosures that led to sharp declines in the market price of the debentures and, eventually, to a total financial collapse.

On July 27, 1987, the corporation reported losses of $10 million for the first quarter of fiscal 1988, ending June 30, 1987. Shortly thereafter, on August 7, 1987, WOW terminated fifteen percent of its domestic workforce (fifty-five employees) and announced reductions in capital expenditures. Two months later, the corporation disclosed that it had laid off another seventeen percent of its workforce (sixty employees) and engaged in further cost-cutting measures. On November 9, 1987, WOW reported net losses of $43 million for the second quarter of fiscal 1988, ending September 30, 1987, and announced price reductions on Teddy Ruxpin and Lazer Tag. Finally, after 1987 Christmas sales fell far below projections, WOW defaulted on the first interest payment of the debentures and, shortly thereafter, filed for bankruptcy on December 21, 1987, rendering the securities worthless.

* * *

II.

We turn first to the plaintiffs' claims against the Officers, the Directors, Smith Barney, and Deloitte under section 11 of the 1933 Act, which creates a private right of action in favor of securities purchasers who rely upon a materially false or misleading prospectus. See 15 U.S.C. § 77k(a). The district court held that (1) except for possible errors in the certified 1987 financial statements that were appended to the document, "there are no statements in, or omissions from, the Debenture Prospectus that would give rise to an inference that any part of the document was false or misleading," WOW, 814 F.Supp. at 866, and (2) even assuming that the 1987 financial statements were false or misleading, each defendant had established an affirmative defense to section 11 liability as a matter of law.

A.

In concluding that the "textual part" of the Debenture Prospectus was not false or misleading, the district court analyzed the plaintiffs' claims of misrepresentation under the rubric of the "bespeaks caution" doctrine: " * * * The doctrine holds that economic projections, estimates of future performance, and similar optimistic statements in a prospectus are not actionable when precise cautionary language elsewhere in the document adequately discloses the risks involved. It does not matter if the optimistic statements are later found to have been inaccurate or based on erroneous assumptions when made, provided that the risk disclosure was conspicuous, specific, and adequately disclosed the assumptions upon which the optimistic language was based * * *. In the context of a summary judgment motion, * * * [t]he doctrine holds that where a prospectus contains adequate cautionary language disclosing specific risks, no reasonable inference can be drawn that a statement regarding those risks was misleading. Id. at 858, 859 (footnote omitted)." The court also analyzed the plaintiffs' claims in the context of information about WOW known to the market at the time of the offering:

" * * * [T]he major rating agencies classified [WOW's] debentures as 'junk bonds.' That this fact was widely disseminated throughout the market is reflected by the 9% interest rate for the debentures, which was substantially higher than the market rate for lower risk securities. Since WOW was widely considered in the marketplace to be a risky investment, Plaintiffs' allegations that statements in or omissions from the Debenture Prospectus were misleading deserve especially careful scrutiny * * *." Id. at 864.

On appeal, the plaintiffs contend that the district court erred by adopting and applying the bespeaks caution doctrine and by granting summary judgment despite evidence indicating that the textual part of the Debenture Prospectus contained material misstatements and omissions. We consider these contentions in order.

1.

"The bespeaks caution doctrine provides a mechanism by which a court can rule as a matter of law (typically in a motion to dismiss for failure to state a cause of action or a motion for summary judgment) that defendants' forward-looking representations contained enough cautionary language or risk disclosure to protect the defendant against claims of securities fraud." Donald C. Langevoort, Disclosures that "Bespeak Caution", 49 Bus.Law. 481, 482–83 (1994) [Disclosures]. At least six circuits have adopted some form of the doctrine. [Citations omitted] Moreover, since the district court's opinion in this case, several trial courts in this circuit have also embraced the doctrine. * * *

Despite this wealth of authority, the plaintiffs breathlessly attempt to portray the bespeaks caution doctrine as a radical departure from settled law and as contrary to the letter and spirit of federal securities statutes. In reality, it is neither. Rather, the doctrine, when properly construed, merely represents the pragmatic application of two fundamental concepts in the law of securities fraud: materiality and reliance. The Fifth Circuit recently explained: "The 'bespeaks caution' doctrine * * * reflects a relatively recent, ongoing, and somewhat uncertain evolution in securities law, an evolution driven by the increase in and the unique nature of fraud actions based on predictive statements. In essence, predictive statements are just what the name implies: predictions. As such, any optimistic projections contained in such statements are necessarily contingent. Thus, the 'bespeaks caution' doctrine has developed to address situations in which optimistic projections are coupled with cautionary language—in particular, relevant specific facts or assumptions—affecting the reasonableness of reliance on and the materiality of those projections. To put it another way, the 'bespeaks caution' doctrine reflects the unremarkable proposition that statements must be analyzed in context." Rubinstein, 20 F.3d at 167 (footnotes omitted). Accord Trump Casino, 7 F.3d at 364 ("[The doctrine] represents new nomenclature rather than substantive change in the law."); see generally Disclosures, 46 Bus.Law. at 487 (explaining materiality and reliance components of the doctrine).

In this light, the district court's measured application of the bespeaks caution doctrine was entirely consistent with the above-noted authority and established Ninth Circuit precedent. * * *

In this case, the district court applied the doctrine narrowly: " * * * [A]n overbroad application of the doctrine would encourage management to conceal deliberate misrepresentations beneath the mantle of broad cautionary language. To prevent this from occurring, the bespeaks caution doctrine applies only to precise cautionary language which directly addresses itself to future projections, estimates or forecasts in a prospectus. By contrast, blanket warnings that securities involve a high degree of risk [are] insufficient to ward against a federal securities fraud claim." WOW, 814 F.Supp. at 858 (citations and quotations omitted); see Kline v. First W. Gov't Sec., Inc., 24 F.3d 480, 489 (3d Cir.1994) ("application of the 'bespeaks caution' doctrine * * * requires that the language bespeaking caution relate directly to that to which plaintiffs claim to have been misled"). As a result, notwithstanding the plaintiffs' shrill arguments to the contrary, the court's context-specific approach entirely comports with Virginia Bankshares, Inc. v. Sandberg, 501 U.S. 1083, 111 S.Ct. 2749, 115 L.Ed.2d 929 (1991), in which the Supreme Court noted that "[w]hile a misleading statement will not always lose its deceptive edge simply by joinder with others that are true, the true statements may discredit the other one so obviously that the risk of real deception drops to nil * * *. [Therefore,] publishing accurate facts * * * can render a misleading proposition too unimportant to ground liability," id. at 1097, 111 S.Ct. at 2760–61; * * *.

In our view, the bespeaks caution doctrine helps "to minimize the chance that a plaintiff with a largely groundless claim will bring a suit and conduct extensive discovery in the hopes of obtaining an increased settlement." Romani, 929 F.2d at 878 (quotation omitted); see generally Blue Chip Stamps v. Manor Drug Stores, 421 U.S. 723, 740, 95 S.Ct. 1917, 1927–28, 44 L.Ed.2d 539 (1975) ("in the field of federal securities laws governing disclosure of information[,] even a complaint which by objective standards may have very little chance of success at trial has a settlement value to the plaintiff out of any proportion to its prospect of success at trial so long as [the plaintiff] may prevent the suit from being resolved against him by dismissal or summary judgment"). Therefore, because it is consistent both with precedent from this circuit and with well-settled principles of securities law articulated by courts across the country, we adopt the district court's formulation of the doctrine.[3]

---

3. The plaintiffs appear to contend that, if the bespeaks caution doctrine is viable, it applies only to section 10(b) claims and not to section 11 claims. This argument is plainly wrong. As noted, the doctrine is primarily an application of the materiality concept, which applies equally to both statutory provisions. E.g., Halkin v. VeriFone Inc. (In re VeriFone Sec. Litig.), 11 F.3d 865, 868–69 (9th Cir.1993). Accordingly, courts have applied the doctrine to section 11 claims as well as section 10(b) claims. See, e.g., Trump, 7 F.3d at 365; I. Meyer Pincus, 936 F.2d at 761; see generally Disclosures, 49 Bus. Law. at 483.

2.

Turning to the merits, the plaintiffs claim the textual disclosures in the Debenture Prospectus were false or misleading in four general areas: liquidity, internal controls, revenue recognition, and sales performance. We consider each in order.

a.

The plaintiffs first contend that the prospectus was false and misleading because it stated that WOW expected to have sufficient cash to operate through March 31, 1988. The prospectus made the following disclosures regarding liquidity: Seasonality of Quarterly Results * * *. There can be no assurance that the Company can maintain sufficient flexibility with respect to its working capital needs, manufacturing capacity and supplies of raw materials, tools and components to be able to minimize the adverse effects of an unanticipated shortfall in seasonal demand * * *. Capital Requirements * * *. To meet seasonal working capital requirements, the Company has borrowed, and expects to continue to borrow, substantial amounts * * *. The Company anticipates that the proceeds of this offering, together with cash flow from operations, existing lines of credit and new bank credit facilities presently being negotiated, will provide sufficient funds to meet the Company's capital needs through March 31, 1988. However, if the Company is unable to obtain adequate capital from this offering and such new bank credit facilities on acceptable terms, its operations would be adversely affected * * *. Liquidity and Capital Resources. Since its inception, the Company's internally generated cash flow has not been sufficient to finance accounts receivable, inventory and capital equipment needs, as well as support growth * * *. To meet seasonal working capital requirements, management expects to continue to borrow substantial amounts under its bank line of credit and its import financing line, both of which it expects to replace or extend prior to expiration. Based on its current plan of operations, management anticipates that existing credit facilities and new bank facilities presently being negotiated, together with the proceeds of the offering of the Debentures and funds from operations, will be sufficient to meet the Company's short-term cash requirements through March 31, 1988.

After reviewing the document, the district court concluded that the prospectus "clearly bespoke caution on the serious risks WOW's liquidity crisis posed to investors * * *. Plaintiffs are not entitled to an inference that they were misled in the face of such disclosures." WOW, 814 F.Supp. at 866. We agree.

* * *

Given the plaintiffs' lack of probative evidence and the Debenture Prospectus' specific references to WOW's continuing cash shortfall and borrowing requirements, the district court was correct to conclude that the prediction of liquidity was not materially misleading as a matter of law. * * *

b.

The plaintiffs next argue that the following Debenture Prospectus description of WOW's internal controls was materially misleading: Information Systems and Control Procedures. The Company's business has grown dramatically in the last year, and the Company's development of its management information system and other systems and control procedures has at times lagged behind this growth. While the Company continues to upgrade its systems, procedures and controls to meet the demand of its expansion, there can be no assurance that the Company can successfully implement these enhancements or that these enhancements will keep pace with the growth.

The plaintiffs contend that, in fact, WOW's internal controls at the time of the offering had "crippling deficiencies" and that "no reasonable investor reading the Prospectus would have concluded that there were any existing problems with controls." The district court disagreed: "Plaintiffs ignore the fact that the Prospectus included an express disclaimer that 'there can be no assurances' that WOW's existing internal controls would continue to be adequate given the rapid pace at which the company was growing. The Prospectus made no predictions to the contrary. Thus, the Prospectus adequately bespoke caution regarding this potential risk to WOW's investors. As a matter of law, Plaintiffs cannot have been misled." WOW, 814 F.Supp. at 865. This conclusion is correct for several reasons. First, contrary to the plaintiffs' assertions, the Debenture Prospectus did not state or imply that WOW's internal control problems were "in the past" and not ongoing. Rather, the prospectus clearly warned that the company's attempt to improve internal controls could prove to be inadequate. Second, the plaintiffs presented no evidence that WOW's internal controls at the time of the offering were materially deficient. Indeed, the allegedly "devastating" management letter issued by Deloitte (two-and-a-half months after the Debenture Offering) concluded that, although "significant problems" existed, WOW's internal controls had no material weaknesses. And, third, WOW probably would not have needed to disclose even serious internal-control deficiencies. Cf. Monroe v. Hughes, 31 F.3d 772, 776 (9th Cir.1994) (holding that an auditor need not disclose internal controls).

The Debenture Prospectus, which noted that WOW had struggled to maintain sufficient internal controls, clearly erred on the side of over disclosure and was therefore not misleading. We affirm the district court on this point.

c.

The plaintiffs next argue that the Debenture Prospectus was misleading because it failed to disclose that WOW engaged in various tactics to "pump up" revenue figures without completing actual sales. Specifically, the plaintiffs contend the prospectus misleadingly omitted WOW's observance of "price protection" (the right to reimbursement in the event of post-sale price reductions), "stock balancing" (the post-sale right to exchange non-defective products for different merchandise), and "guaranteed sales" (the unqualified right to return non-defective products).

The argument regarding price protection and stock balancing is without merit for several reasons. First, the plaintiffs introduced "no evidence that, at the time of the Debenture offering, WOW's management could have foreseen that WOW would have to reduce prices to [the extent it actually did so in late 1987]. Thus, the alleged practice of price protection did not pose a foreseeable risk to WOW's investors at the time of the Debenture offering, so WOW had no duty to disclose it." WOW, 814 F.Supp. at 865. The speculative impact of future exchanges and price reductions was not material. See Hanon, 976 F.2d at 506 ("potential action to be taken sometime in the distant future is not an item appropriately made a part of a public disclosure because of its speculativeness"). And, second, the plaintiffs concede that price protection is a common practice in the toy industry. The undisputed evidence also indicates that stock balancing is commonplace in the industry. As a result, WOW had no duty to disclose its observance of those practices. * * *

Although a slightly closer call, the plaintiffs' contention regarding guaranteed sales fares no better. We agree that a company that "substantially overstate[s] its revenues by reporting consignment transactions as sales * * * mak[es] false or misleading statements of material fact." Malone v. Microdyne Corp., 26 F.3d 471, 478 (4th Cir.1994). And we acknowledge that the plaintiffs did present some evidence that WOW engaged in guaranteed sales prior to the Debenture Offering, particularly in the final quarter of fiscal 1987.

The evidence indicates, however, that Deloitte analyzed WOW's sales practices and concluded that, "[w]hile it is true that on a few occasions prior to the 1987 audit, WOW made the business decision to permit customers to return or exchange nondefective products, these returns were minimal in number, and did not have a material impact on WOW's financial statements taken as a whole." As the district court noted, "[j]ust because some of WOW's customers were allowed a refund does not mean that * * * WOW had a practice of offering guaranteed sales to all its customers. Giving an unsatisfied customer a refund is a normal business method of dealing with an unsatisfied customer. It is not a violation of securities laws for WOW to fail to disclose such an obvious practice to potential investors." WOW, 814 F.Supp. at 862.

The plaintiffs' evidence of guaranteed sales is speculative, nebulous, and nowhere purports to quantify the degree to which WOW engaged in this "normal business" practice. As such, it does not rise to the level of a material omission. * * *

d.

Finally, the plaintiffs argue that the following Debenture Prospectus disclosures misstated WOW's performance in the first quarter of fiscal 1988 and generally hid the fact that, at the time of the Debenture Offering, sales of and demand for WOW products had declined precipitously: Seasonality of Quarterly Results * * *. The Company anticipates that net sales for the quarter ending June 30, 1987 will be less than those for each of the prior three quarters, and the Company expects to report a loss for the quarter * * *. Net Sales * * *. Because sales of toys are highly seasonal, the Company would generally expect net sales to be lower in the first half of the calendar year. The Company's net sales in the first quarter of fiscal 1987 were lower than net sales in each of the preceding two quarters. Similarly, the Company expects net sales for the first quarter of fiscal 1988 to be lower than sales for each of the prior three quarters. At the same time, the Company is continuing to expand its operations in anticipation of the Christmas selling season. As a result, the Company expects to report a net loss for the first quarter of fiscal 1988 proportionally greater than the net loss reported for the first quarter of fiscal 1987.

The plaintiffs contend the prospectus was misleading because it did not state that (1) WOW's performance in the first quarter (which ended a month after the Debenture Offering) would be "substantially" lower than the first quarter of the preceding year or (2) WOW's net quarterly loss would be "disproportionally greater" than that of the prior year. We reject this argument for several reasons.

First, as Smith Barney explains, "[t]he only reasonable reading [of the prospectus] is that, in light of the lower first quarter sales and the higher first quarter operating expenses the company was then expecting, WOW's net loss

* * * was expected to constitute a 'greater proportion' of net revenue than * * * during the first quarter of 1987." The prospectus did not imply that WOW's first quarter 1988 losses would be proportional to its first quarter 1987 losses.

Second, the prospectus clearly warned that WOW expected lower net sales. WOW was under no duty to disclose the precise extent of the anticipated revenue drop. * * *. The plaintiffs complain that the prospectus failed to disclose the extent to which first quarter sales lagged behind WOW's internal projections. The quarter, however, was not yet complete; had WOW actually disclosed its internal business plan, the plaintiffs probably would now be contending that no basis existed for such a prediction. Cf. Convergent Technologies, 948 F.2d at 516 ("It is just good general business practice to make * * * projections for internal corporate use. There is no evidence, however, that the estimates were made with such reasonable certainty even to allow them to be disclosed to the public.") (quotation omitted).

The plaintiffs also argue that the Debenture Prospectus violated section 11 by failing generally to reveal "WOW's crisis of sales and demand." The district court disagreed: "Plaintiffs submit no admissible evidence to show that WOW's sales had decreased so dramatically at the time of the Debenture Offering that WOW's management could have known about, and thus would have had a duty to disclose, the impending collapse of Lazer Tag sales. Plaintiffs cannot use the benefit of 20–20 hindsight to turn management's business judgment into securities fraud." WOW, 814 F.Supp. at 865. We agree.

The plaintiffs argue that WOW's sales, for Lazer Tag in particular, began a dramatic collapse in January 1987 and that, because revenues prior to the Debenture Offering fell below WOW's internal business plan, WOW was required to disclose that "fact" in the Debenture Prospectus. The prospectus, however, fully disclosed WOW's sales for each of the eight completed fiscal quarters of its existence (through March 31, 1987). This disclosure revealed a significant decline in both net sales and net income for the first three months of 1987. The plaintiffs' complaint that WOW should have disclosed the ramifications of that drop in sales (i.e., that the decline was due to more than "normal seasonality") is without merit. See Convergent Technologies, 948 F.2d at 513 ("The challenged statements do not imply any comparison between the rate of past and future growth. They simply report past performance and assert specific limited predictions for the future."); see generally Trump Casino, 7 F.3d at 375 ("The federal securities laws do not ordain that the issuer of a security compare itself in myriad ways to its competitors, whether favorably or unfavorably.").

　　　　* * *

Just four days prior to the Debenture Offering, WOW commenced a production schedule implementing the corporation's optimistic business plan, which projected $542 million in sales. As the Officers note, if demand actually had dried up, the "[p]laintiffs cannot explain why WOW's entire senior and middle management would have lied to themselves about the Company's business outlook." See Apple Computer, 886 F.2d at 1117 ("[the corporation]'s massive investment in [a new product] demonstrates this good faith" belief that it will succeed). The plaintiffs presented no admissible evidence to the contrary. In sum, their argument distills to a contention that WOW should have predicted the collapse in sales that occurred in late 1987, long after the Debenture Offering. The corporation had no duty to do so. See VeriFone, 11

F.3d at 869 ("These alleged nondisclosures are, in substance, failures to make a forecast of future events. Put another way, what the complaint states is that [the issuer] omitted to state the 'fact' that future prospects were not as bright as past performance. Absent allegations that [the issuer] withheld financial data or other existing facts from which forecasts are typically derived, the alleged omissions are not of material, actual facts. Therefore, the forecasts need not have been disclosed, and the failure to make the omitted forecasts did not render the other statements that were made misleading."). We affirm the district court on this point.

e.

The avalanche of documents presented by the plaintiffs does little more than illustrate the fact that, at the time of the Debenture Offering, WOW's future was uncertain. The Debenture Prospectus adequately disclosed this fact and the market, which characterized the debentures as "junk bonds," realized it. As a result, we agree with the district court's summary of the plaintiffs' section 11 case: "When a company fails, it does not automatically mean that a violation of the securities laws has occurred. There are a number of risks involved whenever one invests in any company * * *. The securities laws do not insulate investors against stock downturns which are caused by events not foreseeable to the company's management, nor do they provide insurance against risks that were disclosed to investors at the time they purchased the securities. In this case, WOW's investors took a gamble, as do all investors. They lost. Holders of shares and Debentures knew that WOW was not a diversified company. Its success was based on only two major products * * *. And, WOW's precarious cash position was not concealed from these investors * * *. It was obvious to any reasonable investor that if either of WOW's two products were to lose favor with consumers, the company would be devastated * * *. Plaintiffs have submitted hundreds of pages to this court in an effort to create a genuine issue of fact. Using tortured reasoning, convolution of the issues, and the benefit of hindsight, they point to the most innocuous of optimistic language, and the most immaterial of omitted facts, and claim that they were somehow misled as to the nature of their investment. [That is not sufficient]." WOW, 814 F.Supp. at 873. We affirm the district court's summary judgment in favor of the defendants regarding the textual part of the Debenture Prospectus. * * *

THE BESPEAKS CAUTION DOCTRINE

While a majority of circuits adopted the bespeaks caution doctrine in the period before the 1995 Private Securities Litigation Reform Act, there was considerable variation in how the circuits developed this doctrine.

In the First Circuit, it was held that the doctrine immunized from liability an alleged omission—"that the saddlebred horse industry was entering a recessionary period, making past performance an imperfect indicator of the future," in light of a detailed attached report describing "a number of specific problems facing the saddlebred industry, including overbreeding, declining attendance at races and an average decline in yearling prices."[1] In this

---

1. Romani v. Shearson Lehman Hutton, 929 F.2d 875, 879 (1st Cir.1991). Cf. Shaw v. Digital Equip. Corp., 82 F.3d 1194, 1213 (1st Cir.1996) ("to the extent that plaintiffs allege that the 'adequacy' statement implies a hiatus on new restructuring charges

application of the bespeaks caution doctrine, there was no challenge to an express forward looking statement, merely a dismissal of an alleged omission.

In the Second Circuit, a complaint was dismissed which was alleged to be materially misleading because of two sentences in a prospectus that could be read to suggest that shares of closed end investment were as likely to trade at a premium as a discount in light of a somewhat more detailed discussion elsewhere in the prospectus, that stated that shares of closed end investment companies frequently trade at a discount from their net asset value.[2]

Neither the First Circuit nor the Second Circuit in these opinions provided guidance as to how detailed a discussion of a risk factor had to be to immunize an allegedly misleading material misrepresentation or omission.

A more detailed analysis appeared in the Third Circuit opinion in Donald J. Trump Casino Sec. Litig.:[3]

[A]s a general matter * * * when an offering document's forecasts, opinions or projections are accompanied by meaningful cautionary statements, the forward-looking statements will not form the basis for a securities fraud claim if those statements did not affect the "total mix" of information the document provided investors. In other words, cautionary language, if sufficient, renders the alleged omissions or misrepresentations immaterial as a matter of law.

The bespeaks caution doctrine is, as an analytical matter, equally applicable to allegations of both affirmative misrepresentations and omissions concerning soft information. Whether the plaintiffs allege a document contains an affirmative prediction/opinion which is misleading or fails to include a forecast or prediction whose failure is misleading, the cautionary statements included in the document may render the challenged predictive statements or opinions immaterial as a matter of law. Of course, a vague or blanket (boilerplate) disclaimer which merely warns the reader that the investment has risks will ordinarily be inadequate to prevent misinformation. To suffice, the cautionary statements must be substantive and tailored to the specific future projections, estimates or opinions in the prospectus which the plaintiffs challenge.

The *Trump* opinion contains two significant limitations on its articulation of the doctrine. First, it is limited to prospective information. The bespeaks caution doctrine in this view cannot be used to insulate from liability a

---

for the near future, we do not think that the surrounding context warns against such an implication with sufficient clarity to be thought to bespeak caution"). See also id. at 1217–1221 (nonactionability of loosely optimistic statements).

2. I. Meyer Pincus & Assoc. v. Oppenheimer & Co., Inc., 936 F.2d 759, 760–763 (2d Cir.1991). A subsequent Second Circuit case emphasized: "The cautionary language, however, must relate directly to that by which plaintiffs claim to have been misled." Hunt v. Alliance N. Am. Gov't Income Trust, Inc., 159 F.3d 723, 729 (2d Cir.1998).

"[S]tatements regarding the future payment of dividends were predictions or opinions and not guarantees." International Bus. Mach. Corp. Sec. Litig., 163 F.3d 102, 107 (2d Cir.1998). This case followed Raab v. General Physics Corp., 4 F.3d 286, 290 (4th Cir.1993), and held: "Statements regarding projections of future performance may be actionable under Section 10(b) or Rule 10b–5 if they are worded as guarantees or are supported by specific statements of fact [citation omitted] or if the speaker does not genuinely or reasonably believe them." Ibid.

3. 7 F.3d 357, 371–372 (3d Cir.1993), *cert. denied sub nom.* Gollomp v. Trump, 510 U.S. 1178 (1994).

defendant who misrepresents or omits a historical fact. Second, *Trump* cautions against invocation of the doctrine when the risk factors or disclosures are vague or boilerplate.[4]

A boilerplate warning that a certain process "has only speculative value at the present time and may prove to be totally worthless" is the sort of generic warning that does not "enlighten investors about the status of patent applications, negotiations to sell the business, and the like; [it] do[es] nothing to disabuse an investor influenced by false oral statements."[5]

The Fifth Circuit in Rubinstein v. Collins[6] took a more skeptical view of the bespeaks caution doctrine than the First, Second, or Third Circuits. The court stated:

> Under our precedent, cautionary language is not necessarily sufficient, in and of itself, to render predictive statements immaterial as a matter of law. Rather, as we have proclaimed, "[m]ateriality is not judged in the abstract, but in light of the surrounding circumstances." The appropriate inquiry is whether, under all the circumstances, the omitted fact or the prediction without a reasonable basis "is one [that] a reasonable investor would consider significant in [making] the decision to invest, such that it alters the total mix of information available about the proposed investment." Inclusion of cautionary language—along with disclosure of any firm-specific adverse facts or assumptions—is, of course, relevant to the materiality inquiry, for such inclusion or disclosure is part of the "total mix of information." Nevertheless, cautionary language as such is not per se dispositive of this inquiry.[7]

A different type of skepticism was articulated by the Sixth Circuit. Modifying Sinay v. Lamson & Sessions Co.,[8] an earlier bespeaks caution case, which had held categorically that a claim is insufficient as a matter of law if optimistic opinions are coupled with cautionary statements, the Sixth Circuit in Mayer v. Mylod,[9] relied on the Supreme Court decision in Virginia Bankshares. Virginia Bankshares had stated: "But not every mixture with the true will neutralize the deceptive. If it would take a financial analyst to spot the tension between the one and the other, whatever is misleading will remain materially so, and liability should follow."[10] Accordingly the Sixth Circuit concluded: "Virginia Bankshares contemplates a weighing of the true with the untrue statements in an announcement for liability to result."[11]

In Parnes v. Gateway 2000, Inc.,[12] the Eighth Circuit followed the Third Circuit and added: "The cautionary language must 'relate directly to that by which plaintiffs claim to have been misled.'"

---

4. *See* Harden v. Raffensperger, Hughes & Co., Inc., 65 F.3d 1392, 1406 (7th Cir.1995) (the bespeaks caution doctrine, as a matter of law, does not address the materiality of "hard facts").

5. Pommer v. Medtest Corp., 961 F.2d 620, 624–625 (7th Cir.1992).

6. 20 F.3d 160 (5th Cir.1994).

7. Id. at 167–168.

8. 948 F.2d 1037, 1040 (6th Cir.1991).

9. 988 F.2d 635 (6th Cir.1993).

10. 501 U.S. at 1097

11. 988 F.2d at 639.

12. 122 F.3d 539, 548 (8th Cir.1997).

See also NationsMart Corp. Sec. Litig., 130 F.3d 309, 317 (8th Cir.1997), *cert. denied*, 524 U.S. 927 (1998):

> Many of the warnings of short-term risks to investors, however, were generic and nonspecific. The complaint alleges that the defendants did not adequately warn investors of the potential risks faced by NationsMart between the time of the offering and October 1994, when

In 1997 the Tenth Circuit adopted the bespeaks caution doctrine, after citing cases from eight earlier Circuits that had adopted the doctrine.[13]

The Eleventh Circuit adopted also the bespeaks caution doctrine in Saltzberg v. TM Sterling/Austin Assoc.[14] This brief *per curiam* decision explicitly followed the *Trump* decision.

Other circuits had not adopted the bespeaks caution doctrine, but have employed different analytical approaches. The Seventh and District of Columbia Circuits focused on whether a forward looking statement had a reasonable basis when made.[15]

The Fourth Circuit, in contrast,

> had taken a more extreme position, determining that, even without cautionary language, some predictions are not material. For example, referring to "soft," "puffing" statements, upon which no reasonable investor would rely, the Court of Appeals for the Fourth Circuit stated that, "Projections of future performance not worded as guarantees are generally not actionable under the federal securities laws."[16]

The most hotly contested provision in The 1995 Private Securities Reform Act was the new safe harbor for forward looking statements ultimately enacted in identical language in § 21E of the Securities Exchange Act and § 27A of the Securities Act.

This provision, like much of the Act, is reticulate. The Section only applies to a forward looking statement made by

(1) an issuer that, at that time that the statement is made, is subject to the reporting requirements of § 13(a) or § 15(d);

(2) a person acting on behalf of such issuer;

(3) an outside reviewer retained by such issuer making a statement on behalf of such issuer; or

(4) an underwriter, with respect to information provided by such issuer or information derived from information provided by the issuer.[17]

---

the Prospectus admitted that the company would have to find new sources of revenue. Many statements in the Risk Factors section—such as the warning that "[t]here can be no assurance that any of the Company's Centers or that the Company as a whole will generate income from operations or provide cash from operating activities in the future"— do not provide the sort of detail that would "bespeak caution" to a potential investor.

13. Grossman v. Novell, Inc., 120 F.3d 1112 (10th Cir.1997).

14. 45 F.3d 399 (11th Cir.1995).

15. Wielgos v. Commonwealth Edison Co., 892 F.2d 509, 513–514 (7th Cir.1989); Kowal v. MCI Communications Corp., 16 F.3d 1271, 1277 (D.C.Cir.1994). Cf. Searls v. Glasser, 64 F.3d 1061, 1066 (7th Cir.1995)

(holding that the phrase "recession-resistant" is simply too vague to constitute a material statement of fact). Presumably a forward looking statement that ignored negative prospective material information would not have a reasonable basis.

16. Sec. Act Rel. 7101, 57 SEC Dock. 1999, 2007 (1994), *quoting* Raab v. General Physics Corp., 4 F.3d 286, 290 (4th Cir.1993). This Release added, 57 SEC Dock. at 2007 n. 61:

> In Malone v. Microdyne Corp., 26 F.3d 471, 479–480 (4th Cir.1994), the Court of Appeals relied on Raab in finding that a forward-looking statement was not actionable because the "statement obviously did not constitute a guarantee and was certainly not specific enough to perpetrate a fraud on the market."

17. Sec. Exch. Act § 21E(a).

The safe harbor contained in Securities Act § 27A(c) and Securities Exchange Act § 21E(c) involves three different types of safe harbors:

(1) Securities Act § 27(c)(1)(A) and Securities Exchange Act § 21E(c)(1)(A) may immunize a false forward looking statement if the court concludes it was accompanied "by meaningful cautionary statements." How significant a change this will make in the bespeaks caution doctrine is an open question. If courts narrowly construe the term "meaningful cautionary statement" language when confronted with false statements, much mischief can be avoided.

(2) The defendant is given a second safe harbor in Securities Act § 27A(c)(1)(B) and Securities Exchange Act § 21E(c)(1)(B) if he or she cannot offer and prove sufficient meaningful cautionary statements because the plaintiff is still required to prove the higher culpability standard of "actual knowledge" rather than the lower recklessness or negligence standard available today under the Securities Exchange Act § 10(b) and Rule 14a–9.[18]

(3) There is then a novel safe harbor for oral forward looking statements when appropriate reference is made to a readily available written document. It is unclear whether this will make any meaningful difference given the earlier judicial justifiable reliance doctrine.[19]

The safe harbors are then buttressed by provisions that allow the Commission to further exempt forward looking statements,[20] and that require the court to stay discovery during any motion for summary judgment concerning a covered forward looking statement.[21]

The term forward looking statement is defined in Securities Act § 27A(I) and Securities Exchange Act § 21E(I) in terms similar to Securities Act Rule 175 and Securities Exchange Act Rule 3b–6. The new safe harbors, however, add:[22]

(E) any report issued by an outside reviewer retained by an issuer, to the extent that the report assesses a forward-looking statement made by the issuer; or

(F) a statement containing a projection or estimate of such other items as may be specified by rule or regulation of the Commission.

The Managers Statement emphasized the significance of the bespeaks caution cases when it stated: "As part of the analysis of what constitutes a meaningful cautionary statement, courts should consider the factors identified in the statements. 'Important' factors means the stated factors identified in the cautionary statement must be relevant to the projection and must be of a nature that the factor or factors could actually affect whether the forward-looking statement is realized."[23]

---

18. We will discuss these culpability standards later in this chapter.

19. Sec. Act § 27A(c)(2); Sec. Ex. Act § 21E(c)(2).

20. *See* Sec. Act § 27A(c)(4); Sec. Ex. Act § 21E(c)(4); *see also* Sec. Act §§ 27A(g)–(h); Sec.Ex. Act §§ 21E(g)–(h).

21. Sec. Act § 27A(f); Sec. Ex. Act § 21E(f).

22. Sec. Act §§ 27A(i)(E)–(F) and Sec. Ex. Act §§ 21E(i)(E)–(F).

23. 1995–1996 Fed. Sec. L. Rep. (CCH) ¶ 85,710 at 87,209.

Harris v. Ivax Corp.

United States Court of Appeals, Eleventh Circuit, 1999.
182 F.3d 799

■ Before COX and HULL, CIRCUIT JUDGES, and COHILL, SENIOR DISTRICT JUDGE.

■ COX, CIRCUIT JUDGE:

This appeal invites application of the safe harbor for forward-looking statements added to the Securities Exchange Act of 1934 by the Private Securities Litigation Reform Act of 1995, Pub. L. 104–67, 109 Stat. 737 (1995) (PSLRA). We affirm the district court's dismissal of the complaint under Fed R. Civ. P. 12(b)(6).

According to the complaint—our only source of the facts—the defendant Ivax Corporation is a manufacturer of generic drugs, a highly volatile business. Ivax was profitable in 1995, but lost money in the second quarter of 1996. On August 2, 1996 Ivax issued a press release that, while acknowledging business problems, also showed some optimism. Ivax stock rose. On September 30, the last day of the quarter, Ivax announced in another press release that it anticipated a $43 million loss. On November 11, Ivax announced a $179 million loss for the third quarter, $104 million of which was a reduction in the carrying value of the goodwill ascribed to certain of Ivax's businesses. Neither of the earlier press releases had mentioned the possibility of this goodwill writedown based on third-quarter results. The price of Ivax stock plummeted.

Investors hoping to represent a class of purchasers of Ivax Corporation stock between August 2, 1996 and November 11, 1996 sued Ivax, its chairman and chief executive officer, and its chief financial officer. They claimed that the defendants had committed fraud under the securities Exchange Act § 10(b), 15 U.S.C. § 78j, and Securities and Exchange Commission Rule 10b–5, 17 C.F.R. § 210.10b–5, as well as common law negligent misrepresentation. There are two theories of liability: first, that Ivax's economic projections were fraudulent, and second, that Ivax's disclosure of factors affecting its projections misled by omitting the possibility of a goodwill writedown. The defendants moved to dismiss based on the safe-harbor provision and heightened pleading requirements added to the Securities and Exchange Act of 1934 by the PSLRA.

In a thoughtful opinion, the district court dismissed the complaint under Fed. R. Civ. P. 12(b)(6). * * *

The district court concluded that all of the statements alleged in the complaint to be fraudulent were forward-looking, and that the statements' "cautionary language" was "meaningful." *See Harris v. IVAX Corp.*, 998 F. Supp. 1449, 1453–54 (S.D.Fla.1998). The court thus concluded Ivax's statements were anchored within the statutory safe harbor, and that the cautionary language shielded Ivax from liability. * * *

All of the statements that the plaintiffs claim to be false or misleading are forward-looking. They were accompanied, moreover, by "meaningful cautionary language." Because we reach this conclusion, we need not in this case enter the thicket of the PLSRA's new pleading requirements for scienter; if a statement is accompanied by "meaningful cautionary language," the defendants' state of mind is irrelevant. * * *

Settling on a level of specificity for the forward-looking analysis is the first problem here. In the argument section of their brief, the plaintiffs have specifically mentioned only one of the fraudulent statements alleged in the complaint. From that, we gather that they urge us to treat the August 2 and September 30 press releases with a broad brush, in effect concluding that the releases as a whole were either forward-looking or not. Such an approach would not, however, comport with the Act's demand of articulate pleading: The PLSRA closes the universe of supposedly false statements under scrutiny to those "specified" in the complaint. PLSRA § 101(b), *codified at* 15 U.S.C. § 78u–4(b)(1). While the legislative history does not explain this particular pleading requirement, it implies piecemeal examination of the statements found in a company communication.

The complaint quotes, with added emphasis apparently meant to indicate the misleading statements, seven passages from these two press releases. Two of those passages are, however, outside the sphere of the plaintiffs' allegations of falsehood. First, there is a statement in the August 2, 1996 press release that "we have taken a hard look at our generic drug business," and that "[w]e have instituted actions to enhance the profitability of our U.S. generics business." (r.2–36 ¶ 37.) (The press release goes on to describe restructuring meant to increase efficiency.) Second, there is a statement in the September 30, 1996 press release that "we have scrutinized our generic drug business" and that "we created a task force ... to rapidly identify and implement strategies to reduce costs and improve efficiencies in our U.S. generic drug business." (*Id.* ¶ 49.) As far as we can tell from the complaint, the plaintiffs believe it to be true that Ivax management reevaluated its generic drug business, and the plaintiffs do not allege that Ivax failed in fact to plan to restructure the business to improve efficiency. The plaintiff's core theories appear rather to be two: first, that Ivax's hopeful outlooks concealed an intent to write down goodwill by $104 million in the third quarter of 1996, and second, that a limited list of clouds on the horizon deliberately omitted the risk of a goodwill writedown. In judging whether the statements on which alleged liability rests are forward-looking, our focus is accordingly on the remaining four excerpts from the press releases, discussed below, that contain those outlooks and that list.

1. *Improving reorders.*

The August 2, 1996 press release contained the following sentence: "Reorders are expected to improve as customer inventories are depleted." (r.2–36 ¶ 35.) This statement falls squarely in the middle of one of the categories of "forward-looking statements," as Congress has defined them: it is "a statement of the assumptions underlying" "a statement of future economic performance." 15 U.S.C. § 78u–5(i)(1)(D), (C). The text that follows in the press release (which we discuss below) is a general outlook for the third quarter. The arrangement of the text makes clear that an expected increase in reorders was one of the bases of the optimism. This was therefore a forward-looking statement within the statutory safe harbor.

2. *The "unique challenges."*

The August 2, 1996 press release also announced optimistically that "the challenges unique to this period in our history are now behind us." (r.2–36 ¶ 36.) Taken in context, this statement is forward-looking. The two paragraphs of the press release preceding this statement describe two problems that contributed to a loss in the second quarter: excessive customer inventories, which reduced new orders, and a technical default in a revolving credit facility. Both problems, the statement said, were being resolved; inventories were becoming depleted, and the bank syndicate was expected to waive the default. Thus, the chairman and CEO announced that things were looking up.

"Forward-looking statement[s]" include "statements of future economic performance." 15 U.S.C. § 78u–5(*i*)(1)(c). The chairman and CEO's hopeful conclusion that conditions are better because of two anticipated improvements in business conditions is a prediction of economic performance, however couched. The plaintiffs' purely grammatical argument to the contrary—that a present-tense statement cannot predict the future—is unpersuasive; a statement about the state of a company whose truth or falsity is discernible only after it is made necessarily refers only to future performance. Whether the worst of Ivax's challenges were behind it was a matter verifiable only after the chairman so declared. This statement was thus forward-looking and in the safe harbor.

3. Intact strategies.

The August 2, 1996 press release continued with another hopeful outlook from Ivax's chairman and CEO, Phillip Frost, that "our fundamental business and its underlying strategies remain intact.... Only a limited number of companies are positioned to meaningfully participate in this rapidly growing market and, among them, IVAX is certainly very well positioned." (r.2–36 ¶ 38.) Like the previous statement, this one is a prediction "of future economic performance." 15 U.S.C. § 78u–5(*i*)(1)(c). While it is true that the *state* of Ivax's "fundamental business" and "underlying strategies" is a question of present condition, whether they are intact is a fact only verifiable by seeing how they hold up in the future. Likewise, whether Ivax is "well positioned" is a statement whose truth can only be known after seeing how Ivax's future plays out. That puts this statement in the safe harbor, as well.

4. The laundry list.

The September 30, 1996 press release, which predicted third quarter results, contained a list of factors "relating to [Ivax's] generic drug business [that] will influence [Ivax's] third quarter results." (r.2–36 ¶ 47.) Those five factors included high customer inventory levels and low orders; declining prices; "shelf stock adjustments" for existing customers; higher reserves for returns; and the bankruptcy of a major customer who owed Ivax $16 million. The list is a mixed bag, with some sentences that are forward-looking and some that are not. The statement's choice of language suggests that three of the factors had already been observed: "customer re-orders remain depressed"; "prices have continued to decline"; and "a wholesaler customer who owed us approximately $16 million filed a Chapter 11 bankruptcy petition." (*Id.*) Observed facts of this kind are not "assumptions," and they are not any kind of prediction, either, that would put them within the definition of a forward-looking statement. These sentences are not, therefore, forward-looking. Two other factors, however, are worded as assumptions about future events: "we expect reserves for returns and inventory writeoffs to be well above typical quarters" and "lower prices ... will increase shelf stock adjustments." (*Id.*) As "assumptions underlying" the predictions elsewhere in the press release, these sentences are forward-looking. 15 U.S.C. § 78u–5(*i*)(1)(D).

The mixed nature of this statement raises the question whether the safe harbor benefits the entire statement or only parts of it. Of course, if any of the individual sentences describing known facts (such as the customer's bankruptcy) were allegedly false, we could easily conclude that that smaller, non-forward-looking statement falls outside the safe harbor. But the allegation here is that the list *as a whole* misleads anyone reading it for an explanation of Ivax's projections, because the list omits the expectation of a goodwill write-down. If the allegation is that the whole list is misleading, then it makes no sense to slice the list into separate sentences. Rather, the list becomes a "statement" in the statutory sense, and a basis of liability, as a unit. It must therefore be either forward-looking or not forward-looking in its entirety. The next issue is what the character of the list is as a whole—forward-looking or not.

We conclude that the entire list is due forward-looking treatment. To begin with, there is no question under the statute that a material and misleading omission can fall within the forward-looking safe harbor. *See* 15 U.S.C. § 78u–15(c)(1) ("[I]n any private action arising under this chapter that is based on an untrue statement of material fact or *omission of a material fact necessary to make the statement not misleading*, a person referred to in subsection (a) of this section shall not be liable....") (emphasis added). And while the statute does not tell us exactly what to do with a mixed statement, extrinsic sources of congressional intent point strongly toward treating the entire list as forward-looking. Congress enacted the safe-harbor provision in order to loosen the "muzzling effect" of potential liability for forward-looking statements, which often kept investors in the dark about what management foresaw for the company. *See* H.R. Conf. Rep. 104–369, at 42 (1995), *reprinted in* 1995 U.S.C.C.A.N. 730, 741. Forward-looking conclusions often rest both on historical observations and assumptions about future events. Thus, were we to banish from the safe harbor lists that contain both factual and forward-looking factors, we would inhibit corporate officers from fully explaining their outlooks. Indeed, liability-conscious officers would be relegated to citing only the factors that could individually be called forward-looking. That would hamper the communication that Congress sought to foster.

Treating mixed lists as forward-looking may open a loophole for misleading omissions, but there are two circumstances that should put investors on guard, anyway. First, a list or explanation will only qualify for this treatment if it contains assumptions underlying a forward-looking statement. Investors should know, under the current statutory scheme, that relying on assumptions is dangerous; there will often be no legal recourse even if the assumption is false. Second, a defendant can fully benefit from the safe harbor's shelter only when it has disclosed risk factors in a warning accompanying the forward-looking statement. This disclosure as well should warn investors against blind reliance on mixed lists.

For these reasons, we hold that when the factors underlying a projection or economic forecast include both assumptions and statements of known fact, and a plaintiff alleges that a material factor is missing, the entire list of factors is treated as a forward-looking statement. This list is therefore in the safe harbor.

C. *Cautionary Language*

The district court was correct that adequate cautionary language accompanies the forward-looking statements here. The italicized warning that Ivax appended to both press releases is detailed and informative; it tells the reader in detail what kind of misfortunes could befall the company and what the effect could be. * * * We can reject out of hand, therefore, the plaintiffs' arguments that the cautionary statements are "mere boilerplate." That leaves, however, another question: the plaintiffs here allege fraud by material omission. Neither of the statements mentions the possibility of a large goodwill write-down. To be "meaningful," 15 U.S.C. § 78u–5(c)(I)(A)(i), must the cautionary language explicitly mention *the* factor that ultimately belies a forward-looking statement?

We think not. The statute requires the warning only to mention "important factors that could cause actual results to differ materially from those in the forward-looking statement." 15 U.S.C. § 78u–5(c)(1)(A)(i). It does not require a listing of *all* factors. The conference report, moreover, that accompanied the PSLRA specified that "failure to include the particular factor that ultimately causes the forward-looking statement not to come true with not mean that the statement is not protected by the safe harbor." H.R. Conf. Rep. 104–369, at 44 (1995), *reprinted at* 1995 U.S.C.C.A.N. 730, 743. In short, when an investor has been warned of risks of a significance similar to that actually realized, she is sufficiently on notice of the danger of the investment to make an intelligent decision about it according to her own preferences for risk and reward. This statement satisfies Ivax's burden to warn under the statute, and it excuses Ivax from liability. * * *

For the foregoing reasons, we affirm the district court's dismissal of the complaint.

AFFIRMED.

(d) Reasons, Opinions and Beliefs

Virginia Bankshares, Inc. v. Sandberg

Supreme Court of the United States, 1991.
501 U.S. 1083, 111 S.Ct. 2749, 115 L.Ed.2d 929.

■ Justice Souter delivered the opinion of the Court.

Section 14(a) of the Securities Exchange Act of 1934 authorizes the Securities and Exchange Commission to adopt rules for the solicitation of proxies, and prohibits their violation. In J.I. Case Co. v. Borak, 377 U.S. 426 (1964), we first recognized an implied private right of action for the breach of § 14(a), as implemented by SEC Rule 14a–9, which prohibits the solicitation of proxies by means of materially false or misleading statements.

The questions before us are whether a statement couched in conclusory or qualitative terms purporting to explain directors' reasons for recommending certain corporate action can be materially misleading within the meaning of Rule 14a–9, and whether causation of damages compensable under § 14(a) can be shown by a member of a class of minority shareholders whose votes are not required by law or corporate by-law to authorize the corporate action subject to the proxy solicitation. We hold that knowingly false statements of reasons may be actionable even though conclusory in form, but that respondents have failed to demonstrate the equitable basis required to extend the § 14(a) private action to such shareholders when any indication of congressional intent to do so is lacking.

I

In December 1986, First American Bankshares, Inc., (FABI), a bank holding company, began a "freeze-out" merger, in which the First American

Bank of Virginia (Bank) eventually merged into Virginia Bankshares, Inc., (VBI), a wholly owned subsidiary of FABI. VBI owned 85% of the Bank's shares, the remaining 15% being in the hands of some 2,000 minority shareholders. FABI hired the investment banking firm of Keefe, Bruyette & Woods (KBW) to give an opinion on the appropriate price for shares of the minority holders, who would lose their interests in the Bank as a result of the merger. Based on market quotations and unverified information from FABI, KBW gave the Bank's executive committee an opinion that $42 a share would be a fair price for the minority stock. The executive committee approved the merger proposal at that price, and the full board followed suit.

* * *

Although Virginia law required only that such a merger proposal be submitted to a vote at a shareholders' meeting, and that the meeting be preceded by circulation of a statement of information to the shareholders, the directors nevertheless solicited proxies for voting on the proposal at the annual meeting set for April 21, 1987.[3] In their solicitation, the directors urged the proposal's adoption and stated they had approved the plan because of its opportunity for the minority shareholders to achieve a "high" value, which they elsewhere described as a "fair" price, for their stock.

Although most minority shareholders gave the proxies requested, respondent Sandberg did not, and after approval of the merger she sought damages in the United States District Court for the Eastern District of Virginia from VBI, FABI, and the directors of the Bank. She pleaded two counts, one for soliciting proxies in violation of § 14(a) and Rule 14a–9, and the other for breaching fiduciary duties owed to the minority shareholders under state law. Under the first count, Sandberg alleged, among other things, that the directors had not believed that the price offered was high or that the terms of the merger were fair, but had recommended the merger only because they believed they had no alternative if they wished to remain on the board. At trial, Sandberg invoked language from this Court's opinion in Mills v. Electric Auto–Lite Co., 396 U.S. 375, 385 (1970), to obtain an instruction that the jury could find for her without a showing of her own reliance on the alleged misstatements, so long as they were material and the proxy solicitation was an "essential link" in the merger process.

The jury's verdicts were for Sandberg on both counts, after finding violations of Rule 14a–9 by all defendants and a breach of fiduciary duties by the Bank's directors. The jury awarded Sandberg $18 a share, having found that she would have received $60 if her stock had been valued adequately.

* * *

On appeal, the United States Court of Appeals for the Fourth Circuit affirmed the judgments, holding that certain statements in the proxy solicitation were materially misleading for purposes of the Rule, and that respondents could maintain their action even though their votes had not been needed to effectuate the merger. 891 F.2d 1112 (1989). We granted certiorari because of the importance of the issues presented. 495 U.S. 903 (1990).

---

3. Had the directors chosen to issue a statement instead of a proxy solicitation, they would have been subject to an SEC antifraud provision analogous to Rule 14a–9. See 17 CFR 240.14c–6 (1990). See also 15 U.S.C. § 78n(c).

II

The Court of Appeals affirmed petitioners' liability for two statements found to have been materially misleading in violation of § 14(a) of the Act, one of which was that "The Plan of Merger has been approved by the Board of Directors because it provides an opportunity for the Bank's public shareholders to achieve a high value for their shares." App. to Pet. for Cert. 53a. Petitioners argue that statements of opinion or belief incorporating indefinite and unverifiable expressions cannot be actionable as misstatements of material fact within the meaning of Rule 14a–9, and that such a declaration of opinion or belief should never be actionable when placed in a proxy solicitation incorporating statements of fact sufficient to enable readers to draw their own, independent conclusions.

A

We consider first the actionability *per se* of statements of reasons, opinion or belief. Because such a statement by definition purports to express what is consciously on the speaker's mind, we interpret the jury verdict as finding that the directors' statements of belief and opinion were made with knowledge that the directors did not hold the beliefs or opinions expressed, and we confine our discussion to statements so made.[5] That such statements may be materially significant raises no serious question. The meaning of the materiality requirement for liability under § 14(a) was discussed at some length in TSC Industries, Inc. v. Northway, Inc., 426 U.S. 438 (1976), where we held a fact to be material "if there is a substantial likelihood that a reasonable shareholder would consider it important in deciding how to vote." Id., at 449. We think there is no room to deny that a statement of belief by corporate directors about a recommended course of action, or an explanation of their reasons for recommending it, can take on just that importance. Shareholders know that directors usually have knowledge and expertness far exceeding the normal investor's resources, and the directors' perceived superiority is magnified even further by the common knowledge that state law customarily obliges them to exercise their judgment in the shareholders' interest. Cf. Day v. Avery, 179 U.S.App.D.C. 63, 71, 548 F.2d 1018, 1026 (1976) (action for misrepresentation). Naturally, then, the share owner faced with a proxy request will think it important to know the directors' beliefs about the course they recommend, and their specific reasons for urging the stockholders to embrace it.

B

I

But, assuming materiality, the question remains whether statements of reasons, opinions, or beliefs are statements "with respect to * * * material fact[s]" so as to fall within the strictures of the Rule. Petitioners argue that we would invite wasteful litigation of amorphous issues outside the readily provable realm of fact if we were to recognize liability here on proof that the directors did not recommend the merger for the stated reason and they * * *

---

5. In TSC Industries, Inc. v. Northway, Inc., 426 U.S. 438, 444, n. 7 (1976), we reserved the question whether scienter was necessary for liability generally under § 14(a). We reserve it still.

[urge] us to recognize sound policy grounds for placing such statements outside the scope of the Rule.

* * *

Attacks on the truth of directors' statements of reasons or belief, however, need carry no such threats. * * * Reasons for directors' recommendations or statements of belief are, in contrast, characteristically matters of corporate record subject to documentation, to be supported or attacked by evidence of historical fact outside a plaintiff's control. Such evidence would include not only corporate minutes and other statements of the directors themselves, but circumstantial evidence bearing on the facts that would reasonably underlie the reasons claimed and the history of any statement that those reasons are the basis for a recommendation or other action, a point that becomes especially clear when the reasons or beliefs go to valuations in dollars and cents.

It is no answer to argue, as petitioners do, that the quoted statement on which liability was predicated did not express a reason in dollars and cents, but focused instead on the "indefinite and unverifiable" term, "high," value, much like the similar claim that the merger's terms were "fair" to shareholders. The objection ignores the fact that such conclusory terms in a commercial context are reasonably understood to rest on a factual basis that justifies them as accurate, the absence of which renders them misleading. * * * In this case, whether $42 was "high," and the proposal "fair" to the minority shareholders depended on whether provable facts about the Bank's assets, and about actual and potential levels of operation, substantiated a value that was above, below, or more or less at the $42 figure, when assessed in accordance with recognized methods of valuation.

Respondents adduced evidence for just such facts in proving that the statement was misleading about its subject matter and a false expression of the directors' reasons. Whereas the proxy statement described the $42 price as offering a premium above both book value and market price, the evidence indicated that a calculation of the book figure based on the appreciated value of the Bank's real estate holdings eliminated any such premium. The evidence on the significance of market price showed that KBW had conceded that the market was closed, thin and dominated by FABI, facts omitted from the statement. There was, indeed, evidence of a "going concern" value for the Bank in excess of $60 per share of common stock, another fact never disclosed. However conclusory the directors' statement may have been, then, it was open to attack by garden-variety evidence, subject neither to a plaintiff's control nor ready manufacture, and there was no undue risk of open-ended liability or uncontrollable litigation in allowing respondents the opportunity for recovery on the allegation that it was misleading to call $42 "high."

This analysis comports with the holding that marked our nearest prior approach to the issue faced here, in TSC Industries, 426 U.S., at 454–55. There, to be sure, we reversed summary judgment for a Borak plaintiff who had sued on a description of proposed compensation for minority shareholders as offering a "substantial premium over current market values." But we held only that on the case's undisputed facts the conclusory adjective "substantial" was not materially misleading as a necessary matter of law, and our remand for trial assumed that such a description could be both materially misleading within the meaning of Rule 14a–9 and actionable under § 14(a). See TSC Industries, *supra*, at 458–460, 463–464.

2

Under § 14(a), then, a plaintiff is permitted to prove a specific statement of reason knowingly false or misleadingly incomplete, even when stated in conclusory terms. In reaching this conclusion we have considered statements of reasons of the sort exemplified here, which misstate the speaker's reasons and also mislead about the stated subject matter (e.g., the value of the shares). A statement of belief may be open to objection only in the former respect, however, solely as a misstatement of the psychological fact of the speaker's belief in what he says. In this case, for example, the Court of Appeals alluded to just such limited falsity in observing that "the jury was certainly justified in believing that the directors did not believe a merger at $42 per share was in the minority stockholders' interest but, rather, that they voted as they did for other reasons, e.g., retaining their seats on the board." 891 F.2d, at 1121.

The question arises, then, whether disbelief, or undisclosed belief or motivation, standing alone, should be a sufficient basis to sustain an action under § 14(a), absent proof by the sort of objective evidence described above that the statement also expressly or impliedly asserted something false or misleading about its subject matter. We think that proof of mere disbelief or belief undisclosed should not suffice for liability under § 14(a), and if nothing more had been required or proven in this case we would reverse for that reason.

On the one hand, it would be rare to find a case with evidence solely of disbelief or undisclosed motivation without further proof that the statement was defective as to its subject matter. While we certainly would not hold a director's naked admission of disbelief incompetent evidence of a proxy statement's false or misleading character, such an unusual admission will not very often stand alone, and we do not substantially narrow the cause of action by requiring a plaintiff to demonstrate something false or misleading in what the statement expressly or impliedly declared about its subject.

On the other hand, to recognize liability on mere disbelief or undisclosed motive without any demonstration that the proxy statement was false or misleading about its subject would authorize § 14(a) litigation confined solely to what one skeptical court spoke of as the "impurities" of a director's "unclean heart." Stedman v. Storer, 308 F.Supp. 881, 887 (S.D.N.Y.1969) (dealing with § 10(b)). This, we think, would cross the line that *Blue Chip Stamps* sought to draw. While it is true that the liability, if recognized, would rest on an actual, not hypothetical, psychological fact, the temptation to rest an otherwise nonexistent § 14(a) action on psychological enquiry alone would threaten just the sort of strike suits and attrition by discovery that *Blue Chip Stamps* sought to discourage. We therefore hold disbelief or undisclosed motivation, standing alone, insufficient to satisfy the element of fact that must be established under § 14(a).

C

Petitioners' fall-back position assumes the same relationship between a conclusory judgment and its underlying facts that we described in Part II–B–1, *supra*. Thus, citing Radol v. Thomas, 534 F. Supp. 1302, 1315, 1316 (S.D.Ohio 1982), petitioners argue that even if conclusory statements of reason or belief can be actionable under § 14(a), we should confine liability to instances where the proxy material fails to disclose the offending statement's factual basis. There would be no justification for holding the shareholders entitled to judicial relief, that is, when they were given evidence that a stated reason for a proxy recommendation was misleading, and an opportunity to draw that conclusion themselves.

The answer to this argument rests on the difference between a merely misleading statement and one that is materially so. While a misleading statement will not always lose its deceptive edge simply by joinder with others that are true, the true statements may discredit the other one so obviously that the risk of real deception drops to nil. Since liability under § 14(a) must rest not only on deceptiveness but materiality as well (*i.e.,* it has to be significant enough to be important to a reasonable investor deciding how to vote, see *TSC Industries,* 426 U.S., at 449, 96 S.Ct., at 2132), petitioners are on perfectly firm ground insofar as they argue that publishing accurate facts in a proxy statement can render a misleading proposition too unimportant to ground liability.

But not every mixture with the true will neutralize the deceptive. If it would take a financial analyst to spot the tension between the one and the other, whatever is misleading will remain materially so, and liability should follow. Gerstle v. Gamble–Skogmo, Inc., 478 F.2d 1281, 1297 (C.A.2 1973) ("[I]t is not sufficient that overtones might have been picked up by the sensitive antennae of investment analysts"). Cf. Milkovich v. Lorain Journal Co., 497 U.S. 1, 110 S.Ct. 2695, 2708, 111 L.Ed.2d 1 (1990) (a defamatory assessment of facts can be actionable even if the facts underlying the assessment are accurately presented). The point of a proxy statement, after all, should be to inform, not to challenge the reader's critical wits. Only when the inconsistency would exhaust the misleading conclusion's capacity to influence the reasonable shareholder would a § 14(a) action fail on the element of materiality.

Suffice it to say that the evidence invoked by petitioners in the instant case fell short of compelling the jury to find the facial materiality of the misleading statement neutralized. The directors claim, for example, to have made an explanatory disclosure of further reasons for their recommendation when they said they would keep their seats following the merger, but they failed to mention what at least one of them admitted in testimony, that they would have had no expectation of doing so without supporting the proposal, App. at 281–82. And although the proxy statement did speak factually about the merger price in describing it as higher than share prices in recent sales, it failed even to mention the closed market dominated by FABI. None of these disclosures that the directors point to was, then, anything more than a half-truth, and the record shows that another fact statement they invoke was arguably even worse. The claim that the merger price exceeded book value was controverted, as we have seen already, by evidence of a higher book value than the directors conceded, reflecting appreciation in the Bank's real estate portfolio. Finally, the solicitation omitted any mention of the Bank's value as a going concern at more than $60 a share, as against the merger price of $42. There was, in sum, no more of a compelling case for the statement's immateriality than for its accuracy. * * *

■ JUSTICE SCALIA, concurring in part and concurring in the judgment.

I

As I understand the Court's opinion, the statement "In the opinion of the Directors, this is a high value for the shares" would produce liability if in fact it was not a high value and the Directors knew that. It would not produce liability if in fact it was not a high value but the Directors honestly believed otherwise.

The statement "The Directors voted to accept the proposal because they believe it offers a high value" would not produce liability if in fact the Directors' genuine motive was quite different—except that it would produce liability if the proposal in fact did not offer a high value and the Directors knew that.

I agree with all of this. However, not every sentence that has the word "opinion" in it, or that refers to motivation for Directors' actions, leads us into this psychic thicket. Sometimes such a sentence actually represents facts as facts rather than opinions—and in that event no more need be done than apply the normal rules for § 14(a) liability. I think that is the situation here. In my view, the statement at issue in this case is most fairly read as affirming separately both the fact of the Directors' opinion and the accuracy of the facts upon which the opinion was assertedly based. It reads as follows:

"The Plan of Merger has been approved by the Board of Directors because it provides an opportunity for the Bank's public shareholders to achieve a high value for their shares." App. to Pet. for Cert. 53a.

Had it read "because in their estimation it provides an opportunity, etc." it would have set forth nothing but an opinion. As written, however, it asserts both that the Board of Directors acted for a particular reason and that that reason is correct. This interpretation is made clear by what immediately follows: "The price to be paid is about 30% higher than the [last traded price immediately before announcement of the proposal] * * *. [T]he $42 per share that will be paid to public holders of the common stock represents a premium of approximately 26% over the book value * * *. [T]he bank earned $24,767,000 in the year ended December 31, 1986 * * *." Id., at 53a–54a. These are all facts that support—and that are obviously introduced for the purpose of supporting—the factual truth of the "because" clause, i.e., that the proposal gives shareholders a "high value."

If the present case were to proceed, therefore, I think the normal § 14(a) principles governing misrepresentation of fact would apply. * * *

PUFFING

After *Virginia Bankshares* a number of cases have taken the position that "soft" "puffing" statements such as one characterizing a marketplace for a particular group of products "with an expected annual growth rate of 10% to 30% over the next several years" generally lack materiality "because the market price of a share is not inflated by vague statements predicting growth."[1] In San Leandro Emergency Medical Group Profit Sharing Plan v. Philip Morris Company, Inc.,[2] for example, the court concluded:

> In any event, even the most positive statements by Philip Morris representatives at that time consisted of relatively subdued general comments, such as the company "*should* deliver income growth consistent with its historically superior performance" (emphasis added) and "we are optimistic about 1993." These statements "lack the sort of definite positive projections that

1. Raab v. General Physics Corp., 4 F.3d 286, 289 (4th Cir.1993); Longman v. Food Lion, Inc., 197 F.3d 675, 685 (4th Cir. 1999), *cert. denied*, 529 U.S. 1067 (2000) ("[T]hese statements are the kind of puffery and generalizations that reasonable investors could not have relied upon when deciding whether to buy stock"). See generally Jennifer O'Hare, The Resurrection of the Dodo: The Unfortunate Re-emergence of the Puffery Defense in Private Securities Fraud Actions, 59 Ohio St. L.J. 1697 (1998).

2. 75 F.3d 801 (2d Cir.1996).

might require later correction." *Time Warner*, 9 F.3d at 267. As noted above, such puffery is not actionable.[3]

Compare Lasker v. New York State Electricity & Gas Corp.:[4]

By telling its investors that it would not "compromise its financial integrity," NYSEG was not representing that its actions would in no way impact the company's finances. Nor did it certify that the company would not suffer losses when it touted its "commitment to create earnings opportunities." Likewise, by proffering its conviction that these "business strategies [would] lead to continued prosperity," NYSEG was in no way insuring that dividend rates would remain constant, or that the stock price would not decline. These statements consist of precisely the type of "puffery" that this and other circuits have consistently held to be inactionable.[5]

On the other hand puffing is a somewhat bounded argument. As the Supreme Court wrote in *Virginia Bankshares*: "But not every mixture with the true will neutralize the deceptive. If it would take a financial analyst to spot the tension between the one and the other, whatever is misleading will remain materially so."

Virginia Bankshares suggested also that a statement of opinions, reasons, or beliefs was most likely to be material and actionable when it was accompanied by indicia of reliability. For example, in *Virginia Bankshares* the statements questioned were made by the board of directors in a proxy statement. It is less likely that statements that an offer was "high" or "fair" would have been actionable had they been made by a single director or officer to a news reporter or financial analyst, particularly if the statement appeared to be a personal opinion not based on an earlier internal or external valuation.

PROBLEM 14–3

Tel–Cel is a corporation comprised of local telephone companies and cellular phone systems. In 1999, the cellular phone business was hot, and the local telephone business cool, and Tel–Cel's board believed that the combination was unlovely to investors and that the firm's assets would be worth more if the company were sold.

Rather than just seek out a possible purchaser and negotiate privately, Tel–Cel decided to organize an auction at which bidders could bid on the whole company or on parts of it as they wished. The auction was intimated in a public announcement by Tel–Cel on January 23, 1999, that it had hired two prominent investment banks to "explore strategic alternatives to maximize shareholder value, including the possible sale of the company." On the day of the announcement, the price of Tel–Cel's shares rose from $37 to almost $48.

On March 5, GTE announced that it would not participate in the auction. Although Tel–Cel responded by bravely claiming that "[w]e believe that this [GTE's statement] has no impact on our process [and w]e continue to move along," a week later it met with its investment bankers in private to consider the viability of a "survivor entity" consisting of those assets of Tel–Cel that would not fetch an attractive price at the auction. The conclusion (not publicly announced) of the participants on the meeting was that any such entity would "very clearly bear the

---

3. Id. at 811.   **5.** Id. at 59.

4. 85 F.3d 55 (2d Cir.1996).

taint of a nonsaleable Tel–Cel property which has been aggressively (and publicly) marketed to 'the world.' "

On March 25, Pacific Telesis, one of the Baby Bells and a potential bidder for Tel–Cel's Nevada properties, a major asset, announced that it also wouldn't bid for them after all. Tel–Cel reacted with a public statement that "the bidding process continues to go very smoothly." By this time, several other large potential purchasers had expressed a lack of interest as well. The price of Tel–Cel's stock drifted lower than its peak on January 23, but it was still above $40.

April 16 was the deadline for the submission of bids. On April 13, Tel–Cel's chief executive officer announced publicly that there was "widespread interest almost down to every [Tel–Cel telecommunications] exchange."

The auction was held on April 16 as scheduled but it was a bust. Only seven bids were submitted, none for the whole company. Although Tel–Cel kept mum, it accepted none of the bids. Instead it approached Sprint hat in hand and quickly negotiated a sale of the entire company to Sprint at a price equivalent to $33.50 a share, which was $9 below the then current market price and roughly 10 percent below the market price before the auction was first intimated. As soon as the deal with Sprint was announced, on May 27, 1999, the value of Tel–Cel's shares plummeted, from $42.50 to $32.

1.   Did Tel–Cel make a material misrepresentation or omission in violation of Rule 10b–5?

2.   What effect on liability would there be if Tel–Cel had added to its January 23rd announcement: "Of course, we can not guarantee that any strategic alternative will succeed or will generate an offer in excess of current market price"?

4.   CULPABILITY

Adams v. Standard Knitting Mills

United States Court of Appeals, Sixth Circuit, 1980.
623 F.2d 422, *cert. denied*, 449 U.S. 1067 (1980).

■ Before: Weick, Engel, and Merritt, Circuit Judges.

■ Merritt, Circuit Judge, delivered the opinion of the Court in which Engel, Circuit Judge, joined. Weick, Circuit Judge, filed a separate dissenting opinion.

Merritt, Circuit Judge: In this securities fraud case, Peat, Marwick, Mitchell & Co., herein referred to as "Peat," a firm of certified public accountants, appeals from a judgment of the District Court in the amount of $3.4 million, plus pre-judgment interest, plus attorneys' fees of $1.2 million. The suit is a class action based upon causes of action implied under §§ 10(b) and 14(a) of the Securities Exchange Act of 1934 and SEC Rules 10b–5 and 14a–9. It is based on an allegedly false proxy solicitation issued in order to gain shareholder approval of a merger between two corporations, Chadbourn, Inc. and Standard Knitting Mills, Inc., herein referred to as "Chadbourn" and "Standard." The primary issue is whether Peat is liable for a negligent error—the failure to point out in the proxy statement sent to stockholders of the acquired corporation that certain restrictions on the payment of dividends by the acquiring corporation applied to preferred as well as common stock. We hold that in the context of this case Peat is not liable for such conduct and reverse the District Court on the issue of liability.

I. STATEMENT OF FACTS RESPECTING RESTRICTIONS ON PAYMENT OF DIVIDENDS

A. General Terms and Purpose of the Merger

In April 1970, Chadbourn, Inc., a relatively profitable North Carolina hosiery manufacturer listed on the New York Stock Exchange, acquired all of the common stock of Standard Knitting Mills, Inc., a smaller, publicly-held, Knoxville, Tennessee, textile manufacturer, whose stock traded from time to time, although infrequently, in the over-the-counter market. On April 22, 1970, Standard's stockholders at a special meeting agreed to exchange their stock for a package of Chadbourn securities. The meeting occurred after the stockholders received the proxy statement a month earlier from Standard transmitting information about the proposed merger and Chadbourn's financial condition. The proxy statement contained a recommendation by Standard's management favoring the merger as well as financial statements of Chadbourn prepared by its accountants, Peat Marwick.

Before the merger, Standard's stock traded at around $12.00 a share, although its book value was carried at approximately $21.00 a share, and Chadbourn's stock fluctuated between $8.00 and $14.00 a share. Standard's stockholders exchanged each share of Standard common for $\frac{1}{10}$ of a share of Chadbourn common, plus $1\frac{1}{2}$ shares of Chadbourn convertible, cumulative, preferred stock. The Chadbourn preferred was the main part of the package. According to the terms of the merger agreement, each share of Chadbourn preferred stock given in exchange was supposed to pay annual cash dividends of $.46$\frac{2}{3}$ a share, and Chadbourn was supposed to redeem 20% of these preferred shares each year at $11.00 a share, beginning in 1975. Each preferred share carried a conversion privilege allowing the preferred stockholder to convert a share of preferred into $\frac{6}{10}$ of a share of Chadbourn common. The general purpose of the package appears to have been to give each Standard shareholder a set of Chadbourn securities with approximately the same market value as their Standard shares but with more liquidity and higher dividends.

Approximately a year after the merger, Chadbourn's sales of hosiery plummeted unexpectedly, and it suffered a loss of $17 million. This loss wiped out its retained earnings and left it with a capital deficit of $7 million. Chadbourn now was unable to redeem or pay dividends on the preferred stock. In October 1972, the former Standard stockholders sued Chadbourn, Standard, their management, their lawyers and the appellant, Peat, which was, as previously stated, the accounting firm that prepared and certified Chadbourn's financial statements in the proxy materials. Plaintiffs entered into a settlement agreement with the defendants other than Peat, under which the former Standard shareholders were awarded control of Chadbourn, renamed "Stanwood Corporation." The District Court did not take into account the value of the settlement received by the plaintiffs in determining damages against Peat. Since we reverse the findings of the District Court on liability, we need not reach questions concerning the measure of damages and the award of attorneys' fees.

B. Restrictions on the Use of Retained Earnings Contained in the Chadbourn Loan Agreements

The first restriction on retained earnings is in a 5–year term loan agreement Chadbourn made with three banks in September, 1969. Chadbourn borrowed $6 million from the banks repayable in installments over the 5–year period. In order to protect the banks, the loan agreement contained a provision which prohibited Chadbourn and its subsidiaries in any year during the term of the loan from redeeming or paying dividends "on its *capital* shares of any class" in an amount in excess of $2 million, less the amount of the repayments on the loan, plus future earnings after the 1968–1969 fiscal year.[5] These restrictions would apply to dividend payments on Chadbourn preferred shares issued to Standard shareholders (amounting annually to approximately $450,000) and would apply as well to any distributions to redeem these shares.

The second debt agreement was a little less restrictive. The second contractual restriction on paying out retained earnings is in another debt agreement which Chadbourn also entered into in 1969. Chadbourn borrowed $12.5 million in exchange for an issue of convertible, subordinated debentures. The effect of these restrictions on dividends and distributions was similar, except that under this agreement Chadbourn was free to use its 1968–69 net earnings of $3.1 million, as well as future earnings, for the payment of dividends and stock redemptions.

The net effect of both sets of restrictions on dividends and redemptions, when taken together, was that Chadbourn would either have to continue to make money or refinance its indebtedness in order to meet fully its future dividend and redemption obligations on the preferred stock issued to Standard's shareholders. As is explained above, when the bottom dropped out of its hosiery market and its retained earnings a year after the merger, it could do neither.

C. The Description of the Restrictions on Retained Earnings in the Proxy Statement

Standard's proxy statement dated March 27, 1970, contained a 35-page description of the terms of the transaction and its tax-free nature, comparative earnings and stock prices of Standard and Chadbourn and a description of their history, business, managements and properties. The text was followed by 18 pages of financial statements of both companies, including the opinions of Peat with respect to the Chadbourn financial statements and of Ernst & Ernst with respect to the Standard financial statements.

The plan for the exchange of Standard stock for Chadbourn stock was set out at pages 4–8 of the text under the heading "SUMMARY OF PLAN." Pages 6–7 of this portion of the proxy statement accurately describe the two sets of restrictions as follows:

> Under the provisions of a term loan with three banks maturing October 1, 1974, Chadbourn cannot, without the consent of such banks, [1] declare any dividend or [2] make any distribution (other than common stock dividends), or [3] acquire any of its stock if, after such action, the aggregate of all dividends (other than stock dividends), other distributions to stockholders and all amounts paid for the acquisition of its stock plus

---

5. In August, 1967, at the beginning of Chadbourn's 1967–68 fiscal year, Chadbourn had retained earnings of $4.7 million. Its net earnings during the 1967–68 year were $1.6 million so that retained earnings in August, 1968, at the beginning of the fiscal year 1968–69 were approximately $6.3 million. Its net earnings during the 1968–69 fiscal year were $3.1 million so that retained earnings in August, 1969, at the beginning of the 1969–70 fiscal year were approximately $9.3 million. At this time stockholder equity, consisting of total capital of approximately $18.3 million plus these retained earnings, was $27.7 million.

the amounts of all payments made on the term loan, would exceed $2,000,000 plus Chadbourn's consolidated net earnings since August 2, 1969. The Indenture dated as of March 15, 1969 hereinabove referred to contains certain restrictions on the payment of dividends on capital stock, however, such are less restrictive than those contained in the term loan agreement.

Chadbourn's financial statements as of August 2, 1969, and Peat's opinion, dated October 21, 1969, were published in the back of the March 27, 1970, Standard proxy statement. The liabilities and stockholders' equity side of the balance sheet was shown on page F–5 of the proxy statement. This page sets out amounts for current installments of long-term debt, and the non-current portion of long-term debt, "stockholders' equity," which referred in turn to certain notes, including footnote 7.

Footnote 7, paragraphs (c) and (d) erroneously described the two sets of restrictions as follows:

> (c) As to the note payable to three banks, the Company has agreed to various restrictive provisions including those relating to maintenance of minimum stockholders' equity and working capital, the purchase, sale or encumbering of fixed assets, incurrence [sic] of indebtedness, the leasing of additional assets and the payment of dividends *on common stock* in excess of $2,000,000 plus earnings subsequent to August 2, 1969.

> (d) * * * Further, the indenture has certain restrictive covenants but they are less restrictive than those contained in the note agreement with the three banks. (Emphasis added.)

The word "common" in paragraph (c) referring to the loan agreement was wrong because the relevant provision of the loan agreement restricted the use of retained earnings for the payment of dividends on "*capital* stock of any class," not just "common." Thus the restriction on retained earnings would apply to all distributions to pay dividends or redeem the preferred shares issued to Standard stockholders should they approve the merger.

D. Facts Respecting Peat's Negligence

The facts demonstrate that Peat's omissions were the result of negligence but did not arise from an intent to deceive, or *scienter,* as found by the District Court.

Peat failed to disclose fully in the financial statement the restrictive effect of the loan agreement and indenture on Chadbourn preferred stock. After each entry relating to long-term capitalization, the financial statement directs the attention of the reader to explanatory note 7. Note 7 alone pertains to Chadbourn's long-term debt. Missing from the note is any reference to limitations that the debt agreements placed on Chadbourn preferred stock.

Only in notes 7(c) and 7(d) does Peat mention the restrictive provisions. Note 7(c), which discusses the loan agreement, reports only that "the Company has agreed to various restrictive provisions including * * * the payment of dividends on common stock in excess of $2 million plus earnings subsequent to August 2, 1969." Note 7(d) describes the indenture. It says that "the indenture has certain restrictive covenants, but they are less restrictive than those contained in the [loan] agreement." Thus, there is no indication in either note that the long-term debt restrictions affected the redemption and earnings of preferred stock.

From notes 7(c) and 7(d), a reader easily could derive the following mistaken impression: The loan agreement contains certain restrictions on the payment of dividends by Chadbourn. As note 7(c) explicitly says, the loan agreement restrictions relate to the payment of dividends "on common stock." The indenture contains limitations that are "less restrictive" than those created by the loan agreement. Since the limitations of the loan agreement apply only to common stock, the reader mistakenly could reason that the "less restrictive" indenture constraints appear to have no broader sweep. What note 7 conveys to the reader is the erroneous notion that neither the loan agreement nor the indenture restrictions apply to Chadbourn preferred stock.

The remainder of the proxy solicitation does not entirely correct the misunderstanding created by the financial statement notes. Peat argues that the textual language from the body of the proxy statement, quoted above in subsection C, adequately advised Standard shareholders that long-term debt agreements restricted certain aspects of Chadbourn's preferred stock. We conclude, however, that contrary to Peat's claim, the text is equivocal.

The text states that Chadbourn cannot "declare any dividends" or "make any distributions" under certain conditions specified by the loan agreement. These phrases are placed under the heading "The Chadbourn Common Stock." It would not be irrational to conclude from the location of these statements that the restrictions applied solely to the common stock of Chadbourn. This conclusion would be confirmed by note 7(c), which explicitly states that the loan agreement restricts the payment of dividends on common stock. Moreover, under the section of the text labeled "Provisions Relating to the $.46⅔ Preferred Stock," there is no indication that any debt restrictions exist, much less that they apply to the dividends or redemption of preferred stock.

Nor does the language in the text regarding indenture restrictions correct the misleading impression of note 7(d). The text reports that the indenture contains "certain restrictions on the payment of dividends on capital stock." Like note 7(d), the text fails to mention restrictions on the redemption of Chadbourn preferred stock. The language regarding dividend payment restrictions on capital stock is found in the "Chadbourn Common Stock" section. Its location casts doubt on the argument that "capital stock," the restrictions on which are mentioned in part by the text, was meant in this context to include preferred stock. Adding to the doubt is the absence of any information about the indenture from the "Preferred Stock" section of the text. At best the textual discussion of indenture restrictions is equivocal regarding their reach.

The finding of the District Court that Peat acted with scienter in making the omissions is nevertheless clearly erroneous. We find in the record nothing to indicate that a desire to deceive, defraud or manipulate motivated Peat to omit from the financial statement information regarding the applicability of long-term debt restrictions. Indeed, Stanwood Corporation, the successor to Chadbourn controlled by the former Standard shareholders, hired and retained as vice president and treasurer the Peat associate, Hugh Freeze, who the shareholders' counsel now claim sought to defraud them. If the shareholders and their representatives really believed Freeze intended to defraud them, it seems doubtful that they would have put him in charge of the financial affairs of the corporation.

At most the evidence supports a finding that Peat acted negligently in preparing the financial statements. Peat became aware that note 7 incorrectly described the debt limitation several weeks before the merger vote occurred.

The Standard proxy statement was mailed to its stockholders on March 27, 1970. Between March 23, 1970, and April 1, 1970, Chadbourn's outside counsel telephoned Freeze, the Peat manager in charge of the Chadbourn audit, and told him that a description of restrictions relating to Chadbourn's stock had been inserted in the forepart of the Standard proxy statement prior to mailing. The lawyer called to his attention the difference in the description in the proxy statement and the footnote, pointing out that the footnote said "common" rather than "capital stock of any class." In the course of this conversation, Freeze took a copy of the preliminary Standard proxy statement and noted the change by hand in note 7(c). Thereafter, footnote 7(c) was not amended, and no effort was made to call the discrepancy to the attention of Standard stockholders or officials. Freeze did not foresee that the bottom would drop out of Chadbourn's earnings and that what appeared to be a minor error at the time would become a major bone of contention.

The evidence simply suggests a mistake, an oversight, the failure to foresee a problem. We find nothing in the record indicating an intent to deceive or a motive for deception. J.B. Woolsey, Standard's vice president for financial affairs, and presumably other Standard officers, knew of the restrictions and recommended the merger anyway. No stockholder testified that he was deceived. An erroneous statement cannot *ipso facto* prove fraud, and here we find no evidence of anything other than a negligent error.

II. LIABILITY FOR NEGLIGENT MISREPRESENTATION UNDER SEC RULES 10b–5 AND 14a–9

In view of our conclusion that the District Court's findings of scienter are clearly erroneous, we reverse the imposition of liability under Rule 10b–5. In Ernst & Ernst v. Hochfelder, 425 U.S. 185 (1976), the Supreme Court settled the issue. It unequivocally held that liability under Rule 10b–5 requires "intentional misconduct." Id. at 201. The Court said that 10b–5 requires "intentional or willful conduct designed to deceive or defraud investors." Id. at 199.

We turn to the question of the standard of liability under Rule 14a–9 pertaining to statements made in proxy solicitations. There has been relatively little case law on the standard of liability following the Supreme Court decision in J.I. Case Co. v. Borak, 377 U.S. 426 (1964), which established a private right of action under 14(a) and Rule 14a–9. Two circuits have examined the issue. Both have prescribed a negligence standard for the corporation issuing the proxy statement. One held that the negligence standard also applies to outside, nonmanagement directors, Gould v. American–Hawaiian Steamship Co., 535 F.2d 761, 777–78 (3d Cir.1976); and the other intimated in dicta, without deciding the issue, that a *scienter* standard probably should apply to outside directors and accountants, Gerstle v. Gamble–Skogmo, Inc., 478 F.2d 1281, 1300–1301 (2d Cir.1973).

In view of the overall structure and collective legislative histories of the securities laws, as well as important policy considerations, we conclude that scienter should be an element of liability in private suits under the proxy provisions as they apply to outside accountants.

It is not simply a question of statutory interpretation. Federal courts created the private right of action under section 14, and they have a special responsibility to consider the consequences of their rulings and to mold liability fairly to reflect the circumstances of the parties. Although we are not called on in this case to decide the standard of liability of the corporate issuer of proxy material, we are influenced by the fact that the accountant here, unlike the corporate issuer, does not directly benefit from the proxy vote and is not in privity with the stockholder. Unlike the corporate issuer, the preparation of financial statements to be appended to proxies and other reports is the daily fare of accountants, and the accountant's potential liability for relatively minor mistakes would be enormous under a negligence standard. In contrast to section 12(2) of the 1933 Act which imposes liability for negligent misrepresentation in a prospectus, Rule 14a–9 does not require privity. In contrast to section 11 of the 1933 Act which imposes liability for negligent misrepresentation in registration statements, Rule 14a–9 does not require proof of actual investor reliance on the misrepresentation. Rule 14a–9, like 10b–5, substitutes the less exacting standard of materiality for reliance, TSC Ind., Inc. v. Northway, Inc., 426 U.S. 438 (1976), and in the instant case there was no proof of investor reliance on the notes to the financial statements which erroneously described the restriction on payment of dividends. We can see no reason for a different standard of liability for accountants under the proxy provisions than under 10(b).[6]

We may not end our consideration there, however. We must turn to the legislative history of the proxy provisions. Section 14(a) and Rule 14a–9 are silent regarding the proper standard of liability. The Senate Report to the 1934 Act, commonly known as the Fletcher Report, discussed the sort of proxy abuse that Congress was trying to stop, that of corporate officers using the proxy mechanism to ratify their own frauds upon the shareholders, or outsiders soliciting shareholders' approval to plunder a ripe company. The Report cited one example, * * *. The nature of each wrong deed depicted by the Report evidenced scienter.

An even more informative section of the Report is one describing the scope of 14(a):

> It is contemplated that the rules and regulations promulgated by the Commission will protect investors from *promiscuous* solicitation of their proxies, on the one hand, by irresponsible outsiders seeking to wrest control of a corporation away from honest and conscientious corporation officials; and, on the other hand, by *unscrupulous* corporate officials

---

6. Indeed section 18 of the 1934 Act, dealing with misstatements in reports filed with the SEC, requires *both* scienter *and* reliance for civil liability. Section 14 is much more similar to section 18 than it is to section 11 of the 1933 Act. Under the current regulatory scheme, proxy materials must be filed in advance of the solicitation with the SEC, see 17 C.F.R. § 240.14A–6, and are therefore subject to the provisions of section 18. In contrast, proxy solicitations *per se* do not put the solicitor within the ambit of section 11.

The District Court found that the plaintiffs could not recover under section 18 because they had not shown the reliance which is required by that section. This was, of course, true. At the same time, the defendants argue that the specific remedy provided by section 18 precludes implication of a cause of action under either section 10 or section 14, when the requirements of section 18 are not met. Only one circuit has directly discussed this question, finding that inability to satisfy the requirements of section 18 does not bar a less restrictive implied action brought under section 10, Ross v. A.H. Robins Co., Inc., 607 F.2d 545 (2d Cir.1979). This question was not specifically addressed by the District Court and, because we find that in all events, the plaintiffs cannot recover under sections 10 or 14, we need not decide this question here.

seeking to retain control of the management by *concealing* and *distorting* facts. (emphasis added)

Senate Committee on Banking & Currency, S.Rep. No. 1455, 73d Cong., 2d Sess. 77 (1934).

The words "unscrupulous," "concealing," and "distorting" all imply knowledge or scienter; and we interpret "promiscuous" to mean reckless. In addition the characterization of irresponsible outsiders trying to "wrest control * * * from *honest* * * * corporate officials," implies dishonesty—and hence scienter—on the part of the outsiders. Consequently, the Report leads us to believe that its authors contemplated that 14(a) would be applied only against the knowing or reckless wrongdoing of outsiders.

The few times the proxy section was discussed in debate paint a similar picture of the type of misconduct against which 14(a) was directed. Roosevelt's aid, Corcoran, who drafted the original version of the 1934 Act, spoke of "*unscrupulous* proxy committees" (emphasis added). See 78 Cong.Rec. 6544 (1934). Everett Dirksen, then a Representative from Illinois, stated, "[t]here is little doubt that there has been grave abuse of this authority to solicit proxies and the use of such proxies for *manipulation* "(emphasis added) 78 Cong.Rec. 7961 (1934). Further debate indicates Congress' concern that directors and officers should not be able to complete their fraud upon a company by means of a proxy solicitation that seeks ratification of their illegal acts. See 78 Cong.Rec. 7712–14 (1934). Congressman Pettengill of Indiana stated during Committee hearings exactly what he thought such undesirable activity amounted to: "larceny." See Hearings on H.R. 7852 Before the House Comm. on Interstate & Foreign Commerce, 73d Cong., 2d Sess. 480 (1934). The common denominator of all these depictions of the problem is wrongdoing with some degree of knowledge, *i.e.* scienter; and nowhere, not in the committee reports nor in the House or Senate debates, does it appear that Congress desired to protect the investor against negligence of accountants as well.

Another important consideration is Congressional intent regarding subsequent amendments that are indirectly linked to 14(a). In passing the Williams Act of 1968 governing tender offers, Congress expressed the desire that proxy statements and tender offers be governed by the *same* rules and regulations. This would logically extend to standards of liability. Because 14(e) pertaining to tender offers requires scienter, we believe there is a strong policy reason for imposing a similar standard on 14(a).

According to the House Report for the Williams Act, "[t]he cash tender offer is similar to a proxy contest, and the committee could find no reason to continue the present gap in the federal securities laws which leaves the cash tender offer exempt from disclosure provisions." H.R.Rep. No. 1711, 90th Cong., 2d Sess., reprinted in [1968] U.S.Code Cong. & Ad.News 2811, 2813. Tender offers and proxy solicitations are two alternative methods of achieving the same result, corporate control; and Congress perceived that both were subject to the same type of abuse. It therefore acted to eliminate an existing loophole in the old law so that wrongful usurpation of control would not escape securities regulation whenever one combatant chooses to seize control by tender offer rather than by proxy fight. Id.

Senator Williams of New Jersey, the sponsor of the bill, stated

"What this bill would do is to provide the *same kind of disclosure requirements which now exist,* for example, *in contests through proxies* for controlling ownership in a company." (emphasis added)

113 Cong.Rec. 24665 (1967).

Senator Javits echoed this view.

The Senator [Williams] represents to the Senate, and I accept his representation fully, that this is analogous to the proxy rules. Id.

And Senator Williams repeated that "[t]his legislation is patterned on the present law and regulations which govern proxy contests." Id. Logically the above testimony implies similar standards of liability for both proxy statements and tender offers. Otherwise some misleading solicitations which would trigger liability if shaped in the form of one transaction, would be immune if shaped as the other, or *vice versa.*

The language of the Williams Act clearly demonstrates that Congress envisioned scienter to be an element of 14(e). Congress used the words "fraudulent," "deceptive," and "manipulative." This language indicates, in light of *Ernst & Ernst,* that 14(e) requires scienter. Although *Ernst & Ernst* was decided several years after the enactment of 14(e), we are bound by its holding that Congress intends scienter when it uses the above quoted language.

We conclude that 14(a) and 14(e) should be governed by the same standard of liability insofar as accountants' liability is concerned, and that an action under 14(a) requires proof of scienter. Finding no evidence of scienter, we reverse the imposition of liability under 14(a) and Rule 14a–9.

THE REQUIRED CULPABILITY OF THE DEFENDANT UNDER SECTIONS 14(a)

Section 14(a) of the 1934 Act simply authorizes the Commission to adopt such rules and regulations relating to proxy solicitations as are "necessary or appropriate in the public interest or for the protection of investors." There are no substantive provisions whatever in the statute regarding the form or content of any proxy statement. Rule 14a–9, which is quoted in the *Adams* case, merely prohibits any "false or misleading" statement in a proxy statement, without any hint as to what the required culpability of a defendant must be in order for him to become liable for a violation of that rule. In Gerstle v. Gamble–Skogmo, Inc.,[1] the Second Circuit held, in an opinion by Judge Friendly, that simple negligence is a sufficient basis for liability under Rule 14a–9, at least so far as the corporate issuer of the proxy statement is concerned.[2] Judge Friendly noted the absence of any "evil-sounding language" in either Section 14(a) or Rule 14a–9 and explained the basis of the decision as follows:

"In contrast [to the language of § 10(b)], the scope of the rulemaking authority granted under section 14(a) is broad, extending to all proxy regulation 'necessary or appropriate in the public interest or for the protection of investors' and not limited by any words connoting fraud or deception. This language suggests that rather than emphasizing the prohibition of fraudulent conduct on the part of insiders to a securities transac-

---

1.   478 F.2d 1281 (2d Cir.1973).

2.   See, also, Gould v. American–Hawaiian Steamship Co., 535 F.2d 761 (3d Cir. 1976); National Home Products, Inc. v. Gray, 416 F.Supp. 1293 (D.Del.1976).

tion, as we think section 10(b) does, in section 14(a) Congress was somewhat more concerned with protection of the outsider whose proxy is being solicited. Indeed, it was this aspect of the statute that the Supreme Court emphasized in recognizing a private right of action for violation of section 14(a) in *Borak,* 377 U.S. at 431–432. We note also that while an open-ended reading of Rule 10b–5 would render the express civil liability provisions of the securities acts largely superfluous, and be inconsistent with the limitations Congress built into these sections, * * * a reading of Rule 14a–9 as imposing liability without scienter in a case like the present is completely compatible with the statutory scheme."[3]

As Judge Friendly points out, there would hardly be any difference between this standard and that of intentional misstatement if the corporation is to be charged with the knowledge of all of its officers and employees. However, he suggests, without definitively deciding the question, that perhaps the corporation would be put in the shoes of those charged with drafting the proxy statement and might be exonerated if they made no intentional misstatements and were not negligent in drafting the document. It should be noted that the *Adams* case is not necessarily inconsistent with the *Gerstle* case. Judge Friendly there limited his holding to the liability of the corporate issuer of the proxy statement and did not rule on the culpability required with respect to a collateral participant, whereas in the *Adams* case the Third Circuit limited its holding to the fault required of such a collateral participant (i.e., the accountant who had certified the financial statements included in the proxy statement). Is there a sound basis for this distinction, if it is one? The shareholders of the corporation, upon whom any loss will fall if it is held liable, would seem to be less at fault than anyone else in any way associated with the proxy statement or the transaction to which it relates.

In Wilson v. Great American Industries, Inc.,[4] the Second Circuit reaffirmed the *Gerstle* case and extended its holding to directors and officers of the issuer who drafted, or had knowledge of, the false or misleading statements in the proxy statement. The court stated that "the preparation of a proxy statement by corporate insiders containing materially false or misleading statements or omitting a material fact is sufficient to satisfy the *Gerstle* negligence standard."[5] The court found, however, that the corporate directors and officers *knew* that the statements in the proxy statement were false or misleading at the time the proxy statement was issued; and therefore this statement of the court might be characterized as *dictum.*

In Shidler v. All American Life & Financial Corp.,[6] the Eighth Circuit held that there was no liability without fault in an action under Section 14(a) (the trial court had expressly found in that case that there was no negligence, although there was a material misstatement in the proxy statement). The court said: "A strict liability rule would impose liability for fully innocent misstatements. It is too blunt a tool to ferret out the kind of deceptive practices Congress sought to prevent in enacting section 14(a)."[7]

Is there any justification for a distinction between the liability of a corporation under Rule 10b–5 for issuing a misleading offering circular (in a transaction exempt from registration under the 1933 Act) and its liability for

---

3. 478 F.2d at 1299.
4. 855 F.2d 987 (2d Cir.1988).
5. 855 F.2d at 995.

6. 775 F.2d 917 (8th Cir.1985).
7. Id. at 927.

issuing a misleading proxy statement in a transaction that is functionally indistinguishable? The language of the sections may be different, as pointed out by Judge Friendly (and as relied upon exclusively by the Supreme Court in the *Aaron* case), but after all Congress didn't create any civil liability for violation of either one; the courts did that.

We will explore later the different culpability standard under Rule 10b–5.

B.   Rule 10b–5: Fraud in Connection With a Purchase or Sale of a Security

Rule 10b–5 is the basic federal securities antifraud provision of the federal securities laws. The Rule reaches fraud "in connection with a purchase or sale of a security" in contrast to §§ 11 and 12 of the Securities Act which address fraud involved in securities distributions or Rule 14a–9 which is limited to fraud in a proxy solicitation.

As a practical matter Rule 10b–5 primarily has been applied to three types of fraud: (1) misrepresentations or omissions in corporate statements; (2) trading while in possession of material nonpublic information, euphemistically called "insider trading"; and (3) manipulation. The basic elements of proving a Rule 10b–5 violation overlap for each type of fraud.

We have earlier explored material misrepresentations or omissions in this Chapter in the context of Rule 14a–9.

The origins of Rule 10b–5 are humble enough. Section 10(b) of the Securities Exchange Act was a residual provision following far more specific prohibitions in §§ 9 and 10 against specific forms of market manipulation. As one of the drafters stated of the somewhat broader version that was initially denominated § 9(c) in the Securities Exchange Bill: "Subsection (c) says, 'Thou shalt not devise any other cunning devices.' "[1]

Section 10(b) was not self enforcing. Until 1942 there was no need for the Securities and Exchange Commission to adopt a rule under § 10(b) prohibiting fraud in the sale of a security because § 17(a) of the Securities Act of 1933 employed similar language to prohibit fraud "in the offer or sale of any securities. * * * "

Then, as the Rule's drafter, attorney Milton V. Freeman memorably recalled:

> It was one day in the year [1942], I believe. I was sitting in my office in the S.E.C. building in Philadelphia and I received a call from Jim Treanor who was then the Director of the Trading and Exchange Division. He said, "I have just been on the telephone with Paul Rowen," who was then the S.E.C. Regional Administrator in Boston, "and he has told me about the president of some company in Boston, who is going around buying up the stock of his company from his own shareholders at $4.00 a share, and he has been telling them that the company is doing very badly, whereas, in fact, the earnings are going to be quadrupled and will be $2.00 a share for this coming year. Is there anything we can do about it?" So he came upstairs and I called in my secretary and I looked at Section 10(b) and I looked at Section 17, and I put them together, and the only discussion we

---

1. Stock Exchange Regulation, Hearings before House Comm. on Interstate & Foreign Commerce, 73d Cong., 2d Sess. 115 (1934) (testimony of Thomas Corcoran).

had there was where "in connection with the purchase or sale" should be, and we decided it should be at the end.

We called the Commission and we got on the calendar, and I don't remember whether we got there that morning or after lunch. We passed a piece of paper around to all the commissioners. All the commissioners read the rule and they tossed it on the table, indicating approval. Nobody said anything except Sumner Pike who said, "Well," he said, "we are against fraud, aren't we?" That is how it happened.[2]

Rule 10b–5 is one long sentence:

It shall be unlawful for any person, directly or indirectly, by the use of any means or instrumentality of interstate commerce, or of the mails, or of any facility of any national securities exchange,

(1) to employ any device, scheme, or artifice to defraud,

(2) to make any untrue statement of a material fact or to omit to state a material fact necessary in order to make the statements made, in the light of the circumstances under which they were made, not misleading, or

(3) to engage in any act, practice, or course of business which operates or would operate as a fraud or deceit upon any person, in connection with the purchase or sale of any security.

The significance of Rule 10b–5 was recognized quickly. In 1943 the Commission published a report concluding that two officers in the company Milton Freeman described in his recollection had violated the Rule.[3]

In 1947 a federal district court implied a private cause of action.[4] The Supreme Court subsequently acknowledged also that a cause of action can be implied from Rule 10b–5,[5] although a large majority of circuits today hold that a private cause of action cannot be implied from § 17(a).[6]

1. THE REQUIREMENT THAT THERE BE FRAUD

Santa Fe Industries, Inc. v. Green

Supreme Court of the United States, 1977.
430 U.S. 462, 97 S.Ct. 1292, 51 L.Ed.2d 480.

■ MR. JUSTICE WHITE delivered the opinion of the Court.

The issue in this case involves the reach and coverage of § 10(b) of the Securities Exchange Act of 1934 and Rule 10b–5 thereunder in the context of a Delaware short-form merger transaction used by the majority stockholder of a corporation to eliminate the minority interest.

2. ABA Sec. Corp., Banking & Bus. Law, Conference on Codification of the Federal Securities Laws, 22 Bus. Law. 793, 921–923, esp. at 922 (1967). For an exhaustive examination of the historical context of § 10(b), *see* Steve Thel, The Original Conception of Section 10(b) of the Securities Exchange Act, 42 Stan. L. Rev. 385 (1990).

3. Ward La France Truck Corp., 13 SEC 373 (1943).

4. Kardon v. National Gypsum Co., 73 F.Supp. 798 (E.D.Pa.1947).

5. Superintendent of Ins. of State of N.Y. v. Bankers Life & Casualty Co., 404 U.S. 6, 13 n. 9 (1971).

6. *See, e.g.,* Finkel v. Stratton Corp., 962 F.2d 169, 174–175 (2d Cir.1992).

I

In 1936 petitioner Santa Fe Industries, Inc. ("Santa Fe") acquired control of 60% of the stock of Kirby Lumber Corporation ("Kirby"), a Delaware corporation. Through a series of purchases over the succeeding years, Santa Fe increased its control of Kirby's stock to 95%; the purchase prices during the period 1968–1973 ranged from $65 to $92.50 per share. In 1974, wishing to acquire 100% ownership of Kirby, Santa Fe availed itself of § 253 of the Delaware Corporation Law, known as the "short-form merger" statute. Section 253 permits a parent corporation owning at least 90% of the stock of a subsidiary to merge with that subsidiary, upon approval by the parent's board of directors, and to make payment in cash for the shares of the minority stockholders. The statute does not require the consent of, or advance notice to, the minority stockholders. However, notice of the merger must be given within 10 days after its effective date, and any stockholder who is dissatisfied with the terms of the merger may petition the Delaware Court of Chancery for a decree ordering the surviving corporation to pay him the fair value of his shares, as determined by a court-appointed appraiser subject to review by the court. Del.Gen.Corp.Law §§ 253, 262.

Santa Fe obtained independent appraisals of the physical assets of Kirby—land, timber, buildings, and machinery—and of Kirby's oil, gas, and mineral interests. These appraisals, together with other financial information, were submitted to Morgan, Stanley & Company ("Morgan Stanley"), an investment banking firm retained to appraise the fair market value of Kirby stock. Kirby's physical assets were appraised at $320 million (amounting to $640 for each of the 500,000 shares); Kirby's stock was valued by Morgan Stanley at $125 per share. Under the terms of the merger, minority stockholders were offered $150 per share.

The provisions of the short-form merger statute were fully complied with. The minority stockholders of Kirby were notified the day after the merger became effective and were advised of their right to obtain an appraisal in Delaware court if dissatisfied with the offer of $150 per share. They also received an information statement containing, in addition to the relevant financial data about Kirby, the appraisals of the value of Kirby's assets and the Morgan Stanley appraisal concluding that the fair market value of the stock was $125 per share.

Respondents, minority stockholders of Kirby, objected to the terms of the merger, but did not pursue their appraisal remedy in the Delaware Court of Chancery. Instead, they brought this action in federal court on behalf of the corporation and other minority stockholders, seeking to set aside the merger or to recover what they claimed to be the fair value of their shares. The amended complaint asserted that, based on the fair market value of Kirby's physical assets as revealed by the appraisal included in the Information Statement sent to minority shareholders, Kirby's stock was worth at least $772 per share. The complaint alleged further that the merger took place without prior notice to minority stockholders; that the purpose of the merger was to appropriate the difference between the "conceded pro rata value of the physical assets" and the offer of $150 per share—to "freez[e] out the minority stockholders at a wholly inadequate price," app. 103a, 100a; and that Santa Fe, knowing the appraised value of the physical assets, obtained a "fraudulent appraisal" of the stock from Morgan Stanley and offered $25 above that appraisal "in order to lull the minority stockholders into erroneously believing that [Santa Fe was] generous." Id., at 103a. This course of conduct was alleged to be "a violation of Rule 10b–5 because defendants employed a 'device, scheme or artifice to defraud' and engaged in an 'act, practice or course of business which operates or would operate as a fraud or deceit upon any person, in connection with the purchase or sale of any security.'" Ibid. Morgan Stanley assertedly participated in the fraud as an accessory by submitting its appraisal of $125 per share although knowing the appraised value of the physical assets.

The District Court dismissed the complaint for failure to state a claim upon which relief could be granted. 391 F. Supp. 849 (S.D.N.Y.1975). As the District Court understood the complaint, respondents' case rested on two distinct grounds. First, federal law was assertedly violated because the merger was for the sole purpose of eliminating the minority from the company, therefore lacking any justifiable business purpose, and because the merger was undertaken without prior notice to the minority shareholders. Second, the low valuation placed on the shares in the cash exchange offer was itself said to be a fraud actionable under Rule 10b–5. In rejecting the first ground for recovery, the District Court reasoned that Delaware law required neither a business purpose for a short-form merger nor prior notice to the minority shareholders who the statute contemplated would be removed from the company, and that Rule 10b–5 did not override these provisions of state corporate law by independently placing a duty on the majority not to merge without prior notice and without a justifiable business purpose.

As for the claim that actionable fraud inhered in the allegedly gross undervaluation of the minority shares, the District Court observed that respondents valued their shares at a minimum of $772 per share, "basing this figure on the pro rata value of Kirby's physical assets." Id., at 853. Accepting this valuation for purposes of the motion to dismiss, the District Court further noted that, as revealed by the complaint, the physical asset appraisal, along with other information relevant to Morgan Stanley's valuation of the shares, had been included with the Information Statement sent to respondents within the time required by state law. It thought that if "full and fair disclosure is made, transactions eliminating minority interests are beyond the purview of Rule 10b–5," and concluded that "the complaint fail[ed] to allege an omission, misstatement or fraudulent course of conduct that would have impeded a shareholder's judgment of the value of the offer." Id., at 854. The complaint therefore failed to state a claim and was dismissed.

A divided Court of Appeals for the Second Circuit reversed. 533 F.2d 1283 (1976). It first agreed that there was a double aspect to the case: first, the claim that gross undervaluation of the minority stock itself violated Rule 10b–5; and second, that "without any misrepresentation or failure to disclose relevant facts, the merger itself constitutes a violation of Rule 10b–5" because it was accomplished without any corporate purpose and without prior notice to the minority stockholders. Id., at 1285. As to the first aspect of the case, the Court of Appeals did not disturb the District Court's conclusion that the complaint did not allege a material misrepresentation or nondisclosure with respect to the value of the stock; and the court declined to rule that a claim of gross undervaluation itself would suffice to make out a Rule 10b–5 case. With respect to the second aspect of the case, however, the court fundamentally disagreed with the District Court as to the reach and coverage of Rule 10b–5. The Court of Appeals' view was that, although the Rule plainly reached material misrepresentations and nondisclosures in connection with the purchase or sale of securities, neither misrepresentation nor nondisclosure was a necessary element of a Rule 10b–5 action; the Rule reached "breaches of fiduciary duty by a majority against minority shareholders without any charge of misrepresentation or lack of disclosure." Id., at 1287.[8] The court went on to hold that the complaint, taken as a whole, stated a cause of action under the Rule:

> "We hold that a complaint alleges a claim under Rule 10b–5 when it charges, in connection with a Delaware short-form merger, that the majority has committed a breach of its fiduciary duty to deal fairly with minority shareholders by effecting the merger without any justifiable business purpose. The minority shareholders are given no prior notice of the merger, thus having no opportunity to apply for injunctive relief, and the proposed price to be paid is substantially lower than the appraised value reflected in the Information Statement." Id., at 1291.

* * *

We granted the petition for certiorari challenging this holding because of the importance of the issue involved to the administration of the federal securities laws. 429 U.S. 814 (1976). We reverse.

II

* * * The Court of Appeals' approach to the interpretation of Rule 10b–5 is inconsistent with that taken by the Court last Term in Ernst & Ernst v. Hochfelder, 425 U.S. 185 (1976).

* * *

To the extent that the Court of Appeals would rely on the use of the term "fraud" in Rule 10b–5 to bring within the ambit of the Rule all breaches of fiduciary duty in connection with a securities transaction, its interpretation would, like the interpretation rejected by the Court in *Ernst & Ernst,* "add a gloss to the operative language of the statute quite different from its commonly accepted meaning." Id., at 199. But as the Court there held, the language of the statute must control the interpretation of the Rule: * * *[12]

---

8. The court concluded its discussion thus:

> "Whether full disclosure has been made is not the crucial inquiry since it is the merger and the undervaluation which constituted the fraud, and not whether or not the majority determines to lay bare their real motives. If there is no valid corporate purpose for the merger, then even the most brazen disclosure of that fact to the minority shareholders in no way mitigates the fraudulent conduct." 533 F.2d at 1292.

12. The case for adhering to the language of the statute is even stronger here than in *Ernst & Ernst,* where the interpretation of Rule 10b–5 rejected by the Court was strongly urged by the Commission. See also Piper v. ChrisCraft Industries, Inc., ante, p. 1, and Blue Chip Stamps v. Manor Drug Stores, 421 U.S. 723 (1975) (rejecting interpretations of Rule 10b–5 urged by the SEC as *amicus curiae*). By contrast, the Commission apparently has not concluded that Rule 10b–5 should be used to reach "going private" transactions where the majority stockholder eliminates the minority at an allegedly unfair price. See SEC Securities Act Release No. 5567 (Feb. 6, 1975), CCH Fed.Sec.L.Rep. ¶ 80,104 (proposing Rules 13e–3A and 13e–3B dealing with "going private" transactions, pursuant to six sections of the 1934 Act including § 10(b), but stating that the Commission "has reached no conclusions with respect to the proposed rules"). Because we are concerned here only with § 10(b), we intimate no view as to the Commission's authority to promulgate such rules under other sections of the Act.

The language of § 10(b) gives no indication that Congress meant to prohibit any conduct not involving manipulation or deception. Nor have we been cited to any evidence in the legislative history that would support a departure from the language of the statute. "When a statute speaks so specifically in terms of manipulation and deception, * * * and when its history reflects no more expansive intent, we are quite unwilling to extend the scope of the statute * * *." Id., at 214 (footnote omitted). Thus the claim of fraud and fiduciary breach in this complaint states a cause of action under any part of Rule 10b–5 only if the conduct alleged can be fairly viewed as "manipulative or deceptive" within the meaning of the statute.

III

It is our judgment that the transaction, if carried out as alleged in the complaint, was neither deceptive nor manipulative and therefore did not violate either § 10(b) of the Act or Rule 10b–5.

As we have indicated, the case comes to us on the premise that the complaint failed to allege a material misrepresentation or material failure to disclose. The finding of the District Court, undisturbed by the Court of Appeals, was that there was no "omission" or "misstatement" in the Information Statement accompanying the notice of merger. On the basis of the information provided, minority shareholders could either accept the price offered or reject it and seek an appraisal in the Delaware Court of Chancery. Their choice was fairly presented, and they were furnished with all relevant information on which to base their decision.[14]

We therefore find inapposite the cases relied upon by respondents and the court below, in which the breaches of fiduciary duty held violative of Rule 10b–5 included some element of deception.[15] Those cases forcefully reflect the

14. In addition to their principal argument that the complaint alleges a fraud under clauses (a) and (c) of Rule 10b–5, respondents also argue that the complaint alleges nondisclosure and misrepresentation in violation of clause (b) of the Rule. Their major contention in this respect is that the majority stockholder's failure to give the minority advance notice of the merger was a material nondisclosure, even though the Delaware short-form merger statute does not require such notice. Brief for Respondents, at 27. But respondents do not indicate how they might have acted differently had they had prior notice of the merger. Indeed, they accept the conclusion of both courts below that under Delaware law they could not have enjoined the merger because an appraisal proceeding is their sole remedy in the Delaware courts for any alleged unfairness in the terms of the merger. Thus the failure to give advance notice was not a material nondisclosure within the meaning of the statute or the Rule. Cf. TSC Industries, Inc. v. Northway, Inc., 426 U.S. 438 (1976).

15. The decisions of this Court relied upon by respondents all involved deceptive conduct as part of the Rule 10b–5 violation alleged. Affiliated Ute Citizens v. United States, 406 U.S. 128 (1972) (misstatements of material fact used by bank employees in position of market maker to acquire stock at less than fair value); Superintendent of Insurance v. Bankers Life & Cas. Co., 404 U.S. 6, 9 (1971) ("seller [of bonds] was duped into believing that it, the seller, would receive the proceeds"). Cf. SEC v. Capital Gains Research Bureau, 375 U.S. 180 (1963) (injunction under Investment Advisers Act of 1940 to compel registered investment adviser to disclose to his clients his own financial interest in his recommendations).

We have been cited to a large number of cases in the Courts of Appeals, all of which involved an element of deception as part of the fiduciary misconduct held to violate Rule 10b–5. E.g., Schoenbaum v. Firstbrook, 405 F.2d 215, 220 (C.A.2 1968) (en banc), cert. denied, 395 U.S. 906 (1969) (majority stockholder and board of directors "were guilty of deceiving" the minority stockholders); Drachman v. Harvey, 453 F.2d 722, 733, 736, 737 (C.A.2 1971) (en banc) (Rule 10b–5 violation

principle that "[s]ection 10(b) must be read flexibly, not technically and restrictively" and that the statute provides a cause of action for any plaintiff who "suffer[s] an injury as a result of deceptive practices touching its sale [or purchase] of securities. * * *." Superintendent of Insurance v. Bankers Life & Casualty Co., 404 U.S. 6, 12–13 (1971). But the cases do not support the proposition, adopted by the Court of Appeals below and urged by respondents here, that a breach of fiduciary duty by majority stockholders, without any deception, misrepresentation, or nondisclosure, violates the statute and the Rule.

It is also readily apparent that the conduct alleged in the complaint was not "manipulative" within the meaning of the statute. Manipulation is "virtually a term of art when used in connection with securities markets." Ernst & Ernst, 425 U.S., at 199. The term refers generally to practices, such as wash sales, matched orders, or rigged prices, that are intended to mislead investors by artificially affecting market activity. See, e.g., § 9 of the 1934 Act (prohibiting specific manipulative practices); *Ernst & Ernst, supra*; Piper v. Chris–Craft Industries, Inc., 430 U.S., at 43 (Rule 10b–6, also promulgated under § 10(b), is "an antimanipulative provision designed to protect the orderliness of the securities market during distributions of stock" and "to prevent stimulative trading by an issuer in its own securities in order to create an unnatural and unwarranted appearance of market activity"); 2 A. Bromberg, Securities Law: Fraud § 7.3 (1975); 3 L. Loss, Securities Regulation 1541–70 (2d ed. 1961); 6 id., at 3755–3763 (2d ed. Supp.1969). Section 10(b)'s general prohibition of practices deemed by the SEC to be "manipulative"—in this technical sense of artificially affecting market activity in order to mislead investors—is fully consistent with the fundamental purpose of the 1934 Act "to substitute a philosophy of full disclosure for the philosophy of *caveat emptor* * * *." Affiliated Ute Citizens v. United States, 406 U.S. 128, 151 (1972), quoting SEC v. Capital Gains Research Bureau, 375 U.S. 180, 186 (1963). Indeed, nondisclosure is usually essential to the success of a manipulative scheme. 3 L. Loss, *supra*, at 1565. No doubt Congress meant to prohibit the full range of ingenious devices that might be used to manipulate securities prices. But we do not think

alleged on facts found "indistinguishable" from Superintendent of Insurance v. Bankers Life & Cas. Co.); Schlick v. Penn–Dixie Cement Corp., 507 F.2d 374 (C.A.2 1974), cert. denied, 421 U.S. 976 (1975) (scheme of market manipulation and merger on unfair terms, one aspect of which was misrepresentation); Pappas v. Moss, 393 F.2d 865, 869 (C.A.3 1968) ("if a 'deception' is required in the present context [of § 10(b) and Rule 10b–5], it is fairly found by viewing this fraud as though the 'independent' stockholders were standing in the place of the defrauded corporate entity," where the board of directors passed a resolution containing at least two material misrepresentations and authorizing the sale of corporate stock to the directors at a price below fair market value); Shell v. Hensley, 430 F.2d 819, 825 (C.A.5 1970) (derivative suit alleging that corporate officers used misleading proxy materials and other reports to deceive shareholders regarding a bogus employment contract intended to conceal improper payments to the corporation president and regarding purchases by the corporation of certain securities at excessive prices); Rekant v. Desser, 425 F.2d 872, 882 (C.A.5 1970) (as part of scheme to cause corporation to issue Treasury shares and a promissory note for grossly inadequate consideration, corporate officers deceived shareholders by making affirmative misrepresentations in the corporation's annual report and by failing to file any such report the next year). See Recent Cases, 89 Harv.L.Rev. 1917, 1926 (1976) (stating that no appellate decision before that of the Court of Appeals in this case and in Marshel v. AFW Fabric Corp., 533 F.2d 1277 (CA2), vacated and remanded for a determination of mootness, 429 U.S. 881 (1976), "had permitted a 10b–5 claim without some element of misrepresentation or nondisclosure") (footnote omitted).

it would have chosen this "term of art" if it had meant to bring within the scope of § 10(b) instances of corporate mismanagement such as this, in which the essence of the complaint is that shareholders were treated unfairly by a fiduciary.

IV

The language of the statute is, we think, "sufficiently clear in its context" to be dispositive here, Ernst & Ernst, 425 U.S., at 201; but even if it were not, there are additional considerations that weigh heavily against permitting a cause of action under Rule 10b–5 for the breach of corporate fiduciary duty alleged in this complaint. Congress did not expressly provide a private cause of action for violations of § 10(b). Although we have recognized an implied cause of action under that section in some circumstances, Superintendent of Insurance v. Bankers Life & Cas. Co., *supra*, 404 U.S. at 13 n. 9, we have also recognized that a private cause of action under the anti-fraud provisions of the Securities Exchange Act should not be implied where it is "unnecessary to ensure the fulfillment of Congress' purposes" in adopting the Act. Piper v. Christ–Craft Industries, 430 U.S. at 41. Cf. J.I. Case Co. v. Borak, 377 U.S. 426, 431–433 (1964). As we noted earlier, p. 1302, *supra*, the Court repeatedly has described the "fundamental purpose" of the Act as implementing a "philosophy of full disclosure"; once full and fair disclosure has occurred, the fairness of the terms of the transaction is at most a tangential concern of the statute. Cf. Mills v. Electric Auto–Lite Co., 396 U.S. 375, 381–385 (1970). As in Cort v. Ash, 422 U.S. 66, 78, 80 (1975), we are reluctant to recognize a cause of action here to serve what is "at best a subsidiary purpose" of the federal legislation.

A second factor in determining whether Congress intended to create a federal cause of action in these circumstances is "whether 'the cause of action [is] one traditionally relegated to state law. * * *'" Piper v. Chris–Craft Industries, Inc., 430 U.S., at 949, quoting Cort v. Ash, 422 U.S., at 78. The Delaware Legislature has supplied minority shareholders with a cause of action in the Delaware Court of Chancery to recover the fair value of shares allegedly undervalued in a short-form merger. See p. 2, *supra*. Of course, the existence of a particular state law remedy is not dispositive of the question whether Congress meant to provide a similar federal remedy, but as in *Piper* and *Cort*, we conclude that "it is entirely appropriate in this instance to relegate respondent and others in his situation to whatever remedy is created by state law." 422 U.S., at 84; 430 U.S., at 962.

The reasoning behind a holding that the complaint in this case alleged fraud under Rule 10b–5 could not be easily contained. It is difficult to imagine how a court could distinguish, for purposes of Rule 10b–5 fraud, between a majority stockholder's use of a short-form merger to eliminate the minority at an unfair price and the use of some other device, such as a long-form merger, tender offer, or liquidation, to achieve the same result; or indeed how a court could distinguish the alleged abuses in these going private transactions from other types of fiduciary self-dealing involving transactions in securities. The result would be to bring within the Rule a wide variety of corporate conduct traditionally left to state regulation. In addition to posing a "danger of vexatious litigation which could result from a widely expanded class of plaintiffs under Rule 10b–5," Blue Chip Stamps v. Manor Drug Stores, 421 U.S. 723, 740 (1975), this extension of the federal securities laws would overlap and quite possibly interfere with state corporate law. Federal courts applying a "federal fiduciary principle" under Rule 10b–5 could be expected to depart from state fiduciary standards at least to the extent necessary to ensure uniformity within the federal system.[16] Absent a clear indication of congressional intent, we are reluctant to federalize the substantial portion of the law of corporations that deals with transactions in securities, particularly where established state policies of corporate regulation would be overridden. As the Court stated in Cort v. Ash, *supra*, "Corporations are creatures of state law, and investors commit their funds to corporate directors on the understanding that, except where federal law *expressly* requires certain responsibilities of directors with respect to stockholders, state law will govern the internal affairs of the corporation." 422 U.S., at 84 (emphasis added).

We thus adhere to the position that "Congress by § 10(b) did not seek to regulate transactions which constitute no more than internal corporate mismanagement." Superintendent of Insurance v. Bankers Life & Cas. Co., 404 U.S., at 12. There may well be a need for uniform federal fiduciary standards to govern mergers such as that challenged in this complaint. But those standards should not be supplied by judicial extension of § 10(b) and Rule 10b–5 to "cover the corporate universe."

The judgment of the Court of Appeals is reversed, and the case is remanded for further proceedings consistent with this opinion.

So ordered.

■ MR. JUSTICE BRENNAN dissents and would affirm for substantially the reasons stated in the majority and concurring opinions in the Court of Appeals, 2 Cir., 533 F.2d 1283 (1976).

■ MR. JUSTICE BLACKMUN, concurring in part.

Like Mr. Justice Stevens, I refrain from joining Part IV of the Court's opinion. I, too, regard that part as unnecessary for the decision in the instant case and, indeed, as exacerbating the concerns I expressed in my dissents in Blue Chip Stamps v. Manor Drug Stores, 421 U.S. 723, 761 (1975), and in Ernst & Ernst v. Hochfelder, 425 U.S. 185, 215 (1976). I, however, join the remainder of the Court's opinion and its judgment.

■ MR. JUSTICE STEVENS, concurring in part.

For the reasons stated by Mr. Justice Blackmun in his dissenting opinion in Blue Chip Stamps v. Manor Drug Stores, 421 U.S. 723, 761, and those stated in my dissent in Piper v. Chris–Craft Industries, 97 S.Ct. 926, 955 (1977), I believe both of those cases were incorrectly decided. I foresee some danger that Part IV of the Court's opinion in this case may incorrectly be read as extending the holdings of those cases. Moreover, the entire discussion in Part IV is unnecessary to the decision of this case. Accordingly, I join only Parts I, II and III of the Court's opinion. I would also add further emphasis to the fact that

---

16. For example, some States apparently require a "valid corporate purpose" for the elimination of the minority interest through a short-form merger, whereas other States do not. Compare Bryan v. Brock & Blevins Co., 490 F.2d 563 (CA5), *cert. denied,* 419 U.S. 844 (1974) (merger arranged by controlling stockholder for no business purpose except to eliminate 15% minority stockholder violated Georgia short-form merger statute) with Stauffer v. Standard Brands, Inc., 41 Del.Ch. 7, 187 A.2d 78 (Sup. Ct. 1962) (Delaware short-form merger statute allows majority stockholder to eliminate the minority interest without any corporate purpose and subject only to an appraisal remedy). Thus to the extent that Rule 10b–5 is interpreted to require a valid corporate purpose for elimination of minority shareholders as well as a fair price for their shares, it would impose a stricter standard of fiduciary duty than that required by the law of some States.

the controlling stockholders in this case did not breach any duty owed to the minority shareholders because (a) there was complete disclosure of the relevant facts, and (b) the minority are entitled to receive the fair value of their shares. The facts alleged in the complaint do not constitute "fraud" within the meaning of Rule 10b–5.

RULE 10b–5 AS A REMEDY FOR MISMANAGEMENT

The practical consequence of Santa Fe v. Green was to largely end a movement in the Second Circuit to establish a "new fraud" under which it was possible for a corporation to be defrauded by a majority or all of its board without a material misrepresentation or omission to its shareholders.[1]

Santa Fe Industries, however, was not the last word. Six months after it was decided the Second Circuit in Goldberg v. Meridor,[2] addressed a derivative action on behalf of UGO charging that its parent, Maritimecor, had caused it to issue shares to the parent for all its assets and liabilities in an unfair transaction and on the basis of nondisclosure or misleading disclosure of material facts that were known to all the directors. Judge Friendly stated for the majority:[3]

> The problem with the application of § 10(b) and Rule 10b–5 to derivative actions has lain in the degree to which the knowledge of officers and directors must be attributed to the corporation, thereby negating the element of deception. * * *

> * * * [There is no requirement that there be] one virtuous or ignorant lamb among the directors in order for liability to arise under § 10(b) or Rule 10b–5 on a deception theory as to securities transactions with a controlling stockholder. * * *

> *Schoenbaum*, then can rest solidly on the now widely recognized ground that there is deception of the corporation (in effect, of its minority shareholders) when the corporation is influenced by its controlling shareholder to engage in a transaction adverse to the corporation's interests (in effect, the minority shareholders' interests) and *there is nondisclosure or misleading disclosures as to the material facts of the transaction* (italics supplied). Assuming that, in light of the decision in *Green*, the existence of "controlling influence" and "wholly inadequate consideration"—an aspect of the *Schoenbaum* decision that perhaps attracted more attention, see 405 F.2d at 219–20—can no longer alone form the basis for Rule 10b–5 liability, we do not read *Green* as ruling that no action lies under Rule 10b–5 when a controlling corporation causes a partly owned subsidiary to sell its securities to the parent in a fraudulent transaction and fails to make a disclosure or, as can be alleged here, makes a misleading disclosure. * * *

> * * * The nub of the matter is that the conduct attacked in *Green* did not violate the " 'fundamental purpose' of the Act as implementing a 'philosophy of full disclosure,' " 430 U.S. at 478; the conduct here attacked does.

---

1. See Ruckle v. Roto Am. Corp., 339 F.2d 24 (2d Cir.1964); O'Neill v. Maytag, 339 F.2d 764 (2d Cir.1964); Schoenbaum v. Firstbrook, 405 F.2d 215 (2d Cir. *en banc* 1968), *cert. denied sub nom.* Manley v. Schoenbaum, 395 U.S. 906 (1969).

2. 567 F.2d 209 (2d Cir.1977), *cert. denied*, 434 U.S. 1069 (1978).

3. Id. at 215–220.

Defendants contend that even if all this is true, the failure to make a public disclosure or even the making of a misleading disclosure would have no effect, since no action by stockholders to approve the UGO–Maritimecor transaction was required. * * *

* * * When, as in a derivative action, the deception is alleged to have been practiced on the corporation, even though all the directors were parties to it, the test [of materiality] must be whether the facts that were not disclosed or were misleadingly disclosed to the shareholders "would have assumed actual significance in the deliberations" of reasonable and disinterested directors or created "a substantial likelihood" that such directors would have considered the "total mix" of information available to have been "significantly altered." * * *

Beyond this Goldberg and other minority shareholders would not have been without remedy if the alleged facts had been disclosed. * * *

The availability of injunctive relief if the defendants had not lulled the minority stockholders of UGO into security by a deceptive disclosure, as they allegedly did, is in sharp contrast to *Green*, where the disclosure following the merger transaction was full and fair, and, as to the pre-merger period, respondents accepted "the conclusion of both courts below that under Delaware law they could not have enjoined the merger because an appraisal proceeding is their sole remedy in the Delaware courts for any alleged unfairness in the terms of the merger," * * *[4]

Subsequent cases followed Judge Friendly's lead in Goldberg and held that if a plaintiff was deceived as to a remedy under state law, the plaintiff would have a cause of action under Rule 10b–5.

As Judge Friendly stated in Mayer v. Oil Field Systems Corp.,[5] the courts of appeals have "unanimously" read Footnote 14 in the *Santa Fe Industries* case "to mean that plaintiffs may prove the existence of a means of self-protection by showing that they could have pursued some available state remedy if they had not been deceived."

SECTION 14(e)

Section 14(e) makes it unlawful for any person to make any untrue statement of a material fact "or to engage in any fraudulent, deceptive, or manipulative acts or practices," in connection with any tender offer or any solicitation in opposition to or in favor of a tender offer. This Section, in the tradition of the general fraud provisions of the 1933 and 1934 Acts, applies to all securities without regard to registration.[1]

Although § 14(e) adds "fraudulent" to the "manipulative or deceptive" of § 10(b), the two Sections have been treated as similar, if not identical. In *Schreiber v. Burlington Northern, Inc.*, the Court concluded that the term *manipulative* in § 14(e) required a misrepresentation or omission. This, the Court held, was consistent with both the common law concept of manipulation as affecting market activity by means of practices such as wash sales and rigged

---

4. Cf. Virginia Bankshares, Inc. v. Sandberg, 501 U.S. 1083 (1991) (causation could not be established when there was no link between alleged misrepresentations to minority shareholder and any state remedy).

5. 721 F.2d 59 (2d Cir.1983).

1. We have earlier discussed implied causes of action and standing under §§ 14(d) and (e) of the Securities Exchange Act.

prices,[2] and the earlier holding in *Santa Fe Industries, Inc. v. Green*[3] that § 10(b) did not cover mismanagement without some sort of misrepresentation. The Court also overruled a Sixth Circuit precedent, *Mobil Corp. v. Marathon Oil Co.,*[4] that had earlier held that manipulation in the context of a lockup does not always require an element of misrepresentation or nondisclosure.[5]

Wharf (Holdings) Limited v. United International Holdings, Inc.

Supreme Court of the United States, 2001.
532 U.S. 588, 121 S.Ct. 1776, 149 L.Ed.2d 845.

■ JUSTICE BREYER delivered the opinion of the Court.

This securities fraud action focuses upon a company that sold an option to buy stock while secretly intending never to honor the option. The question before us is whether this conduct violates § 10(b) of the Securities Exchange Act of 1934, which prohibits using "any manipulative or deceptive device or contrivance" "in connection with the purchase or sale of any security." . . . 15 U.S.C. § 78j(b); see also 17 CFR § 240.10b–5 (2000). We conclude that it does.

I

Respondent United International Holdings, Inc., a Colorado-based company, sued petitioner The Wharf (Holdings) Limited, a Hong Kong firm, in Colorado's Federal District Court. United said that in October 1992 Wharf had sold it an option to buy 10% of the stock of a new Hong Kong cable system. But, United alleged, at the time of the sale Wharf secretly intended not to permit United to exercise the option. United claimed that Wharf's conduct amounted to a fraud "in connection with the . . . sale of [a] security," prohibited § 10(b), and violated numerous state laws as well. A jury found in United's favor. The Court of Appeals for the Tenth Circuit upheld that verdict. 210 F.3d 1207 (2000). And we granted certiorari to consider whether the dispute fell within the scope of § 10(b).

The relevant facts, viewed in the light most favorable to the verdict winner, United, are as follows. In 1991, the Hong Kong government announced that it would accept bids for the award of an exclusive license to operate a cable television system in Hong Kong. Wharf decided to prepare a bid. Wharf's chairman, Peter Woo, instructed one of its managing directors, Stephen Ng, to find a business partner with cable system experience. Ng found United. And United sent several employees to Hong Kong to help prepare Wharf's application, negotiate contracts, design the system, and arrange financing.

United asked to be paid for its services with a right to invest in the cable system if Wharf should obtain the license. During August and September 1992, while United's employees were at work helping Wharf, Wharf and United negotiated about the details of that payment. Wharf prepared a draft letter of intent that contemplated giving United the right to become a co-investor, owning 10% of the system. But the parties did not sign the letter of intent. And in September, when Wharf submitted its bid, it told the Hong Kong authorities

2. 472 U.S. 1, 7 (1985).

3. 430 U.S. 462 (1977).

4. 669 F.2d 366 (6th Cir.1981), *cert. denied,* 455 U.S. 982 (1982).

5. 472 U.S. at 5 n.3.

that Wharf would be the system's initial sole owner. Lodging to App. AY–4, although Wharf would also "consider" allowing United to become an investor, id., at AY–6.

In early October 1992, Ng met with a United representative, who told Ng that United would continue to help only if Wharf gave United an enforceable right to invest. Ng then orally granted United an option with the following terms: (1) United had the right to buy 10% of the future system's stock; (2) the price of exercising the option would be 10% of the system's capital require-ments minus the value of United's previous services (including expenses); (3) United could exercise the option only if it showed that it could fund its 10% share of the capital required for at least the first 18 months; and (4) the option would expire if not exercised within six months of the date that Wharf received the license. The parties continued to negotiate about how to write documents that would embody these terms, but they never reduced the agreement to writing.

In May 1993, Hong Kong awarded the cable franchise to Wharf. United raised $66 million designed to help finance its 10% share. In July or August 1993, United told Wharf that it was ready to exercise its option. But Wharf refused to permit United to buy any of the system's stock. Contemporaneous internal Wharf documents suggested that Wharf had never intended to carry out its promise. For example, a few weeks before the key October 1992 meeting. Ng had prepared a memorandum stating that United wanted a right to invest that it could exercise if it was able to raise the necessary capital. A handwritten note by Wharf's Chairman Woo replied, "No, no, no, we don't accept that." App. DT–187; Lodging to App. A1–1. In September 1993, after meeting with the Wharf board to discuss United's investment in the cable system, Ng wrote to another Wharf executive, "How do we get out?" Id., at CY–1. In December 1993, after United had filed documents with the Securities Exchange Commis-sion representing that United was negotiating the acquisition of a 10% Interest in the cable system, an internal Wharf memo stated that "our next move should be to claim that our directors got quite upset over these representa-tions.... Publicly, we do not acknowledge [United's] opportunity" to acquire the 10% interest. Id., at DF–I (emphasis in original). In the margin of a December 1993 letter from United discussing its expectation of investing in the cable system, Ng wrote, "Be careful, must deflect this! Now?" Id., at DI–I. Other Wharf documents referred to the need to "back pedal," id., at DG–1, and "stall," id., at DJ–1.

These documents, along with other evidence, convinced the jury that Wharf, through Ng, had orally sold United an option to purchase a 10% interest in the future cable system while secretly intending not to permit United to exercise its option, in violation of § 10(b) of the Securities Exchange Act and various state laws. The jury awarded United compensatory damages of $67 million and, in light of circumstances of fraud, malice, or willful and wanton conduct, App. EM–1, 8, punitive damages of $58.5 million on the state-law claims. As we have said, the Court of Appeals upheld the jury's award. 210 F.3d 1207 (C.A.10 2000). And we granted certiorari to determine whether Wharf's oral sale of an option it intended not to honor is prohibited by § 10(b).

II

Section 10(b) of the Securities Exchange Act makes it "unlawful for any person ... to use or employ, in connection with the purchase or sale of any security . . ., any manipulative or deceptive device or contrivance in contravention of such rules and regulations as the [SEC] may prescribe." 15 U.S.C. § 78j.

Pursuant to this provision, the SEC has promulgated Rule 10b–5. That Rule forbids the use, "in connection with the purchase or sale of any security," of (1) "any device, scheme, or artifice to defraud"; (2) "any untrue statement of a material fact"; (3) the omission of "a material fact necessary in order to make the statements made . . . not misleading"; or (4) any other "act, practice, or course of business that operates * * * as a fraud or deceit." 17 CFR §§ 240.10b–5 (2000).

To succeed in a Rule 10b–5 suit, a private plaintiff must show that the defendant used, in connection with the purchase or sale of a security, one of the four kinds of manipulative or deceptive devices to which the Rule refers, and must also satisfy certain other requirements not at issue here. * * *

Wharf argues that it conduct falls outside the Rule's scope for two basic reasons. First, Wharf points out that its agreement to grant United an option to purchase shares in the cable system was an oral agreement. And it says that § 10(b) does not cover oral contracts of sale. Wharf points to *Blue Chip Stamps*, in which this Court construed the Act's "purchase or sale" language to mean that only "actual purchasers and sellers of securities" have standing to bring a private action for damages. See 421 U.S. at 730–731. Wharf notes that the Court's interpretation of he Act flowed in part from the need to protect defendants against lawsuits that "turn largely on which oral version of a series of occurrences the jury may decide to credit." *Blue Chip Stamps, supra,* at 742. And it claims that an oral purchase or sale would pose a similar problem of proof and thus should not satisfy the Rule's "purchase or sale" requirement.

Blue Chip Stamps, however, involved the very different question whether the Act protects a person who did not actually buy securities, but who might have done so had the seller told the truth. The Court held that the Act does not cover such a potential buyer, in part for the reason that Wharf states. But United is not a potential buyer, by providing Wharf with its services, it actually bought the option that Wharf sold. And Blue Chip Stamps said nothing to suggest that oral purchases or sales fall outside the scope of the Act. Rather, the Court's concern was about "the abuse potential and proof problems inherent in suits by investors who neither bought nor sold, but asserted they would have traded absent fraudulent conduct by others." United States v. O'Hagan, 521 U.S. 642, 664 (1997). Such a "Potential purchase" claim would rest on facts, including the plaintiff's state of mind, that might be "totally unknown and unknowable to the defendant," depriving the jury of "the benefit of weighing the plaintiff's version against the defendant's version." *Blue Chip Stamps, supra,* at 746. An actual sale, even if oral, would not create this problem, because both parties would be able to testify as to whether the relevant events had occurred.

Neither is there any other convincing reason to interpret the Act to exclude oral contracts as a class. The Act itself says that it applies to "any contract" for the purchase or sale of a security. 15 U.S.C. §§ 78c(a)(13), (14). Oral contracts for the sale of securities are sufficiently common that the Uniform Commercial Code and statutes of frauds in every State now consider them enforceable. See U.C.C. § 8–113 (Supp. 2000) ("A contract * * * for the sale or purchase of a security is enforceable whether or not there is a writing signed or record authenticated by a party against whom enforcement is sought"); see also 2C U. L. A. 77–81 (Supp. 2000) (table of enactments of U. C. C. Revised Art. 8

(amended 1994)) (noting adoption of § 8–113, with minor variations, by all States except Rhode Island and South Carolina). * * *

Second, Wharf argues that a secret reservation not to Permit the exercise of an Option falls outside § 10(b) because it does not "relate to the value of a security purchase or the consideration paid"; hence it does "not implicate [§ 10(b)'s] policy of full disclosure." Brief for Petitioners 25, 26 (emphasis deleted). But even were it the case that the Act covers only misrepresentations likely to affect the value of securities, Wharf's secret reservation was such a misrepresentation. To sell an option while secretly intending not to permit the option's exercise is misleading, because a buyer normally presumes good faith. Cf., e.g., Restatement (Second) of Torts § 530, Comment c (1976) ("Since a promise necessarily carries with it the implied assertion of an intention to perform [,] it follows that a promise made without such an intention is fraudulent"). For similar reasons, the secret reservation misled United about the option's value. Since Wharf did not intend to honor the option, the option was, unbeknownst to United, valueless.

Finally, Wharf supports its claim for an exemption from the statute by characterizing this case as a "dispute over the ownership of securities." Brief for Petitioners 24. Wharf expresses concern that interpreting the Act to allow recovery in a case like this one will permit numerous plaintiffs to bring federal securities claims that are in reality no more than ordinary state breach-of-contract claims—actions that lie outside the Act's basic objectives. United's claim, however, is not simply that Wharf failed to carry out a promise to sell it securities. It is a claim that Wharf sold it a security (the option) while secretly intending from the very beginning not to honor the option. And United proved that secret with documentary evidence that went well beyond evidence of a simple failure to perform. Moreover, Wharf has not shown us that its concern has proven serious as a practical matter in the past. Cf. Threadgill v. Black, 730 F.2d 810, 811–812 (C.A.D.C.) (per curiam); (suggesting in 1984 that contracting to sell securities with the secret reservation not to perform one's obligations under the contract violates § 10(b)). Nor does Wharf persuade us that it is likely to prove serious in the future. Cf. Private Securities Litigation Reform Act of 1995, Pub. L. 104–67, § 21D(b)(2), ML 15 U.S.C. § 78u–4(b)(2) (1994 ed., Supp. V) (imposing, beginning in 1995, stricter pleading requirements in private securities fraud actions that, among other things, require that a complaint "state with particularly acts giving rise to a strong inference that the defendant acted with the required [fraudulent] state of mind").

For these reasons, the judgment of the Court of Appeals is

Affirmed.

2.   THE DUTY TO UPDATE AND THE DUTY TO CORRECT

Clause (2) of Rule 10b–5 prohibits the "[omission] to state a material fact necessary in order to make the statement made, in the light of the circumstances under which they were made, not misleading. * * * " The Commission "believes that, depending on the circumstances, there is a duty to correct statements made in any filing * * * if the statements either have become inaccurate by virtue of subsequent events, or are later discovered to have been false and misleading from the outset, and the issuer knows or should know that persons are continuing to rely on all or any material portion of the statements."[1]

---

1. Sec. Act Rel. 6084, 17 SEC Dock. 1048, 1054 (1979); *see also* Sec. Ex. Act Rel.   8995 (1970) (a company that has complied with the reporting requirements "still has an

The courts have addressed both a duty to update or correct issuer statements *and* a separate duty to correct statements made by others that can be attributed to the issuer.

In re Time Warner Inc. Securities Litigation

United States Court of Appeals, Second Circuit, 1993.
9 F.3d 259.

■ Before NEWMAN, CHIEF JUDGE, WINTER and MINER, CIRCUIT JUDGES.

■ JON O. NEWMAN, CHIEF JUDGE:

This appeal from the dismissal of a securities fraud complaint requires us to consider the recurring issue of whether stock fraud claims are sufficiently pleaded to warrant at least discovery and perhaps trial. Three separate issues are presented: (1) whether a corporation has a duty to update somewhat optimistic predictions about achieving a business plan when it appears that the plan might not be realized, (2) whether a corporation has a duty to disclose a specific alternative to an announced business plan when that alternative is under active consideration, and (3) whether a corporation is responsible for statements in newspapers and security analyst reports that are attributed to unnamed corporate personnel. * * *

Plaintiffs' complaint alleged that defendant Time Warner, Inc. and four of its officers had misled the investing public by statements and omissions made in the course of Time Warner's efforts to reduce its debt. The District Court dismissed the complaint with prejudice for failure to adequately plead material misrepresentations or omissions attributable to the defendants and for failure to adequately plead scienter. We hold that the complaint's allegations of scienter and certain of its allegations concerning omissions are adequate to survive a motion to dismiss, and we accordingly reverse the order of dismissal and remand.

Background

On June 7, 1989, Time, Inc. received a surprise tender offer for its stock from Paramount Communications. Paramount's initial offer was $175 per share, in cash, and was eventually increased to $200 per share. *See* Paramount Communications, Inc. v. Time Inc., 571 A.2d 1140, 1147–49 (Del.1989). Time's directors declined to submit this offer to the shareholders and continued discussions that had begun somewhat earlier concerning a merger with Warner Communications, Inc. Eventually, Time and Warner agreed that Time would acquire all of Warner's outstanding stock for $70 per share, even though this acquisition would cause Time to incur debt of over $10 billion. Time shareholders and Paramount were unsuccessful in their effort to enjoin the Warner acquisition, which was completed in July 1989.

Thus, in 1989, Time Warner, Inc., the entity resulting from the merger, found itself saddled with over $10 billion in debt, an outcome that drew criticism from many shareholders. The company embarked on a highly publi-

obligation to make full and prompt announcement of facts regarding the company's financial condition"); Sec. Act Rel. 5699, 9 SEC Dock. 472, 474 (1976) ("this responsibility may extend to situations where management knows its previously disclosed assessments no longer have a reasonable basis").

cized campaign to find international "strategic partners" who would infuse billions of dollars of capital into the company and who would help the company realize its dream of becoming a dominant worldwide entertainment conglomerate. Ultimately, Time Warner formed only two strategic partnerships, each on a much smaller scale than had been hoped for. Faced with a multi-billion dollar balloon payment on the debt, the company was forced to seek an alternative method of raising capital—a new stock offering that substantially diluted the rights of the existing shareholders. The company first proposed a variable price offering on June 6, 1991. This proposal was rejected by the SEC, but the SEC approved a second proposal announced on July 12, 1991. Announcement of the two offering proposals caused a substantial decline in the price of Time Warner stock. From June 5 to June 12, the share price fell from $117 to $94. By July 12, the price had fallen to $89.75.

* * *

Discussion

Cases of this sort present an inevitable tension between two powerful interests. On the one hand, there is the interest in deterring fraud in the securities markets and remedying it when it occurs. That interest is served by recognizing that the victims of fraud often are unable to detail their allegations until they have had some opportunity to conduct discovery of those reasonably suspected of having perpetrated a fraud. Consistent with that interest, modern pleading rules usually permit a complaint to survive dismissal unless, in the familiar phrase, "it appears beyond doubt that the plaintiff can prove no set of facts in support of his claim which would entitle him to relief." *See* Conley v. Gibson, 355 U.S. 41, 45–46, 78 S.Ct. 99, 101–02, 2 L.Ed.2d 80 (1957).

On the other hand, there is the interest in deterring the use of the litigation process as a device for extracting undeserved settlements as the price of avoiding the extensive discovery costs that frequently ensue once a complaint survives dismissal, even though no recovery would occur if the suit were litigated to completion. It has never been clear how these competing interests are to be accommodated, and the adjudication process is not well suited to the formulation of a universal resolution of the tensions between them. In the absence of a more refined statutory standard than the vague contours of section 10(b) or a more detailed attempt at rule-making than the SEC has managed in Rule 10b–5, despite 50 years of unavailed opportunity, courts must adjudicate the precise cases before them, striking the balance as best they can.

In doing so, we do well to recognize several consequences of this common law approach to what is supposed to be a statutory standard. First, our outcomes will not necessarily evolve a discernible pattern. Second, the absence of a clear pattern will inevitably create uncertainty in the fields of both securities and litigation. Third, however sensitively we strike the balance in a particular case, we will not avoid the risks of adverse consequences: in the aftermath of any ruling that upholds the dismissal of a 10b–5 suit, there will be some opportunity for unremedied fraud; in the aftermath of any ruling that permits a 10b–5 suit to progress beyond a motion to dismiss, there will be some opportunity to extract an undeserved settlement. Unattractive as those prospects are, they neither indicate a sound basis for decision nor permit avoidance of decision.

* * *

I. Existence of an actionable misrepresentation or omission

A. Anonymous statements to reporters and analysts

We first consider whether the District Court properly concluded that Rule 9(b) required dismissal of allegations of fraudulent statements when the complaint failed to identify the speaker. The complaint contains excerpts from a variety of newspaper stories and security analyst reports. Some of these accounts contain anonymous quotes or paraphrases of statements from alleged Time Warner insiders. Others merely report upon Time Warner's activities. In both cases, plaintiffs allege that some as yet unknown agents of Time Warner made misleading statements (or omitted to disclose material information) in discussions with the reporter or analyst. These reports and stories, excerpted in the complaint at ¶¶ 42, 44–47, 49, 54, 58–62, 65, 69, 72, generally confirm that negotiations concerning strategic alliances are ongoing and add little to the statements for which Time Warner is concededly responsible. But some of the statements implied in the reports and stories would bolster plaintiffs' case considerably. * * *

Rule 9(b) requires that "[i]n all averments of fraud or mistake, the circumstances constituting fraud or malice shall be stated with particularity." Judge Lasker understood Rule 9(b) to require, at a minimum, that the plaintiff identify the speaker of the allegedly fraudulent statements. We believe that he was correct. Plaintiffs rely on several district court decisions that they claim apply a less strict rule for statements attributed to corporate "spokespersons," *see* In re AnnTaylor Stores Securities Litigation, 807 F.Supp. 990, 1004 (S.D.N.Y.1992); Cytryn v. Cook, Fed.Sec.L.Rep. (CCH) ¶ 95,409, 1990 WL 128233 (N.D.Cal. July 2, 1990), and for statements by newspapers and analysts allegedly caused by corporate employees, *see* Alfus v. Pyramid Technology Corp., 764 F. Supp. 598, 603 (N.D.Cal.1991); In re Columbia Securities Litigation, 747 F. Supp. 237, 245 (S.D.N.Y.1990). These cases are distinguishable on their facts, in that they involve official press releases, *see* AnnTaylor, 807 F.Supp. at 1004–05; *see also* DiVittorio v. Equidyne Extractive Industries, Inc., 822 F.2d 1242, 1247 (2d Cir.1987) (offering statement), statements by named individuals to analysts or reporters, *see* Columbia, 747 F. Supp. at 245; Cytryn, Fed.Sec.L.Rep. (CCH) at 97,016, or the defendant's placing its "imprimatur" on analyst's reports, *see* Alfus, 764 F. Supp. at 603; *see also* Elkind v. Liggett & Myers, Inc., 635 F.2d 156, 163–64 (2d Cir.1980). None of these cases sanctions the pleading of fraud through completely unattributed statements, even when the plaintiff alleges on information and belief that the unattributed statement was made by an agent of the defendant.

Just as 10b–5 litigation, however resolved, risks adverse consequences, as we have noted, a strict application of Rule 9(b) in the context of unattributed statements also risks unfortunate effects. A scheming corporation could inflate its stock price through fraudulent statements whispered to reporters or analysts. If the reporters or analysts refused to reveal their sources and if no one inside the corporation leaked to the stockholders or to regulators the identity of the speakers, the corporation would have perpetuated a fraud that could not be remedied by a private civil action under the federal securities laws. For several reasons, however, we have some confidence that this is not a sufficiently likely scenario to justify a rule that would permit a suit alleging unattributed statements to survive a motion to dismiss. * * *

As an initial matter, the function of financial reporters and security analysts is to determine the truth about the affairs of publicly traded companies. Few reporters or analysts would knowingly abet a fraud, and many will detect and reveal a corporation's efforts to use them as a channel for fraudulent statements. Additionally, investors tend to discount information in newspaper articles and analyst reports when the author is unable to cite specific, attributable information from the company. Thus, the opportunity to manipulate stock prices through the planting of false stories is somewhat limited. Finally, the effect of a less strict construction of Rule 9(b) would be only to allow discovery on the issue of the linkage between the corporation and the newspaper stories or analyst reports. Sometimes, of course, plaintiff's counsel would be able to use discovery to determine the identity of the speaker, and would find that this speaker was a person for whom the corporation was responsible. But far more often, we suspect, this would not be the case. Either the corporation is not responsible for the statements, in which case it has been unnecessarily burdened either by the expense of discovery or by a settlement extracted under threat of such discovery, or it is responsible, and having exhibited sufficient devotion to a fraudulent scheme so as to prevent attribution of statements in advance of discovery, it will often attempt and sometimes succeed in stonewalling discovery.

Alternatively, the District Court found that the unattributed statements, even if attributable to Time Warner, were not actionable. We do not reach this issue, since we find that dismissal with prejudice under Fed.R.Civ.P. 9(b) was proper as to these statements. It is true that dismissal under Rule 9(b) is usually without prejudice, see Luce v. Edelstein, 802 F.2d 49, 56–57 (2d Cir.1986), but plaintiffs, though offered the opportunity by the District Court, have presented nothing to suggest that they could amend the complaint to adequately plead a link between the defendants and the unattributed statements.

B.   Attributed statements and corporate press releases

We next focus on those statements as to which there is no issue of attribution. While plaintiffs claim that these statements were misleading, in that they exaggerated the likelihood that strategic alliances would be made, plaintiffs primarily fault these statements for what they did not disclose. The nondisclosure is of two types: failure to disclose problems in the strategic alliance negotiations, and failure to disclose the active consideration of an alternative method of raising capital. * * *

1.   *Affirmative misrepresentations.* We agree with the District Court that none of the statements constitutes an *affirmative* misrepresentation. Most of the statements reflect merely that talks are ongoing, and that Time Warner hopes that the talks will be successful. There is no suggestion that the factual assertions contained in any of these statements were false when the statements were made. As to the expressions of opinion and the projections contained in the statements, while not beyond the reach of the securities laws, see Virginia Bankshares, Inc. v. Sandberg, 501 U.S. 1083, 1088–1098, 111 S.Ct. 2749, 2756–61 (1991) (proxy statements actionable under section 14(a)); Goldman v. Belden, 754 F.2d 1059, 1068–69 (2d Cir.1985) (positive predictions actionable under section 10(b)), the complaint contains no allegations to support the inference that the defendants either did not have these favorable opinions on future prospects when they made the statements or that the favorable opinions were without a basis in fact.

2. *Nondisclosure of problems in the strategic alliance negotiations.* The allegations of nondisclosure are more serious. Plaintiffs' first theory of nondisclosure is that the defendants' statements hyping strategic alliances gave rise to a duty to disclose problems in the alliance negotiations as those problems developed. We agree that a duty to update opinions and projections may arise if the original opinions or projections have become misleading as the result of intervening events. *See* In re Gulf Oil/Cities Service Tender Offer Litigation, 725 F.Supp. 712, 745–49 (S.D.N.Y.1989) (material misstatements or omissions adequately set forth alleging that defendants had expressed a strong interest in consummating a merger and had not disclosed a later "change of heart"); In re Warner Communications Securities Litigation, 618 F.Supp. 735, 752 (S.D.N.Y. 1985) (approving settlement), *aff'd,* 798 F.2d 35 (2d Cir.1986). But, in this case, the attributed public statements lack the sort of definite positive projections that might require later correction. The statements suggest only the hope of any company, embarking on talks with multiple partners, that the talks would go well. No identified defendant stated that he thought deals would be struck by a certain date, or even that it was likely that deals would be struck at all. Cf. In re Apple Computer Securities Litigation, 886 F.2d 1109, 1118–19 (9th Cir.1989) (Chairman of the Board stated that new computer product would be "phenomenally successful the first year out of the chute," etc.), *cert. denied,* 496 U.S. 943, 110 S.Ct. 3229, 110 L.Ed.2d 676 (1990). These statements did not become materially misleading when the talks did not proceed well.[4]

3. *Nondisclosure of alternative methods of raising capital.* Still more serious is the allegation of a failure to disclose the simultaneous consideration of the rights offering as an alternative method of raising capital. As an initial matter, of course, a reasonable investor would probably have wanted to know of consideration of the rights offering. Though both the rights offering and strategic alliances would have brought capital into the corporation, the two acts would have directly opposite effects on the price of Time Warner stock. A successful strategic alliance, simultaneously opening new markets and reducing debt, would have improved the corporation's expected profit stream, and should have served to drive up the share price. An offering of new shares, in contrast, would dilute the ownership rights of existing shareholders, likely decrease dividends, and drive down the price of the stock.

But a corporation is not required to disclose a fact merely because a reasonable investor would very much like to know that fact. Rather, an omission is actionable under the securities laws only when the corporation is subject to a duty to disclose the omitted facts. *See* Basic Inc. v. Levinson, 485 U.S. 224, 239 n. 17, 108 S.Ct. 978, 987 n. 17, 99 L.Ed.2d 194 (1988); Glazer v. Formica Corp., 964 F.2d 149, 157 (2d Cir.1992). As Time Warner pointedly reminds us, we have not only emphasized the importance of ascertaining a duty to disclose when omissions are at issue but have also drawn a distinction between the concepts of a duty to disclose and materiality. *See Glazer,* 964 F.2d at 157. It appears, however, that the distinction has meaning only in certain contexts. For example, where the issue is whether an individual's relationship to information imposed upon him a duty to disclose, the inquiry as to his duty

---

4. Although the statements are generally open-ended, there is one sense in which they have a solid core. The statements represent as fact that serious talks with multiple parties were ongoing. If this factual assertion ceased to be true, defendants would have had an obligation to update their earlier statements. But the complaint does not allege that the talks ever stopped or ceased to be "serious," just that they eventually went poorly.

is quite distinct from the inquiry as to the information's materiality. *See* Dirks v. SEC, 463 U.S. 646, 103 S.Ct. 3255, 77 L.Ed.2d 911 (1983). On the other hand, where the disclosure duty arises from the combination of a prior statement and a subsequent event, which, if not disclosed, renders the prior statement false or misleading, the inquiries as to duty and materiality coalesce. The undisclosed information is material if there is "a substantial likelihood that the disclosure of the omitted fact would have been viewed by the reasonable investor as having significantly altered the 'total mix' of information available." TSC Industries, Inc. v. Northway, Inc., 426 U.S. 438, 449, 96 S.Ct. 2126, 2132, 48 L.Ed.2d 757 (1976). If a reasonable investor would so regard the omitted fact, it is difficult to imagine a circumstance where the prior statement would not be rendered misleading in the absence of the disclosure. As *Glazer* makes clear, one circumstance creating a duty to disclose arises when disclosure is necessary to make prior statements not misleading. *Glazer,* 964 F.2d at 157 (citing Roeder v. Alpha Industries, Inc., 814 F.2d 22, 26 (1st Cir.1987)).

We have previously considered whether disclosure of one business plan required disclosure of considered alternatives in Kronfeld v. Trans World Airlines, Inc., 832 F.2d 726 (2d Cir.1987), *cert. denied,* 485 U.S. 1007, 108 S.Ct. 1470, 99 L.Ed.2d 700 (1988). In *Kronfeld,* the defendant, TWA's parent corporation, failed to disclose in the prospectus for a new issue of TWA stock that it was contemplating termination of its relationship with TWA. Because the prospectus discussed "in some detail the relationship between TWA" and the parent, *id.* at 735, we held that a fact question was presented as to whether it was materially misleading not to disclose the possibility of termination, *id.* at 736–37. In effect, the alternative, if disclosed, would have suggested to investors that the various guarantees extended from the parent to TWA might be meaningless. In the pending case, the District Court understood the obligation to disclose alternate business plans to be limited to the context of mutually exclusive alternatives. It is true that *Kronfeld* involved such alternatives—the TWA parent could not both maintain and terminate its relations with TWA—and that this case does not. Time Warner potentially could have raised all its needed capital from either strategic alliances or a rights offering, or it could have raised some part of the necessary capital using each approach.

We believe, however, that a disclosure duty limited to mutually exclusive alternatives is too narrow. A duty to disclose arises whenever secret information renders prior public statements materially misleading, not merely when that information completely negates the public statements. Time Warner's public statements could have been understood by reasonable investors to mean that the company hoped to solve the *entire* debt problem through strategic alliances. Having publicly hyped strategic alliances, Time Warner may have come under a duty to disclose facts that would place the statements concerning strategic alliances in a materially different light.

It is important to appreciate the limits of our disagreement with the District Court. We do not hold that whenever a corporation speaks, it must disclose every piece of information in its possession that could affect the price of its stock. Rather, we hold that when a corporation is pursuing a specific business goal and announces that goal as well as an intended approach for reaching it, it may come under an obligation to disclose other approaches to reaching the goal when those approaches are under active and serious consideration. Whether consideration of the alternate approach constitutes material information, and whether nondisclosure of the alternate approach renders the original disclosure misleading, remain questions for the trier of fact, and may be resolved by summary judgment when there is no disputed issue of material fact. We conclude here only that the allegations in this complaint of nondisclosure of the rights offering are sufficient to survive a motion to dismiss. * * *

In re Burlington Coat Factory Securities Litigation

United States Court of Appeals, Third Circuit, 1997.
114 F.3d 1410.

Burlington Coat Factory Warehouse Corporation ("BCF"), a Delaware corporation based in New Jersey, announced its fourth quarter and full fiscal year results for 1994 on September 20, 1994. The results were below the investment community's expectations, and BCF's common stock fell sharply, losing approximately 30% in one day. Within a day of the initial announcement, the first investor suit was filed. In the next few days, the company made additional explanatory disclosures, and the stock price fell even further. More investor suits were filed. The action at hand is the product of the consolidation of these suits.

* * *

The district court dismissed the case both for failure to state claims on which relief could be granted and for failure to plead those claims with adequate particularity.

* * *

BCF is one of the leading retailers of coats in the United States. Its specialty is selling brand name clothes at discount prices. By mid–1993, BCF was operating a total of 185 stores in 39 states. The stores ranged in size from 16,000 to 133,000 square feet and featured outerwear (coats, jackets, and raincoats) and complete lines of clothing for men, women, and children.

* * *

On September 20, 1994, BCF reported its year-end revenues and earnings for fiscal 1994. These results were below the market's expectations, with the earnings per share for fiscal 1994 being $1.12 as compared to the $1.37 that analysts had been predicting. On September 20 itself, the price of BCF stock fell almost 30%, from $23.25 to $15.75 per share. Between September 20 and September 23 both BCF and outside analysts attempted to explain the reasons for the worse-than-expected results. By the close of the market on September 23, 1994, the price of BCF stock had fallen to $13.63.

* * *

Duties to Update and Correct

Plaintiffs * * * assert that BCF had a duty to correct the November 1, 1993, expression of comfort with the analysts' projections. In particular, plaintiffs point to the refusal of BCF's CEO, Monroe Milstein, in an interview given to Reuters—reported on March 22, 1994—to comment on analysts' earnings projections for both the third quarter of 1994 and the full year. Plaintiffs assert that on March 22, 1994, and at other unspecified points in time after November 1, 1993, defendants had had a duty to correct the November 1 earnings projection. Although plaintiffs characterize their claim as a "duty to correct" claim, they appear to be asserting both a duty to correct and a duty to update.

The Seventh Circuit explained in Stransky v. Cummins Engine Co., Inc., 51 F.3d 1329 (7th Cir.1995), that the duty to correct is analytically different from the duty to update, although litigants, as appears to be the case here, often fail to distinguish between the two. *Id. at 1331.*

* * *

(a) Duty to Correct

The Stransky court articulated the duty to correct as applying:

when a company makes a historical statement that, at the time made, the company believed to be true, but as revealed by subsequently discovered information actually was not. The company then must correct the prior statement within a reasonable time.

51 F.3d at 1331–32 (emphasis added); see also *Backman v. Polaroid Corp., 910 F.2d 10, 16–17 (1st Cir.1990)* (in banc) ("Obviously, if a disclosure is in fact misleading when made, and the speaker thereafter learns of this, there is a duty to correct it.") (emphasis added). We have no quarrel with the Stransky articulation, except to note that we think the duty to correct can also apply to a certain narrow set of forward-looking statements. We will attempt to illustrate the kinds of circumstances we have in mind with an example.

Imagine the following situation. A public company in Manhattan makes a forecast that appears to it to be reasonable at the time made. Subsequently, the company discovers that it misread a vital piece of data that went into its forecast. Perhaps a fax sent by the company's factory manager in some remote location was blurry and was reasonably misread by management in Manhattan as representing sales for the past quarter as 100,000 units as opposed 10,000 units. Manhattan management then makes an erroneous forecast based on the information it has at the time. A few weeks later, management receives the correct sales figures by mail. So long as the correction in the sales figures was material to the forecast that was disclosed earlier, we think there would likely be a duty on the part of the company to disclose either the corrected figures or a corrected forecast. In other words, there is an implicit representation in any forecast (or statement of historical fact) that errors of the type we have identified will be corrected. This duty derives from the implicit factual representation that a public company makes whenever it makes a forecast, i.e., that the forecast was reasonable at the time made. What is crucial to recognize is that the error, albeit an honest one, was one that had to do with information available at the time the forecast was made and that the error in the information was subsequently discovered. * * *

Plaintiffs phrase their claim as based on a "duty to correct." * * * [A]s to the "duty to correct" claim, plaintiffs have failed to allege how and what the specific error or set of errors might have been that went into the November 1, 1993, forecast. Nor have the plaintiffs identified the specific times at which those errors were discovered, so as to allow correction and trigger defendants' alleged duty. Therefore, the "duty to correct" claim (to the extent one is being made) fails Rule 9(b)'s pleading standards. In any event, we think plaintiffs' claim is better characterized as a "duty to update" claim.

(b) Duty to Update

The duty to update, in contrast to the duty to correct, concerns statements that, although reasonable at the time made, become misleading when viewed in the context of subsequent events. See *Greenfield v. Heublein, Inc., 742 F.2d 751, 758 (3d Cir.1984); Backman, 910 F.2d at 17.* In Greenfield, we explained that updating might be required if a prior disclosure "[had] become materially misleading in light of subsequent events." *742 F.2d at 758;* cf. *Time Warner, 9 F.3d at 267.* However, although we have generally recognized that a duty to update might exist under certain circumstances, we have not clarified when such circumstances might exist. Cf. *Phillips, 881 F.2d at 1245; Greenfield, 742 F.2d at 758–60; Backman, 910 F.2d at 17* (the duty arises only under "special circumstances").

Specifically, we have not addressed the question whether a duty to update might exist for ordinary, run-of-the-mill forecasts, such as the earnings projection in this case. At issue here is the statement of BCF's CAO on November 1, 1993, that he was comfortable with analyst projections of $1.20 to $1.30 as a mid-range for earnings per share in fiscal 1994. Plaintiffs' argument appears to be that, as BCF obtained information in the period subsequent to November 1, 1993, that would have produced a material change in the earnings projection for fiscal 1994, there was an ongoing duty to disclose this information. In essence then, the claim is that the disclosure of a single specific forecast produced a continuous duty to update the public with either forecasts or hard information that would in any way change a reasonable investor's perception of the originally forecasted range. We decline to hold that the disclosure of a single, ordinary earnings forecast can produce such an expansive set of disclosure obligations.

For a plaintiff to allege that a duty to update a forward-looking statement arose on account of an earlier-made projection, the argument has to be that the projection contained an implicit factual representation that remained "alive" in the minds of investors as a continuing representation. * * * Determining whether such a representation is implicit in an ordinary forecast is a function of what a reasonable investor expects as a result of the background regulatory structure. In particular, we note three features of the existing federal securities disclosure apparatus:

1. Except for specific periodic reporting requirements (primarily the requirements to file quarterly and annual reports), there is no general duty on the part of a company to provide the public with all material information. See *Time Warner, 9 F.3d at 267* ("a corporation is not required to disclose a fact merely because a reasonable investor would very much like to know that fact"). Thus, possession of material nonpublic information alone does not create a duty to disclose it. [Citations omitted.]

2. Equally well settled is the principle that an accurate report of past successes does not contain an implicit representation that the trend is going to continue, and hence does not, in and of itself, obligate the company to update the public as to the state of the quarter in progress. [Citations omitted.]

3. Finally, the existing regulatory structure is aimed at encouraging companies to make and disclose internal forecasts by protecting them from liability for disclosing internal forecasts that, although reasonable when made, turn out to be wrong in hindsight. See *Stransky, 51 F.3d at 1333.* Companies are not obligated either to produce or disclose internal forecasts, and if they do, they are protected from liability, except to the extent that the forecasts were unreasonable when made. See *Glassman, 90 F.3d at 631.* The regulatory structure seeks to encourage companies to disclose forecasts by providing companies with some protection from liability. However, where it comes to

affirmative disclosure requirements, the current regulatory scheme focuses on backward-looking "hard" information, not forecasts. See id. (citing Frank H. Easterbrook and Daniel R. Fischel, The Economic Structure of Corporate Law, 305–06 (1991)). Increasing the obligations associated with disclosing reasonably made internal forecasts is likely to deter companies from providing this information—a result contrary to the SEC's goal of encouraging the voluntary disclosure of company forecasts. Cf. *Stransky, 51 F.3d at 1333;* Raab, 4 F.3d at 290.

Based on features one and two, we do not think it can be said that an ordinary earnings projection contains an implicit representation on the part of the company that it will update the investing public with all material information that relates to that forecast. Under existing law, the market knows that companies have neither a specific obligation to disclose internal forecasts nor a general obligation to disclose all material information. *Shaw, 82 F.3d at 1202 & 1209.* We conclude that ordinary, run-of-the-mill forecasts contain no more than the implicit representation that the forecasts were made reasonably and in good faith. Cf. *Stransky, 51 F.3d at 1333; Kowal, 16 F.3d at 1277.* Just as the accurate disclosure of a line of past successes has been ruled not to contain the implication that the current period is going just as well, see *Gross, 93 F.3d at 994,* disclosure of a specific earnings forecast does not contain the implication that the forecast will continue to hold good even as circumstances change.

Finally, the federal securities laws, as they stand today, aim at encouraging companies to disclose their forecasts. A judicially created rule that triggers a duty of continuous disclosure of all material information every time a single specific earnings forecast is disclosed would likely result in a drastic reduction in the number of such projections made by companies. It is these specific earnings projections that are the most useful to investors in deciding whether to invest in a firm's securities. * * * The only types of projections that would be exempt from the duty of continuous disclosure advocated by plaintiffs, and hence the only types of projections that would likely be disclosed under the rule proposed by plaintiffs, would be vague expressions of hope and optimism that are of little use to investors. * * * Therefore, apart from the fact that plaintiffs' disclosure theory has no support in the existing regulatory structure, adopting it would severely undermine the goal of encouraging the maximal disclosure of information useful to investors. Cf. *Hillson, 42 F.3d at 219* (increasing the level of liability for projections would produce a result contrary to the goals of full disclosure that underlie the federal securities laws). In sum, under the existing disclosure apparatus, the voluntary disclosure of an ordinary earnings forecast does not trigger any duty to update.

THE DUTY TO UPDATE AND THE DUTY TO CORRECT

As both *Time Warner* and *Burlington Coat* suggest, the courts have long recognized that a corporation owes a duty to correct a statement that it believed was true when made but subsequent events reveal that the statement in fact was not true when made. As a leading First Circuit case explained:

> Obviously, if a disclosure is in fact misleading when made, and the speaker thereafter learns of this, there is a duty to correct it. In Greenfield v. Heublein, Inc., 742 F.2d 751, 758 (3d Cir.1984), *cert. denied*, 469 U.S. 1215, * * * (1985), * * * the court called for disclosure if a prior disclosure "becomes materially misleading in light of subsequent events," a quite different duty. We may agree that, in special circumstances, a statement,

correct at the time, may have a forward intent and connotation upon which parties may be expected to rely. If this is a clear meaning, and there is a change, correction, more exactly, further disclosure, may be called for.[1]

This duty to correct persists as long as the prior statements remain "alive." As the District Court in Ross v. A.H. Robins Co., Inc.[2] explained:

Both Section 10(b) and Rule 10b–5 are silent as to the effect of time on the duty to correct, but logic compels the conclusion that time may render statements immaterial and end any duty to correct or revise them. In measuring the effect of time in a particular instance, the type of later information and the importance of earlier information contained in a prior statement must be considered. Thus, general financial information in a two-year-old annual report may be stale and immaterial. [Citation omitted.] However, no general rule of time can be applied to all circumstances. Rather, a "particular duty to correct a specific prior statement exists as long as traders in the market could reasonably rely on the statement." [Citation omitted.]

Burlington Coat illustrates that the courts are divided whether a corporation also has a duty to update a statement that was true when made but because of subsequent events became untrue. Some recent cases have suggested that this duty does not exist under Rule 10b–5.[3]

In limited circumstances an issuer may also be responsible for correcting or updating third party statements when the issuer is the source of the inaccuracies or is responsible for their dissemination. Normally, however, the mere presence of rumors or publicly circulating inaccuracies concerning the issuer does not require a response from the issuer.[4]

---

1.   Backman v. Polaroid Corp., 910 F.2d 10, 16–17 (1st Cir.1990).

In Rudolph v. Arthur Andersen & Co., 800 F.2d 1040, 1043 (11th Cir.1986), *cert. denied*, 480 U.S. 946 (1987), the Eleventh Circuit stated that "accountants 'have a duty to take reasonable steps to correct misstatements they have discovered in previous financial statements on which they know the public is relying' " quoting from IIT, International Inv. Trust v. Cornfeld, 619 F.2d 909, 927 (2d Cir.1980).

2.   465 F.Supp. 904, 908 (S.D.N.Y.1979), *rev'd on other grounds*, 607 F.2d 545 (2d Cir.1979), *cert. denied*, 446 U.S. 946 (1980).

3.   In Grassi v. Information Resources, Inc., 63 F.3d 596, 599 (7th Cir.1995), the court highlighted: "a company has no duty to update forward-looking statements merely because changing circumstances have proven them wrong."

Cf. San Leandro Emergency Med. Group Profit Sharing Plan v. Philip Morris Co., Inc., 75 F.3d 801 (2d Cir.1996), which declined to find a material omission when a cigarette manufacturer considered a marketing plan to discover cigarette prices and increase market share while publicly stating that the company was committed to increased prices to sustain profits. In this case, unlike *Time Warner*, there was uncertainty whether the company had in fact committed itself to a new marketing strategy and foreclosed all alternatives.

But cf. Shaw v. Digital Equip. Corp., 82 F.3d 1194, 1205 (1st Cir.1996), analyzing Item 11(a) of Form S–3:

The primary purpose of the "material changes" disclosure requirement of Item 11(a), then, is to ensure that the prospectus provides investors with an update of the information required to be disclosed in the incorporated Exchange Act filings, including the information provided in those filings concerning "known trends and uncertainties" with respect to "net sales or revenues or income from continuing operations." 17 C.F.R. § 229.303(a)(3)(ii).

4.   *See, e.g.*, Electronic Specialty Co. v. International Controls Corp., 409 F.2d 937, 949 (2d Cir.1969), item in *Wall Street Journal* column "Heard on the Street" held not attributable to the issuer: "While a company may choose to correct a misstatement in the press not attributable to it, cf. SEC v. Texas Gulf Sulphur Co., 401 F.2d 833, 857–859,

For example, in Elkind v. Liggett & Myers, Inc.,[5] the Second Circuit observed:

> We have no doubt that a company may so involve itself in the preparation of reports and projections by outsiders as to assume a duty to correct material errors in those projections. This may occur when officials of the company have, by their activity, made an implied representation that the information they have reviewed is true or at least in accordance with the company's views.[6]

But a company assumes no duty to disclose its own internal earnings forecasts or to warn analysts that their optimistic view was not shared by the company if it merely reviewed analyst reports and made suggestions as to factual and descriptive matters while adhering to a policy not to comment on earnings forecasts.[7]

Regarding the duty to up date and the duty to correct, see generally 7 Louis Loss & Joel Seligman, Securities Regulation 3519–3523 (3d ed. 1991); Robert H. Rosenblum, An Issuer's Duty under Rule 10b–5 to Correct and Update Materially Misleading Statements, 40 Cath. U. L. Rev. 289 (1991); Gregory S. Porter, What Did You Know and When Did You Know It?: Public Company Disclosure and the Mythical Duties to Correct and Update, 68 Fordham L. Rev. 2199 (2000).

PROBLEM 14–4

In 2001 Mondo Electronics secured a patent for a new type of "multi-thermal" battery (MTB). Its CEO, Mitch Mondo announced in a December 2001 press conference that the MTB was a "breakthrough" for the battery powered automobile. On the basis of "systematic 6 month tests," he announced that the MTB would allow the "typical United States or foreign made automobile to drive up to 50 hours without recharging at speeds of up to 90 miles per hour."

Mondo's CFO explained that when full production of 10,000 batteries was achieved at Mondo's plant in late 2002, the cost per battery would be $250, which would permit retail sales of the battery at $500 per battery and approximately double Mondo's net income.

By early 2002, Mondo's engineers had learned that:

866–869 (concurring opinion) (2d Cir. 1968), we find nothing in the securities legislation requiring it to do so." *See also* State Teachers Retirement Bd. v. Fluor Corp., 654 F.2d 843, 850 (2d Cir.1981): "A company has no duty to correct or verify rumors in the marketplace unless these rumors can be attributed to the company."

5. 635 F.2d 156 (2d Cir.1980).

6. Id. at 163; *see also* Goldman v. Belden, 754 F.2d 1059, 1069 (2d Cir.1985); Cooper v. Pickett, 137 F.3d 616, 623–624 (9th Cir.1997); Winkler v. Wigley, 242 F.3d 369 (2d Cir.2000).

7. Elkind v. Liggett & Myers, 635 F.2d 156, 163 (2d Cir.1980). Cf. In re Time Warner Inc. Sec. Litig., 794 F.Supp. 1252, 1258–1259 (S.D.N.Y.1992), *aff'd* in part & rev'd in part, 9 F.3d 259 (2d Cir.1993), *cert. denied sub nom* ZVI Trading Corp. Employees' Money Purchase Pension Plan & Trust v. Ross, 511 U.S. 1017 (1994):

Only statements attributable to the defendants, or omissions by them, can support the claims against them. * * * [N]either the alleged statements by anonymous Time Warner sources which are quoted in the complaint nor analysts' and journalists' reports allegedly based on information gleaned from Time Warner sources may be attributed to the defendants.

(1) They had underestimated the weight of the typical sedan and minivan, with the consequence that the typical battery driven could achieve top speeds up to 60 miles per hour.

(2) Tests over 18 months disclosed that the MTD deteriorated over time and between 12 and 18 months needed to be recharged an average of once every 28 hours.

(3) More comprehensive engineering data revealed an average cost per battery of $260.

(4) The same engineering study revealed that full production at Mondo's plant could only produce 8000 batteries per year.

Which, if any, of those data would Mondo be required to reveal under Rule 10b–5?

3. "INSIDER" TRADING

The SEC in *In re* Cady, Roberts & Co.,[1] and the Second Circuit in SEC v. Texas Gulf Sulphur Co.,[2] popularized what came to be known as the "disclose or abstain" duty. As the court in Texas Gulf Sulphur phrased this duty:

> The essence of the Rule is that anyone who, trading for his own account in the securities of a corporation has "access, directly or indirectly, to information intended to be available only for a corporate purpose and not for the personal benefit of anyone" may not take "advantage of such information knowing it is unavailable to those with whom he is dealing," i.e., the investing public. Matter of Cady, Roberts & Co., 40 SEC 907, 912 (1961). Insiders, as directors or management officers are, of course, by this Rule, precluded from so unfairly dealing, but the Rule is also applicable to one possessing the information who may not be strictly termed an "insider" within the meaning of Sec. 16(b) of the Act. Cady, Roberts, *supra*. Thus, anyone in possession of material inside information must either disclose it to the investing public, or, if he is disabled from disclosing it in order to protect a corporate confidence, or he chooses not to do so, must abstain from trading in or recommending the securities concerned while such inside information remains undisclosed.[3]

While the concept of a disclose or abstain duty has endured, the *Texas Gulf Sulphur* intimation that the duty was universal has not. In three subsequent Supreme Court decisions, that Court has sharpened the scope of who is subject to the disclose or abstain duty.

Chiarella v. United States

Supreme Court of the United States, 1980.
445 U.S. 222, 100 S.Ct. 1108, 63 L.Ed.2d 348.

■ Mr. Justice Powell delivered the opinion of the Court.

The question in this case is whether a person who learns from the confidential documents of one corporation that it is planning an attempt to secure control of a second corporation violates § 10(b) of the Securities Ex-

---

1. 40 SEC 907 (1961).

2. 401 F.2d 833 (2d Cir.1968), *cert. denied sub nom.* Coates v. SEC, 394 U.S. 976 (1969).

3. Id. at 848.

change Act of 1934 if he fails to disclose the impending takeover before trading in the target company's securities.

I

Petitioner is a printer by trade. In 1975 and 1976, he worked as a "markup man" in the New York composing room of Pandick Press, a financial printer. Among documents that petitioner handled were five announcements of corporate takeover bids. When these documents were delivered to the printer, the identities of the acquiring and target corporations were concealed by blank spaces or false names. The true names were sent to the printer on the night of the final printing.

The petitioner, however, was able to deduce the names of the target companies before the final printing from other information contained in the documents. Without disclosing his knowledge, petitioner purchased stock in the target companies and sold the shares immediately after the takeover attempts were made public. By this method, petitioner realized a gain of slightly more than $30,000 in the course of 14 months. Subsequently, the Securities and Exchange Commission (Commission or SEC) began an investigation of his trading activities. In May 1977, petitioner entered into a consent decree with the Commission in which he agreed to return his profits to the sellers of the shares. On the same day, he was discharged by Pandick Press.

In January 1978, petitioner was indicted on 17 counts of violating § 10(b) of the Securities Exchange Act of 1934 (1934 Act) and SEC Rule 10b–5. After petitioner unsuccessfully moved to dismiss the indictment, he was brought to trial and convicted on all counts.

The Court of Appeals for the Second Circuit affirmed petitioner's conviction. 588 F.2d 1358 (1978). We granted certiorari, 441 U.S. 942 (1979), and we now reverse.

II

Section 10(b) of the 1934 Act prohibits the use "in connection with the purchase or sale of any security * * * [of] any manipulative or deceptive device or contrivance in contravention of such rules and regulations as the Commission may prescribe." Pursuant to this section, the SEC promulgated Rule 10b–5 * * *.

This case concerns the legal effect of the petitioner's silence. The District Court's charge permitted the jury to convict the petitioner if it found that he willfully failed to inform sellers of target company securities that he knew of a forthcoming takeover bid that would make their shares more valuable. In order to decide whether silence in such circumstances violates § 10(b), it is necessary to review the language and legislative history of that statute as well as its interpretation by the Commission and the federal courts.

Although the starting point of our inquiry is the language of the statute, Ernst & Ernst v. Hochfelder, 425 U.S. 185, 197 (1976), § 10(b) does not state whether silence may constitute a manipulative or deceptive device. Section 10(b) was designed as a catchall clause to prevent fraudulent practices. Id., at 202, 206. But neither the legislative history nor the statute itself affords specific guidance for the resolution of this case. When Rule 10b–5 was promulgated in 1942, the SEC did not discuss the possibility that failure to provide information might run afoul of § 10(b).

* * *

The Federal courts have found violations of § 10(b) where corporate insiders used undisclosed information for their own benefit. E.g., SEC v. Texas Gulf Sulphur Co., 401 F.2d 833 (C.A.2 1968), cert. denied, 404 U.S. 1005 (1971). The cases also have emphasized, in accordance with the common-law rule, that "[t]he party charged with failing to disclose market information must be under a duty to disclose it." Frigitemp Corp. v. Financial Dynamics Fund, Inc., 524 F.2d 275, 282 (C.A.2 1975). Accordingly, a purchaser of stock who has no duty to a prospective seller because he is neither an insider nor a fiduciary has been held to have no obligation to reveal material facts. See General Time Corp. v. Talley Industries, Inc., 403 F.2d 159, 164 (C.A.2 1968), *cert. denied,* 393 U.S. 1026 (1969).

* * *

Thus, administrative and judicial interpretations have established that silence in connection with the purchase or sale of securities may operate as a fraud actionable under § 10(b) despite the absence of statutory language or legislative history specifically addressing the legality of nondisclosure. But such liability is premised upon a duty to disclose arising from a relationship of trust and confidence between parties to a transaction. Application of a duty to disclose prior to trading guarantees that corporate insiders, who have an obligation to place the shareholder's welfare before their own, will not benefit personally through fraudulent use of material nonpublic information.[12]

III

In this case, the petitioner was convicted of violating § 10(b) although he was not a corporate insider and he received no confidential information from the target company. Moreover, the "market information" upon which he relied did not concern the earning power or operations of the target company, but only the plans of the acquiring company.[13] Petitioner's use of that information was not a fraud under § 10(b) unless he was subject to an affirmative duty to disclose it before trading. In this case, the jury instructions failed to specify any such duty. In effect, the trial court instructed the jury that petitioner owed a duty to everyone; to all sellers, indeed, to the market as a whole. The jury simply was told to decide whether petitioner used material, nonpublic information at a time when "he knew other people trading in the securities market did not have access to the same information." Record, at 677.

The Court of Appeals affirmed the conviction by holding that "[a]nyone— corporate insider or not—who regularly receives material nonpublic informa-

---

12. "Tippees" of corporate insiders have been held liable under § 10(b) because they have a duty not to profit from the use of inside information that they know is confidential and know or should know came from a corporate insider, Shapiro v. Merrill Lynch, Pierce, Fenner & Smith, 495 F.2d 228, 237–238 (C.A.2 1974). The tippee's obligation has been viewed as arising from his role as a participant after the fact in the insider's breach of a fiduciary duty. Subcommittees of American Bar Association Section of Corporation, Banking, and Business Law, Comment Letter on Material, Non–Public Information (Oct. 15, 1973) reprinted in BNA, Securities Regulation & Law Report No. 233, at D–1, D–2 (Jan. 2, 1974).

13. See Fleischer, Mundheim & Murphy, An Initial Inquiry into the Responsibility to Disclose Market Information, 121 U.Pa. L.Rev. 798, 799 (1973).

tion may not use that information to trade in securities without incurring an affirmative duty to disclose." 588 F.2d 1358, 1365 (C.A.2 1978) (emphasis in original). Although the court said that its test would include only persons who regularly receive material nonpublic information, id., at 1366, its rationale for that limitation is unrelated to the existence of a duty to disclose. The Court of Appeals, like the trial court, failed to identify a relationship between petitioner and the sellers that could give rise to a duty. Its decision thus rested solely upon its belief that the federal securities laws have "created a system providing equal access to information necessary for reasoned and intelligent investment decisions." 588 F.2d, at 1362. The use by anyone of material information not generally available is fraudulent, this theory suggests, because such information gives certain buyers or sellers an unfair advantage over less informed buyers and sellers.

This reasoning suffers from two defects. First not every instance of financial unfairness constitutes fraudulent activity under § 10(b). See Santa Fe Industries, Inc. v. Green, 430 U.S. 462, 474–477 (1977). Second, the element required to make silence fraudulent—a duty to disclose—is absent in this case. No duty could arise from petitioner's relationship with the sellers of the target company's securities, for petitioner had no prior dealings with them. He was not their agent, he was not a fiduciary, he was not a person in whom the sellers had placed their trust and confidence. He was, in fact, a complete stranger who dealt with the sellers only through impersonal market transactions.

We cannot affirm petitioner's conviction without recognizing a general duty between all participants in market transactions to forgo actions based on material, nonpublic information. Formulation of such a broad duty, which departs radically from the established doctrine that duty arises from a specific relationship between two parties * * * should not be undertaken absent some explicit evidence of congressional intent.

As we have seen, no such evidence emerges from the language or legislative history of § 10(b). Moreover, neither the Congress nor the Commission ever has adopted a parity-of-information rule. Instead the problems caused by misuse of market information have been addressed by detailed and sophisticated regulation that recognizes when use of market information may not harm operation of the securities markets. For example, the Williams Act limits but does not completely prohibit a tender offeror's purchases of target corporation stock before public announcement of the offer. Congress' careful action in this and other areas contrasts, and is in some tension, with the broad rule of liability we are asked to adopt in this case.

Indeed, the theory upon which the petitioner was convicted is at odds with the Commission's view of § 10(b) as applied to activity that has the same effect on sellers as the petitioner's purchases. "Warehousing" takes place when a corporation gives advance notice of its intention to launch a tender offer to institutional investors who then are able to purchase stock in the target company before the tender offer is made public and the price of shares rises. In this case, as in warehousing, a buyer of securities purchases stock in a target corporation on the basis of market information which is unknown to the seller. In both of these situations, the seller's behavior presumably would be altered if he had the nonpublic information. Significantly, however, the Commission has acted to bar warehousing under its authority to regulate tender offers after recognizing that action under § 10(b) would rest on a "somewhat different theory" than that previously used to regulate insider trading as fraudulent activity.

We see no basis for applying such a new and different theory of liability in this case. As we have emphasized before, the 1934 Act cannot be read " 'more broadly than its language and the statutory scheme reasonably permit.' " Touche Ross & Co. v. Redington, 442 U.S. 560, 578 (1979), quoting SEC v. Sloan, 436 U.S. 103, 116 (1978). Section 10(b) is aptly described as a catch-all provision, but what it catches must be fraud. When an allegation of fraud is based upon nondisclosure, there can be no fraud absent a duty to speak. We hold that a duty to disclose under § 10(b) does not arise from the mere possession of nonpublic market information. The contrary result is without support in the legislative history of § 10(b) and would be inconsistent with the careful plan that Congress has enacted for regulation of the securities markets. Cf. Santa Fe Industries Inc. v. Green, 430 U.S., at 479.

IV

In its brief to this Court the United States offers an alternative theory to support petitioner's conviction. It argues that petitioner breached a duty to the acquiring corporation when he acted upon information that he obtained by virtue of his position as an employee of a printer employed by the corporation. The breach of this duty is said to support a conviction under § 10(b) for fraud perpetrated upon both the acquiring corporation and the sellers.

We need not decide whether this theory has merit for it was not submitted to the jury. The jury was told, in the language of Rule 10b-5, that it could convict the petitioner if it concluded that he either (i) employed a device, scheme or artifice to defraud or (ii) engaged in an act, practice, or course of business which operated or would operate as a fraud or deceit upon any person. Record, at 681. The trial judge stated that a "scheme to defraud" is a plan to obtain money by trick or deceit and that "a failure by Chiarella to disclose material, non-public information in connection with his purchase of stock would constitute deceit." Id., at 683. Accordingly, the jury was instructed that the petitioner employed a scheme to defraud if he "did not disclose * * * material non-public information in connection with the purchases of the stock." Id., at 685–686.

Alternatively, the jury was instructed that it could convict if "Chiarella's alleged conduct of having purchased securities without disclosing material, nonpublic information would have or did have the effect of operating as a fraud upon a seller." Id., at 686. The judge earlier had stated that fraud "embraces all the means which human ingenuity can devise and which are resorted to by one individual to gain an advantage over another by false misrepresentation, suggestions or by suppression of the truth." Id., at 683.

The jury instructions demonstrate that petitioner was convicted merely because of his failure to disclose material, nonpublic information to sellers from whom he bought the stock of target corporations. The jury was not instructed on the nature or elements of a duty owed by petitioner to anyone other than the sellers. Because we cannot affirm a criminal conviction on the basis of a theory not presented to the jury, Rewis v. United States, 401 U.S. 808, 814 (1971), see Dunn v. United States, 442 U.S. 100, 106 (1979), we will not speculate upon whether such a duty exists, whether it has been breached, or whether such a breach constitutes a violation of § 10(b).

The judgment of the Court of Appeals is

Reversed.

■ MR. JUSTICE BRENNAN, concurring in the judgment.

The Court holds, correctly in my view, that "a duty to disclose under § 10(b) does not arise from the mere possession of nonpublic market information." Ante, at 1118. Prior to so holding, however, it suggests that no violation of § 10(b) could be made out absent a breach of some duty arising out of a fiduciary relationship between buyer and seller. I cannot subscribe to that suggestion. On the contrary, it seems to me that Part I of The Chief Justice's dissent, post, at 1120–1122, correctly states the applicable substantive law—a person violates § 10(b) whenever he improperly obtains or converts to his own benefit nonpublic information which he then uses in connection with the purchase or sale of securities.

While I agree with Part I of The Chief Justice's dissent, I am unable to agree with Part II. Rather, I concur in the judgment of the majority because I think it clear that the legal theory sketched by The Chief Justice is not the one presented to the jury. * * *

■ MR. CHIEF JUSTICE BURGER, dissenting.

I believe that the jury instructions in this case properly charged a violation of § 10(b) and Rule 10b–5, and I would affirm the conviction.

I

As a general rule, neither party to an arm's length business transaction has an obligation to disclose information to the other unless the parties stand in some confidential or fiduciary relation. See Prosser, The Law of Torts § 106. This rule permits a businessman to capitalize on his experience and skill in securing and evaluating relevant information; it provides incentive for hard work, careful analysis, and astute forecasting. But the policies that underlie the rule also should limit its scope. In particular, the rule should give way when an informational advantage is obtained, not by superior experience, foresight, or industry, but by some unlawful means. One commentator has written:

> "[T]he way in which the buyer acquires the information which he conceals from the vendor should be a material circumstance. The information might have been acquired as the result of his bringing to bear a superior knowledge, intelligence, skill or technical judgment; it might have been acquired by chance; or it might be acquired by means of some tortious action on his part. * * * *Any time information is acquired by an illegal act it would seem that there should be a duty to disclose that information.*" Keeton, Fraud—Concealment and Non–Disclosure, 15 Tex.L.Rev. 1, 25–26 (1936) (emphasis added).

I would read § 10(b) and Rule 10b–5 to encompass and build on this principle: to mean that a person who has misappropriated nonpublic information has an absolute duty to disclose that information or to refrain from trading.

* * *

■ MR. JUSTICE BLACKMUN, with whom MR. JUSTICE MARSHALL joins, dissenting.

Although I agree with much of what is said in Part I of the dissenting opinion of The Chief Justice, ante, I write separately because, in my view, it is unnecessary to rest petitioner's conviction on a "misappropriation" theory. The fact that petitioner Chiarella purloined, or, to use The Chief Justice's word, ante, p. 1123, "stole," information concerning pending tender offers certainly is the most dramatic evidence that petitioner was guilty of fraud. He has conceded that he knew it was wrong, and he and his co-workers in the print shop were specifically warned by their employer that actions of this kind were improper and forbidden. But I also would find petitioner's conduct fraudulent within the meaning of § 10(b) of the Securities Exchange Act of 1934 and the Securities and Exchange Commission's Rule 10b–5, even if he had obtained the blessing of his employer's principals before embarking on his profiteering scheme. Indeed, I think petitioner's brand of manipulative trading, with or without such approval, lies close to the heart of what the securities laws are intended to prohibit.

* * *

Dirks v. SEC

Supreme Court of the United States, 1983.
463 U.S. 646, 103 S.Ct. 3255, 77 L.Ed.2d 911.

■ JUSTICE POWELL delivered the opinion of the Court.

Petitioner Raymond Dirks received material nonpublic information from "insiders" of a corporation with which he had no connection. He disclosed this information to investors who relied on it in trading in the shares of the corporation. The question is whether Dirks violated the antifraud provisions of the federal securities laws by this disclosure.

I

In 1973, Dirks was an officer of a New York broker-dealer firm who specialized in providing investment analysis of insurance company securities to institutional investors. On March 6, Dirks received information from Ronald Secrist, a former officer of Equity Funding of America. Secrist alleged that the assets of Equity Funding, a diversified corporation primarily engaged in selling life insurance and mutual funds, were vastly overstated as the result of fraudulent corporate practices. Secrist also stated that various regulatory agencies had failed to act on similar charges made by Equity Funding employees. He urged Dirks to verify the fraud and disclose it publicly.

Dirks decided to investigate the allegations. He visited Equity Funding's headquarters in Los Angeles and interviewed several officers and employees of the corporation. The senior management denied any wrongdoing, but certain corporation employees corroborated the charges of fraud. Neither Dirks nor his firm owned or traded any Equity Funding stock, but throughout his investigation he openly discussed the information he had obtained with a number of clients and investors. Some of these persons sold their holdings of Equity Funding securities, including five investment advisers who liquidated holdings of more than $16 million.

While Dirks was in Los Angeles, he was in touch regularly with William Blundell, the *Wall Street Journal's* Los Angeles bureau chief. Dirks urged Blundell to write a story on the fraud allegations. Blundell did not believe, however that such a massive fraud could go undetected and declined to write the story. He feared that publishing such damaging hearsay might be libelous.

During the two-week period in which Dirks pursued his investigation and spread word of Secrist's charges, the price of Equity Funding stock fell from $26 per share to less than $15 per share. This led the New York Stock

Exchange to halt trading on March 27. Shortly thereafter California insurance authorities impounded Equity Funding's records and uncovered evidence of the fraud. Only then did the Securities and Exchange Commission (SEC) file a complaint against Equity Funding and only then, on April 2, did the *Wall Street Journal* publish a front-page story based largely on information assembled by Dirks. Equity Funding immediately went into receivership.

The SEC began an investigation into Dirks' role in the exposure of the fraud. After a hearing by an administrative law judge, the SEC found that Dirks had aided and abetted violations of § 17(a) of the Securities Act of 1933, § 10(b) of the Securities Exchange Act of 1934, and SEC Rule 10b–5, by repeating the allegations of fraud to members of the investment community who later sold their Equity Funding stock. The SEC concluded: "Where 'tippees'—regardless of their motivation or occupation—come into possession of material 'information that they know is confidential and know or should know came from a corporate insider,' they must either publicly disclose that information or refrain from trading." 21 S.E.C. Docket 1401, 1407 (1981) (footnote omitted) (quoting Chiarella v. United States, 445 U.S. 222, 230 n. 12 (1980)). Recognizing, however, that Dirks "played an important role in bringing [Equity Funding's] massive fraud to light," 21 S.E.C. Docket, at 1412, the SEC only censured him.

Dirks sought review in the Court of Appeals for the District of Columbia Circuit. The court entered judgment against Dirks "for the reasons stated by the Commission in its opinion." App. to Pet. for Cert. C–2. Judge Wright, a member of the panel, subsequently issued an opinion. Judge Robb concurred in the result and Judge Tamm dissented; neither filed a separate opinion. Judge Wright believed that "the obligations of corporate fiduciaries pass to all those to whom they disclose their information before it has been disseminated to the public at large." 220 U.S.App.D.C. 309, 324, 681 F.2d 824, 839 (1982). Alternatively, Judge Wright concluded that, as an employee of a broker-dealer, Dirks had violated "obligations to the SEC and to the public completely independent of any obligations he acquired" as a result of receiving the information. Id., at 325, 681 F.2d, at 840.

In view of the importance to the SEC and to the securities industry of the question presented by this case, we granted a writ of certiorari. 459 U.S. 1014 (1982). We now reverse.

II

In the seminal case of In re Cady, Roberts & Co., 40 S.E.C. 907 (1961), the SEC recognized that the common law in some jurisdictions imposes on "corporate 'insiders,' particularly officers, directors, or controlling stockholders" an "affirmative duty of disclosure * * * when dealing in securities." Id., at 911, and n. 13.[10] The SEC found that not only did breach of this common-law duty

---

10. The duty that insiders owe to the corporation's shareholders not to trade on inside information differs from the common-law duty that officers and directors also have to the corporation itself not to mismanage corporate assets, of which confidential information is one. See 3 Fletcher Cyclopedia of the Laws of Private Corporations §§ 848, 900 (1975 ed. and Supp. 1982); 3A Fletcher §§ 1168.1, 1168.2. In holding that breaches of this duty to shareholders violated the Securities Exchange Act, the *Cady, Roberts* Commission recognized, and we agree, that "[a] significant purpose of the Exchange Act was to eliminate the idea that use of inside information for personal advantage was a normal emolument of corporate office." See 40 S.E.C., at 912, n. 15.

also establish the elements of a Rule 10b–5 violation, but that individuals other than corporate insiders could be obligated either to disclose material nonpublic information before trading or to abstain from trading altogether. Id., at 912. In *Chiarella,* we accepted the two elements set out in *Cady, Roberts* for establishing a Rule 10b–5 violation: "(i) the existence of a relationship affording access to inside information intended to be available only for a corporate purpose, and (ii) the unfairness of allowing a corporate insider to take advantage of that information by trading without disclosure." 445 U.S., at 227. In examining whether Chiarella had an obligation to disclose or abstain, the Court found that there is no general duty to disclose before trading on material nonpublic information, and held that "a duty to disclose under § 10(b) does not arise from the mere possession of nonpublic market information." Id., at 235. Such a duty arises rather from the existence of a fiduciary relationship. See id., at 227–235.

Not "all breaches of fiduciary duty in connection with a securities transaction," however, come within the ambit of Rule 10b–5. Santa Fe Industries, Inc. v. Green, 430 U.S. 462, 472 (1977). There must also be "manipulation or deception." Id., at 473. In an inside-trading case this fraud derives from the "inherent unfairness involved where one takes advantage" of "information intended to be available only for a corporate purpose and not for the personal benefit of anyone." In re Merrill Lynch, Pierce, Fenner & Smith, Inc., 43 S.E.C. 933, 936 (1968). Thus, an insider will be liable under Rule 10b–5 for inside trading only where he fails to disclose material nonpublic information before trading on it and thus makes "secret profits." *Cady, Roberts,* 40 S.E.C., at 916, n. 31.

III

We were explicit in *Chiarella* in saying that there can be no duty to disclose where the person who has traded on inside information "was not [the corporation's] agent, * * * was not a fiduciary, [or] was not a person in whom the sellers [of the securities] had placed their trust and confidence." 445 U.S., at 232. Not to require such a fiduciary relationship, we recognized, would "depar[t] radically from the established doctrine that duty arises from a specific relationship between two parties" and would amount to "recognizing a general duty between all participants in market transactions to forgo actions based on material, nonpublic information." Id., at 232, 233. This requirement of a specific relationship between the shareholders and the individual trading on inside information has created analytical difficulties for the SEC and courts in policing tippees who trade on inside information. Unlike insiders who have independent fiduciary duties to both the corporation and its shareholders, the typical tippee has no such relationships.[14] In view of this absence, it has been

---

14. Under certain circumstances, such as where corporate information is revealed legitimately to an underwriter, accountant, lawyer, or consultant working for the corporation, these outsiders may become fiduciaries of the shareholders. The basis for recognizing this fiduciary duty is not simply that such persons acquired nonpublic corporate information, but rather that they have entered into a special confidential relationship in the conduct of the business of the enter- prise and are given access to information solely for corporate purposes. See SEC v. Monarch Fund, 608 F.2d 938, 942 (C.A.2 1979); In re Investors Management Co., 44 S.E.C. 633, 645 (1971); In re Van Alystne, Noel & Co., 43 S.E.C. 1080, 1084–1085 (1969); In re Merrill Lynch, Pierce, Fenner & Smith, Inc., 43 S.E.C. 933, 937 (1968); Cady, Roberts, 40 S.E.C., at 912. When such a person breaches his fiduciary relationship, he may be treated more properly as a tipper

unclear how a tippee acquires the *Cady, Roberts* duty to refrain from trading on inside information.

A

The SEC's position, as stated in its opinion in this case, is that a tippee "inherits" the *Cady, Roberts* obligation to shareholders whenever he receives inside information from an insider. * * *

This view differs little from the view that we rejected as inconsistent with congressional intent in *Chiarella*. In that case, the Court of Appeals agreed with the SEC and affirmed Chiarella's conviction, holding that " '[a]nyone—corporate insider or not—who regularly receives material nonpublic information may not use that information to trade in securities without incurring an affirmative duty to disclose.' " United States v. Chiarella, 588 F.2d 1358, 1365 (C.A.2 1978) (emphasis in original). Here, the SEC maintains that anyone who knowingly receives nonpublic material information from an insider has a fiduciary duty to disclose before trading.[15]

In effect, the SEC's theory of tippee liability in both cases appears rooted in the idea that the antifraud provisions require equal information among all traders. This conflicts with the principle set forth in *Chiarella* that only some persons, under some circumstances, will be barred from trading while in possession of material nonpublic information.[16] Judge Wright correctly read our opinion in *Chiarella* as repudiating any notion that all traders must enjoy equal

---

than a tippee. See Shapiro v. Merrill Lynch, Pierce, Fenner & Smith, Inc., 495 F.2d 228, 237 (C.A.2 1974) (investment banker had access to material information when working on a proposed public offering for the corporation). For such a duty to be imposed, however, the corporation must expect the outsider to keep the disclosed nonpublic information confidential, and the relationship at least must imply such a duty.

15. Apparently the SEC believes this case differs from *Chiarella* in that Dirks' receipt of inside information from Secrist, an insider, carried Secrist's duties with it, while Chiarella received the information without the direct involvement of an insider and thus inherited no duty to disclose or abstain. The SEC fails to explain, however, why the receipt on nonpublic information from an insider automatically carries with it the fiduciary duty of the insider. As we emphasized in *Chiarella*, mere possession of nonpublic information does not give rise to a duty to disclose or abstain; only a specific relationship does that. And we do not believe that the mere receipt of information from an insider creates such a special relationship between the tippee and the corporation's shareholders.

Apparently recognizing the weakness of its argument in light of *Chiarella*, the SEC

attempts to distinguish that case factually as involving not "inside" information, but rather "market" information, i.e., "information generated within the company relating to its assets or earnings." Brief for Respondent 23. This Court drew no such distinction in *Chiarella* and, as The Chief Justice noted, "[i]t is clear that § 10(b) and Rule 10b–5 by their terms and by their history make no such distinction." 445 U.S., at 241, n. 1 (dissenting opinion). See ALI Fed.Sec.Code § 1603, Comment (2)(j) (Proposed Official Draft 1978).

16. In *Chiarella*, we noted that formulation of an absolute equal information rule "should not be undertaken absent some explicit evidence of congressional intent." 445 U.S., at 233, 100 S.Ct., at 1117. Rather than adopting such a radical view of securities trading, Congress has expressly exempted many market professionals from the general statutory prohibition set forth in § 11(a)(1) of the Securities Exchange Act, 15 U.S.C. § 78k(a)(1), against members of a national securities exchange trading for their own account. See id., at 233, n. 16, 100 S.Ct., at 1117, n. 16. We observed in *Chiarella* that "[t]he exception is based upon Congress' recognition that [market professionals] contribute to a fair and orderly marketplace at the same time they exploit the informational advantage that comes from their possession of [nonpublic information]." Ibid.

information before trading: "[T]he 'information' theory is rejected. Because the disclose-or-refrain duty is extraordinary, it attaches only when a party has legal obligations other than a mere duty to comply with the general antifraud proscriptions in the federal securities laws." 220 U.S.App.D.C., at 322, 681 F.2d, at 837. See *Chiarella*, 445 U.S., at 235, n. 20. We reaffirm today that "[a] duty [to disclose] arises from the relationship between parties * * * and not merely from one's ability to acquire information because of his position in the market." 445 U.S., at 232–233, n.14.

Imposing a duty to disclose or abstain solely because a person knowingly receives material nonpublic information from an insider and trades on it could have an inhibiting influence on the role of market analysts, which the SEC itself recognizes is necessary to the preservation of a healthy market.[17] It is commonplace for analysts to "ferret out and analyze information," 21 S.E.C., at 1406,[18] and this often is done by meeting with and questioning corporate officers and others who are insiders. And information that the analysts obtain normally may be the basis for judgments as to the market worth of a corporation's securities. The analyst's judgment in this respect is made available in market letters or otherwise to clients of the firm. It is the nature of this type of information, and indeed of the markets themselves, that such information cannot be made simultaneously available to all of the corporation's stockholders or the public generally.

B

The conclusion that recipients of inside information do not invariably acquire a duty to disclose or abstain does not mean that such tippees always are free to trade on the information. The need for a ban on some tippee trading is clear. Not only are insiders forbidden by their fiduciary relationship from personally using undisclosed corporate information to their advantage, but they may not give such information to an outsider for the same improper purpose of

17. The SEC expressly recognized that "[t]he value to the entire market of [analysts'] efforts cannot be gainsaid; market efficiency in pricing is significantly enhanced by [their] initiatives to ferret out and analyze information, and thus the analyst's work redounds to the benefit of all investors." 21 S.E.C., at 1406. The SEC asserts that analysts remain free to obtain from management corporate information for purposes of "filling in the 'interstices in analysis' * * *." Brief for Respondent 42 (quoting *Investors Management Co.*, 44 S.E.C., at 646). But this rule is inherently imprecise, and imprecision prevents parties from ordering their actions in accord with legal requirements. Unless the parties have some guidance as to where the line is between permissible and impermissible disclosures and uses, neither corporate insiders nor analysts can be sure when the line is crossed. Cf. *Adler v. Klawans*, 267 F.2d 840, 845 (C.A.2 1959) (Burger, J., sitting by designation).

18. On its facts, this case is the unusual one. Dirks is an analyst in a broker-dealer firm, and he did interview management in the course of his investigation. He uncovered, however, startling information that required no analysis or exercise of judgment as to its market relevance. Nonetheless, the principle at issue here extends beyond these facts. The SEC's rule—applicable without regard to any breach by an insider—could have serious ramifications on reporting by analysts of investment views.

Despite the unusualness of Dirks' "find," the central role that he played in uncovering the fraud at Equity Funding, and that analysts in general can play in revealing information that corporations may have reason to withhold from the public, is an important one. Dirks' careful investigation brought to light a massive fraud at the corporation. And until the Equity Funding fraud was exposed, the information in the trading market was grossly inaccurate. But for Dirks' efforts, the fraud might well have gone undetected longer. * * *

exploiting the information for their personal gain. See 15 U.S.C. § 78t(b) (making it unlawful to do indirectly "by means of any other person" any act made unlawful by the federal securities laws). Similarly, the transactions of those who knowingly participate with the fiduciary in such a breach are "as forbidden" as transactions "on behalf of the trustee himself." Mosser v. Darrow, 341 U.S. 267, 272 (1951). * * * As the court explained in *Mosser,* a contrary rule "would open up opportunities for devious dealings in the name of the others that the trustee could not conduct in his own." 341 U.S., at 271. See SEC v. Texas Gulf Sulphur Co., 446 F.2d 1301, 1308 (CA2), cert. denied, 404 U.S. 1005 (1971). Thus, the tippee's duty to disclose or abstain is derivative from that of the insider's duty. See Tr. of Oral Ar. 38. Cf. *Chiarella,* 445 U.S., at 246, n. 1 (Blackmun, J., dissenting). As we noted in *Chiarella,* "[t]he tippee's obligation has been viewed as arising from his role as a participant after the fact in the insider's breach of a fiduciary duty." 445 U.S., at 230, n. 12.

Thus, some tippees must assume an insider's duty to the shareholders not because they receive inside information, but rather because it has been made available to them *improperly.*[19] And for Rule 10b–5 purposes, the insider's disclosure is improper only where it would violate his *Cady, Roberts* duty. Thus, a tippee assumes a fiduciary duty to the shareholders of a corporation not to trade on material nonpublic information only when the insider has breached his fiduciary duty to the shareholders by disclosing the information to the tippee and the tippee knows or should know that there has been a breach.[20] As Commissioner Smith perceptively observed in *Investors Management Co.:* "[T]ippee responsibility must be related back to insider responsibility by a necessary finding that the tippee knew the information was given to him in breach of a duty by a person having a special relationship to the issuer not to disclose the information * * *." 44 S.E.C., at 651 (concurring in the result). Tipping thus properly is viewed only as a means of indirectly violating the *Cady, Roberts* disclose-or-abstain rule.[21]

---

19. The SEC itself has recognized that tippee liability properly is imposed only in circumstances where the tippee knows, or has reason to know, that the insider has disclosed improperly inside corporate information. In *Investors Management Co., supra,* the SEC stated that one element of tippee liability is that the tippee knew or had reason to know "that [the information] was non-public and had been obtained *improperly* by selective revelation or otherwise." 44 S.E.C., at 641 (emphasis added). Commissioner Smith read this test to mean that a tippee can be held liable only if he received information in breach of an insider's duty not to disclose it. Id., at 650 (concurring in the result).

20. Professor Loss has linked tippee liability to the concept in the law of restitution that " '[w]here a fiduciary in violation of his duty to the beneficiary communicates confidential information to a third person, the third person, if he had notice of the violation of duty, holds upon a constructive trust for the beneficiary any profit which he makes through the use of such information.' " 3 L. Loss, Securities Regulation 1451 (2d ed. 1961) (quoting Restatement of Restitution § 201(2) (1937)). Other authorities likewise have expressed the view that tippee liability exists only where there has been a breach of trust by an insider of which the tippee had knowledge. * * *

21. We do not suggest that knowingly trading on inside information is ever "socially desirable or even that it is devoid of moral considerations." Dooley, Enforcement of Insider Trading Restrictions, 66 Va.L.Rev. 1, 55 (1980). Nor do we imply an absence of responsibility to disclose promptly indications of illegal actions by a corporation to the proper authorities—typically the SEC and exchange authorities in cases involving securities. Depending on the circumstances, and even where permitted by law, one's trading on material nonpublic information is behavior that may fall below ethical standards of conduct. But in a statutory area of the law

C

In determining whether a tippee is under an obligation to disclose or abstain, it thus is necessary to determine whether the insider's "tip" constituted a breach of the insider's fiduciary duty. All disclosures of confidential corporate information are not inconsistent with the duty insiders owe to shareholders. In contrast to the extraordinary facts of this case, the more typical situation in which there will be a question whether disclosure violates the insider's *Cady, Roberts* duty is when insiders disclose information to analysts. * * * In some situations, the insider will act consistently with his fiduciary duty to shareholders, and yet release of the information may affect the market. For example, it may not be clear—either to the corporate insider or to the recipient analyst—whether the information will be viewed as material nonpublic information. Corporate officials may mistakenly think the information already has been disclosed or that it is not material enough to affect the market. Whether disclosure is a breach of duty therefore depends in large part on the purpose of the disclosure. This standard was identified by the SEC itself in *Cady, Roberts:* a purpose of the securities laws was to eliminate "use of inside information for personal advantage." 40 S.E.C., at 912, n. 15. See n. 10, *supra.* Thus, the test is whether the insider personally will benefit, directly or indirectly, from his disclosure. Absent some personal gain, there has been no breach of duty to stockholders. And absent a breach by the insider, there is no derivative breach. As Commissioner Smith stated in *Investors Management Co.:* "It is important in this type of case to focus on policing insiders and what they do * * * rather than on policing information *per se* and its possession. * * * " 44 S.E.C., at 648 (concurring in the result).

The SEC argues that, if inside-trading liability does not exist when the information is transmitted for a proper purpose but is used for trading, it would be a rare situation when the parties could not fabricate some ostensibly legitimate business justification for transmitting the information. We think the SEC is unduly concerned. In determining whether the insider's purpose in making a particular disclosure is fraudulent, the SEC and the courts are not required to read the parties' minds. Scienter in some cases is relevant in determining whether the tipper has violated his *Cady, Roberts* duty.[23] But to

such as securities regulation, where legal principles of general application must be applied, there may be "significant distinctions between actual legal obligations and ethical ideals." SEC, Report of the Special Study of Securities Markets, H.R.Doc. No. 95, 88th Cong., 1st Sess., pt. 1, pp. 237–238 (1963). The SEC recognizes this. At oral argument, the following exchange took place:

"QUESTION: So, it would not have satisfied his obligation under the law to go to the SEC first?

"[SEC's counsel]: That is correct. That an insider has to observe what has come to be known as the abstain or disclosure rule. Either the information has to be disclosed to the market if it is inside information * * * or the insider must abstain." Tr. of Oral Arg. 27.

Thus, it is clear that Rule 10b–5 does not impose any obligation simply to tell the SEC about the fraud before trading.

23. *Scienter*—"a mental state embracing intent to deceive, manipulate, or defraud," Ernst & Ernst v. Hochfelder, 425 U.S. 185, 193, n. 12, 96 S.Ct. 1375, 1381, n. 12, 47 L.Ed.2d 668 (1976)—is an independent element of a Rule 10b–5 violation. See Aaron v. SEC, 446 U.S. 680, 695, 100 S.Ct. 1945, 1955, 64 L.Ed.2d 611 (1980). Contrary to the dissent's suggestion, see post, at p. 3271, n.10, motivation is not irrelevant to the issue of *scienter.* It is not enough that an insider's conduct results in harm to investors; rather, a violation may be found only where there is "intentional or willful conduct designed to deceive or defraud investors by controlling or artificially affecting the price of securities." Ernst & Ernst v. Hochfelder, *supra*, 425 U.S.,

determine whether the disclosure itself "deceive[s], manipulate[s], or defraud[s]" shareholders, Aaron v. SEC, 446 U.S. 680, 686 (1980), the initial inquiry is whether there has been a breach of duty by the insider. This requires courts to focus on objective criteria, i.e., whether the insider receives a direct or indirect personal benefit from the disclosure, such as a pecuniary gain or a reputational benefit that will translate into future earnings. Cf. 40 S.E.C., at 912, n. 15; Brudney, Insiders, Outsiders, and Informational Advantages Under the Federal Securities Laws, 93 Harv.L.Rev. 324, 348 (1979) ("The theory * * * is that the insider, by giving the information out selectively, is in effect selling the information to its recipient for cash, reciprocal information, or other things of value for himself. * * * "). There are objective facts and circumstances that often justify such an inference. For example, there may be a relationship between the insider and the recipient that suggests a *quid pro quo* from the latter, or an intention to benefit the particular recipient. The elements of fiduciary duty and exploitation of nonpublic information also exist when an insider makes a gift of confidential information to a trading relative or friend. The tip and trade resemble trading by the insider himself followed by a gift of the profits to the recipient.

Determining whether an insider personally benefits from a particular disclosure, a question of fact, will not always be easy for courts. But it is essential, we think, to have a guiding principle for those whose daily activities must be limited and instructed by the SEC's inside-trading rules, and we believe that there must be a breach of the insider's fiduciary duty before the tippee inherits the duty to disclose or abstain. In contrast, the rule adopted by the SEC in this case would have no limiting principle.

IV

Under the inside-trading and tipping rules set forth above, we find that there was no actionable violation by Dirks. It is undisputed that Dirks himself was a stranger to Equity Funding, with no pre-existing fiduciary duty to its shareholders. He took no action, directly or indirectly, that induced the shareholders or officers of Equity Funding to repose trust or confidence in him. There was no expectation by Dirks' sources that he would keep their information in confidence. Nor did Dirks misappropriate or illegally obtain the information about Equity Funding. Unless the insiders breached their *Cady, Roberts* duty to shareholders in disclosing the nonpublic information to Dirks, he breached no duty when he passed it on to investors as well as to the *Wall Street Journal*.

It is clear that neither Secrist nor the other Equity Funding employees violated their *Cady, Roberts* duty to the corporation's shareholders by providing information to Dirks.[27] The tippers received no monetary or personal benefit

---

at 199, 96 S.Ct., at 1383. The issue in this case, however, is not whether Secrist or Dirks acted with *scienter,* but rather whether there was any deceptive or fraudulent conduct at all, i.e., whether Secrist's disclosure constituted a breach of his fiduciary duty and thereby caused injury to shareholders. See n.27, *infra.* Only if there was such a breach did Dirks, a tippee, acquire a fiduciary duty to disclose or abstain.

27. In this Court, the SEC appears to contend that an insider invariably violates a fiduciary duty to the corporation's shareholders by transmitting nonpublic corporate information to an outsider when he has reason to believe that the outsider may use it to the disadvantage of the shareholders. "Thus, regardless of any ultimate motive to bring to public attention the derelictions at Equity Funding, Secrist breached his duty to Equity

for revealing Equity Funding's secrets, nor was their purpose to make a gift of valuable information to Dirks. As the facts of this case clearly indicate, the tippers were motivated by a desire to expose the fraud. See *supra*, at 1–2. In the absence of a breach of duty to shareholders by the insiders, there was no derivative breach by Dirks. See n. 20, *supra*. Dirks therefore could not have been "a participant after the fact in [an] insider's breach of a fiduciary duty." *Chiarella*, 445 U.S., at 230, n. 12.

V

We conclude that Dirks, in the circumstances of this case, had no duty to abstain from use of the inside information that he obtained. The judgment of the Court of Appeals therefore is

Funding shareholders." Brief for Respondent 31. This perceived "duty" differs markedly from the one that the SEC identified in *Cady, Roberts* and that has been the basis for federal tippee-trading rules to date. In fact, the SEC did not charge Secrist with any wrongdoing, and we do not understand the SEC to have relied on any theory of a breach of duty by Secrist in finding that Dirks breached his duty to Equity Funding's shareholders. See App. 250 (decision of administrative law judge) ("One who knows himself to be a beneficiary of non-public, selectively disclosed inside information must fully disclose or refrain from trading."); SEC's Reply to Notice of Supplemental Authority before the SEC 4 ("If Secrist was acting properly, Dirks inherited a duty to [Equity Funding]'s shareholders to refrain from improper private use of the information."); Brief on behalf of the SEC in the Court of Appeals, at 47–50; id., at 51 ("[K]nowing possession of inside information by any person imposes a duty to abstain or disclose."); id., at 52–54; id., at 55 ("[T]his obligation arises not from the manner in which such information is acquired * * *."); 220 U.S. App. D.C., at 322–323, 681 F.2d, at 838 (Wright, J.).

The dissent argues that "Secrist violated his duty to Equity Funding shareholders by transmitting material nonpublic information to Dirks with the intention that Dirks would cause his clients to trade on that information." *Post*, at 3274. By perceiving a breach of fiduciary duty whenever inside information is intentionally disclosed to securities traders, the dissenting opinion effectively would achieve the same result as the SEC's theory below, i.e., mere possession of inside information while trading would be viewed as a Rule 10b–5 violation. But *Chiarella* made it explicitly clear there is no general duty to forgo market transactions "based on material, nonpublic information." 445 U.S., at 233, 100

S.Ct., at 1117. Such a duty would "depar[t] radically from the established doctrine that duty arises from a specific relationship between two parties." Ibid. See p. 3261, *supra*.

Moreover, to constitute a violation of Rule 10b–5, there must be fraud. See *Ernst & Ernst v. Hochfelder*, 425 U.S. 185, 199, 96 S.Ct. 1375, 1383, 47 L.Ed.2d 668 (1976) (statutory words "manipulative," "device," and "contrivance * * * connot[e] intentional or willful conduct designed to *deceive or defraud* investors by controlling or artificially affecting the price of securities") (emphasis added). There is no evidence that Secrist's disclosure was intended to or did in fact "deceive or defraud" anyone. Secrist certainly intended to convey relevant information that management was unlawfully concealing, and—so far as the record shows—he believed that persuading Dirks to investigate was the best way to disclose the fraud. Other efforts had proved fruitless. Under any objective standard, Secrist received no direct or indirect personal benefit from the disclosure.

The dissenting opinion focuses on shareholder "losses," "injury," and "damages," but in many cases there may be no clear causal connection between inside trading and outsiders' losses. In one sense, as market values fluctuate and investors act on inevitably incomplete or incorrect information, there always are winners and losers; but those who have "lost" have not necessarily been defrauded. On the other hand, inside trading for personal gain is fraudulent, and is a violation of the federal securities laws. See Dooley, *supra*, at 39–41, 70. Thus, there is little legal significance to the dissent's argument that Secrist and Dirks created new "victims" by disclosing the information to persons who traded. In fact, they prevented the fraud from continuing and victimizing many more investors.

Reversed.

■ Justice Blackmun, with whom Justice Brennan and Justice Marshall join, dissenting.

The Court today takes still another step to limit the protections provided investors by § 10(b) of the Securities Exchange Act of 1934. See Chiarella v. United States, 445 U.S. 222, 246 (1980) (dissenting opinion). The device employed in this case engrafts a special motivational requirement on the fiduciary duty doctrine. This innovation excuses a knowing and intentional violation of an insider's duty to shareholders if the insider does not act from a motive of personal gain. Even on the extraordinary facts of this case, such an innovation is not justified.

* * *

II

A

No one questions that Secrist himself could not trade on his inside information to the disadvantage of uninformed shareholders and purchasers of Equity Funding securities. See Brief for United States as *Amicus Curiae* 19, n. 12. Unlike the printer in *Chiarella,* Secrist stood in a fiduciary relationship with these shareholders. As the Court states, ante, at 5, corporate insiders have an affirmative duty of disclosure when trading with shareholders of the corporation. See *Chiarella,* 445 U.S., at 227. This duty extends as well to purchasers of the corporation's securities. Id., at 227, n. 8, citing Gratz v. Claughton, 187 F.2d 46, 49 (CA2), cert. denied, 341 U.S. 920 (1951).

The Court also acknowledges that Secrist could not do by proxy what he was prohibited from doing personally. Ante, at 12; Mosser v. Darrow, 341 U.S. 267, 272 (1951). But this is precisely what Secrist did. Secrist used Dirks to disseminate information to Dirks' clients, who in turn dumped stock on unknowing purchasers. Secrist thus intended Dirks to injure the purchasers of Equity Funding securities to whom Secrist had a duty to disclose. Accepting the Court's view of tippee liability, it appears that Dirk's knowledge of this breach makes him liable as a participant in the breach after the fact. Ante, at 12, 19; *Chiarella,* 445 U.S., at 230, n. 12.

B

The Court holds, however, that Dirks is not liable because Secrist did not violate his duty; according to the Court, this is so because Secrist did not have the improper purpose of personal gain. Ante, at 15–16, 18–19. In so doing, the Court imposes a new, subjective limitation on the scope of the duty owed by insiders to shareholders. The novelty of this limitation is reflected in the Court's lack of support for it.

* * *

IV

In my view, Secrist violated his duty to Equity Funding shareholders by transmitting material nonpublic information to Dirks with the intention that Dirks would cause his clients to trade on that information. Dirks, therefore, was under a duty to make the information publicly available or to refrain from actions that he knew would lead to trading. Because Dirks caused his clients to trade, he violated § 10(b) and Rule 10b–5. Any other result is a disservice to this country's attempt to provide fair and efficient capital markets. I dissent.

United States v. O'Hagan

Supreme Court of the United States, 1997.
521 U.S. 642, 117 S.Ct. 2199, 138 L.Ed.2d 724.

■ JUSTICE GINSBURG delivered the opinion of the Court.

This case concerns the interpretation and enforcement of § 10(b) and § 14(e) of the Securities Exchange Act of 1934, and rules made by the Securities and Exchange Commission pursuant to these provisions, Rule 10b–5 and Rule 14e–3(a). Two prime questions are presented. The first relates to the misappropriation of material, nonpublic information for securities trading; the second concerns fraudulent practices in the tender offer setting. In particular, we address and resolve these issues: (1) Is a person who trades in securities for personal profit, using confidential information misappropriated in breach of a fiduciary duty to the source of the information, guilty of violating § 10(b) and Rule 10b–5? (2) Did the Commission exceed its rulemaking authority by adopting Rule 14e–3(a), which proscribes trading on undisclosed information in the tender offer setting, even in the absence of a duty to disclose? Our answer to the first question is yes, and to the second question, viewed in the context of this case, no.

I

Respondent James Herman O'Hagan was a partner in the law firm of Dorsey & Whitney in Minneapolis, Minnesota. In July 1988, Grand Metropolitan PLC (Grand Met), a company based in London, England, retained Dorsey & Whitney as local counsel to represent Grand Met regarding a potential tender offer for the common stock of the Pillsbury Company, headquartered in Minneapolis. Both Grand Met and Dorsey & Whitney took precautions to protect the confidentiality of Grand Met's tender offer plans. O'Hagan did no work on the Grand Met representation. Dorsey & Whitney withdrew from representing Grand Met on September 9, 1988. Less than a month later, on October 4, 1988, Grand Met publicly announced its tender offer for Pillsbury stock.

On August 18, 1988, while Dorsey & Whitney was still representing Grand Met, O'Hagan began purchasing call options for Pillsbury stock. Each option gave him the right to purchase 100 shares of Pillsbury stock by a specified date in September 1988. Later in August and in September, O'Hagan made additional purchases of Pillsbury call options. By the end of September, he owned 2,500 unexpired Pillsbury options, apparently more than any other individual investor. See App. 85, 148. O'Hagan also purchased, in September 1988, some 5,000 shares of Pillsbury common stock, at a price just under $39 per share. When Grand Met announced its tender offer in October, the price of Pillsbury stock rose to nearly $60 per share. O'Hagan then sold his Pillsbury call options and common stock, making a profit of more than $4.3 million.

The Securities and Exchange Commission (SEC or Commission) initiated an investigation into O'Hagan's transactions, culminating in a 57–count indictment. The indictment alleged that O'Hagan defrauded his law firm and its client, Grand Met, by using for his own trading purposes material, nonpublic information regarding Grand Met's planned tender offer. *Id., at* 8. According to the indictment, O'Hagan used the profits he gained through this trading to conceal his previous embezzlement and conversion of unrelated client trust funds. *Id.,* at 10. O'Hagan was charged with 20 counts of mail fraud, in violation of 18 U.S.C. § 1341; 17 counts of securities fraud, in violation of § 10(b) of the Securities Exchange Act of 1934 (Exchange Act), 48 Stat. 891, 15 U.S.C. § 78j(b), and SEC Rule 10b–5, 17 CFR § 240.10b–5 (1996); 17 counts of fraudulent trading in connection with a tender offer, in violation of § 14(e) of the Exchange Act, 15 U.S.C. § 78n(e), and SEC Rule 14e–3(a), 17 CFR § 240.14e–3(a) (1996); and 3 counts of violating federal money laundering statutes, 18 U.S.C. §§ 1956(a)(1)(B)(i), 1957. See App. 13–24. A jury convicted O'Hagan on all 57 counts, and he was sentenced to a 41–month term of imprisonment.

A divided panel of the Court of Appeals for the Eighth Circuit reversed all of O'Hagan's convictions. 92 F.3d 612 (1996). Liability under § 10(b) and Rule 10b–5, the Eighth Circuit held, may not be grounded on the "misappropriation theory" of securities fraud on which the prosecution relied. Id., at 622. The Court of Appeals also held that Rule 14e–3(a)—which prohibits trading while in possession of material, nonpublic information relating to a tender offer— exceeds the SEC's § 14(e) rulemaking authority because the rule contains no breach of fiduciary duty requirement. Id., at 627. The Eighth Circuit further concluded that O'Hagan's mail fraud and money laundering convictions rested on violations of the securities laws, and therefore could not stand once the securities fraud convictions were reversed. Id., at 627–628. Judge Fagg, dissenting, stated that he would recognize and enforce the misappropriation theory, and would hold that the SEC did not exceed its rulemaking authority when it adopted Rule 14e–3(a) without requiring proof of a breach of fiduciary duty. Id., at 628.

Decisions of the Courts of Appeals are in conflict on the propriety of the misappropriation theory under § 10(b) and Rule 10b–5, see *infra* this page and n. 3, and on the legitimacy of Rule 14e–3(a) under § 14(e), see *infra,* at 25. We granted certiorari, 519 U.S. 1087, 117 S.Ct. 759, 136 L.Ed.2d 695 (1997), and now reverse the Eighth Circuit's judgment.

II

We address first the Court of Appeals' reversal of O'Hagan's convictions under § 10(b) and Rule 10b–5. Following the Fourth Circuit's lead, see United States v. Bryan, 58 F.3d 933, 943–959 (1995), the Eighth Circuit rejected the misappropriation theory as a basis for s 10(b) liability. We hold, in accord with several other Courts of Appeals, that criminal liability under § 10(b) may be predicated on the misappropriation theory.[4]

---

4. Twice before we have been presented with the question whether criminal liability for violation of § 10(b) may be based on a misappropriation theory. In Chiarella v. United States, 445 U.S. 222, 235–237, 100 S.Ct. 1108, 1118–1119, 63 L.Ed.2d 348 (1980), the jury had received no misappropriation theory instructions, so we declined to address the question. See *infra,* at 17. In Carpenter v. United States, 484 U.S. 19, 24, 108 S.Ct. 316, 319–320, 98 L.Ed.2d 275 (1987), the Court divided evenly on whether, under the circumstances of that case, convictions resting on the misappropriation theory should be affirmed. See Aldave, The Misappropriation Theory: Carpenter and Its Aftermath, 49 Ohio St. L.J. 373, 375 (1988) (observing that "Carpenter was, by any reckoning, an unusual case," for the information there misappropriated belonged not

A

In pertinent part, § 10(b) of the Exchange Act provides:

"It shall be unlawful for any person, directly or indirectly, by the use of any means or instrumentality of interstate commerce or of the mails, or of any facility of any national securities exchange—

* * *

"(b) To use or employ, in connection with the purchase or sale of any security registered on a national securities exchange or any security not so registered, any manipulative or deceptive device or contrivance in contravention of such rules and regulations as the [Securities and Exchange] Commission may prescribe as necessary or appropriate in the public interest or for the protection of investors." 15 U.S.C. § 78j(b).

The statute thus proscribes (1) using any deceptive device (2) in connection with the purchase or sale of securities, in contravention of rules prescribed by the Commission. The provision, as written, does not confine its coverage to deception of a purchaser or seller of securities, see United States v. Newman, 664 F.2d 12, 17 (C.A.2 1981); rather, the statute reaches any deceptive device used "in connection with the purchase or sale of any security." * * *

Under the "traditional" or "classical theory" of insider trading liability, § 10(b) and Rule 10b–5 are violated when a corporate insider trades in the securities of his corporation on the basis of material, nonpublic information. Trading on such information qualifies as a "deceptive device" under § 10(b), we have affirmed, because "a relationship of trust and confidence [exists] between the shareholders of a corporation and those insiders who have obtained confidential information by reason of their position with that corporation." Chiarella v. United States, 445 U.S. 222, 228, 100 S.Ct. 1108, 1114, 63 L.Ed.2d 348 (1980). That relationship, we recognized, "gives rise to a duty to disclose [or to abstain from trading] because of the 'necessity of preventing a corporate insider from * * * tak[ing] unfair advantage of * * * uninformed * * * stockholders.'" Id., at 228–229, 100 S.Ct., at 1115 (citation omitted). The classical theory applies not only to officers, directors, and other permanent insiders of a corporation, but also to attorneys, accountants, consultants, and others who temporarily become fiduciaries of a corporation. See Dirks v. SEC, 463 U.S. 646, 655, n. 14, 103 S.Ct. 3255, 3262, 77 L.Ed.2d 911 (1983).

The "misappropriation theory" holds that a person commits fraud "in connection with" a securities transaction, and thereby violates § 10(b) and Rule 10b–5, when he misappropriates confidential information for securities trading purposes, in breach of a duty owed to the source of the information. See Brief for United States 14. Under this theory, a fiduciary's undisclosed, self-serving use of a principal's information to purchase or sell securities, in breach of a duty of loyalty and confidentiality, defrauds the principal of the exclusive use of that information. In lieu of premising liability on a fiduciary relationship between company insider and purchaser or seller of the company's stock, the misappropriation theory premises liability on a fiduciary-turned-trader's deception of those who entrusted him with access to confidential information.

The two theories are complementary, each addressing efforts to capitalize on nonpublic information through the purchase or sale of securities. The

to a company preparing to engage in securities transactions, e.g., a bidder in a corporate acquisition, but to the Wall Street Journal).

classical theory targets a corporate insider's breach of duty to shareholders with whom the insider transacts; the misappropriation theory outlaws trading on the basis of nonpublic information by a corporate "outsider" in breach of a duty owed not to a trading party, but to the source of the information. The misappropriation theory is thus designed to "protect the integrity of the securities markets against abuses by 'outsiders' to a corporation who have access to confidential information that will affect the corporation's security price when revealed, but who owe no fiduciary or other duty to that corporation's shareholders." Ibid.

In this case, the indictment alleged that O'Hagan, in breach of a duty of trust and confidence he owed to his law firm, Dorsey & Whitney, and to its client, Grand Met, traded on the basis of nonpublic information regarding Grand Met's planned tender offer for Pillsbury common stock. App. 16. This conduct, the Government charged, constituted a fraudulent device in connection with the purchase and sale of securities.[5]

B

We agree with the Government that misappropriation, as just defined, satisfies § 10(b)'s requirement that chargeable conduct involve a "deceptive device or contrivance" used "in connection with" the purchase or sale of securities. We observe, first, that misappropriators, as the Government describes them, deal in deception. A fiduciary who "[pretends] loyalty to the principal while secretly converting the principal's information for personal gain," Brief for United States 17, "dupes" or defrauds the principal. See Aldave, Misappropriation: A General Theory of Liability for Trading on Nonpublic Information, 13 Hofstra L.Rev. 101, 119 (1984).

We addressed fraud of the same species in Carpenter v. United States, 484 U.S. 19, 108 S.Ct. 316, 98 L.Ed.2d 275 (1987), which involved the mail fraud statute's proscription of "any scheme or artifice to defraud," 18 U.S.C. § 1341. Affirming convictions under that statute, we said in Carpenter that an employee's undertaking not to reveal his employer's confidential information "became a sham" when the employee provided the information to his co-conspirators in a scheme to obtain trading profits. 484 U.S., at 27. A company's confidential information, we recognized in Carpenter, qualifies as property to which the company has a right of exclusive use. Id., at 25–27. The undisclosed misappropriation of such information, in violation of a fiduciary duty, the Court said in Carpenter, constitutes fraud akin to embezzlement—" 'the fraudulent appropriation to one's own use of the money or goods entrusted to one's care by another.' " Id., at 27, 108 S.Ct., at 317 (quoting Grin v. Shine, 187 U.S. 181, 189, 23 S.Ct. 98, 101–102, 47 L.Ed. 130 (1902)); see Aldave, 13 Hofstra L.Rev., at 119. Carpenter's discussion of the fraudulent misuse of confidential information, the Government notes, "is a particularly apt source of guidance here, because [the mail fraud statute] (like Section 10(b)) has long been held to

---

5. The Government could not have prosecuted O'Hagan under the classical theory, for O'Hagan was not an "insider" of Pillsbury, the corporation in whose stock he traded. Although an "outsider" with respect to Pillsbury, O'Hagan had an intimate association with, and was found to have traded on confidential information from, Dorsey & Whitney, counsel to tender offeror Grand Met. Under the misappropriation theory, O'Hagan's securities trading does not escape Exchange Act sanction, as it would under the dissent's reasoning, simply because he was associated with, and gained nonpublic information from, the bidder, rather than the target.

require deception, not merely the breach of a fiduciary duty." Brief for United States 18, n.9 (citation omitted).

Deception through nondisclosure is central to the theory of liability for which the Government seeks recognition. As counsel for the Government stated in explanation of the theory at oral argument: "To satisfy the common law rule that a trustee may not use the property that [has] been entrusted [to] him, there would have to be consent. To satisfy the requirement of the Securities Act that there be no deception, there would only have to be disclosure." Tr. of Oral Arg. 12; see generally Restatement (Second) of Agency §§ 390, 395 (1958) (agent's disclosure obligation regarding use of confidential information).[6]

The misappropriation theory advanced by the Government is consistent with Santa Fe Industries, Inc. v. Green, 430 U.S. 462, 97 S.Ct. 1292, 51 L.Ed.2d 480 (1977), a decision underscoring that § 10(b) is not an all-purpose breach of fiduciary duty ban; rather, it trains on conduct involving manipulation or deception. See id., at 473–476. In contrast to the Government's allegations in this case, in Santa Fe Industries, all pertinent facts were disclosed by the persons charged with violating § 10(b) and Rule 10b–5, see id., at 474; therefore, there was no deception through nondisclosure to which liability under those provisions could attach, see id., at 476. Similarly, full disclosure forecloses liability under the misappropriation theory: Because the deception essential to the misappropriation theory involves feigning fidelity to the source of information, if the fiduciary discloses to the source that he plans to trade on the nonpublic information, there is no "deceptive device" and thus no § 10(b) violation—although the fiduciary-turned-trader may remain liable under state law for breach of a duty of loyalty.

We turn next to the § 10(b) requirement that the misappropriator's deceptive use of information be "in connection with the purchase or sale of [a] security." This element is satisfied because the fiduciary's fraud is consummated, not when the fiduciary gains the confidential information, but when, without disclosure to his principal, he uses the information to purchase or sell securities. The securities transaction and the breach of duty thus coincide. This is so even though the person or entity defrauded is not the other party to the trade, but is, instead, the source of the nonpublic information. See Aldave, 13 Hofstra L.Rev., at 120 ("a fraud or deceit can be practiced on one person, with resultant harm to another person or group of persons"). A misappropriator who trades on the basis of material, nonpublic information, in short, gains his advantageous market position through deception; he deceives the source of the information and simultaneously harms members of the investing public. See id., at 120–121, and n. 107.

The misappropriation theory targets information of a sort that misappropriators ordinarily capitalize upon to gain no-risk profits through the purchase or sale of securities. Should a misappropriator put such information to other use, the statute's prohibition would not be implicated. The theory does not

---

6. Under the misappropriation theory urged in this case, the disclosure obligation runs to the source of the information, here, Dorsey & Whitney and Grand Met. Chief Justice Burger, dissenting in Chiarella, advanced a broader reading of § 10(b) and Rule 10b–5; the disclosure obligation, as he envisioned it, ran to those with whom the misappropriator trades. 445 U.S., at 240, 100 S.Ct., at 1120–1121 ("a person who has misappropriated nonpublic information has an absolute duty to disclose that information or to refrain from trading"); see also id., at 243, n. 4, 100 S.Ct., at 1122 n. 4. The Government does not propose that we adopt a misappropriation theory of that breadth.

catch all conceivable forms of fraud involving confidential information; rather, it catches fraudulent means of capitalizing on such information through securities transactions.

The Government notes another limitation on the forms of fraud § 10(b) reaches: "The misappropriation theory would not . . . apply to a case in which a person defrauded a bank into giving him a loan or embezzled cash from another, and then used the proceeds of the misdeed to purchase securities." Brief for United States 24, n. 13. In such a case, the Government states, "the proceeds would have value to the malefactor apart from their use in a securities transaction, and the fraud would be complete as soon as the money was obtained." Ibid. In other words, money can buy, if not anything, then at least many things; its misappropriation may thus be viewed as sufficiently detached from a subsequent securities transaction that § 10(b)'s "in connection with" requirement would not be met. Ibid.

The dissent's charge that the misappropriation theory is incoherent because information, like funds, can be put to multiple uses, see post, at 4–8, misses the point. The Exchange Act was enacted in part "to insure the maintenance of fair and honest markets," 15 U.S.C. § 78b, and there is no question that fraudulent uses of confidential information fall within § 10(b)'s prohibition if the fraud is "in connection with" a securities transaction. It is hardly remarkable that a rule suitably applied to the fraudulent uses of certain kinds of information would be stretched beyond reason were it applied to the fraudulent use of money.

The dissent does catch the Government in overstatement. Observing that money can be used for all manner of purposes and purchases, the Government urges that confidential information of the kind at issue derives its value *only* from its utility in securities trading. See Brief for United States 10, 21; *post*, at 4–6 (several times emphasizing the word "only"). Substitute "ordinarily" for "only," and the Government is on the mark. * * *

The misappropriation theory comports with § 10(b)'s language, which requires deception "in connection with the purchase or sale of any security," not deception of an identifiable purchaser or seller. The theory is also well-tuned to an animating purpose of the Exchange Act: to insure honest securities markets and thereby promote investor confidence. See 45 Fed.Reg. 60412 (1980) (trading on misappropriated information "undermines the integrity of, and investor confidence in, the securities markets"). Although informational disparity is inevitable in the securities markets, investors likely would hesitate to venture their capital in a market where trading based on misappropriated nonpublic information is unchecked by law. As investor's informational disadvantage vis-a-vis a misappropriator with material, nonpublic information stems from contrivance, not luck; it is a disadvantage that cannot be overcome with research or skill. See Brudney, Insiders, Outsiders, and Informational Advantages Under the Federal Securities Laws, 93 Harv. L.Rev. 322, 356 (1979) ("If the market is thought to be systematically populated with * * * transactors [trading on the basis of misappropriated information] some investors will refrain from dealing altogether, and others will incur costs to avoid dealing with such transactors or corruptly to overcome their unerodable informational advantages."); Aldave, 13 Hofstra L.Rev., at 122–123.

In sum, considering the inhibiting impact on market participation of trading on misappropriated information, and the congressional purposes underlying § 10(b), it makes scant sense to hold a lawyer like O'Hagan a § 10(b) violator if he works for a law firm representing the target of a tender offer, but not if he works for a law firm representing the bidder. The text of the statute requires no such result.[9] The misappropriation at issue here was properly made the subject of a § 10(b) charge because it meets the statutory requirement that there be "deceptive" conduct "in connection with" securities transactions.

C

The Court of Appeals rejected the misappropriation theory primarily on two grounds. First, as the Eighth Circuit comprehended the theory, it requires neither misrepresentation nor nondisclosure. See 92 F.3d, at 618. As we just explained, however, see *supra*, at 8–10, deceptive nondisclosure is essential to the § 10(b) liability at issue. Concretely, in this case, "it [was O'Hagan's] failure to disclose his personal trading to Grand Met and Dorsey, in breach of his duty to do so, that made his conduct 'deceptive' within the meaning of [§]10(b)." Reply Brief 7.

Second and "more obvious," the Court of Appeals said, the misappropriation theory is not moored to § 10(b)'s requirement that "the fraud be 'in connection with the purchase or sale of any security.'" See 92 F.3d, at 618 (quoting 15 U.S.C. § 78j(b)). According to the Eighth Circuit, three of our decisions reveal that § 10(b) liability cannot be predicated on a duty owed to the source of nonpublic information: Chiarella v. United States, 445 U.S. 222, 100 S.Ct. 1108, 63 L.Ed.2d 348 (1980); Dirks v. SEC, 463 U.S. 646, 103 S.Ct. 3255, 77 L.Ed.2d 911 (1983); and Central Bank of Denver, N.A. v. First Interstate Bank of Denver, N. A., 511 U.S. 164, 114 S.Ct. 1439, 128 L.Ed.2d 119 (1994). "Only a breach of a duty to parties to the securities transaction," the Court of Appeals concluded, "or, at the most, to other market participants such as investors, will be sufficient to give rise to § 10(b) liability." 92 F.3d, at 618. We read the statute and our precedent differently, and note again that § 10(b) refers to "the purchase or sale of any security," not to identifiable purchasers or sellers of securities.

Chiarella involved securities trades by a printer employed at a shop that printed documents announcing corporate takeover bids. See 445 U.S., at 224, 100 S.Ct., at 1112. Deducing the names of target companies from documents he handled, the printer bought shares of the targets before takeover bids were announced, expecting (correctly) that the share prices would rise upon announcement. In these transactions, the printer did not disclose to the sellers of the securities (the target companies' shareholders) the nonpublic information on which he traded. See ibid. For that trading, the printer was convicted of violating § 10(b) and Rule 10b–5. We reversed the Court of Appeals judgment that had affirmed the conviction. See id., at 225.

---

9. As noted earlier, however, see *supra*, at 9–10, the textual requirement of deception precludes § 10(b) liability when a person trading on the basis of nonpublic information has disclosed his trading plans to, or obtained authorization from, the principal—even though such conduct may affect the securities markets in the same manner as the conduct reached by the misappropriation theory. Contrary to the dissent's suggestion, see *post*, at 11–13, the fact that § 10(b) is only a partial antidote to the problems it was designed to alleviate does not call into question its prohibition of conduct that falls within its textual proscription. Moreover, once a disloyal agent discloses his imminent breach of duty, his principal may seek appropriate equitable relief under state law. Furthermore, in the context of a tender offer, the principal who authorizes an agent's trading on confidential information may, in the Commission's view, incur liability for an Exchange Act violation under Rule 14e–3a.

The jury in *Chiarella* had been instructed that it could convict the defendant if he willfully failed to inform sellers of target company securities that he knew of a takeover bid that would increase the value of their shares. See id., at 226, 100 S.Ct., at 1113–1114. Emphasizing that the printer had no agency or other fiduciary relationship with the sellers, we held that liability could not be imposed on so broad a theory. See id., at 235, 100 S.Ct., at 1118. There is under § 10(b), we explained, no "general duty between all participants in market transactions to forgo actions based on material, nonpublic information." Id., at 233, 100 S.Ct., at 1117. Under established doctrine, we said, a duty to disclose or abstain from trading "arises from a specific relationship between two parties." Ibid.

The Court did not hold in *Chiarella* that the only relationship prompting liability for trading on undisclosed information is the relationship between a corporation's insiders and shareholders. That is evident from our response to the Government's argument before this Court that the printer's misappropriation of information from his employer for purposes of securities trading—in violation of a duty of confidentiality owed to the acquiring companies—constituted fraud in connection with the purchase or sale of a security, and thereby satisfied the terms of § 10(b). Id., at 235–236, 100 S.Ct., at 1118–1119. The Court declined to reach that potential basis for the printer's liability, because the theory had not been submitted to the jury. See id., at 236–237, 100 S.Ct., at 1118–1119. But four Justices found merit in it. See id., at 239, 100 S.Ct., at 1120 (Brennan, J., concurring in judgment); id., at 240–243, 100 S.Ct., at 1120–1122 (Burger, C. J., dissenting); id., at 245, 100 S.Ct., at 1123 (Blackmun, J., joined by Marshall, J., dissenting). And a fifth Justice stated that the Court "wisely le[ft] the resolution of this issue for another day." Id., at 238, 100 S.Ct., at 1120 (STEVENS, J., concurring).

Chiarella thus expressly left open the misappropriation theory before us today. Certain statements in *Chiarella,* however, led the Eighth Circuit in the instant case to conclude that § 10(b) liability hinges exclusively on a breach of duty owed to a purchaser or seller of securities. See 92 F.3d, at 618. The Court said in *Chiarella* that § 10(b) liability "is premised upon a duty to disclose arising from a relationship of trust and confidence between parties to a transaction," 445 U.S., at 230 (emphasis added), and observed that the print-shop employee defendant in that case "was not a person in whom the sellers had placed their trust and confidence," see id., at 232, 100 S.Ct., at 1117. These statements rejected the notion that § 10(b) stretches so far as to impose "a general duty between all participants in market transactions to forgo actions based on material, nonpublic information," id., at 233, 100 S.Ct., at 1117, and we confine them to that context. The statements highlighted by the Eighth Circuit, in short, appear in an opinion carefully leaving for future resolution the validity of the misappropriation theory, and therefore cannot be read to foreclose that theory.

Dirks, too, left room for application of the misappropriation theory in cases like the one we confront. *Dirks* involved an investment analyst who had received information from a former insider of a corporation with which the analyst had no connection. See 463 U.S., at 648–649. The information indicated that the corporation had engaged in a massive fraud. The analyst investigated the fraud, obtaining corroborating information from employees of the corporation. During his investigation, the analyst discussed his findings with clients and investors, some of whom sold their holdings in the company the analyst suspected of gross wrongdoing. See *id.*, at 649.

The SEC censured the analyst for, *inter alia,* aiding and abetting § 10(b) and Rule 10b–5 violations by clients and investors who sold their holdings based on the nonpublic information the analyst passed on. See *id.*, at 650–652. In the SEC's view, the analyst, as a "tippee" of corporation insiders, had a duty under § 10(b) and Rule 10b–5 to refrain from communicating the nonpublic information to persons likely to trade on the basis of it. See *id.*, at 651, 655–656. This Court found no such obligation, see *id.*, at 665–667, and repeated the key point made in *Chiarella:* There is no " 'general duty between all participants in market transactions to forgo actions based on material, nonpublic information.' " *Id.*, at 655 (quoting *Chiarella,* 445 U.S., at 233); see Aldave, 13 Hofstra L.Rev., at 122 (misappropriation theory bars only "trading on the basis of information that the wrongdoer converted to his own use in violation of some fiduciary, contractual, or similar obligation to the owner or rightful possessor of the information").

No showing had been made in *Dirks* that the "tippers" had violated any duty by disclosing to the analyst nonpublic information about their former employer. The insiders had acted not for personal profit, but to expose a massive fraud within the corporation. See *Dirks,* 463 U.S., at 666–667. Absent any violation by the tippers, there could be no derivative liability for the tippee. See *id.*, at 667. Most important for purposes of the instant case, the Court observed in *Dirks:* "There was no expectation by [the analyst's] sources that he would keep their information in confidence. Nor did [the analyst] misappropriate or illegally obtain the information * * *." *Id.*, at 665. *Dirks* thus presents no suggestion that a person who gains nonpublic information through misappropriation in breach of a fiduciary duty escapes § 10(b) liability when, without alerting the source, he trades on the information.

Last of the three cases the Eighth Circuit regarded as warranting disapproval of the misappropriation theory, *Central Bank* held that "a private plaintiff may not maintain an aiding and abetting suit under § 10(b)." 511 U.S., at 191. We immediately cautioned in *Central Bank* that secondary actors in the securities markets may sometimes be chargeable under the securities Acts: "Any person or entity, including a lawyer, accountant, or bank, who employs a manipulative device or makes a material misstatement (or omission) *on which a purchaser or seller of securities relies* may be liable as a primary violator under 10b–5, assuming * * * the requirements for primary liability under Rule 10b–5 are met." *Ibid.* (emphasis added). The Eighth Circuit isolated the statement just quoted and drew from it the conclusion that § 10(b) covers only deceptive statements or omissions on which purchasers and sellers, and perhaps other market participants, rely. See 92 F.3d, at 619. It is evident from the question presented in *Central Bank,* however, that this Court, in the quoted passage, sought only to clarify that secondary actors, although not subject to aiding and abetting liability, remain subject to primary liability under § 10(b) and Rule 10b–5 for certain conduct.

Furthermore, *Central Bank*'s discussion concerned only private civil litigation under § 10(b) and Rule 10b–5, not criminal liability. *Central Bank*'s reference to purchasers or sellers of securities must be read in light of a longstanding limitation on private § 10(b) suits. In *Blue Chip Stamps* v. *Manor Drug Stores,* 421 U.S. 723 (1975), we held that only actual purchasers or sellers of securities may maintain a private civil action under § 10(b) and Rule 10b–5.

We so confined the § 10(b) private right of action because of "policy considerations." *Id.*, at 737. In particular, *Blue Chip Stamps* recognized the abuse potential and proof problems inherent in suits by investors who neither bought nor sold, but asserted they would have traded absent fraudulent conduct by others. See *id.*, at 739–747; see also Holmes v. Securities Investor Protection Corporation, 503 U.S. 258, 285 (1992) (O'CONNOR, J., concurring in part and concurring in judgment); *id.*, at 289–290 (SCALIA, J., concurring in judgment). Criminal prosecutions do not present the dangers the Court addressed in *Blue Chip Stamps,* so that decision is "inapplicable" to indictments for violations of § 10(b) and Rule 10b–5. United States v. Naftalin, 441 U.S. 768, 774, n. 6 (1979); see also *Holmes,* 503 U.S. at 281 (O'CONNOR, J., concurring in part and concurring in judgment) ("The purchaser/seller standing requirement for private civil actions under § 10(b) and Rule 10b–5 is of no import in criminal prosecutions for willful violations of those provisions.").

In sum, the misappropriation theory, as we have examined and explained it in this opinion, is both consistent with the statute and with our precedent.[11] Vital to our decision that criminal liability may be sustained under the misappropriation theory, we emphasize, are two sturdy safeguards Congress has provided regarding scienter. To establish a criminal violation of Rule 10b–5, the Government must prove that a person "willfully" violated the provision. See 15 U.S.C. § 78ff(a). Furthermore, a defendant may not be imprisoned for violating Rule 10b–5 if he proves that he had no knowledge of the rule. See *ibid.*[13] O'Hagan's charge that the misappropriation theory is too indefinite to permit the imposition of criminal liability, see Brief for Respondent 30–33, thus fails not only because the theory is limited to those who breach a recognized duty. In addition, the statute's "requirement of the presence of culpable intent as a necessary element of the offense does much to destroy any force in the argument that application of the [statute]" in circumstances such as O'Hagan's is unjust. *Boyce Motor Lines, Inc.* v. *United States,* 342 U.S. 337, 342 (1952).

The Eighth Circuit erred in holding that the misappropriation theory is inconsistent with § 10(b). The Court of Appeals may address on remand O'Hagan's other challenges to his convictions under § 10(b) and Rule 10b–5.

III

We consider next the ground on which the Court of Appeals reversed O'Hagan's convictions for fraudulent trading in connection with a tender offer,

---

11. The United States additionally argues that Congress confirmed the validity of the misappropriation theory in the Insider Trading and Securities Fraud Enforcement Act of 1988 (ITSFEA), § 2(1), 102 Stat. 4677, note following 15 U.S.C. § 78u–1. See Brief for United States 32–35. ITSFEA declares that "the rules and regulations of the Securities and Exchange Commission under the Securities Exchange Act of 1934 * * * governing trading while in possession of material, nonpublic information are, as required by such Act, necessary and appropriate in the public interest and for the protection of investors." Note following 15 U.S.C. § 78u–1. ITSFEA also includes a new § 20A(a) of the Exchange Act expressly providing a private cause of action against persons who violate the Exchange Act "by purchasing or selling a security while in possession of material, nonpublic information"; such an action may be brought by "any person who, contemporaneously with the purchase or sale of securities that is the subject of such violation, has purchased * * * or sold * * * securities of the same class." 15 U.S.C. § 78t–1(a). Because we uphold the misappropriation theory on the basis of § 10(b) itself, we do not address ITSFEA's significance for cases of this genre.

13. The statute provides no such defense to imposition of monetary fines. See *ibid.*

in violation of § 14(e) of the Exchange Act and SEC Rule 14e–3(a). A sole question is before us as to these convictions: Did the Commission, as the Court of Appeals held, exceed its rulemaking authority under § 14(e) when it adopted Rule 14e–3(a) without requiring a showing that the trading at issue entailed a breach of fiduciary duty? We hold that the Commission, in this regard and to the extent relevant to this case, did not exceed its authority.

The governing statutory provision, § 14(e) of the Exchange Act, reads in relevant part:

> "It shall be unlawful for any person to engage in any fraudulent, deceptive, or manipulative acts or practices, in connection with any tender offer. * * * The [SEC] shall, for the purposes of this subsection, by rules and regulations define, and prescribe means reasonably designed to prevent, such acts and practices as are fraudulent, deceptive, or manipulative." 15 U.S.C. § 78n(e).

Section 14(e)'s first sentence prohibits fraudulent acts in connection with a tender offer. This self-operating proscription was one of several provisions added to the Exchange Act in 1968 by the Williams Act, 82 Stat. 454. The section's second sentence delegates definitional and prophylactic rulemaking authority to the Commission. Congress added this rulemaking delegation to § 14(e) in 1970 amendments to the Williams Act. See § 5, 84 Stat. 1497.

Through § 14(e) and other provisions on disclosure in the Williams Act, Congress sought to ensure that shareholders "confronted by a cash tender offer for their stock [would] not be required to respond without adequate information." *Rondeau* v. *Mosinee Paper Corp.*, 422 U.S. 49, 58 * * * (1975); see *Lewis* v. *McGraw*, 619 F.2d 192, 195 (C.A.2 1980) (*per curiam*) ("very purpose" of Williams Act was "informed decisionmaking by shareholders"). As we recognized in *Schreiber* v. *Burlington Northern, Inc.*, 472 U.S. 1 * * * (1985), Congress designed the Williams Act to make "disclosure, rather than court-imposed principles of 'fairness' or 'artificiality,' * * * the preferred method of market regulation." *Id.*, at 9, n. 8. Section 14(e), we explained, "supplements the more precise disclosure provisions found elsewhere in the Williams Act, while requiring disclosure more explicitly addressed to the tender offer context than that required by § 10(b)." *Id.*, at 10–11.

Relying on § 14(e)'s rulemaking authorization, the Commission, in 1980, promulgated Rule 14e–3(a). That measure provides:

> "(a) If any person has taken a substantial step or steps to commence, or has commenced, a tender offer (the 'offering person'), it shall constitute a fraudulent, deceptive or manipulative act or practice within the meaning of section 14(e) of the [Exchange] Act for any other person who is in possession of material information relating to such tender offer which information he knows or has reason to know is nonpublic and which he knows or has reason to know has been acquired directly or indirectly from:

> "(1) The offering person,

> "(2) The issuer of the securities sought or to be sought by such tender offer, or

> "(3) Any officer, director, partner or employee or any other person acting on behalf of the offering person or such issuer, to purchase or sell or cause to be purchased or sold any of such securities or any securities convertible into or exchangeable for any such securities or any option or

right to obtain or to dispose of any of the foregoing securities, unless within a reasonable time prior to any purchase or sale such information and its source are publicly disclosed by press release or otherwise." 17 CFR § 240.14e–3(a) (1996).

As characterized by the Commission, Rule 14e–3(a) is a "disclose or abstain from trading" requirement. 45 Fed.Reg. 60410 (1980).[15] The Second Circuit concisely described the rule's thrust:

"One violates Rule 14e–3(a) if he trades on the basis of material nonpublic information concerning a pending tender offer that he knows or has reason to know has been acquired 'directly or indirectly' from an insider of the offeror or issuer, or someone working on their behalf. Rule 14e–3(a) is a disclosure provision. It creates a duty in those traders who fall within its ambit to abstain or disclose, *without regard to whether the trader owes a preexisting fiduciary duty* to respect the confidentiality of the information." *United States* v. *Chestman,* 947 F.2d 551, 557 (1991) (en banc) (emphasis added), cert. denied, 503 U.S. 1004 * * * (1992).

See also *SEC* v. *Maio,* 51 F.3d 623, 635 (C.A.7 1995) ("Rule 14e–3 creates a duty to disclose material nonpublic information, or abstain from trading in stocks implicated by an impending tender offer, *regardless of whether such information was obtained through a breach of fiduciary duty.*") (emphasis added); *SEC* v. *Peters,* 978 F.2d 1162, 1165 (C.A.10 1992) (as written, Rule 14e–3(a) has no fiduciary duty requirement).

In the Eighth Circuit's view, because Rule 14e–3(a) applies whether or not the trading in question breaches a fiduciary duty, the regulation exceeds the SEC's § 14(e) rulemaking authority. See 92 F.3d, at 624, 627. Contra, *Maio,* 51 F.3d, at 634–635 (CA7); *Peters,* 978 F.2d, at 1165–1167 (CA10); *Chestman,* 947 F.2d, at 556–563 (CA2) (all holding Rule 14e–3(a) a proper exercise of SEC's statutory authority). In support of its holding, the Eighth Circuit relied on the text of § 14(e) and our decisions in *Schreiber* and *Chiarella.* See 92 F.3d, at 624–627.

The Eighth Circuit homed in on the essence of § 14(e)'s rulemaking authorization: "[T]he statute empowers the SEC to 'define' and 'prescribe means reasonably designed to prevent' 'acts and practices' which are 'fraudulent.'" *Id.,* at 624. All that means, the Eighth Circuit found plain, is that the SEC may "identify and regulate," in the tender offer context, "acts and practices" the law already defines as "fraudulent"; but, the Eighth Circuit maintained, the SEC may not "create its own definition of fraud." *Ibid.* (internal quotation marks omitted).

This Court, the Eighth Circuit pointed out, held in *Schreiber* that the word "manipulative" in the § 14(e) phrase "fraudulent, deceptive, or manipulative acts or practices" means just what the word means in § 10(b): Absent misrepresentation or nondisclosure, an act cannot be indicated as manipulative. See 92 F.3d, at 625 (citing *Schreiber,* 472 U.S., at 7–8, and n. 6). Section 10(b) interpretations guide construction of § 14(e), the Eighth Circuit added, see 92 F.3d at 625, citing this Court's acknowledgment in *Schreiber* that § 14(e)'s "'broad antifraud prohibition' * * * [is] modeled on the antifraud provisions of

15. The rule thus adopts for the tender offer context a requirement resembling the one Chief Justice Burger would have adopted in *Chiarella* for misappropriators under § 10(b). See *supra,* at 10, n. 6.

§ 10(b) * * * and Rule 10b–5,'' 472 U.S., at 10 (citation omitted); see *id.,* at 10–11, n. 10.

For the meaning of "fraudulent" under § 10(b), the Eighth Circuit looked to *Chiarella.* See 92 F.3d, at 625. In that case, the Eighth Circuit recounted, this Court held that a failure to disclose information could be "fraudulent" under § 10(b) only when there was a duty to speak arising out of " 'a fiduciary or other similar relationship of trust and confidence.' " *Chiarella,* 445 U.S., at 228 (quoting Restatement (Second) of Torts § 551(2)(a) (1976)). Just as § 10(b) demands a showing of a breach of fiduciary duty, so such a breach is necessary to make out a § 14(e) violation, the Eighth Circuit concluded.

As to the Commission's § 14(e) authority to "prescribe means reasonably designed to prevent" fraudulent acts, the Eighth Circuit stated: "Properly read, this provision means simply that the SEC has broad regulatory powers in the field of tender offers, but the statutory terms have a fixed meaning which the SEC cannot alter by way of an administrative rule." 92 F.3d, at 627.

The United States urges that the Eighth Circuit's reading of § 14(e) misapprehends both the Commission's authority to define fraudulent acts and the Commission's power to prevent them. "The 'defining' power," the United States submits, "would be a virtual nullity were the SEC not permitted to go beyond common law fraud (which is separately prohibited in the first [self-operative] sentence of Section 14(e))." Brief for United States 11; see *id.,* at 37.

In maintaining that the Commission's power to define fraudulent acts under § 14(e) is broader than its rulemaking power under § 10(b), the United States questions the Court of Appeals' reading of *Schreiber.* See *id.,* at 38–40. Parenthetically, the United States notes that the word before the *Schreiber* Court was "manipulative"; unlike "fraudulent," the United States observes, " 'manipulative' . . . is 'virtually a term of art when used in connection with the securities markets.' " *Id.,* at 38, n. 20 (quoting *Schreiber,* 472 U.S., at 6). Most tellingly, the United States submits, *Schreiber* involved acts alleged to violate the self-operative provision in § 14(e)'s first sentence, a sentence containing language similar to § 10(b). But § 14(e)'s second sentence, containing the rulemaking authorization, the United States points out, does not track § 10(b), which simply authorizes the SEC to proscribe "manipulative or deceptive devices or contrivances." Brief for United States 38. Instead, § 14(e)'s rulemaking prescription tracks § 15(c)(2)(D) of the Exchange Act, 15 U.S.C. § 78o(c)(2)(D), which concerns the conduct of broker-dealers in over-the-counter markets. See Brief for United States 38–39. Since 1938, see 52 Stat. 1075, § 15(c)(2) has given the Commission authority to "define, and prescribe means reasonably designed to prevent, such [broker-dealer] acts and practices as are fraudulent, deceptive, or manipulative." 15 U.S.C. § 78o(c)(2)(D). When Congress added this same rulemaking language to § 14(e) in 1970, the Government states, the Commission had already used its § 15(c)(2) authority to reach beyond common law fraud. See Brief for United States 39, n. 22.

We need not resolve in this case whether the Commission's authority under § 14(e) to "define * * * such acts and practices as are fraudulent" is broader than the Commission's fraud-defining authority under § 10(b), for we agree with the United States that Rule 14e–3(a), as applied to cases of this genre, qualifies under § 14(e) as a "means reasonably designed to prevent" fraudulent trading on material, nonpublic information in the tender offer context.[17] A prophylactic measure, because its mission is to prevent, typically encompasses more than the core activity prohibited. As we noted in *Schreiber*, § 14(e)'s rulemaking authorization gives the Commission "latitude," even in the context of a term of art like "manipulative," "to regulate nondeceptive activities as a 'reasonably designed' means of preventing manipulative acts, without suggesting any change in the meaning of the term 'manipulative' itself." 472 U.S., at 11, n. 11. We hold, accordingly, that under § 14(e), the Commission may prohibit acts, not themselves fraudulent under the common law or § 10(b), if the prohibition is "reasonably designed to prevent * * * acts and practices [that] are fraudulent." 15 U.S.C. § 78n(e).[18]

Because Congress has authorized the Commission, in § 14(e), to prescribe legislative rules, we owe the Commission's judgment "more than mere deference or weight." Batterton v. Francis, 432 U.S. 416, 424–426 (1977). Therefore, in determining whether Rule 14e–3(a)'s "disclose or abstain from trading" requirement is reasonably designed to prevent fraudulent acts, we must accord the Commission's assessment "controlling weight unless [it is] arbitrary, capricious, or manifestly contrary to the statute." Chevron U.S.A. Inc. v. Natural Resources Defense Council, Inc., 467 U.S. 837, 844 * * * (1984). In this case, we conclude, the Commission's assessment is none of these.

In adopting the "disclose or abstain" rule, the SEC explained:

> "The Commission has previously expressed and continues to have serious concerns about trading by persons in possession of material, nonpublic information relating to a tender offer. This practice results in unfair disparities in market information and market disruption. Security holders who purchase from or sell to such persons are effectively denied the benefits of disclosure and the substantive protections of the Williams Act. If furnished with the information, these security holders would be able to make an informed investment decision, which could involve deferring the purchase or sale of the securities until the material information had been disseminated or until the tender offer has been commenced or terminated." 45 Fed.Reg. 60412 (1980) (footnotes omitted).

The Commission thus justified Rule 14e–3(a) as a means necessary and proper to assure the efficacy of Williams Act protections.

The United States emphasizes that Rule 14e–3(a) reaches trading in which "a breach of duty is likely but difficult to prove." Reply Brief 16. "Particularly in the context of a tender offer," as the Tenth Circuit recognized, "there is a fairly wide circle of people with confidential information," *Peters*, 978 F.2d, at 1167, notably, the attorneys, investment bankers, and accountants involved in structuring the transaction. The availability of that information may lead to

---

17. We leave for another day, when the issue requires decision, the legitimacy of Rule 14e–3(a) as applied to "warehousing," which the Government describes as "the practice by which bidders leak advance information of a tender offer to allies and encourage them to purchase the target company's stock before the bid is announced." Reply Brief 17. As we observed in *Chiarella*, one of the Commission's purposes in proposing Rule 14e–3(a) was "to bar warehousing under its authority to regulate tender offers." 445 U.S., at 234.

The Government acknowledges that trading authorized by a principal breaches no fiduciary duty. See Reply Brief 17. The instant case, however, does not involve trading authorized by a principal: therefore, we need not here decide whether the Commission's proscription of warehousing falls within its § 14(e) authority to define or prevent fraud.

18. The Commission's power under § 10(b) is more limited. See *supra*, at 6 (Rule 10b–5 may proscribe only conduct that § 10(b) prohibits).

abuse, for "even a hint of an upcoming tender offer may send the price of the target company's stock soaring." *SEC v. Materia,* 745 F.2d 197, 199 (C.A.2 1984). Individuals entrusted with nonpublic information, particularly if they have no long-term loyalty to the issuer, may find the temptation to trade on that information hard to resist in view of "the very large short-term profits potentially available [to them]." *Peters,* 978 F.2d, at 1167.

"It may be possible to prove circumstantially that a person [traded on the basis of material, nonpublic information], but almost impossible to prove that the trader obtained such information in breach of a fiduciary duty owed either by the trader or by the ultimate insider source of the information." *Ibid.* The example of a "tippee" who trades on information received from an insider illustrates the problem. Under Rule 10b–5, "a tippee assumes a fiduciary duty to the shareholders of a corporation not to trade on material nonpublic information only when the insider has breached his fiduciary duty to the shareholders by disclosing the information to the tippee and the tippee knows or should know that there has been a breach." *Dirks,* 463 U.S., at 660. To show that a tippee who traded on nonpublic information about a tender offer had breached a fiduciary duty would require proof not only that the insider source breached a fiduciary duty, but that the tippee knew or should have known of that breach. "Yet, in most cases, the only parties to the [information transfer] will be the insider and the alleged tippee." *Peters,* 978 F.2d, at 1167.

In sum, it is a fair assumption that trading on the basis of material, nonpublic information will often involve a breach of a duty of confidentiality to the bidder or target company or their representatives. The SEC, cognizant of the proof problem that could enable sophisticated traders to escape responsibility, placed in Rule 14e–3(a) a "disclose or abstain from trading" command that does not require specific proof of a breach of fiduciary duty. That prescription, we are satisfied, applied to this case, is a "means reasonably designed to prevent" fraudulent trading on material, nonpublic information in the tender offer context. See *Chestman,* 947 F.2d, at 560 ("While dispensing with the subtle problems of proof associated with demonstrating fiduciary breach in the problematic area of tender offer insider trading, [Rule 14e–3(a)] retains a close nexus between the prohibited conduct and the statutory aims."); accord, *Maio,* 51 F.3d, at 635, and n. 14; *Peters,* 978 F.2d, at 1167.[21] Therefore, insofar as it serves to prevent the type of misappropriation charged against O'Hagan, Rule 14e–3(a) is a proper exercise of the Commission's prophylactic power under § 14(e).

As an alternate ground for affirming the Eighth Circuit's judgment, O'Hagan urges that Rule 14e–3(a) is invalid because it prohibits trading in advance of a tender offer—when "a substantial step * * * to commence" such an offer has been taken—while § 14(e) prohibits fraudulent acts "in connection with any tender offer." See Brief for Respondent 41–42. O'Hagan further contends that, by covering pre-offer conduct, Rule 14e–3(a) "fails to comport with due process on two levels": The rule does not "give fair notice as to when, in advance of a tender offer, a violation of § 14(e) occurs," *id.,* at 42; and it "disposes of any scienter requirement," *id.,* at 43. The Court of Appeals did not address these arguments, and O'Hagan did not raise the due process points in

---

21. The dissent insists that even if the misappropriation of information from the bidder about a tender offer is fraud, the Commission has not explained why such fraud is "in connection with" a tender offer. *Post,* at 19. What else, one can only wonder, might such fraud be "in connection with"?

his briefs before that court. We decline to consider these contentions in the first instance. The Court of Appeals may address on remand any arguments O'Hagan has preserved.

IV

Based on its dispositions of the securities fraud convictions, the Court of Appeals also reversed O'Hagan's convictions, under 18 U.S.C. § 1341, for mail fraud. See 92 F.3d, at 627–628. Reversal of the securities convictions, the Court of Appeals recognized, "did not as a matter of law require that the mail fraud convictions likewise be reversed." *Id.,* at 627 (citing *Carpenter,* 484 U.S., at 24, in which this Court unanimously affirmed mail and wire fraud convictions based on the same conduct that evenly divided the Court on the defendants' securities fraud convictions). But in this case, the Court of Appeals said, the indictment was so structured that the mail fraud charges could not be disassociated from the securities fraud charges, and absent any securities fraud, "there was no fraud upon which to base the mail fraud charges." 92 F.3d, at 627–628.

The United States urges that the Court of Appeals' position is irreconcilable with *Carpenter:* Just as in *Carpenter,* so here, the "mail fraud charges are independent of [the] securities fraud charges, even [though] both rest on the same set of facts." Brief for United States 46–47. We need not linger over this matter, for our rulings on the securities fraud issues require that we reverse the Court of Appeals judgment on the mail fraud counts as well.

O'Hagan, we note, attacked the mail fraud convictions in the Court of Appeals on alternate grounds; his other arguments, not yet addressed by the Eighth Circuit, remain open for consideration on remand.

* * *

The judgment of the Court of Appeals for the Eighth Circuit is reversed, and the case is remanded for further proceedings consistent with this opinion.

It is so ordered.

■ JUSTICE SCALIA, concurring in part and dissenting in part.

I join Parts I, III, and IV of the Court's opinion. I do not agree, however, with Part II of the Court's opinion, containing its analysis of respondent's convictions under § 10(b) and Rule 10b–5. * * *

While the Court's explanation of the scope of § 10(b) and Rule 10b–5 would be entirely reasonable in some other context, it does not seem to accord with the principle of lenity we apply to criminal statutes (which cannot be mitigated here by the Rule, which is no less ambiguous than the statute). See Reno v. Koray, 515 U.S. 50, 64–65 * * * (1995) (explaining circumstances in which rule of lenity applies); United States v. Bass, 404 U.S. 336, 347–348 * * * (1971) (discussing policies underlying rule of lenity). In light of that principle, it seems to me that the unelaborated statutory language: "to use or employ in connection with the purchase or sale of any security * * * any manipulative or deceptive device or contrivance," § 10(b) must be construed to require the manipulation or deception of a party to a securities transaction.

■ JUSTICE THOMAS, with whom THE CHIEF JUSTICE joins, concurring in the judgment in part and dissenting in part.

Today the majority upholds respondent's convictions for violating § 10(b) of the Securities Exchange Act of 1934, and Rule 10b–5 promulgated thereunder, based upon the Securities and Exchange Commission's "misappropriation theory." Central to the majority's holding is the need to interpret § 10(b)'s requirement that a deceptive device be "use[d] or employ[ed], in connection with the purchase or sale of any security." 15 U.S.C. § 78j(b). Because the Commission's misappropriation theory fails to provide a coherent and consistent interpretation of this essential requirement for liability under § 10(b), I dissent.

The majority also sustains respondent's convictions under § 14(e) of the Securities Exchange Act, and Rule 14e–3(a) promulgated thereunder, regardless of whether respondent violated a fiduciary duty to anybody. I dissent too from that holding because, while § 14(e) does allow regulations prohibiting nonfraudulent acts as a prophylactic against certain fraudulent acts, neither the majority nor the Commission identifies any relevant underlying fraud against which Rule 14e–3(a) reasonably provides prophylaxis. With regard to the respondent's mail fraud convictions, however, I concur in the judgment of the Court.

I

I do not take issue with the majority's determination that the undisclosed misappropriation of confidential information by a fiduciary can constitute a "deceptive device" within the meaning of § 10(b). Nondisclosure where there is a pre-existing duty to disclose satisfies our definitions of fraud and deceit for purposes of the securities laws. See Chiarella v. United States, 445 U.S. 222, 230 (1980).

Unlike the majority, however, I cannot accept the Commission's interpretation of when a deceptive device is "use[d] * * * in connection with" a securities transaction. Although the Commission and the majority at points seem to suggest that *any* relation to a securities transaction satisfies the "in connection with" requirement of § 10(b), both ultimately reject such an overly expansive construction and require a more integral connection between the fraud and the securities transaction. The majority states, for example, that the misappropriation theory applies to undisclosed misappropriation of confidential information "for securities trading purposes," *ante,* at 7, thus seeming to require a particular intent by the misappropriator in order to satisfy the "in connection with" language. See also *ante,* at 11 (the "misappropriation theory targets information of a sort that misappropriators *ordinarily* capitalize upon to gain no-risk profits through the purchase or sale of securities") (emphasis added); *ante,* at 11–12 (distinguishing embezzlement of money used to buy securities as lacking the requisite connection). The Commission goes further, and argues that the misappropriation theory satisfies the "in connection with" requirement because it "depends on an *inherent* connection between the deceptive conduct and the purchase or sale of a security." Brief for United States 21 (emphasis added); see also *ibid.* (the "misappropriated information had personal value to respondent *only* because of its utility in securities trading") (emphasis added).

The Commission's construction of the relevant language in § 10(b), and the incoherence of that construction, become evident as the majority attempts to describe why the fraudulent theft of information falls under the Commission's misappropriation theory, but the fraudulent theft of money does not. The majority correctly notes that confidential information "qualifies as property to which the company has a right of exclusive use." *Ante,* at 9. It then observes that the "undisclosed misappropriation of such information, in violation of a fiduciary duty, * * * constitutes fraud akin to embezzlement—the fraudulent appropriation to one's own use of the money or goods entrusted to one's care by another." *Ibid.* (citations and internal quotation marks omitted). So far the majority's analogy to embezzlement is well taken, and adequately demonstrates that undisclosed misappropriation can be a fraud on the source of the information.

What the embezzlement analogy does not do, however, is explain how the relevant fraud is "used or employed, in connection with" a securities transaction. And when the majority seeks to distinguish the embezzlement of funds from the embezzlement of information, it becomes clear that neither the Commission nor the majority has a coherent theory regarding § 10(b)'s "in connection with" requirement. * * *

The Government's construction of the "in connection with" requirement—and its claim that such requirement precludes coverage of financial embezzlement—also demonstrates how the majority's described distinction of financial embezzlement is incomplete. Although the majority claims that the fraud in a financial embezzlement case is complete as soon as the money is obtained, and before the securities transaction is consummated, that is not uniformly true, and thus cannot be the Government's basis for claiming that such embezzlement does not violate the securities laws. It is not difficult to imagine an embezzlement of money that takes place via the mechanism of a securities transaction—for example where a broker is directed to purchase stock for a client and instead purchases such stock—using client funds—for his own account. The unauthorized (and presumably undisclosed) transaction is the very act that constitutes the embezzlement and the "securities transaction and the breach of duty thus coincide." What presumably distinguishes monetary embezzlement for the Government is thus that it is not *necessarily* coincident with a securities transaction, not that it *never* lacks such a "connection."

Once the Government's construction of the misappropriation theory is accurately described and accepted—along with its implied construction of § 10(b)'s "in connection with" language—that theory should no longer cover cases, such as this one, involving fraud on the source of information where the source has no connection with the other participant in a securities transaction. It seems obvious that the undisclosed misappropriation of confidential information is not necessarily consummated by a securities transaction. In this case, for example, upon learning of Grand Met's confidential takeover plans, O'Hagan could have done any number of things with the information: He could have sold it to a newspaper for publication, see Tr. of Oral Arg. 36; he could have given or sold the information to Pillsbury itself, see *id.,* at 37; or he could even have kept the information and used it solely for his personal amusement, perhaps in a fantasy stock trading game.

Any of these activities would have deprived Grand Met of its right to "exclusive use," *ante,* at 9, of the information and, if undisclosed, would constitute "embezzlement" of Grand Met's informational property. Under *any* theory of liability, however, these activities would not violate § 10(b) and, according to the Commission's monetary embezzlement analogy, these possibilities are sufficient to preclude a violation under the misappropriation theory even where the informational property *was* used for securities trading. That O'Hagan actually did use the information to purchase securities is thus no more significant here than it is in the case of embezzling money used to purchase securities. In both cases the embezzler *could have* done something else with the property, and hence the Commission's necessary "connection" under the securities laws would not be met. If the relevant test under the "in connection with" language is whether the fraudulent act is *necessarily* tied to a securities transaction, then the misappropriation of confidential information used to trade no more violates § 10(b) than does the misappropriation of funds used to trade. As the Commission concedes that the latter is not covered under its theory, I am at a loss to see how the same theory can coherently be applied to the former. * * *

I need not address the coherence, or lack thereof, of the majority's new theory, for it suffers from a far greater, and dispositive, flaw: It is not the theory offered by the Commission. Indeed, as far as we know from the majority's opinion, this new theory has *never* been proposed by the Commission, much less adopted by rule or otherwise. It is a fundamental proposition of law that this Court "may not supply a reasoned basis for the agency's action that the agency itself has not given." Motor Vehicle Mfrs. Assn. of United States, Inc. v. State Farm Mut. Automobile Ins. Co., 463 U.S. 29, 43 * * * (1983). We do not even credit a "*post hoc* rationalization" of counsel for the agency, *id.,* at 50, so one is left to wonder how we could possibly rely on a *post hoc* rationalization invented by this Court and never even presented by the Commission for our consideration.

Whether the majority's new theory has merit, we cannot possibly tell on the record before us. There are no findings regarding the "ordinary" use of misappropriated information, much less regarding the "ordinary" use of other forms of embezzled property. The Commission has not opined on the scope of the new requirement that property must "ordinarily" be used for securities trading in order for its misappropriation to be "in connection with" a securities transaction. We simply do not know what would or would not be covered by such a requirement, and hence cannot evaluate whether the requirement embodies a consistent and coherent interpretation of the statute. Moreover, persons subject to this new theory, such as respondent here, surely could not and cannot regulate their behavior to comply with the new theory because, until today, the theory has never existed. In short, the majority's new theory is simply not presented by this case, and cannot form the basis for upholding respondent's convictions.

WHO HAS A DUTY TO DISCLOSE?

Chiarella, Dirks, and *O'Hagan* are consistent that only one with a duty to disclose is subject to the Rule 10b-5 disclose or abstain rule. *Chiarella* emphatically rejected the "egalitarian" or parity-of-information theory implicit in the Second Circuit's holding that "[a]nyone, corporate insider or not, who regularly receives material nonpublic information may not use that information to trade in securities without incurring an affirmative duty to disclose."[1]

---

1. United States v. Chiarella, 588 F.2d 1358, 1365 (2d Cir.1978). Necessarily this also amounted to a rejection of the similar egalitarian theory articulated in SEC v. Tex- as Gulf Sulphur Co., 401 F.2d 833, 848 (2d Cir.1968), *cert. denied sub nom.* Coates v. SEC, 394 U.S. 976 (1969).

Insiders: It had long been clear that officers and directors[2] and majority or other controlling shareholders[3] were subject to the disclose or abstain rule.

Constructive Insiders: *Dirks* was significant for footnote 14 which transforms such "outsiders" as an underwriter, accountant, lawyer, or corporate consultant into constructive insiders ("fiduciaries of the shareholders") when they "[enter] into a special confidential relationship in the conduct of the business of the enterprise and are given access to information solely for corporate purposes."[4]

The Court underlined that "[f]or such a duty to be imposed * * * the corporation must expect the outsider to keep the disclosed nonpublic information confidential and the relationship at least must imply such a duty." The Court in *Dirks* then offered two contrasting illustrations of the reach of the constructive insider concept. In footnote 14, the Court cited Shapiro v. Merrill Lynch, Pierce, Fenner & Smith, Inc.,[5] where the duty was properly applied to an investment banker who had access to material information when working on a proposed public offering for a corporation. On the other hand, in *Dirks* footnote 22, the Court described Walton v. Morgan Stanley & Co.,[6] a common law action on behalf of the issuer, in which an investment bank was not held liable when it represented a client, corporation *A*, in an investigation of a separate corporation *B*, a possible takeover target. The investment bank received on a confidential basis unpublished material information from corporation *B*. After corporation *A* abandoned the proposed takeover, the investment bank relied on the confidential information in trading in corporation *B*'s stock. "For purposes of the decision, it was assumed that the firm knew the information was confidential, but that it had been received in arm's length negotiations." The Supreme Court appeared to approve the Court of Appeals conclusion that there was "no basis for imposing tippee liability on the investment firm." Even with the limitation implicit in the Walton case, *Dirks* footnote 14 represents a significant broadening of the insider category.

Dirks did not, however, define what it meant by a special confidential relationship beyond observing that a constructive insider is "given access to information solely for corporate purposes" *and* "the corporation must expect the outsider to keep the disclosed information confidential, and the relationship at least must imply such a duty."

For a legislative egalitarian proposal, *see* Joel Seligman, The Reformulation of Federal Securities Law Concerning Nonpublic Information, 73 Geo. L.J. 1083 (1985). Professor Brudney earlier had advanced another theory that falls somewhat short of egalitarianism: that there should be a universal ban on trading by persons who obtain material, nonpublic information through "unerodable informational advantages"—which is to say, advantages that normally arise because of a person's position giving access to information not legally available to public investors however diligent. Victor Brudney, Insiders, Outsiders, and Informational Advantages under the Federal Securities Laws, 93 Harv. L. Rev. 322 (1979).

2. *See, e.g.*, List v. Fashion Park, Inc., 340 F.2d 457 (2d Cir.1965), *cert. denied sub nom.* List v. Lerner, 382 U.S. 811 (1965); Kardon v. National Gypsum Co., 69 F.Supp. 512 (E.D.Pa.1946), 73 F.Supp. 798 (E.D.Pa. 1947), 83 F.Supp. 613 (E.D.Pa.1947); Northern Trust Co. v. Essaness Theatres Corp., 103 F.Supp. 954 (N.D.Ill.1952).

3. *See, e.g.*, Rogen v. Ilikon Corp., 361 F.2d 260 (1st Cir.1966); Speed v. Transamerica Corp., 99 F.Supp. 808 (D.Del.1951), 135 F.Supp. 176 (D.Del.1955), *aff'd*, 235 F.2d 369 (3d Cir.1956).

4. 463 U.S. at 655 n.14.

5. 495 F.2d 228 (2d Cir.1974).

6. 623 F.2d 796 (2d Cir.1980).

In SEC v. Lund,[7] a district court held, in effect, that the constructive insider duty will attach upon proof of access to information given solely for corporate purposes with an expectation that the disclosed information be kept confidential. In *Lund*, Horowitz, the chief executive of P & F Industries, informed Lund, the chief executive of Verit Industries, that P & F was negotiating a new joint venture involving a gambling casino. The executives were friends and had a long standing business relationship. Horowitz had been a member of Verit's board of directors for at least seven years. The court concluded that Lund was a temporary P & F insider when he traded on the basis of information concerning the casino project:

> The information was made available to Lund solely for corporate purposes. It was not disclosed in idle conversation or for some other purpose. The relationship between Horowitz and Lund was such as to imply that the information was to be kept confidential. Horowitz clearly did not expect Lund to make the information public or to use the information for his personal gain. Lund knew or should have known that the information he received was confidential and that it had been disclosed to him solely for legitimate corporate purposes.[8]

This may reach too far. The information in Walton v. Morgan Stanley & Co. was also provided with an implicit expectation of confidentiality or limited use, but the Supreme Court approved the exoneration of the outsider in that case.

The Court in *Dirks* Footnote 14 added one more point concerning constructive insiders. "When such a person breaches his fiduciary relationship, he may be treated more properly as a tipper than a tippee." This eliminates the need to prove (1) that the constructive insider received material nonpublic information in violation of a traditional insider's fiduciary duties—normally, of course, the constructive insider will receive the data without violating a traditional insider's duties—and (2) that the constructive insider knew or should have known that the data were given to him or her in violation of a traditional insider's duties. *Dirks* requires these proofs in a case against a tippee.

Tippers and Tippees: In a Second Circuit case preceding *Dirks* the court had held that an insider can be held liable for conveying nonpublic material information to outsiders who trade even when the insider does not trade.[9]

In *Dirks* the Supreme Court similarly held: "Not only are insiders forbidden by their fiduciary relationship from personally using undisclosed corporate information to their advantage, but they also may not give such information to an outsider for the same improper purpose of exploiting the information for their personal gain."[10] That is to say, an insider may not use a tippee as a surrogate or agent for illegal trading. But this does not address information that is communicated consistently with fiduciary duties, for example, to secure a corporate loan or business relationship. Granted that the tipper no longer may be held liable for communicating this information, are all "tippees" then free to trade while in possession of appropriately communicated information?

In *Dirks* the Court's response was equivocal. In certain circumstances these types of outsiders may become constructive insiders under the logic of

---

7. 570 F.Supp. 1397 (C.D.Cal.1983).

8. Id. at 1403.

9. Shapiro v. Merrill Lynch, Pierce, Fenner & Smith, Inc., 495 F.2d 228, 237–238 (2d Cir.1974).

10. 463 U.S. at 659.

footnote 14. But the general rule is that "[t]ippees must assume an insider's duty to the shareholders not because they receive inside information, but rather because it has been made available to them *improperly*."[11] [Emphasis in original.] The key to the test "is whether the insider personally will benefit, directly or indirectly, from his disclosure. Absent some personal gain, there has been no breach of duty to stockholders. And absent a breach by the insider, there is no derivative breach."[12]

Dirks also has complicated proof of a Rule 10b–5 violation, as SEC v. *Switzer*,[13] illustrates. In *Switzer*, a university football coach, while sitting in the stands at a track meet, overheard a business executive give his wife material nonpublic information concerning a firm in which the executive served as a director. To prove a violation of Rule 10b–5, a plaintiff must show that the tip was made with scienter. In *Switzer* the Commission was unable to persuade an Oklahoma jury that the business executive had intentionally or recklessly tipped the coach, with the result that the coach and other more remote tippees were allowed to retain substantial profits.

In United States v. Chestman[14] a tipper-tippee theory also proved unsuccessful when a corporate insider informed his sister about a pending tender offer for the presumably innocent purpose of helping her tender her shares. The sister informed her daughter who in turn told her husband who told his stockbroker, Chestman. In this context, the Second Circuit held that "marriage does not, without more, create a fiduciary relationship." Since the tips from the insider to his sister and her tip to her daughter and her daughter's tip to her husband could not establish the requisite fiduciary relationship, the *Dirks* tipper-tippee analysis did not result in liability.

The *O'Hagan* case alluded to these types of evidentiary difficulty when Justice Ginsburg wrote for the majority:

"[I]t may be possible to prove circumstantially that a person [traded on the basis of material, nonpublic information], but almost impossible to prove that the trader obtained such information in breach of a fiduciary duty owed either by the trader or by the ultimate insider source of the information." [Citation omitted]. The example of a "tippee" who trades on information received from an insider illustrates the problem. * * * To show that a tippee who traded on nonpublic information about a tender offer had breached a fiduciary duty would require proof not only that the insider source breached a fiduciary duty, but that the tippee knew or should have known of that breach. "Yet, in most cases, the only parties to the [information transfer] will be the insider and the alleged tippee."[15]

The Misappropriation Theory: As *O'Hagan* explained in Footnote 4, the Supreme Court twice before had been presented with the question of whether an outsider who misappropriated nonpublic information could be held liable under Rule 10b–5. In neither *Chiarella* nor Carpenter v. United States,[16] had the Court resolved the question. *O'Hagan* also underlies that the lower federal courts were divided over the question.

11.   Id. at 660.

12.   Id. at 662.

13.   590 F.Supp. 756 (W.D.Okla.1984).

14.   947 F.2d 551 (2d Cir. *en banc* 1991), *cert. denied*, 503 U.S. 1004 (1992).

15.   521 U.S. 642, 675 (1997).

16.   484 U.S. 19, 24 (1987).

In *O'Hagan* the Court held that "a person commits fraud 'in connection with' a securities transaction, and thereby violates § 10(b) and Rule 10b–5 when he misappropriates confidential information for securities trading purposes, in breach of a duty to the source of the information. * * * In lieu of premising liability on a fiduciary relationship between company insider and purchaser or seller of the company's stock, the misappropriation theory premises liability on a fiduciary-turned-trader's deception of those who entrusted him with access to confidential information."[17]

This theory is bounded. There must be deception of the source of the information. Here O'Hagan was held to have deceived both his law firm and Grand Met, the firm that employed the law firm. The misappropriation theory does not create a duty that runs to those with whom the misappropriator traded. Although not directly addressed in *O'Hagan*, the Supreme Court's approach would seem capable of reaching "a judge's law clerk who trades on information in an unpublished opinion or a Government employee who trades on a secret report."[18]

The *O'Hagan* version of the misappropriation theory will subsume the alternative duty to employer doctrine activated by Justice Stevens in *Chiarella*. That duty could apply to any employer and could necessarily include traditional and constructive insiders as well as employees of tender offer bidders, judges, and governments. The misappropriation theory, in contrast has been applied in instances that did not involve a violation of a duty to an employer.[19]

Under the misappropriation theory the plaintiff's burden is simplified. Proving a tippee's scienter can be a major stumbling block. The tippee must know of a benefit to the tipper. The same tippee, however, can be held liable under the misappropriation theory if it can be shown that the misappropriator knew that he or she wrongly took another's information. The misappropriation scienter element seems far more appropriate for certain types of wrongdoing. For example, if a businessperson in Corporation *A* proposes a transaction to a second businessperson in Corporation *B* solely for the purpose of fraudulently securing Corporation *B*'s proprietary information, it would be highly difficult to establish tipping liability. Disclosure of these data by the Corporation *B* businessperson would appear to be consistent with his other underlying fiduciary duties. Under tipping analysis, since the Corporation *A* businessperson would know that the Corporation *B* businessperson had not violated a fiduciary duty, he or she would appear to be free to trade. This, however, is a highly troubling result, because the *A* businessperson had engaged in a fraud or deceit to secure the data. Under misappropriation analysis, it would be remediable if the plaintiff could prove that *A* businessperson secretly traded on the basis of the confidential data. This type of scienter analysis better aligns the proof of a fraud or deceit with the knowledge of a wrong than tippee liability under the *Dirks* paradigm, which may give tippees a free ride to trade for person of benefit whenever the tipper has not also secured a personal benefit.

---

17. 521 U.S. at 652.

18. These had been Burger's concerns in *Chiarella. See* 445 U.S. at 242.

19. SEC v. Willis, 777 F.Supp. 1165 (S.D.N.Y.1991) (holding liable a psychiatrist who traded on the basis of a patient's disclo-sures about her husband's inside information). See generally Joel Seligman, A Mature Synthesis: *O'Hagan* Resolves "Insider" Trading's Most Vexing Problems, 23 Del. J. Corp. L. 1 (1998).

Rule 14e–3. In 1980, after the *Chiarella* decision, the Securities and Exchange Commission adopted Rule 14e–3, applicable when (1) any person has taken a substantial step or steps to commence, or has commenced a tender offer *and* another person is in possession of material information relating to the tender offer; (2) the information the other person knows or has reason to know is nonpublic; (3) that information has been acquired directly or indirectly from the offeror, from the issuer of the securities sought or to be sought by the tender offer (the target), or from any officer, director, partner, employee, or any other person acting on behalf of the offeror or the target; and (4) the other person purchases or sells or causes the purchase or sale of any security to be sought or in fact sought in the tender offer *or* any other security convertible into or exchangeable for that security *or* any option or right to obtain or to dispose of that security, unless (5) within a reasonable time before any purchase or sale the information *and* its source are publicly disclosed by a press release or otherwise.[20]

O'Hagan resolved that Rule 14e–3 was validly adopted. The Court did not address the meaning of such concepts as a "substantial step * * * to commence" a tender offer.The Rule 14e–3 adoption Release articulated the Commission's belief

> that a substantial step or steps to commence a tender offer include, but are not limited to, voting on a resolution by the offering person's board of directors relating to the tender offer; the formulation of a plan or proposal to make a tender offer by the offering person or the person(s) acting on behalf of the offering person; or activities which substantially facilitate the tender offer such as: arranging financing for a tender offer; preparing or directing or authorizing the preparation of tender offer materials; or authorizing negotiations, negotiating or entering into agreements with any person to act as a dealer manager, soliciting dealer, forwarding agent or depository in connection with the tender offer.[21]

In *O'Connor & Assoc. v. Dean Witter Reynolds, Inc.*,[22] the court found that allegedly fraudulent conduct when the offer was still in a proposed state could violate Rule 14e–3 even if the offer never became effective because it was conditioned upon the target board's approval and the board rejected the proposal at the same time that it publicly announced it.[23] A substantial step to commence a tender offer can be taken even if no tender offer is actually made. A court had no difficulty in concluding that a substantial step had been taken to accomplish a tender offer when the two firms had hired a consulting firm, signed confidentiality agreements, and held meetings between top officials.[24] Similarly when a potential bidder had acquired a large portion in a target from which it could launch a tender offer, this could constitute a substantial step even if this occurred before any meetings between the bidder and the target.[25]

20. *See generally* 8 Louis Loss & Joel Seligman, Securities Regulation 3729–3739 (3d ed. 1991). The Second Circuit has held that there is simply no language in [Rule 14e–3] indicating that "a defendant must know that the nonpublic information in his possession relates to a tender offer." SEC v. Sargent, 229 F.3d 68, 78 (1st Cir.2000).

21. Sec. Ex. Act Rel. 17,120, 20 SEC Dock. 1241, 1248 n.33 (1980).

22. 529 F.Supp. 1179 (S.D.N.Y.1981).

23. Id. at 1188–1193.

24. SEC v. Mayhew, 121 F.3d 44, 52–53 (2d Cir.1997).

25. SEC v. Warde, 151 F.3d 42, 49 (2d Cir.1998).

In *SEC v. Maio*,[26] the court held that a meeting before the parties signed a confidentiality agreement was a substantial step toward commencing a tender offer, because one of the two corporations had earlier solicited a tender offer.

PROBLEM 14–5

Wyoming was employed as Director of Fiduciary Services by the St. Louis law firm of Larsen & Gould ("Larsen & Gould"). She controlled the selection of stockbrokers for the placing of securities trades on behalf of the trust accounts managed by Larsen & Gould. Murtagh was employed as a stockbroker by Morgan Merrill. Wyoming directed a large share of Larsen & Gould's business to Murtagh. Murtagh and Wyoming also shared a personal and financial relationship.

From December 7, 2001 until December 12, 2001, Larsen & Gould represented the Bank of St. Louis in connection with a potential merger with MoBanks. This was a highly confidential transaction. Though few lawyers at Larsen & Gould were involved in the transactions, Wyoming had daily contact with at least one, John Green. Green visited Wyoming's office frequently to check stock prices and monitor his personal account. Computer records indicate that Wyoming opened Green's account summary on Wyoming's computer at 3:27 p.m. and 3:28 p.m. on December 12, 2001.

At 3:29 p.m., one minute after opening Green's account summary, Wyoming placed a call to Murtagh. The call lasted one minute and twelve seconds. Immediately after Wyoming's call, Murtagh called his trading assistant, Krista Kreme, and entered orders to purchase approximately 11,000 shares of MoBanks stock, priced at $85 per share, for his own account, and those of other family members. Kreme also purchased 400 shares of MoBanks stock for her own account. To her knowledge, Murtagh never had bought across all of his family accounts at once.

Kreme on December 12th also telephoned her fiancee, Nord Bagel, and said "buy MoBanks." Bagel instantly bought 1000 shares.

After the market closed on December 12, 2001, Bank of St. Louis and MoBanks announced their merger. As a result of the merger, MoBanks stock price increased by $8 a share (or 28 percent) before the market opened on December 13, 2001.

Have (1) Wyoming, (2) Murtagh, (3) Kreme, or (4) Bagel violated Rule 10b–5? If so, why?

PROBLEM 14–6

Former business school classmates, Sirhan Dippity and Mella Prop, share a one room business office in Silicon Valley. Each operates a separate financial consulting firm. Recently Dippity overheard Prop discuss with a client "the Incubator deal." Dippity knew that Prop was on retainer to Incubator, Inc. Dippity telephoned his broker, Kelley Sharn, and asked for a research report on Incubator, a local biotech firm. Sharn telephoned later that day with an upbeat report and Dippity bought 1,000 shares of Incubator.

The next day Macrohard announced a friendly tender offer for Incubator at a 50 percent premium above the prior day's stock market.

Has Mella Prop or Sirhan Dippity violated Rule 10b–5?

Has Sirhan Dippity violated Rule 14e–3?

26. 51 F.3d 623, 636 (7th Cir.1995).

NEW DEVELOPMENTS IN INSIDER TRADING AND SELECTIVE DIS-
CLOSURE

Regulation FD: In August, 2000 the SEC adopted Regulation FD. The
adoption Release succinctly explained:

> Regulation FD (Fair Disclosure) is a new issuer disclosure rule that
> addresses selective disclosure. The regulation provides that when an issuer,
> or person acting on its behalf, discloses material nonpublic information to
> certain enumerated persons (in general, securities market professionals
> and holders of the issuer's securities who may well trade on the basis of the
> information), it must make public disclosure of that information. The
> timing of the required public disclosure depends on whether the selective
> disclosure was intentional or non-intentional; for an intentional selective
> disclosure, the issuer must make public disclosure simultaneously; for a
> non-intentional disclosure, the issuer must make public disclosure prompt-
> ly. Under the regulation, the required public disclosure may be made by
> filing or furnishing a Form 8–K, or by another method or combination of
> methods that is reasonably designed to effect broad, non-exclusionary
> distribution of the information to the public.[1]

The SEC's decision to adopt Regulation FD in the face of considerable
opposition from securities analysts and investment banking firms (but much
vocal support from individual investors) was based on several different and
independent policy considerations:

First, the SEC recognized that there was considerable legal doubt as to
whether Rule 10b–5 could be stretched to reach corporate disclosure to securities analysts or institutional investors that were not accompanied by actual
bribes or other tangible inducements.

Second, in addition to giving unequal access to material information to
privileged investors, selective disclosure involved an independent danger not
generally associated with insider trading: it could be used to undermine the
independence of securities analysts, upon whose efforts market efficiency might
substantially depend. That is, information can be used as a means of securing
the acquiescence and support of securities analysts because management can
cut off a critical analyst from the flow of future sensitive information.

Third, the SEC believed that selective disclosure was becoming pervasive
and in the words of the adoption release that "voluntary steps" to remedy the
problem "have been far from effective."

Against these considerations favoring regulation, the Commission balanced
the acknowledged danger that a rule against selective disclosure might "chill"
issuer communications and result in less information reaching the market.
Although the Commission did not accept this claim, it did narrow the scope of
Regulation FD in several important respects from the Rule that it had originally proposed:

> (1) As adopted, Regulation FD applies only to communications made
> to a limited number of persons (securities market professionals and holders
> of the issuer's securities under circumstances where it was reasonably
> foreseeable that the holder would trade on the basis of the information);

---

1. Sec. Ex. Act Rel. 43,154, 73 SEC
Dock. 3 (2000).

(2) The Rule applies only to certain issuer personnel (senior officials and lower-ranking persons regularly engaged in communications with securities market professionals or securities holders);

(3) Private liability cannot result from a Regulation FD violation;

(4) Expressly excluded from the Rule's coverage were statements made in connection with marketing securities offerings (such as at road-shows).

As so narrowed, Rule 100 of Regulation FD applies, as explained in the adoption Release:

Whenever: (1) an issuer, or person acting on its behalf,

(2) discloses material nonpublic information,

(3) to certain enumerated persons (in general, securities market professionals or holders of the issuer's securities who may well trade on the basis of the information),

(4) the issuer must make public disclosure of that same information: (a) simultaneously (for intentional disclosures), or (b) promptly (for non-intentional disclosures).

As a whole, the regulation requires that when an issuer makes an intentional disclosure of material nonpublic information to a person covered by the regulation, it must do so in a manner that provides general public disclosure, rather than through a selective disclosure. For a selective disclosure that is non-intentional, the issuer must publicly disclose the information promptly after it knows (or is reckless in not knowing) that the information selectively disclosed was both material and nonpublic.[2]

Despite these limitations, Regulation F–D alarmed some issuers, analysts, and investment banking firms. In particular, the Release warned:

One common situation that raises special concerns about selective disclosure has been the practice of securities analysts seeking "guidance" from issuers regarding earnings forecasts. *When an issuer official engages in a private discussion with an analyst who is seeking guidance about earnings estimates, he or she takes on a high degree of risk under Regulation FD.* If the issuer official communicates selectively to the analyst nonpublic information that the company's anticipated earnings will be higher than, lower than, or even the same as what analysts have been forecasting, the issuer likely will have violated Regulation FD. This is true whether the information about earnings is communicated expressly or through indirect "guidance," the meaning of which is apparent though implied. Similarly, an issuer cannot render material information immaterial simply by breaking it into ostensibly non-material pieces.[3] (emphasis added)

This warning is, however, counterbalanced in the Release's next paragraph by a clear statement of traditional "mosaic theory:"

At the same time, an issuer is not prohibited from disclosing a non-material piece of information to an analyst, even if, unbeknownst to the issuer, that piece helps the analyst complete a "mosaic" of information that, taken together, is material. Similarly, since materiality is an objective

---

2. Id. at 7.   **3.** Id. at 11.

test keyed to the reasonable investor, Regulation FD will not be implicated where an issuer discloses immaterial information whose significance is discerned by the analyst. Analysts can provide a valuable service in sifting through and extracting information that would not be significant to the ordinary investor to reach material conclusions. We do not intend, by Regulation FD, to discourage this sort of activity. The focus of Regulation FD is on whether the issuer discloses material nonpublic information, not on whether an analyst, through some combination of persistence, knowledge, and insight, regards as material information whose significance is not apparent to the reasonable investor.[4]

Regulation FD applies only to reporting companies. In addition, Rule 100(b)(2) of Regulation FD sets out four specific exclusions from coverage: (1) communications made to persons who owe the issuer a duty of trust or confidence (for example, lawyers or investment bankers working for the issuer); (2) communications to persons who expressly agree to maintain the information in confidence (for example, selective disclosure might be made to offerees in a private placement if they agree to maintain the information so disclosed in confidence); (3) communications to credit ratings organizations (whose own purpose is ultimately public disclosure); and (4) communications made in connection with securities offerings. This last exclusion raises special problems which the Commission will ultimately have to resolve: why should selective disclosure be permitted at a roadshow, for example, where the audience consists of institutional investors and analysts who are likely to trade promptly in the secondary market upon learning of material information? Put differently, if selective disclosure is undesirable, why should Regulation FD exempt it in the public offering process?

Although Rule 100(a)(2) gives the issuer an opportunity to make "prompt" public disclosure after a non-intentional selective disclosure, Rule 101(a) defines "intentional" to include statements that are made "recklessly." On this basis, some commentators have concluded that most selective disclosures made by senior corporate officials, who are typically well aware of their corporations' condition and competitive position, will likely be found to be reckless. Hence, the possibility of a corrective after-the-fact disclosure may be illusory in practice—except perhaps in the case of impromptu oral statements made, for example, at a conference with a limited audience.

Rule 101(e) defines the type of "public disclosure" that will satisfy the requirements of Regulation FD. As adopted, it says that issuers can make public disclosure for purposes of Regulation FD by filing or furnishing a Form 8-K, or by disseminating information "through another method (or by a combination of methods) of disclosure that is reasonably designed to provide broad, non-exclusionary distribution of the information to the public." In the adoption Release, the Commission recommended (but did not require) the following "model":

First, issue a press release, distributed through regular channels, containing the information;

Second, provide adequate notice, by a press release and/or website posting, of a scheduled conference call to discuss the announced results, giving investors both the time and date of the conference call, and instructions on how to access the call; and

4. Ibid.

Third, hold the conference call in an open manner, permitting investors to listen in either by telephonic means or through Internet webcasting.

By following these steps, an issuer can use the press release to provide the initial broad distribution of the information, and then discuss its release with analysts in the subsequent conference call, without fear that if it should disclose additional material details related to the original disclosure it will be engaging in a selective disclosure of material information.[5]

At present, the SEC does not consider the posting of information on the issuer's website to be a "sufficient method of public disclosure" for purposes of Rule 101(e). However, the Commission noted that

As technology evolves and as more investors have access to and use the Internet, however, we believe that some issuers, whose websites are widely followed by the investment community, could use such a method. Moreover, while the posting of information on an issuer's website may not now, by itself, be a sufficient means of public disclosure, we agree with commenters that the issuer websites can be an important component of an effective disclosure process. Thus, in some circumstances an issuer may be able to demonstrate that disclosure made on its website could be part of a combination of methods, 'reasonably designed to provide broad, non-exclusionary distribution' of information to the public.[6]

Currently, issuers generally appear to be adopting the public press conference approach over the Form 8–K filing approach, as their preferred means for making public disclosure for purposes of Rule 101(e).

An early empirical study of company disclosure after Regulation FD suggested little "chilling effect" on information dissemination. The National Investor Relations Institute (NIRI) reported in a February 2001 survey that 28 percent of companies were disclosing more information than they had before Regulation FD and 24 percent were disclosing less.[7]

Rule 10b5–1: The SEC Responds to the "Use or Possession" Debate.

An unsettled issue in insider trading law had surrounded the need, if any, to show a causal connection between the trader's possession of inside information and the trader's decision to trade. While the SEC long argued that it need show only "knowing possession," some cases have required a showing of "use" (although they also have recognized that possession may establish a strong inference of use). See SEC v. Adler, 137 F.3d 1325, 1337 (11th Cir. 1998, *cert. denied,* 525 U.S. 1071 (1999)); United States v. Smith, 155 F.3d 1051, 1069 & n. 27 (9th Cir.1998) ("use" must be proven in a criminal case). To resolve this conflict (and in its favor), the SEC has adopted new Rule 10b5–1 ("Trading 'on the basis of' materials nonpublic information in insider trading cases").

Rule 10b5–1 defines a trade or sale to have occurred "on the basis of" material nonpublic information at the time of the purchase or sale. However, the rule also created an important safe harbor from liability when the trade results from a preexisting plan, contract, or instruction that was made in good faith.

---

5. Id. at 14–15.

6. Id. at 15.

7. NIRI Finds that Divisive Regulation FD Prompts Varied Disclosure Results So Far, 33 Sec. Reg. & L. Rep. (BNA) 335 (2001).

Specifically, Rule 10b5–1(c)(1)(i) creates an affirmative defense from the general rule of liability if the following factors can be established:

1.   Before becoming aware of the information, the person entered into a binding contract to purchase or sell the security, provided instructions to another person to execute the trade for its account, or adopted a written plan for trading securities;

2.   The contract, instruction or plan either expressly specified the amount, price, and date or provided a written formula or algorithm, and dates, or did not permit the person to exercise any subsequent influence.

3.   No alteration or deviation from the prior contract, instruction, or plan occurred after the time that the person became aware of the material nonpublic information.

Thus, if (i) a corporate executive were to establish a written plan with his broker under which the broker was instructed to sell 10% of the executive's holdings in the company each year (or quarter), (ii) the broker was not itself aware of the material nonpublic information, and (iii) the executive did not modify the plan after becoming aware of material, nonpublic information or otherwise exercise influence over the broker's trading, such written plan or instruction would enable the executive to buy or sell his company's stock without fear of incurring insider trading liability. Such Rule 10b5–1 plans are becoming a standard part of corporate life, as they enable executives to assure themselves that they can meet expected financial commitments through stock sales and they simplify the need for pre-clearance by corporate counsel. In addition, they permit the executive to exercise stock options and immediately sell the underlying stock on a pre-arranged timetable. The corporation, itself, can also use such a plan to effect stock repurchases without having to halt them when it becomes aware of material information.

Rule 10b5–2

Another unsettled issue in insider trading law has involved the circumstances under which non-business relationships, such as family and personal relationships, give rise to the duty to trust or confidence required under misappropriation theory. In United States v. Chestman, 947 F.2d 551 (2d Cir.1991) (en banc), a wife passed information about an approaching merger and tender offer to her husband, who then tipped his broker who traded. Nonetheless, an en banc, but closely divided, Second Circuit found no liability under Rule 10b–5, because it said no fiduciary relationship existed between the husband and wife with respect to confidential business information. Rule 10b5–2 effectively overrules *Chestman* and curtails the need in many instances to inquire into the minute details of personal relationships. It specifies three non-exclusive situations in which a duty of trust or confidence arises for purposes of misappropriation theory and Rule 10b–5:

1.   Whenever a person agrees to maintain information in trust or confidence;

2.   When two people have a history, pattern or practice of sharing confidences such that the recipient of the information knows or reasonably should know that the person communicating the material nonpublic information expects that the recipient will maintain its confidentiality; and

3.   When a person receives or obtains material nonpublic information from certain enumerated close family members: spouses, parents, children,

and siblings. An affirmative defense is, however, recognized under which the defendant may show that under the specific facts of the actual family relationship, no duty of trust or confidence existed.

Effectively, Rule 10b5–2 "federalizes" the state law of family relationships for purposes of Rule 10b–5. Note also that long-time domestic partners who are unmarried will only be reached under clause 2 above, not the automatic language of clause 3.

4. CULPABILITY

Ernst & Ernst v. Hochfelder

Supreme Court of the United States, 1976.
425 U.S. 185, 96 S.Ct. 1375, 47 L.Ed.2d 668.

■ Mr. Justice Powell delivered the opinion of the Court.

The issue in this case is whether an action for civil damages may lie under § 10(b) of the Securities Exchange Act of 1934 (1934 Act) and Securities and Exchange Commission Rule 10b–5, in the absence of an allegation of intent to deceive, manipulate, or defraud on the part of the defendant.

I

Petitioner, Ernst & Ernst, is an accounting firm. From 1946 through 1967 it was retained by First Securities Company of Chicago (First Securities), a small brokerage firm and member of the Midwest Stock Exchange and of the National Association of Securities Dealers, to perform periodic audits of the firm's books and records. In connection with these audits Ernst & Ernst prepared for filing with the Securities and Exchange Commission (the Commission) the annual reports required of First Securities under § 17(a) of the 1934 Act. It also prepared for First Securities responses to the financial questionnaires of the Midwest Stock Exchange (the Exchange).

Respondents were customers of First Securities who invested in a fraudulent securities scheme perpetrated by Leston B. Nay, president of the firm and owner of 92% of its stock. Nay induced the respondents to invest funds in "escrow" accounts that he represented would yield a high rate of return. Respondents did so from 1942 through 1966, with the majority of the transactions occurring in the 1950's. In fact, there were no escrow accounts as Nay converted respondents' funds to his own use immediately upon receipt. These transactions were not in the customary form of dealings between First Securities and its customers. The respondents drew their personal checks payable to Nay or a designated bank for his account. No such escrow accounts were reflected on the books and records of First Securities, and none was shown on its periodic accounting to respondents in connection with their other investments. Nor were they included in First Securities' filings with the Commission or the Exchange.

This fraud came to light in 1968 when Nay committed suicide, leaving a note that described First Securities as bankrupt and the escrow accounts as "spurious." Respondents subsequently filed this action for damages against Ernst & Ernst in the United States District Court for the Northern District of Illinois under § 10(b) of the 1934 Act. The complaint charged that Nay's escrow scheme violated § 10(b) and Commission Rule 10b–5, and that Ernst &

Ernst had "aided and abetted" Nay's violations by its "failure" to conduct proper audits of First Securities. As revealed through discovery, respondents' cause of action rested on a theory of negligent nonfeasance. The premise was that Ernst & Ernst had failed to utilize "appropriate auditing procedures" in its audits of First Securities, thereby failing to discover internal practices of the firm said to prevent an effective audit. The practice principally relied on was Nay's rule that only he could open mail addressed to him at First Securities or addressed to First Securities to his attention, even if it arrived in his absence. Respondents contended that if Ernst & Ernst had conducted a proper audit, it would have discovered this "mail rule." The existence of the rule then would have been disclosed in reports to the Exchange and to the Commission by Ernst & Ernst as an irregular procedure that prevented an effective audit. This would have led to an investigation of Nay that would have revealed the fraudulent scheme. Respondents specifically disclaimed the existence of fraud or intentional misconduct on the part of Ernst & Ernst.

After extensive discovery the District Court granted Ernst & Ernst's motion for summary judgment and dismissed the action. The court rejected Ernst & Ernst's contention that a cause of action for aiding and abetting a securities fraud could not be maintained under § 10(b) and Rule 10b–5 merely on allegations of negligence. It concluded, however, that there was no genuine issue of material fact with respect to whether Ernst & Ernst had conducted its audits in accordance with generally accepted auditing standards.

The Court of Appeals for the Seventh Circuit reversed and remanded, holding that one who breaches a duty of inquiry and disclosure owed another is liable in damages for aiding and abetting a third party's violation of Rule 10b–5 if the fraud would have been discovered or prevented but for the breach. 503 F.2d 1100 (1974).[7] The court reasoned that Ernst & Ernst had a common-law and statutory duty of inquiry into the adequacy of First Securities' internal control system because it had contracted to audit First Securities and to prepare for filing with the Commission the annual report of its financial condition required under § 17 of the 1934 Act and Rule 17a–5. The Court further reasoned that respondents were beneficiaries of the statutory duty to inquire and the related duty to disclose any material irregularities that were discovered. Id., at 1105–1111. The court concluded that there were genuine

---

7. In support of this holding, the Court of Appeals cited its decision in Hochfelder v. Midwest Stock Exchange, *supra*, where it detailed the elements necessary to establish a claim under Rule 10b–5 based on a defendant's aiding and abetting a securities fraud solely by inaction. * * *. In such a case the plaintiff must show "that the party charged with aiding and abetting had knowledge of or, but for the breach of a duty of inquiry, should have had knowledge of the fraud, and that possessing such knowledge the party failed to act due to an improper motive or breach of a duty of disclosure." * * *. The court explained in the instant case that these "elements constitute a flexible standard of liability which should be amplified according to the peculiarities of each case." 503 F.2d, at 1104. In view of our holding that an intent to deceive, manipulate, or defraud is required for civil liability under § 10(b) and Rule 10b–5, we need not consider whether civil liability for aiding and abetting is appropriate under the section and the rule, nor the elements necessary to establish such a cause of action. See, e.g., Brennan v. Midwestern United Life Ins. Co., 259 F.Supp. 673 (1966), 286 F.Supp. 702 (N.D.Ind.1968), aff'd, 417 F.2d 147 (C.A.7 1969), cert. denied, 397 U.S. 989 (1970) (defendant held liable for giving active and knowing assistance to a third party engaged in violations of the securities laws). See generally Ruder, Multiple Defendants in Securities Law Fraud Cases: Aiding and Abetting, Conspiracy, In Pari Delicto, Indemnification and Contribution, 120 U.Pa.L.Rev. 597, 620–645 (1972).

issues of fact as to whether Ernst & Ernst's failure to discover and comment upon Nay's mail rule constituted a breach of its duties of inquiry and disclosure, id., at 1111, and whether inquiry and disclosure would have led to the discovery or prevention of Nay's fraud. Id., at 1115.

We granted certiorari to resolve the question whether a private cause of action for damages will lie under § 10(b) and Rule 10b–5 in the absence of any allegation of "scienter"—intent to deceive, manipulate, or defraud.[12] 421 U.S. 909 (1975). We conclude that it will not and therefore we reverse.

II

Federal regulation of transactions in securities emerged as part of the aftermath of the market crash in 1929. The Securities Act of 1933 (1933 Act), as amended was designed to provide investors with full disclosure of material information concerning public offerings of securities in commerce, to protect investors against fraud and, through the imposition of specified civil liabilities, to promote ethical standards of honesty and fair dealing. See H.R.Rep. No. 85, 73d Cong., 1st Sess., 1–5 (1933). The 1934 Act was intended principally to protect investors against manipulation of stock prices through regulation of transactions upon securities exchanges and in over-the-counter markets, and to impose regular reporting requirements on companies whose stock is listed on national securities exchanges. See S.Rep. No. 792, 73d Cong., 2d Sess., 1–5 (1934). Although the Acts contain numerous carefully drawn express civil remedies and criminal penalties, Congress recognized that efficient regulation of securities trading could not be accomplished under a rigid statutory program. As part of the 1934 Act Congress created the Commission, which is provided with an arsenal of flexible enforcement powers. See, e.g., 1933 Act §§ 8, 19, 20; 1934 Act §§ 9, 19, 21.

* * *

12. Although the verbal formulations of the standard to be applied have varied, several courts of appeals have held in substance that negligence alone is sufficient for civil liability under § 10(b) and Rule 10b–5. See, e.g., White v. Abrams, 495 F.2d 724, 730 (C.A.9 1974) ("flexible duty" standard); Myzel v. Fields, 386 F.2d 718, 735 (C.A.8 1967), cert. denied 390 U.S. 951 (1968) (negligence sufficient); Kohler v. Kohler Co., 319 F.2d 634 (C.A.7 1963) (knowledge not required). Other courts of appeals have held that some type of scienter—i.e., intent to defraud, reckless disregard for the truth, or knowing use of some practice to defraud—is necessary in such an action. See, e.g., Clegg v. Conk, 507 F.2d 1351, 1361–1362 (C.A.10 1974), cert. denied, 422 U.S. 1007 (1975) (an element of "scienter or conscious fault"); Lanza v. Drexel & Co., 479 F.2d 1277, 1306 (C.A.2 1973) ("willful or reckless disregard" of the truth). But few of the decisions announcing that some form of negligence suffices for civil liability under § 10(b) and Rule 10b–5 actually have involved only negligent conduct. Small-

wood v. Pearl Brewing Co., 489 F.2d 579, 606 (CA5), cert. denied, 419 U.S. 873 (1974); Kohn v. American Metal Climax, Inc., 458 F.2d 255, 286 (C.A.3 1972) (Adams, J., concurring); Bucklo, Scienter and Rule 10b–5, 67 Nw.U.L.Rev. 562, 568–570 (1972).

In this opinion the term "scienter" refers to a mental state embracing intent to deceive, manipulate, or defraud. In certain areas of the law recklessness is considered to be a form of intentional conduct for purposes of imposing liability for some act. We need not address here the question whether, in some circumstances, reckless behavior is sufficient for civil liability under § 10(b) and Rule 10b–5.

Since this case concerns an action for damages we also need not consider the question whether scienter is a necessary element in an action for injunctive relief under § 10(b) and Rule 10b–5. Cf. SEC v. Capital Gains Research Bureau, Inc., 375 U.S. 180 (1963).

Although § 10(b) does not by its terms create an express civil remedy for its violation, and there is no indication that Congress, or the Commission when adopting Rule 10b–5, contemplated such a remedy, the existence of a private cause of action for violations of the statute and the rule is now well established. Blue Chip Stamps v. Manor Drug Stores, 421 U.S. 723, 730 (1975); Affiliated Ute Citizens v. United States, 406 U.S. 128, 150–154 (1972); Superintendent of Insurance v. Bankers Life and Casualty Co., 404 U.S. 6, 13 n. 9 (1971). During the 30–year period since a private cause of action was first implied under § 10(b) and Rule 10b–5, a substantial body of case law and commentary has developed as to its elements. Courts and commentators long have differed with regard to whether scienter is a necessary element of such a cause of action, or whether negligent conduct alone is sufficient. In addressing this question, we turn first to the language of § 10(b), for "[t]he starting point in every case involving construction of a statute is the language itself." *Blue Chip Stamps, supra,* at 756 (Powell, J., concurring); e.g., FTC v. Bunte Brothers, Inc., 312 U.S. 349, 350 (1941).

A

Section 10(b) makes unlawful the use or employment of "any manipulative or deceptive device or contrivance" in contravention of Commission rules. The words "manipulative or deceptive" used in conjunction with "device or contrivance" strongly suggest that § 10(b) was intended to proscribe knowing or intentional misconduct. See SEC v. Texas Gulf Sulphur Co., 401 F.2d 833, 868 (C.A.2 1968) (Friendly, J., concurring), cert. denied sub nom., Kline v. SEC, 394 U.S. 976 (1969); Loss, Summary Remarks, 30 Bus.Lawyer 163, 165 (1975). See also Kohn v. American Metal Climax, Inc., 458 F.2d 255, 280 (C.A.3 1972) (Adams, J., concurring).

In its *amicus curiae* brief, however, the Commission contends that nothing in the language "manipulative or deceptive device or contrivance" limits its operation to knowing or intentional practices. In support of its view, the Commission cites the overall congressional purpose in the 1933 and 1934 Acts to protect investors against false and deceptive practices that might injure them. See Affiliated Ute Citizens v. United States, *supra,* at 151; Superintendent of Insurance v. Bankers Life & Casualty Co., 404 U.S., at 11–12; J.I. Case Co. v. Borak, 377 U.S. 426, 432–433 (1964). See also SEC v. Capital Gains Research Bureau, Inc., 375 U.S. 180, 195 (1963). The Commission then reasons that since the "effect" upon investors of given conduct is the same regardless of whether the conduct is negligent or intentional, Congress must have intended to bar all such practices and not just those done knowingly or intentionally. The logic of this effect-oriented approach would impose liability for wholly faultless conduct where such conduct results in harm to investors, a result the Commission would be unlikely to support. But apart from where its logic might lead, the Commission would add a gloss to the operative language of the statute quite different from its commonly accepted meaning. See, e.g., Addison v. Holly Hill Fruit Products, Inc., 322 U.S. 607, 617–618 (1944). The argument simply ignores the use of the words "manipulative," "device," and "contrivance," terms that make unmistakable a congressional intent to proscribe a type of conduct quite different from negligence. Use of the word "manipulative" is especially significant. It is and was virtually a term of art when used in connection with securities markets. It connotes intentional or willful conduct designed to deceive or defraud investors by controlling or artificially affecting the price of securities.

In addition to relying upon the Commission's argument with respect to the operative language of the statute, respondents contend that since we are dealing with "remedial legislation," Tcherepnin v. Knight, 389 U.S. 332, 336 (1967), it must be construed " 'not technically and restrictively, but flexibly to effectuate its remedial purposes.' " Affiliated Ute Citizens v. United States, *supra*, at 151, quoting SEC v. Capital Gains Research Bureau, *supra*, at 186. They argue that the "remedial purposes" of the Acts demand a construction of § 10(b) that embraces negligence as a standard of liability. But in seeking to accomplish its broad remedial goals, Congress did not adopt uniformly a negligence standard even as to express civil remedies. In some circumstances and with respect to certain classes of defendants, Congress did create express liability predicated upon a failure to exercise reasonable care. E.g., 1933 Act § 11(b)(3)(B) (liability of "experts," such as accountants, for misleading statements in portions of registration statements for which they are responsible). But in other situations good faith is an absolute defense. 1934 Act § 18 (misleading statements in any document filed pursuant to the 1934 Act). And in still other circumstances Congress created express liability regardless of the defendant's fault, 1933 Act § 11(a) (issuer liability for misleading statements in the registration statement).

It is thus evident that Congress fashioned standards of fault in the express civil remedies in the 1933 and 1934 Acts on a particularized basis. Ascertainment of congressional intent with respect to the standard of liability created by a particular section of the Acts must therefore rest primarily on the language of that section. Where, as here, we deal with a judicially implied liability, the statutory language certainly is no less important. In view of the language of § 10(b) which so clearly connotes intentional misconduct, and mindful that the language of a statute controls when sufficiently clear in its context, United States v. Oregon, 366 U.S. 643, 648 (1961); Packard Motor Car Co. v. NLRB, 330 U.S. 485, 492 (1947), further inquiry may be unnecessary. We turn now, nevertheless, to the legislative history of the 1934 Act to ascertain whether there is support for the meaning attributed to § 10(b) by the Commission and respondents.

B

Although the extensive legislative history of the 1934 Act is bereft of any explicit explanation of Congress' intent, we think the relevant portions of that history support our conclusion that § 10(b) was addressed to practices that involve some element of scienter and cannot be read to impose liability for negligent conduct alone.

* * *

Neither the intended scope of § 10(b) nor the reasons for the changes in its operative language are revealed explicitly in the legislative history of the 1934 Act, which deals primarily with other aspects of the legislation. There is no indication, however, that § 10(b) was intended to proscribe conduct not involving scienter. The extensive hearings that preceded passage of the 1934 Act touched only briefly on § 10, and most of the discussion was devoted to the enumerated devices that the Commission is empowered to proscribe under § 10(a). The most relevant exposition of the provision that was to become § 10(b) was by Thomas G. Corcoran, a spokesman for the drafters. Corcoran indicated:

"Subsection (c) [§ 9(c) of H.R. 7852—later § 10(b)] says, 'Thou shalt not devise any other cunning devices.' * * *

"Of course subsection (c) is a catch-all clause to prevent manipulative devices. I do not think there is any objection to that kind of clause. The Commission should have the authority to deal with new manipulative devices."

Hearings on H.R. 7852 and H.R. 8720 before the House Comm. on Interstate and Foreign Commerce, 73d Cong., 2d Sess., 115 (1934). This brief explanation of § 10(b) by a spokesman for its drafters is significant. The section was described rightly as a "catch-all" clause to enable the Commission "to deal with new manipulative [or cunning] devices." It is difficult to believe that any lawyer, legislative draftsman, or legislator would use these words if the intent was to create liability for merely negligent acts or omissions. Neither the legislative history nor the briefs supporting respondents identify any usage or authority for construing "manipulative [or cunning] devices" to include negligence.

* * *

C

The 1933 and 1934 Acts constitute interrelated components of the federal regulatory scheme governing transactions in securities. See *Blue Chip Stamps,* 421 U.S., at 727–730. As the Court indicated in SEC v. National Securities, Inc., 393 U.S. 453 (1969), "the interdependence of the various sections of the securities laws is certainly a relevant factor in any interpretation of the language Congress has chosen. * * * Recognizing this, respondents and the Commission contrast § 10(b) to other sections of the Acts to support their contention that civil liability may be imposed upon proof of negligent conduct. We think they misconceive the significance of the other provisions of the Acts."

The Commission argues that Congress has been explicit in requiring willful conduct when that was the standard of fault intended, citing § 9 of the 1934 Act, which generally proscribes manipulation of securities prices. Sections 9(a)(1) and (a)(2), for example, respectively prohibit manipulation of security prices "[f]or the purpose of creating a false or misleading appearance of actual trading in a security * * * or * * * with respect to the market for any such security," and "for the purpose of inducing the purchase or sale of such security by others." See also § 9(a)(4). Section 9(e) then imposes upon "[a]ny person who willfully participates in any act or transaction in violation of" other provisions of § 9 civil liability to anyone who purchased or sold a security at a price affected by the manipulative activities. From this the Commission concludes that since § 10(b) is not by its terms explicitly restricted to willful, knowing, or purposeful conduct, it should not be construed in all cases to require more than negligent action or inaction as a precondition for civil liability.

The structure of the Acts does not support the Commission's argument. In each instance that Congress created express civil liability in favor of purchasers or sellers of securities it clearly specified whether recovery was to be premised on knowing or intentional conduct, negligence, or entirely innocent mistake. See 1933 Act, §§ 11, 12, 15; 1934 Act §§ 9, 18, 20. For example, § 11 of the 1933 Act unambiguously creates a private action for damages when a registration statement includes untrue statements of material facts or fails to state material facts necessary to make the statements therein not misleading. Within the limits specified by § 11(e), the issuer of the securities is held absolutely liable for any damages resulting from such misstatement or omission. But experts such as accountants who have prepared portions of the registration statement are accorded a "due diligence" defense. In effect, this is a negligence standard. An expert may avoid civil liability with respect to the portions of the registration statement for which he was responsible by showing that "after reasonable investigation" he had "reasonable ground[s] to believe" that the statements for which he was responsible were true and there was no omission of a material fact.[26] § 11(b)(3)(B)(i). See, e.g., Escott v. BarChris Construction Corp., 283 F.Supp. 643, 697–703 (S.D.N.Y.1968). The express recognition of a cause of action premised on negligent behavior in § 11 stands in sharp contrast to the language of § 10(b), and significantly undercuts the Commission's argument.

We also consider it significant that each of the express civil remedies in the 1933 Act allowing recovery for negligent conduct, see §§ 11, 12(2), 15, is subject to significant procedural restrictions not applicable under § 10(b).[28] Section 11(e) of the 1933 Act, for example, authorizes the court to require a plaintiff bringing a suit under § 11, § 12(2), or § 15 thereof to post a bond for costs, including attorneys' fees and in specified circumstances to assess costs at the conclusion of the litigation. Section 13 specifies a statute of limitations of one year from the time the violation was or should have been discovered, in no event to exceed three years from the time of offer or sale, applicable to actions brought under § 11, § 12(2), or § 15. These restrictions, significantly, were imposed by amendments to the 1933 Act adopted as part of the 1934 Act. Prior to amendment § 11(e) contained no provision for payment of costs. The amendments also substantially shortened the statute of limitations provided by § 13. Compare Pub.L. No. 22, *supra*, § 13, 48 Stat. 84, with 15 U.S.C. § 77m. See 1934 Act, § 207, 48 Stat. 908. We think these procedural limitations

---

26. Other individuals who sign the registration statement, directors of the issuer, and the underwriter of the securities similarly are accorded a complete defense against civil liability based on the exercise of reasonable investigation and a reasonable belief that the registration statement was not misleading. §§ 11(b)(3)(A), (C), (D), (C). See, e.g., Feit v. Leasco Data Processing Equipment Corp., 332 F.Supp. 544, 575–583 (E.D.N.Y. 1971) (underwriters, but not officer-directors, established their due diligence defense). See generally R. Jennings & H. Marsh, Securities Regulation 1018–1027 (3d ed. 1972), and sources cited therein; Folk, Civil Liabilities under the Federal Securities Acts: The Bar-Chris Case, 55 Va.L.Rev. 199 (1969).

28. Each of the provisions of the 1934 Act that expressly create civil liability, except those directed to specific classes of individuals such as directors, officers, or 10% beneficial holders of securities, see § 16(b), Foremost–McKesson, Inc. v. Provident Securities Co., *supra*; Kern County Land Co. v. Occidental Petroleum Corp., 411 U.S. 582 (1973), contains a state-of-mind condition requiring something more than negligence. Section 9

creates potential civil liability for any person who "willfully participates" in the manipulation of securities on a national exchange. § 9(e). Section 18 creates potential civil liability for misleading statements filed with the Commission, but provides the defendant with the defense that "he acted in good faith and had no knowledge that such statement was false or misleading." And § 20, which imposes liability upon "controlling persons" for violations of the Act by those they control, exculpates a defendant who "acted in good faith and did not * * * induce the act * * * constituting the violation * * *." Emphasizing the important difference between the operative language and purpose of § 14(a) of the 1934 Act as contrasted with § 10(b), however, some courts have concluded that proof of scienter is unnecessary in an action for damages by the shareholder recipients of a materially misleading proxy statement against the issuer corporation. Gerstle v. Gamble–Skogmo, Inc., 478 F.2d 1281, 1299 (C.A.2 1973). See also Kohn v. American Metal Climax, Inc., *supra*, at 289–290.

indicate that the judicially created private damage remedy under § 10(b)—which has no comparable restrictions—cannot be extended, consistently with the intent of Congress, to actions premised on negligent wrongdoing. Such extension would allow causes of action covered by § 11, § 12(2), and § 15 to be brought instead under § 10(b) and thereby nullify the effectiveness of the carefully drawn procedural restrictions on these express actions. See e.g., Fischman v. Raytheon Manufacturing Co., 188 F.2d 783, 786–787 (C.A.2 1951); SEC v. Texas Gulf Sulphur Co., 401 F.2d at 867–868 (Friendly, J., concurring); Rosenberg v. Globe Aircraft Corp., 80 F.Supp. 123, 124 (E.D.Pa.1948); 3 L. Loss, Securities Regulation 1787–1788 (2d ed. 1961); R. Jennings & H. Marsh, Securities Regulation 1070–1074 (3d ed. 1972). We would be unwilling to bring about this result absent substantial support in the legislative history, and there is none.[31]

D

We have addressed, to this point, primarily the language and history of § 10(b). The Commission contends, however, that subsections (2) and (3) of Rule 10b–5 are cast in language which—if standing alone—could encompass both intentional and negligent behavior. These subsections respectively provide that it is unlawful "[t]o make any untrue statement of a material fact or to omit to state a material fact necessary in order to make the statements made, in light of the circumstances under which they were made, not misleading * * *" and "to engage in any act, practice, or course of business which operates or would operate as a fraud or deceit upon any person. * * *" Viewed in isolation the language of subsection (2), and arguably that of subsection (3), could be read as proscribing, respectively, any type of material misstatement or omission, and any course of conduct, that has the effect of defrauding investors, whether the wrongdoing was intentional or not.

We note first that such a reading cannot be harmonized with the administrative history of the rule, a history making clear that when the Commission adopted the rule it was intended to apply only to activities that involved scienter. More importantly, Rule 10b–5 was adopted pursuant to authority

---

31. Section 18 of the 1934 Act creates a private cause of action against persons, such as accountants, who "make or cause to be made" materially misleading statements in reports or other documents filed with the Commission. We need not consider the question whether a cause of action may be maintained under § 10(b) on the basis of actions that would constitute a violation of § 18. Under § 18 liability extends to persons who, in reliance on such statements, purchased or sold a security whose price was affected by the statements. Liability is limited, however, in the important respect that the defendant is accorded the defense that he acted in "good faith and had no knowledge that such statement was false or misleading." Consistent with this language, the legislative history of the section suggests something more than negligence on the part of the defendant is required for recovery. The original version of § 18(a), § 17(a) of S. 2693, H.R. 7852 and H.R. 7855, see pp. 14–15, *supra*, provided that the defendant would not be liable if "he acted in good faith and in the exercise of reasonable care had no ground to believe that such statement was false or misleading." The accounting profession objected to this provision on the ground that liability would be created for honest errors in judgment. See Senate Hearings on Stock Exchange Practices, *supra*, at 7175–7183; House Hearings on H.R. 7852 and H.R. 8720, *supra*, at 653. In subsequent drafts the current formulation was adopted. It is also significant that actions under § 18 are limited by a relatively short statute of limitations similar to that provided in § 13 of the 1933 Act, § 18(c). Moreover, as under § 11(e) of the 1933 Act the District Court is authorized to require the plaintiff to post a bond for costs, including attorney's fees, and to assess such costs at the conclusion of the litigation. § 18(a).

granted the Commission under § 10(b). The rulemaking power granted to an administrative agency charged with the administration of a federal statute is not the power to make law. Rather, it is " 'the power to adopt regulations to carry into effect the will of Congress as expressed by the statute.' " Dixon v. United States, 381 U.S. 68, 74 (1965), quoting Manhattan General Equipment Co. v. Commissioner, 297 U.S. 129, 134 (1936). Thus, despite the broad view of the Rule advanced by the Commission in this case, its scope cannot exceed the power granted the Commission by Congress under § 10(b). For the reasons stated above, we think the Commission's original interpretation of Rule 10b–5 was compelled by the language and history of § 10(b) and related sections of the Acts. See, e.g., Gerstle v. Gamble–Skogmo, Inc., 478 F.2d 1281, 1299 (C.A.2 1973); Lanza v. Drexel & Co., 479 F.2d 1277, 1304–1305 (C.A.2 1973); SEC v. Texas Gulf Sulphur Co., *supra*, at 868; 3 L. Loss, *supra*, 1766; 6 id., at 3883–3885 (Sup.1969). When a statute speaks so specifically in terms of manipulation and deception, and of implementing devices and contrivances—the commonly understood terminology of intentional wrongdoing—and when its history reflects no more expansive intent, we are quite unwilling to extend the scope of the statute to negligent conduct.

III

Recognizing that § 10(b) and Rule 10b–5 might be held to require proof of more than negligent nonfeasance by Ernst & Ernst as a precondition to the imposition of civil liability, respondents further contend that the case should be remanded for trial under whatever standard is adopted. Throughout the lengthy history of this case respondents have proceeded on a theory of liability premised on negligence, specifically disclaiming that Ernst & Ernst had engaged in fraud or intentional misconduct. In these circumstances, we think it inappropriate to remand the action for further proceedings.

The judgment of the Court of Appeals is Reversed.

■ MR. JUSTICE STEVENS took no part in the consideration or decision of this case.

■ MR. JUSTICE BLACKMUN, with whom MR. JUSTICE BRENNAN joins, dissenting.

Once again—see Blue Chip Stamps v. Manor Drug Stores, 421 U.S. 723, 730 (1975)—the Court interprets § 10(b) of the Securities Exchange Act of 1934 and the Securities and Exchange Commission's Rule 10b–5 restrictively and narrowly and thereby stultifies recovery for the victim. This time the Court does so by confining the statute and the Rule to situations where the defendant has "scienter," that is, the "intent to deceive, manipulate, or defraud." Sheer negligence, the Court says, is not within the reach of the statute and the Rule, and was not contemplated when the great reforms of 1933, 1934, and 1942 were effectuated by Congress and the Commission.

Perhaps the Court is right, but I doubt it. The Government and the Commission doubt it too, as is evidenced by the thrust of the brief filed by the Solicitor General on behalf of the Commission as *amicus curiae*. The Court's opinion, ante, to be sure has a certain technical consistency about it. It seems to me, however, that an investor can be victimized just as much by negligent conduct as by positive deception, and that it is not logical to drive a wedge between the two, saying that Congress clearly intended the one but certainly not the other.

No one questions the fact that the respondents here were the victims of an intentional securities fraud practiced by Leston B. Nay. What is at issue, of course, is the petitioner-accountant firm's involvement and that firm's responsibility under Rule 10b–5. The language of the Rule, making it unlawful for any person "in connection with the purchase or sale of any security"

> "(b) To make any untrue statement of a material fact or to omit to state a material fact necessary in order to make the statements made, in the light of the circumstances under which they were made, not misleading, or

> "(c) To engage in any act, practice, or course of business which operates or would operate as a fraud or deceit upon any person,"

seems to me, clearly and succinctly, to prohibit negligent as well as intentional conduct of the kind proscribed, to extend beyond common law fraud, and to apply to negligent omission and commission. This is consistent with Congress' intent, repeatedly recognized by the Court, that securities legislation enacted for the purpose of avoiding frauds be construed "not technically and restrictively, but flexibly to effectuate its remedial purposes." SEC v. Capital Gains Research Bureau, Inc., 375 U.S. 180, 195 (1963); Superintendent of Insurance v. Bankers Life & Casualty Co., 404 U.S. 6, 12 (1971); Affiliated Ute Citizens v. United States, 406 U.S. 128, 151 (1972).

* * *

THE REQUIRED CULPABILITY OF THE DEFENDANT UNDER RULE 10b–5

In Aaron v. SEC[1] the Supreme Court addressed the questions of whether the *scienter* requirement of the *Hochfelder* case applied in an injunction action by the Commission as well as a private damage action and whether that requirement existed under Section 17(a) of the 1933 Act as well as under Rule 10b–5. The Court held, first, that the same requirements regarding the fault of the defendant must be shown by the Commission in an injunction action as by a private plaintiff in an action for damages or other relief, but that the *scienter* requirement does not exist under two of the three clauses of Section 17(a) although it does under Rule 10b–5 with respect to any action. The Court said:

"In determining whether proof of scienter is a necessary element of a violation of § 17(a), there is less precedential authority in this Court to guide us. But the controlling principles are well settled. Though cognizant that 'Congress intended securities legislation enacted for the purpose of avoiding frauds to be construed "not technically and restrictively, but flexibly to effectuate its remedial purposes,"' "Affiliated Ute Citizens v. United States, 406 U.S. at 151 quoting, SEC v. Capital Gains Research Bureau, 375 U.S. at 195, the Court has also noted that 'generalized references to the "remedial purposes" of the securities laws will not justify reading a provision "more broadly than its language and statutory scheme reasonably permit." Touche Ross & Co. v. Redington, 442 U.S. 560, 578, quoting, SEC v. Sloan, 436 U.S. 103, 116. Thus, if the language of a provision of the securities laws is sufficiently clear in its context and not at odds with the legislative history, it is unnecessary 'to examine the additional considerations of "policy" * * * that may have influenced the lawmakers in their formulation of the statute.' Ernst & Ernst v. Hochfelder, 425 U.S. at 214, n. 33.

---

1.   446 U.S. 680 (1980).

"The language of § 17(a) strongly suggests that Congress contemplated a scienter requirement under § 17(a)(1), but not under § 17(a)(2) or § 17(a)(3). The language of § 17(a)(1) which makes it unlawful 'to employ any device, scheme, or artifice to defraud,' plainly evinces an intent on the part of Congress to proscribe only knowing or intentional misconduct. Even if it be assumed that the term 'defraud' is ambiguous, given its varied meanings at law and in equity, the terms 'device', 'scheme,' and 'artifice' all connote knowing or intentional practices. Indeed, the term 'device,' which also appears in § 10(b), figured prominently in the Court's conclusion in *Hochfelder* that the plain meaning of § 10(b) embraces a scienter requirement. Id., at 199.

"By contrast, the language of § 17(a)(2), which prohibits any person from obtaining money or property 'by means of any untrue statement of a material fact or any omission to state a material fact,' is devoid of any suggestion whatsoever of a scienter requirement. As a well-known commentator has noted, '[there] is nothing on the face of Clause (2) itself which smacks of *scienter* or intent to defraud.' 3 L.Loss, Securities Regulation 1442 (2d ed. 1961). In fact, this Court in *Hochfelder* pointed out that the similar language of Rule 10b–5(b) 'could be read as proscribing * * * any type of material misstatement or omission * * * that has the effect of defrauding investors, whether the wrong-doing was intentional or not.' 425 U.S., at 212.

"Finally, the language of § 17(a)(3), under which it is unlawful for any person 'to engage in any transaction, practice, or course of business which *operates* or *would operate* as a fraud or deceit,' (emphasis added) quite plainly focuses upon the *effect* of particular conduct on members of the investing public, rather than upon the culpability of the person responsible. This reading follows directly from *Capital Gains,* which attributed to a similarly worded provision in § 206(2) of the Investment Advisers Act of 1940 a meaning that does not require a 'showing [of] deliberate dishonesty as a condition precedent to protecting investors.' 375 U.S. at 200.

"It is our view, in sum, that the language of § 17(a) requires scienter under § 17(a)(1), but not under § 17(a)(2) or § 17(a)(3). Although the parties have urged the Court to adopt a uniform culpability requirement for the three subparagraphs of § 17(a), the language of the section is simply not amenable to such an interpretation. This is not the first time that this Court has had occasion to emphasize the distinctions among the three subparagraphs of § 17(a). In United States v. Naftalin, 441 U.S. 768, 774, the Court noted that each subparagraph of § 17(a) 'proscribes a distinct category of misconduct. Each succeeding prohibition is meant to cover additional kinds of illegalities—not to narrow the reach of the prior sections.' (Footnote omitted.) Indeed, since Congress drafted § 17(a) in such a manner as to compel the conclusion that scienter is required under one subparagraph but not under the other two, it would take a very clear expression in the legislative history of congressional intent to the contrary to justify the conclusion that the statute does not mean what it so plainly seems to say.

"We find no such expression of congressional intent in the legislative history."[2]

The Court did not clearly confront the question of how the identical language in Section 17(a) and in Rule 10b–5 (which was copied from Section 17(a)) could mean two different things. The Court's emphasis upon the lan-

---

2. 446 U.S. at 695–697.

guage of Section 10(b) rather than that of Rule 10b–5 suggests, however, that the Court may have been holding that the Commission exceeded its authority in adopting Rule 10b–5 to the extent that it purports to prohibit conduct which is merely negligent or entirely without fault on the part of the defendant. The Court said:

"The conclusion in *Hochfelder* that allegations of simple negligence could not sustain a private cause of action for damages under § 10(b) and Rule 10b–5 rested on several grounds. It was the view of the Court that the terms 'manipulative,' 'device,' and 'contrivance'—whether given their commonly accepted meaning or read as terms of art—quite clearly evinced a congressional intent to proscribe only 'knowing or intentional misconduct.' Id., at 197–199. This meaning, in fact, was thought to be so unambiguous as to suggest that 'further inquiry may be unnecessary.' Id., at 201.

* * *

"In our view the rationale of *Hochfelder* ineluctably leads to the conclusion that scienter is an element of a violation of § 10(b) and Rule 10b–5, regardless of the identity of the plaintiff or the nature of the relief sought. Two of the three factors relied upon in *Hochfelder*—the language of § 10(b) and its legislative history—are applicable whenever a violation of § 10(b) or Rule 10b–5 is alleged, whether in a private cause of action for damages or in a Commission injunctive action under § 21(d). In fact, since *Hochfelder* involved an implied cause of action that was not within the contemplation of the Congress that enacted § 10(b), id., at 196, it would be quite anomalous in a case like the present one, involving as it does the express remedy Congress created for § 10(b) violations, not to attach at least as much significance to the fact that the statutory language and its legislative history support a scienter requirement."[3]

Sections 11 and 12(a)(2) of the Securities Act of 1933 proscribe, in connection with the transactions covered by those sections, untrue statements of material facts and omissions of material facts necessary to make the statements made not misleading, as we have seen in Chapter 13. Rule 10b–5, like Section 17(a) of the Securities Act of 1933 from which it was copied, uses identical language in clause (2). However, Sections 11 and 12(a)(2) provide a defense if the defendant (other than the issuer under Section 11) establishes lack of knowledge of the untruth or omission and the use of due care. No such defense is expressly recognized in Section 17(a) and Rule 10b–5. This raises the question whether the latter provisions are intended to establish absolute liability for a misstatement or omission regardless of due care or the lack thereof.

This question was resolved by the Supreme Court with respect to Rule 10b–5 in the *Ernst & Ernst* case. The Supreme Court even reserved the question as to whether "reckless" behavior might be a sufficient basis of culpability to found an action under Rule 10b–5, being willing to concede in that case only that a conscious "intent to deceive, manipulate, or defraud" was sufficient.

At least 11 of the 12 circuits in the period after *Ernst & Ernst* adopted the view that "recklessness" is a sufficient basis for liability, answering the

---

3.   446 U.S. at 690–691. See also SEC v. Dain Rauscher, Inc., 254 F.3d 852, 856 (9th Cir.2001) (Section 17(a)(1), like Rule 10b–5, requires scienter; §§ 17(a)(2)–(3) only require negligence).

question left open by the Supreme Court in *Ernst & Ernst's* soon famous Footnote 12.[4] These circuits generally followed the definition of "recklessness" which was first set out by the Seventh Circuit in Sundstrand Corp. v. Sun Chemical Corp.,[5] as follows: "Reckless conduct may be defined as * * * a highly unreasonable [conduct], involving not merely simple, or even inexcusable negligence, but an extreme departure from the standards of ordinary care, and which presents a danger of misleading buyers or sellers that is either known to the defendant or is so obvious that the actor must have been aware of it."[6] Whether phrased as "a lesser form of intent," "an extreme departure from the standards of ordinary care," or "severe recklessness," the Seventh Circuit

4. *1st Circuit*: Cook v. Avien, Inc., 573 F.2d 685, 692 (1st Cir.1978); Hoffman v. Estabrook & Co., Inc., 587 F.2d 509, 516 (1st Cir.1978) (approving district court instruction defining recklessness as "carelessness approaching indifference"); Cleary v. Perfectune, Inc., 700 F.2d 774, 777 (1st Cir.1983); SEC v. Lehman Bros., 157 F.3d 2, 7 (1st Cir.1998) (scienter could be established when someone "deliberately averted his eyes from evident misconduct").

2nd Circuit: Rolf v. Blyth, Eastman Dillon & Co., Inc., 570 F.2d 38, 45–46 (2d Cir. 1978), *cert. denied*, 439 U.S. 1039 (1978) (at least when defendant owed a fiduciary duty); Reiss v. Pan Am. World Airways, Inc., 711 F.2d 11, 14 (2d Cir.1983); SEC v. U.S. Envt'l, Inc., 155 F.3d 107, 111 (2d Cir.1998), *cert. denied sub nom.* Romano v. SEC, 526 U.S. 1111 (1999).

3d Circuit: Coleco Indus., Inc. v. Berman, 567 F.2d 569, 574 (3d Cir.1977), *cert. denied*, 439 U.S. 830 (1978); McLean v. Alexander, 599 F.2d 1190, 1198 (3d Cir.1979) ("with reckless disregard for its truth or falsity" or without a "genuine belief" in the truth of information disclosed); Eisenberg v. Gagnon, 766 F.2d 770, 776 (3d Cir.1985), *cert. denied sub nom.* Wasserstrom v. Eisenberg, 474 U.S. 946 (1985); Phillips Petroleum Sec. Litig., 881 F.2d 1236, 1244 (3d Cir.1989) ("an extreme departure from the standards of ordinary care").

5th Circuit: G.A. Thompson & Co., Inc. v. Partridge, 636 F.2d 945, 961 (5th Cir.1981); Warren v. Reserve Fund, Inc., 728 F.2d 741, 745 (5th Cir.1984); Shivangi v. Dean Witter Reynolds, Inc., 825 F.2d 885, 889 (5th Cir. 1987).

6th Circuit: Mansbach v. Prescott, Ball & Turben, 598 F.2d 1017, 1023–1025 (6th Cir. 1979) (recklessness is "highly unreasonable conduct which is an extreme departure from the standards of ordinary care"); Ohio Drill & Tool Co. v. Johnson, 625 F.2d 738, 741 (6th Cir.1980).

7th Circuit: Sundstrand Corp. v. Sun Chem. Corp., 553 F.2d 1033, 1044–1045 (7th Cir.1977), *cert. denied*, 434 U.S. 875 (1977); Sanders v. John Nuveen & Co., Inc., 554 F.2d 790, 792–793 (7th Cir.1977); Rankow v. First Chicago Corp., 870 F.2d 356, 366–367 (7th Cir.1989); Goldberg v. Household Bank, F.S.B., 890 F.2d 965, 967 (7th Cir.1989).

8th Circuit: Van Dyke v. Coburn Enter., Inc., 873 F.2d 1094, 1100 (8th Cir.1989).

9th Circuit: Hollinger v. Titan Capital Corp., 914 F.2d 1564, 1569–1570 (9th Cir. 1990), *cert. denied*, 499 U.S. 976 (1991).

10th Circuit: Hackbart v. Holmes, 675 F.2d 1114, 1117–1118 (10th Cir.1982) (quoting standard in Sunstrand Corp. v. Sun Chem. Corp., 553 F.2d at 1045); Zobrist v.Coal–X, Inc., 708 F.2d 1511, 1516 (10th Cir.1983); C.E. Carlson, Inc. v. SEC, 859 F.2d 1429, 1435 (10th Cir.1988); Board of County Comm'r of San Juan County v. Liberty Group, 965 F.2d 879, 884 (10th Cir.1992), *cert. denied*, 506 U.S. 918 (1992).

11th Circuit: SEC v. Carriba Air, Inc., 681 F.2d 1318, 1324 (11th Cir.1982) (knowing misconduct or severe recklessness); Kennedy v. Tallant, 710 F.2d 711, 720 (11th Cir.1983); McDonald v. Alan Bush Brokerage Co., 863 F.2d 809, 814 (11th Cir.1989); Ross v. Bank South, N.A., 885 F.2d 723, 730 n. 10 (11th Cir.1989), *cert. denied*, 495 U.S. 905 (1990).

D.C. Circuit: Dirks v. SEC, 681 F.2d 824, 844 (D.C.Cir.1982), *rev'd on other grounds*, 463 U.S. 646 (1983) ("the overwhelming rule in the Courts of Appeals"); SEC v. Steadman, 967 F.2d 636, 641–642 (D.C.Cir.1992) (applying "extreme departure from the standards of ordinary care" test).

5. 553 F.2d 1033 (7th Cir.1977), *cert. denied*, 434 U.S. 875 (1977).

6. Id. at 1045.

standard has been followed by panels in a majority of the other circuits.[7] Compare Board of County Comm'r of San Juan County v. Liberty Group:[8] "[T]he line between gross negligence and recklessness is a fine one at best."

Then in 1994 the Supreme Court again granted *certiorari* in the *Central Bank* case[9] to address whether recklessness would suffice against a defendant who aided and abetted a Rule 10b–5 claim. Instead, the Court concluded that there was no implied private claim for aiding and abetting under § 10(b). The Court did not reach the culpability question.

In 1995 Congress did. As part of the Private Securities Litigation Reform Act of 1995, § 17A of the Securities Act and § 21E of the Securities Exchange Act were amended to create a safe harbor when a plaintiff alleged a fraudulent forward looking statement unless the statement was made with "actual knowledge." This means that plaintiffs now can only rely on a defendants' recklessness in alleging claims concerning historical facts. After the 1995 Act, several courts, however, have affirmed that the Act did not alter the prevailing recklessness standard for historical facts.[10]

PROBLEM 14–7

(1) Rexford is the Chief Executive Officer of Hughes Gyros Inc. Bachman is the Chief Financial Officer. Early in 2002 Rexford was criminally convicted for a scheme in which he secretly sold gyroscope parts from Hughes inventory. The SEC has now commenced a civil action under Rule 10b–5 against Bachman.

Bachman argues that he did not act with the required culpability when he assisted Rexford and the others to purchase and resell inventory. He obtained cashier's checks with which to purchase the inventory but directed that his name not appear on these checks. The cashier's checks bore the names of a nominee account holder. Bachman transferred the proceeds of the sale among various noncorporate accounts held by Rexford, even though he concedes that these transactions had no apparent business purpose. Bachman has employed a Nuremberg defense by arguing that he simply did what he was told and was not in a position to question the orders given to him by his employer. What result?

(2) Hughes Gyros also published an earnings forecast in its latest Form 10–K annual report based on a linear extrapolation of prior year earnings, including those artificially inflated as a result of the secret inventory sales. What result if Bachman is sued and asserts § 21E of the Securities Exchange Act in defense?

---

7. Cook v. Avien, Inc., 573 F.2d 685, 692 (1st Cir.1978); Phillips Petroleum Sec. Litig., 881 F.2d 1236, 1244 (3d Cir.1989); Broad v. Rockwell Int'l Corp., 642 F.2d 929, 961–962 (5th Cir.*en banc* 1981), *cert. denied*, 454 U.S. 965 (1981); Mansbach v. Prescott, Ball & Turben, 598 F.2d 1017, 1023–1025 (6th Cir.1979); Hollinger v. Titan Capital Corp., 914 F.2d 1564, 1569–1570 (9th Cir. 1990), *cert. denied*, 499 U.S. 976 (1991); Hackbart v. Holmes, 675 F.2d 1114, 1117–1118 (10th Cir.1982); McDonald v. Alan Bush Brokerage Co., 863 F.2d 809, 814 (11th Cir. 1989).

8. 965 F.2d 879, 884 (10th Cir.1992), *cert. denied*, 506 U.S. 918 (1992).

9. 511 U.S. 164 (1994). *See generally* 8 Louis Loss & Joel Seligman 3653–3677 (3d ed. 1991).

10. See, e.g., Nathenson v. Zonagen Inc., 267 F.3d 400 (5th Cir.2001) ("It seems clear to us that the PSLRA has not generally altered the substantial scienter requirement for claims brought under section 10(b) and Rule 10b–5 ..."), citing Greebel v. FTP Software, Inc., 194 F.3d 185, 198–201 (1st Cir. 1999); Advanta Corp. Sec. Litig., 180 F.3d 525, 534 (3d Cir.1999); Comshare, Inc. Sec. Litig., 183 F.3d 542, 548–49 (6th Cir.1999); Bryant v. Avado Brands, Inc., 187 F.3d 1271, 1283–1284 (11th Cir.1999); Novak v. Kasaks, 216 F.3d 300, 306 (2d Cir.2000).

5. RELIANCE AND CAUSATION

Basic Incorporated v. Levinson

Supreme Court of the United States, 1988.
485 U.S. 224, 108 S.Ct. 978, 99 L.Ed.2d 194.

■ BLACKMUN, J., delivered the opinion of the Court, in which BRENNAN,

MARSHALL, and STEVENS, JJ., joined, and in Parts I, II, and III of which WHITE and O'CONNOR, JJ., joined. WHITE, J., filed an opinion concurring in part and dissenting in part, in which O'CONNOR, J., joined. REHNQUIST, C.J. and SCALIA and KENNEDY, JJ., took no part in the consideration or decision of the case.

■ JUSTICE BLACKMUN:

* * *

IV

A

We turn to the question of reliance and the fraud-on-the-market theory. Succinctly put:

> "The fraud on the market theory is based on the hypothesis that, in an open and developed securities market, the price of a company's stock is determined by the available material information regarding the company and its business. * * * Misleading statements will therefore defraud purchasers of stock even if the purchasers do not directly rely on the misstatements. * * * The causal connection between the defendants' fraud and the plaintiffs' purchase of stock in such a case is no less significant than in a case of direct reliance on misrepresentations." Peil v. Speiser, 806 F.2d 1154, 1160–1161 (C.A.3 1986).

Our task, of course, is not to assess the general validity of the theory, but to consider whether it was proper for the courts below to apply a rebuttable presumption of reliance, supported in part by the fraud-on-the-market theory. Cf. the comments of the dissent, post, at 3–5.

This case required resolution of several common questions of law and fact concerning the falsity or misleading nature of the three public statements made by Basic, the presence or absence of scienter, and the materiality of the misrepresentations, if any. In their amended complaint, the named plaintiffs alleged that in reliance on Basic's statements they sold their shares of Basic stock in the depressed market created by petitioners. See Amended Complaint in No. C79–1220 (ND Ohio) ¶¶ 27, 29, 35, 40; see also id., at ¶ 33 (alleging effect on market price of Basic's statements). Requiring proof of individualized reliance from each member of the proposed plaintiff class effectively would have prevented respondents from proceeding with a class action, since individual issues then would have overwhelmed the common ones. The District Court found that the presumption of reliance created by the fraud-on-the-market theory provided "a practical resolution to the problem of balancing the substantive requirement of proof of reliance in securities cases against the procedural requisites of [Fed. Rule Civ.Proc.] 23." The District Court thus concluded that with reference to each public statement and its impact upon the open market for Basic shares, common questions predominated over individual questions, as required by Fed. Rule Civ.Proc. 23(a)(2) and (b)(3).

Petitioners and their *amici* complain that the fraud-on-the-market theory effectively eliminates the requirement that a plaintiff asserting a claim under Rule 10b–5 prove reliance. They note that reliance is and long has been an element of common-law fraud, see e.g., Restatement (Second) of Torts § 525 (1977); Prosser and Keeton on The Law of Torts § 108 (5th ed.1984), and argue that because the analogous express right of action includes a reliance requirement, see, e.g., § 18(a) of the 1934 Act, as amended, 15 U.S.C. § 78r(a), so too must an action implied under § 10(b).

We agree that reliance is an element of a Rule 10b–5 cause of action. See Ernst & Ernst v. Hochfelder, 425 U.S., at 206 (quoting Senate Report). Reliance provides the requisite causal connection between a defendant's misrepresentation and a plaintiff's injury. * * * There is, however, more than one way to demonstrate the causal connection. Indeed, we previously have dispensed with a requirement of positive proof of reliance, where a duty to disclose material information had been breached, concluding that the necessary nexus between the plaintiffs' injury and the defendant's wrongful conduct had been established. See Affiliated Ute Citizens v. United States, 406 U.S., at 153—154. Similarly, we did not require proof that material omissions or misstatements in a proxy statement decisively affected voting, because the proxy solicitation itself, rather than the defect in the solicitation materials, served as an essential link in the transaction. See Mills v. Electric Auto—Lite Co., 396 U.S. 375, 384—385 (1970).

The modern securities markets, literally involving millions of shares changing hands daily, differ from the face-to-face transactions contemplated by early fraud cases, and our understanding of Rule 10b—5's reliance requirement must encompass these differences.

> "In face-to-face transactions, the inquiry into an investor's reliance upon information is into the subjective pricing of that information by that investor. With the presence of a market, the market is interposed between seller and buyer and, ideally, transmits information to the investor in the processed form of a market price. Thus the market is performing a substantial part of the valuation process performed by the investor in a face-to-face transaction. The market is acting as the unpaid agent of the investor, informing him that given all the information available to it, the value of the stock is worth the market price." In re LTV Securities Litigation, 88 F.R.D. 134, 143 (N.D.Tex.1980).

Accord, e.g., Peil v. Speiser, 806 F.2d, at 1161 ("In an open and developed market, the dissemination of material misrepresentations or withholding of material information typically affects the price of the stock, and purchasers generally rely on the price of the stock as a reflection of its value"); Blackie v. Barrack, 524 F.2d 891, 908 (C.A.9 1975) ("the same causal nexus can be adequately established indirectly, by proof of materiality coupled with the common sense that a stock purchaser does not ordinarily seek to purchase a loss in the form of artificially inflated stock"), cert. denied, 429 U.S. 816 (1976).

B

Presumptions typically serve to assist courts in managing circumstances in which direct proof, for one reason or another, is rendered difficult. See, e.g., D. Louisell & C. Mueller, Federal Evidence 541—542 (1977). The courts below accepted a presumption, created by the fraud-on-the-market theory and subject to rebuttal by petitioners, that persons who had traded Basic shares had done so in reliance on the integrity of the price set by the market, but because of petitioners' material misrepresentations that price had been fraudulently depressed. Requiring a plaintiff to show a speculative state of facts, i.e., how he would have acted if omitted material information had been disclosed, see Affiliated Ute Citizens v. United States, 406 U.S., at 153—154, or if the misrepresentation had not been made, see Sharp v. Coopers & Lybrand, 649 F.2d 175, 188 (C.A.3 1981), cert. denied, 455 U.S. 938 (1982), would place an unnecessarily unrealistic evidentiary burden on the Rule 10b—5 plaintiff who has traded on an impersonal market. Cf. Mills v. Electric Auto—Lite Co., 396 U.S., at 385.

Arising out of considerations of fairness, public policy, and probability, as well as judicial economy, presumptions are also useful devices for allocating the burdens of proof between parties. See E. Cleary, McCormick on Evidence 968—969 (3rd ed.1984); see also Fed.Rule Evid. 301 and notes. The presumption of reliance employed in this case is consistent with, and, by facilitating Rule 10b—5 litigation, supports, the congressional policy embodied in the 1934 Act. In drafting that Act, Congress expressly relied on the premise that securities markets are affected by information, and enacted legislation to facilitate an investor's reliance on the integrity of those markets:

> "No investor, no speculator, can safely buy and sell securities upon the exchanges without having an intelligent basis for forming his judgment as to the value of the securities he buys or sells. The idea of a free and open public market is built upon the theory that competing judgments of buyers and sellers as to the fair price of a security brings [*sic*] about a situation where the market price reflects as nearly as possible a just price. Just as artificial manipulation tends to upset the true function of an open market, so the hiding and secreting of important information obstructs the operation of the markets as indices of real value." H.R.Rep.No. 1383, *supra*, at 11.

See Lipton v. Decimation, Inc., 734 F.2d 740, 748 (C.A.11 1984), cert. denied, 469 U.S. 1132 (1985).

The presumption is also supported by common sense and probability. Recent empirical studies have tended to confirm Congress' premise that the market price of shares traded on well-developed markets reflects all publicly available information, and, hence, any material misrepresentations.[11] It has been noted that "it is hard to imagine that there ever is a buyer or seller who does not rely on market integrity. Who would knowingly roll the dice in a crooked crap game?" Schlanger v. Four—Phase Systems Inc., 555 F.Supp. 535, 538 (S.D.N.Y.1982). Indeed, nearly every court that has considered the proposition has concluded that where materially misleading statements have been disseminated into an impersonal, well-developed market for securities, the

---

11. See In re LTV Securities Litigation, 88 F.R.D. 134, 144 (N.D.Tex.1980) (citing studies); Fischel, Use of Modern Finance Theory in Securities Fraud Cases Involving Actively Traded Securities, 38 Bus.Law. 1, 4, n.9 (1982) (citing literature on efficient-capital-market theory); Dennis, Materiality and the Efficient Capital Market Model: A Recipe for the Total Mix, 25 Wm. & Mary L.Rev. 373, 374–381, and n.1 (1984). We need not determine by adjudication what economists and social scientists have debated through the use of sophisticated statistical analysis and the application of economic theory. For purposes of accepting the presumption of reliance in this case, we need only believe that market professionals generally consider most publicly announced material statements about companies, thereby affecting stock market prices.

reliance of individual plaintiffs on the integrity of the market price may be presumed. Commentators generally have applauded the adoption of one variation or another of the fraud-on-the-market theory. An investor who buys or sells stock at the price set by the market does so in reliance on the integrity of that price. Because most publicly available information is reflected in market price, an investor's reliance on any public material misrepresentations, therefore, may be presumed for purposes of a Rule 10b–5 action.

C

The Court of Appeals found that petitioners "made public, material misrepresentations and [respondents] sold Basic stock in an impersonal, efficient market. Thus the class, as defined by the district court, has established the threshold facts for proving their loss." 786 F.2d, at 751.[27] The court acknowledged that petitioners may rebut proof of the elements giving rise to the presumption, or show that the misrepresentation in fact did not lead to a distortion of price or that an individual plaintiff traded or would have traded despite his knowing the statement was false. Id., at 750, n.6.

Any showing that severs the link between the alleged misrepresentation and either the price received (or paid) by the plaintiff, or his decision to trade at a fair market price, will be sufficient to rebut the presumption of reliance. For example, if petitioners could show that the "market makers" were privy to the truth about the merger discussions here with Combustion, and thus that the market price would not have been affected by their misrepresentations, the causal connection could be broken: the basis for finding that the fraud had been transmitted through market price would be gone.[28] Similarly, if, despite petitioners' allegedly fraudulent attempt to manipulate market price, news of the merger discussions credibly entered the market and dissipated the effects of the misstatements, those who traded Basic shares after the corrective statements would have no direct or indirect connection with the fraud.[29] Petitioners also could rebut the presumption of reliance as to plaintiffs who would have divested themselves of their Basic shares without relying on the integrity of the

---

27. The Court of Appeals held that in order to invoke the presumption, a plaintiff must allege and prove: (1) that the defendant made public misrepresentations; (2) that the misrepresentations were material; (3) that the shares were traded on an efficient market; (4) that the misrepresentations would induce a reasonable, relying investor to misjudge the value of the shares; and (5) that the plaintiff traded the shares between the time the misrepresentations were made and the time the truth was revealed. See 786 F.2d, at 750.

Given today's decision regarding the definition of materiality as to preliminary merger discussions, elements (2) and (4) may collapse into one.

28. By accepting this rebuttable presumption, we do not intend conclusively to adopt any particular theory of how quickly and completely publicly available information is reflected in market price. Furthermore, our decision today is not to be interpreted as

addressing the proper measure of damages in litigation of this kind.

29. We note there may be a certain incongruity between the assumption that Basic shares are traded on a well-developed, efficient, and information-hungry market, and the allegation that such a market could remain misinformed, and its valuation of Basic shares depressed, for 14 months, on the basis of the three public statements. Proof of that sort is a matter for trial, throughout which the District Court retains the authority to amend the certification order as may be appropriate. See Fed.Rule Civ.Proc. 23(c)(1) and (c)(4). See 7B C. Wright, A. Miller & M. Kane, Federal Practice and Procedure 128–132 (1966). Thus, we see no need to engage in the kind of factual analysis the dissent suggests that manifests the "oddities" of applying a rebuttable presumption of reliance in this case. See post, at 10–13.

market. For example, a plaintiff who believed that Basic's statements were false and that Basic was indeed engaged in merger discussions, and who consequently believed that Basic stock was artificially underpriced, but sold his shares nevertheless because of other unrelated concerns, e.g., potential antitrust problems, or political pressures to divest from shares of certain businesses, could not be said to have relied on the integrity of a price he knew had been manipulated.

V

In summary:

* * *

5. It is not inappropriate to apply a presumption of reliance supported by the fraud-on-the-market theory.

6. That presumption, however, is rebuttable.

7. The District Court's certification of the class here was appropriate when made but is subject on remand to such adjustment, if any, as developing circumstances demand.

The judgment of the Court of Appeals is vacated and the case is remanded to that court for further proceedings consistent with this opinion.

It is so ordered.

■ THE CHIEF JUSTICE, JUSTICE SCALIA, and JUSTICE KENNEDY took no part in the consideration or decision of this case.

■ JUSTICE WHITE, with whom JUSTICE O'CONNOR joins, concurring in part and dissenting in part.

I join Parts I–III of the Court's opinion, as I agree that the standard of materiality we set forth in TSC Industries, Inc. v. Northway, Inc., 426 U.S. 438, 449 (1976), should be applied to actions under § 10(b) and Rule 10b–5. But I dissent from the remainder of the Court's holding because I do not agree that the "fraud-on-the-market" theory should be applied in this case.

I

Even when compared to the relatively youthful private cause-of-action under § 10(b), see Kardon v. National Gypsum Co., 69 F.Supp. 512 (E.D.Pa. 1946), the fraud-on-the-market theory is a mere babe. Yet today, the Court embraces this theory with the sweeping confidence usually reserved for more mature legal doctrines. In so doing, I fear that the Court's decision may have many adverse, unintended effects as it is applied and interpreted in the years to come.

A

At the outset, I note that there are portions of the Court's fraud-on-the-market holding with which I am in agreement. Most importantly, the Court rejects the version of that theory, heretofore adopted by some courts,[2] which equates "causation" with "reliance," and permits recovery by a plaintiff who claims merely to have been *harmed* by a material misrepresentation which

---

2. See, e.g., Zweig v. Hearst Corp., 594 F.2d 1261, 1268–1271 (C.A.9 1979); Arthur Young & Co. v. United States District Court, 549 F.2d 686, 694–695 (CA9), cert. denied, 434 U.S. 829 (1977); Pellman v. Cinerama, Inc., 89 F.R.D. 386, 388 (S.D.N.Y.1981).

altered a market price, notwithstanding proof that the plaintiff did not in any way *rely* on that price. Ante, at 23. I agree with the Court that if Rule 10b–5's reliance requirement is to be left with any content at all, the fraud-on-the-market presumption must be capable of being rebutted by a showing that a plaintiff did not "rely" on the market price. For example, a plaintiff who decides, months in advance of an alleged misrepresentation, to purchase a stock; one who buys or sells a stock for reasons unrelated to its price; one who actually sells a stock "short" days before the misrepresentation is made— surely none of these people can state a valid claim under Rule 10b–5. Yet, some federal courts have allowed such claims to stand under one variety or another of the fraud-on-the-market theory.

Happily, the majority puts to rest the prospect of recovery under such circumstances. A nonrebuttable presumption of reliance—or even worse, allowing recovery in the face of "affirmative evidence of nonreliance," Zweig v. Hearst Corp., 594 F.2d 1261, 1272 (C.A.9 1979) (Ely, J., dissenting)—would effectively convert Rule 10b–5 into "a scheme of investor's insurance." Shores v. Sklar, 647 F.2d 462, 469, n. 5 (C.A.5 1981) (en banc), cert. denied, 459 U.S. 1102 (1983). There is no support in the Securities Act, the Rule, or our cases for such a result.

B

But even as the Court attempts to limit the fraud-on-the-market theory it endorses today, the pitfalls in its approach are revealed by previous uses by the lower courts of the broader versions of the theory. Confusion and contradiction in court rulings are inevitable when traditional legal analysis is replaced with economic theorization by the federal courts.

In general, the case law developed in this Court with respect to § 10(b) and Rule 10b–5 has been based on doctrines with which we, as judges, are familiar: common-law doctrines of fraud and deceit. See, e.g., Santa Fe Industries, Inc. v. Green, 430 U.S. 462, 471–477 (1977). Even when we have extended civil liability under Rule 10b–5 to a broader reach than the common law had previously permitted, see ante, at 19, n. 22, we have retained familiar legal principles as our guideposts. See, e.g. Herman & MacLean v. Huddleston, 459 U.S. 375, 389–390 (1983). The federal courts have proved adept at developing an evolving jurisprudence of Rule 10b–5 in such a manner. But with no staff economists, no experts schooled in the "efficient-capital-market hypothesis," no ability to test the validity of empirical market studies, we are not well equipped to embrace novel constructions of a statute based on contemporary microeconomic theory.[4]

The "wrong turns" in those Court of Appeals and district court fraud-on-the-market decisions which the Court implicitly rejects as going too far should

---

4. This view was put well by two commentators who wrote a few years ago:

"Of all recent developments in financial economics, the efficient capital market hypothesis ('ECMH') has achieved the widest acceptance by the legal culture. * * *

"Yet the legal culture's remarkably rapid and broad acceptance of an economic concept that did not exist twenty years ago is not matched by an equivalent degree of *understanding*." Gilson & Kraakman, The Mechanisms of Market Efficiency, 70 Va.L.Rev. 549, 549–550 (1984) (footnotes omitted; emphasis added).

While the fraud-on-the-market theory has gained even broader acceptance since 1984, I doubt that it has achieved any greater understanding.

be ample illustration of the dangers when economic theories replace legal rules as the basis for recovery. Yet the Court today ventures into this area beyond its expertise, beyond—by its own admission—the confines of our previous fraud cases. See ante, at 18–19. Even if I agreed with the Court that "modern securities markets * * * involving millions of shares changing hands daily" require that the "understanding of Rule 10b–5's reliance requirement" be changed, ibid., I prefer that such changes come from Congress in amending § 10(b). The Congress, with its superior resources and expertise, is far better equipped than the federal courts for the task of determining how modern economic theory and global financial markets require that established legal notions of fraud be modified. In choosing to make these decisions itself, the Court, I fear, embarks on a course that it does not genuinely understand, giving rise to consequences it cannot foresee.

For while the economists' theories which underpin the fraud-on-the-market presumption may have the appeal of mathematical exactitude and scientific certainty, they are—in the end—nothing more than theories which may or may not prove accurate upon further consideration. Even the most earnest advocates of economic analysis of the law recognize this. See, e.g., Easterbrook, Afterword: Knowledge and Answers, 85 Colum. L. Rev. 1117, 1118 (1985). Thus, while the majority states that, for purposes of reaching its result it need only make modest assumptions about the way in which "market professionals generally" do their jobs, and how the conduct of market professionals affects stock prices, ante, at 21, n. 23, I doubt that we are in much of a position to assess which theories aptly describe the functioning of the securities industry.

Consequently, I cannot join the Court in its effort to reconfigure the securities laws, based on recent economic theories, to better fit what it perceives to be the new realities of financial markets. I would leave this task to others more equipped for the job than we.

C

At the bottom of the Court's conclusion that the fraud-on-the-market theory sustains a presumption of reliance is the assumption that individuals rely "on the integrity of the market price" when buying or selling stock in "impersonal, well-developed market[s] for securities." Ante, at 21–22. Even if I was prepared to accept (as a matter of common sense or general understanding) the assumption that most persons buying or selling stock do so in response to the market price, the fraud-on-the-market theory goes further. For in adopting a "presumption of reliance," the Court *also* assumes that buyers and sellers rely—not just on the market price—but on the *"integrity"* of that price. It is this aspect of the fraud-on-the-market hypothesis which most mystifies me.

To define the term "integrity of the market price," the majority quotes approvingly from cases which suggest that investors are entitled to " 'rely on the price of a stock as a reflection of its value.' " Ante, at 19 (quoting Peil v. Speiser, 806 F.2d 1154, 1161 (C.A.3 1986)). But the meaning of this phrase eludes me, for it implicitly suggests that stocks have some "true value" that is measurable by a standard other than their market price. While the Scholastics of Medieval times professed a means to make such a valuation of a commodity's "worth," I doubt that the federal courts of our day are similarly equipped.

Even if securities had some "value"—knowable and distinct from the market price of a stock—investors do not always share the Court's presumption that a stock's price is a "reflection of [this] value." Indeed, "many investors purchase or sell stock because they believe the price *inaccurately* reflects the corporation's worth." See Black, Fraud on the Market: A Criticism of Dispensing with Reliance Requirements in Certain Open Market Transactions, 62 N.C. L.Rev. 435, 455 (1984) (emphasis added). If investors really believed that stock prices reflected a stock's "value," many sellers would never sell, and many buyers never buy (given the time and cost associated with executing a stock transaction). As we recognized just a few years ago: "[I]nvestors act on inevitably incomplete or inaccurate information, [consequently] there are always winners and losers; but those who have 'lost' have not necessarily been defrauded." Dirks v. SEC, 463 U.S. 646, 667, n. 27 (1983). Yet today, the Court allows investors to recover who can show little more than that they sold stock at a lower price than what might have been.[7]

I do not propose that the law retreat from the many protections that § 10(b) and Rule 10b–5, as interpreted in our prior cases, provide to investors. But any extension of these laws, to approach something closer to an investor insurance scheme, should come from Congress, and not from the courts.

II

Congress has not passed on the fraud-on-the-market theory the Court embraces today. That is reason enough for us to abstain from doing so. But it is even more troubling that, to the extent that any view of Congress on this question can be inferred indirectly, it is contrary to the result the majority reaches.

* * *

III

Finally, the particular facts of this case make it an exceedingly poor candidate for the Court's fraud-on-the-market theory, and illustrate the illogic achieved by that theory's application in many cases.

Respondents here are a class of sellers who sold Basic stock between October, 1977 and December 1978, a fourteen-month period. At the time the class period began, Basic's stock was trading at $20 a share (at the time, an all-time high); the last members of the class to sell their Basic stock got a price of just over $30 a share. App. 363, 423. It is indisputable that virtually every member of the class made money from his or her sale of Basic stock.

The oddities of applying the fraud-on-the-market theory in this case are manifest. First, there are the facts that the plaintiffs are sellers and the class period is so lengthy—both are virtually without precedent in prior fraud-on-the-market cases. * * *

---

7. This is what the Court's rule boils down to in practical terms. For while, in theory, the Court allows for rebuttal of its "presumption of reliance"—a proviso with which I agree, * * *, in practice the Court must realize, as other courts applying the fraud-on-the-market theory have, that such rebuttal is virtually impossible in all but the most extraordinary case. See Blackie v. Barrack, 524 F.2d at 906–907, n. 22; In re LTV Securities Litigation, 88 F.R.D. 134, 143, n. 4 (N.D.Tex.1980).

Consequently, while the Court considers it significant that the fraud-on-the-market presumption it endorses is a rebuttable one, ante, at 17, 23, the majority's implicit rejection of the "pure causation" fraud-on-the-market theory rings hollow. In most cases, the Court's theory will operate just as the causation theory would, creating a non-rebuttable presumption of "reliance" in future 10b–5 actions.

Second, there is the fact that in this case, there is no evidence that petitioner's officials made the troublesome misstatements for the purpose of manipulating stock prices, or with any intent to engage in underhanded trading of Basic stock. Indeed, during the class period, petitioners do not appear to have purchased or sold *any* Basic stock whatsoever. App. to Pet. for Cert. 27a. I agree with *amicus* who argues that "[i]mposition of damages liability under Rule 10b–5 makes little sense * * * where a defendant is neither a purchaser nor a seller of securities." See Brief for American Corporate Counsel Association as *Amicus Curiae* 13. In fact, in previous cases, we had recognized that Rule 10b–5 is concerned primarily with cases where the fraud is committed by one trading the security at issue. See e.g., Blue Chip Stamps v. Manor Drug Stores, 421 U.S. 723, 736, n. 8 (1975). And it is difficult to square liability in this case with § 10(b)'s express provision that it prohibits fraud *"in connection with"* the purchase or sale of any security." See 15 U.S.C. § 78j(b) (emphasis added).

Third, there are the peculiarities of what kinds of investors will be able to recover in this case. As I read the District Court's class certification order, App. to Pet. for Cert. 123a–126a; ante, at 3–4, n. 5, there are potentially many persons who did not purchase Basic stock until *after* the first false statement (October 1977), but who nonetheless *will* be able to recover under the Court's fraud-on-the-market theory. Thus, it is possible that a person who heard the first corporate misstatement and *disbelieved* it—i.e., someone who purchased Basic stock thinking that petitioners' statement was false—may still be included in the plaintiff-class on remand. How a person who undertook such a speculative stock-investing strategy—and made $10 a share doing so (if he bought on October 22, 1977, and sold on December 15, 1978)—can say that he was "defrauded" by virtue of his reliance on the "integrity" of the market price is beyond me. And such speculators may not be uncommon, at least in this case. See App. to Pet. for Cert. 125a.

Indeed, the facts of this case lead a casual observer to the almost inescapable conclusion that many of those who bought or sold Basic stock during the period in question flatly disbelieved the statements which are alleged to have been "materially misleading." Despite three statements denying that merger negotiations were underway, Basic stock hit record-high after record-high during the 14–month class period. It seems quite possible that, like Casca's knowing disbelief of Caesar's "thrice refusal" of the Crown, clever investors were skeptical of petitioners' three denials that merger talks were going on. Yet such investors, the savviest of the savvy, will be able to recover under the Court's opinion, as long as they now claim that they believed in the "integrity of the market price" when they sold their stock (between September and December, 1978). Thus, persons who bought after hearing and relying on the *falsity* of petitioner's statements may be able to prevail and recover money damages on remand.

And who will pay the judgments won in such actions? I suspect that all too often the majority's rule will "lead to large judgments, payable in the last analysis by innocent investors, for the benefit of speculators and their lawyers." Cf. SEC v. Texas Gulf Sulphur Co., 401 F.2d 833, 867 (C.A.2 1968) (en banc) (Friendly, J., concurring), cert. denied, 394 U.S. 976 (1969). This Court and others have previously recognized that "inexorably broadening * * * the class of plaintiff[s] who may sue in this area of the law will ultimately result in more harm than good." Blue Chip Stamps v. Manor Drug Stores, *supra*, at 747–748.

See also *Ernst v. Ernst v. Hochfelder,* 425 U.S., at 214; Ultramares Corp. v. Touche, 255 N.Y. 170, 179–180, 174 N.E. 441, 444–445 (1931) (Cardozo, C.J.). Yet such a bitter harvest is likely to be reaped from the seeds sown by the Court's decision today.

IV

In sum, I think the Court's embracement of the fraud-on-the-market theory represents a departure in securities law that we are ill-suited to commence—and even less equipped to control as it proceeds. As a result, I must respectfully dissent.

THE FRAUD ON THE MARKET THEORY

The Ninth Circuit, in Blackie v. Barrack,[1] originated the "fraud on the market" theory.

The court in the *Blackie* case said: "A purchaser on the stock exchanges * * * relies generally on the supposition that the market price is validly set and that no unsuspected manipulation has artificially inflated the price, and thus indirectly on the truth of the representations underlying the stock price— whether he is aware of it or not, the price he pays reflects material misrepresentations. Requiring direct proof from each purchaser that he relied on a particular representation when purchasing would defeat recovery by those whose reliance was indirect, despite the fact that the causational chain is broken only if the purchaser would have purchased stock even had he known of the misrepresentation." Several other circuits adopted the fraud on the market theory in the period before *Basic v. Levinson.*[2]

The fraud on the market theory also received favorable treatment from some commentators.[3] The theory was endorsed when it was used in the context of class actions to eliminate the necessity of each class member proving subjective reliance and where the securities were traded on a developed and open market, so that market prices reflect available information about the corporation. The theory, however, was criticized when courts applied it to undeveloped markets,[4] or used the theory to eliminate the reliance requirement entirely rather than to merely create a rebuttable presumption of reliance.

In the *Basic* case the Supreme Court adopted the fraud-on-the-market theory. It should be carefully noted, however, that this was a four to two decision with three justices not participating and therefore it cannot be considered to have definitively resolved this question. The Court defined the question

---

1. 524 F.2d 891 (9th Cir.1975), *cert. denied,* 429 U.S. 816 (1976).

2. See Panzirer v. Wolf, 663 F.2d 365 (2d Cir.1981), *vacated as moot sub nom.* Price Waterhouse v. Panzirer, 459 U.S. 1027 (1982); Shores v. Sklar, 647 F.2d 462 (5th Cir.1981), *cert. denied,* 459 U.S. 1102 (1983); Harris v. Union Elec. Co., 787 F.2d 355 (8th Cir.1986); T. J. Raney & Sons, Inc. v. Fort Cobb, Okla. Irrigation Fuel Auth., 717 F.2d 1330 (10th Cir.1983), *cert. denied,* 465 U.S. 1026 (1984); Lipton v. Documation, Inc., 734 F.2d 740, 743 (11th Cir.1984).

3. See Barbara Black, Fraud on the Market: A Criticism of Dispensing with Reliance Requirements in Certain Open Market Transactions, 62 N.C.L.Rev. 435 (1984); Robert N. Rapp, Rule 10b–5 and "Fraud-On-the-Market"—Heavy Seas Meet Tranquil Shores, 39 Wash. & Lee L.Rev. 861 (1982); Note, Fraud-On-the-Market: An Emerging Theory of Recovery Under SEC Rule 10b–5, 50 Geo. W.L.Rev. 627 (1982); Note, The Fraud-On-the-Market Theory, 95 Harv.L.Rev. 1143 (1982).

4. See, e.g., Note, 95 Harv. L. Rev. at 1156–58.

for the purposes of the opinion as whether the court should establish a "rebuttable presumption that, in trading, he [the plaintiff] relied on the integrity of the price set by the market" as satisfying this requirement of reliance in order for the plaintiff to prevail. The plurality opinion concedes that "reliance is an element of a Rule 10b–5 cause of action," and limits the holding to this question of whether a rebuttable presumption should be established to satisfy that requirement.

This question is the most important one in any Rule 10b–5 *class action*. A repudiation of this theory would virtually put an end to all class actions under Rule 10b–5. As the plurality opinion notes, without such a presumption, in almost all Rule 10b–5 class actions "it would be impractical to certify a class." The Court further states that "Requiring proof of individualized reliance from each member of the proposed plaintiff class effectively would have prevented respondents from proceeding with a class action, since individual issues then would have overwhelmed the common ones." On the other hand, as the dissent points out, the application of the "fraud-on-the-market theory" does not as a practical matter permit any rebuttal of the "presumption" since "such rebuttal is virtually impossible in all but the most extraordinary case."

In Freeman v. Laventhol & Horwath[5] the court stated that among the factors which should be considered in determining whether there is an "efficient market" for the purpose of applying the fraud-on-the-market theory are a large weekly trading volume; the existence of a significant number of reports by security analysts; the existence of market makers and arbitrageurs in the security; the company's eligibility to file an S–3 Registration Statement; and a history of immediate movement of the stock price caused by unexpected corporate events or financial releases.

The lower courts have generally held that the over-the-counter securities markets, like the stock exchanges, are efficient markets for the purposes of the fraud on the market doctrine.[6]

The most difficult application of the fraud on the market doctrine is whether the doctrine reaches new securities issues sold before there is an established market for the trading of the securities. In Shores v. Sklar,[7] decided before *Basic*, the Fifth Circuit declined to hold that the fraud on the market theory was applicable to a new issue of municipal bonds, but held that a plaintiff could recover if the bonds were "fraudulently" marketed. "The securities laws allow an investor to rely on the integrity of the market to the extent that the securities it offers to him for purchase are entitled to be in the market place."[8] On the other hand, a plaintiff could not recover in a new issue context if all that he or she could prove was "that the bonds would have been offered at

---

5. 915 F.2d 193 (6th Cir.1990).

6. See, e.g., Cammer v. Bloom, 711 F.Supp. 1264 (D.N.J.1989); Hurley v. Federal Deposit Ins. Corp., 719 F.Supp. 27, 33–34 (D.Mass.1989) (fraud on the market theory applies equally to New York Stock Exchange, American Stock Exchange, and over-the counter trading); Rospatch Sec. Litig., 1991 Fed.Sec.L.Rep. (CCH) ¶ 96,160 at 90,873–90,-874 (W.D.Mich.1991).

Stocks traded in the over-the-counter "pink sheets" have been held not to be trad-

ed in an efficient market. Binder v. Gillespie, 184 F.3d 1059, 1064–1065 (9th Cir.1999), *cert. denied sub nom.,* Binder v. Wilson, 528 U.S. 1154. See also Krogman v. Sterritt, 202 F.R.D. 467 (N.D.Tex.2001) (a stock traded in the OTC bulletin board held not to be traded in a sufficiently efficient market to justify fraud-on-the-market presumption).

7. 647 F.2d 462 (5th Cir.1981), *cert. denied,* 459 U.S. 1102 (1983).

8. Id. at 471.

a lower price or a higher rate, rather than that they would never have been issued or market."[9] It is not clear why a plaintiff should be deprived of a remedy if the securities could only have been sold at a materially lower price.

In *Basic* the Court had no occasion to address the *Shores v. Sklar* "fraud created the market" variation of the theory to cover the nonmarketable of the new issue situation. Subsequent lower court decisions have wrestled with the implications of *Shores.* In *Joseph v. Wiles,*[10] the Tenth Circuit reasoned:

> Cases discussing the issue define "unmarketable" strictly. The Sixth Circuit breaks the term into two categories: (1) "economic unmarketability," which occurs when a security is patently worthless, and (2) "legal unmarketability," which occurs when a regulatory or municipal agency would have been required by law to prevent or forbid the issuance of the security. *Ockerman v. May Zima & Co.,* 27 F.3d 1151, 1160 (6th Cir.1994). *Cf. Ross v. Bank South,* 885 F.2d 723, 729 (11th Cir.1989) (en banc) ("[T]he fraud must be so pervasive that it goes to the very existence of the bonds and the validity of their presence on the market.").[11]

Judge Easterbrook separately aptly criticized the oversimplification of *Shores v. Sklar*:

> Full disclosure of adverse information may lower the price, but it does not exclude the security from the market. Securities of bankrupt corporations trade freely; some markets specialize in penny stocks. Thus the linchpin of *Shores*—that disclosing bad information keeps securities off the market, entitling investors to rely on the presence of the securities just as they would rely on statements in a prospectus—is simply false.[12]

Basic held that the fraud on the market presumption could be rebutted. A 1995 law review article found that in no reported post-*Basic* case had a defendant succeeded in rebutting the presumption of reliance, nor had any court allowed a defendant to use any defense other than the three listed by the Supreme Court in *Basic* to rebut that presumption.[13] Subsequently the presumption was successfully rebutted when a defendant showed that a plaintiff actually knew relevant information that was not disclosed to the market.[14]

Other defenses to the *Basic* presumption have been presented. In Kaplan v. Rose,[15] for example, the court reasoned: "If, however, the information that defendants are alleged to have withheld from or misrepresented to the market has entered the market through other channels, the market will not have been misled, and the stock price will reflect the full universe of information, despite the defendants' misrepresentations." This has been called the "truth on the market" defense.[16]

Regarding the fraud on the market theory generally, *see* Louis Loss & Joel Seligman, Securities Regulation 4385–4408 (3d ed. rev. 1992); Robert N. Sobol,

9. Id. at 470.

10. 223 F.3d 1155 (10th Cir.2000).

11. Id. at 1164.

12. Eckstein v. Balcor Film Investors, 8 F.3d 1121, 1131 (7th Cir.1993), *cert. denied,* 510 U.S. 1073 (1994).

13. Elliott, J.Weiss & John S. Beckerman, Let the Money Do the Monitoring: How Institutional Investors Can Reduce Agency

Costs in Securities Class Actions, 104 Yale L.J. 2053, 2077 n. 128 (1995).

14. Gurary v. Winehouse, 190 F.3d 37, 45–46 (2d Cir.1999).

15. 49 F.3d 1363, 1376 (9th Cir.1994), *cert. denied sub nom.* Payne v. Kaplan, 516 U.S. 810 (1995).

16. Schaffer v. Timberland Co., 924 F.Supp. 1298, 1308–1309 (D.N.H.1996).

The Benefit of the Internet: The World Wide Web and the Securities Law Doctrine of Truth-on-the-Market, 25 J. Corp. L. 85 (1999).

JUSTIFIABLE RELIANCE AND NONRELIANCE CLAUSES

Several recent Rule 10b–5 decisions have also articulated a "justifiable reliance" requirement.[1] As described by the Fourth Circuit in Myers v. Finkle:[2]

A determination of whether an investor may be justified in relying on oral representations that conflict with contemporaneous written statements in the investor's possession requires a consideration of all relevant factors, including:

(1) [T]he sophistication and expertise of the plaintiff in financial and securities matters; (2) the existence of long standing business or personal relationships; (3) access to relevant information; (4) the existence of a fiduciary relationship; (5) concealment of the fraud; (6) the opportunity to detect the fraud; (7) whether the plaintiff initiated the stock transaction or sought to expedite the transaction; and (8) the generality or specificity of the misrepresentations.

* * * Because no single factor is dispositive, consideration of all factors is necessary.

The justifiable reliance requirement, if applicable, is essentially limited to instances when there have been oral communications, typically in addition to— or in contradiction of—written statements. Justifiable reliance need not be proven when the plaintiff is entitled to the fraud on the market presumption of reliance.

A different view of the justifiable reliance doctrine was articulated in Astor Chauffeured Limousine Co. v. Runnfeldt Inv. Corp.,[3] where the court rejected an argument

that a buyer's failure to investigate the statements made to it means that any reliance is unreasonable. The securities laws are designed to induce the person who possesses information to reveal it accurately. The obligation rests with the speaker, not with the listener.

Although, as many cases hold, "reliance" is an element of the plaintiff's case under Rule 10b–5, e.g., Basic Inc. v. Levinson, 485 U.S. 224, 243 * * * (1988), "reliance" in securities law is no more than the combination of a material misstatement (or omission) and causation. * * * [Therefore,] we concluded in [Rowe v. Maremont Corp., 850 F.2d 1226, 1233 (7th Cir.1988)], that justifiable reliance is not an *independent* element in securities litigation.

But the court conceded that "an investor cannot close his eyes to a known risk. [Citations omitted.] This follows from the definition of materiality. No reasonable investor, knowing that statements are false or probably so, should consider the information important in determining whether to buy or sell."[4]

---

1. *See, e.g.,* Kennedy v. Josephthal & Co., Inc., 814 F.2d 798, 814 (1st Cir.1987) (citing factors used by courts in examining whether reliance on misrepresentations is justified).

2. 950 F.2d 165, 167 (4th Cir.1991).

3. 910 F.2d 1540, 1546 (7th Cir.1990).

4. Id. at 1547.

In face-to-face transactions, the equivalent of a justifiable reliance requirement has been applied by the courts through the misnamed plaintiff's due diligence requirement which we will explore later. After *Ernst & Ernst*, this in essence means that the defendant can establish a defense if he or she can show that the plaintiff lacked due diligence *and* the plaintiff's scienter was the same as that applied to defendants. The defense is misnamed in the sense that due diligence suggests a negligent standard, while the *Ernst & Ernst* culpability standard requires intentional or reckless misconduct.[5]

Recent cases have also explored potentially more far reaching nonreliance clauses in stock purchase agreements which attempt to preclude damages under the federal securities laws for prior oral statements.[6] In Rissman v. Rissman,[7] Judge Easterbrook concluded:

> [W]e now follow those cases by holding that a written anti-reliance clause precludes any claim of deceit by prior representations. The principle is functionally the same as a doctrine long accepted in this circuit: that a person who has received written disclosure of the truth may not claim to rely on contrary oral falsehoods. [citations omitted.] A non-reliance clause is not identical to a truthful disclosure, but it has a similar function: it ensures that both the transaction and any subsequent litigation proceed on the basis of the parties' writings, which are less subject to the vagaries of memory and the risks of fabrication.
>
> Memory plays tricks. Acting in the best of faith, people may "remember" things that never occurred but now serve their interests. Or they may remember events with a change of emphasis or nuance that makes a substantial difference to meaning. Express or implied qualifications may be lost in the folds of time. A statement such as "I won't sell at current prices" may be recalled years later as "I won't sell." Prudent people protect themselves against the limitations of memory (and the temptation to shade the truth) by limiting their dealings to those memorialized in writing, and promoting the privacy of the written word in a principal function of the federal securities laws.
>
> Failure to enforce agreements such as the one between Arnold and Randall could not make sellers of securities better off in the long run. Faced with an unavoidable risk of claims based on oral statements, persons transacting in securities would reduce the price they pay, setting aside the difference as a reserve for risk. If, as Arnold says, Randall was willing to pay $17 million and not a penny more, then a legal rule entitling Arnold to an extra $95 million if Tiger should be sold in the future would have scotched the deal (the option value of the deferred payment exceeds 1 cent), leaving Arnold with no cash and the full risk of the venture. Arnold can't have both $17 million with certainty and a continuing right to 1/3 of any premium Randall negotiates for the firm, while bearing no risk from the fickle toy business; that would make him better off than if he had held his shares throughout. * * *

---

5. Cf. also Bateman Eichler, Hill Richards, Inc. v. Berner, 472 U.S. 299 (1985) (the defendant is also entitled to the *in pari delicto* defense but only when the plaintiff bears at least substantially equal responsibility for the violations for which he or she seeks redress). We will examine *in pari delicto* later.

6. See, e.g., Jackvony v. RIHT Fin. Corp., 873 F.2d 411 (1st Cir.1989); One–O–One Enter., Inc. v. Caruso, 848 F.2d 1283 (D.C.Cir.1988).

7. 213 F.3d 381 (7th Cir.2000).

Arnold calls the no-reliance clauses "boilerplate," and they were; transactions lawyers have language of this sort stored up for reuse. But the fact that language has been used before does not make it less binding when used again. Phrases become boilerplate when many parties find that the language serves their ends. That's a reason to enforce the promises, not to disregard them. * * * Judges need not speculate about the reason a clause appears or is omitted, however; what matters when litigation breaks out is what the parties actually signed.[8]

Semerenko v. Cendant Corp.

United States Court of Appeals, Third Circuit, 2000.
223 F.3d 165.

■ BEFORE: MANSMANN AND GREENBERG, CIRCUIT JUDGES and ALARCON, SENIOR CIRCUIT JUDGE.*

I

The P. Schoenfeld Asset Management LLC and the class of similarly situated investors (collectively, the "Class") appeal from the order of the district court dismissing their claims for securities fraud pursuant to Rule 12(b)(6) of the Federal Rules of Civil Procedure. The Class's complaint was filed under § 10(b) of the Securities Exchange Act of 1934 (the "Exchange Act") and Rule 10b–5. The complaint also alleged that the individual defendants were liable for the underlying violations of § 10(b) and Rule 10b–5 as control persons under § 20(a) of the Exchange Act.

We conclude that the complaint alleges sufficient facts to establish the elements of reliance and loss causation, and that the district court applied the incorrect analysis for determining whether the complaint alleges that the purported misrepresentations were made "in connection with" the purchase or the sale of a security. Because the standard that we have articulated for the "in connection with" requirement is different from the one applied by the district court, we vacate the judgment below and remand the matter for further proceedings. Given that we do not resolve whether the dismissal was proper under § 10(b) and Rule 10b–5, we do not address the dismissal of the Class's claim under § 20(a).

II

The Class filed this action against the Cendant Corporation ("Cendant"), its former officers and directors Walter A. Forbes, E. Kirk Shelton, Christopher K. McLeod, and Cosmo Corigliano (the "individual defendants"), and its accountant Ernst & Young LLP ("Ernst & Young") (collectively, the "defendants"). The Class alleges that the defendants violated § 10(b) and Rule 10b–5 by making certain misrepresentations about Cendant during a tender offer for

---

8. Id. at 384–385. Judge Rover concurred in this result but wrote separately to urge that in fact the two cases that the majority relies upon, Jackvony v. RIHT Fin. Corp., 873 F.2d 411 (1st Cir.1989) and One–O–One Enter. v. Caruso, 848 F.2d 1283 (D.C.Cir.1988), were conventional justifiable reliance cases and did not base their conclu-

sions on written antireliance clauses but on a broader review of surrounding circumstances. Id. at 384–389.

* The Honorable Arthur L. Alarcon, Senior Judge of the United States Court of Appeals for the Ninth Circuit, sitting by designation.

shares of American Bankers Insurance Group, Inc. ("ABI") common stock. The Class consists of persons who purchased shares of ABI common stock during the course of the tender offer. The class period runs from January 27, 1998 to October 13, 1998. The complaint does not allege that any member of the Class purchased securities issued by Cendant, or that any member of the Class tendered shares of ABI common stock to Cendant. Instead, it alleges that the defendants made certain misrepresentations about Cendant that artificially inflated the price at which the Class purchased their shares of ABI common stock, and that the Class suffered a corresponding loss when those misrepresentations were disclosed to the public and the merger agreement was terminated. In light of the procedural posture of this case, we must assume the truth of the facts alleged in the complaint. See *In re Burlington Coat Factory Sec. Litig.*, 114 F.3d 1410, 1420 (3d Cir.1997).

On December 22, 1997, the American International Group, Inc. ("AIG") announced that it would acquire one hundred percent of the outstanding shares of ABI common stock for $47 per share. On January 27, 1998, Cendant made a competing tender offer to purchase the same shares at a price of $58 per share, or a total price of approximately $2.7 billion. In conjunction with its tender offer, Cendant filed with the Securities and Exchange Commission (the "SEC") a Schedule 14D–1 that overstated its income during prior financial reporting periods.

On March 3, 1998, AIG matched Cendant's bid and offered to pay ABI shareholders $58 for each share of outstanding ABI common stock. Cendant eventually raised its bid price to $67 per share. It then executed an agreement to purchase ABI for approximately $3.1 billion, payable in part cash and in part shares of Cendant common stock. Cendant filed an amendment to its Schedule 14D–1 on March 23, 1998 reporting the terms of the merger agreement. Eight days later, Cendant filed a Form 10–K reporting its financial results for the 1997 fiscal year.

After the close of trading on April 15, 1998, Cendant announced that it had discovered potential accounting irregularities, and that its Audit Committee had engaged Willkie, Farr & Gallagher and Arthur Andersen LLP to perform an independent investigation. Cendant also announced that it had retained Deloitte & Touche LLP to reaudit its financial statements, and that "in accordance with [Statement of Accounting Standards] No. 1, the Company's previously issued financial statements and auditors' reports should not be relied upon." Nevertheless, the April 15, 1998 announcement reported that the irregularities occurred in a single business unit that "accounted for less than one third" of Cendant's net income, and it indicated that Cendant would restate its annual and quarterly earnings for the 1997 fiscal year by $0.11 to $0.13 per share. Immediately after Cendant disclosed the accounting irregularities, the price of ABI common stock dropped from $64–7/8 to $57–3/4, representing an eleven percent decrease from the price at which the shares had been trading.

Following the April 15 announcement, Cendant made several public statements in which it represented that it was committed to completing the merger with ABI notwithstanding the discovery of the accounting irregularities. On April 27, 1998, Walter A. Forbes, the chairman of the board of directors of Cendant, and Henry R. Silverman, the president and the chief executive officer of Cendant, issued a letter to Cendant shareholders, which was published in the financial press. That letter states:

We are outraged that the apparent misdeeds of a small number of individuals within a limited part of our company has adversely affected the value of your investment—and ours—in Cendant. We are working together diligently to clear this matter up as soon as possible. We fully support the Audit Committee's investigation and continue to believe that the strategic rationale and industrial logic of the HFS/CUC merger that created Cendant is as compelling as ever.

Cendant is strong, highly liquid, and extremely profitable. The vast majority of Cendant's operating businesses and earnings are unaffected and the prospects for the Company's future growth and success are excellent.

We have reaffirmed our commitment to completing all pending acquisitions: American Bankers, National Parking Corporation and Providian Insurance.

In a press release issued on May 5, 1998, Cendant stated that "over eighty percent of the Company's net income for the first quarter of 1998 came from Cendant business units not impacted by the potential accounting irregularities."

On July 14, 1998, Cendant revealed that the April 15, 1998 announcement anticipating the restatement of its financial results for the 1997 fiscal year was inaccurate, and that the actual reduction in income would be twice as much as previously announced. Cendant further acknowledged that its investigation had uncovered several accounting irregularities that had not previously been disclosed, and that those accounting irregularities affected additional Cendant business units and other fiscal years. Cendant estimated that earnings would be reduced by as much as $0.28 per share in 1997. After the July 14, 1998 disclosure, the price of ABI common stock dropped until Cendant issued several public statements indicating that it intended to continue the tender offer and that it was "contractually committed" to completing the ABI merger. Thereafter, the market price of ABI common stock was "buoyed" by Cendant's repeated statements that it was committed to completing the merger.

On August 13, 1998, Cendant issued a press release announcing that its investigation into the accounting irregularities was complete. The release stated that Cendant would restate its earnings by $0.28 per share in 1997, by $0.19 per share in 1996, and by $0.14 per share in 1995. On August 27, 1998, Cendant issued a statement that the board of directors had adopted the audit report. The audit report was publicly filed with the SEC on August 28, 1998, and a copy was forwarded to the United States Attorney for the District of New Jersey. The report included findings that "fraudulent financial reporting" and other "errors" inflated Cendant's pretax income by approximately $500 million from 1995 to 1997, and that Forbes and Shelton were "among those who must bear responsibility." After the audit report was filed with the SEC, the price of ABI common stock closed at $53–1/2 per share on August 28, 1998 and fell further to a closing price of $51–7/8 per share on August 31, 1998, the first day of trading following the disclosure.

On September 29, 1998, Cendant filed an amended Form 10–K for the 1997 fiscal year announcing that Cendant had actually lost $217.2 million in 1997 rather than earning $55.5 million, as previously reported. That announcement caused the price of ABI common stock to drop further to $43 per share by the close of trading. On October 13, 1998, Cendant and ABI announced that they were terminating the merger agreement, and that Cendant would pay ABI a

$400 million dollar break up fee, despite the fact that it was not contractually bound to do so. The termination agreement, which was executed the same day, provided that the termination of the merger would not result in liability on the part of Cendant or ABI, or on the part of any of their directors, officers, employees, agents, legal and financial advisors, or shareholders. In response to the disclosure, the price of ABI common stock dropped to $35-1/2 per share by the end of the day.

On October 14, 1998, the day after Cendant and ABI disclosed the termination of the planned merger, the Class filed a complaint in the United States District Court for the District of New Jersey alleging that Cendant and the individual defendants violated § 10(b) and Rule 10b-5 by making fraudulent misrepresentations concerning Cendant's financial condition, its willingness to complete the tender offer, and its willingness to complete the proposed merger. The complaint also alleged that the individual defendants were liable for those violations as control persons under § 20(a). The Class subsequently amended its complaint to expand the class period and to name Ernst & Young as an additional defendant in its claims under § 10(b) and Rule 10(b)(5).

The defendants filed a motion to dismiss the Class's complaint pursuant to Rule 12(b)(6) and Rule 9(b) of the Federal Rules of Civil Procedure. The district court granted the motion and entered an order dismissing the complaint under Rule 12(b)(6). In explaining its dismissal order, the district court stated that the complaint failed to establish that the alleged misrepresentations were made "in connection with" the Class's purchases of ABI common stock, that the Class reasonably relied on the purported misrepresentations, and that the Class suffered a loss as the proximate result of the purported misrepresentations. The order also dismissed the Class's § 20(a) claim against the individual defendants on the basis that a claim for control person liability cannot be maintained in the absence of an underlying violation of the Exchange Act. In light of its decision to dismiss the complaint pursuant to Rule 12(b)(6), the district court declined to consider whether the Class's complaint also failed to satisfy the heightened pleading requirements of Rule 9(b).

* * *

IV

* * *

A.

* * *

We must first decide whether the Class's complaint pleads sufficient facts to satisfy the "in connection with" requirement of § 10(b) and Rule 10b-5. The parties have expressed much disagreement over the standard that this court applies in determining whether an alleged misrepresentation was made "in connection with" the purchase or the sale of a security. The defendants, in varying respects, contend that the alleged misrepresentations must speak directly to the investment value of the security that is bought or sold, and that they must have been made with the specific purpose or objective of influencing an investor's decision. In contrast, the Class and the SEC, as amicus curiae, argue that the "in connection with" requirement is satisfied whenever a misrepresentation is made in a manner that is reasonably calculated to influence the investment decisions of market participants. Recognizing that "the 'in connection with' phrase is not the least difficult aspect of the 10b-5 complex to tie down," we take this opportunity to clarify the standard that governs this matter. Chemical Bank v. Arthur Andersen & Co., 726 F.2d 930, 942 (2d Cir.1984) (noting the difficulty in establishing a test for the "in connection with" requirement) (quotations and citations omitted).

In Ketchum v. Green, 557 F.2d 1022 (1977), this court considered the question whether certain misrepresentations arising out of an internal contest for the control of a closely held corporation were made "in connection with" the subsequent forced redemption of the losing parties' stock. There, a group of minority shareholders secretly conspired to remove the two majority shareholders from their respective positions as the chairman of the board of directors and as the president of the corporation. See *Ketchum*, 557 F.2d at 1023–24. By misrepresenting their intentions concerning the election of corporate officers, the minority shareholders were able to persuade the majority shareholders to elect them to a majority of the seats on the board of directors. See id. After gaining control of the board of directors, the minority shareholders immediately voted to remove the two majority shareholders from their officerships. See id. To entrench themselves, they also passed resolutions terminating the majority shareholders' employment and authorizing the mandatory repurchase of the majority shareholders' stock pursuant to a stock retirement agreement. The majority shareholders brought an action pursuant to § 10(b) and Rule 10b–5 to enjoin their ouster from the corporation and to obtain damages. See *id.* at 1024. On review, this court held that the majority shareholders failed to establish that the complained of misrepresentations were made "in connection with" the purchase or the sale of a security. See *id.* at 1027–29. In addition to noting that the case fell within an "internal corporate mismanagement" exception to § 10(b) and Rule 10b–5, the court reasoned that the degree of proximity between the claimed fraud and the securities transaction was simply too attenuated for the case to fall within the scope of the federal securities laws. See *id.* at 1028–29.

This court again considered the contours of the "in connection with" requirement in Angelastro v. Prudential–Bache Sec., Inc., 764 F.2d 939 (3d Cir.1985), when it addressed the question whether a brokerage firm could be held liable under § 10(b) and Rule 10b–5 for making misrepresentations concerning the terms of its margin accounts. In that case, a class of investors sued a national brokerage firm for misrepresenting both the specific interest rates that it would charge in connection with a margin purchase and the formula that it would apply in calculating those rates. See *Angelastro*, 764 F.2d at 941. The district court dismissed the investors' complaint on the basis that the alleged misrepresentations were not made "in connection with" the purchase or the sale of a security. See id. This court reversed, holding that the investors could pursue their claims under § 10(b) and Rule 10b–5. The court reasoned that the requisite causal connection was satisfied by the brokerage firm's fraudulent course of dealing, notwithstanding the fact that the alleged misrepresentations did not relate to the merits of a security. See *id.* at 944–45. In holding in favor of the class, the court specifically noted that "Rule 10b–5 also encompasses misrepresentations beyond those implicating the investment value of a particular security." Id.

While the decisions in *Ketchum* and *Angelastro* are illustrative of the point that the "in connection with" language requires a causal connection between the claimed fraud and the purchase or the sale of a security, and that the misrepresentations need not refer to a particular security, they are not helpful in applying the standard to the facts of this case. This case does not present a claim based on allegations of internal corporate misconduct arising from a contest for the control of a closely held corporation. See *Ketchum*, 557 F.2d at 1028. Nor does it concern a fraudulent course of dealing by a brokerage firm. See *Angelastro*, 764 F.2d at 944. Rather, it involves the public dissemination of allegedly misleading information into an efficient securities market. In light of the law of this circuit that the scope of the "in connection with" requirement must be determined on a case-by-case basis, we are compelled to look elsewhere in deciding the standard that governs this matter. See *Ketchum*, 557 F.2d at 1027; *Angelastro*, 764 F.2d at 942–43, 945.

In resolving the issue before us, we are persuaded by recent decisions in the Second Circuit and the Ninth Circuit that have addressed the scope of the "in connection with" requirement when the alleged fraud involves the public dissemination of false and misleading information. See In re Ames Dep't Stores Inc. Stock Litig., 991 F.2d 953, 956, 965–66 (2d Cir.1993) (involving the public dissemination of false information in publicly filed offering documents, press releases, and research reports); McGann v. Ernst & Young, 102 F.3d 390, 392–93 (9th Cir.1996) (involving the public dissemination of false information in a publicly filed annual report). Those courts have generally adopted the standard articulated in Securities & Exch. Comm'n v. Texas Gulf Sulphur Co., 401 F.2d 833, 862 (2d Cir.1968) (in banc), and applied an objective analysis that considers the alleged misrepresentation in the context in which it was made. They have held that, where the fraud alleged involves the public dissemination of information in a medium upon which an investor would presumably rely, the "in connection with" element may be established by proof of the materiality of the misrepresentation and the means of its dissemination. See In re Ames Dep't Stores Inc. Stock Litig., 991 F.2d at 963, 965; Securities & Exch. Comm'n v. Rana Research, Inc., 8 F.3d 1358, 1362 (9th Cir.1993); In re Leslie Fay Cos. Sec. Litig., 871 F. Supp. 686, 697 (S.D.N.Y.1995). Under that standard, it is irrelevant that the misrepresentations were not made for the purpose or the object of influencing the investment decisions of market participants. See In re Ames Dep't Stores Inc. Stock Litig., 991 F.2d at 965 (holding that an investor's reliance need not be envisioned to give rise to liability under § 10(b) and Rule 10b–5).

We conclude that the materiality and public dissemination approach should apply in this case. The purpose underlying § 10(b) and Rule 10b–5 is to ensure that investors obtain fair and full disclosure of material facts in connection with their decisions to purchase or sell securities. See *Angelastro*, 764 F.2d at 942. That purpose is best satisfied by a rule that recognizes the realistic causal effect that material misrepresentations, which raise the public's interest in particular securities, tend to have on the investment decisions of market participants who trade in those securities. See In re Ames Dep't Stores Inc. Stock Litig., 991 F.2d at 966. We therefore adopt the reasoning of the Second Circuit and the Ninth Circuit and hold that the Class may establish the "in connection with" element simply by showing that the misrepresentations in question were disseminated to the public in a medium upon which a reasonable investor would rely, and that they were material when disseminated. We also point out that, under the standard which we adopt, the Class is not required to establish that the defendants actually envisioned that members of the Class would rely upon the alleged misrepresentations when making their investment decisions. See In re Ames Dep't Stores Inc. Stock Litig., 991 F.2d at 965; In re Leslie Fay Cos. Sec. Litig., 871 F. Supp. at 697–98. Rather, it must only show that the alleged misrepresentations were reckless. See *In re Advanta Corp. Sec. Litig.*, 180 F.3d 525, 535 (3d Cir.1999) (reaffirming that § 10(b) and Rule 10b–5 cover reckless misrepresentations).

* * *

We emphasize, though, that it is no defense that the alleged misrepresentations were made in the context of a tender offer and a proposed merger, or that they did not specifically refer to the investment value of the security that was bought or sold. It is well established that information concerning a tender offer or a proposed merger may be material to persons who trade in the securities of the target company, despite the highly contingent nature of both types of transactions. [citations omitted.] So long as the alleged misrepresentations were material, the "in connection with" requirement may be satisfied simply by showing that they were publicly disseminated in a medium upon which investors tend to rely. * * *

We do not resolve, however, whether the "in connection with" requirement is satisfied in the present case. Because the standard that we have set forth is different from the one applied by the district court, and because the parties have not been afforded a full opportunity to brief the issues of materiality and public dissemination, we will remand this matter to allow the district court to consider, in the first instance, the question whether the Class's complaint pleads sufficient facts to satisfy the requirements of Rule 12(b)(6). We note, however, that the issue of materiality typically presents a mixed question of law and fact, and that the delicate assessment of inferences is generally best left to the trier of fact. See *Shapiro*, 964 F.2d at 281 n.11. The district court should decide the issue of materiality as a matter of law only if the alleged misrepresentations are so clearly and obviously unimportant that reasonable minds could not differ in their answers to the question. See *Weiner*, 129 F.3d at 317; *In re Craftmatic Sec. Litig.*, 890 F.2d 628, 641 (3d Cir.1989).

B.

We next turn to the question whether the Class's complaint alleges sufficient facts to establish the element of reliance. It is axiomatic that a private action for securities fraud must be dismissed when a plaintiff fails to plead that he or she reasonably and justifiably relied on an alleged misrepresentation. See *Weiner*, 129 F.3d at 315 (setting forth reliance as an element of a private right of action under § 10(b) and Rule 10–5); *In re Burlington Coat Factory Sec. Litig.*, 114 F.3d at 1417 (same). The defendants claim that the complaint fails to establish the element of reliance, because it alleges that the defendants' misrepresentations were made in the context of a tender offer and a proposed merger, that AIG made a competing tender offer to purchase shares of ABI common stock at $58 per share, and that Cendant issued a press release on April 15, 1998 warning investors not to rely on its prior representations concerning its financial condition.

Traditionally, purchasers and sellers of securities were required to establish that they were aware of, and directly misled by, an alleged misrepresentation to state a claim for securities fraud under § 10(b) and Rule 10b–5. See *Peil v. Speiser*, 806 F.2d 1154, 1160 (3d Cir.1986) (discussing theories of reliance). Recognizing that the requirement of showing direct reliance presents an unreasonable evidentiary burden in a securities market where face-to-face transactions are rare and where lawsuits are brought by classes of investors, however, this court has adopted a rule that creates a presumption of reliance in certain cases. See id. Under the fraud on the market theory, a plaintiff in a securities action is generally entitled to a rebuttable presumption of reliance if he or she purchased or sold securities in an efficient market. See *In re Burlington Coat Factory Sec. Litig.*, 114 F.3d at 1419 n.8 (holding that a purchaser of securities in an open and developed market is entitled to a presumption of reliance).

The fraud on the market theory of reliance is, in essence, a theory of indirect actual reliance under which a plaintiff is entitled to three separate presumptions in attempting to establish the element of direct reliance. See *Zlotnick v. Tie Communications*, 836 F.2d 818, 822 (3d Cir.1988). Under the fraud on the market theory of reliance, the court presumes (1) that the market price of the security actually incorporated the alleged misrepresentations, (2) that the plaintiff actually relied on the market price of the security as an indicator of its value, and (3) that the plaintiff acted reasonably in relying on the market price of the security. See id. The fraud on the market theory of reliance, however, creates only a presumption, which a defendant may rebut by raising any defense to actual reliance. See *Basic, Inc.*, 485 U.S. at 248–49. This court has pointed out that the presumption of reliance may be rebutted by showing that the market did not respond to the alleged misrepresentations, or that the plaintiff did not actually rely on the market price when making his or her investment decision. See *Zlotnik*, 836 F.2d at 822; *Peil*, 806 F.2d at 1161. This court has also held that a defendant may defeat the presumption of reliance by showing that the plaintiff 's reliance on the market price was actually unreasonable. See *Zlotnik*, 836 F.2d at 822; *Peil*, 806 F.2d at 1161.

In the present case, we are persuaded that the Class has sufficiently pleaded the element of reliance to withstand a challenge under Rule 12(b)(6) with respect to at least some of the alleged misrepresentations. The complaint alleges that ABI common stock traded in an open and developed market throughout the class period, that the market price of ABI common stock incorporated the alleged misrepresentations, and that the Class members purchased shares of ABI common stock in reliance on that price. The complaint also states that the Class was directly misled by the alleged misrepresentations. Those allegations, if true, are sufficient to establish direct reliance and to create a presumption of indirect actual reliance so long as the Class's reliance on the purported misrepresentations or the market price of ABI common stock was not unreasonable as a matter of law.

We conclude that it was reasonable for the Class members who purchased shares prior to March 3, 1998 to rely on the alleged misrepresentations occurring prior to that date. The defendants have not provided us with a legitimate reason for us to conclude to the contrary. Their arguments concern only the reasonableness of the reliance of the Class members who purchased shares of ABI common stock after March 3, 1998. They have no bearing on the investment decisions of persons who purchased shares of ABI common stock prior to that date, because the reasonableness of reliance is determined at the time of the transaction in question. See *Hayes v. Gross*, 982 F.2d 104, 107 (3d Cir.1992) (requiring an investor to rely on an alleged misrepresentation at the time of the purchase or the sale of securities); *Zlotnik, 836 F.2d at 823* (same); *Gannon v. Continental Ins. Co.*, 920 F. Supp. 566, 578 (D.N.J.1996) (holding that an investor cannot rely on statements that are made subsequent to the purchase of securities).

To the extent that the defendant's arguments suggest that it is unreasonable as a matter of law to rely on information concerning a tender offer or a merger before the transaction is finalized, we disagree. The Supreme Court has cautioned that "no particular event or factor short of closing the transaction need be either necessary or sufficient by itself to render merger discussions material." *Basic, Inc.*, 485 U.S. at 239. And, other courts have similarly held that information concerning a tender offer may be material while the transaction is still in the planning stage. *Maio*, 51 F.3d at 637; *Mayhew*, 916 F. Supp. at 131. If it may be reasonable for an investor to find information concerning a tentative tender offer or a merger important when making an investment decision, we see no reason why the conditional nature of those transactions should necessarily prevent the investor from reasonably relying on that information as well. See 2 Thomas Lee Hazen, The Law of Securities Regulation § 13.5B, at 527 (3d ed. 1995) (stating that "the reliance requirement is a corollary of materiality").

We are also persuaded that the Class members who purchased shares of ABI common stock between March 3, 1998 and April 15, 1998 alleged sufficient facts to satisfy the element of reliance. With respect to those purchasers, the defendants maintain that AIG's $58 tender offer provided an independent valuation of ABI common stock upon which the Class members directly or indirectly relied. In effect, the defendants suggest that the market did not incorporate the alleged misrepresentations into the price of ABI common stock during the competing tender offer, and that the Class members would have purchased shares of ABI common stock to tender to AIG even if they had known the truth about Cendant. See *Basic, Inc.*, 485 U.S. at 249 (noting that the presumption of indirect actual reliance may be rebutted by showing that the plaintiff would have completed the transaction regardless of the alleged misrepresentations); *Zlotnik*, 836 F.2d at 822 (stating that the presumption of indirect actual reliance may be rebutted by showing that the market price was not affected by the alleged misrepresentations). While those arguments are facially appealing, we do not find them persuasive given the procedural posture of this case.

In reviewing a motion to dismiss under Rule 12(b)(6), we must accept the allegations of the complaint as true and draw all reasonable inferences in the light most favorable to the plaintiffs. See *Wiener*, 129 F.3d at 315. In this case, the Class's complaint alleges that the market price of ABI common stock was inflated due to the alleged misrepresentations, and it states that the Class purchased "ABI shares believing they would receive $58 per share ... in a combination of cash and Cendant stock." Though we agree with the defendants that the market price of ABI common stock incorporated information concerning AIG's $58 tender offer, we may not assume for the present purposes that it did not also incorporate information concerning a potential acquisition by Cendant, or that Cendant's tender offer did not have an actual effect on the Class. Indeed, it is likely that the shares of ABI common stock traded at a relative premium during the competing tender offer based on the fact that two purportedly willing and able suitors sought to acquire the company. It is also possible that members of the Class would not have purchased shares of ABI common stock had they been unable to exchange them for shares of Cendant. Because we must assume the truth of the allegations of the complaint, and resolve all competing allegations and inferences in favor of the Class, we agree that the existence of a competing tender offer did not effect the Class's reliance on the defendants' alleged misrepresentations. See *In re Burlington Coat*

Factory Sec. Litig., 114 F.3d at 1420 (stating that a court must credit the allegations of the complaint and not the defendant's responses when resolving conflicting allegations on a motion to dismiss). We also note that the effect of the $58 tender offer would have been limited to those members of the Class who purchased shares from March 3, 1998, when the tender offer was made, and March 17, 1998, when Cendant raised its bid price to $67 per share.

We agree that the Class has failed to demonstrate that it was reasonable for its members to rely on the defendants' prior financial statements and auditors' reports following the April 15, 1998 disclosure of the accounting irregularities. The complaint states that Cendant disclosed on April 15, 1998 that it had uncovered accounting irregularities, and that it warned investors not to rely on its prior financial statements and auditor's reports when making an investment decision. The complaint further alleges that the common stock of both Cendant and ABI traded in an efficient market, and that the market price of each stock instantly dropped after Cendant issued the warning. In light of the curative nature of the warning statement, and given the instantaneous decline in the market price of both companies' common stock, we conclude that the announcement immediately rendered the prior misrepresentations concerning Cendant's financial condition thereafter immaterial as a matter of law. See *Weiner*, 129 F.3d at 321 (holding that a public statement curing the misleading effect of a prior misrepresentation renders the prior misrepresentation immaterial); In re Burlington Coat Factory Sec. Litig., 114 F.3d at 1425 (stating that an efficient market immediately incorporates information into the price of a security); Teamsters Local 282 Pension Trust Fund v. Angelos, 762 F.2d 522, 530 (7th Cir.1985) (dicta) (stating that an investor may not ask a court to focus on a misrepresentation and ignore information that has already been disseminated). Thus, neither the market nor the Class members could have reasonably relied upon Cendant's prior financial statements or its audit reports after April 15, 1998. Because it made no misrepresentations after the curative statement was issued, Ernst & Young may not be held liable to members of the Class who purchased shares of ABI common stock after April 15, 1998.

Nevertheless, we do not accept the defendants' contention that the Class could not have reasonably relied on the alleged misrepresentations that were included in the April 15, 1998 announcement. The Class claims that the April 15, 1998 announcement misrepresented Cendant's financial condition by stating that the company expected to restate its 1997 earnings by $0.11 to $0.13 per share and to reduce its net income prior to restructuring and unusual charges by approximately $100 to $115 million. The defendants claim that the Class was not entitled to rely on those statements or on any subsequent statements, because the announcement warned that the representations were subject to "known and unknown risks and uncertainties including, but not limited to, the outcome of the Audit Committee's investigation." Their argument is based upon both the bespeaks caution doctrine, which renders alleged misrepresentations immaterial, and the common sense principle that investors do not act reasonably in relying on statements that are accompanied by meaningful cautionary language.

The parties disagree as to whether the bespeaks caution doctrine applies to the statements made in the April 15, 1998 announcement that predicted the amount by which Cendant would restate its results for the 1997 year. The Class and the SEC maintain that the "bespeaks caution" doctrine is inapplicable, because the statements related to present and historical facts that were capable of verification and, as such, not forward-looking. See Grossman v. Novell, Inc., 120 F.3d 1112, 1123 (10th Cir.1997) (holding that the bespeaks caution doctrine applies only to forward-looking information). The defendants, in contrast, characterize the statements concerning the restatement as forward-looking, and thus subject to the bespeaks caution doctrine, because Cendant had not completed a reaudit when it disclosed the amount of the anticipated restatement. See Harris v. Ivax Corp., 182 F.3d 799, 802–3 (11th Cir.1999) (holding that statements made on the last day of a quarter concerning the results for the quarter are forward-looking).

We need not decide whether the alleged misrepresentations in the April 15, 1998 announcement were forward-looking statements, however, because we conclude that the accompanying warnings were not sufficiently cautionary to warn against the danger of relying on the specific numbers identified in the announcement. In re Trump Casino Sec. Litig., 7 F.3d 357, 369 (3d Cir.1993), this court instructed that cautionary language must be "extensive yet specific" to prevent a reasonable investor from relying on specific projections. There, the court explained:

> a vague or blanket (boilerplate) disclaimer which merely warns the reader that the investment has risks will ordinarily be inadequate to prevent misinformation. To suffice, the cautionary statements must be substantive and tailored to the specific future projections, estimates or opinions in the prospectus which the plaintiffs challenge.

Id. at 371–72.

In Kline v. First Western Gov't Sec., Inc., 24 F.3d 480, 489 (3d Cir.1994), this court clarified that "Trump requires that the language bespeaking caution relate directly to that by which plaintiffs claim to have been misled."

In the present case, the cautionary language set forth in the April 15, 1998 announcement generally pertains only to the risk that the results of operations could vary in future fiscal years. In fact, the only risk factor that is apparently applicable to the restatement of Cendant's results for the 1997 fiscal year relates to the risk that the announcement's calculations might differ from those made by the Audit Committee. We are not persuaded that such a general statement of risk is sufficiently substantive and tailored to satisfy the requirements of the bespeaks caution doctrine. See In re Trump Casino Sec. Litig., 7 F.3d at 371–72. Nor are we persuaded that it is adequate to give investors reasonable notice that the projected restatement of Cendant's financial statements should not be trusted so as to make any reliance unreasonable as a matter of law. In our opinion, a reasonable investor may be willing to rely on the announcement's specific calculations concerning the restatement in the absence of a more detailed explanation of the reasons that the calculations might be incorrect and of the effect of any error. The announcement's blanket warning—that the amount of the restatement could later turn out to be wrong—was simply not sufficient to caution reasonable investors against relying on the defendants' representations. See Kline, 24 F.3d at 489–90 (holding that cautionary statements in an opinion letter were not sufficiently cautionary to preclude reliance where they suggested nothing more than the possibility that the speaker "might have gotten the law wrong or incorrectly assessed the risk that the IRS would deny deductions"); see, e.g., Harris, 182 F.3d at 810, 813–14 (setting forth meaningful and specific cautionary language as an appendix to the opinion). Because we conclude that the alleged misrepresentations concerning the restatement of Cendant's 1997 financial information did not include sufficient cautionary language, we agree that the Class could reasonably rely on the anticipated restatement in the April 15, 1998 announcement. For the same reason, we conclude that the Class members were not necessarily prevented from reasonably relying on the defendants' subsequent statements concerning Cendant's intent to merge with ABI.

The Class was not entitled, however, to rely indefinitely upon the April 15, 1998 misrepresentations. Cendant announced on July 14, 1998 that it had revised the restatement of its 1997 income, and it disseminated the formal results of the Audit Committee's investigation one month later. We think that it is possible that either, if not both, of those announcements might have cured the effect of the alleged misrepresentations in the April 15, 1998 announcement and rendered the disclosure thereafter unreliable. However, in light of our decision to remand this case, and given that the parties have not discussed the issue, we leave it for the district court to decide in the first instance the point at which the particular misrepresentations could no longer be trusted.

C.

Finally, we must decide whether the Class's complaint adequately pleads the element of loss causation. The defendants contend that the complaint failed to allege sufficient facts to support an inference that the alleged misrepresentations were the proximate cause of the Class's loss. They maintain that the complaint shows that several intervening events, and not the alleged misrepresentations, led first to the artificial inflation and then to the decline in the market price of ABI common stock. In particular, they assert that the price of ABI common stock was inflated by AIG's $58 tender offer and by the approval of the merger agreement by the board of directors of ABI. They also suggest that the Class's loss was actually caused by the mutual termination of the merger agreement by the board of directors of both ABI and Cendant. We disagree.

In Scattergood v. Perelman, 945 F.2d 618, 624 (3d Cir.1991), this court held that a plaintiff may establish the element of loss causation simply by showing that he or she purchased a security at a market price that was artificially inflated due to a fraudulent misrepresentation. Id. In that case, the defendants issued a press release stating that they were considering acquiring the outstanding shares of another company at the prevailing market price. See *id. at 623*. The press release also warned that the defendants had "not yet determined to proceed with such transaction," and it cautioned that there could "be no assurance that [the defendants] will ultimately decide to make such an offer or that the [board of directors of the target corporation] would recommend such an offer to the stockholders." Id. Some of the plaintiffs purchased shares of the target company's stock at price below the tender offer price expecting that the stock would be acquired at the tender offer price in the near future. See *id. at 624*. The defendants moved to dismiss the complaint pursuant to Rule 12(b)(6), because the complaint lacked an assertion that "the plaintiffs experienced an economic loss as a proximate result of the alleged Rule 10b–5 violation." Id. The district court granted the motion to dismiss, and this court reversed. This court held that "the fair inference of the complaint, if one assumes—as we must—the truth of its allegations, is that the market price paid by the plaintiffs exceeded the value of the stock at the time of purchase based on the facts." Id. It reasoned that the dismissal was improper, because the complaint suggested that the price paid exceeded the value that the market would have established for the target company's shares had the truth been known. See id. The court expressed no opinion concerning the proper method for measuring the plaintiffs' injury. See *id. at 624 n.2.*

This court reached a similar conclusion in Hayes v. Gross, 982 F.2d 104, 107 (3d Cir.1992). There, an investor filed a class action lawsuit against the directors and officers of a savings and loan association pursuant to § 10(b) and Rule 10b–5 claiming that the class members were injured when they purchased the association's stock at an inflated price. See *id. at 105.* At the urging of the directors, the officers, and the Resolution Trust Company, the district court dismissed the action for failure to state a claim. See *id. at 105.* This court reversed the dismissal and remanded the matter for further proceedings. It concluded that the class had established the element of reliance, and it expressly found "no merit" in the Resolution Trust Company's contention that the complaint failed to allege the element of loss causation. See *id. at 107 & n.2.* In holding that the complaint stated a claim under § 10(b) and Rule 10b–5, the court explained:

> Plaintiff alleges that defendants knowingly or recklessly made material misrepresentations which inflated the market price for Bell stock, and that he relied on the market price as reflecting Bell's true value. As a result, plaintiff claims to have suffered injury as a stock purchaser.

Id. at 107.

We interpret *Scattergood* and *Hayes* as holding that, where the claimed loss involves the purchase of a security at a price that is inflated due to an alleged misrepresentation, there is a sufficient causal nexus between the loss and the alleged misrepresentation to satisfy the loss causation requirement. Cf. Sowell v. Butcher & Singer, Inc., 926 F.2d 289, 297 (3d Cir.1991) (stating that the difference between the purchase price and the "true value" of the security at the time of the purchase is the "proper measure of damages to reflect the loss proximately caused by the defendants' deceit") (quoting Huddleston v. Herman & MacLean, 640 F.2d 534, 555 (5th Cir.1981) modified on other grounds, 459 U.S. 375, 103 S. Ct. 683, 74 L. Ed. 2d 548 (1983)). We note, however, that those decisions assume that the artificial inflation was actually "lost" due to the alleged fraud. Where the value of the security does not actually decline as a result of an alleged misrepresentation, it cannot be said that there is in fact an economic loss attributable to that misrepresentation. In the absence of a correction in the market price, the cost of the alleged misrepresentation is still incorporated into the value of the security and may be recovered at any time simply by reselling the security at the inflated price. See Green v. Occidental Petroleum Corp., 541 F.2d 1335, 1345 (9th Cir.1976) (Sneed, J., concurring) (stating that an investor's proximate losses are limited to those amounts that are attributable to the unrecovered inflation in the purchase price). Because a plaintiff in an action under § 10(b) and Rule 10b–5 must prove that he or she suffered an actual economic loss, we are persuaded that an investor must also establish that the alleged misrepresentations proximately caused the decline in the security's value to satisfy the element of loss causation.

We find the Eleventh Circuit's decision in Robbins v. Koger Properties, Inc., 116 F.3d 1441, 1448 (11th Cir.1997), instructive of this point. In that case, a group of investors filed a class action lawsuit against Kroger Properties, Inc. ("KPI"), its officers, and its independent accountant pursuant to § 10(b) and Rule 10b–5 when the price of KPI stock dropped following a dividend cut. See *id. at 1445.* Only the suit against the independent accountant proceeded to trial. See id. At trial, the investors presented evidence that the independent accounting firm made fraudulent statements which inflated the price at which they purchased KPI stock. See *id. at 1445–46*. It was also shown, however, that the dividend cut and the drop in the price of KPI stock occurred more than one year before the fraud was uncovered, and that the board of directors cut the dividend for reasons unrelated to the alleged fraud. See *id. at 1445, 1448*. The independent accountant moved for judgment as a matter of law, contending that the investors had failed to prove the essential element of loss causation. See *id. at 1446*. The district court denied the accountant's motion, and the Eleventh Circuit reversed. See *id. at 1446, 1449*. The Eleventh Circuit held that the investors had failed to satisfy the loss causation requirement, because they did not present evidence that the artificial inflation was removed from the market price of KPI stock, thereby causing a loss. See *id. at 1446*. In entering judgment in favor of the accountant, the court noted that the misrepresentations were not discovered until more than one year after the drop in the stock price, and that the investors had not presented any evidence that the cut in dividends, which led to the drop in price, was related to the alleged misrepresentations. See *id. at 1446–47*.

Turning to the complaint at issue in this case, we are persuaded that the Class has alleged sufficient facts to show that the alleged misrepresentations proximately caused the claimed loss. The Class contends that it purchased shares of ABI common stock at a price that was inflated due to the alleged misrepresentations, and that it suffered a loss when the truth was made known and the price of ABI common stock returned to its true value. The complaint states, in relevant part:

> 94. As a result of the Cendant Defendants' fraudulent conduct as alleged herein, the prices at which ABI securities traded were artificially inflated throughout the Class Period. When plaintiff and the other members of the Class purchased their ABI securities, the true value of such securities was substantially lower than the prices paid by plaintiff and the other members of the Class. The market price of ABI common stock declined sharply from its March 23, 1998, $64–7/16 per share closing price, to its September 29, 1998, $43 per share closing price. By October 13, 1998, ABI's closing price dropped to $35–1/2. In ignorance of the materially false and misleading nature of the statements and documents complained of herein, as well as of the adverse, undisclosed information known to defendants, plaintiff and the other members of the Class relied, to their detriment on such statements and documents, and/or on the integrity of the market, in purchasing their ABI common stock at artificially inflated prices during the Class Period. Had plaintiff and the other members of the Class known the truth, they would not have taken such action.

> 95. At all relevant times, the misrepresentations and omissions particularized in this Amended Complaint directly or proximately caused, or were a substantial contributing cause of, the damages sustained by plaintiff and the other members of the Class. The misstatements and omissions complained of herein had the effect of creating in the market an unrealistically positive assessment of Cendant, as well as of its financial condition, causing ABI's common stock to be overvalued and artificially inflated at all relevant times. Defendants' false portrayal, during the Class Period, of the Company's operations and prospects, as well as of Cendant's financial condition, resulted in purchases of ABI securities by plaintiff and by the other members of the Class at artificially inflated prices measured by the

difference between the market prices and the actual value of such securities at the time of purchase, thus causing the damages complained of
herein.

* * *97. As a direct and proximate result of defendants' aforesaid
wrongful conduct during the Class Period, plaintiff and other members of
the Class have suffered substantial damages in connection with their
purchases of ABI common stock.

The complaint further indicates that the price of ABI common stock was
"buoyed" by the defendants alleged misrepresentations, and that it dropped in
response to disclosure of the alleged misrepresentations and the termination of
the merger agreement. Assuming the truth of those allegations, and taking all
reasonable inferences in the light most favorable to the Class, we agree that the
Class is entitled to offer evidence to support its claim.

Notwithstanding the allegations of the complaint, however, the defendants
maintain that the price of ABI common stock was inflated, not by the alleged
misrepresentations, but rather by AIG's $58 tender offer and by the approval of
the merger agreement by the board of directors of ABI. We do not agree. The
Class period covers persons who purchased shares of ABI common stock prior
to both events. For those purchasers, neither the competing tender offer nor
the board approval of the merger agreement could have provided an independent valuation that would have inflated the price of ABI common stock.

Nor can we say, for the Class members who purchased shares of ABI
common stock after that time, that the announcement of AIG's $58 bid and the
approval of the merger agreement were sufficient to destroy the causal connection between the alleged misrepresentations and the artificial inflation in the
price of ABI common stock. It is well established that not every intervening
event is sufficient to break the chain of causation. See Rankow v. First Chicago
Corp., 870 F.2d 356, 367 (7th Cir.1989) (stating that to allow any intervening
change in market conditions not directly caused by the defendant to break the
chain of causation and exempt the defendant from liability would eviscerate
Rule 10b–5); W. Page Keeton et al., Prosser & Keeton on the Law of Torts § 44
(5th ed. 1984) (explaining that proximate causation is not destroyed by every
intervening event). So long as the alleged misrepresentations were a substantial
cause of the inflation in the price of a security and in its subsequent decline in
value, other contributing forces will not bar recovery. See Robbins, 116 F.3d at
1447 n.5. While we are mindful that the defendants may disprove that the Class
suffered a loss as a result of the alleged misrepresentations by showing that the
misrepresentations were not a substantial factor in setting the price of ABI
common stock during the Class period, we disagree that the defendants may do
so at this stage of the proceedings. See In re Burlington Coat Factory Sec.
Litig., 114 F.3d at 1420 (setting forth the standard for reviewing a motion to
dismiss). It is possible that one portion of the inflation was attributable to both
the competing tender offer and the board approval of the merger agreement,
and that the remaining portion of the inflation was attributable to the alleged
misrepresentations. It is equally reasonable to infer that the alleged misrepresentations played a substantial role in the decision of the board of directors of
ABI to approve the merger agreement, especially considering the fact that ABI
shareholders were to receive Cendant common stock in exchange for their
shares of ABI common stock.

We also disagree with the defendants' contention that the mutual termination of the merger agreement was an intervening event that caused the

Class's loss. The complaint alleges that the market price of the common stock of both ABI and Cendant declined in response to the alleged fraud. From that allegation, it is reasonable to conclude that the disclosure of the falsity of the alleged misrepresentations played a substantial factor in the termination of the merger agreement. Indeed, it is possible that the board of directors of ABI no longer found it beneficial for its shareholders to exchange shares of ABI common stock for shares of Cendant common stock following the discovery of Cendant's true financial condition. In light of the sharp decline in the price of Cendant common stock, it is also reasonable to infer that the board of directors of Cendant sought to cancel the merger to avoid diluting the shares of its existing shareholders. We therefore agree with the contentions of the Class and conclude that the complaint alleges sufficient facts to establish the element of loss causation.

CONCLUSION

In sum, we conclude that the complaint alleges sufficient facts to establish the elements of reliance and loss causation. We do not resolve, however, whether the complaint also satisfies the "in connection with" requirement; nor do we consider whether the complaint complies with the heightened pleading requirements of Rule 9(b). Rather, we vacate the judgment of the district court and remand this matter so that the district court may determine, in the first instance, whether the alleged misrepresentations were material and publicly disseminated in a reliable medium and, in the case of Ernst & Young, whether it was reasonably foreseeable that Cendant would use its financial statements and audit reports in its tender offer for shares of ABI common stock. We also instruct the district court to consider whether the complaint nevertheless should be dismissed for a failure to plead scienter with particularity. Because we do not resolve whether the dismissal was proper under § 10(b) and Rule 10b–5, we do not address the merits of the dismissal of the Class's claim under § 20(a).

SEC v. Zandford

United States Supreme Court, 2002.
___ U.S. ___, 122 S.Ct. 1899, 153 L.Ed.2d 1.

■ STEVENS, J., delivered the opinion for a unanimous Court.

The Securities and Exchange Commission (SEC) filed a civil complaint alleging that a stockbroker violated both § 10(b) of the Securities Exchange Act of 1934, 48 Stat. 891, as amended, 15 U.S.C. § 78j(b), and the SEC's Rule 10b–5, by selling his customer's securities and using the proceeds for his own benefit without the customer's knowledge or consent. The question presented is whether the alleged fraudulent conduct was "in connection with the purchase or sale of any security" within the meaning of the statute and the rule.

I

Between 1987 and 1991, respondent was employed as a securities broker in the Maryland branch of a New York brokerage firm. In 1987, he persuaded William Wood, an elderly man in poor health, to open a joint investment account for himself and his mentally retarded daughter. According to the SEC's complaint, the "stated investment objectives for the account were 'safety of principal and income.'" App. to Pet. for Cert. 27a. The Woods granted respondent discretion to manage their account and a general power of attorney to engage in securities transactions for their benefit without prior approval. Relying on respondent's promise to "conservatively invest" their money, the Woods entrusted him with $419,255. Before Mr. Wood's death in 1991, all of that money was gone.

In 1991, the National Association of Securities Dealers (NASD) conducted a routine examination of respondent's firm and discovered that on over 25 separate occasions, money had been transferred from the Woods' account to accounts controlled by respondent. In due course, respondent was indicted in the United States District Court for the District of Maryland on 13 counts of wire fraud in violation of 18 U.S.C. § 1343. App. to Pet. for Cert. 40a. The first count alleged that respondent sold securities in the Woods' account and then made personal use of the proceeds. *Id.*, at 42a. Each of the other counts alleged that he made wire transfers between Maryland and New York that enabled him to withdraw specified sums from the Woods' accounts. *Id.*, at 42a–50a. Some of those transfers involved respondent writing checks to himself from a mutual fund account held by the Woods, which required liquidating securities in order to redeem the checks. Respondent was convicted on all counts, sentenced to prison for 52 months, and ordered to pay $10,800 in restitution.

After respondent was indicted, the SEC filed a civil complaint in the same District Court alleging that respondent violated § 10(b) and Rule 10b–5 by engaging in a scheme to defraud the Woods and by misappropriating approximately $343,000 of the Woods' securities without their knowledge or consent. *Id.*, at 27a. * * *

* * * In its role enforcing the Act, the SEC has consistently adopted a broad reading of the phrase "in connection with the purchase or sale of any security." It has maintained that a broker who accepts payment for securities that he never intends to deliver, or who sells customer securities with intent to misappropriate the proceeds, violates § 10(b) and Rule 10b–5. See, *e.g., In re Bauer*, 26 S. E. C. 770 (1947); *In re Southeastern Securities Corp.*, 29 S. E. C. 609 (1949). This interpretation of the ambiguous text of § 10(b), in the context of formal adjudication, is entitled to deference if it is reasonable, see *United States* v. *Mead Corp.*, 533 U.S. 218, 229–230, and n. 12 (2001). For the reasons set forth below, we think it is. While the statute must not be construed so broadly as to convert every common-law fraud that happens to involve securities into a violation of § 10(b), *Marine Bank* v. *Weaver*, 455 U.S. 551, 556, 71 L. Ed. 2d 409, 102 S. Ct. 1220 (1982) ("Congress, in enacting the securities laws, did not intend to provide a broad federal remedy for all fraud"), neither the SEC nor this Court has ever held that there must be a misrepresentation about the value of a particular security in order to run afoul of the Act.

The SEC claims respondent engaged in a fraudulent scheme in which he made sales of his customer's securities for his own benefit. Respondent submits that the sales themselves were perfectly lawful and that the subsequent misappropriation of the proceeds, though fraudulent, is not properly viewed as having the requisite connection with the sales; in his view, the alleged scheme is not materially different from a simple theft of cash or securities in an investment account. We disagree.

According to the complaint, respondent "engaged in a scheme to defraud" the Woods beginning in 1988, shortly after they opened their account, and that scheme continued throughout the 2–year period during which respondent made a series of transactions that enabled him to convert the proceeds of the sales of the Woods' securities to his own use. App. to Pet. for Cert. 27a–29a. The securities sales and respondent's fraudulent practices were not independent events. This is not a case in which, after a lawful transaction had been consummated, a broker decided to steal the proceeds and did so. Nor is it a case in which a thief simply invested the proceeds of a routine conversion in the stock market. Rather, respondent's fraud coincided with the sales themselves.

Taking the allegations in the complaint as true, each sale was made to further respondent's fraudulent scheme; each was deceptive because it was neither authorized by, nor disclosed to, the Woods. With regard to the sales of shares in the Woods' mutual fund, respondent initiated these transactions by writing a check to himself from that account, knowing that redeeming the check would require the sale of securities. Indeed, each time respondent "exercised his power of disposition for his own benefit," that conduct, "without more," was a fraud. *United States* v. *Dunn,* 268 U.S. 121 (1925). In the aggregate, the sales are properly viewed as a "course of business" that operated as a fraud or deceit on a stockbroker's customer.

Insofar as the connection between respondent's deceptive practices and his sale of the Woods' securities is concerned, the case is remarkably similar to *Superintendent of Ins. of N. Y.* v. *Bankers Life & Casualty Co.,* 404 U.S. 6 (1971). In that case the directors of Manhattan Casualty Company authorized the sale of the company's portfolio of treasury bonds because they had been "duped" into believing that the company would receive the proceeds of the sale. *Id.,* at 9. We held that "Manhattan was injured as an investor through a deceptive device which deprived it of any compensation for the sale of its valuable block of securities." *Id.,* at 10. In reaching this conclusion, we did not ask, as the Fourth Circuit did in this case, whether the directors were misled about the value of a security or whether the fraud involved "manipulation of a particular security." 238 F.3d, at 565. In fact, we rejected the Second Circuit's position in *Superintendent of Ins. of N. Y.* v. *Bankers Life & Casualty Co.,* 430 F.2d 355, 361 (1970), that because the fraud against Manhattan did not take place within the context of a securities exchange it was not prohibited by § 10(b). 404 U.S., at 10. We refused to read the statute so narrowly, noting that it "must be read flexibly, not technically and restrictively." *Id.,* at 12. Although we recognized that the interest in " 'preserving the integrity of the securities markets,' " was one of the purposes animating the statute, we rejected the notion that § 10(b) is limited to serving that objective alone. *Ibid.* ("We agree that Congress by § 10(b) did not seek to regulate transactions which constitute no more than internal corporate mismanagement. But we read § 10(b) to mean that Congress meant to bar deceptive devices and contrivances in the purchase or sale of securities whether conducted in the organized markets or face to face").

Like the company directors in *Bankers Life*, the Woods were injured as investors through respondent's deceptions, which deprived them of any compensation for the sale of their valuable securities. They were duped into believing respondent would "conservatively invest" their assets in the stock market and that any transactions made on their behalf would be for their benefit for the " 'safety of principal and income.' " App. to Pet. for Cert. 27a. The fact that respondent misappropriated the proceeds of the sales provides persuasive evidence that he had violated § 10(b) when he made the sales, but misappropriation is not an essential element of the offense. Indeed, in *Bankers Life,* we flatly stated that it was "irrelevant" that "the proceeds of the sale that were due the seller were misappropriated." 404 U.S. 6 at 10. It is enough that the scheme to defraud and the sale of securities coincide.

The Court of Appeals below distinguished *Bankers Life* on the ground that it involved an affirmative misrepresentation, whereas respondent simply failed to inform the Woods of his intent to misappropriate their securities. 238 F.3d, at 566. We are not persuaded by this distinction. Respondent was only able to carry out his fraudulent scheme without making an affirmative misrepresentation because the Woods had trusted him to make transactions in their best interest without prior approval. Under these circumstances, respondent's fraud represents an even greater threat to investor confidence in the securities industry than the misrepresentation in *Bankers Life*. Not only does such a fraud prevent investors from trusting that their brokers are executing transactions for their benefit, but it undermines the value of a discretionary account like that held by the Woods. The benefit of a discretionary account is that it enables individuals, like the Woods, who lack the time, capacity, or know-how to supervise investment decisions, to delegate authority to a broker who will make decisions in their best interests without prior approval. If such individuals cannot rely on a broker to exercise that discretion for their benefit, then the account loses its added value. Moreover, any distinction between omissions and misrepresentations is illusory in the context of a broker who has a fiduciary duty to her clients. See *Chiarella* v. *United States,* 445 U.S. 222, 230 (1980) (noting that "silence in connection with the purchase or sale of securities may operate as a fraud actionable under § 10(b)" when there is "a duty to disclose arising from a relationship of trust and confidence between parties to a transaction"); *Affiliated Ute Citizens of Utah* v. *United States,* 406 U.S., at 153.

More recently, in *Wharf (Holdings) Ltd.* v. *United Int'l Holdings, Inc.,* 532 U.S. 588 (2001), our decision that the seller of a security had violated § 10(b) focused on the secret intent of the seller when the sale occurred. The purchaser claimed "that Wharf sold it a security (the option) while secretly intending from the very beginning not to honor the option." *Id.,* at 597. Although Wharf did not specifically argue that the breach of contract underlying the complaint lacked the requisite connection with a sale of securities, it did assert that the case was merely a dispute over ownership of the option, and that interpreting § 10(b) to include such a claim would convert every breach of contract that happened to involve a security into a violation of the federal securities laws. *Id.,* at 596. We rejected that argument because the purchaser's claim was not that the defendant failed to carry out a promise to sell securities; rather, the claim was that the defendant sold a security while never intending to honor its agreement in the first place. *Id.,* at 596–597. Similarly, in this case the SEC claims respondent sold the Woods' securities while secretly intending from the very beginning to keep the proceeds. In *Wharf,* the fraudulent intent deprived the purchaser of the benefit of the sale whereas here the fraudulent intent deprived the seller of that benefit, but the connection between the deception and the sale in each case is identical.

In *United States* v. *O'Hagan,* 521 U.S. 642 (1997), we held that the defendant had committed fraud "in connection with" a securities transaction when he used misappropriated confidential information for trading purposes. We reasoned that "the fiduciary's fraud is consummated, not when the fiduciary gains the confidential information, but when, without disclosure to his principal, he uses the information to purchase or sell securities. The securities transaction and the breach of duty thus coincide. This is so even though the person or entity defrauded is not the other party to the trade, but is, instead, the source of the nonpublic information." *Id.*, at 655–656. The Court of Appeals distinguished *O'Hagan* by reading it to require that the misappropriated information or assets not have independent value to the client outside the securities market, 238 F.3d, at 565. We do not read *O'Hagan* as so limited. In the chief passage cited by the Court of Appeals for this proposition, we discussed the Government's position that "the misappropriation theory would not . . . apply to a case in which a person defrauded a bank into giving him a loan or embezzled cash from another, and then used the proceeds of the misdeed to purchase securities," because in that situation "the proceeds would have value to the malefactor apart from their use in a securities transaction, and the fraud would be complete as soon as the money was obtained." 521 U.S., at 656 (internal quotation marks omitted). Even if this passage could be read to introduce a new requirement into § 10(b), it would not affect our analysis of this case, because the Woods' securities did not have value for respondent apart from their use in a securities transaction and the fraud was not complete before the sale of securities occurred.

As in *Bankers Life, Wharf,* and *O'Hagan,* the SEC complaint describes a fraudulent scheme in which the securities transactions and breaches of fiduciary duty coincide. Those breaches were therefore "in connection with" securities sales within the meaning of § 10(b).[4] Accordingly, the judgment of the Court of Appeals is reversed, and the case is remanded for further proceedings consistent with this opinion.

THE IN CONNECTION WITH AND CAUSATION REQUIREMENTS

Few securities law topics are more complicated than the in connection with and causation requirements of Rule 10b–5. To some extent the complexity is semantic. Torts law is complicated enough with its requirements of "causation in fact," "but for causation" (which is really reliance), and "legal" or "proximate cause." Recent cases under Rule 10b–5 have also adopted an alternative vocabulary employing the terms "loss causation" and "transaction causation."[1]

---

4. Contrary to the Court of Appeals' prediction, 238 F.3d 559, 566 (C.A.4 2001), our analysis does not transform every branch of fiduciary duty into a federal securities violation. If, for example, a broker embezzles cash from a client's account or takes advantage of the fiduciary relationship to induce his client into a fraudulent real estate transaction, then the fraud would not include the requisite connection to a purchase or sale of securities. Tr. of Oral Arg. 16. Likewise if the broker told his client he was stealing the client's assets, that breach of fiduciary duty might be in connection with a sale of securities, but it would not involve a deceptive device or fraud. Cf. *Santa Fe Industries, Inc. v. Green,* 430 U.S. 462, 474–476 (1977).

1. In LHLC Corp. v. Cluett, Peabody & Co., Inc., 842 F.2d 928, 931 (7th Cir.1988), *cert. denied,* 488 U.S. 926 (1988), Judge Easterbrook, while conceding that the terms are "confusing," stated that: "The plaintiff must show both [transaction causation and loss causation]. 'Loss Causation' means that the investor would not have suffered a loss if the facts were what he believed them to be; 'transaction causation' means that the investor would not have engaged in the transaction had the other party made truthful statements at the time required." He also stated that: "Used without care, these terms hinder rather than facilitate understanding." Ibid. See also Bastian v. Petren Resources Corp., 892 F.2d 680, 683–685 (7th Cir.1990), *cert. denied,* 496 U.S. 906 (1990): "'Loss causation' is an exotic name—perhaps an unhappy one, LHLC Corp. v. Cluett, Peabody & Co., 842 F.2d 928, 931 (7th Cir.1988)—for the standard rule of tort law that the plaintiff must allege and prove that, but for the defendant's wrongdoing, the plaintiff would not have incurred the harm of which he complains."

To some extent the complexity is a product of the phraseology of § 10b–5 and Rule 10b–5. Both require that a fraud be "in connection with the purchase or sale of any security." A good deal of the difficulty is traceable to Justice Douglas' reference in an early Supreme Court Rule 10b–5 case (involving a complex fraud in which an insurance company was bought with its own assets) to the plaintiff's having "suffered an injury as a result of deceptive practices touching its sale of securities as an investor."[2] Professor Louis Loss has popularized the idea that Justice Douglas' use of "touching" was nothing more than a variation of "in connection with" as a matter of literary style.[3]

Be that as it may, the lower courts have generally construed the "in connection with" element as adumbrated by *Superintendent of Insurance* to require "some nexus but not necessarily a direct and close relationship" between the fraud and the purchase or sale of a security.[4] The difficulty has been in identifying how close a nexus.

In Chemical Bank v. Arthur Andersen & Co.,[5] where Frigitemp pledged 100 percent of the stock in its wholly owned subsidiary, Elsters, as security for bank loans, it was not enough to allege a misstatement by the *parent's* auditor with respect to the financial condition of the parent. Judge Friendly wrote:

> The purpose of § 10(b) and Rule 10b–5 is to protect persons who are deceived in securities transactions—to make sure that buyers of securities get what they think they are getting and that sellers of securities are not tricked into parting with something for a price known to the buyer to be inadequate or for a consideration not to be what it purports to be. Andersen is not alleged to have deceived the Banks with respect to the pledge of the Elsters' stock; the Banks got exactly what they expected. Their showing is simply that but for Andersen's description of Frigitemp they would not have renewed the Frigitemp loans or made the Elsters' loan which Frigitemp guaranteed, and that if they had not done this, there would have been no pledge of Elsters' stock. Such "but-for" causation is not enough. The Act and Rule impose liability for a proscribed act in connection with the purchase or sale of a security; it is not sufficient to allege that a defendant has committed a proscribed act in a transaction of which the pledge of a security is a part.

The Second Circuit subsequently distinguished *Chemical Bank* where misrepresentations about the financial condition of a broker-dealer that were held to be in connection with loan transactions concerned the broker-dealer's financial strength and were directly related to its ability to carry out its contractual obligations.[6] "[I]n the instant case, securities were transferred as a direct result of a misrepresentations, whereas in Chemical Bank the direct result of the misrepresentations was a loan and not a securities transfer."[7]

2. Superintendent of Ins. of State of N.Y. v. Bankers Life & Casualty Co., 404 U.S. 6, 12–13 (1971).

3. *See, e.g.,* Chemical Bank v. Arthur Andersen & Co., 726 F.2d 930, 942 (2d Cir. 1984), *cert. denied,* 469 U.S. 884 (1984) ("We are inclined to agree with Professor Loss, that 'there is no reason to believe that the Justice's use of 'touching' was anything more than his variation of 'in connection with' as a matter of literary style'").

4. *See, e.g.,* Abrams v. Oppenheimer Gov't Sec., Inc., 737 F.2d 582 (7th Cir.1984).

5. 726 F.2d 930, 943 (2d Cir.1984), *cert. denied,* 469 U.S. 884 (1984).

6. SEC v. Drysdale Sec. Corp., 785 F.2d 38, 41–43 (2d Cir.1986), *cert. denied sub nom.* Essner v. SEC, 476 U.S. 1171 (1986).

7. Id. at 43. In Ames Dep't Stores, Inc. Stock Litig., 991 F.2d 953, 963 (2d Cir.1993), the Second Circuit reversed a district court

Some courts, willing to go further than the Second Circuit did in *Chemical Bank*, have construed the "in connection with" element to "contemplate a causal connection between the alleged fraud and the purchase or sale of stock."[8] One lower court rationalized the less demanding standard Justice Douglas articulated in Superintendent of Insurance v. Bankers Life by observing:

> While it may be that *Bankers Life* suggests that the "connection" element of § 10(b) is not precisely the same as causation, since the bond sale only *made possible* the accomplishment of the fraud as opposed to having caused it, the two concepts are similar to one another. This is so because both the "connection" and "causation" principles speak to the degree of proximity required between a misrepresentation and a securities transaction.[9]

Semerenko is typical of recent cases in recognizing that in addition to the connection with element a plaintiff also may have to separately prove transaction causation (often, as in *Semerenko*, called reliance) and loss causation (invariably meaning proximate causation).

Transaction causation or reliance is often presumed, either by dint of the fraud or the market doctrine or under cases at least dating back to the Supreme Court decision in Affiliated Ute Citizens v. United States[10] when a plaintiff's claim is based on a defendant's material omission.[11] The basis for a presumption with respect to a material omission was aptly articulated by a later Second Circuit decision: "Because, in such situations, the plaintiff is unaware of the omitted information, the record generally fails to provide a basis from which a finder of fact may evaluate how the plaintiff would have reacted if he or she had been aware of the withheld information. * * * To saddle a plaintiff with proving the generally indeterminable fact of what would have happened but for the omission [or the misrepresentations that skewed the market value of stock] would reduce the protection against fraud afforded by Section 10(b)."[12]

dismissal for failure to state a claim, stating in part:

> [T]he district court evidently assumed that the only statements that are made in connection with the sale of stock are those made in the issuing documents. This reasoning would eliminate the vast majority of private Rule 10b–5 actions and subvert the 1934 Act's efforts to protect investors from deliberate fraud. The securities markets are highly sensitive to press releases and to information contained in all sorts of publicly released corporate documents, and the investor is foolish who would ignore such releases. In light of this, defendants have been held liable for misrepresentations in press releases, Basic Inc. v. Levinson, 485 U.S. 224 (1988), and for misrepresentations in corporate documents other than those issued to shareholders, Fischman v. Raytheon, 188 F.2d 783.

Similarly, in United States v. Russo, 74 F.3d 1383, 1391–1392 (2d Cir.1996), *cert. denied,* 519 U.S. 927 (1996), the court relied on *Ames* to conclude that fraudulent short sales made for the express purpose of financing a stock kiting scheme were sufficiently "in connection with" a manipulation to violate § 10(b) and Rule 10b–5.

8. See, e.g., Tully v. Mott Supermarkets, Inc., 540 F.2d 187, 194 (3d Cir.1976).

9. Ketchum v. Green, 557 F.2d 1022, 1029 (3d Cir.1977), *cert. denied*, 434 U.S. 940 (1977).

10. 406 U.S. 128, 153–154 (1972).

11. Affiliated Ute referred to this requirement as "causation in fact."

12. Litton Indus., Inc. v. Lehman Bros. Kuhn Loeb, Inc., 967 F.2d 742, 747–748 (2d Cir.1992).

Difficult questions have been posed with respect to transaction causation when a presumption is not appropriate. For example, do investors rely on an outside accountant's certificate when purchasing privately placed securities from an issuer? In AUSA Life Ins. Co. v. Ernst & Young,[13] a divided Second Circuit ruled against the Ernst & Young (E & Y) accounting firm on this issue: "This was not a situation where the notes were marketed en masse, and E & Y had a barely tangential role in the transaction. Rather, the purchasers of these private placement notes specifically required the audits of E & Y before purchasing the notes and as a condition of their purchase."[14]

Loss causation or proximate cause posed other complexities in Litton Industries, Inc. v. Lehman Brothers Kuhn Loeb Inc.[15] Litton Industries alleged that the price it paid for the acquisition of Itek Corporation was artificially inflated by insider trading in Itek's common stock. The Second Circuit wrote in part:

> Litton * * * argues that the same concerns that spawn a transaction causation presumption militate for a presumption that the Itek Board relied on the market—which, in the present context, would mean a presumption of one component of what Litton must prove to establish loss causation.
>
> Proof whether the Itek Board relied on the market, however, involves few of the evidentiary uncertainties exhibited in either the omission or fraud-on-the-market context. In the case at hand—unlike the omission situation—Itek knew of the crucial information, that the market price of Itek stock had risen and that Litton had plans to acquire Itek. And—unlike the fraud-on-the-market context—the face-to-face negotiations between the acquirer and the target boards in a friendly tender offer situation, as here, make the question of the target board's reliance an issue of determinable fact.
>
> Litton argues, relying on *Chris-Craft Industries*, that when loss causation requires proof of third-party reliance a presumption of third-party reliance is appropriate. In *Chris-Craft Industries*, we recognized that to establish the defendant's wrongful interference with plaintiff's tender offer to third-party shareholders, the plaintiff need not show that *it* relied upon defendant's violation. 480 F.2d at 373. We noted that when the harmful effect of the defendant's violation depends on the volition of third parties, the plaintiff need only demonstrate that the *third party* relied on the violation. Because it would have been "unduly burdensome" and "impractical" to require the plaintiff to prove that each shareholder relied on defendant's violation, in *Chris-Craft* we presumed the shareholders' reliance as well. *Id.* at 375. Litton claims that this amounted to a presumption of loss causation and, being a similarly situated plaintiff, it too should be accorded such a presumption. We disagree. In the case at hand, proof that the Itek Board relied on the market does not involve a *Chris-Craft*-like burden of establishing the inclinations of a large number of shareholders. We, therefore, affirm the district court's finding that Litton must prove actual reliance on the part of the Itek Board.
>
> To satisfy the loss causation requirement, Litton must establish that absent insider trading in Itek stock, Litton would have acquired Itek at a

13. 206 F.3d 202 (2d Cir.2000). **15.** 967 F.2d 742 (2d Cir.1992).
14. Id. at 209.

lower price per share. To demonstrate this, Litton must show that the appellees' trading caused the market price of Itek stock to rise *and* that the market price was a substantial factor in the Itek Board's assessment of Litton's offers. For the purposes of summary judgment, the appellees accepted the proposition that the trader defendants caused the market price of Itek stock to rise; therefore, the district court focused on whether, absent artificial inflation of the stock price, the Itek Board would have been willing to accept less than $48 per share. For the purposes of reviewing the district court's grant of summary judgment, we need only consider whether there is a genuine issue of whether the then-current market price of Itek stock played a substantial role in the Itek Board's decision. * * *

The district court decision probably has to be read as accepting the proposition that market price considerations played no role or a very insubstantial role in the Itek Board's decision. 709 F. Supp. at 447. It is difficult to imagine, however, any pricing decision by a responsible target board in which market price considerations played no role. The essential question in a tender offer, after all, is whether the offer is more attractive than the available alternatives. In assessing the alternative of continued independence, the market price of the stock is the central consideration, at least for the public shareholders in the usual situation. *See* Stout, *supra*, 99 Yale L.J. at 1282. From the record there is every indication that the Itek Board was aware of its responsibility to the shareholders. The most favorable interpretation of the district court's determination is that the Itek Board believed that the value of Itek stock was higher than any "market price plus premium" that Litton might have offered based on a market untainted by insider trading; thus the market price did not play a substantial role in the Itek Board's decision-making. *See* 709 F. Supp. at 446.

The district court based its decision on affidavits from members of Itek's Board—affidavits detailing the Board members' recollections of the transaction. These affidavits, indeed, provide evidence that the majority of the Board members in assessing the value of Itek stock looked primarily to what they referred to as the inherent value of the company, which they thought to be greater than the $46 per share initially offered by Litton. The question before us is whether these affidavits establish that there is no genuine issue of fact concerning whether, absent insider trading, Litton might have acquired Itek for less than $48 per share.

Litton argues that the fairness report prepared by First Boston, Itek's investment banker, reveals that the Itek Board was both aware of the market price plus premium method of pricing and itself relied on such a pricing method to evaluate Litton's offers. On January 12–13, 1983, First Boston presented a study to the Itek Board concerning Litton's offer. The study, which was fully explained to the Board in a series of presentations, detailed the market price of Itek stock between September 1, 1982 and January 10, 1983 and compared Litton's bid with bids for similarly situated companies with respect to the ratio of premium to market price. It also included a Value Line report on Itek that prominently displayed Itek's "recent price" of $32 and price/earnings ratio of 23.9. On the basis of its study, First Boston concluded that Litton's offer was fair. Although the Board members now deny that they relied on the methods set forth by the study, the schedule 14D–9 "Solicitation/Recommendation Statement" sent to the shareholders in connection with the $48 offer stated that the Board had relied in part on First Boston's report in reaching its recommendation. Itek Chairman Robert Henderson's letter to the shareholders recommending acceptance of the tender offer also indicated that careful consideration was given to First Boston's advice. Furthermore, the final price recommended by the Itek Board provides some circumstantial evidence that the Board may have relied on the market price plus premium. The closing price on January 11, 1983 was $32.50 per share. Calculating on the basis of this price, the market price plus 50% premium totals to $48.75—almost the exact price that the Itek Board approved on January 13.

In addition, although many of the Itek Board members recite that they relied on Itek's inherent value, there appears to have been neither a discussion of the inherent value of the company at the relevant Board meetings nor a report determining that value. In fact, the only assessment of Itek that might be construed as positing that the company's true value diverged from its market value was a three-year strategic plan, like others before it, did not discuss market price of the stock. Although the plan did not assess the company's value, Henderson and other Board members concluded, based on the plan that, if all went well, Itek stock would be selling at perhaps $50–$52 per share in three years. When faced with Litton's initial offer, however, Henderson himself determined that $46 was a fair offer when his valuation was discounted for risk. Although the majority of the Itek Board members now avow they would not have accepted the $46 offer, the record indicates that they did not reject Litton's initial offer. Instead, they sent Henderson back to the negotiating table to see if he could work out a better deal. When Litton offered $48 per share the Itek Board unanimously voted to recommend the offer to the shareholders, which suggests that the other Board members who believed that Itek stock was worth upwards of $50 per share also were willing to discount that value for market considerations. The Itek Board's conduct, thus, is open to more than one interpretation. The Itek Board's failure to reject the $46 offer and its willingness to accept $48 suggest that the Board members might have been in search of the best offer the market would bear instead of waiting for a bidder to match either what they believed was their company's inherent value or what the market price might reach in three to five years. The market price and current pricing practices may have been central to any assessment of what the market will bear.

In a situation such as this, in which thought processes of the Itek Board and the theory that best characterizes their conduct are at issue, caution must be exercised in granting summary judgment. *See* Wechsler v. Steinberg, 733 F.2d 1054, 1058–59 (2d Cir.1984) (concluding that in a section 10(b) scienter analysis "[i]ssues of motive and intent are usually inappropriate for disposition on summary judgment"). Exercising such caution, we find, when viewing the record in the light most favorable to Litton, that a reasonable jury might find market price was a substantial factor in the Itek Board's assessment of Litton's offer and that absent insider trading the Itek Board would have accepted less than $48 per share.[16]

---

16. Id. at 748–751.

A subsequent Second Circuit case went far towards harmonizing loss causation with the traditional torts law analysis of proximate cause:

The loss causation inquiry typically examines how directly the subject of the fraudulent statement caused the loss, and whether the resulting was a foreseeable outcome of the fraudulent statement. [Citations omitted.] Related factors include whether intervening causes are present [citations omitted] (and the lapse of time between defendant's actions and plaintiff's injury increases the likelihood that the loss occurred due to events in the interim). In the end, whether loss causation has been demonstrated presents a public policy question, the resolution of which is predicated upon notions of equity because it establishes who, if anyone, along the causal chain should be liable for the plaintiffs' losses. [Citation omitted.] A finding of foreseeability must satisfy the judicial mind that such result conforms to "a rough sense of justice." *Palsgraf v. L.I.R.R. Co.*, 248 N.Y. 339, 352, 162 N.E. 99 (1928) (Andrews, J., dissenting).[17]

In recent cases loss causation has been adequately alleged when a principal executive of a corporation provided investors with a modified background report on him and other principal executives that omitted negative events concerning their business and financial history.[18] The court elaborated:

A comparison of *Marbury Management, Inc. v. Kohn*, 629 F.2d 705 (2d Cir.1980) and *Bennett v. United States Trust Co.*, 770 F.2d 308 (2d Cir.1985), elucidates why the plaintiffs' allegations of loss causation are sufficiently particular. In *Marbury Management*, a trainee at a brokerage firm had falsely claimed that he was a stockbroker and "portfolio management specialist," and persuaded several clients to invest in his recommended stocks, overcoming the clients' own reservations. 629 F.2d at 707. We affirmed the jury verdict for the plaintiffs, stating that "only the loss that might reasonably be expected to result from action or inaction in reliance on a fraudulent misrepresentation is legally, that, proximately, caused by the misrepresentation." *Id.* at 708. In *Bennett*, conversely, we affirmed the dismissal of a complaint that alleged that the defendants had misrepresented to the plaintiffs that the Federal Reserve's margin rules did not apply to public utility shares pledged to a bank as collateral. The plaintiffs had alleged that they would not have invested if they knew the rules did in fact apply, and thus defendants were responsible for their losses when the value of the stock declined. *See* 770 F.2d at 310, 311.

We distinguished *Marbury Management* on the grounds that in that case the misrepresentation related to the value of the shares—specifically, the reliability of the trainee's valuation—while in *Bennett*, the misrepresentation related to rules extrinsic to the decline in the securities' value. *Id.* at 314. We went on to observe that had plaintiffs known the seller in *Marbury Management* was an inexperienced trainee without expertise they would not have accepted his recommendations to buy stock. *Id.* Such a misrepresentation, we thought, misled plaintiffs with respect to the "investment quality" of the stock, although the misrepresentation was not directly related to the stock's intrinsic investment characteristics. *Id.* Thus, because the misrepresentation in *Marbury Management* induced the pur-

17. Suez Equity Investors, L.P. v. Toronto–Dominion Bank, 250 F.3d 87, 96 (2d Cir.2001).

18. Id. at 93–94.

chase (transaction loss) and related to the stock's value (loss causation), it was causally related to the loss. In *Bennett*, since the margin rules were intrinsic to the stock, the complaint failed to allege loss causation. *See id.; see also Mfrs. Hanover Trust*, 801 F.2d at 22 (holding that misrepresentations by defendant accounting firm about the financial status of its client— a company trading in repurchase agreements—proximately caused the plaintiff's loss, those misrepresentations pertained to the "investment quality" of the repurchase agreement selected).

The rule derived from the holdings of *Marbury Management* and *Bennett* is that plaintiffs may allege transaction and loss causation by averring both that they would not have entered the transaction but for the misrepresentations *and* that the defendants' misrepresentations induced a disparity between the transaction price and the true "investment quality" of the securities at the time of transaction.[19]

PROBLEM 14–8

Larry Abel, the chief executive officer, of Kain, Inc., a closely held corporation, recently had dinner with his business school classmate, Margaret Jones, chief executive officer of Franklin Press, a thinly traded over-the-counter corporation. At the conclusion of dinner, they agreed to merge Kain, Inc. and Franklin Press. Three days later a formal merger agreement was signed with a press conference to make the announcement public scheduled one week later.

The day after the merger agreement signed, Afterman, a shareholder in Franklin Press, telephoned Franklin's public relations officer, and asked about "rumors of an impending major event." The public relations officer emphatically denied the rumors. Afterman promptly sold her Franklin stock at $20. After the merger was announced Franklin's stock rose to $30.

1. Can Afterman rely on the fraud on the market presumption to prove reliance?

2. Could Afterman prove reliance if her stock sale order had been placed before the conversation with the public relations officer?

3. Would an earlier originated stock sale order be "in connection with" a stock sale that occurred after Franklin's public relations officer made a material misrepresentation about Franklin's future?

4. Suppose Afterman could satisfy the reliance and in connection with requirements. Could Afterman establish loss causation for the difference between her $20 sales price per Franklin share and $30 price at which Franklin was quoted after the merger announcement if the relevant stock market index was up 25 percent?

5. Could Afterman establish loss causation if the Baucus Brothers decided the day after the merger agreement was signed to seek control of Franklin Press and their open market purchases pushed the trading price of Franklin to $25?

See generally 8 Louis Loss & Joel Seligman, Securities Regulation 3680–3687 (3d ed. 1991); 9 Louis Loss & Joel Seligman, Securities Regulation 4404–4408 (3d ed. 1992).

---

19. Id. at 97–98. Accord: Castellano v. Young & Rubicam, Inc., 257 F.3d 171, 187– 190 (2d Cir.2001).

6. STANDING

Blue Chip Stamps v. Manor Drug Stores

Supreme Court of the United States, 1975.
421 U.S. 723, 95 S.Ct. 1917, 44 L.Ed.2d 539.

■ MR. JUSTICE REHNQUIST delivered the opinion of the Court.

This case requires us to consider whether the offerees of a stock offering, made pursuant to an antitrust consent decree and registered under the Securities Act of 1933, 15 U.S.C. § 77a et seq. ("the 1933 Act"), may maintain a private cause of action for money damages where they allege that the offeror has violated the provisions of Rule 10b–5 of the Securities and Exchange Commission, but where they have neither purchased nor sold any of the offered shares. See Birnbaum v. Newport Steel Corp., 193 F.2d 461 (CA2), cert. denied, 343 U.S. 956 (1952).

I

In 1963 the United States filed a civil antitrust action against Blue Chip Stamp Company ("Old Blue Chip") a company in the business of providing trading stamps to retailers, and nine retailers who owned 90% of its shares. In 1967 the action was terminated by the entry of a consent decree. United States v. Blue Chip Stamp Co., 272 F.Supp. 432 (C.D.Cal.1967), aff'd sub nom. Thrifty Shoppers Scrip Co. v. United States, 389 U.S. 580 (1968). The decree contemplated a plan of reorganization whereby Old Blue Chip was to be merged into a newly formed corporation "New Blue Chip." The holdings of the majority shareholders of Old Blue Chip were to be reduced, and New Blue Chip, one of the petitioners here, was required under the plan to offer a substantial number of its shares of common stock to retailers who had used the stamp service in the past but who were not shareholders in the old company. Under the terms of the plan, the offering to nonshareholder users was to be proportional to past stamp usage and the shares were to be offered in units consisting of common stock and debentures.

The reorganization plan was carried out, the offering was registered with the SEC as required by the 1933 Act, and a prospectus was distributed to all offerees as required by § 5 of that Act. Somewhat more than 50% of the offered units were actually purchased. In 1970, two years after the offering, respondent, a former user of the stamp service and therefore an offeree of the 1968 offering, filed this suit in the United States District Court for the Central District of California. Defendants below and petitioners here are Old and New Blue Chip, eight of the nine majority shareholders of Old Blue Chip, and the directors of New Blue Chip (collectively called "Blue Chip").

Respondent's complaint alleged, *inter alia,* that the prospectus prepared and distributed by Blue Chip in connection with the offering was materially misleading in its overly pessimistic appraisal of Blue Chip's status and future prospects. It alleged that Blue Chip intentionally made the prospectus overly pessimistic in order to discourage respondent and other members of the allegedly large class whom it represents from accepting what was intended to be a bargain offer, so that the rejected shares might later be offered to the public at a higher price. The complaint alleged that class members because of and in reliance on the false and misleading prospectus failed to purchase the offered units. Respondent therefore sought on behalf of the alleged class some $21,400,000 in damages representing the lost opportunity to purchase the units; the right to purchase the previously rejected units at the 1968 price, and in addition, it sought some $25,000,000 in exemplary damages.

The only portion of the litigation thus initiated which is before us is whether respondent may base its action on Rule 10(b)(5) of the Securities and Exchange Commission without having either bought or sold the shares described in the allegedly misleading prospectus. * * *

     * * *

Despite the contrast between the provisions of Rule 10b–5 and the numerous carefully drawn express civil remedies provided in both the Acts of 1933 and 1934, it was held in 1946 by the United States District Court for the Eastern District of Pennsylvania that there was an implied private right of action under the Rule. Kardon v. National Gypsum Co., 69 F.Supp. 512 (1946). This Court had no occasion to deal with the subject until 20–odd years later, and at that time we confirmed with virtually no discussion the overwhelming consensus of the district courts and courts of appeals that such a cause of action did exist. Superintendent of Insurance v. Bankers Life and Casualty Co., 404 U.S. 6, 13 n. 9 (1971); Affiliated Ute Citizens v. United States, 406 U.S. 128, 150–154 (1972). Such a conclusion was, of course, entirely consistent with the Court's recognition in J.I. Case Co. v. Borak, 377 U.S. 426, 432 (1964), that private enforcement of Commission rules may "[provide] a necessary supplement to Commission action."

Within a few years after the seminal *Kardon* decision the Court of Appeals for the Second Circuit concluded that the plaintiff class for purposes of a private damage action under § 10(b) and Rule 10b–5 was limited to actual purchasers and sellers of securities. Birnbaum v. Newport Steel Corp., *supra*.

The Court of Appeals in this case did not repudiate *Birnbaum;* indeed, another panel of that court (in an opinion by Judge Ely) had but a short time earlier affirmed the rule of that case. Mount Clemens Industries v. Bell, 464 F.2d 339 (C.A.9 1972). But in this case a majority of the Court of Appeals found that the facts warranted an exception to the *Birnbaum* rule. For the reasons hereinafter stated, we are of the opinion that *Birnbaum* was rightly decided, and that it bars respondent from maintaining this suit under Rule 10b–5.

III

The panel which decided *Birnbaum* consisted of Chief Judge Swan and Judges Learned Hand and Augustus Hand: the opinion was written by the latter. Since both § 10(b) and Rule 10b–5 proscribed only fraud "in connection with the purchase or sale" of securities, and since the history of § 10(b) revealed no congressional intention to extend a private civil remedy for money damages to other than defrauded purchasers or sellers of securities in contrast to the express civil remedy provided by § 16(b) of the 1934 Act, the court concluded that the plaintiff class in a Rule 10b–5 action was limited to actual purchasers and sellers. 193 F.2d 461, 463–464.

Just as this Court had no occasion to consider the validity of the *Kardon* holding that there was a private cause of action under Rule 10b–5 until 20–odd years later, nearly the same period of time has gone by between the *Birnbaum* decision and our consideration of the case now before us. As with *Kardon,* virtually all lower federal courts facing the issue in the hundreds of reported cases presenting this question over the past quarter century have reaffirmed *Birnbaum's* conclusion that the plaintiff class for purposes of § 10(b) and Rule 10b–5 private damage action is limited to purchasers and sellers of securities. * * *

In 1957 and again in 1959, the Securities and Exchange Commission sought from Congress amendment of § 10(b) to change its wording from "in connection with the purchase of sale of any security" to "in connection with the purchase or sale of, *or any attempt to purchase or sell,* any security." (Emphasis added.) 103 Cong.Rec. 11636 (1957); SEC Legislation, Hearings before Subcom. of Sen.Com. on Banking & Currency on S. 1178–1182, 86th Cong., 1st Sess., 367–368 (1959); S. 2545, 85th Cong., 1st Sess. (1957); S. 1179, 86th Cong., 1st Sess. (1959). In the words of a memorandum submitted by the Commission to a congressional committee, the purpose of the proposed change was "to make section 10(b) also applicable to manipulative activities in connection with any attempt to purchase or sell any security." Hearings on S. 1178–1182, *supra,* at 331. Opposition to the amendment was based on fears of the extension of civil liability under § 10(b) that it would cause. Id., at 368. Neither change was adopted by Congress.

The longstanding acceptance by the courts, coupled with Congress' failure to reject *Birnbaum's* reasonable interpretation of the wording of § 10(b), wording which is directed towards injury suffered "in connection with the purchase or sale" of securities, argues significantly in favor of acceptance of the *Birnbaum* rule by this Court. Blau v. Lehman, 368 U.S. 403, 413 (1962).

Available extrinsic evidence from the texts of the 1933 and 1934 Acts as to the congressional scheme in this regard, though not conclusive, supports the result reached by the *Birnbaum* court. The wording of § 10(b) directed at fraud "in connection with the purchase or sale" of securities stands in contrast with the parallel antifraud provision of the 1933 Act, § 17(a)[6] reaching fraud "in the offer or sale" of securities. Cf. § 5 of the 1933 Act. When Congress wished to provide a remedy to those who neither purchase nor sell securities, it had little trouble in doing so expressly. Cf. § 16(b) of the 1934 Act, 15 U.S.C. § 78p.

Section 28(a) of the 1934 Act which limits recovery in any private damage action brought under the 1934 Act to "actual damages," likewise provides some support for the purchaser-seller rule. See, e.g., A. Bromberg, Securities Law: Fraud—SEC Rule 10b–5, § 8.8, at 221 (1968). While the damages suffered by purchasers and sellers pursuing a § 10(b) cause of action may on occasion be difficult to ascertain, Affiliated Ute Citizens v. United States, *supra,* 406 U.S. at 155, in the main such purchasers and sellers at least seek to base recovery on a demonstrable number of shares traded. In contrast, a putative plaintiff, who neither purchases nor sells securities, but sues instead for intangible economic injury such as loss of a noncontractual opportunity to buy or sell, is more likely to be seeking a largely conjectural and speculative recovery in which the number of shares involved will depend on the plaintiff's subjective hypothesis. Cf. Estate Counseling Service v. Merrill Lynch, Pierce, Fenner & Smith, 303

6. * * * We express, of course, no opinion on whether § 17(a) in light of the express civil remedies of the 1933 Act gives rise to an implied cause of action. Compare Greater Iowa Corp. v. McLendon, 378 F.2d 783, 788, 791 (C.A.8 1967), with Fischman v. Raytheon Mfg. Corp., 188 F.2d 783, 787 (C.A.2 1951). See, e.g., SEC v. Texas Gulf Sulphur Co., 401 F.2d 833, 867 (C.A.2 1968) (Opinion of Friendly, J., concurring), cert. denied, 394 U.S. 976 (1969); 3 L. Loss, Securities Regulation 1785 (1961).

F.2d 527, 533 (C.A.10 1962); Levine v. Seilon, Inc., 439 F.2d 328, 335 (C.A.2 1971); Wolf v. Frank, 477 F.2d 467, 478 (C.A.5 1973).

One of the justifications advanced for implication of a cause of action under § 10(b) lies in § 29(b) of the 1934 Act providing that a contract made in violation of any provision of the 1934 Act is voidable at the option of the deceived party. See e.g., Kardon v. National Gypsum Co., 69 F.Supp. 512, 514 (E.D.Pa.1946); Slavin v. Germantown Fire Insurance Co., 174 F.2d 799, 815 (C.A.3 1949); Fischman v. Raytheon Manufacturing Co., 188 F.2d 783, 787 n. 4 (C.A.2 1951); A. Bromberg, Securities Regulation: Fraud—SEC Rule 10b–5 § 2.4(1)(b) (1968). But that justification is absent when there is no actual purchase or sale of securities, or a contract to do so, affected or tainted by a violation of § 10(b). Cf. Mount Clemens Industries, Inc. v. Bell, *supra.*

The principal express nonderivative private civil remedies, created by Congress contemporaneously with the passage of § 10(b), for violations of various provisions of the 1933 and 1934 Acts are by their terms expressly limited to purchasers or sellers of securities. Thus § 11(a) of the 1933 Act confines the cause of action it grants to "any person acquiring the security" while the remedy granted by § 12 of that Act is limited to the "person purchasing the said security." Section 9 of the 1934 Act, prohibiting a variety of fraudulent and manipulative devices, limits the express civil remedy provided for its violation to "any person who shall purchase or sell any security" in a transaction affected by a violation of the provision. Section 18 of the 1934 Act, prohibiting false or misleading statements in reports or other documents required to be filed by the 1934 Act, limits the express remedy provided for its violation to "any person * * * who * * * shall have purchased or sold a security at a price which was affected by such statement * * *." It would indeed be anomalous to impute to Congress an intention to expand the plaintiff class for a judicially implied cause of action beyond the bounds it delineated for comparable express causes of action.

Having said all this, we would by no means be understood as suggesting that we are able to divine from the language of § 10(b) the express "intent of Congress" as to the contours of a private cause of action under Rule 10b–5. When we deal with private actions under Rule 10b–5, we deal with a judicial oak which has grown from little more than a legislative acorn. Such growth may be quite consistent with the congressional enactment and with the role of the federal judiciary in interpreting it, see J.I. Case v. Borak, *supra*, but it would be disingenuous to suggest that either Congress in 1934 or the Securities and Exchange Commission in 1942 foreordained the present state of the law with respect to Rule 10b–5. It is therefore proper that we consider, in addition to the factors already discussed, what may be described as policy considerations when we come to flesh out the portions of the law with respect to which neither the congressional enactment nor the administrative regulations offer conclusive guidance.

Three principal classes of potential plaintiffs are presently barred by the *Birnbaum* rule. First are potential purchasers of shares, either in a new offering or on the Nation's post-distribution trading markets, who alleged that they decided not to purchase because of an unduly gloomy representation or the omission of favorable material which made the issuer appear to be a less favorable investment vehicle than it actually was. Second are actual shareholders in the issuer who allege that they decided not to sell their shares because of an unduly rosy representation or a failure to disclose unfavorable material.

Third are shareholders, creditors, and perhaps others related to an issuer who suffered loss in the value of their investment due to corporate or insider activities in connection with the purchase or sale of securities which violate Rule 10b–5. It has been held that shareholder members of the second and third of these classes may frequently be able to circumvent the *Birnbaum* limitation through bringing a derivative action on behalf of the corporate issuer if the latter is itself a purchaser or seller of securities. See, e.g., Schoenbaum v. Firstbrook, 405 F.2d 215, 219 (C.A.2d.1968), cert. denied sub nom. Manley v. Schoenbaum, 395 U.S. 906 (1969). But the first of these classes, of which respondent is a member, can not claim the benefit of such a rule.

A great majority of the many commentators on the issue before us have taken the view that the *Birnbaum* limitation on the plaintiff class in a Rule 10b–5 action for damages is an arbitrary restriction which unreasonably prevents some deserving plaintiffs from recovering damages which have in fact been caused by violations of Rule 10b–5. See, e.g., Lowenfels, The Demise of the *Birnbaum* Doctrine: A New Era for Rule 10b–5, 54 Va.Law Rev. 268 (1968). The Securities and Exchange Commission has filed an *amicus* brief in this case espousing that same view. We have no doubt that this is indeed a disadvantage of the *Birnbaum* rule, and if it had no countervailing advantages it would be undesirable as a matter of policy, however much it might be supported by precedent and legislative history. But we are of the opinion that there are countervailing advantages to the *Birnbaum* rule, purely as a matter of policy, although those advantages are more difficult to articulate than is the disadvantage.

There has been widespread recognition that litigation under Rule 10b–5 presents a danger of vexatiousness different in degree and in kind from that which accompanies litigation in general. This fact was recognized by Judge Browning in his opinion for the majority of the Court of Appeals in this case, 492 F.2d 141, and by Judge Hufstedler in her dissenting opinion when she said:

> "The purchaser-seller rule has maintained the balances built into the congressional scheme by permitting damage actions to be brought only by those persons whose active participation in the marketing transaction promises enforcement of the statute without undue risk of abuse of the litigation process and without distorting the securities market." 492 F.2d 147.

Judge Friendly in commenting on another aspect of Rule 10b–5 litigation has referred to the possibility that unduly expansive imposition of civil liability "will lead to large judgments, payable in the last analysis by innocent investors, for the benefit of speculators and their lawyers. * * *." SEC v. Texas Gulf Sulphur Co., 401 F.2d 833, 867 (C.A.2 1968) (concurring opinion). See also Boone and McGowan, Standing to Sue under Rule 10b–5, 49 Tex.L.Rev. 617, 648–649 (1971).

We believe that the concern expressed for the danger of vexatious litigation which could result from a widely expanded class of plaintiffs under Rule 10b–5 is founded in something more substantial than the common complaint of the many defendants who would prefer avoiding lawsuits entirely to either settling them or trying them. These concerns have two largely separate grounds.

The first of these concerns is that in the field of federal securities laws governing disclosure of information even a complaint which by objective standards may have very little chance of success at trial has a settlement value to the plaintiff out of any proportion to its prospect of success at trial so long as he may prevent the suit from being resolved against him by dismissal or summary judgment. The very pendency of the lawsuit may frustrate or delay normal business activity of the defendant which is totally unrelated to the lawsuit. * * *

* * *

The second ground for fear of vexatious litigation is based on the concern that, given the generalized contours of liability, the abolition of the *Birnbaum* rule would throw open to the trier of fact many rather hazy issues of historical fact the proof of which depended almost entirely on oral testimony. We in no way disparage the worth and frequent high value of oral testimony when we say that dangers of its abuse appear to exist in this type of action to a peculiarly high degree. * * *

* * *

But in the absence of the *Birnbaum* rule, it would be sufficient for a plaintiff to prove that he had failed to purchase or sell stock by reason of a defendant's violation of Rule 10b–5. The manner in which the defendant's violation caused the plaintiff to fail to act could be as a result of the reading of a prospectus, as respondent claims here, but it could just as easily come as a result of a claimed reading of information contained in the financial pages of a local newspaper. Plaintiff's proof would not be that he purchased or sold stock, a fact which would be capable of documentary verification in most situations, but instead that he decided *not* to purchase or sell stock. Plaintiff's entire testimony could be dependent upon uncorroborated oral evidence of many of the crucial elements of his claim, and still be sufficient to go to the jury. The jury would not even have the benefit of weighing the plaintiff's version against the defendant's version, since the elements to which the plaintiff would testify would be in many cases totally unknown and unknowable to the defendant. The very real risk in permitting those in respondent's position to sue under Rule 10b–5 is that the door will be open to recovery of substantial damages on the part of one who offers only his own testimony to prove that he ever consulted a prospectus of the issuer, that he paid any attention to it, or that the representations contained in it damaged him. The virtue of the *Birnbaum* rule, simply stated, in this situation, is that it limits the class of plaintiffs to those who have at least dealt in the security to which the prospectus, representation, or omission relates. And their dealing in the security, whether by way of purchase or sale, will generally be an objectively demonstrable fact in an area of the law otherwise very much dependent upon oral testimony. In the absence of the *Birnbaum* doctrine, bystanders to the securities marketing process could await developments on the sidelines without risk, claiming that inaccuracies in disclosure caused non-selling in a falling market and that unduly pessimistic predictions by the issuer followed by a rising market caused them to allow retrospectively golden opportunities to pass.

* * *

IV

The majority of the Court of Appeals in this case expressed no disagreement with the general proposition that one asserting a claim for damages based on the violation of Rule 10b–5 must be either a purchaser or seller of securities. However, it noted that prior cases have held that persons owning contractual rights to buy or sell securities are not excluded by the *Birnbaum* rule. Relying on these cases, it concluded that respondent's status as an offeree pursuant to the terms of the consent decree served the same function, for purposes of delimiting the class of plaintiffs, as is normally performed by the requirement of a contractual relationship. 492 F.2d, at 142.

* * *

Even if we were to accept the notion that the *Birnbaum* rule could be circumvented on a case-by-case basis through particularized judicial inquiry into the facts surrounding a complaint, this respondent and the members of his alleged class would be unlikely candidates for such a judicially created exception. While the *Birnbaum* rule has been flexibly interpreted by lower federal courts, we have been unable to locate a single decided case from any court in the 20–odd years of litigation since the *Birnbaum* decision which would support the right of persons who were in the position of respondent here to bring a private suit under Rule 10b–5. Respondent was not only not a buyer or seller of any security but it was not even a shareholder of the corporate petitioners.

* * *

Reversed.

■ Mr. Justice Powell, with whom Mr. Justice Stewart and Mr. Justice Marshall join, concurring.

* * *

Mr. Justice Blackmun's dissent charges the Court with a "preternatural solicitousness for corporate well-being and a seeming callousness toward the investing public." Our task in this case is to construe a statute. In my view, the answer is plainly compelled by the language as well as the legislative history of the Securities Acts. But even if the language is not "plain" to all, I would have thought none could doubt that the statute can be read fairly to support the result the Court reaches. Indeed, if one takes a different view—and imputes callousness to all who disagree—he must attribute a lack of legal and social perception to the scores of federal judges who have followed *Birnbaum* for two decades.

The dissenting opinion also charges the Court with paying "no heed to the unremedied wrong" arising from the type of "fraud" that may result from reaffirmance of the *Birnbaum* rule. If an issue of statutory construction is to be decided on the basis of assuring a *federal* remedy—in addition to state remedies—for every perceived fraud, at least we should strike a balance between the opportunities for fraud presented by the contending views. It may well be conceded that *Birnbaum* does allow some fraud to go unremedied under the federal Securities Acts. But the construction advocated by the dissent could result in wider opportunities for fraud. As the Court's opinion makes plain, abandoning the *Birnbaum* construction in favor of the rule urged by the dissent would invite any person who failed to purchase a newly offered security that subsequently enjoyed substantial market appreciation to file a claim alleging that the offering prospectus understated the company's potential. The number of possible plaintiffs with respect to a public offering would be virtually unlimited. As noted above * * *, an honest offeror could be confronted with subjective claims by plaintiffs who had neither purchased its securities nor seriously considered the investment. It frequently would be impossible to refute a plaintiff's assertion that he relied on the prospectus, or even that he made a decision not to buy the offered securities. A rule allowing this type of open-ended litigation would itself be an invitation to fraud.[5]

■ MR. JUSTICE BLACKMUN, with whom MR. JUSTICE DOUGLAS and MR. JUSTICE BRENNAN join, dissenting.

* * *

Cowin v. Bresler

United States Court of Appeals, District of Columbia Circuit, 1984.
741 F.2d 410.

■ Before WRIGHT, WILKEY and BORK, CIRCUIT JUDGES.

■ BORK, CIRCUIT JUDGE:

Bresler & Reiner, Inc. is a publicly-owned company incorporated in the State of Delaware and engaged in the development and management of residential and commercial properties in the District of Columbia. In late 1980, Daniel Cowin, a Bresler & Reiner shareholder, sued the company and its directors on his own behalf. Cowin has a minority interest in the company. The individual directors-appellees, with their families, own in excess of 79% of the company's stock. Appellees Bresler and Reiner together hold more than 70% of the company's outstanding shares, and their control of the corporation is undisputed.

The thrust of Cowin's charges is that the appellees have manipulated the business for their personal profit at the expense of the minority shareholders. The complaint alleges numerous instances of corporate mismanagement, fraud, and self-dealing, all in breach of the common law fiduciary duty owed by the directors of the company to the appellant as a shareholder. Several of the challenged transactions involve deals between the company and certain limited partnerships in which the appellees, including Bresler and Reiner, have significant interests. The complaint also charges Bresler and Reiner with forcing the company to engage in a stock repurchase program at a time when the company was in default on its notes payable and having severe cash flow problems. Cowin alleges that appellees used, and are still using, the repurchase plan to "severely limit[ ] the public market for trading in Company stock"; according to appellant, their ultimate intent is to "[convert] the Company to a private corporation owned solely by" them for their own benefit. Brief for Plaintiff-Appellant at 14. To remedy the alleged common law violations, Cowin seeks damages for the diminished value of his stock and injunctions against the allegedly wrongful transactions. He also requests the appointment of a receiver to liquidate the company for his benefit and the benefit of the other shareholders.

---

5. The dissent also charges that we are callous toward the "investing public"—a term it does not define. It would have been more accurate, perhaps, to have spoken of the noninvesting public, because the Court's decision does not abandon the investing public. The great majority of registered issues of securities are offered by established corporations that have shares outstanding and held by members of the investing public. The types of suits that the dissent would encourage could result in large damage claims, costly litigation, generous settlements to avoid such cost, and often—where the litigation runs its course—in large verdicts. The shareholders of the defendant corporations—the "investing public"—would ultimately bear the burden of this litigation, including the fraudulent suits that would not be screened out by the dissent's bare requirement of a "logical nexus between the alleged fraud and the sale or purchase of a security."

The remainder of the complaint charges appellees with violations of the federal securities laws, primarily in connection with the transactions detailed above. Specifically, Cowin claims that Bresler and Reiner caused the company to "disseminate reports to the public shareholders which were materially deceptive" and concealed material information in violation of Rule 10b–5 and section 10(b) of the Securities Exchange Act of 1934 (1982). Brief for Plaintiff–Appellant at 15. The complaint also charges appellees with violating section 14(a) of the 1934 Act, by causing the company to issue deceptive proxy materials. Cowin seeks to require the disclosure of the material concealed in alleged violation of the Act and, among other things, to invalidate the elections for directors based on the alleged proxy violations.

* * *

The district court also dismissed most of appellant's Rule 10b–5 claims.
* * *

Appellees answered those portions of the complaint that survived the lower court's order and moved for summary judgment on the section 14(a) claim. In its second order, entered April 21, 1983, the district court granted summary judgment for appellees on that claim, holding that Cowin had no standing to challenge, on an individual basis, the allegedly misleading nature of proxy solicitations because he had not personally relied on them.[2]

This appeal followed.

I.

* * *

B.

Cowin's request for the appointment of a receiver to liquidate the company, as distinct from his state law claims for damages and injunctive relief, was properly before the district court in a personal action. See, e.g., Lichens Co. v. Standard Commercial Tobacco Co., 28 Del.Ch. 220, 228–32, 40 A.2d 447, 451–52 (1944); Salnita Corp. v. Walter Holding Corp., 19 Del.Ch. 426, 431, 168 A. 74, 76 (1933). The court found, however, that Cowin had failed to meet the pleading requirements necessary to support such relief. R.E. at 33. We disagree. Although a request for a court-appointed receiver "to wind up a solvent going business is rarely granted," Berwald v. Mission Development Co., 40 Del.Ch. 509, 512, 185 A.2d 480, 482 (Sup.Ct.1962), and the court's power to do so must "always [be] exercised with great restraint," Hall v. John S. Isaacs & Sons Farms, Inc., 39 Del.Ch. 244, 253, 163 A.2d 288, 293 (Sup.Ct.1960), we believe that Cowin has sufficiently plead the requisite elements to support his claim.

* * *

2. The court ruled, alternatively, that Cowin could not demonstrate "loss causation" or economic injury and that the equitable relief appellant sought on his § 14(a) claim—the invalidation of the 1980 directors' election—would "constitute an exercise of futility" because of appellees' unquestionable control over a significant majority of votes. R.E. at 53 (citing Schlick v. Penn–Dixie Cement Corp., 507 F.2d 374, 380 (2d Cir.1974), cert. denied, 421 U.S. 976 (1975)).

With respect to that portion of Cowin's § 10(b) claim that survived the motion to dismiss, the lower court dismissed "without prejudice * * * to facilitate an expeditious appeal of this action." R.E. at 55. The court based this action on what it deemed the expectations of both parties.

II.

Appellant's federal claims raise novel questions under the Securities Exchange Act of 1934, 15 U.S.C. § 78a et seq. (1982). Although Cowin did not buy or sell his stock in connection with the allegedly misleading reports issued by the company, he relies upon section 10(b) of the Act and Rule 10b–5 in seeking to prevent appellees from "depress[ing] the value of [his] stock and * * * eliminat[ing] the public market in that stock through dissemination of deceptive statements." Reply Brief for Plaintiff–Appellant at 18. In short, appellant claims not that he was wrongfully induced to buy or sell stock by appellees' misrepresentations but rather that his stock was made less valuable by appellees' misrepresentations to the investing public generally. He does not seek damages but an injunction requiring an end to the alleged misrepresentations and disclosure of past misrepresentations. It is clear from Blue Chip Stamps v. Manor Drug Stores, 421 U.S. 723 (1975), that appellant could not maintain an action for damages under section 10(b) or Rule 10b–5. The question before us is whether he may bring suit for an injunction.

* * *

A.

In *Blue Chip*, the Supreme Court held that only purchasers or sellers of securities have standing to pursue private claims for damages under section 10(b) and Rule 10b–5. The only difference between that case and this is that appellant seeks only injunctive relief. The question is whether that difference means that plaintiff's action survives *Blue Chip*. We think that it does not.

* * *

B.

Cowin argues that the purchaser-seller limitation does not apply to actions seeking equitable relief. He points to a pre-*Blue Chip* line of cases holding that a private party who seeks only injunctive relief need not have bought or sold securities to sue under Rule 10b–5, see, e.g., Kahan v. Rosenstiel, 424 F.2d 161 (3d Cir.), cert. denied, 398 U.S. 950 (1970); Mutual Shares Corp. v. Genesco, Inc., 384 F.2d 540 (2d Cir.1967), and contends that the "exception" to the purchaser-seller rule in those cases survives *Blue Chip* because the Supreme Court limited its holding in that case to private damage actions. Brief for Plaintiff–Appellant at 19–24. We appear to be the first court of appeals squarely to address this issue,[17] and we think *Blue Chip* cannot be so limited.

17. The Eleventh Circuit recently discussed a related issue in Liberty Nat'l Ins. Holding Co. v. Charter Co., 734 F.2d 545 (1984). There the court held that the shareholder plaintiffs did not have a private cause of action under § 10(b) to force the controlling shareholder to divest itself of its holdings, or to remove voting power from the controlling shareholder. At 558–59. In Tully v. Mott Supermarkets, Inc., 540 F.2d 187 (3d Cir.1976), the court assumed for "present purposes" only, that the "relaxed standing rule of *Kahan* retains its validity after *Blue Chip Stamps* in appropriate cases where only injunctive relief is sought to prevent incipient 10b–5 violations" but then held that the case

before it did not fit into the "*Kahan* exception." Id. at 194. In Davis v. Davis, 526 F.2d 1286 (5th Cir.1976), the court, in dicta, did approve the "approach taken by the Second Circuit [in Mutual Shares Corp. v. Genesco] with regard to injunctive relief" but only after it had ruled that the plaintiff was "clearly a 'seller' under the [ ] definitional provisions of the Act." Id. at 1289–90.

The only other appellate court to reach this issue directly was a pre-*Blue Chip* case from the Eighth Circuit which adopted the view we take in this case. See Greater Iowa Corp. v. McLendon, 378 F.2d 783, 791 (8th Cir.1967).

It is true, as the Court in *Blue Chip* acknowledged, that the question of what constitutes the proper plaintiff class under section 10(b) and Rule 10b–5 cannot be conclusively determined by resort to the text of those enactments; as one might expect, neither the statute nor the rule speaks directly to the question of who may sue since the right to sue was created afterwards by the judiciary. See *Blue Chip,* 421 U.S. at 737. Still, in the process of implying private rights judges must take account of the statutory scheme. See generally Schneider, Implying Private Rights and Remedies Under the Federal Securities Act, 62 N.C.L.Rev. 853, 884–96 (1984); Frankel, Implied Rights of Action, 67 Va.L.Rev. 553, 559–70 (1981). No better guidance exists than the language of the relevant statute and regulation. See *Blue Chip,* 421 U.S. at 756 (Powell, J., concurring) ("The starting point in every case involving construction of a statute is the language itself.").

The relaxed standing requirement urged on us by appellant would be contrary to the rationale of section 10(b) and Rule 10b–5 as perceived by the Supreme Court in *Blue Chip.* While it may be possible to discern differences between an action for damages and a suit for an injunction, most of the Supreme Court's argument in *Blue Chip* applies quite as much to the latter as to the former. The scope of section 10(b) and Rule 10b–5 is limited to fraud "in connection with the purchase or sale of a security." Congress was asked on two different occasions to expand the jurisdictional reach of those provisions but chose not to. In contrast, Congress did choose to define the scope of other provisions in the 1933 and 1934 Acts in terms that clearly reflected a broader jurisdictional reach. Congress also limited standing in those instances where it did create express remedies under the Act to a class of persons including only purchasers or sellers. Thus, the purchaser-seller limitation is "sufficiently supported by the statutory structure of the Securities Act." The Supreme Court, 1974 Term, *supra,* 89 Harv.L.Rev. at 269. See also Northland Capital Corp., at 1426–27 (*Blue Chip*'s holding based primarily on the "language of the Act and its legislative history"). These features also constrain us to accept, in the context of an injunctive suit, the common meaning of the terms "purchase or sale" and reject an expansive construction of the Rule, as *Blue Chip* did for damage actions.

Attempting to fashion a different concept of standing for cases like this would involve us in distinctions altogether too awkward to be persuasive. As *Blue Chip* noted, the "wording of § 10(b) * * * is surely badly strained when construed to provide a cause of action, not to purchasers and sellers of securities, but to the world at large." 421 U.S. at 733 n. 5. The Court also stated that it "would indeed be anomalous to impute to Congress an intention to expand the plaintiff class for a judicially implied cause of action beyond the bounds it delineated for comparable express causes of action." Id. at 737. See also id. at 755 (noting "consistency of [Birnbaum] rule with the statutes involved and their legislative history").

Our analysis might well end here. However, because *Blue Chip* went beyond statutory analysis to examine certain "policy considerations," 421 U.S. at 737, Cowin argues that relaxing the purchaser-seller requirement in his case is proper because that would not contradict the several policies relied upon by *Blue Chip.* Several lower courts, including the lower court in this case, have distinguished the Supreme Court's opinion in this fashion. See, e.g., Fuchs v.

Swanton Corp., 482 F.Supp. 83, 89–90 (S.D.N.Y.1979); Hundahl v. United Benefit Life Insurance Co., 465 F.Supp. 1349, 1357–59 (N.D.Tex.1979).

If we thought this question open, we might conclude that injunctive suits present many of the same problems of vexatiousness, "strike" suits, abuse of discovery, and the like that damage actions do. We need not decide that, however, for we think the approach appellant suggests is foreclosed by *Blue Chip* itself. There, the plaintiff had contended that two policies articulated by the Court—the difficulties in corroborating the elements of Rule 10b–5 proof and the potential for an unlimited class of plaintiffs—were simply not raised on the facts of the case. If plaintiffs were allowed to sue, the Court said, "it would mean that the lesser practical difficulties of corroborating at least some elements of their proof would be regarded as sufficient to avoid the *Birnbaum* rule." 421 U.S. at 754–55, 95 S.Ct. at 1934–35. The Court rejected this result stating that while its decision to affirm *Birnbaum* was in part based on these "practical difficulties," the consistency of the rule with "the statutes involved and their legislative history [were] likewise bases for retaining the rule." Id. at 755, 95 S.Ct. at 1934. To take such arguments into account "would leave the *Birnbaum* rule open to endless case-by-case erosion." Id. Thus, while "policy considerations" did play a role in the *Blue Chip* decision, when those policy considerations were inconsistent with the retention of a flat rule and with the other grounds on which the decision rested—the statute and its history—they were not strong enough to create an exception.

In cases of doubt, the institutional role of the Supreme Court weighs in favor of considering its rulings to be general rather than limited to the particular facts. The Supreme Court, unlike the lower federal courts, is given a largely discretionary jurisdiction which is used when areas of the law require clarification. As Judge Marshall put it in holding that *Blue Chip* forecloses injunctive suits by plaintiffs who have neither purchased nor sold securities, "[W]e must be mindful of the [Supreme] Court's function in hearing and deciding * * * cases. It does not sit to adjudicate individual disputes; that is the business of the district courts and courts of appeal. Rather it uses individual cases and controversies to shape and guide the development of the law. This is particularly true where, as here, it speaks in an area of judge made law." Wright v. Heizer Corp., 411 F.Supp. 23, 34 (N.D.Ill.1975), aff'd in part and rev'd in part, 560 F.2d 236 (7th Cir.1977), cert. denied, 434 U.S. 1066 (1978). When the Court wishes to make a narrow, fact-bound holding, typically it says so. When it does not say so, the rebuttable presumption is that a general rule has been enunciated. Here there is more than that presumption, for the Court gave every indication that it wished to speak broadly. *Blue Chip* expressly acknowledged that the rule it adopted in that case operated as a bar to Rule 10b–5 actions brought by "shareholders, creditors, and perhaps others related to an issuer who suffered loss in the value of their investment due to corporate or insider activities in connection with the purchase or sale of securities which violate Rule 10b–5." 421 U.S. at 737–38. Appellant falls directly within this group and we may not allow him to proceed on his Rule 10b–5 claims against the company.

THE PURCHASER SELLER REQUIREMENT UNDER RULE 10b–5

As with causation, much of the complexity of defining Rule 10b–5 standing requirements is a consequence of the somewhat imprecise term, "in connection with a purchase or sale" of securities. Several applications of this concept have been settled by the courts, both before and after *Blue Chip Stamps*.

Issuance of Its Own Securities: In the leading case of Hooper v. Mountain States Securities Corp.,[1] it was decided that the issuance of its own securities by a corporation was a "sale" within the meaning of Rule 10b–5 (and, of course, a "purchase" by the other party to the transaction), and this holding has been followed by cases where the issue has subsequently arisen.[2]

Repurchase of Its Own Securities: Clearly the repurchase by a corporation of its own outstanding securities involves a purchase and sale. Cochran v. Channing Corp.[3] held that a repurchase by a corporation of its own shares could be the basis of an action under Rule 10b–5. In fact, many of the early nondisclosure cases involved a purchase of minority shares by the issuing corporation, rather than by the controlling shareholders, while there existed allegedly material, nondisclosed inside information. Obviously, whether the "insiders" purchase shares themselves, or have the corporation purchase and increase their percentage ownership, should not make any difference in that type of case.

Privity: In its first case involving a private action under Rule 10b–5, the Supreme Court "read § 10(b) to mean that Congress meant to bar deceptive devices and contrivances in the purchase or sale of securities whether conducted in the organized markets or [as in that case] face-to-face."[4]

Contemporaneous Traders: In the 1988 Insider Trading and Securities Fraud Enforcement Act, Congress adopted § 20A of the Securities Exchange Act to provide standing for "contemporaneous traders." Section 20A(a) specifically provides a private right of action "to any person who, contemporaneously with the purchase or sale of securities that is the subject of [a violation of any provision of the 1934 Act or its rules by purchasing or selling a security while in possession of material nonpublic information], has purchased * * * or sold * * * securities *of the same class*." [Emphasis added.]

While the Act did not define "contemporaneous traders," the House Committee on Energy and Commerce explained that the term "has developed through case law."[5] The Committee cited Shapiro v. Merrill Lynch, Pierce, Fenner & Smith, Inc.,[6] which held defendants liable "not only to the purchasers of the actual shares sold by defendants (in the unlikely event they can be identified) but to all persons who during the same period purchased Douglas Stock in the open market without knowledge of the material inside information which was in the possession of defendants."[7] The Committee also cited Wilson

---

1. Hooper v. Mountain States Sec. Corp., 282 F.2d 195, 200–203 (5th Cir.1960), *cert. denied*, 365 U.S. 814 (1961).

2. *See, e.g.*, Ruckle v. Roto Am. Corp., 339 F.2d 24, 27–28 (2d Cir.1964); Dasho v. Susquehanna Corp., 380 F.2d 262, 270 (7th Cir.1967), *cert. denied sub nom.* Bard v. Dasho, 389 U.S. 977 (1967); Schoenbaum v. Firstbrook, 405 F.2d 215, 219 (2d Cir.1968), cert. *denied sub nom.* Manley v. Schoenbaum, 395 U.S. 906 (1969); Miller v. San Sebastian Gold Mines, Inc., 540 F.2d 807, 809 (5th Cir.1976); Harris v. Union Elec. Co., 787 F.2d

355, 368 (8th Cir.1986), *cert. denied*, 479 U.S. 823 (1986).

3. *See, also*, Mutual Shares Corp. v. Genesco, Inc., 384 F.2d 540 (2d Cir.1967) (the problem there was that the plaintiffs had not been the ones who had sold).

4. Superintendent of Ins. of State of N.Y. v. Bankers Life & Casualty Co., 404 U.S. 6, 12 (1971).

5. H.R. Rep. No. 100–910, 100th Cong., 2d Sess. 27 n. 22 (1988).

6. 495 F.2d 228 (2d Cir.1974).

7. Id. at 237.

v. Comtech Telecommunications Corp.,[8] which observed of the "during the same period" concept in *Shapiro* that "the entire period * * * was only four days."[9] *Wilson* then added significantly:

> To extend the period of liability well beyond the time of the insider's trading simply because disclosure was never made could make the insider liable to all the world. * * * Any duty of disclosure is owed only to those investors trading contemporaneously with the insider; non-contemporaneous traders do not require the protection of the "disclose or abstain" rule because they do not suffer the disadvantage of trading with someone who has superior access to information.[10]

Finally the Committee cited O'Connor & Assoc. v. Dean Witter Reynolds, Inc.,[11] which quoted *Shapiro* and *Wilson* and reiterated two earlier principles: (1) There need not be strict privity between a buyer and a seller in a Rule 10b–5 claim, and (2) liability does not extend to those who traded before the defendant's trades or breach of the disclose or abstain duty.[12]

Private Plaintiffs: As held earlier by Birnbaum v. Newport Steel Corp.,[13] and reiterated by *Blue Chip Stamps*, a private plaintiff does have to be an actual buyer or seller.[14] The *Birnbaum* case itself was a so called sale of control case. In such a case, the controlling shareholder may be held liable, either to the corporation or to the minority shareholders, for his or her sale of the control block to a third party. Because neither the corporation nor the other shareholders in the typical case have purchased or sold any securities, it is clear that most of such actions cannot be maintained under Rule 10b–5. It is also clear that a shareholder who has not tendered in a tender offer has no standing to sue the offeror or the target company under Rule 10b–5.[15] Certainly a shareholder who merely claims that the value of his or her stock was depreciated by acts of the defendant has no standing under Rule 10b–5 individually,[16] nor derivatively unless the wrongful acts of the defendant involved some purchase or sale of securities by the corporation.

Who is a purchaser or seller for the purpose of applying this limitation? It has been held that a trust beneficiary has standing to bring an action against the trustee alleging fraud in selling securities of the trust corpus, because the beneficial interest of the beneficiary was sold and therefore he was a "seller."[17] It has also been held that a secured party is a seller in a case where the

---

8.   648 F.2d 88 (2d Cir.1981).

9.   Id. at 94.

10.   Id. at 94–95.

11.   559 F.Supp. 800 (S.D.N.Y.1983).

12.   Id. at 803. See also id. at 805: "This rationale for the contemporaneous trading standard applies equally to options cases, regardless whether particular sales can be matched with particular purchases." *See also* Neubronner v. Milken, 6 F.3d 666, 670 (9th Cir.1993) (adopting Second Circuit's approach in *Wilson*).

13.   193 F.2d 461 (2d Cir.1952), *cert. denied*, 343 U.S. 956 (1952).

14.   In a criminal or Commission action the "in connection with" requirement merely requires that someone buy or sell during the period of allegedly fraudulent activity. *See, e.g.*, SEC v. National Sec., Inc., 393 U.S. 453 (1969), cited in *Blue Chip Stamps*, 421 U.S. at 751 n. 14; United States v. Carpenter, 791 F.2d 1024, 1033 (2d Cir.1986), *aff'd by evenly divided court*, 484 U.S. 19 (1987).

15.   *See* Petersen v. Federated Dev. Co., 387 F.Supp. 355 (S.D.N.Y.1974).

16.   Sargent v. Genesco, Inc., 492 F.2d 750 (5th Cir.1974).

17.   Norris v. Wirtz, 719 F.2d 256 (7th Cir.1983); Kirshner v. United States, 603 F.2d 234 (2d Cir.1978), *cert. denied*, 444 U.S. 995 (1979); James v. Gerber Products Co., 483 F.2d 944 (6th Cir.1973).

securities were sold on foreclosure by the sheriff[18] and that the pledgor is a seller when the pledgee sells the securities on foreclosure,[19] since in both cases they have an interest in the proceeds of the sale (although the pledgor does, of course, only if a surplus over the amount of the debt is produced by the sale). It has also been held by the Supreme Court that a pledge of stock is itself a "sale" for the purposes of Rule 10b–5.[20]

In a stockholders' derivative action it is the corporation, not the private plaintiff that must have bought or sold the relevant security.[21] In contrast it has been held that the dissolution of a partnership involves a sale by a limited partner of their limited partnership interests.[22]

The "Forced Seller:" In Vine v. Beneficial Finance Co., Inc.,[23] the Second Circuit held that a minority shareholder in a corporation who was "cashed out" by the effectuation of a short-form merger of his or her corporation with its corporate parent was a "forced seller" and entitled to sue under Rule 10b–5. This same rationale has been applied to a liquidation[24] and to an ordinary merger.[25] The *Vine* case was reaffirmed in Mayer v. Oil Field Systems Corp.,[26] in an opinion by Judge Friendly. In that case, a limited partner was forced to accept stock in a corporation in exchange for his limited partnership interest in a transaction which only had to be approved by the general partner. The court said that the fact that he had no choice in the matter, as in the *Vine* case, did not prevent him from being a "seller" under the forced seller doctrine. It would appear that he was also a "purchaser" of the stock of the corporation which he received, although the court does not analyze that side of the transaction.

On the other hand, the doctrine has been limited to instances where the plaintiff is forced to surrender a security for cash or a fundamentally different security. It does not reach, for example, an instance where the plaintiff retains shares in a going concern but the issuance of new shares dilutes the value of the plaintiff's investment.[27] Similarly while the courts have treated an arm's

---

18. Falls v. Fickling, 621 F.2d 1362 (5th Cir.1980); Bosse v. Crowell Collier and Macmillan, 565 F.2d 602 (9th Cir.1977).

19. Dopp v. Franklin National Bank, 374 F.Supp. 904 (S.D.N.Y.1974).

20. Rubin v. United States, 449 U.S. 424 (1981).

21. *See, e.g.,* Blue Chip Stamps v. Manor Drug Stores, 421 U.S. 723, 738 (1975); Frankel v. Slotkin, 984 F.2d 1328, 1332–1334 (2d Cir.1993).

22. 7547 Corp. v. Parker & Parsley Dev. Partners, L.P., 38 F.3d 211, 228–229 (5th Cir.1994); Bolger v. Laventhol, Krekstein, Horwath & Horwath, 381 F.Supp. 260 (S.D.N.Y.1974); Houlihan v. Anderson–Stokes, Inc., 434 F.Supp. 1330 (D.D.C.1977).

23. 374 F.2d 627 (2d Cir.1967), *cert. denied,* 389 U.S. 970 (1967). *Cf.* Isquith v. Caremark Int'l, Inc., 136 F.3d 531 (7th Cir. 1998), *cert. denied,* 525 U.S. 920 (1998), where the court held that a spinoff was not a sale of securities since it did not effect a fundamental change in the plaintiff's hold-ings. *Isquith* criticized the "defunct forced seller doctrine" and charactered it as succeeded by a related "fundamental change" doctrine. Id. at 535–537.

24. Coffee v. Permian Corp., 434 F.2d 383 (5th Cir.1970); Dudley v. Southeastern Factor and Fin. Corp., 446 F.2d 303 (5th Cir.1971), *cert. denied,* 404 U.S. 858 (1971); Alley v. Miramon, 614 F.2d 1372 (5th Cir. 1980).

25. Mader v. Armel, 402 F.2d 158 (6th Cir.1968), *cert. denied,* 394 U.S. 930 (1969).

26. 721 F.2d 59 (2d Cir.1983).

27. *See* Sargent v. Genesco, Inc., 492 F.2d 750, 764–765 (5th Cir.1974); Jeanes v. Henderson, 703 F.2d 855, 860 (5th Cir.1983); Ray v. Karris, 780 F.2d 636, 640 n. 1 (7th Cir.1985); Mosher v. Kane, 784 F.2d 1385, 1389 (9th Cir.1986), *rev'd on other grounds sub nom.* Washington Pub. Power Supply Sys. Sec. Litig., 823 F.2d 1349 (9th Cir. en banc 1987).

length stock-for-assets exchange between two independent corporation as constituting a purchase or sale for the purposes of § 10(b),[28] a transfer of securities from a *wholly* owned subsidiary to its parent or between two corporations wholly controlled by a third corporation has been held to amount not to a purchase or sale but rather to "a mere transfer between corporate pockets."[29]

Contracts to Buy or Sell Securities: A contract to sell securities is itself a "sale" for the purposes of the rule in the *Blue Chip* case;[30] however, parties who negotiate for the purchase and sale of securities but never arrive at any enforceable contract can not sue under Rule 10b–5.[31] It has been held that an oral agreement to sell is not sufficient to satisfy the purchase or sale requirement of Rule 10b–5 if it is unenforceable under the statute of frauds.[32] In A.T. Brod & Co. v. Perlow[33] the court held that a contract of purchase entered into without the intention of paying for the securities was a "sale" within the Rule; and Commerce Reporting Co. v. Puretec, Inc.[34] held that a contract of sale entered into by the defendant without any intention of performing it, but merely for the purpose of getting a better offer from a third party, was a "purchase" by the other party within the Rule. These cases have been followed in the Tenth Circuit[35] and the Seventh Circuit has held that a breach of a contract by a person who has agreed to sell securities, accompanied by "conversion" of the securities, title to which had allegedly passed to a plaintiff, amounted to "fraud" permitting an action under Rule 10b–5.[36]

The Injunction Plaintiff: Mutual Shares Corp. v. Genesco, Inc.,[37] illustrates one situation where an exception to the rule that the plaintiff must be a purchaser or seller had clearly been established before the *Blue Chip* case. If the plaintiff is merely seeking an injunction against the continuance by the defendant of market manipulation or other conduct violative of Rule 10b–5, his or her status as a shareholder of the corporation was held to give him or her standing to bring such action and the plaintiff need not allege that he or she is a purchaser or seller. This decision was followed by the Third Circuit[38] and the Sixth Circuit.[39] However, in Wright v. Heizer Corp.[40] Judge Marshall stated

---

28.   *See, e.g.*, Swanson v. American Consumer Indus. Inc., 415 F.2d 1326, 1330 (7th Cir.1969).

29.   Blau v. Mission Corp., 212 F.2d 77, 80 (2d Cir.1954), *cert. denied*, 347 U.S. 1016 (1954); International Controls Corp. v. Vesco, 490 F.2d 1334, 1343 (2d Cir.1974), *cert. denied*, 417 U.S. 932 (1974); Rathborne v. Rathborne, 683 F.2d 914, 918–919 (5th Cir.1982); Gelles v. TDA Indus., Inc., 44 F.3d 102, 105 (2d Cir.1994) ("Gelles held literally the exact same shares before and after the transaction").

30.   Mosher v. Kane, 784 F.2d 1385 (9th Cir.1986); Griggs v. Pace Am. Group, Inc., 170 F.3d 877, 880 (9th Cir.1999).

31.   Reprosystem, B.V. v. SCM Corp., 727 F.2d 257 (2d Cir.1984), *cert. denied*, 469 U.S. 828 (1984); Northland Capital Corp. v. Silver, 735 F.2d 1421 (D.C.Cir.1984).

32.   Kagan v. Edison Bros. Stores, Inc., 907 F.2d 690 (7th Cir.1990); Pelletier v.

Stuart–James Co., Inc., 863 F.2d 1550 (11th Cir.1989).

33.   375 F.2d 393 (2d Cir.1967).

34.   290 F.Supp. 715 (S.D.N.Y.1968).

35.   Richardson v. MacArthur, 451 F.2d 35 (10th Cir.1971).

36.   Allico National Corp. v. Amalgamated Meat Cutters & Butcher Workmen of N. Am., 397 F.2d 727 (7th Cir.1968).

37.   384 F.2d 540 (2d Cir.1967).

38.   Kahan v. Rosenstiel, 424 F.2d 161 (3d Cir.1970), *cert. denied*, 398 U.S. 950 (1970).

39.   Britt v. The Cyril Bath Co., 417 F.2d 433 (6th Cir.1969).

40.   411 F.Supp. 23, 34 (N.D.Ill.1975). *See also* Greater Iowa Corp. v. McLendon, 378 F.2d 783 (8th Cir.1967); Liberty Nat'l Ins. Holding Co. v. Charter Co., 734 F.2d 545, 555–559 (11th Cir.1984). Cf. Advanced Re-

that he did not believe that this exception survived the Supreme Court decision in *Blue Chip*. He said: "In this regard we note that at no point in *Blue Chip* did the Court cite, let alone discuss or disapprove a cluster of courts of appeals decisions which appear to have declined to apply the structures of *Birnbaum* to private 10b–5 actions seeking solely equitable relief. * * * But we must be mindful of the Court's function in hearing and deciding such cases * * * it uses individual cases and controversies to shape and guide the development of the law. * * * Thus, we have concluded that we would not be justified in drawing a distinction here between an action at law and one in equity." In the *Cowin* case the District of Columbia Circuit Court of Appeals has now endorsed this conclusion of Judge Marshall.

See generally 8 Louis Loss & Joel Seligman, Securities Regulation 3680–3726 (3d ed. 1991); Francesca Muratori, The Boundaries of the "In Connection With" Requirement of Rule 10b–5: Should Advertising Be Actionable as Securities Fraud?, 56 Bus. Law. 1057 (2001).

C.   SECTION 16(b): LIABILITY FOR SHORT SWING PROFITS

Section 16 was the original and only express "insider" trading provisions in the 1934 Act. The 1934 report of the Senate Banking and Currency Committee explained:

> Among the most vicious practices unearthed at the hearings before the subcommittee was the flagrant betrayal of their fiduciary duties by directors and officers of corporations who used their positions of trust and the confidential information which came to them in such positions, to aid them in their market activities. Closely allied to this type of abuse was the unscrupulous employment of inside information by large stockholders who, while not directors and officers, exercised sufficient control over the destinies of their companies to enable them to acquire and profit by information not available to others.[1]

In one case described in the Committee's report on the bill, "the president of a corporation testified that he and his brothers controlled the company with a little over 10 percent of the shares; that shortly before the company passed a dividend, they disposed of their holdings for upward of $16 million and later repurchased them for about $7 million, showing a profit of approximately $9 million on the transaction."[2]

Section 16(a) provides that every officer or director of a company with an equity security registered under § 12, as well as every person "who is directly or indirectly the beneficial owner of more than 10 per centum of any class of any equity security" so registered, shall file with the Commission, as well as any exchange on which the security is listed, an initial report of his or her holdings of *all* the issuer's equity securities, and a further report within two days after the close of each calendar month in which there has been any change in his or her holdings.[3] The factor that touches off the reporting requirement is

---

sources Int'l Inc. v. Tri–Star Petroleum Co., 4 F.3d 327, 333 (4th Cir.1993).

In Trump Hotels & Casino Resorts, Inc. v. Mirage Resorts, Inc., 140 F.3d 478 (3d Cir.1998), the court declined to resolve whether a nonpurchasing or nonselling plaintiff could bring a Rule 10b–5 injunctive claim, but instead dismissed on causation grounds.

1. S. Rep. No. 1455, 73d Cong., 2d Sess. 55 (1934).

2. S. Rep. No. 792, 73d Cong., 2d Sess. 9 (1934).

3. Section 403 of the Sarbanes–Oxley Act of 2002 amended § 16(a) to require insider reports to be filed within ten days after a

the registration of an *equity* security. If a particular company has only its common stock registered, § 16 applies also to its preferred stock. But the Section does not apply to any of the securities—even equity securities—of a company that has only a nonconvertible bond issue registered. Similarly a 10 + percent owner of an *unregistered* equity security who is neither a director nor an officer is not subject to § 16 even with respect to equity securities that are registered. This is pure disclosure, except that § 16(a) serves the further function of facilitating the enforcement of § 16(b).[4]

Section 16(b) was designed to protect "outside" stockholders against short swing speculation by "insiders" with advance information. It was described by the Administration's spokesman in the 1934 hearings as a "crude rule of thumb."[5]

Nonetheless § 16(b) has proven to be quite controversial. Because § 16(b) will impose a form of strict liability on those statutory insiders who buy and sell (or sell and buy) any equity security within any period of less than six months, the Section is vulnerable to criticism that it can impose liability upon entirely innocent persons.[6] It would seem that any moderately bright manipulator should be able to string out his or her activities over a period of more than six months and escape any penalty under the Section.

At the same time, the provision's very simplicity (in the usual case) has undoubtedly had a substantial deterrent effect.[7] Since the elements of the action are so simple, the defendant is apt to find that he or she has no practical alternative but to pay up; "the liability is, as a practical matter, inexorable."[8] Consequently the number of reported decisions is probably no indicator of the total amount of short term profits recaptured or, once the Section became well

person becomes a beneficial owner, director, or officer and within two days after a change of ownership.

Within one year after enactment of the Sarbanes–Oxley Act change of ownership reports must be made electronically. § 16(a)(4).

4. Because compliance with § 16(a) was a longstanding problem, the Commission in the 1991 rules revision adopted Item 405 of Regulation S–K, which requires the *registrant* to disclose, in its proxy and information statements and annual reports, the names of delinquents together with the number of transactions and number of delinquent filings for each such person.

5. 15 Stock Exchange Practices, Hearings before Senate Comm. on Banking & Currency, 73d Cong., 2d Sess. 6557 (1934) (testimony of Thomas G. Corcoran).

6. In Western Auto Supply Co. v. Gamble–Skogmo, Inc., 348 F.2d 736 (8th Cir. 1965), *cert. denied,* 382 U.S. 987 (1966), Gamble–Skogmo purchased 25,942 shares of the stock of its subsidiary, Western Auto Supply Company at $32.35 per share, and simultaneously contributed these shares to its profit-sharing trust for the benefit of its employees. Within less than six months it

sold all of its previous holdings in Western Auto, over 1,200,000 shares, to Beneficial Finance Co. for $36.00 per share. Beneficial through its new subsidiary, Western Auto, recovered from Gamble–Skogmo over $94,000 representing the "profit" obtained by matching the purchase of the 25,942 shares with the sale of that number of shares to Beneficial. The court stated: "We * * * have noted the reference to the ethical position of Beneficial in seeking to recover, in effect, a part of the purchase price it willingly paid for the stock. The punctilios of the parties are not an issue here." Id. at 743.

The Western Auto Supply Company case is typical of many reported § 16(b) litigation. The courts themselves have employed such phrases as "draconian" and "purposeless harshness" in connection with § 16(b).

7. *See* Whiting v. Dow Chem. Co., 523 F.2d 680, 689 (2d Cir.1975). In 1987 an ABA Task Force endorsed retention of § 16(b) on deterrent grounds. Report of the Task Force on Regulation of Insider Trading Part II: Reform of Section 16, 42 Bus. Law. 1087 (1987).

8. Anderson v. Commissioner, 480 F.2d 1304, 1308 (7th Cir.1973).

known, simply foregone.[9] Conversely, although there have been quite a few reported cases, they all involved some legal question that counsel obviously thought was worth the expense of a defense. "There is no rule so 'objective' ('automatic' would be a better word) that it does not require some mental effort in applying it on the part of the person or persons entrusted by law with its application."[10]

Kern County Land Co. v. Occidental Petroleum Corp.

Supreme Court of the United States, 1973.
411 U.S. 582, 93 S.Ct. 1736, 36 L.Ed.2d 503.

■ MR. JUSTICE WHITE delivered the opinion of the Court.

Section 16(b) of the Securities Exchange Act of 1934 * * * provides that officers, directors, and holders of more than 10% of the listed stock of any company shall be liable to the company for any profits realized from any purchase and sale or sale and purchase of such stock occurring within a period of six months. Unquestionably, one or more statutory purchases occurs when one company, seeking to gain control of another, acquires more than 10% of the stock of the latter through a tender offer made to its shareholders. But is it a § 16(b) "sale" when the target of the tender offer defends itself by merging into a third company and the tender offeror then exchanges his stock for the stock of the surviving company and also grants an option to purchase the latter stock that is not exercisable within the statutory six months period? This is the question before us in this case.

I

On May 8, 1967, after unsuccessfully seeking to merge with Kern County Land Company (Old Kern), Occidental Petroleum Corporation (Occidental) announced an offer, to expire on June 8, 1967, to purchase on a first-come, first-served basis 500,000 shares of Old Kern common stock at a price of $83.50 per share plus a brokerage commission of $1.50 per share. By May 10, 1967, 500,000 shares, more than 10% of the outstanding shares of Old Kern, had been tendered. On May 11, Occidental extended its offer to encompass an additional 500,000 shares. At the close of the tender offer, on June 8, 1967, Occidental owned 887,549 shares of Old Kern.

Immediately upon the announcement of Occidental's tender offer, the Old Kern management undertook to frustrate Occidental's takeover attempt. A management letter to all stockholders cautioned against tender and indicated that Occidental's offer might not be the best available, since the management was engaged in merger discussions with several companies. When Occidental extended its tender offer, the president of Old Kern sent a telegram to all stockholders again advising against tender. In addition, Old Kern undertook merger discussions with Tenneco, Inc. (Tenneco), and, on May 19, 1967, the Board of Directors of Old Kern announced that it had approved a merger proposal advanced by Tenneco. Under the terms of the merger, Tenneco would acquire the assets, property, and goodwill of Old Kern, subject to its liabilities,

---

9. *See* Arrow Distrib. Corp. v. Baumgartner, 783 F.2d 1274, 1278 (5th Cir.1986), *amended per curiam on other grounds & reh'g denied*, 783 F.2d 1274 (5th Cir.1986).

10. Blau v. Lamb, 363 F.2d 507, 520 (2d Cir.1966), *cert. denied*, 385 U.S. 1002 (1967).

through "Kern County Land Company" (New Kern), a new corporation to be formed by Tenneco to receive the assets and carry on the business of Old Kern. The shareholders of Old Kern would receive a share of Tenneco cumulative convertible preference stock in exchange for each share of Old Kern common stock which they owned. On the same day, May 19, Occidental, in a quarterly report to stockholders, appraised the value of the new Tenneco stock at $105 per share.

Occidental, seeing its tender offer and takeover attempt being blocked by the Old Kern–Tenneco "defensive" merger, countered on May 25 and 31 with two mandamus actions in the California courts seeking to obtain extensive inspection of Old Kern books and records. Realizing that, if the Old Kern–Tenneco merger were approved and successfully closed, Occidental would have to exchange its Old Kern shares for Tenneco stock and would be locked into a minority position in Tenneco, Occidental took other steps to protect itself. Between May 30 and June 2, it negotiated an arrangement with Tenneco whereby Occidental granted Tenneco Corporation, a subsidiary of Tenneco, an option to purchase at $105 per share all of the Tenneco preference stock to which Occidental would be entitled in exchange for its Old Kern stock when and if the Old Kern–Tenneco merger was closed. The premium to secure the option, at $10 per share, totaled $8,866,230 and was to be paid immediately upon the signing of the option agreement. If the option were exercised, the premium was to be applied to the purchase price. By the terms of the option agreement, the option could not be exercised prior to December 9, 1967, a date six months and one day after expiration of Occidental's tender offer. On June 2, 1967, within six months of the acquisition by Occidental of more than 10% ownership of Old Kern, Occidental and Tenneco Corporation executed the option. Soon thereafter, Occidental announced that it would not oppose the Old Kern–Tenneco merger and dismissed in a state court suits against Old Kern.

The Old Kern–Tenneco merger plan was presented to and approved by Old Kern shareholders at their meeting on July 17, 1967. Occidental refrained from voting its Old Kern shares, but in a letter read at the meeting Occidental stated that it had determined prior to June 2 not to oppose the merger and that it did not consider the plan unfair or inequitable. Indeed, Occidental indicated that had it been voting, it would have voted in favor of the merger.

* * *

The Old Kern–Tenneco merger transaction was closed on August 30. Old Kern shareholders thereupon became irrevocably entitled to receive Tenneco preference stock, share-for-share in exchange for their Old Kern stock. Old Kern was dissolved and all of its assets including "all claims, demands, rights and choses in action accrued or to accrue under and by virtue of the Securities Exchange Act of 1934 * * * " were transferred to New Kern.

The option granted by Occidental on June 2, 1967, was exercised on December 11, 1967. Occidental, not having previously availed itself of its rights, exchanged certificates representing 887,549 shares of Old Kern stock for a certificate representing a like number of shares of Tenneco preference stock. The certificate was then endorsed over to the optionee-purchaser, and in return $84,129,185 was credited to Occidental's accounts at various banks. Adding to this amount the $8,886,230 premium paid in June, Occidental received $93,905,415 for its Old Kern stock (including the 1,900 shares acquired prior to issuance of its tender offer). In addition, Occidental received dividends totaling

$1,793,439.22. Occidental's total profit was $19,506,419.22 on the shares obtained through its tender offer.

On October 17, 1967, New Kern instituted a suit under § 16(b) against Occidental to recover the profits which Occidental had realized as a result of its dealings in Old Kern stock. The complaint alleged that the execution of the Occidental–Tenneco option on June 2, 1967, and the exchange of Old Kern shares for shares of Tenneco to which Occidental became entitled pursuant to the merger closed on August 30, 1967, were both "sales" within the coverage of § 16(b). Since both acts took place within six months of the date on which Occidental became the owner of more than 10% of the stock of Old Kern, New Kern asserted that § 16(b) required surrender of the profits realized by Occidental. * * *

Although traditional cash-for-stock transactions that result in a purchase and sale or a sale and purchase within the six-month, statutory period are clearly encompassed within the purview of § 16(b), the courts have wrestled with the question of inclusion or exclusion of certain "unorthodox" transactions. The statutory definitions of "purchase" and "sale" are broad and, at least arguably, reach many transactions not ordinarily deemed a sale or purchase. In deciding whether borderline transactions are within the reach of the statute, the courts have come to inquire whether the transaction may serve as a vehicle for the evil which Congress sought to prevent—the realization of short-swing profits based upon access to inside information—thereby endeavoring to implement congressional objectives without extending the reach of the statute beyond its intended limits. The statute requires the inside, short-swing trader to disgorge all profits realized on all "purchases" and "sales" within the specified time period, without proof of actual abuse of insider information, and without proof of intent to profit on the basis of such information. Under these strict terms, the prevailing view is to apply the statute only when its application would serve its goals. "[W]here alternative constructions of the terms of § 16(b) are possible, those terms are to be given the construction that best serves the congressional purpose of curbing short-swing speculation by corporate insiders." Reliance Electric Co. v. Emerson Electric Co., *supra*, at 424. See Blau v. Lamb, 363 F.2d 507 (C.A.2 1966), cert. denied 385 U.S. 1002 (1967). Thus, "[i]n interpreting the terms 'purchase' and 'sale,' courts have properly asked whether the particular type of transaction involved is one that gives rise to speculative abuse." Reliance Electric Co. v. Emerson Electric Co., *supra*, at 424, n. 4.

In the present case, it is undisputed that Occidental became a "beneficial owner" within the terms of § 16(b) when, pursuant to its tender offer, it "purchased" more than 10% of the outstanding shares of Old Kern. We must decide, however, whether a "sale" within the ambit of the statute took place either when Occidental became irrevocably bound to exchange its shares of Old Kern for shares of Tenneco pursuant to the terms of the merger agreement between Old Kern and Tenneco or when Occidental gave an option to Tenneco to purchase from Occidental the Tenneco shares so acquired.[28]

---

28. Both events occurred within six months of Occidental's first acquisition of Old Kern shares pursuant to its tender offer. Although Occidental did not exchange its Old Kern shares until December 11, 1967, it is not contended that that date, rather than the date on which Occidental became irrevocably bound to do so, should control. Similarly, although the option was not exercised until December 11, 1967, no liability is asserted with respect to that event, because it occurred more than six months after Occidental's last acquisition of Old Kern stock.

III

On August 30, 1967, the Old Kern–Tenneco merger agreement was signed, and Occidental became irrevocably entitled to exchange its shares of Old Kern stock for shares of Tenneco preference stock. Concededly the transaction must be viewed as though Occidental had made the exchange on that day. But even so, did the exchange involve a "sale" of Old Kern shares within the meaning of § 16(b)? We agree with the Court of Appeals that it did not, for we think it totally unrealistic to assume or infer from the facts before us that Occidental either had or was likely to have access to inside information, by reason of its ownership of more than 10% of the outstanding shares of Old Kern, so as to afford it an opportunity to reap speculative, short-swing profits from its disposition within six months of its tender offer purchases.

It cannot be contended that Occidental was an insider when, on May 8, 1967, it made an irrevocable offer to purchase 500,000 shares of Old Kern stock at a price substantially above market. At that time, it owned only 1,900 shares of Old Kern stock, far fewer than the 432,000 shares needed to constitute the 10% ownership required by the statute. There is no basis for finding that, at the time the tender offer was commenced, Occidental enjoyed an insider's opportunity to acquire information about Old Kern's affairs.

It is also wide of the mark to assert that Occidental, as a sophisticated corporation knowledgeable in matters of corporate affairs and finance, knew that its tender offer would either succeed or would be met with a "defensive merger." If its takeover efforts failed, it is argued, Occidental knew it could sell its stock to the target company's merger partner at a substantial profit. Calculations of this sort, however, whether speculative or not and whether fair or unfair to other stockholders or to Old Kern, do not represent the kind of speculative abuse at which the statute is aimed, for they could not have been based on inside information obtained from substantial stockholdings that did not yet exist. Accepting both that Occidental made this very prediction and that it would recurringly be an accurate forecast in tender-offer situations, we nevertheless fail to perceive how the fruition of such anticipated events would require, or in any way depend upon the receipt and use of inside information. If there are evils to be redressed by way of deterring those who would make tender offers, § 16(b) does not appear to us to have been designed for this task.

By May 10, 1967, Occidental had acquired more than 10% of the outstanding shares of Old Kern. It was thus a statutory insider when, on May 11, it extended its tender offer to include another 500,000 shares. We are quite unconvinced, however, that the situation had changed materially with respect to the possibilities of speculative abuse of inside information by Occidental. Perhaps Occidental anticipated that extending its offer would increase the likelihood of the ultimate success of its takeover attempt or the occurrence of a defensive merger. But again, the expectation of such benefits was unrelated to the use of information unavailable to other stockholders or members of the public with sufficient funds and the intention to make the purchases Occidental had offered to make before June 8, 1967.

The possibility that Occidental had, or had the opportunity to have, any confidential information about Old Kern before or after May 11, 1967, seems extremely remote. Occidental was, after all, a tender offeror, threatening to seize control of Old Kern, displace its management, and use the company for its own ends. The Old Kern management vigorously and immediately opposed Occidental's efforts. Twice it communicated with its stockholders, advising against acceptance of Occidental's offer and indicating prior to May 11 and prior to Occidental's extension of its offer, that there was a possibility of an imminent merger and a more profitable exchange. Old Kern's management refused to discuss with Occidental officials the subject of an Old Kern–Occidental merger. Instead, it undertook negotiations with Tenneco and forthwith concluded an agreement, announcing the merger terms on May 19. Requests by Occidental for inspection of Old Kern records were sufficiently frustrated by Old Kern's management to force Occidental to litigation to secure the information it desired.

There is, therefore, nothing in connection with Occidental's acquisition of Old Kern stock pursuant to its tender offer to indicate either the possibility of inside information being available to Occidental by virtue of its stock ownership or the potential for speculative abuse of such inside information by Occidental. Much the same can be said of the events leading to the exchange of Occidental's Old Kern stock for Tenneco preferred, which is one of the transactions that is sought to be classified a "sale" under § 16(b). The critical fact is that the exchange took place and was required pursuant to a merger between Old Kern and Tenneco. That merger was not engineered by Occidental but was sought by Old Kern to frustrate the attempts of Occidental to gain control of Old Kern. Occidental obviously did not participate in or control the negotiations or the agreement between Old Kern and Tenneco. Cf. Newmark v. RKO General, 425 F.2d 348 (C.A.2), cert. denied 400 U.S. 854 (1970); Park & Tilford v. Schulte, 160 F.2d 984 (C.A.2), cert. denied 332 U.S. 761 (1947). Once agreement between those two companies crystalized, the course of subsequent events was out of Occidental's hands. Old Kern needed the consent of its stockholders, but as it turned out, Old Kern's management had the necessary votes without the affirmative vote of Occidental. The merger agreement was approved by a majority of the stockholders of Old Kern, excluding the votes to which Occidental was entitled by virtue of its ownership of Old Kern shares. See generally Ferraiolo v. Newman, 259 F.2d 342 (C.A.6 1958), cert. denied 359 U.S. 927 (1959); Roberts v. Eaton, 212 F.2d 82 (C.A.2 1954). Occidental, although registering its opinion that the merger would be beneficial to Old Kern shareholders, did not in fact vote at the stockholders' meeting at which merger approval was obtained. Under California law, its abstention was tantamount to a vote against approval of the merger. Moreover, at the time of stockholder ratification of the merger, Occidental's previous dealing in Old Kern stock was, as it had always been, fully disclosed.

Once the merger and exchange were approved, Occidental was left with no real choice with respect to the future of its shares of Old Kern. Occidental was in no position to prevent the issuance of a ruling by the Internal Revenue Service that the exchange of Old Kern stock for Tenneco preferred would be tax-free; and, although various lawsuits were begun in state and federal courts seeking to postpone the merger closing beyond the statutory six months period, those efforts were futile. The California Corporation Commissioner issued the necessary permits for the closing that took place on August 30, 1967.[a] The

---

a. [Eds.] This cryptic reference to "various lawsuits" and to the proceedings before the California Commissioner of Corporations conceals a monumental legal battle initiated when Occidental woke up after the shareholders' meeting to the fact that it had a Section 16(b) problem if the sale of assets was consummated within six months of its

merger left no right in dissenters to secure appraisal of their stock. Occidental could, of course, have disposed of its shares of Old Kern for cash before the merger was closed. Such an act would have been a § 16(b) sale and would have left Occidental with a prima facie § 16(b) liability. It was not, therefore, a realistic alternative for Occidental as long as it felt that it could successfully defend a suit like the present one. See generally Petteys v. Butler, 367 F.2d 528 (C.A.8 1966), cert. denied 385 U.S. 1006 (1967); Ferraiolo v. Newman, *supra*; Lynam v. Livingston, 276 F.Supp. 104 (Del.1967); Blau v. Hodgkinson, 100 F.Supp. 361 (S.D.N.Y.1951). We do not suggest that an exchange of stock pursuant to a merger may never result in § 16(b) liability. But the involuntary nature of Occidental's exchange, when coupled with the absence of the possibility of speculative abuse of inside information, convinces us that § 16(b) should not apply to transactions such as this one.

IV

Petitioner also claims that the Occidental–Tenneco option agreement should itself be considered a sale either because it was the kind of transaction the statute was designed to prevent or because the agreement was an option in form but in fact a sale. But the mere execution of an option to sell is not generally regarded as a "sale." See Booth v. Varian Associates, 334 F.2d 1 (C.A.1 1964), cert. denied 379 U.S. 961 (1965); Allis–Chalmers Mfg. Co. v. Gulf & Western Industries, 309 F.Supp. 75 (Wis.1970); Marquette Cement Mfg. Co. v. Andreas, 239 F.Supp. 962 (S.D.N.Y.1965). And we do not find in the execution of the Occidental–Tenneco option agreement a sufficient possibility for the speculative abuse of inside information with respect to Old Kern's affairs to warrant holding that the option agreement was itself a "sale" within the meaning of § 16(b). The mutual advantages of the arrangement appear quite clear. As the District Court found, Occidental wanted to avoid the position of a minority stockholder with a huge investment in a company over which it had no control and in which it had not chosen to invest. On the other hand, Tenneco did not want a potentially troublesome minority stockholder

purchases of stock of Old Kern, although it would seem that it would have been relatively easy for Occidental to have negotiated a postponement of the closing at the time it made its option deal with Tenneco if it had recognized the problem then. A flurry of lawsuits were filed all over the United States to enjoin the transaction until the six months had passed; an attempt was made to get the California Commissioner of Corporations to deny the permit necessary for the closing on the basis that the transaction was not "fair, just and equitable" to the shareholders of Old Kern, although Occidental had publicly read a letter to the shareholders' meeting stating that in its opinion the transaction was the "best deal" that those shareholders could get; and application was made to the Securities and Exchange Commission for a special exemptive rule to relieve Occidental of its potential Section 16(b) liability. In one county in Texas where an injunction action had been filed, Louis Nizer was flown in from New York City to represent Occidental and local counsel for Tenneco wrote a classic brief in which the country bumpkin lawyer took on the city slicker and illustrated each point of his argument with a quotation from one of Mr. Nizer's published literary efforts extolling his own exploits as an attorney. (Occidental and Mr. Nizer of course had the last laugh, when the Second Circuit reversed a $23,500,000 judgment against Occidental and the Supreme Court affirmed.) None of this effort succeeded and the transaction closed on schedule; and then the race by the 16(b) Bar to the courthouse began, initiating six years of litigation over the liability question. If the judgment against Occidental had been affirmed, the result would have been that the public shareholders of Occidental would have been forced to make a gift of $23,500,000 to the public shareholders of Tenneco. Total fees paid to lawyers throughout this fiasco are unknown, but undoubtedly ran into the millions. *Cui bono?*

that had just been vanquished in a fight for the control of Old Kern. Motivations like these do not smack of insider trading; and it is not clear to us, as it was not to the Court of Appeals, how the negotiation and execution of the option agreement gave Occidental any possible opportunity to trade on inside information it might have obtained from its position as a major stockholder of Old Kern. Occidental wanted out, but only at a date more than six months hence. It was willing to get out at a price of $105 per share, a price at which it had publicly valued Tenneco preferred on May 19 when the Tenneco–Old Kern agreement was announced. In any event, Occidental was dealing with the putative new owners of Old Kern who undoubtedly knew more about Old Kern and Tenneco's affairs than did Occidental. If Occidental had leverage in dealing with Tenneco, it is incredible that its source was inside information rather than the fact of its large stock ownership itself.

Neither does it appear that the option agreement, as drafted and executed by the parties, offered measurable possibilities for speculative abuse. What Occidental granted was a "call" option. Tenneco had the right to buy after six months, but Occidental could not force Tenneco to buy. The price was fixed at $105 for each share of Tenneco preferred. Occidental could not share in a rising market for the Tenneco stock. See Silverman v. Landa, 306 F.2d 422 (C.A.2 1966). If the stock fell more than $10 per share, the option might not be exercised, and Occidental might suffer a loss if the market further deteriorated to a point where Occidental was forced to sell. Thus, the option, by its very form, left Occidental with no choice but to sell if Tenneco exercised the option, which it was almost sure to do if the value of Tenneco stock remained relatively steady. On the other hand, it is difficult to perceive any speculative value to Occidental if the stock declined and Tenneco chose not to exercise its option. See generally Note, Put and Call Options Under Section 16 of the Securities Exchange Act, 69 Yale L.Rev. 868 (1960); Filer, Understanding Put and Call Options, 96–111 (1959); Leffler, The Stock Market, 363–378 (2d ed. 1957).

The option, therefore, does not appear to have been an instrument with potential for speculative abuse, whether or not Occidental possessed inside information about the affairs of Old Kern. In addition, the option covered Tenneco preference stock, a stock as yet unissued, unregistered, and untraded. It was the value of this stock that underlay the option and that determined whether the option would be exercised, whether Occidental would be able to profit from the exercise, and whether there was any real likelihood of the exploitation of inside information. If Occidental had inside information when it negotiated and signed the option agreement it was inside information with respect to Old Kern. Whatever it may have known or expected as to the future value of Old Kern stock, Occidental had no ownership position in Tenneco giving it any actual or presumed insights into the future value of Tenneco stock. That was the critical item of intelligence if Occidental was to use the option for purposes of speculation. Also, the date for exercise of the option was over six months in the future, a period that, under the statute itself, is assumed to dissipate whatever trading advantage that might be imputed to a major stockholder with inside information. See Note, Stock Exchanges Pursuant to Corporation Consolidation: A Section 16(b) "Purchase or Sale?," 217 U.Pa. L.Rev. 1034, 1054 (1969); Silverman v. Landa, 306 F.2d 422 (C.A.2 1962). By enshrining the statutory period into the option, Occidental also, at least if the statutory period is taken to accomplish its intended purpose, limited its speculative possibilities. Nor should it be forgotten that there was no absolute assurance that the merger, which was not controlled by Occidental, would be consummated. In the event the merger did not close, the option itself would become null and void.

Nor can we agree that we must reverse the Court of Appeals on the ground that the option agreement was in fact a sale because the premium paid was so large as to make the exercise of the option almost inevitable, particularly when coupled with Tenneco's desire to rid itself of a potentially troublesome stockholder. The argument has force, but resolution of the question is very much a matter of judgment, economic and otherwise, and the Court of Appeals rejected the argument. That court emphasized that the premium paid was what experts had said the option was worth, the possibility that the market might drop sufficiently in the six months following execution of the option to make exercise unlikely, and the fact that here, unlike the situation in Bershad v. McDonough, 428 F.2d 693 (C.A.7 1970), the optionor did not surrender practically all emoluments of ownership by executing the option. Nor did any other special circumstances indicate that the parties understood and intended that the option was in fact a sale. We see no satisfactory basis or reason for disagreeing with the judgment of the Court of Appeals in this respect.

The judgment of the Court of Appeals is affirmed.

So ordered.

■ Mr. Justice Douglas, with whom Mr. Justice Brennan and Mr. Justice Stewart concur, dissenting.

* * *

The very construction of § 16(b) reinforces the conclusion that the section is based in the first instance on a totally objective appraisal of the relevant transactions. See Smolowe v. Delendo Corp., *supra*, at 236. Had the draftsmen intended that the operation of the section hinge on abuse of access to inside information it would have been anomalous to limit the section to purchases and sales occurring within six months. Indeed, the purpose of the six-month limitation, coupled with the definition of an insider, was to create a *conclusive presumption* that an insider who turns a short-swing profit in the stock of his corporation had access to inside information *and* capitalized on that information by speculating in the stock. But, the majority departs from the benign effects of this presumption when it assumes that it is "totally unrealistic to assume or infer from the facts before us that Occidental either had or was likely to have access to inside information * * *." Ante, at 201. The majority abides by this assumption even for that period after which Occidental became a 10% shareholder and then extended its tender offer in order to purchase additional Old Kern shares.

The majority takes heart from those decisions of lower federal courts which endorse a "pragmatic" approach to § 16(b). Many involved the question whether a conversion of one security of an issurer into another security of the same issuer constituted a purchase or a sale. It would serve no purpose to parse their holdings because, as Louis Loss describes, they have a "generalization-defying nature." In 1966 the Securities and Exchange Commission exercised its exemptive power under § 16(b) to adopt Rule 16b–9, which under specified conditions excludes a conversion from the operation of § 16(b). This rule will relieve the courts of much of the burden that has developed from *ad hoc* analysis in this narrow area. But, by sanctioning the approach of these cases, the majority brings to fruition Louis Loss's prophecy that they will "continue to rule us from their graves,'' for henceforth they certainly will be applied by analogy to the area of mergers and other consolidations.

Thus, the courts will be caught up in an *ad hoc* analysis of each transaction, determining both from the economics of the transaction and the *modus operandi* of the insider whether there exists the possibility of speculative abuse of inside information. Instead of a section that is easy to administer and by its clear-cut terms discourages litigation, we have instead a section that fosters litigation because the Court's decision holds out the hope for the insider that he may avoid § 16(b) liability. In short, the majority destroys much of the section's prophylactic effect. I would be the first to agree that "[e]very transaction which can be reasonably defined as a purchase [should] be so defined, if the transaction is of a kind which can possibly lend itself to the speculation encompassed by Section 16(b)." Ferraiolo v. Newman, 259 F.2d 342, 345 (C.A.6 1958) (Stewart, J.). See also Reliance Electric Co. v. Emerson Electric Co., *supra*, at 424. Certainly we cannot allow transactions which present the possibility of abuse but do not fall within the classic conception of a purchase or sale to escape the confines of § 16(b). It is one thing to interpret the terms "purchase" and "sale" liberally in order to include those transactions which evidence the evil Congress sought to eliminate; it is quite another to abandon the bright-line test of § 16(b) for those transactions which clearly fall within its literal bounds. Section 16(b), because of the six-month limitation, allows some to escape who have abused their inside information. It should not be surprising, given the objective nature of the rule, if some are caught unwittingly.

* * *

It is this "objective standard" that the Court hung to so tenaciously in Reliance Electric, but now apparently would abandon to a large extent. In my view the Court improperly takes upon itself the task of refashioning the contours of § 16(b) and changing its essential thrust.

* * *

"PURCHASE" AND "SALE"

The unorthodox transaction analysis in *Kern* is limited to involuntary transactions. For example, in Colan v. Mesa Petroleum Co.,[1] where Mesa abandoned its tender offer for Unocal and participated in a recapitalization incident to Unocal's self-tender offer by exchanging Unocal stock that it had bought in the market three months earlier for Unocal bonds created in the recapitalization, the court distinguished *Kern County* on the ground that Mesa's exchange was voluntary.

The broader issue implicated by *Kern* is the meaning of "purchase" and "sale."

A "purchase" or "sale" for the purposes of Section 16(b) may occur even though there is not a cash transaction, but an exchange of stock for property or for other stock. The courts long struggled with when convertible securities transactions would involve a "purchase" or "sale."[2] Similarly, with respect to

---

1. 951 F.2d 1512 (9th Cir.1991), *cert. denied*, 504 U.S. 911 (1992). See also C.R.A. Realty Corp. v. Fremont Gen. Corp., 5 F.3d 1341 (9th Cir.1993).

2. Cf. Park & Tilford v. Schulte, 160 F.2d 984 (2d Cir.1947), *cert. denied*, 332 U.S. 761 (1947) (conversion of senior security into common stock was a "purchase"). Ferraiolo v. Newman, 259 F.2d 342 (6th Cir.1958), *cert.*

the options, *Kern* rejected the acquisition of an option, in contrast to exercise of the option, as a purchase under § 16(b). This approach was subject to sharp criticism. Judge Duff wrote in Seinfeld v. Hospital Corporation of America[3]:

"Virtually all courts to consider the issue have held that 'an exercise of a [ ] [call] option is a purchase of the underlying stock for purposes of § 16(b).' [citations omitted] Thus, according to these cases, if a person exercises an option for stock and then, within six months, sells the stock, he is liable under § 16(b) regardless of whether he was a statutory insider on the date he acquired the option and regardless of whether that date was more than six months prior to the sale of the stock.

"This judicial rule cannot withstand careful analysis. A person who acquires a call option acquires the right to purchase the underlying stock at a given price. If the price of the stock subsequently rises and the person exercises the option and then sells the stock, the 'profit' he earns represents the 'swing' in the price, not between the date of exercise of the option and later sale of the stock, but rather between the time he originally purchases the option and the time he sells the stock."

Derivative Securities: In 1991 the Commission adopted Rule 16a–1(c), which generally defines the term "derivative securities" to mean "an option, warrant, convertible security, stock appreciation right, or similar right with an exercise or conversion privilege at a price related to an equity security."[4] Call options are options to purchase; put options are options to sell.

Both under the 1991 rules and earlier the purchase *and* sale of a derivative security can be actionable under § 16(b), whether derivative securities are purchased in the open market, from the issuer, or in any other way.[5]

As *Kern County* suggests, section 16(b) attaches also to any purchase or sale of stock through exercise of a derivative security.[6]

denied, 359 U.S. 927 (1959) (conversion of preferred stock into common stock did not involve "purchase").

In Gund v. First Florida Banks, Inc., 726 F.2d 682 (11th Cir.1984), the Eleventh Circuit held that a director who sold convertible debentures and within six months purchased common stock by using the proceeds of the sale to purchase stock would be liable under § 16(b).

In contrast, the owner of preferred stock, which is not presently convertible because of material contingencies beyond the owner's control, was held not to be a beneficial owner under § 16(b) when the owner would otherwise have owned over 10 percent of a corporation's common stock had the preferred been immediately convertible. Levner v. Saud, 61 F.3d 8 (2d Cir.1995).

3. 685 F.Supp. 1057, 1065–1067 (N.D.Ill.1988) (footnotes omitted).

4. Sec. Ex. Act Rel. 28,869, 48 SEC Dock. 216 (1991). There are several exceptions.

A "blocker" provision limiting a shareholder's ability to convert shares into common stock to 4.99 percent prevented a defendant from being subject to § 16(b). Levy v. Marshall Capital Management, Inc., 2000–2001 Fed.Sec.L.Rep. (CCH) ¶ 91,230 (E.D.N.Y.2000). See also Schaffer v. CC Inv., LDC, 115 F.Supp.2d 440 (S.D.N.Y.2000) (similar conversion cap).

5. See Rule 16a–4; see generally 5 Louis Loss & Joel Seligman, Securities Regulation 2366–2379 (3d ed. rev. 2001).

Several other items are defined in the 1991 rules. See Rules 16a–1(b) ("call equivalent position"); 16a–1(h) ("put equivalent position"); 16a–1(d) ("equity security of such issuer").

In Magma Power Co. v. Dow Chem. Co., 136 F.3d 316, 322–323 (2d Cir.1998), the court concluded: "The establishment of a 'call establishment position' constitutes a purchase of the underlying security under section 16(b). [Citation deleted.]"

6. See, e.g., Seinfeld v. Hospital Corp. of Am., 685 F.Supp. 1057, 1065 (N.D.Ill. 1988).

In 1991 the Commission adopted Rule 16b–6 based on the premise "that holding derivative securities is functionally equivalent to holding the underlying equity securities for purposes of Section 16:"[7]

The former Commission Section 16 rules and case law, by failing to recognize the functional equivalence of derivative securities and the underlying equity securities, and by therefore focusing on the exercise, rather than the acquisition, of the derivative security, have left open a significant potential for short-swing abuse in trading derivative securities, while permitting recovery in situations that represent long-term investments.[8] For example, an insider with knowledge of a positive material development, to be announced shortly, determines that while he wants to retain his existing equity position, he wants to take advantage of the information, so he purchases issuer warrants. After the public announcement and rise in stock price the insider sells his common stock, obtaining a short-swing profit, knowing that he holds the warrants. Under the former rules, he could simply wait six months and a day to exercise the warrants so the profit would not be subject to Section 16(b) and not recoverable by the company. Ironically, however, an insider who purchased a warrant for investment purposes, exercised the warrant after a year and sold the underlying stock five months later—17 months after the purchase of the warrant, far beyond the six month period the statute defines as short-swing—would be subject to short-swing profit recovery.

Given the short-swing profit potential presented by transactions in derivative securities, the Commission has amended the rules to make it clear that ownership of derivative securities constitutes beneficial ownership of the underlying equity securities for purposes of Section 16. Therefore, transactions in options, convertible securities, warrants and similar derivative securities will be matchable with transactions in other derivative securities and in the underlying equity, and the profits recoverable by the corporation.[9]

Mergers and Tender Offers. The SEC has impliedly ruled that statutory mergers and consolidations are covered generally by exempting certain of them in Rule 16b–7. That rule provides that where one of the corporations involved in a merger or consolidation owns 85 percent or more of the stock of the other corporation before the merger or had 85 percent or more of the combined assets of all corporations involved in the merger or consolidation, any acquisition or disposition of securities by *its* shareholders in connection with the merger or consolidation is not to be treated as a purchase or sale under Section 16(b). In

In Gwozdzinsky v. Zell/Chilmark Fund, L.P., 156 F.3d 305, 308–309 (2d Cir.1998), the court concluded:

> In the case of derivative securities, the SEC has defined the terms "purchase" and "sale" broadly. See, e.g., 17 C.F.R. § 16(b)–6(a). Thus, under Rule 16b–6(d), any insider who writes a put option on securities of the issuer is liable under Section 16(b) to the extent of any premium received for writing the option if the option is either canceled or expires unexercised within six months of its writing, an event that is designed to pre-

vent a scheme whereby an insider with inside information favorable to the issuer writes a put option, and receives a premium for doing so, knowing, by virtue of his inside information, that the option will not be exercised within six months.

7. Sec. Ex. Act Rel. 28,869, 48 SEC Dock. 216, 226 (1991).

8. Nonetheless *Kern County* held that the mere grant of an option is not a sale, or, implicitly, a purchase. 411 U.S. at 601.

9. Id. at 229.

other words, if there is a "downstairs" merger of a corporation into its own subsidiary, or a merger of a "giant" corporation into a "pigmy," and in either case the percentage test is met, the shareholders of the merging corporation have not made a sale of their stock in the merging corporation nor a purchase of the stock received by them in the continuing corporation, for the purpose of Section 16(b). There is a qualification, however, to the effect that the rule does not apply if the person makes both a purchase of a security of a corporation involved in the merger and a sale of a security of any other corporation involved in the merger (other than the merger transaction itself) during a period of six months within which the merger occurs.

Where the merger or sale of assets falls outside the terms of this exemptive rule, the *Kern County Land Co.* case holds that it *may be* a sale of the stock of the acquired corporation (and presumably a purchase of stock of the acquiring corporation), but that in the case of such an "unorthodox" transaction it will not be held to be a purchase or sale if there is no "possibility" that the transaction could "lend itself" to the abuses which Section 16(b) was designed to prevent. In American Standard, Inc. v. Crane Co.[10] the Second Circuit held that where an unsuccessful tender offeror was forced to exchange its holdings for those of another company with which the target company had arranged a "defensive merger", that exchange was not a sale of the securities purchased nor a purchase of the securities received in the merger which could be matched with its sale of those securities within six months. The court also held that the tender offeror's original purchases of stock of the target company which disappeared in the merger could not be matched with its sale of the securities received in the merger, although those also were within a period of six months, because they were securities of different issuers.

In Gold v. Sloan[11] the Fourth Circuit held that the receipt of securities in a merger was a purchase as to one officer-director of the acquired corporation who had complete control of the negotiations, but was not a purchase with respect to another director sued in the same case because he was on the outs with the management of the acquired corporation and had no knowledge of the negotiations beyond what was publicly released, even though he cast the deciding vote for the transaction (which was only approved by a 4–3 vote on the board).[12]

A cash merger under which the shareholders of the acquired corporation are simply paid in cash for their shares would seem to be functionally equivalent to a simple purchase for cash (aside from the involuntary nature of the sale as to those who vote against the merger), and it is doubtful whether it would be considered to be an "unorthodox" transaction within the *Kern County Land Co.* case. The issuer of the securities is extinguished, however, by such a transaction. Such a transaction is usually carried out with a subsidiary of the acquiring corporation (or a subsidiary of a subsidiary) and the surviving corporation has only one shareholder—its new parent.

The cases have generally held that a transaction in which a hostile tender offeror tenders the shares acquired by him to a "white knight" or sells them back to the issuer in a "greenmail" transaction is not an "unorthodox transac-

---

10. 510 F.2d 1043 (2d Cir.1974), *cert. denied*, 421 U.S. 1000 (1975).

11. 486 F.2d 340 (4th Cir.1973), *cert. denied*, 419 U.S. 873 (1974).

12. Compare Morales v. Arlen Realty & Development Corp., 352 F.Supp. 941 (S.D.N.Y.1973); Makofsky v. Ultra Dynamics Corp., 383 F.Supp. 631 (S.D.N.Y.1974).

tion" within the meaning of the *Kern County Land Company* case, since it is merely a voluntary sale for cash.[13] On the other hand, it was held by the Second Circuit that a defeated tender offeror which was forced to accept securities of a rival bidder, when the target company was merged with a subsidiary of the White Knight, was not liable under Section 16(b) under the rationale of the *Kern County Land Company* case, since the exchange of securities was involuntary (the defendant voted against the merger) and there was no possibility of access to inside information in view of the relationship of the defendant to the issuer.[14] However, in Sterman v. Ferro Corporation,[15] the Sixth Circuit upheld the ultimate end-run around potential liability under Section 16(b) by ruling that, where the shareholder sold stock back to the issuer in a greenmail transaction, the issuer simply added on to the purchase price the potential liability under Section 16(b) of the seller and the seller immediately acknowledged such liability and repaid that portion of the consideration back to the issuer, any liability under Section 16(b) had been satisfied. This ploy would of course only work, if at all, where the sale is to the issuing corporation.

The Supreme Court in Gollust v. Mendell[16] held that where a merger of a subsidiary corporation into its parent was carried out after the institution of a suit under Section 16(b) by a shareholder of the subsidiary, and the plaintiff shareholder received stock of the parent corporation in the merger, the plaintiff shareholder was not divested of standing to pursue the litigation. The Court emphasized the fact that the literal language of the statute only requires that the plaintiff be a shareholder of the "issuer" at the time the suit is *instituted*." It is not clear, however, how the court would rule in a case where the merger is carried out before the Section 16(b) action is filed, as it normally would be in this type of case since the merger itself usually furnishes the second half of the transaction which allegedly violated Section 16(b). The court states flatly that the definition of "issuer" in the 1934 Act "does not include parent or subsidiary corporations," but it also refused to rule on the question of whether a plaintiff shareholder of the parent corporation is entitled to bring a "double derivative action" under Section 16(b). It is clear, however, that a cash-out merger which divests the plaintiff of any interest in the parent corporation or the subsidiary, whether carried out before or after the institution of the action under Section 16(b), would deprive the shareholder of any standing to bring that action. The court says that the plaintiff must have a "continuing interest" in the litigation until judgment in order to avoid raising a serious question under the Constitutional requirement in Article III of a "case or controversy."

"ANY PERIOD OF LESS THAN SIX MONTHS"

Any purchase or sale may be matched under § 16(b) with any sale or purchase within six months before or after its date, not merely three months before or after such date.[1] A "period of less than six months" means, since the

---

13.   Texas Int'l Airlines v. National Airlines, Inc., 714 F.2d 533 (5th Cir.1983), *cert. denied*, 465 U.S. 1052 (1984); Super Stores, Inc. v. Reiner, 737 F.2d 962 (11th Cir.1984).

14.   Heublein, Inc. v. General Cinema Corp., 722 F.2d 29 (2d Cir.1983).

15.   785 F.2d 162 (6th Cir.1986).

16.   501 U.S. 115 (1991).

1.   Gratz v. Claughton, 187 F.2d 46 (2d Cir.1951), *cert. denied*, 341 U.S. 920 (1951). To calculate "how long is six months" when measured from the last day of a month with 31 days to a month with no corresponding 31st day, the court in Jammies Int'l, Inc. v.

law does not take account of fractions of days, a period commencing at 0001 hours on one day and ending at midnight on the day two days before the corresponding date in the sixth succeeding month; *e.g.*, from January 15, through July 13, inclusive, in any year. On the other hand, a purchase at 8:00 a.m. on January 15 followed by a sale at 4:00 p.m. on July 14 would be in a period of exactly six months (since January 15 and July 14 are counted as full days), and not within a period of "less than" six months.[2]

"PROFIT REALIZED"

The 1943 Second Circuit opinion, Smolowe v. Delendo Corp.,[1] has long been the controlling precedent on how to calculate the "profit realized" when there is more than one pair of transactions within a six month period:

> We must suppose that the statute was intended to be thoroughgoing, to squeeze all possible profits out of stock transactions, and thus to establish a standard so high as to prevent any conflict between the selfish interest of a fiduciary officer, director, or stockholder and the faithful performance of his duty. * * * The only rule whereby all possible profits can be surely recovered is that of lowest price in, highest price out—within six months—as applied by the district court.

More specifically the calculation proceeds as follows:

> Listed in one column are all the purchases made during the period for which recovery of profits is sought. In another column are listed all of the sales during that period. Then the shares purchased at the lowest price are matched against an equal number of the shares sold at the highest price within six months of such purchase, and the profit computed. After that the next lowest prices matched against the next highest price and that profit is computed. Then, the same process is repeated until all the shares in the purchase column which may be matched against shares sold for higher prices in the sale column have been matched off. Where necessary to accurate computation it would seem proper to split a larger denomination or lot of shares in order to match off part of the lot against an equal amount on the other side. The gross recovery is the sum of the profits thus determined.[2]

But "obviously no transaction can figure in more than one equation."[3] That is to say, if there is a purchase of 100 shares on February 1 followed by a sale of 100 shares on March 1 and another purchase of 100 shares on April 1, the sale on March 1 can be matched against either purchase (the plaintiff, of

Nowinski, 700 F.Supp. 189 (S.D.N.Y.1988), picked the last day of the sixth month rather than the first day of the seventh month. The "draconian penalties" of § 16(b) should not be applied when confusion exists regarding whether its terms have been violated. Id. at 192.

2. Stella v. Graham–Paige Motors Corp., 132 F.Supp. 100 (S.D.N.Y.1955), *rev'd on other grounds*, 232 F.2d 299 (2d Cir.1956), *cert. denied*, 352 U.S. 831 (1956); Colonial Realty Corp. v. MacWilliams, 381 F.Supp. 26 (S.D.N.Y.1974), *aff'd*, 512 F.2d 1187 (2d Cir. 1975), *cert. denied*, 423 U.S. 867 (1975); Mor-

ales v. Reading & Bates Offshore Drilling Co., 392 F.Supp. 41 (N.D.Okla.1975) (citing this casebook).

1. 136 F.2d 231, 239 (2d Cir.1943), *cert. denied*, 320 U.S. 751 (1943).

2. Robert S. Rubin & Myer Feldman, Statutory Inhibitions upon Unfair Use of Corporate Information by Insiders, 95 U. Pa. L. Rev. 468, 482–483 (1947).

3. Gratz v. Claughton, 187 F.2d 46, 52 (2d Cir.1951), *cert. denied*, 341 U.S. 920 (1951).

course, will pick the one at the lower price) but not both. On the other hand, if the case were the same except that 200 shares were sold on March 1, presumably 100 of that figure could be match against the February 1 purchase and the other 100 against the April 1 purchase.

Feder v. Martin Marietta Corp.

United States Court of Appeals, Second Circuit, 1969.
406 F.2d 260, *cert. denied*, 396 U.S. 1036 (1970).

■ Before Waterman, Smith and Hays, Circuit Judges.

■ Waterman, Circuit Judge. Plaintiff-appellant, a stockholder of the Sperry Rand Corporation ("Sperry") after having made the requisite demand upon Sperry which was not complied with, commenced this action pursuant to § 16(b) of the Securities Exchange Act of 1934, 15 U.S.C.A. § 78p(b) (1964), to recover for Sperry "short-swing" profits realized upon Sperry stock purchases and sales by the Martin Marietta Corporation ("Martin"). Plaintiff alleged that George M. Bunker, the President and Chief Executive of Martin Marietta, was deputized by, or represented, Martin Marietta when he served as a member of the Sperry Rand Board of Directors and therefore during his membership Martin Marietta was a "director" of Sperry Rand within the meaning of Section 16(b). The United States District Court for the Southern District of New York, Cooper, J., sitting without a jury, finding no deputization, dismissed plaintiff's action. 286 F.Supp. 937 (S.D.N.Y.1968). We hold to the contrary and reverse the judgment below.

The purpose of § 16(b) as succinctly expressed in the statute itself is to prevent "unfair use of information" by insiders and thereby to protect the public and outside stockholders. The only remedy which the framers of § 16(b) deemed effective to curb insider abuse of advance information was the imposition of a liability based upon an objective measure of proof, e.g., Smolowe v. Delendo Corp., 136 F.2d 231, 235 (2 Cir.), cert. denied 320 U.S. 751 * * * (1943). Thus, application of the act is not conditional upon proof of an insider's intent to profit from unfair use of information, e.g., Blau v. Lamb, 363 F.2d 507, 515 (2 Cir.1966), cert. denied 385 U.S. 1002 * * * (1967), or upon proof that the insider was privy to any confidential information, e.g., Ferraiolo v. Newman, 259 F.2d 342, 344 (6 Cir.1958), cert. denied, 359 U.S. 927 * * * (1959). Rather, Section 16(b) liability is automatic, and liability attaches to any profit by an insider on any short-swing transaction embraced within the arbitrarily fixed time limits of the statute.

The judicial tendency, especially in this circuit, has been to interpret Section 16(b) in ways that are most consistent with the legislative purpose, even departing where necessary from the literal statutory language. See, e.g., cases cited in Blau v. Oppenheim, 250 F.Supp. 881, 884–885 (S.D.N.Y.1966) (Weinfeld, J.). But the policy underlying the enactment of § 16(b) does not permit an expansion of the statute's scope to persons other than directors, officers, and 10% shareholders. Blau v. Lehman, 368 U.S. 403, 410–411 (1962). * * * Through the creation of a legal fiction, however, our courts have managed to remain within the limits of § 16(b)'s literal language and yet have expanded the Act's reach.

In Rattner v. Lehman, 193 F.2d 564 (2 Cir.1952), Judge Learned Hand in his concurring opinion planted the seed for a utilization of the theory of deputization upon which plaintiff here proceeds. In discussing the question whether a partnership is subject to Section 16(b) liability whenever a partner is a director of a corporation whose stock the partnership traded, Judge Hand stated:

> I agree that § 16(b) does not go so far; but I wish to say nothing as to whether, if a firm deputed a partner to represent its interests as a director on the board, the other partners would not be liable. True, they would not even then be formally "directors"; but I am not prepared to say that they could not be so considered; for some purposes the common law does treat a firm as a jural person. 193 F.2d at 567.

The Supreme Court in Blau v. Lehman, 368 U.S. 403, 408–410 (1962), affirming 286 F.2d 786 (2 Cir.1960), affirming 173 F.Supp. 590 (S.D.N.Y.1959) more firmly established the possibility of an entity, such as a partnership or a corporation, incurring Section 16(b) liability as a "director" through the deputization theory. Though the Court refused to reverse the lower court decisions that had held no deputization, it stated:

> Although admittedly not "literally designated" as one, it is contended that Lehman is a director. No doubt Lehman Brothers, though a partnership, could for purposes of § 16 be a "director" of Tide Water and function through a deputy * * *. 368 U.S. at 409 * * *.

In Marquette Cement Mfg. Co. v. Andreas, 239 F. Supp. 962, 967 (S.D.N.Y. 1965), relying upon Blau v. Lehman, the availability of the deputization theory to impose § 16(b) liability was again recognized. * * *

In light of the above authorities, the validity of the deputization theory, presumed to be valid here by the parties and by the district court, is unquestionable. Nevertheless, the situations encompassed by its application are not as clear. The Supreme Court in Blau v. Lehman intimated that the issue of deputization is a question of fact to be settled case by case and not a conclusion of law. See 368 U.S. at 408–409. Therefore, it is not enough for appellant to show us that inferences to support appellant's contentions should have been drawn from the evidence. Id. at 409. Rather our review of the facts and inferences found by the court below is imprisoned by the "unless clearly erroneous" standard. Fed.R.Civ.P. 52(a). In the instant case, applying that standard, though there is some evidence in the record to support the trial court's finding of no deputization, we, upon considering the entire evidence, are left with the definite and firm conviction that a mistake was committed. Guzman v. Pichirilo, 369 U.S. 698, 702 (1962); United States v. United States Gypsum Co., 333 U.S. 364, 394–395 (1948). Consequently, we reverse the result reached below.

Bunker served as a director of Sperry from April 29, 1963 to August 1, 1963, when he resigned. During the period December 14, 1962 through July 24, 1963, Martin Marietta accumulated 801,300 shares of Sperry stock of which 101,300 shares were purchased during Bunker's directorship. Between August 29, 1963 and September 6, 1963, Martin Marietta sold all of its Sperry stock. Plaintiff seeks to reach, on behalf of the Sperry Rand Corporation, the profits made by Martin Marietta from the 101,300 shares of stock acquired between April 29 and August 1, all of which, of course, were sold within six months after purchase.

The district court, in determining that Bunker was not a Martin deputy, made the following findings of fact to support its decision: (1) Sperry initially invited Bunker to join its Board two and a half months before Martin began its accumulation of Sperry stock; (2) Bunker turned down a second offer by Sperry at a time when Martin already held 400,000 shares of Sperry stock; (3) Sperry, not Martin, took the initiative to encourage Bunker to accept the directorship; (4) no other Martin man was ever mentioned for the position in the event Bunker absolutely declined; and (5) Bunker's fine reputation and engineering expertise was the prime motivation for Sperry's interest in him. In addition, the testimony of the only two witnesses who testified at trial, Mr. Bunker and a Mr. Norman Frost, a Sperry director and its chief counsel, were fully believed and accepted as truthful by the court. We assume all of the foregoing findings have a basis of fact in the evidence, but we find there was additional, more germane, uncontradicted evidence, overlooked or ignored by the district court, which we are firmly convinced require us to conclude that Martin Marietta was a "director" of Sperry Rand.

First and foremost is Bunker's testimony that as chief executive of Martin Marietta he was "ultimately responsible for the total operation of the corporation" including personal approval of all the firm's financial investments, and, in particular, all of Martin's purchases of Sperry stock. As the district court aptly recognized, Bunker's control over Martin Marietta's investments, coupled with his position on the Board of Directors of Sperry Rand, placed him in a position where he could acquire inside information concerning Sperry and could utilize such data for Martin Marietta's benefit without disclosing this information to any other Martin Marietta personnel. Thus, the district court's findings that Bunker "never disclosed inside information relevant to investment decisions" and that the "information that he obtained while a director 'simply wasn't germane to that question at all' " are not significant. 286 F.Supp. at 946. Nor are these findings totally supported by the evidence. Bunker's testimony revealed that while he was a Sperry director three Sperry officials had furnished him with information relating to the "short-range outlook" at Sperry, and, in addition, Bunker admitted discussing Sperry's affairs with two officials at Martin Marietta and participating in sessions when Martin's investment in Sperry was reviewed. Moreover, an unsigned document concededly originating from the Martin Marietta files, entitled "Notes on Exploratory Investment in Sperry Rand Corporation," describing the Sperry management, evaluating their abilities, and analyzing the merit of Sperry's forecasts for the future, further indicates that Martin Marietta may have benefited, or intended to benefit, from Bunker's association with Sperry Rand.

In contrast, in Blau v. Lehman, *supra*, where Lehman Brothers was the alleged "director," the Lehman partner exercised no power of approval concerning the partnership's investment; was not consulted for advice; had no advance knowledge of Lehman Brothers' intention to purchase the stock of the corporation of which he was a member of the board of directors; and never discussed the operating details of that corporation's affairs with any member of Lehman Brothers. 368 U.S. at 406. Similarly, in Rattner v. Lehman, *supra*, the court's decision was premised on the assumption that the defendant's purchases and sales were made without any advice or concurrence from the defendant's partner sitting on the Board of the company in whose stock the defendant traded.

It appears to us that a person in Bunker's unique position could act as a deputy for Martin Marietta even in the absence of factors indicating an intention or belief on the part of both companies that he was so acting. We do not hold that, without more, Bunker's control over Martin Marietta, see Marquette Cement Mfg. Co. v. Andreas, *supra* at 967, or the possibility that inside information was obtained or disclosed, mandates that Bunker was Martin's deputy. However, additional evidence detailed hereafter which indicates that the managements of Sperry Rand and of Martin Marietta intended that Bunker should act as Martin's deputy on the Sperry Board, and believed he was so acting, lends valuable support to our factual conclusion.

First, in Bunker's letter of resignation to General MacArthur, the Chairman of the Board of Directors of Sperry Rand, he stated:

> When I became a member of the Board in April, it appeared to your associates that the Martin Marietta ownership of a substantial number of shares of Sperry Rand should have representation on your Board. This representation does not seem to me really necessary and I prefer not to be involved in the affairs of Sperry Rand when there are so many other demands on my time * * *.

Martin Marietta urges that we should not read this letter to mean what it so clearly says. They would have us believe that this letter was so phrased because Bunker intended "to write a gentle letter of resignation to a great (but elderly) man whom he admired, in terms that he would understand." No matter how advanced in years the Chairman of the Sperry Board may have been, we are puzzled by defendant's contention that he, and only he, of all those on the Sperry Board, considered Bunker to be representing Martin's interests. Furthermore, if, throughout Bunker's service, the Chairman of the Board misunderstood the purpose of Bunker's directorship, why Bunker upon resignation would want this misunderstanding perpetuated is even more perplexing. Certainly the more logical inference from the wording of Bunker's letter of resignation is the inference that Bunker served on the Sperry Board as a representative of Martin Marietta so as to protect Martin's investment in Sperry.

Second, the Board of Directors of Martin Marietta formally consented to and approved Bunker's directorship of Sperry prior to Bunker's acceptance of the position. While Martin's organizational policy required that Bunker secure that Board's approval of any corporate directorship he were offered, the approval was not obtained until, significantly, the Board had been informed by Bunker that Martin had a 10 million dollar investment in Sperry stock at the time. Bunker testified that he "thought the Board would draw the inference that his presence on Sperry's Board would be to Martin's interest." Indeed, as noted by the district court, "the logic behind such an inference is obvious when we stop to consider that a directorship, by its very nature, carries with it potential access to information unavailable to the ordinary investor." 286 F.Supp. at 945. Surely such conduct by the Martin Board supports an inference that it deputized Bunker to represent its interests on Sperry's Board. The trial court's finding to the contrary leaves us with the definite and firm conviction that a mistake was indeed committed.

Finally, Bunker's testimony clearly established that the Martin Marietta Corporation had representatives or deputies who served on the boards of other corporations. The only distinctions drawn by the court below to differentiate Bunker's Sperry relationship from the relationship to Martin Marietta of other Martin Marietta deputies on other corporate boards were that Bunker had no duty to report back to Martin what was going on at Sperry and there was a lesser degree of supervision over Bunker's actions than over the actions of the others. Otherwise Bunker was a typical Martin deputy. In view of Bunker's position of almost absolute authority over Martin's affairs, such differences hardly suffice to refute the evidentiary value of the similarities between the functions of Bunker and those of Martin's representatives on other corporate boards.

In summary, it is our firm conviction that the district court erred in apportioning the weight to be accorded the evidence before it. The control possessed by Bunker, his letter of resignation, the approval by the Martin Board of Bunker's directorship with Sperry, and the functional similarity between Bunker's acts as a Sperry director and the acts of Martin's representatives on other boards, as opposed to the factors relied upon by the trial court, are all definite and concrete indicatives that Bunker, in fact, was a Martin deputy, and we find that indeed he was.

The trial court's disposition of the case obviated the need for it to determine whether § 16(b) liability could attach to the corporate director's short-swing profits realized after the corporation's deputy had ceased to be a member of the board of directors of the corporation whose stock had been so profitably traded in. It was not until after Bunker's resignation from the Sperry Board had become effective that Martin Marietta sold any Sperry stock. The issue is novel and until this case no court has ever considered the question. We hold that the congressional purpose dictates that Martin must disgorge all short-swing profits made from Sperry stock purchased during its Sperry directorship and sold after the termination thereof if sold within six months of purchase. * * *

"OFFICER OR DIRECTOR"

The term "officer" is defined by the SEC to mean "an issuer's president, principal financial officer, or principal accounting officer (or, if there is no such accounting officer, the controller), any vice-president of the issuer in charge of a principal business unit, division or function (such as sales, administration or finance), any other officer who performs a policy-making function, or any other person who performs similar policy-making functions for the issuer. Officers of the issuer's parent(s) or subsidiaries shall be deemed officers of the issuer if they perform such policy-making functions for the issuer."[1] An officer of a subsidiary of the issuer has been held not to be subject to Section 16(b), unless he or she is in fact performing the functions of an officer of the parent corporation.[2]

In Merrill Lynch, Pierce, Fenner & Smith, Inc. v. Livingston[3] the Ninth Circuit held that a securities salesman who was given the "honorary" title of vice president was not an officer with access to inside information within the coverage of Section 16(b).[4] The court said that it must look behind the title of

1. Rule 16a–1(f).

2. Lee Nat'l Corp. v. Segur, 281 F.Supp. 851 (E.D.Pa.1968). However, a person who was the "Executive Vice–President of International Operations" of a corporation and "one of the more active members of the executive committee" did not get anywhere with the argument that he was "merely a figurehead" and should not be liable under Section 16(b). Selas Corp. of Am. v. Voogd, 365 F.Supp. 1268 (E.D.Pa.1973).

3. 566 F.2d 1119 (9th Cir.1978).

4. This holding was limited, however, in the subsequent Ninth Circuit case of National Medical Enterprises, Inc. v. Small, 680 F.2d 83 (9th Cir.1982), to a situation where the person's title "is essentially honorary or ceremonial."

the person to ascertain his real duties and that "A person who does not have the title of an officer may, in fact, have a relationship to the company which gives him the very access to insider information that the statute was designed to reach." The *Livingston* case was followed in the Sixth Circuit and the Second Circuit.[5] In the case of C.R.A. Realty Corp. v. Crotty[6] the Second Circuit stated that "it is an employee's duties and responsibilities—rather than his actual title—that determine whether he is an officer within the purview of § 16(b)."

The SEC rules adopted in 1991, however, have embodied the approach of these cases in making the determination of whether an individual is an officer depend upon function rather than title. In a note to Rule 16a–1(f), the Commission indicated that " 'policy-making function' is not intended to include policy-making functions that are not significant."

While the Supreme Court in the case of Blau v. Lehman[7] indicated that one person may be "deputed" to act for another on the board of directors, thereby making the principal a "director" for the purposes of Section 16(b), it also made clear that the actual fact of such "deputizing" must be proven by the plaintiff. To what extent, if any, does the court in the *Feder* case broaden this principle?

It has been held that an officer or director is liable under Section 16(b) for short-swing profits even though he only holds such office at the time of the sale and not at the time of the prior purchase.[8] It has also been held that an officer or director may be liable for short-swing profits on stock which was registered at the time of the purchase or sale, although not at the time of the matching transaction less than six months earlier.[9] The same result was reached in the *Feder* case where the defendant was only an officer or director at the time of the purchase and not at the time of the subsequent sale after he leaves office. Both the Second Circuit[10] and the Third Circuit[11] have held, however, that there is no liability imposed upon a director or officer where both ends of the transaction occurred *after* he left office, even though within six months thereafter.

The 1991 Section 16 Rules have overruled the first result of the cases mentioned above by exempting the front end of any transaction which occurs before a person becomes an officer or director, on the theory that the person could not normally have had any access to inside information before he became an insider; and if in fact he did, a remedy would exist under Rule 10b–5. Those rules, however, have adopted all of the other results of the cases cited above.

Feder v. Frost

United States Court of Appeals for the Second Circuit, 2000.
220 F.3d 29.

■ Before: WINTER, CHIEF JUDGE, CARDAMONE, and STRAUB, CIRCUIT JUDGES.

■ WINTER, CHIEF JUDGE:

Mark Feder appeals from Judge Owen's dismissal of his complaint, which alleged a violation of Section 16(b) of the Securities Exchange Act of 1934, 15

---

5. Winston v. Federal Express Corporation, 853 F.2d 455 (6th Cir.1988); C.R.A. Realty Corp. v. Crotty, 878 F.2d 562 (2d Cir. 1989).

6. 878 F.2d at 566.

7. 368 U.S. 403 (1962).

8. Adler v. Klawans, 267 F.2d 840 (2d Cir.1959); Marquette Cement Manufacturing Co. v. Andreas, 239 F.Supp. 962 (S.D.N.Y. 1965).

9. Arrow Distributing Corp. v. Baumgartner, 783 F.2d 1274 (5th Cir.1986).

10. Lewis v. Varnes, 505 F.2d 785 (2d Cir.1974).

11. Lewis v. Mellon Bank, 513 F.2d 921 (3d Cir.1975).

U.S.C. § 78p(b). Feder is a shareholder of IVAX Corporation and brought the suit derivatively on its behalf. His complaint alleged that appellee Philip Frost is a statutory insider of IVAX and that Frost and Frost–Nevada Limited Partnership ("FNLP"), a firm controlled by Frost, are controlling shareholders of North American Vaccine, Inc. ("NAVI"). He claims that Frost/FNLP must disgorge short-swing profits under Section 16(b) as a result of sales by NAVI of IVAX common stock and purchases by Frost/FNLP of IVAX stock.

The district court concluded as a matter of law that Frost/FNLP did not "realize" any profits from NAVI's sale of IVAX stock. Feder v. Frost, 1999 U.S. Dist. LEXIS 3463, No. 98 CV 4744, 1999 WL 163174, at *2–3 (S.D.N.Y. Mar.24, 1999). We disagree and reverse.

BACKGROUND

* * *

Frost is Chairman and CEO of IVAX, a publicly owned corporation. The sole general partner of FNLP is a corporation, all of whose shares are owned by Frost. Frost, with FNLP, is the beneficial owner of 12.8% of IVAX's stock. Frost is also a director of NAVI, whose stock is publicly traded as well. Frost, with FNLP, owns 17.3% of NAVI's common stock.

In addition, Frost and FNLP are parties to a shareholders' agreement. The combined holdings of the parties to this agreement amount to 50.8% of NAVI's common stock. The parties nominate individuals to NAVI's board of directors and have "effective control" over NAVI. The complaint states, "As a result of these contractual arrangements and ... rights at law, Frost ... has: (1) Voting power which includes the power to vote, or to direct the voting of, NAVI securities; and/or (2) Investment power which includes the power to dispose, or to direct the disposition, of NAVI securities."

During various times in late 1995 and early 1996, Frost and FNLP purchased IVAX shares and NAVI sold IVAX shares. Appellant claims that Frost/FNLP were beneficial owners of the IVAX shares sold by NAVI for purposes of Section 16(b). He also contends that all purchases and sales by Frost, FNLP, and NAVI within six months of each other can be matched to determine profits, if any, by the standards applicable under Section 16(b). When matched, he alleges, they disclose substantial short-swing profits. Although these profits accrued to NAVI, appellant claims that they are attributable to Frost/FNLP on a pro rata basis as a result of the increase in value of their NAVI holdings.

* * *

The district court dismissed the complaint because it concluded that Frost/FNLP did not "realize" any profits from NAVI's sales of IVAX stock. Conceding that the transactions increased the value of NAVI—and that Frost/FNLP may have benefitted from this increased value, see *Feder, 1999 U.S. Dist. LEXIS 3463, 1999 WL 163174,* at *2—the court held that "in a traditional section 16(b) case, the defendant would have cash in hand which the court might require him to disgorge. It is not entirely clear to me how this defendant could be required to disgorge this 'economic effect.'" Id.

The district court also rejected appellant's argument that Rule 16a–1(a)(2)'s definition of "beneficial owner" applies to the determination of whether profits from various purchases and sales have been realized for purposes of Section 16(b). *1999 U.S. Dist. LEXIS 3463,* at *7, Id. at *2 n.6. The district court held that the Rule 16a–1(a)(2) definition "is to be used solely for determining whether a person" is a statutory insider and, because there was no dispute that Frost/FNLP is a statutory insider of NAVI, that definition was irrelevant.

* * *

DISCUSSION

* * *

a) Rule 16a–1

The Exchange Act does not define the term "beneficial owner." However, in 1988, the SEC proposed rules under Section 16 that, inter alia, contained such a definition. [Citation Omitted.] The accompanying SEC release explained that the rules were being proposed in part because "uncertainty as to the status of indirect interests in securities of the issuer, such as ownership of derivative securities and holdings of the immediate family, trusts, corporations, and partnerships, has raised requests for a definition." [Citations Omitted.] Two definitions of "beneficial owner" were deemed necessary by the Commission because of the different uses to which the term is put in Section 16. The first use is to determine who is a ten-percent beneficial owner and therefore a statutory insider. The second use is the determination of which transactions must be reported under Section 16(a) as effecting a change in beneficial ownership or as triggering liability under Section 16(b). [Citations Omitted.]

The rules were adopted in final form in 1991. * * *

Rule 16a–1(a)(1) * * * provides the definition of beneficial owner that "is used only to determine [insider] status as a ten percent holder." Exchange Act Release No. 34–28869, *56 Fed. Reg. at 7244* (using standards set forth in Section 13(d) of Exchange Act); see also Exchange Act Release No. 34–26333, *53 Fed. Reg. at 50001* (explaining that analysis of beneficial owner for purposes of ascertaining who is ten-percent holder turns on person's potential for control so that proposed new rule relies on Section 13(d) for deciding who is ten-percent holder). Once ten-percent status—or, of course, status as an officer or director—is determined, the definition of beneficial owner provided by Rule 16a–1(a)(2) comes into play for purposes of the reporting and short-swing profit provisions of Section 16. Under Rule 16a–1(a)(2), "the term beneficial owner shall mean any person who, directly or indirectly ... has or shares a direct or indirect pecuniary interest in the equity securities...." *17 C.F.R. § 240.16a–1(a)(2).* The term "pecuniary interest" is defined as "the opportunity, directly or indirectly, to profit or share in any profit derived from a transaction in the subject securities." *17 C.F.R. § 240.16a–1(a)(2)(i).* The pecuniary interest test was designed to "codify the courts' emphasis on pecuniary interests and deem that indirect pecuniary interests are sufficient to establish a reporting obligation and the potential for short-swing profit recovery with respect to those securities." [Citation Omitted.]

Securities owned by a corporation are assets affecting the value of that corporation's shares, and a shareholder does in that meaningful sense have at least an indirect pecuniary interest in portfolio securities. However, attributing a corporation's transactions in portfolio securities to all shareholders would clearly cast the net far too wide, and thus the Rule provides a "safe harbor"— actually a provision more in the nature of an exception—under which a shareholder is deemed not to have a pecuniary interest in a corporation's portfolio securities. Under the safe harbor, corporate transactions in portfolio securities are not attributed to a shareholder "if the shareholder is not a controlling shareholder of the entity and does not have or share investment control over the entity's portfolio." *17 C.F.R. § 240.16a–1(a)(2)(iii).*

According to the SEC release accompanying the adoption of the Rule, the term "controlling shareholder" refers only to a shareholder with the power to exercise control over the corporation by virtue of his or her securities holdings. * * *

b) *The Merits*

The merits turn essentially on the answer to three questions: (i) does Rule 16a–1(a) render Frost/FNLP a beneficial owner of the IVAX stock sold by NAVI for purposes of triggering Section 16(b) liability; (ii) does the safe harbor protect Frost/FNLP from Section 16(b) liability as a matter of law; and (iii) if (i) is answered in the affirmative, and (ii) in the negative, is the Rule beyond the SEC's rule-making authority? We answer (i) in the affirmative and (ii) and (iii) in the negative.

With regard to whether Frost/FNLP was a beneficial owner of the IVAX stock traded by NAVI, we cannot agree with the district court that Rule 16a–1(a)(2) is irrelevant because Frost/FNLP's status as a statutory insider in NAVI is undisputed. Under the plain language of the Rule, its definition of beneficial owner applies for purposes "other than" determining whether a person is a beneficial owner of more than ten percent of any class of equity securities. *17 C.F.R. § 240.16a–1(a)(2).* It is, therefore, of direct relevance to the issue of whether Frost/FNLP was a beneficial owner of the IVAX stock sold by NAVI for purposes of Section 16(b).

Rule 16a–1(a)(2)'s definition of "beneficial ownership" clearly encompasses the facts alleged in the complaint. The complaint alleged purchases and sales of IVAX's stock by Frost/FNLP and NAVI within a period of less than six months that resulted in a profit to NAVI. Given Frost/FNLP's ownership of stock in NAVI, Frost/FNLP had an indirect pecuniary interest in NAVI's IVAX stock because it shared indirectly in NAVI's profit through an increase in the value of their NAVI holdings.

We must also reject Frost/FNLP's claim that Rule 16a–1(a)(2)(iii)'s safe-harbor provision—or exception—exempts Frost/FNLP from the definition of beneficial owner as a matter of law. We simply cannot determine at this stage in the litigation whether the safe harbor applies because appellant has alleged a shareholders' agreement that would support a finding that Frost/FNLP had working control, with others, over NAVI's portfolio. See Rule 16a–1(a)(2)(iii). Frost claims to have had no actual involvement in NAVI's decision to sell the IVAX stock, but that is clearly not a matter to be determined on a Fed. R. Civ. P. 12(b)(6) motion.

The argument that Rule 16a–1(a)(2) is invalid because any profit to Frost/FNLP was not "realized" relies heavily upon our decision in *Mayer v. Chesapeake Ins. Co., 877 F.2d 1154 (2d Cir.1989).* In Mayer, we affirmed the dismissal of a Section 16(b) claim against an individual defendant as well as against certain companies that the individual defendant either owned or controlled. See *877 F.2d at 1155–56*. As to the Section 16(b) liability of a shareholder of a corporation that trades in the securities of another corporation in which the shareholder is an insider, we stated:

> [I]n considering § 16(b) claims against an individual shareholder of a corporation that engaged in short-swing transactions in the shares of a registered company of which the individual was a director and hence an insider, the district courts have generally held that the insider's benefit as a director or as a shareholder of the transacting corporation was too indirect to make him responsible for disgorgement of profits under § 16(b).

Id. at 1160–61 (citing and discussing two district court cases). Based on the authorities discussed, including several SEC releases, we framed the issue as whether the defendants received any "direct benefit" from the sale of shares. We concluded that no "direct benefit" was received. *Id. at 1162.*

In so concluding, we specifically rejected plaintiff's contention that because of the individual defendant's position and the interrelationships among all the defendants that they should collectively be deemed "joint beneficial owners" of the stock at issue. We rejected that argument because it would require us, "in effect, [to] engraft onto § 16(b) the contours of § 13(d) ... [and] since the focus of § 13(d) is control, we have not viewed the group of persons who are subject to the strict liability imposed by § 16(b) for disgorgement of profits as congruent with the group of persons to whom ... § 13(d) applies." Id.

We specifically acknowledged, however, that the SEC had not "in the past viewed the different thrusts of the two sections as warranting defining the two groups identically ... [and a]s a result, different determinations of beneficial ownership under the section and rule are possible." Id. (internal quotations and citations omitted). We also noted that the SEC had recently proposed a "new rule [16a–1(a)], which would extend § 16(b) liability to insiders having merely an indirect pecuniary interest, thereby changing existing law, and perhaps unifying the concepts of beneficial ownership under §§ 16(a), 16(b), and 13(d)...." Id. (internal citations omitted and emphasis added). But we determined that "the proposed rule does not govern the present case." Id. Mayer does not, therefore, suggest in any way that the proposed rule would be invalid as beyond the SEC's power.

* * *

CONCLUSION

We therefore reverse.

TEN PERCENT HOLDER

In 1976 the Supreme Court decided the case of Foremost–McKesson, Inc. v. Provident Securities Co.[1] holding that the defendant had to be a 10% holder *before* the purchase in order to impose liability upon it under Section 16(b). The Court stated:

"Our construction of § 16(b) also is supported by the distinction Congress recognized between short-term trading by mere stockholders and such trading by directors and officers. The legislative discourse revealed that Congress thought that all short-swing trading by directors and officers was vulnerable to abuse because of their intimate involvement in corporate affairs. But trading by

---

1. 423 U.S. 232 (1976).

mere stockholders was viewed as being subject to abuse only when the size of their holdings afforded the potential for access to corporate information. These different perceptions simply reflect the realities of corporate life.

"It would not be consistent with this perceived distinction to impose liability on the basis of a purchase made when the percentage of stock ownership requisite to insider status had not been acquired. To be sure, the possibility does exist that one who becomes a beneficial owner by a purchase will sell on the basis of information attained by virtue of his newly acquired holdings. But the purchase itself was not one posing dangers that Congress considered intolerable, since it was made when the purchaser owned no shares or less than the percentage deemed necessary to make one an insider. Such a stockholder is more analogous to the stockholder who never owns more than 10% and thereby is excluded entirely from the operation of § 16(b), than to a director or officer whose every purchase and sale is covered by the statute. While this reasoning might not compel our construction of the exemptive provision, it explains why Congress may have seen fit to draw the line it did. Cf. Adler v. Klawans, 267 F.2d 840, 845 (C.A.2 1959)."[2]

In Reliance Electric Co. v. Emerson Electric Co.[3] the Supreme Court held that where a 10% holder sold an amount of stock sufficient to bring him below the 10% level and then sold the remainder of his holdings, both sales being within six months of a purchase, only the first sale could be matched with the purchase to produce Section 16(b) liability, even though the sales were arranged in this way for the express purpose of avoiding such liability with respect to the second sale. The Court said: "In this case, the respondent, the owner of 13.2% of a corporation's shares, disposed of its entire holdings in two sales, both of them within six months of purchase. The first sale reduced the respondent's holdings to 9.96% and the second disposed of the remainder. The question presented is whether the profits derived from the second sale are recoverable by the Corporation under § 16(b). We hold that they are not."

In Chemical Fund, Inc. v. Xerox Corp.[4] a mutual fund purchased more than 10% of an outstanding issue of convertible debentures of Xerox Corp. The debentures were a registered security and an "equity security" as defined in the 1934 Act, but these debentures were convertible only into approximately 2.72% of the Xerox common stock if they had all been converted. While it was in this position, the fund purchased convertible debentures of Xerox and sold common stock of Xerox within a six months period, and the District Court held it liable for the profit computed by matching these transactions. The Second Circuit reversed. Judge Lumbard said:

"Thus the question is: are the Debentures by themselves a 'class of any equity security,' or does the class consist of the common stock augmented, as to any beneficial holder in question, by the number of shares into which the Debentures it owns are convertible? We think that the Debentures are not a class by themselves; the total percentage of common stock which a holder would own following a hypothetical conversion of the Debentures it holds is the test of liability under section 16(b). The history of the legislation, the stated purpose of the Act, and the anomalous consequences of any other meaning all support this conclusion."[5]

---

2.   423 U.S. at 253, 254.

3.   404 U.S. 418, 419–420 (1972).

4.   377 F.2d 107 (2d Cir.1967).

5.   377 F.2d at 110. Compare with the *Chemical Fund* case, Ellerin v. Massachusetts Mut. Life Ins. Co., 270 F.2d 259 (2d

While a person who falls within Section 16(b) is liable for short-swing profits in *"any* equity security" of the issuer, regardless of whether it is registered or not, in order for the section to apply the corporation must have *some* equity security registered, and in order to be brought within the section as a 10% holder (as distinguished from an officer or director) the person must be a 10% holder of a *registered* security.

PROBLEM 14–9

(1) If a person acquires 120,000 shares of a registered security, of which there are 1,000,000 shares outstanding, on May 1; purchases an additional 50,000 shares on July 1; sells 70,001 shares on September 1; and sells all of his remaining 99,999 shares on September 5; for which, if any, shares would the person be liable under § 16(b)?

(2) Suppose that a corporation has a listed common stock outstanding and also a convertible preferred which is neither listed nor registered under Section 12(g) (because not held by more than 500 persons). A owns 90% of the preferred issue, which is convertible into more than 10% of the common, assuming complete conversion. The owner purchases and sells preferred within a period of six months. Under the *Chemical Fund* rationale, is the owner subject to liability under Section 16(b) as a 10% holder of a *registered* security?

RULE 16b–3

There are several statutory and rule exemptions from §§ 16(a) and (b). The most frequently amended and litigated of these exemptive rules is Rule 16b–3 which exempts certain employee benefit plans from § 16(b).

In 1996 a new version of Rule 16b–3 was adopted. The adoption Release explained in part:

> New Rule 16b–3 exempts from short-swing profit recovery any acquisitions and dispositions of issuer equity securities (including those that occur upon the exercise or conversion of a derivative security, whether in-or out-of-the money) between an officer or director and the issuer, subject to simplified conditions. A transaction with an employee benefit plan sponsored by the issuer will be treated the same as a transaction with the issuer. However, unlike the current rule, a transaction need not be pursuant to an employee benefit plan or any compensatory program to be exempt, nor need it specifically have a compensatory element.

> A transaction will be exempt if it satisfies the appropriate conditions set forth among four alternative categories: Tax–Conditioned and Related Plans; Discretionary Transactions; Grants, Awards and Other Acquisitions from the Issuer; and Dispositions to the Issuer. New Rule 16b–3 eliminates many of the conditions of current Rule 16b–3, such as general written plan conditions, the prohibition against transfer of derivative securities, shareholder approval as a general condition for plan exemption, the six-month holding period as a general condition for the exemption of grant and award transactions, the disinterested administration or formula plan require-

---

Cir.1959), in which the court held that two "series" of preferred stock, differing as to dividend rates, redemption prices and sinking fund provisions, nevertheless constituted a single "class" for the purpose of determining whether a person was a 10% holder under Section 16(b).

ments regarding grant transactions, and the window period requirement for fund-switching transactions and stock appreciation right exercises.[1]

Under the 1996 rules derivative securities will get two bites at the apple. Under Note (1) to Rule 16b–3, if they do not satisfy that Rule they may be exempt if they satisfy Rule 16b–6(b). On the other hand, under the Note to Rule 16b–6(b), the exercise or conversion of a derivative security that does not satisfy Rule 16b–6(b) may be exempted under Rule 16b–3.

With regard to § 16, *see generally* 5 Louis Loss & Joel Seligman, Securities Regulation 2321–2482 (3d ed. rev. 2001); Steve Thel, The Genius of Section 16: Regulating the Management of Publicly Held Companies, 42 Hastings L.J. 391 (1991); Merritt B. Fox, Insider Trading Deterrence versus Managerial Incentives: A Unified Theory of Section 16(b), 92 Mich. L. Rev. 2088 (1994); but see Michael H. Dessent, Weapons to Fight Insider Trading in the 21st Century: A Call for the Repeal of Section 16(b), 33 Akron L. Rev. 481 (2000).

THE SARBANES–OXLEY ACT

Section 306 of the Sarbanes–Oxley Act prohibits director or executive officer trades during pension fund blackout periods.

Section 306(a)(4) defines a blackout period with respect to an issuer's equity securities

(A) means any period of more than 3 consecutive business days during which the ability of not fewer than 50 percent of the participants or beneficiaries under all individual account plans maintained by the issuer to purchase, sell, or otherwise acquire or transfer an interest in any equity of such issuer held in such fiduciary of the plan; and

(B) does not include, under regulations which shall be prescribed by the Commission—

(i) a regularly scheduled period in which the participants and beneficiaries may not purchase, sell, or otherwise acquire or transfer an interest in any equity of such issuer, if such period is—

(1) incorporated into the individual account plan; and

(2) timely disclosed to employees before becoming participants under the individual account plan or as a subsequent amendment to the plan; or

(ii) any suspension described in subparagraph (A) that is imposed solely in connection with person becoming participants or beneficiaries, or ceasing to be participants or beneficiaries, in an individual account plan by reason of a corporate merger, acquisition, divestiture, or similar transaction involving the plan or plan sponsor.

---

1. Sec. Ex. Act Rel. 37,260, 62 SEC Dock. 138, 143 (1996).

CHAPTER 15

GENERAL CIVIL LIABILITY PROVISIONS

A. THE PRIVATE SECURITIES LITIGATION REFORM ACT OF 1995

1. THE DILEMMA OF PRIVATE SECURITIES LITIGATION

The passage of the Private Securities Litigation Reform Act of 1995 (the "1995 Act") reflected a number of political and social developments, including the election of Republican majorities in both Houses of Congress for the first time in over forty years and the increasing disenchantment of much of the public with securities class actions (and possibly with private enforcement of law in general). The 1995 Act also sought to respond to academic critiques of securities litigation.

During the course of the Congressional hearings that led up to the passage of the 1995 Act,[1] much of the critical testimony directed at securities class actions went beyond "war stories" of specific abuses and called into question the overall social utility of the securities class action. The following charges (with various qualifications and refinements) were made by a number of witnesses and contemporaneous academic critics:

1. The volume of securities class actions was increasing to "epidemic" proportions, with securities class actions being triggered almost automatically by any 10% or greater one-day decline in a stock's price; as a result, class actions succeeded less at deterring fraud than at penalizing companies with high volatility.

2. In securities class actions, the benefits to individual class members were negligible, seldom exceeding a very small percentage of their losses.

3. Securities class actions were lawyer-driven, because plaintiffs' attorneys reaped millions in fees while class members received only pennies. Often, such high fees were the result of collusive deals between plaintiffs' attorneys and defense counsel that left the class members undercompensated.

4. Securities class actions settled not on the basis of their merits, but based on their "nuisance value" (that is, the direct and indirect costs of defending against them). Hence, the easy availability of securities class actions tended mainly to encourage the filing of highly speculative claims.

Each of these claims was robustly denied by proponents of securities class actions, and each side presented to Congress their own empirical studies. Although little consensus has yet emerged, and the empirical data still remains

---

1. Both the Senate and the House held extensive hearings. See "Private Litigation Under the Federal Securities Laws: Hearings Before the Subcomm. on Securities of the Senate Committee on Banking, Housing and Urban Affairs," 103rd Congress, 1st Sess. (June 17 and July 21, 1993) (hereinafter, "Senate Hearings") and "Securities Litigation Reform Hearings Before the House Subcommittee on Telecommunications and Finance of the Committee on Energy and Commerce," 103rd Congress, 2nd Sess. (July 22 and August 10, 1994) (hereinafter "House Hearings").

less than ideal, subsequent studies and research has clarified some of the issues and introduced new evidence.

Of all the criticisms directed at securities litigation, the claim that the volume of securities litigation was dramatically accelerating has proven the least tenable. While anecdotal impressions were abundant, hard data did not establish any significant increase in volume over time, but rather revealed very high variance from year to year. SEC Director of Enforcement, William R. McLucas, presented the only hard statistics at the Congressional hearings, and these showed an irregular pattern of peaks and valleys: for example, 235 securities class actions had been filed in 1973, 268 in 1992 (the last year before his testimony), but only 108 in 1987.[2] Still, even this data indicated that annual class action filings in the early 1990's were running well ahead of the pace in the 1980's (but no higher than in some years during the 1970's). Both sides could thus take some comfort. However, before any inferences are drawn from this data, it should be understood that subsequent researchers have found much of this data on aggregate filings to be unreliable.[3] One problem that confounded the effort to measure volume was the tendency for a dozen or more parallel class actions to be filed against the same issuer, often within a matter of days or even hours, and then to be consolidated into a single class action proceeding by the Panel on Multi–District Litigation. Thus, to avoid double counting, some later studies have focused on the number of issuers sued during a period, not the number of actions filed. For example, a subsequent study that looked to the issuers sued produced the following numbers on the average annual filing rate for securities class actions:[4]

Average Annual Litigation Rates
Pre-Reform Act

	Federal Court Findings	Total Dispositions
1991	153	138
1992	192	156
1993	158	173
1994	220	191
1995	162	220
TOTAL	885	878
Annual Average:	177	176

In light of this more recent data, which chiefly illustrates the period-to-period fluctuations in class action filings, even critics of securities litigation have

---

2. See Senate Hearings at 121.

3. A Federal Judicial Center study of class actions has found that the actual number of class actions filed may be significantly higher than those reported to the Administrative Office of the Federal Courts, and the actual annual filing rate being as much as two to five times higher. See Thomas E. Willging, et al., EMPIRICAL STUDY OF CLASS ACTIONS IN FOUR FEDERAL DISTRICTS, pp. 198–199 (1996). This tendency may be attributable to poor record-keeping or the tendency for an action initially filed as an individual action to be later amended into a class action.

4. Denise Martin, et al. *Recent Trends IV: What Explains Filings and Settlements in Shareholder Class Actions?* (National Economic Research Associates, 1996) at Table 1 and Table 5; see also, Joseph A. Grundfest and Michael A. Perino, SECURITIES LITIGATION REFORM: The First Year's Experience (1987) at Table 2. The premise of the above chart is that over the long run, annual dispositions (after an initial lag) should more or less match annual filings (as they seem to do in this table).

largely abandoned the claim that there was any exponential rise in the volume of securities class actions during the 1990's.[5]

The claim that any 10% drop in stock price would lead automatically to the filing of a securities class action was made by several Silicon Valley executives at the Senate Hearings preceding the 1995 Act. In response, plaintiffs' attorneys commissioned a financial economist to compute the total number of one-day stock price drops of 10% or greater on the New York, American, and NADSAQ stock markets and compare them with the number of subsequent class actions against those issuers. The data showed 33,206 such one-day stock drops of 10% or greater, but only 1,584 subsequent class actions—or a relatively modest 4.4% rate.[6]

Still, even if the claim that class actions automatically follow a stock drop has been debunked as a myth, subsequent surveys do show that securities class actions are most frequently brought against high-technology companies. Arguably, such disproportionate exposure may chill the capital formation process in these industries.

Another argument repeatedly made to Congress was that class members in securities class actions received only negligible recoveries on an individual basis. The fullest study at the time of the hearings showed that, in some 254 settlements of securities class actions between 1991 and 1993, the median payment to class members was about 5% of their losses (or a median settlement of around $4 million).[7] Such evidence was consistent either with the interpretation that securities class actions were disproportionately frivolous suits, brought for their harassment value, or with the view that such actions were settled collusively in a manner that subordinated the interests of the class to the goal of maximizing the plaintiffs' attorneys fees.[8]

The problem in evaluating securities class actions based on the relationship between settlement size and investor "losses" is that it is extremely difficult to develop an accurate measure of the losses that were legally caused by the defendant. Although it is comparatively simple to measure the total decline in a stock's price over a specified period, the decline that is attributable to the defendant's misconduct (i.e., any material misstatement or omission) may be only a small fraction of the total decline that the stock experienced. Basically, a defendant is liable only for that portion of the plaintiff's economic losses that the plaintiff can show were proximately caused by the defendant's actionable misrepresentations or omissions. Thus, for example, a stock may fall fifty points in a single day following disclosure of previously undisclosed material information, but much of this decline may be attributable to external developments in the world or in the financial markets or to a general industry decline. As a result, a methodology that simply compares the settlement size to the total

---

5. See, e.g., Joseph A. Grundfest, Why Disimply?, 108 Harv L. Rev. 727, 734–735 (1995) (acknowledging that there had not been any dramatic increase but suggesting debate should focus on the quality, not quantity, of securities litigation).

6. See Joel Seligman, The Merits Do Matter: A Comment on Professor Grundfest's "Disimplying Private Rights of Action Under the Federal Securities Laws: The Commis-

sion's Authority", 108 Harv. L. Rev. 438, 443, n.19 (1994).

7. See Fred Dunbar & Vinith Juneja, Recent Trends III: What Explains Settlements in Shareholder Actions?, (National Economic Research Associates, 1993) (cited in Senate Hearings at 739).

8. In the same Dunbar & Juneja study, *supra* note 7, average attorneys' fees came to over 31% of the settlement. Id. at 754, tbl. 7.

investors' economic losses on their investment tends systematically to overstate the losses that were legally recoverable.[9] To correct for this problem that the defendants are not liable for the plaintiffs' full economic losses, subsequent researchers have used techniques that seek to net out the industry wide decline from the individual stock's price drop. These researchers have also recognized that investors do not simply buy and hold, but may be in-and-out traders during the class period. To the extent that class members trade both ways during the class period, class members will experience both gains and losses as a result of defendant's alleged misrepresentations, which again need to be netted.[10] In the fullest study done to date on this basis, Professors Carleton, Weisbach and Weiss examined 340 class actions settled between 1989 and 1994 and estimated (using the more sophisticated "two-trader model") that 24.1% of all settlements recovered at least one half of their estimated damages, and another 19.3% recovered at least one-fourth of their estimated damages, while 31.8% recovered less than 10% of their estimated damages.[11] This evidence is inconsistent with any global characterization of securities class actions as "frivolous" or as "nuisance" litigation, because recoveries of over 50% would compare favorably with most other forms of litigation. Still, the finding that 31% of securities class actions settled for less than 10% of estimated damages certainly suggests that some significant portion of securities class actions may have minimal settlement value and could be considered "frivolous."[12]

This data, which shows high variance in the outcomes in securities class actions, also conflicts with the frequently heard claim that the "merits do not merit" in securities class actions.[13] Indeed, more recent research has suggested that there is a range of cases in which it is simply uneconomic for plaintiffs' attorneys to seek to enforce the federal securities laws. Professors Bohn and Choi found that few securities class actions involved companies with initial public offerings for less that $10 million or with aftermarket losses of under $5

---

9. This appears to be a problem with the above-cited Dunbar & Juneja study, which measured class losses by measuring the difference between what the class earned on their investment and what they would have earned on the same funds invested in the Standard & Poor's Industrial 500 Index. The entire industry may have underperformed the S & P 500, but these losses are not recoverable.

10. Economists distinguish between a "single trader" and a "two trader model." Under the former, it is assumed that investors only purchase during the fraud interval; under the latter, they both buy and sell and thus benefit to a degree from any fraud by the issuer. See generally, Mark L. Mitchell & Jeffrey M. Netter, The Role of Financial Economics in Securities Fraud Cases: Applications at the Securities and Exchange Commission, 49 Bus. Law. 545 (1994); see also Bradford Cornell & R. Gregory Morgan, Using Finance Theory to Measure Damages in Fraud on the Market Cases, 37 UCLA L. Rev. 883 (1990).

11. See Willard T. Carleton, et al., Securities Class Action Lawsuits: A Descriptive Study, 38 Ariz. L. Rev 491, 494–499 (1996).

12. Other possibilities could also explain *some* of these cases: (1) defendants may have insufficient assets to pay more than 10% of damages, (2) subsequent adverse changes in the law may have rendered initially meritorious actions no longer viable, or (3) plaintiff's attorneys were unable to finance or bear the costs of litigating a meritorious action and so settled cheaply.

13. This hypothesis was first expounded in a provocative article by Stanford Professor Janet Cooper Alexander. See Janet Cooper Alexander, Do the Merits Matter? A Study of Settlements in Securities Class Actions, 43 Stan. L. Rev. 497 (1991) (estimating that securities class actions involving initial public offerings settled for around 25% of estimated damages, but employing a small sample of only eight cases).

million.[14] Although multiple explanations can attempt to account for this apparent underenforcement, the simplest hypothesis is that plaintiffs' attorneys determined that losses of under $5 million would not sufficiently compensate them for the risk and expense involved in bringing suit. Remember that if the typical plaintiffs attorney's fee in securities class actions is roughly 30% of the settlement and if the typical settlement is for less that half the estimated losses, then $5 million in losses would produce a settlement of under $2.5 million and a plaintiff's fee award of less than $750,000. This expected $750,000 recovery to the attorneys may be the breakeven point, below which plaintiffs' attorneys will not go forward with the suit.

Academic skeptics have doubted that the securities class action can play an important compensatory role, even if the typical action is meritorious.[15] Their chief concern is the basic circularity of the payments in securities litigation. Most settlements in securities class actions appear to be funded out of insurance policies and payments by the defendant corporation.[16] Assume then that the plaintiff class consists of the 50% of XYZ Corporation's shareholders who allegedly purchased XYZ's stock at an inflated price based on misleading statements in its annual report. If the full cost of the settlement is paid by XYZ Corporation (directly or indirectly through insurance), then the settlement's cost is borne indirectly by all of XYZ Corporation's shareholders proportionately. Hence, 50% of the settlement is borne by the supposedly victimized class members (because they constitute 50% of all shareholders); even the balance of the settlement may fall largely on diversified shareholders. Throughout the universe of publicly held corporations, diversified shareholders probably divide roughly equally between these two subgroups: the group that pays the settlement, and the plaintiff class that receives the settlement. Thus, in some actions, diversified shareholders win, and in others, they lose, but on average they just break even—except for the fact that attorneys deduct substantial transaction costs, which in this view amount to a dead weight social loss. In short, from this perspective, money can be said to be simply moving from one shareholder pocket to another (minus the tax that the legal system subtracts).

The rival perspective sees insurance as fostering preventive monitoring and guaranteeing the availability of compensation. By some estimates, insurance may account for as much as 96% of securities class action settlements.[17] If the cost of insurance premiums leads issuers to install preventive controls against securities fraud, thus reducing the incidence of loss, the securities class action may still perform an important deterrent and compensatory function. But this

---

14. See James Bohn & Stephen Choi, Fraud in the New–Issues Market: Empirical Evidence on Securities Class Actions, 144 U. Pa. L. Rev, 903 (1996). It should be understood that a significant fraction of initial public offerings are for less than $10 million.

15. For a good summary of these arguments, see Donald L. Langevoort, Capping Damages for Open–Market Securities Fraud, 38 Ariz. L. Rev. 639 (1996) (recommending a deterrent rather than compensatory rationale for securities litigation). For the contrary view that securities class actions can (and probably do) perform a socially valuable compensatory function, see James D. Cox, Mak-

ing Securities Fraud Class Actions Virtuous, 39 Ariz. L. Rev. 497 (1997)

16. See Senate Hearings at 139 (Statement of Vincent O'Brien estimating that 96% of the settlement comes from insurance proceeds). Little empirical research has, however, been done on this issue, and this estimate may not be reliable. Historically, the typical Officers and Directors insurance policy did not cover securities law liabilities. More recently, policy coverage has been expanded, but surveys as to coverage have not been conducted.

17. See note 16 *supra*.

hypothesis leads to a more open-ended question: does insurance further or retard the deterrent and compensatory purposes of the federal securities laws? Although in a perfectly efficient world insurers may compel issuers to install adequate monitoring and preventive controls to reduce the risk of securities fraud (e.g., through audit committees and independent boards), some close analysts of the insurance industry see this as a very idealized description of actual practices. In their view, the insurance industry is content simply to fund settlements and raise premiums, thereby causing more litigation to be brought and, in turn, more insurance to be purchased at higher prices.[18] Proponents of this view would presumably favor liability being shifted from the entity (the corporation) to other defendants (accountants, corporate officers, underwriters, etc.), who could not be insured. Little prospect exists, however, of such a system being adopted.

Perhaps the most frequently voiced criticism about securities class actions is that plaintiffs attorneys make too much and often do so at the expense of the class by trading a low class recovery fee for a high fee award. Although some quantitative research has reported that class action settlements tend to result in bonuses for the attorneys at the expense of class members,[19] most of the research is qualitative and arguably anecdotal. The finding that plaintiffs' attorneys do receive on average 31% of the settlement (and that this percentage does not decline with the amount of the settlement)[20] does seem somewhat out of line with the norms in other class actions (although it can be argued that the plaintiffs' securities bar is a highly sophisticated and a national bar that can command higher fees based on merit). Instances of possibly collusive settlements have been analyzed in the law reviews[21] and a few judicial opinions.[22]

What causes (and what can correct) this tendency for "cheap" settlements in class actions is a more debatable question. Academic commentary has suggested that prevailing methods of calculating fee awards (whether on an hourly basis or a fixed percentage of the recovery) may lead counsel to settle for too little.[23] Although academic theorists have made a variety of proposals to regulate attorney fees in order to reduce the potential for collusion,[24] the basic approach of the 1995 Act was to limit fee awards, while also increasing the riskiness and expense of the litigation. The natural consequence of this policy approach is to reduce the incentive for the plaintiff's attorney to invest in the class action and to make the economically motivated attorney more willing to settle early (and for a reduced amount).

18. See Kent D. Syverud, On the Demand for Liability Insurance, 72 Tex. L. Rev. 1629 (1994). For the counter-view that insurance does encourage monitoring, see Randall R. Bovbjeg, Liability and Liability Insurance: Chicken and Egg, Destructive Spiral, or Risk and Reaction, 72 Tex. L Rev. 1655 (1996).

19. See A. Rosenfeld, An Empirical Test of Class–Action Settlement, 5. J. Legal Stud. 113 (1976).

20. See note 8 *supra*.

21. See John C. Coffee, The Unfaithful Champion: The Plaintiff As Monitor in Shareholder Litigation, 48 Law & Contemp. Probs. 5 (1985).

22. For a recent example, see Epstein v. MCA, Inc., 126 F.3d 1235 (9th Cir.1997).

23. See John C. Coffee, Understanding the Plaintiff's Attorney: The Implications of Economic Theory for Private Enforcement of Law, 86 Colum. L. Rev. 669, 717 (1986); Jonathan R. Macey & Geoffrey P. Miller, The Plaintiffs' Attorney's Role in Class Actions and Derivative Actions: Economic Analysis and Recommendations for Reform, 58 U. Chi. L. Rev. 1 (1991).

24. See, e.g., Bruce L. Hay, The Theory of Fee Regulation in Class Action Settlements, 46 U. L. Rev. 1429 (1997).

Since the 1995 Act was passed, there have been several major studies that have broadly sought to measure its impact.[25] For the most part, these studies (and more recent updates of them) agree on the following major trends:

1. *Overall Filing Rates.* The initial study completed—the 1997 Stanford Study—found a decline of between 30% to 38% in filings in federal court of securities class actions during 1996 (the first year after the passage of the 1995 Act) in comparison to the average rate prior to the 1995 Act.[26] Much of this decline appeared, however, to be the result of a substitution effect: plaintiffs filed in state court instead of in federal court (or filed in both courts).

After Congress in 1998 enacted the Securities Litigation Uniform Standards Act of 1998,[27] state securities class actions effectively were ended.

In 2000 PricewaterhouseCoopers LLP published its 2000 Securities Litigation study. The Study summarized the number of securities class action lawsuits filed by year:

Years Filed	Federal Cases	State only Cases	Total
Private Securities Litigation Reform Act (December 22, 1995)			
1996	122	25	147
1997	169	13	182
1998	247	13	260
Securities Litigation Uniform Standards Act (November 22, 1998)			
1999	207	—	207
2000	201	—	201

After substantial NYSE and Nasdaq stock price declines in 2000–2001, Stanford Law School Security Class Action Clearinghouse subsequently reported 295 securities class actions through September 2001.

2. *Characteristics of Securities Class Actions After the 1995 Act.* In the aftermath of the 1995 Act there have been significant changes in the characteristics of securities class actions.

a. In 1995 39% of all cases alleged accounting fraud. The percentage of cases involving accounting fraud climbed to 53% in 2000.[28] Accompanying this surge has been a significant increase in earnings restatements. According to Arthur Andersen, total restatements in 1997 were 176. By 1999 there were more than 200. Restatement often occurred because of improperly recognized

25. See, e.g., Joseph Grundfest & Michael Perino, "Securities Litigation Reform: The First Year's Experience" (John M. Olin Program in Law and Economics, Stanford Law School Working Paper no. 140, Feb. 1997) (hereinafter "Stanford Study"); Denise Martin, et al., Recent Trends IV: What Explains Filings and Settlements in Shareholder Class Actions? (National Economic Research Associates, Nov. 1996) (hereinafter "NERA Study"); U.S. Securities and Exchange Comm. Office of General Counsel, Report to the President and the Congress on the First Year of Practice Under The Private Securities Litigation Reform Act of 1995 (Apr. 1997); PricewaterhouseCooper 2000 Securities Litigation Study; Stanford Law School, Securities Class Action Clearinghouse (Sept. 12, 2001).

26. See Stanford Study, *supra* note 25, at 4–6.

27. 112 Stat. 3227.

28. PricewaterhouseCoopers 2000 Securities Litigation Study at 2.

revenue.[29]

b.   Insider Trading had been alleged initially in 57% of the post–1995 Act cases as compared to only 21% of pre–1995 Act cases.[30] In all likelihood this is a consequence of the 1995 Act's pleading rules, which required the plaintiff to plead facts raising a "strong inference of fraud."

c.   Forecasts and other forward-looking statements were contested in a much smaller percentage of cases after the 1995 Act. Complaints alleging false forward-looking statements as the sole basis for liability accounted for only about 12% of all post–1995 Act complaints in a study by the SEC Office of General Counsel.[31] Again, the "safe harbor" for forward-looking information in the 1995 Act seems most likely responsible.

3.   *The Lead Plaintiff Concept.* As later discussed, the lead plaintiff provisions of the 1995 Act sought to encourage more active participation by institutional and other large investors in class actions to counteract the perceived tendency for lawyers to prefer their own interests.[32] Yet, the SEC Study found only eight cases (out of a sample of 105 cases) in the first year after the 1995 Act's passage in which institutions did seek to be named lead counsel.[33] In 1997 in only 9 of 175 cases did institutions seek the role of the lead plaintiff.[34]

4.   *The Race to the Courthouse.* Much criticism in the Congressional hearings preceding the 1995 Act focused on the tendency for securities class actions to be filed within a day or two after a stock drop, sometimes with multiple class actions being filed in different courts that were virtual carbon copies of each other. The motive for such rushed filings appears to have been the inevitable jockeying for position among rival counsel for the important position of lead counsel (the premise being that the first attorney to file a securities class action gained a procedural advantage). The consequence of these races was inevitably hastily drafted, and sometimes poorly researched, formulaic complaints, which courts viewed skeptically.

In the wake of the 1995 Act, this race to the courthouse appears to have slowed. The SEC study found that the average lag time between the end of the class period and the filing of the complaint was 79 days (up from 45 days prior to the 1995 Act).[35] This change seems to be the result of both procedural provisions in the 1995 Act[36] and a general sense within the plaintiff's bar that it is better to organize the plaintiff's team before filing the class action in order to reduce the possibility that the action will be "stolen" by an unfriendly lead plaintiff or rival law firm. Also, the heightened pleading standards in the 1995

---

29.   Arthur Andersen, An Analysis of the Industries and Accounting Issues Underlying Public Company Restatements for the Four Years Ended December 31, 2000, at 10–12.

30.   Grundfest & Perino, *supra* n.25.

31.   SEC study, *supra* n.25.

32.   Section 21D(a)(3) of the 1934 Act.

33.   See SEC Study at 51.

34.   Institutional Investors Not Opting to Lead Class Suits, Despite Potential Recoveries, 30 Sec. Reg. & L. Rep. (BNA) 405 (1998). Cf. Mat. W. Berger, John P. Coffey &

Gerald H. Silk, Institutional Investors as Lead Plaintiffs: Is There a New and Changing Landscape?, 23 Sec. Reg. L.J. 127 (2000) (predicting greater institutional investor interest after Cendant Corporation agreed to pay $3.2 billion in cash in action in which three institutional investors were lead plaintiffs).

35.   See SEC Study at 23.

36.   Section 21D(a)(3)(A) requires an "early notice" to class members which invites a lead plaintiff to take control of the action.

Act make it extremely dangerous for a plaintiff's attorney to file a hastily prepared complaint, as it can easily be dismissed.

5. *Secondary Defendants.* The 1995 Act clearly reduced the exposure of secondary defendants to liability, both by enhancing the pleading standards and by adopting a system of proportionate liability to replace the former regime of joint and several liability. In the first year after the 1995 Act's passage, the SEC Study found in its sample of 105 class actions that accounting firms had been named in only six cases, corporate counsel in no cases, and underwriters in 19 cases.[37] In sharp contrast, prior to 1995, the number of actions that named "Big Six" accounting firms as defendants in audit-related suits was 192 in 1990, 172 in 1991, and 141 in 1992.[38] Clearly, there has been a marked drop, but much of it may be attributable to a Supreme Court decision in 1994 that rejected the use of "aiding and abetting" theories of liability under Section 10(b) of the 1934 Act.[39] For whatever reason, secondary defendants, including the principal gatekeepers who monitor the corporation (accountants, directors, and underwriters), appear to face significantly reduced liability under 1934 Act today.[40]

6. *Settlements.* Both before and after the 1995 Act a significant proportion of federal securities class actions have been settled. A 2000 study of 255 post–1995 Act settlements reported over $6.6 billion had been paid to plaintiffs and nearly 50% of all cases had resulted in a payment of over $5 million. In 2000 the average settlement was $15.4 million, which is reduced to an average of $8.8 when "extreme cases" such as Cendant Corporation (which accounted for approximately one half of all settlement dollars for the post–1995 Act period) are removed.[41]

7. *Proceduralization.* After its first years' experience, the 1995 Act appears to have had little impact on the number of federal securities class actions filed, although the Securities Litigation Uniform Standard Act of 1998 has effectively ended state securities class actions.

The 1995 Act has had a significant impact on the nature of class actions filed, notably reducing class actions based on forward looking statements and against secondary defendants. The race to the courthouse has slowed and the value of settlement appears to be up, both of which suggest more carefully drafted complaints are being filed.

The most striking result of the 1995 Act to date has been the proceduralization of federal securities class actions. An increased proportion of federal securities class actions appear to address such matters as the stricter 1995 Act standards, the lead plaintiff provisions, or pretrial discovery stays.

The basic policy issue suggested by these developments is whether a dispute resolution system in which litigation on the merits is increasingly remote makes sense. To be sure, a nontrial system reduces the costs and burdens of litigation on corporations, reduces nonmeritorious litigation, and may strengthen desirable entrepreneurial risk-taking. But a nontrial system

---

37. SEC Study at 23.

38. Id. Not all these actions were necessarily class actions. Also, some may have been filed in state court, where the 1995 Act.

39. See Central Bank of Denver v. First Interstate Bank, 511 U.S. 164 (1994).

40. This conclusion does not apply, however, to the 1933 Act, where Section 11 still applies to secondary defendants in registered public offerings and was not significantly affected by the 1995 Act.

41. PricewaterhouseCoopers 2000 Securities Litigation Study, at 6.

also may systematically reduce incentives to comply with a mandatory disclosure system and reduce the deterrent impact of fraud remedies.

B. PLEADING

The Conference Report on The Private Securities Litigation Reform Act of 1995 characterized the heightened pleading standard in §§ 21D(b)(1)–(2) of the Securities Exchange Act in these terms:[1]

"Naming a party in a civil suit for fraud is a serious matter. Unwarranted fraud claims can lead to serious injury to reputation for which our legal system effectively offers no redress. For this reason, among others, Rule 9(b) of the Federal Rules of Civil Procedure requires that plaintiffs plead allegations of fraud with "particularity." The Rule has not prevented abuse of the securities laws by private litigants. Moreover, the courts of appeals have interpreted Rule 9(b)'s requirement in conflicting ways, creating distinctly different standards among the circuits. The House and Senate hearings on securities litigation reform included testimony on the need to establish uniform and more stringent pleading requirements to curtail the filing of meritless lawsuits.

"The Conference Committee language is based in part on the pleading standard of the Second Circuit. The standard also is specifically written to conform the language to Rule 9(b)'s notion of pleading with "particularity."

"Regarded as the most stringent pleading standard, the Second Circuit requirement is that the plaintiff state facts with particularity, and that these facts, in turn, must give rise to a "strong inference" of the defendant's fraudulent intent. Because the Conference Committee intends to strengthen existing pleading requirements, it does not intend to codify the Second Circuit's case law interpreting this pleading standard. The plaintiff must also specifically plead with particularity each statement alleged to have been misleading. The reason or reasons why the statement is misleading must also be set forth in the complaint in detail. If an allegation is made on information and belief, the plaintiff must state with particularity all facts in the plaintiff's possession on which the belief is formed."

Subsequently President Clinton vetoed the 1995 Act on three grounds, the first of which involved the Act's new pleading standards. With respect to the pleading standards, the Presidential veto message stated:

I believe that the pleading requirements of the Conference Report with regard to a defendant's state of mind impose an unacceptable procedural hurdle to meritorious claims being heard in Federal courts. I am prepared to support the high pleading standard of the U.S. Court of Appeals for the Second Circuit—the highest pleading standard of any Federal circuit court. But the conferees make crystal clear in the Statement of Managers their intent to raise the standard even beyond that level. I am not prepared to accept that.

The conferees deleted an amendment offered by Senator Specter and adopted by the Senate that specifically incorporated Second Circuit case law with respect to pleading a claim of fraud. Then they specifically indicated that they were not adopting Second Circuit case law but instead intended to "strengthen" the existing pleading requirements of the Second Circuit. All this shows that the conferees meant to erect a higher barrier to

---

1. H.R. Rep. No. 104–369, 104th Cong., 1st Sess. (1995).

bringing suit than any now existing—one so high that even the most aggrieved investors with the most painful losses may get tossed out of court before they have a chance to prove their case.

The Presidential veto was overridden by a vote in the Senate of 68 to 30 and a vote in the House of 319 to 100, and the Act became law on December 22, 1995.[2]

In the years before the 1995 Act, the number of federal securities actions dismissed for failure to plead fraud with sufficient particularity appeared to significantly increase.[3] Underlying this apparent increase was a split among the circuits in how to address defendants Rule 9(b) motions. On one side, the Second Circuit adopted a strong inference of fraud pleading standard.[4] Under this standard a plaintiff could establish this strong inference by "either (a) alleging facts to show that defendants had both motive and opportunity to commit fraud, or (b) by alleging facts that constitute strong circumstantial evidence of conscious misbehavior or recklessness."[5]

On the other side the Ninth Circuit rejected the strong inference of fraud requirement. In GlenFed, Inc. Sec. Litig.,[6] the Circuit *en banc* concluded: "We are not permitted to add new requirements to Rule 9(b) simply because we like the effects of doing so. This is a job for Congress * * *."[7]

In 1995 Congress took on this job. The unresolved question was whether Congress codified the Second Circuit standard or adopted a tougher one. The courts soon divided.

Novak v. Kasaks

United States Court of Appeals for the Second Circuit, 2000.
216 F.3d 300.

JUDGES:

■ Before: WALKER, LEVAL, and POOLER, CIRCUIT JUDGES.

■ JOHN M. WALKER, JR., CIRCUIT JUDGE:

[The district court had dismissed plaintiffs' initial complaint based on Rule 10b–5 and an amended complaint, both times for failure to plead its allegations with sufficient particularity to support a strong inference that the defendants had acted fraudulently. *See* Novak v. Kasaks, 997 F. Supp. 425 (S.D.N.Y.1998) ("Novak I") and Novak v. Kasaks, 26 F. Supp. 2d 658 (S.D.N.Y.1998) ("Novak II").]

In 1996, plaintiffs-appellants filed this securities fraud class action, alleging violations of sections 10(b) and 20(a) of the Securities Exchange Act ("the 1934 Act") and Rule 10b–5 promulgated thereunder. In two opinions issued in 1998, the district court dismissed both the original complaint. * * *

In light of Second Circuit precedent and the provisions of the Private Securities Litigation Reform Act ("PSLRA"), we hold that the district court

---

2. Pub. L. 104–67, 109 Stat. 737.

3. *See* Joel Seligman, The Merits Do Matter, 108 Harv. L. Rev. 438, 445–448 (1994).

4. *See, e.g.*, Shields v. Citytrust Bancorp, Inc., 25 F.3d 1124, 1129 (2d Cir.1994).

5. Chill v. General Elec. Co., 101 F.3d 263, 267 (2d Cir.1996).

6. 42 F.3d 1541 (9th Cir. *en banc* 1994).

7. Id. at 1546.

erred in: (1) concluding that the plaintiffs had failed to plead sufficient facts to support a strong inference of fraudulent intent; and (2) imposing an exceedingly onerous burden on the plaintiffs with respect to their obligation to plead facts with particularity. We see no persuasive alternative grounds for upholding the district court's dismissal of the complaint. Accordingly, we vacate the judgment of the district court and remand for further proceedings consistent with these determinations. In addition, we instruct the district court to allow the plaintiffs to replead to the extent they wish to do so in light of this opinion.

BACKGROUND

On April 25, 1996, plaintiffs Carol Novak and Robert Nieman brought this action on behalf of all purchasers of the common stock of the AnnTaylor Stores Corporation between February 3, 1994, and May 4, 1995 (the "Class Period"). In their complaint, the plaintiffs named two groups of defendants: (1) the AnnTaylor defendants, both the corporation itself—which, through its wholly-owned subsidiary, defendant AnnTaylor, Inc., is a specialty retailer of women's clothing, shoes, and accessories—and several officers at the highest level of management; and (2) the Merrill Lynch defendants, a group of entities and individuals that collectively held a dominant share of AnnTaylor stock and sold a significant fraction of their holdings during the Class Period.

The complaint—in both its original and amended forms—essentially alleges that, during the Class Period, the defendants made, or controlled others who made, materially false and misleading statements and omissions concerning the financial performance of AnnTaylor ("the Company"), primarily by failing properly to account for millions of dollars of inventory. According to the plaintiffs, the defendants knowingly and intentionally issued financial statements that overstated AnnTaylor's financial condition by accounting for inventory that they knew to be obsolete and nearly worthless at inflated values and by deliberately failing to adhere to the Company's publicly stated markdown policy. The following facts are taken largely from the plaintiffs' complaint.

The plaintiffs' specific allegations focus on AnnTaylor's so-called "Box and Hold" practice, whereby a substantial and growing quantity of out-of-date inventory was stored in several warehouses during the Class Period without being marked down. Internal Company documents ("Weekly Reports")—distributed at regular Monday morning merchandise meetings in which the AnnTaylor defendants participated—distinguished between regular inventory and "Box and Hold" inventory. According to the complaint, these reports demonstrated that: (1) much of the "Box and Hold" inventory was several years old and thus unlikely to be sold at full price, if at all; and (2) the levels of such inventory grew significantly during the Class Period, from about 10% to about 34% of total inventory. However, AnnTaylor's public financial statements did not distinguish between types of inventory, nor did AnnTaylor write off any of the "Box and Hold" inventory during the Class Period, allegedly in violation of Generally Accepted Accounting Principles ("GAAP") that required markdowns under these circumstances. Instead, the defendants made or caused to be made a series of positive statements to the public about the status of AnnTaylor's inventories, describing them at various points during the Class Period as "under control," "in good shape," and at "reasonable" or "expected" levels; stating that "no major or unusual markdowns were anticipated"; and attributing rising levels of inventory to growth, expansion, and planned future sales.

The plaintiffs contend that this course of conduct amounts to securities fraud. Had AnnTaylor taken appropriate write-downs, they argue, the Company's earnings would have been substantially lower than reported. Thus, the AnnTaylor defendants' alleged deception painted too rosy a picture of the Company's current performance and future prospects and kept the company's stock price at an artificially high level during the Class Period. According to the amended complaint, during this time, many AnnTaylor executives demanded that the individual AnnTaylor defendants * * * end the Box & Hold practice as it made no business sense and was growing out of control. Defendants' response * * * was that AnnTaylor could not "afford" to eliminate or write-down the Box & Hold inventory because doing so would "kill" the Company's reported financial results and/or profit margins and damage the Company on "Wall Street."

Ultimately, the defendants were forced to publicly acknowledge serious inventory problems—i.e., that inventories were too high and liquidation would result in much lower fiscal 1995 earnings than expected—at which point AnnTaylor stock prices fell precipitously, to the plaintiffs' detriment.

On July 1, 1996, in response to these allegations, the defendants moved to dismiss the action, and on August 16, 1996, the district judge granted a motion by the defendants to stay all discovery pending a ruling on the motions to dismiss pursuant to 15 U.S.C. § 78u–4(b)(3)(B).

On March 10, 1998, the district court issued an opinion and order granting the defendants' motions to dismiss the complaint. *See* Novak I, 997 F. Supp. at 426. The court concluded that "the fatal defect in the complaint lies in its allegations of scienter." *Id.* at 430. Specifically, the plaintiffs had "failed to plead facts giving rise to a strong inference of fraudulent intent" in that they did not "allege with sufficient specificity that * * * defendants * * * were aware that much of their inventory was worthless or seriously overvalued, or were reckless as to whether that was the case." *Id.* at 430–31. According to the district court, in order to meet the pleading requirement, the plaintiffs needed to identify the confidential sources of their information, see *id.* at 431–32, include written documentation of the "Box and Hold" practice in their complaint, see *id.* at 432, and allege facts showing that the Merrill Lynch defendants actually knew about "Box and Hold," see *id.* at 434.

On April 9, 1998, the plaintiffs filed an amended complaint. The defendants thereafter served motions to dismiss. On November 9, 1998, the district court dismissed the plaintiffs' amended complaint with prejudice. *See* Novak II, 26 F. Supp. 2d at 660. In the district court's view, the amended complaint failed to remedy the defects of the original one, including lack of particularity in pleading, unnamed sources, and lack of specific evidence of the Merrill Lynch defendants' knowledge of the "Box and Hold" practice. *See* id. at 660–62. In addition, the district court found "that it would be futile to permit further amendment" of the complaint and thus dismissed it with prejudice. *Id.* at 663. This appeal followed.

* * *

DISCUSSION

We review de novo a district court's order dismissing a complaint on the pleadings and accept as true all facts alleged in the complaint. *See* Stevelman v. Alias Research Inc., 174 F.3d 79, 83 (2d Cir.1999) (*citing* Chill v. General Elec. Co., 101 F.3d 263, 267 (2d Cir.1996)). In this case, we are called upon to decide principally whether the district court, in assessing the sufficiency of the pleadings, applied appropriate standards in light of our precedents and the provisions of the PSLRA and whether it erred in concluding that the plaintiffs had failed to state a claim. We must also decide whether, even if the district court erred, there are alternative grounds for affirming the dismissal of the plaintiffs' § 10(b) claims.

I.   Sufficiency of the Pleadings

The landscape of securities fraud litigation has been transformed in recent years by the passage of the PSLRA. This case requires us to determine the impact of two provisions in this legislation on the pleading standard for scienter and the required degree of particularity in pleading in this circuit.

A.   The PSLRA and Anti–Fraud Provisions in Federal Securities Laws

Section 10(b) of the 1934 Act, 15 U.S.C. § 78j(b), and Rule 10b–5 promulgated thereunder, 17 C.F.R. § 240.10b–5, prohibit fraudulent activities in connection with securities transactions. Section 10(b) makes it unlawful

> to use or employ, in connection with the purchase or sale of any security * * *, any manipulative or deceptive device or contrivance in contravention of such rules and regulations as the Commission may prescribe as necessary or appropriate in the public interest or for the protection of investors. * * *

Rule 10b–5 specifies the following actions among the types of behavior proscribed by the statute:

> To make any untrue statement of a material fact or to omit to state a material fact necessary in order to make the statements made, in the light of the circumstances under which they were made, not misleading. * * *

In order to state a claim under these provisions, a complaint must allege that the defendants acted with scienter. *See, e.g.*, Chill, 101 F.3d at 266. This scienter requirement for a private action under Rule 10b–5 has been firmly established for at least a generation. *See* Ernst & Ernst v. Hochfelder, 425 U.S. 185, 193, 47 L. Ed. 2d 668, 96 S. Ct. 1375 (1976) (holding that no "private cause of action for damages will lie under § 10(b) and Rule 10b–5 in the absence of any allegation of 'scienter'—intent to deceive, manipulate, or defraud"); Lanza v. Drexel & Co., 479 F.2d 1277, 1301 (2d Cir.1973) (en banc) ("Other cases in this circuit clearly indicate that 'facts amounting to scienter, intent to defraud, reckless disregard for the truth, or knowing use of a device, scheme or artifice to defraud' are essential to the imposition of liability.") (quoting Shemtob v. Shearson, Hammill & Co., 448 F.2d 442, 445 (2d Cir. 1971)). This case pertains not to the scienter requirement itself, but rather to the pleading requirement for scienter in the securities fraud context. Prior to the passage of the PSLRA, we had decided that, in order to state a claim for securities fraud, plaintiffs had to allege facts giving rise to "a strong inference of fraudulent intent." Acito v. Imcera Group, Inc., 47 F.3d 47, 52 (2d Cir.1995).

In addition to pleading scienter, it is well-established that a securities fraud complaint must also plead certain facts with particularity in order to state a claim. Fed. R. Civ. P. 9(b) requires that, whenever a complaint contains allegations of fraud, "the circumstances constituting fraud * * * shall be stated with particularity." *See also* Chill, 101 F.3d at 267 (noting that "the actual fraudulent statements or conduct and the fraud alleged must be stated with particularity") (internal citations omitted). "A complaint making such allegations must '(1) specify the statements that the plaintiff contends were fraudulent, (2) identify the speaker, (3) state where and when the statements were made, and (4) explain why the statements were fraudulent.'" Shields v. Citytrust Bancorp, Inc., 25 F.3d 1124, 1128 (2d Cir.1994) (quoting Mills v. Polar Molecular Corp., 12 F.3d 1170, 1175 (2d Cir.1993)).

In 1995, Congress amended the 1934 Act through passage of the PSLRA. [Citations omitted.] Legislators were apparently motivated in large part by a perceived need to deter strike suits wherein opportunistic private plaintiffs file securities fraud claims of dubious merit in order to exact large settlement recoveries. See H.R. Conf. Rep. No. 104–369, at 31 (1995) (noting "significant evidence of abuse in private securities lawsuits," including "the routine filing of lawsuits against issuers of securities and others whenever there is a significant change in an issuer's stock price, without regard to any underlying culpability of the issuer," and "the abuse of the discovery process to impose costs so burdensome that it is often economical for the victimized party to settle"), reprinted in 1995 U.S.C.C.A.N. 730, 730.

In order "to curtail the filing of meritless lawsuits," the PSLRA imposed stringent procedural requirements on plaintiffs pursuing private securities fraud actions. See id. at 41. This case concerns two of these provisions in particular. First, the statute requires that,

> in any private action arising under this chapter in which the plaintiff may recover money damages only on proof that the defendant acted with a particular state of mind, the complaint shall, with respect to each act or omission alleged to violate this chapter, state with particularity facts giving rise to a strong inference that the defendant acted with the required state of mind.

15 U.S.C. § 78u–4(b)(2) (emphasis added) hereinafter "paragraph (b)(2)." Second, the statute requires that,

> in any private action arising under this chapter in which the plaintiff alleges that the defendant—
>
> (A) made an untrue statement of a material fact; or
>
> (B) omitted to state a material fact necessary in order to make the statements made, in the light of the circumstances in which they were made, not misleading;
>
> the complaint shall specify each statement alleged to have been misleading, the reason or reasons why the statement is misleading, and, if an allegation regarding the statement or omission is made on information and belief, the complaint shall state with particularity all facts on which that belief is formed.

15 U.S.C. § 78u–4(b)(1) (emphasis added) hereinafter "paragraph (b)(1)." In addition, § 21D(b)(3)(A) of the PSLRA requires courts to dismiss complaints that fail to meet the pleading requirements of paragraphs (b)(1) and (b)(2). See 15 U.S.C. § 78u–4(b)(3)(A). We must determine the impact of these new requirements in order to decide whether the plaintiffs in this case have pleaded sufficient facts with enough particularity to state a claim under the 1934 Act.

B. The Pleading Standard for Scienter

1. The Second Circuit's Pre–PSLRA Pleading Standard

We can easily summarize the pleading standard for scienter that prevailed in this circuit prior to the PSLRA:

Plaintiffs must allege facts that give rise to a strong inference of fraudulent intent. "The requisite 'strong inference' of fraud may be established either (a) by alleging facts to show that defendants had both motive and opportunity to commit fraud, or (b) by alleging facts that constitute strong circumstantial evidence of conscious misbehavior or recklessness."

Acito, 47 F.3d at 52 (*quoting* Shields, 25 F.3d 1124 at 1128) (internal citations omitted). However, this statement of the standard conceals the complexity and uncertainty that often surround its application. This difficulty in application stems, at least in part, from the "inevitable tension" between the interests in deterring securities fraud and deterring strike suits. See In re Time Warner Inc. Sec. Litig., 9 F.3d 259, 263 (2d Cir.1993). As a result, different courts applying the pleading standard to differing factual circumstances may reach seemingly disparate results. *See id.* at 264. Nevertheless, we discern some basic patterns in our case law under § 10(b) and Rule 10b–5 that help to provide substance to the general language of the standard itself.

We described the type of motive and opportunity required to plead scienter under our pre-reform standard as follows:

Motive would entail concrete benefits that could be realized by one or more of the false statements and wrongful nondisclosures alleged. Opportunity would entail the means and likely prospect of achieving concrete benefits by the means alleged.

Shields, 25 F.3d at 1130. Plaintiffs could not proceed based on motives possessed by virtually all corporate insiders, including: (1) the desire to maintain a high corporate credit rating, see San Leandro Emergency Med. Group Profit Sharing Plan v. Philip Morris Cos., Inc., 75 F.3d 801, 814 (2d Cir.1996), or otherwise sustain "the appearance of corporate profitability, or of the success of an investment," *Chill,* 101 F.3d at 268; and (2) the desire to maintain a high stock price in order to increase executive compensation, see *Acito,* 47 F.3d at 54, or prolong the benefits of holding corporate office, see *Shields,* 25 F.3d at 1130. Rather, plaintiffs had to allege that defendants benefitted in some concrete and personal way from the purported fraud. This requirement was generally met when corporate insiders were alleged to have misrepresented to the public material facts about the corporation's performance or prospects in order to keep the stock price artificially high while they sold their own shares at a profit. *See, e.g.,* Stevelman, 174 F.3d at 85; Goldman v. Belden, 754 F.2d 1059, 1070 (2d Cir.1985). Accordingly, in the ordinary case, adequate motive arose from the desire to profit from extensive insider sales.

Plaintiffs could also meet the pre-PSLRA pleading standard by alleging facts that constituted strong circumstantial evidence of conscious misbehavior or recklessness on the part of defendants. Intentional misconduct is easily identified since it encompasses deliberate illegal behavior, such as securities trading by insiders privy to undisclosed and material information, *see* Simon DeBartolo Group, L.P. v. Richard E. Jacobs Group, Inc., 186 F.3d 157, 168–69 (2d Cir.1999), or knowing sale of a company's stock at an unwarranted discount, *see* Schoenbaum v. Firstbrook, 405 F.2d 215, 219 (2d Cir.1968) (en banc).

Recklessness is harder to identify with such precision and consistency. In 1978, when we first held that recklessness suffices to plead scienter under § 10(b) and Rule 10b–5, we defined reckless conduct as:

at the least, conduct which is "highly unreasonable" and which represents "an extreme departure from the standards of ordinary care * * * to the extent that the danger was either known to the defendant or so obvious that the defendant must have been aware of it."

Rolf v. Blyth, Eastman Dillon & Co., Inc., 570 F.2d 38, 47 (2d Cir.1978) (quoting Sanders v. John Nuveen & Co., 554 F.2d 790, 793 (7th Cir.1977)) (ellipsis in original). Similarly, we later noted that " 'an egregious refusal to see the obvious, or to investigate the doubtful, may in some cases give rise to an inference of * * * recklessness.' " *Chill,* 101 F.3d at 269 (*quoting* Goldman v. McMahan, Brafman, Morgan & Co., 706 F. Supp. 256, 259 (S.D.N.Y. 1989)) (ellipsis in original).

However, these general standards offer little insight into precisely what actions and behaviors constitute recklessness sufficient for § 10(b) liability. It is the actual facts of our securities fraud cases that provide the most concrete guidance as to the types of allegations required to meet the pre-PSLRA pleading standard in this circuit.

According to these cases, securities fraud claims typically have sufficed to state a claim based on recklessness when they have specifically alleged defendants' knowledge of facts or access to information contradicting their public statements. Under such circumstances, defendants knew or, more importantly, should have known that they were misrepresenting material facts related to the corporation. Thus, for example, the pleading standard was met where the plaintiffs alleged that the defendants made or authorized statements that sales to China would be "an important new source of revenue" when they knew or should have known that Chinese import restrictions in place at the time would severely limit such sales. *See* Cosmas v. Hassett, 886 F.2d 8, 12 (2d Cir.1989). Similarly, the pleading standard was met where the plaintiffs alleged that the defendants released to the investing public several highly positive predictions about the marketing prospects of a computer system to record hotel guests' long-distance telephone calls when they knew or should have known several facts about the system and its consumers that revealed "grave uncertainties and problems concerning future sales of" the system. *Goldman,* 754 F.2d at 1063, 1070.

Under certain circumstances, we have found allegations of recklessness to be sufficient where plaintiffs alleged facts demonstrating that defendants failed to review or check information that they had a duty to monitor, or ignored obvious signs of fraud. Thus, the pleading standard was met where the plaintiff alleged that the defendant, his broker, consistently reassured the plaintiff that the investment advisor responsible for the plaintiff's portfolio "knew what he was doing" but never actually investigated the advisor's decisions to determine "whether there was a basis for the defendant's assertions." *Rolf,* 570 F.2d at 47–48. Similarly, the pleading standard was met where the defendant allegedly included false statements in SEC filings despite "the obviously evasive and suspicious statements made to him" by the corporate officials upon whom he was relying for this information and despite outside counsel's recommendation that these statements not be included. *SEC v. McNulty,* 137 F.3d 732, 741 (2d Cir.1998).

At the same time, however, we have identified several important limitations on the scope of liability for securities fraud based on reckless conduct. First, we have refused to allow plaintiffs to proceed with allegations of "fraud by hindsight." *See Stevelman,* 174 F.3d at 85. Corporate officials need not be clairvoyant; they are only responsible for revealing those material facts reasonably available to them. *See* Denny v. Barber, 576 F.2d 465, 470 (2d Cir.1978). Thus, allegations that defendants should have anticipated future events and made certain disclosures earlier than they actually did do not suffice to make out a claim of securities fraud. *See Acito,* 47 F.3d at 53.

Second, as long as the public statements are consistent with reasonably available data, corporate officials need not present an overly gloomy or cautious picture of current performance and future prospects. *See Stevelman,* 174 F.3d at 85; Shields, 25 F.3d at 1129–30. Where plaintiffs contend defendants had access to contrary facts, they must specifically identify the reports or statements containing this information. *See San Leandro,* 75 F.3d at 812 ("Plaintiffs' unsupported general claim of the existence of confidential company sales reports that revealed the larger decline in sales is insufficient to survive a motion to dismiss.").

Third, there are limits to the scope of liability for failure adequately to monitor the allegedly fraudulent behavior of others. Thus, the failure of a non-fiduciary accounting firm to identify problems with the defendant-company's internal controls and accounting practices does not constitute reckless conduct sufficient for § 10(b) liability. *See* Decker v. Massey–Ferguson, Ltd., 681 F.2d 111, 120 (2d Cir.1982). Similarly, the failure of a parent company to interpret extraordinarily positive performance by its subsidiary—specifically, the "unprecedented and dramatically increasing profitability" of a particular form of trading—as a sign of problems and thus to investigate further does not amount to recklessness under the securities laws. See *Chill,* 101 F.3d at 269–70.

Finally, allegations of GAAP violations or accounting irregularities, standing alone, are insufficient to state a securities fraud claim. *See Stevelman,* 174 F.3d at 84; Chill, 101 F.3d at 270. Only where such allegations are coupled with evidence of "corresponding fraudulent intent," *Chill,* 101 F.3d at 270, might they be sufficient.

We now examine to what extent these lessons from our prior case law have survived the recent reform of the securities laws.

2. Implications of the PSLRA for the Pleading Standard for Scienter in this Circuit

Courts have disagreed on the proper interpretation of the new pleading requirement imposed by paragraph (b)(2) in light of the text of the PSLRA and its legislative history. They have generally come to one of two conclusions:

(1) The statute effectively adopts the Second Circuit's pleading standard for scienter wholesale, and thus plaintiffs may continue to state a claim by pleading either motive and opportunity or strong circumstantial evidence of recklessness or conscious misbehavior. *See* In re Advanta Corp. Sec. Litig., 180 F.3d 525 (3d Cir.1999); Press v. Chemical Invest. Servs. Corp., 166 F.3d 529, 538 (2d Cir.1999) (dicta); Rubinstein v. Skyteller, Inc., 48 F. Supp. 2d 315, 320 (S.D.N.Y.1999) (following Press).

(2) The statute strengthens the Second Circuit's standard by rejecting the simple pleading of motive and opportunity. *See* Bryant v. Avado Brands, Inc., 187 F.3d 1271, 1283 (11th Cir.1999); In re Silicon Graphics Inc. Sec. Litig., 183 F.3d 970, 979 (9th Cir.1999); In re Comshare, Inc. Sec. Litig., 183 F.3d 542, 550–51 (6th Cir.1999); Novak I, 997 F. Supp. at 430; In re Glenayre Tech., Inc.

Sec. Litig., 982 F. Supp. 294, 298 (S.D.N.Y.1997); In re Baesa Sec. Litig., 969 F. Supp. 238, 241–42 (S.D.N.Y.1997).

Our own review of the text and legislative history leads us to a middle ground. We conclude that the PSLRA effectively raised the nationwide pleading standard to that previously existing in this circuit and no higher (with the exception of the "with particularity" requirement). At the same time, however, we believe that Congress's failure to include language about motive and opportunity suggests that we need not be wedded to these concepts in articulating the prevailing standard. We are led to these conclusions by the considerations that follow.

In order to gauge the implications of paragraph (b)(2), we apply familiar canons of statutory construction. We look first to the text of the statute. If that language is plain and its meaning sufficiently clear, we need look no further. *See* Connecticut Nat'l Bank v. Germain, 503 U.S. 249, 254, 117 L. Ed. 2d 391, 112 S. Ct. 1146 (1992). Only if the text of the statute is not unambiguous do we turn for guidance to legislative history and the purposes of the statute. *See* Dowling v. United States, 473 U.S. 207, 218, 87 L. Ed. 2d 152, 105 S. Ct. 3127 (1985). Applying these principles, we conclude that the enactment of paragraph (b)(2) did not change the basic pleading standard for scienter in this circuit.

In this case, our interpretive task begins and ends with the text of the statute. In drafting paragraph (b)(2), Congress specifically incorporated this circuit's "strong inference" language to define the pleading standard for securities fraud cases. Compare 15 U.S.C. § 78u–4(b)(2) (requiring plaintiffs to "state with particularity facts giving rise to a strong inference that the defendant acted with the required state of mind"), with *Acito*, 47 F.3d at 52 ("Plaintiffs must allege facts that give rise to a strong inference of fraudulent intent."). We agree with the Third Circuit that this "use of the Second Circuit's language compels the conclusion that the Reform Act establishes a pleading standard approximately equal in stringency to that of the Second Circuit." *In re Advanta Corp.*, 180 F.3d at 534. *Cf.* United States v. Johnson, 14 F.3d 766, 770 (2d Cir.1994) (finding that Congress's use of "substantially identical language" to that of an earlier statute "bespeaks an intention to import" judicial interpretations of that language into the new statute).

Given the absence of ambiguity in the statutory text, no resort to legislative history or the purposes of the PSLRA is required. In any event, there is nothing in these sources that would alter our conclusion. As far as the general purposes of the PSLRA are concerned, Congress plainly sought to impose a stricter nationwide pleading standard and did so. But this purpose does not require raising the standard above that of this circuit, particularly in light of the explicit Congressional recognition that our pre-PSLRA standard was the most stringent in the nation. See H.R. Conf. Rep. No. 104–369, at 41. "In many jurisdictions, adoption of a 'strong inference' standard will substantially heighten the barriers to pleading scienter, a result Congress expressly intended. Moreover, even in jurisdictions already employing the Second Circuit standard, the additional requirement that plaintiffs state facts 'with particularity' represents a heightening of the standard." *In re Advanta Corp.*, 180 F.3d at 534.

Meanwhile, in our view, as is so often the case with legislative history generally, the legislative history of the PSLRA contains "conflicting expressions of legislative intent" with respect to the pleading requirement. *Id. at 533.* For example, while the Conference Committee rejected language from the Senate bill that would have adopted the Second Circuit rule wholesale, including language about motive and opportunity and recklessness, see H.R. Conf. Rep. No. 104–369, at 41 & 48 n.23, the Senate Committee reporting the bill stated that it was proposing not "a new and untested pleading standard that would generate additional litigation," but rather "a uniform standard modeled upon the pleading standard of the Second Circuit." S. Rep. No. 104–98, at 15 (1995), reprinted in 1995 U.S.C.C.A.N. 679, 694 (noting that courts interpreting the proposed "strong inference" pleading standard might find Second Circuit case law "instructive").

When all is said and done, we believe that the enactment of paragraph (b)(2) did not change the basic pleading standard for scienter in this circuit (except by the addition of the words "with particularity"). Accordingly, we hold that the PSLRA adopted our "strong inference" standard: In order to plead scienter, plaintiffs must "state with particularity facts giving rise to a strong inference that the defendant acted with the required state of mind," as required by the language of the Act itself. Although litigants and lower courts need and should not employ or rely on magic words such as "motive and opportunity," we believe that our prior case law may be helpful in providing guidance as to how the "strong inference" standard may be met. Therefore, in applying this standard, district courts should look to the cases and factors discussed in Section I.B.1 above to determine whether plaintiffs have pleaded facts giving rise to the requisite "strong inference." These cases suggest, in brief, that the inference may arise where the complaint sufficiently alleges that the defendants: (1) benefitted in a concrete and personal way from the purported fraud, see supra at * * *; (2) engaged in deliberately illegal behavior, see supra at * * * ; (3) knew facts or had access to information suggesting that their public statements were not accurate, see supra at * * * ; or (4) failed to check information they had a duty to monitor, see supra at * * *. We now turn to the complaint in this case to determine whether the plaintiffs have met their burden to plead scienter.

3.   Strong Inference of Fraudulent Intent on the Part of the AnnTaylor Defendants

The district court concluded that the plaintiffs had failed to plead facts giving rise to a strong inference of the defendants' fraudulent intent, as required to state a claim under § 10(b). We disagree.

According to the complaint, the AnnTaylor defendants knew at all relevant times that the Company had serious inventory problems that they sought to disguise by adopting the "Box and Hold" scheme. By refusing to mark down inventory they knew to be "worthless," "obsolete," and "unsalable," the defendants acted "intentionally and deliberately" to artificially inflate AnnTaylor's reported financial results. They discussed the need to mark down inventory but refused to do so because that would damage the Company's financial prospects. Further, in approving the inventory management practices of "Box and Hold," the defendants knowingly sanctioned procedures that violated the Company's own markdown policy, as stated in the Company's public filings. In doing so, they caused those filings to be materially misleading in that the disclosed policy no longer reflected actual practice. Lastly, despite knowledge of the true reasons for rising inventory levels, the defendants made repeated statements to the investment community either offering false reassurances that inventory was under control or giving false explanations for its growth. In short, the Complaint alleges that the defendants engaged in conscious misstatements with the intent to deceive. There is no doubt that this pleading satisfies the standard for scienter under Hochfelder, and the requirement of the PSLRA that plaintiffs state facts with particularity that give rise to a strong inference of the required state of mind.

In the end, we believe that the district court applied the correct standard but erroneously found that this standard was not met on these pleadings. According to the district court, the scienter requirement can be satisfied by pleading either "conscious recklessness"—i.e., a state of mind "approximating actual intent, and not merely a heightened form of negligence"—or "actual intent." *Novak I,* 997 F. Supp. at 430. This was an accurate statement of the law. However, the district court believed that the facts pleaded by the plaintiffs supported nothing more than an inference that the managers of AnnTaylor disagreed over matters of business judgment, such as the valuation of inventory and the timing of markdowns. *See Novak II,* 26 F. Supp. 2d at 660. This was incorrect as a matter of law. When managers deliberately make materially false statements concerning inventory with the intent to deceive the investment community, they have engaged in conduct actionable under the securities laws.

C.   Particularity of the Facts Pleaded

The district court also found the facts pleaded by the plaintiffs insufficiently particularized, in large part because they did not reveal the identity of the personal sources of their critical factual allegations. We disagree with the district court's reasoning and accordingly vacate and remand for further proceedings consistent with the discussion that follows.

As discussed above, Rule 9(b) has long required plaintiffs in securities fraud cases to state "the circumstances constituting fraud * * * with particularity." The PSLRA imposed an additional requirement: whenever plaintiffs allege, on information and belief, that defendants made material misstatements or omissions, the complaint must "state with particularity all facts on which that belief is formed." *15 U.S.C. § 78u–4*(b)(1). This requirement plainly applies in this case. In numerous places in their complaint, the plaintiffs allege, based on information and belief, that the AnnTaylor defendants made materially misleading statements or omissions. Most importantly, they allege that the defendants made false statements concerning the value of inventory because "Box and Hold" merchandise was "unsalable," "obsolete," and "nearly worthless," and its "actual value was nearly zero." In order to survive at this stage, the complaint must state with particularity sufficient facts to support the belief that the "Box and Hold" inventory was of limited value, and accordingly that the defendants' positive public statements concerning inventory growth were false and misleading.

The district court concluded that the plaintiffs had failed to meet these particularity requirements, in substantial part because they failed to reveal their confidential sources for some of the facts on which their belief in the essential worthlessness of the "Box and Hold" inventory was based. *See Novak I,* 997 F. Supp. at 431–32; *Novak II,* 26 F. Supp. 2d at 660–61. The lower court found the plaintiffs' allegations in this respect at worst "conclusory, unsupported and inflammatory," and at best "based upon reports by * * * anonymous 'former employees' " who should have been identified by name. *Novak II,* 26 F. Supp. 2d at 661. The district court's reasoning and conclusions were flawed in several respects.

For one thing, the complaint provides specific facts concerning the Company's significant write-off of inventory directly following the Class Period, which tends to support the plaintiffs' contention that inventory was seriously over-valued at the time the purportedly misleading statements were made. Specifi-cally, the plaintiffs allege that: (1) in AnnTaylor's May 1995 reporting of its first quarter fiscal 1995 results, the Company "admitted to analysts that its inventories were too high" and that "inventory liquidation" would follow; (2) in AnnTaylor's July 29, 1995 10–Q filed with the SEC, it "admitted that the decrease in the Company's gross profit percentage was attributable to 'in-creased cost of goods sold as a percentage of net sales, primarily resulting from markdowns' "; and (3) a January 22, 1996 Weekly Report showed that even six months after the Class Period, substantial amounts of "Box and Hold" invento-ry still dated from 1993 and 1994, which supports the inference that inventory during the Class Period was similarly dated. Thus, the complaint identifies with particularity several documentary sources that support the plaintiffs' belief that serious inventory problems existed during the Class Period itself.

We recognize that the complaint does not state with particularity every fact upon which this belief was based, since it is apparent that there were also personal sources who were not specifically identified. However, plaintiffs who rely on confidential sources are not always required to name those sources, even when they make allegations on information and belief concerning false or misleading statements, as here.

First, there is nothing in the case law of this circuit that requires plaintiffs to reveal confidential sources at the pleading stage. The defendants rely heavily on Segan v. Dreyfus Corp., 513 F.2d 695 (2d Cir.1975), in which we held that a plaintiff's complaint was insufficiently specific and rejected the argument that further disclosure would, among other things, identify a confidential informant. *See id.* at 696. But in Dreyfus, we held only that the plaintiff had to plead additional facts, not that the plaintiff was required to reveal the name of the informant. *See id.* ("A suit charging fraud may not be based on facts so secret that the defendants cannot be told what they are.") (emphasis added). Some district courts in this circuit have on occasion stated that Rule 9(b) requires plaintiffs in securities fraud cases to allege the "sources that support the alleged specific facts," *e.g.*, Blanchard v. Katz, 705 F. Supp. 1011, 1012 (S.D.N.Y.1989); Crystal v. Foy, 562 F. Supp. 422, 425 (S.D.N.Y.1983), but in no case have they dismissed a complaint for failure to identify confidential sources.

Second, while paragraph (b)(1) may compel revelation of confidential sources under certain circumstances, such circumstances are not necessarily present in this case. The defendants point to district court decisions outside this circuit that hold or imply that the PSLRA generally requires plaintiffs to include the names of their confidential sources. *See* In re Silicon Graphics Inc. Sec. Litig., 970 F. Supp. 746, 763 (N.D.Cal.1997); In re Aetna Inc. Sec. Litig., No. CIV. A. MDL 1219, 1999 WL 354527, at *4 (E.D.Pa. May 26, 1999). However, this rule is based on a misreading of the legislative history of the PSLRA. Specifically, the court in Silicon Graphics relied primarily on the hyperbolic statements of legislators attempting (unsuccessfully) to amend the proposed Act to lighten plaintiffs' pleading burden. *See* Silicon Graphics, 970 F. Supp. at 763–64. In fact, the applicable provision of the law as ultimately enacted requires plaintiffs to plead only facts and makes no mention of the sources of these facts. *See* 15 U.S.C. § 78u–4(b)(1).

More fundamentally, our reading of the PSLRA rejects any notion that confidential sources must be named as a general matter. In our view, notwith-standing the use of the word "all," paragraph (b)(1) does not require that plaintiffs plead with particularity every single fact upon which their beliefs concerning false or misleading statements are based. Rather, plaintiffs need only plead with particularity sufficient facts to support those beliefs. Accordingly, where plaintiffs rely on confidential personal sources but also on other facts, they need not name their sources as long as the latter facts provide an adequate basis for believing that the defendants' statements were false. Moreover, even if personal sources must be identified, there is no requirement that they be named, provided they are described in the complaint with sufficient particularity to support the probability that a person in the position occupied by the source would possess the information alleged. In both of these situations, the plaintiffs will have pleaded enough facts to support their belief, even though some arguably relevant facts have been left out. Accordingly, a complaint can meet the new pleading requirement imposed by paragraph (b)(1) by providing documentary evidence and/or a sufficient general description of the personal sources of the plaintiffs' beliefs.

Thus, we find no requirement in existing law that, in the ordinary course, complaints in securities fraud cases must name confidential sources, and we see no reason to impose such a requirement under the circumstances of this case. "The primary purpose of Rule 9(b) is to afford defendant fair notice of the plaintiff's claim and the factual ground upon which it is based." Ross v. Bolton, 904 F.2d 819, 823 (2d Cir.1990). This purpose, which also underlies paragraph (b)(1), can be served without requiring plaintiffs to name their confidential sources as long as they supply sufficient specific facts to support their allegations. Imposing a general requirement of disclosure of confidential sources serves no legitimate pleading purpose while it could deter informants from providing critical information to investigators in meritorious cases or invite retaliation against them.

We express no view as to whether the plaintiffs' allegations in this case were sufficiently particularized. Instead, we remand to the district court with instructions to: (1) allow the plaintiffs to replead in light of our discussion above; and (2) reconsider the particularity of the plaintiffs' pleadings in light of the proper standards.

* * *

CONCLUSION

For the foregoing reasons, we hold, first, that: (a) in order to plead scienter in securities fraud cases, plaintiffs must "state with particularity facts giving rise to a strong inference that the defendant acted with the required state of mind"; and (b) the plaintiffs here pleaded sufficient facts to establish a strong inference of fraudulent intent on the part of the AnnTaylor defendants. Second, we hold that the district court erred, under the circumstances of this case, by requiring the plaintiffs to reveal the names of their confidential sources in order to meet the particularity requirements of the PSLRA. On remand, we instruct the district court to: (a) permit the plaintiffs to replead; and (b) evaluate their pleadings anew in light of our interpretation of these requirements. * * * Accordingly, the judgment of the district court is vacated and the case remanded for further proceedings consistent with these rulings.

PLEADING AFTER THE 1995 ACT

In the aftermath of the 1995 Act the circuits wrestled with several different pleading questions, most notably including:

(1) Did the 1995 Act raise the substantive culpability standard under Rule 10b–5 from the pre–1995 Act intentionally or recklessness to a heightened "deliberate recklessness" standard which the Ninth Circuit defined as reflecting "some degree of intentional or conscious misconduct?"[1] The Conference Report accompanying the Securities Litigation Uniform Standards Act of 1998 expressly rejected the conclusion that the 1995 Act had intended to change the prevailing scienter standard[2] and most subsequent federal circuit court decisions have agreed that the 1995 Act does not alter the Rule 10b–5 culpability standard.[3]

(2) How does a plaintiff satisfy the strong inference of scienter pleading standard in § 21D(b)(2) of the 1934 Act? This was the pivotal issue that *Novak v. Kasaks* addressed. The Second Circuit concluded in *Novak*: "[T]he PSLRA effectively raised the nationwide pleading standard to that previously existing in this circuit and no higher, with the exception of the 'with particularity' requirement."[4]

The other circuits have reached a variety of views.

The Third Circuit has largely followed the Second Circuit interpretation of § 21D(b)(2).[5]

In contrast in *Silicon Graphics Inc. Sec. Litig.*[6] the Ninth Circuit ruled:

> We hold that a private securities plaintiff proceeding under the PSLRA must plead, in great detail, facts that constitute strong circumstantial evidence of deliberately reckless or conscious misconduct. Our holding rests, in part, on our conclusion that Congress intended to elevate the pleading requirement above the Second Circuit standard requiring plaintiffs merely to provide facts showing simple recklessness or a motive to commit fraud and opportunity to do so. We hold that although facts showing mere recklessness or a motive to commit fraud and opportunity to do so may provide some reasonable inference of intent, they are not sufficient to establish a strong inference of deliberate recklessness. In order to show a strong inference of deliberate recklessness, plaintiffs must state facts that come closer to demonstrating intent, as opposed to mere motive and opportunity.

1. In re Silicon Graphics Inc. Sec. Litig., 183 F.3d 970, 977 (9th Cir.1999).

2. Conf. Rep. 105–803, 105th Cong., 2d Sess. 30 (1998):

> The managers understand, however, that certain federal district courts have interpreted the Reform Act as having altered the scienter requirement. In that regard, the managers again emphasize that the clear intent in 1995 and our continuing intent in this legislation is that neither the Reform Act nor S. 1260 in any way alters the scienter standard in federal securities fraud suits.

3. See, e.g., Sterlin v. Biomune Sys., 154 F.3d 1191 (10th Cir.1998); Berry v. Valence Tech., Inc., 175 F.3d 699 (9th Cir.1999); Rothman v. Gregor, 220 F.3d 81, 96–98 (2d Cir.2000).

4. 216 F.3d at 310.

5. In re Advanta Corp. Sec. Litig., 180 F.3d 525, 533–534 (3d Cir.1999)

> The text of section 21D(b)(2) closely mirrors language employed by the Second Circuit, particularly as it requires the plaintiff to allege facts supporting a "strong inference" of scienter. In fact, with the exception of the Act's "state with particularity" requirement, the two standards are virtually identical. [Citations omitted.] We believe Congress's use of the Second Circuit's language compels the conclusion that the Reform Act establishes a pleading standard approximately equal in stringency to that of the Second Circuit.

6. 183 F.3d 970 (9th Cir.1999).

Accordingly, we hold that particular facts giving rise to a strong inference of deliberate recklessness, at a minimum, is required to satisfy the heightened pleading standard under the PSLRA. We think that our holding represents the best way to reconcile Congress' express adoption of the Second Circuit's so-called "strong inference standard" with its express refusal to codify that circuit's case law interpreting the standard.[7]

Applying this approach the court in *Silicon Graphics* (SGI) dismissed a complaint concerning plans to produce graphic design computers called the Indigo2 Impact Workstation (Indigo2), which SGI had assured investors would help sustain a 40% growth rate in the 1996 fiscal year. This projection drove its stock to an all time high of $44 7/8 or August 21, 1995.

According to the complaint by mid-September 1995 SGI began encountering quality control problems with a primary component, the Toshiba Asic chip. Nonetheless, McCracken, SGI's chief executive officer, made repeated optimistic statements:

September 19, 1995: McCracken told Morgan Stanley that there were "no supply constraints" on the Indigo2.

September 21, 1995: McCracken announced at an industry conference that Indigo2 sales growth "was accelerating."

September 22, 1995: McCracken told Morgan Stanley that "that there is no problem with [Indigo2], nor is there an engineering halt."

September 26, 1995: SGI announced "volume shipments" of the Indigo2 workstation.

The shortage of Asic chips compounded other major problems for SGI, as the Ninth Circuit explained:

The company was suffering through declining sales to the United States government and Original Equipment Manufacturers ("OEM"), languishing demand in Europe, and complications resulting from the reorganization of its sales force. As these problems became apparent, investors began to lose confidence in SGI's ability to maintain its high growth rate, and as a result, SGI's stock dropped to a low of $29 7/8 on October 9, 1995.

On October 19, 1995, SGI announced that its revenue had grown just 33% during the first quarter of FY96, well below the projected growth of 40%. The disappointing first quarter performance, according to [the Brody complaint], caused SGI's officers to fear another drop in the value of SGI stock. To prevent such a drop, Brody asserts that SGI's officers allegedly conspired to restore investor confidence by downplaying SGI's problems. In furtherance of their alleged "conspiracy," SGI's officers made the following statements which were intended to artificially inflate the value of SGI stock:

October 19, 1995: SGI issued a press release reporting that the Indigo2 was shipping in volume.

October 19, 1995: In a conference call, McCracken and other officers told securities analysts and institutional investors that SGI's sales force reorganization had been successful. The officers attributed the shortcoming in the first quarter growth to a "temporary pause" in

---

7. Id. at 974. Judge Browning dissented and would follow the Second and Third Circuit approach to the strong inference standard. Id. at 991.

OEM sales, and a brief drop in demand from the U.S. Government and French businesses. SGI assured investors that (1) there were no manufacturing problems with or supply constraints on the Indigo2; (2) demand was strong for the workstation, and it was being shipped in volume; (3) the Indigo2 upgrade was on schedule and would be introduced in January 1996 as planned; and (4) the goal of 40% revenue growth for FY 96 would be achieved.

October 19, 1995: McCracken stated during an interview that SGI's first quarter performance was "probably less" than the growth the company would see during FY 96.

To further inflate the value of SGI stock, the company announced its plan to repurchase 1.3 million of its own shares immediately and another 5.7 million over a longer period. According to Brody, the statements had their intended effect: SGI's stock price dropped only slightly despite its disappointing first quarter results.

SGI's problems continued throughout October 1995. SGI again failed to ship the Indigo2 in volume and its sales continued to decline because the sales force reorganization had been ineffective. Moreover, demand for the Indigo2 remained low among OEM and European customers. As a result, SGI fell even farther below its target of 40% growth for FY 96.

Brody alleges that SGI's officers learned of these problems through internal company reports. Notwithstanding the negative reports, the officers continued to make positive public statements in their allegedly conscious effort to mislead investors:

November 2, 1995: SGI officers held a press conference for securities analysts and investors, stating that (1) SGI would still achieve its goal of 40% revenue growth; (2) the failure to meet growth expectations for the first quarter resulted from temporary sales force reorganization problems and a temporary pause in OEM sales; (3) Indigo2 sales were beating expectations, and the product was now shipping in volume afer some initial problems with the Toshiba ASIC chips; (4) development of the Indigo2 upgrade was proceeding as scheduled; and (5) SGI's second quarter performance would exceed its first quarter performance.

Early November 1995: SGI's first quarter report to shareholders included a letter from McCracken stating that the Indigo2 "began shipping in volume in September."

Again, Brody contends that these false and misleading statements had their intended effect: SGI's stock rose from $31 on November 1, 1995 to $36 on November 3, 1995. During the month of November, the individually named SGI officers allegedly took advantage of SGI's inflated stock value by selling 388,188 shares of SGI stock at prices as high as $37. On December 5, 1995, SGI stock reached a class-period high of $38. By mid-December, however, rumors began to circulate that SGI would again fall short of projected growth in the second quarter and its stock price began to drop.

* * *

Soon thereafter, SGI began to publicly confirm the negative rumors about its performance. On January 2, 1996, the company announced its disappointing second quarter results and acknowledged that revenue growth for the year would be much lower than expected. The next day,

SGI's stock fell to $21 1/8. On January 17, 1996, SGI's officers admitted to securities analysts that SGI had been unable to fill Indigo2 orders because of a shortage of ASIC chips and other primary components. They also acknowledged that OEM, North American, and European sales had all been down.

* * *

In dismissing the Brody complaint, the Ninth Circuit concluded:

[Under the PSLRA] * * * Brody is required to state with particularity all facts giving rise to a "strong inference" of the required state of mind. See 15 U.S.C. § 78u–4(b)(1), (2). * * * Brody must state with particularity facts demonstrating deliberate recklessness. In order to plead "with particularity," Brody must provide all the facts forming the basis for her belief in great detail.

* * *

Here, Brody neither states facts with sufficient particularity nor raises a strong inference of deliberate recklessness. In her First Amended Complaint, Brody advances two primary grounds for her information and belief: (1) the existence of internal SGI reports that contradicted positive public statements made by the officers; and (2) the unusual sale of a massive amount of SGI stock by the officers. Specifically, Brody alleges that the SGI officers received SGI internal reports notifying them of serious production and sales problems with the Indigo2.

Notwithstanding the alleged negative reports, the SGI officers continued to make positive representations to investors regarding production and sales of the Indigo2. Brody contends that the SGI officers intended for their positive comments to mislead investors and temporarily restore their faith in the company. According to Brody, the positive comments had their intended effect: SGI's stock remained artificially inflated long enough for the officers to profit from massive and improper insider trading.

Although Brody's complaint suggests an inference of deliberate recklessness, it lacks sufficient detail and foundation necessary to meet either the particularity or strong inference requirements of the PSLRA. For example, Brody fails to state facts relating to the internal reports, including their contents, who prepared them, which officers reviewed them and from whom she obtained the information. In short, Brody's complaint is not sufficiently specific to raise a strong inference of deliberate recklessness. As the district court recognized, mere boilerplate pleadings will rarely, if ever, raise a strong inference of deliberate recklessness or otherwise satisfy the PSLRA's particularity requirement. The district court also concluded that the sales of stock were not so suspicious as to create a strong inference of deliberate recklessness. We agree with the district court.[8]

Other circuits have sought standards similar to the pre–1995 Second Circuit standard, but strengthened the Second Circuit standard in specific incremental ways. In Greebel v. FTP Software, Inc.,[9] the First Circuit reasoned:

From the words of the Act, certain conclusions can be drawn. First, Congress plainly contemplated that scienter could be proven by inference,

---

8. Id. at 981–984.   **9.** 194 F.3d 185 (1st Cir.1999).

thus acknowledging the role of indirect and circumstantial evidence. See 15 U.S.C. § 78u–4(b)(2) (requiring that "the complaint * * * state with particularity facts giving rise to a strong inference that the defendant acted with the required state of mind") (emphasis added). Second, the words of the Act neither mandate nor prohibit the use of any particular method to establish an inference of scienter. Third, Congress has effectively mandated a special standard for measuring whether allegations of scienter survive a motion to dismiss. While under Rule 12(b)(6) all inferences must be drawn in plaintiffs' favor, inferences of scienter do not survive if they are merely reasonable, as is true when pleadings for other causes of action are tested by motion to dismiss under Rule 12(b)(6). See Conley v. Gibson, 355 U.S. 41, 45–46 (1957). Rather, inferences of scienter survive a motion to dismiss only if they are both reasonable and *"strong"* inferences.

* * *

This court has considered many different types of evidence as relevant to show scienter. Examples include: insider trading (discussed below); divergence between internal reports and external statements on the same subject (see Serabian v. Amoskeag Bank Shares, Inc., 24 F.3d 357, 361 (1st Cir.1994)); closeness in time of an allegedly fraudulent statement or omission and the later disclosure of inconsistent information (see *Shaw*, 82 F.3d at 1224–25); evidence of bribery by a top company official (see Greenstone v. Cambex Corp., 975 F.2d 22, 26 (1st Cir.1992)); existence of an ancillary lawsuit charging fraud by a company and the company's quick settlement of that suit (see id.); disregard of the most current factual information before making statements (see Glassman v. Computervision Corp., 90 F.3d 617, 627 (1st Cir.1996)); disclosure of accrual basis information in a way which could only be understood by a sophisticated person with a high degree of accounting skill (see Holmes v. Bateson, 583 F.2d 542, 552 (1st Cir.1978)); the personal interest of certain directors in not informing disinterested directors of impending sale of stock (see Estate of Soler v. Rodriguez, 63 F.3d 45, 54 (1st Cir.1995); and the self-interested motivation of defendants in the form of saving their salaries or jobs (see *Serabian*, 24 F.3d at 368). While a number of these cases could be thought of as falling into motive and opportunity patterns, this court continues to prefer a more fact-specific inquiry. See, e.g., *Glassman*, 90 F.3d at 624 (fact that lead underwriter may have had incentive to inflate the offering price was significant, but overall, complaint failed to state a claim on which relief could be granted).

The most salient feature of the PSLRA is that whatever the characteristic pattern of the facts alleged, those facts must now present a *strong* inference of scienter. A mere reasonable inference is insufficient to survive a motion to dismiss. * * *

It is clear that scienter allegations now must be judged under the "strong inference" standard at the motion to dismiss stage.

Our view of the Act is thus close to that articulated by the Sixth Circuit. That court held that a plaintiff could survive a motion to dismiss by "pleading facts that give rise to a strong inference of [scienter]." *In re Comshare, Inc. Sec. Litig.*, 183 F.3d 542, 550 (6th Cir.1999) (internal quotation marks omitted). * * *

Without adopting any pleading litany of motive and opportunity, we reject defendants' argument that facts showing motive and opportunity can never be enough to permit the drawing of a strong inference of scienter. But, as we cautioned in *Maldanado*, 137 F.3d at 10 n.6, merely pleading motive and opportunity, regardless of the strength of the inferences to be drawn of scienter, is not enough.[10]

Cases involving insider trading allegations generally are easier to successfully plead, but success is not inevitable. In Ronconi v. Larkin,[11] the Ninth Circuit stated:

We have considered insider trading as circumstantial evidence that a statement was false when made.

But not every sale of stock by a corporate insider shows that the share price is about to decline. A corporate insider may sell stock to fund major family expenses, diversify his portfolio, or arrange his estate plan. He may sell stock in a pattern that has nothing to do with any inside information, such as selling stock twice a year when the college tuition for his children is due. Our cases dealing with pleading insider trading to prove scienter are instructive. They require a plaintiff to allege "unusual" or "suspicious" stock sales. "Insider trading is suspicious only when it is 'dramatically out of line with prior trading practices at times calculated to maximize the personal benefit from undisclosed insider information.'" We have identified three relevant factors: "(1) the amount and percentage of shares sold by insiders; (2) the timing of the sales; and (3) whether the sales were consistent with the insider's prior trading history."[12]

(3) Did the group pleading doctrine survive the enactment of the 1995 Act. As a recent District Court decision explained:

The group pleading doctrine is an exception to the requirement that the fraudulent acts of each defendant be identified separately in the complaint. [Citations omitted.] The doctrine allows plaintiffs to rely on a presumption that statements in prospectuses, registration statements, annual reports, press releases,, or other *group-published information*, are the collective work of those individuals with direct involvement in the everyday business of the company. [Citations omitted] Where the defendants are insiders, no specific connection between them and the fraudulent representations is necessary.[13]

One commentator urged in 2001 that the 1995 Act's "command that plaintiff plead scienter with particularity should end the erroneous reliance that some courts have placed on 'group pleading' to satisfy that element of a 10(b) case."[14] So far a majority of cases addressing the issue have determined

---

10. Id. at 195–197. See similar articulations in Nathenson v. Zonagen, Inc., 267 F.3d 400 (5th Cir.2001); In re Comshare Inc. Sec. Litig., 183 F.3d 542, 551–553 (6th Cir.1999); Florida St. Bd. of Admin. v. Green Tree Fin. Corp., 270 F.3d 645, 652 (8th Cir.2001); City of Philadelphia v. Fleming Co., Inc., 264 F.3d 1245, 1259–1263 (10th Cir.2001); Bryant v. Avado Brands, Inc., 187 F.3d 1271, 1283 (11th Cir.1999).

11. 253 F.3d 423 (9th Cir.2001).

12. Id. at 435.

13. Elliott Assoc., L.P. v. Hayes, 141 F.Supp.2d 344, 354 (S.D.N.Y.2000).

14. William O. Fisher, Don't Call Me a Securities Law Groupie: The Rise and Possible Demise of the "Group Pleading" Protocol in 10b–5 Cases, 56 Bus. Law. 991, 1046 (2001). More colorfully the author suggested: "courts would do best to put this pleading protocol to the sword." Id. at 1055.

that the group pleading doctrine does in fact survive the passage of the 1995 Act.[15]

PROBLEM 15–1

Plaintiffs' have alleged that Academic is a leading publisher and distributor of classroom and professional magazines, and other educational products, which it sells through retail distributors, book clubs, book fairs, classrooms and libraries. In the years leading up to 1999–2000, Academic's best-selling product was "Platonics," a series of college level study guides. Before December 2000, defendants had expanded Platonics distribution to high school and middle school classes. This change in strategy was presented to the public as a significant positive development.

What the public did not know was that Academic shipped books to retailers and distributors with full right of return.

Before 2001, Academic boasted one of the lowest book return rates in the college book publishing industry. On September 12, 2000 stock broker Lyman Stark issued a report on Academic's return rates that incorporated statements made at a meeting with senior Academic officers, including defendant Chipmunk. These officers represented that company's return rate historically ran at 15 to 20 percent, as compared to 35 percent rates at other book publishers. Platonics books were being returned at even less than 20 percent, and while the expansion into the high school and middle school market could cause the return rate to rise, it would rise only "modestly." Academic officials added the "the issue of managing return exposure is one that gets considerable management attention."

First quarter results, ending August 31, 2001, recorded a loss worse than had been experienced in the same quarter the previous year. Nevertheless, on September 19, 2001 Lyman Stark issued another report derived from statements by company officials that Academic's "return rates remain among the lowest in the industry at less than 20 percent, which suggests that Platonic has been somewhat underdistributed."

In the February 2001 Academic issued a press release announcing a third quarter 2000 loss of 80 cents per share and that Academic would take a $13 million pre-tax charge to cover a reserve for now anticipated additional book returns. The next day Academic's stock fell 40 percent.

(1) Given these facts will plaintiffs be able to plead with sufficient particularity, as required by § 21D(b)(1) "each statement alleged to have been misleading, the reason or reasons why the statement is misleading, and, if an allegation regarding the statement or omission is made on information and belief * * * all facts on which that belief is based."

(2) What facts can plaintiff plead to satisfy the "strong inference that defendant acted with the required state of mind" required by § 21D(b)(2)?

(3) Would plaintiffs' case be stronger if Chipmunk, Academic's chief executive officer, had sold 2 percent of her total stock holdings in January 2001?

In re Cendant Corp. Litig.

United States Court of Appeals for the Third Circuit, 2001.
264 F.3d 201.

■ Before: BECKER, CHIEF JUDGE, SLOVITER and AMBRO, CIRCUIT JUDGES.

---

15. Raytheon Sec. Litig., 157 F.Supp.2d 131, 152–153 (D.Mass.2001).

OPINION OF THE COURT

■ BECKER, CHIEF JUDGE.

I.   INTRODUCTION & SUMMARY

These are consolidated appeals from the District Court's approval of a $3.2 billion settlement of a securities fraud class action brought against Cendant Corporation and its auditors, Ernst & Young, and the Court's award of $262 million in fees to counsel for the plaintiff class. Both the settlement and the fee award are challenged in these appeals. The enormous size of both the settlement and the fee award presages a new generation of "mega cases" that will test our previously developed jurisprudence. * * *

In this case, the District Court selected as lead plaintiff a group made up of three pension funds (the CalPERS Group or Lead Plaintiff). Following the dictates of the Reform Act, the court first identified that Group, which is made up of three huge government pension funds, as being the movant with the largest financial interest in the relief sought by the class. The court then made a preliminary determination that the CalPERS Group satisfied Federal Rule of Civil Procedure 23's typicality and adequacy requirements, which, under the PSLRA, made it the presumptive lead plaintiff. The District Court ultimately appointed the CalPERS Group as lead plaintiff because it determined that no member of the plaintiff class had succeeded in rebutting the statutory presumption. We find no fault with the court's decisions on this score.

The Lead Plaintiff then asked the District Court to appoint as lead counsel two firms with which it had previously negotiated a Retainer Agreement, Bernstein, Litowitz, Berger, & Grossmann of New York City, and Barrack, Rodos & Bacine of Philadelphia. The court declined initially to approve the Lead Plaintiff's choice, deciding instead to select lead counsel via an auction, but giving the CalPERS Group's chosen counsel the option to match what the court determined to be the lowest qualified bid. Those firms exercised this option and were appointed as lead counsel. Following the settlement of the case, and consonant with the results of the auction, Lead Counsel petitioned for and was awarded a sum of $262 million in counsel fees, even though that amount was at least $76 million higher than that provided for under the Retainer Agreement.

We conclude that the court's decision to hold an auction to select lead counsel was inconsistent with the Reform Act, which is designed to infuse lead plaintiffs with the responsibility (and motivation) to drive a hard bargain with prospective lead counsel and to give deference to their stewardship. Although we believe that there are situations under which the PSLRA would permit a court to employ the auction technique, this was not one of them. Here, inasmuch as the Lead Plaintiff conducted its counsel search with faithful observance to the letter and spirit of the Reform Act, it was improper for the District Court to supplant the CalPERS Group's statutorily-conferred right to select and retain lead counsel by deciding to hold an auction. In sum, we hold that the District Court erred in using an auction to appoint lead counsel; rather it should have done so pursuant to the terms of the Retainer Agreement.

Because the District Court's process resulted in the firms chosen by the Lead Plaintiff being appointed lead counsel anyway, this error was harmless (with regard to the selection of lead counsel).

* * *

IV. Counsel Selection and Counsel Fees

* * * The Reform Act establishes detailed and interrelated procedures for choosing a lead plaintiff and selecting lead counsel. We first address the District Court's appointment of the CalPERS Group as lead plaintiff, and then its choice to use an auction to select lead counsel. With respect to legal questions— including whether the District Court applied the correct standards in selecting the lead plaintiff and when, if ever, a court may hold an auction to select lead counsel in cases governed by the PSLRA—we review de novo. *See Brytus v. Spang & Co.,* 203 F.3d 238, 244 (3d Cir.2000). If the court committed no legal errors, we review its award of attorneys fees for abuse of discretion. *See id.*

A.   Introduction: Attorney–Client Tension in the Class Action Context

Lawyers operate under ethical rules that require them to serve only their clients' interests. When a representation involves a single client, the ability to select, retain and monitor counsel gives clients reason to be confident that their lawyers will live it up to this obligation. The power to select counsel lets clients choose lawyers with whom they are comfortable and in whose ability and integrity they have confidence. The power to negotiate the terms under which counsel is retained confers upon clients the ability to craft fee agreements that promise to hold down lawyers' fees and that work to align their lawyers' economic interests with their own. And the power to monitor lawyers' performance and to communicate concerns allows clients to police their lawyers' conduct and thus prevent shirking. This regime has served the American legal system well for a very long time.

1.   The Problem With Class Action

Most of the safeguards we have described vanish in the class action context, where "the client" is a sizeable, often far-flung, group. Logistical and coordination problems invariably preclude class members from meeting and agreeing on anything, and, at all events, most class members generally lack the economic incentive or sophistication to take an active role. There is simply no way for "the class" to select, retain, or monitor counsel.

Although class counsel has an ethical duty of undivided loyalty to the interests of the class, reason for concern remains. This is in large measure because a rational, self-interested client seeks to maximize net recovery; he or she wants the representation to terminate when his or her gross recovery minus his or her counsel's fee is largest. In contrast, at least in theory and often in practice, a rational, self-interested lawyer looks to maximize his or her net fee, and thus wants the representation to end at the moment where the difference between his or her fees and costs—which include not only the opportunities for other work that the lawyer gives up by pursuing it—is greatest. These two points rarely converge. As a result, there is often a conflict between the economic interests of clients and their lawyers, and this fact creates reason to fear that class counsel will be highly imperfect agents for the class.

Because of this conflict (and because "the class" cannot counteract its effects via counsel selection, retention, and monitoring), an agent must be located to oversee the relationship between the class and its lawyers. Traditionally, that agent has been the court. Although some courts have played an active role with regard to selecting lead counsel in securities cases, most have traditionally appointed the person who filed the first suit as lead plaintiff, and generally selected that person's lawyer to serve as lead counsel (assuming, of course, that the lawyer possessed sufficient competence and experience). [Citation omitted.] In addition, time and institutional constraints have generally prevented courts from actively monitoring the performance of lead counsel during the pendency of litigation.

Under such a regime, it was essential for courts to scrutinize fee requests to protect the interests of absent class members. Lead plaintiffs were often unsophisticated investors who held small claims, and, according to some reports, they were sometimes paid "bounties" by lead counsel in exchange for their "services." [Citation omitted.] In such situations, it was unlikely that the lead plaintiff had undertaken a meaningful counsel selection process; indeed it was suspected that lead counsel generally selected the lead plaintiff rather than vice versa. [Citations omitted.] Moreover, there was generally little reason to believe that the lead plaintiff had the incentive or inclination to engage in aggressive or effective bargaining over lead counsel's fee, or that a typical lead plaintiff could be counted on to engage in meaningful monitoring of lead counsel's performance.

* * * The first major attempt to address counsel selection as well as fees came in Judge Vaughn R. Walker's application of the auction technique in *In re Oracle Securities Litigation*, 131 F.R.D. 688 (N.D.Cal.1990), which has since been used in a number of cases * * *. The basic concept is simple: the judge solicits bids from law firms to serve as lead counsel and selects the lowest bidder that the court determines will adequately represent the class. In theory, an auction will mimic a market transaction and result in reasonable quality, low-cost representation for the class.

The auction method offers several potential advantages. First, unlike all of the methods previously discussed, it deals with counsel selection in addition to counsel retention. When an auction is used, counsel are no longer "selected" by the race-to-the-courthouse method, and this means that courts can exercise greater control over counsel quality. Second, auctions may lead to lower-priced representation. Under the traditional method, lead counsel (who has already been appointed) tries to get as much as it can from the court in terms of fees. Under the auction method, in contrast, prospective lead counsel compete to submit the lowest reasonable bid. Third, assuming a sufficiently large number of bidders, an auction will likely better approximate a market transaction than having a judge set attorneys fees after the fact. Fourth, auctions may provide a way for new firms to enter the market for plaintiff-side securities class action lawyers, thus rendering the overall market more competitive. Fifth, the auction method may require a smaller investment of judicial time than the time-consuming lodestar method, and could minimize the dangers of hindsight biases associated with the traditional, after-the-fact approach to determining fees. * * *

Auctions may not be a panacea, however. One persistent criticism is that courts generally identify the "lowest" bidder and appoint that bidder as lead counsel, without performing the cost/quality weighing in the way a real client would. Another fear is that because auctions do not reward the attorneys who discover legal violations, they may reduce lawyers' incentives to seek out and disclose illegality (because unless they are selected as lead counsel, they may not be compensated for the time they spent doing so). Moreover, bids in large, potentially high-recovery, cases are likely to be quite complex and it may be difficult for courts to assess their relative costs to the class. This risk is especially strong in cases where the bids consist of a complicated set of alternate fees that vary depending on the size of the recovery and the stage of the proceedings at which recovery is obtained. In such situations, a court cannot assess which bid is the cheapest without first assessing the likely amount of recovery. Additionally, if there are too few bidders, the degree to which an auction will actually simulate the market is questionable. Finally, there is a risk that auctions could result in a "winner's curse," systematically selecting bidders who overestimate the odds or amount of a likely recovery. Such a "winning" bidder might then find itself litigating an unprofitable case, which may then give it an incentive to settle early and cheaply.

* * *

3.   The PSLRA

In *Let the Money Do the Monitoring: How Institutional Investors Can Reduce Agency Costs in Securities Class Actions,* Professors Elliott J. Weiss and John S. Beckerman argued that institutional investors are well suited to select, retain, and monitor lead counsel in securities class actions. *See* 104 Yale L.J. 2053 (1995). Their article explained how then-current practices deterred institutional investors from taking a more active role, and recommended legislation to encourage them to serve as lead plaintiffs.

The Weiss and Beckerman proposal had three parts. First, to ensure that institutional investors found out about pending class actions, they argued that courts should require that meaningful notices be sent out soon after the filing of a complaint. *See id.* at 2108. Second, "because the named plaintiff or group of plaintiffs with the largest financial stake in the outcome of an action has the greatest economic incentive to monitor class counsel's performance effectively," Weiss and Beckerman suggested that courts "adopt a presumption that that plaintiff or group will 'most adequately' represent class members' interests." *Id.* at 2105. They recommended that "[c]ourts * * * provide other putative plaintiffs with an opportunity to rebut this presumption, but should allow them to do so only by demonstrating that the presumptively 'most adequate' plaintiff has a significant disqualifying conflict of interest or is subject to unique defenses that would render it incapable of adequately representing the class." *Id.* at 2105–06. Weiss and Beckerman further suggested that only putative class members should be permitted to file adequacy and typicality objections against the presumptive lead plaintiff, and recommended that even those parties be entitled to discovery "only where they can demonstrate some reasonable basis for believing that a presumptively adequate plaintiff would not be capable of representing the class adequately." *Id.* at 2109.

* * *

Third, once such a lead plaintiff was selected, Weiss and Beckerman submitted that courts should "appoint as lead counsel the attorney for the 'most adequate plaintiff' " and should defer to that plaintiff's discretion in setting attorneys fees, noting that institutional investors are "experienced and sophisticated consumers of legal services." *Id.* at 2105–06. Weiss and Beckerman speculated that if institutional investors frequently served as lead plaintiffs, plaintiff-side securities law firms would grow increasingly concerned about their long-term reputations with such investors and thus might have less incentive to shirk in particular cases. *See id.* at 2106–07. The authors acknowledged that fee structures negotiated by institutional lead plaintiffs might "differ substantially from the fee structure that courts currently employ," but suggested that courts "might well feel confident in assuming that a fee arrangement an institutional investor had negotiated with its lawyers before initiating a class action maximized those lawyers' incentives to represent diligently the class's interests, reflected the deal a fully informed client would negotiate, and thus presumptively was reasonable." *Id.* at 2105.

Soon after Weiss and Beckerman's article was published, Congress enacted the PSLRA. The statute establishes a detailed and integrated procedure for selecting a lead plaintiff and for choosing and retaining lead counsel in securities class actions that is unquestionably based on Weiss and Beckerman's proposal. * * *

B.   The Reform Act's Procedures; Selection of the CalPERS Group As Lead Plaintiff

The Reform Act establishes a two-step process for appointing a lead plaintiff: the court first identifies the presumptive lead plaintiff, and then determines whether any member of the putative class has rebutted the presumption. *See* 15 U.S.C. § 78u–4(a)(3)(B)(iii)(I) & (II). * * *

1.   Legal Standards

a.   *Identifying the Presumptive Lead Plaintiff*

In appointing a lead plaintiff, the court's first duty is to identify the movant that is presumptively entitled to that status. The process begins with the identification of the movant with "the largest financial interest in the relief sought by the class." 15 U.S.C. § 78u–4(a)(3)(B)(iii)(I)(bb). In many cases (such as this one, *see supra* Part II.B), this determination will be relatively easy, but in others it may prove difficult. The Reform Act provides no formula for courts to follow in making this assessment, but we agree with the many district courts that have held that courts should consider, among other things: (1) the number of shares that the movant purchased during the putative class period; (2) the total net funds expended by the plaintiffs during the class period; and (3) the approximate losses suffered by the plaintiffs. [Citations omitted.]

Any time the question appears genuinely contestable, we think that a district court would be well within its discretion in requiring that competing movants submit documentation as to their holdings in the defendant company or companies and in seeking further information if it deems the original submissions to be an inadequate basis for an informed decision. Once the court has identified the movant with "the largest financial interest in the relief sought by the class," it should then turn to the question whether that movant "otherwise satisfies the requirements of Rule 23 of the Federal Rules of Civil Procedure," and is thus the presumptively most adequate plaintiff. 15 U.S.C. § 78u–4(a)(3)(B)(iii)(I)(cc).

        * * *

In making the initial adequacy assessment in this context, courts should also consider two additional factors. Because one of a lead plaintiff's most important functions is to "select and retain" lead counsel, *see* 15 U.S.C. § 78u–4(a)(3)(B)(v), one of the best ways for a court to ensure that it will fairly and adequately represent the interests of the class is to inquire whether the movant has demonstrated a willingness and ability to select competent class counsel and to negotiate a reasonable retainer agreement with that counsel, *see, e.g.,* In re Quintus Sec. Litig., 201 F.R.D. 475 (N.D.Cal.2001). Thus, a court might conclude that the movant with the largest losses could not surmount the threshold adequacy inquiry if it lacked legal experience or sophistication, intended to select as lead counsel a firm that was plainly incapable of undertaking the representation, or had negotiated a clearly unreasonable fee agreement with its chosen counsel. [Citations omitted]. We stress, however, that the question at this stage is not whether the court would "approve" that movant's choice of counsel or the terms of its retainer agreement or whether another movant may have chosen better lawyers or negotiated a better fee agreement; rather, the question is whether the choices made by the movant with the largest losses are so deficient as to demonstrate that it will not fairly and adequately represent the interests of the class, thus disqualifying it from serving as lead plaintiff at all.

The second additional factor that the court should consider in making the threshold adequacy determination will arise only when the movant with the largest interest in the relief sought by the class is a group rather than an individual person or entity. The PSLRA explicitly permits a "group of persons" to serve as lead plaintiff. See 15 U.S.C. § 78u–4(a)(3)(B)(iii)(I); see also id. § 78u–4(a)(3)(B)(i) (providing that the court "shall appoint as lead plaintiff the member or members of the purported plaintiff class that the court determines to be the most capable of adequately representing the interests of class members") (emphasis added). But the goal of the Reform Act's lead plaintiff provision is to locate a person or entity whose sophistication and interest in the litigation are sufficient to permit that person or entity to function as an active agent for the class, see, e.g., H.R. Conf. Rep. No. 104–369, at 32 (1995) reprinted in 1995 U.S.C.C.A.N. 730, 731; S. Rep. No. 104–98, at 10 (1995), reprinted in 1995 U.S.C.C.A.N. 679, 689; Weiss & Beckerman, 104 Yale L.J. at 2105–06, and a group is not entitled to presumptive lead plaintiff status unless it "otherwise satisfies" Rule 23, which in turn requires that it be able to "fairly and adequately protect the interests of the class." If the court determines that the way in which a group seeking to become lead plaintiff was formed or the manner in which it is constituted would preclude it from fulfilling the tasks assigned to a lead plaintiff, the court should disqualify that movant on the grounds that it will not fairly and adequately represent the interests of the class.

We note at this juncture that we disagree with those courts that have held that the statute invariably precludes a group of "unrelated individuals" from serving as a lead plaintiff. [Citations omitted.] The statute contains no requirement mandating that the members of a proper group be "related" in some manner; it requires only that any such group "fairly and adequately protect the interests of the class." We do not intimate that the extent of the prior relationships and/or connection between the members of a movant group should not properly enter into the calculus of whether that group would "fairly and adequately protect the interests of the class," but it is this test, not one of relatedness, with which courts should be concerned.

If, for example, a court were to determine that the movant "group" with the largest losses had been created by the efforts of lawyers hoping to ensure their eventual appointment as lead counsel, it could well conclude, based on this history, that the members of that "group" could not be counted on to monitor counsel in a sufficient manner. [Citations omitted.]

Courts must also inquire whether a movant group is too large to represent the class in an adequate manner. At some point, a group becomes too large for its members to operate effectively as a single unit. [Citations omitted.] When that happens, the PSLRA's goal of having an engaged lead plaintiff actively supervise the conduct of the litigation and the actions of class counsel will be impossible to achieve, and the court should conclude that such a movant does not satisfy the adequacy requirement. [Citations omitted.]

Like many of the district courts that have considered this question, we do not establish a hard-and-fast rule; instead, we note only that a kind of "rule of reason prevails." *See, e.g., Advanced Tissue*, 184 F.R.D. at 352; *Chill*, 181 F.R.D. at 409. We do, however, agree with the Securities and Exchange Commission that courts should generally presume that groups with more than five members are too large to work effectively. *See Brief for the Securities and Exchange Commission as Amicus Curiae* at 17 n. 13.

* * *

b. *Determining Whether the Presumption Has Been Rebutted*

Once a presumptive lead plaintiff is located, the court should then turn to the question whether the presumption has been rebutted. The Reform Act is quite specific on this point, providing that the presumption "may be rebutted only upon proof by a member of the purported plaintiff class that the presumptively most adequate plaintiff—(aa) will not fairly and adequately protect the interests of the class; or (bb) is subject to unique defenses that render such plaintiff incapable of adequately representing the class." 15 U.S.C. § 78u–4(a)(3)(B)(iii)(II) (emphasis added). This language makes two things clear. First, only class members may seek to rebut the presumption, and the court should not permit or consider any arguments by defendants or non-class members. [Citations omitted.] Second, once the presumption is triggered, the question is not whether another movant might do a better job of protecting the interests of the class than the presumptive lead plaintiff; instead, the question is whether anyone can prove that the presumptive lead plaintiff will not do a "fair[ ] and adequate[ ]" job. We do not suggest that this is a low standard, but merely stress that the inquiry is not a relative one.

If no class member succeeds in rebutting the presumption, then the district court should appoint the presumptive lead plaintiff as the lead plaintiff. If the presumption has been rebutted, the court must begin the process anew (i.e., identifying which of the remaining movants has the highest financial interest in the class's recovery, assessing whether that movant satisfies the threshold typicality and adequacy requirements, and determining whether the presumption has been rebutted) until a lead plaintiff is selected.

2. Application of the Standards Here

Under these standards, we believe that the District Court correctly identified the CalPERS Group as the presumptively most adequate plaintiff. The Group filed a motion to serve as lead plaintiff, and no party has questioned that of all the movants it has the largest financial interest in the relief sought by the Class. The District Court expressly found that the CalPERS Group satisfied Rule 23(a)'s typicality requirement. See *In re Cendant Corp. Litig.*, 182 F.R.D. 144, 149–50 (D.N.J.1998). * * *

The District Court also found no obvious reason to doubt that a group composed of the three largest pension funds in the United States could adequately protect the class's interests. The CalPERS Group's members are legally sophisticated entities, their chosen counsel are well-qualified, and the

Retainer Agreement that they negotiated was not plainly unreasonable. Moreover, although it is a group, there is no indication that the CalPERS Group was artificially created by its lawyers, and the fact that it contains three members offers no obvious reason to doubt that its members could operate effectively as a single unit. We therefore find no abuse of discretion in the District Court's determination that the CalPERS Group was the presumptive lead plaintiff.

We also conclude that the District Court was correct in holding that the CalPERS Group's presumptive lead plaintiff status had not been rebutted. Appellant Aboff and Douglas Wilson (who is not before us on appeal) offered three reasons why the statutory presumption in favor of the CalPERS Group had been rebutted. First, Aboff and Wilson represented that "they had negotiated a reduced fee schedule with their attorneys." *Id.* at 148. As we stressed above, the question at this stage is not whether Aboff and Wilson would have done a better job of securing high-quality, low-cost counsel than the CalPERS Group; the question is whether the former have put forward "proof" that the latter would "not fairly and adequately represent the class." Had Aboff and Wilson shown that: (1) their fee agreement was substantially lower than that negotiated by the CalPERS Group; (2) their chosen counsel were as qualified or more qualified than those chosen by the presumptive lead plaintiff; and (3) the CalPERS Group had no adequate explanation for why it made the choice that it did, then the presumption may have been rebutted. But this would only happen if the facts suggested that the CalPERS Group had performed inadequately in an objective sense. But Aboff and Wilson did not make this showing simply by alleging that they negotiated a lower fee; hence we hold that the District Court did not abuse its discretion in rejecting this argument.

Aboff and Wilson's second contention was that the presumption had been rebutted because "considerations other than the interests of the class might have influenced the CalPERS group when it retained its attorneys." *Id.* at 148. Specifically, they alleged that "counsel for the CalPERS group had made substantial contributions to the campaign of the New York State Comptroller, who, as sole trustee of the NYSCRF [a member of the CalPERS Group], has substantial influence over the decisions of the fund," and they argued that this "created an appearance of impropriety because the contributions may have played a role in the selection of the group's counsel—a practice known as 'pay-to-play.'" *Id.* at 148–49. We likewise find no abuse of discretion in the District Court's decision to reject this argument.

Lest we be misunderstood, we observe that actual *proof* of pay-to-play would constitute strong (and, quite probably, dispositive) evidence that the presumption had been rebutted. A movant that was willing to base its choice of class counsel on political contributions instead of professional considerations would, it seems to us, have quite clearly demonstrated that it would "not fairly and adequately protect the interests of the class." Thus, had Aboff and Wilson backed up their claims, the District Court would have likely been justified in holding that the presumption had been rebutted and disqualifying the CalPERS Group from serving as lead plaintiff.

The problem for Aboff and Wilson is that the District Court expressly found that they had not provided evidence in support of their pay-to-play allegations, see *id.* at 149, and we have no basis upon which to disagree. * * *

Aboff and Wilson's last submission was that the court "should select lead plaintiff through a process of competitive bidding." *Id.* at 149. The District Court refused, noting that "the PSLRA permits no such thing." Id. We agree.

See supra Part IV.B.1 (discussing the procedures that the Reform Act establishes for selecting a lead plaintiff). We therefore hold that the District Court was correct to appoint the CalPERS Group as lead plaintiff.

C. The Auction

We turn now to NYCPF's objection to the District Court's decision to employ an auction to select lead counsel.

* * *

2. Does the Reform Act Ever Permit an Auction?

The statutory section most directly on point provides that "the most adequate plaintiff shall, subject to the approval of the court, select and retain counsel to represent the class." 15 U.S.C. § 78u–4(a)(3)(B)(v). This language makes two things clear. First, the lead plaintiff's right to select and retain counsel is not absolute—the court retains the power and the duty to supervise counsel selection and counsel retention. But second, and just as importantly, the power to "select and retain" lead counsel belongs, at least in the first instance, to the lead plaintiff, and the court's role is confined to deciding whether to "approve" that choice. Because a court-ordered auction involves the court rather than the lead plaintiff choosing lead counsel and determining the financial terms of its retention, this latter determination strongly implies that an auction is not generally permissible in a Reform Act case, at least as a matter of first resort.

This conclusion gains support when we examine the overall structure of the PSLRA's lead plaintiff section. The Reform Act contains detailed procedures for choosing the lead plaintiff, see supra Part IV.B.1, indicating that Congress attached great importance to ensuring that the right person or group is selected. The only powers expressly given to the lead plaintiff, however, are to "select and retain" counsel. If those powers are seriously limited, it would seem odd for Congress to have established such a specific means for choosing the lead plaintiff. But if the powers to "select and retain" lead counsel carry a great deal of discretion and responsibility, it makes perfect sense that Congress attached great significance to the identity of the person or group that would be making those choices.

Adding support to our view that auctions are not generally permitted is the fact that the Reform Act's lead plaintiff provisions were clearly modeled after the Weiss and Beckerman proposal. The statutory language is almost identical to that suggested in Weiss and Beckerman's article, compare 15 U.S.C. § 78u–4(a)(3), with Weiss & Beckerman, 104 Yale L.J. at 2105–09, and this view is confirmed by the Senate Report, see S. Rep. No. 104–98, at 11 n.32 (1995), reprinted in 1995 U.S.C.C.A.N. 679, 690 n.32. The entire thrust of Weiss and Beckerman's argument was that large investors would do a better job at counsel selection, retention, and monitoring than judges have traditionally done, and their proposal sought to encourage such investors to serve as lead plaintiff for that purpose. This goal would be significantly undermined were we to interpret the Reform Act as permitting courts to take decisions involving counsel selection and retention away from the lead plaintiff by ordering an auction.

Lastly, our belief that the PSLRA does not allow an auction in the ordinary case is well supported in the Reform Act's legislative history. Both the Conference Committee Report and the Senate Report state that the purpose of the legislation was to encourage institutional investors to serve as lead plaintiff, predicting that their involvement would significantly benefit absent class members. See H.R. Conf. Rep. No. 104–369, at 34 (1995), reprinted in 1995 U.S.C.C.A.N. 730, 733; S. Rep. No. 104–98, at 11 (1995), reprinted in 1995 U.S.C.C.A.N. 679, 690. Both Reports begin by acknowledging that lead counsel have historically chosen the lead plaintiff rather than vice versa, and by outlining the significant problems created by that phenomenon. See H.R. Conf. Rep. No. 104–369, at 32–33 (1995), reprinted in 1995 U.S.C.C.A.N. 730, 731–32; S. Rep. No. 104–98, at 11 (1995), reprinted in 1995 U.S.C.C.A.N. 679, 690. Later, both Reports contain a brief discussion of the lead plaintiff's power to choose lead counsel:

> [The] lead plaintiff provision solves the dilemma of who will serve as class counsel. Subject to court approval, the most adequate plaintiff retains class counsel. As a result, the Conference Committee expects that the plaintiff will choose counsel rather than, as is true today, counsel choosing the plaintiff. The Conference Committee does not intend to disturb the court's discretion under existing law to approve or disapprove lead plaintiff's choice of counsel when necessary to protect the interests of the plaintiff class.

H.R. Conf. Rep. No. 104–369, at 35 (1995), reprinted in 1995 U.S.C.C.A.N. 730, 734; S. Rep. No. 104–98, at 11–12 (1995), reprinted in 1995 U.S.C.C.A.N. 679, 690.

The second sentence of the above-quoted language emphasizes that the choice belongs to the lead plaintiff, and the third is significant for two reasons. First, it confirms that the court's role is generally limited to "approving or disapproving lead plaintiff's choice of counsel;" and that it is not the court's responsibility to make that choice itself. Second, it indicates that the court should generally employ a deferential standard in reviewing the lead plaintiff's choices. It is not enough that the lead plaintiff selected counsel or negotiated a retainer agreement that is different than what the court would have done; the question is whether judicial intervention is "necessary to protect the interests of the plaintiff class."

We respect the arguments advanced by Judge Shadur—a jurist of extraordinary distinction, who * * * is one of the primary judicial advocates in favor of the auction method—as to why auctions are not inconsistent with the Reform Act, but we ultimately find them unpersuasive. Judge Shadur notes that the PSLRA provides that a movant's status as presumptive lead plaintiff may be overcome if it can be shown that the movant will not fairly and adequately represent the class, and observes that the statute makes the lead plaintiff's right to select and retain counsel "subject to the approval of the court." [Citations omitted.] Based on these two provisions, Judge Shadur writes:

> Suppose for instance a plaintiff in such a presumptive status has agreed that its own lawyers, if acting as class counsel, are to receive one-third of any class recovery. Suppose further that another highly reputable law firm that has appeared of record for another putative plaintiff or plaintiffs, having demonstrated excellent credentials in earlier securities class action litigation and being clearly capable of handling the complexities of the current lawsuit, is willing to handle the case for half of that percentage fee—or to provide even a greater contrast, is willing to work for that lesser percentage and also to impose a cap on the firm's total fee payment. In that circumstance the presumptive lead plaintiff could certainly bind itself

contractually to pay one-third of its share of the class recovery to its own lawyer, but any court would be remiss if it were to foist that one-third contingency arrangement on all of the other class members who had not themselves chosen that law firm to be their advocate. * * *

In this Court's view, if the presumptive lead plaintiffs were to insist on their class counsel handling the action on the hypothesized materially less favorable contractual basis, that insistence would effectively rebut the presumption that the putative class representatives, despite the amounts that they have at stake personally, were indeed the "most adequate plaintiffs"—that is, the class members "most capable of adequately representing the interests of class members" (Subsection (a)(3)(B)(i)). If on the other hand the presumptive class representative were willing to be represented by the most favorable qualified bidder among the lawyers submitting bids, with that bidder either supplanting the presumptive lead plaintiff's original choice of counsel or working together with that original counsel (but with the total lawyers' fees to be circumscribed by the low bidder's proposal), the presumption would clearly remain unrebutted and the presumptive most adequate plaintiffs would properly be appointed as lead plaintiffs.

[Citation omitted.]

As should be clear from our discussion of the proper means of appointing a lead plaintiff, * * * we concur with the first portion of Judge Shadur's analysis. In a situation like the one he describes, we think it quite clear that the presumptive lead plaintiff's actions (especially if it could offer no persuasive reason for preferring the first, more expensive firm, to the second, equally-qualified but less expensive one) would demonstrate that it would not fairly and adequately represent the interests of the class. This, of course, would require the court to disqualify that movant from serving as the lead plaintiff and to locate another movant that could serve in that capacity. It would not, in our view, require the court to appoint the movant whose lawyer had offered to work for half as much as the lawyers for the first movant.

As the foregoing makes clear, we part company with Judge Shadur insofar as he argues that his hypothetical shows that the Reform Act necessarily permits an auction. Judge Shadur's view appears to be that any movant who is unwilling to be represented by the firm or firms that a court determines to be the lowest qualified bidder in a court-conducted auction has necessarily shown that it will not fairly and adequately represent the interests of the class. We disagree for two reasons. First, this approach is in considerable tension with the text of the PSLRA. As we explained above, the Reform Act makes clear that it is the lead plaintiff's job to "select and retain" lead counsel and it is the court's duty to decide whether to "approve" that choice. But under Judge Shadur's approach, a presumptive lead plaintiff's only option is to assent to the counsel and the fee terms that were chosen by the court via a court-ordered auction (because otherwise the movant will be disqualified from serving as lead plaintiff on the grounds that it will not fairly and adequately represent the interests of the class). Judge Shadur's reading of the statute in effect confers upon the court the right to "select and retain" counsel and limits the lead plaintiff to deciding whether to acquiesce in those choices, thus eliminating any discretion on the part of the lead plaintiff. We simply do not think that such a result is consistent with the statutory text.

Moreover, we do not agree that the fact that a presumptive lead plaintiff refuses to accede to the counsel or fee terms set via an auction demonstrates that it will not fairly and adequately represent the interests of the absent class members. As we explained earlier, the Reform Act's lead plaintiff provisions (which include the section that confers on the lead plaintiff the rights to select and retain lead counsel) were based on Weiss and Beckerman's article. A central thrust of Weiss and Beckerman's argument was that institutional investors would likely do a better job than courts at selecting, retaining, and monitoring counsel than courts have traditionally done. *See* 104 Yale L.J. at 2105–07. Whether we (or Judge Shadur) would agree with this proposition is irrelevant; what is clear is that Congress did. And if institutional investors are as good or better than courts at balancing quality and cost in selecting class counsel, then it follows that the fact that those investors may choose different lawyers and negotiate different fee arrangements than the court does not demonstrate that those investors will not fairly and adequately represent the interests of the class. We therefore respectfully disagree with Judge Shadur that the use of court-ordered auctions can be squared with the PSLRA in the ordinary case.

Instead, we think that the Reform Act evidences a strong presumption in favor of approving a properly-selected lead plaintiff's decisions as to counsel selection and counsel retention. When a properly-appointed lead plaintiff asks the court to approve its choice of lead counsel and of a retainer agreement, the question is not whether the court believes that the lead plaintiff could have made a better choice or gotten a better deal. Such a standard would eviscerate the Reform Act's underlying assumption that, at least in the typical case, a properly-selected lead plaintiff is likely to do as good or better job than the court at these tasks. Because of this, we think that the court's inquiry is appropriately limited to whether the lead plaintiff's selection and agreement with counsel are reasonable on their own terms.

In making this determination, courts should consider: (1) the quantum of legal experience and sophistication possessed by the lead plaintiff; (2) the manner in which the lead plaintiff chose what law firms to consider; (3) the process by which the lead plaintiff selected its final choice; (4) the qualifications and experience of counsel selected by the lead plaintiff; and (5) the evidence that the retainer agreement negotiated by the lead plaintiff was (or was not) the product of serious negotiations between the lead plaintiff and the prospective lead counsel. [Citation omitted.]

We do not mean for this list to be exhaustive, or to intimate that district courts are required to give each of these factors equal weight in a particular case; at bottom, the ultimate inquiry is always whether the lead plaintiff's choices were the result of a good faith selection and negotiation process and were arrived at via meaningful arms-length bargaining. Whenever it is shown that they were not, it is the court's obligation to disapprove the lead plaintiff's choices. [Citation omitted.]

Although we think, for reasons explained above, that an auction is impermissible in most Reform Act cases, we do not rule out the possibility that it could be validly used. If the court determines that the lead plaintiff 's initial choice of counsel or negotiation of a retainer agreement is inadequate, it should clearly state why (for both the benefit of the lead plaintiff and for the record) and should direct the lead plaintiff to undertake an acceptable selection process. If the lead plaintiff's response demonstrates that it is unwilling or unable to do so, then the court will, of necessity, be required to take a more active role.

At that point, a court will have several options. If a litigant were to have repeatedly undertaken a flawed process of selecting and retaining lead counsel, that may be enough to show that it will not fairly and adequately protect the interests of the class. In such a situation, the court would be justified in disqualifying that litigant from serving as lead plaintiff, selecting a new lead plaintiff, and directing that newly-appointed lead plaintiff to undertake an acceptable search.

On the other hand, it is possible that the court could conclude that, perhaps due to the nature of the case at hand, none of the possible lead plaintiffs is capable of fulfilling the model contemplated by the Reform Act, i.e., a sophisticated investor who has suffered sizeable losses and can be counted on to serve the interests of the class in an aggressive manner. In such a situation, it would be permissible for a court to conclude that its obligation to protect the interests of the plaintiff class makes it necessary for the court to assume direct control over counsel selection and counsel retention, and, were the court to so conclude, an auction would be one permissible means by which the court could select and retain counsel on behalf of the class. We stress, however, that it is not sufficient justification for an auction in a case governed by the Reform Act that the court prefers a process of counsel selection or counsel retention that it, rather than the lead plaintiff, controls, nor is it enough that the court thinks that an auction is an inherently superior mechanism for determining a reasonable fee.

3. Was the Auction in this Case Permissible?

We now analyze whether, under these precepts, the District Court's decision to conduct an auction was justified. We begin by rejecting the contention that the court's willingness to permit counsel chosen by Lead Plaintiff to match what the District Court determined to be the lowest qualified bid fully protected the CalPERS Group's right to "select and retain" lead counsel. First, because the court's order gave the matching power to the Group's choice of counsel rather than to the Group itself, this approach did not, in fact, preserve the Group's ability to "select" lead counsel. Moreover, because the court's order meant that Lead Plaintiff's choice would be honored only if it was made pursuant to fee terms set by the District Court, the court's approach also undermined the CalPERS Group's ability to "retain" counsel.

In its written opinion, the District Court gave several reasons for holding an auction. First, it noted that the PSLRA makes Lead Plaintiff's decision "subject to the approval of the court." The court stressed that "given the opportunity, absent class members would try to secure the most qualified representation at the lowest cost," and then observed that, at the end of the case, it would be required to ensure that the "total attorneys' fees and expenses" that it awarded to lead counsel did "not exceed a reasonable percentage of the amount of any damages and prejudgment interest actually paid to the class." *In re Cendant Corp. Litig.,* 182 F.R.D. 144, 150 (D.N.J.1998). The court concluded that holding an auction would aid it in making this determination and in protecting the class's interests because it would simulate the market, thus providing a "benchmark of reasonableness." *Id.* at 150–52. Second, the District Court stated that holding an auction would have the "salutary" effect of "removing any speculative doubt" about Aboff and Wilson's pay-to-play allegations. *Id.* at 152.

These reasons are not sufficient justification for holding an auction. The first (i.e., a generalized desire to hold down costs by "simulating" the market) would apply in every case, and thus cannot be enough to justify a procedure that we have concluded may only be used rarely. Further, there is no need to "simulate" the market in cases where a properly-selected lead plaintiff conducts a good-faith counsel selection process because in such cases—at least under the theory supporting the PSLRA—the fee agreed to by the lead plaintiff is the market fee.

Nor do we think that the laudable desire to dispel mere allegations of impropriety as to one member of the CalPERS Group is enough to justify holding an auction. Were it sufficient, then any disgruntled class member (or lawyer seeking to be appointed lead counsel) could disable the lead plaintiff from exercising its statutorily-conferred power by making unsupported allegations of impropriety.

It could also be argued that two of the District Court's statements during the August 4 and August 19, 1998, hearings support its decision to hold an auction. To begin with, we doubt that any of these musings could properly be seen as "findings" sufficient to justify the court's actions. But even if they could, we find these proffered reasons simply inadequate. During the August 4 hearing, the District Court suggested that institutional investors may not do a good job of selecting lead counsel because "at times familiarity or a long time association between a client and a lawyer * * * may limit arms length bargaining." These "concerns" cannot justify the court's decision to hold an auction because there was simply no evidence of "familiarity or a long time association" between any member of the CalPERS Group and either of the firms that the Group proposed retaining, nor was there any evidence of or finding by the District Court that arms-length bargaining had not, in fact, taken place.

We are similarly unable to conclude that the auction was justified based on the District Court's statement during the August 19 hearing that "one can make the argument * * * that because of [their] economic power that at times [large investors] get a little complacent economically and therefore * * * they are not as cost effective as they should be." First, as a generic supposition, this intuition is directly at odds with the principles that animated the Reform Act. Second, the court never made findings that the CalPERS Group had been "complacent economically" or had demonstrated that it would not be "as cost effective as [it] should be."

                    * * *

For the foregoing reasons, we hold that the District Court abused its discretion by conducting an auction because its decision to do so was founded upon an erroneous understanding of the legal standards undergirding the propriety of conducting an auction under the PSLRA. With regard to counsel selection, however, this error was harmless because the counsel selected via the auction process were the same as those whom the Lead Plaintiff sought to have appointed in the first place.

See generally William S. Lerach & Eric A. Isaacson, Pleading Scienter under Section 21D(b)(2) of the Securities Exchange Act of 1934: Motive, Opportunity, Recklessness, and the Private Securities Litigation Reform Act of 1995, 33 San Diego L. Rev. 893 (1996); Hillary A. Sale, Heightened Pleading and Discovery Stays: An Analysis of the PSLRA's Internal–Information Standard on '33 and '34 Act Claims, 76 Wash. U. L. Q. 537 (1998); Elliott J. Weiss, Complex Litigation at the Millennium: Pleading Securities Fraud, 64 Law & Contemp. Probs. Nos. 2–3 5 (Spr./Sum. 2001).

LEAD PLAINTIFF PROVISION

As the *Cendant Corp.* case aptly illustrates the 1995 Act's lead plaintiff provision has been extraordinarily productive of litigation. To date most cases have addressed:

1. What standard should be used to select the lead plaintiff with the "largest financial interest"?

In Critical Path, Inc. Sec. Litig.[1], the court compared two methods of determining "the largest financial interest" in selecting a lead plaintiff:

The first looks to four factors:

(1) the number of shares purchased; (2) the number of net shares purchased; (3) the total net funds expended by the plaintiffs during the class period; and (4) the approximate losses suffered by the plaintiffs. [citing cases.]

The second equates "largest financial interest" with potential recovery.

Here the court created a hybrid of both methods focusing on "the most straightforward financial interest in the recovery sought, but considers that it should be supplemented with in/out losses, i.e., losses suffered by selling shares during the class period."[2]

2. How large a group may be aggregated to serve as lead counsel? In *Cendant Corp. Litig.*, Judge Becker correctly explained that the 1995 Act contemplates a "group" serving as lead plaintiff and noted that the SEC had urged "that groups with more than five members are too large to work effectively."[3]

While other courts generally have agreed that more than one plaintiff may be appointed as lead plaintiff,[4] there has been less precision as to how large an

---

1. 156 F.Supp.2d 1102, 1107 (N.D.Cal. 2001).

2. Id. at 1108.

In Olsten Corp. Sec. Litig., 3 F.Supp.2d 286, 295 (E.D.N.Y.1998), the party with the largest potential damages, not the largest number of shares, was held to be the party with "the largest financial interest."

In Switzenbaum v. Orbital Sciences Corp., 187 F.R.D. 246 (E.D.Va.1999), the court did not appoint the lead plaintiff applicant with the largest damages, when the group chose not to provide meaningful information about the identity of its members.

Cf. Steven M. Pesner & Andrew J. Rossman, Choosing Lead Plaintiffs under the Private Securities Litigation Reform Act: Who Shall Lead?, 27 Sec. Reg. L. J. 195 (1999).

3. 264 F.3d at 267. See generally Jill E. Fisch, Aggregation, Auctions, and Other Developments in the Selection of Lead Counsel Under the PSLRA, 64 Law & Contemp. Probs. 53, 65–78 (Spr.-Sum. 2001).

4. See, e.g., Zuckerman v. Foxmeyer Health Corp., 4 F.Supp.2d 618 (N.D.Tex. 1998). Cf. Network Assoc., Inc., Sec. Litig., 76 F.Supp.2d 1017, 1023–1024 (N.D.Cal.1999) ("aggregation is improper").

aggregation is unreasonable under the 1995 Act.[5]

The courts have also divided over whether aggregation of unrelated plaintiffs is permissible.[6]

3. Who can oppose the selection of lead plaintiffs? Some courts have ruled that a defendant may not oppose a plaintiff's motion regarding satisfaction of the lead plaintiff provision, but may object to the adequacy of certification and notice when these are prerequisites to consideration of a motion for lead plaintiff.[7]

Other courts have ruled that nothing in the 1995 Act precludes or limits the right of the defendants to challenge a motion to appoint lead plaintiff and class counsel.[8]

The courts generally have not permitted interlocutory appeals to lead plaintiff appointments.[9]

4. How should lead counsel be selected? Judge Becker's decision in *Cendant Corp.* may reduce judicial enthusiasm for auctions, but before *Cendant* they were frequently employed.[10] In *Wenderhold v. Cylink Corp.*,[11] Judge Walker ordered a sealed auction procedure and requested:

> The submitted proposals shall identify each defendant from which recovery is sought and set forth:
>
> (1) the firm's experience in securities class action litigation and the background and experience of those lawyers in the firm who, it is anticipated, will be engaged in representing the class in the present litigation, including the terms and fee arrangements under which such representation took place;
>
> (2) the bona fide qualifications of the firm to complete the work necessary for representation of the class, including the willingness of the

---

5. Cf. Tumolo v. Cymer, 1999 Fed.Sec. L.Rep. (CCH) ¶ 90,453 (S.D.Cal.1999), (rejecting approximately 339 unrelated investors as lead plaintiff).

In Yousefi v. Lockheed Martin Corp., 70 F.Supp.2d 1061 (C.D.Cal.1999), the court acknowledged that "the majority of courts addressing the issue have permitted the aggregation of claims," id. at 1067 [citations omitted], but declined to appoint 137 lead plaintiffs.

6. See, e.g., Aronson v. McKesson HBOC, Inc., 79 F.Supp.2d 1146, 1153–1154 (N.D.Cal.1999) (adopting a "narrow" or "strict" approach to aggregation).

7. See, e.g., Greebel v. FTP Software, Inc., 939 F.Supp. 57, 61 (D.Mass.1996), *aff'd*, 194 F.3d 185 (1st Cir.1999).

In Takeda v. Turbodyne Tech., Inc., 67 F.Supp.2d 1129 (C.D.Cal.1999) the court ruled that the defendants have no standing to oppose the appointment of a lead plaintiff, but addressed their concerns *sua sponte*.

In Fields v. Biomatrix, Inc., 198 F.R.D. 451 (D.N.J.2000), the court held that even if a defendant does not have standing, a court may *sua sponte* consider the issuer raised by them.

8. King v. Livent, Inc., 36 F.Supp.2d 187, 190 (S.D.N.Y.1999).

9. Pindus v. Fleming Co., Inc., 146 F.3d 1224, 1227 (10th Cir.1998); Metro Serv. Inc. v. Wiggins, 158 F.3d 162 (2d Cir.1998); Florida State Bd. of Admin. v. Brick, 210 F.3d 371 (6th Cir.2000); Z–Seven Fund, Inc. v. Motorcar Parts & Accessories, 231 F.3d 1215 (9th Cir.2000).

10. See Fisch, supra n. 3, at 78–95. See also Rubin, Auctioning Class Actions: Turning the Tables on Plaintiffs' Lawyers' Abuse or Stripping the Plaintiff Wizards of Their Curtain, 52 Bus. Law. 1441 (1997).

11. 188 F.R.D. 577 (N.D.Cal.1999).

firm to post a completion bond or other security for the faithful completion of its services to the class, and the terms of any such bond or security;

(3) the firm's insurance coverage for malpractice;

(4) evidence that the firm has evaluated the case, including specifically the range and probability of recovery;

(5) the percentage of any recovery the firm will charge in the event of a recovery as fees and costs for all work performed in connection with the case set forth on the Fee Schedule Grid, affixed as Appendix A below. This shall include an explanation of the percentage fee arrangement involving a straight, increasing or decreasing fee percentage based on the overall amount of recovery through monetary increments and/or stage of recovery at which litigation is reached;

(6) a certification on behalf of the firm that (a) its proposal was prepared independently of any other firm, entity or person not affiliated with the firm, (b) no part of the proposal was disclosed to anyone outside the firm prior to filing with the court and (c) the proposal was prepared without direct or indirect consultation with other firms that have filed actions on behalf of the proposed class in this matter, or entered on behalf of the proposed class in this matter, or entered an appearance in any fashion.

The court notes that counsel located within this district will not necessarily receive more favorable consideration simply because of their location.[12]

In *Wenderhold*,[13] Judge Walker then rejected the sole competitive bid because it failed to comply with his request that a percentage of recovery fee schedule include litigation expenses. A new round of competitive bids was held. The selection of a small firm with no prior litigation experience in the circuit raised questions as to the extent to which nonprice factors, such as experience or litigation success, are appropriately taken into account in actions to choose lead counsel.[14]

There have been other issues concerning selection of courses. For instance, in Vincelli v. National Home Health Care Corp., the court declined to appoint an Executive Committee of five law firms to work with lead counsel since this seemed "contrary to the PSLRA's goal of turning control from the litigator to the lead plaintiff."[15]

NOTICE AND STAY PROVISIONS

A veritable banquet of other procedural provisions were enacted by the Private Securities Litigation Reform Act of 1995.[1] To date much attention has focused on the notice and stay provisions.

12. Id. at 587–588.

13. 189 F.R.D. 570 (N.D.Cal.1999).

14. 191 F.R.D. 600 (N.D.Cal.2000) (competitive bid process).

15. 112 F.Supp.2d 1309, 1317 (M.D.Fla. 2000). Similarly in Weltz v. Lee, 199 F.R.D. 129 (S.D.N.Y.2001), the court rejected appointment of an executive committee to serve as lead counsel. "[T]he court finds that the PSLRA would be better served by the appointment of one law firm to manage the case." Id. at 134. Cf. Holley v. Kitty Hawk, Inc., 200 F.R.D. 275, 282–283 (N.D.Tex.2001) (appointment of two lead co-counsel).

1. We addressed the Act's new forward looking statement pleading standards. Regarding the procedural requirements, see

(1) Under § 21D(a)(3)(A) early notice to class members must be published in a widely circulated national business-oriented publication or wire service. A notice filed in the Business Wire will satisfy the "widely circulated" requirement of § 21D(a)(3)(A) because this provision was not designed to ensure notice to the entire class "but merely to those sophisticated and institutional investors that Congress deemed presumptively most adequate to serve as lead plaintiffs."[2]

The description of the claims in a notice must be congruent with the claims alleged in the pleadings.[3]

There are limits as to what notice may be communicated. In McKesson HBOC, Inc. Sec. Litig.,[4] a court ordered curative notice when two law firms that were not selected as lead counsel initiated a solicitation campaign to recruit individual shareholders to assert nonclass claims.

The court stated in part:

[T]he court finds that the policies of the Reform Act and Rule 23 are best served by limiting solicitations that are distributed in the same manner as official court-ordered notices and that induce class members to provide authorizations to opt out of the class without a clear understanding of the costs and benefits of a class membership. . . .

There may be circumstances in which putative class members would seek separate representation and enter into agreements with their attorneys that give the attorneys, authorization to opt out of a class. However, when the agreements are solicited by mass mailings and over the Internet, and when retaining separate counsel is as easy as pressing a "Click Here" button on a web page, the prospects for abuse are simply too great. This is particularly true when the agreement—such as this one—is made on a contingency fee basis and without the benefit of an understanding of the class action process and the court's supervision of fees. Locking putative class members into such representations would needlessly multiply this litigation and severely disrupt the effectiveness of the class-action device.[5]

When inadequate notice was provided of class members' ability or need to move to act as lead plaintiff, the court appointed temporary lead plaintiffs and ordered a new notice to be published.[6]

Courts have enforced the requirement that a motion to serve as lead plaintiff must be filed within 60 days of the date on which the notice advising of the pendency of the action is published.[7]

(2) In general, all discovery and other proceedings shall be stayed during the pendency of any motion to dismiss "unless the court finds * * * that

---

generally 10 Louis Loss & Joel Seligman, Securities Regulation 4636–4669 (3d ed. rev. 1996).

2. Greebel v. FTP Software, Inc., 939 F.Supp. 57, 62–64 (D.Mass.1996), *aff'd*, 194 F.3d 185 (1st Cir.1999).

A notice in the *Investors Business Daily* satisfied the notice requirement of this Section. Seamans v. Aid Auto Stores, Inc., 2000 Fed.Sec.L.Rep. (CCH) ¶ 90,902 at 93,807 (E.D.N.Y.2000).

3. Wenderhold v. Cylink Corp., 188 F.R.D. 577, 579 (N.D.Cal.1999), citing Ravens v. Iftikar, 174 F.R.D. 651, 656–661 (N.D.Cal. 1997).

4. 126 F.Supp.2d 1239 (N.D.Cal.2000).

5. Id. at 1244.

6. Holley v. Kitty Hawk, Inc., 200 F.R.D. 275 (N.D.Tex.2001).

7. See, e.g., Netsky v. Capstead Mortgage Corp., 2000 Fed.Sec.L. Rep. (CCH) ¶ 91,-020 (N.D.Tex.2000).

particularized discovery is necessary to preserve evidence or to prevent undue prejudice to any party."[8] Section 21D(b)(3)(B) has been held to stay discovery required by Rule 26 of the Federal Rules of Civil Procedure.[9]

In SG Cowen Sec. Corp. v. U.S. Dist. Ct. for N.D. of Cal.,[10] the court held that limited discovery may not be permitted so that a plaintiff might uncover facts sufficient to satisfy the Act's pleading requirements. As the court earlier stated: "Congress clearly intended that complaints in these securities actions should stand or fall based on the actual knowledge of the plaintiffs rather than information produced by the defendants after the action has been filed."[11]

In an appropriate case the court will lift the automatic stay of discovery to the limited extent of permitting plaintiffs to preserve the *status quo* by serving on defendants and third parties subpoenas *duces tecum* for the purpose of preserving evidence.[12]

C. SECONDARY LIABILITY

1. CONTROL PERSON LIABILITY

Hollinger v. Titan Capital Corp.

United States Court of Appeals, Ninth Circuit *en banc*, 1990.
914 F.2d 1564, *cert. denied*, 499 U.S. 976 (1991).

■ Before GOODWIN, CHIEF JUDGE, SCHROEDER, ALARCON, NORRIS, NELSON, CANBY, HALL, WIGGINS, BRUNETTI, THOMPSON, and RYMER, CIRCUIT JUDGES.

■ WILLIAM A. NORRIS, CIRCUIT JUDGE:

Emil Wilkowski, a dishonest securities salesman, embezzled money entrusted to him by four clients. As a result, Wilkowski was convicted of criminal securities fraud and grand theft. In this civil action for alleged violations of federal securities and state laws, the victimized investors seek to recover their losses from a brokerage firm and a financial counseling firm with which

---

8. Sec. Act § 27(b)(i); Sec. Ex. Act § 21D(b)(3)(B).

9. Medhekar v. U.S. Dist. Ct., 99 F.3d 325 (9th Cir.1996). The stay also applies to period during which a motion for reconsideration of a dismissal decision was under review. Powers v. Eichen, 961 F.Supp. 233 (S.D.Cal.1997).

The stay provision in § 21D(b)(3)(A) need not delay a motion to seek class certification. Diamond Multimedia Sys., Inc., Sec. Litig., 1997 Fed.Sec.L.Rep. (CCH) ¶ 99,561 (N.D.Cal.1997).

Section 21D(b)(3)(B) applies to shareholder derivative actions under § 14(a) as well as class actions. Trump Hotel Shareholder Derivative Litig., 1997 Fed.Sec.L.Rep. (CCH) ¶ 99,537 (S.D.N.Y.1997).

10. 189 F.3d 909 (9th Cir.1999).

11. Medhekar v. U.S. Dist. Ct., 99 F.3d at 328.

12. Grand Casinos, Inc., Sec. Litig., 988 F.Supp. 1270 (D.Minn.1997). Cf. Randell S. Thomas & Kenneth J. Martin, Using State Inspection Statutes for Discovery in Federal Securities Fraud Actions, 77 B.U.L. Rev. 69 (1997). See generally Hillary A. Sale, Heightened Pleading and Discovery Stays: An Analysis of the Effect of the PSLRAs Internal–Information Standard on '33 and '34 Act Claims, 76 Wash. U. L.Q. 537 (1998).

In Transcrypt Int'l. Sec. Litig., 57 F.Supp.2d 836 (D.Neb.1999), the court declined to stay an individual claim in state court, concluding that only class actions were addressed by the 1995 Act.

In Vacold LLC v. Cerami, 2000–2001 Fed.Sec.L.Rep. (CCH) ¶ 91,334 (S.D.N.Y. 2001), the court ordered expedited discovery under § 21D(b)(3)(B) when the date of an alleged nondisclosure was uncertain.

Wilkowski was associated. The district court granted summary judgment to both defendants, which plaintiffs now appeal. * * *

I

Defendant/appellee Painter Financial Group, Ltd. ("Painter") was formed in May 1983 to provide financial counseling and to sell insurance to individuals and small businesses. Shortly thereafter, Emil Wilkowski rented space in Painter's office in Bellevue, Washington, from which he sold insurance and counseled individuals as a Painter representative. During the summer of 1983, Wilkowski met appellants Judy D'Arcy and Kay Hollinger, two business partners who were seeking financial advice. Wilkowski assisted them with a real estate transaction and was soon doing their bookkeeping, advising them on tax matters, and offering them investment advice.

In November 1983, Wilkowski and several other Painter representatives in the Bellevue office applied to the National Association of Securities Dealers ("NASD") for registration as securities salesmen for defendant/appellee Titan Capital Corporation ("Titan"), a registered broker-dealer firm regulated by the Securities and Exchange Commission ("SEC") and by the NASD. Sales representatives of broker-dealers must be registered with the NASD if the broker-dealer is a member of this self-regulatory organization.

When Wilkowski filled out his application for registration with the NASD, he answered "no" to questions asking whether he had ever willfully made a false statement, been the subject of a major legal proceeding, or been convicted or pleaded guilty to a felony. He supplied a photo and fingerprints as requested. The NASD registered Wilkowski as a securities salesman for Titan on December 12, 1983, and on January 26, 1984, Wilkowski entered into a contract in which Titan authorized him to engage in the securities business as a registered representative of Titan, operating out of Painter's office in Bellevue. That office became a Titan branch office: Titan provided Wilkowski with business cards and stationery and required the office to display a sign with Titan's logo.

As part of its usual registration process, the NASD requested the FBI to run a fingerprint check on Wilkowski. The FBI report, which was not completed until after the NASD had approved Wilkowski's registration, revealed that he had pleaded guilty in 1972 to three counts of felony forgery, for which he received a five-year suspended sentence. The NASD immediately sent a copy of the rap sheet to Titan and requested that Titan return to the NASD a written statement from Wilkowski, providing details about the conviction and an explanation of his failure to disclose the information on the registration form.

When Titan asked Wilkowski for an explanation, he responded with a letter explaining that he believed that pursuant to his plea agreement, his forgery conviction would be expunged upon his making restitution of $16,000. Without saying so explicitly, Wilkowski gave the impression that he had in fact made restitution by indicating that he believed the conviction had been removed from his record before he prepared the application for the NASD. Along with this explanation, Wilkowski submitted a new application form, on which he disclosed the forgery conviction. The NASD did not revoke Wilkowski's registration and Titan did not terminate him as a registered representative. Painter, however, did terminate Wilkowski as a financial counselor.

During the time that Wilkowski worked as a registered representative of Titan, he received funds from appellants to invest. Wilkowski legitimately invested some of the funds in securities through Titan. Sometimes, however,

Wilkowski instructed appellants to make the checks payable to him personally, and they complied. Rather than investing these funds, Wilkowski diverted them for his own use. He used Titan stationery to generate bogus receipts and financial statements that indicated that the stolen funds had been used to purchase securities and mutual funds through Titan. Ultimately, Wilkowski's activities were discovered and he was convicted of criminal securities fraud and grand theft.

In this civil action, appellants seek to recover their losses under various antifraud provisions of the federal securities laws and under state law. The district court awarded summary judgment to both Titan and Painter on all of appellants' federal claims and dismissed appellants' pendent state claims. We affirm summary judgment in favor of Painter on all federal claims. We affirm summary judgment in favor of Titan on all federal claims, except three: 1) the claim that Titan is liable for Wilkowski's wrongdoing as a "controlling person" under § 20(a) of the 1934 Act, 15 U.S.C. § 78t(a); 2) the claim that Titan is liable as a "controlling person" under § 15 of the Securities Act of 1933 Act ("1933 Act"), 15 U.S.C. § 77o; and 3) the claim that Titan is liable as Wilkowski's employer under the common law theory of respondeat superior.
* * *

III

We next consider whether Titan can be held vicariously liable as a "controlling person" under § 20(a) of the 1934 Act for Wilkowski's violations of the securities laws. Section 20(a) provides:

> Every person who, directly or indirectly, controls any person liable under any provision of this chapter or of any rule or regulation thereunder shall also be liable jointly and severally with and to the same extent as such controlled person to any person to whom such controlled person is liable, unless the controlling person acted in good faith and did not directly or indirectly induce the act or acts constituting the violation or cause of action.

15 U.S.C. § 78t(a).

To hold Titan liable under § 20(a), appellants must first establish that Titan was a "controlling person" within the meaning of the statute.[16]

The district court interpreted the law of this circuit as requiring appellants to prove that Titan exercised "actual power or influence" over Wilkowski's fraudulent dealings and that Titan was a "culpable participant" in the alleged illegal activity in order to establish that Titan was a "controlling person" for the purpose of § 20(a). R.E. at 32 (citing *Buhler*, 807 F.2d at 835). The district court, after applying this test, granted Titan summary judgment on appellants' § 20(a) claim. First, the court reasoned that Titan had no "power or influence" over Wilkowski because Wilkowski was an independent contractor and Titan did not exercise any control over Wilkowski's defalcation of funds; did not benefit from the defalcation of funds; and did not authorize Wilkowski to receive personal checks. *See id.* Second, the court concluded that because Titan and Wilkowski had contractually agreed that Wilkowski would be an indepen-

---

16. The SEC has defined "control" to mean: [T]he possession, direct or indirect, of the power to direct or cause the direction of the management and policies of a person, whether through ownership of voting securities, by contract, or otherwise. 17 C.F.R. § 230.405.

dent contractor, Titan had no duty to supervise unauthorized and unknown transactions and therefore could not have been a "culpable participant" in Wilkowski's misdeeds. *See id.* at 34. In applying the language in *Buhler*, the District Court made the question of whether Titan controlled Wilkowski turn on the particular business arrangement of the parties.

A

The SEC, as amicus curiae, joins appellants in arguing that the district court erred in holding that Titan could not be held vicariously liable as a "controlling person" under § 20(a) for Wilkowski's misdeeds. We agree. Today we hold that a broker-dealer is a controlling person under § 20(a) with respect to its registered representatives.

First, the SEC notes that this circuit and other circuits have interpreted the securities laws to impose a duty on broker-dealers to supervise their registered representatives.[17] In *Zweig*, we noted that Congress adopted § 20(a) in an attempt to protect the investing public from representatives who were inadequately supervised or controlled:

> Purchasers of securities frequently rely heavily for investment advice on the broker-representative handling the purchaser's portfolio. Such representatives traditionally are compensated by commissions in direct proportion to sales. The opportunity and temptation to take advantage of the client is ever present. To ensure the diligence of supervision and control, the broker-dealer is held vicariously liable if the representative injures the investor through violations of Section 10(b) or the rules thereunder promulgated. The very nature of the vast securities business, as it has developed in this country, militates for such a rule as public policy and would seem to suggest strict court enforcement.

521 F.2d at 1135.

The SEC argues that the representative/broker-dealer relationship is necessarily one of controlled and controlling person because the broker-dealer is required to supervise its representatives. This requirement arises from § 15 of the 1934 Act, which the SEC has interpreted as authority to impose sanctions on broker-dealers who have failed to provide adequate supervision of their registered representatives. *See, e.g., In re Reynolds & Co.*, 39 S.E.C. 902, 916–17 (1960); *In re Bond & Goodwin, Inc.*, 15 S.E.C. 584, 601 (1944).

Second, the SEC argues that as a practical matter the broker-dealer exercises control over its registered representatives because the representatives need the broker-dealer to gain access to the securities markets. Again, the SEC points to § 15(a) of the 1934 Act, which provides that a person cannot lawfully engage in the securities business unless he or she is either registered with the NASD as a broker-dealer or as a person associated with a broker-dealer. Because a sales representative must be associated with a registered broker-dealer in order to have legal access to the trading markets, the broker-dealer always has the power to impose conditions upon that association, or to terminate it. The broker-dealer's ability to deny the representative access to the markets gives the broker-dealer effective control over the representative at

---

17. See, e.g., Zweig v. Hearst Corp., 521 F.2d 1129, 1134–35 (9th Cir.), *cert. denied*, 423 U.S. 1025, 96 S. Ct. 469, 46 L. Ed. 2d 399 (1975); accord Paul F. Newton & Co. v. Texas Commerce Bank, 630 F.2d 1111, 1120 (5th Cir.1980); Marbury Management, Inc. v. Kohn, 629 F.2d 705, 716 (2d Cir.), *cert. denied*, 449 U.S. 1011(1980).

the most basic level. Moreover, because the broker-dealer is required by statute to establish and enforce a reasonable system of supervision to control its representatives' activities, the broker-dealer necessarily exerts ongoing control over the types of transactions made by the representative and her ways of handling clients' accounts.

In contrast to the SEC's position, the district court's reasoning implied that even if Titan had the power to deny Wilkowski access to the trading markets or was required by statute to supervise his securities transactions, Titan still should not be considered a controlling person under § 20(a) because Wilkowski was an independent contractor, not an agent. We find no support in the statutory scheme for such a restrictive definition of controlling person that would exclude independent contractors, and thus, we do not distinguish for purposes of § 20(a) between registered representatives who are employees or agents and those who might meet the definition of independent contractors.

In sum, § 20(a) of the Act provides that a person cannot lawfully engage in the securities business unless he is either registered as or associated with a broker-dealer, and we see no basis in the statutory scheme to distinguish between those associated persons who are employees and agents on the one hand, and those who are independent contractors on the other. To exclude from the definition of controlling person those registered representatives who might technically be called independent contractors would be an unduly restrictive reading of the statute and would tend to frustrate Congress' goal of protecting investors. Thus, we reject the argument that broker-dealers can avoid a duty to supervise simply by entering into a contract that purports to make the representative, who is not himself registered under the Act as a broker-dealer, an "independent contractor."

To summarize, we hold that a broker-dealer is a controlling person under § 20(a) with respect to its registered representatives. This result is consistent with Zweig, where we said that "[t]o ensure the diligence of supervision and control, the broker-dealer is held vicariously liable if the representative injures the investor through violations of Section 10(b) or the rules thereunder promulgated." 521 F.2d at 1135. Thus, for appellants to establish that Titan was a controlling person, they need only show that Wilkowski was not himself a registered broker-dealer but was a representative employed by or associated with a registered broker-dealer. This they have done. The facts are not in dispute that Wilkowski was a registered representative associated with Titan. Accordingly, Titan was, as a matter of law, a "controlling person" under § 20(a) with respect to Wilkowski.

B

Titan also argues that it was not a controlling person because it was not a "culpable participant" in Wilkowski's deeds as required by *Buhler*, 807 F.2d at 835–36, and *Christoffel v. E.F. Hutton & Co.*, 588 F.2d 665, 668–69 (9th Cir.1978).

The district court, citing earlier cases from our circuit, agreed with Titan and ruled that a broker-dealer is not a "controlling person" under § 20(a) unless the plaintiff proves that the broker-dealer was a "culpable participant" in the violation.

Today, however, we hold that a plaintiff is *not* required to show "culpable participation" to establish that a broker-dealer was a controlling person under

§ 20(a).[24] The statute does not place such a burden on the plaintiff. Section 20(a) provides that a "controlling person" is liable "unless [he] acted in good faith and did not directly or indirectly induce the act or acts constituting the violation or cause of action." 15 U.S.C. § 78t(a). Thus, the statute premises liability solely on the control relationship, subject to the good faith defense. According to the statutory language, once the plaintiff establishes that the defendant is a "controlling person," then the defendant bears the burden of proof to show his good faith.

* * *

To summarize, a broker-dealer controls a registered representative for the purposes of § 20(a). By recognizing this control relationship, we do not mean that a broker-dealer is vicariously liable under § 20(a) for all actions taken by its registered representatives. Nor are we making the broker-dealer the "insurer" of its representatives, which is a result we rejected in *Christoffel* as going beyond the scope of the vicarious liability imposed upon a broker-dealer by § 20(a). The mere fact that a controlling person relationship exists does not mean that vicarious liability necessarily follows. Section 20(a) provides that the "controlling person" can avoid liability if she acted in good faith and did not directly or indirectly induce the violations. By making the good faith defense available to controlling persons, Congress was able to avoid what it deemed to be an undesirable result, namely that of insurer's liability, and instead it made vicarious liability under § 20(a) dependent upon the broker-dealer's good faith.[26]

C

Contrary to the district court's ruling, the broker-dealer cannot satisfy its burden of proving good faith merely by saying that it has supervisory procedures in place, and therefore, it has fulfilled its duty to supervise. A broker-dealer can establish the good faith defense only by proving that it "maintained and enforced a reasonable and proper system of supervision and internal control." Zweig, 521 F.2d at 1134–35; see also Paul F. Newton & Co., 630 F.2d at 1120 (broker-dealer must show it "diligently enforce[d] a proper system of supervision and control"). Accordingly, the district court erred in ruling that because "Titan had adopted rules for accepting investment payments and for supervising a contractor's compliance with securities laws and regulations," it had satisfied its duty to supervise. R.E. at 34. Should Titan choose to rely upon the good faith defense, then it must carry its burden of persuasion that its supervisory system was adequate and that it reasonably discharged its responsibilities under the system. The evidence below raised material issues of fact as to

---

24. Today's holding, however, is reached in the context of the broker-dealer/registered representative relationship exclusively. We do not address the question of whether in other contexts the first prong of the *Buhler* and *Christoffel* test for determining a "controlling person," namely that of power and influence, may be applied. A person may, of course, be a controlling person without being a broker-dealer. *See, e.g., Zweig*, 521 F.2d at 1132.

26. The broker-dealer may also, of course, rely on a contention that the representative was acting outside of the broker-dealer's statutory "control." For example, Titan could argue that when appellants entrusted their money to Wilkowski they were not reasonably relying upon him as a registered representative of Titan, but were placing the money with Wilkowski for purposes other than investment in markets to which Wilkowski had access only by reason of his relationship with broker-dealer Titan.

whether Titan's supervision of Wilkowski was sufficient to entitle Titan to the good faith defense. Summary judgment was, accordingly, improper.

CONTROL PERSON LIABILITY

Section 15 of the 1933 Act provides that "Every person who * * * controls any person liable under section 11 or 12, shall also be liable jointly and severally with and to the same extent as such controlled person to any person to whom such controlled person is liable, unless the controlling person had no knowledge of or reasonable grounds to believe in the existence of the facts by reason of which the liability of the controlled person is alleged to exist." Section 20(a) of the 1934 Act provides that "every person who * * * controls any person liable under any provision of this title * * * shall also be liable jointly and severally with and to the same extent as such controlled person to any person to whom such controlled person is liable, unless the controlling person acted in good faith and did not directly or indirectly induce the act or acts constituting the violation or cause of action."

The reason for this difference in language is hard to fathom, especially since Section 15 of the 1933 Act was amended in the bill which enacted the 1934 Act, and harder still to interpret. Section 15 would seem to make ignorance a complete defense; whereas, Section 20(a) requires a showing of "good faith", which would certainly include lack of knowledge of the violation but arguably might require more. In addition, Section 20(a) requires a showing that the controlling person did not "induce" the acts constituting the violation, but it is difficult to imagine a situation where the controlling person induced the act but was ignorant of it.

The concept of control is both broad and fact specific under the federal securities laws. The House Committee report stated with reference to the definition of "underwriter" in the Securities Act:

> The concept of control herein involved is not a narrow one, depending upon a mathematical formula of 51 percent of voting power, but it is broadly defined to permit the provisions of the act to become effective wherever the fact of control actually exists.[1]

The same Committee stated, in speaking of the concept of control as used in the registration and civil liability provisions of the Exchange Act:

> [W]hen reference is made to "control," the term is intended to include actual control as well as what has been called legally enforceable control. * * * It was thought undesirable to attempt to define the term. It would be difficult if not impossible to enumerate or to anticipate the many ways in which actual control may be exerted. A few examples of the methods used are stock ownership, lease, contract, and agency. It is well known that actual control sometimes may be exerted through ownership of much less than a majority of the stock of a corporation either by the ownership of such stock alone or through such ownership in combination with other factors.[2]

1. H.R. Rep. No. 85, 73d Cong., 1st Sess. 14 (1933).

2. H.R. Rep. No. 1383, 73d Cong., 2d Sess. 26 (1934).

A 1982 law review article generalized:

[C]ontrol is defined to include: (1) majority ownership of equity and voting stock; (2) the ability to control the decision making processes as to policy; (3) the power to select and influence directors

In Burgess v. Premier Corporation[3] the court held that a director who was not involved in the day-to-day operations of a company and who did not participate in the preparation of the company's prospectus was not liable as a controlling person for alleged misrepresentations made to investors in connection with tax shelter investments and cattle herds offered by the company. In San Francisco–Oklahoma Petroleum Exploration Corp. v. Carstan Oil Co., Inc.,[4] however, the court held that a director and sole stockholder was liable as a "controlling person" in connection with the unregistered sale of fractional interest in oil and gas wells which were not exempted from registration. The defendant claimed that he was simply a figurehead, that his name was used because his son could not use his and that he did not participate in any way and made no effort to learn what the corporation was doing. The court said that even if this testimony were accepted, it demonstrated that he "must have made a conscious effort not to know."

With respect to broker-dealers, *Hollinger* is significant for its holding that (1) a broker-dealer is a controlling person under § 20(a) with respect to its registered representatives and (2) there is no support in the statutory scheme for a definition of "controlling person" that would exclude independent contractors.[5]

Under the controlling person provisions of the federal securities laws there were several other interpretative issues.

An unsettled question endures whether the controlling person must be a culpable participant in the alleged violation.[6] The 1934 Act's § 20(a) does provide that lack of participation in the violation and good faith are an affirmative defense for a controlling person,[7] but "the plain meaning of [the

---

and officers; (4) the prerogative to guard or disseminate internal business information at the individual's discretion; (5) relative independence from shareholders and fiduciary responsibilities due to the existence of only a few friendly shareholders, or no other shareholders at all; and (6) the power to determine and implement steps for the future of the company.

Bradley Forst, Going Public and the Implications to Corporate Control: The Modern Lawyer's Role as Counselor, 23 S. Tex. L.J. 71, 76 (1982). For a classic study of the evolution of control, *see* Adolf A. Berle & Gardiner C. Means, The Modern Corporation and Private Property ch. 5 (Rev. ed. 1968).

3. 727 F.2d 826 (9th Cir.1984).

4. 765 F.2d 962 (10th Cir.1985).

5. See also Martin v. Shearson Lehman Hutton, Inc., 986 F.2d 242, 244 (8th Cir. 1993), *cert. denied*, 510 U.S. 861 (1993) ("Shearson's status as employer is sufficient to establish it as a controlling person"). With respect to the other permutations of the meaning of control, see 4 Louis Loss & Joel Seligman, Securities Regulation ch. 5 (3d ed. rev. 2000).

6. A minority of circuits have held that culpable participation is required. *See, e.g.*, Boguslavsky v. Kaplan, 159 F.3d 715, 720 (2d Cir.1998); Ash v. Ameritreat, Inc., 189 F.3d 463 (3d Cir.1999).

Judge Sweet in Dietrich v. Bauer, 126 F.Supp.2d 759, 764 (S.D.N.Y.2001) summarized the Second Circuit law:

"In order to establish a prima facie case of liability under § 20(a), a plaintiff must show: (1) a primary violation by a controlled person; (2) control of the primary violator by the defendant; and (3) that the controlling person was in some meaningful sense a culpable participant in the primary violation." *Boguslavsky v. Kaplan,* 159 F.3d 715, 720 (2d Cir.1998) (internal quotation marks omitted) (*citing SEC v. First Jersey Sec., Inc.,* 101 F.3d 1450, 1472–73 (2d Cir.1996)). Once a *prima facie* case has been made out, the defendant may still escape liability if he shows that he acted in good faith. *First Jersey,* 101 F.3d at 1473 (citations omitted).

7. *See, e.g.*, G.A. Thompson & Co., Inc. v. Partridge, 636 F.2d 945, 958 (5th Cir. 1981).

statute] does not require participation in the wrongful transaction."[8] With the trend of recent cases following *Hollinger* [9]and rejecting culpable participation as an extrastatutory requirement, the courts have placed greater stress on the good faith defense. This defense generally requires some supervisory procedures and perhaps other precautionary measures, depending on the circumstances.[10] Thus a newspaper publisher does not have the same duty to supervise a financial columnist[11] that a broker-dealer has to supervise its employees.[12] For one thing the broker-dealer is subject to § 15(b)(4)(E),

8. Metge v. Baehler, 762 F.2d 621, 631 (8th Cir.1985), *cert. denied sub nom.* Metge v. Bankers Trust Co., 474 U.S. 1057 (1986). "In addition, good faith and lack of participating are affirmative defenses in a controlling person action, and requiring them as part of the plaintiff's prima facie case while allowing them as affirmative defenses, confuses the parties' responsibilities and unnecessarily burdens the plaintiffs contrary to the plain meaning of the statute."

9. See, e.g., Dellastatious v. Williams, 242 F.3d 191 (4th Cir.2001); Abbott v. Equity Group, Inc., 2 F.3d 613, 619–621 (5th Cir. 1993), *cert. denied sub nom.* Turnbull v. Home Ins. Co., 510 U.S. 1177 (1994); Harrison v. Dean Witter Reynolds, Inc., 974 F.2d 873, 881 (7th Cir.1992), *on the merits*, 79 F.3d 609 (7th Cir.1996), *cert. denied*, 519 U.S. 825 (1996); Farley v. Henson, 11 F.3d 827, 835–837 (8th Cir.1993); Howard v. Everex Sys., Inc., 228 F.3d 1057, 1065–1066 (9th Cir.2000); Maher v. Durango Metals, Inc., 144 F.3d 1302, 1305 (10th Cir.1998).

In the Eleventh Circuit, a panel formulated the applicable standard in these terms:

[A] defendant is liable as a controlling person under section 20(a) if he or she "had the power to control the general affairs of the entity primarily liable at the time the entity violated the securities laws * * * [and] had the requisite power to directly or indirectly control or influence the specific corporate policy which resulted in the primary liability."

Brown v. Enstar Group, Inc., 84 F.3d 393, 396 (11th Cir.1996), *cert. denied sub nom.* Brown v. Mendel, 519 U.S. 1112.

10. *See, e.g.,* Richardson v. MacArthur, 451 F.2d 35, 42 (10th Cir.1971); Sanders v. John Nuveen & Co., Inc., 524 F.2d 1064, 1072 (7th Cir.1975), *vacated on other grounds sub nom.* John Nuveen & Co., Inc. v. Sanders, 425 U.S. 929 (1976) ("The 'act' involved here is Nuveen's failure to make a proper investigation * * * "); Carpenter v. Harris, Upham & Co., Inc., 594 F.2d 388, 394 (4th

Cir.1979), *cert. denied sub nom.* Carpenter v. Edwards & Warren, 444 U.S. 868 (1979) ("It is required of the controlling person only that he maintain an adequate system of internal control, and that he maintain the system in a diligent manner"); San Francisco–Oklahoma Petroleum Exploration Corp. v. Carstan Oil Co., Inc., 765 F.2d 962, 965 (10th Cir.1985). Cf. SEC v. First Jersey Sec., Inc., 101 F.3d 1450, 1474 (2d Cir.1996), *cert. denied*, 552 U.S. 812 (1997): "The district court's findings that First Jersey's training and compliance methods were not bona fide attempts to comply with the securities laws were a permissible view of the evidence, and hence are not clearly erroneous. * * * "

11. Zweig v. Hearst Corp., 521 F.2d 1129, 1132–1135 (9th Cir.1975), *cert. denied*, 423 U.S. 1025 (1975).

Secondary liability for breach of a duty to supervise is not limited to broker-dealers under the Securities Exchange Act, *see, e.g.,* Kersh v. General Council of Assemblies of God, 804 F.2d 546, 550 (9th Cir.1986), an inevitable result given the origins of the controlling person provisions with specific legislative reference to "dummy directors."

12. See, e.g., Hollinger v. Titan Capital Corp., 914 F.2d 1564, 1573–1574 (9th Cir. *en banc* 1990), *cert. denied*, 499 U.S. 976 (1991).

In Davis v. Avco Fin. Serv., Inc., 739 F.2d 1057, 1068 (6th Cir.1984), *reh'g & reh'g en banc denied*, 739 F.2d 1057 (6th Cir.1984), *cert. denied*, 470 U.S. 1005 (1985), 472 U.S. 1012 (1985), the court listed the following considerations as pertinent in establishing the defense:

(1) the question of decisional (planning) and facilitative (promotional) participation, such as designing the deal and contracting and attempting to persuade potential purchasers, (2) access to source data against which the truth or falsity of representations can be tested, (3) relative skill in ferreting out the truth * * *, (4) pecuniary interest in the completion of the transaction, and (5) the existence of

which authorizes the Commission to discipline broker-dealers who fail reasonably to supervise those they control.[13] A Second Circuit decision generalized:

> [W]here * * * the erring salesman completes the transactions through the employing brokerage house and the brokerage house receives a commission on the transactions, the burden of proving good faith is shifted to the brokerage house, * * * and requires it to show at least that it has not been negligent in supervision, * * * and that it has maintained and enforced a reasonable and proper system of supervision and internal control over sales personnel.[14]

It is not sufficient for a broker-dealer merely to have supervisory procedures in place; the broker-dealer must also prove that the supervisory system was diligently enforced.[15]

Given the Supreme Court's 1994 decision, Central Bank of Denver, N.A. v. First Interstate Bank of Denver, N.A.,[16] holding that a private plaintiff may not maintain an aiding and abetting suit under § 10(b), it appears highly unlikely that a private plaintiff or the Commission may maintain a § 10(b) *respondeat superior* claim. Nonetheless, *respondeat superior* claims can still be asserted against brokerage firms under state law.[17]

Regarding controlling person and respondeat superior liability, *see generally* 9 Louis Loss & Joel Seligman, Securities Regulation 4466–4479 (3d ed. 1992); Jennifer H. Arlen & William J. Carney, Vicarious Liability for Fraud on Securities Markets; Theory and Evidence, 1992 U. Ill. L. Rev. 691; Alfred F. Conard, Enterprise Liability and Insider Trading, 49 Wash. & Lee L. Rev. 913 (1992); Loftus C. Carson, The Liability of Controlling Persons under the Federal Securities Acts, 72 Notre Dame L. Rev. 263 (1997).

PROBLEM 15–2

LaserTechnologies (LaserTech), Inc., developed a camera system that created souvenirs for fans at sporting events. In 2001, LaserVision formed TechVision Advanced Imaging, LLC. ("Tail"), to finance the marketing of technology. LaserTech was TAIL's corporate parent and a managing member of TAIL. Ariana Luck, the president of LaserTech, served as CEO, president, and director of TAIL. Defendant Dana Jones, a director of LaserTech, served as a manager of TAIL. Defendant Ramona O'Malley had no connection to TAIL except by virtue of her role as an outside director of LaserTech.

In October 2001, Luck invited plaintiff Rochelle Delicious to become an equity investor in Tail. In November 2001, TAIL sent Delicious offering documents

---

a relationship of trust and confidence between the plaintiff and the alleged "seller."

13. See Zweig v. Hearst Corp., 521 F.2d 1129, 1135 (9th Cir.1975), *cert. denied*, 423 U.S. 1025 (1975); Hollinger v. Titan Capital Corp., 914 F.2d 1564, 1573–1574 (9th Cir. *en banc* 1990), *cert. denied*, 499 U.S. 976 (1991).

14. Marbury Management, Inc. v. Kohn, 629 F.2d 705, 716 (2d Cir.1980), *cert. denied sub nom.* Wood Walker & Co. v. Marbury Management, Inc., 449 U.S. 1011 (1980).

15. Hollinger v. Titan Capital Corp., 914 F.2d 1564, 1576 (9th Cir. *en banc* 1990), *cert. denied*, 499 U.S. 976 (1991), *quoting* Paul F. Newton & Co. v. Texas Commerce Bank, 630 F.2d 1111, 1120 (5th Cir.1980).

16. 511 U.S. 164 (1994).

17. *See, e.g.,* Bates v. Shearson Lehman Bros., Inc., 42 F.3d 79 (1st Cir.1994). See also Robert A. Prentice, Conceiving the Inconceivable and Judicially Implementing the Preposterous: The Premature Demise of Respondeat Superior Liability under Section 10(b), 58 Ohio St. L.J. 1325 (1997).

regarding the sale of the TAIL securities ("November Offering Memorandum"). On December 3, 2001, Delicious invested $201,000 in TAIL.

In reaching her decision to invest in TAIL, Delicious relied, at least in part, on the November Offering Memorandum. Sometime before November 2001, one of LaserTech's directors, Gary Burke, reviewed and criticized the draft memorandum. Burke had previously been a securities lawyer with the Securities and Exchange Commission. LaserTech's directors were informed that the problems with the memorandum were technical in nature and would be corrected in accordance with Burke's wishes. The memorandum was revised before being sent to Delicious. There is no evidence that, after this revision, Burke had any further objections to the November Offering Memorandum.

Delicious' shares soon were worthless. Assume that the Offering Memorandum violated both § 11 of the 1933 Act and Rule 10b–5 of the 1934 Act by grossly overstating TAIL's projected revenues and misrepresenting the value of TAIL's assets.

Jones, O'Malley and Burke have been sued as "control persons" under § 15 of the 1933 Act and § 20 of the 1934 Act.

(1) How, if at all, would proof of control person liability be different under the 1933 and 1934 Acts?

(2) Are Jones, O'Malley and Burke "control persons"?

(3) Would Jones, O'Malley, and Burke be "culpable participants" if that was required?

(4) Would Jones, O'Malley, and Burke be entitled to a "good faith" defense?

2.   AIDING AND ABETTING

Central Bank of Denver, N.A. v. First Interstate Bank of Denver, N.A.

Supreme Court of the United States, 1994.
511 U.S. 164, 114 S.Ct. 1439, 128 L.Ed.2d 119.

■ KENNEDY, J., delivered the opinion of the Court, in which REHNQUIST, C.J., and O'CONNOR, SCALIA, and THOMAS, JJ., joined. STEVENS, J., filed a dissenting opinion, in which BLACKMUN, SOUTER, and GINSBURG, JJ., joined.

■ JUSTICE KENNEDY:

As we have interpreted it, § 10(b) of the Securities Exchange Act of 1934 imposes private civil liability on those who commit a manipulative or deceptive act in connection with the purchase or sale of securities. In this case, we must answer a question reserved in two earlier decisions: whether private civil liability under § 10(b) extends as well to those who do not engage in the manipulative or deceptive practice but who aid and abet the violation. See Herman & MacLean v. Huddleston, 459 U.S. 375, 379, n. 5 (1983); Ernst & Ernst v. Hochfelder, 425 U.S. 185, 191–192, n. 7 (1976).

I

In 1986 and 1988, the Colorado Springs–Stetson Hills Public Building Authority (Authority) issued a total of $26 million in bonds to finance public improvements at Stetson Hills, a planned residential and commercial development in Colorado Springs. Petitioner Central Bank served as indenture trustee for the bond issues.

The bonds were secured by landowner assessment liens, which covered about 250 acres for the 1986 bond issue and about 272 acres for the 1988 bond issue. The bond covenants required that the land subject to the liens be worth at least 160% of the bonds' outstanding principal and interest. The covenants required AmWest Development, the developer of Stetson Hills, to give Central Bank an annual report containing evidence that the 160% test was met.

In January 1988, AmWest provided Central Bank an updated appraisal of the land securing the 1986 bonds and of the land proposed to secure the 1988 bonds. The 1988 appraisal showed land values almost unchanged from the 1986 appraisal. Soon afterwards, Central Bank received a letter from the senior underwriter for the 1986 bonds. Noting that property values were declining in Colorado Springs and that Central Bank was operating on an appraisal over 16 months old, the underwriter expressed concern that the 160% test was not being met.

Central Bank asked its in-house appraiser to review the updated 1988 appraisal. The in-house appraiser decided that the values listed in the appraisal appeared optimistic considering the local real estate market. He suggested that Central Bank retain an outside appraiser to conduct an independent review of the 1988 appraisal. After an exchange of letters between Central Bank and AmWest in early 1988, Central Bank agreed to delay independent review of the appraisal until the end of the year, six months after the June 1988 closing on the bond issue. Before the independent review was complete, however, the Authority defaulted on the 1988 bonds.

Respondents First Interstate and Jack Naber had purchased $2.1 million of the 1988 bonds. After the default, respondents sued the Authority, the 1988 underwriter, a junior underwriter, an AmWest director, and Central Bank for violations of § 10(b) of the Securities Exchange Act of 1934. The complaint alleged that the Authority, the underwriter defendants, and the AmWest director had violated § 10(b). The complaint also alleged that Central Bank was "secondarily liable under § 10(b) for its conduct in aiding and abetting the fraud." App. 26.

The United States District Court for the District of Colorado granted summary judgment to Central Bank. The United States Court of Appeals for the Tenth Circuit reversed. First Interstate Bank of Denver, N.A. v. Pring, 969 F.2d 891 (1992).

     * * *

We granted certiorari to resolve the continuing confusion over the existence and scope of the § 10(b) aiding and abetting action. * * *

II

In the wake of the 1929 stock market crash and in response to reports of widespread abuses in the securities industry, the 73d Congress enacted two landmark pieces of securities legislation: the Securities Act of 1933 (1933 Act) and the Securities Exchange Act of 1934 (1934 Act). 48 Stat. 74, as amended, 15 U.S.C. § 77a et seq.; 48 Stat. 881, 15 U.S.C. § 78a et seq. The 1933 Act regulates initial distributions of securities, and the 1934 Act for the most part regulates post-distribution trading. Blue Chip Stamps v. Manor Drug Stores, 421 U.S. 723, 752 (1975). Together, the Acts "embrace a fundamental purpose

* * * to substitute a philosophy of full disclosure for the philosophy of caveat emptor." Affiliated Ute Citizens of Utah v. United States, 406 U.S. 128, 151 (1972) (internal quotation marks omitted).

The 1933 and 1934 Acts create an extensive scheme of civil liability. The Securities and Exchange Commission (SEC) may bring administrative actions and injunctive proceedings to enforce a variety of statutory prohibitions. Private plaintiffs may sue under the express private rights of action contained in the Acts. They may also sue under private rights of action we have found to be implied by the terms of § 10(b) and § 14(a) of the 1934 Act. Superintendent of Ins. of New York v. Bankers Life & Casualty Co., 404 U.S. 6, 13, n. 9 (1971) (§ 10(b)); J.I. Case Co. v. Borak, 377 U.S. 426, 430–435 (1964) (§ 14(a)). This case concerns the most familiar private cause of action: the one we have found to be implied by § 10(b), the general antifraud provision of the 1934 Act. * * *

In our cases addressing § 10(b) and Rule 10b–5, we have confronted two main issues. First, we have determined the scope of conduct prohibited by § 10(b). See, e.g., Dirks v. SEC, 463 U.S. 646 (1983); Aaron v. SEC, 446 U.S. 680 (1980); Chiarella v. United States, 445 U.S. 222 (1980); Santa Fe Industries, Inc. v. Green, 430 U.S. 462 (1977); Ernst & Ernst v. Hochfelder, 425 U.S. 185 (1976). Second, in cases where the defendant has committed a violation of § 10(b), we have decided questions about the elements of the 10b–5 private liability scheme: for example, whether there is a right to contribution, what the statute of limitations is, whether there is a reliance requirement, and whether there is an in pari delicto defense. See Musick, Peeler & Garrett v. Employers Ins. of Wausau, 508 U.S. 286 (1993); Lampf, Pleva, Lipkind, Prupis & Petigrow v. Gilbertson, 501 U.S. 350 (1991); Basic Inc. v. Levinson, 485 U.S. 224 (1988); Bateman Eichler, Hill Richards, Inc. v. Berner, 472 U.S. 299 (1985); see also Blue Chip Stamps, *supra*; Schlick v. Penn–Dixie Cement Corp., 507 F.2d 374 (C.A.2 1974); cf. Virginia Bankshares, Inc. v. Sandberg, 501 U.S. 1083 (1991) (§ 14); Schreiber v. Burlington Northern, Inc., 472 U.S. 1 (1985) (same).

The latter issue, determining the elements of the 10b–5 private liability scheme, has posed difficulty because Congress did not create a private § 10(b) cause of action and had no occasion to provide guidance about the elements of a private liability scheme. We thus have had "to infer how the 1934 Congress would have addressed the issues had the 10b–5 action been included as an express provision in the 1934 Act." Musick, Peeler, *supra*, at ___ (slip op., at 8).

With respect, however, to the first issue, the scope of conduct prohibited by § 10(b), the text of the statute controls our decision. In § 10(b), Congress prohibited manipulative or deceptive acts in connection with the purchase or sale of securities. It envisioned that the SEC would enforce the statutory prohibition through administrative and injunctive actions. Of course, a private plaintiff now may bring suit against violators of § 10(b). But the private plaintiff may not bring a 10b–5 suit against a defendant for acts not prohibited by the text of § 10(b). To the contrary, our cases considering the scope of conduct prohibited by § 10(b) in private suits have emphasized adherence to the statutory language, " 'the starting point in every case involving construction of a statute.' " Ernst & Ernst, *supra*, at 197 (quoting Blue Chip Stamps, 421 U.S., at 756 (Powell, J., concurring)); see Chiarella, *supra*, at 226; Santa Fe Industries, *supra*, at 472. We have refused to allow 10b–5 challenges to conduct not prohibited by the text of the statute.

In Ernst & Ernst, we considered whether negligent acts could violate § 10(b). We first noted that "the words 'manipulative' or 'deceptive' used in conjunction with 'device or contrivance' strongly suggest that § 10(b) was intended to proscribe knowing or intentional misconduct." 425 U.S., at 197. The SEC argued that the broad congressional purposes behind the Act—to protect investors from false and misleading practices that might injure them— suggested that § 10(b) should also reach negligent conduct. Id., at 198. We rejected that argument, concluding that the SEC's interpretation would "add a gloss to the operative language of the statute quite different from its commonly accepted meaning." Id., at 199.

In Santa Fe Industries, another case involving "the reach and coverage of § 10(b)," 430 U.S., at 464, we considered whether § 10(b) "reached breaches of fiduciary duty by a majority against minority shareholders without any charge of misrepresentation or lack of disclosure." Id., at 470 (internal quotation marks omitted). We held that it did not, reaffirming our decision in Ernst & Ernst and emphasizing that the "language of § 10(b) gives no indication that Congress meant to prohibit any conduct not involving manipulation or deception." Id., at 473.

Later, in Chiarella, we considered whether § 10(b) is violated when a person trades securities without disclosing inside information. We held that § 10(b) is not violated under those circumstances unless the trader has an independent duty of disclosure. In reaching our conclusion, we noted that "not every instance of financial unfairness constitutes fraudulent activity under § 10(b)." 445 U.S., at 232. We stated that "the 1934 Act cannot be read more broadly than its language and the statutory scheme reasonably permit," and we found "no basis for applying * * * a new and different theory of liability" in that case. Id., at 234 (internal quotation marks omitted). "Section 10(b) is aptly described as a catchall provision, but what it catches must be fraud. When an allegation of fraud is based upon nondisclosure, there can be no fraud absent a duty to speak." Id., at 234–235.

Adherence to the text in defining the conduct covered by § 10(b) is consistent with our decisions interpreting other provisions of the securities Acts. In Pinter v. Dahl, 486 U.S. 622 (1988), for example, we interpreted the word "seller" in § 12(1) of the 1934 Act by "looking first at the language of § 12(1)." Id., at 641. Ruling that a seller is one who solicits securities sales for financial gain, we rejected the broader contention "grounded in tort doctrine," that persons who participate in the sale can also be deemed sellers. Id., at 649. We found "no support in the statutory language or legislative history for expansion of § 12(1)," id., at 650, and stated that "the ascertainment of congressional intent with respect to the scope of liability created by a particular section of the Securities Act must rest primarily on the language of that section." Id. at 653.

* * *

The federal courts have not relied on the "directly or indirectly" language when imposing aiding and abetting liability under § 10(b), and with good reason. There is a basic flaw with this interpretation. According to respondents and the SEC, the "directly or indirectly" language shows that "Congress * * * intended to reach all persons who engage, even if only indirectly, in proscribed activities connected with securities transactions." Brief for SEC 8. The problem, of course, is that aiding and abetting liability extends beyond persons who engage, even indirectly, in a proscribed activity; aiding and abetting liability reaches persons who do not engage in the proscribed activities at all, but who give a degree of aid to those who do. A further problem with respondents' interpretation of the "directly or indirectly" language is posed by the numerous provisions of the 1934 Act that use the term in a way that does not impose aiding and abetting liability. See § 7(f)(2)(c), 15 U.S.C. § 78g(f)(2)(c) (direct or indirect ownership of stock); § 9(b)(2)–(3), 15 U.S.C. § 78i(b)(2)–(3) (direct or indirect interest in put, call, straddle, option, or privilege); § 13(d)(1), 15 U.S.C. § 78m(d)(1) (direct or indirect ownership); § 16(a), 15 U.S.C. § 78p(a) (direct or indirect ownership); § 20, 15 U.S.C. § 78t (direct or indirect control of person violating Act). In short, respondents' interpretation of the "directly or indirectly" language fails to support their suggestion that the text of § 10(b) itself prohibits aiding and abetting. See 5B A. Jacobs, Litigation and Practice Under Rule 10b–5 § 40.07, p. 2–465 (rev. 1993).

Congress knew how to impose aiding and abetting liability when it chose to do so. See, e.g., Act of Mar. 4, 1909, § 332, 35 Stat. 1152, as amended, 18 U.S.C. § 2 (general criminal aiding and abetting statute); Packers and Stockyards Act, 1921, ch. 64, § 202, 42 Stat. 161, as amended, 7 U.S.C. § 192(g) (civil aiding and abetting provision); see generally *infra*, at 16–20. If, as respondents seem to say, Congress intended to impose aiding and abetting liability, we presume it would have used the words "aid" and "abet" in the statutory text. But it did not. Cf. Pinter v. Dahl, 486 U.S., at 650 ("When Congress wished to create such liability, it had little trouble doing so"); Blue Chip Stamps, 421 U.S., at 734 ("When Congress wished to provide a remedy to those who neither purchase nor sell securities, it had little trouble in doing so expressly").

We reach the uncontroversial conclusion, accepted even by those courts recognizing a § 10(b) aiding and abetting cause of action, that the text of the 1934 Act does not itself reach those who aid and abet a § 10(b) violation. Unlike those courts, however, we think that conclusion resolves the case. It is inconsistent with settled methodology in § 10(b) cases to extend liability beyond the scope of conduct prohibited by the statutory text. To be sure, aiding and abetting a wrongdoer ought to be actionable in certain instances. Cf. Restatement (Second) of Torts § 876(b) (1977). The issue, however, is not whether imposing private civil liability on aiders and abettors is good policy but whether aiding and abetting is covered by the statute.

As in earlier cases considering conduct prohibited by § 10(b), we again conclude that the statute prohibits only the making of a material misstatement (or omission) or the commission of a manipulative act. See Santa Fe Industries, 430 U.S., at 473 ("language of § 10(b) gives no indication that Congress meant to prohibit any conduct not involving manipulation or deception"); Ernst & Ernst, 425 U.S., at 214 ("When a statute speaks so specifically in terms of manipulation and deception * * *, we are quite unwilling to extend the scope of the statute"). The proscription does not include giving aid to a person who commits a manipulative or deceptive act. We cannot amend the statute to create liability for acts that are not themselves manipulative or deceptive within the meaning of the statute.

III

Because this case concerns the conduct prohibited by § 10(b), the statute itself resolves the case, but even if it did not, we would reach the same result. When the text of § 10(b) does not resolve a particular issue, we attempt to infer "how the 1934 Congress would have addressed the issue had the 10b–5 action been included as an express provision in the 1934 Act." Musick, Peeler, 508 U.S., at ___ (slip op., at 8). For that inquiry, we use the express causes of action in the securities Acts as the primary model for the § 10(b) action. The reason is evident: Had the 73d Congress enacted a private § 10(b) right of action, it likely would have designed it in a manner similar to the other private rights of action in the securities Acts. See Musick, Peeler, 508 U.S., at ___ (slip op., at 7–11).

In Musick, Peeler, for example, we recognized a right to contribution under § 10(b). We held that the express rights of contribution contained in §§ 9 and 18 of the Acts were "important * * * features of the federal securities laws and that consistency required us to adopt a like contribution rule for the right of action existing under Rule 10b–5." 508 U.S., at ___ (slip op., at 10). In Basic Inc. v. Levinson, 485 U.S. 224, 243 (1988), we decided that a plaintiff in a 10b–5 action must prove that he relied on the defendant's misrepresentation in order to recover damages. In so holding, we stated that the "analogous express right of action"—§ 18(a) of the 1934 Act—"includes a reliance requirement." Ibid. And in Blue Chip Stamps, we held that a 10b–5 plaintiff must have purchased or sold the security to recover damages for the defendant's misrepresentation. We said that "the principal express private nonderivative civil remedies, created by Congress contemporaneously with the passage of § 10(b) * * * are by their terms expressly limited to purchasers or sellers of securities." 421 U.S., at 735–736.

Following that analysis here, we look to the express private causes of action in the 1933 and 1934 Acts. See, e.g., Musick, Peeler, *supra*, at ___ (slip op., at 9–11); Blue Chip Stamps, *supra*, at 735–736. In the 1933 Act, § 11 prohibits false statements or omissions of material fact in registration statements; it identifies the various categories of defendants subject to liability for a violation, but that list does not include aiders and abettors. 15 U.S.C. § 77k. Section 12 prohibits the sale of unregistered, nonexempt securities as well as the sale of securities by means of a material misstatement or omission; and it limits liability to those who offer or sell the security. 15 U.S.C. § 77l. In the 1934 Act, § 9 prohibits any person from engaging in manipulative practices such as wash sales, matched orders, and the like. 15 U.S.C. § 78i. Section 16 prohibits short-swing trading by owners, directors, and officers. 15 U.S.C. § 78p. Section 18 prohibits any person from making misleading statements in reports filed with the SEC. 15 U.S.C. § 78r. And § 20A, added in 1988, prohibits any person from engaging in insider trading. 15 U.S.C. § 78t–1.

This survey of the express causes of action in the securities Acts reveals that each (like § 10(b)) specifies the conduct for which defendants may be held liable. Some of the express causes of action specify categories of defendants who may be liable; others (like § 10(b)) state only that "any person" who commits one of the prohibited acts may be held liable. The important point for present purposes, however, is that none of the express causes of action in the 1934 Act further imposes liability on one who aids or abets a violation. Cf. 7 U.S.C. § 25(a)(1) (1988 ed. and Supp. IV) (Commodity Exchange Act's private civil aiding and abetting provision).

From the fact that Congress did not attach private aiding and abetting liability to any of the express causes of action in the securities Acts, we can infer that Congress likely would not have attached aiding and abetting liability to § 10(b) had it provided a private § 10(b) cause of action. See Musick, Peeler, 508 U.S., at ___ (slip op., at 10) ("Consistency requires us to adopt a like contribution rule for the right of action existing under Rule 10b–5"). There is no reason to think that Congress would have attached aiding and abetting liability only to § 10(b) and not to any of the express private rights of action in the Act. In Blue Chip Stamps, we noted that it would be "anomalous to impute to Congress an intention to expand the plaintiff class for a judicially implied cause of action beyond the bounds it delineated for comparable express causes of action." 421 U.S., at 736. Here, it would be just as anomalous to impute to Congress an intention in effect to expand the defendant class for 10b–5 actions beyond the bounds delineated for comparable express causes of action.

Our reasoning is confirmed by the fact that respondents' argument would impose 10b–5 aiding and abetting liability when at least one element critical for recovery under 10b–5 is absent: reliance. A plaintiff must show reliance on the defendant's misstatement or omission to recover under 10b–5. Basic Inc. v. Levinson, *supra*, at 243. Were we to allow the aiding and abetting action proposed in this case, the defendant could be liable without any showing that the plaintiff relied upon the aider and abettor's statements or actions. See also Chiarella, 445 U.S., at 228 (omission actionable only where duty to disclose arises from specific relationship between two parties). Allowing plaintiffs to circumvent the reliance requirement would disregard the careful limits on 10b–5 recovery mandated by our earlier cases.

IV

Respondents make further arguments for imposition of § 10(b) aiding and abetting liability, none of which leads us to a different answer.

A

The text does not support their point, but respondents and some amici invoke a broad-based notion of congressional intent. They say that Congress legislated with an understanding of general principles of tort law and that aiding and abetting liability was "well established in both civil and criminal actions by 1934." Brief for SEC 10. Thus, "Congress intended to include" aiding and abetting liability in the 1934 Act. Id., at 11. A brief history of aiding and abetting liability serves to dispose of this argument.

Aiding and abetting is an ancient criminal law doctrine. See United States v. Peoni, 100 F.2d 401, 402 (C.A.2 1938); 1 M. Hale, Pleas of the Crown 615 (1736). Though there is no federal common law of crimes, Congress in 1909 enacted what is now 18 U.S.C. § 2, a general aiding and abetting statute applicable to all federal criminal offenses. Act of Mar. 4, 1909, § 332, 35 Stat. 1152. The statute decrees that those who provide knowing aid to persons committing federal crimes, with the intent to facilitate the crime, are themselves committing a crime. Nye & Nissen v. United States, 336 U.S. 613, 619 (1949).

The Restatement of Torts, under a concert of action principle, accepts a doctrine with rough similarity to criminal aiding and abetting. An actor is liable for harm resulting to a third person from the tortious conduct of another "if he * * * knows that the other's conduct constitutes a breach of duty and gives substantial assistance or encouragement to the other * * *." Restatement (Second) of Torts § 876(b) (1977); see also W. Keeton, D. Dobbs, R. Keeton, & D. Owen, Prosser and Keeton on Law of Torts 322–324 (5th ed. 1984). The doctrine has been at best uncertain in application, however. As the Court of Appeals for the District of Columbia Circuit noted in a comprehensive opinion on the subject, the leading cases applying this doctrine are statutory securities cases, with the common-law precedents "largely confined to isolated acts of adolescents in rural society." Halberstam v. Welch, 705 F.2d 472, 489 (1983). Indeed, in some States, it is still unclear whether there is aiding and abetting tort liability of the kind set forth in § 876(b) of the Restatement. See, e.g., FDIC v. S. Prawer & Co., 829 F.Supp. 453, 457 (D.Me.1993) (in Maine, "it is clear * * * that aiding and abetting liability did not exist under the common law, but was entirely a creature of statute"); In re Asbestos School Litigation, 1991 U.S.Dist. LEXIS 10471 (ED Pa.1991) (cause of action under Restatement § 876 "has not yet been applied as a basis for liability" by Pennsylvania courts); Meadow Limited Partnership v. Heritage Savings and Loan Assn., 639 F.Supp. 643, 653 (E.D.Va.1986) (aiding and abetting tort based on Restatement § 876 "not expressly recognized by the state courts of the Commonwealth" of Virginia); Sloan v. Fauque, 239 Mont. 383, 385, 784 P.2d 895, 896 (1989) (aiding and abetting tort liability is issue "of first impression in Montana").

More to the point, Congress has not enacted a general civil aiding and abetting statute—either for suits by the Government (when the Government sues for civil penalties or injunctive relief) or for suits by private parties. Thus, when Congress enacts a statute under which a person may sue and recover damages from a private defendant for the defendant's violation of some statutory norm, there is no general presumption that the plaintiff may also sue aiders and abettors. See, e.g., Electronic Laboratory Supply Co. v. Cullen, 977 F.2d 798, 805–806 (C.A.3 1992).

     * * *

With this background in mind, we think respondents' argument based on implicit congressional intent can be taken in one of three ways. First, respondents might be saying that aiding and abetting should attach to all federal civil statutes, even laws that do not contain an explicit aiding and abetting provision. But neither respondents nor their amici cite, and we have not found, any precedent for that vast expansion of federal law. It does not appear Congress was operating on that assumption in 1934, or since then, given that it has been quite explicit in imposing civil aiding and abetting liability in other instances. We decline to recognize such a comprehensive rule with no expression of congressional direction to do so.

Second, on a more narrow ground, respondents' congressional intent argument might be interpreted to suggest that the 73d Congress intended to include aiding and abetting only in § 10(b). But nothing in the text or history of § 10(b) even implies that aiding and abetting was covered by the statutory prohibition on manipulative and deceptive conduct.

Third, respondents' congressional intent argument might be construed as a contention that the 73d Congress intended to impose aiding and abetting liability for all of the express causes of action contained in the 1934 Act—and thus would have imposed aiding and abetting liability in § 10(b) actions had it enacted a private § 10(b) right of action. As we have explained, however, none of the express private causes of action in the Act imposes aiding and abetting liability, and there is no evidence that Congress intended that liability for the express causes of action.

Even assuming, moreover, a deeply rooted background of aiding and abetting tort liability, it does not follow that Congress intended to apply that kind of liability to the private causes of action in the securities Acts. Cf. Mertens, 508 U.S., at ___ (slip op., at 6) (omission of knowing participation liability in ERISA "appears all the more deliberate in light of the fact that 'knowing participation' liability on the part of both cotrustees and third persons was well established under the common law of trusts"). In addition, Congress did not overlook secondary liability when it created the private rights of action in the 1934 Act. Section 20 of the 1934 Act imposes liability on "controlling persons"—persons who "control any person liable under any provision of this chapter or of any rule or regulation thereunder." 15 U.S.C. § 78t(a). This suggests that "when Congress wished to create such [secondary] liability, it had little trouble doing so." Pinter v. Dahl, 486 U.S., at 650; cf. Touche Ross & Co. v. Redington, 442 U.S. 560, 572 (1979) ("Obviously, then, when Congress wished to provide a private damages remedy, it knew how to do so and did so expressly"); see also Fischel, 69 Calif.L.Rev., at 96–98. Aiding and abetting is "a method by which courts create secondary liability" in persons other than the violator of the statute. Pinter v. Dahl, *supra*, at 648, n. 24. The fact that Congress chose to impose some forms of secondary liability, but not others, indicates a deliberate congressional choice with which the courts should not interfere.

We note that the 1929 Uniform Sale of Securities Act contained a private aiding and abetting cause of action. And at the time Congress passed the 1934 Act, the blue sky laws of 11 States and the Territory of Hawaii provided a private right of action against those who aided a fraudulent or illegal sale of securities. See Abrams, The Scope of Liability Under Section 12 of the Securities Act of 1933: "Participation" and the Pertinent Legislative Materials, 15 Ford.Urb.L.J. 877, 945, and n. 423 (1987) (listing provisions). Congress enacted the 1933 and 1934 Acts against this backdrop, but did not provide for aiding and abetting liability in any of the private causes of action it authorized.

In sum, it is not plausible to interpret the statutory silence as tantamount to an implicit congressional intent to impose § 10(b) aiding and abetting liability.

B

When Congress reenacts statutory language that has been given a consistent judicial construction, we often adhere to that construction in interpreting the reenacted statutory language. See, e.g., Keene Corp. v. United States, 508 U.S. ___ (1993) (slip op., at 12); Pierce v. Underwood, 487 U.S. 552, 567 (1988); Lorillard v. Pons, 434 U.S. 575, 580–581 (1978). Congress has not reenacted the language of § 10(b) since 1934, however, so we need not determine whether the other conditions for applying the reenactment doctrine are present. Cf. Fogerty v. Fantasy, Inc., 510 U.S. ___ (1994) (slip op., at 10–16).

Nonetheless, the parties advance competing arguments based on other post–1934 legislative developments to support their differing interpretations of § 10(b). Respondents note that 1983 and 1988 committee reports, which make oblique references to aiding and abetting liability, show that those Congresses interpreted § 10(b) to cover aiding and abetting. H.R.Rep. No. 100–910, pp. 27–28 (1988); H.R.Rep. No. 355, p. 10 (1983). But "we have observed on more than one occasion that the interpretation given by one Congress (or a committee or Member thereof) to an earlier statute is of little assistance in discerning the meaning of that statute." Public Employees Retirement System v. Betts, 492 U.S. 158, 168 (1989); see Weinberger v. Rossi, 456 U.S. 25, 35 (1982); Consumer Product Safety Comm'n v. GTE Sylvania, Inc., 447 U.S. 102, 118, and n. 13 (1980).

Respondents observe that Congress has amended the securities laws on various occasions since 1966, when courts first began to interpret § 10(b) to cover aiding and abetting, but has done so without providing that aiding and abetting liability is not available under § 10(b). From that, respondents infer that these Congresses, by silence, have acquiesced in the judicial interpretation of § 10(b). We disagree. This Court has reserved the issue of 10b–5 aiding and abetting liability on two previous occasions. Herman & MacLean v. Huddleston, 459 U.S., at 379, n. 5; Ernst & Ernst, 425 U.S., at 191–192, n. 7. Furthermore, our observations on the acquiescence doctrine indicate its limitations as an expression of congressional intent. "It does not follow * * * that Congress' failure to overturn a statutory precedent is reason for this Court to adhere to it." It is "impossible to assert with any degree of assurance that congressional failure to act represents" affirmative congressional approval of the [courts'] statutory interpretation. * * * Congress may legislate, moreover, only through passage of a bill which is approved by both Houses and signed by the President. See U.S. Const. Art. I, § 7, cl. 2. Congressional inaction cannot amend a duly enacted statute." Patterson v. McLean Credit Union, 491 U.S. 164, 175, n. 1 (1989) (quoting Johnson v. Transportation Agency, Santa Clara County, 480 U.S. 616, 671–672 (1987) (Scalia, J., dissenting)); see Helvering v. Hallock, 309 U.S. 106, 121 (1940) (Frankfurter, J.) ("We walk on quicksand when we try to find in the absence of corrective legislation a controlling legal principle").

* * *

It is true that our cases have not been consistent in rejecting arguments such as these. Compare Flood v. Kuhn, 407 U.S. 258, 281–282 (1972), with Pension Benefit Guaranty Corp., *supra*, at 650; compare Merrill Lynch, Pierce, Fenner & Smith, Inc. v. Curran, 456 U.S. 353, 381–382 (1982), with Aaron v. SEC, 446 U.S. 680, 694, n. 11 (1980). As a general matter, however, we have stated that these arguments deserve little weight in the interpretive process. Even were that not the case, the competing arguments here would not point to a definitive answer. We therefore reject them. As we stated last Term, Congress has acknowledged the 10b–5 action without any further attempt to define it. Musick, Peeler, 508 U.S., at ___ (slip op., at 7). We find our role limited when the issue is the scope of conduct prohibited by the statute. Id., at ___ (slip op., at 5). That issue is our concern here, and we adhere to the statutory text in resolving it.

C

The SEC points to various policy arguments in support of the 10b–5 aiding and abetting cause of action. It argues, for example, that the aiding and abetting cause of action deters secondary actors from contributing to fraudulent activities and ensures that defrauded plaintiffs are made whole. Brief for SEC 16–17.

Policy considerations cannot override our interpretation of the text and structure of the Act, except to the extent that they may help to show that adherence to the text and structure would lead to a result "so bizarre" that Congress could not have intended it. Demarest v. Manspeaker, 498 U.S. 184, 191 (1991); cf. Pinter v. Dahl, 486 U.S., at 654 ("We need not entertain Pinter's policy arguments"); Santa Fe Industries, 430 U.S., at 477 (language sufficiently clear to be dispositive). That is not the case here.

* * *

In addition, "litigation under Rule 10b–5 presents a danger of vexatiousness different in degree and in kind from that which accompanies litigation in general." Blue Chip Stamps, *supra*, at 739; see Virginia Bankshares, 501 U.S., at ___; S.Rep. No. 792, 73d Cong., 2d Sess., p. 21 (1934) (attorney's fees provision is protection against strike suits). Litigation under 10b–5 thus requires secondary actors to expend large sums even for pretrial defense and the negotiation of settlements. See 138 Cong.Rec. S12605 (Aug. 12, 1992) (remarks of Sen. Sanford) (asserting that in 83% of 10b–5 cases major accounting firms pay $8 in legal fees for every $1 paid in claims).

This uncertainty and excessive litigation can have ripple effects. For example, newer and smaller companies may find it difficult to obtain advice from professionals. A professional may fear that a newer or smaller company may not survive and that business failure would generate securities litigation against the professional, among others. In addition, the increased costs incurred by professionals because of the litigation and settlement costs under 10b–5 may be passed on to their client companies, and in turn incurred by the company's investors, the intended beneficiaries of the statute. See Winter, Paying Lawyers, Empowering Prosecutors, and Protecting Managers: Raising the Cost of Capital in America, 42 Duke L.J. 945, 948–966 (1993).

* * *

D

At oral argument, the SEC suggested that 18 U.S.C. § 2 is "significant" and "very important" in this case. Tr. of Oral Arg. 41, 43. At the outset, we note that this contention is inconsistent with the SEC's argument that recklessness is a sufficient scienter for aiding and abetting liability. Criminal aiding and abetting liability under § 2 requires proof that the defendant "in some sort associated himself with the venture, that he participated in it as in something that he wished to bring about, that he [sought] by his action to make it succeed." Nye & Nissen, 336 U.S., at 619 (internal quotation marks omitted). But recklessness, not intentional wrongdoing, is the theory underlying the aiding and abetting allegations in the case before us.

Furthermore, while it is true that an aider and abettor of a criminal violation of any provision of the 1934 Act, including § 10(b), violates 18 U.S.C. § 2, it does not follow that a private civil aiding and abetting cause of action must also exist. We have been quite reluctant to infer a private right of action from a criminal prohibition alone; in Cort v. Ash, 422 U.S. 66, 80 (1975), for example, we refused to infer a private right of action from "a bare criminal statute." And we have not suggested that a private right of action exists for all injuries caused by violations of criminal prohibitions. See Touche Ross, 442 U.S., at 568 ("question of the existence of a statutory cause of action is, of course, one of statutory construction"). If we were to rely on this reasoning now, we would be obliged to hold that a private right of action exists for every provision of the 1934 Act, for it is a criminal violation to violate any of its provisions. 15 U.S.C. § 78ff. And thus, given 18 U.S.C. § 2, we would also have to hold that a civil aiding and abetting cause of action is available for every provision of the Act. There would be no logical stopping point to this line of reasoning: Every criminal statute passed for the benefit of some particular class of persons would carry with it a concomitant civil damages cause of action.

* * *

V

Because the text of § 10(b) does not prohibit aiding and abetting, we hold that a private plaintiff may not maintain an aiding and abetting suit under § 10(b). The absence of § 10(b) aiding and abetting liability does not mean that secondary actors in the securities markets are always free from liability under the securities Acts. Any person or entity, including a lawyer, accountant, or bank, who employs a manipulative device or makes a material misstatement (or omission) on which a purchaser or seller of securities relies may be liable as a primary violator under 10b–5, assuming all of the requirements for primary liability under Rule 10b–5 are met. See Fischel, 69 Calif.L.Rev., at 107–108. In any complex securities fraud, moreover, there are likely to be multiple violators; in this case, for example, respondents named four defendants as primary violators. App. 24–25.

Respondents concede that Central Bank did not commit a manipulative or deceptive act within the meaning of § 10(b). Tr. of Oral Arg. 31. Instead, in the words of the complaint, Central Bank was "secondarily liable under § 10(b) for its conduct in aiding and abetting the fraud." App. 26. Because of our conclusion that there is no private aiding and abetting liability under § 10(b), Central Bank may not be held liable as an aider and abettor. The District Court's grant of summary judgment to Central Bank was proper, and the judgment of the Court of Appeals is

Reversed.

■ JUSTICE STEVENS, with whom JUSTICE BLACKMUN, JUSTICE SOUTER, and JUSTICE GINSBURG join, dissenting.

The main themes of the Court's opinion are that the text of § 10(b) of the Securities Exchange Act of 1934, 15 U.S.C. § 78j(b), does not expressly mention aiding and abetting liability, and that Congress knows how to legislate. Both propositions are unexceptionable, but neither is reason to eliminate the private right of action against aiders and abettors of violations of § 10(b) and the Securities and Exchange Commission's Rule 10b–5. Because the majority gives short shrift to a long history of aider and abettor liability under § 10(b) and Rule 10b–5, and because its rationale imperils other well established forms of secondary liability not expressly addressed in the securities laws, I respectfully dissent.

In hundreds of judicial and administrative proceedings in every circuit in the federal system, the courts and the SEC have concluded that aiders and abettors are subject to liability under § 10(b) and Rule 10b–5. See 5B A. Jacobs, Litigation and Practice Under Rule 10b–5 § 40.02 (rev. ed. 1993) (citing cases). While we have reserved decision on the legitimacy of the theory in two cases that did not present it, all 11 Courts of Appeals to have considered the question have recognized a private cause of action against aiders and abettors under § 10(b) and Rule 10b–5. The early aiding and abetting decisions relied upon principles borrowed from tort law; in those cases, judges closer to the times and climate of the 73d Congress than we concluded that holding aiders and abettors liable was consonant with the 1934 Act's purpose to strengthen the antifraud remedies of the common law. One described the aiding and abetting theory, grounded in "general principles of tort law," as a "logical and natural complement" to the private § 10(b) action that furthered the Exchange Act's purpose of "creation and maintenance of a post-issuance securities market that is free from fraudulent practices." Brennan v. Midwestern United Life Ins. Co., 259

F.Supp. 673, 680 (N.D.Ind.1966) (borrowing formulation from the Restatement of Torts § 876(b) (1939)), later opinion, 286 F.Supp. 702 (1968), aff'd, 417 F.2d 147 (C.A.7 1969), cert. denied, 397 U.S. 989 (1970). See also Pettit v. American Stock Exchange, 217 F.Supp. 21, 28 (S.D.N.Y.1963).

The Courts of Appeals have usually applied a familiar three-part test for aider and abettor liability, patterned on the Restatement of Torts formulation, that requires (i) the existence of a primary violation of § 10(b) or Rule 10b–5, (ii) the defendant's knowledge of (or recklessness as to) that primary violation, and (iii) "substantial assistance" of the violation by the defendant. See, e.g., Cleary v. Perfectune, Inc., 700 F.2d 774, 776–777 (C.A.1 1983); IIT, An Int'l Investment Trust v. Cornfeld, 619 F.2d 909, 922 (C.A.2 1980). If indeed there has been "continuing confusion" concerning the private right of action against aiders and abettors, that confusion has not concerned its basic structure, still less its "existence." See ante, at 1444. Indeed, in this case, petitioner assumed the existence of a right of action against aiders and abettors, and sought review only of the subsidiary questions whether an indenture trustee could be found liable as an aider and abettor absent a breach of an indenture agreement or other duty under state law, and whether it could be liable as an aider and abettor based only on a showing of recklessness. These questions, it is true, have engendered genuine disagreement in the Courts of Appeals. But instead of simply addressing the questions presented by the parties, on which the law really was unsettled, the Court sua sponte directed the parties to address a question on which even the petitioner justifiably thought the law was settled, and reaches out to overturn a most considerable body of precedent.

Many of the observations in the majority's opinion would be persuasive if we were considering whether to recognize a private right of action based upon a securities statute enacted recently. Our approach to implied causes of action, as to other matters of statutory construction, has changed markedly since the Exchange Act's passage in 1934. At that time, and indeed until quite recently, courts regularly assumed, in accord with the traditional common law presumption, that a statute enacted for the benefit of a particular class conferred on members of that class the right to sue violators of that statute. Moreover, shortly before the Exchange Act was passed, this Court instructed that such "remedial" legislation should receive "a broader and more liberal interpretation than that to be drawn from mere dictionary definitions of the words employed by Congress." Piedmont & Northern R. Co. v. ICC, 286 U.S. 299, 311 (1932). There is a risk of anachronistic error in applying our current approach to implied causes of action, ante, at 12, to a statute enacted when courts commonly read statutes of this kind broadly to accord with their remedial purposes and regularly approved rights to sue despite statutory silence.

Even had § 10(b) not been enacted against a backdrop of liberal construction of remedial statutes and judicial favor toward implied rights of action, I would still disagree with the majority for the simple reason that a "settled construction of an important federal statute should not be disturbed unless and until Congress so decides." Reves v. Ernst & Young, 494 U.S. 56, 74 (1990) (Stevens, J., concurring). See Blue Chip Stamps v. Manor Drug Stores, 421 U.S. 723, 733 (1975) (the "longstanding acceptance by the courts" and "Congress' failure to reject" rule announced in landmark Court of Appeals decision favored retention of the rule). A policy of respect for consistent judicial and administrative interpretations leaves it to elected representatives to assess settled law and to evaluate the merits and demerits of changing it. Even when there is no affirmative evidence of ratification, the Legislature's failure to reject a consistent judicial or administrative construction counsels hesitation from a court asked to invalidate it. Cf. Burnet v. Coronado Oil & Gas Co., 285 U.S. 393, 406 (1932) (Brandeis, J., dissenting). Here, however, the available evidence suggests congressional approval of aider and abettor liability in private § 10(b) actions. In its comprehensive revision of the Exchange Act in 1975, Congress left untouched the sizeable body of case law approving aiding and abetting liability in private actions under § 10(b) and Rule 10b–5. The case for leaving aiding and abetting liability intact draws further strength from the fact that the SEC itself has consistently understood § 10(b) to impose aider and abettor liability since shortly after the rule's promulgation. See Ernst & Young, 494 U.S., at 75 (Stevens, J., concurring). In short, one need not agree as an original matter with the many decisions recognizing the private right against aiders and abettors to concede that the right fits comfortably within the statutory scheme, and that it has become a part of the established system of private enforcement. We should leave it to Congress to alter that scheme.

The Court would be on firmer footing if it had been shown that aider and abettor liability "detracts from the effectiveness of the 10b–5 implied action or interferes with the effective operation of the securities laws." See Musick, Peeler & Garrett v. Employers Ins. of Wausau, 508 U.S. ___, ___ (1993) (slip op., at 11). However, the line of decisions recognizing aider and abettor liability suffers from no such infirmities. The language of both § 10(b) and Rule 10b–5 encompasses "any person" who violates the Commission's anti-fraud rules, whether "directly or indirectly"; we have read this "broad" language "not technically and restrictively, but flexibly to effectuate its remedial purposes." Affiliated Ute Citizens of Utah v. United States, 406 U.S. 128, 151 (1972). In light of the encompassing language of § 10(b), and its acknowledged purpose to strengthen the anti-fraud remedies of the common law, it was certainly no wild extrapolation for courts to conclude that aiders and abettors should be subject to the private action under § 10(b). Allowing aider and abettor claims in private § 10(b) actions can hardly be said to impose unfair legal duties on those whom Congress has opted to leave unregulated: Aiders and abettors of § 10(b) and Rule 10b–5 violations have always been subject to criminal liability under 18 U.S.C. § 2. See 15 U.S.C. § 78ff (criminal liability for willful violations of securities statutes and rules promulgated under them). Although the Court canvasses policy arguments against aider and abettor liability, ante, at 24–25, it does not suggest that the aiding and abetting theory has had such deleterious consequences that we should dispense with it on those grounds. The agency charged with primary responsibility for enforcing the securities laws does not perceive such drawbacks, and urges retention of the private right to sue aiders and abettors. See Brief for the Securities and Exchange Commission as Amicus Curiae in Support of Respondents 5–17.

As framed by the Court's order redrafting the questions presented, this case concerns only the existence and scope of aiding and abetting liability in suits brought by private parties under § 10(b) and Rule 10b–5. The majority's rationale, however, sweeps far beyond even those important issues. The majority leaves little doubt that the Exchange Act does not even permit the Commission to pursue aiders and abettors in civil enforcement actions under § 10b and Rule 10b–5. See ante ___, at 12 (finding it dispositive that "the text of the 1934 Act does not itself reach those who aid and abet a § 10(b) violation"). Aiding and abetting liability has a long pedigree in civil proceedings brought by the SEC under § 10(b) and Rule 10b–5, and has become an important part of the

Commission's enforcement arsenal. Moreover, the majority's approach to aiding and abetting at the very least casts serious doubt, both for private and SEC actions, on other forms of secondary liability that, like the aiding and abetting theory, have long been recognized by the SEC and the courts but are not expressly spelled out in the securities statutes. The principle the Court espouses today—that liability may not be imposed on parties who are not within the scope of § 10(b)'s plain language—is inconsistent with long-established Commission and judicial precedent.

As a general principle, I agree, "the creation of new rights ought to be left to legislatures, not courts." Musick, Peeler, 508 U.S., at ___ (slip op., at 5). But judicial restraint does not always favor the narrowest possible interpretation of rights derived from federal statutes. While we are now properly reluctant to recognize private rights of action without an instruction from Congress, we should also be reluctant to lop off rights of action that have been recognized for decades, even if the judicial methodology that gave them birth is now out of favor. Caution is particularly appropriate here, because the judicially recognized right in question accords with the longstanding construction of the agency Congress has assigned to enforce the securities laws. Once again the Court has refused to build upon a " 'secure foundation * * * laid by others,' " Patterson v. McLean Credit Union, 491 U.S. 164, 222 (1989) (Stevens, J., dissenting) (quoting B. Cardozo, The Nature of the Judicial Process 149 (1921)).

I respectfully dissent.

THE RISE, FALL, AND PARTIAL REVIVAL OF AIDING AND ABETTING

As Justice Stevens wrote in his dissent in *Central Bank*:

In hundreds of judicial and administrative proceedings in every circuit in the federal system, the courts and the SEC have concluded that aiders and abettors are subject to liability under § 10(b) and Rule 10b–5. [Citation omitted.] While we have reserved decision on the legitimacy of the theory in two cases that did not present it, all 11 Courts of Appeals to have considered the question have recognized a private cause of action against aiders and abettors under § 10(b) and Rule 10b–5.[1]

In one fell swoop *Central Bank* ended a frequently employed theory of derivative liability.

Initially *Central Bank* appeared to resolve many issues not before the Supreme Court. It seemed likely, as Justice Stevens stated in his *Central Bank* dissent, that the majority interpretation of Rule 10b–5 would not permit the SEC "to pursue aiders and abettors in civil enforcement actions under § 10(b) and Rule 10b–5."[2]

In 1995, however, Congress restored the Commission's authority to bring aiding and abetting actions when it enacted § 20(f) of the 1934 Act. Note, however, that § 20(f) applies only to persons who "knowingly provide substantial assistance" to the primary violator.

One of the first decisions to apply this new provision was SEC v. Fehn.[3] There, Fehn, an attorney, was retained by a company which was being

---

1. 511 U.S. at 192.

2. Id. at 200.

3. 97 F.3d 1276 (9th Cir.1996), *cert. denied*, 522 U.S. 813 (1997).

investigated by the SEC in connection with its earlier initial public offering. After learning that the company's true promoter had not been disclosed, he initially advised that the company should disclose the omitted material facts in its quarterly Form 10–Q, but later reversed himself when pressured to do so by the firm's promoter. Fehn later testified that he had advised the promoter that such disclosures were unnecessary and would impair the promoter's ability to assert his Fifth Amendment privilege against self-incrimination. Fehn also reviewed and edited a revised Form 10–Q that made partial, but not materially complete, disclosure of the promoter's role in the formation of the company and the syndication of its initial public offering. Fehn also reviewed and edited a later Form 10–Q filed by the issuer.

Based upon this conduct, the district court and the Ninth Circuit both found that Fehn had knowingly aided and abetted securities law violations and that § 20(f) could be applied retroactively to conduct occurring before its enactment. Despite the use of the, term "knowingly" in § 20(f), the Ninth Circuit relied on the legislative history to the provision and found that § 20(f) was intended by Congress "to preserve the definition of aiding and abetting as it existed pre-Central Bank."

Finally, even if there were primary violations, Fehn asserted that he could not be liable for professional advice provided to a client in good faith. After holding that the reporting requirements of the federal securities law did not violate the defendant's privilege against self-incrimination, the Ninth Circuit rejected Fehn's "good faith" defense by finding that "his efforts were not 'reasonable' in light of the well established disclosure requirements imposed by the * * * [federal securities laws]."[4]

Central Bank appears to leave little room for implying other forms of derivative liability such as *respondeat superior* or conspiracy.

Many types of individuals who earlier had been held liable as aiders and abettors in earlier § 10(b) cases, such as accountants and attorneys, potentially could be held liable as primary violators of § 10(b).

In Anixter v. Home–Stake Prod. Co.,[5] the Tenth Circuit attempted to sharpen the distinction between primary and derivative liability, stating in part:

> To establish a primary liability claim under § 10(b), a plaintiff must prove the following facts: (1) that the defendant made an untrue statement of material fact, or failed to state a material fact; (2) that the conduct occurred in connection with the purchase or sale of a security; (3) that the defendant made the statement or omission with scienter; and (4) that plaintiff relied on the misrepresentation, and sustained damages as a proximate result of the misrepresentation. *Farlow v. Peat, Marwick, Mitchell & Co.*, 956 F.2d 982, 986 (10th Cir.1992). This contrasts with aider and abettor liability, which required plaintiff to prove (1) the existence of a primary violation of the securities laws by another; (2) knowledge of the primary violation by alleged aider and abettor; and (3) substantial assistance by the alleged aider and abettor in achieving the primary violation. Id. The critical element separating primary from aiding and abetting violations is the existence of a representation, either by statement or

---

4. Id. at 1294.

5. 77 F.3d 1215, 1225–1227 (10th Cir. 1996).

omission, made by the defendant, that is relied upon by the plaintiff. Reliance only on representations made by another cannot itself form the basis of liability. See *Central Bank of Denver*, 511 U.S. at 177, 114 S. Ct. at 1448.

Clearly, accountants may make representations in their role as auditor to a firm selling securities. *See, e.g.*, Herman & MacLean v. Huddleston, 459 U.S. 375, 103 S.Ct. 683, 74 L.Ed.2d 548 (1983) (defendant accountant found primarily liable for violating § 10(b) based on representations made in registration statements filed with the SEC). Typical representations include certifications of financial statements and opinion letters. [Citation omitted.] An accountant's false and misleading representations in connection with the purchase or sale of any security, if made with the proper state of mind and if relied upon by those purchasing or selling a security, can constitute a primary violation. [Citation omitted.] There is no requirement that the alleged violator directly communicate misrepresentations to plaintiffs for primary liability to attach. [Citation omitted.] Nevertheless, for an accountant's misrepresentation to be actionable as a primary violation, there must be a showing that he knew or should have known that his representation would be communicated to investors because § 10(b) and Rule 10b–5 focus on fraud made "in connection with the sale or purchase" of a security. [Citation omitted.]

Reading the language of § 10(b) and 10b–5 through the lens of Central Bank of Denver, we conclude that in order for accountants to "use or employ" a "deception" actionable under the antifraud law, they must themselves make a false or misleading statement (or omission) that they know or should know will reach potential investors. In addition to being consistent with the language of the statute, this rule, though far from a bright line, provides more guidance to litigants than a rule allowing liability to attach to an accountant or other outside professional who provided "significant" or "substantial" assistance to the representations of others. [Citations omitted.]

In SEC v. First Jersey Sec., Inc.,[6] the Second Circuit added: "Primary liability may be imposed 'not only on persons who made fraudulent misrepresentations but also on those who had knowledge of the fraud and assisted in its perpetration.' Azrielli v. Cohen Law Offices, 21 F.3d 512, 517 (2d Cir.1994)." The same Second Circuit in Wright v. Ernst & Young LLP held, however, that only a defendant who actually made a false or misleading statement could be held liable under § 10(b) after *Central Bank*.[7]

Certain types of legal actors appear more likely than others to be primarily liable. For example, accountants sign a report expressing an opinion as to whether corporate financial statements are presented in accordance with generally accepted accounting principles. If the financial statements are fraudulent, the signing of this report could subject the accountant to primary liability. On the other hand, other aspects of corporate reports are not covered by the accountant's report, and presumably an accountant would normally not be held

---

6.   101 F.3d 1450, 1471 (2d Cir.1996). *See also* McGann v. Ernst & Young, 102 F.3d 390, 396–397 (9th Cir.1996), *cert. denied*, 520 U.S. 1181 (1997).

7.   152 F.3d 169, 175, 178 (2d Cir.1998). A corporate officer who signs an SEC filing can be held primarily liable. Howard v. Everex Sys., Inc., 228 F.3d 1057, 1061–1063 (9th Cir.2000).

liable for fraud in these nonfinancial parts of corporate filings. The fact that accountants can be held liable as "experts" under § 11, strengthens the argument that they could be held primarily liable as signers of reports in Form 10–K annual reports under Rule 10b–5. Tax attorneys appear to run a similar risk of being held liable for § 10(b) primary liability when they prepare opinion letters concerning tax consequences that are distributed to investors.[8]

Other aspects of the legal landscape were not changed by *Central Bank*. The SEC before and after the case can bring Rule 102(e) disciplinary actions against attorneys and accountants who aid and abet a securities violation while practicing before the Commission. The Justice Department retains its criminal aiding and abetting authority.[9] Private securities litigants may continue to rely on other forms of derivative liability such as controlling person or "expert" liability under § 11.

PROBLEM 15–3

Arthur & Hayes LLP is the outside auditor for QT Gourmet Food Products, a corporation engaged in the franchising of high end quick food restaurants. In January 2002 partner Melisa Hayes orally approved QT's 3d quarter Management Discussion and Analysis (MD & A) statement (Reg. S–K Item 303(b)) which contained several materially false statements including a material misstatement of the last two years earnings per share and a material misstatement of the likely effect on QT's balance sheet from its pending merger with the popular Taste of Russia Gourmet Blini food chain. Because the MD & A Item is the responsibility of management, it is not audited by Arthur & Hayes. Nonetheless it is a common practice at QT and other firms to have the outside auditor review the MD & A Item. QT's January 2002 statement concludes: "As always we are grateful to Arthur & Hayes LLP for their review of this and other accounting statements in this report."

(1) Can a private investor hold Arthur & Hayes primarily liable under Rule 10b–5?

(2) Could the SEC hold Arthur & Hayes liable under § 20(f) of the Securities Act?

D. Defenses

We have earlier explored what today is the most frequently successfully invoked securities law defense, the failure to plead with sufficient particularity, as well as the due diligence defense under § 11, the reasonable care defense under § 12, and the good faith defense in controlling person liability actions. Here we explore other defenses that can be raised generally under the federal securities laws.

1. STATUTES OF LIMITATION

Until the Sarbanes–Oxley Act of 2002 amended 28 U.S.C. § 1658(b) the statute of limitations for implied causes of action such as Rule 10b–5 had been established by the United States Supreme Court in the following *Lampf* decision as one year after discovery of the facts constituting a violation or three years after the violation. The Sarbanes–Oxley Act extended those limits so that

8. Kline v. First Western Gov't Sec., Inc., 24 F.3d 480 (3d Cir.1994), *cert. denied sub nom.* Arvey, Hodes, Costello & Burman v. Kline, 513 U.S. 1032 (1994).

9. 18 U.S.C. § 2.

no private securities right of action may be brought later than the earlier of *two* years after the discovery of the facts constituting the violation or *five* years after such violation. The reversal of *Lampf* represents one of the most eagerly sought goals of the private plaintiffs bar. The Sarbanes–Oxley Act did not directly address the repeal of the Private Securities Litigation Reform Act of 1995 on the grounds that it had deterred or needlessly delayed meritorious private litigation or permitting aiding and abetting actions against attorneys and auditors and reverse through legislation the 1994 United States Supreme Court decision in *Central Bank,* which held that such actions could not be implied from the key federal securities law fraud remedy, Rule 10b–5.

The reversal of *Lampf* nonetheless is quite significant. It represents a return to the general approach of Congress before the 1995 Act that private litigation performs an important role in deterring securities fraud. It is likely to lead to more private claims, particularly through its extension of the one year to two years after discovery standard. In 1995 Congress declined to adopt this type of approach because of a greater concern about frivolous litigation. The pendulum appears to have swung, at least temporarily, to a greater concern about wrongdoing by corporate insiders and certified public accountants.

The basic Supreme Court philosophy towards the federal securities law statute of limitations in *Lampf* continues to have force.

Lampf, Pleva, Lipkind, Prupis & Petigrow v. Gilbertson

Supreme Court of the United States, 1991.
501 U.S. 350, 111 S.Ct. 2773, 115 L.Ed.2d 321.

■ Justice Blackmun delivered the opinion of the Court, except as to Part II–A.

In this litigation we must determine which statute of limitations is applicable to a private suit brought pursuant to § 10(b) of the Securities Exchange Act of 1934 and to Securities and Exchange Commission Rule 10b–5, promulgated thereunder.

I

The controversy arises from the sale of seven Connecticut limited partnerships formed for the purpose of purchasing and leasing computer hardware and software. Petitioner Lampf, Pleva, Lipkind, Prupis & Petigrow is a West Orange, N.J., law firm that aided in organizing the partnerships and that provided additional legal services, including the preparation of opinion letters addressing the tax consequences of investing in the partnerships. The several plaintiff-respondents purchased units in one or more of the partnerships during the years 1979 through 1981 with the expectation of realizing federal income tax benefits therefrom.

The partnerships failed, due in part to the technological obsolescence of their wares. In late 1982 and early 1983, plaintiff-respondents received notice that the United States Internal Revenue Service was investigating the partnerships. The IRS subsequently disallowed the claimed tax benefits because of overvaluation of partnership assets and lack of profit motive.

On November 3, 1986, and June 4, 1987, plaintiff-respondents filed their respective complaints in the United States District Court for the District of Oregon, naming as defendants petitioner and others involved in the preparation of offering memoranda for the partnerships. The complaints alleged that plaintiff-respondents were induced to invest in the partnerships by misrepresentations in the offering memoranda, in violation of, among other things, § 10(b) of the 1934 Act and Rule 10b–5. The claimed misrepresentations were said to include assurances that the investments would entitle the purchasers to substantial tax benefits; that the leasing of the hardware and software packages would generate a profit; that the software was readily marketable; and that certain equipment appraisals were accurate and reasonable. Plaintiff-respondents asserted that they became aware of the alleged misrepresentations only in 1985 following the disallowance by the IRS of the tax benefits claimed.

After consolidating the actions for discovery and pretrial proceedings, the District Court granted summary judgment for the defendants on the ground that the complaints were not timely filed. App. to Pet. for Cert. 22A. Following precedent of its controlling court, see, e.g., Robuck v. Dean Witter & Co., 649 F.2d 641 (C.A.9 1980), the District Court ruled that the securities claims were governed by the state statute of limitations for the most analogous forum-state cause of action. The court determined this to be Oregon's 2–year limitations period for fraud claims, Ore.Rev.Stat. § 12.110(1) (1989). The court found that reports to plaintiff-respondents detailing the declining financial status of each partnership and allegations of misconduct made known to the general partners put plaintiff-respondents on "inquiry notice" of the possibility of fraud as early as October 1982. App. to Pet. for Cert. 43A. The court also ruled that the distribution of certain fiscal reports and the installation of a general partner previously associated with the defendants did not constitute fraudulent concealment sufficient to toll the statute of limitations. Applying the Oregon statute to the facts underlying plaintiff-respondents' claims, the District Court determined that each complaint was time barred.

The Court of Appeals for the Ninth Circuit reversed and remanded the cases. See Reitz v. Leasing Consultants Associates, 895 F.2d 1418 (1990) (judgment entry). In its unpublished opinion, the Court of Appeals found that unresolved factual issues as to when plaintiff-respondents discovered or should have discovered the alleged fraud precluded summary judgment. Then, as did the District Court, it selected the 2–year Oregon limitations period. In so doing, it implicitly rejected petitioner's argument that a federal limitations period should apply to Rule 10b–5 claims. App. to Pet. for Cert. 8A. In view of the divergence of opinion among the Circuits regarding the proper limitations period for Rule 10b–5 claims,[1] we granted certiorari to address this important issue. * * *

II

Plaintiff-respondents maintain that the Court of Appeals correctly identified common-law fraud as the source from which § 10(b) limitations should be derived. They submit that the underlying policies and practicalities of § 10(b) litigation do not justify a departure from the traditional practice of "borrowing" analogous state-law statutes of limitations. Petitioner, on the other hand,

---

1. See, e.g., Nesbit v. McNeil, 896 F.2d 380 (C.A.9 1990) (applying state limitations period governing common-law fraud); Bath v. Bushkin, Gaims, Gaines and Jonas, 913 F.2d 817 (C.A.10 1990) (same); O'Hara v. Kovens, 625 F.2d 15 (C.A.4 1980), cert. denied, 449 U.S. 1124 (1981) (applying state blue sky limitations period); Forrestal Village, Inc. v. Graham, 179 U.S.App.D.C. 225, 551 F.2d 411 (1977) (same); In re Data Access Systems Securities Litigation, 843 F.2d 1537 (CA3), cert. denied sub nom. Vitiello v. I. Kahlowsky & Co., 488 U.S. 849 (1988) (establishing uniform federal period); Short v. Belleville Shoe Mfg. Co., 908 F.2d 1385 (C.A.7 1990), cert. pending, No. 90–526 (same).

argues that a federal period is appropriate, contending that we must look to the "1–and–3–year" structure applicable to the express causes of action in § 13 of the Securities Act of 1933, and to certain of the express actions in the 1934 Act.[2] The Solicitor General, appearing on behalf of the Securities Exchange Commission, agrees that use of a federal period is indicated, but urges the application of the 5–year statute of repose specified in § 20A of the 1934 Act, as added by § 5 of the Insider Trading and Securities Fraud Enforcement Act of 1988, 102 Stat. 4681. The 5–year period, it is said, accords with "Congress's most recent views on the accommodation of competing interests, provides the closest federal analogy, and promises to yield the best practical and policy results in Rule 10b–5 litigation." Brief for Securities and Exchange Commission as *Amicus Curiae* 8. For the reasons discussed below, we agree that a uniform federal period is indicated, but we hold that the express causes of action contained in the 1933 and 1934 Acts provide the source.

A

It is the usual rule that when Congress has failed to provide a statute of limitations for a federal cause of action, a court "borrows" or "absorbs" the local time limitation most analogous to the case at hand. Wilson v. Garcia, 471 U.S. 261, 266–267 (1985); Auto Workers v. Hoosier Cardinal Corp., 383 U.S. 696, 704 (1966); Campbell v. Haverhill, 155 U.S. 610, 617 (1895). This practice, derived from the Rules of Decision Act, 28 U.S.C. § 1652, has enjoyed sufficient longevity that we may assume that, in enacting remedial legislation, Congress ordinarily "intends by its silence that we borrow state law." Agency Holding Corp. v. Malley–Duff & Associates, Inc., 483 U.S. 143, 147 (1987).

The rule, however, is not without exception. We have recognized that a state legislature rarely enacts a limitations period with federal interests in mind, Occidental Life Ins. Co. v. EEOC, 432 U.S. 355, 367 (1977), and when the operation of a state limitations period would frustrate the policies embraced by the federal enactment, this Court has looked to federal law for a suitable period. See, e.g., DelCostello v. Teamsters, 462 U.S. 151 (1983); *Agency Holding Corp.*, *supra*; McAllister v. Magnolia Petroleum Co., 357 U.S. 221, 224 (1958). These departures from the state-borrowing doctrine have been motivated by this Court's conclusion that it would be "inappropriate to conclude that Congress would choose to adopt state rules at odds with the purpose or operation of federal substantive law." *DelCostello,* 462 U.S., at 161.

Rooted as it is in the expectations of Congress, the "state-borrowing doctrine" may not be lightly abandoned. We have described federal borrowing as "a closely circumscribed exception," to be made "only 'when a rule from elsewhere in federal law clearly provides a closer analogy than available state statutes, and when the federal policies at stake and the practicalities of litigation make that rule a significantly more appropriate vehicle for interstitial lawmaking.'" Reed v. United Transportation Union, 488 U.S. 319, 324 (1989), quoting *DelCostello,* 462 U.S., at 172.

Predictably, this determination is a delicate one. Recognizing, however, that a period must be selected,[3] our cases do provide some guidance as to

2. Although not identical in language, all these relate to one year after discovery and to three years after violation.

3. On rare occasions, this Court has found it to be Congress' intent that no time limitation be imposed upon a federal cause of action. See, e.g., Occidental Life Ins. Co. v.

whether state or federal borrowing is appropriate and as to the period best suited to the cause of action under consideration. From these cases we are able to distill a hierarchical inquiry for ascertaining the appropriate limitations period for a federal cause of action where Congress has not set the time within which such an action must be brought.

First, the court must determine whether a uniform statute of limitations is to be selected. Where a federal cause of action tends in practice to "encompass numerous and diverse topics and subtopics," Wilson v. Garcia, 471 U.S., at 273, such that a single state limitations period may not be consistently applied within a jurisdiction, we have concluded that the federal interests in predictability and judicial economy counsel the adoption of one source, or class of sources, for borrowing purposes. Id., at 273–275. This conclusion ultimately may result in the selection of a single federal provision, see *Agency Holding Corp., supra*, or of a single variety of state actions. See *Wilson v. Garcia* (characterizing all actions under 42 U.S.C. § 1983 as analogous to a state-law personal injury action).

Second, assuming a uniform limitations period is appropriate, the court must decide whether this period should be derived from a state or a federal source. In making this judgment, the court should accord particular weight to the geographic character of the claim:

> "The multistate nature of [the federal cause of action at issue] indicates the desirability of a uniform federal statute of limitations. With the possibility of multiple state limitations, the use of state statutes would present the danger of forum shopping and, at the very least, would 'virtually guarante[e] * * * complex and expensive litigation over what should be a straightforward matter.' " *Agency Holding Corp.,* 483 U.S., at 154, quoting Report of the Ad Hoc Civil RICO Task Force of the ABA Section of Corporation, Banking and Business Law 392 (1985).

Finally, even where geographic considerations counsel federal borrowing, the aforementioned presumption of state borrowing requires that a court determine that an analogous federal source truly affords a "closer fit" with the cause of action at issue than does any available state-law source. Although considerations pertinent to this determination will necessarily vary depending upon the federal cause of action and the available state and federal analogues, such factors as commonality of purpose and similarity of elements will be relevant.

B

In the present litigation, our task is complicated by the nontraditional origins of the § 10(b) cause of action. The text of § 10(b) does not provide for private claims. Such claims are of judicial creation, having been implied under the statute for nearly half a century. * * * Although this Court repeatedly has recognized the validity of such claims, * * * we have made no pretense that it was Congress' design to provide the remedy afforded. See *Ernst & Ernst,* 425 U.S., at 196 ("[T]here is no indication that Congress, or the Commission when adopting Rule 10b–5, contemplated such a remedy.") (footnotes omitted). It is therefore no surprise that the provision contains no statute of limitations.

EEOC, 432 U.S. 355 (1977). No party in the present litigation argues that this was Congress' purpose in enacting § 10(b), and we agree that there is no evidence of such intent.

In a case such as this, we are faced with the awkward task of discerning the limitations period that Congress intended courts to apply to a cause of action it really never knew existed. Fortunately, however, the drafters of § 10(b) have provided guidance.

We conclude that where, as here, the claim asserted is one implied under a statute that also contains an express cause of action with its own time limitation, a court should look first to the statute of origin to ascertain the proper limitations period. We can imagine no clearer indication of how Congress would have balanced the policy considerations implicit in any limitations provision than the balance struck by the same Congress in limiting similar and related protections. See *DelCostello,* 462 U.S., at 171; United Parcel Service, Inc. v. Mitchell, 451 U.S. 56, 69–70 (1981) (opinion concurring in judgment). When the statute of origin contains comparable express remedial provisions, the inquiry usually should be at an end. Only where no analogous counterpart is available should a court then proceed to apply state-borrowing principles.

In the present litigation, there can be no doubt that the contemporaneously enacted express remedial provisions represent "a federal statute of limitations actually designed to accommodate a balance of interests very similar to that at stake here—a statute that is, in fact, an analogy to the present lawsuit more apt than any of the suggested state-law parallels." *DelCostello,* 462 U.S., at 169. The 1934 Act contained a number of express causes of action, each with an explicit limitations period. With only one more restrictive exception,[5] each of these includes some variation of a 1–year period after discovery combined with a 3–year period of repose.[6] In adopting the 1934 Act, the 73d Congress also amended the limitations provision of the 1933 Act, adopting the 1–and–3–year structure for each cause of action contained therein.

Section 9 of the 1934 Act, pertaining to the willful manipulation of security prices, and § 18, relating to misleading filings, target the precise dangers that are the focus of § 10(b). Each is an integral element of a complex web of regulations. Each was intended to facilitate a central goal: "to protect investors against manipulation of stock prices through regulation of transactions upon securities exchanges and in over-the-counter markets, and to impose regular reporting requirements on companies whose stock is listed on national securities exchanges." *Ernst & Ernst,* 425 U.S., at 195, citing S.Rep. No. 792, 73d Cong., 2d Sess., 1–5 (1934).

C

We therefore conclude that we must reject the Commission's contention that the 5–year period contained in § 20A, added to the 1934 Act in 1988, is

---

5. Section 16(b) sets a 2–year rather than a 3–year period of repose. Because that provision requires the disgorgement of unlawful profits and differs in focus from § 10(b) and from the other express causes of action, we do not find § 16(b) to be an appropriate source from which to borrow a limitations period here.

6. Section 9(e) of the 1934 Act provides:

"No action shall be maintained to enforce any liability created under this section, unless brought within one year after the discovery of the facts constituting the violation and within three years after such violation."

Section 18(c) of the 1934 Act provides:

"No action shall be maintained to enforce any liability created under this section unless brought within one year after the discovery of the facts constituting the cause of action and within three years after such cause of action accrued."

more appropriate for § 10(b) actions than is the 1–and–3–year structure in the Act's original remedial provisions. The Insider Trading and Securities Fraud Enforcement Act of 1988, which became law more than 50 years after the original securities statutes, focuses upon a specific problem, namely, the "purchasing or selling [of] a security while in possession of material, nonpublic information," 15 U.S.C. § 78t–1(a), that is, "insider trading." Recognizing the unique difficulties in identifying evidence of such activities, the 100th Congress adopted § 20A as one of "a variety of measures designed to provide greater deterrence, detection and punishment of violations of insider trading." H.R.Rep. No. 100–910, p. 7 (1988). There is no indication that the drafters of § 20A sought to extend that enhanced protection to other provisions of the 1934 Act. Indeed, the text of § 20A indicates the contrary. Section 20A(d) states: "Nothing in this section shall be construed to limit or condition the right of any person to bring an action to enforce a requirement of this chapter or the availability of any cause of action implied from a provision of this chapter."

The Commission further argues that because some conduct that is violative of § 10(b) is also actionable under § 20A, adoption of a 1–and–3–year structure would subject actions based on § 10(b) to two different statutes of limitations. But § 20A also prohibits insider-trading activities that violate sections of the 1934 Act with express limitations periods. The language of § 20A makes clear that the 100th Congress sought to alter the remedies available in insider trading cases, and *only* in insider trading cases. There is no inconsistency.

Finally, the Commission contends that the adoption of a 3–year period of repose would frustrate the policies underlying § 10(b). The inclusion, however, of the 1–and–3–year structure in the broad range of express securities actions contained in the 1933 and 1934 Acts suggests a congressional determination that a 3–year period is sufficient. See Ceres Partners v. GEL Associates, 918 F.2d 349, 363 (C.A.2 1990).

Thus, we agree with every Court of Appeals that has been called upon to apply a federal statute of limitations to a § 10(b) claim that the express causes of action contained in the 1933 and 1934 Acts provide a more appropriate statute of limitations than does § 20A. * * *

Necessarily, we also reject plaintiff-respondents' assertion that state-law fraud provides the closest analogy to § 10(b). The analytical framework we adopt above makes consideration of state-law alternatives unnecessary where Congress has provided an express limitations period for correlative remedies within the same enactment.[8]

III

Finally, we address plaintiff-respondents' contention that, whatever limitations period is applicable to § 10(b) claims, that period must be subject to the doctrine of equitable tolling. Plaintiff-respondents note, correctly, that "[t]ime

---

8. Justice Kennedy would borrow the one-year limitations period contained in the 1934 Act but not the accompanying period of repose. In our view, the one-and-three-year scheme represents an indivisible determination by Congress as to the appropriate cutoff point for claims under the statute. It would disserve that legislative determination to sever the two periods. Moreover, we find no support in our cases for the practice of borrowing only a portion of an express statute of limitations. Indeed, such a practice comes close to the type of judicial policymaking that our borrowing doctrine was intended to avoid.

requirements in law suits * * * are customarily subject to 'equitable tolling.' " Irwin v. Department of Veterans Affairs, 498 U.S. 89, 95 (1990) (slip op. 5), citing Hallstrom v. Tillamook County, 493 U.S. 20, 27 (1989) (slip op. 6). Thus, this Court has said that in the usual case, "where the party injured by the fraud remains in ignorance of it without any fault or want of diligence or care on his part, the bar of the statute does not begin to run until the fraud is discovered, though there be no special circumstances or efforts on the part of the party committing the fraud to conceal it from the knowledge of the other party." Bailey v. Glover, 21 Wall. 342, 348 (1874); see also Holmberg v. Armbrecht, 327 U.S. 392, 396–397 (1946). Notwithstanding this venerable principle, it is evident that the equitable tolling doctrine is fundamentally inconsistent with the 1–and–3–year structure.

The 1–year period, by its terms, begins after discovery of the facts constituting the violation, making tolling unnecessary. The 3–year limit is a period of repose inconsistent with tolling. One commentator explains: "[T]he inclusion of the three-year period can have no significance in this context other than to impose an outside limit." Bloomenthal, The Statute of Limitations and Rule 10b–5 Claims: A Study in Judicial Lassitude, 60 U.Colo.L.Rev. 235, 288 (1989). See also ABA Committee on Federal Regulation of Securities, Report of the Task Force on Statute of Limitations for Implied Actions 645, 655 (1986) (advancing "the inescapable conclusion that Congress did not intend equitable tolling to apply in actions under the securities laws"). Because the purpose of the 3–year limitation is clearly to serve as a cutoff, we hold that tolling principles do not apply to that period.

IV

Litigation instituted pursuant to § 10(b) and Rule 10b–5 therefore must be commenced within one year after the discovery of the facts constituting the violation and within three years after such violation.[9] As there is no dispute that the earliest of plaintiff-respondents' complaints was filed more than three years after petitioner's alleged misrepresentations, plaintiff-respondents' claims were untimely.

The judgment of the Court of Appeals is reversed.

It is so ordered.

■ JUSTICE SCALIA, concurring in part and concurring in the judgment.

Although I accept the *stare decisis* effect of decisions we have made with respect to the statutes of limitations applicable to particular federal causes of action, I continue to disagree with the methodology the Court has very recently adopted for purposes of making those decisions. In my view, absent a congressionally created limitations period state periods govern, or, if they are inconsistent with the purposes of the federal act, no limitations period exists. See Agency Holding Corp. v. Malley–Duff & Associates, Inc., 483 U.S. 143, 157–170 (1987) (Justice Scalia, concurring in judgment), see also Reed v. United Transportation Union, 488 U.S. 319, 334 (1989) (Justice Scalia, concurring in judgment).

---

9. The Commission notes, correctly, that the various 1–and–3–year periods contained in the 1934 and 1933 Acts differ slightly in terminology. To the extent that these distinctions in the future might prove significant, we select as the governing standard for an action under § 10(b) the language of § 9(e) of the 1934 Act.

The present case presents a distinctive difficulty because it involves one of those so-called "implied" causes of action that, for several decades, this Court was prone to discover in—or, more accurately, create in reliance upon—federal legislation. See Thompson v. Thompson, 484 U.S. 174, 190 (1988) (Justice Scalia, concurring in judgment). Raising up causes of action where a statute has not created them may be a proper function for common-law courts, but not for federal tribunals. See id., at 191–192; Cannon v. University of Chicago, 441 U.S. 677, 730–749 (1979) (Powell, J., dissenting). We have done so, however, and thus the question arises what statute of limitations applies to such a suit. Congress has not had the opportunity (since it did not itself create the cause of action) to consider whether it is content with the state limitations or would prefer to craft its own rule. That lack of opportunity is particularly apparent in the present case, since Congress *did* create special limitations periods for the Securities Exchange Act causes of actions that it actually enacted. See 15 U.S.C. §§ 78p(b), 78i(e), 78r(c); see also § 77m.

When confronted with this situation, the only thing to be said for applying my ordinary (and the Court's pre–1983 traditional) rule is that the unintended and possibly irrational results will certainly deter judicial invention of causes of action. That is not an unworthy goal, but to pursue it in that fashion would be highly unjust to those who must litigate past inventions. An alternative approach would be to say that since we "implied" the cause of action we ought to "imply" an appropriate statute of limitations as well. That is just enough, but too lawless to be imagined. It seems to me the most responsible approach, where the enactment that has been the occasion for our creation of a cause of action contains a limitations period for an analogous cause of action, is to use that. We are imagining here. And I agree with the Court that "[w]e can imagine no clearer indication of how Congress would have balanced the policy considerations implicit in any limitations provision than the balance struck by the same Congress in limiting similar and related protections." Ante, at 8.

I join the judgment of the Court, and all except Part IIA of the Court's opinion.

■ [Justices Stevens and Souter dissented on the basis that the courts should continue to "borrow" state statutes of limitations for Rule 10b–5, as they have until recently. Justices Kennedy and O'Connor dissented on the basis that, while it was all right to "borrow" the 1–year period after discovery in the 1934 Act, the 3–year period of repose should not be included, and that, in any event, the new limitations period should not be applied "retroactively" to this case.— Eds.] * * *

STATUTES OF LIMITATION

Section 13 of the Securities Act of 1933 establishes a federal statute of limitations for all civil actions under §§ 11 and 12. Under § 12(a)(2) the period of limitations is one year after discovery of the false statement but not more than three years after the sale.[1] Under § 12(a)(1) the period of limitations is one year after "the violation", for example, the sale in violation of § 5. Under § 11 the statute prescribes an overall limitation of three years after "the security was bona fide offered to the public." This apparently means that as to a portion of an unsold allotment purchased by the plaintiff more than three years after the original public offering, a possible action under § 12(a)(1) (if the

---

1. Cook v. Avien, Inc., 573 F.2d 685 (1st Cir.1978).

issue was unregistered) or under § 11 (if the issue was registered) was barred before it accrued. While this result is ridiculous, it seems to be what the statute says. In 1954 Congress amended the Investment Company Act to eliminate this problem in connection with the sale of mutual fund shares, where it was most acute. The Commission by the device of an "undertaking" has attempted to achieve the same result in other situations involving continuous or "shelf" registrations.

There is no period of limitations prescribed in the statute for actions under § 10(b). Sections 9 and 18 of the 1934 Act include their own limitations periods for express actions under the 1934 Act. In the absence of any express statute of limitation the courts generally held until a few years before *Lampf* that the most "analogous" state statute of limitations should be applied.[2] Then the Third Circuit in 1988,[3] followed by the Seventh Circuit[4] and the Second Circuit[5] in 1990, held that the express statutes of limitations specified for other causes of action in the 1933 Act and the 1934 Act should be adopted for actions under Rule 10b–5, because these were more "analogous" than any state statutes of limitations. The result of these cases was adopted by the Supreme Court in *Lampf*, although the Supreme Court stated that this should be the statute of limitations specified in § 9(e) of the 1934 Act rather than § 13 of the 1933 Act which had been applied in the Third and Seventh Circuit decisions. It is not apparent that which Section is applied makes any substantial difference in result, as the *Lampf* case indicates, since they generally specify the same two time periods of one year after discovery and three years after the violation.

After the lower courts began applying *Lampf*'s one and three year limitations periods retroactively,[6] Congress added § 27A to the Securities Exchange Act which specifies that the limitation period for any § 10(b) private civil action begun on or before June 19, 1991—the day before *Lampf* was decided—would be the limitation period provided in the relevant jurisdiction as of that date, and plaintiffs were allowed no more than 60 days to reinstate earlier dismissed or unfiled actions.[7] The new Section did not apply to actions filed after June 19, 1991.

There soon developed a virtual cottage industry challenging the constitutionality of § 27A(a). At least nine circuits have now upheld the constitutionality of § 27(a) (applying to cases pending on December 19, 1991).[8]

---

2. Initially, the most "analogous" state statute of limitations was held to be the period for "fraud" actions. In Wachovia Bank & Trust Co. v. National Student Marketing Corp., 650 F.2d 342 (D.C.Cir.1980), the court stated that until December 1971, there were only two cases which had applied the state Blue Sky Law limitations period to federal securities actions, while there had been 46 applying a forum state's general fraud statute. After that date there was a strong trend towards applying the state statute of limitations in its Blue Sky Law to actions brought under Rule 10b–5.

3. Data Access Sys. Sec. Litig., 843 F.2d 1537 (3d Cir. *en banc* 1988), *cert. denied*, 488 U.S. 849 (1988).

4. Short v. Belleville Shoe Manufacturing Co., 908 F.2d 1385 (7th Cir.1990), *cert. denied*, 501 U.S. 1250 (1991).

5. Ceres Partners v. GEL Assoc., 918 F.2d 349 (2d Cir.1990).

6. *See, e.g.,* Anixter v. Home–Stake Prod. Co., 939 F.2d 1420, 1440–1442 (10th Cir.1991), *amended in part & reh'g denied in part,* 947 F.2d 897 (10th Cir.1991); Boudreau v. Deloitte, Haskins & Sells, 942 F.2d 497 (8th Cir.1991); Welch v. Cadre Capital, 946 F.2d 185 (2d Cir.1991).

7. Pub. L. No. 102–242 § 476, 105 Stat. 2387.

8. Henderson v. Scientific–Atlanta, Inc., 971 F.2d 1567 (11th Cir.1992); Anixter v.

On the other hand, the Supreme Court in Plaut v. Spendthrift Farm, Inc.,[9] held in 1995 that § 27A(b), which allowed § 10(b) private civil actions dismissed earlier as time barred to be reinstated, was a violation of the Constitution's separation of powers doctrine.

Of more moment for private litigants is the significance of inquiry notice discussed in the following case.[10]

Law v. Medco Research, Inc.

United States Court of Appeals, Seventh Circuit, 1997.
113 F.3d 781.

■ Before Posner, Chief Judge, and Eschbach and Manion, Circuit Judges.

■ Posner, Chief Judge.

When this securities fraud case was last before us, we held that the district judge had erred when he granted the defendants' motion to dismiss on the ground that it was apparent from the face of the complaint that the suit had been filed after the one-year statute of limitations applicable to suits under the SEC's Rule 10b–5 had run. *LaSalle v. Medco Research, Inc.,* 54 F.3d 443 (7th Cir.1995) (same case, different lead named plaintiff). We rejected the proposition "that the conjunction of optimistic forecasts with a sharp drop in price establishes inquiry notice as a matter of law." *Id.* at 447. On remand, the district judge again granted summary judgment for the defendants on the basis of the statute of limitations. We had left open the possibility that this might be appropriate if, when Medco's stock price had been plummeting notwithstanding the optimistic forecasts, the prices of its competitors' shares had been holding steady or rising. But in granting summary judgment the second time the judge did not allude to these price movements. The defendants had on remand presented some evidence concerning them—but it was evidence that Medco's stock price had moved in tandem with the prices of its competitors' stocks. The defendants could not use this evidence to show that the statute of limitations had run, but they could and did use it to support an alternative ground for dismissal of the suit, to which the judge however did not allude, that there was no causal relation between the alleged fraud and the loss to the members of the plaintiff class. To support their statute of limitations defense, the defendants presented another kind of evidence, which the district judge found convincing— articles published in the trade press that should have made the plaintiffs suspicious. * * *

Home–Stake Prod. Co., 977 F.2d 1533 (10th Cir.1992), *on reh'g,* 977 F.2d 1549 (10th Cir. 1992), *cert. denied sub nom.* Dennler v. Trippet, 507 U.S. 1029 (1993); Berning v. A.G. Edwards & Sons, Inc., 990 F.2d 272 (7th Cir.1993); Gray v. First Winthrop Corp., 989 F.2d 1564 (9th Cir.1993); Cooperativa de Ahorro y Credito Aguada v. Kidder, Peabody & Co., 993 F.2d 269 (1st Cir.1993); Pacific Mut. Life Ins. Co. v. First RepublicBank Corp., 997 F.2d 39 (5th Cir.1993), *aff'd sub nom.* Morgan Stanley & Co., Inc. v. Pacific Mut. Life Ins. Co., 511 U.S. 658 (1994); Cooke v. Manufactured Homes, Inc., 998 F.2d 1256, 1264–1265 (4th Cir.1993); Axel Johnson Inc. v. Arthur Andersen & Co., 6 F.3d 78 (2d Cir.1993); Freeman v. Laventhol & Horwath, 34 F.3d 333, 342 (6th Cir.1994).

9. 514 U.S. 211 (1995).

10. The courts are divided whether the SEC itself can be bound by a statute of limitations. Cf. SEC v. Rind, 991 F.2d 1486 (9th Cir.1993) (Commission not bound); Johnson v. SEC, 87 F.3d 484 (D.C.Cir.1996) (holding that five year statute of limitations of 28 U.S.C. § 2462 is applicable to SEC administrative proceedings).

In June, the FDA recalled several batches of a very similar drug called Adenocard that was being manufactured in the same plant by the same firm, LyphoMed, that Medco had licensed to manufacture Adenoscan, the successor product to Adenocard. It was plausible to suppose that the problems that LyphoMed had encountered in manufacturing Adenocard might lap over to Adenoscan and delay the approval of that drug. In April of 1993, with Adenoscan still not approved, Medco announced that it was going to sue FujisawaUSA, LyphoMed's parent. The suit was filed the next month, and revealed that the problems at the LyphoMed plant had caused Medco to withdraw temporarily its application for the approval of Adenoscan a week before it had told the investing public that the application was on track. On these facts—all we had to go on when the case was last here—we held that not until April 1993 did investors have enough information to start the statute of limitations running; the suit filed in September was well within a year of that date.

The evidence presented by the defendants on remand consists primarily of articles published before September 1992 that posted "storm warnings," in the district judge's phrase (a cliche in opinions about investors' diligence, e.g., *Dodds v. Cigna Securities, Inc.,* 12 F.3d 346, 350 (2d Cir.1993)), of trouble ahead for Medco. One investment newsletter said in December 1990 that Medco was "an overpriced hype job" and "does not reveal bad news." The market disagreed; Medco's stock price rose from $6.75 in the following month to more than $30 a year later. In May 1991, a business journal reported that Medco had "found a whole new crew of idiots to buy [its] stock." Again the market disagreed. All the storm warnings posted before April of the following year were premature. An idiot who bought stock in Medco in January 1991 and sold it in June 1992, at the very bottom of Medco's plunge, would still have made a profit of more than 100 percent.

Throughout this period Medco was one of the most shorted stocks on the American Stock Exchange. The judge thought this should have warned investors that Medco was in trouble. Not so. For every short seller—a pessimist about the value of the stock that he's selling short—there is, on the other side of the transaction, an optimist, who thinks the stock worth more than the short-sale price. Unless the shorts are trading on insider information, all that a large volume of short selling proves is a diversity of opinions about the company's future—a diversity hardly surprising when the company's future depends on when the Food and Drug Administration will permit it to sell a new drug. Of course, if there were more pessimists, all wanting to sell short, than there were optimists, the price of a stock would plunge; but the important thing would not be the short selling, but the price plunge, and we made clear in our previous opinion that a price plunge, without more, is not a reasonable basis for suspecting fraud.

The strongest evidence submitted by Medco in support of its motion for summary judgment was a series of articles published in August of 1992 reporting that Fujisawa had sued the principal owner of the company that had sold it LyphoMed. (That suit was decided against Fujisawa in *Fujisawa Pharmaceutical Co. v. Kapoor,* 936 F.Supp. 455 (N.D.Ill.1996), now pending on appeal to this court.) In part the articles merely repeated what had been reported in June—that Fujisawa had had to recall some batches of Adenocard. But they also reported that the former LyphoMed (now Fujisawa) was having quality-control and regulatory-assurance problems with a number of LyphoMed drugs. Coming only four months after Medco had represented to the investing public that its application for FDA approval of Adenoscan was proceeding smoothly, these reports of trouble, in conjunction with the plunge in Medco's stock price, created grounds for suspicion that Medco's representation about being "on track" might have been false. Missing, however, was any indication in the articles published in August of 1992 that Medco had been aware of the problems at Fujisawa–LyphoMed, or aware of their bearing on the prospects for early approval of Adenoscan, when four months earlier it had announced that everything was going smoothly. One of the plaintiffs' claims of fraud is that Medco did know then. But nothing in the trade press indicated that. An innocently false representation is not actionable under Rule 10b–5. Ernst & Ernst v. Hochfelder, 425 U.S. 185, 193, 96 S.Ct. 1375, 1380–81, 47 L.Ed.2d 668 (1976); Eckstein v. Balcor Film Investors, 8 F.3d 1121, 1131 (7th Cir.1993); *Goldberg v. Household Bank,* F.S.B., 890 F.2d 965, 967 (7th Cir.1989). When the representation is false for reasons likely to have been within the knowledge of the company when making it, investors upon learning of the falsity should smell the possibility of fraud, but not when the representation concerns conditions internal to a customer, supplier, licensee, licensor, or other outsider to the firm making the representation, conditions that moreover may have arisen after the representation was made.

Another claim of fraud is that back in August of 1991, when Medco had characterized the FDA's request for additional data as a sign that approval was imminent, it knew that the request signified that there would probably be a substantial delay. Nothing in the trade press would have alerted investors to this fraud either. Taken as a whole, the media reports on Medco revealed widely different assessments of the value of the stock and (what was basically the same thing) the likely date of approval of Adenoscan, but did not scatter clues that Medco had been lying about its dealings with the FDA.

But suppose it were true that before September 1992 investors knew enough to suspect fraud. Would the statute of limitations have begun to run then? As an original matter, one might well answer "yes" but then quickly add that the running of the statute of limitations would be tolled (interrupted), as permitted by the doctrine of equitable tolling, until the investors had enough facts in hand to enable them to file a complaint that would comply with the requirements of the Federal Rules of Civil Procedure for pleading fraud. These requirements include pleading the fraud with particularity (a requirement that has been stiffened for securities fraud cases filed after December 22, 1995, see Private Securities Litigation Reform Act of 1995, Pub.L. No. 104–67, § 101(b), § 21D(b)(2), 109 Stat. 737, 747, codified at 15 U.S.C. § 78u–4(b)(2)) and having a reasonable evidentiary basis for all factual allegations in the complaint. Fed.R.Civ.P. 9(b), 11(b)(3); *In re HealthCare Compare Corp. Securities Litigation v. HealthCare Compare Corp.,* 75 F.3d 276, 280–81 (7th Cir.1996); *In re Donald J. Trump Casino Securities Litigation,* 7 F.3d 357, 373 n. 17 (3d Cir.1993). However, the Supreme Court has held that, given the discovery rule, there is no defense of equitable tolling to the statute of limitations in a Rule 10b–5 case. *Lampf, Pleva, Lipkind, Prupis & Petigrow v. Gilbertson,* 501 U.S. 350, 363–64, 111 S.Ct. 2773, 2782–83, 115 L.Ed.2d 321 (1991). This holding makes it extremely important to decide what exactly it is that the investors must discover (or should have discovered) to start the statute of limitations running. Is mere suspicion discovery? Or, at the other extreme, must the investor have learned (or have been in a position where he should have learned) all the facts he needs in order to file a suit? Language can be found in the case law to support either formula, and although more cases use the former, see, e.g., *LaSalle v. Medco Research, Inc., supra,* 54 F.3d at 444, and *Whirlpool Financial Corp. v. GN Holdings, Inc.,* 67 F.3d 605, 609 (7th Cir.1995), than the latter, see *Dodds v. Cigna Securities, Inc., supra,* 12 F.3d at 350, none of the cases treats the difference between the two formulas as an issue. See also *Norris v. Wirtz,* 818 F.2d 1329, 1334 (7th Cir.1987), overruled on other grounds in *Short v. Belleville Shoe Mfg. Co.,* 908 F.2d 1385 (7th Cir.1990). Perhaps it made no difference in those cases or the parties had chosen not to make it an issue.

We think it is time to resolve the issue. The most sensible approach, it seems to us, is to adapt the formula that section 13 of the Securities Act of 1933 uses for its one-year statute of limitations for suits complaining of false registration statements: "after the discovery of the untrue statement ... or after such discovery should have been made by the exercise of reasonable diligence." 15 U.S.C. § 77m. In other words, the plaintiff gets a year after he learned or should have learned the facts that he must know to know that he has a claim. In the case of a suit complaining of a false registration statement, all he has to know is that the statement was untrue; so, as soon as he knows or should know that, the one-year period begins to run. In a fraud case, he needs to know more: that the defendant has made a representation that was knowingly false. When the plaintiff knows or should know this, the statute of limitations begins to run. This approach is implied in *Lampf* itself. The Court said not that equitable tolling was inconsistent with the one-year statute of limitations (as it was, the Court held, with the three-year statute of repose), but that it was "unnecessary" because of the discovery rule. 501 U.S. at 363, 111 S.Ct. at 2782. This formulation implies that the rule should be so interpreted as to make equitable tolling unnecessary to protect investors' interest in having a reasonable, a practical, time within which to sue. It may not have been an accident, therefore, that the Court described the discovery rule as requiring that suit be "commenced within one year after the discovery of *the facts constituting the violation.*" Id. at 364, 111 S.Ct. at 2782 (emphasis added).

The test is an objective one, as the statutory language makes clear: not whether the plaintiffs did know more than a year before they sued that the defendant had committed fraud, but whether they should have known. Suspicious circumstances, coupled with ease of discovering, without the use of legal process, whether the suspicion is well grounded, may cause the statute of limitations to start to run before the plaintiffs discover the actual fraud, as in *Renz v. Beeman,* 589 F.2d 735, 751–52 (2d Cir.1978). The defendants in our case, however, have not explained what investors could have done before Medco sued Fujisawa in May of 1993, less than three months before this suit was filed, to obtain the necessary facts. We pressed the defendants' lawyer on this point at argument, and he suggested that the plaintiffs should have hired a lawyer to investigate, called their broker, or called Medco. These do not strike us as serious suggestions. The lawyer would not be able to subpoena the correspondence between Medco and the FDA which when it finally came to light in Medco's suit against Fujisawa established the factual predicate for the claim of fraud. The defendants do not argue that the lawyer could have obtained the documents from the FDA under the Freedom of Information Act, which has an exception for trade secrets and commercial information. 5 U.S.C. § 552(b)(4).

The statute of limitations in securities fraud cases serves, as we have emphasized in other opinions, important public purposes. *Tregenza v. Great*

American Communications Co., 12 F.3d 717, 722 (7th Cir.1993); *Short v. Belleville Shoe Mfg. Co., supra*, 908 F.2d at 1392. But too much emphasis on the statute of limitations can precipitate premature and groundless suits, as plaintiffs rush to beat the deadline without being able to obtain good evidence of fraud; and the three-year statute of repose gives defendants a definite limit beyond which they needn't fear being sued. On the record compiled so far, the defendants in this case, who have the burden of proving an affirmative defense, such as that the statute of limitations has run, have failed to show that a reasonably diligent investor would have brought suit before this suit was actually filed.

The defendants' alternative ground for affirmance is based on a study by a finance expert that compared the price movements in Medco's stock from November 1990 to June 1992—the period in which it first rose by 375 percent to its peak value in January of 1992 and then plunged by 61 percent from that value—with the price movements in Medco's competitors' stocks. The prices of those stocks had risen and fallen in tandem with Medco's, and the expert concluded that general market forces, rather than anything special to Medco, specifically the representations in May 1991 and April 1992 that exaggerated the prospects of early approval of Adenoscan, had been responsible for Medco's decline. If this is right, the fraud caused no harm, and the suit fails. *Bastian v. Petren Resources Corp.*, 892 F.2d 680, 685–86 (7th Cir.1990); *Roots Partnership v. Lands' End, Inc.*, 965 F.2d 1411, 1419 (7th Cir.1992); *Caremark, Inc. v. Coram Healthcare Corp.*, 113 F.3d 645, 648–49 (7th Cir.1997); *Citibank, N.A. v. K–H Corp.*, 968 F.2d 1489, 1495–96 (2d Cir.1992); *McGonigle v. Combs*, 968 F.2d 810, 821 (9th Cir.1992); see also Private Securities Litigation Reform Act of 1995, § 101(b), § 21D(b)(4), 109 Stat. at 747 (15 U.S.C.§ 78u–4(b)(4)) (codifying the judge-made "loss causation" rule). It may or may not be right; but the plaintiffs' reply brief does not mention the study, even though the defendants rely on it in their brief to provide the factual basis for the argument that the alleged fraud did not cause the plaintiffs' loss.

Failure to contest a point is not necessarily a waiver, but it is a risky tactic, and sometimes fatal. See *Hardy v. City Optical Inc.*, 39 F.3d 765, 771 (7th Cir.1994); *Singletary v. Continental Ill. Nat'l Bank & Trust Co.*, 9 F.3d 1236, 1240 (7th Cir.1993). Here it leaves us without any basis for questioning the soundness of the defendants' study. It is true that the plaintiffs presented some contrary evidence in the district court. But they do not mention that evidence in this court. By their silence the plaintiffs imply either that they think evidence on causation irrelevant—which would bespeak a fundamental misunderstanding of the law governing private damages actions for securities fraud—or that they have lost faith in their own study but hope to find better evidence if the case is remanded. They could have said simply that given their own study, the defendants' evidence on causation is thrown sufficiently into doubt to warrant a trial. But they have not said that. We conclude that the suit was properly dismissed, although not on the basis of the statute of limitations.

Affirmed.

PROBLEM 15–4

Biomune is a biotech company which, during the relevant time period, was developing a protein called Immuno–C to be used in enhancing human immune systems. David Derrick was Biomune's President, CEO, Chairman of the Board and main spokesperson.

Plaintiff asserts this "action arises from a fraud of massive proportions," generally consisting of a "scheme to obtain Biomune's listing on NASDAQ, manipulate Biomune's finances and inflate the price of Biomune stock in order to dump thousands of Biomune shares on the market and earn millions of dollars in profits."

With respect to the manipulation of Biomune's capital and surplus, Plaintiff alleges that a "fraud network" consisting of relatives and friends of Derrick effectuated a "cleanup" of Biomune's balance sheet. Plaintiff alleges that several transactions were entered into for the purpose of manipulating Biomune's finances so that Biomune could obtain a NASDAQ listing. Plaintiff further alleges that during 1993 and 1994, Defendants made false and misleading statements regarding the financial stability and commercial success of Biomune.

On October 12, 1995, Plaintiff brought this class action Complaint on behalf of two classes: all persons who purchased Biomune common stock during the period September 15, 1993 through January 12, 1995 ("fraud class").

After Plaintiff filed his Complaint, Defendants moved to dismiss arguing *inter alia*, the suit was barred by the applicable one year statute of limitations. The district court agreed and dismissed the action.

The district court determined that an article published in *Barron's* on August 1, 1994, entitled "A Question of Immunity" put Plaintiff on inquiry notice of his claims. In support of its conclusion, the district court quoted the following passages from the article.

"The story you're about to read is true. And in its broad outlines, alas, ofttold. Not even the names have been changed. Maybe its retelling will protect a few innocents.

Concludes Hatch, who studied under one of Biomune's founders at Brigham Young University in the mid-Seventies, "I don't rule out the one in 100 chance that Biomune actually has something. But if I were betting, I'd say the other 99% is going to rule."

And that's a bet, it turns out, based on considerably more than the scientific evidence. As Hatch knows—and anyone else who cares to take the trouble to research Biomune's corporate history can discover—ever since its December 1981 founding as New Age Corp.—the company's true raison d'etre hasn't been shrimp farming in Ecuador or tomato cultivation in Egypt or immunity enhancers or any of the ventures it's run through. It's been to sell shares as currency to keep any number of its promoters' ventures afloat.

And who are those promoters? The list is long and their connections colorful, but we will list only one. Biomune founder and consultant of long-standing is a Salt Lake City philanthropist, Jack D. Solomon. He owns no Biomune shares, according to the company's SEC filings. But a byzantine array of entities in one way or another affiliated with Solomon own more than 35% of its stock. As it happens, way back when—in 1983—the federal district court in Nevada permanently enjoined Solomon from violations of the registration, antifraud, stock ownership reporting and proxy solicitation provisions of the securities laws. Without admitting or denying the charges, Solomon consented to the filing of that injunction rather than fight SEC charges that, as president and chairman of Advanced Patent Technology Inc., he had illegally sold about 8.7 million shares of unregistered stock in purported private placements between 1975 and late 1980 to raise money for AT's purchase of a Las Vegas slot machine route business and other gaming-related enterprises. Over that span, APT's shares climbed from pennies to just under $10—and they subsequently went back to pennies, before being delisted from NASDAQ.

There's a lesson there somewhere.

(1) Should an article in a financial news magazine put plaintiffs on inquiry notice?

(2) If an article criticizes certain unpublished medical tests of Immuno–C, what dangers would there be in holding that inquiry notice had begun?

(3) If an article criticizes the past practices of promoters, does that supply inquiry notice?

(4) Should it make any difference that Derrick, Biomune's CEO, sent a letter rebutting each point in this article?

INQUIRY NOTICE, LACHES, ESTOPPEL, AND WAIVER BY CONDUCT

As Judge Posner notes in his reference to Dodds v. Cigna Securities, inquiry notice has been around long enough so that there are now "cliches" about investors diligence.[1]

In Howard v. Haddad,[2] decided in 1992, Justice Powell, sitting by designation, stated the concept of "within one year after discovery limitations period thus began running either when [the plaintiff] had notice of these facts or when, exercising reasonable diligence, he would have discovered them."

Today it is a commonplace that the federal securities laws one year statutes of limitations begin to run from constructive or inquiry notice as well as actual notice.[3]

While *Lampf, Pleva, Lipkind, Prupis & Petigrow v. Gilbertson*[4] rejected the extension of the federal securities statutes of limitations by the doctrine of equitable tolling, *Lampf* did not address whether a plaintiff could be barred *before* the expiration of a statutory period if he or she was not reasonably diligent or, worse, if he or she were shown to have earlier acquired knowledge of the fraud before bringing suit. Among other doctrines that might be invoked in addition to inquiry notice are laches,[5] estoppel,[6] and waiver by conduct.[7]

---

1.   Law v. Medco Research, Inc., 113 F.3d at 784.

2.   962 F.2d 328, 330 (4th Cir.1992).

3.   See, e.g., Sterlin v. Biomune Sys., 154 F.3d 1191 (10th Cir.1998); Berry v. Valence Tech., Inc., 175 F.3d 699 (9th Cir.1999), *cert. denied,* 528 U.S. 1019 (1999); Rothman v. Gregor, 220 F.3d 81, 96–98 (2d Cir.2000).

4.   501 U.S. at 363.

5.   "To invoke laches as a defense there must be (1) a lack of diligence by the party against whom the defense is asserted, and (2) prejudice to the party asserting the defense. * * * [w]here these elements are present, the damage to the party asserting the defense is caused by his detrimental reliance on his adversary's conduct." Hecht v. Harris, Upham & Co., 430 F.2d 1202, 1208 (9th Cir. 1970).

6.   Hecht v. Harris, Upham & Co., 430 F.2d 1202, 1208 (9th Cir.1970), also offered a definition of estoppel, quoting Hampton v. Paramount Pictures Corp., 279 F.2d 100, 104 (9th Cir.1960), *cert. denied,* 364 U.S. 882 (1960):

Four elements must be present to establish the defense of estoppel: (1) The party to be estopped must know the facts; (2) he must intend that his conduct shall be acted on or must so act that the party asserting the estoppel has a right to believe it is so intended; (3) the latter must be ignorant of the true facts; and (4) he must rely on the former's conduct to his injury.

7.   It has been held that the defenses of estoppel and waiver by conduct are available to a § 12(a)(1) defendant. Straley v. Universal Uranium & Milling Corp., 289 F.2d 370, 373–374 (9th Cir.1961).

In Davis v. Merrill Lynch, Pierce, Fenner & Smith, Inc., 906 F.2d 1206, 1213–1214 (8th Cir.1990), under the heading, "Ratification, Waiver and Estoppel," the court held (1) that ratification and waiver arguments "bear a heavy burden in the churning context"; (2) that the question is whether the customer's "apparent assent was given voluntarily and

Before *Lampf*, when the federal statute of limitations could be extended to protect a reasonably diligent plaintiff suing on a fraud charge even in an action at law (unless a particular statute provided otherwise), it did not follow that a plaintiff who sought a legal remedy on a federal cause of action within the period specified in the applicable statute of limitations should be barred under any circumstances short of expiration of the statutory period.[8]

After *Lampf*, with statutes of limitations for both express and implied causes of action federalized, the argument against shortening the statute is strengthened. It is one thing for a court of equity to apply the traditional doctrine of laches to an action whose outside limitation period is referred to state law. But we have seen that this is explained by simply not referring to state law beyond the point of necessity. That is to say, when Congress has not bothered to write its own limitation period, there is normally no evidence of a statutory purpose to exclude so basic an equitable doctrine as laches.

But when Congress does prescribe a specific and relatively short statute of limitations for a federal action as it has done in §§ 13 of the 1933 Act and 9(e), 16(b), 18(c), and 29(b) of the 1934 Act—especially when it has rather uniformly provided that the action may be enforced "at law or in equity" as it has done in §§ 12 of the 1933 Act and 9(e), 16(b), and 18(a) of the 1934 Act—there is a strong inference that the prescribed limitation period is not to be cut short, whether in an action sounding in fraud or *a fortiori* in an action under § 12 (a)(1) of the 1933 Act for violation of § 5.

2.   PLAINTIFFS' DUE DILIGENCE

Stephenson v. Paine Webber Jackson & Curtis, Inc.

United States Court of Appeals for the Fifth Circuit, 1988.
839 F.2d 1095, *cert. denied*, 488 U.S. 926 (1988).

■ Before WISDOM, GARWOOD, and JONES, CIRCUIT JUDGES.

■ EDITH H. JONES, CIRCUIT JUDGE:

In May 1984, Monroe Stephenson brought suit against Paine, Webber, Jackson & Curtis, Inc. ("Paine, Webber"), and James Welch ("Welch"), a former Paine Webber broker, for trading securities on his behalf without authorization, which he alleged constituted a violation of the Securities Act of

---

intelligently with full knowledge of the facts," so that the broker is not relieved of liability by the customer's failure to report the unauthorized trading after receiving written confirmations and monthly statements; (3) that the "voluntarily and intelligently" test was not met by an elderly woman customer, unsophisticated with respect to investments, who relied completely on a Merrill Lynch employee's advice; (4) that, in any event, questions of ratification and waiver are factual issues, so that the jury chose to reject the argument about failure to report the unauthorized trading; and (5) that the contention that the nature of the securities industry is such that it should be excused from churning liability when the customer fails to report unauthorized trades must be rejected.

Equitable estoppel is not permissible against the SEC when neither the Commission nor the NASD made any representations to defendants on which they relied. Graham v. SEC, 222 F.3d 994, 1006–1008 (D.C.Cir. 2000).

8. *See, e.g.,* Stevens v. Abbott, Proctor & Paine, 288 F.Supp. 836, 845 (E.D.Va.1968); Norte & Co. v. Krock, 1967–1969 Fed.Sec. L.Rep. (CCH) ¶ 92,295 at 94,410 (S.D.N.Y. 1968).

1933, 15 U.S.C. § 77a, et. seq.; the Securities Exchange Act of 9134, 15 U.S.C. § 78a, *et. seq.,* the Racketeer Influenced and Corrupt Organizations Act ("RICO"); 18 U.S.C. § 1961, *et. seq.*; and state law. The district court dismissed the § 17(a), RICO, and state law claims as a matter of law pursuant to Fed.R.Civ.P. 12(b)(6), and dismissed the 10b–5 claim pursuant to Fed.R.Civ.P. 41(b) after finding that plaintiff had not carried his burden of proof and that the claim was otherwise barred by equitable defenses. * * *

We affirm the district court's judgment.

* * *

I.

BACKGROUND

In 1979, Stephenson, a tax attorney, opened several accounts in New Orleans with Paine Webber and shortly thereafter began trading in options with the assistance of James Sanders, a Paine Webber account executive. When, in early 1982, Sanders left Paine Webber, Stephenson's account was transferred to Welch, another broker in the local Paine Webber office. Stephenson resumed options trading through Welch and continued such trading until late 1983. After each trade in his account, Stephenson received a confirmation slip for the transaction from Paine Webber, and for each month there was activity in his account, he received a monthly account statement which provided detailed information about that activity, including the amount of each trade, the identity of each item traded, whether the trade was in a margin account, and the rate of interest charged on the margin account.

In October 1982, Stephenson was informed by telegram that he owed over $4,000 for a trade made on his behalf by Welch in September. According to Stephenson, that trade was clearly unauthorized, but he challenged only Welch, and not Paine Webber, about it. Welch allegedly promised to correct the error but failed in the following months to do so.

Stephenson ignored his December 1982 monthly statement from Paine Webber, looking only at the interest figure for his tax return. He did nothing at this point to see whether the purportedly improper trade of September 1982 had been corrected. Had he done so, he would have been alerted to what he now asserts were other unauthorized trades. Stephenson was aware in January 1983, however, that he had not received a promised positive interest spread on GNMA margin purchases.

In April 1983, Stephenson was informed by Welch that alleged errors in his account had not been corrected and in June, he received a mailgram confirming a bond purchase that he asserts was not authorized. Again, Stephenson complained only to Welch, and not to Paine Webber, of the "mistake." Nevertheless, Stephenson's account remained active and numerous trades were executed on Stephenson's behalf from May—August 1983, the period during which Stephenson's greatest losses were incurred. Stephenson admitted at trial, however, that he never opened a single confirmation slip or account statement until August of 1983 because, as he testified, he regarded them as "junk mail."

Not until August 24, 1983 did Stephenson issue his first formal written complaint, in the form of a letter hand-delivered to Welch regarding the handling of his account. The letter objected to only eleven (11) transactions, all of which had been made subsequent to June 21, 1983.

On August 31, 1983, Stephenson wrote a second letter similar to the first which was also hand-delivered to Welch. Finally, on September 15, Stephenson wrote a third letter which identified fifty-nine (59) allegedly unauthorized transactions in his account. Each of these transactions had been reported in account statements and in confirmation slips transmitted to Stephenson between August 9, 1982 and August 22, 1983. Paine Webber was not aware of Stephenson's allegations until it received this third letter dated September 15, 1983.

At trial, evidence was introduced to show that Paine Webber had not exercised sufficient supervision over Welch and that had it done so, the unauthorized transactions would have been brought to the attention of Paine Webber at a much earlier date so that further unlawful trading could have been prevented.

The district court concluded that Stephenson had failed to carry his burden of establishing the alleged violations of Rule 10b–5 by a preponderance of the evidence. In so finding, the court determined that in light of Stephenson's extensive financial training and experience, his failure to take corrective action upon learning that his broker had made an error constituted reckless conduct. The court also relied on its observation of Stephenson's testimony as "simply not believable."

The court further held that Stephenson's securities claim was barred by the equitable defenses of laches, waiver, and ratification. Stephenson's disregard of the confirmation slips and monthly statements was found to constitute waiver of his right to sue for the allegedly unauthorized transactions, and it was held that his delay of at least eleven months in complaining of Welch's conduct from October 1982 to September 1983 resulted in prejudice to Paine Webber and Welch so as to invoke the defense of laches.

II.

ANALYSIS

A.   The 10b–5 claim

At the close of appellant's case, the trial court dismissed his 10b–5 claim pursuant to Rule 41(b) of the Federal Rules of Civil Procedure. * * *

In order to demonstrate a violation of Rule 10b–5, the plaintiff must prove (1) a material misrepresentation or omission by the defendant, (2) scienter on the part of the defendant, (3) reliance, and (4) due diligence by the plaintiff to pursue his or her own interest with care and good faith. *Dupuy v. Dupuy*, 551 F.2d 1005, 1014 (5th Cir.1977), *cert. denied*, 434 U.S. 911, 98 S. Ct. 312, 54 L. Ed. 2d 197 (1977). Our analysis in this case focuses on the due diligence element of the claim.

Prior to the Supreme Court's holding in *Ernst and Ernst v. Hochfelder*, 425 U.S. 185, 96 S. Ct. 1375, 47 L. Ed. 2d 668 (1976), *reh'g denied*, 425 U.S. 986, 96 S. Ct. 2194, 48 L. Ed. 2d 811 (1976), many courts adopted a negligence standard in determining whether a plaintiff's duty of due diligence had been met. *See, e.g. Clement A. Evans & Co. v. McAlpine*, 434 F.2d 100, 103 (5th Cir.1970); *City National Bank of Fort Smith Ark. v. Vanderboom*, 422 F.2d 221, 230 (8th Cir.1970), *cert. denied*, 399 U.S. 905, 90 S. Ct. 2196, 26 L. Ed. 2d 560 (1970). In *Ernst*, the Supreme Court held that mere negligence on the part of a defendant cannot satisfy the scienter requirement for liability under 10b–5.

This ruling prompted several circuit courts to reevaluate the appropriateness of a negligence standard in the due diligence context in view of the fact that negligence had been held inadequate to satisfy the defendant's intent requirement. The Fifth Circuit undertook this task in *Dupuy*, 551 F.2d 1005, and held that after *Ernst*, the relevant inquiry in determining due diligence is whether the plaintiff has "intentionally refused to investigate in disregard of a risk known to him or so obvious that he must be taken to have been aware of it, and so great as to make it highly probable that harm would follow." *Dupuy*, 551 F.2d 1005 at 1020 (citing W. Prosser, § 34 at 185 (1971)). This "recklessness" standard has been followed without exception in the Fifth Circuit.

Stephenson principally contends that the Supreme Court's decision in *Bateman Eichler, Hill Richards, Inc. v. Berner*, 472 U.S. 299, 105 S. Ct. 2622, 86 L. Ed. 2d 215 (1985) essentially abolished the due diligence requirement for private 10b–5 actions as well as the equitable defenses of estoppel, waiver, and ratification. Without citing any apposite language from *Bateman Eichler*, appellant asserts that because *Bateman Eichler* narrowed the availability of the *in pari delicto* defense in securities fraud cases brought by tippees, it correlatively expanded the scope of all private 10b–5 causes of action. We disagree.

Bateman Eichler neither discussed the elements of the plaintiff's cause of action under Rule 10b–5 (as it assumed they existed in the case) nor suggested that its principles govern any other equitable defenses than *in pari delicto*. In the absence of support from the holding or even dictum of *Bateman Eichler*, Stephenson must rely solely on analogy to defeat the requirement of a plaintiff's diligence and the possibility of other equitable defenses. His analogy, founded on general references to the deterrent aspects of the federal securities laws, fails.

Although due diligence, equitable defenses and the *in pari delicto* doctrine are arguably related in that they inquire into a plaintiff's conduct, they are applied in decidedly different contexts. The doctrine of due diligence and equitable defenses, like waiver, laches, estoppel or ratification, require an investor to be attentive to *self-protection*, whereas *in pari delicto* applies where the plaintiff has failed in his duty of disclosure to *others*, e.g., where a tippee trades on the basis of inside information without disclosing that information. *Bateman Eichler's* holding results from the concern that insider trading may go largely undiscovered by law enforcement officials if tippees are *altogether precluded by in pari delicto* from bringing suit against tippers. Thus, *Bateman Eichler* specifically limits its holding regarding the inapplicability of the *in pari delicto* defense to situations where preclusion of suit would interfere with the enforcement of the securities laws. *See Bateman Eichler*, 472 U.S. at 310, 105 S. Ct. at 2629, 86 L. Ed. 2d at 224.

The due diligence standard and the equitable defenses, contrary to Stephenson's reasoning, ultimately foster the same law enforcement goal as *Bateman Eichler*, but from a different perspective. We have rightly stated, "by requiring plaintiffs to invest carefully, the Court promotes the anti-fraud policies of the Acts and engenders stability in the markets."*Dupuy*, 551 F.2d at 1014. These standards relating to a plaintiff's conduct encourage an investor to complain promptly about violations of his or her rights and, in so doing, to enable those with authority to control wrongdoing before additional investors are injured. The SEC has from its inception encouraged diligence in stock transactions. *Straub v. Vaisman & Co.*, 540 F.2d 591, 597 (3d Cir.1976); *see also* Wheeler, *Plaintiff's Duty of Due Care under Rule 10b–5: An Implied*

Defense to an Implied Remedy, 70 Nw.U.L.Rev. 561, 564–68 (1976). To elimi-nate diligence-promoting standards in private Rule 10b–5 causes of action by a false analogy with *Bateman Eichler*, would seriously undercut the objectives of the SEC and the securities law. *Bateman Eichler* does not eliminate the existing due diligence requirements nor does it contravene our continued recognition of the equitable defenses in Rule 10b–5 cases.

This case demonstrates the wisdom of retaining the recklessness-due diligence standard for plaintiffs. Although it is not clear that Stephenson challenges the district court's finding of his recklessness, the district court's finding was not clearly erroneous. We agree with the district court that Stephenson's delay in reporting the allegedly unlawful trades and his failure to read Paine Webber correspondence containing accurate and detailed informa-tion about his accounts, even after he became fully aware that those accounts were not being properly handled, rose above mere negligence to the level of recklessness. Stephenson's high level of education, experience, and demonstrat-ed prowess in financial and securities matters are a critical factor in our decision. Stephenson is well-versed in securities transactions. He has traded securities with personal funds for over twenty years, has participated in securities fraud litigation, and has had wide exposure to investment issues in his capacity as a tax attorney. Further, Stephenson had ample opportunity to attempt to rectify the alleged errors in his account. It was uncontroverted at trial that he knew of an "unauthorized" transaction in October 1982, that he knew it had not yet been corrected in April, 1983, and that an interest spread promised for Spring 1983 had not materialized. Throughout the entire period of alleged unauthorized trades, he received statements which he knew would have revealed the status of his accounts. He never read them. This is not a case in which an unsophisticated or trusting investor relied upon a broker's superior expertise or a close friend's accommodation. *Compare Petrites*, 646 F.2d 1033; *Dupuy*, 551 F.2d 1005; *Siebel*, 725 F.2d 995. Stephenson was sufficiently knowledgeable and in control of his affairs to have reviewed his Paine Webber statements, as most people do their monthly bank statements, and discern a pattern of error. These facts, together with the district court's expressed doubt about Stephenson's credibility at trial, are sufficient to support its finding of recklessness. * * *

For the foregoing reasons, the judgment of the district court is AF-FIRMED.

PLAINTIFF'S LACK OF DILIGENCE

The first cousin to the inquiry notice concept that has developed under recent court interpretations of the federal securities laws statutes of limitations is the plaintiffs lack of diligence or the Rule 10b–5 due diligence defense.[1]

Before the Supreme Court rejected negligence as a basis of Rule 10b–5 liability in *Ernst & Ernst* the courts were in the process of developing a defense to an action under Rule 10b–5 based upon the failure of the plaintiff to make any investigation of the facts relating to the corporation to protect himself in the transaction in which he claims that he was defrauded by the defendant. One of the first results of the *Ernst & Ernst* case, initially considered a tremendous victory for defendants, was ironically to curtail sharply the devel-

---

1. *See* Wheeler, Plaintiff's Duty of Due Care under Rule 10b–5: An Implied Defense to an Implied Remedy, 70 Nw. U. L. Rev. 561 (1975).

opment of this defense. In Holdsworth v. Strong,[2] the Tenth Circuit sitting *en banc* held that since the *Ernst & Ernst* case required "scienter" on the part of the defendant, it would be inappropriate any longer to permit a defense based upon lack of diligence by the plaintiff. The court said: "If the negligence standard were being applied it might be appropriate to allow due diligence to be exacted from the victim, but where liability of the defendant requires proof of intentional misconduct, the exaction of a due diligence standard from the plaintiff becomes irrational and unrelated." The court said, however, that reliance is required on the part of the plaintiff, at least in the case of an affirmative misrepresentation, and that "the plaintiff would not be heard to say that he relied on misrepresentations which were obviously false."

The Seventh Circuit in Teamsters Local 282 Pension Trust Fund v. Angelos[3] reached basically the same conclusion. The court stated:

> A violation of Section 17(a)(1) or Rule 10b–5 is an intentional tort, requiring wilful or at least reckless misstatement. Ernst & Ernst v. Hochfelder, 425 U.S. 185 (1976); Aaron v. SEC, 446 U.S. 680 (1980). We therefore concluded in Sundstrand Corp. v. Sun Chemical Corp., 553 F.2d 1033, 1040 (7th Cir.), *cert. denied*, 434 U.S. 875 (1977), that in a case under Rule 10b–5 the defense of the buyer's "failure to exercise due care or diligence * * * is not available in an intentional fraud case." See also Competitive Associates, Inc. v. Laventhol Krekstein, Horwath & Horwath, 516 F.2d 811 (2d Cir.1975); but cf. Dupuy v. Dupuy, 551 F.2d 1005, 1015 (5th Cir.1977), *cert. denied*, 434 U.S. 911 (1977). We drew a line between fraud and negligent nondisclosure: "In a nondisclosure case, reliance is vitiated if the plaintiff is chargeable with the omitted information. * * * But under a reckless or *Hochfelder scienter* standard," "[i]f contributory fault of plaintiff is to cancel out wanton or intentional fraud, it ought to be gross conduct somewhat comparable to that of defendant." Id. at 1048, quoting from Holdsworth v. Strong, 545 F.2d 687, 693 (10th Cir.1976) (en banc). See also Goodman v. Epstein, 582 F.2d 388, 405 & n. 47 (7th Cir.1978), *cert. denied,* 440 U.S. 939 (1979), stating in dictum that in light of *Hochfelder* the victim's want of "due diligence" is no longer a defense in actions under Rule 10b–5.[4]

The *Dupuy* case followed in *Stephenson* takes basically the same position, although the Fifth Circuit does concede that since "reckless conduct" has been established as a basis for liability on the part of the defendant, the plaintiff's recklessness might be a sufficient basis for denying him recovery.[5] On the other hand, in Zobrist v. Coal–X, Inc.[6] the court held that an investor could not claim that he relied upon alleged oral misrepresentations regarding the "riskless" nature of the transaction where the offering circular delivered to him, but which he did not read, clearly spelled out the risks involved in the investment

---

2. 545 F.2d 687 (10th Cir.1976), *cert. denied*, 430 U.S. 955 (1977).

3. 762 F.2d 522 (7th Cir.1985).

4. 762 F.2d at 528–529.

5. See, also, Mallis v. Bankers Trust Co., 615 F.2d 68 (2d Cir.1980), *cert. denied*, 449 U.S. 1123 (1981). In that case the Second Circuit said that the defense of "unclean hands" will only be permitted in a Rule 10b–5 action where the plaintiff's reprehensible conduct is directly related to the subject matter in litigation and the party seeking to invoke the doctrine was injured by the conduct. Also, the plaintiff must have "equal guilt" with the defendant. So far as the due diligence defense is concerned, the court said that "A plaintiff's burden is simply to negate recklessness when the defendant puts that in issue, not to establish due care."

6. 708 F.2d 1511 (10th Cir.1983).

(presumably in the standard "risk factors" section). While not framed in terms of a requirement of "due diligence", this decision in effect says that the plaintiff must at least exercise enough diligence to read the written material furnished to him by the seller, or he will be charged with knowledge of it. The Seventh Circuit in the *Teamsters Local* case specifically stated that it agreed with the result reached in the *Zobrist* case.[7]

The Third Circuit took a somewhat different tack in Straub v. Vaisman and Co.,[8] in which that court refused to abandon entirely the due diligence defense. The court said: "In Rule 10b–5 cases, where the defendant acts intentionally, the line should be drawn between the extremes of making the plaintiff's lack of diligence, regardless of degree, a complete bar or at the other limit—completely irrelevant. * * * The latter option fails to encourage investor caution and, under the former view, Rule 10b–5 would provide less assistance to the trusting or gullible than does the common law. * * * The obligation of due care must be a flexible one, dependent upon the circumstances of each case. We require only that the plaintiff act reasonably. Since the failure to meet that standard is in the nature of an affirmative defense, the burden of proof rests upon the defendant. Such matters as fiduciary relationship, opportunity to detect the fraud, sophistication of the plaintiff, the existence of long-standing business or personal relationships, and access to the relevant information, are all worthy of consideration."

It thus appears that the due diligence defense has been largely eliminated so far as any requirement that the plaintiff investigate the truth of intentional misrepresentations made to him, but it may partially survive in a requirement that the plaintiff must have "justifiably" relied upon the truth of the representation.[9]

To the extent that this defense survives, it should be applied (as it has been in the past) only in the case of face-to-face dealings between the plaintiff and the defendant, often in the stock of corporations which are not publicly traded. It would, obviously, be inappropriate to require a person purchasing or selling stock in the organized market to launch an investigation of the corporation whose stock he is buying or of the truth of public statements made by the persons in control of the corporation.

IN PARI DELICTO

On two occasions the Supreme Court has addressed the common law *in pari delicto* defense.

7. *Accord*: Kennedy v. Josephthal & Co., Inc., 814 F.2d 798 (1st Cir.1987). See also Royal Am. Managers, Inc. v. IRC Holding Corp., 885 F.2d 1011 (2d Cir.1989). On the other hand, the Eleventh Circuit in Bruschi v. Brown, 876 F.2d 1526 (11th Cir.1989), held that an investor's failure to read disclosure documents that conflicted with her broker's oral representations did not preclude her from justifiably relying on the oral statements. The court stated that the fact that some information in the disclosure documents would have indicated that some of the broker's alleged oral misstatements were un-

reliable was only one factor in deciding if the reliance was justified.

If it is affirmatively proven that the plaintiff did not rely on the alleged misrepresentations, then of course plaintiff cannot prevail under Rule 10b–5. Smolen v. Deloitte, Haskins & Sells, 921 F.2d 959 (9th Cir.1990).

8. 540 F.2d 591 (3d Cir.1976).

9. See Thompson v. Smith Barney, Harris Upham & Co., 709 F.2d 1413 (11th Cir.1983).

In a 1985 case, Bateman Eichler, Hill Richards, Inc. v. Berner,[1] the Court was confronted with a Rule 10b–5 case in which a tippee complained that the defendant tippers had falsely stated that they were conveying inside information. Reminding that "pari" means "equal," Justice Brennan stated:

> a private action for damages in these circumstances may be barred on the grounds of the plaintiff's own culpability only where (1) as a direct result of his own actions, the plaintiff bears at least substantially equal responsibility for the violations he seeks to redress, and (2) preclusion of suit would not significantly interfere with the effective enforcement of the securities laws and protection of the investing public.[2]

Significantly Justice Brennan added: "In the context of insider trading, we do not believe that a person [the tippee] whose liability is solely derivative [from the tipper] can be said to be as culpable as one whose breach of duty gave rise to that liability in the first place."[3]

Denying the doctrine in these circumstances "will best promote * * * 'a high standard of business ethics * * * in every facet of the securities industry.' [Citation deleted.] Although a number of lower courts have reasoned that a broad rule of caveat tippee would better serve this goal, we believe the contrary position adopted by other courts represents the better view."[4]

Three years later in Pinter v. Dahl,[5] the Supreme Court held that "the Court of Appeals' notion that the *in pari delicto* defense should not be allowed in actions involving strict liability offenses [§ 12(a)(1)] is without support in history or logic," and that *Bateman Eichler* provides the appropriate test for allowance of the in pari delicto defense in a private action under any of the federal securities laws." Further:[6]

> As the parties and the Commission agree, a purchaser's knowledge that the securities are unregistered cannot, by itself, constitute equal culpability, even where the investor is a sophisticated buyer who may not necessarily need the protection of the Securities Act. Barring the investor's recovery under the *in pari delicto* doctrine, "at least on the basis solely of the buyer's knowledge of the violation, is so foreign to the purpose of the section that there is hardly a trace of it in the decisions under * * * [§ 12(a)(1)]."

> * * * Because the Act is specifically designed to protect investors, even where a plaintiff actively participates in the distribution of unregistered securities, his suit should not be barred where his promotional efforts are incidental to his role as an investor. * * * [T]hus, the *in pari delicto* defense may defeat recovery in a [§ 12(a)(1)] action only where the plaintiff's role in the offering or sale of nonexempted, unregistered securities is more as a promoter than as an investor.

> Whether the plaintiff in a particular case is primarily an investor or primarily a promoter depends upon a host of factors, all readily accessible to trial courts. These factors include the extent of the plaintiff's financial involvement compared to that of third parties solicited by the plaintiff; the incidental nature of the plaintiff's promotional activities; the benefits

1. 472 U.S. 299 (1985).

2. Id. at 310–311.

3. 486 U.S. at 313.

4. Id. at 315.

5. 486 U.S. 622, 632–634 (1988).

6. 486 U.S. at 636–639.

received by the plaintiff from his promotional activities; and the extent of the plaintiff's involvement in the planning stages of the offering (such as whether the plaintiff has arranged an understanding or prepared the offering materials).

PROBLEM 15–5

Clarence and Dudley Milton were raised in poverty in a poor section of New Orleans. They worked as children and as youths and always on a share and share alike basis. By 2001 they had accumulated certain valuable properties held by Les Freres Corporation. The stock and the partnerships were divided equally between Clarence and Dudley. Clarence was the older brother and dominated their personal relationships. Dudley did not finish college, but acquired firsthand knowledge of the construction business and real estate development.

In late 2001, the Miltons organized the Lori Corporation to acquire a valuable long-term lease on land bounded by Toulouse, Burgundy, Rampart, and St. Peter streets in the City of New Orleans. To form the Lori Corporation, each brother contributed $10,000 to the enterprise and received 50 percent of the company's stock.

All went well until March 30, 2002, when Clarence abruptly cut off Dudley's management fee. Clarence always controlled the checkbook. Clarence claimed that Dudley turned his back on the project. At the time, however, Dudley had serious kidney trouble causing increasing medical expenses; and he was supporting his present wife and child and his former wife and children.

After his management was terminated and having no personal contacts with the development of the Lori property, Dudley had to rely on Clarence for information as to what was happening to the financing of the projected hotel. Dudley testified that whenever he spoke to Clarence over the telephone Clarence told him that the Lori Hotel "was having a rough time; everything is going downhill"; that "it's just practically worthless."

Shortly after Clarence cut off Dudley's income, Clarence began negotiations with William Monteleone, owner of a well-known and long-successful French Quarter hotel.

Clarence's negotiations with Monteleone and his representatives were extensive. A letter to the New Monteleone Hotel from Arthur L. Ballin, an attorney who represented Monteleone, shows that instead of "everything going downhill", prospects were favorable. Ultimately Monteleone agreed to put up $600,000 in cash, for which he would receive a 20 percent interest. The Lori Corporation would receive a 40 percent interest, for its lease to the land on which the hotel was to be built. Clarence would receive a 40 percent interest. For two months before Clarence bought Dudley's stock and for one month before the putative directors' meeting approving the partnership with Monteleone, Clarence knew that the Lori stock was worth a small fortune, but not Dudley, although he lived in the same apartment complex with Clarence and they shared a patio.

Indeed, during the time he was negotiating with Ballin and Monteleone Clarence assured Dudley that the development of the hotel had been stalled by a failure to obtain financing. Not knowing of Clarence's bright future for the hotel, never having been informed of the need for a bona fide or non-existent directors' meeting, and hard pressed financially, Dudley sold his stock to Clarence for $10,000 in July 2002.

When Dudley subsequently learned that Clarence had negotiated a deal with Monteleone that might have increased his 50 percent stock interest in Lori

Corporation to over $1 million he brought a Rule 10b–5 lawsuit against Clarence. Clarence has asserted the defense of Dudley's failure of due diligence. How would a court rule on Clarence's defense?

E.   Remedies

1.   RESCISSION

Randall v. Loftsgaarden

Supreme Court of the United States, 1986.
478 U.S. 647, 106 S.Ct. 3143, 92 L.Ed.2d 525.

■ Justice O'Connor delivered the opinion of the Court.

The question presented is whether the recovery available to a defrauded tax shelter investor, entitled under § 12(2) of the Securities Act of 1933 or § 10(b) of the Securities Exchange Act of 1934 to rescind the fraudulent transaction or obtain rescissory damages, must be reduced by any tax benefits the investor has received from the tax shelter investment.

I

In 1973, petitioners purchased interests in Alotel Associates (Associates), a limited partnership organized by respondent B.J. Loftsgaarden to build and operate a motel in Rochester, Minnesota. Loftsgaarden was the president and sole shareholder of respondent Alotel, Inc. (Alotel), which, together with Loftsgaarden, was to be a general partner in the venture.

Loftsgaarden marketed this $3.5 million project as a "tax shelter," which would result in " 'significantly greater returns for persons in relatively high income tax brackets.' " *Austin v. Loftsgaarden,* 675 F.2d 168, 173 (C.A.8 1982) *(Austin I).* As a partnership, Associates would not be taxed as an entity. Rather, its taxable income and losses would pass through to the limited partners, who would then be entitled to claim their individual shares of the partnership's deductible losses to the extent of their adjusted basis in their partnership interests. 26 U.S.C. § 704(d). Especially attractive from the high-income investor's perspective was the fact that "in a real estate investment such as the one contemplated by Loftsgaarden, the limited partner's basis is not restricted to the amount of his actual investment (the amount 'at risk'); rather, it may be increased by the partner's proportional share of any nonrecourse loans made to the partnership." 675 F.2d, at 173. See 26 U.S.C. § 465(c)(3)(D). Consequently, the individual limited partner may be able to claim deductible partnership losses in amounts greatly in excess of the funds invested, and offset those losses against other income.

The initial offering memorandum indicated that Associates would employ financing techniques designed to provide large and immediate tax savings to the limited partners: a nonrecourse loan would finance the bulk of the project, and rapid depreciation methods would be used to throw off large initial losses. Nonetheless, the initial offering was unsuccessful, and Loftsgaarden revised the plan and the offering memorandum to propose that Associates would rent land instead of purchasing it, thereby incurring another deductible expense. Petitioners subscribed to the second offering, investing from $35,000 to $52,500 each. Associates soon began to experience financial difficulties, and in February 1975 Loftsgaarden asked the limited partners to make additional loans to

Associates; they complied, but initiated an investigation into the partnership. Associates eventually defaulted on its obligations, and in 1978 the motel was foreclosed on by its creditors.

Petitioners brought suit in the District Court in 1976, alleging securities fraud and raising federal claims under § 12(2) of the Securities Act of 1933, 48 Stat. 84, as amended, 15 U.S.C. § 77l (2), § 10(b) of the Securities Exchange Act of 1934, 48 Stat. 891, 15 U.S.C. § 78j(b), and SEC Rule 10b–5, 17 CFR 240.10b–5 (1985), as well as pendent state law claims. The jury found that respondents had knowingly made material misrepresentations and omissions in the revised offering memorandum, and that petitioners had reasonably relied on these material misstatements, which caused their damages. Among other misstatements, respondents had mischaracterized the financing available, the terms of the land lease, and the manner and extent of their compensation for services rendered. These findings made respondents liable under § 10(b), Rule 10b–5, and state law. The District Court also accepted the jury's advisory verdict that respondents were liable under § 12(2) for knowingly making material misrepresentations and omissions in the offering memorandum which induced their purchases. App. to Pet. for Cert. E–1.

Finding that petitioners' investments were worthless by the time they discovered the fraud in 1975, the District Court held that the remedy of rescission was proper under § 12(2), which provides that an investor harmed by prospectus fraud may sue "to recover the consideration paid for such security with interest thereon, less the amount of any income received thereon, upon the tender of such security, or for damages if he no longer owns the security." 15 U.S.C. § 77l(2). Rescission was permissible, the court ruled, notwithstanding that petitioners had not made a tender of their securities to respondents until shortly before trial. App. to Pet. for Cert. E–15. Accordingly, the District Court entered judgment for petitioners in the amount of the consideration paid for the limited partnership units, together with prejudgment interest; it also noted that each of the counts found by the jury would independently support respondents' liability, but that "each plaintiff is entitled only to a single recovery." Id., at E–16. The District Court rejected respondents' contention that petitioners' recovery should be offset by tax benefits received, concluding that "[a]bsent [respondents'] fraud, which induced their purchases, [petitioners] would probably have made other investments which produced temporary tax savings, but without the total loss of their investment." Id., at F–9—F–10.

A panel of the Court of Appeals for the Eighth Circuit sustained respondents' liability under § 12(2) and § 10(b), but reversed the rescissory award and remanded for a new trial on that issue. The panel rejected respondents' claim that petitioners were not entitled to rescission under § 12(2) because they had made no tender of their partnership interests until shortly before trial, 675 F.2d, at 179, agreeing with the District Court's "decision to apply what was essentially a rescissory measure of damages in this case." Id., at 181. The panel held, however, that the District Court had erred in refusing to reduce "the damage award" by an amount equal to any tax benefits received by petitioners "on account of the investment." Ibid.

In the panel's view, an "actual damages principle," applicable both to § 12(2) and § 10(b), required that an award of rescission or of rescissory damages be " 'reduced by any value received as a result of the fraudulent transaction.' " Id., at 181 (quoting Garnatz v. Stifel, Nicolaus & Co., 559 F.2d 1357, 1361 (C.A.8 1977), cert. denied, 435 U.S. 951, 98 S.Ct. 1578, 55 L.Ed.2d

801 (1978)). The panel observed that the benefits anticipated from a successful real estate tax shelter typically include tax savings to the limited partner in the early years, followed by income in later years, and reasoned that "unlike a corporate shareholder, . . . even if the enterprise fails to become profitable, the limited partner clearly may have something of value because of the investment's unique tax treatment." 675 F.2d, at 182. In light of "the value of the tax deductions generated by such an investment," the panel held that "the strictly compensatory nature of damages awardable in private securities fraud actions requires that such value be taken into account in determining whether and to what extent damages were inflicted upon plaintiffs." *Id.*, at 183. Finally, the panel rejected petitioners' objection that "because there are tax consequences to any investment one makes, evidence of those consequences will now figure in every securities fraud case," and asserted that its holding was limited to "cases involving investments that are expressly marketed and sold as tax shelters." Ibid.

On remand, the District Court held a bench trial on the issue of tax benefits, and calculated each petitioner's damages as the purchase price of his partnership interest plus simple interest, minus net tax benefits. App. to Pet. for Cert. C–5. Both petitioners and respondents appealed from the District Court's judgment, and, after a second panel ruled on various subsidiary issues, the Court of Appeals reconsidered the case en banc. *Austin v. Loftsgaarden*, 768 F.2d 949 (C.A.8 1985), *(Austin II)*.

Relying in part on the law of the case, and noting that the Second Circuit had reached a similar result in *Salcer v. Envicon Equities Corp.*, 744 F.2d 935 (1984), vacated and remanded, 478 U.S. 1015, 106 S.Ct. 3324, 92 L.Ed.2d 731 (1986), the Court of Appeals adhered to the Austin I panel's holding that an award of rescission or of rescissory damages to a defrauded tax shelter investor should be reduced by any tax benefits actually received. This offset, moreover, was required whether the award stemmed from liability under § 10(b) or § 12(2). 768 F.2d, at 953–954. As to § 10(b), the Court of Appeals relied on § 28(a) of the 1934 Act, which provides that "no person permitted to maintain a suit for damages under the provisions of this chapter shall recover, through satisfaction of judgment in one or more actions, a total amount in excess of his actual damages on account of the act complained of." 15 U.S.C. § 78bb(a). As to § 12(2), the court acknowledged that "the words 'actual damages' do not appear in the 1933 Act," but suggested that the rescission remedy provided by § 12(2) had been, and should be, construed as

> "substantially equivalent to the damages permitted under section 28(a). Cf. *Affiliated Ute Citizens v. United States*, 406 U.S. 128, 155, 92 S.Ct. 1456, 1473, 31 L.Ed.2d 741 (1972). . . . The goal of rescission under section 12(2) is to return the parties to the status quo *ante*, 'and hence a plaintiff can recover no more than his or her "net economic loss," i.e., 'actual damages.' " 768 F.2d, at 954 (quoting *Salcer, supra*, at 940).

Although the Court of Appeals recognized that "tax benefits received" are not "a form of income in a strict accounting sense," 768 F.2d, at 955, it nonetheless concluded, in light of its interpretation of § 28(a) and of the purposes of the rescission remedy, that tax benefits are "income received" within the meaning of § 12(2). 768 F.2d, at 954–955.

The Court of Appeals then proceeded to engage in a detailed analysis of the manner in which petitioners' rescissory damages should be determined. The court ruled that prejudgment interest should not have been based on the total consideration paid by each petitioner, but rather on the amount by which each was " 'out-of-pocket' during each year of the investment." *Id.*, at 958. The court then determined that under its theory the tax consequences flowing from petitioners' recovery of damages, as well as the tax benefits themselves, should be taken into account in determining damages. Accordingly, it doubled the total damages award, including prejudgment interest, to reflect the fact that each petitioner was in the 50% income tax bracket. *Id.*, at 960–961. The combined effect of the *Austin II* court's several rulings was this: under the rescissory approach originally employed by the District Court, petitioners would have been entitled to total recoveries ranging from $64,610 to $96,385, App. to Pet. for Cert. B–1—B–2; under the Court of Appeals' final ruling, petitioners could recover only amounts ranging from $506 to $7,666. 768 F.2d, at 961.

Two judges dissented from the Court of Appeals' adherence to the panel's holding in *Austin I*. In their view, tax benefits could not plausibly be viewed as "income received" within the meaning of § 12(2), and the effect of allowing a tax benefit offset was to provide "a windfall to the defendant—the fraudulent party." 768 F.2d, at 963 (Lay, C.J., dissenting). We granted certiorari because of the question's importance to the administration of the federal tax and securities laws, and because the Courts of Appeals are divided in their treatment of tax benefits for purposes of calculating damages in federal securities fraud litigation. 474 U.S. 978, 106 S.Ct. 379, 88 L.Ed.2d 333 (1985). See *Burgess v. Premier Corp.*, 727 F.2d 826, 838 (C.A.9 1984) (refusing to reduce damages by tax benefits received in an action under § 10(b)). We now reverse.

II

Section 12(2) specifies the conduct that gives rise to liability for prospectus fraud and expressly creates a private right of action in favor of the defrauded investor, who "may sue either at law or in equity in any court of competent jurisdiction, to recover the consideration paid for such security with interest thereon, less the amount of any income received thereon, upon the tender of such security, or for damages if he no longer owns the security." 15 U.S.C. § 77*l* (2). Thus, § 12(2) prescribes the remedy of rescission except where the plaintiff no longer owns the security. See *Wigand v. Flo-Tek, Inc.*, 609 F.2d 1028, 1035 (C.A.2 1979). Even in the latter situation, we may assume that a rescissory measure of damages will be employed; the plaintiff is entitled to a return of the consideration paid, reduced by the amount realized when he sold the security and by any "income received" on the security. See H.R.Rep. No. 85, 73d Cong., 1st Sess., 9 (1933) (under § 12, the buyer can "sue for recovery of his purchase price, or for damages not exceeding such price"); L. Loss, Fundamentals of Securities Regulation 1020 (1983) (hereinafter Loss) ("[W]hen the plaintiff in § 12 no longer owns the security, damages are to be measured so as to result in the substantial equivalent of rescission").

Petitioners contend that § 12(2)'s "income received" language clearly excludes tax benefits received pursuant to a tax shelter investment because tax benefits are not "a form of income in a strict accounting sense," *Austin II*, 768 F.2d, at 955 (footnote omitted), and are not taxed as such. Accordingly, petitioners argue that tax benefits cannot offset a rescissory award under § 12(2).

Here, as in other contexts, the starting point in construing a statute is the language of the statute itself. *E.g.*, *Santa Fe Industries, Inc. v. Green*, 430 U.S. 462, 477, 97 S.Ct. 1292, 1303, 51 L.Ed.2d 480 (1977). Moreover, "if the language of a provision of the securities laws is sufficiently clear in its context and not at odds with the legislative history, it is unnecessary 'to examine the additional considerations of "policy" * * * that may have influenced the lawmakers in their formulation of the statute.' " *Aaron v. SEC*, 446 U.S. 680, 695, 100 S.Ct. 1945, 1955, 64 L.Ed.2d 611 (1980) (quoting *Ernst & Ernst v. Hochfelder*, 425 U.S. 185, 214, n. 33, 96 S.Ct. 1375, 1391, n. 33, 47 L.Ed.2d 668 (1976)). Section 12(2), we think, speaks with the clarity necessary to invoke this "plain language" canon: § 12(2)'s offset for "income received" on the security does not encompass the tax benefits received by defrauded investors by virtue of their ownership of the security, because such benefits cannot, under any reasonable definition, be termed "income."

The tax benefits attributable to ownership of a security initially take the form of tax deductions or tax credits. These have no value in themselves; the economic benefit to the investor—the true "tax benefit"—arises because the investor may offset tax deductions *against* income received from other sources or use tax credits to reduce the taxes otherwise payable on account of such income. Unlike payments in cash or property received by virtue of ownership of a security—such as distributions or dividends on stock, interest on bonds, or a limited partner's distributive share of the partnership's capital gains or profits—the "receipt" of tax deductions or credits is not itself a taxable event, for the investor has received no money or other "income" within the meaning of the Internal Revenue Code. See 26 U.S.C. § 61. Thus, we would require compelling evidence before imputing to Congress an intent to describe the tax benefits an investor derives from tax deductions or credits attributable to ownership of a security as "income received thereon."

This Court's decision in *United Housing Foundation, Inc. v. Forman*, 421 U.S. 837, 95 S.Ct. 2051, 44 L.Ed.2d 621 (1975), lends additional support to our conclusion that the economic value of tax deductions and tax credits in the hands of a particular investor is not "income received" on a security for purposes of § 12(2). In *Forman*, the Court rejected a claim that shares in certain housing projects must be deemed to be "securities" because of "the deductibility for tax purposes of the portion of the monthly rental charge applied to interest on the mortgage," which was said to constitute "an expectation of 'income.' " *Id.*, at 854–855, 95 S.Ct., at 2062. To the contrary, the Court found "no basis in law for the view that the payment of interest, with its consequent deductibility for tax purposes, constitutes income or profits." *Id.*, at 855, 95 S.Ct., at 2062. In this case, we reject the analogous suggestion that the tax deductions petitioners were entitled to take by virtue of their partnership interests "constitut[e] income or profits." *Ibid.*

Respondents have produced no specific evidence from the sparse legislative history of § 12(2) to establish that Congress intended tax benefits to be treated as "income received." Instead, respondents urge that we look to the nature of the equitable remedy of rescission, which they say is exclusively "an effort to restore the *status quo ante*." Brief for Respondents 27. Under this interpretation of rescission, respondents maintain, " 'any person demanding the rescission of a contract to which he is a party must restore or offer to restore to the other party whatever he may have received under the contract in the way of money, property, or other consideration or benefit.' " *Ibid.* (quoting 2 H. Black, Rescission of Contracts and Cancellation of Written Instruments § 617, p. 1417 (1916)). Petitioners' tax benefits, respondents argue, constitute such "consideration or benefit."

Generalities such as these—which come to us unsupported by any instance in which a common law court treated tax benefits as consideration or property that must be returned or offset against the plaintiff's recovery in rescission— fall far short of the showing required to overcome the plain language of § 12(2). Moreover, even at common law, it is quite likely that tax benefits would be ignored for purposes of a rescissory remedy. Under the "direct product" rule, the party seeking rescission was required to credit the party against whom rescission was sought only with gains that were the "direct product" of the property the plaintiff had acquired under the transaction to be rescinded: "The phrase 'direct product' means that which is derived from the ownership or possession of the property without the intervention of an independent transaction by the possessor." Restatement of Restitution § 157, Comment *b* (1937). We agree with amici, the United States and the Securities and Exchange Commission, that tax benefits, because they accrue only if the tax deductions or credits the investment throws off are combined with income generated by the investor or taxes owed on such income, would in all likelihood not have been deemed a "direct product" of the security at common law. See Brief for United States and SEC as *Amici Curiae 13.* Cf. *Cereal Byproducts Co. v. Hall,* 16 Ill.App.2d 79, 147 N.E.2d 383, aff'd, 15 Ill.2d 313, 155 N.E.2d 14 (1958) (refusing to reduce damages for an accountant's negligence in not discovering an embezzlement of plaintiff by the amount of the tax benefits plaintiff received by virtue of the theft). Respondents offer no reason to think that in enacting § 12(2) Congress intended to curtail the investor's recovery by relaxing the limit on offsets imposed by the "direct product" rule.

Respondents' view of the purposes served by § 12(2)'s rescission remedy is likewise flawed. Certainly a restoration of the plaintiff to his position prior to the fraud is one goal that will generally be served by § 12(2), as by common law rescission or restitution. But the 1933 Act is intended to do more than ensure that defrauded investors will be compensated: the Act also "aim[s] * * * to prevent further exploitation of the public by the sale of unsound, fraudulent, and worthless securities through misrepresentation [and] to place adequate and true information before the investor." S.Rep. No. 47, 73d Cong., 1st Sess., 1 (1933). See also *United States v. Naftalin,* 441 U.S. 768, 775–776, 99 S.Ct. 2077, 2082–2083, 60 L.Ed.2d 624 (1979). We may therefore infer that Congress chose a rescissory remedy when it enacted § 12(2) in order to deter prospectus fraud and encourage full disclosure as well as to make investors whole. Indeed, by enabling the victims of prospectus fraud to demand rescission upon tender of the security, Congress shifted the risk of an intervening decline in the value of the security to defendants, whether or not that decline was actually caused by the fraud. See Thompson, The Measure of Recovery under Rule 10b–5: A Restitution Alternative to Tort Damages, 37 Vand.L.Rev. 349, 369 (1984) (hereinafter Thompson); Loss, at 1133. Thus, rescission adds an additional measure of deterrence as compared to a purely compensatory measure of damages.

We also reject, as did the Court of Appeals, 768 F.2d, at 958, respondents' alternative contention that tax benefits constitute "a return of, or a reduction in, 'consideration.'" Brief for Respondents 29–30. There is no indication that Congress intended the word "consideration" in § 12(2) to mean anything other than what the context would suggest—the money or property given by the investor in exchange for the security. And, in view of the express offset for "income received," we think any implicit offset for a return of consideration must be confined to the clear case in which such money or property is returned to the investor. Here, the consideration given by petitioners in exchange for their partnership interests took the form of money, not tax deductions, and the fact that petitioners received tax deductions from which they were able to derive tax benefits therefore cannot constitute a return of that consideration. Accordingly, we hold that § 12(2) does not authorize an offset of tax benefits received by a defrauded investor against the investor's rescissory recovery, either as "income received" or as a return of "consideration," and that this is so whether or not the security in question is classified as a tax shelter.

III

We now consider whether § 28(a) should alter our conclusion that § 12(2) does not authorize a reduction in the plaintiff's recovery in the amount of tax benefits received, and whether § 28(a) requires such an offset when a rescissory measure of damages is applied to a plaintiff's § 10(b) claim. Respondents suggest that § 12(2) and § 28(a) should be construed *in pari materia*, arguing that the Court of Appeals correctly determined that § 28(a) stands for a broad principle that recovery under the federal securities laws is strictly limited to the defrauded investor's "actual damages," and hence that anything of economic value received by the victim of fraud as a result of the investment must be used to reduce the victim's recovery. This principle, they say, requires us to construe § 12(2)'s express offset for "income received" on the security as encompassing any tax benefits received by petitioners.

The Court of Appeals relied on *Globus v. Law Research Service, Inc.*, 418 F.2d 1276 (C.A.2 1969), cert. denied, 397 U.S. 913, 90 S.Ct. 913, 25 L.Ed.2d 93 (1970), which read § 17(a) of the 1933 Act in pari materia with § 28(a) insofar as the latter provision is deemed to bar punitive damages. See 768 F.2d, at 954. Assuming, arguendo, that *Globus* was correctly decided, it is clearly distinguishable, for any private right of action under § 17(a) would be an implied one, and § 17(a) makes no reference to damages, whether punitive or compensatory. See 418 F.2d, at 1283–1284. By contrast, Congress addressed the matter of prospectus fraud with considerable specificity in § 12(2), which not only antedates § 28(a), but was also left untouched by Congress when it passed the 1934 Act. See Loss, at 1024. We therefore decline to read § 28(a) as mandating a limit on the rescission remedy created by Congress in the 1933 Act by enactment of § 12(2). To hold otherwise would be to effect a partial repeal of § 12(2) by implication, and " '[i]t is, of course, a cardinal principle of statutory construction that repeals by implication are not favored.' " *Radzanower v. Touche Ross & Co.*, 426 U.S. 148, 154, 96 S.Ct. 1989, 1993, 48 L.Ed.2d 540 (1976) (quoting *United States v. United Continental Tuna Corp.*), 425 U.S. 164, 168, 96 S.Ct. 1319, 1322–1323, 47 L.Ed.2d 653 (1976). There is no "irreconcilable conflict" here between the two Acts, nor is this a case in which " 'the later act covers the whole situation of the earlier one and is clearly intended as a substitute.' " 426 U.S., at 154, 96 S.Ct., at 1993, quoting *Posadas v. National City Bank*, 296 U.S. 497, 503, 56 S.Ct. 349, 352, 80 L.Ed. 351 (1936). Cf. *Herman & MacLean v. Huddleston*, 459 U.S. 375, 384, 103 S.Ct. 683, 688, 74 L.Ed.2d 548 (1983) (adopting a "cumulative construction of the remedies under the 1933 and 1934 Acts").

The issue whether and under what circumstances rescission or a rescissory measure of damages is available under § 10(b) is an unsettled one. In *Affiliated Ute Citizens v. United States*, 406 U.S. 128, 155, 92 S.Ct. 1456, 1473, 31 L.Ed.2d 741 (1972), which involved violations of § 10(b) and Rule 10b–5 by a buyer of securities, this Court held that ordinarily "the correct measure of damages under § 28 of the Act, 15 U.S.C. § 78bb(a), is the difference between the fair value of all that the [plaintiff] received and the fair value of what he would have received had there been no fraudulent conduct." Courts have also generally applied this "out-of-pocket" measure of damages in § 10(b) cases involving fraud by a seller of securities, see, *e.g., Harris v. American Investment Co.*, 523 F.2d 220, 225 (C.A.8 1975), cert. denied, 423 U.S. 1054, 96 S.Ct. 784, 46 L.Ed.2d 643 (1976); Thompson, at 365. But there is authority for allowing the § 10(b) plaintiff, at least in some circumstances, to choose between "undoing the bargain (when events since the transaction have not made rescission impossible) or holding the defendant to the bargain by requiring him to pay [out-of-pocket] damages." Loss, at 1133. See, *e.g., Blackie v. Barrack*, 524 F.2d 891, 909 (C.A.9 1975) ("While out of pocket loss is the ordinary standard in a 10b–5 suit, it is within the discretion of the district judge in appropriate circumstances to apply a rescissory measure"), cert. denied, 429 U.S. 816, 97 S.Ct. 57, 50 L.Ed.2d 75 (1976).

Respondents do not dispute that rescission or a rescissory measure of damages may sometimes be appropriate under § 10(b), nor do they dispute that in this case a rescissory recovery is appropriate on petitioners' § 10(b) claims as well as on their § 12(2) claims. Instead, they contend that § 28(a) strictly limits any such rescissory recovery to the plaintiff's net economic harm. We shall therefore assume, arguendo, that a rescissory recovery may sometimes be proper on a § 10(b) claim, and that this is such a case.

In enacting § 28(a), Congress did not specify what was meant by "actual damages." It is appropriate, therefore, to look to "the state of the law at the time the legislation was enacted" for guidance in defining the scope of this limitation. *Merrill Lynch, Pierce, Fenner & Smith v. Curran*, 456 U.S. 353, 378, 102 S.Ct. 1825, 1839, 72 L.Ed.2d 182 (1982). When § 28(a) was enacted § 12(2) stood as a conspicuous example of a rescissory remedy, and we have found that Congress did not intend that a recovery in rescission under § 12(2) be reduced by tax benefits received. Accordingly, we think § 28(a) should not be read to compel a different result where rescissory damages are obtained under § 10(b).

Even apart from the analogy furnished by § 12(2), this Court has never interpreted § 28(a) as imposing a rigid requirement that every recovery on an express or implied right of action under the 1934 Act must be limited to the net economic harm suffered by the plaintiff. To be sure, this Court has noted that "Section 28(a) of the 1934 Act * * * limits recovery in any private damages action brought under the 1934 Act to 'actual damages,'" *Blue Chip Stamps v. Manor Drug Stores*, 421 U.S. 723, 734, 95 S.Ct. 1917, 1925, 44 L.Ed.2d 539 (1975), and *Affiliated Ute Citizens* clearly interpreted § 28(a) as governing the measures of damages that are permissible under § 10(b). 406 U.S., at 155, 92 S.Ct., at 1473. But the Court in *Affiliated Ute Citizens* also indicated that "where the defendant received more than the seller's actual loss * * * damages are the amount of the defendant's profit." Ibid. This alternative standard aims at preventing the unjust enrichment of a fraudulent buyer, and it clearly does more than simply make the plaintiff whole for the economic loss proximately caused by the buyer's fraud. Indeed, the accepted rationale underlying this alternative is simply that "[i]t is more appropriate to give the defrauded party the benefit even of windfalls than to let the fraudulent party keep them." *Janigan v. Taylor*, 344 F.2d 781, 786 (CA1), cert. denied, 382 U.S. 879, 86 S.Ct. 163, 15 L.Ed.2d 120 (1965). See also *Falk v. Hoffman*, 233 N.Y. 199, 135 N.E. 243 (1922) (Cardozo, J.). Thus, the mere fact that the receipt of tax benefits, plus a full recovery under a rescissory measure of damages, may place a § 10(b) plaintiff in a better position than he would have been in absent the fraud, does not establish that the flexible limits of § 28(a) have been exceeded.

In any case, respondents' contention that plaintiffs will receive undeserved "windfalls" absent an offset for tax benefits is greatly overstated. Even if tax benefits could properly be characterized as a windfall—which we doubt—the tax laws will serve to reduce, although not necessarily to eliminate, the extent of plaintiffs' net economic gain as compared to the status quo ante. We are told that the "tax benefit rule" will apply in cases of rescission, thus making the recovery taxable as ordinary income. See *Hillsboro National Bank v. Commissioner*, 460 U.S. 370, 103 S.Ct. 1134, 75 L.Ed.2d 130 (1983); Brief for United States and SEC as *Amici Curiae* 25. Any residual gains to plaintiffs thus emerge more as a function of the operation of the Internal Revenue Code's complex provisions than of an unduly generous damages standard for defrauded investors.

Respondents also overlook the fact that Congress' aim in enacting the 1934 Act was not confined solely to compensating defrauded investors. Congress intended to deter fraud and manipulative practices in the securities markets, and to ensure full disclosure of information material to investment decisions. *Affiliated Ute Citizens, supra*, 406 U.S., at 151, 92 S.Ct., at 1471; see also *Herman & MacLean*, 459 U.S., at 386–387, 103 S.Ct., at 1144–1145. This deterrent purpose is ill served by a too rigid insistence on limiting plaintiffs to recovery of their "net economic loss." Salcer, 744 F.2d, at 940. The effect of allowing a tax benefit offset would often be substantially to insulate those who commit securities frauds from any appreciable liability to defrauded investors. The resulting diminution in the incentives for tax shelter promoters to comply with the federal securities laws would seriously impair the deterrent value of private rights of action, which, we have emphasized, "provide 'a most effective weapon in the enforcement' of the securities laws and are a 'necessary supplement to Commission action.'" *Bateman Eichler, Hill Richards, Inc. v. Berner*, 472 U.S. 299, 310, 105 S.Ct. 2622, 2628, 86 L.Ed.2d 215 (1985) (quoting *J.I. Case Co. v. Borak*, 377 U.S. 426, 432, 84 S.Ct. 1555, 1560, 12 L.Ed.2d 423 (1964)).

The Court of Appeals' elaborate method for calculating damages and interest so as to offset tax benefits supplies an additional reason for rejecting its tax benefit offset rule. We need not inquire whether evidence concerning tax benefits is ordinarily so speculative as to be beyond the jury's province. Cf. *Norfolk & Western Ry. Co. v. Liepelt*, 444 U.S. 490, 100 S.Ct. 755, 62 L.Ed.2d 689 (1980). It is enough that there are formidable difficulties in predicting the ultimate treatment of the investor's claimed tax benefits, whether or not an audit has commenced, and that the burdens associated with reconstruction of the investor's tax history for purposes of calculating interest are substantial. We think that § 28(a) cannot fairly be read to require such a full-scale inquiry into a defrauded investor's dealings with the tax collector lest the investor escape with anything more than his "net economic loss."

Respondents' sole remaining contention is that a rule requiring the offset of tax benefits is required in view of "the economic reality of tax benefits produced by tax shelters." Brief for Respondents 14. They maintain that since "tax benefits to the partner represent an important tangible economic advantage expected to be derived from his investment," *Salcer, supra*, at 940, Congress must have intended that tax benefits would reduce the plaintiff's allowable recovery under § 28(a). In support of their version of "economic reality," respondents note that the return from a tax shelter investment may be analyzed as consisting of cash flow, tax benefits, and equity value, Brief for Respondents 11, and that some courts have held that investors may sue for fraud where a tax shelter investment has not produced promised tax benefits. See *Sharp v. Coopers & Lybrand*, 649 F.2d 175 (C.A.3 1981), cert. denied, 455 U.S. 938, 102 S.Ct. 1427, 71 L.Ed.2d 648 (1982).

We have already established that Congress did not design § 12(2) to accommodate these arguments, and that § 28(a) does not place them on a surer footing. Respondents essentially ask us to treat tax benefits as a separate asset that is acquired when a limited partner purchases a share in a tax shelter partnership. But the legal form of the transaction does not reflect this treatment. Petitioners purchased securities, thereby acquiring freely alienable rights to any income that accrued to them by virtue of their ownership. They did not, however, also acquire a separate, freely transferable bundle of tax losses that would have value apart from petitioners' status as partners. For obvious reasons, tax deductions and tax credits are not, in the absence of a statutory provision to the contrary, freely transferable from one person to another if wholly severed from the property or activity to which they relate: "[t]he statutes pertaining to the determination of taxable income * * * disclos[e] a general purpose to confine allowable losses to the taxpayer sustaining them, *i.e.*, to treat them as personal to him and not transferable to or usable by another." *New Colonial Ice Co. v. Helvering*, 292 U.S. 435, 440, 54 S.Ct. 788, 790, 78 L.Ed. 1348 (1934). Accordingly, we decline to treat these tax losses as so much property created by the promoters of the partnership. It is for Congress, not this Court, to decide whether the federal securities laws should be modified to comport with respondents' version of economic reality.

We acknowledge that, absent an offset for tax benefits, plaintiffs may have an incentive to wait to raise their § 12(2) claims until they have received the bulk of the tax benefits available from a tax shelter, since after their securities are tendered they will cease to receive tax benefits. We are not persuaded, however, that courts lack adequate means to deal with any potential for abuse on this score. In cases under § 10(b), some courts have barred plaintiffs from electing rescission, or a rescissory measure of damages, where they delayed tender or suit in order to increase their expected recovery should the market decline. See, *e.g., Baumel v. Rosen*, 412 F.2d 571, 574–575 (C.A.4 1969), cert. denied, 396 U.S. 1037, 90 S.Ct. 681, 24 L.Ed.2d 681 (1970); Loss, at 1133, n. 127; Thompson, at 369–370. A similar rule may well be appropriate where plaintiffs delay tender or suit in order to obtain additional tax benefits, although we need not so decide today.

We also have no occasion in this case to decide whether, assuming that a rescissory recovery may sometimes be proper under § 10(b), plaintiffs in such cases should invariably be free to elect a rescissory measure of damages rather than out-of-pocket damages. Consequently, we do not consider whether courts may ever refuse to allow a rescissory recovery under § 10(b) where the "premium" for expected tax benefits represented a large portion of the purchase price, in which event the out-of-pocket measure might yield a significantly smaller recovery. See *Salcer*, 744 F.2d, at 940, and n. 5. In this case, a rescissory measure of damages was determined to be proper, and respondents have abandoned their initial challenge to that ruling.

We conclude, then, that the Court of Appeals erred in holding that § 28(a) requires a rescissory recovery under § 12(2) or § 10(b) to be reduced by tax benefits received from a tax shelter investment. The judgment is reversed, and the case is remanded for further proceedings consistent with this opinion.

It is so ordered.

RESCISSION AND RESCISSORY DAMAGES

Section 12 of the 1933 Act expressly provides for a remedy of rescission, which is indeed the only remedy available to the plaintiff if he or she still owns the security. That Section provides that the plaintiff may sue "to recover the consideration paid for such security with interest thereon, less the amount of any income received thereon, upon the tender of such security," and that he or she may, in the alternative, sue for damages only "if he no longer owns the security." On the other hand, § 11 of the 1933 Act expressly provides only for the recovery of damages by the plaintiff. Although § 11(e) says that the suit authorized under that Section "may be" to recover damages as specified in that subsection, the cases have not suggested that the plaintiff has any alternative to the recovery of the damages.

The law relating to the remedies which can be obtained by a plaintiff who establishes a cause of action under Rule 10b–5 or Rule 14a–9 or § 14(e) is less settled. As the Supreme Court majority wrote in *Loftsgaarden*, it was only willing to conclude "that rescission or a rescissory measure of damages may sometimes be appropriate under § 10(b)" * * *[1] The Court did not resolve when or whether the right to rescission could be lost by a plaintiff because of laches, estoppel, or waiver by conduct. Moreover, rescission may not be available because of events which have transpired after the original transaction. For example, if the defendant purchased securities in a transaction which violated Rule 10b–5 and has subsequently disposed of them before the institution of an action by the plaintiff, rescission is no longer possible as a practical matter.[2]

When rescission is unavailable as a practical matter, rescissory damages may be awarded that provide the equivalent to rescission. Rescissory damages measure the difference between the plaintiff's purchase price and the plaintiff's resale price, plus interest, and less any dividends or other corporate distributions (with interest) that the plaintiff received.[3] Several courts have awarded rescissory damages (although these damages are sometimes labeled "rescissionary" or "restitution" damages).[4] A few courts have taken the position in Rule 10b–5 litigation that certain cases are inappropriate for rescission or rescissory

---

1.   478 U.S. at 661.

2.   *See* Gottlieb v. Sandia Am. Corp., 304 F.Supp. 980 (E.D.Pa.1969), *aff'd*, 452 F.2d 510 (3d Cir.1971), *cert. denied*, 404 U.S. 938 (1971) where the defendant corporation had spun-off the securities acquired from the plaintiff to its shareholders before the suit.

In Gordon v. Burr, 506 F.2d 1080 (2d Cir.1974), the court held that a plaintiff purchaser of shares was entitled to the remedy of rescission against a defendant not in privity with him, that is, a salesperson selling on behalf of a principal. However, a defrauded *seller* obviously could not actually obtain re-

scission against such a defendant, since the defendant doesn't have the stock to give back, although it is possible that a court might apply a rescissory measure of damages.

3.   *See generally* Thompson, The Measure of Recovery under Rule 10b–5: A Restitution Alternative to Tort Damages, 37 Vand. L. Rev. 349 (1984).

4.   *See e.g.,* Myzel v. Fields, 386 F.2d 718, 740–741 (8th Cir.1967), *cert. denied*, 390 U.S. 951 (1968); Rolf v. Blyth Eastman Dillon & Co., Inc., 570 F.2d 38, 49 (2d Cir.1978), *cert. denied*, 439 U.S. 1039 (1978); Robertson v. White, 81 F.3d 752 (8th Cir.1996).

damages.[5] As a general proposition a plaintiff who seeks rescissory damages must act promptly.[6] Whether or not rescission, rescissory or some other measure of damages will be awarded is today within the court's discretion. Unlike Rule 10b–5, under § 12(a)(2) a plaintiff would appear to have a right to rescissory damages, but after 1995, § 12(b) requires a loss causation modification to traditional rescissory damages.[7]

The holding in *Loftsgaarden* that offsetting tax benefits may not reduce a rescissory damages recovery under § 12(a)(2) has been followed generally under Rule 10b–5 damages calculations.[8]

2. DAMAGES

Section 10(b) and Rule 10b–5 specify no damages or rescission standards, prompting the courts to take an ad hoc approach that often uses the common law out of pocket measure as an initial reference point and allows appellate courts to exercise "the discretion traditionally left to the trial courts in finding damages appropriate to the facts of the case."[1]

The out-of-pocket measure of damages may be expected to yield the difference between the value of the security (not necessarily market value at the time of the defendant's purchase but presumably value at that time as judged in the light of the issuer's subsequent history) and the price paid by the plaintiff for it (or the value of anything that the defendant may have given in exchange). Often this measure is calculated in securities cases by comparing the price the plaintiff paid with the market value after corrective disclosure.[2]

5. *See, e.g.,* Huddleston v. Herman & MacLean, 640 F.2d 534, 555 (5th Cir.1981), *modified on other grounds,* 650 F.2d 815 (5th Cir.1981), *aff'd in part & rev'd in part on other grounds,* 459 U.S. 375 (1983). "A bank, unless it is acting as a broker or in a situation closely analogous to that of a broker, is not within the category of parties against whom rescissional damages may be awarded." Letterman Bros. Energy Sec. Litig., 799 F.2d 967, 972 (5th Cir.1986), *cert. denied sub nom.* Letterman Bros. Energy Program 1980–2 v. BancTexas Dallas, N.A., 480 U.S. 918 (1987). See also Ambassador Hotel Co., Ltd. v. Wei–Chuan Inv., 189 F.3d 1017, 1030–1031 (9th Cir.1999), where the court was unwilling to allow rescission without return of the stock, but did permit rescissory damages.

6. Feldman v. Pioneer Petroleum, Inc., 813 F.2d 296, 301–302 n. 10 (10th Cir.1987), *cert. denied,* 484 U.S. 954 (1987).

7. Rowe v. Maremont Corp., 850 F.2d 1226, 1240–1241 (7th Cir.1988).

8. *See, e.g.,* Volk v. D.A. Davidson & Co., 816 F.2d 1406, 1414 (9th Cir.1987); but *see* Medcom Holding Co. v. Baxter Travenol Lab, Inc., 106 F.3d 1388 (7th Cir.1997).

1. 2 American L. Inst., Federal Securities Code 789 (1990).

2. *See, e.g.,* Harris v. American Inv. Co., 523 F.2d 220, 226–228 (8th Cir.1975), *cert. denied,* 423 U.S. 1054 (1976).

Section 11(e) of the Securities Act of 1933 provides a modified out of pocket measure of damages. Generally purchase price less value at the time of *suit* rather than at *delivery.* Section 11(g) limits the amount that may be recovered to the price at which the security was offered to the public; this primarily limits the plaintiff who purchased in the open market rather than in the course of the distribution. When the security has been disposed of in the open market before suit, the measure of damages is purchase price less resale price (with no mention of interest or of deducting income damages as in § 12). If the market goes up pending suit and the security is disposed of before judgment, the defendant gets the benefit of the increase over the value at the time of suit; but if the market goes *down* and the security is disposed of *pending suit* the plaintiff still gets only the difference between the purchase price and the value at the time of suit. In other words it is to the plaintiff's advantage not to hold the security after filing suit if he or she wants to be sure of being made whole.

One court explained a measure of damages after corrective disclosure by observing: "When markets are liquid and respond quickly to news, the drop when the truth appears is a good measure of the value of the information, making it the appropriate measure of damages."[3]

In Akerman v. Oryx Communications, Inc.,[4] a registered issue was brought out on June 30, 1981 at a price of $4.75 per unit (consisting of one share of common stock and a warrant to purchase an additional share). The prospectus contained an erroneous *pro forma* unaudited financial statement for an interim period of eight months (although this misstatement was innocently included). The corporation disclosed this misstatement to the SEC on October 13, 1981, at which time the unit price had declined to $4.00 and the misstatement was disclosed to the public on November 9, 1981, by which time there had been a further decline in price to $3.25 This § 11 action was filed on November 25, 1981, and the price after the public disclosure had *risen* to $3.50 by that date. The court held that the defendants had established "negative causation" under § 11 because the entire decline in price occurred before the public disclosure of the misstatement in the prospectus and the price only rose after that disclosure before the filing of the action.

In addition when damages are calculated after corrective measure, the defendants should be given the opportunity to show that part or all of the securities price movement was caused by factors other than the alleged fraud and market movements.[5]

These are the general principles, typically applicable to corporate misrepresentation or omission cases. The law of federal securities law damages is one dominated today by exceptions. Consider the special rules that are discussed in the following three cases for claims involving churning, a two tier tender offer, and insider trading.

Miley v. Oppenheimer & Co., Inc.

United States Court of Appeals, Fifth Circuit, 1981.
637 F.2d 318.

■ Before GOLDBERG, POLITZ and SAM D. JOHNSON, CIRCUIT JUDGE.

■ GOLDBERG, CIRCUIT JUDGE:

* * * The jury in this case concluded that defendant Oppenheimer had churned plaintiff Miley's account in violation of both the federal securities law and the Texas common law fiduciary duty of investment brokers. Although Oppenheimer strongly protests the jury's finding of liability in this case, we feel that there is sufficient evidence in the record to support finding each of the three requisite elements of a federal securities law churning violation and to support a finding that Oppenheimer breached its Texas common law fiduciary duty.

---

3. Goldberg v. Household Bank, F.S.B., 890 F.2d 965, 966–967 (7th Cir.1989). *See also* Steinberg v. Chem–Tronics, Inc., 786 F.2d 1429 (9th Cir.1986); Pidcock v. Sunnyland Am., Inc., 854 F.2d 443, 447–448 (11th Cir.1988); Home Theater Sec. Litig., 1997 Fed.Sec.L.Rep. (CCH) ¶ 99,576 (C.D.Cal. 1997).

4. 810 F.2d 336 (2d Cir.1987).

5. See Gerstle v. Gamble–Skogmo, Inc., 478 F.2d 1281, 1306 (2d Cir.1973), where Judge Friendly noted that "[t]he passage of time introduces so many elements * * * that extreme prolongation of the period for calculating damages may be grossly unfair."

In addition to contesting the sufficiency of the evidence supporting the finding of liability, defendant Oppenheimer has raised several difficult questions of law concerning the compensatory and punitive damages award, the charge to the jury, and the refusal to order arbitration of the pendent state claims in this case. It is to these challenges that we now turn.

II. *Compensatory Damages: Crying Over Spilt Milk*

In instructing the jury on the elements of the actual damages in this case and by awarding over $54,000 in such damages, Judge Mahon allowed Miley to recover for both the commission and interest paid as a result of the excessive trading and for the decline in the value of her portfolio in excess of the average decline in the stock market during the time in which Oppenheimer handled her account. Oppenheimer argues that allowing recovery for both excess commissions and excess portfolio decline constitutes double recovery and sets an improper floor on damages for breach of fiduciary duty.

Once the gravamen of the churning complaint is clearly identified, the argument that awarding both excess commissions and excess portfolio decline constitutes double recovery appears to be without merit. The willful misconduct at the core of a churning complaint is the broker's excessive trading of an account in an effort to amass commissions. While excessive commissions represent the sole source of gain to the broker from his misconduct, there are in fact two distinct harms which may be proximately caused by the broker's churning of an account. It is necessary to remedy both harms in order to fully compensate the victimized investor.

First, and perhaps foremost, the investor is harmed by having had to pay the excessive commissions to the broker the "skimmed milk" of the churning violation. The broker's wrongful collection of commissions generated by the intentional, excessive trading of the account constitutes a compensable violation of both the federal securities laws and the broker's common law fiduciary duty, regardless of whether the investor's portfolio increased or decreased in value as a result of such trading. Second, the investor is harmed by the decline in the value of his portfolio, the "spilt milk" of the churning violation, as a result of the broker's having intentionally and deceptively concluded transactions, aimed at generating fees, which were unsuitable for the investor. The intentional and deceptive mismanagement of a client's account, resulting in a decline in the value of that portfolio, constitutes a compensable violation of both the federal securities laws and the broker's common law fiduciary duty, regardless of the amount of the commissions paid to the broker. In sum, once a jury finds that the broker has churned an investor's account, it may also find that the investor would have paid less commissions and that his portfolio would have had a greater value had the broker not committed the churning violation.[7] See Nichols, *The Broker's Duty to His Customer Under Federal Fiduciary and Suitability Standards*, 26 Buff.L.Rev. 435, 445 (1977) ("Where there is excessive trading in an account ('churning'), the customer can be damaged in many ways. He must pay the brokerage commissions on both purchases and sales, he may miss dividends, incur unnecessary capital gain or ordinary income taxes depending on the holding period, and, most difficult to measure, he may lose the benefits that a well-managed portfolio in long-term holdings might have

---

7. These two distinct and compensable harms were clearly alleged in Miley's complaint, and there could be little doubt based on the evidence presented at trial that she was seeking redress for both forms of loss.

brought him.''); Brodsky, *Measuring Damages in Churning and Suitability Cases,* 6 Sec.Reg. Law J. 157, 159–160 (1978) (''Most often, the customer complains that the broker churned unsuitable securities. Then, both causes of action are appropriate and both damage theories (excess commissions and excess decline in portfolio value) should be considered.'')

Defendant Oppenheimer fails to cite a single case in which a court refused to award both excess commissions and excess decline in portfolio value on the ground that such recovery would constitute double compensation. In fact, those courts and authorities which have considered the issue have concluded that, in an attempt to excessively trade an account so as to generate commissions, a broker may enter into unsuitable transactions, thereby simultaneously damaging the value of the portfolio. *E.g., Mihara v. Dean Witter & Co., supra,* 619 F.2d at 826 (affirming a damage award as properly compensating for both commissions earned through the excessive trading and trading losses resulting from the unsuitable transactions entered into as the result of such trading); *Hecht v. Harris, Upham & Co., supra,* 430 F.2d at 1211 (finding actual damages from churning to be both excess commissions and trading losses, but refusing to grant recovery for trading losses due to waiver and estoppel); *Carras v. Burns, supra,* 516 F.2d at 259; Note, *Churning By Securities Dealers,* 80 Harv.L.Rev. 869, 883–87 (1967); Nichols, *supra* at 445; Brodsky, *supra* at 159–160.

Although not briefed by defendant Oppenheimer, it appears that the real problem with compensating the victimized investor for the decline in the value of his portfolio (as well as for the excess commissions) is not the fear of double recovery, but rather, the difficulty in accurately measuring the loss in portfolio value proximately caused by the excessive trading and unsuitable transactions. The task of fully compensating the investor without being unduly speculative at the expense of the broker has never been undertaken by this court, and has plagued and divided other courts which have faced the problem. *See McNeal v. Paine, Webber, Jackson & Curtis, Inc., supra,* 598 F.2d at 894 n. 14 (5th Cir. 1979). It is and has been clear that, in theory, the plaintiff is entitled to recover the difference between what he would have had if the account has been handled legitimately and what he in fact had at the time the violation ended with the transfer of the account to a new broker. However, the nature of the churning offense as well as the inherent uncertainties of the operation of the stock market make exact implementation of this elementary legal theory impossible.

Churning is a unified offense: there is no single transaction, or limited, identifiable group of trades, which can be said to constitute churning. Rather, a finding of churning, by the very nature of the offense, can only be based on a hindsight analysis of the entire history of a broker's management of an account and of his pattern of trading that portfolio, in comparison to the needs and desires of an investor. A corollary of the principle that churning is a unified offense of the notion that no set group of transactions can be specifically identified as ''but for'' causes of churning is that there are many ''legitimate'' ways of handling any given account. Each of the countless legitimate ways to manage every account would yield a different portfolio value. Thus, it is impossible to compute the exact amount of trading losses caused by the churning of an account.

However, neither the difficulty of the task nor the guarantee of imprecision in results can be a basis for judicial abdication from the responsibility to set fair and reasonable damages in a case. It is clear that awarding full ''out of pocket'' recovery i. e. the difference between the original and final values of Miley's portfolio would be to assume, in effect, that none of Oppenheimer's transactions were legitimate, and to disregard the ordinary hazards of the stock market. *See* Note, *Churning By Securities Dealers,* 80 Harv.L.Rev. 869, 884 (1969). Such compensation would clearly constitute a windfall for the plaintiff. However, a refusal to grant any compensation for the decline in portfolio value would be to assume, in effect, that all of Oppenheimer's transactions were legitimate and to disregard the jury's finding that the broker wrongly concluded unsuitable transactions to the detriment of the investor. See id. at 883–84. Such a refusal to grant any compensation for trading losses would clearly constitute a windfall for the defendant.

As demonstrated above, a refusal by a court to estimate the amount of trading losses caused by the churning of an account could only yield a certain windfall for either the investor or the broker. However, the essence of the judicial power to set damages, the source and maintenance of its legitimacy, is not the power to choose between alternative windfalls, but is rather the duty to attempt to correct existing windfalls. Thus, a court in a churning case must attempt to approximate the trading losses sustained as a result of the broker's misconduct. *See Fey v. Walston & Co., Inc.,* 493 F.2d 1036, 1055 (7th Cir.1974). ("It is now elementary that when precise damage measurements are precluded by wrongful acts, the wrongdoer cannot insist upon exact measurements and the precise tracing of causal lines to an impractical extent; fair approximations are in order."); Brodsky, *supra* at 158–159.

In order to approximate the trading losses caused by the broker's misconduct, it is necessary to estimate how the investor's portfolio would have fared in the absence of the such misconduct. The trial judge must be afforded significant discretion to choose the indicia by which such estimation is to be made, based primarily on the types of securities comprising the portfolio.[10] However, in the absence of either a specialized portfolio or a showing by either party that a different method is more accurate, it seems that the technique discussed by Judge Oakes in *Rolf v. Blyth, Eastman, Dillon & Co., Inc.,* 570 F.2d 38, 49 (2d Cir.), *cert. denied,* 439 U.S. 1039, 99 S.Ct. 642, 58 L.Ed.2d 698 (1978) and employed by Judge Mahon in this case is preferable. *See* Brodsky, *supra* at 157. ("Given the recognized difficulty in computing damages in these cases, that [the *Rolf*] formula is a logical approach toward compensating a customer for loss.") This mode of estimation utilizes the average percentage performance in the value of the Dow Jones Industrials or the Standard and Poor's Index during the relevant period as the indicia of how a given portfolio would have performed in the absence of the broker's misconduct.

In the case at bar, Judge Mahon instructed the jury to compute trading loss damages by finding:

> "by a preponderance of the evidence the difference between the amount of plaintiff's original investment and dividends therefrom less any withdrawals received by Mrs. Miley and less the ending value of her account with defendants. This amount is to then be reduced by the average percentage decline in value of the Dow Jones Industrials or the Standard and Poor's Index during the relevant period of time.

---

10.   For example, a judge could decide to use a different figure for portfolios consisting of stock in oil companies as opposed to stock of domestic automobile producers, given the unusual performance of such securities for reasons unrelated to the broker's performance of his job. See Brodsky, *supra* at 165–166.

Answer in dollars and cents, if any, or none."

In addition, as part of this same instruction Judge Mahon told the jury that they could award "only such damages as will reasonably compensate her for such injury and damage * * * You are not permitted to award speculative damages." We feel that this instruction was both correct and sufficient on the issue of trading losses caused by churning.

DAMAGES NET OF THE MARKET

A plaintiff in a churning case can recover both the diminution in the portfolio's value *and* the brokerage commissions.[1] The diminution in the portfolio value should be calculated "net of the market." That is, a defendant is not responsible for stock price drops caused by forces other than his or her own misconduct. This offset concept is implicitly required under § 11(e) which provides:

> that if the defendant proves that any portion or all of such damages represents other than the depreciation in value of such security resulting from such part of the registration statement, with respect to which his liability is asserted, not being true or omitting to state a material fact required to be stated therein or necessary to make the statements therein not misleading, such portion of or all such damages shall not be recoverable.[2]

The net of the market concept is equally applicable to corporate misrepresentation or omission cases and in essence has become a part of the legal landscape, often today subsumed in the term "loss causation."

The typical calculation of damages net of the market requires judicial acceptance of an appropriate market index. For example if a portfolio declined by 25 percent while an appropriate market index declined 10 percent, damages should equal 15 percent. The courts, as suggested by *Miley*, have often used the Dow Jones Industrial or Standard & Poor's index as the market index.[3] By calculating portfolio value net of the market a plaintiff can be awarded damages even when the value of the portfolio increases. For example if the plaintiff's portfolio increased in value five percent while the appropriate market index increased by 50 percent, damages in a churning case should equal 45 percent.[4] The courts, however, have not always been willing to increase damages based on market movement when the value of a portfolio increased.[5]

1. Miley v. Oppenheimer, 637 F.2d 318, 326–329 (5th Cir.1981); McGinn v. Merrill Lynch, Pierce, Fenner & Smith, Inc., 736 F.2d 1254, 1257 (8th Cir.1984); Hatrock v. Edward D. Jones & Co., 750 F.2d 767, 773–774 (9th Cir.1984); Nesbit v. McNeil, 896 F.2d 380, 385–386 (9th Cir.1990); Davis v. Merrill Lynch, Pierce, Fenner & Smith, Inc., 906 F.2d 1206, 1217–1219 (8th Cir.1990).

2. In Feit v. Leasco Data Processing Equip. Corp., 332 F.Supp. 544, 586 (E.D.N.Y. 1971), the court took judicial notice of "the very drastic general decline in the stock market in 1969" and adjusted the damage figure accordingly.

3. Rolf v. Blyth, Eastman Dillon & Co., Inc., 570 F.2d 38, 49 (2d Cir.1978), *cert. denied*, 439 U.S. 1039 (1978); Miley v. Oppenheimer & Co., Inc., 637 F.2d 318, 328 (5th Cir.1981).

4. *See* VMS Sec. Litig., 136 F.R.D. 466, 481–482 (N.D.Ill.1991).

5. Nesbit v. McNeil, 896 F.2d 380, 385 (9th Cir.1990) (not analyzing portfolio value net of the market when portfolio value increased). From the point-of-view of financial economics, increasingly the source of expertise in damages calculations, damages in securities class actions involve two quite different methodological problems: (1) How to calculate the price at which a security

Churning damages involves a feature that is more idiosyncratic. Because the portfolio's value will diminish, in part, because of the payment of brokerage commissions, churning damages appear to involve a form of double counting or, in any event, the recovery of more than actual damages. For example, if a portfolio with an initial value of $100,000 is reduced to $50,000, some amount of the reduction will be in the form of brokerage commissions. The plaintiff recovers the brokerage commissions both in the recovery of the value of the portfolio and again in a separate damage recovery for the commissions. Hence if the initial portfolio of $100,000 would recover $110,000 ignoring, for the moment, market movements. This can be justified on the premise propounded in cases such as Janigan v. Taylor,[6] that "it is more appropriate to give the defrauded party the benefit even of windfalls than to let the fraudulent party keep them." For the choice is between allowing a broker to retain commissions while engaging in fraudulent excessive trading and giving the plaintiff a windfall. The law favors the latter solution because it is more likely to deter churning.[7]

PROBLEM 15–6

On August 7, 2001 Endrun Corp., an oil and gas exploration firm, issued a press release, asserting that it had purchased a major foreign oil field with probable reserves of 100 million barrels. Endrun was traded on the New York Stock Exchange and between August 7 and August 12th its stock rose from $12 per share to $20 per share during a period when the Dow Jones Industrial Average declined 2 percent and the leading oil and gas stock price index declined 5 percent.

On August 15th California announced new pollution control standards for automobiles which caused the oil and gas stock price index to decline a further 10 percent; the Dow Jones industrial average, in fact, rose 2 percent that day.

On August 18 Endrun published a second press release concerning its new foreign oil field, disclosing that it was required to provide 75 percent of potential profits to the foreign country as an oil royalty.

By August 21st Endrun stock had declined to $12; between August 15 and 21 neither the oil and gas stock index or the Dow Jones industrial average, in fact, changed.

What damages for a stock purchaser who bought Endrun at $20 on August 12 and sold at $12 on August 22?

would have traded absent securities fraud during the class period; and (2) How to calculate the number and dollar amounts investors were injured during that period. See generally Mark L. Mitchell & Jeffrey M. Netter, The Role of Financial Economics in Securities Fraud Cases: Applications at the Securities and Exchange Commission, 49 Bus. Law. 545, 557–570 (1994); Janet C. Alexander, Rethinking Damages in Securities Class Actions, 48 Stan. L. Rev. 1487 (1996);

Michael Barclay & Frank L. Torchio, A Comparison of Trading Models Used for Calculating Aggregate Damages in Securities Litigation, 64 Law & Contemp. Probs. 105 (2001).

6. 344 F.2d 781, 786 (1st Cir.1965), *cert. denied*, 382 U.S. 879 (1965).

7. Cf. Randall v. Loftsgaarden, 478 U.S. 647 (1986).

Elkind v. Liggett & Myers, Inc.

United States Court of Appeals, Second Circuit, 1980.
635 F.2d 156.

■ Before: Mansfield and Newman, Circuit Judges.*

■ Mansfield, Circuit Judge:

This case presents a number of issues arising out of what has become a form of corporate brinkmanship—non-public disclosure of business-related information to financial analysts. The action is a class suit by Arnold B. Elkind on behalf of certain purchasers (more fully described below) of the stock of Liggett & Myers, Inc. (Liggett) against it. They seek damages for alleged failure of its officers to disclose certain material information with respect to its earnings and operations and for their alleged wrongful tipping of inside information to certain persons who then sold Liggett shares on the open market.

After a non-jury trial Judge Constance Baker Motley held in post-trial findings and conclusions that Liggett did not violate Section 10(b) of the Securities Exchange Act of 1934 or Rule 10b–5 promulgated thereunder by failing prior to July 18, 1972, to release figures showing a substantial downturn in earnings or to correct erroneous projections of financial analysts which it had allegedly fostered. The court found, however, that on July 10, 1972, and July 17, 1972, officers of Liggett disclosed material inside information to individual financial analysts, leading to sale of Liggett stock by investors to whom this information was conveyed. Damages were computed on the basis of the difference between the price which members of the plaintiff class (uninformed buyers of Liggett stock between the time of the first tip and subsequent public disclosure) paid and what the stock sold for after the later disclosure. See 472 F.Supp. 123 (S.D.N.Y.1978). We affirm the dismissal of the counts alleging failure to disclose or correct. We reverse the finding of liability based on the alleged July 10, 1972, tip for want of materiality and scienter. We remand the determination of liability based on the July 17, 1972, tip for determination of damages. In all other respects the judgment is affirmed.

* * *

Liggett is a diversified company, with traditional business in the tobacco industry supplemented by acquisitions in such industries as liquor (Paddington Corp., importer of J & B Scotch), pet food (Allen Products Co. and Perk Foods Co., manufacturer of Alpo dog food), cereal, watchbands, cleansers and rugs. Its common stock is listed on the New York Stock Exchange.

In 1969 Liggett officers concluded that the company's stock was underpriced, due in part to lack of appreciation in the financial community for the breadth of its market activity. To cure this perceived deficiency, Liggett initiated an "analyst program," hiring a public relations firm and encouraging closer contact between analysts and company management. This included meetings with analysts at which Liggett officials discussed operations. Liggett also reviewed and commented on reports which the analysts were preparing, to correct errors and other misunderstandings.

---

* Pursuant to § 0.14 of the Rules of this Court, this appeal is being determined by Judges Mansfield and Newman, who are in agreement on this opinion.

Liggett had a record year in 1971, with earnings of $4.22 per share (up from $3.56 in 1970). The first quarter of 1972 was equally auspicious. On March 22, Liggett issued a press release reporting that sales of the non-tobacco lines had continued to increase in the first two months, but noting that current stockpiling of J & B Scotch by customers (in anticipation of a price increase) could affect sales. On May 3, 1972, the company released its first quarter figures, showing earnings of $1.00 per share (compared to $.81 in the first quarter of 1971).

This quarterly operations report led to considerable optimism in the financial community over Liggett's prospects. Management did nothing to deflate the enthusiasm. A number of reports containing predictions that 1972 earnings would increase about 10% over 1971 earnings were reviewed by officials of Liggett during the first five months of 1972. While company personnel corrected factual errors in these reports, they did not comment (or made noncommittal or evasive comments) on the earnings projections, according to the findings below, which are supported by the record. At group meetings with analysts in February and March, management indicated that it was making "good progress" with certain products and that it was "well-positioned" to take advantage of industry trends. At the end of March, Liggett successfully made a public offering of $50 million of debentures. At an April 25 stockholders' meeting, Liggett's Executive Vice President expressed general optimism that the company was continuing to make good progress. On May 3, the first quarter earnings were released. At a May 16 meeting with analysts in New York, officials reiterated their vague but quieting pronouncements. Similar comments, to the effect that 1972 was expected to be a "good year," were voiced at a June 5 presentation in London.

Despite the company's outward appearance of strength, Liggett's management was less sanguine intramurally. Internal budget projections called for only a two percent increase in earnings in 1972. In April and May, a full compilation of updated figures was ordered, and new projections were presented to the Board of Directors on May 15. April was marked by a sharp decline, with earnings of only $.03 per share (compared to $.30 the previous April). The 1972 earnings projection was revised downward from $4.30 to $3.95 per share. May earnings, which the Board received on June 19, rebounded somewhat to $.23 per share (compared to $.27 in May 1971 and original budget projections of $.34). At meetings with analysts during this period, Liggett officials took a more negative tone, emphasizing, for example, various cost pressures. There was no public disclosure of the adverse financial developments at this time. Beginning in late June, 1972, the price of Liggett's common stock steadily declined.

On July 17, preliminary earnings data for June and six-month totals became available to the Board of Directors. June earnings were $.20 per share (compared to $.44 in June 1971). The first half earnings for 1972 were approximately $1.46 per share, down from $1.82 the previous year. The Board decided to issue a press release the following day. That release, issued at about 2:15 P.M. on July 18, disclosed the preliminary earnings figures and attributed the decline to shortcomings in all of Liggett's product lines.

The district court found two "tips" of material inside information in the days before the July 18 press release. On July 10, analyst Peter Barry of Kuhn Loeb & Co. spoke by telephone with Daniel Provost, Liggett's Director of Corporate Communications. According to Barry's deposition testimony, apparently adopted by the court below, Provost confirmed Barry's suggestions that J & B sales were slowing due to earlier stockpiling and that a new competing dog food was affecting Alpo sales adversely. Barry asked if a projection of a 10% earnings decline would be realistic, and received what he characterized as a noncommittal response. Barry testified that Provost told him that a preliminary earnings statement would be coming out in a week or so. Since Barry knew of no prior instances in which Liggett had issued such a preliminary statement, he deduced that the figures would be lower than expected. Barry sent a wire * * * to Kuhn Loeb's offices. The information was conveyed to three clients. Two of them, holders of a total of over 600,000 shares, did not sell. A third client sold the 100 shares he owned. No other Kuhn Loeb customers sold between the time of the July 10 "tip" and the release of preliminary earnings figures on July 18; Kuhn Loeb customers bought some 5,000 shares during this period.

The second "tip" occurred on July 17, one day before the preliminary earnings figures for the first half were released. Analyst Robert Cummins of Loeb Rhoades & Co. questioned Ralph Moore, Liggett's chief financial officer, about the recent decline in price of Liggett's common stock, as well as performance of the various subsidiaries. According to Cummins' deposition, he asked Moore whether there was a good possibility that earnings would be down, and received an affirmative ("grudging") response. Moore added that this information was confidential. Cummins sent a wire to his firm, spoke with a stockbroker who promptly sold 1,800 shares of Liggett stock on behalf of his customers.

The district court held that each of these disclosures was a tip of material information in violation of Rule 10b–5, rendering Liggett liable to all persons who bought the company's stock during the period from July 11 to July 18, 1972, inclusive, without knowledge of the tipped information. However, the court rejected plaintiff's claims that Liggett was under a legal obligation to correct the analysts' earlier erroneous predictions, relying on this court's decision in Electronic Specialty Co. v. International Controls Corp., 409 F.2d 937 (2d Cir.1969). It also rejected plaintiff's claims that Liggett's earlier statements to analysts and stockholders were misrepresentations and that Liggett was under a duty to issue a preliminary earnings statement in June when it received its May figures.

In computing damages for the July 10 and 17 tips, the court attempted to award the difference between the amount plaintiff class members paid for their stock and the value they received. The latter was interpreted to be the price at which the stock would have sold had there been public disclosure of the tipped information. The court ruled that plaintiff's expert testimony on this point was speculative and unsupported by the record. Instead, following Mitchell v. Texas Gulf Sulphur Co., 446 F.2d 90 (10th Cir.), cert. denied, 404 U.S. 1004 (1971), it looked to the actual market price at the end of "a reasonable period" (eight trading days) following the July 18 release of earning figures as an approximation of what the price would have been had the tipped information been disclosed publicly. Thus damages amounted to the difference between the plaintiff class members' purchase prices (generally in the vicinity of $60 per share) and $43, the price of the stock eight trading days after disclosure. Based on the total volume of trading transactions from July 11 to July 18, the court awarded damages amounting to $740,000 on condition that any unclaimed portion would revert to Liggett. To this the court added prejudgment interest of approximately $300,000.

      * * *

4. Damages

This case presents a question of measurement of damages which we have previously deferred, believing that damages are best addressed in a concrete setting. See Shapiro v. Merrill Lynch, Pierce, Fenner & Smith, Inc., *supra*, 495 F.2d at 241–42; Heit v. Weitzen, 402 F.2d 909, 917 & n. 8 (2d Cir.1968), cert. denied, 395 U.S. 903 (1969). We ruled in *Shapiro* that defendants selling on inside information would be liable to those who bought on the open market and sustained, "substantial losses" during the period of insider trading.[23]

The district court looked to the measure of damages used in cases where a buyer was induced to purchase a company's stock by materially misleading statements or omissions. In such cases of fraud by a fiduciary intended to induce others to buy or sell stock the accepted measure of damages is the "out-of-pocket" measure.[24] This consists of the difference between the price paid and the "value" of the stock when brought (or when the buyer committed himself to buy, if earlier).[25] Except in rare face-to-face transactions, however, uninformed traders on an open, impersonal market are not induced by representations on the part of the tipper or tippee to buy or sell. Usually they are wholly unacquainted with and uninfluenced by the tippee's misconduct. They trade independently and voluntarily but without the benefit of information known to the trading tippee.

In determining what is the appropriate measure of damages to be awarded to the outside uninformed investor as the result of tippee-trading through use of information that is not equally available to all investors it must be remembered that investors who trade in a stock on the open market have no absolute right to know inside information. They are, however, entitled to an honest market in which those with whom they trade have no confidential corporate information. See SEC v. Texas Gulf Sulphur Co., *supra*, 401 F.2d at 848, 851–52.

    "The primary object of the exchange is to afford facilities for trading in securities under the safest and fairest conditions attainable. In order that

---

23. The Sixth Circuit has since reached the opposite conclusion, Fridrich v. Bradford, 542 F.2d 307, 318 (6th Cir.1976), *cert. denied*, 429 U.S. 1053 (1977).

24. Affiliated Ute Citizens v. United States, 406 U.S. 128, 155 (1972); Blackie v. Barrack, 524 F.2d 891, 909 (9th Cir.1975), *cert. denied* 429 U.S. 816 (1976); Fershtman v. Schectman, 450 F.2d 1357, 1361 (2d Cir. 1971), *cert. denied*, 405 U.S. 1066 (1972); Note, The Measurement of Damages in Rule 10b–5 Cases Involving Actively Traded Securities, 26 Stan.L. Rev. 371, 383–84 & n. 65 (1974).

25. Some cases have suggested the availability as an alternative measure of damages of a modified rescissionary measure, consisting of the difference between the price

the defrauded party paid and the price at the time he learned or should have learned the true state of affairs. The theory of this measure is to restore the plaintiff to the position where he would have been had he not been fraudulently induced to trade. See, e.g., Mitchell v. Texas Gulf Sulphur Co., 446 F.2d 90, 104–06 (10th Cir.), *cert. denied*, 404 U.S. 1004 (1971). The soundness of this measure has been vigorously disputed in the case of open market trading. Green v. Occidental Petroleum Corp., 541 F.2d 1335, 1341–44 (9th Cir.1976) (Sneed, J., concurring). While the district court cited to *Mitchell*, its opinion makes clear that it was applying the out-of-pocket measure of damages. Since the district court did not apply this modified rescissionary measure, we need not pass on it here.

parties may trade on even terms they should have, as far as practicable, the same opportunities for knowledge in regard to the subject matter of the trade." H.R.Rep. No. 1383, 73d Cong., 2d Sess. 12 (1934).

It is the combination of the tip and the tippee's trading that poses the evil against which the open market investor must be protected, 2 Bromberg, Securities Law: Fraud § 7.5(3)(b), at 190.9 (1979); Cary, Insider Trading in Stocks, 21 Bus.Law 1009 (1966). The reason for the "disclose or abstain" rule is the unfairness in permitting an insider to trade for his own account on the basis of material inside information not available to others. The tipping of material information is a violation of the fiduciary's duty but no injury occurs until the information is used by the tippee. The entry into the market of a tippee with superior knowledge poses the threat that if he trades on the basis of the inside information he may profit at the expense of investors who are disadvantaged by lack of the inside information. For this both the tipper and the tippee are liable. See SEC v. Texas Gulf Sulphur Co., 312 F.Supp. 77, 95 (S.D.N.Y.1970), affd., 446 F.2d 1301, 1308 (2d Cir.1971). If the insider chooses not to trade, on the other hand, no injury may be claimed by the outside investor, since the public has no right to the undisclosed information.

Recognizing the foregoing, we in *Shapiro* suggested that the district court must be accorded flexibility in assessing damages, after considering

"the extent of the selling defendants' trading in Douglas stock, whether such trading effectively impaired the integrity of the market, * * * what profits or other benefits were realized by defendants [and] what expenses were incurred and what losses were sustained by plaintiffs. * * * More-over, we do not foreclose the possibility that an analysis by the district court of the nature and character of the Rule 10b–5 violations committed may require limiting the extent of liability imposed on either class of defendants." 495 F.2d at 242.

We thus gave heed to the guidance provided by the Supreme Court in Affiliated Ute Citizens v. United States, 406 U.S. 128, 151 (1972), to the effect that "Congress intended securities legislation enacted for the purpose of avoiding frauds to be construed 'not technically and restrictively, but flexibly to effectu-ate its remedial purposes.' Id., at 195. This was recently said once again in Superintendent of Insurance v. Bankers Life & Casualty Co., 404 U.S. 6, 12 (1971)." See also Mills v. Electric Auto–Lite Co., 396 U.S. 375, 386, 391 (1970) (1934 Act does not "circumscribe the courts' power to grant appropriate remedies").

Within the flexible framework thus authorized for determining what amounts should be recoverable by the uninformed trader from the tipper and tippee trader, several measures are possible. First, there is the traditional out-of-pocket measure used by the district court in this case. For several reasons this measure appears to be inappropriate. In the first place, as we have noted, it is directed toward compensating a person for losses directly traceable to the defendant's fraud upon him. No such fraud or inducement may be attributed to a tipper or tippee-trading on an impersonal market. Aside from this the measure poses serious proof problems that may often be insurmountable in a tippee-trading case. The "value" of the stock traded during the period of nondisclosure of the tipped information (i.e., the price at which the market would have valued the stock if there had been a disclosure) is hypothetical. Expert testimony regarding that "value" may, as the district court found in the present case, be entirely speculative. This has led some courts to conclude that the drop in price of the stock after actual disclosure and after allowing a period of time to elapse for the market to absorb the news may sometimes approximate the drop which would have occurred earlier had the tip been disclosed. See Harris v. American Investment Company, 523 F.2d 220, 227 (8th Cir.1975), cert. denied, 432 U.S. 1054 (1976). The court below adopted this approach of using post-public disclosure market price as *nunc pro tunc* evidence of the "value" of the stock during the period of non-disclosure.

Whatever may be the reasonableness of the *nunc pro tunc* "value" method of calculating damages in other contexts, it has serious vulnerabilities here. It rests on the fundamental assumptions (1) that the tipped information is substantially the same as that later disclosed publicly, and (2) that one can determine how the market would have reacted to the public release of the tipped information at an earlier time by its reaction to that information at a later, proximate time. This theory depends on the parity of the "tip" and the "disclosure." When they differ, the basis of the damage calculation evaporates. One could not reasonably estimate how the public would have reacted to the news that the Titanic was near an iceberg from how it reacted to news that the ship had struck an iceberg and sunk. In the present case, the July 10 tip that preliminary earnings would be released in a week is not comparable to the later release of the estimated earnings figures on July 18. Nor was the July 17 tipped information that there was a good possibility that earnings would be down comparable to the next day's release of the estimated earnings figures.

An equally compelling reason for rejecting the theory is its potential for imposition of Draconian, exorbitant damages, out of all proportion to the wrong committed, lining the pockets of all interim investors and their counsel at the expense of innocent corporate stockholders. Logic would compel application of the theory to a case where a tippee sells only 10 shares of a heavily traded stock (e.g., IBM), which then drops substantially when the tipped information is publicly disclosed. To hold the tipper and tippee liable for the losses suffered by every open market buyer of a stock as a result of the later decline in value of the stock after the news became public would be grossly unfair. While the securities laws do occasionally allow for potentially ruinous recovery, we will not readily adopt a measure mandating "large judgments, payable in the last instance by innocent investors [here, Liggett shareholders], for the benefit of speculators and their lawyers," SEC v. Texas Gulf Sulphur Co., *supra*, 401 F.2d at 867 (Friendly, J., concurring); cf. Blue Chip Stamps v. Manor Drug Stores, 421 U.S. 723, 739–40 (1975), unless the statute so requires.

An alternative measure would be to permit recovery of damages caused by erosion of the market price of the security that is traceable to the tippee's wrongful trading, i.e., to compensate the uninformed investor for the loss in market value that he suffered as a direct result of the tippee's conduct. Under this measure an innocent trader who bought Liggett shares at or after a tippee sold on the basis of inside information would recover any decline in value of his shares caused by the tippee's trading. Assuming the impact of the tippee's trading on the market is measurable, this approach has the advantage of limiting the plaintiffs to the amount of damage actually caused in fact by the defendant's wrongdoing and avoiding windfall recoveries by investors at the expense of stockholders other than the tippee trader, which could happen in the present action against Liggett. The rationale is that if the market price is not affected by the tippee's trading, the uninformed investor is in the same position as he would have been had the insider abstained from trading. In such event the equilibrium of the market has not been disturbed and the outside investor has not been harmed by the informational imbalance. Only where the market has been contaminated by the wrongful conduct would damages be recoverable.

This causation-in-fact approach has some disadvantages. It allows no recovery for the tippee's violation of his duty to disclose the inside information before trading. Had he fulfilled this duty, others, including holders of the stock, could then have traded on an equal informational basis. Another disadvantage of such a measure lies in the difficult if not impossible burden it would impose on the uninformed trader of proving the time when and extent to which the integrity of the market was affected by the tippee's conduct. In some cases, such as *Mitchell, supra,* and *Shapiro, supra,* the existence of very substantial trading by the tippee, coupled with a sharp change in market price over a short period, would provide the basis for measuring a market price movement attributable to the wrongful trading. On the other hand, in a case where there was only a modest amount of tippee trading in a heavy-volume market in the stock, accompanied by other unrelated factors affecting the market price, it would be impossible as a practical matter to isolate such rise or decline in market price, if any, as was caused by the tippee's wrongful conduct. Moreover, even assuming market erosion caused by this trading to be provable and that the uninformed investor could show that it continued after his purchase, there remains the question of whether the plaintiff would not be precluded from recovery on the ground that any post-purchase decline in market price attributable to the tippee's trading would not be injury to him as a purchaser, i.e., "in connection with the purchase and sale of securities," but injury to him as a stockholder due to a breach of fiduciary duty by the company's officers, which is not actionable under § 10(b) of the 1934 Act or Rule 10b–5 promulgated thereunder. Blue Chip Stamps v. Manor Drug Stores, 421 U.S. 723 (1975); Birnbaum v. Newport Steel Corp., 193 F.2d 461 (2d Cir.), cert. denied, 343 U.S. 956 (1952). For these reasons, we reject this strict direct market-repercussion theory of damages.

A third alternative is (1) to allow any uninformed investor, where a reasonable investor would either have delayed his purchase or not purchased at all if he had had the benefit of the tipped information, to recover any post-purchase decline in market value of his shares up to a reasonable time after he learns of the tipped information or after there is a public disclosure of it but (2) limit his recovery to the amount gained by the tippee as a result of his selling at the earlier date rather than delaying his sale until the parties could trade on an equal informational basis. Under this measure if the tippee sold 5,000 shares at $50 per share on the basis of inside information and the stock thereafter declined to $40 per share within a reasonable time after public disclosure, an uninformed purchaser buying shares during the interim (e.g., at $45 per share) would recover the difference between his purchase price and the amount at which he could have sold the shares on an equal informational basis (i.e., the market price within a reasonable time after public disclosure of the tip), subject to a limit of $50,000, which is the amount gained by the tippee as a result of his trading on the inside information rather than on an equal basis. Should the intervening buyers, because of the volume and price of their purchases, claim more than the tippee's gain, their recovery (limited to that gain) would be shared *pro rata.*

This third alternative, which may be described as the disgorgement measure, has in substance been recommended by the American Law Institute in its

1978 Proposed Draft of a Federal Securities Code, §§ 1603, 1703(b), 1708(b), 1711(j). It offers several advantages. To the extent that it makes the tipper and tippees liable up to the amount gained by their misconduct, it should deter tipping of inside information and tippee-trading. On the other hand, by limiting the total recovery to the tippee's gain, the measure bars windfall recoveries of exorbitant amounts bearing no relation to the seriousness of the misconduct. It also avoids the extraordinary difficulties faced in trying to prove traditional out-of-pocket damages based on the true "value" of the shares purchased or damages claimed by reason of market erosion attributable to tippee trading. A plaintiff would simply be required to prove (1) the time, amount and price per share of his purchase, (2) that a reasonable investor would not have paid as high a price or made the purchase at all if he had had the information in the tippee's possession, and (3) the price to which the security had declined by the time he learned the tipped information or at a reasonable time after it became public, whichever event first occurred. He would then have a claim and, up to the limits of the tippee's gain, could recover the decline in market value of his shares before the information became public or known to him. In most cases the damages recoverable under the disgorgement measure would be roughly commensurate to the actual harm caused by the tippee's wrongful conduct. In a case where the tippee sold only a few shares, for instance, the likelihood of his conduct causing any substantial injury to intervening investors buying without benefit of his confidential information would be small. If, on the other hand, the tippee sold large amounts of stock, realizing substantial profits, the likelihood of injury to intervening uninformed purchasers would be greater and the amount of potential recovery thereby proportionately enlarged.

We recognize that there cannot be any perfect measure of damages caused by tippee-trading. The disgorgement measure, like others we have described, does have some disadvantages. It modifies the principle that ordinarily gain to the wrongdoer should not be a prerequisite to liability for violation of Rule 10b–5. See Myzel v. Fields, 386 F.2d 718, 750 (8th Cir.1967); Fischer v. Kletz, 266 F.Supp. 180, 183 (S.D.N.Y.1967); Comment, Insiders' Liability Under Rule 10b–5 for the Illegal Purchase, 78 Yale L.J. 864, 876 (1969). It partially duplicates disgorgement remedies available in proceedings by the SEC or others. Under some market conditions such as where the market price is depressed by wholly unrelated causes, the tippee might be vulnerable to heavy damages, permitting some plaintiffs to recover underserved windfalls. In some instances the total claims could exceed the wrongdoer's gain, limiting each claimant to a pro rata share of the gain. In other situations, after deducting the cost of recovery, including attorneys' fees, the remainder might be inadequate to make a class action worthwhile. However, as between the various alternatives we are persuaded, after weighing the pros and cons, that the disgorgement measure, despite some disadvantages, offers the most equitable resolution of the difficult problems created by conflicting interests.

In the present case the sole Rule 10b–5 violation was the tippee-trading of 1,800 Liggett shares on the afternoon of July 17, 1972. Since the actual preliminary Liggett earnings were released publicly at 2:15 P.M. on July 18 and were effectively disseminated in a Wall Street Journal article published on the morning of July 19, the only outside purchasers who might conceivably have been damaged by the insider-trading were those who bought Liggett shares between the afternoon of July 17 and the opening of the market on July 19. Thereafter all purchasers bought on an equal informational footing, and any outside purchaser who bought on July 17 and 18 was able to decide within a reasonable time after the July 18–19 publicity whether to hold or sell his shares in the light of the publicly-released news regarding Liggett's less favorable earnings.

The market price of Liggett stock opened on July 17, 1972, at $55⅝, and remained at substantially the same price on that date, closing at $55¼. By the close of the market on July 18 the price declined to $52½ per share. Applying the disgorgement measure, any member of the plaintiff class who bought Liggett shares during the period from the afternoon of July 17 to the close of the market on July 18 and met the reasonable investor requirement would be entitled to claim a *pro rata* portion of the tippee's gain, based on the difference between their purchase price and the price to which the market price declined within a reasonable time after the morning of July 19. By the close of the market on July 19 the market price had declined to $46⅜ per share. The total recovery thus would be limited to the gain realized by the tippee from the inside information, i.e., 1,800 shares multiplied by approximately $9.35 per share.

The finding of liability based on the July 10, 1972, tip is reversed. The award of damages is also reversed and the case is remanded for a determination of damages recoverable for tippee-trading based on the July 17, 1972, tip, to be measured in accordance with the foregoing. Each party will bear its own costs.

DAMAGES RECOVERABLE UNDER RULE 10b–5

There are a number of permutations in federal securities law damages cases, particularly under Rule 10b–5.

The out of pocket formula endures as the most frequently awarded measure of damages. But it has long been subject to the important qualification, as illustrated by Mitchell v. Texas Gulf Sulphur Co.,[1] that the calculation will be made with reference to a reasonable period of time after the discovery by the plaintiff of the fraud, so that he or she is given an opportunity after all of the facts are known to repurchase where he or she is a defrauded seller or to dispose of the securities purchased where he or she is a defrauded buyer. Under this approach the defendant is not liable for any depreciation in value of the securities after that time where the defendant is a buyer or any depreciation in value after that time where the defendant is a seller.

Given the deterrent goal of damages articulated in *Loftsgaarden*, it should be no surprise that a number of cases apply a measure of damages based upon the defendant's profits rather than the plaintiff's loss. If the defendant buyer's profit on resale is greater than the out of pocket measure, the plaintiff is entitled to the profit.[2] Once it is found that the defendant acquired the property by fraud and that the profit was the proximate consequence of the fraud, whether foreseeable or not, "it is more appropriate to give the defrauded party the benefit even of windfalls than to let the fraudulent party keep them."[3] The damages ceiling imposed by § 28(a) in terms of "actual damages on account of the act complained of" does not foreclose a windfall recovery

1. 446 F.2d 90 (10th Cir.1971), *cert. denied*, 404 U.S. 1004 (1971).

2. Affiliated Ute Citizens of Utah v. United States, 406 U.S. 128, 155 (1972); Randall v. Loftsgaarden, 478 U.S. 647, 663 (1986).

3. Janigan v. Taylor, 344 F.2d 781, 786 (1st Cir.1965), *cert. denied*, 382 U.S. 879 (1965); Myzel v. Fields, 386 F.2d 718, 748–749 (8th Cir.1967), *cert. denied*, 390 U.S. 951 (1968).

based on the defendant's benefit rather than the plaintiff's loss.[4] In *Randall v. Loftsgaarden*, the Court said it had "never interpreted § 28(a) as imposing a rigid requirement that every recovery on an express or implied right of action under the 1934 Act must be limited to the net economic harm suffered by the plaintiff."[5]

Consequential damages (which are "actual damages") are recoverable on top of everything else—for example the plaintiff's cost of investigating the transaction before he or she entered into it.[6] Rescission does not preclude consequential damages for prerescission losses.[7] But "[a] plaintiff seeking consequential damages for fraud, at common law or under federal securities legislation, must establish the causal nexus with a good deal of certainty," varying "somewhat inversely with the depth of the fraud."[8]

In limited circumstances the "actual damages" of § 28(a) can include benefit of the bargain damages "when they can be established with reasonable certainty.[9]" Since the price paid by the successful offeror in a tender offer contest often exceeds the fair market value of the securities surrendered by the shareholders, defrauded shareholders or a target company would hardly ever, under the out-of-pocket measure of damages, have redress."[10] Similarly in *Abell v. Potomac Ins. Co.* the court held that Rule 10b–5 might compensate bondholders "for the loss of a contracted right to a guaranteed stream of income," which is "a property right distinguishable from possessory interests in the bonds themselves."[11]

It is clear that punitive damages are precluded by the limitation in § 28(a) to actual damages in private federal securities cases. But punitive damages may be recovered under state law[12] and the SEC can seek treble damages.

The cases have evolved a ceiling on insider trading damages. In the *Elkind* case Judge Mansfield put a cap on the liability of a nontrading tipper (or rather the liability of his employing corporation), limiting it to an obligation to return pro rata to the public traders in the market the profits made by his tippees.

4. Myzel v. Fields, 386 F.2d 718, 748–749 (8th Cir.1967), *cert. denied*, 390 U.S. 951 (1968). The courts have granted recovery also of fraudulent windfall profits reaped by fraudulent *sellers*, although they are harder to prove. Zeller v. Bogue Elec. Mfg. Corp., 476 F.2d 795, 801–803 (2d Cir.1973), *cert. denied*, 414 U.S. 908 (1973); Ohio Drill & Tool Co. v. Johnson, 498 F.2d 186, 190–191 (6th Cir.1974); Hackbart v. Holmes, 675 F.2d 1114, 1122 (10th Cir.1982).

5. 478 U.S. 647, 663 (1986).

6. Esplin v. Hirschi, 402 F.2d 94 (10th Cir.1968), *cert. denied*, 394 U.S. 928 (1969); Zeller v. Bogue Elec. Mfg. Corp., 476 F.2d 795, 803 (2d Cir.1973), *cert. denied sub nom.* Bogue Elec. Mfg. Corp. v. Zeller, 414 U.S. 908 (1973); James v. Meinke, 778 F.2d 200, 205–206 (5th Cir.1985); Grubb v. Federal Deposit Ins. Corp., 868 F.2d 1151, 1165 (10th Cir. 1989).

7. Foster v. Financial Technology Inc., 517 F.2d 1068, 1072 (9th Cir.1975).

8. Zeller v. Bogue Elec. Mfg. Corp., 476 F.2d 795, 803 & n. 11 (2d Cir.1973), *cert. denied sub nom.* Bogue Elec. Mfg. Corp. v. Zeller, 414 U.S. 908 (1973).

9. Osofsky v. Zipf, 645 F.2d 107, 114 (2d Cir.1981).

10. Id. at 114.

11. 858 F.2d 1104, 1137 (5th Cir.1988), *cert. denied sub nom.* Abell v. Wright, Lindsey & Jennings, 492 U.S. 918 (1989).

12. Young v. Taylor, 466 F.2d 1329, 1337–1338 (10th Cir.1972); Miley v. Oppenheimer & Co., Inc., 637 F.2d 318, 330 (5th Cir.1981); Hatrock v. Edward D. Jones & Co., 750 F.2d 767, 771 (9th Cir.1984); Davis v. Merrill Lynch, Pierce, Fenner & Smith, 906 F.2d 1206, 1219–1229 (8th Cir.1990); Hunt v. Miller, 908 F.2d 1210, 1216 n. 13 (4th Cir. 1990).

Congress by the addition of § 20A to the 1934 Act in the Insider Trading and Securities Fraud Enforcement Act of 1988, which created an express cause of action in favor of contemporaneous market traders for violations of the insider trading rules, has now adopted the decision of the *Elkind* case and has applied it to both insiders and their tippees. Subsection (b)(1) provides that "the total amount of damages imposed [in favor of such traders] * * * shall not exceed the profit gained or loss avoided [by the defendant] in the transaction or transactions that are the subject of the violation." Furthermore, it has provided that there shall be deducted from that recovery any amount which has been "disgorged" by the defendant as a result of action by the SEC.[13] Therefore, if the defendant has settled with the Commission by giving up all of his profit, the class action lawyers are out of luck.

Even before the 1988 Act the disgorgement of profits formula was often employed in SEC insider trading cases. Beginning with SEC v. Texas Gulf Sulphur Co.[14] in 1971, the courts have ordered restitution or disgorgement of profits in several Commission injunctive actions for trading while in possession of material nonpublic information.

The purpose of disgorgement is to deprive defendants "of the gains of their wrongful conduct."[15] As a subsequent Second Circuit decision put it, "the primary purpose of disgorgement is not to compensate investors. Unlike damages, it is a method of forcing a defendant to give up the amount by which he was unjustly enriched."[16] At the same time, "[d]isgorgement is remedial and not punitive. The court's power to order disgorgement extends only to the amount with interest by which the defendant profited from his wrongdoing. Any further sum would constitute a penalty assessment."[17]

In *SEC v. MacDonald*,[18] the court concluded that the appropriate period for determining the profit realized by an insider was "a reasonable time after public dissemination of the inside information" rather than when the insider later ultimately sold the stock. The court reasoned that the value of the stock at a subsequent sale date would be influenced by other developments unrelated to the defendant's wrongful conduct. "When a fraudulent buyer has reached the point of his full gain from the fraud, viz; the market price a reasonable time after the undisclosed information has become public, any consequence of a subsequent decision be it to sell or to retain the stock is not causally related to the fraud."[19] Hence if an insider in possession of material nonpublic information bought when the stock was at $4, and the price rose to $5 a reasonable time after that information was made public, and the insider sold one year later at $10, the *MacDonald* decision would limit disgorgement to $1 per share.[20]

Regarding damages see generally 8 Louis Loss & Joel Seligman, Securities Regulation 3740–3746 (3d ed. 1991), 9 id. 4408–4427 (3d ed. 1992).

---

13. § 20A(b)(2).

14. 446 F.2d 1301, 1307–1308 (2d Cir. 1971), *cert. denied*, 404 U.S. 1005 (1971).

15. Id. at 1308.

16. SEC v. Commonwealth Chem. Sec., Inc., 574 F.2d 90, 102 (2d Cir.1978) (stock price manipulation).

17. SEC v. Blatt, 583 F.2d 1325, 1335 (5th Cir.1978).

18. 699 F.2d 47, 52–55 (1st Cir.1983).

19. Id. at 54.

20. See also SEC v. MacDonald, 568 F.Supp. 111, 113 (D.R.I.1983), *aff'd per curiam*, 725 F.2d 9 (1st Cir.1984) (determining that reasonable period after publication of material information extended form December 24, 1975 until at least 16 days later); SEC v. Ingoldsby, 1990 Fed.Sec.L.Rep. (CCH) ¶ 95,351 at 96,695 (D.Mass.1990) (nine days after publication).

3. INJUNCTIVE RELIEF

In Rondeau v. Mosinee Paper Corp., 422 U.S. 49 (1975), the Supreme Court held that the traditional equitable requirements for the issuance of an injunction, including the showing by the plaintiff of irreparable injury, applied to an action under the federal securities laws. (This requirement of "irreparable injury" to the plaintiff of course does not apply where the plaintiff is the Securities and Exchange Commission, as it most often is.) The court rejected the argument that an injunction could issue automatically simply upon the showing of a violation of the Williams Act as held by the court below and urged by the three dissenting justices. Chief Justice Burger said:

"We turn, therefore, to the Court of Appeals' conclusion that respondent's claim was not to be judged according to traditional equitable principles and that the bare fact that petitioner violated the Williams Act justified entry of an injunction against him. This position would seem to be foreclosed by Hecht Co. v. Bowles, 321 (1944). There, the administrator of the Emergency Price Control Act of 1942 brought suit to redress violations of that statute. The fact of the violations was admitted, but the District Court declined to enter an injunction because they were inadvertent and the defendant had taken immediate steps to rectify them. This Court held that such an exercise of equitable discretion was proper despite § 205(a) of the Act, which provided that an injunction or other order "shall be granted" upon a showing of violation, observing:

" 'We are dealing with the requirements of equity practice with a background of several hundred years of history * * *. *The historic injunctive process was designed to deter, not to punish.* The essence of equity jurisdiction has been the power of the Chancellor to do equity and to mold each decree to the necessities of the particular case. Flexibility rather than rigidity has distinguished it. The qualities of mercy and practicality have made equity the instrument for nice adjustment and reconciliation between the public interest and private needs as well as between competing private claims. We do not believe that such a major departure from that long tradition as is here proposed should be lightly implied. 321 U.S., at 329–330. (Emphasis added).'

"This reasoning applies *a fortiori* to actions involving only 'competing private claims,' and suggests that the District Court here was entirely correct in insisting that respondent satisfy the traditional prerequisites of extraordinary equitable relief by establishing irreparable harm. Moreover, the District Judge's conclusions that petitioner acted in good faith and that he promptly filed a Schedule 13D when his attention was called to this obligation support the exercise of its sound judicial discretion to deny an application for an injunction, relief which is historically 'designed to deter, not to punish' and to permit the court 'to mold each decree to the necessities of the particular case.' 321 U.S. at 329. As Mr. Justice Douglas aptly pointed out in *Hecht Co.,* the 'grant of *jurisdiction* to issue compliance orders hardly suggests an absolute duty to do so under any and all circumstances.' Ibid. (emphasis by Court)."

The private plaintiff in a Rule 10b–5 action usually has no interest in obtaining an injunction against the alleged violation. In most cases, the plaintiff does not know what has happened until it is too late to stop it. Where the plaintiff claims to know in advance of the alleged violation, then he or she obviously would have a standing problem in bringing any action. The plaintiff cannot have relied upon the false or misleading statement or omission, when it is alleged that he or she knows the truth. In one situation, however, that involving a corporate transaction which can be carried out by a vote of a board of directors allegedly dominated by the defendant or by a vote of the shareholders when the defendant has a majority of the votes, the most efficacious form of relief would be to stop the transaction at its inception. Private plaintiffs, however, have usually not pressed for that form of relief, even when the action is filed before the consummation of the transaction and the complaint contains a pro forma count for injunctive relief. The reason is that if the plaintiff were successful in thus nipping the fraud in the bud, at relatively little cost and effort, his or her lawyer would not get a fee commensurate with that which might be obtained if the plaintiff secured a judgment for damages after the fact. The same is true with respect to an action under § 14(a) or § 13(e) or § 14(e) where there are not two contesting factions and the complaint is essentially about alleged derelictions of the management of the corporation.

On the other hand, in the context of a fight for control of the corporation, either in a proxy contest or with respect to a hostile tender offer, the favorite judicial weapon of the contestants has been an action for an injunction against the opponent, which will disrupt his or her timetable and, perhaps, cripple efforts to secure proxies or tenders by the shareholders. Most of the early cases under the proxy rules and the tender offer rules were injunctive actions to restrain alleged violations on the part of the opposite side in the contest. Many of these cases took the position of the dissenters in the *Rondeau* case that an injunction could issue merely on the basis of the finding of a violation, in the discretion of the trial judge, without the necessity of applying the traditional principles of equity relating to such relief. In particular, these courts did not consider it necessary to find, in order to issue a *temporary* injunction, that there was a "probability of success" on the merits on the part of the plaintiff and the likelihood of "irreparable harm" to the plaintiff if the temporary injunction were not issued.

After *Rondeau* the lower courts have wrestled with the effect of that case on the issuance of a preliminary, as opposed to a permanent injunction.

The case itself dealt only with a permanent injunction. But if a showing of irreparable harm is a prerequisite to the issuance of an injunction after a trial on the merits, it would seem to follow that a showing of the likelihood of irreparable harm should be required before an injunction is issued without a trial, especially if, as a practical matter, it is a final and conclusive determination of the litigation in favor of the plaintiff.

In General Aircraft Corp. v. Lampert,[1] the First Circuit quoted and applied the *Rondeau* case in connection with the issuance of a preliminary injunction for a violation of § 13(d). The District Court, on the basis of its finding that the defendants were late in filing their Schedule 13D and that it was materially false and misleading, had issued a temporary injunction prohibiting the defendants from soliciting proxies for the upcoming annual meeting, from acquiring any more shares of stock of the target company and from voting their own stock at the upcoming annual meeting. The Circuit Court affirmed the granting of the preliminary injunction that prohibited the solicitation of proxies or the acquisition of additional shares "*until the Schedule 13D is* amended to reflect accurately" the information called for; however, it reversed that portion of the preliminary injunction which disenfranchised the defendants with respect to the annual meeting insofar as the voting of their own shares was concerned. The court said: "In the circumstances disclosed by this record, sterilization of

---

1.   556 F.2d 90 (1st Cir.1977).

appellants' legally acquired shares would be punishment, not deterrence, since it would deprive appellants of previously acquired voting rights without sound reason. While it may be appropriate for the courts to enjoin the voting of shares rapidly acquired just before a contest for control following a Section 13(d) violation, * * * absent a clear showing of irreparable injury, disenfranchisement should not extend to prior holdings legally acquired.''

Before and after *Rondeau* the courts have also addressed what type of injunctive relief a plaintiff may seek. Besides the formula in *Lampert* restraining further purchases until a corrected schedule has been filed, or in some instances for a specified period after that,[2] relief under §§ 14(d)–(e) has included extension of the depositing security holders' statutory right to withdraw,[3] preliminary restraint against transferring or hypothecating deposited shares in order to permit their return if it should ultimately be ordered,[4] and requiring both sides to start over when both have violated.[5] The courts, while conceiving of the possibility of divestiture or disenfranchisement, usually have rejected these remedies as unreasonably harsh.[6]

In Chapter 18 we shall address the more frequently employed standards for SEC injunctions.

4.   INDEMNIFICATION AND CONTRIBUTION

The right of a corporate officer or director to obtain indemnification for litigation expenses or for liabilities and fines incurred either in direct or derivative actions brought on behalf of the corporation or in third party actions arising from activities undertaken in a representative capacity is generally dependent on state law.

State Indemnification Statutes. A number of states have enacted director and officer indemnification statutes. Among the most expansive is Delaware Corporation Law § 145. This statute encompasses both third party actions and derivative actions brought against a director, an officer, an employee or an

2. See, e.g., Kirsch Co. v. Bliss & Laughlin Indus., Inc., 495 F.Supp. 488, 502 (W.D.Mich.1980); Pabst Brewing Co. v. Kalmanovitz, 551 F.Supp. 882, 895 (D.Del.1982); Irving Bank Corp. v. Bank of N.Y. Co., Inc., 692 F.Supp. 163, 172 (S.D.N.Y.1988) (ten days); cf. Corenco Corp. v. Schiavone & Sons, Inc., 488 F.2d 207 (2d Cir.1973) (court concluded that a "cooling off" period would not be justified on the facts); Chromalloy Am. Corp. v. Sun Chem. Corp., 611 F.2d 240, 248–249 (8th Cir.1979) (no 90 day injunction against purchases while information was disseminated top public).

3. Butler Aviation Int'l, Inc. v. Comprehensive Designers, Inc., 425 F.2d 842 (2d Cir.1970); Prudent Real Estate Trust v. Johncamp Realty, Inc., 599 F.2d 1140, 1149 (2d Cir.1979) (injunction until necessary corrections are made in Schedule 14D–1 and a reasonable period is allowed for withdrawal of stock already tendered).

4. North Am. Car Corp. v. Flying Tiger Corp., 1969–1970 Fed.Sec.L.Rep. (CCH) ¶ 92,-757 (N.D.Ill.1970).

5. Cauble v. White, 360 F.Supp. 1021 (E.D.La.1973).

6. Bath Indus., Inc. v. Blot, 427 F.2d 97 (7th Cir.1970); Management Assistance Inc. v. Edelman, 584 F.Supp. 1021, 1025–1031 (S.D.N.Y.1984); American Carriers, Inc. v. Baytree Investors, Inc., 685 F.Supp. 800, 812–813 (D.Kan.1988).

In SEC v. Scott, 565 F.Supp. 1513, 1537 (S.D.N.Y.1983), *aff'd per curiam sub nom.* SEC v. Cayman Islands Reinsurance Corp., Ltd., 734 F.2d 118 (2d Cir.1984), the court, though ordering disgorgement against one of the defendants, denied an injunction largely because "the grave collateral consequences of an injunction" against a broker-dealer "would result in punishing [him] instead of merely deterring him." *See also* Gearhart Indus., Inc. v. Smith Int'l, Inc., 741 F.2d 707 (5th Cir.1984).

agent. In both types of action, a successful defendant has an absolute right to indemnification for his or her expenses, including attorney's fees. In derivative actions, a director or officer may be indemnified against expenses, including attorney's fees, except where such person was adjudged to be liable for negligence or misconduct, but not for judgments and probably not for settlement payments. On the other hand, in third party actions, a defendant may be reimbursed for all expenses, including attorney's fees, judgments and settlement payments actually and reasonably incurred. In both derivative and third party actions, a statutory standard of conduct must be met. The defendant may be indemnified only if such individual "acted in good faith and in a manner he reasonably believed to be in or not opposed to the best interests of the corporation," and, with respect to criminal actions, only if such person had no reasonable cause to believe that the conduct was unlawful. This determination may be made by a majority of the directors who are not parties to the action, by shareholders, by independent counsel or by a court. Furthermore, the statute expressly provides that the statutory indemnification provisions shall not be deemed exclusive of any other rights conferred under any bylaw, agreement, or stockholder or director action.

Federal Securities Laws: The SEC statutes are silent on indemnification except for provisions in the Trust Indenture and Investment Company Acts. The civil liability provisions of the 1933 and 1934 acts that contemplate more than one defendant do contain provisions on contribution. Section 11(f) of the 1933 Act provides:

> All or any one or more of the persons specified in subsection (a) shall be jointly and severally liable, and every person who becomes liable to make any payment under this section may recover contribution as in cases of contract from any person who, if sued separately, would have been liable to make the same payment, unless the person who has become liable was, and the other was not, guilty of fraudulent misrepresentation.

In 1995 a new § 21D(g) was added to the Securities Exchange Act to preserve joint and several liability for persons who knowingly commit securities fraud,[1] but otherwise to proportionately limit liability to the "portion of the judgment that corresponds to the percentage of responsibility of that covered person.[2] The percentage of responsibility is to be determined by jury special interrogatories:[3]

> In determining the percentage of responsibility under this paragraph, the trier of fact shall consider—
>
> (i) the nature of the conduct of each covered person found to have caused or contributed to the loss incurred by the plaintiff or plaintiffs; and
>
> (ii) the nature and extent of the causal relationship between the conduct of each such person and the damages incurred by the plaintiff or plaintiffs."[4]

There is an elaborate provision for uncollectible shares limited to plaintiffs with a net worth of less than $200,000.[5]

---

1. Sec. Ex. Act § 21D(g)(2)(A).
2. Sec. Ex. Act § 21D(g)(2)(B).
3. Sec. Ex. Act § 21D(g)(3).

4. Sec. Ex. Act § 21D(g)(3)(C).
5. Sec. Ex. Act § 21D(g)(4).

Any covered person, essentially a defendant under § 11 of the 1933 Act or generally under the 1934 Act, or any other person who could have been joined in the original action,[6] is subject to contribution and to any continuing liability to the plaintiff on the judgement.[7]

Section 21D(g) codified a key holding in the Supreme Court's 1993 decision, *Musick, Peeler & Garrett v. Employers Ins. of Wausau.*[8] In *Musick, Peeler* the Court addressed the question whether defendants in a Rule 10b–5 action have an implied right to seek contribution. The Court wrote in part:

> We now turn to the question whether a right to contribution is within the contours of the 10b–5 action. * * * Our task is not to assess the relative merits of the competing rules, but rather to attempt to infer how the 1934 Congress would have addressed the issue had the 10b–5 action been included as an express provision in the 1934 Act. See Lampf, Pleva, *supra,* * * *; Ernst & Ernst v. Hochfelder, 425 U.S. 185, 200–201, 96 S.Ct. 1375, 47 L.Ed.2d 668 (1976). We do this not as an exercise in historical reconstruction for its own sake, but to ensure that the rules established to govern the 10b–5 action are symmetrical and consistent with the overall structure of the Act and, in particular, with those portions of the Act most analogous to the private 10b–5 right of action that is of judicial creation. Although we have narrowed our discretion in this regard over the years, our goals in establishing limits for the 10b–5 action have remained the same: to ensure the action does not conflict with Congress' own express rights of action, Ernst & Ernst, *supra,* at 210, to promote clarity, consistency and coherence for those who rely upon or are subject to 10b–5 liability, cf. Blue Chip Stamps, *supra,* at 737–744, and to effect Congress' objectives in enacting the securities laws, Santa Fe Industries, Inc. v. Green, 430 U.S. 462, 477–478, 97 S.Ct. 1292, 51 L.Ed.2d 480 (1977).

> Inquiring about what a given Congress might have done, though not a promising venture as a general proposition, does in this case yield an answer we find convincing. It is true that the initial step, drawing some inference of congressional intent from the language of § 10(b) itself, id., at 472; Ernst & Ernst, *supra,* at 197, yields no answer. The text of § 10(b) provides little guidance where we are asked to specify elements or aspects of the 10b–5 apparatus unique to a private liability arrangement, including a statute of limitations, Lampf, Pleva, *supra,* at 1293, a reliance requirement, Basic Inc. v. Levinson, 485 U.S. 224, 243, 108 S.Ct. 978, 99 L.Ed.2d 194 (1988), a defense to liability, Bateman Eichler, Hill Richards, Inc. v. Berner, 472 U.S. 299, 105 S.Ct. 2622, 86 L.Ed.2d 215 (1985), or a right to contribution. Having made no attempt to define the precise contours of the private cause of action under § 10(b), Congress had no occasion to address how to limit, compute or allocate liability arising from it.

> There are, however, two sections of the 1934 Act, §§ 9 and 18 * * *, that, as we have noted, are close in structure, purpose and intent to the 10b–5 action. Lampf, Pleva, *supra,* * * *. See also Basic Inc., *supra,* at 243; Bateman Eichler, *supra,* at 316, n.28; Ernst & Ernst, *supra,* at 209, n. 28. Each confers an explicit right of action in favor of private parties and, in so doing, discloses a congressional intent regarding the definition and apportionment of liability among private parties. For two distinct reasons, these

---

6. Sec. Ex. Act §§ 21D(g)(10)(C), 21D(g)(8).

7. Sec. Ex. Act § 21D(g)(5).

8. 508 U.S. 286 (1993).

express causes of action are of particular significance in determining how Congress would have resolved the question of contribution had it provided for a private cause of action under § 10(b). First, §§ 9 and 18 are instructive because both "target the precise dangers that are the focus of § 10(b)," Lampf, Pleva, *supra*, * * *, and the intent motivating all three sections is the same—"to deter fraud and manipulative practices in the securities market, and to ensure full disclosure of information material to investment decisions." Randall v. Loftsgaarden, 478 U.S. 647, 664, 106 S.Ct. 3143, 92 L.Ed.2d 525 (1986).

Second, of the eight express liability provisions contained in the 1933 and 1934 Acts, §§ 9 and 18 impose liability upon defendants who stand in a position most similar to 10b–5 defendants for the sake of assessing whether they should be entitled to contribution. All three causes of action impose direct liability on defendants for their own acts as opposed to derivative liability for the acts of others; all three involve defendants who have violated the securities law with scienter, Ernst & Ernst, *supra*, at 209, n. 28; all three operate in many instances to impose liability on multiple defendants acting in concert, 3 L. Loss, Securities Regulation 1739–1740, n. 178 (2d ed. 1961); and all three are based on securities provisions enacted into law by the 73rd Congress. The Acts' six other express liability provisions, on the other hand, stand in marked contrast to the implied § 10 remedy: § 15 of the 1933 Act * * * and § 20 of the 1934 Act * * * impose derivative liability only; §§ 11 and 12 of the 1933 Act * * * and § 16 of the 1934 Act * * * do not require scienter in all instances, see Ernst & Ernst, *supra*, at 208; Kern County Land Co. v. Occidental Petroleum Corp., 411 U.S. 582, 595, 93 S.Ct. 1736, 36 L.Ed.2d 503 (1973); § 12 of the 1933 Act and § 16 of the 1934 Act do not often create joint defendant liability, see Pinter v. Dahl, 486 U.S. 622, 650, 108 S.Ct. 2063, 100 L.Ed.2d 658 (1988); Kern County, *supra*, at 591; and § 20A of the 1934 Act * * * was not an original liability provision in that Act, having been added to the securities laws in 1988, see Lampf, Pleva, *supra*, * * *.

Sections 9 and 18 contain nearly identical express provisions for a right to contribution, each permitting a defendant to "recover contribution as in cases of contract from any person who, if joined in the original suit, would have been liable to make the same payment." * * * These were forward-looking provisions at the time. The course of tort law in this century has been to reverse the old rule against contribution, but this movement has been confined in large part to actions in negligence. 3 F. Harper, F. James, & O. Gray, Law of Torts § 10.2, p. 42, and n. 10 (2d ed. 1986). The express contribution provisions in §§ 9 and 18 were, and still are, cited as important precedents because they permit contribution for intentional torts. See id., § 10.2, p. 43, and n.11; Ruder, Multiple Defendants in Securities Law Fraud Cases, 120 U.Pa.L.Rev. 597, 650–651 (1972). We think that these explicit provisions for contribution are an important, not an inconsequential, feature of the federal securities laws and that consistency requires us to adopt a like contribution rule for the right of action existing under Rule 10b–5. Given the identity of purpose behind §§ 9, 10(b) and 18, and similarity in their operation, we find no ground for ruling that allowing contribution in 10b–5 actions will frustrate the purposes of the statutory section from which it is derived.

Our conclusion is consistent with the rule adopted by the vast majority of courts of appeals and district courts that have considered the question. * * * We consider this to be of particular importance because in the more than twenty years since a right to contribution was first recognized for 10b–5 defendants, deHass v. Empire Petroleum Co., 286 F.Supp. 809, 815–816 (D.Colo.1968), aff'd in part, vacated in part on other grounds, 435 F.2d 1223 (C.A.10 1970), neither the Securities and Exchange Commission nor the federal courts have suggested that the contribution right detracts from the effectiveness of the 10b–5 implied action or interferes with the effective operation of the securities laws. See Brief for the Securities and Exchange Commission as Amicus Curiae 25–26. Absent any showing that the implied § 10(b) liability structure or the 1934 Act as a whole will be frustrated by finding a right to contribution paralleling the right to contribution in analogous express liability provisions, our task is complete and our resolution clear: Those charged with liability in a 10b–5 action have a right to contribution against other parties who have joint responsibility for the violation. * * *

Musick, Peeler did not, however, address how to administer contribution payments. The commentators and courts had limited this debate to a choice between a contractual or a pro rata method[9] which assigns each defendant an equal share of the judgment, regardless of fault *or* a fault basis.[10] Section 21D(g)(8) adopts a relative fault approach when it provides: "A claim for contribution shall be based on the percentage of responsibility of the claimant and of each person against whom a claim for contribution is made."[11]

Conceivably the greatest significance of the contribution provision of the 1995 Act was clarifying the law of settlement discharges. Before the Act, the courts generally allowed settlement for orders but were divided as to how to apply the value of a settlement to a subsequent judgment. A few courts simply reduced the judgment by the dollar value of the settlement (the *pro tanto* method); other courts reduced the dollar value of the judgment by the percentage of the fault not attributable to the non-settling defendants (the proportionate fault method).[12] In § 21D(g)(7) the 1995 Act adopted the greater of either method.[13]

As a practical matter *Central Bank* which ended private aiding and abetting claims under Rule 10b–5 and § 21D(g)(7) reverse the tactical balance of power in settlements. Before *Central Bank* and § 21D(g)(7), a plaintiff could attempt to persuade a derivative defendant such as an accountant firm to settle for fear of joint and several liability. After 1995, if an action can be brought against such defendants at all, the plaintiff bears the entire risk of undercom-

---

9. *See, e.g.*, William O. Douglas & Gregory E. Bates, The Federal Securities Act of 1933, 43 Yale L.J. 171, 178–181 (1933). Cf. David S. Ruder, Multiple Defendants in Securities Law Fraud Cases: Aiding and Abetting, Conspiracy, *In Pari Delicto*, Indemnification, and Contribution, 120 U. Pa. L. Rev. 597, 647–651 (1972).

10. Smith v. Mulvaney, 827 F.2d 558 (9th Cir.1987) (recognizing relative culpability form of contribution under Rule 10b–5).

11. Although *Musick* did not resolve how contribution should be allocated, the Supreme Court in a 1994 admiralty case approved use of a proportionate share approach to determine the liability of nonsettling defendants. McDermott, Inc. v. AmClyde & River Don Castings Ltd., 511 U.S. 202 (1994).

12. Franklin v. Kaypro, 884 F.2d 1222 (9th Cir.1989), *cert. denied sub nom.* Franklin v. Peat Marwick Main & Co., 498 U.S. 890.

13. See Del–Val Fin. Corp., 868 F.Supp. 547 (S.D.N.Y.1994).

pensation if a court subsequently concludes that the dollar value of a settlement was proportionately too low and the plaintiff receives no benefit if the defendant settles too high.[14]

Under 21D(g)(7) a covered person who settles any private action before a final verdict is discharged from all claims for contribution brought by other persons. Upon entry of the settlement by the court, the court "shall enter a bar order constituting the final discharge of all obligations of the settling covered person arising out of the action."[15] Moreover, when a plaintiff enters into a settlement before a final verdict or judgment, the verdict or first judgement is reduced by the greater of "(i) an amount that corresponds to the percentage of responsibility of that covered person or (ii) the amount paid to the plaintiff by the person."[16]

The most significant issue that *Musick Peeler* and § 21D(g) did not resolve is whether there is an implied right to indemnification? Earlier court decisions had addressed this.

In Globus v. Law Research Service, Inc., 418 F.2d 1276 (2d Cir.1969), cert. denied, 397 U.S. 913 (1970) [Globus I], private actions based on § 17(a) and Rule 10b–5 were brought against LRS, the issuer, Hoppenfeld, its president, and Blair, the underwriter, alleging defects in an offering circular used in connection with a public offering of securities under Regulation A (the small issues exemption) promulgated under § 3(b) of the 1933 Act. Blair cross-claimed against LRS pursuant to an indemnification agreement, indemnifying it for any loss arising out of defects in the offering circular, except for "wilful misfeasance, bad faith or gross negligence * * * or * * * reckless disregard of its obligations under the agreement." The court concluded that since the underwriter had actual knowledge of the material misstatements and omissions, it would be contrary to the public policy embodied in the federal securities laws to permit the underwriter to enforce the indemnification agreement.

In connection with its opinion the court considered the policy considerations as to indemnity under § 11 of the 1933 Act (which applies to registered securities, but not to Regulation A offerings) and expressed its views in these terms at pages 1288–1289:

"Although the 1933 Act does not deal expressly with the question before us, provisions in that Act confirm our conclusion that Blair should not be entitled to indemnity from LRS. See generally Note, Indemnification of Underwriters and § 11 of the Securities Act of 1933, 72 Yale L.J. 406. For example, § 11 of the Act, makes underwriters jointly liable with directors, experts and signers of the registration statement. And, the SEC has announced its view

14. See Lucas v. Hackett Assoc., Inc., 18 F.Supp.2d 531 (E.D.Pa.1998): "By asserting that the provisions of the PSLRA apply for purposes of settlement, the settling defendants gain a significant advantage in this litigation. They may not, in the future, pursue a different, and wholly inconsistent, advantage by contending that viatical settlements are not securities without running afoul of the doctrine of judicial estoppel." Id. at 534.

15. § 21D(g)(7)(A). The 1995 Act contribution section is limited to covered persons ("(1) a defendant in any private action arising under this chapter; or (2) a defendant in any private action arising under section 77k of this title, who is an outside director of the issuer of the securities that are the subject of the action") and does not otherwise apply. Neuberger v. Shapiro, 110 F.Supp.2d 373, 381–382 (E.D.Pa.2000).

16. § 21D(g)(7)(B).

that indemnification of directors, officers and controlling persons for liabilities arising under the 1933 Act is against the public policy of the Act. [The SEC's view now appears in Regulation S–K, Item 510.] If we follow the syllogism through to its conclusion, underwriters should be treated equally with controlling persons and hence prohibited from obtaining indemnity from the issuer. * * * *

"Civil liability under section 11 and similar provisions was designed not so much to compensate the defrauded purchaser as to promote enforcement of the Act and to deter negligence by providing a penalty for those who fail in their duties. And Congress intended to impose a 'high standard of trusteeship' on underwriters. Kroll, [Some Reflections on Indemnification Provisions & S.E.C. Liability Insurance in the Light of BarChris and Globus, 24 Bus.Law. 685] *supra*, at 687. Thus, what Professor Loss terms the 'in terrorem effect' of civil liability, 3 Loss, *supra*, at 1831, might well be thwarted if underwriters were free to pass their liability on to the issuer. Underwriters who knew they could be indemnified simply by showing that the issuer was 'more liable' than they (a process not too difficult when the issuer is inevitably closer to the facts) would have a tendency to be lax in their independent investigations. * * * Cases upholding indemnity for negligence in other fields are not necessarily apposite. The goal in such cases is to compensate the injured party. But the Securities Act is more concerned with prevention than cure.

"Finally, it has been suggested that indemnification of the underwriter by the issuer is particularly suspect. Although in form the underwriter is reimbursed by the issuer, the recovery ultimately comes out of the pockets of the issuer's stockholders. Many of these stockholders may be the very purchasers to whom the underwriter should have been initially liable. The 1933 Act prohibits agreements with purchasers which purport to exempt individuals from liability arising under the Act [§ 14]. The situation before us is at least reminiscent of the evil this section was designed to avoid."

Because *Globus I* involved "actual knowledge," it left open the question whether indemnification is available for merely negligent violations of the federal securities laws. The preponderance of subsequent cases, particularly recent cases, have denied indemnification for indemnification claims not arising under § 11.[17] After *Globus* indemnification has generally been held to be unavailable under Rule 10b–5,[18] or what is now § 12(a)(2).[19]

Globus sets forth the SEC's position on indemnification of directors, officers and controlling persons under the 1933 and 1934 Acts. That policy is presently expressed in SEC Regulation S–K, Items 702, 510 and 512.

Item 702, where applicable, requires a statement of the general effect of any statute, provision or arrangement under which any director, officer or controlling person of the registrant is insured or indemnified against Securities Act liability. Under Item 512(h), if the registrant requests acceleration of the effectiveness of a registration statement pursuant to § 8(a) of the 1933 Act, and waivers have not been obtained, a reference to such indemnification provisions

17. Eichenholtz v. Brennan, 52 F.3d 478, 484 (3d Cir.1995); Gould v. American–Hawaiian Steamship Co., 387 F.Supp. 163, 168–172 (D.Del.1974), *remanded on other grounds*, 535 F.2d 761 (3d Cir.1976) (Rule 14a–9, the proxy fraud Rule).

18. See, e.g., Asdar Group v. Pillsbury, Madison & Sutro, 99 F.3d 289, 291 (9th Cir. 1996).

19. Baker, Watts & Co. v. Miles & Stockbridge, 876 F.2d 1101 (4th Cir.1989).

must be made in the registration statement along with a statement that in the opinion of the Commission such provisions are against public policy and will not be relied upon by any beneficiary without adjudication by a court of their validity. This statement with respect to SEC policy must substantially follow the form set forth in the Item.

Under Item 510, if acceleration of the effective date of the registration statement is not being requested so that Item 512(h) is inoperative, and if waivers have not been obtained, a description of the indemnification provisions relating to such persons and the Commission's policy on indemnification must be set forth in the registration statement. If the director, officer or controlling person of the registrant is also a member or controlling person of one of the underwriters of the issue, any applicable indemnification provisions must also be described.

These provisions do not prohibit a selling shareholder in a secondary offering from indemnifying the issuer, officers or directors, experts and underwriters from § 11 liabilities arising from his or her misstatements or omissions appearing in the registration statement. Although the registration statement is that of the issuer, registration of a selling shareholder's securities are for the shareholder's benefit and the issuer and other shareholders are entitled to indemnification. The cross-indemnification provisions between the issuer and underwriters which are contained in the typical underwriting agreement are also permitted, provided that the Item 512(h) undertaking contains a disclaimer against utilization until the validity of such provisions has been adjudicated. Finally, it is to be noted that there is no objection to insuring against § 11 liability, regardless of who pays the premiums.[20]

See generally 10 Louis Loss & Joel Seligman, Securities Regulation 4685–4701 (3d ed. rev. 1996).

SETTLEMENT RELEASES

Can a state law settlement release federal securities class action claims that arise under federal statutes within the exclusive jurisdiction of the federal courts? In Matsushita Electric Industrial Co., Ltd. v. Epstein,[1] the Supreme Court answered with a qualified "Yes." Justice Thomas wrote in part for a 5–4 majority:

This case presents the question whether a federal court may withhold full faith and credit from a state-court judgment approving a class-action settlement simply because the settlement releases claims within the exclusive jurisdiction of the federal courts. The answer is no. Absent a partial repeal of the Full Faith and Credit Act, 28 U.S.C. § 1738, by another federal statute, a federal court must give the judgment the same effect that it would have in the courts of the State in which it was rendered.

I

In 1990, petitioner Matsushita Electric Industrial Co. made a tender offer for the common stock of MCA, Inc., a Delaware corporation. The tender offer

---

20. This position has been formalized since 1982 in Securities Act Rule 461(c).

1. 516 U.S. 367 (1996).

Justice Ginsburg dissented in part, but notably observed: "I write separately to em-

phasize a point key to the application of § 1738: A state-court judgment generally is not entitled to full faith and credit unless it satisfies the requirements of the Fourteenth Amendment's Due Process Clause."

not only resulted in Matsushita's acquisition of MCA, but also precipitated two lawsuits on behalf of the holders of MCA's common stock. First, a class action was filed in the Delaware Court of Chancery against MCA and its directors for breach of fiduciary duty in failing to maximize shareholder value. The complaint was later amended to state additional claims against MCA's directors for, inter alia, waste of corporate assets by exposing MCA to liability under the federal securities laws. In addition, Matsushita was added as a defendant and was accused of conspiring with MCA's directors to violate Delaware law. The Delaware suit was based purely on state-law claims.

While the state class action was pending, the instant suit was filed in Federal District Court in California. The complaint named Matsushita as a defendant and alleged that Matsushita's tender offer violated Securities Exchange Commission (SEC) Rules 10b–3 and 14d–10. These Rules were created by the SEC pursuant to the 1968 Williams Act Amendments to the Securities Exchange Act of 1934 (Exchange Act), 48 Stat. 881, as amended, 15 U.S.C. § 78a et seq. Section 27 of the Exchange Act confers exclusive jurisdiction upon the federal courts for suits brought to enforce the Act or rules and regulations promulgated thereunder. See 15 U.S.C. § 78aa. The District Court declined to certify the class, entered summary judgment for Matsushita, and dismissed the case. The plaintiffs appealed to the Court of Appeals for the Ninth Circuit.

After the federal plaintiffs filed their notice of appeal but before the Ninth Circuit handed down a decision, the parties to the Delaware suit negotiated a settlement. In exchange for a global release of all claims arising out of the Matsushita–MCA acquisition, the defendants would deposit $2 million into a settlement fund to be distributed pro rata to the members of the class. As required by Delaware Chancery Rule 23, which is modeled on Federal Rule of Civil Procedure 23, the Chancery Court certified the class for purposes of settlement and approved a notice of the proposed settlement. The notice informed the class members of their right to request exclusion from the settlement class and to appear and present argument at a scheduled hearing to determine the fairness of the settlement. In particular, the notice stated that "by filing a valid Request for Exclusion, a member of the Settlement Class will not be precluded by the Settlement from individually seeking to pursue the claims alleged in the * * * California Federal Actions, * * * or any other claim relating to the events at issue in the Delaware Actions." App. to Pet. for Cert. 96a. Two such notices were mailed to the class members and the notice was also published in the national edition of the Wall Street Journal. The Chancery Court then held a hearing. After argument from several objectors, the Court found the class representation adequate and the settlement fair.

The order and final judgment of the Chancery Court incorporated the terms of the settlement agreement, providing:

"All claims, rights and causes of action (state or federal, including but not limited to claims arising under the federal securities law, any rules or regulations promulgated thereunder, or otherwise), whether known or unknown that are, could have been or might in the future be asserted by any of the plaintiffs or any member of the Settlement Class (other than those who have validly requested exclusion therefrom), * * * in connection with or that arise now or hereafter out of the Merger Agreement, the Tender Offer, the Distribution Agreement, the Capital Contribution Agreement, the employee compensation arrangements, the Tender Agreements, the Initial Proposed Settlement, this Settlement * * * and including without limitation the claims asserted in the

California Federal Actions * * * are hereby compromised, settled, released and discharged with prejudice by virtue of the proceedings herein and this Order and Final Judgment." In re *MCA, Inc. Shareholders Litigation,* C.A. No. 11740 (Feb. 22, 1993), reprinted in App. to Pet. for Cert. 74a–75a (emphasis added).

The judgment also stated that the notice met all the requirements of due process. The Delaware Supreme Court affirmed. In re *MCA, Inc., Shareholders Litigation,* 633 A.2d 370 (1993) (judgment order).

Respondents were members of both the state and federal plaintiff classes. Following issuance of the notice of proposed settlement of the Delaware litigation, respondents neither opted out of the settlement class nor appeared at the hearing to contest the settlement or the representation of the class. On appeal in the Ninth Circuit, petitioner Matsushita invoked the Delaware judgment as a bar to further prosecution of that action under the Full Faith and Credit Act, 28 U.S.C. § 1738.

The Ninth Circuit rejected petitioner's argument, ruling that § 1738 did not apply. Epstein v. MCA, Inc., 50 F.3d 644, 661–666 (1995). * * *

A

The state court judgment in this case differs in two respects from the judgments that we have previously considered in our cases under the Full Faith and Credit Act. As respondents and the Court of Appeals stressed, the judgment was the product of a class action and incorporated a settlement agreement releasing claims within the exclusive jurisdiction of the federal courts. Though respondents urge "the irrelevance of section 1738 to this litigation," Brief for Respondents 25, we do not think that either of these features exempts the judgment from the operation of § 1738.

That the judgment at issue is the result of a class action, rather than a suit brought by an individual, does not undermine the initial applicability of § 1738. * * *

* * * Section 27 provides that "the district courts of the United States * * * shall have exclusive jurisdiction * * * of all suits in equity and actions at law brought to enforce any liability or duty created by this chapter or the rules and regulations thereunder." 15 U.S.C. § 78aa. There is no suggestion in § 27 that Congress meant for plaintiffs with Exchange Act claims to have more than one day in court to challenge the legality of a securities transaction. Though the statute plainly mandates that suits alleging violations of the Exchange Act may be maintained only in federal court, nothing in the language of § 27 "remotely expresses any congressional intent to contravene the common-law rules of preclusion or to repeal the express statutory requirements of * * * 28 U.S.C. § 1738." Allen v. McCurry, *supra,* at 97–98.

Nor does § 27 evince any intent to prevent litigants in state court—whether suing as individuals or as part of a class—from voluntarily releasing Exchange Act claims in judicially approved settlements. While § 27 prohibits state courts from adjudicating claims arising under the Exchange Act, it does not prohibit state courts from approving the release of Exchange Act claims in the settlement of suits over which they have properly exercised jurisdiction, i.e., suits arising under state law or under federal law for which there is concurrent jurisdiction. In this case, for example, the Delaware action was not "brought to enforce" any rights or obligations under the Act. The Delaware court asserted judicial power over a complaint asserting purely state law causes of action and, after the parties agreed to settle, certified the class and approved the settlement pursuant to the requirements of Delaware Rule of Chancery 23 and the Due Process Clause. Thus, the Delaware court never trespassed upon the exclusive territory of the federal courts, but merely approved the settlement of a common-law suit pursuant to state and nonexclusive federal law. See Abramson v. Pennwood Investment Corp., 392 F.2d 759, 762 (2d Cir.1968) ("Although the state court could not adjudicate the federal claim, it was within its powers over the corporation and the parties to approve the release of that claim as a condition of settlement of the state action"). While it is true that the state court assessed the general worth of the federal claims in determining the fairness of the settlement, such assessment does not amount to a judgment on the merits of the claims. See TBK Partners, Ltd. v. Western Union Corp., 675 F.2d 456, 461 (2d Cir.1982) ("'Approval of a settlement does not call for findings of fact regarding the claims to be compromised. The court is concerned only with the likelihood of success or failure; the actual merits of the controversy are not to be determined'") (quoting Haudek, The Settlement and Dismissal of Stockholders' Actions–Part II: The Settlement, 23 Sw.L.J. 765, 809 (1969) (footnotes omitted)). The Delaware court never purported to resolve the merits of the Exchange Act claims in the course of appraising the settlement; indeed, it expressly disavowed that purpose. See In re MCA, Inc. Shareholders Litigation, Fed.Sec.L.Rep. p 7749 (1993), reprinted in App. to Pet. for Cert. 68a ("In determining whether a settlement should be approved, a court should not try the merits of the underlying claims. This principle would seem to be especially appropriate where the underlying claims, like the federal claims here, are outside the jurisdiction of this Court" (citation omitted)).

The legislative history of the Exchange Act elucidates no specific purpose on the part of Congress in enacting § 27. See Murphy v. Gallagher, 761 F.2d 878, 885 (2d Cir.1985) (noting that the legislative history of the Exchange Act provides no readily apparent explanation for the provision of exclusive jurisdiction in § 27) (citing 2 & 3 L. Loss, Securities Regulation 997, 2005 (2d ed. 1961)). We may presume, however, that Congress intended § 27 to serve at least the general purposes underlying most grants of exclusive jurisdiction: "to achieve greater uniformity of construction and more effective and expert application of that law." Murphy v. Gallagher, *supra*, at 885. When a state court upholds a settlement that releases claims under the Exchange Act, it threatens neither of these policies. There is no danger that state court judges who are not fully expert in federal securities law will say definitively what the Exchange Act means and enforce legal liabilities and duties thereunder. And the uniform construction of the Act is unaffected by a state court's approval of a proposed settlement because the state court does not adjudicate the Exchange Act claims but only evaluates the overall fairness of the settlement, generally by applying its own business judgment to the facts of the case. See, e.g., Polk v. Good, 507 A.2d 531, 535 (Del.1986).

* * *

In the end, §§ 27 and 1738 "do not pose an either-or proposition." Connecticut Nat. Bank v. Germain, 503 U.S. 249, 253, 112 S.Ct. 1146, 117 L.Ed.2d 391 (1992). They can be reconciled by reading § 1738 to mandate full faith and credit of state court judgments incorporating global settlements, provided the rendering court had jurisdiction over the underlying suit itself, and by reading § 27 to prohibit state courts from exercising jurisdiction over suits arising under the Exchange Act. Cf. C. Wright, A. Miller, & E. Cooper,

Federal Practice and Procedure § 4470 pp. 688–689 (1981) ("Settlement of state court litigation has been held to defeat a subsequent federal action if the settlement was intended to apply to claims in exclusive federal jurisdiction as well as other claims. * * * These rulings are surely correct"). Congress' intent to provide an exclusive federal forum for adjudication of suits to enforce the Exchange Act is clear enough. But we can find no suggestion in § 27 that Congress meant to override the "principles of comity and repose embodied in § 1738," Kremer v. Chemical Constr. Corp., 456 U.S. at 463, by allowing plaintiffs with Exchange Act claims to release those claims in state court and then litigate them in federal court. We conclude that the Delaware courts would give the settlement judgment preclusive effect in a subsequent proceeding and, further, that § 27 did not effect a partial repeal of § 1738. * * *

In Epstein v. MCA, Inc.,[1] a Ninth Circuit panel by a 2–1 vote withdrew an earlier opinion on remand and gave full faith and credit to the Delaware Chancery Court judgment.[2]

F. ARBITRATION OF SECURITIES LAW CLAIMS

Rodriguez de Quijas v. Shearson/American Express, Inc.

Supreme Court of the United States, 1989.
490 U.S. 477, 109 S.Ct. 1917, 104 L.Ed.2d 526.

■ JUSTICE KENNEDY delivered the opinion of the Court.

The question here is whether a predispute agreement to arbitrate claims under the Securities Act of 1933 is unenforceable, requiring resolution of the claims only in a judicial forum.

I

Petitioners are individuals who invested about $400,000 in securities. They signed a standard customer agreement with the broker, which included a clause stating that the parties agreed to settle any controversies "relating to [the] accounts" through binding arbitration that complies with specified procedures. The agreement to arbitrate these controversies is unqualified, unless it is found to be unenforceable under federal or state law. Customer's Agreement ¶ 13. The investments turned sour, and petitioners eventually sued respondent and its broker-agent in charge of the accounts, alleging that their money was lost in unauthorized and fraudulent transactions. In their complaint they pleaded various violations of federal and state law, including claims under § 12(2) of the Securities Act of 1933, 15 U.S.C. § 77l(2), and claims under three sections of the Securities Exchange Act of 1934.

The District Court ordered all the claims to be submitted to arbitration except for those raised under § 12(2) of the Securities Act. It held that the latter claims must proceed in the court action under our clear holding on the point in Wilko v. Swan, 346 U.S. 427, 74 S.Ct. 182, 98 L.Ed. 168 (1953). The

1. 179 F.3d 641 (9th Cir.1999), *cert. denied sub nom.* Epstein v. Matsushita Elec. Indus. Co., 528 U.S. 1004 (1999).

2. See also Hall v. Coram Healthcare Corp., 157 F.3d 1286 (11.th Cir.1998), *cert. denied,* 526 U.S. 1114 (1999) (a settlement agreement contained a merger clause specifically stating that the settlement constituted the entire agreement and here where plaintiffs challenged the contract, rather than suing in tort, the merger clause governed).

District Court reaffirmed its ruling upon reconsideration, and also entered a default judgment against the broker, who is no longer in the case. The Court of Appeals reversed, concluding that the arbitration agreement is enforceable because this Court's subsequent decisions have reduced *Wilko* to "obsolescence." Rodriguez de Quijas v. Shearson/Lehman Bros., Inc., 845 F.2d 1296, 1299 (C.A.5 1988). We granted certiorari, 488 U.S. 954 (1988).

II

The *Wilko* case, decided in 1953, required the Court to determine whether an agreement to arbitrate future controversies constitutes a binding stipulation "to waive compliance with any provision" of the Securities Act, which is nullified by § 14 of the Act. 15 U.S.C. § 77n. The Court considered the language, purposes, and legislative history of the Securities Act, and concluded that the agreement to arbitrate was void under § 14. But the decision was a difficult one in view of the competing legislative policy embodied in the Arbitration Act, which the Court described as "not easily reconcilable," and which strongly favors the enforcement of agreements to arbitrate as a means of securing "prompt, economical and adequate solution of controversies." 346 U.S., at 438, 74 S.Ct., at 188.

It has been recognized that *Wilko* was not obviously correct, for "the language prohibiting waiver of 'compliance with any provision of this title' could easily have been read to relate to substantive provisions of the Act without including the remedy provisions." Alberto–Culver Co. v. Scherk, 484 F.2d 611, 618, n. 7 (C.A.7 1973) (Stevens, J., dissenting), rev'd, 417 U.S. 506 (1974). The Court did not read the language this way in *Wilko*, however, and gave two reasons. First, the Court rejected the argument that "arbitration is merely a form of trial to be used in lieu of a trial at law." 346 U.S., at 433. The Court found instead that § 14 does not permit waiver of "the right to select the judicial forum" in favor of arbitration, id., at 435, because "arbitration lacks the certainty of a suit at law under the Act to enforce [the buyer's] rights," id., at 432. Second, the Court concluded that the Securities Act was intended to protect buyers of securities, who often do not deal at arm's length and on equal terms with sellers, by offering them "a wider choice of courts and venue" than is enjoyed by participants in other business transactions, making "the right to select the judicial forum" a particularly valuable feature of the Securities Act. Id., at 435.

We do not think these reasons justify an interpretation of § 14 that prohibits agreements to arbitrate future disputes relating to the purchase of securities. The Court's characterization of the arbitration process in *Wilko* is pervaded by what Judge Jerome Frank called "the old judicial hostility to arbitration." Kulukundis Shipping Co. v. Amtorg Trading Corp., 126 F.2d 978, 985 (C.A.2 1942). That view has been steadily eroded over the years, beginning in the lower courts. See *Scherk,* 484 F.2d, at 616 (Stevens, J., dissenting) (citing cases). The erosion intensified in our most recent decisions upholding agreements to arbitrate federal claims raised under the Securities Exchange Act of 1934, see Shearson/American Express Inc. v. McMahon, 482 U.S. 220 (1987), under the RICO statutes, see *ibid.,* and under the antitrust laws, see Mitsubishi Motors Corp. v. Soler Chrysler–Plymouth, Inc., 473 U.S. 614 (1985). * * * To the extent that *Wilko* rested on suspicion of arbitration as a method of weakening the protections afforded in the substantive law to would-be complainants, it has fallen far out of step with our current strong endorsement of the federal statutes favoring this method of resolving disputes.

Once the outmoded presumption of disfavoring arbitration proceedings is set to one side, it becomes clear that the right to select the judicial forum and the wider choice of courts are not such essential features of the Securities Act that § 14 is properly construed to bar any waiver of these provisions. Nor are they so critical that they cannot be waived under the rationale that the Securities Act was intended to place buyers of securities on an equal footing with sellers. *Wilko* identified two different kinds of provisions in the Securities Act that would advance this objective. Some are substantive, such as placing on the seller the burden of proving lack of scienter when a buyer alleges fraud. See 346 U.S., at 431, 74 S.Ct., at 184, citing 15 U.S.C. § 77l(2). Others are procedural. The specific procedural improvements highlighted in *Wilko* are the statute's broad venue provisions in the federal courts; the existence of nation-wide service of process in the federal courts; the extinction of the amount-in-controversy requirement that had applied to fraud suits when they were brought in federal courts under diversity jurisdiction rather than as a federal cause of action; and the grant of concurrent jurisdiction in the state and federal courts without possibility of removal. See 346 U.S., at 431, citing 15 U.S.C. § 77v(a).

There is no sound basis for construing the prohibition in § 14 on waiving "compliance with any provision" of the Securities Act to apply to these procedural provisions. Although the first three measures do facilitate suits by buyers of securities, the grant of concurrent jurisdiction constitutes explicit authorization for complainants to waive those protections by filing suit in state court without possibility of removal to federal court. These measures, more-over, are present in other federal statutes which have not been interpreted to prohibit enforcement of predispute agreements to arbitrate. See *Shearson/American Express Inc. v. McMahon, supra* (construing the Securities Exchange Act of 1934; see 15 U.S.C. § 78aa); ibid. (construing the RICO statutes; see 18 U.S.C. § 1965); *Mitsubishi Motors Corp. v. Soler Chrysler Plymouth, Inc., supra* (construing the antitrust laws; see 15 U.S.C. § 15).

Indeed, in *McMahon* the Court declined to read § 29(a) of the Securities Exchange Act of 1934, the language of which is in every respect the same as that in § 14 of the 1933 Act, compare 15 U.S.C. § 77v(a) with § 78aa, to prohibit enforcement of predispute agreements to arbitrate. The only conceivable distinction in this regard between the Securities Act and the Securities Exchange Act is that the former statute allows concurrent federal-state jurisdiction over causes of action and the latter statute provides for exclusive federal jurisdiction. But even if this distinction were thought to make any difference at all, it would suggest that arbitration agreements, which are "in effect, a specialized kind of forum-selection clause," Scherk v. Alberto–Culver Co., 417 U.S. 506, 519 (1974), should not be prohibited under the Securities Act, since they, like the provision for concurrent jurisdiction, serve to advance the objective of allowing buyers of securities a broader right to select the forum for resolving disputes, whether it be judicial or otherwise. And in *McMahon* we explained at length why we rejected the *Wilko* Court's aversion to arbitration as a forum for resolving disputes over securities transactions, especially in light of the relatively recent expansion of the Securities and Exchange Commission's authority to oversee and to regulate those arbitration procedures. 482 U.S., at 231–234, 107 S.Ct., at 2339–2342. We need not repeat those arguments here.

Finally, in *McMahon* we stressed the strong language of the Arbitration Act, which declares as a matter of federal law that arbitration agreements "shall be valid, irrevocable, and enforceable, save upon such grounds as exist at law or in equity for the revocation of any contract." 9 U.S.C. § 2. Under that statute, the party opposing arbitration carries the burden of showing that Congress intended in a separate statute to preclude a waiver of judicial remedies, or that such a waiver of judicial remedies inherently conflicts with the underlying purposes of that other statute. 482 U.S., at 226–227. But as Justice Frankfurter said in dissent in *Wilko,* so it is true in this case: "There is nothing in the record before us, nor in the facts of which we can take judicial notice, to indicate that the arbitral system * * * would not afford the plaintiff the rights to which he is entitled." 346 U.S., at 439, 74 S.Ct., at 189. Petitioners have not carried their burden of showing that arbitration agreements are not enforceable under the Securities Act.

The language quoted above from § 2 of the Arbitration Act also allows the courts to give relief where the party opposing arbitration presents "well-supported claims that the agreement to arbitrate resulted from the sort of fraud or overwhelming economic power that would provide grounds 'for the revocation of any contract.' " *Mitsubishi,* 473 U.S., at 627. This avenue of relief is in harmony with the Securities Act's concern to protect buyers of securities by removing "the disadvantages under which buyers labor" in their dealings with sellers. *Wilko,* 346 U.S., at 435. Although petitioners suggest that the agreement to arbitrate here was adhesive in nature, the record contains no factual showing sufficient to support that suggestion.

III

We do not suggest that the Court of Appeals on its own authority should have taken the step of renouncing *Wilko.* If a precedent of this Court has direct application in a case, yet appears to rest on reasons rejected in some other line of decisions, the Court of Appeals should follow the case which directly controls, leaving to this Court the prerogative of overruling its own decisions. We now conclude the *Wilko* was incorrectly decided and is inconsistent with the prevailing uniform construction of other federal statutes governing arbitration agreements in the setting of business transactions. Although we are normally and properly reluctant to overturn our decisions construing statutes, we have done so to achieve a uniform interpretation of similar statutory language, Commissioner v. Estate of Church, 335 U.S. 632, 649–650, and to correct a seriously erroneous interpretation of statutory language that would undermine congressional policy as expressed in other legislation, see, e.g., Boys Markets, Inc. v. Retail Clerks, 398 U.S. 235, 240–241 (1970) (overruling Sinclair Refining Co. v. Atkinson, 370 U.S. 195 (1962)). Both purposes would be served here by overruling the *Wilko* decision.

It also would be undesirable for the decisions in *Wilko* and *McMahon* to continue to exist side by side. Their inconsistency is at odds with the principle that the 1933 and 1934 Acts should be construed harmoniously because they "constitute interrelated components of the federal regulatory scheme governing transactions in securities." Ernst & Ernst v. Hochfelder, 425 U.S. 185, 206 (1976). In this case, for example, petitioners' claims under the 1934 Act were subjected to arbitration, while their claim under the 1933 Act was not permitted to go to arbitration, but was required to proceed in court. That result makes little sense for similar claims, based on similar facts, which are supposed to arise within a single federal regulatory scheme. In addition, the inconsistency between *Wilko* and *McMahon* undermines the essential rationale for a harmonious construction of the two statutes, which is to discourage litigants from manipulating their allegations merely to cast their claims under one of the securities laws rather than another. For all of these reasons, therefore, we overrule the decision in *Wilko*.

Petitioners argue finally that if the Court overrules *Wilko,* it should not apply its ruling retroactively to the facts of this case. We disagree. The general rule of long standing is that the law announced in the Court's decision controls the case at bar. See, e.g., Saint Francis College v. Al–Khazraji, 481 U.S. 604, 608 (1987); United States v. Schooner Peggy, 5 U.S. (1 Cranch) 103, 109 (1801). In some civil cases, the Court has restricted its rulings to have prospective application only, where specific circumstances are present. Chevron Oil v. Huson, 404 U.S. 97, 106–107 (1971). Under the *Chevron* approach, the customary rule of retroactive application is appropriate here. Although our decision to overrule *Wilko* establishes a new principle of law for arbitration agreements under the Securities Act, this ruling furthers the purposes and effect of the Arbitration Act without undermining those of the Securities Act. Today's ruling, moreover, does not produce "substantial inequitable results," id., at 107, 92 S.Ct., at 355, for petitioners do not make any serious allegation that they agreed to arbitrate future disputes relating to their investment contracts in reliance on *Wilko*'s holding that such agreements would be held unenforceable by the courts. Our conclusion is reinforced by our assessment that resort to the arbitration process does not inherently undermine any of the substantive rights afforded to petitioners under the Securities Act.

The judgment of the Court of Appeal is *affirmed*.

■ JUSTICE STEVENS, with whom JUSTICE BRENNAN, JUSTICE MARSHALL, and JUSTICE BLACKMUN join, dissenting.

The Court of Appeals refused to follow Wilko v. Swan, 346 U.S. 427 (1953), a controlling precedent of this Court. As the majority correctly acknowledges, ante, at 1921, the Court of Appeals therefore engaged in an indefensible brand of judicial activism. We, of course, are not subject to the same restraint when asked to upset one of our own precedents. But when our earlier opinion gives a statutory provision concrete meaning, which Congress elects not to amend during the ensuing 3½ decades, our duty to respect Congress' work product is strikingly similar to the duty of other federal courts to respect our work product.

In the final analysis, a Justice's vote in a case like this depends more on his or her views about the respective lawmaking responsibilities of Congress and this Court than on conflicting policy interests. Judges who have confidence in their own ability to fashion public policy are less hesitant to change the law those of us who are inclined to give wide latitude to the views of the voters' representatives on nonconstitutional matters. Cf. Boyle v. United Technologies Corp., 487 U.S. 500, 108 S.Ct. 2510, 101 L.Ed.2d 442 (1988). As I pointed out years ago, Alberto–Culver Co. v. Scherk, 484 F.2d 611, 615–620 (C.A.7 1973) (dissenting opinion), rev'd, 417 U.S. 506 (1974), there are valid policy and textual arguments on both sides regarding the interrelation of federal securities and arbitration Acts. See ante, at 1919–1921. None of these arguments, however, carries sufficient weight to tip the balance between judicial and legislative authority and overturn an interpretation of an Act of Congress that has been settled for many years.

I respectfully dissent.

ARBITRATION OF SECURITIES LAW CLAIMS

In Wilko v. Swan[1] the United States Supreme Court held in 1953 that a claim under what is now § 12(a)(2) of the 1933 Act would not be sent to arbitration, despite an agreement of the parties that any dispute between them would be subject to arbitration, because this would conflict with the "nonwaiver" provision in § 14 of the 1933 Act declaring that any provision "to waive compliance with any provision of this title or of the rules and regulations of the Commission shall be void." The Court reasoned that the agreement to arbitrate attempted to "waive" the right of the plaintiff to have his statutory cause of action decided exclusively by the federal court (it was, of course, always the defendant who wanted to arbitrate rather than litigate). The 1934 Act has a similar "nonwaiver" provision in § 29(a). It was thought for decades that the *Wilko* case precluded any compulsory arbitration of *any* federal security law claims.

In 1987, however, the Supreme Court in Shearson/American Express, Inc. v. McMahon[2] held that the *Wilko* case did not apply to an action under the 1934 Act and in 1989 in the *Rodriguez* case completely overruled the *Wilko* case as to actions brought under the 1933 Act.

The practical impact of *McMahon* and *Rodriguez* is to create a world in which arbitration of broker-customer disputes is the norm, not the exception. In recent years over 6,000 broker-customer disputes have been received by the National Association of Securities Dealers (before which a substantial majority are arbitrated) and the stock exchanges.[3]

In 1992 the NASD and principal securities exchanges resolved a long standing issue when they unanimously voted that class claims filed in arbitration are not eligible for arbitration. Later that year the Commission approved NASD and New York Stock Exchange rule changes in effect requiring that (1) securities law class actions solely be litigated, not arbitrated, and (2) predispute arbitration agreements contain a statement prohibiting persons from bringing class actions to arbitration or from attempting to enforce an agreement to arbitrate against a class member. "The Commission agrees with the NASD's position that, in all cases, class actions are better handled by the courts and the investors should have access to the courts to resolve class actions efficiently."[4]

In September 1994 the NASD appointed an Arbitration Policy Task Force chaired by former SEC Chairman David Ruder. To address the complexities caused by the growth in securities arbitration, in early 1996, the Task Force published a 156 page report entitled Securities Arbitration Reform,[5] known as the Ruder Report.

At its core, the Ruder Task Force focused on three basic questions: (1) When should a customer's relinquishment of rights to litigate federal securities

---

1.   346 U.S. 427 (1953).

2.   482 U.S. 220 (1987).

3.   *See, e.g.*, 10 Louis Loss & Joel Seligman, Securities Regulation 4590 n.296 (3d ed. rev. 1996).

4.   Sec. Ex. Act Rels. 31,371, 52 SEC Dock. 2189 (1992); 33,939, 56 SEC Dock. 1392 (1994) (adopting rule change). The New

York Stock Exchange also adopted similar rule changes. Sec. Ex. Act Rel. 31,097, 52 SEC Dock. 1160 (1992) (Rule 600(d)).

5.   *Reprinted in* 1995–1996 Fed. Sec. L. Rep. (CCH) ¶ 85,735 (1996). *See generally* Joel Seligman, The Quiet Revolution: Securities Arbitration Confronts the Hard Questions, 33 Hous. L. Rev. 327 (1996).

claims be binding? (2) Who should arbitrate securities customer claims? (3) What remedies should be available?

When Should a Customer's Relinquishment of Rights to Litigate Federal Securities Claims Be Binding?

The Ruder Report began its analysis of this issue with a candid acknowledgment:

> Customers * * * are not required by SRO rules to arbitrate disputes. They point out, however, that they often cannot open brokerage accounts unless they first execute a predispute arbitration agreement. The predispute arbitration agreement generally is part of a firm drafted, non-negotiated customer agreement. * * *
>
> Data collected by the GAO suggest that large broker-dealer firms (which hold approximately 75 percent of individual investor accounts) universally require predispute arbitration agreements for margin and option accounts, but usually do not require them for cash accounts. Increasingly, such agreements also are being required for accounts with a checking account or money market feature. As a consequence, most individual investors have entered into agreements that contain predispute arbitration clauses. In addition, it expected that as an increasing number of custody accounts are opened, these accounts will also require predispute arbitration agreements.[6]

Nevertheless, the Ruder Report rejected a prohibition of predispute arbitration clauses, stating in part:

[T]he Task Force believes that member firms should continue to be permitted to utilize predispute arbitration agreements with their customers. We do so primarily for three reasons:

> First, we conclude, along with the vast majority of those who presented their views to us, that, even with its flaws, securities arbitration is clearly preferable to civil litigation. Arbitration offers investors a more efficient, faster, and cheaper process than court litigation.
>
> Second, although many investor representatives claim that SRO sponsored securities arbitration is unfair, neither the independent studies conducted, nor the statistics on the results of customer-broker arbitrations, support this conclusion. In 1992, for example, the GAO concluded, after an extensive survey, that arbitration results at SRO sponsored forums "show no indication of a pro-industry bias." Between 1991 and 1995, arbitrators awarded damages to customer claimants in 50 percent of all cases they decided. These results are not consistent with a systemic bias in favor of industry parties.
>
> Third, the Task Force believes that our recommendations set forth in this Report concerning predispute arbitration issues and other arbitrations process issues will significantly address the concerns that investors have raised.[7]

Who Should Arbitrate Securities Customer Claims?

With limited exceptions, the securities exchanges and the NASD have required arbitration to be subjected to arbitration by a specific exchange or the NASD.

---

6. Ruder Report at 12–13.   **7.** Id. at 18.

The Ruder Report did recommend that the NASD along with other industry SROs, the SEC, and state regulators study whether a new single securities industry arbitration forum should be established.[8]

The emphasis in the Report, however, was on a series of proposals to improve the NASD arbitration process.

The NASD has three systems of arbitration. First, a small claims system limited to claims not exceeding $25,000, after later amendment, which has a simplified procedure.[9] Second, a pilot program for large and complex claims above $1 million. This has been little used to date.[10] And third, a standard system, which hears the majority of cases for cases now above $25,000 (except those that chose the new pilot rules for large and complex cases).[11]

Two significant reforms were proposed for the standard NASD arbitration process. First, the much criticized system of discovery would in part be replaced with a system of mandatory production of designated essential documents early in the arbitration process without awaiting a specific request.[12] In 1999 the Commission approved a Discovery Guide for use in NASD arbitrations.[13] Second, a new system of party selection of arbitrators from lists of qualified individuals to replace the appointment of arbitrators by the NASD staff.[14] This too was adopted.[15]

What Remedies Should Be Available?

The fundamental question here is whether arbitrators should have the power to award punitive damages.

The Rudder Report adopted a statesman-like approach to punitive damages, conceding that both the securities industry's and the investor's views of punitive damages had "merit":

8. Id. at 145–151.

9. Id. at 64–67. In 1997 the small claims ceiling was raised from $10,000 to $25,000. Sec. Ex. Act Rel. 38,635, 64 SEC Dock. 1399 (1997). In 2000 the Commission approved a voluntary single arbitrator pilot for cases involving claims of $50,000.01 to $200,000. Sec. Ex. Act Rel. 42,426, 71 SEC Dock. 1616 (2000).

10. Ruder Report at 68–69.

In 1996 the Commission extended for a second year the NASD procedures for large and complex cases. During the first year 578 cases were filed that were eligible for these procedures, but in only 25 of these cases did the parties agree to proceed under these procedures. Sec. Ex. Act Rel. 37,513, 62 SEC Dock. 1246, 1247 (1996).

11. Ruder Report at 69–70.

12. Id. at 77–79.

13. Sec. Ex. Act Rel. 41,833, 70 SEC Dock. 1139 (1999). The adoption Release stated in part:

The Discovery Guide consists of introductory and instructional text, and fourteen Document Production Lists. The first two lists, one for firms or associated persons and one for customers, contain documents that are presumptively discoverable in all customer cases, unless the arbitrator(s), in the exercise of discretion, determines that some or all of the documents in the two lists should not be produced. The next twelve lists, which are dispute specific, contain additional documents that should be produced by both customers and firms or associated persons for respectively, claims of churning, failure to supervise, misrepresentation/omissions, negligence/breach of fiduciary duty, unauthorized trading, and unsuitability. For example, a party involved in a churning claim should produce documents from either List One or Two, which apply to all customer cases, and documents from List Three or Four, which apply to churning claims.

14. Ruder Report at 89–90.

15. Sec. Ex. Act Rel. 40,555, 68 SEC Dock. 430 (1998).

The public policy argument underlying the industry's position is that punitive damages are intended to serve a broad societal purpose of deterring misconduct; they are not intended to compensate individual claimants. As such, punitive damages derive from the exclusive authority of the state to define and punish wrongdoing. In contrast, arbitration is a private mechanism designed to resolve particular disputes in an inexpensive, efficient, and expedited forum. A private forum, without the safeguards and procedures of the judicial system, does not have the capacity to impose penalties intended to protect that public welfare.

The industry contends that to vest in a private forum the authority to impose such penalties raises serious questions of due process and fairness. * * * For example, unlike punitive damages awarded in civil litigation, the grounds on which to challenge an award of punitive damages in arbitration are extremely narrow. The right to appeal is not only an essential element in the due process right afforded to those who have been punished, but it also provides a measure of consistency and judiciousness in the award of punitive damages. Also, in contrast to civil litigation, there are no reasoned opinions as there would be in bench trials, no right to a jury trial, and no differentiation as to the standard to be applied in granting the award.[16]

In contrast:

The investor community points out that, since the Supreme Court's decision in *McMahon*, investors have been effectively denied the ability to select the court system to resolve disputes with their brokers. Generally, the investor's only choice is to select an industry sponsored arbitration forum because the [American Arbitration Association] is infrequently included in the predispute arbitration agreement as an alternative forum. Consequently, if the SRO forum does not permit arbitrators to award those punitive damages that are available in court, investors will be deprived of their rights to claim them.

Investors thus argue that the failure of the SRO arbitration system to permit punitive damages would constitute a serious deprivation of rights they would have had in civil litigation. Retaining punitive damages therefore should be an essential part of the bargain under which investors agree to waive their rights to sue in court.[17]

Against this background, the Ruder Report made two principal recommendations with respect to punitive damages.

First, there should be a cap of the lesser of two times compensatory damages or $750,000.[18]

Second, the Ruder Report recommended that when punitive damages are awarded, a written award should clearly specify what portion is for compensatory damages and what portion is for punitive damages.[19]

Neither proposal was adopted.[20] With respect to punitive damages, as the following case illustrates, the courts have not been inactive.

---

16. Id. at 36–37.

17. Id. at 38–39.

18. Id. at 42.

19. Id. at 44.

20. In 1997 the Commission circulated a NASD proposal to adopt the two times compensatory damages or $750,000 cap. Sec. Ex. Act Rel. 39,371, 65 SEC Dock. 2170 (1997). See generally Symposium on Punitive Damages and the Consumerization of Arbi-

Mastrobuono v. Shearson Lehman Hutton, Inc.

Supreme Court of the United States, 1995.
514 U.S. 52, 115 S.Ct. 1212, 131 L.Ed.2d 76.

■ JUSTICE STEVENS delivered the opinion of the Court.

New York law allows courts, but not arbitrators, to award punitive damages. In a dispute arising out of a standard-form contract that expressly provides that it "shall be governed by the laws of the State of New York," a panel of arbitrators awarded punitive damages. The District Court and Court of Appeals disallowed that award. The question presented is whether the arbitrators' award is consistent with the central purpose of the Federal Arbitration Act to ensure "that private agreements to arbitrate are enforced according to their terms." Volt Information Sciences, Inc. v. Board of Trustees of Leland Stanford Junior Univ., 489 U.S. 468, 479, 109 S.Ct. 1248, 1256, 103 L.Ed.2d 488 (1989).

I

In 1985 petitioners, Antonio Mastrobuono, then an assistant professor of medieval literature, and his wife Diana Mastrobuono, an artist, opened a securities trading account with respondent Shearson Lehman Hutton, Inc. (Shearson), by executing Shearson's standard-form Client's Agreement. Respondent Nick DiMinico, a vice president of Shearson, managed the Mastrobuonos' account until they closed it in 1987. In 1989, petitioners filed this action in the United States District Court for the Northern District of Illinois, alleging that respondents had mishandled their account and claiming damages on a variety of state and federal law theories.

Paragraph 13 of the parties' agreement contains an arbitration provision and a choice-of-law provision. Relying on the arbitration provision and on §§ 3 and 4 of the Federal Arbitration Act (FAA), 9 U.S.C. §§ 3, 4, respondents filed a motion to stay the court proceedings and to compel arbitration pursuant to the rules of the National Association of Securities Dealers. The District Court granted that motion, and a panel of three arbitrators was convened. After conducting hearings in Illinois, the panel ruled in favor of petitioners.

In the arbitration proceedings, respondents argued that the arbitrators had no authority to award punitive damages. Nevertheless, the panel's award included punitive damages of $400,000, in addition to compensatory damages of $159,327. Respondents paid the compensatory portion of the award but filed a motion in the District Court to vacate the award of punitive damages. The District Court granted the motion, 812 F.Supp. 845 (N.D.Ill.1993), and the Court of Appeals for the Seventh Circuit affirmed. 20 F.3d 713 (1994). Both courts relied on the choice-of-law provision in Paragraph 13 of the parties' agreement, which specifies that the contract shall be governed by New York law. Because the New York Court of Appeals has decided that in New York the power to award punitive damages is limited to judicial tribunals and may not be exercised by arbitrators, Garrity v. Lyle Stuart, Inc., 40 N.Y.2d 354, 386 N.Y.S.2d 831, 353 N.E.2d 793 (1976), the District Court and the Seventh Circuit held that the panel of arbitrators had no power to award punitive damages in this case.

tration: Articles by Stipanowich, Ruder & Spiedel, 92 Nw. U. L. Rev. 1 (1997); SEC Sends Back for Revisions NASD Proposal on Punitive Damages, 30 Sec. Reg. & L. Rep. (BNA) 286 (1998).

We granted certiorari, 513 U.S. 921, 115 S.Ct. 305, 130 L.Ed.2d 218 (1994), because the Courts of Appeals have expressed differing views on whether a contractual choice-of-law provision may preclude an arbitral award of punitive damages that otherwise would be proper. Compare Barbier v. Shearson Lehman Hutton, Inc., 948 F.2d 117 (C.A.2 1991), and Pierson v. Dean Witter Reynolds, Inc., 742 F.2d 334 (C.A.7 1984), with Bonar v. Dean Witter Reynolds, Inc., 835 F.2d 1378, 1386–1388 (C.A.11 1988), Raytheon Co. v. Automated Business Systems, Inc., 882 F.2d 6 (C.A.1 1989), and Lee v. Chica, 983 F.2d 883 (C.A.8 1993). We now reverse.

II

* * *

* * * Petitioners ask us to hold that the FAA pre-empts New York's prohibition against arbitral awards of punitive damages because this state law is a vestige of the "ancient" judicial hostility to arbitration. See Allied–Bruce, 513 U.S., at 270, 115 S.Ct. at 838, quoting Bernhardt v. Polygraphic Co. of America, Inc., 350 U.S. 198, 211, n. 5, 76 S.Ct. 273, 281, n. 5, 100 L.Ed. 199 (1956) (Frankfurter, J., concurring). Petitioners rely on Southland Corp. v. Keating, 465 U.S. 1, 104 S.Ct. 852, 79 L.Ed.2d 1 (1984), and Perry v. Thomas, 482 U.S. 483, 107 S.Ct. 2520, 96 L.Ed.2d 426 (1987), in which we held that the FAA pre-empted two California statutes that purported to require judicial resolution of certain disputes. In Southland, we explained that the FAA not only "declared a national policy favoring arbitration," but actually "withdrew the power of the states to require a judicial forum for the resolution of claims which the contracting parties agreed to resolve by arbitration." 465 U.S., at 10, 104 S.Ct. at 858.

Respondents answer that the choice-of-law provision in their contract evidences the parties' express agreement that punitive damages should not be awarded in the arbitration of any dispute arising under their contract. Thus, they claim, this case is distinguishable from Southland and Perry, in which the parties presumably desired unlimited arbitration but state law stood in their way. Regardless of whether the FAA pre-empts the Garrity decision in contracts not expressly incorporating New York law, respondents argue that the parties may themselves agree to be bound by Garrity, just as they may agree to forgo arbitration altogether. In other words, if the contract says "no punitive damages," that is the end of the matter, for courts are bound to interpret contracts in accordance with the expressed intentions of the parties—even if the effect of those intentions is to limit arbitration.

We have previously held that the FAA's pro-arbitration policy does not operate without regard to the wishes of the contracting parties. In Volt Information Sciences, Inc. v. Board of Trustees of Leland Stanford Junior Univ., 489 U.S. 468, 109 S.Ct., 1248, 103 L.Ed.2d 488 (1989), the California Court of Appeal had construed a contractual provision to mean that the parties intended the California rules of arbitration, rather than the FAA's rules, to govern the resolution of their dispute. Id., at 472, 109 S.Ct., at 1252. Noting that the California rules were "manifestly designed to encourage resort to the arbitral process," id., at 476, 109 S.Ct., at 1254, and that they "generally foster[ed] the federal policy favoring arbitration," id., at 476, n.5, 109 S.Ct., at 1254 n. 5, we concluded that such an interpretation was entirely consistent with the federal policy "to ensure the enforceability, according to their terms, of private agreements to arbitrate." Id., at 476, 109 S.Ct., at 1254. After referring to the holdings in Southland and Perry, which struck down state laws limiting agreed-upon arbitrability, we added: "But it does not follow that the FAA prevents the enforcement of agreements to arbitrate under different rules than those set forth in the Act itself. Indeed, such a result would be quite inimical to the FAA's primary purpose of ensuring that private agreements to arbitrate are enforced according to their terms. Arbitration under the Act is a matter of consent, not coercion, and parties are generally free to structure their arbitration agreements as they see fit. Just as they may limit by contract the issues which they will arbitrate, see Mitsubishi [v. Soler Chrysler–Plymouth, 473 U.S. 614, 628, 105 S.Ct. 3346, 3354–55, 87 L.Ed.2d 444 (1985)], so too may they specify by contract the rules under which that arbitration will be conducted." Volt, 489 U.S., at 479, 109 S.Ct., at 1256.

Relying on our reasoning in Volt, respondents thus argue that the parties to a contract may lawfully agree to limit the issues to be arbitrated by waiving any claim for punitive damages. On the other hand, we think our decisions in Allied–Bruce, Southland, and Perry make clear that if contracting parties agree to include claims for punitive damages within the issues to be arbitrated, the FAA ensures that their agreement will be enforced according to its terms even if a rule of state law would otherwise exclude such claims from arbitration. Thus, the case before us comes down to what the contract has to say about the arbitrability of petitioners' claim for punitive damages.

III

Shearson's standard-form "Client Agreement," which petitioners executed, contains 18 paragraphs. The two relevant provisions of the agreement are found in Paragraph 13. The first sentence of that paragraph provides, in part, that the entire agreement "shall be governed by the laws of the State of New York." App. to Pet. for Cert. 44. The second sentence provides that "any controversy" arising out of the transactions between the parties "shall be settled by arbitration" in accordance with the rules of the National Association of Securities Dealers (NASD), or the Boards of Directors of the New York Stock Exchange and/or the American Stock Exchange. Ibid. The agreement contains no express reference to claims for punitive damages. To ascertain whether Paragraph 13 expresses an intent to include or exclude such claims, we first address the impact of each of the two relevant provisions, considered separately. We then move on to the more important inquiry: the meaning of the two provisions taken together. See Restatement (Second) of Contracts § 202(2) (1979) ("A writing is interpreted as a whole").

The choice-of-law provision, when viewed in isolation, may reasonably be read as merely a substitute for the conflict-of-laws analysis that otherwise would determine what law to apply to disputes arising out of the contractual relationship. Thus, if a similar contract, without a choice-of-law provision, had been signed in New York and was to be performed in New York, presumably "the laws of the State of New York" would apply, even though the contract did not expressly so state. In such event, there would be nothing in the contract that could possibly constitute evidence of an intent to exclude punitive damages claims. Accordingly, punitive damages would be allowed because, in the absence of contractual intent to the contrary, the FAA would pre-empt the Garrity rule. See *supra*, at 4.

Even if the reference to "the laws of the State of New York" is more than a substitute for ordinary conflict-of-laws analysis and, as respondents urge, includes the caveat, "detached from otherwise-applicable federal law," the provision might not preclude the award of punitive damages because New York allows its courts, though not its arbitrators, to enter such awards. See Garrity, 40 N.Y.2d, at 358, 386 N.Y.S.2d at 834, 353 N.E.2d, at 796. In other words, the provision might include only New York's substantive rights and obligations, and not the State's allocation of power between alternative tribunals. Respondents' argument is persuasive only if "New York law" means "New York decisional law, including that State's allocation of power between courts and arbitrators, notwithstanding otherwise-applicable federal law." But, as we have demonstrated, the provision need not be read so broadly. It is not, in itself, an unequivocal exclusion of punitive damages claims.

The arbitration provision (the second sentence of Paragraph 13) does not improve respondents' argument. On the contrary, when read separately this clause strongly implies that an arbitral award of punitive damages is appropriate. It explicitly authorizes arbitration in accordance with NASD rules; the panel of arbitrators in fact proceeded under that set of rules. The NASD's Code of Arbitration Procedure indicates that arbitrators may award "damages and other relief." NASD Code of Arbitration Procedure P 3741(e) (1993). While not a clear authorization of punitive damages, this provision appears broad enough at least to contemplate such a remedy. Moreover, as the Seventh Circuit noted, a manual provided to NASD arbitrators contains this provision:

"B. Punitive Damages. The issue of punitive damages may arise with great frequency in arbitrations. Parties to arbitration are informed that arbitrators can consider punitive damages as a remedy." 20 F.3d, at 717. Thus, the text of the arbitration clause itself surely does not support—indeed, it contradicts—the conclusion that the parties agreed to foreclose claims for punitive damages.

Although neither the choice-of-law clause nor the arbitration clause, separately considered, expresses an intent to preclude an award of punitive damages, respondents argue that a fair reading of the entire Paragraph 13 leads to that conclusion. On this theory, even if "New York law" is ambiguous, and even if "arbitration in accordance with NASD rules" indicates that punitive damages are permissible, the juxtaposition of the two clauses suggests that the contract incorporates "New York law relating to arbitration." We disagree. At most, the choice-of-law clause introduces an ambiguity into an arbitration agreement that would otherwise allow punitive damages awards. As we pointed out in Volt, when a court interprets such provisions in an agreement covered by the FAA, "due regard must be given to the federal policy favoring arbitration, and ambiguities as to the scope of the arbitration clause itself resolved in favor of arbitration." 489 U.S., at 476, 109 S.Ct., at 1254. See also Moses H. Cone Memorial Hospital v. Mercury Constr. Corp., 460 U.S. 1, 24–25, 103 S.Ct. 927, 941–42, 74 L.Ed.2d 765 (1983).

Moreover, respondents cannot overcome the common-law rule of contract interpretation that a court should construe ambiguous language against the interest of the party that drafted it. See, e.g., United States Fire Ins. Co. v. Schnackenberg, 88 Ill.2d 1, 4, 57 Ill.Dec. 840, 842, 429 N.E.2d 1203, 1205 (1981); Graff v. Billet, 64 N.Y.2d 899, 902, 487 N.Y.S.2d 733, 734–735, 477 N.E.2d 212, 213–214 (1984); Restatement (Second) of Contracts § 206 (1979); United States v. Seckinger, 397 U.S. 203, 210, 90 S.Ct. 880, 884–85, 25 L.Ed.2d 224 (1970). Respondents drafted an ambiguous document, and they cannot now claim the benefit of the doubt. The reason for this rule is to protect the party who did not choose the language from an unintended or unfair result. That rationale is well-suited to the facts of this case. As a practical matter, it seems unlikely that petitioners were actually aware of New York's bifurcated approach to punitive damages, or that they had any idea that by signing a standard-form agreement to arbitrate disputes they might be giving up an important substantive right. In the face of such doubt, we are unwilling to impute this intent to petitioners.

Finally the respondents' reading of the two clauses violates another cardinal principle of contract construction: that a document should be read to give effect to all its provisions and to render them consistent with each other. See, e.g., In re Halas, 104 Ill.2d 83, 92, 83 Ill.Dec. 540, 546, 470 N.E.2d 960, 964 (1984); Crimmins Contracting Co. v. City of New York, 74 N.Y.2d 166, 172–173, 544 N.Y.S.2d 580, 583–84, 542 N.E.2d 1097, 1100 (1989); Trump–Equitable Fifth Avenue Co. v. H.R.H. Constr. Corp., 106 App.Div.2d 242, 244, 485 N.Y.S.2d 65, 67 (1985); Restatement (Second) of Contracts § 203(a) and Comment b (1979); id. § 202(5). We think the best way to harmonize the choice-of-law provision with the arbitration provision is to read "the laws of the State of New York" to encompass substantive principles that New York courts would apply, but not to include special rules limiting the authority of arbitrators. Thus, the choice-of-law provision covers the rights and duties of the parties, while the arbitration clause covers arbitration; neither sentence intrudes upon the other. In contrast, respondents' reading sets up the two clauses in conflict with one another: one foreclosing punitive damages, the other allowing them. This interpretation is untenable.

We hold that the Court of Appeals misinterpreted the parties' agreement. The arbitral award should have been enforced as within the scope of the contract. The judgment of the Court of Appeals is, therefore, reversed.

It is so ordered.

IS MANDATORY ARBITRATION ALWAYS MANDATORY?

As *Mastrobuono* states, the Federal Arbitration Act's "proarbitration policy does not operate without regard to the wishes of the contracting parties."[1] Nonetheless the question of whether securities actions must be submitted to arbitration has been quite frequently litigated.

In *Securities Industry Ass'n v. Connolly*[2] the court emphatically held that a Massachusetts rule that barred broker-dealers from including mandatory arbitration clauses in customer agreements was preempted by the Federal Arbitration Act because the rule singled out arbitration agreements for more demanding standards than those imposed by the general law of contracts in Massachusetts.

Although a challenge to the validity of the entire contract is subject to arbitration, a challenge specifically directed to fraud in the inducement of the arbitration clause itself must be addressed by the court.[3]

In *First Options of Chicago, Inc. v. Kaplan*,[4] the Supreme Court held that when the parties agree to submit the arbitrability question itself to arbitration, a court should review an arbitrator's decision about arbitrability like any other

---

1. 514 U.S. at 52, 57 (1995).

2. 883 F.2d 1114 (1st Cir.1989), *cert. denied*, 495 U.S. 956 (1990).

3. Prima Paint Corp. v. Flood & Conklin Mfg. Co., 388 U.S. 395, 403–404 (1967); see also Perry v. Thomas, 482 U.S. 483, 491 n. 8 (1987).

4. 514 U.S. 938 (1995).

matter the parties have agreed to arbitrate. "If, on the other hand, the parties did not agree to submit the arbitrability question itself to arbitration, then the court should decide that question just as it would decide any other question that the parties did not submit to arbitration, namely independently."[5] To resolve whether the parties agreed to arbitrate arbitrability, generally the courts should apply ordinary state law principles that govern contract formation.[6]

There must, of course, be a *contractual intention* to arbitrate before *Shearson* or *Rodriguez* attaches.[7] But all doubts are to be resolved in favor of arbitration.[8]

A customer-broker arbitration clause is not *per se* unconscionable as a contract of adhesion.[9] Nor is an agreement to arbitrate in accordance with SEC approved procedures "unconscionable as a matter of law."[10]

Nonetheless the courts do retain a limited power to review arbitration awards on such grounds as an award being made in "manifest disregard of the law," or its being "completely irrational," or "arbitrary and capricious,"[11]

In 1998 the Commission approved NASD and NYSE rule changes requiring mandatory predispute agreements to arbitrate employment discrimination or sexual harassment claims.[12]

In recent years a particularly difficult issue concerning securities arbitration involves brokerage firm dispute with their employees, particularly when employment discrimination or sexual harassment claims are alleged.

With respect to securities arbitration generally, see 10 Louis Loss & Joel Seligman, Securities Regulation 4559–4605 (3rd ed. rev. 1996); Kenneth R. Davis, The Arbitration Claws: Unconscionability in the Securities Industry, 78 B.U. L. Rev. 255 (1998);Cheryl Nichols, Arbitrator Selection at the NASD: Investor Perception of a Pro–Securities Industry Bias, 15 Ohio St. J. on Disp. Resol. 63 (1999); Steven A. Ramirez, Arbitration and Reform in Private Securities Litigation; Dealing with the Meritorious as Well as the Frivolous. 40 Wm. & Mary L. Rev. 1055 (1999).

5. Id. at 943.

6. Ibid. Under *First Options*, when the parties had agreed that only a particular exchange could arbitrate and that exchange declines to do so, the case should proceed to trial and not be heard by substitute arbitrators. Salomon Inc. Shareholders' Derivative Litig., 68 F.3d 554 (2d Cir.1995).

7. *See* Leicht v. Bateman Eichler, Hill Richards, Inc., 848 F.2d 130 (9th Cir.1988).

8. Mitsubishi Motors Corp. v. Soler Chrysler–Plymouth, Inc., 473 U.S. 614, 626 (1985), *quoting* Moses H. Cone Mem. Hosp. v. Mercury Constr. Corp., 460 U.S. 1, 24–25 (1983).

9. Cohen v. Wedbush, Noble, Cooke, Inc., 841 F.2d 282, 285–286 (9th Cir.1988); Adams v. Merrill Lynch, Pierce, Fenner & Smith, Inc., 888 F.2d 696, 700 (10th Cir. 1989); Dillard v. Merrill Lynch, Pierce, Fenner & Smith, Inc., 961 F.2d 1148, 1154 (5th Cir.1992) ("[a] party to an arbitration agreement cannot obtain a jury trial merely by demanding one").

10. Cohen v. Wedbush, Noble, Cooke, Inc., 841 F.2d 282, 286 (9th Cir.1988); Gonick v. Drexel Burnham Lambert, Inc., 711 F.Supp. 981, 984 (N.D.Cal.1988).

11. *See, e.g.*, Advest, Inc., v. McCarthy, 914 F.2d 6, 8 (1st Cir.1990), citing cases; Raiford v. Merrill Lynch, Pierce, Fenner & Smith, Inc., 903 F.2d 1410 (11th Cir.1990); Greenberg v. Bear, Stearns & Co., 220 F.3d 22, 28 (2d Cir.2000).

12. Sec. Ex. Act Rels. 40,109, 67 SEC Dock. 824 (1998) (NASD); 40,858, 68 SEC Dock. 2491 (1998) (NYSE). Absent these amendments practically every court has held that the arbitration clause in Form U–4 reached Title VII sexual discrimination or sexual harassment claims. Desiderio v. NASD, Inc., 191 F.3d 198, 203 (2d Cir.1999), *cert. denied*, 531 U.S. 1069 (2001).

CHAPTER 16

Civil Liability Under the Investment Company Act

A. Background

By 2000 nearly $7 trillion was held by mutual funds, the most popular form of investment company, approximately 14 times the total in 1985.[1] By 1998 the proportion of United States households owning mutual funds had risen to 44 percent.[2]

To regulate all types of investment companies the Securities and Exchange Commission enforces the Investment Company Act of 1940.[3]

Investment companies engage primarily in the business of investing and reinvesting in securities of other companies. They are basically institutions that provide a medium for public investment in pools of corporate securities. Their *raison d'être* is diversification of risk.

The several types of investment companies are classified by the statute into three basic groups. Some of the Act's provisions apply to all investment companies, others only to one or two classes or subclasses.

(i) Face–Amount Certificate Companies: These companies issue face-amount installment certificates, which, in essence, are unsecured obligations to pay either (1) a specified amount to the holder at a fixed future date if all the required payments are made or (2) a cash surrender value upon surrender of the certificate prior to maturity.[4]

(ii) Unit Investment Trusts: In the "unit" or "fixed" investment trusts there is no obligation to pay any specified amount. Typically the holder of a share in such a trust has merely an undivided interest in a package of specified securities that are held by a trustee or custodian. There is no board of directors, and management discretion in the management of the portfolio is entirely

---

1. 2001 Securities Industry Fact Book at 59. In 1998 there had been 7,300 mutual funds offered by over 510 investment companies. Levitt Calls on Mutual Fund Industry for Further Education Efforts on Fees, 30 Sec. Reg. & L. Rep. (BNA) 1430 (1998).

2. GAO, Mutual Fund Fees: Additional Disclosure Could Encourage Price Competition 4 (GAO/GGD–OO–126 2000).

3. See generally 1 Louis Loss & Joel Seligman, Securities Regulation 242–272 (3d ed. rev. 1998); 9 id. 4447–4453 (3d ed. 1992); Tamar Frankel, Trends in the Regulation of Investment Companies and Investment Advisers, 1 Vill. J. L. & Inv. Management 3 (1999); Symposium: Mutual Fund Regulation in the Next Millennium, 44 N.Y.L. Sch. L. Rev. 431 (2001).

4. §§ 2(a)(15), 4(1). A cemetery and mortuary company that issued face-amount certificates of the installment type was an investment company under § 3(a)(2) of the Investment Company Act, even though its primary business was the funeral industry and it did not reinvest the proceeds from sale of the certificates in securities but rather used most of the proceeds for its own operating expenses. Section 3(a)(2) defines an investment company on the basis of the issuance of a face-amount certificate without regard to either the issuer's primary business or the reinvestment of sales proceeds. SEC v. Mount Vernon Memorial Park, 664 F.2d 1358, 1363 (9th Cir.1982).

eliminated or reduced to a minimum.[5] Indeed, the trust's sole asset is almost always the share of a single open-end investment company, and the unit investment trust issues "periodic payment plan certificates" that represent the indirect interest of its investors in the shares of the underlying investment company.[6] The recent, highly popular exchange-traded funds, or ETFs, issued by several stock markets are unit investment trusts.[7]

(iii) Management Companies: The residual and largest group of investment companies—all those that are not face-amount certificate companies or unit investment trusts—consists of the "management companies."[8]

Management investment companies are subdivided into "open-end" companies (popularly called "mutual funds") and "closed-end" companies; each of these is in turn divided into "diversified" and "non-diversified" companies.[9] An open-end company is one that is offering or has outstanding any "redeemable security"—defined as a security that entitles the holder on demand to receive approximately his proportionate share of the issuer's net assets or its cash equivalent.[10] Almost all open-end companies continuously offer new shares to the public so as to cover redemptions and to increase their funds available for investment. Closed-end companies do not have redeemable securities; they may occasionally offer new securities to the public as any industrial company does, but the usual way to acquire their shares is on the open market. The definition of a "diversified" management company is based on a mathematical test of the degree of diversification of the portfolio. Most open-end companies are in fact diversified.

Investment companies had a period of phenomenal growth in the late 1920s. By 1929, they were being created at the rate of one a day and the American public had invested almost $7 billion in investment companies of all types. After the stock market crash, closed-end management companies fell into disrepute and the rise of other types of companies accelerated. The fixed or unit trusts had their day between 1930 and 1935, and the more recent growth has been primarily in the open-end management companies—the "mutual funds" and, in recent years, the money market funds.[11] These funds charge no initial sales load.

Perhaps because the statute was the result of a compromise—but in a greater measure, probably, because of the different types of companies it covers

---

5. § 4(2). There has been tremendous growth in the unit investment trust (UIT) industry over the last two decades.

6. § 2(a)(27).

7. See generally Tuuli–Ann Ristkok, Exchange–Traded Funds, 34 Rev. Securities & Commodities Reg. 109 (2001).

8. § 4(3).

9. § 5.

10. § 2(a)(32).

11. "[M]oney market funds are open-end investment companies which invest primarily in short-term debt instruments. They provide a vehicle to permit investors to take advantage of what, at times, may be the higher short-term interest rates earned on large investments ... [by] the purchase of larger denomination instruments than could normally be bought by the individual small investor." Inv. Co. Act Rel. 8786 (1977), *quoted in* 4 T. Frankel, The Regulation of Money Managers: The Investment Company Act and the Investment Advisers Act 308 (1980).

In 1991 the Commission adopted several amendments to rules and forms that affect money market funds, notably including Rule 2a–7. See Inv. Co. Act Rel. 17,589, 46 SEC Dock. 970 (1990) (proposal); 18,005, 48 SEC Dock. 346 (1991) (adoption).

In 2000 $1.845 trillion was invested in money market funds, approximately 26.5 percent of all mutual fund assets. 2001 Securities Industry Fact Book at 59.

and the intricacies of the problems it presents—the Investment Company Act is the most complex of the entire SEC series.

In March 1990 the Commission formed a task force to reexamine the regulation of investment companies and make recommendations for legislation and rules in order to reform the regulatory structure, including among the subject matters, internationalization, alternative structures, securitization, distribution of open-end company shares, repurchase of closed-end company shares, and bank involvement with investment companies.[12]

Then, in 1992, the Commission's Division of Investment Management published a 525 page report, Protecting Investors: A Half Century of Investment Company Regulation. The Report described the rapid growth of the industry:

> Increasingly, mutual funds are organized in investment company "complexes," *i.e.,* large groups of mutual funds associated with common advisers or underwriters, typically with liberal exchange privileges among the funds. The one hundred largest mutual fund complexes account for eighty-five percent of total investment company assets....

> In recent years, continued industry growth has been fueled in large part by dramatic changes in the financial marketplace. Institutional demand for collective investment products accounts for a significant portion of that growth. When the Investment Company Act was passed, few, if any, institutional investors invested in investment companies. Institutional assets, which accounted for only eleven percent of investment company assets in 1970, now account for over twenty-five percent of total investment company assets.

> In addition, in recent years, an international market for professional asset management has emerged. Investment companies have proved to be attractive vehicles for investors who wish to invest in diversified portfolios of foreign securities. Internationalization of the securities markets also has sparked interest in eliminating barriers to cross-border sales of investment company services.

> Marketplace innovations also have led to a host of new pooled securities products that either were not anticipated or whose significance was not fully appreciated when the Investment Company Act was passed in 1970. Many of these products are constrained by the framework of a statute that originally was designed to deal with only those limited forms of pooled investment vehicles that existed in the marketplace in the 1930s.

> For example, a relatively new financial technique called structured finance or securitization is revolutionizing corporate finance, enabling companies to borrow at low cost while providing investors with high quality debt insulated from the credit risk of the company. This technique has gained widespread acceptance. In fact, structured finance volume now constitutes more than half of all United States corporate bond new issue volume. This technique was not anticipated when the Investment Company Act was enacted. Thus, some but not all structured financings fall within the Act's definition of investment company but, as a practical matter, those offerings that fall within the definition of investment company cannot

12. SEC Ann. Rep. 48 (1990).

operate as registered investment companies within the regulatory framework of the Act as currently written.[13]

In 1996 the National Securities Markets Improvement Act defined as a "covered security": A security issued by a registered investment company (or one that has filed a registration statement under the Investment Company Act of 1940).[14] For these investment company securities, there is now partial preemption of state law in the securities offering and shareholder report areas. Title II of the 1996 also made several amendments to the Investment Company Act.

B.   REGISTRATION AND REGULATORY PROVISIONS

As under the other SEC statutes, the technique of the Investment Company Act is first of all to require registration—in this case, registration of all investment companies that make use of the mail or interstate facilities—so as to have a basis for the regulatory scheme.[1] Most of the required information is similar to that contained in registration statements filed under the 1933 and 1934 Acts, from which investment companies are not exempted. But the 1940 Act registration statement must also recite the registrant's policy about specified subjects—e.g., diversification, issuance of senior securities, borrowing and lending money, engaging in underwriting, and investing in real estate or commodities—that may not be changed without the vote of a majority of the outstanding voting securities.[2]

In the Act the definition of "investment company" distinguishes companies subject to the registration requirement from holding companies on one hand and operating companies on the other. This is done through a quantitative definition in terms of the portion of a company's assets that are "investment securities." Thus, one of the several definitions is that an investment company "is engaged or proposes to engage in the business of investing, reinvesting, owning, holding, or trading in securities" and owns "investment securities" exceeding 40 percent of its total assets (exclusive of government securities and cash); the term *investment securities* in turn is defined to exclude securities of majority owned subsidiaries that are not themselves investment companies.[3]

Several categories are automatically excluded from the definition of "investment company." One covers any "issuer whose outstanding securities (other than short term paper) are beneficially owned by not more than one hundred persons and which is not making and does not presently propose to make a public offering of its securities."[4] The Act contains a number of exemptions in addition to giving the Commission broad authority to exempt

---

13. SEC, Div. of Inv. Management, Protecting Investors: A Half Century of Investment Company Regulation xviii-xx (1992).

14. Securities Act § 18(b)(2).

1. § 7.

2. §§ 8(b), 13; cf. § 21.

3. § 3(a), (b).

4. § 3(c)(1).

In 1996 Title II of the National Securities Markets Improvement Act amended § 3(c)(1) and added new § 3(c)(7) to harmonize the § 3(c)(1) exemption for issuers whose

securities are owned by no more than 100 persons with the § 3(c)(7) exemption for private investment company offerings to qualified purchasers. Subsequently the Commission adopted new Rules to define terms (Rules 2a51-1 to 2a51-3), address beneficial ownership by knowledgeable employees or other persons (Rule 3c-5), and permit transfers of interest in §§ 3(c)(1) and 3(c)(7) funds (Rule 3c-6). Inv. Co. Act Rels. 22,405, 63 SEC Dock. 1084 (1996) (proposal); 22,597, 64 SEC Dock. 550 (1997) (adoption).

any person, security, or transaction or any class of persons, securities, or transactions—by rule or order, conditionally or unconditionally—from any or all of the provisions of the Act.[5]

The regulatory provisions of the Investment Company Act of 1940, as significantly amended in 1970, are designed to accomplish six main objectives: (1) Correction of abuses in sales practices;[6] (2) annual investment advisory fees;[7] (3) independent management;[8] (4) greater electoral participation in management by security holders;[9] (5) adequate and feasible capital structures;[10]

---

5. §§ 6, 6(c).

6. This addresses initial sales charges or "front end loads." Currently NASD Manual Rule 2830(d) provides for a ceiling of 8.5 percent on the sale of open-end investment company shares and registered unit investment company single-payment contract plans with lower ceilings on large orders.

7. § 36(b).

8. Limitations on director affiliations are in § 10. "Interested person" is broadly defined in § 2(a)(19).

In 1999 SEC Chairman Arthur Levitt proposed four measures to strengthen mutual fund broad independence:

· that fund boards have a majority of independent directors;

· that independent directors nominate any new independent directors;

· that outside counsel for directors be independent from management to ensure that directors get objective and accurate information; and

· that fund shareholders have more specific information on which to judge the independence of their fund directors.

Levitt Unveils Four–Step Plan to Boost Mutual Fund Governance, 31 Sec. Reg. & L. Rep. (BNA) 393 (1999).

In 2001 the Commission adopted new investment company director independence rules. Inv. Co. Act Rels. 24,082, 70 SEC 1867 (1999) (proposal); 24,816, 74 SEC Dock. 3 (2001) (adoption); 24,816A, 74 SEC Dock. 973 (2001) (corrections to adopted rules).

First, new rule amendments require that:

· independent directors constitute a majority of the fund's board of directors;

· independent directors select and nominate other independent directors; and

· any legal counsel for the fund's independent directors be an independent legal counsel.

Second, the new rules and amendments will also:

· prevent qualified individuals from being unnecessarily disqualified from serving as independent directors;

· permit [the SEC] to monitor the independence of directors by requiring funds to keep records of their assessments of director independence;

· temporarily suspend the independent director minimum percentage requirements if a fund falls below a required percentage due to an independent director's death or resignation; and

· exempt funds from the requirement that shareholders ratify or reject the directors' selection of an independent public accountant, if the fund establishes an audit committee composed entirely of independent directors.

Finally, [the Commission requires] that funds provide better information about directors, including:

· basic information about the identity and business experience of directors;

· fund shares owned by directors;

· information about directors that may raise conflict of interest concerns; and

· the board's role in governing the fund.

Id. at 4.

Since 1940 the Investment Company Act § 17 has prohibited specific types of self-dealing and excessive commissions by affiliated persons. This Section, before and after amendments, is among the most complicated in federal securities law. See generally 1 T. Frankel, The Regulation of Money Managers: The Investment Company Act and The Investment Advisers Act 529–532 (1978) (definition of affiliated person); 2 id. 408–606 (1978).

9. §§ 13, 15, 16(a), 18, 20, 32(a).

10. §§ 18, 28.

and (6) required financial statements and accounting.[11]

C. CIVIL LIABILITY

Gartenberg v. Merrill Lynch Asset Management, Inc.

United States Court of Appeals, Second Circuit, 1982.
694 F.2d 923, *cert. denied sub nom.* Andre v. Merrill Lynch Ready Assets Trust, 461 U.S. 906 (1983).

■ BEFORE MANSFIELD, VAN GRAAFEILAND AND NEWMAN, CIRCUIT JUDGES.

■ MANSFIELD, CIRCUIT JUDGE:

Irving L. Gartenberg and Simone C. Andre, two shareholders of the Merrill Lynch Ready Assets Trust, a money market fund (the "Fund"), appeal from a judgment of the Southern District of New York, Milton Pollack, *Judge*, entered after a non-jury trial, dismissing their consolidated derivative actions against the Fund and its affiliates, Merrill Lynch Asset Management, Inc., the adviser and manager of the Fund (the "Manager") and Merrill Lynch, Pierce, Fenner & Smith, Inc. (the "Broker"). The plaintiffs claimed violations of § 36(b) of the Investment Company Act of 1940, 15 U.S.C. § 80a–35(b) (the "Act"). 528 F. Supp. 1038, 1040. The principal claim is that the fees paid by the Fund to the Manager for various services, including investment advice and processing of daily orders of the Fund's shareholders, were so disproportionately large as to constitute a breach of fiduciary duty in violation of § 36(b). We affirm the judgment dismissing the complaint.

Since the facts are fully set forth in detail in Judge Pollack's opinion, 528 F. Supp. 1038, only a brief summary here is necessary. The Fund, organized in 1975 as a no-load, diversified, open-end investment company, invests in short-term money market securities expected to pay the highest current income consistent with preservation of capital and maintenance of liquidity, such as short-term securities of the U.S. Government or its agencies, bank certificates of deposit, and commercial paper. An investor may purchase and redeem shares of the Fund without any charges or penalties. There is a daily declaration of dividends, reflecting the net income of the Fund's portfolio. As the district court noted, the purchaser's investment in the Fund is more like a bank account than the traditional investment in securities. Idle money can be invested in the Fund for as little as a day and put to work earning interest. The ease of entrance and egress for the investor, coupled with the ability to share in high yields which the modest investor could not obtain through a bank deposit and might not be able to realize alone, has with the rise (until recently) of interest rates attracted an increasing number of investors. As a result the size of the Fund increased enormously over a few years, from $288 million in April 1977 to over $19 billion as of September 1981.

The Fund has an 8–person Board of Trustees, of whom 2 are interested and 6 are independent and unaffiliated. The operations of the Fund are conducted by the Manager, which provides the Fund with office space and facilities, administrative staff, equipment, portfolio management, compliance with SEC and state record-keeping and reporting requirements, and services to Fund shareholders. For the processing of approximately 80% of the purchases and redemptions of shares of the Fund the Manager uses the Broker, another

---

11. §§ 30–31.

Merrill Lynch affiliate, which is the largest registered broker-dealer in the United States, with 408 domestic offices located in numerous cities and towns, in which more than 7,000 account executives are located. In addition, the Manager uses the vast facilities of the Merrill Lynch organization and its affiliates to render special services to the Fund. For example, Merrill Lynch Economics, Inc. provides economic research and forecasting services while Merrill Lynch Government Securities, Inc. provides expertise with respect to U.S. government and agency securities. A customer located anywhere in the United States can call the nearest office of the Broker or the Bank of New York, the Fund's custodian and transfer agent, order the purchase or redemption without charge of shares of the Fund, and through use of wires and computers the transaction will be carried out immediately. An average of 30,000 such orders are processed daily by the Broker's large organization.

Under the foregoing management the Fund has performed reasonably well in terms of average percentage yields for its shareholders. Its average percentage yields from 1978 through 1980 were slightly above the average for all similar funds. In 1980 it ranked 37th out of 76 money funds in terms of yield.

For all of these services the Manager charges the Fund an advisory fee based on a percentage of the average daily value of the Fund's net assets. The fee rate is graduated downward as the Fund's total assets increase in value. Since 1979 the schedule called for payment of 0.50% (½ of 1%) of the Fund's average daily value of net assets under $500 million and for various intermediate percentages as the value of the net assets increases down to 0.275% for assets in excess of $2.5 billion, resulting in an effective rate of 0.288%. This schedule is the product of a series of negotiations by the 6 independent Fund Trustees with the Manager over the period from 1977 to 1979, which resulted in reductions in the effective rate as the Fund grew in size.

Three studies were made at the Fund's insistence to determine the estimated cost of the processing services provided by the Broker through the Manager to the Fund, two by the Merrill Lynch organization's internal accounting staff and one by the independent accounting firm of Peat, Marwick, Mitchell & Co. ("PMM"). The estimates ranged from $2.02 to $7.50 per Fund order. The earlier internal study which produced the lowest figure did so mainly because it used a modified "incremental" cost method of accounting, based on the assumption that most costs would have been incurred by the Broker even if it had processed no Fund orders. By the time the PMM study was conducted in late 1979, however, modified full cost accounting methods were used for the reason that Fund orders represented a sizeable proportion of all business processed by the Broker; indeed, by April 1981 Fund orders accounted for 37% of all Broker business, necessitating the hiring by the Broker of close to 3,000 non-sales personnel. Had the Manager been required to reimburse the Broker for these costs instead of their being absorbed by the Broker as another Merrill Lynch affiliate, the Broker's net profit after taxes would have been greatly reduced, resulting in a figure ranging from a 38.4% profit to a substantial loss depending on which cost accounting study was used. In 1980, for instance, the last calendar year for which full figures are available, the Manager's fee was slightly over $33 million on the Fund's average net assets of $11.16 billion. Based on the volume of orders generated by 675,324 purchasers, the Broker's processing costs, estimated according to the PMM study, were so large that the Manager suffered a loss during 1980. 528 F. Supp. at 1053–54.

Judge Pollack, construing the legislative history of the Act, decided that the standard for determining whether the Manager had been guilty of a breach of fiduciary duty in violation of § 36(b) was not whether its fees were "reasonable" as urged by plaintiffs but whether they were unfair to the Fund and shareholders, which was to be determined by reference to the nature, quality and extent of the manager's services to the Fund, the money market fund industry practice and level of management fees, and to a lesser extent the Manager's net earnings as a result of providing the services. After reviewing the evidence and appraising the live witnesses who testified, he concluded that the compensation paid to the Manager was fair. *Id.* at 1055.

The package of services described above was found to be extensive and valuable, providing Fund customers with the vast facilities of the Merrill Lynch organization, which were not available to non-Merrill Lynch funds.

The Manager's fee schedule was found by Judge Pollack to "bear a fair relation to the subject matter from which they are derived." *Id.* at 1068. He further found that "the total fee was fair to the Fund" after taking into consideration the nature and extent of the services, the fees charged by other advisers to other money market funds, the overall cost to the Merrill Lynch organization of providing the services, and the fee schedule's allowance for economies of scale by reducing the rate as the Fund's net assets increased. *Id.* at 1055. Judge Pollack also gave weight to the process by which the 6 noninterested trustees of the Fund approved of its management agreement with the Manager. The trustees, who were represented by capable independent counsel, were found to be competent, independent and conscientious in the performance of their duties. They were furnished with sufficient information to evaluate the contract. They thoroughly reviewed and weighed all facts pertinent to the fee, many of which are now part of the record, before approving the Manager's fee after negotiations.

The district court rejected plaintiffs' argument that in determining the fairness of the Manager's compensation the court must take into account as an offset to the Manager's fee the value to the Merrill Lynch organization of "fall-out" business generated by Fund customers who, after opening up a no-charge Fund account, transact other financial business with the Merrill Lynch Broker, such as purchases of stocks and bonds, for which the customer is charged a fee or commission. Thirty-eight percent of new Fund customers for the third quarter of 1979 transacted some non-Fund business through the Broker by January 1980. The fall-out benefit argument was rejected on the ground that any such offset could not be measured since it could not be established with certainty and without heavy expense what portion of the increase in brokerage business would have gone to the Broker without regard to the Fund. Judge Pollack further reasoned that the idea of an offset lacked logic since the customer would in any event have to pay a brokerage fee on non-Fund business. The possible benefit to the Merrill Lynch organization from a "float" resulting from its having the use of redemption funds before paying them to the redeeming Fund customer was found unpersuasive since it was obvious to all concerned. Plaintiffs' claim that there was unnecessary duplication in the Manager's services based on the Bank of New York's obligation to perform them was rejected for lack of proof.

The district court further found that an adequate disclosure of the pertinent facts needed to determine the fairness of the Manager's fee had been made to the Fund's trustees and shareholders.

DISCUSSION

Section 36(b) of the Investment Act of 1940, 15 U.S.C. § 80a–35(b), which governs this case, provides that "the investment adviser of a registered investment company shall be deemed to have a fiduciary duty with respect to the receipt of compensation for services" paid by the investment company or its security holders and that in an action by a security holder on behalf of the investment company against the adviser or affiliate "it shall not be necessary to allege or prove that any defendant engaged in personal misconduct" but "the plaintiff shall have the burden of proving a breach of fiduciary duty."

Appellants contend that the district court erred in rejecting a "reasonableness" standard for determining whether the Manager performed its "fiduciary duty" in compliance with § 36(b). They further urge that the district court erred in relying primarily, in determining whether there was a breach of fiduciary duty, on other money market funds' level of management fees and on the Broker's costs. They argue that since each investment company fund is a captive of its manager, from which it cannot as a practical matter divorce itself, and since there is no possibility that a competitor will take the fund's business from its manager by offering a lower rate, the manager sets its own fee and the fund has no practical alternative but to pay it. It is contended that the test should therefore be what rate would have resulted from arm's-length negotiations in light of the services to be rendered. Appellants further contend that under this standard the fee in this case would have been substantially lower because of economies of scale, the Fund's massive bargaining power as the largest fund in history, and the Broker's duplication of services which the Bank of New York was already required to render. In short it is argued that a fee percentage which may have been reasonable when the Fund was freshly-launched became unreasonable when the Fund grew to its present huge size. See, e.g., *Fogel v. Chestnutt*, 668 F.2d 100, 111 (2d Cir.1981), *cert. denied*, 459 U.S. 828, 103 S. Ct. 65, 74 L. Ed. 2d 66, 51 U.S.L.W. 3254 (1982).

In support of their advocacy of a "reasonableness" standard as the test by which a fiduciary's conduct under § 36(b) should be governed, appellants point to excerpts from the Act's tortuous legislative history, just as the district court relied on other portions of the same history apparently rejecting that criterion in favor of a "breach of fiduciary duty" standard. The legislative history contains statements of legislators and legislative reports pointing in both directions. Bills introduced in 1967 and 1968, which would have imposed a "reasonableness" test, failed of passage. See H.R. 9510, H.R. 9511, and S. 1659, 90th Cong., 1st Sess. (1967) and S. 3724, 90th Cong., 2d Sess. (1968). When the mutual fund industry objected to this standard, a bill (S. 2224) was introduced in 1969 containing § 36(b) in its present form, which was enacted in 1970. The Senate Report on the bill and the House Committee Report accompanying the companion bill do not define the term "fiduciary duty" as used in the bill or how it was to be distinguished from the term "reasonable" that had been used in predecessor bills. See *Investment Company Amendments Act of 1970*, S. Rep. No. 91–184, 91st Cong., 2d Sess. (1970), reprinted in [1970] U.S. Code Cong. & Ad. News 4897, and *Investment Company Amendments Act of 1970*, H.R. Rep. No. 91–1382, 91st Cong., 2d Sess. (1970). The Senate Report does state that an adviser-manager would not be precluded from earning a profit on services provided by it to a fund, that a "cost-plus" type of contract is not required, and that the court is not authorized "to substitute its business judgment for that of a mutual fund's board of directors in the area of management fees," *id.* at 4902–03. On the other hand, the same Report states that a "corporate waste" standard would be "unduly restrictive," [1970] U.S. Code Cong. & Ad. News at 4901, and Congressman Moss, Chairman of the Committee on Interstate and Foreign Commerce, who was one of the chief sponsors of § 36(b), explained to the House that "this [bill], by imposition of the fiduciary duty, would in effect require a standard of reasonableness in the charges," 116 Cong. Rec. 33281 (Sept. 23, 1970). Thus there was no attempt to set forth a definitive test by which observance or breach of fiduciary duty was to be determined.

In short, the legislative history of § 36(b) indicates that the substitution of the term "fiduciary duty" for "reasonable," while possibly intended to modify the standard somewhat, was a more semantical than substantive compromise, shifting the focus slightly from the fund directors to the conduct of the investment adviser-manager. As the district court and all parties seem to recognize, the test is essentially whether the fee schedule represents a charge within the range of what would have been negotiated at arm's-length in the light of all of the surrounding circumstances. (Gartenberg Br. 15, 23, 24; Merrill Lynch Br. 27; Judge Pollack's opinion, 528 F. Supp. at 1047.) The Senate recognized that as a practical matter the usual arm's length bargaining between strangers does not occur between an adviser and the fund, stating:

"Since a typical fund is organized by its investment adviser which provides it with almost all management services and because its shares are bought by investors who rely on that service, a mutual fund cannot, as a practical matter sever its relationship with the adviser. Therefore, the forces of arm's-length bargaining do not work in the mutual fund industry in the same manner as they do in other sectors of the American economy." S. Rep. No. 91–184, *supra*, [1970] U.S. Code Cong. & Ad. News at 4901.

To be guilty of a violation of § 36(b), therefore, the adviser-manager must charge a fee that is so disproportionately large that it bears no reasonable relationship to the services rendered and could not have been the product of arm's-length bargaining. *Fogel v. Chestnutt, supra*, 668 F.2d at 112 (2d Cir. 1981), *cert. denied*, 459 U.S. 828, 103 S. Ct. 65, 74 L. Ed. 2d 66, 51 U.S.L.W. 3254 (1982); *In re Gartenberg*, 636 F.2d 16, 18 (2d Cir.1980), *cert. denied*, 451 U.S. 910, 68 L. Ed. 2d 298, 101 S. Ct. 1979 (1981). To make this determination all pertinent facts must be weighed.

We disagree with the district court's suggestions that the principal factor to be considered in evaluating a fee's fairness is the price charged by other similar advisers to funds managed by them, that the "price charged by advisers to those funds establishes the free and open market level for fiduciary compensation," that the "market price * * * serves as a standard to test the fairness of the investment advisory fee," and that a fee is fair if it "is in harmony with the broad and prevailing market choice available to the investor," 528 F. Supp. at 1049, 1067–68. Competition between money market funds for shareholder business does not support an inference that competition must therefore also exist between adviser-managers for fund business. The former may be vigorous even though the latter is virtually non-existent. Each is governed by different forces. Reliance on prevailing industry advisory fees will not satisfy § 36(b).

We do not suggest that rates charged by other adviser-managers to other similar funds are not a factor to be taken into account. Indeed, to the extent that other managers have tended "to reduce their effective charges as the fund grows in size," the Senate Committee noted that such a reduction represents "the best industry practice [which] will provide a guide," S. Rep. No. 91–184, *supra*, [1970] U.S. Code Cong. & Ad. News at 4902. However, the existence in most cases of an unseverable relationship between the adviser-manager and the fund it services tends to weaken the weight to be given to rates charged by advisers of other similar funds. Report of the Securities and Exchange Commission on the Public Policy Implications of Investment Company Growth, H.R. Rep. No. 2337, 89th Cong., 2d Sess. (1966) 131, 148. A fund cannot move easily from one adviser-manager to another. Therefore "investment advisers seldom, if ever, compete with each other for advisory contracts with mutual funds." *Id.* at 126.

One reason why fund competition for shareholder business does not lead to competition between adviser-managers for fund business is the relative insignificance of the adviser's fee to each shareholder. The fund customer's shares of the advisory fee is usually too small a factor to lead him to invest in one fund rather than in another or to monitor adviser-manager's fees. "Cost reductions in the form of lower advisory fees * * * do not figure significantly in the battle for investor favor." *Id.* Hence money market funds do not generally advertise that their advisory fees may be lower than those charged by advisers to other funds. The disparity is competitively insignificant. In the present case, for instance, the alleged excessive Manager's fee amounts to $2.88 *a year* for each $1,000 invested. If rates charged by the many other advisers were an affirmative competitive criterion, there would be little purpose in § 36(b). Congress, however, recognized that because of the potentially incestuous relationships between many advisers and their funds, other factors may be more important in determining whether a fee is so excessive as to constitute a "breach of fiduciary duty." These include the adviser-manager's cost in providing the service, the nature and quality of the service, the extent to which the adviser-manager realizes economies of scale as the fund grows larger, and the volume of orders which must be processed by the manager. The legislative history of § 36(b) makes clear that Congress "intended that the court look at all the facts in connection with the determination and receipt of such compensation, including all services rendered to the fund or its shareholders and all compensation and payments received, in order to reach a decision as to whether the adviser has properly acted as a fiduciary in relation to such compensation." S. Rep. No. 91–184, *supra*, [1970] U.S. Code Cong. & Ad. News at 4910.

As the district court recognized, the expertise of the independent trustees of a fund, whether they are fully informed about all facts bearing on the adviser-manager's service and fee, and the extent of care and conscientiousness with which they perform their duties and important factors to be considered in deciding whether they and the adviser-manager are guilty of a breach of fiduciary duty in violation of § 36(b). But even if the trustees of a fund endeavored to act in a responsible fashion, an adviser-manager's fee could be so disproportionately large as to amount to a breach of fiduciary duty in violation of § 36(b). Moreover, an intent to defraud need not be proved to establish a violation. Section 36(b)(1), 15 U.S.C. § 80a–35(b)(1), expressly relieves the plaintiffs of the necessity of alleging or proving that any defendant engaged in personal misconduct.

Nor do we subscribe to the district court's suggestion, 528 F. Supp. at 1044, that because § 36(b) was adopted in response to public concern over fees charged to investors in front-end load equity funds, the standard for determining whether there has been a breach of duty in avoiding excessive fees should be different or lower for managers of no-load money market funds, which are a recent, post-statute phenomenon. A potential for abuse of fiduciary relationship regarding fees charged for management and advisory services exists with respect to both types of fund since the adviser-manager's fee remains insignificant to each shareholder, whether or not a load factor inhibits redemption of shares.

Application of the foregoing standards to this case confirms that plaintiffs have failed to meet their burden of proving that the fees charged by the Manager to the Fund were so excessive or unfair as to amount to a breach of fiduciary duty within the meaning of § 36(b). There is no evidence that the services rendered by the Manager have not been of the highest quality, bringing to bear the expertise and facilities of the huge, far-flung Merrill Lynch organization. The average investor in the Fund, while not realizing the highest possible yield for his investment, has enjoyed a better-than-average return.

The substantial increase in the Manager's fee, from $1,578,476 in 1977 to $39,369,587 for the year ending June 1981, resulted from the tremendous increase in the size of the Fund, from $428 million to over $19 billion during the same period. This increase multiplied the number of customers, daily transactions and other activities which the Manager and the Merrill Lynch organization handled as part of the service for the fee, thereby increasing costs proportionately. The orders processed annually by the Manager for the Fund increased from 2,486,782 in 1979 to 6,096,537 for the 12–month period ending June 30, 1981. Appellants' contention that since the Manager's own administrative expenses did not increase proportionately during the period after 1978, its profit margin was 96 percent for the 12–month period ending September 30, 1981, is unrealistic and was properly rejected by the district court. Proceeding on the erroneous theory that only the administrative costs incurred by the Manager itself may be considered, appellants ignore the heavy costs incurred by other Merrill Lynch affiliates in processing the increased volume of purchases and redemptions of Fund shares which were under the Manager's guidance. Since the Manager and Broker were divisions of one economic unit, the district court was entitled to deduct these costs in calculating the Manager's net profits. To limit consideration to the Manager's own administrative expenses would be to exalt form over substance and disregard the expressed Congressional intent that "all the facts in connection with the determination and receipt of such compensation" be considered.

Although the court reduced the after-tax profits by determining the Manager's tax liability before deducting the processing costs, deduction of the costs before determining after-tax liability would nevertheless result in profits that could hardly be labeled so excessive as to constitute a breach of fiduciary duty. For instance, when processing costs are deducted before determining tax liability, the Manager's fee of $39,369,587 for the year ending June 30, 1981, would result in a 38.4 percent after-tax profit if the Fitz–Gerald estimate of processing costs were adopted, 9.8 percent after-tax profit under the Diemer estimate and a $7.7 million loss under the PMM estimate. No cost studies showing a higher after-tax profit were offered by appellants, who had the burden of proof. Moreover, after good-faith bargaining at arm's length between the 6 independent Fund trustees and the Manager, the latter's rate was graduated downward to reflect the economies that might be realized from the increase in value of the net assets. In view of these circumstances we cannot label clearly erroneous the district court's finding that no breach of fiduciary duty was shown.

Faced with these facts appellants respond that the Fund and the Manager, by having the processing of purchasing and redemption orders done by the Broker, were wastefully duplicating the services of its transfer agent, the Bank of New York, which was obligated, among its other duties, to accept Fund purchase and redemption orders. For these services the Bank of New York charged the Fund $13 per shareholder's account per year regardless of the number of transactions. For its services as transfer agent in the year 1980 the bank received $12,404,444 from the Fund. The services rendered to shareholders by the Merrill Lynch organization, however, greatly exceeded those that could be furnished by the Bank of New York, which performs the duties required of it as Transfer Agent under its agreement with the Fund at only one main office located in New York City. Purchasers of shares are attracted to the Fund by the convenience and flexibility of the huge Merrill Lynch Broker's organization with its network of over 400 offices and 7,000 account executives in the United States alone. A simple telephone call or visit by a Fund customer to an account executive in the nearest Merrill Lynch branch office is all that is needed to effectuate in-person Fund services. Most of the transactions through the bank, on the other hand, apparently are effectuated by mail or wire and involve other complications. Thus, although customers could open Fund accounts through the Bank of New York, approximately 80 percent of the 1980 Fund purchase and redemption orders were initiated through the Broker and approximately 99 percent of the half-million new Fund accounts in 1980 were opened through the Broker's branch office system. If the Fund did not have the Broker's network to provide the in-person services sought by customers and to handle the millions of orders executed annually but instead were restricted to use of the limited facilities of the Bank of New York, it would be unable to function effectively at its present high-volume level. There is no evidence that the Bank of New York is prepared to expand its location and services to the level provided by the Broker.

A more serious problem is posed by appellants' claim that in negotiating the Manager's fee the Merrill Lynch Fund and Manager failed to take into account that the Merrill Lynch Broker has gained large "fall-out" financial benefits annually in the form of commissions on non-Fund securities business generated by Fund customers and interest income on funds (known as the "float") held by the Broker from the date when a redemption check is issued by the Fund to its customer until the date it clears. If these benefits were taken into consideration, the argument goes, they would constitute a very substantial offset calling for a lower fee to the Manager than that paid by the Fund. Therefore, appellants contend, the Manager and the Fund, by failing to offset these benefits, were guilty of a breach of fiduciary duty in violation of § 36(b).

The record reveals that a large percentage of persons who opened accounts with the Broker as Fund customers, e.g., some 38 percent of those who opened such accounts in the third quarter of 1979, later did some non-Fund business with Merrill Lynch, generating commissions for the Broker. Robert Diemer, the Broker's Director of Financial Services, testified that processing of Fund accounts helped to attract new equity security business which increased the Broker's commission revenue. These benefits to an affiliate in the Merrill Lynch organization, to the extent quantifiable, should be taken into account in determining whether the Manager's fee meets the standard of § 36(b). Although the independent trustees may have been aware of these benefits, we are unpersuaded by the district court's suggestion that they cannot be measured or quantified because of inability to determine "whether customers who normally did an above-average level of brokerage business also tended to have Fund accounts" or to ascertain "what portion of the [increased brokerage business] would . . . have gone to Merrill Lynch in any event." It would not seem impossible, through use of today's sophisticated computer equipment and statistical techniques, to obtain estimates of such "fall-out" and "float benefits" which, while not precise, could be a factor of sufficient substance to give the Funds' trustees a sound basis for negotiating a lower Manager's fee. However, the burden was on appellants, not the defendants, to adduce evidence demonstrating that the benefits were so substantial that they rendered the Manager's fee so disproportionately large as to label its negotiation a "breach of fiduciary duty" within the meaning of § 36(b). Since appellants failed to offer such evidence, the dismissal of their contention must be affirmed.

Since the district court properly took into consideration the fact that the Merrill Lynch organization's costs of processing Fund orders are substantial and the record fails to show that the Manager's profits were so disproportionately large as to amount to a breach of fiduciary duty, we find no merit in appellants' further argument that the Manager violated § 36(b) by failing to disclose to the Fund's trustees relevant cost information and potential benefits. As Judge Pollack found, the Trustees were aware of or could obtain the essential facts needed to negotiate a reasonable fee. Similarly the Fund stockholders, before approving the management agreement between the Manager and the Fund, were made aware through proxy materials that the non-affiliated Fund trustees, who were the shareholders' watchdog representatives, *Burks v. Lasker*, 441 U.S. 471, 484–85, 60 L. Ed. 2d 404, 99 S. Ct. 1831 (1979), had considered extensive relevant information before continuing in effect the Fund's agreement with the Manager. Since the trustees have the primary responsibility under the Act, § 36(b) does not require that the Fund shareholders be furnished with additional information over and above that provided.

Our affirmance is not a holding that the fee contract between the Fund and the Manager is fair and reasonable. We merely conclude that on this record appellants failed to prove by a preponderance of the evidence a breach of fiduciary duty. Whether a violation of § 36(b) might be established through more probative evidence of (1) the Broker's processing costs, (2) the offsetting commission benefits realized by the Broker from non-Fund securities business generated by Fund accounts, and (3) the "float" interest income gained by the Broker from its method of handling payment on Fund redemptions, must therefore remain a matter of speculation. Indeed, the independent trustees of the Fund might well be advised, in the interests of Fund investors, to initiate such studies.

* * *

The judgment of the district court is affirmed.

PROBLEM 16–1

A cash management account (CMA) consists of a bundle of financial services administered through a central asset account that combines (1) a securities trading account, (2) a savings vehicle, consisting of one of three money market funds or an insured savings account, (3) a debit card, (4) check-writing privileges and (5) a detailed monthly statement. The focal point of the CMA program is the securities account, which generates substantial revenue for the securities firm that organizes the CMA. The program links the securities account to the savings vehicle through a "sweep" feature that automatically transfers idle cash into the savings vehicle—credit balances of $1,000 or more are transferred into savings the day after receipt; balances of less than $1,000 are swept weekly. An initial deposit of $20,000 is required to open a CMA program account, but a minimum balance thereafter need not be maintained.

By 2001 Ferrel Finch's (FF) CMA fund, an investment company registered under the Investment Company Act, was the largest in the United States with $19 billion in assets and over 850,000 shareholders. Investors in the Fund hold their investment as shares, on which dividends are declared and reinvested daily. Participation in the CMA program is required in order to invest in the Fund.

FF, the sponsor of the CMA program, is the largest securities firm in the United States. It acts as a distributor of the Fund and services the individual CMA program accounts. The day-to-day management of the Fund is performed by FF Asset Management, Inc. ("FFAM"), which serves as investment adviser to approximately 40 to 50 mutual funds as well as to institutional and individual investors. The Fund's investment adviser is Fund Asset Management, Inc. ("FAM"), a wholly-owned subsidiary of FFAM.

Direct compensation for services and management comes from three fees: (1) a $65 annual service fee paid by each CMA program participant to FF; (2) an investment advisory fee paid by the Fund to FAM based on the Fund's asset level; and (3) payments made by the Fund to FF under a Rule 12b–1 plan, under which the payments are passed on almost entirely to financial consultants.

Although all program participants are obliged to pay the service fee, approximately 25 percent of them do not invest in the Fund. The second fee, the advisory fee, is based on a schedule of declining percentages as assets increase beyond certain breakpoints: 1.5 percent of the average daily value of net assets under $500 million; 1 percent of that amount between $500 million and $1 billion, and 0.375 percent of that amount in excess of $1 billion. The third fee, paid under the Rule 12b–1 plan, is based on a distribution each month at an annual rate of 12.5 basis points (0.125 percent of the Fund's assets), which FF passes through to the financial consultants, save for 1 basis point that it pays to sales management and up to .50 of a basis point retained for administrative costs of the program.

The Fund is governed by a Board of Trustees, comprised of one affiliated trustee and six independent trustees. The unaffiliated trustees have joined the Board at the invitation of FF, and each acts as a trustee or director of one or more of FF's other mutual funds. The Board oversees the investments and administration of the Fund, and evaluates the advisory fee annually and the Rule 12b–1 plan quarterly.

The investment advisory fees of the Fund have been approved by the shareholders. The proxy statement set forth the three-tier schedule of the Fund's advisory fee. It listed also all the other investment companies for which FFAM acts as investment advisers. The list included two columns, indicated for each of the listed companies its "Rate" and "First Breakpoint." The first of the listed money market funds was FFAT's Ready Asset Trust ("FRAT"), with a listed rate of 0.5 percent and first breakpoint at $500 million.

Has FF violated § 36(b)?

Richard Meyer v. Oppenheimer Management Corp.

United States Court of Appeals for the Second Circuit, 1990.
895 F.2d 861.

■ Before NEWMAN and WINTER, CIRCUIT JUDGES, and TENNEY,* DISTRICT JUDGE.

■ WINTER, CIRCUIT JUDGE:

This case involves a challenge to a money market mutual fund distribution plan on the grounds, inter alia, that it violates several provisions of the Investment Company Act of 1940, 15 U.S.C. § 80a–1 et seq. (1988) ("the 1940 Act" or "the Act"). The plan was adopted under Rule 12b–1, 17 C.F.R. § 270.12b–1 (1989), promulgated in 1980 by the Securities and Exchange Commission. Plaintiff-appellant Richard Meyer contends that the directors and shareholders should have been informed of preliminary negotiations concerning the sale by one of the owners of its interest in the investment adviser to the fund. Meyer also claims that the distribution plan constituted an unfair burden imposed by the sale of the investment adviser under Section 15(f) of the 1940 Act, that the advisory and distribution fees are unfair under Section 36(b) of the Act, and that the plan violates the stipulation of settlement in a previous lawsuit. We disagree and affirm.

BACKGROUND

Defendant Daily Cash Accumulation Fund, Inc. ("the Fund"), is a money market mutual fund regulated by the 1940 Act, and Pamela Meyer, for whom Richard Meyer brought suit as custodian (collectively "Meyer"), is a shareholder in the Fund. At all pertinent times, the Fund's investment adviser was defendant Centennial Capital Corporation ("Centennial"). The defendants Oppenheimer & Co. and its subsidiaries (collectively "Oppenheimer") owned over half of the voting shares and about 30 percent of the total equity of Centennial. The other 70 percent of Centennial's equity was owned by four stockbroker entities, A.G. Edwards & Sons, Inc., Thomson McKinnon Securities, Inc., Bateman Eichler, Hill, Richards, Inc., and J.C. Bradford & Co. (collectively "the Brokers"). Since beginning operations in 1978, the Fund has served primarily as a vehicle for the Brokers to offer safe, liquid investments to their customers. The Brokers and their customers thus own over 90 percent of the outstanding shares of the Fund. Centennial, in exchange for a fee based on the Fund's total net assets, has provided investment advisory services to the Fund, including general management and supervision of the Fund's investment portfolio. The Brokers have promoted the sale of Fund shares and have served as the distribution link between their customers and the Fund.

Promulgated in 1980, Rule 12b–1 permits an open-end investment company to use fund assets to cover sale and distribution expenses pursuant to a written plan approved by a majority of the fund's board of directors, including a majority of the disinterested directors, and a majority of the fund's outstanding voting shares. See 17 C.F.R. § 270.12b–1(b). Prior to this Rule, brokers had to bear these expenses themselves.

In the fall of 1981, two of the Brokers, A.G. Edwards & Sons, Inc. ("Edwards") and Thomson McKinnon Securities, Inc. ("McKinnon"), informed Centennial that several other funds had offered them payments under the new

---

* The Honorable Charles H. Tenney, District Judge, United States District Court for the Southern District of New York, sitting by designation.

Rule 12b–1 to reimburse the distribution costs resulting from ownership of money market fund shares by their customers. Edwards and McKinnon also indicated that they were considering withdrawing their customers from the Fund unless it adopted a similar Rule 12b–1 distribution plan. Shortly thereafter, Centennial recommended to the directors of the Fund that they consider adopting a 12b–1 plan.

In February 1982, the directors of the Fund decided to propose to the shareholders a 12b–1 plan providing for payments to the Brokers and others of distribution expenses up to 0.20 percent of the net assets of the Fund. On March 25, the directors of the Fund issued a proxy statement concerning the 12b–1 plan, and the shareholders approved the plan at the annual meeting on April 27. After issuance of the proxy statement but before the shareholders' meeting, Meyer instituted the present action.

Meanwhile, without the knowledge of either the Centennial directors or the Fund directors, Oppenheimer & Co. decided to sell several of Oppenheimer's interests, including its share in Centennial. On February 26, 1982, Oppenheimer & Co. retained Lazard Freres to assist in such a sale, and, shortly thereafter, Oppenheimer began negotiations with the British firm Mercantile House Holdings and its subsidiary Mercantile House (collectively "Mercantile"). On May 31, 1982, Oppenheimer and Mercantile entered into an agreement by which Mercantile paid $162 million in exchange for the Oppenheimer holdings, including its interest in Centennial. The agreement was publicly announced on June 1. The directors of the Fund first learned of the proposed sale of Oppenheimer's interest in Centennial to Mercantile around the time of the June 1 public announcement. None of the Fund's independent directors had knowledge of the proposed Oppenheimer sale, therefore, when they approved the 12b–1 plan in February 1982.

On June 7, 1982, pursuant to Section 15(f) of the 1940 Act, 15 U.S.C. § 80a–15(f), the Fund's board of directors approved a new investment advisory agreement between the Fund and Centennial to reflect the change in ownership of Centennial. As required by Section 15(f), the board found that the sale to Mercantile would not impose an unfair burden on the Fund. On June 21, the board issued a proxy statement describing Oppenheimer's sale of its interest in Centennial and the new advisory agreement, and on July 2 Meyer amended his complaint to seek to enjoin the sale or to require in the alternative that the profits of the sale accrue to the Fund and not to Oppenheimer. On July 27, the board of the Fund considered Meyer's claims and concluded that they were baseless. The shareholders approved the new agreement on July 29, 1982.

* * *

DISCUSSION

We turn first to Meyer's argument that the Fund directors and the shareholders should have been informed of the potential Oppenheimer sale of its interest in Centennial before they approved the 12b–1 plan. In particular, Meyer claims that failure of Oppenheimer to inform the Fund's directors of the sale and the omission of information about that sale from the proxy statement are material non-disclosures that invalidate the 12b–1 plan.

Rule 20a–1, promulgated under the 1940 Act, 17 C.F.R. § 270.20a–1, makes Section 14(a) and related provisions of the Securities Exchange Act of 1934, * * * applicable to proxy statements issued under the 1940 Act. Moreover, Rule 12b–1(d), also promulgated under the 1940 Act, states that

[T]he directors of [an investment advisory] company *shall* have a duty to request and evaluate, and any person who is a party to any agreement with such company relating to [a 12b–1 distribution plan] *shall* have a duty to furnish, *such information as may reasonably be necessary to an informed determination* of whether such plan should be implemented or continued; * * * the directors *should* consider and give appropriate weight to all pertinent factors. * * * 7 C.F.R. § 270.12b–1(d) (emphasis added).

If the potential sale was material to consideration of the adoption of a 12b–1 plan, then Oppenheimer should have informed the Fund's directors about the sale, and the proxy statement should have included pertinent information. *Cf. Basic Inc. v. Levinson,* 485 U.S. 224 * * * (1988); *Kronfeld v. Trans World Airlines, Inc.,* 832 F.2d 726 (2d Cir.1987), *cert. denied,* 485 U.S. 1007 * * * (1988). However, the sale of Oppenheimer's interest in Centennial was irrelevant so far as approval of the 12b–1 plan was concerned. The district court found that the plan was "proposed to meet the competition and to counter the intention of the Brokers who accounted for 90percent of the Fund's assets to leave the Fund." 707 F. Supp. at 1407. The record amply supports this finding. Approval of such a plan had become a matter of sheer economic necessity as a result of the promulgation of Rule 12b–1. A drastic and rapid reduction of the Fund's asset value by withdrawals would have forced the investment adviser to make financially damaging decisions and would have raised costs to the individual shareholders. Meyer may or may not be correct in his assertion that shareholders in a money market mutual fund are indifferent to asset size, but it cannot be denied that an enormous and rapid shrinkage in asset size is potentially very damaging. The Fund might, for example, be forced to dispose of assets prematurely or to make other decisions reducing the financial return in order to meet redemption calls. Lower total assets would also result in a higher effective advisory charge to remaining shareholders because of the economies of scale of fund management. In short, adoption of the 12b–1 plan was essential to the financial well-being of the Fund.

The potential sale of Oppenheimer's interest in Centennial was thus irrelevant to the shareholders' and directors' decisions to adopt the 12b–1 plan. It is true, as Meyer argues, that Oppenheimer's interest in Centennial would have been worth less if the 12b–1 plan were not adopted because the loss of virtually all of the Fund's assets would necessarily reduce the advisory fees. The fact that Oppenheimer might also have suffered from the Fund's loss of assets, however, would in no way affect the consideration of the merits of such a plan by the shareholders and directors because that plan was independently essential to the Fund's well-being whether or not the sale of Centennial facilitated its adoption.

For similar reasons, we reject the contention that the sale of Centennial imposed an unfair burden on the Fund in violation of Section 15(f) of the 1940 Act. Congress enacted Section 15(f) in 1975 to limit the impact of our decision in *Rosenfeld v. Black,* 445 F.2d 1337 (2d Cir.1971), *cert. dismissed,* 409 U.S. 802, 93 S. Ct. 24, 34 L. Ed. 2d 62 (1972), which held that a fund could recover the profits realized by a former investment adviser from the transfer of its business to its successor. *See* S.Rep. No. 75, 94th Cong., 1st Sess. 71, *reprinted in* 1975 U.S. Code Cong. & Admin. News 179, 249. In Section 15(f), Congress provided a means by which investment advisers might earn a profit upon the sale of the fund to another adviser, subject to two safeguards.

The first safeguard, which is not pertinent to this appeal, is a requirement that 75 percent of the adviser's directors be independent for three years after the transaction. *See* 15 U.S.C. § 80a–15(f)(1)(A). The second safeguard, which is very much at issue, requires that there is not imposed an unfair burden on such company as a result of such transaction or any express or implied terms, conditions, or understandings applicable thereto. 15 U.S.C. § 80a–15(f)(1)(B).

Section 15(f) also provides that an unfair burden * * * includes any arrangement, during the two-year period after the date on which any such transaction occurs, whereby the investment adviser * * * receives or is entitled to receive any compensation directly or indirectly * * * for other than bona fide investment advisory or other services. 15 U.S.C. § 80a–15(f)(2)(B).

Meyer argues that the 12b–1 plan in this case constitutes just such an "arrangement" under Section 15(f).

Section 15(f) states that the alleged unfair burden must be "a result of" the sale. To succeed, therefore, Meyer must demonstrate that the 12b–1 plan was adopted "as a result of" the Oppenheimer–Mercantile transaction. As discussed above, that showing cannot be made in the instant case. Adoption of the 12b–1 plan by the Fund's directors and shareholders was a matter of economic necessity. The Fund directors approved the 12b–1 plan in February 1982 in ignorance of Oppenheimer's plans to sell its interest in Centennial and were reacting solely to the risk that the Brokers would withdraw from the Fund. This risk was, as stated, completely independent of the proposed sale of Oppenheimer's interest in Centennial. The plan was thus in no way "a result of" that sale.

We now turn to the question whether the advisory fees and the 12b–1 fees were excessive under Section 36(b) of the Act. We reiterate that the relevant judgment on appeal is the judgment entered on June 23, 1989, entered pursuant to the opinion dated June 13. In that opinion, the district court held that aggregation of the fees was not necessary and that the individual fees were not excessive. 715 F. Supp. at 577. We agree.

Section 36(b) of the Act imposes a fiduciary duty on investment advisers and "affiliated persons" regarding "the receipt of compensation for services, or of payments of a material nature." 15 U.S.C. § 80a–35(b). An advisory fee violates Section 36(b) if it "is so disproportionately large that it bears no reasonable relationship to the services rendered and could not have been the product of arm's-length bargaining." *Gartenberg v. Merrill Lynch Asset Management, Inc.*, 694 F.2d 923, 928 (2d Cir.1982), *cert. denied*, 461 U.S. 906 * * * (1983).

In [*Meyer v. Oppenheimer Management Corp.*, 764 F.2d 76 (2d Cir.1985)], we stated that "[a] claim that payments made under Rule 12b–1 are excessive when combined with advisory fees, where both payments are made to 'affiliated persons' of an investment adviser, is cognizable under section 36(b)." 764 F.2d at 83. This statement stands only for the proposition that the costs of 12b–1 plans involving such affiliates as well as advisory fees are subject to review under Section 36(b). Were such review not available, investment advisers might be able to extract additional compensation for advisory services by excessive distributions under a 12b–1 plan. The statement does not, however, stand for the additional proposition that 12b–1 payments to an adviser's affiliates are to be aggregated with advisory fees to determine the merits of a Section 36(b) claim. The two kinds of payments are for entirely different services, namely advice on the one hand and sales and distribution on the other. If the fee for each service viewed separately is not excessive in relation to the service rendered, then the sum of the two is also permissible.

In the instant case, the district court found that neither payment was excessive. In its June 15, 1989, opinion, it incorporated the factual findings of its earlier opinion that no evidence existed to show that the amounts paid to Centennial were "atypical or excessive," 707 F. Supp. at 1405. *See* 715 F. Supp. at 575 (adopting prior factual findings). It further found that the 12b–1 payments were "a matter of economic survival and fair in light of the objectives of the settlement." 707 F. Supp. at 1404. In its June 15, 1989, opinion, the district court amplified its findings with profit and cost figures drawn from testimony credited by the court. *See* 715 F. Supp. at 575–76. Although Meyer challenges the figures, the district court found them reliable, a finding that was not clearly erroneous.

* * *

Affirmed.

PROBLEM 16–2

The Allegiance Mutual Fund Complex is the largest in the United States, with 237 registered investment companies. As with virtually all mutual fund complexes, two aspects of its corporate governance are quite distinctive. First, each investment company has outside investment advisers that make all relevant investment decisions. Second, the same 12 individuals sit on the board of directors of each of Allegiance's 237 corporations.

Under § 10(a) each registered investment company must have at least 40 percent of its directors financially independent of the investment adviser. Allegiance has complied with this requirement by selecting nine nonemployee directors.

In 2001 all 237 Allegiance firms were advised by an Allegiance affiliate. The nine outside directors received total annual compensation ranging from $220,500 to $273,500 from the 237 companies they direct. On no occasion in 2001 did the directors replace the investment adviser in any of the 237 investment companies or reject an adviser proposal.

Can a shareholder prove that the outside directors were "interested persons" ineligible to be directors under § 10(a)? See §§ 2(a)(19)(A)(i); 2(a)(3)(C); 2(a)(9).

CHAPTER 17

STATE LAW

A. PARTIAL FEDERAL PREEMPTION

Earlier we discussed the extent to which the National Securities Market Improvement Act of 1996 has partially preempted several aspects of state securities regulation, but not the state law fraud remedies, including the civil liability provisions.

Two years later, the Securities Litigation Uniform Standards Act of 1998, in fact did preempt any class action (and certain consolidated proceedings that resemble a class action) based on either state statutory law or common law that alleges in substance (i) a misrepresentation or omission of a material fact, or (ii) the use of manipulation, a deceptive device, or a contrivance in connection with the purchase or sale of a security. Such actions are barred in both state and federal court. The effect is to eliminate any private cause of action under state "Blue Sky" fraud statutes that might be asserted by a class or any aggregation of 50 or more persons. Individual suits may still be maintained under state statutes or based on common law, and a statutory exemption permits state and local government units, or their pension funds, to sue as a class.

The legislation was a response to a sudden migration of securities class actions to state court in 1996, the year following the passage of the Private Securities Litigation Reform Act of 1995 (the "PSLRA").[1] Possibly in order to avoid the stay of discovery, heightened pleading requirements, increased sanctions or safe harbor provisions of the PSLRA, plaintiffs' attorneys experimented with state courts (where, however, the "fraud on the market" doctrine is generally not recognized—thus making for an uncertain tradeoff). Ironically, the migration of securities class actions to state court proved to be a one year phenomenon, as several studies have found the number of 1997 levels. Still, industry groups pressed hard for the 1998 legislation, claiming in part that, absent such protection, they would not dare to make use of the safe harbor for forward-looking statements in the PSLRA (because the safe harbor does not apply in state courts).

Technically, the 1998 proposed legislation preempts only class actions, but the definition of class action broadly reaches related individual actions having predominantly common issues of law or fact (if, under the Senate bill, 50 or more individuals sue). The legislation also only applies to a "covered security," which term is borrowed from Section 18(b)(i) of the 1933 Act and includes (i) all securities listed on the New York Stock Exchange, NASDAQ, or the American Stock Exchange and (ii) senior securities of the same issuer.[2] Several exemptions are set forth in the legislation, most notably to permit state class actions involving traditional corporate governance issues (such as in the takeover defense or "going private" areas).

---

1. For a discussion of the backdrop to this legislation, see Richard Painter, Responding to a False Alarm: Federal Preemption of State Securities Fraud Causes of Action, 84 Cornell L. Rev. 1 (1998).

2. See, e.g., Lander v. Hartford Life & Annuity Ins. Co., 251 F.3d 101 (2d Cir.2001) (dismissal of state claims under 1998 Act).

B.   Common Law

State common law offers a variety of different types of claims in the securities context including breach of warranty (but typically only when an instrument is sold that is not a genuine security, there is no implied warranty of quality or value); rescission (which requires a plaintiff to be in privity and to prove justifiable reliance on a material fact); and deceit (which does not require strict privity and does not require the plaintiff to show that the plaintiff was one to whom the third party made a representation).[1]

None of these remedies is a panacea. But claims of negligence or negligent misrepresentation (which are modern variants of rescission or deceit) are increasingly asserted because the culpability standard is easier to satisfy than Rule 10b–5 with its limitation to "intent to defraud" which has been judicially construed to include recklessness.[2]

Negligence or negligent misrepresentation also may be asserted by borrowers against accountants or lawyers when no security was purchased or sold and no Rule 10b–5 claims would be possible. Nonetheless the scope of negligence or negligent misrepresentation varies by state.

---

1. *See* summary of doctrines and citations in 9 Louis Loss & Joel Seligman Ch.11.A (3d ed. 1992).

2. Cf. Trust Co. of La. v. N.N.P. Inc., 104 F.3d 1478, 1487–1488 (5th Cir.1997):

Under Louisiana law, the elements of a claim for negligent misrepresentation are: (1) the existence of a legal duty on the part of the defendant to supply correct information or to refrain from supplying incorrect information; (2) breach of that duty; and (3) damages caused to the plaintiff as a result of that breach. [Citation deleted.] In order for an attorney to have a legal duty to supply correct information so that he is liable to a non-client for malpractice, the plaintiff must show that the attorney provided legal services and that the attorney knew the third party intended to rely upon those legal services. [Citations deleted.] An attorney's liability to the third party flows from the codal provision that establishes liability for a *stipulation pour autrui* pursuant to which one may bind himself to a contract for the benefit of a third party. [Citation deleted.] Where an attorney contracts to provide a professional opinion for the benefit of a third person, privity of contract results, and the agreement becomes binding and effective in favor of the third party upon his acceptance. [Citation deleted.]

In Perenco Nigeria Ltd. v. Ashland, Inc., 242 F.3d 299 (5th Cir.2001), the court held:

Under Texas law, a plaintiff alleging fraud must establish (1) a material misrepresentation, (2) which was false, and (3) which was either known to be false when made or was asserted without knowledge of its truth, (4) which was intended to be acted upon, (5) which was relied upon, and (6) which caused injury. The absence of proof of any element, of course, will prevent recovery. The elements of statutory fraud in the sale of stock are substantially the same, except that to recover actual damages, a plaintiff does not have to prove that the defendant knew a statement was false. Similarly, the primary difference between the cause of action for negligent misrepresentation and one for fraud is that a negligent misrepresentation claim does not require an actual intent to defraud, only that in doing so the party making the false statement acted negligently in doing so. All three tort causes of action asserted by Perenco—common-law fraud, statutory fraud in the sales of stock, and negligent misrepresentation—require a showing of both reliance and damages.

Id. at 306.

"Under New York law, the essential elements of a common law fraud include 'a material false representation, an intent to defraud thereby, and reasonable reliance on the representation, causing damage to the plaintiff.' " Turtur v. Rothschild Registry Int'l, Inc., 26 F.3d 304, 310 (2d Cir.1994), quoting Katara v. D.E. Jones Commodities, Inc., 835 F.2d 966, 970–971 (2d Cir.1987).

Because of Chief Judge Cardozo's holding in *Ultramares*, New York law has been frequently cited in this sphere. New York cases have somewhat expanded the *Ultramares* standard to encompass liability to third parties when reliance was reasonably foreseeable and liability lies "within the contemplation of the parties to the accounting retainer."[3] Subsequently the New York Court of Appeals created what has been called the "Credit Alliance" test:

> Before accountants may be held liable in negligence to noncontractual parties who rely to their detriment on inaccurate financial reports, certain prerequisites must be satisfied: (1) the accountants must have been aware that the financial reports were to be used for a particular purpose or purposes; (2) in the furtherance of which a known party or parties was intended to rely; and (3) there must have been some conduct on the part of the accountants linking them to that party or parties, which evinces the accountants' understanding of that party or parties' reliance.[4]

In *Security Pacific* Judge Hancock dissented, stating: "New York's existing privity rule under *Credit Alliance* is already the country's most exacting, * * *. Most jurisdictions now adopt the more lenient Restatement [(Second) of Torts § 552] approach allowing recovery whenever a particular party's reliance is foreseen * * * or some less restrictive variant."[5]

In contrast, in Bily v. Arthur Young & Co.[6], the California Supreme Court declined to permit all merely foreseeable third party users of audit reports to sue the auditor on a theory of professional negligence.

C.   BLUE SKY LAW

THE UNIFORM SECURITIES ACT

Until the adoption of the Uniform Securities Act of 1956 by 37 states, virtually no state had any statutory provisions imposing civil liability for fraud in the sale of securities. The 1956 Uniform Act in § 101 includes a general fraud provision based on Rule 10b–5. This provision was not intended to provide a civil remedy.[1]

---

3. White v. Guarente, 43 N.Y.2d 356, 361, 401 N.Y.S.2d 474, 478, 372 N.E.2d 315 (1977).

4. Credit Alliance Corp. v. Arthur Andersen & Co., 65 N.Y.2d 536, 493 N.Y.S.2d 435, 443, 483 N.E.2d 110 (1985); *accord*: Security Pac. Bus. Credit, Inc. v. Peat Marwick Main & Co., 79 N.Y.2d 695, 586 N.Y.S.2d 87, 90–92, 597 N.E.2d 1080 (1992); Schick v. Ernst & Young, 808 F.Supp. 1097, 1105 (S.D.N.Y.1992).

5. 586 N.Y.S. 2d at 101. *See also* Phar–Mor, Inc. Sec. Litig., 892 F.Supp. 676, 689–694 (W.D.Pa.1995) (in Pennsylvania privity is a requisite element of a professional negligence claim). Cf. Frymire–Brinati v. KPMG Peat Marwick, 2 F.3d 183, 190 (7th Cir.1993): "Illinois does not follow *Ultramares*, * * * so Peat Marwick may be liable even if it did not know that Pepco would use the financial statement to sell new stock. Illinois does, however, insist that the plaintiff prove, by clear and convincing evidence, that Peat Marwick made a materially incorrect statement, with knowledge of falsity (or reckless disregard of its falsity), and that the investors reasonably relied to their detriment." See generally John A. Siliciano, Negligent Accounting and the Limits of Instrumental Tort Reform, 86 Mich. L. Rev. 1929 (1988).

6. 3 Cal.4th 370, 11 Cal.Rptr.2d 51, 834 P.2d 745 (1992).

1. But *see* Shermer v. Baker, 2 Wash. App. 845, 472 P.2d 589 (1970) (permitting civil remedy based on § 101); Kittilson v. Ford, 93 Wash.2d 223, 608 P.2d 264 (1980) (same); cf. Goodman v. Poland, 395 F.Supp. 660 (D.Md.1975) (no civil cause of action under § 101 in Maryland).

Instead § 410 establishes civil liabilities for violations of the 1956 Uniform Arbitration Act. This provision is modeled on what is now § 12(a)(2) of the 1933 Act. Civil enforcement is limited to *buyers* of securities, a limitation that is explained in the Draftsman's Commentary to § 101 as appropriate in light of "the common-law and equitable remedies of deceit and rescission which are available to the state courts without benefit of statute."[2] Section 410(a) permits a buyer to sue either at law or in equity to recover the consideration paid for the security, together with interest at six percent per year from the date of payment, costs, and reasonable attorneys' fees, less the amount of any income received on the security, upon the tender of the security, or for damages if he no longer owns the security.

Section 410(b) defines the persons liable:

> Every person who directly or indirectly controls a seller liable under subsection (a), *every partner, officer, or director of such a seller, every person occupying a similar status or performing similar functions, every employee of such a seller who materially aids in the sale,* and every broker-dealer or agent who materially aids in the sale are also liable jointly and severally with and to the same extent as the seller, unless the non-seller who is so liable sustains the burden of proof that he did not know, and in exercise of reasonable care could not have known, of the existence of the facts by reason of which the liability is alleged to exist. There is contribution as in cases of contract among the several persons so liable.

The defendants potentially liable under § 410(b) appear to be broader than the potential defendants under a Rule 10b–5 action. This breadth plus the lesser culpability requirement often available under the state blue sky statutes inspired the belief that blue sky civil liability was showing signs of a new buoyancy in recent years.[3]

There have been two efforts to revise the Uniform Securities Act of 1956.

The Revised Uniform Securities Act of 1985 ("RUSA") was adopted by only a handful of states and was generally viewed as a failure because of a lack of support from the American Bar Association Corporation, Banking, and Business Law Section, which voted not to approve RUSA in January 1986. In June 1985 both the Securities Industry Association and the North American Securities Administrators Association (NASAA) had requested a two year moratorium on further action, with the NASAA specifically complaining that "the vast number of changes was unjustified." The National Conference of Commissioners on Uniform States Laws (NCCUSL) nonetheless unanimously adopted RUSA in August 1985, but alert to the significant industry and securities administrator opposition, did not withdraw the 1956 Act.[4]

The stalemate over revision is widely credited with building Congressional enthusiasm for the National Securities Markets Improvements Act of 1996.[5] That Act may also have cleared the air for the third version of the Uniform Securities Act.

---

2. Louis Loss, Commentary on the Uniform Securities Act 5–8 (1976).

3. See generally 1 Louis Loss & Joel Seligman 70–86 (3d ed. rev. 1998); 9 Louis Loss & Joel Seligman Ch. 11.B (3d ed. 1992).

4. 1 Louis Loss & Joel Seligman, Securities Regulation 49–50 (3d ed. rev. 1998).

5. Symposium, The National Securities Markets Improvement Act–One Year Later, 53 Bus. Law. 507 (1998).

In 1998 NCCUSL initiated a new effort to revise the Uniform Securities Act, selecting one of this book's co-authors as Reporter. In July 2002 the NCCUSL annual meeting adopted the new Uniform Securities Act (2002). The need for a new version of the Act is a consequence of a combination of the new federal preemptive legislation, significant recent changes in the technology of securities trading and regulation, and the increasingly interstate and international aspects of securities transactions.

Changes in the civil liability provisions were anticipated to be augmentative. A basic fraud provision virtually identical to § 101 of the 1956 Act was anticipated to be retained. New civil liabilities provisions were anticipated to be added to the analogue to § 410 of the 1956 Act to reach defrauded sellers, as well as defrauded buyers and those defrauded by investment advice. It is anticipated that decisions under the 1956 Act may often be cited as precedents for the unrevised aspects of the 2002 proposed Act.

CALIFORNIA

The California Corporate Securities Law of 1968 establishes the most detailed civil liability provisions of any similar statute. Under §§ 25,400 and 25,500 (modeled upon § 9 of the Securities Exchange Act of 1934) any broker-dealer or other person selling or offering for sale or buying or offering to buy a security, who willfully makes a false or misleading statement for the purpose of inducing the purchase or sale of such security by others, is liable to any other person who purchases or sells any security at a price which was affected by such act, for damages equal to the difference between the price paid or received and the price which would have obtained in the absence of the illegal manipulation. Similar liability results from matched orders or other transactions effected for the purpose of manipulation.[1]

Under §§ 25,401 and 25,501, any person who sells or purchases a security by means of any false or misleading statement is liable to the person who purchases the security from him or her or sells the security either for rescission or for damages, unless the defendant proves that the plaintiff knew the facts concerning the untruth or omission or proves that the defendant exercises reasonable care and did not know (or if he or she had exercised reasonable care would not have known) of the untruth or omission.[2]

Under §§ 25,402 and 25,502, any "insider" who purchases or sells a security at a time when he or she knows material information about the issuer which would significantly affect the market price of the security and which is

---

1. In StorMedia, Inc. v. Superior Ct., 20 Cal.4th 449, 84 Cal.Rptr.2d 843, 976 P.2d 214 (1999), the California Supreme Court held that § 25,400 applies both to securities sold in an open market and to other securities such as sales to employees or insiders.

2. Section 25,401 (when read with § 25,501) differs from common law misrepresentation in California in that (1) proof of reliance is not required, (2) proof of causation is not required, and (3) the plaintiff need not plead the defendant's negligence. The two Sections are not intended to establish strict liability. A defendant may prove or plead (1) that he or she exercised reasonable care and did not know of the untruth or omission, (2) that, even if he or she had exercised reasonable care, he or she would not have know of the untruth or omission, and (3) that the plaintiff knew the facts concerning the untruth or omission. Bowden v. Robinson, 67 Cal.App.3d 705, 136 Cal.Rptr. 871, 878 (1977).

Section 25,501, however, requires privity; "liability is limited to actual sellers." Admiralty Fund v. Jones, 677 F.2d 1289, 1296 (9th Cir.1982).

not generally available to the public is liable to the other party to the transaction, unless the insider has reason to believe that the other party is also in possession of the information or unless the defendant proves that the plaintiff in fact knew the information or that the plaintiff would have purchased or sold at the same price even if the information had been revealed to him or her. An "insider" is defined as an issuer or any officer, director or controlling person of the issuer or any other person whose relationship to the issuer gives him or her access, directly or indirectly, to material information about the issuer not generally available to the public. Damages recoverable are the difference between the price paid and the market value which the security would have had if the information known to the defendant had been publicly disseminated before the transaction and a reasonable time had elapsed for the market to absorb the information.

Under § 25,503, a right of action is given to any person who purchases a security sold in violation of the qualification requirements. However, this Section also provides that there is no cause of action under the Section if the security is qualified before the receipt of any part of the consideration, even though an offer or a contract of sale may have been made before that time, thus abolishing the so-called "infection" doctrine in California under which it was seemingly impossible to avoid civil liability, once an illegal offer had been made before qualification, by any means (other than by not carrying out the transaction).[3]

With respect to persons liable, California substitutes the phrase "every principal officer" for the Uniform Act's "every officer."[4] California also has a provision to the effect that a person who "with intent to deceive or defraud" materially assists in a violation of the securities registration or the general fraud provisions or an order suspending trading in an over-the-counter security is jointly and severally liable with any other person liable for the violation.[5]

There is a further "professional person" provision along the lines of § 11 of the federal 1933 Act to the effect that any accountant, engineer, appraiser, or other person who with his or her written consent has been named in a prospectus or offering circular as having prepared or certified any part of a prospectus, offering circular, or accompanying document is jointly and severally liable under the California equivalent of the Uniform Securities Act § 410(a)(2) if (1) part of the relevant document contains a material falsehood, and (2) the plaintiff acquired the security in reliance on that falsehood.[6] The California

---

3. Section 25,503 does not require proof of scienter, negligence, or the plaintiff's reliance. Bowden v. Robinson, 67 Cal.App.3d 705, 136 Cal.Rptr. 871, 876 (1977).

4. Cf. Unif. Sec. Act § 410(b); Cal. § 25,504. See Sherman v. Lloyd, 181 Cal. App.3d 693, 226 Cal.Rptr. 495, 501–502 (1986). "The control person statute under California law is substantially the same as the federal statute." Underhill v. Royal, 769 F.2d 1426, 1433 (9th Cir.1985); Durham v. Kelly, 810 F.2d 1500, 1505 (9th Cir.1987).

5. § 25,504.1. This has been construed to extend liability to aiders and abettors.

Hudson v. Capital Management Int'l, Inc., 565 F.Supp. 615, 628 (N.D.Cal.1983). Section 25,504.1 by its terms requires proof of "intent to deceive or defraud." See Diasonics Sec. Litig., 599 F.Supp. 447, 459 n. 13 (N.D.Cal.1984); Koehler v. Pulvers, 614 F.Supp. 829, 844 (S.D.Cal.1985).

6. § 25,504.2(a). There are limited defenses in §§ 25,504.2(b)–(c). See Koehler v. Pulvers, 614 Supp. 829, 846–847 (S.D. Cal. 1985) (imposing a standard of care under § 25,504.2).

blue sky provisions have been held not to supersede common law remedies related to securities transactions.[7]

NEW YORK

At the opposite extreme is New York which has no blue sky civil liability of any type, although courts have implied private actions under § 1204 of its insurance law[1] and its Martin Act has a distinctive pattern of state fraud enforcement.[2]

1.   CAUSATION AND RELIANCE

Ritch v. Robinson–Humphrey Co.

Supreme Court of Alabama, 1999.
748 So.2d 861.

■ PER CURIAM.

The United States Court of Appeals for the Eleventh Circuit has certified to this Court the question whether in an action brought pursuant to Ala. Code 1975, § 8–6–19(a)(1), a portion of the Alabama Securities Act, for a violation of Rule 830–X–3–.12 of the Alabama Securities Commission, the plaintiff must prove causation.

This is not the first time we have interpreted § 8–6–19(a). See, e.g., Gilford Partners v. Pizitz, 630 So. 2d 404 (Ala.1993); Banton v. Hackney, 557 So. 2d 807 (Ala.1989); and Clark v. Cowart, 445 So. 2d 884 (Ala.1984). However, we have not dealt with the issue whether the cause of action recognized by § 8–6–19(a)(1) contains a causation element.

In IMED Corp. v. Systems Engineering Associates Corp., 602 So. 2d 344, 346 (Ala.1992), this Court discussed one of the cardinal rules of statutory construction:

> "Words used in a statute must be given their natural, plain, ordinary, and commonly understood meaning, and where plain language is used a court is bound to interpret that language to mean exactly what it says. If the language of the statute is unambiguous, then there is no room for judicial construction and the clearly expressed intent of the legislature must be given effect."

See also DeKalb County LP Gas Co. v. Suburban Gas, Inc., 729 So. 2d 270, 275 (Ala.1998). We conclude that this rule governs our resolution of this certified question.

The pertinent part of § 8–6–19(a) reads: "Any person who (1) Sells * * * a security in violation of * * * any rule * * * imposed under this article . . . is liable to the person buying the security from him * * *." The question, as we understand it, is whether in an action under § 8–6–19(a)(1) the buyer must prove that the seller's violation of the applicable rule (here, Rule 830–X–3–.12)

---

7. Bowden v. Robinson, 67 Cal.App.3d 705, 136 Cal.Rptr. 871, 879 (1977); Eisenbaum v. Western Energy Resources, Inc., 218 Cal.App.3d 314, 267 Cal.Rptr. 5, 12 (1990).

1. See 9 Louis Loss & Joel Seligman, Securities Regulation 4134–4135 (3d ed. 1992).

2. See 1 Louis Loss & Joel Seligman, Securities Regulation 75–83 (3d ed. rev. 1998).

induced or caused the buyer to purchase the security. After examining the statute, we can conclude only that § 8–6–19(a)(1) does not impose such a requirement. For the buyer to recover, the statute requires only that the buyer prove that the seller violated the rule when the buyer purchased a security from the seller. Of course, if the Legislature had intended for § 8–6–19(a)(1) to contain a causation element, then it could have easily included one in the statute. For example, the Legislature could have written the statute so that it read: "Any person who sells a security in violation of any rule imposed under this article is liable to the person buying the security from him if the person purchased the security because of the seller's violation of the rule." Whether the Legislature should have written a causation element into § 8–6–19(a)(1) is not for us to say. We do not pass judgment on the wisdom of statutes. It is well established that it "is our job to say what the law is, not what the law should be." DeKalb County LP Gas Co. v. Suburban Gas, supra, at 275. We hold, therefore, that § 8–6–19(a)(1) does not require a plaintiff to prove that he or she purchased a security because of the seller's violation of the rule.

The defendant argues that federal law should be persuasive in our consideration of § 8–6–19(a)(1) and should lead us to construe that statute as containing a causation element. However, it is a long-held rule in Alabama that statutory construction is necessary only in cases in which the language of the statute creates doubt. Kreutner v. State, 202 Ala. 287, 80 So. 125 (1918). Because § 8–6–19(a)(1) is clear on its face, this is not a situation in which we need to turn to federal law for assistance.

A cause of action based on § 8–6–19(a)(1), part of the Alabama Securities Act, related to a violation of Rule 830–X–3–.12 of the Alabama Securities Commission does not contain a causation element.

QUESTION ANSWERED.

■ Houston, Cook, See, Lyons, Brown, and England, JJ., concur.

■ Hooper, C.J., and Maddox and Johnstone, JJ., dissent.

FRAUD ON THE MARKET

In Basic Inc. v. Levinson,[1] the United States Supreme Court held that plaintiffs in a Rule 10b–5 case can prove reliance through the a fraud on the market presumption.

In Mirkin v. Wasserman,[2] the California Supreme Court declined to allow a plaintiff to rely on the fraud on the market presumption rather than actual reliance in pleading a cause of action for common law deceit. Delaware[3] and New Jersey[4] have also declined to adopt the fraud on the market presumption.

2. DERIVATIVE LIABILITY

Taylor v. Perdition Minerals Group, Ltd.

Supreme Court of Kansas, 1988.
244 Kan. 126, 766 P.2d 805.

■ Six, Justice:

This first impression statutory construction case involves the interpretation of K.S.A.1987 Supp. 17–1268(b) of the Kansas Securities Act. Must a

1. 485 U.S. 224 (1988).

2. 5 Cal.4th 1082, 23 Cal.Rptr.2d 101, 858 P.2d 568 (1993).

3. Malone v. Brincat, 722 A.2d 5, 12–13 (Del.1998).

4. Kaufman v. i-Stat Corp., 165 N.J. 94, 754 A.2d 1188 (2000).

director have materially aided in the sale of unregistered securities to be liable for their illegal sale?

The plaintiffs, W.W. Taylor, Mrs. W.W. Taylor or A. Genevieve Taylor, Michael C. Taylor, John S. Taylor, David J. Taylor, and Mark B. Taylor, a partnership known as Taylor Family Real Estate Trust, (Taylors) appeal from a summary judgment in favor of the director defendants Charles Harris, Leo L. Meeker, Marvin Echols, and Jack Griggs.

The trial court found that, under K.S.A.1987 Supp. 17–1268(b), a director of a corporation is not liable for the illegal sale of the corporation's securities unless the plaintiff can show that the director materially aided in the sale. The trial court ruled that the four director defendants did not materially aid in the securities sale to the Taylors.

We disagree with the trial court's analysis. * * *

We hold that K.S.A.1987 Supp. 17–1268(b) is substantially similar to § 410(b) of the Uniform Securities Act, 7B U.L.A. 643 (1958). Strict liability is imposed on partners, officers, and directors to purchasers of unregistered securities sold in violation of the statute regardless of whether the partner, officer, or director materially aided in the sale unless he or she proves that he or she could not reasonably have had knowledge of the facts by reason of which liability is alleged to exist.

1. *The Facts of the Investment*

In early November of 1981, W.W. Taylor discussed an oil and gas exploration investment, Perdition Minerals Group, Ltd., (Perdition) with his neighbor, Donald Schrag. Taylor became interested and the two men placed a call to Bob Fondren, a securities broker, who had previously supplied Schrag with information on the corporation. Taylor spoke with Fondren who told him: (1) The stock was worth $1.34 a share and would be worth more soon; (2) the company had a lot of oil and gas in Montana; (3) the company was going to do an audit, and (4) the company was preparing to go public. Schrag indicated to Taylor that he was going to buy $200,000 worth of stock at $.50 a share.

Soon after Taylor's discussions with Schrag and Fondren, Schrag arranged a meeting between Taylor and Henry Mulvihill, who was Perdition's chief executive officer. Taylor was supplied with a financial statement and Mulvihill's personal resume. Mulvihill also described the production and value of the acreage held by Perdition in Montana. Taylor did not ask to see any drilling reports or geographical information. Mulvihill told Taylor that several hundred thousand dollars was needed to meet current drilling and lease expenses. Mulvihill gave Taylor a list of references, several of whom Taylor knew, including defendant Charles Harris. Taylor did not contact any of the references. Taylor told Mulvihill that he would purchase 400,000 shares of Perdition for $200,000; $100,000 on behalf of himself and his wife, and $100,000 on behalf of his children.

Taylor attended a Perdition shareholders' meeting on November 20, 1981. He met privately with Mulvihill prior to the meeting. At this private meeting, Mulvihill reassured Taylor that the stock was worth more than $1.34 a share and that he was going to do an audit. There is no evidence in the record indicating that any directors or shareholders of Perdition, other than Mulvihill,

Schrag, and Fondren, made any representations to Taylor or were in any way involved with the sale of stock to him.

At the November 20, 1981, shareholders' meeting, Mulvihill introduced Taylor as a potential Perdition investor. No one inquired as to the circumstances surrounding the issuance of the stock. Defendant Harris was present at the meeting and moved to hire Elmer Fox to audit the company. Harris said that he made the motion based on a recommendation by Mulvihill. Taylor testified at his deposition that prior to the shareholders' meeting, Mulvihill had never given any indication that Harris was Perdition's attorney.

Mulvihill, for tax purposes, had incorporated Perdition in Nevada. Mulvihill and Harris were close friends. In November of 1981, Harris agreed to purchase 2,500 shares of Perdition. Harris is a Wichita attorney. He testified at his deposition that the only legal work he had done on behalf of Perdition was to draw up an employment agreement between Perdition and Milan Ayers. Ayers managed the Montana properties. Mulvihill retained a Denver law firm which specializes in securities and oil and gas law to handle the corporation's other legal matters.

At the time Harris bought his shares, Mulvihill was the sole director and the parent of Perdition. In January 1981, a shareholders' meeting was held at which defendants Marvin Echols, Jack Griggs, Charles Harris, Leo Meeker, and Henry Mulvihill were elected directors. With the exception of Jack Griggs, all the director defendants invested money in Perdition and lost their investment when Perdition became insolvent. The shareholders voted to increase the authorized common stock from 500,000 shares to 4,000,000 shares and to split the outstanding 500,000 shares four for one, into 2,000,000 shares.

Early in 1982, when no audit was forthcoming, Taylor became concerned about his investment. Mulvihill assured Taylor that the audit was being done. Taylor then spoke to a friend who did business with the Elmer Fox accounting firm and asked him to check into Perdition. His friend told him: (1) Fox had no business relationship with Perdition, (2) the SEC had been investigating the Montana properties, and (3) Perdition's current financial statements did not reflect Taylor's $200,000 investment. The 400,000 shares of stock of Perdition purchased by the Taylors were never registered in accordance with K.S.A. 17–1256, –1257, or –1258. The sale of these 400,000 shares of stock of Perdition was not the sale of an exempt security under K.S.A.1987 Supp. 17–1261, nor was it an exempt transaction under K.S.A.1987 Supp. 17–1262.

The Taylors filed the instant lawsuit against Perdition, Mulvihill, Fondren, and the director defendants to rescind the purchase and recover the purchase price based upon violations of registration and misrepresentations under the Kansas Securities Act. The petition alleged that the Perdition stock was not registered pursuant to Kansas law and that Mulvihill and Fondren made misleading and false statements upon which Taylor relied in purchasing the stock.

The trial court entered summary judgment in favor of the director defendants Harris, Echols, Meeker, and Griggs, finding that, under K.S.A.1987 Supp. 17–1268(b), an innocent director must be shown to have materially aided in the sale of securities to be liable. The trial court further found that the facts of the case did not establish that the four directors materially aided in the sale to Taylor.

2. *The Statute, K.S.A.1987 Supp. 17–1268*

K.S.A.1987 Supp. 17–1268(a) establishes the liability of any person who sells a security which is required to be registered under K.S.A. 17–1255 but is not registered, or any person who sells a security by means of untrue statements of material facts. Such a person may be liable to the person buying the security for the consideration paid for the security plus interest, costs, and attorney fees.

The alleged liability of the director defendants is based on K.S.A.1987 Supp. 17–1268(b), which provides:

"Every person who directly or indirectly controls a seller liable under subsection (a), *every partner, officer, or director (or person occupying a similar status or performing similar functions) or employee of such a seller who materially aids in the sale,* and every broker-dealer or agent who materially aids in the sale is also liable jointly and severally with and to the same extent as the seller, unless the nonseller who is so liable sustains the burden of proof that such nonseller did not know, and in the exercise of reasonable care could not have known, of the existence of the facts by reason of which the liability is alleged to exist. There is contribution as in cases of contract among the several persons so liable." (Emphasis added.)

The Taylors contend that the Kansas statute is a "substantially verbatim" enactment of § 410(b) of the 1956 Uniform Securities Act as amended in 1958. A comparison of the two reveals minor differences in punctuation and phrasing.
* * *

K.S.A.1987 Supp. 77–201 establishes rules for statutory construction and requires that words and phrases be construed according to the context and approved usage of the language.

The director defendants, in comparing K.S.A.1987 Supp. 17–1268(b) and § 410(b) of the Uniform Act, reason as follows: The legislature by (1) removing the modifying phrase "of such a seller" after the word director; (2) placing the phrase "or person occupying a similar status or performing similar functions" in parenthesis, (3) and adding an "or" before the word employee intended the phrase "of such a seller who materially aids in the sale" to modify the entire clause "every partner, officer, or director (or person occupying a similar status or performing similar functions) or employee." We do not agree.

The National Conference of Commissioners on Uniform State Laws approved the Uniform Securities Act in 1956. In 1957, Kansas, using the Uniform Act as a model, enacted the Kansas Securities Act. Lovitch, *Securities Registration Under the Kansas Securities Act*, 22 Kan.L.Rev. 565, 566 (1974).

The changes in punctuation and phrasing effected by the legislature in transforming § 410(b) of the Uniform Act into K.S.A.1987 Supp. 17–1268(b) do not insulate directors from strict liability when unregistered securities are sold.

The states that have passed § 410(b) of the Uniform Securities Act have consistently interpreted the statute to impose strict liability on partners, officers, and directors unless the statutory defense of lack of knowledge is proven. [Citations omitted.]

We question the trial court's reliance on *Lanza v. Drexel & Co.*, 479 F.2d 1277 (2d Cir.1973). Lanza arose under federal, not state, securities laws. The plaintiffs in Lanza sought compensatory and punitive damages against former officers and directors of a corporation based on violations of federal securities acts and common-law fraud. The Second Circuit Court of Appeals was construing Rule 10b–5 of the Securities and Exchange Commission, 17 C.F.R. § 240.10b–5 (1988); and § 10(b) of the Securities Exchange Act of 1934, 15 U.S.C. § 78j(b) (1982). The court in Lanza discussed state "blue sky laws" in a footnote.

> "State blue sky laws universally exempt directors from liability for fraud perpetrated by corporate officers unless the directors are in some meaningful sense culpable participants in the fraud." 479 F.2d at 1308 n. 105.

The *Lanza* court identified two types of state laws. The first are those modeled after § 410(b) of the Uniform Act and the second are those in which a director is exempt from liability unless he or she participates in the sale. The Lanza court in footnote 105 refers to fraud; nevertheless, the court correctly characterized the Kansas statute as belonging to the first category.

K.S.A.1987 Supp. 17–1268(b) does not require that a director materially aid in the illegal sale of securities in order to be held jointly and severally liable for the sale.

Our analysis of legislative intent commences with the observation that "Blue Sky" provisions are to be liberally interpreted in favor of purchasers to prevent fraud. *Daniels v. Craiglow*, 131 Kan. 500, 292 Pac. 771 (1930).

Kansas has required registration of securities since 1911. L.1911, ch. 133.

The first securities statute with teeth was passed in Kansas. Loss, Fundamentals of Securities Regulation 8 (2d ed. 1988). According to Professor Louis Loss, Kansas had been a "stronghold" of populist philosophy. The resulting carryover today is to be found in the relative strictness of Midwestern securities statutes. "Indeed, it was in Kansas, apparently, that the term 'blue sky law' first came into general use to describe legislation aimed at promoters who 'would sell building lots in the blue sky in fee simple.' " Loss, Fundamentals of Securities Regulation 8.

The drafters comment to § 410(b) of the Uniform Securities Act observes, "This section is now in the Kansas act substantially verbatim, and Virginia has adopted it with modifications." Loss and Cowett, Blue Sky Law 393 (1958).

We have in past cases identified rules to assist in statutory construction:

(1) "The fundamental rule of statutory construction is that the purpose and intent of the legislature governs when the intent can be ascertained from the statute. In construing statutes, the legislative intention is to be determined from a general consideration of the entire act. Effect must be given, if possible, to the entire act and every part thereof. To this end, it is the duty of the court, as far as practicable, to reconcile the different provisions so as to make them consistent, harmonious, and sensible." *State v. Adee,* 241 Kan. 825, 829, 740 P.2d 611 (1987).

(2) "Interpretation of a statute is a question of law, and it is the function of the court to interpret a statute to give it the effect intended by the legislature. *State, ex rel., v. Unified School District,* 218 Kan. 47, 49, 542 P.2d 664 (1975). It is a fundamental rule of statutory construction to which all other rules are subordinate that the intent of the legislature governs when that intent can be ascertained. *State v. Sexton,* 232 Kan. 539, 657 P.2d 43 (1983)." *Director of Taxation v. Kansas Krude Oil Reclaiming Co.,* 236 Kan. 450, 455, 691 P.2d 1303 (1984).

What did the legislature intend the phrase, "of such a seller who materially aids in the sale" following the word "employee" to modify? Was the phrase intended to modify only an "employee" of such seller, or was it intended to reach back further into the language of the statute and also modify "every partner, officer, or director"? We are persuaded the critical phrase modifies only "employee" of such seller.

If the legislature had intended to make directors liable only in the event they had materially aided in the sale, the Kansas language could easily have read, "every partner, officer, or director *of such a seller who materially aids in the sale*." (Emphasis added.)

In our K.S.A.1987 Supp. 17–1268(b) search for legislative intent we note 2A Sutherland Statutory Construction § 47.33 (4th ed. rev. 1984):

> "Referential and qualifying words and phrases, where no contrary intention appears, refer solely to the last antecedent. The last antecedent is 'the last word, phrase, or clause that can be made an antecedent without impairing the meaning of the sentence.' Thus a proviso usually is construed to apply to the provision of clause immediately preceding it. The rule is another aid to discovery of intent or meaning and is not inflexible and uniformly binding. Where the sense of the entire act requires that a qualifying word or phrase apply to several preceding or even succeeding sections, the word or phrase will not be restricted to its immediate antecedent.

> "Evidence that a qualifying phrase is supposed to apply to all antecedents instead of only to the immediately preceding one may be found in the fact that it is separated from the antecedents by a comma."

No comma was inserted in K.S.A.1987 Supp. 17–1268(b) separating the critical qualifying phrase, "who materially aids in the sale" from the antecedents partner, officer, or director or employee.

The Kansas version of the Uniform Act was adopted in 1957. L.1957, ch. 145. The K.S.A.1987 Supp. 17–1268(b) equivalent section of the prior law, G.S.1949, 17–1240, was found in the securities section of the corporation code. G.S.1949, 17–1240 provided, in part:

> "Every sale or contract for sale made in violation of any of the provisions of this act shall be voidable at the election of the purchasers; and the person making such sale or contract for sale and *every director, officer or agent of or for such seller who shall have participated or aided in any way in making such sale shall be jointly and severally liable* to such purchaser in an action at law in any court of competent jurisdiction...." (Emphasis added.)

Prior to the adoption of K.S.A.1987 Supp. 17–1268(b), a director of a seller was liable only if he or she "participated or aided in any way in making such sale."

Section 410(b) of the Uniform Act altered a director's liability status. Strict director liability was imposed by § 410(b) unless the statutory defense of lack of knowledge was proven. If the Kansas Legislature in 1957 had intended to continue to provide the "materially aids in the sale" shield to Kansas directors it could easily have used the G.S.1949, 17–1240 concept that had been in place since 1929. L.1929, ch. 140. * * *

Johnson v. Colip

Supreme Court of Indiana, 1995.
658 N.E.2d 575.

■ Sullivan, Justice.

This case requires us to explore the circumstances under which a securities lawyer who attends a meeting of prospective investors can be held to be an "agent" of the securities' issuer as that term is defined in the Indiana Securities Act (the "Act").

Facts

Gary Colip, an attorney, was retained in early 1983 to incorporate and represent a corporation established to serve as general partner in several limited partnerships comprising interests in oil properties. He was also responsible for drafting the prospectus used to solicit investors in the partnerships.

This action was commenced in April of 1985 by two complaints in which Allen and Li Yen Johnson alleged that the partnership interests they contracted to buy were sold in violation of the Indiana Securities Act, Ind.Code § 23–2–1–1 et seq. (1982 & 1983 Supp.). They contended that the prospectuses utilized in the sale contained misleading, untrue statements of material fact, or omitted to state material facts. The complaints were subsequently amended to allege that Colip acted "in concert with" the other defendants in preparing or drafting the misleading prospectuses. Colip moved for summary judgment on both of the Johnsons' complaints; the trial court then consolidated the Johnsons' actions.

The complaint was amended again to allege that Colip "further acted in concert with the other Defendants herein, and effectuated or attempted to effect purchases or sales of securities herein." After a hearing, the trial court granted Colip's motion for summary judgment, "pursuant to Ackerman v. Schwartz (N.D.Ind.1989), 733 F.Supp. 1231." The Johnsons appealed and the Court of Appeals reversed in a non-published opinion, Johnson v. Colip (1994), Ind.App. 627 N.E.2d 454. We will state additional facts where necessary.

I

This case arises under the Indiana Securities Act, our state's contribution to the body of Blue Sky laws adopted by each state. Although not as well known as their federal counterparts, these statutes for the most part pre-date by many years the enactment of the first federal securities acts in 1933 and 1934[1] and in many cases provide more rigorous standards for the offer and sale of securities than does the federal regime. And in a time apparently characterized by federal retrenchment in this area, state regulation of securities may serve an increasingly important role both in protecting investors and assuring issuers of a level playing field when they compete for capital.

II

The Indiana Securities Act as in effect in December, 1983, the date of the conduct at issue in this case, provided a private cause of action against every "agent" of a seller or purchaser of securities "who materially aids in the sale or

---

1. *See generally* Louis Loss and Joel Seligman, 1 *Securities Regulation* 29–41 (3d ed, 1989); Louis Loss and Edward M. Cowett, Blue Sky Law 3–10 (1958).

purchase ... unless that person who is so liable sustains the burden of proof that he did not know, and in the exercise of reasonable care, could not have known of the existence of the facts by reason of which the liability is alleged to exist." Ind.Code § 23–2–1–19 (1982). Another section of our Securities Act defines the term "agent" to be:

> Any individual, other than a broker-dealer, who represents a broker-dealer or issuer in effecting or attempting to effect purchasers or sales of securities. A partner, officer, or director of a broker-dealer or issuer or a person occupying a similar status or performing similar functions is an agent only if he effects or attempts to effect a purchase or sale of securities in Indiana.

Ind.Code § 23–2–1–1(b) (1983 Supp.). At issue is whether a genuine issue of material fact exists as to whether Colip was an agent of the other defendants and, if so, whether he "materially aided in the sale of securities herein" and was, therefore, liable to plaintiffs under the Act.

A

The provisions of the Act quoted above, Indiana Code §§ 23–2–1–1(b) and 19, are based substantially upon §§ 401(b) and 410 of the Uniform Securities Act of 1956. The comment to § 401 of the Uniform Act notes that whether a particular individual who represents an issuer is an "agent" depends "upon much the same factors which create an agency relationship at common law. That is to say, the question turns essentially on whether the individual has manifested a consent to the * * * issuer to act subject to his control." Unif.Sec.Act § 401, 7B U.L.A. 581 (1985). Indiana courts have long made the same inquiry to determine the existence of an agency relationship. *Dep't of Treasury v. Ice Service* (1942), 220 Ind. 64, 67–68, 41 N.E.2d 201, 203; *Mullen v. Cogdell* (1994), Ind.App., 643 N.E.2d 390, 398. This determination is usually a question of fact, *Ice Service*, 220 Ind. at 68, 41 N.E.2d at 203. Given the extensive amount of work that Colip performed for the corporation, we see little basis for granting Colip summary judgment if a common law agency relationship is all that is required to create an "agent" for purposes of the Act.

B

But while one must be a common law agent to be an "agent" under the Act, we perceive the Act as containing additional requirements as well. That is, whether Colip is an agent within the meaning of the Act turns on whether he effected or attempted to effect purchases or sales of securities.

This question has not been previously addressed by Indiana appellate courts but has been examined by Judge Miller in federal district court. In *Ackerman v. Schwartz*, 733 F.Supp. 1231 (N.D.Ind.1989), *aff'd in part and rev'd in part on other grounds*, 947 F.2d 841 (7th Cir.1991), investors in an equipment leasing program brought suit against an attorney who wrote a tax opinion letter and the attorney's firm. The defendants moved for summary judgment, claiming that they were not agents within the meaning of the Indiana Securities Act. In construing the definition of "agent" in the Act, the district court examined the meaning of the verb "effect." The court held that liability under the Act requires "more than the mere drafting of an opinion letter," but that liability could be imposed if the attorney and his firm had "personally and actively employed the opinion letter to solicit investors." *Id.* at 1252.

In *Baker v. Miles & Stockbridge*, 95 Md.App. 145, 620 A.2d 356 (1993), the Maryland Court of Special Appeals conducted an extensive survey of the law in other jurisdictions in addressing this question. On appeal in the Maryland case was defendant lawyer's motion for summary judgment on the Blue Sky act contribution claims of plaintiff dealer-manager of a private offering of securities. Resolution of this issue turned on whether the dealer-manager had presented sufficient facts to establish the existence of an agency relationship between the parties. After reviewing the cases cited in footnote 5, *supra*, the Maryland court observed,

> Although the definition of "agent'" in the state securities laws discussed above may vary to differing degrees from the definition [of agent in the Maryland Blue Sky Act], they each have one thing in common: they do not impose liability upon an attorney who merely provides legal services or prepares documents for his or her client. To impose liability, the attorney must do something more than act as legal counsel.

Id., 620 A.2d at 368. The court then held that "an attorney could conceivably be considered an agent if he or she represents a broker-dealer or issuer in *effecting or attempting to effect* the purchase or sale of securities." In order to be considered an agent, an attorney must

> act in a manner that goes beyond legal representation. The definition of "agent" in § 11–101(b) does not include attorneys who merely provide legal services, draft documents for use in the purchase or sale of securities, or engage in their profession's traditional advisory functions. To rise to the level of "effecting" the purchase or sale of securities, the attorney must actively assist in offering securities for sale, solicit offers to buy, or actually perform the sale.

Id.

We agree with the approaches taken by the courts in these cases and hold that an attorney is an agent if his or her affirmative conduct or failure to act when reasonably expected to do so at a meeting of prospective investors made it more likely than not that the investors would purchase the securities than they would have been without such conduct or failure to act.

C

In reversing the summary judgment entered in favor of Colip, the Court of Appeals wrote:

> In attending meetings of prospective investors to answer legal questions concerning the prospectuses, Colip left the realm of an attorney-client relationship to advise third-parties on partnership matters which, one can infer, constituted an attempt to persuade or reassure potential investors and to effect the sale of securities. By "explaining the legal ramifications of the limited partnerships" to prospective investors, Colip was not acting as legal counsel to the Corporation but may have "personally and actively" participated in marketing the limited partnerships. Therefore, the Johnsons have shown that a genuine issue of material fact exists upon undisputed facts regarding whether Colip was an agent of the issuer who materially aided in the sale of securities and, thus, violated the Act. *See McGee v. Bonaventura* (1993), Ind.App., 605 N.E.2d [792,] 793–94. A question of fact remains whether the nature and extent of Colip's participation would make him liable.

While we agree with the Court of Appeals that summary judgment was not appropriate, our analysis differs somewhat. Specifically, we are unable to infer with the same degree of certainty of the Court of Appeals that Colip's attendance at meetings of perspective investors constituted an attempt to effect the sale of securities. Certainly it may have done so and we believe that the determination as to whether or not it did constitutes an issue of fact inappropriate for resolution at summary judgment. For example, if when called upon at the meetings, Colip primarily reassured investors that risks about which they expressed concern were unlikely to materialize, such behavior made it more likely than not that the investors would purchase the securities and constituted an attempt to effect a purchase or sale. On the other hand, if Colip's principal function at the meeting was to either temper the exuberance of the principal promoters (a frequent reason why lawyers are asked to accompany "road shows" promoting new securities' offerings) or to discuss the technical aspects of the partnership agreement or its tax consequences with counsel for prospective investors (much as would occur in the negotiations in any reasonably sophisticated business transaction), we think these facts are not susceptible to the inference that an attempt to effect the purchase or sale of a security occurred. We hold that a genuine issue of material fact remains as to whether Colip's affirmative conduct or failure to act when reasonably expected to do so at a meeting with prospective investors made it more likely than not that the investors would purchase the securities and therefore constituted an attempt to effect the purchase or sale of the securities. Finally, we note that under Indiana Code § 23–2–1–19 Colip does have the opportunity to demonstrate to the finder of fact that he did not know, and in the exercise of reasonable care could not have known, of the existence of the facts by reason of which the liability is alleged to exist.

Conclusion

We reverse the grant of summary judgment in favor of Colip and remand this matter to the trial court for further proceedings consistent with this opinion.

■ SHEPARD, C.J., and DeBRULER, DICKSON, and SELBY, JJ., concur.

3. JURISDICTION

A.S. Goldmen & Co., Inc. v. New Jersey Bureau of Securities

United States Court of Appeals for the Third Circuit, 1999.
163 F.3d 780.

OPINION OF THE COURT

■ GARTH, CIRCUIT JUDGE: This case raises a dormant commerce clause challenge to one aspect of the New Jersey Uniform Securities Law. The appellee, A.S. Goldmen & Co., Inc. ("Goldmen"), claims that N.J.S.A. § 49:3–60 (" § 60") violates the dormant commerce clause insofar as it authorizes the appellant New Jersey Bureau of Securities to prevent Goldmen from selling securities from New Jersey to buyers in other states where purchase of the securities was authorized by state regulators. The district court agreed, and granted summary judgment in favor of Goldmen. We hold that § 60 does not run afoul of the dormant commerce clause, and therefore reverse.

I.

A.

Because of the noted potential for fraud and deception in the buying and selling of securities, securities markets are among the most heavily regulated markets in the United States. Regulation of securities first flourished at the state level in the 1910s, when states began enacting laws that required the registration of a securities offering before the sale of the security was permitted. The purpose of these so-called "blue sky" laws was to allow state authorities to prevent unknowing buyers from being defrauded into buying securities that appeared valuable but in fact were worthless. By 1933, all but one state had passed blue sky laws; today, all fifty states, the District of Columbia, Guam, and Puerto Rico have blue sky laws in force. See Louis Loss & Joel Seligman, 1 Securities Regulation 40–41 (3d ed. Rev. 1998) (hereinafter, "Loss & Seligman").

Aggressive federal regulation of securities markets began in the early 1930s with the passage of the Securities Act of 1933 and the Securities Exchange Act of 1934. Today, the Securities and Exchange Commission ("SEC") administers these and five other federal statutes, which altogether form a complex web of federal regulations. See id. at 224–81. Despite this complex federal scheme, Congress, the courts, and the SEC have made explicit that federal regulation was not designed to displace state blue sky laws that regulate interstate securities transactions. See, e.g., 15 U.S.C. § 77r(c) (1997) (preserving state jurisdiction "to investigate and bring enforcement actions with respect to . . . unlawful conduct by a broker or dealer") (National Securities Markets Improvement Act of 1996); Merrill Lynch, Pierce, Fenner & Smith, Inc. v. Ware, 414 U.S. 117, 137 * * * (1973) ("Congress intended to subject [securities] exchanges to state regulation that is not inconsistent with the federal [laws]."); Loss & Seligman at 275–281. Although the enactment of the National Securities Markets Improvement Act of 1996 narrowed the role of state blue sky laws by expanding the range of federal preemption, federal and state regulations each continue to play a vital role in eliminating securities fraud and abuse. See Loss & Seligman at 60–62; Manning G. Warren III, Reflections on Dual Regulation of Securities Regulation: A Case Against Preemption, 25 B.C. L. Rev. 495, 497, 501–27 (1984) (describing how Congress, the courts, and the SEC have expressly authorized the enforcement of state blue sky laws).

B.

Among blue sky laws, the most common regulatory approach is the mixed disclosure and merit regulation scheme offered by the Uniform Securities Act ("Uniform Act"). Drafted in large part by the late Professor Louis Loss, the Uniform Act has been adopted with some modification in nearly forty states, including New Jersey. See N.J.S.A. § 49:3–47 to 76. The Act contains three essential parts: provisions requiring the registrations of securities sold within the state; provisions requiring the registration of persons involved in the securities industry; and various antifraud provisions. See id; see also Joseph C. Long, 12 Blue Sky Law § 1.07 (1997) (hereinafter, "Long").

This case raises a constitutional challenge to N.J.S.A. § 49:3–60 ("§ 60"), which is New Jersey's codification of the portion of the Uniform Act that makes it "unlawful for any security to be offered or sold in this State" unless the security is either registered by state authorities, is exempt under N.J.S.A. § 49:3–50, or is a federally covered security. When read in conjunction with

N.J.S.A. § 49:3–51(c), which states that "an offer to sell or buy is made in this State ... when the offer ... originates in this State," § 60 grants New Jersey regulatory authorities the power to regulate the offer or sale of all non-exempt, non-covered securities whenever the offer is made within the state of New Jersey. Under N.J.S.A. § 49:3–64 and the 1985 amendments to the New Jersey statute, this authority permits the chief of the New Jersey Bureau of Securities ("Bureau") to exercise broad powers to regulate sale of such securities in New Jersey when it is deemed in the public interest and various statutory requirements have been met.

II.

A.

A.S. Goldmen & Co. is a securities broker-dealer with its sole office located in Iselin, New Jersey. At the time of proceedings before the District Court, Goldmen's sole office was located in New Jersey. Since that time, it has opened at least one other office out of state.

Goldmen specializes in underwriting the public offerings of low priced, over-the-counter securities, and then selling those securities in the secondary market. During the first several months of 1996, Goldmen planned the initial public offering of Imatec, Ltd. ("Imatec"). Imatec is a Delaware corporation, located in New York, that was formed in 1988 to develop, design, market, and license image enhancement technologies. Goldmen planned for the Imatec securities to be traded as a NASDAQ Small Cap stock because such stocks are exempt from initial federal registration requirements, see 15 U.S.C. § 77(d) (1997). The primary regulation of the Imatec security during the first 25 calendar days of the offering would occur at the state level. See 17 C.F.R. § 230.174(d) (1992). Accordingly, in May 1996, Goldmen concurrently filed registration statements with the SEC, and also attempted to register the offering "by qualification" with state regulatory authorities in over a dozen states, including New Jersey.[7]

The prospectus filed by Goldmen with the New Jersey Bureau of Securities ("the Bureau") listed Goldmen as the sole underwriter, and also indicated that Goldmen would own the shares to be offered to the public. Reviewing Goldmen's application, the Bureau expressed various concerns regarding the Imatec offering to Goldmen's counsel. Although the Bureau was not prepared to make allegations of fraud, it had already been investigating Goldmen's business practices at that time, and was concerned that the combination of Goldmen's practices and the bleak financial prospects of Imatec made the offering a high-risk investment that was likely to be associated with abusive and manipulative sales practices.

On August 7, 1996, the Bureau informed Goldmen's counsel that it was considering the issuance of a stop order that would block the Imatec offering from being registered in New Jersey. Goldmen's counsel and the Bureau then entered into negotiations concerning the future of the Imatec offering. On October 23, 1996, these negotiations resulted in a Consent Order signed by the

---

7. Registration "by qualification" is the most comprehensive form of blue sky registration, and is generally necessary when the security is exempt from initial federal registration requirements. The other types of registration, registration "by notification" and registration "by coordination," are much simpler and are reserved for securities that carry a higher indicia of reliability than securities that must be registered by qualification. See N.J.S.A. § 49:3–61 (describing requirements for registration by qualification).

CEO of Imatec and the Bureau chief. According to the Consent Order, Goldmen withdrew its application to register the Imatec offering in New Jersey, and agreed that the Imatec offering did not qualify for N.J.S.A. § 49:3–50(b) exemptions to the registration rule of § 60. Goldmen was permitted to make unsolicited sales from New Jersey or to sell to certain financial institutions or to other broker-dealers. However, the Consent Order specifically denied Goldmen exemptions that would have allowed it to solicit members of the public to purchase Imatec stock in the secondary market. App. 38–41; App. 156–57.

Five days after Goldmen entered into the Consent Order, on October 28, 1996, the registration statement that Goldmen had filed with the SEC became effective. As of that date, Goldmen had managed to register the Imatec offering in sixteen states, but had been forced to withdraw its registration in several others, including New Jersey.

On the morning of October 29, 1996, Goldmen commenced the initial public offering from its office in Iselin, New Jersey. By telephone, Goldmen solicited sales to individuals outside of New Jersey, but did not solicit any sales to individuals within New Jersey. By 3 p.m. of that day, Goldmen had sold the entire public offering. Subsequently, Goldmen continued to buy and sell Imatec securities in the interdealer market from its New Jersey office.

The Bureau learned of Goldmen's sales on November 7, 1996. Because the window for state regulation of the Imatec offering closed 25 days after the offering began,[10] the Bureau acted immediately, notifying Goldmen that it believed that the sales violated the Securities Act and the Consent Order. Goldmen took the position that its sales violated neither state law nor the consent order, and informed the Bureau that it intended to continue to buy and sell securities from its New Jersey office. The Bureau responded by issuing a Cease and Desist Order dated November 12, 1996, which ordered Goldmen to "cease and desist from the solicitation of customers, offer and sale of Imatec in or from the State of New Jersey to any members of the public." App. 91.

B.

On the same day that the Bureau issued the Cease and Desist Order, Goldmen filed this declaratory judgment action against the Bureau in federal district court. Goldmen's complaint claimed that "the New Jersey Securities Act, as applied to securities that were not registered or exempt from registration in New Jersey and were sold by brokers located in New Jersey to residents of states (other than New Jersey) in which the securities were qualified for sale, violates the Commerce Clause of the United States Constitution." The complaint also alleged that even if the Securities Act was constitutional, the Act and the Consent Order did not apply to block Goldmen's sales of Imatec securities from New Jersey. According to Goldmen, the sole legal effect of the Act and the Consent Order was to prohibit Goldmen from selling the securities to buyers located in New Jersey.

The district court issued an Order to Show Cause, and held a hearing on November 20, 1996. The district court issued a preliminary injunction the same day, enjoining the Bureau from taking any action that would prohibit Goldmen from "soliciting, offering or selling securities that are not registered or exempt

---

10. Under 15 U.S.C. § 77r(b)(4)(A) and 17 C.F.R. § 230.174(d), the Imatec security became a "covered security" 25 days after the initial public offering. At that time, state regulation was pre-empted. See 15 U.S.C. § 77r(a)(1)(A) (1997).

from registration in New Jersey to residents of states (other than New Jersey) in which the securities are qualified for sale." App. 402–03.

The case then proceeded to cross-motions for summary judgment. On August 21, 1997, the district court granted Goldmen's motion for summary judgment and denied the Bureau's summary judgment motion. The sole issue addressed was whether the New Jersey Uniform Securities Law violated the dormant commerce clause by authorizing the Bureau to block the sale of securities from New Jersey to buyers in other states where the security was registered. The district court concluded that it did. According to the district court, the law directly regulated interstate commerce because it effectively allowed the Bureau "to impose New Jersey securities regulations onto other states." The district court argued that "[t]o allow the Bureau to preclude consumers in other states from receiving solicitations to purchase securities which their own state regulators have deemed appropriate for purchase is, in essence, to allow the Bureau to substitute its own regulatory judgment for that of other states." Further, the district court argued that absent allegations of fraud, the Bureau had no interest in regulating such transaction. Accordingly, the New Jersey Uniform Securities Law imposed an excessive burden on interstate commerce in relation to New Jersey's local benefits. App. 581 (citing Pike v. Bruce Church, 397 U.S. 137 * * * (1970)).

The Bureau filed a timely appeal.

III.

A. Legal Framework

The Supreme Court has long construed the Commerce Clause as implying a judicial power to invalidate state laws that interfere improperly with interstate commerce. See, e.g., Cooley v. Board of Wardens, 53 U.S. (12 How.) 299 * * * (1851). One consistent strain of these cases authorizes courts to invalidate state regulations when their extra-territorial impact is so great that their "practical effect . . . is to control conduct beyond the boundaries of the state." Healy v. The Beer Institute, 491 U.S. 324, 336 * * * (1989). As Justice Cardozo explained in Baldwin v. G.A.F. Seelig, 294 U.S. 511, 523 * * * (1935), such a power is necessary to prevent states from applying "parochial" laws that can bring about "a speedy end of our national solidarity." "The Constitution," Justice Cardozo stated, "was framed upon the theory that the peoples of the several states must sink or swim together, and that in the long run prosperity and salvation are in union and not division." Id.

According to these "extraterritorial effects" cases, a state may not attempt to regulate commerce that takes place "wholly outside" of its borders: such a "projection of one state regulatory regime into the jurisdiction of another State" is impermissible. Healy, 491 U.S. at 336–37 * * *. Under this rubric, the Supreme Court has invalidated state laws that restricted interstate movement of goods based on the price paid for them in out-of-state transactions. See, e.g., Baldwin, 294 U.S. at 521 * * * (invalidating New York law that banned the importation of milk into New York when the price paid outside of New York to the out-of-state producer was lower than that permitted under then-existing laws regulating milk purchases from New York producers); Lemke v. Farmers' Grain Co., 258 U.S. 50, 61 * * * (invalidating North Dakota law requiring exported wheat to be sold outside of North Dakota at price set by North Dakota state inspector). Similarly, the Court has struck down state laws that prohibited the importation of out-of-state goods unless the importer guaranteed that its in-state prices were no higher than elsewhere. See, e.g., Healy, 491 U.S. at 337 * * * (invalidating Connecticut law prohibiting beer imports unless seller guaranteed that prices offered in Connecticut were no higher than in neighboring states); Brown–Forman Distillers Corp. v. New York State Liquor Auth., 476 U.S. 573, 579 * * * (1986) (invalidating New York law requiring liquor importers to affirm that prices offered to New York wholesalers were lowest nationwide). Finally, the Court has invalidated laws granting officials in one state the authority to block multistate transactions that only marginally involve in-state interests. See Edgar v. MITE Corp., 457 U.S. 624, 643–46 * * * (1982) (invalidating Illinois law that authorized Illinois officials to block substantively unfair takeovers of multistate companies that had connections to Illinois and also other states).

Of course, these cases do not establish that the states are forbidden categorically to regulate transactions that involve interstate commerce. See H.P. Hood & Sons v. Du Mond, 336 U.S. 525, 532–33 * * * (1949) (Jackson, J.) (recognizing that States have "broad power ... to protect its inhabitants against ... fraudulent traders ... even by use of measures which bear adversely upon interstate commerce"). Rather, states are permitted to regulate in-state components of interstate transactions so long as the regulation furthers legitimate in-state interests. A particularly relevant example of this is Hall v. Geiger–Jones Co., 242 U.S. 539 * * * (1917), and its companion cases, Caldwell v. Sioux Falls Stock Yards Co., 242 U.S. 559 * * * (1917) and Merrick v. N.W. Halsey & Co., 242 U.S. 568 * * * (1917) (collectively, the "Blue Sky Cases"). In the Blue Sky Cases, the Court considered dormant commerce clause challenges to then-recently enacted Blue Sky laws in Ohio, South Dakota, and Michigan. Although the three statutes differed somewhat, each granted state securities commissions the authority to block the in-state sale or purchase of unlicensed securities. The laws were challenged both by unlicensed in-state securities sellers and the out-of-state purchasers who had traveled in-state to make their purchases, but the Court rejected their claims that the laws violated the dormant commerce clause. The key to the laws' constitutionality, the Court held, was that "[t]he provisions of the law ... apply to dispositions of securities within the state." Hall, 242 U.S. at 557 * * * (emphasis in original). By limiting the scope of the statute to dispositions of securities "within the State," the Court announced, the states had merely enacted "police regulation[s]," that "affect[ed] interstate commerce ... only incidentally." Id. at 558 * * *; see also CTS Corp. v. Dynamics Corp., 481 U.S. 69, 93 * * * (1987) (rejecting challenge by out-of-state company to Indiana law conditioning acquisition of corporate control of Indiana corporation on approval of a majority of the pre-existing disinterested shareholders, reasoning that law regulated in state corporations); cf. Shafer v. Farmers' Grain Co., 268 U.S. 189, 200 * * * (1925) (invalidating North Dakota law that regulated in-state handling of wheat headed for interstate commerce that served no legitimate in-state interests).

B.   Territoriality

As these cases indicate, the constitutionality of state regulations of interstate commerce depends largely on the territorial scope of the transaction that the state law seeks to regulate. If the transaction to be regulated occurs "wholly outside" the boundaries of the state, the regulation is unconstitutional. MITE Corp, 457 U.S. at 642. If the transaction occurs "within" the boundaries of the state, it is constitutional so long as the regulation furthers legitimate in-state interests. See id. at 643–46; CTS Corp, 481 U.S. at 93.

Therefore, the first issue we must address is the territorial scope of the transaction that New Jersey has attempted to regulate. The question is, what is the territorial basis of a contract entered into by telephone between a New Jersey broker soliciting sales of Imatec securities from New Jersey, and an out-of-state buyer who agrees to purchase them outside of New Jersey? More particularly, can it fairly be said that such a transaction occurs "wholly outside" New Jersey? As this is a legal question, our review is plenary. See Ciarlante v. Brown & Williamson Tobacco Corp., 143 F.3d 139, 145 (3d Cir.1998).

Goldmen and the Bureau offer divergent views of § 60's territorial scope. Goldmen argues that § 60 permits New Jersey to reach out beyond its borders and block willing buyers from completing transactions authorized by their home states. According to Goldmen, "the effects of the Bureau's application of Section 60 is not to regulate in-state brokers, but to preclude out-of-state residents from purchasing a product deemed appropriate for sale by their own regulators." Br. at 20. Goldmen suggests that the offer's origin in New Jersey is not relevant to the transaction's territoriality, because "the 'practical effect' of permitting New Jersey to bar the sale of securities from New Jersey into states where those securities have been qualified for sale is that those out-of-state residents will be precluded altogether from receiving the opportunity to purchase these securities." Id. at 16.

The Bureau's position is that § 60 regulates the offering of securities entirely within the state of New Jersey. According to the Bureau, Section 60 simply regulates how brokers located in New Jersey conduct business from their New Jersey offices. In this instance, these were Imatec securities ... offered for sale by the underwriter through solicitations of the public from New Jersey. The offer and sale arose in New Jersey. Goldmen chose to domicile its highly-regulated business in New Jersey and to conduct that business from within the State. * * *

The Bureau concedes that § 60 may affect interstate commerce, to the extent that sellers such as Goldmen try to sell securities to buyers in other states. However, the Bureau contends that this is merely an indirect effect of what is essentially New Jersey's regulation of New Jersey parties seeking to sell securities in New Jersey.

In resolving this question, we begin by noting that notions of the territorial scope of contracts between citizens of different states have evolved in the past century. At one time, it was fashionable to conceive of contracts between diverse parties as being rooted in a single geographical location, such as the place the offer was accepted. See, e.g., Joseph H. Beale, What Law Governs Validity of a Contract, 23 Harv. L. Rev. 260, 270–71 (1910). Under this traditional approach, it was believed that when a contract offer made in New Jersey was accepted in New York, the contract was "made" in New York, and thus implicated New York's sovereignty. See id; cf. Perrin v. Pearlstein, 314 F.2d 863, 867 (2d Cir.1963).

The contrasting modern approach is to recognize that contracts formed between citizens in different states implicate the regulatory interests of both states. Thus, when an offer is made in one state and accepted in another, we now recognize that elements of the transaction have occurred in each state, and that both states have an interest in regulating the terms and performance of the contract. See, e.g., General Ceramics Inc. v. Firemen's Fund Ins. Co., 66 F.3d 647, 656–59 (3d Cir.1995) (comparing the regulatory interests of New

Jersey and Pennsylvania to a contract formed between a New Jersey company and a Pennsylvania company in the course of determining applicable law). See generally Joseph W. Singer, A Pragmatic Guide to Conflicts, 70 B.U. L. Rev. 731, 785–802 (1990) (describing the regulatory interests of states in contract disputes between diverse parties).

This notion that the sovereignty of both the state of the offeror and offeree are implicated by contracts entered into by citizens in different states is the key to understanding the territorial scope of the contract between Goldmen and the prospective buyers of Imatec in another state such as New York. A contract between Goldmen in New Jersey and a buyer in New York does not occur "wholly outside" New Jersey, just as it does not occur "wholly outside" New York. Rather, elements of the transaction occur in each state, and each state has an interest in regulating the aspect of the transaction that occurs within its boundaries.

Accordingly, § 60 simply allows the Bureau to regulate its "half" of the transaction—the offer that occurs entirely within the state of New Jersey—and thus its territorial scope is indistinguishable from that in Hall v. Geiger–Jones Co., 242 U.S. 539 * * * (1917), Caldwell v. Sioux Falls Stock Yards Co., 242 U.S. 559 * * * (1917) and Merrick v. N.W. Halsey & Co., 242 U.S. 568 * * * (1917).

Viewed in this light, Goldmen's view that § 60 violates the dormant commerce clause because it projects its ban into jurisdictions that would allow the transaction is logically flawed and simply proves too much. If New Jersey seeks to block Goldmen's offering but the buyer's state (say, New York) would allow it, one state must prevail. One state can in effect "force its judgment" upon the other. Under New Jersey's Blue Sky law, New Jersey can block the transaction even if New York would permit it.

Goldmen's alternative is no better, however: under its view of the dormant commerce clause, New York's approval would permit the transaction, over New Jersey's objection. Thus, the difference between New Jersey's Blue Sky law and Goldmen's proposal is simply the market's default rule: should the transaction be allowed if either state permits, or blocked if either side objects? Such questions of the market's "structure" and its "method of operation" are quite simply beyond the concern of the Commerce Clause, as they "relate to the wisdom of the statute, not to its burden on commerce." Exxon Corp. v. Governor of Maryland, 437 U.S. 117, 127–28 * * * (1978).

C. Legitimate Interests

Having concluded that § 60 regulates the in-state component of an interstate transaction, we next consider whether the statute reasonably furthers a "legitimate interest" within the boundaries of New Jersey. MITE Corp., 457 U.S. at 644 * * *; CTS Corp., 481 U.S. at 93.

Goldmen claims that New Jersey has no legitimate interest in regulating Goldmen's non-fraudulent sales to out-of-state residents. If Goldmen's business practices are manipulative, Goldmen argues, the harm will be suffered entirely by out-of-state consumers. Br. at 29. Because the protection of out-of-state consumers from potentially manipulative sales practices is not New Jersey's legitimate concern, Goldmen contends, its regulation of Goldmen's non-fraudulent sales to out-of-state consumers does not implicate any legitimate regulatory interests within the state of New Jersey.

The Bureau responds by arguing that its regulation of in-state sales of securities to out-of-state purchasers furthers important New Jersey interests. We agree. In particular, we consider two legitimate state interests to be particularly strong ones. First, preventing New Jersey companies from offering suspect securities to out-of-state buyers helps preserve the reputation of New Jersey's legitimate securities issuers. States that have failed to monitor out-of-state sales by in-state broker-dealers have suffered in the past, as their legitimate broker-dealers suffered from association with suspect firms offering questionable securities. See Long, § 3.04[3][a] at 3–51 to 3–52 (providing examples); see also Stevens v. Wrigley Pharma. Co., 154 A. 403, 403 (N.J. Ch. Div. 1931) (noting that New Jersey's interest in regulating in-state offers to out-of-state buyers is "not so much to protect the citizens of other states, as to prevent this state from being used as a base of operations for crooks marauding outside the state."); Simms Inv. Co. v. E.F. Hutton & Co., 699 F. Supp. 543, 545 (M.D.N.C.1988) ("[T]he laws protect legitimate resident issuers by exposing illegitimate resident issuers."). Although this state interest is heightened when the state can prove that the in-state firm has engaged in outright fraud, the interest is nonetheless legitimate when the state seeks to block sales of securities that it believes might be associated with dubious or manipulative sales practices. The difference between a state's (i.e., New Jersey's) interest in preventing fraud and preventing questionable practices is a difference in degree, not a difference in kind.

The dissent contends that absent proof of actual fraud, New Jersey has an insufficient interest in regulating securities dealers who sell to out-of-state buyers. It is undisputed that the purpose of securities registration laws is to prevent fraud before it happens, and § 60 serves such a prophylactic purpose. Merrick v. N.W. Halsey & Co., 242 U.S. 568, 587 * * * (1917); Caldwell v. Sioux Falls Stock Yards Co., 242 U.S. 559, 564 * * * (1917) (upholding Blue Sky Law designed "to prevent fraud in the sale and disposition of stocks, bonds or other securities sold or offered for sale within the state"); Hall v. Geiger–Jones Co., 242 U.S. 539, 551 * * * (1917) (upholding Blue Sky Law designed to "prevent deception and save credulity and ignorance from imposition") * * *.

Regulating in-state offers to out-of-state buyers also serves New Jersey interests by protecting New Jersey residents from dubious securities that enter the state in the secondary market. This risk is particularly great because a broker-dealer such as Goldmen could otherwise delay or even avoid the Bureau's scrutiny through an initial sale to a cooperative party outside New Jersey. Because there is no filing requirement for secondary transactions, Goldmen could arrange to "sell" a security to a friendly out-of-state party, immediately buy back the security, and then sell it freely to New Jersey residents using possibly questionable sales practices. App. 77–78. New Jersey's most effective means of preventing such an undesirable result would be to block the initial public offering. See Long, § 3.04[3][b–c] at 3–52 to 3–53.

In conclusion, the Bureau's application of § 60 to Goldmen's Imatec offering furthers two legitimate state interests: preserving the reputation of New Jersey broker-dealers, and protecting New Jersey buyers in the secondary market.

IV.

Because the Bureau's application of § 60 regulates the in-state portion of an interstate transaction and furthers legitimate in-state interests, the application of § 60 to regulate the Imatec offering does not violate the dormant commerce clause. In so holding, we note that our conclusion is in accordance with the overwhelming majority of courts that have considered dormant commerce clause challenges to blue sky laws . . .

Indeed, the established heritage and near universality of the provision that Goldmen has challenged itself underscores its constitutionality. See Healy, 491 U.S. 336–37. * * * Goldmen has challenged a state provision that is an established strand in the legal fabric of securities regulation. The power that Goldmen claims would unduly burden interstate commerce is one that most states have long exercised, and that Congress has for decades expressly allowed to continue. This is not the sort of "parochial" state power that Justice Cardozo warned of in Baldwin, the broad exercise of which "would . . . invite a speedy end of our national solidarity." Baldwin, 294 U.S. at 523.

We will therefore reverse the order of the district court dated August 21, 1997, and remand for proceedings consistent with this opinion.

■ McKEE, CIRCUIT JUDGE, dissenting.

I respectfully dissent from the opinion of my colleagues. The majority recognizes New Jersey's right to regulate that portion of a multi-state transaction occurring within its borders because "one state must prevail" in a dispute that extends beyond its borders and involves residents of other states. * * * The approach the majority uses would be helpful to resolving a choice of law dispute, but it is of only limited assistance in adjudicating this dispute under the Commerce Clause. New Jersey does not allege that Goldmen's sale of Imatec stock involved fraud, and the district court concluded that fraud was not involved. See Dist. Ct. Op. at 7 ("The Bureau does not advance a single allegation of fraud"). Thus, the issue is not which state will win, but whether New Jersey's interest here is sufficient to allow it to prevent Goldmen from soliciting residents of other states. The district court concluded, "the Bureau is reaching out to prohibit a sale, not made to New Jersey residents, which takes place in a national securities market, and which is regulated by each state to protect its own citizens." Id. The district court concluded that New Jersey's interest was not sufficient to allow that result. I agree, and would affirm the well reasoned decision of the district court. * * *

The Supreme Court "has adopted what amounts to a two-tiered approach to analyzing state economic regulation under the Commerce Clause." Brown–Forman Distillers Corp. v. New York State Liquor Authority, 476 U.S. 573, 578–79 * * * (1986). "When a state statute directly regulates or discriminates against interstate commerce, or when its effect is to favor in-state economic interests over out-of-state interests, [the Supreme Court] has generally struck down the statute without further inquiry." Id. at 579. * * * "When, however, a statute has only indirect effects on interstate commerce and regulates even-handedly, [the Court] has examined whether the State's interest is legitimate and whether the burden on interest commerce clearly exceeds the local benefits." Id. (citing Pike v. Bruce Church, Inc., 397 U.S. 137, 142 * * * (1970)).

Although I believe a strong case can be made that § 60 falls within the first tier of inquiry and therefore could be struck down as a per se violation of the Commerce Clause, I think our inquiry should, more appropriately, be conducted under the Pike balancing test that guides inquiry under the second tier.

Although the majority does not directly refer to Pike v. Bruce Church, it is obvious that, by discussing New Jersey's local interests, it is engaging in a balancing of interests as required by Pike. In Pike, the Court wrote:

Where the statute regulates even-handedly to effectuate a legitimate local public interest, and its effects on interstate commerce are only incidental, it will be upheld unless the burden imposed on such commerce is clearly excessive in relation to the local putative benefits. If a legitimate local purpose is found, then the question becomes one of degree. And the extent of the burden that will be tolerated will of course depend on the nature of the local interest involved, and on whether it could be promoted as well with a lesser impact on interstate activities. Occasionally the Court has candidly undertaken a balancing approach in resolving these issues, but more frequently it has spoken in terms of "direct" and "indirect" effects and burdens.

Moreover, a state cannot impose its regulatory scheme on another state in an effort to "control conduct beyond the boundaries of the state." Healy v. Beer Institute, 491 U.S. 324, 326 * * * (1989). This prohibition against extraterritoriality "reflect[s] the Constitution's special concern both with the maintenance of a national economic union unfettered by state-imposed limitations on interstate commerce and with the autonomy of the individual states with their respective spheres." Id. The Supreme Court has summarized the application of the limitations inherent in the Commerce Clause as follows:

Our cases concerning the extraterritorial effects of state economic regulation stand at a minimum for the following propositions: First, the Commerce Clause ... precludes the application of a state statute to commerce that takes place wholly outside of the State's borders, whether or not the commerce has effects within the State. ...Second, a statute that directly controls commerce occurring wholly outside the boundaries of a State exceeds the inherent limits of the enacting State's authority and is invalid regardless of whether the statute's extraterritorial reach was intended by the legislature. The critical inquiry is whether the practical effect of the regulation is to control conduct beyond the boundaries of the State. Third, the practical effect of the statute must be evaluated not only by considering the consequences of the statute itself, but also by considering how the challenged statute may interact with the legitimate regulatory regimes of other States and what effect would arise if not one, but many or every, State adopted similar legislation. Generally speaking, the Commerce Clause protects against inconsistent legislation arising from the projection of one state regulatory regime into the jurisdiction of another.

Id., 491 U.S. at 336–37 (citations and internal quotations omitted).

I agree that Goldmen's telephone solicitation of out-of-state buyers for shares of Imatec would not be a transaction occurring "wholly outside" of New Jersey. However, the majority's view that the Bureau is only regulating its "half" of a transaction by prohibiting Goldmen from soliciting out-of-state buyers, * * * is accurate in theory, but not accurate in the jurisprudential reality of the Commerce Clause. Goldmen is not the issuer of these securities. It is only the underwriter. Imatec, a Delaware corporation whose main office is in New York, is the issuer. Imatec's only connection with New Jersey is that its offering was underwritten by a broker-dealer who happens to be located there, and that broker dealer planned to solicit out-of-state sales from its New Jersey office. It may be reasonably assumed that out of state buyers would purchase these shares from funds held in financial institutions outside of New Jersey, and that any profits would be deposited into those same financial institutions. Moreover, the growth and fiscal strength of Imatec, the Delaware corporation, is related to the value of its shares. Thus, New Jersey's only connection with this interstate transaction lies in the fortuitous circumstance that a broker-dealer would be sitting at a desk somewhere in New Jersey making telephone calls to residents of the 16 states where Imatec securities are appropriately registered and authorized for purchase.

Goldmen has satisfied the registration requirements of 16 states and those states allow their residents to be solicited to purchase shares of Imatec. Each of those states could have enacted a regulatory scheme that only allowed the sale of securities properly registered in the state where the seller maintains its principal office. None of the 16 states have chosen to do so. Our holding has the practical effect of reading § 60 into the regulations of each of those states despite the absence of such a restriction in the regulatory schemes of the 16 states. The majority concludes that this result is consistent with the Commerce Clause because it furthers two "particularly strong" local interests, viz., preserving the reputation of New Jersey broker-dealers and protecting New Jersey buyers in the secondary market. * * * My colleagues can reach this conclusion by viewing § 60 as having only an "incidental" impact on interstate commerce. As I state above, § 60 imposes an absolute ban on interstate commerce that consists of soliciting individual buyers of Imatec stock from New Jersey. If we analyzed the regulation from the perspective of that absolute ban on the solicited sale of Imatec securities to residents of the states where the securities have been approved for sale, the burden on interstate commerce would be far more substantial than the majority suggests.

However, even assuming arguendo that the regulations at issue here have only an "incidental" effect on interstate commerce, New Jersey's interest is still not sufficient to justify prohibiting solicitations in 16 states where these securities are registered. I believe that finding such an interest requires more than the asserted need to protect potential purchasers residing elsewhere from the risks of penny stocks and sellers such as Goldmen. It requires some showing that the interests New Jersey seeks to further would be advanced by applying § 60 to solicitations of Imatec. If the Bureau can establish that Goldmen is engaging in false and misleading sales practices or fraud, New Jersey has an interest sufficient to survive scrutiny under the Commerce Clause. But, the Bureau concedes that "[t]his is not a fraud case." App. at 558. Therefore, I am at a loss to understand how the majority can conclude on the record before us that New Jersey has shown a "particularly strong" interest.

Since New Jersey's interest absent fraudulent business activities is minimal at least, the federal interests are paramount. it is not a question of allowing one state's regulatory scheme to prevail over that of another state. "the balance here must be struck in favor of the federal interests." Kassell, 450 U.S. at 667. * * * Accordingly, I believe we should affirm the decision of the district court.

JURISDICTION IN INTERSTATE TRANSACTIONS

Under the conflict of laws provisions of the Uniform Securities Act, which have been adopted in a number of states including California,[1] the question

---

1. Unif. Sec. Act § 414; cf. Cal. § 25,-008.

whether a particular state's Blue Sky Law applies to a transaction involving a sale by an out-of-state seller to one of its residents turns upon the location of the offer and acceptance under the definitions in that statute and whether the transaction involves an offer to sell which is accepted by the buyer or an offer to buy which is accepted by the seller. The location of an offer or acceptance is defined to include *both* the state from which it is transmitted and the state to which it is directed.[2] If an offer to *sell* is made in a state, that gives jurisdiction regardless of where the acceptance may be made.[3] However, if the transaction is initiated by an offer to *buy*, then both the offer and the acceptance must be "in this state" in order for it to have jurisdiction.[4]

Under these provisions, if an out-of-state seller directs an offer to sell (by mail or telephone, or in person) to a buyer in State A, then the jurisdiction of State A attaches at that moment and there may have already been a violation of State A's Blue Sky Law if the issue was not qualified or exempted. However, in the *Kreis v. Mates Inv. Fund, Inc.* case the advertisement in the national magazine seen by the plaintiff did not confer jurisdiction because there is an exclusion from the definition of "offer" for this purpose of such an advertisements in a newspaper or magazine "which has had more than two-thirds of its circulation outside this state during the last 12 months" or carried on a radio or television program originating outside the state.[5]

Accordingly, in the *Kreis* case it was necessary to base jurisdiction upon the offer to buy sent by the plaintiff to the fund in New York and to find that both the offer to buy *and its acceptance* were in Missouri. Since the offer to buy was directed from Missouri and the acceptance was communicated to the plaintiff in Missouri, the court holds that the jurisdiction of Missouri attached even though the acceptance in a contractual sense may have occurred in New York and the contract performed in New York by the issuance of the shares before any communication to the plaintiff in Missouri.[6]

There would seem to be little doubt as illustrated by *A.S. Goldmen*, that a state has jurisdiction, if it chooses to exercise it, over sellers located in that state even though they are selling to out-of-state buyers. There is also no doubt that the definitions in the Uniform Securities Act make that state's Blue Sky Law applicable whenever the seller directs any offers to sell from that state to

---

2. In Ah Moo v. A.G. Becker Paribas, Inc., 857 F.2d 615, 620 (9th Cir.1988), the court generalized: "Hawaii's blue sky laws are applicable if there was a physical nexus between the 'sale or offer to sell' and the State of Hawaii." Blue sky decisions will often follow the minimum contacts test of International Shoe Co. v. State of Wash., 326 U.S. 310 (1945) to determine personal jurisdiction.

3. Benjamin v. Cablevision Programming Inv., 114 Ill.2d 150, 102 Ill.Dec. 296, 499 N.E.2d 1309 (1986); Getter v. R. G. Dickinson & Co., 366 F.Supp. 559, 573–574 (S.D.Iowa 1973); Feitler v. Midas Assoc., 418 F.Supp. 735, 738 (E.D.Wis.1976) (both §§ 414(c)(1) and (2)); Ansbro v. Southeast Energy Group, Ltd., 658 F.Supp. 566 (N.D.Ill. 1987).

4. *See, e.g.,* Underhill Assoc., Inc. v. Bradshaw, 674 F.2d 293, 295 (4th Cir.1982). Application of the § 414(c)(2) formula affords due process of law. Green v. Weis, Voisin, Cannon, Inc., 479 F.2d 462 (7th Cir.1973).

5. 473 F.2d 1308 (8th Cir.1973).

6. In Haberman v. Washington Pub. Power Supply Sys., 109 Wash.2d 107, 744 P.2d 1032, 1053–1054 (Wash. *en banc* 1987), *appeal dismissed sub nom.* American Express Travel Related Serv. Co. v. Washington Pub. Power Supply Sys., 488 U.S. 805 (1988), which grew out of a bond issue by the System to finance two nuclear power plants, the court applied the "most significant relationship" standard to conclude that Washington was clearly the state with the most substantial contacts with the subject matter of the case.

persons out of the state. This scope of the provisions was justified on the basis that a state should not permit itself to be used as the base for the manufacture of fraudulent devices for export to other states.

The Internet raises new jurisdictional issues, as one commentator theorizes because application of state blue sky laws to securities transactions has traditionally been based on location, i.e., the laws of a given state seek to regulate transactions occurring within the state's boundaries.[7] It is uncertain whether the existing statutory approach will remain adequate. "Despite the additional complexities, existing principles can be used to view e-mail over the Internet as similar to traditional postal mail and phone calls in providing a basis for jurisdiction."[8]

In Booth v. Verity,[9] however, the court held that the mere ability to view a passive web page or mass media report was an insufficient contact with a state to render an out-of-state defendant subject to that state's jurisdiction.

The Uniform Securities Act contains a consent to service of process provision in § 414(g) to address every application for registration and every issuer which proposes to offer a security.

The Act also contains a substituted service of process provision in § 414(h) that will reach a nonresident who engages in illegal conduct and has not filed a consent to a service of process.[10] The inspiration for § 414(h) were state nonresident motorist statutes, whose constitutionality appeared to be conclusively determined by the Supreme Court in 1957.[11]

PROBLEM 17–1

Trident, Inc., a Delaware corporation solely doing business in Florida has a website that includes an "In the News" feature that includes recent news articles and financial analyst opinions of Trident.

Wise, a citizen of Maine, was impressed by a news article describing the "unlimited potential" of a new Trident product and bought 10,000 shares of Trident.

One month later Trident, Inc. filed for bankruptcy reorganization and Wise brought an action based on the Maine blue sky law which includes a provision identical to § 414 of the Uniform Securities Act of 1956. Can Wise establish jurisdiction?

7. Denis T. Rice, The Regulatory Response to the New World of Cybersecurities, 51 Admin. L. Rev. 901, 930–931 (1999).

8. Id. at 933. See also id. at 944–945; ABA Global Cyberspace Jurisdiction Project, 55 Bus. Law. 1801, 1931–1937 (2000).

9. 124 F.Supp.2d 452, 459 (W.D.Ky. 2000).

10. In Piantes v. Hayden–Stone, Inc., 30 Utah 2d 110, 514 P.2d 529 (1973), the court held that jurisdiction could be based either on a state blue sky provision like § 414(h) or on a state's long arm statute.

11. McGee v. International Life Ins. Co., 355 U.S. 220 (1957). See generally 10 Louis Loss & Joel Seligman, Securities Regulation Ch. 14.B (3d ed. rev. 1996).

PART V

ENFORCEMENT OF THE FEDERAL SECURITIES LAWS

CHAPTER 18

SEC ENFORCEMENT ACTIONS

The SEC can bring enforcement actions against broker-dealers, investment adviser, securities attorneys and accountants, and corporate registrants, officers, and directors employing causes of action unavailable to private litigants. The most significant of these actions are considered in the initial four parts of this chapter. The Commission also has an extraordinarily broad panoply of remedies available to it and a distinctive pattern of procedures. These issues conclude this chapter.

The SEC, however, has no power to bring criminal actions for willful violation of the federal securities laws. The Commission's authority is limited to referring potential criminal actions to the Justice Department. Criminal enforcement of the federal securities laws is considered in Chapter 19.

Finally, both the SEC and the Justice Department face similar jurisdictional and choice of law problems when they seek to enforce the federal securities laws extraterritorially. These topics are addressed in Chapter 20.

A. BROKER–DEALERS

In the Matter of John H. Gutfreund, et al.

51 SEC 93 (1992).

Order Instituting Proceedings Pursuant to Section 15(b) of the Securities Exchange Act of 1934, Making Findings, and Imposing Remedial Sanctions and Report of Investigation Pursuant to Section 21(a) of the Securities Exchange Act of 1934.

I.

The Commission deems it appropriate and in the public interest that public administrative proceedings be and they hereby are instituted against John H. Gutfreund, Thomas W. Strauss, and John W. Meriwether pursuant to Section 15(b) of the Securities Exchange Act of 1934 ("Exchange Act").

II.

In anticipation of the institution of these administrative proceedings, Gutfreund, Strauss, and Meriwether have each submitted Offers of Settlement which the Commission has determined to accept. Solely for the purposes of these proceedings and any other proceedings brought by or on behalf of the Commission or to which the Commission is a party, prior to a hearing pursuant to the Commission's Rules of Practice, and without admitting or denying the facts, findings, or conclusions herein, Gutfreund, Strauss, and Meriwether each consent to entry of the findings, and the imposition of the remedial sanctions, set forth below.

III.

The Commission also deems it appropriate and in the public interest that a report of investigation be issued pursuant to Section 21(a) of the Exchange Act with respect to the supervisory responsibilities of brokerage firm employees in certain circumstances. Donald M. Feuerstein consents to the issuance of this Report, without admitting or denying any of the statements contained herein.

IV.

On the basis of this Order and the Respondents' Offers of Settlement, the Commission finds the following:

A. *FACTS*

1. *Brokerage Firm Involved*

Salomon Brothers Inc ("Salomon") is a Delaware corporation with its principal place of business in New York, New York. At all times relevant to this proceeding, Salomon was registered with the Commission as a broker-dealer pursuant to Section 15(b) of the Exchange Act. Salomon has been a government-designated dealer in U.S. Treasury securities since 1939 and a primary dealer since 1961.

2. *Respondents*

John H. Gutfreund was the Chairman and Chief Executive Officer of Salomon from 1983 to August 18, 1991. He had worked at Salomon since 1953.

Thomas W. Strauss was the President of Salomon from 1986 to August 18, 1991. During that time period, Strauss reported to Gutfreund. He had worked at Salomon since 1963.

John W. Meriwether was a Vice Chairman of Salomon and in charge of all fixed income trading activities of the firm from 1988 to August 18, 1991. During that period, Meriwether reported to Strauss. During the same period, Paul W. Mozer, a managing director and the head of Salomon's Government Trading Desk, reported directly to Meriwether.

3. *Other Individual*

Donald M. Feuerstein was the chief legal officer of Salomon Inc. and the head of the Legal Department of Salomon until August 23, 1991. From 1987 until August 23, 1991, the head of Solomon's Compliance Department reported directly to Feuerstein.

4. *Summary*

In late April of 1991, three members of the senior management of Salomon—John Gutfreund, Thomas Strauss, and John Meriwether—were informed that Paul Mozer, the head of the firm's Government Trading Desk, had submitted a false bid in the amount of $3.15 billion in an auction of U.S. Treasury securities on February 21, 1991. The executives were also informed by Donald Feuerstein, the firm's chief legal officer, that the submission of the false bid appeared to be a criminal act and, although not legally required, should be reported to the government. Gutfreund and Strauss agreed to report the matter to the Federal Reserve Bank of New York. Mozer was told that his actions might threaten his future with the firm and would be reported to the government. However, for a period of months, none of the executives took action to investigate the matter or to discipline or impose limitations on Mozer. The information was also not reported to the government for a period of months. During that same period, Mozer committed additional violations of the federal securities laws in connection with two subsequent auctions of U.S. Treasury securities.

The Respondents in this proceeding are not being charged with any participation in the underlying violations. However, as set forth herein, the Commission believes that the Respondents' supervision was deficient and that this failure was compounded by the delay in reporting the matter to the government.

5. *The Submission of Two False Bids in the February 21, 1991 Five-Year U.S. Treasury Note Auction*

For a considerable period of time prior to the February 21, 1991 auction, the Treasury Department had limited the maximum bid that any one bidder could submit in an auction of U.S. Treasury securities at any one yield to 35% of the auction amount. On February 21, 1991, the Treasury Department auctioned $9 billion of five-year U.S. Treasury notes. Salomon submitted a bid in its own name in that auction at a yield of 7.51% in the amount of $3.15 billion, or 35% of the auction amount.[3] In the same auction, Salomon submitted

---

3. The Treasury Department adopted the 35% limitation in July of 1990 after Salomon submitted several large bids in amounts far in excess of the amount of securities to be auctioned. Prior to July of 1990, the Treasury Department had not placed limitations on the

two additional $3.15 billion bids at the same yield in the names of two customers: Quantum Fund and Mercury Asset Management. Both accounts were those of established customers of Salomon, but the bids were submitted without the knowledge or authorization of either customer. Both bids were in fact false bids intended to secure additional securities for Salomon. Each of the three $3.15 billion bids was prorated 54% and Salomon received a total of $5.103 billion of the five-year notes from the auction, or 56.7% of the total amount of securities sold at that auction.

After the auction results were announced, Paul Mozer, then a managing director in charge of Salomon's Government Trading Desk, directed a clerk to write trade tickets "selling" the $1.701 billion auction allocations received in response to the two unauthorized bids to customer accounts in the names of Mercury Asset Management and Quantum Fund at the auction price. Mozer at the same time directed the clerk to write trade tickets "selling" the same amounts from those accounts back to Salomon at the same price. These fictitious transactions were intended to create the appearance that the customers had received the securities awarded in response to the unauthorized bids and had sold those securities to Salomon.

Under Salomon's internal procedures, the trade tickets written by the clerk resulted in the creation of customer confirmations reflecting the purported transactions. Mozer directed the clerk to prevent the confirmations from being sent to either Mercury Asset Management or Quantum Fund. As a result, the normal procedures of Salomon were overridden and confirmations for the fictitious transactions were not sent to either Mercury Asset Management or Quantum Fund.

6. *The Submission of a Bid in the February 21, 1991 Auction by S.G. Warburg and the Treasury Department's Investigation of That Bid and the Salomon False Bid*

In the February 21, 1991 five-year note auction, S.G. Warburg, a primary dealer in U.S. Treasury securities, submitted a bid in its own name in the amount of $100 million at a yield of 7.51%. The 7.51% yield was the same yield used for the unauthorized $3.15 billion Mercury bid submitted by Salomon. At the time the bids were submitted, S.G. Warburg and Mercury Asset Management were subsidiaries of the same holding company, S.G. Warburg, PLC. Because the unauthorized Mercury bid was for the maximum 35% amount, the submission of the $100 million bid in the name of S.G. Warburg meant that two bids had apparently been submitted by affiliated entities in an amount in excess of 35% of the auction.

amount of bids that could be submitted but had limited the maximum amount that any single bidder could purchase in an auction to 35% of the auction amount.

The Salomon bids which led to the adoption of the 35% bidding limitation were submitted at the direction of Paul Mozer. Mozer was angered by the adoption of the new bidding limitation and he expressed his disagreement with the decision to adopt the new rule to officials at the Treasury Department and

in several news articles. Mozer also registered his anger through his bidding activity in the Treasury auction the following day. In an auction for $8 billion of seven-year U.S. Treasury notes on July 11, 1990, Mozer entered 11 bids at the maximum 35% amount at successive yields between 8.60% and 8.70%. The successful bids in the auction were between 8.55% and 8.58%, and the bids submitted by Mozer were intended as protest bids.

The submission of the bids was noticed by officials of the Federal Reserve Bank of New York and brought to the attention of officials of the Treasury Department in Washington, D.C. The Treasury Department officials did not know that one of the bids had been submitted by Salomon without authorization from Mercury. Because the bids were to be significantly prorated, officials of the Treasury Department decided not to reduce the amount of either bid for purposes of determining the results of the February 21, 1991 auction. The Treasury Department began to review whether the relationship between S.G. Warburg and Mercury Asset Management was such that the bids should be aggregated for determination of how the 35% limitation should be applied to those entities in future auctions.

After reviewing facts concerning the corporate relationship between Mercury Asset Management and S.G. Warburg, the Treasury Department determined to treat the two firms as a single bidder in future auctions of U.S. Treasury securities. The Treasury Department conveyed that decision in a letter dated April 17, 1991 from the Acting Assistant Commissioner for Financing to a Senior Director of Mercury Asset Management in London. The April 17 letter noted that a $3.15 billion bid had been submitted by Salomon on behalf of Mercury Asset Management in the five-year U.S. Treasury note auction on February 21, 1991, and that S.G. Warburg had also submitted a bid in the same auction, at the same yield, in the amount of $100 million. The letter noted that Mercury Asset Management and S.G. Warburg were subsidiaries of the same holding company and stated that the Treasury Department would thereafter "treat all subsidiaries of S.G. Warburg, PLC as one single entity for purposes of the 35 percent limitation rule." Copies of the letter were sent to Mozer and to a managing director of S.G. Warburg in New York.

7. *Receipt of the April 17, 1991 Treasury Department Letter by Salomon*

Mozer received the April 17 letter during the week of April 21, 1991. On April 24, he spoke with the Senior Director at Mercury Asset Management who had also received the April 17 letter. Mozer told the Senior Director that the submission of the $3.15 billion bid in the name of Mercury Asset Management was the result of an "error" by a clerk who had incorrectly placed the name of Mercury on the tender form. Mozer told the Senior Director that he was embarrassed by the "error," which he said had been "corrected" internally, and he asked the Senior Director to keep the matter confidential to avoid "problems." The Senior Director indicated that such a course of action would be acceptable. The Mercury Senior Director was not aware that the submission of the bid was an intentional effort by Salomon to acquire additional securities for its own account.

8. *Mozer's Disclosure to John Meriwether of the Submission of One False Bid*

Mozer then went to the office of John Meriwether, his immediate supervisor, and handed him the April 17 letter. When Meriwether was finished reading the letter, Mozer told him that the Mercury Asset Management bid referred to in the letter was in fact a bid for Salomon and had not been authorized by Mercury. After expressing shock at Mozer's conduct, Meriwether told him that his behavior was career-threatening, and he asked Mozer why he had submitted the bid. Mozer told Meriwether that the Government Trading Desk had needed a substantial amount of the notes, that there was also demand from the Government Arbitrage Desk for the notes, and that he had submitted the false bid to satisfy those demands.

Meriwether then asked Mozer if he had ever engaged in that type of conduct before or since. Mozer responded that he had not. Meriwether told Mozer that he would have to take the matter immediately to Thomas Strauss. Mozer then told Meriwether of his conversation with the Mercury Senior Director in which he had told that individual that the bid was an "error" and had asked him to keep the matter confidential. Meriwether listened to Mozer's description of the conversation, but did not respond. He then gave the letter back to Mozer and Mozer left the office.

9.   *Discussions Among Senior Management*

Meriwether then called Thomas Strauss. Strauss was not in, but he returned Meriwether's call later that day. Meriwether told Strauss that Mozer had informed him that he had submitted an unauthorized customer bid in an auction of U.S. Treasury securities. Strauss indicated that they should meet to discuss the matter first thing the next morning.

Meriwether met with Strauss at 9:15 a.m. the following morning, April 25, in Strauss' office. Prior to the meeting, Strauss had arranged for Donald Feuerstein, the firm's chief legal officer, to attend, and Feuerstein was in Strauss' office when Meriwether arrived. Meriwether began the meeting by describing his conversation with Mozer the previous day. He told Strauss and Feuerstein that Mozer had come to him and had informed him that he had submitted an unauthorized customer bid in an auction of U.S. Treasury securities. He said that he had informed Mozer that his conduct was career-threatening and that Mozer had denied that he had ever before or since engaged in that type of conduct. He indicated that Mozer had received a letter from the Treasury Department inquiring about the bid and that Mozer had shown him a copy of that letter. Meriwether also reported that Mozer had said that he had submitted the bid to satisfy demand for the securities from the Government Trading Desk and from Salomon's Government Arbitrage Desk. Finally, he told Strauss and Feuerstein that Mozer had informed him that he had contacted an individual at Mercury Asset Management who had also received the letter from the Treasury Department. Meriwether indicated that Mozer had told that individual that the submission of the bid was an error, and had attempted to persuade him not to inform the government of that fact.

When Meriwether was finished, Feuerstein said that Mozer's conduct was a serious matter and should be reported to the government. Feuerstein asked to see a copy of the April 17 letter. Meriwether returned to the trading floor and retrieved the letter from Mozer. He then returned to Strauss' office and provided the letter to Feuerstein. After some discussion about the letter, Strauss said he wanted to discuss the matter with Gutfreund, who was then out of town, and the meeting ended.

A meeting was then held early the following week, on either Monday, April 29 or Tuesday, April 30, with Gutfreund. The meeting was attended by Meriwether, Feuerstein, Strauss and Gutfreund and was held in Strauss' office. Meriwether summarized his conversation with Mozer. Meriwether also indicated that he believed that the incident was an aberration and he expressed his hope that it would not end Mozer's career at Salomon.

After Meriwether's description, Feuerstein told the group that he believed that the submission of the false bid was a criminal act. He indicated that, while there probably was not a legal duty to report the false bid, he believed that they had no choice but to report the matter to the government. The group then discussed whether the bid should be reported to the Treasury Department or to the Federal Reserve Bank of New York. The hostile relationship that had developed between Mozer and the Treasury Department over the adoption of the 35% bidding limitation in the Summer of 1990 was noted, as was the role of the Federal Reserve Bank of New York as Salomon's regulator in the area of U.S. Treasury securities, and the group concluded that the preferable approach would be to report the matter to the Federal Reserve Bank of New York. The meeting then ended.

At the conclusion of the meeting, each of the four executives apparently believed that a decision had been made that Strauss or Gutfreund would report the false bid to the government, although each had a different understanding about how the report would be handled. Meriwether stated that he believed that Strauss would make an appointment to report the matter to Gerald Corrigan, the President of the Federal Reserve Bank of New York. Feuerstein stated that he believed that Gutfreund wanted to think further about how the bid should be reported. He then spoke with Gutfreund the next morning. Although the April 17 letter had been sent from the Treasury Department, Feuerstein told Gutfreund that he believed the report should be made to the Federal Reserve Bank of New York, which could then, if it wanted, pass the information on to the Treasury Department. Strauss stated that he believed that he and Gutfreund would report the matter in a personal visit with Corrigan, although he believed that Gutfreund wanted to think further about how the matter should be handled. Gutfreund stated that he believed that a decision had been made that he and Strauss, either separately or together, would speak to Corrigan about the matter.

Aside from the discussions referred to above regarding reporting the matter to the government, there was no discussion at either meeting in later April about investigating what Mozer had done, about disciplining him, or about placing limits on his activities. There was also no discussion about whether Mozer had acted alone or had been assisted by others on the Government Trading Desk, about whether false records had been created, about the involvement of the Government Arbitrage Desk, which Mozer had said had sought securities from the auction, or about what had happened with the securities obtained pursuant to the bid. Similarly, there was no discussion about whether Salomon had violated the 35% bidding limitation by also submitting a bid in its own name.

For almost three months, no action was taken to investigate Mozer's conduct in the February 21 auction. That conduct was investigated only after other events prompted an internal investigation by an outside law firm, as is discussed below. During the same period, no action was taken to discipline Mozer or to place appropriate limitations on his conduct. Mozer's employment by Salomon was terminated on August 9, 1991, after an internal investigation had discovered that he had been involved in additional improper conduct.

Each of the four executives who attended the meetings in late April placed the responsibility for investigating Mozer's conduct and placing limits on his activities on someone else. Meriwether stated that he believed that, once he had taken the matter of Mozer's conduct to Strauss and Strauss had brought Feuerstein and Gutfreund into the process, he had no further responsibility to take action with respect to the false bid unless instructed to do so by one of those individuals. Meriwether stated that he also believed that, though he had the authority to recommend that action be taken to discipline Mozer or limit his activities, he had no authority to take such action unilaterally. Strauss stated that he believed that Meriwether, who was Mozer's direct supervisor, and Feuerstein, who was responsible for the legal and compliance activities of the firm, would take whatever steps were necessary or required as a result of Mozer's disclosure. Feuerstein stated that he believed that, once a report to the government was made, the government would instruct Salomon about how to investigate the matter. Gutfreund stated that he believed that the other executives would take whatever steps were necessary to properly handle the matter. According to the executives, there was no discussion among them about any action that would be taken to investigate Mozer's conduct or to place limitations on his activities.

10. *Violations After Disclosure by Mozer to Management*

After Mozer's disclosure of one unauthorized bid on April 24, 1991, he submitted two subsequent unauthorized bids in auctions of U.S. Treasury securities.

* * *

11. *The Delay In Reporting the False Bid to the Government*

There was no disclosure to the government of the false bid in the February 21, 1991 auction prior to August 9, 1991, when the results of the internal investigation were first made public.

In mid-May, after it had become clear to Feuerstein that the false bid had not yet been reported, Feuerstein met with Gutfreund and Strauss and urged them to proceed with disclosure as soon as possible. He was told by both that they still intended to report the matter. Feuerstein also learned from the in-house attorney who worked with the Government Trading Desk of a proposal by Mozer that Salomon finance in excess of 100% of the amount of the two-year U.S. Treasury notes auctioned on May 22, 1991. Feuerstein expressed his disapproval of the proposal to the attorney. Feuerstein believed that Mozer's support for this proposal, his submission of the unauthorized bid in the February auction, and his conduct during the Summer of 1990 which led to the adoption of the 35% bidding limitation combined to indicate that he had an "attitudinal problem." Prior to leaving for Japan on May 23, 1991, Feuerstein spoke with Strauss and conveyed these concerns to him. He also again discussed with Strauss his belief that the bid should be reported to the government as soon as possible. Feuerstein also spoke with Gutfreund in early June and again urged him to report the matter to the government.

* * *

12. *The Internal Investigation*

In early July, Salomon retained a law firm to conduct an internal investigation of the firm's role in the May 22, 1991 two-year note auction. On July 2, a lawyer with that law firm had received a call from the general counsel of a brokerage firm who indicated that an FBI agent and a representative from the Antitrust Division of the Department of Justice had made a request to speak with representatives of the firm about the May two-year note auction. Before agreeing to be retained by the firm, the lawyer indicated that he wished to determine whether Salomon, which was a regular client of the firm, also wanted representation in connection with the matter. The lawyer then spoke with employees of Salomon and was told that Salomon might wish to be represented in connection with the matter and that the firm should hold itself available. Prior to that time, in late June of 1991, Salomon had received inquiries from the Commission and from another government agency concerning activities in the two-year U.S. Treasury notes auctioned on May 22, 1991. Several days after the lawyer contacted Salomon, Feuerstein decided to retain the law firm and directed that it begin an internal investigation of the firm's activities in the May 22, 1991 two-year note auction.

At the time the law firm was retained, it was asked only to investigate facts concerning the May two-year notes. The law firm was not informed of the false bid submitted in the February 21, 1991 auction. On July 8, attorneys from the law firm began interviewing employees on the Government Trading Desk at Salomon. The interviews were attended by several attorneys from the law firm and by the in-house attorney working with the Government Trading Desk. Sometime during the week of July 8, the attorneys learned that one of Salomon's customers in the May two-year note auction, Tiger Management Corporation, had apparently sold $500 million of a $2 billion auction award to Salomon on the day of the auction at the auction price, and that trade tickets for the transaction did not exist.

On July 12, attorneys from the law firm interviewed Thomas Murphy, who was then the head trader on the Government Trading Desk. In connection with questions about customer authorization for the $500 million portion of the $2 billion Tiger award sold to Salomon on the day of the auction, Murphy was asked whether there had been similar types of problems in the past. Murphy said that he could not answer the question without speaking to the Salomon attorney who was present. Murphy and the attorney then left the room. When they returned, Murphy did not answer the question but continued with the interview.

When the interview was over, Feuerstein met with the attorneys from the law firm for a previously-scheduled status meeting. During that meeting, Feuerstein and the attorneys discussed the questions concerning authorization for the $500 million portion of the Tiger award. Feuerstein then informed the attorneys that Salomon had submitted an unauthorized customer bid in the February 21, 1991 five-year note auction. The attorneys and Feuerstein agreed that the scope of the internal investigation should be broadened, and a decision was made that the law firm would expand the investigation to include a review of all auctions for U.S. Treasury notes and bonds since the July 1990 adoption by the Treasury Department of a 35% bidding limitation.[8]

On the following Monday, July 15, the attorneys from the law firm began the expanded internal investigation agreed upon at the meeting. During the review that was conducted between July 15 and early August, the law firm discovered a $1 billion false bid in the December 27, 1990 auction of four-year U.S. Treasury notes, a second $3.15 billion false bid in the February 21, 1991 auction, a $1 billion false bid in the February 7, 1991 auction of thirty-year U.S. Treasury bonds,[9] the failure to disclose the $485 million when-issued position

---

8. Feuerstein also told the lawyers that he had advised senior management that for business reasons the false bid should be reported to the government. He then asked the lawyers to research the question of Salomon's legal duty to report the false bid. Several weeks later, the law firm advised Salomon that, based on the research it had conducted, it was unable to provide any conclusive answer to the question.

9. The bid submitted by Salomon in the February 7, 1991 auction was the result of a failed practical joke which employees of the

in the May 22, 1991 auction, and questions concerning customer authorization for the bid submitted in the name of Tudor in the April 25, 1991 auction.[10] The results of the internal investigation were reported to Feuerstein on August 6 and to other members of senior management of Salomon, including Gutfreund, Strauss, and Meriwether, on August 7.

On August 9, 1991, after consultation with and review by outside counsel, Salomon issued a press release stating that it had "uncovered irregularities and rule violations in connection with its submission of bids in certain auctions of Treasury securities." The release described several of the violations and stated that Salomon had suspended two managing directors on the Government Trading Desk and two other employees.

In telephone conversations on August 9, 1991 in which they reported on the results of the internal investigation, Gutfreund and Strauss disclosed to government officials for the first time that the firm had known of a false bid in a U.S. Treasury auction since late April of 1991. On August 14, 1991, Salomon issued a second press release which publicly disclosed for the first time that Gutfreund, Strauss and Meriwether had been "informed in late April by one of the suspended managing directors that a single unauthorized bid had been submitted in the February 1991 auction of five-year notes."

On Sunday, August 18, at a special meeting of the Board of Directors of Salomon Inc, Gutfreund and Strauss resigned their positions with Salomon and Salomon Inc, and Meriwether resigned his position with Salomon. On August 23, 1991, Feuerstein resigned his position as Chief Legal Officer of Salomon.

* * *

B.   *FINDINGS*

1.   *Legal Principles*

Section 15(b)(4)(E) of the Exchange Act authorizes the Commission to impose sanctions against a broker-dealer if the firm has:

> failed reasonably to supervise, with a view to preventing violations [of federal securities laws], another person who commits such a violation, if such person is subject to his supervision.

Section 15(b)(6) of the Exchange Act incorporates Section 15(b)(4)(E) by reference and authorizes the Commission to impose sanctions for deficient supervision on individuals associated with broker-dealers.

The principles which govern this proceeding are well-established by the Commission's cases involving failure to supervise. The Commission has long emphasized that the responsibility of broker-dealers to supervise their employees is a critical component of the federal regulatory scheme.[14] As the Commis-

---

firm had intended to play against a sales manager in the San Francisco office of Salomon who was scheduled to retire on the day after the auction.

10. As with the false bids submitted in the February 21, 1991 auction, the false bids in the December 27, 1990 and February 7, 1991 auctions were accompanied by fictitious sales of auction allocations received in response to the false bids to accounts in the

names of customers and then back to Salomon, all at the auction price. In addition, in each of those instances, the normal procedures of Salomon were also overridden and confirmations for the fictitious transactions were not sent to the customers.

14. Smith Barney, Harris Upham & Co., Exchange Act Release No. 21,813 (March 5, 1985).

sion stated in *Wedbush Securities, Inc.:*[15]

> In large organizations it is especially imperative that those in authority exercise particular vigilance when indications of irregularity reach their attention.

The supervisory obligations imposed by the federal securities laws require a vigorous response even to indications of wrongdoing. Many of the Commission's cases involving a failure to supervise arise from situations where supervisors were aware only of "red flags" or "suggestions" of irregularity, rather than situations where, as here, supervisors were explicitly informed of an illegal act.

Even where the knowledge of supervisors is limited to "red flags" or "suggestions" of irregularity, they cannot discharge their supervisory obligations simply by relying on the unverified representations of employees.[17] Instead, as the Commission has repeatedly emphasized, "[t]here must be adequate follow-up and review when a firm's own procedures detect irregularities or unusual trading activity * * *."[18] Moreover, if more than one supervisor is involved in considering the actions to be taken in response to possible misconduct, there must be a clear definition of the efforts to be taken and a clear assignment of those responsibilities to specific individuals within the firm.[19]

> * * *

2.   *The Failure to Supervise*

As described above, in late April of 1991 three supervisors of Paul Mozer—John Meriwether, Thomas Strauss, and John Gutfreund—learned that Mozer had submitted a false bid in the amount of $3.15 billion in an auction of U.S. Treasury securities. Those supervisors learned that Mozer had said that the bid had been submitted to obtain additional securities for another trading area of the firm. They also learned that Mozer had contacted an employee of the customer whose name was used on the bid and falsely told that individual that the bid was an error. The supervisors also learned that the bid had been the subject of a letter from the Treasury Department to the customer and that Mozer had attempted to persuade the customer not to inform the Treasury Department that the bid had not been authorized. The supervisors were also informed by Salomon's chief legal officer that the submission of the false bid appeared to be a criminal act.

The information learned by the supervisors indicated that a high level employee of the firm with significant trading discretion had engaged in extremely serious misconduct. As the cases described above make clear, this information required, at a minimum, that the supervisors take action to investigate what had occurred and whether there had been other instances of unreported misconduct. While they could look to counsel for guidance, they had

---

15.   48 S.E.C. 963, 967 (1988).

17.   See Shearson Lehman Hutton Inc., Exchange Act Release No. 26,766 (April 28, 1989); Prudential–Bache Securities, Inc., Exchange Act Release No. 22,755 (January 2, 1986).

18.   Prudential–Bache Securities, Inc., *supra.*

19.   *See, e.g.,* William E. Parodi, Sr., Exchange Act Release No. 27,299 (September 27, 1989); Gary W. Chambers, Exchange Act Release No. 27,963 (April 30, 1990). Supervisors who know of wrongdoing cannot escape liability for failure to supervise simply because they have failed to delegate or assign responsibility to take appropriate action.

an affirmative obligation to undertake an appropriate inquiry. If they were unable to conduct the inquiry themselves or believed it was more appropriate that the inquiry be conducted by others, they were required to take prompt action to ensure that others in fact undertook those efforts. Such an inquiry could have been conducted by the legal or compliance departments of the firm, outside counsel, or others who had the ability to investigate the matter adequately. The supervisors were also required, pending the outcome of such an investigation, to increase supervision of Mozer and to place appropriate limitations on his activities.

The failure to recognize the need to take action to limit the activities of Mozer in light of his admitted misconduct is particularly troubling because Gutfreund and Strauss did place limitations on Mozer's conduct in connection with the June two-year U.S. Treasury note auction at a time when they thought the firm had not engaged in misconduct, but press reports had raised questions about the firm's activities. Although they had previously been informed that a serious violation had in fact been committed by Mozer, they failed for over three months to take any action to place limitations on his activities to deal with that misconduct.

The need to take prompt action was all the more critical in view of the fact that the potential unlawful conduct had taken place in the market for U.S. Treasury securities. The integrity of that market is of vital importance to the capital markets of the United States, as well as to capital markets worldwide, and Salomon occupied a privileged role as a government-designated primary dealer. The failure of the supervisors to take vigorous action to address known misconduct by the head of the firm's Government Trading Desk caused unnecessary risks to the integrity of this important market.

To discharge their obligations, the supervisors should at least have taken steps to ensure that someone within the firm questioned other employees on the Government Trading Desk, such as the desk's clerk or the other managing director on the Desk. Since the supervisors were informed that Mozer had said that he submitted the false bid to obtain additional securities for another trading desk of the firm, they should also have specifically investigated any involvement of that area of the firm in the matter. The supervisors should also have reviewed, or ensured that others reviewed, documentation concerning the February 21, 1991 auction. Such a review would have revealed, at a minimum, that a second false bid had been submitted in the auction and that false trade tickets and customer confirmations had been created in connection with both false bids. Those facts would have raised serious questions about the operations of the Government Trading Desk, and inquiries arising from those questions might well have led to discovery of the additional false bids described above. For instance, two of the other false bids, those submitted in the December 27, 1990 and February 7, 1991 auctions, involved the same pattern of fictitious sales to and from customer accounts and the suppression of customer confirmations used in connection with the February 21, 1991 auction. Inasmuch as Mozer had admitted to committing one apparently criminal act, the supervisors had reason to be skeptical of Mozer's assurances that he had not engaged in other misconduct.

Each of the three supervisors apparently believed that someone else would take the supervisory action necessary to respond to Mozer's misconduct. There was no discussion, however, among any of the supervisors about what action should be taken or about who would be responsible for taking action. Instead, each of the supervisors assumed that another would act. In situations where supervisors are aware of wrongdoing, it is imperative that they take prompt and unequivocal action to define the responsibilities of those who are to respond to the wrongdoing. The supervisors here failed to do that. As a result, although there may be varying degrees of responsibility, each of the supervisors bears some measure of responsibility for the collective failure of the group to take action.

After the disclosure of one unauthorized bid to Meriwether, Mozer committed additional violations in connection with the submission of two subsequent unauthorized customer bids. Had limits been placed on his activities after the one unauthorized bid was disclosed, these violations might have been prevented. While Mozer was told by Meriwether that his conduct was career-threatening and that it would be reported to senior management and to the government, these efforts were not a sufficient supervisory response under the circumstances. The supervisors were required to take action reasonably designed to prevent a repetition of the misconduct that had been disclosed to them. They could, for instance, have temporarily limited Mozer's activities so that he was not involved in the submission of customer bids pending an adequate review of what had occurred in the February 21, 1991 auction, or they could have instituted procedures to require verification of customer bids.

Under the circumstances of this case, the failure of the supervisors to take action to discipline Mozer or to limit his activities constituted a serious breach of their supervisory obligations. Gutfreund, Strauss and Meriwether thus each failed reasonably to supervise Mozer with a view to preventing violations of the federal securities laws.[20]

As Chairman and Chief Executive Officer of Salomon, Gutfreund bore ultimate responsibility for ensuring that a prompt and thorough inquiry was undertaken and that Mozer was appropriately disciplined. A chief executive officer has ultimate affirmative responsibility, upon learning of serious wrongdoing within the firm as to any segment of the securities market, to ensure that steps are taken to prevent further violations of the securities laws and to determine the scope of the wrongdoing. He failed to ensure that this was done. Gutfreund also undertook the responsibility to report the matter to the government, but failed to do so, although he was urged to make the report on several occasions by other senior executives of Salomon. The disclosure was made only after an internal investigation prompted by other events. Gutfreund's failure to report the matter earlier is of particular concern because of Salomon's role in the vitally-important U.S. Treasury securities market. The reporting of the matter to the government was also the only action under consideration within the firm to respond to Mozer's actions. The failure to make the report thus meant that the firm failed to take any action to respond to Mozer's misconduct.

Once improper conduct came to the attention of Gutfreund, he bore responsibility for ensuring that the firm responded in a way that recognized the seriousness and urgency of the situation. In our view, Gutfreund did not discharge that responsibility.

---

20. Salomon did not have established procedures, or a system for applying those procedures, which together reasonably could have been expected to detect and prevent the violations. The affirmative defense provisions of Section 15(b)(4)(E) thus do not apply in this case.

Strauss, as the President of Salomon, was the official within the firm to whom Meriwether first took the matter of Mozer's misconduct for appropriate action. As its president, moreover, Strauss was responsible for the operations of Salomon as a brokerage firm.[21] Though he arranged several meetings to discuss the matter, Strauss failed to direct that Meriwether, Feuerstein, or others within the firm take the steps necessary to respond to the matter. Even if Strauss assumed that Meriwether or Feuerstein had taken the responsibility to address the matter, he failed to follow-up and ascertain whether action had in fact been taken. Moreover, it subsequently became clear that no meaningful action was being taken to respond to Mozer's misconduct. Under these circumstances, Strauss retained his supervisory responsibilities as the president of the brokerage firm, and he failed to discharge those responsibilities.

Meriwether was Mozer's direct supervisor and the head of all fixed-income trading activities at Salomon. Meriwether had also been designated by the firm as the person responsible for supervising the firm's fixed-income trading activities, including the activities of the Government Trading Desk.

When he first learned of Mozer's misconduct, Meriwether promptly took the matter to senior executives within the firm. In so doing, he took appropriate and responsible action. However, Meriwether's responsibilities did not end with communication of the matter to more senior executives. He continued to bear direct supervisory responsibility for Mozer after he had reported the false bid to others within the firm. As a result, until he was instructed not to carry out his responsibilities as Mozer's direct supervisor, Meriwether was required to take appropriate supervisory action. Meriwether's efforts in admonishing Mozer and telling him that his misconduct would be reported to the government were not sufficient under the circumstances to discharge his supervisory responsibilities.

C. DONALD M. FEUERSTEIN

Donald Feuerstein, Salomon's chief legal officer, was informed of the submission of the false bid by Paul Mozer in late April of 1991, at the same time other senior executives of Salomon learned of that act. Feuerstein was present at the meetings in late April at which the supervisors named as respondents in this proceeding discussed the matter. In his capacity as a legal adviser, Feuerstein did advise Strauss and Gutfreund that the submission of the bid was a criminal act and should be reported to the government, and he urged them on several occasions to proceed with disclosure when he learned that the report had not been made. However, Feuerstein did not direct that an inquiry be undertaken, and he did not recommend that appropriate procedures, reasonably designed to prevent and detect future misconduct, be instituted, or that other limitations be placed on Mozer's activities. Feuerstein also did not inform the Compliance Department, for which he was responsible as Salomon's chief legal officer, of the false bid.[22]

---

21. As we noted in Universal Heritage Investments Corporation, 47 S.E.C. 839, 845 (1982):

> The president of a corporate broker-dealer is responsible for compliance with all of the requirements imposed on his firm unless and until he reasonably delegates particular functions to another person in that firm, and neither knows nor has reason to know that such person's performance is deficient.

22. In late May or early June, Feuerstein did speak with the head of the Compliance Department about the need to develop compliance procedures with respect to the firm's activities in government securities.

Unlike Gutfreund, Strauss and Meriwether, however, Feuerstein was not a direct supervisor of Mozer at the time he first learned of the false bid. Because we believe this is an appropriate opportunity to amplify our views on the supervisory responsibilities of legal and compliance officers in Feuerstein's position, we have not named him as a respondent in this proceeding.[23] Instead, we are issuing this report of investigation concerning the responsibilities imposed by Section 15(b)(4)(E) of the Exchange Act under the circumstances of this case.

Employees of brokerage firms who have legal or compliance responsibilities do not become "supervisors" for purposes of Sections 15(b)(4)(E) and 15(b)(6) solely because they occupy those positions. Rather, determining if a particular person is a "supervisor" depends on whether, under the facts and circumstances of a particular case, that person has a requisite degree of responsibility, ability or authority to affect the conduct of the employee whose behavior is at issue.[24] Thus, persons occupying positions in the legal or compliance departments of broker-dealers have been found by the Commission to be "supervisors" for purposes of Sections 15(b)(4)(E) and 15(b)(6) under certain circumstances.[25]

In this case, serious misconduct involving a senior official of a brokerage firm was brought to the attention of the firm's chief legal officer. That individual was informed of the misconduct by other members of senior management in order to obtain his advice and guidance, and to involve him as part of management's collective response to the problem. Moreover, in other instances of misconduct, that individual had directed the firm's response and had made recommendations concerning appropriate disciplinary action, and management had relied on him to perform those tasks.

Given the role and influence within the firm of a person in a position such as Feuerstein's and the factual circumstances of this case, such a person shares in the responsibility to take appropriate action to respond to the misconduct. Under those circumstances, we believe that such a person becomes a "supervisor" for purposes of Sections 15(b)(4)(E) and 15(b)(6). As a result, that person is responsible, along with the other supervisors, for taking reasonable and appropriate action. It is not sufficient for one in such a position to be a mere bystander to the events that occurred.

Once a person in Feuerstein's position becomes involved in formulating management's response to the problem, he or she is obligated to take affirmative steps to ensure that appropriate action is taken to address the misconduct. For example, such a person could direct or monitor an investigation of the conduct at issue, make appropriate recommendations for limiting the activities of the employee or for the institution of appropriate procedures, reasonably

---

23. We note that Feuerstein has represented that he does not intend to be employed in the securities industry in the future.

24. Although it did not represent an opinion of the Commission, the concurring opinion in Arthur James Huff, Exchange Act Release No. 29,017 (March 28, 1991), is consistent with this principle. The operative portion of that opinion, Part VI, explains that in each situation a person's actual responsibili-

ties and authority, rather than, for example, his or her "line" or "non-line" status, will determine whether he or she is a "supervisor" for purposes of Sections 15(b)(4)(E) and (6).

25. *See, e.g.,* First Albany Corporation, Exchange Act Release No. 30,515 (March 25, 1992); Gary W. Chambers, Exchange Act Release No. 27,963 (April 30, 1990); Michael E. Tennenbaum, Exchange Act Release No. 18,-429 (January 19, 1982).

designed to prevent and detect future misconduct, and verify that his or her recommendations, or acceptable alternatives, are implemented. If such a person takes appropriate steps but management fails to act and that person knows or has reason to know of that failure, he or she should consider what additional steps are appropriate to address the matter. These steps may include disclosure of the matter to the entity's board of directors, resignation from the firm, or disclosure to regulatory authorities.[26]

These responsibilities cannot be avoided simply because the person did not previously have direct supervisory responsibility for any of the activities of the employee. Once such a person has supervisory obligations by virtue of the circumstances of a particular situation, he must either discharge those responsibilities or know that others are taking appropriate action.

V. *ORDER*

In view of the foregoing, the Commission deems it appropriate and in the public interest to impose the sanctions specified in the Offers of Settlement submitted by John H. Gutfreund, Thomas W. Strauss, and John W. Meriwether.

BROKER–DEALER DISCIPLINARY PROCEEDINGS

Section 15(b)(4) of the 1934 Act empowers the SEC to censure, place limits on activities, functions or operation, suspend for a period not exceeding 12 months or revoke the registration on any of the six grounds, which can be characterized as (A) misstatements in an application; (B) criminal convictions; (C) injunctions with respect to specified securities or commodities activities; (D) willful violations of the federal securities laws; (E) aiding and abetting or failure to supervise; and (F) bars or suspension of an associated person. Section 15(b)(6) establishes a parallel enforcement mechanism allowing the SEC to directly discipline an associate of a broker-dealer firm.[1]

In recent years § 15(b)(4)(E) failure to supervise cases have been frequently employed by the Commission to inspire more rigorous compliance by broker-dealer firms.[2] Among other spectacular cases in recent years were SEC actions against Prudential Securities for its failure to adequately supervise the sale of approximately $8 billion of limited partnership interests in more than 700 offerings between 1980 and 1990. The Commission alleged that Prudential "made material misstatements and omissions in the sale of limited partnership interests relating, among other things to the nature, potential yields, safety, and purported liquidity of the investments."[3]

---

26. Of course, in the case of an attorney, the applicable Code of Professional Responsibility and the Canons of Ethics may bear upon what course of conduct that individual may properly pursue.

1. *See generally* 6 Louis Loss & Joel Seligman, Securities Regulation 3028–3086 (3d ed. rev. 2002).

2. *See, e.g.,* Graham v. SEC, 222 F.3d 994 (D.C.Cir.2000); Shearson Lehman Bros., Inc., 49 SEC 619 (1986) ("a system of supervisory procedures which rely solely on the branch manager is insufficient"); Dean Wit-

ter Reynolds, Inc., 49 SEC 956 (1988) (a firm's failure to establish guidelines to ensure that its Compliance Department's directives are enforced "is symptomatic of a failure to reasonably supervise").

There are also parallel SRO rules such as NYSE Rule 342(a), which can give rise to sanctions for failure to adequately supervise. See Patrick v. SEC, 19 F.3d 66 (2d Cir.1994), *cert. denied,* 513 U.S. 807 (1994).

3. Prudential Sec. Inc., 51 SEC 726 (1993); Litig. Rel. 13,840, 55 SEC Dock. 709

The most egregious recent failure to supervise cases have involved "rogue brokers." As the GAO reported: "Of the almost 470,000 active brokers listed in CRD as of November 30, 1993, about 10,000 had at least 1 formal disciplinary action against them for a variety of violations, including sales practice abuse violations and such criminal acts as driving while intoxicated, and 816 had 3 or more disciplinary actions."[4]

Among other practices that have been the subject of recent SEC failure to supervise cases have been preannounced, rather then surprise compliance examinations,[5] failure to adequately review new hires,[6] and failure to dismiss or institute heightened supervision of a registered representative when the supervisor learns that the representative has engaged in misconduct.[7]

The Commission, in Gutfreund, emphasized the supervisor's responsibility. Often the supervisor will be a branch manager with responsibilities or review of several registered representatives in a specific office. The Commission has also focused on the quality of compliance procedures in place. When a violation is found a broker-dealer may make restitution to a customer and subject the registered representative or supervisor to sanctions, including education, special supervision, censure, full disclosure to customers, or dismissal.

PROBLEM 18–1

Finance Franchises (FF) is a registered broker-dealer that has adopted a series of cutting edge approaches to supervision. Virtually all of its registered representatives are independent contractors, rather than employees. Most operate in single person offices. Much supervision is done by computer programs that review daily trading records.

Pam Backman, chief of compliance, recently became concerned that John Caviness, a FF independent contractor, may have been excessively trading six specific accounts.

Should she:

(1993). *See also* 55 SEC Dock. 624, 631 (1993).

Similar shortcomings were later found in PaineWebber's offer and sale of approximately $3 billion in limited partnership and direct investment interests between 1986 and 1992. PaineWebber Inc., Sec. Ex. Act Rel. 36,724. 61 SEC Dock. 121 (1996).

For another account of a breakdown in supervision, see Lynch, Report of Inquiry into False Trading Profits at Kidder Peabody & Co., Inc. 11 (Aug. 4, 1994) ("The principal shortcoming that contributed to the non-detection of Jett's false profits was the failure of Jett's immediate supervisors to understand the nature of his trading activity").

4. GAO, Actions Needed to Better Protect Investors against Unscrupulous Brokers 3 (1994). See also Special Report, "Rogue Broker" Problem Raises Troubling Issues for Firms, Regulators, 26 Sec. Reg. & L. Rep. (BNA) 1207 (1994); Testimony of SEC Chairman Arthur Levitt Concerning the Large Firm Project, Subcomm. on Telecommunica-

tions & Fin., House Comm. on Energy & Commerce (Sept. 14, 1994), *reprinted in* 1994–1995 Fed. Sec. L. Rep. (CCH) ¶ 85,433 (1994). See also Joint Regulatory Sales Practice Sweep Report, 1995–1996 Fed. Sec. L. Rep. (CCH) ¶ 85,742 (1996); GAO, Responses to GAO and SEC Recommendations Related to Microcap Stock Fraud (GAO/GGD–98–204) (Sept. 1998).

Later the Justice Department announced in May 1997 that it had charged or convicted 17 rogue brokers in ten states. Justice Announces Prosecutions of 17 "Rogue" Brokers in 10 States, 29 Sec. Reg. & L. Rep. (BNA) 739 (1997).

5. Royal Alliance Assoc., Inc., Sec. Ex. Act Rel. 38,174, 63 SEC Dock. 1606 (1997).

6. Cf. Clarence Z. Wurts, Sec. Ex. Act Rel. 43,842, 74 SEC Dock. 281 (2001).

7. Quest Capital Strategies, Inc., Sec. Ex. Act Rel. 44,935, 76 SEC Dock. 102 (2001).

    (1) telephone Caviness and ask for an explanation?

    (2) plan an unscheduled examination of his office?

    (3) report the pattern of trading to Caviness's line supervisor?

    (4) report the trading pattern to Paul Gorgen, FF's chief executive officer?

    (5) Review FF's compliance procedures?

    (6) Seek to fire Caviness if he is found to have excessively traded?

Andrews v. Prudential Sec., Inc.

United States Court of Appeals, Sixth Circuit, 1998.
160 F.3d 304.

OPINION

■ KENNEDY, CIRCUIT JUDGE.

Plaintiffs, Kyle Andrews, John Meehan, and J. Stephen Stout, appeal the District Court's order granting summary judgment on behalf of the defendant, Prudential Securities, in this diversity action alleging that defendant filed false Uniform Termination Notice of Securities Industry Registration forms ("U–5 forms") with the National Association of Securities Dealers. For the reasons that follow, we **AFFIRM** the judgment of the District Court.

I.

A.   Factual Background

The plaintiffs' suit against Prudential Securities, Inc. ("Prudential") arises out of a requirement imposed upon brokerage firms by the National Association of Securities Dealers ("NASD"). When a brokerage firm terminates the employment of a broker, the firm is required to file with the NASD a Uniform Notice of Termination for Securities Industry Registration. *See* NASD By-laws, Art. IV, § 3(a). In the industry, the form is commonly referred to as the "U–5" form. Item 13 of the U–5 form requires a firm to make the following disclosure:

WHILE EMPLOYED BY OR ASSOCIATED WITH YOUR FIRM, WAS THE INDIVIDUAL:

———

B.   The subject of an investment-related, consumer-initiated complaint that:

    (1) alleged compensatory damages of $10,000 or more, fraud, or wrongful taking of property?

    (2) was settled or decided against the individual for $5,000 or more, or found fraud, or the wrongful taking of property.

See Ex. 1 to Prudential's Motion for Summary Judgment. Firms are additionally required to file an amended U–5 after a broker departs if it learns of facts or circumstances which would require an affirmative response to Item 13. *See* NASD By–Laws, Art. IV, § 3(b). As explained by the NASD, the required disclosure enables the NASD "to detect violations and subsequently sanction persons for violations of the NASD's rules and other applicable federal statutes and regulations." Further, "failure to provide this information may ... subject members of the investing public to repeated misconduct and may deprive member firms of the ability to make informed hiring decisions.'' *See* NASD Notices to Members, No. 88–67 at p. 291. The NASD cautions that failure to provide complete and accurate information in a U–5 form may subject firms to administrative, civil, and even criminal penalties. Id.

Kyle Andrews, John Meehan, and J. Stephen Stout, the plaintiffs in the instant action, were employed with Prudential as registered representatives when the Securities and Exchange Commission (''SEC'') filed suit against Prudential for misconduct in connection with the sale of interests in limited partnerships. A settlement agreement between the SEC and Prudential resulted in a claims resolution process during which several of Prudential's customers filed claims naming plaintiffs as their registered representatives for their purchases of the limited partnerships. The submitted claims were all settled for various amounts over $5,000.

At the time the customer claims were submitted, plaintiffs were no longer working for Prudential; Andrews, Stout, and Meehan departed Prudential in 1989 to work for another brokerage firm. Despite their cessation of employment with Prudential, NASD By-laws required Prudential to file amended U–5 forms if it believed that Item 13 required an amended response. Accordingly, Prudential filed amended forms on December 2, 1994 (plaintiff Meehan), May 24, 1995 (plaintiff Stout), and June 22, 1995 (plaintiff Andrews).

B.   U–5 Amendment: Plaintiff Andrews

On June 22, 1995, Prudential filed an amended U–5 form for Andrews disclosing three complaints filed against Andrews. The amended U–5 form reads as follows:

> * * * clients submitted claim form(s) to the Claims Resolution Process relating to limited partnership purchase(s) during the period: 7/87–10/88; 2/88–4/88; 9/86–1/89. [Andrews] was the broker of record at the time of the purchase(s). No damages were alleged but the amount(s) of actual loss (out-of-pocket) is/are approximately $18,017; $14,478; $14,853.
>
> Settlement(s) with the ... client(s) has/have been reached in the Claims Resolution Process. The dollar amount(s) of the settlements(s) is/are approximately $15,990; $14,670; $31,605.
>
> This matter resulted from the unprecedented, unsolicited mailing of claim forms by Prudential to over 340,000 investors who purchased Limited Partnerships through Prudential from January 1, 1980 to January 1, 1991. The ... client(s) submitted claim form(s) in response to this mailing ...

See Ex. 2 to Prudential's Motion for Summary Judgment.

A review of the customer complaints that formed the basis for the U–5 amendment reveals that the complaints alleged not only unhappiness with the purchases of the limited partnership but also specific dissatisfaction with the representations made by Andrews concerning the partnerships.

See Ex. 7 to Prudential's Motion for Summary Judgment.

C.   U–5 Amendment: Plaintiff Stout

On May 24, 1995, Prudential filed an amendment to the U–5 form filed upon Stout's departure from the firm. The amendment disclosed two complaints brought by consumers during the Claims Resolution Process. The language of the Stout Amendment resembled the Andrews Amendment except for the customer names, out-of-pocket losses and settlement amounts. Like the complaints filed by customers of Andrews, the complaints filed by several of Stout's clients alleged specific dissatisfaction with Stout's representations of the partnerships. Also like the Andrews complaints, Stout's customers complained that the partnerships were not suitable to their financial situations and that they were not fully informed regarding the nature of the partnerships or of the risky nature of the limited partnerships.

D.   Procedural History

As a result of Prudential's filing of the amended U–5 forms, plaintiffs, on March 22, 1996, filed a complaint against Prudential asserting seven counts: (1) fraud/misrepresentation; (2) breach of fiduciary duty and violation of NASD and New York Stock Exchange rules; (3) defamation; (4) intentional infliction of emotional distress; (5) tortious interference with business relations; (6) gross negligence; and (7) violation of due process. In response to a motion to dismiss the complaint, the District Court dismissed the fraud, breach of fiduciary duty, tortious interference, and due process counts. However, the court granted plaintiffs leave to file an amended complaint in order to plead the defamation count with specificity and to identify the U–5 forms upon which they based their allegations.

Following the plaintiffs' filing of an amended complaint on October 1, 1996, the District Court dismissed Meehan's defamation claim on statute of limitations grounds. Thus, the claims which remained to be litigated included the defamation claims of Andrews and Stout and all of the plaintiffs' claims for intentional infliction of emotional distress and gross negligence.

Following the close of discovery, Prudential filed a motion for summary judgment on the remaining three claims. On June 4, 1997, the District Court granted Prudential's motion. Regarding the defamation claims, the court held that the U–5 forms were protected by a qualified privilege which could be defeated only upon a showing of actual malice. Because plaintiffs failed to adduce any evidence that the reports were published with actual malice, the court held that the defamation claims could not withstand Prudential's motion. Alternatively, the court held that the defamation claims could not be maintained because the U–5 forms contained only true statements. Regarding plaintiffs' causes of action for intentional infliction of emotional distress, the court concluded that the filing of the U–5s did not constitute extreme and outrageous conduct. Lastly, the court dismissed the gross negligence claims because, in its view, such a cause of action was not viable in Michigan under the facts alleged and, alternatively, because defendant's actions did not amount to gross negligence.

Plaintiffs now appeal from the order granting summary judgment on behalf of Prudential.

* * *

III.

A.   Defamation

Plaintiffs assert that there is an issue of fact as to whether the statements on the U–5 form are true and thus the District Court erred in granting summary judgment on behalf of Prudential on their defamation claims. Under Michigan law, a plaintiff must establish each of the following four elements to maintain a defamation action: "(a) a false and defamatory statement concerning plaintiff; (b) an unprivileged publication to a third party; (c) fault amounting at least to negligence on the part of the publisher; and (d) either actionability of the statement irrespective of special harm, (defamation per se) or the existence of special harm caused by the publication (defamation per quod)." [Citations omitted.]

As is evident by the first requirement of falsity, truth is a complete defense to a defamation action. [Citations omitted.] We conclude that the District Court properly granted summary judgement on behalf of Prudential on the basis that plaintiffs could not adduce any evidence that the U–5 forms submitted by Prudential were substantively false. Plaintiffs do not allege that they were not the brokers of record at the time of the limited partnership purchases, that the amount of actual losses reported was inaccurate, that the dollar amounts of the settlements lacked a factual basis, or that the claims did not, as reported, result from the mailings of claim forms to investors who purchased limited partnerships between 1980 and 1991. Thus, no statement contained within any of the U–5 forms is false and no defamatory statement was ever uttered.

Plaintiffs, however, allege that the defamatory statement was made when defendant checked affirmatively section (2) of following question asked on the U–5 form:

WHILE EMPLOYED BY OR ASSOCIATED WITH YOUR FIRM, WAS THE INDIVIDUAL:

* * *

B. The subject of an investment-related, *consumer-initiated complaint* that:

(1) alleged compensatory damages of $10,000 or more, fraud, or wrongful taking of property?

(2) was settled or decided against the individual for $5,000 or more, or found fraud, or the wrongful taking of property?

See Item 13 of U–5 Form (emphasis added). Plaintiffs claim Prudential's answer of "Yes" to section (2) of that question on the plaintiffs' amended U–5 forms was defamatory because the claims were not initiated by consumers but were filed in response to Prudential's solicitation and, further, that the clients' submissions were not complaints but merely claim forms. We decline to adopt plaintiffs' narrow interpretation of "consumer-initiated complaint" for several reasons. First, while the primary purpose of Prudential's solicitation of claims was to compensate clients who had been harmed in connection with the purchase of limited partnerships, the information returned by several clients in connection with the solicitation revealed that not only had clients been financially harmed by Prudential's sales of limited partnerships but also that brokerage representatives engaged in conduct which may have amounted to misrepresentation or suitability complaints. The U–5 form enables the NASD "to detect violations and subsequently sanction persons for violations of the NASD's rules and other applicable federal statutes and regulations." *See* NASD Notices to Members, No. 88–67 at p. 291. Thus, the responses to defendant's solicitation of claims initiated discussion and disclosed claims of alleged improper conduct of individual brokers. Prudential furthered the NASD's purpose of the U–5 form filing requirement by informing the NASD of the conduct brought to its attention. The complaints were no less consumer-initiated simply because they followed the SEC investigation and general solicitation by Prudential. We, thus, agree with the District Court's conclusion that an NASD member was required to report a broker against whom such a complaint has been filed even though the complaint was also against the brokerage firm and was made in response to a solicitation resulting from litigation against the brokerage firm.

To the extent that the affirmative answer to the "consumer-initiated complaint" inquiry is claimed to be in any way misleading, the remainder of the U–5 explained the process by which Prudential learned of the plaintiffs' conduct so that the NASD could independently evaluate whether the plaintiffs were the subject of an investment-related, consumer-initiated complaint that was settled against the individual for $5,000 or more, or found fraud, or the wrongful taking of property.[5]

For these reasons, we cannot conclude that plaintiffs could carry their burden of establishing that any statements in the U–5 forms were false. The District Court therefore properly granted summary judgment on plaintiffs' defamation claims.

IV.

For the foregoing reasons, the judgement of the District Court is **AFFIRMED**.

QUALIFIED IMMUNITY

Some have suggested that "rogue brokers" (really, registered representatives) often are too easily employed by other broker-dealers because earlier broker-dealers are reluctant to candidly acknowledge the reason for a registered representative's departure in the joint SEC–State Form 4U–5, Uniform Termination Notice for Securities Industry Registration.

In 1998 the National Association of Securities Dealers, Inc. (NASD) proposed qualified immunity in securities arbitration proceedings for statements made on Form U–5 and Form U–4, the Uniform Application for Securities Registration or Transfer.[1] The proposal was not adopted by the Commission, in part, because of a belief that it was better addressed by the states.

An alternative approach would be a standard providing for absolute immunity.[2]

---

5. In his unrebutted affidavit, Hugh H. Makens, former Director of the Corporation and Securities Bureau of the State of Michigan, past president of the North American Securities Administrators Association, and member of the Legal Advisory Board to the NASD, attested that Prudential "had the obligation and the responsibility under applicable NASD rules to file the amended Form U–5s based on the statements of the customers in the Claim Process Submission forms." Makens further stated that the U–5 reports "fairly represent the customer complaints reflected in the corresponding Claim Process Submission forms." Thus, in his opinion, the fact that the consumer complaints were submitted in response to Prudential's solicitation did not absolve Prudential of its obligation of amending the U–5 forms and did not render false any of the statements therein.

1. Sec. Ex. Act Rel. 39,892, 60 SEC Dock. 2473 (1998).

2. See generally Anne H. Wright, Form U–5 Defamation, 52 Wash. & Lee L. Rev. 1299 (1995); Acciardo v. Millennium Sec. Corp., 83 F.Supp.2d 413 (S.D.N.Y.2000) (discussing both New York qualified and absolute immunity cases).

Securities administrators or self-regulatory organizations generally are subject to absolute or qualified immunity for actions of their employees within the course of their official duties.[3]

To date no state had adopted an immunity provision in its securities statute, although the new Uniform Securities Act (2002) adopted such a provision in the summer of 2002. No state has rejected immunity in this context by judicial decision. A number of states have adopted qualified immunity by judicial decision.[4]

An agent who has been the subject of a Form U–5, Uniform Termination Notice for Securities Industry Registration, may respond to specified adverse disclosures and have responses included in the Form U–5.

B. INVESTMENT ADVISERS

As initially adopted the Investment Advisers Act of 1940 was little more than a continuing census of the nation's investment advisers.[1] But it was substantially tightened by a series of amendments in 1960–15 years after the Commission had first urged such action in a special report to Congress[2]—and was again amended in the Investment Company Amendments Act of 1970 and the Securities Acts Amendments of 1975.

The 1975 Amendments were designed essentially to conform the registration and disciplinary *procedures* more closely to those concurrently prescribed for broker-dealers in the same legislation.

A more significant development occurred in 1996 when Title III of the National Securities Markets Improvement Act, separately titled The Investment Advisers Supervision Coordination Act, generally solely subjected to state regulation advisers with assets under management of $25 million or less (later raised to $30 million).[3] Any adviser with assets under management of $30 million or more or who is an investment adviser to an investment company registered under the Investment Company Act of 1940 will register solely under § 203 of the Investment Advisers Act and not state law. In essence this new division of labor largely eliminated duplicative regulation of investment advisers.

In two significant respects the Investment Advisers Act is limited.

First, unlike state securities statutes, only investment advisers, not investment adviser representatives, must register.

Second, private rights of action are quite limited. In 1979 the Supreme Court held there could be no implied action for damages under § 206, the Investment Advisers Act's equivalent to Rule 10b–5.[4]

---

3. See 10 Louis Loss & Joel Seligman, Securities Regulation 4818–4821 (3d ed. rev. 1996).

4. See, e.g., Eaton Vance Distrib., Inc. v. Ulrich, 692 So.2d 915 (Fla.Dist.Ct.App. 1997); Baravati v. Josephthal, Lyon & Ross, Inc., 28 F.3d 704 (7th Cir.1994) (Illinois); Andrews v. Prudential Sec., Inc., 160 F.3d 304 (6th Cir.1998) (Michigan); Prudential Sec., Inc. v. Dalton, 929 F.Supp. 1411 (N.D.Okla.1996) (Oklahoma); Glennon v. Dean Witter Reynolds Inc., 83 F.3d 132 (6th Cir.1996) (Tennessee).

1. See generally 7 Louis Loss & Joel Seligman, Securities Regulation ch. 8.C (3d ed. 1991).

2. SEC, Protection of Clients' Securities and Funds in Custody of Investment Advisers (1945), *summarized in* Inv. Adv. Act Rel. 39 (1945).

3. Rule 203A–1.

4. Transamerica Mortgage Advisors, Inc. v. Lewis, 444 U.S. 11 (1979).

Each investment adviser who registers under the Investment Advisers Act after 2001, more electronically file Form ADV[5] through the Investment Adviser Registration Depository (IARD).[6] Under the Investment Adviser Act there are other substantive requirements addressing (1) recordkeeping;[7] (2) inspection;[8] (3) performance fees (that is, a statutory prohibition on an investment adviser sharing capital gains);[9] assignment of advisory compacts;[10] and (5) use of the title "investment counsel."[11]

Much litigation under the Act has focused on the definition of investment adviser and on novel forms of advisory fraud.

1.   DEFINITION OF "INVESTMENT ADVISER"

Lowe v. SEC

Supreme Court of the United States, 1985.
472 U.S. 181, 105 S.Ct. 2557, 86 L.Ed.2d 130.

OPINION:

■ JUSTICE STEVENS delivered the opinion of the Court.

The question is whether petitioners may be permanently enjoined from publishing nonpersonalized investment advice and commentary in securities newsletters because they are not registered as investment advisers under § 203(c) of the Investment Advisers Act of 1940 (Act), 54 Stat. 850, 15 U.S.C. § 80b–3(c).

Christopher Lowe is the president and principal shareholder of Lowe Management Corporation. From 1974 until 1981, the corporation was registered as an investment adviser under the Act. During that period Lowe was convicted of misappropriating funds of an investment client, of engaging in business as an investment adviser without filing a registration application with New York's Department of Law, of tampering with evidence to cover up fraud of an investment client, and of stealing from a bank. Consequently, on May 11, 1981, the Securities and Exchange Commission (Commission), after a full hearing before an Administrative Law Judge, entered an order revoking the registration of the Lowe Management Corporation, and ordering Lowe not to associate thereafter with any investment adviser.

In fashioning its remedy, the Commission took into account the fact that petitioners "are now solely engaged in the business of publishing advisory publications." The Commission noted that unless the registration was revoked, petitioners would be "free to engage in all aspects of the advisory business" and that even their publishing activities afforded them "opportunities for dishonesty and self-dealing."

---

5. See 7 Louis Loss & Joel Seligman, Securities Regulation 3332–3344 (3d ed. 1991).

6. Inv. Adv. Act Rel. 1897, 73 SEC Dock. 595 (2000). Simultaneously IARD can be used to file Form ADV with appropriate states.

7. See 7 Louis Loss & Joel Seligman, Securities Regulation 3376–3382 (3d ed. 1991).

8. Id. at 3383–3384.

9. Id. at 3385–3392. There are several exceptions that have been adopted, by rule or, in 1996, by statute.

10. Id. at 3393–3395.

11. Id. at 3396.

A little over a year later, the Commission commenced this action by filing a complaint in the United States District Court for the Eastern District of New York, alleging that Lowe, the Lowe Management Corporation, and two other corporations, were violating the Act, and that Lowe was violating the Commission's order. The principal charge in the complaint was that Lowe and the three corporations (petitioners) were publishing two investment newsletters and soliciting subscriptions for a stock-chart service. The complaint alleged that, through those publications, the petitioners were engaged in the business of advising others "as to the advisability of investing in, purchasing, or selling securities . . . and as a part of a regular business . . . issuing reports concerning securities." Because none of the petitioners was registered or exempt from registration under the Act, the use of the mails in connection with the advisory business allegedly violated § 203(a) of the Act. The Commission prayed for a permanent injunction restraining the further distribution of petitioners' investment advisory publications; for a permanent injunction enforcing compliance with the order of May 11, 1981; and for other relief.

Although three publications are involved in this litigation, only one need be described. A typical issue of the Lowe Investment and Financial Letter contained general commentary about the securities and bullion markets, reviews of market indicators and investment strategies, and specific recommendations for buying, selling, or holding stocks and bullion. The newsletter advertised a "telephone hotline" over which subscribers could call to get current information. The number of subscribers to the newsletter ranged from 3,000 to 19,000. It was advertised as a semimonthly publication, but only eight issues were published in the 15 months after the entry of the 1981 order.

Subscribers who testified at the trial criticized the lack of regularity of publication, but no adverse evidence concerning the quality of the publications was offered. There was no evidence that Lowe's criminal convictions were related to the publications; no evidence that Lowe had engaged in any trading activity in any securities that were the subject of advice or comment in the publications; and no contention that any of the information published in the advisory services had been false or materially misleading.

For the most part, the District Court denied the Commission the relief it requested. 556 F.Supp. 1359, 1371 (E.D.N.Y.1983). The court did enjoin petitioners from giving information to their subscribers by telephone, individual letter, or in person, but it refused to enjoin them from continuing their publication activities or to require them to disgorge any of the earnings from the publications. The District Court acknowledged that the face of the statute did not differentiate between persons whose only advisory activity is the "publication of impersonal investment suggestions, reports and analyses," and those who rendered person-to-person advice, but concluded that constitutional considerations suggested the need for such a distinction. After determining that petitioners' publications were protected by the First Amendment, the District Court held that the Act must be construed to allow a publisher who is willing to comply with the existing reporting and disclosure requirements to register for the limited purpose of publishing such material and to engage in such publishing.

A splintered panel of the Court of Appeals for the Second Circuit reversed. 725 F.2d 892 (1984). The majority first held that petitioners were engaged in business as "investment advisers" within the meaning of the Act. It concluded that the Act does not distinguish between person-to-person advice and impersonal advice given in printed publications. Rather, in its view, the key statutory question was whether the exclusion in § 202(a)(11)(D), 15 U.S.C. § 80b–2(a)(11)(D), for "the publisher of any bona fide newspaper, new magazine, or business or financial publication of general and regular circulation" applied to the petitioners. Relying on its decision in SEC v. *Wall Street Transcript Corp.*, 422 F.2d 1371 (CA2), *cert. denied*, 398 U.S. 958 * * * (1970), the Court of Appeals concluded that the exclusion was inapplicable.

Next, the Court of Appeals rejected petitioners' constitutional claim, reasoning that this case involves "precisely the kind of regulation of commercial activity permissible under the First Amendment." Moreover, it held that Lowe's history of criminal conduct while acting as an investment adviser justified the characterization of his publications "as potentially deceptive commercial speech." The Court of Appeals reasoned that a ruling that petitioners "may not sell their views as to the purchase, sale, or holding of certain securities is no different from saying that a disbarred lawyer may not sell legal advice." Finally, the court noted that its holding was limited to a prohibition against selling advice to clients about specific securities. Thus, the Court of Appeals apparently assumed that petitioners could continue publishing their newsletters if their content was modified to exclude any advice about specific securities.

One judge concurred separately, although acknowledging his agreement with the court's opinion. The dissenting judge agreed that Lowe may not hold himself out as a registered investment adviser and may not engage in any fraudulent activity in connection with his publications, but concluded that the majority had authorized an invalid prior restraint on the publication of constitutionally protected speech. To avoid the constitutional question, he would have adopted the District Court's construction of the Act.

I

We granted certiorari to consider the important constitutional question whether an injunction against the publication and distribution of petitioners' newsletters is prohibited by the First Amendment. 469 U.S. 816 * * * (1984). Petitioners contend that such an injunction strikes at the very foundation of the freedom of the press by subjecting it to license and censorship, see, *e. g.*, *Lovell* v. *City of Griffin*, 303 U.S. 444, 451 * * * (1938). Brief for Petitioners 15–19. In response the Commission argues that the history of abuses in the securities industry amply justified Congress' decision to require the registration of investment advisers, to regulate their professional activities, and, as an incident to such regulation, to prohibit unregistered and unqualified persons from engaging in that business. Brief for Respondent 10; cf. *Konigsberg* v. *State Bar of California*, 366 U.S. 36, 50–51 * * * (1961). In reply, petitioners acknowledge that person-to-person communication in a commercial setting may be subjected to regulation that would be impermissible in a public forum, cf. *Ohralik* v. *Ohio State Bar Assn.*, 436 U.S. 447, 455 (1978), but contend that the regulated class—investment advisers—may not be so broadly defined as to encompass the distribution of impersonal investment advice and commentary in a public market. Reply Brief for Petitioners 1–4.

* * *

III

The basic definition of an "investment adviser" in the Act reads as follows:

" 'Investment adviser' means any person who, for compensation, engages in the business of advising others, either directly or through publications or writings, as to the value of securities or as to the advisability of investing in, purchasing, or selling securities, or who, for compensation and as part of a regular business, issues or promulgates analyses or reports concerning securities...."

Petitioners' newsletters are distributed "for compensation and as part of a regular business" and they contain "analyses or reports concerning securities." Thus, on its face, the basic definition applies to petitioners. The definition, however, is far from absolute. The Act excludes several categories of persons from its definition of an investment adviser, lists certain investment advisers who need not be registered, and also authorizes the Commission to exclude "such other person" as it may designate by rule or order.

One of the statutory exclusions is for "the publisher of any bona fide newspaper, news magazine or business or financial publication of general and regular circulation." Although neither the text of the Act nor its legislative history defines the precise scope of this exclusion, two points seem tolerably clear. Congress did not intend to exclude publications that are distributed by investment advisers as a normal part of the business of servicing their clients. The legislative history plainly demonstrates that Congress was primarily interested in regulating the business of rendering personalized investment advice, including publishing activities that are a normal incident thereto. On the other hand, Congress, plainly sensitive to First Amendment concerns, wanted to make clear that it did not seek to regulate the press through the licensing of nonpersonalized publishing activities.

Congress was undoubtedly aware of two major First Amendment cases that this Court decided before the enactment of the Act. The first, *Near* v. *Minnesota ex rel. Olson*, 283 U.S. 697 * * * (1931), established that "liberty of the press, and of speech, is within the liberty safeguarded by the due process clause of the Fourteenth Amendment from invasion by state action." *Id.*, at 707 * * *. In *Near*, the Court emphatically stated that the "chief purpose" of the press guarantee was "to prevent previous restraints upon publication," *id.*, at 713, and held that the Minnesota nuisance statute at issue in that case was unconstitutional because it authorized a prior restraint on publication.

Almost seven years later, the Court decided *Lovell* v. *City of Griffin*, 303 U.S. 444 * * * (1938), a case that was expressly noted by the Commission during the Senate Subcommittee hearings. In striking down an ordinance prohibiting the distribution of literature within the city without a permit, the Court wrote:

"We think that the ordinance is invalid on its face. Whatever the motive which induced its adoption, its character is such that it strikes at the very foundation of the freedom of the press by subjecting it to license and censorship. The struggle for the freedom of the press was primarily directed against the power of the licensor. It was against that power that John Milton directed his assault by his 'Appeal for the Liberty of Unlicensed Printing.' And the liberty of the press became initially a right to publish 'without a license what formerly could be published only with one.' While this freedom from previous restraint upon publication cannot be regarded as exhausting the guaranty of liberty, the prevention of that restraint was a leading purpose in the adoption of the constitutional provision...."

"The liberty of the press is not confined to newspapers and periodicals. It necessarily embraces pamphlets and leaflets. These indeed have been historic weapons in the defense of liberty, as the pamphlets of Thomas Paine and others in our own history abundantly attest. The press in its historic connotation comprehends every sort of publication which affords a vehicle of information and opinion. What we have had recent occasion to say with respect to the vital importance of protecting this essential liberty from every sort of infringement need not be repeated. *Near* v. *Minnesota....*" *Id.*, at 451–452 * * * (emphasis in original) (footnote omitted).

The reasoning of *Lovell*, particularly since the case was cited in the legislative history, supports a broad reading of the exclusion for publishers.

The exclusion itself uses extremely broad language that encompasses any newspaper, business publication, or financial publication provided that two conditions are met. The publication must be "bona fide," and it must be "of regular and general circulation." Neither of these conditions is defined, but the two qualifications precisely differentiate "hit and run tipsters" and "touts" from genuine publishers. Presumably a "bona fide" publication would be genuine in the sense that it would contain disinterested commentary and analysis as opposed to promotional material disseminated by a "tout." Moreover, publications with a "general and regular" circulation would not include "people who send out bulletins from time to time on the advisability of buying and selling stocks," see Hearings on H. R. 10065, at 87, or "hit and run tipsters." *Ibid.* Because the content of petitioners' newsletters was completely disinterested, and because they were offered to the general public on a regular schedule, they are described by the plain language of the exclusion.

The Court of Appeals relied on its opinion in *SEC* v. *Wall Street Transcript Corp.*, 422 F.2d 1371 (CA2), *cert. denied*, 398 U.S. 958 (1970), to hold that petitioners were not bona fide newspapers and thus not exempt from the Act's registration requirement. In *Wall Street Transcript*, the majority held that the "phrase 'bona fide' newspapers ... means those publications which do not deviate from customary newspaper activities to such an extent that there is a likelihood that the wrongdoing which the Act was designed to prevent has occurred." It reasoned that whether "a given publication fits within this exclusion must depend upon the nature of its practices rather than upon the purely formal 'indicia of a newspaper' which it exhibits on its face and in the size and nature of its subscription list." 422 F.2d, at 1377. The court expressed its concern that an investment adviser "might choose to present [information to clients] in the guise of traditional newspaper format." *Id.*, at 1378. The Commission, citing *Wall Street Transcript*, has interpreted the exclusion to apply "only where, based on the content, advertising material, readership and other relevant factors, a publication is not primarily a vehicle for distributing investment advice."

These various formulations recast the statutory language without capturing the central thrust of the legislative history, and without even mentioning the apparent intent of Congress to keep the Act free of constitutional infirmities. The Act was designed to apply to those persons engaged in the investment-advisory profession—those who provide personalized advice attuned to a client's concerns, whether by written or verbal communication. The mere fact that a publication contains advice and comment about specific securities does not give it the personalized character that identifies a professional investment adviser. Thus, petitioners' publications do not fit within the central purpose of the Act because they do not offer individualized advice attuned to any specific portfolio or to any client's particular needs. On the contrary, they circulate for sale to the public at large in a free, open market—a public forum in which typically anyone may express his views.

The language of the exclusion, read literally, seems to describe petitioners' newsletters. Petitioners are "publishers of any bona fide newspaper, news magazine or business or financial publication." The only modifier that might arguably disqualify the newsletters are the words "bona fide." Notably, however, those words describe the publication rather than the character of the publisher; hence Lowe's unsavory history does not prevent his newsletters from being "bona fide." In light of the legislative history, this phrase translates best to "genuine"; petitioners' publications meet this definition: they are published by those engaged solely in the publishing business and are not personal communications masquerading in the clothing of newspapers, news magazines, or financial publications. Moreover, there is no suggestion that they contained any false or misleading information, or that they were designed to tout any security in which petitioners had an interest. Further, petitioners' publications are "of general and regular circulation." Although the publications have not been "regular" in the sense of consistent circulation, the publications have been "regular" in the sense important to the securities market: there is no indication that they have been timed to specific market activity, or to events affecting or having the ability to affect the securities industry.

The dangers of fraud, deception, or overreaching that motivated the enactment of the statute are present in personalized communications but are not replicated in publications that are advertised and sold in an open market. To the extent that the chart service contains factual information about past transactions and market trends, and the newsletters contain commentary on general market conditions, there can be no doubt about the protected character of the communications, a matter that concerned Congress when the exclusion was drafted. The content of the publications and the audience to which they are directed in this case reveal the specific limits of the exclusion. As long as the communications between petitioners and their subscribers remain entirely impersonal and do not develop into the kind of fiduciary, person-to-person relationships that were discussed at length in the legislative history of the Act and that are characteristic of investment adviser-client relationships, we believe the publications are, at least presumptively, within the exclusion and thus not subject to registration under the Act.

We therefore conclude that petitioners' publications fall within the statutory exclusion for bona fide publications and that none of the petitioners is an "investment adviser" as defined in the Act. It follows that neither their unregistered status, nor the Commission order barring Lowe from associating with an investment adviser, provides a justification for restraining the future publication of their newsletters. It also follows that we need not specifically address the constitutional question we granted certiorari to decide.

The judgment of the Court of Appeals is reversed.

It is so ordered.

■ JUSTICE WHITE, with whom THE CHIEF JUSTICE and JUSTICE REHNQUIST join, concurring in the result.

The issue in this case is whether the Securities and Exchange Commission may invoke the injunctive remedies of the Investment Advisers Act, 15 U.S.C.

§§ 80b–1 to 80b–21, to prevent an unregistered adviser from publishing news-letters containing investment advice that is not specifically tailored to the needs of individual clients. The Court holds that it may not because the activities of petitioner Lowe (hereafter petitioner) do not make him an investment adviser covered by the Act. For the reasons that follow, I disagree with this improvident construction of the statute. In my view, petitioner is an investment adviser subject to regulation and sanction under the Act. I concur in the judgment, however, because to prevent petitioner from publishing at all is inconsistent with the First Amendment.

WHO IS AN INVESTMENT ADVISER?

The definition in §§ 202(a)(11) is broad enough to cover every person who for compensation gives advice with respect to securities, from the highest grade investment counselor who renders personalized service to the publisher of the lowliest tipster sheet.[1]

That said a considerable gray area survives the exclusions in § 202(a)(11) (A)–(F).

(1) **Financial Planners:** In recent years both the SEC and state securities administrators have particularly focused on financial planners. Financial planners provide advisory services as a component of other financially related services—for example, financial or pension consultants or sports or entertainment representatives, as distinct from the lawyers and brokers and others whose advisory services may also be incidental, but are not specifically excluded by Clauses (B) and (C). The SEC staff wrote in a 1987 interpretative release:

> Financial planning typically involves providing a variety of services, principally advisory in nature, to individuals or families regarding the management of their financial resources based upon an analysis of individual client needs. Generally, financial planning services involve preparing a financial program for a client based on the client's financial circumstances and objectives. This information normally would cover present and anticipated assets and liabilities, including insurance, savings, investments, and anticipated retirement or other employee benefits. The program developed for the client usually includes general recommendations for a course of activity, or specific actions, to be taken by the client. For example, recommendations may be made that the client obtain insurance or revise existing coverage, establish an individual retirement account, increase or decrease funds held in savings accounts, or invest funds in securities. A financial planner may develop tax or estate plans for clients or refer clients to an accountant or attorney for these services. * * *

Whether a person providing financially related services of the type discussed in this release is an investment adviser within the meaning of the Advisers Act depends upon all the relevant facts and circumstances. As a general matter, if the activities of any person providing integrated advisory services satisfy the elements of the definition, the person would be an investment adviser within the meaning of the Advisers Act, unless entitled to rely on one of the exclusions from the definition of investment adviser in clauses (A) to (F) of Section 202(a)(11). A determination as to whether a person providing financial planning, pension consulting, or other

---

1. See generally 7 Louis Loss & Joel (3d ed. rev. 1991).
Seligman, Securities Regulation 3344–3375

integrated advisory services is an investment adviser will depend upon whether such person: (1) provides advice, or issues reports or analyses, regarding securities; (2) is in the business of providing such services; and (3) provides such services for compensation.[2]

(2) Brokers and Dealers: Two related questions are presented under § 202(a)(11)(C): The meaning of "solely incidental" and what constitutes "special compensation."

So far as the first phrase is concerned, it is the Commission's view that a broker or dealer whose business consists *almost exclusively* of managing discretionary accounts is an investment adviser.

With respect to the meaning of "special compensation," the Commission's General Counsel stated early:

> Clause (C) of Section 202(a)(11) amounts to a recognition that brokers and dealers commonly give a certain amount of advice to their customers in the course of their regular business, and that it would be inappropriate to bring them within the scope of the Investment Advisers Act merely because of this aspect of their business. On the other hand, that portion of clause (C) which refers to "special compensation" amounts to an equally clear recognition that a broker or dealer who is specially compensated for the rendition of advice should be considered an investment adviser and not be excluded from the purview of the Act merely because he is also engaged in effecting market transactions in securities. It is well known that many brokers and dealers have investment advisory departments which furnish investment advice for compensation in the same manner as does an investment adviser who operates solely in an advisory capacity. The essential distinction to be borne in mind in considering borderline cases ... is the distinction between compensation for advice itself and compensation for services of another character to which advice is merely incidental.[3]

This approach is equally applicable in principle to dealers as well as brokers, except that, since historically dealers did not ordinarily disclose their profits or spreads, it was more difficult as a practical matter to determine whether the profit or spread in a particular case was greater because of the amount of incidental investment advice rendered. Similar problems have resulted from the "unbundling" of rates and the discounting that followed the abolition of fixed stock exchange commissions in 1975. It would be fatal, not surprisingly, for a firm to make two general fee schedules available whose difference is attributable primarily to the presence or absence of investment advice. But the staff does not consider that there is "special compensation" merely because a "full service" firm, for example, charges higher rates than a "discount" firm, or a firm negotiates different fees with different clients for similar transactions.[4]

(3) Professional Persons: A lawyer or accountant or engineer or a teacher of any kind *can* be an investment adviser if the advice rendered is not solely incidental to the practice of the profession.[5] Much of what will be said with reference to the exclusion of certain brokers and dealers by Clause (C) is equally applicable here. Arguably, however, it is not essential that every advisory client of the lawyer be a legal client as well if the lawyer does not hold

---

2. Inv. Adv. Act Rel. 1092, 39 SEC Dock. 494, 495–496 (1987).

3. Inv. Adv. Act Rel. 2 (1940).

4. Inv. Adv. Act Rel. 626, 14 SEC Dock. 946, 950–951 (1978).

5. Section 202(a)(11)(B). "The term 'solely incidental' has been interpreted to

himself or herself out to the public as an investment adviser and is first and foremost a lawyer whose advisory services are "solely incidental" to his or her law practice.

PROBLEM 18–2

The SEC has filed a four count complaint against Defendants Yun Soo Oh Park, a.k.a. Tokyo Joe ("Park"), and Tokyo Joe's Societe Anonyme Corp. (collectively, the "Defendants"), as a result of Defendants' conduct on their web site, which allegedly violates various SEC regulations.

In 1999 Park incorporated Tokyo Joe's Society Anonyme Corp. (hereinafter "Societe Anonyme"). Societe Anonyme was never under the Investment Advisers Act of 1940.

In 1997, Park began posting messages on various public financial Internet bulletin boards, which allow people to electronically post and reply to messages regarding stocks, investing, and other financial subjects. During 1998, Park posted thousands of messages under the names "Tokyo Joe" or "TokyoMex." In early 1998, individuals from these bulletin boards began directly contacting Park, soliciting further information about stock picks and trading. As a result, in March 1998, Park created an e-mail list and sent individuals on the list his stock picks.

In July 1998, Park set up Tokyo Joe's Internet site, at tokyo-joe.com, which operated under Park's control. From July 1998 to December 1998, Tokyo Joe's consisted of two areas. One was a limited area of the web site accessible to the general public, and the other consisted of a more expanded area of the web site accessible only to fee paying members. From about July 1998 to about November 1998, the fee was $299 per year to become a Societe Anonyme member. Members received, among other things, exclusive e-mails of Park's daily stock picks and unlimited access to the members only areas of Park's web site. On or about December 1998, Park added a "chat room" to the members-only area of the web site. The chat room served as a forum in which Park conducted two-way electronic dialogues with Societe Anonyme members about Park's stock picks and other investment advice. Between July 1998 and May 1999, Societe Anonyme's membership increased from about 200 to 3,800 subscribers.

The SEC has brought suit, for among other reasons, Park's failure to register under the Investment Advisers Act. Park has moved to dismiss claiming that he is not subject to the Investment Advisers Act after *Lowe*.

What result should a court reach on Park's motion?

2.   SCALPING

SEC v. Capital Gains Research Bureau, Inc., et al.

Supreme Court of the United States, 1963.
375 U.S. 180, 84 S.Ct. 275, 11 L.Ed.2d 237.

■ Mr. Justice GOLDBERG delivered the opinion of the Court.

We are called upon in this case to decide whether under the Investment Advisers Act of 1940 the Securities and Exchange Commission may obtain an

---

mean that the exclusion will be lost if a professional holds itself out to the public as an adviser or financial planner; provides advisory services that are not reasonably related to other professional activities; or calculates advisory service charges differently from usual professional charges." SEC Staff Report on Financial Planners, Subcomm. On Telecommunications & Fin., House Comm. on Energy & Commerce, 101st Cong., 1st Sess. B–4 (1988).

Cf. Zinn v. Parrish, 644 F.2d 360 (7th Cir.1981) (isolated screening of stock recommendations by sports agent was considering incidental to the agent's principal duty of negotiating football contracts).

injunction compelling a registered investment adviser to disclose to his clients a practice of purchasing shares of a security for his own account shortly before recommending that security for long-term investment and then immediately selling the shares at a profit upon the rise in the market price following the recommendation. The answer to this question turns on whether the practice—known in the trade as "scalping"—"operates as a fraud or deceit upon any client or prospective client" within the meaning of the Act. We hold that it does and that the Commission may "enforce compliance" with the Act by obtaining an injunction requiring the adviser to make full disclosure of the practice to his clients.

The Commission brought this action against respondents in the United States District Court for the Southern District of New York. At the hearing on the application for a preliminary injunction, the following facts were established. Respondents publish two investment advisory services, one of which—"A Capital Gains Report"—is the subject of this proceeding. The Report is mailed monthly to approximately 5,000 subscribers who each pay an annual subscription price of $18. It carries the following description:

> "An Investment Service devoted exclusively to (1) The protection of investment capital. (2) The realization of a steady and attractive income therefrom. (3) The accumulation of CAPITAL GAINS thru the timely purchase of corporate equities that are proved to be undervalued."

Between March 15, 1960, and November 7, 1960, respondents, on six different occasions, purchased shares of a particular security shortly before recommending it in the Report for long-term investment. On each occasion, there was an increase in the market price and the volume of trading of the recommended security within a few days after the distribution of the Report. Immediately thereafter, respondents sold their shares of these securities at a profit. They did not disclose any aspect of these transactions to their clients or prospective clients.

On the basis of the above facts, the Commission requested a preliminary injunction as necessary to effectuate the purposes of the Investment Advisers Act of 1940. The injunction would have required respondents, in any future Report, to disclose the material facts concerning, *inter alia*, any purchase of recommended securities "within a very short period prior to the distribution of a recommendation * * *," and "the intent to sell and the sale of said securities * * * within a very short period after distribution of said recommendation * * *."

The District Court denied the request for a preliminary injunction, holding that the words "fraud" and "deceit" are used in the Investment Advisers Act of 1940 "in their technical sense" and that the Commission had failed to show an intent to injure clients or an actual loss of money to clients. 191 F.Supp. 897. The Court of Appeals for the Second Circuit, sitting *en banc*, by a 5–to–4 vote accepted the District Court's limited construction of "fraud" and "deceit" and affirmed the denial of injunctive relief. * * *

The decision in this case turns on whether Congress, in empowering the courts to enjoin any practice which operates "as a fraud or deceit upon any client or prospective client," intended to require the Commission to establish fraud and deceit "in their technical sense," including intent to injure and actual injury to clients, or whether Congress intended a broad remedial construction of the Act which would encompass nondisclosure of material facts. For resolution of this issue we consider the history and purpose of the Investment Advisers Act of 1940.

I.

The Investment Advisers Act of 1940 was the last in a series of Acts designed to eliminate certain abuses in the securities industry, abuses which were found to have contributed to the stock market crash of 1929 and the depression of the 1930's. * * *

The Public Utility Holding Company Act of 1935 "authorized and directed" the Securities and Exchange Commission "to make a study of the functions and activities of investment trusts and investment companies * * *." Pursuant to this mandate, the Commission made an exhaustive study and report which included consideration of investment counsel and investment advisory services. This aspect of the study and report culminated in the Investment Advisers Act of 1940.

The report reflects the attitude—shared by investment advisers and the Commission—that investment advisers could not "completely perform their basic function—furnishing to clients on a personal basis competent, unbiased, and continuous advice regarding the sound management of their investments—unless all conflicts of interest between the investment counsel and the client were removed." The report stressed that affiliations by investment advisers with investment bankers, or corporations might be "an impediment to a disinterested, objective, or critical attitude toward an investment by clients. * * *"

This concern was not limited to deliberate or conscious impediments to objectivity. Both the advisers and the Commission were well aware that whenever advice to a client might result in financial benefit to the adviser—other than the fee for his advice—"that advice to a client might in some way be tinged with that pecuniary interest [whether consciously or] subconsciously motivated. * * *" The report quoted one leading investment adviser who said that he "would put the emphasis * * * on subconscious" motivation in such situations. It quoted a member of the Commission staff who suggested that a significant part of the problem was not the existence of a "deliberate intent" to obtain a financial advantage, but rather the existence "subconsciously [of] a prejudice" in favor of one's own financial interests. The report incorporated the Code of Ethics and Standards of Practice of one of the leading investment counsel associations, which contained the following canon:

> "[An investment adviser] should continuously occupy an impartial and disinterested position, as free as humanly possible from the *subtle* influence of prejudice, *conscious or unconscious*; he should scrupulously avoid any affiliation, or any act, which subjects his position to challenge in this respect." (Emphasis added.)

Other canons appended to the report announced the following guiding principles: that compensation for investment advice "should consist exclusively of direct charges to clients for services rendered"; that the adviser should devote his time "exclusively to the performance" of his advisory function; that he should not "share in profits" of his clients; and that he should not "directly or indirectly engage in any activity which may jeopardize [his] ability to render unbiased investment advice." These canons were adopted "to the end that the quality of services to be rendered by investment counselors may measure up to the high standards which the public has a right to expect and to demand."

One activity specifically mentioned and condemned by investment advisers who testified before the Commission was *"trading by investment counselors for their own account in securities in which their clients were interested * * *."*

This study and report—authorized and directed by statute—culminated in the preparation and introduction by Senator Wagner of the bill which, with some changes, became the Investment Advisers Act of 1940. * * *

Although certain changes were made in the bill following the hearings, there is nothing to indicate an intent to alter the fundamental purposes of the legislation. The broad proscription against "any * * * practice * * * which operates * * * as a fraud or deceit upon any client or prospective client" remained in the bill from beginning to end. And the Committee Reports indicate a desire to preserve "the personalized character of the services of investment advisers," and to eliminate conflicts of interest between the investment adviser and the clients as safeguards both to "unsophisticated investors" and to "bona fide investment counsel." The Investment Advisers Act of 1940 thus reflects a congressional recognition "of the delicate fiduciary nature of an investment advisory relationship," as well as a congressional intent to eliminate, or at least to expose, all conflicts of interest which might incline an investment adviser—consciously or unconsciously—to render advice which was not disinterested. It would defeat the manifest purpose of the Investment Advisers Act of 1940 for us to hold, therefore, that Congress, in empowering the courts to enjoin any practice which operates "as a fraud or deceit," intended to require proof of intent to injure and actual injury to clients.

This conclusion moreover, is not in derogation of the common law of fraud, as the District Court and the majority of the Court of Appeals suggested. To the contrary, it finds support in the process by which the courts have adapted the common law of fraud to the commercial transactions of our society. It is true that at common law intent and injury have been deemed essential elements in a damage suit between parties to an arm's-length transaction. But this is not such an action. This is a suit for a preliminary injunction in which the relief sought is, as the dissenting judges below characterized it, the "mild prophylactic," 306 F.2d, at 613, of requiring a fiduciary to disclose to his clients, not all his security holdings, but only his dealings in recommended securities just before and after the issuance of his recommendations.

The content of common-law fraud has not remained static as the courts below seem to have assumed. It has varied, for example, with the nature of the relief sought, the relationship between the parties, and the merchandise in issue. It is not necessary in a suit for equitable or prophylactic relief to establish all the elements required in a suit for monetary damages. * * *

Nor is it necessary in a suit against a fiduciary, which Congress recognized the investment adviser to be, to establish all the elements required in a suit against a party to an arm's-length transaction. Courts have imposed on a fiduciary an affirmative duty of "utmost good faith, and full and fair disclosure of all material facts," as well as an affirmative obligation "to employ reasonable care to avoid misleading" his clients. There has also been a growing recognition by common-law courts that the doctrines of fraud and deceit which developed around transactions involving land and other tangible items of wealth are ill-suited to the sale of such intangibles as advice and securities, and that, accordingly, the doctrines must be adapted to the merchandise in issue. The 1909 New York case of *Ridgely* v. *Keene*, 134 App. Div. 647, 119 N.Y. 451, illustrates this continuing development. An investment adviser who, like respondents, published an investment advisory service, agreed, for compensation, to influence his clients to buy shares in a certain security. He did not disclose the agreement to his client but sought "to excuse his conduct by asserting that * * * he honestly believed, that his subscribers would profit by his advice * * *." The court, holding that "his belief in the soundness of his advice is wholly immaterial," declared the act in question "a palpable fraud."

We cannot assume that Congress, in enacting legislation to prevent fraudulent practices by investment advisers, was unaware of these developments in the common law of fraud. Thus, even if we were to agree with the courts below that Congress had intended, in effect, to codify the common law of fraud in the Investment Advisers Act of 1940, it would be logical to conclude that Congress codified the common law "remedially" as the courts had adapted it to the prevention of fraudulent securities transactions by fiduciaries, not "technically" as it has traditionally been applied in damage suits between parties to arm's-length transactions involving land and ordinary chattels.

The foregoing analysis of the judicial treatment of common-law fraud reinforces our conclusion that Congress, in empowering the courts to enjoin any practice which operates "as a fraud or deceit" upon a client, did not intend to require proof of intent to injure and actual injury to the client. Congress intended the Investment Advisers Act of 1940 to be construed like other securities legislation "enacted for the purpose of avoiding frauds," not technically and restrictively, but flexibly to effectuate its remedial purposes.

II.

We turn now to a consideration of whether the specific conduct here in issue was the type which Congress intended to reach in the Investment Advisers Act of 1940. It is arguable—indeed it was argued by "some investment counsel representatives" who testified before the Commission—that any "trading by investment counselors for their own account in securities in which their clients were interested * * *." creates a potential conflict of interest which must be eliminated. We need not go that far in this case, since here the Commission seeks only disclosure of a conflict of interests with significantly greater potential for abuse than in the situation described above. An adviser who, like respondents, secretly trades on the market effect of his own recommendation may be motivated—consciously or unconsciously—to recommend a given security not because of its potential for long-run price increase (which would profit the client), but because of its potential for short-run price increase in response to anticipated activity from the recommendation (which would profit the adviser). An investor seeking the advice of a registered investment adviser must, if the legislative purpose is to be served, be permitted to evaluate such overlapping motivations, through appropriate disclosure, in deciding whether an adviser is serving "two masters" or only one, "especially * * * if one of the masters happens to be economic self-interest." *United States* v. *Mississippi Valley Generating Co.*, 364 U.S. 520, 549. Accordingly, we hold that the Investment Advisers Act of 1940 empowers the courts, upon a showing such as that made here, to require an adviser to make full and frank disclosure of his practice of trading on the effect of his recommendations.

III.

Respondents offer three basic arguments against this conclusion. They argue first that Congress could have made, but did not make, failure to disclose material facts unlawful in the Investment Advisers Act of 1940, as it did in the Securities Act of 1933, and that absent specific language, it should not be assumed that Congress intended to include failure to disclose in its general proscription of any practice which operates as a fraud or deceit. But considering the history and chronology of the statutes, this omission does not seem significant. The Securities Act of 1933 was the first experiment in federal regulation of the securities industry. It was understandable, therefore, for Congress, in declaring certain practices unlawful, to include both a general proscription against fraudulent and deceptive practices and, out of an abundance of caution, a specific proscription against nondisclosure. It soon became clear, however, that the courts, aware of the previously outlined developments in the common law of fraud, were merging the proscription against nondisclosure into the general proscription against fraud, treating the former, in effect, as one variety of the latter. * * * In light of this, and in light of the evident purpose of the Investment Advisers Act of 1940 to substitute a philosophy of disclosure for the philosophy of *caveat emptor*, we cannot assume that the omission in the 1940 Act of a specific proscription against nondisclosure was intended to limit the application of the antifraud and antideceit provisions of the Act so as to render the Commission impotent to enjoin suppression of material facts. The more reasonable assumption, considering what had transpired between 1933 and 1940, is that Congress, in enacting the Investment Advisers Act of 1940 and proscribing any practice which operates "as a fraud or deceit," deemed a specific proscription against nondisclosure surplusage.

Respondents also argue that the 1960 amendment to the Investment Advisers Act of 1940 justifies a narrow interpretation of the original enactment. The amendment made two significant changes which are relevant here. "Manipulative" practices were added to the list of those specifically proscribed. There is nothing to suggest, however, that with respect to a requirement of disclosure, "manipulative" is any broader than fraudulent or deceptive. Nor is there any indication that by adding the new proscription Congress intended to narrow the scope of the original proscription. The new amendment also authorizes the Commission "by rules and regulations [to] define, and prescribe means reasonably designed to prevent, such acts, practices, and courses of business as are fraudulent, deceptive, or manipulative." The legislative history offers no indication, however, that Congress intended such rules to substitute for the "general and flexible" antifraud provisions which have long been considered necessary to control "the versatile inventions of fraud-doers." Moreover, the intent of Congress must be culled from the events surrounding the passage of the 1940 legislation. "Opinions attributed to a Congress twenty years after the event cannot be considered evidence of the intent of the Congress of 1940." *Securities & Exchange Comm'n* v. *Capital Gains Research Bureau, Inc.*, 306 F.2d 606, 615 (dissenting opinion). * * *

Respondents argue, finally, that their advice was "honest" in the sense that they believed it was sound and did not offer it for the purpose of furthering personal pecuniary objectives. This, of course, is but another way of putting the rejected argument that the elements of technical common-law fraud—particularly intent—must be established before an injunction requiring disclosure may be ordered. It is the practice itself, however, with its potential for abuse, which "operates as a fraud or deceit" within the meaning of the Act when relevant information is suppressed. The Investment Advisers Act of 1940 was "directed not only at dishonor, but also at conduct that tempts dishonor." *United States* v. *Mississippi Valley Generating Co.*, 364 U.S. 520, 549. Failure to disclose material facts must be deemed fraud or deceit within its intended meaning, for, as the experience of the 1920's and 1930's amply reveals, the darkness and ignorance of commercial secrecy are the conditions upon which predatory practices best thrive. To impose upon the Securities and Exchange Commission the burden of showing deliberate dishonesty as a condition precedent to protecting investors through the prophylaxis of disclosure would effectively nullify the protective purposes of the statute. Reading the Act in light of its background we find no such requirement commanded. Neither the Commission nor the courts should be required "to separate the mental urges," *Peterson* v. *Greenville*, 373 U.S. 244, 248, of an investment adviser, for "[t]he motives of man are too complex * * * to separate.* * * *" *Mosser* v. *Darrow*, 341 U.S. 267, 271. The statute, in recognition of the adviser's fiduciary relationship to his clients, requires that his advice be disinterested. To insure this it empowers the courts to require disclosure of material facts. It misconceives the purpose of the statute to confine its application to "dishonest" as opposed to "honest" motives. As Dean Shulman said in discussing the nature of securities transactions, what is required is "a picture not simply of the show window, but of the entire store ... not simply truth in the statements volunteered, but disclosure." The high standards of business morality exacted by our laws regulating the securities industry do not permit an investment adviser to trade on the market effect of his own recommendations without fully and fairly revealing his personal interests in these recommendations to his clients.

Experience has shown that disclosure in such situations, while not onerous to the adviser, is needed to preserve the climate of fair dealing which is so essential to maintain public confidence in the securities industry and to preserve the economic health of the country.

The judgment of the Court of Appeals is reversed and the case is remanded to the District Court for proceedings consistent with this opinion.

Reversed and remanded.

PROBLEM 18–3

A commentator on a financial news TV show made highly laudatory statements about Zweig, Inc., the day after purchasing 5000 shares of Zweig's stock. The next day the Zweig stock rose 15 percent. Has the commentator violated the Investment Advisers Act? Has the commentator violated Rule 10b–5 of the Securities Exchange Act? In either case, is it a defense that every statement made was believed to be true?

C. SECURITIES ATTORNEYS AND ACCOUNTANTS

Rule 102(e) (until 1995 Rule 2(e)) of the Commission's Rules of Practice provides that the SEC may deny, temporarily or permanently, the privilege of appearing or practicing before it in any way. The bases specified in Rule 102(e)(i)–(iii) for such a suspension or disbarment of an attorney or accountant from practice before the Commission are that the person is found by the Commission:

"(i) not to possess the requisite qualifications to represent others; or (ii) to be lacking in character or integrity or to have engaged in unethical or improper professional conduct, or (iii) to have willfully violated, or willfully aided and abetted the violation of any provision of the Federal securities laws, or the rules and regulations thereunder."

In addition, attorneys who have been suspended or disbarred, or other persons whose professional licenses have been revoked or suspended, or who have been convicted of a felony, or of a misdemeanor "involving moral turpitude" are automatically suspended.[1]

The basic provisions of Rule 102(e)(i)–(iii) have been in effect since 1935. During the first 40 years of its existence, this Rule generated very little discussion or controversy. During the 1980s, however, it became a very serious bone of contention between the Securities and Exchange Commission and the accounting and legal professions. Originally, the Commission instituted such proceedings only where the respondent's conduct constituted a direct and egregious interference with the functioning of the processes of the Commission. In the late 1970s and early 1980s the Commission sometimes used this Rule as a basis for asserting jurisdiction to regulate the practice by attorneys and accountants of their professions, even where there was no proceeding before the Commission, as long as the alleged conduct of the respondent allegedly facilitated in some fashion a violation of the federal securities laws.

Although the Commission's authority to promulgate such a Rule has been questioned, courts consistently upheld it as necessary to protect the integrity of the SEC's processes.[2] Still, the use of Rule 102(e) proceedings has remained controversial both within the bar and within the Commission. In the case of In the Matter of Keating, Muething & Klekamp,[3] then Commissioner Robert Karmel dissented from the imposition of sanctions under Rule 2(e) on a law firm (even though it had consented to the order), on the basis that the Commission had no statutory authorization to discipline attorneys who practice before it. She wrote:

"When Rule 2(e) is invoked to discipline attorneys for misconduct which does not directly obstruct the administrative process, in my opinion it is done so improperly as a matter of law and as a matter of policy. In the *Emanuel Fields* case[4] the Commission barred an attorney on the theory that the Commission can regulate the manner in which lawyers counsel clients and render opinions in securities transactions in order to protect investors. A primary rationale for so using Rule 102(e) had been that 'the task of enforcing the securities laws rests in overwhelming measure on the bar's shoulders' and that given 'its small staff, limited resources, and onerous tasks, the Commission is peculiarly dependent on the probity and diligence of the professionals who practice before it.' However, Congress did not authorize the Commission to conscript attorneys to enforce their clients' responsibilities under the federal securities laws. Furthermore, institutional limitations alone cannot justify the creation of a new remedy not contemplated by the Congress."

---

1. Rule 102(e)(2).

2. *See* Davy v. SEC, 792 F.2d 1418 (9th Cir.1986); Touche Ross & Co. v. SEC, 609 F.2d 570 (2d Cir.1979); Checkosky v. SEC, 23 F.3d 452, 455 (D.C.Cir.1994); Sheldon v. SEC, 45 F.3d 1515, 1518 (11th Cir.1995).

3. 47 SEC 95 (1979).

4. 45 SEC 262 (1973).

I am firmly convinced that such conscription, or the promulgation and enforcement of regulatory standards of conduct for securities lawyers by the Commission, is very bad policy. It undermines the willingness and ability of the bar to exercise professional responsibility and sows the seeds for government abuse of power.

Two years later, matters came to a head in the following case.

Carter & Johnson

47 SEC 471 (1981).

OPINION OF THE COMMISSION

William R. Carter and Charles J. Johnson, Jr., respondents, appeal from the initial decision of the Administrative Law Judge in this proceeding brought under Rule 2(e) of the Commission Rules of Practice. In an opinion dated March 7, 1979, the Administrative Law Judge found that, in connection with their representation of National Telephone Company, Inc. during the period from May 1974 to May 1975, Carter and Johnson willfully violated and willfully aided and abetted violations of Sections 10(b) and 13(a) of the Securities Exchange Act of 1934 (the "Exchange Act") and Rules 10b–5, 12b–20 and 13a–11 thereunder and that they engaged in unethical and improper professional conduct. In light of these findings, the Administrative Law Judge concluded that Carter and Johnson should be suspended from appearing or practicing before the Commission for periods of one year and nine months, respectively.

For the reasons stated more fully below, we reverse the decision of the Administrative Law Judge with respect to both respondents. We have concluded that the record does not adequately support the Administrative Law Judge's findings of violative conduct by respondents. Moreover, we conclude that certain concepts of proper ethical and professional conduct were not sufficiently developed, at the time of the conduct here at issue, to permit a finding that either respondent breached applicable ethical or professional standards. In addition, we are today giving notice of an interpretation by the Commission of the term "unethical or improper professional conduct," as that term is used in Rule 2(e)(1)(ii). This interpretation will be applicable prospectively in cases of this kind.

* * *

III.   RESPONDENTS' CONDUCT

* * * The conduct [at] issue in these proceedings occurred in connection with respondents' legal representation of National Telephone Company, Inc. ("National") during the period from mid–1974 through mid–1975. National, a Connecticut corporation with its principal offices located in East Hartford, Connecticut, was founded in 1971 to lease sophisticated telephone equipment systems to commercial customers pursuant to long-term (5–to 10–year) leases. National enjoyed an impressive growth rate in its first three years, increasing its total assets from $320,123 to $19,028,613 and its net income from $2,390 to $633,485 during this period. At the same time, the company's backlog grew from $66,000 to $2,610,000 and the value of equipment leases written by it increased from $255,422 to $13,292,549.

The architect of National's meteoric rise was Sheldon L. Hart, one of its founders and, at all times relevant to these proceedings, its controlling stockholder. From its incorporation until his resignation on May 24, 1975, Hart was National's chief executive officer, chairman of the board of directors, president and treasurer. National's chief in-house counsel was Mark I. Lurie who, assisted by Brian Kay, was one of respondents' principal contacts with the company.

In large measure, National was a prisoner of its own success. As is commonly the case with equipment leasing companies, the greater part of National's costs in connection with a new lease, including equipment, marketing and installation expenses, was incurred well before rental payments commenced. Since rental payments were National's only significant source of revenues, the company's cash flow situation worsened with each new lease, and continued growth and operations could only be sustained through external financing. Between 1971 and 1973, National managed to obtain needed capital from an initial public offering of stock under Regulation A, short-term loans from local banks, and an offering of convertible debentures in September of 1973.

National's last successful effort to secure significant outside financing resulted in the execution, in May and June of 1974, of a $15 million credit agreement (the "Credit Agreement") with a group of five banks. Although the Credit Agreement was not closed (in amended form) until December 1974, the banks were willing to advance substantial sums to National under a variety of demand arrangements prior to the closing. In fact, by the time of the closing on December 20, 1974, these advances totaled some $16.8 million. The Credit Agreement was amended to cover this amount, plus $2.2 million for general corporate purposes and an additional $2 million available only upon the implementation of a special business plan limiting National's business growth if other sources of money could not be located. Unfortunately, funds available under the Credit Agreement, as amended, were not sufficient to finance National's expansion and operations much beyond the closing, and the pressure on National's cash flow continued.

National finally ran out of time in July of 1975, after being unable to secure sufficient external financing after the closing of the Credit Agreement. On July 2, 1975, National was forced to file a petition for an arrangement under Chapter XI of the Bankruptcy Act, 11 U.S.C. 701, et seq.; in March of 1976 this proceeding was converted into a reorganization under Chapter X of the Bankruptcy Act, 11 U.S.C. 501, et seq.

    * * *

* * * Carter, an attorney admitted to practice in the State of New York, was born in 1917. He received his law degree from Harvard Law School and has been working for the law firm known as Brown, Wood, Ivey, Mitchell & Petty ("Brown, Wood") since 1945, having become a partner of the firm in 1954. Carter's principal areas of practice have been securities, general corporate and antitrust law. Johnson, also admitted to practice as an attorney in the State of New York, as well as in the State of Connecticut, was born in 1932. He received his legal education at Harvard Law School and joined Brown, Wood's predecessor firm in 1956, becoming a partner in 1967. Johnson's principal areas of practice have been corporate and securities law.

Kenneth M. Socha worked with Carter and Johnson on a variety of legal matters affecting National, including all of the matters which are the basis of these proceedings. Socha joined Brown, Wood as an associate in 1970 and continued in that capacity during all periods relevant to these proceedings.

* * *

During 1974 and 1975, Brown, Wood, principally through Carter, Johnson and Socha, provided a wide range of legal services to National, including the preparation of a Form S–8 registration statement, proxy materials and an annual report for the company's 1974 annual stockholders meeting, other Commission filings, press releases and communications to National's stockholders. Johnson was charged with the overall coordination of Brown, Wood's legal efforts on National's behalf and was generally kept aware of progress on all significant projects. In March of 1974, after another Brown, Wood partner left the firm, Johnson asked Carter to assist Socha in working on the Credit Agreement. Thereafter Carter assumed primary responsibility for that project.

* * *

In May and June of 1974, negotiations with a consortium of five banks, in which Carter, Johnson and Socha were all participants, culminated in the execution of the Credit Agreement, which was dated as of April 30, 1974. The Credit Agreement provided for an interim revolving loan of up to $15 million, evidenced by rolling 90–day notes, until November 29, 1974, at which time National had the option to convert the principal amount then outstanding into six-year term notes. As discussed below, the Credit Agreement (as amended) was not formally closed until December 20, 1974, in part because National was unable to satisfy the closing conditions relating to its liquidity and debt-to-net-worth ratios. Ultimately the banks agreed to waive these conditions.

Since the Credit Agreement contemplated that the loans thereunder would be secured by substantially all of National's assets, it was necessary for National to transfer these assets to Systems; a transfer which in turn required the approval of National's stockholders. In order to secure this approval, National called its annual stockholders meeting for June 27, 1974, and Brown, Wood was asked to prepare the proxy materials for this meeting. Carter and Johnson also participated in the preparation of National's 1974 Annual Report. These proxy materials, along with National's 1974 Annual Report, were sent to National's stockholders on June 17 and filed with the Commission on June 19.

In urging approval of the asset transfers necessitated by the Credit Agreement, National's proxy statement disclosed that

> [t]he future growth and operations of the Company are dependent upon its ability to obtain financing such as is supplied by the Credit Agreement.

National's 1974 Annual Report contained projections of future lease installations which showed, by each quarter, a doubling of annual installations from approximately $13.3 million in fiscal 1974 to approximately $27 million in fiscal 1975. In response to a specific request from Hart, Carter advised National orally and in writing that, in light of Securities Act Release No. 5362 (Feb. 2, 1973), a copy of which Carter sent to Hart, it was permissible to include projections in the Annual Report, but that the assumptions underlying the projections should also be disclosed. Hart ignored this advice and the Annual Report was distributed without assumptions. This incident is the first example in the record of Hart's uncooperative reaction to respondents' advice concerning the disclosure demands of the federal securities laws.

* * *

At the September 11 meeting with the banks, Hart indicated that the projected equity offering had been ruled out by National's investment bankers, due to deteriorating market conditions. He further reported that National's cash flow problems had caused the company voluntarily to institute a "wind-down" program, effective September 1. As he described it, this program, projected to last five months, was a severe retrenchment, designed to protect the banks' existing investment. Under it, National would limit its operations to the conversion of present inventory—approximately $5 million—into installed systems under new leases, phase out further marketing and installation efforts and reduce the company to a "pure maintenance organization." Hart requested an increase in the total amount of the banks' planned loan from $15 to $21 million in order to finance this wind-down program. The banks, however, hesitated, agreeing only that no decision would be made on lending National additional funds until the pending $15 million Credit Agreement was closed.

Hart, in fact, had lied to the banks. No wind-down program had been instituted or, as it turned out, would be until almost eight months later, in May of 1975. There is, however, no evidence in the record that respondents were, or ever became, aware of Hart's September 11, 1974 deception.

* * *

In light of his presence at the July 1, August 19 and October 15 board meetings, as well as the October 18 bank meeting, Johnson was well aware of National's cash crisis, its continuing failure to obtain needed financing and its purported "wind-down" program. This, in addition to the well-known depressed state of the credit markets and the fact that National had projected, confirmed and continued to report, without obviously relevant qualifications, rapidly growing sales and earnings, undoubtedly prompted Johnson to instruct Socha to draft a disclosure letter to National's stockholders approximately two days after the October 18 bank meeting.

The proposed stockholders letter, which was reviewed by both Carter and Johnson and sent to the company in early November, was a candid summary of National's financial predicament, noting that National would "in the near future" have to obtain significant financing in addition to the Credit Agreement. It concluded:

> The Company's efforts to obtain additional financing have been adversely affected by tight credit conditions, increased interest costs, a generally unfavorable equity market and certain factors that are peculiar to its business such as the negative cash flow described above. In view of these factors the Company has determined that it would be prudent to curtail its sales operations and, therefore, to emphasize the liquidity rather than growth until such time as additional debt or equity financing can be obtained.

Johnson subsequently told Lurie that this was the type of communication "that a company * * * interested in keeping its stockholders advised on a regular basis should be making." Despite this advice, National's management declined to issue the letter. Neither respondent elected to pursue the matter.

* * *

It is important to note, at this point, that both Carter and Johnson must have been aware that, if National were to implement the wind-down plan, the company would have no reasonable opportunity to meet the projections of $27 million in lease installations which were set forth in the 1974 Annual Report and indirectly reconfirmed in the company's September 12 letter to its stockholders. The wind-down plan, which Socha summarized in a December 2 memorandum to Johnson, provided that National would not be permitted to enter into any further leases. Obviously, under these circumstances, the company's sales and earnings growth would be halted—short of projected levels.

In early December, Socha received from National a draft of the company's quarterly report to its stockholders for the second fiscal quarter ended September 30, 1974. The report contained a series of graphs, illustrating the successful results of National's operations, but once again made no mention of the dire financial straits in which the company found itself in December. Such an omission was especially significant in light of the disclosure recommendations which Brown, Wood had by then made to National. When Socha inquired whether the use of the graphs had been cleared by Johnson, Lurie informed him that they had. This was not true, as Johnson noted on the copy of the draft report circulated to him by Socha. The quarterly report was mailed as proposed, and neither respondent ever spoke with the company's management about the disclosure problems it presented or about Lurie's misrepresentation to Socha.

* * *

* * * In the final days leading to the closing, National's "wind-down" plan was renegotiated somewhat and finally emerged with a new name, the lease maintenance plan ("LMP"). All the witnesses speaking to the question agreed that the term "lease maintenance plan" had no generally accepted meaning in the industry and that they had never used or heard this term before. Moreover, the terms "wind-down plan," "contingency plan," and "lease maintenance plan," were all intended to refer to the same thing.

The need to revise the original wind-down plan emerged when the consulting firm hired by National to evaluate the plan reported to the banks that, in its original form, the plan was neither feasible nor in the best interests of the banks. Rather, the independent consultants advised that the best course would be to allow National limited continuing growth, financed with additional bank borrowings, and that a wind-down should be implemented only as a last resort and only if the company were unable to obtain additional outside financing.

At a meeting held on December 11, with Carter and representatives of National and the banks present, final details of the Amendment were negotiated. A draft of the Amendment dated December 13, 1974, which was prepared by White & Case, contemplated an arrangement under which the banks would permit Systems to borrow up to $19 million at any time on or before April 30, 1975. These borrowings were to be secured by the telephone leases and equipment transferred to Systems by National and guaranteed by National. If either (1) National and/or Systems attempted to borrow in excess of $19 million from the existing bank group or (2) National failed to meet a specified liquidity test, National and Systems were required to implement the LMP. Their failure to do so in accordance with the provisions of the LMP was an event of default under the Credit Agreement, as modified by the Amendment (the "Amended Credit Agreement"), and resulted in all outstanding indebtedness under that Agreement becoming due and payable upon demand.

The December 13 draft of the Amendment for the first time contained a reference to a "lease maintenance plan" and indicated that the LMP was to be attached as an exhibit to the Amendment. The effect of the implementation of the LMP on National's operations and growth would obviously be both dramatic and devastating. Indeed, as one expert called by respondents testified, the LMP was "a sort of a holding pattern short of bankruptcy or levy by the creditors." The LMP required National to terminate all sales activities, dismiss all sales personnel, and limit its operations to those necessary to service existing leases. In effect, the company would be transformed into a mere service agency, maintaining existing leases, but writing no new ones. Moreover, the final $2 million of the funds to be provided by the banks was only available until June 30, 1975 and could only be used to implement the LMP, principally by financing the installation of equipment already in inventory to complete existing orders.

* * *

On December 19, the day immediately preceding the closing under the Amended Credit Agreement, at a day-long pre-closing meeting, Hart told Carter that he did not want the terms of the LMP made public or filed with the Commission. Although Carter testified that he could not recall the reason for this request, he speculated that Hart sought not to publicize the LMP because he was concerned that the disclosure of the LMP's effects on the company's business would have a negative impact on the morale of National's sales personnel. After reading the LMP, Carter advised Hart that the LMP would have to be filed with the Commission if it were an exhibit to the Amendment, as originally had been contemplated. However, Carter added that the LMP need not be filed with the Commission or publicized if it were not an exhibit but rather merely referred to in the Amendment. Hart agreed, and the Amendment was modified to delete the LMP as an exhibit.

Also at the December 19 pre-closing conference, Carter reviewed and extensively revised a press release prepared by National announcing the closing of the Amended Credit Agreement. The revised press release was reviewed by all parties at the meeting, including the company's management. No one raised any objections to the revisions proposed by Carter.

On December 20, the Amended Credit Agreement was closed and National immediately borrowed $18 million from the banks. Of this amount, over $16.8 million was used to repay existing demand indebtedness based on advances the banks had made to National since the original Credit Agreement had been signed six months earlier. * * *

Immediately after the closing, National issued the press release that Carter had redrafted the day before. The release stated, in its entirety:

PRESS RELEASE—FOR IMMEDIATE RELEASE
EAST HARTFORD, CONN., DECEMBER 20, 1974

National Telephone Company today announced the execution of a $6,000,000 extension of a $15,000,000 Credit Agreement with a group of banks headed by Bankers Trust Company of New York. Included in the $21 million is a contingency fund of $2 million which is available until June 30, 1975 and which may be utilized by the Company only for the purpose of funding a lease maintenance program in the event additional financing is not otherwise available.

Of the $21 million, the Company has borrowed $18 million pursuant to a seven-year term loan, of which approximately $16,500,000 was used to repay outstanding short-term loans. The balance will be used for general operating expenses. Participating in the loans are Bankers Trust Company of New York, Mellon Bank N.A. of Pittsburgh, Central National Bank of Cleveland, The Connecticut Bank and Trust Company and The Hartford National Bank and Trust Company of Hartford, Connecticut.

The press release did not discuss either of the following matters each of which was then within the knowledge of Carter and Johnson.

(1) The precise nature and effects on National's business of the LMP and the likelihood that National would be required to implement the LMP within a short period of time; and

(2) The substantial limitations placed on National's operations by the Amended Credit Agreement.

It is also apparent from the record that the press release's statement indicating that the balance of the financing remaining after the repayment of outstanding bank debt "will be used for general operating expenses" was misleading, in light of the substantial overdue obligations of National then existing.

The second major item of public disclosure concerning the closing was a stockholders' letter mailed, without respondents' knowledge, by National on or about December 23. This letter, which was issued in the face of Socha's advice to National that no further public statements should be issued concerning the Amended Credit Agreement unless such statements were cleared by Brown, Wood, contained numerous misstatements and omissions, including the following:

(1) The letter indicated that the company "was stronger now than ever before in its history" and that it had "a greater availability of capital, expanding productivity and growing earnings" and was "looking forward to an outstanding year in calendar 1975."

(2) The letter indicated that the entire additional $6 million loan to National could be used for future operating expenses.

(3) The letter made no reference to National's repayment of existing bank loans and other pre-existing debts with the proceeds of the financing, its continuing cash needs and shortages, or the LMP.

Respondents first learned of the letter on December 27, when Brian Kay, who was aware that National had ignored Socha's advice that all public disclosure should be reviewed by them, voluntarily telephoned Socha and dictated the letter to him. Socha thought that the letter's description of the Amended Credit Agreement was "seriously inadequate" and immediately gave a copy of it to Johnson. Carter, too, was consulted. While respondents felt that the letter did not make "adequate disclosure" with respect to the Amended Credit Agreement, they concluded that, when read together with the earlier December 20 press release which Carter had revised, it was not materially false or misleading, and that no corrective action by National was therefore required. Johnson later did, however, orally express his dissatisfaction with the letter to Lurie.

* * *

* * * On January 9, 1975, National filed a current report on Form 8–K for the month of December 1974, reporting on the closing under the Amended

Credit Agreement. This document was drafted by Carter, who accepted full responsibility for it.

The Amended Credit Agreement, which was attached to the Form 8–K as an exhibit, made frequent reference to the LMP. And the 8–K itself stated that $2 million of National's recent $21 million loan arrangement was "a contingency fund available until June 30, 1975 only for the purpose of financing a lease maintenance program in the event additional financing is not otherwise available." As previously requested by Hart, however, the LMP itself was not included as an exhibit to the Agreement or the filing; nor was the term "lease maintenance plan" specifically defined or the effects which it would have on the company discussed.

Between the January 9, 1975 filing of National's Form 8–K and mid-March, National's financial condition deteriorated even further, to a degree requiring the implementation of the LMP. In addition, the gap between National's public disclosure posture and its private financial condition continued to widen and National's board of directors was becoming increasingly uncomfortable with the situation. There is no indication in the record that either respondent directly or indirectly became aware of the growing seriousness of the situation until a March 17 telephone call from the banks' counsel, described below. * * *

On March 17—nearly one month after the February 20 consultants report, and over six weeks after the LMP had in fact been triggered—Brown, Wood was informed for the first time, by the *banks'* lawyers, White & Case, that events requiring implementation of the LMP had occurred. The White & Case lawyers had received a telephone call from a vice president of one of the banks informing them of this fact and reporting that no public disclosure had been made by National. The bank vice president also sought White & Case's advice on how to respond to trade creditors of National who were making inquiries to the banks about the company.

During their March 17 conversation, the White & Case lawyers advised Carter that National and its counsel, Brown, Wood, had the responsibility to determine what disclosure, if any, would be appropriate under the circumstances, and they sought assurances that, if proper disclosure were deemed necessary, it would be forthcoming. Carter, who admittedly considered the triggering of the LMP clearly material, assured White & Case that, if what they said were true, Brown, Wood would contact National and "get a statement out." The White & Case lawyers then called the bank's vice president and relayed the content of their conversation with Carter.

On the following day, March 18, Carter telephoned Lurie and informed him of the call from the White & Case lawyers. Lurie neither confirmed nor denied that the LMP had been triggered. Rather, he dissembled, stating that the situation was "tight," but adding that, "if they were careful, they would be all right." Carter advised Lurie that, if the LMP had indeed been triggered, the fact should be disclosed publicly, although he did not press Lurie for a definite answer on whether the LMP had in fact been triggered, or on whether National's management was in fact implementing the LMP as required by the Amended Credit Agreement.

    * * *

On April 23, 1975 both respondents met with Hart and advised him in no uncertain terms that immediate disclosure was required. In response to Hart's protestations that National would soon obtain additional financing, respondents advised him that these hopes, as well as any negotiations for a waiver of the LMP by the banks, did not serve to excuse National's legal obligation to make prompt disclosure.

Shortly before the April 23 meeting, the vice president of one of the lending banks had written to Hart requesting, among other things, a "written response from your counsel regarding [National's] obligation to make public disclosure regarding significant transactions which may have transpired during the last several months, particularly with regard to the implementing of the lease maintenance plan." Presumably as a result of this request, Hart telephoned Johnson on April 28—only five days after having received the unambiguous and forceful advice that disclosure was required—to request that Johnson issue a legal opinion for the banks to the effect that disclosure of the triggering of the LMP was *not* necessary. Johnson testified that he replied as follows:

> I'm incredulous. I just can't believe this. You sat in my office last week and I told you as clearly and positively and precisely as I could that my advice was that you should disclose that you had gone into the lease maintenance mode.

Ultimately, Hart responded to the bank's request for an opinion of counsel with a letter from National stating that no disclosure had been made because, "in the opinion of the company," none was required.

In late April, after the telephone encounter with Hart described above, Johnson instructed Socha to draft a disclosure document for National to issue, either in its next report to the Commission or in a special letter to the stockholders. In doing so, Johnson specified that the draft should be one that would be "acceptable to a person as emotionally involved as Hart." Both respondents reviewed and approved the draft prepared by Socha and it was forwarded to Hart on or about May 1, with the suggestion that Hart call Carter or Johnson about it.

* * * National did not issue this disclosure document in any form and the record does not indicate any response to Brown, Wood's disclosure advice. Neither respondent questioned anyone at the company about management's failure to make the suggested disclosure.

On May 9, Kay called Socha to seek his approval of a draft of the company's proposed current report on Form 8–K for the month of April. Socha reiterated Brown, Wood's earlier advice that disclosure should be made concerning National's present status under the Amended Credit Agreement and of the event of default that resulted from the company's failure to implement the LMP. Although Kay agreed to include the suggested disclosure, the report actually filed with the Commission did not contain any such disclosure, because Lurie would not permit it.

* * *

Later the same day, Socha called Kay and asked for a copy of the company's April Form 8–K. Kay replied that Lurie would not permit him to mail a copy to Brown, Wood or to the Commission. The April Form 8–K was eventually filed with the Commission on May 15, 1975. Socha testified that he was required to obtain a copy of it from the Commission.

* * *

The internal and external tensions which had been developing around National came to a head on Saturday afternoon, May 24, at the special meeting of the board of directors in Hartford, Connecticut. Johnson was there, acting as secretary, having been asked to attend by Hart. Also present at the meeting was independent counsel who had been consulted by the outside directors and asked to attend the meeting in the expectation that Johnson would not be there. It was at this meeting that the outside directors learned for the first time that, for over a month, Brown, Wood had been recommending disclosure and Johnson read a draft of the letter which Brown, Wood had sent to Hart on May 1, disclosing that the LMP had been triggered and its effect on the company. One of the nonmanagement directors testified that he had no prior indication that Brown, Wood had been recommending this disclosure to Hart and that when he heard the letter read by Johnson he "was shocked to the core."

At the May 24 meeting, Hart resigned each of his corporate offices, although he remained a director of the company, Johnson prepared a press release which was unanimously approved by the Board and it was decided that Brown, Wood would continue as company counsel. Johnson, however, resigned as secretary of the company.

＊ ＊ ＊

IV. AIDING AND ABETTING

Rule 2(e)(1)(iii) provides that the Commission may deny, temporarily or permanently, the privilege of appearing or practicing before it to any person who is found by the Commission, after notice of and opportunity for hearing, to have *willfully violated,* or *willfully aided and abetted the violation of,* any provision of the federal securities laws or the rules and regulations thereunder.

A. *The Findings Below.* The Administrative Law Judge summarized the bases for his findings that respondents had "willfully violated and aided and abetted violations" of Sections 10(b) and 13(a) of the Exchange Act and Rules 10b–5, 12b–20 and 13a–11 thereunder as follows:

(i) that the December 20, 1974 press release, revised by Carter, in describing the closing under the Amended Credit Agreement was materially false and misleading in its failure to disclose adequately the nature of the LMP and that Carter was responsible for preparing it;

(ii) that the December 23, 1974 letter which Hart sent to National's stockholders was materially false and misleading, and that neither respondent took action to correct it, or to see that adequate disclosure would be made to clear up the misperceptions created by it, after they learned of the letter on December 27;

(iii) that National's Form 8–K for December 1974 was materially false and misleading in its failure to describe adequately the nature of the LMP, and that Carter has accepted full responsibility for preparing it;

(iv) that respondents failed to communicate with the board of directors of National, or otherwise take steps to insure that adequate disclosures were made in filings with the Commission, in press releases, and in letters to stockholders, despite the optimistic information about the company which they knew had been disseminated to the marketplace; and

(v) that respondents (a) from May 1974 to May 1975, assisted National's management in its efforts to conceal material facts concerning the company's financial condition, and (b) at least from October 1974 to May 1975, failed to inform the company's board of directors concerning management's unwillingness to make required disclosures.

* * * Given the circumstances of this case, we do not believe that respondents' involvement in the affairs or decisionmaking processes of the company was sufficient to justify a finding against them as direct, primary violators of Section 10(b) or Rule 10b–5 as a result of the antifraud violations growing out of National's statements. We therefore will consider respondents' conduct only as it may constitute willful aiding and abetting of a federal securities law violation by National.

B. *Securities Law Violations by National.* We have no doubt that National's failure to disclose the nature of the LMP in the December 20 press release and the December Form 8–K constituted a violation of Sections 10(b) and 13(a) of the Exchange Act and Rules 10b–5, 12b–20 and 13a–11 thereunder. Respondents' position to the contrary rests on the purported knowledge of the marketplace that a leasing company must have new infusions of capital to grow, and that the press release and Form 8–K adequately disclosed that the closing of the Amended Credit Agreement in December made no substantial funds available to finance new leases.

Whatever our doubts about that proposition, it is clear that the LMP involved a great deal more than merely confirming the temporary absence of funds for new leases. It required, among other things, the cessation of all leasing activity and the termination of substantially all sales personnel. * * *

These limiting provisions were highly unusual and their import is not conveyed by the mere repetition of the words "lease maintenance plan" in the press release and in the December Form 8–K. Nor do we find persuasive respondents' argument that the likelihood of the LMP being triggered was so remote that its provisions were not material. * * *

Respondents assert that the disclosure system deals with facts, not contingencies. But the existence of *this* contingency—the uncertainty of additional financing and its relationship to the LMP—*is itself a fact* about which investors are entitled to make their own judgments. * * *

C. *Aiding and Abetting.* Our primary concern, however, is with the respondents' relationship to these violations of the securities laws. Although "[t]he elements of an aiding and abetting claim have not yet crystallized into a set pattern,"[56] we have examined the decisions of the various circuits and conclude that certain legal principles are common to all the decisions.

In the context of the federal securities laws, these principles hold generally that one may be found to have aided and abetted a violation when the following three elements are present:

1. there exists an independent securities law violation committed by some other party;

2. the aider and abettor knowingly and substantially assisted the conduct that constitutes the violation; and

56. Woodward v. Metro Bank of Dallas, 522 F.2d 84, 94 (C.A.5 1975).

3. the aider and abettor was aware or knew that his role was part of an activity that was improper or illegal.

As noted above, we have no difficulty in finding that National committed numerous substantial securities law violations. The second element—substantial assistance—is generally satisfied in the context of a securities lawyer performing professional duties, for he is inevitably deeply involved in his client's disclosure activities and often participates in the drafting of the documents, as was the case with Carter. And he does so knowing that he is participating in the preparation of disclosure documents—that is his job.

In this connection, we do not distinguish between the professional advice of a lawyer given orally or in writing and similar advice which is embodied in drafting documents to be filed with the Commission. Liability in these circumstances should not turn on such artificial distinctions, particularly in light of the almost limitless range of forms which legal advice may take. Moreover, the opposite approach, which would permit a lawyer to avoid or reduce his liability simply by avoiding participation in the drafting process, may well have the undesirable effect of reducing the quality of the disclosure by the many to protect against the defalcations of the few.

For these reasons, the crucial inquiry in a Rule 2(e) proceeding against a lawyer inevitably tends to focus on the awareness or the intent element of the offense of aiding and abetting. It is that element which has been the source of the most disagreement among commentators and the courts. We do not seek to resolve that disagreement today. We do hold, however, that a finding of *willful aiding and abetting* within the meaning of Rule 2(e)(2)(iii) requires a showing that respondents were aware or knew that their role was part of an activity that was improper or illegal.

It is axiomatic that a lawyer will not be liable as an aider and abettor merely because his advice, followed by the client, is ultimately determined to be wrong. What is missing in that instance is a wrongful intent on the part of the lawyer. It is that element of intent which provides the basis for distinguishing between those professionals who may be appropriately considered as subjects of professional discipline and those who, acting in good faith, have merely made errors of judgment or have been careless.

Significant public benefits flow from the effective performance of the securities lawyer's role. The exercise of independent, careful and informed legal judgment on difficult issues is critical to the flow of material information to the securities markets. Moreover, we are aware of the difficulties and limitations attendant upon that role. In the course of rendering securities law advice, the lawyer is called upon to make difficult judgments, often under great pressure and in areas where the legal signposts are far apart and only faintly discernible.

If a securities lawyer is to bring his best independent judgment to bear on a disclosure problem, he must have the freedom to make innocent—or even, in certain cases, careless—mistakes without fear of legal liability or loss of the ability to practice before the Commission. Concern about his own liability may alter the balance of his judgment in one direction as surely as an unseemly obeisance to the wishes of his client can do so in the other. While one imbalance results in disclosure rather than concealment, neither is, in the end, truly in the public interest. Lawyers who are seen by their clients as being motivated by fears for their personal liability will not be consulted on difficult issues.

Although it is a close judgment, after careful review we conclude that the available evidence is insufficient to establish that either respondent acted with sufficient knowledge and awareness or recklessness to satisfy the test for willful aiding and abetting liability. Our conclusion in this regard applies to each of the Administrative Law Judge's findings as to respondents' aiding and abetting National's violations of the federal securities laws.

D. *The December Press Release and Form 8–K.* In drafting the December press release and Form 8–K, Carter advised National that the provisions of the LMP were not required to be disclosed. There is ample evidence in the record indicating both respondents' knowledge about National's financial condition and the importance of the LMP. Johnson attended the Board meetings held on July 1, August 19, and October 15, 1974 at which the directors emphasized the importance of new financing and reviewed Socha's draft shareholders' letter in October that explained the significance of a proposed informal "wind-down" phase in National's corporate life. Johnson informed Carter of these matters in connection with their joint responsibilities for the representation of National. Carter focused on the details of the LMP when he advised Hart that the document embodying the plan did not have to be filed with the Commission if it were not an exhibit to the Amended Credit Agreement. Respondents were clearly aware of the company's lack of success in raising new capital, and the increasingly critical impact of its negative cash flow.

On the other hand, the record also contains no direct evidence of Carter's knowledge that the details of the LMP were material and we decline to infer such knowledge because of facts in the record on which Carter's erroneous judgment as to its immateriality is claimed to have been based. Carter had been told by Hart and others about numerous potential sources for additional financing. * * *

Moreover, the banks were willing to close the Amended Credit Agreement and convert their $16.8 million in demand debt to six-year notes, which suggests they did not believe that National was in serious and immediate financial difficulty.

It is also significant that the December 20 press release, while originally drafted by National's management, was entirely rewritten by Carter in long-hand at the December 19 pre-closing meeting. Having thus revised the document, Carter showed it to all present at the pre-closing and no one suggested any change. In fact, the only comment recalled by Carter was to the effect of, "Boy, that's full disclosure."

In view of the foregoing, we are unable to conclude that it has been demonstrated by sufficient evidence that Carter willfully aided and abetted violations of the securities laws in connection with the December 20 press release and the December Form 8–K.[59]

---

59. The Administrative Law Judge appears to have based his findings of violation in part upon the conclusion that respondents failed to act to correct the public misperceptions created by National's December 23 stockholders letter and, perhaps, by the company's earlier growth predictions and continued optimistic public disclosure. Without deciding the precise extent of National's obligation to dispel the misleading public image of the company which it had previously created, we are unwilling to conclude that *respondents* had an affirmative obligation to do so in the context of the December press release and the December Form 8–K, or that their failure to do so itself constituted willful aiding and abetting of National's violation.

E. *Subsequent Conduct.* The Administrative Law Judge found that, in addition to the violations resulting from the December 20, 1974 press release and the Form 8–K filed on January 8, 1975, National violated the federal securities laws through its continued failure to make adequate disclosures in public statements and Commission filings regarding its deteriorating cash position, its inability to meet earlier growth projections, the triggering of the LMP, and the impact the LMP would have on National. The Administrative Law Judge also found that respondents willfully aided and abetted these violations by failing to ensure that the required disclosures were made or to communicate to National's board of directors concerning management's refusal to make such disclosures. Our review of the record does not reveal a sufficient basis for sustaining respondents' liability as aiders and abettors of these violations.

Respondents' behavior with regard to these violations by National poses an issue that was not present in our earlier discussion of Carter's conduct. There, Carter actively assisted commission of the violations. Here, respondents' behavior was in the nature of inaction and silence.

The courts have differed with respect to the circumstances under which inaction or silence may constitute the requisite assistance to the primary wrongdoer.[60] Some cases require a showing that the alleged aider and abettor deliberately intended to assist the primary violation by his silence or inaction.[61] Other cases have held that inaction or silence may constitute "substantial assistance" when the alleged aider and abettor was under a duty to act or disclose, but failed to do so.[62]

Finally, some courts synthesize the two approaches as follows:

When it is impossible to find any duty of disclosure, an aider and abettor should be found liable only if scienter of the high "conscious intent" variety can be found. Where some special duty of disclosure exists, then liability should be possible with a lesser degree of scienter.[63]

Accordingly, in order to sustain the law judge's finding, we must find that respondents either consciously intended to assist National's violation, or that they breached a duty to disclose or act and had some degree of scienter.

On the basis of the record before us, we think that it is a close question, but in the final analysis we are unable to infer that respondents intended to aid the violations by not acting. The level of intent required by this test is higher

---

60. We note, however, that at least one court has held that mere inaction can never give rise to liability for aiding and abetting a violation of Rule 10b–5. Wessel v. Buhler, 437 F.2d 279, 283 (C.A.9 1971).

61. Rochez Brothers, Inc. v. Rhoades, 527 F.2d 880, 889 (C.A.3 1975): * * * See also S.E.C. v. Coffey, 493 F.2d 1304, 1317 (C.A.6), cert. denied, 420 U.S. 908 (1975).

62. Strong v. France, 474 F.2d 747, 752 (C.A.9 1973); Kerbs v. Fall River Industries, Inc., 502 F.2d 731, 740 (C.A.10 1974). In a factually similar situation in which the court considered whether inaction or silence constitutes substantial assistance for the purposes of aiding and abetting, the court held that

there was a duty * * * S.E.C. v. National Student Marketing Corp., 457 F.Supp. 682, 713 (D.D.C.1978). See also Rolf v. Blyth, Eastman Dillon & Co., Inc., 570 F.2d 38, 45 (C.A.2 1978).

63. Woodward v. Metro Bank of Dallas, 522 F.2d 84, 97 (C.A.5 1975). See also IIT, An International Investment Trust v. Cornfeld, 619 F.2d 909, 922 (C.A.2 1980); Hochfelder v. Midwest Stock Exchange, 503 F.2d 364, 374 (C.A.7), cert. denied, 419 U.S. 875 (1974); Woods v. Homes & Structures of Pittsburg, Kansas, 489 F.Supp. 1270, 1278 (D.Kan. 1980).

than that required by some courts to show the appropriate mental state for the third element of aiding and abetting. There, some courts require only that an aider and abettor be "aware" that his role was part of an illegal or improper activity. Here, the test requires a showing that he "intended" to foster the illegal activity. This is a fine distinction, but we think it is an important one.

Our review of the record, which includes respondents' periodic exhortations to Hart to improve the quality of National's disclosure, leads us to believe that respondents did not intend to assist the violations by their inaction or silence. Rather, they seemed to be at a loss for how to deal with a difficult client.

Association of a law firm with a client lends an air of legitimacy and authority to the actions of a client. There are occasions when, but for the law firm's association, a violation could not have occurred. Under those circumstances, if the firm were cognizant of how it was being used and acquiesced, or if it gained some benefit from the violation beyond that normally obtained in a legal relationship, inaction would probably give rise to an inference of intent. This, however, is not such a case, and we find that respondents did not intend to assist the violation by their inaction.

V.   ETHICAL AND PROFESSIONAL RESPONSIBILITIES

A.   *The Findings of the Administrative Law Judge.* The Administrative Law Judge found that both respondents "failed to carry out their professional responsibilities with respect to appropriate disclosure to all concerned, including stockholders, directors and the investing public * * * and thus knowingly engaged in unethical and improper professional conduct, as charged in the Order." In particular, he held that respondents' failure to advise National's board of directors of Hart's refusal to disclose adequately the company's perilous financial condition was itself a violation of ethical and professional standards referred to in Rule 2(e)(1)(ii).

Respondents argue that the Commission has never promulgated standards of professional conduct for lawyers and that the Commission's application in hindsight of new standards would be fundamentally unfair. Moreover, even if it is permissible for the Commission to apply—without specific adoption or notice—generally recognized professional standards, they argue that no such standards applicable to respondents' conduct existed in 1974–75, nor do they exist today.

We agree that, in general, elemental notions of fairness dictate that the Commission should not establish new rules of conduct and impose them retroactively upon professionals who acted at the time without reason to believe that their conduct was unethical or improper. At the same time, however, we perceive no unfairness whatsoever in holding those professionals who practice before us to generally recognized norms of professional conduct, whether or not such norms had previously been explicitly adopted or endorsed by the Commission. To do so upsets no justifiable expectations, since the professional is already subject to those norms.[64]

The ethical and professional responsibilities of lawyers who become aware that their client is engaging in violations of the securities laws have not been so

---

64. For example, the universally recognized requirement that a lawyer refrain from acting in an area where he does not have an adequate level of preparation or care, e.g., ABA Code of Professional Responsibility, Disciplinary Rule ("ABA D.R.") 6–101.

firmly and unambiguously established that we believe all practicing lawyers can be held to an awareness of generally recognized norms.[65] We also recognize that the Commission has never articulated or endorsed any such standards. That being the case, we reverse the Administrative Law Judge's findings under subparagraph (ii) of Rule 2(e)(1) with respect to both respondents. Nevertheless, we believe that respondents' conduct raises serious questions about the obligations of securities lawyers, and the Commission is hereby giving notice of its interpretation of "unethical or improper professional conduct" as that term is used in Rule 2(e)(1)(ii). The Commission intends to issue a release soliciting comment from the public as to whether this interpretation should be expanded or modified.

B. *Interpretive Background.* Our concern focuses on the professional obligations of the lawyer who gives essentially correct disclosure advice to a client that does not follow that advice and as a result violates the federal securities laws. The subject of our inquiry is not a new one by any means and has received extensive scholarly treatment[66] as well as consideration by a number of local bar ethics committees and disciplinary bodies. Similar issues are also presently under consideration by the ABA's Commission on Evaluation of Professional Standards in connection with the review and proposed revision of the ABA's Code of Professional Responsibility.

While precise standards have not yet emerged, it is fair to say that there exists considerable acceptance of the proposition that a lawyer must, in order to discharge his professional responsibilities, make all efforts within reason to persuade his client to avoid or terminate proposed illegal action. Such efforts could include, where appropriate, notification to the board of directors of a corporate client. In this connection, it is noteworthy that a number of commentators responding to the Commission's request, in Securities Exchange Act Release No. 16045, for written comments on a rulemaking petition concerning the disclosure of relationships between registrants and their lawyers (the "Georgetown Petition"), volunteered their beliefs that such a professional

---

65. We are aware that ABA D.R. 1–102(A)(4) provides that "a lawyer shall not * * * engage in conduct involving dishonesty, fraud, deceit or misrepresentation" and that ABA D.R. 7–102(A)(7) provides that a lawyer may not, in the course of his representation, "counsel or assist his client in conduct that the lawyer knows to be illegal or fraudulent." Although we believe the prohibitions embodied in ABA D.R. 1–102(A)(4) and 7–102(A)(7) to be of such a fundamental nature that we would not hesitate to hold that their coverage plainly falls within the area of conduct prohibited by Rule 2(e)(1)(ii), two factors convince us not to apply them in this case. First, it is unclear whether the operative terms used in these Disciplinary Rules are coextensive with the use of such terms in the statutory prohibitions of Section 10(b) of the Exchange Act. Second, it is not apparent that the reach of ABA D.R. 1–102(A)(4) or 7–102(A)(7) is greater or any different from the reach of Rule 2(e)(1)(ii) in the case of a lawyer who willfully aids and abets a viola-

tion of Section 10(b). Accordingly, in this opinion, we have elected to analyze respondents' actions in the context of the provisions of subparagraph (iii), as discussed above, rather than under subparagraph (ii) of Rule 2(e)(1).

66. E.g., Hoffman, On Learning of a Corporate Client's Crime or Fraud—The Lawyer's Dilemma, 33 Bus. Lawyer 1389 (1978); Association of the Bar of The City of New York, Report By Special Committee on The Lawyers' Role in Securities Transactions, 32 Bus. Lawyer 1879 (1977); Cooney, The Registration Process: The Role of the Lawyer in Disclosure, 33 Bus. Lawyer 1329 (1978); Cutler, The Role of the Private Law Firm, 33 Bus. Lawyer 1549 (1978); Sonde, The Responsibility of Professionals under the Federal Securities Laws—Some Observations, 68 Nw.U.L.Rev. 1 (1973); New York Law Journal, "Expanding Responsibilities under the Securities Laws" (1972), 29 (remarks of Manuel F. Cohen, Esq.).

obligation already exists. This informal expression of views is, of course, not conclusive, and there continues to be a lively debate surrounding the lawyer's proper reaction to his client's wrongdoings.

We are mindful that, when a lawyer represents a corporate client, the client—and the entity to which he owes his allegiance—is the corporation itself and not management or any other individual connected with the corporation. Moreover, the lawyer should try to "insure that decisions of his client are made only after the client has been informed of relevant considerations." These unexceptionable principles take on a special coloration when a lawyer becomes aware that one or more specific members of a corporate client's management is deciding not to follow his disclosure advice, especially if he knows that those in control, such as the board of directors, may not have participated in or been aware of that decision. Moreover, it is well established that no lawyer, even in the most zealous pursuit of his client's interests, is privileged to assist his client in conduct the lawyer knows to be illegal. The application of these recognized principles to the special role of the securities lawyer giving disclosure advice, however, is not a simple task.

The securities lawyer who is an active participant in a company's ongoing disclosure program will ordinarily draft and revise disclosure documents, comment on them and file them with the Commission. He is often involved on an intimate, day-to-day basis in the judgments that determine what will be disclosed and what will be withheld from the public markets. When a lawyer serving in such a capacity concludes that his client's disclosures are not adequate to comply with the law, and so advises his client, he is "aware," in a literal sense, of a continuing violation of the securities laws. On the other hand, the lawyer is only an adviser, and the final judgment—and, indeed, responsibility—as to what course of conduct is to be taken must lie with the client. Moreover, disclosure issues often present difficult choices between multiple shades of gray, and while a lawyer's judgment may be to draw the disclosure obligation more broadly than his client, both parties recognize the degree of uncertainty involved.

The problems of professional conduct that arise in this relationship are well-illustrated by the facts of this case. In rejecting Brown, Wood's advice to include the assumptions underlying its projections in its 1974 Annual Report, in declining to issue two draft stockholders letters offered by respondents and in ignoring the numerous more informal urgings by both respondents and Socha to make disclosure, Hart and Lurie indicated that they were inclined to resist any public pronouncements that were at odds with the rapid growth which had been projected and reported for the company.

If the record ended there, we would be hesitant to suggest that any unprofessional conduct might be involved. Hart and Lurie were, in effect, pressing the company's lawyers hard for the minimum disclosure required by law. That fact alone is not an appropriate basis for a finding that a lawyer must resign or take some extraordinary action. Such a finding would inevitably drive a wedge between reporting companies and their outside lawyers; the more sophisticated members of management would soon realize that there is nothing to gain in consulting outside lawyers.

However, much more was involved in this case. In sending out a patently misleading letter to stockholders on December 23 in contravention of Socha's plain and express advice to clear all such disclosure with Brown, Wood, in deceiving respondents about Johnson's approval of the company's quarterly report to its stockholders in early December and in dissembling in response to respondents' questions about the implementation of the LMP, the company's management erected a wall between National and its outside lawyers—a wall apparently designed to keep out good legal advice in conflict with management's improper disclosure plans.

Any ambiguity in the situation plainly evaporated in late April and early May of 1975 when Hart first asked Johnson for a legal opinion flatly contrary to the express disclosure advice Johnson had given Hart only five days earlier, and when Lurie soon thereafter prohibited Kay from delivering a copy of the company's April 1975 Form 8–K to Brown, Wood.

These actions reveal a conscious desire on the part of National's management no longer to look to Brown, Wood for independent disclosure advice, but rather to embrace the firm within Hart's fraud and use it as a shield to avoid the pressures exerted by the banks toward disclosure. Such a role is a perversion of the normal lawyer-client relationship, and no lawyer may claim that, in these circumstances, he need do no more than stubbornly continue to suggest disclosure when he knows his suggestions are falling on deaf ears.

C.   *"Unethical or Improper Professional Conduct."* The Commission is of the view that a lawyer engages in "unethical or improper professional conduct" under the following circumstances: When a lawyer with significant responsibilities in the effectuation of a company's compliance with the disclosure requirements of the federal securities laws becomes aware that his client is engaged in a substantial and continuing failure to satisfy those disclosure requirements, his continued participation violates professional standards unless he takes prompt steps to end the client's noncompliance. The Commission has determined that this interpretation will be applicable only to conduct occurring after the date of this opinion.

We do not imply that a lawyer is obliged, at the risk of being held to have violated Rule 2(e), to seek to correct every isolated disclosure action or inaction which he believes to be at variance with applicable disclosure standards, although there may be isolated disclosure failures that are so serious that their correction becomes a matter of primary professional concern. It is also clear, however, that a lawyer is not privileged to unthinkingly permit himself to be co-opted into an ongoing fraud and cast as a dupe or a shield for a wrong doing client.

Initially, counseling accurate disclosure is sufficient, even if his advice is not accepted. But there comes a point at which a reasonable lawyer must conclude that his advice is not being followed, or even sought in good faith, and that his client is involved in a continuing course of violating the securities laws. At this critical juncture, the lawyer must take further, more affirmative steps in order to avoid the inference that he has been co-opted, willingly or unwillingly, into the scheme of non-disclosure.

The lawyer is in the best position to choose his next step. Resignation is one option, although we recognize that other considerations, including the protection of the client against foreseeable prejudice, must be taken into account in the case of withdrawal. A direct approach to the board of directors or one or more individual directors or officers may be appropriate; or he may choose to try to enlist the aid of other members of the firm's management.

What is required, in short, is some prompt action[77] that leads to the conclusion that the lawyer is engaged in efforts to correct the underlying problem, rather than having capitulated to the desires of a strong-willed, but misguided client.

Some have argued that resignation is the only permissible course when a client chooses not to comply with disclosure advice. We do not agree. Premature resignation serves neither the end of an effective lawyer-client relationship nor, in most cases, the effective administration of the securities laws. The lawyer's continued interaction with his client will ordinarily hold the greatest promise of corrective action. So long as a lawyer is acting in good faith and exerting reasonable efforts to prevent violations of the law by his client, his professional obligations have been met. In general, the best result is that which promotes the continued, strong-minded and independent participation by the lawyer.

We recognize, however, that the "best result" is not always obtainable, and that there may occur situations where the lawyer must conclude that the misconduct is so extreme or irretrievable, or the involvement of his client's management and board of directors in the misconduct is so thoroughgoing and pervasive that any action short of resignation would be futile. We would anticipate that cases where a lawyer has no choice but to resign would be rare and of an egregious nature.[78]

D. *Conclusion.* As noted above, because the Commission has never adopted or endorsed standards of professional conduct which would have applied to respondents' activities during the period here in question, and since generally accepted norms of professional conduct which existed outside the scope of Rule 2(e) did not, during the relevant time period, unambiguously cover the situation in which respondents found themselves in 1974–75, no finding of unethical or unprofessional conduct would be appropriate. That being the case, we reverse the findings of the Administrative Law Judge under Rule 2(e)(1)(ii). In future proceedings of this nature, however, the Commission will apply the interpretation of subparagraph (ii) of Rule 2(e)(1) set forth in this opinion.

An appropriate order will issue.

■ By the Commission (CHAIRMAN WILLIAMS and COMMISSIONERS LOOMIS and FRIED-MAN); COMMISSIONER EVANS concurring in part and dissenting in part; and COMMISSIONER THOMAS not participating.

RULE 102(e)

Although it was expected that the *Carter and Johnson* case would result in judicial review and clarification of the SEC's authority under what is now Rule 102(e), the Commission neatly sidestepped any judicial test of its power by

---

77. In those cases where resignation is not the only alternative, should a lawyer choose not to resign, we do not believe the action taken *must be successful* to avoid the inference that the lawyer had improperly participated in his client's fraud. Rather, the acceptability of the action must be considered in the light of all relevant surrounding circumstances. Similarly, what is "prompt" in any one case depends on the situation then facing the lawyer.

78. This case does not involve, nor do we here deal with, the additional question of when a lawyer, aware of his client's intention to commit fraud or an illegal act, has a professional duty to disclose that fact either publicly or to an affected third party. Our interpretation today does not require such action at any point, although other existing standards of professional conduct might be so interpreted. See, e.g., ABA D.R. 7–102(B).

declining to impose any sanction on the respondents (while threatening to do so in future cases). Some of the controversy was defused, however, when the Commission's general counsel indicated in 1982 that the Commission would normally limit its discipline of attorneys to instances where the conduct also violated established ethical rules of state bar organizations.[1] The Commission ratified this policy in 1988, stating:

> With respect to attorneys, the Commission generally has not sought to develop or apply independent standards of professional conduct. The great majority of Rule 2(e) proceedings against attorneys involve allegations of violations of law (not of professional standards); thus, the Commission as a matter of policy, generally refrains from using its administrative forum to conduct *de novo* determinations of the professional obligations of attorneys.[2]

Since the Commission's 1981 proceeding against *Carter and Johnson* all, or virtually all, Rule 102(e) proceedings against lawyers have followed injunctions (or occasionally convictions) for securities law violations.[3]

While this denouement ended one Rule 102(e) controversy, it did not end all controversy.

In Checkosky v. SEC,[4] ("Checkosky I") the court remanded to the SEC *per curiam* a Rule 2(e) proceeding so that the Commission could state unequivocally whether it regarded negligent acts without more as constituting a violation of Rule 2(e).

Judge Silberman wrote in his opinion: "If the Commission were to determine that an accountant's negligence is a *per se* violation of Rule 2(e), it would have to consider not only the administrative burden such a position would entail but also whether it would constitute a *de facto* substantive regulation of the profession and thus raise questions as to the legitimacy of Rule 2(e)(1)(ii)— or at least its scope."[5]

Judge Randolph conceded that the Commission did regard negligence as a sufficient basis for a Rule 2(e) violation, but would have vacated and remanded the order to give the SEC the opportunity to adequately justify this aspect of its order.[6]

Judge Reynolds believed that the SEC concluded that the defendants were "*at least* negligent,"[7] but would have affirmed. "The SEC did not have to find

---

1. See Greene, Lawyer Disciplinary Proceedings Before the Securities and Exchange Commission, 14 Sec. Reg. L. Rep. 168 (1982).

2. Sec. Ex. Act Rel. 25,893, 41 SEC Dock. 388 (1988); see also Goelzer & Wyderko, Rule 2(e): Securities and Exchange Commission Discipline of Professionals, 85 Nw. U.L.Rev. 652 (1991).

In 1999 Enforcement Director Richard Walker stated that he anticipated the Commission is likely to continue its policy of not naming lawyers in "original" actions under Rule 102(e). Walker Sees SEC Continuing Restraint in Charging Lawyers over Legal Conduct, 31 Sec. Reg. & L. Rep. (BNA) 1067 (1999).

3. Robert W. Emerson, Rule 2(e) Revisited: SEC Disciplining of Attorneys Since *In re Carter*, 29 Am. Bus. L.J. 155, 213 (1991); Ann Maxey, SEC Enforcement Actions against Securities Lawyers: New Remedies vs. Old Policies, 22 Del. J. Corp. L. 537 (1997).

4. 23 F.3d 452 (D.C.Cir.1994).

5. Id. at 459.

6. Id. at 467.

7. Id. at 494.

scienter to invoke Rule 2(e)(1)(ii) in this case."[8]

On remand in 1997 the Commission concluded:

We believe that Rule 2(e)(1)(ii) does not mandate a particular mental state and that negligent actions by a professional may, under certain circumstances, constitute improper professional conduct. Unlike Rule 2(e)(1)(iii), Rule 2(e)(1)(ii) does not require that the conduct be "willful." Nor do we believe that Respondents are correct that the overall structure of the securities laws mandates that *scienter* is an element of Rule 2(e)(1)(ii). Respondents observe that Section 10(b) of the Exchange Act requires *scienter*. However, other provisions of the securities laws that can involve accountants do not. The Office of the Chief Accountant directs our attention to Section 11 of the Securities Act of 1933, which imposes civil liability on auditors in the absence of *scienter*. Moreover, other provisions of the Exchange Act that may impose liability based on audited financial reports filed with us, such as Sections 15(c)(3) and 13(a) similarly do not contain a *scienter* requirement.[9]

Commissioner Johnson dissented: "I think that this Commission's processes can be protected sufficiently by disciplining professionals under Rule 2(e)(1)(ii) only when it is demonstrated that they acted with scienter."[10]

The following year the District of Columbia Circuit returned to the fray. In Checkosky v. SEC ("Checkosky II"),[11] the Court of Appeals expressed displeasure at the Commission 1997 Opinion stating that it again "failed adequately to explain its interpretation of [Rule 102(e)]",[12] "voicing instead a multiplicity of inconsistent interpretations."[13] The court then took the rare step of remanding the case with instructions to dismiss the proceeding.

The court took particular exception to the standard in the Commission's 1997 Opinion: "We believe that Rule 2(e)(1)(ii) does not mandate a particular mental state and that negligent actions by a professional may, *under certain circumstances,* constitute improper professional conduct."[14] As the court explained: "Elementary administrative law norms of fair notice and reasoned decision making demand that the Commission define those circumstances with some degree of specificity. It has not done so."[15]

In 1998, the Commission amended Rule 102(e), again over a lengthy dissent by Commissioner Johnson. As amended Rule 102(e) adds a new paragraph (iv):

(iv) with respect to persons licensed to practice as accountants, "improper professional conduct" under § 201.102(e)(1)(ii) means:

(A) Intentional or knowing conduct, including reckless conduct, that results in a violation of applicable professional standards: or

---

8. Ibid.

9. David J. Checkosky, AAER 871, 63 SEC Dock. 1691, 1700–1701 (1997).

10. Id. at 1704.

11. 139 F.3d 221 (D.C.Cir.1998).

In Robert D. Potts, CPA, 53 SEC 187 (1997), the Commission divided 2–2 as to whether negligence is a sufficient basis for liability under Rule 102(e)(1), with Commissioners Johnson and Wallman dissenting on this point. The Eighth Circuit affirmed the SEC's ultimate finding of reckless professional conduct for a concurring reviewer. Potts v. SEC, 151 F.3d 810 (8th Cir.1998), *cert. denied,* 526 U.S. 1097 (1999).

12. Id. at 222.

13. Ibid.

14. Id. at 224.

15. Ibid.

(B) Either of the following two types of negligent conduct:

(1) A single instance of highly unreasonable conduct that results in a violation of applicable professional standards in circumstances in which an accountant knows, or should know, that heightened scrutiny is warranted.

(2) Repeated instances of unreasonable conduct, each resulting in a violation of applicable professional standards, that indicate a lack of competence to practice before the Commission.[16]

The Commission majority viewed this standard as responding to the *Checkovsky II* criticism that it had not clearly articulated when an accountant would have engaged in "improper professional conduct."[17]

Commissioner Johnson urged in dissent his view that the Commission lacks authority to promulgate Rule 102(e) and that in any event lacks the authority to adopt a negligence standard under Rule 102(e).[18]

In 2002 § 602 of the Sarbanes–Oxley Act codified Rule 102(e), thus removing any question as to the Commission's ability to adopt the Rule or its culpability standard.

See generally 10 Louis Loss & Joel Seligman, Securities Regulation ch. 13.A (3d ed. rev. 1996); ABA Comm. on Fed. Reg. of Sec., Report of the Task Force on Rule 102(e) Proceedings: Rule 102(e) Sanctions against Accountants, 52 Bus. Law. 965 (1997) (recommending at 985 that the SEC impose a Rule 102(e) sanction for improper professional conduct only upon a finding by the Commission that the accountant is presently "substantially unfit" to practice before the Commission); David B. Hardison & Evan J. Falchuk, *Checkosky v. SEC:* The SEC's New Home Court Disadvantage, 12 Insights No. 7 at 2 (1998); Norman S. Johnson & Ross A. Albert, "Deja Vu All over Again": The Securities and Exchange Commission Once More Attempts to Regulate the Accounting Profession through Rule 102(e) of Its Rules of Practice, 1999 Utah L. Rev. 553.

THE PROFESSIONAL RESPONSIBILITIES OF SECURITIES LAWYERS

Do the professional responsibilities of lawyers to their clients, and to others, differ from those normally applicable because they are advising their clients with respect to compliance with the federal securities laws? This question was the subject of an intense national debate, which was triggered by the filing by the Securities and Exchange Commission of the complaint against National Student Marketing Corporation and the prestigious New York law firm of White & Case in 1972. The principal transaction attacked in that complaint was a merger of National Student Marketing Corporation with another corporation, where the accountants refused to give a "comfort letter" which was a condition of the closing of the transaction. The party entitled to insist upon that condition nevertheless waived it, and the closing proceeded. The SEC asserted in the complaint that White & Case should have insisted upon a resolicitation of the proxies for the merger and, if its client had refused, it should have resigned *and* informed the SEC of the facts. It is this final

---

16. Sec. Act Rel. 7593, 68 SEC Dock. 489 (1998) (adoption). Cf. Russell Ponce, AAER 1297, 73 SEC Dock. 358 (2000) (auditor knew or was reckless in not knowing about false statements).

17. Sec. Act Rel. 7593, 68 SEC Dock. at 491–492.

18. Id. at 510–516.

assertion which provoked much of the controversy. The Commission abandoned this particular assertion in the *Carter and Johnson* case.

The *National Student Marketing* case involved the acquisition in a merger transaction by National Student Marketing Corporation (NSMC) of Interstate National Corporation (INC) for stock of NSMC. As indicated above, the accountants refused to give the "comfort letter" at the closing which was required by the merger agreement and instead provided a letter which detailed material misstatements in the interim financial statements of NSMC which had been furnished to the shareholders of INC when they voted on the merger. NSMC was represented by White & Case while INC was represented by Lord, Bissell & Brooks (LBB), an equally prestigious Chicago law firm. The INC representatives who were present at the closing agreed to waive the requirement of a clean comfort letter from the accountants; they constituted a majority of the Board of Directors of INC and themselves held a majority of its stock (and would receive more than half of the stock being issued by NSMC in the merger transaction). The SEC asserted that the lawyers had violated Rule 10b–5 by their failure to put a stop to the closing of the transaction after receipt of the "noncomfort" letter (which they could have done by refusing to give the opinions required of them at the closing) and to insist upon a resolicitation of the shareholders of INC with corrected financial information regarding NSMC.

In SEC v. National Student Marketing Corp.,[1] Judge Parker in the Federal District court held that LBB and its partners (White & Case in the meantime had settled with the SEC out of court) had been guilty of aiding and abetting a violation of Rule 10b–5. Judge Parker said:

> Upon receipt of the unsigned comfort letter, it became clear that the merger had been approved by the Interstate shareholders on the basis of materially misleading information. In view of the obvious materiality of the information, especially to attorneys learned in securities law, the attorneys' responsibilities to their corporate client required them to take steps to ensure that the information would be disclosed to the shareholders. However, it is unnecessary to determine the precise extent of their obligations here, since it is undisputed that they took no steps whatsoever to delay the closing pending disclosure to and resolicitation of the Interstate shareholders. But, at the very least, they were required to speak out at the closing concerning the obvious materiality of the information and the concomitant requirement that the merger not be closed until the adjustments were disclosed and approval of the merger was again obtained from the Interstate shareholders. Their silence was not only a breach of this duty to speak, but in addition lent the appearance of legitimacy to the closing, see Kerbs v. Fall River Industries, Inc., supra. [502 F.2d 731 (10th Cir.1974)]. The combination of these factors clearly provided substantial assistance to the closing of the merger.
>
> Contrary to the attorney-defendants' contention, imposition of such a duty will not require lawyers to go beyond their accepted role in securities transactions, nor will it compel them to "err on the side of conservation, * * * thereby inhibiting clients' business judgments and candid attorney-client communications." Courts will not lightly overrule an attorney's determination of materiality and the need for disclosure. However, where, as here, the significance of the information clearly removes any doubt

---

1.   457 F.Supp. 682 (D.D.C.1978).

concerning the materiality of the information, attorneys cannot rest on asserted "business judgments" as justification for their failure to make a legal decision pursuant to their fiduciary responsibilities to client shareholders.[2]

The judge, however, refused to issue an injunction against the lawyers, saying that there was no likelihood that they were going to repeat the type of conduct of which they had been found guilty:

> "The Commission has not demonstrated that the defendants engaged in the type of repeated and persistent misconduct which usually justifies the issuance of injunctive relief. * * * Instead, it has shown violations which principally occurred within a period of a few hours at the closing of the merger in 1969. The Commission has not charged, or even suggested, that the defendants were involved in similar misconduct either before or after the events involved in this proceeding. Thus, the violations proved by the SEC appear to be part of an isolated incident, unlikely to recur and insufficient to warrant an injunction."[3]

In a related case against a different lawyer, the District Court held that it would not grant summary judgment to a lawyer with respect to an opinion that he rendered to National Student Marketing in order to permit its accountants to record a transfer of a subsidiary in a certain fashion, although the court also denied the motion of the SEC for summary judgment.[4] In that case the attorney had rendered an opinion that "all of the risks and benefits of ownership" of the subsidiary had passed to the purchaser as of the end of the fiscal year, so as to permit the elimination of the subsidiary's losses on the consolidated statements of National Student Marketing. This opinion was rendered although the attorney knew that the transaction had actually been carried out after the end of the fiscal year and antedated and that the transaction had no economic substance since the purchaser assumed no obligation whatever to pay the purchase price.

After the decision of the Commission in the *Carter and Johnson* case, the Commission followed up on its statement in the opinion that it would propose standards of conduct for lawyers under what is now Rule 102(e) by issuing for comment on September 21, 1981, a proposal to adopt a "Standard of Conduct Constituting Unethical or Improper Professional Practice Before the Commission." That proposed standard read as follows:

> When a lawyer with significant responsibilities in the effectuation of a company's compliance with the disclosure requirements of the federal securities laws becomes aware that his client is engaged in a substantial and continuing failure to satisfy those disclosure requirements, his continued participation violates professional standards unless he takes prompt steps to end the client's noncompliance.

The Commission stated in its Release that it would not solicit comments on the Commission's authority to adopt and to administer what is now Rule 102(e). Despite this assertion by the Commission, the proposal was greeted with withering criticism by the Bar, primarily on the issue of whether the Commission had authority to adopt any "standards of professional conduct" for lawyers

---

2. Id. at 713.

3. Id. at 716.

4. SEC v. National Student Marketing Corp., 402 F.Supp. 641 (D.D.C.1975).

practicing before it. In particular, the Section of Corporation, Banking and Business Law established a special committee to prepare a letter of comment and this letter was officially approved by the Board of Governors of the American Bar Association on November 20, 1981.[5] The letter of comment concluded:

> We regret that the Commission chose to publish the Proposal for public comment. We especially regret that the Commission chose to discourage comments on what we regard as the most important issue it raises. Resolution of that issue is so clearly beyond the Commission's authority, and the notion that the Commission has the power or the responsibility to become a putative bar association is such a poor approach to a complex and difficult set of problems that, in our view, it is not advisable for the Commission to adopt or further consider this or any related proposal. In our view it would be better for the Commission to direct its legal staff to continue their traditional and constructive dialogue with the ABA and other professional groups, including state bar authorities. Dialogues of this nature have served the Commission and the public interest well for nearly fifty years. This is not the time, nor is this issue the cause, to abandon that approach.

After a change in the chairmanship and other personnel of the Commission, this proposal was quietly buried and it has not been heard from since.

In Barker v. Henderson, Franklin, Starnes & Holt,[6] the Seventh Circuit stated as follows concerning the assertion by the plaintiff that a law firm representing a charitable foundation (and an accounting firm working for the foundation) should have "blown the whistle" on the activities of the client:

> The extent to which lawyers and accountants should reveal their clients' wrongdoing—and to whom they should reveal—is a question of great moment. There are proposals to change the rules of legal ethics and the SEC's regulations governing accountants. The professions and the regulatory agencies will debate questions raised by cases such as this one for years to come. We express no opinion on whether the firms did what they should, whether there was malpractice under state law, or whether the rules of ethics (or other fiduciary doctrines) ought to require lawyers and accountants to blow the whistle in equivalent circumstances. We are satisfied, however, that an award of damages under the securities laws is not the way to blaze the trail toward improved ethical standards in the legal and accounting professions. Liability depends on an *existing* duty to disclose. The securities law therefore must lag behind changes in ethical and fiduciary standards. The plaintiffs have not pointed to any rule imposing on either Firm a duty to blow the whistle.[7]

Professor Morgan Shipman earlier asserted[8] that the securities lawyer does not really have any client, but is the attorney to "the situation." This has prompted one lawyer to inquire whether he should send his bill to "the situation"; and, if he did, would the situation pay it?

---

5. 36 Bus. Law. 915 (1982).

6. 797 F.2d 490 (7th Cir.1986).

7. Id. at 497.

8. Morgan Shipman, The Need for SEC Rules to Govern the Duties and Civil Liabilities of Attorneys under the Federal Securities Statutes, 34 Ohio St. L.J. 231, at 257 (1973).

On the other hand, Dean Monroe Freedman asserted[9] that, even without any further development in this direction, the Securities Bar was already a "wholly-owned subsidiary of the Securities and Exchange Commission."

In 1983 the American Bar Association adopted Model Rules of Professional Conduct notably more constricted than the SEC's already abandoned 1981 proposal. Rule 1.6, Confidentiality of Information, specifically provides:

RULE 1.6.   CONFIDENTIALITY OF INFORMATION

(a) A lawyer shall not reveal information relating to representation of a client unless the client consents after consultation, except for disclosures that are impliedly authorized in order to carry out the representation, and except as stated in paragraph (b).

(b) A lawyer may reveal such information to the extent the lawyer reasonably believes necessary:

(1) to prevent the client from committing a criminal act that the lawyer believes is likely to result in imminent death or substantial bodily harm; or

(2) to establish a claim or defense on behalf of the lawyer in a controversy between the lawyer and the client, to establish a defense to a criminal charge or civil claim against the lawyer based upon conduct in which the client was involved, or to respond to allegations in any proceeding concerning the lawyer's representation of the client.

COMMENT:

    * * *

A fundamental principle in the client-lawyer relationship is that the lawyer maintain confidentiality of information relating to the representation. The client is thereby encouraged to communicate fully and frankly with the lawyer even as to embarrassing or legally damaging subject matter. * * *

Disclosure Adverse to Client

The confidentiality rule is subject to limited exceptions. In becoming privy to information about a client, a lawyer may foresee that the client intends serious harm to another person. However, to the extent a lawyer is required or permitted to disclose a client's purposes, the client will be inhibited from revealing facts which would enable the lawyer to counsel against a wrongful course of action. The public is better protected if full and open communication by the client is encouraged than if it is inhibited.

Several situations must be distinguished.

First, the lawyer may not counsel or assist a client in conduct that is criminal or fraudulent. See Rule 1.2(d). Similarly, a lawyer has a duty under Rule 3.3(a)(4) not to use false evidence. This duty is essentially a special instance of the duty prescribed in Rule 1.2(d) to avoid assisting a client in criminal or fraudulent conduct.

9. Monroe Freedman, A Civil Libertarian Looks at Securities Regulation, 35 Ohio   St. L.J. 280, 285 (1974).

Second, the lawyer may have been innocently involved in past conduct by the client that was criminal or fraudulent. In such a situation the lawyer has not violated Rule 1.2(d), because to "counsel or assist" criminal or fraudulent conduct requires knowing that the conduct is of that character.

Third, the lawyer may learn that a client intends prospective conduct that is criminal and likely to result in imminent death or substantial bodily harm. As stated in paragraph (b)(1), the lawyer has professional discretion to reveal information in order to prevent such consequences. The lawyer may make a disclosure in order to prevent homicide or serious bodily injury which the lawyer reasonably believes is intended by a client. It is very difficult for a lawyer to "know" when such a heinous purpose will actually be carried out, for the client may have a change of mind.

The lawyer's exercise of discretion requires consideration of such factors as the nature of the lawyer's relationship with the client and with those who might be injured by the client, the lawyer's own involvement in the transaction and factors that may extenuate the conduct in question. Where practical, the lawyer should seek to persuade the client to take suitable action. In any case, a disclosure adverse to the client's interest should be no greater than the lawyer reasonably believes necessary to the purpose. A lawyer's decision not to take preventive action permitted by paragraph (b)(1) does not violate this Rule.

Withdrawal

If the lawyer's services will be used by the client in materially furthering a course of criminal or fraudulent conduct, the lawyer must withdraw, as stated in Rule 1.16(a)(1).

After withdrawal the lawyer is required to refrain from making disclosure of the clients' confidences, except as otherwise provided in Rule 1.6. Neither this rule nor Rule 1.8(b) nor Rule 1.16(d) prevents the lawyer from giving notice of the fact of withdrawal, and the lawyer may also withdraw or disaffirm any opinion, document, affirmation, or the like. * * *

The professional responsibilities of a securities lawyer are also informed by the securities laws themselves and by specific ethics committee guidelines and opinions.

We have earlier addressed the liability of lawyers under § 11 of the 1933 Act when they serve as directors.[10] The *Central Bank* decision has precluded attorney liability as an aider and abettor in private lawsuits, but after subsequent amendments to the 1934 Act, the SEC may bring Rule 10b–5 aiding and abetting claims. Rule of Practice 102(e)(iii) expressly permits an SEC disciplinary claim against a lawyer (or an accountant) for aiding and abetting a securities violation.

In 2002 Senator Edwards successfully sponsored an amendment to the Sarbanes–Oxley Act to provide in § 307:

> RULES FOR PROFESSIONAL RESPONSIBILITY FOR ATTORNEYS.—Not later than 180 days after the date of enactment of this section, the Commission shall establish rules, in the public interest and for the protection of investors, setting forth minimum standards of professional conduct for attorneys appearing and practicing before the Commission in any way in the representation of public companies, including a rule

---

10. See Escott v. BarChris Constr. Corp., 283 F.Supp. 643 (S.D.N.Y.1968).

(1) requiring an attorney to report evidence of a material violation of securities law or breach of fiduciary duty or similar violation by the company, or any agent thereof to the chief legal counsel or the chief executive officer of the company (or the equivalent thereof); and

(2) if the counsel or officer does not appropriately respond to the evidence (adopting, as necessary, appropriate remedial measures or sanctions with respect to the violation), requiring the attorney to report the evidence to the audit committee of the board of directors comprised solely of directors not employed directly or indirectly by the company, or to the board of directors.

This, as adopted, was not among the most felicitously drafted provisions of the new Act. It did limit the reporting attorney's burden to *material* violations of securities law or breach of fiduciary duty or similar violation and limited the reporting burden to a report within the corporation. On the other hand the reference to Commission power to establish rules "setting forth minimum standards of professional conduct for attorneys" sounded as if the SEC was empowered to supplant state authority over attorneys. This may not have been the intent. The Section may have been intended to codify existing Commission power to adopt Rule 102(e) of its Rules of Practice, a power that has been periodically and unsuccessfully challenged.[11] The reference in § 307 to "appearing and practicing before the Commission in any way" is directly derived from Rule 102(e). Since Congress separately codified the SEC authority to adopt Rule 102(e) in § 602, the reference to "minimum standards of professional conduct for attorneys" may be unnecessary.

In a different sense, § 307 is too narrow. Surely an attorney should have an equal burden to report an antitrust, environmental, health, or safety law violation. The limitations to violations of "securities laws or breach of fiduciary duty or similar violation" was drafted on the floor when a question was posed as to whether earlier introduced language referring to "material violations of law" was germane to a securities act.

A Committee of the Association of the Bar of the City of New York prepared guidelines for attorney preparation of written opinions.[12] These include:

Guideline One

Before rendering an opinion, a lawyer should ascertain the purpose for which the opinion is sought; whether the opinion is to be addressed to the client or another recipient; whether any persons other than the client or other addressee are intended to be entitled to rely on the opinion and, if so, their identity; and whether use by and reliance on the opinion should be expressly limited to a specific person or group of persons or to a particular purpose. * * *

Guideline Two

A lawyer should not give an opinion (including one based on hypothetical facts or one that is legally correct as to the limited matters to which it is

---

11.   10 Louis Loss & Joel Seligman, Securities Regulation 4870–4884 (3d ed. Rev. 1996 & 2002 Supp.).

12.   ABCNY, Report by Special Committee on Lawyers' Role in Securities Trans-

actions, 32 Bus. Law. 1879 (1977). In the context of written opinions involving *unregistered* securities, see also ABA Op. No. 335, 60 ABA J. 488 (1974).

addressed), if he knows or suspects that the opinion is being sought to further an illegal securities transaction.

Guideline Three

The lawyer should identify, consider and reach a conclusion concerning the legal questions posed by the requested opinion, performing such legal research as is reasonable to enable the lawyer to reach the opinion. In order to do so, he will in most instances have to identify and obtain factual information on which his legal analysis will depend. The lawyer generally obtains such factual information through inquiry of the client and, where appropriate, from others, and by reviewing materials provided to him for this purpose by the client or others. The lawyer should, therefore, satisfy himself that the client (and, if appropriate, others providing the lawyer with factual information or materials) is aware of the extent to which the lawyer is relying upon such information or materials in rendering the opinion and that there could be serious consequences if such information and materials are inaccurate or incomplete and, as a result, the legal opinion proves inapplicable or incorrect.

Guideline Four

A lawyer should not render an opinion based on factual information or material which he knows or suspects to be inaccurate in any material respect. Subject to the foregoing and except as stated in (a) and (b) below, a lawyer has no obligation independently to verify factual matters underlying his legal opinion, but in such opinion or otherwise he should make clear to the client and any other intended recipients of the opinion that he has not done so and, where appropriate, he should identify the factual information he has accepted or assumed without verification. A statement in the opinion as to reliance on officers' certificates and other documents will normally serve as adequate notice of the absence of independent verification by the lawyer of the factual matters to which such documents relate.

(a) A lawyer has no obligation to verify statements made, or other information provided to him by a client or other intended recipient of an opinion unless he is aware of inconsistent information, or of experience or circumstances which reasonably alert him that such statements and information may be erroneous or incomplete in a material respect. Where he is aware of such inconsistencies, experience or circumstances, the doubts which they create should be resolved to the lawyer's satisfaction through further inquiry or other appropriate investigation before an opinion is given which is based on such statements or other information.

(b) When the lawyer's opinion requires his interpretation or checking of legal documents, such as contracts, certificates of incorporation, or the terms of securities, he should examine the relevant documents (or copies thereof) and should not rely on the client or others to summarize or paraphrase documents for this purpose unless otherwise warranted by accepted legal practice (such as reliance on real estate title abstracts) and disclosed in the opinion.

In SEC v. Spectrum, Ltd.,[13] the Second Circuit held that an attorney was liable in an injunction action by the Commission for the negligent issuance of legal opinions permitting the distribution of unregistered securities in violation of the 1933 Act. The court said: "In assessing liability as an aider and abettor,

---

13.   489 F.2d 535 (2d Cir.1973).

however, the district judge formulated a requisite standard of culpability—actual knowledge of the improper scheme plus an intent to further that scheme—which we find to be a sharp and unjustified departure from the negligent standard which we have repeatedly held to be sufficient in the context of enforcement proceedings seeking equitable or prophylactic relief." The Supreme Court in the *Aaron* case,[14] has apparently confirmed the actual results of these cases, although that decision will require the Commission to proceed under § 17(a) of the 1933 Act rather than Rule 10b–5, which it had long alleged as an alternate basis for an injunction.

In a 1981 Securities Exchange Act Release,[15] the Commission criticized an attorney for an underwriter in connection with an exempt offering of industrial revenue bonds for failing to make any investigation of the issuer or to protest the failure to include in the offering circular any financial statements regarding the past operations of the issuer. The attorney's opinion rendered in connection with the transaction merely went to the questions of exemptions from the 1933 Act and the Trust Indenture Act of 1939. The Commission stated, however, that "although the opinion letter states that the signator has not independently checked or verified most of the material statements in the offering circular, Mr. Gotten [the underwriter's counsel], who knew that the issuer was a going concern that had been in operation for a number of years, signed and issued the opinion letter without questioning the omission from the offering circular of financial statements concerning the issuer's prior operating history, reviewing any documents as to the financial status of the issuer, or making inquiry as to results of the operations of prior years. This inquiry was totally inadequate and facilitated the bond closing and the bond sales to the public."

The issuer's counsel can be viewed as the "quarterback" in preparing the nonfinancial portions of a 1933 Act registration statement.

For this reason, the Commission has repeatedly cautioned that "the task of enforcing the securities laws rests in overwhelming measure on the Bar's shoulders."[16] If a Commissioner's statement in an address to a Bar group that "a lawyer preparing a registration statement has an obligation to do more than simply act as the blind scrivener of the thoughts of his client" can be discounted as an able lawyer's rhetoric, it is not quite so easy to discount the further suggestion that "in securities matters (other than those where advocacy is clearly proper) the attorney will have to function in a manner more akin to that of the auditor than to that of the advocate."[17]

The question of how far this responsibility of a lawyer as "akin to an auditor" was again raised with considerable controversy in the George C. Kern case,[18] an administrative proceeding brought under § 15(c)(4) of the 1934 Act.

---

14. But *see* SEC v. Haswell, 654 F.2d 698 (10th Cir.1981).

15. Sec. Ex. Act Rel. 17,831, 22 SEC Dock. 1200 (1981).

16. Emanuel Fields, 45 SEC 262, 266 n. 20 (1973), *aff'd without op. sub nom.* Fields v. SEC, 495 F.2d 1075 (D.C.Cir.1974).

17. See generally Richard W. Painter & Jennifer E. Duggan, Lawyer Disclosure of Corporate Fraud: Establishing a Firm Foundation 50 SMU L. Rev. 225 (1996); Donald C.

Langevoort, The Epistemology of Corporate Securities Lawyering: Beliefs, Biases and Organizational Behavior, 63 Brook. L. Rev. 629 (1997); Edward Cohen, Lawyers Investing in Their Clients: The Rules of Professional Responsibility, 14 Insights No. 8 at 2 (2000); Michael S. Sackheim, Ethical Standards for New York Brokerage House Attorneys, 33 Rev. Sec. & Commodities Reg., 199 (2000).

18. 50 SEC 596 (1991).

Section 15(c)(4) was not in the original 1934 Act, but was added in 1964, chiefly to give the SEC an administrative remedy for late or tardy filings. Its scope was significantly expanded in 1984 so that it currently reaches "any person subject to the provisions of Section 12, 13 or 14 or subsection (d) of Section 15" of the 1934 Act (which Sections cover the periodic reporting, proxy and tender offer rules) who "has failed to comply with any such provision, rule or regulation in any material respect." The 1984 amendments also increased its importance by extending its reach to cover any person who "was the cause" of a violation of those Sections. As a result, it seemingly gives the SEC authority equivalent to an administrative injunction over not only the corporate issuer, but also its officers, directors, employees, and even its outside counsel, where such person "was the cause" of a violation.

In 1987, the Commission instituted a proceeding under § 15(c)(4) against George Kern, a director of Allied Stores Corporation and a prominent "mergers and acquisitions" attorney in New York City. Its theory was that Kern caused Allied Stores to fail to comply with its reporting obligations under the Williams Act when it undertook defensive negotiations with a potential "white knight" in response to a hostile takeover bid from Campeau Corporation. Specifically, Kern, as the lawyer principally responsible for Allied Stores' SEC filings, failed on repeated occasions, SEC charged, to amend its Schedule 14D–9 to reflect ongoing material negotiations by which Allied Stores was arranging to sell its real estate to a major developer in order to thwart Campeau.[19] In 1988, the Administrative Law Judge sustained the SEC's position on the merits,[20] but found that because Allied Stores no longer existed as a public company (Campeau had taken it over in a successful tender offer), there was no basis on which he could grant an order against Kern. In his view, it would be pointless to order Kern to cause future compliance by Allied Stores and no authority existed under § 15(c)(4) to grant generalized compliance orders with respect to Kern's conduct regarding other issuers. On its own motion, the Commission decided to review the *Kern* decision, but delayed three years until mid–1991 before releasing its decision. Essentially, the Commission (which had a very different composition in 1991 from the Commission that took the appeal in 1988) affirmed the ALJ's determination to discontinue the proceeding, and it vacated the opinion below, based on its decision that it lacked the power to issue general, forward looking compliance orders under § 15(c)(4).[21] This was a reversal of prior Commission statements, but the Commission's retreat appeared to have been based on the new "cease and desist" powers that the Congress gave it in 1990 under the Remedies Act, which expressly authorized administrative orders against future violations of any provision, rule, or regulation.

19. Section 14(d)(4) of the 1934 Act requires that any solicitation or recommendation to holders of a security to accept or reject a tender offer be made in accordance with rules and regulations promulgated by the Commission. Rule 14d–9 requires the filing of a Schedule 14D–9 as soon as practicable after the solicitation or recommendation is sent or given to security holders. Rule 14d–9(b) then requires that an amendment be filed to the Schedule 14D–9 disclosing any material change "promptly." Thus, Kern was charged under § 15(c)(4) with failing to cause Allied Stores to file such a prompt amendment.

20. *See* George C. Kern, Jr. (Allied Stores Corp.), Admin. Proc. File No. 3–6869 (Mar. 21, 1988) (Opinion by Chief Administrative Law Judge Blair), 1988–1989 Fed. Sec. L. Rep. (CCH) ¶ 84,342 (1988).

21. George C. Kern, Jr., 50 SEC 596 (1991).

In any event a 1990 American Bar Association Report concluded that § 15(c)(4) was not being used as the Commission and Congress had originally envisioned—as an *expeditious* means of correcting public disclosure documents. Rather it was discovered by both the Commission and the private Bar to be an extremely useful vehicle for settling enforcement cases short of injunction.[22]

Compare the Office of Thrift Supervision (OTS) litigation against the firm of Kay, Scholer, Fierman, Hayes & Handler, attorneys to the failed thrift, Lincoln Savings & Loan Association. After Judge Sporkin, former Director of the Commission's Division of Enforcement, sharply queried in a case involving that Association, "[w]here * * * were the * * * attorneys when these transactions were effectuated?",[23] the OTS filed an 83 page notice of charges, seeking to freeze Kay, Scholer's assets and seeking at least $275 million in restitution. The OTS claim against Kaye, Scholer was later settled for $41 million,[24] sparking considerable controversy.[25]

SEC v. Fehn

United States Court of Appeals for the Ninth Circuit, 1996.
97 F.3d 1276, *cert. denied*, 522 U.S. 813 (1997).

■ Before: GOODWIN and HAWKINS, CIRCUIT JUDGES, and FITZGERALD, DISTRICT JUDGE.

OPINION BY:

■ MICHAEL DALY HAWKINS, CIRCUIT JUDGE:

* * *

California attorney H. Thomas Fehn appeals the district court's final judgment and permanent injunction order of April 1, 1994, which ordered Fehn to refrain from aiding and abetting violations of Section 10(b) and Section 15(d) of the Securities Exchange Act of 1934 and related regulations. Fehn advances three distinct challenges to the district court's injunction. He first contends that the Supreme Court's decision in *Central Bank of Denver v. First Interstate Bank of Denver,* 511 U.S. 164 * * * (1994), which held that a private plaintiff may not maintain an action for aiding and abetting violations of Section 10(b) of the Securities Exchange Act, should extend to SEC injunctive actions like the one that precipitated this case. Fehn argues, in the alternative, that even if *Central Bank* does not preclude the SEC's injunctive action against him, the district court erroneously concluded that he aided and abetted violations of Section 10(b) and Section 15(d) and related regulations. Finally, Fehn contends

---

22. Report of the ABA's Section of Business Law Task Force on SEC Section 15(c)(4) Proceedings, 46 Bus. Law. 253 (1990).

23. See Lincoln Sav. & Loan Ass'n v. Wall, 743 F.Supp. 901, 920 (D.D.C.1990).

24. *See* Law Firm Agrees to Pay U.S. Regulators $41 Million, 24 Sec. Reg. & L. Rep. (BNA) 335 (1992).

25. *See generally* Lawrence J. Fox, *OTS v. Kaye, Scholer*: An Assault on the Citadel, 48 Bus. Law. 1521 (1993); Howell E. Jackson,

Reflections On *Kaye, Scholer*: Enlisting Lawyers to Improve the Regulation of Financial Institutions, 66 S. Cal. L. Rev. 1019 (1993); Harris Weinstein, Attorney Liability in the Savings and Loan Crisis, 1993 U. Ill. L. Rev. 53; Ted Scheyer, From Self–Regulation to Bar Corporatism: What the S&L Crisis Means for the Regulation of Lawyers, 35 S. Tex. L. Rev. 639 (1994) (criticizing vagueness of Model Rules as they relate to attorneys in banking law).

that the district court abused its discretion in entering a permanent injunction against him.

* * *

We affirm the district court's permanent injunction order because we conclude that the court correctly found that Fehn had aided and abetted violations of Section 10(b) and Section 15(d) of the Securities Exchange Act and related regulations, and did not abuse its discretion in permanently enjoining him from future aiding and abetting violations.

FACTUAL AND PROCEDURAL BACKGROUND

I.   The Initial Public Offering by CTI Technical, Inc.

CTI Technical, Inc. was incorporated in Nevada in January 1987 by its promoter, Las Vegas resident Edwin "Bud" Wheeler. Although Wheeler directed CTI's operations from the date of its incorporation, his status as company president and chief executive officer was not disclosed publicly until August 1988. In June 1987, seeking to raise capital to acquire other businesses, CTI conducted a $200,000 "blind pool" initial public offering of securities ("IPO").

The CTI offering was tainted by violations of state and federal securities laws. First, CTI violated state blue sky laws by failing to register its securities with the states in which those securities were sold. Second, although CTI filed a Form S–18 registration statement with the SEC, it violated the Securities Act of 1933 and SEC regulations by failing to disclose that Wheeler was the promoter of the company and controlled its nominal directors. Finally, Wheeler and Stoneridge Securities, Inc., underwriter for the IPO, attempted to defraud investors by manipulating the price of the securities in aftermarket trading.

II.   The SEC Investigation of CTI's Initial Public Offering

In early 1988, the SEC launched a formal investigation of CTI's IPO. That investigation was to culminate in the SEC's September 1989 complaint against CTI and Wheeler. As a result of the SEC's action, the defendants consented to a permanent injunction against future securities laws violations, and Wheeler was convicted of securities fraud for misstatements and omissions in CTI's registration statement.

In connection with the SEC investigation, defendant-appellant Fehn was retained to represent CTI and Wheeler, as well as CTI's underwriter and various CTI officers and directors. Fehn is a California attorney who has specialized in securities law during nearly three decades of practice. He has represented clients in connection with the registration and offering of securities under the Securities Act of 1933, compliance with reporting and disclosure requirements under the Securities Exchange Act of 1934, and litigation of various securities matters. Prior to Fehn's retention in connection with the SEC investigation, Fehn's law firm had represented underwriter Stoneridge Securities during CTI's IPO.

During the SEC investigation of CTI and Wheeler, Fehn became aware that CTI was not in compliance with certain reporting requirements of the Securities Exchange Act of 1934. First, Fehn learned that after the IPO, CTI had failed to file Form 10–Q quarterly reports as required by Section 15(d) of the Securities Exchange Act and related regulations. Second, Wheeler's investigative testimony before the SEC revealed that the Food and Drug Administration had banned sales of a diet product known as "Accupatch," CTI's main product and the source of gross sales of $1 million a month, and had impounded CTI's existing inventory of the product. CTI's registration documents, however, failed to disclose these FDA actions.

Fehn advised Wheeler that CTI was required to file the quarterly Form 10–Q's, and that it must disclose, in particular, the FDA's restriction of its Accupatch product. He also discussed with Wheeler whether the Securities Exchange Act required disclosure, in the Form 10–Q's, of Wheeler's and CTI's apparent violations of the Securities Act of 1933 in connection with the IPO. Wheeler flatly refused to make such disclosures. Fehn later testified that he told Wheeler it was his professional opinion that such disclosures were unnecessary under the regulations, and furthermore could impair Wheeler's ability to assert his Fifth Amendment privilege against self-incrimination with respect to those earlier violations.

Because Wheeler wished to limit CTI's expenses, he had a non-lawyer employee of CTI—rather than Fehn—draft the Form 10–Q's. Fehn gave Wheeler a copy of Regulation S–K, which outlines disclosure requirements for Form 10–Q, an instruction booklet describing how to fill out a Form 10–Q, and a sample Form 10–Q. The employee prepared a draft of the Form 10–Q for the quarter ending March 31, 1988, which disclosed the FDA's ban on CTI's Accupatch product. However, the Form 10–Q mischaracterized Wheeler's true role in CTI, describing him as CTI's recently appointed CEO and president rather than the individual who in fact had promoted, incorporated, and controlled the company since its inception. The form also failed to disclose the potential civil liability stemming from Wheeler's and CTI's earlier violations of state and federal securities laws. Fehn reviewed and edited the draft of the Form 10–Q, incorporating financial statements he had obtained from CTI's accountant. Fehn maintains that he made no substantive changes to the document, and, in particular, did not delete from the report any information the SEC later contended was improperly omitted. Fehn's secretary mailed the final Form 10–Q to the SEC, where it was filed in August 1988.

Based on CTI's Form 10–Q for the quarter ending March 31, 1988, Fehn's law firm prepared and mailed two other Form 10–Q's, for the quarters ending December 31, 1987, and June 30, 1988, respectively. These forms, too, mischaracterized Wheeler's relationship to CTI, and failed to mention contingent liabilities stemming from CTI's and Wheeler's earlier securities law violations. Fehn insists that his involvement in the preparation of these later Form 10–Q's was minimal, but the SEC points out that editing notations in Fehn's handwriting appeared on drafts of these Form 10–Q's. These Form 10–Q's were filed in November 1988.

III.   *The SEC Injunctive Action Against Fehn*

In November 1992, the SEC filed a complaint against Fehn, alleging that in preparing and filing the three Form 10–Q's, Fehn had aided and abetted violations of Sections 10(b) and 15(d) of the Securities Exchange Act, 15 U.S.C. §§ 78j(b) and 78o(d), and violations of Rules 10b–5, 12b–20, and 15d–13, 17 C.F.R. §§ 240.10b–5, 240.12b–20, and 240.15d–13. Pursuant to Section 20(b) of the Securities Act of 1933, 15 U.S.C. § 77t(b), and Sections 21(d) and 21(e) of the Securities Exchange Act of 1934, 15 U.S.C. §§ 78u(d) and 78u(e), the SEC brought an action to permanently enjoin Fehn from future securities laws violations. The SEC alleged that CTI and Wheeler had violated Section 10(b) and Section 15(d) by preparing and filing Form 10–Q's that contained false accounts of Wheeler's role in the promotion, formation and management of CTI and his control over CTI stock and directors, and failed to disclose "material contingent liabilities" stemming from CTI's violations of state and federal securities laws in connection with its 1987 IPO. Additionally, the SEC alleged that Fehn had knowingly lent "substantial assist[ance]" to Wheeler and CTI in the preparation and filing of the faulty Form 10–Q's.

On April 1, 1994, following a bench trial, the district court entered final judgment against Fehn, based on its findings that Fehn had aided and abetted violations of Sections 10(b) and 15(d) of the Securities Exchange Act, the Act's antifraud and reporting provisions, respectively, along with Rules 10b–5, 12b–20, and 15d–13. Because it concluded that there was a reasonable likelihood of future violations on Fehn's part, the district court entered an order permanently enjoining Fehn from future aiding and abetting violations of the securities laws. Fehn timely appealed.

ANALYSIS

* * *

II.   *Whether the District Court Erred in Finding Fehn Liable for Aiding and Abetting Violations of Section 10(b) and Section 15(d) of the Securities Exchange Act and Related Regulations*

* * *

A.   *The Elements of Aiding and Abetting Liability under Section 104 of the Private Securities Litigation Act of 1995*

In authorizing the SEC to pursue injunctive actions for aiding and abetting violations of certain securities laws, Congress provided that Section 104 governs the "liability of controlling persons *and persons who aid and abet violations.*" Section 104 provides:

> ***(f) Prosecution of persons who aid and abet violations.*** For purposes of any action brought by the Commission under paragraph (1) or (3) of Section 78u(d) of this title, *any person that knowingly provides substantial assistance to another person in violation of a provision of this chapter, or of any rule or regulation issued under this chapter,* shall be deemed to be in violation of such provision to the same extent as the person to whom such assistance is provided. (emphasis added)

We note that Congress employed language identical to that used by lower federal courts in articulating the elements of aiding and abetting under Section 10(b) *before Central Bank* eliminated private causes of action for aiding and abetting. Before *Central Bank,* the elements of aiding and abetting under Section 10(b) were: (1) the existence of an independent primary violation; (2) actual knowledge by the alleged aider and abettor of the primary violation and of his or her own role in furthering it; and (3) "substantial assistance" by the defendant in the commission of the primary violation. *Hauser,* 14 F.3d at 1343. The new Section 104 defines aiding and abetting as follows: (1) the defendant acted "knowingly," (2) the defendant "provid[ed] substantial assistance," and (3) that assistance was given "to another person in violation of a provision of this chapter, or of any rule or regulation issued under this chapter." The elements of the new Section 104 clearly mirror the elements this Court and others traditionally used to define aiding and abetting under Section 10(b). In our view, the symmetry between the elements of aiding and abetting *before* *Central Bank* and *after* Section 104 is a strong indication that Congress intended Section 104 to preserve the definition of aiding and abetting as it existed pre-*Central Bank*.

　　* * *

1. *The Existence of a Primary Violation*

a. *Disclosure Requirements under Section 10(b) and Section 15(d)*

　　* * *

Section 15(d) is a key reporting and disclosure provision of the Securities Exchange Act, 15 U.S.C. § 78o(d). It provides that issuers that have filed registration statements with the SEC shall file with the Commission, in accordance with such rules and regulations as the Commission may prescribe as necessary or appropriate in the public interest or for the protection of investors, such *supplementary and periodic information,* documents, and reports as may be required by other provisions of the securities laws and SEC regulations. 15 U.S.C. § 78o(d) (emphasis added).

Rule 15d–13 implements Section 15(d)'s disclosure provision by requiring issuers to file quarterly 10–Q reports. Rule 12b–20 requires that, in addition to information explicitly required by other securities regulations, there shall be added such further material information, if any, as may be necessary to make the required statements, in the light of the circumstances under which they are made not misleading.

Rule 12b–20, 17 C.F.R. § 240.12b–20.

Fehn insists that the securities laws impose no duty to disclose, in a quarterly Form 10–Q, a failure to identify a company's promoter at the time of an initial public offering or the existence of prior securities law violations.

We disagree. Read against the backdrop of events in this case, these provisions required CTI and Wheeler to describe correctly Wheeler's role at CTI and to disclose the contingent liabilities stemming from earlier securities law violations.

　　* * *

2. Fehn's "Substantial Assistance" in the Primary Violation

The term "substantial assistance" has been interpreted to include "participation in the editing" of information for the purpose of marketing securities. *Molecular Technology Corp. v. Valentine,* 925 F.2d 910, 918 (6th Cir.1991). Fehn admits that he reviewed the initial draft Form 10–Q prepared by Wheeler's non-lawyer employee, and admits that he personally altered that document. Although he claims to have had less involvement in the preparation of subsequent Form 10–Q's, these documents, too, reflect Fehn's editing notations, and were prepared by Fehn's law firm. Because Fehn had a hand in the editing the Form 10–Q's, and because he failed to properly advise Wheeler and CTI of the material omissions in the Form 10–Q's, instead submitting those forms to the SEC for filing, we conclude that Fehn lent the requisite "substantial assistance" to the primary violation of Section 10(b) and Section 15(d) of the Securities Exchange Act and related regulations.

Fehn urges us that he acted in good faith in rendering professional advice to CTI and Wheeler, and that this alleged good faith precludes a finding that he rendered "substantial assistance" in the primary violations of Sections 10(b) and 15(d). He relies on *In re Carter and Johnson,* [1981] Fed. Sec. L. Rptr. (CCH) Par. 82,847 (Feb. 28, 1981), in which the SEC explained that "so long as a lawyer is acting in good faith and exerting reasonable efforts to prevent violations of the law by his client, his professional obligations have been met." *Carter,* at Par. Par. 84,172–73. We reject Fehn's argument because we find that his efforts were not "reasonable" in light of the well-established disclosure requirements imposed by the aforementioned SEC regulations. Rules 10b–5 and 12b–20 clearly prohibited the misstatements and omissions contained in CTI's Form 10–Q's.

We observe, furthermore, that effective regulation of the issuance and trading of securities depends, fundamentally, on securities lawyers such as Fehn properly advising their clients of the disclosure requirements and other relevant provisions of the securities regulations. Securities regulation in this country is premised on open disclosure, and it is therefore incumbent upon practitioners like Fehn to be highly familiar with the disclosure requirements and to insist that their clients comply with them.

* * *

We express no opinion as to whether Fehn's representation of Wheeler and CTI in connection with the SEC investigation was "compatible" with counseling these same parties about compliance with SEC disclosure requirements. What *is* clear, however, is that the SEC disclosure requirements mandated disclosure of Wheeler's role as CTI's promoter and of the contingent liabilities stemming from CTI's and Wheeler's earlier securities law violations. In failing to make the Form 10–Q's comply with these disclosure requirements, Fehn "substantially assist[ed]" in the primary disclosure violations.

3. Fehn's Scienter in Aiding and Abetting the Primary Violation

The new Section 104, in authorizing SEC injunctive actions against aiders and abettors of the securities laws, makes clear that the requisite scienter for aiding and abetting liability is "knowingly." This requirement is in keeping with the traditional scienter necessary to give rise to aiding and abetting liability under Section 10(b). See Hauser, 14 F.3d at 1343 (requiring "actual knowledge" of the primary wrong and of the aider and abettor's "role in furthering [that violation]").

Fehn's knowledge of the primary violations was plainly established in this case. First, Fehn knew that the representations in CTI's registration statement with respect to Wheeler's role as promoter were inaccurate. In light of the information Fehn possessed when he undertook to review and edit the Form 10–Q's, Fehn must have known that the Form 10–Q's he helped to prepare perpetuated this inaccuracy and, furthermore, contained additional untrue statements about Wheeler's historical relationship with CTI. Second, Fehn knew there was material information about CTI that Wheeler did not wish to disclose in the quarterly Form 10–Q reports, since Wheeler informed Fehn in no uncertain terms of his refusal to disclose in the Form 10–Q's his potential liability for past securities law violations. The "knowledge" element was therefore clearly established in this case.

* * *

CONCLUSION

We affirm the district court's final judgment against Fehn and its order permanently enjoining Fehn from future aiding and abetting of violations of Sections 10(b) and 15(d) of the Securities Exchange Act of 1934 and related regulations.

PROBLEM 18–4

June Lui, an associate of the major Wall Street firm of Smith & Folk ["S&F"] has been asked by partner Richard B. Ito to research the proper response to a "client problem."

S&F's largest client, World Bank, has hired S&F to complete due diligence, on a $1.2 billion debt underwriting to be filed on the SEC's abbreviated Form S–3.

Currently interest rates are extremely favorable. World Bank would like Ito to complete his due diligence within three days.

Lui is concerned that World Bank has not produced Board of Directors Executive Committee Minutes for the previous year. She has repeatedly requested these Minutes and repeatedly been informed, "They are in illegible handwritten form. There isn't time to type them up. There is nothing of significance in them."

Lui is aware of rumors that the Internal Revenue Service is conducting an investigation of World Bank, but has found no document to substantiate the rumors. World Bank's Chief Financial Officer has specifically denied such an IRS investigation.

(1) If Ito signs off on the World Bank without review of the Executive Committee Meeting Minutes, what risk is there of an S&F Rule 102(e) violation?

(2) Assuming that World Bank refuses to produce the Minutes, what can Ito do that would be consistent with both applicable ABA Model Rules of Professional Conduct and the federal securities laws?

ACCOUNTANTS' INDEPENDENCE

The SEC has long expressed strong views with respect to the independence of the outside certifying accountant.[1]

In order to fortify the independence of certified public accountants, the Commission in 1974 required that whenever the auditor for a registered company is dismissed or resigns, a report must be filed on Form 8–K of any "disagreements" between the auditor and the management of the company within the prior two years.[2]

---

1. An accountant, as we have seen, can be liable under § 11 of the Securities Act of 1933; in an SEC aiding and abetting action; under Rule 102(e); or state common law. See generally 2 Louis Loss & Joel Seligman, Securities Regulation 751–766 (3d ed. rev. 1999), Douglas M. Schwab, Jerry L. Marks & Jeffrey A. Richmond, Claims between Auditors and Their Clients, 32 Rev. Sec. & Commodities Reg. 139 (1999); Paul A. Brown, Jeanne A. Calderon & Baruch Lev, Administrative and Judicial Approaches to Auditor Independence, 30 Seton Hall L. Rev. 443 (2000); cf. Ross D. Fuerman, The Role of Auditor Culpability in Naming Auditor Defendants in United States Securities Class Actions, 10 Crit. Perspectives on Acct. 315 (1999) (nonculpable auditors were not routinely named defendants in securities class actions before the 1995 Act); Ross D. Fuerman, Auditors and the Post–Litigation Reform Act Environment. 14 Research Acct. Reg. 1999 (2000) (auditors are named as defendants less frequently in federal securities class actions than in parallel proceedings).

2. Sec. Act Rel. 5550, 5 SEC Dock. 799 (1974).

In 1995, as part of the Private Securities Reform Act, § 10A was added to the Securities Exchange Act to authorize the Commission to modify or supplement generally accepted auditing standards to establish:

(1) procedures designed to provide reasonable assurance of detecting illegal acts that would have a direct and material effect on the determination of financial statement amounts;

(2) procedures designed to identify related party transactions that are material to the financial statements or otherwise require disclosure therein; and

(3) an evaluation of whether there is substantial doubt about the ability of the issuer to continue as a going concern during the ensuring fiscal year.

If an independent public accountant detects or otherwise becomes aware of information indicating that an illegal act (whether or not material) has or may occur, the accountant must inform the appropriate level of management of the issuer and assure that the audit committee or the board is adequately informed with respect to the illegal acts.[3] Failure to respond to a *material* illegal act will require the accountant to report its conclusions to the board,[4] or to resign or to furnish to the Commission a copy of its report.[5]

As adopted in 1997, Rule 10A–1(a) requires an issuer who receives a report requiring a notice to the Commission in accordance with § 10A(b)(3) to provide the notice to the Office of Chief Accountant with the issuer having the option to provide either a summary of the report or a copy of the report itself. If a summary is provided, it must describe "the act that the independent accountant has identified as a likely illegal act and the possible effect of this act on all affected financial statements of the issuer or those related to the most current three-year period, whichever is shorter."[6] Separately the independent accountant must provide the Office of the Chief Accountant a copy of its report (or documentation of any oral report).[7]

By the late 1990s the extent to which management consulting and other services had become more significant to many outside auditor-corporate relationships than auditing itself emerged as the most significant SEC accounting issue.[8]

---

3. Sec. Ex. Act § 10A(b)(1).

4. See Sec. Ex. Act § 10A(b)(2)

5. Sec. Ex. Act § 10A(b)(3).

6. Rule 10A–1(a)(2)(iii)(A).

7. Rule 10A–1(b)(1). See also Edward Cohen, New Section 10A: Illegal Conduct Identified in an Audit, 14 Insights No. 3 at 2 (2000).

8. Cf. Address by Arthur Levitt, Reviewing the Covenant with Investors (N.Y.U. Center for Law and Bus. May 10, 2000):

In fact, today auditing no longer dominates the practices of the largest firms. It accounts for just 30 percent of total revenues—down from 70 percent in 1977. Consulting and other management advisory services now represent over half—up from 12 percent in 1977. Since 1993, auditing revenues have been growing by 9 percent per year on average—while consulting and similar services have been growing at a rate of 27 percent each year.

Id. at 3.

Later in 2000, the Commission proposed rule amendments concerning auditor indepen-

In its 2000 proposed rule amendments concerns auditor independence, the Commission stated in part:

How Non–Audit Services Can Affect Auditor Independence.

The dramatic expansion of non-audit services may fundamentally alter the relationships between auditors and their audit clients in two principal ways. First, as auditing becomes an ever-smaller portion of a firm's business with its audit clients, auditors become increasingly vulnerable to economic pressures from audit clients. Second, certain non-audit services, by their very nature, raise independence issues. These concerns * * * have led us to consider whether our rules should limit—or even completely bar—an auditor's provision of non-audit services to audit clients.[9]

In August 2000 the Panel on Audit Effectiveness issued a report and recommendations. The Panel, which was chaired by Shaun O'Malley, former Chair of Price Waterhouse LLP, was created by the Public Oversight Board at the request of SEC Chairman Arthur Levitt.

The Panel divided on whether to support or reject an exclusionary rule that would prohibit an audit firm generally from providing nonaudit and nontax services to public audit clients.[10]

In November 2000 the Commission adopted a revision of Rule 2–01 of Regulation S–X, the auditor's independence requirements.[11] The Commission chose *not* to adopt a total ban on nonaudit services and instead identified certain nonaudit services that render the auditor not independent of the client.[12]

A preliminary Note to Rule 2–01 of Regulation S–X explains:

Rule 2–01(b) sets forth the general standard of auditor independence. Paragraphs (c)(1) to (c)(5) reflect the application of the general standard to particular circumstances. The rule does not purport to, and the Commission could not, consider all circumstances that raise independence concerns, and these are subject to the general standard in paragraph 2–01(b). In considering this standard, the Commission looks in the first instance to whether a relationship or the provision of a service: (a) creates a mutual or conflicting interest between the accountant and the audit client; (b) places

dence. Sec. Ex Act. Rel. 42,994, 72 SEC Dock. 1901 (2000). Appendix B amplified the trend away from accounting and advisory services (A&A) towards management consulting and other services (MCS) for what are now the "Big 5" Public Accounting Firms.

Estimated U.S. Revenues for Big 5/Big 6 Public Accounting Firms

	1999	1998	1997	1996	1995	1994	1993
Total	$30,616	$25,917	$20,492	$17,305	$15,051	$13,291	$12,162

Estimated revenue mix by service line

	1999	1998	1997	1996	1995	1994	1993
A&A	30%	30%	33%	36%	38%	44%	45%
Tax	19%	19%	20%	20%	20%	20%	22%
MCS	51%	51%	47%	44%	42%	36%	32%

9. Id. at 1908.

10. POB, Panel on Audit Effectiveness 3 (2000).

11. Sec. Ex. Act Rel. 43,602, 73 SEC Dock. 1885 (2000) (adoption).

12. Id. at 1888–1889.

the accountant in the position of auditing his or her own work; (c) results in the accountant acting as management or an employee of the audit client; or (d) places the accountant in a position of being an advocate for the audit client.

The most significant addition was Rule 2–01(c)(4), which defines when an accountant will be independent with respect to nonaudit services. Rule 2–01(c)(4) begins:

> (4) *Non-audit services.* An accountant is not independent if, at any point during the audit and professional engagement period, the accountant provides the following non-audit services to an audit client.

The Rule then elaborates at length concerning (i) bookkeeping or other services relating to the audit client's accounting records or other financial statements; (ii) financial information systems design and implementation; (iii) appraisal or valuation services; (iv) actuarial services; (v) internal audit services; (vi) management functions; (vii) human resources; (viii) broker-dealer services; and (ix) legal services.[13]

In the period following adoption of the revised Rule 2–01 the Commission has brought high profile cases against Big Five accounting firms.

Early in 2001 the Commission ruled in a Rule 102(e) proceeding that KPMG Peat Marwick could not be considered independent when it conducted an audit of a registrant while a loan from the accounting firm to an officer of the registrant was outstanding.[14]

THE SARBANES–OXLEY ACT

In Congressional hearings preceding the Sarbanes–Oxley Act, particular attention was devoted to the wisdom of separating accounting firm audit services from consulting. One early result of Enron had been an acceleration of this process by voluntary means in the Big Five accounting firms. Former SEC Chairman David Ruder thoughtfully explained:

> One of the substantial worries regarding the Andersen audit of Enron has been that Andersen not only audited Enron, but also was paid approximately the same amount for non-audit services. It has been reported that in the year 2000 Andersen was paid audit fees of approximately $25 million and non-audit fees of approximately $27 million. Comparisons of the amounts of audit fees to non-audit fees for a range of companies and auditors have revealed ratios of non-audit to audit fees ranging as high as nine to one. The expressed general concern is that an audit cannot be objective if the auditor is receiving substantial non-audit fees.

> The accounting profession seems to have recognized that management consulting services, which involve accounting firms in helping management make business decisions, should not be performed for an audit client. Three of the Big Five accounting firms (Andersen, Ernst & Young, and KPMG) have now separated their management consulting units from their

---

13. Simultaneously the Commission reinstated earlier proxy statement disclosure in Item 9(e) of Proxy Schedule 14A to require independent public accountants to disclose aggregate fees for audit and nonaudit services.

14. KMPG Peat Marwick LLP, AAER 1374, 74 SEC Dock. 1147 (2001) (former Rule 2–01(b)).

audit units by contractual splits and spinoffs, and a fourth (Pricewater-houseCoopers) has announced its intention to split off its management consulting unit in a public offering. (Wall Street Journal, p3, January 31, 2002) The fifth firm should also do so, or at least refrain from offering management consulting services to audit clients.[1]

The Sarbanes–Oxley Act is quite prohibitive. Section 201 would amend § 10A of the 1934 Act to provide:

(g) PROHIBITED ACTIVITIES.—Except as provided in subsection (h), it shall be unlawful for a registered public accounting firm (and any associated person of that firm, to the extent determined appropriate by the Commission) that performs for any issuer any audit required by this title or the rules of the Commission under this title or, beginning 180 days after the date of commencement of the operations of the Public Company Accounting Oversight Board ... to provide to that issuer, contemporaneously with the audit, any non-audit service, including—

(1) bookkeeping or other services related to the accounting records or financial statements of the audit client;

(2) financial information systems design and implementation;

(3) appraisal or valuation services, fairness opinions, or contribution-in-kind reports;

(4) actuarial services;

(5) internal audit outsourcing services;

(6) management functions or human resources;

(7) broker or dealer, investment adviser, or investment banking services;

(8) legal services and expert services unrelated to the audit; and

(9) any other service that the Board determines, by regulation, is impermissible.

(h) PREAPPROVAL REQUIRED FOR NON–AUDIT SERVICES.—A registered public accounting firm may engage in any non-audit service, including tax services, that is not described in any of paragraphs (1) through (9) of subsection (g) for an audit client, only if the activity is approved in advance by the audit committee of the issuer, in accordance with subsection (i).

The Board is authorized in § 201(b) to exempt any person, issuer, public accounting firm or transaction from the prohibitions in § 10A(g) on a case by case basis.

Section 202 then adds a new § 10A(i) to create a preapproval requirement for audit committees both with respect to audit and nonaudit services provided to the issuer by an auditor. Under the new § 10A(i)(B) preapproval is waived with respect to nonaudit services that constitute not more than 5 percent of the total amount of revenues paid by the issuer to the auditor.

---

1. Senate Comm. On Banking, Housing & Urban Affairs, Hearing on "Accounting and Investor Protection Issues Raised in En-ron and Other Public Companies," Feb. 12, 2002 (testimony of David S. Ruder), at 2.

Section 206 further prohibits a public accounting firm from performing any audit service for an issuer if a senior officer of the issuer was employed by the auditor within the prior year.

In essence the Sarbanes–Oxley Act does not so much totally prohibit auditors from providing nonaudit services, but does limit such services to immaterial amounts.

To the Senate Committee on Banking, Housing & Urban Affairs, "[t]he issue of auditor independence is at the center of this legislation."[2] The Senate Committee Report emphasized it took a middle course neither completely prohibiting all nonaudit consulting services nor totally leaving the issue to the SEC or the new Board:

> The intention of this provision is to draw a clear line around a limited list of non-audit services that accounting firms may not provide to public company audit clients because their doing so creates a fundamental conflict of interest for the accounting firms. The list is based on simple principles. An accounting firm, in order to be independent of its audit client, should not audit its own work, which would be involved in providing bookkeeping services, financial information systems design, appraisal or valuation services, actuarial services, and internal audit outsourcing services to an audit client. The accounting firm should not function as part of management or as an employee of the audit client, which would be required if the accounting firm provides human resources services such as recruiting, hiring, and designing compensation packages for the officers, directors, and managers of an audit client. The accounting firm should not act as an advocate of the audit client, which would be involved in providing legal and expert services to an audit client in legal, administrative, or regulatory proceedings, or serving as a broker-dealer, investment adviser, or investment banker to an audit client, which places the auditor in the role of promoting a client's stock or other interests.[3]

Perhaps of greater significance is the fact that the Sarbanes–Oxley Act does not require the division of an accounting firm into an audit firm and a separate nonaudit firm. It requires instead that for each audit client there is a prohibition of nine nonaudit services and a preapproval requirement for other nonaudit services. This means an audit firm can continue to provide nonaudit services to other clients.

In Arthur Andersen LLP,[4] the Commission settled a Rule 102(e) action with a major accounting firm after the Commission found that the firm failed "to stand up to management in the face of improper accounting practices but instead issued qualified audit reports on financial statements that it knew or is reckless in not knowing are misstated."[5]

D.   Corporate Registrants, Officers, and Directors

In recent years the Commission has also increasingly relied on the internal accounting controls required by § 13(b)(2) of the Securities Exchange Act and the corporate audit committee to ensure accurate corporate reporting.

---

2. S. Rep. No. 107–205, 107th Cong., 2d Sess. (2002).

3. Id. at 18; see generally id. at 15–18.

4. AAER 1405, 75 SEC Dock. 501 (2001).

5. Id. at 511. See also Litig. Rel. 17,039, 75 SEC Dock. 612 (2001).

In 1977, as part of the Foreign Corrupt Practices Act, Congress enacted § 13(b)(2). That Section requires every corporation subject to § 12 or § 15(d) of the 1934 Act to

(A) make and keep books, records, and accounts, which, in reasonable detail, accurately and fairly reflect the transactions and dispositions of the assets of the issuer; and

(B) devise and maintain a system of internal accounting controls sufficient to provide reasonable assurances that

(i) transactions are executed in accordance with management's general or specific authorization;

(ii) transactions are recorded as necessary (I) to permit preparation of financial statements in conformity with generally accepted accounting principles or any other criteria applicable to such statements, and (II) to maintain accountability for assets;

(iii) access to assets is permitted only in accordance with management's general or specific authorization; and

(iv) the recorded accountability for assets is compared with the existing assets at reasonable intervals and appropriate action is taken with respect to any differences.

In 1988 Congress adopted the Foreign Corrupt Practices Act Amendments, which added §§ 13(b)(4)–(7).[1] These new Sections limit criminal liability to persons who *knowingly* violate § 13(b)(2); discharge the liability of an issuer owning 50 percent or less of a subsidiary when the issuer makes a good faith effort to cause the subsidiary to comply with § 13(b)(2); and define the terms *reasonable assurances* and *reasonable detail* to mean "such level of detail and degree of assurance as would satisfy prudent officials in the conduct of their own affairs."[2]

SEC § 13(b)(2) proceedings are against the corporate registrant or its officers and directors. In effect this creates a second set of individuals—in addition to the corporation's auditors—with responsibility for corporate books and records.

Consider the following.

SEC v. World–Wide Coin Investments, Ltd.

567 F.Supp. 724 (N.D.Ga.1983).

■ VINING, DISTRICT JUDGE.

This is a securities fraud action in which the Securities and Exchange Commission (SEC) seeks a permanent injunction against World–Wide Coin Investments, Ltd. (World–Wide) and the individual defendants as well as an

---

1. *See* H.R. Rep. No. 100–576, 100th Cong., 2d Sess. 916–917 (1988).

2. See generally Symposium, The Foreign Corrupt Practices Act on Its Twentieth Anniversary: Its Application, Defense and International Aftermath, 18 Nw. J. Int'l L. & Bus. 269 (1998); Kathleen A. Lacey & Barbara C. George, Expansion of SEC Authority into Internal Corporate Governance: The Accounting Provisions of the Foreign Corrupt Practices Act (A Twentieth Anniversary Review), 7 J. Transnat'l L. & Pol'y 119 (1998); Kenneth B. Winer, Securities Firms and the Foreign Corrupt Practices Act, 33 Rev. Sec. & Commodities Reg. 61 (2000).

order for a full accounting and disclosure of wrongfully received benefits. In an order entered March 29, 1983, this court directed the clerk to enter judgment for the SEC on all counts of the complaint and further directed defendants Hale and Seibert to (1) retain an independent auditor to perform a full accounting of World–Wide of all receipts and disbursements of cash and all purchases and sales and other acquisitions and dispositions of inventory and assets since July 1, 1979, and (2) return whatever shares of World–Wide stock they might hold to World–Wide. Finally, the court ordered World–Wide to make a full disclosure to its present shareholders with respect to all material information relating to its operations since July 1, 1979. The following memorandum opinion will constitute this court's findings of fact and conclusions of law as required by Fed.R.Civ.P. 52(a).

Factual Background

World–Wide Coin Investments, Ltd., is a Delaware corporation with its principal offices in Atlanta, Georgia, and is engaged primarily in the wholesale and retail sale of rare coins, precious metals, gold and silver coins, bullion, and, until 1979, in the retail sale of camera equipment. Its operations also include the sale of Coca–Cola collector items and certain commemorative items. Its inventory of rare coins comes from its purchases of collections from estates and private individuals, purchases from dealers, purchases on domestic commodities exchanges, and purchases at coin shows. Sales are transacted at the Atlanta office and at many major coin shows held in the United States. For some time it published a trade journal, The Coin Wholesaler, which carried both news and feature stories of special interest to coin collectors and investors, who comprised the majority of subscribers. Until August 1979, through its subsidiary World–Wide Camera Fair, Inc., World–Wide operated retail stores in Augusta, Athens, Savannah, Columbus, Georgia, and Jacksonville, Florida, selling camera and photographic equipment. All five stores were sold during the first quarter of fiscal year 1980.

World–Wide's common stock is registered with the SEC pursuant to the Securities Exchange Act of 1934, 15 U.S.C. § 78l(b), and until late 1981 was listed on the Boston Stock Exchange. Prior to July 1979, the company's assets totaled over $2,000,000, and it had over 40 employees. In August 1981, the time of the filing of this lawsuit, the company's assets amounted to less than $500,000, and it had only three employees.

Defendant Joseph H. Hale took over the management and control of World–Wide on July 24, 1979, as the controlling shareholder, chairman of the board, chief executive officer, and president. * * *

On November 5, 1979, Kanes, Benator, as World–Wide's independent auditor, warned Hale and World–Wide that a good and sound internal accounting control system was necessary to ensure the safeguarding of assets against losses from unauthorized use of dispositions and of financial records for preparing financial statements and maintaining accountability for assets. Although the company was notified of the importance of a good system of internal controls, this warning was ignored, and any control system that had existed at World–Wide ceased to exist. The problems that occurred at the company with respect to internal controls and accounting procedures can be divided into three areas: (1) inventory problems, (2) problems with separation of duties and the lack of documentation of transactions, and (3) problems with the books, records, and accounting procedures of the company.

(1) Inventory Problems

The safeguarding of World–Wide's physical inventory was one of its most severe problems; there was considerable testimony at trial to the effect that the company's vault, where most of the rare coins were kept, was unguarded and left open all day to all employees. Furthermore, no one employee was responsible for the issuance of coins from the vault, according to the accountants from May, Zima, who performed the 1980 audit. Scrap silver and bags of silver coins were left unattended in the hallways and in several cluttered, unlocked rooms at World–Wide's offices. During the trial, Hale admitted that he was worried about thefts due both to faulty record-keeping and the system of safeguarding the assets.

Hale also failed to initiate an adequate system of itemizing World–Wide's physical inventory. Rather than maintaining a perpetual inventory system, the company relied on a manual quarterly system, which, in light of the company's inadequate securities measures, was not effective in safeguarding the assets or in keeping an accurate account of the inventory. World–Wide's system made it relatively simple for an employee to improperly value and/or misappropriate large items of inventory undetected. Furthermore, employees were allowed to take large amounts of inventory off the premises of World–Wide for purposes of effecting a sale without giving a receipt.

An accurate valuation of World–Wide's inventory was never accomplished, and Clifford Haygood, the accountant from May, Zima who performed the field work for the 1980 audit, testified that a major reason for the disclaimed opinion in 1980 was the inability to determine the valuation of the cost inventory. Haygood also testified that he was unable to determine the cost of inventory, since World–Wide failed to have adequate purchase orders as documentation to determine the correct cost.[22]

Haygood, along with Robert Nofal, a coin expert hired by May, Zima to determine the value of World–Wide's coin inventory, inspected the offices of World–Wide for approximately 4 ½ days beginning July 30, 1980. After Nofal's examination of the coins, Haygood concluded that the value of inventory by Hale required a substantial write-down of 10% of the value at which they were being carried on World–Wide's books. With respect to the $225,000 "appraisal" of the medallions involved in the 1979 stock swap, Haygood stated that no actual appraisal was ever done since the items were never actually physically inspected, which is necessary for an accurate appraisal.

Nofal testified that he could not determine how much was actually paid for the coins in World–Wide's inventory, since there were no backup documents and only a few coins were cost-coded.[23] Nofal further testified that there was no organization of the inventory and that the vault was open without a guard when he came into the store.

22. Under GAAP (generally accepted accounting principles), a company's inventory must be stated at the lower of cost price or market price. Since World–Wide had no records or purchase orders with respect to its inventory, Haygood was unable to determine the cost under either method.

23. Cost-coding is a form of internal control device used in the coin business; coins are marked with a special code indicating their purchase price and date of purchase. Nofal testified that this type of device is an excellent control over theft problems, which are prevalent in a business with a large inventory such as coins.

(2) Separation of Duties

The lack of qualified personnel working in World–Wide's offices and the company's policy of allowing one individual to accomplish numerous transactions was another primary reason for May, Zima's disclaimed opinion, and was a major concern of Kanes, Benator in its letter of November 5, 1979. This court has previously noted the lack of supervision over the accounting department, managed by Patricia Allen, and her lack of expertise in the area. World–Wide maintains no separation of duties in the area of purchase and sales transactions, and valuation procedures for ending inventory. For instance, a single salesperson can do all the following tasks without supervision or review by another employer or officer: appraise a particular coin offered for purchase by a customer, purchase that coin with a check that the salesperson alone has drawn, count that same coin into inventory, value the coin for inventory purposes, and sell the coin to another purchaser.

Employees, none of whom was bonded, were also allowed to take large amounts of inventory off the company's premises for purposes of effecting a sale without giving a receipt, as well as being given cash to purchase the precious metals and coins at various locations, also without giving a receipt. Nor were employees required to write source documents relating to the purchase and sale of coins, bullion, and other inventory, making it impossible, as Haygood testified, to ascertain whether a particular inventory item had been sold at a profit or loss, or whether it had even been sold. Although pre-numbered invoices could have been used to help alleviate this problem, they were not; there was a complete lack of control over any retail countersales, and Haygood testified that he could not match cash coming in or out with the merchandise going out. The company apparently did have a daily report of cash coming in, but there was no record of items purchased or sold. Hale himself admitted that he told his employees to write down the sales of total bullion rather than writing receipts for individual coins.

Additionally, there were no procedures enforced with respect to writing checks; for instance, no system has been implemented to ensure that the purpose for which a check is written can be ascertained. Since employees have been allowed to write checks without noting the purpose of the transaction on the instrument or on any other document, source documents for most checks do not exist. All employees have had access to presigned checks, and there has been no dollar limit over which an employee cannot write a check. Furthermore, employees have not been required to get approval before writing a check. These policies have caused World–Wide to bounce over 100 checks since Hale took over the management of the company. Because of World–Wide's propensity for having their checks returned due to insufficient funds, the National Bank of Georgia, the company's transfer agent, requested World–Wide to close its account and take its business elsewhere.

Evidence introduced at trial further revealed that approximately $1.7 million worth of checks were written to Hale, his affiliates, or to cash, all without supporting documentation or any indication of the purpose of the checks. Hale testified that approximately $250,000 worth of these checks were repayments of loans he had personally made to the company, but he failed to introduce any executed promissory notes or any document to support that claim. The SEC also introduced various checks to and/or bills from local bars and restaurants written by Hale and reimbursed by either World–Wide or East Coast Coin. Numerous checks written to Hale on World–Wide's account were superimposed over purchase orders, supposedly as source documentation for the transactions.

(3) Books and Records

The lack of qualified accounting personnel not only created problems with World–Wide's inventory but also resulted in completely inaccurate and incomplete books and records. World–Wide, Hale, and Seibert have failed to make and keep books, records, and accounts which accurately and clearly reflect the transactions and dispositions of World–Wide's assets. As discussed previously, World–Wide employees have not been required to write purchase orders or any source document relating to the purchase and sale of coins and bullion, rendering it impossible to arrive at an accurate count or valuation of the inventory.

During his inspection of World–Wide's offices, Haygood stated that the records of operations for Hale's subsidiaries, such as World–Wide Camera Fair, were scattered throughout the office and were not in any order. Although Haygood was aware of the existence of World–Wide Camera Fair following a review of Kanes, Benator's work papers from 1979, he stated that he was unsure about the documentation and the sale of other companies such as World–Wide Rare Metals and Chattanooga Coin and Stamp. With respect to this latter subsidiary, Haygood was unable to identify it as a separate and existing corporation since it had been merged into World–Wide's balance sheet, making it impossible to differentiate between the good will of World–Wide and that of Chattanooga Coin and Stamp. Furthermore, this failure to consolidate the subsidiaries into the form and financial statements rendered the 10Q reports incorrect for fiscal year 1980.

Haygood also testified the company's books were chaotic with respect to the deferred revenue received from subscriptions to the company newspaper, The Coin Wholesaler. There were no accurate records setting out the dates of subscriptions; therefore, the amount of deferred revenue simply had to be estimated on the company's books.

During May, Zima's inspection at the premises, on July 31, 1980, Haygood and other representatives from May, Zima met with Jones and Seibert to express their concern about the state of World–Wide's control procedures and accounting methods. Each item of concern was discussed in detail including questions from Seibert and Jones relative to the evaluation of the potential effects on the company and the continued trading of the common stock. May, Zima explained the position of Robert Nofal and offered to have a second opinion in order to confirm his initial evaluation that the grading policy and inventory values were significantly higher than was appropriate. Seibert and Jones acknowledged the problems noted and agreed that a totally separate inventory would be prepared by Nofal and later compared to the inventory prepared by the company's employee with appropriate reconciliation of differences in order to establish an acceptable, reasonable valuation of inventory. Robert Johnson, a partner at May, Zima, suggested that the company immediately obtain and consult with a securities attorney relative to the necessary action that should be taken as a result of the information May, Zima provided concerning its evaluation of the company's internal accounting control system and the effect on May, Zima's opinion. Johnson further indicated that there was a possible violation of the Foreign Corrupt Practices Act and that World–Wide should seek advice concerning that possibility. Johnson explained that the

May, Zima would be willing to assist World–Wide through further discussions of these matters and/or offer suggestions to remedy the situations noted. Furthermore, Haygood offered to go to the Securities and Exchange Commission with the company to resolve their problems, but Seibert stated that he would rather take his chances and not contact the SEC in the hope that the SEC would not contact him.

World–Wide eventually agreed to retain the law firm of Jones, Bird & Howell and met with Frank Bird of that firm on August 18, 1980. At that meeting, there was a discussion of how World–Wide should communicate to the SEC. Bird agreed that the disclosure should be made immediately and that a Form 8K should be filed on the report received from the company's auditors advising it of a possible problem with the provisions of the Foreign Corrupt Practices Act, a possible disclaimer of opinion on the company's financial statements and the effects on the company's estimated net income resulting from the write-off of investments and subsidiaries. Seibert agreed to draft a Form 8K to disclose these items and to make a press release on the revised estimated income.

Following the initial meeting on July 31, 1980, May, Zima wrote a letter to World–Wide on August 21, 1980, detailing the weaknesses noted in its system of internal accounting controls. In this letter, May, Zima listed the following deficiencies: (1) a lack of supervision in the accounting department, (2) a lack of reliability in the bookkeeping department because of no supervision, (3) a lack of segregation of duties in the accounting department, emphasizing that the segregation of duties would allow for proper checks and balances in the company's accounting system, (4) a lack of control over retail counter sales in that there were no prenumbered invoices and the company could not match cash coming in with merchandise going out, (5) a lack of segregation of duties in the department of purchases and sales of coins, (6) the lack of determined value on some of the items of inventory such as the Coca–Cola memorabilia, (7) problems with "related-party" transactions (transactions between World–Wide and insiders or stockholders).

On October 22, 1980, May, Zima wrote a memorandum to the board of directors of World–Wide, setting forth certain recommendations of procedures which the accounting firm felt would improve and strengthen the company's present system. May, Zima suggested (1) a change in the company's system of cash received and disbursements, suggesting that a listing of mail receipts be prepared by the individual who opens the mail and compared to the bank deposit slip and amounts recorded in the cash receipts journal, (2) petty cash reimbursements should be drawn to the petty cash custodian and not to cash, (3) aging accounts receivable should be reviewed on a periodic basis by an appropriate official separate from the accounting department, (4) an improvement in the safeguarding of the assets of the company, and a provision for regular inspection of the assets, (5) routine procedures to be developed providing for prompt and adequate reporting to the accounting department of sales and/or disposals of property and equipment, (6) utilization of prenumbered inventory tags to facilitate accounting for, and control of, the inventory, (7) obtaining cancelled notes payable from creditors when paid, (8) the maintenance of personnel files for all employees and the rotation of the distribution of payroll checks among appropriate officials, (9) the bonding of employees who receive, disburse, or handle cash or who have access to assets and records, (10) full documentation of travel and entertainment expenses, and (11) a mathematical check for sales and vendor invoices.

Although notified of a possible violation of the Foreign Corrupt Practices Act and of severe problems in the company's internal controls system and accounting procedures, World–Wide did little, if anything, to change its methods of operation. Steve Watson, a staff accountant with the SEC, reviewed World–Wide's accounting records in September 1981 and concluded that there was still inadequate documentation to support purchases made and that the internal controls of the company were inadequate. Watson indicated at trial that the company currently issues receipts for cash sales and has started taking quarterly inventories but that the controls of the company are still inadequate since there are no controls over the inventory itself. He further stated that he was unable to determine the cost of inventory in accordance with generally accepted accounting principles. * * *

APPLICATION OF LAW

I. FOREIGN CORRUPT PRACTICES ACT

The Foreign Corrupt Practices Act, 15 U.S.C. § 78m(b)(2) (Amend. 1977) ("FCPA") was enacted by Congress as an amendment to the 1934 Securities Exchange Act and was the legislative response to numerous questionable and illegal foreign payments by United States corporations in the 1970's. Although one of the major substantive provisions of the FCPA is to require corporate disclosure of assets as a deterrent to foreign bribes, the more significant addition of the FCPA is the accounting controls or "books and records" provision, which gives the SEC authority over the entire financial management and reporting requirements of publicly held United States corporations.

The FCPA was enacted on the principle that accurate recordkeeping is an essential ingredient in promoting management responsibility and is an affirmative requirement for publicly held American corporations to strengthen the accuracy of corporate books and records, which are "the bedrock elements of our system of corporate disclosure and accountability." A motivating factor in the enactment of the FCPA was a desire to protect the investor, as was the purpose behind the enactment of the Securities Acts. It is apparent that investors are entitled to rely on the implicit representations that corporations will account for their funds properly and will not channel funds out of the corporation or omit to include such funds in the accounting system so that there are no checks possible on how much of the corporation's funds are being expended in the manner management later claims.

Like the anti-fraud provisions of the 1934 Securities Exchange Act, the FCPA's provisions on accounting controls are short and deceptively straightforward. Section 13(b)(2) of the FCPA provides that every issuer having a class of securities registered pursuant to section 12 of the Exchange Act shall:

> (a) Make and keep books, records, and accounts which, in reasonable detail, accurately and fairly reflect the transactions and dispositions of the assets of the issuer; and

> (b) Devise and maintain a system of internal accounting controls sufficient to provide reasonable assurances that

>> (i) transactions are executed in accordance with management's general or specific authorization;

(ii) transactions are recorded as necessary (I) to permit preparation of financial statements in conformity with generally accepted accounting principles or any other criteria applicable to such statements, and (II) to maintain accountability for assets;

(iii) access to assets is permitted only in accordance with management's general or specific authorization; and

(iv) the recorded accountability for assets is compared with the existing assets at reasonable intervals and appropriate action is taken with respect to any differences.

Moreover, SEC Regulation 13b–2 was promulgated pursuant to section 13(b)(2) and is entitled "Maintenance of Records and Preparation of Required Reports," contains the following rules:

Rule 13b2–1: No person shall, directly or indirectly, falsify or cause to be falsified, any book, record or account subject to Section 13(b)(2)(A) of the Securities Exchange Act.

Rule 13b2–2: No director or officer of an issuer shall, directly or indirectly,

(a) make or cause to be made a materially false or misleading statement, or

(b) omit to state, or cause another person to omit to state, any material fact necessary in order to make statements made, in light of the circumstances under which such statements were made, not misleading to an accountant in connection with (1) any audit or examination of the financial statements of the issuer required to be made pursuant to this subpart or (2) the preparation or filing of any document or report required to be filed with the Commission pursuant to this subpart or otherwise.

It is clear that section 13(b)(2) and the rules promulgated thereunder are rules of general application which were enacted to (1) assure that an issuer's books and records accurately and fairly reflect its transactions and the disposition of assets, (2) protect the integrity of the independent audit of issuer financial statements that are required under the Exchange Act, and (3) promote the reliability and completeness of financial information that issuers are required to file with the Commission or disseminate to investors pursuant to the Exchange Act.

The accounting provisions of the FCPA will undoubtedly affect the governance and accountability mechanisms of most major and minor corporations, the work of their independent auditors, and the role of the Securities and Exchange Commission. The maintenance of financial records and internal accounting controls are major every-day activities of every registered and/or reporting company. The FCPA also has important implications for the SEC, since the incorporation of the accounting provisions into the federal securities laws confers on the SEC new rulemaking and enforcement authority over the control and record-keeping mechanisms of its registrants. The FCPA reflects a congressional determination that the scope of the federal securities laws and the SEC's authority should be expanded beyond the traditional ambit of disclosure requirements. The consequence of adding these substantive requirements governing accounting control to the federal securities laws will significantly augment the degree of federal involvement in the internal management of public corporations.

Since the FCPA became effective, the SEC has interpreted its authority to enforce the act's requirements quite broadly, taking the position that "it is important that issuers * * * review their accounting procedures, systems of internal accounting controls and business practices in order that they may take any actions necessary to comply with the requirements contained in the Act." The SEC has three basic tools to enforce the requirements of the FCPA: (1) judicial injunctions to prevent violations pursuant to section 21(d) of the 1934 Securities Exchange Act, 15 U.S.C. § 78u(d), (2) the ability to institute administrative proceedings to compel issuer compliance with the provisions of the FCPA or to discipline certain categories of persons who cause violations pursuant to section 15(c)(4) of the 1934 Act, 15 U.S.C. § 78o (c)(4), and Rule 2(e) of the SEC's Rules of Practice, 17 C.F.R. § 201.2e, and (3) the opportunity to refer the case to the Department of Justice for criminal proceedings.

From 1977 to 1979, the SEC was primarily preoccupied with the prevention of the foreign bribery provisions of the FCPA; however, the thrust of its enforcement proceedings at present are with the section 13(b)(2) violations. The FCPA actions currently being litigated by the SEC indicate that it apparently intends to rely heavily on the Act to address management misfeasance, misuse of corporate assets and other conduct reflecting adversely on management's integrity. The instant case is the first action to be litigated throughout trial; most of the other cases have been settled prior to trial or have not been brought to trial.

Section 13(b)(2) contains two separate requirements for issuers in complying with the FCPA's accounting provisions: (1) a company must keep accurate books and records reflecting the transactions and dispositions of the assets of the issuer, and (2) a company must maintain a reliable and adequate system of internal accounting controls. In applying these two separate requirements to the instant case, the court will examine the requirements of each provision and the problems inherent in their interpretation.

The "books and records" provision, contained in section 13(b)(2)(A) of the FCPA has three basic objectives: (1) books and records should reflect transactions in conformity with accepted methods of reporting economic events, (2) misrepresentation, concealment, falsification, circumvention, and other deliberate acts resulting in inaccurate financial books and records are unlawful, and (3) transactions should be properly reflected on books and records in such a manner as to permit the preparation of financial statements in conformity with GAAP and other criteria applicable to such statements.

Congress' use of the term "records" suggests that virtually any tangible embodiment of information made or kept by an issuer is within the scope of section 13(b)(2)(A) of the FCPA, such as tape recordings, computer print-outs, and similar representations. As indicated above, the purpose of this provision is to strengthen the accuracy of records and the reliability of audits.

During congressional consideration of the accounting provisions, there were numerous objections to the requirement that records be "accurate," which noted, for example, that inventories are typically valued on either the assumption that costs are recognized on a first-in, first-out basis or a last-in, first-out basis. Both of these theories, if correctly and honestly applied, produce "accurate" records, even though each may yield considerably different results in terms of the monetary value of inventories. Several objecting groups recommended that the accuracy requirement be subject to a materiality test so that inaccuracies involving small dollar amounts would not be actionable. This view is not accepted, but Congress did make it clear that:

> The term "accurately" in the bill does not mean exact precision as measured by some abstract principle. Rather, it means that an issuer's records should reflect transactions in conformity with accepted methods of recording economic events.

The only express congressional requirement for accuracy is the phrase "in reasonable detail." Although section 13(b)(2) expects management to see that the corporation's recordkeeping system is adequate and effectively implemented, how the issuer goes about this task is up to management; the FCPA provides no guidance, and this court cannot issue any kind of advisory opinion.

Just as the degree of error is not relevant to an issuer's responsibility for any inaccuracies, the motivations of those who erred are not relevant. There are no words in section 13(b)(2)(A) indicating that Congress intended to impose a scienter requirement, although there is some support among officials at the Securities and Exchange Commission for the addition of a scienter requirement and a form of a materiality standard to the FCPA. Senate Bill No. 708, a proposal which would impose a scienter requirement on the accounting provisions of the FCPA, has met with substantial opposition in Congress, and it does not appear that it will be enacted as an amendment to the FCPA in the near future. The concept that the books and records provision of the Act embodies a scienter requirement would be inconsistent with the language of section 13(b)(2)(A), which contains no words indicating that Congress intended to impose such a requirement. Furthermore, either inadvertent or intentional errors could cause the misapplication or unauthorized use of corporate assets that Congress seeks to prevent. Also, a scienter requirement is inappropriate because the difficulty of proving intent would render enforcement extremely difficult. As a practical matter, the standard of accuracy in records will vary with the nature of the transaction involved.

The second branch of the accounting provisions—the requirement that issuers maintain a system of internal accounting controls—appears in section 13(b)(2)(B). Like the recordkeeping provisions of the Act, the internal controls provision is not limited to material transactions or to those above a specific dollar amount. While this requirement is supportive of accuracy and reliability in the auditor's review and financial disclosure process, this provision should not be analyzed solely from that point of view. The internal controls requirement is primarily designed to give statutory content to an aspect of management stewardship responsibility, that of providing shareholders with reasonable assurances that the business is adequately controlled.

Internal accounting control is, generally speaking, only one aspect of a company's total control system; in order to maintain accountability for the disposition of its assets, a business must attempt to make it difficult for its assets to be misappropriated. The internal accounting controls element of a company's control system is that which is specifically designed to provide reasonable, cost-effective safeguards against the unauthorized use or disposition of company assets and reasonable assurances that financial records and accounts are sufficiently reliable for purposes of external reporting. "Internal accounting controls" must be distinguished from the accounting system typically found in a company. Accounting systems process transactions and recognize, calculate, classify, post, summarize, and report transactions. Internal controls safeguard assets and assure the reliability of financial records, one of their main jobs being to prevent and detect errors and irregularities that arise in the accounting systems of the company. Internal accounting controls are basic indicators of the reliability of the financial statements and the accounting system and records from which financial statements are prepared.

Among the factors that determine the internal accounting control environment of a company are its organizational structure, including the competence of personnel, the degree and manner of delegation and responsibility, the quality of internal budgets and financial reports, and the checks and balances that separate incompatible activities. The efficiency of the internal control system of a company cannot be evaluated without considering the company's organizational structure, the caliber of its employees, the strength of its audit committee, the effectiveness of its internal audit operation, and a host of other factors which, while not part of the internal control system itself, have an impact on the function of the system.

Although not specifically delineated in the Act itself, the following directives can be inferred from the internal controls provisions: (1) Every company should have reliable personnel, which may require that some be bonded, and all should be supervised. (2) Account functions should be segregated and procedures designed to prevent errors or irregularities. The major functions of recordkeeping, custodianship, authorization, and operation should be performed by different people to avoid the temptation for abuse of these incompatible functions. (3) Reasonable assurances should be maintained that transactions are executed as authorized. (4) Transactions should be properly recorded in the firm's accounting records to facilitate control, which would also require standardized procedures for making accounting entries. Exceptional entries should be investigated regularly. (5) Access to assets of the company should be limited to authorized personnel. (6) At reasonable intervals, there should be a comparison of the accounting records with the actual inventory of assets, which would usually involve the physical taking of inventory, the counting of cash, and the reconciliation of accounting records with the actual physical assets. Frequency of these comparisons will usually depend on the cost of the process and upon the materiality of the assets involved.

The main problem with the internal accounting controls provision of the FCPA is that there are no specific standards by which to evaluate the sufficiency of controls; any evaluation is inevitably a highly subjective process in which knowledgeable individuals can arrive at totally different conclusions. Any ruling by a court with respect to the applicability of both the accounting provisions and the internal accounting control provisions should be strictly limited to the facts of each case.

The defendants in the instant case contend that the SEC has misconstrued the provisions of the FCPA relating to a knowledge requirement, contending that the SEC must show scienter. The defendants further state that the SEC does not allege a knowing attempt to circumvent for an improper purpose an internal control system required by law and that the complaint ignores all considerations of the costs and benefits of internal accounting controls and seeks to require World–Wide to maintain a system of controls that would destroy the company.

The definition of accounting controls does comprehend reasonable, but not absolute, assurances that the objectives expressed in it will be accomplished by the system. The concept of "reasonable assurances" contained in section 13(b)(2)(B) recognizes that the costs of internal controls should not exceed the benefits expected to be derived. It does not appear that either the SEC or Congress, which adopted the SEC's recommendations, intended that the statute should require that each affected issuer install a fail-safe accounting control system at all costs. It appears that Congress was fully cognizant of the cost-effective considerations which confront companies as they consider the institution of accounting controls and of the subjective elements which may lead reasonable individuals to arrive at different conclusions. Congress has demanded only that judgment be exercised in applying the standard of reasonableness. The size of the business, diversity of operations, degree of centralization of financial and operating management, amount of contact by top management with day-to-day operations, and numerous other circumstances are factors which management must consider in establishing and maintaining an internal accounting controls system. However, an issuer would probably not be successful in arguing a cost-benefit defense in circumstances where the management, despite warnings by its auditors or significant weaknesses of its accounting control system, had decided, after a cost benefit analysis, not to strengthen them, and then the internal accounting controls proved to be so inadequate that the company was virtually destroyed. It is also true that the internal accounting controls provisions contemplate the financial principle or proportionality—what is material to a small company is not necessarily material to a large company.

This court has already declined to adopt the defense offered by the defendants that the accounting controls provisions of the FCPA require a scienter requirement. The remainder of World–Wide's defense appears to be that such a small operation should not be required to maintain an elaborate and sophisticated internal control system, since the costs of implementing and maintaining it would financially destroy the company. It is true that a cost/benefit analysis is particularly relevant here, but it remains undisputed that it was the lack of any control over the inventory and inadequate accounting procedures that primarily contributed to World–Wide's demise. No organization, no matter how small, should ignore the provisions of the FCPA completely, as World–Wide did. Furthermore, common sense dictates the need for such internal controls and procedures in a business with an inventory as liquid as coins, medals, and bullion.

The evidence in this case reveals that World–Wide, aided and abetted by Hale and Seibert, violated the provisions of section 13(b)(2) of the FCPA. As set forth in the factual background portion of this order, the internal recordkeeping and accounting controls of World–Wide has been sheer chaos since Hale took over control of the company. For example, there has been no procedure implemented with respect to writing checks: employees have had access to presigned checks; source documents were not required to be prepared when a check was drawn; employees have not been required to obtain approval before writing a check; and, even when a check was drawn to "cash," supporting documentation was usually not prepared to explain the purpose for which the check was drawn. In addition to extremely lax security measures such as leaving the vault unguarded, there has been no separation of duties in the areas of purchase and sales transactions, and valuation procedures for ending inventory. Furthermore, no promissory notes or other supporting documentation has been prepared to evidence purported loans to World–Wide by Hale or by his affiliate companies.

Since Hale obtained control of World–Wide, employees have not been required to write source documents relating to the purchase and sale of coins, bullion, or other inventory. Because of this total lack of an audit trail with respect to these transactions and the disposition of World–Wide's assets, it has been virtually impossible to determine if an item has been sold at a profit or at a loss. Furthermore, there are more than $1,700,000 worth of checks drawn to Hale or to Hale's affiliates, or to cash, for which no adequate source documentation exists. Furthermore, Hale and Seibert knew that the medallions that were sold to World–Wide by Hale in 1979 were overvalued and unmarketable. Even so, they allowed the incorrect value of the medallions to be entered on the books of World–Wide. They also knew that the company's books and records were neither accurate nor complete. Pursuant to their directives, source documents were not prepared with respect to the transfer of funds; additionally, no audit trail was maintained for the acquisition and disposition of inventory. Furthermore, it appears that there were numerous false and misleading statements and omissions in the company's numerous reports to the SEC, many of which were filed late or not at all.

Individually, the acts of these defendants do not appear so egregious as to warrant the full panoply of relief requested by the SEC nor to impose complete liability under the FCPA. However, the court cannot ignore the all-pervasive effect of the combined failure to act, failure to keep accurate records, failure to maintain any type of inventory control, material omissions and misrepresentations, and other activities which caused World–Wide to decrease from a company of 40 employees and assets over $2,000,000 to a company of only three employees and assets of less than $500,000. It is evident that World–Wide, Hale, and Seibert violated all provisions contained in section 13(b)(2)(A) and (B) and the SEC's rules promulgated thereunder.

THE SARBANES–OXLEY ACT

Much of the Sarbanes–Oxley Act addressed breakdowns in the system of corporate responsibility. As the fervor of Congress increased in late July 2002 the dimensions of the legislative response increased exponentially.

Section 302 of the new Act requires each quarterly and annual report filed under § 13(a) or 15(d) of the 1934 Act to be certified by the principal executive officer or officers *and* the principal financial officer or officers. Each signing officer must certify that

> (1) the signing officer has reviewed the report;

> (2) based on the officer's knowledge, the report does not contain any untrue statement of a material fact or omit to state a material fact necessary in order to make the statements made, in light of the circumstances under which such statements were made, not misleading;

> (3) based on such officer's knowledge, the financial statements, and other financial information included in the report, fairly present in all material respects the financial condition and results of operations of the issuer as of, and for, the periods presented in the report;

> (4) the signing officers—

>> (A) are responsible for establishing and maintaining internal controls;

(B) have designed such internal controls to ensure that material information relating to the issuer and its consolidated subsidiaries is made known to such officers by others within those entities, particularly during the period in which the periodic reports are being prepared;

(C) have evaluated the effectiveness of the issuer's internal controls as of a date within 90 days prior to the report; and

(D) have presented in the report their conclusions about the effectiveness of their internal controls based on their evaluation as of that date;

(5) the signing officers have disclosed to the issuer's auditors and the audit committee of the board of directors (or persons fulfilling the equivalent function)—

(A) all significant deficiencies in the design or operation of internal controls which could adversely affect the issuer's ability to record, process, summarize, and report financial data and have identified for the issuer's auditors any material weaknesses in internal controls; and

(B) any fraud, whether or not material, that involves management or other employees who have a significant role in the issuer's internal controls; and

(6) the signing officers have indicated in the report whether or not there were significant changes in internal controls or in other factors that could significantly affect internal controls subsequent to the date of their evaluation, including any corrective actions with regard to significant deficiencies and material weaknesses.

The personal responsibility imposed on the signing officers in this Section makes this among the most draconian sections of the new Act. While the Act does not go so far as to require certification by board chairs, as earlier considered, the demand for personal responsibility virtually screams from the legislative page. In this instance, Congress may have gone too far. While personal responsibility in the abstract is commendable, the way in which this burden was imposed may prove either to be unduly burdensome or satisfied by pro forma responses. Why, for example, must a signing officer "design" an internal control system if an effective system was earlier designed by another? Is it realistic that a signing officer will always be able to identify every significant deficiency? Can a signing officer rely on an outside accountant to evaluate internal controls?

Section 303, with similar fervor, creates a new violation for any officer or director or any person acting under the direction of any officer or director to take *any* action in contradiction of SEC rules "to fraudulently influence, coerce, manipulate, or mislead any independent public or certified accountant engaged in the performance of an audit of the financial statements of that issuer for the purpose of rendering such financial statements materially misleading." This is a far more defensible standard than § 302 in that it directly precludes inappropriate behavior.

CORPORATE AUDIT COMMITTEES

In 1977, the Commission approved a rule change in the listing requirements of the New York Stock Exchange to require each domestic company with common stock listed on that exchange, "as a condition of intial and and continued listing of its securities . . ., to establish not later than June 30, 1978, and maintain thereafter an audit committee composed solely of directors independent of management and free from any relationship that, in the opinion of the board of directors, would interfere with the exercise of independent judgment as a committee member."[1]

In 1999, a Blue Ribbon Committee on Improving the Effectiveness of Corporate Audit Committees chaired by John C. Whitehead, retired co-chair of Goldman Sachs, and Ira Milstein, partner, Weil, Gotschal & Managees published a report with ten recommendations.[2] The Commission in response approved new disclosure standards to help improve the functioning of corporate audit committees.[3]

Specifically the Commission adopted amendments of Rule 10–01 of Regulation S–X, Item 310 of Regulation S–B, Item 7 of Schedule 14A and Item 302 of Regulation S–K. The Commission also adopted new Item 306 of Regulations S–K *and* S–B.

Collectively, the new rules and regulations:

- require [under Rule 10–01(d) of Regulation S–X] that companies' independent auditors review the financial information included on the companies' Quarterly Reports on Form 10–Q or 10–QSB prior to the companies filing such reports with the Commission;

- extend the requirements of Item 302(a) of Regulation S–K (requiring at fiscal year end appropriate reconciliations and descriptions of any adjustments to the quarterly information previously reported in a Form 10–Q for any quarter) to a wider range of companies;

- require [under new Item 306 of Regulations S–K *and* S–B] that companies include reports of their audit committees in their proxy statements;
  * * *

- require that the report of the audit committee also include a statement by the audit committee whether, based on the review and discussions noted above, the audit committee recommended to the Board of Directors that the audited financial statements be included in the company's Annual Report on Form 10–K or 10–KSB (as applicable) for the last fiscal year for filing with the Commission * * *;

---

1. Sec. Ex. Act Rel. 13,346, 11 SEC Dock. 1945 (1977).

2. Blue Ribbon Comm. on Improving the Effectiveness of Corporate Audit Committees, Report and Recommendations 10–16 (1999), *reprinted in* Report and Recommendations of the Blue Ribbon Committee on Improving the Effectiveness of Corporate Audit Committees, 54 Bus. Law. 1067 (1999); see also Ira M. Milstein, Introduction to the Report and Recommendations of the Blue Ribbon Committees, 54 id. 1057; John F. Olson, How to Really Make Audit Committees More Effective, 54 id. 1097; Lynn E. Turner, Audit Committees: A Roadmap for Establishing Accountability, 15 Insights No. 5 at 17 (2001).

In 1999 the New York Stock Exchange, Sec. Ex. Act Rel. 42,233, 71 SEC Dock. 639 (1999) (adoption); the American Stock Exchange; Sec. Ex. Act Rel. 42,232, 71 SEC Dock. 632 (1999) (adoption); and the NASD, Sec. Ex. Act Rel. 42,231, 71 SEC Dock. 624 (1999) (adoption), approved new audit requirements in response to the Blue Ribbon Committee.

3. Sec. Ex. Act Rels. 41,987, 70 SEC Dock. 1773 (proposal); 42,266, 71 SEC Dock. 787 (1999) (adoption). See John F. Olson, Amy L. Goodman & Michael J. Scanlon, Proposals to Implement Audit Committee Recommendations, 13 Insights No. 11 at 12 (1999).

- require [under Item 7 of Schedule 14A] that companies disclose in their proxy statements whether their Board of Directors has adopted a written charter for the audit committee, and if so, include a copy of the charter as an appendix to the company's proxy statements at least once every three years * * *;

- require that companies, including small business issuers, whose securities are quoted on NASDAQ or listed on the American Stock Exchange ("AMEX") or New York Stock Exchange ("NSYE"), disclose in their proxy statements whether the audit committee members are "independent" as defined in the applicable listing standards, and disclose certain information regarding any director on the audit committee who is not "independent", require that companies, including small business issuers, whose securities are not quoted on NASDAQ or listed on the AMEX or NYSE disclose in their proxy statements whether, if they have an audit committee, the members are "independent" as defined in the NASD's, AMEX's or NYSE's listing standards, and which definition was used; and

- provide "safe harbors" for the new proxy statement disclosures to protect companies and their directors from certain liabilities under the federal securities laws.[4]

The Enron bankruptcy late in 2001 led to sharp criticism of the ineffectuality of the audit committee. Former SEC Chairman Roderick Hills, during whose term in 1977, the New York Stock Exchange adopted the requirement of the independent audit committee was both detailed in his delineation of shortcomings and in his proposed solutions:

- Audit committees may consist of people who satisfy the objective criteria of independence, but their election to the board is too often the whim of the CEO, who decides each year who will sit on the audit committee and who will chair it.

- Audit committees too often seek only to reduce the cost of the audit rather than to seek ways to improve its quality. They do not play a sufficient role in determining what the fair fee should be.

- Audit committees seldom ask the auditor if there is a better, fairer, way to present the company's financial position.

- Audit committees seldom play a role in selecting a new audit firm or in approving a change in the partner in charge of the audit. They may well endorse an engagement or the appointment of a new team, but they are not seen as material to the selection process.

- Audit committees seldom establish themselves as the party in charge of the audit. . . .

Congress may wish . . . to require that:

- Corporations of a certain size with publicly traded stock have an effective, independent audit committee in order to avoid a finding that there is a material weakness in the corporation's internal controls;

- Corporations of a certain size have an independent nominating committee with the authority to secure new directors and appoint all members of the audit committee;

---

4. Sec. Ex. Act Rel. 42,266 at 788–789. See generally Gerald S. Backman, The New   Audit Committee Rules, 28 Sec. Reg. L.J. 3 (2000).

- Audit committees be solely responsible for the retention of accounting firms and be responsible for the fees paid them.[5]

Section 301 of the Sarbanes–Oxley Act adds § 10A(m) of the 1934 Act and expressly directs:

> The audit committee of each issuer, in its capacity as a committee of each issuer, in its capacity as a committee of the board of directors, shall be directly responsible for the appointment, compensation, and oversight of the work of any registered public accounting firm employed by that issuer (including resolution of disagreements between management and the auditor regarding financial reporting) for the purpose of preparing or issuing an audit report or related work, and each registered public accounting firm shall report directly to the audit committee.

The audit committee is required to be comprised entirely of independent directors and be authorized to engage independent counsel and other advisors.

The New York Stock Exchange (NYSE) Corporate Accountability and Listing Standards Committee "in the aftermath of the 'meltdown' of significant companies due to following due diligence ethics and controls," recommended a broader set of corporate governance reforms to the New York Stock Exchange Board of Directors which, in turn, adopted the recommendations and will propose them to the SEC as amendments to the NYSE's rules.[8]

E.   REMEDIES

Few areas of securities law have changed as dramatically in recent years as has the panoply of remedies available to the SEC. Traditionally the SEC relied heavily on two principal enforcement tools: civil injunctions and administrative proceedings. These two tools persist as the backbone of the Commission's enforcement arsenal. In 2000 the SEC initiated 223 civil injunction proceedings and 244 administrative proceedings.[1] Both judicial and administrative proceedings were usually settled by a consent decree that the parties negotiate and that is implemented through a court or SEC order. The incentives for such a negotiated resolution are strong on both sides. The defendants avoid the embarrassment of being found to have violated the securities law and, in cases of lesser gravity, typically consent to the entry of an injunction that only orders them not to commit future violations of the federal securities laws. More importantly, defendants avoid the collateral estoppel effect of an adverse judgment in the SEC's action, which judgment private plaintiffs could use offensively in an action for damages.[2] As a practical matter, the risk that an SEC victory in an injunctive action would entail high financial liability to plaintiffs in a securities class action often dissuades defendants from litigating with the SEC.

From the SEC's standpoint, the advantages of the consent decree procedure were primarily economic. Both in terms of financial cost and staff resources, the SEC could not realistically hope to litigate annually over 100 cases (many with multiple defendants) through trial. Instead, by settling for an

---

5. Senate Comm. on Banking, Housing & Urban Affairs, Hearing on "Accounting and Investor Protection Issues Raised in Enron and Other Public Companies," Feb. 12, 2002 (testimony of Roderick M. Hills), at 4, 8.

8. The NYSE Corporate Accountability and Listing Standards Committee (July 26, 2002).

1. SEC Ann. Rep. 1 (2000).

2. See Parklane Hosiery Co. v. Shore, 439 U.S. 322 (1979).

order barring future violations of the securities laws (plus disgorgement of any profits from the violation) in most cases and by seeking special ancillary relief in a limited number of significant cases, the SEC has sought to employ its enforcement resources efficiently to maximize their impact.

In 1990 the Securities Law Enforcement Remedies and Penny Stock Reform Act dramatically expanded the Commission's enforcement arsenal by adding three significant new tools: civil fines; cease and desist orders; and corporate bar orders.

Increasingly these new tools have had effect. In 2000 SEC civil penalties totaled over $43 million with another $445 million in disgorged illegal profits.[3] Cease and desist orders now rival civil injunction actions in the frequency with which they are invoked.[4]

1.   INJUNCTIONS AND ANCILLARY RELIEF

We have earlier discussed stop order proceedings under the 1933 Act and civil injunctive relief. The Commission is empowered to sue for an injunction under each federal securities statute.[1]

In most Commission injunction actions the practical problem often concerns whether a violation occurred recently enough to warrant the conclusion that there is a threat of recurrence:[2]

> Among the factors that courts have considered in assessing the likelihood of future violations are (1) whether the defendant committed a past violation; (2) the degree of scienter involved in the past violation; (3) whether the past violation can be properly characterized as an isolated occurrence; (4) whether the defendant has acknowledged the wrongfulness of the past conduct and given assurance that the violation will not be repeated; and (5) whether the defendant's occupation puts him or her in a position to commit further violations.[3]

The courts have added: "To obtain injunctive relief the Commission must offer positive proof of the likelihood that the wrongdoing will recur. * * * The Commission needs to go beyond the mere fact of past violations."[4]

It is not inevitable that the Commission can equal this threshold, as the following case illustrates.

SEC v. Unifund, SAL

United States Court of Appeals, Second Circuit, 1990.
910 F.2d 1028.

■ Before Van Graafeiland, Newman and Kearse, Circuit Judges.

■ Jon O. Newman, Circuit Judge:

This is an appeal by two securities purchasers from a preliminary injunction obtained by the Securities and Exchange Commission in a case of alleged

---

3.   SEC Ann. Rep. 1 (2000).

4.   *See, e.g.,* 10 Louis Loss & Joel Seligman, Securities Regulation 4981–4995 (3d ed. rev. 1996).

1.   *See, e.g.,* Sec. Act § 20(b); Sec. Ex. Act § 21(d)(1).

2.   *See, e.g.,* Rondeau v. Mosinee Paper Corp., 422 U.S. 49, 59 (1975), characterizing "the usual basis for injunctive relief, 'that there exists some cognizable danger of recurrent violation' * * * "*See also* SEC v. Manor Nursing Centers, Inc., 458 F.2d 1082, 1100–1101 (2d Cir.1972).

3.   Quoting 10 Louis Loss & Joel Seligman, Securities Regulation 4737 (3d ed. rev. 1996).

4.   SEC v. Caterinicchia, 613 F.2d 102, 105 (5th Cir.1980). See generally Daniel J. Morrissey, SEC Injunctions, 68 Tenn. L. Rev. 427 (2001).

insider trading. This case is unusual in that, as the Commission acknowledged at oral argument, it is the first insider trading case in which the Commission has sought relief against alleged tippees before identifying the alleged tipper. Unifund SAL ("Unifund") and Tamanaco Saudi & Gulf Investment Group ("Tamanaco") appeal, respectively, from * * * orders of the District Court for the Southern District of New York (Shirley Wohl Kram, Judge) granting a preliminary injunction at the request of the Commission. The injunction (a) prohibits violation of section 10(b) of the Securities and Exchange Act * * *, and rule 10b–5 * * *, (b) freezes appellants' accounts, subject to trading approved by the Commission, and (c) bars disposal or alteration of appellants' books and records. * * *

Background

The case concerns trading in the stock and stock options of Rorer Group, Inc. ("Rorer"), a United States pharmaceutical company incorporated in Pennsylvania. Rorer common stock is listed on the New York Stock Exchange, and option contracts for its common stock are listed on the American Stock Exchange. In the summer of 1989, Rorer began confidential merger negotiations with Rhone–Poulenc, S.A. ("Rhone"), a French corporation. The discussions intensified in December and in early January 1990. In mid-January, prior to any public announcement of merger negotiations, massive trading occurred in Rorer stock and options. * * *

The heavy trading volume prompted the Commission to investigate. It quickly identified unusually large Rorer stock and option transactions in brokerage accounts maintained by foreign investors, including appellants Unifund and Tamanaco. Unifund is an investment company based in Lebanon and incorporated under Lebanese law. Tamanaco is an investment company incorporated in Panama. On January 4 Unifund purchased 40,000 shares of Rorer for approximately $2 million through the Beirut office of Merrill Lynch, Pierce, Fenner & Smith, Inc. ("Merrill Lynch"). From January 4 through 12 it bought 810 Rorer call option contracts for approximately $300,000. After the merger announcement, Unifund liquidated its position, making $564,000 on the stock and $980,000 on the options. On January 10, Tamanaco purchased 500 Rorer call options for approximately $150,000 through Compagnie Financiere Esperito Santo ("Esperito Santo"), a Swiss bank in Lausanne. Two days later Tamanaco bought an additional 100 call options through the same bank. The purchases were made through Esperito Santo's account at the Lausanne branch of Dean Witter Reynolds Inc. ("Dean Witter"). Within one week the value of the options quadrupled, producing a profit of approximately $660,000.

On January 17, two days after the merger announcement, the Commission filed this lawsuit against Unifund and other purchasers of Rorer stock and obtained a temporary restraining order. Tamanaco had not yet been identified as the name of one of the purchasers. The TRO barred future violations of section 10(b) and rule 10b–5, required retention of unsold Rorer stock and options as well as the proceeds from those securities that had already been sold, and froze defendants' accounts. The TRO permitted trading in Rorer options and in the frozen accounts with the Commission's permission. * * *

In an opinion dated March 2, Judge Kram detailed the basis for issuing [a preliminary] injunction. * * * On the merits, Judge Kram stated that the standard for a preliminary injunction requested by the Commission is a strong prima facie case of a violation of section 10(b) and a reasonable likelihood that the wrong will be repeated. She found this standard met by various items of circumstantial evidence. Initially, she relied on the unusual trading activity in Rorer securities by Tamanaco and Unifund. There was evidence that in the Espirito Santo account at Dean Witter in Lausanne, through which the Tamanaco's Rorer options had been purchased, no other options had been traded since August 1989. Unifund's January 4 purchase of 40,000 Rorer shares represented 13 percent of the total Rorer shares traded that day. Unifund's stock purchase was nearly twice the size of its next largest investment in any company, even when those investments were aggregated over time. Moreover, its prior equity positions had been partially hedged, but its position in Rorer was not.

To show that the purchases were based on inside information, Judge Kram relied on the following circumstances. On January 10, 1990, Espirito Santo, through which Tamanaco purchased its Rorer options, purchased 3,000 shares of Rorer through the Nyon, Switzerland office of Raymond Jones & Associates, Inc. ("Raymond Jones"), stockbrokers based in Tampa, Florida. Espirito Santo's broker at Raymond Jones, Candid Peyer, told Commission investigators in a telephone interview that in mid-December 1989 a close friend, identified only as an independent money manager in Geneva, had told him that "if you want a Christmas gift, buy February 60 calls in Rorer." Peyer said that in his opinion his friend had "inside information" concerning a takeover of Rorer. Peyer said his friend received the information from an unnamed stockbroker at a Canadian brokerage firm in Lausanne. After a pause in the interview, during which Peyer consulted with a Raymond Jones compliance officer, Peyer said he thought the recommendation was based on inside information because the price of Rorer stock continued to go up. In a subsequent interview after the lawsuit was filed, Peyer revealed that his friend had said that the information came from "the direction" of one of the entities mentioned in connection with the lawsuit.

Judge Kram found that the Peyer "admission" was pertinent not only to Tamanaco but also to Unifund. As the link to Unifund, she pointed to Bank Audi, a Lebanese bank. The connection Judge Kram relied upon was that Ralph Audi, the principal shareholder of Unifund, is related to individuals who run Bank Audi and its Swiss affiliate, Bank Audi Suisse, and that Bank Audi Suisse had purchased Rorer call options in the week prior to the merger announcement and had made the purchases through Raymond Jones, the brokerage firm that employed Candid Peyer. Ralph Audi's relatives, George W. Audi and Raymond W. Audi, are, respectively, chairman and director of Bank Audi; Raymond is also chairman of Bank Audi Suisse. Ralph Audi has borrowed funds from Bank Audi.

* * *

Judge Kram explicitly declined to credit Unifund's innocent explanation for its Rorer purchases. In an affidavit, Ralph Audi stated that Unifund frequently invests in possible takeover targets, that Rorer had been the subject of takeover speculation since August 1989, that his bank in Paris had informed him in the last week of December that additional collateral was needed to secure Unifund's line of credit, and that the "first stock that came to mind for me was

Rorer," because of the prior takeover rumors. Judge Kram found this explanation unconvincing because Audi had not bought Rorer in August, when he claims to have first heard takeover rumors, but did so on January 4, 1990, just after Merrill Lynch had advised against a purchase in December.

Having found a "strong prima facie" case of rule 10b–5 violations by both Unifund and Tamanaco, Judge Kram also found a sufficient likelihood of future violations, a conclusion based primarily on the fact that both defendants regularly trade securities. She therefore issued the preliminary injunction.

* * *

IV. Sufficiency of the Evidence for Preliminary Injunctive Relief.

The major issue on appeal is whether the evidence presented by the Commission sufficed to warrant a preliminary injunction. We begin our consideration of that issue with an examination of the pertinent statute and the standards that have evolved in applying it. Section 21(d) of the Exchange Act provides:

Whenever it shall appear to the Commission that any person is engaged or is about to engage in acts or practices constituting a violation of any provision of this chapter, the rules or regulations thereunder, [or rules of exchanges and other designated entities], it may in its discretion bring an action in the proper district court * * * to enjoin such acts or practices, and upon a proper showing a permanent or temporary injunction or restraining order shall be granted without bond.

* * *

In our earliest encounters with injunction requests by the Commission, we relieved the Commission of the obligation, imposed on private litigants, to show risk of irreparable injury, SEC v. Torr, 87 F.2d 446, 450 (2d Cir.1937), or the unavailability of remedies at law, SEC v. Jones, 85 F.2d 17 (2d Cir.), cert. denied, 299 U.S. 581 * * * (1936). That rule remains the law of this Circuit. See SEC v. Management Dynamics, Inc., 515 F.2d 801, 808–09 (2d Cir.1975).

Though the Commission faces a reduced burden in these respects, compared to private litigants, there is some uncertainty whether in other respects its burden in obtaining a preliminary injunction is the same as or greater than that of private litigants. The uncertainty concerns (1) whether the Commission's showing on the merits must be more than the "likelihood of success" standard required of private litigants, see Jackson Dairy, Inc. v. H.P. Hood & Sons, Inc., 596 F.2d 70, 72 (2d Cir.1979), and (2) whether the alternative test for a preliminary injunction—irreparable harm plus an issue that is a fair ground for litigation and a balance of hardships that tips decidedly to the plaintiff, id.—is available to the Commission. The statutory standard set forth in section 21(d) of the Exchange Act—"a proper showing"—is singularly unenlightening in resolving these issues.

A. *Required Showing on the Merits.* Appellants contend that in this Circuit the Commission can secure a preliminary injunction only upon evidence that establishes a "strong prima facie case," a standard expressed in SEC v. Management Dynamics, Inc., 515 F.2d at 807. The provenance of this somewhat odd formulation puts its authoritativeness in considerable doubt. [The court then reviewed the history of subsequent decisions in the Second Circuit.]

* * *

We find this history an unsubstantial basis for concluding that the Commission's burden on the merits in obtaining a preliminary injunction is any greater than the traditional "likelihood of success" standard we have regularly applied to private litigants, and we see little virtue in enshrining the phrase "strong prima facie case" to serve along with the traditional standard. "Prima facie case" has a clear meaning: evidence of an amount and quality sufficient to send a case to the trier of fact. Functionally, that standard does not serve well at the preliminary injunction stage, where the plaintiff, whether private litigant or Government agency, is usually seeking to preserve the status quo while completing discovery and preparing for a trial at which it will be required to present a prima facie case or suffer a directed verdict. Adding the adjective "strong" only complicates matters further, introducing a qualitative assessment of uncertain meaning with no operational significance. We have never ruled in a preliminary injunction action that the SEC has presented a "prima facie case" but not a "strong prima facie case."

* * *

Though the "clear showing" qualifier appears to have been abandoned for injunctions that serve the traditional purpose of preserving the status quo, plaintiffs have been put to a more rigorous burden in obtaining preliminary injunctions that order some form of mandatory relief. We have said that a "clear showing" is required where the injunction is mandatory. * * * Thus, even when applying the traditional standard of "likelihood of success," a district court, exercising its equitable discretion, should bear in mind the nature of the preliminary relief the Commission is seeking, and should require a more substantial showing of likelihood of success, both as to violation and risk of recurrence, whenever the relief sought is more than preservation of the status quo. Like any litigant, the Commission should be obliged to make a more persuasive showing of its entitlement to a preliminary injunction the more onerous are the burdens of the injunction it seeks. In some cases a preliminary injunction can have very serious consequences, see SEC v. Commonwealth Chemical Securities, Inc., 574 F.2d 90, 99 (2d Cir.1978); SEC v. Geon Industries, Inc., 531 F.2d 39, 55 (2d Cir.1976), yet in other cases may be fairly described as only a " 'mild prophylactic,' " see SEC v. Capital Gains Research Bureau, Inc., 375 U.S. 180, 193 (1963) (quoting with approval from SEC v. Capital Gains Research Bureau, Inc., 306 F.2d 606, 613 (2d Cir.1962) (in banc) (dissenting opinion)).

B. *"Serious Questions on the Merits" Test.* The Commission urges that it is entitled to obtain a preliminary injunction under section 21(d) on the alternative test, available to private litigants, of irreparable injury plus both sufficiently serious questions going to the merits and a balance of hardships tipping decidedly to the party requesting preliminary relief. See Jackson Dairy, Inc. v. H.P. Hood & Sons, Inc., 596 F.2d at 72. However, in the analogous context of a statutory preliminary injunction sought by the Government to enforce the antitrust laws, we have ruled that the "serious questions on the merits" test is not available. See United States v. Siemens Corp., 621 F.2d at 505–06. * * *

* * *

In any event, we have never applied the "serious questions on the merits" test to a preliminary injunction sought by the Commission or, for that matter, by any governmental agency, and we are not disposed to do so now. In practice, the absence of the alternative test as an articulated standard may not have much significance, since, as we have indicated, the degree to which the Commission must show likelihood of success will be reduced where the interim relief sought is not especially onerous.

C. *Application of Preliminary Injunction Standards.* Having labored so extensively to identify the relevant standard for assessing the sufficiency of the Commission's evidence, we find its application to the facts of this case an easier task. Since the test of sufficiency varies with the nature of the relief sought, we consider separately each of the two principal forms of relief that were ordered— the prohibition against future insider trading violations and the freeze order.

(i) *Prohibition Against Future Securities Law Violations.* The prohibition against future securities law violations is among the sanctions that we have characterized as having grave consequences. Such an order subjects the defendant to contempt sanctions if its subsequent trading is deemed unlawful and also has serious collateral effects. See Andre, The Collateral Consequences of SEC Injunctive Relief: Mild Prophylactic or Perpetual Hazard? [1981] Ill.L.Rev. 625. Though the order is prohibitory in form, rather than mandatory, it accomplishes significantly more than preservation of the status quo. For this form of relief, the Commission has to make a substantial showing of likelihood of success as to both a current violation and the risk of repetition. An insider trading violation requires proof not only that the defendant traded on the basis of material nonpublic information but also that in doing so he knew or should have known that he was breaching a fiduciary duty. See Dirks v. SEC, 463 U.S. 646, 660 (1983); Chiarella v. United States, 445 U.S. 222, 230–32 (1980).

In this case, the Commission has not identified the person or entity alleged to have conveyed inside information to either appellant. It is therefore more difficult than in the typical tipping case to determine whether, even if the appellants obtained inside information, they traded upon it in breach of a fiduciary duty that they knew or should have known existed. Though a "tippee's duty to disclose or abstain is derivative from that of the insider's duty," Dirks v. SEC, 463 U.S. at 659, we do not know from whom such a duty might derive in this case.

The Commission attempts to bridge this fundamental gap in its evidence with speculation. Even if we assume that it has sufficiently shown an adequate probability that Candid Peyer, Espirito Santo's broker at Raymond Jones, had material nonpublic information from an insider, we are then asked to infer the requisite relationship to Unifund and Tamanaco from wholly inadequate circumstances. The evidence showed that Unifund's principal is related, familially and financially, to a bank that bought Rorer securities through Raymond Jones. The link to Unifund assumes that Peyer's information was conveyed to Raymond Jones, then to Bank Audi, and then to Unifund, under circumstances where Unifund knew or should have known of a nondisclosure obligation. These assumptions are unsupported on this record. Nor are they provided by the commonality of surnames between an officer of Bank Audi and a shareholder of Unifund (both named Karam), or between an executive of Rhone and an incorporator of Unifund (both named Khoury).

The linkage is no better with respect to Tamanaco. It assumes that Peyer's information was conveyed to Raymond Jones, then to Espirito Santo, and then to Tamanaco. These assumptions are also unsupported.

What the record discloses is unusual trading by both Unifund and Tamanaco on the eve of the merger announcement. They may well have had inside information, but possession of such information without more does not give rise to a duty to disclose or abstain from trading, *Dirks v. SEC*, supra, at least where the recipient of the information is an ordinary investor. Whatever adverse inferences might be drawn from the recalcitrance to discovery that Judge Kram attributed to appellants are not sufficient to remedy the gap in the Commission's showing of a probable insider trading violation.

(ii) *Freeze Order*. We reach a different conclusion with respect to the freeze order, though we modify the terms of the order. In seeking to freeze appellants' accounts, the Commission is requesting ancillary relief to facilitate enforcement of any disgorgement remedy that might be ordered in the event a violation is established at trial. Unlike the injunction against securities law violations, the freeze order does not place appellants at risk of contempt in all future securities transactions. It simply assures that any funds that may become due can be collected. The order functions like an attachment. That does not mean, however, that its issuance must be tested against state law standards, as would be the case if the relief were sought pursuant to rule 64 of the Federal Rules of Civil Procedure. Congress has authorized the Commission to obtain preliminary injunctive relief upon a "proper showing," and it is a matter of federal law whether the showing the Commission has made is sufficient to support an interlocutory freeze order. Cf. FTC v. H.N. Singer, Inc., 668 F.2d 1107, 1112 (9th Cir.1982) (unavailability of attachment does not preclude other provisional remedies). Moreover, an ancillary remedy may be granted, even in circumstances where the elements required to support a traditional SEC injunction have not been established, see SEC v. Commonwealth Chemical Securities, Inc., 574 F.2d at 103 n. 13 (approving disgorgement remedy despite failure to show likelihood of recurring violation), and such a remedy is especially warranted where it is sought for a limited duration, see SEC v. Levine, 881 F.2d 1165, 1177 (2d Cir.1989).

Though the Commission has not presented at this stage sufficient evidence to warrant a preliminary injunction of traditional scope, its evidence suffices to warrant some form of freeze order. There is a basis to infer that the appellants traded on inside information, and while the Commission is endeavoring to prove at trial the requisite element of trading in breach of a fiduciary duty of which the defendants were or should have been aware, the Commission should be able to preserve its opportunity to collect funds that may yet be ordered disgorged.

Three aspects of the freeze order in this case require further consideration. First, the order freezes funds in an amount sufficient to cover not just the profits that might have to be disgorged but the civil penalty, equal to three times the profits, that the Commission may recover under section 21A of the Exchange Act upon proof of a violation. * * * Appellants challenge this aspect of the order, relying on SEC v. Manor Nursing Centers, Inc., 458 F.2d 1082 (2d Cir.1972), where we said that a freeze order could be imposed so long as it orders " 'remedial relief and is not a penalty assessment.' " Id. at 1104 (quoting SEC v. Texas Gulf Sulphur Co., 446 F.2d 1301, 1308 (2d Cir.), *cert. denied*, 404 U.S. 1005 * * * (1971)). That observation was made in setting aside that portion of an order requiring surrender of the income earned on proceeds required to be disgorged. Though recognizing that surrendering the earned income might add to the deterrent effect of securities law enforcement, we concluded that this incremental remedy would be arbitrary in the circumstances presented. Id.

With the enactment of section 21A in 1988, Congress has made the judgment that a civil penalty equal to three times the profits of insider trading should be an available remedy for the Commission. Our reluctance in *Manor Nursing Centers* to permit a freeze order to reach funds not normally forfeitable is not authority for denying the Commission the opportunity to collect funds that Congress has expressly determined are appropriate for forfeiture. * * *

Second, and more troublesome, is the fact that the freeze order obliges appellants not merely to maintain in their accounts funds sufficient to pay the amounts that might eventually be due but also to refrain from any trading in the accounts without the Commission's approval. The Commission understandably prefers such a remedy, which enables it to insist upon high-grade investments to maximize the prospect that sufficient funds will be available in the accounts to pay the civil penalties. But bearing in mind the basic principle that burdensome forms of interim relief require correspondingly substantial justification, we conclude that the Commission's showing in this case is inadequate to support the extensive trading restriction in the freeze order. The Commission has presented a thin case for any ancillary relief. At most, its meager showing entitles it to an order that provides reasonable security for collecting a judgment, with a trading restriction imposed only if that security becomes deficient. The freeze order should be modified to provide that the appellants shall maintain in their accounts funds and securities in an amount equal to three times the profits earned on the Rorer trades, with the proviso that, should either appellant's account balance, at fair market values, decrease to a level at or below twice that appellant's Rorer profits, that appellant must restore the account to a level equal to three times its Rorer profits, failing which the Commission may reimpose its restriction on permissible trading. Though this modified remedy tolerates a risk that unsuccessful trading might erode some of the value of the accounts from which the Commission hopes to collect any penalties that may be assessed, it gives the Commission substantial security without unduly burdening the appellants by denying them the opportunity to invest as they see fit. Presumably, they are as anxious to see their account balances grow as is the Commission, though we acknowledge that the appellants will now have the opportunity to make their more risky investments from the accounts previously frozen so extensively. In any event, we are satisfied that this mild thaw in the freeze order approximately adjusts it to the maximum interim relief to which the Commission is entitled in view of its minimal showing of a violation.

Third, though we are willing to approve a modified freeze order, we do not believe that the Commission is entitled to keep even the modified order in force for whatever period of time the Commission may take to prepare for trial. In view of the Commission's meager showing on the merits, it should not be entitled to interfere with the appellants' unrestricted use of their accounts for more than a brief interval. In view of the time that has already elapsed since the injunction issued, we will direct that the freeze order, as modified, shall terminate thirty days after the issuance of our mandate, unless within such time the Commission advises the District Court of its readiness for immediate trial.

The orders of the District Court are vacated in part and modified in part, and the cause is remanded for entry of orders revised in conformity with this opinion.

SEC v. First Jersey Securities, Inc.

United States Court of Appeals, Second Circuit, 1996.
101 F.3d 1450.

■ KEARSE, CIRCUIT JUDGE:

Defendants First Jersey Securities, Inc. ("First Jersey" or the "Firm"), and Robert E. Brennan appeal from a judgment entered in the United States District Court for the Southern District of New York following a bench trial before Richard Owen, *Judge*, holding defendants liable for violations of § 17(a) of the Securities Act of 1933 ("1933 Act"), 15 U.S.C. § 77q(a) (1994); § 10(b) of the Securities Exchange Act of 1934 ("1934 Act"), 15 U.S.C. § 78j(b) (1994); and Securities and Exchange Commission ("SEC" or the "Commission") Rule 10b–5, 17 C.F.R. s 240.10b–5 (1995), in the sale, repurchase, and resale of six securities. The district court ordered defendants jointly and severally to disgorge the sum of $22,288,099, plus $52,689,894 in prejudgment interest; enjoined them from further securities laws violations; and appointed a special agent (the "Special Agent") to determine whether, in 1982–1987, defendants had committed securities law violations beyond those proven at trial. On appeal, defendants contend principally that the present action was barred by res judicata and that the court erred in imposing liability and in fashioning relief. Brennan also challenges, *inter alia*, the district court's order that he be held jointly and severally liable for the entire amount of disgorgement ordered by the court. For the reasons below, we reverse so much of the judgment as appointed the Special Agent, and in all other respects we affirm.

I. BACKGROUND

The present action was commenced by the SEC in 1985, based on allegations that, beginning in November 1982 and continuing into 1985, First Jersey, with Brennan at the helm, had employed a massive and coordinated system of fraudulent practices to induce its customers to buy certain securities from the Firm at excessive prices unrelated to prevailing market prices, resulting in defendants' gaining more than $27 million in illegal profits from their fraudulent scheme. The following facts were found by the district court to have been established at trial and are not challenged by defendants.

A. *First Jersey's Business Practices*

First Jersey was founded in 1974 as a discount broker-dealer specializing in the underwriting, trading, and distribution of low-priced securities. The vast majority of securities traded by First Jersey were sold primarily in the over-the-counter market and not listed on any national exchange. By 1985, the Firm operated 32 branch offices throughout the United States and 36 offices in foreign countries, and had more than 500,000 retail-customer accounts. It employed approximately 1,200 salespersons or "registered representatives." In hiring such sales personnel, First Jersey typically sought individuals who had no prior experience in the securities business.

A First Jersey registered representative's working month consisted of a three-part cycle. The first two weeks of the month were spent "cold calling," i.e., telephoning individuals who were not customers of the Firm and whose names were found in general directories, to identify persons who might be interested in purchasing a security recommended by the Firm. The second phase began around the third week of the month, when the manager of the branch informed the sales personnel that a recommendation would be forthcoming from the research department in about a week; the manager at that time gave the salespersons no specific information about the security. The salespersons then renewed contacts with their potential customers, informing them that the Firm's research department was about to make a recommendation and seeking to determine how much money a customer would be willing to invest in a First Jersey-recommended security.

The third phase of the cycle began during the fourth week of the month, with the branch manager conducting a sales meeting to disclose to the branch's salespersons the name of the recommended security; only one security at a time was recommended to a given branch; but not all of the branches received the same recommendation. The branch manager relayed information received from the Firm's main office in New York about the recommended security, including its price and the sales commission to be paid. The branch manager also gave the salespersons a scripted sales pitch, which they were required to record and were expected to use virtually verbatim in offering the security to customers. The sales pitch usually described the security as reflecting "a spectacular turn-around situation."

At various times, salespersons were given written materials that included First Jersey research reports, annual reports of the recommended company, and newspaper articles. There generally was no discussion, however, of negative factors such as risks inherent in a recommended security. Further, salespersons were discouraged from conducting independent research on Firm-recommended securities and were not even permitted to contact the Firm's research department about a security without getting permission from the branch manager. In addition, for reasons that will become apparent below, the salespersons at any given branch were prohibited from discussing the Firm's recommendations for their branch with salespersons from other First Jersey branches.

Following the sales meeting, salespersons were to spend the remainder of the month attempting to sell the recommended security—and only that security—to their clients. Salespersons who chose not to sell the recommended security were berated and often censured by First Jersey's management. Further, the compensation structure placed a premium on selling the recommended security. If a client bought the recommended security, the salesperson received a commission in the range of 5%–10% of the price. If the client instead bought a different security, the salesperson received a commission of one percent or less. And for the client's sale of a security, the salesperson received no commission at all. When clients sold previously purchased First Jersey-recommended securities back to the Firm, they were urged to roll the proceeds over into another First Jersey-recommended security. As a result of the commission structure, First Jersey salespersons rarely recommended that their customers purchase any securities other than the one currently recommended by the Firm.

First Jersey received the vast majority of its revenues from trading securities for its own accounts, including securities that it had underwritten. Between November 1982 and August 1986, First Jersey acted as the sole underwriter for at least 31 new issues of securities that were sold in "units" consisting of a combination of shares of common stock and warrants that could later be redeemed for common stock. It was the Firm's regular practice to have sales personnel in a group of branch offices first sell a particular unit and then, shortly thereafter, urge the clients who had purchased those securities to resell them to First Jersey at a slight profit to the client. Then the Firm split the repurchased units and sold the components separately through other branch offices to new customers, at a significantly higher total price than the Firm had paid the original customer.

For example, in November 1982, First Jersey was the underwriter for 1,100,000 units of Sovereign Chemical and Petroleum Products, Inc. ("Sovereign"). Each unit consisted of three shares of common stock and one warrant; the units were not to be split prior to May 1, 1993, except at First Jersey's option. On November 9, 1982, the first day of the offering, First Jersey oversold, selling to customers of certain of its branches approximately 1,700,000 units at the offering price of $3 per unit, for a total price of $5,100,000. Within days, First Jersey bought back more than 1,300,000 units, paying $3.50 per unit; it immediately split the units into their components and priced each of the three shares of stock at $2.25–$2.50 and the warrant at $1. Thus, a unit purchased by First Jersey for $3.50 could be promptly resold, after the unbundling of the components, for a total of approximately $8. First Jersey immediately resold more than 3,000,000 shares of Sovereign common stock and 1,000,000 Sovereign warrants to customers of Firm branches other than the branches that had originally sold and repurchased the units. First Jersey's profit on the resale of the Sovereign securities totaled $5,172,292. The same pattern was followed with respect to securities of five other issuers: Quasar Microsystems, Inc. ("Quasar"), QT&T, Inc. ("QT&T"), Rampart General, Inc. ("Rampart"), Sequential Information Systems, Inc. ("Sequential"), and Trans Net Corp. ("Trans Net").

The Firm did not inform the salespersons who were to suggest that customers resell recommended units to First Jersey that the Firm would immediately split the repurchased units into their component securities and sell the components separately for more than twice what it paid the selling customer. The salespersons who thereafter sold the individual components were not advised of the Firm's original underwriting of the unit. Nor were they provided with a prospectus or advised of the risks disclosed in the prospectus. The reason that First Jersey sales personnel were forbidden to discuss the recommendations for their branch with their counterparts at other First Jersey branches was to prevent them from learning that some branches were buying back units cheaply while other branches were selling components from those units to other Firm clients at inflated markups.

At all relevant times, Brennan was a director and the 100% owner of First Jersey. Between January 1982 and August 1985, he was its president; in September 1985, he became its chairman and chief executive officer. In his capacity as sole shareholder and president or chief executive officer, Brennan met regularly with the heads of First Jersey's departments, made the final decisions concerning which securities the Firm would underwrite, and frequently participated in negotiations concerning the prices at which First Jersey sold the securities. Brennan testified at trial that he periodically received reports on First Jersey's positions in various securities, regularly reviewed the research reports issued to the branch offices, and "typically was aware of most of the research reports that went out, if not all." He also participated in meetings at which the Firm's pricing policies were formulated, and he regularly discussed the Firm's compliance, see Part III.C.2. below, with rules promulgated by the National Association of Securities Dealers, Inc. ("NASD"). Although at trial, Brennan denied any wrongdoing, he did not indicate that the actions challenged here were unauthorized acts of other executives.

B.   *The Present Litigation*

The SEC commenced the present action in October 1985, alleging that the above practices constituted illegal markups and frauds on First Jersey's customers in violation of § 17(a) of the 1933 Act, § 10(b) of the 1934 Act, and Rule 10b–5. The complaint sought disgorgement of the profits gained from those practices, as well as injunctive and other equitable relief.

Defendants moved to dismiss the complaint on the grounds, inter alia, that it was barred by principles of res judicata in light of an administrative proceeding initiated by the SEC in May 1979 and settled in November 1984. The district court rejected the res judicata defense, noting that the administrative proceeding, discussed in greater detail in Part II below, concerned First Jersey's trades in a certain group of securities during the 1970s, whereas the present case involved its trades in different securities in the 1980s. The court concluded that the two sets of claims were not identical for purposes of res judicata.

A 41–day bench trial was held in 1994, at which the court received voluminous documents and extensive testimony, including live, videotaped, or transcribed deposition testimony of 12 former First Jersey salespersons called by the SEC, 22 former First Jersey branch managers and salespersons called by defendants, and several First Jersey officers, including Brennan. In a written opinion dated June 19, 1995, reported at 890 F.Supp. 1185, the court concluded that the SEC had overwhelmingly proven that defendants First Jersey and Brennan with respect to the sales and resales of securities involved herein to First Jersey customers violated § 17(a), § 10(b), and Rule 10b–5 in that with scienter, they deliberately used fraudulent devices in those transactions. Specifically, First Jersey's sales practices were intended by defendants to operate, and did operate, as a pervasive fraud on First Jersey's hundreds of thousands of retail customers.... 890 F.Supp. at 1209. The court found that in selling and repurchasing the unit securities, and reselling the components, First Jersey violated those provisions in two ways, to wit, by withholding material information from customers and by making excessive markups in the prices of the unbundled securities.

As to the first type of violation, the court found that defendants engaged in "a massive and continuing fraud on its customers," *id.* at 1195, both on the initial group of First Jersey customers, i.e., those who resold to the Firm at a small profit without being informed that the units were about to be unbundled and sold at a much higher price, and on the second group of First Jersey customers, i.e., those who purchased the unit components for prices that, in light of the price of the units, were artificially inflated. The court found that the goal

> of the scheme was to leave both the customers selling securities back to [First Jersey] (usually "units") and the customers purchasing securities from [First Jersey] (usually "unit" components), completely ignorant of the way in which First Jersey had in all other respects dealt in those securities, and as to the sales of the components, First Jersey's salesmen knew almost nothing about the companies, and knew they were selling to buyers who knew even less.

Id. The court found that

[d]efendants First Jersey's and Brennan's conduct[ ] was entirely purposeful. It was planned this way. This is clear not only from the patterned and repeated format of the trading, but also from the simple programmed structure of First Jersey's marketing system. Defendants orchestrated every facet of First Jersey's branch office network to ensure that the firm's underwritings and other low-priced stock recommendations were sold *when* they wanted—*where* they wanted—at prices determined not by market forces but by First Jersey itself. Its salesmen themselves, with minimal information and the incentive of earning as much as ten percent (plus a five percent managers' override) on a customer's investment dollar, were accordingly able to sell to the firm's customers securities at illegal mark-ups up to as much as 150 percent.

Id. (emphasis in original) (footnote omitted).

The court concluded that, particularly in light of First Jersey's domination and control of the markets for the securities in question, its conduct constituted securities fraud under precedents dating back half a century.

As to the second type of violation, the district court found that "the evidence overwhelmingly established that the defendants wilfully and deliberately violated established law forbidding excessive markups" in the sale price of the securities. *Id.* at 1197. The court stated that:

[t]he starting point in determining the legality or illegality of a broker's markup on a sale of stock is the establishment, from the best available evidence, of the prevailing market price* * *. This is a factual, not a legal search.

Id. Concluding that First Jersey was not a "market maker" in any of the securities because it did not "hold[ ] itself out to the broker-dealer community as standing ready to purchase and sell that security at particular quoted bid and asked prices," *id.*, the court quoted the applicable SEC guidelines for determining prevailing market price as follows:

"The best evidence of the prevailing market price for a broker-dealer who is not making a market in the security is that dealer's contemporaneous cost of acquiring a security.* * * Where * * * a security is not only inactively traded between dealers, but a competitive market does not exist because that market is 'dominated' by a single dealer, the use of market maker sales or quotations is likely to be impractical or misleading. In such a 'dominated' market, the best evidence of prevailing market price is the dealer's contemporaneous cost, which is either the price that the dealer paid to other dealers, or the price that the dealer paid to its retail customers to acquire the security, after an adjustment that allows the dealer a markdown on purchases from customers."

Id. at 1197–98 (footnote omitted) (quoting Zero–Coupon Securities Release No. 34–24368, 38 S.E.C. Docket 158, 1987 WL 112328 (Apr. 21, 1987)). The court found that First Jersey dominated and controlled the markets for the six securities at issue because the vast majority of the transactions in those securities were conducted by First Jersey. The court further noted that although the Firm made some purchases in the interdealer market, those trades were insignificant because their volume was tiny in comparison to the Firm's "massive retail trading" in those securities with its own customers. 890 F.Supp. at 1200. Having determined that First Jersey was not a market maker in any of those securities, the court concluded that, under the SEC guidelines, the best measure of the securities' prevailing market price was the Firm's cost of acquiring the units from its customers.

To calculate the contemporaneous cost of the units' components, given the prevailing market price of the units, and hence the markup enjoyed by First Jersey, the court adopted an allocation formula proposed by the SEC, which the court described using the following example:

> If a unit consists of two shares of common and one warrant, and First Jersey buys [the unit] back from a customer for $1 and then sells the common at $.75 a share and the warrant at $.50, the First Jersey sales price for a unit equivalent is [a total of $1.50 for the common plus .50 for the warrant, for a total of $2]. Thus, under the allocation formula, 1 share of common is 37.5% of the unit equivalent and 1 warrant is 25%. Applying that percentage to the acquisition cost of the unit, each share of common has a cost basis of $.375 . . . .

890 F.Supp. at 1200 n. 23. Whether the focus be on a single share of the common stock (essentially purchased for $.375 and resold for $.75) or on all of the elements comprised by the unit (purchased for $1 and resold for a total of $2), First Jersey's markup would have been 100%. In the securities at issue here, the court concluded that First Jersey enjoyed markups of up to 150%.

The court noted that First Jersey did not call either its head trader or its head of sales to testify as to how the Firm arrived at its markups. Nor had the expert who testified on First Jersey's behalf posed that question to anybody at First Jersey. The court concluded that the markups were plainly excessive.

The district court ruled that Brennan was primarily liable with First Jersey for the securities violations committed by the Firm. The court based its finding on trial evidence that

> showed plainly that Brennan was a "hands-on" manager who was intimately involved in the operations of First Jersey, including all significant decisions regarding the firm's underwriting, retail sales and trading activities. Brennan signed every one of the underwriting agreements at issue in this case and admitted that he "typically" participated in the key decision to split "units" into their component securities.
>
> In his trial testimony Brennan * * * never denied knowing that First Jersey had repeatedly underwritten "units", and bought the units back from its customers, and had broken up the units, and resold the components to other customers without disclosing the price at which it had repurchased the units. To the contrary, he defended those transactions, taking the position that First Jersey's massive and repeated oversales and repurchases of units were, essentially, accidental, and that the firm's unit repurchases and the prices at which they were acquired, were not material to the customers who bought the components.

Id. at 1201. The court observed that, as the 100% owner of First Jersey during the relevant period, Brennan received periodic reports on the Firm's positions in the securities it traded and, with regard to the Firm's commission policy, that "he could have made any decision he wanted to," *id.* (internal quotation marks omitted). The court concluded that Brennan's control over First Jersey's activity made him liable as a principal for the Firm's fraudulent conduct.

The court also concluded that the evidence of First Jersey's violations and Brennan's position and conduct established Brennan's joint and several liability for the violations as a "controlling person" of the Firm under § 20(a) of the 1934 Act, 15 U.S.C. § 78t(a) (1994). It noted that "as president, chief executive officer, and sole shareholder of First Jersey, Brennan possessed control over every aspect of First Jersey's operations," 890 F.Supp. at 1202. Applying the burden-shifting scheme articulated by this Court in *Marbury Management, Inc. v. Kohn*, 629 F.2d 705 (2d Cir.), *cert. denied*, 449 U.S. 1011 * * * (1980), the court held that the burden had shifted to Brennan to show that he had in good faith "maintained and enforced a reasonable and proper system of supervision and internal control over sales personnel," 890 F.Supp. at 1202 (internal quotation marks omitted), and hence should not be held liable for violations by the Firm. The court found that Brennan had not met that burden. Reviewing the evidence as to the compliance procedures adopted by First Jersey, described in greater detail in Part III.C.2. below, the court found that those procedures were more cosmetic than real, and that they "were never intended for more than appearances should an occasion such as this arise." *Id.* at 1203.

As relief for the proven violations, the court ordered, *inter alia*, that First Jersey and Brennan disgorge the profits gained by the Firm as a result of the frauds with respect to the six securities at issue, and pay prejudgment interest on those sums from the dates of the gains through the entry of judgment—a period of up to 12+ years. The court calculated the Firm's unlawful profits with respect to each issuer as follows:

Issuer	First Jersey's Profit
QT & T	$ 581,659
Quasar	6,302,659
Rampart	2,110,617
Sequential	12,111,384
Sovereign	5,172,292
Trans Net	1,009,488
Total	**$27,288,099**

Id. at 1211. Giving defendants credit for a $5 million payment they made in January 1987 to settle a class action based on transactions in some of these securities, *see id.* at 1211 n. 35, the court ordered defendants to disgorge $22,288,099 in unlawful profits. After excluding interest on the $5 million from the date of the payment, *see id.* at 1212, the court ordered defendants to pay prejudgment interest in the total amount of $52,689,894, *see* Judgment dated July 17, 1995.

In addition, the district court permanently enjoined defendants from further violations of the securities laws, finding that it was "highly likely" that such future violations would occur. 890 F.Supp. at 1210. This finding was based in part on defendants' history of "[b]rushes" with regulatory agencies in the securities industry, *see* Part IV.C. below, which had already resulted in censures, fines, and suspensions, and injunctions. The court observed that, while First Jersey had sold most of its retail branches in 1987, the Firm continued to operate on a day-to-day basis and that at the time of trial Brennan was still the 100% owner of First Jersey's stock, as well as the sole or majority shareholder of a number of other corporations "through which he has the power to and does continue his activities in the securities field." 890 F.Supp. at 1208.

Finally, noting the evidence of violations during a two-year period with respect to the securities of Sovereign, Rampart, Quasar, Trans Net, Sequential, and QT&T, and noting "the background of defendants' sales and business practices," the district court stated that it was "thoroughly convinced under any standard that the particular violations proved at trial are in all probability only the tip of the iceberg." *Id.* at 1212. The court stated that it would therefore appoint a Special Agent to determine whether in 1982–1987 there had been other violations as well and to recommend to the court further disgorgements. The court premised this order on its general equity powers:

> Under the law, "[o]nce the equity jurisdiction of the district court has been properly invoked by a showing of a securities law violation, the court possesses the necessary power to fashion an appropriate remedy." *SEC v. Manor Nursing Centers, Inc.*, 458 F.2d [1082, 1103 (2d Cir.1972)]; *see also SEC v. Posner*, 16 F.3d 520, 521 (2d Cir.1994). Accordingly, I conclude that under the Court's general equitable powers, a special agent should be appointed to examine the records of defendant First Jersey Securities for the period from November 1, 1982 through January 31, 1987, for the purpose of determining whether there exists [sic] excessive markups and/or markdowns charged to [Firm] customers, beyond those proved at trial. Should any such excessive markups or markdowns be determined, the special agent shall recommend to the Court that defendants disgorge and pay over, as the Court may direct, all illegally-obtained profits.

890 F.Supp. at 1212–13.

Judgment was entered accordingly, and this appeal followed.

On appeal, defendants do not challenge the court's factual findings as to First Jersey's business practices, but they make a variety of challenges to the court's rulings as to procedure, liability and relief. * * *

IV.   REMEDIES

Defendants challenge all aspects of the relief ordered by the district court. They contend principally that the injunction and order of disgorgement were improper because the SEC failed to prove that such relief is necessary to prevent future violations; in addition, Brennan contends that he should not be held liable for the full amount of the disgorgement ordered. Defendants also contend that the award of prejudgment interest was unjustified and that the appointment of a Special Agent was impermissible. We find merit only in the challenge to the appointment of the Special Agent.

A.   *Disgorgement*

Once the district court has found federal securities law violations, it has broad equitable power to fashion appropriate remedies, including ordering that culpable defendants disgorge their profits. *See, e.g., SEC v. Lorin*, 76 F.3d 458, 461–62 (2d Cir.1996) (per curiam); *SEC v. Patel*, 61 F.3d 137, 139 (2d Cir. 1995); *SEC v. Manor Nursing Centers, Inc.*, 458 F.2d 1082, 1104 (2d Cir.1972). The primary purpose of disgorgement as a remedy for violation of the securities laws is to deprive violators of their ill-gotten gains, thereby effectuating the deterrence objectives of those laws. *See, e.g., SEC v. Wang*, 944 F.2d 80, 85 (2d Cir.1991); *SEC v. Commonwealth Chemical Securities, Inc.*, 574 F.2d 90, 102 (2d Cir.1978). "The effective enforcement of the federal securities laws requires that the SEC be able to make violations unprofitable. The deterrent effect of an SEC enforcement action would be greatly undermined if securities law violators were not required to disgorge illicit profits." *SEC v. Manor Nursing Centers, Inc.*, 458 F.2d at 1104; *see SEC v. Texas Gulf Sulphur Co.*, 446 F.2d 1301, 1308

(2d Cir.1971) ("It would severely defeat the purposes of the Act if a violator of Rule 10b–5 were allowed to retain the profits from his violation.").

The district court has broad discretion not only in determining whether or not to order disgorgement but also in calculating the amount to be disgorged. *See, e.g., SEC v. Lorin*, 76 F.3d at 462. The amount of disgorgement ordered "need only be a reasonable approximation of profits causally connected to the violation," *SEC v. Patel*, 61 F.3d at 139 (internal quotation marks omitted); "any risk of uncertainty [in calculating disgorgement] should fall on the wrongdoer whose illegal conduct created that uncertainty," *id.* at 140 (internal quotation marks omitted). We review the district court's order of disgorgement for abuse of discretion. *See, e.g., SEC v. Posner*, 16 F.3d 520, 522 (2d Cir.1994), *cert. denied*, 513 U.S. 1077 * * * (1995).

Defendants, relying on *United States v. Carson*, 52 F.3d 1173 (2d Cir.1995), *cert. denied*, 516 U.S. 1122 * * * (1996), argue that disgorgement was not proper here because the SEC did not show that that relief was necessary to prevent future violations. Even assuming the validity of defendants' premise, their reliance on *Carson* is misplaced. Carson was a case brought under the Racketeer Influenced and Corrupt Organizations Statute ("RICO"), 18 U.S.C. § 1961 *et seq.* (1994), which states that "[t]he district courts * * * shall have jurisdiction" to impose civil penalties such as divestiture in order "to prevent and restrain violations of [RICO]," *id.* § 1964(a). In light of that language and the "forward looking" examples given in that jurisdictional section, we held that a divestiture order under RICO must be designed to prevent future conduct rather than to remedy past wrongdoing. See 52 F.3d at 1181–82. The analysis in Carson is inapposite here, since the primary purpose of disgorgement as a remedy for federal securities laws violation is deterrence, through prevention of unjust enrichment on the part of the violator.

Defendants also contend that disgorgement is not needed to reimburse defrauded customers because defendants settled a class action, without objection by the SEC, brought by and on behalf of those customers. This argument too is wide of the mark. Since disgorgement is a method of forcing a defendant to give up the amount by which he was unjustly enriched, it is unlike an award of damages, *see, e.g., SEC v. Commonwealth Chemical Securities, Inc.*, 574 F.2d at 102, and is neither foreclosed nor confined by an amount for which injured parties were willing to settle. A settlement payment may properly, however, be taken into account by the court in calculating the amount to be disgorged, and the district court did so here. It acknowledged the $5 million that defendants paid in settlement of the class action but found that the unlawful profits gained by defendants in the six securities at issue here exceeded $27 million. It was well within the court's discretion to give defendants credit for the $5 million paid out to reimburse victims of their frauds and to require defendants to disgorge the rest of those profits. We also conclude that the amount of disgorgement ordered is a reasonable approximation of First Jersey's unlawful profits from its fraudulent transactions and is not punitive in nature.

Brennan contends that the district court erred in making him jointly and severally liable for disgorgement of the total amount of First Jersey's profits and should not have ordered him to disgorge more than the profits he personally received from the transactions in question. We conclude that that order too was within the court's discretion. As discussed in the previous sections, Brennan is primarily liable for the frauds at issue here, having been "intimately involved" in their perpetration, and is also liable as a controlling person of First Jersey. Under the express terms of § 20(a), a controlling person who has failed to establish his good-faith defense is to be held "liable jointly and severally with and to the same extent as" the controlled person. 15 U.S.C. § 78t. Accordingly, where a firm has received gains through its unlawful conduct, where its owner and chief executive officer has collaborated in that conduct and has profited from the violations, and where the trial court has, within the proper bounds of discretion, determined that an order of disgorgement of those gains is appropriate, it is within the discretion of the court to determine that the owner-officer too should be subject, on a joint and several basis, to the disgorgement order. *See, e.g., Hateley v. SEC*, 8 F.3d 653, 656 (9th Cir.1993) (affirming disgorgement order imposed jointly and severally against broker-dealer securities firm, its president, and its executive vice-president for violations of NASD rules where defendants "acted collectively in violating the association's rules and because of the close relationship among the three of them"); *see also SEC v. Hughes Capital Corp.*, 917 F.Supp. 1080, 1088 (D.N.J.1996) (finding joint and several liability of corporation and individual defendants because all were "knowing participants who acted closely and collectively").

Brennan's contention that he should be required to disgorge only amounts that he withdrew from the Firm might be more persuasive if he had owned less than all of First Jersey's stock. But he was the Firm's sole owner; not surprisingly, he testified at trial that he could request a check in any amount at any time and the Firm would issue one to him. As he owned 100% of the Firm, to the extent that the Firm's net worth was increased by its unlawful activities, so was Brennan's personal wealth.

No more than the total amount of First Jersey's unlawful profits, plus interest on those amounts, is to be disgorged. We see no abuse of discretion in making Brennan individually liable for those sums, jointly and severally with the company he owns. Accordingly, we decline to overturn the order for joint and several disgorgement. * * *

C. *The Permanent Injunction*

We also reject as meritless defendants' contention that the district court erred in permanently enjoining them from future violations of § 17(a), § 10(b), and Rule 10b–5. An injunction prohibiting a party from violating statutory provisions is appropriate where "there is a likelihood that, unless enjoined, the violations will continue." *Commodity Futures Trading Commission v. American Board of Trade, Inc.*, 803 F.2d 1242, 1250–51 (2d Cir.1986); *see also SEC v. Posner*, 16 F.3d at 521–22. Such an injunction is particularly within the court's discretion where a violation was "founded on systematic wrongdoing, rather than an isolated occurrence," *United States v. Carson*, 52 F.3d at 1184 (internal quotation marks omitted), and where the court views the defendant's degree of culpability and continued protestations of innocence as indications that injunctive relief is warranted, since "persistent refusals to admit any wrongdoing ma[k]e it rather dubious that [the offenders] are likely to avoid such violations of the securities laws in the future in the absence of an injunction." *SEC v. Lorin*, 76 F.3d at 461 (internal quotation marks omitted); *see also SEC v. Posner*, 16 F.3d at 521 (where defendants violated securities laws with "high degree of scienter" and failed to assure court that future violations were not likely to recur, injunction was warranted).

In determining that a permanent injunction was warranted in the present case, the district court noted that First Jersey continued to be a broker-dealer owned by Brennan and that it employed a number of key personnel who worked at First Jersey between 1982 and 1985. Brennan himself has remained an active participant in the securities markets. *See, e.g., Hibbard, Brown & Co.,* 58 S.E.C. Docket 2561, 1995 WL 116488, at *1 (Mar. 13, 1995) (describing Brennan's purchase in 1991 of 1,450,000 units of securities). The district court also noted that First Jersey and Brennan had a history of engaging in activities that led to misconduct charges, followed by sanctions imposed by various regulatory agencies or courts, followed by new misconduct charges. Thus, the record showed, inter alia, that for a month in 1973, Brennan was suspended from the sale of mutual funds by the New Jersey Bureau of Securities. In 1974, Anthony Nadino, Brennan's brother-in-law and First Jersey's head trader at all times relevant to this case, was federally enjoined from further violations of the antifraud provisions of the securities laws based on his promulgation of false and misleading quotations and manipulation of the market while employed at another broker-dealer prior to coming to First Jersey. *See SEC v. Management Dynamics, Inc.,* 515 F.2d 801, 810–11, 814 (2d Cir.1975). In 1984, in settlement of the SEC's 1979 Proceeding and its Geosearch action, defendants were enjoined against engaging in certain transactions with regard to securities underwritten by First Jersey and a special consultant was appointed to monitor the Firm's practices. In 1986, NASD commenced and settled a proceeding entitled *Market Surveillance Committee v. First Jersey Securities, Inc., Robert E. Brennan, and Anthony Nadino,* Complaint No. MS–261 (Feb. 7, 1986), concerning markups in Trans Net warrants; First Jersey, Nadino, and Brennan were censured, First Jersey was fined $300,000, and Nadino and Brennan were fined $25,000 each and suspended for 10 days from association with any NASD member. In 1990, NASD commenced and settled a proceeding entitled *District Business Conduct Committee v. First Jersey Securities, Inc., Robert E. Brennan, John E. Dell, Frederick A. Eyerman, et al.,* Complaint No. NEW–619 (Sept. 24, 1990), concerning violations of the NASD's Rules of Fair Practice, in which First Jersey was fined $50,000 and Brennan et al. were censured.

The district court also observed that Brennan, whose trial testimony the court characterized as "belligerent[ly] evasive[ ]," 890 F.Supp. at 1207, took the position in the present case that defendants had done nothing wrong and that if there had been any violations they were merely accidental. In light of defendants' disciplinary record, their deliberate and systematic frauds in the present case, and their continued protestations of innocence, it was well within the discretion of the district court to conclude that permanent injunctive relief is warranted.

D.   *The Appointment of a Special Agent*

Finally, defendants challenge that part of the judgment which provided for the appointment of a Special Agent to determine whether, during the period between 1982 and 1987, First Jersey engaged in fraudulent activity beyond that proved at trial. The district court, in its opinion, stated that it was convinced that the violations pleaded and proven with respect to the six securities at issue in the present litigation were but "the tip of the iceberg." 890 F.Supp. at 1212. Citing its general equity powers, the court stated that a Special Agent would therefore be appointed to investigate the possibility that, in 1982–1987, First Jersey had committed additional violations of the securities laws that the SEC had not pleaded or proven. The Special Agent would be directed, in the event that he found excessive markups or markdowns, to "recommend to the Court that defendants disgorge and pay over, as the Court may direct, all illegally-obtained profits." 890 F.Supp. at 1213. The final judgment stated that the Special Agent would be appointed thereafter, with his powers and duties delineated in a subsequent order. We find merit in defendants' challenge to this part of the judgment.

Section 21(a) of the 1934 Act gives the SEC authority to

> make such investigations as it deems necessary to determine whether any person has violated, is violating, or is about to violate any provision of [the securities laws], the rules and regulations thereunder, the rules of a national securities exchange or registered securities association of which such person is a member * * *.

15 U.S.C. § 78u(a)(1). The Commission is given limited authority to delegate these investigatory powers; § 4(b) allows it to "appoint * * * such officers, attorneys, examiners, and other experts as may be necessary for carrying out its functions under [the securities laws]." *Id.* § 78d(b)(1). This authority, which needed no court order for its exercise, provides no basis for the appointment of the Special Agent envisioned by the judgment in this case, for the agent was not to be one appointed by the SEC, but one appointed by the court.

The court itself, of course, has authority to make appointments of special personnel to assist in the court's judicial functions, such as special masters to assist in the adjudication of complicated factual issues, see Fed.R.Civ.P. 53, or trustees to oversee compliance with the court's final judgment, *see, e.g., SEC v. S&P National Corp.*, 360 F.2d 741, 750 (2d Cir.1966). The appointment of a Special Agent in this case, however, is not for the purpose of assisting in adjudication of a case before the court. Though the SEC argues that appointment of the Special Agent is appropriate because his appointment "is merely a mechanism to assist the court in ascertaining the appropriate amount of disgorgement" (SEC brief on appeal at 49), this argument disregards the fact that the claims brought by the SEC in this case have now been adjudicated, and the appropriate amount of disgorgement to deprive defendants of the unlawful gains from the transactions pleaded and proven in this litigation has been determined. Disgorgement is permissible relief for a valid claim of violation of the securities laws; but disgorgement is not a claim in itself. *See generally Franklin v. Gwinnett County Public Schools*, 503 U.S. 60, 69 * * * (1992) (The " 'question whether a litigant has a "cause of action" is analytically distinct [from] and prior to the question of what relief, if any, a litigant may be entitled to receive.' ") (quoting Davis v. Passman, 442 U.S. 228, 239 * * * (1979)). We do not regard the appointment of an investigator, whose instructions are to unearth claims not previously pursued by the SEC, as ancillary to the adjudication that has been completed.

Nor is the appointment in this case for the purpose of ensuring compliance with the court's judgment. The Special Agent's role, as described by the district court, is not to ensure that defendants' comply with the terms of the permanent injunction in the future. Rather, his role is purely retrospective and investigative. While the court indisputably has some inherent power to make appointments ancillary to its judicial function, we cannot conclude that the investigation of past acts with a view to the recommendation of new charges is a judicial function. Nor can we have confidence that the appointment of an agent to pursue such an investigation would, with respect to any recommended charges resulting from the investigation, preserve for the court the appearance of impartiality.

The parties to an action may themselves agree, of course, subject to court approval, that a special officer is to be appointed to make such investigations. *See, e.g., Handler v. SEC*, 610 F.2d 656, 659–60 (9th Cir.1979). But we are not aware of any case, other than one in which a judgment has been entered on consent, in which an investigative agent has been appointed by the court for the purpose of unearthing past wrongs in addition to those encompassed by the pleadings and proven at trial and recommending new charges to the court. *See id.* at 659 (emphasizing that "the district court did not impose special counsel upon" the corporation).

In sum, though "if a right of action exists to enforce a federal right and Congress is silent on the question of remedies, a federal court may order any appropriate relief," *Franklin v. Gwinnett County Public Schools*, 503 U.S. at 69 * * * we do not regard the appointment of an investigator to determine whether or not the plaintiff had an additional right of action as either appropriate relief for the rights asserted or a proper exercise of the judicial function. Accordingly, we reverse so much of the court's judgment as appointed the Special Agent.

CONCLUSION

We have considered all of defendants' contentions on this appeal and, except to the extent indicated above, have found them to be without merit. So much of the judgment as appointed a Special Agent is reversed. In all other respects, the judgment of the district court is affirmed.

PROBLEM 18–5

In 2000 Hottentot, a securities broker licensed by the National Association of Securities Dealers, was affiliated with two companies, FCN Financial Services and Burnett Grey & Co. These companies were approached by the principals of a company called EDP to help create a market for EDP stock. The stock was not registered with the SEC. At the time, Hottentot was President of Burnett Grey, a broker-dealer firm, and Secretary of FCN, a company that advised clients on taking private companies public, meeting regulatory and compliance requirements relating to such undertakings, and promoting such companies to brokerage firms. In these capacities, she became involved in marketing EDP stock. In 2000, Burnett Grey and FCN made four trades of unregistered EDP stock, in blocks ranging from 75 to 4200 shares.

In marketing the stock, Hottentot did not ensure that EDP had registered its offering with the SEC. Hottentot relied on advice from Peterson, her personal attorney, who heard her oral description of EDP, then stated "this sounds like an exempt transaction to me." Neither Hottentot nor Petersen learned that EDP was apparently a "sham" corporation, which had overstated the value of its assets and which had no real headquarters or employees.

Can the SEC permanently enjoin Hottentot from future violations of the securities laws?

DISGORGEMENT AND ANCILLARY RELIEF

Several statutory provisions in both the federal and state securities laws disqualify a person who has been enjoined from violating the securities law from engaging in almost any aspect of the securities business, at least without the prior consent of the appropriate regulatory agency. For example, professionals, including attorneys, who "practice" before the Commission may be suspended from practice under Rule 102(e) if they have been permanently enjoined from violating the securities laws; brokers and dealers may be similarly disciplined under § 15(b)(4) of the 1934 Act.[1]

An SEC injunction is often accompanied by an asset freeze.[2]

An SEC injunction is also often followed by a private securities class action. If the injunction was the result of a litigated decision (and not a negotiated settlement), the defendant will be collaterally estopped from denying any facts determined by the court. Under Parklane Hosiery Co. v. Shore,[3] private plaintiffs can make offensive use of collateral estoppel even though they were not parties to the earlier proceeding.

Frequently, an SEC injunction will require disgorgement of illegal gains. In insider trading cases, courts typically require the violator to return all profits made on the illegal trades. However, in other cases involving more regulatory violations, complicated issues of causation can surface. For example, suppose a takeover bidder fails to file the requisite Schedule 13D after it crosses the 5 percent threshold at which such a filing is required under the Williams Act. Later, it sells its stock back at an inflated price to the target in a "greenmail" transaction. What profits should be disgorged? In SEC v. First City Financial Corp., Ltd.,[4] the defendants were required to disgorge the $2.7 million profit they received on shares acquired after they were required, but failed, to file their Schedule 13D, even though they argued that extrinsic market factors were responsible for much of the stock's appreciation. The D.C. Circuit found that "disgorgement need only be a reasonable approximation of profits causally connected to the violation."[5]

The Commission has sought and obtained in many of its civil injunctive actions a variety of other ancillary remedies designed to remedy the consequences of past violations or to reduce the likelihood of future violations or both. Sometimes, it may seek the appointment of a receiver for the corporation where the affairs of the corporation are in such a condition as a result of past violations that drastic remedy is considered necessary to protect the rights of investors.[6] In SEC v. Wencke,[7] the Ninth Circuit held that, in connection with such a receivership, the court has jurisdiction to issue a general stay of all state court actions against the corporation by any persons, even though not involved in any way in the violations of the securities laws, as in a bankruptcy proceeding.

The most controversial of these ancillary relief measures have been those designed to give the Commission (or the court) a certain control over the future conduct of the corporation and its business, short of imposing a receivership.

1. For a fuller discussion, see Thomas J. Andre, Jr., The Collateral Consequences of SEC Injunctive Relief: Mild Prophylactic or Perpetual Hazard?, 1981 U. Ill. L. Rev. 625.

2. SEC v. Black, 163 F.3d 188 (3d Cir. 1998); SEC v. Infinity Group Co., 212 F.3d 180, 197 (3d Cir.2000).

3. 439 U.S. 322 (1979).

4. 890 F.2d 1215 (D.C.Cir.1989).

5. Id. at 1231.

6. See, e.g., Los Angeles Trust Deed & Mortgage Exch. v. SEC, 285 F.2d 162 (9th Cir.1960), *cert. denied*, 366 U.S. 919 (1961); SEC v. Manor Nursing Centers, Inc., 458 F.2d 1082 (2d Cir.1972); SEC v. Bilzerian, 127 F.Supp.2d 232 (D.D.C.2000).

7. 622 F.2d 1363 (9th Cir.1980).

Typical of these measures have been: (1) the appointment of "special counsel," as illustrated by the First Jersey case, who is required to be satisfactory to or approved by the Commission, to make an investigation of the past misdeeds of management and report, not only to the board of directors of the corporation, but also to the Commission (or the court);[8] (2) the required resignation of officers and directors;[9] and (3) the election to the board of directors of one or more "independent directors" who are not beholden to the existing management, to control the future conduct of the corporation in specific areas or generally. Such independent director or directors are usually required to be approved (i.e., in effect nominated) by the Securities and Exchange Commission. In SEC v. Mattel, Inc.,[10] the Commission negotiated a consent injunction under which for five years a majority of the directors on both the board of directors and the executive committee were to be chosen from a list selected by the Commission. In addition, a special counsel was to be selected to investigate and prosecute litigation against the old management for securities law violations.

While the types of remedies mentioned in the last paragraph have been employed in a number of cases, this procedure has usually been done with the consent of the defendant corporation either in a provision of a consent injunction or pursuant to an "undertaking" given by the corporation to the Commission as the price of avoiding further litigation. In SEC v. Falstaff Brewing Corp.,[11] the district court refused to order a restructuring of the board of directors of the corporation and stated that "the court should not, without considerable justification, impose a remedy which would in effect regulate areas traditionally left to internal corporate management." Some commentators have questioned whether ancillary remedies of the character employed in *Mattel* intrude upon both the rights of shareholders to elect their own directors and of the states to regulate corporate governance.[12]

Regarding SEC ancillary relief, see 10 L. Loss & J. Seligman, Securities Regulation 4675–4684 (3d ed. rev. 1996).

2.   NEW STATUTORY REMEDIES

The Securities Enforcement Remedies and Penny Stock Reform Act of 1990 (the "Remedies Act") arms the SEC with three new types of civil remedies: (a) civil fines; (b) cease and desist orders; and (c) corporate bar orders.

---

8. In SEC v. Materia, 745 F.2d 197 (2d Cir.1984), *cert. denied*, 471 U.S. 1053 (1985), the court said that once equity jurisdiction is properly invoked, the court has power to order all equitable relief necessary under the circumstances. For cases in which such a special counsel has been appointed, *see* Handler v. SEC, 610 F.2d 656 (9th Cir.1979); SEC v. Medic–Home Enter., Inc., 1979–1980 Fed.Sec.L.Rep. (CCH), ¶ 97,291 (S.D.N.Y. 1980).

9. Such relief has usually been negotiated by a consent decree, but in one litigated case the court did conditionally bar the defendant from future service with the corporation. See SEC v. Techni–Culture, Inc., 1973–

1974 Fed.Sec.L. Rep. (CCH), ¶ 94,501 (D.Ariz. 1974); see also SEC v. Florafax Int'l, Inc., Litig. Rel. 10,617 (N.D.Okla.1984).

10. 1974–1975 Fed.Sec.L.Rep. (CCH), ¶ 94,807 (D.D.C.1974).

11. Fed.Sec.L.Rep. (CCH), ¶ 96,583 (D.D.C.1978), *aff'd*, 629 F.2d 62 (D.C.Cir. 1980); *cert. denied sub nom.* Kalmanovitz v. SEC, 449 U.S. 1012 (1980).

12. See George W. Dent, Jr., Ancillary Relief in Federal Securities Law: A Study in Federal Remedies, 67 Minn. L. Rev. 865 (1983). But *see* James R. Farrand, Ancillary Remedies in SEC Enforcement Suits, 89 Harv. L. Rev. 1779 (1976).

(a) Civil Fines

The Remedies Act amended § 20 of the Securities Act, § 21 of the Exchange Act, § 42 of the Investment Company Act, and § 209 of the Investment Advisers Act, to allow the SEC to seek a monetary penalty in any civil injunctive action brought by it under these acts. In addition to disgorgement of profits, the SEC can now obtain the following civil penalties:

(1) up to $5,000 per violation for individuals and $50,000 per violation for a corporation;

(2) up to $50,000 per violation for individuals and $250,000 for corporations for misconduct involving "fraud, deceit, manipulation, or deliberate or reckless disregard of a regulatory requirement"; or

(3) up to $100,000 per violation for individuals and $500,000 for corporations if, in addition to misconduct involving "fraud, deceit, manipulation, or deliberate or reckless disregard of a regulatory requirement," the "violation directly of indirectly resulted in substantial losses or created a significant risk of substantial losses to other persons."

These provisions extend the Commission's earlier authority to seek civil fines in the context of insider trading[1] so that it covers "such areas as the fraudulent sales techniques and price manipulation of the penny stock market, violations of beneficial ownership disclosure rules including 'parking,' and trading violations such as those that occurred during the market break of 1987."[2] Particular concern was expressed about the "disturbingly low level of compliance" with the insider reporting requirement in § 16(a) of the 1934 Act.[3]

Alternatively the Commission, in any proceeding against a registered broker-dealer or other regulated person subject to the Exchange Act's § 15(b)(4), § 15(b)(6), § 15B, § 15C, or § 17A may impose a civil penalty if it finds that the broker-dealer has committed any of a series of acts of the general kind specified in § 15(b)(4).[4]

The Commission may consider six factors in determining whether a penalty is in the public interest whether: (1) the act or omission involves "fraud, deceit, manipulation, or deliberate or reckless disregard of a regulatory requirement"; (2) the resulting harm to other persons; (3) the extent of any person's unjust enrichment (any restitution being taken into account); (4) the degree of recidivism; (5) the need to "deter such person and other persons from committing such acts or omissions"; and (6) "such other matters as justice may require" (a factor borrowed from the Federal Trade Commission Act).[5]

---

1. This was initially adopted in the Insider Trading Sanctions Act of 1984 and re-enacted in the Insider Trading and Securities Fraud Enforcement Act of 1988. *See* 8 Louis Loss & Joel Seligman, Securities Regulation 3746–3758 (3d ed. 1991).

2. H.R. Rep. No. 101–616, 101st Cong., 2d Sess. 17 (1990).

3. Id. at 23; S. Rep. No. 101–337, 101st Cong., 2d Sess. 17 (1990).

4. Sec. Ex. Act § 21B; Inv. Co. Act § 9(d); Inv. Adv. Act § 203(i).

5. Sec. Ex. Act § 21B(c); Inv. Co. Act § 9(d)(3); Inv. Adv. Act § 203(i)(3). Consideration of these factors is "permissive and not mandatory, because not all of the factors would apply in any given case." H.R. Rep. No. 101–616, 101st Cong. 2d Sess. 20 (1990).

In SEC v. Downe, 969 F.Supp. 149, 159 (S.D.N.Y.1997), *aff'd sub nom.* SEC v. Warde, 151 F.3d 42 (2d Cir.1998), a court applied a civil penalty of 100 percent when an insider trader had no prior history "and his illicit transactions * * * although repealed, involved only one security."

(b) Cease and Desist Orders

The Remedies Act also amended § 8 of the 1933 Act, § 9 of the Investment Company Act, and § 203 of the Investment Advisers Act, and added a new § 21C to the 1934 Act, to provide the SEC with an administrative cease and desist authority. Under this new remedy, the Commission may proceed against any respondent the Commission suspects has violated or is about to violate the federal securities laws, and order the respondent to cease the violation, disgorge profits, and take affirmative steps to comply with the securities laws. The Commission is also authorized by the Remedies Act to issue a temporary cease and desist order without notice to the respondent *without* a hearing. This temporary order will remain in effect until the administrative proceeding for the permanent order is resolved, unless the respondent appeals the temporary order to the Commission and, in turn, to a federal district court.

A theoretical advantage of the administrative cease and desist procedure is that it does not require the Commission—as it must in an injunction proceeding—to show a likelihood of future violation. Nonetheless in 2001 the Commission concluded that there must be some likelihood of future violations when it issues a cease and desist order.[1] Since enactment of the Remedies Act, the SEC has made frequent use of the cease and desist order.[2]

Valicenti Advisory Serv., Inc. v. SEC

United States Court of Appeals for the Second Circuit, 1999.
198 F.3d 62, *cert. denied*, 530 U.S. 1276 (2000).

■ Before: FEINBERG, CALABRESI and SOTOMAYOR, CIRCUIT JUDGES.

PER CURIAM:

Petitioners Valicenti Advisory Services, Inc. ("VAS") and Vincent R. Valicenti appeal from an opinion and order of the Securities and Exchange

---

Cf. Meadows v. SEC, 119 F.3d 1219, 1228 (5th Cir.1997), in which the court affirmed a cease and desist order and a $100,000 fine: "[W]e will affirm the Commission's imposition of sanctions absent arbitrariness or an abuse of discretion."

For an illustration of a court rejecting an SEC proposed fine as "too severe," see SEC v. Moran, 944 F.Supp. 286, 296 (S.D.N.Y. 1996).

1. KPMG Peat Marwick, LLP, AAER 1360, 74 SEC Dock. 357, 380 (2001). But the Commission concluded that this likelihood is less than necessary to issue an injunction:

> Though "some" risk is necessary, it need not be very great to warrant issuing a cease and desist order. Absent evidence to the contrary, a finding of violation raises a sufficient risk of future violation. To put it another way, evidence showing that a respondent violated the law probably also shows a risk of repetition that

merits our ordering to cease and desist. Our conclusion is suggested, though not compelled, by the statutory language. The statute specifies that we may impose a cease and desist order on a person who "has violated" the securities laws. This contrasts with our authority to seek injunctive relief in those instances when a person "is engaged or about to engage" in violative conduct.

Ibid. See also Andrew M. Smith, SEC Cease-and-Desist Orders, 51 Admin. L. Rev. 1197 (1999); Larry S. Gondelman & Thais R. Rencher, What the SEC Won't Tell You about Cease-and-Desist Orders, 28 Sec. Reg. L.J. 163 (2000); Stephen J. Crimmins & Mitchell E. Herr, SEC Resolves Long–Standing Questions about Its Cease-and-Desist Remedy, 33 Sec. Reg. & L. Rep. (BNA) 1084 (2001).

2. *See* 10 Louis Loss & Joel Seligman, Securities Regulation 4987–4993 (3d ed. rev. 1996). See also S. Rep. No. 101–337, 101st Cong., 2d Sess. 20–21 (1990).

Commission ("SEC" or "Commission") finding that VAS, aided and abetted by Valicenti, willfully violated various anti-fraud provisions of the Investment Advisers Act ("IAA"), 15 U.S.C. § 80b–1 *et seq.* (1994 & Supp. 1999), and imposing various sanctions. For the reasons to be discussed, we affirm.

BACKGROUND

Valicenti is the president and sole owner of VAS, an advisory organization registered with the SEC. Throughout 1992, petitioners distributed a packet of marketing materials to prospective clients. That packet contained a chart developed by petitioners which purported to show VAS's rates of return on its "Total Portfolio" between 1987 and 1991 (the "Chart"). On the Chart, a footnote next to "Total Portfolio" indicated that the displayed figures represented a "composite of discretionary accounts with a balanced objective."

In December 1993, the SEC commenced an inspection of VAS, at which time the Commission became aware of the Chart. The SEC found the Chart to be materially misleading because: (1) a reasonable investor would have understood a "composite" to include *all* "discretionary accounts with a balanced objective"; (2) the Chart reflected the performance of only a selected *portion* of VAS's "balanced" accounts; and (3) the rate of return ("ROR") for 1991 indicated on the Chart was more than seven percentage points higher than it would have been had the Chart incorporated all of VAS's balanced accounts for that year.

The Commission also found that petitioners acted with a deliberate intent to defraud. * * * upon the following facts:

Accordingly, the SEC found that both petitioners had violated § 206(1), § 206(2), and § 206(4) of the IAA, 15 U.S.C. §§ 80b–6(1), 80b–6(2), 80(b)–6(4), as well as SEC Rule 206(4)–1(a)(5), 17 C.F.R. § 275.206(4)–1(a)(5). In light of these findings, the SEC sanctioned petitioners with a censure, a cease and desist order, and fines of $50,000 against VAS and $25,000 against Valicenti. The Commission also required petitioners to send copies of the Commission's opinion and order to all existing clients of VAS and, in the following year, to all prospective clients.

Valicenti and VAS petition this court for review of the SEC's opinion and order pursuant to 5 U.S.C. §§ 702–706 (1994) and 15 U.S.C. § 80b–13 (1994). They argue * * * that petitioners violated the securities laws offended due process, because they had insufficient notice that their conduct was unlawful. Finally, petitioners argue that the sanctions exceeded the SEC's statutory authority and constituted an abuse of discretion. For the reasons that follow, we reject these arguments.

DISCUSSION

In reviewing the SEC's opinion and order, we must affirm "the findings of the Commission as to the facts, if supported by substantial evidence." 15 U.S.C. § 80b–13(a). The "traditional standard used for judicial review of agency actions * * * is deferential, and we may neither engage in our own fact-finding nor supplant the [SEC's] reasonable determinations." *Cellular Tel. Co. v. Town of Oyster Bay*, 166 F.3d 490, 494 (2d Cir.1999) (citation and internal quotation marks omitted).

* * *

IV. Sanctions

Petitioners challenge the SEC's imposition of monetary sanctions, the issuance of a cease and desist order, and the requirement that current and future clients be provided with a copy of the Commission's opinion and order ("the distribution requirement"). We review the Commission's imposition of sanctions for abuse of discretion. *See Markowski v. SEC*, 34 F.3d 99, 105 (2d Cir.1994).

We will find an abuse of discretion if the sanctions imposed are either unwarranted in law or without justification in fact. *See United States v. International Bhd. of Teamsters*, 170 F.3d 136, 144 (2d Cir.1999) (citation omitted). The sanctions imposed in this case are both within the SEC's statutory authority and justified under the circumstances. The Commission is empowered to assess monetary penalties of $50,000 against a natural person or $250,000 against a company for willful and fraudulent violations of the IAA. 15 U.S.C. § 80b–3(i)(2)(B) (1994). The Commission may also issue cease and desist orders that would "require [a violator] to comply, or take steps to effect compliance" with the provisions they violated. 15 U.S.C. § 80b–3(k)(1) (1994). Moreover, the Commission is empowered to "place limitations on the activities" of violators, suspend them for up to twelve months, or bar them entirely from the investment advising business. 15 U.S.C. § 80b–3(e), (f) (1994 & Supp. 1999). In determining whether to impose any or all of these statutorily authorized penalties, the Commission is to consider "whether the act or omission for which such penalty is assessed involved fraud, deceit, manipulation, or deliberate or reckless disregard of a regulatory requirement." 15 U.S.C. § 80b–3(i)(3)(A) (1994). Having upheld the SEC's finding that petitioners acted with an intent to defraud, we conclude that the monetary sanctions, the cease and desist order, and the distribution requirement were all justified under the circumstances.

Petitioners argue further that the Commission abused its discretion by imposing the distribution requirement because the imposition of such a sanction was "excessive" and "bore no rational relationship to the violations found." Although we recognize that the imposition of a sanction that is "palpably disproportionate to the violation" may be an abuse of discretion, *see Reddy v. Commodity Futures Trading Comm'n*, 191 F.3d 109, 124 (2d Cir. 1999), the distribution requirement here was rationally connected to the particular conduct at issue, *see id.* As we observed above, the IAA authorizes the SEC to "place limitations on the activities" of violators of the statute. 15 U.S.C. § 80b–3(e), (f). We see no reason why the distribution requirement might not be an appropriate and reasonable "limitation" in certain circumstances. In this regard, we note that the IAA explicitly permits the imposition of sanctions that are plausibly *more severe* than the distribution requirement, including revocation of the petitioners' registration and suspension for up to 12 months, *see id.*, each of which would likely result in greater loss of income and stigmatization than having to furnish copies of the SEC's opinion and order to existing and prospective clients for one year.

Moreover, the SEC has provided at least two reasonable explanations justifying the imposition of the distribution requirement as a reasonable "limitation" on petitioners' investment adviser activities. First, the distribution requirement will apprise present and prospective clients of the Commission's findings so that these investors may be fully informed in deciding whether they wish to do business with petitioners. Second, the distribution requirement may discourage petitioners from committing further violations. Given the serious nature of the petitioners' violations, we cannot deny that the distribution requirement is a rational means to alert actual and prospective clients of petitioners' misconduct and to discourage any further such conduct. *See Reddy*, 191 F.3d at 124 ("'[S]o long as an agency has articulate[d] a satisfactory explanation for its action including a rational connection between the facts found and the choice made, we will uphold its choice of sanctions.'") (citations and internal quotation marks omitted); *County Produce, Inc. v. United States Dep't of Agric.*, 103 F.3d 263, 266 (2d Cir.1997) (noting the "fundamental principle that where Congress has entrusted an administrative agency with the responsibility of selecting the means of achieving the statutory policy[,] the relation of remedy to policy is peculiarly a matter for administrative competence") (citation and internal quotation marks omitted).

Finally, petitioners argue that the distribution requirement was an abuse of discretion because the Commission has never before imposed such a sanction against an investment adviser in a litigated case. The Commission, however, has previously imposed sanctions similar to the distribution requirement here in investment adviser advertising cases that have been settled. [Cases Omitted.] We find no indication that the SEC singled out petitioners for particularly severe punishment. *Cf. Winkler v. SEC*, 377 F.2d 517, 518 (2d Cir.1967) (warning that the court must be "watchful" of whether sanctions have been applied in an "unduly harsh" or "discriminatory" manner). Moreover, petitioners have not identified any particular instances in which persons who intentionally misled their clients received more lenient treatment. Accordingly, we find that the sanctions imposed by the Commission do not constitute an abuse of discretion.

CONCLUSION

Having reviewed the record and examined petitioners' arguments and having found those arguments to be without merit, we affirm the opinion and order of the Securities and Exchange Commission.

(c) Corporate Bar Orders

The Remedies Act amended also § 20(e) of the 1933 Act and § 21(d)(1) of the 1934 Act to enable courts to bar an individual from serving as an officer or director of any publicly reporting corporation. The Senate Report explained, in part: "Although this remedy represents a potentially severe sanction for individual misconduct, persons who have demonstrated a blatant disregard for the requirements of the Federal securities laws should not be placed in a position of trust with a publicly held corporation."[1]

SEC v. Patel

United States Court of Appeals, Second Circuit, 1995.
61 F.3d 137.

■ MINER, CIRCUIT JUDGE:

Defendant-appellant Ratilal K. Patel appeals from a judgment entered in the United States District Court for the Southern District of New York

1. S. Rep. No. 101–337, 101st Cong., 2d Sess. 21–22 (1990). Cf. SEC v. Posner, 16 F.3d 520 (2d Cir.1994), *cert. denied,* 513 U.S. 1077 (1995) (director and officer bar based on District Court's general equitable powers); SEC v. First Pac. Bancorp., 142 F.3d 1186, 1193–1194 (9th Cir.1998), *cert. denied sub nom.* Sands v. SEC, 525 U.S. 1121 (1999) (following *Posner*). Regarding SEC corporate bar orders, see generally 10 Louis Loss & Joel Seligman, Securities Regulation 4993–4995 (3d ed. rev. 1996).

(Patterson, J.) in an action brought against him by plaintiff-appellee Securities and Exchange Commission ("SEC") for violations of federal securities laws. The judgment permanently enjoins Patel from future violations, orders him to disgorge $453,203 in illegal profits plus prejudgment interest and bars him from serving as an officer or director of any public company. On appeal, Patel contends that the district court erred in calculating the "avoided losses" that it ordered him to disgorge. He also contends that the district court considered improper factors in barring him permanently from serving as an officer or director of any public company.

BACKGROUND

The parties have no dispute regarding the factual background of this case. Patel was a founder, director and senior vice president for research and development of Par Pharmaceutical, Inc. ("Par"), a manufacturer of generic drugs. In November of 1987, Par submitted to the Food and Drug Administration ("FDA") an Abbreviated New Drug Application ("the Application") for a generic version of the drug known as Maxzide, which is used for the treatment of hypertension. The Application falsely represented that Par's generic Maxzide, of which sodium bicarbonate was an ingredient, had been tested in bioequivalency studies required by the FDA. This misrepresentation came in the form of a certificate of analysis for sodium bicarbonate. The certificate was backdated to conceal the fact that the bioequivalency studies were performed with a formulation of Maxzide that did not contain the sodium bicarbonate. Patel knew that the Application was false and, in February and March of 1988, sold 75,000 shares of common stock in Par. The average sale price was approximately $21.00 per share, and Patel realized a total of $1,576,358. It was not until July 24, 1989 that Par publicly disclosed that it was recalling its Maxzide tablets.

Par had experienced a number of adverse events before it revealed its problems with Maxzide. In July of 1988, a congressional subcommittee (the Dingell Subcommittee), which had begun an investigation into the generic pharmaceutical industry, focused on Par. A subcommittee subpoena for Par records was served on July 5, 1988, and the press later reported that Par was involved in the Dingell Subcommittee's inquiry into allegations of bribes and payoffs to FDA officials. It seems certain that this information had a negative impact on the price of Par's stock. Another, more serious, decline in the price of the stock occurred in October of 1988, following Par's announcement that it was a target of a grand jury investigation into various improprieties, including bribery, in the generic drug industry.

In April of 1989, the press reported that Ashok Patel, another Senior Vice President of Par, had resigned his position with Par and had agreed to plead guilty to unspecified charges. Later that month, the press reported the indictment of two FDA officials on bribery charges, in an article that referred to Par, Ashok Patel and Dilip Shah. Shah later resigned from the Board of Directors of a Par subsidiary known as Quad Pharmaceuticals, Inc. In May of 1989, the Dingell Subcommittee held public hearings in connection with its investigation into the generic drug approval process. The following month, there were negative press reports on the relationship between FDA officials and Ashok Patel and Dilip Shah. Thereafter, on July 11, it was reported that a third FDA employee had been criminally charged and, on July 17, it was reported that Par had agreed to plead guilty to a charge of providing an unlawful gratuity to an FDA employee. As was to be expected, all the negative news resulted in depressions in the price of Par stock.

When Par announced on July 24, 1989 that it was recalling its Maxzide product and suspending all shipments of the drug, it also announced that it had intentionally furnished a false report to the FDA during a recent inspection; that Ratilal Patel was taking a leave of absence from the company; that its vice president for regulatory affairs and its executive vice-president were taking leaves of absence from the Board of Directors; and that the company was postponing its annual shareholders' meeting in light of the ongoing investigation. Following that announcement, the price of Par stock closed on July 24 at $8.375 per share, down $1.625 from the $10 closing price on Friday, July 21, the previous trading day. On July 25, the next trading day, the stock closed at $7.125 per share. The total decline from the July 21 closing price was $2.875 or 28.75%. On July 26, 1989, the third day after the disclosure, Par stock rallied from $7.125 to close at $7.625.

On September 8, 1989, Patel resigned as a director and senior vice president of Par and as a director of its subsidiary, Quad Pharmaceuticals, Inc. In March of 1992, he settled a securities fraud class action claim with the payment of 500,000 shares of Par stock valued at approximately $3,000,000. In January of 1993, Patel pled guilty to conspiracy to defraud the FDA in connection with the generic Maxzide Application and thereafter was sentenced to a 27–month term of imprisonment, two years of supervised release and a $25,000 fine. * * *

II. Injunction Against Service as Officer and Director

> For violations of the antifraud provisions of the securities laws, the court may prohibit, conditionally or unconditionally, and permanently or for such period of time as it shall determine, any person who violated [the applicable provisions] from acting as an officer or director [of a public company] if the person's conduct demonstrates substantial unfitness to serve as an officer or director. * * *

15 U.S.C. §§ 77t(e) and 78u(d)(2) (enacted in 1990).

In permanently enjoining Patel from serving as an officer or director of any public company at the behest of the SEC, the district court necessarily determined that Patel was substantially unfit to hold such positions. The court identified six factors that it considered in resolving the issue of substantial unfitness: "'(1) the 'egregiousness' of the underlying securities law violation; (2) the defendant's 'repeat offender' status; (3) the defendant's 'role' or position when he engaged in the fraud; (4) the defendant's degree of scienter; (5) the defendant's economic stake in the violation; and (6) the likelihood that misconduct will recur." These factors were suggested in a law review article by Jayne W. Barnard entitled *When is a Corporate Executive "Substantially Unfit to Serve"?*, 70 N.C.L.Rev. 1489, 1492–93 (1992).

Applying the factors suggested by Professor Barnard, the district court found: that Patel's violations were not egregious in comparison with those of others and in view of the size of the loss avoided; that Patel was a first-time offender; that in his position as officer and director of Par, Patel allowed the false Application to be submitted and obstructed the FDA investigation of the Application by providing a "switched sample" of Maxzide to an FDA inspector;

that Patel "showed some scienter in his actions, although he did not engage in clandestine trading"; that he was the sole economic beneficiary of his insider trading; and that, because he was a founder of Par and abused his position as officer and director, "the likelihood of future misconduct is sufficient to warrant the imposition of the injunctive relief requested."

Patel contends that the district court improperly applied the factors it considered "by 'mixing' Patel's 'insider trading' with Par's submission of the false [Application] to the FDA." He further contends that, although his "conduct in the Maxzide affair gave rise to his 'insider' knowledge, it was not part of any 'scheme' to commit the securities law violation[s], and is not relevant to an analysis of his conduct" in respect of the violations. Patel claims that the district court's application of the six-factor test results in an almost even "split" between those factors that cut in his favor and those factors that cut against him. Moreover, Patel thinks that the district court should have taken into account the fact that criminal sanctions were imposed upon him and that he voluntarily settled the class action suit brought against him.

The district court properly considered Patel's involvement in the "Maxzide affair" as part and parcel of his conduct in the securities law violations. His deception of the FDA, although perhaps not originally designed to obtain profits or avoid losses in the sale of his stock, set in motion the scheme that culminated in his breach of fiduciary duties and in the resultant detriment to investors. Also, the district court properly took into account the six factors that it identified in evaluating substantial unfitness. These factors are useful in making the unfitness assessment, although we do not mean to say that they are the only factors that may be taken into account or even that it is necessary to apply all these factors in every case. A district court should be afforded substantial discretion in deciding whether to impose a bar to employment in a public company.

We do find a problem in this case, however, with the district court's finding regarding the likelihood of future misconduct, which is always an important element in deciding whether the substantial unfitness found justifies the imposition of a lifetime ban. The only findings that the district court made in this regard were that "Patel was a founder of Par and used his position as an officer and director to engage in misconduct." This is merely a general statement of events and can in no way justify the prediction that future misconduct will occur.

Moreover, we think that it was error for the district court to say that the likelihood of future misconduct based on the foregoing statement "is sufficient to warrant the imposition of the injunctive relief requested." The loss of livelihood and the stigma attached to permanent exclusion from the corporate suite certainly requires more. In a case in which we approved lifetime banishment as a common law remedy, we noted that the defendants "had committed securities law violations with a 'high degree of scienter' and that their past securities law violations and lack of assurances against future violations demonstrated that such violations were likely to continue." *Posner*, 16 F.3d at 521–22. Although it is not essential for a lifetime ban that there be past violations, we think that it is essential, in the absence of such violations, that a district court articulate the factual basis for a finding of the likelihood of recurrence.

Finally, we take note of the fact that the governing statute provides that a bar on service as an officer or director that is based on substantial unfitness may be imposed "conditionally or unconditionally" and "permanently or for such period of time as [the court] shall determine." We take these provisions to suggest that, before imposing a permanent bar, the court should consider whether a conditional bar (e.g., a bar limited to a particular industry) and/or a bar limited in time (e.g., a bar of five years) might be sufficient, especially where there is no prior history of unfitness. In this connection, we do not think that it would be improper for the district court to take into account any prior punishment that may have been imposed in a criminal proceeding. If the district court decides that a conditional ban or a ban limited in time is not warranted, it should give reasons why a lifetime injunction is imposed.

CONCLUSION

We affirm the judgment to the extent that it enjoins future securities law violations and orders the disgorgement of avoided losses.

(d) The Sarbanes–Oxley Act

There are several new remedial provisions added by the Sarbanes–Oxley Act of 2002.

Section 304 of the new Act requires the forfeiture by the chief executive and financial officers of bonuses or other incentive based compensation received during the 12 months following a financial disclosure that later requires an accounting restatement as a result of the issuer's misconduct.

Section 308 provides that specified civil penalties shall be added to disgorgement funds for investors.

Section 1103 authorizes the SEC to seek from a Federal District Court a temporary freeze order whenever it appears that a corporation may make extraordinary payments to a corporate officer, director, partner, control person, agent or employee.

Section 1105 authorizes the SEC to issue its own order in a cease and desist proceeding prohibiting persons from acting as officers or directors of any company registered under § 12.

F. Procedures

An SEC investigation into a possible violation of the federal securities laws is typically divided into two stages. The first stage is an "informal" inquiry initiated by the SEC staff into allegations of misconduct or as a result of information coming to the staff through many different sources (e.g., suggestions from other SEC divisions, referrals from self-regulatory organizations, complaints from market professionals of manipulation, newspaper reports, or anonymous informants). At this stage, while the staff investigators may interview prospective witnesses, the staff may not issue subpoenas, administer oaths, or otherwise compel testimony. The staff will seek the voluntary cooperation of the issuer and the other objects of its investigation. Defense counsel often face difficult tactical issues at this juncture, balancing their desire to cooperate in order to allay the staff's suspicions against the dangers of a wholesale disclosure of confidential corporate information.

In order to progress to the second or "formal" stage, the Commission staff must present to the Commission itself a request for an order instituting a "formal investigation." While not a formal adjudication or fact finding, this order of investigation authorizes the staff to issue subpoenas and to examine witnesses under oath. However, if a witness refuses to testify or to respond to a subpoena *duces tecum*, Commission investigative subpoenas are not self-enforcing. Rather, the Commission staff must apply under § 21(c) of the 1934 Act to the federal district court "within the jurisdiction in which such investigation or proceeding is carried on, or where such person resides or carries on business" to enforce the subpoena. However, the staff is not required to demonstrate that probable cause exists to believe that the securities laws have been violated.[1] Such a resort is seldom necessary, as few defendants want to infuriate the SEC's staff, given the typical pattern of negotiated resolution of SEC enforcement actions. Although a respondent can challenge the subpoena on the ground that the investigation is not for a legitimate purpose or that the information is not relevant to the investigation (or is already known to the SEC),[2] instances are rare in which such a challenge will be successful. More importantly, there is no requirement that the SEC notify the target of an investigation before it directs a subpoena to third parties.[3]

Special Issues: Proper Purpose

One issue that can arise at this stage is whether the Commission's investigation is the product of improper influence or political pressure on it. In SEC v. Wheeling–Pittsburgh Steel Corp.,[4] Wheeling sought to quash an SEC subpoena on the ground that the investigation into its proxy disclosures was the coerced result of pressure on the Commission from a United States Senator Lowell Weicker, who was allied with one of Wheeling Pittsburgh's principal competitors. The Senator had introduced legislation in the Senate that would have barred the granting of certain federal loan guarantees to any corporation that was under SEC investigation and he repeatedly contacted the SEC to urge an investigation of Wheeling Pittsburgh. In response, Wheeling Pittsburgh sought a motion for a protective order against the SEC's attempt to gather information from its officers. The District Court found that the SEC had permitted the "abuse of its investigating function," but declined to find that the SEC was acting in bad faith.

On appeal, the Third Circuit focused on the issue of "bad faith," saying that judicial enforcement of an administrative subpoena "would constitute an abuse of the court's process" in such circumstances. In remanding the case to the District Court for further findings, it framed the issue, as follows:

> "At bottom, this case raises the question whether, based on objective factors, the SEC's decision to investigate reflected its independent determination, or whether that decision was the product of external influences. The reality of prosecutorial experience, that most investigations originate on the basis of tips, suggestions or importunings of third parties, including commercial competitors, need hardly be noted. That the SEC commenced these proceedings as a result of the importunings of Senator Weicker * * * even with malice on [his] part, is not a sufficient basis to deny enforcement of the subpoena * * * But beginning an informal investigation by collecting facts at the request of a third party, even one harboring ulterior

1. *See* United States v. Morton Salt Co., 338 U.S. 632 (1950); SEC v. Brigadoon Scotch Distrib. Co., 480 F.2d 1047, 1052–53 (2d Cir.1973), *cert. denied*, 415 U.S. 915 (1974).

2. *See* United States v. Powell, 379 U.S. 48 (1964); SEC v. Arthur Young & Co., 584 F.2d 1018, 1020–31 (D.C.Cir.1978), *cert. denied*, 439 U.S. 1071 (1979).

3. *See* SEC v. Jerry T. O'Brien, Inc., 467 U.S. 735 (1984).

4. 648 F.2d 118 (3d Cir.1981).

motives, is much different from entering an order directing a private formal investigation * * * without an objective determination by the Commission and only because of political pressure. The respondents are not free from an informal investigation instigated by anyone, in or out of government. But they *are* entitled to a decision by the SEC, itself, free from third-party political pressure. * * * The SEC order must be supported by an independent agency determination, not one dictated or pressured by external forces."[5]

Right to Counsel

A witness who is subpoenaed to testify at an SEC investigation has the right to be "accompanied, represented and advised by counsel."[6] However, the persons who are being investigated have no right to be represented by counsel during the taking of testimony from other witnesses.[7] Counsel, however, may circumvent this rule by seeking to represent multiple witnesses (for example, the corporation and each of its subpoenaed officers). The SEC long sought to prevent such joint representation by taking the position that an attorney could not represent two or more witnesses, because this would give one defense attorney access to most of the evidence taken through witnesses in an investigation. Courts refused to accept the SEC's attempt to extend legal ethics in this regard and have held that the Commission may bar a counsel from representing multiple witnesses (or may sequester the attorney while any of the clients testify) only when it has "concrete evidence" that the attorney's presence would obstruct or impede the investigation.[8]

Confidentiality

The Commission has always insisted upon the secrecy of its investigations, even after the formal order of investigation has been issued, and typically the SEC attorney conducting the investigation will warn witnesses that they are not permitted to reveal to anyone the testimony they have given. Unlike grand jury proceedings, whose secrecy is mandated by law, there appears to be no statutory basis for the Commission's position.[9] The right of the Commission to refuse to release information acquired in the course of an investigation is, however, recognized by the Freedom of Information Act, subject to limited exceptions.[10]

Wells Submissions

After the staff completes its investigation, it must secure Commission approval to initiate any enforcement action. Although the Commission's decision will be made at a nonpublic meeting, with no right on the target's part to

---

5. Id. at 130.

6. *See* 17 C.F.R. § 203.7(b).

7. The Commission has a "sequestration" rule that denies both the witness, even if the witness is the target of the investigation, and its counsel the right to hear the testimony of other witnesses. *See* 17 C.F.R. § 203.7(b). This rule was upheld in SEC v. Meek, 1979–1980 Fed. Sec. L. Rep. (CCH) ¶ 97,323 (10th Cir. 1980).

8. *See* SEC v. Higashi, 359 F.2d 550 (9th Cir.1966); SEC v. Csapo, 533 F.2d 7 (D.C.Cir.1976); SEC v. Whitman, 613 F.Supp. 48 (D.D.C.1985).

9. The secrecy of grand jury proceedings is established by Rule 6(e) of the Federal Rules of Criminal Procedure. See United States v. DiBona, 601 F.Supp. 1162, 1166 (E.D.Pa.1984), *aff'd on reconsideration*, 610 F.Supp. 449 (1985).

10. *See* 5 U.S.C. § 552(b)(7).

appear or receive advance notice, the staff, as a matter of discretion, customarily informs the subjects of its recommendation and offers them an opportunity to file a written statement, known as a "Wells submission," with the Commission. The term comes from the recommendations of the SEC's Advisory Committee on Enforcement Policies (called the "Wells Committee" after its chairman).[11] In theory, a Wells submission is supposed to address the legal and policy issues in the case that should incline the Commission not to initiate an enforcement action, as opposed to factual issues. In practice, however, most attorneys address factual issues as well. The decision to file a Wells submission must be made carefully by defense counsel, particularly when a criminal reference is possible, because statements made in it may be taken as admissions, may be used for impeachment purposes, and arguably may be discoverable in later civil litigation with private plaintiffs.

RULES OF PRACTICE

The Commission has promulgated formal Rules of Practice to govern the conduct of administrative hearings.[1] An SEC hearing is initiated by the issuance of a Commission order—known as the Order of Proceedings—which is analogous to a complaint in a civil action. Once the Commission's order is served on the named respondents, they have 20 days to answer.[2] If the case is not resolved by settlement, an evidentiary hearing is typically held before an Administrative Law Judge (or "ALJ"). The hearing is conducted much like a civil trial, with the Commission's staff and respondents each having the right to present evidence and testimony and cross-examine witnesses. At the conclusion of the hearing, the ALJ will file an "initial decision," including findings and conclusions and an appropriate order.[3] Once this decision is rendered, any party to the proceeding may file a petition for Commission review of the initial decision,[4] or the Commission, itself, may order a review on its own initiative.

The factual findings made by the Commission in its decision are conclusive if supported by substantial evidence.[5] A party aggrieved by a final order entered by the Commission may obtain judicial review in the United States Court of Appeals for the District of Columbia or in the circuit where the party resides or has its principal place of business.[6]

Because of the broad discretion given the Commission and the severe penalties authorized by some provisions of the federal securities laws, a series of cases in the late 1970s held that the Commission could not impose certain severe sanctions, such as expulsion and suspension, except upon a showing of "clear and convincing evidence" of a securities violation.[7] Eventually, this

---

11. These recommendations were adopted in Sec. Act Rels. 5310 (1972); 5320 (1972). See generally 10 Louis Loss & Joel Seligman, Securities Regulation 4888–4891 (3d ed. rev. 1996); Kenneth B. Winer & Samuel J. Winer, Effective Representation in the SEC Wells Process, 34 Rev. Sec. & Commodities Reg. 59 (2001).

1. The current Rules of Practice were adopted in 1995. See 17 C.F.R. § 201.100 et seq. See generally 10 Louis Loss & Joel Seligman, Securities Regulation ch. 13.C (3d ed. rev. 1996).

2. 17 C.F.R. § 201.220.

3. 17 C.F.R. § 201.410.

4. 17 C.F.R. § 201.411.

5. See § 9(a) of the 1933 Act and § 25(a)(4) of the 1934 Act.

6. See § 9 of the 1933 Act; § 25 of the 1934 Act.

7. See Collins Sec. Corp. v. SEC, 562 F.2d 820 (D.C.Cir.1977).

position produced a split among the Circuits that attracted the Supreme Court's attention.

Steadman v. SEC

Supreme Court of the United States, 1981.
450 U.S. 91, 101 S.Ct. 999, 67 L.Ed.2d 69.

■ JUSTICE BRENNAN delivered the opinion of the Court.

In administrative proceedings, the Securities and Exchange Commission applies a preponderance of the evidence standard of proof in determining whether the antifraud provisions of the federal securities laws have been violated. The question presented is whether such violations must be proved by clear and convincing evidence rather than by a preponderance of the evidence.

I

In June 1971, the Commission initiated a disciplinary proceeding against petitioner and certain of his wholly-owned companies. The proceeding against petitioner was brought pursuant to § 9(b) of the Investment Company Act of 1940 and § 203(f) of the Investment Advisers Act of 1940. The Commission alleged that petitioner had violated numerous provisions of the federal securities laws in his management of several mutual funds registered under the Investment Company Act.

After a lengthy evidentiary hearing before an Administrative Law Judge and review by the Commission in which the preponderance of the evidence standard was employed, the Commission held that between December 1965 and June 1972, petitioner had violated antifraud, reporting, conflict of interest, and proxy provisions of the federal securities laws. Accordingly, it entered an order permanently barring petitioner from associating with any investment adviser or affiliating with any registered investment company, and suspending him for 1 year from associating with any broker or dealer in securities.

Petitioner sought review of the Commission's order in the United States Court of Appeals for the Fifth Circuit on a number of grounds, only one of which is relevant for our purposes. Petitioner challenged the Commission's use of the preponderance of the evidence standard of proof in determining whether he had violated antifraud provisions of the securities laws. He contended that, because of the potentially severe sanctions that the Commission was empowered to impose and because of the circumstantial and inferential nature of the evidence that might be used to prove intent to defraud, the Commission was required to weigh the evidence against a clear and convincing standard of proof. The Court of Appeals rejected petitioner's argument, holding that in a disciplinary proceeding before the Commission violations of the antifraud provisions of the securities laws may be established by a preponderance of the evidence. 603 F.2d 1126, 1143 (C.A.5 1979). See n. 8, supra. Because this was contrary to the position taken by the United States Court of Appeals for the District of Columbia, see Whitney v. SEC, 196 U.S.App.D.C. 12, 604 F.2d 676 (1979); Collins Securities Corp. v. SEC, 183 U.S.App.D.C. 301, 562 F.2d 820 (1977), we granted certiorari to resolve the conflict. 446 U.S. 917 * * * (1980). We affirm.

II

Where Congress has not prescribed the degree of proof which must be adduced by the proponent of a rule or order to carry its burden of persuasion in an administrative proceeding, this Court has felt at liberty to prescribe the standard, for "[i]t is the kind of question which has traditionally been left to the judiciary to resolve." Woodby v. Immigration and Naturalization Service, 385 U.S. 276, 284 (1966). However, where Congress has spoken, we have deferred to "the traditional powers of Congress to prescribe rules of evidence and standards of proof in the federal courts" absent countervailing constitutional constraints. Vance v. Terrazas, 444 U.S. 252, 265 * * * (1980). For Commission disciplinary proceedings initiated pursuant to * * * [§ 9(b) of the Investment Company Act of 1940 and § 211 of the Investment Advisers Act of 1940] we conclude that Congress has spoken, and has said that the preponderance of the evidence standard should be applied.

The securities laws provide for judicial review of Commission disciplinary proceedings in the federal courts of appeals and specify the scope of such review. Because they do not indicate which standard of proof governs Commission adjudications, however, we turn to § 5 of the Administrative Procedure Act (APA), 5 U.S.C. § 554, which "applies * * * in every case of adjudication required by statute to be determined on the record after opportunity for an agency hearing," except in instances not relevant here. Section 5(b), 5 U.S.C. § 554(c)(2) makes the provisions of § 7, 5 U.S.C. § 556, applicable to adjudicatory proceedings. The answer to the question presented in this case turns therefore on the proper construction of § 7.

The search for Congressional intent begins with the language of the statute. Andrus v. Allard, 444 U.S. 51, 56 * * * (1979); Reiter v. Sonotone Corp., 442 U.S. 330, 337 * * * (1979); 62 Cases of Jam v. United States, 340 U.S. 593, 596 * * * (1951). Section 7(c), 5 U.S.C. § 556(d), states in pertinent part:

> Except as otherwise provided by statute, the proponent of a rule or order has the burden of proof. Any oral or documentary evidence may be received, but the agency as a matter of policy shall provide for the exclusion of irrelevant, immaterial, or unduly repetitious evidence. A sanction may not be imposed or rule or order issued except on consideration of the whole record or those parts thereof cited by a party and supported by and *in accordance with* the reliable, probative, and *substantial evidence*. (Emphasis added.)

The language of the statute itself implies the enactment of a standard of proof.

By allowing sanctions to be imposed only when they are "in accordance with * * * *substantial* evidence," Congress implied that a sanction must rest on a *minimum quantity* of evidence. The word "substantial" denotes quantity. The phrase "in accordance with * * * substantial evidence" thus requires that a decision be based on a certain quantity of evidence. Petitioner's contention that the phrase "reliable, probative and substantial evidence" sets merely a standard of *quality* of evidence is, therefore, unpersuasive.[17]

---

17. Section 7(c), of course, also sets minimum quality of evidence standards. For example, the provision directing agency exclusion of "irrelevant, immaterial, or unduly repetitious evidence," and the further requirement that an agency sanction rest on "reliable" and "probative" evidence mandate that agency decisionmaking be premised on evidence of a certain level of quality. Thus, while the words "reliable" and "probative" may imply quality of evidence concerns, the word "substantial" implies quantity of evidence.

The phrase "in accordance with" lends further support to a construction of § 7(c) as establishing a standard of proof. Unlike § 10(e), the APA's explicit "Scope of review" provision that declares that agency action shall be held unlawful if "unsupported by substantial evidence," § 7(c) provides that an agency may issue an order only if that order is "supported by and *in accordance with* * * * substantial evidence" (emphasis added). The additional words "in accordance with" suggest that the adjudicating agency must weigh the evidence and decide, based on the weight of the evidence, whether a disciplinary order should be issued. The language of § 7(c), therefore, requires that the agency decision must be "in accordance with" the weight of the evidence, not simply supported by enough evidence " 'to justify, if the trial were to a jury, a refusal to direct a verdict when the conclusion sought to be drawn from it is one of fact for the jury.' " Consolo v. Federal Maritime Commission, 383 U.S. 607, 620 * * * (1966), quoting National Labor Relations Board v. Columbian Enameling & Stamping Co., 306 U.S. 292, 300 * * * (1939). Obviously, weighing evidence has relevance only if the evidence on each side is to be measured against a standard of proof which allocates the risk of error. See Addington v. Texas, 441 U.S. 418, 423 * * * (1979). Section 10(e), by contrast, does not permit the reviewing court to weigh the evidence, but only to determine that there is in the record " 'such relevant evidence as a reasonable mind might accept as adequate to support a conclusion,' " Consolo v. Federal Maritime Commission, supra, 383 U.S., at 620, quoting Consolidated Edison Co. v. National Labor Relations Board, 305 U.S. 197, 229 (1938). It is not surprising, therefore, in view of the entirely different purposes of § 7(c) and § 10(e), that Congress intended the words "substantial evidence" to have different meanings in context. Thus, petitioner's argument that § 7(c) merely establishes the scope of judicial review of agency orders is unavailing.

While the language of § 7(c) suggests, therefore, that Congress intended the statute to establish a standard of proof, the language of the statute is somewhat opaque concerning the precise standard of proof to be used. The legislative history, however, clearly reveals the Congress' intent. The original Senate version of § 7(c) provided that "no sanction shall be imposed * * * except as supported by relevant, reliable, and probative evidence." S. 7, 79th Cong., 1st Sess. (1945). After the Senate passed this version, the House passed the language of the statute as it reads today, and the Senate accepted the amendment. Any doubt as to the intent of Congress is removed by the House Report, which expressly adopted a preponderance of the evidence standard:

> [W]here a party having the burden of proceeding has come forward with a prima facie and substantial case, he will prevail unless his evidence is discredited or rebutted. In any case the agency must decide "in accordance with the evidence." Where there is evidence pro and con, the agency must weigh it and decide *in accordance with the preponderance*. In short, these provisions require a conscientious and rational judgment on the whole record in accordance with the proofs adduced. H.R. Rep. No. 1980, 79th Cong., 2d Sess. 37 (1946) (emphasis added).

Nor is there any suggestion in the legislative history that a standard of proof higher than a preponderance of the evidence was ever contemplated, much less intended. Congress was primarily concerned with the elimination of agency decisionmaking premised on evidence which was of poor quality—irrelevant, immaterial, unreliable and nonprobative—and of insufficient quantity—less than a preponderance. See H.R. Rep. No. 1980, supra, at 36–37 and 45; S. Doc. No. 248, supra, at 320–322 and 376–378; n. 21, supra.

The language and legislative history of § 7(c) lead us to conclude, therefore, that § 7(c) was intended to establish a standard of proof and that the standard adopted is the traditional preponderance of the evidence standard.

III

Our view of Congressional intent is buttressed by the Commission's long standing practice of imposing sanctions according to the preponderance of the evidence. * * * The Commission's consistent practice, which is in harmony with § 7(c) and its legislative history, is persuasive authority that Congress intended that Commission disciplinary proceedings, subject to § 7 of the APA, be governed by a preponderance of the evidence standard. See Andrus v. Sierra Club, 442 U.S. 347, 358 * * * (1979); United States v. National Association of Securities Dealers, Inc., 422 U.S. 694, 719 * * * (1975) * * *

* * * *

Affirmed.

■ JUSTICE POWELL, with whom JUSTICE STEWART joins, dissenting.

* * *

———

Ex Parte Sanctions. The Commission is authorized to employ one remedial sanction without notice or a hearing to the issuer affected thereby. Under Section 12(k) of the 1934 Act, the Commission "is authorized summarily to suspend trading in any security (other than an exempted security) for a period not exceeding 10 business days," or to suspend all trading on any national securities exchange for a period not to exceed 90 calendar days, although in the latter case only with the approval of the President. Until 1978, the Commission used this authority to effect a permanent suspension of trading (unless lifted by the Commission) in the stock of a particular company, by simply routinely renewing the suspension of trading for another ten days at the end of each ten-day period. In one case the suspension of trading was continued in this fashion for thirteen years.[1]

In SEC v. Sloan,[2] the United States Supreme Court held that such action by the Commission was unauthorized and illegal where the subsequent suspensions of trading were not based on any new circumstances arising after the initial suspension. Justice Brennan in his concurring opinion stated that:

> [T]he SEC's procedural implementation of its § 12(k) power mocks any conclusion other than that the SEC simply could not care whether its § 12(k) orders are justified. So far as this record shows, the SEC never reveals the reasons for its suspension orders. To be sure, here respondent was able long after the fact to obtain some explanation through a Freedom of Information Act request, but even the information tendered was heavily excised and none of it even purports to state the reasoning of the Commissioners under whose authority § 12(k) orders issue. Nonetheless, when the SEC finally agreed to give respondent a hearing on the suspension of Canadian Javelin stock, it required respondent to state, in a verified

---

1. See the concurring opinion of Justice Brennan in SEC v. Sloan, 436 U.S. 103, 123 (1978).

2. 436 U.S. 103 (1978).

petition (that is, under oath) why he thought the unrevealed conclusions of the SEC to be wrong. This is obscurantism run riot.[3]

In the wake of *Sloan,* the Commission will still employ back-to-back suspension orders under Section 12(k), but it is now "very careful to find a different ground for a second order."[4]

3.   436 U.S. at 124–125.

4.   See 4 Louis Loss & Joel Seligman, Securities Regulation 1912 (3d ed. rev. 2000).

CHAPTER 19

CRIMINAL ENFORCEMENT OF THE FEDERAL SECURITIES LAWS

Introductory Note

Criminal prosecutions under the federal securities laws have become increasingly common, most notably in response to the insider trading scandals of the 1980s. However, the criminal provisions of the federal securities laws do not focus on insider trading or even on fraud offenses. Both § 24 of the 1933 Act and § 32(a) or the 1934 Act are considerably broader in scope, each making it a felony for any person "willfully" to violate any statutory provision of either statute, or any rule or regulation promulgated thereunder. Any SEC rule or regulation, or any false filing with the SEC, can support a criminal prosecution (with § 24 providing for a sentence of up to five years and § 32(a) authorizing a sentence of up to 20 years).[1]

Federal prosecutors are not limited to the use of the federal securities laws in seeking to prosecute either financial frauds or insider trading. Indeed, a popular weapon is their traditional standby, the federal mail and wire fraud statutes.[2] We have already seen this provision in action in the *O'Hagan* case.

1. Many provisions in the Sarbanes–Oxley Act addressed criminal remedies.

Title VIII of the new Act, which may be cited as the Corporate and Criminal Fraud Accountability Act of 2002, begins with § 802 which amends chapter 73 of title 18 of the United States Code to add a new § 1519, a criminal provision with up to a 20 year term of imprisonment to address alteration or falsification of records in federal investigations and bankruptcy. Section 802 also adds § 1520 to create a criminal provision with up to ten years imprisonment for destruction of corporate audit records. The provisions were inspired by Arthur Andersen, which on March 7, 2002 was indicted, the first criminal indictment of a Big Five accounting firm. In July 2002 Arthur Andersen was convicted.

Section 807 adds a provision that provides up to a 25 year term of imprisonment for securities fraud.

Title IX, also known as the White Collar Crime Penalty Enforcement Act of 2002, also augments several criminal penalties. Notably § 906 creates criminal penalties for violation of the written certification required by the chief executive officer and chief financial officer. A knowing violation can result in a fine up to $1 million and imprisonment up to ten years.

Section 1106 amends § 32(a) of the 1934 Act to increase specified criminal penalties up to $5 or $25 million and imprisonment up to 20 years.

Section 1107 amends 18 U.S.C. § 1513(e) to add a generic prohibition against person who, "knowingly, with the intent to retaliate, takes any action harmful to any person, including interference with the lawful employment or livelihood of any person, for providing to a law enforcement officer any truthful information relating to the commission or possible commission of any Federal offense, shall be fined under this title or imprisoned not more than 10 years, or both."

2. 18 U.S.C. §§ 1341, 1343. Regarding the federal mail and wire fraud statutes, see John C. Coffee, Jr., The Metastasis of Mail Fraud: The Continuing Story of the "Evolution" of a White Collar Crime, 21 Amer. Crim. L. Rev. 1 (1983); John C. Coffee, Jr., The Federalization of Fraud: Mail and Wire Fraud Statutes, in Otto G. Obermaier & Robert G. Morvillo, White Collar Crime: Business and Regulatory Offenses (1989).

For criminalists, the observation of Judge Rakoff is particularly memorable: "To federal prosecutors of white collar crime, the mail fraud statute is our Stradivarius, our Colt 45, our Louisville Slugger, our Cuisinart—and our true love. We may flirt with RICO, show off with 10b–5, and call the conspiracy law darling, but we always come

Prosecutors can also seek substantially harsher sentences, a special forfeiture sanction and a pretrial freeze of the defendant's assets under the RICO statute.[3] In 1995 Congress, however, ended an earlier express private cause of action for securities violations under RICO.

A. PROCEDURAL ISSUES

Criminal prosecutions in the federal system are brought by United States Attorneys, and the Securities and Exchange Commission has neither authority nor practical control over the decision of a U.S. Attorney to initiate a criminal prosecution. Section 21(d) of the 1934 Act does authorize the Commission to "transmit such evidence as may be available concerning such acts or practices as may constitute a violation of any provision of this [title] or the rules or regulations thereunder to the Attorney General, who may, in his discretion, institute the necessary criminal proceedings under this [title]."

While some criminal prosecutions for securities law violations can originate in a U.S. Attorney's office (often as the result of plea bargain negotiations with defendants in other cases who have an incentive to "cooperate" by revealing other crimes, including those by third parties), the typical pattern is for the initial investigative work in a criminal prosecution to be performed by personnel within the SEC's Division of Enforcement. At some point, personnel within the Division of Enforcement or a regional office may decide that the matter under investigation is sufficiently serious to warrant a criminal prosecution. One of several different courses of action may then be followed: First, a formal "criminal reference" may be made. This requires a vote by the Commission, requesting the Department of Justice to commence an investigation and transmitting any evidence in the Commission's possession pursuant to § 21(d). More often an informal reference will be made. This means that staff of the Commission will informally advise their counterparts in a U.S. Attorney's office (with whom they may have frequent contact on other pending matters) about a case and invite them to request to see the Commission's file. The SEC will invariably comply with such a request.[1] Such informal references without a Commission vote have been held not to violate any rights of the accused.[2]

A criminal reference does not mean the Commission suspends its own enforcement activity. It may still pursue injunctive or administrative relief (such as disgorgement or civil penalties). From defense counsel's perspective, the most important consideration in any SEC investigation is often to protect the client from a criminal reference. Once, defense counsel would bargain in its negotiations for an express promise by the staff that it would not make a criminal reference in return for whatever relief was agreed upon. The practice of the SEC changed, however, following the case of United States v. Fields.[3] There, enforcement staff gave the impression to defense counsel that they

home to the virtues of 18 U.S.C. § 1341, with its simplicity, adaptability and comfortable familiarity." Jed S. Rakoff, The Federal Mail Fraud Statute (Part I), 18 Duquesne L. Rev. 771 (1980).

3. 18 U.S.C. §§ 1961–1968.

1. The Commission's policy is that it does not have "the authority or responsibility for initiating, conducting, settling, or otherwise disposing of criminal proceedings. That authority and responsibility are vested in the Attorney General and representatives of the Department of Justice." See 17 C.F.R. § 202.5(f).

2. See United States v. Bloom, 450 F.Supp. 323 (E.D.Pa.1978).

3. 1977–1978 Fed.Sec.L.Rep. (CCH) ¶ 96,074 (S.D.N.Y.1977), *aff'd in part, rev'd in part*, 592 F.2d 638 (2d Cir.1978).

would not make an informal criminal reference in return for a civil settlement, but in fact they did recommend criminal prosecution and the defendant was indicted. Although the Second Circuit found this implicit promise not to be binding on the U.S. Attorney (who had no notice of it), it condemned the SEC staff attorneys' conduct as unprofessional and indicated that under some circumstances such a promise could be binding. In response, the SEC adopted a formal policy of refusing to comment on whether a criminal reference would be made.[4] This rule has greatly complicated life for defense counsel, who still naturally desire "global" settlements of all pending SEC and criminal charges (and who fear even making Wells submissions if the material in them might be turned over to a U.S. Attorney). Sometimes, before settling potentially criminal charges with the SEC (such as insider trading charges), defense counsel will even approach the U.S. Attorney's staff and ask it to sign off by indicating its lack of interest in criminal prosecution. The premise here is that the U.S. Attorney will read the SEC's staff silence as indicating its implied consent to a noncriminal resolution of the case (although, of course, the staff or the Commission could make a post-settlement request).

A different problem surfaces when parallel SEC and criminal investigations overlap. Discovery in the federal criminal process is limited and is essentially conducted through the mechanism of the grand jury. Before the grand jury, the defendant has a Fifth Amendment right, which defense counsel will strongly encourage the defendant to take. Yet, as discussed below, the Fifth Amendment supplies much less protection in a civil proceeding before the SEC (at which the defendant could be barred from the securities business for life or fined a substantial amount). An incentive therefore arises to use civil discovery to supplement the criminal investigatory process.

SEC v. Dresser Industries, Inc.

United States Court of Appeals, District of Columbia Circuit, 1980.
628 F.2d 1368, *cert. denied*, 449 U.S. 993 (1980).

■ Before Wright, Chief Judge, and McGowan, Tamm, Robinson, MacKinnon, Robb, Wilkey, Wald, Mikva, and Edwards, Circuit Judges.

■ J. Skelly Wright, Chief Judge: Dresser Industries, Inc. (Dresser) appeals from a decision of the District Court requiring obedience to a subpoena *duces tecum* issued by the Securities and Exchange Commission (SEC) on April 21, 1978, and denying Dresser's motion to quash the subpoena. The subpoena was issued in connection with an SEC investigation into Dresser's use of corporate funds to make what are euphemistically called "questionable foreign payments," and into the adequacy of Dresser's disclosures of such payments under the securities laws.

The principal issue facing this en banc court is whether Dresser is entitled to special protection against this SEC subpoena because of a parallel investigation into the same questionable foreign payments now being conducted by a federal grand jury under the guidance of the United States Department of

---

4. See 17 C.F.R. § 202.5(f): "Any person involved in an enforcement matter before the Commission who consents, or agrees to consent, to any judgment or order does so solely for the purpose of resolving the claims against him in that investigative, civil, or administrative matter and not for the purpose of resolving any criminal charges that have been, or might be, brought against him."

Justice (Justice). Dresser argues principally that the SEC subpoena abuses the civil discovery process of the SEC for the purpose of criminal discovery and infringes the role of the grand jury in independently investigating allegations of criminal wrongdoing. On November 19, 1979 a panel of this court issued a decision affirming the District Court but, with Judge Robb dissenting, attaching a condition prohibiting the SEC from providing Justice with the information received from Dresser under this subpoena. Because of the importance of this issue to enforcement of the regulatory laws of the United States, this court voted to vacate the panel opinions and rehear the case en banc.

I.   BACKGROUND

A.   *Origin of the Investigations*

Illegal and questionable corporate payments surfaced as a major public problem in late 1973, when several major scandals implicated prominent American corporations in improper use of corporate funds to influence government officials in the United States and foreign countries. The exposure of these activities disrupted public faith in the integrity of our political system and eroded international trust in the legitimacy of American corporate operations abroad.[3] SEC investigation revealed that many corporate officials were falsifying financial records to shield questionable foreign and domestic payments from exposure to the public and even, in many cases, to corporate directors and accountants. Since the completeness and accuracy of corporate financial reporting is the cornerstone of federal regulation of the securities markets, such falsification became a matter of grave concern to the SEC.

Beginning in the spring of 1974 the SEC brought a series of injunctive actions against certain American corporations. It obtained consent decrees prohibiting future violations of the securities laws and establishing internal corporate procedures for investigation, disclosure, and prevention of illegal corporate payments. However, the problem of questionable foreign payments proved so widespread that the SEC devised a "Voluntary Disclosure Program" to encourage corporations to conduct investigations of their past conduct and make appropriate disclosures without direct SEC coercion. Participation in the Voluntary Disclosure Program would not insulate a corporation from an SEC enforcement action, but the Commission would be less likely to exercise its discretion to initiate enforcement actions against participants. The most important elements of the Voluntary Disclosure Program were (1) an independent committee of the corporation would conduct a thorough investigation into questionable foreign and domestic payments made by the corporation; (2) the committee would disclose the results of this investigation to the board of directors in full; (3) the corporation would disclose the substance of the report to the public and the SEC on Form 8–K; and (4) the corporation would issue a

---

3. The Senate Committee on Banking, Housing, and Urban Affairs reported in May 1977:

> Recent investigations by the SEC have revealed corrupt foreign payments by over 300 U.S. companies involving hundreds of millions of dollars. These revelations have had severe adverse effects. Foreign governments friendly to the United States in Japan, Italy, and the Netherlands have come under intense pressure from their own people. The image of American democracy abroad has been tarnished. Confidence in the financial integrity of our corporations has been impaired. The efficient functioning of our capital markets has been hampered.

S. Rep. No. 114, 95th Cong., 1st Sess. 3 (1977).

policy statement prohibiting future questionable and illegal payments and maintenance of false or incomplete records in connection with them. Except in "egregious cases" the SEC would not require that public disclosures include specific names, dates and places. Rather, the disclosure might be "generic" in form. Thus companies participating in the Voluntary Disclosure Program would ordinarily be spared the consequences to their employees, property, and business that might result from public disclosure of specific instances of foreign bribery or kickbacks. However, companies participating in the Voluntary Disclosure Program had to agree to grant SEC requests for access to the final report and to the unexpurgated underlying documentations.

B.   *The Dresser Investigations*

On January 27, 1976 an attorney and other representatives of Dresser met with members of the SEC staff to discuss a proposed filing. At the meeting Dresser agreed to conduct an internal inquiry into questionable foreign payments, in accordance with the terms of the Voluntary Disclosure Program. The next day Dresser submitted a Form 8–K describing, in generic terms, one questionable foreign payment. Joint Appendix (JA) 100–102. On November 11, 1976 Dresser filed a second Form 8–K reporting the results of the internal investigation. JA 103–108. On February 10, 1977 the company supplemented this report with a third Form 8–K concerning a questionable payment not reported in the earlier reports. JA 109–113. The reports concerned Dresser's foreign activities after November 1, 1973. All disclosures were in generic, not specific, terms.

As part of its general monitoring program the SEC staff requested access to the documents underlying Dresser's report. On July 15, 1977 Dresser refused to grant such access. The company argued that allowing the staff to make notes or copies might subject its documents to public disclosure through the Freedom of Information Act. Dresser stated that such disclosure could endanger certain of its employees working abroad. During the ensuing discussions with the staff Dresser attempted to impose conditions of confidentiality upon any SEC examination of its documents, but the staff did not agree. Instead, it issued a recommendation to the Commission for a formal order of investigation in the Dresser case. * * *

Meanwhile, the Department of Justice had established a task force on transnational payments to investigate possible criminal violations arising from illegal foreign payments. Two SEC attorneys participated in the task force. In the summer of 1977 the Justice task force requested access to SEC files on the approximately 400 companies, including Dresser, that had participated in the Voluntary Disclosure Program. Pursuant to Commission authorization the SEC staff transmitted all such files to the Justice task force in August 1977. After its preliminary investigation of the Form 8–K's submitted by Dresser under the Voluntary Disclosure Program, Justice presented Dresser's case to a grand jury in the District of Columbia on January 25, 1978.

Before any summons or subpoena had issued in either the SEC or the grand jury investigation, Dresser filed suit in the Southern District of Texas against the SEC and Justice to enjoin any further investigation of it by either agency. While Dresser's suit was pending in the Southern District of Texas, the District of Columbia grand jury subpoenaed Dresser's documents on April 21, 1978. At roughly the same time the SEC issued a formal order of private investigation, authorizing the staff to subpoena the documents and to obtain other relevant evidence. JA 7–9 (April 11, 1978). Pursuant to that order the staff issued a subpoena *duces tecum,* returnable on May 4, 1978. JA 14–16 (April 21, 1978). This subpoena covered substantially the same documents and materials subpoenaed by the grand jury, and more. Dresser did not respond to the subpoena.

* * *

II.   GENERAL PRINCIPLES

A.   Parallel Investigations

The civil and regulatory laws of the United States frequently overlap with the criminal laws, creating the possibility of parallel civil and criminal proceedings, either successive or simultaneous. In the absence of substantial prejudice to the rights of the parties involved, such parallel proceedings are unobjectionable under our jurisprudence. As long ago as 1912 the Supreme Court recognized that under one statutory scheme—that of the Sherman Act—a transaction or course of conduct could give rise to both criminal proceedings and civil suits. Standard Sanitary Manufacturing Co. v. United States, 226 U.S. 20, 52 * * * (1912). The Court held that the government could initiate such proceedings either "simultaneously or successively," with discretion in the courts to prevent injury in particular cases. * * *

* * *

The Constitution, therefore, does not ordinarily require a stay of civil proceedings pending the outcome of criminal proceedings. See Baxter v. Palmigiano, 425 U.S. 308 * * * (1976); DeVita v. Sills, 422 F.2d 1172, 1181 (3d Cir.1970). Nevertheless, a court may decide in its discretion to stay civil proceedings, postpone civil discovery, or impose protective orders and conditions "when the interests of justice seem[ ] to require such action, sometimes at the request of the prosecution, * * * sometimes at the request of the defense[.]" United States v. Kordel, supra, 397 U.S. at 12 n.27 (citations omitted); see Horne Brothers, Inc. v. Laird, 463 F.2d 1268, 1271–1272 (D.C.Cir.1972). The court must make such determinations in the light of the particular circumstances of the case.

Other than where there is specific evidence of agency bad faith or malicious governmental tactics, the strongest case for deferring civil proceedings until after completion of criminal proceedings is where a party under indictment for a serious offense is required to defend a civil or administrative action involving the same matter. The noncriminal proceeding, if not deferred, might undermine the party's Fifth Amendment privilege against self-incrimination, expand rights of criminal discovery beyond the limits of Federal Rule of Criminal Procedure 16(b), expose the basis of the defense to the prosecution in advance of criminal trial, or otherwise prejudice the case. If delay of the noncriminal proceeding would not seriously injure the public interest, a court may be justified in deferring it. See, e.g., United States v. Henry, 491 F.2d 702 (6th Cir.1974); Texaco, Inc. v. Borda, 383 F.2d 607, 608–609 (3d Cir.1967); Silver v. McCamey, 221 F.2d 873, 874–875 (D.C.Cir.1955). * * * In some such cases, however, the courts may adequately protect the government and the private party by merely deferring civil discovery or entering an appropriate protective order. Gordon v. FDIC, 427 F.2d 578, 580–581 (D.C.Cir.1970). The case at bar is a far weaker one for staying the administrative investigation. No indictment has been returned; no Fifth Amendment privilege is threatened; Rule 16(b) has not come into effect and the SEC subpoena does not require Dresser to reveal the basis for its defense.

B.   *SEC Investigations*

The case at bar concerns enforcement of the securities laws of the United States, especially the Securities Act of 1933 ('33 Act) and the Securities Exchange Act of 1934 ('34 Act). These statutes explicitly empower the SEC to investigate possible infractions of the securities laws with a view to both civil and criminal enforcement, and to transmit the fruits of its investigations to Justice in the event of potential criminal proceedings. The '34 Act provides in relevant part: "The Commission may, in its discretion, make such investigations as it deems necessary to determine whether any person has violated, is violating, or is about to violate any provision of this chapter[.]" Section 21(a) of the '34 Act (1976). This investigative authority includes the power to administer oaths and affirmations, subpoena witnesses, take evidence, and require production of any books, papers, correspondence, memoranda, or other records which the SEC deems relevant or material. Id., Section 21(b). If it determines that a person "is engaged or is about to engage in acts or practices constituting a violation" of the Act, the SEC may bring an action in federal district court to enjoin such acts or practices. Id., Section 21(d). Under the same subsection of the '34 Act the SEC may "transmit such evidence as may be available concerning such acts or practices * * * to the Attorney General, who may, in his discretion, institute the necessary criminal proceedings under this chapter." Id. The '33 Act is to similar effect. See Sections 19(b), 20(a), (b) of the '33 Act.

Effective enforcement of the securities laws requires that the SEC and Justice be able to investigate possible violations simultaneously. Dissemination of false or misleading information by companies to members of the investing public may distort the efficient workings of the securities markets and injure investors who rely on the accuracy and completeness of the company's public disclosures. If the SEC suspects that a company has violated the securities laws, it must be able to respond quickly: it must be able to obtain relevant information concerning the alleged violation and to seek prompt judicial redress if necessary. Similarly, Justice must act quickly if it suspects that the laws have been broken. Grand jury investigations take time, as do criminal prosecutions. If Justice moves too slowly the statute of limitations may run, witnesses may die or move away, memories may fade, or enforcement resources may be diverted. See United States v. Fields, 592 F.2d 638, 646 (2d Cir.1978), cert. denied 442 U.S. 917 * * * (1979). The SEC cannot always wait for Justice to complete the criminal proceedings if it is to obtain the necessary prompt civil remedy; neither can Justice always await the conclusion of the civil proceeding without endangering its criminal case. Thus we should not block parallel investigations by these agencies in the absence of "special circumstances" in which the nature of the proceedings demonstrably prejudices substantial rights of the investigated party or of the government. See United States v. Kordel, supra, 397 U.S. at 11–13.

* * *

In essence, Dresser has launched this attack on the parallel SEC and Justice proceedings in order to obtain protection against the bare SEC proceeding, which it fears will result in public disclosure of sensitive corporate documents. The prejudice Dresser claims it will suffer from the parallel nature of the proceedings is speculative and undefined if indeed Dresser would suffer any prejudice from it at all. Any entitlement to confidential treatment of its documents must arise under the laws pertaining to the SEC; the fortuity of a parallel grand jury investigation cannot expand Dresser's rights in this SEC enforcement action. Thus Dresser's invocation of *LaSalle* [United States v. LaSalle National Bank, 437 U.S. 298 (1978)] can avail the company nothing.

IV.   COOPERATION BETWEEN SEC AND JUSTICE

In its initial decision in this case a panel of this court ruled that "the broad prophylactic rule enunciated in *LaSalle* is inappropriate where the SEC and the Justice Department are simultaneously pursuing civil and criminal investigations." Slip opinion at 18. The panel therefore affirmed the District Court and ordered enforcement of the SEC subpoena. Out of a concern that the SEC subpoena might somehow "subvert the limitations of criminal discovery," id., however, the panel, with one judge dissenting, modified the terms of the subpoena enforcement order. It required that "once the Justice Department initiates criminal proceedings by means of a grand jury, the SEC may not provide the Justice Department with the fruits of the Commission's civil discovery gathered after the decision to prosecute." Id. at 22. We affirm the judgment of the District Court and reject the panel's modification.

First, we note that no party to this case had suggested or requested a modification such as that imposed by the panel majority, either in the District Court or in this court. * * *

Second, we note that there is no support for the panel's modification in either the relevant statutes or legislative history. Both the '33 Act and the '34 Act and other statutes related to securities law enforcement as well expressly authorize the SEC to "transmit such evidence as may be available * * * to the Attorney General, who may, in his discretion, institute the necessary criminal proceedings under this subchapter." Section 20(b) of the '33 Act; Section 21(d) of the '34 Act. The statutes impose no limitation on when this transmittal may occur. The parties have not cited any portions of the legislative histories of these Acts relevant to this question, nor have we found any. But the SEC and Justice find considerable support for their interpretation in the legislative history of the Foreign Corrupt Practices Act of 1977, 91 Stat. 1494, Title I, 15 U.S.C. §§ 78a, 78m, 78dd–1, 78dd–2, 78ff (Supp. I 1977).

* * *

Congress manifestly did not intend that the SEC be forbidden to share information with Justice at this stage of the investigation. Under the panel majority's theory of the case the SEC would be foreclosed from sharing the fruits of its investigation with Justice as soon as Justice begins its own investigation through a grand jury. Only by waiting until the close of the SEC proceeding before initiating its own grand jury investigation could Justice obtain access to the evidence procured by the SEC. In view of Congress' concern that the agencies share information "at the earliest stage of any investigation in order to insure that the evidence needed for a criminal prosecution does not become stale," S.Rep. No. 114, supra, at 12, and that the agencies avoid "a costly duplication of effort," H.R.Rep. No. 640, supra, at 9, it would be unreasonable to prevent a sharing of information at this point in the investigation.

Third, we note that there is little or no judicial precedent for the panel's modification. * * *

* * *

Finally, we note that the panel's modification would serve no compelling purpose, and might interfere with enforcement of the securities laws by the SEC and Justice. As the Second Circuit has said, the procedure permitting the SEC to communicate with Justice during the preliminary stages of an investigation has "significant advantages." United States v. Fields, supra, 592 F.2d at 646.

> Allowing early participation in the case by the United States Attorney minimizes statute of limitations problems. The more time a United States Attorney has, the easier it is for him to become familiar with the complex facts of a securities fraud case, to prepare the case, and to present it to a grand jury before expiration of the applicable statute of limitations. Earlier initiation of criminal proceedings moreover is consistent with a defendant's right to a speedy trial. * * *

Id. The panel's modification would "interfere with this commendable example of inter-agency cooperation," id., to the detriment of securities law enforcement and in contravention of the will of Congress. On the other side of the balance, the panel's concern for preserving the limitations on criminal discovery is largely irrelevant at this stage of the proceedings, as Dresser agrees. Thus this would be an inappropriate situation to impose a "prophylactic" rule against cooperation between the agencies. We believe the courts can prevent any injustice that may arise in the particular circumstances of parallel investigations in the future. We decline to adopt the position of the panel majority.

* * *

The judgments of the District Court are Affirmed.

Concurring Opinion of Circuit Judge Edwards: I concur in the opinion of the court in this case. I wish to point out, however, that I do not read the court's opinion as expressing any view as to the proper outcome in a case of this sort once an indictment has issued. * * * Once an indictment has issued, the policy interest expressed in United States v. LaSalle National Bank, 437 U.S. 298, 312 * * * (1978), concerning the impermissibility of broadening the scope of criminal discovery through the summons authority of an agency, may come into play. I express no opinion as to whether or not the summons authority of a government agency may continue once an indictment has been issued or, if it may, whether protective conditions need be placed on the exercise of that power. These issues raise questions which are not presented here. The resolution of these questions, therefore, must await another day.

Parallel Proceedings. In one sense, all SEC proceedings are potentially "parallel," because the U.S. Attorney can commence a criminal prosecution at any time within the statute of limitations and the SEC will never agree to discuss the issue of a criminal reference with the target of its investigation. In the usual sense of the term, however, the phrase "parallel proceeding" refers to a situation where the SEC investigation is continuing at the same time that the Justice Department is conducting a grand jury investigation with respect to the same subject matter. In United States v. LaSalle National Bank,[1] the Supreme Court held that a summons issued by the Internal Revenue Service after a recommendation for prosecution had been made by it to the Department of Justice was unenforceable: "Nothing in § 7602 [of the Internal Revenue Code] or its legislative history suggests that Congress intended the summons authority to broaden the Justice Department's right of criminal litigation discovery or to infringe on the role of the grand jury as the principal tool of criminal accusation."[2] Yet in *Dresser Industries,* the D.C. Circuit distinguished *LaSalle* and earlier cases on the ground that different statutory provisions were involved. Is there a sound basis for distinguishing an SEC subpoena from an IRS summons once a criminal referral has been made? What if the SEC feared that investors would continue to be misled by fraudulent financial statements? Is *Dresser* such a case?

A defendant who testifies at an SEC investigation effectively forfeits the privilege against self-incrimination because a transcript of the testimony will in all likelihood be made available to the prosecutor and the grand jury and may be used for impeachment purposes at trial. If the defendant invokes the Fifth Amendment at a civil hearing or trial, the court or administrative law judge may permissibly draw an adverse inference,[3] and it is likely that the defendant will lose the case. In short, the defendant faces Hobson's choice when there are parallel proceedings.

A defendant faced with simultaneous civil litigation and a criminal investigation (or a pending trial) can seek to stay the civil proceedings (or at least any deposition or scheduled testimony of the defendant in the civil case) pending the resolution of the criminal case. Such stays are discretionary with the court, but, in the securities law context, defendants have not been noticeably successful in obtaining stays.[4]

B. CRIMINAL PROSECUTIONS UNDER THE FEDERAL SECURITIES LAWS

Section 24 of the 1933 Act and Section 32(a) of the 1934 Act each criminalize any "willful" violation of the statutory provisions in their respective statutes or of any rule or regulation adopted thereunder. However, there is one significant difference between these two provisions: Section 32 criminalizes a false filing only if it is made "willfully and knowingly." This phrasing raises an interpretive issue: What does "knowingly" add to "willfully?" Does it require some knowledge of guilt or at least bad faith? The problem of construing § 32(a) is compounded by its final clause, which adds that, even if convicted, "no person shall be subject to imprisonment under this section for the violation of any rule or regulation if he proves that he had no knowledge of such rule or regulation." But how can one have "no knowledge" if one must act "knowingly" (in the case of a false filing) to be convicted in the first instance?

---

1. 437 U.S. 298 (1978).

2. 437 U.S. at 312 (1978).

3. See Baxter v. Palmigiano, 425 U.S. 308 (1976).

4. See United States v. Kordel, 397 U.S. 1 (1970); SEC v. Drucker, 1979 Fed.Sec.

L.Rep. (CCH), ¶ 96,821 (S.D.N.Y.1979); see generally Note, Unjust Justice in Parallel Proceedings: Preventing Circumvention of Criminal Discovery Rules, 27 Hofstra L. Rev. 109 (1998).

United States v. Dixon

United States Court of Appeals, Second Circuit, 1976.
536 F.2d 1388.

■ Before: LUMBARD, FRIENDLY and MULLIGAN.

■ FRIENDLY, CIRCUIT JUDGE: [Lloyd Dixon, Jr., the president of AVM Corporation, a "reporting" company under the 1934 Act, was convicted under § 32(a) based on the failure of AVM's proxy statement and Form 10–K to disclose that it had lent him amounts in excess of $65,000 during 1970. Under the then applicable requirements, disclosure was required on the proxy statement if the officer's indebtedness exceeded $10,000 and on the Form 10–K if it exceeded $20,000. Just before the close of its fiscal year, Dixon caused AVM to switch some of his indebtedness to his father's account and Dixon also temporarily paid down the loan from AVM by taking out a bank loan. Thus, on December 31, 1970, the loan balance to AVM was only $19,100. In February, 1971, Dixon took out a new loan with AVM and used it to repay the bank loan. AVM's filings were made by its general counsel, Entwisle, who did not know of Dixon's indebtedness to AVM]. * * * The evidence thus established that the proxy statement sent out March 19, 1971 and the 10–K report filed on March 25, 1971 did not contain the information on Dixon's indebtedness that was required. Dixon's principal defense was that he thought the "SEC rules" provided for a $20,000 exemption, determined on the basis of *year-end* indebtedness, rather than by the highest aggregate balance during the year. Since Dixon's year-end balance still exceeded the $10,000 exemption in the proxy rules, it seems, although the record and briefs are not altogether clear on this, that the defense encompassed an assertion that Dixon thought a $20,000 year-end balance was the test for exemption from both rules. * * *

The most important exculpatory item was testimony by Lewis that Sam Hale, the Ernst & Ernst account executive, had said "sometime around 1967", probably in connection with the 10–K report, that Dixon's loans had to be reduced below $20,000 by year-end in order to avoid having to file a Schedule II. As against this Lewis testified that at some time Lyons, an AVM financial officer, had given him the correct information and that it was Lewis' practice to pass information regarding the accounts to Dixon. * * *

The preparation of the proxy statement was primarily the work of Entwisle. He would prepare a draft based on such information as he had "and then submit it to Mr. Lewis with a copy to Mr. Dixon for input." The first draft would have, "many, many blanks" which would call for information including a paragraph on "Transactions" which was to disclose those transactions between the officers and employees of AVM and AVM itself; stock options and purchases, salaries and vested retirement benefits, were, for example, included by the AVM staff to be written up in the final copy by Entwisle. But Dixon did not inform Entwisle of the loans; the latter learned of them only in 1972 when a grand jury was investigating possible bribery of municipal officials and Entwisle examined the books. After this, AVM in October 1972 filed an 8–K report with the SEC stating that:

> Due to a misunderstanding of the rule, the Company has failed to report publicly outstanding loans to two of its executives.

> * * *

We shall deal first with Dixon's convictions on the two counts, II and VI, of violating the Securities Exchange Act. The failure to include a statement of

Dixon's indebtedness in the proxy statement and a Schedule II in the 10–K report were clear violations of "any provision of this chapter, or any rule or regulation thereunder the violation of which is made unlawful or the observance of which is required under the terms of this chapter," the language of the first clause of § 32(a). The principal questions before us are whether Dixon was shown to have had the state of mind required for a conviction and whether the jury was properly charged.

In United States v. Peltz, 433 F.2d 48, 54–55 (2 Cir.1970), *cert. denied,* 401 U.S. 955 * * * (1971), we pointed out that in regard to violations of the statute or applicable rules or regulations, § 32(a) requires only willfulness; that the "willfully and knowingly" language occurs only in the second clause of § 32(a) relating to false or misleading statements in various papers required to be filed; that the final proviso that "no person shall be subject to imprisonment under this section for the violation of any rule or regulation if he proves that he had no knowledge of such rule or regulation" shows that "A person can willfully violate an SEC rule even if he does not know of its existence"; and that whatever may be true in other contexts,[6] "willfully" thus has a more restricted meaning in § 32(a). However, since the term must have some meaning, we held, as the late Judge Herlands wrote in the very year the statute was passed and long before his appointment to the federal bench, the prosecution need only establish "a realization on the defendant's part that he was doing a wrongful act," Criminal Law Aspects of the Securities Exchange Act of 1934, 21 U. of Va.L.Rev. 139, 144–49 (1934); it is necessary, we added, only that the act be "wrongful under the securities laws and that the knowingly wrongful act involve a significant risk of effecting the violation that has occurred."

While evidence was scarcely needed to show that the chief officer of a corporation required to file 10–K reports and issue proxy statements knew that the content of these was prescribed by statute or rule, the testimony of Lewis and Entwisle sufficed to meet any burden the Government had on that score. Indeed, Dixon does not deny his knowledge that there were SEC rules requiring the reporting of loans to officers, of which there clearly was sufficient evidence; his contention is that he was incorrectly informed of their content. As the sentencing minutes show, Chief Judge Curtin believed Dixon knew that the exemptive provisions of those rules were not satisfied by a sufficiently low balance at year-end, however high the figure had previously been. Dixon contends the evidence of the latter was not sufficient to convince a reasonable juror beyond a reasonable doubt, United States v. Taylor, 464 F.2d 240 (2 Cir.1972). Both the factual issue and the question of the effect of a decision on it favorable to Dixon may be close ones, but we need not resolve them. We do not have here the case of a defendant manifesting an honest belief that he was complying with the law. Dixon did a "wrongful act," in the sense of our decision in *Peltz,* when he caused the corporate books to show, as of December 31, 1970, debts of his father and of Lewis which in fact were his own. True, Dixon may have thought his year-end thimblerig would provide escape from a rule different from the one that existed. But such acts are wrongful "under the Securities Acts" if they lead, as here, to the very violations that would have

---

6. As the Supreme Court has pointed out, " '[W]illful' is a word 'of many meanings, its construction often being influenced by its context,' " Screws v. United States, 325 U.S. 91, 101 * * * (1945), quoting Spies v. United States, 317 U.S. 492 * * * (1943). The Model Penal Code would have requirements of "willfulness" satisfied by proof that the person had acted "knowingly." ALI Proposed Official Draft § 2.02 (1962).

been prevented if the defendant had acted with the aim of scrupulously obeying the rules (which would have necessarily involved correctly ascertaining them) rather than of avoiding them. Such an intention to deceive is enough to meet the modest requirements of the first clause of § 32(a) when violations occur. * * *

Knowing versus Willful. Dixon was convicted under the first clause of § 32(a), which applies to a failure to comply with an SEC rule or regulation (here, the failure to disclose the indebtedness). What if the prosecution had instead been for a false filing so that the "willfully and knowingly" language of the second clause of § 32(a) became applicable? Some commentators have said that the word "knowingly" in the second clause is redundant.[1] However, Judge Friendly in *Dixon* notes that "the difference seems to have been deliberate."[2] Assuming that the defendant requested a jury charge on the meaning of "knowingly," would it have been necessary for the prosecution to prove more than voluntary and intentional conduct, for example, that the defendant knew he was acting illegally?[3] A subsequent Second Circuit decision held that the terms willfully and knowingly do not require that the government prove the element of specific intent to defraud.[4] Other courts have held that a conviction under § 32(a) can be both "willful" and done knowingly when based upon "reckless, deliberate indifference to or disregard for truth and falsity"[5]—a standard under § 21(a) similar to the culpability standard under § 10(b).

The final clause of Section 32(a) of the Securities Exchange Act of 1934 provides: "[N]o person shall be subject to imprisonment under this section in violation of any rule or regulation if he proves that he had no knowledge of such rule or regulation." The "no knowledge" clause was interpreted in the United States v. Lilley[6] to mean that

> Congress intended to charge every man with knowledge of the standards prescribed in the securities acts themselves. It would frustrate the intent of Congress to permit a person whose conduct is expressly prohibited by statute to attempt to prove no knowledge of a parallel rule provision. Allowing these defendants to invoke the "no knowledge" clause would have precisely this effect. * * * It was not intended by the Congress that the "no knowledge" clause of the penalty statute should be available to persons who were charged with knowing their conduct to be in violation of

1. 10 Louis Loss & Joel Seligman, Securities Regulation 4757–4759 (3d ed. rev. 1996).

2. 536 F.2d at 1396.

3. See United States v. Simon, 425 F.2d 796, 798 (2d Cir.1969), *cert. denied*, 397 U.S. 1006 (1970) ("Nothing turns on the different phrasing in the * * * statutes. The Government concedes it had the burden of offering proof * * * not merely that the financial statement was false or misleading in a material respect, but that defendants knew it to be and deliberately sought to mislead.").

4. United States v. Chiarella, 588 F.2d 1358, 1370–1371 (2d Cir.1978), *rev'd on other grounds*, 445 U.S. 222 (1980). Cf. United States v. DeSantis, 134 F.3d 760, 764 (6th Cir.1998) (a specific intent to defraud and recklessness are alternative standards).

5. United States v. Weiner, 578 F.2d 757, 786–787 (9th Cir.1978), *cert. denied*, 439 U.S. 981; United States v. Boyer, 694 F.2d 58 (3d Cir.1982).

6. 291 F.Supp. 989, 992–993 (S.D.Tex. 1968).

law, but did not happen to know it was in violation of a particular rule or regulation of the SEC such as Rule 10b–5. * * *

* * * Proof of no knowledge cannot mean proof that defendants did not know, for example, the precise number or common name of the rule, the book and page where it was to be found, or the date upon which it was promulgated. It does not even mean proof of a lack of knowledge that their conduct was proscribed by rule rather than by statute. Proof of "no knowledge" of the rule can only mean proof of an ignorance of the substance of the rule, proof that they did not know that their conduct was contrary to law.

The "no knowledge" clause is only relevant to sentencing. The person convicted has the burden of persuasion to prove no knowledge at sentencing. Because this does not impose a burden on the defendant to disprove the elements of a crime, Section 32(a) of the Securities Exchange Act of 1934 has been held not to raise a constitutional problem.[7]

United States v. Bilzerian

United States Court of Appeals, Second Circuit, 1991.
926 F.2d 1285.

■ Before: LUMBARD, CARDAMONE and WINTER, Circuit Judges.

■ CARDAMONE, CIRCUIT JUDGE:

One of the principal questions posed by this appeal is whether the availability of civil proceedings—often used to enforce the securities laws—forecloses the government from instituting criminal prosecution for the violation of these same laws. The complex contrivances revealed in the present record, such as "parking" stock at a brokerage firm in order to create the impression that the stock has been sold, or having a broker "accumulate" stock on an investor's behalf in order to delay disclosure of the purchase, carry home the meaning of Scott's "O, what a tangled web we weave, When first we practice to deceive!" 2 Sir Walter Scott, Marmion, Canto VI, XVII (Little Brown & Co. 1857). Although these schemes are not specifically dealt with in the securities laws, the Securities Exchange Act nonetheless contains a general antifraud provision and other federal laws prohibit conspiracy, fraud, and making false statements to United States agencies. This appeal addresses the propriety of enforcing the complained of trading methods through these general fraud and false statement provisions.

Appellant Paul A. Bilzerian (hereafter referred to as Bilzerian or defendant) was convicted on nine counts of an indictment charging violations of securities fraud, making false statements to the Securities and Exchange Commission (SEC), and conspiracy to commit specific offenses, and to defraud the SEC and the Internal Revenue Service (IRS). The charges relate to transactions defendant made between May 1985 and October 1986 in the common stock of four companies: Cluett, Peabody and Company, Inc. (Cluett), Hammermill Paper Company (Hammermill), H.H. Robertson Company (Robertson) and Armco Steel (Armco). On September 29, 1989, the United States District Court for the Southern District of New York (Ward, J.), entered a

---

7. United States v. Mandel, 296 F.Supp. 1038, 1040 (S.D.N.Y.1969).

judgment of conviction and sentenced Bilzerian to four years in prison and a $1.5 million fine.

FACTS

A. *The Underlying Transactions*

1. The Cluett Transactions

The indictment charged three fraudulent schemes relating to trades in Cluett. These involved misrepresenting the source of funds used to purchase stock, secretly accumulating stock through nominee, and misrepresenting an "open market" purchase. By agreeing to share any profits and by guaranteeing against any loss, Bilzerian in April and May of 1985 raised $9 million to buy Cluett stock from various individual investors. The funds were transferred to him through a series of trusts set up for that purpose. Defendant was required to disclose purchase of this large block of stock on a form filed with the SEC known as a Schedule 13D. On the 13D, and its amendment, respecting the Cluett purchase, defendant stated that the stock was purchased with "personal funds," and did not disclose that they were raised from other investors with whom he had a profit-sharing and guarantee-against-loss agreement.

Bilzerian also engaged an employee of Jeffries & Company, Inc. (Jeffries), a registered broker-dealer, to accumulate stock on his behalf. Under stock accumulation, a broker-dealer purchases stock in its own account with the understanding that the customer will buy it at a later date at the broker's cost plus interest and commissions. In such a transaction the prearranged sale involves no risk of loss to the broker-dealer, who acts as a nominee for the true purchaser. On May 28, 1985 defendant purchased the accumulated stock without revealing the accumulation arrangement to the SEC. The indictment charged that the agreement was fraudulently designed to delay the reporting requirements of the securities laws.

Bilzerian also agreed to purchase 347,567 shares of Cluett common stock from a group of shareholders in contemplation of making a tender offer for that company, offering between $38 and $40 per share depending on the price of his tender offer. This proposed purchase was made with the understanding that the trade would not settle for 45 days and that defendant would cancel the purchase proposal if a third party offered more for the shares. Although he learned that 66,667 of the shares included in this block were already under his control, defendant advised the shareholder group to proceed with the sale. The offering statement claimed that 347,567 shares were purchased "in an open market transaction." The existence and terms of the privately-negotiated transaction were not disclosed.

The indictment alleged that the Cluett transactions violated §§ 10(b) and 32 of the Securities Exchange Act of 1934 (Exchange Act), (Count One), and the federal false statements statute, 18 U.S.C. § 1001 (Counts Two, Three, and Four). Defendant was also charged with conspiring to defraud the SEC and to commit specific offenses in violation of 18 U.S.C. § 371 (Count Eight).

2. The Hammermill Transactions

In June 1986 defendant raised $8 million from an individual investor for the purpose of purchasing Hammermill stock. These funds were made available to him through a trust upon his agreeing to share any profits from the eventual sale of the stock. Bilzerian turned the funds over to a limited partnership—of which he was the general partner—and the partnership made the tender offer for Hammermill. The disclosure relating to the stock purchase and tender offer stated that defendant's contribution to the partnership was from "personal funds."

Once again, defendant arranged to have an employee of Jeffries accumulate Hammermill stock on his behalf. On July 21, 1986 he purchased 551,000 accumulated shares of Hammermill. Although he was required to disclose the acquisition as of July 7, he failed to file until July 25, and at that time did not disclose the accumulation agreement. The Hammermill transactions were alleged to violate 15 U.S.C. §§ 78j(b) and 78ff (Count Five), 18 U.S.C. § 1001 (Counts Six and Seven) and 18 U.S.C. § 371 (Count Eight).

3.   The Robertson and Armco Transactions

Defendant also engaged in "stock parking" transactions in shares of Robertson and Armco. "Parking" refers to a transaction in which a broker-dealer buys stock from a customer with the understanding that the customer will buy the stock back at a later date for the purchase price plus interest and commissions. As with "accumulation" there is no market risk to the broker-dealer who is the owner of the shares in name only.

Bilzerian arranged to park 58,000 shares of Robertson with Jeffries for 30 days. Although he assured Jeffries he would repurchase the stock, the stock price fell substantially in the interim and he refused to honor his commitment. As a result, Jeffries incurred a $250,000 loss. Defendant compensated Jeffries in part for this loss by generating approximately $125,000 in commissions for the broker. He paid the remaining $125,000 with the understanding that it would be refunded when an additional $125,000 of commissions was generated. Jeffries sent Bilzerian a false invoice in the amount of $125,000 for "financial services" that were never performed, and the latter deducted the payment on a 1985 tax return. When additional commissions were generated in 1986 he sent Jeffries fictitious invoices for "consulting services" seeking a refund of the $125,000.

Defendant also arranged to park 306,600 shares of Armco with Jeffries for a 30–day period beginning September 2, 1986. In addition, Jeffries agreed to accumulate Armco stock in its own account on defendant's behalf and then sell him the accumulated stock when he repurchased the 306,600 shares. On October 2 defendant purchased 818,900 shares of Armco from Jeffries at the prevailing market price of $8 per share. Although the broker realized a $575,000 gain on the sale, the profits belonged to defendant by virtue of the stock parking and accumulation agreements. Defendant sent his broker an invoice for fictitious "consulting services" in order to account for the profits he realized on the trade.

For his part in the Robertson and Armco trades, Bilzerian was charged with conspiring to defraud the SEC and the IRS and to commit specific offenses including violations of 15 U.S.C. §§ 78g, 78q, and 78ff (1988) and 18 U.S.C. § 1001, in violation of 18 U.S.C. § 371 (Count Nine).

B.   *The Trial*

At trial defendant argued that he did not intend to violate the securities laws, but believed the financing structure of the transactions, utilizing trusts to borrow funds, would allow him legally to avoid disclosure regarding other investors, and that describing the source of his funds as "personal" was lawful.

A motion was made *in limine* seeking a ruling permitting him to testify regarding his belief in the lawfulness of describing the source of his funds as "personal" without being subjected to cross-examination on communications he had with his attorney on this subject, discussions ordinarily protected by the attorney-client privilege.

Declining to rule on the issue in the abstract, Judge Ward stated that if defendant testified regarding his good faith regarding the legality of the disclosure, it would open the door to cross-examination with respect to the basis for his belief, and that such cross-examination would allow inquiry into communications with his attorney. Thus, defendant did not testify regarding his good faith, and now claims the trial court's ruling prejudiced his defense and infringed his constitutional right to deny each element of the charge against him. * * *

I. CHALLENGES TO THE CONDUCT OF THE TRIAL

A. *Attorney–Client Privilege*

Defendant contends the testimony he sought to introduce regarding his good faith attempt to comply with the securities laws would not have disclosed the content or even the existence of any privileged communications or asserted a reliance on counsel defense. As such, he continues, the attorney-client privilege would not be waived by his testimony and, therefore, the trial court committed reversible error when it denied his motion *in limine* seeking to protect the privilege. He alleges that this ruling, together with similar rulings made during the course of the trial, prevented him from refuting the charge that he acted with criminal intent—a central element of the government's case—and that his constitutional right to "the fullest opportunity to meet the accusation against him. * * * [and] to deny all the elements of the case against him," Walder v. United States, 347 U.S. 62, 65 * * * (1954), was thereby encroached upon.

* * *

The purposes for the privilege are twofold: first, it assures that a person seeking legal advice may do so safely. Its existence therefore encourages the full and truthful revelation by the client of all the facts in his possession. Second, no attorney can represent a client effectively unless the client discloses fully all the facts in his possession. Thus, the privilege "recognizes that sound legal advice or advocacy serves public ends and that such advice or advocacy depends upon the lawyer's being fully informed by the client." Upjohn Co. v. United States, 449 U.S. 383, 389 * * * (1981). The fundamental purpose of the privilege is to " 'encourage full and frank communication between attorneys and their clients.' " United States v. Zolin, 491 U.S. 554 * * * (1989) (quoting Upjohn, 449 U.S. at 389).

Although the underlying rationale for the privilege has changed over time, it has retained its importance in the common law tradition. Id. 109 S.Ct. at 2625–26; see United States v. Schwimmer, 892 F.2d 237, 243 (2d Cir.1989). The potential societal benefit may be great in cases like the one at bar, where defendant seeks legal advice in order to act within the confines of highly complex federal securities laws. Often the importance of the interests promoted by the privilege justify the exclusion of otherwise relevant evidence. See McCormick on Evidence § 72 at 152 (E. Cleary 2d ed. 1972).

However, the attorney-client privilege cannot at once be used as a shield and a sword. See In re von Bulow, 828 F.2d 94, 103 (2d Cir.1987); see also Clark v. United States, 289 U.S. 1, 15 * * * (1933) ("The privilege takes flight if the relation is abused."). A defendant may not use the privilege to prejudice his opponent's case or to disclose some selected communications for self-serving purposes. See von Bulow, 828 F.2d at 101–02. Thus, the privilege may implicitly be waived when defendant asserts a claim that in fairness requires examination of protected communications. See United States v. Exxon Corp., 94 F.R.D. 246, 249 (D.D.C.1981) (claim of good faith reliance on governmental representations waived attorney-client privilege); Hearn v. Rhay, 68 F.R.D. 574, 581 (E.D.Wash. 1975) (assertion of qualified immunity defense waived attorney-client privilege). This waiver principle is applicable here for Bilzerian's testimony that he thought his actions were legal would have put his knowledge of the law and the basis for his understanding of what the law required in issue. His conversations with counsel regarding the legality of his schemes would have been directly relevant in determining the extent of his knowledge and, as a result, his intent.

In support of his argument that asserting a good faith defense does not waive the attorney-client privilege, Bilzerian points to United States v. White, 887 F.2d 267 (D.C.Cir.1989). In that case attorney-client communications were admitted at trial over defense counsel's objection, in part because defendant's assertion of lack of intent was deemed to have waived the privilege. In reversing White's conviction the court stated: "[a] rule thus forfeiting the privilege upon denial of *mens rea* would deter individuals from consulting with their lawyers to ascertain the legality of contemplated actions. * * * " 887 F.2d at 270. Because intent is an element of the case that the government must prove, the court continued, waiver of the attorney-client privilege based in denial of intent "would cut short both the privilege and the right." Id.

Denial of an essential element of the crime charged—here criminal intent—is a constitutional right to be carefully safeguarded. But *White* is distinguishable because the district court's ruling in the instant case did not prevent defendant from denying criminal intent; the district judge merely said that Bilzerian's own testimony as to his good faith would open the door to cross-examination, possibly including inquiry into otherwise privileged communications with his attorney. Defendant was free to deny criminal intent either without asserting good faith or to argue his good faith defense by means of defense counsel's opening and closing statements and by his examination of witnesses.

Another important distinction between *White* and the case at bar is that in the former the privileged communications were actually admitted at trial, allowing the appellate court an opportunity to examine whether defendant's case was or was not prejudiced. See *White*, 887 F.2d at 272. Because defendant did not testify as to his good faith, the privileged communications were not introduced at trial. Hence, the trial court's ruling and our review of defendant's claims lack a specific factual context within which to determine if the defense was actually prejudiced. * * *

* * *

A district court's finding that a defendant has waived the attorney-client privilege is reviewed under the abuse of discretion standard. See In re von Bulow, 828 F.2d at 101. Here the district court's ruling did not prevent the defense from urging lack of intent. Accordingly, the refusal to grant Bilzerian blanket protection from an implied waiver of the attorney-client privilege was not an abuse of discretion.

Bilzerian asserts the court ruled that even his own testimony regarding the steps he took to change the structure of his financing arrangements would waive the privilege. He argues that testimony about underlying facts cannot waive the privilege, because the attorney-client privilege does not extend to underlying facts. See *Upjohn,* 449 U.S. at 395–96 * * *. To the contrary, the trial court held only that Bilzerian's testimony about the changes would open the door on cross-examination to inquiry into Bilzerian's reasons for making the changes, because the topic would necessarily involve Bilzerian's state of mind. Even defendant's trial counsel knew the testimony about the changes would be inextricably intertwined with Bilzerian's assertion of good faith. Counsel said: "Mr. Bilzerian's response would be in substance that he directed these changes to be made so that—in order to enable himself to be able to report as personal funds on the 13D the funds that he received from the trust that he would not have to disclose any of the investors' names and that he thought that doing that, that he believed that was appropriate and proper." The trial court's ruling left defendant free to testify without getting into his state of mind, but correctly held that if he asserted his good faith, the jury would be entitled to know the basis of his understanding that his actions were legal.

Reliance on the Advice of Counsel. In United States v. Crosby,[1] the Second Circuit reversed the convictions of four broker-dealers who sold unregistered stock of a control person, "which * * * made the broker defendants technically 'underwriters'."[2] The defendants had relied on their counsel's advise that the shares were exempt from registration under former Rule 133. Given this advice, the Second Circuit said that the "knowingly" requirement of § 32(a) had not been satisfied: "While such a theory is probably invalid * * *, we cannot say that on its face the legal opinions tendered were so patently erroneous as to permit the jury to speculate on the good faith of the defendants."[3]

Bilzerian presents the mirror image of the reliance on counsel defense. By seeking to testify as to his good faith, Bilzerian put into possible issue whether he might have received contrary indications from his counsel. Although neither the trial court nor the Second Circuit held that he waived his attorney/client privilege, they both suggested that it was in some jeopardy. In such a world, should a securities lawyer give the client reverse "Miranda" warnings to the effect that anything the lawyer says could be held against the client?

Stock Parking. Bilzerian is not the only case in which stock parking has been prosecuted. In United States v. Regan,[4] the general partners of Prince-

1. 294 F.2d 928 (2d Cir.1961).

2. 294 F.2d at 940–41. See also United States v. Wolfson, 405 F.2d 779 (2d Cir.1968) (affirming a criminal conviction for similar conduct).

3. 294 F.2d at 942. Cf. United States v. Peterson, 101 F.3d 375, 381–383 (5th Cir. 1996): "A good faith reliance on the advice of counsel is not a defense to securities fraud. It is simply a means of demonstrating good faith and represents possible evidence of an absence of any intent to defraud."

4. 713 F.Supp. 629 (S.D.N.Y.1989). The criminal convictions of the Princeton/Newport partners were later partially reversed by the Second Circuit. See United States v. Re-

ton/Newport Partners, L.P., an investment firm, were also convicted in connection with a stock parking scheme. The schemes in *Bilzerian* and *Regan* were entirely different, however, and thus reveal the breadth of behavior that stock parking covers. In *Bilzerian,* the motive was to outflank the Section 13(d) requirements of the Williams Act and to hide the identity of the silent partner financing Bilzerian. In *Regan,* it was alleged that Princeton/Newport Partners arranged to sell securities to Drexel Burnham Lambert, Inc. subject to secret repurchase agreements by which it would buy back the securities without regard to their market value at the time of the repurchase; one alleged purpose of this scheme was to permit Princeton/Newport to retain effective economic ownership of the securities while appearing to sell them for tax purposes. Another alleged motive for the stock parking transactions in *Regan* was to allow Drexel to hide its stock ownership in other companies, either, in one case, to permit Drexel to hold a larger ownership percentage than management of the company would have tolerated or, in the other case, to manipulate the company's stock price downward (allegedly so that Drexel could negotiate a better price on an underwriting of convertible bonds it was handling for the company).

"Stock parking" is not itself an independent criminal offense. Rather, specific 1934 Act rules must be found to have been violated. In the case of a broker-dealer, however, such proof is relatively simple. Rules 17a–3 and 17a–4 under the 1934 Act require a broker-dealer to keep accurate financial records—known as "blotters" and "ledger accounts"—showing all transactions in securities, including any repurchase agreements.

At this point, a too easily ignored policy question surfaces: should violations of such technical rules be prosecuted as federal felonies? Did Congress really intend that every SEC regulation, however technical or mundane, could be the subject of a federal criminal prosecution under which sentences of up to ten years are authorized? Particularly in *Regan,* the principal stock parking transactions were designed to achieve a tax purpose (which was subject to independent criminal prosecution if unlawful) and did not seek to defraud investors. While none dispute that the SEC would and should be entitled to injunctive or administrative relief on detecting such a violation, a continuing debate has surrounded the question of whether "overcriminalization" results from the use of criminal sanctions in such cases.[5] Defense counsel have repeatedly asserted that Princeton/Newport was informed that it and its partners would not have been criminally prosecuted if they had cooperated in the Government's investigation of Drexel Burnham. In this light, does attaching criminal sanctions to every SEC regulation give the prosecution too much leverage in plea bargaining? In a more recent stock parking case, the Ninth Circuit appeared to tighten the standard.[6]

gan, 937 F.2d 823 (2d Cir.1991), *cert. denied sub nom.* Zarzecki v. United States, 504 U.S. 940 (1992). Although the Second Circuit reversed the tax fraud counts, it left standing the conviction on the securities fraud charge.

5. These issues are reconsidered in light of the 1980s insider trading scandals in John C. Coffee, Jr., Hush! The Criminal Status of Confidential Business Information After *McNally* and *Carpenter* and the Enduring Problem of Overcriminalization, 26 Amer. Crim. L. Rev. 121 (1988).

6. In Yoshikawa v. SEC, 192 F.3d 1209, 1214 (9th Cir.1999), the court concluded:

Based on our review and analysis of the "parking" caselaw, we conclude that securities "parking" is, at a minimum, comprised of the following elements:

United States v. Mulheren

United States Court of Appeals, Second Circuit, 1991.
938 F.2d 364.

■ Before Van Graafeiland, Meskill and McLaughlin, Circuit Judges.

■ McLaughlin, Circuit Judge:

In the late 1980s a wide prosecutorial net was cast upon Wall Street. Along with the usual flotsam and jetsam, the government's catch included some of Wall Street's biggest, brightest, and now infamous—Ivan Boesky, Dennis Levine, Michael Milken, Robert Freeman, Martin Siegel, Boyd L. Jeffries, and Paul A. Bilzerian—each of whom either pleaded guilty to or was convicted of crimes involving illicit trading scandals. Also caught in the government's net was defendant-appellant John A. Mulheren, Jr., the chief trader at and general partner of Jamie Securities Co. ("Jamie"), a registered broker-dealer.

Mulheren was charged in a 42–count indictment handed-up on June 13, 1989. The indictment alleged that he conspired to and did manipulate the price on the New York Stock Exchange (the "NYSE") of the common stock of Gulf & Western Industries, Inc. ("G&W" or the "company") * * * by purchasing 75,000 shares of G&W common stock on October 17, 1985 for the purpose of raising the price thereof to $45 per share (Counts One through Four); that he engaged in "stock parking" transactions to assist the Seemala Corporation, a registered broker-dealer controlled by Boesky, in evading tax and other regulatory requirements * * *; that he committed mail fraud in connection with the stock parking transactions * * *; and that Mulheren caused Jamie to make and keep false books and records * * *.

* * *

This appeal thus focuses solely on the convictions concerning Mulheren's alleged manipulation of G&W common stock. The government sought to prove that on October 17, 1985, Mulheren purchased 75,000 shares of G&W common stock with the purpose and intent of driving the price of that stock to $45 per share. This, the government claimed, was a favor to Boesky, who wanted to sell his enormous block of G&W common stock back to the company at that price. Mulheren assails the convictions on several grounds.

First, Mulheren claims that the government failed to prove beyond a reasonable doubt that when he purchased the 75,000 shares of G&W common stock on October 17, 1985, he did it for the sole purpose of raising the price at which it traded on the NYSE, rather than for his own investment purposes. Second, Mulheren argues that even if his sole intent had been to raise the price of G&W stock, that would not have been a crime because, he claims, (1) he neither misrepresented any fact nor failed to disclose any fact that he was under a duty to disclose concerning his G&W purchases; (2) his subjective intent in purchasing G&W stock is not "material"; and (3) he did not act for the purpose of deceiving others. Finally, Mulheren cites various alleged eviden-

(1) a pre-arrangement to sell and then buy back securities (to conceal true ownership);

(2) on the same, or substantially the same, terms (thus keeping the market risk entirely on the seller);

(3) for a bad-faith purpose, accomplished through a sham transaction in which nominal title is transferred to the purported buyer while the economic incidents of ownership are left with the purported seller.

tiary and sentencing errors that he believes entitle him to either a new trial or resentencing.

Although we harbor doubt about the government's theory of prosecution, we reverse on Mulheren's first stated ground because we are convinced that no rational trier of fact could have found the elements of the crimes charged here beyond a reasonable doubt.

BACKGROUND

Reviewing the evidence "in the light most favorable to the government, and construing all permissible inferences in its favor," * * * the following facts were established at trial.

In 1985, at the suggestion of his long-time friend, Carl Icahn, a prominent arbitrageur and corporate raider, Ivan Boesky directed his companies to buy G & W stock, a security that both Icahn and Boesky believed to be "significantly undervalued." Between April and October 1985, Boesky's companies accumulated 3.4 million shares representing approximately 4.9 percent of the outstanding G&W shares. According to Boesky, Icahn also had a "position of magnitude."

On September 5, 1985, Boesky and Icahn met with Martin Davis, the chairman of G&W. At the meeting, Boesky expressed his interest in taking control of G&W through a leveraged buyout or, failing that, by increasing his position in G & W stock and securing seats on the G&W board of directors. Boesky told Davis that he held 4.9 percent of G&W's outstanding shares. Davis said he was not interested in Boesky's proposal, and he remained adamant in subsequent telephone calls and at a later meeting on October 1, 1985.

At the October 1, 1985 meeting, which Icahn also attended, Boesky added a new string to his bow: if Davis continued to reject Boesky's attempts at control, then G&W should buy-out his position at $45 per share. At that time, G&W was, indeed, reducing the number of its outstanding shares through a repurchase program, but, the stock was trading below $45 per share. Davis stated that, although he would consider buying Boesky's shares, he could not immediately agree to a price. Icahn, for his part, indicated that he was not yet sure whether he would sell his G&W stock.

During—and for sometime before—these negotiations, Mulheren and Boesky also maintained a relationship of confidence and trust. The two had often shared market information and given each other trading tips. At some point during the April–October period when Boesky was acquiring G&W stock, Mulheren asked Boesky what he thought of G&W and whether Icahn held a position in the stock. Boesky responded that he "thought well" of G&W stock and that he thought Icahn did indeed own G&W stock. Although Boesky told Mulheren that G & W stock was "a good purchase and worth owning," Boesky never told Mulheren about his meetings or telephone conversations with Davis because he considered the matter "very confidential." Speculation in the press, however, was abound. Reports in the August 19, 1985 issue of *Business Week* and the September 27, 1985 issue of the *Wall Street Journal* indicated that Boesky and Icahn each owned close to five percent of G&W and discussed the likelihood of a take-over of the company. Mulheren, however, testifying in his own behalf, denied reading these reports and denied knowing whether Boesky and Icahn held positions in G&W.

On October 3, 1985, two days after his meeting with Boesky and Icahn, Davis met with Mulheren. Mulheren stated that he had a group of investors interested in knowing whether G&W would join them in acquiring CBS. According to Davis, Mulheren also volunteered that he could be "very helpful in monitoring the activities of Ivan Boesky [in G&W stock;] [Mulheren] knew that [Davis] considered Mr. Boesky adversarial;" and Mulheren agreed with Davis' unflattering assessment of Boesky. In a telephone conversation sometime between this October 3 meeting and a subsequent meeting between the two on October 9, 1985, Mulheren told Davis that he believed that Boesky did not own any G&W securities. Mulheren also said that he did not own any G&W stock either. When Davis and Mulheren met again on October 9, they spoke only about Mulheren's CBS proposal.

In the meantime, Boesky continued to press Davis to accept his proposals to secure control of G&W. When Boesky called Davis after their October 1, 1985 meeting, Davis "told [Boesky] as clearly as [he] could again that [G&W] had no interest whatsoever in doing anything with [Boesky]." Boesky then decided to contact his representative at Goldman, Sachs & Co. to arrange the sale of his massive block of stock to G & W. Boesky advised Goldman, Sachs that G&W common stock was not trading at $45 per share at the time, "but that should it become 45," he wanted to sell. A Goldman, Sachs representative met with Davis shortly thereafter regarding the company's repurchase of Boesky's G&W shares.

Sometime after the close of the market on October 16, 1985, Boesky called Davis, offering to sell his block of shares back to G&W at $45 per share. NYSE trading had closed that day at $44¾ per share, although at one point during that day it had reached $45. Davis told Boesky that the company would buy his shares back, but only at the "last sale"—the price at which the stock traded on the NYSE at the time of the sale—and that Boesky should have his Goldman, Sachs representative contact Kidder Peabody & Co. to arrange the transaction.[1]

After this conversation with Davis, but before 11:00 a.m. on October 17, 1985, Boesky called Mulheren. According to Boesky's testimony, the following, critical exchange took place:

> BOESKY: Mr. Mulheren asked me if I liked the stock on that particular day, and I said yes, I still liked it. At the time it was trading at 44¾. I said I liked it; however, I would not pay more than 45 for it and it would be great if it traded at 45. The design for the comment * * *

> DEFENSE COUNSEL MR. PUCCIO: Objection to the "design of the comment." I would ask only for the conversation.

> A.U.S.A. GILBERT: What if anything did he say to you?

> BOESKY: I understand.

Shortly after 11:00 a.m. on October 17, 1985, Jamie (Mulheren's company) placed an order with Oliver Ihasz, a floor broker, to purchase 50,000 shares of G&W at the market price. Trading in G&W had been sluggish that morning

---

1. Around the same time, Mulheren received a call from a broker at another firm who had failed to execute an order that day to buy 25,000 shares of G&W for an institutional customer. The broker asked Mulheren if Mulheren would sell him the 25,000 shares he needed. Mulheren, who, at the time, did not own any shares of G&W, checked the stock, noted "it was up a dollar that day" and agreed to "short" the broker—sell what he did not own—25,000 shares. Obviously, Mulheren would soon be obligated to cover his short position, i.e. buy 25,000 shares of G&W.

(only 32,200 shares had traded between 9:30 a.m. and 11:03 a.m.), and the market price was holding steady at $44¾, the price at which it had closed the day before. At 11:04 a.m., Ihasz purchased 16,100 shares at $44¾ per share. Unable to fill the entire 50,000 share order at $44¾, Ihasz purchased the remaining 33,900 shares between 11:05 a.m. and 11:08 a.m. at $44⅞ per share.

At 11:09 a.m., Ihasz received another order from Jamie; this time, to purchase 25,000 shares of G&W for no more than $45 per share. After attempting to execute the trade at $44⅞, Ihasz executed the additional 25,000 share purchase at $45 per share at 11:10 a.m. In sum, between 11:04 a.m. and 11:10 a.m., Jamie purchased a total of 75,000 shares of G&W common stock, causing the price at which it traded per share to rise from $44¾ to $45. At 11:17 a.m., Boesky and Icahn sold their G&W stock—6,715,700 shares between them—back to the company at $45 per share. Trading in G&W closed on the NYSE on October 17, 1985 at $43⅝ per share. At the end of the day, Jamie's trading in G&W common stock at Mulheren's direction had caused it to lose $64,406.

DISCUSSION

A convicted defendant, of course, bears "a very heavy burden" to demonstrate that the evidence at trial was insufficient to prove his guilt beyond a reasonable doubt. * * * "A jury's verdict will be sustained if there is *substantial evidence*, taking the view most favorable to the government, to support it." Where " '*any* rational trier of fact could have found the essential elements of the crime,' the conviction must stand." United States v. Badalamenti, 794 F.2d 821, 828 (2d Cir.1986) (quoting Jackson v. Virginia, 443 U.S. 307, 319 * * * (1979)) (emphasis in original).

On this appeal, however, we are reminded that "in America we still respect the dignity of the individual, and [a defendant] * * * is not to be imprisoned except on definite proof of a specific crime." United States v. Bufalino, 285 F.2d 408, 420 (2d Cir.1960) (Clark, J., concurring). To that end, it is "imperative that we not rend the fabric of evidence and examine each shred in isolation; rather, the reviewing court 'must use its experience with people and events in weighing the chances that the evidence correctly points to guilt against the possibility of innocent or ambiguous inference.' " United States v. Redwine, 715 F.2d 315, 319 (7th Cir.1983) (quoting United States v. Kwitek, 467 F.2d 1222, 1226 (7th Cir.1972)).

The government's theory of prosecution in this case is straightforward. In its view, when an investor, who is neither a fiduciary nor an insider, engages in securities transactions in the open market with the sole intent to affect the price of the security, the transaction is manipulative and violates Rule 10b–5.[2] Unlawful manipulation occurs, the argument goes, even though the investor has not acted for the "purpose of inducing the purchase or sale of such security by others," an element the government would have had to prove had it chosen to proceed under the manipulation statute, § 9(a)(2). Mulheren was not charged with violating § 9(a)(2). When the transaction is effected for an

---

2. The government also appears to argue in the alternative that the violation occurs not by simply engaging in a securities transaction with the intent to affect the price of a security, but rather by failing to disclose that subjective intent to the market. The government contends that all investors are under a "general duty" not to manipulate; thus, absent disclosure of an intent to manipulate, Rule 10b–5 is violated. We express no view on this theory.

investment purpose, the theory continues, there is no manipulation, even if an increase or diminution in price was a foreseeable consequence of the investment.

Although we have misgivings about the government's view of the law, we will assume, without deciding on this appeal, that an investor may lawfully be convicted under Rule 10b–5 where the purpose of his transaction is solely to affect the price of a security. The issue then becomes one of Mulheren's subjective intent. The government was obligated to prove beyond a reasonable doubt that when Mulheren purchased 75,000 shares of G&W common stock on October 17, 1985, he did it with the intent to raise its price, rather than with the intent to invest. We conclude that the government failed to carry this burden.

In order to convict, the government had to demonstrate, in the first place, that Mulheren was aware that Boesky had a stake in G&W. In proof of knowledge, the government makes three arguments.

First, the government suggests that Boesky himself told Mulheren of his G&W positions. Boesky, however, never so testified; and the greatest puzzle in this record is why that critical question was never directly put to Boesky.[3]

Second, the government relies on the speculation reported in the media, specifically the *Wall Street Journal* and *Business Week,* and the rumors floating on Wall Street that Boesky and Icahn owned substantial positions in G & W. There was no evidence, however, that Mulheren read these articles or heard these rumors. On the contrary, Mulheren flatly denied knowing of their existence. Moreover, knowledge of a rumor, particularly one on Wall Street, can hardly substitute for knowledge of a fact.

Third, the government contends that Mulheren's knowledge of Boesky's position is evident in the October 3, 1985 meeting between Davis and Mulheren. In that meeting, Mulheren told Davis that he knew that Davis and Boesky had an "adversarial" relationship and Mulheren "understood" Davis' "position" and offered to help Davis "in any way he could" to "monitor" Boesky's G&W transactions. While this evidence, taken in isolation, might create an inference that Mulheren knew of Boesky's G&W holdings (as the source of the Boesky–Davis adversarial relationship), the rest of Davis' testimony casts a considerable shadow on the inference. Davis went on to testify that in a telephone conversation sometime between their October 3 and October 9 meetings Mulheren stated that he did not believe Boesky owned any G&W stock at all. By this time, of course, Boesky had already told Davis (at their September 5 meeting) that he owned 4.9 percent of G&W's outstanding shares. Given that Mulheren was at the time attempting to curry favor from Davis in connection with Mulheren's CBS proposal, it was hardly in Mulheren's best interest to lie to Davis by telling him that Boesky owned *no* shares, if in fact Mulheren knew that Boesky owned 3.4 million shares. In sum, the evidence of

---

3. The closest Boesky came to testifying that he told Mulheren about his G&W holdings is the following exchange on direct examination concerning a telephone conversation between Mulheren and Boesky sometime in the period between April and the end of September 1985:

A.U.S.A. Gilbert: What in fact did you tell [Mulheren] about the stock?

Boesky: As my position was being accumulated, I told him that's how I felt about it, that it was a good purchase and worth owning.

Mulheren's knowledge that Boesky had an interest in G&W rests on a very slender reed.

Even were we to conclude otherwise, however, the convictions still could not be sustained. Assuming that Mulheren knew that Boesky held a substantial position in G&W stock, the government nevertheless failed to prove that Mulheren agreed to and then purchased the 75,000 shares for the sole purpose of raising the price at which G&W common stock traded.

The strongest evidence supporting an inference that Mulheren harbored a manipulative intent, is the telephone conversation between Boesky and Mulheren that occurred either late in the day on October 16 or before 11:00 a.m. on October 17, 1985. In discussing the virtues of G&W stock, Boesky told Mulheren that he "would not pay more than 45 for it and it would be great if it traded at 45." To this Mulheren replied "I understand." The meaning of this cryptic conversation is, at best, ambiguous, and we reject the government's contention that this conversation "*clearly* conveyed Boesky's request that the price of the stock be pushed up to $45 * * * [and Mulheren's] agreement to help." Boesky never testified (again, he was not asked) what he meant by his words.[4]

We acknowledge that, construed as an innocent tip—i.e. G&W would be a "great" buy at a price of $45 or below—the conversation appears contradictory. It seems inconsistent for Boesky to advise, on one hand, that he would not pay more than $45, yet on the other to exclaim that it would be a bargain ("great") at $45. The conversation does not make any more sense, however, if construed as a request for illicit manipulation. That Boesky put a limit on the price he would pay for the stock ("I would not pay more than 45 for it") seems inconsistent with a request to drive up the price of the stock. If a conspiracy to manipulate for his own selfish benefit had been Boesky's intent, and if Davis were poised to repurchase the shares at the "last sale," Boesky would obviously have preferred to see Mulheren drive the trading in G&W stock to a price above $45. In this regard, it is noteworthy that there was *no* evidence whatever that Mulheren knew of Boesky's demand to get $45 per share from G&W. Moreover, during the four to six weeks preceding this conversation, Mulheren repeatedly asked Boesky what he thought of G&W—evincing Mulheren's predisposition (and Boesky's knowledge thereof) to invest in the company. In fact, Mulheren took a position in G&W when he shorted a broker 25,000 shares of G&W after the market closed on October 16.

Clearly, this case would be much less troubling had Boesky said "I want you to bring it up to 45" or, perhaps, even, "I'd like to see it trading at 45." But to hang a conviction on the threadbare phrase "it would be great if it traded at 45," particularly when the government does not suggest that the words were some sort of sinister code, defies reason and a sense of fair play. Any doubt about this is dispelled by the remaining evidence at trial.

First, and perhaps most telling, is that Jamie *lost* over $64,000 on Mulheren's October 17th transactions. This is hardly the result a market manipulator seeks to achieve. One of the hallmarks of manipulation is some profit or personal gain inuring to the alleged manipulator. See, e.g., Baum v. Phillips, Appel & Walden, Inc., 648 F.Supp. 1518, 1531 (S.D.N.Y.1986), aff'd per curiam, 867 F.2d 776 (2d Cir.1989 * * *); Walck v. American Stock Exchange, Inc., 565

---

4. Defense counsel objected after Boesky testified "[t]he design of the comment. * * * " No ruling was made on the objection and the government—for reasons known only to itself—abandoned further inquiry into Boesky's state of mind.

F.Supp. 1051, 1065–66 (E.D.Pa.1981), aff'd, 687 F.2d 778 (3d Cir.1982) * * *; SEC v. Commonwealth Chemical Securities, Inc., 410 F.Supp. 1002, 1013 (S.D.N.Y.1976), aff'd in part, modified on other grounds, 574 F.2d 90 (2d Cir.1978).

Second, the unrebutted trial testimony of the G&W specialist demonstrated that if raising the price of G&W to $45 per share was Mulheren's sole intent, Mulheren purchased significantly more shares (and put Jamie in a position of greater risk) than necessary to achieve the result. The G&W specialist testified that at the time Jamie placed its second order, 5,000 shares would "definitely" have raised the trading price from $44⅞ to $45 per share. Yet, Jamie bought 25,000 shares.

Although there was no evidence that Mulheren received a *quid pro quo* from Boesky for buying G&W stock, the government, nevertheless, claims that Mulheren had a "strong pecuniary interest" in accommodating Boesky in order to maintain the close and mutually profitable relationship they enjoyed. With this argument the government is hoist with its own petard. Precisely because of this past profitable relationship, the more reasonable conclusion is that Mulheren understood Boesky's comment as another tip—this time to buy G&W stock. Indeed, there was no evidence that Boesky had ever asked Mulheren to rig the price of a stock in the past.

None of the traditional badges of manipulation are present in this case. Mulheren conspicuously purchased the shares for Jamie's account in the open market. Compare United States v. Scop, 846 F.2d 135, 137 (matched orders through fictitious nominees), modified on other grounds, 856 F.2d 5 (2d Cir.1988); United States v. Gilbert, 668 F.2d 94, 95 (2d Cir.1981) (matched orders and wash sales)[5], *cert. denied*, 456 U.S. 946 * * * (1982); United States v. Minuse, 114 F.2d 36, 38 (2d Cir.1940) (fictitious accounts, matched orders, wash sales, dissemination of false literature). The government argues that Mulheren's deceptive intent can be inferred from the fact that (1) he purchased the G&W shares through Ihasz, a floor broker whom the government claims was used only infrequently by Jamie; and (2) Ihasz never informed anyone that the purchases were made for Jamie. These arguments are factually flawed.

There was no evidence that there was anything unusual about Ihasz's execution of the trades. Oliver Ihasz testified that Jamie was a customer of his company. There was no testimony that his company was used infrequently, or that Mulheren's request was in any way out of the ordinary. Nor is there anything peculiar about the fact that Ihasz disclosed only the name of the clearing broker and not Jamie, as the purchaser, when he executed the trade. As Ihasz testified, in an open market transaction, the only information the floor broker provides to the seller is the name of the clearing broker, not the ultimate buyer. Jamie was conspicuously identified as the ultimate buyer of the G&W securities on Ihasz's order tickets, where it is supposed to appear.

The government also argues that manipulative intent can be inferred from the fact that Mulheren's purchase on October 17, 1985 comprised 70 percent of the trading in G&W common stock during the period between the opening of the market and 11:10 a.m. Such market domination, the government contends,

---

5. In a wash sale transaction, beneficial ownership of the stock does not change. A matched order involves the prearranged purchase and sale, usually through different brokers, of the same amount of securities at substantially the same price and time. Both practices give the appearance of legitimate market activity.

is indicative of manipulation. While we agree, as a general proposition, that market domination is a factor that supports a manipulation charge, the extent to which an investor controls or dominates the market at any given period of time cannot be viewed in a vacuum. For example, if only ten shares of a stock are bought or sold in a given hour and only by one investor, that investor has created 100 percent of the activity in that stock in that hour. This alone, however, does not make the investor a manipulator. The percent of domination must be viewed in light of the time period involved and other indicia of manipulation. Taken in this context, the cases upon which the government relies, United States v. Gilbert, 668 F.2d 94 (2d Cir.1981 * * *); United States v. Stein, 456 F.2d 844 (2d Cir.1972 * * *); In re Delafield & Delafield, [1967–69 Transfer Binder] Fed.Sec.L.Rep. (CCH) ¶ 77, 648 (SEC 1969), are readily distinguishable.

Gilbert, for example, involved the manipulation of the shares of Conrac Corporation where, over a *one-year period,* the defendant's trading constituted more than 50 percent of the overall trading. See United States v. Gilbert, [1981–82 Transfer Binder] Fed.Sec.L.Rep. (CCH) ¶ 98,244, at 91,602, 91,605 (S.D.N.Y.1981), *aff'd,* 668 F.2d at 95. In *Stein,* the manipulator's transactions accounted for 28.8 percent of the daily exchange volume of transactions in Buckeye Corporation stock over a *four month period.* See *Stein,* 456 F.2d at 846. When domination is sustained over such an extended period of time, evidence of manipulation is strong. But, if the percentage of control be measured in terms of minutes or hours, anyone could find himself labeled a manipulator.

In re Delafield & Delafield is the only case that gives us pause. There, the respondents entered into a consent decree with the Securities and Exchange Commission concerning allegations that they had manipulated the Class A common stock of the Mary Carter Paint Company by selling 17,600 shares of the stock between 2:00 p.m. and the close of the market on January 9, 1968. Respondents' transactions represented 83 percent of the transactions in the stock during that period. Significantly, however, the sales "were effected in the name of two foreign banks to conceal the identity" of the true seller. See In re Delafield & Delafield, ¶ 77,648 at 83,400. No such chicanery exists here. Thus, in the absence of other indicia of manipulation—and there are none—the fact that Mulheren dominated the market between 9:30 a.m. and 11:10 a.m. on October 17, 1985 (noting that Mulheren's purchases represented a small fraction of the total October 17th activity in G&W stock) carries little weight.

The government also urges that Mulheren's manipulative intent—as opposed to investment intent—can be inferred from certain of Mulheren's actions after his purchase of the G&W shares. For example, Mulheren sold G&W call options in the afternoon of October 17, 1985 that were designed to create a hedge in the event of a drop in the price of stock. Had Mulheren known, however, that Boesky and Icahn were going to unload 6.7 million shares of G&W stock—which had the inevitable effect of driving the price down—surely Mulheren would have had the foresight to write the options *before* Boesky and Icahn had a chance to sell. That Mulheren wrote the options in the afternoon suggests only that he was attempting to mitigate his losses.

Finally, the government contends that the fact that Mulheren continued to do favors for Boesky after G&W repurchased Boesky and Icahn's shares is inconsistent with his claim that he was "duped" by Boesky into purchasing the 75,000 G&W shares. We disagree. First, the evidence of "favors" rests largely on the unproven "stock parking" charges. Second, Mulheren's conduct after his G&W purchases is equally consistent with that of a sophisticated businessman who turns the other cheek after being slapped by the hand that usually feeds him.

We acknowledge that this case treads dangerously close to the line between legitimate inference and impermissible speculation. We are persuaded, however, that to come to the conclusion it did, "the jury must have engaged in false surmise and rank speculation." United States v. Wiley, 846 F.2d 150, 155 (2d Cir.1988) (citing United States v. Starr, 816 F.2d 94, 99 (2d Cir.1987)). At best, Mulheren's convictions are based on evidence that is "at least as consistent with innocence as with guilt," United States v. Mankani, 738 F.2d 538, 547 (2d Cir.1984), and "on inferences no more valid than others equally supported by reason and experience." United States v. Bufalino, 285 F.2d 408, 419 (2d Cir.1960). Accordingly, the judgments of conviction are reversed and Counts One through Four of the indictment are dismissed.

———

The Meaning of Manipulation. Only weeks before the *Mulheren* decision, another Second Circuit panel upheld the convictions for stock manipulation of the Princeton/Newport Partners. According to the Government's theory in United States v. Regan,[1] Drexel Burnham arranged with Princeton/Newport, an arbitrage and hedge trading firm, for the latter to sell short the stock of one of its clients, C.O.M.B., Inc., whose convertible bonds Drexel was about to underwrite. Drexel apparently feared that its client, C.O.M.B., Inc., was manipulating the price of its common stock upwards (in order to get a lower interest rate concession on its soon-to-be-issued bonds, because the more attractive the bonds' conversion price, the lower the interest rate necessary to attract purchasers). In response, Drexel sought to drive C.O.M.B.'s stock price downward on the eve of the underwriting. On appeal, the defendants claimed that because they owed no fiduciary duty to the parties they traded with in their sales of C.O.M.B. stock they had no duty to disclose the fact that the market had been manipulated. The Second Circuit panel in *Regan* rejected this theory, concluding:

> Failure to disclose that the market prices are being artificially depressed operates as a deceit on the market place and is an omission of a material fact * * * Appellants' argument that a fiduciary relationship must exist before liability can be found is without merit.[2]

Regan thus seemingly accepted the Government's theory that there is a general obligation to disclose the fact that one has manipulated market prices. But this was precisely the theory as to which the *Mulheren* panel said "we harbor doubt about the Government's theory of prosecution."[3] Interestingly, one judge sat on

---

1. 937 F.2d 823 (2d Cir.1991), *cert. denied sub nom.* Zarzecki v. United States, 504 U.S. 940 (1992).

2. Id. at 829.

3. United States v. Mulheren, 938 F.2d 364, 366 (2d Cir.1991). Some commentors deny that there is any objective meaning to the term "manipulation" and recommend that the entire concept be abandoned as founded on "conceptual confusion." See Daniel R. Fischel & David J. Ross, Should The Law Prohibit "Manipulation" in Financial Markets?, 105 Harv.L.Rev. 503 (1991). Cf. Steve Thel, $850,000 in Six Minutes—The Mechanics of Securities Manipulation, 79 Cornell L. Rev. 219 (1994); Judith R. Starr & David Herman, The Same Old Wine in a

both panels. The issue seems to depend on whether stock manipulation is viewed as a disclosure crime (in which case omissions are normally actionable only if there is a duty to speak) or as a crime of conduct (in which case purchases made with a "manipulative intent" to raise or depress the market price artificially are themselves unlawful without more).[4]

Regarding criminal enforcement of the federal securities laws, *see generally* 10 Louis Loss & Joel Seligman, Securities Regulation ch. 12.B (3d ed. rev. 1996).

Brand New Bottle: Applying Market Manipulation Principles to Internet Stock Scams, 29 Sec. Reg. L.J. 236 (2001).

4. In SEC v. Kimmes, 799 F.Supp. 852, 859 (N.D.Ill.1992), *aff'd on other grounds sub nom.* SEC v. Quinn, 997 F.2d 287 (7th Cir. 1993), the court generalized:

[A]ny activities that falsely persuade the public that activity in an over-the-counter security is "the reflection of a genuine demand instead of a mirage" are outlawed by 1933 Act § 17(a) and 1934 Act § 10(b) (*SEC v. Resch–Cassin & Co.,* 362 F.Supp. 964, 975 (S.D.N.Y.1973)). Such activities may include (1) fraudulent promises of quick profits made by salesmen to friends and customers (*United States v. Blitz,* 533 F.2d 1329, 1338 (2d Cir.1976); (2) directed and controlled trading in a security (*United States v. Cohen,* 518 F.2d 727, 734 (2d Cir.1975); *United States v. Corr,* 543 F.2d 1042, 1045–1046 (2d Cir.1976); (3) the use of wash sales and matched orders (*Edward J. Mawod & Co. v. SEC,* 591 F.2d 588, 595 (10th Cir.1979)); (4) the use of undisclosed nominees (*SEC v. Commonwealth Chemical Securities, Inc.,* 410 F.Supp. 1002, 1017–1018 (S.D.N.Y.1976), *aff'd in part and modified in part on other grounds,* 574 F.2d 90 (2d Cir.1978); and (5) the use of material misrepresentations in newsletters and otherwise (*United States v. Mahler,* 579 F.2d 730, 732 (2d Cir.1978).

In a manipulation case, individual purchases or sales are not the appropriate unit of prosecution; "these retail events were only a step in the advancement of the scheme as a whole. On the facts here, each count properly charged a manipulation of the securities of each of the three separate companies—each involving a discrete scheme." United States v. Haddy, 134 F.3d 542, 549 (3d Cir.1998), *cert. denied,* 525 U.S. 827 (1998).

CHAPTER 20

INTERNATIONAL ENFORCEMENT

Securities markets around the world have become increasingly global as U.S. investors have expanded their holdings of foreign securities and foreign issuers have made greater use of the U.S. capital markets. In 1980, U.S. investors purchased or sold only an estimated $17.9 billion in foreign equities; by 2000 this figure had ballooned to an estimated $3,615.7 billion. Conversely foreign investors bought $7,035.5 billion in United States equities in 2000.[1]

Driving this movement to a globalized securities market is a variety of factors: (1) capital market imbalances caused by national differences in saving rates and investment opportunities, with the result that some nations (the OPEC countries early in the 1980s and Japan later in the decade) became the world's supplier of capital; (2) the development of new technology for international trading (e.g., satellite communications, computer advances, and fiber optics); (3) the desire of institutional investors to hold an internationally diversified portfolio of securities to reduce their exposure to economic downturn in any one country; (4) the need of issuers to tap international equity markets to reduce their cost of capital; and (5) the fear of the United States financial services industry that unless foreign issuers were accommodated, United States dealers would be excluded from profitable business, and foreign securities markets would gradually out distance American markets in terms of their depth and liquidity.

The internationalization of securities markets carries profound implications for the world's securities market regulators. Although the gains to both issuers and investors from reducing the barriers to transnational capital flows seem obvious, so also are the risks. For example, when 24 hour trading in U.S. securities eventually develops and corporations list their stock on stock exchanges in New York, London, and Tokyo, offshore trading (particularly in securities of United States corporations) might provide a haven for insider trading or other manipulative practices that would quickly be detected and prosecuted within the United States. Yet, what is the extraterritorial reach of the United States securities laws?

A. THE EXTRATERRITORIAL APPLICATION OF THE FEDERAL SECURITIES LAWS

It if often said that the securities laws are "silent" on the question of their extraterritorial reach.[1] This is debatable.[2] Section 2(a)(7) of the 1933 Act defines the term "interstate commerce" to include "trade or commerce in securities or any transportation or communication relating thereto * * * between any foreign country and any State, Territory or the District of Colum-

---

1. 2001 Sec. Indus. Ass'n, Fact Book at 78–79.

1. See, e.g., Ronald E. Bornstein & N. Elaine Dugger, Symposium: International Regulation of Insider Trading, 1987 Colum. Bus. L. Rev. 375, 399.

2. For the contrasting view that the securities markets of the 1920s were already internationalized and that Congress understood this well, see Margaret V. Sachs, The International Reach of Rule 10b–5: The Myth of Congressional Silence, 28 Colum. J. of Trans. L. 677 (1990).

bia." As a result, even a phone call from abroad arguably could violate § 5 of the 1933 Act, which forbids the use of "any means or instruments of transportation or communication in interstate commerce" to offer or sell an unregistered security. In contrast § 30(b) of the 1934 Act, makes the provisions of that Act and of any rules adopted thereunder inapplicable to "any person insofar as he transacts a business in securities without the jurisdiction of the United States, unless he transacts such business in contravention of such rules and regulations as the Commission may prescribe as necessary or appropriate for the protection of investors." At least one Circuit Court decision has read this grant of rulemaking authority to imply a Congressional intent to limit the extraterritorial application of the federal securities laws because it shows, it said, that "Congress was concerned with extraterritorial transactions only if they were part of a plan to harm American investors or markets."[3] Compare the following.

Itoba Ltd. v. Lep Group PLC

United States Court of Appeals, Second Circuit, 1995.
54 F.3d 118.

■ Before: FEINBERG, VAN GRAAFEILAND and MINER, CIRCUIT JUDGES.

■ VAN GRAAFEILAND, CIRCUIT JUDGE:

Itoba Limited appeals from a judgment of the United States District Court for the District of Connecticut (Eginton, J.) dismissing its securities fraud action against Lep Group PLC, William Berkley, John Read, Peter Grant and John East for lack of subject matter jurisdiction. For the reasons stated below, we reverse and remand for further proceedings.

The corporate defendant in this case, Lep Group PLC, is a London-based holding company with some fifty subsidiaries operating in thirty countries. It is a true conglomerate, owning businesses in freight forwarding, home security systems, biotechnology, travel services, and real estate speculation. Lep's "ordinary shares", the British equivalent of common stock, are registered in the United Kingdom, obligating the company to comply with United Kingdom securities laws. The primary trading market for Lep's ordinary shares is the International Stock Exchange of the United Kingdom and the Republic of Ireland Ltd. (the "London Exchange").

To create a United States market for its ordinary shares, Lep deposited 12,842,850 of its approximately 136 million shares in an American depository in 1988. The depository in turn issued an American Depository Receipt (ADR) for each five ordinary shares of Lep on deposit. Because these ADRs trade in the form of American Depository Shares (ADSs) on the National Association of Securities Dealers Automated Quotation System ("NASDAQ"), Lep is subject to the reporting and disclosure requirements of United States securities law.

A.D.T. Limited ("ADT") is a transnational holding company based in Bermuda. Its shares are listed on the New York Stock Exchange and approximately fifty percent of its shareholders of record reside in the United States. Itoba, a Channel Islands company, is a wholly-owned subsidiary of ADT. ADT also is the corporate parent of A.D.T. Securities Systems, Inc., a Delaware-

---

3. Zoelsch v. Arthur Andersen & Co.,
824 F.2d 27, 32 (D.C.Cir.1987) (Bork, J.).

based firm and one of America's largest suppliers of security and protection services.

In mulling over expansion plans for A.D.T. Securities Systems, ADT considered the possible acquisition of one of A.D.T. Securities Systems' largest competitors in the American security market, National Guardian, ADT already owned a small interest in that corporation through shares it held of Lep, the parent company of National Guardian. Because ownership of Lep would lead to control of National Guardian, ADT considered increasing its Lep holdings.

At the same time, Canadian Pacific was interested in expanding into the freight forwarding business and also was pondering a sizeable investment in Lep. Learning of their mutual interest, the companies agreed to explore a joint purchase of Lep. Canadian Pacific hired S.G. Warburg, a London investment bank, to evaluate Lep's business operations. Nicholas Wells, ADT's in-house financial analyst, was directed by Michael Ashcroft, ADT's chairman, to perform a valuation of Lep.

In December 1989, S.G. Warburg issued an extensive report assessing Lep's prospects. The analysis in this report was based on Lep's U.K. annual reports, the Form 20-F that Lep filed with the United States Securities and Exchange Commission for the year ended December 31, 1988, Lep's shareholder register, and broker reports. Shortly after the Warburg report was issued, Canadian Pacific abandoned the proposed joint venture.

ADT's interest, on the other hand, did not diminish. Wells continued his examination of Lep, relying heavily on the Warburg report. To supplement his research, he obtained from Canadian Pacific a copy of Lep's Form 20-F for 1988. Wells frequently discussed his analyses of these documents with David Hammond, ADT's vice chairman and the person in charge of acquisitions.

Based on Wells' analyses and their own review of the Warburg report, Hammond and Ashcroft decided to acquire Lep. Soon thereafter, Hammond formulated a plan to increase ADT's Lep holdings by making anonymous purchases on the market through one of ADT's offshore companies, in this case Itoba. Hammond contacted the board members of Itoba and recommended that they approve his purchase plan.

As expected, Itoba's board approved the plan. Itoba's board then requested one of ADT's employees to commence share purchases in Itoba's name; these purchases were made according to Hammond's plan and paid for by ADT. During the second half of 1990, Itoba executed a number of significant purchases on the London Exchange pursuant to the plan. By November 1990, Itoba had acquired over 37 million Lep ordinary shares for approximately $114 million.

Before ADT could complete its planned acquisition, however, Lep disclosed a series of business reversals that decimated its share value; Lep's stock price plummeted 97% and the value of Itoba's Lep holdings declined by nearly $111 million. Lep wrote off approximately $522 million from its books for the fiscal year ended December 31, 1991.

Itoba sued Lep and its officers in the District of Connecticut, asserting violations of sections 10(b) and 20 of the Securities Exchange Act of 1934 (the "Act") and of Rule 10b-5. According to Itoba, the defendants were subject to liability because they failed to disclose material matters in statements filed with the SEC. Specifically, Itoba alleged that Lep made high risk investments and engaged in speculative business ventures without informing the investing public. Itoba claimed that had these matters been properly disclosed, it would not have purchased Lep's stock at artificially inflated prices.

Itoba also asserted claims against Lep director William Berkley for alleged violations of sections 10(b) and 12(2) of the Act and of Rule 10b–5. Berkley, a United States citizen and a resident of Connecticut, had sold a large block of Lep ordinary shares in the United States on the same day that Itoba purchased a large block of shares in London. Itoba alleged that had Berkley properly complied with his duty to disclose material, nonpublic information before trading, it would not have made that purchase.

Defendants moved to dismiss Itoba's claims for lack of subject matter jurisdiction, and Magistrate Judge Jean Margolis, to whom the matter was referred for recommendation and report, issued a report that recommended dismissing Itoba's action on jurisdictional grounds. The district court adopted the magistrate judge's recommendations in toto. It dismissed Itoba's action on Fed.R.Civ.P. 12(b)(1) grounds in a short-form order. This, we conclude, was error.

It is well recognized that the Securities Exchange Act is silent as to its extraterritorial application. See, e.g., Alfadda v. Fenn, 935 F.2d 475, 478 (2d Cir.) (citing 15 U.S.C. § 78aa), cert. denied, 502 U.S. 1005 * * * (1991). However, in determining whether Congress intended that the "precious resources of United States courts" be devoted to a specific transnational securities fraud claim, we are not without guidance. Two jurisdictional tests have emerged under this Court's decisions: the "conduct test", as announced in Leasco Data Processing Equip. Corp. v. Maxwell, 468 F.2d 1326, 1336–37 (2d Cir.1972), and the "effects test", as announced in Schoenbaum v. Firstbrook, 405 F.2d 200, 206–09 (2d Cir.), rev'd with respect to holding on merits, 405 F.2d 215 (2d Cir.1968) (in banc), cert. denied sub nom. Manley v. Schoenbaum, 395 U.S. 906 * * * (1969). There is no requirement that these two tests be applied separately and distinctly from each other. Indeed, an admixture or combination of the two often gives a better picture of whether there is sufficient United States involvement to justify the exercise of jurisdiction by an American court. It is in this manner that we address the issue of jurisdiction in the instant case. Because we believe that the allegations are sufficient to support jurisdiction, we reverse.

Under the conduct test, a federal court has subject matter jurisdiction if (1) the defendant's activities in the United States were more than "merely preparatory" to a securities fraud conducted elsewhere, Bersch v. Drexel Firestone, Inc., 519 F.2d 974, 987 (2d Cir.), cert. denied, 423 U.S. 1018 * * * (1975), and (2) these activities or culpable failures to act within the United States "directly caused" the claimed losses, Alfadda, supra, 935 F.2d at 478. Inherent in the conduct test is the principle that Congress does not want " 'the United States to be used as a base for manufacturing fraudulent security devices for export, even when these are peddled only to foreigners.' " Psimenos v. E.F. Hutton & Co., 722 F.2d 1041, 1045 (2d Cir.1983) (quoting IIT v. Vencap, Ltd., 519 F.2d 1001, 1017 (2d Cir.1975)).

The magistrate judge correctly stated the conduct test when she said that Itoba must prove that Lep's United States-based activities directly caused Itoba's financial losses. However, whether she correctly applied the test is an entirely different matter. The magistrate judge based her recommendation to deny jurisdiction on the following findings:

First, Itoba and ADT did not read the SEC filing and rely on them; it was an investment bank hired by ADT which had reviewed the documents. And second, the SEC filings were filed in connection with LEP's ADS's and ADR's, not the ordinary shares purchased by Itoba, for which annual reports and press releases were generated from England.

The magistrate judge's first finding—that ADT and Itoba did not read and rely on the SEC filing in making their purchase decision—must be rejected in view of the clearly-established fact that the executives of Itoba and ADT based their investment decision on the Warburg report. The analyses and conclusions in this report were predicated on information found in the Form 20–F that Lep filed with the SEC. Nicholas Wells, the ADT executive responsible for assessing investment prospects, made the Warburg report the centerpiece of his Lep valuation. Moreover, he not only relied on the discussion of the SEC filing as contained in the Warburg report, he also used his own copy of the 1988 Form 20–F to formulate his purchase recommendations. According to the affidavit of ADT's vice chairman, the decision to acquire Lep was based upon these recommendations.

The fact that Itoba's board members did not read the SEC filing is not of controlling significance. A party need not personally have read a misleading financial report to establish reliance; derivative reliance is a well-established basis for liability in a Rule 10b–5 action. * * * The acquisition plan that Itoba's directors approved was formulated and funded by ADT, which in turn relied on its financial officer's analysis of the Warburg report and Lep's SEC filing. The contents of Lep's 1988 Form 20–F were thus a "substantial" and "significant contributing cause" to Itoba's purchase decision. There is no requirement, as suggested by the magistrate judge's decision, that Itoba read Lep's filing before it could rely on it.

The magistrate judge's second reason for denying jurisdiction, i.e., that the SEC filings were made in connection with Lep's ADS and ADR, not its ordinary shares, is only fifty percent correct and therefore is one hundred percent wrong. The ADRs were simply a grouping into one security of five ordinary shares. Inevitably, there was a direct linkage between the prices of the ADRs representing five ordinary shares and the prices of the single ordinary shares themselves. If the ordinary share price fell on the London Exchange, the market price of an ADR would decrease in similar manner, and visa versa.

Finally, a Rule 10b–5 action is not barred because a false and misleading statement in an SEC filing pertains to a security that is not the security purchased. See In re Ames Dep't Stores Inc. Stock Litig., 991 F.2d 953, 961–62 (2d Cir.1993). So long as the fraudulent device employed is of the type that would cause reasonable investors to rely thereon and, so relying, cause them to purchase or sell the corporation's securities, a Rule 10b–5 action may lie. See SEC v. Texas Gulf Sulphur Co., 401 F.2d 833, 860 (2d Cir.1968) (in banc), *cert. denied sub nom.* Coates v. Securities & Exchange Comm'n, 394 U.S. 976 * * * (1969). SEC filings generally are the type of "devices" that a reasonable investor would rely on in purchasing securities of the filing corporation. When these United States filings include substantial misrepresentations, they may be a predicate for subject matter jurisdiction. See Psimenos, supra, 722 F.2d at 1045 (citing Leasco, supra, 468 F.2d at 1337).

The fact that the Lep ordinary shares were issued and purchased in England does not change our conclusion. "The conduct test does not center its inquiry on whether domestic investors or markets are affected, but on the nature of conduct within the United States as it relates to carrying out the alleged fraudulent scheme. * * *'' Psimenos, supra, 722 F.2d at 1045; see Leasco, supra, 468 F.2d at 1337.

Moreover, the making of the allegedly false and misleading filings with the SEC was not "merely preparatory to the fraud." Although the magistrate judge refrained from forthrightly stating as much, she tiptoed around that statement as follows:

> It is beyond dispute that SEC filings and press releases are the type of information on which an investor relies in making his or her investment decisions. Securities & Exchange Comm'n v. Texas Gulf Sulphur Co., 401 F.2d 833, 862 (2d Cir.1968), *cert. denied sub nom.* Coates v. Securities & Exchange Comm'n, 394 U.S. 976 (1969). Even beyond the issue of whether the SEC filings were "merely preparatory to the fraud," plaintiff cannot demonstrate that the alleged acts within the United States "directly caused [its] losses" for two reasons.

She then propounded the two reasons we have rejected in the preceding paragraphs and cited two cases whose application here is questionable at best, Koal Industries Corp. v. Asland, S.A., 808 F.Supp. 1143, 1153–55 (S.D.N.Y. 1992) and Nathan Gordon Trust v. Northgate Exploration, Ltd., 148 F.R.D. 105, 107–08 (S.D.N.Y.1993). In Koal Industries, a Panamanian corporation acquired two Netherlands Antilles corporations which owned interests in an Arkansas mining company. The entire transaction took place in Switzerland and the financing was obtained from outside the United States. The only contact with the United States other than the location of the mine was a telephone call seeking additional funds for the acquisition. Northgate involved a motion for class certification. The defendant was a Canadian corporation which owned an interest in a gold mine located in northern Canada, concerning which the defendant filed allegedly false SEC statements. The proposed class was to consist of all persons who purchased Northgate stock on the Toronto, Montreal, London and New York Exchanges. The defendant requested that the class be limited to those who purchased on the New York Exchange, and the district court granted its request. In contrast to the discretionary nature of the district court's class certification ruling and the "fraud on the market" class issues of Northgate, the instant case involves a single plaintiff asserting direct individual fraud.

Appellees address the issue of "preparatory conduct" more directly. They assert that the mere filing of a document with the SEC should not trigger jurisdiction in United States courts. In support of this contention, they point out that Lep's financial statements were prepared in England and contend that the act of filing alone should not confer subject matter jurisdiction in the United States. They say further that the filing was "incidental or preparatory conduct" in whatever wrongdoing may have occurred. With respect to the first contention, we hold that the situs of preparations for SEC filings should not be determinative of jurisdictional questions. Otherwise, the protection afforded by the Securities Exchange Act could be circumvented simply by preparing SEC filings outside the United States. We find no support in the Act for such a result.

The second half of appellees' argument overlooks a basic purpose of the securities law, which is fair disclosure of material facts. A material fact that is undisclosed in an SEC filing remains undisclosed absent public enlightenment. This may bring into play a concomitant duty, i.e., the duty to correct. [citation omitted.] Lep's uncorrected nondisclosure played as much a role in Itoba's purchases as the price listings on the London Exchange and NASDAQ. In view of the deleterious effect this continued nondisclosure had on the thousands of ADT shareholders in the United States, it cannot be described correctly as incidental or preparatory.

This argument, of course, combines pertinent principles of both the conduct and effects tests, the latter one being based on fraud which takes place abroad which impacts on "stock registered and listed on [an American] national securities exchange and [is] detrimental to the interests of American investors." Schoenbaum, supra, 405 F.2d at 208. Here, we have fraud occurring on an American exchange and persisting abroad that has impacted detrimentally upon thousands of United States shareholders in the defrauded company, i.e., over $100 million lost in the shareholders' corporate equity.

The magistrate judge held that "if ADT were the plaintiff, the 'effects test' would be met, in that ADT's stock is traded on the New York Stock Exchange and approximately fifty percent (50%) of its shares are held in this country." See generally Consolidated Gold Fields PLC v. Minorco, S.A., 871 F.2d 252, 262–63 (2d Cir.), amended on other grounds, 890 F.2d 569 (2d Cir.), cert. dismissed, 492 U.S. 939 * * * (1989); Matter of Marc Rich & Co. A.G., 707 F.2d 663, 666–67 (2d Cir.), cert. denied, 463 U.S. 1215 * * * (1983); United States v. Aluminum Co. of Am., 148 F.2d 416, 443 (2d Cir.1945); Restatement (Second) of Law of Foreign Relations § 18(b), cmt. d. We believe this reasoning applies with equal effect where, although Itoba, ADT's wholly-owned subsidiary, was the nominal purchaser and owner of the Lep stock, it was ADT which financed the deal and which, with its shareholders, ultimately must bear the loss. This is not a case in which Lep's acts "simply [had] an adverse affect [sic] on the American economy or American investors generally." See Bersch, supra, 519 F.2d at 989. In short, we hold that a sufficient combination of ingredients of the conduct and effects tests is present in the instant case to justify the exercise of jurisdiction by the district court. See generally Leasco, supra, 468 F.2d at 1338.

For some reason that is not clear to us, the magistrate judge did not consider it necessary to address specifically Itoba's causes of action against any of the individual defendants. She simply recommended a blanket dismissal of the complaint as to all defendants, which recommendation was adopted without discussion by the district court. We find this particularly troublesome with respect to the defendant Berkley.

On October 8, 1990, Berkley, a United States resident and a Lep director, sold 7,300,000 ordinary shares of Lep to his United States-based broker, New York & Foreign Securities Corporation, which in turn sold these shares for its own account on the London Exchange. Berkley received almost $24 million for his shares. That same day, Itoba purchased 7,500,000 shares on the London Exchange through its London-based broker. Whether the close temporal relationship of these two transactions is or is not coincidental presents an interesting question. After executing this purchase, Itoba and ADT executives learned that the shares they had acquired were owned previously by Berkley. When Itoba brought the instant action, it asserted a separate claim against Berkley based on this Court's "disclose or abstain" rule, which imposes on insiders a duty to disclose material information before trading in their company's securities. See SEC v. Texas Gulf Sulphur Co., supra, 401 F.2d at 848. In Shapiro v. Merrill Lynch, Pierce, Fenner & Smith, Inc., 495 F.2d 228, 237 (2d Cir.1974), we held that an insider who fails to comply with his duty to disclose or abstain can be held liable "not only to the purchasers of the actual shares sold by [the insider,] but to all persons who during the same period purchased [the corporation's] stock in the open market without knowledge of the material inside information which was in the possession of [the insider]."

Although we do not presently rule on the issue, it would seem that Berkley's failure to disclose material, nonpublic information prior to selling his Lep shares is the type of behavior that falls under this Rule 10b–5 rubric. Because antifraud provisions are designed to prevent corporate insiders from taking unfair advantage of uninformed outsiders, Shapiro v. Merrill Lynch, supra, 495 F.2d at 235 (citing Radiation Dynamics, Inc. v. Goldmuntz, 464 F.2d 876, 890 (2d Cir.1972)), Berkley's alleged nondisclosure during a sales transaction executed by two parties within the United States—Berkley and his broker—is the type of conduct that should trigger jurisdiction. See Roth v. Fund of Funds, Ltd., 279 F.Supp. 935, 936–37 (S.D.N.Y.), aff'd, 405 F.2d 421 (2d Cir.1968), cert. denied, 394 U.S. 975 * * * (1969).

Moreover, it is not clear that Itoba is disabled from asserting its claim because it purchased its shares on a foreign market—the London Exchange. In Shapiro v. Merrill Lynch, supra, we held that an inside trader is subject to liability to all purchasers of his corporation's stock on the "open market." 495 F.2d at 237. Whether the "open market" encompasses foreign exchanges is an issue we leave for remand.

We conclude that Itoba's claim against Berkley should not have been incorporated without discussion into Itoba's claim against the non-resident defendants and just as silently dismissed.

CONCLUSION

Unlike some securities actions brought to recover questionable damages on behalf of optimistically described classes, we are met here with a single plaintiff which suffered direct substantial losses. A plaintiff such as this should not be deprived of its day in an American court by a Rule 12(b)(1) order based on erroneous facts and questionable law. We conclude that the issues now before us best can be resolved by a trial on the merits in which the facts relevant to jurisdiction may be more fully developed. See Bersch, supra, 519 F.2d at 992–93 (quoting Leasco, supra, 468 F.2d at 1330). We reverse the judgment below and remand for such a trial.

THE CONDUCT OR EFFECT TEST

A. *The "Effect" Test.* The first significant decision to consider the extra-territorial application of the federal securities laws was Schoenbaum v. First-brook.[1] There, an American shareholder of Banff Oil Ltd. brought an action alleging that its parent corporation, Acquitaine, had purchased shares of Banff based on inside information and at an unfairly low price. Both Banff and Acquitaine were Canadian corporations, and the challenged transactions occurred entirely in Canada. Although the District Court dismissed the action for lack of subject matter jurisdiction, the Second Circuit reversed on the ground that the listing and trading of Banff's stock on the American Stock Exchange implied that the challenged transactions had sufficient effect on American investors to sustain subject matter jurisdiction. It said:

1. 405 F.2d 200 (2d Cir.1968), *rev'd on other grounds on reh'g en banc*, 405 F.2d 215 (2d Cir.1968), *cert. denied sub nom.* Manley v. Schoenbaum, 395 U.S. 906 (1969).

We believe that Congress intended the Exchange Act to have extraterritorial application in order to protect domestic investors who have purchased foreign securities on American exchanges and to protect the domestic securities market from the effects of improper foreign transactions in American securities. In our view, neither the usual presumption against extraterritorial application of legislation nor the specific language of Section 30(b) show Congressional intent to preclude application of the Exchange Act to transactions regarding stocks traded in the United States which are effected outside the United States when extraterritorial application of the Act is necessary to protect American investors.[2]

Subsequent decisions have uniformly followed *Schoenbaum*'s holding that a listing on an American exchange effectively gives rise to subject matter jurisdiction in U.S. courts over an anti-fraud complaint. For example, in SEC v. Unifund SAL,[3] information leaked from a French bidder about its approaching tender offer for an American target (Rorer Group), and various investors in Europe began purchasing Rorer's stock and options, which were listed exclusively on American exchanges. Although the locus of the misconduct was outside the United States, the trading occurred in the United States; as a result, the Second Circuit found that "the activity created the near certainty that United States shareholders, who could reasonably be expected to hold Rorer securities, would be adversely affected."[4]

How far can the "effects test" be stretched? Suppose the Rorer securities in *Unifund* were traded principally on foreign exchanges, but that the issuing corporation was still a U.S. firm. Judge Friendly suggested in IIT v. Cornfeld that the "American nationality of the issuer" can be a factor that "points strongly toward applying the anti-fraud provisions of our securities laws. * * * "[5]Still, if neither plaintiffs nor defendants in a securities fraud suit are U.S. citizens or residents, it is highly unlikely that subject matter jurisdiction will be found to exist.[6] Although it is possible that the SEC could still bring an enforcement action on these facts, its current policy is not to challenge insider trading when the transaction occurs wholly outside the United States and over a foreign exchange.[7]

The "Conduct" Test. In Bersch v. Drexel Firestone, Inc.[8] and Leasco Data Processing Equipment Corp. v. Maxwell,[9] Judge Friendly framed a "conduct" test as an alternative to the "effect" test of *Schoenbaum*. Applying a more sophisticated two step analysis, he asked, first, whether "considerations of foreign relations law * * * preclude our reading [the Acts] as applicable," and, second, "whether Congress would have wished the precious resources of United States courts and law enforcement agencies to be devoted to them." The first

---

2.   405 F.2d at 206.

3.   910 F.2d 1028 (2d Cir.1990). *See also* Des Brisay v. Goldfield Corp., 549 F.2d 133 (9th Cir.1977).

4.   910 F.2d at 1033.

5.   619 F.2d 909, 918 (2d Cir.1980).

6.   See Fidenas AG v. Compagnie Int'l Pour L'Informatique CII Honeywell Bull, S.A., 606 F.2d 5 (2d Cir.1979). The result might be different, however, if fraudulent conduct occurred within the United States. Note that even if subject matter jurisdiction

were found to exist, other procedural obstacles might remain, such as the doctrine of forum non conveniens.

7.   For the suggestion that subject matter jurisdiction is more easily found when the SEC is the plaintiff, see Zoelsch v. Arthur Andersen & Co., 824 F.2d 27, 33 n. 3 (D.C.Cir.1987).

8.   519 F.2d 974 (2d Cir.1975).

9.   468 F.2d 1326 (2d Cir.1972).

question led him to rely on the Restatement (Second) of the Foreign Relations Law of the United States (1965), and the second question led him to speculate—with remarkable candor in *Bersch*—about what Congress likely would have done had it focused on the issue.[10]

The same day that *Bersch* was handed down, the Second Circuit also decided IIT v. Vencap, Ltd.,[11] another opinion written by Judge Friendly. The plaintiff in *Vencap* was a Luxembourg investment firm that had invested in a Bahamas venture capital firm organized by an American citizen residing in the Bahamas. Americans owned less than 1 percent of the plaintiff trust's shares, and the Second Circuit found that neither this trivial percentage of ownership nor the defendant's status as an American citizen was sufficient to give the court jurisdiction. Instead, it focused on the fact that certain actions essential to the consummation of the fraud had taken place in the New York City offices of the attorneys for the defendant. It then explained why this conduct was sufficient to support subject matter jurisdiction:

> We do not think Congress intended to allow the United States to be used as a base for manufacturing fraudulent security devices for export, even when these are peddled only to foreigners. This country would surely look askance if one of our neighbors stood by silently and permitted misrepresented securities to be poured into the United States. By the same token it is hard to believe Congress meant to prohibit the SEC from policing similar activities within this country. * * * If there would be subject matter jurisdiction over a suit by the SEC to prevent the concoction of securities frauds in the United States for export, there would also seem to be jurisdiction over a suit for damages or rescission by a defrauded foreign individual. Our ruling on this basis of jurisdiction is limited to the perpetration of fraudulent acts themselves and does not extend to mere preparatory activities or the failure to prevent fraudulent acts where the bulk of the activity was performed in foreign countries, such as in *Bersch*. Admittedly the distinction is a fine one. But the position we are taking here itself extends the application of the securities laws to transnational transactions beyond prior decisions and the line has to be drawn somewhere if the securities laws are not to apply in every instance where something has happened in the United States, however large the gap between the something and a consummated fraud and however negligible the effect in the United States or on its citizens.[12]

What conduct must occur within the United States when the securities are not themselves traded here? In Travis v. Anthes Imperial Ltd.[13] a Canadian corporation made an exchange offer to the shareholders of another Canadian corporation, but excluded U.S. shareholders to avoid compliance with U.S. securities law. When the excluded U.S. shareholders complained, negotiations

---

10. In Zoelsch v. Arthur Andersen & Co., 824 F.2d 27, 32 (D.C.Cir.1987), Judge Bork (perhaps alone unintimidated by the aura of Judge Friendly) wrote: "It is somewhat odd to say, as in *Bersch* * * *, that courts must determine their jurisdiction by divining what 'Congress would have wished" if it had addressed the problem.' A more natural inquiry might be what jurisdiction Congress in fact thought about and conferred."

11. 519 F.2d 1001 (2d Cir.1975).

12. 519 F.2d at 1017–18. For another finding by Judge Friendly that conduct was more than "merely preparatory" and satisfied the *Bersch* test, see IIT v. Cornfeld, 619 F.2d 909 (2d Cir.1980).

13. 473 F.2d 515 (8th Cir.1973).

and communications into the United States followed, and eventually the company agreed to purchase their shares for cash. The closing of this cash purchase transaction occurred within the United States. Plaintiffs contended that the Canadian bidder had told them to retain their shares for approximately a year, at which point it would make an offer for the U.S. shares on terms that would give them an after tax result essentially equivalent to those given the Canadian shareholders. After the Canadian tender offer had been completed, giving the bidder over 90 percent of the target and destroying the public market for the stock, it indicated that it would not make an offer to the United States shareholders after all; instead it eventually offered them a price, which the plaintiffs accepted, that was considerably below what the plaintiffs claimed they could have obtained had they sold their shares at the time of the original offer. The plaintiffs sued, claiming that the promise to make a second offer had been made fraudulently, and that the officers of both corporations had engaged in self-dealing in carrying out the deal in a manner that excluded the United States shareholders. Although the District Court found subject matter jurisdiction lacking, characterizing the question as "whether a tender offer by one Canadian corporation for the shares of another Canadian corporation, not extended to United States resident shareholders is within the subject matter jurisdiction of this Court,"[14] the Eighth Circuit reversed, noting that a series of letters and telephone calls between the parties discussing both the Canadian tender offer and the proposed United States offer constituted "significant conduct with respect to the alleged violations in the United States."[15]

Whether the sending of documents into a jurisdiction is considered "conduct" or an "effect," *Travis* shows the significance of Judge Friendly's decisions in *Bersch* and *Vencap*: if a suit is brought by United States residents against nonresidents with regard to a transaction predominantly occurring outside the United States, United States courts may still find the requisite "conduct" of "effect" necessary to confer jurisdiction on them if any communications are directed into the United States from abroad that contain alleged material misrepresentations or omissions.

The harder cases under the "conduct" test come when the facts in *Travis* are reversed and nonresidents sue U.S. residents, claiming that the defendants' conduct went beyond the merely "preparatory" stage and "directly caused" their losses. Here, circuits have disagreed. In MCG, Inc. v. Great Western Energy Corp.,[16] the Fifth Circuit summarized the current state of the law thus:

> [O]ur colleagues in the Second Circuit have exercised jurisdiction in cases in which foreign investors alleged fraudulent acts in the United States * * *, but declined jurisdiction when the acts occurring in the United States were merely preparatory to the alleged fraud. This approach has been viewed as requiring that the domestic conduct needed to trigger subject matter jurisdiction must satisfy the elements of a violation of Rule 10b–5 * * * The Third, Eighth and Ninth Circuits have adopted a more relaxed standard, requiring that conduct, not necessarily fraudulent itself, be alleged to have occurred in the United States in furtherance of a fraudulent scheme.[17]

14. Travis v. Anthes Imperial Ltd., 331 F.Supp. 797, 800 (E.D.Mo.1971).

15. 473 F.2d at 524.

16. 896 F.2d 170 (5th Cir.1990).

17. Id. at 174–75. In Robinson v. TCI/US West Communications Inc., 117 F.3d 900, 906 (5th Cir.1997), the Fifth Circuit adopted the Second Circuit test as the better

Kauthar SDN BHD v. Sternberg

United States Court of Appeals for the Seventh Circuit, 1998.
149 F.3d 659, *cert. denied,* 525 U.S. 1114 (1999).

■ Before CUMMINGS, RIPPLE and ROVNER, CIRCUIT JUDGES.

OPINION:

■ RIPPLE, CIRCUIT JUDGE.

Plaintiff, a Malaysian corporation based on Kuala Lumpur, Malaysia, invested $38 million in the stock of Rimsat, Ltd., a corporation incorporated in the Carribean Island of Nevis but with a principal place of business in exotic Fort Wayne, Indiana. Rimsat's business plan was to provide satellite communications services to customers in the Pacific Rim region by means of satellites that Rimsat had contracted to purchase from a Russian satellite company, which satellites were to be placed in a geosynchronous orbit position that Rimsat was to lease from a company incorporated in Pacific Rim island of Tonga. Rimsat was eventually forced into bankruptcy by its Russian creditors and filed for bankruptcy in Federal District Court in Indiana. Kauther thereupon also brought suit in the same Indiana court, alleging that all of the participants that solicited it to invest in Rimsat knowingly misled it. The district court dismissed the suit finding that the securities violations were outside the statutory protection of the federal securities laws because insufficient conduct was alleged to have occurred in the United States. The Seventh Circuit reversed and explained its version of the conduct test and its application to these facts as follows:

In contrast with the effects analysis, which examines actions occurring outside of the United States, the conduct analysis focuses on actions occurring in this country as they "relate[ ] to the alleged scheme to defraud." *Tamari,* 730 F.2d at 1107. The chronic difficulty with such a methodology has been describing, in sufficiently precise terms, the sort of conduct occurring in the United States that ought to be adequate to trigger American regulation of the transaction. Indeed, the circuits that have confronted the matter have articulated a number of methodologies.

The predominant difference among the circuits, it appears, is the degree to which the American-based conduct must be related causally to the fraud and

reasoned one in applying the conduct test. See also Joseph P. Garland & Brian P. Murray, Subject Matter Jurisdiction under the Federal Securities Law: The State of Affairs afer *Itoba,* 20 Md. J. Int'l L. & Trade 235 (1996).

For a major article propounding an alternative approach, see Merritt B. Fox, Securities Disclosure in a Globalizing Market: Who Should Regulate Whom, 95 Mich. L. Rev. 2498 (1997). In this article, Professor Fox concluded:

> The analysis that this article employs, however, shows that neither the traditional investor protection approach nor the proposed market protection approach is in the enlightened self-interest

of the United States. In contrast, I conclude that the United States should apply its regime only to issuers of U.S. nationality, but do so regardless of the location of transactions in the issuer's shares and regardless of who the buyers are. This set of issuers, of course, is exactly the same set of issuers the United States would regulate under the optimal apportionment authority at the international level recommended here.

Id. at 2505. See also Merritt B. Fox, The Political Economy of Statutory Reach: U.S. Disclosure Rules in a Globalizing Market for Securities, 97 Mich. L. Rev. 696 (1998); Merritt B. Fox, The Securities Globalization Disclosure Debate, 78 Wash. U.L.Q. 567 (2001).

the resultant harm to justify the application of American securities law. At one end of the spectrum, the District of Columbia Circuit appears to require that the domestic conduct at issue must itself constitute a securities violation. *See Zoelsch*, 824 F.2d at 31 ("Jurisdiction will lie in American courts where the domestic conduct comprises all the elements of a defendant's conduct necessary to establish a violation of section 10(b) and Rule 10b–5."). At the other end of the spectrum, the Third, Eighth and Ninth Circuits, although also focusing on whether the United States-based conduct caused the plaintiffs' loss, to use the Fifth Circuit's words, "generally require some lesser quantum of conduct." *Robinson v. TCI/US West Communications, Inc.*, 117 F.3d 900, 906 (5th Cir.1997). In *SEC v. Kasser*, 548 F.2d 109, 114 (3d Cir.), *cert. denied*, 431 U.S. 938 * * * (1977), the Third Circuit stated that the conduct came within the scope of the statute if "at least some activity designed to further a fraudulent scheme occurs within this country." The Eighth Circuit, in *Continental Grain (Australia) Pty. Ltd. v. Pacific Oilseeds, Inc.*, 592 F.2d 409, 421 (8th Cir.1979), held that the antifraud provisions were applicable when the domestic conduct "was in furtherance of a fraudulent scheme and was significant with respect to its accomplishment." The Ninth Circuit adopted the *Continental Grain* approach in *Grunenthal GmbH v. Hotz*, 712 F.2d 421, 425 (9th Cir.1983).

Our colleagues in the Second and Fifth Circuits have set a course between the two extremes that we have just discussed. That approach requires a higher quantum of domestic conduct than do the Third, Eighth and Ninth Circuits. *See Robinson*, 117 F.3d 900, 905–06 (5th Cir.1997). The Second Circuit has stated that foreign plaintiffs' suits under the antifraud provisions of the securities laws, such as Kauthar's, will be "heard only when substantial acts in furtherance of the fraud were committed within the United States." *Psimenos v. E.F. Hutton & Co., Inc.*, 722 F.2d 1041, 1045 (2d Cir.1983). Furthermore, if the United States-based activities were merely preparatory in nature, or if the " 'bulk of the activity was performed in foreign countries,' " jurisdiction will not exist. Id. at 1046 (quoting *IIT v. Vencap, Ltd.*, 519 F.2d 1001, 1018 (2d Cir.1975)). In addition, only "where conduct 'within the United States directly caused' the loss will a district court have jurisdiction over suits by foreigners who have lost money through sales abroad." *Id.* (quoting *Bersch v. Drexel Firestone, Inc.*, 519 F.2d 974, 993 (2d Cir.), cert. denied, 423 U.S. 1018 * * * (1975)); *see also Vencap*, 519 F.2d at 1018.

Although this court has not had occasion to articulate an approach to the extraterritorial application of the securities laws, we have employed these concepts with respect to analogous actions brought under the Commodity Exchange Act. *See Mak*, 112 F.3d at 288–89; *Tamari*, 730 F.2d at 1107 & n.11. In that context, we have stated that "[w]hen the conduct occurring in the United States is material to the successful completion of the alleged scheme, jurisdiction is asserted based on the theory that Congress would not have intended the United States to be used as a base for effectuating the fraudulent conduct of foreign companies." *Tamari*, 730 F.2d at 1108. We think that our approach under the Commodities Act ought to be followed with respect to the securities laws and, although stated more generally, that it represents the same midground as that identified by the Second and Fifth Circuits. In our view, the absence of all but the most rudimentary Congressional guidance counsels that federal courts should be cautious in determining that transnational securities matters are within the ambit of our antifraud statutes. Nevertheless, we would do serious violence to the policies of these statutes if we did not recognize our Country's manifest interest in ensuring that the United States is not used as a "base of operations" from which to "defraud foreign securities purchasers or sellers." *Kasser,* 548 F.2d at 116. This interest is amplified by the fact that we live in an increasingly global financial community. The Second and Fifth Circuit's iterations of the test embody a satisfactory balance of these competing considerations. This analytical pattern will enable the courts to address situations in which the United States is being used as a launching pad for fraudulent international securities schemes. At the same time, it will cause us to refrain from adjudicating disputes which have little in the way of a significant connection to the United States.

We believe, therefore, that federal courts have jurisdiction over an alleged violation of the antifraud provisions of the securities laws when the conduct occurring in the United States directly causes the plaintiff's alleged loss in that the conduct forms a substantial part of the alleged fraud and is material to its success. This conduct must be more than merely preparatory in nature; however, we do not go so far as to require that the conduct occurring domestically must itself satisfy the elements of a securities violation.

We turn now to an application of these principles to Kauthar's allegations. Kauthar argues that a host of alleged general activities undertaken by various of the defendants constitutes conduct that was part of the scheme to defraud Kauthar and to solicit Kauthar's investment in Rimsat. Kauthar alleges that various documents containing fraudulent misrepresentations and omissions were prepared in the United States and were sent to it by wire and by the United States mail in an effort to obtain Kauthar's investment. Kauthar also alleges that phone calls were made from Fort Wayne, Indiana, and from San Diego, California, for the same purpose. Kauthar further alleges that the defendants had meetings and phone conversations in the United States to discuss the deceptive information contained in the prospectus and to "ultimately agree upon a plan to obtain equity funding from Kauthar by means of false and deceptive statements of fact." R.111 Para. 60. Thus, according to the complaint, the United States was utilized as a base of operations from which to launch the defendants' fraudulent scheme to defraud Kauthar. Moreover, Kauthar also alleges a set of specific acts that, in combination with those already mentioned, satisfy the conduct analysis. Specifically, Kauthar alleges that it wired the payment for the Rimsat securities, over $38 million, in six installments to Rimsat's bank account in Fort Wayne, Indiana. Therefore, Kauthar has alleged that the defendants conceived and planned a scheme to defraud Kauthar in the United States, that they prepared materials in support of the scheme to solicit the payment in the United States and sent those materials from the United States via the United States mail, and that they received in the United States the fraudulently solicited payment for the securities—the final step in the alleged fraud. We think these allegations sufficient to bring the alleged conduct within the ambit of the securities laws. * * *

PROBLEM 20–1

The sole business of Southeast Asian and European Overseas Traders (SAED), a Panamanian Corporation, is to invest in securities. It is wholly owned by Allen Truck, a citizen of Canada. In 2002, while vacationing in Florida, Truck made offers by telephone and e-mail to sell SAED securities to a French bank, located in Paris.

(1) Would such telephone calls and e-mail be sufficient to establish jurisdiction under the Securities Exchange Act?

(2) Assuming all facts are the same, but an electronic fund transfer was made by a French purchaser to Truck's Florida bank account, would that establish jurisdiction?

B.   PERSONAL JURISDICTION

Both § 22(a) of the 1933 Act and § 27 of the 1934 Act provide that process may be served on a defendant "wherever the defendant may be found." This provision has been found to "extend personal jurisdiction [under the Act] to the full reach permitted by the due process clause."[1] Under Supreme Court decisions on personal jurisdiction, this constitutional standard is satisfied when the defendant has taken purposeful action directed toward the United States and its effects were foreseeable.[2] Thus, it is possible that in a given case there could be subject matter jurisdiction, but not personal jurisdiction (at least not against some peripheral defendants), if the effect on United States securities markets was real, but was not intended or foreseen by the particular defendant.

Still, consider the facts of a 1990 insider trading case where the primary contact between the foreign defendant and the United States was its use of the medium of an American securities exchange to effect its transactions. In SEC v. Unifund SAL,[3] the Second Circuit found personal jurisdiction to exist against two foreign companies, who were alleged to have purchased the shares of an American company traded exclusively on the American Stock Exchange by placing their orders from abroad. In some instances, the orders were placed by a Swiss bank, acting as agent, to a foreign office of a United States brokerage firm. No conduct by the defendants was alleged to have occurred within the United States. In *Unifund*, the Second Circuit emphasized the harmful effects of insider trading on United States securities markets, and the district court specifically found that the defendants had "taken purposeful action directed toward the United States, and that any effects of this action in the United States are foreseeable."[4] But what made this action "purposeful toward the United States"? Was it that a United States corporation was involved? If so, would it make a difference if the actual trading had occurred on a European exchange when an impact on a United States exchange was still foreseeable? Does the decision imply that personal jurisdiction exists any time there is insider trading in the stock of a United States corporation anywhere around the world (even in the case of a face-to-face transaction between two foreign nationals)? Or, is the Second Circuit assuming that the defendant must have actually known that the transaction would be effected over a United States exchange? Once multiple international listings become common, would most traders know (or even want to know) this detail?

In SEC v. Tome,[5] the Second Circuit upheld service of process against various *unknown* foreign defendants who allegedly participated in an insider trading scheme, based only on publication of the complaint in the International Herald Tribune. The case involved the hostile tender offer by Joseph E.

---

1. See Leasco Data Processing Equip. Corp. v. Maxwell, 468 F.2d 1326, 1339 (2d Cir.1972).

2. See Asahi Metal Industry Co. v. Superior Court, 480 U.S. 102 (1987) (where Japanese manufacturer sold product to Taiwanese assembler).

3. 910 F.2d 1028 (2d Cir.1990).

4. SEC v. Foundation Hai, 736 F.Supp. 465, 469 (S.D.N.Y.1990).

5. 833 F.2d 1086 (2d Cir.1987), *cert. denied sub nom.* Lombardfin S.p.A. v. SEC, 486 U.S. 1014 (1988).

Seagram & Co. For St. Joe Minerals Corporation. The trades were effected through several European financial institutions (including Swiss banks protected by bank secrecy statutes). *Tome* probably is best read as holding that a United States court may obtain personal jurisdiction over a foreign national trading in United States securities over a United States exchange, when the foreign citizen has significant additional United States contacts. Defendant Tome had resided from time to time and did significant business in the United States.

C. INTERNATIONAL ENFORCEMENT

SEC v. Banca Della Svizzera Italiana

United States District Court, Southern District of New York, 1981.
92 F.R.D. 111.

■ MILTON POLLACK, DISTRICT JUDGE.

Plaintiff, Securities Exchange Commission ("SEC"), moves this Court for an appropriate order pursuant to Fed.R.Civ.P. 37 for the failure and refusal of defendant, Banca Della Svizzera Italiana ("BSI") to provide the SEC with information relative to the identities of the principals for whom it purchased stock and stock options on American exchanges in St. Joe Minerals Corporation ("St. Joe"), a New York corporation which produces natural resources.

The underlying law suit is an action by the SEC against the said defendant and unnamed others for an injunction and an accounting for violations of the insider trading provisions of the Securities Exchange Act of 1934, Sections 10(b) and 14(e), and Rules 10b–5 and 14e–3 promulgated thereunder.

Authority to bring this action resides in Section 21(d) of the Exchange Act, 15 U.S.C. § 78u(d). Jurisdiction of the Court is posited under Sections 21(e) and 27 of the Exchange Act.

Jurisdiction over BSI exists by virtue of BSI's doing business here. There is evidence in the record that BSI operates in New York at 44 Wall Street through a subsidiary corporation. This was denied by counsel for BSI at the hearing but a letter to the contrary signed some time ago by BSI, a copy of which was furnished to the Court by the SEC indicates that the denial was erroneous and obviously was inadvertent.

The issue posed to the Court is whether to compel a foreign party which transacted purchases on American securities exchanges to make discovery and answer interrogatories concerning its undisclosed principals where the acts of disclosure might subject that party to criminal liability in its home country. The Court has carefully balanced the interests at stake and considered the resisting party's professed good faith. It concludes that compelling the complete discovery demanded is not only justified in the instant case but required to preserve our vital national interest in maintaining the integrity of the securities markets against violations committed and/or aided and assisted by parties located abroad. Accordingly, an order should issue requiring full responses to the SEC's interrogatories.

The Facts

This action alleges insider trading on the part of BSI and its principals in the purchase and sale of call options for the common stock as well as the common stock itself of St. Joe. The options were traded through the Philadelphia Stock Exchange and the stock was traded on the New York Stock Exchange both of which are registered national exchanges. The purchases in question were made immediately prior to the announcement on March 11, 1981 of a cash tender offer by a subsidiary of Joseph E. Seagram & Sons, Inc. ("Seagram"), an Indiana corporation for all of the common stock of St. Joe at $45 per share. Prior to the announcement of the tender offer St. Joe stock traded on the market at $30 per share, (approximately).

The orders for the call options and the stock were placed close to the opening of trading on the exchanges on March 10, 1981, one day prior to Seagram's offer and announcement, at prices above the last quoted market price for the options and the stock. The options were due to expire in ten days, thereby significantly indicating an expectation that the price of St. Joe common stock would rise substantially and imminently.

BSI succeeded in purchasing approximately 1055 call options which carried the right to purchase 105,500 shares of St. Joe common stock and in purchasing 3,000 shares of the St. Joe common stock. On the next day the stock opened sharply higher in price and the bank shortly instructed its brokers to close out the purchases of the options and sell 2,000 of the 3,000 shares of common stock acquired. These transactions resulted in a virtually overnight profit just short of $2 million.

Promptly on noticing the undue activity in the options market, the SEC investigated and based on its findings brought this suit. The SEC contends that there is a strong probability that the purchasers were unlawfully using material non-public information which could only have been obtained or misappropriated from sources charged with a confidential duty not to disclose information prior to the public announcement of the tender offer.

The SEC applied for and obtained a Temporary Restraining Order against the Irving Trust Company which held the proceeds of the sales of the options and of the common stock in BSI's bank account with Irving Trust. The Temporary Restraining Order also directed immediate discovery proceedings including the requirement that "insofar as permitted by law" BSI should disclose within three business days the identity of its principals. The effect of the Temporary Restraining Order was to immobilize the profits derived from the questioned transactions.

The SEC endeavored by one or another procedural means, here and abroad, to obtain the identity of those who, along with the bank, were involved in the particular options purchases. No disclosure was forthcoming. Explanatory but uninformative letters so far as concerned the identity of the principals were received by the SEC from time to time. The SEC served formal interrogatories which were refined at the Court's suggestion to target the demanded disclosure in simplest terms. Conferences were held with the Court at which explanations were supplied and it was made clear at these that if need be an appropriate order enforceable by appropriate but, to the bank, unpalatable sanctions, might follow any continued impasse. Nonetheless, BSI declined to furnish the requested information voluntarily, adhering to its assertion of banking secrecy law. Eight months elapsed in the efforts to obtain the requisite disclosure by cooperative measures.

The bank regularly suggested, in the interim, a variety of alternative means by which the SEC might proceed to seek the disclosure. Some of these were doomed to failure in the opinion of the bank's own experts. It appeared to the Court that the proposals would only send the SEC on empty excursions, with little to show for them except more delay, more expense, more frustration, and possibly also, the inexorable operation of time bars against the claims by statutory limits for the assertion thereof. The proposed alternatives were not viable substitutes for direct discovery.

The matter came before the Court for crystallization on November 6, 1981 and after hearing counsel, the Court announced an informal opinion that it had determined to enter an order requiring disclosure, to be followed by severe contempt sanctions if it was not complied with. One week was fixed for submission of the order by the SEC. Apparently, the decision of the Court had a catalytic effect. A waiver of Swiss confidentiality was secured by the bank and reported to the Court. Also reported was that the bank had furnished some but not all the answers to the demanded interrogatories. A further period was requested to endeavor to complete the requisite responses with leave to show that any omissions were either not within the bank's ability to respond or were due to inappropriate demands. This moved finality forward to November 20, 1981.

Since the Court is unable to predict whether ultimate compliance will be secured or whether other notions of confidentiality may be developed on behalf of the disclosed Panamanian customers of the bank, applicable to Switzerland or elsewhere, it becomes useful to analyze the legal situation posited. The principles to be applied will be similar and will serve the further purposes of this case.

The authorities and commentators

1. The Supreme Court's Opinion in *Societe*

Any discussion of the issue posed here must begin with the Supreme Court's opinion in Societe Internationale Pour Participations Industrielles et Commerciales, S.A. v. Rogers, 357 U.S. 197 * * * (1958) which is the Court's latest decision on the subject. *Societe* holds that the good faith of the party resisting discovery is a key factor in the decision whether to impose sanctions when foreign law prohibits the requested disclosure.

In *Societe* a Swiss holding company was suing for the return of property seized by the Alien Property Custodian during World War II. The district court dismissed plaintiff's complaint as a sanction for its refusal to comply with the Court's order to produce bank records, despite a finding that the Swiss government had constructively seized the documents and that plaintiff had shown good faith efforts to comply with the production order. Id. at 201–02.

The Court of Appeals affirmed.

The Supreme Court reversed. It held that where plaintiff was prohibited by Swiss law from complying with the discovery order and there was no showing of bad faith, the sanction of dismissal without prejudice was not justified. The Court indicated that a party who had made deliberate use of foreign law to evade American law might be subject to sanctions.

[T]he Government suggests that petitioner stands in the position of one who deliberately courted legal impediments to production of the Sturzenegger records, and who thus cannot now be heard to assert its good faith after this expectation was realized. Certainly these contentions, if supported by the facts, would have a vital bearing on justification for dismissal of the action, but they are not open to the Government here. The findings below reach no such conclusions. * * * Id. at 208–09 * * *. Under *Societe,* then, a foreign law's prohibition of discovery is not decisive of the issue. A noncomplying party's good or bad faith is a vital factor to consider.

* * *

Application of the law to the Facts of this Case

BSI claims that it may be subject to criminal liability under Swiss penal and banking law if it discloses the requested information. However, this Court finds the factors in § 40 of the Restatement of Foreign Relations to tip decisively in favor of the SEC. Moreover, it holds BSI to be "in the position of one who deliberately courted legal impediments * * * and who thus cannot now be heard to assert its good faith after this expectation was realized." *Societe, supra* at 208–09 * * *. BSI acted in bad faith. It made deliberate use of Swiss nondisclosure law to evade in a commercial transaction for profit to it, the strictures of American securities law against insider trading. Whether acting solely as an agent or also as a principal (something which can only be clarified through disclosure of the requested information), BSI invaded American securities markets and profited in some measure thereby.[4] It cannot rely on Swiss nondisclosure law to shield this activity.

1.   The vital national interests at stake

The first of the § 40 factors is the vital national interest of each of the States. The strength of the United States interest in enforcing its securities laws to ensure the integrity of its financial markets cannot seriously be doubted. That interest is being continually thwarted by the use of foreign bank accounts. Congress, in enacting legislation on bank record-keeping, expressed its concern over the problem over a decade ago:

> Secret foreign bank accounts and secret foreign financial institutions have permitted a proliferation of "white collar" crime * * * and have allowed Americans and others to avoid the law and regulations concerning securities and exchanges. * * * The debilitating effects of the use of these secret institutions on Americans and the American economy are vast.

H.R.Rep. No. 975, 91 Cong., 2d Sess. 12, *reprinted in* 1970 U.S.Code Cong. & Admin.News 4394, 4397.

The evisceration of the United States interest in enforcing its securities laws continues up to the present. *See, e.g.,* Wall Street Journal, Oct. 29, 1981, at 1, col. 5 ("some Wall Street sources believe the SEC faces an insurmountable problem: obtaining from foreign sources the information that often is necessary to identify violators").

The Swiss government, on the other hand, though made expressly aware of the litigation, has expressed no opposition. In response to BSI's lawyers inquiries, the incumbent Swiss Federal Attorney General, Rudolf Gerber, said

---

4. BSI's contention that it is only a "nominal" party and therefore that it is wrong to place it in the predicament of having conflicting legal obligations is further answered by the well-established rule of agency law that an agent is liable as principal for the acts of an undisclosed principal. See, e.g., Bottorff v. Ault, 374 F.2d 832 (7th Cir.1967); Siegel v. Council of Long Island Educators, Inc., 75 Misc.2d 750, 348 N.Y.S.2d 816 (Sup. Ct. 1973) (per curiam).

only that a foreign court could not change the rule that disclosure required the consent of the one who imparted the secret and that BSI might thus be subject to prosecution. The Swiss government did not "confiscate" the Bank records to prevent violations of its law, as it did in *Societe*. NEITHER THE UNITED STATES NOR THE SWISS GOVERNMENT has suggested that discovery be halted. * * *

It is also of significance that the secrecy privilege * * * is one belonging to the bank customers and may be waived by them. It is not something required to protect the Swiss government itself or some other public interest. * * *

2.   Hardship considerations and the element of good faith

The second factor of § 40 of the Restatement of Foreign Relations is the extent and nature of the hardship that inconsistent enforcement actions would impose upon the party subject to both jurisdictions. It is true that BSI may be subject to fines and its officers to imprisonment under Swiss law. However, this Court notes that there is some flexibility in the application of that law. Not only may the particular bank involved obtain waivers from its customers to avoid prosecution, but Article 34 of the Swiss Penal Code contains a "State of Necessity" exception that relieves a person of criminal liability for acts committed to protect one's own good, including one's fortune, from an immediate danger if one is not responsible for the danger and one cannot be expected to give up one's good. * * *

Of course, given BSI's active part in the insider trading transactions alleged here, the Swiss government might well conclude—as this Court has—that BSI is responsible for the conflict it is in and that therefore the "State of Necessity" exception should not apply. However, that is certainly no cause for this Court to withhold its sanctions since the dilemma would be a result of BSI's bad faith. A party's good or bad faith is an important factor to consider, and this Court finds that BSI, which deposited the proceeds of these transactions in an American bank account in its name and which certainly profited in some measure from the challenged activity, undertook such transactions fully expecting to use foreign law to shield it from the reach of our laws. Such "deliberate courting" of foreign legal impediments will not be countenanced.

3.   The remaining § 40 factors

The last three of the § 40 Restatement of Foreign Relations Law factors— the place of performance, the nationality of the resisting party, and the extent to which enforcement can be expected to achieve compliance with the rule prescribed by that state—appear to be less important in this Circuit. It is significant nevertheless that they too tip in favor of the SEC. Performance may be said to occur here as well as in Switzerland since the actual answering of the interrogatories will presumably take place in the United States, where BSI's lawyers are. As for citizenship, it is true that BSI is a Swiss corporation. However, its transnational character, as evidenced by its large number of foreign affiliates, * * * and its New York "subsidiary" (so styled by it), render this Court less reluctant to order BSI to conform to our laws even where such an order may cause conflict with Swiss law. Last, with respect to enforcement, this Court believes that an appropriate formal order directing the demanded disclosure, to the extent that compliance has been incomplete, will serve as the requisite foundation for any further actions that may be needed in the form of sanctions and should serve to bring home the obligations a foreign entity undertakes when it conducts business on the American securities exchanges.

Conclusion

It would be a travesty of justice to permit a foreign company to invade American markets, violate American laws if they were indeed violated, withdraw profits and resist accountability for itself and its principals for the illegality by claiming their anonymity under foreign law. * * *

International Amendments and Globalization. More recently, the Commission has primarily relied on enforcement within the United States and the Memoranda of Understanding (MOU) approach.[1] By 2000 the SEC has entered into over 30 information sharing arrangements with foreign counterparts.[2] This resulted that year in 345 SEC requests to foreign authorities for enforcement assistance and 519 requests from foreign authorities for foreign enforcement assistance.[3]

MOUs vary a great deal in their breadth. For example, the Dutch, French, Norwegian, and Swedish memoranda are phrased as binding agreements that go beyond the earlier statement of intent formula to biding commitments to investigate and prosecute fraud, manipulation, and other securities violations. Others, particularly the Costa Rican, Hungarina, and Mexican memoranda, emphasize the SEC's technical assistance. Insider trading is a popular theme. Most of the MOUs are not for the most part binding agreements under international law. But "they serve as statements of intent between like-minded regulators to provide mutual assistance and cooperation in a variety of matters."[4]

In 1990 Congress enacted the International Securities Enforcement Cooperation Act which amended § 24 if the Securities Exchange Act. In § 24(d) the SEC can withhold disclosure under the Freedom of Information Act of records obtained from a foreign securities authority.

There are now also a limited number of treaties for mutual assistance in criminal matters.[5] The first treaty, the 1977 Treaty on Mutual Assistance on Criminal Matters between the Swiss Confederation and the United States, which "provides for broad assistance in criminal matters, including assistance in locating witnesses, production and authentication of business records, and

---

1. See 10 Louis Loss & Joel Seligman, Securities Regulation 5122–5123 (3d ed. rev. 1996); Michael D. Mann, Paul A. Leder & Elizabeth Jacobs, The Establishment of International Mechanisms for Enforcing Provisional Orders and Final Judgments Arising from Securities Law Violations, 55 Law & Contemp. Probs. 303 (Autumn 1992); Michael D. Mann, Joseph G. Mari & George Lavdas, International Agreements and Understandings for the Production of Information and Other Mutual Assistance, 29 Int'l L. 780 (1995); Hendrik F. Jordaan, "Has IOSCO Advanced International Securities Law Enforcement?": An Analysis in Light of SEC MOUs with Emerging Markets, 26 Sec. Reg. L. J. 269 (1998).

2. SEC, Ann. Rep. 14 (2000).

3. Ibid.

4. Sec. Act Rel. 6841, 44 SEC Dock. 56, 65 n.54 (1989).

5. See SEC, Staff Report on Internationalization of the Securities Markets VII–49 to VII–60 (1987) (describing four treaties for mutual assistance in criminal matters with Italy, the Netherlands, Switzerland, and Turkey).

service of judicial and administrative documents," but not extradition, has been enforced, with quite limited success, after agonizing delays.[6]

In 1982 the United States entered into a "memorandum of understanding" with the Swiss Government for improving international law enforcement cooperation in the field of insider trading, to which was attached an agreement with the Swiss Bankers' Association with respect to requests for information from the SEC on the misuse of inside information.[7] In December 1987 the Swiss Federal Assembly adopted a new 1–1/2 page Article 161 of the Penal Code with respect to insider trading. This treaty went into effect in December 1988.[8]

6. Id. at VII–50; see, e.g., SEC v. Certain Unknown Purchasers, 1984–1985 Fed. Sec. L. Rep. (CCH) ¶ 91,951 (S.D.N.Y. 1985); cf. SEC v. Banca della Svizzera Italiana, 92 F.R.D. 111 (S.D.N.Y.1981).

The Swiss Federal Office for Police Matters has taken the position that the rule of specialty implicit in Article IX of the Treaty for the Extradition of Criminals between the United States and Switzerland, 31 Stat. 1928 (May 14, 1900), will not block a civil enforcement action filed by the SEC. SEC v. Eurobond Exch., Ltd., 13 F.3d 1334, 1336, 1337 (9th Cir.1994).

Cf. Colello v. SEC, 908 F. Supp. 738 (C.D.Cal.1995) (holding it is a violation of the Fifth Amendment to freeze assets under the Mutual Assistance in Criminal Matters treaty without affording defendants a notice of an asset freeze or a hearing and that the Swiss asset freeze constituted an unreasonable search under the Fourth Amendment).

7. Int'l Sec. Rel. 2, 43 SEC Dock. 123 (1982).

8. Lionel Frei & Stefan Treschsel Origins and Applications of the United States–Switzerland Treaty on Mutual Assistance in Criminal Matters, 31 Harv. Int'l L. J. 77 (1990).

*

INDEX

References are to Pages

DEGREES OF REGULATION
Generally, 1

DERIVATIVE ACTIONS
Indemnification statutes protecting directors and officers, 1349
Rule 10b–5 actions compared, 1053 et seq.

DERIVATIVES AND DERIVATIVE EXCHANGES
Generally, 15
See also Futures and Futures Exchanges, this index
Commodity Futures Modernization Act of 2000 (CFMA), 62
Equity derivatives, 48
Hedging, use for, 1
Security interests, characterization as, 385 et seq.

DIRECTORS AND OFFICERS
See also Corporations, this index
Conspiracy to violate registration requirements, 554 et seq.
Corporate reporting violations, 1506 et seq.
Criminal liabilities, 1349
Executive compensation, disclosure of in prospectus, 214
Fiduciary duties, takeover contests and, 811 et seq.

†

1–58778–214–6

90000

9 781587 782145